Essential
Dictionary
&Thesaurus

Plus Language in Action
supplement

Essential

Dictionary

&Thesaurus

Plus Language in Action
supplement

Collins

An Imprint of HarperCollins*Publishers*

first edition 2004

© HarperCollins Publishers 2004

HarperCollins Publishers
Westerhill Road, Bishopbriggs, Glasgow G64 2QT
Great Britain

www.collins.co.uk

Collins® and Bank of English® are registered trademarks of
HarperCollins Publishers Limited

ISBN 0-00-716331-2

Acknowledgements
We would like to thank those authors and publishers who kindly gave
permission for copyright material to be used in the Bank of English. We would
also like to thank Times Newspapers Ltd for providing valuable data.

Note
Entered words that we have reason to believe constitute trademarks have
been designated as such. However, neither the presence nor absence of
such designation should be regarded as affecting the legal status of
any trademark.

A catalogue record for this book is available from the British Library

Computing support by Thomas Widmann

Typeset by Morton Word Processing Ltd, Scarborough

Supplement typeset by Wordcraft

Printed by William Clowes Ltd., Beccles and London

Editorial Staff

BANK *of* ENGLISH

This book has been compiled with constant reference to the Bank of English, a unique database containing over 524 million words of written and spoken English, enabling Collins lexicographers to analyse how the language is actually used and how it is changing. The Bank of English was set up to be a resource for language research and lexicography, and contains a very wide range of material from books, newspapers, radio, TV, magazines, letters and talks, thereby reflecting the whole spectrum of English today. Its size and range make it an unequalled resource, and the purpose-built software for its analysis is unique to Collins dictionaries.

This ensures that Collins dictionaries accurately reflect English as it is used today in a way that is most helpful to the dictionary or thesaurus user.

Contents

Foreword

This book is an immensely practical and helpful language resource. It provides two kinds of language help, arranged on the same page for quick and easy look-up. In the top section of each page you will find a dictionary text which gives help with spellings and meanings, while the lower section of each page provides a matching thesaurus with a choice of synonyms.

The dictionary includes spelling help for all irregular forms of words. Pronunciation help is also given for words considered difficult or confusing, and up-to-date spelling and language tips throughout the dictionary text provide additional advice on spelling and using English correctly and effectively.

The synonym lists of the thesaurus text are divided into numbered categories, each relating to the particular meaning of the word in the dictionary text, so that it is easy to identify the sense that most closely relates to the context required. In addition, the most useful synonym for each sense is given first and highlighted in bold type. This is particularly helpful when a main entry word has a number of different senses. It also gives you an idea of which synonym is the closest alternative to the word you have looked up.

The thesaurus text also includes key opposites (antonyms) at many of the main entry words. These opposites provide you with another way of expressing yourself. For instance, if you want to say that something is *difficult*, it can sometimes be effective to use a negative construction and, using the word's opposite, you may think of a phrase such as "*by no means easy*".

The symbol ❶ appears after the headword of every dictionary entry which has matching thesaurus text, to draw the user's attention to the fact that additional synonym help is included for that entry.

The Language in Action Supplement will help you to write in a style that will smoothly communicate your message to your audience, in any situation.

This book is thus a uniquely helpful reference tool, providing spelling, meaning, language help, a wide choice of alternatives and opposites, and a writing guide, all together in a single source. This makes it an invaluable language resource, and an ideal companion for anyone who wants to increase their command of English.

Guide to the Text

DICTIONARY

Entry words ●

policy of racial segregation in S Africa.
apartment ⓘ *noun* **1** room in a building. **2** flat.

apathy ⓘ *noun* lack of interest or enthusiasm. **apathetic** *adjective* **apathetically** *adverb*

Part of speech labels

ape *noun* **1** tailless monkey such as the chimpanzee or gorilla. **2** stupid, clumsy, or ugly man. ◆ *verb* **3** imitate. **apeman** *noun* extinct primate thought to have been the forerunner of true humans.

aperient [ap-**peer**-ee-ent] *adjective* **1** having a mild laxative effect. ◆ *noun* **2** mild laxative.

aperitif [ap-per-rit-**teef**] *noun* alcoholic drink taken before a meal.

aperture *noun* **1** opening or hole. **2** opening in a camera or telescope that controls the amount of light entering it.

apex ⓘ *noun* highest point.

APEX Advance Purchase Excursion: reduced fare for journeys booked a specified period in advance.

aphasia *noun* disorder of the central nervous system that affects the ability to speak and understand words.

aphelion [ap-**heel**-lee-on] *noun, pl* **-lia** [-lee-a] point of a planet's orbit that is farthest from the sun.

Variant spellings ●

aphid [**eh**-fid], **aphis** [**eh**-fiss] *noun* small insect which sucks the sap from plants.

aphorism *noun* short clever saying expressing a general truth.

aphrodisiac [af-roh-**diz**-zee-ak] *noun* **1** substance that arouses sexual desire. ◆ *adjective* **2** arousing sexual desire.

apiary [**ape**-yar-ee] *noun, pl* **-ries** place where bees are kept. **apiarist** *noun* beekeeper.

apiculture *noun* breeding and care of bees.

Examples ●
show how the entry word is used

apiece ⓘ *adverb* each, e.g. *they were given two*

Thesaurus symbols
identify dictionary entries with matching thesaurus text

Sense numbers

Definitions

Spelling help
given for all irregular and difficult forms of words

THESAURUS

by oneself, isolated, to one side
apart from *preposition* = **except for**, aside from, besides, but, excluding, not counting, other than, save

apartment *noun* **1** = **room**, accommodation, living quarters, quarters, rooms, suite **2** = **flat**, penthouse, duplex (*US & Canada*)

International English
from all regions of the world where English is spoken

apathetic *adjective* = **uninterested**, cool, indifferent, passive, phlegmatic, unconcerned OPPOSITE interested

apathy *noun* = **lack of interest**, coolness, indifference, inertia, nonchalance, passivity, torpor, unconcern OPPOSITE interest

apex *noun* = **highest point**, crest, crown, culmination, peak, pinnacle, point, summit, top

Opposites ●

OPPOSITE base
apiece *adverb* = **each**, for each, from each,

Synonyms
offer a wide range of alternatives

Dictionary sense numbers
show which dictionary sense the synonym list matches

Guide to the Text

apples apiece.

aplomb 🟠 [ap-**plom**] *noun* calm self-possession.

apocalypse *noun* **1** end of the world. **2** event of great destruction. **the Apocalypse** book of Revelation, the last book of the New Testament. **apocalyptic** *adjective*

Apocrypha [ap-**pok**-rif-fa] *plural noun* **the Apocrypha** collective name for the 14 books of the Old Testament which are not accepted as part of the Hebrew scriptures.

apocryphal 🟠 *adjective* (of a story) of questionable authenticity.

apogee [**ap**-oh-jee] *noun* **1** point of the moon's or a satellite's orbit that is farthest from the earth. **2** highest point.

apolitical *adjective* not concerned with political matters.

apologia *noun* formal written defence of a cause.

apology 🟠 *noun, pl* **-gies 1** expression of regret for wrongdoing. **2** (foll. by *for*) poor example (of). **3** same as APOLOGIA. **apologetic** *adjective* showing or expressing regret. **apologetically** *adverb* **apologetics** *noun* branch of theology concerned with the reasoned defence of Christianity. **apologist** *noun* person who formally defends a cause. **apologize** *verb* make an apology.

> **SPELLING TIP**
>
> Remember that the correct way to spell **apology** is with one *p* and one *l*.

apoplexy *noun Med* stroke. **apoplectic** *adjective* **1** of apoplexy. **2** *Informal* furious.

- **Derived words**
- **Pronunciation help** given for all difficult words
- **Cross references**
- **Language notes** give spelling tips and advice on good English
- **Subject field labels** identify words or senses used in a specialist or technical field
- **Usage labels** identify areas of usage

individually, respectively, separately OPPOSITE all together

aplomb *noun* = **self-possession**, calmness, composure, confidence, level-headedness, poise, sang-froid, self-assurance, self-confidence OPPOSITE self-doubt

apocryphal *adjective* = **dubious**, doubtful, legendary, mythical, questionable, unauthenticated, unsubstantiated OPPOSITE factual

apologetic *adjective* = **regretful**, contrite, penitent, remorseful, rueful, sorry

apologize *verb* = **say sorry**, ask forgiveness, beg pardon, express regret

apology *noun* **1** = **defence**, acknowledgment, confession, excuse, explanation, justification, plea **2** (foll. by *for*) = **mockery**, caricature,

- **Part of speech labels**
- **Key synonyms** given first

Abbreviations Used in This Book

AD	Anno Domini	*Med*	Medicine
adj	adjective	*masc*	masculine
adv	adverb	*Meteorol*	Meteorology
Amer	America(n)	*Mil*	Military
Anat	Anatomy	*Myth*	Mythology
Arch	Archaic	*n*	noun
Archit	Architecture	*N*	North(ern)
Astrol	Astrology	*Naut*	Nautical
Aust	Australia(n)	*NW*	Northwest(ern)
BC	before Christ	*NZ*	New Zealand
Biol	Biology	*Obs*	Obsolete
Bot	Botany	*Offens*	Offensive
Brit	British	*orig.*	originally
Canad	Canadian	*Path*	Pathology
Chem	Chemistry	*Photog*	Photography
C of E	Church of England	*pl*	plural
conj	conjunction	*Poet*	Poetic
Derog	Derogatory	*prep*	preposition
Dial	Dialect	*pron*	pronoun
E	East(ern)	*Psychol*	Psychology
e.g.	for example	®	Trademark
Eng	English	*RC*	Roman Catholic
esp.	especially	*S*	South(ern)
etc.	et cetera	*S Afr*	South Africa(n)
fem	feminine	*Scot*	Scottish
foll.	followed	*sing*	singular
Geom	Geometry	*US*	United States
Hist	History	*usu.*	usually
Hum	Humorous	*v*	verb
Inf	Informal	*W*	West(ern)
interj	interjection	*Zool*	Zoology
Lit	Literary		

Aa

a *adjective* indefinite article, used before a noun being mentioned for the first time.
A *noun, pl* **A's, As** highest grade in an examination. **from A to Z** from start to finish.
Å angstrom unit.
a- *prefix* not or without, e.g. *apolitical; amoral.*
A1 *adjective Informal* first-class, excellent.
AA 1 Alcoholics Anonymous. **2** Automobile Association.
aardvark *noun* S African anteater with long ears and snout.
AB 1 able-bodied seaman. **2** Alberta.
aback *adverb* **taken aback** startled or disconcerted.
abacus [ab-a-cuss] *noun* beads on a wire frame, used for doing calculations.
abaft *adjective, adverb Naut* closer to the rear of (a ship).
abalone [ab-a-**lone**-ee] *noun* edible sea creature with a shell lined with mother of pearl.
abandon ❶ *verb* **1** desert or leave (one's wife, children, etc.). **2** give up (hope etc.) altogether.
♦ *noun* **3** lack of inhibition. **abandoned** *adjective* **1** deserted. **2** uninhibited.
abandonment *noun*
abase *verb* humiliate or degrade (oneself).
abasement *noun*
abashed ❶ *adjective* embarrassed and ashamed.
abate ❶ *verb* make or become less strong.
abatement *noun*
abattoir [ab-a-twahr] *noun* slaughterhouse.
abbess *noun* nun in charge of a convent.
abbey ❶ *noun* dwelling place of, or a church belonging to, a community of monks or nuns.
abbot *noun* head of an abbey of monks.
abbreviate ❶ *verb* shorten (a word) by leaving out some letters. **abbreviation** *noun* shortened form of a word or words.
ABC *noun* **1** alphabet. **2** basics of a subject.
abdicate ❶ *verb* give up (the throne or a responsibility). **abdication** *noun*
abdomen *noun* part of the body containing the stomach and intestines. **abdominal** *adjective*
abduct ❶ *verb* carry off, kidnap. **abduction** *noun* **abductor** *noun*
aberration ❶ *noun* **1** sudden change from what is normal, accurate, or correct. **2** brief lapse in control of one's thoughts or feelings. **aberrant** *adjective* showing aberration.
abet ❶ *verb* **abetting, abetted** help or encourage in wrongdoing. **abettor** *noun*
abeyance ❶ *noun* **in abeyance** not in use.
abhor ❶ *verb* **-horring, -horred** detest utterly. **abhorrent** *adjective* hateful, loathsome.

THESAURUS

abandon *verb* **1 =leave**, desert, forsake, strand OPPOSITE **maintain**. **2 =give up**, relinquish, surrender, yield OPPOSITE **take**
♦*noun* **3 =wildness**, recklessness OPPOSITE **control**
abandonment *noun* **1 =leaving**, dereliction, desertion, forsaking
abashed *adjective* **=embarrassed**, ashamed, chagrined, disconcerted, dismayed, humiliated, mortified, shamefaced, taken aback
abate *verb* **=decrease**, decline, diminish, dwindle, fade, lessen, let up, moderate, outspan (S Afr), relax, slacken, subside, weaken OPPOSITE **increase**
abbey *noun* **=monastery**, convent, friary, nunnery, priory
abbreviate *verb* **=shorten**, abridge, compress, condense, contract, cut, reduce,

summarize OPPOSITE **expand**
abbreviation *noun* **=shortening**, abridgment, contraction, reduction
abdicate *verb* **=give up**, abandon, quit, relinquish, renounce, resign, step down (*inf*)
abdication *noun* **=giving up**, abandonment, quitting, renunciation, resignation, retirement, surrender
abduct *verb* **=kidnap**, carry off, seize, snatch (*sl*)
abduction *noun* **=kidnapping**, carrying off, seizure
aberration *noun* **1 =oddity**, abnormality, anomaly, defect, irregularity, peculiarity, quirk **2 =lapse**
abet *verb* **=help**, aid, assist, connive at, support
abeyance *noun* **in abeyance =shelved**,

abhorrence noun
abide ⊕ verb **1** endure, put up with. **2** Obs
stay or dwell, e.g. abide with me. **abide by** verb
obey (the law, rules, etc.). **abiding** adjective
lasting.
ability ⊕ noun, pl **-ties 1** competence, power.
2 talent.
abject ⊕ adjective **1** utterly miserable. **2**
lacking all self-respect. **abjectly** adverb
abjure verb deny or renounce on oath.
ablative [ab-lat-iv] noun case of nouns in Latin
and other languages, indicating source, agent,
or instrument of action.
ablaze ⊕ adjective **1** burning fiercely. **2**
emotionally aroused, e.g. ablaze with desire.
able ⊕ adjective capable, competent. **ably**
adverb **able-bodied** adjective strong and
healthy. **able-bodied seaman** seaman who is
trained in certain skills.
-able adj suffix able to be acted on as
specified, e.g. washable. **-ably** adv suffix **-ability**
n suffix
ablutions plural noun act of washing.
ABM antiballistic missile.
abnormal ⊕ adjective not normal or usual.
abnormally adverb **abnormality** noun

aboard adverb, preposition on, in, onto, or into
(a ship, train, or plane).
abode ⊕ noun home, dwelling.
abolish ⊕ verb do away with. **abolition** noun
abolitionist noun person who wishes to do
away with something, esp. slavery.
A-bomb noun short for ATOMIC BOMB.
abominable ⊕ adjective detestable, very bad.
abominable snowman large apelike creature
said to live in the Himalayas. **abominably**
adverb
abomination noun **1** someone or something
that is detestable. **2** strong dislike.
aborigine [ab-or-**rij**-in-ee], **aboriginal** noun
original inhabitant of a country or region, esp.
(A-) Australia. **aboriginal** adjective
abort ⊕ verb **1** have an abortion or perform
an abortion on. **2** have a miscarriage. **3** end a
plan or process before completion. **abortion**
noun **1** operation to end a pregnancy. **2**
Informal something grotesque. **abortionist**
noun **1** person in favour of legal abortion. **2**
person who performs abortions, esp. illegally.
abortive adjective unsuccessful.
abound ⊕ verb be plentiful. **abounding**
adjective

——————— THESAURUS ———————

hanging fire, on ice (inf), pending, suspended
abhor verb =**hate**, abominate, detest, loathe,
shrink from, shudder at OPPOSITE love
abhorrent adjective =**hateful**, abominable,
disgusting, distasteful, hated, horrid, loathsome,
offensive, repulsive
abide verb **1** =**tolerate**, accept, bear, endure,
put up with, stand, suffer
abide by verb =**obey**, adhere to, agree to,
carry out, comply with, conform to, discharge,
follow, fulfil, keep to, observe, submit to
abiding adjective =**everlasting**, continuing,
enduring, lasting, permanent, persistent,
unchanging OPPOSITE brief
ability noun **1** =**skill**, aptitude, capability,
competence, expertise, proficiency OPPOSITE
inability. **2** =**talent**
abject adjective **1** =**miserable**, deplorable,
forlorn, hopeless, pitiable, wretched **2** =**servile**,
cringing, degraded, fawning, grovelling,
submissive OPPOSITE dignified
ablaze adjective **1** =**on fire**, aflame, alight,
blazing, burning, fiery, flaming, ignited, lighted
able adjective =**capable**, accomplished,
competent, efficient, proficient, qualified, skilful
OPPOSITE incapable
able-bodied adjective =**strong**, fit, healthy,
robust, sound, sturdy OPPOSITE weak
abnormal adjective =**unusual**, atypical,

exceptional, extraordinary, irregular, munted
(NZ sl), odd, peculiar, strange, uncommon
OPPOSITE common
abnormality noun =**oddity**, deformity,
exception, irregularity, peculiarity, singularity,
strangeness
abode noun =**home**, domicile, dwelling,
habitat, habitation, house, lodging, pad (sl),
quarters, residence
abolish verb =**do away with**, annul, cancel,
destroy, eliminate, end, eradicate, put an end
to, quash, rescind, revoke, stamp out OPPOSITE
continue
abolition noun =**ending**, cancellation,
destruction, elimination, end, extermination,
termination, wiping out
abominable adjective =**terrible**, despicable,
detestable, disgusting, hateful, horrible, horrid,
repulsive, revolting, vile OPPOSITE good
abort verb **1** =**terminate** (a pregnancy) **2**
=**miscarry 3** =**stop**, arrest, axe (inf), call off,
check, end, fail, halt, terminate
abortion noun **1** =**termination**, deliberate
miscarriage, miscarriage
abortive adjective =**failed**, fruitless, futile,
ineffectual, miscarried, unsuccessful, useless,
vain
abound verb =**be plentiful**, flourish,
proliferate, swarm, swell, teem, thrive

about ⊙ *preposition* **1** concerning, on the subject of. **2** in or near (a place). ◆ *adverb* **3** nearly, approximately. **4** nearby. **about to** shortly going to, e.g. *about to leave*. **not about to** determined not to, e.g. *I'm not about to give up now*. **about-turn** *noun* **1** turn to the opposite direction. **2** complete change of attitude.

above ⊙ *adverb, preposition* **1** over or higher (than). **2** greater (than). **3** superior (to). **above board** in the open, without dishonesty.

abracadabra *noun* supposedly magic word.

abrasion ⊙ *noun* scraped area on the skin.

abrasive *adjective* harsh and unpleasant in manner.

abrasive ⊙ *adjective* **1** harsh and unpleasant in manner. **2** tending to rub or scrape. ◆ *noun* **3** substance for cleaning or polishing by rubbing.

abreast ⊙ *adverb, adjective* side by side. **abreast of** up to date with.

abridge ⊙ *verb* shorten by using fewer words. **abridgment, abridgement** *noun*

abroad ⊙ *adverb* **1** to or in a foreign country. **2** at large.

abrogate *verb* cancel (a law or agreement) formally. **abrogation** *noun*

abrupt ⊙ *adjective* **1** sudden, unexpected. **2** blunt and rude. **abruptly** *adverb* **abruptness** *noun*

abs *plural noun Informal* abdominal muscles.

abscess [ab-sess] *noun* inflamed swelling containing pus.

abscond ⊙ *verb* leave secretly.

abseil [ab-sale] *verb* go down a steep drop by a rope fastened at the top and tied around one's body.

absent ⊙ *adjective* **1** not present. **2** lacking. **3** inattentive. ◆ *verb* **4** stay away. **absently** *adverb* **absence** *noun* **1** being away. **2** lack. **absentee** *noun* person who should be present but is not. **absenteeism** *noun* persistent absence from work or school. **absent-minded** *adjective* inattentive or forgetful. **absent-mindedly** *adverb*

absinthe *noun* strong green aniseed-flavoured liqueur.

absolute ⊙ *adjective* **1** complete, perfect. **2** not limited, unconditional. **3** pure, e.g. *absolute alcohol*. **absolute zero** *Physics* lowest possible temperature, -273.15°C. **absolutely** *adverb* **1** completely. ◆ *interjection* **2** certainly, yes. **absolutism** *noun* government by a ruler with unrestricted power.

——————————— T H E S A U R U S ———————————

about *preposition* **1** = **regarding**, as regards, concerning, dealing with, on, referring to, relating to **2** = **near**, adjacent to, beside, circa (*used with dates*), close to, nearby ◆*adverb* **3** = **nearly**, almost, approaching, approximately, around, close to, more or less, roughly

above *preposition* **1** = **over**, higher than, on top of, upon OPPOSITE **under**. **2** = **greater than**, beyond, exceeding OPPOSITE **less than**

abrasion *noun* = **graze**, chafe, scrape, scratch, scuff, surface injury

abrasive *adjective* **1** = **unpleasant**, caustic, cutting, galling, grating, irritating, rough, sharp **2** = **rough**, chafing, grating, scraping, scratchy

abreast *adverb, adjective* = **alongside**, beside, side by side

abreast of *adjective* = **informed about**, acquainted with, *au courant* (with), *au fait* (with), conversant with, familiar with, in the picture about, in touch with, keeping one's finger on the pulse of, knowledgeable about, up to date with, up to speed with

abridge *verb* = **shorten**, abbreviate, condense, cut, decrease, reduce, summarize OPPOSITE **expand**

abroad *adverb* **1** = **overseas**, in foreign lands, out of the country

abrupt *adjective* **1** = **sudden**, precipitate,

quick, surprising, unexpected OPPOSITE **slow**. **2** = **curt**, brusque, gruff, impatient, rude, short, terse OPPOSITE **polite**

abscond *verb* = **flee**, clear out, disappear, escape, make off, run off, steal away

absence *noun* **1** = **nonattendance**, absenteeism, truancy **2** = **lack**, deficiency, need, omission, unavailability, want

absent *adjective* **1** = **missing**, away, elsewhere, gone, nonexistent, out OPPOSITE **present**. **2** = **lacking**, unavailable OPPOSITE **present**. **3** = **absent-minded**, blank, distracted, inattentive, oblivious, preoccupied, vacant, vague OPPOSITE **aware** ◆*verb* **4 absent oneself** = **stay away**, keep away, play truant, withdraw

absent-minded *adjective* = **vague**, distracted, dreaming, forgetful, inattentive, preoccupied, unaware OPPOSITE **alert**

absolute *adjective* **1** = **total**, complete, outright, perfect, pure, sheer, thorough, utter **2** = **supreme**, full, sovereign, unbounded, unconditional, unlimited, unrestricted

absolutely *adverb* **1** = **totally**, completely, entirely, fully, one hundred per cent, perfectly, utterly, wholly OPPOSITE **fairly**

absolution *noun* = **forgiveness**, deliverance, exculpation, exoneration, mercy, pardon, release

A

absolve ⊕ *verb* declare to be free from blame or sin. **absolution** *noun*
absorb ⊕ *verb* **1** soak up (a liquid). **2** take in. **3** engage the interest of (someone).
absorption *noun* **absorbent** *adjective* able to absorb liquid. **absorbency** *noun*
abstain ⊕ *verb* **1** choose not to do something. **2** choose not to vote. **abstainer** *noun*
abstention *noun* abstaining, esp. from voting.
abstinence *noun* abstaining, esp. from drinking alcohol. **abstinent** *adjective*
abstemious ⊕ [ab-**steem**-ee-uss] *adjective* taking very little alcohol or food.
abstemiousness *noun*
abstract ⊕ *adjective* **1** existing as a quality or idea rather than a material object. **2** theoretical. **3** (of art) using patterns of shapes and colours rather than realistic likenesses. ♦ *noun* **4** summary. **5** abstract work of art. **6** abstract word or idea. ♦ *verb* **7** summarize. **8** remove.
abstracted *adjective* lost in thought.
abstractedly *adverb* **abstraction** *noun*
abstruse ⊕ *adjective* not easy to understand.
absurd ⊕ *adjective* incongruous or ridiculous.
absurdly *adverb* **absurdity** *noun*
abundant ⊕ *adjective* plentiful. **abundantly** *adverb* very, e.g. *it is abundantly clear.*
abundance *noun*
abuse ⊕ *verb* **1** use wrongly. **2** ill-treat violently. **3** speak harshly and rudely to. ♦ *noun* **4** prolonged ill-treatment. **5** harsh and vulgar comments. **6** wrong use. **abuser** *noun* **abusive** *adjective* **abusively** *adverb* **abusiveness** *noun*
abut *verb* **abutting, abutted** be next to or

——————— THESAURUS ———————

absolve *verb* =**forgive**, deliver, exculpate, excuse, let off, pardon, release, set free OPPOSITE> **condemn**
absorb *verb* **1** =**soak up**, suck up **2** =**take in**, consume, digest, imbibe, incorporate, receive **3** =**preoccupy**, captivate, engage, engross, fascinate, rivet
absorbed *adjective* **1** =**soaked up 2** =**taken in**, assimilated, digested, incorporated, received **3** =**preoccupied**, captivated, engrossed, fascinated, immersed, involved, lost, rapt, riveted, wrapped up
absorbent *adjective* =**permeable**, porous, receptive, spongy
absorbing *adjective* **3** =**fascinating**, captivating, engrossing, gripping, interesting, intriguing, riveting, spellbinding OPPOSITE> **boring**
absorption *noun* **1** =**soaking up**, sucking up **2** =**taking in**, assimilation, consumption, digestion, incorporation **3** =**concentration**, fascination, immersion, intentness, involvement, preoccupation
abstain *verb* **1** =**refrain**, avoid, decline, deny yourself, desist, fast, forbear, forgo, give up, keep from OPPOSITE> **abandon yourself**
abstemious *adjective* =**self-denying**, ascetic, austere, frugal, moderate, sober, temperate
abstention *noun* =**refusal**, abstaining, abstinence, avoidance, forbearance, refraining, self-control, self-denial, self-restraint
abstinence *noun* =**self-denial**, abstemiousness, avoidance, forbearance, moderation, self-restraint, soberness, teetotalism, temperance
abstinent *adjective* =**self-denying**, abstaining, abstemious, forbearing, moderate, self-controlled, sober, temperate

abstract *adjective* **1** =**indefinite**, general OPPOSITE> **specific. 2** =**theoretical**, hypothetical, notional OPPOSITE> **real** ♦*noun* **4** =**summary**, abridgment, digest, epitome, outline, précis, résumé, synopsis OPPOSITE> **expansion** ♦*verb* **7** =**summarize**, abbreviate, abridge, condense, digest, epitomize, outline, précis, shorten **8** =**remove**, detach, extract, isolate, separate, take away, take out, withdraw OPPOSITE> **add**
abstraction *noun* **1** =**idea**, concept, generalization, notion, thought **2** =**theory**, formula, hypothesis, theorem
abstruse *adjective* =**obscure**, arcane, complex, deep, enigmatic, esoteric, recondite, unfathomable, vague
absurd *adjective* =**ridiculous**, crazy (*inf*), farcical, foolish, idiotic, illogical, inane, incongruous, irrational, ludicrous, nonsensical, preposterous, senseless, silly, stupid, unreasonable OPPOSITE> **sensible**
absurdity *noun* =**ridiculousness**, farce, folly, foolishness, incongruity, joke, nonsense, silliness, stupidity
abundance *noun* =**plenty**, affluence, bounty, copiousness, exuberance, fullness, profusion OPPOSITE> **lack**
abundant *adjective* =**plentiful**, ample, bountiful, copious, exuberant, filled, full, luxuriant, profuse, rich, teeming OPPOSITE> **scarce**
abuse *verb* **1** =**misuse 2** =**ill-treat**, damage, exploit, harm, hurt, injure, maltreat, take advantage of OPPOSITE> **protect. 3** =**insult**, castigate, curse, defame, disparage, malign, rouse on (*Aust*), scold, vilify OPPOSITE> **respect** ♦*noun* **4** =**ill-treatment**, damage, exploitation, harm, hurt, injury, maltreatment, manhandling

touching.
abuzz *adjective* noisy, busy with activity etc.
abysmal ⊕ *adjective Informal* extremely bad,
awful. **abysmally** *adverb*
abyss ⊕ *noun* very deep hole or chasm.
Ac *Chem* actinium.
AC alternating current.
a/c account.
acacia [a-**kay**-sha] *noun* tree or shrub with
yellow or white flowers.
academy ⊕ *noun, pl* -**mies 1** society to
advance arts or sciences. **2** institution for
training in a particular skill. **3** *Scot* secondary
school. **academic** *adjective* **1** of an academy or
university. **2** of theoretical interest only. ♦ *noun*
3 lecturer or researcher at a university.
academically *adverb* **academician** *noun*
member of an academy.
acanthus *noun* **1** prickly plant. **2** ornamental
carving in the shape of an acanthus leaf.
ACAS Advisory Conciliation and Arbitration
Service.
acc. account.

accede ⊕ *verb* **1** consent or agree (to). **2** take
up (an office or position).
accelerate ⊕ *verb* (cause to) move faster.
acceleration *noun* **accelerator** *noun* pedal in a
motor vehicle to increase speed.
accent ⊕ *noun* **1** distinctive style of
pronunciation of a local, national, or social
group. **2** mark over a letter to show how it is
pronounced. **3** stress on a syllable or musical
note. ♦ *verb* **4** place emphasis on.
accentuate ⊕ *verb* stress, emphasize.
accentuation *noun*
accept ⊕ *verb* **1** receive willingly. **2** agree to.
3 consider to be true. **accepted** *adjective*
generally approved. **acceptance** *noun*
acceptable *adjective* **1** tolerable. **2** satisfactory.
acceptably *adverb* **acceptability** *noun*
access ⊕ *noun* **1** means of or right to
approach or enter. ♦ *verb* **2** obtain (data) from
a computer. **accessible** *adjective* **1** easy to
reach. **2** easy to understand. **accessibility** *noun*
accession *noun* taking up of an office or
position.

———————— THESAURUS ————————

5 =**insults**, blame, castigation, censure,
defamation, derision, disparagement, invective,
reproach, scolding, vilification **6** =**misuse**,
misapplication
abusive *adjective* **2** =**harmful**, brutal, cruel,
destructive, hurtful, injurious, rough OPPOSITE
kind. 3 =**insulting**, censorious, defamatory,
disparaging, libellous, offensive, reproachful,
rude, scathing OPPOSITE **approving**
abysmal *adjective Inf* =**terrible**, appalling,
awful, bad, dire, dreadful
abyss *noun* =**pit**, chasm, crevasse, fissure,
gorge, gulf, void
academic *adjective* **1** =**scholarly**, bookish,
erudite, highbrow, learned, literary, studious **2**
=**hypothetical**, abstract, conjectural,
impractical, notional, speculative, theoretical
♦*noun* **3** =**scholar**, academician, don, fellow,
lecturer, master, professor, tutor
accede *verb* **1** =**agree**, accept, acquiesce,
admit, assent, comply, concede, concur,
consent, endorse, grant **2** =**inherit**, assume,
attain, come to, enter upon, succeed, succeed
to (*as heir*)
accelerate *verb* =**speed up**, advance,
expedite, further, hasten, hurry, quicken
OPPOSITE **slow down**
acceleration *noun* =**speeding up**, hastening,
hurrying, quickening, stepping up (*inf*)
accent *noun* **1** =**pronunciation**, articulation,
brogue, enunciation, inflection, intonation,
modulation, tone **3** =**emphasis**, beat, cadence,

force, pitch, rhythm, stress, timbre ♦*verb* **4**
=**emphasize**, accentuate, stress, underline,
underscore
accentuate *verb* =**emphasize**, accent, draw
attention to, foreground, highlight, stress,
underline, underscore OPPOSITE **minimize**
accept *verb* **1** =**receive**, acquire, gain, get,
obtain, secure, take OPPOSITE **reject. 2** =**agree
to**, approve, concur with, consent to, cooperate
with **3** =**believe**, admit, recognize
acceptable *adjective* **1** =**tolerable** OPPOSITE
unacceptable. 2 =**satisfactory**, adequate,
admissible, all right, fair, moderate, passable,
suitable
acceptance *noun* **1** =**accepting**, acquiring,
gaining, getting, obtaining, receipt, securing,
taking **2** =**agreement**, acknowledgment,
acquiescence, approval, assent, concurrence,
consent, cooperation **3** =**belief**, admission,
recognition
accepted *adjective* =**agreed**, acknowledged,
approved, common, conventional, customary,
established, normal, recognized, traditional
OPPOSITE **unconventional**
access *noun* **1** =**entrance**, admission,
admittance, approach, entry, passage, path,
road
accessibility *noun* **1** =**handiness**, availability,
nearness, possibility, readiness
accessible *adjective* **1** =**handy**, achievable, at
hand, attainable, available, near, nearby,
obtainable, reachable OPPOSITE **unavailable**

A

accessory ❶ *noun, pl* **-ries** **1** supplementary part or object. **2** person involved in a crime although not present when it is committed.
accident ❶ *noun* **1** mishap, usu. one causing injury or death. **2** event happening by chance.
accidental *adjective* **1** happening by chance or unintentionally. ◆ *noun* **2** *Music* symbol indicating that a sharp, flat, or natural note is not a part of the key signature. **accidentally** *adverb* **accident-prone** *adjective* often having accidents.
acclaim ❶ *verb* **1** applaud, praise. ◆ *noun* **2** enthusiastic approval. **acclamation** *noun*
acclimatize ❶ *verb* adapt to a new climate or environment. **acclimatization** *noun*
accolade ❶ *noun* **1** award, honour, or praise. **2** award of knighthood.
accommodate ❶ *verb* **1** provide with lodgings. **2** have room for. **3** oblige, do a favour for. **4** adapt or adjust (to something).
accommodation *noun* house or room for living in. **accommodating** *adjective* obliging.

SPELLING TIP

The Bank of English shows that people usually remember that **accommodation** and **accommodate** have two *c*s, but they often forget that these words have two *m*s as well.

---

accompany ❶ *verb* **-nying, -nied** **1** go along with. **2** occur with. **3** provide a musical accompaniment for. **accompaniment** *noun* **1** something that accompanies. **2** *Music* supporting part that goes with a solo. **accompanist** *noun*
accomplice ❶ *noun* person who helps another to commit a crime.
accomplish ❶ *verb* **1** manage to do. **2** finish. **accomplishment** *noun* **1** completion. **2** personal ability or skill. **accomplished** *adjective* expert, proficient.

——— T H E S A U R U S ———

accessory *noun* **1** = **addition**, accompaniment, adjunct, adornment, appendage, attachment, decoration, extra, supplement, trimming **2** = **accomplice**, abettor, assistant, associate (*in crime*), colleague, confederate, helper, partner
accident *noun* **1** = **misfortune**, calamity, collision, crash, disaster, misadventure, mishap **2** = **chance**, fate, fluke, fortuity, fortune, hazard, luck
accidental *adjective* **1** = **unintentional**, casual, chance, fortuitous, haphazard, inadvertent, incidental, random, unexpected, unforeseen, unlooked-for, unplanned OPPOSITE planned
accidentally *adverb* **1** = **unintentionally**, by accident, by chance, fortuitously, haphazardly, inadvertently, incidentally, randomly, unwittingly OPPOSITE deliberately
acclaim *verb* **1** = **praise**, applaud, approve, celebrate, cheer, clap, commend, exalt, hail, honour, salute ◆ *noun* **2** = **praise**, acclamation, applause, approval, celebration, commendation, honour, kudos OPPOSITE criticism
acclamation *noun* = **praise**, acclaim, adulation, approval, ovation, plaudit, tribute
acclimatization *noun* = **adaptation**, adjustment, habituation, inurement, naturalization
acclimatize *verb* = **adapt**, accommodate, accustom, adjust, get used to, habituate, inure, naturalize
accolade *noun* **1** = **praise**, acclaim, applause, approval, commendation, compliment, ovation,

recognition, tribute
accommodate *verb* **1** = **house**, cater for, entertain, lodge, put up, shelter **3** = **help**, aid, assist, oblige, serve **4** = **adapt**, adjust, comply, conform, fit, harmonize, modify, reconcile, settle
accommodating *adjective* = **helpful**, considerate, cooperative, friendly, hospitable, kind, obliging, polite, unselfish, willing OPPOSITE unhelpful
accommodation *noun* = **housing**, board, digs (*Brit inf*), house, lodging(s), quarters, shelter
accompaniment *noun* **1** = **supplement**, accessory, companion, complement **2** *Music* = **backing music**, backing
accompany *verb* **1** = **go with**, attend, chaperon, conduct, convoy, escort, hold (someone's) hand **2** = **occur with**, belong to, come with, follow, go together with, supplement
accompanying *adjective* **2** = **additional**, associated, attached, attendant, complementary, related, supplementary
accomplice *noun* = **helper**, abettor, accessory, ally, assistant, associate, collaborator, colleague, henchman, partner
accomplish *verb* **1** = **do**, achieve, attain, bring about, carry out, effect, execute, fulfil, manage, perform, produce OPPOSITE fail. **2** = **finish**, complete
accomplished *adjective* = **skilled**, expert, gifted, masterly, polished, practised, proficient,

A

accord ❶ *noun* **1** agreement, harmony. ♦ *verb* **2** fit in with. **3** grant or give. **of one's own accord** voluntarily.

accordance *noun* **in accordance with** conforming to or according to.

according ❶ *adverb* **according to 1** as stated by. **2** in conformity with. **accordingly** *adverb* **1** in an appropriate manner. **2** consequently.

accordion *noun* portable musical instrument played by moving the two sides apart and together, and pressing a keyboard or buttons toproduce the notes. **accordionist** *noun*

accost ❶ *verb* approach and speak to.

account ❶ *noun* **1** report, description. **2** business arrangement making credit available. **3** record of money received and paid out with the resulting balance. **4** person's money held in a bank. **5** importance, value. ♦ *verb* **6** judge to be. **on account of** because of. **accountable** *adjective* responsible to someone or for something. **accountability** *noun* **account for** *verb* **1** explain. **2** make up, constitute.

accounting ❶ *noun* skill or practice of maintaining and auditing business accounts. **accountant** *noun* person who maintains and audits business accounts. **accountancy** *noun*

accoutrements [ak-**koo**-tra-ments] *plural noun* clothing and equipment for a particular activity.

accredited ❶ *adjective* authorized, officially recognized.

accretion [ak-**kree**-shun] *noun* **1** gradual growth. **2** something added.

accrue ❶ *verb* **-cruing, -crued** increase gradually. **accrual** *noun*

accumulate ❶ *verb* gather together in increasing quantity. **accumulation** *noun* **accumulative** *adjective* **accumulator** *noun* rechargeable electric battery.

accurate ❶ *adjective* exact, correct. **accurately** *adverb* **accuracy** *noun*

accursed ❶ [a-**curse**-id] *adjective* **1** under a curse. **2** detestable.

accusative *noun* grammatical case indicating

—————————— T H E S A U R U S ——————————

talented OPPOSITE⟩ **incompetent**

accomplishment *noun* **1** = **completion**, bringing about, carrying out, conclusion, execution, finishing, fulfilment, performance

accord *noun* **1** = **agreement**, conformity, correspondence, harmony, rapport, sympathy, unison OPPOSITE⟩ **conflict** ♦*verb* **2** = **agree**, conform, correspond, fit, harmonize, match, suit, tally

accordingly *adverb* **1** = **appropriately**, correspondingly, fitly, properly, suitably **2** = **consequently**, as a result, ergo, hence, in consequence, so, therefore, thus

according to *adverb* **1** = **as stated by**, as believed by, as maintained by, in the light of, on the authority of, on the report of **2** = **in keeping with**, after, after the manner of, consistent with, in accordance with, in compliance with, in line with, in the manner of

accost *verb* = **approach**, buttonhole, confront, greet, hail

account *noun* **1** = **description**, explanation, narrative, report, statement, story, tale, version **3** = **statement**, balance, bill, books, charge, invoice, reckoning, register, score, tally **5** = **importance**, consequence, honour, note, significance, standing, value, worth ♦*verb* **6** = **consider**, count, estimate, judge, rate, reckon, regard, think, value

accountability *noun* = **responsibility**, answerability, chargeability, culpability, liability

accountable *adjective* = **responsible**, amenable, answerable, charged with, liable,

obligated, obliged

accountant *noun* = **auditor**, bean counter (*inf*), book-keeper

account for *verb* **1** = **explain**, answer for, clarify, clear up, elucidate, illuminate, justify, rationalize

accredited *adjective* = **authorized**, appointed, certified, empowered, endorsed, guaranteed, licensed, official, recognized

accrue *verb* = **increase**, accumulate, amass, arise, be added, build up, collect, enlarge, flow, follow, grow

accumulate *verb* = **collect**, accrue, amass, build up, gather, hoard, increase, pile up, store OPPOSITE⟩ **disperse**

accumulation *noun* = **collection**, build-up, gathering, heap, hoard, increase, mass, pile, stack, stock, stockpile, store

accuracy *noun* = **exactness**, accurateness, authenticity, carefulness, closeness, correctness, fidelity, precision, strictness, truthfulness, veracity OPPOSITE⟩ **inaccuracy**

accurate *adjective* = **exact**, authentic, careful, close, correct, faithful, precise, scrupulous, spot-on (*Brit inf*), strict, true, unerring OPPOSITE⟩ **wrong**

accurately *adverb* = **exactly**, authentically, closely, correctly, faithfully, precisely, scrupulously, strictly, to the letter, truly, unerringly

accursed *adjective* **1** = **cursed**, bewitched, condemned, damned, doomed, hopeless, ill-fated, ill-omened, jinxed, unfortunate, unlucky,

A

the direct object.

accuse ❶ *verb* charge with wrongdoing.
accused *noun Law* person or people accused of
a crime in a court. **accuser** *noun* **accusing**
adjective **accusation** *noun* **accusatory** *adjective*
accustom ❶ *verb* make used to. **accustomed**
adjective **1** usual. **2** used (to). **3** in the habit
(of).

ace ❶ *noun* **1** playing card with one symbol on
it. **2** *Informal* expert. **3** *Tennis* unreturnable
serve. ♦ *adjective* **4** *Informal* excellent.

acerbic [ass-**sir**-bik] *adjective* harsh or bitter.
acerbity *noun*

acetate [**ass**-it-tate] *noun* **1** *Chem* salt or ester
of acetic acid. **2** (also **acetate rayon**) synthetic
textile fibre.

acetic [ass-**see**-tik] *adjective* of or involving
vinegar. **acetic acid** colourless liquid used to
make vinegar.

acetone [**ass**-it-tone] *noun* colourless liquid
used as a solvent.

acetylene [ass-**set**-ill-een] *noun* colourless
flammable gas used in welding metals.

ache ❶ *noun* **1** dull continuous pain. ♦ *verb* **2**
be in or cause continuous dull pain. **aching**
adjective, noun **achingly** *adverb*

achieve ❶ *verb* gain by hard work or ability.
achievement *noun* something accomplished.

achiever *noun*

> **LANGUAGE TIP**
>
> Remember the 'ie'. This word is
> very commonly misspelled.

Achilles heel [ak-**kill**-eez] *noun* small but fatal
weakness.

Achilles tendon *noun* cord connecting the
calf to the heel bone.

achromatic *adjective* **1** colourless. **2** *Music*
with no sharps or flats.

acid ❶ *noun* **1** *Chem* one of a class of
compounds, corrosive and sour when dissolved
in water, that combine with a base to form a
salt. **2** *Slang* LSD. ♦ *adjective* **3** containing acid.
4 sour-tasting. **5** sharp or sour in manner.
acidly *adverb* **acidic** *adjective* **acidify** *verb*
-fying, -fied. acidity *noun* **Acid (House)** *noun*
type of funk-based electronically edited disco
music with hypnotic sound effects. **acid rain**
rain containing acid from atmospheric
pollution. **acid test** conclusive test of value.

acknowledge ❶ *verb* **1** admit, recognize. **2**
indicate recognition of (a person). **3** say one
has received. **acknowledgment**,
acknowledgement *noun*

———— THESAURUS ————

wretched OPPOSITE favoured. **2** = **hateful**,
abominable, despicable, detestable, execrable,
hellish, horrible OPPOSITE **wonderful**

accusation *noun* = **charge**, allegation,
complaint, denunciation, incrimination,
indictment, recrimination

accuse *verb* = **charge**, blame, censure,
denounce, impeach, impute, incriminate, indict
OPPOSITE **absolve**

accustom *verb* = **adapt**, acclimatize, acquaint,
discipline, exercise, familiarize, train

accustomed *adjective* **1** = **usual**, common,
conventional, customary, established, everyday,
expected, habitual, normal, ordinary, regular,
traditional OPPOSITE **odd**. **2** = **used**,
acclimatized, acquainted, adapted, familiar,
familiarized, trained OPPOSITE **unfamiliar**. **3**
= **in the habit of**, given to

ace *noun* **1** = **one**, single point **2** *Inf* = **expert**,
champion, dab hand (*Brit inf*), fundi (*S Afr*),
master, star, virtuoso, wizard (*inf*) ♦ *adjective* **4**
Inf = **excellent**, awesome (*sl*), brilliant, fine,
great, outstanding, superb

ache *noun* **1** = **pain**, hurt, pang, pounding,
soreness, suffering, throbbing ♦ *verb* **2** = **hurt**,
pain, pound, smart, suffer, throb, twinge

achieve *verb* = **attain**, accomplish, acquire,

bring about, carry out, complete, do, execute,
fulfil, gain, get, obtain, perform

achievement *noun* = **accomplishment**, act,
deed, effort, exploit, feat, feather in one's cap,
stroke

acid *adjective* **4** = **sour**, acerbic, acrid,
pungent, tart, vinegary OPPOSITE **sweet**. **5**
= **sharp**, biting, bitter, caustic, cutting, harsh,
trenchant, vitriolic OPPOSITE **kindly**

acidity *noun* **4** = **sourness**, acerbity,
pungency, tartness **5** = **sharpness**, bitterness,
harshness

acknowledge *verb* **1** = **accept**, admit, allow,
concede, confess, declare, grant, own, profess,
recognize, yield OPPOSITE **deny**. **2** = **greet**,
address, hail, notice, recognize, salute OPPOSITE
ignore. **3** = **reply to**, answer, notice, react to,
recognize, respond to, return OPPOSITE **deny**

acknowledged *adjective* **1** = **accepted**,
accredited, approved, confessed, declared,
professed, recognized

acknowledgment *noun* **1** = **acceptance**,
admission, allowing, confession, declaration,
profession, realization, yielding **2** = **greeting**,
addressing, hail, hailing, notice, recognition,
salutation, salute **3** = **appreciation**, answer,
credit, gratitude, reaction, recognition, reply,

acme [**ak**-mee] *noun* highest point of achievement or excellence.

acne [**ak**-nee] *noun* pimply skin disease.

acolyte *noun* **1** follower or attendant. **2** *Christianity* person who assists a priest.

aconite *noun* **1** poisonous plant with hoodlike flowers. **2** poison obtained from this plant.

acorn *noun* nut of the oak tree.

acoustic *adjective* **1** of sound and hearing. **2** (of a musical instrument) not electronically amplified. **acoustics** *noun* **1** science of sounds. ♦ *plural* **2** features of a room or building determining how sound is heard within it. **acoustically** *adverb*

acquaint ❶ *verb* make familiar, inform.

acquainted *adjective* **acquaintance** *noun* **1** person known. **2** personal knowledge.

acquiesce ❶ [ak-wee-**ess**] *verb* agree to what someone wants. **acquiescence** *noun* **acquiescent** *adjective*

acquire ❶ *verb* gain, get. **acquisition** *noun* **1** thing acquired. **2** act of getting. **acquired taste 1** liking for something at first considered unpleasant. **2** the thing liked.

acquisitive ❶ *adjective* eager to gain material possessions. **acquisitiveness** *noun*

acquit ❶ *verb* **-quitting, -quitted 1** pronounce (someone) innocent. **2** behave in a particular way. **acquittal** *noun*

acre *noun* measure of land, 4840 square yards.

acreage [**ake**-er-rij] *noun* land area in acres.

acrid ❶ [**ak**-rid] *adjective* pungent, bitter.

acridity *noun*

acrimonious ❶ *adjective* bitter in speech or manner. **acrimony** *noun*

acrobat *noun* person skilled in gymnastic feats requiring agility and balance. **acrobatic** *adjective* **acrobatics** *plural noun* acrobatic feats.

acronym *noun* word formed from the initial letters of other words, such as NASA.

acrophobia *noun* fear of heights.

acropolis [a-**crop**-pol-liss] *noun* citadel of an ancient Greek city.

across *adverb, preposition* **1** from side to side (of). **2** on or to the other side (of). **across the board** applying equally to all.

acrostic *noun* lines of writing in which the first or last letters of each line spell a word or saying.

acrylic *noun, adjective* (synthetic fibre, paint, etc.) made from acrylic acid. **acrylic acid** strong-smelling corrosive liquid.

act ❶ *noun* **1** thing done. **2** law or decree. **3** section of a play or opera. **4** one of several short performances in a show. **5** pretended attitude. ♦ *verb* **6** do something. **7** behave in a particular way. **8** perform in a play, film, etc. **act of God** unpredictable natural event. **acting** *noun* **1** art of an actor. ♦ *adjective* **2** temporarily performing the duties of. **action** *noun* process of doing something. **active** *adjective* moving, working. **actor, actress** *noun* person who acts in a play, film, etc.

ACT Australian Capital Territory.

——————— THESAURUS ———————

response, return, thanks

acquaint *verb* =**tell**, disclose, divulge, enlighten, familiarize, inform, let (someone) know, notify, reveal

acquaintance *noun* **1** =**associate**, colleague, contact OPPOSITE **good friend**. **2** =**knowledge**, awareness, experience, familiarity, fellowship, relationship, understanding OPPOSITE **ignorance**

acquainted with *adjective* =**familiar with**, alive to, apprised of, *au fait* (with), aware of, conscious of, experienced in, informed of, knowledgeable about, versed in

acquiesce *verb* =**agree**, accede, accept, allow, approve, assent, comply, concur, conform, consent, give in, go along with, submit, yield OPPOSITE **resist**

acquiescence *noun* =**agreement**, acceptance, approval, assent, compliance, conformity, consent, giving in, obedience, submission, yielding

acquire *verb* =**get**, amass, attain, buy, collect, earn, gain, gather, obtain, receive, secure, win

OPPOSITE **lose**

acquisition *noun* **1** =**possession**, buy, gain, prize, property, purchase **2** =**acquiring**, attainment, gaining, procurement

acquisitive *adjective* =**greedy**, avaricious, avid, covetous, grabbing, grasping, predatory, rapacious OPPOSITE **generous**

acquit *verb* **1** =**clear**, discharge, free, liberate, release, vindicate OPPOSITE **sentence**. **2** =**behave**, bear, comport, conduct, perform

acquittal *noun* **1** =**clearance**, absolution, deliverance, discharge, exoneration, liberation, release, relief, vindication

acrid *adjective* =**pungent**, bitter, caustic, harsh, sharp, vitriolic

acrimonious *adjective* =**bitter**, caustic, irascible, petulant, rancorous, spiteful, splenetic, testy OPPOSITE **good-tempered**

acrimony *noun* =**bitterness**, harshness, ill will, irascibility, rancour, virulence OPPOSITE **goodwill**

act *noun* **1** =**deed**, accomplishment, achievement, action, exploit, feat, performance,

A

actinide series *noun* series of 15 radioactive elements with increasing atomic numbers from actinium to lawrencium.

actinium *noun Chem* radioactive chemical element.

action ❶ *noun* **1** process of doing something. **2** thing done. **3** lawsuit. **4** operating mechanism. **5** events forming the plot of a story or play. **6** *Slang* main activity in a place. **7** minor battle. **actionable** *adjective* giving grounds for a lawsuit. **action replay** rerun of an event on a television tape.

active ❶ *adjective* **1** moving, working, e.g. *he remained active in public affairs.* **2** busy, energetic. **3** *Grammar* (of a verb) in a form indicating that the subject is performing the action, e.g. *threw* in *Kim threw the ball.* **actively** *adverb* **activity** *noun* **1** state of being active. **2** *pl* **-ties** leisure pursuit. **activate** *verb* make active. **activation** *noun* **activator** *noun*

activist *noun* person who works energetically to achieve political or social goals. **activism** *noun*

active service military duty in an operational area.

actual ❶ *adjective* existing in reality. **actually** *adverb* really, indeed. **actuality** *noun*

> **LANGUAGE TIP**
>
> Avoid using *actual* or *actually* when it adds nothing to the sense of the sentence.

actuary *noun, pl* **-aries** statistician who calculates insurance risks. **actuarial** *adjective*

actuate *verb* start up (a device).

acuity [ak-**kew**-it-ee] *noun* keenness of vision or thought.

acumen ❶ [ak-**yew**-men] *noun* ability to make good judgments.

acupuncture *noun* medical treatment involving the insertion of needles at various points on the body. **acupuncturist** *noun*

acute ❶ *adjective* **1** severe. **2** keen, shrewd. **3** sharp, sensitive. **4** (of an angle) less than 90°. ◆ *noun* **5** accent ( ) over a letter to indicate the quality or length of its sound, as in café. **acutely** *adverb* **acuteness** *noun*

ad *noun Informal* advertisement.

AD anno Domini.

adage [**ad**-ij] *noun* wise saying, proverb.

adagio [ad-**dahj**-yo] *noun, pl* **-gios**, *adverb Music* (piece to be played) slowly and

——————— T H E S A U R U S ———————

undertaking **2** =**law**, bill, decree, edict, enactment, measure, ordinance, resolution, statute **4** =**performance**, routine, show, sketch, turn **5** =**pretence**, affectation, attitude, front, performance, pose, posture, show ◆*verb* **6** =**do**, carry out, enact, execute, function, operate, perform, take effect, work **8** =**perform**, act out, impersonate, mimic, play, play *or* take the part of, portray, represent

acting *noun* **1** =**performance**, characterization, impersonation, performing, playing, portrayal, stagecraft, theatre ◆*adjective* **2** =**temporary**, interim, pro tem, provisional, substitute, surrogate

action *noun* **1** =**act**, accomplishment, achievement, performance **2** =**deed**, accomplishment, achievement, act, exploit, feat **3** =**lawsuit**, case, litigation, proceeding, prosecution, suit **4** =**movement**, activity, functioning, motion, operation, process, working **7** =**battle**, clash, combat, conflict, contest, encounter, engagement, fight, skirmish, sortie

activate *verb* =**start**, arouse, energize, galvanize, initiate, mobilize, move, rouse, set in motion, stir OPPOSITE> **stop**

active *adjective* **1** =**in operation**, acting, at work, effectual, in action, in force, operative,

working **2** =**busy**, animated, bustling, energetic, hard-working, industrious, involved, lively, occupied, on the go (*inf*), on the move, vigorous OPPOSITE> **slow**

activist *noun* =**militant**, organizer, partisan

activity *noun* **1** =**action**, animation, bustle, exercise, exertion, hustle, labour, motion, movement OPPOSITE> **inertia**. **2** =**pursuit**, hobby, interest, pastime, project, scheme

actor, actress *noun* =**performer**, player, Thespian

actual *adjective* =**definite**, concrete, factual, physical, positive, real, substantial, tangible OPPOSITE> **supposed**

actually *adverb* =**really**, as a matter of fact, indeed, in fact, in point of fact, in reality, in truth, literally, truly

acumen *noun* =**judgment**, astuteness, cleverness, ingenuity, insight, intelligence, perspicacity, shrewdness

acute *adjective* **1** =**sharp**, excruciating, fierce, intense, piercing, powerful, severe, shooting, violent **2** =**perceptive**, astute, clever, insightful, keen, observant, sensitive, sharp, smart OPPOSITE> **slow**

acuteness *noun* **1** =**seriousness**, severity **2** =**perceptiveness**, astuteness, cleverness, discrimination, insight, perspicacity, sharpness gracefully.

adamant ⊕ *adjective* unshakable in determination or purpose. **adamantly** *adverb*

Adam's apple *noun* projecting lump of thyroid cartilage at the front of the throat.

adapt ⊕ *verb* alter for new use or new conditions. **adaptable** *adjective* **adaptability** *noun* **adaptation** *noun* **1** thing produced by adapting something. **2** adapting. **adaptor**, **adapter** *noun* device for connecting several electrical appliances to a single socket.

ADC aide-de-camp.

add ⊕ *verb* **1** combine (numbers or quantities). **2** join (to something). **3** say or write further. **addition** *noun* thing added. **add up** *verb* **1** calculate the sum of (two or more numbers). **2** *Informal* make sense. **add up to** *verb* amount to.

addendum ⊕ *noun, pl* **-da** **1** an addition. **2** appendix to a book etc.

adder *noun* small poisonous snake.

addict ⊕ *noun* **1** person who is unable to stop taking drugs. **2** *Informal* person devoted to something. **addicted** *adjective* **addiction** *noun* **addictive** *adjective* causing addiction.

addition ⊕ *noun* **1** adding. **2** thing added. **in addition** besides, as well. **additional** *adjective*

additionally *adverb* **additive** *noun* something added, esp. to a foodstuff, to improve it or prevent deterioration.

addled *adjective* confused or unable to think clearly.

address ⊕ *noun* **1** place where a person lives. **2** direction on a letter. **3** location. **4** formal public speech. ♦ *verb* **5** mark the destination, as on an envelope. **6** speak to. **7** give attention to (a problem, task, etc.). **addressee** *noun* person addressed.

> **SPELLING TIP**
>
> If you spell **address** wrongly, you probably miss out one *d*. Remember to double the *d* and the *s*.

adduce *verb* mention something as evidence or proof.

adenoids [ad-in-oidz] *plural noun* mass of tissue at the back of the throat. **adenoidal** *adjective* having a nasal voice caused by swollen adenoids.

adept ⊕ *adjective, noun* very skilful (person).

adequate ⊕ *adjective* **1** sufficient, enough. **2**

————————————— THESAURUS —————————————

adamant *adjective* =**determined**, firm, fixed, obdurate, resolute, stubborn, unbending, uncompromising OPPOSITE flexible

adapt *verb* =**adjust**, acclimatize, accommodate, alter, change, conform, convert, modify, remodel, tailor

adaptability *noun* =**flexibility**, changeability, resilience, versatility

adaptable *adjective* =**flexible**, adjustable, changeable, compliant, easy-going, plastic, pliant, resilient, versatile

adaptation *noun* **1** =**conversion**, adjustment, alteration, change, modification, transformation, variation, version **2** =**acclimatization**, familiarization, naturalization

add *verb* **1** =**count up**, add up, compute, reckon, total, tot up OPPOSITE remove. **2** =**include**, adjoin, affix, append, attach, augment, supplement

addendum *noun* **1** =**addition**, appendage, attachment, extension, extra **2** =**appendix**, postscript, supplement

addict *noun* **1** =**junkie**, fiend (*inf*), freak (*inf*) **2** *Inf* =**fan**, adherent, buff (*inf*), devotee, enthusiast, follower, nut (*sl*)

addicted *adjective* **1** =**dependent**, habituated, hooked (*sl*) **2** *Inf* =**devoted**, absorbed, dedicated

addiction *noun* **1** =**dependence**, craving, enslavement, habit **2** *Inf* =**obsession**, dedication, devotion

addition *noun* **1** =**counting up**, adding up, computation, totalling, totting up OPPOSITE reduction. **2** =**extra**, addendum, additive, appendage, appendix, attachment, augmentation, enlargement, extension, gain, increase, increment, supplement OPPOSITE removal ♦ **in addition** =**as well**, additionally, also, besides, into the bargain, moreover, over and above, to boot, too

additional *adjective* =**extra**, added, fresh, further, new, other, spare, supplementary

address *noun* **3** =**location**, abode, dwelling, home, house, residence, situation, whereabouts **4** =**speech**, discourse, dissertation, lecture, oration, sermon, talk ♦*verb* **6** =**speak to**, approach, greet, hail, talk to **7** =**concentrate on**, apply (oneself) to, attend to, devote (oneself) to, engage in, focus on, take care of

add up *verb* **1** =**count up**, add, compute, count, reckon, total, tot up

adept *adjective* =**skilful**, able, accomplished, adroit, expert, practised, proficient, skilled, versed OPPOSITE inept ♦*noun* =**expert**, dab hand (*Brit inf*), fundi (*S Afr*), genius, hotshot (*inf*), master

A

not outstanding. **adequately** *adverb* **adequacy** *noun*

à deux [ah **der**] *adverb French* of or for two people.

adhere ❶ *verb* **1** stick (to). **2** be devoted (to). **adherence** *noun* **adherent** *noun* devotee, follower. **adhesion** *noun* **1** sticking (to). **2** joining together of parts of the body that are normally separate, as after surgery.

adhesive ❶ *noun* **1** substance used to stick things together. ◆ *adjective* **2** able to stick to things.

ad hoc *adjective, adverb Latin* for a particular purpose only.

adieu ❶ [a-**dew**] *interjection* farewell, goodbye.

ad infinitum *adverb Latin* endlessly.

adipose *adjective* of or containing fat.

adj. adjective.

adjacent ❶ *adjective* **1** near or next (to). **2** having a common boundary. **3** *Geom* (of a side in a right-angled triangle) lying between a specified angle and the right angle.

adjective *noun* word that adds information about a noun or pronoun. **adjectival** *adjective*

adjoin ❶ *verb* be next to. **adjoining** *adjective*

adjourn ❶ *verb* **1** close (a court) at the end of a session. **2** postpone temporarily. **3** *Informal* go elsewhere. **adjournment** *noun*

adjudge *verb* declare (to be).

adjudicate ❶ *verb* **1** give a formal decision on (a dispute). **2** judge (a competition). **adjudication** *noun* **adjudicator** *noun*

adjunct *noun* subordinate or additional person or thing.

adjure *verb* **1** command (to do). **2** appeal earnestly. **adjuration** *noun*

adjust ❶ *verb* **1** adapt to new conditions. **2** alter slightly so as to be suitable. **adjustable** *adjective* **adjuster** *noun* **adjustment** *noun*

adjutant [aj-oo-tant] *noun* army officer in charge of routine administration.

ad-lib ❶ *verb* **-libbing, -libbed 1** improvise a speech etc. without preparation. ◆ *noun* **2** improvised remark.

Adm. Admiral(ty).

admin *noun Informal* administration.

administer ❶ *verb* **1** manage (business affairs). **2** organize and put into practice. **3** give (medicine or treatment).

administrate ❶ *verb* manage (an organization). **administration** *noun* **administrative** *adjective* **administrator** *noun*

——————— THESAURUS ———————

adequacy *noun* **1** = **sufficiency 2** = **fairness**, capability, competence, suitability, tolerability

adequate *adjective* **1** = **enough**, satisfactory, sufficient OPPOSITE **lacking**. **2** = **fair**, competent, satisfactory, tolerable, up to scratch (*inf*) OPPOSITE **inadequate**

adhere *verb* **1** = **stick**, attach, cleave, cling, fasten, fix, glue, hold fast, paste

adherent *noun* = **supporter**, admirer, devotee, disciple, fan, follower, upholder OPPOSITE **opponent**

adhesive *noun* **1** = **glue**, cement, gum, paste ◆*adjective* **2** = **sticky**, clinging, cohesive, gluey, glutinous, tenacious

adieu *interjection* = **goodbye**, farewell

adjacent *adjective* **1** = **next**, adjoining, beside, bordering, close, near, neighbouring, next door, touching OPPOSITE **separated**

adjoin *verb* = **connect**, border, join, link, touch

adjoining *adjective* = **connecting**, abutting, adjacent, bordering, neighbouring, next door, touching

adjourn *verb* **2** = **postpone**, defer, delay, discontinue, interrupt, put off, suspend OPPOSITE **continue**

adjournment *noun* **2** = **postponement**, delay, discontinuation, interruption, putting off, suspension

adjudicate *verb* **1** = **judge**, adjudge, arbitrate, decide, determine, mediate, referee, settle, umpire

adjudication *noun* **1** = **judgment**, arbitration, conclusion, decision, finding, pronouncement, ruling, settlement, verdict

adjust *verb* **1** = **adapt**, accustom **2** = **alter**, make conform, modify

adjustable *adjective* **2** = **alterable**, adaptable, flexible, malleable, modifiable, movable

adjustment *noun* **1** = **acclimatization**, orientation, settling in **2** = **alteration**, adaptation, modification, redress, regulation, tuning

ad-lib *verb* **1** = **improvise**, busk, extemporize, make up, speak off the cuff, wing it (*inf*)

administer *verb* **1, 2** = **manage**, conduct, control, direct, govern, handle, oversee, run, supervise **3** = **give**, apply, dispense, impose, mete out, perform, provide

administration *noun* = **management**, application, conduct, control, direction, government, running, supervision

administrative *adjective* = **managerial**, directorial, executive, governmental, organizational, regulatory, supervisory

administrator *noun* = **manager**, bureaucrat, executive, official, organizer, supervisor

admirable *adjective* = **excellent**, commendable, exquisite, fine, laudable,

A

admiral *noun* highest naval rank. **Admiralty** *noun* former government department in charge of the Royal Navy.

admire ❶ *verb* regard with esteem and approval. **admirable** [ad-mer-a-bl] *adjective* **admirably** *adverb* **admiration** *noun* **admirer** *noun* **admiring** *adjective* **admiringly** *adverb*

admissible ❶ *adjective* allowed to be brought in as evidence in court. **admissibility** *noun*

admission ❶ *noun* 1 permission to enter. 2 permission to join (an organization). 3 entrance fee. 4 confession.

admit ❶ *verb* -mitting, -mitted 1 confess, acknowledge. 2 concede the truth of. 3 allow in. **admission** *noun* permission to enter. **admittance** *noun* permission to enter. **admittedly** *adverb* it must be agreed.

admixture *noun* 1 mixture. 2 ingredient.

admonish ❶ *verb* reprove sternly. **admonition** *noun*

ad nauseam [ad naw-zee-am] *adverb Latin* to a boring or sickening extent.

ado *noun* fuss, trouble.

adobe [ad-oh-bee] *noun* sun-dried brick.

adolescence ❶ *noun* period between puberty and adulthood. **adolescent** *noun, adjective* (person) between puberty and adulthood.

Adonis *noun* handsome young man.

adopt ❶ *verb* 1 take (someone else's child) as one's own. 2 take up (a plan or principle). **adoption** *noun* **adoptive** *adjective* related by adoption.

adore ❶ *verb* 1 love intensely. 2 worship. 3 *Informal* like very much, e.g. *I adore being in the country.* **adorable** *adjective* **adoration** *noun* **adoring** *adjective* **adoringly** *adverb*

adorn ❶ *verb* decorate, embellish. **adornment** *noun*

ADP automatic data processing.

adrenal [ad-reen-al] *adjective* near the kidneys. **adrenal glands** glands covering the top of the kidneys.

adrenalin, adrenaline *noun* hormone secreted by the adrenal glands in response to stress.

adrift ❶ *adjective, adverb* 1 drifting. 2 without a clear purpose.

adroit ❶ *adjective* quick and skilful. **adroitly** *adverb* **adroitness** *noun*

adsorb *verb* (of a gas or vapour) condense

—————————— THESAURUS ——————————

praiseworthy, wonderful, worthy OPPOSITE deplorable

admiration *noun* =**regard**, amazement, appreciation, approval, esteem, praise, respect, wonder

admire *verb* =**respect**, appreciate, approve, esteem, look up to, praise, prize, think highly of, value OPPOSITE despise

admirer *noun* =**fan**, devotee, disciple, enthusiast, follower, partisan, supporter

admissible *adjective* =**permissible**, acceptable, allowable, passable, tolerable OPPOSITE inadmissible

admission *noun* 1 =**entrance**, access, admittance, entry 2 =**acceptance**, entrée, entry, initiation, introduction 4 =**confession**, acknowledgment, allowance, declaration, disclosure, divulgence, revelation

admit *verb* 1 =**confess**, acknowledge, declare, disclose, divulge, own, reveal 2 =**allow**, agree, grant, let, permit, recognize OPPOSITE deny. 3 =**let in**, accept, allow, give access, initiate, introduce, receive, take in OPPOSITE exclude

admonish *verb* =**reprimand**, berate, chide, rebuke, rouse on (*Aust*), scold, slap on the wrist, tell off (*inf*) OPPOSITE praise

adolescence *noun* =**youth**, boyhood, childishness, girlhood, immaturity, minority, teens, youthfulness

adolescent *noun* =**youth**, juvenile, minor, teenager, youngster ◆*adjective* =**young**, boyish, girlish, immature, juvenile, puerile, teenage, youthful

adopt *verb* 1 =**foster**, take in OPPOSITE give up. 2 =**choose**, assume, espouse, follow, maintain, take up OPPOSITE reject

adoption *noun* 1 =**fostering**, adopting, taking in 2 =**choice**, appropriation, assumption, embracing, endorsement, espousal, selection, taking up

adorable *adjective* 1, 3 =**lovable**, appealing, attractive, charming, cute, dear, delightful, fetching, pleasing, sweet OPPOSITE hateful

adore *verb* 1 =**love**, admire, cherish, dote on, esteem, honour OPPOSITE hate. 2 =**worship**, exalt, glorify, idolize, revere

adoring *adjective* 1 =**loving**, admiring, affectionate, devoted, doting, fond OPPOSITE hating

adorn *verb* =**decorate**, array, embellish, festoon

adornment *noun* =**decoration**, accessory, embellishment, festoon, frill, frippery, ornament, supplement, trimming

adrift *adjective* 1 =**drifting**, afloat, unanchored, unmoored 2 =**aimless**, directionless, goalless, purposeless

adroit *adjective* =**skilful**, adept, clever, deft, dexterous, expert, masterful, neat, proficient, skilled OPPOSITE unskilful

and form a thin film on a surface. **adsorbent** *adjective* **adsorption** *noun*
adulation ❂ *noun* uncritical admiration.
adult ❂ *adjective* **1** fully grown, mature. ◆ *noun* **2** adult person or animal. **adulthood** *noun*
adulterate *verb* spoil something by adding inferior material. **adulteration** *noun*
adultery *noun, pl* **-teries** sexual unfaithfulness of a husband or wife. **adulterer, adulteress** *noun* **adulterous** *adjective*
adv. adverb.
advance ❂ *verb* **1** go or bring forward. **2** further (a cause). **3** propose (an idea). **4** lend (a sum of money). ◆ *noun* **5** forward movement. **6** improvement. **7** loan. ◆ *plural* **8** approaches to a person with the hope of starting a romantic or sexual relationship. ◆ *adjective* **9** done or happening before an event. **in advance** ahead.
advanced *adjective* **1** at a late stage in development. **2** not elementary. **advancement** *noun* promotion.
advantage ❂ *noun* **1** more favourable position or state. **2** benefit or profit. **3** *Tennis* point scored after deuce. **take advantage of 1** use (a person) unfairly. **2** use (an opportunity).

advantageous *adjective* **advantageously** *adverb* **advantaged** *adjective* in a superior social or financial position.
advent *noun* **1** arrival. **2** (**A-**) season of four weeks before Christmas. **Adventist** *noun* member of a Christian sect that believes in the imminent return of Christ.
adventitious *adjective* added or appearing accidentally.
adventure ❂ *noun* exciting and risky undertaking or exploit. **adventurer, adventuress** *noun* **1** person who unscrupulously seeks money or power. **2** person who seeks adventures. **adventurous** *adjective* **adventurously** *adverb*
adverb *noun* word that adds information about a verb, adjective, or other adverb. **adverbial** *adjective*
adversary ❂ [ad-verse-er-ree] *noun, pl* **-saries** opponent or enemy.
adverse ❂ *adjective* **1** unfavourable. **2** antagonistic or hostile. **adversely** *adverb*
adversity *noun* very difficult or hard circumstances.
advert ❂ *noun Informal* advertisement.

———————— THESAURUS ————————

adulation *noun* =**worship**, fawning, fulsome praise, servile flattery, sycophancy OPPOSITE ridicule
adult *adjective* **1** =**fully grown**, full grown, fully developed, grown-up, mature, of age, ripe ◆*noun* **2** =**grown-up**, grown or grown-up person (man or woman), person of mature age
advance *verb* **1** =**progress**, accelerate, bring forward, come forward, go on, hasten, make inroads, proceed, speed OPPOSITE retreat. **2** =**benefit**, further, improve, prosper **3** =**suggest**, offer, present, proffer, put forward, submit OPPOSITE withhold. **4** =**lend**, pay beforehand, supply on credit OPPOSITE defer payment ◆*noun* **5** =**progress**, advancement, development, forward movement, headway, inroads, onward movement **6** =**improvement**, breakthrough, gain, growth, progress, promotion, step **7** =**loan**, credit, deposit, down payment, prepayment, retainer ◆*plural* **8** =**overtures**, approach, approaches, moves, proposals, proposition ◆*adjective* **9** =**prior**, beforehand, early, forward, in front **in advance** =**beforehand**, ahead, earlier, previously
advanced *adjective* =**foremost**, ahead, avant-garde, forward, higher, leading, progressive OPPOSITE backward
advancement *noun* =**promotion**, betterment, gain, improvement, preferment, progress, rise

advantage *noun* **1** =**superiority**, ascendancy, dominance, lead, precedence, sway **2** =**benefit**, good, help, profit OPPOSITE disadvantage
advantageous *adjective* **1** =**superior**, dominant, dominating, favourable **2** =**beneficial**, convenient, expedient, helpful, of service, profitable, useful, valuable, worthwhile OPPOSITE useless
adventure *noun* =**escapade**, enterprise, experience, exploit, incident, occurrence, undertaking, venture
adventurer *noun* **1** =**mercenary**, charlatan, fortune-hunter, gambler, opportunist, rogue, speculator **2** =**hero**, daredevil, heroine, knight-errant, traveller, voyager
adventurous *adjective* **2** =**daring**, bold, daredevil, enterprising, intrepid, reckless OPPOSITE cautious
adversary *noun* =**opponent**, antagonist, competitor, contestant, enemy, foe, rival OPPOSITE ally
adverse *adjective* **1** =**unfavourable**, contrary, detrimental, inopportune, negative OPPOSITE favourable. **2** =**hostile**, antagonistic, opposing
adversity *noun* =**hardship**, affliction, bad luck, disaster, distress, hard times, misfortune, reverse, trouble
advert *noun Inf* =**advertisement**, ad (*inf*), announcement, blurb, commercial, notice, plug (*inf*), poster

A

advertise ⊕ *verb* **1** present or praise (goods or services) to the public in order to encourage sales. **2** make (a vacancy, event, etc.) known publicly. **advertisement** *noun* public announcement to sell goods or publicize an event. **advertiser** *noun* **advertising** *adjective, noun*

SPELLING TIP

Some verbs can be spelt ending in either *-ise* or *-ize*, but **advertise** and **advise** always have an *s*.

---

advice ⊕ *noun* recommendation as to what to do. **advise** *verb* **1** offer advice to. **2** notify (someone). **adviser, advisor** *noun* **advisable** *adjective* prudent, sensible. **advisability** *noun* **advisory** *adjective* giving advice. **advised** *adjective* considered, thought-out, e.g. *ill-advised*. **advisedly** [ad-**vize**-id-lee] *adverb* deliberately.

SPELLING TIP

The Bank of English shows that people sometimes write **advise** with an *s* where they ought to write **advice** with a *c*. The verb is **advise** and the noun is **advice**.

---

advocaat *noun* liqueur with a raw egg base.
advocate ⊕ *verb* **1** propose or recommend. ♦ *noun* **2** person who publicly supports a cause. **3** *Scot* barrister. **advocacy** *noun*
adze *noun* tool with an arched blade at right angles to the handle.

aegis [**ee**-jiss] *noun* sponsorship, protection.
aeolian harp [ee-**oh**-lee-an] *noun* musical instrument that produces sounds when the wind passes over its strings.
aeon [**ee**-on] *noun* immeasurably long period of time.
aerate *verb* put gas into (a liquid), as when making a fizzy drink. **aeration** *noun*
aerial *adjective* **1** in, from, or operating in the air. **2** relating to aircraft. ♦ *noun* **3** metal pole, wire, etc., for receiving or transmitting radio or TV signals.
aero- *combining form* air or aircraft, e.g. *aeronautics*.
aerobatics *plural noun* stunt flying. **aerobatic** *adjective*
aerobics *noun* exercises designed to increase the amount of oxygen in the blood. **aerobic** *adjective* **aerobically** *adverb*
aerodrome *noun* small airport.
aerodynamics *noun* study of how air flows around moving solid objects. **aerodynamic** *adjective*
aerofoil *noun* part of an aircraft, such as the wing, designed to give lift.
aerogram *noun* airmail letter on a single sheet of paper that seals to form an envelope.
aeronautics *noun* study or practice of aircraft flight. **aeronautical** *adjective*
aeroplane *noun* powered flying vehicle with fixed wings.
aerosol *noun* pressurized can from which a substance can be dispensed as a fine spray.

LANGUAGE TIP

Be careful not to confuse the spelling 'aer-' with 'air-'.

——————————————— THESAURUS ———————————————

advertise *verb* **1** = **publicize**, plug (*inf*), promote, tout **2** = **announce**, make known
advertisement *noun* = **advert** (*inf*), ad (*inf*), announcement, blurb, commercial, notice, plug (*inf*), poster
advice *noun* = **guidance**, counsel, help, opinion, recommendation, suggestion
advisability *noun* = **wisdom**, appropriateness, aptness, desirability, expediency, fitness, propriety, prudence, suitability
advisable *adjective* = **wise**, appropriate, desirable, expedient, fitting, politic, prudent, recommended, seemly, sensible OPPOSITE> **unwise**
advise *verb* **1** = **recommend**, admonish, caution, commend, counsel, prescribe, suggest,

urge **2** = **notify**, acquaint, apprise, inform, let (someone) know, make known, report, tell, warn
adviser *noun* = **guide**, aide, confidant, consultant, counsellor, guru, helper, mentor, right-hand man
advisory *adjective* = **advising**, consultative, counselling, helping, recommending
advocate *verb* **1** = **recommend**, advise, argue for, campaign for, champion, commend, encourage, promote, propose, support, uphold OPPOSITE> **oppose** ♦*noun* **2** = **supporter**, campaigner, champion, counsellor, defender, promoter, proponent, spokesman, upholder **3** *Scot* = **lawyer**, attorney, barrister, counsel, solicitor

aerospace noun 1 earth's atmosphere and space beyond. ◆ adjective 2 of rockets or space vehicles, e.g. the aerospace industry.
aesthetic [iss-**thet**-ik] adjective relating to the appreciation of art and beauty. **aesthetics** noun study of art, beauty, and good taste. **aesthetically** adverb **aesthete** [**eess**-theet] noun person who has or affects an extravagant love of art. **aestheticism** noun
aether noun same as ETHER.
aetiology [ee-tee-**ol**-a-jee] noun same as ETIOLOGY.
afar adverb **from afar** from or at a great distance.
affable ❶ adjective friendly and easy to talk to. **affably** adverb **affability** noun
affair ❶ noun 1 event or happening. 2 sexual relationship outside marriage. 3 thing to be done or attended to. ◆ plural 4 personal or business interests. 5 matters of public interest.
affect¹ ❶ verb 1 act on, influence. 2 move (someone) emotionally.

> **LANGUAGE TIP**
>
> Do not confuse affect meaning 'influence' with effect meaning 'accomplish'.

affect² ❶ verb 1 put on a show of. 2 wear or use by preference. **affectation** noun attitude or manner put on to impress. **affected** adjective 1 displaying affectation. 2 pretended. **affection** noun fondness or love.
affection ❶ noun fondness or love.
affectionate adjective loving. **affectionately** adverb
affianced [af-**fie**-anst] adjective Old-fashioned engaged to be married.
affidavit [af-fid-**dave**-it] noun written statement made on oath.
affiliate ❶ verb (of a group) link up with a larger group. **affiliation** noun
affinity ❶ noun, pl -**ties** 1 close connection or liking. 2 close resemblance. 3 chemical attraction.
affirm ❶ verb 1 declare to be true. 2 uphold or confirm (an idea or belief). **affirmation** noun
affirmative noun, adjective (word or phrase) indicating agreement.
affix verb 1 attach or fasten. ◆ noun 2 word or syllable added to a word to change its meaning.
afflict ❶ verb give pain or grief to. **affliction** noun
affluent ❶ adjective having plenty of money.

———— THESAURUS ————

affable adjective =**friendly**, amiable, amicable, approachable, congenial, cordial, courteous, genial, pleasant, sociable, urbane OPPOSITE **unfriendly**
affair noun 1 =**event**, activity, business, episode, happening, incident, matter, occurrence 2 =**relationship**, amour, intrigue, liaison, romance
affect¹ verb 1 =**influence**, act on, alter, bear upon, change, concern, impinge upon, relate to 2 =**move**, disturb, overcome, perturb, stir, touch, upset
affect² verb 1 =**put on**, adopt, aspire to, assume, contrive, feign, imitate, pretend, simulate
affectation noun =**pretence**, act, artificiality, assumed manners, facade, insincerity, pose, pretentiousness, show
affected adjective 1 =**mannered**, contrived, unnatural OPPOSITE **natural**. 2 =**pretended**, artificial, feigned, insincere, phoney or phony (inf), put-on OPPOSITE **genuine**
affection noun =**fondness**, attachment, care, feeling, goodwill, kindness, liking, love, tenderness, warmth
affectionate adjective =**fond**, attached, caring, devoted, doting, friendly, kind, loving, tender, warm-hearted OPPOSITE **cool**
affiliate verb =**join**, ally, amalgamate, associate, band together, combine, incorporate, link, unite
affinity noun 1 =**attraction**, fondness, inclination, leaning, liking, partiality, rapport, sympathy OPPOSITE **hostility**. 2 =**similarity**, analogy, closeness, connection, correspondence, kinship, likeness, relationship, resemblance OPPOSITE **difference**
affirm verb 1 =**declare**, assert, maintain, state, swear OPPOSITE **reject**. 2 =**confirm**, certify, pronounce, testify OPPOSITE **deny**
affirmation noun 1 =**declaration**, assertion, oath, statement 2 =**confirmation**, certification, pronouncement, testimony
affirmative adjective =**agreeing**, approving, assenting, concurring, confirming, consenting, corroborative, favourable, positive OPPOSITE **negative**
afflict verb =**torment**, distress, grieve, harass, hurt, oppress, pain, plague, trouble
affliction noun =**suffering**, adversity, curse, disease, hardship, misfortune, ordeal, plague, scourge, torment, trial, trouble, woe
affluence noun =**wealth**, abundance, fortune, opulence, plenty, prosperity, riches

A

affluence *noun* wealth.
afford ⓘ *verb* **1** have enough money to buy. **2** be able to spare (the time etc.). **3** give or supply. **affordable** *adjective*
afforest *verb* plant trees on. **afforestation** *noun*
affray *noun* noisy fight, brawl.
affront ⓘ *verb, noun* insult.
Afghan *noun* **1** language of Afghanistan. **2** person from Afghanistan. ◆ *adjective* **3** of Afghanistan or its language. **Afghan hound** large slim dog with long silky hair.
aficionado [af-fish-yo-**nah**-do] *noun, pl* **-dos** enthusiastic fan of something or someone.
afield *adverb* **far afield** far away.
aflame ⓘ *adjective* burning.
afloat *adverb, adjective* **1** floating. **2** at sea.
afoot ⓘ *adverb, adjective* happening, in operation.
aforesaid, aforementioned *adjective* referred to previously.
aforethought *adjective* premeditated, e.g. *with malice aforethought.*
a fortiori [eh for-tee-**or**-rye] *adverb* for a stronger reason.
Afr. Africa(n)
afraid ⓘ *adjective* **1** frightened. **2** regretful.
afresh ⓘ *adverb* again, anew.
African *adjective* **1** of Africa. ◆ *noun* **2** person from Africa. **African-American** *noun* **1** American of African descent. ◆ *adjective* **2** of African-Americans. **African violet** house plant with pink or purple flowers and hairy leaves.
Afrikaans *noun* language used in S Africa, related to Dutch.
Afrikaner *noun* White S African whose mother

tongue is Afrikaans.
Afro- *combining form* African, e.g. *Afro-Caribbean.*
aft *adverb* at or towards the rear of a ship or aircraft.
after ⓘ *preposition* **1** following in time or place. **2** in pursuit of. **3** in imitation of. ◆ *conjunction* **4** at a later time than. ◆ *adverb* **5** at a later time. **afters** *plural noun Informal* dessert.
afterbirth *noun* material expelled from the womb after childbirth.
aftercare *noun* **1** support given to a person discharged from a hospital or prison. **2** regular care required to keep something in good condition.
aftereffect *noun* result occurring some time after its cause.
afterglow *noun* **1** glow left after a source of light has gone. **2** pleasant feeling left after an enjoyable experience.
afterlife *noun* life after death.
aftermath ⓘ *noun* results of an event considered together.
afternoon *noun* time between noon and evening.
afterpains *plural noun* pains caused by the contraction of the womb after childbirth.
aftershave *noun* lotion applied to the face after shaving.
afterthought *noun* **1** idea occurring later. **2** something added later.
afterwards, afterward *adverb* later.
Ag *Chem* silver.
again ⓘ *adverb* **1** once more. **2** in addition.
against ⓘ *preposition* **1** in opposition or contrast to. **2** in contact with. **3** as a protection from.

———————————— THESAURUS ————————————

affluent *adjective* =**wealthy**, loaded (*sl*), moneyed, opulent, prosperous, rich, well-heeled (*inf*), well-off, well-to-do OPPOSITE **poor**
afford *verb* **2** =**spare**, bear, manage, stand, sustain **3** =**give**, offer, produce, provide, render, supply, yield
affordable *adjective* **1** =**inexpensive**, cheap, economical, low-cost, moderate, modest, reasonable OPPOSITE **expensive**
affront *verb* =**offend**, anger, annoy, displease, insult, outrage, provoke, slight ◆*noun* =**insult**, offence, outrage, provocation, slap in the face (*inf*), slight, slur
aflame *adjective* =**burning**, ablaze, alight, blazing, fiery, flaming, lit, on fire
afoot *adjective* =**going on**, abroad, brewing, current, happening, in preparation, in progress, on the go (*inf*), up (*inf*)

afraid *adjective* **1** =**scared**, apprehensive, cowardly, faint-hearted, fearful, frightened, nervous OPPOSITE **bold**. **2** =**sorry**, regretful, unhappy OPPOSITE **happy**
afresh *adverb* =**again**, anew, newly, once again, once more, over again
after *adverb* **5** =**following**, afterwards, behind, below, later, subsequently, succeeding, thereafter OPPOSITE **before**
aftermath *noun* =**effects**, aftereffects, consequences, end result, outcome, results, sequel, upshot, wake
again *adverb* **1** =**once more**, afresh, anew, another time **2** =**also**, besides, furthermore, in addition, moreover
against *preposition* **1** =**opposed to**, anti (*inf*), averse to, hostile to, in defiance of, in opposition to, resisting, versus **2** =**beside**,

agape *adjective* **1** (of the mouth) wide open. **2** (of a person) very surprised.

agaric *noun* fungus with gills on the underside of the cap, such as a mushroom.

agate [ag-git] *noun* semiprecious form of quartz with striped colouring.

agave [a-**gave**-vee] *noun* tropical American plant with tall flower stalks and thick leaves.

age ❶ *noun* **1** length of time a person or thing has existed. **2** time of life. **3** latter part of human life. **4** period of history. **5** long time. ◆ *verb* **ageing** *or* **aging, aged 6** make or grow old. **aged** *adjective* **1** [ay-jid] old. **2** [rhymes with **raged**] being at the age of. **ageing, aging** *noun, adjective* **ageless** *adjective* **1** apparently never growing old. **2** seeming to have existed for ever. **age-old** *adjective* very old.

agency ❶ *noun, pl* **-cies 1** organization providing a service. **2** business or function of an agent. **3** *Old-fashioned* power or action by which something happens.

agenda ❶ *noun* list of things to be dealt with, esp. at a meeting.

agent ❶ *noun* **1** person acting on behalf of another. **2** person or thing producing an effect. **agency** *noun* organization providing a service. **agent provocateur** [azh-on prov-vok-at-**tur**] *noun, pl* **agents provocateurs** [azh-on prov-vok-at-**tur**] person employed by the authorities to tempt people to commit illegal acts and so be discredited or punished.

agglomeration *noun* confused mass or cluster.

aggrandize *verb* make greater in size, power, or rank. **aggrandizement** *noun*

aggravate ❶ *verb* **1** make worse. **2** *Informal* annoy. **aggravating** *adjective* **aggravation** *noun*

SPELLING TIP

The biggest problem with spelling **aggravate** is not how many *g*s there are at the beginning, but that there is an *a* (not an *e*) in the middle.

---

aggregate ❶ *noun* **1** total. **2** rock consisting of a mixture of minerals. **3** sand or gravel used to make concrete. ◆ *adjective* **4** gathered into a mass. **5** total or final. ◆ *verb* **6** combine into a whole. **aggregation** *noun*

aggression ❶ *noun* **1** hostile behaviour. **2** unprovoked attack. **aggressive** *adjective* **1** showing aggression. **2** forceful. **aggressively** *adverb* **aggressiveness** *noun* **aggressor** *noun*

SPELLING TIP

The Bank of English shows that **aggressive** is quite a common word and that *agressive* is a common way of misspelling it.

---

aggrieved ❶ *adjective* upset and angry.

---

abutting, facing, in contact with, on, opposite to, touching, upon **3 = in preparation for**, in anticipation of, in expectation of, in provision for

age 1 = lifetime, generation *noun* **3 = old age**, advancing years, decline (*of life*), majority, maturity, senescence, senility, seniority OPPOSITE **youth. 4 = time**, date, day(s), duration, epoch, era, period, span

aged *adjective* **1 = old**, ancient, antiquated, antique, elderly, getting on, grey OPPOSITE **young**

agency *noun* **1 = business**, bureau, department, office, organization **3** *Old-fashioned* **= medium**, activity, means, mechanism

agenda *noun* **= list**, calendar, diary, plan, programme, schedule, timetable

agent *noun* **1 = representative**, envoy, go-between, negotiator, rep (*inf*), surrogate **2 = force**, agency, cause, instrument, means, power, vehicle

aggravate *verb* **1 = make worse**, exacerbate, exaggerate, increase, inflame, intensify, magnify, worsen OPPOSITE **ease. 2** *Inf* **= annoy**, bother, get on one's nerves (*inf*), irritate, nettle, provoke OPPOSITE **please**

aggravation *noun* **1 = worsening**, exacerbation, exaggeration, heightening, increase, inflaming, intensification, magnification **2** *Inf* **= annoyance**, exasperation, gall, grief (*inf*), hassle (*inf*), irritation, provocation

aggregate *noun* **1 = total**, accumulation, amount, body, bulk, collection, combination, mass, pile, sum, whole ◆*adjective* **4 = accumulated**, collected, combined, composite, mixed **5 = total**, cumulative ◆*verb* **6 = combine**, accumulate, amass, assemble, collect, heap, mix, pile

aggression *noun* **1 = hostility**, antagonism, belligerence, destructiveness, pugnacity **2 = attack**, assault, injury, invasion, offensive, onslaught, raid

aggressive *adjective* **1 = hostile**, belligerent,

aggro *noun Slang* aggressive behaviour.
aghast ❶ *adjective* overcome with amazement or horror.
agile ❶ *adjective* **1** nimble, quick-moving. **2** mentally quick. **agilely** *adverb* **agility** *noun*
agin *preposition Dialect* against, opposed to.
agitate ❶ *verb* **1** disturb or excite. **2** stir or shake (a liquid). **3** stir up public opinion for or against something. **agitated** *adjective* anxious or worried. **agitatedly** *adverb* **agitation** *noun* **agitator** *noun*
agitprop *noun* political agitation and propaganda.
aglitter *adjective* sparkling, glittering.
aglow *adjective* glowing.
AGM annual general meeting.
agnostic *noun* **1** person who believes that it is impossible to know whether God exists. ♦ *adjective* **2** of agnostics. **agnosticism** *noun*
ago *adverb* in the past.
agog ❶ *adjective* eager or curious.
agony ❶ *noun, pl* **-nies** extreme physical or mental pain. **agonize** *verb* **1** worry greatly. **2** (cause to) suffer agony. **agonizing** *adjective* **agonizingly** *adverb* **agony aunt** journalist who gives advice in an agony column. **agony column** newspaper or magazine feature offering advice on personal problems.
agoraphobia *noun* fear of open spaces. **agoraphobic** *noun, adjective*
agrarian *adjective* of land or agriculture.
agree ❶ *verb* **agreeing, agreed 1** be of the same opinion. **2** consent. **3** reach a joint decision. **4** be consistent. **5** (foll. by *with*) be suitable to (one's health or digestion).
agreeable *adjective* **1** pleasant and enjoyable. **2** prepared to consent. **agreeably** *adverb*
agreement *noun* **1** agreeing. **2** contract.
agriculture ❶ *noun* raising of crops and livestock. **agricultural** *adjective* **agriculturalist** *noun*
agrimony *noun* yellow-flowered plant with bitter-tasting fruits.
agronomy [ag-**ron**-om-mee] *noun* science of soil management and crop production. **agronomist** *noun*
aground ❶ *adverb* onto the bottom of shallow water.
ague [**aig**-yew] *noun* periodic fever with shivering.

——————————— THESAURUS ———————————

destructive, offensive, pugnacious, quarrelsome OPPOSITE **friendly**. **2 = forceful**, assertive, bold, dynamic, energetic, enterprising, militant, pushy (*inf*), vigorous OPPOSITE **retiring**
aggressor *noun* **= attacker**, assailant, assaulter, invader
aggrieved *adjective* **= hurt**, afflicted, distressed, disturbed, harmed, injured, unhappy, wronged
aghast *adjective* **= horrified**, amazed, appalled, astonished, astounded, awestruck, confounded, shocked, startled, stunned
agile *adjective* **1 = nimble**, active, brisk, lithe, quick, sprightly, spry, supple, swift OPPOSITE **slow**. **2 = acute**, alert, bright (*inf*), clever, lively, quick-witted, sharp
agility *noun* **1 = nimbleness**, litheness, liveliness, quickness, suppleness, swiftness
agitate *verb* **1 = upset**, disconcert, distract, excite, fluster, perturb, trouble, unnerve, worry OPPOSITE **calm**. **2 = stir**, beat, convulse, disturb, rouse, shake, toss
agitation *noun* **1 = turmoil**, clamour, commotion, confusion, disturbance, excitement, ferment, trouble, upheaval **2 = turbulence**, convulsion, disturbance, shaking, stirring, tossing
agitator *noun* **3 = troublemaker**, agent provocateur, firebrand, instigator, rabble-rouser, revolutionary, stirrer (*inf*)

agog *adjective* **= eager**, avid, curious, enthralled, enthusiastic, excited, expectant, impatient, in suspense
agonize *verb* **1 = suffer**, be distressed, be in agony, be in anguish, go through the mill, labour, strain, struggle, worry
agony *noun* **= suffering**, anguish, distress, misery, pain, throes, torment, torture
agree *verb* **1 = concur**, assent, be of the same opinion, comply, consent, see eye to eye OPPOSITE **deny**. **4 = match**, coincide, conform, correspond, tally
agreeable *adjective* **1 = pleasant**, delightful, enjoyable, gratifying, likable *or* likeable, pleasing, satisfying, to one's taste OPPOSITE **unpleasant**. **2 = consenting**, amenable, approving, complying, concurring, in accord, onside (*inf*), sympathetic, well-disposed, willing
agreement *noun* **1 = concurrence**, agreeing, assent, compliance, concord, consent, harmony, union, unison OPPOSITE **disagreement**. **2 = contract**, arrangement, bargain, covenant, deal (*inf*), pact, settlement, treaty, understanding
agricultural *adjective* **= farming**, agrarian, country, rural, rustic
agriculture *noun* **= farming**, cultivation, culture, husbandry, tillage
aground *adverb* **= beached**, ashore, foundered, grounded, high and dry, on the

A

ah *interjection* exclamation of pleasure, pain, etc.

aha *interjection* exclamation of triumph, surprise, etc.

ahead ❶ *adverb* **1** in front. **2** forwards.

ahem *interjection* clearing of the throat to attract attention etc.

ahoy *interjection* shout used at sea to attract attention.

AI 1 artificial insemination. **2** artificial intelligence.

aid ❶ *verb, noun* (give) assistance or support.

AID formerly, artificial insemination by donor: see DI.

aide ❶ *noun* assistant.

aide-de-camp [aid-de-**kom**] *noun, pl* **aides-de-camp** [aid-de-**kom**] military officer serving as personal assistant to a senior.

AIDS acquired immunodeficiency syndrome, a viral disease that destroys the body's ability to fight infection.

AIH artificial insemination by husband.

ail ❶ *verb* **1** trouble, afflict. **2** be ill. **ailing** *adjective* **1** sickly. **2** unsuccessful over a long time. **ailment** *noun* illness.

aileron [**ale**-er-on] *noun* movable flap on an aircraft wing which controls rolling.

aim ❶ *verb* **1** point (a weapon or missile) or direct (a blow or remark) at a target. **2** propose or intend. ◆ *noun* **3** aiming. **4** intention, purpose. **aimless** *adjective* having no purpose. **aimlessly** *adverb*

ain't *Not standard* **1** am not. **2** is not. **3** are not. **4** has not. **5** have not.

air ❶ *noun* **1** mixture of gases forming the earth's atmosphere. **2** space above the ground, sky. **3** breeze. **4** quality or manner. **5** tune. ◆

plural **6** affected manners. ◆ *verb* **7** make known publicly. **8** expose to air to dry or ventilate. **on the air** in the act of broadcasting on radio or television. **airless** *adjective* stuffy. **air base** centre from which military aircraft operate. **airborne** *adjective* **1** carried by air. **2** (of aircraft) flying. **airbrush** *noun* atomizer spraying paint by compressed air. **airfield** *noun* place where aircraft can land and take off. **air force** branch of the armed forces responsible for air warfare. **air gun** gun fired by compressed air. **air hostess** stewardess on an aircraft. **airlift** *noun* **1** transport of troops or cargo by aircraft when other routes are blocked. ◆ *verb* **2** transport by airlift. **airlock** *noun* **1** air bubble blocking the flow of liquid in a pipe. **2** airtight chamber. **airmail** *noun* **1** system of sending mail by aircraft. **2** mail sent in this way. **airman** *noun* member of the air force. **air miles** miles of free air travel that can be earned by buying airline tickets and various other products. **airplane** *noun US* aeroplane. **airplay** *noun* broadcast performances of a record on radio. **airport** *noun* airfield for civilian aircraft, with facilities for aircraft maintenance and passengers. **air raid** attack by aircraft. **airship** *noun* lighter-than-air self-propelled aircraft. **airsick** *adjective* nauseated from travelling in an aircraft. **airspace** *noun* atmosphere above a country, regarded as its territory. **airstrip** *noun* cleared area where aircraft can take off and land. **airtight** *adjective* sealed so that air cannot enter.

air conditioning *noun* system that controls the temperature and humidity of the air in a building. **air-conditioned** *adjective* **air conditioner**

———————— T H E S A U R U S ————————

rocks, stranded, stuck

ahead *adverb* **1** = **in front**, at an advantage, at the head, before, in advance, in the lead, leading, to the fore

aid *verb* = **help**, assist, encourage, favour, promote, serve, subsidize, support, sustain OPPOSITE **obstruct** ◆*noun* = **help**, assistance, benefit, encouragement, favour, promotion, relief, service, support OPPOSITE **hindrance**

aide *noun* = **assistant**, attendant, helper, right-hand man, second, supporter

ailing *adjective* **1** = **ill**, crook (*Aust & NZ sl*), indisposed, infirm, poorly, sick, under the weather (*inf*), unwell, weak

ailment *noun* = **illness**, affliction, complaint, disease, disorder, infirmity, malady, sickness

aim *verb* **2** = **intend**, attempt, endeavour, mean, plan, point, propose, seek, set one's

sights on, strive, try ◆*noun* **4** = **intention**, ambition, aspiration, desire, goal, objective, plan, purpose, target

aimless *adjective* = **purposeless**, directionless, pointless, random, stray OPPOSITE **purposeful**

air *noun* **1, 2** = **atmosphere**, heavens, sky **3** = **wind**, breeze, draught, zephyr **4** = **manner**, appearance, atmosphere, aura, demeanour, impression, look, mood **5** = **tune**, aria, lay, melody, song ◆*plural* **6** = **affectation**, arrogance, haughtiness, hauteur, pomposity, pretensions, superciliousness, swank (*inf*) ◆*verb* **7** = **publicize**, circulate, display, exhibit, express, give vent to, make known, make public, reveal, voice **8** = **ventilate**, aerate, expose, freshen

airborne *adjective* = **flying**, floating, gliding, hovering, in flight, in the air, on the wing

aircraft *noun* any machine that flies, such as an aeroplane. **aircraft carrier** warship for the launching and landing of aircraft.

Airedale *noun* large rough-coated terrier.

airing ๑ *noun* **1** exposure to air for drying or ventilation. **2** exposure to public debate.

airline *noun* company providing scheduled flights for passengers and cargo. **airliner** *noun* large passenger aircraft.

airworthy *adjective* (of aircraft) fit to fly. **airworthiness** *noun*

airy ๑ *adjective* **airier, airiest 1** well-ventilated. **2** light-hearted and casual. **airily** *adverb*

aisle ๑ [rhymes with **mile**] *noun* passageway separating seating areas in a church, theatre, etc., or row of shelves in a supermarket.

ajar *adjective, adverb* (of a door) partly open.

AK Alaska.

akimbo *adverb* **with arms akimbo** with hands on hips and elbows outwards.

akin *adjective* **akin to** similar, related.

Al *Chem* aluminium.

AL Alabama.

à la *preposition* in the manner of.

alabaster *noun* soft white translucent stone.

à la carte *adjective, adverb* (of a menu) having dishes individually priced.

alacrity ๑ *noun* speed, eagerness.

à la mode *adjective* fashionable.

alarm ๑ *noun* **1** sudden fear caused by awareness of danger. **2** warning sound. **3** device that gives this. **4** alarm clock. ♦ *verb* **5** fill with fear. **alarming** *adjective* **alarmingly** *adverb* **alarmist** *noun* person who alarms others needlessly. **alarm clock** clock which sounds at a set time to wake someone up.

alas *adverb* unfortunately, regrettably.

alb *noun* long white robe worn by a Christian priest.

albacore *noun* tuna found in warm seas, eaten for food.

albatross *noun* large sea bird with very long wings.

albeit *conjunction* even though.

albino *noun, pl* **-nos** person or animal with white skin and hair and pink eyes. **albinism** *noun*

Albion *noun Poetic* **1** Britain. **2** England.

album *noun* **1** book with blank pages for keeping photographs or stamps in. **2** long-playing record.

albumen *noun* egg white.

albumin, albumen *noun* protein found in blood plasma, egg white, milk, and muscle.

alchemy *noun* medieval form of chemistry concerned with trying to turn base metals into gold and to find the elixir of life. **alchemist** *noun*

alcohol ๑ *noun* **1** colourless flammable liquid present in intoxicating drinks. **2** intoxicating drinks generally. **alcoholic** *adjective* **1** of alcohol. ♦ *noun* **2** person addicted to alcohol. **alcoholism** *noun* addiction to alcohol.

alcopop *noun Informal* alcoholic drink that tastes like a soft drink.

alcove ๑ *noun* recess in the wall of a room.

aldehyde *noun* one of a group of chemical compounds derived from alcohol by oxidation.

alder *noun* tree related to the birch.

alderman *noun* formerly, senior member of a local council.

ale *noun* kind of beer.

alembic *noun* anything that distils or purifies, esp. an obsolete vessel used for distillation.

alert ๑ *adjective* **1** watchful, attentive. ♦ *noun* **2** warning of danger. ♦ *verb* **3** warn of danger. **4** make (someone) aware of (a fact). **on the alert** watchful. **alertness** *noun*

A level *noun* (pass in a subject at) the

T H E S A U R U S

---

airing *noun* **1** = **ventilation**, aeration, drying, freshening **2** = **exposure**, circulation, display, dissemination, expression, publicity, utterance, vent

airy *adjective* **1** = **well-ventilated**, fresh, light, open, spacious, uncluttered OPPOSITE suffocating. **2** = **light-hearted**, blithe, cheerful, high-spirited, jaunty, lively, sprightly OPPOSITE miserable

aisle *noun* = **passageway**, alley, corridor, gangway, lane, passage, path

alacrity *noun* = **eagerness**, alertness, enthusiasm, promptness, quickness, readiness, speed, willingness, zeal OPPOSITE reluctance

alarm *noun* **1** = **fear**, anxiety, apprehension, consternation, fright, nervousness, panic, scare, trepidation OPPOSITE calm. **2, 3** = **danger signal**, alarm bell, alert, bell, distress signal, hooter, siren, warning ♦*verb* **5** = **frighten**, daunt, dismay, distress, give (someone) a turn (*inf*), panic, scare, startle, unnerve OPPOSITE comfort

alarming *adjective* = **frightening**, daunting, distressing, disturbing, scaring, shocking, startling, unnerving

alcoholic *adjective* **1** = **intoxicating**, brewed, distilled, fermented, hard, strong ♦*noun* **2** = **drunkard**, dipsomaniac, drinker, drunk, inebriate, tippler, toper, wino (*inf*)

alcove *noun* = **recess**, bay, compartment,

A

advanced level of the GCE.

alfalfa noun kind of plant used to feed livestock.

alfresco adverb, adjective in the open air.

algae [al-jee] plural noun plants which live in or near water and have no true stems, leaves, or roots.

algebra noun branch of mathematics using symbols to represent numbers. **algebraic** adjective

ALGOL noun Computers computer programming language designed for mathematical and scientific purposes.

Algonquin, Algonkin noun a member of a North American Indian people formerly living along Lawrence and Ottawa Rivers in Canada.

algorithm noun logical arithmetical or computational procedure for solving a problem.

alias ⊕ adverb 1 also known as, e.g. William Bonney, alias Billy the Kid. ♦ noun 2 false name.

alibi ⊕ noun 1 plea of being somewhere else when a crime was committed. 2 Informal excuse.

Alice band noun band worn across the head to hold the hair back from the face.

alien ⊕ adjective 1 foreign. 2 repugnant (to). 3 from another world. ♦ noun 4 foreigner. 5 being from another world. **alienable** adjective Law able to be transferred to another owner. **alienate** verb cause to become hostile. **alienation** noun

alight[1] ⊕ verb 1 step out of (a vehicle). 2 land.

alight[2] ⊕ adjective 1 on fire. 2 lit up.

align ⊕ [a-line] verb 1 bring (a person or group) into agreement with the policy of another. 2 place in a line. **alignment** noun

alike ⊕ adjective 1 like, similar. ♦ adverb 2 in the same way.

alimentary adjective of nutrition. **alimentary canal** food passage in the body.

alimony noun allowance paid under a court order to a separated or divorced spouse.

A-line adjective (of a skirt) slightly flared.

aliped [al-lee-ped] noun animal, like the bat, whose toes are joined by membrane that serves as wing.

aliphatic adjective (of an organic compound) having an open chain structure.

aliquot Maths adjective 1 of or denoting an exact divisor of a number. ♦ noun 2 exact divisor.

alive ⊕ adjective 1 living, in existence. 2 lively. **alive to** aware of. **alive with** swarming with.

alkali [alk-a-lie] noun substance which combines with acid and neutralizes it to form a salt. **alkaline** adjective **alkalinity** noun **alkaloid** noun any of a group of organic compounds containing nitrogen.

all ⊕ adjective 1 whole quantity or number (of). ♦ adverb 2 wholly, entirely. 3 (in the score of games) each. **give one's all** make the greatest possible effort. **all in** adjective 1 exhausted. 2

──────── T H E S A U R U S ────────

corner, cubbyhole, cubicle, niche, nook

alert adjective 1 = **watchful**, attentive, awake, circumspect, heedful, observant, on guard, on one's toes, on the lookout, vigilant, wide-awake OPPOSITE slow ♦noun 2 = **warning**, alarm, signal, siren OPPOSITE all clear ♦verb 3 = **warn**, alarm, forewarn, signal OPPOSITE lull. 4 = **inform**, notify OPPOSITE lull

alertness noun 1 = **watchfulness**, attentiveness, heedfulness, liveliness, vigilance

alias adverb 1 = **also known as**, also called, otherwise, otherwise known as ♦noun 2 = **pseudonym**, assumed name, nom de guerre, nom de plume, pen name, stage name

alibi noun 2 Inf = **excuse**, defence, explanation, justification, plea, pretext, reason

alien adjective 1 = **strange**, exotic, foreign, unfamiliar OPPOSITE like ♦noun 4 = **foreigner**, newcomer, outsider, stranger OPPOSITE citizen

alienate verb = **set against**, disaffect, estrange, make unfriendly, turn away

alienation noun = **setting against**, disaffection, estrangement, remoteness, separation, turning away

alight[1] verb 1 = **get off**, descend, disembark, dismount, get down 2 = **land**, come down, come to rest, descend, light, perch, settle, touch down OPPOSITE rise

alight[2] adjective 1 = **on fire**, ablaze, aflame, blazing, burning, fiery, flaming, lighted, lit 2 = **lit up**, bright, brilliant, illuminated, shining

align verb 1 = **ally**, affiliate, agree, associate, cooperate, join, side, sympathize 2 = **line up**, even up, order, range, regulate, straighten

alignment noun 1 = **alliance**, affiliation, agreement, association, cooperation, sympathy, union 2 = **lining up**, adjustment, arrangement, evening up, order, straightening up

alike adjective 1 = **similar**, akin, analogous, corresponding, identical, of a piece, parallel, resembling, the same OPPOSITE different ♦adverb 2 = **similarly**, analogously, correspondingly, equally, evenly, identically, uniformly OPPOSITE differently

alive adjective 1 = **living**, animate, breathing, existing, extant, in existence, in the land of the living (inf), subsisting OPPOSITE dead. 2 = **lively**, active, alert, animated, energetic, full (of wrestling) with no style forbidden. ♦ *adverb* **3** with all expenses included. **all-clear** *noun* signal indicating that danger is over. **all right** *adjective* **1** adequate, satisfactory. **2** unharmed. ♦ *interjection* **3** expression of approval or agreement. **all-rounder** *noun* person with ability in many fields.

Allah *noun* name of God in Islam.

allay *verb* reduce (fear or anger).

allege ❶ *verb* state without proof. **alleged** *adjective* **allegedly** [al-**lej**-id-lee] *adverb*

allegation *noun* unproved accusation.

allegiance ❶ *noun* loyalty to a person, country, or cause.

allegory ❶ *noun, pl* **-ries** story with an underlying meaning as well as the literal one. **allegorical** *adjective*

allegretto *noun, pl* **-tos**, *adverb Music* (piece to be played) fairly quickly or briskly.

allegro *noun, pl* **-gros**, *adverb Music* (piece to be played) in a brisk lively manner.

alleluia *interjection* same as HALLELUJAH.

allergy ❶ *noun, pl* **-gies** extreme sensitivity to a substance, which causes the body to react to it. **allergic** *adjective* having or caused by an allergy. **allergic to** having a strong dislike of, e.g. *allergic to work.* **allergen** [**al**-ler-jen] *noun* substance capable of causing an allergic reaction.

alleviate ❶ *verb* lessen (pain or suffering). **alleviation** *noun*

alley ❶ *noun* **1** narrow street or path. **2** long

narrow enclosure in which tenpin bowling or skittles is played.

alliance ❶ *noun* **1** state of being allied. **2** formal relationship between countries or groups for a shared purpose.

alligator *noun* reptile of the crocodile family, found in the southern US and China.

alliteration *noun* use of the same sound at the start of words occurring together. **alliterative** *adjective*

allocate ❶ *verb* assign to someone or for a particular purpose. **allocation** *noun*

allopathy [al-**lop**-ath-ee] *noun* orthodox method of treating disease, by using drugs that produce an effect opposite to the effect of the disease beingtreated, as contrasted with homeopathy. **allopathic** *adjective*

allot ❶ *verb* **-lotting, -lotted** assign as a share or for a particular purpose. **allotment** *noun* **1** distribution. **2** portion allotted. **3** small piece of public land rented to grow vegetables on.

allotrope *noun* any of two or more physical forms in which an element can exist. **allotropic** *adjective* **allotropy** *noun*

allow ❶ *verb* **1** permit. **2** set aside. **3** acknowledge (a point or claim). **allow for** *verb* take into account. **allowable** *adjective*

allowance *noun* **1** amount of money given at regular intervals. **2** amount permitted. **make allowances for 1** treat or judge (someone) less severely because he or she has special problems. **2** take into account.

——————————— T H E S A U R U S ———————————

of life, vital, vivacious OPPOSITE lifeless

all *adjective* **1** = **entire**, complete, each, each and every, every, every bit of, every one of, every single, full, the whole of, total ♦*adverb* **2** = **completely**, altogether, entirely, fully, totally, utterly, wholly

allegation *noun* = **claim**, accusation, affirmation, assertion, charge, declaration, statement

allege *verb* = **claim**, affirm, assert, charge, declare, maintain, state OPPOSITE deny

alleged *adjective* = **stated**, affirmed, asserted, declared, described, designated, ostensible, professed, purported, so-called, supposed, unproved

allegiance *noun* = **loyalty**, constancy, devotion, faithfulness, fidelity, obedience OPPOSITE disloyalty

allegorical *adjective* = **symbolic**, emblematic, figurative, symbolizing

allegory *noun* = **symbol**, fable, myth, parable, story, symbolism, tale

allergic *adjective* = **sensitive**, affected by,

hypersensitive, susceptible

allergy *noun* = **sensitivity**, antipathy, hypersensitivity, susceptibility

alleviate *verb* = **ease**, allay, lessen, lighten, moderate, reduce, relieve, soothe

alley *noun* **1** = **passage**, alleyway, backstreet, lane, passageway, pathway, walk

alliance *noun* **1** = **connection**, affiliation, agreement, association, combination, marriage, partnership OPPOSITE **break**. **2** = **union**, coalition, confederation, federation, league, pact, treaty OPPOSITE **division**

allied *adjective* = **united**, affiliated, associated, combined, connected, in league, linked, related

allocate *verb* = **assign**, allot, allow, apportion, budget, designate, earmark, mete, set aside, share out

allocation *noun* = **assignment**, allotment, allowance, lot, portion, quota, ration, share

allot *verb* = **assign**, allocate, apportion, budget, designate, earmark, mete, set aside, share out

allotment *noun* **2** = **share**, allocation, allowance, grant, portion, quota, ration, stint **3**

A

alloy ⊕ *noun* **1** mixture of two or more metals. ♦ *verb* **2** mix (metals).

allspice *noun* spice made from the berries of a tropical American tree.

allude ⊕ *verb* (foll. by *to*) refer indirectly to.

allusion *noun* indirect reference. **allusive** *adjective*

> **LANGUAGE TIP**
>
> *Allude* is followed by *to*. Be careful not to confuse this word with *elude* meaning 'escape'. Also be careful not to confuse *allusion* with *illusion* meaning 'fallacy' or 'fantasy'.

allure ⊕ *noun* **1** attractiveness. ♦ *verb* **2** entice or attract. **alluring** *adjective*

alluvium *noun* fertile soil deposited by flowing water. **alluvial** *adjective*

ally ⊕ *noun, pl* **-lies 1** country, person, or group with an agreement to support another. ♦ *verb* **-lying, -lied 2 ally oneself with** join as an ally. **allied** *adjective*

alma mater *noun* school, university, or college that one attended.

almanac *noun* yearly calendar with detailed information on anniversaries, phases of the moon, etc.

almighty ⊕ *adjective* **1** having absolute power. **2** *Informal* very great. ♦ *noun* **3 the Almighty** God.

almond *noun* edible oval-shaped nut which grows on a small tree.

almoner *noun* formerly, a hospital social worker.

almost ⊕ *adverb* very nearly.

alms [ahmz] *plural noun Old-fashioned* gifts to the poor.

aloe *noun* **1** plant with fleshy spiny leaves. ♦ *plural* **2** bitter drug made from aloe leaves. **aloe vera** plant producing a juice used for skin and hair care.

aloft *adverb* **1** in the air. **2** in a ship's rigging.

alone ⊕ *adjective, adverb* without anyone or anything else.

along *preposition* **1** over part or all the length of. ♦ *adverb* **2** forward. **3** in company with others, e.g. *come along for the ride.* **alongside** *preposition, adverb* beside (something).

aloof ⊕ *adjective* distant or haughty in manner. **aloofness** *noun*

alopecia [al-loh-**pee**-sha] *noun* loss of hair.

———————— T H E S A U R U S ————————

=plot, kitchen garden, patch, tract

allow *verb* **1 =permit**, approve, authorize, enable, endure, let, sanction, stand, suffer, tolerate OPPOSITE> prohibit. **2 =set aside**, allocate, allot, assign, give, grant, provide, spare **3 =acknowledge**, admit, concede, confess, grant, own

allowable *adjective* **1 =permissible**, acceptable, admissible, all right, appropriate, suitable, tolerable

allowance *noun* **2 =portion**, allocation, amount, grant, lot, quota, ration, share, stint

allow for *verb* **=take into account**, consider, make allowances for, make concessions for, make provision for, plan for, provide for, take into consideration

alloy *noun* **1 =mixture**, admixture, amalgam, blend, combination, composite, compound, hybrid ♦*verb* **2 =mix**, amalgamate, blend, combine, compound, fuse

all right *adjective* **1 =satisfactory**, acceptable, adequate, average, fair, O.K. *or* okay (*inf*), standard, up to scratch (*inf*) OPPOSITE> bad. **2 =well**, healthy, O.K. *or* okay (*inf*), safe, sound, unharmed, uninjured, whole OPPOSITE> bad

allude *verb* (foll. by *to*) **=refer**, hint, imply, intimate, mention, suggest, touch upon

allure *noun* **1 =attractiveness**, appeal,

attraction, charm, enchantment, enticement, glamour, lure, persuasion, seductiveness, temptation ♦*verb* **2 =attract**, captivate, charm, enchant, entice, lure, persuade, seduce, tempt, win over

alluring *adjective* **=attractive**, beguiling, captivating, come-hither, fetching, glamorous, seductive, tempting OPPOSITE> unattractive

allusion *noun* **=reference**, casual remark, hint, implication, innuendo, insinuation, intimation, mention, suggestion

ally *noun* **1 =partner**, accomplice, associate, cobber (*Aust or old-fashioned NZ inf*), collaborator, colleague, friend, helper OPPOSITE> rival ♦*verb* **2 ally oneself with =unite with**, associate with, collaborate with, combine with, join forces with, join with

almighty *adjective* **1 =all-powerful**, absolute, invincible, omnipotent, supreme, unlimited OPPOSITE> weak. **2** *Inf* **=great**, enormous, excessive, intense, loud, severe, terrible OPPOSITE> poor

almost *adverb* **=nearly**, about, approximately, close to, just about, not quite, on the brink of, practically, virtually

alone *adjective* **=by oneself**, apart, detached, isolated, lonely, lonesome (*chiefly US & Canad*), only, on one's tod (*sl*), separate, single, solitary,

aloud ❶ *adverb* in an audible voice.
alp *noun* high mountain. **the Alps** high mountain range in S central Europe.
alpaca *noun* **1** Peruvian llama. **2** wool or cloth made from its hair.
alpenstock *noun* iron-tipped stick used by climbers.
alpha *noun* **1** first letter in the Greek alphabet. **2** highest grade in an examination. **alpha and omega** the first and last. **alpha particle** positively charged particle emitted during some radioactive transformations. **alpha ray** stream of alpha particles.
alphabet *noun* set of letters used in writing a language. **alphabetical** *adjective* in the conventional order of the letters of an alphabet. **alphabetically** *adverb* **alphabetize** *verb* put in alphabetical order. **alphabetization** *noun*
alphanumeric *adjective* consisting of alphabetical and numerical symbols.
alpine *adjective* **1** of high mountains. **2** (**A-**) of the Alps. ♦ *noun* **3** mountain plant.
already ❶ *adverb* **1** before the present time. **2** sooner than expected.
alright *adjective, interjection* all right.

> **LANGUAGE TIP**
>
> The form *alright*, though very common, is still considered by many people to be wrong or less acceptable than *all right*.

Alsatian *noun* large wolflike dog.
also ❶ *adverb* in addition, too. **also-ran** *noun* loser in a race, competition, or election.

alt. *combining form Informal* alternative e.g. *alt. rock*.
altar *noun* **1** table used for Communion in Christian churches. **2** raised structure on which sacrifices are offered and religious rites are performed. **altarpiece** *noun* work of art above and behind the altar in some Christian churches.
alter ❶ *verb* make or become different.
alteration *noun*
altercation *noun* heated argument.
alter ego *noun* **1** second self. **2** very close friend.
alternate ❶ *verb* **1** (cause to) occur by turns. ♦ *adjective* **2** occurring by turns. **3** every second (one) of a series, e.g. *alternate Fridays*.
alternately *adverb* **alternation** *noun*
alternative *noun* one of two choices.
alternator *noun* electric generator for producing alternating current. **alternating current** electric current that reverses direction at frequent regular intervals.
alternative ❶ *noun* **1** one of two choices. ♦ *adjective* **2** able to be done or used instead of something else. **3** (of medicine, lifestyle, etc.) not conventional. **alternatively** *adverb*
although ❶ *conjunction* despite the fact that.
altimeter [al-**tim**-it-er] *noun* instrument that measures altitude.
altitude *noun* height above sea level.
alto *noun, pl* **-tos** *Music* **1** short for CONTRALTO. **2** (singer with) the highest adult male voice. **3** instrument with the second-highest pitch in its group.
altogether ❶ *adverb* **1** entirely. **2** on the whole. **3** in total.

——————— THESAURUS ———————

unaccompanied OPPOSITE accompanied
aloof *adjective* =**distant**, detached, haughty, remote, standoffish, supercilious, unapproachable, unfriendly OPPOSITE **friendly**
aloud *adverb* =**out loud**, audibly, clearly, distinctly, intelligibly, plainly
already *adverb* **1** =**before now**, at present, before, by now, by then, even now, heretofore, just now, previously
also *adverb* =**too**, additionally, and, as well, besides, further, furthermore, in addition, into the bargain, moreover, to boot
alter *verb* =**change**, adapt, adjust, amend, convert, modify, reform, revise, transform, turn, vary
alteration *noun* =**change**, adaptation, adjustment, amendment, conversion, difference, modification, reformation, revision, transformation, variation

alternate *verb* **1** =**change**, act reciprocally, fluctuate, interchange, oscillate, rotate, substitute, take turns ♦*adjective* **3** =**every other**, alternating, every second
alternative *noun* **1** =**choice**, option, other (of two), preference, recourse, selection, substitute ♦*adjective* **2** =**different**, alternate, another, other, second, substitute
alternatively *adverb* =**or**, as an alternative, if not, instead, on the other hand, otherwise
although *conjunction* =**though**, albeit, despite the fact that, even if, even though, notwithstanding, while
altogether *adverb* **1** =**completely**, absolutely, fully, perfectly, quite, thoroughly, totally, utterly, wholly OPPOSITE **relatively**. **2** =**on the whole**, all in all, all things considered, as a whole, collectively, generally, in general **3** =**in total**, all told, everything included, in all, in

altruism ⊕ *noun* unselfish concern for the welfare of others. **altruist** *noun* **altruistic** *adjective* **altruistically** *adverb*
alum *noun* double sulphate of aluminium and potassium.
aluminium *noun Chem* light silvery-white metal that does not rust.
alumnus [al-**lumm**-nuss] *noun, pl* **-ni** [-nie] *Chiefly US* graduate of a college. **alumna** [al-**lumm**-na] *n fem, pl* **-nae** [-nee]
always ⊕ *adverb* **1** at all times. **2** for ever. **3** in any case, e.g. *you could always work abroad*.
alyssum *noun* garden plant with small yellow or white flowers.
am *verb see* BE.
Am *Chem* americium.
AM 1 amplitude modulation. **2** (in Britain) Member of the National Assembly for Wales.
Am. America(n).
a.m. ante meridiem: before noon.
amalgam *noun* **1** blend or combination. **2** alloy of mercury and another metal.
amalgamate ⊕ *verb* combine or unite. **amalgamation** *noun*
amanuensis [am-man-yew-**en**-siss] *noun, pl* **-ses** [-seez] person who writes from dictation.
amaranth *noun* **1** imaginary flower that never fades. **2** lily-like plant with red, green, or purple flowers.
amaryllis *noun* lily-like plant with large red, pink, or white flowers.
amass ⊕ *verb* collect or accumulate.
amateur ⊕ *noun* **1** person who engages in a sport or activity as a pastime rather than as a profession. **2** person unskilled in something. ♦ *adjective* **3** not professional. **amateurish** *adjective* lacking skill. **amateurishly** *adverb* **amateurism** *noun*
amatory *adjective* relating to romantic or sexual love.
amaut, amowt *noun Canad* a hood on an Eskimo woman's parka for carrying a child.
amaze ⊕ *verb* surprise greatly, astound. **amazing** *adjective* **amazingly** *adverb* **amazement** *noun*
Amazon *noun* **1** strong and powerful woman. **2** legendary female warrior. **Amazonian** *adjective*
ambassador ⊕ *noun* senior diplomat who represents his or her country in another country. **ambassadorial** *adjective*
amber *noun* **1** clear yellowish fossil resin. ♦ *adjective* **2** brownish-yellow.
ambergris [**am**-ber-greece] *noun* waxy substance secreted by the sperm whale, used in making perfumes.
ambidextrous *adjective* able to use both hands with equal ease.
ambience, ambiance *noun* atmosphere of a place.
ambient *adjective* surrounding.
ambiguous ⊕ *adjective* having more than one possible meaning. **ambiguously** *adverb*
ambiguity *noun, pl* **-ties**
ambit *noun* limits or boundary.
ambition ⊕ *noun* **1** desire for success. **2** something so desired, goal. **ambitious** *adjective* **ambitiously** *adverb*

———————— T H E S A U R U S ————————

sum, taken together
altruistic *adjective* =**selfless**, benevolent, charitable, generous, humanitarian, philanthropic, public-spirited, self-sacrificing, unselfish OPPOSITE **self-interested**
always *adverb* **1** =**continually**, consistently, constantly, every time, invariably, perpetually, repeatedly, twenty-four-seven (*inf*), without exception OPPOSITE **hardly**. **2** =**forever**, eternally, evermore
amalgamate *verb* =**combine**, ally, blend, fuse, incorporate, integrate, merge, mingle, unite OPPOSITE **divide**
amalgamation *noun* =**combination**, blend, coalition, compound, fusion, joining, merger, mixture, union
amass *verb* =**collect**, accumulate, assemble, compile, gather, hoard, pile up
amateur *noun* **1** =**nonprofessional**, dabbler, dilettante, layman
amateurish *adjective* =**unprofessional**, amateur, bungling, clumsy, crude, inexpert, unaccomplished OPPOSITE **professional**
amaze *verb* =**astonish**, alarm, astound, bewilder, dumbfound, shock, stagger, startle, stun, surprise
amazement *noun* =**astonishment**, admiration, bewilderment, confusion, perplexity, shock, surprise, wonder
amazing *adjective* =**astonishing**, astounding, breathtaking, eye-opening, jaw-dropping, overwhelming, staggering, startling, stunning, surprising
ambassador *noun* =**representative**, agent, consul, deputy, diplomat, envoy, legate, minister
ambiguity *noun* =**vagueness**, doubt, dubiousness, equivocation, obscurity, uncertainty
ambiguous *adjective* =**unclear**, dubious, enigmatic, equivocal, inconclusive, indefinite, indeterminate, obscure, vague OPPOSITE **clear**

ambivalence ❶ [am-**biv**-a-lenss] *noun* state of feeling two conflicting emotions at the same time. **ambivalent** *adjective* **ambivalently** *adverb*

amble ❶ *verb* **1** walk at a leisurely pace. ♦ *noun* **2** leisurely walk or pace.

ambrosia *noun* **1** anything delightful to taste or smell. **2** *Myth* food of the gods. **ambrosial** *adjective*

ambulance *noun* motor vehicle designed to carry sick or injured people.

ambulatory *adjective* **1** of or relating to walking. **2** able to walk. ♦ *noun, pl* **-ries 3** place for walking in, such as a cloister.

ambush ❶ *noun* **1** act of waiting in a concealed position to make a surprise attack. **2** attack from a concealed position. ♦ *verb* **3** attack from a concealed position.

ameliorate [am-**meal**-yor-rate] *verb* make (something) better. **amelioration** *noun*

amen *interjection* so be it: used at the end of a prayer.

amenable ❶ [a-**mean**-a-bl] *adjective* likely or willing to cooperate.

amend ❶ *verb* make small changes to correct or improve (something). **amendment** *noun*

amends ❶ *plural noun* **make amends for** compensate for.

amenity ❶ *noun, pl* **-ties** useful or enjoyable feature.

American *adjective* **1** of the United States of America or the American continent. ♦ *noun* **2** person from America or the American continent. **Americanism** *noun* expression or custom characteristic of Americans. **Americanize** *verb* make American in outlook, form, etc.

americium *noun Chem* white metallic element artificially produced from plutonium.

amethyst [am-myth-ist] *noun* bluish-violet variety of quartz used as a gemstone.

Amharic *noun* official language of Ethiopia.

amiable ❶ *adjective* friendly, pleasant-natured. **amiably** *adverb* **amiability** *noun*

amicable ❶ *adjective* friendly. **amicably** *adverb* **amicability** *noun*

amid, amidst ❶ *preposition* in the middle of, among. **amidships** *adverb* at or towards the middle of a ship.

amino acid [am-**mean**-oh] *noun* organic compound found in protein.

amiss ❶ *adverb* **1** wrongly, badly. ♦ *adjective* **2** wrong, faulty. **take something amiss** be offended by something.

amity *noun* friendship.

ammeter *noun* instrument for measuring electric current.

ammo *noun Informal* ammunition.

ammonia *noun* **1** strong-smelling alkaline gas containing hydrogen and nitrogen. **2** solution of this in water.

ammonite *noun* fossilized spiral shell of an extinct sea creature.

ammunition ❶ *noun* **1** bullets, bombs, and

———————— T H E S A U R U S ————————

ambition *noun* **1** = **enterprise**, aspiration, desire, drive, eagerness, longing, striving, yearning, zeal **2** = **goal**, aim, aspiration, desire, dream, hope, intent, objective, purpose, wish

ambitious *adjective* = **enterprising**, aspiring, avid, eager, hopeful, intent, purposeful, striving, zealous OPPOSITE **lazy**

ambivalent *adjective* = **undecided**, contradictory, doubtful, equivocal, in two minds, uncertain, unsure, wavering

amble *verb* **1** = **stroll**, dawdle, meander, mosey (*inf*), ramble, saunter, walk, wander

ambush *noun* **1** = **trap**, lying in wait, waylaying ♦*verb* **3** = **trap**, attack, bushwhack (*US*), ensnare, surprise, waylay

amenable *adjective* = **receptive**, able to be influenced, acquiescent, agreeable, compliant, open, persuadable, responsive, susceptible OPPOSITE **stubborn**

amend *verb* = **change**, alter, correct, fix, improve, mend, modify, reform, remedy, repair, revise

amendment *noun* = **change**, addendum, addition, alteration, correction, emendation, improvement, modification, reform, remedy, repair, revision

amends *plural noun* **make amends for** = **compensate for**, atone for, give satisfaction for, make reparation for, make restitution for, recompense, redress

amenity *noun* = **facility**, advantage, comfort, convenience, service

amiable *adjective* = **pleasant**, affable, agreeable, charming, congenial, engaging, friendly, genial, likable *or* likeable, lovable OPPOSITE **unfriendly**

amicable *adjective* = **friendly**, amiable, civil, cordial, courteous, harmonious, neighbourly, peaceful, sociable OPPOSITE **unfriendly**

amid, amidst *preposition* = **in the middle of**, among, amongst, in the midst of, in the thick of, surrounded by

amiss *adverb* **1** = **wrongly**, erroneously, improperly, inappropriately, incorrectly, mistakenly, unsuitably ♦*adjective* **2** = **wrong**, awry, faulty, incorrect, mistaken, untoward shells that can be fired from or as a weapon. **2** facts that can be used in an argument.

amnesia *noun* loss of memory. **amnesiac** *adjective, noun*

amnesty ❶ *noun, pl* **-ties** general pardon for offences against a government.

amniocentesis *noun, pl* **-ses** removal of some amniotic fluid to test for possible abnormalities in a fetus.

amniotic fluid *noun* fluid surrounding a fetus in the womb.

amoeba [am-**mee**-ba] *noun, pl* **-bae** [-bee] **-bas** microscopic single-celled animal able to change its shape.

amok ❶ *adverb* **run amok** run about in a violent frenzy.

among, amongst ❶ *preposition* **1** in the midst of. **2** in the group or number of. **3** to each of, e.g. *divide it among yourselves.*

amoral [aim-**mor**-ral] *adjective* without moral standards. **amorality** *noun*

> **LANGUAGE TIP**
>
> *Amoral* is often wrongly used where *immoral* is meant. You would use *amoral* to talk about people who have no moral standards, or about a place or situation where moral rules do not apply, as in *a violent and amoral criminal* or *the amoral world of big business*, while *immoral* should be used to talk about the breaking of rules, as in *criminal or immoral activities.*

amorous ❶ *adjective* feeling, showing, or relating to sexual love or desire. **amorously** *adverb*

amorphous *adjective* **1** without distinct shape.

2 of no recognizable character or type.

amortize *verb* pay off (a debt) gradually by periodic transfers to a sinking fund.

amount ❶ *noun* **1** extent or quantity. ◆ *verb* **2** (foll. by *to*) be equal or add up to.

amour *noun* (secret) love affair.

amour-propre [am-**moor**-**prop**-ra] *noun* French self-respect.

amp *noun* **1** ampere. **2** *Informal* amplifier.

amperage *noun* strength of an electrical current measured in amperes.

ampere [am-pair] *noun* basic unit of electric current.

ampersand *noun* the character (&), meaning *and.*

> **LANGUAGE TIP**
>
> It is best to avoid using an *ampersand* (&) to replace the word *and* in formal writing.

amphetamine [am-**fet**-am-mean] *noun* drug used as a stimulant.

amphibian *noun* **1** animal that lives on land but breeds in water. **2** vehicle that can travel on both land and water. **amphibious** *adjective* **1** living or operating both on land and in water. **2** relating to a military attack launched from the sea against a shore.

amphitheatre *noun* open oval or circular building with tiers of seats rising round an arena.

amphora [am-for-ra] *noun, pl* **-phorae** [-for-ree] ancient Greek or Roman jar with two handles and a narrow neck.

ample ❶ *adjective* **1** more than sufficient e.g. *there is already ample evidence.* **2** large e.g. *ample helpings of stewed pears and pomegranates.* **amply** *adverb*

amplify ❶ *verb* **-fying, -fied 1** increase the

——————— THESAURUS ———————

OPPOSITE **right**

ammunition *noun* **1** = **munitions**, armaments, explosives, powder, rounds, shells, shot

amnesty *noun* = **general pardon**, absolution, dispensation, forgiveness, immunity, remission (*of penalty*), reprieve

amok *adverb* **run amok** = **madly**, berserk, destructively, ferociously, in a frenzy, murderously, savagely, uncontrollably, violently, wildly

among, amongst *preposition* **1** = **in the midst of**, amid, amidst, in the middle of, in the thick of, surrounded by, together with, with **2** = **in the group of**, in the class of, in the

company of, in the number of, out of **3** = **to each of**, between

amorous *adjective* = **loving**, erotic, impassioned, in love, lustful, passionate, tender OPPOSITE **cold**

amount *noun* **1** = **quantity**, expanse, extent, magnitude, mass, measure, number, supply, volume ◆ *verb* **2** (foll. by *to*) = **add up to**, become, come to, develop into, equal, mean, total

ample *adjective* **1** = **plenty**, abundant, bountiful, copious, expansive, extensive, full, generous, lavish, plentiful, profuse OPPOSITE **little**

strength of (a current or sound signal). **2** explain in more detail. **3** increase the size or effect of. **amplification** noun **amplifier** noun device used to amplify a current or sound signal.

amplitude noun greatness of extent.

ampoule noun small sealed glass vessel containing liquid for injection.

amputate 𝕆 verb cut off (a limb or part of a limb) for medical reasons. **amputation** noun **amputee** noun person who has had a limb amputated.

amuck 𝕆 adverb same as AMOK.

amulet noun something carried or worn as a protection against evil.

amuse 𝕆 verb **1** cause to laugh or smile. **2** entertain or divert. **amusing** adjective **amusingly** adverb **amusement** noun **1** state of being amused. **2** something that amuses.

amylase noun enzyme, present in saliva, that helps to change starch into sugar.

an adjective form of **a** used before vowels, and sometimes beforeh, e.g. an hour.

> **LANGUAGE TIP**
>
> This form of the indefinite article is also used with abbreviations which have a vowel sound when read aloud: an MA. It is old-fashioned to use an before words like hotel or historic.

anabolic steroid noun synthetic steroid hormone used to stimulate muscle and bone growth.

anabolism noun Biol metabolic process in which body tissues are synthesized from food.

anachronism [an-**nak**-kron-iz-zum] noun person or thing placed in the wrong historical period or seeming to belong to another time. **anachronistic** adjective

anaconda noun large S American snake which kills by constriction.

anaemia 𝕆 [an-**neem**-ee-a] noun deficiency in the number of red blood cells. **anaemic** adjective **1** having anaemia. **2** pale and sickly. **3** lacking vitality.

anaerobic adjective Biol not requiring oxygen.

anaesthetic 𝕆 [an-niss-**thet**-ik] noun, adjective (substance) causing loss of bodily feeling. **anaesthesia** [an-niss-**theez**-ee-a] noun loss of bodily feeling. **anaesthetist** [an-**neess**-thet-ist] noun doctor trained to administer anaesthetics. **anaesthetize** verb

Anaglypta noun ® thick embossed wallpaper, designed to be painted.

anagram noun word or phrase made by rearranging the letters of another word or phrase.

anal [**ain**-al] adjective of the anus.

analgesic [an-nal-**jeez**-ik] noun, adjective (drug) relieving pain. **analgesia** noun absence of pain.

analogous adjective similar in some respects.

analogue noun **1** something that is similar in some respects to something else. ♦ adjective **2** displaying information by means of a dial, e.g. analogue speedometers.

analogy 𝕆 noun, pl **-gies 1** similarity in some respects. **2** comparison made to show such a similarity. **analogical** adjective **analogize** verb **1** use analogy. **2** show analogy between.

analysis 𝕆 [an-**nal**-liss-iss] noun, pl **-ses** [-seez] **1** separation of a whole into its parts for study and interpretation. **2** psychoanalysis. **analyse**

———————————— THESAURUS ————————————

amplify verb **2** = **go into detail**, develop, elaborate, enlarge, expand, explain, flesh out OPPOSITE **simplify**. **3** = **expand**, enlarge, extend, heighten, increase, intensify, magnify, strengthen, widen OPPOSITE **reduce**

amply adverb **1** = **fully**, abundantly, completely, copiously, generously, profusely, richly OPPOSITE **insufficiently**

amputate verb = **cut off**, curtail, lop, remove, separate, sever, truncate

amuck same as AMOK

amuse verb **2** = **entertain**, charm, cheer, delight, interest, please OPPOSITE **bore**

amusement noun **1** = **entertainment**, cheer, enjoyment, fun, merriment, mirth, pleasure OPPOSITE **sadness**. **2** = **pastime**, diversion, entertainment, game, hobby, joke, recreation,

sport

amusing adjective **1** = **funny**, comical, droll, humorous, witty **2** = **entertaining**, enjoyable, interesting OPPOSITE **boring**

anaemic adjective **2** = **pale**, ashen, colourless, pallid, wan OPPOSITE **glowing** OPPOSITE **rosy**. **3** = **feeble**, sickly, weak

anaesthetic noun = **painkiller**, analgesic, anodyne, narcotic, opiate, sedative, soporific ♦adjective = **pain-killing**, analgesic, anodyne, deadening, dulling, numbing, sedative, soporific

analogy noun **1** = **similarity**, correlation, correspondence, likeness, parallel, relation, resemblance **2** = **comparison**

analyse verb **1** = **examine**, evaluate, investigate, research, test, think through, work over

A

[**an**-nal-lize] *verb* **1** make an analysis of (something). **2** psychoanalyse. **analyst** *noun* **1** person skilled in analysis. **2** psychoanalyst. **analytical, analytic** *adjective* **analytically** *adverb*
anarchism ⊕ *noun* doctrine advocating the abolition of government. **anarchist** *noun* **anarchistic** *adjective*
anarchy ⊕ [**an**-ark-ee] *noun* **1** lawlessness and disorder. **2** lack of government in a state. **anarchic** *adjective*
anastigmat *noun* lens corrected for astigmatism. **anastigmatic** *adjective* (of lens) not astigmatic.
anathema [an-**nath**-im-a] *noun* detested person or thing. **anathematize** *verb* curse (a person or thing).
anatomy ⊕ *noun, pl* **-mies 1** science of the structure of the body. **2** physical structure. **3** person's body, e.g. *a delicate part of his anatomy*. **4** detailed analysis. **anatomical** *adjective* **anatomically** *adverb* **anatomist** *noun* expert in anatomy.
ancestor ⊕ *noun* **1** person from whom one is descended. **2** forerunner. **ancestral** *adjective* **ancestry** *noun* lineage or descent.
anchor *noun* **1** heavy hooked device attached to a boat by a cable and dropped overboard to fasten the ship to the sea bottom. **2** source of stability or security. ◆ *verb* **3** fasten with or as if with an anchor. **anchorage** *noun* place where boats can be anchored. **anchorman,** **anchorwoman** *noun* **1** broadcaster in a central studio who links up and presents items from outside camera units and other studios. **2** last person to compete in a relay team.
anchorite *noun* religious recluse.
anchovy [an-chov-ee] *noun, pl* **-vies** small strong-tasting fish.

ancien régime [on-syan ray-**zheem**] *noun* *French* a former system, esp. the political and social system in France before the 1789 Revolution.
ancient ⊕ *adjective* **1** dating from very long ago. **2** very old. **ancients** *plural noun* people who lived very long ago.
ancillary ⊕ *adjective* **1** supporting the main work of an organization. **2** used as an extra or supplement.
and ⊕ *conjunction* **1** in addition to. **2** as a consequence. **3** then, afterwards. **and/or** *conjunction* either or both.
andante [an-**dan**-tay] *noun, adverb Music* (piece to be played) moderately slowly.
andantino [an-dan-**tee**-no] *noun, pl* **-nos,** *adverb Music* (piece to be played) slightly faster or slower than andante.
andiron *noun* iron stand for supporting logs in a fireplace.
androgynous *adjective* having both male and female characteristics.
android *noun* robot resembling a human.
anecdote ⊕ *noun* short amusing account of an incident. **anecdotal** *adjective*
anemometer *noun* instrument for recording wind speed.
anemone [an-**nem**-on-ee] *noun* plant with white, purple, or red flowers.
aneroid barometer *noun* device for measuring air pressure, consisting of a partially evacuated chamber in which variations in pressure cause apointer on the lid to move.
aneurysm, aneurism [an-new-riz-zum] *noun* permanent swelling of a blood vessel.
anew *adverb* **1** once more. **2** in a different way.
angel ⊕ *noun* **1** spiritual being believed to be an attendant or messenger of God. **2** person

——————— THESAURUS ———————

analysis *noun* **1** = **examination**, breakdown, dissection, inquiry, investigation, scrutiny, sifting, test
analytical, analytic *adjective* **1** = **rational**, inquiring, inquisitive, investigative, logical, organized, problem-solving, systematic
anarchic *adjective* = **lawless**, chaotic, disorganized, rebellious, riotous, ungoverned OPPOSITE> **law-abiding**
anarchist *noun* = **revolutionary**, insurgent, nihilist, rebel, terrorist
anarchy *noun* = **lawlessness**, chaos, confusion, disorder, disorganization, revolution, riot OPPOSITE> **order**
anatomy *noun* **2** = **structure**, build, composition, frame, framework, make-up **4**

= **examination**, analysis, dissection, division, inquiry, investigation, study
ancestor *noun* = **forefather**, forebear, forerunner, precursor, predecessor OPPOSITE> **successor**
ancient *adjective* = **old**, aged, antique, archaic, old-fashioned, primeval, primordial, timeworn OPPOSITE> **new**
ancillary *adjective* **1** = **supporting**, auxiliary, secondary, subordinate, subsidiary OPPOSITE> **major**. **2** = **supplementary**, additional, extra
and *conjunction* **1** = **also**, along with, as well as, furthermore, in addition to, including, moreover, plus, together with
anecdote *noun* = **story**, reminiscence, short story, sketch, tale, urban legend, urban myth,

who is kind, pure, or beautiful. **angelic** *adjective*
angelically *adverb*
angelica [an-**jell**-ik-a] *noun* **1** aromatic plant.
2 its candied stalks, used in cookery.
Angelus [an-**jell**-uss] *noun* **1** (in the Roman
Catholic Church) prayers recited in the
morning, at midday, and in the evening. **2** bell
signalling the times of these prayers.
anger ⊕ *noun* **1** fierce displeasure or extreme
annoyance. ♦ *verb* **2** make (someone) angry.
angina [an-**jine**-a] *noun* heart disorder causing
sudden severe chest pains (also **angina
pectoris**).
angle¹ ⊕ *noun* **1** space between or shape
formed by two lines or surfaces that meet. **2**
divergence between these, measured in
degrees. **3** corner. **4** point of view. ♦ *verb* **5**
bend or place (something) at an angle.
angle² ⊕ *verb* **1** fish with a hook and line. **2**
(foll. by *for*) try to get by hinting. **angler** *noun*
angling *noun*
Anglican *noun, adjective* (member) of the
Church of England. **Anglicanism** *noun*
anglicize *verb* make or become English in
outlook, form, etc. **Anglicism** *noun* expression
or custom characteristic of the English.
Anglo *noun, pl* **-glos** *Canad* English-speaking
Canadian.
Anglo- *combining form* **1** English, e.g. *Anglo-
Scottish.* **2** British, e.g. *Anglo-American.*
Anglophile *noun* person who admires
England or the English. **Anglophilia** *noun*
Anglophobe *noun* person who dislikes
England or the English. **Anglophobia** *noun*
Anglo-Saxon *noun* **1** member of any of the
W Germanic tribes that settled in England from
the fifth century AD. **2** language of the Anglo-
Saxons. ♦ *adjective* **3** of the Anglo-Saxons or

their language.
angora *noun* **1** variety of goat, cat, or rabbit
with long silky hair. **2** hair of the angora goat
or rabbit. **3** cloth made from this hair.
Angostura Bitters *plural noun* ® bitter
tonic, used as a flavouring in alcoholic drinks.
angry ⊕ *adjective* **-grier, -griest 1** full of
anger. **2** inflamed, e.g. *an angry wound.*
angrily *adverb*
angst ⊕ *noun* feeling of anxiety.
angstrom *noun* unit of length used to
measure wavelengths.
anguish ⊕ *noun* great mental pain.
anguished *adjective*
angular *adjective* **1** (of a person) lean and
bony. **2** having angles. **3** measured by an
angle. **angularity** *noun*
anhydrous *adjective Chem* containing no
water.
anil *noun* West Indian shrub, from which
indigo is obtained.
aniline *noun* colourless oily liquid obtained
from coal tar and used for making dyes,
plastics, and explosives.
animal ⊕ *noun* **1** living creature with
specialized sense organs and capable of
voluntary motion, esp. one other than a human
being. **2** quadruped. ♦ *adjective* **3** of animals. **4**
sensual, physical. **animality** *noun* animal
instincts of human beings. **animalcule** *noun*
microscopic animal.
animate ⊕ *verb* **1** give life to. **2** make lively. **3**
make a cartoon film of. ♦ *adjective* **4** having life.
animated *adjective* **animatedly** *adverb*
animation *noun* **1** technique of making cartoon
films. **2** liveliness and enthusiasm. **animator**
noun
animism *noun* belief that natural objects

———————— THESAURUS ————————

yarn
angel *noun* **1** =**divine messenger**, archangel,
cherub, seraph **2** =**dear**, beauty, darling, gem,
jewel, paragon, saint, treasure
angelic *adjective* **1** =**heavenly**, celestial,
cherubic, ethereal, seraphic OPPOSITE **satanic.**
2 =**pure**, adorable, beautiful, entrancing,
lovely, saintly, virtuous
anger *noun* **1** =**rage**, annoyance, displeasure,
exasperation, fury, ire, outrage, resentment,
temper, wrath OPPOSITE **calmness** ♦*verb* **2**
=**enrage**, annoy, displease, exasperate, gall,
incense, infuriate, madden, outrage, rile, vex
OPPOSITE **soothe**
angle¹ *noun* **1** =**intersection**, bend, crook,
elbow, nook **2** =**corner**, edge, point **4** =**point
of view**, approach, aspect, outlook, perspective,

position, side, slant, standpoint, viewpoint
angle² *verb* **1** =**fish**, cast
angry *adjective* **1** =**furious**, annoyed, cross,
displeased, enraged, exasperated, incensed,
infuriated, irate, mad (*inf*), outraged, resentful
OPPOSITE **calm**
angst *noun* =**anxiety**, apprehension, unease,
worry OPPOSITE **peace of mind**
anguish *noun* =**suffering**, agony, distress,
grief, heartache, misery, pain, sorrow, torment,
woe
animal *noun* **2** =**creature**, beast, brute
♦*adjective* **4** =**physical**, bestial, bodily, brutish,
carnal, gross, sensual
animate *verb* **2** =**enliven**, energize, excite,
fire, inspire, invigorate, kindle, move, stimulate
OPPOSITE **inhibit** ♦*adjective* **4** =**living**, alive,

possess souls. **animist** noun, adjective **animistic** adjective

animosity ⊙ noun, pl **-ties** hostility, hatred.

animus noun hatred, animosity.

anion [an-eye-on] noun ion with negative charge.

anise [an-niss] noun plant with liquorice-flavoured seeds.

aniseed noun liquorice-flavoured seeds of the anise plant.

ankle noun joint between the foot and leg.

anklet noun ornamental chain worn round the ankle.

ankylosis [ang-kill-loh-siss] noun abnormal immobility of a joint, caused by a fibrous growth.

anna noun former Indian coin worth one sixteenth of rupee.

annals ⊙ plural noun yearly records of events. **annalist** noun

anneal verb toughen (metal or glass) by heating and slow cooling.

annelid noun worm with a segmented body, such as an earthworm.

annex ⊙ verb **1** seize (territory). **2** take (something) without permission. **3** join or add (something) to something larger. **annexation** noun

annexe noun **1** extension to a building. **2** nearby building used as an extension.

annihilate ⊙ verb destroy utterly. **annihilation** noun

anniversary noun, pl **-ries 1** date on which

something occurred in a previous year. **2** celebration of this.

anno Domini adverb Latin (indicating years numbered from the supposed year of the birth of Christ) in the year of our Lord.

annotate verb add notes to (a written work). **annotation** noun

announce ⊙ verb **1** make known publicly. **2** proclaim. **announcement** noun **announcer** noun person who introduces radio or television programmes.

annoy ⊙ verb irritate or displease. **annoyance** noun **annoying** adjective **annoyingly** adverb

annual ⊙ adjective **1** happening once a year. **2** lasting for a year. ◆ noun **3** plant that completes its life cycle in a year. **4** book published once every year. **annually** adverb

annuity noun, pl **-ties** fixed sum paid every year.

annul ⊙ verb **-nulling, -nulled** declare (something, esp. a marriage) invalid. **annulment** noun

annular [an-new-lar] adjective ring-shaped.

Annunciation noun Christianity angel Gabriel's announcement to the Virgin Mary of her conception of Christ.

anode noun Electricity positive electrode in a battery, valve, etc. **anodize** verb coat (metal) with a protective oxide film by electrolysis.

anodyne noun **1** something that relieves pain or distress. ◆ adjective **2** relieving pain or distress.

anoint ⊙ verb smear with oil as a sign of

————— THESAURUS —————

alive and kicking, breathing, live, moving

animated adjective **2** = **lively**, ebullient, energetic, enthusiastic, excited, passionate, spirited, vivacious OPPOSITE listless

animation noun **2** = **liveliness**, ebullience, energy, enthusiasm, excitement, fervour, passion, spirit, verve, vivacity, zest

animosity noun = **hostility**, acrimony, antipathy, bitterness, enmity, hatred, ill will, malevolence, malice, rancour, resentment OPPOSITE **friendliness**

annals plural noun = **records**, accounts, archives, chronicles, history

annex verb **1** = **seize**, acquire, appropriate, conquer, occupy, take over **3** = **join**, add, adjoin, attach, connect, fasten OPPOSITE remove

annihilate verb = **destroy**, abolish, eradicate, exterminate, extinguish, obliterate, wipe out

announce verb = **make known**, advertise, broadcast, declare, disclose, proclaim, report, reveal, tell OPPOSITE hide

announcement noun = **statement**, advertisement, broadcast, bulletin, communiqué, declaration, proclamation, report, revelation

announcer noun = **presenter**, broadcaster, commentator, master of ceremonies, newscaster, newsreader, reporter

annoy verb = **irritate**, anger, bother, displease, disturb, exasperate, get on one's nerves (inf), hassle (inf), madden, molest, pester, plague, trouble, vex OPPOSITE soothe

annoyance noun = **irritation**, anger, bother, hassle (inf), nuisance, trouble

annoying adjective = **irritating**, disturbing, exasperating, maddening, troublesome OPPOSITE **delightful**

annual adjective **1** = **yearly**, once a year **2** = **yearlong**

annually adverb **1** = **yearly**, every year, once a year, per annum, per year

annul verb = **invalidate**, abolish, cancel, declare or render null and void, negate, nullify, consecration.

anomaly ⊕ [an-**nom**-a-lee] *noun, pl* **-lies** something that deviates from the normal, irregularity. **anomalous** *adjective*

anomie [an-oh-mee] *noun Sociology* lack of social or moral standards. **anomic** [an-**nom**-mik] *adjective*

anon *adverb Obs* in a short time, soon.

anon. anonymous.

anonymous ⊕ *adjective* **1** by someone whose name is unknown or withheld. **2** having no known name. **anonymously** *adverb* **anonymity** *noun*

anorak *noun* waterproof hooded jacket.

anorexia *noun* psychological disorder characterized by fear of becoming fat and refusal to eat (also **anorexia nervosa**). **anorexic** *adjective, noun*

another *adjective, pronoun* **1** one more. **2** a different (one).

answer ⊕ *noun* **1** reply to a question, request, letter, etc. **2** solution to a problem. **3** reaction or response. ◆ *verb* **4** give an answer (to). **5** be responsible to (a person). **6** respond or react. **answerable** *adjective* (foll. by *for* or *to*) responsible for or accountable to. **answering machine** device for answering a telephone automatically and recording messages.

ant *noun* small insect living in highly organized colonies. **anteater** *noun* mammal which feeds on ants by means of a long snout. **ant hill** mound built by ants around their nest.

antacid *noun* substance that counteracts acidity, esp. in the stomach.

antagonist ⊕ *noun* opponent or adversary. **antagonism** *noun* open opposition or hostility. **antagonistic** *adjective* **antagonize** *verb* arouse hostility in, annoy.

antalkali [ant-**alk**-a-lie] *noun* substance that

neutralizes alkalis.

Antarctic *noun* **1 the Antarctic** area around the South Pole. ◆ *adjective* **2** of this region.

SPELLING TIP

Almost one in every hundred references to the **Antarctic** in the Bank of English is written without its first *c* as *Antartic*. Note there is a *c* after the *r*.

---

ante *noun* **1** player's stake in poker. ◆ *verb* **-teing, -ted** *or* **-teed 2** place (one's stake) in poker.

ante- *prefix* before in time or position, e.g. *antedate; antechamber.*

antecedent *noun* **1** event or circumstance happening or existing before another. ◆ *adjective* **2** preceding, prior.

antechamber *noun* same as ANTEROOM.

antedate *verb* precede in time.

antediluvian *adjective* **1** of the time before the biblical Flood. **2** old-fashioned.

antelope *noun* deerlike mammal with long legs and horns.

antenatal *adjective* during pregnancy, before birth.

antenna *noun* **1** *pl* **-nae** insect's feeler. **2** *pl* **-nas** aerial.

antepenultimate *adjective* third last.

ante-post *adjective* (of a bet) placed before the runners in a race are confirmed.

anterior *adjective* **1** to the front. **2** earlier.

anteroom *noun* small room leading into a larger one, often used as a waiting room.

anthem ⊕ *noun* **1** song of loyalty, esp. to a country. **2** piece of music for a choir, usu. set to words from the Bible.

THESAURUS

repeal, retract OPPOSITE restore

anoint *verb* =consecrate, bless, hallow, sanctify

anomalous *adjective* =unusual, abnormal, eccentric, exceptional, incongruous, inconsistent, irregular, munted (*NZ sl*), odd, peculiar OPPOSITE **normal**

anomaly *noun* =irregularity, abnormality, eccentricity, exception, incongruity, inconsistency, oddity, peculiarity

anonymous *adjective* **1** =uncredited, unacknowledged, unknown, unsigned OPPOSITE **signed. 2** =unnamed, incognito, nameless, unidentified OPPOSITE **known**

answer *noun* **1** =reply, comeback, defence, rejoinder, response, retort, return, riposte

OPPOSITE question. **2** = solution, explanation **3** = reaction, response ◆*verb* **4** = reply, respond, retort, return OPPOSITE ask. **6** = react, respond

answerable *adjective* (foll. by *for* or *to*) =responsible, accountable, amenable, chargeable, liable, subject, to blame

antagonism *noun* =hostility, antipathy, conflict, discord, dissension, friction, opposition, rivalry OPPOSITE **friendship**

antagonist *noun* =opponent, adversary, competitor, contender, enemy, foe, rival

antagonistic *adjective* =hostile, at odds, at variance, conflicting, incompatible, in dispute, opposed, unfriendly

antagonize *verb* =annoy, anger, get on one's nerves (*inf*), hassle (*inf*), irritate, offend

A

anther *noun* part of a flower's stamen containing pollen.

anthology ⊕ *noun, pl* **-gies** collection of poems or other literary pieces by various authors. **anthologist** *noun*

anthracite *noun* hard coal burning slowly with little smoke or flame but intense heat.

anthrax *noun* dangerous disease of cattle and sheep, communicable to humans.

anthropocentric *adjective* regarding human beings as the most important factor in the universe.

anthropoid *adjective* 1 like a human. ♦ *noun* 2 ape, such as a chimpanzee, that resembles a human.

anthropology *noun* study of human origins, institutions, and beliefs. **anthropological** *adjective* **anthropologist** *noun*

anthropomorphic *adjective* attributing human form or personality to a god, animal, or object. **anthropomorphism** *noun*

anti *adjective, preposition Informal* opposed (to).

anti- *prefix* 1 against, opposed to, e.g. *anti-war*. 2 opposite to, e.g. *anticlimax*. 3 counteracting, e.g. *antifreeze*.

anti-aircraft *adjective* for defence against aircraft attack.

antiballistic missile *noun* missile designed to destroy a ballistic missile in flight.

antibiotic *noun* 1 chemical substance capable of destroying bacteria. ♦ *adjective* 2 of antibiotics.

antibody *noun, pl* **-bodies** protein produced in the blood, which destroys bacteria.

Antichrist *noun* 1 *New Testament* the antagonist of Christ. 2 any enemy of Christ or Christianity.

anticipate ⊕ *verb* 1 foresee and act in advance of. 2 look forward to. 3 make use of (something) before receiving it. **anticipation** *noun* **anticipatory** *adjective*

anticlimax ⊕ *noun* disappointing conclusion to a series of events. **anticlimactic** *adjective*

anticlockwise *adverb, adjective* in the opposite direction to the rotation of the hands of a clock.

antics ⊕ *plural noun* absurd acts or postures.

anticyclone *noun* area of moving air of high pressure in which the winds rotate outwards.

antidote ⊕ *noun* 1 substance that counteracts a poison. 2 anything that counteracts a harmful condition.

antifreeze *noun* liquid added to water to lower its freezing point, used in car radiators.

antigen [an-tee-jen] *noun* substance, usu. a toxin, causing the blood to produce antibodies.

antihero *noun, pl* **-roes** central character in a book, film, etc., who lacks the traditional heroic virtues.

antihistamine *noun* drug used to treat allergies.

antimacassar *noun* cloth put over a chair-back to prevent soiling.

antimony [an-tim-mon-ee] *noun Chem* brittle silvery-white metallic element.

antinuclear *adjective* opposed to nuclear weapons or nuclear power.

antipasto *noun, pl* **-tos** appetizer in an Italian meal.

antipathy ⊕ [an-**tip**-a-thee] *noun* dislike, hostility. **antipathetic** *adjective*

antiperspirant *noun* substance used to reduce or prevent sweating.

antiphon *noun* hymn sung in alternate parts by two groups of singers. **antiphonal** *adjective*

antipodes [an-**tip**-pod-deez] *plural noun* any two places diametrically opposite one another on the earth's surface. **the Antipodes** Australia and New Zealand. **antipodean** *adjective*

antipyretic *adjective* 1 reducing fever. ♦ *noun* 2 drug that reduces fever.

antiquary *noun, pl* **-quaries** student or collector of antiques or ancient works of art.

antiquarian *adjective* 1 of or relating to antiquities or rare books. ♦ *noun* 2 antiquary.

antiquated ⊕ *adjective* out-of-date.

——————— THESAURUS ———————

anthem *noun* 1 = **song of praise**, paean 2 = **hymn**, canticle, carol, chant, chorale, psalm

anthology *noun* = **collection**, compendium, compilation, miscellany, selection, treasury

anticipate *verb* 1 = **expect**, await, foresee, foretell, predict, prepare for 2 = **look forward to**, hope for

anticipation *noun* 1 = **expectation**, expectancy, foresight, forethought, premonition, prescience

anticlimax *noun* = **disappointment**, bathos,

comedown (*inf*), letdown OPPOSITE> **climax**

antics *plural noun* = **clowning**, escapades, horseplay, mischief, playfulness, pranks, tomfoolery, tricks

antidote *noun* = **cure**, countermeasure, remedy

antipathy *noun* = **hostility**, aversion, bad blood, dislike, enmity, hatred, ill will OPPOSITE> affinity

antiquated *adjective* = **obsolete**, antique, archaic, dated, old-fashioned, out-of-date, passé OPPOSITE> **up-to-date**

antique ❶ *noun* **1** object of an earlier period, valued for its beauty, workmanship, or age. ♦ *adjective* **2** made in an earlier period. **3** old-fashioned.

antiquity ❶ *noun* **1** great age. **2** ancient times. **antiquities** *plural noun* objects dating from ancient times.

antiracism *noun* policy of challenging racism and promoting racial tolerance. **antiracist** *noun, adjective*

antirrhinum *noun* two-lipped flower of various colours.

antiscorbutic *adjective* preventing or curing scurvy.

anti-Semitism *noun* discrimination against Jews. **anti-Semite** *noun* person who persecutes or discriminates against Jews. **anti-Semitic** *adjective*

antiseptic ❶ *adjective* **1** preventing infection by killing germs. ♦ *noun* **2** antiseptic substance.

antisocial ❶ *adjective* **1** avoiding the company of other people. **2** (of behaviour) harmful to society.

antistatic *adjective* reducing the effects of static electricity.

antithesis ❶ [an-**tith**-iss-iss] *noun, pl* **-ses** [-seez] **1** exact opposite. **2** placing together of contrasting ideas or words to produce an effect of balance. **antithetical** *adjective*

antitoxin *noun* (serum containing) an antibody that acts against a toxin.

antitrades *plural noun* winds blowing in the opposite direction from and above the trade winds.

antitrust *adjective Aust, S Afr & US* (of laws) opposing business monopolies.

antler *noun* branched horn of male deer.

antonym *noun* word that means the opposite of another.

anus [**ain**-uss] *noun* opening at the end of the alimentary canal, through which faeces are discharged.

anvil *noun* heavy iron block on which metals are hammered into particular shapes.

anxiety ❶ *noun, pl* **-ties** state of being anxious.

anxious ❶ *adjective* **1** worried and tense. **2** intensely desiring. **anxiety** *noun* **anxiously** *adverb*

any *adjective, pronoun* **1** one or some, no matter which. ♦ *adverb* **2** at all, e.g. *it isn't any worse.* **anybody** *pronoun* anyone. **anyhow** *adverb* anyway. **anyone** *pronoun* **1** any person. **2** person of any importance. **anything** *pronoun* any object, event, or action whatever. **anyway** *adverb* **1** at any rate, nevertheless. **2** in any manner. **anywhere** *adverb* in, at, or to any place.

LANGUAGE TIP

It is no longer considered wrong to use *anyone* with a following plural form as in *Has anyone lost their purse?*

Anzac *noun* (in World War 1) a soldier serving with the Australian and New Zealand Army Corps.

AOB (on the agenda for a meeting) any other business.

aorta [eh-**or**-ta] *noun* main artery of the body, carrying oxygen-rich blood from the heart.

apace *adverb Lit* swiftly.

Apache *noun, pl* **Apaches, Apache** Native American of the SW US and N Mexico.

apart ❶ *adverb* **1** to or in pieces. **2** to or at a distance. **3** individual, distinct. **apart from** other than.

apartheid *noun* former official government

————————————— T H E S A U R U S —————————————

antique *noun* **1 = period piece**, bygone, heirloom, relic ♦*adjective* **2 = vintage**, antiquarian, classic, olden **3 = old-fashioned**, archaic, obsolete, outdated

antiquity *noun* **1 = old age**, age, ancientness, elderliness, oldness **2 = distant past**, ancient times, olden days, time immemorial

antiseptic *adjective* **1 = hygienic**, clean, germ-free, pure, sanitary, sterile, uncontaminated OPPOSITE dirty ♦*noun* **2 = disinfectant**, germicide, purifier

antisocial *adjective* **1 = unsociable**, alienated, misanthropic, reserved, retiring, uncommunicative, unfriendly, withdrawn OPPOSITE **sociable. 2 = disruptive**, antagonistic, belligerent, disorderly, hostile, menacing, rebellious, uncooperative

antithesis *noun* **1 = opposite**, contrary, contrast, converse, inverse, reverse

anxiety *noun* **= uneasiness**, angst, apprehension, concern, foreboding, misgiving, nervousness, tension, trepidation, worry OPPOSITE **confidence**

anxious *adjective* **1 = uneasy**, apprehensive, concerned, fearful, in suspense, nervous, on tenterhooks, tense, troubled, worried OPPOSITE **certain. 2 = eager**, desirous, impatient, intent, itching, keen, yearning OPPOSITE **reluctant**

apart *adverb* **1 = to pieces**, asunder, in bits, in pieces, to bits **2 = separate**, alone, aside, away,

A

policy of racial segregation in S Africa.
apartment ⊕ *noun* **1** room in a building. **2** flat.
apathy ⊕ *noun* lack of interest or enthusiasm. **apathetic** *adjective* **apathetically** *adverb*
ape *noun* **1** tailless monkey such as the chimpanzee or gorilla. **2** stupid, clumsy, or ugly man. ♦ *verb* **3** imitate. **apeman** *noun* extinct primate thought to have been the forerunner of true humans.
aperient [ap-**peer**-ee-ent] *adjective* **1** having a mild laxative effect. ♦ *noun* **2** mild laxative.
aperitif [ap-per-rit-**teef**] *noun* alcoholic drink taken before a meal.
aperture *noun* **1** opening or hole. **2** opening in a camera or telescope that controls the amount of light entering it.
apex ⊕ *noun* highest point.
APEX Advance Purchase Excursion: reduced fare for journeys booked a specified period in advance.
aphasia *noun* disorder of the central nervous system that affects the ability to speak and understand words.
aphelion [ap-**heel**-lee-on] *noun, pl* **-lia** [-lee-a] point of a planet's orbit that is farthest from the sun.
aphid [**eh**-fid], **aphis** [**eh**-fiss] *noun* small insect which sucks the sap from plants.
aphorism *noun* short clever saying expressing a general truth.
aphrodisiac [af-roh-**diz**-zee-ak] *noun* **1** substance that arouses sexual desire. ♦ *adjective* **2** arousing sexual desire.
apiary [**ape**-yar-ee] *noun, pl* **-ries** place where bees are kept. **apiarist** *noun* beekeeper.
apiculture *noun* breeding and care of bees.
apiece ⊕ *adverb* each, e.g. *they were given two*

apples apiece.
aplomb ⊕ [ap-**plom**] *noun* calm self-possession.
apocalypse *noun* **1** end of the world. **2** event of great destruction. **the Apocalypse** book of Revelation, the last book of the New Testament. **apocalyptic** *adjective*
Apocrypha [ap-**pok**-rif-fa] *plural noun* **the Apocrypha** collective name for the 14 books of the Old Testament which are not accepted as part of the Hebrew scriptures.
apocryphal ⊕ *adjective* (of a story) of questionable authenticity.
apogee [ap-oh-jee] *noun* **1** point of the moon's or a satellite's orbit that is farthest from the earth. **2** highest point.
apolitical *adjective* not concerned with political matters.
apologia *noun* formal written defence of a cause.
apology ⊕ *noun, pl* **-gies 1** expression of regret for wrongdoing. **2** (foll. by *for*) poor example (of). **3** same as APOLOGIA. **apologetic** *adjective* showing or expressing regret. **apologetically** *adverb* **apologetics** *noun* branch of theology concerned with the reasoned defence of Christianity. **apologist** *noun* person who formally defends a cause. **apologize** *verb* make an apology.

> **SPELLING TIP**
>
> Remember that the correct way to spell **apology** is with one *p* and one *l*.

apoplexy *noun Med* stroke. **apoplectic** *adjective* **1** of apoplexy. **2** *Informal* furious.

——— THESAURUS ———

by oneself, isolated, to one side
apart from *preposition* =**except for**, aside from, besides, but, excluding, not counting, other than, save
apartment *noun* **1** =**room**, accommodation, living quarters, quarters, rooms, suite **2** =**flat**, penthouse, duplex (*US & Canad*)
apathetic *adjective* =**uninterested**, cool, indifferent, passive, phlegmatic, unconcerned OPPOSITE interested
apathy *noun* =**lack of interest**, coolness, indifference, inertia, nonchalance, passivity, torpor, unconcern OPPOSITE interest
apex *noun* =**highest point**, crest, crown, culmination, peak, pinnacle, point, summit, top OPPOSITE base
apiece *adverb* =**each**, for each, from each,

individually, respectively, separately OPPOSITE all together
aplomb *noun* =**self-possession**, calmness, composure, confidence, level-headedness, poise, sang-froid, self-assurance, self-confidence OPPOSITE self-doubt
apocryphal *adjective* =**dubious**, doubtful, legendary, mythical, questionable, unauthenticated, unsubstantiated OPPOSITE factual
apologetic *adjective* =**regretful**, contrite, penitent, remorseful, rueful, sorry
apologize *verb* =**say sorry**, ask forgiveness, beg pardon, express regret
apology *noun* **1** =**defence**, acknowledgment, confession, excuse, explanation, justification, plea **2** (foll. by *for*) =**mockery**, caricature,

A

apostasy [ap-**poss**-stass-ee] *noun, pl* **-sies** abandonment of one's religious faith or other belief. **apostate** *noun, adjective*

a posteriori [eh poss-steer-ee-**or**-rye] *adjective* involving reasoning from effect to cause.

Apostle *noun* **1** one of the twelve disciples chosen by Christ to preach his gospel. **2** (**a-**) ardent supporter of a cause or movement. **apostolic** [ap-poss-**stoll**-ik] *adjective*

apostrophe [ap-**poss**-trof-fee] *noun* **1** punctuation mark (') showing the omission of a letter or letters in a word, e.g. *don't* , or forming the possessive,e.g. *Jill's car*. **2** digression from a speech to address an imaginary or absent person or thing.

apothecary *noun, pl* **-caries** *Obs* chemist.

apotheosis ❶ [ap-poth-ee-**oh**-siss] *noun, pl* **-ses** [-seez] **1** perfect example. **2** elevation to the rank of a god.

appal ❶ *verb* **-palling, -palled** dismay, terrify. **appalling** *adjective* dreadful, terrible.

> **SPELLING TIP**
>
> The verb **appal** has two *ps*, but only one *l*. If you extend it with an ending beginning with a vowel, you must add another *l*, as in **appalling**.

apparatus ❶ *noun* equipment for a particular purpose.

apparel [ap-**par**-rel] *noun Old-fashioned* clothing.

apparent ❶ *adjective* **1** readily seen, obvious. **2** seeming as opposed to real. **apparently** *adverb*

> **SPELLING TIP**
>
> It's quite common to spell **apparently** with three *as*, but there should only be two - and then an *e*.

apparition ❶ *noun* ghost or ghostlike figure.

appeal ❶ *verb* **1** make an earnest request. **2** attract, please, or interest. **3** request a review of a lower court's decision by a higher court. ♦ *noun* **4** earnest request for money or help. **5** power to attract, please, or interest people. **6** request for a review of a lower court's decision by a higher court.

appealing *adjective* **appealingly** *adverb*

appear ❶ *verb* **1** become visible or present. **2** seem. **3** be seen in public. **appearance** *noun* **1** sudden or unexpected arrival of someone or something at a place. **2** an appearing. **3** outward aspect.

appease ❶ *verb* **1** pacify (a person) by

———————————— THESAURUS ————————————

excuse, imitation, travesty

Apostle *noun* **1** = **evangelist**, herald, messenger, missionary, preacher **2** (not cap.) = **supporter**, advocate, champion, pioneer, propagandist, proponent

apotheosis *noun* **2** = **deification**, elevation, exaltation, glorification, idolization

appal *verb* = **horrify**, alarm, daunt, dishearten, dismay, frighten, outrage, shock, unnerve

appalling *adjective* = **horrifying**, alarming, awful, daunting, dreadful, fearful, frightful, horrible, shocking, terrifying OPPOSITE encouraging

apparatus *noun* = **equipment**, appliance, contraption (*inf*), device, gear, machinery, mechanism, tackle, tools

apparent *adjective* **1** = **obvious**, discernible, distinct, evident, manifest, marked, unmistakable, visible OPPOSITE uncertain. **2** = **seeming**, ostensible, outward, superficial OPPOSITE real

apparently *adverb* **2** = **it appears that**, it seems that, on the face of it, ostensibly, outwardly, seemingly, superficially

apparition *noun* = **ghost**, chimera, phantom, spectre, spirit, wraith

appeal *verb* **1** = **plead**, ask, beg, call upon, entreat, pray, request OPPOSITE refuse. **2** = **attract**, allure, charm, entice, fascinate, interest, please, tempt ♦ *noun* **4** = **plea**, application, entreaty, petition, prayer, request, supplication OPPOSITE refusal. **5** = **attraction**, allure, beauty, charm, fascination OPPOSITE repulsiveness

appealing *adjective* **2** = **attractive**, alluring, charming, desirable, engaging, lekker (*S Afr sl*), winsome OPPOSITE repellent

appear *verb* **1** = **come into view**, be present, come out, come to light, crop up (*inf*), emerge, occur, show up (*inf*), surface, turn up OPPOSITE disappear. **2** = **look (like** or **as if)**, occur, seem, strike one as

appearance *noun* **1** = **arrival**, coming, emergence, introduction, presence **2** = **look**, demeanour, expression, figure, form, looks, manner, mien (*lit*) **3** = **impression**, front, guise, illusion, image, outward show, pretence, semblance

A

yielding to his or her demands. **2** satisfy or relieve (a feeling). **appeasement** *noun*
appellant *noun* person who makes an appeal to a higher court.
appellation *noun* name, title.
append ⊕ *verb* join on, add. **appendage** *noun* thing joined on or added.
appendicitis *noun* inflammation of the appendix.
appendix ⊕ *noun, pl* **-dices, -dixes 1** separate additional material at the end of a book. **2** *Anat* short closed tube attached to the large intestine.

LANGUAGE TIP

Extra sections at the end of a book are *appendices*. The plural *appendixes* is used in medicine.

---

appertain *verb* (foll. by *to*) **1** belong to. **2** be connected with.
appetite ⊕ *noun* **1** desire for food or drink. **2** liking or willingness. **appetizer** *noun* thing eaten or drunk to stimulate the appetite.
appetizing *adjective* stimulating the appetite.
applaud ⊕ *verb* **1** show approval of by clapping one's hands. **2** approve strongly.
applause *noun* approval shown by clapping one's hands.

apple *noun* round firm fleshy fruit that grows on trees. **in apple-pie order** *Informal* very tidy.
appliance ⊕ *noun* device with a specific function.
applicable ⊕ *adjective* relevant, appropriate. **applicability** *noun*
applicant ⊕ *noun* person who applies for something.
application ⊕ *noun* **1** formal request. **2** act of applying something to a particular use. **3** diligent effort. **4** act of putting something onto a surface.
applicator *noun* simple device for applying cosmetics, medication, etc.
appliqué [ap-plee-kay] *noun* kind of decoration in which one material is cut out and attached to another.
apply ⊕ *verb* **-plying, -plied 1** make a formal request. **2** put to practical use. **3** put onto a surface. **4** be relevant or appropriate. **apply oneself** concentrate one's efforts. **applicant** *noun* **application** *noun* formal request. **applied** *adjective* (of a skill, science, etc.) put to practical use.
appoint ⊕ *verb* **1** assign to a job or position. **2** fix or decide, e.g. *appoint a time.* **3** equip or furnish. **appointee** *noun* **appointment** *noun* **1** arrangement to meet a person. **2** act of placing someone in a job. **3** the job itself. ♦ *plural* **4** fixtures or fittings.

————— T H E S A U R U S —————

appease *verb* **1** = **pacify**, calm, conciliate, mollify, placate, quiet, satisfy, soothe OPPOSITE upset. **2** = **ease**, allay, alleviate, calm, relieve, soothe
appeasement *noun* **1** = **pacification**, accommodation, compromise, concession, conciliation, mollification, placation **2** = **easing**, alleviation, lessening, relieving, soothing
appendage *noun* = **attachment**, accessory, addition, supplement
appendix *noun* **1** = **supplement**, addendum, addition, adjunct, appendage, postscript
appetite *noun* **1** = **desire**, craving, demand, hunger, relish, stomach, taste OPPOSITE disgust. **2** = **liking**, longing, passion, yearning
appetizing *adjective* = **delicious**, appealing, inviting, mouthwatering, palatable, succulent, tasty, tempting
applaud *verb* **1** = **clap**, cheer OPPOSITE boo. **2** = **approve**, acclaim, commend, compliment, encourage, extol, praise OPPOSITE criticize
applause *noun* = **ovation**, big hand, cheers, clapping, hand
appliance *noun* = **device**, apparatus, gadget, implement, instrument, machine, mechanism,

tool
applicable *adjective* = **appropriate**, apt, fitting, pertinent, relevant, suitable, useful OPPOSITE inappropriate
applicant *noun* = **candidate**, claimant, inquirer
application *noun* **1** = **request**, appeal, claim, inquiry, petition, requisition **3** = **effort**, commitment, dedication, diligence, hard work, industry, perseverance
apply *verb* **1** = **request**, appeal, claim, inquire, petition, put in, requisition **2** = **use**, bring to bear, carry out, employ, exercise, exert, implement, practise, utilize **3** = **put on**, cover with, lay on, paint, place, smear, spread on **4** = **be relevant**, be applicable, be appropriate, bear upon, be fitting, fit, pertain, refer, relate
apply oneself *verb* = **try**, be diligent, buckle down (*inf*), commit oneself, concentrate, dedicate oneself, devote oneself, persevere, work hard
appoint *verb* **1** = **assign**, choose, commission, delegate, elect, name, nominate, select OPPOSITE fire. **2** = **decide**, allot, arrange, assign, choose, designate, establish, fix, set

A

apportion ⊕ *verb* divide out in shares.
apposite ⊕ *adjective* suitable, apt. **apposition**
noun grammatical construction in which two
nouns or phrases referring to the same thing
are placed one after anotherwithout a
conjunction, e.g. *my son the doctor.*
appraise ⊕ *verb* estimate the value or quality
of. **appraisal** *noun* **appraising** *adjective*
appraisingly *adverb*
appreciate ⊕ *verb* 1 value highly. 2 be aware
of and understand. 3 be grateful for. 4 rise in
value. **appreciable** *adjective* enough to be
noticed. **appreciably** *adverb* **appreciation**
noun **appreciative** *adjective* feeling or showing
appreciation. **appreciatively** *adverb*
apprehend ⊕ *verb* 1 arrest and take into
custody. 2 grasp (something) mentally.

apprehension *noun* 1 dread, anxiety. 2 arrest.
3 understanding. **apprehensive** *adjective*
fearful or anxious. **apprehensively** *adverb*
apprentice ⊕ *noun* 1 someone working for a
skilled person for a fixed period in order to
learn his or her trade. ◆ *verb* 2 take or place
(someone) as an apprentice. **apprenticeship**
noun
apprise *verb* make aware (of).
appro *noun* **on appro** *Informal* on approval.
approach ⊕ *verb* 1 come near or nearer (to).
2 make a proposal or suggestion to. 3 begin to
deal with (a matter). ◆ *noun* 4 approaching or
means of approaching. 5 proposal or
suggestion made to someone. 6 approximation.
approachable *adjective* 1 friendly. 2 accessible.
approbation *noun* approval.

———————— THESAURUS ————————

OPPOSITE> cancel. 3 = **equip**, fit out, furnish,
provide, supply
appointed *adjective* 1 = **assigned**, chosen,
delegated, elected, named, nominated, selected
2 = **decided**, allotted, arranged, assigned,
chosen, designated, established, fixed, set 3
= **equipped**, fitted out, furnished, provided,
supplied
appointment *noun* 1 = **meeting**,
arrangement, assignation, date, engagement,
interview, rendezvous 2 = **selection**,
assignment, choice, election, naming,
nomination 3 = **job**, assignment, office, place,
position, post, situation ◆*plural* 4 = **fittings**,
fixtures, furnishings, gear, outfit, paraphernalia,
trappings
apportion *verb* = **divide**, allocate, allot,
assign, dispense, distribute, dole out, give out,
ration out, share
apposite *adjective* = **appropriate**, applicable,
apt, fitting, pertinent, relevant, suitable, to the
point OPPOSITE> **inappropriate**
appraisal *noun* = **assessment**, estimate,
estimation, evaluation, judgment, opinion
appraise *verb* = **assess**, estimate, evaluate,
gauge, judge, rate, review, value
appreciable *adjective* = **significant**,
considerable, definite, discernible, evident,
marked, noticeable, obvious, pronounced,
substantial OPPOSITE> **insignificant**
appreciate *verb* 1 = **value**, admire, enjoy,
like, prize, rate highly, respect, treasure
OPPOSITE> **scorn**. 2 = **be aware of**, perceive,
realize, recognize, sympathize with, take
account of, understand OPPOSITE>
misunderstand. 3 = **be grateful for**, be
appreciative, be indebted, be obliged, be
thankful for, give thanks for OPPOSITE> **be**

ungrateful for. 4 = **increase**, enhance, gain,
grow, improve, rise OPPOSITE> **fall**
appreciation *noun* 2 = **awareness**,
admiration, comprehension, enjoyment,
perception, realization, recognition, sensitivity,
sympathy, understanding OPPOSITE> **ignorance**.
3 = **gratitude**, acknowledgment, gratefulness,
indebtedness, obligation, thankfulness, thanks
OPPOSITE> **ingratitude**. 4 = **increase**,
enhancement, gain, growth, improvement, rise
OPPOSITE> **fall**
appreciative *adjective* = **grateful**, beholden,
indebted, obliged, thankful
apprehend *verb* 1 = **arrest**, capture, catch,
nick (*sl, chiefly Brit*), seize, take prisoner
OPPOSITE> **free**. 2 = **understand**, comprehend,
conceive, get the picture, grasp, perceive,
realize, recognize OPPOSITE> **miss**
apprehension *noun* 1 = **anxiety**, alarm,
concern, dread, fear, foreboding, suspicion,
trepidation, worry OPPOSITE> **confidence**. 2
= **arrest**, capture, catching, seizure, taking
OPPOSITE> **release**. 3 = **awareness**,
comprehension, grasp, perception,
understanding OPPOSITE> **incomprehension**
apprehensive *adjective* = **anxious**,
concerned, foreboding, nervous, uneasy,
worried OPPOSITE> **confident**
apprentice *noun* 1 = **trainee**, beginner,
learner, novice, probationer, pupil, student
OPPOSITE> **master**
approach *verb* 1 = **move towards**, come
close, come near, draw near, near, reach 2
= **make a proposal to**, appeal to, apply to,
make overtures to, sound out 3 = **set about**,
begin work on, commence, embark on, enter
upon, make a start, undertake ◆*noun* 4
= **coming**, advance, arrival, drawing near,

A

appropriate ❶ *adjective* **1** suitable, fitting. ◆
verb **2** take for oneself. **3** put aside for a
particular purpose. **appropriately** *adverb*
appropriateness *noun* suitability.
appropriation *noun* act of putting (something)
aside for a particular purpose.
approve ❶ *verb* **1** consider good or right. **2**
authorize, agree to. **approval** *noun* **1** consent.
2 favourable opinion. **on approval** (of goods)
with an option to be returned without payment
if unsatisfactory. **approving** *adjective*
approvingly *adverb*
approx. approximate(ly).
approximate ❶ *adjective* **1** almost but not
quite exact. ◆ *verb* (foll. by *to*) **2** come close to.
3 be almost the same as. **approximately**
adverb **approximation** *noun*
appurtenances *plural noun* minor or
additional features.
Apr. April.
après-ski [ap-ray-**skee**] *noun* social activities
after a day's skiing.
apricot *noun* **1** yellowish-orange juicy fruit like
a small peach. ◆ *adjective* **2** yellowish-orange.
April *noun* fourth month of the year. **April
fool** victim of a practical joke played on April 1
(**April Fools' Day**).
a priori [eh pry-**or**-rye] *adjective* involving
reasoning from cause to effect.
apron ❶ *noun* **1** garment worn over the front
of the body to protect the clothes. **2** area at an
airport or hangar for manoeuvring and loading

aircraft. **3** part of a stage in front of the curtain.
apropos [ap-prop-**poh**] *adjective, adverb*
appropriate(ly). **apropos of** with regard to.
apse *noun* arched or domed recess, esp. in a
church.
apt ❶ *adjective* **1** having a specified tendency.
2 suitable. **3** quick to learn. **aptly** *adverb*
aptness *noun* **aptitude** *noun* natural ability.
APT Advanced Passenger Train.
aqua *adjective* short for AQUAMARINE (sense 2).
aqualung *noun* mouthpiece attached to air
cylinders, worn for underwater swimming.
aquamarine *noun* **1** greenish-blue gemstone.
◆ *adjective* **2** greenish-blue.
aquaplane *noun* **1** board on which a person
stands to be towed by a motorboat. ◆ *verb* **2**
ride on an aquaplane. **3** (of a motor vehicle)
skim uncontrollably on a thin film of water.
aquarium *noun, pl* **aquariums, aquaria 1**
tank in which fish and other underwater
creatures are kept. **2** building containing such
tanks.
Aquarius *noun* (the water bearer) eleventh
sign of the zodiac.
aquatic *adjective* **1** living in or near water. **2**
done in or on water. **aquatics** *plural noun*
water sports.
aquatint *noun* print like a watercolour,
produced by etching copper.
aqua vitae [ak-wa **vee**-tie] *noun Obs* brandy.
aqueduct *noun* structure carrying water across
a valley or river.

———— THESAURUS ————

nearing **5** = **proposal**, appeal, application,
invitation, offer, overture, proposition **6**
= **likeness**, approximation, semblance
approachable *adjective* **1** = **friendly**, affable,
congenial, cordial, open, sociable OPPOSITE
reserved. **2** = **accessible**, attainable, reachable
OPPOSITE **remote**
appropriate *adjective* **1** = **suitable**, apt,
befitting, fitting, pertinent, relevant, to the
point, well-suited OPPOSITE **irrelevant** ◆*verb* **2**
= **seize**, commandeer, confiscate, embezzle,
filch, impound, misappropriate, pilfer, pocket,
steal, take possession of, usurp OPPOSITE **give**.
3 = **allocate**, allot, apportion, assign, devote,
earmark, set aside OPPOSITE **withhold**
approval *noun* **1** = **consent**, agreement,
assent, authorization, blessing, endorsement,
permission, recommendation, sanction **2**
= **favour**, acclaim, admiration, applause,
appreciation, esteem, good opinion, praise,
respect OPPOSITE **disapproval**
approve *verb* **1** = **favour**, admire, commend,
have a good opinion of, like, praise, regard

highly, respect **2** = **agree to**, allow, assent to,
authorize, consent to, endorse, pass, permit,
recommend, sanction OPPOSITE **veto**
approximate *adjective* **1** = **close**, estimated,
inexact, loose, near, rough OPPOSITE **specific**
◆*verb* (foll. by *to*) **2** = **come close**, approach,
border on, come near, reach, touch, verge on **3**
= **resemble**
approximately *adverb* = **almost**, about,
around, circa (*used with dates*), close to, in the
region of, just about, more or less, nearly,
roughly
approximation *noun* = **guess**, conjecture,
estimate, estimation, guesswork, rough
calculation, rough idea
apron *noun* **1** = **pinny**, pinafore (*inf*)
apt *adjective* **1** = **inclined**, disposed, given,
liable, likely, of a mind, prone, ready **2**
= **appropriate**, fitting, pertinent, relevant,
suitable, to the point OPPOSITE **irrelevant**. **3**
= **gifted**, clever, quick, sharp, smart, talented
OPPOSITE **slow**
aptitude *noun* = **gift**, ability, capability,

A

aqueous *adjective* of, like, or containing water.

aquiline *adjective* **1** (of a nose) curved like an eagle's beak. **2** of or like an eagle.

Ar *Chem* argon.

AR Arkansas.

Arab *noun* **1** member of a Semitic people originally from Arabia. ♦ *adjective* **2** of the Arabs. **Arabian** *adjective* of Arabia or the Arabs. **Arabic** *noun* **1** language of the Arabs. ♦ *adjective* **2** of Arabic, Arabs, or Arabia. **Arabic numerals** the symbols 1, 2, 3, 4, 5, 6, 7, 8, 9, 0, used to represent numbers.

arabesque [ar-ab-**besk**] *noun* **1** ballet position in which one leg is raised behind and the arms are extended. **2** elaborate ornamental design.

arable ⊙ *adjective* suitable for growing crops on.

arachnid [ar-**rak**-nid] *noun* eight-legged invertebrate, such as a spider, scorpion, tick, or mite.

arak *noun* same as ARRACK.

Aramaic *noun* an ancient Semitic language of the Middle East.

Aran *adjective* (of sweaters etc.) knitted in a complicated pattern traditional to the Aran Islands, usu. with natural unbleachedwool.

arbiter ⊙ *noun* **1** person empowered to judge in a dispute. **2** person with influential opinions about something.

arbitrary ⊙ *adjective* based on personal choice or chance, rather than reason. **arbitrarily** *adverb* **arbitrariness** *noun*

SPELLING TIP

The spelling *arbitary* appears 22 times in the Bank of English. But the correct spelling, **arbitrary**, appears 1959 times: it has three rs.

---

arbitration ⊙ *noun* hearing and settling of a dispute by an impartial referee chosen by both sides. **arbitrate** *verb* **arbitrator** *noun*

arboreal [ahr-**bore**-ee-al] *adjective* of or living in trees.

arboretum [ahr-bore-**ee**-tum] *noun, pl* **-ta** [-ta] place where rare trees or shrubs are cultivated.

arboriculture *noun* cultivation of trees or shrubs. **arboriculturist** *noun*

arbour *noun* glade sheltered by trees.

arbutus [ar-**byew**-tuss] *noun, pl* **-tuses** evergreen shrub with strawberry-like berries.

arc ⊙ *noun* **1** part of a circle or other curve. **2** luminous discharge of electricity across a small gap between two electrodes. ♦ *verb* **3** form an arc.

arcade ⊙ *noun* **1** covered passageway lined with shops. **2** set of arches and their supporting columns.

Arcadian *adjective* rustic in an idealized way.

arcane ⊙ *adjective* mysterious and secret.

arch¹ ⊙ *noun* **1** curved structure supporting a bridge or roof. **2** something curved. **3** curved lower part of the foot. ♦ *verb* **4** (cause to) form an arch. **archway** *noun* passageway under an arch.

arch² ⊙ *adjective* **1** superior, knowing. **2** coyly playful. **archly** *adverb* **archness** *noun*

arch- *combining form* chief, principal, e.g. *archenemy.*

archaeology *noun* study of ancient cultures from their physical remains. **archaeological** *adjective* **archaeologist** *noun*

archaeopteryx *noun* extinct bird with teeth, a long tail, and well-developed wings.

archaic ⊙ [ark-**kay**-ik] *adjective* **1** ancient. **2** out-of-date. **archaism** [ark-kay-iz-zum] *noun* archaic word or phrase.

archangel [ark-ain-jell] *noun* chief angel.

THESAURUS

---

faculty, intelligence, proficiency, talent

arable *adjective* =**productive**, farmable, fertile, fruitful

arbiter *noun* **1** =**judge**, adjudicator, arbitrator, referee, umpire **2** =**authority**, controller, dictator, expert, governor, lord, mana (*NZ*), master, pundit, ruler

arbitrary *adjective* =**random**, capricious, chance, erratic, inconsistent, personal, subjective, whimsical OPPOSITE reasoned

arbitrate *verb* =**settle**, adjudicate, decide, determine, judge, mediate, pass judgment, referee, umpire

arbitration *noun* =**settlement**, adjudication,

decision, determination, judgment

arbitrator *noun* =**judge**, adjudicator, arbiter, referee, umpire

arc *noun* **1** =**curve**, arch, bend, bow, crescent, half-moon

arcade *noun* =**gallery**, cloister, colonnade, portico

arcane *adjective* =**mysterious**, esoteric, hidden, occult, recondite, secret

arch¹ *noun* **1** =**archway**, curve, dome, span, vault **2** =**curve**, arc, bend, bow, hump, semicircle ♦*verb* **4** =**curve**, arc, bend, bow, bridge, span

arch² *adjective* **2** =**playful**, frolicsome,

A

archbishop *noun* chief bishop.
archdeacon *noun* priest ranking just below a bishop.
archdiocese *noun* diocese of an archbishop.
archduke *noun* duke of specially high rank.
archduchess *n fem* **archduchy** *noun* territory of an archduke or archduchess.
archer *noun* person who shoots with a bow and arrow. **archery** *noun*
archetype ❶ [ark-ee-type] *noun* **1** perfect specimen. **2** original model. **archetypal** *adjective*
archipelago [ark-ee-**pel**-a-go] *noun, pl* **-gos 1** group of islands. **2** sea full of small islands.
architect ❶ *noun* person qualified to design and supervise the construction of buildings.
architecture *noun* **1** style in which a building is designed and built. **2** designing and construction of buildings. **architectural** *adjective* **architecturally** *adverb*
architrave *noun Archit* **1** beam that rests on columns. **2** moulding round a doorway or window.
archive ❶ [ark-ive] *noun* **1** (often pl) collection of records or documents. **2** place where these are kept. **archival** *adjective* **archivist** [ark-iv-ist] *noun* person in charge of archives.
Arctic ❶ *noun* **1 the Arctic** area around the North Pole. ◆ *adjective* **2** of this region. **3** (a-) *Informal* very cold.
ardent ❶ *adjective* **1** passionate. **2** eager, zealous. **ardently** *adverb* **ardour** *noun* **1** passion. **2** enthusiasm, zeal.
arduous ❶ *adjective* hard to accomplish, strenuous. **arduously** *adverb*
are[1] *verb* see BE.
are[2] *noun* unit of measure, 100 square metres.
area ❶ *noun* **1** part or region. **2** size of a two-dimensional surface. **3** subject field. **4** small sunken yard giving access to a basement.
arena ❶ *noun* **1** seated enclosure for sports events. **2** area of a Roman amphitheatre where gladiators fought. **3** sphere of intense activity.
aren't are not.
areola *noun, pl* **-lae, -las** small circular area, such as the coloured ring around the human nipple.
arête *noun* sharp ridge separating valleys.
argon *noun Chem* inert gas found in the air.
argosy *noun, pl* **-sies** *Poetic* large merchant ship.
argot [**ahr**-go] *noun* slang or jargon.
argue ❶ *verb* **-guing, -gued 1** try to prove by giving reasons. **2** debate. **3** quarrel, dispute.
arguable *adjective* **arguably** *adverb* **argument** *noun* **1** quarrel. **2** discussion. **3** point presented for or against something. **argumentation** *noun* process of reasoning methodically.
argumentative *adjective* given to arguing.

> **SPELLING TIP**
>
> There's an *e* at the end of **argue**, but you should leave it out when you write **argument**. A lot of people get that wrong.

argy-bargy *noun, pl* **-bargies** *Informal*

———— T H E S A U R U S ————

mischievous, pert, roguish, saucy, sly, waggish
archaic *adjective* **1 =old**, ancient, antique, bygone, olden (*arch*), primitive OPPOSITE new.
2 =old-fashioned, antiquated, behind the times, obsolete, outmoded, out of date, passé OPPOSITE new
archetypal *adjective* **1 =typical**, classic, ideal, model, standard **2 =original**
archetype *noun* **1 =standard**, model, paradigm, pattern, prime example **2 =original**, prototype
architect *noun* **=designer**, master builder, planner
architecture *noun* **1 =structure**, construction, design, framework, make-up, style **2 =design**, building, construction, planning
archive *noun* **1** (often pl) **=records**, annals, chronicles, documents, papers, rolls **2 =record office**, museum, registry, repository
Arctic *adjective* **2 =polar**, far-northern, hyperborean **3** (not cap.) *Inf* **=freezing**, chilly,
cold, frigid, frozen, glacial, icy
ardent *adjective* **1 =passionate**, amorous, hot-blooded, impassioned, intense, lusty OPPOSITE cold. **2 =enthusiastic**, avid, eager, keen, zealous OPPOSITE indifferent
ardour *noun* **1 =passion**, fervour, intensity, spirit, vehemence, warmth **2 =enthusiasm**, avidity, eagerness, keenness, zeal
arduous *adjective* **=difficult**, exhausting, fatiguing, gruelling, laborious, onerous, punishing, rigorous, strenuous, taxing, tiring OPPOSITE easy
area *noun* **1 =region**, district, locality, neighbourhood, part, portion, section, sector, zone **3 =field**, department, domain, province, realm, sphere, territory
arena *noun* **1 =ring**, bowl, enclosure, field, ground, stadium **2 =amphitheatre 3** **=sphere**, area, domain, field, province, realm, sector, territory
argue *verb* **1 =maintain**, assert, claim,

squabbling argument.

aria [ah-ree-a] *noun* elaborate song for solo voice, esp. one from an opera.

arid ⊙ *adjective* 1 parched, dry. 2 uninteresting. **aridity** *noun*

Aries *noun* (the ram) first sign of the zodiac.

aright *adverb* rightly.

arise ⊙ *verb* **arising, arose, arisen** 1 come about. 2 come into notice. 3 get up.

aristocracy ⊙ *noun, pl* **-cies** 1 highest social class. 2 government by this class. **aristocrat** *noun* member of the aristocracy. **aristocratic** *adjective* **aristocratically** *adverb*

arithmetic *noun* 1 calculation by or of numbers. ◆ *adjective* 2 of arithmetic. **arithmetical** *adjective* **arithmetically** *adverb* **arithmetician** *noun*

ark *noun* 1 *Old Testament* boat built by Noah, which survived the Flood. 2 (**A-**) *Judaism* chest containing the writings of Jewish Law.

arm[1] ⊙ *noun* 1 upper limb from the shoulder to the wrist. 2 sleeve of a garment. 3 side of a chair. **armful** *noun* as much as can be held in the arms. **armlet** *noun* band worn round the arm. **armchair** *noun* upholstered chair with side supports for the arms. **armhole** *noun* opening in a garment through which the arm passes. **armpit** *noun* hollow under the arm at the shoulder.

arm[2] ⊙ *verb* 1 supply with weapons. 2 prepare (a bomb etc.) for use. **arms** *plural noun* 1 weapons. 2 military exploits. 3 heraldic emblem.

armada ⊙ *noun* large number of warships.

armadillo *noun, pl* **-los** small S American mammal covered in strong bony plates.

Armageddon *noun* 1 *New Testament* final battle between good and evil at the end of the world. 2 catastrophic conflict.

armament ⊙ *noun* 1 military weapons. 2 preparation for war.

armature *noun* revolving structure in an electric motor or generator, wound with coils carrying the current.

armistice ⊙ [arm-miss-stiss] *noun* agreed suspension of fighting.

armour ⊙ *noun* 1 metal clothing formerly worn to protect the body in battle. 2 metal plating of tanks, warships, etc. **armoured** *adjective* 1 having a protective covering. 2 consisting of armoured vehicles. **armourer** *noun* maker, repairer, or keeper of arms or armour. **armoury** *noun* place where weapons are stored.

army ⊙ *noun, pl* **armies** 1 military land forces of a nation. 2 great number.

aroma ⊙ *noun* pleasant smell. **aromatic** *adjective* **aromatherapy** *noun* massage with

———————— THESAURUS ————————

dispute, remonstrate 2 = **debate**, discuss, reason 3 = **quarrel**, bicker, disagree, dispute, fall out (*inf*), fight, squabble

argument *noun* 1 = **quarrel**, clash, controversy, disagreement, dispute, feud, fight, row, squabble OPPOSITE **agreement**. 2 = **discussion**, debate 3 = **reason**, argumentation, assertion, case, claim, defence, dialectic, ground(s), line of reasoning, logic, plea, polemic, reasoning

argumentative *adjective* = **quarrelsome**, belligerent, combative, contentious, contrary, disputatious, litigious, opinionated OPPOSITE **easy-going**

arid *adjective* 1 = **dry**, barren, desert, parched, sterile, torrid, waterless OPPOSITE **rich**. 2 = **boring**, dreary, dry, dull, tedious, tiresome, uninspired, uninteresting OPPOSITE **interesting**

arise *verb* 1 = **happen**, begin, emerge, ensue, follow, occur, result, start, stem 3 = **get up**, get to one's feet, go up, rise, stand up, wake up

aristocracy *noun* 1 = **upper class**, elite, gentry, nobility, patricians, peerage, ruling class OPPOSITE **commoners**

aristocrat *noun* = **noble**, grandee, lady, lord, patrician, peer, peeress

aristocratic *adjective* = **upper-class**, blue-blooded, elite, gentlemanly, lordly, noble, patrician, titled OPPOSITE **common**

arm[1] *noun* 1 = **upper limb**, appendage, limb

arm[2] *verb* 1 = **equip**, accoutre, array, deck out, furnish, issue with, provide, supply 2 = **prime**

armada *noun* = **fleet**, flotilla, navy, squadron

armament *noun* 1 = **weapons**, ammunition, arms, guns, materiel, munitions, ordnance, weaponry

armed *adjective* 1 = **carrying weapons**, equipped, fitted out, protected 2 = **primed**

armistice *noun* = **truce**, ceasefire, peace, suspension of hostilities

armour *noun* = **protection**, armour plate, covering, sheathing, shield

armoured *adjective* 1 = **protected**, armour-plated, bombproof, bulletproof, ironclad, mailed, steel-plated

arms *plural noun* 1 = **weapons**, armaments, firearms, guns, instruments of war, ordnance, weaponry 3 = **heraldry**, blazonry, crest, escutcheon, insignia

army *noun* 1 = **soldiers**, armed force, legions, military, military force, soldiery, troops 2 = **vast number**, array, horde, host, multitude, pack,

A

fragrant oils to relieve tension.

arose *verb* past tense of ARISE.

around ❶ *preposition, adverb* **1** on all sides (of). **2** from place to place (in). **3** somewhere in or near. **4** approximately.

arouse ❶ *verb* **1** stimulate, make active. **2** awaken. **arousal** *noun*

arpeggio [arp-**pej**-ee-oh] *noun, pl* **-gios** *Music* notes of a chord played or sung in quick succession.

arr. 1 arranged (by). **2** arrival. **3** arrive(d).

arrack *noun* alcoholic drink distilled from grain or rice.

arraign [ar-**rain**] *verb* **1** bring (a prisoner) before a court to answer a charge. **2** accuse. **arraignment** *noun*

arrange ❶ *verb* **1** plan. **2** agree. **3** put in order. **4** adapt (music) for performance in a certain way. **arrangement** *noun*

arrant *adjective* utter, downright.

arras *noun* tapestry wall-hanging.

array ❶ *noun* **1** impressive display or collection. **2** orderly arrangement, esp. of troops. **3** *Poetic* rich clothing. ◆ *verb* **4** arrange in order. **5** dress in rich clothing.

arrears *plural noun* money owed. **in arrears** late in paying a debt.

arrest ❶ *verb* **1** take (a person) into custody. **2** stop the movement or development of. **3** catch and hold (the attention). ◆ *noun* **4** act of taking a person into custody. **5** slowing or stopping.

arresting *adjective* attracting attention, striking.

arrive ❶ *verb* **1** reach a place or destination. **2** happen, come. **3** *Informal* be born. **4** *Informal* attain success. **arrival** *noun* **1** arriving. **2** person or thing that has just arrived.

arrivederci [ar-reeve-a-**der**-chee] *interjection Italian* goodbye.

arrogant ❶ *adjective* proud and overbearing. **arrogantly** *adverb* **arrogance** *noun*

arrogate *verb* claim or seize without justification.

——————— THESAURUS ———————

swarm, throng

aroma *noun* =**scent**, bouquet, fragrance, odour, perfume, redolence, savour, smell

aromatic *adjective* =**fragrant**, balmy, perfumed, pungent, redolent, savoury, spicy, sweet-scented, sweet-smelling OPPOSITE **smelly**

around *preposition* **1** =**surrounding**, about, encircling, enclosing, encompassing, on all sides of, on every side of **4** =**approximately**, about, circa (*used with dates*), roughly ◆*adverb* **1** =**everywhere**, about, all over, here and there, in all directions, on all sides, throughout **3** =**near**, at hand, close, close at hand, nearby, nigh (*arch or dial*)

arouse *verb* **1** =**stimulate**, excite, incite, instigate, provoke, spur, stir up, summon up, whip up OPPOSITE **quell**. **2** =**awaken**, rouse, waken, wake up

arrange *verb* **1** =**plan**, construct, contrive, devise, fix up, organize, prepare **2** =**agree**, adjust, come to terms, compromise, determine, settle **3** =**put in order**, classify, group, line up, order, organize, position, sort OPPOSITE **disorganize**. **4** =**adapt**, instrument, orchestrate, score

arrangement *noun* **1** =**plan**, organization, planning, preparation, provision, schedule **2** =**agreement**, adjustment, compact, compromise, deal, settlement, terms **3** =**order**, alignment, classification, form, organization, structure, system **4** =**adaptation**, instrumentation, interpretation, orchestration, score, version

array *noun* **1, 2** =**arrangement**, collection,

display, exhibition, formation, line-up, parade, show, supply **3** *Poet* =**clothing**, apparel, attire, clothes, dress, finery, garments, regalia ◆*verb* **4** =**arrange**, display, exhibit, group, parade, range, show **5** =**dress**, adorn, attire, clothe, deck, decorate, festoon

arrest *verb* **1** =**capture**, apprehend, catch, detain, nick (*sl, chiefly Brit*), seize, take prisoner OPPOSITE **release**. **2** =**stop**, block, delay, end, inhibit, interrupt, obstruct, slow, suppress OPPOSITE **speed up**. **3** =**grip**, absorb, engage, engross, fascinate, hold, intrigue, occupy ◆*noun* **4** =**capture**, bust (*inf*), cop (*sl*), detention, seizure OPPOSITE **release**. **5** =**stopping**, blockage, delay, end, hindrance, interruption, obstruction, suppression OPPOSITE **acceleration**

arresting *adjective* =**striking**, engaging, impressive, noticeable, outstanding, remarkable, stunning, surprising OPPOSITE **unremarkable**

arrival *noun* **1** =**coming**, advent, appearance, arriving, entrance, happening, occurrence, taking place **2** =**newcomer**, caller, entrant, incomer, visitor

arrive *verb* **1** =**come**, appear, enter, get to, reach, show up (*inf*), turn up OPPOSITE **go**. **4** *Inf* =**succeed**, become famous, make good, make it (*inf*), make the grade (*inf*)

arrogance *noun* =**conceit**, disdainfulness, haughtiness, high-handedness, insolence, pride, superciliousness, swagger OPPOSITE **modesty**

arrogant *adjective* =**conceited**, disdainful, haughty, high-handed, overbearing, proud, scornful, supercilious OPPOSITE **modest**

arrow ❶ *noun* **1** pointed shaft shot from a bow. **2** arrow-shaped sign or symbol used to show direction. **arrowhead** *noun* pointed tip of an arrow.

arrowroot *noun* nutritious starch obtained from the root of a W Indian plant.

arse *noun Taboo* buttocks or anus. **arsehole** *noun Taboo* **1** anus. **2** stupid or annoying person.

arsenal ❶ *noun* place where arms and ammunition are made or stored.

arsenic *noun* **1** toxic grey element. **2** highly poisonous compound of this. **arsenical** *adjective*

arson *noun* crime of intentionally setting property on fire. **arsonist** *noun*

art ❶ *noun* **1** creation of works of beauty, esp. paintings or sculpture. **2** works of art collectively. **3** skill. ◆ *plural* **4** nonscientific branches of knowledge. **artist** *noun* **1** person who produces works of art, esp. paintings or sculpture. **2** person skilled at something. **3** artiste. **artiste** *noun* professional entertainer such as a singer or dancer. **artistic** *adjective* **artistically** *adverb* **artistry** *noun* artistic skill. **arty** *adjective* **artier, artiest** *Informal* having an affected interest in art.

artefact *noun* something made by human beings.

arteriosclerosis [art-ear-ee-oh-skler-**oh**-siss] *noun* hardening of the arteries.

artery *noun, pl* **-teries 1** one of the tubes carrying blood from the heart. **2** major road or means of communication. **arterial** *adjective* **1** of an artery. **2** (of a route) major.

artesian well [art-**teez**-yan] *noun* well bored vertically so that the water is forced to the surface by natural pressure.

Artex *noun* ® textured plaster-like covering for ceilings and walls.

artful ❶ *adjective* cunning, wily. **artfully** *adverb* **artfulness** *noun*

arthritis *noun* painful inflammation of a joint or joints. **arthritic** *adjective, noun*

arthropod *noun* animal, such as a spider or insect, with jointed limbs and a segmented body.

artic *noun Informal* articulated lorry.

artichoke *noun* flower head of a thistle-like plant, cooked as a vegetable.

article ❶ *noun* **1** written piece in a magazine or newspaper. **2** item or object. **3** clause in a document. **4** *Grammar* any of the words the, a, or an.

articled *adjective* bound (as an apprentice) by a written contract.

articulate ❶ *adjective* **1** able to express oneself clearly and coherently. **2** (of speech) clear, distinct. **3** *Zool* having joints. ◆ *verb* **4** speak or say clearly and coherently. **articulately** *adverb* **articulated** *adjective* jointed. **articulated lorry** large lorry in two separate sections joined by a pivoted bar. **articulation** *noun*

artifact *noun* same as ARTEFACT.

artifice ❶ *noun* **1** clever trick. **2** cleverness, skill. **artificer** [art-**tiff**-iss-er] *noun* craftsman.

artificial *adjective* man-made, not occurring naturally.

artificial ❶ *adjective* **1** man-made, not occurring naturally. **2** made in imitation of something natural. **3** not sincere. **artificial insemination** introduction of semen into the womb by means other than sexual intercourse. **artificial intelligence** branch of computer science aiming to produce machines which can imitate intelligent human behaviour. **artificial respiration** method of restarting a person's breathing after it has stopped. **artificially** *adverb* **artificiality** *noun*

——————— THESAURUS ———————

arrow *noun* **1** = **dart**, bolt, flight, quarrel, shaft (*arch*) **2** = **pointer**, indicator

arsenal *noun* = **armoury**, ammunition dump, arms depot, ordnance depot, stockpile, store, storehouse, supply

art *noun* **3** = **skill**, craft, expertise, ingenuity, mastery, virtuosity

artful *adjective* = **cunning**, clever, crafty, shrewd, sly, smart, wily OPPOSITE **open**

article *noun* **1** = **piece**, composition, discourse, essay, feature, item, paper, story, treatise **2** = **thing**, commodity, item, object, piece, substance, unit **3** = **clause**, item, paragraph, part, passage, point, portion, section

articulate *adjective* **1, 2** = **expressive**, clear, coherent, eloquent, fluent, lucid, well-spoken OPPOSITE **incoherent** ◆ *verb* **4** = **express**, enunciate, pronounce, say, speak, state, talk, utter, voice

artifice *noun* **1** = **trick**, contrivance, device, machination, manoeuvre, stratagem, subterfuge, tactic **2** = **cleverness**, ingenuity, inventiveness, skill

artificial *adjective* **1** = **synthetic**, man-made, manufactured, non-natural, plastic **2** = **fake**, bogus, counterfeit, imitation, mock, sham, simulated OPPOSITE **authentic**. **3** = **insincere**, affected, contrived, false, feigned, forced, phoney *or* phony (*inf*), unnatural OPPOSITE **true**

A

artillery ◐ noun 1 large-calibre guns. 2 branch of the army who use these.

artisan ◐ noun skilled worker, craftsman.

artless ◐ adjective 1 free from deceit or cunning. 2 natural, unpretentious. **artlessly** adverb

arum lily [air-rum] noun plant with a white funnel-shaped leaf surrounding a spike of flowers.

Aryan [air-ree-an] noun 1 (in Nazi Germany) non-Jewish person of the Nordic type. 2 person supposedly of Indo-European descent. ◆ adjective 3 of Aryans.

as ◐ conjunction 1 while, when. 2 in the way that. 3 that which, e.g. do as you are told. 4 since, seeing that. 5 for instance. ◆ adverb, conjunction 6 used to indicate amount or extent in comparisons, e.g. he is as tall as you. ◆ preposition 7 in the role of, being, e.g. as a mother, I am concerned.

As Chem arsenic.

ASA Advertising Standards Authority.

asafoetida noun strong-smelling plant resin used as a spice in Eastern cookery.

a.s.a.p. as soon as possible.

asbestos noun fibrous mineral which does not burn. **asbestosis** noun lung disease caused by inhalation of asbestos fibre.

ascend ◐ verb go or move up. **ascent** noun 1 ascending. 2 upward slope. **ascendant** adjective 1 dominant or influential. ◆ noun 2 **in the ascendant** increasing in power or influence. **ascendancy** noun condition of being dominant. **the Ascension** Christianity passing of Jesus Christ from earth into heaven.

ascertain ◐ verb find out definitely.

ascertainable adjective **ascertainment** noun

ascetic ◐ [ass-set-tik] noun, adjective (person) abstaining from worldly pleasures and comforts. **asceticism** noun

ascorbic acid [ass-core-bik] noun vitamin C.

ascribe ◐ verb attribute, as to a particular origin. **ascription** noun

aseptic [eh-sep-tik] adjective free from harmful bacteria. **asepsis** [eh-sep-siss] noun aseptic condition.

asexual [eh-sex-yew-al] adjective without sex. **asexually** adverb

ash¹ ◐ noun 1 powdery substance left when something is burnt. ◆ plural 2 remains after burning, esp. of a human body after cremation. **the Ashes** cricket trophy competed for in test matches by England and Australia. **ashen** adjective pale with shock. **ashtray** noun receptacle for tobacco ash and cigarette butts. **Ash Wednesday** first day of Lent.

ash² noun tree with grey bark.

ashamed ◐ adjective feeling shame.

ashlar noun square block of hewn stone used in building.

ashore ◐ adverb towards or on land.

ashram noun religious retreat where a Hindu holy man lives.

Asian adjective 1 (also **Asiatic**) of the

———————— THESAURUS ————————

artillery noun 1 = **big guns**, battery, cannon, cannonry, gunnery, ordnance

artisan noun = **craftsman**, journeyman, mechanic, skilled workman, technician

artistic adjective = **creative**, aesthetic, beautiful, cultured, elegant, refined, sophisticated, stylish, tasteful OPPOSITE tasteless

artistry noun = **skill**, brilliance, craftsmanship, creativity, finesse, mastery, proficiency, virtuosity

artless adjective 1 = **straightforward**, frank, guileless, open, plain OPPOSITE artful. 2 = **natural**, plain, pure, simple, unadorned, unaffected, uncontrived, unpretentious OPPOSITE affected

as conjunction 1 = **when**, at the time that, during the time that, just as, while 2 = **in the way that**, in the manner that, like 3 = **what**, that which 4 = **since**, because, considering that, seeing that 5 = **for instance**, like, such as ◆preposition 7 = **being**, in the character of, in the role of, under the name of

ascend verb = **move up**, climb, go up, mount, scale OPPOSITE fall

ascent noun 1 = **rise**, ascending, ascension, climb, mounting, rising, scaling, upward movement 2 = **upward slope**, gradient, incline, ramp, rise, rising ground

ascertain verb = **find out**, confirm, determine, discover, establish, learn

ascetic noun = **monk**, abstainer, hermit, nun, recluse OPPOSITE hedonist ◆adjective = **self-denying**, abstinent, austere, celibate, frugal, puritanical, self-disciplined OPPOSITE self-indulgent

ascribe verb = **attribute**, assign, charge, credit, impute, put down, refer, set down

ashamed adjective = **embarrassed**, distressed, guilty, humiliated, mortified, remorseful, shamefaced, sheepish, sorry OPPOSITE proud

ashen adjective = **pale**, colourless, grey, leaden, like death warmed up (inf), pallid, wan, white OPPOSITE rosy

ashore adverb = **on land**, aground, landwards, on dry land, on the beach, on the shore,

A

continent of Asia or any of its peoples or languages. **2** of the Indian subcontinent. ◆ *noun* **3** person from Asia or a descendant of one. **4** person from the Indian subcontinent or a descendant of one. **Asian pear** apple-shaped pear with crisp juicy flesh.

> **LANGUAGE TIP**
>
> Use *Asian* for 'someone who comes from Asia'. *Asiatic* in this context can be offensive.

aside ❶ *adverb* **1** to one side. **2** out of other people's hearing, e.g. *he took me aside to tell me his plans.* ◆ *noun* **3** remark not meant to be heard by everyone present.
asinine ❶ [**ass**-in-nine] *adjective* stupid, idiotic.
ask ❶ *verb* **1** say or write (something) in a form that requires an answer. **2** make a request or demand. **3** invite.
askance [ass-**kanss**] *adverb* **look askance at 1** look at with an oblique glance. **2** regard with suspicion.
askew ❶ *adverb, adjective* to one side, crooked.
aslant *adverb, preposition* at a slant (to), slanting (across).
asleep ❶ *adjective* **1** sleeping. **2** (of limbs) numb.
asp *noun* small poisonous snake.
asparagus *noun* plant whose shoots are cooked as a vegetable.

aspect ❶ *noun* **1** feature or element. **2** position facing a particular direction. **3** appearance or look.
aspen *noun* kind of poplar tree.
asperity [ass-**per**-rit-ee] *noun* roughness of temper.
aspersion *noun* **cast aspersions on** make derogatory remarks about.
asphalt *noun* **1** black hard tarlike substance used for road surfaces etc. ◆ *verb* **2** cover with asphalt.
asphodel *noun* plant with clusters of yellow or white flowers.
asphyxia ❶ [ass-**fix**-ee-a] *noun* suffocation.
asphyxiate *verb* suffocate. **asphyxiation** *noun*
aspic *noun* savoury jelly used to coat meat, eggs, fish, etc.
aspidistra *noun* plant with long tapered leaves.
aspirate *Phonetics verb* **1** pronounce with an *h* sound. ◆ *noun* **2** an *h* sound.
aspire ❶ *verb* (foll. by *to*) yearn (for), hope (to do or be). **aspirant** *noun* person who aspires.
aspiration *noun* strong desire or aim. **aspiring** *adjective*
aspirin *noun* **1** drug used to relieve pain and fever. **2** tablet of this.
ass ❶ *noun* **1** donkey. **2** stupid person.
assagai *noun* same as ASSEGAI.
assail ❶ *verb* attack violently. **assailant** *noun*
assassin ❶ *noun* person who murders a prominent person. **assassinate** *verb* murder (a prominent person). **assassination** *noun*

———————————— THESAURUS ————————————

shorewards, to the shore
aside *adverb* **1** = **to one side**, apart, beside, on one side, out of the way, privately, separately, to the side ◆*noun* **3** = **interpolation**, parenthesis
asinine *adjective* = **stupid**, fatuous, foolish, idiotic, imbecilic, moronic, senseless
ask *verb* **1** = **inquire**, interrogate, query, question, quiz OPPOSITE answer. **2** = **request**, appeal, beg, demand, plead, seek **3** = **invite**, bid, summon
askew *adverb* = **crookedly**, aslant, awry, obliquely, off-centre, to one side OPPOSITE straight ◆*adjective* = **crooked**, awry, cockeyed (*inf*), lopsided, oblique, off-centre, skewwhiff (*Brit inf*) OPPOSITE even
asleep *adjective* **1** = **sleeping**, dormant, dozing, fast asleep, napping, slumbering, snoozing (*inf*), sound asleep
aspect *noun* **1** = **feature**, angle, facet, side **2** = **position**, outlook, point of view, prospect, scene, situation, view **3** = **appearance**, air,

attitude, bearing, condition, demeanour, expression, look, manner
asphyxiate *verb* = **suffocate**, choke, smother, stifle, strangle, strangulate, throttle
aspiration *noun* = **aim**, ambition, desire, dream, goal, hope, objective, wish
aspire *verb* (foll. by *to*) = **aim**, desire, dream, hope, long, seek, set one's heart on, wish
aspiring *adjective* = **hopeful**, ambitious, eager, longing, wannabe (*inf*), would-be
ass *noun* **1** = **donkey**, moke (*sl*) **2** = **fool**, blockhead, halfwit, idiot, jackass, numbskull *or* numskull, oaf, twit (*inf*, *chiefly Brit*)
assail *verb* = **attack**, assault, fall upon, lay into (*inf*), set upon
assailant *noun* = **attacker**, aggressor, assailer, assaulter, invader
assassin *noun* = **murderer**, executioner, hatchet man (*sl*), hit man (*sl*), killer, liquidator, slayer
assassinate *verb* = **murder**, eliminate (*sl*), hit (*sl*), kill, liquidate, slay, take out (*sl*)

assault ❶ *noun* **1** violent attack. ◆ *verb* **2** attack violently. **assault course** series of obstacles used in military training.

assay *noun* **1** analysis of a substance, esp. a metal, to ascertain its purity. ◆ *verb* **2** make such an analysis.

assegai *noun* slender spear used in S Africa.

assemble ❶ *verb* **1** collect or congregate. **2** put together the parts of (a machine).

assemblage *noun* **1** collection or group. **2** assembling. **assembly** *noun* **1** *pl* **-blies** assembled group. **2** assembling. **assembly line** sequence of machines and workers in a factory assembling a product.

assent ❶ *noun* **1** agreement or consent. ◆ *verb* **2** agree or consent.

assert ❶ *verb* **1** declare forcefully. **2** insist upon (one's rights etc.). **assert oneself** put oneself forward forcefully. **assertion** *noun* **1** positive statement, usu. made without evidence. **2** act of asserting. **assertive** *adjective* **assertively** *adverb* **assertiveness** *noun*

assess ❶ *verb* **1** judge the worth or importance of. **2** estimate the value of (income or property) for taxation purposes. **assessment** *noun* **assessor** *noun*

asset ❶ *noun* **1** valuable or useful person or thing. ◆ *plural* **2** property that a person or firm can sell, esp. to pay debts.

asseverate *verb* declare solemnly.

asseveration *noun*

assiduous ❶ *adjective* **1** hard-working. **2** done with care. **assiduously** *adverb* **assiduity** *noun*

assign ❶ *verb* **1** appoint (someone) to a job or task. **2** allot (a task). **3** attribute. **assignation** [ass-sig-**nay**-shun] *noun* **1** assigning. **2** secret arrangement to meet. **assignment** *noun* **1** task assigned. **2** assigning.

assimilate ❶ *verb* **1** learn and understand (information). **2** absorb or be absorbed or incorporated. **assimilable** *adjective* **assimilation** *noun*

assist ❶ *verb* give help or support. **assistance** *noun* **assistant** *noun* **1** helper. ◆ *adjective* **2** junior or deputy.

assizes *plural noun* court sessions formerly

———————— THESAURUS ————————

assault *noun* **1** = **attack**, charge, invasion, offensive, onslaught OPPOSITE **defence** ◆*verb* **2** = **attack**, beset, fall upon, lay into (*inf*), set about, set upon, strike at OPPOSITE **protect**

assemble *verb* **1** = **gather**, amass, bring together, call together, collect, come together, congregate, meet, muster, rally OPPOSITE **dismiss**. **2** = **put together**, build up, connect, construct, fabricate, fit together, join, piece together, set up OPPOSITE **divide**

assembly *noun* **1** = **gathering**, collection, company, conference, congress, council, crowd, group, mass, meeting **2** = **putting together**, building up, connecting, construction, piecing together, setting up

assent *noun* **1** = **agreement**, acceptance, approval, compliance, concurrence, consent, permission, sanction OPPOSITE **refusal** ◆*verb* **2** = **agree**, allow, approve, consent, grant, permit

assert *verb* **1** = **state**, affirm, declare, maintain, profess, pronounce, swear OPPOSITE **deny**. **2** = **insist upon**, claim, defend, press, put forward, stand up for, stress, uphold OPPOSITE **retract** ◆ **assert oneself** = **be forceful**, exert one's influence, make one's presence felt, put oneself forward, put one's foot down (*inf*)

assertion *noun* **1** = **statement**, claim, declaration, pronouncement **2** = **insistence**, maintenance, stressing

assertive *adjective* = **confident**, aggressive, domineering, emphatic, feisty (*inf, chiefly US & Canad*), forceful, insistent, positive, pushy (*inf*), strong-willed OPPOSITE **meek**

assess *verb* **1** = **judge**, appraise, estimate, evaluate, rate, size up (*inf*), value, weigh **2** = **evaluate**, fix, impose, levy, rate, tax, value

assessment *noun* **1** = **judgment**, appraisal, estimate, evaluation, rating, valuation **2** = **evaluation**, charge, fee, levy, rating, toll, valuation

asset *noun* **1** = **benefit**, advantage, aid, blessing, boon, feather in one's cap, help, resource, service OPPOSITE **disadvantage** ◆*plural* **2** = **property**, capital, estate, funds, goods, money, possessions, resources, wealth

assiduous *adjective* **1** = **diligent**, hard-working, indefatigable, industrious, persevering, persistent, unflagging OPPOSITE **lazy**

assign *verb* **1** = **select**, appoint, choose, delegate, designate, name, nominate **2** = **give**, allocate, allot, apportion, consign, distribute, give out, grant **3** = **attribute**, accredit, ascribe, put down

assignation *noun* **1** = **selection**, appointment, assignment, choice, delegation, designation, nomination **2** = **secret meeting**, clandestine meeting, illicit meeting, rendezvous, tryst (*arch*)

assignment *noun* **1** = **task**, appointment, commission, duty, job, mission, position, post, responsibility

assimilate *verb* **1** = **learn**, absorb, digest, take in **2** = **adjust**, adapt, blend in, digest, incorporate, mingle, take in

assist *verb* = **help**, abet, aid, cooperate, lend a

held in each county of England and Wales.
assoc. association.

associate ❶ *verb* **1** connect in the mind. **2** mix socially. ◆ *noun* **3** partner in business. **4** friend or companion. ◆ *adjective* **5** having partial rights or subordinate status, e.g. *associate member.* **association** *noun* **1** society or club. **2** associating.

assonance *noun* rhyming of vowel sounds but not consonants, as in *time* and *light.* **assonant** *adjective*

assorted ❶ *adjective* consisting of various types mixed together. **assortment** *noun* assorted mixture.

asst assistant.

assuage [ass-**wage**] *verb* relieve (pain, grief, thirst, etc.).

assume ❶ *verb* **1** take to be true without proof. **2** take upon oneself, e.g. *he assumed command.* **3** pretend, e.g. *I assumed indifference.* **assumption** *noun* **1** thing assumed. **2** assuming.

assure ❶ *verb* **1** promise or guarantee. **2** convince. **3** make (something) certain. **4** insure against loss of life. **assured** *adjective* **1** confident. **2** certain to happen. **assuredly** [a-**sure**-id-lee] *adverb* definitely. **assurance** *noun* assuring or being assured.

astatine *noun Chem* radioactive nonmetallic element.

aster *noun* plant with daisy-like flowers.

asterisk *noun* **1** star-shaped symbol (*) used in printing or writing to indicate a footnote etc. ◆ *verb* **2** mark with an asterisk.

astern *adverb* **1** at or towards the stern of a ship. **2** backwards.

asteroid *noun* any of the small planets that orbit the sun between Mars and Jupiter.

asthma [**ass**-ma] *noun* illness causing difficulty in breathing. **asthmatic** *adjective, noun*

astigmatism [eh-**stig**-mat-tiz-zum] *noun* inability of a lens, esp. of the eye, to focus properly. **astigmatic** *adjective*

astir *adjective* **1** out of bed. **2** in motion.

astonish ❶ *verb* surprise greatly.
astonishment *noun* **astonishing** *adjective*
astonishingly *adverb*

astound ❶ *verb* overwhelm with amazement.

——————— THESAURUS ———————

helping hand, serve, support OPPOSITE **hinder**
assistance *noun* =**help**, aid, backing, cooperation, helping hand, support OPPOSITE **hindrance**
assistant *noun* **1** =**helper**, accomplice, aide, ally, colleague, right-hand man, second, supporter
associate *verb* **1** =**connect**, ally, combine, identify, join, link, lump together OPPOSITE **separate. 2** =**mix**, accompany, consort, hobnob, mingle, socialize OPPOSITE **avoid**
◆*noun* **3** =**partner**, collaborator, colleague, confederate, co-worker **4** =**friend**, ally, cobber (*Aust or old-fashioned NZ inf*), companion, comrade, mate (*inf*)
association *noun* **1** =**group**, alliance, band, club, coalition, federation, league, organization, society **2** =**connection**, blend, combination, joining, juxtaposition, mixture, pairing, union
assorted *adjective* =**various**, different, diverse, miscellaneous, mixed, motley, sundry, varied OPPOSITE **similar**
assortment *noun* =**variety**, array, choice, collection, jumble, medley, mixture, selection
assume *verb* **1** =**take for granted**, believe, expect, fancy, imagine, infer, presume, suppose, surmise, think OPPOSITE **know. 2** =**take on**, accept, enter upon, put on, shoulder, take, take over **3** =**put on**, adopt, affect, feign, imitate, impersonate, mimic, pretend to, simulate

assumed *adjective* **1** =**taken for granted**, accepted, expected, hypothetical, presumed, presupposed, supposed, surmised **3** =**false**, bogus, counterfeit, fake, fictitious, made-up, make-believe OPPOSITE **real**
assumption *noun* **1** =**presumption**, belief, conjecture, guess, hypothesis, inference, supposition, surmise **2** =**taking on**, acceptance, acquisition, adoption, entering upon, putting on, shouldering, takeover, taking up
assure *verb* **1** =**promise**, certify, confirm, declare confidently, give one's word to, guarantee, pledge, swear, vow **2** =**convince**, comfort, embolden, encourage, hearten, persuade, reassure **3** =**make certain**, clinch, complete, confirm, ensure, guarantee, make sure, seal, secure
assured *adjective* **1** =**confident**, certain, poised, positive, self-assured, self-confident, sure of oneself OPPOSITE **self-conscious. 2** =**certain**, beyond doubt, confirmed, ensured, fixed, guaranteed, in the bag (*sl*), secure, settled, sure OPPOSITE **uncertain**
astonish *verb* =**amaze**, astound, bewilder, confound, daze, dumbfound, stagger, stun, surprise
astonishing *adjective* =**amazing**, astounding, bewildering, breathtaking, brilliant, jaw-dropping, sensational (*inf*), staggering, stunning, surprising
astonishment *noun* =**amazement**, awe,

A

astounding *adjective* **astoundingly** *adverb*
astrakhan *noun* **1** dark curly fleece of lambs from Astrakhan in Russia. **2** fabric resembling this.
astral *adjective* **1** of stars. **2** of the spirit world.
astray ❶ *adverb* off the right path.
astride *adverb, preposition* with a leg on either side (of).
astringent *adjective* **1** causing contraction of body tissue. **2** checking the flow of blood from a cut. **3** severe or harsh. ◆ *noun* **4** astringent substance. **astringency** *noun*
astro- *combining form* star.
astrolabe *noun* instrument formerly used to measure the altitude of stars and planets.
astrology *noun* study of the alleged influence of the stars, planets, and moon on human affairs. **astrologer** *noun* **astrological** *adjective*
astronaut *noun* person trained for travelling in space.
astronautics *noun* science and technology of space flight. **astronautical** *adjective*
astronomy *noun* scientific study of heavenly bodies. **astronomer** *noun* **astronomical** *adjective* **1** very large. **2** of astronomy. **astronomically** *adverb*
astrophysics *noun* science of the physical and chemical properties of stars, planets, etc. **astrophysical** *adjective* **astrophysicist** *noun*
astute ❶ *adjective* perceptive or shrewd. **astutely** *adverb* **astuteness** *noun*
asunder *adverb* into parts or pieces.
asylum ❶ *noun* **1** refuge or sanctuary. **2** old name for a mental hospital.
asymmetry *noun* lack of symmetry. **asymmetrical, asymmetric** *adjective*
asymptote [ass-im-tote] *noun* straight line closely approached but never met by a curve.
at *preposition* indicating position in space or time, movement towards an object, etc., e.g. *at midnight; throwing stones at windows.*
At *Chem* astatine.
atavism [at-a-viz-zum] *noun* recurrence of a trait present in distant ancestors. **atavistic** *adjective*
ate *verb* past tense of EAT.
atelier [at-tell-yay] *noun* workshop, artist's studio.
atheism ❶ [aith-ee-iz-zum] *noun* belief that there is no God. **atheist** *noun* **atheistic** *adjective*
atherosclerosis *noun, pl* **-ses** disease in which deposits of fat cause the walls of the arteries to thicken.
athlete ❶ *noun* person trained in or good at athletics. **athletic** *adjective* **1** physically fit or strong. **2** of an athlete or athletics. **athletics** *plural noun* track-and-field sports such as running, jumping, throwing, etc. **athletically** *adverb* **athleticism** *noun*
at-home *noun* social gathering in a person's home.
athwart *preposition* **1** across. ◆ *adverb* **2** transversely.
atigi *noun* a type of parka worn by the Inuit in Canada.
atlas *noun* book of maps.
atmosphere ❶ *noun* **1** mass of gases surrounding a heavenly body, esp. the earth. **2** prevailing tone or mood (of a place etc.). **3** unit of pressure. **atmospheric** *adjective*
atmospherics *plural noun* radio interference due to electrical disturbance in the atmosphere.
atoll *noun* ring-shaped coral reef enclosing a lagoon.
atom ❶ *noun* **1** smallest unit of matter which can take part in a chemical reaction. **2** very small amount. **atom bomb** same as ATOMIC

———————— T H E S A U R U S ————————

bewilderment, confusion, consternation, surprise, wonder, wonderment
astounding *adjective* =**amazing**, astonishing, bewildering, breathtaking, brilliant, impressive, jaw-dropping, sensational (*inf*), staggering, stunning, surprising
astray *adverb* =**off the right track**, adrift, amiss, lost, off, off course, off the mark
astute *adjective* =**intelligent**, canny, clever, crafty, cunning, perceptive, sagacious, sharp, shrewd, subtle OPPOSITE> stupid
asylum *noun* **1** =**refuge**, harbour, haven, preserve, retreat, safety, sanctuary, shelter **2** *Old-fashioned* =**mental hospital**, hospital, institution, madhouse (*inf*), psychiatric hospital
atheism *noun* =**nonbelief**, disbelief,

godlessness, heathenism, infidelity, irreligion, paganism, scepticism, unbelief
atheist *noun* =**nonbeliever**, disbeliever, heathen, infidel, pagan, sceptic, unbeliever
athlete *noun* =**sportsperson**, competitor, contestant, gymnast, player, runner, sportsman, sportswoman
athletic *adjective* **1** =**fit**, active, energetic, muscular, powerful, strapping, strong, sturdy OPPOSITE> feeble
athletics *plural noun* =**sports**, contests, exercises, gymnastics, races, track and field events
atmosphere *noun* **1** =**air**, aerosphere, heavens, sky **2** =**feeling**, ambience, character, climate, environment, mood, spirit,

BOMB.

atomic *adjective* **1** of or using atomic bombs or atomic energy. **2** of atoms. **atomic bomb** bomb in which the energy is provided by nuclear fission. **atomic energy** nuclear energy. **atomic number** number of protons in the nucleus of an atom. **atomic weight** ratio of the mass per atom of an element to one twelfth of the mass of a carbon atom.

atomize *verb* reduce to atoms or small particles. **atomizer** *noun* device for discharging a liquid in a fine spray.

atonal [eh-**tone**-al] *adjective* (of music) not written in an established key. **atonality** *noun*

atone ⊕ *verb* make amends (for sin or wrongdoing). **atonement** *noun*

atop *preposition* on top of.

atrium *noun, pl* **atria 1** upper chamber of either half of the heart. **2** central hall extending through several storeys of a modern building. **3** main courtyard of an ancient Roman house.

atrocious ⊕ *adjective* **1** extremely cruel or wicked. **2** horrifying or shocking. **3** *Informal* very bad. **atrociously** *adverb* **atrocity** *noun* **1** wickedness. **2** *pl* **-ties** act of cruelty.

atrophy [at-trof-fee] *noun, pl* **-phies 1** wasting away of an organ or part. **2** failure to grow. ♦ *verb* **-phying, -phied 3** (cause to) waste away.

atropine *noun* poisonous alkaloid obtained from deadly nightshade.

attach ⊕ *verb* **1** join, fasten, or connect. **2** attribute or ascribe, e.g. *he attaches great importance to his looks*. **attached** *adjective* (foll. by *to*) fond of. **attachment** *noun*

attaché [at-**tash**-shay] *noun* specialist attached to a diplomatic mission. **attaché case** flat rectangular briefcase for papers.

attack ⊕ *verb* **1** launch a physical assault (against). **2** criticize. **3** set about (a job or problem) with vigour. **4** affect adversely. ♦ *noun* **5** act of attacking. **6** sudden bout of illness. **attacker** *noun*

attain ⊕ *verb* **1** achieve or accomplish (a task or aim). **2** reach. **attainable** *adjective* **attainment** *noun* accomplishment.

attar *noun* fragrant oil made from roses.

attempt ⊕ *verb* **1** try, make an effort. ♦ *noun* **2** effort or endeavour.

attend ⊕ *verb* **1** be present at. **2** go regularly to a school, college, etc. **3** look after. **4** pay attention. **5** apply oneself (to). **attendance** *noun* **1** attending. **2** number attending. **attendant** *noun* **1** person who assists, guides, or provides a service. ♦ *adjective* **2** accompanying. **attention** *noun* **1** concentrated direction of the mind. **2** consideration. **3** care. **4** alert position in military drill. **attentive** *adjective* **1** giving attention. **2** considerately helpful. **attentively** *adverb* **attentiveness** *noun*

attenuated *adjective* **1** weakened. **2** thin and

——————— THESAURUS ———————

surroundings, tone

atom *noun* **2** = **particle**, bit, dot, speck, spot, trace

atone *verb* = **make amends**, compensate, do penance, make redress, make reparation, make up for, pay for, recompense, redress

atonement *noun* = **amends**, compensation, penance, recompense, redress, reparation, restitution

atrocious *adjective* **1** = **cruel**, barbaric, brutal, fiendish, infernal, monstrous, savage, vicious, wicked OPPOSITE **good. 2** = **shocking**, appalling, detestable, grievous, horrible, horrifying, terrible OPPOSITE **fine**

atrocity *noun* **1** = **cruelty**, barbarity, brutality, fiendishness, horror, savagery, viciousness, wickedness **2** = **act of cruelty**, abomination, crime, evil, horror, outrage

attach *verb* **1** = **connect**, add, couple, fasten, fix, join, link, secure, stick, tie OPPOSITE **remove. 2** = **put**, ascribe, assign, associate, attribute, connect

attached *adjective* (foll. by *to*) = **fond of**, affectionate towards, devoted to, full of regard

for

attack *verb* **1** = **assault**, invade, lay into (*inf*), raid, set upon, strike (at) OPPOSITE **defend. 2** = **criticize**, abuse, blame, censure, have a go (at) (*inf*), put down, vilify ♦ *noun* **5 a** = **assault**, campaign, charge, foray, incursion, invasion, offensive, onslaught, raid, strike OPPOSITE **defence. b** = **criticism**, abuse, blame, censure, denigration, stick (*sl*), vilification **6** = **bout**, convulsion, fit, paroxysm, seizure, spasm, stroke

attacker *noun* **1** = **assailant**, aggressor, assaulter, intruder, invader, raider

attain *verb* **1** = **achieve**, accomplish, acquire, complete, fulfil, gain, get, obtain

attainment *noun* = **achievement**, accomplishment, completion, feat

attempt *verb* **1** = **try**, endeavour, seek, strive, undertake, venture ♦ *noun* **2** = **try**, bid, crack (*inf*), effort, go (*inf*), shot (*inf*), stab (*inf*), trial

attend *verb* **1** = **be present**, appear, frequent, go to, haunt, put in an appearance, show oneself, turn up, visit OPPOSITE **be absent. 3** = **look after**, care for, mind, minister to, nurse,

A

extended. **attenuation** *noun*

attest *verb* affirm the truth of, be proof of. **attestation** *noun*

attic ❶ *noun* space or room within the roof of a house.

attire ❶ *noun* fine or formal clothes. **attired** *adjective* dressed in a specified way.

attitude ❶ *noun* 1 way of thinking and behaving. 2 posture of the body. 3 *Informal* hostile manner.

attorney *noun* 1 person legally appointed to act for another. 2 *US* lawyer.

attract ❶ *verb* 1 arouse the interest or admiration of. 2 draw (something) closer by exerting a force on it. **attraction** *noun* 1 power to attract. 2 something that attracts. **attractive** *adjective* **attractively** *adverb* **attractiveness** *noun*

attribute ❶ *verb* 1 (usu. foll. by *to*) regard as belonging to or produced by. ♦ *noun* 2 quality or feature representative of a person or thing. **attributable** *adjective* **attribution** *noun* **attributive** *adjective Grammar* (of an adjective)

preceding the noun modified.

attrition *noun* constant wearing down to weaken or destroy, e.g. *war of attrition*.

attune ❶ *verb* adjust or accustom (a person or thing).

atypical [eh-**tip**-ik-al] *adjective* not typical.

Au *Chem* gold.

aubergine [**oh**-bur-zheen] *noun* dark purple tropical fruit, cooked and eaten as a vegetable.

aubrietia [aw-**bree**-sha] *noun* trailing plant with purple flowers.

auburn *adjective* (of hair) reddish-brown.

auction *noun* 1 public sale in which articles are sold to the highest bidder. ♦ *verb* 2 sell by auction. **auctioneer** *noun* person who conducts an auction.

audacious ❶ *adjective* 1 recklessly bold or daring. 2 impudent. **audaciously** *adverb* **audacity** *noun*

audible ❶ *adjective* loud enough to be heard. **audibly** *adverb* **audibility** *noun*

audience ❶ *noun* 1 group of spectators or listeners. 2 formal interview.

——————— THESAURUS ———————

take care of, tend **4 = pay attention**, hear, heed, listen, mark, note, observe, pay heed OPPOSITE **ignore**. **5 attend to = apply oneself to**, concentrate on, devote oneself to, get to work on, look after, occupy oneself with, see to, take care of

attendance *noun* **1 = presence**, appearance, attending, being there **2 = turnout**, audience, crowd, gate, house, number present

attendant *noun* **1 = assistant**, aide, companion, escort, follower, guard, helper, servant ♦*adjective* **2 = accompanying**, accessory, associated, concomitant, consequent, related

attention *noun* **1 = concentration**, deliberation, heed, intentness, mind, scrutiny, thinking, thought **2 = notice**, awareness, consciousness, consideration, observation, recognition, regard OPPOSITE **inattention**. **3 = care**, concern, looking after, ministration, treatment

attentive *adjective* **1 = careful**, alert, awake, concentrating, heedful, intent, mindful, observant, studious, watchful OPPOSITE **heedless**. **2 = considerate**, courteous, helpful, kind, obliging, polite, respectful, thoughtful OPPOSITE **negligent**

attic *noun* **= loft**, garret

attire *noun* **= clothes**, apparel, costume, dress, garb, garments, outfit, robes, wear

attitude *noun* **1 = disposition**, approach, frame of mind, mood, opinion, outlook,

perspective, point of view, position, stance **2 = position**, pose, posture, stance

attract *verb* **1 = appeal to**, charm, enchant OPPOSITE **repel**. **2 = draw**, allure, entice, lure, pull (*inf*), tempt OPPOSITE **disgust**

attraction *noun* **1 = appeal**, allure, charm, enticement, fascination, lure, magnetism, pull (*inf*), temptation

attractive *adjective* **= appealing**, alluring, charming, fair, fetching, good-looking, handsome, inviting, lekker (*S Afr sl*), lovely, pleasant, pretty, tempting OPPOSITE **unattractive**

attribute *verb* **1** (usu. foll. by *to*) **= ascribe**, charge, credit, put down to, set down to ♦*noun* **2 = quality**, aspect, character, characteristic, facet, feature, peculiarity, property, trait

attune *verb* **= accustom**, adapt, adjust, familiarize, harmonize, regulate

audacious *adjective* **1 = daring**, bold, brave, courageous, fearless, intrepid, rash, reckless OPPOSITE **timid**. **2 = cheeky**, brazen, defiant, impertinent, impudent, insolent, presumptuous, shameless OPPOSITE **tactful**

audacity *noun* **1 = daring**, boldness, bravery, courage, fearlessness, nerve, rashness, recklessness **2 = cheek**, chutzpah (*US & Canad inf*), effrontery, impertinence, impudence, insolence, nerve

audible *adjective* **= clear**, detectable, discernible, distinct, hearable, perceptible

audio *adjective* **1** of sound or hearing. **2** of or for the transmission or reproduction of sound. **audiotypist** *noun* typist trained to type from a dictating machine. **audiovisual** *adjective* (esp. of teaching aids) involving both sight and hearing.

audit *noun* **1** official examination of business accounts. ◆ *verb* **auditing, audited 2** examine (business accounts) officially. **auditor** *noun*

audition *noun* **1** test of a performer's ability for a particular role or job. ◆ *verb* **2** test or be tested in an audition.

auditorium *noun, pl* **-toriums, -toria** area of a concert hall or theatre where the audience sits.

auditory *adjective* of or relating to hearing.

au fait [oh **fay**] *adjective French* **1** fully informed. **2** expert.

auf Wiedersehen [owf **vee**-der-zay-en] *interjection German* goodbye.

Aug. August.

auger *noun* carpenter's tool for boring holes.

aught *pronoun Old-fashioned* anything whatever.

augment *verb* increase or enlarge. **augmentation** *noun*

au gratin [oh **grat**-tan] *adjective* covered and cooked with breadcrumbs and sometimes cheese.

augur *verb* be a sign of (future events).

augury *noun* **1** foretelling of the future. **2** *pl* **-ries** omen.

august *adjective* dignified and imposing.

August *noun* eighth month of the year.

auk *noun* northern sea bird with short wings and black-and-white plumage.

auld lang syne *noun* times past.

aunt *noun* **1** father's or mother's sister. **2** uncle's wife. **auntie, aunty** *noun, pl* **aunties** *Informal* aunt. **Aunt Sally 1** figure used in fairgrounds as a target. **2** target of abuse or criticism.

au pair *noun* young foreign woman who does housework in return for board and lodging.

aura ❶ *noun* distinctive air or quality of a person or thing.

aural *adjective* of or using the ears or hearing.

aureate *adjective* **1** covered with gold, gilded. **2** (of style of writing or speaking) excessively elaborate.

aureole, aureola *noun* halo.

au revoir [oh riv-**vwahr**] *interjection French* goodbye.

auricle *noun* **1** upper chamber of the heart. **2** outer part of the ear. **auricular** *adjective*

auriferous *adjective* containing gold.

aurochs *noun, pl* **aurochs** recently extinct European wild ox.

aurora *noun, pl* **-ras, -rae** bands of light sometimes seen in the sky in polar regions. **aurora australis** aurora seen near the South Pole. **aurora borealis** aurora seen near the North Pole.

auscultation *noun* listening to the internal sounds of the body, usu. with a stethoscope, to help with diagnosis.

auspices [**aw**-spiss-siz] *plural noun* **under the auspices of** with the support and approval of.

auspicious ❶ *adjective* showing signs of future success, favourable. **auspiciously** *adverb*

Aussie *noun, adjective Informal* Australian.

austere ❶ *adjective* **1** stern or severe. **2** ascetic or self-disciplined. **3** severely simple or plain. **austerely** *adverb* **austerity** *noun*

austral *adjective* southern.

Australasian *noun, adjective* (person) from Australia, New Zealand, and neighbouring islands.

Australian *noun, adjective* (person) from Australia.

Austrian *noun, adjective* (person) from Austria.

autarchy [**aw**-tar-kee] *noun* absolute power or autocracy.

autarky [**aw**-tar-kee] *noun* policy of economic self-sufficiency.

authentic ❶ *adjective* known to be real, genuine. **authentically** *adverb* **authenticity** *noun* **authenticate** *verb* establish as genuine.

THESAURUS

OPPOSITE⟩ inaudible

audience *noun* **1** = **spectators**, assembly, crowd, gallery, gathering, listeners, onlookers, turnout, viewers **2** = **interview**, consultation, hearing, meeting, reception

aura *noun* = **air**, ambience, atmosphere, feeling, mood, quality, tone

auspicious *adjective* = **favourable**, bright, encouraging, felicitous, hopeful, promising OPPOSITE⟩ **unpromising**

austere *adjective* **1** = **stern**, forbidding,

formal, serious, severe, solemn, strict OPPOSITE⟩ **kindly**. **2** = **ascetic**, abstemious, puritanical, self-disciplined, sober, solemn, strait-laced, strict OPPOSITE⟩ **abandoned**. **3** = **plain**, bleak, harsh, simple, spare, Spartan, stark OPPOSITE⟩ **luxurious**

austerity *noun* **1** = **sternness**, formality, inflexibility, rigour, seriousness, severity, solemnity, stiffness, strictness **2** = **asceticism**, puritanism, self-denial, self-discipline, sobriety **3** = **plainness**, simplicity, starkness

A

authentication *noun*
author ❶ *noun* **1** writer of a book etc. **2** originator or creator. **authorship** *noun*
authority ❶ *noun, pl* **-ties 1** power to command or control others. **2** (often pl) person or group having this power. **3** expert in a particular field. **authoritarian** *noun, adjective* (person) insisting on strict obedience to authority. **authoritative** *adjective* **1** recognized as being reliable, e.g. *the authoritative book on Shakespeare.* **2** possessing authority. **authoritatively** *adverb* **authorize** *verb* **1** give authority to. **2** give permission for. **authorization** *noun*
autism *noun Psychiatry* disorder, usu. of children, characterized by lack of response to people and limited ability to communicate. **autistic** *adjective*
auto- *combining form* self-, e.g. *autobiography.*
autobahn *noun* German motorway.
autobiography *noun, pl* **-phies** account of a person's life written by that person. **autobiographical** *adjective*
autobiographically *adverb*
autocrat ❶ *noun* **1** ruler with absolute authority. **2** dictatorial person. **autocratic** *adjective* **autocratically** *adverb* **autocracy** *noun* government by an autocrat.
autocross *noun* motor-racing over a rough

course.
Autocue *noun* ® electronic television prompting device displaying a speaker's script, unseen by the audience.
autogiro, autogyro *noun, pl* **-ros** self-propelled aircraft resembling a helicopter but with an unpowered rotor.
autograph *noun* **1** handwritten signature of a (famous) person. ♦ *verb* **2** write one's signature on or in.
automat *noun US* vending machine.
automate *verb* make (a manufacturing process) automatic. **automation** *noun*
automatic ❶ *adjective* **1** (of a device) operating mechanically by itself. **2** (of a process) performed by automatic equipment. **3** done without conscious thought. **4** (of a firearm) self-loading. ♦ *noun* **5** self-loading firearm. **6** vehicle with automatic transmission.
automatically *adverb* **automatic transmission** transmission system in a motor vehicle in which the gears change automatically.
automaton *noun* **1** robot. **2** person who acts mechanically.
automobile *noun US* motor car.
automotive *adjective* relating to motor vehicles.
autonomy ❶ *noun* self-government.
autonomous *adjective*

——————— THESAURUS ———————

authentic *adjective* =**genuine**, actual, authoritative, bona fide, legitimate, pure, real, true-to-life, valid OPPOSITE **fake**
authenticity *noun* =**genuineness**, accuracy, certainty, faithfulness, legitimacy, purity, truthfulness, validity
author *noun* **1** =**writer**, composer, creator **2** =**creator**, architect, designer, father, founder, inventor, originator, producer
authoritarian *noun* =**disciplinarian**, absolutist, autocrat, despot, dictator, tyrant ♦*adjective* =**strict**, autocratic, dictatorial, doctrinaire, dogmatic, severe, tyrannical OPPOSITE **lenient**
authoritative *adjective* **1** =**reliable**, accurate, authentic, definitive, dependable, trustworthy, valid OPPOSITE **unreliable**. **2** =**commanding**, assertive, imperious, imposing, masterly, self-assured OPPOSITE **timid**
authority *noun* **1** =**power**, command, control, direction, influence, mana (*NZ*), supremacy, sway, weight **2** (often pl) =**powers that be**, administration, government, management, officialdom, police, the Establishment **3** =**expert**, connoisseur, guru, judge, master, professional, specialist

authorization *noun* **1** =**permission**, a blank cheque, approval, leave, licence, permit, warrant
authorize *verb* **1** =**empower**, accredit, commission, enable, entitle, give authority **2** =**permit**, allow, approve, give authority for, license, sanction, warrant OPPOSITE **forbid**
autocracy *noun* =**dictatorship**, absolutism, despotism, tyranny
autocrat *noun* **1** =**dictator**, absolutist, despot, tyrant
autocratic *adjective* =**dictatorial**, absolute, all-powerful, despotic, domineering, imperious, tyrannical
automatic *adjective* **1, 2** =**mechanical**, automated, mechanized, push-button, self-propelling OPPOSITE **done by hand**. **3** =**involuntary**, instinctive, mechanical, natural, reflex, spontaneous, unconscious, unwilled OPPOSITE **conscious**
autonomous *adjective* =**self-ruling**, free, independent, self-determining, self-governing, sovereign
autonomy *noun* =**independence**, freedom, home rule, self-determination, self-government, self-rule, sovereignty OPPOSITE **dependency**

autopsy *noun, pl* **-sies** examination of a corpse to determine the cause of death.
autoroute *noun* French motorway.
autostrada *noun* Italian motorway.
autosuggestion *noun* process in which a person unconsciously influences his or her own behaviour or beliefs.
autumn *noun* season between summer and winter. **autumnal** *adjective*
auxiliary ⊕ *adjective* **1** secondary or supplementary. **2** supporting. ◆ *noun, pl* **-ries 3** person or thing that supplements or supports.
auxiliary verb verb used to form the tense, voice, or mood of another, such as *will in I will go.*
avail ⊕ *verb* **1** be of use or advantage (to). ◆ *noun* **2** use or advantage, esp. in *to no avail*.
avail oneself of make use of. **available** obtainable or accessible.
available ⊕ *adjective* obtainable or accessible. **availability** *noun*
avalanche ⊕ *noun* **1** mass of snow or ice falling down a mountain. **2** sudden overwhelming quantity of anything.
avant-garde ⊕ [av-ong-**gard**] *noun* **1** group of innovators, esp. in the arts. ◆ *adjective* **2** innovative and progressive.
avarice ⊕ [**av**-a-riss] *noun* greed for wealth. **avaricious** *adjective*

avast *interjection Naut* stop.
avatar *noun Hinduism* appearance of a god in animal or human form.
Ave. Avenue.
Ave Maria [ah-vay ma-**ree**-a] *noun* same as HAIL MARY.
avenge ⊕ *verb* take revenge in retaliation for (harm done) or on behalf of (a person harmed). **avenger** *noun*
avenue ⊕ *noun* **1** wide street. **2** road between two rows of trees. **3** way of approach.
aver [av-**vur**] *verb* **averring, averred** state to be true.
average ⊕ *noun* **1** typical or normal amount or quality. **2** result obtained by adding quantities together and dividing the total by the number of quantities. ◆ *adjective* **3** usual or typical. **4** calculated as an average. ◆ *verb* **5** calculate the average of. **6** amount to as an average.
averse ⊕ *adjective* (usu. foll. by *to*) disinclined or unwilling. **aversion** *noun* **1** strong dislike. **2** person or thing disliked.
avert ⊕ *verb* **1** turn away. **2** ward off.
aviary *noun, pl* **aviaries** large cage or enclosure for birds.
aviation ⊕ *noun* art of flying aircraft. **aviator** *noun*
avid ⊕ *adjective* **1** keen or enthusiastic. **2**

———— THESAURUS ————

auxiliary *adjective* **1 = supplementary**, back-up, emergency, fall-back, reserve, secondary, subsidiary, substitute OPPOSITE **primary. 2 = supporting**, accessory, aiding, ancillary, assisting, helping OPPOSITE **primary** ◆*noun* **3 = helper**, assistant, associate, backup, companion, reserve, subordinate, supporter
avail *verb* **1 = benefit**, aid, assist, be of advantage, be useful, help, profit ◆*noun* **2 = benefit**, advantage, aid, good, help, profit, use
availability *noun* **= accessibility**, attainability, handiness, readiness
available *adjective* **= accessible**, at hand, at one's disposal, free, handy, on tap, ready, to hand OPPOSITE **in use**
avalanche *noun* **1 = snow-slide**, landslide, landslip **2 = flood**, barrage, deluge, inundation, torrent
avant-garde *adjective* **2 = progressive**, experimental, ground-breaking, innovative, pioneering, unconventional OPPOSITE conservative
avarice *noun* **= greed**, covetousness, meanness, miserliness, niggardliness, parsimony, stinginess OPPOSITE **liberality**

avaricious *adjective* **= grasping**, covetous, greedy, mean, miserly, niggardly, parsimonious, stingy
avenge *verb* **= get revenge for**, get even for (*inf*), get one's own back, hit back, punish, repay, retaliate
avenue *noun* **1 = street**, boulevard, course, drive, passage, path, road, route, way
average *noun* **1 = usual**, norm, normal, par, standard **2 = mean**, medium, midpoint ◆ *adjective* **3 = usual**, commonplace, fair, general, normal, ordinary, regular, standard, typical OPPOSITE **unusual. 4 = mean**, intermediate, median, medium, middle OPPOSITE **minimum** ◆*verb* **6 = make on average**, balance out to, be on average, do on average, even out to
averse *adjective* (usu. foll. by *to*) **= opposed**, disinclined, hostile, ill-disposed, loath, reluctant, unwilling OPPOSITE **willing**
aversion *noun* **1 = hatred**, animosity, antipathy, disinclination, dislike, hostility, revulsion, unwillingness OPPOSITE **love**
avert *verb* **1 = turn away**, turn aside **2 = ward off**, avoid, fend off, forestall, frustrate, preclude, prevent, stave off
aviator *noun* **= pilot**, aeronaut, airman, flyer

A

greedy (for). **avidly** adverb **avidity** noun
avocado noun, pl **-dos** pear-shaped tropical
fruit with a leathery green skin and yellowish-
green flesh.
avocation noun Old-fashioned **1** occupation. **2**
hobby.
avocet noun long-legged wading bird with a
long slender upward-curving bill.
avoid ❶ verb **1** prevent from happening. **2**
refrain from. **3** keep away from. **avoidable**
adjective **avoidance** noun
avoirdupois [av-er-de-**poise**] noun system of
weights based on pounds and ounces.
avow ❶ verb **1** state or affirm. **2** admit openly.
avowal noun **avowed** adjective **avowedly** [a-
vow-id-lee] adverb
avuncular adjective (of a man) friendly,
helpful, and caring towards someone younger.
await ❶ verb **1** wait for. **2** be in store for.
awake ❶ verb **awaking, awoke, awoken 1**
emerge or rouse from sleep. **2** (cause to)
become alert. ◆ adjective **3** not sleeping. **4** alert.
awaken ❶ verb awake. **awakening** noun

award ❶ verb **1** give (something, such as a
prize) formally. ◆ noun **2** something awarded,
such as a prize.
aware ❶ adjective having knowledge,
informed. **awareness** noun
awash adverb washed over by water.
away ❶ adverb **1** from a place, e.g. go away. **2**
to another place, e.g. put that gun away. **3** out
of existence, e.g. fade away. **4** continuously,
e.g. laughing away. ◆ adjective **5** not present. **6**
distant, e.g. two miles away. **7** Sport played on
an opponent's ground.
awe ❶ noun **1** wonder and respect mixed with
dread. ◆ verb **2** fill with awe. **awesome**
adjective **1** inspiring awe. **2** Slang excellent or
outstanding. **awestruck** adjective filled with
awe.
aweigh adjective Naut (of an anchor) no
longer hooked into the bottom.
awful ❶ adjective **1** very bad or unpleasant. **2**
Informal very great. **3** Obs inspiring awe.
awfully adverb **1** in an unpleasant way. **2**
Informal very. **awfulness** noun

——————— T H E S A U R U S ———————

avid adjective **1 = enthusiastic**, ardent,
devoted, eager, fanatical, intense, keen,
passionate, zealous OPPOSITE indifferent. **2**
= insatiable, grasping, greedy, hungry,
rapacious, ravenous, thirsty, voracious
avoid verb **1 = prevent**, avert **2 = refrain
from**, dodge, duck (out of) (inf), eschew, fight
shy of, shirk **3 = keep away from**, bypass,
dodge, elude, escape, evade, shun, steer clear
of OPPOSITE seek out
avoidance noun **3 = evasion**, dodging,
eluding, escape, keeping away, shunning,
steering clear
avowed adjective **1 = declared**, open,
professed, self-proclaimed, sworn **2**
= confessed, acknowledged, admitted
await verb **1 = wait for**, abide, anticipate,
expect, look for, look forward to, stay for **2**
= be in store for, attend, be in readiness for,
be prepared for, be ready for, wait for
awake verb **1 = wake up**, awaken, rouse,
wake **2 = alert**, arouse, kindle, provoke, revive,
stimulate, stir up ◆adjective **3 = not sleeping**,
aroused, awakened, aware, conscious, wakeful,
wide-awake OPPOSITE sleeping. **4 = alert**,
alive, attentive, aware, heedful, observant, on
the lookout, vigilant, watchful
awaken verb **= awake**, arouse, revive, rouse,
wake
award verb **1 = give**, bestow, confer, endow,
grant, hand out, present ◆noun **2 = prize**,
decoration, gift, grant, trophy

aware adjective **= knowing**, acquainted with,
conscious of, conversant with, enlightened,
familiar with, informed, in the loop, in the
picture, knowledgeable, mindful of OPPOSITE
ignorant
awareness noun **= knowledge**, consciousness,
familiarity, perception, realization, recognition,
understanding
away adverb **1 = from here**, abroad, apart, at
a distance, elsewhere, far, from home, hence,
off, remote **2 = aside**, out of the way, to one
side **4 = continuously**, incessantly,
interminably, relentlessly, repeatedly,
uninterruptedly, unremittingly ◆adjective **5**
= not present, abroad, absent, elsewhere,
gone, not at home, not here, out
awe noun **1 = wonder**, admiration,
amazement, astonishment, dread, fear, horror,
respect, reverence, terror OPPOSITE contempt
◆verb **2 = impress**, amaze, astonish, frighten,
horrify, intimidate, stun, terrify
awesome adjective **= awe-inspiring**, amazing,
astonishing, breathtaking, formidable,
impressive, intimidating, stunning
awful adjective **1 = terrible**, abysmal,
appalling, deplorable, dreadful, frightful,
ghastly, horrendous OPPOSITE wonderful. **3**
Obs **= awe-inspiring**, awesome, fearsome,
majestic, solemn
awfully adverb **1 = badly**, disgracefully,
dreadfully, reprehensibly, unforgivably,
unpleasantly, woefully, wretchedly **2** Inf **= very**,

awhile *adverb* for a brief time.
awkward ⊙ *adjective* **1** clumsy or ungainly. **2** embarrassed. **3** difficult to use or handle. **4** inconvenient. **awkwardly** *adverb* **awkwardness** *noun*
awl *noun* pointed tool for piercing wood, leather, etc.
awning *noun* canvas roof supported by a frame to give protection against the weather.
awoke *verb* past tense of AWAKE. **awoken** *verb* past participle of AWAKE.
AWOL [eh-woll] *adjective Mil* absent without leave.
awry [a-rye] *adverb, adjective* **1** with a twist to one side, askew. **2** amiss.
axe ⊙ *noun* **1** tool with a sharp blade for felling trees or chopping wood. **2** *Informal* dismissal from employment etc. ◆ *verb* **3** *Informal* dismiss (employees), restrict (expenditure), or terminate (a project).
axil *noun* angle where the stalk of a leaf joins a stem.
axiom ⊙ *noun* **1** generally accepted principle. **2** self-evident statement. **axiomatic** *adjective* **1** containing axioms. **2** self-evident.
axis ⊙ *noun, pl* **axes 1** (imaginary) line round which a body can rotate or about which an object or geometrical figure is symmetrical. **2** one of two fixed lines on a graph, against which quantities or positions are measured. **axial** *adjective*
axle ⊙ *noun* shaft on which a wheel or pair of wheels turns.
axolotl *noun* aquatic salamander of central America.
ayah *noun* (in parts of the former British Empire) native maidservant or nursemaid.
ayatollah *noun* Islamic religious leader in Iran.
aye, ay *interjection* **1** yes. ◆ *noun* **2** affirmative vote or voter.
AZ Arizona.
azalea [az-**zale**-ya] *noun* garden shrub grown for its showy flowers.
azimuth *noun* **1** arc of the sky between the zenith and the horizon. **2** horizontal angle of a bearing measured clockwise from the north.
Aztec *noun, adjective* (person) of the race ruling Mexico before the Spanish conquest in the 16th century.
azure *adjective, noun* (of) the colour of a clear blue sky.

———————— T H E S A U R U S ————————

dreadfully, exceedingly, exceptionally, extremely, greatly, immensely, terribly
awkward *adjective* **1** = **clumsy**, gauche, gawky, inelegant, lumbering, uncoordinated, ungainly OPPOSITE **graceful**. **2** = **embarrassed**, ill at ease, uncomfortable OPPOSITE **comfortable**. **3** = **difficult**, cumbersome, troublesome, unmanageable, unwieldy **4** = **inconvenient** OPPOSITE **convenient**
awkwardness *noun* **1** = **clumsiness**, gawkiness, inelegance, ungainliness **3** = **unwieldiness**, difficulty **4** = **inconvenience**

axe *noun* **1** = **hatchet**, adze, chopper **2** *Inf* = **the sack**, dismissal, termination, the boot (*sl*), the chop (*sl*) (*inf*) ◆*verb* **3** *Inf* = **cut back**, cancel, dismiss, dispense with, eliminate, fire (*inf*), get rid of, remove, sack (*inf*)
axiom *noun* **1** = **principle**, adage, aphorism, dictum, maxim, precept **2** = **truism**
axiomatic *adjective* **2** = **self-evident**, accepted, assumed, certain, given, granted, manifest, understood
axis *noun* **1** = **pivot**, axle, centre line, shaft, spindle
axle *noun* = **shaft**, axis, pin, pivot, rod, spindle

Bb

B *Chem* boron.

Ba *Chem* barium.

BA Bachelor of Arts.

baa *verb* **baaing, baaed 1** make the characteristic bleating sound of a sheep. ♦ *noun* **2** cry made by a sheep.

baas *noun S Afr* boss.

babble ⊕ *verb* **1** talk excitedly or foolishly. **2** (of streams) make a low murmuring sound. ♦ *noun* **3** muddled or foolish speech.

babe *noun* **1** baby. **2** *Slang* an attractive girl.

babel [**babe**-el] *noun* confused mixture of noises or voices.

babiche *noun Canad* thongs or lacings of rawhide.

baboon *noun* large monkey with a pointed face and a long tail.

baby ⊕ *noun, pl* **-bies 1** very young child or animal. **2** *Slang* sweetheart. ♦ *adjective* **3** comparatively small of its type. **babyish** *adjective* **baby-sit** *verb* take care of a child while the parents are out. **baby-sitter** *noun*

baccarat [**back**-a-rah] *noun* card game involving gambling.

bacchanalia *noun* wild drunken party or orgy.

bach *noun NZ* small holiday cottage.

bachelor *noun* **1** unmarried man. **2** person who holds the lowest university or college degree, e.g. *a Bachelor of Science.*

SPELLING TIP

We find *batchelor* spelt with a *t* 14 times in the Bank of English. The correct spelling has no *t*: **bachelor**.

---

bacillus [bass-**ill**-luss] *noun, pl* **-li** [-lie] rod-shaped bacterium, esp. one causing disease. **bacillary** *adjective* of or caused by bacilli.

back ⊕ *noun* **1** rear part of the human body, from the neck to the pelvis. **2** spinal column. **3** part or side of an object opposite the front. **4** part of anything less often seen or used. **5** *Ball games* defensive player or position. ♦ *verb* **6** (cause to) move backwards. **7** provide money for (a person or enterprise). **8** bet on the success of. **9** (foll. by *onto*) have the back facing towards. ♦ *adjective* **10** situated behind, e.g. *back garden.* **11** owing from an earlier date, e.g. *back pay.* ♦ *adverb* **12** at, to, or towards the rear. **13** to or towards the original starting point or condition. **backer** *noun* person who gives financial support. **backfire** *verb* fail to have the desired effect. **background** *noun* space behind chief figures of a picture, etc. **backing** *noun* **1** support. **2** musical accompaniment for a pop singer. **backlash** *noun* sudden and adverse reaction. **backward** *adjective* **1** directed towards the rear. **2** retarded in physical, material, or intellectual development. **backwardness** *noun* **backwards** *adverb* **1** towards the rear. **2** with the back foremost. **3** in the reverse of the usual direction. **back door** secret or underhand means of entry to a job etc. **back down** *verb* withdraw an earlier claim. **back number** old issue of a newspaper or magazine. **back out** *verb* withdraw (from an agreement). **back room** place where secret research or planning is done. **back up** *verb* support. **backup** *noun* **1** support or reinforcement. **2** reserve or substitute.

THESAURUS

babble *verb* **1** =**gabble**, burble, chatter, gibber, jabber, prattle, waffle (*inf, chiefly Brit*) **2** =**gurgle** ♦*noun* **3** =**gabble**, burble, drivel, gibberish, waffle (*inf, chiefly Brit*)

baby *noun* **1** =**infant**, babe, babe in arms, bairn (*Scot*), child, newborn child ♦*adjective* **3** =**small**, little, mini, miniature, minute, teeny-weeny, tiny, wee

babyish *adjective* **1** =**childish**, foolish, immature, infantile, juvenile, puerile, sissy, spoiled

back *noun* **1** =**rear**, end, hindquarters OPPOSITE head. **3** =**end**, far end, hind part, rear, reverse, stern, tail end OPPOSITE front ♦*verb* **7** =**support**, advocate, assist, champion, endorse, promote, sponsor OPPOSITE oppose ♦*adjective* **10** =**rear**, end, hind, hindmost, posterior, tail OPPOSITE front. **11** =**previous**,

backbencher *noun* Member of Parliament who does not hold office in the government or opposition.

backbiting ⊙ *noun* spiteful talk about an absent person.

backbone ⊙ *noun* 1 spinal column. 2 strength of character.

backbreaking ⊙ *adjective* (of work or effort) exhausting.

backchat *noun Informal* impudent replies.

backcloth, backdrop *noun* painted curtain at the back of a stage set.

backdate *verb* make (a document) effective from a date earlier than its completion.

backfire ⊙ *verb* 1 (of a plan) fail to have the desired effect. 2 (of an engine) make a loud noise like an explosion.

backgammon *noun* game played with counters and dice.

background ⊙ *noun* 1 events or circumstances that help to explain something. 2 person's social class, education, or experience. 3 part of a scene or picture furthest from the viewer.

backhand *noun Tennis etc.* stroke played with the back of the hand facing the direction of the stroke. **backhanded** *adjective* ambiguous or implying criticism, e.g. *a backhanded compliment.* **backhander** *noun Slang* bribe.

backlash ⊙ *noun* sudden and adverse reaction.

backlog ⊙ *noun* accumulation of things to be dealt with.

backpack *noun* 1 rucksack. ♦ *verb* 2 go hiking with a backpack. **backpacker** *noun*

back-pedal *verb* retract or modify a previous statement.

back-seat driver *noun Informal* person who offers unwanted advice.

backside *noun Informal* buttocks.

backslide ⊙ *verb* relapse into former bad habits. **backslider** *noun*

backstage *adverb, adjective* behind the stage in a theatre.

backstairs *adjective* underhand, e.g. *backstairs deals.*

backstreet *noun* 1 street far from any main road. ♦ *adjective* 2 secret or illegal, e.g. *a backstreet abortion.*

backstroke *noun* swimming stroke performed on the back.

backtrack *verb* 1 return by the same route by which one has come. 2 retract or reverse one's opinion or policy.

backwash *noun* 1 water washed backwards by the motion of a boat. 2 repercussion.

backwater *noun* isolated or backward place or condition.

backwoods *plural noun* remote sparsely populated area.

bacon *noun* salted or smoked pig meat.

bacteria ⊙ *plural noun, sing* **-rium** large group of microorganisms, many of which cause disease. **bacterial** *adjective* **bacteriology** *noun* study of bacteria. **bacteriologist** *noun*

——————— T H E S A U R U S ———————

delayed, earlier, elapsed, former, overdue, past
[OPPOSITE] **later**
backbiting *noun* =**slander**, bitchiness (*sl*), cattiness (*inf*), defamation, disparagement, gossip, malice, spitefulness
backbone *noun* 1 =**spinal column**, spine, vertebrae, vertebral column 2 =**strength of character**, character, courage, determination, fortitude, grit, nerve, pluck, resolution
backbreaking *adjective* =**exhausting**, arduous, crushing, gruelling, hard, laborious, punishing, strenuous
back down *verb* =**give in**, accede, admit defeat, back-pedal, cave in (*inf*), concede, surrender, withdraw, yield
backer *noun* =**supporter**, advocate, angel (*inf*), benefactor, patron, promoter, second, sponsor, subscriber
backfire *verb* 1 =**fail**, boomerang, disappoint, flop (*inf*), miscarry, rebound, recoil
background *noun* 1 =**circumstances**, culture, environment, history, tradition 2

=**upbringing**, education, grounding
backing *noun* 1 =**support**, aid, assistance, encouragement, endorsement, moral support, patronage, sponsorship
backlash *noun* =**reaction**, counteraction, recoil, repercussion, resistance, response, retaliation
backlog *noun* =**build-up**, accumulation, excess, hoard, reserve, stock, supply
back out *verb* =**withdraw**, abandon, cancel, give up, go back on, resign, retreat
backslide *verb* =**relapse**, go astray, go wrong, lapse, revert, slip, stray, weaken
backslider *noun* =**relapser**, apostate, deserter, recidivist, recreant, renegade, turncoat
back up *verb* =**support**, aid, assist, bolster, confirm, corroborate, reinforce, second, stand by, substantiate
backward *adjective* 2 =**slow**, behind, dull, retarded, subnormal, underdeveloped, undeveloped
backwards *adverb* 1 =**towards the rear**,

LANGUAGE TIP

Note that the word *bacteria* is already plural and does not need an '-s'. The singular form is *bacterium*.

bad ❶ *adjective* **worse, worst 1** of poor quality. **2** lacking skill or talent. **3** harmful. **4** immoral or evil. **5** naughty or mischievous. **6** rotten or decayed. **7** unpleasant. **badly** *adverb* **badness** *noun* **bad blood** feeling of intense hatred.

bade *verb* a past tense of BID.

badge ❶ *noun* emblem worn to show membership, rank, etc.

badger ❶ *noun* **1** nocturnal burrowing mammal with a black and white head. ◆ *verb* **2** pester or harass.

badinage ❶ [**bad**-in-nahzh] *noun* playful and witty conversation.

badminton *noun* game played with rackets and a shuttlecock, which is hit back and forth over a high net.

baffle ❶ *verb* **1** perplex or puzzle. ◆ *noun* **2** device to limit or regulate the flow of fluid, light, or sound. **bafflement** *noun*

bag ❶ *noun* **1** flexible container with an opening at one end. **2** handbag or piece of luggage. **3** loose fold of skin under the eyes. **4** *Offens* ugly or bad-tempered woman. **5** amount of game killed by a hunter. ◆ *verb* **bagging, bagged 6** put into a bag. **7** succeed in capturing, killing or scoring, e.g. *he has bagged*

over 40 goals this season. **bags of** *Informal* lots (of). **baggy** *adjective* **-gier, -giest** (of clothes) hanging loosely.

bagatelle *noun* **1** something of little value. **2** board game in which balls are struck into holes.

bagel *noun* hard ring-shaped bread roll.

baggage ❶ *noun* **1** suitcases packed for a journey. **2** *Informal* previous knowledge or experience that affects contemporary behaviour, e.g. *ideological baggage*.

bagpipes *plural noun* musical wind instrument with reed pipes and an inflatable bag.

bah *interjection* expression of contempt or disgust.

bail¹ ❶ *noun* **1** *Law* money deposited with a court as security for a person's reappearance in court. **2** person giving such security. ◆ *verb* **3** pay bail for (a person).

bail², bale ❶ *verb* (foll. by *out*) **1** remove (water) from (a boat). **2** *Informal* help (a person or organization) out of a predicament. **3** make an emergency parachute jump from an aircraft.

bail³ *noun Cricket* either of two wooden bars across the tops of the stumps.

bailey *noun* outermost wall or court of a castle.

bailiff *noun* **1** sheriff's officer who serves writs and summonses. **2** landlord's agent.

bailiwick *noun* area a person is interested in or operates in.

bairn *noun Scot* child.

bait ❶ *noun* **1** piece of food on a hook or in a trap to attract fish or animals. **2** enticement or temptation. ◆ *verb* **3** put a piece of food on or

———— T H E S A U R U S ————

behind, rearward **3 = in reverse**
bacteria *plural noun* **= microorganisms**, bacilli, bugs (*sl*), germs, microbes, pathogens, viruses
bad *adjective* **1 = inferior**, defective, faulty, imperfect, inadequate, poor, substandard, unsatisfactory OPPOSITE **satisfactory**. **3 = harmful**, damaging, dangerous, deleterious, detrimental, hurtful, ruinous, unhealthy OPPOSITE **beneficial**. **4 = wicked**, corrupt, criminal, evil, immoral, mean, sinful, wrong OPPOSITE **virtuous**. **5 = naughty**, disobedient, mischievous, unruly OPPOSITE **well-behaved**. **6 = rotten**, decayed, mouldy, off, putrid, rancid, sour, spoiled **7 = unfavourable**, adverse, distressing, gloomy, grim, troubled, unfortunate, unpleasant
badge *noun* **= mark**, brand, device, emblem, identification, insignia, sign, stamp, token
badger *verb* **2 = pester**, bully, goad, harass, hound, importune, nag, plague, torment

badinage *noun* **= wordplay**, banter, mockery, pleasantry, repartee, teasing
badly *adverb* **2 = poorly**, carelessly, imperfectly, inadequately, incorrectly, ineptly, wrongly OPPOSITE **well**
baffle *verb* **1 = puzzle**, bewilder, confound, confuse, flummox, mystify, nonplus, perplex, stump OPPOSITE **explain**
bag *noun* **1 = container**, receptacle, sac, sack ◆*verb* **7 = catch**, acquire, capture, kill, land, shoot, trap
baggage *noun* **1 = luggage**, accoutrements, bags, belongings, equipment, gear, paraphernalia, suitcases, things
baggy *adjective* **= loose**, bulging, droopy, floppy, ill-fitting, oversize, roomy, sagging, slack OPPOSITE **tight**
bail¹ *noun* **1** *Law* **= security**, bond, guarantee, pledge, surety, warranty
bail², bale *verb* (foll. by *out*) **2** *Inf* **=help**, aid, relieve, rescue, save (someone's) bacon (*inf*,

in (a hook or trap). **4** persecute or tease.

baize noun woollen fabric used to cover billiard and card tables.

bake verb **1** cook by dry heat as in an oven. **2** make or become hardened by heat. **3** Informal be extremely hot. **baker** noun person whose business is to make or sell bread, cakes, etc. **baker's dozen** thirteen. **bakery** noun, pl -eries place where bread, cakes, etc. are baked or sold. **baking powder** powdered mixture containing sodium bicarbonate, used as a raising agent in baking.

bakeapple noun cloudberry.

bakkie noun S Afr small truck.

baksheesh noun (in some Eastern countries) money given as a tip.

balaclava, balaclava helmet noun close-fitting woollen hood that covers the ears and neck.

balalaika noun guitar-like musical instrument with a triangular body.

balance ⊕ noun **1** stability of mind or body. **2** state in which a weight or amount is evenly distributed. **3** amount that remains, e.g. the balance of what you owe. **4** weighing device. **5** difference between the credits and debits of an account. ◆ verb **6** weigh in a balance. **7** make or remain steady. **8** consider or compare. **9** compare or equalize the money going into or coming out of an account. **balance of payments** difference between the payments for the imports and exports of a country. **balance of power** equal distribution of military and economic power among countries. **balance of trade** difference in value between a country's imports and exports. **balance sheet** statement showing the financial position of a business.

balcony ⊕ noun, pl -nies **1** platform on the outside of a building with a rail along the outer edge. **2** upper tier of seats in a theatre or cinema.

bald ⊕ adjective **1** having little or no hair on the scalp. **2** plain or blunt, e.g. the bald facts. **3** (of a tyre) having a worn tread. **balding** adjective becoming bald. **baldly** adverb **baldness** noun

balderdash ⊕ noun stupid talk.

bale¹ noun **1** large bundle of hay or goods tightly bound together. ◆ verb **2** make or put into bales.

bale² verb same as BAIL².

baleen noun whalebone.

baleful adjective vindictive or menacing. **balefully** adverb

balk, baulk ⊕ verb **1** be reluctant to (do something). **2** thwart or hinder.

Balkan adjective of any of the countries of the Balkan Peninsula: Romania, Bulgaria, Albania, Greece, the former Yugoslavia, and theEuropean part of Turkey.

ball¹ ⊕ noun **1** round or nearly round object, esp. one used in games. **2** single delivery of the ball in a game. **3** bullet. **4** more or less rounded part of the body, e.g. the ball of the foot. ◆ plural Taboo slang **5** testicles. **6** nonsense. ◆ verb **7** form into a ball, e.g. he balled his fist. **ball bearings** steel balls between moving parts of a machine to reduce friction. **ball cock** device with a floating ball and a valve for regulating the flow of water. **ballpoint, ballpoint pen** noun pen with a tiny ball bearing as a writing point.

ball² noun formal social function for dancing. **ballroom** noun

———————————————— THESAURUS ————————————————

chiefly Brit) **3** = **escape**, quit, retreat, withdraw

bait noun **2** = **lure**, allurement, attraction, decoy, enticement, incentive, inducement, snare, temptation ◆verb **4** = **tease**, annoy, bother, harass, hassle (inf), hound, irritate, persecute, torment, wind up (Brit sl)

baked adjective **2** = **dry**, arid, desiccated, parched, scorched, seared, sun-baked, torrid

balance noun **1** = **stability**, composure, equanimity, poise, self-control, self-possession, steadiness **2** = **equilibrium**, correspondence, equity, equivalence, evenness, parity, symmetry OPPOSITE⟩ **instability**. **3** = **remainder**, difference, residue, rest, surplus ◆verb **6** = **weigh 7** = **stabilize**, level, match, parallel, steady OPPOSITE⟩ **upset**. **8** = **compare**, assess, consider, deliberate, estimate, evaluate **9** = **calculate**, compute, settle, square, tally, total

balcony noun **1** = **terrace**, veranda **2** = **upper circle**, gallery, gods

bald adjective **1** = **hairless**, baldheaded, depilated **2** = **plain**, blunt, direct, forthright, straightforward, unadorned, unvarnished

balderdash noun = **nonsense**, claptrap (inf), drivel, garbage (inf), gibberish, hogwash, hot air (inf), kak (S Afr sl), rubbish

baldness noun **1** = **hairlessness**, alopecia (Path), baldheadedness **2** = **plainness**, austerity, bluntness, severity, simplicity

balk, baulk verb **1** = **recoil**, evade, flinch, hesitate, jib, refuse, resist, shirk, shrink from OPPOSITE⟩ **accept**. **2** = **foil**, check, counteract, defeat, frustrate, hinder, obstruct, prevent, thwart

ball¹ noun **1** = **sphere**, drop, globe, globule, orb, pellet, spheroid

B

ballad *noun* **1** narrative poem or song. **2** slow sentimental song.

ballast ⊕ *noun* **1** substance, such as sand, used to stabilize a ship when it is not carrying cargo. **2** crushed rock used for road or railway foundation. ◆ *verb* **3** give stability or weight to.

ballet *noun* **1** classical style of expressive dancing based on conventional steps. **2** theatrical performance of this. **ballerina** *noun* female ballet dancer.

ballistics *noun* study of the flight of projectiles, such as bullets. **ballistic** *adjective* **ballistic missile** missile guided automatically in flight but which falls freely at its target.

balloon ⊕ *noun* **1** inflatable rubber bag used as a plaything or decoration. **2** large bag inflated with air or gas, designed to float in the atmosphere with passengers in a basket underneath. ◆ *verb* **3** fly in a balloon. **4** swell or increase rapidly in size, e.g. *his weight ballooned.* **balloonist** *noun*

ballot ⊕ *noun* **1** method of voting secretly. **2** actual vote or paper indicating a person's choice. ◆ *verb* **-loting, -loted 3** vote or ask for a vote from.

ballyhoo ⊕ *noun* exaggerated fuss.

balm ⊕ *noun* **1** aromatic substance used for healing and soothing. **2** anything that comforts or soothes.

balmy ⊕ *adjective* **balmier, balmiest** (of weather) mild and pleasant.

baloney *noun Informal* nonsense.

balsa [bawl-sa] *noun* very light wood from a tropical American tree.

balsam *noun* **1** aromatic resin obtained from various trees and shrubs. **2** soothing ointment.

3 flowering plant.

Baltic *adjective* of the Baltic Sea in N Europe or the states bordering it.

baluster *noun* set of posts supporting a rail.

balustrade *noun* ornamental rail supported by balusters.

bamboo *noun* tall treelike tropical grass with hollow stems.

bamboozle ⊕ *verb Informal* **1** cheat or mislead. **2** confuse, puzzle.

ban ⊕ *verb* **banning, banned 1** prohibit or forbid officially. ◆ *noun* **2** official prohibition.

banal ⊕ [ban-**nahl**] *adjective* ordinary and unoriginal. **banality** *noun*

banana *noun* yellow crescent-shaped fruit.

banana republic small politically unstable country whose economy is dominated by foreign interests.

band¹ ⊕ *noun* **1** group of musicians playing together. **2** group of people having a common purpose. **bandmaster** *noun* conductor of a band. **bandsman** *noun* **bandstand** *noun* roofed outdoor platform for a band. **band together** *verb* unite.

band² ⊕ *noun* **1** strip of some material, used to hold objects. **2** strip of contrasting colour or texture. **3** *Physics* range of frequencies or wavelengths between two limits.

bandage ⊕ *noun* **1** piece of material used to cover a wound or wrap an injured limb. ◆ *verb* **2** cover with a bandage.

bandanna, bandana *noun* large brightly coloured handkerchief or neckerchief.

bandicoot *noun* ratlike Australian marsupial.

bandit ⊕ *noun* robber, esp. a member of an armed gang. **banditry** *noun*

——————————————— T H E S A U R U S ———————————————

ballast *noun* **1** = **counterbalance**, balance, counterweight, equilibrium, sandbag, stability, stabilizer, weight

balloon *verb* **4** = **swell**, billow, blow up, dilate, distend, expand, grow rapidly, inflate, puff out

ballot *noun* **1** = **vote**, election, poll, polling, voting

ballyhoo *noun* = **fuss**, babble, commotion, hubbub, hue and cry, hullabaloo, noise, racket, to-do

balm *noun* **1** = **ointment**, balsam, cream, embrocation, emollient, lotion, salve, unguent **2** = **comfort**, anodyne, consolation, curative, palliative, restorative, solace

balmy *adjective* = **mild**, clement, pleasant, summery, temperate OPPOSITE **rough**

bamboozle *verb Inf* **1** = **cheat**, con (*inf*), deceive, dupe, fool, hoodwink, swindle, trick **2** = **puzzle**, baffle, befuddle, confound, confuse,

mystify, perplex, stump

ban *verb* **1** = **prohibit**, banish, bar, block, boycott, disallow, disqualify, exclude, forbid, outlaw OPPOSITE **permit** ◆ *noun* **2** = **prohibition**, boycott, disqualification, embargo, restriction, taboo OPPOSITE **permission**

banal *adjective* = **unoriginal**, hackneyed, humdrum, mundane, pedestrian, stale, stereotyped, trite, unimaginative OPPOSITE **original**

band¹ *noun* **1** = **ensemble**, combo, group, orchestra **2** = **gang**, body, company, group, party, posse (*inf*)

band² *noun* **1** = **strip**, belt, bond, chain, cord, ribbon, strap

bandage *noun* **1** = **dressing**, compress, gauze, plaster ◆ *verb* **2** = **dress**, bind, cover, swathe

bandit *noun* = **robber**, brigand, desperado,

B

bandolier *noun* shoulder belt for holding cartridges.

bandwagon *noun* **jump, climb on the bandwagon** join a party or movement that seems assured of success.

bandy *adjective* **-dier, -diest 1** (also **bandy-legged**) having legs curved outwards at the knees. ♦ *verb* **-dying, -died 2** exchange (words) in a heated manner. **3** use (a name, term, etc.) frequently.

bane ⊕ *noun* person or thing that causes misery or distress. **baneful** *adjective*

bang ⊕ *noun* **1** short loud explosive noise. **2** hard blow or loud knock. ♦ *verb* **3** hit or knock, esp. with a loud noise. **4** close (a door) noisily. ♦ *adverb* **5** precisely, e.g. *bang in the middle*. **6** with a sudden impact.

banger *noun* **1** *Informal* old decrepit car. **2** *Slang* sausage. **3** firework that explodes loudly.

bangle *noun* bracelet worn round the arm or the ankle.

banish ⊕ *verb* **1** send (someone) into exile. **2** drive away, e.g. *she has banished all thoughts of retirement*. **banishment** *noun*

banisters ⊕ *plural noun* railing supported by posts on a staircase.

banjo *noun*, *pl* **-jos, -joes** guitar-like musical instrument with a circular body.

bank¹ ⊕ *noun* **1** institution offering services such as the safekeeping and lending of money. **2** any supply, store, or reserve. ♦ *verb* **3** deposit (cash or cheques) in a bank. **4** transact business with a bank. **banking** *noun* **bank holiday** public holiday when banks are closed by law.

banknote *noun* piece of paper money. **bank on** *verb* rely on.

bank² ⊕ *noun* **1** raised mass, esp. of earth. **2** slope, as of a hill. **3** sloping ground at the side of a river. ♦ *verb* **4** form into a bank. **5** cover (a fire) with ashes and fuel so that it will burn slowly. **6** cause (an aircraft) or (of an aircraft) to tip to one side on turning.

bank³ ⊕ *noun* arrangement of switches, keys, oars, etc. in a row or in tiers.

banker *noun* **1** manager or owner of a bank. **2** keeper of the bank in gambling games.

bankrupt ⊕ *noun* **1** person declared by a court to be unable to pay his or her debts. ♦ *adjective* **2** financially ruined. **3** completely lacking a particular quality, e.g. *morally bankrupt*. ♦ *verb* **4** make bankrupt. **bankruptcy** *noun*

banner ⊕ *noun* **1** long strip of cloth displaying a slogan, advertisement, etc. **2** placard carried in a demonstration or procession.

bannisters *plural noun* same as BANISTERS.

banns *plural noun* public declaration, esp. in a church, of an intended marriage.

banquet ⊕ *noun* **1** elaborate formal dinner. ♦ *verb* **-queting, -queted 2** hold or take part in a banquet.

banshee *noun* (in Irish folklore) female spirit whose wailing warns of a coming death.

bantam *noun* small breed of chicken.

bantamweight *noun* boxer weighing up to 118lb (professional) or 54kg (amateur).

banter ⊕ *verb* **1** tease jokingly. ♦ *noun* **2** teasing or joking conversation.

——————————— T H E S A U R U S ———————————

highwayman, marauder, outlaw, thief

bane *noun* = **plague**, bête noire, curse, nuisance, pest, ruin, scourge, torment
OPPOSITE▷ **blessing**

bang *noun* **1** = **explosion**, clang, clap, clash, pop, slam, thud, thump **2** = **blow**, bump, cuff, knock, punch, smack, stroke, whack ♦*verb* **3** = **hit**, belt (*inf*), clatter, knock, slam, strike, thump ♦*adverb* **5** = **straight**, precisely, slap, smack **6** = **hard**, abruptly, headlong, noisily, suddenly

banish *verb* **1** = **expel**, deport, eject, evict, exile, outlaw OPPOSITE▷ **receive**. **2** = **get rid of**, ban, cast out, discard, dismiss, oust, remove

banishment *noun* **1** = **expulsion**, deportation, exile, expatriation, transportation

banisters *plural noun* = **railing**, balusters, balustrade, handrail, rail

bank¹ *noun* **1** = **storehouse**, depository, repository **2** = **store**, accumulation, fund, hoard, reserve, reservoir, savings, stock,

stockpile ♦*verb* **3** = **save**, deposit, keep

bank² *noun* **1** = **mound**, banking, embankment, heap, mass, pile, ridge **3** = **side**, brink, edge, margin, shore ♦*verb* **4** = **pile**, amass, heap, mass, mound, stack **6** = **tilt**, camber, cant, heel, incline, pitch, slant, slope, tip

bank³ *noun* = **row**, array, file, group, line, rank, sequence, series, succession

bankrupt *adjective* **2** = **insolvent**, broke (*inf*), destitute, impoverished, in queer street, in the red, munted (*NZ sl*), ruined, wiped out (*inf*)
OPPOSITE▷ **solvent**

bankruptcy *noun* **2** = **insolvency**, disaster, failure, liquidation, ruin

banner *noun* **1** = **flag**, colours, ensign, pennant, standard, streamer **2** = **placard**

banquet *noun* **1** = **feast**, dinner, meal, repast, revel, treat

banter *verb* **1** = **joke**, jest, kid (*inf*), rib (*inf*), taunt, tease ♦*noun* **2** = **joking**, badinage,

B

Bantu *noun* **1** group of languages of Africa. **2** *Offens* Black speaker of a Bantu language.

banyan *noun* Indian tree whose branches grow down into the soil forming additional trunks.

baobab [**bay**-oh-bab] *noun* African tree with a thick trunk and angular branches.

bap *noun Brit* large soft bread roll.

baptism ⊙ *noun* Christian religious ceremony in which a person is immersed in or sprinkled with water as a sign of being cleansed from sinand accepted into the Church. **baptismal** *adjective* **baptize** *verb* **1** perform baptism on. **2** give a name to.

Baptist *noun* member of a Protestant denomination that believes in adult baptism by immersion.

bar¹ ⊙ *noun* **1** rigid length of metal, wood, etc. **2** solid, usu. rectangular block, of any material. **3** anything that obstructs or prevents. **4** counter or room where drinks are served. **5** heating element in an electric fire. **6** place in court where the accused stands during trial. **7** *Music* group of beats repeated throughout a piece of music. ◆ *verb* **barring, barred 8** secure with a bar. **9** obstruct. **10** ban or forbid. ◆ *preposition* **11** (also **barring**) except for. **the Bar** barristers collectively. **barman, barmaid, bartender** *noun*

bar² *noun* unit of atmospheric pressure.

barachois [bar-ah-**shwah**] *noun* (in the Atlantic Provinces of Canada) a shallow lagoon formed by a sand bar.

barb ⊙ *noun* **1** cutting remark. **2** point facing in the opposite direction to the main point of a fish-hook etc. **barbed** *adjective* **barbed wire** strong wire with protruding sharp points.

barbarian ⊙ *noun* member of a primitive or uncivilized people. **barbaric** *adjective* cruel or brutal. **barbarism** *noun* condition of being backward or ignorant. **barbarity** *noun* **1** state of being barbaric or barbarous. **2** *pl* **-ties** vicious act. **barbarous** *adjective* **1** uncivilized. **2** brutal or cruel.

barbecue *noun* **1** grill on which food is cooked over hot charcoal, usu. outdoors. **2** outdoor party at which barbecued food is served. ◆ *verb* **3** cook (food) on a barbecue.

barber *noun* person who cuts men's hair and shaves beards.

barbican *noun* walled defence to protect a gate or drawbridge of a fortification.

barbiturate *noun* drug used as a sedative.

bard *noun Lit* poet. **the Bard** William Shakespeare.

bare ⊙ *adjective* **1** unclothed, naked. **2** without the natural or usual covering. **3** unembellished, simple. **4** just sufficient, e.g. *the bare minimum.* ◆ *verb* **5** uncover. **barely** *adverb* only just. **bareness** *noun*

bareback *adjective, adverb* (of horse-riding) without a saddle.

barefaced ⊙ *adjective* shameless or obvious.

barefoot, barefooted *adjective, adverb* with the feet uncovered.

bareheaded *adjective, adverb* with the head uncovered.

bargain ⊙ *noun* **1** agreement establishing

——————— THESAURUS ———————

jesting, kidding (*inf*), repartee, teasing, wordplay

baptism *noun* =**christening**, immersion, purification, sprinkling

baptize *verb* **1** = **purify**, cleanse, immerse

bar¹ *noun* **1** =**rod**, paling, palisade, pole, rail, shaft, stake, stick **3** = **obstacle**, barricade, barrier, block, deterrent, hindrance, impediment, obstruction, stop OPPOSITE help. **4** = **public house**, boozer (*Brit, Aust & NZ inf*), beer parlour (*Canad*), beverage room (*Canad*), canteen, counter, inn, pub (*inf, chiefly Brit*), saloon, tavern, watering hole (*facetious sl*) ◆*verb* **8** = **fasten**, barricade, bolt, latch, lock, secure **9** = **obstruct**, hinder, prevent, restrain **10** = **exclude**, ban, black, blackball, forbid, keep out, prohibit OPPOSITE admit ◆ **the Bar** = **barristers**, body of lawyers, counsel, court, judgment, tribunal

barb *noun* **1** = **dig**, affront, cut, gibe, insult, sarcasm, scoff, sneer **2** = **point**, bristle, prickle, prong, quill, spike, spur, thorn

barbarian *noun* =**savage**, boor, brute, lout, philistine, yahoo OPPOSITE cultured

barbaric *adjective* =**brutal**, barbarous, coarse, crude, cruel, fierce, inhuman, savage

barbarous *adjective* **1** =**uncivilized**, barbarian, brutish, primitive, rough, rude, savage, uncouth, wild **2** =**brutal**, barbaric, cruel, ferocious, heartless, inhuman, monstrous, ruthless, vicious

barbed *adjective* **1** =**cutting**, critical, hostile, hurtful, nasty, pointed, scathing, unkind **2** =**spiked**, hooked, jagged, prickly, spiny, thorny

bare *adjective* **1** =**naked**, nude, stripped, unclad, unclothed, uncovered, undressed, without a stitch on (*inf*) OPPOSITE covered. **3** =**plain**, austere, basic, sheer, simple, spare, spartan, stark, unadorned, unembellished OPPOSITE adorned

barefaced *adjective* =**obvious**, blatant, bold, brazen, flagrant, open, shameless what each party will give, receive, or perform in a transaction. **2** something bought or offered at a low price. ♦ *verb* **3** negotiate the terms of an agreement. **into the bargain** besides, in addition. **bargain for** *verb* anticipate or take into account.

barge ⊕ *noun* **1** flat-bottomed boat used to transport freight. ♦ *verb* **2** *Informal* push violently. **bargee** *noun* person in charge of a barge. **barge in, into** *verb* interrupt rudely.

barista *noun* person who makes and sells coffee in a coffee bar.

baritone *noun* (singer with) the second lowest adult male voice.

barium [bare-ee-um] *noun Chem* soft white metallic element. **barium meal** preparation of barium sulphate swallowed by a patient before an x-ray of the alimentary canal.

bark¹ ⊕ *noun* **1** loud harsh cry of a dog. ♦ *verb* **2** (of a dog) make its typical cry. **3** shout in an angry tone. **barker** *noun* person at a fairground who calls loudly to passers-by in order to attract customers.

bark² ⊕ *noun* **1** tough outer layer of a tree. ♦ *verb* **2** scrape or rub off skin.

barking *adjective Slang* mad.

barley *noun* **1** tall grasslike plant cultivated for grain. **2** grain of this plant used in making malt and whisky and in soups. **barley sugar** brittle clear amber-coloured sweet. **barley water** drink made from an infusion of barley.

bar mitzvah *noun Judaism* ceremony marking the 13th birthday of a boy, who then assumes full religious obligations.

barmy ⊕ *adjective* -mier, -miest *Slang* insane.

barn *noun* large building on a farm used for storing grain. **barn dance** informal party with country dancing. **barn owl** owl with pale brown and white plumage. **barnstorm** *verb US* tour rural districts putting on shows or making speeches in a political campaign.

barnacle *noun* shellfish that lives attached to rocks, ship bottoms, etc. **barnacle goose** goose with a black-and-white head and body.

barney *noun Informal* noisy fight or argument.

barometer *noun* instrument for measuring atmospheric pressure. **barometric** *adjective*

baron *noun* **1** member of the lowest rank of nobility. **2** powerful businessman, e.g. *a press baron.* **baroness** *noun* **baronial** *adjective*

baronet *noun* commoner who holds the lowest hereditary British title.

baroque [bar-**rock**] *noun* **1** highly ornate style of art, architecture, or music from the late 16th to the early 18th century. ♦ *adjective* **2** ornate in style.

barque [bark] *noun* sailing ship, esp. one with three masts.

barrack *verb* criticize loudly or shout against (a team or speaker).

barracks ⊕ *plural noun* building used to accommodate military personnel.

barracouta *noun* large Pacific fish with a protruding lower jaw and strong teeth.

barracuda [bar-rack-**kew**-da] *noun* fierce tropical sea fish.

barrage ⊕ [bar-rahzh] *noun* **1** continuous delivery of questions, complaints, etc. **2** continuous artillery fire. **3** artificial barrier across a river to control the water level.

barrel *noun* **1** cylindrical container with rounded sides and flat ends. **2** amount that a barrel can hold. **3** tube in a firearm through which the bullet is fired. **barrel organ** musical instrument played by turning a handle.

barren ⊕ *adjective* **1** (of a woman or female animal) incapable of producing offspring. **2** (of land) unable to support the growth of crops, fruit, etc. **3** unprofitable, e.g. *a barren period.* **barrenness** *noun*

barricade ⊕ *noun* **1** barrier, esp. one erected hastily for defence. ♦ *verb* **2** erect a barricade

—————— THESAURUS ——————

barely *adverb* = **only just**, almost, at a push, by the skin of one's teeth, hardly, just, scarcely OPPOSITE **completely**

bargain *noun* **1** = **agreement**, arrangement, contract, pact, pledge, promise **2** = **good buy**, (cheap) purchase, discount, giveaway, good deal, reduction, snip (*inf*), steal (*inf*) ♦ *verb* **3** = **negotiate**, agree, contract, covenant, cut a deal, promise, stipulate, transact

barge *noun* **1** = **canal boat**, flatboat, lighter, narrow boat

bark¹ *noun* **1** = **yap**, bay, howl, woof, yelp ♦ *verb* **2** = **yap**, bay, howl, woof, yelp

bark² *noun* **1** = **covering**, casing, cortex (*Anat*,

bot), crust, husk, rind, skin

barmy *adjective Sl* = **insane**, crazy, daft (*inf*), foolish, idiotic, nuts (*sl*), out of one's mind, stupid OPPOSITE **sane**

barracks *plural noun* = **camp**, billet, encampment, garrison, quarters

barrage *noun* **1** = **torrent**, burst, deluge, hail, mass, onslaught, plethora, stream **2** = **bombardment**, battery, cannonade, fusillade, gunfire, salvo, shelling, volley

barren *adjective* **1** = **infertile**, childless, sterile OPPOSITE **fertile**. **2** = **unproductive**, arid, desert, desolate, dry, empty, unfruitful, waste OPPOSITE **rich**

B

across (an entrance).

barrier ⊕ *noun* anything that prevents access, progress, or union. **barrier cream** cream that protects the skin. **barrier reef** long narrow coral reef lying close to the shore.

barrister *noun* lawyer qualified to plead in a higher court.

barrow[1] *noun* 1 wheelbarrow. 2 movable stall used by street traders.

barrow[2] *noun* mound of earth over a prehistoric tomb.

barter ⊕ *verb* 1 trade (goods) in exchange for other goods. ◆ *noun* 2 trade by the exchange of goods.

basal *adjective* 1 of, at, or constituting a base. 2 fundamental.

basalt [**bass**-awlt] *noun* dark volcanic rock. **basaltic** *adjective*

bascule *noun* drawbridge that operates by a counterbalanced weight.

base[1] ⊕ *noun* 1 bottom or supporting part of anything. 2 fundamental part. 3 centre of operations, organization, or supply. 4 starting point. 5 chemical compound that combines with an acid to form a salt. 6 *Maths* the number of units in a counting system that is equivalent to one in the next higher counting place. ◆ *verb* 7 (foll. by *on* or *upon*) use as a basis (for). 8 (foll. by *at* or *in*) station or place. **baseless** *adjective* **basement** *noun* partly or wholly underground storey of a building. **base rate** rate of interest as a basis for bank lending rates.

base[2] ⊕ *adjective* 1 dishonourable or immoral. 2 of inferior quality or value. 3 debased or

counterfeit. **basely** *adverb* **baseness** *noun*

baseball *noun* 1 team game in which runs are scored by hitting a ball with a bat then running round four bases. 2 ball used for this.

basement *noun* partly or wholly underground storey of a building.

bases *noun* plural of BASIS.

bash ⊕ *Informal verb* 1 hit violently or forcefully. ◆ *noun* 2 heavy blow. **have a bash** *Informal* make an attempt.

bashful ⊕ *adjective* shy or modest. **bashfully** *adverb* **bashfulness** *noun*

basic ⊕ *adjective* 1 of or forming a base or basis. 2 elementary or simple. 3 *Chem* of or containing a base. **basics** *plural noun* fundamental principles, facts, etc. **basically** *adverb*

BASIC *noun* computer programming language that uses common English words.

basil *noun* aromatic herb used in cooking.

basilica *noun* rectangular church with a rounded end and two aisles.

basilisk *noun* legendary serpent said to kill by its breath or glance.

basin *noun* 1 round open container. 2 sink for washing the hands and face. 3 sheltered area of water where boats may be moored. 4 catchment area of a particular river.

basis ⊕ *noun, pl* **-ses** fundamental principles etc. from which something is started or developed.

bask ⊕ *verb* 1 lie in or be exposed to something, esp. pleasant warmth. 2 enjoy (approval or favourable conditions).

basket *noun* container made of interwoven

———————— THESAURUS ————————

barricade *noun* 1 = **barrier**, blockade, bulwark, fence, obstruction, palisade, rampart, stockade ◆*verb* 2 = **bar**, block, blockade, defend, fortify, obstruct, protect, shut in

barrier *noun* a = **barricade**, bar, blockade, boundary, fence, obstacle, obstruction, wall b = **hindrance**, difficulty, drawback, handicap, hurdle, obstacle, restriction, stumbling block

barter *verb* 1 = **trade**, bargain, drive a hard bargain, exchange, haggle, sell, swap, traffic

base[1] *noun* 1 = **bottom**, bed, foot, foundation, pedestal, rest, stand, support ⌐OPPOSITE⌐ top. 2 = **basis**, core, essence, heart, key, origin, root, source 3 = **centre**, camp, headquarters, home, post, settlement, starting point, station ◆*verb* 7 (foll. by *on* or *upon*) = **found**, build, construct, depend, derive, establish, ground, hinge 8 (foll. by *at* or *in*) = **place**, locate, post, station

base[2] *adjective* 1 = **dishonourable**, contemptible, despicable, disreputable, evil,

immoral, scungy (*Aust & NZ inf*), shameful, sordid, wicked ⌐OPPOSITE⌐ honourable. 3 = **counterfeit**, alloyed, debased, fake, forged, fraudulent, impure

bash *Inf verb* 1 = **hit**, belt (*inf*), smash, sock (*sl*), strike, wallop (*inf*)

bashful *adjective* = **shy**, blushing, coy, diffident, reserved, reticent, retiring, timid ⌐OPPOSITE⌐ forward

basic *adjective* 1 = **essential**, fundamental, key, necessary, primary, vital ⌐OPPOSITE⌐ secondary. 2 = **elementary**, simple

basically *adverb* 1 = **essentially**, at heart, fundamentally, inherently, in substance, intrinsically, mostly, primarily

basics *plural noun* = **essentials**, brass tacks (*inf*), fundamentals, nitty-gritty (*inf*), nuts and bolts (*inf*), principles, rudiments

basis *noun* = **foundation**, base, bottom, footing, ground, groundwork, support

strips of wood or cane. **basketwork** *noun*
basketball *noun* **1** team game in which
points are scored by throwing the ball through
a high horizontal hoop. **2** ball used for this.
basque *noun* tight-fitting bodice for women.
Basque *noun, adjective* (member or language)
of a people living in the W Pyrenees in France
and Spain.
bas-relief *noun* sculpture in which the figures
project slightly from the background.
bass¹ ⊕ [base] *noun* **1** (singer with) the lowest
adult male voice. **2** *Informal* same as BASS GUITAR
or DOUBLE BASS. ♦ *adjective* **3** of the lowest range
of musical notes. **bass guitar** electric guitar
with same pitch and tuning as a double bass.
bass² *noun* edible sea fish.
basset hound *noun* smooth-haired dog with
short legs and long ears.
bassoon *noun* low-pitched woodwind
instrument.
bastard ⊕ *noun* **1** *Offens* obnoxious or
despicable person. **2** person born of parents
not married to each other. **bastardize** *verb*
debase or corrupt.
baste¹ *verb* moisten (meat) during cooking
with hot fat.
baste² *verb* sew with loose temporary stitches.
bastion ⊕ *noun* **1** projecting part of a
fortification. **2** thing or person regarded as
defending a principle.
bat¹ ⊕ *noun* **1** any of various types of club
used to hit the ball in certain sports. ♦ *verb*
batting, batted 2 strike with or as if with a
bat. **3** *Cricket* take a turn at batting. **batsman**
noun Cricket person who bats or specializes in
batting.
bat² *noun* nocturnal mouselike flying animal.
bat³ *verb* **not bat an eyelid** *Informal* show no
surprise.
batch ⊕ *noun* group of people or things dealt
with at the same time.

bated *adjective* **with bated breath** in
suspense or fear.
bath ⊕ *noun* **1** large container in which to
wash the body. **2** act of washing in such a
container. ♦ *plural* **3** public swimming pool. ♦
verb **4** wash in a bath. **bathroom** *noun* room
with a bath, sink, and usu. a toilet.
Bath chair *noun* wheelchair for an invalid.
bathe ⊕ *verb* **1** swim in open water for
pleasure. **2** apply liquid to (the skin or a
wound) in order to cleanse or soothe. **3** (foll.
by *in*) fill (with), e.g. *bathed in sunlight*. ♦ *noun*
4 *Brit* instance of bathing. **bather** *noun*
bathos [bay-thoss] *noun* sudden ludicrous
change in speech or writing from a serious
subject to a trivial one.
bathyscaph, bathyscaphe, bathysphere
noun deep-sea diving vessel for observation.
batik [bat-**teek**] *noun* **1** process of printing
fabric using wax to cover areas not to be dyed.
2 fabric printed in this way.
batman *noun* officer's servant in the armed
forces.
baton ⊕ *noun* **1** thin stick used by the
conductor of an orchestra. **2** short bar
transferred in a relay race. **3** police officer's
truncheon.
batrachian [bat-**tray**-kee-an] *noun* **1**
amphibian, esp. a frog or toad. ♦ *adjective* **2** of
or relating to frogs and toads.
battalion *noun* army unit consisting of three
or more companies.
batten¹ ⊕ *noun* strip of wood fixed to
something, esp. to hold it in place. **batten**
down *verb* secure with battens.
batten² ⊕ *verb* **batten on** thrive at the
expense of (someone else).
batter¹ ⊕ *verb* **1** hit repeatedly. **2** damage or
injure, as by blows, heavy wear, etc., e.g.
battered by gales. **battering ram** large beam
used to break down fortifications.

——————————— T H E S A U R U S ———————————

bask *verb* **1** = **lie in**, laze, loll, lounge, outspan
(*S Afr*), relax, sunbathe
bass¹ *adjective* **3** = **deep**, deep-toned, low,
low-pitched, resonant, sonorous
bastard *noun* **1** *Offens* = **rogue**, blackguard,
miscreant, reprobate, scoundrel, villain, wretch
2 = **illegitimate child**, love child, natural child
bastion *noun* **1** = **stronghold**, bulwark,
citadel, defence, fortress **2** = **tower of**
strength, mainstay, prop, rock, support
bat¹ *verb* **2** = **hit**, bang, smack, strike, swat,
thump, wallop (*inf*), whack
batch *noun* = **group**, amount, assemblage,
bunch, collection, crowd, lot, pack, quantity,

set
bath *noun* **2** = **wash**, cleansing, douche,
scrubbing, shower, soak, tub ♦*verb* **4** = **wash**,
bathe, clean, douse, scrub down, shower, soak
bathe *verb* **1** = **swim 2** = **wash**, cleanse, rinse
3 (foll. by *in*) = **cover**, flood, immerse, steep,
suffuse
baton *noun* **1** = **stick**, wand **3** = **truncheon**,
club, rod
batten¹ **batten down** *verb* = **fasten**, board
up, clamp down, cover up, fix, nail down,
secure, tighten
batten² *verb* **batten on** = **thrive**, fatten,
flourish, gain, grow, increase, prosper

B

batter² *noun* mixture of flour, eggs, and milk, used in cooking.

battery ❶ *noun, pl* **-teries 1** device that produces electricity in a torch, radio, etc. **2** number of similar things occurring together. **3** *Law* assault by beating. **4** group of heavy guns operating as a single unit. ◆ *adjective* **5** kept in series of cages for intensive rearing, e.g. *battery hens.*

battle ❶ *noun* **1** fight between large armed forces. **2** conflict or struggle. ◆ *verb* **3** struggle.

battle-axe *noun* **1** *Informal* domineering woman. **2** (formerly) large heavy axe.

battledress *noun* ordinary uniform of a soldier.

battlefield, battleground ❶ *noun* place where a battle is fought.

battlement *noun* wall with gaps along the top for firing through.

battleship ❶ *noun* large heavily armoured warship.

batty ❶ *adjective* **-tier, -tiest** *Slang* eccentric or crazy.

bauble ❶ *noun* trinket of little value.

baulk ❶ *verb* same as BALK.

bauxite *noun* claylike substance that is the chief source of aluminium.

bawdy ❶ *adjective* **bawdier, bawdiest** (of writing etc.) containing humorous references to sex. **bawdiness** *noun*

bawl ❶ *verb* **1** shout or weep noisily. ◆ *noun* **2** loud shout or cry.

bay¹ ❶ *noun* stretch of coastline that curves inwards.

bay² ❶ *noun* **1** recess in a wall. **2** area set aside for a particular purpose, e.g. *loading bay.* **3** compartment in an aircraft, e.g. *bomb bay.* **bay window** window projecting from a wall.

bay³ ❶ *noun* **1** deep howl of a hound or wolf. ◆ *verb* **2** howl in deep prolonged tones. **at bay 1** forced to turn and face attackers. **2** at a safe distance.

bay⁴ *noun* Mediterranean laurel tree. **bay leaf** its dried leaf, used in cooking.

bay⁵ *adjective, noun* reddish-brown (horse).

bayonet *noun* **1** sharp blade that can be fixed to the end of a rifle. ◆ *verb* **-neting, -neted 2** stab with a bayonet.

bazaar ❶ *noun* **1** sale in aid of charity. **2** market area, esp. in Eastern countries.

bazooka *noun* portable rocket launcher that fires an armour-piercing projectile.

B & B bed and breakfast.

BB Boys' Brigade.

BBC British Broadcasting Corporation.

BC 1 before Christ. **2** British Columbia.

BCG antituberculosis vaccine.

BD Bachelor of Divinity.

BDS Bachelor of Dental Surgery.

be ❶ *verb, present sing 1st person* **am**. *2nd person* **are**. *3rd person* **is**. *present pl* **are**. *past sing 1st person* **was**. *2nd person* **were**. *3rd person* **was**. *past pl* **were**. *present participle* **being**. *past participle* **been 1** exist or live. **2** pay a visit, e.g. *have you been to Spain?* **3** take place, e.g. *my birthday was last Monday.* **4** used as a linking between the subject of a sentence and its complement, e.g. *John is a musician.* **5** forms the progressive present tense, e.g. *the man is running.* **6** forms the passive voice of all transitive verbs, e.g. *a good film is being shown on television tonight.*

Be *Chem* beryllium.

BE Bachelor of Engineering.

be- *prefix* **1** surround or cover, e.g. *befog.* **2** affect completely, e.g. *bedazzle.* **3** consider as

——————— THESAURUS ———————

batter¹ *verb* **1 = beat**, buffet, clobber (*sl*), pelt, pound, pummel, thrash, wallop (*inf*)

battery *noun* **4 = artillery**, cannon, cannonry, gun emplacements, guns

battle *noun* **1 = fight**, action, attack, combat, encounter, engagement, hostilities, skirmish OPPOSITE **peace**. **2 = conflict**, campaign, contest, crusade, dispute, struggle ◆*verb* **3 = struggle**, argue, clamour, dispute, fight, lock horns, strive, war

battlefield *noun* **= battleground**, combat zone, field, field of battle, front

battleship *noun* **= warship**, gunboat, man-of-war

batty *adjective Sl* **= crazy**, daft (*inf*), dotty (*sl, chiefly Brit*), eccentric, mad, munted (*NZ sl*), odd, peculiar, potty (*Brit inf*), touched

bauble *noun* **= trinket**, bagatelle, gewgaw, gimcrack, knick-knack, plaything, toy, trifle

baulk see BALK

bawdy *adjective* **= rude**, coarse, dirty, indecent, lascivious, lecherous, lewd, ribald, salacious, scungy (*Aust & NZ inf*), smutty OPPOSITE **clean**

bawl *verb* **a = shout**, bellow, call, clamour, howl, roar, yell **b = cry**, blubber, sob, wail, weep

bay¹ *noun* **= inlet**, bight, cove, gulf, natural harbour, sound

bay² *noun* **2 = recess**, alcove, compartment, niche, nook, opening

bay³ *noun* **1 = howl**, bark, clamour, cry, yelp ◆*verb* **2 = howl**, bark, clamour, cry, yelp

bazaar *noun* **1 = fair**, bring-and-buy, fete, sale

B

or cause to be, e.g. *befriend*. **4** provide or cover with, e.g. *bejewelled*. **5** at, for, against, on, or over, e.g. *bewail*.

beach ❶ *noun* **1** area of sand or pebbles on a shore. ♦ *verb* **2** run or haul (a boat) onto a beach. **beachcomber** *noun* person who searches shore debris for anything or worth.

beachhead *noun* beach captured by an attacking army on which troops can be landed.

beacon ❶ *noun* **1** fire or light on a hill or tower, used as a warning. **2** lighthouse. **3** radio or other signal used in air navigation.

bead ❶ *noun* **1** small piece of plastic, wood, etc., pierced for threading on a string to form a necklace etc. **2** small drop of moisture. **3** small metal knob acting as the sight of a firearm. **beaded** *adjective* **beading** *noun* strip of moulding used for edging furniture. **beady** *adjective* **beadier, beadiest** small, round, and glittering, e.g. *beady eyes*.

beagle *noun* small hound with short legs and drooping ears.

beak¹ ❶ *noun* **1** projecting horny jaws of a bird. **2** *Slang* nose. **beaky** *adjective* **beakier, beakiest**

beak² *noun Slang* judge, magistrate, or headmaster.

beaker *noun* **1** large drinking cup. **2** lipped glass container used in laboratories.

beam ❶ *noun* **1** broad smile. **2** ray of light. **3** narrow flow of electromagnetic radiation or particles. **4** long thick piece of wood, metal, etc., used in building. **5** breadth of a ship at its widest part. ♦ *verb* **6** smile broadly. **7** divert or aim (a radio signal, light, etc.) in a certain direction.

bean *noun* seed or pod of various plants, eaten

as a vegetable or used to make coffee etc. **full of beans** *Informal* full of energy and vitality.

beansprout *noun* small edible shoot grown from a bean seed.

beanie *noun Brit, Aust & NZ* close-fitting woolen hat.

beano *noun, pl* **beanos** *Brit slang* celebration or party.

bear¹ ❶ *verb* **bearing, bore, borne 1** support or hold up. **2** bring, e.g. *to bear gifts*. **3** *passive* **born** give birth to. **4** produce as by natural growth. **5** tolerate or endure. **6** stand up to, e.g. *his story does not bear scrutiny*. **7** hold in the mind, e.g. *to bear a grudge*. **8** show or be marked with, e.g. *he still bears the scars*. **9** have or be in (relation or comparison), e.g. *her account bears no relation to the facts*. **10** move in a specified direction, e.g. *bring to bear*. **bearable** *adjective* **bear down on** *verb* **1** press down on. **2** approach (someone) in a determined manner. **bear out** *verb* show to be truthful.

bear² *noun* large heavy mammal with a shaggy coat. **bear hug** rough tight embrace. **bearskin** *noun* tall fur helmet worn by some British soldiers.

beard *noun* **1** hair growing on the lower parts of a man's face. ♦ *verb* **2** oppose boldly. **bearded** *adjective*

bearer ❶ *noun* person who carries, presents, or upholds something.

bearing ❶ *noun* **1** relevance (to). **2** person's general social conduct. **3** part of a machine that supports another part, esp. one that reduces friction. ♦ *plural* **4** sense of one's own relative position, e.g. *I lost my bearings in the fog*.

———————— THESAURUS ————————

of work **2** = **market**, exchange, marketplace

be *verb* **1** = **exist**, be alive, breathe, inhabit, live

beach *noun* **1** = **shore**, coast, sands, seashore, seaside, water's edge

beacon *noun* **1** = **signal**, beam, bonfire, flare, sign **2** = **lighthouse**, watchtower

bead *noun* **2** = **drop**, bubble, droplet, globule

beady *adjective* = **bright**, gleaming, glinting, glittering, sharp, shining

beak *noun* **1** = **bill**, mandible, neb (*arch or dial*), nib **2** *Sl* = **nose**, proboscis, snout

beam *noun* **1** = **smile**, grin **2** = **ray**, gleam, glimmer, glint, glow, shaft, streak, stream **4** = **rafter**, girder, joist, plank, spar, support, timber ♦*verb* **6** = **smile**, grin **7** = **send out**, broadcast, emit, transmit

bear¹ *verb* **1** = **support**, have, hold, maintain, possess, shoulder, sustain, uphold OPPOSITE⟩

give up. 2 = **carry**, bring, convey, hump (*Brit sl*), move, take, transport OPPOSITE⟩ **put down. 3, 4** = **produce**, beget, breed, bring forth, engender, generate, give birth to, yield **5** = **tolerate**, abide, allow, brook, endure, permit, put up with (*inf*), stomach, suffer

bearable *adjective* **5** = **tolerable**, admissible, endurable, manageable, passable, sufferable, supportable, sustainable OPPOSITE⟩ **intolerable**

bearer *noun* = **carrier**, agent, conveyor, messenger, porter, runner, servant

bearing *noun* **1** = **relevance**, application, connection, import, pertinence, reference, relation, significance OPPOSITE⟩ **irrelevance. 2** = **manner**, air, aspect, attitude, behaviour, demeanour, deportment, posture ♦*plural* **4** = **position**, aim, course, direction, location, orientation, situation, track, way, whereabouts

B

beast ⊕ *noun* **1** large wild animal. **2** brutal or uncivilized person. **beastly** *adjective* unpleasant or disagreeable.

beat ⊕ *verb* **beating, beat, beaten** *or* **beat 1** hit hard and repeatedly. **2** move (wings) up and down. **3** throb rhythmically. **4** stir or mix vigorously. **5** *Music* indicate (time) by one's hand or a baton. **6** overcome or defeat. **7** (foll. by *back* or *off*) drive, push, or thrust. **8** *Slang* puzzle or baffle. ◆ *noun* **9** (sound made by) a stroke or blow. **10** regular throb. **11** assigned route, as of a policeman. **12** basic rhythmic unit in a piece of music. **beat up** *verb* injure (someone) by repeated blows or kicks.

beatify [bee-at-if-fie] *verb* **-fying, -fied** *RC Church* declare (a dead person) to be among the blessed in heaven: the first step towards canonization. **beatific** *adjective* displaying great happiness. **beatification** *noun* **beatitude** *noun Christianity* any of the blessings on the poor, meek, etc., in the Sermon on the Mount.

beatnik *noun* young person in the late 1950s who rebelled against conventional attitudes etc.

beau ⊕ [boh] *noun, pl* **beaux, beaus 1** boyfriend or admirer. **2** man greatly concerned with his appearance.

Beaufort scale *noun* scale for measuring wind speeds.

Beaujolais *noun* wine, usu. red, from southern Burgundy in France.

beauteous *adjective Lit* beautiful.

beautician *noun* person who gives beauty treatments professionally.

beautiful ⊕ *adjective* **1** very attractive to look at. **2** very pleasant. **beautifully** *adverb*

beautify ⊕ *verb* **-fying, -fied** make beautiful. **beautification** *noun*

beauty ⊕ *noun, pl* **-ties 1** combination of all the qualities of a person or thing that delight the senses and mind. **2** very attractive woman. **3** *Informal* something outstanding of its kind. **beautiful** *adjective* very attractive to look at. **beauty queen** woman who has been judged the most beautiful in a contest. **beauty spot 1** place of outstanding beauty. **2** small black spot formerly worn on a lady's face as decoration.

beaver *noun* **1** amphibious rodent with a big flat tail. **2** (hat made of) its fur. **beaver away** *verb* work industriously.

becalmed ⊕ *adjective* (of a sailing ship) motionless through lack of wind.

became *verb* past tense of BECOME.

because ⊕ *conjunction* on account of the fact that. **because of** on account of.

beck[1] *noun* **at someone's beck and call** having to be constantly available to do as someone asks.

beck[2] *noun N English* stream.

beckon ⊕ *verb* summon with a gesture.

become ⊕ *verb* **-coming, -came, -come 1** come to be. **2** (foll. by *of*) happen to, e.g. *what became of him?* **3** suit, e.g. *that dress really becomes you.* **becoming** *adjective* **1** attractive or pleasing. **2** appropriate or proper.

bed ⊕ *noun* **1** piece of furniture on which to

——————— T H E S A U R U S ———————

bear out *verb* =**support**, confirm, corroborate, endorse, justify, prove, substantiate, uphold, vindicate

beast *noun* **1** =**animal**, brute, creature **2** =**brute**, barbarian, fiend, monster, ogre, sadist, savage, swine

beastly *adjective* =**unpleasant**, awful, disagreeable, horrid, mean, nasty, rotten OPPOSITE> **pleasant**

beat *verb* **1** =**hit**, bang, batter, buffet, knock, pound, strike, thrash **2** =**flap**, flutter **3** =**throb**, palpitate, pound, pulsate, quake, thump, vibrate **6** =**defeat**, conquer, outdo, overcome, overwhelm, surpass, vanquish ◆*noun* **10** =**throb**, palpitation, pulsation, pulse **11** =**route**, circuit, course, path, rounds, way **12** =**rhythm**, accent, cadence, metre, stress, time

beaten *adjective* **4** =**stirred**, blended, foamy, frothy, mixed, whipped, whisked **6** =**defeated**, cowed, overcome, overwhelmed, thwarted, vanquished

beat up *verb* =**assault**, attack, batter, beat the living daylights out of (*inf*), knock about *or* around, thrash

beau *noun* **1** =**boyfriend**, admirer, fiancé, lover, suitor, sweetheart **2** =**dandy**, coxcomb, fop, gallant, ladies' man

beautiful *adjective* **1** =**attractive**, exquisite, fair, fine, gorgeous, handsome, lekker (*S Afr sl*), lovely OPPOSITE> **ugly**. **2** =**pleasant**, charming, delightful, pleasing

beautify *verb* =**make beautiful**, adorn, decorate, embellish, festoon, garnish, glamorize, ornament

beauty *noun* **1** =**attractiveness**, charm, comeliness, elegance, exquisiteness, glamour, grace, handsomeness, loveliness OPPOSITE> **ugliness**. **2** =**belle**, good-looker, lovely (*sl*), stunner (*inf*)

becalmed *adjective* =**still**, motionless, settled, stranded, stuck

because *conjunction* =**since**, as, by reason of, in that, on account of, owing to, thanks to

beckon *verb* =**gesture**, bid, gesticulate,

sleep. **2** garden plot. **3** bottom of a river, lake, or sea. **4** layer of rock. ♦ *verb* **bedding, bedded 5** plant in a bed. **go to bed with** have sexual intercourse with. **bed and breakfast** overnight accommodation plus breakfast. **bedclothes** *plural noun* coverings for a bed. **bed down** *verb* go to or put into a place to sleep or rest. **bedpan** *noun* shallow bowl used as a toilet by bedridden people. **bedridden** *adjective* confined to bed because of illness or old age. **bedrock** *noun* **1** solid rock beneath the surface soil. **2** basic facts or principles. **bedroom** *noun* **bedsit, bedsitter** *noun* furnished sitting room with a bed. **bedspread** *noun* top cover on a bed. **bedstead** *noun* framework of a bed. **BEd** Bachelor of Education. **bedaub** *verb* smear with something sticky or dirty. **bedding** *noun* **1** sheets and covers that are used on a bed. **2** litter, such as straw, for animals. **bedeck** *verb* cover with decorations. **bedevil** ⊕ [bid-**dev**-ill] *verb* **-illing, -illed** harass, confuse, or torment. **bedlam** ⊕ *noun* noisy confused situation. **Bedouin** *noun, pl* **-in, -ins** member of a nomadic Arab race. **bedraggled** ⊕ *adjective* untidy, wet, or dirty. **bee**[1] *noun* insect that makes wax and honey. **have a bee in one's bonnet** be obsessed with an idea. **beehive** *noun* structure in which bees live. **beeswax** *noun* wax secreted by bees, used in polishes etc.

bee[2] *noun US* social gathering to carry out a communal task, e.g. *quilting bee.*
Beeb *noun Informal* the BBC.
beech *noun* European tree with a smooth greyish bark.
beef ⊕ *noun* **1** flesh of a cow, bull, or ox. **2** *Informal* complaint. ♦ *verb* **3** *Informal* complain. **beefy** *adjective* **beefier, beefiest 1** like beef. **2** *Informal* strong and muscular. **beefburger** *noun* flat grilled or fried cake of minced beef. **beefeater** *noun* yeoman warder at the Tower of London. **beef tomato, beefsteak tomato** large fleshy tomato. **beef up** *verb* make stronger or more effective.
been *verb* past participle of BE.
beep *noun* **1** high-pitched sound, like that of a car horn. ♦ *verb* **2** (cause to) make this noise.
beer *noun* alcoholic drink brewed from malt and hops. **beery** *adjective*
beer parlour ⊕ *noun Canad* tavern.
beet *noun* plant with an edible root and leaves. **beetroot** *noun* type of beet plant with a dark red root.
beetle[1] *noun* insect with a hard wing cover on its back.
beetle[2] *adjective* overhang or jut. **beetling** *adjective* **beetle-browed** *adjective* having bushy or overhanging eyebrows.
befall ⊕ *verb Old-fashioned* happen to (someone).
befit ⊕ *verb* be appropriate or suitable for. **befitting** *adjective*

B

---

motion, nod, signal, summon, wave at
become *verb* **1 = come to be,** alter to, be transformed into, change into, develop into, grow into, mature into, ripen into **3 = suit,** embellish, enhance, fit, flatter, set off
becoming *adjective* **1 = flattering,** attractive, comely, enhancing, graceful, lekker (*S Afr sl*), neat, pretty, tasteful OPPOSITE ugly. **2 = appropriate,** compatible, fitting, in keeping, proper, seemly, suitable, worthy OPPOSITE inappropriate
bed *noun* **1 = bedstead,** berth, bunk, cot, couch, divan **2 = plot,** area, border, garden, patch, row, strip **3 = bottom,** base
bedevil *verb* **= torment,** afflict, confound, confuse, distress, harass, plague, trouble, vex, worry
bedlam *noun* **= pandemonium,** chaos, commotion, confusion, furore, tumult, turmoil, uproar
bedraggled *adjective* **= messy,** dirty, dishevelled, disordered, muddied, unkempt, untidy
bedridden *adjective* **= confined to bed,** confined, flat on one's back, incapacitated, laid up (*inf*)
bedrock *noun* **1 = bottom,** bed, foundation, rock bottom, substratum, substructure **2 = basics,** basis, core, essentials, fundamentals, nuts and bolts (*inf*), roots
beefy *adjective* **2** *Inf* **= brawny,** bulky, hulking, muscular, stocky, strapping, sturdy, thickset OPPOSITE **scrawny**
beer parlour *noun* (*Canad*) **= tavern,** inn, bar, pub (*informal, chiefly Brit*), public house, watering hole (*facetious slang*), boozer (*Brit, Austral & NZ informal*), beverage room (*Canad*), hostelry, alehouse (*archaic*), taproom
befall *verb Old-fashioned* **= happen,** chance, come to pass, fall, occur, take place, transpire (*inf*)
befitting *adjective* **= appropriate,** apposite, becoming, fit, fitting, proper, right, seemly, suitable OPPOSITE **unsuitable**

B

before ⊕ *conjunction, preposition, adverb* indicating something earlier in time, in front of, or preferred to, e.g. *before the war; brought before a judge; death before dishonour.*
beforehand *adverb* in advance.
befriend ⊕ *verb* become friends with.
befuddled *adjective* stupefied or confused, as through alcoholic drink.
beg ⊕ *verb* **begging, begged 1** solicit (for money or food), esp. in the street. **2** ask formally or humbly. **beg the question** assume the thing under examination as proved. **go begging** be unwanted or unused.
began *verb* past tense of BEGIN.
beget *verb* **-getting, -got** or **-gat, -gotten** or **-got** *Old-fashioned* **1** cause or create. **2** father.
beggar ⊕ *noun* **1** person who lives by begging. **2** *Brit* fellow. ◆ *verb* **3 beggar description** be impossible to describe.
beggarly *adjective*
begin ⊕ *verb* **-ginning, -gan, -gun 1** start. **2** bring or come into being. **beginner** *noun* person who has just started learning to do something. **beginning** *noun*
begone *interjection* go away!
begonia *noun* tropical plant with waxy flowers.
begot *verb* a past of BEGET. **begotten** *verb* a past participle of BEGET.

begrudge ⊕ *verb* **1** envy (someone) the possession of something, e.g. *I don't begrudge him his success.* **2** give or allow unwillingly, e.g. *he begrudged her an apology.*
beguile ⊕ [big-**gile**] *verb* **1** cheat or mislead. **2** charm or amuse. **beguiling** *adjective*
beguine [big-**geen**] *noun* **1** S American dance. **2** music for this.
begum [**bay**-gum] *noun* Muslim woman of high rank.
begun *verb* past participle of BEGIN.
behalf *noun* **on behalf of** in the interest of or for the benefit of.
behave ⊕ *verb* **1** act or function in a particular way. **2** conduct (oneself) properly. **behaviour** *noun* manner of behaving.
behaviour ⊕ *noun* manner of behaving.
behead *verb* remove the head from.
beheld *verb* past of BEHOLD.
behemoth [bee-**hee**-moth] *noun* huge person or thing.
behest *noun* order or earnest request, e.g. *I came at her behest.*
behind ⊕ *preposition, adverb* **1** indicating position to the rear, lateness, responsibility, etc., e.g. *behind the wall; behind schedule; the reasons behind her departure.* ◆ *noun* **2** *Informal* buttocks.
behold ⊕ *verb* **-holding, -held** *Old-fashioned*

———— T H E S A U R U S ————

before *preposition* **a** = earlier than, in advance of, prior to OPPOSITE after. **b** = ahead of, in advance of, in front of ◆*adverb* **a** = previously, ahead, earlier, formerly, in advance, sooner **b** = in front, ahead
beforehand *adverb* = in advance, ahead of time, already, before, earlier, in anticipation, previously, sooner
befriend *verb* = help, aid, assist, back, encourage, side with, stand by, support, welcome
beg *verb* **1** = scrounge, bludge (*Aust & NZ*), cadge, seek charity, solicit charity, sponge on, touch (someone) for (*sl*) OPPOSITE give. **2** = implore, beseech, entreat, petition, plead, request, solicit
beggar *noun* **1** = tramp, bag lady (*chiefly US*), bum (*inf*), down-and-out, pauper, vagrant
beggarly *adjective* **1** = poor, destitute, impoverished, indigent, needy, poverty-stricken
begin *verb* **1** = start, commence, embark on, initiate, instigate, institute, prepare, set about OPPOSITE stop. **2** = happen, appear, arise, come into being, emerge, originate, start OPPOSITE end
beginner *noun* = novice, amateur, apprentice,

learner, neophyte, starter, trainee, tyro OPPOSITE expert
beginning *noun* **1** = start, birth, commencement, inauguration, inception, initiation, onset, opening, origin, outset OPPOSITE end. **2** = seed, fount, germ, root
begrudge *verb* **1** = resent, be jealous, envy, grudge
beguile *verb* **1** = fool, cheat, deceive, delude, dupe, hoodwink, mislead, take for a ride (*inf*), trick OPPOSITE enlighten. **2** = charm, amuse, distract, divert, engross, entertain, occupy
beguiling *adjective* **2** = charming, alluring, attractive, bewitching, captivating, enchanting, enthralling, intriguing
behave *verb* **1** = act, function, operate, perform, run, work **2** = conduct oneself properly, act correctly, keep one's nose clean, mind one's manners OPPOSITE carry on (*inf*) OPPOSITE misbehave
behaviour *noun* = conduct, actions, bearing, demeanour, deportment, manner, manners, ways
behind *preposition* **a** = after, at the back of, at the heels of, at the rear of, following, later than OPPOSITE in front of. **b** = causing, at the

look (at). **beholder** *noun*

beholden ⊕ *adjective* indebted or obliged.

behove *verb Old-fashioned* be necessary or fitting for.

beige *adjective* pale brown.

being ⊕ *noun* 1 state or fact of existing. 2 something that exists or is thought to exist. 3 human being. ◆ *verb* 4 present participle of BE.

belabour *verb* attack verbally or physically.

belated ⊕ *adjective* late or too late. **belatedly** *adverb*

belch ⊕ *verb* 1 expel wind from the stomach noisily through the mouth. 2 expel or be expelled forcefully, e.g. *smoke belched from the factory*. ◆ *noun* 3 act of belching.

beleaguered ⊕ *adjective* 1 struggling against difficulties or criticism. 2 besieged by an enemy.

belfry *noun, pl* **-fries** part of a tower where bells are hung.

belie *verb* 1 show to be untrue. 2 misrepresent.

belief ⊕ *noun* 1 faith or confidence. 2 opinion. 3 principle accepted as true, often without proof. **believe** *verb* 1 accept as true or real. 2 think, assume, or suppose. 3 accept (someone's) statement or opinion as true, e.g. *I don't believe you!* **believe in** be convinced of the truth or existence of. **believable** *adjective* **believer** *noun*

Belisha beacon [bill-**lee**-sha] *noun* flashing orange globe mounted on a post, marking a pedestrian crossing.

belittle ⊕ *verb* treat as having little value or importance.

bell *noun* 1 hollow, usu. metal, cup-shaped instrument that emits a ringing sound when struck. 2 device that rings or buzzes as a signal. **ring a bell** bring to mind something previously known or experienced. **bell-bottoms** *plural noun* trousers that flare from the knee.

belladonna *noun* (drug obtained from) deadly nightshade.

belle *noun* beautiful woman, esp. the most attractive woman at a function.

belles-lettres [bell-**let**-tra] *noun* literary works, esp. essays and poetry.

bellicose *adjective* warlike and aggressive.

belligerent ⊕ *adjective* 1 hostile and aggressive. 2 engaged in war. ◆ *noun* 3 person or country engaged in war. **belligerence** *noun*

bellow ⊕ *verb* 1 make a low deep cry like that of a bull. 2 shout in anger. ◆ *noun* 3 loud deep roar.

bellows *plural noun* instrument for pumping a stream of air into something.

belly ⊕ *noun, pl* **-lies** 1 part of the body of a vertebrate which contains the intestines. 2 stomach. 3 front, lower, or inner part of something. ◆ *verb* **-lying, -lied** 4 (cause to) swell out. **bellyful** *noun Slang* more than one can tolerate. **belly laugh** loud deep laugh.

———————— THESAURUS ————————

bottom of, initiating, instigating, responsible for ◆*adverb* **a** = **after**, afterwards, following, in the wake (of), next, subsequently OPPOSITE **in advance of**. **b** = **overdue**, behindhand, in arrears, in debt

behold *verb Old-fashioned* = **look at**, observe, perceive, regard, survey, view, watch, witness

beholden *adjective* = **indebted**, bound, grateful, obliged, owing, under obligation

being *noun* 1 = **existence**, life, reality OPPOSITE **nonexistence**. 2 = **nature**, entity, essence, soul, spirit, substance 3 = **human being**, creature, individual

belated *adjective* = **late**, behindhand, behind time, delayed, late in the day, overdue, tardy

belch *verb* 1 = **burp** (*inf*), hiccup 2 = **emit**, discharge, disgorge, erupt, give off, spew forth, vent

beleaguered *adjective* 1 = **harassed**, badgered, hassled (*inf*), persecuted, pestered, plagued, put upon, vexed 2 = **besieged**, assailed, beset, blockaded, hemmed in, surrounded

belief *noun* 1 = **faith**, assurance, confidence, conviction, trust OPPOSITE **doubt**. 2 = **opinion**, feeling, impression, judgment, notion 3 = **faith**, credo, creed, doctrine, dogma, ideology, principles, tenet

believable *adjective* 1 = **credible**, authentic, imaginable, likely, plausible, possible, probable, trustworthy OPPOSITE **unbelievable**

believe *verb* 1 = **accept**, be certain of, be convinced of, credit, depend on, have faith in, rely on, swear by, trust OPPOSITE **disbelieve**. 2 = **think**, assume, gather, imagine, judge, presume, reckon, speculate, suppose

belittle *verb* = **disparage**, decry, denigrate, deprecate, deride, scoff at, scorn, sneer at OPPOSITE **praise**

belligerent *adjective* 1 = **aggressive**, bellicose, combative, hostile, pugnacious, unfriendly, warlike, warring OPPOSITE **friendly** ◆*noun* 3 = **fighter**, combatant, warring nation

bellow *verb* 2 = **shout**, bawl, cry, howl, roar, scream, shriek, yell ◆*noun* 3 = **shout**, bawl, cry, howl, roar, scream, shriek, yell

belly *noun* 1, 2 = **stomach**, abdomen, corporation (*inf*), gut, insides (*inf*), paunch,

B

belong ⊙ *verb* **1** (foll. by *to*) be the property of. **2** (foll. by *to*) be a part or member of. **3** (foll. by *to* or *with*) be classified with.
belongings *plural noun* personal possessions.
beloved ⊙ *adjective* **1** dearly loved. ◆ *noun* **2** person dearly loved.
below ⊙ *preposition, adverb* at or to a position lower than, under.
belt ⊙ *noun* **1** band of cloth, leather, etc., worn usu. around the waist. **2** long narrow area, e.g. *a belt of trees*. **3** circular strip of rubber that drives moving parts in a machine. ◆ *verb* **4** fasten with a belt. **5** *Slang* hit very hard. **6** *Slang* move very fast. **belt out** *verb* sing (a song) loudly.
bemoan ⊙ *verb* express sorrow or dissatisfaction about.
bemused ⊙ *adjective* puzzled or confused.
ben *noun Scot & Irish* mountain peak.
bench ⊙ *noun* **1** long seat. **2** long narrow work table. **the bench 1** judge or magistrate sitting in court, or judges and magistrates collectively. **2** place where substitutes sit during a sports match. **benchmark** *noun* criterion by which to measure something.
bend ⊙ *verb* **bending, bent 1** (cause to) form a curve. **2** (often foll. by *down*) etc. incline the body. **3** (cause to) submit. ◆ *noun* **4** curved part. ◆ *plural* **5** *Informal* decompression sickness.

bend the rules *Informal* ignore or change rules to suit oneself. **bendy** *adjective* **bendier, bendiest**
beneath ⊙ *adverb, preposition* **1** below. **2** not worthy of.
Benedictine *adjective* **1** of an order of Christian monks and nuns founded by Saint Benedict. ◆ *noun* **2** liqueur first made by Benedictine monks.
benediction *noun* prayer for divine blessing. **benedictory** *adjective*
benefactor, benefactress ⊙ *noun* someone who supports a person or institution by giving money. **benefaction** *noun* **1** act of doing good. **2** gift to charity.
benefice *noun Christianity* church office providing its holder with an income.
beneficent [bin-eff-iss-ent] *adjective* charitable or generous. **beneficence** *noun*
beneficial ⊙ *adjective* helpful or advantageous.
beneficiary ⊙ *noun, pl* **-ciaries** person who gains or benefits.
benefit ⊙ *noun* **1** something that improves or promotes. **2** advantage or sake, e.g. *I'm doing this for your benefit*. **3** payment made by a government to a poor, ill, or unemployed person. **4** theatrical performance or sports event to raise money for charity. ◆ *verb* **-fiting,**

——————— THESAURUS ———————

potbelly, tummy ◆*verb* **4** = **swell out**, billow, bulge, fill, spread, swell
bellyful *noun Sl* = **surfeit**, enough, excess, glut, plenty, satiety, too much
belong *verb* **1** (foll. by *to*) = **be the property of**, be at the disposal of, be held by, be owned by **2** (foll. by *to*) = **be a member of**, be affiliated to, be allied to, be associated with, be included in
belonging *noun* **2** = **relationship**, acceptance, affinity, association, attachment, fellowship, inclusion, loyalty, rapport
belongings *plural noun* = **possessions**, accoutrements, chattels, effects, gear, goods, paraphernalia, personal property, stuff, things
beloved *adjective* **1** = **dear**, admired, adored, darling, loved, pet, precious, prized, treasured, valued, worshipped
below *preposition* = **lower than**, inferior, lesser, less than, subject, subordinate ◆*adverb* = **lower**, beneath, down, under, underneath
belt *noun* **1** = **waistband**, band, cummerbund, girdle, girth, sash **2** = **zone**, area, district, layer, region, stretch, strip, tract
bemoan *verb* = **lament**, bewail, deplore, grieve for, mourn, regret, rue, weep for

bemused *adjective* = **puzzled**, at sea, bewildered, confused, flummoxed, muddled, nonplussed, perplexed
bench *noun* **1** = **seat**, form, pew, settle, stall **2** = **worktable**, board, counter, table, trestle table, workbench **the bench 1** = **court**, courtroom, judges, judiciary, magistrates, tribunal
benchmark *noun* = **reference point**, criterion, gauge, level, measure, model, norm, par, standard, yardstick
bend *verb* **1** = **curve**, arc, arch, bow, turn, twist, veer **2** = **lean**, bow ◆*noun* **4** = **curve**, angle, arc, arch, bow, corner, loop, turn, twist
beneath *adverb* **1** = **underneath**, below, in a lower place ◆*preposition* **1** = **under**, below, lower than, underneath OPPOSITE> **over**. **2** = **unworthy of**, below, inferior to, less than, unbefitting
benefactor *noun* = **supporter**, backer, donor, helper, patron, philanthropist, sponsor, well-wisher
beneficial *adjective* = **helpful**, advantageous, benign, favourable, profitable, useful, valuable, wholesome OPPOSITE> **harmful**
beneficiary *noun* = **recipient**, heir, inheritor, payee, receiver

B

-fited 5 do or receive good. **beneficial**
adjective
benevolence ❶ *noun* **1** inclination to do
good. **2** act of kindness. **benevolent** *adjective*
benevolently *adverb*
Bengali *noun, adjective* (member or language)
of a people living chiefly in Bangladesh and W
Bengal.
benighted *adjective* ignorant or uncultured.
benign ❶ [bin-**nine**] *adjective* **1** showing
kindliness. **2** favourable or propitious. **3** (of a
tumour) not threatening to life. **benignly**
adverb
bent ❶ *verb* **1** past of BEND. ◆ *adjective* **2**
curved. **3** *Slang* dishonest or corrupt, e.g. *a
bent cop.* **4** *Offens slang* homosexual. ◆ *noun* **5**
personal inclination or aptitude. **bent on**
determined to pursue (a course of action).
bento, bento box *noun* thin lightweight
box divided into compartments, which contain
small separate dishes comprising a Japanese
meal.
benumb *verb* **1** make numb or powerless. **2**
stupefy (the mind etc.).
benzene *noun* flammable poisonous liquid
used as a solvent, insecticide, etc.
benzine *noun* volatile liquid used as a solvent.
bequeath ❶ *verb* **1** dispose of (property) as in
a will. **2** hand down. **bequest** *noun* legal gift of
money or property by someone who has died.
berate ❶ *verb* scold harshly.
berberis *noun* shrub with red berries.
bereaved ❶ *adjective* having recently lost a
close friend or relative through death.

bereavement *noun*
bereft ❶ *adjective* (foll. by *of*) deprived.
beret [**ber**-ray] *noun* round flat close-fitting
brimless cap.
berg¹ *noun* S Afr mountain.
berg² *noun* iceberg.
bergamot *noun* small Asian tree, the fruit of
which yields an oil used in perfumery.
beri-beri *noun* disease caused by vitamin B
deficiency.
berk *noun Brit, Aust & NZ slang* stupid person.
berkelium *noun Chem* radioactive element.
berm *noun NZ* narrow grass strip between the
road and the footpath in a residential area.
Bermuda shorts *plural noun* shorts that
come down to the knees.
berry *noun, pl* **-ries** small soft stoneless fruit.
berserk ❶ *adjective* **go berserk** become
violent or destructive.
berth ❶ *noun* **1** bunk in a ship or train. **2**
place assigned to a ship at a mooring. ◆ *verb* **3**
dock (a ship). **give a wide berth to** keep clear
of.
beryl *noun* hard transparent mineral.
beryllium *noun Chem* toxic silvery-white
metallic element.
beseech ❶ *verb* **-seeching, -sought** or
-seeched ask earnestly; beg.
beset ❶ *verb* **1** trouble or harass constantly. **2**
attack from all sides.
beside ❶ *preposition* **1** at, by, or to the side
of. **2** as compared with. **3** away from, e.g.
beside the point. **beside oneself** overwhelmed
or overwrought. **besides** *adverb, preposition* in

——————— T H E S A U R U S ———————

benefit *noun* **1** = **help**, advantage, aid, asset,
assistance, favour, good, profit OPPOSITE **harm**
◆*verb* **5** = **help**, aid, assist, avail, enhance,
further, improve, profit OPPOSITE **harm**
benevolent *adjective* = **kind**, altruistic,
benign, caring, charitable, generous,
philanthropic
benign *adjective* **1** = **kindly**, amiable, friendly,
genial, kind, obliging, sympathetic OPPOSITE
unkind. **3** = **harmless**, curable, remediable
OPPOSITE **malignant**
bent *adjective* **2** = **curved**, angled, arched,
bowed, crooked, hunched, stooped, twisted
OPPOSITE **straight** ◆*noun* **5** = **inclination**,
ability, aptitude, leaning, penchant, preference,
propensity, tendency
bent on *adjective* = **determined to**, disposed
to, fixed on, inclined to, insistent on,
predisposed to, resolved on, set on
bequeath *verb* **1** = **leave**, endow, entrust,
give, grant, will **2** = **hand down**, bestow,

impart, pass on
bequest *noun* = **legacy**, bestowal,
endowment, estate, gift, inheritance, settlement
berate *verb* = **scold**, castigate, censure, chide,
criticize, harangue, rebuke, reprimand, reprove,
rouse on (*Aust*), tell off (*inf*), upbraid OPPOSITE
praise
bereavement *noun* = **loss**, affliction, death,
deprivation, misfortune, tribulation
bereft *adjective* (foll. bu *of*) = **deprived**,
devoid, lacking, parted from, robbed of,
wanting
berserk *adjective* **go berserk** = **go crazy**, go
mad, go wild, raging, rampage, run amok
berth *noun* **1** = **bunk**, bed, billet, hammock **2**
= **anchorage**, dock, harbour, haven, pier, port,
quay, wharf ◆*verb* **3** = **anchor**, dock, drop
anchor, land, moor, tie up
beseech *verb* = **beg**, ask, call upon, entreat,
implore, plead, pray, solicit
beset *verb* **1** = **plague**, bedevil, harass, pester,

addition.
besiege ⊕ *verb* **1** surround with military forces. **2** hem in. **3** overwhelm, as with requests.
besmirch *verb* tarnish (someone's name or reputation).
besom *noun* broom made of twigs.
besotted ⊕ *adjective* infatuated.
besought *verb* a past of BESEECH.
bespatter *verb* splash, e.g. with dirty water.
bespeak *verb* indicate or suggest. **bespoke** *adjective* **1** (esp. of a suit) made to the customer's specifications. **2** making or selling such suits, e.g. *a bespoke tailor.*
bespoke *adjective* (esp. of a suit) made to the customer's specifications.
best ⊕ *adjective* **1** most excellent of a particular group etc. ♦ *adverb* **2** in a manner surpassing all others. ♦ *noun* **3** the utmost effort, e.g. *I did my best.* **4** most outstanding or excellent person, thing, or group in a category. ♦ *verb* **5** defeat. **best man** groom's attendant at a wedding. **bestseller** *noun* book or other product that has sold in great numbers. **bestselling** *adjective*
bestial ⊕ *adjective* **1** brutal or savage. **2** of or like a beast. **bestiality** *noun*
bestir *verb* cause (oneself) to become active.
bestow ⊕ *verb* present (a gift) or confer (an honour). **bestowal** *noun*
bestride *verb* have or put a leg on either side of.

bet ⊕ *noun* **1** the act of staking a sum of money or other stake on the outcome of an event. **2** stake risked. **3** course of action, e.g. *your best bet is to go by train.* ♦ *verb* **betting, bet** or **betted 4** make or place (a bet). **5** *Informal* predict.
beta *noun* second letter in the Greek alphabet.
beta-blocker *noun* drug used to treat high blood pressure and angina. **beta particle** electron or positron emitted by a nucleus during radioactive decay or nuclear fission.
betake *verb* **betake oneself** *Formal* go or move.
betel [bee-tl] *noun* Asian climbing plant, the leaves and nuts of which can be chewed.
bête noire [bet nwahr] *noun, pl* **bêtes noires** person or thing that one particularly dislikes.
betide *verb* happen (to).
betoken ⊕ *verb* indicate or signify.
betray ⊕ *verb* **1** hand over or expose (one's nation, friend, etc.) treacherously to an enemy. **2** disclose (a secret or confidence) treacherously. **3** reveal unintentionally.
betrayal *noun* **betrayer** *noun*
betrothed *adjective* engaged to be married.
betrothal *noun*
better ⊕ *adjective* **1** more excellent than others. **2** improved or fully recovered in health. ♦ *adverb* **3** in a more excellent manner. **4** in or to a greater degree. ♦ *plural noun* **5** one's superiors. ♦ *verb* **6** improve upon. **get the**

trouble
beside *preposition* **1** = **next to**, abreast of, adjacent to, alongside, at the side of, close to, near, nearby, neighbouring
beside oneself *adjective* = **distraught**, apoplectic, at the end of one's tether, demented, desperate, frantic, frenzied, out of one's mind, unhinged
besides *adverb* = **too**, also, as well, further, furthermore, in addition, into the bargain, moreover, otherwise, what's more ♦ *preposition* = **in addition to**, apart from, barring, excepting, excluding, other than, over and above, without
besiege *verb* **1, 2** = **surround**, blockade, encircle, hem in, lay siege to, shut in **3** = **harass**, badger, harry, hassle (*inf*), hound, nag, pester, plague
besotted *adjective* = **infatuated**, doting, hypnotized, smitten, spellbound
best *adjective* **1** = **finest**, foremost, leading, most excellent, outstanding, pre-eminent, principal, supreme, unsurpassed ♦ *adverb* **2**

= **most highly**, extremely, greatly, most deeply, most fully ♦ *noun* **4** = **finest**, cream, elite, flower, pick, prime, top
bestial *adjective* **1** = **brutal**, barbaric, beastly, brutish, inhuman, savage
bestow *verb* = **present**, award, commit, give, grant, hand out, impart, lavish OPPOSITE obtain
bet *noun* **1** = **gamble**, long shot, risk, speculation, venture, wager **2** = **stake** ♦ *verb* **4** = **gamble**, chance, hazard, risk, speculate, stake, venture, wager
betoken *verb* = **indicate**, bode, denote, promise, represent, signify, suggest
betray *verb* **1** = **be disloyal**, be treacherous, be unfaithful, break one's promise, double-cross (*inf*), inform on *or* against, sell out (*inf*), stab in the back **2, 3** = **give away**, disclose, divulge, let slip, reveal
betrayal *noun* **1** = **disloyalty**, deception, double-cross (*inf*), sell-out (*inf*), treachery, treason, trickery OPPOSITE loyalty. **2, 3** = **giving away**, disclosure, divulgence,

B

better of defeat or outwit. **betterment** *noun* improvement. **better off** in more favourable circumstances, esp. financially. **better-off** *adjective* reasonably wealthy.
between ❼ *preposition, adverb* indicating position in the middle, alternatives, etc.

> **LANGUAGE TIP**
>
> *Between* is used when two people or things are mentioned: *the trade war between Europe and America.* Otherwise use *among.*

betwixt *preposition, adverb Old-fashioned* between.
bevel *noun* **1** slanting edge. ♦ *verb* **-elling, -elled 2** slope. **3** cut a bevel on (a piece of timber etc.).
beverage ❼ *noun* drink.
beverage room ❼ *noun Canad* tavern.
bevy ❼ *noun, pl* **bevies** flock or group.
bewail ❼ *verb* express great sorrow over.
beware ❼ *verb* be on one's guard (against).
bewilder ❼ *verb* confuse utterly. **bewildering** *adjective* **bewilderment** *noun*
bewitch ❼ *verb* **1** attract and fascinate. **2** cast a spell over. **bewitching** *adjective*

beyond ❼ *preposition* **1** at or to a point on the other side of. **2** outside the limits or scope of. ♦ *adverb* **3** at or to the far side of something. ♦ *noun* **4** the unknown, esp. life after death.
bezique *noun* card game for two or more players.
bhaji *noun, pl* **bhaji, bhajis** Indian deep-fried savoury of chopped vegetables in spiced batter.
bhp brake horsepower.
Bi *Chem* bismuth.
bi- *combining form* two or twice, e.g. *bifocal; biweekly.*
biannual *adjective* occurring twice a year. **biannually** *adverb*
bias ❼ *noun* **1** mental tendency, esp. prejudice. **2** diagonal cut across the weave of a fabric. **3** *Bowls* bulge or weight on one side of a bowl that causes it to roll in a curve. ♦ *verb* **-asing, -ased** *or* **-assing, -assed 4** cause to have a bias. **biased, biassed** *adjective* **bias binding** strip of material used for binding hems.
bib *noun* **1** piece of cloth or plastic worn to protect a young child's clothes when eating. **2** upper front part of dungarees etc.
Bible *noun* **1** sacred writings of the Christian religion. **2** (**b-**) book regarded as authoritative. **biblical** *adjective*
bibliography *noun, pl* **-phies 1** list of books

———————————————— T H E S A U R U S ————————————————

revelation
better *adjective* **1 = superior**, excelling, finer, greater, higher-quality, more desirable, preferable, surpassing ⟨OPPOSITE⟩ **worse. 2 = well**, cured, fully recovered, on the mend (*inf*), recovering, stronger ⟨OPPOSITE⟩ **worse** ♦*adverb* **3 = in a more excellent manner**, in a superior way, more advantageously, more attractively, more competently, more effectively ⟨OPPOSITE⟩ **worse. 4 = to a greater degree**, more completely, more thoroughly ♦*verb* **6 = improve**, enhance, further, raise ⟨OPPOSITE⟩ **lower**
between *preposition* **= amidst**, among, betwixt, in the middle of, mid
beverage *noun* **= drink**, liquid, liquor, refreshment
beverage room *noun* (*Canad*) **= tavern**, inn, bar, pub (*informal, chiefly Brit*), public house, watering hole (*facetious slang*), boozer (*Brit, Austral & NZ informal*), beer parlour (*Canad*), hostelry, alehouse (*archaic*), taproom
bevy *noun* **= group**, band, bunch (*inf*), collection, company, crowd, gathering, pack, troupe
bewail *verb* **= lament**, bemoan, cry over,

deplore, grieve for, moan, mourn, regret
beware *verb* **= be careful**, be cautious, be wary, guard against, heed, look out, mind, take heed, watch out
bewilder *verb* **= confound**, baffle, bemuse, confuse, flummox, mystify, nonplus, perplex, puzzle
bewildered *adjective* **= confused**, at a loss, at sea, baffled, flummoxed, mystified, nonplussed, perplexed, puzzled
bewitch *verb* **= enchant**, beguile, captivate, charm, enrapture, entrance, fascinate, hypnotize ⟨OPPOSITE⟩ **repulse**
bewitched *adjective* **= enchanted**, charmed, entranced, fascinated, mesmerized, spellbound, under a spell
beyond *preposition* **1 = past**, above, apart from, at a distance, away from, over **2 = exceeding**, out of reach of, superior to, surpassing
bias *noun* **1 = prejudice**, favouritism, inclination, leaning, partiality, tendency ⟨OPPOSITE⟩ **impartiality** ♦*verb* **4 = prejudice**, distort, influence, mana (*NZ*), predispose, slant, sway, twist, warp, weight
biased *adjective* **1 = prejudiced**, distorted,

B

on a subject. **2** list of sources used in a book etc. **bibliographer** *noun*

bibliophile *noun* person who collects or is fond of books.

bibulous *adjective* addicted to alcohol.

bicameral *adjective* (of a legislature) consisting of two chambers.

bicarbonate *noun* salt of carbonic acid.

bicarbonate of soda powder used in baking or as medicine.

bicentenary *US* **bicentennial** *adjective* **1** marking a 200th anniversary. ◆ *noun, pl* **-naries** **2** 200th anniversary.

biceps *noun* muscle with two origins, esp. the muscle that flexes the forearm.

bicker ❶ *verb* argue over petty matters.

bicycle *noun* **1** vehicle with two wheels, one behind the other, pedalled by the rider. ◆ *verb* **2** ride a bicycle.

bid ❶ *verb* **bidding, bade, bidden 1** say (a greeting), e.g. *to bid farewell.* **2** command. **3** *past* **bid** offer (an amount) in an attempt to buy something. ◆ *noun* **4** offer of a specified amount. **5** attempt. **bidder** *noun* **biddable** *adjective* obedient. **bidding** *noun* **1** command. **2** invitation.

bide *verb* **bide one's time** wait patiently for an opportunity.

bidet [**bee**-day] *noun* low basin for washing the genital area.

biennial *adjective* **1** occurring every two years. ◆ *noun* **2** plant that completes its life cycle in two years.

bier *noun* stand on which a corpse or coffin rests before burial.

biff *Slang noun* **1** blow with the fist. ◆ *verb* **2** give (someone) such a blow.

bifocals *plural noun* spectacles with lenses permitting near and distant vision. **bifocal** *adjective* having two different focuses.

bifurcate *verb* fork into two branches.

big ❶ *adjective* **bigger, biggest 1** of considerable size, height, number, or capacity. **2** important through having power, wealth, etc. **3** elder. **4** generous. ◆ *adverb* **5** on a grand scale, e.g. *think big.* **bighead** *noun Informal* conceited person. **big-headed** *adjective* **big shot, bigwig** *noun Informal* important person. **big top** *Informal* main tent of a circus.

bigamy *noun* crime of marrying a person while still legally married to someone else. **bigamist** *noun* **bigamous** *adjective*

bight *noun* **1** long curved shoreline. **2** curve or loop in a rope.

bigot ❶ *noun* person who is intolerant, esp. regarding religion or race. **bigoted** *adjective* **bigotry** *noun*

bijou [**bee**-zhoo] *adjective* (of a house) small but elegant.

bike *noun Informal* bicycle or motorcycle.

bikini *noun* woman's brief two-piece swimming costume.

bilateral *adjective* affecting or undertaken by two parties.

bilberry *noun* bluish-black edible berry.

bile *noun* **1** bitter yellow fluid secreted by the liver. **2** irritability or peevishness.

bilge *noun* **1** *Informal* nonsense. **2** ship's bottom. **3** dirty water that collects in a ship's bilge.

bilingual *adjective* involving or using two languages.

———————————— THESAURUS ————————————

one-sided, partial, slanted, weighted

bicker *verb* =**quarrel**, argue, disagree, dispute, fight, row (*inf*), squabble, wrangle OPPOSITE> agree

bid *verb* **1** = **say**, call, greet, tell, wish **2** = **tell**, ask, command, direct, instruct, order, require **3** = **offer**, proffer, propose, submit, tender ◆*noun* **4** = **offer**, advance, amount, price, proposal, sum, tender **5** = **attempt**, crack (*inf*), effort, go (*inf*), stab (*inf*), try

bidding *noun* **1** = **order**, beck and call, command, direction, instruction, request, summons

big *adjective* **1** = **large**, enormous, extensive, great, huge, immense, massive, substantial, vast OPPOSITE> little. **2** = **important**, eminent, influential, leading, main, powerful, prominent, significant, skookum (*Canad*) OPPOSITE> unimportant. **3** = **grown-up**, adult, elder,

grown, mature OPPOSITE> young. **4** = **generous**, altruistic, benevolent, gracious, magnanimous, noble, unselfish

bighead *noun Inf* = **boaster**, braggart, know-all (*inf*)

bigheaded *adjective Inf* = **boastful**, arrogant, cocky, conceited, egotistic, immodest, overconfident, swollen-headed

bigot *noun* = **fanatic**, racist, sectarian, zealot

bigoted *adjective* = **intolerant**, biased, dogmatic, narrow-minded, opinionated, prejudiced, sectarian OPPOSITE> tolerant

bigotry *noun* = **intolerance**, bias, discrimination, dogmatism, fanaticism, narrow-mindedness, prejudice, sectarianism OPPOSITE> tolerance

big shot, bigwig *noun Inf* = **important person**, celebrity, dignitary, mogul, personage, somebody, V.I.P. OPPOSITE> nonentity

B

bilious *adjective* **1** sick, nauseous. **2** *Informal* bad-tempered or irritable.

bilk *verb* cheat, esp. by not paying.

bill¹ ⊕ *noun* **1** statement of money owed for goods or services supplied. **2** draft of a proposed new law. **3** poster. **4** *US & Canad* banknote. **5** list of events, such as a theatre programme. ♦ *verb* **6** send or present a bill to. **7** advertise by posters. **bill of fare** menu. **clean bill of health** favourable account of a person or thing's physical or financial condition. **fit, fill the bill** *Informal* be suitable or adequate.

bill² ⊕ *noun* bird's beak. **bill and coo** (of lovers) kiss and whisper amorously.

billabong *noun Aust* stagnant pool in an intermittent stream.

billboard *noun Chiefly US & Canad* hoarding.

billet ⊕ *verb* **-leting, -leted 1** assign a lodging to (a soldier). ♦ *noun* **2** accommodation for a soldier in civil lodgings.

billet-doux [bill-ee-**doo**] *noun, pl* **billets-doux** love letter.

billhook *noun* tool with a hooked blade, used for chopping etc.

billiards *noun* game played on a table with balls and a cue.

billion *noun* **1** one thousand million. **2** formerly, one million million. **billionth** *adjective*

billionaire *noun* person who owns at least a billion pounds, dollars, etc.

billow ⊕ *noun* **1** large sea wave. **2** swelling or surging mass, as of smoke or sound. ♦ *verb* **3** rise up or swell out. **billowy, billowing** *adjective*

billy, billycan *noun, pl* **-lies, -lycans** metal can or pot for cooking on a camp fire.

billy goat *noun* male goat.

biltong *noun S Afr* strips of dried meat.

bimbo *noun Slang* attractive but empty-headed young person, esp. a woman.

bimonthly *adverb, adjective* **1** every two months. **2** twice a month.

bin *noun* **1** container for rubbish or for storing grain, coal, etc. **2** a large container for bulk storage. ♦ *verb* **3** put in a rubbish bin.

binary [**bine**-a-ree] *adjective* **1** composed of two parts. **2** *Maths, computers* of or in a counting system with only two digits, 0 and 1.

bind ⊕ *verb* **binding, bound 1** make secure with or as if with a rope. **2** place (someone) under obligation. **3** place under certain constraints, e.g. *bound by the rules.* **4** stick together or cause to stick, e.g. *egg binds fat and flour.* **5** enclose and fasten (the pages of a book) between covers. ♦ *noun* **6** *Informal* annoying situation. **binder** *noun* **1** firm cover for holding loose sheets of paper together. **2** something used to fasten or hold together. **3** *Obs* machine for cutting and binding sheaves. **binding** *noun* **1** anything that binds or fastens. **2** book cover. ♦ *adjective* **3** imposing an obligation or duty.

bindweed *noun* plant that twines around a support.

binge ⊕ *noun Informal* bout of excessive indulgence, esp. in drink.

bingo *noun* gambling game in which numbers are called out and covered by the players on their individual cards.

binnacle *noun* box holding a ship's compass.

binoculars *plural noun* optical instrument consisting of two small telescopes joined together. **binocular** *adjective* involving both eyes.

binomial *noun, adjective* (mathematical expression) consisting of two terms.

bio- *combining form* life or living organisms, e.g. *biology.*

biochemistry *noun* study of the chemistry of living things. **biochemist** *noun*

biodegradable *adjective* capable of being

——————— T H E S A U R U S ———————

bill¹ *noun* **1** =**charges**, account, invoice, reckoning, score, statement, tally **2** =**proposal**, measure, piece of legislation, projected law **3** =**advertisement**, bulletin, circular, handbill, hand-out, leaflet, notice, placard, poster **5** =**list**, agenda, card, catalogue, inventory, listing, programme, roster, schedule ♦*verb* **6** =**charge**, debit, invoice **7** =**advertise**, announce, give advance notice of, post

bill² *noun* =**beak**, mandible, neb (*arch or dial*), nib

billet *verb* **1** =**quarter**, accommodate, berth, station ♦*noun* **2** =**quarters**, accommodation, barracks, lodging

billow *noun* **1** =**wave**, breaker, crest, roller, surge, swell, tide ♦*verb* **3** =**surge**, balloon, belly, puff up, rise up, roll, swell

bind *verb* **1** =**tie**, fasten, hitch, lash, secure, stick, strap, wrap OPPOSITE **free**. **2** =**oblige**, compel, constrain, engage, force, necessitate, require ♦*noun* **6** *Inf* =**nuisance**, bore, difficulty, dilemma, drag (*inf*), pain in the neck (*inf*), quandary, spot (*inf*)

binding *adjective* **3** =**compulsory**, indissoluble, irrevocable, mandatory, necessary, obligatory, unalterable OPPOSITE **optional**

binge *noun Inf* =**bout**, bender (*inf*), feast, fling, orgy, spree

B

decomposed by natural means.
biodiversity *noun* existence of a wide variety of species in their natural environment.
biography ❶ *noun, pl* **-phies** account of a person's life by another person. **biographical** *adjective* **biographer** *noun*
biological *adjective* **1** of or relating to biology. **2** (of a detergent) containing enzymes that remove natural stains. **biological warfare** use of living organisms or their toxic products to kill or disable.
biology *noun* study of living organisms. **biologist** *noun*
bionic *adjective* having a part of the body that is operated electronically.
biopsy *noun, pl* **-sies** examination of tissue from a living body.
biosphere *noun* part of the earth's surface and atmosphere inhabited by living things.
biotechnology *noun* use of microorganisms, such as cells or bacteria, in industry and technology.
bioterrorism *noun* use of viruses, bacteria, etc., by terrorists. **bioterrorist** *noun*
bipartite *adjective* **1** consisting of two parts. **2** affecting or made by two parties.
biped [**bye**-ped] *noun* animal with two feet.
biplane *noun* aeroplane with two sets of wings, one above the other.
bipolar *adjective* **1** having two poles. **2** having two extremes.
birch *noun* **1** tree with thin peeling bark. **2** birch rod or twigs used, esp. formerly, for flogging offenders. ◆ *verb* **3** flog with a birch.
bird *noun* **1** creature with feathers and wings, most types of which can fly. **2** *Slang* young woman. **bird's-eye view 1** view seen from above. **2** general or overall impression.
birdie *noun Golf* score of one stroke under par for a hole.
biretta *noun* stiff square cap worn by the Catholic clergy.
Biro *noun* ® ballpoint pen.
birth ❶ *noun* **1** process of bearing young; childbirth. **2** act of being born. **3** origin or beginning. **4** ancestry. **give birth to** bear (offspring). **birth control** any method of

contraception. **birthday** *noun* anniversary of the day of one's birth. **birthmark** *noun* blemish on the skin formed before birth. **birth rate** ratio of live births to population. **birthright** *noun* privileges or possessions that someone is entitled to as soon as he or she is born.
biscuit *noun* **1** small flat dry sweet or plain cake. **2** porcelain that has been fired but not glazed. ◆ *adjective* **3** pale brown.
bisect ❶ *verb* divide into two equal parts.
bisexual *adjective* **1** sexually attracted to both men and women. **2** showing characteristics of both sexes. ◆ *noun* **3** bisexual person. **bisexuality** *noun*
bishop *noun* **1** clergyman who governs a diocese. **2** chessman which is moved diagonally. **bishopric** *noun* diocese or office of a bishop.
bismuth *noun Chem* pinkish-white metallic element.
bison *noun, pl* **-son** large hairy animal of the cattle family.
bisque[1] *noun* thick rich soup made from shellfish.
bisque[2] *adjective* pinkish-tan.
bistro *noun, pl* **-tros** small restaurant.
bit[1] ❶ *noun* **1** small piece, portion, or quantity. **2** short time or distance. **a bit** rather, somewhat. **bit by bit** gradually.
bit[2] ❶ *noun* **1** metal mouthpiece on a bridle. **2** cutting or drilling part of a tool.
bit[3] *verb* past tense of BITE.
bit[4] *noun Maths, computers* **1** single digit of binary notation, either 0 or 1. **2** smallest unit of information.
bitch ❶ *noun* **1** female dog, fox, or wolf. **2** *Offens* spiteful woman. ◆ *verb* **3** *Informal* complain or grumble. **bitchy** *adjective* **bitchier, bitchiest. bitchiness** *noun*
bite ❶ *verb* **biting, bit, bitten 1** grip, tear, or puncture the skin, as with the teeth or jaws. **2** take firm hold of or act effectively upon. **3** (of corrosive material) eat away or into. ◆ *noun* **4** act of biting. **5** wound or sting inflicted by biting. **6** snack. **biter** *noun* **biting** *adjective* **1** piercing or keen. **2** sarcastic.
bitter ❶ *adjective* **1** having a sharp unpleasant

———— T H E S A U R U S ————

biography *noun* =**life story**, account, curriculum vitae, CV, life, memoir, profile, record
birth *noun* **1** =**childbirth**, delivery, parturition OPPOSITE **death. 2** =**nativity 4** =**ancestry**, background, blood, breeding, lineage, parentage, pedigree, stock
bisect *verb* =**cut in two**, cross, cut across,

divide in two, halve, intersect, separate, split
bit[1] *noun* **1** =**piece**, crumb, fragment, grain, morsel, part, scrap, speck
bit[2] *noun* **1** =**curb**, brake, check, restraint, snaffle
bitchy *adjective* **2** *Inf* =**spiteful**, backbiting, catty (*inf*), mean, nasty, snide, vindictive OPPOSITE **nice**

taste. **2** showing or caused by hostility or resentment. **3** extremely cold. ◆ *noun* **4** beer with a slightly bitter taste. ◆ *plural* **5** bitter-tasting alcoholic drink. **bitterly** *adverb* **bitterness** *noun* **bittersweet** *adjective* **1** tasting of bitterness and sweetness. **2** pleasant but tinged with sadness.

bittern *noun* wading marsh bird with a booming call.

bitty *adjective* **-tier, -tiest** lacking unity, disjointed. **bittiness** *noun*

bitumen *noun* black sticky substance obtained from tar or petrol.

bivalve *noun, adjective* (marine mollusc) with two hinged segments to its shell.

bivouac *noun* **1** temporary camp in the open air. ◆ *verb* **-acking, -acked** **2** camp in a bivouac.

bizarre ⊕ *adjective* odd or unusual.

Bk *Chem* berkelium.

blab ⊕ *verb* **blabbing, blabbed** reveal (secrets) indiscreetly.

blabber *verb* talk without thinking.

black ⊕ *adjective* **1** of the darkest colour, like coal. **2** without light. **3** (**B-**) dark-skinned. **4** without hope. **5** angry or resentful, e.g. *black looks*. **6** unpleasant in a macabre manner, e.g. *black comedy*. **7** (of coffee or tea) without milk or cream. ◆ *noun* **8** darkest colour. **9** (**B-**) member of a dark-skinned race. **10** complete darkness. ◆ *verb* **11** make black. **12** (of trade unionists) boycott (goods or people).

blackness *noun* **blacken** *verb* **1** make or become black. **2** defame or slander. **blacking**

noun preparation for giving a black finish to shoes, metals, etc. **black-and-blue** *adjective* bruised, as from a beating. **black-and-white** *adjective* **1** not in colour. ◆ *noun* **in black and white 2** in print or writing. **black box** *Informal* flight recorder. **black eye** bruising round the eye. **black hole** *Astronomy* hypothetical region of space from which neither matter nor radiation can escape. **black ice** thin transparent layer of new ice on a road. **black magic** magic used for evil purposes. **Black Maria** police van for transporting prisoners. **black market** illegal trade in goods or currencies. **black pudding** sausage made from blood, suet, etc. **black sheep** person who is regarded as a disgrace by his or her family. **black spot** place on a road where accidents frequently occur. **black widow** American spider, the female of which eats its mate.

blackball *verb* exclude from a group.

blackberry *noun* small blackish edible fruit.

blackbird *noun* common European thrush.

blackboard *noun* hard black surface used for writing on with chalk.

blackcurrant *noun* very small blackish edible fruit that grows in bunches.

blackguard ⊕ [blag-gard] *noun* unprincipled person.

blackhead *noun* small black spot on the skin.

blackleg *noun* person who continues to work during a strike.

blacklist ⊕ *noun* **1** list of people or organizations considered untrustworthy etc. ◆ *verb* **2** put on a blacklist.

———————— T H E S A U R U S ————————

bite *verb* **1** = **cut**, chew, gnaw, nip, pierce, pinch, snap, tear, wound ◆*noun* **5** = **wound**, nip, pinch, prick, smarting, sting, tooth marks **6** = **snack**, food, light meal, morsel, mouthful, piece, refreshment, taste, tucker (*Aust & NZ inf*)

biting *adjective* **1** = **piercing**, bitter, cutting, harsh, penetrating, sharp **2** = **sarcastic**, caustic, cutting, incisive, mordant, scathing, stinging, trenchant, vitriolic

bitter *adjective* **1** = **sour**, acid, acrid, astringent, harsh, sharp, tart, unsweetened, vinegary OPPOSITE> sweet. **2** = **resentful**, acrimonious, begrudging, hostile, sore, sour, sullen OPPOSITE> happy. **3** = **freezing**, biting, fierce, intense, severe, stinging OPPOSITE> gentle

bitterness *noun* **1** = **sourness**, acerbity, acidity, sharpness, tartness **2** = **resentment**, acrimony, animosity, asperity, grudge, hostility, rancour, sarcasm

bizarre *adjective* = **strange**, eccentric,

extraordinary, fantastic, freakish, ludicrous, munted (*NZ sl*), outlandish, peculiar, unusual, weird, zany OPPOSITE> normal

blab *verb* = **tell**, blurt out, disclose, divulge, give away, let slip, let the cat out of the bag, reveal, spill the beans (*inf*)

black *adjective* **1** = **dark**, dusky, ebony, jet, pitch-black, raven, sable, swarthy OPPOSITE> light. **4** = **gloomy**, depressing, dismal, foreboding, hopeless, ominous, sad, sombre OPPOSITE> happy. **5** = **angry**, furious, hostile, menacing, resentful, sullen, threatening OPPOSITE> happy ◆*verb* **12** = **boycott**, ban, bar, blacklist

blacken *verb* **1** = **darken**, befoul, begrime, cloud, dirty, make black, smudge, soil **2** = **discredit**, defame, denigrate, malign, slander, smear, smirch, vilify

blackguard *noun* = **scoundrel**, bastard (*offens*), bounder (*old-fashioned Brit sl*), rascal, rogue, swine, villain

B

B

blackmail ⊕ *noun* **1** act of attempting to extort money by threats. ♦ *verb* **2** (attempt to) obtain money by blackmail.

blackout ⊕ *noun* **1** extinguishing of all light as a precaution against an air attack. **2** momentary loss of consciousness or memory. **black out** *verb* **1** extinguish (lights). **2** lose consciousness or memory temporarily.

blacksmith *noun* person who works iron with a furnace, anvil, etc.

blackthorn *noun* thorny shrub with white flowers and small sour plumlike fruits.

black-tie *adjective* denoting an occasion when a dinner jacket should be worn.

bladder *noun* **1** sac in the body where urine is held. **2** hollow bag which may be filled with air or liquid.

blade *noun* **1** cutting edge of a weapon or tool. **2** thin flattish part of a propeller, oar, etc. **3** leaf of grass.

blame ⊕ *verb* **1** consider (someone) responsible for, e.g. *I blame her for the failure.* **2** (foll. by *on*) put responsibility for (something) on (someone), e.g. *she blames the failure on me.* ♦ *noun* **3** responsibility for something that is wrong. **4** expression of condemnation. **blameless** *adjective* **blameworthy** *adjective* deserving blame.

blanch *verb* **1** become white or pale. **2** prepare (vegetables etc.) by plunging them in boiling water.

blancmange [blam-monzh] *noun* jelly-like dessert made with milk.

bland ⊕ *adjective* **1** dull and uninteresting. **2** smooth in manner. **blandly** *adverb*

blandishments *plural noun* flattery intended to coax or persuade.

blank ⊕ *adjective* **1** not written on. **2** with spaces left for details to be filled in. **3** without decoration. **4** showing no interest or expression, e.g. *a blank stare.* **5** lacking ideas or inspiration, e.g. *his mind went blank.* ♦ *noun* **6** empty space. **7** condition of not understanding. **8** cartridge containing no bullet. **blankly** *adverb* **blank cheque 1** signed cheque without the amount payable specified. **2** complete freedom of action. **blank verse** unrhymed verse.

blanket ⊕ *noun* **1** large thick cloth used as covering for a bed. **2** concealing cover, as of snow. ♦ *adjective* **3** applying to a wide group of people, situations, conditions, etc. ♦ *verb* **4** cover as with a blanket.

blare ⊕ *verb* **1** sound loudly and harshly. ♦ *noun* **2** loud harsh noise.

blarney ⊕ *noun* flattering talk.

blasé [blah-zay] *adjective* indifferent or bored through familiarity.

blaspheme ⊕ *verb* **1** speak disrespectfully of (God or sacred things). **2** utter curses.

————————— T H E S A U R U S —————————

blacklist *verb* **2** = **exclude**, ban, bar, boycott, debar, expel, reject, snub

black magic *noun* = **witchcraft**, black art, diabolism, necromancy, sorcery, voodoo, wizardry

blackmail *noun* **1** = **threat**, extortion, hush money (*sl*), intimidation, ransom ♦*verb* **2** = **threaten**, coerce, compel, demand, extort, hold to ransom, intimidate, squeeze

blackness *noun* **1** = **darkness**, duskiness, gloom, murkiness, swarthiness OPPOSITE> **light**

blackout *noun* **2** = **unconsciousness**, coma, faint, loss of consciousness, oblivion, swoon

black sheep *noun* = **disgrace**, bad egg (*old-fashioned inf*), dropout, ne'er-do-well, outcast, prodigal, renegade, reprobate

blame *verb* **1** = **hold responsible**, accuse, censure, chide, condemn, criticize, find fault with, reproach OPPOSITE> **clear** ♦*noun* **3** = **responsibility**, accountability, accusation, culpability, fault, guilt, liability, onus OPPOSITE> **credit**

blameless *adjective* = **innocent**, above suspicion, clean, faultless, guiltless, immaculate, impeccable, irreproachable, perfect, unblemished, virtuous OPPOSITE> **guilty**

blameworthy *adjective* = **reprehensible**, discreditable, disreputable, indefensible, inexcusable, iniquitous, reproachable, shameful

bland *adjective* **1** = **dull**, boring, flat, humdrum, insipid, tasteless, unexciting, uninspiring, vapid OPPOSITE> **interesting**

blank *adjective* **1** = **unmarked**, bare, clean, clear, empty, void, white OPPOSITE> **full**. **4** = **expressionless**, deadpan, empty, impassive, poker-faced (*inf*), vacant, vague OPPOSITE> **interested** ♦*noun* **6** = **empty space**, emptiness, gap, nothingness, space, vacancy, vacuum, void

blanket *noun* **1** = **cover**, coverlet, rug **2** = **covering**, carpet, cloak, coat, layer, mantle, sheet ♦*verb* **4** = **cover**, cloak, coat, conceal, hide, mask, obscure, suppress

blare *verb* **1** = **sound out**, blast, clamour, clang, resound, roar, scream, trumpet

blarney *noun* = **flattery**, blandishments, cajolery, coaxing, soft soap (*inf*), spiel, sweet talk (*inf*), wheedling

blasé *adjective* = **indifferent**, apathetic, lukewarm, nonchalant, offhand, unconcerned

blasphemy *noun* **blasphemous** *adjective* **blasphemer** *noun*

blast ⊕ *noun* **1** explosion. **2** sudden strong gust of air or wind. **3** sudden loud sound, as of a trumpet. **4** *US slang* very enjoyable or thrilling experience. ♦ *verb* **5** blow up (a rock etc.) with explosives. **6** make a loud harsh noise. **7** criticize severely. ♦ *interjection* **8** *Slang* expression of annoyance. **blasted** *adjective, adverb Slang* extreme or extremely. **blast furnace** furnace for smelting, using a preheated blast of air. **blastoff** *noun* launching of a rocket.

blatant ⊕ [blay-tant] *adjective* glaringly obvious. **blatantly** *adverb*

blather *verb, noun* same as BLETHER.

blaze¹ ⊕ *noun* **1** strong fire or flame. **2** very bright light. **3** outburst of passion. ♦ *verb* **4** burn or shine brightly. **5** become stirred with anger or excitement.

blaze² *noun* **1** mark made on a tree to indicate a route. **2** light-coloured marking on the face of an animal. ♦ *verb* **3** mark (a tree etc.) with a blaze.

blaze³ *verb* **blaze something abroad** make something widely known.

blazer *noun* lightweight jacket, often in the colours of a school etc.

blazon *verb* proclaim publicly.

bleach ⊕ *verb* **1** make or become white or colourless. ♦ *noun* **2** bleaching agent.

bleak ⊕ *adjective* **1** exposed and barren. **2** offering little hope.

bleary ⊕ *adjective* -rier, -riest with eyes dimmed, as by tears or tiredness. **blearily** *adverb*

bleat *verb* **1** (of a sheep, goat, or calf) utter its plaintive cry. **2** whine. ♦ *noun* **3** cry of sheep, goats, and calves.

bleed ⊕ *verb* **bleeding, bled 1** lose or emit blood. **2** draw blood from (a person or animal). **3** *Informal* obtain money by extortion. **4** draw off or emit liquid or gas.

bleep *noun* **1** short high-pitched sound made by an electrical device. ♦ *verb* **2** make a bleeping sound. **bleeper** *noun* small portable radio receiver that makes a bleeping signal.

blemish ⊕ *noun* **1** defect or stain. ♦ *verb* **2** spoil or tarnish.

blench *verb* shy away, as in fear.

blend ⊕ *verb* **1** mix or mingle (components or ingredients). **2** look good together. ♦ *noun* **3** mixture. **blender** *noun* electrical appliance for puréeing vegetables etc.

blende *noun* mineral consisting mainly of zinc sulphide.

blenny *noun, pl* -nies small fish with a tapering scaleless body.

———————————————— THESAURUS ————————————————

OPPOSITE⟩ interested

blaspheme *verb* **1** = profane, desecrate **2** = curse, abuse, damn, execrate, revile, swear

blasphemous *adjective* **1** = irreverent, godless, impious, irreligious, profane, sacrilegious, ungodly OPPOSITE⟩ reverent

blasphemy *noun* **1** = irreverence, desecration, impiety, profanity, sacrilege **2** = cursing, execration, profanity, swearing

blast *noun* **1** = explosion, bang, burst, crash, detonation, discharge, eruption, outburst, salvo, volley **2** = gust, gale, squall, storm, strong breeze, tempest **3** = blare, blow, clang, honk, peal, scream, toot, wail ♦*verb* **5** = blow up, break up, burst, demolish, destroy, explode, put paid to, ruin, shatter

blastoff *noun* = launch, discharge, expulsion, firing, launching, liftoff, projection, shot

blatant *adjective* = obvious, brazen, conspicuous, flagrant, glaring, obtrusive, ostentatious, overt OPPOSITE⟩ subtle

blaze¹ *noun* **1** = fire, bonfire, conflagration, flames **2** = glare, beam, brilliance, flare, flash, gleam, glitter, glow, light, radiance ♦*verb* **4** = burn, beam, fire, flame, flare, flash, glare, gleam, glow, shine

bleach *verb* **1** = whiten, blanch, fade, grow pale, lighten, wash out

bleak *adjective* **1** = exposed, bare, barren, desolate, unsheltered, weather-beaten, windswept OPPOSITE⟩ sheltered. **2** = dismal, cheerless, depressing, discouraging, dreary, gloomy, grim, hopeless, joyless, sombre OPPOSITE⟩ cheerful

bleary *adjective* = dim, blurred, blurry, foggy, fuzzy, hazy, indistinct, misty, murky

bleed *verb* **1** = lose blood, flow, gush, ooze, run, shed blood, spurt **2** = draw *or* take blood, extract, leech **3** *Inf* = extort, drain, exhaust, fleece, milk, squeeze

blemish *noun* **1** = mark, blot, defect, disfigurement, fault, flaw, imperfection, smudge, stain, taint OPPOSITE⟩ improvement ♦*verb* **2** = mark, damage, disfigure, impair, injure, mar, spoil, stain, sully, taint, tarnish OPPOSITE⟩ improve

blend *verb* **1** = mix, amalgamate, combine, compound, merge, mingle, unite **2** = go well, complement, fit, go with, harmonize, suit ♦*noun* **3** = mixture, alloy, amalgamation, combination, compound, concoction, mix, synthesis, union

B

bless ❶ *verb* **1** make holy by means of a religious rite. **2** call upon God to protect. **3** give thanks to. **4** endow with health, talent, etc.
blessed *adjective* **1** holy. **2** *RC Church* beatified by the Pope. **3** *Euphemistic* damned. **blessing** *noun* **1** invoking of divine aid. **2** approval. **3** happy event.
blether *Scot verb* **1** talk, esp. foolishly or at length. ♦ *noun* **2** conversation. **3** talkative person.
blew *verb* past tense of BLOW¹.
blight ❶ *noun* **1** person or thing that spoils or prevents growth. **2** withering plant disease. ♦ *verb* **3** cause to suffer a blight. **4** frustrate or disappoint.
blighter *noun Informal* irritating person.
blimey *interjection Slang* exclamation of surprise or annoyance.
blimp *noun* small airship.
blind ❶ *adjective* **1** unable to see. **2** unable or unwilling to understand. **3** not determined by reason, e.g. *blind hatred*. ♦ *verb* **4** deprive of sight. **5** deprive of good sense, reason, or judgment. ♦ *noun* **6** covering for a window. **7** something that serves to conceal the truth. **blindly** *adverb* **blindness** *noun* **blind alley** alley open at one end only. **blind date** *Informal* prearranged social meeting between two people who have not met. **blind man's buff** game in which a blindfolded person tries to catch and identify other players. **blind spot 1** area of the retina where vision is not

experienced. **2** place where vision is obscured. **3** subject about which a person is ignorant.

> **LANGUAGE TIP**
>
> The use of *the blind, the disabled*, etc. can be offensive and should be avoided. Instead you should talk about *blind people, disabled people*, etc.

blindfold *verb* **1** prevent (a person) from seeing by covering the eyes. ♦ *noun* **2** piece of cloth used to cover the eyes. ♦ *adjective, adverb* **3** with the eyes covered by a cloth.
blink ❶ *verb* **1** close and immediately reopen (the eyes). **2** shine intermittently. ♦ *noun* **3** act of blinking. **on the blink** *Slang* not working properly.
blinkers *plural noun* leather flaps on a horse's bridle to prevent sideways vision. **blinkered** *adjective* considering only a narrow point of view.
blip *noun* **1** spot of light on a radar screen indicating the position of an object. **2** temporary irregularity in performance.
bliss ❶ *noun* perfect happiness. **blissful** *adjective* **blissfully** *adverb*
blister ❶ *noun* **1** small bubble on the skin. **2** swelling, as on a painted surface. ♦ *verb* **3** (cause to) have blisters. **blistering** *adjective* **1** (of weather) very hot. **2** (of criticism) extremely

———————————— T H E S A U R U S ————————————

bless *verb* **1** = **sanctify**, anoint, consecrate, dedicate, exalt, hallow, ordain OPPOSITE> **curse**. **4** = **endow**, bestow, favour, give, grace, grant, provide OPPOSITE> **afflict**
blessed *adjective* **1, 2** = **holy**, adored, beatified, divine, hallowed, revered, sacred, sanctified
blessing *noun* **1** = **benediction**, benison, commendation, consecration, dedication, grace, invocation, thanksgiving OPPOSITE> **curse**. **2** = **approval**, backing, consent, favour, good wishes, leave, permission, sanction, support OPPOSITE> **disapproval**. **3** = **benefit**, favour, gift, godsend, good fortune, help, kindness, service, windfall OPPOSITE> **disadvantage**
blight *noun* **1** = **curse**, affliction, bane, contamination, corruption, evil, plague, pollution, scourge, woe OPPOSITE> **blessing**. **2** = **disease**, canker, decay, fungus, infestation, mildew, pest, pestilence, rot ♦ *verb* **4** = **frustrate**, crush, dash, disappoint, mar, ruin, spoil, undo, wreck
blind *adjective* **1** = **sightless**, eyeless, unseeing,

unsighted, visionless OPPOSITE> **sighted**. **2** = **unaware of**, careless, heedless, ignorant, inattentive, inconsiderate, indifferent, insensitive, oblivious, unconscious of OPPOSITE> **aware**. **3** = **unreasoning**, indiscriminate, prejudiced ♦ *noun* **7** = **cover**, camouflage, cloak, facade, feint, front, mask, masquerade, screen, smoke screen
blindly *adverb* **2** = **thoughtlessly**, carelessly, heedlessly, inconsiderately, recklessly, senselessly **3** = **aimlessly**, at random, indiscriminately, instinctively
blink *verb* **1** = **wink**, bat, flutter **2** = **flicker**, flash, gleam, glimmer, shine, twinkle, wink **on the blink** *Sl* = **not working (properly)**, faulty, malfunctioning, out of action, out of order, playing up
bliss *noun* = **joy**, beatitude, blessedness, blissfulness, ecstasy, euphoria, felicity, gladness, happiness, heaven, nirvana, paradise, rapture OPPOSITE> **distress**
blissful *adjective* = **joyful**, ecstatic, elated, enraptured, euphoric, happy, heavenly (*inf*),

harsh.

blithe ⊕ *adjective* **1** casual and indifferent. **2** very happy. **blithely** *adverb*

blithering *adjective Informal* stupid.

blitz ⊕ *noun* **1** violent and sustained attack by aircraft. **2** intensive attack or concerted effort. ◆ *verb* **3** attack suddenly and intensively.

blizzard ⊕ *noun* blinding storm of wind and snow.

bloat ⊕ *verb* cause to swell, as with liquid or air.

bloater *noun* salted smoked herring.

blob ⊕ *noun* **1** soft mass or drop. **2** indistinct or shapeless form.

bloc ⊕ *noun* people or countries combined by a common interest.

block ⊕ *noun* **1** large solid piece of wood, stone, etc. **2** large building of offices, flats, etc. **3** group of buildings enclosed by intersecting streets. **4** obstruction or hindrance. **5** piece of wood or metal engraved for printing. **6** one of a set of wooden or plastic cubes used as a toy. **7** *Slang* person's head. ◆ *verb* **8** obstruct or impede by introducing an obstacle. **blockage** *noun* **blockbuster** *noun* highly successful film, novel, etc. **blockhead** *noun* stupid person. **block letter** plain capital letter.

blockade ⊕ *noun* **1** sealing off of a place to prevent the passage of goods. ◆ *verb* **2** impose a blockade on.

blog *noun* short for WEBLOG.

bloke ⊕ *noun Informal* man.

blonde ⊕ (*masc*) **blond** *adjective, noun* fair-haired (person).

blood ⊕ *noun* **1** red fluid that flows around the body. **2** bloodshed. **3** race or kinship. ◆ *verb* **4** initiate (a person) to war or hunting. **in cold blood** done deliberately. **bloodless** *adjective* **1** without blood or bloodshed. **2** pale. **3** lacking vitality. **blood bath** massacre. **bloodcurdling** *adjective* terrifying. **bloodhound** *noun* large dog formerly used for tracking. **blood poisoning** same as SEPTICAEMIA. **blood pressure** pressure exerted by the blood on the inner walls of the blood vessels. **bloodshed** *noun* slaughter or killing. **bloodshot** *adjective* (of an eye) inflamed. **blood sport** sport involving the killing of animals. **bloodstream** *noun* flow of blood round the body. **bloodsucker** *noun* **1** animal that sucks blood. **2** *Informal* person who extorts money from other people. **bloodthirsty** *adjective* taking pleasure in violence. **blood vessel** tube that carries the blood in the body.

bloody ⊕ *adjective* **1** covered with blood. **2** marked by much killing. ◆ *adjective, adverb* **3** *Slang* extreme or extremely. ◆ *verb* **4** stain with blood. **bloody-minded** *adjective* deliberately unhelpful.

bloom ⊕ *noun* **1** blossom on a flowering plant. **2** period when flowers open. **3**

——————— THESAURUS ———————

rapturous

blister *noun* **1** = **sore**, abscess, boil, carbuncle, cyst, pimple, pustule, swelling

blithe *adjective* **1** = **heedless**, careless, casual, indifferent, nonchalant, thoughtless, unconcerned, untroubled OPPOSITE concerned

blitz *noun* **1** = **attack**, assault, blitzkrieg, bombardment, offensive, onslaught, raid, strike

blizzard *noun* = **snowstorm**, blast, gale, squall, storm, tempest

bloat *verb* = **puff up**, balloon, blow up, dilate, distend, enlarge, expand, inflate, swell OPPOSITE contract

blob *noun* **1** = **drop**, ball, bead, bubble, dab, droplet, globule, lump, mass

bloc *noun* = **group**, alliance, axis, coalition, faction, league, union

block *noun* **1** = **piece**, bar, brick, chunk, hunk, ingot, lump, mass **4** = **obstruction**, bar, barrier, hindrance, impediment, jam, obstacle ◆ *verb* **8** = **obstruct**, bung up (*inf*), choke, clog, close, impede, plug, stem the flow, stop up OPPOSITE open

blockade *noun* **1** = **stoppage**, barricade, barrier, block, hindrance, impediment, obstacle,

obstruction, restriction, siege

blockage *noun* **8** = **obstruction**, block, impediment, occlusion, stoppage

blockhead *noun* = **idiot**, chump (*inf*), dunce, fool, nitwit, numbskull *or* numskull, thickhead, twit (*inf, chiefly Brit*)

bloke *noun Inf* = **man**, chap, character (*inf*), fellow, guy (*inf*), individual, person

blonde *adjective* = **fair**, fair-haired, fair-skinned, flaxen, golden-haired, light, tow-headed

blood *noun* **1** = **lifeblood**, gore, vital fluid **3** = **family**, ancestry, birth, descent, extraction, kinship, lineage, relations

bloodcurdling *adjective* = **terrifying**, appalling, chilling, dreadful, fearful, frightening, hair-raising, horrendous, horrifying, scaring, spine-chilling

bloodshed *noun* = **killing**, blood bath, blood-letting, butchery, carnage, gore, massacre, murder, slaughter, slaying

bloodthirsty *adjective* = **cruel**, barbarous, brutal, cut-throat, ferocious, gory, murderous, savage, vicious, warlike

bloody *adjective* **1** = **bloodstained**, bleeding, blood-soaked, blood-spattered, gaping, raw **2**

B

flourishing condition. **4** youthful or healthy glow. **5** whitish coating on fruit, leaves, etc. ◆ verb **6** (of flowers) open. **7** bear flowers. **8** be in a healthy, glowing condition.
bloomer noun Informal stupid mistake.
bloomers plural noun woman's baggy knickers.
blossom ⓘ noun **1** flowers of a plant. ◆ verb **2** (of plants) flower. **3** come to a promising stage.
blot ⓘ noun **1** spot or stain. **2** something that spoils. ◆ verb **blotting, blotted 3** cause a blemish in or on. **4** soak up (ink) by using blotting paper. **blotter** noun **blot out** verb darken or hide completely. **blotting paper** soft absorbent paper for soaking up ink.
blotch noun discoloured area or stain. **blotchy** adjective **blotchier, blotchiest**
blotto adjective Slang extremely drunk.
blouse noun woman's shirtlike garment.
blouson noun short loose jacket with a tight waist.
blow¹ ⓘ verb **blowing, blew, blown 1** (of air, the wind, etc.) move. **2** move or be carried as if by the wind. **3** expel (air etc.) through the mouth or nose. **4** cause (a musical instrument) to sound by forcing air into it. **5** burn out (a fuse etc.). **6** Slang spend (money) freely. **7** Slang use (an opportunity) ineffectively. **blower** noun **blowy** adjective windy. **blow-dry** verb style (the hair) with a hand-held dryer. **blowfly** noun fly that lays its eggs in meat. **blowtorch** noun small burner producing a very hot flame. **blowout** noun **1** sudden loss of air in a tyre. **2** escape of oil or gas from a well. **3** Slang filling meal. **blowpipe** noun long tube from which

darts etc. are shot by blowing. **blow up** verb **1** explode. **2** fill with air. **3** Informal lose one's temper. **4** exaggerate the importance of. **5** Informal enlarge (a photograph).
blow² ⓘ noun **1** hard hit. **2** sudden setback. **3** attacking action, e.g. a blow for freedom.
blowie noun Aust informal bluebottle.
blown verb past participle of BLOW¹.
blowsy adjective fat, untidy, and red-faced.
blubber noun **1** fat of whales, seals, etc. ◆ verb **2** sob without restraint.
bludge verb **1** Aust & NZ informal evade work. **2** scrounge. **bludger** noun person who scrounges.
bludgeon ⓘ noun **1** short thick club. ◆ verb **2** hit with a bludgeon. **3** force or bully.
blue ⓘ noun **1** colour of a clear unclouded sky. **2** sportsman representing Oxford or Cambridge University. ◆ plural **3** feeling of depression. **4** type of folk music of Black American origin. ◆ adjective **bluer, bluest 5** of the colour blue. **6** depressed. **7** pornographic. **out of the blue** unexpectedly. **bluish** adjective **bluebell** noun flower with blue bell-shaped flowers. **bluebottle** noun large fly with a dark-blue body. **blue cheese** cheese containing a blue mould. **blue-collar** adjective denoting manual industrial workers. **blue heeler** Aust & NZ informal dog that controls cattle by biting their heels. **blueprint** noun **1** photographic print of a plan. **2** description of how a plan is expected to work. **blue ribbon** first prize in a competition. **bluestocking** noun intellectual woman. **bluetongue** noun Australian lizard with a blue tongue.

———— T H E S A U R U S ————

= **cruel**, ferocious, fierce, sanguinary, savage
bloom noun **2** = **flower**, blossom, blossoming, bud, efflorescence, opening **3** = **prime**, beauty, flourishing, health, heyday, vigour **4** = **glow**, freshness, lustre, radiance OPPOSITE **whiteness**
◆verb **6, 7** = **blossom**, blow, bud, burgeon, open, sprout OPPOSITE **wither**. **8** = **flourish**, develop, fare well, grow, prosper, succeed, thrive, wax OPPOSITE **fail**
blossom noun **1** = **flower**, bloom, bud, floret, flowers ◆verb **2** = **flower**, bloom, burgeon **3** = **grow**, bloom, develop, flourish, mature, progress, prosper, thrive
blot noun **1** = **spot**, blotch, mark, patch, smear, smudge, speck, splodge **2** = **stain**, blemish, defect, fault, flaw, scar, spot, taint
◆verb **3** = **stain**, disgrace, mark, smirch, smudge, spoil, spot, sully, tarnish **4** = **soak up**, absorb, dry, take up
blot out verb = **obliterate**, darken, destroy,

eclipse, efface, obscure, shadow
blow¹ verb **2** = **carry**, drive, fling, flutter, move, sweep, waft **3** = **exhale**, breathe, pant, puff **4** = **play**, blare, mouth, pipe, sound, toot, trumpet, vibrate
blow² noun **1** = **knock**, bang, clout (inf), punch, smack, sock (sl), stroke, thump, wallop (inf), whack **2** = **setback**, bombshell, calamity, catastrophe, disappointment, disaster, misfortune, reverse, shock
blow up verb **1** = **explode**, blast, blow sky-high, bomb, burst, detonate, rupture, shatter **2** = **inflate**, bloat, distend, enlarge, expand, fill, puff up, pump up, swell **3** Inf = **lose one's temper**, become angry, erupt, fly off the handle (inf), hit the roof (inf), rage, see red (inf)
bludgeon noun **1** = **club**, cosh (Brit), cudgel, truncheon ◆verb **2** = **club**, beat up, cosh (Brit), cudgel, knock down, strike **3** = **bully**, bulldoze (inf), coerce, force, railroad (inf), steamroller

bluff¹ ❶ *verb* **1** pretend to be confident in order to influence (someone). ♦ *noun* **2** act of bluffing.
bluff² ❶ *noun* **1** steep cliff or bank. ♦ *adjective* **2** good-naturedly frank and hearty.
blunder ❶ *noun* **1** clumsy mistake. ♦ *verb* **2** make a blunder. **3** act clumsily.
blunderbuss *noun* obsolete gun with a wide flared muzzle.
blunt ❶ *adjective* **1** not having a sharp edge or point. **2** (of people, speech, etc.) straightforward or uncomplicated. ♦ *verb* **3** make less sharp. **bluntly** *adverb*
blur ❶ *verb* **blurring, blurred 1** make or become vague or less distinct. **2** smear or smudge. ♦ *noun* **3** something vague, hazy, or indistinct. **blurry** *adjective* **-rier, -riest**
blurb *noun* promotional description, as on the jacket of a book.
blurt ❶ *verb* (foll. by *out*) utter suddenly and involuntarily.
blush ❶ *verb* **1** become red in the face, esp. from embarrassment or shame. ♦ *noun* **2** reddening of the face. **blusher** *noun* cosmetic for giving the cheeks a rosy colour.
bluster ❶ *verb* **1** speak loudly or in a bullying way. ♦ *noun* **2** empty threats or protests.
blustery *adjective* (of weather) rough and

windy.
BMA British Medical Association.
B-movie *noun* film originally made as a supporting film, now considered a genre in its own right.
BO *Informal* body odour.
boa *noun* **1** large nonvenomous snake. **2** long scarf of fur or feathers. **boa constrictor** large snake that kills its prey by crushing.
boab [boh-ab] *noun Aust informal* short for BAOBAB.
boar *noun* **1** uncastrated male pig. **2** wild pig.
board ❶ *noun* **1** long flat piece of sawn timber. **2** smaller flat piece of rigid material for a specific purpose, e.g. *ironing board*; *chess board*. **3** group of people who administer a company, trust, etc. **4** meals provided for money. ♦ *plural* **5** the stage. ♦ *verb* **6** go aboard (a train, aeroplane, etc.). **7** cover with boards. **8** receive meals and lodgings in return for money. **on board** on or in a ship, aeroplane, etc.
boarder *noun* pupil who lives at school during the school term. **boarding house** private house that provides meals and accommodation for paying guests. **boarding school** school providing living accommodation for pupils.
boardroom *noun* room where the board of a company meets.

——————— THESAURUS ———————

blue *noun* **1** = **azure**, cobalt, cyan, navy, sapphire, ultramarine ♦*plural* **3** = **depression**, doldrums, dumps (*inf*), gloom, low spirits, melancholy, unhappiness ♦*adjective* **5** = **azure**, cerulean, cobalt, cyan, navy, sapphire, sky-coloured, ultramarine **6** = **depressed**, dejected, despondent, downcast, low, melancholy, sad, unhappy OPPOSITE happy. **7** = **smutty**, indecent, lewd, obscene, risqué, X-rated (*inf*) OPPOSITE decent
blueprint *noun* = **plan**, design, draft, outline, pattern, pilot scheme, prototype, sketch
bluff¹ *verb* **1** = **deceive**, con, delude, fake, feign, mislead, pretend, pull the wool over someone's eyes ♦*noun* **2** = **deception**, bluster, bravado, deceit, fraud, humbug, pretence, sham, subterfuge
bluff² *noun* **1** = **precipice**, bank, cliff, crag, escarpment, headland, peak, promontory, ridge ♦*adjective* **2** = **hearty**, blunt, blustering, genial, good-natured, open, outspoken, plain-spoken OPPOSITE sensitive
blunder *noun* **1** = **mistake**, bloomer (*Brit inf*), clanger (*inf*), error, fault, faux pas, gaffe, howler (*inf*), inaccuracy, indiscretion, oversight, slip, slip-up (*inf*) OPPOSITE accuracy ♦*verb* **2** = **make a mistake**, botch, bungle, err, put

one's foot in it (*inf*), slip up (*inf*) OPPOSITE be correct. **3** = **stumble**, bumble, flounder
blunt *adjective* **1** = **dull**, dulled, edgeless, pointless, rounded, unsharpened OPPOSITE pointed. **2** = **forthright**, bluff, brusque, frank, outspoken, plain-spoken, rude, straightforward, tactless OPPOSITE sensitive ♦*verb* **3** = **dull**, dampen, deaden, numb, soften, take the edge off, water down, weaken OPPOSITE stimulate
blur *verb* **1** = **make indistinct**, cloud, darken, make hazy, make vague, mask, obscure ♦*noun* **3** = **indistinctness**, confusion, fog, haze, obscurity
blurt *verb* (foll. by *out*) = **exclaim**, disclose, let the cat out of the bag, reveal, spill the beans (*inf*), tell all, utter suddenly
blush *verb* **1** = **turn red**, colour, flush, go red (as a beetroot), redden, turn scarlet OPPOSITE pale ♦*noun* **2** = **reddening**, colour, flush, glow, pink tinge, rosiness, rosy tint, ruddiness
bluster *verb* **1** = **roar**, bully, domineer, hector, rant, storm ♦*noun* **2** = **hot air**, bluff, bombast, bravado (*inf*)
blustery *adjective* = **gusty**, boisterous, inclement, squally, stormy, tempestuous, violent, wild, windy
board *noun* **1** = **plank**, panel, piece of timber,

boast ⊕ *verb* **1** speak too proudly about one's talents etc. **2** possess (something to be proud of). ◆ *noun* **3** bragging statement. **4** something that is bragged about. **boastful** *adjective*

boat *noun* **1** small vehicle for travelling across water. **2** *Informal* ship. **3** boat-shaped dish, e.g. *gravy boat.* ◆ *verb* **4** travel in a boat. **boater** *noun* flat straw hat. **boating** *noun* **boat train** train scheduled to take passengers to or from a ship.

boatswain *noun* same as BOSUN.

bob¹ ⊕ *verb* **bobbing, bobbed 1** move up and down repeatedly. ◆ *noun* **2** short abrupt movement.

bob² *noun* **1** hairstyle in which the hair is cut short evenly all round the head. **2** weight on a pendulum or plumb line. ◆ *verb* **bobbing, bobbed 3** cut (the hair) in a bob.

bob³ *noun, pl* **bob** *Brit informal* (formerly) shilling.

bobbin *noun* reel on which thread is wound.

bobble *noun* small ball of material, usu. for decoration.

bobby *noun, pl* **-bies** *Informal* policeman.

bobotie *noun S Afr* dish of curried mince.

bobsleigh *noun* **1** sledge for racing down an icy track. ◆ *verb* **2** ride on a bobsleigh.

bod *noun Informal* person.

bode ⊕ *verb* be an omen of (good or ill).

bodega *noun* shop in a Spanish-speaking country that sells wine.

bodge *verb Informal* make a mess of.

bodice *noun* upper part of a dress.

bodkin *noun* blunt large-eyed needle.

body ⊕ *noun, pl* **bodies 1** entire physical structure of an animal or human. **2** trunk or torso. **3** corpse. **4** group regarded as a single entity. **5** main part of anything. **6** separate mass of water or land. **7** person. **8** woman's one-piece undergarment. **bodily** *adjective* **1** relating to the body. ◆ *adverb* **2** by taking hold of the body. **body-board** *noun Aust, NZ, S Afr & US* small polystyrene surfboard. **bodyguard** *noun* person or group of people employed to protect someone. **body shop** place where vehicle bodywork is repaired. **body stocking** woman's one-piece undergarment, covering the torso. **bodywork** *noun* outer shell of a motor vehicle.

Boer *noun* descendant of the Dutch settlers in S Africa.

boffin ⊕ *noun Brit informal* scientist or expert.

bog ⊕ *noun* **1** wet spongy ground. **2** *Slang* toilet. **boggy** *adjective* **-gier, -giest. bog down** *verb* **bogging, bogged** impede physically or mentally.

bogan *noun Aust dated & NZ slang* youth who dresses and behaves rebelliously.

bogey, bogy ⊕ *noun* **1** evil or mischievous spirit. **2** something that worries or annoys. **3** *Golf* score of one stroke over par on a hole.

boggle *verb* **1** be surprised, confused, or alarmed. **2** hesitate when confronted with a problem.

bogie, bogy *noun* set of wheels, as on a railway carriage.

bog-standard *adjective Slang* completely ordinary.

bogus ⊕ [boh-**guss**] *adjective* not genuine.

bogy *noun, pl* **-gies** same as BOGEY or BOGIE.

bohemian *noun, adjective* (person) leading an unconventional life.

——— THESAURUS ———

slat, timber **3 = directors,** advisers, committee, conclave, council, panel, trustees **4 = meals,** daily meals, provisions, victuals ◆*verb* **6 = get on,** embark, enter, mount OPPOSITE **land. 8 = lodge,** put up, quarter, room

boast *verb* **1 = brag,** blow one's own trumpet, crow, skite (*Aust & NZ*), strut, swagger, talk big (*sl*), vaunt OPPOSITE **cover up. 2 = possess,** be proud of, congratulate oneself on, exhibit, flatter oneself, pride oneself on, show off ◆*noun* **3 = brag,** avowal OPPOSITE **disclaimer**

boastful *adjective* **1 = bragging,** cocky, conceited, crowing, egotistical, full of oneself, swaggering, swollen-headed, vaunting

bob¹ *verb* **1 = duck,** bounce, hop, nod, oscillate, waggle, wobble

bode *verb* **= portend,** augur, be an omen of, forebode, foretell, predict, signify, threaten

bodily *adjective* **1 = physical,** actual, carnal, corporal, corporeal, material, substantial, tangible

body *noun* **1 = physique,** build, figure, form, frame, shape **2 = torso,** trunk **3 = corpse,** cadaver, carcass, dead body, remains, stiff (*sl*) **4 = organization,** association, band, bloc, collection, company, confederation, congress, corporation, society **5 = main part,** bulk, essence, mass, material, matter, substance

boffin *noun Brit inf* **= expert,** brainbox, egghead, fundi (*S Afr*), genius, intellectual, inventor, mastermind

bog *noun* **1 = marsh,** fen, mire, morass, quagmire, slough, swamp, wetlands, muskeg (*Canad*)

bogey *noun* **1 = bugbear,** bête noire, bugaboo, nightmare

bogus *adjective* **= fake,** artificial, counterfeit, false, forged, fraudulent, imitation, phoney or

boil¹ ❶ *verb* **1** (cause to) change from a liquid to a vapour so quickly that bubbles are formed. **2** reach or cause to reach boiling point. **3** cook by the process of boiling. **4** bubble like something boiling. **5** be extremely angry. ◆ *noun* **6** state or action of boiling. **boiler** *noun* piece of equipment which provides hot water. **boiler suit** one-piece overall. **boiling point** temperature at which a liquid boils.

boil² ❶ *noun* red pus-filled swelling on the skin.

boisterous ❶ *adjective* **1** noisy and lively. **2** turbulent or stormy. **boisterously** *adverb*

bold ❶ *adjective* **1** confident and fearless. **2** immodest or impudent. **3** standing out distinctly. **boldly** *adverb* **boldness** *noun*

bole *noun* tree trunk.

bolero *noun, pl* **-ros 1** (music for) traditional Spanish dance. **2** short open jacket.

boll *noun* rounded seed capsule of cotton, flax, etc.

bollard *noun* **1** short thick post used to prevent the passage of motor vehicles. **2** post on a quay etc. for securing mooring lines.

boloney *noun* same as BALONEY.

Bolshevik *noun* (formerly) Russian Communist. **bolshie, bolshy** *adjective Informal* difficult or rebellious.

bolshie, bolshy *adjective Informal* difficult or rebellious.

bolster ❶ *verb* **1** support or strengthen. ◆ *noun* **2** long narrow pillow.

bolt ❶ *noun* **1** sliding metal bar for fastening a door etc. **2** metal pin which screws into a nut. **3** flash (of lightning). **4** sudden movement, esp. in order to escape. **5** arrow for a crossbow. ◆ *verb* **6** run away suddenly. **7** fasten with a bolt. **8** eat hurriedly. **bolt upright** stiff and rigid. **bolt hole** place of escape.

bomb ❶ *noun* **1** container fitted with explosive material. **2** *Slang* large amount of money. ◆ *verb* **3** attack with bombs. **4** move very quickly. **the bomb** nuclear bomb. **bomber** *noun* **1** aircraft that drops bombs. **2** person who throws or puts a bomb in a particular place. **bombshell** *noun* shocking or unwelcome surprise.

bombard ❶ *verb* **1** attack with heavy gunfire or bombs. **2** attack verbally, esp. with questions. **bombardier** *noun* noncommissioned rank in the Royal Artillery. **bombardment** *noun*

bombast ❶ *noun* pompous language. **bombastic** *adjective*

bona fide ❶ [**bone**-a **fide**-ee] *adjective* genuine.

bonanza *noun* sudden good luck or wealth.

bonbon *noun* sweet.

bond ❶ *noun* **1** something that binds, fastens or holds together. **2** something that unites people, e.g. *a bond of friendship*. **3** written or spoken agreement. **4** *Finance* certificate of debt issued to raise funds. **5** *S Afr* conditional pledging of property, esp. a house, as security for the repayment of a loan. ◆ *plural* **6** something that restrains or imprisons. ◆ *verb* **7** bind. **bonded** *adjective*

bondage ❶ *noun* **1** slavery. **2** subjection to

——————————— T H E S A U R U S ———————————

phony (*inf*), sham OPPOSITE genuine

bohemian *noun* =**nonconformist**, beatnik, dropout, hippy, iconoclast ◆*adjective* =**unconventional**, alternative, artistic, arty (*inf*), left bank, nonconformist, offbeat, unorthodox OPPOSITE **conservative**

boil¹ *verb* **1** =**bubble**, **4** =**froth**, bubble, effervesce, fizz, foam, seethe

boil² *noun* =**pustule**, blister, carbuncle, gathering, swelling, tumour, ulcer

boisterous *adjective* **1** =**unruly**, disorderly, loud, noisy, riotous, rollicking, rowdy, unrestrained, vociferous, wild OPPOSITE **self-controlled**

bold *adjective* **1** =**fearless**, adventurous, audacious, brave, courageous, daring, enterprising, heroic, intrepid, valiant OPPOSITE timid. **2** =**impudent**, barefaced, brazen, cheeky, confident, forward, feisty (*US & Canad*), insolent, rude, shameless OPPOSITE **shy**

bolster *verb* **1** =**support**, augment, boost, help, reinforce, shore up, strengthen

bolt *noun* **1** =**bar**, catch, fastener, latch, lock, sliding bar **2** =**pin**, peg, rivet, rod ◆*verb* **6** =**run away**, abscond, dash, escape, flee, fly, make a break (for it), run for it **7** =**lock**, bar, fasten, latch, secure **8** =**gobble**, cram, devour, gorge, gulp, guzzle, stuff, swallow whole, wolf

bomb *noun* **1** =**explosive**, device, grenade, mine, missile, projectile, rocket, shell, torpedo ◆*verb* **3** =**blow up**, attack, blow sky-high, bombard, destroy, shell, strafe, torpedo

bombard *verb* **1** =**bomb**, assault, blitz, fire upon, open fire, pound, shell, strafe **2** =**attack**, assail, beset, besiege, harass, hound, pester

bombardment *noun* **1** =**bombing**, assault, attack, barrage, blitz, fusillade, shelling

bombastic *adjective* =**grandiloquent**, grandiose, high-flown, inflated, pompous, verbose, wordy

bona fide *adjective* =**genuine**, actual, authentic, honest, kosher (*inf*), legitimate, real, true OPPOSITE **bogus**

bond *noun* **1** =**fastening**, chain, cord, fetter,

B

some influence or duty. **3** sexual practice in which one partner is tied or chained up.
bone ⊕ *noun* **1** any of the hard parts in the body that form the skeleton. ◆ *plural* **2** human skeleton. ◆ *verb* **3** remove the bones from (meat for cooking etc.). **boneless** *adjective* **bony** *adjective* **bonier, boniest 1** having many bones. **2** thin or emaciated. **bone china** porcelain containing powdered bone. **bone-dry** *adjective* completely dry. **bone-idle** *adjective* extremely lazy. **bone meal** ground bones used as a fertilizer.
bonfire *noun* large outdoor fire.
bongo *noun, pl* **-gos, -goes** small drum played with the fingers.
bonhomie [**bon**-om-ee] *noun* cheerful friendliness.
bonito [ba-**nee**-toh] *noun, pl* **-os 1** small tunny-like marine food fish. **2** related fish, whose flesh is dried and flaked and used in Japanese cookery.
bonk *verb Informal* **1** have sex with. **2** hit. **bonking** *noun*
bonkers *adjective Slang* crazy.
bon mot [bon moh] *noun, pl* **bons mots** clever and fitting remark.
bonnet *noun* **1** metal cover over a vehicle's engine. **2** hat which ties under the chin. **3** *Scot* soft cloth cap.
bonny *adjective* **-nier, -niest** *Scot* **1** beautiful. **2** good or fine.
bonsai *noun, pl* **-sai** ornamental miniature tree or shrub.
bonus ⊕ *noun* something given, paid, or received above what is due or expected.
bon voyage *interjection* phrase used to wish a traveller a pleasant journey.
boo *interjection* **1** shout of disapproval. **2** shout to startle someone. ◆ *verb* **booing, booed 3** shout 'boo' to show disapproval.
boob *Slang noun* **1** foolish mistake. **2** female

breast. ◆ *verb* **3** make a foolish mistake.
boobook [**boo**-book] *noun* small spotted Australian brown owl.
booby *noun, pl* **-bies** foolish person. **booby prize** prize given for the lowest score in a competition. **booby trap 1** hidden bomb primed to be set off by an unsuspecting victim. **2** trap for an unsuspecting person, intended as a joke.
boogie *verb Informal* dance to fast pop music.
book ⊕ *noun* **1** number of pages bound together between covers. **2** long written work. **3** number of tickets, stamps, etc. fastened together. **4** libretto of a musical etc. **5** record of betting transactions. ◆ *plural* **6** record of transactions of a business or society. ◆ *verb* **7** reserve (a place, passage, etc.) in advance. **8** record the name of (a person) who has committed an offence. **bookcase** *noun* piece of furniture containing shelves for books. **bookish** *adjective* **1** fond of reading. **2** forming opinions through reading rather than experience.
booklet *noun* thin book with paper covers.
bookie *noun Informal* short for BOOKMAKER.
book-keeping *noun* systematic recording of business transactions. **book-keeper** *noun*
bookmaker *noun* person whose occupation is taking bets.
bookmark *verb Computers* store (a website) so that one can return to it easily.
bookworm *noun* **1** person devoted to reading. **2** small insect that feeds on books.
boom[1] ⊕ *verb* **1** make a loud deep echoing sound. **2** prosper vigorously and rapidly. ◆ *noun* **3** loud deep echoing sound. **4** period of high economic growth. **boomer** *noun Aust* large male kangaroo.
boom[2] *noun* **1** pole to which the foot of a sail is attached. **2** pole carrying an overhead microphone. **3** barrier across a waterway.
boomerang *noun* **1** curved wooden missile

——————— THESAURUS ———————

ligature, manacle, shackle, tie **2 = tie**, affiliation, affinity, attachment, connection, link, relation, union **3 = agreement**, contract, covenant, guarantee, obligation, pledge, promise, word ◆*verb* **6 = hold together**, bind, connect, fasten, fix together, glue, paste
bondage *noun* **1 = slavery**, captivity, confinement, enslavement, imprisonment, subjugation
bonus *noun* = **extra**, dividend, gift, icing on the cake, plus, premium, prize, reward
bony *adjective* **2 = thin**, emaciated, gaunt, lean, scrawny, skin and bone, skinny
book *noun* **1 = notebook**, album, diary,

exercise book, jotter, pad **2 = work**, publication, title, tome, tract, volume ◆*verb* **7 = reserve**, arrange for, charter, engage, make reservations, organize, programme, schedule **8 = note**, enter, list, log, mark down, put down, record, register, write down
booklet *noun* = **brochure**, leaflet, pamphlet
boom[1] *verb* **1 = bang**, blast, crash, explode, resound, reverberate, roar, roll, rumble, thunder **2 = flourish**, develop, expand, grow, increase, intensify, prosper, strengthen, swell, thrive
OPPOSITE fall ◆*noun* **3 = bang**, blast, burst, clap, crash, explosion, roar, rumble, thunder **4 = expansion**, boost, development, growth,

which can be made to return to the thrower. ◆ *verb* **2** (of a plan) recoil unexpectedly.

boon¹ ❶ *noun* something helpful or beneficial.

boon² ❶ *adjective* close or intimate.

boongary [boong-gar-ree] *noun, pl* **-garies** tree kangaroo of NE Queensland, Australia.

boor ❶ *noun* rude or insensitive person. **boorish** *adjective*

boost ❶ *noun* **1** encouragement or help. **2** upward thrust or push. **3** increase. ◆ *verb* **4** improve. **5** increase. **booster** *noun* **1** small additional injection of a vaccine. **2** radio-frequency amplifier to strengthen signals. **3** first stage of a multistage rocket.

boot¹ ❶ *noun* **1** outer covering for the foot that extends above the ankle. **2** space in a car for luggage. **3** *Informal* kick. **4** *Slang* dismissal from employment. ◆ *verb* **5** *Informal* kick. **6** start up (a computer). **bootee** *noun* baby's soft shoe. **boot camp** centre for young offenders, with strict discipline and hard physical exercise.

boot² *noun* **to boot** in addition.

booth *noun* **1** small partly enclosed cubicle. **2** stall at a fair or market.

bootleg *adjective* **1** produced, distributed, or sold illicitly. ◆ *verb* **-legging, -legged 2** make, carry, or sell (illicit goods). **bootlegger** *noun*

booty ❶ *noun, pl* **-ties** valuable articles obtained as plunder.

booze *verb, noun Informal* (consume) alcoholic drink. **boozy** *adjective* **boozer** *noun Informal* **1** person who is fond of drinking. **2** pub. **booze-up** *noun Informal* drinking spree.

bop *verb* **bopping, bopped** *Informal* dance to pop music.

borage *noun* Mediterranean plant with star-shaped blue flowers.

borax *noun* white mineral used in making glass. **boracic** *adjective*

Bordeaux *noun* red or white wine from SW France.

border ❶ *noun* **1** dividing line between political or geographical regions. **2** band around or along the edge of something. ◆ *verb* **3** provide with a border. **4** be adjacent to. **5** be nearly the same as, e.g. *resentment that borders on hatred.*

bore¹ ❶ *verb* **1** make (a hole) with a drill etc. ◆ *noun* **2** hole or tunnel drilled in search of oil, minerals, etc. **3** (diameter of) the hollow of a gun barrel.

bore² ❶ *verb* **1** make weary by being dull or repetitious. ◆ *noun* **2** dull or repetitious person or thing. **bored** *adjective* **boredom** *noun*

bore³ *noun* high wave in a narrow estuary, caused by the tide.

bore⁴ *verb* past tense of BEAR¹.

boree [baw-ree] *noun Aust* same as MYALL.

boric *adjective* of or containing boron. **boric acid** white soluble solid used as a mild antiseptic.

born *verb* **1** a past participle of BEAR¹. ◆ *adjective* **2** possessing certain qualities from birth, e.g. *a born musician.*

born-again *adjective* **1** having experienced conversion, esp. to evangelical Christianity. **2** showing the enthusiasm of someone newly converted to a cause, e.g. *a born-again romantic.*

borne *verb* a past participle of BEAR¹.

improvement, increase, jump, upsurge OPPOSITE **decline** upswing, upturn

boon¹ *noun* =**benefit**, advantage, blessing, favour, gift, godsend, manna from heaven, windfall

boon² *adjective* =**intimate**, close, special

boorish *adjective* =**loutish**, churlish, coarse, crude, oafish, uncivilized, uncouth, vulgar OPPOSITE **refined**

boost *noun* **1** =**help**, encouragement, gee-up, praise, promotion OPPOSITE **knock**. **3** =**rise**, addition, expansion, improvement, increase, increment, jump OPPOSITE **fall** ◆*verb* **4** =**promote**, advertise, encourage, foster, further, gee up, hype, improve, plug (*inf*), praise **5** =**increase**, add to, amplify, develop, enlarge, expand, heighten, raise OPPOSITE **cut**

boot¹ *verb Inf* **5** =**kick**, drive, drop-kick, knock, punt, put the boot in(to) (*sl*), shove

booty *noun* =**plunder**, gains, haul, loot, prey,

spoils, swag (*sl*), takings, winnings

border *noun* **1** =**frontier**, borderline, boundary, line, march **2** =**edge**, bounds, brink, limits, margin, rim, verge ◆*verb* **3** =**edge**, bind, decorate, fringe, hem, rim, trim

bore¹ *verb* **1** =**drill**, burrow, gouge out, mine, penetrate, perforate, pierce, sink, tunnel

bore² *verb* **1** =**tire**, be tedious, fatigue, jade, pall on, send to sleep, wear out, weary OPPOSITE **interest** ◆*noun* **2** =**nuisance**, anorak (*inf*), pain (*inf*), yawn (*inf*)

bored *adjective* =**fed up**, listless, tired, uninterested, wearied

boredom *noun* =**tedium**, apathy, ennui, flatness, monotony, sameness, tediousness, weariness, world-weariness OPPOSITE **excitement**

boring *adjective* =**uninteresting**, dull, flat, humdrum, mind-numbing, monotonous, tedious, tiresome

boron *noun Chem* element used in hardening steel.

boronia *noun* Australian aromatic flowering shrub.

borough *noun* town or district with its own council.

borrow ⊕ *verb* **1** obtain (something) temporarily. **2** adopt (ideas etc.) from another source. **borrower** *noun*

borscht, borsch *noun* Russian soup based on beetroot.

borstal *noun* (formerly) prison for young criminals.

borzoi *noun* tall dog with a long silky coat.

bosh *noun Informal* empty talk, nonsense.

Bosnian *noun, adjective* (person) from Bosnia.

bosom ⊕ *noun* **1** chest of a person, esp. the female breasts. ♦ *adjective* **2** very dear, e.g. *a bosom friend*.

boss¹ ⊕ *noun* **1** person in charge of or employing others. ♦ *verb* **2 boss around, about** be domineering towards. **bossy** *adjective* **bossier, bossiest**

boss² ⊕ *noun* raised knob or stud.

bosun *noun* officer responsible for the maintenance of a ship.

bot. **1** botanical. **2** botany.

botany *noun* study of plants. **botanical, botanic** *adjective* **botanist** *noun*

botch ⊕ *verb* **1** spoil through clumsiness. **2** repair badly. ♦ *noun* **3** (also **botch-up**) badly done piece of work or repair.

both *adjective, pronoun* two considered together.

bother ⊕ *verb* **1** take the time or trouble. **2** give annoyance or trouble to. **3** pester. ♦ *noun* **4** trouble, fuss, or difficulty. ♦ *interjection* **5** *Chiefly Brit* exclamation of slight annoyance. **bothersome** *adjective*

bothy *noun, pl* **-ies** *Chiefly Scot* hut used for temporary shelter.

bottle ⊕ *noun* **1** container for holding liquids. **2** *Slang* courage. ♦ *verb* **3** put in a bottle. **bottle bank** container into which people can throw glass bottles for recycling. **bottle-green** *adjective* dark green. **bottleneck** *noun* narrow stretch of road where traffic is held up. **bottle tree** Australian tree with a bottle-shaped swollen trunk. **bottle up** *verb* restrain (powerful emotion).

bottom ⊕ *noun* **1** lowest, deepest, or farthest removed part of a thing. **2** least important or successful position. **3** ground underneath a sea, lake, or river. **4** buttocks. ♦ *adjective* **5** lowest or last. **bottomless** *adjective* **bottom out** *verb* reach the lowest point and level out.

botulism *noun* severe food poisoning.

bouclé *noun* looped yarn giving a knobbly effect.

boudoir [boo-dwahr] *noun* woman's bedroom or private sitting room.

bouffant [boof-fong] *adjective* (of a hairstyle) having extra height through backcombing.

bougainvillea *noun* climbing plant with red or purple flowers.

bough *noun* large branch of a tree.

bought *verb* past of BUY.

─────────── THESAURUS ───────────

borrow *verb* **1** = **take on loan**, bludge (*Aust & NZ*), cadge, scrounge (*inf*), touch (someone) for (*sl*), use temporarily OPPOSITE **lend**. **2** = **steal**, adopt, copy, obtain, plagiarize, take, usurp

bosom *noun* **1** = **breast**, bust, chest ♦*adjective* **2** = **intimate**, boon, cherished, close, confidential, dear, very dear

boss¹ *noun* **1** = **head**, chief, director, employer, gaffer (*inf, chiefly Brit*), leader, manager, master, supervisor

boss² *noun* = **stud**, knob, point, protuberance, tip

boss around (also **about**) *verb* = **domineer**, bully, dominate, oppress, order, push around (*sl*)

bossy *adjective Inf* = **domineering**, arrogant, authoritarian, autocratic, dictatorial, hectoring, high-handed, imperious, overbearing, tyrannical

botch *verb* **1** = **spoil**, blunder, bungle, cock up (*Brit sl*), make a pig's ear of (*inf*), mar, mess up, screw up (*inf*) ♦*noun* **3** = **mess**, blunder, bungle,

cock-up (*Brit sl*), failure, hash, pig's ear (*inf*)

bother *verb* **3** = **trouble**, disturb, harass, hassle (*inf*), inconvenience, pester, plague, worry OPPOSITE **help** ♦*noun* **4** = **trouble**, difficulty, fuss, hassle (*inf*), inconvenience, irritation, nuisance, problem, worry OPPOSITE **help**

bottleneck *noun* = **hold-up**, block, blockage, congestion, impediment, jam, obstacle, obstruction, snarl-up (*inf, chiefly Brit*)

bottle up *verb* = **suppress**, check, contain, curb, keep back, restrict, shut in, trap

bottom *noun* **1** = **lowest part**, base, bed, depths, floor, foot, foundation, lower side, sole, underneath, underside OPPOSITE **top**. **4** = **buttocks**, backside, behind (*inf*), posterior, rear, rump, seat ♦*adjective* **5** = **lowest**, last OPPOSITE **higher**

bottomless *adjective* = **unlimited**, boundless, deep, fathomless, immeasurable, inexhaustible, infinite, unfathomable

LANGUAGE TIP

Be careful not to confuse the past forms *bought* (from *buy*) with *brought* (from *bring*).

B

bouillon [**boo**-yon] *noun* thin clear broth or stock.

boulder *noun* large rounded rock.

boulevard *noun* wide, usu. tree-lined, street.

bounce ❶ *verb* **1** (of a ball etc.) rebound from an impact. **2** *Slang* (of a cheque) be returned uncashed owing to a lack of funds in the account. ♦ *noun* **3** act of rebounding. **4** springiness. **5** *Informal* vitality or vigour. **bouncer** *noun* person employed at a disco etc. to remove unwanted people. **bouncing** *adjective* vigorous and robust. **bouncy** *adjective* **bouncier, bounciest**

bound¹ *verb* **1** past of BIND. ♦ *adjective* **2** destined or certain. **3** compelled or obliged.

bound² ❶ *verb* **1** move forwards by jumps. ♦ *noun* **2** jump upwards or forwards.

bound³ ❶ *verb* **1** limit or place restrictions on. **2** form a boundary of. ♦ *plural noun* **3** limit, e.g. *his ignorance knows no bounds.* **boundary** *noun*, *pl* **-aries** dividing line that indicates the farthest limit.

bound⁴ *adjective* going or intending to go towards, e.g. *homeward bound.*

bounder *noun Old-fashioned Brit slang* morally reprehensible person.

bounty ❶ *noun*, *pl* **-ties 1** generosity. **2** generous gift or reward. **bountiful, bounteous** *adjective*

bouquet ❶ *noun* **1** bunch of flowers. **2** aroma of wine. **bouquet garni** bunch of herbs tied together and used for flavouring soups etc.

bourbon [**bur**-bn] *noun* whiskey made from maize.

bourgeois ❶ [**boor**-zhwah] *adjective, noun Offens* middle-class (person). **bourgeoisie** *noun* middle classes.

bourn *noun* (in S Britain) stream.

Bourse [**boorss**] *noun* stock exchange, esp. of Paris.

bout ❶ *noun* **1** period of activity or illness. **2** boxing or wrestling match.

boutique *noun* small clothes shop.

bouzouki *noun* Greek stringed musical instrument.

bovine *adjective* **1** relating to cattle. **2** rather slow and stupid.

bow¹ ❶ [rhymes with **now**] *verb* **1** lower (one's head) or bend (one's knee or body) as a sign of respect or shame. **2** comply or accept. ♦ *noun* **3** movement made when bowing.

bow² [rhymes with **go**] *noun* **1** knot with two loops and loose ends. **2** weapon for shooting arrows. **3** something curved, bent, or arched. **4** long stick stretched with horsehair for playing stringed instruments. **bow-legged** *adjective* having legs that curve outwards at the knees. **bow window** curved bay window.

bow³ ❶ [rhymes with **now**] *noun* front end of a ship.

——————— T H E S A U R U S ———————

bounce *verb* **1** = **rebound**, bob, bound, jump, leap, recoil, ricochet, spring ♦*noun* **4** = **springiness**, elasticity, give, recoil, resilience, spring **5** *Inf* = **life**, dynamism, energy, go (*inf*), liveliness, vigour, vivacity, zip (*inf*)

bound¹ *adjective* **1** = **tied**, cased, fastened, fixed, pinioned, secured, tied up **2** = **certain**, destined, doomed, fated, sure **3** = **obliged**, beholden, committed, compelled, constrained, duty-bound, forced, pledged, required

bound² *verb* **1** = **leap**, bob, bounce, gambol, hurdle, jump, skip, spring, vault ♦*noun* **2** = **leap**, bob, bounce, gambol, hurdle, jump, skip, spring, vault

bound³ *verb* **1, 2** = **limit**, confine, demarcate, encircle, enclose, hem in, restrain, restrict, surround ♦*plural noun* **3** = **boundary**, border, confine, edge, extremity, limit, rim, verge

boundary *noun* = **limits**, barrier, border, borderline, brink, edge, extremity, fringe, frontier, margin

bountiful *adjective* = **generous**, liberal, magnanimous, open-handed, prodigal, unstinting

bounty *noun* **1** = **generosity**, benevolence, charity, kindness, largesse *or* largess, liberality, philanthropy **2** = **reward**, bonus, gift, present

bouquet *noun* **1** = **bunch of flowers**, buttonhole, corsage, garland, nosegay, posy, spray, wreath **2** = **aroma**, fragrance, perfume, redolence, savour, scent

bourgeois *adjective Offens* = **middle-class**, conventional, hidebound, materialistic, traditional

bout *noun* **1** = **period**, fit, spell, stint, term, turn **2** = **fight**, boxing match, competition, contest, encounter, engagement, match, set-to, struggle

bow¹ *verb* **1** = **bend**, bob, droop, genuflect, nod, stoop **2** = **give in**, acquiesce, comply, concede, defer, kowtow, relent, submit, succumb, surrender, yield ♦*noun* **3** = **bending**, bob, genuflexion, kowtow, nod, obeisance

bow³ *noun* = **prow**, beak, fore, head, stem

B

bowdlerize *verb* remove words regarded as indecent from (a play, novel, etc.).
bowdlerization *noun*
bowel *noun* **1** intestine, esp. the large intestine. ♦ *plural* **2** innermost part.
bower *noun* shady leafy shelter. **bowerbird** *noun* songbird of Australia and New Guinea, the males of which build bower-like display grounds to attract females.
bowie knife *noun* stout hunting knife.
bowl¹ ⊙ *noun* **1** round container with an open top. **2** hollow part of an object.
bowl² ⊙ *noun* **1** large heavy ball. ♦ *plural* **2** game played on smooth grass with wooden bowls. ♦ *verb* **3** roll smoothly along the ground. **4** *Cricket* send (a ball) towards the batsman. **5** *Cricket* dismiss (a batsman) by delivering a ball that breaks his wicket. **6** play bowls. **bowler** *noun* **bowling** *noun* game in which bowls are rolled at a group of pins.
bowler *noun* stiff felt hat with a rounded crown.
box¹ ⊙ *noun* **1** container with a firm flat base and sides. **2** separate compartment in a theatre, stable, etc. **3** place to which mail is sent and from which it is collected or redistributed, e.g. *a post-office box.* ♦ *verb* **4** put into a box. **the box** *Informal* television. **boxy** *adjective* **boxier, boxiest** squarish or chunky. **box in** *verb* prevent from moving freely. **box jellyfish** highly venomous jellyfish of Australian tropical waters with a cuboidal body. **box junction** road junction marked with yellow lines which may only be entered if the exit is clear. **box lacrosse** *Canad* lacrosse played indoors. **box office** place where theatre or cinema tickets are sold. **box pleat** flat double pleat.
box² ⊙ *verb* **1** fight (an opponent) in a boxing match. **2** hit (a person's ears) with the fist.
boxer *noun* **1** person who participates in the sport of boxing. **2** medium-sized dog with smooth hair and a short nose. **boxer shorts,**

boxers *plural noun* men's underpants shaped like shorts but with a front opening. **boxing** *noun* sport of fighting with the fists.
box³ *noun* **1** evergreen tree with shiny leaves. **2** eucalyptus with similar timber and foliage, and with rough bark.
Boxing Day *noun* first weekday after Christmas.
boy ⊙ *noun* male child. **boyish** *adjective* **boyhood** *noun* **boyfriend** *noun* male friend with whom a person is romantically or sexually involved.
boycott ⊙ *verb* **1** refuse to deal with (an organization or country). ♦ *noun* **2** instance of boycotting.

> **SPELLING TIP**
>
> The word **boycott** has two *ts*, whether or not it has an ending such as in **boycotting**.

BP blood pressure.
Br *Chem* bromine.
bra *noun* woman's undergarment for supporting the breasts.
braaivlies, braai *S Afr noun* **1** grill on which food is cooked over hot charcoal, usu. outdoors. ♦ *verb* **2** cook (food) in this way.
brace ⊙ *noun* **1** object fastened to something to straighten or support it. **2** pair, esp. of game birds. ♦ *plural* **3** straps worn over the shoulders to hold up trousers. ♦ *verb* **4** steady or prepare (oneself) for something unpleasant. **5** strengthen or fit with a brace. **bracing** *adjective* refreshing and invigorating.
bracelet *noun* ornamental chain or band for the wrist.
bracken *noun* large fern.
bracket *noun* **1** pair of characters used to enclose a section of writing. **2** group falling within certain defined limits. **3** support fixed to

———————————— T H E S A U R U S ————————————

bowels *plural noun* **1** = **guts**, entrails, innards (*inf*), insides (*inf*), intestines, viscera, vitals **2** = **depths**, belly, core, deep, hold, inside, interior
bowl¹ *noun* **1** = **basin**, dish, vessel
bowl² *verb* **4** *Cricket* = **throw**, fling, hurl, pitch
box¹ *noun* **1** = **container**, carton, case, casket, chest, pack, package, receptacle, trunk ♦*verb* **4** = **pack**, package, wrap
box² *verb* **1** = **fight**, exchange blows, spar
boxer *noun* **1** = **fighter**, prizefighter, pugilist, sparring partner
boy *noun* = **lad**, fellow, junior, schoolboy, stripling, youngster, youth

boycott *verb* **1** = **embargo**, ban, bar, black, exclude, outlaw, prohibit, refuse, reject
OPPOSITE> **support**
boyfriend *noun* = **sweetheart**, admirer, beau, date, lover, man, suitor
boyish *adjective* = **youthful**, adolescent, childish, immature, juvenile, puerile, young
brace *noun* **1** = **support**, bolster, bracket, buttress, prop, reinforcement, stay, strut, truss ♦*verb* **5** = **support**, bolster, buttress, fortify, reinforce, steady, strengthen
bracing *adjective* = **refreshing**, brisk, crisp, exhilarating, fresh, invigorating, stimulating

a wall. ◆ *verb* **-eting, -eted 4** put in brackets. **5** class together.

brackish *adjective* (of water) slightly salty.

bract *noun* leaf at the base of a flower.

bradawl *noun* small boring tool.

brae *noun Scot* hill or slope.

brag ❶ *verb* **bragging, bragged 1** speak arrogantly and boastfully. ◆ *noun* **2** boastful talk or behaviour. **3** card game similar to poker.

braggart *noun* person who boasts loudly.

Brahma *noun* Hindu god, the Creator.

Brahman, Brahmin *noun* member of the highest Hindu caste.

braid ❶ *verb* **1** interweave (hair, thread, etc.). ◆ *noun* **2** length of hair etc. that has been braided. **3** narrow ornamental tape of woven silk etc.

Braille *noun* system of writing for the blind, consisting of raised dots interpreted by touch.

brain ❶ *noun* **1** soft mass of nervous tissue in the head. **2** intellectual ability. ◆ *verb* **3** hit (someone) hard on the head. **brainless** *adjective* stupid. **brainy** *adjective* **brainier, brainiest** *Informal* clever. **brainchild** *noun* idea produced by creative thought. **braindead** *adjective* **1** having suffered irreversible stoppage of breathing due to brain damage. **2** *Informal* not using or showing intelligence. **brainstorm** *noun* sudden mental aberration. **brain up** *verb* make (something) more intellectually demanding or sophisticated. **brainwash** *verb* cause (a person) to alter his or her beliefs, esp. by methods based on isolation, sleeplessness, etc. **brainwave** *noun* sudden idea.

braise *verb* cook slowly in a covered pan with a little liquid.

brake¹ ❶ *noun* **1** device for slowing or stopping a vehicle. ◆ *verb* **2** slow down or stop by using a brake. **brake horsepower** rate at which an engine does work. **brake light** red light at the rear of a motor vehicle that comes on when the brakes are applied.

brake² *noun* area of dense undergrowth.

bramble *noun* **1** prickly shrub that produces blackberries. **2** *Scot* blackberry.

bran *noun* husks of cereal grain.

branch ❶ *noun* **1** secondary stem of a tree. **2** offshoot or subsidiary part of something larger or more complex. ◆ *verb* **3** (of stems, roots, etc.) divide, then develop in different directions. **branch out** *verb* expand one's interests.

brand ❶ *noun* **1** particular product. **2** particular kind or variety. **3** identifying mark burnt onto the skin of an animal. **4** *Lit* burning piece of wood. ◆ *verb* **5** mark with a brand. **6** denounce as being, e.g. *he was branded a fascist*. **brand-new** *adjective* absolutely new.

brandish ❶ *verb* wave (a weapon etc.) in a threatening way.

brandy *noun, pl* **-dies** alcoholic spirit distilled from wine. **brandy snap** tube-shaped crisp sweet biscuit.

brash ❶ *adjective* offensively loud, showy, or self-confident. **brashness** *noun*

brass *noun* **1** alloy of copper and zinc. **2** family of wind instruments made of brass. **3** engraved brass memorial tablet in a church. **4** *N English dialect* money. **5** *Informal* bold self-confidence. **brassy** *adjective* **brassier, brassiest 1** brazen or flashy. **2** like brass, esp. in colour. **brass hat** *Informal* top-ranking military officer.

brasserie *noun* restaurant serving drinks and cheap meals.

───────── T H E S A U R U S ─────────

OPPOSITE **tiring**

brag *verb* **1** = **boast**, blow one's own trumpet, bluster, crow, skite (*Aust & NZ*), swagger, talk big (*sl*), vaunt

braggart *noun* = **boaster**, bigmouth (*sl*), bragger, show-off (*inf*)

braid *verb* **1** = **interweave**, entwine, interlace, intertwine, lace, plait, twine, weave

brain *noun* **2** = **intelligence**, intellect, sense, understanding

brainless *adjective* = **stupid**, foolish, idiotic, inane, mindless, senseless, thoughtless, witless

brainwave *noun* = **idea**, bright idea, stroke of genius, thought

brainy *adjective Inf* = **intelligent**, bright, brilliant, clever, smart

brake¹ *noun* **1** = **control**, check, constraint, curb, rein, restraint ◆*verb* **2** = **slow**, check,

decelerate, halt, moderate, reduce speed, slacken, stop

branch *noun* **1** = **bough**, arm, limb, offshoot, shoot, spray, sprig **2** = **division**, chapter, department, office, part, section, subdivision, subsection, wing

brand *noun* **1** = **label**, emblem, hallmark, logo, mark, marker, sign, stamp, symbol, trademark **2** = **kind**, cast, class, grade, make, quality, sort, species, type, variety ◆*verb* **5** = **mark**, burn, burn in, label, scar, stamp **6** = **stigmatize**, censure, denounce, discredit, disgrace, expose, mark

brandish *verb* = **wave**, display, exhibit, flaunt, flourish, parade, raise, shake, swing, wield

brash *adjective* = **bold**, brazen, cocky, impertinent, impudent, insolent, pushy (*inf*), rude OPPOSITE **timid**

B

brassica *noun* any plant of the cabbage and turnip family.

brassiere *noun* bra.

brat *noun* unruly child.

bravado ❶ *noun* showy display of self-confidence.

brave ❶ *adjective* **1** having or showing courage, resolution, and daring. **2** splendid. ◆ *noun* **3** Native American warrior. ◆ *verb* **4** confront with resolution or courage. **bravery** *noun*

bravo *interjection* well done!

bravura *noun* **1** display of boldness or daring. **2** *Music* brilliance of execution.

brawl ❶ *noun* **1** noisy fight. ◆ *verb* **2** fight noisily.

brawn ❶ *noun* **1** physical strength. **2** pressed meat from the head of a pig or calf. **brawny** *adjective*

bray *verb* **1** (of a donkey) utter its loud harsh sound. ◆ *noun* **2** donkey's loud harsh sound.

braze *verb* join (two metal surfaces) with brass.

brazen ❶ *adjective* **1** shameless and bold. ◆ *verb* **2 brazen it out** overcome a difficult situation boldly or shamelessly. **brazenly** *adverb*

brazier [**bray**-zee-er] *noun* portable container for burning charcoal or coal.

brazil nut *noun* large three-sided nut of a tropical American tree.

breach ❶ *noun* **1** breaking of a promise, obligation, etc. **2** serious quarrel or separation. **3** gap or break. ◆ *verb* **4** break (a promise, law, etc.). **5** make a gap in.

bread ❶ *noun* **1** food made by baking a mixture of flour and water or milk. **2** *Slang* money. **breadwinner** *noun* person whose

earnings support a family.

breadline *noun* **on the breadline** living at subsistence level.

breadth ❶ *noun* **1** extent of something from side to side. **2** lack of restriction, esp. of viewpoint or interest.

break ❶ *verb* **breaking, broke, broken 1** separate or become separated into two or more pieces. **2** damage or become damaged so as to be inoperative. **3** fail to observe (an agreement etc.). **4** disclose or be disclosed, e.g. *he broke the news*. **5** bring or come to an end, e.g. *the good weather broke at last*. **6** weaken or be weakened, as in spirit. **7** cut through or penetrate, e.g. *silence broken by shouts*. **8** improve on or surpass, e.g. *break a record*. **9** accustom (a horse) to being ridden. **10** (of the male voice) become permanently deeper at puberty. ◆ *noun* **11** act or result of breaking. **12** gap or interruption in continuity. **13** sudden rush, esp. to escape. **14** *Informal* fortunate opportunity. **15** *Billiards, snooker* series of successful shots during one turn. **break even** make neither a profit nor a loss. **breakable** *adjective* **breakage** *noun* **breaker** *noun* large wave. **breakaway** *adjective, noun* **1** (consisting of) a dissenting group who have left a larger unit. ◆ *noun* **2** *Aust.* stampede of cattle, esp. at the smell of water. **break down** *verb* **1** cease to function. **2** yield to strong emotion. **3** decompose or separate into component parts. **breakdown** *noun* **1** act or instance of breaking down. **2** nervous breakdown. **3** separation of something into its component parts. **break-in** *noun* illegal entering of a building, esp. by thieves. **break into** *verb* start doing, esp. suddenly, e.g. *she broke into song*. **breakneck** *adjective* fast and dangerous. **break off** *verb* **1**

———— THESAURUS ————

bravado *noun* =**swagger**, bluster, boastfulness, boasting, bombast, swashbuckling, vaunting

brave *adjective* **1** =**courageous**, bold, daring, fearless, heroic, intrepid, plucky, resolute, valiant OPPOSITE timid ◆*verb* **4** =**confront**, defy, endure, face, stand up to, suffer, tackle, withstand OPPOSITE **give in to**

bravery *noun* **1** =**courage**, boldness, daring, fearlessness, fortitude, heroism, intrepidity, mettle, pluck, spirit, valour OPPOSITE **cowardice**

brawl *noun* **1** =**fight**, affray, altercation, clash, dispute, fracas, fray, mêlée, punch-up (*inf*), rumpus, scuffle, skirmish ◆*verb* **2** =**fight**, scrap (*inf*), scuffle, tussle, wrestle

brawn *noun* **1** =**muscle**, beef (*inf*), might,

muscles, power, strength, vigour

brawny *adjective* **1** =**muscular**, beefy (*inf*), hefty (*inf*), lusty, powerful, strapping, strong, sturdy, well-built

brazen *adjective* **1** =**bold**, audacious, barefaced, brash, defiant, impudent, insolent, shameless, unabashed, unashamed OPPOSITE **modest**

breach *noun* **1** =**nonobservance**, contravention, infraction, infringement, noncompliance, transgression, trespass, violation OPPOSITE **compliance**. **3** =**crack**, cleft, fissure, gap, opening, rift, rupture, split

bread *noun* **2** *Sl* =**money**, cash, dough (*sl*), lolly (*Aust & NZ sl*)

breadth *noun* **1** =**width**, broadness, latitude, span, spread, wideness **2** =**extent**, compass,

sever or detach. **2** end (a relationship etc.).
break out *verb* begin or arise suddenly.
breakthrough *noun* important development or
discovery. **break up** *verb* **1** (cause to) separate.
2 come to an end. **3** (of a school) close for the
holidays. **breakwater** *noun* wall that extends
into the sea to protect a harbour or beach from
the force of waves.
breakfast *verb, noun* (eat) the first meal of
the day.
bream *noun* freshwater silvery fish.
breast ⊙ *noun* **1** either of the two soft fleshy
milk-secreting glands on a woman's chest. **2**
chest. **3** source of human emotions. ♦ *verb* **4** *Lit*
reach the summit of. **breastbone** *noun* long
flat bone in the front of the body, to which
most of the ribs are attached. **breast-feed** *verb*
feed (a baby) with milk from the breast.
breaststroke *noun* swimming stroke in which
the arms are extended in front of the head and
swept back on either side.
breath ⊙ *noun* **1** taking in and letting out of
air during breathing. **2** air taken in and let out
during breathing. **3** slight gust of air.
breathless *adjective* **breathtaking** *adjective*
causing awe or excitement. **breathe** *verb* **1**

take in oxygen and give out carbon dioxide. **2**
be alive. **3** whisper. **4** impart or instil, e.g. *the
move breathed new life into his career.* **breather**
noun Informal short rest. **breathing** *noun*
Breathalyser *noun* ® device for estimating
the amount of alcohol in the breath.
breathalyse *verb*
bred *verb* past of BREED.
breech *noun* **1** buttocks. **2** part of a firearm
behind the barrel. **breech birth, breech
delivery** birth of a baby with the feet or
buttocks appearing first.
breeches *plural noun* trousers extending to
just below the knee.
breed ⊙ *verb* **breeding, bred 1** produce new
or improved strains of (domestic animals or
plants). **2** bear (offspring). **3** bring up, e.g. *he
was born and bred in Hull.* **4** produce or be
produced, e.g. *breed trouble.* ♦ *noun* **5** group of
animals etc. within a species that have certain
clearly defined characteristics. **6** kind or sort.
breeder *noun* **breeder reactor** nuclear
reactor that produces more fissionable material
than it uses. **breeding** *noun* result of good
upbringing or training.
breeze ⊙ *noun* **1** gentle wind. ♦ *verb* **2** move

——————— THESAURUS ———————

expanse, range, scale, scope
break *verb* **1** = **separate**, burst, crack, destroy,
disintegrate, fracture, fragment, shatter, smash,
snap, split, tear OPPOSITE unite. **3** = **disobey**,
breach, contravene, disregard, infringe, renege
on, transgress, violate OPPOSITE follow. **4**
= **reveal**, announce, disclose, divulge, impart,
inform, let out, make public, proclaim, tell **5**
= **stop**, abandon, cut, discontinue, give up,
interrupt, pause, rest, suspend **6** = **weaken**,
demoralize, dispirit, subdue, tame, undermine **8**
= **beat**, better, exceed, excel, go beyond,
outdo, outstrip, surpass, top ♦ *noun* **11**
= **division**, crack, fissure, fracture, gap, hole,
opening, split, tear **12** = **rest**, breather (*inf*),
hiatus, interlude, intermission, interruption,
interval, let-up (*inf*), lull, pause, respite **14** *Inf*
= **stroke of luck**, advantage, chance, fortune,
opening, opportunity
breakable *adjective* **1** = **fragile**, brittle,
crumbly, delicate, flimsy, frail, frangible, friable
breakdown *noun* **1** = **collapse**, disintegration,
disruption, failure, mishap, stoppage
break down *verb* **1** = **collapse**, come
unstuck, fail, seize up, stop, stop working **2**
= **be overcome**, crack up (*inf*), go to pieces
break-in *noun* = **burglary**, breaking and
entering, robbery
break off *verb* **1** = **detach**, divide, part, pull

off, separate, sever, snap off, splinter **2** = **stop**,
cease, desist, discontinue, end, finish, halt, pull
the plug on, suspend, terminate
break out *verb* = **begin**, appear, arise,
commence, emerge, happen, occur, set in,
spring up, start
breakthrough *noun* = **development**,
advance, discovery, find, invention, leap,
progress, quantum leap, step forward
break up *verb* **1** = **separate**, dissolve, divide,
divorce, part, scatter, sever, split **2** = **stop**,
adjourn, disband, dismantle, end, suspend,
terminate
breast *noun* **1** = **bosom**, bust, chest, front,
teat, udder
breath *noun* **1** = **respiration**, breathing,
exhalation, gasp, gulp, inhalation, pant, wheeze
breathe *verb* **1** = **inhale and exhale**, draw in,
gasp, gulp, pant, puff, respire, wheeze **3**
= **whisper**, murmur, sigh
breather *noun Inf* = **rest**, break, breathing
space, halt, pause, recess, respite
breathless *adjective* **1** = **out of breath**,
gasping, gulping, panting, short-winded, spent,
wheezing
breathtaking *adjective* = **amazing**,
astonishing, awe-inspiring, exciting, impressive,
magnificent, sensational, stunning (*inf*), thrilling
breed *verb* **1** = **cultivate**, develop **2**

B

quickly or casually. **breezy** *adjective* **breezier, breeziest** 1 windy. 2 casual or carefree.
breeze block *noun* light building brick made of ashes bonded by cement.
Bren gun *noun* gas-operated light machine gun.
brent *noun* small goose with a dark grey plumage.
brethren *plural noun Old-fashioned* (used in religious contexts) brothers.
Breton *adjective* 1 of Brittany. ◆ *noun* 2 person from Brittany. 3 language of Brittany.
breviary *noun, pl* **-aries** book of prayers to be recited daily by a Roman Catholic priest.
brevity ① *noun* shortness.
brew ① *verb* 1 make (beer etc.) by steeping, boiling, and fermentation. 2 prepare (a drink) by infusing. 3 be about to happen or forming, e.g. *trouble was brewing.* ◆ *noun* 4 beverage produced by brewing. **brewer** *noun* **brewery** *noun, pl* **-eries** place where beer etc. is brewed.
briar¹, brier *noun* 1 European shrub with a hard woody root. 2 tobacco pipe made from this root.
briar² *noun* same as BRIER¹.
bribe ① *verb* 1 offer or give something to someone to gain favour, influence, etc. ◆ *noun* 2 something given or offered as a bribe. **bribery** *noun*
bric-a-brac ① *noun* miscellaneous small ornamental objects.
brick *noun* 1 (rectangular block of) baked clay

used in building. ◆ *verb* 2 (foll. by *up* or *over*) build, enclose, or fill with bricks. **brickbat** *noun* blunt criticism. **bricklayer** *noun* person who builds with bricks.
bride ① *noun* woman who has just been or is about to be married. **bridal** *adjective*
bridegroom *noun* man who has just been or is about to be married. **bridesmaid** *noun* girl who attends a bride at her wedding.
bridge¹ ① *noun* 1 structure for crossing a river etc. 2 platform from which a ship is steered or controlled. 3 upper part of the nose. 4 dental plate with artificial teeth that is secured to natural teeth. 5 piece of wood supporting the strings of a violin etc. ◆ *verb* 6 build a bridge over (something). 7 connect or reduce the distance between. **bridgehead** *noun* fortified position at the end of a bridge nearest the enemy. **bridging loan** loan made to cover the period between two transactions.
bridge² *noun* card game based on whist, played between two pairs.
bridle ① *noun* 1 headgear for controlling a horse. 2 something that curbs or restrains. ◆ *verb* 3 show anger or indignation. 4 put a bridle on (a horse). **bridle path** path suitable for riding horses.
Brie [bree] *noun* soft creamy white cheese.
brief ① *adjective* 1 short in duration. 2 concise. ◆ *noun* 3 condensed statement or written synopsis. 4 (also **briefing**) set of instructions. ◆ *plural* 5 men's or women's underpants. ◆ *verb* 6

———————————— THESAURUS ————————————

= **reproduce**, bear, bring forth, hatch, multiply, procreate, produce, propagate 3 = **bring up**, nourish, nurture, raise, rear 4 = **produce**, arouse, bring about, cause, create, generate, give rise to, stir up ◆*noun* 5 = **variety**, pedigree, race, species, stock, strain, type 6 = **kind**, brand, sort, stamp, type, variety
breeding *noun* = **refinement**, cultivation, culture, manners, polish, sophistication, urbanity
breeze *noun* 1 = **light wind**, air, breath of wind, current of air, draught, gust, waft, zephyr ◆*verb* 2 = **move briskly**, flit, glide, hurry, pass, sail, sweep
breezy *adjective* 1 = **windy**, airy, blowy, blustery, fresh, gusty, squally OPPOSITE calm. 2 = **carefree**, blithe, casual, easy-going, free and easy, jaunty, light-hearted, lively, sprightly OPPOSITE serious
brevity *noun* = **shortness**, briefness, conciseness, crispness, curtness, economy, impermanence, pithiness, succinctness, terseness, transience, transitoriness OPPOSITE

wordiness
brew *verb* 1, 2 = **make** (*beer*), boil, ferment, infuse (*tea*), soak, steep, stew 3 = **develop**, foment, form, gather, start, stir up ◆*noun* 4 = **drink**, beverage, blend, concoction, infusion, liquor, mixture, preparation
bribe *verb* 1 = **buy off**, corrupt, grease the palm *or* hand of (*sl*), pay off (*inf*), reward, suborn ◆*noun* 2 = **inducement**, allurement, backhander (*sl*), enticement, kickback (*US*), pay-off (*inf*), sweetener (*sl*)
bribery *noun* = **buying off**, corruption, inducement, palm-greasing (*sl*), payola (*inf*)
bric-a-brac *noun* = **knick-knacks**, baubles, curios, ornaments, trinkets
bridal *adjective* = **matrimonial**, conjugal, connubial, marital, marriage, nuptial, wedding
bridge¹ *noun* 1 = **arch**, flyover, overpass, span, viaduct ◆*verb* 7 = **connect**, join, link, span OPPOSITE separate
bridle *noun* 2 = **curb**, check, control, rein, restraint ◆*verb* 3 = **get angry**, be indignant, bristle, draw (oneself) up, get one's back up,

give information and instructions to (a person).
briefly *adverb* **briefcase** *noun* small flat case
for carrying papers, books, etc.
brier¹, briar *noun* wild rose with long thorny
stems.
brier² *noun* same as BRIAR¹.
brig *noun* two-masted square-rigged ship.
Brig. Brigadier.
brigade 𝟎 *noun* **1** army unit smaller than a
division. **2** group of people organized for a
certain task. **brigadier** *noun* high-ranking army
officer.
brigand 𝟎 *noun* bandit.
brigantine *noun* two-masted sailing ship.
bright 𝟎 *adjective* **1** emitting or reflecting
much light. **2** (of colours) intense. **3** full of
promise. **4** lively or cheerful. **5** clever. **brightly**
adverb **brightness** *noun* **brighten** *verb*
brill *noun* edible European flatfish.
brilliant 𝟎 *adjective* **1** shining with light. **2** (of
a colour) vivid. **3** splendid. **4** extremely clever. ◆
noun **5** diamond cut so as to increase its

sparkle. **brilliance, brilliancy** *noun*
brilliantine *noun* perfumed hair oil.
brim 𝟎 *noun* **1** upper rim of a cup etc. **2**
projecting edge of a hat. ◆ *verb* **brimming,
brimmed 3** be full to the brim.
brimstone *noun* *Obs* sulphur.
brindled *adjective* brown or grey streaked
with a darker colour.
brine *noun* salt water. **briny** *adjective* very
salty. **the briny** *Informal* the sea.
bring 𝟎 *verb* **bringing, brought 1** carry,
convey, or take to a designated place or
person. **2** cause to happen. **3** *Law* put forward
(charges) officially. **bring about** *verb* cause to
happen. **bring off** *verb* succeed in achieving.
bring out *verb* **1** publish or have (a book)
published. **2** reveal or cause to be seen. **bring
up** *verb* **1** rear (a child). **2** mention. **3** vomit
(food).
brinjal *noun* *S Afr* dark purple tropical fruit,
cooked and eaten as a vegetable.
brink 𝟎 *noun* edge of a steep place. **on the**

—————————— THESAURUS ——————————

raise one's hackles, rear up
brief *adjective* **1 = short**, ephemeral, fleeting,
momentary, quick, short-lived, swift, transitory
OPPOSITE **long** ◆*noun* **3 = summary**,
abridgment, abstract, digest, epitome, outline,
précis, sketch, synopsis **4 = instructions**,
conference, directions, guidance, information,
preparation, priming, rundown ◆*verb* **6
= inform**, advise, explain, fill in (*inf*), instruct,
keep posted, prepare, prime, put (someone) in
the picture (*inf*)
briefly *adverb* **= shortly**, concisely, hastily,
hurriedly, in a nutshell, in brief, momentarily,
quickly
brigade *noun* **2 = group**, band, company,
corps, force, outfit, squad, team, troop, unit
brigand *noun* **= bandit**, desperado,
freebooter, gangster, highwayman, marauder,
outlaw, plunderer, robber
bright *adjective* **1, 2 = shining**, brilliant,
dazzling, gleaming, glowing, luminous,
lustrous, radiant, shimmering, vivid OPPOSITE
dark. 5 = intelligent, astute, aware, clever,
inventive, quick-witted, sharp, smart, wide-
awake OPPOSITE **stupid**
brighten *verb* **1 = light up**, gleam, glow,
illuminate, lighten, make brighter, shine
OPPOSITE **dim**
brightness *noun* **1, 2 = shine**, brilliance,
glare, incandescence, intensity, light,
luminosity, radiance, vividness OPPOSITE
dullness. 5 = intelligence, acuity, cleverness,
quickness, sharpness, smartness

brilliance, brilliancy *noun* **1, 2
= brightness**, dazzle, intensity, luminosity,
lustre, radiance, sparkle, vividness OPPOSITE
darkness. 3 = splendour, éclat, glamour,
grandeur, illustriousness, magnificence **4
= cleverness**, distinction, excellence, genius,
greatness, inventiveness, talent, wisdom
OPPOSITE **stupidity**
brilliant *adjective* **1, 2 = shining**, bright,
dazzling, glittering, intense, luminous, radiant,
sparkling, vivid OPPOSITE **dark. 3 = splendid**,
celebrated, famous, glorious, illustrious,
magnificent, notable, outstanding, superb **4
= intelligent**, clever, expert, gifted, intellectual,
inventive, masterly, penetrating, profound,
talented OPPOSITE **stupid**
brim *noun* **1 = rim**, border, brink, edge, lip,
margin, skirt, verge ◆*verb* **3 = be full**, fill, fill up,
hold no more, overflow, run over, spill, well
over
bring *verb* **1 = take**, bear, carry, conduct,
convey, deliver, escort, fetch, guide, lead,
transfer, transport **2 = cause**, contribute to,
create, effect, inflict, occasion, produce, result
in, wreak
bring about *verb* **= cause**, accomplish,
achieve, create, effect, generate, give rise to,
make happen, produce
bring off *verb* **= accomplish**, achieve, carry
off, execute, perform, pull off, succeed
bring up *verb* **1 = rear**, breed, develop,
educate, form, nurture, raise, support, teach,
train **2 = mention**, allude to, broach, introduce,

B

brink of very near. **brinkmanship** noun
pressing of a dangerous situation to the limit of
safety in order to win an advantage.
briquette noun block of compressed coal
dust.
brisk ❶ adjective **1** lively and quick. **2**
invigorating or sharp, e.g. a brisk breeze. **3**
practical and businesslike. **briskly** adverb
brisket noun beef from the breast of a cow.
bristle ❶ noun **1** short stiff hair. ◆ verb **2**
(cause to) stand up like bristles. **3** show anger.
bristly adjective **bristlier, bristliest**
Brit noun Informal British person.
Brit. 1 Britain. **2** British.
Britannia noun female warrior personifying
Great Britain.
Britannic adjective of Britain, esp. in Her
Britannic Majesty.
British adjective **1** of Great Britain or the
British Commonwealth. ◆ plural noun **2** people
of Great Britain.
Briton noun native or inhabitant of Britain.
brittle ❶ adjective hard but easily broken.
brittleness noun
broach ❶ verb **1** introduce (a topic) for
discussion. **2** open (a bottle or barrel).
broad ❶ adjective **1** having great breadth or
width. **2** not detailed. **3** extensive, e.g. broad
support. **4** obvious, e.g. broad hints. **5** strongly
marked, e.g. a broad Bristol accent. ◆ noun **6**
Slang chiefly US woman. **broadly** adverb
broaden verb **broadband** noun
telecommunication transmission technique

using a wide range of frequencies. **broad bean**
thick flat edible bean. **broadcast** noun
programme or announcement on radio or
television. **broad-leaved** adjective (of trees)
having broad rather than needle-shaped leaves.
broad-minded adjective tolerant. **broadsheet**
noun newspaper in a large format. **broadside**
noun **1** strong verbal or written attack. **2** Naval
firing of all the guns on one side of a ship at
once.
B-road noun secondary road in Britain.
broadcast ❶ noun **1** programme or
announcement on radio or television. ◆ verb **2**
transmit (a programme or announcement) on
radio or television. **3** make widely known. **4**
scatter (seed etc.). **broadcaster** noun
broadcasting noun
brocade noun rich fabric woven with a raised
design.
broccoli noun type of cabbage with greenish
flower heads.

SPELLING TIP

You might expect a word that
sounds like **broccoli** to have
two ls at the end, but it has
only one because it comes from
Italian and ends with an i.

---

brochure ❶ noun booklet that contains
information about a product or service.
broderie anglaise noun open embroidery on

———— T H E S A U R U S ————

move, propose, put forward, raise
brink noun =**edge**, border, boundary, brim,
fringe, frontier, limit, lip, margin, rim, skirt,
threshold, verge
brisk adjective **1** = **lively**, active, bustling, busy,
energetic, quick, sprightly, spry, vigorous
OPPOSITE **slow**
briskly adverb **1** = **quickly**, actively, apace,
energetically, promptly, rapidly, readily, smartly
bristle noun **1** = **hair**, barb, prickle, spine,
stubble, thorn, whisker ◆verb **2** = **stand up**,
rise, stand on end **3** = **be angry**, bridle, flare
up, rage, see red, seethe
bristly adjective = **hairy**, prickly, rough, stubbly
brittle adjective = **fragile**, breakable, crisp,
crumbling, crumbly, delicate, frail, frangible,
friable OPPOSITE **tough**
broach verb **1** = **bring up**, introduce, mention,
open up, propose, raise the subject, speak of,
suggest, talk of, touch on **2** = **open**, crack,
draw off, pierce, puncture, start, tap, uncork
broad adjective **1** = **wide**, ample, expansive,

extensive, generous, large, roomy, spacious,
vast, voluminous, widespread OPPOSITE
narrow. **3** = **general**, all-embracing,
comprehensive, encyclopedic, inclusive,
overarching, sweeping, wide, wide-ranging
broadcast noun **1** = **transmission**,
programme, show, telecast ◆verb **2** = **transmit**,
air, beam, cable, put on the air, radio, relay,
show, televise **3** = **make public**, advertise,
announce, circulate, proclaim, publish, report,
spread
broaden verb = **expand**, develop, enlarge,
extend, increase, spread, stretch, supplement,
swell, widen OPPOSITE restrict
broad-minded adjective = **tolerant**, free-
thinking, indulgent, liberal, open-minded,
permissive, unbiased, unbigoted, unprejudiced
OPPOSITE **narrow-minded**
broadside noun **1** = **attack**, assault, censure,
criticism, denunciation, diatribe, swipe **2** Naval
= **bombardment**
brochure noun = **booklet**, advertisement,

white cotton etc.
broekies [brook-eez] *plural noun S Afr informal* underpants.
brogue[1] *noun* sturdy walking shoe.
brogue[2] *noun* strong accent, esp. Irish.
broil *verb Aust, NZ, US & Canad* same as GRILL. **broiler** *noun* young tender chicken for roasting.
broke ⊕ *verb* **1** past tense of BREAK. ◆ *adjective* **2** *Informal* having no money.
broken ⊕ *verb* **1** past participle of BREAK. ◆ *adjective* **2** fractured or smashed. **3** (of the speech of a foreigner) noticeably imperfect, e.g. *broken English*. **brokenhearted** *adjective* overwhelmed by grief. **broken home** family where the parents are separated or divorced.
broker ⊕ *noun* agent who buys or sells goods, securities, etc. **brokerage** *noun* commission charged by a broker.
brolga *noun* large grey Australian crane with a trumpeting call (also **native companion**).
brolly *noun, pl* **-lies** *Informal* umbrella.
bromide *noun* **1** chemical compound used in medicine and photography. **2** boring or meaningless remark.
bromine *noun Chem* dark red liquid element that gives off a pungent vapour.
bronchus [bronk-uss] *noun, pl* **bronchi** [bronk-eye] either of the two branches of the windpipe. **bronchial** *adjective* **bronchitis** *noun* inflammation of the bronchi.
bronco *noun, pl* **-cos** (in the US) wild or partially tamed pony.
brontosaurus *noun* very large plant-eating four-footed dinosaur.
bronze ⊕ *noun* **1** alloy of copper and tin. **2**

statue, medal, etc. made of bronze. ◆ *adjective* **3** made of, or coloured like, bronze. ◆ *verb* **4** (esp. of the skin) make or become brown.
Bronze Age era when bronze tools and weapons were used. **bronze medal** medal awarded as third prize.
brooch *noun* ornament with a pin, worn fastened to clothes.
brood ⊕ *noun* **1** number of birds produced at one hatching. **2** all the children of a family. ◆ *verb* **3** (of a bird) sit on or hatch eggs. **4** think long and unhappily. **broody** *adjective* **1** moody and sullen. **2** (of a hen) wishing to hatch eggs. **3** *Informal* (of a woman) wishing to have a baby.
brook[1] **⊕** *noun* small stream.
brook[2] **⊕** *verb* bear or tolerate.
broom *noun* **1** long-handled sweeping brush. **2** yellow-flowered shrub. **broomstick** *noun* handle of a broom.
bros., Bros. brothers.
broth *noun* soup, usu. containing vegetables.
brothel *noun* house where men pay to have sex with prostitutes.
brother ⊕ *noun* **1** boy or man with the same parents as another person. **2** close friend or comrade. **3** member of a male religious order.
brotherly *adjective* **brotherhood** *noun* **1** fellowship. **2** association, such as a trade union.
brother-in-law *noun, pl* **brothers-in-law 1** brother of one's husband or wife. **2** husband of one's sister.
brought *verb* past of BRING.
brouhaha *noun* loud confused noise.
brow *noun* **1** part of the face from the eyes to the hairline. **2** eyebrow. **3** top of a hill.

——————— THESAURUS ———————

circular, folder, handbill, hand-out, leaflet, mailshot, pamphlet
broke *adjective* **2** *Inf* = **penniless**, bankrupt, bust (*inf*), down and out, impoverished, insolvent, in the red, munted (*NZ sl*), ruined, short, skint (*Brit sl*) OPPOSITE> **rich**
broken *adjective* **2** = **smashed**, burst, fractured, fragmented, ruptured, separated, severed, shattered **3** = **imperfect**, disjointed, halting, hesitating, stammering
brokenhearted *adjective* = **heartbroken**, desolate, devastated, disconsolate, grief-stricken, inconsolable, miserable, sorrowful, wretched
broker *noun* = **dealer**, agent, factor, go-between, intermediary, middleman, negotiator
bronze *adjective* **3** = **reddish-brown**, brownish, chestnut, copper, rust, tan
brood *noun* **1** = **offspring**, clutch, family,

issue, litter, progeny ◆*verb* **4** = **think upon**, agonize, dwell upon, mope, mull over, muse, obsess, ponder, ruminate
brook[1] *noun* = **stream**, beck, burn, rill, rivulet, watercourse
brook[2] *verb* = **tolerate**, abide, accept, allow, bear, countenance, endure, hack (*sl*), put up with (*inf*), stand, stomach, suffer, support, swallow, thole (*dial*), withstand
brother *noun* **1** = **sibling**, blood brother, kin, kinsman, relation, relative **3** = **monk**, cleric, friar
brotherhood *noun* **1** = **fellowship**, brotherliness, camaraderie, companionship, comradeship, friendliness, kinship **2** = **association**, alliance, community, fraternity, guild, league, order, society, union
brotherly *adjective* = **kind**, affectionate, altruistic, amicable, benevolent, cordial, fraternal, friendly, neighbourly, philanthropic,

browbeat ๏ *verb* frighten (someone) with threats.

brown ๏ *noun* **1** colour of earth or wood. ◆ *adjective* **2** (of bread) made from wheatmeal or wholemeal flour. **3** of the colour brown. ◆ *verb* **4** make or become brown. **brownish** *adjective* **browned-off** *adjective Informal* bored and depressed.

brownie *noun* **1** elf said to do household chores at night. **2** small square nutty chocolate cake.

Brownie Guide, Brownie *noun* junior Guide. **Brownie point** credit for being seen to do the right thing.

browse ๏ *verb* **1** look through (a book or articles for sale) in a casual manner. **2** nibble on young shoots or leaves. ◆ *noun* **3** instance of browsing. **browser** *noun Computers* software package that enables a user to read hypertext, esp. on the Internet.

brucellosis *noun* infectious disease of animals which can be transmitted to humans.

bruise ๏ *noun* **1** discoloured area on the skin caused by an injury. ◆ *verb* **2** cause a bruise on. **bruiser** *noun* strong tough person.

brumby *noun Aust* **1** wild horse. **2** unruly person.

brunch *noun Informal* breakfast and lunch combined.

brunette *noun* girl or woman with dark brown hair.

brunt ๏ *noun* main force or shock of a blow, attack, etc.

brush¹ ๏ *noun* **1** device made of bristles, wires, etc. used for cleaning, painting, etc. **2** brief unpleasant encounter. **3** fox's tail. ◆ *verb* **4** clean, scrub, or paint with a brush. **5** touch lightly and briefly. **brush off** *verb Slang* dismiss or ignore (someone). **brush up** *verb* refresh one's knowledge of (a subject).

brush² ๏ *noun* thick growth of shrubs. **brushwood** *noun* cut or broken-off tree branches and twigs.

brush turkey *noun* bird of New Guinea and Australia resembling the domestic fowl, with black plumage.

brusque ๏ *adjective* blunt or curt in manner or speech. **brusquely** *adverb* **brusqueness** *noun*

Brussels sprout *noun* vegetable like a tiny cabbage.

brute ๏ *noun* **1** brutal person. **2** animal other than man. ◆ *adjective* **3** wholly instinctive or physical, like an animal. **4** without reason. **brutish** *adjective* of or like an animal. **brutal** *adjective* **1** cruel and vicious. **2** extremely honest in speech or manner. **brutally** *adverb* **brutality** *noun* **brutalize** *verb*

bryony *noun* wild climbing hedge plant.

BSc Bachelor of Science.

BSE bovine spongiform encephalopathy: fatal virus disease of cattle.

BSI British Standards Institution.

BST British Summer Time.

——————— T H E S A U R U S ———————

sympathetic
browbeat *verb* =**bully**, badger, coerce, dragoon, hector, intimidate, ride roughshod over, threaten, tyrannize

brown *adjective* **3** =**brunette**, auburn, bay, bronze, chestnut, chocolate, coffee, dun, hazel, sunburnt, tan, tanned, tawny, umber ◆*verb* **4** =**fry**, cook, grill, sauté, seal, sear

browse *verb* **1** =**skim**, dip into, examine cursorily, flip through, glance at, leaf through, look round, look through, peruse, scan, survey **2** =**graze**, eat, feed, nibble

bruise *noun* **1** =**discoloration**, black mark, blemish, contusion, injury, mark, swelling ◆*verb* **2** =**discolour**, damage, injure, mar, mark, pound

brunt *noun* =**full force**, burden, force, impact, pressure, shock, strain, stress, thrust, violence

brush¹ *noun* **1** =**broom**, besom, sweeper **2** =**encounter**, clash, conflict, confrontation, skirmish, tussle ◆*verb* **4** =**clean**, buff, paint, polish, sweep, wash **5** =**touch**, flick, glance, graze, kiss, scrape, stroke, sweep

brush² *noun* =**shrubs**, brushwood, bushes, copse, scrub, thicket, undergrowth

brush off *verb Sl* =**ignore**, disdain, dismiss, disregard, reject, repudiate, scorn, snub, spurn

brush up *verb* =**revise**, bone up (*inf*), cram, go over, polish up, read up, refresh one's memory, relearn, study

brusque *adjective* =**curt**, abrupt, discourteous, gruff, impolite, sharp, short, surly, terse OPPOSITE> polite

brutal *adjective* **1** =**cruel**, bloodthirsty, heartless, inhuman, ruthless, savage, uncivilized, vicious OPPOSITE> kind. **2** =**harsh**, callous, gruff, impolite, insensitive, rough, rude, severe OPPOSITE> sensitive

brutality *noun* **1** =**cruelty**, atrocity, barbarism, bloodthirstiness, ferocity, inhumanity, ruthlessness, savagery, viciousness

brute *noun* **1** =**savage**, barbarian, beast, devil, fiend, monster, sadist, swine **2** =**animal**, beast, creature, wild animal ◆*adjective* **3** =**physical**, bodily, carnal, fleshly **4** =**mindless**, instinctive, senseless, unthinking

Bt Baronet.

bubble ❶ *noun* **1** ball of air in a liquid or solid. **2** thin film of liquid forming a ball around air or a gas. **3** transparent dome. **4** something initially very pleasing or successful which suddenly disappears or goes wrong. ◆ *verb* **5** form bubbles. **6** move or flow with a gurgling sound. **bubbly** *adjective* **-blier, -bliest 1** excited and lively. **2** full of bubbles. ◆ *noun* **3** *Informal* champagne. **bubble over** *verb* express an emotion freely.

bubonic plague [bew-**bonn**-ik] *noun* acute infectious disease characterized by swellings.

buccaneer ❶ *noun* pirate.

buck[1] *noun* **1** male of the goat, hare, kangaroo, rabbit, and reindeer. ◆ *verb* **2** (of a horse etc.) jump with legs stiff and back arched. **3** *Informal* resist or oppose obstinately, e.g. *to buck a trend.* **buckshot** *noun* large lead pellets used for shooting game. **buck up** *verb* make or become more cheerful.

buck[2] *noun US, Canad & Aust slang* dollar.

buck[3] *noun* **pass the buck** *Informal* shift blame or responsibility onto someone else.

bucket *noun* **1** open-topped round container with a handle. ◆ *verb* **-eting, -eted 2** (also **bucket down**) rain heavily **kick the bucket** *Slang* die. **bucketful** *noun*

buckle ❶ *noun* **1** clasp for fastening a belt or strap. ◆ *verb* **2** fasten or be fastened with a buckle. **3** (cause to) bend out of shape through pressure or heat. **buckle down** *verb Informal* apply oneself with determination.

buckshee *adjective Slang* free.

buckteeth *plural noun* projecting upper front teeth. **buck-toothed** *adjective*

buckwheat *noun* small black grain used for making flour.

bucolic [bew-**koll**-ik] *adjective* of the countryside or country life.

bud ❶ *noun* **1** swelling on a tree or plant that develops into a leaf or flower. **2** partially opened flower. ◆ *verb* **budding, budded 3** produce buds. **budding** *adjective* beginning to develop or grow, e.g. *a budding actor.*

Buddhism *noun* eastern religion founded by Buddha. **Buddhist** *noun, adjective*

buddleia *noun* shrub with long spikes of purple flowers.

buddy *noun, pl* **-dies** *Informal* friend.

budge ❶ *verb* **1** move slightly. **2** change (an opinion).

budgerigar *noun* small cage bird bred in many different-coloured varieties.

budget ❶ *noun* **1** financial plan for a period of time. **2** money allocated for a specific purpose. ◆ *verb* **-eting, -eted 3** plan the expenditure of (money or time). ◆ *adjective* **4** cheap. **the Budget** statement of government's financial plans for the coming year. **budgetary** *adjective*

> **SPELLING TIP**
>
> A lot of verbs ending in *et*, have two *ts* when you add an ending like *-ing*, but **budget** is not one of them: **budgeting** and **budgeted** have a single *t*.

budgie *noun Informal* short for BUDGERIGAR.

buff[1] ❶ *noun* **1** soft flexible undyed leather. ◆ *adjective* **2** dull yellowish-brown. ◆ *verb* **3** clean or polish with soft material. **in the buff** *Informal* naked.

buff[2] ❶ *noun Informal* expert on or devotee of a given subject.

buffalo *noun* **1** type of cattle. **2** *US* bison.

buffer[1] ❶ *noun* something that lessens shock

——— THESAURUS ———

bubble *noun* **1, 2 = air ball**, bead, blister, blob, drop, droplet, globule ◆*verb* **5 = foam**, boil, effervesce, fizz, froth, percolate, seethe, sparkle **6 = gurgle**, babble, burble, murmur, ripple, trickle

bubbly *adjective* **1 = lively**, animated, bouncy, elated, excited, happy, merry, sparky **2 = frothy**, carbonated, effervescent, fizzy, foamy, sparkling

buccaneer *noun* **= pirate**, corsair, freebooter, privateer, sea-rover

buckle *noun* **1 = fastener**, catch, clasp, clip, hasp ◆*verb* **2 = fasten**, clasp, close, hook, secure **3 = distort**, bend, bulge, cave in, collapse, contort, crumple, fold, twist, warp

bud *noun* **1 = shoot**, embryo, germ, sprout

◆*verb* **3 = develop**, burgeon, burst forth, grow, shoot, sprout

budding *adjective* **= developing**, beginning, burgeoning, embryonic, fledgling, growing, incipient, nascent, potential, promising

budge *verb* **1 = move**, dislodge, push, shift, stir

budget *noun* **2 = allowance**, allocation, cost, finances, funds, means, resources ◆*verb* **3 = plan**, allocate, apportion, cost, estimate, ration

buff[1] *adjective* **2 = yellowish-brown**, sandy, straw, tan, yellowish ◆*verb* **3 = polish**, brush, burnish, rub, shine, smooth

buff[2] *noun Inf* **= expert**, addict, admirer, aficionado, connoisseur, devotee, enthusiast,

or protects from damaging impact, circumstances, etc. **buffer state** small state between two rival powers.
buffer² *noun Brit informal* stupid or bumbling man.
buffet¹ ⊕ [boof-ay] *noun* **1** counter where drinks and snacks are served. **2** meal at which guests serve themselves from a range of dishes.
buffet² ⊕ [buff-it] *verb* **-feting, -feted 1** knock against or about. **2** hit, esp. with the fist. ◆ *noun* **3** blow, esp. with the hand.
buffoon ⊕ *noun* clown or fool. **buffoonery** *noun*
bug ⊕ *noun* **1** small insect. **2** *Informal* minor illness. **3** small mistake in a computer program. **4** concealed microphone. ◆ *verb* **bugging, bugged 5** *Informal* irritate (someone). **6** conceal a microphone in (a room or phone).
bugbear ⊕ *noun* thing that causes obsessive anxiety.
bugger *noun* **1** *Taboo slang* unpleasant or difficult person or thing. **2** *Slang* any person, e.g. *poor old bugger*. **3** person who practises buggery. ◆ *verb* **4** *Slang* tire. **5** practise buggery with. **bugger off** *verb Taboo slang* go away. **buggery** *noun* anal intercourse.
buggy *noun, pl* **-gies 1** light horse-drawn carriage having two or four wheels. **2** lightweight folding pram.
bugle *noun* instrument like a small trumpet. **bugler** *noun*
build ⊕ *verb* **building, built 1** make, construct, or form by joining parts or materials. **2** establish and develop. ◆ *noun* **3** shape of the body. **builder** *noun* **building** *noun* structure

with walls and a roof. **building society** organization where money can be borrowed or invested. **build-up** *noun* gradual increase. **build up** *verb* construct or establish gradually.
built ⊕ *verb* past of BUILD. **built-in** *adjective* incorporated as an integral part. **built-up** *adjective* having many buildings.
bulb ⊕ *noun* **1** same as LIGHT BULB. **2** onion-shaped root which grows into a flower or plant. **bulbous** *adjective* round and fat.
bulge ⊕ *noun* **1** swelling on a normally flat surface. **2** sudden increase in number. ◆ *verb* **3** swell outwards. **bulging** *adjective*
bulimia *noun* disorder characterized by compulsive overeating followed by vomiting. **bulimic** *adjective, noun*
bulk ⊕ *noun* **1** size or volume, esp. when great. **2** main part. ◆ *verb* **3 bulk large** be or seem important. **in bulk** in large quantities. **bulky** *adjective*
bulkhead *noun* partition in a ship or aeroplane.
bull¹ ⊕ *noun* male of some animals, such as cattle, elephants, and whales. **bullock** *noun* castrated bull. **bulldog** *noun* thickset dog with a broad head and a muscular body. **bulldozer** *noun* powerful tractor for moving earth. **bulldoze** *verb* **1** demolish or flatten with a bulldozer. **2** *Informal* achieve (something) or persuade (someone) by intimidation, e.g. *the new law was bulldozed through parliament*.
bullfight *noun* public show in which a matador kills a bull. **bullfinch** *noun* common European songbird. **bullfrog** *noun* large American frog with a deep croak. **bull's-eye** *noun* central disc

——————— T H E S A U R U S ———————

fan, fundi (*S Afr*)
buffer¹ *noun* =**safeguard**, bulwark, bumper, cushion, fender, intermediary, screen, shield, shock absorber
buffet¹ *noun* **1** =**snack bar**, brasserie, café, cafeteria, refreshment counter, sideboard
buffet² *verb* **1, 2** =**batter**, beat, bump, knock, pound, pummel, strike, thump, wallop (*inf*)
buffoon *noun* =**clown**, comedian, comic, fool, harlequin, jester, joker, wag
bug *noun* **2** *Inf* =**illness**, disease, infection, virus **3** =**fault**, defect, error, flaw, glitch, gremlin ◆*verb* **5** *Inf* =**annoy**, bother, disturb, get on one's nerves (*inf*), hassle (*inf*), irritate, pester, vex **6** =**tap**, eavesdrop, listen in, spy
bugbear *noun* =**pet hate**, bane, bête noire, bogey, dread, horror, nightmare
build *verb* **1** =**construct**, assemble, erect, fabricate, form, make, put up, raise [OPPOSITE] **dismantle** ◆*noun* **3** =**physique**, body, figure,

form, frame, shape, structure
building *noun* =**structure**, domicile, dwelling, edifice, house
build-up *noun* =**increase**, accumulation, development, enlargement, escalation, expansion, gain, growth [OPPOSITE] **reduce**
bulbous *adjective* =**bulging**, bloated, convex, rounded, swelling, swollen
bulge *noun* **1** =**swelling**, bump, hump, lump, projection, protrusion, protuberance [OPPOSITE] **hollow**. **2** =**increase**, boost, intensification, rise, surge ◆*verb* **3** =**swell out**, dilate, distend, expand, project, protrude, puff out, stick out
bulk *noun* **1** =**size**, dimensions, immensity, largeness, magnitude, substance, volume, weight **2** =**main part**, better part, body, lion's share, majority, mass, most, nearly all, preponderance
bulky *adjective* **1** =**large**, big, cumbersome, heavy, hulking, massive, substantial, unwieldy,

of a target. **bull terrier** terrier with a short smooth coat.

bull[2] noun Informal complete nonsense.

bull[3] noun papal decree.

bullet ⊙ noun small piece of metal fired from a gun.

bulletin ⊙ noun short official report or announcement.

bullion noun gold or silver in the form of bars.

bully ⊙ noun, pl -lies **1** person who hurts, persecutes, or intimidates a weaker person. ◆ verb **-lying, -lied 2** hurt, intimidate, or persecute (a weaker person).

bully beef noun canned corned beef.

bully-off noun Hockey method of restarting play in which opposing players strike their sticks together before trying to hit the ball. **bully off** verb Hockey restart play with a bully-off.

bulrush noun tall stiff reed.

bulwark ⊙ noun **1** wall used as a fortification. **2** person or thing acting as a defence.

bum[1] noun Slang buttocks or anus. **bumbag** noun small bag attached to a belt and worn round the waist.

bum[2] Informal noun **1** disreputable idler. **2** US tramp or hobo. ◆ verb **bumming, bummed 3** get by begging. ◆ adjective **4** of poor quality.

bumble ⊙ verb speak, do, or move in a clumsy way. **bumbling** adjective, noun

bumblebee noun large hairy bee.

bumf, bumph noun Informal official documents or forms.

bump ⊙ verb **1** knock or strike with a jolt. **2** travel in jerks and jolts. ◆ noun **3** dull thud from an impact or collision. **4** lump on the body caused by a blow. **5** raised uneven part.

bumpy adjective **bumpier, bumpiest**. **bump into** verb Informal meet (someone) by chance. **bump off** verb Informal murder.

bumper[1] noun bar on the front and back of a vehicle to protect against damage.

bumper[2] ⊙ noun **1** glass filled to the brim. ◆ adjective **2** unusually large or abundant.

bumph noun same as BUMF.

bumpkin ⊙ noun awkward simple country person.

bumptious ⊙ adjective offensively self-assertive.

bun noun **1** small sweet bread roll or cake. **2** hair gathered into a bun shape at the back of the head.

bunch ⊙ noun **1** number of things growing, fastened, or grouped together. **2** group, e.g. a bunch of cowards. ◆ verb **3** group or be grouped together in a bunch.

bundle ⊙ noun **1** number of things gathered loosely together. ◆ verb **2** cause to go roughly or unceremoniously. **bundle up** verb make into a bundle.

bung noun **1** stopper for a cask etc. ◆ verb **2** (foll. by up) Informal close with a bung. **3** Slang throw (something) somewhere in a careless manner.

bungalow noun one-storey house.

———————— THESAURUS ————————

voluminous, weighty OPPOSITE small

bulldoze verb **1** = **demolish**, flatten, level, raze

bullet noun = **projectile**, ball, missile, pellet, shot, slug

bulletin noun = **announcement**, account, communication, communiqué, dispatch, message, news flash, notification, report, statement

bully noun **1** = **persecutor**, browbeater, bully boy, coercer, intimidator, oppressor, ruffian, tormentor, tough ◆verb **2** = **persecute**, browbeat, coerce, domineer, hector, intimidate, oppress, push around (sl), terrorize, tyrannize

bulwark noun **1** = **fortification**, bastion, buttress, defence, embankment, partition, rampart **2** = **defence**, buffer, guard, mainstay, safeguard, security, support

bumbling adjective = **clumsy**, awkward, blundering, bungling, incompetent, inefficient, inept, maladroit, muddled OPPOSITE efficient

bump verb **1** = **knock**, bang, collide (with), crash, hit, slam, smash into, strike **2** = **jerk**, bounce, jolt, rattle, shake ◆noun **3** = **knock**,

bang, blow, collision, crash, impact, jolt, thud, thump **4** = **lump**, bulge, contusion, hump, nodule, protuberance, swelling

bumper[2] adjective **2** = **exceptional**, abundant, bountiful, excellent, jumbo (inf), massive, whopping (inf)

bumpkin noun = **yokel**, country bumpkin, hick (inf, chiefly US & Canad), hillbilly, peasant, rustic

bumptious adjective = **cocky**, arrogant, brash, conceited, forward, full of oneself, overconfident, pushy (inf), self-assertive

bumpy adjective = **rough**, bouncy, choppy, jarring, jerky, jolting, rutted, uneven

bunch noun **1** = **number**, assortment, batch, bundle, clump, cluster, collection, heap, lot, mass, pile **2** = **group**, band, crowd, flock, gang, gathering, party, team ◆verb **3** = **group**, assemble, bundle, cluster, collect, huddle, mass, pack

bundle noun **1** = **bunch**, assortment, batch, collection, group, heap, mass, pile, stack ◆verb **2** = **push**, hurry, hustle, rush, shove, thrust

bundle up verb = **wrap up**, swathe

bungee jumping, bungy jumping *noun* sport of leaping from a high bridge, tower, etc., to which one is connected by a rubber rope.

bungle ⊕ *verb* **1** spoil through incompetence. ♦ *noun* **2** blunder or muddle. **bungler** *noun* **bungling** *adjective, noun*

bunion *noun* inflamed swelling on the big toe.

bunk¹ *noun* narrow shelflike bed. **bunk bed** one of a pair of beds constructed one above the other.

bunk² ⊕ *noun* same as BUNKUM.

bunk³ *noun* **do a bunk** *Slang* make a hurried and secret departure.

bunker *noun* **1** sand-filled hollow forming an obstacle on a golf course. **2** underground shelter. **3** large storage container for coal etc.

bunkum *noun* nonsense.

bunny *noun, pl* **-nies** child's word for a rabbit.

Bunsen burner *noun* gas burner used in laboratories.

bunting¹ *noun* decorative flags.

bunting² *noun* songbird with a short stout bill.

bunya *noun* tall dome-shaped Australian coniferous tree (also **bunya-bunya**).

bunyip *noun Aust* legendary monster said to live in swamps and lakes.

buoy ⊕ *noun* **1** floating marker anchored in the sea. ♦ *verb* **2** prevent from sinking. **3** encourage or hearten. **buoyant** *adjective* **1** able to float. **2** cheerful or resilient. **buoyancy** *noun*

bur *noun* same as BURR¹.

burble *verb* **1** make a bubbling sound. **2** talk quickly and excitedly.

burden¹ ⊕ *noun* **1** heavy load. **2** something difficult to cope with. ♦ *verb* **3** put a burden on. **4** oppress. **burdensome** *adjective*

burden² *noun* **1** theme of a speech etc. **2** chorus of a song.

burdock *noun* weed with prickly burrs.

bureau ⊕ *noun, pl* **-reaus, -reaux 1** office that provides a service. **2** writing desk with shelves and drawers. **bureaucracy** *noun* administrative system based on complex rules and procedures.

bureaucracy ⊕ *noun, pl* **-cies 1** administrative system based on complex rules and procedures. **2** excessive adherence to complex procedures. **bureaucrat** *noun* **bureaucratic** *adjective*

burette *noun* glass tube for dispensing known volumes of fluids.

burgeon *verb* develop or grow rapidly.

burger *noun Informal* hamburger.

burgess *noun* citizen or freeman of a borough.

burgh *noun* Scottish borough. **burgher** *noun* citizen.

burglar ⊕ *noun* person who enters a building to commit a crime, esp. theft. **burglary** *noun, pl* **-ries. burgle** *verb*

Burgundy *noun* type of French wine. **burgundy** *adjective* dark-purplish red.

burgundy *adjective* dark-purplish red.

burial ⊕ *noun* burying of a dead body.

burlesque ⊕ *noun* artistic work which satirizes a subject by caricature.

burly ⊕ *adjective* **-lier, -liest** (of a person)

—— THESAURUS ——

bungle *verb* **1** = **mess up**, blow (*sl*), blunder, botch, foul up, make a mess of, muff, ruin, spoil
OPPOSITE **accomplish**

bungling *adjective* = **incompetent**, blundering, cack-handed (*inf*), clumsy, ham-fisted (*inf*), inept, maladroit

bunk² same as BUNKUM

bunkum *noun* = **nonsense**, balderdash, baloney (*inf*), garbage (*inf*), hogwash, hot air (*inf*), kak (*S Afr sl*), moonshine, poppycock (*inf*), rubbish, stuff and nonsense, twaddle

buoy *noun* **1** = **marker**, beacon, float, guide, signal ♦*verb* **3** = **encourage**, boost, cheer, cheer up, hearten, lift, raise, support, sustain

buoyant *adjective* **1** = **floating**, afloat, light, weightless **2** = **cheerful**, carefree, chirpy (*inf*), happy, jaunty, light-hearted, upbeat (*inf*)
OPPOSITE **sad**

burden¹ *noun* **1** = **load**, encumbrance, weight **2** = **trouble**, affliction, millstone, onus, responsibility, strain, weight, worry ♦*verb* **3** = **weigh down**, bother, encumber, handicap,

load, oppress, saddle with, tax, worry

bureau *noun* **1** = **office**, agency, branch, department, division, service **2** = **desk**, writing desk

bureaucracy *noun* **1** = **government**, administration, authorities, civil service, corridors of power, officials, the system **2** = **red tape**, officialdom, regulations

bureaucrat *noun* **1** = **official**, administrator, civil servant, functionary, mandarin, officer, public servant

burglar *noun* = **housebreaker**, cat burglar, filcher, pilferer, robber, sneak thief, thief

burglary *noun* = **breaking and entering**, break-in, housebreaking, larceny, robbery, stealing, theft, thieving

burial *noun* = **interment**, funeral

buried *adjective* **1** = **interred**, entombed, laid to rest **3** = **hidden**, concealed, private, sequestered, tucked away

burlesque *noun* = **parody**, caricature, mockery, satire, send-up (*Brit inf*), spoof (*inf*), broad and strong.

burn¹ ❶ *verb* **burning, burnt** *or* **burned 1** be or set on fire. **2** destroy or be destroyed by fire. **3** damage, injure, or mark by heat. **4** feel strong emotion. **5** to record data on (a compact disc). ◆ *noun* **6** injury or mark caused by fire or exposure to heat. **burner** *noun* part of a stove or lamp that produces the flame.

burning *adjective* **1** intense. **2** urgent or crucial.

burn² *noun Scot* small stream.

burnish ❶ *verb* make smooth and shiny by rubbing.

burnous *noun* long circular cloak with a hood, worn esp. by Arabs.

burnt *verb* a past of BURN¹.

burp *verb, noun Informal* belch.

burr¹ *noun* head of a plant with prickles or hooks.

burr² *noun* **1** soft trilling sound given to the letter *r* in some dialects. **2** whirring sound. **3** rough edge left after cutting.

burrawang *noun* Australian plant with fernlike leaves and an edible nut.

burrow ❶ *noun* **1** hole dug in the ground by a rabbit etc. ◆ *verb* **2** dig holes in the ground. **3** delve deeply, e.g. *he burrowed into his coat pocket*.

bursar *noun* treasurer of a school, college, or university. **bursary** *noun, pl* **-ries** scholarship.

burst ❶ *verb* **bursting, burst 1** (cause to) break open or apart noisily and suddenly. **2** come or go suddenly and forcibly. **3** be full to the point of breaking open. ◆ *noun* **4** instance of breaking open suddenly. **5** sudden outbreak or occurrence. **burst into** *verb* give vent to (an emotion) suddenly.

bury ❶ *verb* **burying, buried 1** place in a grave. **2** place in the earth and cover with soil. **3** conceal or hide. **4** occupy (oneself) with deep concentration.

bus *noun* **1** large motor vehicle for carrying passengers. ◆ *verb* **bussing, bussed 2** travel or transport by bus.

busby *noun, pl* **-bies** tall fur hat worn by some soldiers.

bush ❶ *noun* **1** dense woody plant, smaller than a tree. **2** wild uncultivated part of a country. **bushy** *adjective* **bushier, bushiest** (of hair) thick and shaggy. **bushbaby** *noun* small African tree-living mammal with large eyes. **Bushman** *noun* member of a hunting and gathering people of Southern Africa. **bush telegraph** means of spreading gossip.

bushel *noun* obsolete unit of measure equal to 8 gallons.

business ❶ *noun* **1** purchase and sale of goods and services. **2** commercial establishment. **3** trade or profession. **4** proper concern or responsibility. **5** affair, e.g. *it's a dreadful business*. **businesslike** *adjective* efficient and methodical. **businessman, businesswoman** *noun*

——————————— THESAURUS ———————————

takeoff (*inf*), travesty

burly *adjective* =**brawny**, beefy (*inf*), bulky, hefty, stocky, stout, sturdy, thickset, well-built OPPOSITE **scrawny**

burn¹ *verb* **1** =**be on fire**, be ablaze, blaze, flame, flare, glow, go up in flames, smoke **3** =**set on fire**, char, ignite, incinerate, kindle, light, parch, scorch, sear, singe, toast **4** =**be passionate**, be angry, be aroused, be inflamed, fume, seethe, simmer, smoulder

burning *adjective* **1** =**intense**, ardent, eager, fervent, impassioned, passionate, vehement OPPOSITE **cool**. **2** =**crucial**, acute, compelling, critical, essential, important, pressing, significant, urgent, vital

burnish *verb* =**polish**, brighten, buff, furbish, glaze, rub up, shine, smooth OPPOSITE **scuff**

burrow *noun* **1** =**hole**, den, lair, retreat, shelter, tunnel ◆*verb* **2** =**dig**, delve, excavate, hollow out, scoop out, tunnel

burst *verb* **1** =**explode**, blow up, break, crack, puncture, rupture, shatter, split, tear apart **2** =**rush**, barge, break, break out, erupt, gush forth, run, spout ◆*noun* **4** =**explosion**, bang, blast, blowout, break, crack, discharge, rupture, split **5** =**rush**, gush, gust, outbreak, outburst, outpouring, spate, spurt, surge, torrent

bury *verb* **1** =**inter**, consign to the grave, entomb, inhume, lay to rest OPPOSITE **dig up**. **2** =**embed**, engulf, submerge **3** =**hide**, conceal, cover, enshroud, secrete, stow away OPPOSITE **uncover**

bush *noun* **1** =**shrub**, hedge, plant, shrubbery, thicket **2** =**the wild**, backwoods, brush, scrub, scrubland, woodland

bushy *adjective* =**thick**, bristling, fluffy, fuzzy, luxuriant, rough, shaggy, unruly

business *noun* **1** =**trade**, bargaining, commerce, dealings, industry, manufacturing, selling, transaction **2** =**establishment**, company, concern, corporation, enterprise, firm, organization, venture **3** =**profession**, career, employment, function, job, line, occupation, trade, vocation, work, yakka (*Aust & NZ inf*) **4** =**concern**, affair, assignment, duty, pigeon (*inf*), problem, responsibility, task

businesslike *adjective* =**efficient**, methodical, orderly, organized, practical, professional,

B

busker noun street entertainer. **busk** verb act as a busker.

bust¹ ❶ noun **1** woman's bosom. **2** sculpture of the head and shoulders.

bust² ❶ Informal verb **busting, bust** or **busted 1** burst or break. **2** (of the police) raid (a place) or arrest (someone). ♦ adjective **3** broken. **go bust** become bankrupt. **bust-up** noun Informal **1** serious quarrel. **2** brawl or disturbance.

bustard noun bird with long strong legs, a heavy body, a long neck, and speckled plumage.

bustle¹ ❶ verb **1** hurry with a show of activity or energy. ♦ noun **2** energetic and noisy activity. **bustling** adjective

bustle² noun cushion or framework formerly worn under the back of a woman's skirt to hold it out.

busy ❶ adjective **busier, busiest 1** actively employed. **2** crowded or full of activity. ♦ verb **busying, busied 3** keep (someone, esp. oneself) busy. **busily** adverb **busybody** noun meddlesome or nosy person.

but ❶ conjunction **1** contrary to expectation. **2** in contrast. **3** other than. **4** without it happening. ♦ preposition **5** except. ♦ adverb **6** only. **but for** were it not for.

butane [bew-tane] noun gas used for fuel.

butch adjective Slang markedly or aggressively masculine.

butcher ❶ noun **1** person who slaughters animals or sells their meat. **2** brutal murderer. ♦ verb **3** kill and prepare (animals) for meat. **4** kill (people) brutally or indiscriminately. **5** make a mess of. **butcherbird** noun Australian magpie that impales its prey on thorns. **butchery** noun

butler noun chief male servant.

butt¹ ❶ noun **1** thicker end of something. **2** unused end of a cigar or cigarette. **3** Chiefly US & Canad slang buttocks.

butt² ❶ noun **1** person or thing that is the target of ridicule. **2** mound of earth behind a target. ♦ plural **3** target range.

butt³ ❶ verb **1** strike with the head or horns. ♦ noun **2** blow with the head or horns. **butt in** verb interrupt a conversation.

butt⁴ ❶ noun large cask.

butter noun **1** edible fatty solid made by churning cream. ♦ verb **2** put butter on. **buttery** adjective **butter up** verb flatter.

butter bean noun large pale flat edible bean.

buttercup noun small yellow flower.

butterfingers noun Informal person who drops things by mistake.

butterfly noun **1** insect with brightly coloured wings. **2** swimming stroke in which both arms move together in a forward circular action.

buttermilk noun sourish milk that remains after the butter has been separated from milk.

butterscotch noun kind of hard brittle toffee.

buttock noun either of the two fleshy masses

——————— THESAURUS ———————

systematic, thorough, well-ordered OPPOSITE **inefficient**

businessman noun = **executive**, capitalist, employer, entrepreneur, financier, industrialist, merchant, tradesman, tycoon

bust¹ noun = **bosom**, breast, chest, front, torso

bust² Inf verb **1** = **break**, burst, fracture, rupture **2** = **arrest**, catch, fossick (Aust & NZ), raid, search **go bust** = **go bankrupt**, become insolvent, be ruined, fail

bustle¹ verb **1** = **hurry**, fuss, hasten, rush, scamper, scurry, scuttle OPPOSITE **idle** ♦noun **2** = **activity**, ado, commotion, excitement, flurry, fuss, hurly-burly, stir, to-do OPPOSITE **inactivity**

busy adjective **1** = **occupied**, active, employed, engaged, hard at work, industrious, on duty, rushed off one's feet, working OPPOSITE **unoccupied**. **2** = **lively**, energetic, exacting, full, hectic, hustling OPPOSITE **idle** ♦verb **3** = **occupy**, absorb, employ, engage, engross, immerse, interest OPPOSITE **off duty**

busybody noun = **nosy parker** (inf), gossip, meddler, snooper, stirrer (inf), troublemaker, tattletale (chiefly US & Canad)

but conjunction **1** = **however**, further, moreover, nevertheless, on the contrary, on the other hand, still, yet ♦preposition **5** = **except**, bar, barring, excepting, excluding, notwithstanding, save, with the exception of ♦adverb **6** = **only**, just, merely, simply, singly, solely

butcher noun **2** = **murderer**, destroyer, killer, slaughterer, slayer ♦verb **3** = **slaughter**, carve, clean, cut, cut up, dress, joint, prepare **4** = **kill**, assassinate, cut down, destroy, exterminate, liquidate, massacre, put to the sword, slaughter, slay

butt¹ noun **1** = **end**, haft, handle, hilt, shaft, shank, stock **2** = **stub**, fag end (inf), leftover, tip

butt² noun **1** = **target**, Aunt Sally, dupe, laughing stock, victim

butt³ verb **1** = **knock**, bump, poke, prod, push, ram, shove, thrust ♦noun **2** = **knock**, bump, poke, prod, push, ram, shove, thrust

butt⁴ noun = **cask**, barrel

butt in verb = **interfere**, chip in (inf), cut in, interrupt, intrude, meddle, put one's oar in, stick one's nose in that form the human rump.

button ❶ *noun* **1** small disc or knob sewn to clothing, which can be passed through a slit in another piece of fabric to fasten them. **2** knob that operates a piece of equipment when pressed. ◆ *verb* **3** fasten with buttons.

buttonhole *noun* **1** slit in a garment through which a button is passed. **2** flower worn on a lapel. ◆ *verb* **3** detain (someone) in conversation.

buttress ❶ *noun* **1** structure to support a wall. ◆ *verb* **2** support with, or as if with, a buttress.

buxom ❶ *adjective* (of a woman) healthily plump and full-bosomed.

buy ❶ *verb* **buying, bought 1** acquire by paying money for. **2** be capable of purchasing, e.g. *money can't buy love*. **3** acquire by any exchange or sacrifice. **4** *Slang* accept as true. **5** bribe. ◆ *noun* **6** thing acquired through payment. **buyer** *noun* **1** customer. **2** person employed to buy merchandise.

LANGUAGE TIP

Be careful not to confuse the past forms *bought* (from *buy*) with *brought* (from *bring*).

---

buzz *noun* **1** rapidly vibrating humming sound. **2** *Informal* telephone call. **3** *Informal* sense of excitement. ◆ *verb* **4** make a humming sound. **5** be filled with an air of excitement. **6** *Informal* fly an aircraft very low over. **buzzer** *noun* **buzz around** *verb* move around quickly and busily. **buzz word** jargon word which becomes fashionably popular.

buzzard *noun* bird of prey of the hawk family.

by ❶ *preposition* **1** indicating the doer of an action, nearness, movement past, time before or during which, etc., e.g. *bitten by a dog; down by the river; driving by the school; in bed by midnight.* ◆ *adverb* **2** near. **3** past. **by and by** eventually. **by and large** in general.

bye[1] *noun* **1** *Sport* situation where a player or team wins a round by having no opponent. **2** *Cricket* run scored off a ball not touched by the batsman.

bye[2], **bye-bye** *interjection Informal* goodbye.

by-election *noun* election held during parliament to fill a vacant seat.

bygone ❶ *adjective* **1** past or former. ◆ *plural noun* **2 let bygones be bygones** agree to forget past quarrels.

bylaw, bye-law *noun* rule made by a local authority.

by-line *noun* line under the title of a newspaper or magazine article giving the author's name.

bypass ❶ *noun* **1** main road built to avoid a city. **2** operation to divert blood flow away from a damaged part of the heart. ◆ *verb* **3** go round or avoid.

by-product *noun* secondary or incidental product of a process.

byre *noun* shelter for cows.

bystander ❶ *noun* person present but not involved.

byte *noun Computers* group of bits processed as one unit of data.

byway *noun* minor road.

byword ❶ *noun* person or thing regarded as a perfect example of something.

Byzantine *adjective* **1** of Byzantium or the Byzantine Empire. **2** of the style of architecture developed in the Byzantine Empire. **3** complicated.

——————— T H E S A U R U S ———————

buttress *noun* **1** = **support**, brace, mainstay, prop, reinforcement, stanchion, strut ◆*verb* **2** = **support**, back up, bolster, prop up, reinforce, shore up, strengthen, sustain, uphold

buxom *adjective* = **plump**, ample, bosomy, busty, curvaceous, healthy, voluptuous, well-rounded OPPOSITE **slender**

buy *verb* **1** = **purchase**, acquire, get, invest in, obtain, pay for, procure, shop for OPPOSITE **sell** ◆*noun* **6** = **purchase**, acquisition, bargain, deal

by *preposition* **1 a** = **via**, by way of, over **b** = **through**, through the agency of **c** = **near**, along, beside, close to, next to, past ◆*adverb* **2**

= **near**, at hand, close, handy, in reach

bygone *adjective* **1** = **past**, antiquated, extinct, forgotten, former, lost, of old, olden OPPOSITE **future**

bypass *verb* **3** = **go round**, avoid, circumvent, depart from, detour round, deviate from, get round, give a wide berth to, pass round OPPOSITE **meet**

bystander *noun* = **onlooker**, eyewitness, looker-on, observer, passer-by, spectator, viewer, watcher, witness OPPOSITE **participant**

byword *noun* = **saying**, adage, maxim, motto, precept, proverb, slogan

Cc

C 1 *Chem* carbon. **2** Celsius. **3** centigrade. **4** century. **5** the Roman numeral for 100.

c. circa.

Ca *Chem* calcium.

CA 1 California. **2** Chartered Accountant.

ca. circa.

cab ❶ *noun* **1** taxi. **2** enclosed driver's compartment on a train, lorry, etc. **cabbie, cabby** *noun, pl* **-bies** *Informal* taxi driver.

cabal ❶ [kab-**bal**] *noun* **1** small group of political plotters. **2** secret plot.

cabaret [kab-a-ray] *noun* dancing and singing show in a nightclub.

cabbage *noun* **1** vegetable with a large head of green leaves. **2** *Informal* person with no mental faculties.

caber *noun* tree trunk tossed in competition at Highland games.

cabin ❶ *noun* **1** compartment in a ship or aircraft. **2** small hut. **cabin boy** boy who waits on the officers and passengers of a ship. **cabin cruiser** motorboat with a cabin

cabinet ❶ *noun* **1** piece of furniture with drawers or shelves. **2** (C-) committee of senior government ministers. **cabinet-maker** *noun* person who makes fine furniture.

cable *noun* **1** strong thick rope. **2** bundle of wires that carries electricity or electronic signals. **3** telegram sent abroad. ◆ *verb* **4** send (someone) a message by cable. **cable car** vehicle pulled up a steep slope by a moving cable. **cable television** television service conveyed by cable to subscribers.

caboodle *noun* **the whole caboodle** *Informal* the whole lot.

caboose *noun US & Canad* guard's van on a train.

cabriolet [kab-ree-oh-**lay**] *noun* small horse-drawn carriage with a folding hood.

cacao [kak-**kah**-oh] *noun* tropical tree with seed pods from which chocolate and cocoa are made.

cachalot *noun* sperm whale.

cache [kash] *noun* hidden store of weapons or treasure.

cachet [kash-shay] *noun* prestige, distinction.

cachou *noun* lozenge eaten to sweeten the breath.

cack-handed *adjective Informal* clumsy.

cackle *verb* **1** laugh shrilly. **2** (of a hen) squawk with shrill broken notes. ◆ *noun* **3** cackling noise.

cacophony [kak-**koff**-on-ee] *noun* harsh discordant sound. **cacophonous** *adjective*

cactus *noun, pl* **-tuses, -ti** fleshy desert plant with spines but no leaves.

cad ❶ *noun Old-fashioned* dishonourable man. **caddish** *adjective*

cadaver [kad-**dav**-ver] *noun* corpse.

cadaverous *adjective* pale, thin, and haggard.

caddie, caddy *noun, pl* **-dies 1** person who carries a golfer's clubs. ◆ *verb* **-dying, -died 2** act as a caddie.

caddis fly *noun* insect whose larva (**caddis worm**) lives underwater in a protective case of sand and stones.

caddy *noun, pl* **-dies** small container for tea.

cadence [**kade**-enss] *noun* **1** rise and fall in the pitch of the voice. **2** close of a musical phrase.

cadenza *noun* complex solo passage in a piece of music.

cadet *noun* young person training for the armed forces or police.

THESAURUS

---

cab *noun* **1** = **taxi**, hackney carriage, minicab, taxicab

cabal *noun* **1** = **clique**, caucus, conclave, faction, league, party, set **2** = **plot**, conspiracy, intrigue, machination, scheme

cabin *noun* **1** = **room**, berth, compartment, quarters **2** = **hut**, chalet, cottage, lodge, shack, shanty, shed

cabinet *noun* **1** = **cupboard**, case, chiffonier, closet, commode, dresser, escritoire, locker **2** (usu. cap.) = **council**, administration, assembly, counsellors, ministry

cad *noun Old-fashioned* = **scoundrel**, bounder (*old-fashioned Brit sl*), heel (*sl*), rat (*inf*), rotter (*sl, chiefly Brit*)

caddish *adjective Old-fashioned* = **ungentlemanly**, despicable, ill-bred, low, unmannerly

C

cadge *verb Informal* get (something) by taking advantage of someone's generosity. **cadger** *noun*

cadi *noun, pl* **-dis** judge in a Muslim community.

cadmium *noun Chem* bluish-white metallic element used in alloys.

cadre [**kah**-der] *noun* small group of people selected and trained to form the core of a political organization or military unit.

caecum [**seek**-um] *noun, pl* **-ca** [-ka] pouch at the beginning of the large intestine.

Caerphilly *noun* creamy white mild-flavoured cheese.

Caesarean section [see-**zair**-ee-an] *noun* surgical incision into the womb to deliver a baby.

caesium *noun Chem* silvery-white metallic element used in photocells.

caesura [siz-**your**-ra] *noun, pl* **-ras, -rae** [-ree] pause in a line of verse.

café ❶ *noun* **1** small or inexpensive restaurant serving light refreshments. **2** *S Afr* corner shop or grocer. **cafeteria** *noun* self-service restaurant.

caffeine *noun* stimulant found in tea and coffee.

caftan *noun* same as KAFTAN.

cage ❶ *noun* **1** enclosure of bars or wires, for keeping animals or birds. **2** enclosed platform of a lift in a mine. **caged** *adjective* kept in a cage.

cagey ❶ *adjective* **cagier, cagiest** *Informal* reluctant to go into details. **cagily** *adverb*

cagoule [kag-**gool**] *noun* lightweight hooded waterproof jacket.

cahoots *plural noun* **in cahoots** *Informal* conspiring together.

caiman *noun* same as CAYMAN.

cairn *noun* mound of stones erected as a memorial or marker.

cairngorm *noun* yellow or brownish quartz gemstone.

caisson [**kay**-son] *noun* watertight chamber used to carry out construction work under water.

cajole ❶ *verb* persuade by flattery. **cajolery** *noun*

cake ❶ *noun* **1** sweet food baked from a mixture of flour, eggs, etc. **2** flat compact mass of something, such as soap. ◆ *verb* **3** form into a hardened mass or crust.

calabash *noun* **1** type of large round gourd. **2** bowl made from this.

calamine *noun* pink powder consisting chiefly of zinc oxide, used in skin lotions and ointments.

calamity ❶ *noun, pl* **-ties** disaster. **calamitous** *adjective*

calciferol *noun* substance found in fish oils and used to treat rickets.

calcify *verb* **-fying, -fied** harden by the depositing of calcium salts. **calcification** *noun*

calcium *noun Chem* silvery-white metallic element found in bones, teeth, limestone, and chalk.

calculate ❶ *verb* **1** solve or find out by a mathematical procedure or by reasoning. **2** aim to have a particular effect. **calculable** *adjective* **calculated** *adjective* deliberate, premeditated. **calculating** *adjective* selfishly scheming. **calculation** *noun* **calculator** *noun* small electronic device for making calculations.

calculus *noun, pl* **-luses 1** branch of mathematics dealing with infinitesimal changes to a variable number or quantity. **2** *Pathology* hard deposit in kidney or bladder.

caldron *noun* same as CAULDRON.

——————— THESAURUS ———————

café *noun* =**snack bar**, brasserie, cafeteria, coffee bar, coffee shop, lunchroom, restaurant, tearoom

cage *noun* **1** =**enclosure**, pen, pound

cagey *adjective Inf* =**wary**, careful, cautious, chary, discreet, guarded, noncommittal, shrewd, wily OPPOSITE> **careless**

cajole *verb* =**persuade**, coax, flatter, seduce, sweet-talk (*inf*), wheedle

cake *noun* **2** =**block**, bar, cube, loaf, lump, mass, slab ◆*verb* **3** =**encrust**, bake, coagulate, congeal, solidify

calamitous *adjective* =**disastrous**, cataclysmic, catastrophic, deadly, devastating, dire, fatal, ruinous, tragic OPPOSITE> **fortunate**

calamity *noun* =**disaster**, cataclysm,

catastrophe, misadventure, misfortune, mishap, ruin, tragedy, tribulation OPPOSITE> **benefit**

calculate *verb* **1** =**work out**, compute, count, determine, enumerate, estimate, figure, reckon **2** =**plan**, aim, design, intend

calculated *adjective* =**deliberate**, considered, intended, intentional, planned, premeditated, purposeful OPPOSITE> **unplanned**

calculating *adjective* =**scheming**, crafty, cunning, devious, Machiavellian, manipulative, sharp, shrewd, sly OPPOSITE> **direct**

calculation *noun* **1** =**working out**, answer, computation, estimate, forecast, judgment, reckoning, result **2** =**planning**, contrivance, deliberation, discretion, foresight, forethought, precaution

C

Caledonian *adjective* Scottish.
calendar *noun* **1** chart showing a year divided up into months, weeks, and days. **2** system for determining the beginning, length, and division of years. **3** schedule of events or appointments.
calender *noun* machine in which paper or cloth is smoothed by passing it between rollers.
calends *plural noun* first day of each month in the ancient Roman calendar.
calendula *noun* marigold.
calf¹ *noun, pl* **calves 1** young cow, bull, elephant, whale, or seal. **2** leather made from calf skin. **calve** *verb* give birth to a calf. **calf love** adolescent infatuation.
calf² *noun, pl* **calves** back of the leg between the ankle and knee.
calibre ⊕ [kal-lib-ber] *noun* **1** person's ability or worth. **2** diameter of the bore of a gun or of a shell or bullet. **calibrate** *verb* mark the scale or check the accuracy of (a measuring instrument). **calibration** *noun*
calico *noun, pl* **-coes, -cos** white cotton fabric.
californium *noun Chem* radioactive element produced artificially.
caliph *noun Hist* Muslim ruler.
call ⊕ *verb* **1** name. **2** shout to attract attention. **3** telephone. **4** summon. **5** (often foll. by *on*) visit. **6** arrange (a meeting, strike, etc.). ◆ *noun* **7** cry, shout. **8** animal's or bird's cry. **9** telephone communication. **10** short visit. **11** summons, invitation. **12** need, demand.
caller *noun* **calling** *noun* vocation, profession. **call box** kiosk for a public telephone. **call for** *verb* require. **call girl** prostitute with whom appointments are made by telephone. **call off**

verb cancel. **call up** *verb* **1** summon to serve in the armed forces. **2** cause one to remember.
calligraphy *noun* (art of) beautiful handwriting. **calligrapher** *noun*
calliper *noun* **1** metal splint for supporting the leg. **2** instrument for measuring diameters.
callisthenics *plural noun* light keep-fit exercises. **callisthenic** *adjective*
callous ⊕ *adjective* showing no concern for other people's feelings. **calloused** *adjective* (of skin) thickened and hardened. **callously** *adverb* **callousness** *noun*
callow ⊕ *adjective* young and inexperienced.
callus *noun, pl* **-luses** area of thick hardened skin.
calm ⊕ *adjective* **1** not agitated or excited. **2** not ruffled by the wind. **3** windless. ◆ *noun* **4** peaceful state. ◆ *verb* **5** (often foll. by *down*) make or become calm. **calmly** *adverb* **calmness** *noun*
Calor Gas *noun* ® butane gas liquefied under pressure in containers for domestic use.
calorie *noun* **1** unit of measurement for the energy value of food. **2** unit of heat. **calorific** *adjective* of calories or heat.
calumny *noun, pl* **-nies** false or malicious statement. **calumniate** *verb* make false or malicious statements about.
Calvary *noun* place outside the walls of Jerusalem where Jesus was crucified.
calves *noun* plural of CALF.
Calvinism *noun* theological system of Calvin, stressing predestination and salvation solely by God's grace. **Calvinist** *noun, adjective*

———————————— T H E S A U R U S ——————————————

calibre *noun* **1** = **worth**, ability, capacity, distinction, merit, quality, stature, talent **2** = **diameter**, bore, gauge, measure
call *verb* **1** = **name**, christen, describe as, designate, dub, entitle, label, style, term **2** = **cry**, arouse, hail, rouse, shout, yell OPPOSITE whisper. **3** = **phone**, ring up (*inf, chiefly Brit*), telephone **4** = **summon**, assemble, convene, gather, muster, rally OPPOSITE dismiss. **5** (often foll. by *on*) = **visit**, drop in on, look in on, look up, see ◆*noun* **7** = **cry**, hail, scream, shout, signal, whoop, yell OPPOSITE whisper. **11** = **summons**, appeal, command, demand, invitation, notice, order, plea, request **12** = **need**, cause, excuse, grounds, justification, occasion, reason
call for *verb* = **require**, demand, entail, involve, necessitate, need, occasion, suggest
calling *noun* = **profession**, career, life's work, mission, trade, vocation

callous *adjective* = **heartless**, cold, hard-bitten, hardened, hardhearted, insensitive, uncaring, unfeeling OPPOSITE compassionate
callow *adjective* = **inexperienced**, green, guileless, immature, naive, raw, unsophisticated
calm *adjective* **1** = **cool**, collected, composed, dispassionate, relaxed, sedate, self-possessed, unemotional OPPOSITE excited. **2, 3** = **still**, balmy, mild, quiet, serene, smooth, tranquil, windless OPPOSITE wild ◆*noun* **4** = **peacefulness**, hush, peace, quiet, repose, serenity, stillness OPPOSITE disturbance ◆*verb* **5** (often foll. by *down*) = **quieten**, hush, mollify, outspan (*S Afr*), placate, relax, soothe OPPOSITE excite
calmness *noun* **1** = **coolness**, composure, cool (*sl*), equanimity, impassivity, poise, sang-froid, self-possession **2** = **peacefulness**, calm, hush, quiet, repose, restfulness, serenity, stillness, tranquillity

Calvinistic *adjective*
calypso *noun, pl* **-sos** West Indian song with improvised topical lyrics.
calyx *noun, pl* **calyxes, calyces** outer leaves that protect a flower bud.
cam *noun* device that converts a circular motion to a to-and-fro motion. **camshaft** *noun* part of an engine consisting of a rod to which cams are fixed.
camaraderie *noun* comradeship.
camber *noun* slight upward curve to the centre of a surface.
cambric *noun* fine white linen fabric.
camcorder *noun* combined portable video camera and recorder.
came *verb* past tense of COME.
camel *noun* humped mammal that can survive long periods without food or water in desert regions.
camellia [kam-**meal**-ya] *noun* evergreen ornamental shrub with white, pink, or red flowers.
Camembert [**kam**-mem-bare] *noun* soft creamy French cheese.
cameo *noun, pl* **cameos 1** brooch or ring with a profile head carved in relief. **2** small part in a film or play performed by a well-known actor or actress.
camera *noun* apparatus used for taking photographs or pictures for television or cinema. **in camera** in private session.
cameraman *noun* man who operates a camera for television or cinema.
camiknickers *plural noun* woman's undergarment consisting of knickers attached to a camisole.
camisole *noun* woman's bodice-like garment.
camomile *noun* aromatic plant, used to make herbal tea.
camouflage ⊙ [**kam**-moo-flahzh] *noun* **1** use of natural surroundings or artificial aids to conceal or disguise something. ◆ *verb* **2** conceal by camouflage.
camp¹ ⊙ *noun* **1** (place for) temporary lodgings consisting of tents, huts, or cabins. **2** group supporting a particular doctrine. ◆ *verb* **3** stay in a camp. **camper** *noun* **camp follower**

person who supports a particular group without being a member of it.
camp² ⊙ *adjective Informal* **1** effeminate or homosexual. **2** consciously artificial or affected. **camp it up** *Informal* behave in a camp way.
campaign ⊙ *noun* **1** series of coordinated activities designed to achieve a goal. **2** number of military operations aimed at achieving an objective. ◆ *verb* **3** take part in a campaign.
campanile [camp-an-**neel**-lee] *noun* bell tower, usu. one not attached to another building.
campanology *noun* art of ringing bells.
campanologist *noun*
campanula *noun* plant with blue or white bell-shaped flowers.
camphor *noun* aromatic crystalline substance used medicinally and in mothballs.
camphorated *adjective*
campion *noun* red, pink, or white wild flower.
campus *noun, pl* **-puses** grounds of a university or college.
can¹ *verb, past* **could 1** be able to. **2** be allowed to.
can² *noun* **1** metal container for food or liquids. ◆ *verb* **canning, canned 2** put (something) into a can. **canned** *adjective* **1** preserved in a can. **2** (of music) prerecorded.
cannery *noun, pl* **-neries** factory where food is canned.
Canada Day *noun* July 1, the anniversary of the day when Canada became the first British colony to receive dominion status.
Canada goose *noun* large greyish-brown N American goose with a black neck and head and a white throat patch.
Canada jay *noun* a large common jay of North America with a grey body, and a white-and-black crestless head.
Canadian *noun, adjective* (person) from Canada.
canal ⊙ *noun* **1** artificial waterway. **2** passage in the body. **canalize** *verb* **1** give direction to. **2** convert into a canal.
canapé [**kan**-nap-pay] *noun* small piece of bread or toast with a savoury topping.
canard *noun* false report.

——————— THESAURUS ———————

camouflage *noun* **1** = **disguise**, blind, cloak, concealment, cover, mask, masquerade, screen, subterfuge [OPPOSITE] **display** ◆*verb* **2** = **disguise**, cloak, conceal, cover, hide, mask, obfuscate, obscure, screen, veil [OPPOSITE] **reveal**
camp¹ *noun* **1** = **camp site**, bivouac, camping ground, encampment, tents

camp² *adjective Inf* **1** = **effeminate 2** = **affected**, artificial, mannered, ostentatious, posturing
campaign *noun* **1** = **operation**, crusade, drive, movement, push **2** = **attack**, expedition, offensive
canal *noun* **1** = **waterway**, channel, conduit, duct, passage, watercourse

C

canary *noun, pl* **-ries** small yellow songbird often kept as a pet.

canasta *noun* card game like rummy, played with two packs.

cancan *noun* lively high-kicking dance performed by a female group.

cancel ❶ *verb* **-celling, -celled 1** stop (something that has been arranged) from taking place. **2** mark (a cheque or stamp) with an official stamp to prevent further use. **cancellation** *noun* **cancel out** *verb* counterbalance, neutralize.

cancer ❶ *noun* **1** serious disease resulting from a malignant growth or tumour. **2** malignant growth or tumour. **3** evil influence that spreads dangerously. **cancerous** *adjective*

Cancer *noun* (the crab) fourth sign of the zodiac. **tropic of Cancer** see TROPIC.

candela [kan-dee-la] *noun* unit of luminous intensity.

candelabrum *noun, pl* **-bra** large branched candle holder.

candid ❶ *adjective* honest and straightforward. **candidly** *adverb*

candidate ❶ *noun* **1** person seeking a job or position. **2** person taking an examination. **candidacy, candidature** *noun*

candle *noun* stick of wax enclosing a wick, which is burned to produce light. **candlestick** *noun* holder for a candle. **candlewick** *noun* cotton fabric with a tufted surface.

Candlemas *noun Christianity* Feb. 2, Feast of the Purification of the Virgin Mary.

candour ❶ *noun* honesty and straightforwardness.

candy *noun, pl* **-dies** *US* a sweet or sweets. **candied** *adjective* coated with sugar.

candyfloss *noun* light fluffy mass of spun sugar on a stick. **candy-striped** *adjective* having coloured stripes on a white background.

candytuft *noun* garden plant with clusters of white, pink, or purple flowers.

cane *noun* **1** stem of the bamboo or similar plant. **2** flexible rod used to beat someone. **3** slender walking stick. ◆ *verb* **4** beat with a cane.

cane toad large toad used to control insects and other pests of sugar-cane plantations.

canine [kay-nine] *adjective* **1** of or like a dog. ◆ *noun* **2** sharp pointed tooth between the incisors and the molars.

canister *noun* metal container.

canker ❶ *noun* **1** ulceration, ulcerous disease. **2** something evil that spreads and corrupts.

cannabis *noun* **1** Asian plant with tough fibres. **2** drug obtained from the dried leaves and flowers of this plant, which can be smoked or chewed.

cannelloni *plural noun* tubular pieces of pasta filled with meat etc.

cannibal *noun* **1** person who eats human flesh. **2** animal that eats others of its own kind. **cannibalism** *noun* **cannibalize** *verb* use parts from (one machine) to repair another.

cannon ❶ *noun* **1** large gun on wheels. **2** billiard stroke in which the cue ball hits two balls successively. **cannonade** *noun* continuous heavy gunfire. **cannonball** *noun* heavy metal ball fired from a cannon. **cannon into** *verb* collide with.

cannot can not.

canny ❶ *adjective* **-nier, -niest** shrewd, cautious. **cannily** *adverb*

canoe *noun* light narrow open boat propelled by a paddle or paddles. **canoeing** *noun* sport of rowing in a canoe. **canoeist** *noun*

canon[1] *noun* priest serving in a cathedral.

canon[2] ❶ *noun* **1** Church decree regulating morals or religious practices. **2** general rule or standard. **3** list of the works of an author that are accepted as authentic. **4** piece of music in which the same melody is taken up in different parts. **canonical** *adjective* **canonize** *verb* declare (a person) officially to be a saint. **canonization** *noun*

──────── T H E S A U R U S ────────

cancel *verb* **1 = call off**, abolish, abort, annul, delete, do away with, eliminate, erase, expunge, obliterate, repeal, revoke

cancellation *noun* **1 = abandonment**, abolition, annulment, deletion, elimination, repeal, revocation

cancer *noun* **1 = sickness**, pestilence **2 = growth**, malignancy, tumour **3 = corruption**

candid *adjective* **= honest**, blunt, forthright, frank, open, outspoken, plain, straightforward, truthful OPPOSITE **diplomatic**

candidate *noun* **1 = contender**, applicant, claimant, competitor, contestant, entrant,

nominee, runner

candour *noun* **= honesty**, directness, forthrightness, frankness, openness, outspokenness, straightforwardness, truthfulness OPPOSITE **dishonesty**

canker *noun* **1 = disease**, cancer, infection, rot, sore, ulcer **2 = corruption**, blight, rot, scourge

cannon *noun* **1 = gun**, big gun, field gun, mortar

canny *adjective* **= shrewd**, astute, careful, cautious, clever, judicious, prudent, wise OPPOSITE **inept**

canoodle *verb Slang* kiss and cuddle.

canopy ❶ *noun, pl* **-pies 1** covering above a bed, door, etc. **2** any large or wide covering. **canopied** *adjective* covered with a canopy.

cant¹ ❶ *noun* **1** insincere talk. **2** specialized vocabulary of a particular group. ♦ *verb* **3** use cant.

cant² ❶ *noun* **1** tilted position. ♦ *verb* **2** tilt, overturn.

can't can not.

cantaloupe, cantaloup *noun* kind of melon with sweet orange flesh.

cantankerous ❶ *adjective* quarrelsome, bad-tempered.

cantata [kan-tah-ta] *noun* musical work consisting of arias, duets, and choruses.

canteen *noun* **1** restaurant attached to a workplace or school. **2** box containing a set of cutlery.

canter ❶ *noun* **1** horse's gait between a trot and a gallop. ♦ *verb* **2** move at a canter.

canticle *noun* short hymn with words from the Bible.

cantilever *noun* beam or girder fixed at one end only. **cantilever bridge** bridge made of two cantilevers that meet in the middle.

canto [kan-toe] *noun, pl* **-tos** main division of a long poem.

canton *noun* political division of a country, esp. Switzerland.

cantonment [kan-toon-ment] *noun* military camp.

cantor *noun* man employed to lead services in a synagogue.

Canuck *noun, adjective Informal* Canadian.

canvas *noun* **1** heavy coarse cloth used for sails and tents, and for oil painting. **2** an oil painting on canvas. **under canvas** in a tent.

canvass ❶ *verb* **1** try to get votes or support (from). **2** find out the opinions of (people) by conducting a survey. ♦ *noun* **3** canvassing.

canyon *noun* deep narrow valley.

caoutchouc [**cow**-chook] *noun* raw rubber.

cap ❶ *noun* **1** soft close-fitting covering for the head. **2** cap given to player selected for a national team. **3** small lid. **4** small explosive device used in a toy gun. **5** contraceptive device. ♦ *verb* **capping, capped 6** cover or top with something. **7** select (a player) for a national team. **8** impose an upper limit on (a tax). **9** outdo, excel.

CAP (in the EU) Common Agricultural Policy.

cap. capital.

capable ❶ *adjective* **1** (foll. by *of*) having the ability (for). **2** competent and efficient. **capably** *adverb* **capability** *noun, pl* **-ties**

capacity ❶ *noun, pl* **-ties 1** ability to contain, absorb, or hold. **2** maximum amount that can be contained or produced. **3** physical or mental ability. **4** position, function. **capacious** *adjective* roomy. **capacitance** *noun* (measure of) the ability of a system to store electrical charge. **capacitor** *noun* device for storing electrical charge.

caparisoned [kap-**par**-riss-sond] *adjective* magnificently decorated.

cape¹ ❶ *noun* short cloak.

cape² ❶ *noun* large piece of land that juts out

——————— THESAURUS ———————

canon² *noun* **2 = rule**, criterion, dictate, formula, precept, principle, regulation, standard, statute, yardstick **3 = list**, catalogue, roll

canopy *noun* **1 = awning**, covering, shade, sunshade

cant¹ *noun* **1 = hypocrisy**, humbug, insincerity, lip service, pretence, pretentiousness, sanctimoniousness **2 = jargon**, argot, lingo, patter, slang, vernacular

cant² *verb* **2 = tilt**, angle, bevel, incline, rise, slant, slope

cantankerous *adjective* **= bad-tempered**, choleric, contrary, disagreeable, grumpy, irascible, irritable, testy, waspish OPPOSITE cheerful

canter *noun* **1 = jog**, amble, dogtrot, lope ♦*verb* **2 = jog**, amble, lope

canvass *verb* **1 = campaign**, electioneer, solicit, solicit votes **2 = poll**, examine, inspect, investigate, scrutinize, study ♦*noun* **3 = poll**,

examination, investigation, scrutiny, survey, tally

cap *verb* **9 = beat**, better, crown, eclipse, exceed, outdo, outstrip, surpass, top, transcend

capability *noun* **1 = ability**, capacity, means, potential, power, qualification(s), wherewithal **2 = competence**, efficiency, proficiency OPPOSITE inability

capable *adjective* **1 = able**, accomplished, gifted, qualified, talented OPPOSITE **incapable. 2 = competent**, efficient, proficient OPPOSITE **incompetent**

capacious *adjective* **= spacious**, broad, commodious, expansive, extensive, roomy, sizable *or* sizeable, substantial, vast, voluminous, wide OPPOSITE **limited**

capacity *noun* **1 = size**, amplitude, compass, dimensions, extent, magnitude, range, room, scope, space, volume **3 = ability**, aptitude, aptness, capability, competence, facility, genius, gift **4 = function**, office, position, post,

C

into the sea.
caper ❶ *noun* **1** high-spirited prank. ♦ *verb* **2** skip about.
capercaillie, capercailzie [kap-per-**kale**-yee] *noun* large black European grouse.
capers *plural noun* pickled flower buds of a Mediterranean shrub used in sauces.
capillary [kap-**pill**-a-ree] *noun, pl* **-laries 1** very fine blood vessel. ♦ *adjective* **2** (of a tube) having a fine bore.
capital[1] ❶ *noun* **1** chief city of a country. **2** accumulated wealth. **3** wealth used to produce more wealth. **4** large letter, as used at the beginning of a name or sentence. ♦ *adjective* **5** involving or punishable by death. **6** *Old-fashioned* excellent. **capitalize** *verb* **1** write or print (words) in capitals. **2** convert into or provide with capital. **capitalize on** *verb* take advantage of (a situation). **capital gain** profit from the sale of an asset. **capitalism** *noun* economic system based on the private ownership of industry.
capital[2] *noun* top part of a pillar.
capitalism ❶ *noun* economic system based on the private ownership of industry. **capitalist** *adjective* **1** of capitalists or capitalism. **2** supporting capitalism. ♦ *noun* **3** supporter of capitalism. **4** person who owns a business.
capitation *noun* tax of a fixed amount per person.
capitulate ❶ *verb* surrender on agreed terms. **capitulation** *noun*
capon [**kay**-pon] *noun* castrated cock fowl fattened for eating.

cappuccino [kap-poo-**cheen**-oh] *noun, pl* **-nos** coffee with steamed milk, sprinkled with powdered chocolate.
caprice ❶ [kap-**reess**] *noun* sudden change of attitude. **capricious** *adjective* tending to have sudden changes of attitude. **capriciously** *adverb*
Capricorn *noun* (the goat) tenth sign of the zodiac. **tropic of Capricorn** see TROPIC.
capsicum *noun* kind of pepper used as a vegetable or as a spice.
capsize ❶ *verb* overturn accidentally.
capstan *noun* rotating cylinder round which a ship's rope is wound.
capsule ❶ *noun* **1** soluble gelatine case containing a dose of medicine. **2** plant's seed case. **3** *Anat* membrane surrounding an organ. **4** detachable crew compartment of a spacecraft.
Capt. Captain.
captain ❶ *noun* **1** commander of a ship or civil aircraft. **2** middle-ranking naval officer. **3** junior officer in the army. **4** leader of a team or group. ♦ *verb* **5** be captain of. **captaincy** *noun*
caption *noun* **1** title or explanation accompanying an illustration. ♦ *verb* **2** provide with a caption.
captious *adjective* tending to make trivial criticisms.
captivate ❶ *verb* attract and hold the attention of. **captivating** *adjective*
captive ❶ *noun* **1** person kept in confinement. ♦ *adjective* **2** kept in confinement. **3** (of an audience) unable to leave. **captivity** *noun*

——— THESAURUS ———

province, role, sphere
cape[2] *noun* =**headland**, head, peninsula, point, promontory
caper *noun* **1** =**escapade**, antic, high jinks, jape, lark (*inf*), mischief, practical joke, prank, stunt ♦*verb* **2** =**dance**, bound, cavort, frolic, gambol, jump, skip, spring, trip
capital[1] *noun* **2** =**money**, assets, cash, finances, funds, investment(s), lolly (*Aust & NZ sl*), means, principal, resources, wealth, wherewithal ♦*adjective* **6** *Old-fashioned* =**first-rate**, excellent, fine, splendid, sterling, superb
capitalism *noun* =**private enterprise**, free enterprise, laissez faire *or* laisser faire, private ownership
capitalize on *verb* =**take advantage of**, benefit from, cash in on (*inf*), exploit, gain from, make the most of, profit from
capitulate *verb* =**give in**, cave in (*inf*), come to terms, give up, relent, submit, succumb, surrender, yield ⟨OPPOSITE⟩ **resist**

caprice *noun* =**whim**, fad, fancy, fickleness, impulse, inconstancy, notion, whimsy
capricious *adjective* =**unpredictable**, changeful, erratic, fickle, fitful, impulsive, inconsistent, inconstant, mercurial, variable, wayward, whimsical ⟨OPPOSITE⟩ **consistent**
capsize *verb* =**overturn**, invert, keel over, tip over, turn over, turn turtle, upset
capsule *noun* **1** =**pill**, lozenge, tablet **2** =**pod**, case, receptacle, seed case, sheath, shell, vessel
captain *noun* =**leader**, boss, chief, commander, head, master, skipper
captivate *verb* =**charm**, allure, attract, beguile, bewitch, enchant, enrapture, enthral, entrance, fascinate, infatuate, mesmerize ⟨OPPOSITE⟩ **repel**
captive *noun* **1** =**prisoner**, convict, detainee, hostage, internee, prisoner of war, slave ♦*adjective* **2** =**confined**, caged, enslaved, ensnared, imprisoned, incarcerated, locked up, penned, restricted, subjugated

captor *noun* person who captures a person or animal.
capture ✪ *verb* 1 take by force. 2 succeed in representing (something elusive) artistically. ◆ *noun* 3 capturing.
capuchin [kap-yoo-chin] *noun* S American monkey with thick hair on the top of its head.
capybara *noun* very large S American rodent.
car ✪ *noun* 1 motor vehicle designed to carry a small number of people. 2 passenger compartment of a cable car, lift, etc. 3 US railway carriage. **carjack** *verb* attack (a car driver) to rob them or to steal the car. **car park** area or building reserved for parking cars.
carafe [kar-raff] *noun* glass bottle for serving water or wine.
caramel *noun* 1 chewy sweet made from sugar and milk. 2 burnt sugar, used for colouring and flavouring food. **caramelize** *verb* turn into caramel.
carapace *noun* hard upper shell of tortoises and crustaceans.
carat *noun* 1 unit of weight of precious stones. 2 measure of the purity of gold in an alloy.
caravan *noun* 1 large enclosed vehicle for living in, designed to be towed by a car or horse. 2 group travelling together in Eastern countries. **caravanserai** *noun* large inn enclosing a courtyard, providing accommodation for caravans in Eastern countries.
caraway *noun* plant whose seeds are used as a spice.
carbide *noun* compound of carbon with a metal.
carbine *noun* light automatic rifle.
carbohydrate *noun* any of a large group of energy-producing compounds in food, such as sugars and starches.
carbolic acid *noun* disinfectant derived from coal tar.
carbon *noun* nonmetallic element occurring as charcoal, graphite, and diamond, found in all organic matter. **carbonate** *noun* salt or ester of carbonic acid. **carbonated** *adjective* (of a drink) containing carbon dioxide. **carboniferous** *adjective* producing coal or carbon. **carbonize** *verb* 1 turn into carbon as a result of heating. 2

coat with carbon. **carbon copy** 1 copy made with carbon paper. 2 very similar person or thing. **carbon dioxide** colourless gas exhaled by people and animals. **carbonic acid** weak acid formed from carbon dioxide and water.
carbon paper paper coated on one side with a dark waxy pigment, used to make a copy of something as it is typed or written.
Carborundum *noun* ® compound of silicon and carbon, used for grinding and polishing.
carboy *noun* large bottle with a protective casing.
carbuncle *noun* inflamed boil.
carburettor *noun* device which mixes petrol and air in an internal-combustion engine.
carcass, carcase ✪ *noun* 1 dead body of an animal. 2 *Informal* person's body.
carcinogen *noun* substance that produces cancer. **carcinogenic** *adjective* **carcinoma** *noun* malignant tumour.
card[1] *noun* 1 piece of thick stiff paper or cardboard used for identification, reference, or sending greetings or messages. 2 one of a set of cards with a printed pattern, used for playing games. 3 small rectangle of stiff plastic with identifying numbers for use as a credit card, cheque card, or charge card. 4 *Old-fashioned* witty or eccentric person. ◆ *plural* 5 any card game, or card games in general. **cardboard** *noun* thin stiff board made from paper pulp. **cardsharp** *noun* professional card player who cheats.
card[2] *noun* 1 machine or tool for combing wool before spinning. ◆ *verb* 2 process with such a machine or tool.
cardamom *noun* spice obtained from the seeds of a tropical plant.
cardiac *adjective* of the heart. **cardiogram** *noun* electrocardiogram. **cardiograph** *noun* electrocardiograph. **cardiology** *noun* study of the heart and its diseases. **cardiologist** *noun* **cardiovascular** *adjective* of the heart and the blood vessels.
cardigan *noun* knitted jacket.
cardinal ✪ *noun* 1 any of the high-ranking clergymen of the RC Church who elect the Pope and act as his counsellors. ◆ *adjective* 2 fundamentally important. **cardinal number**

——————— THESAURUS ———————

captivity *noun* 2 = confinement, bondage, custody, detention, imprisonment, incarceration, internment, slavery
capture *verb* 1 = catch, apprehend, arrest, bag, collar (*inf*), secure, seize, take, take prisoner OPPOSITE free ◆*noun* 3 = catching, apprehension, arrest, imprisonment, seizure,

taking, taking captive, trapping
car *noun* 1 = vehicle, auto (*US*), automobile, jalopy (*inf*), machine, motor, motorcar, wheels (*inf*) 3 *US* = (railway) carriage, buffet car, cable car, coach, dining car, sleeping car, van
carcass *noun* = body, cadaver (*Med*), corpse, dead body, framework, hulk, remains, shell,

number denoting quantity but not order in a group, for example four as distinct from fourth.
cardinal points the four main points of the compass.
care ❶ *verb* **1** be concerned. **2** like (to do something). **3** (foll. by *for*) like, be fond of. **4** (foll. by *for*) look after. ✦ *noun* **5** careful attention, caution. **6** protection, charge. **7** trouble, worry. **in, into care** made the legal responsibility of a local authority. **carefree** *adjective* **careful** *adjective* **carefully** *adverb* **carefulness** *noun* **careless** *adjective* **carelessly** *adverb* **carelessness** *noun* **caring** *adjective*
careen *verb* tilt over to one side.
career ❶ *noun* **1** series of jobs in a profession or occupation that a person has through their life. **2** part of a person's life spent in a particular occupation. ✦ *verb* **3** rush in an uncontrolled way. **careerist** *noun* person who seeks advancement by any possible means.
carefree ❶ *adjective* without worry or responsibility.
caress ❶ *noun* **1** gentle affectionate touch or embrace. ✦ *verb* **2** touch gently and affectionately.
caret [kar-rett] *noun* symbol (∧) indicating a place in written or printed matter where

something is to be inserted.
caretaker ❶ *noun* person employed to look after a place.
careworn *adjective* showing signs of worry.
cargo ❶ *noun, pl* **-goes** goods carried by a ship, aircraft, etc. **cargo pants, trousers** *plural noun* loose trousers with a large pocket on each leg.
caribou *noun, pl* **-bou** *or* **-bous** large N American reindeer.
caricature ❶ *noun* **1** drawing or description of a person that exaggerates features for comic effect. ✦ *verb* **2** make a caricature of.
caries [**care**-reez] *noun* tooth decay.
carillon [kar-**rill**-yon] *noun* **1** set of bells played by keyboard or mechanically. **2** tune played on such bells.
cark *verb Aust & NZ slang* die.
Carmelite *noun, adjective* (friar or nun) of the Order of Our Lady of Carmel.
carminative *noun, adjective* (drug) able to relieve flatulence.
carmine *adjective* vivid red.
carnage ❶ *noun* extensive slaughter of people.
carnal ❶ *adjective* of a sexual or sensual nature. **carnal knowledge** sexual intercourse.
carnation *noun* cultivated plant with fragrant

———— THESAURUS ————

skeleton
cardinal *adjective* **2** = **principal**, capital, central, chief, essential, first, fundamental, key, leading, main, paramount, primary OPPOSITE **secondary**
care *verb* **1** = **be concerned**, be bothered, be interested, mind **4** (foll. by *for*) = **look after**, attend, foster, mind, minister to, nurse, protect, provide for, tend, watch over ✦*noun* **5** = **caution**, attention, carefulness, consideration, forethought, heed, management, pains, prudence, vigilance, watchfulness OPPOSITE **abandon**. **6** = **protection**, charge, control, custody, guardianship, keeping, management, supervision **7** = **worry**, anxiety, concern, disquiet, perplexity, pressure, responsibility, stress, trouble OPPOSITE **pleasure**
career *noun* **1** = **occupation**, calling, employment, life's work, livelihood, pursuit, vocation ✦*verb* **3** = **rush**, barrel (along) (*inf, chiefly US & Canad*), bolt, dash, hurtle, race, speed, tear
carefree *adjective* = **untroubled**, blithe, breezy, cheerful, easy-going, halcyon, happy-go-lucky, light-hearted OPPOSITE **unhappy**
careful *adjective* = **thorough**, cautious, chary, circumspect, conscientious, discreet, meticulous, painstaking, particular, precise,

prudent, scrupulous, thoughtful OPPOSITE **careless**
careless *adjective* = **negligent**, absent-minded, casual, cavalier, forgetful, irresponsible, lackadaisical, neglectful, nonchalant, offhand, slapdash, slipshod, sloppy (*inf*), thoughtless OPPOSITE **careful**
carelessness *noun* = **negligence**, irresponsibility, laxity, neglect, omission, slackness, sloppiness (*inf*), thoughtlessness
caress *noun* **1** = **stroke**, cuddle, embrace, fondling, hug, kiss, pat ✦*verb* **2** = **stroke**, cuddle, embrace, fondle, hug, kiss, neck (*inf*), nuzzle, pet
caretaker *noun* = **warden**, concierge, curator, custodian, janitor, keeper, porter, superintendent, watchman
cargo *noun* = **load**, baggage, consignment, contents, freight, goods, merchandise, shipment
caricature *noun* **1** = **parody**, burlesque, cartoon, distortion, farce, lampoon, satire, send-up (*Brit inf*), takeoff (*inf*), travesty ✦*verb* **2** = **parody**, burlesque, distort, lampoon, mimic, mock, ridicule, satirize, send up (*Brit inf*), take off (*inf*)
carnage *noun* = **slaughter**, blood bath, bloodshed, butchery, havoc, holocaust,

white, pink, or red flowers.
carnelian *noun* reddish-yellow gemstone.
carnival ✪ *noun* **1** festive period with processions, music, and dancing in the street. **2** travelling funfair.
carnivore *noun* meat-eating animal.
carnivorous *adjective*
carob *noun* pod of a Mediterranean tree, used as a chocolate substitute.
carol ✪ *noun* **1** joyful Christmas hymn. ♦ *verb* **-olling, -olled 2** sing carols. **3** sing joyfully.
carotid [kar-**rot**-id] *adjective, noun* (of) either of the two arteries supplying blood to the head.
carouse *verb* have a merry drinking party.
carousal *noun* merry drinking party.
carousel [kar-roo-**sell**] *noun* **1** revolving conveyor belt for luggage or photographic slides. **2** *US* merry-go-round.
carp[1] *noun* large freshwater fish.
carp[2] ✪ *verb* complain, find fault.
carpal *noun* wrist bone.
carpel *noun* female reproductive organ of a flowering plant.
carpenter ✪ *noun* person who makes or repairs wooden structures. **carpentry** *noun*
carpet *noun* **1** heavy fabric for covering floors. **2** covering like a carpet. ♦ *verb* **carpeting, carpeted 3** cover with a carpet. **on the carpet** *Informal* being reprimanded.
carpetbagger *noun* politician seeking office in a place where he or she has no connections.
carpet snake *or* **python** large nonvenomous Australian snake with a carpet-like pattern on its back.
carpus *noun, pl* **-pi** set of eight bones of the wrist.
carriage ✪ *noun* **1** one of the sections of a train for passengers. **2** way a person holds his or her head and body. **3** four-wheeled horse-drawn vehicle. **4** moving part of a machine that supports and shifts another part. **5** charge made for conveying goods. **carriageway** *noun*

part of a road along which traffic passes in one direction.
carrier *noun* **1** person or thing that carries something. **2** person or animal that does not suffer from a disease but can transmit it to others. **carrier bag** large plastic or paper bag for shopping. **carrier pigeon** homing pigeon used for carrying messages.
carrion *noun* dead and rotting flesh. **carrion crow** scavenging European crow.
carrot *noun* **1** long tapering orange root vegetable. **2** something offered as an incentive.
carroty *adjective* (of hair) reddish-orange.
carry ✪ *verb* **-rying, -ried 1** take from one place to another. **2** have with one habitually, in one's pocket etc. **3** transmit (a disease). **4** have as a factor or result. **5** hold (one's head or body) in a specified manner. **6** secure the adoption of (a bill or motion). **7** (of sound) travel a certain distance. **carrycot** *noun* light portable bed for a baby, with handles and a hood. **carry on** *verb* **1** continue. **2** do, run, or take part in. **3** *Informal* cause a fuss. **carry out** *verb* follow, accomplish. **carry through** *verb* bring to completion.
cart *noun* **1** open two-wheeled horse-drawn vehicle for carrying goods or passengers. **2** small vehicle pulled or pushed by hand. ♦ *verb* **3** carry, usu. with some effort. **carthorse** *noun* large heavily built horse. **cartwheel** *noun* **1** sideways somersault supported by the hands with legs outstretched. **2** large spoked wheel of a cart.
carte blanche *noun French* complete authority.
cartel *noun* association of competing firms formed to fix prices.
Carthusian *noun, adjective* (monk or nun) of a strict monastic order founded in 1084.
cartilage [kar-**till**-ij] *noun* strong flexible tissue forming part of the skeleton. **cartilaginous** *adjective*

C

——————————— THESAURUS ———————————

massacre, mass murder, murder, shambles
carnal *adjective* **=sexual**, erotic, fleshly, lascivious, lewd, libidinous, lustful, sensual
carnival *noun* **1 =festival**, celebration, fair, fete, fiesta, gala, holiday, jamboree, jubilee, merrymaking, revelry
carol *noun* **1 =song**, chorus, ditty, hymn, lay
carp[2] *verb* **=find fault**, cavil, complain, criticize, pick holes, quibble, reproach OPPOSITE **praise**
carpenter *noun* **=joiner**, cabinet-maker, woodworker
carriage *noun* **1 =vehicle**, cab, coach,

conveyance **2 =bearing**, air, behaviour, comportment, conduct, demeanour, deportment, gait, manner, posture
carry *verb* **1 =transport**, bear, bring, conduct, convey, fetch, haul, lug, move, relay, take, transfer **6 =win**, accomplish, capture, effect, gain, secure
carry on *verb* **1 =continue**, endure, keep going, last, maintain, perpetuate, persevere, persist **3** *Inf* **=make a fuss**, create (*sl*), misbehave
carry out *verb* **=perform**, accomplish, achieve, carry through, effect, execute, fulfil,

C

cartography *noun* map making.
cartographer *noun* **cartographic** *adjective*
carton ❶ *noun* container made of cardboard or waxed paper.
cartoon ❶ *noun* **1** humorous or satirical drawing. **2** sequence of these telling a story. **3** film made by drawing a series of drawings which give the illusion of movement when projected. **cartoonist** *noun*
cartouche, cartouch *noun* **1** ornamental tablet or panel in the form of a scroll. **2** oval figure containing royal or divine Egyptian names.
cartridge ❶ *noun* **1** casing containing an explosive charge and bullet for a gun. **2** part of the pick-up of a record player that converts the movements of the stylus into electrical signals. **3** sealed container of film, tape, etc. **cartridge paper** strong thick drawing paper.
carve ❶ *verb* **1** cut to form an object. **2** form (an object or design) by cutting. **3** slice (cooked meat). **carving** *noun* **carve out** *verb Informal* make or create (a career).
caryatid [kar-ree-**at**-id] *noun* supporting column in the shape of a female figure.
Casanova *noun* promiscuous man.
casbah *noun* citadel of a N African city.
cascade ❶ *noun* **1** waterfall. **2** something flowing or falling like a waterfall. ◆ *verb* **3** flow or fall in a cascade.
cascara *noun* bark of a N American shrub, used as a laxative.
case¹ ❶ *noun* **1** instance, example. **2** matter for discussion. **3** condition, state of affairs. **4** set of arguments supporting an action or cause. **5** person or problem dealt with by a doctor, social worker, or solicitor. **6** action, lawsuit. **7** evidence offered in court to support a claim. **8**

Grammar form of a noun, pronoun, or adjective showing its relation to other words in the sentence. **in case** so as to allow for the possibility that.
case² ❶ *noun* **1** container, protective covering. **2** suitcase. ◆ *verb* **3** *Slang* inspect (a building) with the intention of burgling it. **case-hardened** *adjective* having been made callous by experience.
casein *noun* protein found in milk and its products.
casement *noun* window that is hinged on one side.
cash ❶ *noun* **1** banknotes and coins. ◆ *adjective* **2** of, for, or paid in cash. ◆ *verb* **3** obtain cash for. **cash-and-carry** *adjective* operating on a basis of cash payment for goods that are taken away by the buyer. **cash in on** *verb Informal* gain profit or advantage from. **cash register** till that displays and adds the prices of the goods sold.
cashew *noun* edible kidney-shaped nut.
cashier¹ ❶ *noun* person responsible for handling cash in a bank, shop, etc.
cashier² ❶ *verb* dismiss with dishonour from the armed forces.
cashmere *noun* fine soft wool obtained from goats.
casing *noun* protective case, covering.
casino *noun, pl* **-nos** public building or room where gambling games are played.
cask *noun* barrel used to hold alcoholic drink.
casket ❶ *noun* **1** small box for valuables. **2** *US* coffin.
Cassandra *noun* someone whose prophecies of doom are unheeded.
cassava *noun* starch obtained from the roots of a tropical American plant, used to make

——————— T H E S A U R U S ———————

implement, realize
carton *noun* = **box**, case, container, pack, package, packet
cartoon *noun* **1** = **drawing**, caricature, lampoon, parody, satire, sketch **2** = **comic strip 3** = **animation**, animated cartoon, animated film
cartridge *noun* **1** = **shell**, charge, round **3** = **container**, capsule, case, cassette, cylinder, magazine
carve *verb* **1, 2** = **cut**, chip, chisel, engrave, etch, hew, mould, sculpt, whittle **3** = **slice**
cascade *noun* **1** = **waterfall**, avalanche, cataract, deluge, downpour, falls, flood, fountain, outpouring, shower, torrent ◆*verb* **3** = **flow**, descend, fall, flood, gush, overflow, pitch, plunge, pour, spill, surge, teem, tumble

case¹ *noun* **1** = **instance**, example, illustration, occasion, occurrence, specimen **3** = **situation**, circumstance(s), condition, context, contingency, event, position, state **6** = **lawsuit**, action, dispute, proceedings, suit, trial
case² *noun* **1** = **container**, box, canister, capsule, carton, casing, chest, covering, crate, envelope, holder, jacket, receptacle, sheath, shell, wrapper
cash *noun* **1** = **money**, brass (*N Eng dial*), coinage, currency, dough (*sl*), funds, lolly (*Aust & NZ sl*), notes, ready money, silver
cashier¹ *noun* = **teller**, bank clerk, banker, bursar, clerk, purser, treasurer
cashier² *verb* = **dismiss**, discard, discharge, drum out, expel, give the boot to (*sl*)
casket *noun* **1** = **box**, case, chest, coffer, jewel

tapioca.

casserole *noun* **1** covered dish in which food is cooked slowly, usu. in an oven. **2** dish cooked in this way. ◆ *verb* **3** cook in a casserole.

cassette *noun* plastic case containing a reel of film or magnetic tape.

cassia *noun* tropical plant whose pods yield a mild laxative. **cassia bark** cinnamon-like bark used as a spice.

cassock *noun* long tunic, usu. black, worn by priests.

cassowary *noun, pl* **-waries** large flightless bird of Australia and New Guinea.

cast ⊙ *noun* **1** actors in a play or film collectively. **2** object shaped by a mould while molten. **3** mould used to shape such an object. **4** rigid plaster-of-Paris casing for immobilizing broken bones while they heal. **5** sort, kind. **6** slight squint in the eye. ◆ *verb* **casting, cast 7** select (an actor) to play a part in a play or film. **8** give (a vote). **9** let fall, shed. **10** shape (molten material) in a mould. **11** throw with force. **12** direct (a glance). **castaway** *noun* shipwrecked person. **casting vote** deciding vote used by the chairman of a meeting when the votes on each side are equal. **cast-iron** *adjective* **1** made of a hard but brittle type of iron. **2** definite, unchallengeable. **cast-off** *adjective, noun* discarded (person or thing). **cast off** *verb* **1** discard (something no longer wanted). **2** untie a ship from a dock. **3** knot and remove (stitches) from the needle in knitting. **cast on** *verb* make (stitches) on the needle in knitting.

castanets *plural noun* musical instrument, used by Spanish dancers, consisting of curved pieces of hollow wood clicked together in the hand.

caste ⊙ *noun* **1** any of the hereditary classes into which Hindu society is divided. **2** social rank.

castellated *adjective* having battlements.

caster *noun* same as CASTOR.

caster sugar *noun* finely ground white sugar.

castigate ⊙ *verb* reprimand severely.
castigation *noun*

castle ⊙ *noun* **1** large fortified building, often built as a ruler's residence. **2** rook in chess. **castle in the air** daydream.

castor *noun* small swivelling wheel fixed to the bottom of a piece of furniture for easy moving.

castor oil *noun* oil obtained from an Indian plant, used as a lubricant and purgative.

castrate ⊙ *verb* **1** remove the testicles of. **2** deprive of vigour or masculinity. **castration** *noun*

casual ⊙ *adjective* **1** careless, nonchalant. **2** (of work or workers) occasional. **3** shallow, superficial. **4** for informal wear. **5** happening by chance. ◆ *noun* **6** occasional worker. **casually** *adverb* **casualty** *noun* person killed or injured in an accident or war.

casualty ⊙ *noun, pl* **-ties 1** person killed or injured in an accident or war. **2** hospital department treating victims of accidents. **3** person or thing that has suffered as the result of something.

casuistry *noun* reasoning that is misleading or oversubtle. **casuist** *noun*

cat ⊙ *noun* **1** small domesticated furry mammal. **2** related wild mammal, such as the lion or tiger. **catty** *adjective* **-tier, -tiest** *Informal* spiteful. **catkin** *noun* drooping flower spike of certain trees. **catcall** *noun* derisive whistle or cry. **catfish** *noun* fish with whisker-like barbels round the mouth. **catgut** *noun* strong cord used to string musical instruments and sports rackets. **catnap** *noun, verb* doze.

THESAURUS

box

cast *noun* **1** = **actors**, characters, company, dramatis personae, players, troupe **5** = **type**, complexion, manner, stamp, style ◆ *verb* **7, 8** = **choose**, allot, appoint, assign, name, pick, select **9** = **give out**, deposit, diffuse, distribute, emit, radiate, scatter, shed, spread **10** = **form**, found, model, mould, set, shape **11** = **throw**, fling, hurl, launch, pitch, sling, thrust, toss

caste *noun* **2** = **class**, estate, grade, order, rank, social order, status, stratum

castigate *verb* = **reprimand**, berate, censure, chastise, criticize, lambast(e), rebuke, rouse on (*Aust*), scold

cast-iron *adjective* **2** = **certain**, copper-bottomed, definite, established, fixed, guaranteed, settled

castle *noun* **1** = **fortress**, chateau, citadel, keep, palace, stronghold, tower

cast-off *adjective* = **unwanted**, discarded, rejected, scrapped, surplus to requirements, unneeded, useless ◆ *noun* = **reject**, discard, failure, outcast, second

castrate *verb* **1** = **neuter**, emasculate, geld

casual *adjective* **1** = **careless**, blasé, cursory, lackadaisical, nonchalant, offhand, relaxed, unconcerned [OPPOSITE] **concerned**. **2** = **occasional**, irregular **4** = **informal**, non-dressy, sporty [OPPOSITE] **formal**. **5** = **chance**, accidental, incidental, random, unexpected [OPPOSITE] **planned**

casualty *noun* **1** = **victim**, death, fatality, loss,

C

cat-o'-nine-tails *noun* whip with nine knotted thongs. **Catseyes** *plural noun* ® glass reflectors set in the road to indicate traffic lanes. **cat's paw** person used by another to do unpleasant things for him or her. **catwalk** *noun* 1 narrow pathway or platform. 2 narrow platform where models display clothes in a fashion show.

catabolism *noun* breaking down of complex molecules into simple ones.

cataclysm [kat-a-kliz-zum] *noun* 1 violent upheaval. 2 disaster, such as an earthquake. **cataclysmic** *adjective*

catacombs ❶ [kat-a-koomz] *plural noun* underground burial place consisting of tunnels with recesses for tombs.

catafalque [kat-a-falk] *noun* raised platform on which a body lies in state before or during a funeral.

catalepsy *noun* trancelike state in which the body is rigid. **cataleptic** *adjective*

catalogue ❶ *noun* 1 book containing details of items for sale. 2 systematic list of items. ◆ *verb* 3 enter (an item) in a catalogue. 4 make a systematic list of.

catalyst *noun* 1 substance that speeds up a chemical reaction without itself changing. 2 person or thing that causes a change. **catalyse** *verb* speed up (a chemical reaction) by a catalyst. **catalysis** *noun* **catalytic** *adjective*

catamaran *noun* boat with twin parallel hulls.

catapult ❶ *noun* 1 Y-shaped device with a loop of elastic, used by children for firing stones. ◆ *verb* 2 shoot forwards or upwards violently. 3 cause (someone) suddenly to be in a particular situation.

cataract *noun* 1 eye disease in which the lens becomes opaque. 2 opaque area of an eye. 3 large waterfall.

catarrh [kat-tar] *noun* excessive mucus in the nose and throat, during or following a cold. **catarrhal** *adjective*

catastrophe ❶ [kat-ass-trof-fee] *noun* great and sudden disaster. **catastrophic** *adjective*

catatonia *noun* form of schizophrenia characterized by stupor, with outbreaks of excitement. **catatonic** *adjective*

catch ❶ *verb* **catching, caught** 1 seize, capture. 2 surprise in an act, e.g. *two boys were caught stealing*. 3 hit unexpectedly. 4 be in time for (a bus, train, etc.). 5 see or hear. 6 be infected with (an illness). 7 entangle. 8 understand, make out. 9 start burning. ◆ *noun* 10 device for fastening a door, window, etc. 11 total number of fish caught. 12 *Informal* concealed or unforeseen drawback. 13 *Informal* person considered worth having as a husband or wife. **catch it** *Informal* be punished. **catching** *adjective* infectious. **catchy** *adjective* **catchier, catchiest** (of a tune) pleasant and easily remembered. **catchment area** area served by a particular school or hospital. **catch on** *verb Informal* 1 become popular. 2 understand. **catch out** *verb Informal* trap (someone) in an error or lie. **catchpenny** *adjective* designed to have instant appeal without regard for quality. **catch phrase** well-known phrase associated with a particular entertainer. **catch 22** inescapable dilemma. **catch up with** *verb* reach or pass. **catchword** *noun* well-known and frequently used phrase.

catechism [kat-ti-kiz-zum] *noun* instruction on

——————— THESAURUS ———————

sufferer, wounded

cat *noun* 1 =**feline**, kitty (*inf*), moggy (*sl*), puss (*inf*), pussy (*inf*), tabby

catacombs *plural noun* =**vault**, crypt, tomb

catalogue *noun* 1 =**directory**, gazetteer 2 =**list**, index, inventory, record, register, roll ◆*verb* 3 =**register**, file, index 4 =**list**, alphabetize, classify, inventory, tabulate

catapult *noun* 1 =**sling**, slingshot (*US*) ◆*verb* 2, 3 =**shoot**, heave, hurl, pitch, plunge, propel

catastrophe *noun* =**disaster**, adversity, calamity, cataclysm, fiasco, misfortune, tragedy, trouble

catcall *noun* =**jeer**, boo, gibe, hiss, raspberry, whistle

catch *verb* 1 =**seize**, apprehend, arrest, capture, clutch, ensnare, entrap, get, grab, grasp, grip, lay hold of, snare, snatch, take, trap OPPOSITE▷ **release**. 2 =**discover**, catch in the

act, detect, expose, find out, surprise, take unawares, unmask 6 =**contract**, develop, get, go down with, incur, succumb to, suffer from OPPOSITE▷ **avoid**. 8 =**make out**, comprehend, discern, get, grasp, hear, perceive, recognize, sense, take in ◆*noun* 10 =**fastener**, bolt, clasp, clip, latch 12 *Inf* =**drawback**, disadvantage, fly in the ointment, hitch, snag, stumbling block, trap, trick OPPOSITE▷ **benefit**

catching *adjective* =**infectious**, communicable, contagious, transferable, transmittable OPPOSITE▷ **non-infectious**

catch on *verb Inf* 2 =**understand**, comprehend, find out, get the picture, grasp, see, see through, twig (*Brit inf*)

catchword *noun* =**slogan**, byword, motto, password, watchword

catchy *adjective* =**memorable**, captivating, haunting, popular the doctrine of a Christian Church in a series of questions and answers. **catechize** *verb* **1** instruct by using a catechism. **2** question (someone) thoroughly.

category ❶ *noun, pl* **-ries** class, group. **categorical** *adjective* absolutely clear and certain. **categorically** *adverb* **categorize** *verb* put in a category. **categorization** *noun*

cater ❶ *verb* provide what is needed or wanted, esp. food or services. **caterer** *noun*

caterpillar *noun* **1** wormlike larva of a moth or butterfly. **2** ® endless track, driven by cogged wheels, used to propel a heavy vehicle.

caterwaul *verb, noun* wail, yowl.

catharsis [kath-**thar**-siss] *noun, pl* **-ses 1** relief of strong suppressed emotions. **2** evacuation of the bowels, esp. with a laxative. **cathartic** *adjective* **1** causing catharsis. ◆ *noun* **2** drug that causes catharsis.

cathedral *noun* principal church of a diocese.

Catherine wheel *noun* rotating firework.

catheter [**kath**-it-er] *noun* tube inserted into a body cavity to drain fluid.

cathode *noun* negative electrode, by which electrons leave a circuit. **cathode rays** stream of electrons from a cathode in a vacuum tube. **cathode-ray tube** vacuum tube in which a beam of electrons produces a visible image, used in television receivers etc.

catholic *adjective* **1** (of tastes or interests) covering a wide range. ◆ *noun, adjective* **2** (C-) (member) of the Roman Catholic Church. **Catholicism** *noun*

> **LANGUAGE TIP**
>
> Note that the meaning of *catholic* can change depending on whether it begins with a capital letter or not.

cation [**kat**-eye-on] *noun* positively charged ion.

cattle ❶ *plural noun* domesticated cows and bulls. **cattle-grid** *noun* grid over a ditch in the road to prevent livestock crossing.

Caucasian, Caucasoid *noun, adjective* (member) of the light-skinned racial group of humankind.

caucus *noun, pl* **-cuses 1** local committee or faction of a political party. **2** political meeting to decide future plans.

caudal *adjective* at or near an animal's tail.

caught *verb* past of CATCH.

caul *noun Anat* membrane sometimes covering a child's head at birth.

cauldron, caldron *noun* large pot used for boiling.

cauliflower *noun* vegetable with a large head of white flower buds surrounded by green leaves.

caulk *verb* fill in (cracks) with paste etc.

causal *adjective* of or being a cause. **causally** *adverb* **causation, causality** *noun* relationship of cause and effect.

cause ❶ *noun* **1** something that produces a particular effect. **2** (foll. by *for*) reason, motive. **3** aim or principle supported by a person or group. ◆ *verb* **4** be the cause of.

cause célèbre [kawz sill-**leb**-ra] *noun, pl* **causes célèbres** [kawz sill-**leb**-ra] controversial legal case or issue.

causeway *noun* raised path or road across water or marshland.

caustic ❶ *adjective* **1** capable of burning by chemical action. **2** bitter and sarcastic. ◆ *noun* **3** caustic substance. **caustically** *adverb* **caustic soda** same as SODIUM HYDROXIDE.

cauterize *verb* burn (a wound) with heat or a caustic agent to prevent infection. **cauterization** *noun*

caution ❶ *noun* **1** care, esp. in the face of

———————————— THESAURUS ————————————

categorical *adjective* =**absolute**, downright, emphatic, explicit, express, positive, unambiguous, unconditional, unequivocal, unqualified, unreserved OPPOSITE **vague**

category *noun* =**class**, classification, department, division, grade, grouping, heading, section, sort, type

cater *verb* =**provide**, furnish, outfit, purvey, supply

cattle *plural noun* =**cows**, beasts, bovines, livestock, stock

catty *adjective Inf* =**spiteful**, backbiting, bitchy (*inf*), malevolent, malicious, rancorous, shrewish, snide, venomous

cause *noun* **1** =**origin**, agent, beginning, creator, genesis, mainspring, maker, producer, root, source, spring OPPOSITE **result**. **2** (foll. by *for*) =**reason**, basis, grounds, incentive, inducement, justification, motivation, motive, purpose **3** =**aim**, belief, conviction, enterprise, ideal, movement, principle ◆*verb* **4** =**produce**, bring about, create, generate, give rise to, incite, induce, lead to, result in OPPOSITE **stop**

caustic *adjective* **1** =**burning**, acrid, astringent, biting, corroding, corrosive, mordant, vitriolic **2** =**sarcastic**, acrimonious, cutting, pungent, scathing, stinging, trenchant, virulent, vitriolic OPPOSITE **kind**

C

danger. **2** warning. ◆ *verb* **3** warn, advise.
cautionary *adjective* warning. **cautious**
adjective showing caution. **cautiously** *adverb*
cavalcade ⊕ *noun* procession of people on
horseback or in cars.
cavalier ⊕ *adjective* **1** showing haughty
disregard. ◆ *noun* **2** *Old-fashioned* gallant
gentleman. **3** (**C-**) supporter of Charles I in the
English Civil War.
cavalry ⊕ *noun, pl* **-ries** part of the army orig.
on horseback, but now often using fast
armoured vehicles.
cave ⊕ *noun* hollow in the side of a hill or cliff.
caving *noun* sport of exploring caves. **cave in**
verb **1** collapse inwards. **2** *Informal* yield under
pressure. **caveman** *noun* **1** prehistoric cave
dweller. **2** *Informal* man who is primitive in his
behaviour.
caveat [**kav**-vee-at] *noun* warning.
cavern ⊕ *noun* large cave. **cavernous**
adjective
caviar, caviare *noun* salted sturgeon roe,
regarded as a delicacy.
cavil *verb* **-illing, -illed 1** make petty
objections. ◆ *noun* **2** petty objection.
cavity ⊕ *noun, pl* **-ties 1** hollow space. **2**
decayed area on a tooth.
cavort *verb* skip about.
caw *noun* **1** cry of a crow, rook, or raven. ◆
verb **2** make this cry.
cay *noun* low island or bank composed of sand
and coral fragments.
cayenne pepper, cayenne *noun* hot red
spice made from capsicum seeds.
cayman *noun, pl* **-mans** S American reptile
similar to an alligator.

CB Citizens' Band.
CBE Commander of the Order of the British
Empire.
CBI Confederation of British Industry.
cc cubic centimetre.
Cd *Chem* cadmium.
CD compact disc.
CD-ROM compact disc read-only memory.
Ce *Chem* cerium.
cease ⊕ *verb* bring or come to an end.
ceaseless *adjective* **ceaselessly** *adverb*
ceasefire *noun* temporary truce.
cedar *noun* **1** evergreen coniferous tree. **2** its
wood.
cede ⊕ *verb* surrender (territory or legal
rights).
cedilla *noun* character (¸) placed under a *c* in
some languages, to show that it is pronounced
s , not *k*.
Ceefax *noun* ® BBC teletext service.
ceilidh [**kay**-lee] *noun* informal social
gathering for singing and dancing, esp. in
Scotland.
ceiling *noun* **1** inner upper surface of a room.
2 upper limit set on something. **3** upper
altitude to which an aircraft can climb.
celandine *noun* wild plant with yellow
flowers.
celebrate ⊕ *verb* **1** hold festivities to mark (a
happy event, anniversary, etc.). **2** perform (a
religious ceremony). **3** praise publicly.
celebrated *adjective* well known. **celebration**
noun **celebrant** *noun* person who performs a
religious ceremony. **celebrity** *noun, pl* **-rities 1**
famous person. **2** state of being famous.
celeriac [sill-**ler**-ee-ak] *noun* variety of celery

———— T H E S A U R U S ————

caution *noun* **1** = **care**, alertness, carefulness,
circumspection, deliberation, discretion,
forethought, heed, prudence, vigilance,
watchfulness OPPOSITE daring. **2** = **warning**,
admonition, advice, counsel, injunction ◆*verb* **3**
= **warn**, admonish, advise, tip off, urge
cautious *adjective* = **careful**, cagey (*inf*), chary,
circumspect, guarded, judicious, prudent,
tentative, wary OPPOSITE careless
cavalcade *noun* = **parade**, array, march-past,
procession, spectacle, train
cavalier *adjective* **1** = **haughty**, arrogant,
disdainful, lofty, lordly, offhand, scornful,
supercilious
cavalry *noun* = **horsemen**, horse, mounted
troops OPPOSITE infantrymen
cave *noun* = **hollow**, cavern, cavity, den,
grotto
cavern *noun* = **cave**, hollow, pothole

cavernous *adjective* = **deep**, hollow, sunken,
yawning
cavity *noun* **1** = **hollow**, crater, dent, gap,
hole, pit
cease *verb* = **stop**, break off, conclude,
discontinue, end, finish, halt, leave off, refrain,
terminate OPPOSITE start
ceaseless *adjective* = **continual**, constant,
endless, eternal, everlasting, incessant,
interminable, never-ending, nonstop, perpetual,
unremitting OPPOSITE occasional
cede *verb* = **surrender**, concede, hand over,
make over, relinquish, renounce, resign,
transfer, yield
celebrate *verb* **1** = **rejoice**, commemorate,
drink to, keep, kill the fatted calf, observe, put
the flags out, toast **2** = **perform**, bless, honour,
solemnize
celebrated *adjective* = **well-known**,

with a large turnip-like root.

celerity [sill-**ler**-rit-tee] *noun* swiftness.

celery *noun* vegetable with long green crisp edible stalks.

celestial ⊕ *adjective* **1** heavenly, divine. **2** of the sky.

celibate ⊕ *adjective* **1** unmarried or abstaining from sex, esp. because of a religious vow of chastity. ♦ *noun* **2** celibate person. **celibacy** *noun*

cell ⊕ *noun* **1** smallest unit of an organism that is able to function independently. **2** small room for a prisoner, monk, or nun. **3** small compartment of a honeycomb etc. **4** small group operating as the core of a larger organization. **5** device that produces electrical energy by chemical reaction. **cellular** *adjective* **1** of or consisting of cells. **2** woven with an open texture. **3** designed for or using cellular radio. **cellular radio** radio communication, used esp. in car phones, based on a network of transmitters each serving a small area. **cell phone, cellular phone** telephone operating by radio communication via a network of transmitters each serving a small area.

cellar *noun* **1** underground room for storage. **2** stock of wine.

cello [**chell**-oh] *noun, pl* **-los** large low-pitched instrument of the violin family. **cellist** *noun*

Cellophane *noun* ® thin transparent cellulose sheeting used as wrapping.

cellulite *noun* fat deposits under the skin alleged to resist dieting.

celluloid *noun* kind of plastic used to make toys and, formerly, photographic film.

cellulose *noun* main constituent of plant cell walls, used in making paper, plastics, etc.

Celsius *adjective* of the temperature scale in which water freezes at 0° and boils at 100°.

Celt [**kelt**] *noun* person from Scotland, Ireland, Wales, Cornwall, or Brittany. **Celtic** [**kel**-tik, **sel**-tik] *noun* **1** group of languages including Gaelic and Welsh. ♦ *adjective* **2** of the Celts or the Celtic languages.

cement ⊕ *noun* **1** fine grey powder mixed with water and sand to make mortar or concrete. **2** something that unites, binds, or joins. **3** material used to fill teeth. ♦ *verb* **4** join, bind, or cover with cement. **5** make (a relationship) stronger.

cemetery ⊕ *noun, pl* **-teries** place where dead people are buried.

cenotaph *noun* monument honouring soldiers who died in a war.

censer *noun* container for burning incense.

censor ⊕ *noun* **1** person authorized to examine films, books, etc., to ban or cut anything considered obscene or objectionable. ♦ *verb* **2** ban or cut parts of (a film, book, etc.). **censorship** *noun* **censorious** *adjective* harshly critical.

censure ⊕ *noun* **1** severe disapproval. ♦ *verb* **2** criticize severely.

census *noun, pl* **-suses** official count of a population.

cent *noun* hundredth part of a monetary unit such as the dollar or euro.

centaur *noun* mythical creature with the head,

———————— T H E S A U R U S ————————

acclaimed, distinguished, eminent, famous, illustrious, notable, popular, prominent, renowned OPPOSITE **unknown**

celebration *noun* **1** = **festivity**, anniversary, commemoration, festival, gala, jubilee, merrymaking, party, red-letter day, revelry **2** = **honouring**, observance, performance, remembrance, solemnization

celebrity *noun* **1** = **personality**, big name, big shot (*inf*), dignitary, luminary, star, superstar, V.I.P. OPPOSITE **nobody. 2** = **fame**, distinction, notability, prestige, prominence, renown, reputation, repute, stardom OPPOSITE **obscurity**

celestial *adjective* **1** = **heavenly**, angelic, astral, divine, ethereal, spiritual, sublime, supernatural

celibacy *noun* = **chastity**, continence, purity, virginity

cell *noun* **2** = **room**, chamber, compartment, cubicle, dungeon, stall **3** = **compartment**,

cavity **4** = **unit**, caucus, core, coterie, group, nucleus

cement 1 *noun* = **mortar**, plaster **2** = **glue**, adhesive, gum, paste, sealant ♦ *verb* **4** = **stick together**, attach, bind, bond, combine, glue, join, plaster, seal, unite, weld

cemetery *noun* = **graveyard**, burial ground, churchyard, God's acre, necropolis

censor *verb* **2** = **cut**, blue-pencil, bowdlerize, expurgate

censorious *adjective* = **critical**, captious, carping, cavilling, condemnatory, disapproving, disparaging, fault-finding, hypercritical, scathing, severe

censure *noun* **1** = **disapproval**, blame, condemnation, criticism, obloquy, rebuke, reprimand, reproach, reproof, stick (*sl*) OPPOSITE **approval** ♦ *verb* **2** = **criticize**, blame, castigate, condemn, denounce, rap over the knuckles, rebuke, reprimand, reproach, rouse on (*Aust*), scold, slap on the wrist OPPOSITE

C

arms, and torso of a man, and the lower body and legs of a horse.

centenary [sen-**teen**-a-ree] *noun, pl* **-naries** 100th anniversary or its celebration.

centenarian *noun* person at least 100 years old. **centennial** *noun US* centenary.

centi- *prefix* **1** one hundredth, e.g. *centimetre*. **2** a hundred, e.g. *centipede*.

centigrade *adjective* same as CELSIUS.

> **LANGUAGE TIP**
>
> Scientists now use *Celsius* in preference to *centigrade*.

centigram, centigramme *noun* one hundredth of a gram.

centilitre *noun* one hundredth of a litre.

centime [**son**-teem] *noun* monetary unit worth one hundredth of a franc.

centimetre *noun* one hundredth of a metre.

centipede *noun* small wormlike creature with many legs.

central ❶ *adjective* **1** of, at, or forming the centre. **2** main, principal. **centrally** *adverb* **centrality** *noun* **centralism** *noun* principle of central control of a country or organization. **centralize** *verb* bring under central control. **centralization** *noun* **central heating** system for heating a building from one central source of heat. **central processing unit** part of a computer that performs logical and arithmetical operations on the data.

centre ❶ *noun* **1** middle point or part. **2** place for a specified activity. **3** person or thing that is a focus of interest. **4** political party or group favouring moderation. **5** *Sport* player who plays in the middle of the field. ◆ *verb* **6** put in the centre of something. **central** *adjective* **centrist** *noun* person favouring political moderation. **centre on** *verb* have as a centre or main theme.

centrifugal *adjective* moving away from a centre. **centrifuge** *noun* machine that separates

substances by centrifugal force. **centrifugal force** force that acts outwards on any body that rotates or moves along a curved path.

centripetal *adjective* moving towards a centre.

centurion *noun* (in ancient Rome) officer commanding 100 men.

century *noun, pl* **-ries 1** period of 100 years. **2** cricket score of 100 runs.

CEO chief executive officer.

cephalopod [**seff**-a-loh-pod] *noun* sea mollusc with a head and tentacles, such as the octopus.

ceramic *noun* **1** hard brittle material made by heating clay to a very high temperature. **2** object made of this. ◆ *plural* **3** art of producing ceramic objects. ◆ *adjective* **4** made of ceramic.

cereal *noun* **1** grass plant with edible grain, such as oat or wheat. **2** this grain. **3** breakfast food made from this grain, eaten mixed with milk.

cerebellum [serr-rib-**bell**-lum] *noun, pl* **-lums, -la** [-la] back part of the brain.

cerebral [**ser**-rib-ral] *adjective* **1** of the brain. **2** intellectual.

cerebrum [**serr**-rib-rum] *noun, pl* **-brums, -bra** [-bra] main part of the brain.

cerebrospinal *adjective* of the brain and spinal cord.

ceremony ❶ *noun, pl* **-nies 1** formal act or ritual. **2** formally polite behaviour. **ceremonial** *adjective, noun* **ceremonially** *adverb* **ceremonious** *adjective* excessively polite or formal. **ceremoniously** *adverb*

cerise [ser-**reess**] *adjective* cherry-red.

cerium *noun Chem* steel-grey metallic element.

cert *noun Informal* certainty, e.g. *a dead cert*.

certain ❶ *adjective* **1** positive and confident. **2** definite. **3** some but not much. **4** named but not known, e.g. *a certain Miss Watson taught me English.* **certainly** *adverb* **certainty** *noun* **1** state of being sure. **2** *pl* **-ties** something that is inevitable.

certificate ❶ *noun* official document stating

———— THESAURUS ————

applaud

central *adjective* **1** = **middle**, inner, interior, mean, median, mid OPPOSITE **outer**. **2** = **main**, chief, essential, focal, fundamental, key, primary, principal OPPOSITE **minor**

centralize *verb* = **unify**, concentrate, condense, incorporate, rationalize, streamline

centre *noun* **1** = **middle**, core, heart, hub, kernel, midpoint, nucleus, pivot OPPOSITE **edge**. **3** = **focus** ◆*verb* **6** = **focus**, cluster, concentrate, converge, revolve

ceremonial *adjective* **1** = **ritual**, liturgical, ritualistic **2** = **formal**, solemn, stately OPPOSITE **informal** ◆*noun* **1** = **ritual**, ceremony, rite **2** = **formality**, solemnity

ceremonious *adjective* = **formal**, civil, courteous, deferential, dignified, punctilious, solemn, stately, stiff

ceremony *noun* **1** = **ritual**, commemoration, function, observance, parade, rite, service, show, solemnities **2** = **formality**, ceremonial, decorum, etiquette, niceties, pomp, propriety,

the details of a birth, academic course, etc.
certify ❶ *verb* **-fying, -fied 1** confirm, attest
to. **2** guarantee. **3** declare legally insane.
certifiable *adjective* considered legally insane.
certification *noun*
certitude *noun* confidence, certainty.
cervix *noun, pl* **cervixes, cervices 1** narrow
entrance of the womb. **2** neck. **cervical**
adjective
cessation *noun* ceasing.
cession *noun* ceding.
cesspit, cesspool *noun* covered tank or pit
for sewage.
cetacean [sit-**tay**-shun] *noun* fish-shaped sea
mammal such as a whale or dolphin.
cetane [**see**-tane] *noun* colourless liquid
hydrocarbon, used as a solvent.
cf compare.
Cf *Chem* californium.
CFC chlorofluorocarbon.
cg centigram.
CGI computer-generated image(s).
ch. 1 chapter. **2** church.
cha-cha, cha-cha-cha *noun* (music for) a
modern ballroom dance from Latin America.
chafe ❶ *verb* **1** make sore or worn by rubbing.
2 be annoyed or impatient.
chafer *noun* large beetle.
chaff¹ ❶ *noun* **1** grain husks. **2** something of
little worth.
chaff² ❶ *verb* tease good-naturedly.
chaffinch *noun* small European songbird.
chagrin [**shag**-grin] *noun* annoyance and
disappointment. **chagrined** *adjective* annoyed
and disappointed.
chain ❶ *noun* **1** flexible length of connected
metal links. **2** (usu. pl) anything that restricts or
restrains. **3** series of connected facts or events.

4 group of shops, hotels, etc. owned by one
firm. ◆ *verb* **5** restrict or fasten with or as if with
a chain. **chain gang** *US* group of prisoners
chained together. **chain mail** same as MAIL².
chain reaction series of events, each of which
causes the next. **chain-smoke** *verb* smoke
(cigarettes) continuously. **chain smoker**
chair ❶ *noun* **1** seat with a back, for one
person. **2** official position of authority. **3** person
holding this. **4** professorship. ◆ *verb* **5** preside
over (a meeting). **chairlift** series of chairs
suspended from a moving cable for carrying
people up a slope. **chairman, chairwoman**
noun person in charge of a company's board of
directors or a meeting (also **chairperson**)

LANGUAGE TIP

Chairman can seem
inappropriate when applied to a
woman, while *chairwoman* can
be offensive. *Chair* and
chairperson can be applied to
either a man or a woman; *chair* is
generally preferred to *chairperson*.

---

chaise [**shaze**] *noun* light horse-drawn
carriage.
chaise longue [**long**] *noun* couch with a back
and a single armrest.
chalcedony [kal-**sed**-don-ee] *noun, pl* **-nies**
variety of quartz.
chalet *noun* **1** kind of Swiss wooden house
with a steeply sloping roof. **2** similar house,
used as a holiday home.
chalice [**chal**-liss] *noun* **1** large goblet. **2**
goblet containing the wine at Communion.
chalk *noun* **1** soft white rock consisting of

C

—————————— T H E S A U R U S ——————————

protocol
certain *adjective* **1** = **sure**, assured, confident,
convinced, positive, satisfied OPPOSITE
uncertain. 2 = **definite**, conclusive, decided,
established, fixed, incontrovertible, inevitable,
irrefutable, known, settled, sure, true,
undeniable, unequivocal OPPOSITE **indefinite**
certainly *adverb* **2** = **definitely**, assuredly,
indisputably, indubitably, surely, truly,
undeniably, undoubtedly, without doubt
certainty *noun* **1** = **sureness**, assurance,
confidence, conviction, faith, positiveness, trust,
validity OPPOSITE **doubt. 2** = **fact**, banker,
reality, sure thing (*inf*), truth
certificate *noun* = **document**, authorization,
credential(s), diploma, licence, testimonial,
voucher, warrant

certify *verb* **1** = **confirm**, attest, authenticate,
declare, testify, validate, verify **2** = **guarantee**,
assure
chafe *verb* **1** = **rub**, abrade, rasp, scrape,
scratch **2** = **be annoyed**, be impatient, fret,
fume, rage, worry
chaff¹ *noun* **1** = **husks 2** = **rubbish**, dregs,
refuse, remains, trash, waste
chaff² *verb* = **tease**, mock, rib (*inf*), ridicule,
scoff, taunt
chain *noun* **1** = **link**, bond, coupling, fetter,
manacle, shackle **3** = **series**, progression,
sequence, set, string, succession, train ◆*verb* **5**
= **bind**, confine, enslave, fetter, handcuff,
manacle, restrain, shackle, tether
chairman *noun* = **director**, chairperson,
chairwoman, master of ceremonies, president,

C

calcium carbonate. **2** piece of chalk, often coloured, used for drawing and writing on blackboards. ◆ *verb* **3** draw or mark with chalk. **chalky** *adjective*

challenge ❶ *noun* **1** demanding or stimulating situation. **2** call to take part in a contest or fight. **3** questioning of a statement of fact. **4** demand by a sentry for identification or a password. ◆ *verb* **5** issue a challenge to. **challenged** *adjective* disabled as specified *physically challenged; mentally challenged*. **challenger** *noun*

chamber ❶ *noun* **1** hall used for formal meetings. **2** legislative or judicial assembly. **3** *Old-fashioned* bedroom. **4** compartment, cavity. **5** compartment for a cartridge in a gun. ◆ *plural* **6** set of rooms used as offices by a barrister. **chambermaid** *noun* woman employed to clean bedrooms in a hotel. **chamber music** classical music to be performed by a small group of musicians. **chamber pot** bowl for urine, formerly used in bedrooms.

chamberlain *noun Hist* officer who managed the household of a king or nobleman.

chameleon [kam-**meal**-yon] *noun* small lizard that changes colour to blend in with its surroundings.

chamfer [**cham**-fer] *verb* bevel the edge of.

chamois [**sham**-wah] *noun, pl* **-ois 1** small mountain antelope. **2** [**sham**-ee] soft suede leather. **3** piece of this, used for cleaning or polishing.

chamomile [**kam**-mo-mile] *noun* same as CAMOMILE.

champ[1] *verb* chew noisily. **champ at the bit** *Informal* be impatient to do something.

champ[2] *noun* short for CHAMPION.

champagne *noun* sparkling white French wine.

champion ❶ *noun* **1** overall winner of a competition. **2** (foll. by *of*) someone who

defends a person or cause. ◆ *verb* **3** support. ◆ *adjective* **4** *Dialect* excellent. **championship** *noun*

chance ❶ *noun* **1** likelihood, probability. **2** opportunity to do something. **3** risk, gamble. **4** unpredictable element that causes things to happen one way rather than another. ◆ *verb* **5** risk, hazard. **6** (foll. by *to*) do something without planning to. **chancy** *adjective* **chancier, chanciest** uncertain, risky. **by chance** without planning.

chancel *noun* part of a church containing the altar and choir.

chancellery *noun, pl* **-leries 1** residence or office of a chancellor. **2** office of an embassy or consulate.

chancellor *noun* **1** head of government in some European countries. **2** honorary head of a university. **chancellorship** *noun* **Chancellor of the Exchequer** cabinet minister responsible for finance.

Chancery *noun* division of the British High Court of Justice.

chancre [**shang**-ker] *noun* small hard growth which is the first sign of syphilis.

chandelier [shan-dill-**eer**] *noun* ornamental light with branches and holders for several candles or bulbs.

chandler *noun* dealer, esp. in ships' supplies.

change ❶ *noun* **1** becoming different. **2** variety or novelty. **3** different set, esp. of clothes. **4** balance received when the amount paid is more than the cost of a purchase. **5** coins of low value. ◆ *verb* **6** make or become different. **7** give and receive (something) in return. **8** exchange (money) for its equivalent in a smaller denomination or different currency. **9** put on other clothes. **10** leave one vehicle and board another. **changeable** *adjective* changing often. **changeling** *noun* child believed to have been exchanged by fairies for another.

———— THESAURUS ————

speaker, spokesman

challenge *noun* **1** = **trial**, test **2** = **confrontation**, provocation, ultimatum **3** = **question** ◆*verb* **5** = **test**, confront, defy, dispute, object to, question, tackle, throw down the gauntlet

chamber *noun* **1** = **hall**, room **2** = **council**, assembly, legislative body, legislature **3** *Old-fashioned* = **bedroom**, apartment, room **4** = **compartment**, cubicle, enclosure

champion *noun* **1** = **winner**, conqueror, hero, title holder, victor **2** (foll. by *of*) = **defender**, backer, guardian, patron, protector, upholder ◆*verb* **3** = **support**, advocate, back, commend,

defend, encourage, espouse, fight for, promote, uphold

chance *noun* **1** = **probability**, likelihood, odds, possibility, prospect OPPOSITE certainty. **2** = **opportunity**, occasion, opening, time **3** = **risk**, gamble, hazard, jeopardy, speculation, uncertainty **4** = **luck**, accident, coincidence, destiny, fate, fortune, providence OPPOSITE design ◆*verb* **5** = **risk**, endanger, gamble, hazard, jeopardize, stake, try, venture, wager

change *noun* **1** = **alteration**, difference, innovation, metamorphosis, modification, mutation, revolution, transformation, transition **2** = **variety**, break (*inf*), departure, diversion,

channel ❶ *noun* **1** band of broadcasting frequencies. **2** means of access or communication. **3** broad strait connecting two areas of sea. **4** bed or course of a river, stream, or canal. **5** groove. ◆ *verb* **-nelling, -nelled 6** direct or convey through a channel.

chant ❶ *verb* **1** utter or sing (a slogan or psalm). ◆ *noun* **2** rhythmic or repetitive slogan. **3** psalm that has a short simple melody with several words sung on one note.

chanter *noun* (on bagpipes) pipe on which the melody is played.

chanty *noun, pl* **-ties** same as SHANTY[2].

chaos ❶ *noun* complete disorder or confusion.

chaotic *adjective* **chaotically** *adverb*

chap ❶ *noun Informal* man or boy.

chapati, chapatti *noun* (in Indian cookery) flat thin unleavened bread.

chapel *noun* **1** place of worship with its own altar, within a church. **2** similar place of worship in a large house or institution. **3** Nonconformist place of worship. **4** section of a trade union in the print industry.

chaperone [**shap**-per-rone] *noun* **1** older person who accompanies and supervises a young person or young people on a social occasion. ◆ *verb* **2** act as a chaperone to.

chaplain *noun* clergyman attached to a chapel, military body, or institution. **chaplaincy** *noun, pl* **-cies**

chaplet *noun* garland for the head.

chapped *adjective* (of the skin) raw and cracked, through exposure to cold.

chaps *plural noun* leather leggings without a seat, worn by cowboys.

chapter ❶ *noun* **1** division of a book. **2** period in a life or history. **3** sequence of events, e.g. *chapter of accidents*. **4** branch of a society or club.

char[1] *verb* **charring, charred** blacken by partial burning.

char[2] *Informal noun* **1** charwoman. ◆ *verb* **charring, charred 2** clean other people's houses as a job.

char[3] *noun Old-fashioned slang* tea.

char[4] *noun* small troutlike fish.

charabanc [**shar**-rab-bang] *noun Old-fashioned* coach for sightseeing.

character ❶ *noun* **1** combination of qualities distinguishing a person, group, or place. **2** reputation, esp. good reputation. **3** person represented in a play, film, or story. **4** unusual or amusing person. **5** letter, numeral, or symbol used in writing or printing. **characteristic** *noun* **1** distinguishing feature or quality. ◆ *adjective* **2** typical. **characteristically** *adverb* **characterize** *verb* **1** be a characteristic of. **2** (foll. by *as*) describe. **characterization** *noun*

charade ❶ [**shar**-rahd] *noun* **1** absurd pretence. ◆ *plural* **2** game in which one team

—————— THESAURUS ——————

novelty, variation OPPOSITE **monotony** ◆*verb* **6** = **alter**, convert, modify, mutate, reform, reorganize, restyle, shift, transform, vary OPPOSITE **keep. 7** = **exchange**, barter, convert, interchange, replace, substitute, swap, trade

changeable *adjective* = **variable**, erratic, fickle, inconstant, irregular, mobile, mutable, protean, shifting, unsettled, unstable, volatile, wavering OPPOSITE **constant**

channel *noun* **2** = **route**, approach, artery, avenue, canal, conduit, course, duct, means, medium, passage, path, way **3** = **strait 5** = **groove**, furrow, gutter ◆*verb* **6** = **direct**, conduct, convey, guide, transmit

chant *verb* **1** = **sing**, carol, chorus, descant, intone, recite, warble ◆*noun* **3** = **song**, carol, chorus, melody, psalm

chaos *noun* = **disorder**, anarchy, bedlam, confusion, disorganization, lawlessness, mayhem, pandemonium, tumult OPPOSITE **orderliness**

chaotic *adjective* = **disordered**, anarchic, confused, deranged, disorganized, lawless, riotous, topsy-turvy, tumultuous, uncontrolled

chap *noun Inf* = **fellow**, bloke (*Brit inf*),

character, guy (*inf*), individual, man, person

chaperone *noun* **1** = **escort**, companion ◆*verb* **2** = **escort**, accompany, attend, protect, safeguard, shepherd, watch over

chapter *noun* **1** = **section**, clause, division, episode, part, topic **2** = **period**, part, phase, stage

character *noun* **1** = **nature**, attributes, calibre, complexion, disposition, personality, quality, temperament, type **2** = **reputation**, honour, integrity, rectitude, strength, uprightness **3** = **role**, part, persona, portrayal **4** = **eccentric**, card (*inf*), oddball (*inf*), original **5** = **symbol**, device, figure, hieroglyph, letter, mark, rune, sign

characteristic *noun* **1** = **feature**, attribute, faculty, idiosyncrasy, mark, peculiarity, property, quality, quirk, trait ◆*adjective* **2** = **typical**, distinctive, distinguishing, idiosyncratic, individual, munted (*NZ sl*), peculiar, representative, singular, special, symbolic, symptomatic OPPOSITE **rare**

characterize *verb* **1** = **identify**, brand, distinguish, indicate, mark, represent, stamp, typify acts out a word or phrase, which the other team has to guess.

charcoal noun black substance formed by partially burning wood.

charge ❶ verb **1** ask as a price. **2** enter a debit against a person's account for (a purchase). **3** accuse formally. **4** make a rush at or sudden attack upon. **5** fill (a glass). **6** fill (a battery) with electricity. **7** command, assign. ♦ noun **8** price charged. **9** formal accusation. **10** attack. **11** command, exhortation. **12** custody, guardianship. **13** person or thing entrusted to someone's care. **14** cartridge, shell. **15** amount of electricity stored in a battery. **in charge of** in control of. **chargeable** adjective **charger** noun **1** device for charging an accumulator. **2** (in the Middle Ages) warhorse.

chargé d'affaires [shar-zhay daf-**fair**] noun, pl **chargés d'affaires** head of a diplomatic mission in the absence of an ambassador or in a small mission.

chariot noun two-wheeled horse-drawn vehicle used in ancient times in wars and races. **charioteer** noun chariot driver.

charisma ❶ [kar-**rizz**-ma] noun person's power to attract or influence people. **charismatic** [kar-rizz-**mat**-ik] adjective

charity ❶ noun, pl **-ties 1** organization that gives help, such as money or food, to those in need. **2** giving of help to those in need. **3** help given to those in need. **4** kindly attitude towards people. **charitable** adjective **charitably** adverb

charlady noun same as CHARWOMAN.

charlatan ❶ [**shar**-lat-tan] noun person who claims expertise that he or she does not have.

charleston noun lively dance of the 1920s.

charlock noun weed with hairy leaves and yellow flowers.

charlotte noun dessert made with fruit and bread or cake crumbs.

charm ❶ noun **1** attractive quality. **2** trinket worn on a bracelet. **3** small object with supposed magical powers. **4** magic spell. ♦ verb **5** attract, delight. **6** influence by personal charm. **7** protect or influence as if by magic. **charmer** noun **charming** adjective attractive. **charmingly** adverb

charnel house noun building or vault for the bones of the dead.

chart ❶ noun **1** graph, table, or diagram showing information. **2** map of the sea or stars. ♦ verb **3** plot the course of. **4** make a chart of. **the charts** Informal weekly lists of the bestselling pop records.

charter ❶ noun **1** document granting or demanding certain rights. **2** fundamental principles of an organization. **3** hire of transport

———— THESAURUS ————

charade noun **1** = **pretence**, fake, farce, pantomime, parody, travesty

charge verb **3** = **accuse**, arraign, blame, impeach, incriminate, indict OPPOSITE acquit. **4** = **attack**, assail, assault, rush, stampede, storm OPPOSITE retreat. **5** = **fill**, load **7** = **command**, bid, commit, demand, entrust, instruct, order, require ♦noun **8** = **price**, amount, cost, expenditure, expense, outlay, payment, rate, toll **9** = **accusation**, allegation, imputation, indictment OPPOSITE acquittal. **10** = **attack**, assault, onset, onslaught, rush, sortie, stampede OPPOSITE retreat. **11** = **instruction**, command, demand, direction, injunction, mandate, order, precept **12** = **care**, custody, duty, office, responsibility, safekeeping, trust **13** = **ward**

charisma noun = **charm**, allure, attraction, lure, magnetism, personality

charismatic adjective = **charming**, alluring, attractive, enticing, influential, lekker (S Afr sl), magnetic

charitable adjective **2, 3** = **generous**, beneficent, benevolent, bountiful, kind, lavish, liberal, philanthropic OPPOSITE mean. **4** = **kind**, considerate, favourable, forgiving, humane, indulgent, lenient, magnanimous, sympathetic, tolerant, understanding OPPOSITE unkind

charity noun **2** = **help**, assistance, benefaction, philanthropy, relief **3** = **donations**, contributions, endowment, fund, gift, hand-out, largesse or largess OPPOSITE meanness. **4** = **kindness**, altruism, benevolence, compassion, fellow feeling, generosity, goodwill, humanity, indulgence OPPOSITE ill will

charlatan noun = **fraud**, cheat, con man (inf), fake, impostor, phoney or phony (inf), pretender, quack, sham, swindler

charm noun **1** = **attraction**, allure, appeal, fascination, magnetism OPPOSITE unattractiveness. **2** = **trinket 3** = **talisman**, amulet, fetish **4** = **spell**, enchantment, magic, sorcery ♦verb **5** = **attract**, allure, beguile, bewitch, captivate, delight, enchant, enrapture, entrance, fascinate, mesmerize OPPOSITE repel. **6** = **win over**

charming adjective = **attractive**, appealing, captivating, cute, delightful, fetching, lekker (S Afr sl), likable or likeable, pleasing, seductive, winsome OPPOSITE unpleasant

chart noun **1** = **table**, blueprint, diagram, graph, plan **2** = **map** ♦verb **3** = **plot**, map out **4** = **outline**, delineate, draft, shape, sketch

for private use. ✦ *verb* **4** hire by charter. **5** grant
a charter to. **chartered** *adjective* officially
qualified to practise a profession, e.g. *chartered
accountant.*
chartreuse [shar-**trerz**] *noun* sweet-smelling
green or yellow liqueur.
charwoman *noun* woman whose job is to
clean other people's homes.
chary [**chair**-ee] *adjective* **-rier, -riest** wary,
careful. **charily** *adverb*
chase[1] **ⓘ** *verb* **1** run after quickly in order to
catch or drive away. **2** *Informal* rush, run. **3**
Informal try energetically to obtain. ✦ *noun* **4**
chasing, pursuit. **chaser** *noun* milder drink
drunk after another stronger one.
chase[2] *verb* engrave or emboss (metal).
chasm **ⓘ** [**kaz**-zum] *noun* **1** deep crack in the
earth. **2** wide difference.
chassis [**shass**-ee] *noun, pl* **-sis** frame, wheels,
and mechanical parts of a vehicle.
chaste **ⓘ** *adjective* **1** abstaining from sex
outside marriage or altogether. **2** (of style)
simple. **chastely** *adverb* **chastity** *noun*
chasten **ⓘ** [**chase**-en] *verb* subdue by
criticism.
chastise **ⓘ** *verb* **1** scold severely. **2** punish by
beating. **chastisement** *noun*
chasuble [**chazz**-yew-bl] *noun* long sleeveless
robe worn by a priest when celebrating Mass.
chat **ⓘ** *noun* **1** informal conversation. ✦ *verb*
chatting, chatted 2 have an informal
conversation. **chatty** *adjective* **-tier, -tiest.**

chatroom *noun* site on the Internet where
users have group discussions by e-mail.
chateau [**shat**-toe] *noun, pl* **-teaux, -teaus**
French castle.
chatelaine [**shat**-tell-lane] *noun* (formerly)
mistress of a large house or castle.
chattels *plural noun* possessions.
chatter **ⓘ** *verb* **1** speak quickly and
continuously about unimportant things. **2** (of a
bird or monkey) make rapid repetitive high-
pitched noises. **3** (of the teeth) rattle with cold
or fear. ✦ *noun* **4** idle talk. **chatterbox** *noun*
person who chatters a lot.
chauffeur *noun* person employed to drive a
car for someone. **chauffeuse** *n fem*
chauvinism [**show**-vin-iz-zum] *noun* irrational
belief that one's own country, race, group, or
sex is superior. **chauvinist** *noun, adjective*
chauvinistic *adjective*
cheap **ⓘ** *adjective* **1** costing relatively little. **2**
of poor quality. **3** not valued highly. **4** mean,
despicable. **cheaply** *adverb* **cheapen** *verb* **1**
lower the reputation of. **2** reduce the price of.
cheap-jack *noun Informal* person who sells
cheap and shoddy goods. **cheapskate** *noun
Informal* miserly person.
cheat **ⓘ** *verb* **1** act dishonestly to gain profit or
advantage. **2** (usu. foll. by *on*) be unfaithful
(to). ✦ *noun* **3** person who cheats. **4** fraud,
deception.
check **ⓘ** *verb* **1** examine, investigate. **2** slow
the growth or progress of. **3** correspond, agree.

——————————— T H E S A U R U S ———————————

charter *noun* **1** = **document**, contract, deed,
licence, permit ✦*verb* **4** = **hire**, commission,
employ, lease, rent **5** = **authorize**, sanction
chase[1] *verb* **1** = **pursue**, course, drive, drive
away, expel, follow, hound, hunt, put to flight,
run after, track ✦*noun* **4** = **pursuit**, hunt,
hunting, race
chasm *noun* **1** = **gulf**, abyss, crater, crevasse,
fissure, gap, gorge, ravine
chaste *adjective* **1** = **pure**, immaculate,
innocent, modest, unaffected, undefiled,
virtuous OPPOSITE **promiscuous**. **2** = **simple**
chasten *verb* = **subdue**, chastise, correct,
discipline, humble, humiliate, put in one's
place, tame
chastise *verb* **1** = **scold**, berate, castigate,
censure, correct, discipline, rouse on (*Aust*),
upbraid OPPOSITE **praise**. **2** = **beat**, flog, lash,
lick (*inf*), punish, scourge, whip
chastity *noun* **1** = **purity**, celibacy,
continence, innocence, maidenhood, modesty,
virginity, virtue OPPOSITE **promiscuity**
chat *noun* **1** = **talk**, chatter, chinwag (*Brit inf*),

conversation, gossip, heart-to-heart, natter,
tête-à-tête ✦*verb* **2** = **talk**, chatter, gossip, jaw
(*sl*), natter
chatter *verb* **1** = **prattle**, babble, blather, chat,
gab (*inf*), gossip, natter, rabbit (on) (*Brit inf*),
schmooze (*sl*) ✦*noun* **4** = **prattle**, babble,
blather, chat, gab (*inf*), gossip, natter
cheap *adjective* **1** = **inexpensive**, bargain,
cut-price, economical, keen, low-cost, low-
priced, reasonable, reduced OPPOSITE **dear**. **2**
= **inferior**, common, poor, second-rate, shoddy,
tatty, tawdry, two a penny, worthless OPPOSITE
good. **4** = **despicable**, contemptible, mean
OPPOSITE **decent**
cheapen *verb* **1** = **degrade**, belittle, debase,
demean, denigrate, discredit, disparage, lower
2 = **devalue**, depreciate
cheat *verb* **1** = **deceive**, beguile, con (*inf*),
defraud, double-cross (*inf*), dupe, fleece, fool,
mislead, rip off (*sl*), swindle, trick ✦*noun* **3**
= **deceiver**, charlatan, con man (*inf*), double-
crosser (*inf*), shark, sharper, swindler, trickster **4**
= **deception**, deceit, fraud, rip-off (*sl*), scam (*sl*),

C

◆ *noun* **4** test to ensure accuracy or progress. **5** break in progress. **6** *US* cheque. **7** pattern of squares or crossed lines. **8** *Chess* position of a king under attack. **checked** *adjective* having a pattern of squares. **check in** *verb* register one's arrival. **checkmate** *noun* **1** *Chess* winning position in which an opponent's king is under attack and unable to escape. **2** utter defeat. ◆ *verb* **3** *Chess* place the king of (one's opponent) in checkmate. **4** thwart, defeat. **check out** *verb* **1** pay the bill and leave a hotel. **2** examine, investigate. **3** *Informal* have a look at. **checkout** *noun* counter in a supermarket, where customers pay. **checkup** *noun* thorough medical examination.

checkers *noun US* same as DRAUGHTS.

Cheddar *noun* firm orange or yellowy-white cheese.

cheek ⊕ *noun* **1** either side of the face below the eye. **2** *Informal* impudence, boldness. ◆ *verb* **3** *Informal* speak impudently to. **cheeky** *adjective* **cheekier, cheekiest** impudent, disrespectful. **cheekily** *adverb* **cheekiness** *noun*

cheep *noun* **1** young bird's high-pitched cry. ◆ *verb* **2** utter a cheep.

cheer ⊕ *verb* **1** applaud or encourage with shouts. **2** make or become happy. ◆ *noun* **3** shout of applause or encouragement. **4** feeling of happiness. **cheerful** *adjective* **cheerfully** *adverb* **cheerfulness** *noun* **cheerless** *adjective* dreary, gloomy. **cheery** *adjective* **cheerily** *adverb*

cheerio *interjection Informal* goodbye.

cheese *noun* **1** food made from coagulated milk curd. **2** block of this. **cheesy** *adjective* **cheeseburger** *noun* hamburger topped with melted cheese. **cheesecake** *noun* **1** dessert

with a biscuit-crumb base covered with a sweet cream-cheese mixture. **2** *Slang* photographs of naked or near-naked women. **cheesecloth** *noun* light cotton cloth. **cheesed off** bored, annoyed. **cheeseparing** *adjective* mean, miserly.

cheetah *noun* large fast-running spotted African wild cat.

chef *noun* cook in a restaurant.

chef-d'oeuvre [shay-**durv**] *noun, pl* **chefs-d'oeuvre** masterpiece.

chemical *noun* **1** substance used in or resulting from a reaction involving changes to atoms or molecules. ◆ *adjective* **2** of chemistry or chemicals. **chemically** *adverb*

chemise [shem-**meez**] *noun Old-fashioned* woman's loose-fitting slip.

chemistry ⊕ *noun* science of the composition, properties, and reactions of substances.

chemical *noun* substance used in or resulting from a reaction involving changes to atoms or molecules. **chemist** *noun* **1** shop selling medicines and cosmetics. **2** qualified dispenser of prescribed medicines. **3** specialist in chemistry.

chemotherapy *noun* treatment of disease, often cancer, using chemicals.

chenille [shen-**neel**] *noun* (fabric of) thick tufty yarn.

cheque *noun* written order to one's bank to pay money from one's account. **cheque book** book of detachable blank cheques issued by a bank. **cheque card** plastic card issued by a bank guaranteeing payment of a customer's cheques.

chequer *noun* **1** piece used in Chinese chequers. ◆ *plural* **2** game of draughts.

──────── T H E S A U R U S ────────

swindle, trickery

check *verb* **1** = **examine**, inquire into, inspect, investigate, look at, make sure, monitor, research, scrutinize, study, test, vet OPPOSITE **ignore**. **2** = **stop**, delay, halt, hinder, impede, inhibit, limit, obstruct, restrain, retard OPPOSITE **further** ◆*noun* **4** = **examination**, inspection, investigation, once-over (*inf*), research, scrutiny, test

cheek *noun* **2** *Inf* = **impudence**, audacity, chutzpah (*US & Canad inf*), disrespect, effrontery, impertinence, insolence, lip (*sl*), nerve, temerity

cheeky *adjective* = **impudent**, audacious, disrespectful, forward, impertinent, insolent, insulting, pert, saucy OPPOSITE **respectful**

cheer *verb* **1** = **applaud**, acclaim, clap, hail OPPOSITE **boo**. **2** = **cheer up**, brighten, buoy

up, comfort, encourage, gladden, hearten, uplift OPPOSITE **depress** ◆*noun* **3** = **applause**, acclamation, ovation, plaudits

cheerful *adjective* = **happy**, buoyant, cheery, chirpy (*inf*), enthusiastic, jaunty, jolly, light-hearted, merry, optimistic, upbeat (*inf*) OPPOSITE **gloomy**

cheerfulness *noun* = **happiness**, buoyancy, exuberance, gaiety, geniality, good cheer, good humour, high spirits, jauntiness, light-heartedness

cheerless *adjective* = **gloomy**, bleak, desolate, dismal, drab, dreary, forlorn, miserable, sombre, woeful OPPOSITE **bright**

cheery *adjective* = **cheerful**, breezy, carefree, chirpy (*inf*), genial, good-humoured, happy, jovial, upbeat (*inf*)

chemist *noun* **2** = **pharmacist**, apothecary

chequered *adjective* **1** marked by varied fortunes, e.g. *a chequered career.* **2** having a pattern of squares.

cherish ❶ *verb* **1** cling to (an idea or feeling). **2** care for.

cheroot [sher-**root**] *noun* cigar with both ends cut flat.

cherry *noun, pl* **-ries 1** small red or black fruit with a stone. **2** tree on which it grows. ◆ *adjective* **3** deep red. **cherry tomato** miniature tomato.

cherub *noun, pl* **-ubs, -ubim 1** angel, often represented as a winged child. **2** sweet child. **cherubic** [cher-**rew**-bik] *adjective*

chervil *noun* aniseed-flavoured herb.

chess *noun* game for two players with 16 pieces each, played on a chequered board of 64 squares. **chessman** *noun* piece used in chess.

chest ❶ *noun* **1** front of the body, from neck to waist. **2** large strong box. **chest of drawers** piece of furniture consisting of drawers in a frame.

chesterfield *noun* couch with high padded sides and back.

chestnut *noun* **1** reddish-brown edible nut. **2** tree on which it grows. **3** reddish-brown horse. **4** *Informal* old joke. ◆ *adjective* **5** (of hair or a horse) reddish-brown.

chesty *adjective* **chestier, chestiest** *Informal* symptomatic of chest disease.

cheval glass [shev-**val**] *noun* full-length mirror mounted to swivel within a frame.

Cheviot *noun* large British sheep reared for its wool.

chevron [**shev**-ron] *noun* V-shaped pattern, esp. on the sleeve of a military uniform to indicate rank.

chew ❶ *verb* grind (food) between the teeth.

chewy *adjective* **chewier, chewiest** requiring a lot of chewing. **chewing gum** flavoured gum to be chewed but not swallowed. **chew over** *verb* consider carefully.

chianti [kee-**ant**-ee] *noun* dry red Italian wine.

chiaroscuro [kee-ah-roh-**skew**-roh] *noun, pl* **-ros** distribution of light and shade in a picture.

chic ❶ [**sheek**] *adjective* **1** stylish, elegant. ◆ *noun* **2** stylishness, elegance.

chicane [shik-**kane**] *noun* obstacle in a motor-racing circuit.

chicanery *noun* trickery, deception.

chick *noun* **1** baby bird. **2** *Slang* young woman. **chickpea** *noun* edible yellow pealike seed. **chickweed** *noun* weed with small white flowers.

chicken *noun* **1** domestic fowl. **2** its flesh, used as food. **3** *Slang* coward. ◆ *adjective* **4** *Slang* cowardly. **chicken feed** *Slang* trifling amount of money. **chicken out** *verb Informal* fail to do something through cowardice.

chickenpox *noun* infectious disease with an itchy rash.

chicory *noun, pl* **-ries 1** plant whose leaves are used in salads. **2** root of this plant, used as a coffee substitute.

chide ❶ *verb* **chiding, chided** or **chid, chid** or **chidden** rebuke, scold.

chief ❶ *noun* **1** head of a group of people. ◆ *adjective* **2** most important. **chiefly** *adverb* **1** especially. **2** mainly. **chieftain** *noun* leader of a tribe.

chiffchaff *noun* common European warbler.

chiffon [**shif**-fon] *noun* fine see-through fabric.

chignon [**sheen**-yon] *noun* knot of hair pinned up at the back of the head.

chigoe [**chig**-go] *noun* tropical flea that burrows into the skin.

chihuahua [chee-**wah**-wah] *noun* tiny short-haired dog.

chilblain *noun* inflammation of the fingers or

———————— THESAURUS ————————

(*obs*), dispenser

cherish *verb* **1** = **cling to**, cleave to, encourage, entertain, foster, harbour, hold dear, nurture, prize, sustain, treasure OPPOSITE **despise**. **2** = **care for**, comfort, hold dear, love, nurse, shelter, support OPPOSITE **neglect**

chest *noun* **2** = **box**, case, casket, coffer, crate, strongbox, trunk

chew *verb* = **bite**, champ, chomp, crunch, gnaw, grind, masticate, munch

chewy *adjective* = **tough**, as tough as old boots, leathery

chic *adjective* **1** = **stylish**, elegant, fashionable, smart, trendy (*Brit inf*) OPPOSITE **unfashionable**

chide *verb* = **scold**, admonish, berate, censure, criticize, lecture, rebuke, reprimand, reproach, reprove, rouse on (*Aust*), tell off (*inf*), tick off (*inf*)

chief *noun* **1** = **head**, boss (*inf*), captain, commander, director, governor, leader, manager, master, principal, ruler OPPOSITE **subordinate** ◆ *adjective* **2** = **primary**, foremost, highest, key, leading, main, predominant, pre-eminent, premier, prime, principal, supreme, uppermost OPPOSITE **minor**

chiefly *adverb* **1** = **especially**, above all, essentially, primarily, principally **2** = **mainly**, in general, in the main, largely, mostly, on the whole, predominantly, usually

C

toes, caused by exposure to cold.

child ⊕ *noun, pl* **children 1** young human being, boy or girl. **2** son or daughter. **3** product of an influence or environment, e.g. *a child of the Sixties*. **childhood** *noun* **childish** *adjective* **1** immature, silly. **2** of or like a child. **childishly** *adverb* **childless** *adjective* **childlike** *adjective* innocent, trustful. **childbirth** *noun* giving birth to a child. **child's play** very easy task.

> **LANGUAGE TIP**
>
> Note that *childish* has overtones of *foolish* while *childlike* suggests an *innocent* quality.

chill ⊕ *noun* **1** a feverish cold. **2** moderate coldness. ◆ *verb* **3** make (something) cool or cold. **4** cause (someone) to feel cold or frightened. ◆ *adjective* **5** unpleasantly cold. **chilly** *adjective* **chillier, chilliest 1** moderately cold. **2** unfriendly. **chilly-bin** *noun NZ informal* insulated container for carrying food and drink. **chilliness** *noun* **chill out** *Informal vb* to relax, esp. after energetic dancing at a rave.

chilli, chili *noun* **1** small red or green hot-tasting capsicum pod, used in cooking. **2** (also **chilli con carne**) hot-tasting Mexican dish of meat, onions, beans, and chilli powder.

chime ⊕ *noun* **1** musical ringing sound of a bell or clock. ◆ *verb* **2** make a musical ringing sound. **3** indicate (the time) by chiming. **4** (foll. by *with*) be consistent with.

chimera [kime-**meer**-a] *noun* **1** unrealistic hope or idea. **2** fabled monster with a lion's head, goat's body, and serpent's tail. **chimerical** *adjective*

chimney *noun* hollow vertical structure for carrying away smoke from a fire. **chimney**

breast walls surrounding the base of a chimney or fireplace. **chimneypot** *noun* short pipe on the top of a chimney. **chimney sweep** *person who cleans soot from chimneys*

chimp *noun Informal* short for CHIMPANZEE.

chimpanzee *noun* intelligent black African ape.

chin *noun* part of the face below the mouth. **chinwag** *noun Informal* chat.

china ⊕ *noun* **1** fine earthenware or porcelain. **2** dishes or ornaments made of this. **china clay** same as KAOLIN.

chinchilla *noun* **1** S American rodent bred for its soft grey fur. **2** its fur.

chine *noun* **1** cut of meat including part of the backbone. ◆ *verb* **2** cut (meat) along the backbone.

Chinese *adjective* **1** of China. ◆ *noun* **2** *pl* **-nese** person from China. **3** any of the languages of China. **Chinese chequers** game played with marbles or pegs on a star-shaped board. **Chinese lantern** collapsible lantern made of thin paper.

chink[1] ⊕ *noun* small narrow opening, e.g. *a chink of light*.

chink[2] *verb, noun* (make) a light ringing sound.

chintz *noun* printed cotton fabric with a glazed finish.

chip ⊕ *noun* **1** strip of potato, fried in deep fat. **2** tiny wafer of semiconductor material forming an integrated circuit. **3** counter used to represent money in gambling games. **4** small piece removed by chopping, breaking, etc. **5** mark left where a small piece has been broken off something. ◆ *verb* **chipping, chipped 6** break small pieces from. **have a chip on one's shoulder** *Informal* bear a grudge. **chip in** *verb Informal* **1** contribute (money). **2** interrupt with a remark. **chippie** *noun Brit, Aust & NZ informal*

——— THESAURUS ———

child *noun* **1** = **youngster**, babe, baby, bairn (*Scot*), infant, juvenile, kid (*inf*), offspring, toddler, tot

childbirth *noun* = **child-bearing**, confinement, delivery, labour, lying-in, parturition, travail

childhood *noun* = **youth**, boyhood *or* girlhood, immaturity, infancy, minority, schooldays

childish *adjective* **1** = **immature**, foolish, infantile, juvenile, puerile [OPPOSITE] mature. **2** = **young**, boyish *or* girlish, juvenile

childlike *adjective* = **innocent**, artless, guileless, ingenuous, naive, simple, trusting

chill *noun* **2** = **cold**, bite, coldness, coolness, crispness, frigidity, nip, rawness, sharpness ◆*verb*

3 = **cool**, freeze, refrigerate **4** = **dishearten**, dampen, deject, depress, discourage, dismay ◆*adjective* **5** = **cold**, biting, bleak, chilly, freezing, frigid, raw, sharp, wintry

chilly *adjective* **1** = **cool**, brisk, crisp, draughty, fresh, nippy, penetrating, sharp [OPPOSITE] warm. **2** = **unfriendly**, frigid, hostile, unresponsive, unsympathetic, unwelcoming [OPPOSITE] friendly

chime *noun* **1** = **ring**, clang, jingle, peal, sound, tinkle, toll ◆*verb* **2** = **ring**, clang, jingle, peal, sound, tinkle, toll

china *noun* **1** = **pottery**, ceramics, porcelain **2** = **crockery**, service, tableware, ware

chink[1] *noun* **1** = **opening**, aperture, cleft,

carpenter.
chipboard *noun* thin board made of compressed wood particles.
chipmunk *noun* small squirrel-like N American rodent with a striped back.
chipolata *noun* small sausage.
chiropodist [kir-**rop**-pod-ist] *noun* person who treats minor foot complaints. **chiropody** *noun*
chiropractic [kire-oh-**prak**-tik] *noun* system of treating bodily disorders by manipulation of the spine. **chiropractor** *noun*
chirp, chirrup ⊕ *verb* **1** (of a bird or insect) make a short high-pitched sound. **2** speak in a lively fashion. ♦ *noun* **3** chirping sound. **chirpy** *adjective* **chirpier, chirpiest** *Informal* lively and cheerful.
chisel *noun* **1** metal tool with a sharp end for shaping wood or stone. ♦ *verb* **-elling, -elled 2** carve or form with a chisel.
chit¹ *noun* short official note, such as a receipt.
chit² *noun Old-fashioned* pert or impudent girl.
chitchat *noun* chat, gossip.
chitterlings *plural noun* pig's intestines cooked as food.
chivalry ⊕ *noun* **1** courteous behaviour, esp. by men towards women. **2** medieval system and principles of knighthood. **chivalrous** *adjective*
chives *plural noun* herb with a mild onion flavour.
chivvy *verb* **-vying, -vied** *Informal* harass, nag.
chlorine *noun* strong-smelling greenish-yellow gaseous element, used to disinfect water.
chlorinate *verb* disinfect (water) with chlorine.
chlorination *noun* **chloride** *noun* compound of chlorine and another substance.
chlorofluorocarbon *noun* any of various gaseous compounds of carbon, hydrogen, chlorine, and fluorine, used in refrigerators and aerosolpropellants, some of which break down the ozone in theatmosphere.

chloroform *noun* strong-smelling liquid formerly used as an anaesthetic.
chlorophyll *noun* green colouring matter of plants, which enables them to convert sunlight into energy.
chock *noun* **1** block or wedge used to prevent a heavy object from moving. ♦ *verb* **2** secure by a chock. **chock-full, chock-a-block** *adjective* completely full.
chocolate *noun* **1** sweet food made from cacao seeds. **2** sweet or drink made from this. ♦ *adjective* **3** dark brown.
choice ⊕ *noun* **1** choosing. **2** opportunity or power of choosing. **3** person or thing chosen or that may be chosen. **4** alternative action or possibility. ♦ *adjective* **5** of high quality.
choir *noun* **1** organized group of singers, esp. in church. **2** part of a church occupied by the choir.
choke ⊕ *verb* **1** hinder or stop the breathing of (a person) by strangling or smothering. **2** have trouble in breathing. **3** block, clog up. ♦ *noun* **4** device controlling the amount of air that is mixed with the fuel in a petrol engine. **choker** *noun* tight-fitting necklace. **choke back** *verb* suppress (tears or anger).
cholera [kol-ler-a] *noun* serious infectious disease causing severe vomiting and diarrhoea.
choleric [kol-ler-ik] *adjective* bad-tempered. **choler** *noun Old-fashioned* bad temper.
cholesterol [kol-**lest**-er-oll] *noun* fatty substance found in animal tissue, an excess of which can cause heart disease.
chomp *verb* chew noisily.
chook *noun Aust & NZ* hen or chicken.
choose ⊕ *verb* **choosing, chose, chosen 1** select from a number of alternatives. **2** decide (to do something) because one wants to.
choosy *adjective* **choosier, choosiest** *Informal* fussy, hard to please.
chop¹ ⊕ *verb* **chopping, chopped 1** cut with a blow from an axe or knife. **2** cut into pieces.

C

———— THESAURUS ————

crack, cranny, crevice, fissure, gap
chip *noun* **4** = **scratch**, fragment, nick, notch, shard, shaving, sliver, wafer ♦*verb* **6** = **nick**, chisel, damage, gash, whittle
chirp, chirrup *verb* **1** = **tweet**, cheep, peep, pipe, twitter, warble
chivalrous *adjective* **1** = **courteous**, gallant, gentlemanly, honourable **2** = **valiant**, bold, brave, courageous
chivalry *noun* **1** = **courtesy**, gallantry, gentlemanliness, politeness **2** = **knighthood**, courage, knight-errantry
choice *noun* **2** = **option**, alternative, pick,

preference, say **3** = **selection**, range, variety
♦*adjective* **5** = **best**, elite, excellent, exclusive, prime, rare, select
choke *verb* **1** = **strangle**, asphyxiate, gag, overpower, smother, stifle, suffocate, suppress, throttle **3** = **block**, bar, bung, clog, congest, constrict, obstruct, stop
choose *verb* = **pick**, adopt, designate, elect, opt for, prefer, select, settle upon OPPOSITE reject
choosy *adjective Inf* = **fussy**, discriminating, faddy, fastidious, finicky, particular, picky (*inf*), selective OPPOSITE **indiscriminating**

3 *Boxing, karate* hit (an opponent) with a short sharp blow. ♦ *noun* **4** cutting or sharp blow. **5** slice of lamb or pork, usu. with a rib. **chopper** *noun* **1** *Informal* helicopter. **2** small axe. **3** butcher's cleaver. **4** cycle with very high handlebars. **choppy** *adjective* **-pier, -piest** (of the sea) fairly rough.

chop² *verb* **chopping, chopped**. **chop and change** change one's mind repeatedly.

chops *plural noun Informal* jaws, cheeks.

chopsticks *plural noun* pair of thin sticks used to eat Chinese food.

chop suey *noun* Chinese dish of chopped meat and vegetables in a sauce.

choral *adjective* of a choir.

chorale [kor-**rahl**] *noun* slow stately hymn tune.

chord¹ *noun Maths* straight line joining two points on a curve.

chord² *noun* simultaneous sounding of three or more musical notes.

chore ❶ *noun* **1** routine task. **2** unpleasant task.

chorea [kor-**ree**-a] *noun* disorder of the nervous system characterized by uncontrollable brief jerky movements.

choreography *noun* composition of steps and movements for dancing. **choreographer** *noun* **choreographic** *adjective*

chorister *noun* singer in a choir.

chortle ❶ *verb* **1** chuckle in amusement. ♦ *noun* **2** amused chuckle.

chorus ❶ *noun, pl* **-ruses 1** large choir. **2** part of a song repeated after each verse. **3** something expressed by many people at once. **4** group of singers or dancers who perform together in a show. ♦ *verb* **chorusing, chorused 5** sing or say together. **in chorus** in unison.

chose *verb* past tense of CHOOSE. **chosen** *verb* past participle of CHOOSE.

chough [chuff] *noun* large black bird of the crow family.

choux pastry [shoo] *noun* very light pastry made with eggs.

chow *noun* **1** thick-coated dog with a curled tail, orig. from China. **2** *Informal* food.

chowder *noun* thick soup containing clams or fish.

chow mein *noun* Chinese-American dish of chopped meat or vegetables fried with noodles.

chrism *noun* consecrated oil used for anointing in some churches.

Christ *noun* **1** Jesus of Nazareth, regarded by Christians as the Messiah. ♦ *interjection* **2** *Taboo slang* oath of annoyance or surprise.

christen ❶ *verb* **1** baptize. **2** give a name to. **3** *Informal* use for the first time. **christening** *noun*

Christendom *noun* all Christian people or countries.

Christian *noun* **1** person who believes in and follows Christ. ♦ *adjective* **2** of Christ or Christianity. **3** kind, good. **Christianity** *noun* religion based on the life and teachings of Christ. **Christian name** person's first name. **Christian Science** religious system which emphasizes spiritual healing.

Christmas ❶ *noun* **1** annual festival on Dec. 25 commemorating the birth of Christ. **2** period around this time. **Christmassy** *adjective* **Christmas box** tip given at Christmas to postmen or tradesmen. **Christmas Day** Dec. 25. **Christmas Eve** Dec. 24. **Christmas tree** evergreen tree or imitation of one, decorated as part of Christmas celebrations.

chromatic *adjective* **1** of colour or colours. **2** *Music* (of a scale) proceeding by semitones. **chromatically** *adverb*

chromatography *noun* separation and analysis of the components of a substance by slowly passing it through an adsorbing material.

chromium, chrome *noun Chem* grey metallic element used in steel alloys and for electroplating.

chromosome *noun* microscopic gene-carrying body in the nucleus of a cell.

chronic *adjective* **1** (of an illness) lasting a long time. **2** habitual, e.g. *chronic drinking*. **3** *Informal* of poor quality. **chronically** *adverb*

chronicle ❶ *noun* **1** record of events in order of occurrence. ♦ *verb* **2** record in or as if in a chronicle. **chronicler** *noun*

chronology *noun, pl* **-gies** arrangement or list

chop *verb* **1 = cut**, cleave, fell, hack, hew, lop, sever

chore *noun* **1 = task**, duty, errand, job **2 = burden**

chortle *verb* **1 = chuckle**, cackle, crow, guffaw ♦*noun* **2 = chuckle**, cackle, crow, guffaw

chorus *noun* **1 = choir**, choristers, ensemble, singers, vocalists **2 = refrain**, burden, response,

strain **3 = unison**, accord, concert, harmony

christen *verb* **1 = baptize 2 = name**, call, designate, dub, style, term, title

Christmas *noun* **= festive season**, Noel, Xmas (*inf*), Yule (*arch*)

chronicle *noun* **1 = record**, account, annals, diary, history, journal, narrative, register, story ♦*verb* **2 = record**, enter, narrate, put on record, of events in order of occurrence. **chronological** *adjective* **chronologically** *adverb*

chronometer *noun* timepiece designed to be accurate in all conditions.

chrysalis [**kriss**-a-liss] *noun* insect in the stage between larva and adult, when it is in a cocoon.

chrysanthemum *noun* garden flower with a large head made up of thin petals.

chub *noun* freshwater fish of the carp family.

chubby ❶ *adjective* **-bier, -biest** plump and round. **chubbiness** *noun*

chuck¹ ❶ *verb* **1** *Informal* throw. **2** *Informal* give up, reject. **3** touch (someone) affectionately under the chin.

chuck² *noun* **1** cut of beef from the neck to the shoulder. **2** device that holds a workpiece in a lathe or a tool in a drill.

chuckle ❶ *verb* **1** laugh softly. ◆ *noun* **2** soft laugh.

chuff *verb* (of a steam engine) move while making a puffing sound.

chuffed *adjective Informal* very pleased.

chug *noun* **1** short dull sound like the noise of an engine. ◆ *verb* **chugging, chugged 2** operate or move with this sound.

chukka, chukker *noun* period of play in polo.

chum ❶ *Informal noun* **1** close friend. ◆ *verb* **chumming, chummed 2 chum up with** form a close friendship with. **chummy** *adjective* **-mier, -miest**

chump *noun* **1** *Informal* stupid person. **2** thick piece of meat. **3** thick block of wood.

chunk ❶ *noun* **1** thick solid piece. **2** considerable amount. **chunky** *adjective* **chunkier, chunkiest 1** (of a person) broad and heavy. **2** (of an object) large and thick.

church *noun* **1** building for public Christian worship. **2** particular Christian denomination. **3** (**C-**) Christians collectively. **4** clergy.

churchgoer *noun* person who attends church regularly. **churchwarden** *noun* member of a congregation who assists the vicar. **churchyard** *noun* grounds round a church, used as a graveyard.

churlish ❶ *adjective* surly and rude.

churn ❶ *noun* **1** machine in which cream is shaken to make butter. **2** large container for milk. ◆ *verb* **3** stir (cream) vigorously to make butter. **4** move about violently. **churn out** *verb Informal* produce (things) rapidly in large numbers.

chute¹ [**shoot**] *noun* steep slope down which things may be slid.

chute² *noun Informal* short for PARACHUTE.

chutney *noun* pickle made from fruit, vinegar, spices, and sugar.

chyle *noun* milky fluid formed in the small intestine during digestion.

chyme *noun* thick fluid mass of partially digested food that leaves the stomach.

CIA (in the US) Central Intelligence Agency.

cicada [sik-**kah**-da] *noun* large insect that makes a high-pitched drone.

cicatrix [**sik**-a-trix] *noun, pl* **-trices** scar.

CID Criminal Investigation Department.

cider *noun* alcoholic drink made from fermented apple juice.

cigar *noun* roll of cured tobacco leaves for smoking.

cigarette *noun* thin roll of shredded tobacco in thin paper, for smoking.

cilantro *noun* the US and Canadian word for CORIANDER.

cilium *noun, pl* **cilia** *Biol* **1** short thread projecting from a cell, whose rhythmic beating causes movement. **2** eyelash.

cinch [**sinch**] *noun Informal* easy task.

cinchona [sing-**kone**-a] *noun* **1** S American tree with medicinal bark. **2** (drug made from) the dried bark of this tree, which yields quinine.

cinder *noun* piece of material that will not burn, left after burning coal.

Cinderella *noun* poor, neglected, or unsuccessful person.

cine camera *noun* camera for taking moving pictures.

cinema ❶ *noun* **1** place for showing films. **2** films collectively. **cinematic** *adjective* **cinematograph** *noun* combined camera, printer, and projector. **cinematography** *noun*

———— T H E S A U R U S ————

recount, register, relate, report, set down, tell

chubby *adjective* =**plump**, buxom, flabby, podgy, portly, roly-poly, rotund, round, stout, tubby OPPOSITE> skinny

chuck¹ *verb* **1** *Inf* =**throw**, cast, fling, heave, hurl, pitch, sling, toss

chuckle *verb* **1** =**laugh**, chortle, crow, exult, giggle, snigger, titter

chum *Inf noun* **1** =**friend**, cobber (*Aust or old-*fashioned NZ inf*), companion, comrade, crony, mate (*inf*), pal (*inf*)

chunk *noun* **1** =**piece**, block, dollop (*inf*), hunk, lump, mass, nugget, portion, slab

churlish *adjective* =**rude**, brusque, harsh, ill-tempered, impolite, sullen, surly, uncivil OPPOSITE> polite

churn *verb* **4** =**stir up**, agitate, beat, convulse, swirl, toss technique of making films. **cinematographer** *noun*

cineraria *noun* garden plant with daisy-like flowers.

cinerarium *noun, pl* **-raria** place for keeping the ashes of the dead after cremation.

cinnabar *noun* heavy red mineral containing mercury.

cinnamon *noun* spice obtained from the bark of an Asian tree.

SPELLING TIP

Cinnamon is a tricky word to spell. The Bank of English shows at least 3 different ways of getting it wrong. The correct spelling has two *ns* in the middle and only one *m*.

---

cinquefoil *noun* plant with five-lobed leaves.
cipher ❶ [**sife**-er] *noun* **1** system of secret writing. **2** unimportant person. **3** *Obs* numeral zero.
circa [**sir**-ka] *preposition Latin* approximately, about.
circle ❶ *noun* **1** perfectly round geometric figure, line, or shape. **2** group of people sharing an interest or activity. **3** *Theatre* section of seats above the main level of the auditorium. ◆ *verb* **4** move in a circle (round). **5** enclose in a circle. **circular** *adjective* round. **circulate** *verb* move round.
circlet *noun* circular ornament worn on the head.
circuit ❶ *noun* **1** complete route or course, esp. a circular one. **2** complete path through which an electric current can flow. **3** periodical journey round a district, as made by judges. **4** motor-racing track. **5** series of sports

tournaments. **circuitous** [sir-**kew**-it-uss] *adjective* indirect and lengthy. **circuitry** [**sir**-kit-tree] *noun* electrical circuit(s).
circular ❶ *adjective* **1** in the shape of a circle. **2** moving in a circle. ◆ *noun* **3** letter for general distribution. **circularity** *noun*
circulate ❶ *verb* **1** send, go, or pass from place to place or person to person. **2** move about a party, talking to different people.
circulation *noun* **1** flow of blood around the body. **2** number of copies of a newspaper or magazine sold. **3** sending or moving round. **circulatory** *adjective*
circum- *prefix* around, on all sides, e.g. *circumlocution.*
circumcise *verb* **1** remove the foreskin of. **2** cut or remove the clitoris of. **circumcision** *noun*
circumference ❶ *noun* **1** boundary of a specified area or shape, esp. of a circle. **2** distance round this.
circumflex *noun* mark (ˆ) over a vowel to show that it is pronounced in a particular way.
circumlocution *noun* indirect way of saying something. **circumlocutory** *adjective*
circumnavigate *verb* sail right round. **circumnavigation** *noun*
circumscribe *verb* **1** limit, restrict. **2** draw a line round. **circumscription** *noun*
circumspect *adjective* cautious and careful not to take risks. **circumspectly** *adverb* **circumspection** *noun*
circumstance ❶ *noun* (usu. pl) occurrence or condition that accompanies or influences a person or event. **pomp and circumstance** formal display or ceremony. **circumstantial** *adjective* **1** (of evidence) strongly suggesting something but not proving it. **2** very detailed.
circumstantiate *verb* prove by giving details.
circumvent *verb* **1** avoid or get round (a rule etc.). **2** outwit. **circumvention** *noun*

─────── T H E S A U R U S ───────

cinema *noun* **1** = **pictures**, flicks (*sl*), movies **2** = **films**, big screen (*inf*), flicks (*sl*), motion pictures, movies, pictures
cipher *noun* **1** = **code**, cryptograph **2** = **nobody**, nonentity
circle *noun* **1** = **ring**, disc, globe, orb, sphere **2** = **group**, clique, club, company, coterie, set, society ◆*verb* **4** = **go round**, circumnavigate, circumscribe, wheel **5** = **enclose**, circumscribe, encircle, envelop, ring, surround
circuit *noun* **1** = **course**, journey, lap, orbit, revolution, route, tour **4** = **track**
circuitous *adjective* = **indirect**, labyrinthine, meandering, oblique, rambling, roundabout, tortuous, winding OPPOSITE **direct**

circular *adjective* **1** = **round**, ring-shaped, rotund, spherical **2** = **orbital**, circuitous, cyclical ◆*noun* **3** = **advertisement**, notice
circulate *verb* **1** = **spread**, broadcast, disseminate, distribute, issue, make known, promulgate, publicize, publish
circulation *noun* **1** = **bloodstream** **3** = **distribution**, currency, dissemination, spread, transmission
circumference *noun* **1** = **boundary**, border, edge, extremity, limits, outline, perimeter, periphery, rim
circumstance *noun* (usu. pl) = **situation**, condition, contingency, event, happening, incident, occurrence, position, state, state of

circus *noun, pl* **-cuses** (performance given by) a travelling company of acrobats, clowns, performing animals, etc.

cirque *noun* steep-sided semicircular hollow found in mountainous areas.

cirrhosis [sir-roh-siss] *noun* serious liver disease, often caused by drinking too much alcohol.

cirrus *noun, pl* **-ri** high wispy cloud.

CIS Commonwealth of Independent States.

Cistercian *noun, adjective* (monk or nun) of a strict Benedictine order.

cistern ① *noun* water tank, esp. one that holds water for flushing a toilet.

citadel ① *noun* fortress in a city.

cite ① *verb* **1** quote, refer to. **2** bring forward as proof. **3** summon to appear before a court of law. **citation** *noun* **1** commendation for bravery. **2** summons to appear before a court of law. **3** quotation.

citizen ① *noun* **1** native or naturalized member of a state or nation. **2** inhabitant of a city or town. **citizenship** *noun* **Citizens' Band** range of radio frequencies for private communication by the public.

citric acid *noun* weak acid found in citrus fruits.

citron *noun* lemon-like fruit of a small Asian tree.

citrus fruit *noun* juicy sharp-tasting fruit such as an orange or lemon.

city ① *noun, pl* **-ties 1** large or important town. **2** town that has received this title from the Crown. **the City** area of London as a financial centre.

civet [siv-vit] *noun* **1** spotted catlike African mammal. **2** musky fluid from its glands used in perfume.

civic ① *adjective* of a city or citizens. **civics** *noun* study of the rights and responsibilities of citizenship.

civil ① *adjective* **1** relating to the citizens of a state as opposed to the armed forces or the Church. **2** polite, courteous. **civilly** *adverb* **civility** *noun* polite or courteous behaviour. **civilian** *noun, adjective* (person) not belonging to the armed forces. **civil law** law relating to private and civilian affairs. **civil service** service responsible for the administration of the government. **civil servant** member of the civil service. **civil war** war between people of the same country.

civilize ① *verb* **1** refine or educate (a person). **2** make (a place) more pleasant or more acceptable. **civilization** *noun* **1** high level of human cultural and social development. **2** particular society which has reached this level.

civvies *plural noun Slang* ordinary clothes that are not part of a uniform.

cl centilitre.

Cl *Chem* chlorine.

clack *noun* **1** sound made by two hard objects striking each other. ◆ *verb* **2** make this sound.

clad *verb* a past of CLOTHE.

cladding *noun* material used to cover the outside of a building.

claim ① *verb* **1** assert as a fact. **2** demand as a right. **3** need, require. ◆ *noun* **4** assertion that something is true. **5** assertion of a right. **6** something claimed as a right. **7** demand for payment in connection with an insurance policy. **claimant** *noun*

clairvoyance ① *noun* power of perceiving things beyond the natural range of the senses. **clairvoyant** *noun, adjective*

clam *noun* **1** edible shellfish with a hinged

——————— THESAURUS ———————

affairs, status
cistern *noun* =**tank**, basin, reservoir, sink, vat
citadel *noun* =**fortress**, bastion, fortification, keep, stronghold, tower
cite *verb* **1** =**quote**, adduce, advance, allude to, enumerate, extract, mention, name, specify
citizen *noun* =**inhabitant**, denizen, dweller, resident, subject, townsman
city *noun* **1** =**town**, conurbation, metropolis, municipality
civic *adjective* =**public**, communal, local, municipal
civil *adjective* **1** =**civic**, domestic, municipal, political OPPOSITE state. **2** =**polite**, affable, courteous, obliging, refined, urbane, well-mannered OPPOSITE rude
civilization *noun* **1** =**culture**, advancement,

cultivation, development, education, enlightenment, progress, refinement, sophistication **2** =**society**, community, nation, people, polity
civilize *verb* **1** =**cultivate**, educate, enlighten, refine, sophisticate, tame
civilized *adjective* **1** =**cultured**, educated, enlightened, humane, polite, sophisticated, urbane OPPOSITE primitive
claim *verb* **1** =**assert**, allege, challenge, insist, maintain, profess, uphold **2** =**demand**, ask, call for, insist, need, require ◆*noun* **4** =**assertion**, affirmation, allegation, pretension **6** =**demand**, application, call, petition, request, requirement
clairvoyant *noun* =**psychic**, diviner, fortune-teller, visionary
clairvoyant *adjective* =**psychic**, extrasensory,

C

shell. ♦ *verb* **clamming, clammed 2 clam up**
Informal stop talking, esp. through nervousness.
clamber ⊕ *verb* climb awkwardly.
clammy ⊕ *adjective* **-mier, -miest**
unpleasantly moist and sticky. **clamminess**
noun
clamour ⊕ *noun* **1** loud protest. **2** loud
persistent noise or outcry. ♦ *verb* **3** make a loud
noise or outcry. **clamorous** *adjective* **clamour**
for *verb* demand noisily.
clamp ⊕ *noun* **1** tool with movable jaws for
holding things together tightly. **2** short for
WHEEL CLAMP. ♦ *verb* **3** fasten with a clamp. **4**
immobilize (a car) with a wheel clamp. **clamp**
down on *verb* **1** become stricter about. **2**
suppress.
clan ⊕ *noun* **1** group of families with a
common ancestor, esp. among Scottish
Highlanders. **2** close group. **clannish** *adjective*
(of a group) tending to exclude outsiders.
clandestine ⊕ *adjective* secret and concealed.
clang *verb* **1** make a loud ringing metallic
sound. ♦ *noun* **2** ringing metallic sound.
clanger *noun Informal* obvious mistake.
clangour *noun* loud continuous clanging
sound. **clangorous** *adjective*
clank *noun* **1** harsh metallic sound. ♦ *verb* **2**
make such a sound.
clap¹ ⊕ *verb* **clapping, clapped 1** applaud by
hitting the palms of one's hands sharply
together. **2** put quickly or forcibly. **3** strike
(someone) lightly with an open hand, for
example in greeting. ♦ *noun* **4** act or sound of
clapping. **5** sudden loud noise, e.g. *a clap of*
thunder. **clapped out** *Slang* worn out,
dilapidated.
clap² *noun Slang* gonorrhoea.

clapper *noun* piece of metal inside a bell,
which causes it to sound when struck against
the side. **clapperboard** *noun* pair of hinged
boards clapped together during filming to help
in synchronizing sound and picture.
claptrap *noun Informal* foolish or pretentious
talk.
claque *noun* group of people hired to
applaud.
claret [**klar**-rit] *noun* dry red wine from
Bordeaux.
clarify ⊕ *verb* **-fying, -fied 1** make (a matter)
clear and unambiguous. **2** remove the water
from (butter) by heating it. **clarification** *noun*
clarinet *noun* keyed woodwind instrument
with a single reed. **clarinettist** *noun*
clarion *noun* **1** obsolete high-pitched trumpet.
2 its sound. **clarion call** strong encouragement
to do something.
clarity ⊕ *noun* clearness.
clash ⊕ *verb* **1** come into conflict. **2** (of events)
happen at the same time. **3** (of colours) look
unattractive together. **4** (of objects) make a
loud harsh sound by being hit together. ♦ *noun*
5 fight, argument. **6** fact of two events
happening at the same time. **7** loud harsh
noise, esp. of things striking together.
clasp ⊕ *noun* **1** device for fastening things. **2**
firm grasp or embrace. ♦ *verb* **3** grasp or
embrace firmly. **4** fasten with a clasp. **clasp**
knife large knife with blades that fold into the
handle.
class ⊕ *noun* **1** group of people sharing a
similar social position. **2** system of dividing
society into such groups. **3** group of people or
things sharing a common characteristic. **4**
group of pupils or students taught together. **5**

———————————— T H E S A U R U S ————————————

second-sighted, telepathic, visionary
clamber *verb* = **climb**, claw, scale, scrabble,
scramble, shin
clammy *adjective* = **moist**, close, damp, dank,
sticky, sweaty
clamour *noun* **2** = **noise**, commotion, din,
hubbub, outcry, racket, shouting, uproar
clamp *noun* **1** = **vice**, bracket, fastener, grip,
press ♦ *verb* **3** = **fasten**, brace, fix, make fast,
secure
clan *noun* **1** = **family**, tribe **2** = **group**,
brotherhood, faction, fraternity, society
clandestine *adjective* = **secret**, cloak-and-
dagger, concealed, covert, furtive, private,
stealthy, surreptitious, underground
clap¹ *verb* **1** = **applaud**, acclaim, cheer
OPPOSITE> **boo**
clarification *noun* **1** = **explanation**,

elucidation, exposition, illumination,
interpretation, simplification
clarify *verb* **1** = **explain**, clear up, elucidate,
illuminate, interpret, make plain, simplify, throw
or shed light on
clarity *noun* = **clearness**, definition, limpidity,
lucidity, precision, simplicity, transparency
OPPOSITE> **obscurity**
clash *verb* **1** = **conflict**, cross swords, feud,
grapple, lock horns, quarrel, war, wrangle **4**
= **crash**, bang, clang, clank, clatter, jangle, jar,
rattle ♦ *noun* **5** = **conflict**, brush, collision,
confrontation, difference of opinion,
disagreement, fight, showdown (*inf*)
clasp *noun* **1** = **fastening**, brooch, buckle,
catch, clip, fastener, grip, hook, pin **2** = **grasp**,
embrace, grip, hold, hug ♦ *verb* **3** = **grasp**,
clutch, embrace, grip, hold, hug, press, seize,

standard of quality. **6** *Informal* elegance or excellence, e.g. *a touch of class.* ◆ *verb* **7** place in a class.
classic � *adjective* **1** being a typical example of something. **2** of lasting interest because of excellence. **3** attractive because of simplicity of form. ◆ *noun* **4** author, artist, or work of art of recognized excellence. ◆ *plural* **5** study of ancient Greek and Roman literature and culture. **classical** *adjective* **1** of or in a restrained conservative style. **2** denoting serious art music. **3** of or influenced by ancient Greek and Roman culture. **classically** *adverb* **classicism** *noun* artistic style showing emotional restraint and regularity of form. **classicist** *noun*

LANGUAGE TIP

If you are describing Greek and Roman culture, the correct word to use is *classical. Classic* is used to describe highly rated art or literature.

---

classify � *verb* **-fying, -fied 1** divide into groups with similar characteristics. **2** declare (information) to be officially secret. **classifiable** *adjective* **classification** *noun*
classy � *adjective* **classier, classiest** *Informal* stylish and elegant.
clatter *verb, noun* (make) a rattling noise.
clause � *noun* **1** section of a legal document. **2** part of a sentence, containing a verb.

claustrophobia *noun* abnormal fear of confined spaces. **claustrophobic** *adjective*
clavichord *noun* early keyboard instrument.
clavicle *noun* same as COLLARBONE.
claw � *noun* **1** sharp hooked nail of a bird or beast. **2** similar part, such as a crab's pincer. ◆ *verb* **3** tear with claws or nails.
clay *noun* fine-grained earth, soft when moist and hardening when baked, used to make bricks and pottery. **clayey** *adjective* **clay pigeon** baked clay disc hurled into the air as a target for shooting.
claymore *noun* large two-edged sword formerly used by Scottish Highlanders.
clean � *adjective* **1** free from dirt or impurities. **2** not yet used. **3** morally acceptable, inoffensive. **4** (of a reputation or record) free from dishonesty or corruption. **5** complete, e.g. *a clean break.* **6** smooth and regular. ◆ *verb* **7** make (something) free from dirt. ◆ *adverb* **8** *Not standard* completely, e.g. *I clean forgot.* **come clean** *Informal* reveal or admit something.
cleaner *noun* **cleanly** *adverb* **cleanliness** *noun*
clean-cut *adjective* **1** clearly outlined. **2** wholesome in appearance.
cleanse � *verb* make clean. **cleanser** *noun*
clear � *adjective* **1** free from doubt or confusion. **2** easy to see or hear. **3** able to be seen through. **4** free from darkness or obscurity. **5** free of obstruction. **6** (of weather) free from clouds. **7** (of skin) without blemish. **8** (of money) without deduction. ◆ *adverb* **9** in a clear or distinct manner. **10** out of the way,

---

——————————— THESAURUS ———————————

squeeze **4** =**fasten**, connect
class *noun* **3** =**group**, category, division, genre, kind, set, sort, type ◆*verb* **7** =**classify**, brand, categorize, designate, grade, group, label, rank, rate
classic *adjective* **1** =**typical**, archetypal, characteristic, definitive, exemplary, ideal, model, quintessential, standard **2** =**best**, consummate, finest, first-rate, masterly, world-class OPPOSITE **second-rate** ◆*noun* **4** =**standard**, exemplar, masterpiece, model, paradigm, prototype
classical *adjective* **1** =**pure**, elegant, harmonious, refined, restrained, symmetrical, understated, well-proportioned
classification *noun* **1** =**categorization**, analysis, arrangement, grading, sorting, taxonomy
classify *verb* **1** =**categorize**, arrange, catalogue, grade, pigeonhole, rank, sort, systematize, tabulate
classy *adjective* *Inf* =**high-class**, elegant,

exclusive, posh (*inf, chiefly Brit*), stylish, superior, top-drawer, up-market
clause *noun* **1** =**section**, article, chapter, condition, paragraph, part, passage
claw *noun* **1** =**nail**, talon **2** =**pincer** ◆*verb* **3** =**scratch**, dig, lacerate, maul, rip, scrape, tear
clean *adjective* **1** =**pure**, antiseptic, decontaminated, flawless, hygienic, immaculate, impeccable, purified, spotless, sterile, sterilized, unblemished, uncontaminated, unpolluted OPPOSITE **soiled**. **3** =**moral**, chaste, decent, good, honourable, innocent, pure, respectable, upright, virtuous OPPOSITE **indecent**. **5** =**complete**, conclusive, decisive, entire, final, perfect, thorough, total, unimpaired, whole ◆*verb* **7** =**cleanse**, disinfect, launder, purge, purify, rinse, sanitize, scour, scrub, wash OPPOSITE **soil**
cleanse *verb* =**clean**, absolve, clear, purge, purify, rinse, scour, scrub, wash
cleanser *noun* =**detergent**, disinfectant, purifier, scourer, soap, solvent

e.g. *he lifted him clear of the deck.* ◆ *verb* **11** make or become clear. **12** pass by or over (something) without contact. **13** prove (someone) innocent of a crime or mistake. **14** make as profit. **clearly** *adverb* **clearance** *noun* **1** clearing. **2** official permission. **3** space between two parts in motion. **clear-cut** *adjective* easy to understand, not vague. **clearing** *noun* treeless area in a wood. **clear off** *verb Informal* go away. **clear out** *verb* **1** remove and sort the contents of. **2** *Informal* go away. **clear-sighted** *adjective* having good judgment. **clearway** *noun* stretch of road on which motorists may stop in an emergency.
cleat *noun* **1** wedge. **2** piece of wood or iron with two projecting ends round which ropes are fastened.
cleave[1] *verb* **cleaving, cleft, cleaved** *or* **clove, cleft, cleaved** *or* **cloven** split apart. **cleavage** *noun* **1** space between a woman's breasts, as revealed by a low-cut dress. **2** division, split. **cleaver** *noun* butcher's heavy knife with a square blade.
cleave[2] *verb* cling or stick.
clef *noun Music* symbol at the beginning of a stave to show the pitch.
cleft *noun* **1** narrow opening or crack. ◆ *verb* **2** a past of CLEAVE[1]. **in a cleft stick** in a very difficult position.
clematis *noun* climbing plant with large colourful flowers.
clement *adjective* (of weather) mild.
clemency *noun* kind or lenient treatment.

clementine *noun* small orange citrus fruit.
clench *verb* **1** close or squeeze (one's teeth or fist) tightly. **2** grasp firmly.
clerestory [**clear**-store-ee] *noun, pl* **-ries** row of windows at the top of a wall above an adjoining roof.
clergy ⊕ *noun* priests and ministers as a group. **clergyman** *noun*
cleric *noun* member of the clergy.
clerical *adjective* **1** of clerks or office work. **2** of the clergy.
clerk *noun* employee in an office, bank, or court who keeps records, files, and accounts.
clever ⊕ *adjective* **1** intelligent, quick at learning. **2** showing skill. **cleverly** *adverb* **cleverness** *noun*
clianthus [klee-**anth**-us] *noun* Australian or NZ plant with slender scarlet flowers.
cliché [**klee**-shay] *noun* expression or idea that is no longer effective because of overuse. **clichéd** *adjective*
click *noun* **1** short sharp sound. ◆ *verb* **2** make this sound. **3** *Informal* (of two people) get on well together. **4** *Informal* become suddenly clear. **5** *Computers* press and release (a button on a mouse). **6** *Slang* be a success. **7** (also **click on**) *Computers* to select a particular function by pressing a button on a mouse.
client ⊕ *noun* **1** person who uses the services of a professional person or company. **2** *Computers* a program or work station that requests data from a server. **clientele** [klee-on-**tell**] *noun* clients collectively.

———————— THESAURUS ————————

clear *adjective* **1** = **certain**, convinced, decided, definite, positive, resolved, satisfied, sure OPPOSITE **confused. 2** = **obvious**, apparent, blatant, comprehensible, conspicuous, distinct, evident, manifest, palpable, plain, pronounced, recognizable, unmistakable OPPOSITE **hidden. 3** = **transparent**, crystalline, glassy, limpid, pellucid, see-through, translucent OPPOSITE **muddy. 5** = **unobstructed**, empty, free, open, smooth, unhindered, unimpeded OPPOSITE **closed. 6** = **bright**, cloudless, fair, fine, light, luminous, shining, sunny, unclouded OPPOSITE **dark. 7** = **unblemished**, clean, immaculate ◆*verb* **11** = **unblock**, disentangle, extricate, free, open, rid **12** = **pass over**, jump, leap, miss, vault **13** = **absolve**, acquit, excuse, exonerate, justify, vindicate OPPOSITE **blame. 14** = **gain**, acquire, earn, make, reap, secure
clear-cut *adjective* = **straightforward**, black-and-white, cut-and-dried (*inf*), definite, explicit, plain, precise, specific, unambiguous, unequivocal

clearly *adverb* = **obviously**, beyond doubt, distinctly, evidently, markedly, openly, overtly, undeniably, undoubtedly
clergy *noun* = **priesthood**, churchmen, clergymen, clerics, holy orders, ministry, the cloth
clergyman *noun* = **minister**, chaplain, cleric, man of God, man of the cloth, padre, parson, pastor, priest, vicar
clever *adjective* **1** = **intelligent**, bright, ingenious, knowledgeable, quick-witted, resourceful, shrewd, smart OPPOSITE **stupid. 2** = **talented**, gifted OPPOSITE **inept**
cleverness *noun* = **intelligence**, ability, brains, ingenuity, quick wits, resourcefulness, shrewdness, smartness
cliché *noun* = **platitude**, banality, commonplace, hackneyed phrase, stereotype, truism
client *noun* = **customer**, applicant, buyer, consumer, patient, patron, shopper
clientele *noun* = **customers**, business, clients,

C

cliff ⊕ *noun* steep rock face, esp. along the sea shore. **cliffhanger** *noun* film, game, etc., that is tense and exciting because its outcome is uncertain.

climacteric *noun* **1** same as MENOPAUSE. **2** diminishing sex drive and fertility experienced by men in middle age.

climate ⊕ *noun* **1** typical weather conditions of an area. **2** prevailing trend. **climatic** *adjective* **climatically** *adverb*

LANGUAGE TIP

Climatic is sometimes wrongly used where *climactic* is meant. *Climatic* should be used to talk about things relating to climate; *climactic* is used to describe something which forms a climax.

---

climax ⊕ *noun* **1** most intense point of an experience, series of events, or story. **2** same as ORGASM. ◆ *verb* **3** *Not universally accepted* reach a climax. **climactic** *adjective*

climb ⊕ *verb* **1** go up, ascend. **2** rise to a higher point or intensity. ◆ *noun* **3** climbing. **4** place to be climbed. **climber** *noun* **climb down** *verb* retreat from an opinion or position.

clime *noun Poetic* place or its climate.

clinch ⊕ *verb* **1** settle (an argument or agreement) decisively. ◆ *noun* **2** *Boxing, wrestling* movement in which one competitor holds on to the other to avoid punches. **3** *Informal* lover's embrace. **clincher** *noun Informal* something decisive.

cling ⊕ *verb* **clinging, clung** hold tightly or stick closely. **clingfilm** *noun* thin polythene material for wrapping food.

clinic ⊕ *noun* **1** building where outpatients receive medical treatment or advice. **2** private or specialized hospital. **clinical** *adjective* **1** of a clinic. **2** logical and unemotional. **clinically** *adverb*

clink[1] *verb, noun* (make) a light sharp metallic sound.

clink[2] *noun Slang* prison.

clinker *noun* fused coal left over in a fire or furnace.

clinker-built *adjective* (of a boat) made of overlapping planks.

clip[1] **⊕** *verb* **clipping, clipped 1** cut with shears or scissors. **2** *Informal* hit sharply. ◆ *noun* **3** short extract of a film. **4** *Informal* sharp blow. **clipped** *adjective* (of speech) abrupt and disjointed. **clippers** *plural noun* tool for clipping. **clipping** *noun* something cut out, esp. an article from a newspaper.

clip[2] **⊕** *noun* **1** device for attaching or holding things together. ◆ *verb* **clipping, clipped 2** attach or hold together with a clip.

clipper *noun* fast commercial sailing ship.

clique ⊕ [kleek] *noun* small exclusive group. **cliquey** *adjective*

clitoris [klit-or-iss] *noun* small sexually sensitive organ at the front of the vulva. **clitoral** *adjective*

cloak ⊕ *noun* **1** loose sleeveless outer garment. **2** something that covers or conceals. ◆ *verb* **3** cover or conceal. **cloakroom** *noun* room where coats may be left temporarily.

clobber[1] *verb Informal* **1** hit. **2** defeat utterly.

clobber[2] *noun Informal* belongings, esp. clothes.

cloche [klosh] *noun* **1** cover to protect young plants. **2** woman's close-fitting hat.

clock *noun* **1** instrument for showing the time. **2** device with a dial for recording or measuring.

————————— THESAURUS —————————

following, market, patronage, regulars, trade
cliff *noun* = **rock face**, bluff, crag, escarpment, overhang, precipice, scar, scarp
climactic *adjective* **1** = **crucial**, critical, decisive, paramount, peak
climate *noun* **2** = **weather**, temperature
climax *noun* **1** = **culmination**, height, highlight, high point, peak, summit, top, zenith
climb *verb* **1** = **ascend**, clamber, mount, rise, scale, shin up, soar, top
climb down *verb* = **back down**, eat one's words, retract, retreat
clinch *verb* **1** = **settle**, conclude, confirm, decide, determine, seal, secure, set the seal on, sew up (*inf*)
cling *verb* = **stick**, adhere, clasp, clutch,

embrace, grasp, grip, hug
clinical *adjective* **2** = **unemotional**, analytic, cold, detached, dispassionate, impersonal, objective, scientific
clip[1] *verb* **1** = **trim**, crop, curtail, cut, pare, prune, shear, shorten, snip **2** *Inf* = **smack**, clout (*inf*), cuff, knock, punch, strike, thump, wallop (*inf*), whack ◆*noun* **4** *Inf* = **smack**, clout (*inf*), cuff, knock, punch, strike, thump, wallop (*inf*), whack
clip[2] *verb* **2** = **attach**, fasten, fix, hold, pin, staple
clique *noun* = **group**, cabal, circle, coterie, faction, gang, set
cloak *noun* **1** = **cape**, coat, mantle, wrap ◆*verb* **3** = **cover**, camouflage, conceal, disguise, hide,

C

♦ verb **3** record (time) with a stopwatch.
clockwise adverb, adjective in the direction in which the hands of a clock rotate. **clock in** or **on, out** or **off** verb register arrival at or departure from work on an automatic time recorder. **clock up** verb reach (a total).

clockwork noun mechanism similar to the kind in a clock, used in wind-up toys. **like clockwork** with complete regularity and precision.

clod noun **1** lump of earth. **2** stupid person. **cloddish** adjective **clodhopper** noun Informal clumsy person.

clog ⊕ verb **clogging, clogged 1** obstruct. ♦ noun **2** wooden or wooden-soled shoe.

cloisonné [klwah-**zon**-nay] noun design made by filling in a wire outline with coloured enamel.

cloister noun **1** covered pillared arcade, usu. in a monastery. **2** place of religious seclusion. **cloistered** adjective sheltered.

clone noun **1** animal or plant produced artificially from the cells of another animal or plant, and identical to the original. **2** Informal person who closely resembles another. ♦ verb **3** produce as a clone.

close¹ ⊕ verb [rhymes with **nose**] **1** shut. **2** prevent access to. **3** end, terminate. **4** bring or come nearer together. ♦ noun **5** end, conclusion. **6** [rhymes with **dose**] street closed at one end. **7** [rhymes with **dose**] courtyard, quadrangle. **closed-circuit television** television system used within a limited area such as a building. **closed shop** place of work in which all workers must belong to a particular trade union.

close² ⊕ adjective [rhymes with **dose**] **1** near. **2** intimate. **3** careful, thorough. **4** compact, dense. **5** oppressive, stifling. **6** secretive. ♦ adverb **7** closely, tightly. **closely** adverb **closeness** noun **close season** period when it is illegal to kill certain game or fish. **close shave** Informal narrow escape. **close-up** noun photograph or film taken at close range.

closet noun **1** US cupboard. **2** small private room. ♦ adjective **3** private, secret. ♦ verb **closeting, closeted 4** shut (oneself) away in private.

closure noun **1** closing. **2** ending of a debate by immediate vote. **3** a resolution of a significant event or relationship in a person's life.

clot noun **1** soft thick lump formed from liquid. **2** Informal stupid person. ♦ verb **clotting, clotted 3** form soft thick lumps.

cloth ⊕ noun **1** (piece of) woven fabric. **2** (preceded by the) the clergy.

clothe ⊕ verb **clothing, clothed** or **clad 1** put clothes on. **2** provide with clothes. **clothes** plural noun **1** articles of dress. **2** bed coverings. **clothier** noun Old-fashioned maker or seller of clothes or cloth. **clothing** noun clothes collectively.

cloud ⊕ noun **1** mass of condensed water vapour floating in the sky. **2** floating mass of smoke, dust, etc. **3** large number of insects etc. in flight. **4** something that threatens or causes gloom. ♦ verb **5** (foll. by over) become cloudy. **6** confuse. **7** make gloomy or depressed. **cloudless** adjective **cloudy** adjective **1** having a lot of clouds. **2** (of liquid) not clear.

cloudburst noun heavy fall of rain.

——————— THESAURUS ———————

mask, obscure, screen, veil
clog verb **1** = **obstruct**, block, congest, hinder, impede, jam
close¹ verb **1** = **shut**, bar, block, lock, plug, seal, secure, stop up OPPOSITE open. **2** = **end**, cease, complete, conclude, finish, shut down, terminate, wind up OPPOSITE begin. **4** = **connect**, come together, couple, fuse, join, unite OPPOSITE part ♦noun **5** = **end**, completion, conclusion, culmination, denouement, ending, finale, finish
close² adjective **1** = **near**, adjacent, adjoining, at hand, cheek by jowl, handy, impending, nearby, neighbouring, nigh OPPOSITE far. **2** = **intimate**, attached, confidential, dear, devoted, familiar, inseparable, loving OPPOSITE distant. **3** = **careful**, detailed, intense, minute, painstaking, rigorous, thorough **4** = **compact**, congested, crowded, dense, impenetrable,

jam-packed, packed, tight **5** = **stifling**, airless, heavy, humid, muggy, oppressive, stuffy, suffocating, sweltering OPPOSITE airy. **6** = **secretive**, private, reticent, secret, taciturn, uncommunicative
closed adjective **1** = **shut**, fastened, locked, out of service, sealed OPPOSITE open. **2** = **exclusive**, restricted **3** = **finished**, concluded, decided, ended, over, resolved, settled, terminated
cloth noun **1** = **fabric**, material, textiles
clothe verb **1** = **dress**, array, attire, cover, drape, garb, robe OPPOSITE undress. **2** = **fit out**, equip
clothes plural noun **1** = **clothing**, apparel, attire, costume, dress, garb, garments, gear (inf), outfit, wardrobe, wear
clothing noun = **clothes**, apparel, attire, costume, dress, garb, garments, gear (inf), outfit, wardrobe, wear

cloudberry *noun* creeping plant with white flowers and orange berry-like fruits.

clout ❶ *Informal noun* **1** hard blow. **2** power, influence. ◆ *verb* **3** hit hard.

clove¹ *noun* dried flower bud of a tropical tree, used as a spice.

clove² *noun* segment of a bulb of garlic.

clove³ *verb* a past tense of CLEAVE¹. **clove hitch** knot used to fasten a rope to a spar.

cloven *verb* a past participle of CLEAVE¹. **cloven hoof** divided hoof of a cow, goat, etc.

clover *noun* plant with three-lobed leaves. **in clover** in luxury.

clown ❶ *noun* **1** comic entertainer in a circus. **2** amusing person. **3** stupid person. ◆ *verb* **4** behave foolishly. **5** perform as a clown. **clownish** *adjective*

cloying *adjective* sickeningly sweet.

club ❶ *noun* **1** association of people with common interests. **2** building used by such a group. **3** thick stick used as a weapon. **4** stick with a curved end used to hit the ball in golf. **5** playing card with black three-leaved symbols. ◆ *verb* **clubbing, clubbed 6** hit with a club. **club together** *verb* combine resources for a common purpose.

club foot *noun* deformity of the foot causing inability to put the foot flat on the ground.

cluck *noun* **1** low clicking noise made by a hen. ◆ *verb* **2** make this noise.

clue ❶ *noun* something that helps to solve a mystery or puzzle. **not have a clue** be completely baffled. **clueless** *adjective* stupid.

clued-up *adjective* shrewd and well-informed.

clump ❶ *noun* **1** small group of things or people. **2** dull heavy tread. ◆ *verb* **3** walk heavily. **4** form into clumps.

clumsy ❶ *adjective* **-sier, -siest 1** lacking skill or physical coordination. **2** badly made or done. **clumsily** *adverb* **clumsiness** *noun*

clung *verb* past of CLING.

clunk *noun* **1** dull metallic sound. ◆ *verb* **2** make such a sound.

cluster ❶ *noun* **1** small close group. ◆ *verb* **2** gather in clusters.

clutch ❶ *verb* **1** grasp tightly. **2** (foll. by *at*) try to get hold of. ◆ *noun* **3** device enabling two revolving shafts to be connected and disconnected, esp. in a motor vehicle. **4** tight grasp.

clutch² *noun* **1** set of eggs laid at the same time. **2** small group of things.

clutter ❶ *verb* **1** scatter objects about (a place) untidily. ◆ *noun* **2** untidy mess.

Clydesdale *noun* heavy powerful carthorse.

cm centimetre.

Cm *Chem* curium.

CND Campaign for Nuclear Disarmament.

Co *Chem* cobalt.

CO 1 Colorado. **2** Commanding Officer.

Co. 1 Company. **2** County.

co- *prefix* together, joint, or jointly, e.g. *coproduction*.

c/o 1 care of. **2** *Book-keeping* carried over.

coach ❶ *noun* **1** long-distance bus. **2** railway carriage. **3** large four-wheeled horse-drawn carriage. **4** trainer, instructor. ◆ *verb* **5** train, teach. **coachman** *noun* driver of a horse-drawn

C

--- THESAURUS ---

cloud *noun* **1, 2 = mist**, gloom, haze, murk, vapour ◆*verb* **5** (foll. by *over*) **= obscure**, becloud, darken, dim, eclipse, obfuscate, overshadow, shade, shadow, veil **6 = confuse**, disorient, distort, impair, muddle, muddy the waters

cloudy *adjective* **1 = dull**, dim, gloomy, leaden, louring *or* lowering, overcast, sombre, sunless OPPOSITE **clear**. **2 = opaque**, muddy, murky

clout *Inf noun* **2 = influence**, authority, mana (*NZ*), power, prestige, pull, weight ◆*verb* **3 = hit**, clobber (*sl*), punch, sock (*sl*), strike, thump, wallop (*inf*)

clown *noun* **1 = comedian**, buffoon, comic, fool, harlequin, jester **2 = joker**, prankster ◆*verb* **4 = play the fool**, act the fool, jest, mess about

club *noun* **1 = association**, fraternity, group, guild, lodge, set, society, union **3 = stick**, bat, bludgeon, cosh (*Brit*), cudgel, truncheon ◆*verb* **6 = beat**, bash, batter, bludgeon, cosh (*Brit*), hammer, pummel, strike

clue *noun* **= indication**, evidence, hint, lead, pointer, sign, suggestion, suspicion, trace

clueless *adjective* **= stupid**, dim, dozy (*Brit inf*), dull, half-witted, simple, slow, thick, unintelligent, witless

clump *noun* **1 = cluster**, bunch, bundle, group, mass ◆*verb* **3 = stomp**, lumber, plod, thud, thump, tramp

clumsy *adjective* **1 = awkward**, bumbling, gauche, gawky, ham-fisted (*inf*), lumbering, maladroit, ponderous, uncoordinated, ungainly, unwieldy OPPOSITE **skilful**

cluster *noun* **1 = gathering**, assemblage, batch, bunch, clump, collection, group, knot ◆*verb* **2 = gather**, assemble, bunch, collect, flock, group

clutch¹ *verb* **1 = seize**, catch, clasp, cling to, embrace, grab, grasp, grip, snatch

clutter *verb* **1 = litter**, scatter, strew OPPOSITE **arrange** ◆*noun* **2 = untidiness**, confusion, disarray, disorder, hotchpotch, jumble, litter, coach or carriage.

coagulate [koh-**ag**-yew-late] *verb* change from a liquid to a semisolid mass. **coagulation** *noun* **coagulant** *noun* substance causing coagulation.

coal *noun* black rock consisting mainly of carbon, used as fuel. **coalface** *noun* exposed seam of coal in a mine. **coalfield** *noun* area with coal under the ground. **coal gas** mixture of gases produced from coal, used for heating and lighting. **coal tar** black tar made from coal, used for making drugs and chemical products.

coalesce ● [koh-a-**less**] *verb* come together, merge. **coalescence** *noun*

coalition ● [koh-a-**lish**-un] *noun* temporary alliance, esp. between political parties.

coaming *noun* raised frame round a ship's hatchway for keeping out water.

coarse ● *adjective* **1** rough in texture. **2** unrefined, indecent. **3** of inferior quality. **coarsely** *adverb* **coarseness** *noun* **coarsen** *verb* **coarse fish** any freshwater fish not of the salmon family.

coast ● *noun* **1** place where the land meets the sea. ◆ *verb* **2** move by momentum, without the use of power. **3** proceed without great effort. **coastal** *adjective* **coaster** *noun* **1** small mat placed under a glass. **2** small ship.

coastguard *noun* **1** organization that aids ships and swimmers in trouble and prevents smuggling. **2** member of this. **coastline** *noun* outline of a coast.

coat ● *noun* **1** outer garment with long sleeves. **2** animal's fur or hair. **3** covering layer, e.g. *a coat of paint*. ◆ *verb* **4** cover with a layer. **coating** *noun* covering layer. **coat of arms** heraldic emblem of a family or institution.

coax ● *verb* **1** persuade gently. **2** obtain by persistent coaxing.

coaxial [koh-**ax**-ee-al] *adjective* (of a cable) transmitting by means of two concentric conductors separated by an insulator.

cob *noun* **1** stalk of an ear of maize. **2** thickset type of horse. **3** round loaf of bread. **4** male swan.

cobalt *noun Chem* brittle silvery-white metallic element.

cobber *noun Aust or NZ informal* friend.

cobble *noun* cobblestone. **cobbler** *noun* shoe mender. **cobblestone** *noun* rounded stone used for paving. **cobble together** *verb* put together clumsily.

cobblers *plural noun Taboo slang* nonsense.

cobia [koh-**bee**-a] *noun* large dark-striped game fish of tropical and subtropical seas.

COBOL *noun* high-level computer programming language for general commercial use.

cobra *noun* venomous hooded snake of Asia and Africa.

cobweb *noun* spider's web.

coca *noun* dried leaves of a S American shrub which contain cocaine.

Coca-Cola *noun* ® dark brown fizzy soft drink.

cocaine *noun* addictive drug used as a narcotic and as an anaesthetic.

coccyx [kok-six] *noun, pl* **coccyges** [kok-**sije**-eez] bone at the base of the spinal column.

cochineal *noun* red dye obtained from a Mexican insect, used for food colouring.

cochlea [kok-lee-a] *noun, pl* **-leae** [-li-**ee**] spiral tube in the internal ear, which converts sound vibrations into nerve impulses.

cock *noun* **1** male bird, esp. of domestic fowl. **2** *Taboo slang* penis. **3** stopcock. ◆ *verb* **4** draw back (the hammer of a gun) to firing position. **5** lift and turn (part of the body). **cockerel** *noun* young domestic cock. **cock-a-hoop** *adjective* in high spirits. **cock-and-bull story** improbable story.

——— THESAURUS ———

mess, muddle OPPOSITE **order**

coach *noun* **1** = **bus**, car, charabanc, vehicle **3** = **carriage 4** = **instructor**, handler, teacher, trainer, tutor ◆*verb* **5** = **instruct**, drill, exercise, prepare, train, tutor

coalesce *verb* = **blend**, amalgamate, combine, fuse, incorporate, integrate, merge, mix, unite

coalition *noun* = **alliance**, amalgamation, association, bloc, combination, confederation, conjunction, fusion, merger, union

coarse *adjective* **1** = **rough** OPPOSITE **soft**. **2** = **vulgar**, earthy, improper, indecent, indelicate, ribald, rude, smutty OPPOSITE **refined**. **3** = **crude**, homespun, impure, unfinished,

unpolished, unprocessed, unpurified, unrefined OPPOSITE **smooth**

coarseness *noun* **1** = **roughness**, crudity, unevenness **2** = **vulgarity**, bawdiness, crudity, earthiness, indelicacy, ribaldry, smut, uncouthness

coast *noun* **1** = **shore**, beach, border, coastline, seaboard, seaside ◆*verb* **2** = **cruise**, drift, freewheel, glide, sail, taxi

coat *noun* **2** = **fur**, fleece, hair, hide, pelt, skin, wool **3** = **layer**, coating, covering, overlay ◆*verb* **4** = **cover**, apply, plaster, smear, spread

coax *verb* **1** = **persuade**, allure, cajole, entice, prevail upon, sweet-talk (*inf*), talk into, wheedle

cockade noun feather or rosette worn on a hat as a badge.

cockatiel, cockateel noun crested Australian parrot with a greyish-brown and yellow plumage.

cockatoo noun crested parrot of Australia or the East Indies.

cocker spaniel noun small spaniel.

cockeyed adjective **1** Informal crooked, askew. **2** foolish, absurd.

cockie, cocky noun, pl **-kies** Aust & NZ informal farmer.

cockle noun edible shellfish. **cockleshell** noun **1** shell of the cockle. **2** small light boat.

Cockney noun **1** native of the East End of London. **2** London dialect.

cockpit noun **1** pilot's compartment in an aircraft. **2** driver's compartment in a racing car. **3** site of many battles or contests.

cockroach noun beetle-like insect which is a household pest.

cockscomb noun same as COXCOMB.

cocksure adjective overconfident, arrogant.

cocktail ❶ noun **1** mixed alcoholic drink. **2** appetizer of seafood or mixed fruits.

cocky ❶ adjective **cockier, cockiest** conceited and overconfident. **cockily** adverb **cockiness** noun

coco noun coconut palm.

cocoa noun **1** powder made from the seed of the cacao tree. **2** drink made from this powder.

coconut noun **1** large hard fruit of a type of palm tree. **2** edible flesh of this fruit.

cocoon noun **1** silky protective covering of a silkworm. **2** protective covering. ♦ verb **3** wrap up tightly for protection.

cocotte noun small fireproof dish in which individual portions of food are cooked.

cod noun **1** large food fish of the North Atlantic. **2** any other fish of the same family. **cod-liver oil** oil extracted from fish, rich in vitamins A and D.

COD cash on delivery.

coda [kode-a] noun final part of a musical composition.

coddle verb **1** pamper, overprotect. **2** cook (eggs) in water just below boiling point.

code ❶ noun **1** system of letters, symbols, or prearranged signals by which messages can be communicated secretly or briefly. **2** set of principles or rules. ♦ verb **3** put into code.

codify [kode-if-fie] verb **-fying, -fied** organize (rules or procedures) systematically. **codification** noun

codeine [kode-een] noun drug used as a painkiller.

codex noun, pl **codices** volume of manuscripts of an ancient text.

codger noun Informal old man.

codicil [kode-iss-ill] noun addition to a will.

codpiece noun Hist bag covering the male genitals, attached to the breeches.

codswallop noun Slang nonsense.

coeducation noun education of boys and girls together. **coeducational** adjective

coefficient noun **1** Maths number or constant placed before and multiplying a quantity. **2** Physics number or constant used to calculate the behaviour of a substance under specified conditions.

coelacanth [seel-a-kanth] noun primitive marine fish.

coeliac disease [seel-ee-ak] noun disease which hampers digestion of food.

coequal adjective, noun equal.

coerce [koh-urss] verb compel, force. **coercion** noun **coercive** adjective

coeval [koh-eev-al] adjective, noun contemporary.

coexist verb exist together, esp. peacefully despite differences. **coexistence** noun

coextensive adjective covering the same area.

C of E Church of England.

coffee noun **1** drink made from the roasted and ground seeds of a tropical shrub. **2** beanlike seeds of this shrub. ♦ adjective **3** medium-brown. **coffee bar** café, snack bar. **coffee table** small low table. **coffee-table book** large expensive illustrated book.

coffer noun **1** chest for valuables. ♦ plural **2** store of money.

cofferdam noun watertight enclosure pumped dry to enable construction work to be done.

coffin noun box in which a corpse is buried or cremated.

cog noun **1** one of the teeth on the rim of a gearwheel. **2** unimportant person in a big organization.

cogent ❶ [koh-jent] adjective forcefully convincing. **cogency** noun **cogently** adverb

cogitate ❶ [koj-it-tate] verb think deeply

OPPOSITE> **bully**

cocky adjective =**overconfident**, arrogant, brash, cocksure, conceited, egotistical, full of oneself, swaggering, vain OPPOSITE> **modest**

code noun **1** = **cipher**, cryptograph **2** = **principles**, canon, convention, custom, ethics, etiquette, manners, maxim, regulations, rules, system

C

about. **cogitation** noun
cognac [kon-yak] noun French brandy.
cognate adjective derived from a common original form.
cognition noun act or experience of knowing or acquiring knowledge. **cognitive** adjective
cognizance noun knowledge, understanding. **cognizant** adjective
cognomen [kog-noh-men] noun, pl -nomens, -nomina [-nom-min-a] 1 nickname. 2 surname.
cognoscenti [kon-yo-shen-tee] plural noun connoisseurs.
cohabit verb live together as husband and wife without being married. **cohabitation** noun
cohere ❶ verb 1 hold or stick together. 2 be logically connected or consistent. **coherence** noun **coherent** adjective 1 logical and consistent. 2 capable of intelligible speech. 3 sticking together. **coherently** adverb **cohesion** noun sticking together. **cohesive** adjective
cohort noun 1 band of associates. 2 tenth part of an ancient Roman legion.
coif verb **coiffing, coiffed** 1 arrange the hair of. ♦ noun 2 close-fitting cap worn in the Middle Ages.
coiffure noun hairstyle. **coiffeur, coiffeuse** noun hairdresser.
coil ❶ verb 1 wind in loops. 2 move in a winding course. ♦ noun 3 something coiled. 4 single loop of this. 5 coil-shaped contraceptive device inserted in the womb. 6 electrical conductor wound into a spiral.
coin ❶ noun 1 piece of metal money. 2 metal currency collectively. ♦ verb 3 invent (a word or phrase). 4 make or stamp (coins). **coin it in** Informal earn money quickly. **coinage** noun 1 coins collectively. 2 word or phrase coined. 3

coining.
coincide ❶ verb 1 happen at the same time. 2 agree or correspond exactly. **coincidence** noun 1 occurrence of simultaneous or apparently connected events. 2 coinciding. **coincident** adjective in agreement. **coincidental** adjective resulting from coincidence. **coincidentally** adverb
coir noun coconut fibre, used for matting.
coitus [koh-it-uss], **coition** [koh-ish-un] noun sexual intercourse. **coital** adjective
coke[1] noun solid fuel left after gas has been distilled from coal.
coke[2] noun Slang cocaine.
Coke noun ® short for COCA-COLA.
col noun high mountain pass.
Col. Colonel.
cola noun dark brown fizzy soft drink.
colander noun perforated bowl for straining or rinsing foods.
cold ❶ adjective 1 lacking heat. 2 lacking affection or enthusiasm. 3 (of a colour) giving an impression of coldness. 4 (of a scent in hunting) faint. 5 Slang unconscious, e.g. out cold. ♦ noun 6 lack of heat. 7 mild illness causing a runny nose, sneezing, and coughing. **coldly** adverb **coldness** noun **cold-blooded** adjective 1 cruel, unfeeling. 2 having a body temperature that varies according to the surrounding temperature. **cold cream** creamy preparation for softening and cleansing the skin. **cold feet** Slang nervousness, fear. **cold-shoulder** verb treat with indifference. **cold sore** cluster of blisters near the lips, caused by a virus. **cold war** political hostility between countries without actual warfare.
coleslaw noun salad dish of shredded raw

———————— THESAURUS ————————

cogent adjective =**convincing**, compelling, effective, forceful, influential, potent, powerful, strong, weighty
cogitate verb =**think**, consider, contemplate, deliberate, meditate, mull over, muse, ponder, reflect, ruminate
coherent adjective 1 =**consistent**, logical, lucid, meaningful, orderly, organized, rational, reasoned, systematic OPPOSITE> **inconsistent. 2** =**intelligible**, articulate, comprehensible OPPOSITE> **unintelligible**
coil verb 1 =**wind**, curl, loop, snake, spiral, twine, twist, wreathe, writhe
coin noun 1, 2 =**money**, cash, change, copper, silver, specie ♦verb 3 =**invent**, create, fabricate, make up, originate 4 =**mint**, forge, mould
coincide verb 1 =**occur simultaneously**, be

concurrent, coexist, synchronize 2 =**agree**, accord, concur, correspond, harmonize, match, square, tally OPPOSITE> **disagree**
coincidence noun 1 =**chance**, accident, fluke, happy accident, luck, stroke of luck 2 =**coinciding**, concurrence, conjunction, correlation, correspondence
coincidental adjective =**chance**, accidental, casual, fluky (inf), fortuitous, unintentional, unplanned OPPOSITE> **deliberate**
cold adjective 1 =**chilly**, arctic, bleak, cool, freezing, frigid, frosty, frozen, icy, wintry OPPOSITE> **hot. 2** =**unfriendly**, aloof, distant, frigid, indifferent, reserved, standoffish OPPOSITE> **emotional** ♦noun 6 =**coldness**, chill, frigidity, frostiness, iciness
cold-blooded adjective 1 =**callous**, dispassionate, heartless, ruthless, steely, stony-

C

cabbage in a dressing.

coley noun codlike food fish of the N Atlantic.

colic noun severe pains in the stomach and bowels. **colicky** adjective

colitis [koh-**lie**-tiss] noun inflammation of the colon.

collaborate ❶ verb 1 work with another on a project. 2 cooperate with an enemy invader. **collaboration** noun **collaborative** adjective **collaborator** noun

collage [kol-**lahzh**] noun 1 art form in which various materials or objects are glued onto a surface. 2 picture made in this way.

collapse ❶ verb 1 fall down suddenly. 2 fail completely. 3 fold compactly. ♦ noun 4 collapsing. 5 sudden failure or breakdown. **collapsible** adjective

collar ❶ noun 1 part of a garment round the neck. 2 band put round an animal's neck. 3 cut of meat from an animal's neck. ♦ verb 4 Informal seize, arrest. 5 catch in order to speak to. **collarbone** noun bone joining the shoulder blade to the breastbone.

collate verb gather together, examine, and put in order. **collation** noun 1 collating. 2 light meal. **collator** noun

collateral noun 1 security pledged for the repayment of a loan. ♦ adjective 2 descended from a common ancestor but through different lines. 3 additional but subordinate.

colleague ❶ noun fellow worker, esp. in a profession.

collect¹ ❶ verb 1 gather together. 2 accumulate (stamps etc.) as a hobby. 3 fetch. 4 receive payments of (taxes etc.). 5 regain control of (oneself). **collected** adjective calm and controlled. **collection** noun 1 things collected. 2 collecting. 3 sum of money collected. **collective** adjective of or done by a group. **collector** noun

collect² noun short prayer.

collective ❶ adjective 1 of or done by a group. ♦ noun 2 group of people working together on an enterprise and sharing the benefits from it. **collective bargaining** negotiation between a trade union and an employer on the wages etc. of the employees. **collectively** adverb **collectivism** noun theory that the state should own all means of production. **collectivize** verb organize according to the theory of collectivism.

colleen noun Irish girl.

college noun 1 place of higher education. 2 Brit name given to some secondary schools. 3 group of people of the same profession or with special duties. **collegian** noun member of a college. **collegiate** adjective

collide ❶ verb 1 crash together violently. 2 have an argument. **collision** noun

collie noun silky-haired sheepdog.

colliery noun, pl **-lieries** coal mine. **collier** noun 1 coal miner. 2 coal ship.

collocate verb (of words) occur together regularly. **collocation** noun

colloid noun suspension of particles in a solution. **colloidal** adjective

colloquial ❶ adjective suitable for informal speech or writing. **colloquialism** noun

——————— THESAURUS ———————

hearted, unemotional, unfeeling OPPOSITE caring

collaborate verb 1 = **work together**, cooperate, join forces, participate, play ball (inf), team up 2 = **conspire**, collude, cooperate, fraternize

collaboration noun 1 = **teamwork**, alliance, association, cooperation, partnership

collaborator noun 1 = **co-worker**, associate, colleague, confederate, partner, team-mate 2 = **traitor**, fraternizer, quisling, turncoat

collapse verb 1 = **fall down**, cave in, crumple, fall, fall apart at the seams, give way, subside 2 = **fail**, come to nothing, fold, founder, go belly-up (inf) ♦noun 4 = **falling down**, cave-in, disintegration, falling apart, ruin, subsidence 5 = **failure**, downfall, flop, slump

collar verb 4 Inf = **seize**, apprehend, arrest, capture, catch, grab, nab (inf), nail (inf)

colleague noun = **fellow worker**, ally, assistant, associate, collaborator, comrade, helper, partner, team-mate, workmate

collect¹ verb 1 = **assemble**, cluster, congregate, convene, converge, flock together, rally OPPOSITE scatter. 2 = **gather**, accumulate, amass, assemble, heap, hoard, save, stockpile OPPOSITE spread

collected adjective = **calm**, composed, cool, poised, self-possessed, serene, unperturbed, unruffled OPPOSITE nervous

collection noun 1 = **accumulation**, anthology, assembly, assortment, cluster, compilation, group, heap, hoard, mass, pile, set, stockpile, store 3 = **contribution**, alms, offering, offertory

collective adjective 1 = **combined**, aggregate, composite, corporate, cumulative, joint, shared, unified, united OPPOSITE individual

collide verb 1 = **crash**, clash, come into collision, meet head-on 2 = **conflict**, clash

collision noun 1 = **crash**, accident, bump, impact, pile-up (inf), prang (inf), smash 2 = **conflict**, clash, confrontation, encounter, colloquial word or phrase.

colloquium *noun, pl* **-quiums, -quia** academic seminar.

colloquy *noun, pl* **-quies** conversation or conference.

collusion *noun* secret or illegal cooperation.

collude *verb* act in collusion.

collywobbles *plural noun Slang* nervousness.

cologne *noun* mild perfume.

colon[1] *noun* punctuation mark (:).

colon[2] *noun* part of the large intestine connected to the rectum. **colonic** *adjective*

colonel *noun* senior commissioned army or air-force officer.

colonnade *noun* row of columns.

colony ❶ *noun, pl* **-nies 1** group of people who settle in a new country but remain under the rule of their homeland. **2** territory occupied by a colony. **3** group of people or animals of the same kind living together. **colonial** *adjective, noun* (inhabitant) of a colony.

colonialism *noun* policy of acquiring and maintaining colonies. **colonist** *noun* settler in a colony. **colonize** *verb* make into a colony.

colonization *noun*

Colorado beetle *noun* black-and-yellow beetle that is a serious pest of potatoes.

coloration, colouration *noun* arrangement of colours.

coloratura *noun Music* **1** complicated vocal passage. **2** soprano who specializes in such music.

colossal ❶ *adjective* very large.

colossus *noun, pl* **-si, -suses 1** huge statue. **2** huge or important person or thing.

colostomy *noun, pl* **-mies** operation to form an opening from the colon onto the surface of the body, for emptying the bowel.

colour ❶ *noun* **1** appearance of things as a result of reflecting light. **2** substance that gives colour. **3** complexion. **4** vividness, authenticity. ◆ *plural* **5** flag of a country or regiment. **6** *Sport* badge or symbol denoting membership of a team. ◆ *verb* **7** apply colour to. **8** influence (someone's judgment). **9** blush. **coloured** *adjective* **1** having colour. **2** (**C-**) (in S Africa) of mixed White and non-White parentage. **colourful** *adjective* **1** with bright or varied colours. **2** vivid, distinctive. **colourfully** *adverb* **colouring** *noun* **1** application of colour. **2** something added to give colour. **3** complexion. **colourless** *adjective* **1** dull and uninteresting. **2** without colour. **colour-blind** *adjective* unable to distinguish between certain colours.

colt *noun* young male horse.

columbine *noun* garden flower with five petals.

column ❶ *noun* **1** pillar. **2** vertical division of a newspaper page. **3** regular feature in a newspaper. **4** vertical arrangement of numbers. **5** narrow formation of troops. **columnist** *noun* journalist who writes a regular feature in a newspaper.

com-, con- *prefix* together, jointly, e.g. *commingle.*

coma ❶ *noun* state of deep unconsciousness.

comatose *adjective* **1** in a coma. **2** sound asleep.

comb ❶ *noun* **1** toothed implement for arranging the hair. **2** cock's crest. **3** honeycomb. ◆ *verb* **4** use a comb on. **5** search with great care.

combat ❶ *noun, verb* **-bating, -bated** fight, struggle. **combatant** *noun* **1** fighter. ◆ *adjective* **2** fighting. **combative** *adjective*

———— T H E S A U R U S ————

opposition, skirmish

colloquial *adjective* = **informal**, conversational, demotic, everyday, familiar, idiomatic, vernacular

colony *noun* **1** = **settlement**, community, dependency, dominion, outpost, possession, province, satellite state **2** = **territory**

colossal *adjective* = **huge**, enormous, gigantic, immense, mammoth, massive, monumental, prodigious, vast OPPOSITE **tiny**

colour *noun* **1** = **hue**, shade, tint **2** = **pigment**, colorant, dye, paint, tint ◆*verb* **7** = **paint**, dye, stain, tinge, tint **9** = **blush**, flush, redden

colourful *adjective* **1** = **bright**, brilliant, multicoloured, psychedelic, variegated OPPOSITE **drab. 2** = **interesting**, distinctive, graphic, lively, picturesque, rich, vivid OPPOSITE

boring

colourless *adjective* **1** = **uninteresting**, characterless, dreary, dull, insipid, lacklustre, vapid OPPOSITE **interesting. 2** = **drab**, achromatic, anaemic, ashen, bleached, faded, wan, washed out OPPOSITE **radiant**

column *noun* **1** = **pillar**, obelisk, post, shaft, support, upright **5** = **line**, file, procession, rank, row

coma *noun* = **unconsciousness**, oblivion, stupor, trance

comb *verb* **4** = **untangle**, arrange, dress, groom **5** = **search**, forage, fossick, hunt (*Aust & NZ*), rake, ransack, rummage, scour, sift

combat *noun* = **fight**, action, battle, conflict, contest, encounter, engagement, skirmish, struggle, war, warfare OPPOSITE **peace** ◆*verb*

combe *noun* same as COOMB.
combine ❶ *verb* **1** join together. **2** form a chemical compound. ♦ *noun* **3** association of people or firms for a common purpose. **combination** *noun* **1** combining. **2** people or things combined. **3** set of numbers that opens a special lock. ♦ *plural* **4** old-fashioned undergarment with long sleeves and long legs. **combine harvester** machine that reaps and threshes grain in one process.
combo *noun, pl* **-bos** small group of jazz musicians.
combustion *noun* process of burning. **combustible** *adjective* burning easily.
come ❶ *verb* **coming, came, come 1** move towards a place, arrive. **2** occur. **3** reach a specified point or condition. **4** be produced. **5** (foll. by *from*) be born in. **6** become, e.g. *a dream come true.* **come across** *verb* **1** meet or find by accident. **2** (often foll. by *as*) give an impression of (being). **comeback** *noun Informal* **1** return to a former position. **2** retort. **come by** *verb* find, obtain. **comedown** *noun* **1** decline in status. **2** disappointment. **come into** *verb* **1** enter. **2** inherit. **come of** *verb* result from. **come to** *verb* **1** regain consciousness. **2** amount to (a total figure). **come up** *verb* be mentioned, arise.
comeuppance *noun Informal* deserved punishment.

comedy ❶ *noun, pl* **-dies 1** humorous play, film, or programme. **2** humorous aspect of events. **comedian, comedienne** *noun* **1** entertainer who tells jokes. **2** person who performs in comedy.
comely *adjective* **-lier, -liest** *Old-fashioned* nice-looking.
comestibles *plural noun Formal* food.
comet *noun* heavenly body with a long luminous tail.
comfit *noun* sugar-coated sweet.
comfort ❶ *noun* **1** physical ease or wellbeing. **2** consolation. **3** means of consolation. ♦ *verb* **4** soothe, console. **comfortable** *adjective* **1** giving comfort. **2** free from pain. **3** *Informal* well-off financially. **comfortably** *adverb*
comforter *noun* **1** person or thing that comforts. **2** baby's dummy. **3** *Brit* woollen scarf.
comfrey *noun* tall plant with bell-shaped flowers.
comfy *adjective* **-fier, -fiest** *Informal* comfortable.
comic ❶ *adjective* **1** humorous, funny. **2** of comedy. ♦ *noun* **3** comedian. **4** magazine containing strip cartoons. **comical** *adjective* amusing. **comically** *adverb*
comma *noun* punctuation mark (,).

—————— THESAURUS ——————

=**fight**, defy, do battle with, oppose, resist, withstand OPPOSITE **support**
combatant *noun* **1** =**fighter**, adversary, antagonist, enemy, opponent, soldier, warrior
combination *noun* **1** =**mixture**, amalgamation, blend, coalescence, composite, connection, mix **2** =**association**, alliance, coalition, confederation, consortium, federation, syndicate, union
combine *verb* **1** =**join together**, amalgamate, blend, connect, integrate, link, merge, mix, pool, unite OPPOSITE **separate**
come *verb* **1** =**arrive**, advance, appear, approach, draw near, materialize, move towards, near, reach, show up (*inf*), turn up (*inf*) **2** =**happen**, fall, occur, take place **4** =**result**, arise, be produced, emanate, emerge, flow, issue, originate
come across *verb* **1** =**find**, bump into (*inf*), chance upon, discover, encounter, meet, notice, stumble upon, unearth
comeback *noun Inf* **1** =**return**, rally, rebound, recovery, resurgence, revival, triumph **2** =**response**, rejoinder, reply, retaliation, retort, riposte
comedian *noun* =**comic**, card (*inf*), clown, funny man, humorist, jester, joker, wag, wit
comedown *noun* **1** =**decline**, deflation, demotion, reverse **2** =**disappointment**, anticlimax, blow, humiliation, letdown
comedy *noun* **1** =**light entertainment**, farce OPPOSITE **drama**. **2** =**humour**, fun, hilarity, jesting, joking OPPOSITE **seriousness**
comeuppance *noun Inf* =**punishment**, chastening, deserts, due reward, recompense, retribution
comfort *noun* **1** =**luxury**, cosiness, ease, opulence, snugness, wellbeing **2** =**relief**, compensation, consolation, help, succour, support OPPOSITE **annoyance** ♦*verb* **4** =**console**, commiserate with, hearten, reassure, soothe OPPOSITE **distress**
comfortable *adjective* **1** =**pleasant**, agreeable, convenient, cosy, homely, relaxing, restful OPPOSITE **unpleasant**. **2** =**happy**, at ease, at home, contented, gratified, relaxed, serene OPPOSITE **uncomfortable**. **3** *Inf* =**well-off**, affluent, in clover (*inf*), prosperous, well-to-do
comforting *adjective* =**consoling**, cheering, consolatory, encouraging, heart-warming, reassuring, soothing OPPOSITE **upsetting**

command ⊕ *verb* **1** order. **2** have authority over. **3** deserve and get. **4** look down over. ◆ *noun* **5** authoritative instruction that something must be done. **6** authority to command. **7** knowledge. **8** military or naval unit with a specific function. **9** instruction given to a computer. **commandant** *noun* officer commanding a military group. **commandeer** *verb* **1** seize for military use. **2** take (something to which one is not entitled). **commander** *noun* **1** military officer in command of a group or operation. **2** middle-ranking naval officer. **commander-in-chief** *noun, pl* **commanders-in-chief** supreme commander of a nation's armed forces. **commandment** *noun* command from God, esp. one of the Ten Commandments in the Old Testament. **commando** *noun, pl* **-dos, -does** (member of) a military unit trained for swift raids in enemy territory.

commedia dell'arte [kom-mede-ee-a dell-art-tay] *noun* form of improvised comedy popular in Italy in the 16th century, with stock characters and a stereotyped plot.

commemorate ⊕ *verb* honour the memory of: e.g. *a series of events to commemorate the end of the Second World War.* **commemoration**

noun **commemorative** *adjective*

commence ⊕ *verb* begin. **commencement** *noun* **1** beginning, start. **2** *US & Canad* graduation ceremony.

commend ⊕ *verb* **1** praise. **2** recommend. **commendable** *adjective* **commendably** *adverb* **commendation** *noun*

commensurable *adjective* **1** measurable by the same standards. **2** *Maths* **a** having a common factor **b** having units of the same dimensions and being related by whole numbers. **commensurability** *noun*

commensurate *adjective* corresponding in degree, size, or value.

comment ⊕ *noun* **1** remark. **2** talk, gossip. **3** explanatory note. ◆ *verb* **4** make a comment.

commentary *noun, pl* **-taries 1** spoken accompaniment to a broadcast or film. **2** series of explanatory notes on a subject. **commentate** *verb* provide a commentary. **commentator** *noun*

commerce ⊕ *noun* **1** buying and selling, trade. **2** *Lit* social relations. **commercial** *adjective* **1** of commerce. **2** (of television or radio) paid for by advertisers. **3** having profit as the main aim. ◆ *noun* **4** television or radio advertisement. **commercialize** *verb* make

————————— T H E S A U R U S —————————

comic *adjective* **1** = **funny**, amusing, comical, droll, farcical, humorous, jocular, witty OPPOSITE **serious** ◆*noun* **3** = **comedian**, buffoon, clown, funny man, humorist, jester, wag, wit

comical *adjective* = **funny**, amusing, comic, droll, farcical, hilarious, humorous, priceless, side-splitting

coming *adjective* **1** = **approaching**, at hand, forthcoming, imminent, impending, in store, near, nigh ◆*noun* **2** = **arrival**, advent, approach

command *verb* **1** = **order**, bid, charge, compel, demand, direct, require OPPOSITE **ask**. **2** = **have authority over**, control, dominate, govern, handle, head, lead, manage, rule, supervise OPPOSITE **be subordinate to** ◆*noun* **5** = **order**, commandment, decree, demand, directive, instruction, requirement, ultimatum **6** = **authority**, charge, control, government, mana (*NZ*), management, mastery, power, rule, supervision

commandeer *verb* **1** = **seize**, appropriate, confiscate, requisition, sequester, sequestrate

commander *noun* = **officer**, boss, captain, chief, commanding officer, head, leader

commanding *adjective* **2** = **controlling**, advantageous, decisive, dominant, dominating, superior

commemorate *verb* = **remember**, celebrate, honour, immortalize, pay tribute to, recognize, salute OPPOSITE **ignore**

commemoration *noun* = **remembrance**, ceremony, honouring, memorial service, tribute

commence *verb* = **begin**, embark on, enter upon, initiate, open, originate, start OPPOSITE **stop**

commend *verb* **1** = **praise**, acclaim, applaud, approve, compliment, extol, speak highly of OPPOSITE **criticize**. **2** = **recommend**

commendable *adjective* **1** = **praiseworthy**, admirable, creditable, deserving, estimable, exemplary, laudable, meritorious, worthy

commendation *noun* **1** = **praise**, acclaim, acclamation, approbation, approval, credit, good opinion, panegyric **2** = **recommendation**

comment *noun* **1** = **remark**, observation, statement **3** = **note**, annotation, commentary, explanation, exposition, illustration ◆*verb* **4** = **remark**, mention, note, observe, point out, say, utter

commentary *noun* **1** = **narration**, description, voice-over **2** = **notes**, analysis, critique, explanation, review, treatise

commentator *noun* **1** = **reporter**, special correspondent, sportscaster **2** = **critic**, annotator, interpreter

commercial. **commercialization** noun
commercial traveller sales representative.
commie noun, adjective Informal offens
communist.
commingle verb mix or be mixed.
commis noun, pl **-mis** apprentice waiter or
chef.
commiserate ➊ verb (foll. by with) express
sympathy (for). **commiseration** noun

> **SPELLING TIP**
>
> The most popular way to
> misspell **commiserate** and
> **commiseration** is to double the
> s as well as the m. There should
> indeed be two ms, but only one
> s.

commissar noun (formerly) official responsible
for political education in Communist countries.
commissariat noun military department in
charge of food supplies.
commissary noun, pl **-saries** US shop
supplying food or equipment, esp. in a military
camp.
commission ➊ noun **1** piece of work that an
artist is asked to do. **2** duty, task. **3** percentage
paid to a salesperson for each sale made. **4**
group of people appointed to perform certain
duties. **5** committing of a crime. **6** Mil rank or
authority officially given to an officer. ✦ verb **7**
place an order for. **8** Mil give a commission to.
9 grant authority to. **out of commission** not in
working order. **commissioner** noun **1**
appointed official in a government department.
2 member of a commission.
commissionaire noun uniformed doorman at
a hotel, theatre, etc.
commit ➊ verb **-mitting, -mitted 1** perform
(a crime or error). **2** hand over, allocate. **3**
pledge (oneself) to a course of action. **4** send
(someone) to prison or hospital. **committal**
noun sending someone to prison or hospital.
commitment noun **1** dedication to a cause. **2**

responsibility that restricts freedom of action.

> **SPELLING TIP**
>
> The correct spelling of
> **commitment** has three ms
> altogether, but only two ts
> (which are not next to each
> other). Although the Bank of
> English has 176 examples of
> committment, with three ms and
> three ts, this spelling is wrong.

committee noun group of people appointed
to perform a specified service or function.

> **SPELLING TIP**
>
> The commonest misspelling of
> **committee** is commitee, with 81
> occurrences in the Bank of
> English, which also has
> examples of comittee. The
> correct spelling is with two ms
> and two ts.

commode noun **1** seat with a hinged flap
concealing a chamber pot. **2** chest of drawers.
commodious adjective roomy.
commodity noun, pl **-ities** article of trade.
commodore noun senior commissioned
officer in the navy.
common ➊ adjective **1** occurring often. **2**
belonging to two or more people. **3** public,
general. **4** lacking in taste or manners. ✦ noun **5**
area of grassy land belonging to a community.
✦ plural **6** shared food. **House of Commons,
the Commons** lower chamber of the British
parliament. **in common** shared. **commonly**
adverb **commoner** noun person who does not
belong to the nobility. **common-law** adjective
(of a relationship) regarded as a marriage
through being long-standing. **Common
Market** European Union. **commonplace**
adjective **1** ordinary, everyday. ✦ noun **2** trite

———————— THESAURUS ————————

commerce noun **1** = **trade**, business, dealing,
exchange, traffic
commercial adjective **1** = **mercantile**, trading
3 = **materialistic**, mercenary, profit-making
commiserate verb (foll. by with)
= **sympathize**, console, feel for, pity
commission noun **2** = **duty**, errand, mandate,
mission, task **3** = **fee**, cut, percentage, rake-off
(sl), royalties **4** = **committee**, board,
commissioners, delegation, deputation,

representatives ✦verb **7** = **appoint**, contract,
engage, nominate, order, select **9** = **authorize**,
delegate, depute, empower
commit verb **1** = **do**, carry out, enact, execute,
perform, perpetrate **4** = **put in custody**,
confine, imprison OPPOSITE **free**
commitment noun **1** = **dedication**, devotion,
involvement, loyalty OPPOSITE **indecisiveness**.
2 = **responsibility**, duty, engagement, liability,
obligation, tie

C

remark. **common room** sitting room for students or staff in a school or college.
common sense good practical understanding.
commonwealth noun 1 state or nation viewed politically. 2 (C-) association of independent states that used to be ruled by Britain.
commotion ❶ noun noisy disturbance.
commune¹ ❶ noun 1 group of people who live together and share everything. 2 smallest district of local government in some countries. **communal** adjective shared. **communally** adverb
commune² ❶ verb (foll. by with) feel very close (to), e.g. communing with nature.
communion noun 1 sharing of thoughts or feelings. 2 (C-) Christian ritual of sharing consecrated bread and wine. 3 religious group with shared beliefs and practices.
communicate ❶ verb 1 make known or share (information, thoughts, or feelings). 2 receive Communion. **communicable** adjective (of a disease) able to be passed on. **communicant** noun person who receives Communion. **communicating** adjective (of a door) joining two rooms. **communication** noun 1 communicating. 2 thing communicated. ◆ plural 3 means of travelling or sending messages. **communicative** adjective talking

freely.
communiqué [kom-**mune**-ik-kay] noun official announcement.
communism ❶ noun 1 belief that all property and means of production should be shared by the community. 2 (C-) system of state control of the economy and society in some countries.
communist noun, adjective **communistic** adjective
community ❶ noun, pl **-ties** 1 all the people living in one district. 2 group with shared origins or interests. 3 the public, society.
community centre building used by a community for activities.
commute ❶ verb 1 travel daily to and from work. 2 reduce (a sentence) to a less severe one. **commuter** noun person who commutes to and from work. **commutator** noun device used to change alternating electric current into direct current.
compact¹ ❶ adjective 1 closely packed. 2 neatly arranged. 3 concise, brief. ◆ noun 4 small flat case containing a mirror and face powder. ◆ verb 5 pack closely together. **compactly** adverb **compactness** noun **compact disc** small digital audio disc on which the sound is read by an optical laser system.
compact² ❶ noun contract, agreement.
companion ❶ noun 1 person who associates

——————————— THESAURUS ———————————

common adjective 1 = **average**, commonplace, conventional, customary, everyday, familiar, frequent, habitual, ordinary, regular, routine, standard, stock, usual OPPOSITE rare. 2 = **collective**, communal, public OPPOSITE private. 3 = **popular**, accepted, general, prevailing, prevalent, universal, widespread 4 = **vulgar**, coarse, inferior, plebeian OPPOSITE cultured
commonplace adjective 1 = **everyday**, banal, common, humdrum, mundane, obvious, ordinary, run-of-the-mill, widespread OPPOSITE rare ◆noun 2 = **cliché**, banality, platitude, truism
common sense noun = **good sense**, gumption (Brit inf), horse sense, level-headedness, native intelligence, prudence, sound judgment, wit
commotion noun = **disturbance**, disorder, excitement, furore, fuss, hue and cry, rumpus, tumult, turmoil, upheaval, uproar
communal adjective = **public**, collective, general, joint, shared OPPOSITE private
commune¹ noun 1 = **community**, collective, cooperative, kibbutz
commune² verb (foll. by with) = **contemplate**,

meditate on, muse on, ponder, reflect on
communicate verb 1 = **make known**, convey, declare, disclose, impart, inform, pass on, proclaim, transmit OPPOSITE keep secret
communication noun 1 = **passing on**, contact, conversation, correspondence, dissemination, link, transmission 2 = **message**, announcement, disclosure, dispatch, information, news, report, statement, word
communicative adjective = **talkative**, chatty, expansive, forthcoming, frank, informative, loquacious, open, outgoing, voluble OPPOSITE reserved
communism noun (also cap.) = **socialism**, Bolshevism, collectivism, Marxism, state socialism
communist noun (also cap.) = **socialist**, Bolshevik, collectivist, Marxist, Red (inf)
community noun 1 = **populace**, commonwealth, residents, society, state 2 = **public**, general public, people 3 = **group**, brotherhood, company, society
commuter noun = **daily traveller**, straphanger (inf), suburbanite
compact¹ adjective 1 = **closely packed**, compressed, condensed, dense, pressed

with or accompanies someone. **2** woman paid to live with another woman. **companionable** *adjective* friendly. **companionship** *noun*
companionway *noun* ladder linking the decks of a ship.
company ⊙ *noun, pl* **-nies 1** business organization. **2** group of actors. **3** small unit of troops. **4** crew of a ship. **5** fact of being with someone. **6** gathering of people. **7** guest or guests. **8** person's associates.
compare ⊙ *verb* **1** examine (things) and point out the resemblances or differences. **2** (foll. by *to*) declare to be (like). **3** (foll. by *with*) be worthy of comparison. **comparable** *adjective* **1** worthy of comparison. **2** able to be compared. **comparability** *noun* **comparative** *adjective* **1** relative. **2** involving comparison. **3** *Grammar* denoting the form of an adjective or adverb indicating *more*. ♦ *noun* **4** *Grammar* comparative form of a word. **comparatively**

adverb **comparison** *noun* **1** comparing. **2** similarity or equivalence.
compartment ⊙ *noun* **1** section of a railway carriage. **2** separate section.
compass ⊙ *noun* **1** instrument for showing direction, with a needle that points north. **2** limits, range. ♦ *plural* **3** hinged instrument for drawing circles.
compassion ⊙ *noun* pity, sympathy. **compassionate** *adjective*
compatible ⊙ *adjective* able to exist, work, or be used together. **compatibility** *noun*
compatriot *noun* fellow countryman or countrywoman.
compel ⊙ *verb* **-pelling, -pelled** force (to be or do). **compelling** *adjective* **1** convincing. **2** arousing strong interest.
compendium *noun, pl* **-diums, -dia** selection of board games in one box. **compendious** *adjective* brief but comprehensive.

——————— THESAURUS ———————

together, solid, thick OPPOSITE **loose. 3** = **brief**, compendious, concise, succinct, terse, to the point OPPOSITE **lengthy** ♦*verb* **5** = **pack closely**, compress, condense, cram, stuff, tamp OPPOSITE **separate**
compact[2] *noun* = **agreement**, arrangement, bargain, bond, contract, covenant, deal, pact, treaty, understanding
companion *noun* **1** = **friend**, accomplice, ally, associate, cobber (*Aust or old-fashioned NZ inf*), colleague, comrade, consort, mate (*inf*), partner **2** = **escort**, aide, assistant, attendant, chaperon, squire
companionship *noun* **1** = **fellowship**, camaraderie, company, comradeship, conviviality, esprit de corps, friendship, rapport, togetherness
company *noun* **1** = **business**, association, concern, corporation, establishment, firm, house, partnership, syndicate **5** = **companionship**, fellowship, presence, society **6** = **group**, assembly, band, collection, community, crowd, gathering, party, set **7** = **guests**, callers, party, visitors
comparable *adjective* **1** = **on a par**, a match for, as good as, commensurate, equal, equivalent, in a class with, proportionate, tantamount OPPOSITE **different. 2** = **similar**, akin, alike, analogous, cognate, corresponding, cut from the same cloth, of a piece, related
comparative *adjective* **1** = **relative**, by comparison, qualified
compare *verb* **1** = **weigh**, balance, contrast, juxtapose, set against **2** (foll. by *to*) = **liken to**, correlate to, equate to, identify with, mention

in the same breath as, parallel, resemble **3** (foll. by *with*) = **be on a par with**, approach, bear comparison, be in the same class as, be the equal of, compete with, equal, hold a candle to, match
comparison *noun* **1** = **contrast**, distinction, juxtaposition **2** = **similarity**, analogy, comparability, correlation, likeness, resemblance
compartment *noun* **1** = **carriage 2** = **section**, alcove, bay, berth, booth, cubbyhole, cubicle, locker, niche, pigeonhole
compass *noun* **2** = **range**, area, boundary, circumference, extent, field, limit, reach, realm, scope
compassion *noun* = **sympathy**, condolence, fellow feeling, humanity, kindness, mercy, pity, sorrow, tenderness, understanding OPPOSITE **indifference**
compassionate *adjective* = **sympathetic**, benevolent, charitable, humane, humanitarian, kind-hearted, merciful, pitying, tender-hearted, understanding OPPOSITE **uncaring**
compatibility *noun* = **harmony**, affinity, agreement, concord, empathy, like-mindedness, rapport, sympathy
compatible *adjective* = **harmonious**, adaptable, congruous, consistent, in harmony, in keeping, suitable OPPOSITE **inappropriate**
compel *verb* = **force**, coerce, constrain, dragoon, impel, make, oblige, railroad (*inf*)
compelling *adjective* **1** = **convincing**, cogent, conclusive, forceful, irrefutable, powerful, telling, weighty **2** = **fascinating**, enchanting, enthralling, gripping, hypnotic, irresistible, mesmeric, spellbinding OPPOSITE **boring**

C

compensate ❶ *verb* **1** make amends to (someone), esp. for injury or loss. **2** (foll. by *for*) cancel out (a bad effect). **compensation** *noun* payment to make up for loss or injury. **compensatory** *adjective*

compere *noun* **1** person who presents a stage, radio, or television show. ♦ *verb* **2** be the compere of.

compete ❶ *verb* try to win or achieve (a prize, profit, etc.). **competition** *noun* **1** competing. **2** event in which people compete. **3** people against whom one competes. **competitive** *adjective* **1** involving rivalry. **2** eager to be more successful than other people. **3** offering good value compared with commercial rivals. **competitor** *noun*

competent ❶ *adjective* having the skill or knowledge to do something well. **competently** *adverb* **competence** *noun*

compile ❶ *verb* collect and arrange (information), esp. to make a book. **compilation** *noun* **compiler** *noun*

complacent ❶ *adjective* self-satisfied. **complacently** *adverb* **complacency** *noun*

complain ❶ *verb* **1** express resentment or displeasure. **2** (foll. by *of*) say that one is suffering from (an illness). **complaint** *noun* **1** complaining. **2** mild illness. **complainant** *noun* *Law* plaintiff.

complaisant [kom-**play**-zant] *adjective* willing to please. **complaisance** *noun*

complement ❶ *noun* **1** thing that completes something. **2** complete amount or number. **3** *Grammar* word or words added to a verb to complete the meaning. **4** *Maths* angle added to a specified angle to produce a right angle. ♦ *verb* **5** make complete. **complementary** *adjective*

> **LANGUAGE TIP**
>
> Avoid confusing this word with *compliment*.

complete ❶ *adjective* **1** thorough, absolute. **2** finished. **3** having all the necessary parts. ♦ *verb* **4** finish. **5** make whole or perfect. **completely** *adverb* **completeness** *noun* **completion** *noun* finishing.

complex ❶ *adjective* **1** made up of parts. **2**

——————— THESAURUS ———————

compensate *verb* **1** = **recompense**, atone, make amends, make good, refund, reimburse, remunerate, repay **2** (foll. by *for*) = **cancel (out)**, balance, counteract, counterbalance, make up for, offset, redress

compensation *noun* = **recompense**, amends, atonement, damages, reimbursement, remuneration, reparation, restitution, satisfaction

compete *verb* = **contend**, be in the running, challenge, contest, fight, strive, struggle, vie

competence *noun* = **ability**, capability, capacity, expertise, fitness, proficiency, skill, suitability OPPOSITE **incompetence**

competent *adjective* = **able**, adequate, capable, fit, proficient, qualified, suitable OPPOSITE **incompetent**

competition *noun* **1** = **rivalry**, opposition, strife, struggle **2** = **contest**, championship, event, head-to-head, puzzle, quiz, tournament **3** = **opposition**, challengers, field, rivals

competitive *adjective* **1** = **cut-throat**, aggressive, antagonistic, at odds, dog-eat-dog, opposing, rival **2** = **ambitious**, combative

competitor *noun* = **contestant**, adversary, antagonist, challenger, opponent, rival

compilation *noun* = **collection**, accumulation, anthology, assemblage, assortment, treasury

compile *verb* = **put together**, accumulate, amass, collect, cull, garner, gather, marshal, organize

complacency *noun* = **self-satisfaction**, contentment, satisfaction, smugness

complacent *adjective* = **self-satisfied**, contented, pleased with oneself, resting on one's laurels, satisfied, serene, smug, unconcerned OPPOSITE **insecure**

complain *verb* **1** = **find fault**, bemoan, bewail, carp, deplore, groan, grouse, grumble, lament, moan, whine, whinge (*inf*)

complaint *noun* **1** = **criticism**, charge, grievance, gripe (*inf*), grouse, grumble, lament, moan, protest **2** = **illness**, affliction, ailment, disease, disorder, malady, sickness, upset

complement *noun* **1** = **completion**, companion, consummation, counterpart, finishing touch, rounding-off, supplement **2** = **total**, aggregate, capacity, entirety, quota, totality, wholeness ♦ *verb* **5** = **complete**, cap (*inf*), crown, round off, set off

complementary *adjective* = **completing**, companion, corresponding, interdependent, interrelating, matched, reciprocal OPPOSITE **incompatible**

complete *adjective* **1** = **total**, absolute, consummate, outright, perfect, thorough, thoroughgoing, utter OPPOSITE **partial**. **2** = **finished**, accomplished, achieved, concluded, ended OPPOSITE **unfinished**. **3** = **entire**, all, faultless, full, intact, plenary, unbroken, whole complicated. ◆ *noun* **3** whole made up of parts. **4** group of unconscious feelings that influences behaviour. **complexity** *noun*

complexion ❶ *noun* **1** skin of the face. **2** character, nature.

compliance *noun* **1** complying. **2** tendency to do what others want. **compliant** *adjective*

complicate ❶ *verb* make or become complex or difficult to deal with. **complication** *noun*

complicity *noun* fact of being an accomplice in a crime.

compliment ❶ *noun* **1** expression of praise. ◆ *plural* **2** formal greetings. ◆ *verb* **3** praise.

complimentary *adjective* **1** expressing praise. **2** free of charge.

LANGUAGE TIP

Avoid confusing this word with *complement*.

---

compline *noun* last service of the day in the Roman Catholic Church.

comply ❶ *verb* **-plying, -plied** (foll. by *with*) act in accordance (with).

component ❶ *noun, adjective* (being) part of a whole.

comport *verb* behave (oneself) in a specified way.

compose ❶ *verb* **1** put together. **2** be the component parts of. **3** create (a piece of music or writing). **4** calm (oneself). **5** arrange artistically. **composed** *adjective* (of people) in control of their feelings. **composer** *noun* person who writes music. **composition** *noun* way that something is put together or arranged.

composite *noun, adjective* (something) made up of separate parts.

composition ❶ *noun* **1** way that something is put together or arranged. **2** work of art, esp. a musical one. **3** essay. **4** composing.

———————————————— T H E S A U R U S ————————————————

OPPOSITE incomplete ◆*verb* **4** = **finish**, close, conclude, crown, end, finalize, round off, settle, wrap up (*inf*) OPPOSITE **start**

completely *adverb* **1** = **totally**, absolutely, altogether, entirely, every inch, fully, hook, line and sinker, in full, lock, stock and barrel, one hundred per cent, perfectly, thoroughly, utterly, wholly

completion *noun* = **finishing**, bitter end, close, conclusion, culmination, end, fruition, fulfilment

complex *adjective* **1** = **compound**, composite, heterogeneous, manifold, multifarious, multiple **2** = **complicated**, convoluted, elaborate, intricate, involved, labyrinthine, tangled, tortuous OPPOSITE **simple** ◆*noun* **3** = **structure**, aggregate, composite, network, organization, scheme, system OPPOSITE **clear**. **4** = **obsession**, fixation, fixed idea, phobia, preoccupation

complexion *noun* **1** = **skin**, colour, colouring, hue, pigmentation, skin tone **2** = **nature**, appearance, aspect, character, guise, light, look, make-up

complexity *noun* **2** = **complication**, elaboration, entanglement, intricacy, involvement, ramification

complicate *verb* = **make difficult**, confuse, entangle, involve, muddle, ravel

complicated *adjective* = **difficult**, complex, convoluted, elaborate, intricate, involved, perplexing, problematic, puzzling, troublesome OPPOSITE **simple**

complication *noun* **1** = **problem**, difficulty,

drawback, embarrassment, obstacle, snag

compliment *noun* **1** = **praise**, bouquet, commendation, congratulations, eulogy, flattery, honour, tribute OPPOSITE **criticism**. ◆ **2** *plural* = **greetings**, good wishes, regards, remembrances, respects, salutation OPPOSITE **insult** ◆*verb* **3** = **praise**, commend, congratulate, extol, flatter, pay tribute to, salute, speak highly of OPPOSITE **criticize**

complimentary *adjective* **1** = **flattering**, appreciative, approving, commendatory, congratulatory, laudatory OPPOSITE **critical**. **2** = **free**, courtesy, donated, gratis, gratuitous, honorary, on the house

comply *verb* (foll. by *with*) = **obey**, abide by, acquiesce, adhere to, conform to, follow, observe, submit, toe the line OPPOSITE **defy**

component *noun* = **part**, constituent, element, ingredient, item, piece, unit ◆*adjective* = **constituent**, inherent, intrinsic

compose *verb* **1** = **put together**, build, comprise, constitute, construct, fashion, form, make, make up OPPOSITE **destroy**. **3** = **create**, contrive, devise, invent, produce, write **4** = **calm**, collect, control, pacify, placate, quiet, soothe **5** = **arrange**, adjust

composed *adjective* = **calm**, at ease, collected, cool, level-headed, poised, relaxed, sedate, self-possessed, serene, unflappable OPPOSITE **agitated**

composition *noun* **1** = **design**, arrangement, configuration, formation, layout, make-up, organization, structure **3** = **essay**, exercise, literary work, opus, piece, treatise, work **4**

compositor *noun* person who arranges type for printing.

compos mentis ❶ *adjective* Latin sane.

compost *noun* decayed plants used as a fertilizer.

composure ❶ *noun* calmness.

compote *noun* fruit stewed with sugar.

compound[1] ❶ *noun, adjective* **1** (thing, esp. chemical) made up of two or more combined parts or elements. ◆ *verb* **2** combine or make by combining. **3** intensify, make worse. **compound fracture** fracture in which the broken bone pierces the skin. **compound interest** interest paid on a sum and its accumulated interest.

compound[2] *noun* fenced enclosure containing buildings.

comprehend ❶ *verb* understand. **comprehensible** *adjective* **comprehension** *noun* **comprehensive** *adjective* **1** of broad scope, fully inclusive. ◆ *noun* **2** comprehensive school. **comprehensive school** secondary school for children of all abilities.

compress ❶ *verb* [kum-**press**] **1** squeeze together. **2** make shorter. ◆ *noun* [**kom**-press] **3** pad applied to stop bleeding or cool inflammation. **compression** *noun* **compressor** *noun* machine that compresses gas or air.

comprise ❶ *verb* be made up of or make up.

compromise ❶ [**kom**-prom-mize] *noun* **1** settlement reached by concessions on each side. ◆ *verb* **2** settle a dispute by making concessions. **3** put in a dishonourable position.

comptroller *noun* (in titles) financial controller.

compulsion ❶ *noun* **1** irresistible urge. **2** forcing by threats or violence. **compulsive** *adjective* **compulsively** *adverb* **compulsory** *adjective* required by rules or laws.

compunction *noun* feeling of guilt or shame.

compute ❶ *verb* calculate, esp. using a computer. **computation** *noun* **computer** *noun* electronic machine that stores and processes data. **computerize** *verb* **1** adapt (a system) to be handled by computer. **2** store or process in a computer. **computerization** *noun*

comrade ❶ *noun* **1** fellow member of a union or socialist political party. **2** companion. **comradeship** *noun*

con[1] ❶ *Informal noun* **1** short for CONFIDENCE TRICK. ◆ *verb* **conning, conned 2** deceive, swindle.

———— THESAURUS ————

= creation, compilation, fashioning, formation, formulation, making, production, putting together

composure *noun* **= calmness**, aplomb, equanimity, poise, sang-froid, self-assurance, self-possession, serenity OPPOSITE agitation

compound[1] *noun* **1** **= combination**, alloy, amalgam, blend, composite, fusion, medley, mixture, synthesis OPPOSITE **element** ◆*verb* **2** **= combine**, amalgamate, blend, intermingle, mix, synthesize, unite OPPOSITE **divide. 3** **= intensify**, add to, aggravate, augment, complicate, exacerbate, heighten, magnify, worsen OPPOSITE **lessen**

comprehend *verb* **= understand**, apprehend, conceive, fathom, grasp, know, make out, perceive, see, take in OPPOSITE **misunderstand**

comprehensible *adjective* **= understandable**, clear, coherent, conceivable, explicit, intelligible, plain

comprehension *noun* **= understanding**, conception, discernment, grasp, intelligence, perception, realization OPPOSITE incomprehension

comprehensive *adjective* **1** **= broad**, all-embracing, all-inclusive, blanket, complete, encyclopedic, exhaustive, full, inclusive, overarching, thorough OPPOSITE **limited**

compress *verb* **1** **= squeeze**, concentrate, condense, contract, crush, press, squash **2** **= shorten**, abbreviate, contract

comprise *verb* **= be composed of**, compose, consist of, constitute, contain, embrace, encompass, form, include, make up, take in

compromise *noun* **1** **= give-and-take**, accommodation, adjustment, agreement, concession, settlement, trade-off OPPOSITE disagreement ◆*verb* **2** **= meet halfway**, adjust, agree, concede, give and take, go fifty-fifty (*inf*), settle, strike a balance OPPOSITE **disagree. 3** **= weaken**, discredit, dishonour, embarrass, expose, jeopardize, prejudice OPPOSITE support

compulsion *noun* **1** **= urge**, drive, necessity, need, obsession, preoccupation **2** **= force**, coercion, constraint, demand, duress, obligation, pressure, urgency

compulsive *adjective* **1** **= irresistible**, compelling, driving, neurotic, obsessive, overwhelming, uncontrollable, urgent

compulsory *adjective* **= obligatory**, binding, *de rigueur*, forced, imperative, mandatory, required, requisite OPPOSITE **voluntary**

compute *verb* **= calculate**, add up, count, enumerate, figure out, reckon, tally, total

comrade *noun* **2** **= companion**, ally, associate, cobber (*Aust or old-fashioned NZ inf*), colleague, co-worker, fellow, friend, partner

con² *noun* an argument against **pros and cons** see PRO¹.

con³ *noun Slang* convict.

concatenation *noun* series of linked events.

concave ⊕ *adjective* curving inwards.

concavity *noun*

conceal ⊕ *verb* **1** cover and hide. **2** keep secret. **concealment** *noun*

concede ⊕ *verb* **1** admit to be true. **2** acknowledge defeat in (a contest or argument). **3** grant as a right.

conceit ⊕ *noun* **1** too high an opinion of oneself. **2** far-fetched or clever comparison. **conceited** *adjective*

conceive ⊕ *verb* **1** imagine, think. **2** form in the mind. **3** become pregnant. **conceivable** *adjective* imaginable, possible. **conceivably** *adverb*

concentrate ⊕ *verb* **1** fix one's attention or efforts on something. **2** bring or come together in large numbers in one place. **3** make (a liquid) stronger by removing water from it. ◆ *noun* **4** concentrated liquid. **concentration**

noun **1** concentrating. **2** proportion of a substance in a mixture or solution.

concentration camp prison camp for civilian prisoners, esp. in Nazi Germany.

concentric *adjective* having the same centre.

concept ⊕ *noun* abstract or general idea.

conceptual *adjective* of or based on concepts. **conceptualize** *verb* form a concept of.

conception ⊕ *noun* **1** general idea. **2** becoming pregnant.

concern ⊕ *noun* **1** anxiety, worry. **2** something that is of importance to someone. **3** business, firm. ◆ *verb* **4** worry (someone). **5** involve (oneself). **6** be relevant or important to. **concerned** *adjective* **1** interested, involved. **2** anxious, worried. **concerning** *preposition* about, regarding.

concert *noun* musical entertainment. **in concert 1** working together. **2** (of musicians) performing live. **concerted** *adjective* done together.

concertina *noun* **1** small musical instrument similar to an accordion. ◆ *verb* **-naing, -naed 2**

——————————— THESAURUS ———————————

con¹ *Inf noun* **1** = **swindle**, deception, fraud, scam (*sl*), sting (*inf*), trick ◆*verb* **2** = **swindle**, cheat, deceive, defraud, double-cross (*inf*), dupe, hoodwink, rip off (*sl*), trick

concave *adjective* = **hollow**, indented [OPPOSITE] convex

conceal *verb* **1** = **hide**, bury, camouflage, cover, disguise, mask, obscure, screen [OPPOSITE] reveal

concede *verb* **1** = **admit**, accept, acknowledge, allow, confess, grant, own [OPPOSITE] deny. **2** = **give up**, cede, hand over, relinquish, surrender, yield [OPPOSITE] conquer

conceit *noun* **1** = **self-importance**, arrogance, egotism, narcissism, pride, swagger, vanity **2** = **fancy**, fantasy, image, whim, whimsy

conceited *adjective* **1** = **self-important**, arrogant, bigheaded (*inf*), cocky, egotistical, full of oneself, immodest, narcissistic, too big for one's boots *or* breeches, vain [OPPOSITE] modest

conceivable *adjective* = **imaginable**, believable, credible, possible, thinkable [OPPOSITE] inconceivable

conceive *verb* **1** = **imagine**, believe, comprehend, envisage, fancy, suppose, think, understand **2** = **think up**, contrive, create, design, devise, formulate **3** = **become pregnant**, become impregnated

concentrate *verb* **1** = **focus one's attention on**, be engrossed in, put one's mind to, rack one's brains [OPPOSITE] disregard. **2** = **gather**,

accumulate, centre, cluster, collect, congregate, converge, focus, huddle [OPPOSITE] scatter

concentrated *adjective* **1** = **intense**, all-out (*inf*), deep, hard, intensive **2** = **condensed**, boiled down, evaporated, reduced, rich, thickened, undiluted

concentration *noun* **1** = **focusing**, absorption, application, single-mindedness [OPPOSITE] inattention

concept *noun* = **idea**, abstraction, conception, conceptualization, hypothesis, image, notion, theory, view

conception *noun* **1** = **idea**, concept, design, image, notion, plan **2** = **impregnation**, fertilization, germination, insemination

concern *noun* **1** = **worry**, anxiety, apprehension, burden, care, disquiet, distress **2** = **business**, affair, interest, job, responsibility, task **3** = **business**, company, corporation, enterprise, establishment, firm, organization ◆*verb* **4** = **worry**, bother, disquiet, distress, disturb, make anxious, perturb, trouble **6** = **be relevant to**, affect, apply to, bear on, interest, involve, pertain to, regard, touch

concerned *adjective* **1** = **involved**, active, implicated, interested, mixed up, privy to **2** = **worried**, anxious, bothered, distressed, disturbed, troubled, uneasy, upset [OPPOSITE] indifferent

concerning *preposition* = **regarding**, about, apropos of, as regards, on the subject of, re, relating to, respecting, touching, with reference

C

collapse or fold up like a concertina.

concerto [kon-**chair**-toe] *noun, pl* **-tos, -ti** large-scale composition for a solo instrument and orchestra.

concession ❶ *noun* **1** grant of rights, land, or property. **2** reduction in price for a specified category of people. **3** conceding. **4** thing conceded. **concessionary** *adjective*

concession road *noun Canad* (esp. in Ontario) one of a series of roads separating land concessions in a township.

conch *noun* **1** shellfish with a large spiral shell. **2** its shell.

concierge [kon-see-**airzh**] *noun* (in France) caretaker in a block of flats.

conciliate ❶ *verb* try to end a disagreement (with). **conciliation** *noun* **conciliator** *noun* **conciliatory** *adjective*

concise ❶ *adjective* brief and to the point. **concisely** *adverb* **concision, conciseness** *noun*

conclave *noun* **1** secret meeting. **2** private meeting of cardinals to elect a new pope.

conclude ❶ *verb* **1** decide by reasoning. **2** end, finish. **3** arrange or settle finally.

conclusion *noun* **1** decision based on reasoning. **2** ending. **3** final arrangement or settlement. **conclusive** *adjective* ending doubt, convincing. **conclusively** *adverb*

concoct ❶ *verb* **1** make up (a story or plan). **2** make by combining ingredients. **concoction** *noun*

concomitant *adjective* existing along with something else.

concord *noun* state of peaceful agreement, harmony. **concordance** *noun* **1** similarity or consistency. **2** index of words in a book. **concordant** *adjective* agreeing.

concordat *noun* pact or treaty.

concourse *noun* **1** large open public place where people can gather. **2** large crowd.

concrete ❶ *noun* **1** mixture of cement, sand, stone, and water, used in building. ◆ *verb* **2** cover with concrete. ◆ *adjective* **3** made of concrete. **4** particular, specific. **5** real or solid, not abstract.

concubine [**kon**-kew-bine] *noun* woman living with a man as his wife, but not married to him.

concupiscence [kon-**kew**-piss-enss] *noun Formal* lust. **concupiscent** *adjective*

concur ❶ *verb* **-curring, -curred** agree. **concurrence** *noun* **concurrent** *adjective* happening at the same time or place. **concurrently** *adverb* at the same time.

concussion *noun* period of unconsciousness caused by a blow to the head. **concussed** *adjective* having concussion.

condemn ❶ *verb* **1** express disapproval of. **2** sentence, e.g. *he was condemned to death.* **3** force into an unpleasant situation. **4** declare unfit for use. **condemnation** *noun* **condemnatory** *adjective*

condense ❶ *verb* **1** make shorter. **2** turn from

———— T H E S A U R U S ————

to

concession *noun* **1, 2** = **grant**, adjustment, allowance, boon, compromise, indulgence, permit, privilege **3** = **conceding**, acknowledgment, admission, assent, confession, surrender, yielding

conciliate *verb* = **pacify**, appease, clear the air, mediate, mollify, placate, reconcile, soothe, win over

conciliation *noun* = **pacification**, appeasement, mollification, placation, reconciliation, soothing

conciliatory *adjective* = **pacifying**, appeasing, mollifying, pacific, peaceable, placatory

concise *adjective* = **brief**, compendious, condensed, laconic, pithy, short, succinct, terse OPPOSITE **rambling**

conclude *verb* **1** = **decide**, assume, deduce, gather, infer, judge, surmise, work out **2** = **end**, cease, close, complete, finish, round off, terminate, wind up OPPOSITE **start**. **3** = **accomplish**, bring about, carry out, effect, pull off

conclusion *noun* **1** = **decision**, conviction,

deduction, inference, judgment, opinion, verdict **2** = **end**, bitter end, close, completion, ending, finale, finish, result, termination **3** = **outcome**, consequence, culmination, end result, result, upshot

conclusive *adjective* = **decisive**, clinching, convincing, definite, final, irrefutable, ultimate, unanswerable OPPOSITE **inconclusive**

concoct *verb* **1** = **make up**, contrive, devise, formulate, hatch, invent, think up **2** = **prepare**, brew

concoction *noun* **2** = **mixture**, blend, brew, combination, compound, creation, mix, preparation

concrete *adjective* **4** = **specific**, definite, explicit OPPOSITE **vague**. **5** = **real**, actual, factual, material, sensible, substantial, tangible OPPOSITE **abstract**

concur *verb* = **agree**, acquiesce, assent, consent

condemn *verb* **1** = **disapprove**, blame, censure, criticize, damn, denounce, reproach, reprove, upbraid OPPOSITE **approve**. **2** = **sentence**, convict, damn, doom, pass gas into liquid. **condensation** noun **condenser** noun Electricity capacitor.

condescend ❶ verb **1** behave patronizingly towards someone. **2** agree to do something, but as if doing someone a favour. **condescension** noun

condiment noun seasoning for food, such as salt or pepper.

condition ❶ noun **1** particular state of being. **2** necessary requirement for something else to happen. **3** restriction, qualification. **4** state of health, physical fitness. **5** medical problem, e.g. a heart condition. ♦ plural **6** circumstances. ♦ verb **7** train or influence to behave in a particular way. **8** treat with conditioner. **9** control. **on condition that** only if. **conditional** adjective depending on circumstances.

conditioner noun thick liquid used when washing to make hair or clothes feel softer.

condo noun, pl -**dos** informal a condominium building or apartment.

condolence noun **1** sympathy, e.g. a message of condolence. ♦ plural **2** expression of sympathy.

condom noun rubber sheath worn on the penis or in the vagina during sexual intercourse to prevent conception or infection.

condominium noun Aust, US & Canad block of flats in which each flat is owned by the occupant.

condone ❶ verb overlook or forgive (wrongdoing).

condor noun large vulture of S America.

conducive adjective (foll. by to) likely to lead (to).

conduct ❶ noun **1** management of an activity. **2** behaviour. ♦ verb **3** carry out (a task). **4** behave (oneself). **5** direct (musicians) by moving the hands or a baton. **6** lead, guide. **7** transmit (heat or electricity). **conduction** noun transmission of heat or electricity. **conductivity** noun ability to transmit heat or electricity. **conductive** adjective **conductor** noun **1** person who conducts musicians. **2** (fem **conductress**) official on a bus who collects fares. **3** something that conducts heat or electricity.

conduit [kon-dew-it] noun channel or tube for fluid or cables.

cone noun **1** object with a circular base, tapering to a point. **2** cone-shaped ice-cream wafer. **3** plastic cone used as a traffic marker on the roads. **4** scaly fruit of a conifer tree.

coney noun same as CONY.

confab noun Informal conversation (also **confabulation**).

confection noun **1** any sweet food. **2**

C

——————— THESAURUS ———————

sentence on OPPOSITE **acquit**
condemnation noun **1** = **disapproval**, blame, censure, denunciation, reproach, reproof, stricture **2** = **sentence**, conviction, damnation, doom, judgment
condensation noun **1** = **abridgment**, contraction, digest, précis, synopsis **2** = **distillation**, liquefaction, precipitate, precipitation
condense verb **1** = **abridge**, abbreviate, compress, concentrate, epitomize, shorten, summarize OPPOSITE **rxpand**. **2** = **concentrate**, boil down, reduce, thicken OPPOSITE **dilute**
condensed adjective **1** = **abridged**, compressed, concentrated, shortened, shrunken, slimmed-down, summarized **2** = **concentrated**, boiled down, reduced, thickened
condescend verb **1** = **patronize**, talk down to **2** = **lower oneself**, bend, deign, humble or demean oneself, see fit, stoop
condescending adjective **1** = **patronizing**, disdainful, lofty, lordly, snobbish, snooty (inf), supercilious, superior, toffee-nosed (sl, chiefly Brit)
condition noun **1** = **state**, circumstances, lie of the land, position, shape, situation, state of

affairs **2, 3** = **requirement**, limitation, prerequisite, proviso, qualification, restriction, rider, stipulation, terms **4** = **health**, fettle, fitness, kilter, order, shape, state of health, trim **5** = **ailment**, complaint, infirmity, malady, problem, weakness ♦plural **6** = **circumstances**, environment, milieu, situation, surroundings, way of life ♦verb **7** = **accustom**, adapt, equip, prepare, ready, tone up, train, work out
conditional adjective = **dependent**, contingent, limited, provisional, qualified, subject to, with reservations OPPOSITE **unconditional**
condone verb = **overlook**, excuse, forgive, let pass, look the other way, make allowance for, pardon, turn a blind eye to OPPOSITE **condemn**
conduct noun **1** = **management**, administration, control, direction, guidance, handling, organization, running, supervision **2** = **behaviour**, attitude, bearing, demeanour, deportment, manners, ways ♦verb **3** = **carry out**, administer, control, direct, handle, manage, organize, preside over, run, supervise **4** = **behave**, acquit, act, carry, comport, deport **6** = **accompany**, convey, escort, guide, lead, steer, usher

elaborate article of clothing. **confectioner** *noun* maker or seller of confectionery. **confectionery** *noun* sweets.

confederate ❶ *noun* **1** member of a confederacy. **2** accomplice. ◆ *adjective* **3** united, allied. ◆ *verb* **4** unite in a confederacy.

confederacy *noun, pl* **-cies** union of states or people for a common purpose. **confederation** *noun* alliance of political units.

confer ❶ *verb* **-ferring, -ferred 1** discuss together. **2** grant, give. **conference** *noun* meeting for discussion. **conferment** *noun* granting, giving.

confess ❶ *verb* **1** admit (a fault or crime). **2** admit to be true. **3** declare (one's sins) to God or a priest, in hope of forgiveness. **confession** *noun* **1** something confessed. **2** confessing. **3** declaring one's sins to God or a priest, in hope of forgiveness. **confessional** *noun* small stall in which a priest hears confessions. **confessor** *noun* priest who hears confessions.

confetti *noun* small pieces of coloured paper thrown at weddings.

confidant ❶ *noun* person confided in. **confidante** *n fem*

confide ❶ *verb* **1** tell someone (a secret). **2** entrust. **confidence** *noun* **1** trust. **2** self-assurance. **3** something confided. **in confidence** as a secret. **confidence trick** swindle involving gaining a person's trust in order to cheat him or her. **confident** *adjective* sure, esp. of oneself. **confidently** *adverb*

confidential *adjective* **1** private, secret. **2** entrusted with someone's secret affairs. **confidentially** *adverb* **confidentiality** *noun*

configuration *noun* arrangement of parts.

confine ❶ *verb* **1** keep within bounds. **2** restrict the free movement of. **confines** *plural noun* boundaries, limits. **confinement** *noun* **1** being confined. **2** period of childbirth.

confirm ❶ *verb* **1** prove to be true. **2** reaffirm, strengthen. **3** administer the rite of confirmation to. **confirmation** *noun* **1** confirming. **2** something that confirms. **3** *Christianity* rite that admits a baptized person to full church membership. **confirmed** *adjective* firmly established in a habit or condition, e.g. *a confirmed bachelor*.

confiscate ❶ *verb* seize (property) by authority. **confiscation** *noun*

--- T H E S A U R U S ---

confederacy *noun* = **union**, alliance, coalition, confederation, federation, league

confer *verb* **1** = **discuss**, consult, converse, deliberate, discourse, talk **2** = **grant**, accord, award, bestow, give, hand out, present

conference *noun* = **meeting**, colloquium, congress, consultation, convention, discussion, forum, seminar, symposium

confess *verb* **1** = **admit**, acknowledge, come clean (*inf*), concede, confide, disclose, divulge, own up OPPOSITE **cover up. 2** = **declare**, affirm, assert, confirm, profess, reveal

confession *noun* **1, 2** = **admission**, acknowledgment, disclosure, exposure, revelation

confidant *noun* = **close friend**, alter ego, bosom friend, crony, familiar, intimate

confide *verb* **1** = **tell**, admit, confess, disclose, divulge, impart, reveal, whisper **2** = **entrust**, commend, commit, consign

confidence *noun* **1** = **trust**, belief, credence, dependence, faith, reliance OPPOSITE **doubt. 2** = **self-assurance**, aplomb, assurance, boldness, courage, firmness, nerve, self-possession OPPOSITE **shyness** ◆ **in confidence** = **in secrecy**, between you and me (and the gatepost), confidentially, privately

confident *adjective* **a** = **certain**, convinced, counting on, positive, satisfied, secure, sure OPPOSITE **unsure. b** = **self-assured**, assured,

bold, dauntless, fearless, self-reliant OPPOSITE **shy**

confidential *adjective* **1** = **secret**, classified, hush-hush (*inf*), intimate, off the record, private, privy

confidentially *adverb* **1** = **in secret**, behind closed doors, between ourselves, in camera, in confidence, personally, privately, sub rosa

confine *verb* **1** = **imprison**, cage, enclose, incarcerate, intern, shut up **2** = **restrict**, hem in, hold back, keep, limit

confinement *noun* **1** = **imprisonment**, custody, detention, incarceration, internment, porridge (*sl*) **2** = **childbirth**, childbed, labour, lying-in, parturition

confines *plural noun* = **limits**, boundaries, bounds, circumference, edge, precincts

confirm *verb* **1** = **prove**, authenticate, bear out, corroborate, endorse, ratify, substantiate, validate, verify **2** = **strengthen**, buttress, establish, fix, fortify, reinforce

confirmation *noun* **1** = **sanction**, acceptance, agreement, approval, assent, endorsement, ratification OPPOSITE **refusal. 2** = **proof**, authentication, corroboration, evidence, substantiation, testimony, validation, verification OPPOSITE **denial**

confirmed *adjective* = **long-established**, chronic, dyed-in-the-wool, habitual, hardened, ingrained, inveterate, seasoned

conflagration *noun* large destructive fire.
conflate *verb* combine or blend into a whole.
conflation *noun*
conflict ❶ *noun* 1 disagreement. 2 struggle or fight. ♦ *verb* 3 be incompatible.
confluence *noun* 1 place where two rivers join. 2 gathering.
conform ❶ *verb* 1 comply with accepted standards or customs. 2 (foll. by *to* or *with*) be like or in accordance with. **conformist** *noun*, *adjective* (person) complying with accepted standards or customs. **conformity** *noun* compliance with accepted standards or customs.
confound ❶ *verb* 1 astound, bewilder. 2 confuse. **confounded** *adjective Informal* damned, e.g. *what a confounded nuisance!*
confront ❶ *verb* come face to face with. **confrontation** *noun* serious argument.
confuse ❶ *verb* 1 mix up. 2 perplex, disconcert. 3 make unclear. **confusion** *noun*
confute *verb* prove wrong. **confutation** *noun*

conga *noun* 1 dance performed by a number of people in single file. 2 large single-headed drum played with the hands.
congeal *verb* (of a liquid) become thick and sticky.
congenial ❶ *adjective* 1 pleasant, agreeable. 2 having similar interests and attitudes. **congeniality** *noun*
congenital ❶ *adjective* (of a condition) existing from birth. **congenitally** *adverb*
conger *noun* large sea eel.
congested ❶ *adjective* crowded to excess. **congestion** *noun*
conglomerate *noun* 1 large corporation made up of many companies. 2 thing made up of several different elements. ♦ *verb* 3 form into a mass. ♦ *adjective* 4 made up of several different elements. **conglomeration** *noun*
congratulate ❶ *verb* express one's pleasure to (someone) at his or her good fortune or success. **congratulations** *plural noun*, *interjection* **congratulatory** *adjective*

———————————————— T H E S A U R U S ————————————————

confiscate *verb* = **seize**, appropriate, commandeer, impound, sequester, sequestrate OPPOSITE **give back**
confiscation *noun* = **seizure**, appropriation, forfeiture, impounding, sequestration, takeover
conflict *noun* 1 = **opposition**, antagonism, difference, disagreement, discord, dissension, friction, hostility, strife OPPOSITE **accord**. 2 = **battle**, clash, combat, contest, encounter, fight, strife, war OPPOSITE **peace** ♦*verb* 3 = **be incompatible**, be at variance, clash, collide, differ, disagree, interfere OPPOSITE **agree**
conflicting *adjective* 1 = **opposing**, antagonistic, discordant 3 = **incompatible**, clashing, contradictory, contrary, inconsistent, paradoxical OPPOSITE **agreeing**
conform *verb* 1 = **comply**, adapt, adjust, fall in with, follow, obey, toe the line 2 (foll. by *to* or *with*) = **agree**, accord, correspond, harmonize, match, suit, tally
conformist *noun* = **traditionalist**, stick-in-the-mud (*inf*), yes man
conformity *noun* = **compliance**, conventionality, observance, orthodoxy, traditionalism
confound *verb* 1 = **bewilder**, astound, baffle, dumbfound, flummox, mystify, nonplus, perplex
confront *verb* = **face**, accost, challenge, defy, encounter, oppose, stand up to, tackle OPPOSITE **evade**
confrontation *noun* = **conflict**, contest, encounter, fight, head-to-head, set-to (*inf*),

showdown (*inf*)
confuse *verb* 1 = **mix up**, disarrange, disorder, jumble, mingle, muddle, ravel 2 = **bewilder**, baffle, bemuse, faze, flummox, mystify, nonplus, perplex, puzzle
confused *adjective* 1 = **disordered**, chaotic, disorganized, higgledy-piggledy (*inf*), in disarray, jumbled, mixed up, topsy-turvy, untidy OPPOSITE **ordered**. 2 = **bewildered**, at sea, baffled, disorientated, flummoxed, muddled, nonplussed, perplexed, puzzled, taken aback OPPOSITE **enlightened**
confusing *adjective* 2 = **bewildering**, baffling, contradictory, disconcerting, misleading, perplexing, puzzling OPPOSITE **clear**
confusion *noun* 1 = **disorder**, chaos, commotion, jumble, mess, muddle, shambles, turmoil, untidiness, upheaval OPPOSITE **order**. 2 = **bewilderment**, disorientation, mystification, perplexity, puzzlement OPPOSITE **enlightenment**
congenial *adjective* 1 = **pleasant**, affable, agreeable, companionable, favourable, friendly, genial, kindly 2 = **compatible**, kindred, like-minded, sympathetic, well-suited
congenital *adjective* = **inborn**, immanent, inbred, inherent, innate, natural
congested *adjective* = **overcrowded**, crowded, teeming OPPOSITE **clear**
congestion *noun* = **overcrowding**, crowding, jam
congratulate *verb* = **compliment**, pat on the back, wish joy to

congregate ⊙ *verb* gather together in a crowd. **congregation** *noun* people who attend a church. **congregational** *adjective* **Congregationalism** *noun* Protestant denomination in which each church is self-governing. **Congregationalist** *adjective, noun*
congress ⊙ *noun* **1** formal meeting for discussion. **2 (C-)** federal parliament of the US. **congressional** *adjective* **Congressman, Congresswoman** *noun* member of Congress.
congruent *adjective* **1** similar, corresponding. **2** *Geom* identical in shape and size.
congruence *noun*
conical *adjective* cone-shaped.
conic section *noun* *Geom* figure formed by the intersection of a plane and a cone.
conifer *noun* cone-bearing tree, such as the fir or pine. **coniferous** *adjective*
conjecture ⊙ *noun, verb* guess. **conjectural** *adjective*
conjoined twins *plural noun* the technical name for SIAMESE TWINS.
conjugal ⊙ [kon-jew-gal] *adjective* of marriage.
conjugate *verb* give the inflections of (a verb).
conjugation *noun* complete set of inflections of a verb.
conjunction *noun* **1** combination. **2** simultaneous occurrence of events. **3** part of speech joining words, phrases, or clauses.
conjunctivitis *noun* inflammation of the membrane covering the eyeball and inner eyelid. **conjunctiva** *noun* this membrane.
conjuncture *noun* combination of events.

conjure ⊙ *verb* **1** perform tricks that appear to be magic. **2** summon (a spirit) by magic.
conjuror, conjurer *noun* **conjure up** *verb* produce as if by magic.
conk *noun Slang* nose.
conker *noun Informal* nut of the horse chestnut. **conkers** *noun* game played with conkers tied on strings.
conk out *verb Informal* **1** (of a machine) break down. **2** fall asleep suddenly.
connect ⊙ *verb* **1** join together. **2** put into telephone communication with. **3** associate in the mind. **connection, connexion** *noun* **1** relationship, association. **2** link or bond. **3** opportunity to transfer from one public vehicle to another. **4** influential acquaintance.
connective *adjective*
conning tower *noun* raised observation tower containing the periscope on a submarine.
connive ⊙ *verb* **1** (foll. by *at*) allow (wrongdoing) by ignoring it. **2** conspire.
connivance *noun*
connoisseur ⊙ [kon-noss-**sir**] *noun* person with special knowledge of the arts, food, or drink.
connotation *noun* associated idea conveyed by a word. **connote** *verb*
connubial [kon-**new**-bee-al] *adjective* of marriage.
conquer ⊙ *verb* **1** defeat. **2** overcome (a difficulty). **3** take (a place) by force. **conqueror** *noun* **conquest** *noun* **1** conquering. **2** person or thing conquered. **3** person whose affections have been won.

——————————— T H E S A U R U S ———————————

congratulations *plural noun, interjection* =**good wishes**, best wishes, compliments, felicitations, greetings
congregate *verb* =**come together**, assemble, collect, convene, converge, flock, gather, mass, meet OPPOSITE **disperse**
congregation *noun* =**assembly**, brethren, crowd, fellowship, flock, multitude, throng
congress *noun* **1** =**meeting**, assembly, conclave, conference, convention, council, legislature, parliament
conjecture *noun* =**guess**, hypothesis, shot in the dark, speculation, supposition, surmise, theory ◆*verb* =**guess**, hypothesize, imagine, speculate, suppose, surmise, theorize
conjugal *adjective* =**marital**, bridal, connubial, married, matrimonial, nuptial, wedded
conjure *verb* **1** =**perform tricks**, juggle
conjure up *verb* =**bring to mind**, contrive, create, evoke, produce as if by magic, recall, recollect

conjuror, conjurer *noun* **1** =**magician**, illusionist, sorcerer, wizard
connect *verb* **1** =**join**, affix, attach, couple, fasten, link, unite OPPOSITE **separate**
connected *adjective* **1** =**joined**, affiliated, akin, allied, associated, combined, coupled, linked, related, united
connection *noun* **1** =**association**, affinity, bond, liaison, link, relationship, relevance, tie-in **2** =**link**, alliance, association, attachment, coupling, fastening, junction, tie, union **4** =**contact**, acquaintance, ally, associate, friend, sponsor
connivance *noun* **1** =**tacit consent 2** =**collusion**, abetting, complicity, conspiring
connive *verb* **1** (foll. by *at*) =**turn a blind eye to**, abet, disregard, let pass, look the other way, overlook, wink at **2** =**conspire**, collude, cook up (*inf*), intrigue, plot, scheme
connoisseur *noun* =**expert**, aficionado, appreciator, authority, buff (*inf*), devotee, fundi

consanguinity *noun Formal* relationship by blood.

conscience ❶ *noun* sense of right or wrong as regards thoughts and actions. **conscience-stricken** *adjective* feeling anxious or guilty.

conscientious ❶ *adjective* 1 painstaking. 2 governed by conscience. **conscientiously** *adverb* **conscientious objector** person who refuses to serve in the armed forces on moral or religious grounds.

conscious ❶ *adjective* 1 alert and awake. 2 aware. 3 deliberate, intentional. 4 of the part of the mind that determines the choices of action. **consciously** *adverb* **consciousness** *noun*

conscript *noun* 1 person enrolled for compulsory military service. ◆ *verb* 2 enrol (someone) for compulsory military service. **conscription** *noun*

consecrate ❶ *verb* 1 make sacred. 2 dedicate to a specific purpose. **consecration** *noun*

consecutive ❶ *adjective* in unbroken succession. **consecutively** *adverb*

consensus ❶ *noun* general agreement.

SPELLING TIP

The Bank of English has 6694 examples of the word **consensus** and another 112 of *concensus* with a *c* in the middle. The correct spelling is **consensus** and it has only one *c*.

---

consent ❶ *noun* 1 agreement, permission. ◆ *verb* 2 (foll. by *to*) permit, agree to.

consequence ❶ *noun* 1 result, effect. 2 importance. **consequent** *adjective* resulting. **consequently** *adverb* as a result, therefore. **consequential** *adjective* 1 important. 2 following as a result.

conservative ❶ *adjective* 1 opposing change. 2 moderate, cautious. 3 conventional in style. 4 (**C-**) of the Conservative Party, the British right-wing political party which believes in private enterprise and capitalism. ◆ *noun* 5 conservative person. 6 (**C-**) supporter or member of the Conservative Party. **conservatism** *noun*

——————— THESAURUS ———————

(*S Afr*), judge, mana (*NZ*)

conquer *verb* 1 = **defeat**, beat, crush, get the better of, master, overcome, overpower, overthrow, quell, subjugate, vanquish [OPPOSITE] **lose to. 3** = **seize**, acquire, annex, obtain, occupy, overrun, win

conqueror *noun* 1 = **winner**, defeater, vanquisher, victor

conquest *noun* 1 a = **defeat**, mastery, overthrow, rout, triumph, victory **b** = **takeover**, annexation, coup, invasion, occupation, subjugation

conscience *noun* = **principles**, moral sense, scruples, sense of right and wrong, still small voice

conscientious *adjective* 1 = **thorough**, careful, diligent, exact, faithful, meticulous, painstaking, particular, punctilious [OPPOSITE] **careless**

conscious *adjective* 1 = **alert**, awake, responsive [OPPOSITE] **unconscious. 2** = **aware**, alive to, sensible, sentient [OPPOSITE] **unaware. 3** = **deliberate**, calculated, intentional, knowing, premeditated, self-conscious, studied, wilful [OPPOSITE] **unintentional**

consciousness *noun* 2 = **awareness**, apprehension, knowledge, realization, recognition, sensibility

consecrate *verb* 1 = **sanctify**, hallow, ordain, venerate **2** = **dedicate**, devote, set apart

consecutive *adjective* = **successive**, in

sequence, in turn, running, sequential, succeeding, uninterrupted

consensus *noun* = **agreement**, assent, common consent, concord, general agreement, harmony, unanimity, unity

consent *noun* 1 = **agreement**, acquiescence, approval, assent, compliance, go-ahead (*inf*), O.K. *or* okay (*inf*), permission, sanction [OPPOSITE] **refusal** ◆*verb* 2 = **agree**, acquiesce, allow, approve, assent, concur, permit [OPPOSITE] **refuse**

consequence *noun* 1 = **result**, effect, end result, issue, outcome, repercussion, sequel, upshot **2** = **importance**, account, concern, import, moment, significance, value, weight

consequent *adjective* = **following**, ensuing, resultant, resulting, subsequent, successive

consequently *adverb* = **as a result**, accordingly, ergo, hence, subsequently, therefore, thus

conservation *noun* 1 = **protection**, guardianship, preservation, safeguarding, safekeeping **2** = **saving**, husbandry, maintenance, upkeep

conservative *adjective* 1 = **traditional**, conventional, die-hard, hidebound, moderate, reactionary [OPPOSITE] **radical. 2** = **cautious 4** (cap.) = **Tory**, right-wing ◆*noun* **5** = **traditionalist**, die-hard, reactionary, stick-in-the-mud (*inf*) [OPPOSITE] **radical. 6** (cap.) = **Tory**, right-winger

C

conservatoire [kon-**serv**-a-twahr] *noun*
school of music.
conservatory *noun, pl* **-ries 1** room with
glass walls and a glass roof, attached to a
house. **2** conservatoire.
conserve ❶ *verb* **1** protect from harm, decay,
or loss. **2** preserve (fruit) with sugar. ◆ *noun* **3**
jam containing large pieces of fruit.
conservancy *noun* environmental conservation.
conservation *noun* **1** protection of natural
resources and the environment. **2** conserving.
conservationist *noun* **conservative** *adjective*
opposing change.
consider ❶ *verb* **1** regard as. **2** think about. **3**
be considerate of. **4** discuss. **5** look at.
considerable *adjective* large in amount or
degree. **considerably** *adverb* **considerate**
adjective thoughtful towards others.
considerately *adverb* **consideration** *noun* **1**
careful thought. **2** fact that should be
considered. **3** thoughtfulness. **4** payment for a
service. **considered** *adjective* thought out with
care. **considering** *preposition* taking (a specified
fact) into account.
consign ❶ *verb* **1** put somewhere. **2** send
(goods). **consignee** *noun* **consignor** *noun*
consignment *noun* shipment of goods.
consist ❶ *verb* **1 consist of** be made up of. **2**

consist in have as its main or only feature.
consistent *adjective* unchanging, constant.
consistent ❶ *adjective* **1** unchanging,
constant. **2** (foll. by *with*) in agreement.
consistently *adverb* **consistency** *noun, pl* **-cies**
1 being consistent. **2** degree of thickness or
smoothness.
console¹ ❶ *verb* comfort in distress.
consolation *noun* **1** consoling. **2** person or
thing that consoles.
console² *noun* **1** panel of controls for
electronic equipment. **2** cabinet for a television
or audio equipment. **3** ornamental wall bracket.
4 part of an organ containing the pedals, stops,
and keys.
consolidate ❶ *verb* **1** make or become
stronger or more stable. **2** combine into a
whole. **consolidation** *noun*
consommé [kon-**som**-may] *noun* thin clear
meat soup.
consonant *noun* **1** speech sound made by
partially or completely blocking the breath
stream, such as *b* or *f*. **2** letter representing this.
◆ *adjective* **3** (foll. by *with*) agreeing (with).
consonance *noun* agreement, harmony.
consort ❶ *verb* **1** (foll. by *with*) keep company
(with). ◆ *noun* **2** husband or wife of a monarch.
consortium *noun, pl* **-tia** association of

——— T H E S A U R U S ———

conserve *verb* **1** =**protect**, hoard, husband,
keep, nurse, preserve, save, store up, take care
of, use sparingly OPPOSITE **waste**
consider *verb* **1** =**think**, believe, deem, hold
to be, judge, rate, regard as **2** =**think about**,
cogitate, contemplate, deliberate, meditate,
ponder, reflect, ruminate, turn over in one's
mind, weigh **3** =**bear in mind**, keep in view,
make allowance for, reckon with, remember,
respect, take into account
considerable *adjective* =**large**, appreciable,
goodly, great, marked, noticeable, plentiful,
sizable *or* sizeable, substantial OPPOSITE **small**
considerably *adverb* =**greatly**, appreciably,
markedly, noticeably, remarkably, significantly,
substantially, very much
considerate *adjective* =**thoughtful**, attentive,
concerned, kindly, mindful, obliging, patient,
tactful, unselfish OPPOSITE **inconsiderate**
consideration *noun* **1** =**thought**, analysis,
deliberation, discussion, examination, reflection,
review, scrutiny **2** =**factor**, concern, issue, point
3 =**thoughtfulness**, concern, considerateness,
kindness, respect, tact **4** =**payment**, fee,
recompense, remuneration, reward, tip
considering *preposition* =**taking into
account**, in the light of, in view of

consignment *noun* =**shipment**, batch,
delivery, goods
consist *verb* **1 consist of** =**be made up of**,
amount to, be composed of, comprise, contain,
embody, include, incorporate, involve **2**
consist in =**lie in**, be expressed by, be found
or contained in, inhere in, reside in
consistency *noun* **1** =**constancy**, evenness,
regularity, steadfastness, steadiness, uniformity
2 =**texture**, compactness, density, firmness,
thickness, viscosity
consistent *adjective* **1** =**unchanging**,
constant, dependable, persistent, regular,
steady, true to type, undeviating OPPOSITE
erratic. 2 (foll. by *with*) =**agreeing**, coherent,
compatible, congruous, consonant,
harmonious, logical OPPOSITE **contradictory**
consolation *noun* =**comfort**, cheer,
encouragement, help, relief, solace, succour,
support
console¹ *verb* =**comfort**, calm, cheer,
encourage, express sympathy for, soothe
OPPOSITE **distress**
consolidate *verb* **1** =**strengthen**, fortify,
reinforce, secure, stabilize **2** =**combine**,
amalgamate, federate, fuse, join, unite
consort *verb* **1** (foll. by *with*) =**associate**,

business firms.
conspectus *noun Formal* survey or summary.
conspicuous ❶ *adjective* **1** clearly visible. **2** noteworthy, striking. **conspicuously** *adverb*
conspire ❶ *verb* **1** plan a crime together in secret. **2** act together as if by design.
conspiracy *noun* **1** conspiring. **2** *pl* **-cies** plan made by conspiring. **conspirator** *noun* **conspiratorial** *adjective*
constable *noun* police officer of the lowest rank. **constabulary** *noun, pl* **-laries** police force of an area.
constant ❶ *adjective* **1** continuous. **2** unchanging. **3** faithful. ◆ *noun* **4** unvarying quantity. **5** something that stays the same. **constantly** *adverb* **constancy** *noun*
constellation *noun* group of stars.
consternation ❶ *noun* anxiety or dismay.
constipation *noun* difficulty in defecating. **constipated** *adjective* having constipation.
constituent ❶ *noun* **1** member of a constituency. **2** component part. ◆ *adjective* **3** forming part of a whole. **constituency** *noun, pl* **-cies 1** area represented by a Member of Parliament. **2** voters in such an area.
constitute ❶ *verb* **1** be, amount to. **2** form, make up. **constitution** *noun* **1** principles on

which a state is governed. **2** physical condition. **3** structure. **constitutional** *adjective* **1** of a constitution. **2** in accordance with a political constitution. **3** being inherent to a person or thing. ◆ *noun* **4** walk taken for exercise. **constitutionally** *adverb*
constrain ❶ *verb* **1** compel, force. **2** limit, restrict. **constrained** *adjective* embarrassed or unnatural. **constraint** *noun* something that limits or controls a person's actions.
constrict *verb* **1** make narrower by squeezing. **2** limit, restrict. **constriction** *noun* **constrictive** *adjective* **constrictor** *noun* **1** large snake that squeezes its prey to death. **2** muscle that compresses an organ.
construct ❶ *verb* **1** build or put together. **2** *Geom* draw (a figure). **construction** *noun* **1** constructing. **2** thing constructed. **3** interpretation. **4** *Grammar* way in which words are arranged in a sentence, clause, or phrase. **constructive** *adjective* (of advice, criticism, etc.) useful and helpful. **constructively** *adverb*
construe *verb* **-struing, -strued** interpret.
consul *noun* **1** official representing a state in a foreign country. **2** one of the two chief magistrates in ancient Rome. **consular** *adjective* **consulate** *noun* workplace or position of a

————————————— T H E S A U R U S —————————————

fraternize, go around with, hang about, around *or* out with, keep company, mix ◆*noun* **2** = **spouse**, companion, husband, partner, wife
conspicuous *adjective* **1** = **obvious**, blatant, clear, evident, noticeable, patent, salient [OPPOSITE] **inconspicuous**. **2** = **noteworthy**, illustrious, notable, outstanding, prominent, remarkable, salient, signal, striking
conspiracy *noun* **2** = **plot**, collusion, intrigue, machination, scheme, treason
conspirator *noun* = **plotter**, conspirer, intriguer, schemer, traitor
conspire *verb* **1** = **plot**, contrive, intrigue, machinate, manoeuvre, plan, scheme **2** = **work together**, combine, concur, contribute, cooperate, tend
constant *adjective* **1** = **continuous**, ceaseless, incessant, interminable, nonstop, perpetual, sustained, unrelenting [OPPOSITE] **occasional**. **2** = **unchanging**, even, fixed, invariable, permanent, stable, steady, uniform, unvarying [OPPOSITE] **changing**. **3** = **faithful**, devoted, loyal, stalwart, staunch, true, trustworthy, trusty [OPPOSITE] **undependable**
constantly *adverb* **1, 2** = **continuously**, all the time, always, continually, endlessly, incessantly, interminably, invariably, nonstop, perpetually, twenty-four-seven (*inf*) [OPPOSITE] **occasionally**

consternation *noun* = **dismay**, alarm, anxiety, distress, dread, fear, trepidation
constituent *noun* **1** = **voter**, elector **2** = **component**, element, factor, ingredient, part, unit ◆*adjective* **3** = **component**, basic, elemental, essential, integral
constitute *verb* **2** = **make up**, compose, comprise, establish, form, found, set up
constitution *noun* **2** = **health**, build, character, disposition, physique **3** = **structure**, composition, form, make-up, nature
constitutional *adjective* **1** = **statutory**, chartered, vested ◆*noun* **4** = **walk**, airing, stroll, turn
constrain *verb* **1** = **force**, bind, coerce, compel, impel, necessitate, oblige, pressurize **2** = **restrict**, check, confine, constrict, curb, restrain, straiten
constraint *noun* = **restriction**, check, curb, deterrent, hindrance, limitation, rein, restraint
construct *verb* **1** = **build**, assemble, compose, create, fashion, form, make, manufacture, put together, shape [OPPOSITE] **demolish**
construction *noun* **2** = **building**, composition, creation, edifice **3** = **interpretation**, explanation, inference, reading, rendering
constructive *adjective* = **helpful**, positive, practical, productive, useful, valuable [OPPOSITE]

consul. **consulship** noun
consult ❶ verb go to for advice or information.
consultant noun **1** specialist doctor with a senior position in a hospital. **2** specialist who gives professional advice. **consultancy** noun, pl **-cies** work or position of a consultant.
consultation noun (meeting for) consulting.
consultative adjective giving advice.
consume ❶ verb **1** eat or drink. **2** use up. **3** destroy. **4** obsess. **consumer** noun person who buys goods or uses services. **consumerism** noun protection of the rights of consumers.
consumption noun **1** amount consumed. **2** consuming. **3** purchase of goods and services. **4** Old-fashioned tuberculosis. **consumptive** noun, adjective Old-fashioned (person) having tuberculosis.
consummate ❶ [kon-sum-mate] verb **1** make (a marriage) legal by sexual intercourse. **2** complete or fulfil. ◆ adjective [kon-**sum**-mit] **3** supremely skilled. **4** complete, extreme. **consummation** noun
cont. continued.
contact ❶ noun **1** communicating. **2** touching. **3** useful acquaintance. **4** connection between two electrical conductors in a circuit. ◆ verb **5** get in touch with. **contact lens** lens

placed on the eyeball to correct defective vision.
contagion ❶ noun **1** passing on of disease by contact. **2** disease spread by contact. **3** spreading of a harmful influence. **contagious** adjective spreading by contact, catching.
contain ❶ verb **1** hold or be capable of holding. **2** consist of. **3** control, restrain.
container noun **1** object used to hold or store things in. **2** large standard-sized box for transporting cargo by lorry or ship.
containerize verb pack (cargo) into containers.
containment noun prevention of the spread of something harmful.
contaminate ❶ verb **1** make impure, pollute. **2** make radioactive. **contaminant** noun contaminating substance. **contamination** noun
contemn verb Formal regard with contempt.
contemplate ❶ verb **1** think deeply. **2** consider as a possibility. **3** gaze at.
contemplation noun **contemplative** adjective deeply thoughtful.
contemporary ❶ adjective **1** present-day, modern. **2** living or occurring at the same time. **3** of roughly the same age. ◆ noun, pl **-raries 4** person or thing living or occurring at the same time as another. **contemporaneous** adjective

——————— T H E S A U R U S ———————

unproductive
consult verb **=ask**, compare notes, confer, pick (someone's) brains, question, refer to, take counsel, turn to
consultant noun **2 =specialist**, adviser, authority, mana (NZ)
consultation noun **=seminar**, appointment, conference, council, deliberation, dialogue, discussion, examination, hearing, interview, meeting, session
consume verb **1 =eat**, devour, eat up, gobble (up), put away, swallow **2 =use up**, absorb, dissipate, exhaust, expend, spend, squander, waste **3 =destroy**, annihilate, demolish, devastate, lay waste, ravage **4 =obsess**, absorb, dominate, eat up, engross, monopolize, preoccupy
consumer noun **=buyer**, customer, purchaser, shopper, user
consummate verb **2 =complete**, accomplish, conclude, crown, end, finish, fulfil OPPOSITE> start ◆adjective **3 =skilled**, accomplished, matchless, perfect, polished, practised, superb, supreme **4 =complete**, absolute, conspicuous, extreme, supreme, total, utter
consumption noun **2 =using up**, depletion, diminution, dissipation, exhaustion, expenditure, loss, waste **4** Old-fashioned

=tuberculosis, T.B.
contact noun **1 =communication**, association, connection **2 =touch**, contiguity **3 =acquaintance**, connection ◆verb **5 =get** or **be in touch with**, approach, call, communicate with, reach, speak to, write to
contagious adjective **=infectious**, catching, communicable, spreading, transmissible
contain verb **1 =hold**, accommodate, enclose, have capacity for, incorporate, seat **2 =include**, comprehend, comprise, consist of, embody, embrace, involve **3 =restrain**, control, curb, hold back, hold in, keep a tight rein on, repress, stifle
container noun **1 =holder**, receptacle, repository, vessel
contaminate verb **1 =pollute**, adulterate, befoul, corrupt, defile, infect, stain, taint, tarnish OPPOSITE> purify
contamination noun **1 =pollution**, contagion, corruption, defilement, impurity, infection, poisoning, taint
contemplate verb **1 =think about**, consider, deliberate, meditate, muse over, ponder, reflect upon, ruminate (upon) **2 =consider**, envisage, expect, foresee, intend, plan, think of **3 =look at**, examine, eye up, gaze at, inspect, regard, stare at, study, survey, view

happening at the same time.

contempt ⊕ *noun* **1** dislike and disregard. **2** open disrespect for the authority of a court. **contemptible** *adjective* deserving contempt. **contemptuous** *adjective* showing contempt. **contemptuously** *adverb*

contend ⊕ *verb* **1** (foll. by *with*) deal with. **2** state, assert. **3** compete. **contender** *noun*

content¹ ⊕ *noun* **1** meaning or substance of a piece of writing. **2** amount of a substance in a mixture. ◆ *plural* **3** what something contains. **4** list of chapters at the front of a book.

content² ⊕ *adjective* **1** satisfied with things as they are. **2** willing to accept a proposed course of action. ◆ *verb* **3** make (someone) content. ◆

noun **4** happiness and satisfaction. **contented** *adjective* **contentment** *noun*

contention ⊕ *noun* **1** disagreement or dispute. **2** point asserted in argument.

contentious *adjective* **1** causing disagreement. **2** quarrelsome.

contest ⊕ *noun* **1** competition or struggle. ◆ *verb* **2** dispute, object to. **3** fight or compete for. **contestant** *noun*

context ⊕ *noun* **1** circumstances of an event or fact. **2** words before and after a word or sentence that help make its meaning clear. **contextual** *adjective*

contiguous *adjective* very near or touching.

continent¹ *noun* one of the earth's large masses of land. **the Continent** mainland of Europe. **continental** *adjective* **continental breakfast** light breakfast of coffee and rolls. **continental quilt** same as DUVET.

continent² *adjective* **1** able to control one's bladder and bowels. **2** sexually restrained. **continence** *noun*

contingent ⊕ *noun* **1** group of people that represents or is part of a larger group. ◆ *adjective* **2** (foll. by *on*) dependent on (something uncertain). **contingency** *noun, pl* **-cies** something that may happen.

——————— T H E S A U R U S ———————

contemporary *adjective* **1** = **modern**, à la mode, current, newfangled, present, present-day, recent, up-to-date OPPOSITE **old**. **2** = **coexisting**, concurrent, contemporaneous ◆*noun* **4** = **peer**, fellow

contempt *noun* **1** = **scorn**, derision, disdain, disregard, disrespect, mockery, slight OPPOSITE **respect**

contemptible *adjective* = **despicable**, detestable, ignominious, measly, paltry, pitiful, shameful, worthless OPPOSITE **admirable**

contemptuous *adjective* = **scornful**, arrogant, condescending, derisive, disdainful, haughty, sneering, supercilious, withering OPPOSITE **respectful**

contend *verb* **1** (foll. by *with*) = **compete**, clash, contest, fight, jostle, strive, struggle, vie **2** = **argue**, affirm, allege, assert, dispute, hold, maintain

content¹ *noun* **1** = **meaning**, essence, gist, significance, substance **2** = **amount**, capacity, load, measure, size, volume ◆*plural* **3** = **constituents**, elements, ingredients, load

content² *adjective* **1** = **satisfied**, agreeable, at ease, comfortable, contented, fulfilled **2** = **willing to accept** ◆*verb* **3** = **satisfy**, appease, humour, indulge, mollify, placate, please ◆*noun* **4** = **satisfaction**, comfort, contentment, ease,

gratification, peace of mind, pleasure

contented *adjective* **1** = **satisfied**, comfortable, content, glad, gratified, happy, pleased, serene, thankful OPPOSITE **discontented**

contentious *adjective* **2** = **argumentative**, bickering, captious, cavilling, disputatious, quarrelsome, querulous, wrangling

contentment *noun* **1** = **satisfaction**, comfort, content, ease, equanimity, fulfilment, happiness, peace, pleasure, serenity OPPOSITE **discontent**

contest *noun* **1** = **competition**, game, match, tournament, trial ◆*verb* **2** = **dispute**, argue, call in *or* into question, challenge, debate, doubt, object to, oppose, question **3** = **compete**, contend, fight, strive, vie

contestant *noun* = **competitor**, candidate, contender, entrant, participant, player

context *noun* **1** = **circumstances**, ambience, background, conditions, frame of reference, situation

contingency *noun* = **possibility**, accident, chance, emergency, event, eventuality, happening, incident

continual *adjective* **1** = **constant**, frequent, incessant, interminable, unremitting OPPOSITE **erratic**. **2** = **recurrent**, regular, repeated

continue ❶ *verb* **-tinuing, -tinued 1** (cause to) remain in a condition or place. **2** carry on (doing something). **3** resume. **4** go on beyond a place. **continual** *adjective* **1** constant. **2** recurring frequently. **continually** *adverb* **continuance** *noun* continuing. **continuation** *noun* **1** continuing. **2** part added. **continuity** *noun, pl* **-ties 1** smooth development or sequence. **2** arrangement of scenes in a film so that they follow each other logically and without breaks. **continuous** *adjective* continuing uninterrupted. **continuously** *adverb* **continuo** *noun, pl* **-tinuos** *Music* continuous bass part, usu. played on a keyboard instrument.

continuum *noun, pl* **-tinua, -tinuums** continuous series.

contort *verb* twist out of shape. **contortion** *noun* **contortionist** *noun* performer who contorts his or her body to entertain.

contour *noun* **1** outline. **2** (also **contour line**) line on a map joining places of the same height.

contra- *prefix* against or contrasting, e.g. *contraflow.*

contraband ❶ *noun, adjective* smuggled (goods).

contraception *noun* prevention of pregnancy by artificial means. **contraceptive** *noun* **1**

device used or pill taken to prevent pregnancy. ◆ *adjective* **2** preventing pregnancy.

contract ❶ *noun* **1** (document setting out) a formal agreement. ◆ *verb* **2** make a formal agreement (to do something). **3** make or become smaller or shorter. **4** catch (an illness). **5** tighten (muscles) or (of muscles) be tightened. **contraction** *noun* **1** contracting. **2** shortened word. **contractor** *noun* firm that supplies materials or labour, esp. for building. **contractual** *adjective*

contradict ❶ *verb* **1** declare the opposite of (a statement) to be true. **2** be at variance with. **contradiction** *noun* **contradictory** *adjective* **contradistinction** *noun* distinction made by contrasting different qualities.

contraflow *noun* flow of traffic going alongside but in an opposite direction to the usual flow.

contralto *noun, pl* **-tos** (singer with) the lowest female voice.

contraption ❶ *noun* strange-looking device. **contrapuntal** *adjective Music* of or in counterpoint.

contrary ❶ *noun* **1** complete opposite. ◆ *adjective* **2** opposed, completely different. **3** perverse, obstinate. ◆ *adverb* **4** in opposition. **contrarily** *adverb* **contrariness** *noun* **contrariwise** *adverb*

——————— T H E S A U R U S ———————

OPPOSITE ▷ occasional
continually *adverb* **1** = **constantly**, all the time, always, forever, incessantly, interminably, nonstop, persistently, twenty-four-seven (*inf*) **2** = **repeatedly**
continuation *noun* **1** = **continuing**, perpetuation, prolongation, resumption **2** = **addition**, extension, furtherance, postscript, sequel, supplement
continue *verb* **1** = **remain**, abide, carry on, endure, last, live on, persist, stay, survive OPPOSITE ▷ **quit. 2** = **keep on**, carry on, go on, maintain, persevere, persist in, stick at, sustain OPPOSITE ▷ **stop. 3** = **resume**, carry on, pick up where one left off, proceed, recommence, return to, take up OPPOSITE ▷ **stop**
continuing *adjective* **1, 2** = **lasting**, enduring, in progress, ongoing, sustained
continuity *noun* **1** = **sequence**, cohesion, connection, flow, progression, succession
continuous *adjective* = **constant**, extended, prolonged, unbroken, unceasing, undivided, uninterrupted OPPOSITE ▷ **occasional**
contraband *noun* = **smuggling**, black-marketing, bootlegging, trafficking ◆ *adjective* = **smuggled**, banned, bootleg, forbidden, hot

(*inf*), illegal, illicit, prohibited, unlawful
contract *noun* **1** = **agreement**, arrangement, bargain, commitment, covenant, pact, settlement ◆ *verb* **2** = **agree**, bargain, come to terms, commit oneself, covenant, negotiate, pledge OPPOSITE ▷ **refuse. 3** = **shorten**, abbreviate, curtail, diminish, dwindle, lessen, narrow, reduce, shrink, shrivel OPPOSITE ▷ **increase. 4** = **catch**, acquire, be afflicted with, develop, get, go down with, incur OPPOSITE ▷ **avoid**
contraction *noun* **1** = **shortening**, compression, narrowing, reduction, shrinkage, shrivelling, tightening **2** = **abbreviation**
contradict *verb* **1** = **deny**, challenge, rebut **2** = **be at variance with**, belie, controvert, fly in the face of, negate OPPOSITE ▷ **confirm**
contradiction *noun* **1** = **denial 2** = **incongruity**, conflict, contravention, inconsistency, negation, opposite
contradictory *adjective* **2** = **inconsistent**, conflicting, contrary, incompatible, opposed, opposite, paradoxical
contraption *noun Inf* = **device**, apparatus, contrivance, gadget, instrument, mechanism
contrary *noun* **1** = **opposite**, antithesis,

contrast ❶ *noun* **1** obvious difference. **2** person or thing very different from another. **3** degree of difference between colours in a photograph or television picture. ◆ *verb* **4** compare in order to show differences. **5** (foll. by *with*) be very different (from).

contravene *verb* break (a rule or law). **contravention** *noun*

contretemps [kon-tra-tahn] *noun, pl* **-temps** embarrassing minor disagreement.

contribute ❶ *verb* **1** give for a common purpose or fund. **2** (foll. by *to*) be partly responsible (for). **3** write articles for a publication. **contribution** *noun* **contributor** *noun* **contributory** *adjective*

contrite ❶ *adjective* sorry and apologetic. **contritely** *adverb* **contrition** *noun*

contrive ❶ *verb* **1** make happen. **2** devise or construct. **contrivance** *noun* **1** device. **2** plan. **3** contriving. **contrived** *adjective* planned or artificial.

control ❶ *noun* **1** power to direct something. **2** curb or check. **3** standard of comparison in an experiment. ◆ *plural* **4** instruments used to operate a machine. ◆ *verb* **-trolling, -trolled 5** have power over. **6** limit, restrain. **7** regulate,

operate. **controllable** *adjective* **controller** *noun*

controversy ❶ *noun, pl* **-sies** fierce argument or debate. **controversial** *adjective* causing controversy.

> **LANGUAGE TIP**
>
> Note that the stress used always to be on the first syllable, 'kon', but is now more often on the second syllable, 'trov'.

contumely [kon-tume-mill-ee] *noun Lit* scornful or insulting treatment.

contusion *noun Formal* bruise.

conundrum *noun* riddle.

conurbation *noun* large urban area formed by the growth and merging of towns.

convalesce ❶ *verb* recover after an illness or operation. **convalescence** *noun* **convalescent** *noun, adjective*

convection *noun* transmission of heat in liquids or gases by the circulation of currents.

convector *noun* heater that gives out hot air.

convene ❶ *verb* gather or summon for a formal meeting. **convener, convenor** *noun*

——————— THESAURUS ———————

converse, reverse ◆*adjective* **2** = **opposed**, adverse, clashing, contradictory, counter, discordant, hostile, inconsistent, opposite, paradoxical OPPOSITE **consistent**. **3** = **perverse**, awkward, cantankerous, difficult, disobliging, intractable, obstinate, stroppy (*Brit sl*), unaccommodating OPPOSITE **willing**

contrast *noun* **1** = **difference**, comparison, disparity, dissimilarity, distinction, divergence, opposition ◆*verb* **4** = **compare**, differentiate, distinguish, set in opposition, set off **5** (foll. by *with*) = **differ**, oppose

contribute *verb* **1** = **give**, add, bestow, chip in (*inf*), donate, provide, subscribe, supply **2** (foll. by *to*) = **be partly responsible for**, be conducive to, be instrumental in, help, lead to, tend to

contribution *noun* **1** = **gift**, addition, donation, grant, input, offering, subscription

contributor *noun* **1** = **giver**, donor, patron, subscriber, supporter

contrite *adjective* = **sorry**, chastened, conscience-stricken, humble, penitent, regretful, remorseful, repentant, sorrowful

contrivance *noun* **1** = **device**, apparatus, appliance, contraption, gadget, implement, instrument, invention, machine, mechanism **2** = **plan**, intrigue, machination, plot, ruse, scheme, stratagem, trick

contrive *verb* **1** = **bring about**, arrange, effect, manage, manoeuvre, plan, plot, scheme, succeed **2** = **devise**, concoct, construct, create, design, fabricate, improvise, invent, manufacture

contrived *adjective* = **forced**, artificial, elaborate, laboured, overdone, planned, strained, unnatural OPPOSITE **natural**

control *noun* **1** = **power**, authority, charge, command, guidance, mana (*NZ*), management, oversight, supervision, supremacy **2** = **restraint**, brake, check, curb, limitation, regulation ◆*plural* **4** = **instruments**, console, control panel, dash, dashboard, dials ◆*verb* **5** = **have power over**, administer, command, direct, govern, handle, have charge of, manage, manipulate, supervise **6** = **restrain**, check, constrain, contain, curb, hold back, limit, repress, subdue

controversial *adjective* = **disputed**, at issue, contentious, debatable, disputable, open to question, under discussion

controversy *noun* = **argument**, altercation, debate, dispute, quarrel, row, squabble, wrangling

convalescence *noun* = **recovery**, improvement, recuperation, rehabilitation, return to health

convalescent *adjective* = **recovering**, getting better, improving, mending, on the mend,

C

person who calls a meeting.
convenient ❶ *adjective* **1** suitable or opportune. **2** easy to use. **3** nearby. **conveniently** *adverb* **convenience** *noun* **1** quality of being convenient. **2** useful object. **3** *Euphemistic* public toilet.
convent *noun* **1** building where nuns live. **2** school run by nuns.
conventicle *noun* secret or unauthorized religious meeting.
convention ❶ *noun* **1** widely accepted view of proper behaviour. **2** assembly or meeting. **3** formal agreement. **conventional** *adjective* **1** (unthinkingly) following the accepted customs. **2** customary. **3** (of weapons or warfare) not nuclear. **conventionally** *adverb* **conventionality** *noun*
converge ❶ *verb* meet or join. **convergence** *noun* **convergent** *adjective*
conversant *adjective* **conversant with** having knowledge or experience of.
converse¹ ❶ *verb* have a conversation. **conversation** *noun* informal talk. **conversational** *adjective* **conversationalist** *noun* person with a specified ability at conversation.
converse² ❶ *adjective, noun* opposite or

contrary. **conversely** *adverb*
convert ❶ *verb* **1** change in form, character, or function. **2** cause to change in opinion or belief. **3** change (money) into a different currency. **4** *Rugby* make a conversion after (a try). ◆ *noun* **5** person who has converted to a different belief or religion. **conversion** *noun* **1** (thing resulting from) converting. **2** *Rugby* score made after a try by kicking the ball over the crossbar. **convertible** *adjective* **1** capable of being converted. ◆ *noun* **2** car with a folding or removable roof.
convex ❶ *adjective* curving outwards. **convexity** *noun*
convey ❶ *verb* **1** communicate (information). **2** carry, transport. **3** transfer (the title to property). **conveyance** *noun* **1** *Old-fashioned* vehicle. **2** transfer of the legal title to property. **conveyancing** *noun* branch of law dealing with the transfer of ownership of property.
conveyor belt continuous moving belt for transporting things, esp. in a factory.
convict ❶ *verb* **1** declare guilty. ◆ *noun* **2** person serving a prison sentence. **conviction** *noun* **1** firm belief. **2** instance of being convicted.
convince ❶ *verb* persuade by argument or

———————— T H E S A U R U S ————————

recuperating
convene *verb* =**gather**, assemble, bring together, call, come together, congregate, convoke, meet, summon
convenience *noun* **1** =**usefulness**, accessibility, advantage, appropriateness, availability, benefit, fitness, suitability, utility OPPOSITE inconvenience. **2** =**appliance**, amenity, comfort, facility, help, labour-saving device
convenient *adjective* **1** =**suitable**, appropriate, fit, timely **2** =**useful**, handy, helpful, labour-saving, serviceable OPPOSITE useless. **3** =**nearby**, accessible, at hand, available, close at hand, handy, just round the corner, within reach OPPOSITE inaccessible
convention *noun* **1** =**custom**, code, etiquette, practice, propriety, protocol, tradition, usage **2** =**assembly**, conference, congress, convocation, council, meeting **3** =**agreement**, bargain, contract, pact, protocol, treaty
conventional *adjective* **1** =**unoriginal**, banal, hackneyed, prosaic, routine, run-of-the-mill, stereotyped OPPOSITE unconventional. **2** =**ordinary**, accepted, customary, normal, orthodox, regular, standard, traditional, usual
converge *verb* =**come together**, coincide,

combine, gather, join, meet, merge
conversation *noun* =**talk**, chat, conference, dialogue, discourse, discussion, gossip, tête-à-tête
converse¹ *verb* =**talk**, chat, commune, confer, discourse, exchange views
converse² *adjective* =**opposite**, contrary, counter, reverse, reversed, transposed ◆*noun* =**opposite**, antithesis, contrary, obverse, other side of the coin, reverse
conversion *noun* **1** =**change**, adaptation, alteration, metamorphosis, modification, reconstruction, remodelling, reorganization, transformation
convert *verb* **1** =**change**, adapt, alter, customize, modify, remodel, reorganize, restyle, revise, transform, transpose, turn **2** =**reform**, convince, proselytize ◆*noun* **5** =**neophyte**, disciple, proselyte
convex *adjective* =**rounded**, bulging, gibbous, protuberant OPPOSITE concave
convey *verb* **1** =**communicate**, disclose, impart, make known, relate, reveal, tell **2** =**carry**, bear, bring, conduct, fetch, guide, move, send, transport
convict *verb* **1** =**find guilty**, condemn, imprison, pronounce guilty, sentence ◆*noun* **2** =**prisoner**, criminal, culprit, felon, jailbird, lag

C

evidence. **convincing** *adjective* **convincingly** *adverb*

convivial *adjective* sociable, lively. **conviviality** *noun*

convocation *noun* **1** calling together. **2** large formal meeting. **convoke** *verb* call together.

convoluted *adjective* **1** coiled, twisted. **2** (of an argument or sentence) complex and hard to understand. **convolution** *noun*

convolvulus *noun* twining plant with funnel-shaped flowers.

convoy *noun* group of vehicles or ships travelling together.

convulse ⊙ *verb* **1** (of part of the body) undergo violent spasms. **2** (of a person) shake violently. **3** *Informal* (be) overcome with laughter. **convulsion** *noun* **1** violent muscular spasm. ◆ *plural* **2** uncontrollable laughter. **convulsive** *adjective*

cony *noun, pl* **conies 1** rabbit. **2** rabbit fur.

coo *verb* **cooing, cooed** (of a dove or pigeon) make a soft murmuring sound.

cooee *interjection* call to attract attention.

cook *verb* **1** prepare (food) by heating. **2** (of food) be cooked. ◆ *noun* **3** person who cooks food. **cook the books** falsify accounts. **cooker** *noun* **1** apparatus for cooking heated by gas or electricity. **2** apple suitable for cooking.

cookery *noun* art of cooking. **cookie** *noun US* biscuit. **cook up** *verb Informal* devise (a story or scheme).

Cooktown orchid *noun* purple Australian orchid.

cool ⊙ *adjective* **1** moderately cold. **2** calm and unemotional. **3** indifferent or unfriendly. **4** *Informal* sophisticated or excellent. **5** *Informal* (of a large sum of money) without exaggeration, e.g. *a cool million*. ◆ *verb* **6** make

or become cool. ◆ *noun* **7** coolness. **8** *Slang* calmness, composure. **coolly** *adverb* **coolness** *noun* **coolant** *noun* fluid used to cool machinery while it is working. **cool drink** *noun S Afr* nonalcoholic drink. **cooler** *noun* container for making or keeping things cool.

coolie *noun Old-fashioned offens* unskilled Oriental labourer.

coomb, coombe *noun* valley.

coop¹ *noun* cage or pen for poultry. **coop up** *verb* confine in a restricted place.

coop² [**koh**-op] *noun* (shop run by) a cooperative society.

cooper *noun* person who makes or repairs barrels.

cooperate ⊙ *verb* work or act together. **cooperation** *noun* **cooperative** *adjective* **1** willing to cooperate. **2** (of an enterprise) owned and managed collectively. ◆ *noun* **3** cooperative organization.

coopt [koh-**opt**] *verb* add (someone) to a group by the agreement of the existing members.

coordinate ⊙ *verb* **1** bring together and cause to work together efficiently. ◆ *noun* **2** *Maths* any of a set of numbers defining the location of a point. ◆ *plural* **3** clothes designed to be worn together. **coordination** *noun* **coordinator** *noun*

coot *noun* **1** small black water bird. **2** foolish person.

cop *Slang noun* **1** policeman. ◆ *verb* **copping, copped 2** take or seize. **cop it** get into trouble or be punished. **cop out** *verb* avoid taking responsibility or committing oneself. **cop-out** *noun*

copal *noun* resin used in varnishes.

cope¹ ⊙ *verb* (often foll. by *with*) **1** deal

————————————— T H E S A U R U S —————————————

(*sl*)

conviction *noun* **1** = **belief**, assurance, certainty, certitude, confidence, creed, faith, opinion, persuasion, principle, tenet, view

convince *verb* = **persuade**, assure, bring round, prevail upon, satisfy, sway, win over

convincing *adjective* = **persuasive**, cogent, conclusive, credible, impressive, plausible, powerful, telling OPPOSITE **unconvincing**

convulsion *noun* **1** = **spasm**, contraction, cramp, fit, paroxysm, seizure

cool *adjective* **1** = **cold**, chilled, chilly, nippy, refreshing OPPOSITE **warm**. **2** = **calm**, collected, composed, relaxed, sedate, self-controlled, self-possessed, unemotional, unruffled OPPOSITE **troubled**. **3** = **unfriendly**, aloof, distant, indifferent, lukewarm, offhand, standoffish,

unenthusiastic, unwelcoming OPPOSITE **friendly** ◆*verb* **6** = **chill**, cool off, freeze, lose heat, refrigerate OPPOSITE **warm (up)** ◆*noun* **8** *Sl* = **calmness**, composure, control, poise, self-control, self-discipline, self-possession, temper

cooperate *verb* = **work together**, collaborate, combine, conspire, coordinate, join forces, pool resources, pull together OPPOSITE **conflict**

cooperation *noun* = **teamwork**, collaboration, combined effort, esprit de corps, give-and-take, unity OPPOSITE **opposition**

cooperative *adjective* **1** = **helpful**, accommodating, obliging, onside (*inf*), responsive, supportive **2** = **shared**, collective, combined, joint

coordinate *verb* **1** = **bring together**, harmonize, integrate, match, organize,

successfully (with). **2** tolerate, endure.
cope² *noun* large ceremonial cloak worn by
some Christian priests.
cope³ *verb* provide with a coping.
copier *noun* see COPY.
copilot *noun* second pilot of an aircraft.
coping *noun* sloping top row of a wall.
copious ❶ [kope-ee-uss] *adjective* abundant,
plentiful. **copiously** *adverb*
copper¹ *noun* **1** soft reddish-brown metal. **2**
copper or bronze coin. **3** large metal container
used to boil water. ◆ *adjective* **4** reddish-brown.
copper-bottomed *adjective* financially reliable.
copperplate *noun* **1** fine handwriting style. **2**
(print taken from) an engraved copper plate.
copper² *noun Slang* policeman.
coppice, copse *noun* small group of trees
growing close together.
copra *noun* dried oil-yielding kernel of the
coconut.
copula *noun, pl* **-las, -lae** *verb* used to link the
subject and complement of a sentence, e.g.
become in they become chums.
copulate *verb* have sexual intercourse.
copulation *noun*
copy ❶ *noun, pl* **copies 1** thing made to look
exactly like another. **2** single specimen of a
book etc. **3** material for printing. **4** suitable
material for a newspaper article. ◆ *verb*
copying, copied 5 make a copy of. **6** act or
try to be like. **copier** *noun* machine that copies.
copybook *noun* **blot one's copybook**
Informal spoil one's reputation. **copyright** *noun*
1 exclusive legal right to reproduce and control
a book, work of art, etc. ◆ *verb* **2** take out a
copyright on. ◆ *adjective* **3** protected by
copyright. **copywriter** *noun* person who writes
advertising copy.
coquette *noun* woman who flirts. **coquettish**
adjective
coracle *noun* small round boat of wicker
covered with skins.

coral *noun* **1** hard substance formed from the
skeletons of very small sea animals. ◆ *adjective* **2**
orange-pink.
cor anglais *noun, pl* **cors anglais** woodwind
instrument similar to the oboe.
corbel *noun* stone or timber support sticking
out of a wall.
cord ❶ *noun* **1** thin rope or thick string. **2**
cordlike structure in the body. **3** corduroy. **4** *US*
electrical flex. ◆ *plural* **5** corduroy trousers. ◆
adjective **6** (also **corded**) (of fabric) ribbed.
cordate *adjective* heart-shaped.
cordial ❶ *adjective* **1** warm and friendly. ◆
noun **2** drink with a fruit base. **cordially** *adverb*
cordiality *noun*
cordite *noun* explosive used in guns and
bombs.
cordon ❶ *noun* chain of police, soldiers, etc.,
guarding an area. **cordon off** *verb* form a
cordon round.
cordon bleu [**bluh**] *adjective* (of cookery or
cooks) of the highest standard.
corduroy *noun* cotton fabric with a velvety
ribbed surface.
core ❶ *noun* **1** central part of certain fruits,
containing the seeds. **2** central or essential part.
3 region of a nuclear reactor that contains
fissionable material. ◆ *verb* **4** remove the core
from.
corella *noun* white Australian cockatoo.
co-respondent *noun* person with whom
someone being sued for divorce is claimed to
have committed adultery.
corgi *noun* short-legged sturdy dog.
coriander *noun* **1** plant grown for its aromatic
seeds and leaves. **2** its dried seeds, used as a
flavouring.
cork *noun* **1** thick light bark of a
Mediterranean oak. **2** piece of this used as a
stopper. ◆ *verb* **3** seal with a cork. **corked**
adjective (of wine) spoiled through having a
decayed cork. **corkage** *noun* restaurant's

———————— THESAURUS ————————

synchronize, systematize
cope¹ *verb* (often foll. by *with*) **1 = manage,**
carry on, get by (*inf*), hold one's own, make the
grade, struggle through, survive **2 = deal with,**
contend with, grapple with, handle, struggle
with, weather, wrestle with
copious *adjective* **= abundant,** ample,
bountiful, extensive, full, lavish, plentiful,
profuse
copy *noun* **1 = reproduction,** counterfeit,
duplicate, facsimile, forgery, imitation, likeness,
model, replica OPPOSITE> **original** ◆*verb* **5**
= reproduce, counterfeit, duplicate, replicate,

transcribe OPPOSITE> **create. 6 = imitate,** act
like, ape, behave like, emulate, follow, mimic,
mirror, repeat
cord *noun* **1 = rope,** line, string, twine
cordial *adjective* **1 = warm,** affable, agreeable,
cheerful, congenial, friendly, genial, hearty,
sociable OPPOSITE> **unfriendly**
cordon *noun* **= chain,** barrier, line, ring
cordon off *verb* **= surround,** close off,
encircle, enclose, fence off, isolate, picket,
separate
core *noun* **1 = kernel,** pith **2 = centre,** crux,
essence, gist, heart, nub, nucleus

charge for serving wine bought elsewhere.

corkscrew *noun* **1** spiral metal tool for pulling corks from bottles. ◆ *adjective* **2** like a corkscrew in shape.

corm *noun* bulblike underground stem of certain plants.

cormorant *noun* large dark-coloured long-necked sea bird.

corn[1] **ⓘ** *noun* **1** cereal plant such as wheat or oats. **2** grain of such plants. **3** *US* maize. **4** *Slang* something unoriginal or oversentimental. **corny** *adjective* **cornier, corniest** *Slang* unoriginal or oversentimental. **cornflakes** *plural noun* breakfast cereal made from toasted maize. **cornflour** *noun* fine maize flour *NZ* fine wheat flour. **cornflower** *noun* plant with blue flowers.

corn[2] *noun* painful hard skin on the toe.

corncrake *noun* brown bird with a harsh cry.

cornea [korn-ee-a] *noun, pl* **-neas, -neae** transparent membrane covering the eyeball. **corneal** *adjective*

corned beef *noun* beef preserved in salt.

cornelian *noun* same as CARNELIAN.

corner **ⓘ** *noun* **1** area or angle where two converging lines or surfaces meet. **2** place where two streets meet. **3** sharp bend in a road. **4** remote place. **5** *Sport* free kick or shot from the corner of the field. ◆ *verb* **6** force into a difficult or inescapable position. **7** (of a vehicle) turn a corner. **8** obtain a monopoly of.

cornerstone *noun* **1** indispensable part or basis. **2** stone at the corner of a wall.

cornet *noun* **1** brass instrument similar to the trumpet. **2** cone-shaped ice-cream wafer.

cornice [korn-iss] *noun* decorative moulding round the top of a wall.

Cornish *plural noun, adjective* (people) of Cornwall. **Cornish pasty** pastry case with a filling of meat and vegetables.

cornucopia [korn-yew-**kope**-ee-a] *noun* **1** great abundance. **2** symbol of plenty, consisting of a horn overflowing with fruit and flowers.

corolla *noun* petals of a flower collectively.

corollary [kor-**oll**-a-ree] *noun, pl* **-laries** idea, fact, or proposition which is the natural result

of something else.

corona [kor-**rone**-a] *noun, pl* **-nas, -nae** **1** ring of light round the moon or sun. **2** long cigar with blunt ends.

coronary [kor-ron-a-ree] *adjective* **1** of the arteries surrounding the heart. ◆ *noun, pl* **-naries** **2** coronary thrombosis. **coronary thrombosis** condition in which the flow of blood to the heart is blocked by a blood clot.

coronation *noun* ceremony of crowning a monarch.

coroner *noun* official responsible for the investigation of violent, sudden, or suspicious deaths.

coronet *noun* small crown.

corpora *noun* plural of CORPUS.

corporal[1] *noun* noncommissioned officer in an army.

corporal[2] *adjective* of the body. **corporal punishment** physical punishment, such as caning.

corporation **ⓘ** *noun* **1** large business or company. **2** city or town council. **3** *Informal* large paunch. **corporate** *adjective* **1** of business corporations. **2** shared by a group.

corporeal [kore-**pore**-ee-al] *adjective* physical or tangible.

corps **ⓘ** [kore] *noun, pl* **corps** **1** military unit with a specific function. **2** organized body of people.

corpse **ⓘ** *noun* dead body.

corpulent *adjective* fat or plump. **corpulence** *noun*

corpus *noun, pl* **corpora** collection of writings, esp. by a single author.

corpuscle *noun* red or white blood cell.

corral *US noun* **1** enclosure for cattle or horses. ◆ *verb* **-ralling, -ralled** **2** put in a corral.

correct **ⓘ** *adjective* **1** free from error, true. **2** in accordance with accepted standards. ◆ *verb* **3** put right. **4** indicate the errors in. **5** rebuke or punish. **6** make conform to a standard.

correctly *adverb* **correctness** *noun* **correction** *noun* **1** correcting. **2** alteration correcting something. **3** punishment. **corrective** *adjective* intended to put right something wrong.

———————— THESAURUS ————————

corner *noun* **1** = angle, bend, crook, joint **4** = space, hideaway, hide-out, nook, retreat ◆ *verb* **6** = trap, run to earth **8** *as in* **corner the market** = monopolize, dominate, engross, hog (*sl*)

corny *adjective Sl* = unoriginal, hackneyed, old-fashioned, old hat, stale, stereotyped, trite

corporation *noun* **1** = business, association, corporate body, society **2** = town council, civic

authorities, council, municipal authorities **3** *Inf* = paunch, beer belly (*inf*), middle-age spread (*inf*), potbelly, spare tyre (*Brit sl*), spread (*inf*)

corps *noun* **1** = team, band, company, detachment, division, regiment, squadron, troop, unit

corpse *noun* = body, cadaver, carcass, remains, stiff (*sl*)

correct *adjective* **1** = true, accurate, exact,

correlate *verb* place or be placed in a mutual relationship. **correlation** *noun*
correspond ❶ *verb* **1** be consistent or compatible (with). **2** be the same or similar. **3** communicate by letter. **corresponding** *adjective* **correspondingly** *adverb*
correspondence *noun* **1** communication by letters. **2** letters so exchanged. **3** relationship or similarity. **correspondence course** study conducted by post. **correspondent** *noun* **1** person employed by a newspaper etc. to report on a special subject or from a foreign country. **2** letter writer.
corridor ❶ *noun* **1** passage in a building or train. **2** strip of land or airspace providing access through foreign territory.
corrie *noun Scot* circular hollow on a hillside.
corrigendum [kor-rij-**end**-um] *noun, pl* **-da** error to be corrected.
corroborate ❶ *verb* support (a fact or opinion) by giving proof. **corroboration** *noun* **corroborative** *adjective*
corroboree *noun Aust* Aboriginal gathering or dance.

corrode ❶ *verb* **1** eat or be eaten away by chemical action or rust. **2** destroy gradually.
corrosion *noun* **corrosive** *adjective*
corrugate *verb* fold into alternate grooves and ridges. **corrugated** *adjective*
corrupt ❶ *adjective* **1** open to or involving bribery. **2** morally depraved. **3** (of a text or data) unreliable through errors or alterations. ◆ *verb* **4** make corrupt. **corruptly** *adverb* **corruption** *noun* **corruptible** *adjective*
corsage [kor-**sahzh**] *noun* small bouquet worn on the bodice of a dress.
corsair *noun* **1** pirate. **2** pirate ship.
corselet *noun* **1** one-piece undergarment combining a corset and bra. **2** piece of armour to cover the trunk.
corset ❶ *noun* women's close-fitting undergarment worn to shape the torso.
cortege [kor-**tayzh**] *noun* funeral procession.
cortex *noun, pl* **-tices** *Anat* outer layer of the brain or other internal organ. **cortical** *adjective*
cortisone *noun* steroid hormone used to treat various diseases.
corundum *noun* hard mineral used as an

——— THESAURUS ———

faultless, flawless, O.K. *or* okay (*inf*), precise, right OPPOSITE inaccurate. **2** = **proper**, acceptable, appropriate, fitting, kosher (*inf*), O.K. *or* okay (*inf*), seemly, standard OPPOSITE inappropriate ◆*verb* **3** = **rectify**, adjust, amend, cure, emend, redress, reform, remedy, right OPPOSITE damage. **5** = **punish**, admonish, chasten, chastise, chide, discipline, rebuke, reprimand, reprove, rouse on (*Aust*) OPPOSITE praise
correction *noun* **2** = **rectification**, adjustment, alteration, amendment, emendation, improvement, modification **3** = **punishment**, admonition, castigation, chastisement, discipline, reformation, reproof
correctly *adverb* = **rightly**, accurately, perfectly, precisely, properly, right
correctness *noun* **1** = **truth**, accuracy, exactitude, exactness, faultlessness, fidelity, preciseness, precision, regularity **2** = **decorum**, civility, good breeding, propriety, seemliness
correspond *verb* **1** = **be consistent**, accord, agree, conform, fit, harmonize, match, square, tally OPPOSITE differ. **3** = **communicate**, exchange letters, keep in touch, write
correspondence *noun* **1, 2** = **letters**, communication, mail, post, writing **3** = **relation**, agreement, coincidence, comparison, conformity, correlation, harmony, match, similarity
correspondent *noun* **1** = **reporter**,

contributor, journalist **2** = **letter writer**, pen friend *or* pal
corresponding *adjective* **1, 2** = **related**, analogous, answering, complementary, equivalent, matching, reciprocal, similar
corridor *noun* **1** = **passage**, aisle, alley, hallway, passageway
corroborate *verb* = **support**, authenticate, back up, bear out, confirm, endorse, ratify, substantiate, validate OPPOSITE contradict
corrode *verb* **1** = **eat away**, consume, corrupt, erode, gnaw, oxidize, rust, wear away
corrosive *adjective* **1** = **corroding**, caustic, consuming, erosive, virulent, vitriolic, wasting, wearing
corrupt *adjective* **1** = **dishonest**, bent (*sl*), bribable, crooked (*inf*), fraudulent, unprincipled, unscrupulous, venal OPPOSITE honest. **2** = **depraved**, debased, degenerate, dissolute, profligate, vicious OPPOSITE reform. **3** = **distorted**, altered, doctored, falsified ◆*verb* **4 a** = **bribe**, buy off, entice, fix (*inf*), grease (someone's) palm (*sl*), lure, suborn. **b** = **deprave**, debauch, pervert, subvert OPPOSITE reform
corruption *noun* **1** = **dishonesty**, bribery, extortion, fraud, shady dealings (*inf*), unscrupulousness, venality **2** = **depravity**, decadence, evil, immorality, perversion, vice, wickedness **3** = **distortion**, doctoring, falsification

abrasive.

coruscate *verb Formal* sparkle. **coruscation** *noun*

corvette *noun* lightly armed escort warship.

cos¹, **cos lettuce** *noun* long crisp-leaved lettuce.

cos² *Maths* cosine.

cosh *noun* **1** heavy blunt weapon. ◆ *verb* **2** hit with a cosh.

cosine [koh-sine] *noun* (in trigonometry) ratio of the length of the adjacent side to that of the hypotenuse in a right-angled triangle.

cosmetic ❶ *noun* **1** preparation used to improve the appearance of a person's skin. ◆ *adjective* **2** improving the appearance only.

cosmic ❶ *adjective* of the whole universe. **cosmic rays** electromagnetic radiation from outer space.

cosmonaut *noun* Russian name for an astronaut.

cosmopolitan ❶ *adjective* **1** composed of people or elements from many countries. **2** having lived and travelled in many countries. ◆ *noun* **3** cosmopolitan person. **cosmopolitanism** *noun*

cosmos *noun* the universe. **cosmogony** *noun* study of the origin of the universe. **cosmology** *noun* study of the origin and nature of the universe. **cosmological** *adjective*

Cossack *noun* member of a S Russian people famous as horsemen and dancers.

cosset *verb* **cosseting, cosseted** pamper.

cost ❶ *noun* **1** amount of money, time, labour, etc., required for something. ◆ *plural* **2** expenses of a lawsuit. ◆ *verb* **costing, cost 3** have as its cost. **4** involve the loss or sacrifice of. **5** *past* **costed** estimate the cost of. **costly** *adjective* **-lier, -liest 1** expensive. **2** involving great loss or sacrifice. **costliness** *noun* **cost of living** average cost of the basic necessities of life.

costal *adjective* of the ribs.

costermonger *noun* person who sells fruit and vegetables from a street barrow.

costive *adjective Old-fashioned* having or causing constipation.

costume ❶ *noun* **1** style of dress of a particular place or time, or for a particular activity. **2** clothes worn by an actor or performer. **costumier** *noun* maker or seller of costumes. **costume jewellery** inexpensive artificial jewellery.

cosy ❶ *adjective* **-sier, -siest 1** warm and snug. **2** intimate, friendly. ◆ *noun* **3** cover for keeping things warm, e.g. *a tea cosy*. **cosily** *adverb* **cosiness** *noun*

cot¹ *noun* **1** baby's bed with high sides. **2** small portable bed. **cot death** unexplained death of a baby while asleep.

cot² *noun* **1** *Lit* small cottage. **2** cote.

cote *noun* shelter for birds or animals.

coterie [kote-er-ee] *noun* exclusive group, clique.

cotoneaster [kot-tone-ee-**ass**-ter] *noun* garden shrub with red berries.

cottage ❶ *noun* small house in the country. **cottager** *noun* **cottage cheese** soft mild white cheese. **cottage industry** craft industry in which employees work at home. **cottage pie** dish of minced meat topped with mashed potato.

cotter *noun* pin or wedge used to secure machine parts.

cotton *noun* **1** white downy fibre covering the seeds of a tropical plant. **2** cloth or thread made from this. **cottony** *adjective* **cotton on (to)** *verb Informal* understand. **cotton wool** fluffy cotton used for surgical dressings etc.

cotyledon [kot-ill-**ee**-don] *noun* first leaf of a plant embryo.

couch *noun* **1** piece of upholstered furniture for seating more than one person. ◆ *verb* **2** express in a particular way. **couch potato** *Slang* lazy person whose only hobby is

———————————— THESAURUS ————————————

corset *noun* **1** = **girdle**, belt, bodice

cosmetic *adjective* **2** = **beautifying**, nonessential, superficial, surface

cosmic *adjective* = **universal**, stellar

cosmopolitan *adjective* **2** = **sophisticated**, broad-minded, catholic, open-minded, universal, urbane, well-travelled, worldly-wise OPPOSITE unsophisticated ◆ *noun* **3** = **man or woman of the world**, jet-setter, sophisticate

cost *noun* **1** = **price**, amount, charge, damage (*inf*), expense, outlay, payment, worth ◆ *verb* **3** = **sell at**, come to, command a price of, set (someone) back (*inf*) **4** = **lose**, do disservice to,

harm, hurt, injure

costly *adjective* **1** = **expensive**, dear, exorbitant, extortionate, highly-priced, steep (*inf*), stiff OPPOSITE inexpensive. **2** = **damaging**, catastrophic, deleterious, disastrous, harmful, loss-making, ruinous

costume *noun* **1** = **outfit**, apparel, attire, clothing, dress, ensemble, garb, livery, uniform

cosy *adjective* **1** = **snug**, comfortable, comfy (*inf*), homely, sheltered, tucked up, warm **2** = **intimate**, friendly

cottage *noun* = **cabin**, chalet, hut, lodge, shack

C

watching television.

couchette [koo-**shett**] *noun* bed converted from seats on a train or ship.

couch grass *noun* quickly spreading grassy weed.

cougar [**koo**-gar] *noun* puma.

cough ❶ *verb* 1 expel air from the lungs abruptly and noisily. ◆ *noun* 2 act or sound of coughing. 3 illness which causes coughing.

cough up *verb Informal* hand over or pay (money).

could *verb* past tense of CAN¹.

couldn't could not.

coulomb [**koo**-lom] *noun* SI unit of electric charge.

coulter [**kole**-ter] *noun* blade at the front of a ploughshare.

council ❶ *noun* 1 group meeting for discussion or consultation. 2 local governing body of a town or region. ◆ *adjective* 3 of or by a council. **councillor** *noun* member of a council. **council tax** tax based on the value of property, to fund local services.

counsel ❶ *noun* 1 advice or guidance. 2 discussion or consultation. 3 barrister or barristers. ◆ *verb* **-selling, -selled** 4 give guidance to. 5 urge, recommend. **counsellor** *noun*

count¹ ❶ *verb* 1 say numbers in order. 2 find the total of. 3 be important. 4 regard as. 5 take into account. ◆ *noun* 6 counting. 7 number reached by counting. 8 *Law* one of a number of charges. **countless** *adjective* too many to count. **count on** *verb* rely or depend on. **count out** *verb* 1 exclude. 2 declare (a boxer) defeated when he has not risen from the floor

within ten seconds.

count² *noun* European nobleman.

countdown *noun* counting backwards to zero of the seconds before an event.

countenance *noun* 1 (expression of) the face. ◆ *verb* 2 allow or tolerate.

counter¹ *noun* 1 long flat surface in a bank or shop, on which business is transacted. 2 small flat disc used in board games.

counter² ❶ *verb* 1 oppose, retaliate against. ◆ *adverb* 2 in the opposite direction. 3 in direct contrast. ◆ *noun* 4 opposing or retaliatory action.

counter³ *noun* apparatus for counting things.

counter- *prefix* 1 opposite, against, e.g. *counterattack*. 2 complementary, corresponding, e.g. *counterpart*.

counteract ❶ *verb* act against or neutralize.

counteraction *noun*

counterattack *noun, verb* attack in response to an attack.

counterbalance ❶ *noun* 1 weight or force balancing or neutralizing another. ◆ *verb* 2 act as a counterbalance to.

counterblast *noun* aggressive response to a verbal attack.

counterclockwise *adverb, adjective US* anticlockwise.

counterespionage *noun* activities to counteract enemy espionage.

counterfeit ❶ *adjective* 1 fake, forged. ◆ *noun* 2 fake, forgery. ◆ *verb* 3 fake, forge.

counterfoil *noun* part of a cheque or receipt kept as a record.

counterintelligence *noun* activities designed to frustrate enemy espionage.

——————— T H E S A U R U S ———————

cough *verb* 1 = **clear one's throat**, bark, hack ◆*noun* 2 = **frog** *or* **tickle in one's throat**, bark, hack

council *noun* 1, 2 = **governing body**, assembly, board, cabinet, committee, conference, congress, convention, panel, parliament

counsel *noun* 1 = **advice**, direction, guidance, information, recommendation, suggestion, warning 3 = **legal adviser**, advocate, attorney, barrister, lawyer, solicitor ◆*verb* 4 = **advise**, instruct, warn 5 = **urge**, advocate, exhort, recommend

count¹ *verb* 1 = **enumerate** 2 = **add (up)**, calculate, compute, number, reckon, tally, tot up 3 = **matter**, be important, carry weight, rate, signify, tell, weigh 4 = **consider**, deem, judge, look upon, rate, regard, think 5 = **take into account** *or* **consideration**, include,

number among ◆*noun* 6 = **calculation**, computation, enumeration, numbering, poll 7 = **sum**, reckoning, tally

counter² *verb* 1 = **retaliate**, answer, hit back, meet, oppose, parry, resist, respond, ward off OPPOSITE **yield** ◆*adverb* 3 = **opposite to**, against, at variance with, contrariwise, conversely, in defiance of, versus OPPOSITE **similar**

counteract *verb* = **act against**, foil, frustrate, negate, neutralize, offset, resist, thwart

counterbalance *verb* 2 = **offset**, balance, compensate, make up for, set off

counterfeit *adjective* 1 = **fake**, bogus, false, forged, imitation, phoney *or* phony (*inf*), sham, simulated OPPOSITE **real** ◆*noun* 2 = **fake**, copy, forgery, fraud, imitation, phoney *or* phony (*inf*), reproduction, sham OPPOSITE **the real thing** ◆*verb* 3 = **fake**, copy, fabricate, feign, forge,

C

countermand ⊕ *verb* cancel (a previous order).

counterpane *noun* bed covering.

counterpart ⊕ *noun* person or thing complementary to or corresponding to another.

counterpoint *noun Music* **1** technique of combining melodies. **2** part or melody so combined.

counterpoise *noun, verb* counterbalance.

counterproductive *adjective* having an effect opposite to the one intended.

countersign *verb* sign (a document already signed by someone) as confirmation.

countersink *verb* drive (a screw) into a shaped hole so that its head is below the surface.

countertenor *noun* male alto.

countess *noun* **1** woman holding the rank of count or earl. **2** wife or widow of a count or earl.

country ⊕ *noun, pl* **-tries 1** nation. **2** nation's territory. **3** nation's people. **4** part of the land away from cities. **5** person's native land.

countrified *adjective* rustic in manner or appearance. **country and western, country music** popular music based on American White folk music. **country dancing** British folk dancing in rows or circles. **countryman, countrywoman** *noun* **1** person from one's native land. **2** person who lives in the country.

countryside *noun* land away from cities.

county ⊕ *noun, pl* **-ties 1** division of a country. ♦ *adjective* **2** *Informal* upper-class.

coup ⊕ [koo] *noun* **1** successful action. **2** coup d'état.

coup de grâce [koo de **grahss**] *noun* final or decisive action.

coup d'état [koo day-**tah**] *noun* sudden violent overthrow of a government.

coupé [**koo**-pay] *noun* sports car with two doors and a sloping fixed roof.

couple ⊕ *noun* **1** two people who are married or romantically involved. **2** two partners in a dance or game. ♦ *verb* **3** connect, associate. **4** *Lit* have sexual intercourse. **a couple 1** a pair. **2** *Informal* a few. **couplet** *noun* two consecutive lines of verse, usu. rhyming and of the same metre. **coupling** *noun* device for connecting things, such as railway carriages.

coupon ⊕ *noun* **1** piece of paper entitling the holder to a discount or gift. **2** detachable order form. **3** football pools entry form.

courage ⊕ *noun* ability to face danger or pain without fear. **courageous** *adjective* **courageously** *adverb*

courgette *noun* type of small vegetable marrow.

courier ⊕ *noun* **1** person employed to look after holiday-makers. **2** person employed to deliver urgent messages.

course ⊕ *noun* **1** series of lessons or medical treatment. **2** onward movement in space or time. **3** route or direction taken. **4** area where golf is played or a race is run. **5** any of the successive parts of a meal. **6** continuous layer of masonry at one level in a building. **7** mode of conduct or action. **8** natural development of events. ♦ *verb* **9** (of liquid) run swiftly. **10** hunt with hounds that follow the quarry by sight and not scent. **of course** as expected, naturally.

courser *noun Lit* swift horse.

court ⊕ *noun* **1** body which decides legal

———————————— THESAURUS ————————————

imitate, impersonate, pretend, sham, simulate

countermand *verb* =**cancel**, annul, override, repeal, rescind, retract, reverse, revoke

counterpart *noun* =**opposite number**, complement, equal, fellow, match, mate, supplement, tally, twin

countless *adjective* =**innumerable**, endless, immeasurable, incalculable, infinite, legion, limitless, myriad, numberless, untold OPPOSITE limited

count on *verb* =**depend on**, bank on, believe (in), lean on, pin one's faith on, reckon on, rely on, take for granted, take on trust, trust

country *noun* **1** =**nation**, commonwealth, kingdom, people, realm, state **2** =**territory**, land, region, terrain **3** =**people**, citizens, community, inhabitants, nation, populace, public, society **4** =**countryside**, backwoods, farmland, green belt, outback (*Aust & NZ*),

provinces, sticks (*inf*) OPPOSITE town

countryside *noun* =**country**, farmland, green belt, outback (*Aust & NZ*), outdoors, sticks (*inf*)

county *noun* =**province**, shire

coup *noun* **1** =**masterstroke**, accomplishment, action, deed, exploit, feat, manoeuvre, stunt

couple *noun* **1** =**pair**, two, twosome ♦*verb* **3** =**link**, connect, hitch, join, marry, pair, unite, wed, yoke

coupon *noun* **1** =**slip**, card, certificate, ticket, token, voucher

courage *noun* =**bravery**, daring, fearlessness, gallantry, heroism, mettle, nerve, pluck, resolution, valour OPPOSITE cowardice

courageous *adjective* =**brave**, bold, daring, fearless, gallant, gritty, intrepid, lion-hearted, stouthearted, valiant OPPOSITE cowardly

courier *noun* **1** =**guide**, representative **2** =**messenger**, bearer, carrier, envoy, runner

C

cases. **2** place where it meets. **3** marked area for playing a racket game. **4** courtyard. **5** residence, household, or retinue of a sovereign. ◆ *verb* **6** *Old-fashioned* try to gain the love of. **7** try to win the favour of. **8** invite, e.g. *to court disaster*. **courtier** *noun* attendant at a royal court. **courtly** *adjective* **-lier, -liest** ceremoniously polite. **courtliness** *noun* **courtship** *noun* courting of an intended spouse or mate. **court martial** *noun, pl* **courts martial** court for trying naval or military offences. **court shoe** woman's low-cut shoe without straps or laces. **courtyard** *noun* paved space enclosed by buildings or walls.

courtesan [kor-tiz-**zan**] *noun* Hist mistress or high-class prostitute.

courtesy ⊙ *noun* **1** politeness, good manners. **2** *pl* **-sies** courteous act. **(by) courtesy of** by permission of. **courteous** *adjective* polite. **courteously** *adverb*

cousin *noun* child of one's uncle or aunt.

couture [koo-**toor**] *noun* high-fashion designing and dressmaking. **couturier** *noun* person who designs women's fashion clothes.

cove ⊙ *noun* small bay or inlet.

coven [**kuv**-ven] *noun* meeting of witches.

covenant ⊙ [**kuv**-ven-ant] *noun* **1** formal agreement to make an annual (charitable) payment. ◆ *verb* **2** agree by a covenant.

Coventry *noun* **send someone to Coventry** punish someone by refusing to speak to them.

cover ⊙ *verb* **1** place something over, to protect or conceal. **2** extend over or lie on the surface of. **3** travel over. **4** keep a gun aimed at. **5** insure against loss or risk. **6** include. **7** report (an event) for a newspaper. **8** be enough to pay for. ◆ *noun* **9** anything that covers. **10** outside of a book or magazine. **11** pretext or disguise. **12** individual table setting. **13** insurance. **14** shelter or protection. **coverage** *noun* amount or extent covered. **coverlet** *noun* bed cover. **cover charge** fixed service charge in a restaurant.

covert *adjective* **1** concealed, secret. ◆ *noun* **2** thicket giving shelter to game birds or animals. **covertly** *adverb*

covet ⊙ *verb* **coveting, coveted** long to possess (what belongs to someone else). **covetous** *adjective* **covetousness** *noun*

covey [**kuv**-vee] *noun* small flock of grouse or

———— THESAURUS ————

course *noun* **1** = **classes**, curriculum, lectures, programme, schedule **2** = **progression**, development, flow, movement, order, progress, sequence, unfolding **3** = **route**, direction, line, passage, path, road, track, trajectory, way **4** = **racecourse**, cinder track, circuit **7** = **procedure**, behaviour, conduct, manner, method, mode, plan, policy, programme **8** = **period**, duration, lapse, passage, passing, sweep, term, time ◆*verb* **9** = **run**, flow, gush, race, speed, stream, surge **10** = **hunt**, chase, follow, pursue **of course** = **naturally**, certainly, definitely, indubitably, needless to say, obviously, undoubtedly, without a doubt

court *noun* **1** = **law court**, bar, bench, tribunal **4** = **courtyard**, cloister, piazza, plaza, quad (*inf*), quadrangle, square, yard **5 a** = **palace**, hall, manor, royal household **b** = **retinue**, attendants, cortege, entourage, suite, train ◆*verb* **6** *Old-fashioned* = **woo**, date, go (out) with, run after, serenade, set one's cap at, take out, walk out with **7** = **cultivate**, curry favour with, fawn upon, flatter, pander to, seek, solicit **8** = **invite**, attract, bring about, incite, prompt, provoke, seek

courteous *adjective* = **polite**, affable, attentive, civil, gallant, gracious, refined, respectful, urbane, well-mannered [OPPOSITE] **discourteous**

courtesy *noun* **1** = **politeness**, affability,

civility, courteousness, gallantry, good manners, graciousness, urbanity **2** = **favour**, indulgence, kindness

courtier *noun* = **attendant**, follower, squire

courtly *adjective* = **ceremonious**, chivalrous, dignified, elegant, formal, gallant, polished, refined, stately, urbane

courtyard *noun* = **yard**, enclosure, quad, quadrangle

cove *noun* = **bay**, anchorage, inlet, sound

covenant *noun* **1** = **promise**, agreement, arrangement, commitment, contract, pact, pledge ◆*verb* **2** = **promise**, agree, contract, pledge, stipulate, undertake

cover *verb* **1** = **envelop**, cloak, coat, conceal, encase, enshroud, hide, mask, obscure, overlay, put on, shroud, veil, wrap [OPPOSITE] **reveal**. **2** = **submerge**, engulf, flood, overrun, wash over **3** = **travel over**, cross, pass through *or* over, traverse **7** = **report**, describe, investigate, narrate, relate, tell of, write up ◆*noun* **9** = **covering**, canopy, case, coating, envelope, jacket, lid, top, wrapper **11** = **disguise**, camouflage, concealment, facade, front, mask, pretext, screen, smoke screen, veil **13** = **insurance**, compensation, indemnity, protection, reimbursement **14** = **protection**, defence, guard, shelter, shield

covet *verb* = **long for**, aspire to, crave, desire, envy, lust after, set one's heart on, yearn for partridge.

cow[1] ❶ *noun* **1** mature female of cattle and of certain other mammals, such as the elephant or seal. **2** *Informal offens* a disagreeable woman.

cowboy *noun* **1** (in the US) ranch worker who herds and tends cattle, usu. on horseback. **2** *Informal* irresponsible or unscrupulous worker.

cowpat *noun* pool of cow dung. **cowpox** *noun* disease of cows, the virus of which is used in the smallpox vaccine.

cow[2] *verb* intimidate, subdue.

coward ❶ *noun* person who lacks courage. **cowardly** *adjective* **cowardice** *noun* lack of courage.

cower ❶ *verb* cringe in fear.

cowl *noun* **1** loose hood. **2** monk's hooded robe. **3** cover on a chimney to increase ventilation.

cowling *noun* cover on an engine.

cowrie *noun* brightly-marked sea shell.

cowslip *noun* small yellow wild flower.

cox *noun* **1** coxswain. ◆ *verb* **2** act as cox of (a boat).

coxcomb *noun* **1** comb of a domestic cock. **2** *Informal* conceited dandy.

coxswain [**kok**-sn] *noun* person who steers a rowing boat.

coy ❶ *adjective* affectedly shy or modest. **coyly** *adverb* **coyness** *noun*

coyote [koy-**ote**-ee] *noun* prairie wolf of N America.

coypu *noun* beaver-like aquatic rodent, bred for its fur.

cozen *verb Lit* cheat, trick.

CPU *Computers* central processing unit.

Cr *Chem* chromium.

crab *noun* **1** edible shellfish with ten legs, the first pair modified into pincers. **2** crab louse.

crab louse parasitic louse living in the pubic area of humans.

crab apple *noun* small sour apple.

crabbed *adjective* **1** (of handwriting) hard to read. **2** (also **crabby**) bad-tempered.

crack ❶ *verb* **1** break or split partially. **2** break with a sharp noise. **3** (cause to) make a sharp noise. **4** (of the voice) become harsh or change pitch suddenly. **5** break down or yield under strain. **6** hit suddenly. **7** force (a safe) open. **8** solve (a code or problem). **9** tell (a joke). ◆ *noun* **10** sudden sharp noise. **11** narrow gap. **12** sharp blow. **13** *Informal* gibe, joke. **14** *Slang* highly addictive form of cocaine. ◆ *adjective* **15** *Informal* first-rate, excellent, e.g. *a crack shot*.

cracking *adjective* **1** very fast, e.g. *a cracking pace*. **2** very good. **crackdown** *noun* severe disciplinary measures. **crack down on** *verb* take severe measures against. **crack up** *verb Informal* have a physical or mental breakdown.

cracker *noun* **1** thin dry biscuit. **2** decorated cardboard tube, pulled apart with a bang, containing a paper hat and a joke or toy. **3** small explosive firework. **4** *Slang* an outstanding thing or person.

crackers *adjective Slang* insane.

crackle *verb* **1** make small sharp popping noises. ◆ *noun* **2** crackling sound. **crackling** *noun* **1** crackle. **2** crisp skin of roast pork.

crackpot *noun, adjective Informal* eccentric (person).

cradle ❶ *noun* **1** baby's bed on rockers. **2** place where something originates. **3** supporting structure. ◆ *verb* **4** hold gently as if in a cradle.

—————— THESAURUS ——————

covetous *adjective* =**envious**, acquisitive, avaricious, close-fisted, grasping, greedy, jealous, rapacious, yearning

coward *noun* =**wimp** (*inf*), chicken (*sl*), scaredy-cat (*inf*), yellow-belly (*sl*)

cowardice *noun* =**faint-heartedness**, fearfulness, spinelessness, weakness

cowardly *adjective* =**faint-hearted**, chicken (*sl*), craven, fearful, scared, soft, spineless, timorous, weak, yellow (*inf*) OPPOSITE **brave**

cowboy *noun* **1** =**rancher**, cattleman, drover, gaucho (*S Amer*), herdsman, stockman

cower *verb* =**cringe**, draw back, flinch, grovel, quail, shrink, tremble

coy *adjective* =**shy**, bashful, demure, modest, reserved, retiring, shrinking, timid OPPOSITE **bold**

crack *verb* **1** =**break**, burst, cleave, fracture, snap, splinter, split **2, 3** =**snap**, burst, crash,

detonate, explode, pop **5** =**give in**, break down, collapse, give way, go to pieces, lose control, succumb, yield **6** =**hit**, clip (*inf*), clout (*inf*), cuff, slap, smack, whack **8** =**solve**, decipher, fathom, get the answer to, work out ◆*noun* **10** =**snap**, burst, clap, crash, explosion, pop, report **11** =**break**, chink, cleft, cranny, crevice, fissure, fracture, gap, rift **12** =**blow**, clip (*inf*), clout (*inf*), cuff, slap, smack, whack **13** *Inf* =**joke**, dig, funny remark, gag (*inf*), jibe, quip, wisecrack, witticism ◆*adjective* **15** *Inf* =**first-class**, ace, choice, elite, excellent, first-rate, hand-picked, superior, world-class

crackdown *noun* =**suppression**, clampdown, crushing, repression

cracked *adjective* =**broken**, chipped, damaged, defective, faulty, flawed, imperfect, split

cradle *noun* **1** =**crib**, bassinet, cot, Moses

craft ⊕ *noun* **1** occupation requiring skill with the hands. **2** skill or ability. **3** *pl* **craft** boat, ship, aircraft, or spaceship. ◆ *verb* **4** make skilfully. **crafty** *adjective* **craftier, craftiest** skilled in deception. **craftily** *adverb* **craftiness** *noun* **craftsman, craftswoman** *noun* skilled worker. **craftsmanship** *noun*

crag ⊕ *noun* steep rugged rock. **craggy** *adjective*

cram ⊕ *verb* **cramming, crammed 1** force into too small a space. **2** fill too full. **3** study hard just before an examination.

cramp¹ ⊕ *noun* **1** painful muscular contraction. **2** clamp for holding masonry or timber together. ◆ *verb* **3** affect with a cramp.

cramp² ⊕ *verb* confine, restrict. **cramped** *adjective* **1** closed in. **2** (of handwriting) small and irregular.

crampon *noun* spiked plate strapped to a boot for climbing on ice.

cranberry *noun* sour edible red berry.

crane *noun* **1** machine for lifting and moving heavy weights. **2** large wading bird with a long neck and legs. ◆ *verb* **3** stretch (one's neck) to see something.

crane fly *noun* long-legged insect with slender wings.

cranesbill *noun* plant with pink or purple flowers.

cranium *noun, pl* **-niums, -nia 1** skull. **2** part of the skull enclosing the brain. **cranial** *adjective*

crank *noun* **1** arm projecting at right angles

from a shaft, for transmitting or converting motion. **2** *Informal* eccentric person. ◆ *verb* **3** turn with a crank. **4** start (an engine) with a crank. **cranky** *adjective* **crankier, crankiest** *Informal* **1** eccentric. **2** bad-tempered.

crankshaft *noun* shaft driven by a crank.

cranny ⊕ *noun, pl* **-nies** narrow opening.

crap *Slang noun* **1** rubbish, nonsense. **2** *Taboo* faeces. ◆ *verb* **crapping, crapped 3** *Taboo* defecate. **crappy** *adjective*

crape *noun* same as CREPE.

craps *noun* gambling game played with two dice.

crash ⊕ *noun* **1** collision involving a vehicle or vehicles. **2** sudden loud smashing noise. **3** financial collapse. ◆ *verb* **4** (cause to) collide violently with a vehicle, a stationary object, or the ground. **5** (cause to) make a loud smashing noise. **6** (cause to) fall with a crash. **7** collapse or fail financially. **8** *Informal* gate-crash. **crash barrier** safety barrier along a road or racetrack.

crash course short, very intensive course in a particular subject. **crash helmet** protective helmet worn by a motorcyclist. **crash-land** *verb* (of an aircraft) land in an emergency, causing damage. **crash-landing** *noun*

crass ⊕ *adjective* stupid and insensitive. **crassly** *adverb* **crassness** *noun*

crate ⊕ *noun* **1** large wooden container for packing goods. ◆ *verb* **2** put in a crate.

crater ⊕ *noun* **1** very large hole in the ground or in the surface of the moon. **2** mouth of a

——————— T H E S A U R U S ———————

basket **2** = **birthplace**, beginning, fount, fountainhead, origin, source, spring, wellspring ◆*verb* **4** = **hold**, lull, nestle, nurse, rock, support
craft *noun* **1** = **occupation**, business, employment, handicraft, pursuit, trade, vocation, work, yakka (*Aust & NZ inf*) **2** = **skill**, ability, aptitude, art, artistry, expertise, ingenuity, know-how (*inf*), technique, workmanship **3** = **vessel**, aircraft, boat, plane, ship, spacecraft
craftsman *noun* = **skilled worker**, artisan, maker, master, smith, technician, wright
craftsmanship *noun* = **workmanship**, artistry, expertise, mastery, technique
crafty *adjective* = **cunning**, artful, calculating, devious, sharp, shrewd, sly, subtle, wily
OPPOSITE> **open**
crag *noun* = **rock**, bluff, peak, pinnacle, tor
cram *verb* **1** = **stuff**, compress, force, jam, pack in, press, shove, squeeze **3** = **study**, bone up (*inf*), mug up (*sl*), revise, swot
cramp¹ *noun* **1** = **spasm**, ache, contraction, convulsion, pain, pang, stitch, twinge

cramp² *verb* = **restrict**, constrain, hamper, handicap, hinder, impede, inhibit, obstruct
cramped *adjective* **1** = **closed in**, confined, congested, crowded, hemmed in, overcrowded, packed, uncomfortable OPPOSITE> **spacious**
cranny *noun* = **crevice**, chink, cleft, crack, fissure, gap, hole, opening
crash *noun* **1** = **collision**, accident, bump, pile-up (*inf*), prang (*inf*), smash, wreck **2** = **smash**, bang, boom, clang, clash, clatter, din, racket, thunder **3** = **collapse**, debacle, depression, downfall, failure, ruin ◆*verb* **4** = **collide**, bump (into), crash-land (*an aircraft*), drive into, have an accident, hit, plough into, wreck **6** = **hurtle**, fall headlong, give way, lurch, overbalance, plunge, topple **7** = **collapse**, be ruined, fail, fold, fold up, go belly up (*inf*), go bust (*inf*), go to the wall, go under
crass *adjective* = **insensitive**, boorish, gross, indelicate, oafish, stupid, unrefined, witless
OPPOSITE> **sensitive**
crate *noun* **1** = **container**, box, case, packing case, tea chest

volcano.

cravat noun man's scarf worn like a tie.

crave ⊕ verb **1** desire intensely. **2** beg or plead for. **craving** noun

craven adjective cowardly.

craw noun **stick in one's craw** Informal be difficult for one to accept.

crawfish noun same as CRAYFISH.

crawl ⊕ verb **1** move on one's hands and knees. **2** move very slowly. **3** (foll. by to) flatter in order to gain some advantage. **4** feel as if covered with crawling creatures. ◆ noun **5** crawling motion or pace. **6** overarm swimming stroke. **crawler** noun

crayfish noun **1** edible freshwater shellfish like a lobster. **2** any similar shellfish, e.g. the spiny lobster.

crayon verb, noun (draw or colour with) a stick or pencil of coloured wax or clay.

craze ⊕ noun short-lived fashion or enthusiasm. **crazed** adjective **1** wild and uncontrolled. **2** (of porcelain) having fine cracks. **crazy** adjective **crazier, craziest 1** ridiculous. **2** (foll. by about) very fond (of). **3** insane. **craziness** noun **crazy paving** paving made of irregularly shaped slabs of stone.

creak ⊕ verb, noun (make) a harsh squeaking

sound. **creaky** adjective **creakier, creakiest**

cream ⊕ noun **1** fatty part of milk. **2** food or cosmetic resembling cream in consistency. **3** best part (of something). ◆ adjective **4** yellowish-white. ◆ verb **5** beat to a creamy consistency. **6** remove the cream from. **creamer** noun powdered milk substitute for use in coffee. **creamery** noun, pl **-eries** place where dairy products are made or sold. **creamy** adjective **creamier, creamiest. cream cheese** rich soft white cheese. **cream off** verb take the best part from. **cream of tartar** purified tartar used in baking powder.

crease ⊕ noun **1** line made by folding or pressing. **2** wrinkle or furrow. **3** Cricket line marking the bowler's and batsman's positions. ◆ verb **4** crush or line.

create ⊕ verb **1** make, cause to exist. **2** appoint to a new rank or position. **3** Slang make an angry fuss. **creation** noun **creative** adjective **1** imaginative or inventive. ◆ noun **2** person who is creative professionally. **creativity** noun **creator** noun **1** person who creates. **2** (C-) God.

creature ⊕ noun **1** animal, person, or other being. **2** person controlled by another.

crèche noun place where small children are

——————————— THESAURUS ———————————

crater noun **1** = **hollow**, depression, dip

crave verb **1** = **long for**, desire, hanker after, hope for, lust after, want, yearn for **2** = **beg**, ask, beseech, entreat, implore, petition, plead for, pray for, seek, solicit, supplicate

craving noun **1** = **longing**, appetite, desire, hankering, hope, hunger, thirst, yearning, yen (inf)

crawl verb **1, 2** = **creep**, advance slowly, inch, slither, worm one's way, wriggle, writhe OPPOSITE **run. 3** (foll. by to) = **grovel**, creep, fawn, humble oneself, toady **4** = **be full of**, be alive, be overrun (sl), swarm, teem

craze noun = **fad**, enthusiasm, fashion, infatuation, mania, rage, trend, vogue

crazy adjective **1** = **ridiculous**, absurd, foolish, idiotic, ill-conceived, ludicrous, nonsensical, preposterous, senseless OPPOSITE **sensible. 2** (foll. by about) = **fanatical**, devoted, enthusiastic, infatuated, mad, passionate, wild (inf) OPPOSITE **uninterested. 3** = **insane**, crazed, demented, deranged, mad, nuts (sl), out of one's mind, unbalanced OPPOSITE **sane**

creak verb, noun = **squeak**, grate, grind, groan, scrape, scratch, screech

cream noun **2** = **lotion**, cosmetic, emulsion, essence, liniment, oil, ointment, paste, salve, unguent **3** = **best**, elite, flower, pick, prime

◆adjective **4** = **off-white**, yellowish-white

creamy adjective **1** = **milky**, buttery **2** = **smooth**, rich, soft, velvety

crease noun **1, 2** = **line**, corrugation, fold, groove, ridge, wrinkle ◆verb **4** = **wrinkle**, corrugate, crumple, double up, fold, rumple, screw up

create verb **1** = **make**, bring about, cause, compose, devise, formulate, invent, lead to, occasion, originate, produce, spawn OPPOSITE **destroy. 2** = **appoint**, constitute, establish, install, invest, make, set up

creation noun **a** = **making**, conception, development, establishment, formation, foundation, generation, genesis, inception, institution, procreation, production, setting up **b** = **invention**, achievement, brainchild (inf), concoction, handiwork, magnum opus, pièce de résistance

creative adjective = **imaginative**, artistic, clever, gifted, ingenious, inspired, inventive, original, visionary

creativity noun = **imagination**, cleverness, ingenuity, inspiration, inventiveness, originality

creator noun **1** = **maker**, architect, author, designer, father, inventor, originator, prime mover

creature noun **1** = **living thing**, animal, beast,

C

looked after while their parents are working, shopping, etc.

credence [kreed-enss] *noun* belief in the truth or accuracy of a statement.

credentials ❶ *plural noun* document giving evidence of a person's identity or qualifications.

credible ❶ *adjective* **1** believable. **2** trustworthy. **credibly** *adverb* **credibility** *noun*

credit ❶ *noun* **1** system of allowing customers to receive goods and pay later. **2** reputation for trustworthiness in paying debts. **3** money at one's disposal in a bank account. **4** side of an account book on which such sums are entered. **5** (source or cause of) praise or approval. **6** influence or reputation based on the good opinion of others. **7** belief or trust. ◆ *plural* **8** list of people responsible for the production of a film, programme, or record. ◆ *verb* **crediting, credited 9** enter as a credit in an account. **10** (foll. by *with*) attribute (to). **11** believe.

creditable *adjective* praiseworthy. **creditably** *adverb* **creditor** *noun* person to whom money is owed. **credit card** card allowing a person to buy on credit.

credo *noun, pl* **-dos** creed.

credulous ❶ *adjective* too willing to believe. **credulity** *noun*

creed ❶ *noun* statement or system of (Christian) beliefs or principles.

creek ❶ *noun* **1** narrow inlet or bay. **2** *Aust, NZ, US & Canad* small stream.

creel *noun* wicker basket used by anglers.

creep ❶ *verb* **creeping, crept 1** move quietly and cautiously. **2** crawl with the body near to the ground. **3** have a crawling sensation on the skin, from fear or disgust. **4** (of a plant) grow along the ground or over rocks. ◆ *noun* **5** creeping movement. **6** *Slang* obnoxious or servile person. **give one the creeps** *Informal* make one feel fear or disgust. **creeper** *noun* creeping plant. **creepy** *adjective* **creepier, creepiest** *Informal* causing a feeling of fear or disgust. **creepy-crawly** *noun, pl* **-crawlies** *Informal* insect, viewed with fear or disgust.

cremate *verb* burn (a corpse) to ash. **cremation** *noun* **crematorium** *noun* building where corpses are cremated.

crème de menthe *noun* peppermint-flavoured liqueur.

crenellated *adjective* having battlements.

creole *noun* **1** language developed from a mixture of languages. **2** (**C**-) native-born W Indian or Latin American of mixed European and African descent.

creosote *noun* **1** dark oily liquid made from coal tar and used for preserving wood. ◆ *verb* **2** treat with creosote.

crepe [krayp] *noun* **1** fabric or rubber with a crinkled texture. **2** very thin pancake. **crepe paper** *paper with a crinkled texture*

crept *verb* past of CREEP.

crepuscular *adjective* *Lit* of or like twilight.

Cres. Crescent.

crescendo [krish-end-oh] *noun, pl* **-dos 1**

———— THESAURUS ————

being, brute, human being, individual, man, mortal, person, soul, woman

credentials *plural noun* = **certification**, authorization, document, licence, papers, passport, reference(s), testimonial

credibility *noun* = **believability**, integrity, plausibility, reliability, trustworthiness

credible *adjective* **1** = **believable**, conceivable, imaginable, likely, plausible, possible, probable, reasonable, thinkable OPPOSITE **unlikely. 2** = **reliable**, dependable, honest, sincere, trustworthy, trusty OPPOSITE **unreliable**

credit *noun* **1** = **deferred payment**, hire-purchase, (the) H.P., the slate (*inf*), tick (*inf*) **5** = **praise**, acclaim, acknowledgment, approval, commendation, honour, kudos, recognition, tribute **6** = **prestige**, esteem, good name, influence, mana (*NZ*), position, regard, reputation, repute, standing, status **7** = **belief**, confidence, credence, faith, reliance, trust ◆*verb* **10** (foll. by *with*) = **attribute to**, ascribe to, assign to, impute to **11** = **believe**, accept, have faith in, rely on, trust

creditable *adjective* = **praiseworthy**, admirable, commendable, honourable, laudable, reputable, respectable, worthy

credulity *noun* = **gullibility**, blind faith, credulousness, naivety

creed *noun* = **belief**, articles of faith, catechism, credo, doctrine, dogma, principles

creek *noun* **1** = **inlet**, bay, bight, cove, firth *or* frith (*Scot*) **2** *Aust & NZ, US, & Canadian* = **stream**, bayou, brook, rivulet, runnel, tributary, watercourse

creep *verb* **1** = **sneak**, approach unnoticed, skulk, slink, steal, tiptoe **2** = **crawl**, glide, slither, squirm, wriggle, writhe ◆*noun* **6** *Sl* = **bootlicker** (*inf*), crawler (*sl*), sneak, sycophant, toady ◆*plural* **give one the creeps** *Inf* = **disgust**, frighten, make one's hair stand on end, make one squirm, repel, repulse, scare

creeper *noun* = **climbing plant**, rambler, runner, trailing plant, vine (*chiefly US*)

creepy *adjective* *Inf* = **disturbing**, eerie, frightening, hair-raising, macabre, menacing, scary (*inf*), sinister gradual increase in loudness, esp. in music. ♦ *adverb* **2** gradually getting louder.

crescent ❶ *noun* **1** (curved shape of) the moon as seen in its first or last quarter. **2** crescent-shaped street. ♦ *adjective* **3** crescent-shaped.

cress *noun* plant with strong-tasting leaves, used in salads.

crest ❶ *noun* **1** top of a mountain, hill, or wave. **2** tuft or growth on a bird's or animal's head. **3** heraldic design used on a coat of arms and elsewhere. ♦ *verb* **4** come to or be at the top of. **crested** *adjective* **crestfallen** *adjective* disheartened.

cretin *noun* **1** *Informal* stupid person. **2** *Obs* person afflicted with physical and mental retardation caused by a thyroid deficiency. **cretinism** *noun* **cretinous** *adjective*

cretonne *noun* heavy printed cotton fabric used in furnishings.

crevasse *noun* deep open crack in a glacier.

crevice ❶ *noun* narrow crack or gap in rock.

crew¹ ❶ *noun* **1** people who work on a ship or aircraft. **2** group of people working together. **3** *Informal* any group of people. ♦ *verb* **4** serve as a crew member (on). **crew cut** man's closely cropped haircut.

crew² *verb Old-fashioned* past tense of CROW².

crewel *noun* fine worsted yarn used in embroidery.

crib ❶ *noun* **1** piece of writing stolen from elsewhere. **2** translation or list of answers used by students, often illicitly. **3** baby's cradle. **4** rack for fodder. **5** short for CRIBBAGE. ♦ *verb* **cribbing, cribbed 6** copy (someone's work)

dishonestly.

cribbage *noun* card game for two to four players.

crick *noun* **1** muscle spasm or cramp in the back or neck. ♦ *verb* **2** cause a crick in.

cricket¹ *noun* outdoor game played with bats, a ball, and wickets by two teams of eleven. **cricketer** *noun*

cricket² *noun* chirping insect like a grasshopper.

cried *verb* past of CRY.

crier *noun* (formerly) official who made public announcements (also **town crier**).

crime ❶ *noun* **1** unlawful act. **2** unlawful acts collectively. **3** *Informal* disgraceful act. **criminal** *noun* **1** person guilty of a crime. ♦ *adjective* **2** of crime. **3** *Informal* deplorable. **criminalize** *verb* **1** make (an activity) criminal. **2** treat (a person) as a criminal. **criminally** *adverb* **criminality** *noun* **criminology** *noun* study of crime. **criminologist** *noun*

crimp *verb* **1** fold or press into ridges. **2** curl (hair) tightly.

crimson *adjective* deep purplish-red.

cringe ❶ *verb* **1** flinch in fear. **2** behave in a submissive or timid way.

crinkle *verb, noun* wrinkle, crease, or fold. **crinkly** *adjective*

crinoline *noun* hooped petticoat.

cripple ❶ *noun* **1** person who is lame or disabled. **2** person with a mental or social problem, e.g. *an emotional cripple.* ♦ *verb* **3** make lame or disabled. **4** damage (something).

crisis ❶ *noun, pl* **-ses 1** crucial stage, turning point. **2** time of extreme trouble.

—————— THESAURUS ——————

crescent *noun* **1** = **meniscus**, new moon, sickle

crest *noun* **1** = **top**, apex, crown, highest point, peak, pinnacle, ridge, summit **2** = **tuft**, comb, crown, mane, plume **3** = **emblem**, badge, bearings, device, insignia, symbol

crestfallen *adjective* = **disappointed**, dejected, depressed, despondent, discouraged, disheartened, downcast, downhearted OPPOSITE **elated**

crevice *noun* = **gap**, chink, cleft, crack, cranny, fissure, hole, opening, slit

crew¹ *noun* **1** = **(ship's) company**, hands, (ship's) complement **2** = **team**, corps, gang, posse, squad **3** *Inf* = **crowd**, band, bunch (*inf*), gang, horde, mob, pack, set

crib *noun* **2** = **translation**, key **3** = **cradle**, bassinet, bed, cot **4** = **manger**, rack, stall ♦ *verb* **6** = **copy**, cheat, pirate, plagiarize, purloin, steal

crime *noun* **1** = **offence**, felony, misdeed,

misdemeanour, transgression, trespass, unlawful act, violation **2** = **lawbreaking**, corruption, illegality, misconduct, vice, wrongdoing

criminal *noun* **1** = **lawbreaker**, convict, crook (*inf*), culprit, felon, offender, sinner, villain ♦ *adjective* **2** = **unlawful**, corrupt, crooked (*inf*), illegal, illicit, immoral, lawless, wicked, wrong OPPOSITE **lawful**. **3** *Inf* = **disgraceful**, deplorable, foolish, preposterous, ridiculous, scandalous, senseless OPPOSITE **right**

cringe *verb* **1** = **shrink**, cower, draw back, flinch, recoil, shy, wince **2** = **grovel**, bootlick (*inf*), crawl, creep, fawn, kowtow, pander to, toady

cripple *verb* **3** = **disable**, hamstring, incapacitate, lame, maim, paralyse, weaken **4** = **damage**, destroy, impair, put out of action, put paid to, ruin, spoil OPPOSITE **help**

crippled *adjective* **3** = **disabled**, handicapped, incapacitated, laid up (*inf*), lame, paralysed

C

crisp ⊕ *adjective* **1** fresh and firm. **2** dry and brittle. **3** clean and neat. **4** (of weather) cold but invigorating. **5** clear and sharp. **6** lively or brisk. ♦ *noun* **7** very thin slice of potato fried till crunchy. ♦ *verb* **8** make or become crisp. **crisply** *adverb* **crispness** *noun* **crispy** *adjective* **crispier, crispiest** hard and crunchy.

crispbread *noun* thin dry biscuit.

crisscross *verb* **1** move in or mark with a crosswise pattern. ♦ *adjective* **2** (of lines) crossing in different directions.

criterion ⊕ *noun, pl* **-ria** standard of judgment.

critic ⊕ *noun* **1** professional judge of any of the arts. **2** person who finds fault. **critical** *adjective* **1** very important or dangerous. **2** very seriously ill or injured. **3** fault-finding. **4** able to examine and judge carefully. **5** of a critic or criticism. **critically** *adverb* **criticism** *noun* **1** fault-finding. **2** analysis of a work of art. **criticize** *verb* **1** find fault with. **2** analyse. **critique** *noun* critical essay.

croak ⊕ *verb* **1** (of a frog or crow) give a low hoarse cry. **2** utter or speak with a croak. **3** *Slang* die. ♦ *noun* **4** low hoarse sound. **croaky** *adjective* hoarse.

Croatian [kroh-ay-shun], **Croat** *adjective* **1** of Croatia. ♦ *noun* **2** person from Croatia. **3** dialect of Serbo-Croat spoken in Croatia.

crochet [kroh-shay] *verb* **-cheting, -cheted 1** make by looping and intertwining yarn with a hooked needle. ♦ *noun* **2** work made in this way.

crock[1] *noun* earthenware pot or jar. **crockery** *noun* dishes.

crock[2] *noun Informal* old or decrepit person or thing.

crocodile *noun* **1** large amphibious tropical reptile. **2** a line of people, esp. schoolchildren, walking two by two. **crocodile tears** insincere show of grief.

crocus *noun, pl* **-cuses** small plant with yellow, white, or purple flowers in spring.

croft *noun* small farm worked by one family in Scotland. **crofter** *noun*

croissant [krwah-son] *noun* rich flaky crescent-shaped roll.

cromlech *noun* circle of prehistoric standing stones.

crone *noun* witchlike old woman.

crony *noun, pl* **-nies** close friend.

crook ⊕ *noun* **1** *Informal* criminal. **2** bent or curved part. **3** hooked pole. ♦ *verb* **4** bend or curve. ♦ *adjective* **5** *Aust & NZ slang* unwell, injured **go crook** *Aust & NZ slang* become angry. **crooked** *adjective* **1** bent or twisted. **2** set at an angle. **3** *Informal* dishonest.

croon ⊕ *verb* sing, hum, or speak in a soft low tone. **crooner** *noun* male singer of sentimental ballads.

crop ⊕ *noun* **1** cultivated plant. **2** season's total yield of produce. **3** group of things

———————— T H E S A U R U S ————————

crisis *noun* **1 = critical point**, climax, crunch (*inf*), crux, culmination, height, moment of truth, turning point **2 = emergency**, deep water, dire straits, meltdown (*inf*), panic stations (*inf*), plight, predicament, trouble

crisp *adjective* **1 = firm**, crispy, crunchy, fresh OPPOSITE **soft. 2 = brittle**, crumbly **3 = clean**, neat, smart, spruce, tidy, trim, well-groomed, well-pressed **4 = bracing**, brisk, fresh, invigorating, refreshing OPPOSITE **warm**

criterion *noun* **=standard**, bench mark, gauge, measure, principle, rule, test, touchstone, yardstick

critic *noun* **1 = judge**, analyst, authority, commentator, connoisseur, expert, mana (*NZ*), pundit, reviewer **2 = fault-finder**, attacker, detractor, knocker (*inf*)

critical *adjective* **1 = crucial**, all-important, decisive, pivotal, precarious, pressing, serious, urgent, vital OPPOSITE **unimportant. 3 = disparaging**, captious, censorious, derogatory, disapproving, fault-finding, nagging, nit-picking (*inf*), scathing OPPOSITE **complimentary. 4 = analytical**, discerning, discriminating, fastidious, judicious, penetrating, perceptive OPPOSITE **undiscriminating**

criticism *noun* **1 = fault-finding**, bad press, censure, character assassination, disapproval, disparagement, flak (*inf*), stick (*sl*) **2 = analysis**, appraisal, appreciation, assessment, comment, commentary, critique, evaluation, judgment

criticize *verb* **1 = find fault with**, carp, censure, condemn, disapprove of, disparage, knock (*inf*), put down, slate (*inf*) OPPOSITE **praise**

croak *verb* **1, 2 = squawk**, caw, grunt, utter *or* speak huskily, wheeze

crook *noun* **1** *Inf* **=criminal**, cheat, racketeer, robber, rogue, shark, swindler, thief, villain

crooked *adjective* **1 = bent**, curved, deformed, distorted, hooked, irregular, misshapen, out of shape, twisted, warped, zigzag OPPOSITE **straight. 2 = at an angle**, askew, awry, lopsided, off-centre, skewwhiff (*Brit inf*), slanting, squint, uneven **3** *Inf* **=dishonest**, bent (*sl*), corrupt, criminal, fraudulent, illegal, shady (*inf*), underhand, unlawful OPPOSITE **honest**

croon *verb* **=sing**, hum, purr, warble

appearing at one time. **4** (handle of) a whip. **5** pouch in a bird's gullet. **6** very short haircut. ◆ verb **cropping, cropped 7** cut very short. **8** produce or harvest as a crop. **9** (of animals) feed on (grass). **cropper** noun **come a cropper** Informal have a disastrous failure or heavy fall. **crop-top** noun short T-shirt or vest that reveals the wearer's midriff. **crop up** verb Informal happen unexpectedly.

croquet [kroh-kay] noun game played on a lawn in which balls are hit through hoops.

croquette [kroh-kett] noun fried cake of potato, meat, or fish.

crosier noun same as CROZIER.

cross ⊕ verb **1** move or go across (something). **2** meet and pass. **3** draw two lines across (a cheque) to make it payable only into a bank account. **4** mark with a cross. **5** (with out) delete with a cross or lines. **6** place (one's arms or legs) crosswise. **7** make the sign of the cross on (oneself). **8** challenge or oppose. **9** cross-fertilize. ◆ noun **10** structure, symbol, or mark of two intersecting lines. **11** such a structure of wood as a means of execution. **12** representation of the Cross as an emblem of Christianity. **13** crossbred animal or plant. **14** mixture of two things. **15** hindrance or misfortune, e.g. that's my cross to bear. ◆ adjective **16** angry, annoyed. **17** lying or placed across. **the Cross** Christianity the cross on which Christ was crucified. **crossing** noun **1** place where a street may be crossed safely. **2** place where one thing crosses another. **3** journey across water. **crossly** adverb **crossness** noun **crossbar** noun horizontal bar across goalposts or on a bicycle. **cross-bench** noun seat in Parliament for a member belonging to neither the government nor the opposition. **crossbow** noun weapon consisting of a bow fixed across a wooden stock. **crossbred** adjective bred from two different types of animal or plant. **crossbreed** noun crossbred

animal or plant. **crosscheck** verb check using a different method. **cross-country** adjective, adverb **1** by way of open country or fields. ◆ noun **2** race across open ground. **cross-examine** verb Law question (a witness for the opposing side) to check his or her testimony. **cross-examination** noun **cross-eyed** adjective with eyes looking towards each other. **cross-fertilize** verb fertilize (an animal or plant) from one of a different kind. **cross-fertilization** noun **crossfire** noun gunfire crossing another line of fire. **cross-ply** adjective (of a tyre) having the fabric cords in the outer casing running diagonally. **cross-purposes** plural noun **at cross-purposes** misunderstanding each other. **cross-reference** noun reference within a text to another part. **crossroads** noun place where roads intersect. **cross section 1** (diagram of) a surface made by cutting across something. **2** representative sample. **crosswise** adjective, adverb **1** across. **2** in the shape of a cross. **crossword puzzle, crossword** noun puzzle in which words suggested by clues are written into a grid of squares.

crosswalk noun Canad place marked where pedestrians may cross a road.

crotch noun part of the body between the tops of the legs.

crotchet noun musical note half the length of a minim.

crotchety adjective Informal bad-tempered.

crouch ⊕ verb **1** bend low with the legs and body close. ◆ noun **2** this position.

croup[1] [kroop] noun throat disease of children, with a cough.

croup[2] [kroop] noun hind quarters of a horse.

croupier [kroop-ee-ay] noun person who collects bets and pays out winnings at a gambling table in a casino.

crouton noun small piece of fried or toasted bread served in soup.

crow[1] noun large black bird with a harsh call.

———————— THESAURUS ————————

crop noun **2** = **produce**, fruits, gathering, harvest, reaping, vintage, yield ◆verb **7** = **cut**, clip, lop, pare, prune, shear, snip, trim **9** = **graze**, browse, nibble

crop up verb Inf = **happen**, appear, arise, emerge, occur, spring up, turn up

cross verb **1** = **go across**, bridge, cut across, extend over, move across, pass over, span, traverse **2** = **intersect**, crisscross, intertwine **5** (with out) = **strike off** or **out**, blue-pencil, cancel, delete, eliminate, score off or out **8** = **oppose**, block, impede, interfere, obstruct, resist **9** = **interbreed**, blend, crossbreed, cross-

fertilize, cross-pollinate, hybridize, intercross, mix, mongrelize ◆noun **12** = **crucifix**, rood **14** = **mixture**, amalgam, blend, combination **15** = **trouble**, affliction, burden, grief, load, misfortune, trial, tribulation, woe, worry ◆adjective **16** = **angry**, annoyed, grumpy, ill-tempered, in a bad mood, irascible, put out, short OPPOSITE good-humoured. **17** = **transverse**, crosswise, diagonal, intersecting, oblique

cross-examine verb = **question**, grill (inf), interrogate, pump, quiz

crouch verb **1** = **bend down**, bow, duck,

as the crow flies in a straight line. **crow's feet** wrinkles at the corners of the eyes. **crow's nest** lookout platform at the top of a ship's mast **stone the crows!** *Brit & Aust slang* expression of surprise, dismay, etc.

crow² ❶ *verb* **1** (of a cock) make a shrill squawking sound. **2** boast or gloat. **3** (of a baby) utter cries of pleasure.

crowbar *noun* iron bar used as a lever.

crowd ❶ *noun* **1** large group of people or things. **2** particular group of people. ♦ *verb* **3** gather together in large numbers. **4** press together in a confined space. **5** fill or occupy fully.

crown ❶ *noun* **1** monarch's headdress of gold and jewels. **2** wreath for the head, given as an honour. **3** top of the head or of a hill. **4** artificial cover for a broken or decayed tooth. **5** former British coin worth 25 pence. ♦ *verb* **6** put a crown on the head of (someone) to proclaim him or her monarch. **7** put on or form the top of. **8** put the finishing touch to (a series of events). **9** attach a crown to (a tooth). **10** *Informal* hit on the head. **the Crown** power of the monarchy. **crown court** local criminal court in England and Wales. **crown jewels** jewellery used by a sovereign on state occasions. **crown-of-thorns** *noun* starfish with a spiny outer covering that feeds on living

coral. **crown prince, crown princess** heir to a throne.

crozier *noun* bishop's hooked staff.

crucial ❶ *adjective* **1** very important. **2** *Slang* excellent. **crucially** *adverb*

crucible *noun* pot in which metals are melted.

crucify ❶ *verb* **-fying, -fied 1** put to death by fastening to a cross. **2** *Informal* punish severely.

crucifix *noun* model of Christ on the Cross.

crucifixion *noun* crucifying. **the Crucifixion** *Christianity* crucifying of Christ. **cruciform** *adjective* cross-shaped.

crude ❶ *adjective* **1** rough and simple. **2** tasteless, vulgar. **3** in a natural or unrefined state. **crude oil** unrefined petroleum. **crudely** *adverb* **crudity, crudeness** *noun*

cruel ❶ *adjective* **1** delighting in others' pain. **2** causing pain or suffering. **cruelly** *adverb* **cruelty** *noun*

cruet *noun* small container for salt, pepper, etc., at table.

cruise ❶ *noun* **1** sail for pleasure. ♦ *verb* **2** sail from place to place for pleasure. **3** (of a vehicle) travel at a moderate and economical speed.

cruiser *noun* **1** fast warship. **2** motorboat with a cabin. **cruiserweight** *noun* same as LIGHT HEAVYWEIGHT. **cruise missile** low-flying guided missile.

crumb ❶ *noun* **1** small fragment of bread or

─────────── T H E S A U R U S ───────────

hunch, kneel, squat, stoop

crow² *verb* **2 = gloat**, blow one's own trumpet, boast, brag, exult, skite (*Aust & NZ*), strut, swagger, triumph

crowd *noun* **1 = multitude**, army, horde, host, mass, mob, pack, swarm, throng **2 = group**, bunch (*inf*), circle, clique, lot, set ♦*verb* **3 = flock**, congregate, gather, mass, stream, surge, swarm, throng **4 = squeeze**, bundle, congest, cram, pack, pile

crowded *adjective* **= packed**, busy, congested, cramped, full, jam-packed, swarming, teeming

crown *noun* **1 = coronet**, circlet, diadem, tiara **2 = laurel wreath**, garland, honour, laurels, prize, trophy, wreath **3 = high point**, apex, crest, pinnacle, summit, tip, top ♦*verb* **6 = honour**, adorn, dignify, festoon **8 = cap**, be the climax *or* culmination of, complete, finish, perfect, put the finishing touch to, round off, top **10** *Inf* **= strike**, belt (*inf*), biff (*sl*), box, cuff, hit over the head, punch

Crown *noun* **= monarchy**, royalty, sovereignty

crucial *adjective* **1 = vital**, central, critical, decisive, essential, high-priority, important, momentous, pivotal, pressing, urgent

crucify *verb* **1 = execute**, persecute, torment,

torture

crude *adjective* **1 = primitive**, clumsy, makeshift, rough, rough-and-ready, rudimentary, unpolished **2 = vulgar**, coarse, dirty, gross, indecent, obscene, scungy (*Aust & NZ inf*), smutty, tasteless, uncouth OPPOSITE tasteful. **3 = unrefined**, natural, raw, unprocessed OPPOSITE processed

crudely *adverb* **2 = vulgarly**, bluntly, coarsely, impolitely, roughly, rudely, tastelessly

crudity, crudeness *noun* **1 = roughness**, clumsiness **2 = vulgarity**, coarseness, impropriety, indecency, indelicacy, obscenity, smuttiness

cruel *adjective* **1 = brutal**, barbarous, callous, hard-hearted, heartless, inhumane, malevolent, sadistic, spiteful, unkind, vicious OPPOSITE kind

cruelly *adverb* **1 = brutally**, barbarously, callously, heartlessly, in cold blood, mercilessly, pitilessly, sadistically, spitefully **2 = bitterly**, deeply, fearfully, grievously, monstrously, severely

cruelty *noun* **1 = brutality**, barbarity, callousness, depravity, fiendishness, inhumanity, mercilessness, ruthlessness, spitefulness

cruise *noun* **1 = sail**, boat trip, sea trip, voyage

C

other dry food. **2** small amount. **crumby**
adjective **crumbier, crumbiest**
crumble ❶ *verb* **1** break into fragments. **2** fall
apart or decay. ♦ *noun* **3** pudding of stewed
fruit with a crumbly topping. **crumbly** *adjective*
-blier, -bliest
crummy *adjective* **-mier, -miest** *Slang* of poor
quality.
crumpet *noun* **1** round soft yeast cake, eaten
buttered. **2** *Slang* sexually attractive women
collectively.
crumple ❶ *verb* **1** crush, crease. **2** collapse,
esp. from shock. **crumpled** *adjective*
crunch ❶ *verb* **1** bite or chew with a noisy
crushing sound. **2** make a crisp or brittle sound.
♦ *noun* **3** crunching sound. **4** *Informal* critical
moment. **crunchy** *adjective*
crupper *noun* strap that passes from the back
of a saddle under a horse's tail.
crusade ❶ *noun* **1** medieval Christian war to
recover the Holy Land from the Muslims. **2**
vigorous campaign in favour of a cause. ♦ *verb*
3 take part in a crusade. **crusader** *noun*
cruse *noun* small earthenware jug or pot.
crush ❶ *verb* **1** compress so as to injure, break,
or crumple. **2** break into small pieces. **3** defeat
or humiliate utterly. ♦ *noun* **4** dense crowd. **5**
Informal infatuation. **6** drink made by crushing
fruit.
crust ❶ *noun* **1** hard outer part of something,
esp. bread. **2** solid outer shell of the earth. ♦
verb **3** cover with or form a crust. **crusty**
adjective **crustier, crustiest 1** having a crust. **2**
irritable.
crustacean *noun* hard-shelled, usu. aquatic
animal with several pairs of legs, such as the
crab or lobster.

crutch *noun* **1** long sticklike support with a
rest for the armpit, used by a lame person. **2**
person or thing that gives support. **3** crotch.
crux *noun, pl* **cruxes** crucial or decisive point.
cry ❶ *verb* **crying, cried 1** shed tears. **2** call or
utter loudly. ♦ *noun, pl* **cries 3** fit of weeping. **4**
loud utterance. **5** urgent appeal, e.g. *a cry for
help*. **crying** *adjective* **a crying shame**
something demanding immediate attention.
crybaby *noun* person, esp. a child, who cries
too readily. **cry off** *verb Informal* withdraw from
an arrangement. **cry out for** *verb* need
urgently.
cryogenics *noun* branch of physics concerned
with very low temperatures. **cryogenic**
adjective
crypt *noun* vault under a church, esp. one
used as a burial place.
cryptic *adjective* obscure in meaning, secret.
cryptically *adverb* **cryptography** *noun* art of
writing in and deciphering codes.
crystal *noun* **1** (single grain of) a
symmetrically shaped solid formed naturally by
some substances. **2** very clear and brilliant
glass, usu. with the surface cut in many planes.
3 tumblers, vases, etc., made of crystal. ♦
adjective **4** bright and clear. **crystalline**
adjective **1** of or like crystal or crystals. **2** clear.
crystallize *verb* **1** make or become definite. **2**
form into crystals. **crystallization** *noun*
Cs *Chem* caesium.
CS gas *noun* gas causing tears and painful
breathing, used to control civil disturbances.
CT Connecticut.
Cu *Chem* copper.
cu. cubic.
cub ❶ *noun* **1** young wild animal such as a

———————— THESAURUS ————————

♦*verb* **2** = **sail**, coast, voyage **3** = **travel along**,
coast, drift, keep a steady pace
crumb *noun* = **bit**, fragment, grain, morsel,
scrap, shred, *soupçon*
crumble *verb* **1** = **crush**, fragment, granulate,
grind, pound, powder, pulverize **2**
= **disintegrate**, collapse, decay, degenerate,
deteriorate, fall apart, go to pieces, go to wrack
and ruin, tumble down
crumple *verb* **1** = **crush**, crease, rumple, screw
up, wrinkle **2** = **collapse**, break down, cave in,
fall, give way, go to pieces
crunch *verb* **1** = **chomp**, champ, chew noisily,
grind, munch ♦*noun* **4** *Inf* = **critical point**, crisis,
crux, emergency, moment of truth, test
crusade *noun* **2** = **campaign**, cause, drive,
movement, push
crush *verb* **1** = **squash**, break, compress, press,

pulverize, squeeze **3 a** = **overcome**, conquer,
overpower, overwhelm, put down, quell, stamp
out, subdue **b** = **humiliate**, abash, mortify, put
down (*sl*), quash, shame ♦*noun* **4** = **crowd**,
huddle, jam
crust *noun* **1** = **layer**, coating, covering, shell,
skin, surface
crusty *adjective* **1** = **crispy**, hard **2** = **irritable**,
cantankerous, cross, gruff, prickly, short-
tempered, testy
cry *verb* **1** = **weep**, blubber, shed tears, snivel,
sob OPPOSITE **laugh**. **2** = **shout**, bawl, bellow,
call out, exclaim, howl, roar, scream, shriek, yell
OPPOSITE **whisper** ♦*noun* **3** = **weeping**,
blubbering, snivelling, sob, sobbing, weep **4**
= **shout**, bellow, call, exclamation, howl, roar,
scream, screech, shriek, yell **5** = **appeal**, plea
cry off *verb Inf* = **back out**, excuse oneself,

bear or fox. **2** (**C-**) Cub Scout. ◆ *adjective* **3** young or inexperienced, e.g. *a cub reporter.* ◆ *verb* **cubbing, cubbed 4** give birth to cubs. **Cub Scout** member of a junior branch of the Scout Association.

cubbyhole *noun* small enclosed space or room.

cube *noun* **1** object with six equal square sides. **2** number resulting from multiplying a number by itself twice. ◆ *verb* **3** cut into cubes. **4** find the cube of (a number). **cubic** *adjective* **1** having three dimensions. **2** cube-shaped. **3** involving the cubes of numbers. **cubism** *noun* style of art in which objects are represented by geometrical shapes. **cubist** *adjective, noun* **cube root** number whose cube is a given number.

cubicle *noun* enclosed part of a large room, screened for privacy.

cubit *noun* old measure of length based on the length of the forearm.

cuckold *noun* **1** man whose wife has been unfaithful. ◆ *verb* **2** be unfaithful to (one's husband).

cuckoo *noun* **1** migratory bird with a characteristic two-note call, which lays its eggs in the nests of other birds. ◆ *adjective* **2** *Informal* insane or foolish. **cuckoo spit** white frothy mass produced on plants by larvae.

cucumber *noun* long green-skinned fleshy fruit used in salads.

cud *noun* partially digested food which a ruminant brings back into its mouth to chew again. **chew the cud** think deeply.

cuddle ⊙ *verb, noun* hug. **cuddle up** *verb* lie close to and hug someone. **cuddly** *adjective*

cudgel ⊙ *noun* short thick stick used as a weapon.

cue¹ ⊙ *noun* **1** signal to an actor or musician

to begin speaking or playing. **2** signal or reminder. ◆ *verb* **cueing, cued 3** give a cue to.

cue² *noun* **1** long tapering stick used in billiards, snooker, or pool. ◆ *verb* **cueing, cued 2** hit (a ball) with a cue.

cuff¹ *noun* end of a sleeve. **off the cuff** *Informal* without preparation. **cuff link** one of a pair of decorative fastenings for shirt cuffs.

cuff² *verb* **1** hit with an open hand. ◆ *noun* **2** blow with an open hand.

cuisine [quiz-**zeen**] *noun* style of cooking.

cul-de-sac ⊙ *noun* road with one end blocked off.

culinary *adjective* of kitchens or cookery.

cull *verb* **1** choose, gather. **2** remove or kill (inferior or surplus animals) from a herd. ◆ *noun* **3** culling.

culminate ⊙ *verb* reach the highest point or climax. **culmination** *noun*

culottes *plural noun* women's knee-length trousers cut to look like a skirt.

culpable ⊙ *adjective* deserving blame. **culpability** *noun*

culprit ⊙ *noun* person guilty of an offence or misdeed.

cult ⊙ *noun* **1** specific system of worship. **2** sect devoted to the beliefs of a cult. **3** devotion to a person, idea, or activity. **4** popular fashion.

cultivate ⊙ *verb* **1** prepare (land) to grow crops. **2** grow (plants). **3** develop or improve (something). **4** try to develop a friendship with (someone). **cultivated** *adjective* well-educated. **cultivation** *noun* **cultivator** *noun* farm implement for breaking up soil.

culture ⊙ *noun* **1** ideas, customs, and art of a particular society. **2** particular society. **3** developed understanding of the arts. **4** development by special training. **5** cultivation

——— THESAURUS ———

quit, withdraw

cub *noun* **1** = **young**, offspring, whelp

cuddle *verb* = **hug**, bill and coo, cosset, embrace, fondle, pet, snuggle

cudgel *noun* = **club**, baton, bludgeon, cosh (*Brit*), stick, truncheon

cue¹ *noun* = **prompt**, catchword **1 2** = **signal**, hint, reminder, sign, suggestion

cul-de-sac *noun* = **dead end**, blind alley

culminate *verb* = **end up**, climax, close, come to a climax, come to a head, conclude, finish, wind up

culmination *noun* = **climax**, acme, conclusion, consummation, finale, peak, pinnacle, zenith

culpable *adjective* = **blameworthy**, at fault, found wanting, guilty, in the wrong, to blame, wrong [OPPOSITE⟩ **blameless**

culprit *noun* = **offender**, criminal, evildoer, felon, guilty party, miscreant, transgressor, wrongdoer

cult *noun* **2** = **sect**, clique, faction, religion, school **3** = **devotion**, idolization, worship

cultivate *verb* **1** = **farm**, plant, plough, tend, till, work **3** = **develop**, foster, improve, promote, refine **4** = **court**, dance attendance upon, run after, seek out

cultivation *noun* **1** = **farming**, gardening, husbandry, planting, ploughing, tillage **3** = **development**, encouragement, fostering, furtherance, nurture, patronage, promotion, support

cultural *adjective* = **artistic**, civilizing, edifying, educational, enlightening, enriching, humane, liberal of plants or rearing of animals. **6** growth of bacteria for study. ♦ *verb* **7** grow (bacteria) for study. **cultural** *adjective* **cultured** *adjective* showing good taste or manners. **cultured pearl** pearl artificially grown in an oyster shell.

culvert ⊕ *noun* drain under a road or railway.

cum *preposition* with, e.g. *a kitchen-cum-dining room.*

cumbersome, cumbrous ⊕ *adjective* **1** awkward because of size or shape. **2** difficult because of complexity.

cumin, cummin *noun* sweet-smelling seeds of a Mediterranean plant, used in cooking.

cummerbund *noun* wide sash worn round the waist.

cumquat *noun* same as KUMQUAT.

cumulative [kew-myew-la-tiv] *adjective* increasing steadily.

cumulus [kew-myew-luss] *noun, pl* **-li** thick white or dark grey cloud.

cuneiform [kew-nif-form] *noun, adjective* (written in) an ancient system of writing using wedge-shaped characters.

cunjevoi *noun* **1** *Aust* plant of tropical Asia and Australia with small flowers, cultivated for its edible rhizome. **2** sea squirt.

cunning ⊕ *adjective* **1** clever at deceiving. **2** ingenious. ♦ *noun* **3** cleverness at deceiving. **4** ingenuity. **cunningly** *adverb*

cup ⊕ *noun* **1** small bowl-shaped drinking container with a handle. **2** contents of a cup. **3** (competition with) a cup-shaped trophy given as a prize. **4** hollow rounded shape. ♦ *verb* **cupping, cupped 5** form (one's hands) into the shape of a cup. **6** hold in cupped hands. **cupful** *noun* **cup tie** eliminating match between two teams in a cup competition.

cupboard ⊕ *noun* piece of furniture or alcove with a door, for storage.

Cupid *noun* Roman god of love, represented as a winged boy with a bow and arrow.

cupidity [kew-**pid**-it-ee] *noun* greed for money or possessions.

cupola [**kew**-pol-la] *noun* domed roof or ceiling.

cupreous *adjective* of copper.

cur *noun* *Lit* **1** mongrel dog. **2** contemptible person.

curaçao [kew-**rah**-so] *noun* orange-flavoured liqueur.

curare [kew-**rah**-ree] *noun* poisonous resin of a S American tree, used as a muscle relaxant in medicine.

curate *noun* clergyman who assists a parish priest. **curacy** [**kew**-rah-see] *noun, pl* **-cies** work or position of a curate.

curative *adjective, noun* (something) able to cure.

curator *noun* person in charge of a museum or art gallery. **curatorship** *noun*

curb ⊕ *noun* **1** something that restrains. **2** strap under a horse's jaw, used to check it. ♦ *verb* **3** control, restrain.

curd *noun* coagulated milk, used to make cheese. **curdle** *verb* turn into curd, coagulate.

cure ⊕ *verb* **1** get rid of (an illness or problem). **2** make (someone) well again. **3** preserve by salting, smoking, or drying. ♦ *noun* **4** (treatment causing) curing of an illness or person. **5** remedy or solution. **curable** *adjective*

curette *noun* **1** surgical instrument for scraping tissue from body cavities. ♦ *verb* **2** scrape with a curette. **curettage** *noun*

curfew *noun* **1** law ordering people to stay inside their homes after a specific time at night. **2** time set as a deadline by such a law.

Curia *noun, pl* **-riae** court and government of the Roman Catholic Church.

———————————— THESAURUS ————————————

culture *noun* **1** = **civilization**, customs, lifestyle, mores, society, way of life **3** = **refinement**, education, enlightenment, good taste, sophistication, urbanity **5** = **farming**, cultivation, husbandry

cultured *adjective* = **refined**, educated, enlightened, highbrow, sophisticated, urbane, well-informed, well-read

culvert *noun* = **drain**, channel, conduit, gutter, watercourse

cumbersome *adjective* **1** = **awkward**, bulky, burdensome, heavy, unmanageable, unwieldy, weighty OPPOSITE> practical

cunning *adjective* **1** = **crafty**, artful, devious, Machiavellian, sharp, shifty, sly, wily OPPOSITE> frank. **2** = **skilful**, imaginative, ingenious

OPPOSITE> clumsy ♦*noun* **3** = **craftiness**, artfulness, deviousness, guile, slyness, trickery OPPOSITE> candour. **4** = **skill**, artifice, cleverness, ingenuity, subtlety OPPOSITE> clumsiness

cup *noun* **1** = **mug**, beaker, bowl, chalice, goblet, teacup **3** = **trophy**

cupboard *noun* = **cabinet**, press

curb *noun* **1** = **restraint**, brake, check, control, deterrent, limitation **2** = **rein**, bridle ♦*verb* **3** = **restrain**, check, control, hinder, impede, inhibit, restrict, retard, suppress

cure *verb* **1, 2** = **make better**, correct, ease, heal, mend, relieve, remedy, restore **3** = **preserve**, dry, pickle, salt, smoke ♦*noun* **4** = **remedy**, antidote, medicine, nostrum, panacea, treatment

curie *noun* standard unit of radioactivity.

curio [kew-ree-oh] *noun, pl* **-rios** rare or unusual object valued as a collector's item.

curious ➊ *adjective* **1** eager to learn or know. **2** eager to find out private details. **3** unusual or peculiar. **curiously** *adverb* **curiosity** *noun* **1** eagerness to know or find out. **2** *pl* **-ties** rare or unusual object.

curium [kew-ree-um] *noun Chem* radioactive element artificially produced from plutonium.

curl ➊ *noun* **1** curved piece of hair. **2** curved spiral shape. ◆ *verb* **3** make (hair) into curls or (of hair) grow in curls. **4** make into a curved spiral shape. **curly** *adjective* **curler** *noun* pin or small tube for curling hair. **curling** *noun* game like bowls, played with heavy stones on ice.

curlew *noun* long-billed wading bird.

curlicue *noun* ornamental curl or twist.

curmudgeon *noun* bad-tempered person.

currajong *noun* same as KURRAJONG.

currant *noun* **1** small dried grape. **2** small round berry, such as a redcurrant.

current ➊ *adjective* **1** of the immediate present. **2** most recent, up-to-date. **3** commonly accepted. ◆ *noun* **4** flow of water or air in one direction. **5** flow of electricity. **6** general trend. **currently** *adverb* **currency** *noun, pl* **-cies 1** money in use in a particular country. **2** general acceptance or use. **current account** bank account from which money may be drawn at any time by cheque or computerized card.

curriculum *noun, pl* **-la, -lums** all the courses of study offered by a school or college.

curriculum vitae [vee-tie] outline of someone's educational and professional history, prepared for job applications.

> **SPELLING TIP**
>
> You possibly read the word **curriculum** more often than you have to write it. It's easy not to notice that the only letter that is doubled is the *r* in the middle.

curry[1] *noun, pl* **-ries 1** Indian dish of meat or vegetables in a hot spicy sauce. ◆ *verb* **-rying, -ried 2** prepare (food) with mixture of hot spices. **curry powder** mixture of spices for making curry.

curry[2] *verb* **-rying, -ried 1** groom (a horse). **2** dress (leather). **curry favour** ingratiate oneself with an important person. **currycomb** *noun* ridged comb for grooming a horse.

curse ➊ *verb* **1** swear (at). **2** ask a supernatural power to cause harm to. ◆ *noun* **3** swearword. **4** (result of) a call to a supernatural power to cause harm to someone. **5** something causing trouble or harm. **cursed** *adjective* **1** under a curse. **2** (foll. by *with*) having (something unfortunate).

cursive *adjective, noun* (handwriting) done with joined letters.

cursor *noun* movable point of light that shows a specific position on a visual display unit.

cursory *adjective* quick and superficial. **cursorily** *adverb*

curt ➊ *adjective* brief and rather rude. **curtly** *adverb* **curtness** *noun*

curtail ➊ *verb* **1** cut short. **2** restrict.

——— THESAURUS ———

curiosity *noun* **1** = **inquisitiveness**, interest, nosiness (*inf*), prying, snooping (*inf*) **2** = **oddity**, freak, novelty, phenomenon, rarity, sight, spectacle, wonder

curious *adjective* **1** = **inquiring**, inquisitive, interested, questioning, searching OPPOSITE indifferent. **2** = **inquisitive**, meddling, nosy (*inf*), prying **3** = **unusual**, bizarre, extraordinary, munted (*NZ sl*), mysterious, novel, odd, peculiar, rare, strange, unexpected

curl *noun* **2** = **twist**, coil, kink, ringlet, spiral, whorl ◆*verb* **4** = **twirl**, bend, coil, curve, loop, spiral, turn, twist, wind

curly *adjective* = **curling**, crinkly, curled, frizzy, fuzzy, wavy, winding

currency *noun* **1** = **money**, coinage, coins, lolly (*Aust & NZ sl*), notes **2** = **acceptance**, circulation, exposure, popularity, prevalence, vogue

current *adjective* **1** = **present**, contemporary, present-day OPPOSITE past. **2** = **up-to-date**, fashionable, in fashion, in vogue, trendy (*Brit inf*) **3** = **prevalent**, accepted, common, customary, in circulation, popular, topical, widespread ◆*noun* **4** = **flow**, course, draught, jet, progression, river, stream, tide, undertow **6** = **mood**, atmosphere, feeling, tendency, trend, undercurrent

curse *verb* **1** = **swear**, blaspheme, cuss (*inf*), take the Lord's name in vain **2** = **damn**, anathematize, excommunicate ◆*noun* **3** = **oath**, blasphemy, expletive, obscenity, swearing, swearword **4** = **denunciation**, anathema, ban, excommunication, hoodoo (*inf*), jinx **5** = **affliction**, bane, hardship, plague, scourge, torment, trouble

cursed *adjective* **1** = **damned**, accursed, bedevilled, doomed, ill-fated

curtailment *noun*

curtain ⊕ *noun* **1** piece of cloth hung at a window or opening as a screen. **2** hanging cloth separating the audience and the stage in a theatre. **3** fall or closing of the curtain at the end, or the rise or opening of the curtain at the start of a theatricalperformance. **4** something forming a barrier or screen. ◆ *plural* **5** *Informal* death, the end. ◆ *verb* **6** provide with curtains. **7** (foll. by *off*) separate by a curtain. **curtain call** return to the stage by performers to receive applause.

curtsy, curtsey *noun, pl* **-sies, -seys 1** woman's gesture of respect made by bending the knees and bowing the head. ◆ *verb* **-sying, -sied** *or* **-seying, -seyed 2** make a curtsy.

curve ⊕ *noun* **1** continuously bending line with no straight parts. **2** something that curves or is curved. ◆ *verb* **3** form or move in a curve.

curvy *adjective* **curvier, curviest. curvaceous** *adjective Informal* (of a woman) having a shapely body. **curvature** *noun* curved shape. **curvilinear** *adjective* consisting of or bounded by a curve.

cushion ⊕ *noun* **1** bag filled with soft material, to make a seat more comfortable. **2** something that provides comfort or absorbs shock. **3** padded edge of a billiard, snooker, or pool table. ◆ *verb* **4** lessen the effects of. **5** protect from injury or shock.

cushy ⊕ *adjective* **cushier, cushiest** *Informal* easy, e.g. *a cushy job.*

cusp *noun* **1** pointed end, esp. on a tooth. **2** *Astrol* division between houses or signs of the zodiac.

cuss *Informal noun* **1** curse, oath. **2** annoying person. ◆ *verb* **3** swear (at). **cussed** [**kuss**-id] *adjective Informal* obstinate.

custard *noun* sweet yellow sauce made from milk and eggs.

custody ⊕ *noun* **1** keeping safe. **2** imprisonment prior to being tried. **custodial** *adjective* **custodian** *noun* person in charge of a public building.

custom ⊕ *noun* **1** long-established activity or action. **2** usual habit. **3** regular use of a shop or business. ◆ *plural* **4** duty charged on imports or exports. **5** government department which collects these. **6** area at a port, airport, or border where baggage and freight are examined for dutiable goods. **customary** *adjective* **1** usual. **2** established by custom. **customarily** *adverb* **customer** *noun* **1** person who buys goods or services. **2** *Informal* person who behaves in a specified way, e.g. *a cool customer.* **custom-built, custom-made** *adjective* made to the specifications of an individual customer.

cut ⊕ *verb* **cutting, cut 1** open up, penetrate, wound, or divide with a sharp instrument. **2** divide. **3** trim or shape by cutting. **4** abridge, shorten. **5** reduce, restrict. **6** *Informal* hurt the feelings of. **7** pretend not to recognize. **8** *Informal* not attend (classes). **9** grow (teeth) through the gums. **10** call a halt to a shooting sequence in a film. **11** move quickly to another scene in a film. **12** divide (a pack of cards) at random. ◆ *noun* **13** act of cutting. **14** stroke or incision made by cutting. **15** piece cut off. **16** reduction. **17** deletion in a text, film, or play. **18** *Informal* share, esp. of profits. **19** style in which hair or a garment is cut. **cut and dried** *Informal* settled in advance. **cutback** *noun* decrease or reduction. **cut back (on)** *verb* decrease or reduce. **cut in** *verb* **1** interrupt. **2** obstruct another vehicle in overtaking it. **cut off** *verb* **1** separate. **2** stop the supply of. **cut out** *verb* **1** shape by cutting. **2** delete, remove. **3** *Informal* stop doing (something). **4** (of an engine) cease to operate suddenly. **5 be cut**

———————— THESAURUS ————————

curt *adjective* = **short**, abrupt, blunt, brief, brusque, gruff, monosyllabic, succinct, terse

curtail *verb* **1** = **cut short**, cut back, decrease, diminish, dock, lessen, reduce, shorten, truncate

curtain *noun* **1** = **hanging**, drape (*chiefly US*)

curve *noun* **1, 2** = **bend**, arc, curvature, loop, trajectory, turn ◆*verb* **3** = **bend**, arc, arch, coil, hook, spiral, swerve, turn, twist, wind

curved *adjective* = **bent**, arched, bowed, rounded, serpentine, sinuous, twisted

cushion *noun* **1** = **pillow**, beanbag, bolster, hassock, headrest, pad ◆*verb* **4** = **soften**, dampen, deaden, muffle, stifle, suppress

cushy *adjective Inf* = **easy**, comfortable, soft, undemanding

custody *noun* **1** = **safekeeping**, care, charge, keeping, protection, supervision **2** = **imprisonment**, confinement, detention, incarceration

custom *noun* **1** = **tradition**, convention, policy, practice, ritual, rule, usage **2** = **habit**, practice, procedure, routine, way, wont **3** = **customers**, patronage, trade ◆*plural* **4** = **duty**, import charges, tariff, tax, toll

customary *adjective* = **usual**, accepted, accustomed, common, conventional, established, normal, ordinary, routine, traditional [OPPOSITE⟩ unusual

customer *noun* **1** = **client**, buyer, consumer, patron, purchaser, regular (*inf*), shopper

out for be suited for or to. **cut-price** *adjective* at a reduced price. **cut up** *verb* **1** cut into pieces. **2 be cut up** *Informal* be very upset.

cutaneous [kew-**tane**-ee-uss] *adjective* of the skin.

cute ⊕ *adjective* **1** appealing or attractive. **2** *Informal* clever or shrewd. **cutely** *adverb* **cuteness** *noun*

cuticle [**kew**-tik-kl] *noun* skin at the base of a fingernail or toenail.

cutlass *noun* curved one-edged sword formerly used by sailors.

cutlery *noun* knives, forks, and spoons. **cutler** *noun* maker of cutlery.

cutlet *noun* **1** small piece of meat like a chop. **2** flat croquette of chopped meat or fish.

cutter *noun* **1** person or tool that cuts. **2** any of various small fast boats.

cut-throat ⊕ *adjective* **1** fierce or relentless. ◆ *noun* **2** murderer. **3** razor with a long folding blade.

cutting ⊕ *noun* **1** article cut from a newspaper or magazine. **2** piece cut from a plant from which to grow a new plant. **3** passage cut through high ground for a road or railway. ◆ *adjective* **4** (of a remark) hurtful.

cuttlefish *noun* squidlike sea mollusc.

CV curriculum vitae.

cwm [**koom**] *noun* (in Wales) valley.

cwt hundredweight.

cyanide *noun* extremely poisonous chemical compound.

cyanosis *noun* blueness of the skin, caused by a deficiency of oxygen in the blood.

cyber- *combining form* computers, e.g. *cyberspace*.

cybernetics *noun* branch of science in which electronic and mechanical systems are studied and compared to biological systems.

cyberspace *noun* place said to contain all the data stored in computers.

cybersquatting *noun* registering an Internet domain name belonging to another person in the hope of selling it to them for a profit. **cybersquatter** *noun*

cyclamen [**sik**-la-men] *noun* plant with red, pink, or white flowers.

cycle ⊕ *verb* **1** ride a bicycle. ◆ *noun* **2** bicycle. **3** *US* motorcycle. **4** complete series of recurring events. **5** time taken for one such series. **6** single complete movement in an electrical, electronic, or mechanical process. **7** set of plays, songs, or poems about a figure or event. **cyclical, cyclic** *adjective* occurring in cycles. **cyclist** *noun* person who rides a bicycle.

cyclone *noun* violent wind moving clockwise round a central area.

cyclotron *noun* apparatus that accelerates charged particles by means of a strong vertical magnetic field.

cygnet *noun* young swan.

cylinder *noun* **1** solid or hollow body with straight sides and circular ends. **2** container with this shape. **3** chamber within which the piston moves in an internal-combustion engine. **cylindrical** *adjective*

cymbal *noun* percussion instrument consisting of a brass plate which is struck against another or hit with a stick.

Cymric [**kim**-rik] *adjective* Welsh.

cynic ⊕ [**sin**-ik] *noun* person who believes that people always act selfishly. **cynical** *adjective* **cynically** *adverb* **cynicism** *noun*

cynosure [**sin**-oh-zyure] *noun* centre of

——————— T H E S A U R U S ———————

cut *verb* **1** =**penetrate**, chop, pierce, score, sever, slash, slice, slit, wound **2** =**divide**, bisect, dissect, slice, split **3** =**shape**, carve, chisel, clip, fashion, form, hew, lop, mow, pare, prune, sculpt, shave, snip, trim, whittle **4** =**abridge**, abbreviate, condense, curtail, delete, shorten OPPOSITE **extend**. **5** =**reduce**, contract, cut back, decrease, diminish, lower, slash, slim (down) OPPOSITE **increase**. **6** *Inf* =**hurt**, insult, put down, snub, sting, wound **7** =**ignore**, avoid, cold-shoulder, slight, spurn, turn one's back on OPPOSITE **greet** ◆*noun* **14** =**incision**, gash, laceration, nick, slash, slit, stroke, wound **16** =**reduction**, cutback, decrease, fall, lowering, saving **18** *Inf* =**share**, percentage, piece, portion, section, slice **19** =**style**, fashion, look, shape

cutback *noun* =**reduction**, cut, decrease,

economy, lessening, retrenchment

cute *adjective* **1** =**appealing**, attractive, charming, delightful, engaging, lekker (*S Afr sl*), lovable

cut in *verb* **1** =**interrupt**, break in, butt in, intervene, intrude

cut off *verb* **1** =**separate**, isolate, sever **2** =**interrupt**, disconnect, intercept

cut out *verb* **3** *Inf* =**stop**, cease, give up, refrain from

cut-throat *adjective* **1** =**competitive**, dog-eat-dog, fierce, relentless, ruthless, unprincipled ◆*noun* **2** =**murderer**, assassin, butcher, executioner, hit man (*sl*), killer

cutting *adjective* **4** =**hurtful**, barbed, caustic, malicious, sarcastic, scathing, vitriolic, wounding OPPOSITE **kind**

attention.

cypher *noun* same as CIPHER.

cypress *noun* evergreen tree with dark green leaves.

Cypriot *noun, adjective* (person) from Cyprus.

cyst [sist] *noun* (abnormal) sac in the body containing fluid or soft matter. **cystic** *adjective*

cystitis [siss-**tite**-iss] *noun* inflammation of the bladder.

cytology [site-**ol**-a-jee] *noun* study of plant and animal cells. **cytological** *adjective* **cytologist** *noun*

cytoplasm *noun* protoplasm of a cell excluding the nucleus.

czar [zahr] *noun* same as TSAR.

Czech *noun, adjective* **1** (person) from the Czech Republic. ◆ *noun* **2** language of the Czech Republic.

—————————— T H E S A U R U S ——————————

cycle *noun* **4, 5** = **era**, circle, period, phase, revolution, rotation

cynic *noun* = **sceptic**, doubter, misanthrope, misanthropist, pessimist, scoffer

Dd

d *Physics* density.

D 1 *Chem* deuterium. **2** the Roman numeral for 500.

d. 1 *Brit* (before decimalization) penny. **2** died.

dab¹ ⊕ *verb* **dabbing, dabbed 1** pat lightly. **2** apply with short tapping strokes. ◆ *noun* **3** small amount of something soft or moist. **4** light stroke or tap. **dab hand** *Informal* person who is particularly good at something.

dab² *noun* small flatfish with rough scales.

dabble ⊕ *verb* **1** be involved in something superficially. **2** splash about. **dabbler** *noun*

dace *noun* small freshwater fish.

dacha *noun* country cottage in Russia.

dachshund *noun* dog with a long body and short legs.

dad *noun Informal* father.

Dada, Dadaism *noun* early 20th-century artistic movement that systematically used arbitrary and absurd concepts. **Dadaist** *noun, adjective*

daddy *noun, pl* **-dies** *Informal* father.

daddy-longlegs *noun Informal* crane fly.

dado [day-doe] *noun, pl* **-does, -dos** lower part of an interior wall, below a rail, decorated differently from the upper part.

daffodil *noun* yellow trumpet-shaped flower that blooms in spring.

daft ⊕ *adjective Informal* foolish or crazy.

dagga *noun S Afr informal* cannabis.

dagger ⊕ *noun* short knifelike weapon with a pointed blade.

daguerreotype [dag-**gair**-oh-type] *noun* type of early photograph produced on chemically treated silver.

dahlia [day-lya] *noun* brightly coloured garden flower.

Dáil Éireann [doil air-in], **Dáil** *noun* lower chamber of parliament in the Irish Republic.

daily ⊕ *adjective* **1** occurring every day or every weekday. ◆ *adverb* **2** every day. ◆ *noun, pl* **-lies 3** daily newspaper. **4** *Brit informal* person who cleans other people's houses.

dainty ⊕ *adjective* **-tier, -tiest 1** delicate or elegant. ◆ *noun, pl* **-ties 2** small cake or sweet. **daintily** *adverb*

daiquiri [dak-eer-ee] *noun* iced drink containing rum, lime juice, and sugar.

dairy *noun, pl* **dairies 1** place for the processing or sale of milk and its products. **2** *NZ* small shop selling groceries and milk often outside normal trading hours. ◆ *adjective* **3** of milk or its products. **dairy cattle** cows kept mainly for their milk. **dairy farm** farm where cows are kept mainly for their milk. **dairymaid** *noun* (formerly) woman employed to milk cows. **dairyman** *noun* man employed to look after cows.

dais [day-iss] *noun* raised platform in a hall, used by a speaker.

daisy *noun, pl* **-sies** small wild flower with a yellow centre and white petals. **daisy chain** string of daisies joined together by their stems to make a necklace. **daisywheel** *noun* flat disc in a word processor with radiating spokes for printing letters.

Dalai Lama *noun* chief lama and (until 1959) ruler of Tibet.

dale *noun* (esp. in N England) valley.

dally *verb* **-lying, -lied 1** waste time. **2** (foll. by *with*) deal frivolously (with). **dalliance** *noun* flirtation.

Dalmatian *noun* large dog with a white coat and black spots.

dam¹ ⊕ *noun* **1** barrier built across a river to create a lake. **2** lake created by this. ◆ *verb* **damming, dammed 3** build a dam across (a river).

THESAURUS

dab *verb* **1** = **pat**, tap, touch **2** = **daub**, stipple ◆*noun* **3** = **spot**, bit, drop, pat, smudge, speck **4** = **pat**, flick, stroke, tap, touch

dabble *verb* **1** = **play at**, dip into, potter, tinker, trifle (with) **2** = **splash**, dip

daft *adjective Inf* = **foolish**, absurd, asinine, crackpot (*inf*), crazy, idiotic, insane, silly, stupid, witless

dagger *noun* = **knife**, bayonet, dirk, stiletto

daily *adjective* **1** = **everyday**, diurnal, quotidian ◆*adverb* **2** = **every day**, day by day, once a day

dainty *adjective* **1** = **delicate**, charming, elegant, exquisite, fine, graceful, neat, petite, pretty OPPOSITE **clumsy**

dam² *noun* mother of an animal such as a sheep or horse.

damage ❶ *verb* **1** harm, spoil. ♦ *noun* **2** harm to a person or thing. **3** *Informal* cost, e.g. *what's the damage?* ♦ *plural* **4** money awarded as compensation for injury or loss.

damask *noun* fabric with a pattern woven into it, used for tablecloths etc.

dame ❶ *noun* **1** *Slang* woman. **2** (**D-**) title of a woman who has been awarded the OBE or another order of chivalry.

damn ❶ *interjection* **1** *Slang* exclamation of annoyance. ♦ *adverb, adjective* **2** (also **damned**) *Slang* extreme(ly). ♦ *verb* **3** condemn as bad or worthless. **4** (of God) condemn to hell. **damnable** *adjective* annoying. **damnably** *adverb* **damnation** *interjection, noun* **damning** *adjective* proving or suggesting guilt, e.g. *a damning report.*

damp ❶ *adjective* **1** slightly wet. ♦ *noun* **2** slight wetness, moisture. ♦ *verb* (also **dampen**) **3** make damp. **4** (foll. by *down*) reduce the intensity of (feelings or actions). **damply** *adverb* **dampness** *noun* **damper** *noun* **1** movable plate to regulate the draught in a fire. **2** pad in a piano that deadens the vibration of each string. **put a damper on** have a depressing or inhibiting effect on. **damp course, damp-proof course** layer of water-resistant material built into the foot of a wall to stop moisture rising.

damsel *noun Old-fashioned* young woman.

damson *noun* small blue-black plumlike fruit.

dan *noun Martial arts* **1** any of the 10 black-belt grades of proficiency. **2** competitor entitled to a dan grading.

dance ❶ *verb* **1** move the feet and body rhythmically in time to music. **2** perform (a particular dance). **3** skip or leap. **4** move rhythmically. ♦ *noun* **5** series of steps and movements in time to music. **6** social meeting arranged for dancing. **dancer** *noun*

D and C *noun Med* dilatation and curettage: a minor operation in which the neck of the womb is stretched and the lining of the womb scraped, to clear the womb or remove tissue for diagnosis.

dandelion *noun* yellow-flowered wild plant.

dander *noun* **get one's dander up** *Slang* become angry.

dandle *verb* move (a child) up and down on one's knee.

dandruff *noun* loose scales of dry dead skin shed from the scalp.

dandy *noun, pl* **-dies 1** man who is overconcerned with the elegance of his appearance. ♦ *adjective* **-dier, -diest 2** *Informal* very good. **dandified** *adjective*

Dane *noun* person from Denmark. **Danish** *noun, adjective* (language) of Denmark. **Danish blue** strong white cheese with blue veins. **Danish pastry** iced puff pastry filled with fruit, almond paste, etc.

danger ❶ *noun* **1** possibility of being injured or killed. **2** person or thing that may cause injury or harm. **3** likelihood that something unpleasant will happen. **danger money** extra money paid for doing dangerous work. **dangerous** *adjective* **dangerously** *adverb*

dangle ❶ *verb* **1** hang loosely. **2** display as an

——————— T H E S A U R U S ———————

dam¹ *noun* **1** = **barrier**, barrage, embankment, obstruction, wall ♦*verb* **3** = **block up**, barricade, hold back, obstruct, restrict

damage *verb* **1** = **harm**, hurt, impair, injure, ruin, spoil, weaken, wreck OPPOSITE **fix** ♦*noun* **2** = **harm**, destruction, detriment, devastation, hurt, injury, loss, suffering OPPOSITE **improvement. 3** *Inf* = **cost**, bill, charge, expense ♦*plural* **4** = **compensation**, fine, reimbursement, reparation, satisfaction

damaging *adjective* = **harmful**, deleterious, detrimental, disadvantageous, hurtful, injurious, ruinous OPPOSITE **helpful**

dame *noun* **2** (with cap.) = **noblewoman**, baroness, dowager, *grande dame*, lady, peeress

damn *verb* **3** = **criticize**, blast, censure, condemn, denounce, put down OPPOSITE **praise. 4** = **sentence**, condemn, doom

damnation *noun* **4** = **condemnation**, anathema, damning, denunciation, doom

damned *adjective* **3** = **detestable**, confounded, hateful, infernal, loathsome **4** = **doomed**, accursed, condemned, lost

damp *adjective* **1** = **moist**, clammy, dank, dewy, drizzly, humid, soggy, sopping, wet OPPOSITE **dry** ♦*noun* **2** = **moisture**, dampness, dankness, drizzle OPPOSITE **dryness** ♦*verb* **3** = **moisten**, dampen, wet **4** (foll. by *down*) = **curb**, allay, check, diminish, dull, inhibit, lessen, moderate, pour cold water on, reduce, restrain, stifle

damper *noun* **put a damper on** = **discourage**, be a wet blanket (*inf*), hinder, pour cold water on (*inf*), restrain

dance *verb* **1** = **prance**, jig, trip, whirl **3** = **skip**, hop ♦*noun* **6** = **ball**, disco, discotheque, hop (*inf*), knees-up (*Brit inf*), social

dancer *noun* = **ballerina**, Terpsichorean

danger *noun* **1, 2** = **peril**, hazard, jeopardy, menace, pitfall, risk, threat enticement.

dank *adjective* unpleasantly damp and chilly.

dapper ❶ *adjective* (of a man) neat in appearance and slight in build.

dappled *adjective* **1** marked with spots of a different colour. **2** covered in patches of light and shadow. **dapple-grey** *noun* horse with a grey coat and darker coloured spots.

Darby and Joan *noun* happily married elderly couple. **Darby and Joan Club** club for elderly people.

dare ❶ *verb* **1** be courageous enough to try (to do something). **2** challenge to do something risky. ♦ *noun* **3** challenge to do something risky. **I dare say** probably. **daring** *adjective* **1** willing to take risks. ♦ *noun* **2** courage to do dangerous things. **daringly** *adverb* **daredevil** *adjective, noun* recklessly bold (person).

dark ❶ *adjective* **1** having little or no light. **2** (of a colour) reflecting little light. **3** (of hair or skin) brown or black. **4** gloomy, sad. **5** sinister, evil. **6** secret, e.g. *keep it dark*. ♦ *noun* **7** absence of light. **8** night. **in the dark** not knowing, uninformed. **darkly** *adverb* **darkness** *noun* **darken** *verb* **dark age** period of ignorance or barbarism. **Dark Ages** period of European history between 500 and 1000 AD.

dark horse person about whom little is known.

darkroom *noun* darkened room for processing photographic film.

darling ❶ *noun* **1** much-loved person. **2** favourite, e.g. *the darling of the financial press*. ♦ *adjective* **3** much-loved.

darn¹ ❶ *verb* **1** mend (a garment) with a series of interwoven stitches. ♦ *noun* **2** patch of darned work.

darn² *interjection, adverb, adjective, verb Euphemistic* damn.

dart ❶ *noun* **1** small narrow pointed missile that is thrown or shot, esp. in the game of darts. **2** sudden quick movement. **3** tapered tuck made in dressmaking. ♦ *plural* **4** game in which darts are thrown at a circular numbered board. ♦ *verb* **5** move or direct quickly and suddenly.

Darwinism *noun* theory of the origin of animal and plant species by evolution. **Darwinian, Darwinist** *adjective, noun*

dash ❶ *verb* **1** move quickly. **2** hurl or crash. **3** frustrate (someone's hopes). ♦ *noun* **4** sudden quick movement. **5** small amount. **6** mixture of style and courage. **7** punctuation mark (-) indicating a change of subject. **8** longer symbol used in Morse code. **dashing** *adjective* stylish and attractive. **dashboard** *noun* instrument panel in a vehicle. **dash off** *verb* write or produce quickly.

THESAURUS

dangerous *adjective* =**perilous**, breakneck, chancy (*inf*), hazardous, insecure, precarious, risky safe

dangerously *adverb* =**perilously**, alarmingly, hazardously, precariously, recklessly, riskily, unsafely

dangle *verb* **1** =**hang**, flap, hang down, sway, swing, trail

dapper *adjective* =**neat**, natty (*inf*), smart, soigné, spruce, spry, trim, well-groomed, well turned out OPPOSITE **untidy**

dare *verb* **1** =**risk**, hazard, make bold, presume, venture **2** =**challenge**, defy, goad, provoke, taunt, throw down the gauntlet ♦*noun* **3** =**challenge**, provocation, taunt

daredevil *adjective* =**daring**, adventurous, audacious, bold, death-defying, madcap, reckless ♦*noun* =**adventurer**, desperado, exhibitionist, madcap, show-off (*inf*), stunt man

daring *adjective* **1** =**brave**, adventurous, audacious, bold, daredevil, fearless, intrepid, reckless, venturesome OPPOSITE **timid** ♦*noun* **2** =**bravery**, audacity, boldness, bottle (*Brit sl*), courage, fearlessness, nerve (*inf*), pluck, temerity OPPOSITE **timidity**

dark *adjective* **1** =**dim**, dingy, murky,

shadowy, shady, sunless, unlit OPPOSITE **clear 3** =**brunette**, black, dark-skinned, dusky, ebony, sable, swarthy OPPOSITE **fair. 4** =**gloomy**, bleak, dismal, grim, morose, mournful, sad, sombre OPPOSITE **cheerful. 5** =**evil**, foul, infernal, sinister, vile, wicked **6** =**secret**, concealed, hidden, mysterious ♦*noun* **7** =**darkness**, dimness, dusk, gloom, murk, obscurity, semi-darkness **8** =**night**, evening, nightfall, night-time, twilight

darken *verb* =**make dark**, blacken, dim, obscure, overshadow OPPOSITE **brighten**

darkness *noun* =**dark**, blackness, duskiness, gloom, murk, nightfall, shade, shadows

darling *noun* **1** =**beloved**, dear, dearest, love, sweetheart, trueluve ♦*adjective* **3** =**beloved**, adored, cherished, dear, precious, treasured

darn¹ *verb* **1** =**mend**, cobble up, patch, repair, sew up, stitch ♦*noun* **2** =**mend**, invisible repair, patch, reinforcement

dart *verb* **5** =**dash**, fly, race, run, rush, shoot, spring, sprint, tear

dash *verb* **1** =**rush**, bolt, fly, hurry, race, run, speed, sprint, tear OPPOSITE **dawdle. 2** =**throw**, cast, fling, hurl, slam, sling **3** =**frustrate**, blight, foil, ruin, spoil, thwart, undo

dastardly *adjective* wicked and cowardly.
dasyure [**dass**-ee-your] *noun* small marsupial of Australia, New Guinea, and adjacent islands.
data ❶ *noun* **1** information consisting of observations, measurements, or facts. **2** numbers, digits, etc., stored by a computer. **data base** store of information that can be easily handled by a computer. **data capture** process for converting information into a form that can be handled by a computer. **data processing** series of operations performed on data, esp. by a computer, to extract or interpret information.

> **LANGUAGE TIP**
>
> *Data* is a Latin plural word but it is generally used as a singular word in English.

date¹ ❶ *noun* **1** specified day of the month. **2** particular day or year when an event happened. **3** *Informal* appointment, esp. with a person of the opposite sex. **4** *Informal* person with whom one has a date. ◆ *verb* **5** mark with the date. **6** assign a date of occurrence to. **7** become old-fashioned. **8** (foll. by *from*) originate from, e.g. *the church dates from Norman times.* **dated** *adjective* old-fashioned. **dateline** *noun Journalism* information about the place and time a story was written, placed at the top of the article. **Date Line** line, approx. equal to 180°, on the east side of which the date is one day earlier than on the west.
date² *noun* dark-brown sweet-tasting fruit of the date palm. **date palm** tall palm grown in tropical regions for its fruit.

dative *noun* (in certain languages) the form of the noun that expresses the indirect object.
datum ❶ *noun, pl* **data** single piece of information in the form of a fact or statistic.
daub ❶ *verb* smear or spread quickly or clumsily.
daughter *noun* **1** female child. **2** woman who comes from a certain place or is connected with a certain thing, e.g. *daughter of the Catholic church.* **daughterly** *adjective* **daughter-in-law** *noun, pl* **daughters-in-law** son's wife.
daunting ❶ *adjective* intimidating or worrying.
dauntless *adjective* fearless.
dauphin [**doe**-fan] *noun* (formerly) eldest son of the king of France.
davenport *noun* **1** small writing table with drawers. **2** *Aust, US & Canad* large couch.
davit [**dav**-vit] *noun* crane, usu. one of a pair, at a ship's side, for lowering and hoisting a lifeboat.
Davy Jones's locker *noun* the sea, considered as a grave for sailors.
Davy lamp *noun* miner's lamp designed to prevent it from igniting gas.
dawdle ❶ *verb* walk slowly, lag behind.
dawdler *noun*
dawn ❶ *noun* **1** daybreak. **2** beginning (of something). ◆ *verb* **3** begin to grow light. **4** begin to develop or appear. **5** (foll. by *on*) become apparent (to).
day ❶ *noun* **1** period of 24 hours. **2** period of light between sunrise and sunset. **3** part of a day occupied with regular activity, esp. work. **4** period or point in time. **5** time of success.
daybreak *noun* time in the morning when

——————————— THESAURUS ———————————

◆*noun* **4 = rush**, dart, race, run, sortie, sprint, spurt **5 = little**, bit, drop, hint, pinch, *soupçon*, sprinkling, tinge, touch OPPOSITE **lot. 6 = style**, brio, élan, flair, flourish, panache, spirit, verve
dashing *adjective* **= stylish**, debonair, elegant, flamboyant, jaunty, showy, smart, sporty OPPOSITE **boring**
data *noun* **1 = information**, details, facts, figures, statistics
date¹ *noun* **3** *Inf* **= appointment**, assignation, engagement, meeting, rendezvous, tryst **4** *Inf* **= partner**, escort, friend ◆*verb* **6 = put a date on**, assign a date to, fix the period of **7 = become old-fashioned**, be dated, show one's age **8** (foll. by *from*) **= come from**, bear a date of, belong to, exist from, originate in
dated *adjective* **= old-fashioned**, obsolete, old hat, outdated, outmoded, out of date, passé, unfashionable OPPOSITE **modern**

daub *verb* **= smear**, coat, cover, paint, plaster, slap on (*inf*)
daunting *adjective* **= intimidating**, alarming, demoralizing, disconcerting, discouraging, disheartening, frightening, off-putting (*Brit inf*), unnerving OPPOSITE **reassuring**
dauntless *adjective* **= fearless**, bold, doughty, gallant, indomitable, intrepid, resolute, stouthearted, undaunted, unflinching
dawdle *verb* **= waste time**, dally, delay, drag one's feet *or* heels, hang about, idle, loaf, loiter, trail OPPOSITE **hurry**
dawn *noun* **1 = daybreak**, cockcrow, crack of dawn, daylight, morning, sunrise, sunup **2 = beginning**, advent, birth, emergence, genesis, origin, rise, start ◆*verb* **3 = grow light**, break, brighten, lighten **4 = begin**, appear, develop, emerge, originate, rise, unfold **5** (foll. by *on*) **= hit**, become apparent, come into one's

D

light first appears. **day centre** place providing meals etc., where elderly or handicapped people can spend the day. **daydream** noun **1** pleasant fantasy indulged in while awake. ♦ verb **2** indulge in idle fantasy. **daydreamer** noun **daylight** noun light from the sun. **daylight robbery** Informal blatant overcharging. **daylight-saving time** time set one hour ahead of the local standard time, to provide an extra hour of light in the evening in summer. **day release** system in which workers go to college one day a week. **day return** reduced fare for a journey to a place and back again on the same day. **day room** communal living-room in a hospital or similar institution. **day-to-day** adjective routine.

daze ① verb **1** stun, by a blow or shock. ♦ noun **2** state of confusion or shock. **dazed** adjective

dazzle ① verb **1** impress greatly. **2** blind temporarily by sudden excessive light. ♦ noun **3** bright light that dazzles. **dazzling** adjective **dazzlingly** (cut) adv

dB, db decibel(s).

DC 1 direct current. **2** District of Columbia.

DD Doctor of Divinity.

D-day noun day selected for the start of some operation, orig. the Allied invasion of Europe in 1944.

DDT noun kind of insecticide.

DE Delaware.

de- prefix indicating: **1** removal, e.g. dethrone. **2** reversal, e.g. declassify. **3** departure, e.g.

decamp.

deacon noun Christianity **1** ordained minister ranking immediately below a priest. **2** (in some Protestant churches) lay official who assists the minister.

deactivate verb make (a bomb etc.) harmless or inoperative.

dead ① adjective **1** no longer alive. **2** no longer in use. **3** numb, e.g. my leg has gone dead. **4** complete, absolute, e.g. dead silence. **5** Informal very tired. **6** (of a place) lacking activity. ♦ noun **7** period during which coldness or darkness is most intense, e.g. in the dead of night. ♦ adverb **8** extremely. **9** suddenly, e.g. I stopped dead. **the dead** dead people. **dead set** firmly decided, e.g. he really was dead set against it. **deadbeat** noun Informal lazy useless person. **dead beat** Informal exhausted. **dead end** road with one end blocked off. **2** situation in which further progress is impossible. **dead heat** tie for first place between two participants in a contest. **deadline** noun time limit. **deadlock** noun point in a dispute at which no agreement can be reached. **deadlocked** adjective **dead loss** Informal useless person or thing. **deadly** adjective likely to cause death. **deadpan** adjective, adverb showing no emotion or expression. **dead reckoning** method of establishing one's position using the distance and direction travelled. **dead weight** heavy weight. **dead wood** Informal useless people or things. **deaden** ① verb make less intense.

——————— THESAURUS ———————

head, come to mind, occur, register (inf), strike **day** noun **1** = **twenty-four hours 2** daylight, daytime **4** = **point in time**, date, time **5** = **time**, age, epoch, era, heyday, period, zenith **daybreak** noun = **dawn**, break of day, cockcrow, crack of dawn, first light, morning, sunrise, sunup **daydream** noun **1** = **fantasy**, dream, fancy, imagining, pipe dream, reverie, wish ♦verb **2** = **fantasize**, dream, envision, fancy, imagine, muse **daylight** noun = **sunlight**, light of day, sunshine **daze** verb **1** = **stun**, benumb, numb, paralyse, shock, stupefy ♦noun **2** = **shock**, bewilderment, confusion, distraction, stupor, trance, trancelike state **dazed** adjective = **shocked**, bewildered, confused, disorientated, dizzy, muddled, punch-drunk, staggered, stunned **dazzle** verb **1** = **impress**, amaze, astonish, bowl over (inf), overpower, overwhelm, take

one's breath away **2** = **blind**, bedazzle, blur, confuse, daze ♦noun **3** = **splendour**, brilliance, glitter, magnificence, razzmatazz (sl), sparkle **dazzling** adjective **1** = **splendid**, brilliant, glorious, sensational (inf), stunning, virtuoso OPPOSITE> ordinary. **2** = **brilliant**, glittering, scintillating, sparkling **dead** adjective **1** = **deceased**, defunct, departed, extinct, late, passed away, perished OPPOSITE> living. **2** = **not working**, inactive, inoperative, stagnant, unemployed, useless OPPOSITE> working. **3** = **numb**, inert, paralysed OPPOSITE> lively. **4** = **total**, absolute, complete, outright, thorough, unqualified, utter **5** Inf = **exhausted**, dead beat (inf), spent, tired, worn out **6** = **boring**, dull, flat, uninteresting ♦noun **7** = **middle**, depth, midst ♦adverb **8** = **exactly**, absolutely, completely, directly, entirely, totally **deaden** verb = **reduce**, alleviate, blunt, cushion, diminish, dull, lessen, muffle, smother, stifle, suppress, weaken **deadline** noun = **time limit**, cutoff point, limit,

deadly ❶ adjective **-lier, -liest 1** likely to cause death. **2** Informal extremely boring. ♦ adverb **3** extremely. **deadly nightshade** plant with poisonous black berries.

deaf ❶ adjective unable to hear. **deaf to** refusing to listen to or take notice of. **deafen** verb make deaf, esp. temporarily. **deafness** noun **deaf-mute** noun person unable to hear or speak.

LANGUAGE TIP

The use of the deaf, the disabled, etc. can be offensive and should be avoided. Instead you should talk about deaf people, disabled people, etc.

---

deal¹ ❶ noun **1** agreement or transaction. **2** kind of treatment, e.g. a fair deal. **3** large amount. ♦ verb **dealing, dealt** [delt] **4** inflict (a blow) on. **5** Cards give out (cards) to the players. **dealer** noun **1** person whose business involves buying and selling. **2** Slang person who sells illegal drugs. **3** Cards person who gives out the cards. **dealings** plural noun transactions or business relations. **deal in** verb buy or sell (goods). **deal out** verb distribute. **deal with** verb **1** take action on. **2** be concerned with. **deal²** noun plank of fir or pine wood.

dean noun **1** chief administrative official of a college or university faculty. **2** chief

administrator of a cathedral. **deanery** noun, pl **-eries 1** office or residence of a dean. **2** parishes of a dean.

dear ❶ noun **1** someone regarded with affection. ♦ adjective **2** much-loved. **3** costly. **dearly** adverb **dearness** noun

dearth ❶ [dirth] noun inadequate amount, scarcity.

death ❶ noun **1** permanent end of life in a person or animal. **2** instance of this. **3** ending, destruction. **deathly** adjective, adverb like death, e.g. a deathly silence; deathly pale. **deathless** adjective everlasting, because of fine qualities. **deathbed** noun bed where a person is about to die or has just died. **death certificate** document signed by a doctor certifying the death of a person and giving the cause of death if known. **death duty** former name for INHERITANCE TAX. **death knell** something that heralds death or destruction. **death mask** cast taken from the face of a person who has recently died. **death row** US part of a prison where convicts awaiting execution are held. **death's-head** noun human skull or a representation of one. **deathtrap** noun place or vehicle considered very unsafe. **death warrant** official authorization for a death sentence. **deathwatch beetle** beetle that bores into wood and makes a tapping sound.

deb noun Informal debutante.

debacle ❶ [day-**bah**-kl] noun disastrous failure.

debar verb prevent, bar.

THESAURUS

---

target date

deadlock noun =impasse, dead heat, draw, gridlock, stalemate, standoff, standstill, tie

deadly adjective **1** =lethal, dangerous, death-dealing, deathly, fatal, malignant, mortal **2** Inf =boring, dull, mind-numbing, monotonous, tedious, tiresome, uninteresting, wearisome

deadpan adjective =expressionless, blank, impassive, inexpressive, inscrutable, poker-faced, straight-faced

deaf adjective =hard of hearing, stone deaf, without hearing **deaf to** =oblivious, indifferent, unconcerned, unhearing, unmoved

deafen verb =make deaf, din, drown out, split or burst the eardrums

deafening adjective =ear-piercing, booming, ear-splitting, overpowering, piercing, resounding, ringing, thunderous

deal¹ noun **1** =agreement, arrangement, bargain, contract, pact, transaction, understanding **3** =amount, degree, extent, portion, quantity, share

dealer noun **1** =trader, merchant, purveyor,

supplier, tradesman, wholesaler

deal in verb =sell, bargain, buy and sell, do business, negotiate, stock, trade, traffic

deal out verb =distribute, allot, apportion, assign, dispense, dole out, give, mete out, share

deal with verb **1** =handle, attend to, cope with, get to grips with, manage, see to, take care of, treat **2** =be concerned with, consider

dear noun **1** =beloved, angel, darling, loved one, precious, treasure ♦adjective **2** =beloved, cherished, close, favourite, intimate, precious, prized, treasured OPPOSITE hated. **3** =expensive, at a premium, costly, high-priced, overpriced, pricey (inf) OPPOSITE cheap

dearth noun =scarcity, deficiency, inadequacy, insufficiency, lack, paucity, poverty, shortage, want

death noun **1, 2** =dying, demise, departure, end, exit, passing OPPOSITE birth. **3** =destruction, downfall, extinction, finish, ruin, undoing OPPOSITE beginning

deathly adjective =deathlike, ghastly, grim, pale, pallid, wan

debase ❶ *verb* lower in value, quality, or character. **debasement** *noun*

debate ❶ *noun* **1** discussion. **2** formal discussion of a proposition, at the end of which people vote on whether to accept it. ◆ *verb* **3** discuss formally. **4** consider (a course of action). **debatable** *adjective* not absolutely certain.

debauch ❶ [dib-**bawch**] *verb* make (someone) bad or corrupt, esp. sexually. **debauched** *adjective* immoral, sexually corrupt. **debauchery** *noun*

debenture *noun* long-term bond bearing fixed interest, issued by a company or a government agency.

debilitate *verb* weaken, make feeble. **debilitation** *noun* **debility** *noun* weakness, infirmity.

debit *noun* **1** acknowledgment of a sum owing by entry on the left side of an account. ◆ *verb* **debiting, debited** **2** charge (an account) with a debt. **3** record as a debit.

debonair ❶ *adjective* (of a man) charming and refined.

debouch *verb* move out from a narrow place to a wider one.

debrief ❶ *verb* receive a report from (a soldier, diplomat, etc.) after an event. **debriefing** *noun*

debris ❶ [**deb**-ree] *noun* fragments of something destroyed.

debt ❶ *noun* something owed, esp. money. **bad debt** debt that is unlikely to be repaid. **debt of honour** debt that is morally but not legally binding. **in debt** owing money. **debtor** *noun*

debug *verb* **1** *Informal* find and remove defects in (a computer program). **2** remove concealed microphones from (a room or telephone).

debunk ❶ *verb Informal* expose the falseness of.

debut ❶ [**day**-byoo] *noun* first public appearance of a performer. **debutante** [**day**-byoo-tont] *noun* young upper-class woman being formally presented to society.

Dec. December.

decade *noun* period of ten years.

decadence ❶ [**dek**-a-denss] *noun* deterioration in morality or culture. **decadent** *adjective*

decaffeinated [dee-**kaf**-fin-ate-id] *adjective* (of coffee, tea, or cola) with caffeine removed.

decagon *noun* geometric figure with ten faces. **decagonal** *adjective*

decahedron [deck-a-**heed**-ron] *noun* solid figure with ten sides.

Decalogue *noun* the Ten Commandments.

decamp *verb* depart secretly or suddenly.

decant *verb* **1** pour (a liquid) from one container to another. **2** rehouse (people) while their homes are being renovated. **decanter** *noun* stoppered bottle for wine or spirits.

decapitate ❶ *verb* behead. **decapitation** *noun*

decathlon *noun* athletic contest with ten events. **decathlete** *noun*

decay ❶ *verb* **1** become weaker or more corrupt. **2** rot. ◆ *noun* **3** process of decaying. **4** state brought about by this process.

decease ❶ *noun Formal* death. **deceased**

──────── THESAURUS ────────

debacle *noun* =**disaster**, catastrophe, collapse, defeat, fiasco, reversal, rout

debase *verb* =**degrade**, cheapen, devalue, lower, reduce OPPOSITE **exalt**

debatable *adjective* =**doubtful**, arguable, controversial, dubious, moot, problematical, questionable, uncertain

debate *noun* **1** =**discussion**, argument, contention, controversy, dispute ◆*verb* **3** =**discuss**, argue, dispute, question **4** =**consider**, deliberate, ponder, reflect, ruminate, weigh

debauchery *noun* =**depravity**, dissipation, dissoluteness, excess, indulgence, intemperance, lewdness, overindulgence

debonair *adjective* =**elegant**, charming, courteous, dashing, refined, smooth, suave, urbane, well-bred

debrief *verb* =**interrogate**, cross-examine, examine, probe, question, quiz

debris *noun* =**remains**, bits, detritus, fragments, rubble, ruins, waste, wreckage

debt *noun* =**debit**, commitment, liability, obligation **in debt** =**owing**, in arrears, in the red (*inf*), liable

debtor *noun* =**borrower**, mortgagor

debunk *verb Inf* =**expose**, cut down to size, deflate, disparage, mock, ridicule, show up

debut *noun* =**introduction**, beginning, bow, coming out, entrance, first appearance, initiation, presentation

decadence *noun* =**degeneration**, corruption, decay, decline, deterioration, dissipation, dissolution

decadent *adjective* =**degenerate**, abandoned, corrupt, decaying, declining, dissolute, immoral, self-indulgent OPPOSITE **moral**

decapitate *verb* =**behead**, execute, guillotine

decay *verb* **1** =**decline**, crumble, deteriorate, disintegrate, dwindle, shrivel, wane, waste *adjective Formal* dead. **the deceased** dead person.

deceive ❶ *verb* **1** mislead by lying. **2** be unfaithful to (one's sexual partner). **deceiver** *noun* **deceit** *noun* behaviour intended to deceive. **deceitful** *adjective*

decelerate *verb* slow down. **deceleration** *noun*

December *noun* twelfth month of the year.

decent ❶ *adjective* **1** (of a person) polite and morally acceptable. **2** fitting or proper. **3** conforming to conventions of sexual behaviour. **4** *Informal* kind. **decently** *adverb* **decency** *noun, pl* **-cies**

decentralize *verb* reorganize into smaller local units. **decentralization** *noun*

deception ❶ *noun* **1** deceiving. **2** something that deceives, trick. **deceptive** *adjective* likely or designed to deceive. **deceptively** *adverb* **deceptiveness** *noun*

deci- *combining form* one tenth.

decibel *noun* unit for measuring the intensity of sound.

decide ❶ *verb* **1** (cause to) reach a decision. **2** settle (a contest or question). **decided** *adjective* **1** unmistakable. **2** determined. **decidedly** *adverb* **decision** *noun* judgment, conclusion, or resolution.

deciduous *adjective* (of a tree) shedding its leaves annually.

decimal *noun* **1** fraction written in the form of a dot followed by one or more numbers. ◆ *adjective* **2** relating to or using powers of ten. **3** expressed as a decimal. **decimalize** *verb* change (a system or number) to the decimal system. **decimalization** *noun* **decimal currency** system of currency in which the units are parts or powers of ten. **decimal point** dot between the unit and the fraction of a number in the decimal system. **decimal system** number system with a base of ten, in which numbers are expressed by combinations of the digits 0 to 9.

decimate ❶ *verb* destroy or kill a large proportion of. **decimation** *noun*

decipher ❶ *verb* work out the meaning of (something illegible or in code). **decipherable** *adjective*

decision ❶ *noun* **1** judgment, conclusion, or resolution. **2** act of making up one's mind. **3** firmness of purpose. **decisive** *adjective* **1** having a definite influence, e.g. *the decisive factor*. **2** having the ability to make quick decisions. **decisively** *adverb* **decisiveness** *noun*

deck ❶ *noun* **1** area of a ship that forms a

——————— T H E S A U R U S ———————

away, wither OPPOSITE **increase. 2 = rot,** corrode, decompose, perish, putrefy ◆*noun* **3 = decline,** collapse, degeneration, deterioration, fading, failing, wasting, withering OPPOSITE **growth. 4 = rot,** caries, decomposition, gangrene, putrefaction

decease *noun Formal* = **death,** demise, departure, dying, release

deceased *adjective Formal* = **dead,** defunct, departed, expired, former, late, lifeless

deceit *noun* = **dishonesty,** cheating, chicanery, deception, fraud, lying, pretence, treachery, trickery OPPOSITE **honesty**

deceitful *adjective* = **dishonest,** deceptive, false, fraudulent, sneaky, treacherous, two-faced, untrustworthy

deceive *verb* **1 = take in** (*inf*), cheat, con (*inf*), dupe, fool, hoodwink, mislead, swindle, trick

deceiver *noun* **1 = liar,** cheat, con man (*inf*), double-dealer, fraud, impostor, swindler, trickster

decency *noun* = **respectability,** civility, correctness, courtesy, decorum, etiquette, modesty, propriety

decent *adjective* **2 = proper,** appropriate, becoming, befitting, fitting, seemly, suitable OPPOSITE **unsatisfactory. 3 = respectable,**

chaste, decorous, modest, proper, pure **4** *Inf* = **kind,** accommodating, courteous, friendly, generous, gracious, helpful, obliging, thoughtful

deception *noun* **1 = trickery,** cunning, deceit, fraud, guile, legerdemain, treachery OPPOSITE **honesty. 2 = trick,** bluff, decoy, hoax, illusion, lie, ruse, subterfuge

deceptive *adjective* = **misleading,** ambiguous, deceitful, dishonest, false, fraudulent, illusory, unreliable

decide *verb* **1 = reach** *or* **come to a decision,** choose, conclude, determine, make up one's mind, resolve OPPOSITE **hesitate. 2 = adjudge,** adjudicate

decidedly *adverb* **2 = definitely,** clearly, distinctly, downright, positively, unequivocally, unmistakably

decimate *verb* = **devastate,** ravage, wreak havoc on

decipher *verb* = **figure out** (*inf*), crack, decode, deduce, interpret, make out, read, solve

decision *noun* **1 = judgment,** arbitration, conclusion, finding, resolution, ruling, sentence, verdict **3 = decisiveness,** determination, firmness, purpose, resolution, resolve, strength floor. **2** similar area in a bus. **3** platform that supports the turntable and pick-up of a record player. **4** *US* pack (of cards). **deck chair** folding chair made of canvas over a wooden frame. **deck hand** sailor assigned duties on the deck of a ship. **decking** *noun* wooden platform in a garden. **deck out** *verb* decorate.

declaim ❶ *verb* **1** speak loudly and dramatically. **2** protest loudly. **declamation** *noun* **declamatory** *adjective*

declare ❶ *verb* **1** state firmly and forcefully. **2** announce officially. **3** acknowledge for tax purposes. **declaration** *noun* **declaratory** *adjective*

declassify *verb* state officially that (information or a document) is no longer secret. **declassification** *noun*

declension *noun Grammar* changes in the form of nouns, pronouns, or adjectives to show case, number, and gender.

decline ❶ *verb* **1** become smaller, weaker, or less important. **2** refuse politely to accept or do. **3** *Grammar* list the inflections of (a noun, pronoun, or adjective). ◆ *noun* **4** gradual weakening or loss.

declivity *noun, pl* **-ties** downward slope.

declutch *verb* disengage the clutch of a motor vehicle.

decoct *verb* extract the essence from (a substance) by boiling. **decoction** *noun*

decode ❶ *verb* convert from code into ordinary language. **decoder** *noun*

décolleté [day-**kol**-tay] *adjective* (of a woman's garment) low-cut. **décolletage** [day-kol-**tazh**] *noun* low-cut dress or neckline.

decommission *verb* dismantle (a nuclear reactor, weapon, etc.) which is no longer needed.

decompose ❶ *verb* be broken down through chemical or bacterial action. **decomposition** *noun*

decompress *verb* **1** free from pressure. **2** return (a diver) to normal atmospheric pressure. **decompression** *noun* **decompression sickness** severe pain and difficulty in breathing, caused by a sudden change in atmospheric pressure.

decongestant *noun* medicine that relieves nasal congestion.

decontaminate *verb* make safe by removing poisons, radioactivity, etc. **decontamination** *noun*

decor [**day**-core] *noun* style in which a room or house is decorated.

decorate ❶ *verb* **1** make more attractive by adding something ornamental. **2** paint or wallpaper. **3** award a (military) medal to. **decoration** *noun* **decorative** *adjective* **decorator** *noun*

decorous ❶ [**dek**-a-russ] *adjective* polite, calm, and sensible in behaviour. **decorously** *adverb*

decorum ❶ [dik-**core**-um] *noun* polite and

————————————— THESAURUS —————————————

of mind *or* will

decisive *adjective* **1** = **crucial**, conclusive, critical, fateful, influential, momentous, significant OPPOSITE **uncertain**. **2** = **resolute**, decided, determined, firm, forceful, incisive, strong-minded, trenchant OPPOSITE **indecisive**

deck out *verb* = **decorate**, adorn, array, beautify, clothe, dress, embellish, festoon

declaim *verb* **1** = **orate**, harangue, hold forth, lecture, proclaim, rant, recite, speak **2** = **protest against**, attack, decry, denounce, inveigh, rail

declaration *noun* **1** = **statement**, acknowledgment, affirmation, assertion, avowal, disclosure, protestation, revelation, testimony **2** = **announcement**, edict, notification, proclamation, profession, pronouncement

declare *verb* **1** = **state**, affirm, announce, assert, claim, maintain, proclaim, profess, pronounce, swear, utter

decline *verb* **1 a** = **lessen**, decrease, diminish, dwindle, ebb, fade, fall off, shrink, wane, weaken **b** = **deteriorate**, decay, degenerate, sink, worsen OPPOSITE **improve**. **2** = **refuse**, abstain, avoid, reject, say 'no', turn down

OPPOSITE **agree to** ◆ *noun* **4** = **deterioration**, decay, degeneration, downturn, drop, dwindling, failing, falling off, lessening, recession, slump, weakening, worsening OPPOSITE **improvement**

decode *verb* = **decipher**, crack, decrypt, interpret, solve, unscramble, work out OPPOSITE **encode**

decompose *verb* = **rot**, break up, crumble, decay, fall apart, fester, putrefy

decor *noun* = **decoration**, colour scheme, furnishing style, ornamentation

decorate *verb* **1** = **adorn**, beautify, embellish, festoon, grace, ornament, trim **2** = **do up** (*inf*), colour, furbish, paint, paper, renovate, wallpaper **3** = **pin a medal on**, cite, confer an honour on *or* upon

decoration *noun* **1** = **adornment**, beautification, elaboration, embellishment, enrichment, ornamentation, trimming **2** = **ornament**, bauble, frill, garnish, trimmings **3** = **medal**, award, badge, ribbon, star

decorative *adjective* = **ornamental**, beautifying, fancy, nonfunctional, pretty

socially correct behaviour.
decoy ❶ *noun* **1** person or thing used to lure someone into danger. **2** dummy bird or animal, used to lure game within shooting range. ♦ *verb* **3** lure away by means of a trick.
decrease ❶ *verb* **1** make or become less. ♦ *noun* **2** lessening, reduction. **3** amount by which something has decreased.
decree ❶ *noun* **1** law made by someone in authority. **2** court judgment. ♦ *verb* **3** order by decree. **decree absolute** final court order in a divorce case, which leaves the parties free to remarry. **decree nisi** court order in a divorce case, which will become absolute unless valid reasons are produced to oppose it.
decrepit ❶ *adjective* weakened or worn out by age or long use. **decrepitude** *noun*
decretal *noun RC Church* papal decree.
decriminalize *verb* make (an illegal act) no longer a crime. **decriminalization** *noun*
decry ❶ *verb* **-crying, -cried** express disapproval of.
dedicate ❶ *verb* **1** commit (oneself or one's time) wholly to a special purpose or cause. **2** inscribe or address (a book etc.) to someone as a tribute. **dedicated** *adjective* devoted to a particular purpose or cause. **dedication** *noun*

deduce ❶ *verb* reach (a conclusion) by reasoning from evidence. **deducible** *adjective*
deduct ❶ *verb* subtract. **deductible** *adjective*
deduction ❶ *noun* **1** deducting. **2** something that is deducted. **3** deducing. **4** conclusion reached by deducing. **deductive** *adjective*
deed ❶ *noun* **1** something that is done. **2** legal document. **deed box** strong box in which legal documents are stored. **deed poll** *Law* deed made by one party only, esp. to change one's name.
deejay *noun Informal* disc jockey.
deem *verb* consider, judge.
deep ❶ *adjective* **1** extending or situated far down, inwards, backwards, or sideways. **2** of a specified dimension downwards, inwards, or backwards, e.g. *three inches deep.* **3** difficult to understand. **4** of great intensity. **5** (foll. by *in*) absorbed in (an activity). **6** (of a colour) strong or dark. **7** low in pitch. **the deep** *Poetic* the sea. **deeply** *adverb* profoundly or intensely (also **deep down**). **deepen** *verb* **deep-freeze** *noun* same as FREEZER. **deep-fry** *verb* cook in hot oil deep enough to cover the food completely. **deep-rooted** *adjective* (of an idea or belief) firmly fixed or held. **deep-seated** *adjective* (of a problem, fear, etc.) affecting one strongly.

D

—————————— T H E S A U R U S ——————————

decorous *adjective* = **proper**, becoming, correct, decent, dignified, fitting, polite, seemly, well-behaved
decorum *noun* = **propriety**, decency, dignity, etiquette, good manners, politeness, protocol, respectability OPPOSITE> **impropriety**
decoy *noun* **1** = **lure**, bait, enticement, inducement, pretence, trap ♦ *verb* **3** = **lure**, deceive, ensnare, entice, entrap, seduce, tempt
decrease *verb* **1** = **lessen**, cut down, decline, diminish, drop, dwindle, lower, reduce, shrink, subside OPPOSITE> **increase** ♦ *noun* **2** = **lessening**, contraction, cutback, decline, dwindling, falling off, loss, reduction, subsidence OPPOSITE> **increase**
decree *noun* **1** = **law**, act, command, edict, order, proclamation, ruling, statute ♦ *verb* **3** = **order**, command, demand, ordain, prescribe, proclaim, pronounce, rule
decrepit *adjective* **a** = **weak**, aged, doddering, feeble, frail, infirm **b** = **worn-out**, battered, beat-up (*inf*), broken-down, dilapidated, ramshackle, rickety, run-down, tumbledown, weather-beaten
decry *verb* = **condemn**, belittle, criticize, denigrate, denounce, discredit, disparage, put down, run down
dedicate *verb* **1** = **devote**, commit, give over

to, pledge, surrender **2** = **inscribe**, address
dedicated *adjective* = **devoted**, committed, enthusiastic, purposeful, single-minded, wholehearted, zealous OPPOSITE> **indifferent**
dedication *noun* **1** = **devotion**, adherence, allegiance, commitment, faithfulness, loyalty, single-mindedness, wholeheartedness OPPOSITE> **indifference**. **2** = **inscription**, address, message
deduce *verb* = **conclude**, draw, gather, glean, infer, reason, take to mean, understand
deduct *verb* = **subtract**, decrease by, knock off (*inf*), reduce by, remove, take away, take off OPPOSITE> **add**
deduction *noun* **1, 2** = **subtraction**, decrease, diminution, discount, reduction, withdrawal **4** = **conclusion**, assumption, finding, inference, reasoning, result
deed *noun* **1** = **action**, achievement, act, exploit, fact, feat, performance **2** = **document**, contract, title
deep *adjective* **1** = **wide**, bottomless, broad, far, profound, unfathomable, yawning OPPOSITE> **shallow**. **3** = **mysterious**, abstract, abstruse, arcane, esoteric, hidden, obscure, recondite, secret **4** = **intense**, extreme, grave, great, profound, serious (*inf*), unqualified OPPOSITE> **superficial**. **5** (foll. by *in*) = **absorbed**, engrossed, immersed, lost,

deer *noun, pl* **deer** large wild animal, the male of which has antlers. **deerstalker** *noun* cloth hat with peaks at the back and front and earflaps.

deface ❶ *verb* deliberately spoil the appearance of. **defacement** *noun*

de facto ❶ *adverb* **1** in fact. ♦ *adjective* **2** existing in fact, whether legally recognized or not.

defame ❶ *verb* attack the good reputation of. **defamation** *noun* **defamatory** [dif-**fam**-a-tree] *adjective*

default ❶ *noun* **1** failure to do something. **2** *Computers* instruction to a computer to select a particular option unless the user specifies otherwise. ♦ *verb* **3** fail to fulfil an obligation. **by default** (happening) only because something else has not happened. **in default of** in the absence of. **defaulter** *noun*

defeat ❶ *verb* **1** win a victory over. **2** thwart, frustrate. ♦ *noun* **3** defeating. **defeatism** *noun* ready acceptance or expectation of defeat. **defeatist** *adjective, noun*

defecate *verb* discharge waste from the body through the anus. **defecation** *noun*

defect ❶ *noun* **1** imperfection, blemish. ♦ *verb* **2** desert one's cause or country to join the opposing forces. **defective** *adjective* imperfect, faulty. **defection** *noun* **defector** *noun*

defence ❶ *noun* **1** resistance against attack. **2** argument in support of something. **3** a country's military resources. **4** defendant's case in a court of law. **5** *Sport* players whose chief task is to stop the opposition scoring. **defenceless** *adjective*

defend ❶ *verb* **1** protect from harm or danger. **2** support in the face of criticism. **3** represent (a defendant) in court. **4** *Sport* protect (a title) against a challenge. **defendant** *noun* person accused of a crime. **defender** *noun* **defensible** *adjective* capable of being defended because believed to be right. **defensibility** *noun* **defensive** *adjective* **1** intended for defence. **2** overanxious to protect oneself against (threatened) criticism. **on the defensive** protecting oneself, esp. against (threatened) criticism. **defensively** *adverb*

defer[1] ❶ *verb* **-ferring, -ferred** delay

———————— T H E S A U R U S ————————

preoccupied, rapt **6** = **dark**, intense, rich, strong, vivid OPPOSITE **light. 7** = **low**, bass, booming, low-pitched, resonant, sonorous OPPOSITE **high** ♦*noun* **the deep** *Poet* = ocean, briny (*inf*), high seas, main, sea

deepen *verb* **1** = **dig out**, excavate, hollow, scoop out **4** = **intensify**, grow, increase, magnify, reinforce, strengthen

deeply *adverb* **4** = **intensely**, acutely, completely, gravely, profoundly, seriously, severely, thoroughly, to the core, to the heart, to the quick

deface *verb* = **vandalize**, damage, deform, disfigure, mar, mutilate, spoil, tarnish

de facto *adverb* **1** = **in fact**, actually, in effect, in reality, really ♦*adjective* **2** = **actual**, existing, real

defame *verb* = **slander**, bad-mouth (*sl, chiefly US & Canad*), cast aspersions on, denigrate, discredit, disparage, knock (*inf*), libel, malign, smear

default *noun* **1** = **failure**, deficiency, dereliction, evasion, lapse, neglect, nonpayment, omission ♦*verb* **3** = **fail**, dodge, evade, neglect

defeat *verb* **1** = **beat**, conquer, crush, master, overwhelm, rout, trounce, vanquish, wipe the floor with (*inf*) OPPOSITE **lose to. 2** = **frustrate**, baffle, balk, confound, foil, get the better of, ruin, thwart ♦*noun* **3** = **conquest**, beating, overthrow, pasting (*sl*), rout OPPOSITE **victory**

defeatist *adjective* = **pessimistic** ♦*noun* = **pessimist**, prophet of doom, quitter

defect *noun* **1** = **imperfection**, blemish, blotch, error, failing, fault, flaw, spot, taint ♦*verb* **2** = **desert**, abandon, change sides, go over, rebel, revolt, walk out on (*inf*)

defection *noun* = **desertion**, apostasy, rebellion

defective *adjective* = **faulty**, broken, deficient, flawed, imperfect, not working, on the blink (*sl*), out of order OPPOSITE **working**

defector *noun* = **deserter**, apostate, renegade, turncoat

defence *noun* **1** = **protection**, cover, guard, immunity, resistance, safeguard, security, shelter **2** = **argument**, excuse, explanation, justification, plea, vindication **3** = **shield**, barricade, bulwark, buttress, fortification, rampart **4** = **plea**, alibi, denial, rebuttal, testimony

defenceless *adjective* = **helpless**, exposed, naked, powerless, unarmed, unguarded, unprotected, vulnerable, wide open OPPOSITE **safe**

defend *verb* **1** = **protect**, cover, guard, keep safe, preserve, safeguard, screen, shelter, shield **2** = **support**, champion, endorse, justify, speak up for, stand up for, stick up for (*inf*), uphold, vindicate

defendant *noun* = **the accused**, defence, offender, prisoner at the bar, respondent

(something) until a future time. **deferment,
deferral** noun
defer² ❶ verb **-ferring, -ferred** (foll. by to)
comply with the wishes (of). **deference** noun
polite and respectful behaviour. **deferential**
adjective **deferentially** adverb
defiance ❶ noun see DEFY.
deficient ❶ adjective **1** lacking some essential
thing or quality. **2** inadequate in quality or
quantity. **deficiency** noun, pl **-cies 1** state of
being deficient. **2** lack, shortage. **deficiency
disease** condition, such as scurvy, caused by a
lack of vitamins or other nutrients. **deficit** noun
amount by which a sum of money is too small.
defile¹ verb treat (something sacred or
important) without respect. **defilement** noun
defile² noun narrow valley or pass.
define ❶ verb **1** state precisely the meaning
of. **2** show clearly the outline of. **definable**
adjective **definite** adjective **1** firm, clear, and
precise. **2** having precise limits. **3** known for
certain. **definite article** the word the.

definitely adverb **definition** noun **1** statement
of the meaning of a word or phrase. **2** quality
of being clear and distinct. **definitive** adjective
1 providing an unquestionable conclusion. **2**
being the best example of something.
definitively adverb
deflate ❶ verb **1** (cause to) collapse through
the release of air. **2** take away the self-esteem
or conceit from. **3** Economics cause deflation of
(an economy). **deflation** noun **1** Economics
reduction in economic activity resulting in lower
output and investment. **2** feeling of sadness
following excitement. **deflationary** adjective
deflect ❶ verb (cause to) turn aside from a
course. **deflection** noun **deflector** noun
deflower verb Lit deprive (a woman) of her
virginity.
defoliate verb deprive (a plant) of its leaves.
defoliant noun **defoliation** noun
deforestation noun destruction of all the
trees in an area.
deform ❶ verb put out of shape or spoil the

——————— THESAURUS ———————

defender noun **1** = **protector**, bodyguard,
escort, guard **2** = **supporter**, advocate,
champion, sponsor
defensive adjective **1** = **on guard**, protective,
watchful
defer¹ verb = **postpone**, delay, hold over,
procrastinate, put off, put on ice (inf), shelve,
suspend
defer² verb (foll. by to) = **comply**, accede,
bow, capitulate, give in, give way to, submit,
yield
deference noun = **respect**, attention, civility,
consideration, courtesy, honour, politeness,
regard, reverence OPPOSITE **disrespect**
deferential adjective = **respectful**,
ingratiating, obedient, obeisant, obsequious,
polite, reverential, submissive
defiance noun = **resistance**, confrontation,
contempt, disobedience, disregard, insolence,
insubordination, opposition, rebelliousness
OPPOSITE **obedience**
defiant adjective = **resisting**, audacious, bold,
daring, disobedient, insolent, insubordinate,
mutinous, provocative, rebellious OPPOSITE
obedient
deficiency noun **1** = **failing**, defect, demerit,
fault, flaw, frailty, imperfection, shortcoming,
weakness **2** = **lack**, absence, dearth, deficit,
scarcity, shortage OPPOSITE **sufficiency**
deficient adjective **1** = **lacking**, inadequate,
insufficient, meagre, scant, scarce, short,
skimpy, wanting **2** = **unsatisfactory**, defective,
faulty, flawed, impaired, imperfect, incomplete,

inferior, weak
deficit noun = **shortfall**, arrears, deficiency,
loss, shortage
define verb **1** = **describe**, characterize,
designate, explain, expound, interpret, specify,
spell out **2** = **mark out**, bound, circumscribe,
delineate, demarcate, limit, outline
definite adjective **1, 2** = **clear**, black-and-
white, cut-and-dried (inf), exact, fixed, marked,
particular, precise, specific OPPOSITE **vague**. **3**
= **certain**, assured, decided, guaranteed,
positive, settled, sure OPPOSITE **uncertain**
definitely adverb = **certainly**, absolutely,
categorically, clearly, positively, surely,
undeniably, unmistakably, unquestionably,
without doubt
definition noun **1** = **explanation**, clarification,
elucidation, exposition, statement of meaning **2**
= **sharpness**, clarity, contrast, distinctness,
focus, precision
definitive adjective **1** = **final**, absolute,
complete, conclusive, decisive **2**
= **authoritative**, exhaustive, perfect, reliable,
ultimate
deflate verb **1** = **collapse**, empty, exhaust,
flatten, puncture, shrink OPPOSITE **expand**. **2**
= **humiliate**, chasten, disconcert, dispirit,
humble, mortify, put down (sl), squash **3**
Economics = **reduce**, depress, devalue, diminish
deflect verb = **turn aside**, bend, deviate,
diverge, glance off, ricochet, swerve, veer
deflection noun = **deviation**, bend,
divergence, swerve

appearance of. **deformation** *noun* **deformed**
adjective **deformity** *noun, pl* **-ties 1** *Pathology*
distortion of a body part. **2** state of being
deformed.

defraud ⊙ *verb* cheat out of money, property,
etc.

defray *verb* provide money for (costs or
expenses).

defrock *verb* deprive (a priest) of priestly
status.

defrost *verb* **1** make or become free of ice. **2**
thaw (frozen food) by removing it from a
freezer.

deft ⊙ *adjective* quick and skilful in movement.
deftly *adverb* **deftness** *noun*

defunct ⊙ *adjective* no longer existing or
operative.

defuse *verb* **1** remove the fuse of (an
explosive device). **2** remove the tension from (a
situation).

defy ⊙ *verb* **-fying, -fied 1** resist openly and
boldly. **2** make impossible, e.g. *the condition of
the refugees defied description.* **defiance** *noun*
open resistance or disobedience. **defiant**
adjective

degenerate ⊙ *adjective* **1** having deteriorated
to a lower mental, moral, or physical level. ◆
noun **2** degenerate person. ◆ *verb* **3** become
degenerate. **degeneracy** *noun* degenerate
behaviour. **degeneration** *noun* **degenerative**
adjective (of a disease or condition) getting
steadily worse.

degrade ⊙ *verb* **1** reduce to dishonour or

disgrace. **2** reduce in status or quality. **3** *Chem*
decompose into smaller molecules. **degrading**
adjective **degradation** *noun*

degree ⊙ *noun* **1** stage in a scale of relative
amount or intensity. **2** academic award given
by a university or college on successful
completion of a course. **3** unit of measurement
for temperature, angles, or latitude and
longitude.

dehumanize *verb* **1** deprive of human
qualities. **2** make (an activity) mechanical or
routine. **dehumanization** *noun*

dehumidifier *noun* device for removing
moisture from the air.

dehydrate *verb* remove water from (food) to
preserve it. **be dehydrated** become weak
through losing too much water from the body.
dehydration *noun*

de-ice *verb* free of ice. **de-icer** *noun*

deify [day-if-fie] *verb* **-fying, -fied** treat or
worship as a god. **deification** *noun*

deign [dane] *verb* agree (to do something),
but as if doing someone a favour.

deism [dee-iz-zum] *noun* belief in god but not
in divine revelation. **deist** *noun*

deity ⊙ [dee-it-ee] *noun, pl* **-ties 1** god or
goddess. **2** state of being divine.

déjà vu [day-zhah **voo**] *noun* feeling of
having experienced before something that is
actually happening now.

dejected ⊙ *adjective* unhappy. **dejectedly**
adverb **dejection** *noun*

de jure ⊙ *adverb, adjective* according to law.

——————— T H E S A U R U S ———————

deform *verb* =**distort**, buckle, contort, deface,
disfigure, gnarl, maim, mangle, mar, misshape,
mutilate, ruin, spoil, twist, warp

deformity *noun* =**abnormality**, defect,
disfigurement, malformation

defraud *verb* =**cheat**, con (*inf*), diddle (*inf*),
embezzle, fleece, pilfer, rip off (*sl*), swindle, trick

deft *adjective* =**skilful**, adept, adroit, agile,
dexterous, expert, neat, nimble, proficient
OPPOSITE **clumsy**

defunct *adjective* =**dead**, bygone, deceased,
departed, expired, extinct, gone, inoperative,
invalid, nonexistent, obsolete, out of
commission

defy *verb* **1** =**resist**, brave, confront,
disregard, flout, scorn, slight, spurn

degenerate *adjective* **1** =**depraved**, corrupt,
debauched, decadent, dissolute, immoral, low,
perverted ◆*verb* **3** =**worsen**, decay, decline,
decrease, deteriorate, fall off, lapse, sink, slip

degradation *noun* **1** =**disgrace**, discredit,
dishonour, humiliation, ignominy, mortification,

shame **2** =**deterioration**, decline,
degeneration, demotion, downgrading

degrade *verb* **1** =**demean**, debase, discredit,
disgrace, dishonour, humble, humiliate, shame
OPPOSITE **honour. 2** =**demote**, downgrade,
lower OPPOSITE **raise**

degrading *adjective* **1** =**demeaning**,
dishonourable, humiliating, infra dig (*inf*),
shameful, undignified, unworthy

degree *noun* **1** =**stage**, grade, notch, point,
rung, step, unit

deity *noun* **1** =**god**, divinity, goddess,
godhead, idol, immortal, supreme being

dejected *adjective* =**downhearted**, crestfallen,
depressed, despondent, disconsolate,
disheartened, downcast, glum, miserable, sad
OPPOSITE **cheerful**

dejection *noun* =**low spirits**, depression,
despair, despondency, doldrums,
downheartedness, gloom, melancholy, sadness,
sorrow, unhappiness

de jure *adverb* =**legally**, by right, rightfully

dekko *noun Brit & Aust slang* **have a dekko** have a look.

delay ❶ *verb* **1** put off to a later time. **2** slow up or cause to be late. ◆ *noun* **3** act of delaying. **4** interval of time between events.

delectable *adjective* delightful, very attractive.

delectation *noun Formal* great pleasure.

delegate ❶ *noun* **1** person chosen to represent others, esp. at a meeting. ◆ *verb* **2** entrust (duties or powers) to someone. **3** appoint as a delegate. **delegation** *noun* **1** group chosen to represent others. **2** delegating.

delete ❶ *verb* remove (something written or printed). **deletion** *noun*

deleterious [del-lit-**eer**-ee-uss] *adjective* harmful, injurious.

Delft *noun* type of earthenware, orig. from Delft in the Netherlands, usu. with blue decoration on a white background (also **delftware**).

deli *noun Informal* delicatessen.

deliberate ❶ *adjective* **1** planned in advance, intentional. **2** careful and unhurried. ◆ *verb* **3** think something over. **deliberately** *adverb* **deliberation** *noun* **deliberative** *adjective*

delicate ❶ *adjective* **1** fine or subtle in quality or workmanship. **2** having a fragile beauty. **3** (of a taste etc.) pleasantly subtle. **4** easily damaged. **5** requiring tact. **delicately** *adverb* **delicacy** *noun* **1** being delicate. **2** *pl* **-cies** something particularly good to eat.

delicatessen *noun* shop selling imported or unusual foods, often already cooked or prepared.

delicious ❶ *adjective* very appealing to taste or smell. **deliciously** *adverb*

delight ❶ *noun* **1** (source of) great pleasure. ◆ *verb* **2** please greatly. **3** (foll. by *in*) take great pleasure (in). **delightful** *adjective* **delightfully** *adverb*

D

—————————————— THESAURUS ——————————————

delay *verb* **1** = **put off**, defer, hold over, postpone, procrastinate, shelve, suspend **2** = **hold up**, bog down, detain, hinder, hold back, impede, obstruct, set back, slow down [OPPOSITE] speed (up) ◆*noun* **3** = **putting off**, deferment, postponement, procrastination, suspension **4** = **hold-up**, hindrance, impediment, interruption, interval, setback, stoppage, wait

delegate *noun* **1** = **representative**, agent, ambassador, commissioner, deputy, envoy, legate ◆*verb* **2** = **entrust**, assign, consign, devolve, give, hand over, pass on, transfer **3** = **appoint**, accredit, authorize, commission, depute, designate, empower, mandate

delegation *noun* **1** = **deputation**, commission, contingent, embassy, envoys, legation, mission **2** = **devolution**, assignment, commissioning, committal

delete *verb* = **remove**, cancel, cross out, efface, erase, expunge, obliterate, rub out, strike out

deliberate *adjective* **1** = **intentional**, calculated, conscious, planned, prearranged, premeditated, purposeful, wilful [OPPOSITE] accidental. **2** = **unhurried**, careful, cautious, circumspect, measured, methodical, ponderous, slow, thoughtful [OPPOSITE] hurried ◆*verb* **3** = **consider**, cogitate, consult, debate, discuss, meditate, ponder, reflect, think, weigh

deliberately *adverb* **1** = **intentionally**, by design, calculatingly, consciously, in cold blood, knowingly, on purpose, wilfully, wittingly

deliberation *noun* = **consideration**, calculation, circumspection, conference,

consultation, debate, discussion, forethought, meditation, reflection, thought

delicacy *noun* **1 a** = **fineness**, accuracy, daintiness, elegance, exquisiteness, lightness, precision, subtlety **b** = **fragility**, flimsiness, frailty, slenderness, tenderness, weakness **c** = **sensitivity**, sensitiveness, tact **2** = **treat**, dainty, luxury, savoury, titbit

delicate *adjective* **1** = **fine**, deft, elegant, exquisite, graceful, precise, skilled, subtle **3** = **subtle**, choice, dainty, delicious, fine, savoury, tender [OPPOSITE] strong. **4** = **fragile**, flimsy, frail, slender, slight, tender, weak **5** = **considerate**, diplomatic, discreet, sensitive, tactful [OPPOSITE] rough

delicately *adverb* **1** = **finely**, daintily, deftly, elegantly, exquisitely, gracefully, precisely, skilfully, subtly **5** = **tactfully**, diplomatically, sensitively

delicious *adjective* = **delectable**, appetizing, choice, dainty, lekker (*S Afr sl*), mouthwatering, savoury, scrumptious (*inf*), tasty, toothsome [OPPOSITE] unpleasant

delight *noun* **1** = **pleasure**, ecstasy, enjoyment, gladness, glee, happiness, joy, rapture [OPPOSITE] displeasure ◆*verb* **2** = **please**, amuse, charm, cheer, enchant, gratify, thrill [OPPOSITE] displease. **3** (foll. by *in*) = **take pleasure in**, appreciate, enjoy, feast on, like, love, relish, revel in, savour

delighted *adjective* = **pleased**, ecstatic, elated, enchanted, happy, joyous, jubilant, overjoyed, thrilled

delightful *adjective* = **pleasant**, agreeable, charming, delectable, enchanting, enjoyable,

delimit *verb* mark or lay down the limits of.
delimitation *noun*
delineate [dill-**lin**-ee-ate] *verb* **1** show by drawing. **2** describe in words. **delineation** *noun*
delinquent ⊕ *noun* **1** someone, esp. a young person, who repeatedly breaks the law. ◆ *adjective* **2** repeatedly breaking the law. **delinquency** *noun, pl* **-cies**
delirium ⊕ *noun* **1** state of excitement and mental confusion, often with hallucinations. **2** great excitement. **delirium tremens** [treh-menz] trembling and hallucinations caused by chronic alcoholism. **delirious** *adjective* **deliriously** *adverb*
deliver ⊕ *verb* **1** carry (goods etc.) to a destination. **2** hand over. **3** aid in the birth of. **4** present (a lecture or speech). **5** release or rescue. **6** strike (a blow). **deliverance** *noun* rescue from captivity or evil. **delivery** *noun, pl* **-eries 1** delivering. **2** something that is delivered. **3** act of giving birth to a baby. **4** style in public speaking.
dell *noun* small wooded hollow.
Delphic *adjective* ambiguous, like the ancient Greek oracle at Delphi.
delphinium *noun* large garden plant with blue flowers.
delta *noun* **1** fourth letter in the Greek alphabet. **2** flat area at the mouth of some rivers where the main stream splits up into several branches.
delude ⊕ *verb* deceive.
deluge ⊕ [del-lyooj] *noun* **1** great flood. **2** torrential rain. **3** overwhelming number. ◆ *verb* **4** flood. **5** overwhelm.
delusion ⊕ *noun* **1** mistaken idea or belief. **2** state of being deluded. **delusive** *adjective*
de luxe ⊕ *adjective* rich or sumptuous, superior in quality.
delve ⊕ *verb* **1** research deeply (for information). **2** *Old-fashioned* dig.
demagnetize *verb* remove magnetic properties from.
demagogue ⊕ *noun* political agitator who appeals to the prejudice and passions of the mob. **demagogic** *adjective* **demagogy** *noun*
demand ⊕ *verb* **1** request forcefully. **2** require as just, urgent, etc. **3** claim as a right. ◆ *noun* **4** forceful request. **5** *Economics* willingness and ability to purchase goods and services. **6** something that requires special effort or sacrifice. **demanding** *adjective* requiring a lot of time or effort.

——————— T H E S A U R U S ———————

pleasurable, rapturous, thrilling OPPOSITE unpleasant
delinquent *noun* **1 = criminal,** culprit, lawbreaker, miscreant, offender, villain, wrongdoer
delirious *adjective* **1 = mad,** crazy, demented, deranged, incoherent, insane, raving, unhinged OPPOSITE **rational. 2 = ecstatic,** beside oneself, carried away, excited, frantic, frenzied, hysterical, wild OPPOSITE **calm**
delirium *noun* **1 = madness,** derangement, hallucination, insanity, raving **2 = frenzy,** ecstasy, fever, hysteria, passion
deliver *verb* **1 = carry,** bear, bring, cart, convey, distribute, transport **2 = hand over,** commit, give up, grant, make over, relinquish, surrender, transfer, turn over, yield **4 = give,** announce, declare, present, read, utter **5 = release,** emancipate, free, liberate, loose, ransom, rescue, save **6 = strike,** administer, aim, deal, direct, give, inflict, launch
deliverance *noun* **= release,** emancipation, escape, liberation, ransom, redemption, rescue, salvation
delivery *noun* **1 = handing over,** consignment, conveyance, dispatch, distribution, surrender, transfer, transmission **3 = childbirth,** confinement, labour, parturition **4**
= speech, articulation, elocution, enunciation, intonation, utterance
delude *verb* **= deceive,** beguile, dupe, fool, hoodwink, kid (*inf*), mislead, take in (*inf*), trick
deluge *noun* **1 = flood,** cataclysm, downpour, inundation, overflowing, spate, torrent **3 = rush,** avalanche, barrage, flood, spate, torrent ◆*verb* **4 = flood,** douse, drench, drown, inundate, soak, submerge, swamp **5 = overwhelm,** engulf, inundate, overload, overrun, swamp
delusion *noun* **1 = misconception,** error, fallacy, false impression, fancy, hallucination, illusion, misapprehension, mistake
de luxe *adjective* **= luxurious,** costly, exclusive, expensive, grand, opulent, select, special, splendid, superior
delve *verb* **1 = research,** burrow, explore, ferret out, forage, investigate, look into, probe, rummage, search
demagogue *noun* **= agitator,** firebrand, rabble-rouser
demand *verb* **1 = request,** ask, challenge, inquire, interrogate, question **2 = require,** call for, cry out for, entail, involve, necessitate, need, want OPPOSITE **give. 3 = claim,** exact, expect, insist on, order ◆*noun* **4 = request,** inquiry, order, question, requisition **5** *Economics*

demarcation ❶ *noun Formal* establishing limits or boundaries, esp. between the work performed by different trade unions.

demean ❶ *verb* **demean oneself** do something unworthy of one's status or character.

demeanour ❶ *noun* way a person behaves.

demented ❶ *adjective* mad. **dementedly** *adverb* **dementia** [dim-**men**-sha] *noun* state of serious mental deterioration.

demerara sugar *noun* brown crystallized cane sugar.

demerger *noun* separation of two or more companies which have previously been merged.

demerit *noun* fault, disadvantage.

demesne [dim-**mane**] *noun* **1** land surrounding a house. **2** *Law* possession of one's own property or land.

demi- *combining form* half.

demigod *noun* **1** being who is part mortal, part god. **2** godlike person.

demijohn *noun* large bottle with a short neck, often encased in wicker.

demilitarize *verb* remove the military forces from. **demilitarization** *noun*

demimonde *noun* **1** (esp. in the 19th century) class of women considered to be outside respectable society because of promiscuity. **2** group considered not wholly respectable.

demise ❶ *noun* **1** eventual failure (of something successful). **2** *Formal* death.

demist *verb* remove condensation from (a windscreen). **demister** *noun*

demo *noun, pl* **demos** *Informal* **1** demonstration, organized expression of public opinion. **2** demonstration record or tape.

demob *verb Informal* demobilize.

demobilize *verb* release from the armed forces. **demobilization** *noun*

democracy ❶ *noun, pl* **-cies 1** government by the people or their elected representatives. **2** state governed in this way. **democrat** *noun* **1** advocate of democracy. **2** (**D-**) member or supporter of the Democratic Party in the US. **democratic** *adjective* **1** of democracy. **2** upholding democracy. **3** (**D-**) of the Democratic Party, the more liberal of the two main political parties in the US. **democratically** *adverb*

demography *noun* study of population statistics, such as births and deaths. **demographer** *noun* **demographic** *adjective*

demolish ❶ *verb* **1** knock down or destroy (a building). **2** disprove (an argument). **demolisher** *noun* **demolition** *noun*

demon ❶ *noun* **1** evil spirit. **2** person who does something with great energy or skill, e.g. *I worked like a demon.* **demonic** *adjective* evil.

demoniac, demoniacal *adjective* **1** appearing to be possessed by a devil. **2** frenzied. **demoniacally** *adverb* **demonology** *noun* study of demons.

demonetize *verb* withdraw from use as currency. **demonetization** *noun*

demonstrate ❶ *verb* **1** show or prove by reasoning or evidence. **2** display and explain the workings of. **3** reveal the existence of. **4** show support or opposition by public parades or rallies. **demonstrable** *adjective* able to be proved. **demonstrably** *adverb* **demonstration** *noun* **1** organized expression of public opinion. **2** explanation or display of how something

———————— THESAURUS ————————

= **need**, call, claim, market, requirement, want

demanding *adjective* = **difficult**, challenging, exacting, hard, taxing, tough, trying, wearing OPPOSITE **easy**

demarcation *noun Formal* = **delimitation**, differentiation, distinction, division, separation

demean *verb* = **lower**, abase, debase, degrade, descend, humble, stoop

demeanour *noun* = **behaviour**, air, bearing, carriage, comportment, conduct, deportment, manner

demented *adjective* = **mad**, crazed, crazy, deranged, frenzied, insane, maniacal, unbalanced, unhinged OPPOSITE **sane**

demise *noun* **1** = **failure**, collapse, downfall, end, fall, ruin **2** *Formal* = **death**, decease, departure

democracy *noun* **1** = **self-government 2** = **republic**, commonwealth

democratic *adjective* **1, 2** = **self-governing**, autonomous, egalitarian, popular, populist, representative

demolish *verb* **1** = **knock down**, bulldoze, destroy, dismantle, flatten, level, raze, tear down OPPOSITE **build**

demolition *noun* **1** = **knocking down**, bulldozing, destruction, explosion, levelling, razing, tearing down, wrecking

demon *noun* **1** = **evil spirit**, devil, fiend, ghoul, goblin, malignant spirit **2** = **wizard**, ace (*inf*), fiend, master

demoniac, demoniacal *adjective* **2** = **frenzied**, crazed, frantic, frenetic, furious, hectic, maniacal, manic

demonic *adjective* = **evil**, devilish, diabolic, diabolical, fiendish, hellish, infernal, satanic

demonstrable *adjective* = **provable**, evident, irrefutable, obvious, palpable, self-evident,

D

works. **3** proof. **demonstrative** *adjective* tending to show one's feelings unreservedly. **demonstratively** *adverb* **demonstrator** *noun* **1** person who demonstrates how a device or machine works. **2** person who takes part in a public demonstration.

demoralize ⊕ *verb* undermine the morale of. **demoralization** *noun*

demote ⊕ *verb* reduce in status or rank. **demotion** *noun*

demotic *adjective* of the common people.

demur ⊕ *verb* **-murring, -murred 1** show reluctance. ◆ *noun* **2 without demur** without objecting.

demure ⊕ *adjective* quiet, reserved, and rather shy. **demurely** *adverb* **demureness** *noun*

demystify *verb* remove the mystery from. **demystification** *noun*

den ⊕ *noun* **1** home of a wild animal. **2** small secluded room in a home. **3** place where people indulge in criminal or immoral activities, e.g. *a den of thieves.*

denarius *noun, pl* **-narii** ancient Roman silver coin, often called a penny in translation.

denationalize *verb* transfer (an industry) from public to private ownership. **denationalization** *noun*

denature *verb* **1** change the nature of. **2** make (alcohol) unfit to drink.

dengue fever, dengue [**deng**-gee] *noun* infectious tropical fever.

denial ⊕ *noun* see DENY.

denier [**den**-yer] *noun* unit of weight used to measure the fineness of nylon or silk.

denigrate ⊕ *verb* criticize unfairly. **denigration** *noun* **denigrator** *noun*

denim *noun* **1** hard-wearing cotton fabric, usu. blue. ◆ *plural* **2** jeans made of denim.

denizen *noun* inhabitant.

denominate ⊕ *verb* give a specific name to.

denomination *noun* **1** group having a distinctive interpretation of a religious faith. **2** unit in a system of weights, values, or measures. **denominational** *adjective*

denominator *noun* number below the line in a fraction.

denote ⊕ *verb* **1** be a sign of. **2** have as a literal meaning. **denotation** *noun*

denouement [day-**noo**-mon] *noun* final outcome or solution in a play or book.

denounce ⊕ *verb* **1** speak vehemently against. **2** give information against. **denunciation** *noun* open condemnation.

dense ⊕ *adjective* **1** closely packed. **2** difficult to see through. **3** stupid. **densely** *adverb*

density *noun, pl* **-ties 1** degree to which something is filled or occupied. **2** measure of the compactness of a substance, expressed as its mass per unit volume.

dent ⊕ *noun* **1** hollow in the surface of

——— T H E S A U R U S ———

demonstrate *verb* **1 = prove**, display, exhibit, indicate, manifest, show, testify to **2 = show how**, describe, explain, illustrate, make clear, teach **4 = march**, parade, picket, protest, rally

demonstration *noun* **1 = march**, mass lobby, parade, picket, protest, rally, sit-in **2 = explanation**, description, exposition, presentation, test, trial **3 = proof**, confirmation, display, evidence, exhibition, expression, illustration, testimony

demoralize *verb* **= dishearten**, deject, depress, discourage, dispirit, undermine, unnerve, weaken OPPOSITE **encourage**

demote *verb* **= downgrade**, degrade, kick downstairs (*sl*), lower in rank, relegate OPPOSITE **promote**

demur *verb* **1 = object**, balk, dispute, hesitate, protest, refuse, take exception, waver ◆ *noun* **2 without demur = without objection**, without a qualm, without compunction, without hesitation, without misgivings, without protest

demure *adjective* **= shy**, diffident, modest, reserved, reticent, retiring, sedate, unassuming OPPOSITE **forward**

den *noun* **1 = lair**, cave, cavern, haunt, hideout, hole, shelter **2 = study**, cubbyhole, hideaway, retreat, sanctuary, sanctum

denial *noun* **1 = negation**, contradiction, dissent, renunciation, repudiation, retraction OPPOSITE **admission. 2 = refusal**, prohibition, rebuff, rejection, repulse, veto

denigrate *verb* **= disparage**, bad-mouth (*sl, chiefly US & Canad*), belittle, knock (*inf*), malign, rubbish (*inf*), run down, slander, vilify OPPOSITE **praise**

denomination *noun* **1 = religious group**, belief, creed, persuasion, school, sect **2 = unit**, grade, size, value

denote *verb* **1 = indicate**, betoken, designate, express, imply, mark, mean, show, signify

denounce *verb* **1 = condemn**, attack, censure, revile, stigmatize, vilify **2 = accuse**, denunciate

dense *adjective* **1 = thick**, close-knit, compact, condensed, heavy, impenetrable, solid OPPOSITE **light. 2 = opaque 3 = stupid**, dozy (*Brit inf*), dull, dumb (*inf*), obtuse, slow-witted, stolid, thick OPPOSITE **bright**

density *noun* **1 = tightness**, compactness, consistency, denseness, impenetrability, solidity, something, made by hitting it. ◆ *verb* **2** make a dent in.

dental *adjective* of teeth or dentistry. **dental floss** waxed thread used to remove food particles from between the teeth. **dental surgeon** dentist. **dentate** *adjective* having teeth or teethlike notches. **dentifrice** [den-tif-riss] *noun* paste or powder for cleaning the teeth. **dentine** [**den**-teen] *noun* hard dense tissue forming the bulk of a tooth. **dentist** *noun* person qualified to practise dentistry. **dentition** *noun* typical arrangement of teeth in a species. **denture** *noun* false tooth.

dentist *noun* person qualified to practise dentistry. **dentistry** *noun* branch of medicine concerned with the teeth and gums.

denude *verb* remove the covering or protection from. **denudation** *noun*

denunciation *noun* see DENOUNCE.

deny ❶ *verb* **-nying, -nied 1** declare to be untrue. **2** refuse to give or allow. **3** refuse to acknowledge. **deniable** *adjective* **denial** *noun* **1** statement that something is not true. **2** rejection of a request.

deodorize *verb* remove or disguise the smell of. **deodorization** *noun* **deodorant** *noun* substance applied to the body to mask the smell of perspiration.

deoxyribonucleic acid *noun* same as DNA.

depart ❶ *verb* **1** leave. **2** differ, deviate. **departed** *adjective* Euphemistic dead. **the departed** Euphemistic a dead person. **departure** *noun*

department ❶ *noun* **1** specialized division of

a large organization. **2** major subdivision of the administration of a government. **3** administrative division of France and some other countries. **4** *Informal* task for which someone is responsible, e.g. *gardening is my department*. **departmental** *adjective* **department store** large shop selling many kinds of goods.

depend ❶ *verb* (foll. by *on*) **1** put trust (in). **2** be influenced or determined (by). **3** rely (on) for income or support. **dependable** *adjective* **dependably** *adverb* **dependability** *noun* **dependant** *noun* person who depends on another for financial support. **dependence** *noun* state of being dependent. **dependency** *noun, pl* **-cies 1** country controlled by another country. **2** overreliance on another person or on a drug. **dependent** *adjective* depending on someone or something.

depict ❶ *verb* **1** produce a picture of. **2** describe in words. **depiction** *noun*

depilatory [dip-**pill**-a-tree] *noun, pl* **-tories** *adjective* (substance) designed to remove unwanted hair.

——————— T H E S A U R U S ———————

thickness **2** = **mass**, bulk
dent *noun* **1** = **hollow**, chip, crater, depression, dimple, dip, impression, indentation, pit ◆*verb* **2** = **make a dent in**, gouge, hollow, press in, push in
deny *verb* **1** = **contradict**, disagree with, disprove, rebuff, rebut, refute OPPOSITE admit. **2** = **refuse**, begrudge, disallow, forbid, reject, turn down, withhold OPPOSITE let. **3** = **renounce**, disclaim, disown, recant, repudiate, retract
depart *verb* **1** = **leave**, absent (oneself), disappear, exit, go, go away, quit, retire, retreat, withdraw OPPOSITE arrive. **2** = **change**, deviate, differ, digress, diverge, stray, swerve, turn aside, vary, veer
department *noun* **1** = **section**, branch, bureau, division, office, station, subdivision, unit
departure *noun* **1** = **leaving**, exit, exodus, going, going away, leave-taking, removal, retirement, withdrawal OPPOSITE arrival. **2**

= **change**, deviation, difference, digression, divergence, innovation, novelty, shift, variation, whole new ball game (*inf*)
depend *verb* (foll. by *on*) **1** = **trust in**, bank on, count on, lean on, reckon on, rely upon, turn to **2** = **be determined by**, be based on, be contingent on, be subject to, be subordinate to, hang on, hinge on, rest on, revolve around
dependable *adjective* **1** = **reliable**, faithful, reputable, responsible, staunch, steady, sure, trustworthy, trusty, unfailing OPPOSITE undependable
dependent *adjective* = **determined**, conditional, contingent, depending, influenced, subject OPPOSITE independent
depict *verb* **1** = **draw**, delineate, illustrate, outline, paint, picture, portray, sketch **2** = **describe**, characterize, narrate, outline, represent
depiction *noun* **1** = **representation**, delineation, picture, portrayal, sketch **2**

deplete ❶ *verb* **1** use up. **2** reduce in number.
depletion *noun*
deplore ❶ *verb* condemn strongly.
deplorable *adjective* very bad or unpleasant.
deploy ❶ *verb* organize (troops or resources) into a position ready for immediate action.
deployment *noun*
deponent *noun Law* person who makes a statement on oath.
depopulate *verb* reduce the population of.
depopulation *noun*
deport ❶ *verb* remove forcibly from a country.
deport oneself behave in a specified way.
deportation *noun* **deportee** *noun*
deportment *noun* way in which a person moves or stands.
depose ❶ *verb* **1** remove from an office or position of power. **2** *Law* testify on oath.
deposit ❶ *verb* **1** put down. **2** entrust for safekeeping, esp. to a bank. **3** lay down naturally. ◆ *noun* **4** sum of money paid into a bank account. **5** money given in part payment for goods or services. **6** accumulation of sediments, minerals, etc. **deposit account** bank account that earns interest. **depositary** *noun*, *pl* **-taries** person to whom something is entrusted for safety. **depositor** *noun*
depository *noun*, *pl* **-tories** store for furniture etc.
deposition *noun* **1** *Law* sworn statement of a witness used in court in his or her absence. **2** deposing. **3** depositing. **4** something deposited.
depot ❶ [dep-oh] *noun* **1** building where goods or vehicles are kept when not in use. **2** *Chiefly US* bus or railway station.
depraved ❶ *adjective* morally bad. **depravity** *noun*
deprecate *verb* express disapproval of.
deprecation *noun* **deprecatory** *adjective*
depreciate ❶ *verb* **1** decline in value or price. **2** criticize. **depreciation** *noun*
depredation *noun* plundering.
depress ❶ *verb* **1** make sad. **2** lower (prices or wages). **3** push down. **depressing** *adjective*
depressingly *adverb* **depressant** *noun*, *adjective* (drug) able to reduce nervous activity.
depression *noun* **1** mental state in which a person has feelings of gloom and inadequacy. **2** economic condition in which there is high unemployment and low output and investment. **3** area of low air pressure. **4** sunken place. **the Depression** the worldwide economic depression of the early 1930s. **depressive** *adjective* **1** tending to cause depression. ◆ *noun* **2** person who suffers from depression.
deprive ❶ *verb* (foll. by *of*) prevent from

——————— THESAURUS ———————

= description
deplete *verb* **1** = **use up**, consume, drain, empty, exhaust, expend, impoverish [OPPOSITE] increase. **2** = **reduce**, lessen [OPPOSITE] increase
deplorable *adjective* = **terrible**, disgraceful, grievous, lamentable, pitiable, regrettable, sad, scandalous, shameful, unfortunate, wretched [OPPOSITE] excellent
deplore *verb* = **disapprove of**, abhor, censure, condemn, denounce, object to, take a dim view of
deploy *verb* = **position**, arrange, set out, station, use, utilize
deployment *noun* = **position**, arrangement, organization, spread, stationing, use, utilization
deport *verb* = **expel**, banish, exile, expatriate, extradite, oust **deport oneself** = **behave**, acquit oneself, act, bear oneself, carry oneself, comport oneself, conduct oneself, hold oneself
depose *verb* **1** = **remove from office**, demote, dethrone, dismiss, displace, oust **2** *Law* = **testify**, avouch, declare, make a deposition
deposit *verb* **1** = **put**, drop, lay, locate, place **2** = **store**, bank, consign, entrust, lodge ◆ *noun* **5** = **down payment**, instalment, part payment, pledge, retainer, security, stake **6** = **sediment**, accumulation, dregs, lees, precipitate, silt

depot *noun* **1** = **storehouse**, depository, repository, warehouse **2** *Chiefly US* = **bus station**, garage, terminus
depraved *adjective* = **corrupt**, degenerate, dissolute, evil, immoral, sinful, vicious, vile, wicked [OPPOSITE] moral
depravity *noun* = **corruption**, debauchery, evil, immorality, sinfulness, vice, wickedness
depreciate *verb* **1** = **decrease**, deflate, devalue, lessen, lose value, lower, reduce [OPPOSITE] expand. **2** = **disparage**, belittle, denigrate, deride, detract, run down, scorn, sneer at
depreciation *noun* **1** = **devaluation**, deflation, depression, drop, fall, slump **2** = **disparagement**, belittlement, denigration, deprecation, detraction
depress *verb* **1** = **sadden**, deject, discourage, dishearten, dispirit, make despondent, oppress, weigh down [OPPOSITE] cheer. **2** = **lower**, cheapen, depreciate, devalue, diminish, downgrade, lessen, reduce [OPPOSITE] increase. **3** = **press down**, flatten, level, lower, push down
depressed *adjective* **1** = **low-spirited**, blue, dejected, despondent, discouraged, dispirited, ' downcast, downhearted, fed up, sad, unhappy

(having or enjoying). **deprivation** *noun*
deprived *adjective* lacking adequate living
conditions, education, etc.
dept department.
depth ⊕ *noun* **1** distance downwards,
backwards, or inwards. **2** intensity of emotion.
3 profundity of character or thought. **4**
intensity of colour. ◆ *plural* **5** remote
inaccessible place, e.g. *the depths of the
Universe.* **6** most severe point, e.g. *in the depths
of the Depression; the depths of their anguish.*
depth charge bomb used to attack submarines
by exploding at a preset depth of water.
depute ⊕ *verb* appoint (someone) to act on
one's behalf. **deputation** *noun* body of people
appointed to represent others. **deputize** *verb*
act as deputy. **deputy** *noun, pl* **-ties** person
appointed to act on behalf of another.
derail *verb* cause (a train) to go off the rails.
derailment *noun*
derailleur [dee-**rail**-yer] *noun* type of gear-
change mechanism for bicycles.
deranged ⊕ *adjective* **1** insane or
uncontrolled. **2** in a state of disorder.
derangement *noun*
derby[1] [**der**-bee] *noun, pl* **-bies** *US* bowler
hat.
derby[2] [**dah**-bee] *noun, pl* **-bies** sporting
event between teams from the same area. **the**

Derby annual horse race run at Epsom Downs.
deregulate *verb* remove regulations or
controls from. **deregulation** *noun*
derelict ⊕ *adjective* **1** unused and falling into
ruins. ◆ *noun* **2** social outcast, vagrant.
dereliction *noun* state of being abandoned.
dereliction of duty failure to do one's duty.
derestrict *verb* make (a road) free from speed
limits.
deride ⊕ *verb* treat with contempt or ridicule.
derision *noun* **derisive** *adjective* mocking,
scornful. **derisory** *adjective* too small or
inadequate to be considered seriously.
de rigueur [de rig-**gur**] *adjective* required by
fashion.
derive ⊕ *verb* (foll. by *from*) take or develop
(from). **derivation** *noun* **derivative** *adjective* **1**
based on other sources, not original. ◆ *noun* **2**
word, idea, etc., derived from another. **3** *Maths*
rate of change of one quantity in relation to
another.
dermatitis *noun* inflammation of the skin.
dermatology *noun* branch of medicine
concerned with the skin. **dermatologist** *noun*
derogate *verb* (foll. by *from*) detract from.
derogation *noun*
derogatory ⊕ [dir-**rog**-a-tree] *adjective*
intentionally offensive.
derrick *noun* **1** simple crane. **2** framework

D

—————————— THESAURUS ——————————

2 = **lowered**, cheapened, depreciated,
devalued, weakened **3** = **sunken**, concave,
hollow, indented, recessed
depressing *adjective* **1** = **bleak**, discouraging,
disheartening, dismal, dispiriting, gloomy,
harrowing, sad, saddening
depression *noun* **1** = **low spirits**, dejection,
despair, despondency, downheartedness,
dumps (*inf*), gloominess, melancholy, sadness,
the blues **2** = **recession**, economic decline,
hard or bad times, inactivity, slump, stagnation
4 = **hollow**, bowl, cavity, dent, dimple, dip,
indentation, pit, valley
deprivation *noun* = **want**, denial, destitution,
dispossession, hardship, need, privation,
removal, withdrawal, withholding
deprive *verb* (foll. by *of*) = **withhold**, bereave,
despoil, dispossess, rob, strip
deprived *adjective* = **poor**, bereft, destitute,
disadvantaged, down at heel, in need, lacking,
needy OPPOSITE prosperous
depth *noun* **1** = **deepness**, drop, extent,
measure **3** = **profoundness**, astuteness,
discernment, insight, penetration, profundity,
sagacity, wisdom OPPOSITE superficiality
deputation *noun* = **delegation**, commission,

embassy, envoys, legation
deputize *verb* = **stand in for**, act for, take the
place of, understudy
deputy *noun* = **substitute**, delegate, legate,
lieutenant, number two, proxy, representative,
second-in-command, surrogate
deranged *adjective* **1** = **mad**, crazed, crazy,
demented, distracted, insane, irrational,
unbalanced, unhinged OPPOSITE sane
derelict *adjective* **1** = **abandoned**, deserted,
dilapidated, discarded, forsaken, munted (*NZ
sl*), neglected, ruined ◆*noun* **2** = **tramp**, bag
lady, down-and-out, outcast, vagrant
deride *verb* = **mock**, disdain, disparage, insult,
jeer, ridicule, scoff, scorn, sneer, taunt
derisory *adjective* = **ridiculous**, contemptible,
insulting, laughable, ludicrous, outrageous,
preposterous
derivation *noun* = **origin**, beginning,
foundation, root, source
derive *verb* (foll. by *from*) = **come from**, arise
from, emanate from, flow from, issue from,
originate from, proceed from, spring from, stem
from
derogatory *adjective* = **disparaging**,
belittling, defamatory, offensive, slighting,

erected over an oil well.

derring-do *noun Old-fashioned or lit* spirited bravery, boldness.

derringer *noun* small large-bored pistol.

derv *noun* diesel oil, when used for road transport.

dervish *noun* member of a Muslim religious order noted for a frenzied whirling dance.

desalination *noun* process of removing salt, esp. from sea water.

descale *verb* remove a hard coating from inside (a kettle or pipe).

descant *noun Music* **1** tune played or sung above a basic melody. ♦ *adjective* **2** denoting the highest member in a family of musical instruments, e.g. *descant clarinets*.

descend ❶ *verb* **1** move down (a slope etc.). **2** move to a lower level, pitch, etc. **3** (foll. by *to*) stoop to (unworthy behaviour). **4** (foll. by *on*) visit unexpectedly. **be descended from** be connected by a blood relationship to.

descendant *noun* person or animal descended from an individual, race, or species.

descendent *adjective* descending. **descent** *noun* **1** descending. **2** downward slope. **3** derivation from an ancestor.

describe ❶ *verb* **1** give an account of (something or someone) in words. **2** trace the outline of (a circle etc.). **description** *noun* **1** statement that describes something or someone. **2** sort, e.g. *flowers of every description*. **descriptive** *adjective* **descriptively**

adverb

descry *verb* **-scrying, -scried 1** catch sight of. **2** discover by looking carefully.

desecrate *verb* damage or insult (something sacred). **desecration** *noun*

desegregate *verb* end racial segregation in. **desegregation** *noun*

deselect *verb Brit politics* refuse to select (an MP) for re-election. **deselection** *noun*

desensitize *verb* make less sensitive.

desert¹ ❶ *noun* region with little or no vegetation because of low rainfall.

desert² ❶ *verb* **1** abandon (a person or place) without intending to return. **2** *Mil* leave (a post or duty) with no intention of returning. **deserter** *noun* **desertion** *noun*

deserts *plural noun* **get one's just deserts** get the punishment one deserves.

deserve ❶ *verb* be entitled to or worthy of.

deserved *adjective* rightfully earned.

deservedly [dee-**zerv**-id-lee] *adverb* **deserving** *adjective* worthy of help, praise, or reward.

deshabille [day-zab-**beel**] *noun* state of being partly dressed.

desiccate *verb* remove most of the water from. **desiccation** *noun*

SPELLING TIP

The word **desiccate** has two *cs* because it comes from the Latin word *siccus*, which means 'dry'.

———— THESAURUS ————

uncomplimentary, unfavourable, unflattering
OPPOSITE **complimentary**

descend *verb* **1** = **move down**, drop, fall, go down, plummet, plunge, sink, subside, tumble OPPOSITE **rise**. **2** = **slope**, dip, incline, slant **3** = **lower oneself**, degenerate, deteriorate, stoop **4** (foll. by *on*) = **attack**, arrive, invade, raid, swoop **be descended from** = **originate from**, be handed down from, be passed down from, derive from, issue from, proceed from, spring from

descent *noun* **1** = **coming down**, drop, fall, plunge, swoop **2** = **slope**, declivity, dip, drop, incline, slant **3** = **ancestry**, extraction, family tree, genealogy, lineage, origin, parentage

describe *verb* **1** = **relate**, depict, explain, express, narrate, portray, recount, report, tell **2** = **trace**, delineate, draw, mark out, outline

description *noun* **1** = **account**, depiction, explanation, narrative, portrayal, report, representation, sketch **2** = **kind**, brand, category, class, order, sort, type, variety

descriptive *adjective* **1** = **graphic**, detailed,

explanatory, expressive, illustrative, pictorial, picturesque, vivid

desert¹ *noun* = **wilderness**, solitude, waste, wasteland, wilds

desert² *verb* **1** = **abandon**, abscond, forsake, jilt, leave, leave stranded, maroon, quit, strand, walk out on (*inf*) OPPOSITE **take care of**

deserted *adjective* = **abandoned**, derelict, desolate, empty, forsaken, neglected, unoccupied, vacant

deserter *noun* = **defector**, absconder, escapee, fugitive, renegade, runaway, traitor, truant

desertion *noun* = **abandonment**, absconding, apostasy, betrayal, defection, dereliction, escape, evasion, flight, relinquishment

deserve *verb* = **merit**, be entitled to, be worthy of, earn, justify, rate, warrant

deserved *adjective* = **well-earned**, due, earned, fitting, justified, merited, proper, rightful, warranted

deserving *adjective* = **worthy**, commendable, estimable, laudable, meritorious, praiseworthy,

design ⊕ *verb* **1** work out the structure or form of (something), by making a sketch or plans. **2** plan and make artistically. **3** intend for a specific purpose. ◆ *noun* **4** sketch, plan, or preliminary drawing. **5** arrangement or features of an artistic or decorative work. **6** finished artistic or decorative pattern. **7** art of designing. **8** intention, e.g. *by design*. **designedly** [dee-zine-id-lee] *adverb* intentionally. **designer** *noun* **1** person who draws up original sketches or plans from which things are made. ◆ *adjective* **2** designed by a well-known designer. **designing** *adjective* cunning and scheming.

designate ⊕ [dez-zig-nate] *verb* **1** give a name to. **2** select (someone) for an office or duty. ◆ *adjective* **3** appointed but not yet in office, e.g. *the Prime Minister designate*. **designation** *noun* name.

desire ⊕ *verb* **1** want very much. ◆ *noun* **2** wish, longing. **3** sexual appetite. **4** person or thing desired. **desirable** *adjective* **1** worth having. **2** arousing sexual desire. **desirability** *noun* **desirous of** having a desire for.

desist ⊕ *verb* (foll. by *from*) stop (doing something).

desk *noun* **1** piece of furniture with a writing surface and drawers. **2** service counter in a public building. **3** section of a newspaper covering a specific subject, e.g. *the sports desk*. **desktop** *adjective* (of a computer) small enough to use at a desk. **desktop publishing** means of publishing reports etc. using a desktop computer and a laser printer.

desolate ⊕ *adjective* **1** uninhabited and bleak. **2** very sad. ◆ *verb* **3** deprive of inhabitants. **4** make (someone) very sad. **desolation** *noun*

despair ⊕ *noun* **1** total loss of hope. ◆ *verb* **2** lose hope.

despatch ⊕ *verb, noun* same as DISPATCH.

desperado ⊕ *noun, pl* **-does, -dos** reckless person ready to commit any violent illegal act.

desperate ⊕ *adjective* **1** in despair and reckless. **2** (of an action) undertaken as a last resort. **3** having a strong need or desire, **desperately** *adverb* **desperation** *noun*

> **SPELLING TIP**
>
> It's often difficult to decide whether to write an *a* or an *e* when it doesn't seem to affect a word's pronunciation. An example in the Bank of English is *desparate*, which should, of course, be spelt **desperate**.

righteous OPPOSITE **undeserving**

design *verb* **1** = **plan**, draft, draw, outline, sketch, trace **2** = **create**, conceive, fabricate, fashion, invent, originate, think up **3** = **intend**, aim, mean, plan, propose, purpose ◆*noun* **4** = **plan**, blueprint, draft, drawing, model, outline, scheme, sketch **5** = **arrangement**, construction, form, organization, pattern, shape, style **7** = **intention**, aim, end, goal, object, objective, purpose, target

designate *verb* **1** = **name**, call, dub, entitle, label, style, term **2** = **appoint**, assign, choose, delegate, depute, nominate, select

designation *noun* = **name**, description, label, mark, title

designer *noun* **1** = **creator**, architect, deviser, inventor, originator, planner

desirable *adjective* **1** = **agreeable**, advantageous, advisable, beneficial, good, preferable, profitable, worthwhile OPPOSITE **disadvantageous**. **2** = **attractive**, adorable, alluring, fetching, glamorous, lekker (*S Afr sl*), seductive, sexy (*inf*) OPPOSITE **unattractive**

desire *verb* **1** = **want**, crave, hanker after, hope for, long for, set one's heart on, thirst for, wish for, yearn for ◆*noun* **2** = **wish**, aspiration, craving, hankering, hope, longing, thirst, want

3 = **lust**, appetite, libido, passion

desist *verb* (foll. by *from*) = **stop**, break off, cease, discontinue, end, forbear, leave off, pause, refrain from

desolate *adjective* **1** = **uninhabited**, bare, barren, bleak, dreary, godforsaken, solitary, wild OPPOSITE **inhabited**. **2** = **miserable**, dejected, despondent, disconsolate, downcast, forlorn, gloomy, wretched OPPOSITE **happy** ◆*verb* **3** = **lay waste**, depopulate, despoil, destroy, devastate, lay low, pillage, plunder, ravage, ruin **4** = **deject**, depress, discourage, dishearten, dismay, distress, grieve OPPOSITE **cheer**

desolation *noun* **1** = **bleakness**, barrenness, isolation, solitude **2** = **misery**, anguish, dejection, despair, distress, gloom, sadness, woe, wretchedness

despair *noun* **1** = **despondency**, anguish, dejection, depression, desperation, gloom, hopelessness, misery, wretchedness ◆*verb* **2** = **lose hope**, give up, lose heart

despairing *adjective* = **hopeless**, dejected, desperate, despondent, disconsolate, frantic, grief-stricken, inconsolable, miserable, wretched

despatch see DISPATCH

desperado *noun* = **criminal**, bandit, lawbreaker, outlaw, villain

despise 🟊 *verb* regard with contempt.
despicable *adjective* deserving contempt.
despicably *adverb*
despite 🟊 *preposition* in spite of.
despoil *verb Formal* plunder. **despoliation**
noun
despondent 🟊 *adjective* unhappy.
despondently *adverb* **despondency** *noun*
despot 🟊 *noun* person in power who acts
unfairly or cruelly. **despotic** *adjective*
despotically *adverb* **despotism** *noun* unfair or
cruel government or behaviour.
dessert *noun* sweet course served at the
end of a meal. **dessertspoon** *noun* spoon
between a tablespoon and a teaspoon in
size.
destabilize *verb* make (a country or
government) politically or economically
unstable. **destabilization** *noun*
destination 🟊 *noun* place to which someone
or something is going.
destined 🟊 [**dess**-tind] *adjective* **1** certain
to be or to do something, e.g. *destined to
fail.* **2** heading towards a specific
destination, e.g. *destined for Eastern*

Europe.
destiny 🟊 *noun, pl* **-nies 1** future marked out
for a person or thing. **2** the power that
predetermines the course of events.
destitute 🟊 *adjective* having no money or
possessions. **destitution** *noun*
destroy 🟊 *verb* **1** ruin, demolish. **2** put an
end to. **3** kill (an animal). **destroyer** *noun* **1**
small heavily armed warship. **2** person or thing
that destroys. **destruction** *noun* ruin.
destruction 🟊 *noun* **1** destroying. **2** cause of
ruin. **destructible** *adjective* able to be
destroyed. **destructive** *adjective* (capable of)
causing destruction. **destructively** *adverb*
destructiveness *noun*
desuetude [diss-**syoo**-it-tude] *noun* condition
of not being in use.
desultory [**dez**-zl-tree] *adjective* **1** jumping
from one thing to another, disconnected. **2**
random. **desultorily** *adverb*
detach 🟊 *verb* disengage and separate.
detachable *adjective* **detached** *adjective* **1** (of
a house) not joined to another house. **2**
showing no emotional involvement.
detachment *noun* **1** lack of emotional
involvement. **2** small group of soldiers.

———————— T H E S A U R U S ————————

desperate *adjective* **1** = **reckless**, audacious,
daring, frantic, furious, risky **2** = **grave**, drastic,
extreme, urgent
desperately *adverb* **2** = **badly**, appallingly,
dangerously, fearfully, frightfully, gravely,
hopelessly, perilously, seriously, severely
desperation *noun* **a** = **misery**, agony,
anguish, despair, hopelessness, trouble,
unhappiness, worry **b** = **recklessness**,
foolhardiness, frenzy, impetuosity, madness,
rashness
despicable *adjective* = **contemptible**,
detestable, disgraceful, hateful, mean, scungy
(*Aust & NZ inf*), shameful, sordid, vile,
worthless, wretched OPPOSITE admirable
despise *verb* = **look down on**, abhor, detest,
loathe, revile, scorn OPPOSITE admire
despite *preposition* = **in spite of**, against, even
with, in the face of, in the teeth of,
notwithstanding, regardless of, undeterred by
despondency *noun* = **dejection**, depression,
despair, desperation, gloom, low spirits,
melancholy, misery, sadness
despondent *adjective* = **dejected**, depressed,
disconsolate, disheartened, dispirited,
downhearted, glum, in despair, sad, sorrowful
OPPOSITE cheerful
despot *noun* = **tyrant**, autocrat, dictator,
oppressor

despotic *adjective* = **tyrannical**, authoritarian,
autocratic, dictatorial, domineering, imperious,
oppressive
despotism *noun* = **tyranny**, autocracy,
dictatorship, oppression, totalitarianism
destination *noun* = **journey's end**, haven,
resting-place, station, stop, terminus
destined *adjective* = **fated**, bound, certain,
doomed, intended, meant, predestined
destiny *noun* **1** = **fortune**, doom, fate, lot,
portion **2** = **fate**, fortune, karma, kismet
destitute *adjective* = **penniless**, down and
out, impoverished, indigent, insolvent,
moneyless, penurious, poor, poverty-stricken
destroy *verb* **1**, **2** = **ruin**, annihilate, crush,
demolish, devastate, eradicate, shatter, wipe
out, wreck
destruction *noun* **1** = **ruin**, annihilation,
demolition, devastation, eradication,
extermination, havoc, slaughter, wreckage
destructive *adjective* = **damaging**,
calamitous, catastrophic, deadly, devastating,
fatal, harmful, lethal, ruinous
detach *verb* = **separate**, cut off, disconnect,
disengage, divide, remove, sever, tear off,
unfasten OPPOSITE attach
detached *adjective* **1** = **separate**,
disconnected, discrete, unconnected **2**
= **uninvolved**, disinterested, dispassionate,

D

detail ⓿ *noun* **1** individual piece of information. **2** unimportant item. **3** small individual features of something, considered collectively. **4** *Chiefly mil* (personnel assigned) a specific duty. ◆ *verb* **5** list fully. **6** *Chiefly mil* assign to a specific duty.
detain ⓿ *verb* **1** delay (someone). **2** hold (someone) in custody. **detainee** *noun* **detainment** *noun*
detect ⓿ *verb* **1** notice. **2** discover, find. **detectable** *adjective* **detection** *noun* **detective** *noun* policeman or private agent who investigates crime. **detector** *noun* instrument used to find something, e.g. *a metal detector.*
detente [day-**tont**] *noun* easing of tension between nations.
detention ⓿ *noun* **1** imprisonment. **2** form of punishment in which a pupil is detained after school.
deter ⓿ *verb* **-terring, -terred** discourage (someone) from doing something by instilling fear or doubt. **deterrent** *noun* **1** something that deters. **2** weapon, esp. nuclear, intended to deter attack. ◆ *adjective* **3** tending to deter. **deterrence** *noun*
detergent ⓿ *noun* chemical substance for washing clothes or dishes.
deteriorate ⓿ *verb* become worse. **deterioration** *noun*
determine ⓿ *verb* **1** settle (an argument or a question) conclusively. **2** find out the facts about. **3** make a firm decision (to do something). **determinant** *noun* factor that determines. **determinate** *adjective* definitely limited or fixed. **determination** *noun* **1** being determined or resolute. **2** determining. **determined** *adjective* firmly decided, unable to be dissuaded. **determinedly** *adverb* **determiner** *noun Grammar* word that determines the object to which a noun phrase refers, e.g. *all.* **determinism** *noun* theory that human choice is not free, but decided by past events. **determinist** *noun, adjective* **deterministic** *adjective*
detest ⓿ *verb* dislike intensely. **detestable** *adjective* **detestation** *noun*
dethrone *verb* remove from a throne or position of power.
detonate ⓿ *verb* explode. **detonation** *noun* **detonator** *noun* small amount of explosive, or a device, used to set off an explosion.
detour ⓿ *noun* route that is not the most

——————————— THESAURUS ———————————

impartial, impersonal, neutral, objective, reserved, unbiased OPPOSITE **subjective**
detachment *noun* **1** = **indifference**, aloofness, coolness, impartiality, neutrality, nonchalance, objectivity, remoteness, unconcern **2** = **unit**, body, force, party, patrol, squad, task force
detail *noun* **2** = **fine point**, nicety, particular, triviality **3** = **point**, aspect, component, element, fact, factor, feature, particular, respect **4** *Chiefly mil* = **party**, assignment, body, detachment, duty, fatigue, force, squad ◆*verb* **5** = **list**, catalogue, enumerate, itemize, recite, recount, rehearse, relate, tabulate **6** *Chiefly mil* = **appoint**, allocate, assign, charge, commission, delegate, send
detailed *adjective* **1** = **comprehensive**, blow-by-blow, exhaustive, full, intricate, minute, particular, thorough OPPOSITE **brief**
detain *verb* **1** = **delay**, check, hinder, hold up, impede, keep back, retard, slow up (*or* down) **2** = **hold**, arrest, confine, intern, restrain
detect *verb* **1** = **notice**, ascertain, identify, note, observe, perceive, recognize, spot **2** = **discover**, find, track down, uncover, unmask
detective *noun* = **investigator**, cop (*sl*), gumshoe (*US sl*), private eye, private investigator, sleuth (*inf*)

detention *noun* **1** = **imprisonment**, confinement, custody, incarceration OPPOSITE **release**
deter *verb* = **discourage**, dissuade, frighten, inhibit from, intimidate, prevent, put off, stop, talk out of
detergent *noun* = **cleaner**, cleanser
deteriorate *verb* = **decline**, degenerate, go downhill (*inf*), lower, slump, worsen OPPOSITE **improve**
determination *noun* **1** = **resolution**, dedication, doggedness, fortitude, perseverance, persistence, resolve, single-mindedness, steadfastness, tenacity, willpower OPPOSITE **indecision**
determine *verb* **1** = **settle**, conclude, decide, end, finish, ordain, regulate **2** = **find out**, ascertain, detect, discover, establish, learn, verify, work out **3** = **decide**, choose, elect, make up one's mind, resolve
determined *adjective* = **resolute**, dogged, firm, intent, persevering, persistent, single-minded, steadfast, tenacious, unwavering
deterrent *noun* **1** = **discouragement**, check, curb, disincentive, hindrance, impediment, obstacle, restraint OPPOSITE **incentive**
detest *verb* = **hate**, abhor, abominate, despise, dislike intensely, loathe, recoil from OPPOSITE

direct one.

detox *verb, noun Informal* (undergo) treatment to rid the body of poisonous substances.

detoxify *verb* **-fying, -fied** remove poison from. **detoxification** *noun*

detract ● *verb* (foll. by *from*) make (something) seem less good. **detractor** *noun* **detraction** *noun*

detriment ● *noun* disadvantage or damage. **detrimental** *adjective* **detrimentally** *adverb*

detritus [dit-**trite**-uss] *noun* **1** loose mass of stones and silt worn away from rocks. **2** debris.

de trop [de **troh**] *adjective French* unwanted, unwelcome.

detumescence *noun* subsidence of swelling. **detumescent** *adjective*

deuce [**dyewss**] *noun* **1** *Tennis* score of forty all. **2** playing card with two symbols or dice with two spots.

deuterium *noun* isotope of hydrogen twice as heavy as the normal atom.

Deutschmark [**doytch**-mark], **Deutsche Mark** [**doytch**-a] *noun* monetary unit of Germany.

devalue *verb* **-valuing, -valued 1** reduce the exchange value of (a currency). **2** reduce the value of (something or someone). **devaluation** *noun*

devastate ● *verb* destroy. **devastated** *adjective* shocked and extremely upset. **devastation** *noun*

develop ● *verb* **1** grow or bring to a later, more elaborate, or more advanced stage. **2** come or bring into existence. **3** build houses or factories on (an area of land). **4** produce

(photographs) by making negatives or prints from a film. **developer** *noun* **1** person who develops property. **2** chemical used to develop photographs or films. **development** *noun* **1** developing. **2** product of developing. **3** event or incident that changes a situation. **4** area of land that has been developed. **developmental** *adjective* **developing country** poor or nonindustrial country that is trying to develop its resources by industrialization.

deviate ● *verb* **1** differ from others in belief or thought. **2** depart from one's previous behaviour. **deviation** *noun* **deviant** *noun, adjective* (person) deviating from what is considered acceptable behaviour. **deviance** *noun*

device ● *noun* **1** machine or tool used for a specific task. **2** scheme or plan. **leave someone to his, her own devices** let someone do as he or she wishes.

devil ● *noun* **1** evil spirit. **2** evil person. **3** person, e.g. *poor devil*. **4** daring person, e.g. *be a devil!* **5** *Informal* something difficult or annoying, e.g. *a devil of a long time.* ◆ *verb* **-illing, -illed 6** prepare (food) with a highly flavoured spiced mixture. **the Devil** *Theology* chief spirit of evil and enemy of God. **devilish** *adjective* **1** cruel or unpleasant. ◆ *adverb* **2** (also **devilishly**) *Informal* extremely. **devilment** *noun* mischievous conduct. **devilry** *noun* mischievousness. **devil-may-care** *adjective* carefree and cheerful. **devil's advocate** person who takes an opposing or unpopular point of view for the sake of argument.

devious ● *adjective* **1** insincere and dishonest.

———— THESAURUS ————

love

detonate *verb* **= explode**, blast, blow up, discharge, set off, trigger

detour *noun* **= diversion**, bypass, indirect course, roundabout way

detract *verb* (foll. by *from*) **= lessen**, devaluate, diminish, lower, reduce, take away from OPPOSITE **improve**

detriment *noun* **= damage**, disadvantage, disservice, harm, hurt, impairment, injury, loss

detrimental *adjective* **= damaging**, adverse, deleterious, destructive, disadvantageous, harmful, prejudicial, unfavourable OPPOSITE **beneficial**

devastate *verb* **= destroy**, demolish, lay waste, level, ravage, raze, ruin, sack, wreck

devastation *noun* **= destruction**, demolition, desolation, havoc, ruin

develop *verb* **1 = advance**, amplify, augment, broaden, elaborate, enlarge, evolve, expand,

flourish, grow, mature, progress, prosper, ripen **2 = form**, breed, establish, generate, invent, originate

development *noun* **1 = growth**, advance, evolution, expansion, improvement, increase, progress, spread **3 = event**, happening, incident, occurrence, result, turn of events, upshot

deviant *noun* **= pervert**, freak, misfit ◆ *adjective* **= perverted**, kinky (*sl*), sick (*inf*), twisted, warped OPPOSITE **normal**

deviate *verb* **= differ**, depart, diverge, stray, swerve, veer, wander

deviation *noun* **= departure**, digression, discrepancy, disparity, divergence, inconsistency, irregularity, shift, variation

device *noun* **1 = gadget**, apparatus, appliance, contraption, implement, instrument, machine, tool **2 = ploy**, gambit, manoeuvre, plan, scheme, stratagem, trick, wile

D

2 indirect. **deviously** *adverb* **deviousness** *noun*

devise ⊕ *verb* work out (something) in one's mind.

devoid ⊕ *adjective* (foll. by *of*) completely lacking (in).

devolve *verb* (foll. by *on* or *to*) pass (power or duties) or (of power or duties) be passed to a successor or substitute. **devolution** *noun* transfer of authority from a central government to regional governments.

devote ⊕ *verb* apply or dedicate to a particular purpose. **devoted** *adjective* showing loyalty or devotion. **devotedly** *adverb* **devotee** [dev-vote-**tee**] *noun* **1** person who is very enthusiastic about something. **2** zealous follower of a religion. **devotion** *noun* **1** strong affection for or loyalty to someone or something. **2** religious zeal. ♦ *plural* **3** prayers. **devotional** *adjective*

devour ⊕ *verb* **1** eat greedily. **2** (of an emotion) engulf and destroy. **3** read eagerly.

devout ⊕ *adjective* deeply religious. **devoutly** *adverb*

dew *noun* drops of water that form on the ground at night from vapour in the air. **dewy** *adjective* **dewier, dewiest. dewy-eyed** *adjective* innocent and inexperienced.

dewlap *noun* loose fold of skin hanging under the throat in dogs, cattle, etc.

dexterity ⊕ *noun* **1** skill in using one's hands.

2 mental quickness. **dexterous** *adjective* **dexterously** *adverb*

dextrin, dextrine *noun* sticky substance obtained from starch, used as a thickening agent in food.

dextrose *noun* glucose occurring in fruit, honey, and the blood of animals.

dg decigram.

DH Department of Health.

dhal, dal *noun* curry made from lentils or beans.

dharma *noun* **1** *Hinduism* moral law or behaviour. **2** *Buddhism* ideal truth.

dhoti *noun, pl* **-tis** long loincloth worn by men in India.

dhow *noun* Arab sailing ship.

DI donor insemination: method of making a woman pregnant by transferring sperm from a man other than her regular partner using artificial means.

di- *prefix* **1** twice, two, or double, e.g. *dicotyledon*. **2** containing two specified atoms or groups of atoms, e.g. *carbon dioxide*.

diabetes [die-a-**beet**-eez] *noun* disorder in which an abnormal amount of urine containing an excess of sugar is excreted. **diabetic** *noun* **1** person who has diabetes. ♦ *adjective* **2** of or having diabetes. **3** suitable for people with diabetes.

diabolic ⊕ *adjective* of the Devil. **diabolical** *adjective Informal* extremely bad, e.g. *the*

——————————— THESAURUS ———————————

devil *noun* **1** = **brute**, beast, demon, fiend, monster, ogre, terror **2** = **scamp**, rascal, rogue, scoundrel **3** = **person**, beggar, creature, thing, wretch **the Devil** *Theology* = **Satan**, Beelzebub, Evil One, Lucifer, Mephistopheles, Old Nick (*inf*), Prince of Darkness

devilish *adjective* **1** = **fiendish**, atrocious, damnable, detestable, diabolical, hellish, infernal, satanic, wicked

devious *adjective* **1** = **sly**, calculating, deceitful, dishonest, double-dealing, insincere, scheming, surreptitious, underhand, wily OPPOSITE **straightforward. 2** = **indirect**, circuitous, rambling, roundabout OPPOSITE **direct**

devise *verb* = **work out**, conceive, construct, contrive, design, dream up, formulate, invent, think up

devoid *adjective* (foll. by *of*) = **lacking**, bereft, deficient, destitute, empty, free from, wanting, without

devote *verb* = **dedicate**, allot, apply, assign, commit, give, pledge, reserve, set apart

devoted *adjective* = **dedicated**, ardent, committed, constant, devout, faithful, loyal,

staunch, steadfast, true OPPOSITE **disloyal**

devotee *noun* **1** = **enthusiast**, adherent, admirer, aficionado, buff (*inf*), fan, fanatic, supporter **2** = **follower**, disciple

devotion *noun* **1** = **dedication**, adherence, affection, allegiance, attachment, commitment, constancy, faithfulness, fidelity, fondness, love, loyalty, passion OPPOSITE **neglect. 2** = **devoutness**, godliness, holiness, piety, reverence, spirituality OPPOSITE **disrespect** ♦ *plural* **3** = **prayers**, church service, divine office, religious observance

devour *verb* **1** = **eat**, consume, gobble, gulp, guzzle, polish off (*inf*), swallow, wolf **2** = **destroy**, annihilate, consume, ravage, waste, wipe out **3** = **enjoy**, read compulsively *or* voraciously, take in

devout *adjective* = **religious**, godly, holy, orthodox, pious, prayerful, pure, reverent, saintly OPPOSITE **irreverent**

dexterity *noun* **1** = **skill**, adroitness, deftness, expertise, finesse, nimbleness, proficiency, touch OPPOSITE **incompetence. 2** = **cleverness**, ability, aptitude, ingenuity

diaconate

diaconate —————— DICTIONARY —————— 222

conditions were diabolical. **diabolically** adverb
diabolism noun witchcraft, devil worship.
diaconate noun position or period of office of
a deacon.
diacritic noun sign above or below a character
to indicate phonetic value or stress.
diadem noun Old-fashioned crown.
diaeresis noun, pl **-ses** mark ( ) placed over a
vowel to show that it is pronounced separately
from the preceding one, for example in *Noël*.
diagnosis ❶ [die-ag-**no**-siss] noun, pl **-ses**
[-seez] discovery and identification of diseases
from the examination of symptoms. **diagnose**
verb **diagnostic** adjective
diagonal ❶ adjective 1 from corner to corner.
2 slanting. ♦ noun 3 diagonal line. **diagonally**
adverb
diagram ❶ noun sketch showing the form or
workings of something. **diagrammatic** adjective
dial noun 1 face of a clock or watch. 2
graduated disc on a measuring instrument. 3
control on a radio or television set used to
change the station. 4 numbered disc on the
front of some telephones. ♦ verb **dialling,**
dialled 5 operate the dial or buttons on a
telephone in order to contact (a number).
dialling tone continuous sound heard on
picking up a telephone, indicating that a
number can be dialled.
dialect ❶ noun form of a language spoken in a
particular area. **dialectal** adjective
dialectic noun logical debate by question and
answer to resolve differences between two
views. **dialectical** adjective
dialogue ❶ noun 1 conversation between two
people, esp. in a book, film, or play. 2
discussion between representatives of two
nations or groups. **dialogue box** noun small
window on a computer screen prompting the
user to enter information.
dialysis [die-**al**-iss-iss] noun Med filtering of
blood through a membrane to remove waste
products.
diamagnetism noun phenomenon exhibited
by substances that are repelled by both poles of
a magnet.

diamanté [die-a-**man**-tee] adjective decorated
with artificial jewels or sequins.
diameter noun (length of) a straight line
through the centre of a circle or sphere.
diametric, diametrical adjective 1 of a
diameter. 2 completely opposed, e.g. *the
diametric opposite.* **diametrically** adverb
diamond noun 1 exceptionally hard, usu.
colourless, precious stone. 2 Geom figure with
four sides of equal length forming two acute
and two obtuse angles. 3 playing card marked
with red diamond-shaped symbols. 4 Baseball
the playing field. **diamond jubilee** sixtieth
anniversary of an event. **diamond wedding**
sixtieth anniversary of a wedding.
diapason [die-a-**pay**-zon] noun 1 either of
two stops found throughout the range of a
pipe organ. 2 range of an instrument or voice.
diaper US & Canad noun towelling cloth to
absorb baby's excrement.
diaphanous [die-**af**-fan-ous] adjective fine and
almost transparent.
diaphoretic noun, adjective (drug) causing
sweating.
diaphragm [**die**-a-fram] noun 1 muscular
partition that separates the abdominal cavity
and chest cavity. 2 contraceptive device placed
over the neck of the womb.
diarrhoea [die-a-**ree**-a] noun frequent
discharge of abnormally liquid faeces.

> **SPELLING TIP**
>
> It's possibly because people
> don't write the word **diarrhoea**
> very often that there's only one
> example of *diarhoea*, with only
> one r, in the Bank of English. Or
> is it because it's such a difficult
> word to spell, we always look it
> up to get it right?

diary ❶ noun, pl **-ries** (book for) a record of
daily events, appointments, or observations.
diarist noun person who writes a diary.
Diaspora [die-**ass**-spore-a] noun 1 dispersion

————— THESAURUS —————

diabolical adjective Inf =**dreadful**, abysmal,
appalling, atrocious, hellish, outrageous,
shocking, terrible
diagnose verb =**identify**, analyse, determine,
distinguish, interpret, pinpoint, pronounce,
recognize
diagnosis noun =**analysis**, conclusion,
examination, investigation, opinion, scrutiny
diagonal adjective 1 = **crossways**, cross,

crosswise 2 = **slanting**, angled, oblique
diagonally adverb 1 = **crosswise**, cornerwise
2 = **aslant**, at an angle, obliquely
diagram noun = **plan**, chart, drawing, figure,
graph, representation, sketch
dialect noun = **language**, brogue, idiom,
jargon, patois, provincialism, speech, vernacular
dialogue noun 1 = **conversation**,
communication, discourse, exchange 2

of the Jews after the Babylonian conquest of Palestine. **2 (d-)** dispersion of people originally of one nation.

diastole [die-**ass**-stoh-lee] *noun* dilation of the chambers of the heart. **diastolic** *adjective*

diatomic *adjective* containing two atoms.

diatonic *adjective Music* of a regular major or minor scale.

diatribe *noun* bitter critical attack.

dibble *noun* small hand tool used to make holes in the ground for seeds or plants.

dice *noun, pl* **dice 1** small cube each of whose sides has a different number of spots (1 to 6), used in games of chance. **2** game played with dice. ◆ *verb* **3** cut (food) into small cubes. **dice with death** take a risk. **dicey** *adjective* **dicier, diciest** *Informal* dangerous or risky.

dichotomy [die-**kot**-a-mee] *noun, pl* **-mies** division into two opposed groups or parts.

dick *noun Taboo slang* penis. **clever dick** person who likes to show how clever he or she is.

Dickensian *adjective* denoting poverty, distress, and exploitation as depicted in Dickens's novels.

dicky[1] *noun, pl* **dickies** false shirt front.

dicky-bird *noun* child's word for a bird.

dicky[2] ● *adjective* **dickier, dickiest** *Informal* shaky or weak, e.g. *a dicky heart.*

Dictaphone *noun* ® tape recorder for recording dictation for subsequent typing.

dictate ● *verb* **1** say aloud for someone else to write down. **2** (foll. by *to*) seek to impose one's will on (other people). ◆ *noun* **3** authoritative command. **4** guiding principle. **dictation** *noun* **dictator** *noun* **1** ruler who has

complete power. **2** person in power who acts unfairly or cruelly. **dictatorship** *noun* **dictatorial** *adjective* like a dictator.

diction ● *noun* manner of pronouncing words and sounds.

dictionary ● *noun, pl* **-aries 1** book consisting of an alphabetical list of words with their meanings. **2** similar book giving equivalent words in two languages. **3** alphabetically ordered reference book of terms relating to a particular subject.

dictum *noun, pl* **-tums, -ta 1** formal statement. **2** popular saying.

did *verb* past tense of DO[1].

didactic *adjective* **1** intended to instruct. **2** overeager to instruct. **didactically** *adverb*

diddle *verb Informal* swindle.

didgeridoo *noun Music* Australian Aboriginal deep-toned wind instrument.

didn't did not.

die[1] ● *verb* **dying, died 1** (of a person, animal, or plant) cease all biological activity permanently. **2** (of something inanimate) cease to exist or function. **be dying for, to do something** *Informal* be eager for or to do something. **die down** *verb* lose strength or power by degrees. **die-hard** *noun* person who resists change.

die[2] *noun* **1** shaped block used to cut or form metal. **2** same as DICE (sense 1).

dieldrin *noun* highly toxic insecticide.

dielectric *noun* **1** substance which does not conduct electricity well, insulator. ◆ *adjective* **2** not conducting electricity well.

dieresis [die-**air**-iss-iss] *noun, pl* **-ses** [-seez] same as DIAERESIS.

——————— T H E S A U R U S ———————

= **discussion**, conference

diary *noun* = **journal**, appointment book, chronicle, daily record, engagement book, Filofax (*Trademark*)

dicky[2] *adjective Inf* = **weak**, fluttery, shaky, shonky (*Aust & NZ inf*), unreliable, unsound, unsteady

dictate *verb* **1** = **speak**, read out, say, utter **2** (foll. by *to*) = **order**, command, decree, demand, direct, impose, lay down the law, pronounce ◆ *noun* **3** = **command**, decree, demand, direction, edict, fiat, injunction, order **4** = **principle**, code, law, rule

dictator *noun* **1** = **absolute ruler**, autocrat, despot **2** = **tyrant**, oppressor

dictatorial *adjective* **a** = **absolute**, arbitrary, autocratic, despotic, totalitarian, tyrannical, unlimited, unrestricted OPPOSITE **democratic.** **b** = **domineering**, authoritarian, bossy (*inf*),

imperious, oppressive, overbearing OPPOSITE servile

dictatorship *noun* **1** = **absolute rule**, absolutism, autocracy, despotism, totalitarianism **2** = **tyranny**, authoritarianism

diction *noun* = **pronunciation**, articulation, delivery, elocution, enunciation, fluency, inflection, intonation, speech

dictionary *noun* = **wordbook**, glossary, lexicon, vocabulary

die[1] *verb* **1** = **pass away**, breathe one's last, cark *Aust & NZ sl* croak (*sl*), expire, give up the ghost, kick the bucket (*sl*), peg out (*inf*), perish, snuff it (*sl*) OPPOSITE **live. 2** = **stop**, break down, fade out or away, fail, fizzle out, halt, lose power, peter out, run down **be dying for, to do something** *Inf* = **long for**, ache for, eager for, desire, hunger for, pine for, yearn for

die-hard *noun* = **reactionary**, fanatic, old

D

diesel *noun* **1** diesel engine. **2** vehicle driven by a diesel engine. **3** diesel oil. **diesel engine** internal-combustion engine in which oil is ignited by compression. **diesel oil** fuel obtained from petroleum distillation.

diet¹ ⊕ *noun* **1** food that a person or animal regularly eats. **2** specific range of foods, to control weight or for health reasons. ♦ *verb* **3** follow a special diet so as to lose weight. ♦ *adjective* **4** (of food) suitable for a weight-reduction diet. **dietary** *adjective* **dietary fibre** fibrous substances in fruit and vegetables that aid digestion. **dieter** *noun* **dietetic** *adjective* prepared for special dietary requirements. **dietetics** *noun* study of diet and nutrition. **dietician** *noun* person who specializes in dietetics.

diet² ⊕ *noun* parliament of some countries.

differ ⊕ *verb* **1** be unlike. **2** disagree.

difference *noun* **1** state of being unlike. **2** disagreement. **3** remainder left after subtraction. **different** *adjective* **1** unlike. **2** unusual. **differently** *adverb*

LANGUAGE TIP

The accepted idiom is *different from* but *different to* is also used. *Different than* is used in America.

---

differential ⊕ *adjective* **1** of or using a difference. **2** *Maths* involving differentials. ♦ *noun* **3** factor that differentiates between two comparable things. **4** *Maths* tiny difference between values in a scale. **5** difference between rates of pay for different types of work. **differential calculus** branch of calculus concerned with derivatives and differentials. **differential gear** mechanism in a road vehicle that allows one driving wheel to rotate faster than the other when cornering. **differentiate** *verb* **1** perceive or show the difference (between). **2** make (one thing) distinct from other such things. **differentiation** *noun*

difficult ⊕ *adjective* **1** requiring effort or skill to do or understand. **2** not easily pleased. **difficulty** *noun, pl* **-ties**

diffident ⊕ *adjective* lacking self-confidence. **diffidence** *noun* **diffidently** *adverb*

diffract *verb* cause to undergo diffraction. **diffraction** *noun Physics* **1** deviation in the direction of a wave at the edge of an obstacle in its path. **2** formation of light and dark fringes by the passage of light through a small aperture.

diffuse *verb* **1** spread over a wide area. ♦ *adjective* **2** widely spread. **3** lacking concision. **diffusely** *adverb* **diffusion** *noun*

dig ⊕ *verb* **digging, dug 1** cut into, break up,

————————— THESAURUS —————————

fogey, stick-in-the-mud (*inf*)

diet¹ *noun* **1** = **food**, fare, nourishment, nutriment, provisions, rations, sustenance, tucker (*Aust & NZ inf*), victuals **2** = **regime**, abstinence, fast, regimen ♦*verb* **3** = **slim**, abstain, eat sparingly, fast, lose weight [OPPOSITE] **indulge**

diet² *noun* = **council**, chamber, congress, convention, legislature, meeting, parliament

differ *verb* **1** = **be dissimilar**, contradict, contrast, depart from, diverge, run counter to, stand apart, vary [OPPOSITE] **accord. 2** = **disagree**, clash, contend, debate, demur, dispute, dissent, oppose, take exception, take issue [OPPOSITE] **agree**

difference *noun* **1** = **dissimilarity**, alteration, change, contrast, discrepancy, disparity, diversity, variation, variety [OPPOSITE] **similarity**. **2** = **disagreement**, argument, clash, conflict, contretemps, debate, dispute, quarrel [OPPOSITE] **agreement. 3** = **remainder**, balance, rest, result

different *adjective* **1** = **unlike**, altered, changed, contrasting, disparate, dissimilar, divergent, diverse, inconsistent, opposed, sundry, varied, various **2** = **unusual**, atypical,

distinctive, extraordinary, munted (*NZ sl*), peculiar, singular, special, strange, uncommon

differentiate *verb* **1** = **distinguish**, contrast, discriminate, make a distinction, mark off, separate, set off *or* apart, tell apart **2** = **make different**, adapt, alter, change, convert, modify, transform

difficult *adjective* **1 a** = **hard**, arduous, demanding, formidable, laborious, onerous, strenuous, uphill [OPPOSITE] **easy. b** = **problematical**, abstruse, baffling, complex, complicated, intricate, involved, knotty, obscure [OPPOSITE] **simple. 2** = **troublesome**, demanding, fastidious, fussy, hard to please, perverse, refractory, unaccommodating [OPPOSITE] **cooperative**

difficulty *noun* **1** = **laboriousness**, arduousness, awkwardness, hardship, strain, strenuousness, tribulation

diffidence *noun* = **shyness**, bashfulness, hesitancy, insecurity, modesty, reserve, self-consciousness, timidity

diffident *adjective* = **shy**, bashful, doubtful, hesitant, insecure, modest, reserved, self-conscious, timid, unassertive, unassuming and turn over or remove (earth), esp. with a spade. **2** excavate (a hole or tunnel) by digging. **3** (foll. by *out* or *up*) find by effort or searching. **4** (foll. by *in* or *into*) thrust or jab. ◆ *noun* **5** digging. **6** archaeological excavation. **7** thrust or poke. **8** spiteful remark. ◆ *plural* **9** *Informal* lodgings. **digger** *noun* machine used for digging.

digest ❶ *verb* **1** subject to a process of digestion. **2** absorb mentally. ◆ *noun* **3** shortened version of a book, report, or article. **digestible** *adjective* **digestion** *noun* (body's system for) breaking down food into easily absorbed substances. **digestive** *adjective* **digestive biscuit** biscuit made from wholemeal flour.

digit [**dij**-it] *noun* **1** finger or toe. **2** numeral from 0 to 9. **digital** *adjective* **1** displaying information as numbers rather than with hands and a dial, e.g. *a digital clock*. **2** representing data as a series of numerical values. **digital recording** sound-recording process that converts audio or analogue signals into a series of pulses. **digital television** television in which the picture is transmitted in digital form and then decoded. **digitally** *adverb*

digitalis *noun* drug made from foxglove leaves, used as a heart stimulant.

dignity ❶ *noun, pl* **-ties 1** serious, calm, and controlled behaviour or manner. **2** quality of being worthy of respect. **3** sense of self-importance. **dignify** *verb* **-fying, -fied** add distinction to. **dignitary** *noun, pl* **-taries** person of high official position.

digress ❶ *verb* depart from the main subject in speech or writing. **digression** *noun*

dihedral *adjective* having or formed by two intersecting planes.

dike *noun* same as DYKE.

diktat *noun* dictatorial decree.

dilapidated ❶ *adjective* (of a building) having fallen into ruin. **dilapidation** *noun*

dilate ❶ *verb* make or become wider or larger. **dilation, dilatation** *noun*

dilatory ❶ [**dill**-a-tree] *adjective* tending or intended to waste time. **dilatoriness** *noun*

dildo *noun, pl* **-dos** object used as a substitute for an erect penis.

dilemma ❶ *noun* situation offering a choice between two equally undesirable alternatives.

dilettante ❶ [dill-it-**tan**-tee] *noun, pl* **-tantes, -tanti** person whose interest in a subject is superficial rather than serious. **dilettantism** *noun*

diligent ❶ *adjective* **1** careful and persevering in carrying out duties. **2** carried out with care and perseverance. **diligently** *adverb* **diligence** *noun*

——————————————— THESAURUS ———————————————

dig *verb* **1, 2 = excavate**, burrow, delve, hollow out, mine, quarry, scoop, tunnel **3** (foll. by *out* or *up*) **= find**, delve, dig down, discover, expose, fossick (*Aust & NZ*), go into, investigate, probe, research, search, uncover, unearth, uproot **4** (foll. by *in* or *into*) **= poke**, drive, jab, prod, punch, thrust ◆*noun* **7 = poke**, jab, prod, punch, thrust **8 = cutting remark**, barb, crack (*sl*), gibe, insult, jeer, sneer, taunt, wisecrack (*inf*)

digest *verb* **1 = ingest**, absorb, assimilate, dissolve, incorporate **2 = take in**, absorb, consider, contemplate, grasp, study, understand ◆*noun* **3 = summary**, abridgment, abstract, epitome, précis, résumé, synopsis

digestion *noun* **= ingestion**, absorption, assimilation, conversion, incorporation, transformation

dignified *adjective* **= distinguished**, formal, grave, imposing, noble, reserved, solemn, stately OPPOSITE **undignified**

dignitary *noun* **= public figure**, bigwig (*inf*), high-up (*inf*), notable, personage, pillar of society, V.I.P., worthy

dignity *noun* **1 = decorum**, courtliness, grandeur, gravity, loftiness, majesty, nobility, solemnity, stateliness **2 = honour**, eminence, importance, rank, respectability, standing, status **3 = self-importance**, pride, self-esteem, self-respect

digress *verb* **= wander**, depart, deviate, diverge, drift, get off the point *or* subject, go off at a tangent, ramble, stray

digression *noun* **= departure**, aside, detour, deviation, divergence, diversion, straying, wandering

dilapidated *adjective* **= ruined**, broken-down, crumbling, decrepit, in ruins, munted (*NZ sl*), ramshackle, rickety, run-down, tumbledown

dilate *verb* **= enlarge**, broaden, expand, puff out, stretch, swell, widen OPPOSITE **contract**

dilatory *adjective* **= time-wasting**, delaying, lingering, procrastinating, slow, sluggish, tardy, tarrying

dilemma *noun* **= predicament**, difficulty, mess, plight, problem, puzzle, quandary, spot (*inf*)

dilettante *noun* **= amateur**, aesthete, dabbler, trifler

diligence *noun* **= application**, attention, care, industry, laboriousness, perseverance

diligent *adjective* **= hard-working**, assiduous,

dill *noun* sweet-smelling herb.

dilly-dally *verb* **-lying, -lied** *Informal* dawdle, waste time.

dilute ⊕ *verb* **1** make (a liquid) less concentrated, esp. by adding water. **2** make (a quality etc.) weaker in force. ♦ *adjective* **3** (of a liquid) thin and watery. **dilution** *noun*

diluvial, diluvian *adjective* of a flood, esp. the great Flood described in the Old Testament.

dim ⊕ *adjective* **dimmer, dimmest 1** badly lit. **2** not clearly seen. **3** unintelligent. ♦ *verb* **dimming, dimmed 4** make or become dim. **take a dim view of** disapprove of. **dimly** *adverb* **dimness** *noun* **dimmer** *noun* device for dimming an electric light.

dime *noun* coin of the US and Canada, worth ten cents.

dimension ⊕ *noun* **1** measurement of the size of something in a particular direction. **2** aspect, factor.

diminish ⊕ *verb* make or become smaller, fewer, or less. **diminished responsibility** *Law* mental derangement which makes a person unaware that he or she is committing a crime. **diminution** *noun* **diminutive** *adjective* **1** very small. ♦ *noun* **2** word or affix which implies smallness or unimportance. **diminutiveness** *noun*

diminuendo *noun Music* gradual decrease in loudness.

dimple *noun* **1** small natural dent, esp. in the cheeks or chin. ♦ *verb* **2** produce dimples by smiling. **dimpled** *adjective*

dimwit *noun Informal* stupid person. **dim-witted** *adjective*

din ⊕ *noun* **1** loud unpleasant confused noise.

♦ *verb* **dinning, dinned 2** (foll. by *into*) instil (something) into someone by constant repetition.

dinar [dee-nahr] *noun* monetary unit of various Balkan, Middle Eastern, and North African countries.

dine ⊕ *verb* eat dinner. **diner** *noun* **1** person eating a meal. **2** *Chiefly US* small cheap restaurant. **dining car** railway coach where meals are served. **dining room** room where meals are eaten.

ding-dong *noun* **1** sound of a bell. **2** *Informal* lively quarrel or fight.

dinghy [ding-ee] *noun, pl* **-ghies** small boat, powered by sails, oars, or a motor.

dingo *noun, pl* **-goes** Australian wild dog (also **native dog**).

dingy ⊕ [din-jee] *adjective* **-gier, -giest** dull and drab. **dinginess** *noun*

dinkum *adjective Aust & NZ informal* genuine or right.

dinky *adjective* **-kier, -kiest** *Brit & Aust informal* small and neat.

dinner ⊕ *noun* main meal of the day, eaten either in the evening or at midday. **dinner jacket** man's semiformal black evening jacket.

dinosaur *noun* extinct gigantic prehistoric reptile.

dint *noun* **by dint of** by means of.

diocese [die-a-siss] *noun* district over which a bishop has control. **diocesan** *adjective*

diode *noun* semiconductor device for converting alternating current to direct current.

Dionysian [die-on-niz-zee-an] *adjective* wild or unrestrained.

dioptre [die-op-ter] *noun* unit for measuring

———— T H E S A U R U S ————

attentive, careful, conscientious, industrious, painstaking, persistent, studious, tireless OPPOSITE **indifferent**

dilute *verb* **1** = **water down**, adulterate, cut, make thinner, thin (out), weaken OPPOSITE **concentrate**. **2** = **reduce**, attenuate, decrease, diffuse, diminish, lessen, mitigate, temper, weaken OPPOSITE **intensify**

dim *adjective* **1** = **poorly lit**, cloudy, dark, grey, overcast, shadowy, tenebrous OPPOSITE **bright**. **2** = **unclear**, bleary, blurred, faint, fuzzy, ill-defined, indistinct, obscured, shadowy OPPOSITE **clear**. **3** = **stupid**, dense, dozy (*Brit inf*), dull, dumb (*inf*), obtuse, slow on the uptake (*inf*), thick OPPOSITE **bright** ♦*verb* **4** = **dull**, blur, cloud, darken, fade, obscure **take a dim view of** = **disapprove of**, be displeased with, be sceptical of, look askance at, reject, suspect, take exception to, view with disfavour

dimension *noun* **1** = **measurement**, amplitude, bulk, capacity, extent, proportions, size, volume

diminish *verb* = **decrease**, curtail, cut, decline, die out, dwindle, lessen, lower, recede, reduce, shrink, subside, wane OPPOSITE **increase**

diminutive *adjective* **1** = **small**, little, mini, miniature, minute, petite, tiny, undersized OPPOSITE **giant**

din *noun* **1** = **noise**, clamour, clatter, commotion, crash, pandemonium, racket, row, uproar OPPOSITE **silence** ♦*verb* **2** (foll. by *into*) = **instil**, drum into, go on at, hammer into, inculcate, instruct, teach

dine *verb* = **eat**, banquet, feast, lunch, sup

dingy *adjective* = **dull**, dark, dim, drab, dreary, gloomy, murky, obscure, sombre

dinner *noun* = **meal**, banquet, feast, main meal, repast, spread (*inf*)

the refractive power of a lens.
diorama *noun* miniature three-dimensional scene, in which models of figures are seen against a three-dimensional background.
dioxide *noun* oxide containing two oxygen atoms per molecule.
dip ❶ *verb* **dipping, dipped 1** plunge quickly or briefly into a liquid. **2** slope downwards. **3** switch (car headlights) from the main to the lower beam. **4** lower briefly. ◆ *noun* **5** dipping. **6** brief swim. **7** liquid chemical in which farm animals are dipped to rid them of insects. **8** depression in a landscape. **9** creamy mixture into which pieces of food are dipped before being eaten. **dip into** *verb* read passages at random from (a book or journal).
Dip Ed Diploma in Education.
diphtheria [dif-**theer**-ya] *noun* contagious disease producing fever and difficulty in breathing and swallowing.
diphthong *noun* union of two vowel sounds in a single compound sound.
diploma *noun* qualification awarded by a college on successful completion of a course.
diplomacy ❶ *noun* **1** conduct of the relations between nations by peaceful means. **2** tact or skill in dealing with people. **diplomat** *noun* official engaged in diplomacy. **diplomatic** *adjective* **1** of diplomacy. **2** tactful in dealing with people. **diplomatic immunity** freedom from legal action and taxation which diplomats have in the country where they are working. **diplomatically** *adverb*
dipper *noun* **1** ladle used for dipping. **2** (also **ousel, ouzel**) songbird that lives by a river.
diprotodont [die-**pro**-toe-dont] *noun*

marsupial with fewer than three upper incisor teeth on each side of the jaw.
dipsomania *noun* compulsive craving for alcohol. **dipsomaniac** *noun, adjective*
dipstick *noun* notched rod dipped into a container to measure the level of a liquid.
diptych [**dip**-tik] *noun* painting on two hinged panels.
dire ❶ *adjective* disastrous, urgent, or terrible.
direct ❶ *adjective* **1** (of a route) shortest, straight. **2** without anyone or anything intervening. **3** likely to have an immediate effect. **4** honest, frank. ◆ *adverb* **5** in a direct manner. ◆ *verb* **6** lead and organize. **7** tell (someone) to do something. **8** tell (someone) the way to a place. **9** address (a letter, package, remark, etc.). **10** provide guidance to (actors, cameramen, etc.) in (a play or film). **directly** *adverb* **1** in a direct manner. **2** at once. ◆ *conjunction* **3** as soon as. **directness** *noun*
direct current electric current that flows in one direction only. **direct debit** order given to a bank by an account-holder to pay an amount of money directly from the account to a specified person orcompany. **direct object** *noun* or pronoun receiving the direct action of the verb, e.g.*a book in I bought you a book.* **director** *noun* person or thing that directs or controls. **directory** *noun* book listing names, addresses, and telephone numbers. **direct speech** reporting of what someone has said by quoting his or her exact words. **direct tax** tax paid by the person or organization on which it is levied.
direction ❶ *noun* **1** course or line along which a person or thing moves, points, or lies. **2**

—————————— THESAURUS ——————————

dip *verb* **1 = plunge**, bathe, douse, duck, dunk, immerse **2 = slope**, decline, descend, drop (down), fall, lower, sink, subside ◆*noun* **5 = plunge**, douche, drenching, ducking, immersion, soaking **6 = bathe**, dive, plunge, swim **8 = hollow**, basin, concavity, depression, hole, incline, slope
dip into *verb* **= sample**, browse, glance at, peruse, skim
diplomacy *noun* **1 = statesmanship**, international negotiation, statecraft **2 = tact**, artfulness, craft, delicacy, discretion, finesse, savoir-faire, skill, subtlety OPPOSITE> **tactlessness**
diplomat *noun* **= negotiator**, conciliator, go-between, mediator, moderator, politician, tactician
diplomatic *adjective* **2 = tactful**, adept, discreet, polite, politic, prudent, sensitive, subtle

OPPOSITE> **tactless**
dire *adjective* **a = disastrous**, awful, calamitous, catastrophic, horrible, ruinous, terrible, woeful **b = desperate**, critical, crucial, drastic, extreme, now or never, pressing, urgent
direct *adjective* **1 = straight**, nonstop, not crooked, shortest, through, unbroken, uninterrupted OPPOSITE> **circuitous**. **2 = first-hand**, face-to-face, head-on, immediate, personal OPPOSITE> **indirect**. **4 = straightforward**, blunt, candid, downright, explicit, frank, honest, open, plain, plain-spoken, point-blank, straight, unambiguous, unequivocal, upfront (*inf*) OPPOSITE> **ambiguous** ◆*verb* **6 = control**, conduct, guide, handle, lead, manage, oversee, run, supervise **7 = order**, bid, charge, command, demand, dictate, instruct **8 = guide**, indicate, lead, point in the direction of, point the way, show **9**

D

management or guidance. ♦ *plural* **3**
instructions for doing something or for reaching
a place. **directional** *adjective*
directive ❶ *noun* instruction, order.
director ❶ *noun* **1** person or thing that directs
or controls. **2** member of the governing board
of a business etc. **3** person responsible for the
artistic and technical aspects of the making of a
film etc. **directorial** *adjective* **directorship**
noun **directorate** *noun* **1** board of directors. **2**
position of director. **director-general** *noun, pl*
directors-general person in overall charge of a
large organization.
directory *noun, pl* **-tories 1** book listing
names, addresses, and telephone numbers. **2**
Computers area of a disk containing the names
and locations of the files it currently holds.
dirge ❶ *noun* slow sad song of mourning.
dirigible [dir-rij-jib-bl] *adjective* **1** able to be
steered. ♦ *noun* **2** airship.
dirk *noun* dagger, formerly worn by Scottish
Highlanders.
dirndl *noun* full gathered skirt.
dirt ❶ *noun* **1** unclean substance, filth. **2** earth,
soil. **3** obscene speech or writing. **4** *Informal*
harmful gossip. **dirt-cheap** *adjective, adverb* at
a very low price. **dirt track** racetrack made of
packed earth or cinders.
dirty ❶ *adjective* **dirtier, dirtiest 1** covered or
marked with dirt. **2** unfair or dishonest. **3**
obscene. **4** displaying dislike or anger, e.g. *a*

dirty look. ♦ *verb* **dirtying, dirtied 5** make
dirty. **dirtiness** *noun*
dis- *prefix* indicating: **1** reversal, e.g. *disconnect.*
2 negation or lack, e.g. *dissimilar; disgrace.* **3**
removal or release, e.g. *disembowel.*
disable ❶ *verb* make ineffective, unfit, or
incapable. **disabled** *adjective* lacking a physical
power, such as the ability to walk.
disablement *noun* **disability** *noun, pl* **-ties 1**
condition of being disabled. **2** something that
disables someone.

LANGUAGE TIP

The use of *the disabled, the blind*
etc. can be offensive and should
be avoided. Instead you should
talk about *disabled people, blind
people,* etc.

---

disabuse *verb* (foll. by *of*) rid (someone) of a
mistaken idea.
disadvantage ❶ *noun* unfavourable or
harmful circumstance. **disadvantageous**
adjective **disadvantaged** *adjective* socially or
economically deprived.
disaffected *adjective* having lost loyalty to or
affection for someone or something.
disaffection *noun*
disagree ❶ *verb* **-greeing, -greed 1** argue or
have different opinions. **2** be different, conflict.

————— THESAURUS —————

= **address**, label, mail, route, send
direction *noun* **1** = **way**, aim, bearing, course,
line, path, road, route, track **2** = **management**,
administration, charge, command, control,
guidance, leadership, order, supervision ♦*plural*
3 = **instructions**, briefing, guidance, guidelines,
plan, recommendation, regulations
directive *noun* = **order**, command, decree,
edict, injunction, instruction, mandate,
regulation, ruling
directly *adverb* **1** = **straight**, by the shortest
route, exactly, in a beeline, precisely,
unswervingly, without deviation **2** = **at once**, as
soon as possible, forthwith, immediately,
promptly, right away, straightaway
director *noun* **1, 2** = **controller**,
administrator, chief, executive, governor, head,
leader, manager, supervisor
dirge *noun* = **lament**, dead march, elegy,
funeral song, requiem, threnody
dirt *noun* **1** = **filth**, dust, grime, impurity,
muck, mud **2** = **soil**, clay, earth, loam **3**
= **obscenity**, indecency, pornography, sleaze,
smut

dirty *adjective* **1** = **filthy**, foul, grimy, grubby,
messy, mucky, muddy, polluted, soiled, unclean
OPPOSITE clean. **2** = **dishonest**, crooked,
fraudulent, illegal, treacherous, unfair,
unscrupulous, unsporting OPPOSITE honest. **3**
= **obscene**, blue, indecent, pornographic,
salacious, scungy (*Aust & NZ inf*), sleazy, smutty
OPPOSITE decent. **4** *as in* **a dirty look**
= **angry**, annoyed, bitter, choked, indignant,
offended, resentful, scorching ♦*verb* **5** = **soil**,
blacken, defile, foul, muddy, pollute, smirch,
spoil, stain OPPOSITE clean
disability *noun* **1** = **handicap**, affliction,
ailment, complaint, defect, disorder,
impairment, infirmity, malady
disable *verb* = **handicap**, cripple, damage,
enfeeble, immobilize, impair, incapacitate,
paralyse, render *or* declare incapable
disabled *adjective* = **handicapped**, crippled,
incapacitated, infirm, lame, paralysed,
weakened OPPOSITE able-bodied
disadvantage *noun* = **drawback**, damage,
detriment, disservice, downside, handicap,
harm, hurt, inconvenience, injury, loss,

3 (foll. by *with*) cause physical discomfort (to), e.g. *curry disagrees with me.* **disagreement** *noun* **1** refusal or failure to agree. **2** difference between results, totals, etc. which shows that they cannot be true. **3** argument.

disagreeable *adjective* **1** unpleasant. **2** (of a person) unfriendly or unhelpful. **disagreeably** *adverb*

disallow ⊙ *verb* reject as untrue or invalid; cancel.

disappear ⊙ *verb* **1** cease to be visible. **2** go away or become lost, esp. without explanation. **3** cease to exist. **disappearance** *noun*

disappoint ⊙ *verb* **1** fail to meet the expectations or hopes of. **2** prevent the fulfilment of (a plan etc.); frustrate.

disappointment *noun* **1** feeling of being disappointed. **2** person or thing that disappoints.

disapprobation *noun* disapproval.

disapprove ⊙ *verb* (foll. by *of*) consider wrong or bad. **disapproval** *noun*

disarm ⊙ *verb* **1** deprive of weapons. **2** win the confidence or affection of. **3** (of a country) decrease the size of one's armed forces.

disarmament *noun* **disarming** *adjective* removing hostility or suspicion. **disarmingly** *adverb*

disarrange ⊙ *verb* throw into disorder.

disarrangement *noun*

disarray ⊙ *noun* **1** confusion and lack of discipline. **2** extreme untidiness. ◆ *verb* **3** throw into confusion.

disassociate *verb* same as DISSOCIATE.

disassociation *noun*

disaster ⊙ *noun* **1** occurrence that causes great distress or destruction. **2** project etc. that fails. **disastrous** *adjective* **disastrously** *adverb*

D

——————— T H E S A U R U S ———————

nuisance, snag, trouble OPPOSITE **benefit**
disagree *verb* **1** = **differ (in opinion)**, argue, clash, cross swords, dispute, dissent, object, quarrel, take issue with OPPOSITE **agree**. **3** = **conflict**, be dissimilar, contradict, counter, differ, diverge, run counter to, vary **2** (foll. by *with*) = **make ill**, bother, discomfort, distress, hurt, nauseate, sicken, trouble, upset

disagreeable *adjective* **1** = **nasty**, disgusting, displeasing, distasteful, objectionable, obnoxious, offensive, repugnant, repulsive, unpleasant OPPOSITE **nice**. **2** = **ill-natured**, bad-tempered, churlish, difficult, disobliging, irritable, rude, surly, unpleasant OPPOSITE **good-natured**

disagreement *noun* **1** = **argument**, altercation, clash, conflict, dispute, dissent, quarrel, row, squabble OPPOSITE **agreement**. **2** = **incompatibility**, difference, discrepancy, disparity, dissimilarity, divergence, incongruity, variance

disallow *verb* = **reject**, disavow, dismiss, disown, rebuff, refuse, repudiate

disappear *verb* **1** = **vanish**, evanesce, fade away, pass, recede OPPOSITE **appear**. **2** = **cease**, die out, dissolve, evaporate, leave no trace, melt away, pass away, perish

disappearance *noun* **1** = **vanishing**, eclipse, evanescence, passing **2** = **going**, departure, evaporation, melting

disappoint *verb* = **let down**, disenchant, disgruntle, dishearten, disillusion, dismay, dissatisfy, fail

disappointed *adjective* = **let down**, cast down, despondent, discouraged, disenchanted, disgruntled, dissatisfied, downhearted,

frustrated OPPOSITE **satisfied**
disappointing *adjective* = **unsatisfactory**, depressing, disconcerting, discouraging, inadequate, insufficient, sad, sorry

disappointment *noun* **1** = **frustration**, chagrin, discontent, discouragement, disenchantment, disillusionment, dissatisfaction, regret **2** = **letdown**, blow, calamity, choker (*inf*), misfortune, setback

disapproval *noun* = **displeasure**, censure, condemnation, criticism, denunciation, dissatisfaction, objection, reproach

disapprove *verb* (foll. by *of*) = **condemn**, deplore, dislike, find unacceptable, frown on, look down one's nose at (*inf*), object to, reject, take a dim view of, take exception to OPPOSITE **approve**

disarm *verb* **1** = **render defenceless**, disable **2** = **win over**, persuade, set at ease **3** = **demilitarize**, deactivate, demobilize, disband

disarmament *noun* **3** = **arms reduction**, arms limitation, de-escalation, demilitarization, demobilization

disarming *adjective* **2** = **charming**, irresistible, likable *or* likeable, persuasive, winning

disarrange *verb* = **disorder**, confuse, disorganize, disturb, jumble (up), mess (up), scatter, shake (up), shuffle, muss (*US & Canad*)

disarray *noun* **1** = **confusion**, disorder, disorganization, disunity, indiscipline, unruliness OPPOSITE **order**. **2** = **untidiness**, chaos, clutter, hotchpotch, jumble, mess, muddle, shambles OPPOSITE **tidiness**

disaster *noun* **1** = **catastrophe**, adversity, calamity, cataclysm, misfortune, ruin, tragedy, trouble

disavow *verb* deny connection with or responsibility for. **disavowal** *noun*

disband *verb* (cause to) cease to function as a group.

disbelieve ❶ *verb* **1** reject as false. **2** (foll. by *in*) have no faith (in). **disbelief** *noun*

disburse *verb* pay out. **disbursement** *noun*

disc *noun* **1** flat circular object. **2** gramophone record. **3** *Anat* circular flat structure in the body, esp. between the vertebrae. **4** *Computers* same as DISK. **disc brake** brake in which two plates rub against a flat disc. **disc jockey** person who introduces and plays pop records on a radio programme or at a disco.

discard ❶ *verb* get rid of (something or someone) as useless or undesirable.

discern *verb* see or be aware of (something) clearly. **discernible** *adjective* **discernibly** *adverb* **discerning** *adjective* having good judgment. **discernment** *noun*

discharge ❶ *verb* **1** release, allow to go. **2** dismiss (someone) from duty or employment. **3** fire (a gun). **4** pour forth, send out. **5** meet the demands of (a duty or responsibility). **6** relieve oneself of (a debt). ◆ *noun* **7** substance that comes out from a place. **8** discharging.

disciple ❶ [diss-**sipe**-pl] *noun* follower of the doctrines of a teacher, esp. Jesus Christ.

discipline ❶ *noun* **1** practice of imposing strict rules of behaviour. **2** area of academic study. ◆ *verb* **3** attempt to improve the behaviour of (oneself or another) by training or rules. **4** punish. **disciplined** *adjective* able to behave and work in a controlled way. **disciplinarian** *noun* person who practises strict discipline. **disciplinary** *adjective*

disclaim *verb* deny (responsibility for or knowledge of something). **disclaimer** *noun* statement denying responsibility.

disclose ❶ *verb* **1** make known. **2** allow to be seen. **disclosure** *noun*

disco *noun*, *pl* **-cos 1** nightclub where people dance to amplified pop records. **2** occasion at which people dance to amplified pop records. **3** mobile equipment for providing music for a disco.

discography *noun*, *pl* **-phies** classified list of gramophone records.

discolour ❶ *verb* change in colour, fade. **discoloration** *noun*

discomfit *verb* make uneasy or confused. **discomfiture** *noun*

discomfort ❶ *noun* inconvenience, distress, or mild pain.

discommode *verb* cause inconvenience to.

discompose *verb* disturb, upset. **discomposure** *noun*

disconcert ❶ *verb* embarrass or upset.

—————— THESAURUS ——————

disastrous *adjective* =**terrible**, calamitous, cataclysmic, catastrophic, devastating, fatal, ruinous, tragic

disbelief *noun* =**scepticism**, distrust, doubt, dubiety, incredulity, mistrust, unbelief OPPOSITE belief

discard *verb* =**get rid of**, abandon, cast aside, dispense with, dispose of, drop, dump (*inf*), jettison, reject, throw away *or* out OPPOSITE keep

discharge *verb* **1** =**release**, allow to go, clear, free, liberate, pardon, set free **2** =**dismiss**, cashier, discard, expel, fire (*inf*), oust, remove, sack (*inf*) **3** =**fire**, detonate, explode, let loose (*inf*), let off, set off, shoot **4** =**pour forth**, dispense, emit, exude, give off, leak, ooze, release **5** =**carry out**, accomplish, do, execute, fulfil, observe, perform **6** =**pay**, clear, honour, meet, relieve, satisfy, settle, square up ◆ *noun* **7** =**emission**, excretion, ooze, pus, secretion, seepage, suppuration **8 a** =**release**, acquittal, clearance, liberation, pardon **b** =**dismissal**, demobilization, ejection **c** =**firing**, blast, burst, detonation, explosion, report, salvo, shot, volley

disciple *noun* =**follower**, adherent, apostle, devotee, pupil, student, supporter OPPOSITE leader

disciplinarian *noun* =**authoritarian**, despot, martinet, stickler, taskmaster, tyrant

discipline *noun* **1** =**training**, conduct, control, orderliness, practice, regimen, regulation, restraint, self-control, strictness **2** =**field of study**, area, branch of knowledge, course, curriculum, speciality, subject ◆ *verb* **3** =**train**, bring up, drill, educate, exercise, prepare **4** =**punish**, bring to book, castigate, chasten, chastise, correct, penalize, reprimand, reprove

disclose *verb* **1** =**make known**, broadcast, communicate, confess, divulge, let slip, publish, relate, reveal OPPOSITE keep secret. **2** =**show**, bring to light, expose, lay bare, reveal, uncover, unveil OPPOSITE cover

disclosure *noun* **1** =**revelation**, acknowledgment, admission, announcement, confession, declaration, divulgence, leak, publication

discolour *verb* =**stain**, fade, mark, soil, streak, tarnish, tinge

discomfort *noun* **a** =**uneasiness**, annoyance, distress, hardship, irritation, nuisance, trouble OPPOSITE comfort. **b** =**pain**, ache, hurt,

disconnect ⊙ *verb* **1** undo or break the connection between (two things). **2** stop the supply of electricity or gas of. **disconnected** *adjective* (of speech or ideas) not logically connected. **disconnection** *noun*

disconsolate ⊙ *adjective* sad beyond comfort. **disconsolately** *adverb*

discontent ⊙ *noun* lack of contentment. **discontented** *adjective* **discontentedly** *adverb*

discontinue ⊙ *verb* come or bring to an end. **discontinuous** *adjective* characterized by interruptions. **discontinuity** *noun*

discord ⊙ *noun* **1** lack of agreement or harmony between people. **2** harsh confused sounds. **discordant** *adjective* **discordance** *noun*

discotheque *noun* same as DISCO.

discount ⊙ *verb* **1** take no account of (something) because it is considered to be unreliable, prejudiced, or irrelevant. **2** deduct (an amount) from the price of something. ♦ *noun* **3** deduction from the full price of something.

discountenance *verb* make (someone) ashamed or confused.

discourage ⊙ *verb* **1** deprive of the will to persist in something. **2** oppose by expressing disapproval. **discouraging** *adjective* **discouragement** *noun*

discourse ⊙ *noun* **1** conversation. **2** formal treatment of a subject in speech or writing. ♦ *verb* **3** (foll. by *on*) speak or write (about) at length.

discourteous ⊙ *adjective* showing bad manners. **discourteously** *adverb* **discourtesy** *noun*

discover ⊙ *verb* **1** be the first to find or to find out about. **2** learn about for the first time.

D

————————————— T H E S A U R U S —————————————

irritation, malaise, soreness OPPOSITE **ease**
disconcert *verb* = **disturb**, faze, fluster, perturb, rattle (*inf*), take aback, unsettle, upset, worry
disconcerting *adjective* = **disturbing**, alarming, awkward, bewildering, confusing, distracting, embarrassing, off-putting (*Brit inf*), perplexing, upsetting
disconnect *verb* **1** = **cut off**, detach, disengage, divide, part, separate, sever, take apart, uncouple
disconnected *adjective* = **illogical**, confused, disjointed, incoherent, jumbled, mixed-up, rambling, unintelligible
disconsolate *adjective* = **inconsolable**, crushed, dejected, desolate, forlorn, grief-stricken, heartbroken, miserable, wretched
discontent *noun* = **dissatisfaction**, displeasure, envy, regret, restlessness, uneasiness, unhappiness
discontented *adjective* = **dissatisfied**, disaffected, disgruntled, displeased, exasperated, fed up, unhappy, vexed OPPOSITE **satisfied**
discontinue *verb* = **stop**, abandon, break off, cease, drop, end, give up, quit, suspend, terminate
discord *noun* **1** = **disagreement**, conflict, dissension, disunity, division, friction, incompatibility, strife OPPOSITE **agreement**. **2** = **disharmony**, cacophony, din, dissonance, harshness, jarring, racket, tumult
discordant *adjective* **1** = **disagreeing**, at odds, clashing, conflicting, contradictory, contrary, different, incompatible **2** = **inharmonious**, cacophonous, dissonant,

grating, harsh, jarring, shrill, strident
discount *verb* **1** = **leave out**, brush off (*sl*), disbelieve, disregard, ignore, overlook, pass over **2** = **deduct**, lower, mark down, reduce, take off ♦*noun* **3** = **deduction**, concession, cut, rebate, reduction
discourage *verb* **1** = **dishearten**, dampen, deject, demoralize, depress, dispirit, intimidate, overawe, put a damper on OPPOSITE **hearten**. **2** = **put off**, deter, dissuade, inhibit, prevent, talk out of OPPOSITE **encourage**
discouraged *adjective* **1** = **put off**, crestfallen, deterred, disheartened, dismayed, dispirited, downcast, down in the mouth, glum
discouragement *noun* **1** = **loss of confidence**, dejection, depression, despair, despondency, disappointment, dismay, downheartedness **2** = **deterrent**, damper, disincentive, hindrance, impediment, obstacle, opposition, setback
discouraging *adjective* **1** = **disheartening**, dampening, daunting, depressing, disappointing, dispiriting, off-putting (*Brit inf*), unfavourable
discourse *noun* **1** = **conversation**, chat, communication, dialogue, discussion, seminar, speech, talk **2** = **speech**, dissertation, essay, homily, lecture, oration, sermon, treatise ♦*verb* **3** (foll. by *on*) = **hold forth**, expatiate, speak, talk
discourteous *adjective* = **rude**, bad-mannered, boorish, disrespectful, ill-mannered, impolite, insolent, offhand, ungentlemanly, ungracious
discourtesy *noun* = **rudeness**, bad manners, disrespectfulness, impertinence, impoliteness,

3 find after study or search. **discoverer** *noun*
discovery *noun, pl* **-eries 1** discovering. **2**
person, place, or thing that has been
discovered.
discredit ❶ *verb* **1** damage the reputation of.
2 cause (an idea) to be disbelieved or
distrusted. ♦ *noun* **3** damage to someone's
reputation. **discreditable** *adjective* bringing
shame.
discreet ❶ *adjective* **1** careful to avoid
embarrassment, esp. by keeping confidences
secret. **2** unobtrusive. **discreetly** *adverb*
discrepancy ❶ *noun, pl* **-cies** conflict or
variation between facts, figures, or claims.
discrete *adjective* separate, distinct.
discretion ❶ [diss-**kresh**-on] *noun* **1** quality of
behaving in a discreet way. **2** freedom or
authority to make judgments and decide what
to do. **discretionary** *adjective*
discriminate ❶ *verb* **1** (foll. by *against* or *in
favour of*) single out (a particular person or
group) for worse or better treatment than
others. **2** (foll. by *between*) recognize or

understand the difference (between).
discriminating *adjective* showing good taste
and judgment. **discrimination** *noun*
discriminatory *adjective* based on prejudice.
discursive *adjective* passing from one topic to
another.
discus *noun* heavy disc-shaped object thrown
in sports competitions.
discuss ❶ *verb* **1** consider (something) by
talking it over. **2** treat (a subject) in speech or
writing. **discussion** *noun*
disdain ❶ *noun* **1** feeling of superiority and
dislike. ♦ *verb* **2** refuse with disdain. **disdainful**
adjective **disdainfully** *adverb*
disease ❶ *noun* illness, sickness. **diseased**
adjective
disembark ❶ *verb* get off a ship, aircraft, or
bus. **disembarkation** *noun*
disembodied *adjective* **1** lacking a body. **2**
seeming not to be attached to or coming from
anyone.
disembowel *verb* **-elling, -elled** remove the
entrails of.

———— THESAURUS ————

incivility, insolence
discover *verb* **1 = find**, come across, come
upon, dig up, locate, turn up, uncover, unearth
2, 3 = find out, ascertain, detect, learn, notice,
perceive, realize, recognize, uncover
discovery *noun* **1 = finding**, detection,
disclosure, exploration, location, revelation,
uncovering **2 = breakthrough**, find, innovation,
invention, secret
discredit *verb* **1 = disgrace**, bring into
disrepute, defame, dishonour, disparage,
slander, smear, vilify OPPOSITE honour. **2**
= doubt, challenge, deny, disbelieve, discount,
dispute, distrust, mistrust, question ♦*noun* **3**
= disgrace, dishonour, disrepute, ignominy, ill-
repute, scandal, shame, stigma OPPOSITE
honour
discreditable *adjective* **1 = disgraceful**,
dishonourable, ignominious, reprehensible,
scandalous, shameful, unworthy
discreet *adjective* **1 = tactful**, careful, cautious,
circumspect, considerate, diplomatic, guarded,
judicious, prudent, wary OPPOSITE tactless
discrepancy *noun* **= disagreement**, conflict,
contradiction, difference, disparity, divergence,
incongruity, inconsistency, variation
discretion *noun* **1 = tact**, carefulness, caution,
consideration, diplomacy, judiciousness,
prudence, wariness OPPOSITE indiscretion. **2**
= choice, inclination, pleasure, preference,
volition, will
discriminate *verb* **1** (foll. by *against* or *in*

favour of) **= show prejudice**, favour, show bias,
single out, treat as inferior, treat as superior,
treat differently, victimize **2** (foll. by *between*)
= differentiate, distinguish, draw a distinction,
segregate, separate, tell the difference
discriminating *adjective* **= discerning**,
cultivated, fastidious, particular, refined,
selective, tasteful OPPOSITE **undiscriminating**
discrimination *noun* **1 = prejudice**, bias,
bigotry, favouritism, intolerance, unfairness **2**
= discernment, judgment, perception,
refinement, subtlety, taste
discuss *verb* **= talk about**, argue, confer,
consider, converse, debate, deliberate, examine
discussion *noun* **= talk**, analysis, argument,
conference, consultation, conversation, debate,
deliberation, dialogue, discourse
disdain *noun* **1 = contempt**, arrogance,
derision, haughtiness, scorn, superciliousness
♦*verb* **2 = scorn**, deride, disregard, look down
on, reject, slight, sneer at, spurn
disdainful *adjective* **= contemptuous**, aloof,
arrogant, derisive, haughty, proud, scornful,
sneering, supercilious, superior
disease *noun* **= illness**, affliction, ailment,
complaint, condition, disorder, infection,
infirmity, malady, sickness
diseased *adjective* **= sick**, ailing, crook (*Aust &
NZ sl*), infected, rotten, sickly, unhealthy,
unsound, unwell, unwholesome
disembark *verb* **= land**, alight, arrive, get off,
go ashore, step out of

disenchanted ❶ *adjective* disappointed and disillusioned. **disenchantment** *noun*
disenfranchise *verb* deprive (someone) of the right to vote or of other rights of citizenship.
disengage ❶ *verb* release from a connection. **disengagement** *noun*
disentangle ❶ *verb* release from entanglement or confusion. **disentanglement** *noun*
disequilibrium *noun* loss or absence of stability or balance.
disestablish *verb* remove state support from (a church etc.). **disestablishment** *noun*
disfavour ❶ *noun* disapproval or dislike.
disfigure ❶ *verb* spoil the appearance of. **disfigurement** *noun*
disfranchise *verb* same as DISENFRANCHISE.
disgorge ❶ *verb* empty out, discharge.
disgrace ❶ *noun* **1** condition of shame, loss of reputation, or dishonour. **2** shameful person or thing. ♦ *verb* **3** bring shame upon (oneself or others). **disgraceful** *adjective* **disgracefully** *adverb*
disgruntled ❶ *adjective* sulky or discontented. **disgruntlement** *noun*
disguise ❶ *verb* **1** change the appearance or manner in order to conceal the identity of (someone or something). **2** misrepresent (something) in order to obscure its actual nature or meaning. ♦ *noun* **3** mask, costume, or manner that disguises. **4** state of being disguised.
disgust ❶ *noun* **1** great loathing or distaste. ♦ *verb* **2** sicken, fill with loathing. **disgusted** *adjective* **disgusting** *adjective* **disgustingly** *adverb*
dish ❶ *noun* **1** shallow container used for holding or serving food. **2** particular kind of food. **3** short for DISH AERIAL. **4** *Informal* attractive person. **dish aerial** aerial consisting of a concave disc-shaped reflector, used esp. for satellite television. **dishcloth** *noun* cloth for washing dishes. **dish out** *verb Informal* distribute. **dish up** *verb Informal* serve (food).
dishabille [diss-a-**beel**] *noun* same as DESHABILLE.
disharmony *noun* lack of agreement, discord.
dishearten ❶ *verb* weaken or destroy the hope, courage, or enthusiasm of.
dishevelled ❶ *adjective* (of a person's hair, clothes, or general appearance) disordered and untidy.
dishonest ❶ *adjective* not honest or fair. **dishonestly** *adverb* **dishonesty** *noun*

——————————— THESAURUS ———————————

disenchanted *adjective* =**disillusioned**, cynical, disappointed, indifferent, jaundiced, let down, sick of, soured
disenchantment *noun* =**disillusionment**, disappointment, disillusion, rude awakening
disengage *verb* =**release**, disentangle, extricate, free, loosen, set free, unloose, untie
disentangle *verb* =**untangle**, disconnect, disengage, extricate, free, loose, unravel
disfavour *noun* =**disapproval**, disapprobation, dislike, displeasure
disfigure *verb* =**damage**, blemish, deface, deform, distort, mar, mutilate, scar
disgorge *verb* =**vomit**, discharge, eject, empty, expel
disgrace *noun* **1** =**shame**, degradation, dishonour, disrepute, ignominy, infamy, odium, opprobrium OPPOSITE> honour. **2** =**stain**, blemish, blot, reproach, scandal, slur, stigma ♦*verb* **3** =**bring shame upon**, degrade, discredit, dishonour, humiliate, shame, sully, taint OPPOSITE> honour
disgraceful *adjective* =**shameful**, contemptible, detestable, dishonourable, disreputable, ignominious, scandalous, shocking, unworthy
disgruntled *adjective* =**discontented**, annoyed, displeased, dissatisfied, grumpy, irritated, peeved, put out, vexed
disguise *verb* **1** =**hide**, camouflage, cloak, conceal, cover, mask, screen, shroud, veil **2** =**misrepresent**, fake, falsify ♦*noun* **3** =**costume**, camouflage, cover, mask, screen, veil **4** =**facade**, deception, dissimulation, front, pretence, semblance, trickery, veneer
disguised *adjective* **1** =**in disguise**, camouflaged, covert, incognito, masked, undercover **2** =**fake**, false, feigned
disgust *noun* **1** =**loathing**, abhorrence, aversion, dislike, distaste, hatred, nausea, repugnance, repulsion, revulsion OPPOSITE> liking ♦*verb* **2** =**sicken**, displease, nauseate, offend, put off, repel, revolt OPPOSITE> please
disgusted *adjective* =**sickened**, appalled, nauseated, offended, repulsed, scandalized
disgusting *adjective* =**sickening**, foul, gross, loathsome, nauseating, offensive, repellent, repugnant, revolting
dish *noun* **1** =**bowl**, plate, platter, salver **2** =**food**, fare, recipe
dishearten *verb* =**discourage**, cast down, deject, depress, deter, dismay, dispirit, put a damper on
dishevelled *adjective* =**untidy**, bedraggled, disordered, messy, ruffled, rumpled, tousled, uncombed, unkempt OPPOSITE> tidy

dishonour ❶ verb 1 treat with disrespect. 2 refuse to cash (a cheque). ◆ noun 3 lack of respect. 4 state of shame or disgrace. 5 something that causes a loss of honour.
dishonourable adjective **dishonourably** adverb
disillusion verb 1 destroy the illusions or false ideas of. ◆ noun 2 (also **disillusionment**) state of being disillusioned.
disincentive noun something that acts as a deterrent.
disinclined ❶ adjective unwilling, reluctant. **disinclination** noun
disinfect ❶ verb rid of harmful germs, chemically. **disinfectant** noun substance that destroys harmful germs. **disinfection** noun
disinformation noun false information intended to mislead.
disingenuous adjective not sincere. **disingenuously** adverb
disinherit ❶ verb Law deprive (an heir) of inheritance. **disinheritance** noun
disintegrate ❶ verb break up. **disintegration** noun
disinter verb -terring, -terred 1 dig up. 2 reveal, make known. **disinterment** noun
disinterested ❶ adjective free from bias or involvement. **disinterest** noun

> **LANGUAGE TIP**
>
> People sometimes use *disinterested* where they mean *uninterested*. If you want to say that someone shows a lack of interest, use *uninterested*. *Disinterested* would be used in a sentence such as *We asked him to decide because he was a disinterested observer.*

disjointed ❶ adjective having no coherence, disconnected.
disjunction noun disconnection, separation. **disjunctive** adjective
disk noun Computers storage device, consisting of a stack of plates coated with a magnetic layer, which rotates rapidly as a single unit.
dislike ❶ verb 1 consider unpleasant or disagreeable. ◆ noun 2 feeling of not liking something or someone.
dislocate verb 1 displace (a bone or joint) from its normal position. 2 disrupt or shift out of place. **dislocation** noun
dislodge ❶ verb remove (something) from a previously fixed position.
disloyal ❶ adjective not loyal, deserting one's

———— T H E S A U R U S ————

dishonest adjective =**deceitful**, bent (sl), cheating, corrupt, crooked (inf), disreputable, double-dealing, false, lying, treacherous OPPOSITE> **honest**
dishonesty noun =**deceit**, cheating, chicanery, corruption, fraud, treachery, trickery, unscrupulousness
dishonour verb 1 =**disgrace**, debase, debauch, defame, degrade, discredit, shame, sully OPPOSITE> **respect** ◆noun 4 =**disgrace**, discredit, disrepute, ignominy, infamy, obloquy, reproach, scandal, shame OPPOSITE> **honour**. 5 =**insult**, abuse, affront, discourtesy, indignity, offence, outrage, sacrilege, slight
dishonourable adjective 4 =**shameful**, contemptible, despicable, discreditable, disgraceful, ignominious, infamous, scandalous 5 =**untrustworthy**, blackguardly, corrupt, disreputable, shameless, treacherous, unprincipled, unscrupulous
disillusioned adjective =**disenchanted**, disabused, disappointed, enlightened, undeceived
disinclination noun =**reluctance**, aversion, dislike, hesitance, objection, opposition, repugnance, resistance, unwillingness
disinclined adjective =**reluctant**, averse,

hesitating, loath, not in the mood, opposed, resistant, unwilling
disinfect verb =**sterilize**, clean, cleanse, decontaminate, deodorize, fumigate, purify, sanitize OPPOSITE> **contaminate**
disinfectant noun =**antiseptic**, germicide, sterilizer
disinherit verb Law =**cut off**, disown, dispossess, oust, repudiate
disintegrate verb =**break up**, break apart, crumble, fall apart, go to pieces, separate, shatter, splinter
disinterest noun =**impartiality**, detachment, fairness, neutrality
disinterested adjective =**impartial**, detached, dispassionate, even-handed, impersonal, neutral, objective, unbiased, unprejudiced OPPOSITE> **biased**
disjointed adjective =**incoherent**, confused, disconnected, disordered, rambling
dislike verb 1 =**be averse to**, despise, detest, disapprove, hate, loathe, not be able to bear or abide or stand, object to, take a dim view of OPPOSITE> **like** ◆noun 2 =**aversion**, animosity, antipathy, disapproval, disinclination, displeasure, distaste, enmity, hostility, repugnance OPPOSITE> **liking**

D

allegiance. **disloyalty** *noun*

dismal ⊕ *adjective* **1** gloomy and depressing. **2** *Informal* of poor quality. **dismally** *adverb*

dismantle ⊕ *verb* take apart piece by piece.

dismay ⊕ *verb* **1** fill with alarm or depression. ◆ *noun* **2** alarm mixed with sadness.

dismember ⊕ *verb* **1** remove the limbs of. **2** cut to pieces. **dismemberment** *noun*

dismiss ⊕ *verb* **1** remove (an employee) from a job. **2** allow (someone) to leave. **3** put out of one's mind. **4** (of a judge) state that (a case) will not be brought to trial. **dismissal** *noun*

dismissive *adjective* scornful, contemptuous.

dismount *verb* get off a horse or bicycle.

disobey ⊕ *verb* neglect or refuse to obey. **disobedient** *adjective* **disobedience** *noun*

disobliging *adjective* unwilling to help.

disorder ⊕ *noun* **1** state of untidiness and disorganization. **2** public violence or rioting. **3** an illness. **disordered** *adjective* untidy.

disorderly *adjective* **1** untidy and disorganized.

2 uncontrolled, unruly.

disorganize *verb* disrupt the arrangement or system of. **disorganization** *noun*

disorientate, disorient *verb* cause (someone) to lose his or her bearings. **disorientation** *noun*

disown ⊕ *verb* deny any connection with (someone).

disparage ⊕ *verb* speak contemptuously of. **disparagement** *noun*

disparate *adjective* completely different.

disparity *noun, pl* **-ties** inequality or difference.

dispassionate ⊕ *adjective* not influenced by emotion. **dispassionately** *adverb*

dispatch ⊕ *verb* **1** send off to a destination or to perform a task. **2** carry out (a duty or a task) with speed. **3** *Old-fashioned* kill. ◆ *noun* **4** official communication or report, sent in haste. **5** report sent to a newspaper by a correspondent. **dispatch rider** motorcyclist who carries dispatches.

—————— THESAURUS ——————

dislodge *verb* =**displace**, disturb, extricate, force out, knock loose, oust, remove, uproot

disloyal *adjective* =**treacherous**, faithless, false, subversive, traitorous, two-faced, unfaithful, untrustworthy OPPOSITE **loyal**

disloyalty *noun* =**treachery**, breach of trust, deceitfulness, double-dealing, falseness, inconstancy, infidelity, treason, unfaithfulness

dismal *adjective* **1** =**gloomy**, bleak, cheerless, dark, depressing, discouraging, dreary, forlorn, sombre, wretched OPPOSITE **happy**

dismantle *verb* =**take apart**, demolish, disassemble, strip, take to pieces

dismay *verb* **1** =**alarm**, appal, daunt, discourage, dishearten, dispirit, distress, frighten, horrify, paralyse, put off, scare, terrify, unnerve ◆*noun* **2** =**alarm**, anxiety, apprehension, consternation, discouragement, dread, fear, horror, trepidation

dismember *verb* **1** =**amputate 2** =**cut into pieces**, dissect, sever

dismiss *verb* **1** =**sack** (*inf*), axe (*inf*), cashier, discharge, fire (*inf*), give notice to, give (someone) their marching orders, lay off, remove **2** =**let go**, disperse, dissolve, free, release, send away **3** =**put out of one's mind**, banish, discard, dispel, disregard, lay aside, reject, set aside

dismissal *noun* **1** =**the sack** (*inf*), expulsion, marching orders (*inf*), notice, removal, the boot (*sl*), the push (*sl*)

disobedience *noun* =**defiance**, indiscipline, insubordination, mutiny, noncompliance, nonobservance, recalcitrance, revolt, unruliness,

waywardness

disobedient *adjective* =**defiant**, contrary, disorderly, insubordinate, intractable, naughty, refractory, undisciplined, unruly, wayward

disobey *verb* =**refuse to obey**, contravene, defy, disregard, flout, ignore, infringe, rebel, violate

disorder *noun* **1** =**untidiness**, chaos, clutter, confusion, disarray, jumble, mess, muddle, shambles **2** =**disturbance**, commotion, riot, turmoil, unrest, unruliness, uproar **3** =**illness**, affliction, ailment, complaint, disease, malady, sickness

disorderly *adjective* **1** =**untidy**, chaotic, confused, disorganized, higgledy-piggledy (*inf*), jumbled, messy, shambolic (*inf*) OPPOSITE **neat**. **2** =**unruly**, disruptive, indisciplined, lawless, riotous, rowdy, tumultuous, turbulent, ungovernable

disorganized *adjective* =**muddled**, chaotic, confused, disordered, haphazard, jumbled, unsystematic

disown *verb* =**deny**, cast off, disavow, disclaim, reject, renounce, repudiate

disparage *verb* =**run down**, belittle, denigrate, deprecate, deride, malign, put down, ridicule, slander, vilify

dispassionate *adjective* =**unemotional**, calm, collected, composed, cool, detached, disinterested, impersonal, imperturbable, serene, unruffled OPPOSITE **emotional**

dispatch *verb* **1** =**send**, consign, dismiss, hasten **2** =**carry out**, discharge, dispose of, finish, perform, settle **3** *Old-fashioned* =**murder**,

D

dispel ⊙ *verb* **-pelling, -pelled** destroy or remove.

dispense ⊙ *verb* **1** distribute in portions. **2** prepare and distribute (medicine). **3** administer (the law etc.). **dispensable** *adjective* not essential. **dispensation** *noun* **1** dispensing. **2** exemption from an obligation. **dispenser** *noun* **dispensary** *noun, pl* **-saries** place where medicine is dispensed. **dispense with** *verb* do away with, manage without.

disperse ⊙ *verb* **1** scatter over a wide area. **2** (cause to) leave a gathering. **3** separate (light) into its different wavelengths. **dispersal, dispersion** *noun*

dispirit ⊙ *verb* make downhearted. **dispirited** *adjective* **dispiriting** *adjective*

displace ⊙ *verb* **1** move from the usual location. **2** remove from office. **displacement** *noun* **displaced person** person forced from his or her home or country, esp. by war.

display ⊙ *verb* **1** make visible or noticeable. ◆ *noun* **2** displaying. **3** something displayed. **4** exhibition. **5** electronic device for representing information visually. **6** *Zool* pattern of behaviour

an animal uses to draw attention to itself when courting, defending its territory, etc.

displease ⊙ *verb* annoy or upset. **displeasure** *noun*

disport *verb* **disport oneself** indulge oneself in pleasure.

dispose ⊙ *verb* place in a certain order. **disposed** *adjective* **1** willing or eager. **2** having an attitude as specified, e.g. *he felt well disposed towards her.* **disposable** *adjective* **1** designed to be thrown away after use. **2** available for use, e.g. *disposable income.* **disposal** *noun* getting rid of something. **at one's disposal** available for use. **disposition** *noun* **1** person's usual temperament. **2** desire or tendency to do something. **3** arrangement. **dispose of** *verb* **1** throw away, get rid of. **2** deal with (a problem etc.). **3** kill.

dispossess *verb* (foll. by *of*) deprive (someone) of (a possession). **dispossessed** *adjective* **dispossession** *noun*

disproportion ⊙ *noun* lack of proportion or equality. **disproportionate** *adjective* **disproportionately** *adverb*

——————— THESAURUS ———————

assassinate, execute, kill, slaughter, slay ◆*noun* **5** =**message**, account, bulletin, communication, communiqué, news, report, story

dispel *verb* =**drive away**, banish, chase away, dismiss, disperse, eliminate, expel

dispense *verb* **1** =**distribute**, allocate, allot, apportion, assign, deal out, dole out, share **2** =**prepare**, measure, mix, supply **3** =**administer**, apply, carry out, discharge, enforce, execute, implement, operate **dispense with** =**do without**, abolish, abstain from, brush aside, cancel, dispose of, do away with, forgo, get rid of, give up

disperse *verb* **1** =**scatter**, broadcast, diffuse, disseminate, distribute, spread, strew **2** =**break up**, disband, dissolve, scatter, separate OPPOSITE▷ collect

dispirited *adjective* =**disheartened**, crestfallen, dejected, depressed, despondent, discouraged, downcast, gloomy, glum, sad

displace *verb* **1** =**move**, disturb, misplace, shift, transpose **2** =**replace**, oust, succeed, supersede, supplant, take the place of

display *verb* **1** =**show**, demonstrate, disclose, exhibit, expose, flaunt, flourish, manifest, parade, present, reveal, show off, vaunt OPPOSITE▷ conceal ◆*noun* **2, 3** =**exhibition**, array, demonstration, presentation, show **4** =**show**, pageant, parade, spectacle

displease *verb* =**annoy**, anger, irk, irritate,

offend, pique, put out, upset, vex

displeasure *noun* =**annoyance**, anger, disapproval, dissatisfaction, distaste, indignation, irritation, resentment OPPOSITE▷ satisfaction

disposable *adjective* **1** =**throwaway**, biodegradable, nonreturnable **2** =**available**, consumable, expendable

disposal *noun* =**throwing away**, discarding, dumping (*inf*), ejection, jettisoning, removal, riddance, scrapping **at one's disposal** =**available**, at one's service, consumable, expendable, free for use

dispose *verb* =**arrange**, array, distribute, group, marshal, order, place, put

dispose of *verb* **1** =**get rid of**, destroy, discard, dump (*inf*), jettison, scrap, throw out *or* away, unload **2** =**deal with**, decide, determine, end, finish with, settle

disposition *noun* **1** =**character**, constitution, make-up, nature, spirit, temper, temperament **2** =**tendency**, bent, bias, habit, inclination, leaning, proclivity, propensity **3** =**arrangement**, classification, distribution, grouping, ordering, organization, placement

disproportion *noun* =**inequality**, asymmetry, discrepancy, disparity, imbalance, lopsidedness, unevenness

disproportionate *adjective* =**unequal**, excessive, inordinate, out of proportion, unbalanced, uneven, unreasonable

disprove ⊙ *verb* show (an assertion or claim) to be incorrect.
dispute ⊙ *noun* **1** disagreement, argument. ♦ *verb* **2** argue about (something). **3** doubt the validity of. **4** fight over possession of.
disqualify ⊙ *verb* stop (someone) officially from taking part in something for wrongdoing. **disqualification** *noun*
disquiet ⊙ *noun* **1** feeling of anxiety. ♦ *verb* **2** make (someone) anxious. **disquietude** *noun*
disquisition *noun* detailed explanation of a subject.
disregard ⊙ *verb* **1** give little or no attention to. ♦ *noun* **2** lack of attention or respect.
disrepair ⊙ *noun* condition of being worn out or in poor working order.
disrepute ⊙ *noun* loss or lack of good reputation. **disreputable** *adjective* having or causing a bad reputation.

disrespect ⊙ *noun* lack of respect.
disrespectful *adjective* **disrespectfully** *adverb*
disrobe *verb* undress.
disrupt ⊙ *verb* interrupt the progress of.
disruption *noun* **disruptive** *adjective*
dissatisfied ⊙ *adjective* not pleased or contented. **dissatisfaction** *noun*
dissect ⊙ *verb* **1** cut open (a corpse) to examine it. **2** examine critically and minutely. **dissection** *noun*
dissemble *verb* conceal one's real motives or emotions by pretence.
disseminate ⊙ *verb* spread (information).
dissemination *noun*
dissent ⊙ *verb* **1** disagree. **2** *Christianity* reject the doctrines of an established church. ♦ *noun* **3** disagreement. **4** *Christianity* separation from an established church. **dissension** *noun* **dissenter** *noun* **dissentient** *adjective* dissenting.

———————————— THESAURUS ————————————

disprove *verb* =**prove false**, contradict, discredit, expose, give the lie to, invalidate, negate, rebut, refute OPPOSITE **prove**
dispute *noun* **1** =**disagreement**, altercation, argument, conflict, contention, controversy, debate, dissension, feud, quarrel ♦*verb* **2** =**argue**, clash, cross swords, debate, quarrel, squabble **3** =**doubt**, challenge, contest, contradict, deny, impugn, question, rebut
disqualification *noun* =**ban**, elimination, exclusion, ineligibility, rejection
disqualified *adjective* =**ineligible**, debarred, eliminated, knocked out, out of the running
disqualify *verb* =**ban**, debar, declare ineligible, preclude, prohibit, rule out
disquiet *noun* **1** =**uneasiness**, alarm, anxiety, concern, disturbance, foreboding, nervousness, trepidation, worry ♦*verb* **2** =**make uneasy**, bother, concern, disturb, perturb, trouble, unsettle, upset, worry
disregard *verb* **1** =**ignore**, brush aside or away, discount, make light of, neglect, overlook, pass over, pay no heed to, turn a blind eye to OPPOSITE **pay attention to** ♦*noun* **2** =**inattention**, contempt, disdain, disrespect, indifference, neglect, negligence, oversight
disrepair *noun* =**dilapidation**, collapse, decay, deterioration, ruination
disreputable *adjective* =**discreditable**, dishonourable, ignominious, infamous, louche, notorious, scandalous, shady (*inf*), shameful OPPOSITE **respectable**
disrepute *noun* =**discredit**, disgrace, dishonour, ignominy, ill repute, infamy, obloquy, shame, unpopularity

disrespect *noun* =**contempt**, cheek, impertinence, impoliteness, impudence, insolence, irreverence, lack of respect, rudeness, sauce OPPOSITE **respect**
disrespectful *adjective* =**contemptuous**, cheeky, discourteous, impertinent, impolite, impudent, insolent, insulting, irreverent, rude
disrupt *verb* =**disturb**, break up or into, confuse, disorder, disorganize, interfere with, interrupt, intrude, spoil, unsettle, upset
disruption *noun* =**disturbance**, interference, interruption, stoppage
disruptive *adjective* =**disturbing**, disorderly, distracting, troublesome, unruly, unsettling, upsetting OPPOSITE **well-behaved**
dissatisfaction *noun* =**discontent**, annoyance, chagrin, disappointment, displeasure, frustration, irritation, resentment, unhappiness
dissatisfied *adjective* =**discontented**, disappointed, disgruntled, displeased, fed up, frustrated, unhappy, unsatisfied OPPOSITE **satisfied**
dissect *verb* **1** =**cut up** or **apart**, anatomize, dismember, lay open **2** =**analyse**, break down, explore, inspect, investigate, research, scrutinize, study
disseminate *verb* =**spread**, broadcast, circulate, disperse, distribute, publicize, scatter
dissension *noun* **1** =**disagreement**, conflict, discord, dispute, dissent, friction, quarrel, row, strife
dissent *verb* **1** =**disagree**, differ, object, protest, refuse, withhold assent or approval ♦*noun* **3** =**disagreement**, discord, dissension, objection, opposition, refusal, resistance

dissertation ⊕ *noun* **1** written thesis, usu. required for a higher university degree. **2** long formal speech.

disservice ⊕ *noun* harmful action.

dissident ⊕ *noun* **1** person who disagrees with and criticizes the government. ◆ *adjective* **2** disagreeing with the government. **dissidence** *noun*

dissimilar ⊕ *adjective* not alike, different. **dissimilarity** *noun*

dissimulate *verb* conceal one's real feelings by pretence. **dissimulation** *noun*

dissipate ⊕ *verb* **1** waste or squander. **2** scatter, disappear. **dissipated** *adjective* showing signs of overindulgence in alcohol and other physical pleasures. **dissipation** *noun*

dissociate ⊕ *verb* regard or treat as separate. **dissociate oneself from** deny or break an association with. **dissociation** *noun*

dissolute ⊕ *adjective* leading an immoral life.

dissolution ⊕ *noun* **1** official breaking up of an organization or institution, such as Parliament. **2** official ending of a formal agreement, such as a marriage.

dissolve ⊕ *verb* **1** (cause to) become liquid. **2** break up or end officially. **3** break down

emotionally, e.g. *she dissolved into tears.*

dissonance *noun* lack of agreement or harmony. **dissonant** *adjective*

dissuade ⊕ *verb* deter (someone) by persuasion from doing something. **dissuasion** *noun*

distaff *noun* rod on which wool etc. is wound for spinning. **distaff side** female side of a family.

distance ⊕ *noun* **1** space between two points. **2** state of being apart. **3** remoteness in manner. **the distance** most distant part of the visible scene. **distance oneself from** separate oneself mentally from. **distant** *adjective* **1** far apart. **2** separated by a specified distance. **3** remote in manner. **distantly** *adverb*

distaste ⊕ *noun* dislike, disgust. **distasteful** *adjective* unpleasant, offensive. **distastefully** *adverb*

distemper¹ *noun* highly contagious viral disease of dogs.

distemper² *noun* paint mixed with water, glue, etc., used for painting walls.

distend *verb* (of part of the body) swell. **distension** *noun*

distil ⊕ *verb* **-tilling, -tilled 1** subject to or

————————— T H E S A U R U S —————————

OPPOSITE> assent

dissenter *noun* = **objector**, dissident, nonconformist

dissertation *noun* **1** = **thesis**, critique, discourse, disquisition, essay, exposition, treatise

disservice *noun* = **bad turn**, harm, injury, injustice, unkindness, wrong OPPOSITE> **good turn**

dissident *noun* **1** = **protester**, agitator, dissenter, rebel ◆*adjective* **2** = **dissenting**, disagreeing, discordant, heterodox, nonconformist

dissimilar *adjective* = **different**, disparate, divergent, diverse, heterogeneous, unlike, unrelated, various OPPOSITE> **alike**

dissipate *verb* **1** = **squander**, consume, deplete, expend, fritter away, run through, spend, waste **2** = **disperse**, disappear, dispel, dissolve, drive away, evaporate, scatter, vanish

dissipation *noun* = **debauchery**, dissoluteness, excess, extravagance, indulgence, intemperance, prodigality, profligacy, wantonness, waste

dissociate *verb* = **separate**, detach, disconnect, distance, divorce, isolate, segregate, set apart **dissociate oneself from** = **break away from**, break off from, part company from, quit

dissolute *adjective* = **immoral**, debauched,

degenerate, depraved, dissipated, profligate, rakish, wanton, wild

dissolution *noun* **1** = **breaking up**, disintegration, division, parting, separation **2** = **adjournment**, discontinuation, end, finish, suspension, termination OPPOSITE> **union**

dissolve *verb* **1** = **melt**, deliquesce, fuse, liquefy, soften, thaw **2** = **end**, break up, discontinue, suspend, terminate, wind up

dissuade *verb* = **deter**, advise against, discourage, put off, remonstrate, talk out of, warn

distance *noun* **1** = **space**, extent, gap, interval, length, range, span, stretch **3** = **reserve**, aloofness, coldness, coolness, remoteness, restraint, stiffness ◆*verb* **distance oneself from** = **separate oneself from**, be distanced from, dissociate oneself from

distant *adjective* **1** = **far-off**, abroad, apart, far, faraway, far-flung, outlying, out-of-the-way, remote, separate OPPOSITE> **close**. **3** = **reserved**, aloof, cool, reticent, standoffish, unapproachable, unfriendly, withdrawn OPPOSITE> **friendly**

distaste *noun* = **dislike**, aversion, disgust, horror, loathing, odium, repugnance, revulsion

distasteful *adjective* = **unpleasant**, disagreeable, objectionable, offensive, repugnant, repulsive, uninviting, unpalatable, obtain by distillation. **2** give off (a substance) in drops. **3** extract the essence of. **distillation** noun **1** process of evaporating a liquid and condensing its vapour. **2** (also **distillate**) concentrated essence. **distiller** noun person or company that makes strong alcoholic drink, esp. whisky. **distillery** noun, pl **-leries** place where a strong alcoholic drink, esp. whisky, is made.

distinct ❶ adjective **1** not the same. **2** easily sensed or understood. **3** clear and definite. **distinctly** adverb **distinction** noun **1** act of distinguishing. **2** distinguishing feature. **3** state of being different. **4** special honour, recognition, or fame. **distinctive** adjective easily recognizable. **distinctively** adverb **distinctiveness** noun

distinguish ❶ verb **1** (usu. foll. by between) make, show, or recognize a difference (between). **2** be a distinctive feature of. **3** make out by hearing, seeing, etc. **distinguishable**

adjective **distinguished** adjective **1** dignified in appearance. **2** highly respected.

distort ❶ verb **1** misrepresent (the truth or facts). **2** twist out of shape. **3** Electronics reproduce or amplify (a signal) inaccurately. **distortion** noun

distract ❶ verb **1** draw the attention of (a person) away from something. **2** entertain. **distracted** adjective unable to concentrate, preoccupied. **distraction** noun

distrait [diss-**tray**] adjective absent-minded or preoccupied.

distraught ❶ [diss-**trawt**] adjective extremely anxious or agitated.

distress ❶ noun **1** extreme unhappiness. **2** great physical pain. **3** poverty. ♦ verb **4** upset badly. **distressed** adjective **1** extremely upset. **2** in financial difficulties. **3** (of furniture or fabric) made to look old. **distressing** adjective **distressingly** adverb

distribute ❶ verb **1** hand out or deliver. **2**

——————— THESAURUS ———————

unsavoury OPPOSITE **enjoyable**
distil verb **1, 3 = extract**, condense, purify, refine
distinct adjective **1 = different**, detached, discrete, individual, separate, unconnected OPPOSITE **similar. 3 = definite**, clear, decided, evident, marked, noticeable, obvious, palpable, unmistakable, well-defined OPPOSITE **vague**
distinction noun **1 = differentiation**, discernment, discrimination, perception, separation **2 = feature**, characteristic, distinctiveness, individuality, mark, particularity, peculiarity, quality **3 = difference**, contrast, differential, division, separation **4 = excellence**, eminence, fame, greatness, honour, importance, merit, prominence, repute
distinctive adjective **= characteristic**, idiosyncratic, individual, original, peculiar, singular, special, typical, unique OPPOSITE **ordinary**
distinctly adverb **3 = definitely**, clearly, decidedly, markedly, noticeably, obviously, patently, plainly, unmistakably
distinguish verb **1** (usu. foll. by between) **= differentiate**, ascertain, decide, determine, discriminate, judge, tell apart, tell the difference **2 = characterize**, categorize, classify, mark, separate, set apart, single out **3 = make out**, discern, know, perceive, pick out, recognize, see, tell
distinguished adjective **2 = eminent**, acclaimed, celebrated, famed, famous, illustrious, noted, renowned, well-known OPPOSITE **unknown**

distort verb **1 = misrepresent**, bias, colour, falsify, pervert, slant, twist **2 = deform**, bend, buckle, contort, disfigure, misshape, twist, warp
distortion noun **1 = misrepresentation**, bias, falsification, perversion, slant **2 = deformity**, bend, buckle, contortion, crookedness, malformation, twist, warp
distract verb **1 = divert**, draw away, sidetrack, turn aside **2 = amuse**, beguile, engross, entertain, occupy
distracted adjective **= agitated**, at sea, flustered, harassed, in a flap (inf), perplexed, puzzled, troubled
distraction noun **1 = diversion**, commotion, disturbance, interference, interruption **2 = entertainment**, amusement, diversion, pastime, recreation
distraught adjective **= frantic**, agitated, beside oneself, desperate, distracted, distressed, out of one's mind, overwrought, worked-up
distress noun **1 = worry**, grief, heartache, misery, pain, sorrow, suffering, torment, wretchedness **2 = pain**, suffering, torment **3 = need**, adversity, difficulties, hardship, misfortune, poverty, privation, trouble ♦verb **4 = upset**, disturb, grieve, harass, sadden, torment, trouble, worry
distressed adjective **1 = upset**, agitated, distracted, distraught, tormented, troubled, worried, wretched **2 = poverty-stricken**, destitute, down at heel, indigent, needy, poor, straitened
distressing adjective **1 = upsetting**, disturbing, harrowing, heart-breaking, painful,

share out. **distribution** noun **1** distributing. **2** arrangement or spread. **distributor** noun **1** wholesaler who distributes goods to retailers in a specific area. **2** device in a petrol engine that sends the electric current to the spark plugs. **distributive** adjective

district ⊕ noun area of land regarded as an administrative or geographical unit. **district nurse** nurse who attends to patients in their homes.

distrust ⊕ verb **1** regard as untrustworthy. ♦ noun **2** feeling of suspicion or doubt. **distrustful** adjective

disturb ⊕ verb **1** intrude on. **2** worry, make anxious. **3** change the position or shape of. **disturbance** noun **disturbing** adjective **disturbingly** adverb **disturbed** adjective Psychiatry emotionally upset or maladjusted.

disunite verb cause disagreement among. **disunity** noun

disuse ⊕ noun state of being no longer used. **disused** adjective

ditch ⊕ noun **1** narrow channel dug in the earth for drainage or irrigation. ♦ verb **2** Slang abandon.

dither ⊕ verb **1** be uncertain or indecisive. ♦ noun **2** state of indecision or agitation. **ditherer** noun **dithery** adjective

ditto noun, pl **-tos 1** the same. ♦ adverb **2** in the same way.

ditty noun, pl **-ties** short simple poem or song.

diuretic [die-yoor-et-ik] noun drug that increases the flow of urine.

diurnal [die-urn-al] adjective happening during the day or daily.

diva noun distinguished female singer.

divan noun **1** low backless bed. **2** backless sofa or couch.

dive ⊕ verb **diving, dived 1** plunge headfirst into water. **2** (of a submarine or diver) submerge under water. **3** fly in a steep nose-down descending path. **4** move quickly in a specified direction. **5** (foll. by in or into) start doing (something) enthusiastically. ♦ noun **6** diving. **7** steep nose-down descent. **8** Slang disreputable bar or club. **diver** noun **1** person who works or explores underwater. **2** person who dives for sport. **3** water bird that swims and dives. **dive bomber** military aircraft designed to release bombs during a dive. **diving bell** diving apparatus with an open bottom, supplied with compressed air from above. **diving board** platform from which swimmers may dive. **diving suit** diver's waterproof suit, with a helmet and air supply.

diverge ⊕ verb **1** separate and go in different directions. **2** deviate (from a prescribed course). **divergence** noun **divergent** adjective

divers adjective Old-fashioned various.

diverse ⊕ adjective **1** having variety, assorted.

————————— T H E S A U R U S —————————

sad, worrying

distribute verb **1** = **hand out**, circulate, convey, deliver, pass round **2** = **share**, allocate, allot, apportion, deal, dispense, dole out

distribution noun **1 a** = **delivery**, dealing, handling, mailing, transportation **b** = **sharing**, allocation, allotment, apportionment, division **2** = **classification**, arrangement, grouping, organization, placement

district noun = **area**, locale, locality, neighbourhood, parish, quarter, region, sector, vicinity

distrust verb **1** = **suspect**, be suspicious of, be wary of, disbelieve, doubt, mistrust, question, smell a rat (inf) OPPOSITE trust ♦noun **2** = **suspicion**, disbelief, doubt, misgiving, mistrust, question, scepticism, wariness OPPOSITE trust

disturb verb **1** = **interrupt**, bother, butt in on, disrupt, interfere with, intrude on, pester **2** = **upset**, alarm, distress, fluster, harass, perturb, trouble, unnerve, unsettle, worry OPPOSITE calm. **3** = **muddle**, disarrange, disorder

disturbance noun **1** = **interruption**, annoyance, bother, distraction, intrusion **2**

= **disorder**, brawl, commotion, fracas, fray, rumpus

disturbed adjective Psychiatry = **unbalanced**, disordered, maladjusted, neurotic, troubled, upset OPPOSITE balanced

disturbing adjective **2** = **worrying**, alarming, disconcerting, distressing, frightening, harrowing, startling, unsettling, upsetting

disuse noun = **neglect**, abandonment, decay, idleness

ditch noun **1** = **channel**, drain, dyke, furrow, gully, moat, trench, watercourse ♦verb **2** Sl = **get rid of**, abandon, discard, dispose of, drop, dump (inf), jettison, scrap, throw out or overboard

dither verb **1** = **vacillate**, faff about (Brit inf), hesitate, hum and haw, shillyshally (inf), teeter, waver OPPOSITE decide ♦noun **2** = **flutter**, flap (inf), fluster, tizzy (inf)

dive verb **1-3** = **plunge**, descend, dip, drop, duck, nose-dive, plummet, swoop ♦noun **6** = **plunge**, jump, leap **7** = **nose dive**, descent, drop, plummet, plunge, swoop

diverge verb **1** = **separate**, branch, divide, fork, part, split, spread **2** = **deviate**, depart,

2 different in kind. **diversity** *noun, pl* **-ties 1** quality of being different or varied. **2** range of difference. **diversify** *verb* **-fying, -fied**. **diversification** *noun*

divert ❶ *verb* **1** change the direction of. **2** entertain, distract the attention of. **diversion** *noun* **1** official detour used by traffic when a main route is closed. **2** something that distracts someone's attention. **3** diverting. **4** amusing pastime. **diversionary** *adjective*

divest *verb* **1** strip (of clothes). **2** deprive (of a role or function).

divide ❶ *verb* **1** separate into parts. **2** share or be shared out in parts. **3** (cause to) disagree. **4** keep apart, be a boundary between. **5** calculate how many times (one number) can be contained in (another). ♦ *noun* **6** division, split.

dividend *noun* **1** sum of money representing part of the profit made, paid by a company to its shareholders. **2** extra benefit. **3** number to be divided by another number. **divider** *noun* **1** screen used to divide a room into separate areas. ♦ *plural* **2** compasses with two pointed arms, used for measuring or dividing lines.

divine ❶ *adjective* **1** of God or a god. **2** godlike. **3** *Informal* splendid. ♦ *verb* **4** discover (something) by intuition or guessing. **divinely** *adverb* **divination** *noun* art of discovering future events, as though by supernatural powers. **divinity** *noun* **1** study of religion. **2** *pl* **-ties** god. **3** state of being divine. **divining rod** forked twig said to move when held over ground in which water or metal is to be found.

division ❶ *noun* **1** dividing, sharing out. **2** one of the parts into which something is divided. **3** mathematical operation of dividing. **4** difference of opinion. **5** several departments in an organization that are grouped together. **divisional** *adjective* of a division in an organization. **divisible** *adjective* **divisibility** *noun* **divisive** [div-**vice**-iv] *adjective* tending to cause disagreement. **divisor** *noun* number to be divided into another number.

divorce ❶ *noun* **1** legal ending of a marriage. **2** any separation, esp. a permanent one. ♦ *verb* **3** legally end one's marriage (to). **4** separate, consider separately. **divorcée**, (*masc*) **divorcé** *noun* person who is divorced.

divot *noun* small piece of turf.

divulge ❶ *verb* make known, disclose. **divulgence** *noun*

divvy *verb* **-vying, -vied** (foll. by *up*) *Informal* divide and share.

Diwali *noun* annual Hindu festival honouring Lakshmi, the goddess of wealth.

Dixie *noun* southern states of the US (also **Dixieland**).

DIY *Brit, Aust & NZ* do-it-yourself.

———————— THESAURUS ————————

digress, meander, stray, turn aside, wander
diverse *adjective* **1** = **various**, assorted, manifold, miscellaneous, of every description, several, sundry, varied **2** = **different**, discrete, disparate, dissimilar, distinct, divergent, separate, unlike, varying
diversify *verb* = **vary**, branch out, change, expand, have a finger in every pie, spread out
diversion *noun* **1** = **detour**, departure, deviation, digression **2** = **distraction 4** = **pastime**, amusement, entertainment, game, recreation, relaxation, sport
diversity *noun* **1** = **difference**, distinctiveness, diverseness, heterogeneity, multiplicity **2** = **range**, variety
divert *verb* **1** = **redirect**, avert, deflect, switch, turn aside **2 a** = **entertain**, amuse, beguile, delight, gratify, regale **b** = **distract**, draw *or* lead away from, lead astray, sidetrack
diverting *adjective* **2** = **entertaining**, amusing, beguiling, enjoyable, fun, humorous, pleasant
divide *verb* **1** = **separate**, bisect, cut (up), part, partition, segregate, split [OPPOSITE] unite. **2** = **share**, allocate, allot, deal out, dispense, distribute **3** = **cause to disagree**, break up, come between, estrange, split

dividend *noun* **1** = **bonus**, cut (*inf*), divvy (*inf*), portion, share, surplus **2** = **gain**, extra, plus
divine *adjective* **1, 2** = **heavenly**, angelic, celestial, godlike, holy, spiritual, superhuman, supernatural **3** *Inf* = **wonderful**, beautiful, excellent, glorious, marvellous, perfect, splendid, superlative ♦*verb* **4** = **infer**, apprehend, deduce, discern, guess, perceive, suppose, surmise
divinity *noun* **1** = **theology**, religion, religious studies **2** = **god** *or* **goddess**, deity, guardian spirit, spirit **3** = **godliness**, deity, divine nature, holiness, sanctity
divisible *adjective* = **dividable**, separable
division *noun* **1** = **separation**, cutting up, dividing, partition, splitting up **2** = **share**, allotment, apportionment **4** = **disagreement**, difference of opinion, discord, rupture, split, variance [OPPOSITE] **unity**. **5** = **part**, branch, category, class, department, group, section
divorce *noun* **1** = **separation**, annulment, dissolution, split-up ♦*verb* **3** = **separate**, disconnect, dissociate, dissolve (*marriage*), divide, part, sever, split up
divulge *verb* = **make known**, confess, declare, disclose, let slip, proclaim, reveal, tell [OPPOSITE]

dizzy ⊕ *adjective* **-zier, -ziest 1** having or causing a whirling sensation. **2** mentally confused. ♦ *verb* **-zying, -zied 3** make dizzy. **dizzily** *adverb* **dizziness** *noun*

DJ 1 disc jockey. **2** dinner jacket.

djinni *noun, pl* **djinn** same as JINNI.

dl decilitre.

dm decimetre.

DM Deutschmark.

DNA *noun* deoxyribonucleic acid, the main constituent of the chromosomes of all living things.

D-notice *noun Brit* official notice sent to newspapers etc., prohibiting publication of certain security information.

do¹ ⊕ *verb* **does, doing, did, done 1** perform or complete (a deed or action). **2** be adequate, e.g. *that one will do.* **3** provide, serve. **4** make (hair) neat or attractive. **5** suit or improve, e.g. *that style does nothing for you.* **6** find the answer to (a problem or puzzle). **7** cause, produce, e.g. *it does no harm to think ahead.* **8** give, grant, e.g. *do me a favour.* **9** work at, as a course of study or a job. **10** mimic. **11** *Informal* cheat or rob. **12** *Slang* use (illegal drugs). **13** used to form questions, e.g. *how do you know?* **14** used to intensify positive statements and commands, e.g. *I do like port; do go on.* **15** used to form negative statements and commands, e.g. *I do not know her well; do not get up.* **16** used to replace an earlier verb, e.g. *he gets paid more than I do.* ♦ *noun, pl* **do's, do's 17** *Informal* party, celebration. **do away with** *verb* get rid of. **do down** *verb* belittle, criticize. **do for** *verb Informal* cause the death or ruin of. **do-gooder** *noun Informal* well-intentioned but naive or impractical person. **do in** *verb Slang* **1** kill. **2** exhaust. **do-it-yourself** *noun* constructing and repairing things oneself. **do up** *verb* **1** fasten. **2** decorate and repair. **do with** *verb* find useful or benefit from, e.g. *I could do with a rest.* **do without** *verb* manage without.

do² *noun, pl* **dos** same as DOH.

Doberman pinscher, Doberman *noun* large dog with a black-and-tan coat.

dob in *verb* **dobbing, dobbed** *Aust & NZ informal* **1** inform against. **2** contribute to a fund.

docile ⊕ *adjective* (of a person or animal) easily controlled. **docilely** *adverb* **docility** *noun*

dock¹ ⊕ *noun* **1** enclosed area of water where ships are loaded, unloaded, or repaired. ♦ *verb* **2** bring or be brought into dock. **3** link (two spacecraft) or (of two spacecraft) be linked together in space. **docker** *noun* person employed to load and unload ships. **dockyard** *noun* place where ships are built or repaired.

dock² ⊕ *verb* **1** deduct money from (a person's wages). **2** remove part of (an animal's tail) by cutting through the bone.

dock³ ⊕ *noun* enclosed space in a court of law where the accused person sits or stands.

dock⁴ ⊕ *noun* weed with broad leaves.

docket *noun* label on a package or other delivery, stating contents, delivery instructions, etc.

doctor ⊕ *noun* **1** person licensed to practise medicine. **2** person who has been awarded a doctorate. ♦ *verb* **3** alter in order to deceive. **4** poison or drug (food or drink). **5** *Informal* castrate (an animal). **doctoral** *adjective* **doctorate** *noun* highest academic degree in any field of knowledge.

—————— T H E S A U R U S ——————

keep secret

dizzy *adjective* **1 = giddy**, faint, light-headed, off balance, reeling, shaky, swimming, wobbly, woozy (*inf*) **2 = confused**, at sea, befuddled, bemused, bewildered, dazed, dazzled, muddled

do¹ *verb* **1 = perform**, accomplish, achieve, carry out, complete, execute **2 = be adequate**, be sufficient, cut the mustard, pass muster, satisfy, suffice **4 = get ready**, arrange, fix, look after, prepare, see to **6 = solve**, decipher, decode, figure out, puzzle out, resolve, work out **7 = cause**, bring about, create, effect, produce ♦*noun* **17** *Inf* **= event**, affair, function, gathering, occasion, party **do without = manage without**, abstain from, dispense with, forgo, get along without, give up, kick (*inf*)

do away with *verb* **= get rid of**, abolish, discard, discontinue, eliminate, put an end to, put paid to, remove

docile *adjective* **= submissive**, amenable, biddable, compliant, manageable, obedient, pliant OPPOSITE **difficult**

docility *noun* **= submissiveness**, compliance, manageability, meekness, obedience

dock¹ *noun* **1 = wharf**, harbour, pier, quay, waterfront ♦*verb* **2 = moor**, anchor, berth, drop anchor, land, put in, tie up **3** *Of spacecraft* **= link up**, couple, hook up, join, rendezvous, unite

dock² *verb* **1 = deduct**, decrease, diminish, lessen, reduce, subtract, withhold OPPOSITE **increase. 2 = cut off**, clip, crop, curtail, cut short, shorten

doctor *noun* **1 = G.P.**, general practitioner, medic (*inf*), medical practitioner, physician

doctrine ❶ [**dock**-trin] *noun* **1** body of teachings of a religious, political, or philosophical group. **2** principle or body of principles that is taught or advocated. **doctrinal** *adjective* of doctrines. **doctrinaire** *adjective* stubbornly insistent on the application of a theory without regard to practicality.

document ❶ *noun* **1** piece of paper providing an official record of something. ◆ *verb* **2** record or report (something) in detail. **3** support (a claim) with evidence. **documentation** *noun*

documentary *noun*, *pl* -**ries** **1** film or television programme presenting the facts about a particular subject. ◆ *adjective* **2** (of evidence) based on documents.

docu-soap *noun* television documentary series presenting the lives of the people filmed as entertainment.

dodder *verb* move unsteadily. **doddery** *adjective*

doddle *noun Informal* something easily accomplished.

dodecagon [doe-**deck**-a-gon] *noun* geometric figure with twelve sides.

dodecahedron [doe-deck-a-**heed**-ron] *noun* solid figure with twelve faces.

dodge ❶ *verb* **1** avoid (a blow, being seen, etc.) by moving suddenly. **2** evade by cleverness or trickery. ◆ *noun* **3** cunning or deceitful trick. **dodger** *noun* **dodgy** *adjective* **dodgier, dodgiest** *Informal* **1** dangerous, risky. **2** untrustworthy.

Dodgem *noun* ® small electric car driven and bumped against similar cars in a rink at a funfair.

dodo *noun*, *pl* **dodos, dodoes** large flightless extinct bird.

doe *noun* female deer, hare, or rabbit.

does *verb* third person singular of the present tense of DO¹.

doesn't does not.

doff *verb* take off or lift (one's hat) in polite greeting.

dog ❶ *noun* **1** domesticated four-legged mammal of many different breeds. **2** related wild mammal, such as the dingo or coyote. **3** male animal of the dog family. **4** *Informal* person, e.g. *you lucky dog!* ◆ *verb* **dogging, dogged** **5** follow (someone) closely. **6** trouble, plague. **the dogs** *Brit informal* greyhound racing. **go to the dogs** *Informal* go to ruin physically or morally. **let sleeping dogs lie** leave things undisturbed. **doggy, doggie** *noun*, *pl* -**gies** child's word for a dog. **doggy bag** bag in which leftovers from a meal may be taken away. **dogcart** *noun* light horse-drawn two-wheeled cart. **dog collar 1** collar for a dog. **2** *Informal* white collar fastened at the back, worn by members of the clergy. **dog days** hottest part of the summer. **dog-eared** *adjective* **1** (of a book) having pages folded down at the corner. **2** shabby, worn. **dog-end** *noun Informal* cigarette end. **dogfight** *noun* close-quarters combat between fighter aircraft. **dogfish** *noun* small shark. **doghouse** *noun US* kennel. **in the doghouse** *Informal* in disgrace. **dogleg** *noun* sharp bend. **dog paddle** swimming stroke in which the hands are paddled in imitation of a swimming dog. **dog rose** wild rose with pink or white flowers. **dog-tired** *adjective Informal* exhausted.

doge [doje] *noun* (formerly) chief magistrate of Venice or Genoa.

dogged ❶ [**dog**-gid] *adjective* obstinately determined. **doggedly** *adverb* **doggedness** *noun*

doggerel *noun* poorly written poetry, usu. comic.

doggo *adverb* **lie doggo** *Informal* hide and keep quiet.

dogma ❶ *noun* doctrine or system of doctrines proclaimed by authority as true. **dogmatic** *adjective* habitually stating one's opinions forcefully or arrogantly. **dogmatically** *adverb* **dogmatism** *noun*

dogsbody *noun*, *pl* -**bodies** *Informal* person

————————————— THESAURUS —————————————

◆*verb* **3** = **change**, alter, disguise, falsify, misrepresent, pervert, tamper with **4** = **add to**, adulterate, cut, dilute, mix with, spike, water down

doctrinaire *adjective* = **dogmatic**, biased, fanatical, inflexible, insistent, opinionated, rigid

doctrine *noun* = **teaching**, article of faith, belief, conviction, creed, dogma, opinion, precept, principle, tenet

document *noun* **1** = **paper**, certificate, record, report ◆*verb* **3** = **support**, authenticate, certify, corroborate, detail, substantiate, validate, verify

dodge *verb* **1** = **duck**, dart, sidestep, swerve, turn aside **2** = **evade**, avoid, elude, get out of, shirk ◆*noun* **3** = **trick**, device, ploy, ruse, scheme, stratagem, subterfuge, wheeze (*Brit sl*)

dog *noun* **1** = **hound**, canine, cur, man's best friend, pooch (*sl*) ◆*verb* **5** = **trouble**, follow, haunt, hound, plague, pursue, track, trail **go to the dogs** *Inf* = **go to ruin**, degenerate, deteriorate, go down the drain, go to pot

dogged *adjective* = **determined**, indefatigable, obstinate, persistent, resolute, steadfast, stubborn, tenacious, unflagging, unshakable who carries out boring tasks for others.

doh *noun Music* in tonic sol-fa, first degree of any major scale.

doily *noun, pl* **-lies** decorative lacy paper mat, laid on a plate.

Dolby *noun* ® system used in tape recorders that reduces noise level on recorded or broadcast sound.

doldrums ❶ *plural noun* **1** depressed state of mind. **2** state of inactivity. **3** area of sea round the equator where there is hardly any wind.

dole ❶ *noun* **1** *Informal* money received from the state while unemployed. ♦ *verb* **2** (foll. by *out*) distribute in small quantities. **on the dole** *Brit informal* receiving unemployment benefit.

doleful *adjective* dreary, unhappy. **dolefully** *adverb* **dolefulness** *noun*

doll *noun* **1** small model of a human being, used as a toy. **2** *Slang* pretty girl or young woman. **doll up** *verb Slang* dress up smartly or showily.

dollar *noun* standard monetary unit of the US, Canada, and various other countries.

dollop ❶ *noun Informal* lump (of food).

dolly *noun, pl* **-lies 1** child's word for a doll. **2** wheeled support on which a camera may be moved.

dolman sleeve *noun* sleeve that is very wide at the armhole, tapering to a tight wrist.

dolmen *noun* prehistoric monument consisting of a horizontal stone supported by vertical stones.

dolomite *noun* mineral consisting of calcium magnesium carbonate.

dolorous *adjective* sad, mournful.

dolphin *noun* sea mammal of the whale family, with a beaklike snout. **dolphinarium** *noun* aquarium for dolphins.

dolt ❶ *noun* stupid person. **doltish** *adjective*

domain *noun* **1** field of knowledge or activity. **2** land under one ruler or government. **3** *Computers* group of computers with the same name on the Internet. **4** *NZ* public park.

dome *noun* **1** rounded roof built on a circular base. **2** something shaped like this. **domed** *adjective*

domestic ❶ *adjective* **1** of one's own country or a specific country, e.g. *domestic and foreign policy.* **2** of the home or family. **3** enjoying running a home. **4** (of an animal) kept as a pet or to produce food. ♦ *noun* **5** person whose job is to do housework in someone else's house. **domestically** *adverb* **domesticity** *noun*

domesticate *verb* **1** bring or keep (a wild animal or plant) under control or cultivation. **2** accustom (someone) to home life. **domestication** *noun* **domestic science** study of household skills.

domicile [dom-miss-ile] *noun* place where one lives. **domiciliary** *adjective*

dominant ❶ *adjective* **1** having authority or influence. **2** main, chief. **dominance** *noun*

dominate ❶ *verb* **1** control or govern. **2** tower above (surroundings). **3** be very significant in. **domination** *noun*

domineering ❶ *adjective* forceful and arrogant.

Dominican *noun, adjective* (friar or nun) of an order founded by Saint Dominic.

dominion ❶ *noun* **1** control or authority. **2**

——————— T H E S A U R U S ———————

OPPOSITE **irresolute**

dogma *noun* =**doctrine**, belief, credo, creed, opinion, teachings

dogmatic *adjective* =**opinionated**, arrogant, assertive, doctrinaire, emphatic, obdurate, overbearing

doldrums *noun* **1** =**depression**, dumps (*inf*), gloom, malaise **2** =**inactivity**, listlessness

dole *noun* **1** *Inf* =**benefit**, allowance, gift, grant, hand-out, pogey (*Canad*) ♦ *verb* **2** (foll. by *out*) =**give out**, allocate, allot, apportion, assign, dispense, distribute, hand out

dollop *noun Inf* =**lump**, helping, portion, scoop, serving

dolt *noun* =**idiot**, ass, blockhead, chump (*inf*), clot (*Brit inf*), dope (*inf*), dunce, fool, oaf

domestic *adjective* **1** =**native**, indigenous, internal **2** =**home**, family, household, private **3** =**home-loving**, domesticated, homely, housewifely, stay-at-home **4** =**domesticated**,

house-trained, pet, tame, trained ♦ *noun* **5** =**servant**, char (*inf*), charwoman, daily, help, maid

dominant *adjective* **1** =**controlling**, assertive, authoritative, commanding, governing, ruling, superior, supreme **2** =**main**, chief, predominant, pre-eminent, primary, principal, prominent OPPOSITE **minor**

dominate *verb* **1** =**control**, direct, govern, have the whip hand over, monopolize, rule, tyrannize **2** =**tower above**, loom over, overlook, stand head and shoulders above, stand over, survey

domination *noun* **1** =**control**, ascendancy, authority, command, influence, mana (*NZ*), power, rule, superiority, supremacy

domineering *adjective* =**overbearing**, arrogant, authoritarian, bossy (*inf*), dictatorial, high-handed, imperious, oppressive, tyrannical OPPOSITE **submissive**

land governed by one ruler or government. **3** (formerly) self-governing division of the British Empire.

domino *noun, pl* **-noes 1** small rectangular block marked with dots, used in dominoes. ◆ *plural* **2** game in which dominoes with matching halves are laid together.

don¹ ❶ *verb* **donning, donned** put on (clothing).

don² *noun* **1** *Brit* member of the teaching staff at a university or college. **2** Spanish gentleman or nobleman. **3** head of a Mafia family.

donnish *adjective* serious and academic.

donate ❶ *verb* give, esp. to a charity or organization. **donation** *noun* **1** donating. **2** thing donated. **donor** *noun* **1** *Med* person who gives blood or organs for use in the treatment of another person. **2** person who makes a donation.

done *verb* **1** past participle of DO¹. ◆ *adjective* **2** completed. **3** used up. **4** socially acceptable. **5** *Informal* cheated, tricked.

doner kebab *noun* see KEBAB.

Don Juan *noun* man who has seduced many women.

donkey *noun* long-eared member of the horse family. **donkey jacket** man's long thick jacket with a waterproof panel across the shoulders. **donkey's years** *Informal* a long time. **donkey-work** *noun* tedious hard work.

Don Quixote [don kee-**hoe**-tee] *noun* impractical idealist.

don't do not.

doodle *verb* **1** scribble or draw aimlessly. ◆ *noun* **2** shape or picture drawn aimlessly.

doom ❶ *noun* **1** death or a terrible fate. ◆ *verb* **2** destine or condemn to death or a terrible fate. **doomsday** *noun* **1** *Christianity* day on which the Last Judgment will occur. **2** any dreaded day.

door ❶ *noun* **1** hinged or sliding panel for

closing the entrance to a building, room, etc. **2** entrance. **doorjamb, doorpost** *noun* vertical post forming one side of a door frame.

doorman *noun* man employed to be on duty at the entrance to a large public building.

doormat *noun* **1** mat for wiping dirt from shoes before going indoors. **2** *Informal* person who offers little resistance to ill-treatment.

door-to-door *adjective* **1** (of selling) from one house to the next. **2** (of a journey) direct.

doorway *noun* opening into a building or room.

dope ❶ *noun* **1** *Slang* illegal drug, usu. cannabis. **2** medicine, drug. **3** *Informal* stupid person. ◆ *verb* **4** give a drug to, esp. in order to improve performance in a race. **dopey, dopy** *adjective* **1** half-asleep, drowsy. **2** *Slang* silly.

doppelgänger *noun Legend* ghostly double of a living person.

Doppler effect *noun* change in the apparent frequency of a sound or light wave as a result of relative motion between the observer and thesource.

Doric *adjective* **1** of a style of ancient Greek architecture. ◆ *noun* **2** country dialect, esp. a Scots one.

dormant ❶ *adjective* temporarily quiet, inactive, or not being used. **dormancy** *noun*

dormer, dormer window *noun* window that sticks out from a sloping roof.

dormitory *noun, pl* **-ries 1** large room, esp. at a school, containing several beds. ◆ *adjective* **2** (of a town or suburb) having many inhabitants who travel to work in a nearby city.

dormouse *noun, pl* **-mice** small mouselike rodent with a furry tail.

dorp *noun S Afr* small town.

dorsal *adjective* of or on the back.

dory *noun, pl* **-ries 1** (also **John Dory**) spiny-finned edible sea fish. **2** same as WALLEYE.

dose ❶ *noun* **1** specific quantity of a medicine

D

——————————— T H E S A U R U S ———————————

dominion *noun* **1** = **control**, authority, command, jurisdiction, mana (*NZ*), power, rule, sovereignty, supremacy **2** = **kingdom**, country, domain, empire, realm, territory

don¹ *verb* = **put on**, clothe oneself in, dress in, get into, pull on, slip on *or* into

donate *verb* = **give**, contribute, make a gift of, present, subscribe

donation *noun* **2** = **contribution**, gift, grant, hand-out, offering, present, subscription

donor *noun* **2** = **giver**, benefactor, contributor, donator, philanthropist OPPOSITE▷ **recipient**

doom *noun* **1** = **destruction**, catastrophe, downfall, fate, fortune, ruin ◆ *verb* **2**

= **condemn**, consign, damn, destine, sentence

doomed *adjective* = **condemned**, bewitched, cursed, fated, hopeless, ill-fated, ill-omened, luckless, star-crossed

door *noun* = **opening**, doorway, entrance, entry, exit

dope *noun* **1** *Sl* = **drug**, narcotic, opiate **3** *Inf* = **idiot**, dimwit (*inf*), dunce, fool, nitwit (*inf*), numbskull *or* numskull, simpleton, twit (*inf*, chiefly *Brit*) ◆ *verb* **4** = **drug**, anaesthetize, knock out, narcotize, sedate, stupefy

dormant *adjective* = **inactive**, asleep, hibernating, inert, inoperative, latent, sleeping, slumbering, suspended OPPOSITE▷ **active**

taken at one time. **2** *Informal* something
unpleasant to experience, e.g. *a dose of the
jitters.* ✦ *verb* **3** give a dose to. **dosage** *noun*
size of a dose.
dosh *noun Slang* money.
doss *verb* **doss down** *Brit & Aust slang* sleep
in an uncomfortable place. **dosshouse** *noun
Brit slang* cheap lodging house for homeless
people.
dossier [doss-ee-ay] *noun* collection of
documents about a subject or person.
dot ❶ *noun* **1** small round mark. **2** shorter
symbol used in Morse code. ✦ *verb* **dotting,
dotted** **3** mark with a dot. **4** scatter, spread
around. **on the dot** at exactly the arranged
time. **dotty** *adjective* **-tier, -tiest** *Slang* rather
eccentric. **dotcom, dot.com** *noun* company
that does most of its business on the Internet.
dote ❶ *verb* **dote on** love to an excessive
degree. **dotage** *noun* weakness as a result of
old age. **doting** *adjective*
dotterel *noun* rare kind of plover.
dottle *noun* tobacco left in a pipe after
smoking.
double ❶ *adjective* **1** as much again in
number, amount, size, etc. **2** composed of two
equal or similar parts. **3** designed for two users,
e.g. *double room.* **4** folded in two. ✦ *adverb* **5**
twice over. ✦ *noun* **6** twice the number,
amount, size, etc. **7** person who looks almost
exactly like another. ✦ *plural* **8** game between
two pairs of players. ✦ *verb* **9** make or become
twice as much or as many. **10** bend or fold
(material etc.). **11** play two parts. **12** turn
sharply. **at, on the double** quickly or
immediately. **doubly** *adverb* **double agent** spy
employed by two enemy countries at the same
time. **double-barrelled** *adjective* **1** (of a gun)
having two barrels. **2** (of a surname) having
two hyphenated parts. **double bass** stringed
instrument, largest and lowest member of the
violin family. **double-breasted** *adjective* (of a

jacket or coat) having overlapping fronts.
double-check *verb* make certain by checking
again. **double chin** fold of fat under the chin.
double cream thick cream with a high fat
content. **double-cross** *verb* **1** cheat or betray.
✦ *noun* **2** double-crossing. **double-dealing**
noun treacherous or deceitful behaviour.
double-decker *noun* **1** bus with two passenger
decks one on top of the other. ✦ *adjective* **2**
Informal (of a sandwich) made from three slices
of bread with two fillings. **double Dutch**
Informal incomprehensible talk, gibberish.
double-edged *adjective* **1** (of a remark)
malicious in intent though apparently
complimentary. **2** (of a knife) having a cutting
edge on each side of the blade. **double
glazing** two panes of glass in a window, fitted
to reduce heat loss. **double-jointed** *adjective*
(of a person) having unusually flexible joints.
double-park *verb* park (a vehicle) alongside
another, causing an obstruction. **double
standard** set of principles that allows greater
freedom to one person or group than to
another. **double take** esp. in comedy, delayed
reaction by a person to a remark or situation.
double talk deceptive or ambiguous talk.
double whammy *Informal* devastating setback
made up of two elements.
double entendre [doob-bl on-tond-ra] *noun*
word or phrase that can be interpreted in two
ways, one of which is rude.
doublet [dub-lit] *noun Hist* man's close-fitting
jacket, with or without sleeves.
doubloon *noun* former Spanish gold coin.
doubt ❶ *noun* **1** uncertainty about the truth,
facts, or existence of something. **2** unresolved
difficulty or point. ✦ *verb* **3** question the truth
of. **4** distrust or be suspicious of (someone).
doubter *noun* **doubtful** *adjective* **1** unlikely. **2**
feeling doubt. **doubtfully** *adverb* **doubtless**
adverb probably or certainly.
douche [doosh] *noun* **1** (instrument for

———————— THESAURUS ————————

dose *noun* **1** = **quantity**, dosage, draught,
measure, portion, potion, prescription
dot *noun* **1** = **spot**, fleck, jot, mark, point,
speck, speckle ✦ *verb* **3** = **spot**, dab, dabble,
fleck, speckle, sprinkle, stipple, stud **on the dot**
= **on time**, exactly, on the button (*inf*),
precisely, promptly, punctually, to the minute
dotage *noun* = **senility**, decrepitude,
feebleness, imbecility, old age, second
childhood, weakness
dote *verb* **dote on** = **adore**, admire, hold
dear, idolize, lavish affection on, prize, treasure
doting *adjective* = **adoring**, devoted, fond,

foolish, indulgent, lovesick
double *adjective* **1** = **twice**, duplicate, twofold
2 = **dual**, coupled, in pairs, paired, twin ✦ *noun*
7 = **twin**, clone, dead ringer (*sl*), doppelgänger,
duplicate, lookalike, replica, spitting image (*inf*)
✦ *verb* **9** = **multiply**, duplicate, enlarge, grow,
increase, magnify **at** *or* **on the double**
= **quickly**, at full speed, briskly, immediately,
posthaste, without delay
double-cross *verb* **1** = **betray**, cheat, defraud,
hoodwink, mislead, swindle, trick, two-time (*inf*)
doubt *noun* **1** = **uncertainty**, apprehension,
distrust, hesitancy, hesitation, indecision,

applying) a stream of water directed onto or into the body for cleansing or medical purposes. ♦ *verb* **2** cleanse or treat by means of a douche.

dough *noun* **1** thick mixture of flour and water or milk, used for making bread etc. **2** *Slang* money. **doughy** *adjective* **doughier, doughiest**. **doughnut** *noun* small cake of sweetened dough fried in deep fat.

doughty [dowt-ee] *adjective* **-tier, -tiest** *Old-fashioned* brave and determined.

dour ⊕ [doo-er] *adjective* sullen and unfriendly. **dourness** *noun*

douse [rhymes with **mouse**] *verb* **1** drench with water or other liquid. **2** put out (a light).

dove *noun* **1** bird with a heavy body, small head, and short legs. **2** *Politics* person opposed to war. **dovecote, dovecot** *noun* structure for housing pigeons. **dovetail** *noun* **1** joint containing wedge-shaped tenons. ♦ *verb* **2** fit together neatly.

dowager *noun* widow possessing property or a title obtained from her husband.

dowdy ⊕ *adjective* **-dier, -diest** dull and old-fashioned. **dowdily** *adverb* **dowdiness** *noun*

dowel *noun* wooden or metal peg that fits into two corresponding holes to join two adjacent parts.

dower *noun* life interest in a part of her husband's estate allotted to a widow by law.

down¹ ⊕ *preposition, adverb* **1** indicating movement to or position in a lower place. ♦ *adverb* **2** indicating completion of an action, lessening of intensity, etc., e.g. *calm down*. ♦ *adjective* **3** depressed, unhappy. ♦ *verb* **4** *Informal* drink quickly. **have a down on** *Informal* feel hostile towards. **download** *verb* transfer (data) from the memory of one computer to that of another. **down under** *Informal* (in or to) Australia or New Zealand. **downward** *adjective, adverb* (descending) from a higher to a lower level, condition, or position. **downwards** *adverb* from a higher to a lower level, condition, or position. **down-and-out** *noun* **1** person who is homeless and destitute. ♦ *adjective* **2** without any means of support. **down-to-earth** *adjective* sensible or practical. **down²** *noun* soft fine feathers. **downy** *adjective*

downbeat *adjective* **1** *Informal* gloomy. **2** relaxed.

downcast ⊕ *adjective* **1** sad, dejected. **2** (of the eyes) directed downwards.

downfall ⊕ *noun* (cause of) a sudden loss of position or reputation.

downgrade ⊕ *verb* reduce in importance or value.

downhearted ⊕ *adjective* sad and discouraged.

downhill *adjective* **1** going or sloping down. ♦

D

—————————— THESAURUS ——————————

irresolution, lack of conviction, misgiving, mistrust, qualm, scepticism, suspense, suspicion OPPOSITE **certainty** ♦*verb* **3 = be uncertain**, be dubious, demur **4 = suspect**, discredit, distrust, fear, lack confidence in, mistrust, query, question OPPOSITE **believe**

doubtful *adjective* **1 = unlikely**, debatable, dubious, equivocal, improbable, problematic(al), questionable, unclear OPPOSITE **certain**. **2 = unsure**, distrustful, hesitating, in two minds (*inf*), sceptical, suspicious, tentative, uncertain, unconvinced, wavering OPPOSITE **decided**

doubtless *adverb* **a = probably**, apparently, most likely, ostensibly, presumably, seemingly, supposedly **b = certainly**, assuredly, indisputably, of course, surely, undoubtedly, unquestionably, without doubt

dour *adjective* **= gloomy**, dismal, dreary, forbidding, grim, morose, sour, sullen, unfriendly OPPOSITE **cheery**

dowdy *adjective* **= frumpy**, dingy, drab, frowzy, old-fashioned, shabby, unfashionable OPPOSITE **chic**

down¹ *adjective* **3 = depressed**, dejected,

disheartened, downcast, low, miserable, sad, unhappy ♦*verb* **4** *Inf* **= swallow**, drain, drink (down), gulp, put away, toss off **have a down on** *Inf* **= be antagonistic** *or* **hostile to**, bear a grudge towards, be prejudiced against, be set against, have it in for (*sl*)

down-and-out *noun* **1 = tramp**, bag lady, beggar, derelict, dosser (*Brit sl*), pauper, vagabond, vagrant ♦*adjective* **2 = destitute**, derelict, impoverished, on one's uppers (*inf*), penniless, short, without two pennies to rub together (*inf*)

downcast *adjective* **1 = dejected**, crestfallen, depressed, despondent, disappointed, disconsolate, discouraged, disheartened, dismayed, dispirited OPPOSITE **cheerful**

downfall *noun* **= ruin**, collapse, comeuppance (*sl*), destruction, disgrace, fall, overthrow, undoing

downgrade *verb* **= demote**, degrade, humble, lower *or* reduce in rank, take down a peg (*inf*) OPPOSITE **raise**

downhearted *adjective* **= dejected**, crestfallen, depressed, despondent, discouraged, disheartened, dispirited, downcast,

D

adverb **2** towards the bottom of a hill. **go downhill** *Informal* deteriorate.

Downing Street *noun Informal* British prime minister or government.

downpour ⊙ *noun* heavy fall of rain.

downright ⊙ *adjective, adverb* extreme(ly).

downs *plural noun* low grassy hills, esp. in S England.

Down's syndrome *noun* genetic disorder characterized by a flat face, slanting eyes, and mental retardation.

downstage *adverb, adjective* to or at the front part of the stage.

downstairs *adverb* **1** to or on a lower floor. ♦ *noun* **2** lower or ground floor.

downtown *US, Canad & NZ noun* **1** the central or lower part of a city, especially the main commercial area. ♦ *adverb* **2** towards, to, or into this area.

downtrodden ⊙ *adjective* oppressed and lacking the will to resist.

dowry *noun, pl* **-ries** property brought by a woman to her husband at marriage.

dowse [rhymes with **cows**] *verb* search for underground water or minerals using a divining rod. **dowser** *noun*

doxology *noun, pl* **-gies** short hymn of praise to God.

doyen [doy-en] *noun* senior member of a group, profession, or society. **doyenne** [doy-en] *n fem*

doyley *noun* same as DOILY.

doze ⊙ *verb* **1** sleep lightly or briefly. ♦ *noun* **2** short sleep. **dozy** *adjective* **dozier, doziest 1** feeling sleepy. **2** *Informal* stupid. **doze off** *verb* fall into a light sleep.

dozen *adjective, noun* twelve. **dozenth** *adjective*

DPP Director of Public Prosecutions.

Dr 1 Doctor. **2** Drive.

drab ⊙ *adjective* **drabber, drabbest 1** dull and dreary. **2** dull brown. **drabness** *noun*

drachm [dram] *qn Brit* one eighth of a fluid ounce.

drachma *noun, pl* **-mas, -mae** standard monetary unit of Greece.

draconian *adjective* severe, harsh.

draft ⊙ *noun* **1** plan, sketch, or drawing of something. **2** preliminary outline of a book, speech, etc. **3** written order for payment of money by a bank. **4** *US & Aust* selection for compulsory military service. ♦ *verb* **5** draw up an outline or plan of. **6** send (people) from one place to another to do a specific job. **7** *US & Aust* select for compulsory military service.

drag ⊙ *verb* **dragging, dragged 1** pull with force, esp. along the ground. **2** trail on the ground. **3** persuade or force (oneself or someone else) to go somewhere. **4** (foll. by *on* or *out*) last or be prolonged tediously. **5** search (a river) with a dragnet or hook. **6** *Computers* move (an image) on the screen by use of the mouse. ♦ *noun* **7** person or thing that slows up progress. **8** *Informal* tedious thing or person. **9** *Slang* women's clothes worn by a man. **10** resistance to the motion of a body passing through air or a liquid. **dragnet** *noun* net used to scour the bottom of a pond or river to search for something. **drag race** race in which specially built cars or motorcycles are timed over a measured course.

dragoman *noun, pl* **-mans, -men** (in some Middle Eastern countries) professional interpreter or guide.

dragon *noun* **1** mythical fire-breathing monster like a huge lizard. **2** *Informal* fierce woman. **dragonfly** *noun* brightly coloured insect with a long slender body and two pairs of wings.

dragoon ⊙ *noun* **1** heavily armed cavalryman.

——— T H E S A U R U S ———

sad, unhappy
downpour *noun* = **rainstorm**, cloudburst, deluge, flood, inundation, torrential rain
downright *adjective* = **complete**, absolute, out-and-out, outright, plain, thoroughgoing, total, undisguised, unqualified, utter
down-to-earth *adjective* = **sensible**, matter-of-fact, no-nonsense, plain-spoken, practical, realistic, sane, unsentimental
downtrodden *adjective* = **oppressed**, exploited, helpless, subjugated, subservient, tyrannized
downward *adjective* = **descending**, declining, earthward, heading down, sliding, slipping
doze *verb* **1** = **nap**, kip (*Brit sl*), nod off (*inf*),

sleep, slumber, snooze (*inf*) ♦*noun* **2** = **nap**, catnap, forty winks (*inf*), kip (*Brit sl*), shuteye (*sl*), siesta, snooze (*inf*)
drab *adjective* **1** = **dull**, dingy, dismal, dreary, flat, gloomy, shabby, sombre OPPOSITE> **bright**
draft *noun* **1** = **outline**, abstract, plan, rough, sketch, version **3** = **order**, bill (*of exchange*), cheque, postal order ♦*verb* **5** = **outline**, compose, design, draw, draw up, formulate, plan, sketch
drag *verb* **1** = **pull**, draw, haul, lug, tow, trail, tug **4** (foll. by *on* or *out*) = **last**, draw out, extend, keep going, lengthen, persist, prolong, protract, spin out, stretch out ♦*noun* **8** *Inf* = **nuisance**, annoyance, bore, bother, pain (*inf*), pest

D

◆ *verb* **2** coerce, force.

drain ⊕ *noun* **1** pipe or channel that carries off water or sewage. **2** cause of a continuous reduction in energy or resources. ◆ *verb* **3** draw off or remove liquid from. **4** flow away or filter off. **5** drink the entire contents of (a glass or cup). **6** make constant demands on (energy or resources), exhaust. **drainage** *noun* **1** system of drains. **2** process or method of draining.

draining board sloping grooved surface at the side of a sink, used for draining washed dishes.

drainpipe *noun* **1** pipe for carrying off rainwater or sewage. ◆ *plural* **2** trousers with very narrow legs.

drake *noun* male duck.

dram *noun* **1** small amount of a strong alcoholic drink, esp. whisky. **2** one sixteenth of an ounce.

drama ⊕ *noun* **1** serious play for theatre, television, or radio. **2** plays collectively. **3** writing, producing, or acting in plays. **4** situation that is exciting or highly emotional. **dramatic** *adjective* **1** of or like drama. **2** behaving flamboyantly. **dramatically** *adverb* **dramatist** *noun* person who writes plays. **dramatize** *verb* **1** rewrite (a book) in the form of a play. **2** express (something) in a dramatic or exaggerated way. **dramatization** *noun*

dramatis personae [drah-mat-tiss per-**soh**-nigh] *plural noun* characters in a play.

dramaturgy *noun* art and technique of the theatre. **dramaturge** *noun* **1** playwright. **2** literary adviser to a theatre, film company, etc. **dramaturgical, dramaturgic** *adjective*

drank *verb* past tense of DRINK.

drape ⊕ *verb* **1** cover with material, usu. in folds. **2** place casually. ◆ *noun* **3** *Aust, US & Canad* curtain. **draper** *noun Brit, Aust & NZ* person who sells fabrics and sewing materials.

drapery *noun, pl* **-peries 1** fabric or clothing arranged and draped. **2** fabrics and cloth collectively.

drastic ⊕ *adjective* strong and severe.

drastically *adverb*

draught ⊕ *noun* **1** current of cold air, esp. in an enclosed space. **2** portion of liquid to be drunk, esp. medicine. **3** gulp or swallow. **4** one of the flat discs used in the game of draughts. ◆ *plural* **5** game for two players using a chessboard and twelve draughts each. ◆ *adjective* **6** (of an animal) used for pulling heavy loads. **draughty** *adjective* **draughtier, draughtiest** exposed to draughts of air.

draughtsman *noun* **1** person employed to prepare detailed scale drawings of machinery, buildings, etc. **2** person skilled in drawing.

draughtsmanship *noun* **draught beer** beer stored in a cask.

draw ⊕ *verb* **drawing, drew, drawn 1** sketch (a figure, picture, etc.) with a pencil or pen. **2** pull (a person or thing) closer to or further away from a place. **3** move in a specified direction, e.g. *the car drew near.* **4** take from a source, e.g. *draw money from bank accounts.* **5** attract, interest. **6** formulate or decide, e.g. *to draw conclusions.* **7** (of two teams or contestants) finish a game with an equal number of points. ◆ *noun* **8** raffle or lottery. **9** contest or game ending in a tie. **10** event, act, etc., that attracts a large audience. **drawing** *noun* **1** picture or plan made by means of lines on a surface. **2** art of making drawings.

drawing pin short tack with a broad smooth head. **drawing room** *Old-fashioned* room where visitors are received and entertained.

drawback *noun* disadvantage. **drawbridge** *noun* bridge that may be raised to prevent access or to enable vessels to pass. **draw out**

—————— THESAURUS ——————

dragoon *verb* **2** = **force**, browbeat, bully, coerce, compel, constrain, drive, impel, intimidate, railroad (*inf*)

drain *noun* **1** = **pipe**, channel, conduit, culvert, ditch, duct, sewer, sink, trench **2** = **reduction**, depletion, drag, exhaustion, sap, strain, withdrawal ◆*verb* **3** = **remove**, bleed, draw off, dry, empty, pump off *or* out, tap, withdraw **4** = **flow out**, effuse, exude, leak, ooze, seep, trickle, well out **5** = **drink up**, finish, gulp down, quaff, swallow **6** = **exhaust**, consume, deplete, dissipate, empty, sap, strain, use up

drama *noun* **1** = **play**, dramatization, show, stage show **3** = **theatre**, acting, dramaturgy, stagecraft **4** = **excitement**, crisis, histrionics, scene, spectacle, turmoil

dramatic *adjective* **1 a** = **theatrical**, dramaturgical, Thespian **b** = **exciting**, breathtaking, climactic, electrifying, melodramatic, sensational, suspenseful, tense, thrilling **2** = **powerful**, expressive, impressive, moving, striking, vivid OPPOSITE **ordinary**

dramatist *noun* = **playwright**, dramaturge, screenwriter, scriptwriter

dramatize *verb* **2** = **exaggerate**, lay it on (thick) (*sl*), overdo, overstate, play to the gallery

drape *verb* **1** = **cover**, cloak, fold, swathe, wrap

drastic *adjective* = **extreme**, desperate, dire, forceful, harsh, radical, severe, strong

draught *noun* **1** = **breeze**, current, flow, movement, puff **2** = **drink**, cup, dose, potion,

D

verb **1** encourage (someone) to talk freely. **2** make longer. **drawstring** *noun* cord run through a hem around an opening, so that when it is pulled tighter, the opening closes.

draw up *verb* **1** prepare and write out (a contract). **2** (of a vehicle) come to a stop.

drawer *noun* **1** sliding box-shaped part of a piece of furniture, used for storage. ◆ *plural* **2** *Old-fashioned* undergarment worn on the lower part of the body.

drawl *verb* **1** speak slowly, with long vowel sounds. ◆ *noun* **2** drawling manner of speech.

drawn ❶ *verb* **1** past participle of DRAW. ◆ *adjective* **2** haggard, tired, or tense in appearance.

dray *noun* low cart used for carrying heavy loads.

dread ❶ *verb* **1** anticipate with apprehension or fear. ◆ *noun* **2** great fear. **dreadful** *adjective* **1** very disagreeable or shocking. **2** extreme, e.g. *a dreadful anticlimax.* **dreadfully** *adverb*

dreadlocks *plural noun* hair worn in the Rastafarian style of tightly twisted strands.

dream ❶ *noun* **1** imagined series of events experienced in the mind while asleep. **2** daydream. **3** cherished hope. **4** *Informal* wonderful person or thing. ◆ *verb* **dreaming, dreamed** *or* **dreamt 5** see imaginary pictures

in the mind while asleep. **6** (often foll. by *of* or *about*) have an image (of) or fantasy (about). **7** (foll. by *of*) consider the possibility (of). ◆ *adjective* **8** ideal, e.g. *a dream house.* **dreamer** *noun* **dreamy** *adjective* **dreamier, dreamiest 1** vague or impractical. **2** *Informal* wonderful. **dreamily** *adverb* **dream team** *Informal* group of people with the ideal combination of talents.

dream up *verb* invent by imagination and ingenuity.

dreary ❶ *adjective* **drearier, dreariest** dull, boring. **drearily** *adverb* **dreariness** *noun*

dredge¹ *verb* clear or search (a river bed or harbour) by removing silt or mud. **dredger** *noun* boat fitted with machinery for dredging.

dredge up *verb Informal* remember (something) obscure or half-forgotten.

dredge² *verb* sprinkle (food) with flour etc.

dregs ❶ *plural noun* **1** solid particles that settle at the bottom of some liquids. **2** most despised elements, e.g. *the dregs of society.*

drench ❶ *verb* make completely wet.

Dresden china, Dresden *noun* delicate decorative porcelain made near Dresden in Germany.

dress ❶ *noun* **1** one-piece garment for a woman or girl, consisting of a skirt and bodice and sometimes sleeves. **2** complete style of

———— T H E S A U R U S ————

quantity

draw *verb* **1** = **sketch**, depict, design, map out, mark out, outline, paint, portray, trace **2** = **pull**, drag, haul, tow, tug **4** = **take out**, extract, pull out **5** = **attract**, allure, elicit, entice, evoke, induce, influence, invite, persuade **6** = **deduce**, derive, infer, make, take ◆ *noun* **9** = **tie**, dead heat, deadlock, impasse, stalemate **10** = **attraction**, enticement, lure, pull (*inf*)

drawback *noun* = **disadvantage**, deficiency, difficulty, downside, flaw, handicap, hitch, snag, stumbling block OPPOSITE⟩ **advantage**

drawing *noun* **1** = **picture**, cartoon, depiction, illustration, outline, portrayal, representation, sketch, study

drawn *adjective* **2** = **tense**, haggard, pinched, stressed, tired, worn

draw out *verb* **2** = **extend**, drag out, lengthen, make longer, prolong, protract, spin out, stretch, string out

draw up *verb* **1** = **draft**, compose, formulate, frame, prepare, write out **2** = **halt**, bring to a stop, pull up, stop

dread *verb* **1** = **fear**, cringe at, have cold feet (*inf*), quail, shrink from, shudder, tremble ◆ *noun* **2** = **fear**, alarm, apprehension, dismay, fright, horror, terror, trepidation

dreadful *adjective* **1** = **terrible**, abysmal, appalling, atrocious, awful, fearful, frightful, hideous, horrible, shocking

dream *noun* **1** = **vision**, delusion, hallucination, illusion, imagination, trance **2** = **daydream**, fantasy, pipe dream **3** = **ambition**, aim, aspiration, desire, goal, hope, wish **4** *Inf* = **delight**, beauty, gem, joy, marvel, pleasure, treasure ◆ *verb* **6** (often foll. by *of* or *about*) = **daydream**, build castles in the air *or* in Spain, conjure up, envisage, fantasize, imagine, stargaze, visualize

dreamer *noun* **2** = **idealist**, daydreamer, escapist, utopian, visionary, Walter Mitty

dreamy *adjective* **2** = **vague**, absent, abstracted, daydreaming, faraway, pensive, preoccupied, with one's head in the clouds OPPOSITE⟩ **practical**

dreary *adjective* = **dull**, boring, drab, humdrum, monotonous, tedious, tiresome, uneventful, wearisome OPPOSITE⟩ **interesting**

dregs *plural noun* **1** = **sediment**, deposit, dross, grounds, lees, resi, residuum, scum, waste **2** = **scum**, good-for-nothings, rabble, ragtag and bobtail, riffraff

drench *verb* = **soak**, drown, flood, inundate, saturate, souse, steep, swamp, wet clothing. ◆ *verb* **3** put clothes on. **4** put on formal clothes. **5** apply a protective covering to (a wound). **6** arrange or prepare. **dressing** *noun* **1** sauce for salad. **2** covering for a wound. **dressing-down** *noun Informal* severe scolding. **dressing gown** coat-shaped garment worn over pyjamas or nightdress. **dressing room** room used for changing clothes, esp. backstage in a theatre. **dressing table** piece of bedroom furniture with a mirror and drawers. **dressy** *adjective* **dressier, dressiest** (of clothes) elegant. **dress circle** first gallery in a theatre. **dressmaker** *noun* person who makes women's clothes. **dressmaking** *noun* **dress rehearsal** last rehearsal of a play or show, using costumes, lighting, etc. **dress up** *verb* **1** put on glamorous or stylish clothes. **2** put on fancy dress. **3** make (something) seem better than it really is, e.g. *to dress up profits*.

dressage [dress-ahzh] *noun* training of a horse to perform manoeuvres in response to the rider's body signals.

dresser[1] *noun* piece of furniture with shelves and with cupboards, for storing or displaying dishes.

dresser[2] *noun Theatre* person employed to assist actors with their costumes.

drew *verb* past tense of DRAW.

drey *noun* squirrel's nest.

dribble ⊕ *verb* **1** (allow to) flow in drops. **2** allow saliva to trickle from the mouth. **3** *Sport* propel (a ball) by repeatedly tapping it with the foot, hand, or a stick. ◆ *noun* **4** small quantity of liquid falling in drops. **5** dribbling. **dribbler** *noun*

driblet *noun* small amount.

dribs and drabs *plural noun Informal* small occasional amounts.

dried *verb* past of DRY.

drier[1] *adjective* a comparative of DRY.

drier[2] *noun* same as DRYER.

driest *adjective* a superlative of DRY.

drift ⊕ *verb* **1** be carried along by currents of air or water. **2** move aimlessly from one place or activity to another. **3** (of snow) pile up in heaps. ◆ *noun* **4** something piled up by the wind or current, such as a snowdrift. **5** general movement or development. **6** point, meaning, e.g. *catch my drift?* **drifter** *noun* **1** person who moves aimlessly from place to place or job to job. **2** fishing boat equipped with drift nets. **drift net** fishing net that is allowed to drift with the tide. **driftwood** *noun* wood floating on or washed ashore by the sea.

drill[1] ⊕ *noun* **1** tool or machine for boring holes. **2** strict and often repetitious training. **3** *Informal* correct procedure. ◆ *verb* **4** bore a hole in (something) with or as if with a drill. **5** teach by rigorous exercises or training.

drill[2] *noun* **1** machine for sowing seed in rows. **2** small furrow for seed. ◆ *verb* **3** sow (seed) in drills or furrows.

drill[3] *noun* hard-wearing cotton cloth.

drily *adverb* see DRY.

drink ⊕ *verb* **drinking, drank, drunk** **1** swallow (a liquid). **2** consume alcohol, esp. to excess. ◆ *noun* **3** (portion of) a liquid suitable for drinking. **4** alcohol, or its habitual or excessive consumption. **drinkable** *adjective* **drinker** *noun* **drink-driving** *adjective, noun* (of) driving a car after drinking alcohol. **drink in** *verb* pay close attention to. **drink to** *verb* drink a toast to.

drip ⊕ *verb* **dripping, dripped** **1** (let) fall in drops. ◆ *noun* **2** falling of drops of liquid. **3** sound made by falling drops. **4** *Informal* weak

---

THESAURUS

dress *noun* **1** = **frock**, gown, outfit, robe **2** = **clothing**, apparel, attire, clothes, costume, garb, garments, togs ◆*verb* **3** = **put on**, attire, change, clothe, don, garb, robe, slip on *or* into OPPOSITE undress. **5** = **bandage**, bind up, plaster, treat **6** = **arrange**, adjust, align, get ready, prepare, straighten

dressmaker *noun* = **seamstress**, couturier, tailor

dribble *verb* **1** = **run**, drip, drop, fall in drops, leak, ooze, seep, trickle **2** = **drool**, drivel, slaver, slobber

drift *verb* **1** = **float**, be carried along, coast, go (aimlessly), meander, stray, waft, wander **3** = **pile up**, accumulate, amass, bank up, drive, gather ◆*noun* **4** = **pile**, accumulation, bank, heap, mass, mound **6** = **meaning**, direction,

gist, import, intention, purport, significance, tendency, thrust

drifter *noun* **1** = **wanderer**, beachcomber, bum (*inf*), hobo (*US*), itinerant, rolling stone, vagrant

drill[1] *noun* **1** = **boring tool**, bit, borer, gimlet **2** = **training**, discipline, exercise, instruction, practice, preparation, repetition ◆*verb* **4** = **bore**, penetrate, perforate, pierce, puncture, sink in **5** = **train**, coach, discipline, exercise, instruct, practise, rehearse, teach

drink *verb* **1** = **swallow**, gulp, guzzle, imbibe, quaff, sip, suck, sup **2** = **booze** (*inf*), hit the bottle (*inf*), tipple, tope ◆*noun* **3** = **beverage**, cup, draught, glass, liquid, potion, refreshment **4** = **alcohol**, booze (*inf*), hooch *or* hootch (*inf, chiefly US & Canad*), liquor, spirits, the bottle dull person. **5** *Med* device by which a solution is passed in small drops through a tube into a vein. **drip-dry** *adjective* denoting clothing that will dry free of creases if hung up when wet. **drip-feed** *verb* feed (someone) a liquid drop by drop, usu. through a vein.

dripping *noun* fat that comes from meat while it is being roasted or fried.

drive ⊕ *verb* **driving, drove, driven 1** guide the movement of (a vehicle). **2** transport in a vehicle. **3** goad into a specified state. **4** push or propel. **5** *Sport* hit (a ball) very hard and straight. **6** make (people or animals) go to or from a place. ♦ *noun* **7** journey by car, van, etc. **8** (also **driveway**) path for vehicles connecting a building to a public road. **9** united effort towards a common goal, e.g. *a recruitment drive*. **10** energy and ambition. **11** *Psychol* motive or interest, e.g. *sex drive*. **12** means by which power is transmitted in a mechanism. **driver** *noun* **drive at** *verb Informal* intend or mean, e.g. *what was he driving at?* **drive-in** *adjective, noun* (denoting) a cinema, restaurant, etc., used by people in their cars. **driving licence** official document authorizing a person to drive a motor vehicle.

drivel ⊕ *noun* **1** foolish talk. ♦ *verb* **-elling, -elled 2** speak foolishly.

drizzle ⊕ *noun* **1** very light rain. ♦ *verb* **2** rain lightly. **drizzly** *adjective* **-zlier, -zliest**

droll ⊕ *adjective* quaintly amusing. **drolly** *adverb* **drollery** *noun*

dromedary [**drom**-mid-er-ee] *noun, pl* **-daries** camel with a single hump.

drone¹ *noun* male bee.

drone² ⊕ *verb, noun* (make) a monotonous low dull sound. **drone on** *verb* talk for a long time in a monotonous tone.

drongo *noun, pl* **-gos** tropical songbird with a glossy black plumage, a forked tail, and a stout bill.

drool ⊕ *verb* **1** (foll. by *over*) show excessive enthusiasm (for). **2** allow saliva to flow from the mouth.

droop ⊕ *verb* hang downwards loosely. **droopy** *adjective* **droopier, droopiest**

drop ⊕ *verb* **dropping, dropped 1** (allow to) fall vertically. **2** decrease in amount, strength, or value. **3** (of ground) go down to a lower level. **4** mention (a hint or name) casually. **5** drive (someone or something) to a place. **6** discontinue. ♦ *noun* **7** small quantity of liquid forming a round shape. **8** any small quantity of liquid. **9** decrease in amount, strength, or value. **10** vertical distance that something may fall. ♦ *plural* **11** liquid medication applied in small drops. **droplet** *noun* **droppings** *plural noun* faeces of certain animals, such as rabbits or birds. **drop in, by** *verb* pay someone a casual visit. **drop kick** (in rugby etc.) kick in which the ball is dropped from the hands and kicked as it hits the ground. **drop off** *verb* **1** *Informal* fall asleep. **2** same as DROP (sense 5). **3** grow smaller or less. **dropout** *noun* **1** person who rejects conventional society. **2** person who does not complete a course of study. **drop out (of)** *verb* abandon or withdraw from (a school, job, etc.).

(*inf*)

drip *verb* **1 = drop**, dribble, exude, plop, splash, sprinkle, trickle ♦*noun* **2 = drop**, dribble, leak, trickle **4** *Inf* **=weakling**, mummy's boy (*inf*), namby-pamby, softie (*inf*), weed (*inf*), wet (*Brit inf*)

drive *verb* **1 =operate**, direct, guide, handle, manage, motor, ride, steer, travel **3 =goad**, coerce, constrain, force, press, prod, prompt, spur **4 =push**, hurl, impel, propel, ram, send, thrust **6 =herd**, urge ♦*noun* **7 =run**, excursion, jaunt, journey, outing, ride, spin (*inf*), trip **9 =campaign**, action, appeal, crusade, effort, push (*inf*) **10 =initiative**, ambition, energy, enterprise, get-up-and-go (*inf*), motivation, vigour, zip (*inf*)

drivel *noun* **1 =nonsense**, garbage (*inf*), gibberish, hogwash, hot air (*inf*), kak (*S Afr sl*), poppycock (*inf*), rubbish, trash, twaddle, waffle (*inf, chiefly Brit*) ♦*verb* **2 =babble**, blether, gab (*inf*), prate, ramble, waffle (*inf, chiefly Brit*)

drizzle *noun* **1 =fine rain**, Scotch mist ♦*verb* **2 =rain**, shower, spot *or* spit with rain, spray, sprinkle

droll *adjective* **=amusing**, comical, entertaining, funny, humorous, jocular, waggish, whimsical

drone² *verb* **=hum**, buzz, purr, thrum, vibrate, whirr ♦*noun* **=hum**, buzz, murmuring, purr, thrum, vibration, whirring

drool *verb* **1** (foll. by *over*) **=gloat over**, dote on, gush, make much of, rave about (*inf*) **2 =dribble**, drivel, salivate, slaver, slobber, water at the mouth

droop *verb* **=sag**, bend, dangle, drop, fall down, hang (down), sink

drop *verb* **1 =fall**, descend, plummet, plunge, sink, tumble **2 =diminish**, decline, fall, plummet **6 =discontinue**, axe (*inf*), give up, kick (*inf*), quit, relinquish ♦*noun* **7 =droplet**, bead, bubble, drip, globule, pearl, tear **8 =dash**, mouthful, shot (*inf*), sip, spot, tot,

dropsy *noun* illness in which watery fluid collects in the body.

dross *noun* **1** scum formed on the surfaces of molten metals. **2** anything worthless.

drought ⊕ *noun* prolonged shortage of rainfall.

drove[1] *verb* past tense of DRIVE.

drove[2] ⊕ *noun* very large group, esp. of people. **drover** *noun* person who drives sheep or cattle.

drown ⊕ *verb* **1** die or kill by immersion in liquid. **2** forget (one's sorrows) temporarily by drinking alcohol. **3** drench thoroughly. **4** make (a sound) inaudible by being louder.

drowse ⊕ *verb* be sleepy, dull, or sluggish.

drowsy *adjective* **drowsily** *adverb* **drowsiness** *noun*

drubbing *noun* utter defeat in a contest etc.

drudge ⊕ *noun* **1** person who works hard at uninteresting tasks. ◆ *verb* **2** work at such tasks. **drudgery** *noun*

drug ⊕ *noun* **1** substance used in the treatment or prevention of disease. **2** chemical substance, esp. a narcotic, taken for the effects it produces. ◆ *verb* **drugging, drugged 3** give a drug to (a person or animal) to cause sleepiness or unconsciousness. **4** mix a drug with (food or drink). **drugstore** *noun* US pharmacy where a wide range of goods are available.

Druid *noun* member of an ancient order of Celtic priests. **Druidic, Druidical** *adjective*

drum ⊕ *noun* **1** percussion instrument sounded by striking a membrane stretched across the opening of a hollow cylinder. **2** cylindrical object or container. ◆ *verb* **drumming, drummed 3** play (music) on a drum. **4** tap rhythmically or regularly.

drummer *noun* **drum into** *verb* instil into (someone) by constant repetition. **drum machine** synthesizer programmed to reproduce the sound of percussion instruments. **drum major** person in charge of a marching band. **drum out (of)** *verb* force to leave (an organization). **drumstick** *noun* **1** stick used for playing a drum. **2** lower joint of the leg of a cooked chicken etc. **drum up** *verb* obtain (support or business) by making requests or canvassing.

drunk ⊕ *verb* **1** past participle of DRINK. ◆ *adjective* **2** intoxicated with alcohol to the extent of losing control over normal functions. **3** overwhelmed by a strong influence or emotion, e.g. *drunk with success.* ◆ *noun* **4** person who is drunk or who frequently gets drunk. **drunkard** *noun* person who frequently gets drunk. **drunken** *adjective* **1** drunk or frequently drunk. **2** caused by or relating to alcoholic intoxication. **drunkenly** *adverb* **drunkenness** *noun*

dry ⊕ *adjective* **drier, driest** *or* **dryer, dryest 1** lacking moisture. **2** having little or no rainfall.

——————— THESAURUS ———————

trace, trickle **9 = decrease**, cut, decline, deterioration, downturn, fall-off, lowering, reduction, slump **10 = fall**, descent, plunge

drop off *verb* **1** *Inf* **= fall asleep**, doze (off), have forty winks (*inf*), nod (off), snooze (*inf*) **3 = decrease**, decline, diminish, dwindle, fall off, lessen, slacken

drop out (of) *verb* **= leave**, abandon, fall by the wayside, give up, quit, stop, withdraw

drought *noun* **= dry spell**, aridity, dehydration, dryness OPPOSITE flood

drove[2] *noun* **= herd**, collection, company, crowd, flock, horde, mob, multitude, swarm, throng

drown *verb* **3 = drench**, deluge, engulf, flood, go under, immerse, inundate, sink, submerge, swamp **4 = overpower**, deaden, muffle, obliterate, overcome, overwhelm, stifle, swallow up, wipe out

drowsy *adjective* **= sleepy**, dopey (*sl*), dozy, half asleep, heavy, lethargic, somnolent, tired, torpid OPPOSITE awake

drudge *noun* **1 = menial**, dogsbody (*inf*), factotum, servant, skivvy (*chiefly Brit*), slave, toiler, worker

drudgery *noun* **= menial labour**, donkey-work, fag (*inf*), grind (*inf*), hard work, labour, skivvying (*Brit*), slog, toil

drug *noun* **1 = medication**, medicament, medicine, physic, poison, remedy **2 = dope** (*sl*), narcotic, opiate, stimulant ◆ *verb* **3 = dose**, administer a drug, anaesthetize, deaden, dope (*sl*), knock out, medicate, numb, poison, stupefy, treat

drum *verb* **4 = beat**, pulsate, rap, reverberate, tap, tattoo, throb **drum into = drive home**, din into, hammer away, harp on, instil into, reiterate

drunk *adjective* **2 = intoxicated**, drunken, inebriated, legless (*inf*), merry (*Brit inf*), plastered (*sl*), tipsy, under the influence (*inf*) ◆ *noun* **4 = drunkard**, alcoholic, boozer (*inf*), inebriate, lush (*sl*), wino (*inf*)

drunkard *noun* **= drinker**, alcoholic, dipsomaniac, drunk, lush (*sl*), tippler, wino (*inf*)

drunkenness *noun* **= intoxication**, alcoholism, bibulousness, dipsomania, inebriation, insobriety, intemperance

3 *Informal* thirsty. **4** (of wine) not sweet. **5**
uninteresting, e.g. *a dry book*. **6** (of humour)
subtle and sarcastic. **7** prohibiting the sale of
alcohol, e.g. *a dry town*. ♦ *verb* **drying, dried 8**
make or become dry. **9** preserve (food) by
removing the moisture. **drily, dryly** *adverb*
dryness *noun* **dryer** *noun* apparatus for
removing moisture. **dry-clean** *verb* clean
(clothes etc.) with chemicals rather than water.
dry-cleaner *noun* **dry-cleaning** *noun* **dry
dock** dock that can be pumped dry to permit
work on a ship's bottom. **dry ice** solid carbon
dioxide. **dry out** *verb* **1** make or become dry. **2**
(cause to) undergo treatment for alcoholism.
dry rot crumbling and drying of timber,
caused by certain fungi. **dry run** *Informal*
rehearsal. **dry-stone** *adjective* (of a wall) made
without mortar. **dry up** *verb* **1** dry (washed
dishes) with a tea towel. **2** stop being
productive. **3** *Informal* stop speaking.
dryad *noun* wood nymph.
DSc Doctor of Science.
DSS Department of Social Security.
DT's *Informal* delirium tremens.
dual ⊕ *adjective* having two parts, functions, or
aspects. **duality** *noun* **dualism** *noun* state of
having or being believed to have two distinct
parts or aspects. **dual carriageway** *Brit, Aust &
NZ* road on which traffic travelling in opposite
directions is separated by a central strip of grass
or concrete.
dub[1] *verb* **dubbing, dubbed** give (a person or
place) a name or nickname.
dub[2] *verb* **dubbing, dubbed 1** provide (a
film) with a new soundtrack, esp. in a different
language. **2** provide (a film or tape) with a
soundtrack. ♦ *noun* **3** style of reggae record
production involving exaggeration of
instrumental parts, echo, etc.
dubbin *noun* thick grease applied to leather to

soften and waterproof it.
dubious ⊕ [dew-bee-uss] *adjective* feeling or
causing doubt. **dubiously** *adverb* **dubiety**
[dew-by-it-ee] *noun*
ducal [duke-al] *adjective* of a duke.
ducat [duck-it] *noun* former European gold or
silver coin.
duchess *noun* **1** woman who holds the rank
of duke. **2** wife or widow of a duke.
duchy *noun, pl* **duchies** territory of a duke or
duchess.
duck[1] *noun* **1** water bird with short legs,
webbed feet, and a broad blunt bill. **2** its flesh,
used as food. **3** female of this bird. **4** *Cricket*
score of nothing. **duckling** *noun* baby duck.
duck-billed platypus *or* **duckbill** see PLATYPUS.
duck[2] ⊕ *verb* **1** move (the head or body)
quickly downwards, to avoid being seen or to
dodge a blow. **2** plunge suddenly under water.
3 *Informal* dodge (a duty or responsibility).
duct *noun* **1** tube, pipe, or channel through
which liquid or gas is conveyed. **2** bodily
passage conveying secretions or excretions.
ductile *adjective* (of a metal) able to be
shaped into sheets or wires.
dud ⊕ *Informal noun* **1** ineffectual person or
thing. ♦ *adjective* **2** bad or useless, e.g. *dud
cheques*.
dude *noun US informal* **1** man. **2** *Old-fashioned*
dandy. **3** any person.
dudgeon ⊕ *noun* **in high dudgeon** angry,
resentful.
due ⊕ *adjective* **1** expected or scheduled to be
present or arrive. **2** owed as a debt. **3** fitting,
proper. ♦ *noun* **4** something that is owed or
required. ♦ *plural* **5** charges for membership of
a club or organization. ♦ *adverb* **6** directly or
exactly, e.g. *due south*. **due to** attributable to
or caused by.
duel ⊕ *noun* **1** formal fight with deadly

——————— THESAURUS ———————

dry *adjective* **1** =**dehydrated**, arid, barren,
desiccated, dried up, parched, thirsty OPPOSITE
wet. **5** =**dull**, boring, dreary, monotonous,
plain, tedious, tiresome, uninteresting OPPOSITE
interesting. **6** =**sarcastic**, deadpan, droll, low-
key, sly ♦*verb* **8** =**dehydrate**, dehumidify,
desiccate, drain, make dry, parch, sear
OPPOSITE **wet**
dry out *verb* **1** =**become dry**, harden, shrivel
up, wilt, wither, wizen
dual *adjective* =**twofold**, binary, double,
duplex, duplicate, matched, paired, twin
dubious *adjective* **a** =**unsure**, doubtful,
hesitant, sceptical, uncertain, unconvinced,
undecided, wavering OPPOSITE **sure. b**

=**suspect**, fishy (*inf*), questionable, suspicious,
unreliable, untrustworthy OPPOSITE
trustworthy
duck[2] *verb* **1** =**bob**, bend, bow, crouch,
dodge, drop, lower, stoop **2** =**plunge**, dip,
dive, douse, dunk, immerse, souse, submerge,
wet **3** *Inf* =**dodge**, avoid, escape, evade, shirk,
shun, sidestep
dud *Inf noun* **1** =**failure**, flop (*inf*), washout
(*inf*) ♦*adjective* **2** =**useless**, broken, duff (*Brit
inf*), failed, inoperative, worthless
dudgeon *noun* **in high dudgeon**
=**indignant**, angry, choked, fuming, offended,
resentful, vexed
due *adjective* **1** =**expected**, scheduled **2**

weapons between two people, to settle a
quarrel. ◆ verb **duelling, duelled 2** fight in a
duel. **duellist** noun

duenna noun (esp. in Spain) elderly woman
acting as chaperone to a young woman.

duet noun piece of music for two performers.

duff adjective Chiefly Brit broken or useless.

duff up verb Brit informal beat (someone)
severely.

duffel, duffle noun short for DUFFEL COAT.
duffel bag cylindrical canvas bag fastened with
a drawstring. **duffel coat** wool coat with
toggle fastenings, usu. with a hood.

duffer noun Informal dull or incompetent
person.

dug¹ verb past of DIG.

dug² noun teat or udder.

dugite [doo-gyte] noun medium-sized
Australian venomous snake.

dugong noun whalelike mammal of tropical
waters.

dugout noun **1** (at a sports ground) covered
bench where managers and substitutes sit. **2**
canoe made by hollowing out a log. **3** Mil
covered excavation to provide shelter.

duke noun **1** nobleman of the highest rank. **2**
prince or ruler of a small principality or duchy.
dukedom noun

dulcet [dull-sit] adjective (of a sound) soothing
or pleasant.

dulcimer noun tuned percussion instrument
consisting of a set of strings stretched over a
sounding board and struck with hammers.

dull ❶ adjective **1** not interesting. **2** (of an
ache) not acute. **3** (of weather) not bright or
clear. **4** lacking in spirit. **5** not very intelligent.
6 (of a blade) not sharp. ◆ verb **7** make or
become dull. **dullness** noun **dully** adverb

dullard noun dull or stupid person.

dulse noun seaweed with large red edible
fronds.

duly ❶ adverb **1** in a proper manner. **2** at the
proper time.

dumb ❶ adjective **1** lacking the power to
speak. **2** silent. **3** Informal stupid. **dumbly**
adverb **dumbness** noun **dumbbell** noun short
bar with a heavy ball or disc at each end, used
for physical exercise. **dumbfounded** adjective
speechless with astonishment. **dumb show**
meaningful gestures without speech.

dumbwaiter noun **1** lift for carrying food etc.
between floors. **2** stand for holding food at a
dining table.

dumdum noun soft-nosed bullet that expands
on impact and causes serious wounds.

dummy ❶ noun, pl -mies **1** figure
representing the human form, used for
displaying clothes etc. **2** copy of an object,
often lacking some essential feature of the
original. **3** rubber teat for a baby to suck. **4**
Slang stupid person. ◆ adjective **5** imitation,
substitute. **dummy run** rehearsal.

dump ❶ verb **1** drop or let fall in a careless
manner. **2** Informal get rid of (someone or
something no longer wanted). **3** dispose of
(nuclear waste). **4** market (goods) in bulk and

THESAURUS

= **payable**, in arrears, outstanding, owed,
owing, unpaid **3** = **fitting**, appropriate,
deserved, justified, merited, proper, rightful,
suitable, well-earned ◆noun **4** = **right(s)**,
comeuppance (sl), deserts, merits, privilege
◆plural **5** = **membership fee**, charge, charges,
contribution, fee, levy ◆adverb **6** = **directly**,
dead, exactly, straight, undeviatingly

duel noun **1** = **fight**, affair of honour, clash,
competition, contest, encounter, engagement,
head-to-head, single combat ◆verb **2** = **fight**,
clash, compete, contend, contest, lock horns,
rival, struggle, vie with

dull adjective **1** = **boring**, dreary, flat,
humdrum, monotonous, plain, run-of-the-mill,
tedious, uninteresting OPPOSITE interesting. **3**
= **cloudy**, dim, dismal, gloomy, leaden, overcast
OPPOSITE bright. **4** = **lifeless**, apathetic, blank,
indifferent, listless, passionless, unresponsive
OPPOSITE lively. **5** = **stupid**, dense, dim-witted
(inf), dozy (Brit inf), slow, thick, unintelligent **6**
= **blunt**, blunted, unsharpened OPPOSITE sharp

◆verb **7** = **relieve**, allay, alleviate, blunt, lessen,
moderate, soften, take the edge off

duly adverb **1** = **properly**, accordingly,
appropriately, befittingly, correctly, decorously,
deservedly, fittingly, rightfully, suitably **2** = **on
time**, at the proper time, punctually

dumb adjective **1, 2** = **mute**, mum, silent,
soundless, speechless, tongue-tied, voiceless,
wordless OPPOSITE articulate. **3** Inf = **stupid**,
asinine, dense, dim-witted (inf), dull, foolish,
thick, unintelligent OPPOSITE bright

dumbfounded adjective = **amazed**,
astonished, astounded, flabbergasted (inf), lost
for words, nonplussed, overwhelmed,
speechless, staggered, stunned

dummy noun **1** = **model**, figure, form,
manikin, mannequin **2** = **copy**, counterfeit,
duplicate, imitation, sham, substitute **4** Sl
= **fool**, blockhead, dunce, idiot, nitwit (inf),
numbskull or numskull, oaf, simpleton
◆adjective **5** = **imitation**, artificial, bogus, fake,
false, mock, phoney or phony (inf), sham,

at low prices, esp. abroad. ◆ *noun* **5** place where waste materials are left. **6** *Informal* dirty unattractive place. **7** *Mil* place where weapons or supplies are stored. **down in the dumps** *Informal* depressed and miserable.

dumpling *noun* **1** small ball of dough cooked and served with stew. **2** round pastry case filled with fruit.

dumpy *adjective* **dumpier, dumpiest** short and plump.

dun¹ *adjective* brownish-grey.

dun² *verb* **dunning, dunned 1** demand payment from (a debtor). ◆ *noun* **2** demand for payment.

dunce ⊕ *noun* person who is stupid or slow to learn.

dunderhead *noun* slow-witted person.

dune *noun* mound or ridge of drifted sand.

dung *noun* faeces from animals such as cattle.

dungarees *plural noun* trousers with a bib attached.

dungeon ⊕ *noun* underground prison cell.

dunk *verb* **1** dip (a biscuit or bread) in a drink or soup before eating it. **2** put (something) in liquid.

dunlin *noun* small sandpiper with a brown back.

duo *noun, pl* **duos 1** pair of performers. **2** *Informal* pair of closely connected people.

duodenum [dew-oh-**deen**-um] *noun, pl* **-na, -nums** first part of the small intestine, just below the stomach. **duodenal** *adjective*

duologue *noun* (in drama) conversation between only two speakers.

dupe *verb* **1** deceive or cheat. ◆ *noun* **2** person who is easily deceived.

duple *adjective Music* having two beats in a bar.

duplex *noun US & Canad* apartment on two floors.

duplicate ⊕ *adjective* **1** copied exactly from an original. ◆ *noun* **2** exact copy. ◆ *verb* **3** make an exact copy of. **4** do again (something that has already been done). **duplication** *noun* **duplicator** *noun*

duplicity *noun* deceitful behaviour.

durable ⊕ *adjective* long-lasting. **durability** *noun* **durable goods, durables** *plural noun* goods that require infrequent replacement.

duration ⊕ *noun* length of time that something lasts.

duress ⊕ *noun* compulsion by use of force or threats.

during *preposition* throughout or within the limit of (a period of time).

dusk ⊕ *noun* time just before nightfall, when it is almost dark. **dusky** *adjective* **duskier, duskiest 1** dark in colour. **2** shadowy. **duskiness** *noun*

dust ⊕ *noun* **1** small dry particles of earth, sand, or dirt. ◆ *verb* **2** remove dust from (furniture) by wiping. **3** sprinkle (something) with a powdery substance. **duster** *noun* cloth used for dusting. **dusty** *adjective* **dustier, dustiest** covered with dust. **dustbin** *noun* large container for household rubbish. **dust bowl** dry area in which the surface soil is exposed to wind erosion. **dustcart** *noun* lorry for collecting household rubbish. **dust jacket** removable paper cover used to protect a book. **dustman** *noun Brit* man whose job is to collect household rubbish. **dustpan** *noun* short-handled shovel into which dust is swept from floors. **dustsheet** *noun Brit* large cloth cover to protect furniture from dust. **dust-up** *noun Informal* fight or argument.

——————— THESAURUS ———————

simulated

dump *verb* **1** =**drop**, deposit, fling down, let fall, throw down **2** *Inf* =**get rid of**, dispose of, ditch (*sl*), empty out, jettison, scrap, throw away *or* out, tip, unload ◆*noun* **5** =**rubbish tip**, junkyard, refuse heap, rubbish heap, tip **6** *Inf* =**pigsty**, hole (*inf*), hovel, mess, slum

dunce *noun* =**simpleton**, blockhead, duffer (*inf*), dunderhead, ignoramus, moron, nincompoop, numbskull *or* numskull, thickhead

dungeon *noun* =**prison**, cage, cell, oubliette, vault

duplicate *adjective* **1** =**identical**, corresponding, matched, matching, twin, twofold ◆*noun* **2** =**copy**, carbon copy, clone, double, facsimile, photocopy, replica, reproduction ◆*verb* **3** =**copy**, clone, double,

replicate, reproduce **4** =**repeat**

durability *noun* =**durableness**, constancy, endurance, imperishability, permanence, persistence

durable *adjective* =**long-lasting**, dependable, enduring, hard-wearing, persistent, reliable, resistant, strong, sturdy, tough OPPOSITE⟩ fragile

duration *noun* =**length**, extent, period, span, spell, stretch, term, time

duress *noun* =**pressure**, coercion, compulsion, constraint, threat

dusk *noun* =**twilight**, dark, evening, eventide, gloaming (*Scot or poet*), nightfall, sundown, sunset OPPOSITE⟩ dawn

dusky *adjective* **1** =**dark**, dark-complexioned, sable, swarthy **2** =**dim**, cloudy, gloomy, murky,

Dutch *adjective* **1** of the Netherlands. ◆ *noun* **2** language of the Netherlands. **go Dutch** *Informal* share the expenses on an outing. **Dutch auction** auction in which the price is gradually lowered until a buyer is found. **Dutch barn** farm building with a steel frame and a curved roof. **Dutch courage** false courage gained from drinking alcohol. **Dutch elm disease** fungal disease of elm trees.

duty ⊙ *noun, pl* **-ties 1** work or a task performed as part of one's job. **2** task that a person feels morally bound to do. **3** government tax on imports. **on duty** at work. **dutiable** *adjective* (of goods) requiring payment of duty. **dutiful** *adjective* doing what is expected. **dutifully** *adverb* **duty-bound** *adjective* morally obliged. **duty-free** *adjective, adverb* with exemption from customs or excise duties.

duvet [**doo**-vay] *noun* kind of quilt used in bed instead of a top sheet and blankets.

DVD Digital Versatile (or Video) Disk.

DVT deep-vein thrombosis.

dwarf ⊙ *noun, pl* **dwarfs, dwarves 1** person who is smaller than average. **2** (in folklore) small ugly manlike creature, often possessing magical powers. ◆ *adjective* **3** (of an animal or plant) much smaller than the usual size for the species. ◆ *verb* **4** cause (someone or something) to seem small by being much larger.

dwell ⊙ *verb* **dwelling, dwelt** *or* **dwelled** live, reside. **dweller** *noun* **dwelling** *noun* place of residence. **dwell on, upon** *verb* think, speak, or write at length about.

dwindle ⊙ *verb* grow less in size, strength, or number.

Dy *Chem* dysprosium.

dye ⊙ *noun* **1** colouring substance. **2** colour produced by dyeing. ◆ *verb* **dyeing, dyed 3** colour (hair or fabric) by applying a dye. **dyer** *noun* **dyed-in-the-wool** *adjective* uncompromising or unchanging in opinion.

dying ⊙ *verb* present participle of DIE¹.

dyke¹ *noun* wall built to prevent flooding.

dyke² *noun* *Slang* lesbian.

dynamic ⊙ *adjective* **1** full of energy, ambition, and new ideas. **2** *Physics* of energy or forces that produce motion. **dynamically** *adverb* **dynamism** *noun* great energy and enthusiasm.

dynamics *noun* **1** branch of mechanics concerned with the forces that change or produce the motions of bodies. ◆ *plural* **2** forces that produce change in a system.

dynamite *noun* **1** explosive made of nitroglycerine. **2** *Informal* dangerous or exciting person or thing. ◆ *verb* **3** blow (something) up with dynamite.

dynamo *noun, pl* **-mos** device for converting mechanical energy into electrical energy.

dynasty ⊙ *noun, pl* **-ties** sequence of hereditary rulers. **dynastic** *adjective* **dynast** *noun* hereditary ruler.

dysentery *noun* infection of the intestine causing severe diarrhoea.

dysfunction *noun* **1** *Med* disturbance or abnormality in the function of an organ or part. **2** (of a family) failure to show the characteristics accepted as normal. **dysfunctional** *adjective*

dyslexia *noun* disorder causing impaired ability to read. **dyslexic** *adjective*

dysmenorrhoea *noun* painful menstruation.

dyspepsia *noun* indigestion. **dyspeptic** *adjective*

D

——————————— T H E S A U R U S ———————————

obscure, shadowy, shady, tenebrous, twilit

dust *noun* **1 =grime**, grit, particles, powder ◆*verb* **3 =sprinkle**, cover, dredge, powder, scatter, sift, spray, spread

dusty *adjective* =dirty, grubby, sooty, unclean, unswept

dutiful *adjective* =**conscientious**, devoted, obedient, respectful, reverential, submissive OPPOSITE **disrespectful**

duty *noun* **1 = responsibility**, assignment, function, job, obligation, role, task, work, yakka (*Aust & NZ inf*) **2 =loyalty**, allegiance, deference, obedience, respect, reverence **3** **= tax**, excise, levy, tariff, toll **on duty =at** work, busy, engaged, on active service

dwarf *noun* **1 =midget**, Lilliputian, pygmy *or* pigmy, Tom Thumb ◆*adjective* **3 =miniature**, baby, bonsai, diminutive, small, tiny, undersized

◆*verb* **4 = tower above** *or* over, diminish, dominate, overshadow

dwell *verb* =live, abide, inhabit, lodge, reside

dwelling *noun* =home, abode, domicile, habitation, house, lodging, quarters, residence

dwindle *verb* =**lessen**, decline, decrease, die away, diminish, fade, peter out, shrink, subside, taper off, wane OPPOSITE **increase**

dye *noun* **1 = colouring**, colorant, colour, pigment, stain, tinge, tint ◆*verb* **3 = colour**, pigment, stain, tinge, tint

dying *adjective* =expiring, at death's door, failing, in extremis, moribund, not long for this world

dynamic *adjective* **1 =energetic**, forceful, go-ahead, go-getting (*inf*), high-powered, lively, powerful, storming (*inf*), vital

dynasty *noun* =empire, government, house,

dysprosium *noun Chem* metallic element of the lanthanide series.

dystopia *noun* imaginary place where everything is as bad as it can be.

dystrophy [**diss**-trof-fee] *noun* see MUSCULAR DYSTROPHY.

———————— THESAURUS ————————

regime, rule, sovereignty

E 1 East(ern). **2** *Slang* ecstasy (the drug).
e- *prefix* electronic, e.g. *e-mail*.
each ❶ *adjective, pronoun* every (one) taken separately.
eager ❶ *adjective* showing or feeling great desire, keen. **eagerly** *adverb* **eagerness** *noun*
eagle *noun* **1** large bird of prey with keen eyesight. **2** *Golf* score of two strokes under par for a hole. **eaglet** *noun* young eagle.
ear¹ ❶ *noun* **1** organ of hearing, esp. the external part of it. **2** sensitivity to musical or other sounds. **earache** *noun* pain in the ear.
earbash *verb Aust & NZ informal* talk incessantly. **eardrum** *noun* thin piece of skin inside the ear which enables one to hear sounds. **earmark** *verb* **1** set (something) aside for a specific purpose. ◆ *noun* **2** distinguishing mark. **earphone** *noun* receiver for a radio etc., held to or put in the ear. **ear-piercing** *adjective* deafening. **earplug** *noun* piece of soft material placed in the ear to keep out water or noise. **earring** *noun* ornament for the lobe of the ear. **earshot** *noun* hearing range.
ear² *noun* head of corn.
earl *noun* British nobleman ranking next below

a marquess. **earldom** *noun*
early ❶ *adjective, adverb* **-lier, -liest 1** before the expected or usual time. **2** in the first part of a period. **3** in a period far back in time.
earn ❶ *verb* **1** obtain by work or merit. **2** (of investments etc.) gain (interest). **earnings** *plural noun* money earned.
earnest¹ ❶ *adjective* serious and sincere. **in earnest** seriously. **earnestly** *adverb*
earnest² ❶ *noun* part payment given in advance, esp. to confirm a contract.
earth ❶ *noun* **1** planet that we live on. **2** land, the ground. **3** soil. **4** fox's hole. **5** wire connecting an electrical apparatus with the earth. ◆ *verb* **6** connect (a circuit) to earth. **come down to earth** return to reality from a daydream. **earthen** *adjective* made of baked clay or earth. **earthenware** *noun* pottery made of baked clay. **earthly** *adjective* conceivable or possible, e.g. *no earthly reason.* **earthy** *adjective* **1** coarse or crude. **2** of or like earth. **earthquake** *noun* violent vibration of the earth's surface. **earthwork** *noun* fortification made of earth. **earthworm** *noun* worm which burrows in the soil.

THESAURUS

each *adjective* = **every**
each *pronoun* = **every one**, each and every one, each one, one and all
eager *adjective* = **keen**, agog, anxious, athirst, avid, enthusiastic, fervent, hungry, impatient, longing OPPOSITE unenthusiastic
eagerness *noun* = **keenness**, ardour, enthusiasm, fervour, hunger, impatience, thirst, yearning, zeal
ear¹ *noun* **2** = **sensitivity**, appreciation, discrimination, taste
early *adjective* **1** = **premature**, advanced, forward, untimely OPPOSITE overdue. **3** = **primitive**, primeval, primordial, undeveloped, young OPPOSITE developed ◆ *adverb* **1** = **too soon**, ahead of time, beforehand, in advance, in good time, prematurely OPPOSITE late
earmark *verb* **1** = **set aside**, allocate, designate, flag, label, mark out, reserve
earn *verb* **1** = **deserve**, acquire, attain, be entitled to, be worthy of, merit, rate, warrant,

win **2** = **make**, bring in, collect, gain, get, gross, net, receive
earnest¹ *adjective* = **serious**, grave, intent, resolute, resolved, sincere, solemn, thoughtful OPPOSITE frivolous ◆ **in earnest** = **in seriousness**, in sincerity, in truth
earnest² *noun* = **down payment**, assurance, deposit, earnest money (*Law*), foretaste, guarantee, pledge, promise, security, token
earnings *plural noun* = **income**, pay, proceeds, profits, receipts, remuneration, salary, takings, wages
earth *noun* **1** = **world**, globe, orb, planet, sphere **2, 3** = **soil**, clay, dirt, ground, land, turf
earthenware *noun* = **crockery**, ceramics, pots, pottery, terracotta
earthly *adjective* = **possible**, conceivable, feasible, imaginable, likely, practical OPPOSITE spiritual
earthy *adjective* **1** = **crude**, bawdy, coarse, raunchy (*sl*), ribald, robust, uninhibited,

E

earwig *noun* small insect with a pincer-like tail.

ease ❶ *noun* **1** freedom from difficulty, discomfort, or worry. **2** rest or leisure, e.g. *at one's ease*. ◆ *verb* **3** give bodily or mental ease to. **4** lessen (severity, tension, pain, etc.). **5** move carefully or gradually. **ease off** *verb* become less severe.

easel *noun* frame to support an artist's canvas or a blackboard.

east *noun* **1** (direction towards) the part of the horizon where the sun rises. **2** region lying in this direction. ◆ *adjective* **3** to or in the east. **4** (of a wind) from the east. ◆ *adverb* **5** in, to, or towards the east. **easterly** *adjective* **eastern** *adjective* **easterner** *noun* person from the east of a country or area. **eastward** *adjective, adverb* **eastwards** *adverb*

Easter *noun* Christian spring festival commemorating the Resurrection of Jesus Christ. **Easter egg** chocolate egg given at Easter.

easy ❶ *adjective* **easier, easiest 1** not needing much work or effort. **2** free from pain, care, or anxiety. **3** easy-going. **easily** *adverb* **easiness** *noun* **easy chair** comfortable armchair. **easy-going** *adjective* relaxed in attitude, tolerant.

eat ❶ *verb* **eating, ate, eaten 1** take (food)

into the mouth and swallow it. **2** have a meal. **3** (foll. by *away* or *up*) destroy. **eatable** *adjective* fit or suitable for eating.

eau de Cologne [oh de kol-**lone**] *noun* French light perfume.

eaves *plural noun* overhanging edges of a roof.

eavesdrop ❶ *verb* **-dropping, -dropped** listen secretly to a private conversation. **eavesdropper** *noun* **eavesdropping** *noun*

ebb ❶ *verb* **1** (of tide water) flow back. **2** fall away or decline, e.g. *her anger ebbed away.* ◆ *noun* **3** flowing back of the tide. **at a low ebb** in a state of weakness.

ebony *noun, pl* **-onies 1** hard black wood. ◆ *adjective* **2** deep black.

ebullient *adjective* full of enthusiasm or excitement. **ebullience** *noun*

EC 1 European Commission. **2** European Community: a former name for the European Union.

eccentric ❶ *adjective* **1** odd or unconventional. **2** (of circles) not having the same centre. ◆ *noun* **3** eccentric person. **eccentrically** *adverb* **eccentricity** *noun*

ecclesiastic ❶ *noun* **1** clergyman. ◆ *adjective* **2** (also **ecclesiastical**) of the Christian Church or clergy.

ECG electrocardiogram.

——————— T H E S A U R U S ———————

unsophisticated

ease *noun* **1 a** =**effortlessness**, easiness, facility, readiness, simplicity **b** =**peace of mind**, comfort, content, happiness, peace, quiet, serenity, tranquillity OPPOSITE tension. **2** =**leisure**, relaxation, repose, rest, restfulness OPPOSITE **pain** ◆*verb* **3** =**comfort**, calm, outspan (*S Afr*), relax, soothe **4** =**relieve**, alleviate, lessen, lighten, soothe OPPOSITE **aggravate**. **5** =**move carefully**, edge, inch, manoeuvre, slide, slip

easily *adverb* **1** =**without difficulty**, comfortably, effortlessly, readily, smoothly, with ease, with one hand tied behind one's back

easy *adjective* **1** =**not difficult**, a piece of cake (*inf*), child's play (*inf*), effortless, no trouble, painless, plain sailing, simple, straightforward, uncomplicated, undemanding OPPOSITE **hard**. **2** =**carefree**, comfortable, cushy (*inf*), leisurely, peaceful, quiet, relaxed, serene, tranquil, untroubled OPPOSITE **difficult**. **3** =**tolerant**, easy-going, indulgent, lenient, mild, permissive, unoppressive OPPOSITE **strict**

easy-going *adjective* =**relaxed**, carefree, casual, easy, even-tempered, happy-go-lucky, laid-back (*inf*), nonchalant, placid, tolerant,

undemanding OPPOSITE **tense**

eat *verb* **1** =**consume**, chew, devour, gobble, ingest, munch, scoff (*sl*), swallow **2** =**have a meal**, dine, feed, take nourishment **3** (foll. by *away* or *up*) =**destroy**, corrode, decay, dissolve, erode, rot, waste away, wear away

eavesdrop *verb* =**listen in**, earwig (*inf*), monitor, overhear, snoop (*inf*), spy

ebb *verb* **1** =**flow back**, go out, recede, retire, retreat, subside, wane, withdraw **2** =**decline**, decrease, diminish, dwindle, fade away, fall away, flag, lessen, peter out ◆*noun* **3** =**flowing back**, going out, low tide, low water, retreat, subsidence, wane, withdrawal

eccentric *adjective* **1** =**odd**, freakish, idiosyncratic, irregular, munted (*NZ sl*), outlandish, peculiar, quirky, strange, unconventional OPPOSITE **normal** ◆*noun* **3** =**crank** (*inf*), character (*inf*), nonconformist, oddball (*inf*), weirdo *or* weirdie (*inf*)

eccentricity *noun* **1** =**oddity**, abnormality, caprice, capriciousness, foible, idiosyncrasy, irregularity, peculiarity, quirk

ecclesiastic *noun* **1** =**clergyman**, churchman, cleric, holy man, man of the cloth, minister, parson, pastor, priest ◆*adjective* **2** (also

echelon [esh-a-lon] *noun* **1** level of power or responsibility. **2** *Mil* formation in which units follow one another but are spaced out sideways to allow each a line of fire ahead.

echidna [ik-**kid**-na] *noun, pl* **-s, -nae** [-nee] mammal with a protective layer of spines, found in Australia and New Guinea (also **spiny anteater**).

echo ❶ *noun, pl* **-oes 1** repetition of sounds by reflection of sound waves off a surface. **2** close imitation. ◆ *verb* **-oing, -oed 3** repeat or be repeated as an echo. **4** imitate (what someone else has said). **echo sounder** sonar.

éclair *noun* finger-shaped pastry filled with cream and covered with chocolate.

éclat [ake-**lah**] *noun* **1** brilliant success. **2** splendour.

eclectic *adjective* selecting from various styles, ideas, or sources. **eclecticism** *noun*

eclipse ❶ *noun* **1** temporary obscuring of one star or planet by another. ◆ *verb* **2** surpass or outclass. **ecliptic** *noun* apparent path of the sun.

eco- *combining form* ecology or ecological, e.g. *ecotourism.*

ecological *adjective* **1** of ecology. **2** intended to protect the environment, e.g. *an ecological approach to agriculture.* **ecologically** *adverb*

ecology *noun* study of the relationships between living things and their environment. **ecologist** *noun*

e-commerce, ecommerce *noun* business transactions done on the Internet.

economy ❶ *noun, pl* **-mies 1** system of interrelationship of money, industry, and employment in a country. **2** careful use of money or resources to avoid waste. **economic** *adjective* **1** of economics. **2** profitable. **3**

Informal inexpensive or cheap. **economics** *noun* **1** social science concerned with the production and consumption of goods and services. ◆ *plural* **2** financial aspects. **economical** *adjective* not wasteful, thrifty. **economically** *adverb* **economist** *noun* specialist in economics. **economize** *verb* reduce expense or waste.

ecosystem *noun* system involving interactions between a community and its environment.

ecru *adjective* pale creamy-brown.

ecstasy ❶ *noun* **1** state of intense delight. **2** *Slang* powerful drug that can produce hallucinations. **ecstatic** *adjective* **ecstatically** *adverb*

SPELLING TIP

People get confused about how many cs there are in **ecstasy**. The Bank of English has 119 occurrences of *ecstacy*, but 3379 of the correct spelling **ecstasy**.

ECT electroconvulsive therapy.

ectoplasm *noun* *Spiritualism* substance that supposedly is emitted from the body of a medium during a trance.

ecumenical *adjective* of the Christian Church throughout the world, esp. with regard to its unity.

eczema [ek-sim-a] *noun* skin disease causing intense itching.

ed. 1 edition. **2** editor.

Edam *noun* round Dutch cheese with a red waxy cover.

eddy ❶ *noun, pl* **eddies 1** circular movement of air, water, etc. ◆ *verb* **eddying, eddied 2** move with a circular motion.

——————— THESAURUS ———————

ecclesiastical) = **clerical**, divine, holy, pastoral, priestly, religious, spiritual

echo *noun* **1** = **repetition**, answer, reverberation **2** = **copy**, imitation, mirror image, parallel, reflection, reiteration, reproduction ◆*verb* **3** = **repeat**, resound, reverberate **4** = **copy**, ape, imitate, mirror, parallel, recall, reflect, resemble

eclipse *noun* **1** = **obscuring**, darkening, dimming, extinction, shading ◆*verb* **2** = **surpass**, exceed, excel, outdo, outshine, put in the shade (*inf*), transcend

economic *adjective* **1** = **financial**, commercial, industrial **2** = **profitable**, money-making, productive, profit-making, remunerative, viable **3** *Inf* = **inexpensive**, cheap, low-priced, modest, reasonable

economical *adjective* = **thrifty**, careful, cost-effective, efficient, frugal, money-saving, prudent, scrimping, sparing OPPOSITE wasteful

economize *verb* = **cut back**, be economical, be frugal, draw in one's horns, retrench, save, scrimp, tighten one's belt

economy *noun* **2** = **thrift**, frugality, husbandry, parsimony, prudence, restraint

ecstasy *noun* **1** = **rapture**, bliss, delight, elation, euphoria, fervour, joy, seventh heaven OPPOSITE agony

ecstatic *adjective* **1** = **rapturous**, blissful, elated, enraptured, entranced, euphoric, in seventh heaven, joyous, on cloud nine (*inf*), overjoyed

eddy *noun* **1** = **swirl**, counter-current,

E

edelweiss [ade-el-vice] *noun* alpine plant with white flowers.
Eden *noun* **1** *Bible* garden in which Adam and Eve were placed at the Creation. **2** place of delight or contentment.
edge ⊕ *noun* **1** border or line where something ends or begins. **2** cutting side of a blade. **3** sharpness of tone. ◆ *verb* **4** provide an edge or border for. **5** push (one's way) gradually. **have the edge on** have an advantage over. **on edge** nervous or irritable.
edgeways *adverb* with the edge forwards or uppermost. **edging** *noun* anything placed along an edge to finish it. **edgy** *adjective* nervous or irritable.
edible ⊕ *adjective* fit to be eaten. **edibility** *noun*
edict ⊕ [ee-dikt] *noun* order issued by an authority.
edifice ⊕ [ed-if-iss] *noun* large building.
edify ⊕ [ed-if-fie] *verb* **-fying, -fied** improve morally by instruction. **edification** *noun*
edit ⊕ *verb* prepare (a book, film, etc.) for publication or broadcast. **edition** *noun* **1** number of copies of a new publication printed at one time. **2** single television or radio programme which forms part of a series. **editor** *noun* **1** person who edits. **2** person in charge of one section of a newspaper or magazine.
editorial *noun* **1** newspaper article stating the opinion of the editor. ◆ *adjective* **2** of editing or editors.

educate ⊕ *verb* **1** teach. **2** provide schooling for. **education** *noun* **educational** *adjective* **educationally** *adverb* **educationalist** *noun* expert in the theory of education. **educative** *adjective* educating.
Edwardian *adjective* of the reign of King Edward VII of Great Britain and Ireland (1901-10).
EEG electroencephalogram.
eel *noun* snakelike fish.
eerie ⊕ *adjective* **eerier, eeriest** uncannily frightening or disturbing. **eerily** *adverb*
efface ⊕ *verb* **1** remove by rubbing. **2** make (oneself) inconspicuous. **effacement** *noun*
effect ⊕ *noun* **1** change or result caused by someone or something. **2** condition of being operative, e.g. *the law comes into effect next month*. **3** overall impression. ◆ *plural* **4** personal belongings. **5** lighting, sounds, etc. to accompany a film or a broadcast. ◆ *verb* **6** cause to happen, accomplish. **effective** *adjective* **1** producing a desired result. **2** operative. **3** impressive. **effectively** *adverb* **effectual** *adjective* producing the intended result. **effectually** *adverb*

> **LANGUAGE TIP**
>
> Note the difference between *effect* meaning 'accomplish' and *affect* meaning 'influence'.

—————— THESAURUS ——————

undertow, vortex, whirlpool ◆*verb* **2 = swirl**, whirl
edge *noun* **1 = border**, boundary, brink, fringe, limit, outline, perimeter, rim, side, verge ◆*verb* **4 = border**, fringe, hem **5 = inch**, creep, ease, sidle, steal **have the edge on = have the advantage over**, have ascendancy over, have dominance over, have superiority over, have the upper hand over **on edge = nervous**, apprehensive, edgy, ill at ease, impatient, irritable, keyed up, on tenterhooks, tense, wired (*sl*)
edgy *adjective* **= nervous**, anxious, ill at ease, irritable, keyed up, on edge, on tenterhooks, restive, tense, wired (*sl*)
edible *adjective* **= eatable**, digestible, fit to eat, good, harmless, palatable, wholesome OPPOSITE> **inedible**
edict *noun* **= decree**, act, command, injunction, law, order, proclamation, ruling
edifice *noun* **= building**, construction, erection, house, structure
edify *verb* **= instruct**, educate, enlighten,

guide, improve, inform, nurture, school, teach
edit *verb* **= revise**, adapt, condense, correct, emend, polish, rewrite
edition *noun* **1 = version**, copy, impression, issue, number, printing, volume **2 = programme** (*TV, Radio*)
educate *verb* **1 = teach**, discipline, enlighten, improve, inform, instruct, school, train, tutor
educated *adjective* **= taught**, coached, informed, instructed, knowledgeable, learned, schooled, tutored OPPOSITE> **ignorant**
education *noun* **= teaching**, development, discipline, enlightenment, instruction, nurture, schooling, training, tuition
educational *adjective* **= instructive**, cultural, edifying, educative, enlightening, improving, informative
eerie *adjective* **= frightening**, creepy (*inf*), ghostly, mysterious, scary (*inf*), spooky (*inf*), strange, uncanny, unearthly, weird
efface *verb* **1 = obliterate**, blot out, cancel, delete, destroy, eradicate, erase, rub out, wipe out

effeminate ⊙ *adjective* (of a man) displaying characteristics thought to be typical of a woman. **effeminacy** *noun*

effervescent ⊙ *adjective* **1** (of a liquid) giving off bubbles of gas. **2** (of a person) lively and enthusiastic. **effervescence** *noun*

effete ⊙ [if-**feet**] *adjective* powerless, feeble.

efficacious ⊙ *adjective* producing the intended result. **efficacy** *noun*

efficient ⊙ *adjective* functioning effectively with little waste of effort. **efficiently** *adverb* **efficiency** *noun*

effigy ⊙ [**ef**-fij-ee] *noun, pl* **-gies** image or likeness of a person.

efflorescence *noun* flowering.

effluent ⊙ *noun* liquid discharged as waste.

effluvium *noun, pl* **-via** unpleasant smell, as of decaying matter or gaseous waste.

effort ⊙ *noun* **1** physical or mental exertion. **2** attempt. **effortless** *adjective* **effortlessly** *adverb*

effrontery ⊙ *noun* brazen impudence.

effusion ⊙ *noun* **1** unrestrained outburst. **2** sudden pouring out of light or liquid. **effusive** *adjective* openly emotional, demonstrative.

effusively *adverb* **effusiveness** *noun*

EFTA European Free Trade Association.

EFTPOS electronic funds transfer at point of sale.

e.g. ⊙ for example.

egalitarian *adjective* **1** upholding the equality of all people. ◆ *noun* **2** person who holds egalitarian beliefs. **egalitarianism** *noun*

egg[1] *noun* **1** oval or round object laid by the females of birds and other creatures, containing a developing embryo. **2** hen's egg used as food. **3** (also **egg cell**) ovum. **egghead** *noun Informal* intellectual person. **eggplant** *noun US, Canad, & Aust* aubergine. **eggshell** *noun* hard covering round the egg of a bird or animal.

egg timer *noun* device used for measuring the time needed to boil an egg.

egg[2] **⊙** *verb* **egg on** encourage or incite, esp. to do wrong.

ego ⊙ *noun, pl* **egos 1** the conscious mind of an individual. **2** self-esteem. **egoism, egotism** *noun* **1** excessive concern for one's own interests. **2** excessively high opinion of oneself. **egotist, egoist** *noun* **egotistic, egoistic** *adjective* **egocentric** *adjective* self-centred.

E

———————————— T H E S A U R U S ————————————

effect *noun* **1** = **result**, conclusion, consequence, end result, event, outcome, upshot **2** = **operation**, action, enforcement, execution, force, implementation **3** = **impression**, essence, impact, sense, significance, tenor ◆*plural* **4** = **belongings**, gear, goods, paraphernalia, possessions, property, things ◆*verb* **6** = **bring about**, accomplish, achieve, complete, execute, fulfil, perform, produce

effective *adjective* **1** = **efficient**, active, adequate, capable, competent, productive, serviceable, useful OPPOSITE **inadequate. 2** = **in operation**, active, current, in effect, in force, operative OPPOSITE **inoperative. 3** = **powerful**, cogent, compelling, convincing, forceful, impressive, persuasive, telling OPPOSITE **weak**

effeminate *adjective* **1** = **womanly**, camp (*inf*), feminine, sissy, soft, tender, unmanly, weak, womanish£ OPPOSITE **manly**

effervescent *adjective* **1** = **bubbling**, carbonated, fizzy, foaming, frothy, sparkling OPPOSITE **still. 2** = **lively**, animated, bubbly, ebullient, enthusiastic, exuberant, irrepressible, vivacious OPPOSITE **flat**

effete *adjective* = **decadent**, dissipated, enfeebled, feeble, ineffectual, spoiled, weak

efficacious *adjective* = **effective**, adequate, efficient, operative, potent, powerful, productive, successful, useful

efficiency *noun* = **competence**, adeptness, capability, economy, effectiveness, power, productivity, proficiency

efficient *adjective* = **competent**, businesslike, capable, economic, effective, organized, productive, proficient, well-organized, workmanlike OPPOSITE **inefficient**

effigy *noun* = **likeness**, dummy, figure, guy, icon, idol, image, picture, portrait, representation, statue

effluent *noun* = **waste**, effluvium, pollutant, sewage

effort *noun* **1** = **exertion**, application, elbow grease (*facetious*), endeavour, energy, pains, struggle, toil, trouble, work, yakka (*Aust & NZ inf*) **2** = **attempt**, endeavour, essay, go (*inf*), shot (*inf*), stab (*inf*), try

effortless *adjective* = **easy**, painless, plain sailing, simple, smooth, uncomplicated, undemanding OPPOSITE **hard**

effrontery *noun* = **insolence**, arrogance, audacity, brazenness, cheek (*inf*), impertinence, impudence, nerve, presumption, temerity

effusive *adjective* = **demonstrative**, ebullient, expansive, exuberant, gushing, lavish, unreserved, unrestrained

egg[2] *verb* **egg on** = **encourage**, exhort, goad, incite, prod, prompt, push, spur, urge

egocentric *adjective* = **self-centred**, egoistic, egoistical, egotistic, egotistical, selfish

egregious [ig-**greej**-uss] *adjective* outstandingly bad.

egress ➊ [**ee**-gress] *noun* **1** departure. **2** way out.

egret [**ee**-grit] *noun* lesser white heron.

Egyptian *adjective* **1** relating to Egypt. ♦ *noun* **2** person from Egypt.

Egyptology *noun* study of the culture of ancient Egypt.

eider *noun* Arctic duck. **eiderdown** *noun* quilt (orig. stuffed with eider feathers).

eight *adjective*, *noun* **1** one more than seven. ♦ *noun* **2** eight-oared boat. **3** its crew. **eighth** *adjective*, *noun* (of) number eight in a series.

eighteen *adjective*, *noun* eight and ten. **eighteenth** *adjective*, *noun* **eighty** *adjective*, *noun* eight times ten. **eightieth** *adjective*, *noun*

Eire *noun* Ireland or the Republic of Ireland.

eisteddfod [ice-**sted**-fod] *noun* Welsh festival with competitions in music and other performing arts.

either *adjective*, *pronoun* **1** one or the other (of two). **2** each of two. ♦ *conjunction* **3** used preceding two or more possibilities joined by *or*. ♦ *adverb* **4** likewise, e.g. *I don't eat meat and he doesn't either.*

LANGUAGE TIP

When *either* is followed by a plural noun, it is acceptable to make the verb plural too: *Either of these books are useful.*

---

ejaculate *verb* **1** eject (semen). **2** utter abruptly. **ejaculation** *noun*

eject ➊ *verb* force out, expel. **ejection** *noun* **ejector** *noun* **ejector seat** *noun* seat in an aircraft that ejects the occupant in an emergency.

eke out ➊ *verb* **1** make (a supply) last by frugal use. **2** make (a living) with difficulty.

elaborate ➊ *adjective* **1** with a lot of fine detail. ♦ *verb* **2** expand upon. **elaborately** *adverb* **elaboration** *noun*

élan [ale-**an**] *noun* style and vigour.

eland [**eel**-and] *noun* large antelope of southern Africa.

elapse ➊ *verb* (of time) pass by.

elastane synthetic fibre that is able to return to its original shape after being stretched.

elastic ➊ *adjective* **1** capable of resuming normal shape after distortion. **2** adapting easily to change. **3** made of elastic. ♦ *noun* **4** tape or fabric containing interwoven strands of flexible rubber. **elasticity** *noun* **elastic band** rubber band.

elated ➊ *verb* extremely happy and excited. **elatedly** *adverb* **elation** *noun*

elbow ➊ *noun* **1** joint between the upper arm and the forearm. **2** part of a garment that covers this. ♦ *verb* **3** shove or strike with the elbow. **elbow grease** vigorous physical labour. **elbow room** sufficient room to move freely.

elder[1] ➊ *adjective* **1** older. ♦ *noun* **2** older person. **3** (in certain Protestant Churches) lay officer. **elderly** *adjective* (fairly) old. **eldest** *adjective* oldest.

elder[2] *noun* small tree with white flowers and

——————— THESAURUS ———————

egoism, egotism *noun* **1** = **self-centredness**, self-absorption, self-interest, selfishness **2** = **conceit**, narcissism, self-esteem, self-importance, vanity

egotist, egoist *noun* **1** = **egomaniac 2** = **narcissist**, bighead (*inf*), boaster, braggart

egotistic, egoistic *adjective* **1** = **self-centred**, egocentric, self-absorbed **2** = **conceited**, boasting, full of oneself, narcissistic, self-important, vain

egress *noun* **1** = **departure**, exit, exodus, withdrawal **2** = **exit**, way out

eject *verb* = **throw out**, banish, drive out, evict, expel, oust, remove, turn out

ejection *noun* = **expulsion**, banishment, deportation, eviction, exile, removal

eke out *verb* **1** = **be sparing with**, economize on, husband, stretch out

elaborate *adjective* **1** = **detailed**, complex, complicated, intricate, involved OPPOSITE

simple ♦ *verb* **2** = **expand (upon)**, add detail, amplify, develop, embellish, enlarge, flesh out OPPOSITE simplify

elapse *verb* = **pass**, glide by, go by, lapse, roll by, slip away

elastic *adjective* **1** = **flexible**, plastic, pliable, pliant, resilient, rubbery, springy, stretchy, supple, tensile OPPOSITE rigid. **2** = **adaptable**, accommodating, adjustable, compliant, flexible, supple, tolerant, variable, yielding OPPOSITE inflexible

elated *adjective* = **joyful**, cock-a-hoop, delighted, ecstatic, euphoric, exhilarated, gleeful, jubilant, overjoyed OPPOSITE dejected

elation *noun* = **joy**, bliss, delight, ecstasy, euphoria, exhilaration, glee, high spirits, jubilation, rapture

elbow *noun* **1** = **joint**, angle ♦ *verb* **3** = **push**, jostle, knock, nudge, shove

elbow room *noun* = **scope**, freedom, latitude,

black berries.

El Dorado [el dor-**rah**-doe] *noun* fictitious country rich in gold.

eldritch *adjective Scot* weird, uncanny.

elect ❶ *verb* **1** choose by voting. **2** decide (to do something). ◆ *adjective* **3** appointed but not yet in office, e.g. *president elect.* **election** *noun* **1** choosing of representatives by voting. **2** act of choosing. **electioneering** *noun* active participation in a political campaign. **elective** *adjective* **1** chosen by election. **2** optional. **elector** *noun* someone who has the right to vote in an election. **electoral** *adjective* **electorate** *noun* people who have the right to vote.

electricity ❶ *noun* **1** form of energy associated with stationary or moving electrons or other charged particles. **2** electric current or charge. **electric** *adjective* **1** produced by, transmitting, or powered by electricity. **2** exciting or tense. **electrical** *adjective* using or concerning electricity. **electrician** *noun* person trained to install and repair electrical equipment. **electrics** *plural noun* electric appliances. **electric chair** *US* chair in which criminals who have been sentenced to death are electrocuted. **electric shock** effect of an electric current passing through the body.

electrify ❶ *verb* **-fying, -fied 1** adapt for operation by electric power. **2** charge with electricity. **3** startle or excite intensely. **electrification** *noun*

electro- *combining form* operated by or caused by electricity.

electrocardiograph *noun* instrument for recording the electrical activity of the heart. **electrocardiogram** *noun* tracing produced by this.

electroconvulsive therapy *noun* treatment of severe mental disorders by passing an electric current through the brain.

electrocute *verb* kill or injure by electricity. **electrocution** *noun*

electrode *noun* conductor through which an electric current enters or leaves a battery,

vacuum tube, etc.

electrodynamics *noun* branch of physics concerned with the interactions between electrical and mechanical forces.

electroencephalograph [ill-lek-tro-en-**sef**-a-loh-graf] *noun* instrument for recording the electrical activity of the brain. **electroencephalogram** *noun* tracing produced by this.

electrolysis [ill-lek-**troll**-iss-iss] *noun* **1** conduction of electricity by an electrolyte, esp. to induce chemical change. **2** destruction of living tissue such as hair roots by an electric current.

electrolyte *noun* solution or molten substance that conducts electricity. **electrolytic** *adjective*

electromagnet *noun* magnet containing a coil of wire through which an electric current is passed. **electromagnetic** *adjective* **electromagnetism** *noun*

electron *noun* elementary particle in all atoms that have a negative electrical charge. **electron microscope** microscope that uses electrons, rather than light, to produce a magnified image. **electronvolt** *noun* unit of energy used in nuclear physics.

electronic *adjective* **1** (of a device) dependent on the action of electrons. **2** (of a process) using electronic devices. **electronic mail** see E-MAIL. **electronic publishing** publication of information on discs etc., so that it can be accessed by computer. **electronics** *noun* technology concerned with the development of electronic devices and circuits.

electroplate *verb* coat with silver etc. by electrolysis.

elegant ❶ *adjective* **1** pleasing or graceful in dress, style, or design. **2** cleverly simple and clear, e.g. *an elegant summary.* **elegance** *noun* **elegantly** *adverb*

elegy [**el**-lij-ee] *noun, pl* **-egies** mournful poem, esp. a lament for the dead. **elegiac** *adjective* mournful or plaintive.

element ❶ *noun* **1** component part. **2**

——————————— T H E S A U R U S ———————————

leeway, play, room, space

elder¹ *adjective* **1** = **older**, first-born, senior ◆*noun* **2** = **older person**, senior

elect *verb* **1** = **choose**, appoint, determine, opt for, pick, prefer, select, settle on, vote

election *noun* = **voting**, appointment, choice, judgment, preference, selection, vote

elector *noun* = **voter**, constituent, selector

electric *adjective* **2** = **charged**, dynamic, exciting, rousing, stimulating, stirring, tense,

thrilling

electrify *verb* **3** = **startle**, astound, excite, galvanize, invigorate, jolt, shock, stir, thrill
OPPOSITE **bore**

elegance *noun* **1** = **style**, dignity, exquisiteness, grace, gracefulness, grandeur, luxury, refinement, taste

elegant *adjective* **1** = **stylish**, chic, delicate, exquisite, fine, graceful, handsome, polished, refined, tasteful OPPOSITE **inelegant**

E

substance which cannot be separated into other substances by ordinary chemical techniques. **3** section of people within a larger group, e.g. *the rowdy element.* **4** heating wire in an electric kettle, stove, etc. ♦ *plural* **5** basic principles of something. **6** weather conditions, esp. wind, rain, and cold. **in one's element** in a situation where one is happiest. **elemental** *adjective* of primitive natural forces or passions.

elementary *adjective* simple and straightforward. **elementary particle** entity that is less complex than an atom.

elephant *noun* huge four-footed thick-skinned animal with ivory tusks and a long trunk.

elephantine *adjective* unwieldy, clumsy.

elephantiasis [el-lee-fan-**tie**-a-siss] *noun* disease with hardening of the skin and enlargement of the legs etc.

elevate ⊕ *verb* **1** raise in rank or status. **2** lift up. **elevated** *adjective* **1** higher than normal, e.g. *elevated cholesterol levels.* **2** (of ideas or pursuits) dignified or of a high rank. **elevation** *noun* **1** raising. **2** height above sea level. **3** scale drawing of one side of a building. **elevator** *noun Aust, US & Canad* lift for carrying people.

eleven *adjective, noun* **1** one more than ten. ♦ *noun* **2** *Sport* team of eleven people. **eleventh** *adjective, noun* (of) number eleven in a series.

elevenses *noun Informal* mid-morning snack.

eleventh hour the last moment.

elf *noun, pl* **elves** (in folklore) small mischievous fairy. **elfin** *adjective* small and delicate.

elicit ⊕ *verb* **1** bring about (a response or reaction), e.g. *her remarks elicited a sharp retort.* **2** find out (information) by careful questioning.

elide *verb* omit (a vowel or syllable) from a spoken word. **elision** *noun*

eligible ⊕ *adjective* **1** meeting the requirements or qualifications needed. **2** desirable as a spouse. **eligibility** *noun*

eliminate ⊕ *verb* **1** get rid of. **2** remove (a team or competitor) from a contest, esp. following a defeat. **elimination** *noun*

elision *noun* see ELIDE.

elite ⊕ [ill-**eet**] *noun* most powerful, rich, or gifted members of a group. **elitism** *noun* belief that society should be governed by a small group of superior people. **elitist** *noun, adjective*

elixir ⊕ [ill-**ix**-er] *noun* imaginary liquid that can prolong life or turn base metals into gold.

Elizabethan *adjective* of the reign of Elizabeth I of England (1558-1603).

elk *noun* large deer of N Europe and Asia.

ellipse *noun* oval shape. **elliptical** *adjective* **1** oval-shaped. **2** (of speech or writing) obscure or ambiguous.

ellipsis [ill-**lip**-siss] *noun, pl* **-ses** omission of letters or words in a sentence.

elm *noun* tree with serrated leaves.

elocution ⊕ *noun* art of speaking clearly in public. **elocutionist** *noun*

elongate ⊕ [**eel**-long-gate] *verb* make or become longer. **elongation** *noun*

elope ⊕ *verb* (of two people) run away secretly to get married. **elopement** *noun*

eloquence ⊕ *noun* fluent powerful use of language. **eloquent** *adjective* **eloquently** *adverb*

———————— T H E S A U R U S ————————

element *noun* **1** = **component**, constituent, factor, ingredient, part, section, subdivision, unit ♦*plural* **5** = **basics**, essentials, foundations, fundamentals, nuts and bolts (*inf*), principles, rudiments **6** = **weather conditions**, atmospheric conditions, powers of nature

elementary *adjective* = **simple**, clear, easy, plain, rudimentary, straightforward, uncomplicated OPPOSITE **advanced**

elevate *verb* **1** = **promote**, advance, aggrandize, exalt, prefer, upgrade **2** = **raise**, heighten, hoist, lift, lift up, uplift

elevated *adjective* **2** = **high-minded**, dignified, exalted, grand, high-flown, inflated, lofty, noble, sublime OPPOSITE **humble**

elevation *noun* **1** = **promotion**, advancement, aggrandizement, exaltation, preferment, upgrading **2** = **altitude**, height

elicit *verb* **1** = **bring about**, bring forth, bring out, bring to light, call forth, cause, derive,

evolve, give rise to **2** = **obtain**, draw out, evoke, exact, extort, extract, wrest

eligible *adjective* **1** = **qualified**, acceptable, appropriate, desirable, fit, preferable, proper, suitable, worthy OPPOSITE **unsuitable**

eliminate *verb* **1** = **get rid of**, cut out, dispose of, do away with, eradicate, exterminate, remove, stamp out, take out

elite *noun* = **best**, aristocracy, cream, flower, nobility, pick, upper class OPPOSITE **rabble**

elitist *adjective* = **snobbish**, exclusive, selective

elixir *noun* = **panacea**, nostrum

elocution *noun* = **diction**, articulation, declamation, delivery, enunciation, oratory, pronunciation, speech, speechmaking

elongate *verb* = **make longer**, draw out, extend, lengthen, prolong, protract, stretch

elope *verb* = **run away**, abscond, bolt, decamp, disappear, escape, leave, run off, slip away, steal away

else ⊙ *adverb* **1** in addition or more, e.g. *what else can I do?* **2** other or different, e.g. *it was unlike anything else that had happened.*
elsewhere *adverb* in or to another place.
elucidate ⊙ *verb* make (something difficult) clear. **elucidation** *noun*
elude ⊙ *verb* **1** escape from by cleverness or quickness. **2** baffle. **elusive** *adjective* difficult to catch or remember.
elver *noun* young eel.
elves *noun* plural of ELF.
Elysium [ill-**liz**-zee-um] *noun* **1** *Greek myth* (also **Elysian fields**) dwelling place of the blessed after death. **2** state or place of perfect bliss.
emaciated ⊙ [im-**mace**-ee-ate-id] *adjective* abnormally thin. **emaciation** *noun*
e-mail, email *noun* **1** (also **electronic mail**) sending of messages between computer terminals. ♦ *verb* **2** communicate in this way.
emanate ⊙ [**em**-a-nate] *verb* issue, proceed from a source. **emanation** *noun*
emancipate ⊙ *verb* free from social, political, or legal restraints. **emancipation** *noun*
emasculate *verb* deprive of power. **emasculation** *noun*
embalm ⊙ *verb* preserve (a corpse) from decay by the use of chemicals etc.

embankment *noun* man-made ridge that carries a road or railway or holds back water.
embargo ⊙ *noun, pl* **-goes 1** order by a government prohibiting trade with a country. ♦ *verb* **-going, -goed 2** put an embargo on.
embark ⊙ *verb* **1** board a ship or aircraft. **2** (foll. by *on*) begin (a new project).
embarkation *noun*
embarrass ⊙ *verb* cause to feel self-conscious or ashamed. **embarrassed** *adjective*
embarrassing *adjective* **embarrassment** *noun*

> **SPELLING TIP**
>
> There are 32 examples of the misspelling *embarras* in the Bank of English and another mistake, *embarassment*, occurs 64 times. Both these words should have two *r*s and two *s*s.

embassy *noun, pl* **-sies 1** offices or official residence of an ambassador. **2** ambassador and his staff.
embattled *adjective* having a lot of difficulties.
embed *verb* **-bedding, -bedded** fix firmly in something solid.
embellish ⊙ *verb* **1** decorate. **2** embroider (a

———————————— THESAURUS ————————————

eloquence *noun* = expressiveness, expression, fluency, forcefulness, oratory, persuasiveness, rhetoric, way with words
eloquent *adjective* = expressive, articulate, fluent, forceful, moving, persuasive, silver-tongued, stirring, vivid, well-expressed [OPPOSITE] **inarticulate**
elsewhere *adverb* = in *or* to another place, abroad, away, hence (*arch*), not here, somewhere else
elucidate *verb* = clarify, clear up, explain, explicate, expound, illuminate, illustrate, make plain, shed *or* throw light upon, spell out
elude *verb* **1** = escape, avoid, dodge, duck (*inf*), evade, flee, get away from, outrun **2** = baffle, be beyond (someone), confound, escape, foil, frustrate, puzzle, stump, thwart
elusive *adjective* **a** = slippery, difficult to catch, shifty, tricky **b** = indefinable, fleeting, intangible, subtle, transient, transitory
emaciated *adjective* = skeletal, cadaverous, gaunt, haggard, lean, pinched, scrawny, thin, undernourished, wasted
emanate *verb* = flow, arise, come forth, derive, emerge, issue, originate, proceed, spring, stem
emancipate *verb* = free, deliver, liberate,

release, set free, unchain, unfetter [OPPOSITE] **enslave**
emancipation *noun* = freedom, deliverance, liberation, liberty, release [OPPOSITE] **slavery**
embalm *verb* = preserve, mummify
embargo *noun* **1** = ban, bar, boycott, interdiction, prohibition, restraint, restriction, stoppage ♦ *verb* **2** = ban, bar, block, boycott, prohibit, restrict, stop
embark *verb* **1** = go aboard, board ship, take ship [OPPOSITE] **get off. 2** (foll. by *on*) = begin, commence, enter, launch, plunge into, set about, set out, start, take up
embarrass *verb* = shame, discomfit, disconcert, distress, fluster, humiliate, mortify, show up (*inf*)
embarrassed *adjective* = ashamed, awkward, blushing, discomfited, disconcerted, humiliated, mortified, red-faced, self-conscious, sheepish
embarrassing *adjective* = humiliating, awkward, compromising, discomfiting, disconcerting, mortifying, sensitive, shameful, toe-curling (*sl*), uncomfortable
embarrassment *noun* = shame, awkwardness, bashfulness, distress, humiliation, mortification, self-consciousness, showing up (*inf*)

story). **embellishment** *noun*

ember *noun* glowing piece of wood or coal in a dying fire.

embezzle ⊕ *verb* steal money that has been entrusted to one. **embezzlement** *noun* **embezzler** *noun*

embittered ⊕ *adjective* feeling anger as a result of misfortune. **embitterment** *noun*

emblazon [im-**blaze**-on] *verb* **1** decorate with bright colours. **2** proclaim or publicize.

emblem ⊕ *noun* object or design that symbolizes a quality, type, or group. **emblematic** *adjective*

embody ⊕ *verb* **-bodying, -bodied 1** be an example or expression of. **2** comprise, include. **embodiment** *noun*

embolden ⊕ *verb* encourage (someone).

embolism *noun* blocking of a blood vessel by a blood clot or air bubble. **embolus** *noun, pl* **-li** material, such as a blood clot, that blocks a blood vessel.

embossed *adjective* (of a design or pattern) standing out from a surface.

embrace ⊕ *verb* **1** clasp in the arms, hug. **2** accept (an idea) eagerly. **3** comprise. ♦ *noun* **4** act of embracing.

embrasure *noun* **1** door or window having splayed sides so that the opening is larger on the inside. **2** opening like this in a fortified wall, for shooting through.

embrocation *noun* lotion for rubbing into the skin to relieve pain.

embroider *verb* **1** decorate with needlework. **2** make (a story) more interesting with fictitious detail. **embroidery** *noun*

embroil ⊕ *verb* involve (a person) in problems. **embroilment** *noun*

embryo ⊕ [em-bree-oh] *noun, pl* **-bryos 1** unborn creature in the early stages of development. **2** something at an undeveloped stage. **embryonic** *adjective* at an early stage. **embryology** *noun* scientific study of embryos.

emend ⊕ *verb* remove errors from. **emendation** *noun*

emerald *noun* **1** bright green precious stone. ♦ *adjective* **2** bright green.

emerge ⊕ *verb* **1** come into view. **2** (foll. by *from*) come out of. **3** become known. **emergence** *noun* **emergent** *adjective*

emergency ⊕ *noun, pl* **-cies** sudden unforeseen occurrence needing immediate action.

emeritus [im-**mer**-rit-uss] *adjective* retired, but retaining an honorary title, e.g. *emeritus professor.*

emery *noun* hard mineral used for smoothing and polishing. **emery board** cardboard strip coated with crushed emery, for filing the nails.

emetic [im-**met**-ik] *noun* **1** substance that causes vomiting. ♦ *adjective* **2** causing vomiting.

———————— T H E S A U R U S ————————

embellish *verb* **1** = **decorate**, adorn, beautify, enhance, enrich, festoon, ornament **2** = **elaborate**, embroider

embellishment *noun* **1** = **decoration**, adornment, enhancement, enrichment, exaggeration, ornament, ornamentation **2** = **elaboration**, embroidery

embezzle *verb* = **misappropriate**, appropriate, filch, misuse, peculate, pilfer, purloin, rip off (*sl*), steal

embezzlement *noun* = **misappropriation**, appropriation, filching, fraud, misuse, peculation, pilfering, stealing, theft

embittered *adjective* = **resentful**, angry, bitter, disaffected, disillusioned, rancorous, soured, with a chip on one's shoulder (*inf*)

emblem *noun* = **symbol**, badge, crest, image, insignia, mark, sign, token

embodiment *noun* **1** = **personification**, epitome, example, exemplar, expression, incarnation, representation, symbol

embody *verb* **1** = **personify**, exemplify, manifest, represent, stand for, symbolize, typify **2** = **incorporate**, collect, combine, comprise, contain, include

embolden *verb* = **encourage**, fire, inflame, invigorate, rouse, stimulate, stir, strengthen

embrace *verb* **1** = **hug**, clasp, cuddle, envelop, hold, seize, squeeze, take *or* hold in one's arms **2** = **accept**, adopt, espouse, seize, take on board, take up, welcome **3** = **include**, comprehend, comprise, contain, cover, encompass, involve, take in ♦ *noun* **4** = **hug**, clasp, clinch (*sl*), cuddle, squeeze

embroil *verb* = **involve**, enmesh, ensnare, entangle, implicate, incriminate, mire, mix up

embryo *noun* **2** = **germ**, beginning, nucleus, root, rudiment

emend *verb* = **revise**, amend, correct, edit, improve, rectify

emendation *noun* = **revision**, amendment, correction, editing, improvement, rectification

emerge *verb* **1** = **come into view**, appear, arise, come forth, surface OPPOSITE **withdraw**. **2** (foll. by *from*) = **issue**, emanate, rise, spring up OPPOSITE **withdraw**. **3** = **become apparent**, become known, come out, come out in the wash, come to light, crop up, transpire

emergency *noun* = **crisis**, danger, difficulty, extremity, necessity, plight, predicament,

EMF electromotive force.

emigrate ⊙ *verb* go and settle in another country. **emigrant** *noun* **emigration** *noun*

émigré [em-mig-gray] *noun* someone who has left his native country for political reasons.

eminent ⊙ *adjective* distinguished, well-known. **eminently** *adverb* **eminence** *noun* **1** position of superiority or fame. **2** (E-) title of a cardinal.

emir [em-**meer**] *noun* Muslim ruler. **emirate** *noun* his country.

emissary *noun, pl* -**saries** agent sent on a mission by a government.

emit ⊙ *verb* **emitting, emitted 1** give out (heat, light, or a smell). **2** utter. **emission** *noun*

emollient *adjective* **1** softening, soothing. ♦ *noun* **2** substance which softens or soothes the skin.

emolument *noun Formal* fees or wages from employment.

emoticon [i-**mote**-i-kon] *noun Computers* symbol depicting a smile or other facial expression, used in e-mail.

emotion ⊙ *noun* strong feeling. **emotional** *adjective* readily affected by or appealing to the emotions. **emotionally** *adverb* **emotive** *adjective* tending to arouse emotion.

empathy *noun* ability to understand someone else's feelings as if they were one's own. **empathize** *verb*

emperor *noun* ruler of an empire. **empress** *n fem*

emphasis ⊙ *noun, pl* -**ses 1** special importance or significance. **2** stress on a word or phrase in speech. **emphasize** *verb* **emphatic** *adjective* showing emphasis. **emphatically** *adverb*

emphysema [em-fiss-**see**-ma] *noun* condition in which the air sacs of the lungs are grossly enlarged, causing breathlessness.

empire ⊙ *noun* **1** group of territories under the rule of one state or person. **2** large organization that is directed by one person or group.

empirical ⊙ *adjective* relying on experiment or experience, not on theory. **empirically** *adverb* **empiricism** *noun* doctrine that all knowledge derives from experience. **empiricist** *noun*

emplacement *noun* prepared position for a gun.

employ ⊙ *verb* **1** hire (a person). **2** provide work or occupation for. **3** use. ♦ *noun* **4 in the employ of** doing regular paid work for.

employee *noun* **employer** *noun* **employment** *noun* **1** state of being employed. **2** work done by a person to earn money.

E

——————— T H E S A U R U S ———————

quandary, scrape (*inf*)

emigrate *verb* =**move abroad**, migrate, move

emigration *noun* =**departure**, exodus, migration

eminence *noun* **1** =**prominence**, distinction, esteem, fame, greatness, importance, note, prestige, renown, repute

eminent *adjective* =**prominent**, celebrated, distinguished, esteemed, famous, high-ranking, illustrious, noted, renowned, well-known OPPOSITE **unknown**

emission *noun* **1** =**giving off** *or* **out**, discharge, ejection, exhalation, radiation, shedding, transmission

emit *verb* **1** =**give off**, cast out, discharge, eject, emanate, exude, radiate, send out, transmit OPPOSITE **absorb**

emotion *noun* =**feeling**, ardour, excitement, fervour, passion, sensation, sentiment, vehemence, warmth

emotional *adjective* **a** =**sensitive**, demonstrative, excitable, hot-blooded, passionate, sentimental, temperamental OPPOSITE **dispassionate**. **b** =**moving**, affecting, emotive, heart-warming, poignant, sentimental, stirring, touching

emotive *adjective* =**sensitive**, controversial, delicate, touchy

emphasis *noun* **1** =**importance**, accent, attention, force, priority, prominence, significance, stress, weight **2** =**stress**, accent

emphasize *verb* **1** =**highlight**, accentuate, dwell on, give priority to, lay stress on, play up, press home, stress, underline OPPOSITE **play down**. **2** =**stress**, accentuate, lay stress on

emphatic *adjective* =**forceful**, categorical, definite, insistent, positive, pronounced, resounding, unequivocal, unmistakable, vigorous OPPOSITE **weak**

empire *noun* **1** =**kingdom**, commonwealth, domain, realm

empirical *adjective* =**first-hand**, experiential, experimental, observed, practical, pragmatic OPPOSITE **hypothetical**

employ *verb* **1** =**hire**, commission, engage, enlist, retain, take on **2** =**keep busy**, engage, fill, make use of, occupy, take up, use up **3** =**use**, apply, bring to bear, exercise, exert, make use of, ply, put to use, utilize

employed *adjective* **1** =**working**, active, busy, engaged, in a job, in employment, in work, occupied OPPOSITE **out of work**

employee *noun* =**worker**, hand, job-holder, staff member, wage-earner, workman

emporium ⊕ *noun, pl* **-riums, -ria** *Old-fashioned* large general shop.

empower ⊕ *verb* enable, authorize.

empress *noun see* EMPEROR.

empty ⊕ *adjective* **-tier, -tiest 1** containing nothing. **2** unoccupied. **3** without purpose or value. **4** (of words) insincere. ♦ *verb* **-tying, -tied 5** make or become empty. **empties** *plural noun* empty boxes, bottles, etc. **emptiness** *noun*

E

empyrean [em-pie-**ree**-an] *noun Poetic* heavens or sky.

EMS European Monetary System.

emu *noun* large Australian flightless bird with long legs.

EMU European Monetary Union.

emulate ⊕ *verb* attempt to equal or surpass by imitating. **emulation** *noun*

emulsion *noun* **1** light-sensitive coating on photographic film. **2** type of water-based paint. ♦ *verb* **3** paint with emulsion paint. **emulsify** *verb* **-fying, -fied** (of two liquids) join together or join (two liquids) together. **emulsifier** *noun*

enable ⊕ *verb* provide (a person) with the means, opportunity, or authority (to do something). **enabling act** legislative act giving certain powers to a person or organization.

enact ⊕ *verb* **1** establish by law. **2** perform (a story or play) by acting. **enactment** *noun*

enamel *noun* **1** glasslike coating applied to metal etc. to preserve the surface. **2** hard white coating on a tooth. ♦ *verb* **-elling, -elled 3** cover with enamel.

enamoured ⊕ *adjective* inspired with love.

en bloc *adverb French* as a whole, all together.

encamp ⊕ *verb* set up in a camp.

encampment *noun*

encapsulate ⊕ *verb* **1** summarize. **2** enclose as in a capsule.

encase *verb* enclose or cover completely. **encased** *adjective*

encephalitis [en-sef-a-**lite**-iss] *noun* inflammation of the brain.

encephalogram *noun* short for ELECTROENCEPHALOGRAM.

enchant ⊕ *verb* delight and fascinate. **enchanting** *adjective* **enchantment** *noun* **enchanter** *noun* **enchantress** *n fem*

enchilada *noun* Mexican dish of a tortilla filled with meat, served with chilli sauce.

encircle *verb* form a circle around. **encirclement** *noun*

enclave *noun* part of a country entirely surrounded by foreign territory.

enclose ⊕ *verb* **1** surround completely. **2** include along with something else. **enclosure** *noun* **enclosed order** Christian religious order whose members do not go into the outside

———— THESAURUS ————

employer *noun* =**boss** (*inf*), company, firm, gaffer (*inf, chiefly Brit*), owner, patron, proprietor

employment *noun* **1 a** =**taking on**, engagement, enlistment, hire, retaining **b** =**use**, application, exercise, exertion, utilization **2** =**job**, line, occupation, profession, trade, vocation, work, yakka (*Aust & NZ inf*)

emporium *noun Old-fashioned* =**shop**, bazaar, market, mart, store, warehouse

empower *verb* =**enable**, allow, authorize, commission, delegate, entitle, license, permit, qualify, sanction, warrant

emptiness *noun* **1, 2** =**bareness**, blankness, desolation, vacancy, vacuum, void, waste **3** =**purposelessness**, banality, futility, hollowness, inanity, meaninglessness, senselessness, vanity, worthlessness **4** =**insincerity**, cheapness, hollowness, idleness

empty *adjective* **1, 2** =**bare**, blank, clear, deserted, desolate, hollow, unfurnished, uninhabited, unoccupied, vacant, void OPPOSITE full. **3** =**purposeless**, banal, fruitless, futile, hollow, inane, meaningless, senseless, vain, worthless OPPOSITE meaningful. **4** =**insincere**, cheap, hollow, idle ♦*verb* **5**

=**evacuate**, clear, drain, exhaust, pour out, unload, vacate, void OPPOSITE fill

emulate *verb* =**imitate**, compete with, copy, echo, follow, mimic, rival

enable *verb* =**allow**, authorize, empower, entitle, license, permit, qualify, sanction, warrant OPPOSITE stop

enact *verb* **1** =**establish**, authorize, command, decree, legislate, ordain, order, proclaim, sanction **2** =**perform**, act out, depict, play, play the part of, portray, represent

enamoured *adjective* =**in love**, captivated, charmed, enraptured, fond, infatuated, smitten, taken

encampment *noun* =**camp**, base, bivouac, camping ground, camp site, cantonment, quarters, tents

encapsulate *verb* **1** =**sum up**, abridge, compress, condense, digest, epitomize, précis, summarize

enchant *verb* =**fascinate**, beguile, bewitch, captivate, charm, delight, enrapture, enthral, ravish

enchanting *adjective* =**fascinating**, alluring, attractive, bewitching, captivating, charming, delightful, entrancing, lekker (*S Afr sl*), lovely,

E

world.

encomium *noun, pl* **-miums, -mia** formal expression of praise.

encompass ⊙ *verb* **1** surround. **2** include comprehensively.

encore *interjection* **1** again, once more. ♦ *noun* **2** extra performance due to enthusiastic demand.

encounter ⊙ *verb* **1** meet unexpectedly. **2** be faced with. ♦ *noun* **3** unexpected meeting. **4** game or battle.

encourage ⊙ *verb* **1** inspire with confidence. **2** spur on. **encouraging** *adjective* **encouragement** *noun*

encroach ⊙ *verb* intrude gradually on a person's rights or land. **encroachment** *noun*

encrust *verb* cover with a layer of something.

encumber ⊙ *verb* hinder or impede.

encumbrance *noun* something that impedes or is burdensome.

encyclical [en-**sik**-lik-kl] *noun* letter sent by the Pope to all bishops.

encyclopedia, encyclopaedia *noun* book or set of books containing facts about many subjects, usu. in alphabetical order.

encyclopedic, encyclopaedic *adjective* comprehensive.

end ⊙ *noun* **1** furthest point or part. **2** limit. **3** last part of something. **4** fragment. **5** death or destruction. **6** purpose. **7** *Sport* either of the two defended areas of a playing field. ♦ *verb* **8** bring or come to a finish. **make ends meet** have just enough money for one's needs.

ending *noun* **endless** *adjective* endways. ♦ *adverb* having the end forwards or upwards.

end product final result of a process, esp. in manufacturing.

endanger ⊙ *verb* put in danger.

endear ⊙ *verb* cause to be liked. **endearing** *adjective* **endearment** *noun* affectionate word or phrase.

endeavour ⊙ *verb* **1** try. ♦ *noun* **2** effort.

endemic *adjective* present within a localized area or peculiar to a particular group of people.

endive *noun* curly-leaved plant used in salads.

endocardium *noun* lining membrane of the heart.

endocrine *adjective* relating to the glands

———————— THESAURUS ————————

pleasant

enclose *verb* **1** = surround, bound, encase, encircle, fence, hem in, shut in, wall in **2** = send with, include, insert, put in

encompass *verb* **1** = surround, circle, encircle, enclose, envelop, ring **2** = include, admit, comprise, contain, cover, embrace, hold, incorporate, take in

encounter *verb* **1** = meet, bump into (*inf*), chance upon, come upon, run across **2** = face, confront, experience ♦*noun* **3** = meeting, brush, confrontation, rendezvous **4** = battle, clash, conflict, contest, head-to-head, run-in (*inf*)

encourage *verb* **1** = inspire, buoy up, cheer, comfort, console, embolden, hearten, reassure, support OPPOSITE discourage. **2** = spur, advocate, egg on, foster, incite, promote, prompt, urge OPPOSITE dissuade

encouragement *noun* **1** = inspiration, cheer, reassurance, support **2** = incitement, promotion, stimulation, stimulus

encouraging *adjective* **1** = promising, bright, cheerful, comforting, good, heartening, hopeful, reassuring, rosy OPPOSITE discouraging

encroach *verb* = intrude, impinge, infringe, invade, make inroads, overstep, trespass, usurp

encumber *verb* = burden, hamper, handicap, hinder, impede, inconvenience, obstruct, saddle, weigh down

end *noun* **1, 2** = extremity, boundary, edge, extent, extreme, limit, point, terminus, tip **3** = finish, cessation, close, closure, conclusion, culmination, denouement, ending, expiration, expiry, finale, resolution, stop, termination OPPOSITE start. **4** = remnant, butt, fragment, leftover, oddment, remainder, scrap, stub **5** = destruction, death, demise, doom, extermination, extinction, ruin **6** = purpose, aim, goal, intention, object, objective, point, reason ♦*verb* **8** = finish, cease, close, conclude, culminate, stop, terminate, wind up OPPOSITE start

endanger *verb* = put at risk, compromise, imperil, jeopardize, put in danger, risk, threaten OPPOSITE save

endearing *adjective* = attractive, captivating, charming, cute, engaging, lekker (*S Afr sl*), lovable, sweet, winning

endearment *noun* = loving word, sweet nothing

endeavour *verb* **1** = try, aim, aspire, attempt, labour, make an effort, strive, struggle, take pains ♦*noun* **2** = effort, attempt, enterprise, trial, try, undertaking, venture

ending *noun* = finish, cessation, close, completion, conclusion, culmination, denouement, end, finale OPPOSITE start

endless *adjective* = eternal, boundless, continual, everlasting, incessant, infinite, interminable, unlimited OPPOSITE temporary

which secrete hormones directly into the
bloodstream.
endogenous [en-**dodge**-in-uss] *adjective*
originating from within.
endorphin *noun* chemical occurring in the
brain, which has a similar effect to morphine.
endorse ➊ *verb* **1** give approval to. **2** sign the
back of (a cheque). **3** record a conviction on (a
driving licence). **endorsement** *noun*
endow ➊ *verb* provide permanent income for.
endowed with provided with. **endowment**
noun
endure ➊ *verb* **1** bear (hardship) patiently. **2**
last for a long time. **endurable** *adjective*
endurance *noun* act or power of enduring.
enduring *adjective* long-lasting.
enema [en-im-a] *noun* medicine injected into
the rectum to empty the bowels.
enemy ➊ *noun, pl* **-mies** hostile person or
nation, opponent.
energy ➊ *noun, pl* **-gies 1** capacity for intense
activity. **2** capacity to do work and overcome
resistance. **3** source of power, such as
electricity. **energetic** *adjective* **energetically**
adverb **energize** *verb* give vigour to. **energy
drink** soft drink supposed to boost the drinker's

energy levels.
enervate *verb* deprive of strength or vitality.
enervated *adjective* **enervation** *noun*
enfant terrible [on-fon ter-**reeb**-la] *noun, pl*
enfants terribles *French* clever but
unconventional or indiscreet person.
enfeeble *verb* weaken. **enfeebled** *adjective*
enfeeblement *noun*
enfold *verb* **1** cover by wrapping something
around. **2** embrace.
enforce ➊ *verb* **1** impose obedience (to a law
etc.). **2** impose (a condition). **enforceable**
adjective **enforcement** *noun*
enfranchise *verb* grant (a person) the right to
vote. **enfranchised** *adjective* **enfranchisement**
noun
engage ➊ *verb* **1** take part, participate. **2**
involve (a person or his or her attention)
intensely. **3** employ (a person). **4** begin a battle
with. **5** bring (a mechanism) into operation.
engaged *adjective* **1** pledged to be married. **2**
in use. **engagement** *noun* **engaging** *adjective*
charming.
engender ➊ *verb* produce, cause to occur.
engine ➊ *noun* **1** any machine which converts
energy into mechanical work. **2** railway

———— T H E S A U R U S ————

endorse *verb* **1** = **approve**, advocate,
authorize, back, champion, promote, ratify,
recommend, support **2** = **sign**, countersign
endorsement *noun* **1** = **approval**, advocacy,
approbation, authorization, backing, favour,
ratification, recommendation, seal of approval,
support **2** = **signature**, countersignature
endow *verb* = **provide**, award, bequeath,
bestow, confer, donate, finance, fund, give
endowment *noun* = **provision**, award,
benefaction, bequest, donation, gift, grant,
legacy
endurable *adjective* **1** = **bearable**, acceptable,
sufferable, sustainable, tolerable
endurance *noun* **1** = **staying power**,
fortitude, patience, perseverance, persistence,
resolution, stamina, strength, tenacity,
toleration **2** = **permanence**, continuity,
durability, duration, longevity, stability
endure *verb* **1** = **bear**, cope with, experience,
stand, suffer, sustain, undergo, withstand **2**
= **last**, continue, live on, persist, remain, stand,
stay, survive
enduring *adjective* = **long-lasting**, abiding,
continuing, lasting, perennial, persistent,
steadfast, unfaltering, unwavering [OPPOSITE]
brief
enemy *noun* = **foe**, adversary, antagonist,
competitor, opponent, rival, the opposition, the

other side [OPPOSITE] **friend**
energetic *adjective* = **vigorous**, active,
animated, dynamic, forceful, indefatigable,
lively, strenuous, tireless [OPPOSITE] **lethargic**
energy *noun* **1, 2** = **vigour**, drive,
forcefulness, get-up-and-go (*inf*), liveliness, pep,
stamina, verve, vitality
enforce *verb* = **impose**, administer, apply,
carry out, execute, implement, insist on,
prosecute, put into effect
engage *verb* **1** = **participate**, embark on,
enter into, join, set about, take part, undertake
2 = **preoccupy**, absorb, captivate, engross, fix,
grip, involve, occupy **3** = **employ**, appoint,
enlist, enrol, hire, retain, take on [OPPOSITE]
dismiss. **4** = **begin battle with**, assail, attack,
encounter, fall on, join battle with, meet, take
on **5** = **set going**, activate, apply, bring into
operation, energize, switch on
engaged *adjective* **1** = **betrothed** (*arch*),
affianced, pledged, promised, spoken for
[OPPOSITE] **free**. **2** = **occupied**, busy, employed,
in use, tied up, unavailable [OPPOSITE] **free**
engaging *adjective* = **charming**, agreeable,
attractive, fetching (*inf*), lekker (*S Afr sl*), likable
or likeable, pleasing, winning, winsome
[OPPOSITE] **unpleasant**
engender *verb* = **produce**, breed, cause,
create, generate, give rise to, induce, instigate,

locomotive.

engineer ❶ *noun* **1** person trained in any branch of engineering. ♦ *verb* **2** plan in a clever manner. **3** design or construct as an engineer.

engineering *noun* profession of applying scientific principles to the design and construction of engines, cars, buildings, or machines.

English *noun* **1** official language of Britain, the US, most of the Commonwealth, and certain other countries. ♦ *adjective* **2** relating to England. **the English** the people of England.

engorge *verb Pathology* clog with blood. **engorgement** *noun*

engrave ❶ *verb* **1** carve (a design) onto a hard surface. **2** fix deeply in the mind.

engraver *noun* **engraving** *noun* print made from an engraved plate.

engross ❶ [en-**groce**] *verb* occupy the attention of (a person) completely. **engrossing** *adjective*

engulf ❶ *verb* cover or surround completely.

enhance ❶ *verb* increase in quality, value, or attractiveness. **enhancement** *noun*

enigma ❶ *noun* puzzling thing or person.

enigmatic *adjective* **enigmatically** *adverb*

enjoin *verb* order (someone) to do something.

enjoy ❶ *verb* **1** take joy in. **2** have the benefit of. **3** experience. **enjoyable** *adjective* **enjoyment** *noun*

enlarge ❶ *verb* **1** make or grow larger. **2** (foll. by *on*) speak or write about in greater detail. **enlargement** *noun*

enlighten ❶ *verb* give information to.

enlightened *adjective* **1** guided by rational thought. **2** tolerant and unprejudiced. **enlightenment** *noun*

enlist ❶ *verb* **1** enter the armed forces. **2** obtain the support of. **enlistment** *noun*

enliven ❶ *verb* make lively or cheerful.

en masse *adverb French* in a group, all together.

enmeshed *adjective* deeply involved, e.g. *enmeshed in turmoil*.

enmity ❶ *noun, pl* **-ties** ill will, hatred.

ennoble ❶ *verb* make noble, elevate.

E

——————————— T H E S A U R U S ———————————

lead to

engine *noun* **1** = **machine**, mechanism, motor

engineer *verb* **2** = **bring about**, contrive, create, devise, effect, mastermind, plan, plot, scheme

engrave *verb* **1** = **carve**, chisel, cut, etch, inscribe **2** = **fix**, embed, impress, imprint, ingrain, lodge

engraving *noun* = **carving**, etching, inscription, plate, woodcut

engross *verb* = **absorb**, engage, immerse, involve, occupy, preoccupy

engrossed *adjective* = **absorbed**, caught up, enthralled, fascinated, gripped, immersed, lost, preoccupied, rapt, riveted

engulf *verb* = **immerse**, envelop, inundate, overrun, overwhelm, submerge, swallow up, swamp

enhance *verb* = **improve**, add to, boost, heighten, increase, lift, reinforce, strengthen, swell OPPOSITE **reduce**

enigma *noun* = **mystery**, conundrum, problem, puzzle, riddle, teaser

enigmatic *adjective* = **mysterious**, ambiguous, cryptic, equivocal, inscrutable, obscure, puzzling, unfathomable OPPOSITE **straightforward**

enjoy *verb* **1** = **take pleasure in** or **from**, appreciate, be entertained by, be pleased with, delight in, like, relish OPPOSITE **hate**. **2** = **have**, be blessed or favoured with, experience, have the benefit of, own, possess, reap the benefits

of, use

enjoyable *adjective* **1** = **pleasurable**, agreeable, delightful, entertaining, gratifying, pleasant, satisfying, to one's liking OPPOSITE **unpleasant**

enjoyment *noun* **1** = **pleasure**, amusement, delectation, delight, entertainment, fun, gratification, happiness, joy, relish

enlarge *verb* **1** = **increase**, add to, amplify, broaden, expand, extend, grow, magnify, swell, widen OPPOSITE **reduce**. **2** (foll. by *on*) = **expand on**, descant on, develop, elaborate on, expatiate on, give further details about

enlighten *verb* = **inform**, advise, cause to understand, counsel, edify, educate, instruct, make aware, teach

enlightened *adjective* **1** = **informed**, aware, civilized, cultivated, educated, knowledgeable, sophisticated OPPOSITE **ignorant**. **2** = **open-minded**, reasonable, tolerant

enlightenment *noun* **1** = **understanding**, awareness, comprehension, education, insight, instruction, knowledge, learning, wisdom

enlist *verb* **1** = **join up**, enrol, enter (into), join, muster, register, sign up, volunteer **2** = **obtain**, engage, procure, recruit

enliven *verb* = **cheer up**, animate, excite, inspire, invigorate, pep up, rouse, spark, stimulate, vitalize OPPOSITE **subdue**

enmity *noun* = **hostility**, acrimony, animosity, bad blood, bitterness, hatred, ill will, malice OPPOSITE **friendship**

E

ennui [on-**nwee**] *noun* boredom, dissatisfaction.

enormous ❶ *adjective* very big, vast. **enormously** *adverb* **enormity** *noun, pl* **-ties 1** great wickedness. **2** gross offence. **3** *Informal* great size.

enough ❶ *adjective* **1** as much or as many as necessary. ◆ *noun* **2** sufficient quantity. ◆ *adverb* **3** sufficiently. **4** fairly or quite, e.g. *that's a common enough experience.*

en passant [on **pass**-on] *adverb French* in passing, by the way.

enquire ❶ *verb* same as INQUIRE. **enquiry** *noun*

enraptured *adjective* filled with delight and fascination.

enrich ❶ *verb* **1** improve in quality. **2** make wealthy or wealthier. **enriched** *adjective* **enrichment** *noun*

enrol ❶ *verb* **-rolling, -rolled** (cause to) become a member. **enrolment** *noun*

en route ❶ *adverb French* on the way.

ensconce *verb* settle firmly or comfortably.

ensemble ❶ [on-**som**-bl] *noun* **1** all the parts of something taken together. **2** complete outfit of clothes. **3** company of actors or musicians. **4** *Music* group of musicians playing together.

enshrine *verb* cherish or treasure.

enshroud *verb* cover or hide as with a shroud.

ensign ❶ *noun* **1** naval flag. **2** banner. **3** *US* naval officer.

enslave *verb* make a slave of (someone). **enslavement** *noun*

ensnare *verb* catch in or as if in a snare.

ensue ❶ *verb* come next, result. **ensuing** *adjective*

en suite *adverb French* connected to a bedroom and entered directly from it.

ensure ❶ *verb* **1** make certain or sure. **2** make safe or protect.

ENT *Med* ear, nose, and throat.

entablature *noun Archit* part of a classical temple above the columns, with an architrave, frieze, and cornice.

entail ❶ *verb* **1** bring about or impose inevitably. **2** *Law* restrict (ownership of property) to designated heirs.

entangle ❶ *verb* catch or involve in or as if in a tangle. **entanglement** *noun*

entente [on-**tont**] *noun* friendly understanding between nations.

enter ❶ *verb* **1** come or go in. **2** join. **3** become involved in, take part in. **4** record (an item) in a journal etc. **5** begin. **entrance** *noun* **1** way into a place. **2** act of entering. **3** right of entering. **entrant** *noun* person who enters a university, contest, etc. **entry** *noun, pl* **-tries 1** entrance. **2** entering. **3** item entered in a journal etc.

——————— THESAURUS ———————

ennoble *verb* =**dignify**, aggrandize, elevate, enhance, exalt, glorify, honour, magnify, raise

enormity *noun* **1** =**wickedness**, atrocity, depravity, monstrousness, outrageousness, vileness, villainy **2** =**atrocity**, abomination, crime, disgrace, evil, horror, monstrosity, outrage **3** *Inf* =**hugeness**, greatness, immensity, magnitude, vastness

enormous *adjective* =**huge**, colossal, gigantic, gross, immense, mammoth, massive, mountainous, tremendous, vast OPPOSITE⟩ tiny

enough *adjective* **1** =**sufficient**, abundant, adequate, ample, plenty ◆*noun* **2** =**sufficiency**, abundance, adequacy, ample supply, plenty, right amount ◆*adverb* **3** =**sufficiently**, abundantly, adequately, amply, reasonably, satisfactorily, tolerably

enquire see INQUIRE

enquiry see INQUIRY

enrich *verb* **1** =**enhance**, augment, develop, improve, refine, supplement **2** =**make rich**, make wealthy

enrol *verb* =**enlist**, accept, admit, join up, recruit, register, sign up *or* on, take on

enrolment *noun* =**enlistment**, acceptance, admission, engagement, matriculation, recruitment, registration

en route *adverb French* =**on** *or* **along the way**, in transit, on the road

ensemble *noun* **1** =**whole**, aggregate, collection, entirety, set, sum, total, totality **2** =**outfit**, costume, get-up (*inf*), suit **3** =**group**, band, cast, chorus, company, troupe

ensign *noun* **1, 2** =**flag**, banner, colours, jack, pennant, pennon, standard, streamer

ensue *verb* =**follow**, arise, come next, derive, flow, issue, proceed, result, stem OPPOSITE⟩ come first

ensure *verb* **1** =**make certain**, certify, confirm, effect, guarantee, make sure, secure, warrant **2** =**protect**, guard, make safe, safeguard, secure

entail *verb* **1** =**involve**, bring about, call for, demand, give rise to, necessitate, occasion, require

entangle *verb* =**tangle**, catch, embroil, enmesh, ensnare, entrap, implicate, snag, snare, trap OPPOSITE⟩ free

enter *verb* **1** =**come** *or* **go in** *or* **into**, arrive, make an, pass into, penetrate, pierce OPPOSITE⟩ exit. **2** =**join**, enlist, enrol OPPOSITE⟩ leave. **3** =**start**, commence, embark upon, set out on, take up **4** =**record**, inscribe, list, log, note,

enteric [en-**ter**-ik] *adjective* intestinal.
enteritis [en-ter-**rite**-iss] *noun* inflammation of the intestine, causing diarrhoea.
enterprise ❶ *noun* **1** company or firm. **2** bold or difficult undertaking. **3** boldness and energy.
enterprising *adjective* full of boldness and initiative.
entertain ❶ *verb* **1** amuse. **2** receive as a guest. **3** consider (an idea). **entertainer** *noun* **entertaining** *adjective* **entertainment** *noun*
enthral ❶ [en-**thrawl**] *verb* **-thralling, -thralled** hold the attention of. **enthralling** *adjective*
enthrone *verb* **1** place (someone) on a throne. **2** praise or honour (something). **enthronement** *noun*
enthusiasm ❶ *noun* ardent interest, eagerness. **enthuse** *verb* (cause to) show enthusiasm. **enthusiast** *noun* ardent supporter of something. **enthusiastic** *adjective* **enthusiastically** *adverb*
entice ❶ *verb* attract by exciting hope or desire, tempt. **enticing** *adjective* **enticement** *noun*
entire ❶ *adjective* including every detail, part,

or aspect of something. **entirely** *adverb* **entirety** *noun*
entitle ❶ *verb* **1** give a right to. **2** give a title to. **entitlement** *noun*
entity ❶ *noun, pl* **-ties** separate distinct thing.
entomb *verb* **1** place (a corpse) in a tomb. **2** serve as a tomb for. **entombment** *noun*
entomology *noun* study of insects.
entomological *adjective* **entomologist** *noun*
entourage ❶ [on-toor-ahzh] *noun* group of people who assist an important person.
entozoon [en-toe-**zoe**-on] *noun, pl* **-zoa** [-zoe-a] internal parasite. **entozoic** *adjective*
entr'acte [on-**tract**] *noun* interval between acts of a play etc.
entrails ❶ *plural noun* **1** intestines. **2** innermost parts of something.
entrance[1] **❶** *noun* see ENTER.
entrance[2] **❶** *verb* **1** delight. **2** put into a trance. **entrancing** *adjective*
entrap *verb* **1** trick into difficulty etc. **2** catch in a trap, or catch as if in a trap. **entrapment** *noun*
entreat ❶ *verb* ask earnestly. **entreaty** *noun, pl* **-ties** earnest request.

E

register, set down, take down
enterprise *noun* **1** = **firm**, business, company, concern, establishment, operation **2** = **undertaking**, adventure, effort, endeavour, operation, plan, programme, project, venture **3** = **initiative**, adventurousness, boldness, daring, drive, energy, enthusiasm, resourcefulness
enterprising *adjective* = **resourceful**, adventurous, bold, daring, energetic, enthusiastic, go-ahead, intrepid, spirited
entertain *verb* **1** = **amuse**, charm, cheer, delight, please, regale **2** = **show hospitality to**, accommodate, be host to, harbour, have company, lodge, put up, treat **3** = **consider**, conceive, contemplate, imagine, keep in mind, think about
entertaining *adjective* **1** = **enjoyable**, amusing, cheering, diverting, funny, humorous, interesting, pleasant, pleasurable
entertainment *noun* **1** = **enjoyment**, amusement, fun, leisure activity, pastime, pleasure, recreation, sport, treat
enthral *verb* = **fascinate**, captivate, charm, enchant, enrapture, entrance, grip, mesmerize
enthusiasm *noun* = **keenness**, eagerness, fervour, interest, passion, relish, zeal, zest
enthusiast *noun* = **lover**, aficionado, buff (*inf*), devotee, fan, fanatic, follower, supporter
enthusiastic *adjective* = **keen**, avid, eager, fervent, passionate, vigorous, wholehearted,

zealous OPPOSITE **apathetic**
entice *verb* = **attract**, allure, cajole, coax, lead on, lure, persuade, seduce, tempt
entire *adjective* = **whole**, complete, full, gross, total
entirely *adverb* = **completely**, absolutely, altogether, fully, in every respect, thoroughly, totally, utterly, wholly OPPOSITE **partly**
entitle *verb* **1** = **give the right to**, allow, authorize, empower, enable, license, permit **2** = **call**, christen, dub, label, name, term, title
entity *noun* = **thing**, being, creature, individual, object, organism, substance
entourage *noun* = **retinue**, associates, attendants, company, court, escort, followers, staff, train
entrails *plural noun* **1** = **intestines**, bowels, guts, innards (*inf*), insides (*inf*), offal, viscera
entrance[1] *noun* **1** = **way in**, access, door, doorway, entry, gate, opening, passage OPPOSITE **exit**. **2** = **appearance**, arrival, coming in, entry, introduction OPPOSITE **departure**. **3** = **admission**, access, admittance, entrée, entry, permission to enter
entrance[2] *verb* **1** = **enchant**, bewitch, captivate, charm, delight, enrapture, enthral, fascinate OPPOSITE **bore**. **2** = **mesmerize**, hypnotize, put in a trance
entrant *noun* = **competitor**, candidate, contestant, entry, participant, player

entrecôte [on-tra-coat] *noun* beefsteak cut from between the ribs.

entrée [on-tray] *noun* **1** dish served before a main course. **2** main course. **3** right of admission.

entrench ❶ *verb* **1** establish firmly. **2** establish in a fortified position with trenches.

entrenched *adjective* **entrenchment** *noun*

entrepreneur ❶ *noun* business person who attempts to make a profit by risk and initiative.

entropy [en-trop-ee] *noun* **1** lack of organization. **2** *Physics* unavailability of the heat energy of a system for mechanical work.

entrust ❶ *verb* put into the care or protection of.

entwine ❶ *verb* twist together or around.

E number *noun* any of a series of numbers with the prefix E indicating a specific food additive recognized by the EU.

enumerate ❶ *verb* name one by one.

enumeration *noun*

enunciate ❶ *verb* **1** pronounce clearly. **2** state precisely or formally. **enunciation** *noun*

enuresis [en-yoo-reece-iss] *noun* involuntary discharge of urine, esp. during sleep. **enuretic** *adjective*

envelop ❶ *verb* **enveloping, enveloped** wrap up, enclose. **envelopment** *noun*

envelope ❶ *noun* folded gummed paper cover for a letter.

environment ❶ [en-vire-on-ment] *noun* **1** external conditions and surroundings in which people, animals, or plants live. **2** natural world of land, sea, air, plants, and animals.

environmental *adjective* **environmentalist** *noun* person concerned with the protection of the natural environment.

> **SPELLING TIP**
>
> For every thousand correct appearances of the word **environment** in the Bank of English, there is one *enviroment*, without the middle *n*.

environs ❶ *plural noun* surrounding area, esp. of a town.

envisage ❶ *verb* conceive of as a possibility.

envoy ❶ *noun* **1** messenger. **2** diplomat ranking below an ambassador.

envy ❶ *noun* **1** feeling of discontent aroused by another's good fortune. ◆ *verb* **-vying, -vied 2** grudge (another's good fortune, success, or qualities). **enviable** *adjective* arousing envy, fortunate. **envious** *adjective* full of envy.

——————— T H E S A U R U S ———————

entreaty *noun* =**plea**, appeal, earnest request, exhortation, petition, prayer, request, supplication

entrenched *adjective* **1** =**fixed**, deep-rooted, deep-seated, ineradicable, ingrained, rooted, set, unshakable, well-established

entrepreneur *noun* =**businessman** or **businesswoman**, impresario, industrialist, magnate, tycoon

entrust *verb* =**give custody of**, assign, commit, confide, delegate, deliver, hand over, turn over

entry *noun* **1** =**way in**, access, door, doorway, entrance, gate, opening, passage OPPOSITE exit. **2** =**coming in**, appearance, entering, entrance, initiation, introduction OPPOSITE departure. **3** =**admission**, access, entrance, entrée, permission to enter

entwine *verb* =**twist**, interlace, interweave, knit, plait, twine, weave, wind OPPOSITE disentangle

enumerate *verb* =**list**, cite, itemize, mention, name, quote, recite, recount, relate, spell out

enunciate *verb* **1** =**pronounce**, articulate, enounce, say, sound, speak, utter, vocalize, voice **2** =**state**, declare, proclaim, promulgate, pronounce, propound, publish

envelop *verb* =**enclose**, cloak, cover, encase, encircle, engulf, shroud, surround, wrap

envelope *noun* =**wrapping**, case, casing, cover, covering, jacket, wrapper

enviable *adjective* =**desirable**, advantageous, favoured, fortunate, lucky, privileged, to die for (*inf*) OPPOSITE undesirable

envious *adjective* =**covetous**, green with envy, grudging, jealous, resentful

environment *noun* **1** =**surroundings**, atmosphere, background, conditions, habitat, medium, setting, situation

environmental *adjective* **2** =**ecological**, green

environmentalist *noun* =**conservationist**, ecologist, green

environs *plural noun* =**surrounding area**, district, locality, neighbourhood, outskirts, precincts, suburbs, vicinity

envisage *verb* =**imagine**, conceive (of), conceptualize, contemplate, envision, fancy, foresee, picture, see, think up, visualize

envoy *noun* **1** =**messenger**, agent, courier, delegate, emissary, intermediary, representative **2** =**diplomat**, ambassador

envy *noun* **1** =**covetousness**, enviousness, jealousy, resentfulness, resentment ◆*verb* **2**

enzyme noun any of a group of complex proteins that act as catalysts in specific biochemical reactions.

Eolithic adjective of the early part of the Stone Age.

epaulette noun shoulder ornament on a uniform.

ephedrine [**eff**-fid-dreen] noun alkaloid used for treatment of asthma and hay fever.

ephemeral ❶ adjective short-lived.

epic noun **1** long poem, book, or film about heroic events or actions. ◆ adjective **2** very impressive or ambitious.

epicene adjective **1** common to both sexes. **2** effeminate.

epicentre noun point on the earth's surface immediately above the origin of an earthquake.

epicure noun person who enjoys good food and drink. **epicurism** noun **epicurean** adjective **1** devoted to sensual pleasures, esp. food and drink. ◆ noun **2** epicure. **epicureanism** noun

epidemic ❶ noun **1** widespread occurrence of a disease. **2** rapid spread of something.

epidermis noun outer layer of the skin.

epidural [ep-pid-**dure**-al] adjective, noun (of) spinal anaesthetic injected to relieve pain during childbirth.

epiglottis noun thin flap that covers the opening of the larynx during swallowing.

epigram ❶ noun short witty remark or poem. **epigrammatic** adjective

epigraph noun **1** quotation at the start of a book. **2** inscription.

epilepsy noun disorder of the nervous system causing loss of consciousness and sometimes convulsions. **epileptic** adjective **1** of or having epilepsy. ◆ noun **2** person who has epilepsy.

epilogue ❶ noun short speech or poem at the end of a literary work, esp. a play.

Epiphany noun Christian festival held on January 6 commemorating the manifestation of Christ to the Magi.

episcopal [ip-**piss**-kop-al] adjective of or governed by bishops. **episcopalian** adjective **1** advocating Church government by bishops. ◆ noun **2** advocate of such Church government.

episode ❶ noun **1** incident in a series of incidents. **2** section of a serialized book, television programme, etc. **episodic** adjective occurring at irregular intervals.

epistemology [ip-iss-stem-**ol**-a-jee] noun study of the source, nature, and limitations of knowledge. **epistemological** adjective **epistemologist** noun

epistle ❶ noun letter, esp. of an apostle. **epistolary** adjective

epitaph ❶ noun **1** commemorative inscription on a tomb. **2** commemorative speech or passage.

epithet ❶ noun descriptive word or name.

epitome ❶ [ip-**pit**-a-mee] noun typical example. **epitomize** verb be the epitome of.

epoch ❶ [**ee**-pok] noun period of notable events. **epoch-making** adjective extremely important.

eponymous [ip-**pon**-im-uss] adjective after whom a book, play, etc. is named. **eponymously** adverb

EPOS electronic point of sale.

Epsom salts plural noun medicinal preparation of magnesium sulphate and water, used to empty the bowels.

equable ❶ [**ek**-wab-bl] adjective even-tempered. **equably** adverb

equal ❶ adjective **1** identical in size, quantity, degree, etc. **2** having identical rights or status. **3** evenly balanced. **4** (foll. by to) having the necessary ability (for). ◆ noun **5** person or thing equal to another. ◆ verb **equalling, equalled 6** be equal to. **equally** adverb **equality** noun

——————————— T H E S A U R U S ———————————

=**covet**, be envious (of), begrudge, be jealous (of), grudge, resent

ephemeral adjective =**brief**, fleeting, momentary, passing, short-lived, temporary, transient, transitory OPPOSITE> eternal

epidemic noun **1** =**plague**, contagion, outbreak **2** =**spread**, growth, upsurge, wave

epigram noun =**witticism**, aphorism, bon mot, quip

epilogue noun =**conclusion**, coda, concluding speech, postscript OPPOSITE> prologue

episode noun **1** =**event**, adventure, affair, escapade, experience, happening, incident, matter, occurrence **2** =**part**, chapter, instalment, passage, scene, section

epistle noun =**letter**, communication, message, missive, note

epitaph noun **1** =**monument**, inscription

epithet noun =**name**, appellation, description, designation (sl), nickname, sobriquet, tag, title

epitome noun =**personification**, archetype, embodiment, essence, quintessence, representation, type, typical example

epitomize verb =**typify**, embody, exemplify, illustrate, personify, represent, symbolize

epoch noun =**era**, age, date, period, time

equable adjective =**even-tempered**, calm, composed, easy-going, imperturbable, level-headed, placid, serene, unflappable (inf) state of being equal. **equalize** verb **1** make or become equal. **2** reach the same score as one's opponent. **equalization** noun **equal opportunity** nondiscrimination as to sex, race, etc. in employment.

equanimity noun calmness of mind.

equate ❶ verb make or regard as equivalent.

equation noun **1** mathematical statement that two expressions are equal. **2** act of equating. **3** representation of a chemical reaction using symbols of the elements.

equator noun imaginary circle round the earth, equidistant from the poles. **equatorial** adjective

equerry [ek-kwer-ee] noun, pl **-ries** officer who acts as an attendant to a member of a royal family.

equestrian adjective of horses and riding.

equidistant adjective equally distant.

equilateral adjective having equal sides.

equilibrium ❶ noun, pl **-ria** steadiness or stability.

equine adjective of or like a horse.

equinox noun time of year when day and night are of equal length. **equinoctial** adjective

equip ❶ verb **equipping, equipped** provide with supplies, components, etc. **equipment** noun **1** set of tools or devices used for a particular purpose. **2** act of equipping.

equipoise noun perfect balance.

equitation noun riding and horsemanship.

equity ❶ noun, pl **-ties 1** fairness. **2** legal system, founded on the principles of natural justice, that supplements common law. ◆ plural **3** interest of ordinary shareholders in a company. **equitable** adjective fair and reasonable. **equitably** adverb

equivalent ❶ adjective **1** equal in value. **2** having the same meaning or result. ◆ noun **3** something that is equivalent. **equivalence** noun

equivocal ❶ adjective **1** ambiguous. **2** deliberately misleading. **3** of doubtful character or sincerity. **equivocally** adverb **equivocate** verb use vague or ambiguous language to mislead people. **equivocation** noun

er ❶ interjection sound made when hesitating in speech.

Er Chem erbium.

ER Queen Elizabeth.

era ❶ noun period of time considered as distinctive.

eradicate ❶ verb destroy completely. **eradication** noun

erase ❶ verb **1** destroy all traces of, e.g. he could not erase the memory of his earlier defeat.

——— T H E S A U R U S ———

OPPOSITE nervous

equal adjective **1** = **identical**, alike, corresponding, equivalent, regular, symmetrical, the same, uniform OPPOSITE different. **3** = **even**, balanced, evenly matched, fifty-fifty (inf), level pegging (Brit inf) OPPOSITE uneven. **4** (foll. by to) = **capable of**, competent to, fit for, good enough for, ready for, strong enough, suitable for, up to OPPOSITE inadequate ◆noun **5** = **match**, counterpart, equivalent, rival, twin ◆verb **6** = **match**, amount to, be tantamount to, correspond to, equate, level, parallel, tie with OPPOSITE be unequal

equality noun **1** = **sameness**, correspondence, equivalence, evenness, identity, likeness, similarity, uniformity OPPOSITE disparity. **2** = **fairness**, egalitarianism, equal opportunity, parity OPPOSITE discrimination

equalize verb **1** = **make equal**, balance, equal, even up, level, match, regularize, smooth, square, standardize

equate verb = **make** or **be equal**, be commensurate, compare, correspond with or to, liken, mention in the same breath, parallel

equation noun **2** = **equating**, comparison, correspondence, parallel

equilibrium noun = **stability**, balance, equipoise, evenness, rest, steadiness, symmetry

equip verb = **supply**, arm, array, fit out, furnish, kit out, provide, stock

equipment noun **1** = **apparatus**, accoutrements, gear, paraphernalia, stuff, supplies, tackle, tools

equitable adjective = **fair**, even-handed, honest, impartial, just, proper, reasonable, unbiased

equivalence noun = **equality**, correspondence, evenness, likeness, parity, sameness, similarity

equivalent adjective **1, 2** = **equal**, alike, commensurate, comparable, corresponding, interchangeable, of a piece, same, similar, tantamount OPPOSITE different ◆noun **3** = **equal**, counterpart, match, opposite number, parallel, twin

equivocal adjective **1** = **ambiguous**, indefinite, indeterminate, oblique, obscure, uncertain, vague OPPOSITE clear. **2** = **misleading**, evasive OPPOSITE clear

era noun = **age**, date, day or days, epoch, generation, period, time

eradicate verb = **wipe out**, annihilate, destroy, eliminate, erase, exterminate, extinguish, get rid of, obliterate, remove, root out

2 rub out. **3** remove sound or information from (a magnetic tape or disk). **eraser** *noun* object for erasing something written. **erasure** *noun* **1** erasing. **2** place or mark where something has been erased.

erbium *noun Chem* metallic element of the lanthanide series.

ere *preposition, conjunction Poetic* before.

erect ❶ *verb* **1** build. **2** found or form. ◆ *adjective* **3** upright. **4** (of the penis, clitoris, or nipples) rigid as a result of sexual excitement. **erectile** *adjective* capable of becoming erect from sexual excitement. **erection** *noun*

erg *noun* unit of work or energy.

ergo *adverb* therefore.

ergonomics *noun* study of the relationship between workers and their environment. **ergonomic** *adjective* **1** designed to minimize effort. **2** of ergonomics.

ergot *noun* **1** fungal disease of cereal. **2** dried fungus used in medicine.

erica *noun* genus of plants including heathers.

ermine *noun* **1** stoat in northern regions. **2** its white winter fur.

erne, ern *noun* fish-eating sea eagle.

Ernie *noun Brit* machine that randomly selects winning numbers of Premium Bonds.

erode ❶ *verb* wear away. **erosion** *noun*

erogenous [ir-**roj**-in-uss] *adjective* sensitive to sexual stimulation.

erotic ❶ *adjective* relating to sexual pleasure or desire. **eroticism** *noun* **erotica** *noun* sexual literature or art.

err ❶ *verb* **1** make a mistake. **2** sin. **erratum** *noun, pl* **-ta** error in writing or printing.

erroneous *adjective* incorrect, mistaken. **erroneously** *adverb* **error** *noun* mistake, inaccuracy, or misjudgment.

errand ❶ *noun* short trip to do something for someone.

errant *adjective* behaving in a manner considered to be unacceptable.

erratic ❶ *adjective* irregular or unpredictable. **erratically** *adverb*

error ❶ *noun* mistake, inaccuracy, or misjudgment.

ersatz [**air**-zats] *adjective* made in imitation, e.g. *ersatz coffee.*

Erse *noun* **1** Gaelic. ◆ *adjective* **2** of or relating to the Gaelic language.

erstwhile ❶ *adjective* former.

erudite ❶ [**air**-rude-ite] *adjective* having great academic knowledge. **erudition** *noun*

erupt ❶ *verb* **1** eject (steam, water, or volcanic material) violently. **2** burst forth suddenly and violently. **3** (of a blemish) appear on the skin. **eruption** *noun*

erysipelas [err-riss-**sip**-pel-ass] *noun* acute skin infection causing purplish patches.

erythema [err-rith-**theme**-a] *noun* patchy inflammation of the skin.

erythrocyte [ir-**rith**-roe-site] *noun* red blood cell of vertebrates that transports oxygen and carbon dioxide.

Es *Chem* einsteinium.

escalate ❶ *verb* increase in extent or intensity.

E

———————— THESAURUS ————————

erase *verb* **1** = **remove**, blot, cancel, delete, expunge, obliterate **2** = **wipe out**, rub out

erect *verb* **1** = **build**, construct, put up, raise, set up OPPOSITE **demolish**. **2** = **found**, create, establish, form, initiate, institute, organize, set up ◆ *adjective* **3** = **upright**, elevated, perpendicular, straight, vertical OPPOSITE **bent**. **4** = **stiff**

erode *verb* = **wear down** *or* **away**, abrade, consume, corrode, destroy, deteriorate, disintegrate, eat away, grind down

erosion *noun* = **deterioration**, abrasion, attrition, destruction, disintegration, eating away, grinding down, wearing down *or* away

erotic *adjective* = **sexual**, amatory, carnal, lustful, seductive, sensual, sexy (*inf*), voluptuous

err *verb* **1** = **make a mistake**, blunder, go wrong, miscalculate, misjudge, mistake, slip up (*inf*)

errand *noun* = **job**, charge, commission, message, mission, task

erratic *adjective* = **unpredictable**, changeable, inconsistent, irregular, shonky (*Aust & NZ inf*), uneven, unreliable, unstable, variable, wayward OPPOSITE **regular**

erroneous *adjective* = **incorrect**, fallacious, false, faulty, flawed, invalid, mistaken, shonky (*Aust & NZ inf*), unsound, wrong OPPOSITE **correct**

error *noun* = **mistake**, bloomer (*Brit inf*), blunder, howler (*inf*), miscalculation, oversight, slip, solecism

erstwhile *adjective* = **former**, bygone, late, old, once, one-time, past, previous, sometime

erudite *adjective* = **learned**, cultivated, cultured, educated, knowledgeable, scholarly, well-educated, well-read OPPOSITE **uneducated**

erupt *verb* **1, 2** = **explode**, belch forth, blow up, burst out, gush, pour forth, spew forth *or* out, spout, throw off **3** = **break out**, appear

eruption *noun* **1, 2** = **explosion**, discharge, ejection, flare-up, outbreak, outburst **3** = **inflammation**, outbreak, rash

escalation *noun*
escalator *noun* moving staircase.
escalope [**ess**-kal-lop] *noun* thin slice of meat, esp. veal.
escapade ❶ *noun* mischievous adventure.
escape ❶ *verb* **1** get free (of). **2** avoid, e.g. *escape attention.* **3** (of a gas, liquid, etc.) leak gradually. **4** be forgotten by, e.g. *the figure escapes me.* ✦ *noun* **5** act of escaping. **6** means of relaxation. **escapee** *noun* person who has escaped. **escapism** *noun* taking refuge in fantasy to avoid unpleasant reality.
escapologist *noun* entertainer who specializes in freeing himself from confinement.
escapology *noun*
escarpment *noun* steep face of a ridge or mountain.
eschatology [ess-cat-**tol**-loh-jee] *noun* branch of theology concerned with the end of the world. **eschatological** *adjective*
escheat [iss-**cheat**] *Law noun* **1** private possessions that become state property in the absence of an heir. ✦ *verb* **2** attain such property.
eschew [iss-**chew**] *verb* abstain from, avoid.
escort ❶ *noun* **1** people or vehicles accompanying another person for protection or as an honour. **2** person who accompanies a person of the opposite sex to a social event. ✦ *verb* **3** act as an escort to.
escritoire [ess-kree-**twahr**] *noun* type of writing desk.
escudo [ess-**kyoo**-doe] *noun, pl* **-dos** monetary unit of Portugal.
escutcheon *noun* shield with a coat of arms. **blot on one's escutcheon** stain on one's honour.
Eskimo *noun* **1** a member of a group of peoples inhabiting N Canada, Greenland, Alaska, and E Siberia, having a material culture adapted to an extremely cold climate. **2** their language.

> **LANGUAGE TIP**
>
> *Eskimo* is considered by many people to be offensive, and in North America the term *Inuit* is often used.

ESN *Obs* educationally subnormal.
esoteric [ee-so-**ter**-rik] *adjective* understood by only a small number of people with special knowledge.
ESP extrasensory perception.
esp. especially.
espadrille [**ess**-pad-drill] *noun* light canvas shoe with a braided cord sole.
espalier [ess-**pal**-yer] *noun* **1** shrub or fruit tree trained to grow flat. **2** trellis for this.
esparto *noun, pl* **-tos** grass used for making rope etc.
especial ❶ *adjective Formal* special. **especially** *adverb* particularly.
Esperanto *noun* universal artificial language.
espionage ❶ [**ess**-pyon-ahzh] *noun* spying.
esplanade *noun* wide open road used as a public promenade.
espouse ❶ *verb* adopt or give support to (a cause etc.). **espousal** *noun*
espresso *noun, pl* **-sos** strong coffee made by forcing steam or boiling water through ground coffee beans.
esprit [ess-**pree**] *noun* spirit, liveliness, or wit.
esprit de corps [de **core**] pride in and loyalty to a group.

——————— T H E S A U R U S ———————

escalate *verb* =**increase**, expand, extend, grow, heighten, intensify, mount, rise ⟨OPPOSITE⟩ decrease
escapade *noun* =**adventure**, antic, caper, prank, scrape (*inf*), stunt
escape *verb* **1** =**get away**, abscond, bolt, break free *or* out, flee, fly, make one's getaway, run away *or* off, slip away **2** =**avoid**, dodge, duck, elude, evade, pass, shun, slip **3** =**leak**, emanate, exude, flow, gush, issue, pour forth, seep ✦*noun* **5** =**getaway**, break, break-out, flight **6** =**relaxation**, distraction, diversion, pastime, recreation
escort *noun* **1** =**guard**, bodyguard, convoy, cortege, entourage, retinue, train **2** =**companion**, attendant, beau, chaperon, guide, partner ✦*verb* **3** =**accompany**, chaperon, conduct, guide, lead, partner, shepherd, usher
especial *adjective Formal* =**exceptional**, noteworthy, outstanding, principal, special, uncommon, unusual
especially *adverb* =**exceptionally**, conspicuously, markedly, notably, outstandingly, remarkably, specially, strikingly, uncommonly, unusually
espionage *noun* =**spying**, counter-intelligence, intelligence, surveillance, undercover work
espousal *noun* =**support**, adoption, advocacy, backing, championing, defence, embracing, promotion, taking up
espouse *verb* =**support**, adopt, advocate, back, champion, embrace, promote, stand up

espy *verb* **espying, espied** catch sight of.

Esq. esquire.

esquire *noun* courtesy title placed after a man's name.

essay ❶ *noun* **1** short literary composition. **2** short piece of writing on a subject done as an exercise by a student. ♦ *verb* **3** attempt.

essayist *noun*

essence ❶ *noun* **1** most important feature of a thing which determines its identity. **2** concentrated liquid used to flavour food.

essential *adjective* **1** vitally important. **2** basic or fundamental. ♦ *noun* **3** something fundamental or indispensable. **essentially** *adverb*

est. 1 established. **2** estimate(d).

establish ❶ *verb* **1** set up on a permanent basis. **2** make secure or permanent in a certain place, job, etc. **3** prove. **4** cause to be accepted. **establishment** *noun* **1** act of establishing. **2** commercial or other institution. **the Establishment** group of people having authority within a society.

estate ❶ *noun* **1** landed property. **2** large area of property development, esp. of new houses or factories. **3** property of a deceased person.

estate agent agent concerned with the valuation, lease, and sale of property. **estate car** car with a rear door and luggage space

behind the rear seats.

esteem ❶ *noun* **1** high regard. ♦ *verb* **2** think highly of. **3** judge or consider.

ester *noun Chem* compound produced by the reaction between an acid and an alcohol.

estimate ❶ *verb* **1** calculate roughly. **2** form an opinion about. ♦ *noun* **3** approximate calculation. **4** statement from a workman etc. of the likely charge for a job. **5** opinion.

estimable *adjective* worthy of respect.

estimation *noun* considered opinion.

estranged *adjective* no longer living with one's spouse. **estrangement** *noun*

estuary ❶ *noun, pl* **-aries** mouth of a river.

ETA estimated time of arrival.

e-tail *noun* selling of goods via the Internet.

et al. 1 and elsewhere. **2** and others.

etc. ❶ et cetera.

et cetera ❶ [et **set**-ra] *Latin* **1** and the rest, and others. **2** or the like. **etceteras** *plural noun* miscellaneous extra things or people.

——————— THESAURUS ———————

for, take up, uphold

essay *noun* **1** = **composition**, article, discourse, dissertation, paper, piece, tract, treatise ♦ *verb* **3** = **attempt**, aim, endeavour, try, undertake

essence *noun* **1** = **fundamental nature**, being, core, heart, nature, quintessence, soul, spirit, substance **2** = **concentrate**, distillate, extract, spirits, tincture

essential *adjective* **1** = **vital**, crucial, important, indispensable, necessary, needed, requisite [OPPOSITE] unnecessary. **2** = **fundamental**, basic, cardinal, elementary, innate, intrinsic, main, principal [OPPOSITE] secondary ♦ *noun* **3** = **prerequisite**, basic, fundamental, must, necessity, rudiment, *sine qua non*

establish *verb* **1** = **create**, constitute, form, found, ground, inaugurate, institute, settle, set up **3** = **prove**, authenticate, certify, confirm, corroborate, demonstrate, substantiate, verify

establishment *noun* **1** = **creation**, formation, foundation, founding, inauguration, installation, institution, organization, setting up **2** = **organization**, business, company, concern, corporation, enterprise, firm, institution, outfit (*inf*) **the Establishment** = **the authorities**,

ruling class, the powers that be, the system

estate *noun* **1** = **lands**, area, domain, holdings, manor, property, homestead (*US & Canad*) **3** = **property**, assets, belongings, effects, fortune, goods, possessions, wealth

esteem *noun* **1** = **respect**, admiration, credit, estimation, good opinion, honour, regard, reverence, veneration ♦ *verb* **2** = **respect**, admire, love, prize, regard highly, revere, think highly of, treasure, value **3** = **consider**, believe, deem, estimate, judge, reckon, regard, think, view

estimate *verb* **1** = **calculate roughly**, assess, evaluate, gauge, guess, judge, number, reckon, value **2** = **form an opinion**, believe, conjecture, consider, judge, rank, rate, reckon, surmise ♦ *noun* **3** = **approximate calculation**, assessment, ballpark figure (*inf*), guess, guesstimate (*inf*), judgment, valuation **5** = **opinion**, appraisal, assessment, belief, estimation, judgment

estimation *noun* = **opinion**, appraisal, appreciation, assessment, belief, consideration, considered opinion, judgment, view

estuary *noun* = **inlet**, creek, firth, fjord, mouth

et cetera *Latin* = **and so on**, and others, and so forth, and the like, and the rest, et al.

etch ❶ *verb* **1** wear away or cut the surface of (metal, glass, etc.) with acid. **2** imprint vividly (on someone's mind). **etching** *noun* picture printed from an etched metal plate.

eternal ❶ *adjective* **1** without beginning or end. **2** unchanging. **eternally** *adverb* **eternity** *noun* **1** infinite time. **2** seemingly endless period of time. **3** timeless existence after death.

eternity ring ring given as a token of lasting affection.

ethane *noun* odourless flammable gas obtained from natural gas and petroleum.

ether *noun* **1** colourless sweet-smelling liquid used as an anaesthetic. **2** region above the clouds. **ethereal** [eth-**eer**-ee-al] *adjective* extremely delicate.

ethic ❶ *noun* moral principle. **ethical** *adjective* **ethically** *adverb* **ethics** *noun* **1** code of behaviour. **2** study of morals.

Ethiopian *adjective* **1** of Ethiopia, its people, or their languages. ◆ *noun* **2** person from Ethiopia.

ethnic ❶ *adjective* **1** relating to a people or group that shares a culture, religion, or language. **2** belonging or relating to such a group, esp. one that is a minority group in a particular place. **ethnic cleansing** practice, by the dominant ethnic group in an area, of removing other ethnic groups by expulsion or extermination. **ethnology** *noun* study of human races. **ethnological** *adjective* **ethnologist** *noun*

ethos [**eeth**-oss] *noun* distinctive spirit and attitudes of a people, culture, etc.

ethyl [**eeth**-ile] *adjective* of, consisting of, or containing the hydrocarbon group C_2H_5.

ethylene *noun* poisonous gas used as an anaesthetic and as fuel.

etiolate [ee-tee-oh-late] *verb* **1** become pale and weak. **2** *Botany* whiten through lack of sunlight.

etiology *noun* study of the causes of diseases.

etiquette ❶ *noun* conventional code of conduct.

étude [**ay**-tewd] *noun* short musical composition for a solo instrument, esp. intended as a technical exercise.

etymology *noun, pl* **-gies** study of the sources and development of words. **etymological** *adjective* **etymologist** *noun*

Eu *Chem* europium.

EU European Union.

eucalyptus, eucalypt *noun* tree, mainly grown in Australia, that provides timber, gum, and medicinal oil from the leaves.

Eucharist [**yew**-kar-ist] *noun* **1** Christian sacrament commemorating Christ's Last Supper. **2** consecrated elements of bread and wine. **Eucharistic** *adjective*

eugenics [yew-**jen**-iks] *noun* study of methods of improving the human race.

eulogy *noun, pl* **-gies** speech or writing in praise of a person. **eulogize** *verb* praise (a person or thing) highly in speech or writing. **eulogist** *noun* **eulogistic** *adjective*

eunuch *noun* castrated man, esp. (formerly) a guard in a harem.

euphemism *noun* inoffensive word or phrase substituted for one considered offensive or upsetting. **euphemistic** *adjective* **euphemistically** *adverb*

euphony *noun, pl* **-nies** pleasing sound. **euphonious** *adjective* pleasing to the ear.

euphonium *noun* brass musical instrument, tenor tuba.

euphoria ❶ *noun* sense of elation. **euphoric** *adjective*

Eurasian *adjective* **1** of Europe and Asia. **2** of mixed European and Asian parentage. ◆ *noun* **3** person of Eurasian parentage.

eureka [yew-**reek**-a] *interjection* exclamation of triumph at finding something.

———————— THESAURUS ————————

etch *verb* **1** = **cut**, carve, eat into, engrave, impress, imprint, inscribe, stamp

etching *noun* = **print**, carving, engraving, impression, imprint, inscription

eternal *adjective* **1** = **everlasting**, endless, immortal, infinite, never-ending, perpetual, timeless, unceasing, unending [OPPOSITE] **occasional**. **2** = **permanent**, deathless, enduring, immutable, imperishable, indestructible, lasting, unchanging [OPPOSITE] **transitory**

eternity *noun* **1** = **infinity**, ages, endlessness, immortality, perpetuity, timelessness **3** = **the afterlife**, heaven, paradise, the hereafter, the next world

ethical *adjective* = **moral**, conscientious, fair, good, honourable, just, principled, proper, right, upright, virtuous [OPPOSITE] **unethical**

ethics *plural noun* **1** = **moral code**, conscience, morality, moral philosophy, moral values, principles, rules of conduct, standards

ethnic *adjective* = **cultural**, folk, indigenous, national, native, racial, traditional

etiquette *noun* = **good** *or* **proper behaviour**, civility, courtesy, decorum, formalities, manners, politeness, propriety, protocol

euphoria *noun* = **elation**, ecstasy, exaltation, exhilaration, intoxication, joy, jubilation, rapture

euro noun, pl **euros** unit of the single currency of the European Union.

Eurodollar noun US dollar as part of a European holding.

Euroland noun the countries within the European Union that have adopted the euro.

European noun, adjective (person) from Europe. **European Union** association of a number of European nations with some shared monetary and political goals.

europium noun Chem silvery-white element of the lanthanide series.

Eurozone same as EUROLAND.

Eustachian tube noun passage leading from the ear to the throat.

euthanasia noun act of killing someone painlessly, esp. to relieve his or her suffering.

eV electronvolt.

evacuate ➊ verb 1 send (someone) away from a place of danger. 2 empty. **evacuation** noun **evacuee** noun

evade ➊ verb 1 get away from or avoid. 2 elude. **evasion** noun **evasive** adjective not straightforward, e.g. an evasive answer. **evasively** adverb

evaluate ➊ verb find or judge the value of. **evaluation** noun

evanescent adjective quickly fading away. **evanescence** noun

evangelical adjective 1 of or according to gospel teaching. 2 of certain Protestant sects which maintain the doctrine of salvation by faith. ♦ noun 3 member of an evangelical sect. **evangelicalism** noun

evangelist noun 1 writer of one of the four gospels. 2 travelling preacher. **evangelism** noun teaching and spreading of the Christian gospel. **evangelize** verb preach the gospel. **evangelization** noun

evaporate ➊ verb 1 change from a liquid or solid to a vapour. 2 disappear. **evaporation** noun **evaporated milk** thick unsweetened tinned milk.

eve ➊ noun 1 evening or day before some special event. 2 period immediately before an event. **evensong** noun evening prayer.

even ➊ adjective 1 flat or smooth. 2 (foll. by with) on the same level (as). 3 constant. 4 calm. 5 equally balanced. 6 divisible by two. ♦ adverb 7 equally. 8 simply. 9 nevertheless. ♦ verb 10 make even.

evening ➊ noun 1 end of the day or early part of the night. ♦ adjective 2 of or in the evening. **evening class** educational class for adults, held during the evening. **evening dress** attire for a formal occasion during the evening.

event ➊ noun 1 anything that takes place. 2 planned and organized occasion. 3 contest in a sporting programme. **eventful** adjective full of exciting incidents.

eventing noun riding competitions, usu. involving cross-country, jumping, and dressage.

eventual ➊ adjective ultimate. **eventually** adverb **eventuality** noun possible event.

──────── T H E S A U R U S ────────

OPPOSITE **despondency**

evacuate verb 1 = **clear**, abandon, desert, forsake, leave, move out, pull out, quit, vacate, withdraw

evade verb 1 = **avoid**, dodge, duck, elude, escape, get away from, sidestep, steer clear of OPPOSITE **face**. 2 = **avoid answering**, equivocate, fend off, fudge, hedge, parry

evaluate verb = **assess**, appraise, calculate, estimate, gauge, judge, rate, reckon, size up (inf), weigh

evaporate verb 1 = **dry up**, dry, vaporize 2 = **disappear**, dematerialize, dissolve, fade away, melt away, vanish

evasion noun 1 = **avoidance**, dodging, escape 2 = **deception**, equivocation, evasiveness, prevarication

evasive adjective = **deceptive**, cagey (inf), equivocating, indirect, oblique, prevaricating, shifty, slippery OPPOSITE **open**

eve noun 1 = **night before**, day before, vigil 2 = **brink**, edge, point, threshold, verge

even adjective 1 = **level**, flat, horizontal, parallel, smooth, steady, straight, true, uniform OPPOSITE **uneven**. 2 (foll. by with) = **equal**, comparable, fifty-fifty (inf), identical, level, like, matching, neck and neck, on a par, similar, tied OPPOSITE **unequal**. 3 = **regular**, constant, smooth, steady, unbroken, uniform, uninterrupted, unvarying, unwavering OPPOSITE **variable**. 4 = **calm**, composed, cool, even-tempered, imperturbable, placid, unruffled, well-balanced OPPOSITE **emotional**

evening noun 1 = **dusk**, gloaming (Scot or poet), twilight

event noun 1 = **incident**, affair, business, circumstance, episode, experience, happening, occasion, occurrence 3 = **competition**, bout, contest, game, tournament

eventful adjective = **exciting**, active, busy, dramatic, full, lively, memorable, remarkable OPPOSITE **dull**

eventual adjective = **final**, concluding, overall, ultimate

eventuality noun = **possibility**, case, chance, contingency, event, likelihood, probability

E

ever ⊙ adverb 1 at any time. 2 always.
evergreen noun, adjective (tree or shrub) having leaves throughout the year. **everlasting** adjective 1 eternal. 2 lasting for an indefinitely long period. **evermore** adverb for all time to come.
every ⊙ adjective 1 each without exception. 2 all possible. **everybody** pronoun every person. **everyday** adjective usual or ordinary. **everyone** pronoun every person. **everything** pronoun **everywhere** adverb in all places.
evict ⊙ verb legally expel (someone) from his or her home. **eviction** noun
evidence ⊙ noun 1 ground for belief. 2 matter produced before a lawcourt to prove or disprove a point. 3 sign, indication. ◆ verb 4 demonstrate, prove. **in evidence** conspicuous.
evident adjective easily seen or understood.
evidently adverb **evidential** adjective of, serving as, or based on evidence. **evidentially** adverb
evil ⊙ noun 1 wickedness. 2 wicked deed. ◆ adjective 3 harmful. 4 morally bad. 5 very unpleasant. **evilly** adverb **evildoer** noun wicked person. **evil eye** look superstitiously supposed

to have the power of inflicting harm.
evince verb make evident.
eviscerate verb disembowel. **evisceration** noun
evoke ⊙ verb call or summon up (a memory, feeling, etc.). **evocation** noun **evocative** adjective
evolve ⊙ verb 1 develop gradually. 2 (of an animal or plant species) undergo evolution.
evolution noun 1 gradual change in the characteristics of living things over successive generations, esp. to a more complex form. 2 gradual development. **evolutionary** adjective
ewe noun female sheep.
ewer noun large jug with a wide mouth.
ex noun Informal former wife or husband.
ex- prefix 1 out of, outside, from, e.g. exodus. 2 former, e.g. ex-wife.
exacerbate [ig-zass-er-bate] verb make (pain, emotion, or a situation) worse. **exacerbation** noun
exact ⊙ adjective 1 correct and complete in every detail. 2 precise, as opposed to approximate. ◆ verb 3 demand (payment or obedience). **exactly** adverb precisely, in every

———————— THESAURUS ————————

eventually adverb = **in the end**, after all, at the end of the day, finally, one day, some time, ultimately, when all is said and done
ever adverb 1 = **at any time**, at all, at any period, at any point, by any chance, in any case, on any occasion 2 = **always**, at all times, constantly, continually, evermore, for ever, perpetually, twenty-four-seven (inf)
everlasting adjective 1 = **eternal**, endless, immortal, indestructible, never-ending, perpetual, timeless, transitory
evermore adverb = **for ever**, always, eternally, ever, to the end of time
every adjective = **each**, all, each one
everybody pronoun = **everyone**, all and sundry, each one, each person, every person, one and all, the whole world
everyday adjective = **ordinary**, common, customary, mundane, routine, run-of-the-mill, stock, usual, workaday OPPOSITE **unusual**
everyone pronoun = **everybody**, all and sundry, each one, each person, every person, one and all, the whole world
everything pronoun = **all**, each thing, the lot, the whole lot
everywhere adverb = **to** or **in every place**, all around, all over, far and wide or near, high and low, in every nook and cranny, the world over, ubiquitously
evict verb = **expel**, boot out (inf), eject, kick

out (inf), oust, remove, throw out, turf out (inf), turn out
evidence noun 1, 2 = **proof**, confirmation, corroboration, demonstration, grounds, substantiation, testimony 3 = **sign**, indication ◆verb 4 = **show**, demonstrate, display, exhibit, indicate, prove, reveal, signify, witness
evident adjective = **obvious**, apparent, clear, manifest, noticeable, perceptible, plain, unmistakable, visible OPPOSITE **hidden**
evidently adverb = **obviously**, clearly, manifestly, plainly, undoubtedly, unmistakably, without question
evil noun 1 = **wickedness**, badness, depravity, malignity, sin, vice, villainy, wrongdoing 2 = **harm**, affliction, disaster, hurt, ill, injury, mischief, misfortune, suffering, woe ◆adjective 3 = **harmful**, calamitous, catastrophic, destructive, dire, disastrous, pernicious, ruinous 4 = **wicked**, bad, depraved, immoral, malevolent, malicious, sinful, villainous 5 = **offensive**, foul, noxious, pestilential, unpleasant, vile
evoke verb = **arouse**, awaken, call, give rise to, induce, recall, rekindle, stir up, summon up OPPOSITE **suppress**
evolution noun 2 = **development**, expansion, growth, increase, maturation, progress, unfolding, working out
evolve verb 1 = **develop**, expand, grow,

respect. **exactness, exactitude** *noun* **exacting** *adjective* making rigorous or excessive demands.
exaggerate ❶ *verb* **1** regard or represent as greater than is true. **2** make greater or more noticeable. **exaggeratedly** *adverb* **exaggeration** *noun*

SPELLING TIP

Some apparently tricky words, like **exaggerate** for example, appear wrongly spelt relatively rarely in the Bank of English. Similarly, there is only one occurrence of *exagerration*, instead of the correct **exaggeration**.

---

exalt ❶ *verb* **1** praise highly. **2** raise to a higher rank. **exalted** *adjective* **exaltation** *noun*
exam *noun* short for EXAMINATION.
examine ❶ *verb* **1** look at closely. **2** test the

knowledge of. **3** ask questions of. **examination** *noun* **1** examining. **2** test of a candidate's knowledge or skill. **examinee** *noun* person who sits an exam. **examiner** *noun* person who sets or marks an exam.
example ❶ *noun* **1** specimen typical of its group. **2** instance that illustrates a fact or opinion. **3** person or thing worthy of imitation. **4** punishment regarded as a warning to others.
exasperate ❶ *verb* cause great irritation to.
exasperation *noun*
excavate ❶ *verb* **1** unearth buried objects from (a piece of land) methodically to learn about the past. **2** make (a hole) in solid matter by digging. **excavation** *noun* **excavator** *noun* large machine used for digging.
exceed ❶ *verb* **1** be greater than. **2** go beyond (a limit). **exceedingly** *adverb* very.
excel ❶ *verb* **-celling, -celled 1** be superior to. **2** be outstandingly good at something.
excellent *adjective* exceptionally good.
excellence *noun*

E

——————— THESAURUS ———————

increase, mature, progress, unfold, work out
exact *adjective* **1** = **correct**, faultless, right, true, unerring **2** = **accurate**, definite, precise, specific OPPOSITE approximate ◆*verb* **3** = **demand**, claim, command, compel, extort, extract, force
exacting *adjective* = **demanding**, difficult, hard, harsh, rigorous, severe, strict, stringent, taxing, tough OPPOSITE easy
exactly *adverb* **a** = **precisely**, accurately, correctly, explicitly, faithfully, scrupulously, truthfully, unerringly **b** = **in every respect**, absolutely, indeed, precisely, quite, specifically, to the letter
exactness, exactitude *noun* **1** = **scrupulousness**, rigorousness, strictness, veracity **2** = **accuracy**, correctness, precision
exaggerate *verb* = **overstate**, amplify, embellish, embroider, enlarge, overemphasize, overestimate
exaggeration *noun* = **overstatement**, amplification, embellishment, enlargement, hyperbole, overemphasis, overestimation OPPOSITE understatement
exalt *verb* **1** = **praise**, acclaim, extol, glorify, idolize, set on a pedestal, worship **2** = **raise**, advance, elevate, ennoble, honour, promote, upgrade
exaltation *noun* **1** = **praise**, acclaim, glorification, idolization, reverence, tribute, worship **2** = **rise**, advancement, elevation, ennoblement, promotion, upgrading
exalted *adjective* **1** = **high-ranking**, dignified,

eminent, grand, honoured, lofty, prestigious
examination *noun* **1** = **inspection**, analysis, exploration, interrogation, investigation, research, scrutiny, study, test **2** = **questioning**, inquiry, inquisition, probe, quiz, test
examine *verb* **1** = **inspect**, analyse, explore, investigate, peruse, scrutinize, study, survey **2** = **test**, question, quiz **3** = **question**, cross-examine, grill (*inf*), inquire, interrogate
example *noun* **2** = **specimen**, case, illustration, instance, sample **3** = **model**, archetype, ideal, paradigm, paragon, prototype, standard **4** = **warning**, caution, lesson
exasperate *verb* = **irritate**, anger, annoy, enrage, incense, inflame, infuriate, madden, pique OPPOSITE calm
exasperation *noun* = **irritation**, anger, annoyance, fury, pique, provocation, rage, wrath
excavate *verb* **1** = **unearth**, dig out, dig up, mine, quarry, uncover **2** = **dig**, burrow, delve, tunnel
exceed *verb* **1** = **surpass**, beat, better, cap (*inf*), eclipse, outdo, outstrip, overtake, pass, top **2** = **go over the limit of**, go over the top, overstep
exceedingly *adverb* = **extremely**, enormously, exceptionally, extraordinarily, hugely, superlatively, surpassingly, unusually, very
excel *verb* **1** = **be superior**, beat, eclipse, outdo, outshine, surpass, transcend **2** = **be good**, be proficient, be skilful, be talented, shine, show talent

Excellency *noun* title used to address a high-ranking official, such as an ambassador.
except ❶ *preposition* **1** (sometimes foll. by *for*) other than, not including. ♦ *verb* **2** not include.
except that but for the fact that. **excepting** *preposition* except. **exception** *noun* **1** excepting. **2** thing that is excluded from or does not conform to the general rule.
exceptionable *adjective* causing offence.
exceptional *adjective* **1** not ordinary. **2** much above the average. **exceptionally** *adverb*
excerpt ❶ *noun* passage taken from a book, speech, etc.
excess ❶ *noun* **1** state or act of exceeding the permitted limits. **2** immoderate amount. **3** amount by which a thing exceeds the permitted limits. **excessive** *adjective* **excessively** *adverb*
exchange ❶ *verb* **1** give or receive (something) in return for something else. ♦ *noun* **2** act of exchanging. **3** thing given or received in place of another. **4** centre in which telephone lines are interconnected. **5** *Finance* place where securities or commodities are traded. **6** transfer of sums of money of equal value between different currencies.
exchangeable *adjective* **exchange rate** rate at which the currency unit of one country may be exchanged for that of another.
Exchequer *noun Brit* government department in charge of state money.
excise¹ *noun* tax on goods produced for the home market.
excise² *verb* cut out or away. **excision** *noun*
excite ❶ *verb* **1** arouse to strong emotion. **2** arouse or evoke (an emotion). **3** arouse sexually. **excitement** *noun* **excitable** *adjective* easily excited. **excitability** *noun* **exciting** *adjective*
exclaim ❶ *verb* speak suddenly, cry out.
exclamation *noun* **exclamation mark** punctuation mark (!) used after exclamations. **exclamatory** *adjective*
exclude ❶ *verb* **1** keep out, leave out. **2** leave out of consideration. **exclusion** *noun* **exclusive** *adjective* **1** excluding everything else. **2** not shared. **3** catering for a privileged minority. ♦ *noun* **4** story reported in only one newspaper. **exclusively** *adverb* **exclusivity, exclusiveness** *noun*

———————— T H E S A U R U S ————————

excellence *noun* = **high quality**, distinction, eminence, goodness, greatness, merit, pre-eminence, superiority, supremacy
excellent *adjective* = **outstanding**, brilliant, exquisite, fine, first-class, first-rate, good, great, superb, superlative, world-class OPPOSITE> **terrible**
except *preposition* **1** (sometimes foll. by *for*) = **apart from**, barring, besides, but, excepting, excluding, omitting, other than, saving, with the exception of ♦*verb* **2** = **exclude**, leave out, omit, pass over
exception *noun* **1** = **exclusion**, leaving out, omission, passing over **2** = **special case**, anomaly, deviation, freak, inconsistency, irregularity, oddity, peculiarity
exceptional *adjective* **1** = **unusual**, abnormal, atypical, extraordinary, irregular, munted (*NZ sl*), odd, peculiar, special, strange OPPOSITE> **average**. **2** = **remarkable**, excellent, extraordinary, marvellous, outstanding, phenomenal, prodigious, special, superior OPPOSITE> **bad**
excerpt *noun* = **extract**, fragment, part, passage, piece, quotation, section, selection
excess *noun* **1** = **overindulgence**, debauchery, dissipation, dissoluteness, extravagance, intemperance, prodigality OPPOSITE> **moderation**. **2** = **surfeit**, glut, overload, superabundance, superfluity, surplus,
too much OPPOSITE> **shortage**
excessive *adjective* = **immoderate**, disproportionate, exaggerated, extreme, inordinate, overmuch, superfluous, too much, undue, unfair, unreasonable
exchange *verb* **1** = **interchange**, barter, change, convert into, swap, switch, trade ♦*noun* **2** = **interchange**, barter, quid pro quo, reciprocity, substitution, swap, switch, tit for tat, trade
excitable *adjective* = **nervous**, emotional, highly strung, hot-headed, mercurial, quick-tempered, temperamental, volatile, wired (*sl*) OPPOSITE> **calm**
excite *verb* **1, 2** = **arouse**, animate, galvanize, inflame, inspire, provoke, rouse, stir up **3** = **thrill**, electrify, titillate
excitement *noun* = **agitation**, action, activity, animation, commotion, furore, passion, thrill
exciting *adjective* = **stimulating**, dramatic, electrifying, exhilarating, rousing, sensational, stirring, thrilling OPPOSITE> **boring**
exclaim *verb* = **cry out**, call out, declare, proclaim, shout, utter, yell
exclamation *noun* = **cry**, call, interjection, outcry, shout, utterance, yell
exclude *verb* **1** = **keep out**, ban, bar, boycott, disallow, forbid, prohibit, refuse, shut out OPPOSITE> **let in**. **2** = **leave out**, count out, eliminate, ignore, omit, pass over, reject, rule

excommunicate ⊕ *verb* exclude from membership and the sacraments of the Church. **excommunication** *noun*
excoriate *verb* **1** censure severely. **2** strip skin from. **excoriation** *noun*
excrement *noun* waste matter discharged from the body.
excrescence *noun* lump or growth on the surface of an animal or plant. **excrescent** *adjective*
excrete *verb* discharge (waste matter) from the body. **excretion** *noun* **excreta** [ik-**skree**-ta] *noun* excrement. **excretory** *adjective*
excruciating ⊕ *adjective* **1** agonizing. **2** hard to bear, e.g. *he spoke at excruciating length.* **excruciatingly** *adverb*
exculpate ⊕ *verb* free from blame or guilt.
excursion ⊕ *noun* short journey, esp. for pleasure.
excuse ⊕ *noun* **1** explanation offered to justify (a fault etc.). ◆ *verb* **2** put forward a reason or justification for (a fault etc.). **3** forgive (a person) or overlook (a fault etc.). **4** make allowances for. **5** exempt. **6** allow to leave. **excusable** *adjective*
ex-directory *adjective* not listed in a telephone directory by request.

execrable [eks-sik-rab-bl] *adjective* of very poor quality.
execute ⊕ *verb* **1** put (a condemned person) to death. **2** carry out or accomplish. **3** produce (a work of art). **4** render (a legal document) effective, as by signing. **execution** *noun*
executioner *noun* **executive** *noun* person or group in an administrative position.
executive ⊕ *noun* **1** person or group in an administrative position. **2** branch of government responsible for carrying out laws etc. ◆ *adjective* **3** having the function of carrying out plans, orders, laws, etc.
executor, executrix *noun* person appointed to perform the instructions of a will.
exegesis [eks-sij-**jee**-siss] *noun, pl* **-ses** [-seez] explanation of a text, esp. of the Bible.
exemplar ⊕ *noun* **1** person or thing to be copied, model. **2** example. **exemplary** *adjective* **1** being a good example. **2** serving as a warning.
exemplify ⊕ *verb* **-fying, -fied 1** show an example of. **2** be an example of. **exemplification** *noun*
exempt ⊕ *adjective* **1** not subject to an obligation etc. ◆ *verb* **2** release from an obligation etc. **exemption** *noun*

E

——————— THESAURUS ———————

out, set aside OPPOSITE include
exclusion *noun* **1** = **ban**, bar, boycott, disqualification, embargo, prohibition, veto **2** = **elimination**, omission, rejection
exclusive *adjective* **1, 2** = **sole**, absolute, complete, entire, full, total, undivided, whole OPPOSITE **shared. 3** = **select**, chic, cliquish, fashionable, posh (*inf, chiefly Brit*), restricted, snobbish, up-market OPPOSITE **unrestricted**
excommunicate *verb* = **expel**, anathematize, ban, banish, cast out, denounce, exclude, repudiate
excruciating *adjective* **1** = **agonizing**, harrowing, intense, piercing, severe, violent **2** = **unbearable**, insufferable
exculpate *verb* = **absolve**, acquit, clear, discharge, excuse, exonerate, pardon, vindicate
excursion *noun* = **trip**, day trip, expedition, jaunt, journey, outing, pleasure trip, ramble, tour
excusable *adjective* = **forgivable**, allowable, defensible, justifiable, pardonable, permissible, understandable, warrantable
excuse *noun* **1** = **justification**, apology, defence, explanation, grounds, mitigation, plea, reason, vindication OPPOSITE **accusation** ◆*verb* **2** = **justify**, apologize for, defend, explain, mitigate, vindicate OPPOSITE **blame. 3, 4**

= **forgive**, acquit, exculpate, exonerate, make allowances for, overlook, pardon, tolerate, turn a blind eye to **5** = **free**, absolve, discharge, exempt, let off, release, relieve, spare OPPOSITE convict
execute *verb* **1** = **put to death**, behead, electrocute, guillotine, hang, kill, shoot **2** = **carry out**, accomplish, administer, discharge, effect, enact, implement, perform, prosecute
execution *noun* **1** = **killing**, capital punishment, hanging **2** = **carrying out**, accomplishment, administration, enactment, enforcement, implementation, operation, performance, prosecution
executioner *noun* = **killer**, assassin, exterminator, hangman, hit man (*sl*), liquidator, murderer, slayer
executive *noun* **1** = **administrator**, director, manager, official **2** = **administration**, directorate, directors, government, hierarchy, leadership, management ◆*adjective* **3** = **administrative**, controlling, decision-making, directing, governing, managerial
exemplary *adjective* **1** = **ideal**, admirable, commendable, excellent, fine, good, model, praiseworthy **2** = **warning**, cautionary
exemplify *verb* = **show**, demonstrate, display, embody, exhibit, illustrate, represent, serve as

exequies [eks-sik-wiz] *plural noun* funeral rites.

exercise ❶ *noun* **1** activity to train the body or mind. **2** set of movements or tasks designed to improve or test a person's ability. **3** performance of a function. ♦ *verb* **4** make use of, e.g. *to exercise one's rights*. **5** take exercise or perform exercises.

exert ❶ *verb* use (influence, authority, etc.) forcefully or effectively. **exert oneself** make a special effort. **exertion** *noun*

exeunt [eks-see-unt] *Latin* they go out: used as a stage direction.

exfoliate *verb* peel in scales or layers.

ex gratia [eks gray-sha] *adjective* given as a favour where no legal obligation exists.

exhale *verb* breathe out. **exhalation** *noun*

exhaust ❶ *verb* **1** tire out. **2** use up. **3** discuss (a subject) thoroughly. ♦ *noun* **4** gases ejected from an engine as waste products. **5** pipe through which an engine's exhaust fumes pass. **exhaustible** *adjective* **exhaustion** *noun* **1** extreme tiredness. **2** exhausting. **exhaustive** *adjective* comprehensive. **exhaustively** *adverb*

exhibit ❶ *verb* **1** display to the public. **2** show (a quality or feeling). ♦ *noun* **3** object exhibited

to the public. **4** *Law* document or object produced in court as evidence. **exhibitor** *noun*

exhibition *noun* **1** public display of art, skills, etc. **2** exhibiting. **exhibitionism** *noun* **1** compulsive desire to draw attention to oneself. **2** compulsive desire to display one's genitals in public. **exhibitionist** *noun*

exhilarate *verb* make lively and cheerful. **exhilaration** *noun*

SPELLING TIP

It may surprise you that it's the vowels, not the consonants, that are a problem when people try to spell **exhilarate** or **exhilaration**. They often make the mistake of writing an *e* instead of an *a* in the middle.

---

exhort ❶ *verb* urge earnestly. **exhortation** *noun*

exhume ❶ [ig-**zyume**] *verb* dig up (something buried, esp. a corpse). **exhumation** *noun*

exigency ❶ *noun, pl* **-cies** urgent demand or need. **exigent** *adjective*

——————— THESAURUS ———————

an example of

exempt *adjective* **1** =**immune**, excepted, excused, free, not liable, released, spared OPPOSITE liable ♦ *verb* **2** =**grant immunity**, absolve, discharge, excuse, free, let off, release, relieve, spare

exemption *noun* =**immunity**, absolution, discharge, dispensation, exception, exoneration, freedom, release

exercise *noun* **1** =**exertion**, activity, effort, labour, toil, training, work, work-out **2** =**task**, drill, lesson, practice, problem **3** =**use**, application, discharge, fulfilment, implementation, practice, utilization ♦ *verb* **4** =**put to use**, apply, bring to bear, employ, exert, use, utilize **5** =**train**, practise, work out

exert *verb* =**use**, apply, bring to bear, employ, exercise, make use of, utilize, wield **exert oneself** =**make an effort**, apply oneself, do one's best, endeavour, labour, strain, strive, struggle, toil, work

exertion *noun* =**effort**, elbow grease (*facetious*), endeavour, exercise, industry, strain, struggle, toil

exhaust *verb* **1** =**tire out**, debilitate, drain, enervate, enfeeble, fatigue, sap, weaken, wear out **2** =**use up**, consume, deplete, dissipate, expend, run through, spend, squander, waste

exhausted *adjective* **1** =**worn out**, all in (*sl*),

debilitated, done in (*inf*), drained, fatigued, knackered (*sl*), spent, tired out OPPOSITE invigorated. **2** =**used up**, consumed, depleted, dissipated, expended, finished, spent, squandered, wasted OPPOSITE replenished

exhausting *adjective* **1** =**tiring**, backbreaking, debilitating, gruelling, laborious, punishing, sapping, strenuous, taxing

exhaustion *noun* **1** =**tiredness**, debilitation, fatigue, weariness **2** =**depletion**, consumption, emptying, using up

exhaustive *adjective* =**thorough**, all-embracing, complete, comprehensive, extensive, full-scale, in-depth, intensive OPPOSITE superficial

exhibit *verb* **1** =**display**, parade, put on view, show **2** =**show**, demonstrate, express, indicate, manifest, reveal

exhibition *noun* **1** =**display**, demonstration, exposition, performance, presentation, representation, show, spectacle

exhilarating *adjective* =**exciting**, breathtaking, enlivening, invigorating, stimulating, thrilling

exhort *verb* =**urge**, advise, beseech, call upon, entreat, persuade, press, spur

exhume *verb* =**dig up**, disentomb, disinter, unearth OPPOSITE bury

exigency *noun* =**need**, constraint, demand,

exiguous *adjective* scanty or meagre.
exile ❶ *noun* **1** prolonged, usu. enforced, absence from one's country. **2** person banished or living away from his or her country. ◆ *verb* **3** expel from one's country.
exist ❶ *verb* **1** have being or reality. **2** eke out a living. **3** live. **existence** *noun* **existent** *adjective*

SPELLING TIP

People often write *-ance* at the end of a word when it should be *-ence*. The Bank of English shows this is the case for *existance* which occurs 43 times. However, the correct spelling **existence** is over 350 times commoner.

---

existential *adjective* of or relating to existence, esp. human existence.
existentialism *noun* philosophical movement stressing the personal experience and responsibility of the individual, who is seen as a free agent. **existentialist** *adjective, noun*
exit ❶ *noun* **1** way out. **2** going out. **3** actor's going off stage. ◆ *verb* **4** go out. **5** go offstage: used as a stage direction.

exocrine *adjective* relating to a gland, such as the sweat gland, that secretes externally through a duct.
exodus ❶ [eks-so-duss] *noun* departure of a large number of people.
ex officio [eks off-**fish**-ee-oh] *adverb, adjective Latin* by right of position or office.
exonerate ❶ *verb* free from blame or a criminal charge. **exoneration** *noun*
exorbitant ❶ *adjective* (of prices, demands, etc.) excessive, immoderate. **exorbitantly** *adverb*
exorcize ❶ *verb* expel (evil spirits) by prayers and religious rites. **exorcism** *noun* **exorcist** *noun*
exotic ❶ *adjective* **1** having a strange allure or beauty. **2** originating in a foreign country. ◆ *noun* **3** non-native plant. **exotically** *adverb*
exotica *plural noun* (collection of) exotic objects.
expand ❶ *verb* **1** make or become larger. **2** spread out. **3** (foll. by *on*) enlarge (on). **4** become more relaxed, friendly, and talkative.
expansion *noun* **expansionism** *noun* policy of expanding the economy or territory of a country. **expansionist** *adjective* **expanse** *noun* uninterrupted wide area. **expansive** *adjective* **1** wide or extensive. **2** friendly and talkative.
expatiate [iks-**pay**-shee-ate] *verb* (foll. by *on*)

E

———————————— T H E S A U R U S ————————————

necessity, requirement
exile *noun* **1** = **banishment**, deportation, expatriation, expulsion **2** = **expatriate**, deportee, émigré, outcast, refugee ◆*verb* **3** = **banish**, deport, drive out, eject, expatriate, expel
exist *verb* **1** = **be**, be present, occur **2** = **survive**, eke out a living, get along *or* by, keep one's head above water, stay alive, subsist **3** = **live**, endure
existence *noun* **1** = **being**, actuality **2** = **subsistence**, survival **3** = **life**
existent *adjective* **1** = **in existence**, existing, extant, present, standing **2** = **surviving 3** = **alive**, living
exit *noun* **1** = **way out**, door, gate, outlet OPPOSITE **entry**. **2** = **departure**, exodus, farewell, going, goodbye, leave-taking, retreat, withdrawal ◆*verb* **4** = **depart**, go away, go out, leave, make tracks, retire, retreat, take one's leave, withdraw OPPOSITE **enter**. **4** = **go offstage** (*Theatre*)
exodus *noun* = **departure**, evacuation, exit, flight, going out, leaving, migration, retreat, withdrawal
exonerate *verb* = **clear**, absolve, acquit,

discharge, exculpate, excuse, justify, pardon, vindicate
exorbitant *adjective* = **excessive**, extortionate, extravagant, immoderate, inordinate, outrageous, preposterous, unreasonable OPPOSITE **reasonable**
exorcize *verb* = **drive out**, cast out, deliver (from), expel, purify
exotic *adjective* **1** = **unusual**, colourful, fascinating, glamorous, mysterious, strange, striking, unfamiliar OPPOSITE **ordinary**. **2** = **foreign**, alien, external, imported, naturalized
expand *verb* **1** = **increase**, amplify, broaden, develop, enlarge, extend, grow, magnify, swell, widen OPPOSITE **reduce**. **2** = **spread (out)**, diffuse, stretch (out), unfold, unfurl, unravel, unroll **3** (foll. by *on*) = **go into detail about**, amplify, develop, elaborate on, embellish, enlarge on, expatiate on, expound on, flesh out
expanse *noun* = **area**, breadth, extent, range, space, stretch, sweep, tract
expansion *noun* **1** = **increase**, amplification, development, enlargement, growth, magnification **2** = **spread**, opening out
expansive *adjective* **1** = **wide**, broad, extensive, far-reaching, voluminous, wide-

speak or write at great length (on).
expatiation *noun*
expatriate ⊕ [eks-**pat**-ree-it] *adjective* **1** living outside one's native country. ✦ *noun* **2** person living outside his or her native country.
expatriation *noun*
expect ⊕ *verb* **1** regard as probable. **2** look forward to, await. **3** require as an obligation.
expectancy *noun* **1** something expected on the basis of an average, e.g. *life expectancy*. **2** feeling of anticipation. **expectant** *adjective* **1** expecting or hopeful. **2** pregnant. **expectantly** *adverb* **expectation** *noun* **1** act or state of expecting. **2** something looked forward to. **3** attitude of anticipation or hope.
expectorate *verb* spit out (phlegm etc.).
expectoration *noun* **expectorant** *noun* medicine that helps to bring up phlegm from the respiratory passages.
expedient ⊕ [iks-**pee**-dee-ent] *noun* **1** something that achieves a particular purpose. ✦ *adjective* **2** suitable to the circumstances, appropriate. **expediency** *noun*
expedite ⊕ *verb* hasten the progress of.
expedition *noun* **1** organized journey, esp. for exploration. **2** people and equipment comprising an expedition. **3** pleasure trip or excursion. **expeditionary** *adjective* relating to an expedition, esp. a military one. **expeditious** *adjective* done quickly and efficiently.
expel ⊕ *verb* **-pelling, -pelled** **1** drive out with force. **2** dismiss from a school etc. permanently. **expulsion** *noun*
expend ⊕ *verb* spend, use up. **expendable** *adjective* able to be sacrificed to achieve an objective. **expenditure** *noun* **1** something expended, esp. money. **2** amount expended. **expense** *noun* **1** cost. **2** (cause of) spending. ✦ *plural* **3** charges, outlay incurred. **expense account** arrangement by which an employee's expenses are refunded by the employer. **expensive** *adjective* high-priced.
experience ⊕ *noun* **1** direct personal participation. **2** particular incident, feeling, etc. that a person has undergone. **3** accumulated knowledge. ✦ *verb* **4** participate in. **5** be affected by (an emotion). **experienced** *adjective* skilful from extensive participation.
experiment ⊕ *noun* **1** test to provide evidence to prove or disprove a theory. **2**

──────── T H E S A U R U S ────────

ranging, widespread **2** = **talkative**, affable, communicative, effusive, friendly, loquacious, open, outgoing, sociable, unreserved
expatriate *adjective* **1** = **exiled**, banished, emigrant, émigré ✦*noun* **2** = **exile**, emigrant, émigré, refugee
expect *verb* **1** = **think**, assume, believe, imagine, presume, reckon, suppose, surmise, trust **2** = **look forward to**, anticipate, await, contemplate, envisage, hope for, predict, watch for **3** = **require**, call for, demand, insist on, want
expectant *adjective* **1** = **expecting**, anticipating, apprehensive, eager, hopeful, in suspense, ready, watchful **2** = **pregnant**, expecting (*inf*), gravid
expectation *noun* **2** = **probability**, assumption, belief, conjecture, forecast, likelihood, presumption, supposition **3** = **anticipation**, apprehension, expectancy, hope, promise, suspense
expediency *noun* = **suitability**, advisability, benefit, convenience, pragmatism, profitability, prudence, usefulness, utility
expedient *noun* **1** = **means**, contrivance, device, makeshift, measure, method, resort, scheme, stopgap ✦*adjective* **2** = **advantageous**, appropriate, beneficial, convenient, effective, helpful, opportune, practical, suitable, useful OPPOSITE **ineffective**
expedition *noun* **1** = **journey**, excursion, mission, quest, safari, tour, trek, voyage
expel *verb* **1** = **drive out**, belch, cast out, discharge, eject, remove, spew **2** = **dismiss**, ban, banish, drum out, evict, exclude, exile, throw out, turf out (*inf*) OPPOSITE **let in**
expend *verb* = **spend**, consume, dissipate, exhaust, go through, pay out, use (up)
expendable *adjective* = **dispensable**, inessential, nonessential, replaceable, unimportant, unnecessary OPPOSITE **indispensable**
expenditure *noun* = **spending**, consumption, cost, expense, outgoings, outlay, output, payment
expense *noun* **1** = **cost**, charge, expenditure, loss, outlay, payment, spending
expensive *adjective* = **dear**, costly, exorbitant, extravagant, high-priced, lavish, overpriced, steep (*inf*), stiff OPPOSITE **cheap**
experience *noun* **1** = **participation**, contact, exposure, familiarity, involvement **2** = **event**, adventure, affair, encounter, episode, happening, incident, occurrence **3** = **knowledge**, practice, training ✦*verb* **4** = **undergo**, encounter, endure, face, feel, go through, live through, sample, taste
experienced *adjective* = **knowledgeable**, accomplished, expert, practised, seasoned, tested, tried, veteran, well-versed OPPOSITE

attempt at something new. ♦ *verb* **3** carry out an experiment. **experimental** *adjective* **experimentally** *adverb* **experimentation** *noun*
expert ⊙ *noun* **1** person with extensive skill or knowledge in a particular field. ♦ *adjective* **2** skilful or knowledgeable. **expertise** [eks-per-**teez**] *noun* special skill or knowledge. **expertly** *adverb*
expiate *verb* make amends for. **expiation** *noun*
expire ⊙ *verb* **1** finish or run out. **2** breathe out. **3** *Lit* die. **expiration** *noun* **expiry** *noun* end, esp. of a contract period.
explain ⊙ *verb* **1** make clear and intelligible. **2** account for. **explanation** *noun* **explanatory** *adjective*
expletive [iks-**plee**-tiv] *noun* swearword.
explicable *adjective* able to be explained.
explicate *verb* *Formal* explain. **explication** *noun*
explicit ⊙ *adjective* **1** precisely and clearly expressed. **2** shown in realistic detail. **explicitly** *adverb*

explode ⊙ *verb* **1** burst with great violence, blow up. **2** react suddenly with emotion. **3** increase rapidly. **4** show (a theory etc.) to be baseless. **explosion** *noun* **explosive** *adjective* **1** tending to explode. ♦ *noun* **2** substance that causes explosions.
exploit ⊙ *verb* **1** take advantage of for one's own purposes. **2** make the best use of. ♦ *noun* **3** notable feat or deed. **exploitation** *noun* **exploiter** *noun*
explore ⊙ *verb* **1** investigate. **2** travel into (unfamiliar regions), esp. for scientific purposes. **exploration** *noun* **exploratory** *adjective* **explorer** *noun*
expo *noun, pl* **expos** *Informal* exposition, large public exhibition.
exponent ⊙ *noun* **1** person who advocates an idea, cause, etc. **2** skilful performer, esp. a musician.
exponential *adjective* *Informal* very rapid. **exponentially** *adverb*
export *noun* **1** selling or shipping of goods to a foreign country. **2** product shipped or sold to

E

——————— T H E S A U R U S ———————

inexperienced
experiment *noun* **1** = **test**, examination, experimentation, investigation, procedure, proof, research **2** = **trial**, trial run ♦*verb* **3** = **test**, examine, investigate, put to the test, research, sample, try, verify
experimental *adjective* = **test**, exploratory, pilot, preliminary, probationary, provisional, speculative, tentative, trial, trial-and-error
expert *noun* **1** = **master**, authority, connoisseur, dab hand (*Brit inf*), fundi (*S Afr*), guru, mana (*NZ*), past master, professional, specialist, virtuoso OPPOSITE amateur ♦*adjective* **2** = **skilful**, adept, adroit, experienced, masterly, practised, professional, proficient, qualified, virtuoso OPPOSITE unskilled
expertise *noun* = **skill**, adroitness, command, facility, judgment, know-how (*inf*), knowledge, mastery, proficiency
expire *verb* **1** = **finish**, cease, close, come to an end, conclude, end, lapse, run out, stop, terminate **2** = **breathe out**, emit, exhale, expel **3** *Lit* = **die**, cark *Aust & NZ sl* depart, kick the bucket (*inf*), pass away *or* on, perish
explain *verb* **1** = **make clear** *or* **plain**, clarify, clear up, define, describe, elucidate, expound, resolve, teach **2** = **account for**, excuse, give a reason for, justify
explanation *noun* **1** = **description**, clarification, definition, elucidation, illustration, interpretation **2** = **reason**, account, answer, excuse, justification, motive, vindication

explanatory *adjective* **1** = **descriptive**, illustrative, interpretive
explicit *adjective* **1** = **clear**, categorical, definite, frank, precise, specific, straightforward, unambiguous OPPOSITE vague
explode *verb* **1** = **blow up**, burst, detonate, discharge, erupt, go off, set off, shatter **4** = **disprove**, debunk, discredit, give the lie to, invalidate, refute, repudiate
exploit *verb* **1** = **take advantage of**, abuse, manipulate, milk, misuse, play on *or* upon **2** = **make the best use of**, capitalize on, cash in on (*inf*), profit by *or* from, use, utilize ♦*noun* **3** = **feat**, accomplishment, achievement, adventure, attainment, deed, escapade, stunt
exploitation *noun* **1** = **misuse**, abuse, manipulation, using
exploration *noun* **1** = **investigation**, analysis, examination, fossick (*Aust & NZ*), inquiry, inspection, research, scrutiny, search **2** = **expedition**, reconnaissance, survey, tour, travel, trip
explore *verb* **1** = **investigate**, examine, fossick (*Aust & NZ*), inquire into, inspect, look into, probe, research, search **2** = **travel**, reconnoitre, scout, survey, tour
explosion *noun* **1** = **bang**, blast, burst, clap, crack, detonation, discharge, report **2** = **outburst**, eruption, fit, outbreak
explosive *adjective* **1** = **unstable**, volatile
exponent *noun* **1** = **advocate**, backer, champion, defender, promoter, proponent,

a foreign country. ♦ *verb* **3** sell or ship (goods) to a foreign country. **exporter** *noun*

expose ⊕ *verb* **1** uncover or reveal. **2** make vulnerable, leave unprotected. **3** subject (a photographic film) to light. **expose oneself** display one's sexual organs in public. **exposure** *noun* **1** exposing. **2** lack of shelter from the weather, esp. the cold. **3** appearance before the public, as on television. **4** *Photog* act of exposing film or plates to light. **5** *Photog* intensity of light falling on a film or plate multiplied by the time of the exposure.

exposé [iks-**pose**-ay] *noun* bringing of a crime, scandal, etc. to public notice.

exposition *noun* see EXPOUND.

expostulate *verb* (foll. by *with*) reason (with), esp. to dissuade. **expostulation** *noun*

expound ⊕ *verb* explain in detail. **exposition** *noun* **1** explanation. **2** large public exhibition.

express ⊕ *verb* **1** put into words. **2** show (an emotion). **3** indicate by a symbol or formula. **4** squeeze out (juice etc.). ♦ *adjective* **5** explicitly stated. **6** (of a purpose) particular. **7** of or for rapid transportation of people, mail, etc. ♦ *noun* **8** fast train or bus stopping at only a few stations. ♦ *adverb* **9** by express delivery.

expression *noun* **1** expressing. **2** word or phrase. **3** showing or communication of emotion. **4** look on the face that indicates mood. **5** *Maths* variable, function, or some combination of these. **expressionless** *adjective* **expressive** *adjective* **expressiveness** *noun* **expressionism** *noun* early 20th-century artistic movement which sought to express emotions rather than represent the physical

world. **expressionist** *noun, adjective*

expropriate *verb* deprive an owner of (property). **expropriation** *noun*

expulsion ⊕ *noun* see EXPEL.

expunge [iks-**sponge**] *verb* delete, erase, blot out.

expurgate [**eks**-per-gate] *verb* remove objectionable parts from (a book etc.).

exquisite ⊕ *adjective* **1** of extreme beauty or delicacy. **2** sensitive or discriminating, e.g. *exquisite manners*. **3** intense in feeling. **exquisitely** *adverb*

ex-serviceman *noun* man who has served in the armed forces.

extant *adjective* still existing.

extemporize *verb* speak, perform, or compose without preparation.

extend ⊕ *verb* **1** draw out or be drawn out, stretch. **2** last for a certain time. **3** (foll. by *to*) include. **4** increase in size or scope. **5** offer, e.g. *extend one's sympathy*. **extendable** *adjective* **extension** *noun* **1** room or rooms added to an existing building. **2** additional telephone connected to the same line as another. **3** extending. **extensive** *adjective* having a large extent, widespread. **extensor** *noun* muscle that extends a part of the body. **extent** *noun* range over which something extends, area.

SPELLING TIP

Lots of nouns in English end with *-tion*, but **extension** is not one of them.

———— T H E S A U R U S ————

supporter, upholder **2** = **performer**, player

expose *verb* **1** = **uncover**, display, exhibit, present, reveal, show, unveil OPPOSITE hide. **2** = **make vulnerable**, endanger, imperil, jeopardize, lay open, leave open, subject

exposed *adjective* **1** = **unconcealed**, bare, on display, on show, on view, revealed, uncovered **2** = **vulnerable**, in peril, laid bare, open, susceptible, unprotected, unsheltered, wide open

exposure *noun* **1** = **publicity**, display, exhibition, presentation, revelation, showing, uncovering, unveiling

expound *verb* = **explain**, describe, elucidate, interpret, set forth, spell out, unfold

express *verb* **1** = **state**, articulate, communicate, declare, phrase, put into words, say, utter, voice, word **2** = **show**, convey, exhibit, intimate, make known, reveal **3** = **represent**, indicate, signify, stand for,

symbolize ♦ *adjective* **5** = **explicit**, categorical, clear, definite, distinct, plain, unambiguous **6** = **specific**, clear-cut, especial, particular, singular, special **7** = **fast**, direct, high-speed, nonstop, rapid, speedy, swift

expression *noun* **1** = **statement**, announcement, communication, declaration, utterance **2** = **phrase**, idiom, locution, remark, term, turn of phrase, word **3** = **indication**, demonstration, exhibition, manifestation, representation, show, sign, symbol, token **4** = **look**, air, appearance, aspect, countenance, face

expressive *adjective* **2** = **vivid**, eloquent, moving, poignant, striking, telling OPPOSITE impassive

exquisite *adjective* **1** = **beautiful**, attractive, comely, dainty, delicate, elegant, fine, lovely, pleasing OPPOSITE ugly. **3** = **intense**, acute, keen, sharp

extenuate ⊕ *verb* make (an offence or fault) less blameworthy. **extenuating** *adjective* **extenuation** *noun*

exterior ⊕ *noun* **1** part or surface on the outside. **2** outward appearance. ◆ *adjective* **3** of, on, or coming from the outside.

exterminate ⊕ *verb* destroy (animals or people) completely. **extermination** *noun* **exterminator** *noun*

external ⊕ *adjective* of, situated on, or coming from the outside. **externally** *adverb* **externalize** *verb* express (feelings) in words or actions.

extinct ⊕ *adjective* **1** having died out. **2** (of a volcano) no longer liable to erupt. **extinction** *noun*

extinguish ⊕ *verb* **1** put out (a fire or light). **2** remove or destroy entirely. **extinguisher** *noun*

extirpate [eks-ter-pate] *verb* destroy utterly.

extol ⊕ *verb* **-tolling, -tolled** praise highly.

extort ⊕ *verb* get (something) by force or threats. **extortion** *noun* **extortionate** *adjective* (of prices) excessive.

extra ⊕ *adjective* **1** more than is usual, expected or needed. ◆ *noun* **2** additional person or thing. **3** something for which an additional charge is made. **4** *Films* actor hired for crowd scenes. **5** *Cricket* run not scored off the bat. ◆ *adverb* **6** unusually or exceptionally.

extra- *prefix* outside or beyond an area or scope, e.g. *extrasensory; extraterritorial.*

extract ⊕ *verb* **1** pull out by force. **2** remove. **3** derive. **4** copy out (an article, passage, etc.) from a publication. ◆ *noun* **5** something extracted, such as a passage from a book etc. **6** preparation containing the concentrated essence of a substance, e.g. *beef extract.*

extraction *noun* **extractor** *noun* **extractor fan** device for removing stale air or fumes from a room.

extracurricular *adjective* taking place outside the normal school timetable.

extradite *verb* send (an accused person) back to his or her own country for trial. **extradition** *noun*

extramural *adjective* connected with but outside the normal courses of a university or college.

E

——————————— THESAURUS ———————————

extend *verb* **1** = **make longer**, drag out, draw out, lengthen, prolong, spin out, spread out, stretch OPPOSITE cut. **2** = **last**, carry on, continue, go on **4** = **widen**, add to, augment, broaden, enhance, enlarge, expand, increase, supplement OPPOSITE reduce. **5** = **offer**, confer, impart, present, proffer OPPOSITE withdraw

extension *noun* **1** = **annexe**, addition, appendage, appendix, supplement **3** = **lengthening**, broadening, development, enlargement, expansion, increase, spread, widening

extensive *adjective* = **wide**, broad, far-flung, far-reaching, large-scale, pervasive, spacious, vast, voluminous, widespread OPPOSITE limited

extent *noun* = **size**, amount, area, breadth, expanse, length, stretch, volume, width

extenuating *adjective* = **mitigating**, justifying, moderating, qualifying

exterior *noun* **1** = **outside**, coating, covering, facade, face, shell, skin, surface OPPOSITE inside ◆*adjective* **3** = **outside**, external, outer, outermost, outward, surface OPPOSITE inside

exterminate *verb* = **destroy**, abolish, annihilate, eliminate, eradicate

external *adjective* = **outer**, exterior, outermost, outside, outward, surface OPPOSITE internal

extinct *adjective* **1** = **dead**, defunct, gone, lost, vanished OPPOSITE living

extinction *noun* **1** = **dying out**, abolition, annihilation, destruction, eradication, extermination, obliteration, oblivion

extinguish *verb* **1** = **put out**, blow out, douse, quench, smother, snuff out, stifle **2** = **destroy**, annihilate, eliminate, end, eradicate, exterminate, remove, wipe out

extol *verb* = **praise**, acclaim, commend, eulogize, exalt, glorify, sing the praises of

extort *verb* = **force**, blackmail, bully, coerce, extract, squeeze

extortionate *adjective* = **exorbitant**, excessive, extravagant, inflated, outrageous, preposterous, sky-high, unreasonable OPPOSITE reasonable

extra *adjective* **1 a** = **additional**, added, ancillary, auxiliary, further, more, supplementary OPPOSITE vital. **b** = **surplus**, excess, leftover, redundant, spare, superfluous, unused ◆*noun* **2** = **addition**, accessory, attachment, bonus, extension, supplement OPPOSITE essential ◆*adverb* **6** = **exceptionally**, especially, extraordinarily, extremely, particularly, remarkably, uncommonly, unusually

extract *verb* **1** = **pull out**, draw, pluck out, pull, remove, take out, uproot, withdraw **3** = **derive**, draw, elicit, glean, obtain ◆*noun* **5** = **passage**, citation, clipping, cutting, excerpt, quotation, selection **6** = **essence**, concentrate, distillation, juice

E

extraneous ❶ [iks-**train**-ee-uss] *adjective* irrelevant.

extraordinary ❶ *adjective* **1** very unusual. **2** (of a meeting) specially arranged to deal with a particular subject. **extraordinarily** *adverb*

extrapolate [iks-**trap**-a-late] *verb* **1** infer (something not known) from the known facts. **2** *Maths* estimate (a value of a function or measurement) beyond the known values by the extension of a curve. **extrapolation** *noun*

extrasensory *adjective* **extrasensory perception** supposed ability to obtain information other than through the normal senses.

extraterrestrial *adjective* of or from outside the earth's atmosphere.

extravagant ❶ *adjective* **1** spending money excessively. **2** going beyond reasonable limits. **extravagance** *noun* **extravaganza** *noun* elaborate and lavish entertainment, display, etc.

SPELLING TIP

Make sure that **extravagant** ends in -*ant*, even though -*ent* sounds like a possibility.

---

extreme ❶ *adjective* **1** of a high or the highest degree or intensity. **2** severe. **3** immoderate. **4** farthest or outermost. ♦ *noun* **5** either of the two limits of a scale or range. **extremely** *adverb* **extremism** *noun* behaviour or beliefs that are immoderate. **extremist** *noun* **1** person who favours immoderate methods. ♦ *adjective* **2** holding extreme opinions. **extremity** *noun, pl* -**ties 1** farthest point. **2** extreme condition, as of misfortune. ♦ *plural* **3** hands and feet.

extreme sport sport with a high risk of injury or death.

extricate ❶ *verb* free from complication or difficulty. **extrication** *noun*

extrinsic *adjective* not contained or included within. **extrinsically** *adverb*

extrovert ❶ *adjective* **1** lively and outgoing. **2** concerned more with external reality than inner feelings. ♦ *noun* **3** extrovert person.

extroversion *noun*

extrude *verb* squeeze or force out. **extrusion** *noun*

exuberant ❶ *adjective* **1** high-spirited. **2** growing luxuriantly. **exuberance** *noun* **exuberantly** *adverb*

exude *verb* **1** (of a liquid or smell) seep or flow out slowly and steadily. **2** make apparent by mood or behaviour, e.g. *exude confidence.*

exult ❶ *verb* be joyful or jubilant. **exultation** *noun* **exultant** *adjective*

eye ❶ *noun* **1** organ of sight. **2** external part of an eye. **3** (often pl) ability to see. **4** attention, e.g. *his new shirt caught my eye.* **5** ability to judge or appreciate, e.g. *a good eye for detail.* **6** one end of a sewing needle. **7** small area of calm at the centre of a hurricane. **8** dark spot on a potato from which a stem grows. ♦ *verb* **eyeing** *or* **eying, eyed 9** look at carefully or warily. **eyeless** *adjective* **eyelet** *noun* **1** small hole for a lace or cord to be passed through. **2**

————————— THESAURUS —————————

extraneous *adjective* =**irrelevant**, beside the point, immaterial, inappropriate, off the subject, unconnected, unrelated

extraordinary *adjective* **1** =**unusual**, amazing, exceptional, fantastic, outstanding, phenomenal, remarkable, strange, uncommon OPPOSITE **ordinary**

extravagant *adjective* **1** =**wasteful**, lavish, prodigal, profligate, spendthrift OPPOSITE **economical**. **2** =**excessive**, outrageous, over the top (*sl*), preposterous, reckless, unreasonable OPPOSITE **conservative**

extreme *adjective* **1** =**maximum**, acute, great, highest, intense, severe, supreme, ultimate, utmost OPPOSITE **mild**. **2** =**severe**, drastic, harsh, radical, rigid, strict, uncompromising **3** =**excessive**, fanatical, immoderate, radical OPPOSITE **moderate**. **4** =**farthest**, far-off, most distant, outermost, remotest OPPOSITE **nearest** ♦*noun* **5** =**limit**, boundary, edge, end, extremity, pole

extremely *adverb* **1** =**very**, awfully (*inf*), exceedingly, exceptionally, extraordinarily, severely, terribly, uncommonly, unusually

extremist *noun* **1** =**fanatic**, die-hard, radical, zealot

extremity *noun* **1** =**limit**, border, boundary, edge, extreme, frontier, pinnacle, tip **2** =**crisis**, adversity, dire straits, disaster, emergency, exigency, trouble ♦*plural* **3** =**hands and feet**, fingers and toes, limbs

extricate *verb* =**free**, disengage, disentangle, get out, release, remove, rescue, wriggle out of

extrovert *adjective* **1** =**outgoing**, exuberant, gregarious, sociable OPPOSITE **introverted**

exuberant *adjective* **1** =**high-spirited**, animated, cheerful, ebullient, energetic, enthusiastic, lively, spirited, vivacious OPPOSITE **subdued**. **2** =**luxuriant**, abundant, copious, lavish, plentiful, profuse

exult *verb* =**be joyful**, be overjoyed, celebrate, jump for joy, rejoice ring that strengthens this. **eyeball** *noun* ball-shaped part of the eye. **eyebrow** *noun* line of hair on the bony ridge above the eye. **eye-catching** *adjective* attracting attention. **eyeful** *noun Informal* **1** view. **2** attractive sight, esp. a woman. **eyeglass** *noun* lens for aiding defective vision. **eyelash** *noun* short hair that grows out from the eyelid. **eyelid** *noun* fold of skin that covers the eye when it is closed. **eyeliner** *noun* cosmetic used to outline the eyes. **eye-opener** *noun Informal* something startling or revealing. **eye shadow** coloured cosmetic worn on the upper eyelids. **eyesight** *noun* ability to see. **eyesore** *noun* ugly object. **eyetooth** *noun* canine tooth. **eyewash** *noun Informal* nonsense. **eyewitness** *noun* person who was present at an event and can describe what happened.

eyrie *noun* **1** nest of an eagle. **2** high isolated place.

———————————————— THESAURUS ————————————————

eye *noun* **1** = **eyeball**, optic (*inf*) **5** = **appreciation**, discernment, discrimination, judgment, perception, recognition, taste ◆*verb* **9** = **look at**, check out (*inf*), contemplate, inspect, study, survey, view, watch

eyesight *noun* = **vision**, perception, sight
eyesore *noun* = **mess**, blemish, blot, disfigurement, horror, monstrosity, sight (*inf*)
eyewitness *noun* = **observer**, bystander, onlooker, passer-by, spectator, viewer, witness

Ff

f *Music* forte.

F 1 Fahrenheit. **2** farad. **3** *Chem* fluorine. **4** franc(s).

f. and the following (page).

fa *noun* same as FAH.

FA Football Association.

fable ⊕ *noun* **1** story with a moral. **2** false or fictitious account. **3** legend. **fabled** *adjective* made famous in legend. **fabulous** *adjective* amazing.

fabric ⊕ *noun* **1** knitted or woven cloth. **2** framework or structure.

fabricate ⊕ *verb* **1** make up (a story or lie). **2** make or build. **fabrication** *noun*

fabulous ⊕ *adjective* **1** *Informal* excellent. **2** astounding. **3** told of in fables. **fabulously** *adverb*

facade [fas-**sahd**] *noun* **1** front of a building. **2** (false) outward appearance.

face ⊕ *noun* **1** front of the head. **2** facial expression. **3** distorted expression. **4** outward appearance. **5** front or main side. **6** dial of a clock. **7** exposed area of coal or ore in a mine. **8** dignity, self-respect. ◆ *verb* **9** look or turn towards. **10** be opposite. **11** be confronted by. **12** provide with a surface. **set one's face against** oppose determinedly. **faceless** *adjective* impersonal, anonymous. **face-lift** *noun* operation to tighten facial skin, to remove wrinkles. **face-saving** *adjective* maintaining dignity or self-respect. **face up to** *verb* accept (an unpleasant fact or reality). **face value** apparent worth or meaning.

facet ⊕ *noun* **1** aspect. **2** surface of a cut gem.

facetious ⊕ [fas-**see**-shuss] *adjective* funny or trying to be funny, esp. at inappropriate times. **facetiously** *adverb*

facia *noun, pl* **-ciae** same as FASCIA.

facial *adjective* **1** of the face. ◆ *noun* **2** beauty treatment for the face.

facile ⊕ [fas-**sile**] *adjective* **1** (of a remark, argument, etc.) superficial and showing lack of real thought. **2** easily performed or achieved.

facilitate ⊕ *verb* make easy. **facilitation** *noun*

THESAURUS

---

fable *noun* **1** = **story**, allegory, legend, myth, parable, tale **2, 3** = **fiction**, fabrication, fantasy, invention, tall story (*inf*), urban legend, urban myth, yarn (*inf*) OPPOSITE fact

fabric *noun* **1** = **cloth**, material, stuff, textile, web **2** = **framework**, constitution, construction, foundations, make-up, organization, structure

fabricate *verb* **1** = **make up**, concoct, devise, fake, falsify, feign, forge, invent, trump up **2** = **build**, assemble, construct, erect, form, make, manufacture, shape

fabrication *noun* **1** = **forgery**, concoction, fake, falsehood, fiction, invention, lie, myth **2** = **construction**, assembly, building, erection, manufacture, production

fabulous *adjective* **1** *Inf* = **wonderful**, brilliant, fantastic (*inf*), marvellous, out-of-this-world (*inf*), sensational (*inf*), spectacular, superb OPPOSITE ordinary. **2** = **astounding**, amazing, breathtaking, inconceivable, incredible, phenomenal, unbelievable **3** = **legendary**, apocryphal, fantastic, fictitious, imaginary, invented, made-up, mythical, unreal

facade *noun* = **appearance**, exterior, face, front, guise, mask, pretence, semblance, show

face *noun* **1** = **countenance**, features, mug (*sl*), visage **2** = **expression**, appearance, aspect, look **3** = **scowl**, frown, grimace, pout, smirk **4** = **side**, exterior, front, outside, surface **8** *as in* **save** *or* **lose face** = **self-respect**, authority, dignity, honour, image, prestige, reputation, standing, status ◆*verb* **10** = **look onto**, be opposite, front onto, overlook **11** = **confront**, brave, come up against, deal with, encounter, experience, meet, oppose, tackle **12** = **coat**, clad, cover, dress, finish

faceless *adjective* = **impersonal**, anonymous, remote

facet *noun* **1** = **aspect**, angle, face, part, phase, plane, side, slant **2** = **surface**

facetious *adjective* = **funny**, amusing, comical, droll, flippant, frivolous, humorous, jocular, playful, tongue in cheek

face up to *verb* = **accept**, acknowledge, come to terms with, confront, cope with, deal with, meet head-on, tackle

facile *adjective* **1** = **superficial**, cursory, glib, hasty, shallow, slick OPPOSITE difficult

F

facility ❂ *noun, pl* **-ties 1** skill. **2** easiness. ◆ *plural* **3** means or equipment for an activity.
facing *noun* **1** lining or covering for decoration or reinforcement. ◆ *plural* **2** contrasting collar and cuffs on a jacket.
facsimile ❂ [fak-**sim**-ill-ee] *noun* exact copy.
facsimile transmission same as FAX (sense 1).
fact ❂ *noun* **1** event or thing known to have happened or existed. **2** provable truth. **fact of life** inescapable, often unpleasant, truth. **facts of life** details of sex and reproduction. **factual** *adjective*
faction[1] ❂ *noun* **1** (dissenting) minority group within a larger body. **2** dissension. **factious** *adjective* of or producing factions.
faction[2] *noun* dramatized presentation of a factual event.
factitious *adjective* artificial.
factor ❂ *noun* **1** element contributing to a result. **2** *Maths* one of the integers multiplied together to give a given number. **3** level on a scale of measurement, e.g. *suntan oil with a factor of 5.* **4** *Scot* property manager. **factorial** *noun* product of all the integers from one to a given number. **factorize** *verb* calculate the factors of (a number).
factory ❂ *noun, pl* **-ries** building where goods are manufactured. **factory farm** farm on which animals are reared using modern industrial methods. **factory ship** ship that processes fish caught by a fleet.
factotum *noun* person employed to do all sorts of work.
faculty ❂ *noun, pl* **-ties 1** physical or mental ability. **2** department in a university or college.
fad ❂ *noun* **1** short-lived fashion. **2** whim.

faddy, faddish *adjective*
fade ❂ *verb* **1** (cause to) lose brightness, colour, or strength. **2** vanish slowly. **fade-in, -out** *noun* gradual increase or decrease, as of vision or sound in a film or broadcast.
faeces [**fee**-seez] *plural noun* waste matter discharged from the anus. **faecal** [**fee**-kl] *adjective*
faïence [**fie**-ence] *noun* tin-glazed earthenware.
faff *verb* (often foll. by *about*) *Brit informal* dither or fuss.
fag[1] *noun* **1** *Informal* boring task. **2** young public schoolboy who does menial chores for a senior boy. ◆ *verb* **3** do menial chores in a public school.
fag[2] *noun Slang* cigarette. **fag end 1** last and worst part. **2** *Slang* cigarette stub.
fag[3] *noun US offens* male homosexual.
faggot[1] *noun* **1** ball of chopped liver, herbs, and bread. **2** bundle of sticks for fuel.
faggot[2] *noun US & Aust offens* male homosexual.
fah *noun Music* (in tonic sol-fa) fourth degree of any major scale.
Fahrenheit [**far**-ren-hite] *adjective* of a temperature scale with the freezing point of water at 32° and the boiling point at 212°.
fail ❂ *verb* **1** be unsuccessful. **2** stop operating. **3** be or judge to be below the required standard in a test. **4** disappoint or be useless to (someone). **5** neglect or be unable to do (something). **6** go bankrupt. ◆ *noun* **7** instance of not passing an exam or test. **without fail 1** regularly. **2** definitely. **failing** *noun* **1** weak point. ◆ *preposition* **2** in the absence of.

——————— THESAURUS ———————

facilitate *verb* =**promote**, expedite, forward, further, help, make easy, pave the way for, speed up OPPOSITE **prevent**
facility *noun* **1, 2** =**ease**, ability, adroitness, dexterity, efficiency, effortlessness, fluency, proficiency, skill OPPOSITE **difficulty** ◆*plural* **3** =**equipment**, advantage, aid, amenity, appliance, convenience, means, opportunity, resource
facsimile *noun* =**copy**, carbon copy, duplicate, fax, photocopy, print, replica, reproduction, transcript
fact *noun* **1** =**event**, *fait accompli*, act, deed, happening, incident, occurrence, performance **2** =**truth**, certainty, reality OPPOSITE **fiction**
faction[1] *noun* **1** =**group**, bloc, cabal, clique, contingent, coterie, gang, party, set, splinter group **2** =**dissension**, conflict, disagreement, discord, disunity, division, infighting, rebellion

OPPOSITE **accord**
factor *noun* **1** =**element**, aspect, cause, component, consideration, influence, item, part
factory *noun* =**works**, mill, plant
factual *adjective* =**true**, authentic, correct, exact, genuine, precise, real, true-to-life OPPOSITE **fictitious**
faculty *noun* **1** =**ability**, aptitude, capacity, facility, power, propensity, skill **2** =**department**, school OPPOSITE **failing**
fad *noun* **1** =**craze**, fashion, mania, rage, trend, vogue **2** =**whim**
fade *verb* **1** =**pale**, bleach, discolour, lose colour, wash out **2** =**dwindle**, decline, die away, disappear, dissolve, melt away, vanish, wane
faded *adjective* **1** =**discoloured**, bleached, dull, indistinct, pale, washed out
fading *adjective* **2** =**declining**, decreasing,

F

failure noun **1** act or instance of failing. **2** unsuccessful person or thing. **fail-safe** adjective designed to return to a safe condition if something goes wrong.

fain adverb Obs gladly.

faint ❶ adjective **1** lacking clarity, brightness, or volume. **2** feeling dizzy or weak. **3** lacking conviction or force. ◆ verb **4** lose consciousness temporarily. ◆ noun **5** temporary loss of consciousness. **faint-hearted** adjective lacking courage and confidence.

fair¹ ❶ adjective **1** unbiased and reasonable. **2** in agreement with rules. **3** light in colour. **4** beautiful. **5** quite good, e.g. *a fair attempt.* **6** quite large, e.g. *a fair amount of money.* **7** (of weather) fine. ◆ adverb **8** fairly. **9** absolutely. **fairly** adverb **1** moderately. **2** to a great degree or extent. **3** as deserved, reasonably. **fairness** noun **fair copy** neat copy, without mistakes or alterations, of a piece of writing. **fair game** person regarded as a justifiable target for criticism or ridicule. **fair play** conventional standard of honourable behaviour. **fairway** noun Golf smooth area between the

tee and the green. **fair-weather** adjective unreliable in difficult situations, e.g. *a fair-weather friend.*

fair² ❶ noun **1** travelling entertainment with sideshows, rides, and amusements. **2** exhibition of commercial or industrial products.

fairground noun open space used for a fair.

fairing noun curved metal structure fitted round part of a car, aircraft, etc. to reduce drag.

Fair Isle noun intricate multicoloured knitted pattern.

fairy ❶ noun, pl **fairies 1** imaginary small creature with magic powers. **2** Offens male homosexual. **fairy godmother** person who helps in time of trouble. **fairyland** noun **fairy lights** small coloured electric bulbs used as decoration. **fairy penguin** small penguin with a bluish head and back, found on the Australian coast. **fairy ring** ring of dark grass caused by fungi. **fairy tale, story 1** story about fairies or magic. **2** unbelievable story or explanation.

fait accompli [fate ak-**kom**-plee] noun French something already done that cannot be altered.

—————— T H E S A U R U S ——————

disappearing, dying, on the decline, vanishing **fail** verb **1 = be unsuccessful**, bite the dust, break down, come to grief, come unstuck, fall, fizzle out (*inf*), flop (*inf*), founder, miscarry, misfire OPPOSITE **succeed. 2 = give out**, cark (*Aust & NZ sl*), conk out (*inf*), cut out, die, peter out, stop working **4, 5 = disappoint**, abandon, desert, forget, forsake, let down, neglect, omit **6 = go bankrupt**, become insolvent, close down, fold (*inf*), go broke (*inf*), go bust (*inf*), go into receivership, go out of business, go to the wall, go under **without fail 1 = regularly**, like clockwork, religiously **2 = dependably**, conscientiously, constantly, without exception **failing** noun **1 = weakness**, blemish, defect, deficiency, drawback, fault, flaw, imperfection, shortcoming OPPOSITE **strength** ◆preposition **2 = in the absence of**, in default of, lacking **failure** noun **1 a = lack of success**, breakdown, collapse, defeat, downfall, fiasco, miscarriage, overthrow OPPOSITE **success. b = bankruptcy**, crash, downfall, insolvency, liquidation, ruin OPPOSITE **prosperity. 2 = loser**, black sheep, dead duck (*sl*), disappointment, dud (*inf*), flop (*inf*), nonstarter, washout (*inf*)

faint adjective **1 = dim**, distant, faded, indistinct, low, muted, soft, subdued, vague OPPOSITE **clear. 2 = dizzy**, exhausted, giddy, light-headed, muzzy, weak, woozy (*inf*) OPPOSITE **energetic. 3 = slight**, feeble, remote, unenthusiastic, weak ◆verb **4 = pass out**, black

out, collapse, flake out (*inf*), keel over (*inf*), lose consciousness, swoon (*lit*) ◆noun **5 = blackout**, collapse, swoon (*lit*), unconsciousness **fair¹** adjective **1, 2 = unbiased**, above board, equitable, even-handed, honest, impartial, just, lawful, legitimate, proper, unprejudiced OPPOSITE **unfair. 3 = light**, blond, blonde, fair-haired, flaxen-haired, towheaded **4 = beautiful**, bonny, comely, handsome, lovely, pretty OPPOSITE **ugly. 5 = respectable**, adequate, average, decent, moderate, O.K. *or* okay (*inf*), passable, reasonable, satisfactory, tolerable **7 = fine**, bright, clear, cloudless, dry, sunny, unclouded

fair² noun **1 = carnival**, bazaar, festival, fete, gala, show

fairly adverb **1 = moderately**, adequately, pretty well, quite, rather, reasonably, somewhat, tolerably **2 = positively**, absolutely, really **3 = deservedly**, equitably, honestly, impartially, justly, objectively, properly, without fear or favour

fairness noun **= impartiality**, decency, disinterestedness, equitableness, equity, justice, legitimacy, rightfulness

fairy noun **1 = sprite**, brownie, elf, leprechaun, peri, pixie

fairy tale, story noun **1 = folk tale**, romance **2 = lie**, cock-and-bull story (*inf*), fabrication, fiction, invention, tall story, untruth, urban legend, urban myth

faith ❶ *noun* **1** strong belief, esp. without proof. **2** religion. **3** complete confidence or trust. **4** allegiance to a person or cause. **faithful** *adjective* **1** loyal. **2** maintaining sexual loyalty to one's lover or spouse. **4** accurate in detail. **faithfully** *adverb* **faithless** *adjective* disloyal or dishonest. **faith-healing** *noun* healing of bodily ailments by religious rather than medical means. **faith-healer** *noun*
fake ❶ *verb* **1** cause something not genuine to appear real or more valuable by fraud. **2** pretend to have (an illness, emotion, etc.). ◆ *noun* **3** person, thing, or act that is not genuine. ◆ *adjective* **4** not genuine.
fakir [**fay**-keer] *noun* **1** member of any Islamic religious order. **2** Hindu holy man.
falcon *noun* small bird of prey. **falconry** *noun* **1** art of training falcons. **2** sport of hunting with falcons. **falconer** *noun*
fall ❶ *verb* **falling, fell, fallen 1** drop from a higher to a lower place through the force of gravity. **2** collapse to the ground. **3** decrease in number or quality. **4** slope downwards. **5** die in battle. **6** be captured. **7** pass into a specified condition. **8** (of the face) take on a sad expression. **9** occur. **10** yield to temptation. ◆ *noun* **11** falling. **12** thing or amount that falls. **13** decrease in value or number. **14** decline in power or influence. **15** capture or overthrow. **16** *US* autumn. ◆ *plural* **17** waterfall. **fall flat** fail utterly. **fall behind** *verb* **1** fail to keep up. **2**

be in arrears with a payment etc. **fall for** *verb* **1** *Informal* fall in love with. **2** be deceived by (a lie or trick). **fall guy 1** *Informal* victim of a confidence trick. **2** scapegoat. **fall in** *verb* **1** collapse. **2** (of a soldier etc.) take his or her place in a formation. **fall in with** *verb* **1** meet with and join. **2** agree with or support a person or idea. **fallout** *noun* radioactive particles spread as a result of a nuclear explosion. **fall out** *verb* **1** *Informal* stop being friendly, disagree. **2** (of a soldier etc.) leave his or her place in a formation. **fall through** *verb* fail. **fall to** *verb* **1** (of a task or duty) become (someone's) responsibility. **2** begin some activity.
fallacy ❶ *noun, pl* **-cies 1** false belief. **2** unsound reasoning. **fallacious** *adjective*
fallen *verb* past participle of FALL.
fallible ❶ *adjective* (of a person) liable to make mistakes. **fallibility** *noun*
Fallopian tube *noun* either of a pair of tubes through which egg cells pass from the ovary to the womb.
fallow¹ ❶ *adjective* (of land) ploughed but left unseeded to regain fertility.
fallow² *adjective* light yellowish-brown. **fallow deer** reddish-brown deer with white spots in summer.
false ❶ *adjective* **1** not true or correct. **2** artificial, fake. **3** deceptive, e.g. *false promises*. **4** forced or insincere, e.g. *false cheer*. **falsely**

——————— THESAURUS ———————

faith *noun* **1, 3 = confidence**, assurance, conviction, credence, credit, dependence, reliance, trust OPPOSITE **doubt. 2 = religion**, belief, church, communion, creed, denomination, dogma, persuasion OPPOSITE **agnosticism. 4 = allegiance**, constancy, faithfulness, fidelity, loyalty
faithful *adjective* **1-3 = loyal**, constant, dependable, devoted, reliable, staunch, steadfast, true, trusty OPPOSITE **disloyal. 4 = accurate**, close, exact, precise, strict, true
faithless *adjective* **= disloyal**, false, fickle, inconstant, traitorous, treacherous, unfaithful, unreliable
fake *verb* **1 = counterfeit**, copy, fabricate, forge **2 = sham**, feign, pretend, put on, simulate ◆*noun* **3 = impostor**, charlatan, copy, forgery, fraud, hoax, imitation, reproduction, sham ◆*adjective* **4 = artificial**, counterfeit, false, forged, imitation, mock, phoney *or* phony (*inf*), sham OPPOSITE **real**
fall *verb* **1, 2 = descend**, cascade, collapse, dive, drop, plummet, plunge, sink, subside, tumble OPPOSITE **rise. 3 = decrease**, decline,

diminish, drop, dwindle, go down, lessen, slump, subside OPPOSITE **increase. 4 = slope**, fall away, incline **5 = die**, be killed, cark (*Aust & NZ sl*), meet one's end, perish OPPOSITE **survive. 6 = be overthrown**, capitulate, pass into enemy hands, succumb, surrender OPPOSITE **triumph. 9 = occur**, befall, chance, come about, come to pass, happen, take place **10 = lapse**, err, go astray, offend, sin, transgress, trespass ◆*noun* **11 = descent**, dive, drop, nose dive, plummet, plunge, slip, tumble **13 = decrease**, cut, decline, dip, drop, lessening, lowering, reduction, slump **14, 15 = collapse**, capitulation, defeat, destruction, downfall, overthrow, ruin
fallacy *noun* **1 = error**, delusion, falsehood, flaw, misapprehension, misconception, mistake, untruth
fallible *adjective* **= imperfect**, erring, frail, ignorant, uncertain, weak OPPOSITE **infallible**
fall out *verb* **1** *Inf* **= argue**, clash, come to blows, differ, disagree, fight, quarrel, squabble
fallow¹ *adjective* **= uncultivated**, dormant, idle, inactive, resting, unplanted, unused

F

adverb **falseness** noun **falsity** noun, pl -ties **1** state of being false. **2** lie. **falsehood** noun **1** quality of being untrue. **2** lie.
falsetto noun, pl -tos voice pitched higher than one's natural range.
falsify ⊕ verb -fying, -fied alter fraudulently. **falsification** noun
falter ⊕ verb **1** be hesitant, weak, or unsure. **2** lose power momentarily. **3** utter hesitantly. **4** move unsteadily. **faltering** adjective
fame ⊕ noun state of being widely known or recognized. **famed** adjective famous.
familiar ⊕ adjective **1** well-known. **2** frequent or common. **3** intimate, friendly. **4** too friendly. ♦ noun **5** demon supposed to attend a witch. **6** friend. **familiarly** adverb **familiarity** noun, pl -ties. **familiarize** verb acquaint fully with a particular subject. **familiarization** noun
family ⊕ noun, pl -lies **1** group of parents and their children. **2** one's spouse and children. **3** one's children. **4** group descended from a common ancestor. **5** group of related objects or beings. ♦ adjective **6** suitable for parents and children together. **familial** adjective **family doctor** Informal same as GENERAL PRACTITIONER.

family name surname, esp. when seen as representing a family's good reputation. **family planning** control of the number of children in a family by the use of contraception. **family tree** chart showing the relationships between individuals in a family over many generations.
famine ⊕ noun severe shortage of food.
famished ⊕ adjective very hungry.
famous ⊕ adjective very well-known.
famously adverb Informal excellently.
fan¹ ⊕ noun **1** hand-held or mechanical object used to create a current of air for ventilation or cooling. ♦ verb **fanning, fanned 2** blow or cool with a fan. **3** spread out like a fan. **fanbase** noun body of admirers of a particular pop singer, sports team, etc. **fan belt** belt that drives a cooling fan in a car engine. **fan heater** heater which uses a fan to spread warmed air through a room. **fanlight** noun semicircular window over a door or window.
fan² ⊕ noun Informal devotee of a pop star, sport, or hobby.
fanatic ⊕ noun person who is excessively enthusiastic about something. **fanatical** adjective **fanatically** adverb **fanaticism** noun

——————— THESAURUS ———————

false adjective **1** = **incorrect**, erroneous, faulty, inaccurate, inexact, invalid, mistaken, wrong OPPOSITE **right**. **2** = **artificial**, bogus, counterfeit, fake, forged, imitation, sham, simulated OPPOSITE **real**. **3** = **untrue**, deceitful, deceptive, fallacious, fraudulent, hypocritical, lying, misleading, trumped up, unreliable, unsound, untruthful OPPOSITE **true**
falsehood noun **1** = **untruthfulness**, deceit, deception, dishonesty, dissimulation, mendacity **2** = **lie**, fabrication, fib, fiction, story, untruth
falsify verb = **alter**, counterfeit, distort, doctor, fake, forge, misrepresent, tamper with
falter verb **1** = **hesitate**, vacillate, waver OPPOSITE **persevere**. **3** = **stutter**, stammer **4** = **stumble**, totter
faltering adjective **1** = **hesitant**, irresolute, tentative, timid, uncertain, weak **3** = **stammering**, broken
fame noun = **prominence**, celebrity, glory, honour, renown, reputation, repute, stardom OPPOSITE **obscurity**
familiar adjective **1** = **well-known**, recognizable OPPOSITE **unfamiliar**. **2** = **common**, accustomed, customary, frequent, ordinary, routine **3** = **friendly**, amicable, close, easy, intimate, relaxed OPPOSITE **formal**. **4** = **disrespectful**, bold, forward, impudent, intrusive, presumptuous
familiarity noun **1** = **acquaintance**,

awareness, experience, grasp, understanding OPPOSITE **unfamiliarity**. **3** = **friendliness**, ease, informality, intimacy, openness, sociability OPPOSITE **formality**. **4** = **disrespect**, boldness, forwardness, presumption OPPOSITE **respect**
familiarize verb = **accustom**, habituate, instruct, inure, school, season, train
family noun **1, 2** = **relations**, folk (inf), household, kin, kith and kin, one's nearest and dearest, one's own flesh and blood, relatives **4** = **clan**, dynasty, house, race, tribe **5** = **group**, class, genre, network, subdivision, system
famine noun = **hunger**, dearth, scarcity, starvation
famished adjective = **starving**, ravenous, voracious
famous adjective = **well-known**, acclaimed, celebrated, distinguished, eminent, illustrious, legendary, noted, prominent, renowned OPPOSITE **unknown**
fan¹ noun **1** = **blower**, air conditioner, ventilator ♦ verb **2** = **blow**, air-condition, cool, refresh, ventilate
fan² noun Inf = **supporter**, admirer, aficionado, buff (inf), devotee, enthusiast, follower, lover
fanatic noun = **extremist**, activist, bigot, militant, zealot
fanatical adjective = **obsessive**, bigoted, extreme, fervent, frenzied, immoderate, overenthusiastic, passionate, wild, zealous

fancy ⊙ *adjective* **-cier, -ciest 1** elaborate, not plain. **2** (of prices) higher than usual. ♦ *noun, pl* **-cies 3** sudden irrational liking or desire. **4** uncontrolled imagination. ♦ *verb* **-cying, -cied 5** *Informal* be sexually attracted to. **6** *Informal* have a wish for. **7** picture in the imagination. **8** suppose. **fancy oneself** *Informal* have a high opinion of oneself. **fancier** *noun* person who is interested in and often breeds plants or animals, e.g. *a pigeon fancier*. **fanciful** *adjective* **1** not based on fact. **2** excessively elaborate. **fancifully** *adverb* **fancy dress** party costume representing a historical figure, animal, etc. **fancy-free** *adjective* not in love. **fancy goods** small decorative gifts.

fandango *noun, pl* **-gos** lively Spanish dance.

fanfare *noun* short loud tune played on brass instruments.

fang *noun* **1** snake's tooth which injects poison. **2** long pointed tooth.

fanny *noun, pl* **-nies** *Slang* **1** *Brit taboo* female genitals. **2** *US* buttocks.

fantasia *noun* musical composition of an improvised nature.

fantastic ⊙ *adjective* **1** *Informal* very good. **2** unrealistic or absurd. **3** strange or difficult to believe. **fantastically** *adverb*

fantasy ⊙ *noun, pl* **-sies 1** far-fetched notion. **2** imagination unrestricted by reality. **3** daydream. **4** fiction with a large fantasy

content. **fantasize** *verb* indulge in daydreams.

fanzine [fan-zeen] *noun* magazine produced by fans of a specific interest, football club, etc., for fellow fans.

FAQ *Computers* frequently asked question *or* questions.

far ⊙ *adverb* **farther** *or* **further, farthest** *or* **furthest 1** at, to, or from a great distance. **2** at or to a remote time. **3** very much. ♦ *adjective* **4** remote in space or time. **faraway** *adjective* **1** very distant. **2** absent-minded. **Far East** East Asia. **far-fetched** *adjective* hard to believe. **far-flung** *adjective* **1** distributed over a wide area. **2** very distant. **far-reaching** *adjective* extensive in influence, effect, or range. **far-sighted** *adjective* having or showing foresight and wisdom.

farad *noun* unit of electrical capacitance.

farce ⊙ *noun* **1** boisterous comedy. **2** ludicrous situation. **farcical** *adjective* ludicrous. **farcically** *adverb*

fare ⊙ *noun* **1** charge for a passenger's journey. **2** passenger. **3** food provided. ♦ *verb* **4** get on (as specified), e.g. *we fared badly*. **fare stage 1** section of a bus journey for which a set charge is made. **2** bus stop marking the end of such a section.

farewell ⊙ *interjection* **1** goodbye. ♦ *noun* **2** act of saying goodbye and leaving. ♦ *verb NZ* say goodbye.

farinaceous *adjective* containing starch or

——————— THESAURUS ———————

fanciful *adjective* **1** = **unreal**, imaginary, mythical, romantic, visionary, whimsical, wild OPPOSITE **unimaginative**

fancy *adjective* **1** = **elaborate**, baroque, decorative, embellished, extravagant, intricate, ornamental, ornate OPPOSITE **plain** ♦ *noun* **3** = **whim**, caprice, desire, humour, idea, impulse, inclination, notion, thought, urge **4** = **delusion**, chimera, daydream, dream, fantasy, vision ♦ *verb* **5** *Inf* = **be attracted to**, be captivated by, like, lust after, take a liking to, take to **6** *Inf* = **wish for**, crave, desire, hanker after, hope for, long for, thirst for, yearn for **7, 8** = **suppose**, believe, conjecture, imagine, reckon, think, think likely

fantasize *verb* = **daydream**, dream, envision, imagine

fantastic *adjective* **1** *Inf* = **wonderful**, awesome (*sl*), excellent, first-rate, marvellous, sensational (*inf*), superb OPPOSITE **ordinary**. **2** = **unrealistic**, extravagant, far-fetched, ludicrous, ridiculous, wild **3** = **strange**, absurd, cock-and-bull (*inf*), fanciful, grotesque, implausible, incredible, outlandish, preposterous, unlikely OPPOSITE **realistic**

fantasy *noun* **1, 3** = **daydream**, dream, flight of fancy, illusion, mirage, pipe dream, reverie, vision **2** = **imagination**, creativity, fancy, invention, originality

far *adverb* **1** = **a long way**, afar, a good way, a great distance, deep, miles **3** = **much**, considerably, decidedly, extremely, greatly, incomparably, very much ♦ *adjective* **4** = **remote**, distant, faraway, far-flung, far-off, outlying, out-of-the-way OPPOSITE **near**

farce *noun* **1** = **comedy**, buffoonery, burlesque, satire, slapstick **2** = **mockery**, joke, nonsense, parody, sham, travesty

farcical *adjective* = **ludicrous**, absurd, comic, derisory, laughable, nonsensical, preposterous, ridiculous, risible

fare *noun* **1** = **charge**, price, ticket money **3** = **food**, provisions, rations, sustenance, victuals ♦ *verb* **4** = **get on**, do, get along, make out, manage, prosper

farewell *noun* **2** = **goodbye**, adieu, departure, leave-taking, parting, sendoff (*inf*), valediction

far-fetched *adjective* = **unconvincing**, cock-and-bull (*inf*), fantastic, implausible, incredible, preposterous, unbelievable, unlikely, unrealistic having a starchy texture.

farm ❶ *noun* **1** area of land for growing crops or rearing livestock. **2** area of land or water for growing or rearing a specified animal or plant, e.g. *fish farm.* ♦ *verb* **3** cultivate (land). **4** rear (stock). **farmer** *noun* **farm hand** person employed to work on a farm. **farmhouse** *noun* **farm out** *verb* send (work) to be done by others. **farmstead** *noun* farm and its buildings. **farmyard** *noun*

farrago [far-**rah**-go] *noun, pl* **-gos, -goes** jumbled mixture of things.

farrier *noun* person who shoes horses.

farrow *noun* **1** litter of piglets. ♦ *verb* **2** (of a sow) give birth.

fart *Taboo noun* **1** emission of gas from the anus. ♦ *verb* **2** emit gas from the anus.

farther, farthest *adverb, adjective* see FAR.

farthing *noun* former British coin equivalent to a quarter of a penny.

farthingale *noun Obs* hoop worn under skirts in the Elizabethan period.

fascia [**fay**-shya] *noun, pl* **-ciae, -cias 1** outer surface of a dashboard. **2** flat surface above a shop window.

fascinate ❶ *verb* **1** attract and interest strongly. **2** make motionless from fear or awe. **fascinating** *adjective* **fascination** *noun*

> **SPELLING TIP**
>
> Remember that there is a silent *c* after the *s* in **fascinate, fascinated,** and **fascinating.**

fascism [**fash**-iz-zum] *noun* right-wing totalitarian political system characterized by state control and extreme nationalism. **fascist** *adjective, noun*

fashion ❶ *noun* **1** style in clothes, hairstyle, etc., popular at a particular time. **2** way something happens or is done. ♦ *verb* **3** form or make into a particular shape. **fashionable** *adjective* currently popular. **fashionably** *adverb*

fast¹ ❶ *adjective* **1** (capable of) acting or moving quickly. **2** done in or lasting a short time. **3** adapted to or allowing rapid movement. **4** (of a clock or watch) showing a time later than the correct time. **5** dissipated. **6** firmly fixed, fastened, or shut. **7** (of colours and dyes) not likely to fade. ♦ *adverb* **8** quickly. **9** soundly, deeply, e.g. *fast asleep.* **10** tightly and firmly. **pull a fast one** *Informal* trick or deceive someone. **fast food** food, such as hamburgers, prepared and served very quickly. **fast lane 1** outside lane on a motorway. **2** quickest but most competitive route to success. **fast-track** *adjective* **1** taking the quickest but most competitive route to success, e.g. *fast-track executives.* ♦ *verb* **2** speed up the progress of (a project or person).

fast² ❶ *verb* **1** go without food, esp. for religious reasons. ♦ *noun* **2** period of fasting.

fasten ❶ *verb* **1** make or become firmly fixed or joined. **2** close by fixing in place or locking. **3** (foll. by *on*) direct (one's attention) towards. **fastener, fastening** *noun* device that fastens.

fastidious *adjective* **1** very fussy about details. **2** excessively concerned with cleanliness. **fastidiously** *adverb* **fastidiousness** *noun*

——————— THESAURUS ———————

OPPOSITE believable

farm *noun* **1** = **smallholding**, croft (*Scot*), farmstead, grange, homestead, plantation, ranch (*chiefly N Amer*) ♦*verb* **3** = **cultivate**, plant, work

fascinate *verb* **1** = **entrance**, absorb, beguile, captivate, engross, enthral, hold spellbound, intrigue OPPOSITE **bore. 2** = **transfix**, rivet OPPOSITE **bore**

fascinating *adjective* **1** = **captivating**, alluring, compelling, engaging, engrossing, enticing, gripping, intriguing, irresistible, riveting OPPOSITE **boring**

fascination *noun* **1** = **attraction**, allure, charm, enchantment, lure, magic, magnetism, pull

fashion *noun* **1** = **style**, craze, custom, fad, look, mode, rage, trend, vogue **2** = **method**, manner, mode, style, way ♦*verb* **3** = **make**, construct, create, forge, form, manufacture,

mould, shape

fashionable *adjective* = **popular**, à la mode, chic, in (*inf*), in vogue, modern, stylish, trendy (*Brit inf*), up-to-date, with it (*inf*) OPPOSITE **unfashionable**

fast¹ *adjective* **1-3** = **quick**, brisk, fleet, flying, hasty, nippy (*Brit inf*), rapid, speedy, swift OPPOSITE **slow. 5** = **dissipated**, dissolute, extravagant, loose, profligate, reckless, self-indulgent, wanton **6** = **fixed**, close, fastened, firm, immovable, secure, sound, steadfast, tight OPPOSITE **unstable** ♦*adverb* **8** = **quickly**, hastily, hurriedly, in haste, like lightning, rapidly, speedily, swiftly OPPOSITE **slowly. 9** = **soundly**, deeply, firmly, fixedly, securely, tightly

fast² *verb* **1** = **go hungry**, abstain, deny oneself, go without food ♦*noun* **2** = **fasting**, abstinence

fasten *verb* **1, 2** = **fix**, affix, attach, bind,

fastness *noun* fortress, safe place.
fat ❶ *adjective* **fatter, fattest 1** having excess flesh on the body. **2** (of meat) containing a lot of fat. **3** thick. **4** profitable. ♦ *noun* **5** extra flesh on the body. **6** oily substance obtained from animals or plants. **fatness** *noun* **fatten** *verb* (cause to) become fat. **fatty** *adjective* **fattier, fattiest** containing fat. **fathead** *noun Informal* stupid person. **fat-headed** *adjective* **fat stock** livestock fattened and ready for market.
fatal ❶ *adjective* causing death or ruin. **fatally** *adverb* **fatality** *noun, pl* **-ties** death caused by an accident or disaster.
fatalism *noun* belief that all events are predetermined and people are powerless to change their destinies. **fatalist** *noun* **fatalistic** *adjective*
fate ❶ *noun* **1** power supposed to predetermine events. **2** inevitable fortune that befalls a person or thing. **fated** *adjective* **1** destined. **2** doomed to death or destruction. **fateful** *adjective* having important, usu. disastrous, consequences.
father ❶ *noun* **1** male parent. **2** person who founds a line or family. **3** man who starts, creates, or invents something. **4** (F-) God. **5** (F-) title of some priests. ♦ *verb* **6** be the father

of (offspring). **fatherhood** *noun* **fatherless** *adjective* **fatherly** *adjective* **father-in-law** *noun, pl* **fathers-in-law** father of one's husband or wife. **fatherland** *noun* one's native country.
fathom ❶ *noun* **1** unit of measurement of the depth of water, equal to six feet. ♦ *verb* **2** understand. **fathomable** *adjective* **fathomless** *adjective* too deep or difficult to fathom.
fatigue ❶ [fat-**eeg**] *noun* **1** extreme physical or mental tiredness. **2** weakening of a material due to stress. **3** soldier's nonmilitary duty. ♦ *plural* **4** soldier's clothing for nonmilitary duty. ♦ *verb* **5** tire out.
fatuous ❶ *adjective* foolish. **fatuously** *adverb* **fatuity** *noun, pl* **-ties 1** foolish thoughtlessness. **2** fatuous remark.
faucet ❶ [**faw**-set] *noun US & Canad* valve with handle, plug etc. to regulate or stop flow of fluid.
fault ❶ *noun* **1** responsibility for something wrong. **2** defect or flaw. **3** mistake or error. **4** *Geology* break in layers of rock. **5** *Tennis, squash, etc.* invalid serve. ♦ *verb* **6** criticize or blame. **at fault** guilty of error. **find fault with** seek out minor imperfections in. **to a fault** excessively. **faulty** *adjective* **faultless** *adjective* **faultlessly** *adverb*

———————— THESAURUS ————————

connect, join, link, secure, tie
fat *adjective* **1** = **overweight**, corpulent, heavy, obese, plump, podgy, portly, rotund, stout, tubby OPPOSITE thin. **2** = **fatty**, adipose, greasy, oily, oleaginous ♦*noun* **5** = **fatness**, blubber, bulk, corpulence, flab, flesh, obesity, paunch
fatal *adjective* **a** = **lethal**, deadly, final, incurable, killing, malignant, mortal, terminal OPPOSITE harmless. **b** = **disastrous**, baleful, baneful, calamitous, catastrophic, ruinous OPPOSITE minor
fatality *noun* = **death**, casualty, loss, mortality
fate *noun* **1** = **destiny**, chance, divine will, fortune, kismet, nemesis, predestination, providence **2** = **fortune**, cup, horoscope, lot, portion, stars
fated *adjective* **1** = **destined**, foreordained, inescapable, inevitable, predestined, preordained, sure, written **2** = **doomed**
fateful *adjective* **a** = **crucial**, critical, decisive, important, portentous, significant OPPOSITE unimportant. **b** = **disastrous**, deadly, destructive, fatal, lethal, ominous, ruinous
father *noun* **1** = **daddy** (*inf*), dad (*inf*), old man (*inf*), pa (*inf*), papa (*old-fashioned inf*), pater, pop (*inf*) **2** = **forefather**, ancestor, forebear, predecessor, progenitor **3** = **founder**, architect, author, creator, inventor, maker,

originator, prime mover **5** (with cap.) = **priest**, padre (*inf*), pastor ♦*verb* **6** = **sire**, beget, get, procreate
fatherland *noun* = **homeland**, motherland, native land
fatherly *adjective* **1** = **paternal**, affectionate, benevolent, benign, kindly, patriarchal, protective, supportive
fathom *verb* **2** = **understand**, comprehend, get to the bottom of, grasp, interpret
fatigue *noun* **1** = **tiredness**, heaviness, languor, lethargy, listlessness OPPOSITE freshness ♦*verb* **5** = **tire**, drain, exhaust, knacker (*sl*), take it out of (*inf*), weaken, wear out, weary OPPOSITE refresh
fatten *verb* = **grow fat**, expand, gain weight, put on weight, spread, swell, thicken
fatty *adjective* = **greasy**, adipose, fat, oily, oleaginous, rich
fatuous *adjective* = **foolish**, brainless, idiotic, inane, ludicrous, mindless, moronic, silly, stupid, witless
faucet *noun* (*US & Canad*) = **tap**, spout, spigot, stopcock, valve
fault *noun* **1** = **responsibility**, accountability, culpability, liability **2** = **flaw**, blemish, defect, deficiency, failing, imperfection, shortcoming, weakness, weak point OPPOSITE strength. **3**

faun noun (in Roman legend) creature with a human face and torso and a goat's horns and legs.

fauna noun, pl **-nas, -nae** animals of a given place or time.

faux pas [foe pah] noun, pl **faux pas** social blunder.

favour ● noun 1 approving attitude. 2 act of goodwill or generosity. 3 partiality. ◆ verb 4 prefer. 5 regard or treat with especial kindness. 6 support or advocate. **favourable** adjective

favourite noun favoured person or thing.

favourable ● adjective 1 encouraging or advantageous. 2 giving consent. 3 useful or beneficial. **favourably** adverb

favourite ● adjective 1 most liked. ◆ noun 2 preferred person or thing. 3 Sport competitor expected to win. **favouritism** noun practice of giving special treatment to a person or group.

fawn[1] ● noun 1 young deer. ◆ adjective 2 light yellowish-brown.

fawn[2] ● verb 1 (foll. by on) seek attention

from (someone) by insincere flattery. 2 (of a dog) try to please by a show of extreme affection.

fax noun 1 electronic system for sending facsimiles of documents by telephone. 2 document sent by this system. ◆ verb 3 send (a document) by this system.

faze verb Informal disconcert or fluster.

FBI US Federal Bureau of Investigation.

FC Football Club.

Fe Chem iron.

fealty noun (in feudal society) subordinate's loyalty to his ruler or lord.

fear ● noun 1 distress or alarm caused by impending danger or pain. 2 something that causes distress. ◆ verb 3 be afraid of (something or someone). **fear for** feel anxiety about something. **fearful** adjective 1 feeling fear. 2 causing distress. 3 Informal very unpleasant. **fearfully** adverb **fearless** adjective **fearlessly** adverb **fearsome** adjective terrifying.

feasible ● adjective able to be done, possible.

———————— THESAURUS ————————

= mistake, blunder, error, indiscretion, lapse, oversight, slip ◆verb 6 = criticize, blame, censure, find fault with, hold (someone) responsible, impugn **at fault** = guilty, answerable, blamable, culpable, in the wrong, responsible, to blame **find fault with** = criticize, carp at, complain, pick holes in, pull to pieces, quibble, take to task **to a fault** = excessively, immoderately, in the extreme, overmuch, unduly

faultless 1 adjective = flawless, foolproof, impeccable, model, perfect, unblemished 2 = correct, exemplary

faulty adjective 1 = defective, broken, damaged, flawed, impaired, imperfect, malfunctioning, out of order 2 = incorrect, unsound

favour noun 1 = approval, approbation, backing, good opinion, goodwill, patronage, support OPPOSITE disapproval. 2 = good turn, benefit, boon, courtesy, indulgence, kindness, service OPPOSITE wrong ◆verb 4, 5 = prefer, incline towards, indulge, reward, side with, smile upon OPPOSITE object to. 6 = support, advocate, approve, champion, commend, encourage OPPOSITE oppose

favourable adjective 1, 3 = advantageous, auspicious, beneficial, encouraging, helpful, opportune, promising, propitious, suitable OPPOSITE disadvantageous. 2 = positive, affirmative, agreeable, approving, encouraging, enthusiastic, reassuring, sympathetic OPPOSITE disapproving

favourably adverb 1, 3 = advantageously, auspiciously, conveniently, fortunately, opportunely, profitably, to one's advantage, well 2 = positively, approvingly, enthusiastically, helpfully, with approval

favourite adjective 1 = preferred, best-loved, choice, dearest, esteemed, favoured ◆noun 2 = darling, beloved, blue-eyed boy (inf), idol, pet, teacher's pet, the apple of one's eye

fawn[1] adjective 2 = beige, buff, greyish-brown, neutral

fawn[2] verb 1 (foll. by on) = ingratiate oneself, crawl, creep, curry favour, dance attendance, flatter, grovel, kowtow, pander to

fawning adjective 1 = obsequious, crawling, cringing, deferential, flattering, grovelling, servile, sycophantic

fear noun 1 = dread, alarm, apprehensiveness, fright, horror, panic, terror, trepidation 2 = bugbear, bête noire, bogey, horror, nightmare, spectre ◆verb 3 = be afraid, dread, shake in one's shoes, shudder at, take fright, tremble at **fear for** = worry about, be anxious about, feel concern for

fearful adjective 1 = scared, afraid, alarmed, frightened, jumpy, nervous, timid, timorous, uneasy OPPOSITE unafraid. 2, 3 = frightful, awful, dire, dreadful, gruesome, hair-raising, horrendous, horrific, terrible

fearfully adverb 1 = nervously, apprehensively, diffidently, timidly, timorously, uneasily

fearless adjective = brave, bold, courageous,

feasibly *adverb* **feasibility** *noun*
feast ⊕ *noun* **1** lavish meal. **2** something extremely pleasing. **3** annual religious celebration. ♦ *verb* **4** eat a feast. **5** give a feast to. **6** (foll. by *on*) eat a large amount of. **feast one's eyes on** look at (someone or something) with a great deal of pleasure.
feat ⊕ *noun* remarkable, skilful, or daring action.
feather *noun* **1** one of the barbed shafts forming the plumage of birds. ♦ *verb* **2** fit or cover with feathers. **3** turn (an oar) edgeways. **feather in one's cap** achievement one can be pleased with. **feather one's nest** make one's life comfortable. **feathered** *adjective* **feathery** *adjective* **featherbedding** *noun* practice of working deliberately slowly so that more workers are employed than are necessary.
featherweight *noun* **1** boxer weighing up to 126lb (professional) or 57kg (amateur). **2** insignificant person or thing.
feature ⊕ *noun* **1** part of the face, such as the eyes. **2** prominent or distinctive part. **3** special article in a newspaper or magazine. **4** main film in a cinema programme. ♦ *verb* **5** have as a feature or be a feature in. **6** give prominence to. **featureless** *adjective*
Feb. February.
febrile [**fee**-brile] *adjective* **1** very active and nervous, e.g. *increasingly febrile activity at the Stock Exchange.* **2** feverish.
February *noun* second month of the year.

feckless ⊕ *adjective* ineffectual or irresponsible.
fecund *adjective* fertile. **fecundity** *noun*
fed ⊕ *verb* past of FEED. **fed up** *Informal* bored, dissatisfied.
federal ⊕ *adjective* **1** of a system in which power is divided between one central government and several regional governments. **2** of the central government of a federation. **federalism** *noun* **federalist** *noun* **federate** *verb* unite in a federation. **federation** *noun* **1** union of several states, provinces, etc. **2** association.
fedora [fid-**or**-a] *noun* man's soft hat with a brim.
fee ⊕ *noun* **1** charge paid to be allowed to do something. **2** payment for professional services.
feeble ⊕ *adjective* **1** lacking physical or mental power. **2** unconvincing. **feebleness** *noun* **feebly** *adverb* **feeble-minded** *adjective* unable to think or understand effectively.
feed ⊕ *verb* **feeding, fed 1** give food to. **2** give (something) as food. **3** eat. **4** supply or prepare food for. **5** supply (what is needed). ♦ *noun* **6** act of feeding. **7** food, esp. for babies or animals. **8** *Informal* meal. **feeder** *noun* **1** baby's bib. **2** device used to feed an animal, child, or sick person. **3** road or railway line linking outlying areas to the main traffic network. **feedback** *noun* **1** information received in response to something done. **2** return of part of the output of an electrical

——————— THESAURUS ———————

dauntless, indomitable, intrepid, plucky, unafraid, undaunted, valiant
fearsome *adjective* =**terrifying**, awe-inspiring, daunting, formidable, frightening, horrifying, menacing, unnerving
feasible *adjective* =**possible**, achievable, attainable, likely, practicable, reasonable, viable, workable OPPOSITE **impracticable**
feast *noun* **1** =**banquet**, dinner, repast, spread (*inf*), treat **2** =**treat**, delight, enjoyment, gratification, pleasure **3** =**festival**, celebration, fete, holiday, holy day, red-letter day, saint's day ♦*verb* **4** =**eat one's fill**, gorge, gormandize, indulge, overindulge, pig out (*sl*) **5** =**wine and dine**
feat *noun* =**accomplishment**, achievement, act, attainment, deed, exploit, performance
feathers *plural noun* **1** =**plumage**, down, plumes
feature *noun* **2** =**aspect**, characteristic, facet, factor, hallmark, peculiarity, property, quality, trait **3** =**article**, column, item, piece, report, story **4** =**highlight**, attraction, main item,

speciality ♦*verb* **6** =**spotlight**, emphasize, foreground, give prominence to, play up, present, star
features *plural noun* **1** =**face**, countenance, lineaments, physiognomy
feckless *adjective* =**irresponsible**, good-for-nothing, hopeless, incompetent, ineffectual, shiftless, worthless
federation *noun* =**union**, alliance, amalgamation, association, coalition, combination, league, syndicate
fed up *adjective* *Inf* =**dissatisfied**, bored, depressed, discontented, down in the mouth, glum, sick and tired, tired
fee *noun* =**charge**, bill, payment, remuneration, toll
feeble *adjective* **1** =**weak**, debilitated, doddering, effete, frail, infirm, puny, sickly, weedy (*inf*) OPPOSITE **strong**. **2** =**flimsy**, inadequate, insufficient, lame, paltry, pathetic, poor, tame, thin, unconvincing OPPOSITE **effective**
feebleness *noun* **1** =**weakness**, effeteness,

F

circuit or loudspeaker to its source.
feel ❶ *verb* **feeling, felt 1** have a physical or emotional sensation of. **2** become aware of or examine by touch. **3** sense by intuition. **4** believe. ♦ *noun* **5** act of feeling. **6** impression. **7** way something feels. **8** sense of touch. **9** instinctive aptitude. **feeler** *noun* **1** organ of touch in some animals. **2** remark made to test others' opinion. **feeling** *noun* **1** emotional reaction. **2** intuitive understanding. **3** opinion. **4** sympathy, understanding. **5** ability to experience physical sensations. **6** sensation experienced. ♦ *plural* **7** emotional sensitivities. **feel like** wish for, want. **feel for** *verb* **1** attempt to find by touch alone. **2** have sympathy or compassion for someone in trouble. **feel up to** *verb* be fit or energetic enough to.
feet *noun* plural of FOOT.
feign [fane] *verb* pretend. **feigned** *adjective*
feint¹ [faint] *noun* **1** sham attack or blow meant to distract an opponent. ♦ *verb* **2** make a feint.
feint² [faint] *noun* narrow lines on ruled paper.
feisty ❶ *adjective* **1** *Inf* lively, resilient, and self-reliant. **2** *US & Canad* frisky. **3** *US & Canad* irritable.
feldspar *noun* hard mineral that is the main constituent of igneous rocks.
felicity *noun* **1** happiness. **2** *pl* **-ties** appropriate expression or style. **felicitations** *plural noun* congratulations. **felicitous** *adjective*
feline *adjective* **1** of cats. **2** catlike. ♦ *noun* **3** member of the cat family.

fell¹ *verb* past tense of FALL.
fell² ❶ *verb* **1** cut down (a tree). **2** knock down.
fell³ *adjective* **in one fell swoop** in a single action or occurrence.
fell⁴ *noun* *Scot & N English* a mountain, hill, or moor.
fell⁵ *noun* animal's skin or hide with its hair.
felloe *noun* (segment of) the rim of a wheel.
fellow ❶ *noun* **1** *Old-fashioned* man or boy. **2** comrade or associate. **3** person in the same group or condition. **4** member of a learned society or the governing body of a college. ♦ *adjective* **5** in the same group or condition.
fellowship *noun* **1** sharing of aims or interests. **2** group with shared aims or interests. **3** feeling of friendliness. **4** paid research post in a college or university. **fellow feeling** sympathy between people who have undergone the same experience. **fellow traveller** Communist sympathizer who is not a Communist Party member.
felon *noun* *Criminal law* (formerly) person guilty of a felony. **felony** *noun, pl* **-nies** serious crime. **felonious** *adjective*
felspar *noun* same as FELDSPAR.
felt¹ *verb* past of FEEL.
felt² *noun* matted fabric made by bonding fibres by pressure. **felt-tip pen** pen with a writing point made from pressed fibres.
fem. feminine.
female *adjective* **1** of the sex which bears offspring. **2** (of plants) producing fruits. ♦ *noun* **3** female person or animal.
feminine ❶ *adjective* **1** having qualities

——————————— T H E S A U R U S ———————————

frailty, infirmity, languor, lassitude, sickliness
feed *verb* **1, 2, 4 = cater for,** nourish, provide for, provision, supply, sustain, victual, wine and dine **3 = eat,** devour, exist on, live on, partake of ♦*noun* **7 = food,** fodder, pasturage, provender **8** *Inf* **= meal,** feast, nosh (*sl*), repast, spread (*inf*)
feel *verb* **1 = experience,** be aware of, notice, observe, perceive **2 = touch,** caress, finger, fondle, handle, manipulate, paw, stroke **3 = sense,** be convinced, intuit **4 = believe,** consider, deem, hold, judge, think ♦*noun* **6 = impression,** air, ambience, atmosphere, feeling, quality, sense **7 = texture,** finish, surface, touch
feeler *noun* **1 = antenna,** tentacle, whisker **2** *as in* **put out feelers = approach,** advance, probe
feeling *noun* **1 = emotion,** ardour, fervour, intensity, passion, sentiment, warmth **2**

= impression, hunch, idea, inkling, notion, presentiment, sense, suspicion **3 = opinion,** inclination, instinct, point of view, view **4 = sympathy,** compassion, concern, empathy, pity, sensibility, sensitivity, understanding **5 = sense of touch,** perception, sensation **6 = atmosphere,** air, ambience, aura, feel, mood, quality
feisty *adjective* (*Informal, chiefly US & Canad*) **= fiery,** spirited, bold, plucky, vivacious
fell² *verb* **1 = cut down,** cut, hew **2 = knock down,** demolish, level
fellow *noun* **1** *Old-fashioned* **= man,** bloke (*Brit inf*), chap (*inf*), character, guy (*inf*), individual, person **2, 3 = associate,** colleague, companion, comrade, partner, peer
fellowship *noun* **1, 3 = camaraderie,** brotherhood, companionship, sociability **2 = society,** association, brotherhood, club, fraternity, guild, league, order

traditionally regarded as suitable for, or typical of, women. **2** of women. **3** belonging to a particular class of grammatical inflection in some languages. **femininity** *noun* **feminism** *noun* advocacy of equal rights for women. **feminist** *noun, adjective*

femme fatale ❶ [fam fat-**tahl**] *noun, pl* **femmes fatales** alluring woman who leads men into dangerous situations by her charm.

femur [**fee**-mer] *noun* thighbone. **femoral** *adjective* of the thigh.

fen ❶ *noun* low-lying flat marshy land. **fenland** *noun*

fence ❶ *noun* **1** barrier of posts linked by wire or wood, enclosing an area. **2** obstacle for a horse to jump in steeplechasing or showjumping. **3** *Slang* dealer in stolen property. ◆ *verb* **4** enclose with or as if with a fence. **5** fight with swords as a sport. **6** avoid a question. **fencing** *noun* **1** sport of fighting with swords. **2** material for making fences. **fencer** *noun*

fend *verb* **fend for oneself** provide for oneself. **fend off** *verb* defend oneself against (verbal or physical attack).

fender *noun* **1** low metal frame in front of a fireplace. **2** soft but solid object hung over a ship's side to prevent damage when docking. **3** *US & Canad* the part of a car body that surrounds the wheels.

feng shui [fung **shway**] *noun* Chinese art of deciding the best design of a building, etc., in order to bring good luck.

Fenian [**feen**-yan] *noun* member of a 19th-century Irish revolutionary organization founded to fight for an independent Ireland.

fennel *noun* fragrant plant whose seeds, leaves, and root are used in cookery.

fenugreek *noun* Mediterranean plant grown for its heavily scented seeds.

feoff [**feef**] *noun Hist* same as FIEF.

feral *adjective* wild.

ferment ❶ *noun* **1** commotion, unrest. ◆ *verb* **2** undergo or cause to undergo fermentation.

fermentation *noun* reaction in which an organic molecule splits into simpler substances, esp. the conversion of sugar to alcohol.

fermium *noun Chem* element artificially produced by neutron bombardment of plutonium.

fern *noun* flowerless plant with fine fronds.

ferocious ❶ *adjective* savagely fierce or cruel. **ferocity** *noun*

ferret ❶ *noun* **1** tamed polecat used to catch rabbits or rats. ◆ *verb* **ferreting, ferreted 2** hunt with ferrets. **3** search around. **ferret out** *verb* find by searching.

ferric, ferrous *adjective* of or containing iron.

Ferris wheel *noun* large vertical fairground wheel with hanging seats for riding in.

ferrule *noun* metal cap to strengthen the end of a stick.

ferry ❶ *noun, pl* **-ries 1** boat for transporting people and vehicles. **2** route or service operated by such a boat. ◆ *verb* **-rying, -ried 3** carry by ferry. **4** convey (goods or people). **ferryboat** *noun* **ferryman** *noun*

fertile ❶ *adjective* **1** capable of producing young, crops, or vegetation. **2** highly productive, e.g. *a fertile mind.* **fertility** *noun* **fertilize** *verb* **1** provide (an animal or plant) with sperm or pollen to bring about fertilization. **2** supply (soil) with nutrients. **fertilization** *noun* **fertilizer** *noun* substance added to the soil to increase its productivity.

fervent, fervid ❶ *adjective* intensely

F

———————— THESAURUS ————————

feminine *adjective* **1, 2 = womanly**, delicate, gentle, ladylike, soft, tender OPPOSITE **masculine**

femme fatale *noun* **= seductress**, enchantress, siren, vamp (*inf*)

fen *noun* **= marsh**, bog, morass, quagmire, slough, swamp, muskeg (*Canad*)

fence *noun* **1 = barrier**, barricade, defence, hedge, palisade, railings, rampart, wall ◆*verb* **4 = enclose**, bound, confine, encircle, pen, protect, surround **6 = evade**, dodge, equivocate, flannel (*Brit inf*), parry

ferment *noun* **1 = commotion**, disruption, excitement, frenzy, furore, stir, tumult, turmoil, unrest, uproar OPPOSITE **tranquillity**

ferocious *adjective* **= fierce**, bloodthirsty, brutal, cruel, predatory, rapacious, ravening,

ruthless, savage, vicious, violent, wild OPPOSITE **gentle**

ferocity *noun* **= savagery**, bloodthirstiness, brutality, cruelty, fierceness, viciousness, wildness

ferret out *verb* **= track down**, dig up, discover, elicit, root out, search out, trace, unearth

ferry *noun* **1 = ferry boat**, packet, packet boat ◆*verb* **3, 4 = carry**, chauffeur, convey, run, ship, shuttle, transport

fertile *adjective* **= productive**, abundant, fecund, fruitful, luxuriant, plentiful, prolific, rich, teeming OPPOSITE **barren**

fertility *noun* **= fruitfulness**, abundance, fecundity, luxuriance, productiveness, richness

fertilizer *noun* **= compost**, dressing, dung,

passionate and sincere. **fervently** *adverb*
fervour *noun* intensity of feeling.
fescue *noun* pasture and lawn grass with stiff
narrow leaves.
fester ⊕ *verb* **1** grow worse and increasingly
hostile, e.g. *the bitterness which had been
festering beneath the surface.* **2** (of a wound)
form pus. **3** rot and decay, e.g. *rubbish festered
in the heat.*
festival ⊕ *noun* **1** organized series of special
events or performances. **2** day or period of
celebration. **festive** *adjective* of or like a
celebration. **festivity** *noun, pl* **-ties 1** happy
celebration. ♦ *plural* **2** celebrations.
festoon ⊕ *verb* hang decorations in loops.
feta *noun* white salty Greek cheese.
fetal *adjective* see FETUS.
fetch ⊕ *verb* **1** go after and bring back. **2** be
sold for. **3** *Informal* deal (a blow). **fetching**
adjective attractive. **fetch up** *verb Informal*
arrive or end up.
fete [fate] *noun* **1** gala, bazaar, etc., usu. held
outdoors. ♦ *verb* **2** honour or entertain regally.
fetid *adjective* stinking.
fetish ⊕ *noun* **1** form of behaviour in which
sexual pleasure is derived from looking at or
handling an inanimate object. **2** thing with
which one is excessively concerned. **3** object
believed to have magical powers. **fetishism**
noun **fetishist** *noun*
fetlock *noun* projection behind and above a
horse's hoof.
fetter *noun* **1** chain or shackle for the foot. ♦
plural **2** restrictions. ♦ *verb* **3** restrict. **4** bind in
fetters.

fettle *noun* state of health or spirits.
fetus, foetus [fee-tuss] *noun, pl* **-tuses**
embryo of a mammal in the later stages of
development. **fetal, foetal** *adjective*
feu *noun* (in Scotland) right of use of land in
return for a fixed annual payment.
feud ⊕ *noun* **1** long bitter hostility between
two people or groups. ♦ *verb* **2** carry on a feud.
feudalism *noun* medieval system in which
people held land from a lord, and in return
worked and fought for him. **feudal** *adjective* of
or like feudalism.
fever ⊕ *noun* **1** (illness causing) high body
temperature. **2** nervous excitement. **fevered**
adjective **feverish** *adjective* **1** suffering from
fever. **2** in a state of nervous excitement.
feverishly *adverb* **fever pitch** state of great
excitement.
few ⊕ *adjective* not many. **a few** a small
number. **quite a few, a good few** several.

> **LANGUAGE TIP**
>
> *Few(er)* is used of things that
> can be counted: *Fewer than five
> visits.* Compare *less,* which is
> used for quantity: *It uses less
> sugar.*

fey *adjective* **1** whimsically strange. **2** having
the ability to look into the future.
fez *noun, pl* **fezzes** brimless tasselled cap, orig.
from Turkey.
ff *Music* fortissimo.
ff. and the following (pages).

——————— THESAURUS ———————

manure
fervent, fervid *adjective* =**intense**, ardent,
devout, earnest, enthusiastic, heartfelt,
impassioned, passionate, vehement OPPOSITE
apathetic
fervour *noun* =**intensity**, ardour, enthusiasm,
excitement, passion, vehemence, warmth, zeal
fester *verb* **1** =**intensify**, aggravate, smoulder
2 =**suppurate**, ulcerate **3** =**putrefy**, decay
festival *noun* **1** =**celebration**, carnival,
entertainment, fête, gala, jubilee **2** =**holy day**,
anniversary, commemoration, feast, fete, fiesta,
holiday, red-letter day, saint's day
festive *adjective* =**celebratory**, cheery,
convivial, happy, jovial, joyful, joyous, jubilant,
merry OPPOSITE mournful
festivity *noun* (often pl) =**celebration**,
entertainment, festival, party
festoon *verb* =**decorate**, array, deck, drape,
garland, hang, swathe, wreathe

fetch *verb* **1** =**bring**, carry, convey, deliver,
get, go for, obtain, retrieve, transport **2** =**sell
for**, bring in, earn, go for, make, realize, yield
fetching *adjective* =**attractive**, alluring,
captivating, charming, cute, enticing, winsome
fetish *noun* **1, 2** =**fixation**, mania, obsession,
thing (*inf*) **3** =**talisman**, amulet
feud *noun* **1** =**hostility**, argument, conflict,
disagreement, enmity, quarrel, rivalry, row,
vendetta ♦*verb* **2** =**quarrel**, bicker, clash,
contend, dispute, fall out, row, squabble, war
fever *noun* **1** =**delirium 2** =**excitement**,
agitation, ferment, fervour, frenzy, restlessness
feverish *adjective* **1** =**hot**, febrile, fevered,
flushed, inflamed, pyretic (*Med*) **2** =**excited**,
agitated, frantic, frenetic, frenzied,
overwrought, restless OPPOSITE calm
few *adjective* =**not many**, meagre, negligible,
rare, scanty, scarcely any, sparse, sporadic
OPPOSITE many

fiancé [fee-**on**-say] *noun* man engaged to be married. **fiancée** *n fem*

fiasco ❶ *noun, pl* **-cos, -coes** ridiculous or humiliating failure.

fiat [**fee**-at] *noun* **1** arbitrary order. **2** official permission.

fib ❶ *noun* **1** trivial lie. ◆ *verb* **fibbing, fibbed** **2** tell a lie. **fibber** *noun*

fibre ❶ *noun* **1** thread that can be spun into yarn. **2** threadlike animal or plant tissue. **3** fibrous material in food. **4** strength of character. **5** essential substance or nature. **fibrous** *adjective* **fibreboard** *noun* building material made of compressed wood. **fibreglass** *noun* material made of fine glass fibres, used as insulation. **fibre optics** transmission of information by light along very thin flexible fibres of glass.

fibrillation *noun* uncontrollable twitching of muscles, esp. those in the heart.

fibroid [**fibe**-royd] *adjective* **1** *Anat* (of structures or tissues) containing or resembling fibres. ◆ *noun* **2** benign tumour composed of fibrous connective tissue. **fibrositis** [fibe-roh-**site**-iss] *noun* inflammation of the tissues of muscle sheaths.

fibula [**fib**-yew-la] *noun, pl* **-lae, -las** slender outer bone of the lower leg. **fibular** *adjective*

fiche [**feesh**] *noun* sheet of film for storing publications in miniaturized form.

fickle ❶ *adjective* changeable, inconstant. **fickleness** *noun*

fiction ❶ *noun* **1** literary works of the imagination, such as novels. **2** invented story.

fictional *adjective* **fictionalize** *verb* turn into fiction. **fictitious** *adjective* **1** not genuine. **2** of or in fiction.

fiddle ❶ *noun* **1** violin. **2** *Informal* dishonest action or scheme. ◆ *verb* **3** play the violin. **4** falsify (accounts). **5** move or touch something restlessly. **fiddling** *adjective* trivial. **fiddly** *adjective* **-lier, -liest** awkward to do or use.

fiddlesticks *interjection* expression of annoyance or disagreement.

fidelity ❶ *noun* **1** faithfulness. **2** accuracy in detail. **3** quality of sound reproduction.

fidget ❶ *verb* **1** move about restlessly. ◆ *noun* **2** person who fidgets. ◆ *plural* **3** restlessness. **fidgety** *adjective*

fiduciary [fid-**yew**-she-er-ee] *Law noun, pl* **-aries 1** person bound to act for someone else's benefit, as a trustee. ◆ *adjective* **2** of a trust or trustee.

fie *interjection Obs or facetious* exclamation of disapproval.

fief [**feef**] *noun Hist* land granted by a lord in return for war service.

field ❶ *noun* **1** enclosed piece of agricultural land. **2** marked off area for sports. **3** area rich in a specified natural resource. **4** all the competitors in a competition. **5** all the competitors except the favourite. **6** battlefield. **7** sphere of knowledge or activity. **8** place away from the laboratory or classroom where practical work is done. **9** background, as of a flag. **10** area over which electric, gravitational, or magnetic force is exerted. ◆ *verb* **11** *Sport* catch and return (a ball). **12** send (a player or

——————————— T H E S A U R U S ———————————

fiasco *noun* =**flop** (*inf*), catastrophe, cock-up (*Brit sl*), debacle, disaster, failure, mess, washout (*inf*)

fib *noun* **1** = **lie**, fiction, story, untruth, white lie

fibre *noun* =**thread**, filament, pile, strand, texture, wisp **4** *as in* **moral fibre** = **strength of character**, resolution, stamina, strength, toughness **5** = **essence**, nature, quality, spirit, substance

fickle *adjective* =**changeable**, capricious, faithless, inconstant, irresolute, temperamental, unfaithful, variable, volatile OPPOSITE> **constant**

fiction *noun* **1** = **tale**, fantasy, legend, myth, novel, romance, story, yarn (*inf*) **2** = **lie**, cock and bull story (*inf*), fabrication, falsehood, invention, tall story, untruth, urban legend, urban myth

fictional *adjective* =**imaginary**, invented, legendary, made-up, nonexistent, unreal

fictitious *adjective* **1** = **false**, bogus, fabricated, imaginary, invented, made-up,

make-believe, mythical, untrue OPPOSITE> **true**

fiddle *noun* **1** =**violin 2** *Inf* =**fraud**, fix, racket, scam (*sl*), swindle ◆*verb* **4** = **cheat**, cook the books (*inf*), diddle (*inf*), fix, swindle, wangle (*inf*) **5** = **fidget**, finger, interfere with, mess about *or* around, play, tamper with, tinker

fiddling *adjective* =**trivial**, futile, insignificant, pettifogging, petty, trifling

fidelity *noun* **1** = **loyalty**, allegiance, constancy, dependability, devotion, faithfulness, staunchness, trustworthiness OPPOSITE> **infidelity**. **2** = **accuracy**, closeness, correspondence, exactness, faithfulness, precision, scrupulousness OPPOSITE> **inaccuracy**

fidget *verb* **1** = **move restlessly**, fiddle (*inf*), fret, squirm, twitch ◆*plural noun* **3** = **restlessness**, fidgetiness, jitters (*inf*), nervousness, unease, uneasiness

fidgety *adjective* =**restless** (*inf*), impatient, jittery (*inf*), jumpy, nervous, on edge, restive, uneasy team) on to the field. **13** play as a fielder. **14** deal with (a question) successfully. **fielder** noun *Sport* player whose task is to field the ball. **field day** day or time of exciting activity. **field events** throwing and jumping events in athletics. **fieldfare** noun type of large thrush. **field glasses** binoculars. **field hockey** *US* hockey played on grass, as distinguished from ice hockey. **field marshal** army officer of the highest rank. **fieldmouse** noun, pl -**mice** nocturnal mouse that lives in fields and woods. **field sports** hunting, shooting, and fishing. **fieldwork** noun investigation made in the field as opposed to the classroom or the laboratory. **fiend ⊕ [feend]** noun **1** evil spirit. **2** cruel or wicked person. **3** *Informal* person devoted to something, e.g. *fitness fiend.* **fiendish** adjective **fiendishly** adverb

fierce ⊕ adjective **1** wild or aggressive. **2** intense or strong. **fiercely** adverb **fierceness** noun

fiery ⊕ [fire-ee] adjective **fierier, fieriest 1** consisting of or like fire. **2** easily angered. **3** (of food) very spicy.

fiesta noun religious festival, carnival.

FIFA [fee-fa] Fédération Internationale de Football Association (International Association Football Federation).

fife noun small high-pitched flute.

fifteen adjective, noun **1** five and ten. ♦ noun **2** Rugby Union team. **fifteenth** adjective, noun

fifth adjective, noun **1** (of) number five in a series. ♦ noun **2** one of five equal parts of something. **fifth column** group secretly helping the enemy.

fifty adjective, noun, pl -**ties** five times ten. **fifty-fifty** *Informal* adverb **1** equally divided, e.g. *they split the profits fifty-fifty.* ♦ adjective **2** having an equal chance of happening or not happening, e.g. *a fifty-fifty chance of success.* **fiftieth** adjective, noun

fig noun **1** soft pear-shaped fruit. **2** tree bearing it. **fig leaf 1** representation of the leaf of a fig tree, used to cover the genitals of a nude statue or painting. **2** anything used to conceal something thought to be shameful.

fig. 1 figurative(ly). **2** figure.

fight ⊕ verb **fighting, fought 1** struggle (against) in battle or physical combat. **2** struggle to overcome someone or obtain something. **3** carry on (a battle or contest). **4** make (one's way) somewhere with difficulty. ♦ noun **5** aggressive conflict between two (groups of) people. **6** quarrel or contest. **7** resistance. **8** boxing match. **fighter** noun **1** boxer. **2** determined person. **3** aircraft designed to destroy other aircraft. **fight off** verb **1** drive away (an attacker). **2** struggle to avoid.

figment noun **figment of one's imagination** imaginary thing.

figure ⊕ noun **1** numerical symbol. **2** amount expressed in numbers. **3** bodily shape. **4** well-known person. **5** representation in painting or sculpture of a human form. **6** diagram or illustration. **7** set of movements in dancing or skating. **8** *Maths* any combination of lines, planes, points, or curves. ♦ plural **9** calculations with numbers. ♦ verb **10** calculate (sums or amounts). **11** *US & Aust* consider, conclude. **12** (usu. foll. by *in*) be included (in). **figure of**

——————— THESAURUS ———————

field noun **1** = **meadow**, grassland, green, lea (*poet*), pasture **4** = **competitors**, applicants, candidates, competition, contestants, entrants, possibilities, runners **7** = **speciality**, area, department, discipline, domain, line, province, territory ♦verb **11** *Sport* = **retrieve**, catch, pick up, return, stop **14** = **deal with**, deflect, handle, turn aside

fiend noun **1** = **demon**, devil, evil spirit **2** = **brute**, barbarian, beast, ghoul, monster, ogre, savage **3** *Inf* = **enthusiast**, addict, fanatic, freak (*inf*), maniac

fiendish adjective **1** = **devilish**, diabolical, hellish, infernal, satanic **2** = **wicked**, cruel, malignant, monstrous, unspeakable

fierce adjective **1** = **wild**, brutal, cruel, dangerous, ferocious, fiery, furious, menacing, powerful, raging, savage, stormy, strong, tempestuous, vicious, violent OPPOSITE gentle. **2** = **intense**, cut-throat, keen, relentless, strong

fiercely adverb = **ferociously**, furiously, passionately, savagely, tempestuously, tigerishly, tooth and nail, viciously, with no holds barred

fiery adjective **1** = **burning**, ablaze, afire, aflame, blazing, flaming, on fire **2** = **excitable**, fierce, hot-headed, impetuous, irascible, irritable, passionate

fight verb **1** = **battle**, box, clash, combat, do battle, grapple, spar, struggle, tussle, wrestle **2** = **oppose**, contest, defy, dispute, make a stand against, resist, stand up to, withstand **3** = **engage in**, carry on, conduct, prosecute, wage ♦noun **5, 6** = **battle**, clash, conflict, contest, dispute, duel, encounter, struggle, tussle **7** = **resistance**, belligerence, militancy, pluck, spirit

fighter noun **1** = **boxer**, prize fighter, pugilist

fight off verb **1** = **repel**, beat off, drive away, keep *or* hold at bay, repress, repulse, resist, stave off, ward off

speech expression in which words do not have their literal meaning. **figurative** *adjective* (of language) abstract, imaginative, or symbolic. **figuratively** *adverb* **figurine** *noun* statuette. **figurehead** *noun* **1** nominal leader. **2** carved bust at the bow of a ship. **figure out** *verb* solve or understand.

filament *noun* **1** fine wire in a light bulb that gives out light. **2** fine thread.

filbert *noun* hazelnut.

filch ⊕ *verb* steal (small amounts).

file[1] ⊕ *noun* **1** box or folder used to keep documents in order. **2** documents in a file. **3** information about a person or subject. **4** line of people one behind the other. **5** *Computers* organized collection of related material. ♦ *verb* **6** place (a document) in a file. **7** place (a legal document) on official record. **8** bring a lawsuit, esp. for divorce. **9** walk or march in a line. **filing cabinet** piece of office furniture with deep drawers used for storing documents.

file[2] ⊕ *noun* **1** tool with a roughened blade for smoothing or shaping. ♦ *verb* **2** shape or smooth with a file. **filings** *plural noun* shavings removed by a file.

filial *adjective* of or befitting a son or daughter.

filibuster *noun* **1** obstruction of legislation by making long speeches. **2** person who filibusters. ♦ *verb* **3** obstruct (legislation) with such delaying tactics.

filigree *noun* **1** delicate ornamental work of gold or silver wire. ♦ *adjective* **2** made of filigree.

Filipino [fill-lip-**pee**-no] *adjective* **1** of the Philippines. ♦ *noun* **2** (*fem* (**Filipina**) person from the Philippines.

fill ⊕ *verb* **1** make or become full. **2** occupy completely. **3** plug (a gap). **4** satisfy (a need). **5** hold and perform the duties of (a position). **6** appoint to (a job or position). **one's fill** sufficient for one's needs or wants. **filler** *noun* substance that fills a gap or increases bulk. **fill in** *verb* **1** complete (a form or drawing). **2** act as a substitute. **3** *Informal* give (a person) fuller details. **filling** *noun* **1** substance that fills a gap or cavity, esp. in a tooth. ♦ *adjective* **2** (of food) substantial and satisfying. **filling station** garage selling petrol, oil, etc.

fillet *noun* **1** boneless piece of meat or fish. ♦ *verb* **filleting, filleted 2** remove the bones from.

fillip *noun* something that adds stimulation or enjoyment.

filly *noun, pl* -**lies** young female horse.

film ⊕ *noun* **1** sequence of images projected on a screen, creating the illusion of movement. **2** story told in such a sequence of images. **3** thin strip of light-sensitive cellulose used to make photographic negatives and transparencies. **4** thin sheet or layer. ♦ *verb* **5** photograph with a movie or video camera. **6** make a film of (a scene, story, etc.). **7** cover or become covered with a thin layer. ♦ *adjective* **8** connected with films or the cinema. **filmy** *adjective* **filmier, filmiest** very thin, delicate. **film strip** set of pictures on a strip of film, projected separately as slides.

filter ⊕ *noun* **1** material or device permitting

F

——————— T H E S A U R U S ———————

figure *noun* **1** = **number**, character, digit, numeral, symbol **2** = **amount**, cost, price, sum, total, value **3** = **shape**, body, build, frame, physique, proportions **4** = **character**, big name, celebrity, dignitary, personality **5, 6** = **diagram**, design, drawing, illustration, representation, sketch ♦ *verb* **10** = **calculate**, compute, count, reckon, tally, tot up, work out **12** (usu. foll. by *in*) = **feature**, act, appear, be featured, contribute to, play a part

figurehead *noun* **1** = **front man**, mouthpiece, puppet, titular *or* nominal head

figure out *verb* = **understand**, calculate, comprehend, compute, decipher, fathom, make out, reckon, see, work out

filch *verb* = **steal**, embezzle, misappropriate, pilfer, pinch (*inf*), take, thieve, walk off with

file[1] *noun* = **folder**, case, data, documents, dossier, information, portfolio **4** = **line**, column, queue, row ♦ *verb* **6** = **put in place**, document, enter, pigeonhole **7** = **register**, record **9**

= **march**, parade, troop

file[2] *verb* **2** = **smooth**, abrade, polish, rasp, rub, scrape, shape

fill *verb* **1** = **stuff**, cram, crowd, glut, pack, stock, supply, swell **2** = **saturate**, charge, imbue, impregnate, pervade, suffuse **3** = **plug**, block, bung, close, cork, seal, stop **5** = **perform**, carry out, discharge, execute, fulfil, hold, occupy **one's fill** = **sufficient**, all one wants, ample, enough, plenty

filler *noun* = **padding**, makeweight, stopgap

fill in *verb* **1** = **complete**, answer, fill out (*US*), fill up **2** = **replace**, deputize, represent, stand in, sub, substitute, take the place of **3** *Inf* = **inform**, acquaint, apprise, bring up to date, give the facts *or* background

filling *noun* **1** = **stuffing**, contents, filler, inside, insides, padding, wadding ♦ *adjective* **2** = **satisfying**, ample, heavy, square, substantial

film *noun* **1, 2** = **movie**, flick (*sl*), motion picture **4** = **layer**, coating, covering, dusting, fluid to pass but retaining solid particles. **2** device that blocks certain frequencies of sound or light. **3** traffic signal that allows vehicles to turn either left or right while the main signals are at red. ◆ *verb* **4** remove impurities from (a substance) with a filter. **5** pass slowly or faintly. **filter tip** (cigarette with) a built-in filter to reduce the amount of nicotine etc. inhaled by a smoker.

filth ❶ *noun* **1** disgusting dirt. **2** offensive material or language. **filthy** *adjective* **filthier, filthiest. filthily** *adverb* **filthiness** *noun*

filtrate *noun* **1** filtered gas or liquid. ◆ *verb* **2** remove impurities with a filter. **filtration** *noun*

fin *noun* **1** projection from a fish's body enabling it to balance and swim. **2** vertical tailplane of an aircraft.

finagle [fin-**nay**-gl] *verb* get or achieve by craftiness or trickery.

final ❶ *adjective* **1** at the end. **2** having no possibility of further change, action, or discussion. ◆ *noun* **3** deciding contest between winners of previous rounds in a competition. ◆ *plural* **4** last examinations in an educational course. **finally** *adverb* **finality** *noun* **finalist** *noun* competitor in a final. **finalize** *verb* put into final form. **finale** [fin-**nah**-lee] *noun* concluding part of a dramatic performance or musical work.

finance ❶ *verb* **1** provide or obtain funds for. ◆ *noun* **2** system of money, credit, and

investment. **3** management of money, loans, or credits. **4** (provision of) funds. ◆ *plural* **5** money resources. **financial** *adjective* **financially** *adverb* **financier** *noun* person involved in large-scale financial business. **financial year** twelve-month period used for financial calculations.

finch *noun, pl* **finches** small songbird with a short strong beak.

find ❶ *verb* **finding, found 1** discover by chance. **2** discover by search or effort. **3** become aware of. **4** consider to have a particular quality. **5** experience (a particular feeling). **6** *Law* pronounce (the defendant) guilty or not guilty. **7** provide, esp. with difficulty. ◆ *noun* **8** person or thing found, esp. when valuable. **finder** *noun* **finding** *noun* conclusion from an investigation. **find out** *verb* **1** gain knowledge of. **2** detect (a crime, deception, etc.).

fine[1] ❶ *adjective* **1** very good. **2** (of weather) clear and dry. **3** in good health. **4** satisfactory. **5** of delicate workmanship. **6** thin or slender. **7** in small particles. **8** very small, e.g. *fine print*. **9** subtle or abstruse, e.g. *a fine distinction*. **finely** *adverb* **fineness** *noun* **finery** *noun* showy clothing. **fine art** art produced to appeal to the sense of beauty. **fine-tune** *verb* make small adjustments to (something) so that it works really well.

fine[2] ❶ *noun* **1** payment imposed as a penalty. ◆ *verb* **2** impose a fine on.

———— T H E S A U R U S ————

membrane, skin, tissue ◆*verb* **5, 6** = **photograph**, shoot, take, video, videotape **filter** *noun* **1** = **sieve**, gauze, membrane, mesh, riddle, strainer ◆*verb* **4** = **purify**, clarify, filtrate, refine, screen, sieve, sift, strain, winnow **5** = **trickle**, dribble, escape, exude, leak, ooze, penetrate, percolate, seep **filth** *noun* **1** = **dirt**, excrement, grime, muck, refuse, sewage, slime, sludge, squalor **2** = **obscenity**, impurity, indecency, pornography, smut, vulgarity **filthy** *adjective* **1** = **dirty**, begrimed, blackened, foul, grimy, grubby, muddy, polluted, putrid, slimy, squalid, unclean **2** = **obscene**, corrupt, depraved, impure, indecent, lewd, licentious, pornographic, smutty **final** *adjective* **1** = **last**, closing, concluding, latest, terminal, ultimate OPPOSITE first. **2** = **conclusive**, absolute, decided, definite, definitive, incontrovertible, irrevocable, settled **finale** *noun* = **ending**, climax, close, conclusion, culmination, denouement, epilogue OPPOSITE opening **finalize** *verb* = **complete**, clinch, conclude,

decide, settle, tie up, work out, wrap up (*inf*) **finally** *adverb* = **in conclusion**, at last, at length, at long last, eventually, in summary, in the end, lastly, to conclude, ultimately **finance** *verb* **1** = **fund**, back, bankroll (*US*), guarantee, pay for, subsidize, support, underwrite ◆*noun* **2** = **economics**, accounts, banking, business, commerce, investment, money **finances** *plural noun* **5** = **resources**, affairs, assets, capital, cash, funds, money, wherewithal **financial** *adjective* = **economic**, fiscal, monetary, pecuniary **find** *verb* **1** = **discover**, come across, encounter, hit upon, locate, meet, recognize, spot, uncover OPPOSITE lose. **2, 3** = **realise**, detect, discover, learn, note, notice, observe, perceive ◆*noun* **8** = **discovery**, acquisition, asset, bargain, catch, good buy **find out** *verb* **1** = **learn**, detect, discover, note, observe, perceive, realize **2** = **detect**, catch, disclose, expose, reveal, uncover, unmask **fine**[1] *adjective* **1** = **excellent**, accomplished, exceptional, exquisite, first-rate, magnificent,

finesse ❶ [fin-**ness**] *noun* **1** delicate skill. **2** subtlety and tact.

finger ❶ *noun* **1** one of the four long jointed parts of the hand. **2** part of a glove that covers a finger. **3** something that resembles a finger in shape or function. **4** quantity of liquid in a glass as deep as a finger is wide. ◆ *verb* **5** touch or handle with the fingers. **fingering** *noun* technique of using the fingers in playing a musical instrument. **fingerboard** *noun* part of a stringed instrument against which the strings are pressed. **finger bowl** small bowl of water for diners to rinse their hands in at the table. **fingerprint** *noun* **1** impression of the ridges on the tip of the finger. ◆ *verb* **2** take the fingerprints of (someone). **fingerstall** *noun* cover to protect an injured finger.

finial *noun Archit* ornament at the apex of a gable or spire.

finicky *adjective* **1** excessively particular, fussy. **2** overelaborate.

finis *noun Latin* end: used at the end of a book.

finish ❶ *verb* **1** bring to an end, stop. **2** use up. **3** bring to a desired or completed condition. **4** put a surface texture on (wood, cloth, or metal). **5** defeat or destroy. ◆ *noun* **6** end, last part. **7** death or defeat. **8** surface texture. **finishing school** private school for girls that teaches social graces.

finite ❶ [**fine**-ite] *adjective* having limits in space, time, or size.

Finn *noun* native of Finland. **Finnish** *adjective* **1** of Finland. ◆ *noun* **2** official language of Finland.

finnan haddock, haddie *noun* smoked

haddock.

fiord *noun* same as FJORD.

fipple flute *noun* end-blown flute with a plug (**fipple**) at the mouthpiece, such as a recorder.

fir *noun* pyramid-shaped tree with needle-like leaves and erect cones.

fire ❶ *noun* **1** state of combustion producing heat, flames, and smoke. **2** burning coal or wood, or a gas or electric device, used to heat a room. **3** uncontrolled destructive burning. **4** shooting of guns. **5** intense passion, ardour. ◆ *verb* **6** operate (a weapon) so that a bullet or missile is released. **7** *Informal* dismiss from employment. **8** bake (ceramics etc.) in a kiln. **9** (of an internal-combustion engine) start. **10** excite. **firearm** *noun* rifle, pistol, or shotgun. **fireball** *noun* **1** ball of fire at the centre of an explosion. **2** large bright meteor. **3** *Slang* energetic person. **firebrand** *noun* person who causes unrest. **firebreak** *noun* strip of cleared land to stop the advance of a fire. **firebrick** *noun* heat-resistant brick used for lining furnaces, fireplaces, etc. **fire brigade** organized body of people whose job is to put out fires. **firecracker** *noun* firework which produces a loud bang. **firedamp** *noun* explosive gas, composed mainly of methane, formed in mines. **fire drill** rehearsal of procedures for escape from a fire. **fire engine** vehicle with apparatus for extinguishing fires. **fire escape** metal staircase or ladder down the outside of a building for escape in the event of fire. **firefighter** *noun* member of a fire brigade. **firefly** *noun, pl* **-flies** beetle that glows in the dark. **fireguard** *noun* protective grating in front of a fire. **fire irons** tongs, poker, and shovel for

F

———————————— THESAURUS ————————————

masterly, outstanding, splendid, superior OPPOSITE **poor. 2 = sunny**, balmy, bright, clear, clement, cloudless, dry, fair, pleasant OPPOSITE **cloudy. 4 = satisfactory**, acceptable, all right, convenient, good, O.K. *or* okay (*inf*), suitable **5 = delicate**, dainty, elegant, expensive, exquisite, fragile, quality OPPOSITE **coarse. 6 = slender**, diaphanous, flimsy, gauzy, gossamer, light, sheer, thin **9 = subtle**, abstruse, acute, hairsplitting, minute, precise, sharp

fine² *noun* **1 = penalty**, damages, forfeit, punishment ◆*verb* **2 = penalize**, mulct, punish

finery *noun* = **splendour**, frippery, gear (*inf*), glad rags (*inf*), ornaments, showiness, Sunday best, trappings, trinkets

finesse *noun* **1 = skill**, adeptness, adroitness, craft, sophistication **2 = subtlety**, delicacy, diplomacy, discretion, tact

finger *verb* **5 = touch**, feel, fiddle with (*inf*),

handle, manipulate, maul, paw (*inf*), toy with

finish *verb* **1 = stop**, cease, close, complete, conclude, end, round off, terminate, wind up, wrap up (*inf*) OPPOSITE **start. 2 = consume**, devour, dispose of, eat, empty, exhaust, use up **3 = perfect**, polish, refine **4 = coat**, gild, lacquer, polish, stain, texture, veneer, wax **5 = destroy**, bring down, defeat, dispose of, exterminate, overcome, put an end to, put paid to, rout, ruin ◆*noun* **6 = end**, cessation, close, completion, conclusion, culmination, denouement, finale, run-in OPPOSITE **beginning. 7 = defeat**, annihilation, curtains (*inf*), death, end, end of the road, ruin **8 = surface**, lustre, patina, polish, shine, smoothness, texture

finite *adjective* = **limited**, bounded, circumscribed, delimited, demarcated, restricted OPPOSITE **infinite**

tending a domestic fire. **fireplace** *noun* recess in a room for a fire. **fire power** *Mil* amount a weapon or unit can fire. **fire raiser** person who deliberately starts fires. **fire station** building where firefighters are stationed. **fire trap** building which could easily catch fire or which would be difficult to escape from if it did. **firewall** *noun Computers* computer that prevents unauthorized access to a computer network from the Internet. **firework** *noun* **1** device containing chemicals that is ignited to produce spectacular explosions and coloured sparks. ◆ *plural* **2** show of fireworks. **3** *Informal* outburst of temper. **firing line** leading or most vulnerable position. **firing squad** group of soldiers ordered to execute an offender by shooting.

firm¹ ❶ *adjective* **1** not soft or yielding. **2** securely in position. **3** definite. **4** having determination or strength. ◆ *adverb* **5** in an unyielding manner, e.g. *hold firm.* ◆ *verb* **6** make or become firm. **firmly** *adverb* **firmness** *noun*

firm² ❶ *noun* business company.

firmament *noun Lit* sky or the heavens.

first ❶ *adjective* **1** earliest in time or order. **2** graded or ranked above all others. ◆ *noun* **3** person or thing coming before all others. **4** outset or beginning. **5** first-class honours degree at university. **6** lowest forward gear in a motor vehicle. ◆ *adverb* **7** before anything else.

8 for the first time. **firstly** *adverb* **first aid** immediate medical assistance given in an emergency. **first-class** *adjective* **1** of the highest class or grade. **2** excellent. **first-foot** *Scot noun, pl* **first-foots 1** first person to enter a house in the New Year. ◆ *verb* **2** visit (someone) as a first-foot. **first-footing** *noun* **first-hand** *adjective, adverb* (obtained) directly from the original source. **first mate** officer of a merchant ship second in command to the captain. **first person** *Grammar* category of verbs and pronouns used by a speaker to refer to himself or herself. **first-rate** *adjective* excellent. **first refusal** right to buy something before it is offered to others. **first-strike** *adjective* (of a nuclear missile) for use in an opening attack to destroy enemy weapons. **First Nations** *plural noun Canad* Canadian aboriginal communities. **First Peoples** *plural noun Canad* a collective term for the Native Canadian peoples, the Inuit, and the Métis.

firth *noun* narrow inlet of the sea.

fiscal *adjective* **1** of government finances, esp. taxes. ◆ *noun* **2** short for PROCURATOR FISCAL.

fish ❶ *noun, pl* **fish, fishes 1** cold-blooded vertebrate with gills, that lives in water. **2** its flesh as food. ◆ *verb* **3** try to catch fish. **4** fish in (a particular area of water). **5** (foll. by *for*) grope for and find with difficulty. **6** (foll. by *for*) seek indirectly. **fisherman** *noun* person who

———————— THESAURUS ————————

fire *noun* **1, 3** =**flames**, blaze, combustion, conflagration, inferno **4** =**bombardment**, barrage, cannonade, flak, fusillade, hail, salvo, shelling, sniping, volley **5** =**passion**, ardour, eagerness, enthusiasm, excitement, fervour, intensity, sparkle, spirit, verve, vigour ◆*verb* **6** =**shoot**, detonate, discharge, explode, let off, pull the trigger, set off, shell **7** *Inf* =**dismiss**, cashier, discharge, make redundant, sack (*inf*), show the door **10** =**inspire**, animate, enliven, excite, galvanize, impassion, inflame, rouse, stir

firebrand *noun* =**rabble-rouser**, agitator, demagogue, incendiary, instigator, tub-thumper

fireworks *plural noun* **2** =**pyrotechnics**, illuminations **3** *Inf* =**trouble**, hysterics, rage, row, storm, uproar

firm¹ *adjective* **1** =**hard**, dense, inflexible, rigid, set, solid, solidified, stiff, unyielding OPPOSITE> **soft**. **2** =**secure**, embedded, fast, fixed, immovable, rooted, stable, steady, tight, unshakable OPPOSITE> **loose**. **3** =**definite 3** =**determined**, adamant, inflexible, resolute, resolved, set on, unbending, unshakable, unyielding OPPOSITE> **wavering**

firm² *noun* =**company**, association, business, concern, conglomerate, corporation, enterprise, organization, partnership

firmly *adverb* =**securely**, immovably, like a rock, resolutely, staunchly, steadfastly, steadily, tightly, unchangeably, unflinchingly, unshakably, unwaveringly

firmness *noun* **1** =**hardness**, inelasticity, inflexibility, resistance, rigidity, solidity, stiffness **4** =**resolve**, constancy, inflexibility, resolution, staunchness, steadfastness

first *adjective* **1** =**earliest**, cardinal, elementary, fundamental, initial, introductory, key, maiden, opening, original, premier, primary, primordial, rudimentary **2** =**foremost**, chief, head, highest, leading, pre-eminent, prime, principal, ruling ◆*noun* **4** *as in* **from the first** =**start**, beginning, commencement, inception, introduction, outset, starting point ◆*adverb* **7** =**to begin with**, at the beginning, at the outset, beforehand, firstly, initially, in the first place, to start with

first-rate *adjective* =**excellent**, crack (*sl*), elite, exceptional, first class, outstanding, superb, catches fish for a living or for pleasure. **fishery** noun, pl **-eries** area of the sea used for fishing. **fishing** noun job or pastime of catching fish. **fishy** adjective **fishier, fishiest 1** of or like fish. **2** Informal suspicious or questionable.

fishfinger noun oblong piece of fish covered in breadcrumbs. **fishmeal** dried ground fish used as animal feed or fertilizer. **fishmonger** noun seller of fish. **fishnet** noun open mesh fabric resembling netting. **fishwife** noun, pl **-wives** coarse scolding woman.

fishplate noun metal plate holding rails together.

fission noun **1** splitting. **2** Biol asexual reproduction involving a division into two or more equal parts. **3** splitting of an atomic nucleus with the release of a large amount of energy. **fissionable** adjective **fissile** adjective **1** capable of undergoing nuclear fission. **2** tending to split.

fissure ⊙ [fish-er] noun long narrow cleft or crack.

fist noun clenched hand. **fisticuffs** plural noun fighting with the fists.

fistula [fist-yew-la] noun long narrow ulcer.

fit¹ ⊙ verb **fitting, fitted 1** be appropriate or suitable for. **2** be of the correct size or shape (for). **3** adjust so as to make appropriate. **4** try (clothes) on and note any adjustments needed. **5** make competent or ready. **6** correspond with the facts or circumstances. ♦ adjective **7** appropriate. **8** in good health. **9** worthy or deserving. ♦ noun **10** way in which something fits. **fitness** noun **fitted** adjective **1** designed for excellent fit, e.g. a fitted suit. **2** (of a kitchen, bathroom, etc.) having equipment and

furniture built or selected to suit the measurements of the room. **3** (of a carpet) covering a floor completely. **fitter** noun **1** person skilled in the installation and adjustment of machinery. **2** person who fits garments. **fitting** adjective **1** appropriate, suitable. ♦ noun **2** accessory or part. **3** trying on of clothes for size. ♦ plural **4** furnishings and accessories in a building. **fitment** noun **1** accessory attached to a machine. **2** detachable part of the furnishings of a room. **fit in** verb **1** give a place or time to. **2** belong or conform. **fit out** verb provide with the necessary equipment.

fit² ⊙ noun **1** sudden attack or convulsion, such as an epileptic seizure. **2** sudden short burst or spell.

fitful ⊙ adjective occurring in irregular spells. **fitfully** adverb

five adjective, noun one more than four. **fiver** noun Informal five-pound note. **fives** noun ball game resembling squash but played with bats or the hands.

fix ⊙ verb **1** make or become firm, stable, or secure. **2** repair. **3** place permanently. **4** settle definitely. **5** direct (the eyes etc.) steadily. **6** Informal unfairly influence the outcome of. ♦ noun **7** Informal difficult situation. **8** ascertaining of the position of a ship by radar etc. **9** Slang injection of a narcotic drug. **fixed** adjective **fixedly** [fix-id-lee] adverb steadily. **fixer** noun **1** solution used to make a photographic image permanent. **2** Slang person who arranges things. **fix up** verb **1** arrange. **2** provide (with).

fixation ⊙ noun obsessive interest in

————————————— THESAURUS —————————————

superlative, top-notch (inf), world-class

fishy adjective **1** = **fishlike**, piscatorial, piscatory, piscine **2** Inf = **suspicious**, dodgy (Brit, Aust & NZ inf), dubious, funny (inf), implausible, odd, questionable, suspect, unlikely

fissure noun = **crack**, breach, cleft, crevice, fault, fracture, opening, rift, rupture, split

fit¹ verb **1, 2** = **suit**, accord, belong, conform, correspond, match, meet, tally **3** = **adapt**, adjust, alter, arrange, customize, modify, shape, tweak (inf) **5** = **equip**, arm, fit out, kit out, prepare, provide ♦ adjective **7** = **appropriate**, apt, becoming, correct, fitting, proper, right, seemly, suitable OPPOSITE **inappropriate**. **8** = **healthy**, able-bodied, hale, in good shape, robust, strapping, trim, well OPPOSITE **unfit**

fit² noun **1** = **seizure**, attack, bout, convulsion, paroxysm, spasm **2** = **outbreak**, bout, burst, outburst, spell

fitful adjective = **irregular**, broken, desultory, disturbed, inconstant, intermittent, spasmodic, sporadic, uneven OPPOSITE **regular**

fitness noun **7** = **appropriateness**, aptness, competence, eligibility, propriety, readiness, suitability **8** = **health**, good condition, good health, robustness, strength, vigour, wellness

fitting adjective **1** = **appropriate**, apposite, becoming, correct, decent, proper, right, seemly, suitable OPPOSITE **unfitting** ♦ noun **2** = **accessory**, attachment, component, part, piece, unit

fix verb **1** = **fasten**, attach, bind, connect, link, secure, stick, tie **2** = **repair**, correct, mend, patch up, put to rights, see to **3** = **place**, embed, establish, implant, install, locate, plant, position, set **4** = **decide**, agree on, arrange, arrive at, determine, establish, set, settle, specify **5** = **focus**, direct **6** Inf = **rig**, fiddle (inf),

something. **fixated** *adjective* obsessed.
fixative *noun* liquid used to preserve or hold things in place.
fixture *noun* **1** permanently fitted piece of household equipment. **2** person whose presence seems permanent. **3** sports match or the date fixed for it.
fizz ✪ *verb* **1** make a hissing or bubbling noise. **2** give off small bubbles. ◆ *noun* **3** hissing or bubbling noise. **4** releasing of small bubbles of gas by a liquid. **5** effervescent drink. **fizzy** *adjective* **fizzier, fizziest. fizziness** *noun*
fizzle *verb* make a weak hissing or bubbling sound. **fizzle out** *verb Informal* come to nothing, fail.
fjord [fee-**ord**] *noun* long narrow inlet of the sea between cliffs, esp. in Norway.
FL Florida.
flab *noun Informal* unsightly body fat.
flabbergasted ✪ *adjective* completely astonished.
flabby ✪ *adjective* **-bier, -biest 1** having flabby flesh. **2** loose or limp. **flabbiness** *noun*
flaccid [**flas**-sid] *adjective* soft and limp. **flaccidity** *noun*
flag¹ ✪ *noun* **1** piece of cloth attached to a pole as an emblem or signal. ◆ *verb* **flagging, flagged 2** mark with a flag or sticker. **3** (often foll. by *down*) signal (a vehicle) to stop by waving the arm. **flag day** day on which small stickers are sold in the streets for charity.
flagpole, flagstaff *noun* pole for a flag.
flagship *noun* **1** admiral's ship. **2** most

important product of an organization.
flag² ✪ *verb* **flagging, flagged** lose enthusiasm or vigour.
flag³, flagstone *noun* flat paving-stone. **flagged** *adjective* paved with flagstones.
flag⁴ *noun* any of various plants with sword-shaped leaves, esp. the iris.
flagellate [**flaj**-a-late] *verb* whip, esp. in religious penance or for sexual pleasure. **flagellation** *noun* **flagellant** *noun* person who whips himself or herself.
flagellum [flaj-**jell**-lum] *noun, pl* **-la** [-la] **-lums 1** *Biol* whiplike outgrowth from a cell that acts as an organ of movement. **2** *Botany* long thin shoot.
flageolet [flaj-a-**let**] *noun* small instrument like a recorder.
flagon *noun* **1** wide bottle for wine or cider. **2** narrow-necked jug for liquid.
flagrant ✪ [**flayg**-rant] *adjective* openly outrageous. **flagrantly** *adverb* **flagrancy** *noun*
flail ✪ *verb* **1** wave about wildly. **2** beat or thrash. ◆ *noun* **3** tool formerly used for threshing grain by hand.
flair ✪ *noun* **1** natural ability. **2** stylishness.
flak *noun* **1** anti-aircraft fire. **2** *Informal* severe criticism.
flake ✪ *noun* **1** small thin piece, esp. chipped off something. **2** *Aust, NZ & US informal* unreliable person. ◆ *verb* **3** peel off in flakes. **flaky** *adjective* **flakier, flakiest. flake out** *verb Informal* collapse or fall asleep from exhaustion.
flambé [**flahm**-bay] *verb* **flambéing,**

influence, manipulate ◆*noun* **7** *Inf* =**predicament**, difficulty, dilemma, embarrassment, mess, pickle (*inf*), plight, quandary
fixation *noun* =**obsession**, complex, hang-up (*inf*), infatuation, mania, preoccupation, thing (*inf*)
fixed *adjective* **3** =**immovable**, established, permanent, rigid, rooted, secure, set ⟨OPPOSITE⟩ **moving. 4** =**definite**, agreed, arranged, decided, established, planned, resolute, resolved, settled, unwavering
fix up *verb* **1** =**arrange**, agree on, fix, organize, plan, settle, sort out **2** =**provide**, arrange for, bring about, lay on
fizz *verb* **1, 2** =**bubble**, effervesce, fizzle, froth, hiss, sparkle, sputter
fizzy *adjective* =**bubbly**, bubbling, carbonated, effervescent, gassy, sparkling
flabbergasted *adjective* =**astonished**, amazed, astounded, dumbfounded, lost for words, overwhelmed, speechless, staggered,

stunned
flabby *adjective* **1** =**baggy 2** =**limp**, drooping, flaccid, floppy, loose, pendulous, sagging ⟨OPPOSITE⟩ **firm**
flag¹ *noun* **1** =**banner**, colours, ensign, pennant, pennon, standard, streamer ◆*verb* **2** =**mark**, indicate, label, note **3** (often foll. by *down*) =**hail**, signal, warn, wave
flag² *verb* =**weaken**, abate, droop, fade, languish, peter out, sag, wane, weary, wilt
flagging *adjective* =**weakening**, declining, deteriorating, fading, faltering, waning, wilting
flagrant *adjective* =**outrageous**, barefaced, blatant, brazen, glaring, heinous, scandalous, shameless ⟨OPPOSITE⟩ **slight**
flail *verb* **1** =**windmill 2** =**thrash**, beat, thresh
flair *noun* **1** =**ability**, aptitude, faculty, feel, genius, gift, knack, mastery, talent **2** =**style**, chic, dash, discernment, elegance, panache, stylishness, taste
flake *noun* **1** =**chip**, layer, peeling, scale, shaving, sliver, wafer ◆*verb* **2** =**chip**, blister,

flambéed cook or serve (food) in flaming brandy.

flamboyant ❶ adjective **1** behaving in a very noticeable, extravagant way. **2** very bright and showy. **flamboyance** noun

flame ❶ noun **1** luminous burning gas coming from burning material. ◆ verb **2** burn brightly. **3** become bright red. **old flame** Informal former sweetheart.

flamenco noun, pl **-cos 1** rhythmical Spanish dance accompanied by a guitar and vocalist. **2** music for this dance.

flamingo noun, pl **-gos, -goes** large pink wading bird with a long neck and legs.

flammable adjective easily set on fire. **flammability** noun

flan noun open sweet or savoury tart.

flange noun projecting rim or collar.

flank ❶ noun **1** part of the side between the hips and ribs. **2** side of a body of troops. ◆ verb **3** be at or move along the side of.

flannel noun **1** small piece of cloth for washing the face. **2** soft woollen fabric for clothing. **3** Informal evasive talk. ◆ plural **4** trousers made of flannel. ◆ verb **-nelling, -nelled 5** Informal talk evasively. **flannelette** noun cotton imitation of flannel.

flap ❶ verb **flapping, flapped 1** move back and forwards or up and down. ◆ noun **2** action or sound of flapping. **3** piece of something attached by one edge only. **4** hinged section of an aircraft's wing that is raised and lowered to control the speed. **5** Informal state of excitement or panic.

flapjack noun chewy biscuit made with oats.

flare ❶ verb **1** blaze with a sudden unsteady flame. **2** Informal (of temper, violence, or trouble) break out suddenly. **3** (of a skirt or trousers) become wider towards the hem. ◆ noun **4** sudden unsteady flame. **5** signal light. ◆ plural **6** flared trousers. **flared** adjective (of a skirt or trousers) becoming wider towards the hem.

flash ❶ noun **1** sudden burst of light or flame. **2** sudden occurrence (of intuition or emotion). **3** very short time. **4** brief unscheduled news announcement. **5** Photog small bulb that produces an intense flash of light. ◆ adjective **6** (also **flashy**) vulgarly showy. ◆ verb **7** (cause to) burst into flame. **8** (cause to) emit light suddenly or intermittently. **9** move very fast. **10** come rapidly (to mind or view). **11** Informal display ostentatiously. **12** Slang expose oneself indecently. **flasher** noun Slang man who exposes himself indecently. **flashback** noun scene in a book, play, or film, that shows earlier events. **flash flood** sudden short-lived flood. **flashlight** noun US torch. **flash point 1** critical point beyond which a situation will inevitably erupt into violence. **2** lowest temperature at which vapour given off by a liquid can ignite.

flashing noun watertight material used to cover joins in a roof.

flask noun **1** same as VACUUM FLASK. **2** flat bottle for carrying alcoholic drink in the pocket. **3** narrow-necked bottle.

flat¹ ❶ adjective **flatter, flattest 1** level and horizontal. **2** even and smooth. **3** (of a tyre) deflated. **4** outright. **5** fixed. **6** without variation or emotion. **7** (of a drink) no longer fizzy. **8** (of a battery) with no electrical charge. **9** Music below the true pitch. ◆ adverb **10** in or into a flat position. **11** completely or absolutely. **12** exactly. **13** Music too low in pitch. ◆ noun **14** flat surface. **15** Music symbol lowering the pitch of a note by a semitone. **16** punctured car tyre. **17** level ground. **18** mudbank exposed at low tide. **flat out** with maximum speed or effort. **flatly** adverb **flatness** noun **flatten** verb **flatfish** noun sea fish, such as the sole, which has a flat body. **flat-footed** adjective **1** having

———————————————— T H E S A U R U S ————————————————

peel off

flake out verb Inf =**collapse**, faint, keel over, pass out

flamboyant adjective **1** =**theatrical**, dashing, extravagant, ostentatious, swashbuckling **2** =**showy**, brilliant, colourful, dazzling, elaborate, florid, glamorous, glitzy (sl), ornate

flame noun **1** =**fire**, blaze ◆verb **2** =**burn**, blaze, flare, flash, glare, glow, shine

flank noun **1** =**side**, hip, loin, thigh

flap verb **1** =**flutter**, beat, flail, shake, thrash, vibrate, wag, wave ◆noun **2** =**flutter**, beating, shaking, swinging, swish, waving **5** Inf =**panic**, agitation, commotion, fluster, state (inf), sweat

(inf), tizzy (inf)

flare verb **1** =**blaze**, burn up, flicker, glare ◆noun **4** =**flame**, blaze, burst, flash, flicker, glare

flash noun **1** =**gleam**, blaze, burst, dazzle, flare, flicker, shimmer, spark, streak **3** =**moment**, instant, jiffy (inf), second, split second, trice, twinkling of an eye ◆adjective **6** (also **flashy**) =**showy**, flamboyant, garish, gaudy, glitzy (sl), jazzy (inf), ostentatious, snazzy (inf), tacky (inf), tasteless, vulgar ◆verb **7** =**blaze**, flare **8** =**gleam**, flicker, glare, shimmer, sparkle, twinkle **9** =**speed**, dart, dash, fly, race, shoot, streak, whistle, zoom **11** Inf =**show**, display, exhibit, expose, flaunt, flourish a less than usually arched instep. **2** clumsy or insensitive. **flat racing** horse racing over level ground with no jumps.

flat² ⊕ *noun* set of rooms for living in which are part of a larger building. **flatlet** *noun* small flat. **flatmate** *noun* person with whom one shares a flat.

flatter ⊕ *verb* **1** praise insincerely. **2** show to advantage. **3** make (a person) appear more attractive in a picture than in reality. **flatterer** *noun* **flattery** *noun*

flattie *noun NZ & S Afr informal* flat tyre.

flatulent *adjective* suffering from or caused by too much gas in the intestines. **flatulence** *noun*

flaunt ⊕ *verb* display (oneself or one's possessions) arrogantly.

> **LANGUAGE TIP**
>
> Be careful not to confuse this with *flout* meaning 'disobey'.

flautist [**flaw**-tist] *noun* flute player.

flavour ⊕ *noun* **1** distinctive taste. **2** distinctive characteristic or quality. ◆ *verb* **3** give flavour to. **flavouring** *noun* substance used to flavour food. **flavourless** *adjective*

flaw ⊕ *noun* **1** imperfection or blemish. **2** mistake that makes a plan or argument invalid. **flawed** *adjective* **flawless** *adjective*

flax *noun* **1** plant grown for its stem fibres and seeds. **2** its fibres, spun into linen thread.

flaxen *adjective* (of hair) pale yellow.

flay *verb* **1** strip the skin off. **2** criticize severely.

flea *noun* small wingless jumping bloodsucking insect. **flea market** market for cheap goods.

fleapit *noun Informal* shabby cinema or theatre.

fleck *noun* **1** small mark, streak, or speck. ◆ *verb* **2** speckle.

fled *verb* past of FLEE.

fledged *adjective* **1** (of young birds) able to fly. **2** (of people) fully trained. **fledgling, fledgeling** *noun* **1** young bird. ◆ *adjective* **2** new or inexperienced.

flee ⊕ *verb* **fleeing, fled** run away (from).

fleece *noun* **1** sheep's coat of wool. **2** sheepskin used as a lining for coats etc. **3** warm polyester fabric. **4** jacket or top made of this fabric. ◆ *verb* **5** defraud or overcharge. **fleecy** *adjective* made of or like fleece.

fleet¹ ⊕ *noun* **1** number of warships organized as a unit. **2** number of vehicles under the same ownership.

fleet² ⊕ *adjective* swift in movement. **fleeting** *adjective* rapid and soon passing. **fleetingly** *adverb*

Fleet Street *noun* **1** street in London where many newspaper offices were formerly situated. **2** British national newspapers collectively.

———————— T H E S A U R U S ————————

flat¹ *adjective* **1, 2 = even**, horizontal, level, levelled, low, smooth OPPOSITE **uneven**. **3 = punctured**, blown out, burst, collapsed, deflated, empty **4 = absolute**, categorical, downright, explicit, out-and-out, positive, unequivocal, unqualified **6 = dull**, boring, dead, lacklustre, lifeless, monotonous, tedious, tiresome, uninteresting OPPOSITE **exciting** ◆*adverb* **11 = completely**, absolutely, categorically, exactly, point blank, precisely, utterly **flat out = at full speed**, all out, at full tilt, for all one is worth, hell for leather (*inf*)

flat² *noun* **= apartment**, rooms, duplex (*US & Canad*)

flatten *verb* **1 = level**, compress, even out, iron out, raze, smooth off, squash, trample

flatter *verb* **1 = praise**, butter up, compliment, pander to, soft-soap (*inf*), sweet-talk (*inf*), wheedle **2 = suit**, become, do something for, enhance, set off, show to advantage

flattery *noun* **1 = obsequiousness**, adulation, blandishments, fawning, servility, soft-soap (*inf*), sweet-talk (*inf*), sycophancy

flaunt *verb* **= show off**, brandish, display, exhibit, flash about, flourish, parade, sport (*inf*)

flavour *noun* **1 = taste**, aroma, flavouring, piquancy, relish, savour, seasoning, smack, tang, zest OPPOSITE **blandness**. **2 = quality**, character, essence, feel, feeling, style, tinge, tone ◆*verb* **3 = season**, ginger up, imbue, infuse, leaven, spice

flaw *noun* **1 = weakness**, blemish, chink in one's armour, defect, failing, fault, imperfection, weak spot

flawed *adjective* **1 = damaged**, blemished, defective, faulty, imperfect **2 = unsound**, erroneous

flawless *adjective* **1 = perfect**, faultless, impeccable, spotless, unblemished, unsullied

flee *verb* **= run away**, bolt, depart, escape, fly, make one's getaway, scarper (*Brit sl*), take flight, take off (*inf*), take to one's heels, turn tail

fleet¹ *noun* **1 = navy**, armada, flotilla, task force

fleet² *adjective* **= swift**, fast, flying, mercurial, meteoric, nimble, nimble-footed, quick, rapid, speedy, winged

fleeting *adjective* **= momentary**, brief, ephemeral, passing, short-lived, temporary, transient, transitory OPPOSITE **lasting**

Flemish *noun* **1** one of two official languages of Belgium. ◆ *adjective* **2** of Flanders, in Belgium.

flesh ❶ *noun* **1** soft part of a human or animal body. **2** *Informal* excess fat. **3** meat of animals as opposed to fish or fowl. **4** thick soft part of a fruit or vegetable. **5** human body as opposed to the soul. **in the flesh** in person, actually present. **one's own flesh and blood** one's family. **flesh-coloured** *adjective* yellowish-pink. **fleshly** *adjective* **1** carnal. **2** worldly. **fleshy** *adjective* **fleshier, fleshiest 1** plump. **2** like flesh. **flesh wound** wound affecting only superficial tissue.

fleur-de-lys, fleur-de-lis [flur-de-**lee**] *noun, pl* **fleurs-de-lys, fleurs-de-lis** heraldic lily with three petals.

flew *verb* past tense of FLY¹.

flex ❶ *noun* **1** flexible insulated electric cable. ◆ *verb* **2** bend. **flexible** *adjective* **1** easily bent. **2** adaptable. **flexibly** *adverb* **flexibility** *noun* **flexitime** *noun* system permitting variation in starting and finishing times of work.

flick ❶ *verb* **1** touch or move with the finger or hand in a quick movement. **2** move with a short sudden movement, often repeatedly, e.g. *the windscreen wipers flicked back and forth.* ◆ *noun* **3** tap or quick stroke. ◆ *plural* **4** *Slang* the cinema. **flick knife** knife with a spring-loaded blade which shoots out when a button is pressed. **flick through** *verb* look at (a book or magazine) quickly or idly.

flicker ❶ *verb* **1** shine unsteadily or intermittently. **2** move quickly to and fro. ◆ *noun* **3** unsteady brief light. **4** brief faint indication.

flier *noun* see FLY¹.

flight¹ ❶ *noun* **1** journey by air. **2** act or manner of flying through the air. **3** group of birds or aircraft flying together. **4** aircraft flying on a scheduled journey. **5** set of stairs between two landings. **6** stabilizing feathers or plastic fins on an arrow or dart. **flightless** *adjective* (of certain birds or insects) unable to fly. **flight deck 1** crew compartment in an airliner. **2** runway deck on an aircraft carrier. **flight lieutenant** junior commissioned officer in an air force. **flight of fancy** imaginative but impractical idea. **flight recorder** electronic device in an aircraft storing information about its flight.

flight² ❶ *noun* act of running away.

flighty *adjective* **flightier, flightiest** frivolous and fickle.

flimsy ❶ *adjective* **-sier, -siest 1** not strong or substantial. **2** thin. **3** not very convincing. **flimsily** *adverb* **flimsiness** *noun*

flinch ❶ *verb* draw back or wince, as from pain. **flinch from** *verb* shrink from or avoid.

fling ❶ *verb* **flinging, flung 1** throw, send, or move forcefully or hurriedly. ◆ *noun* **2** spell of self-indulgent enjoyment. **3** brief romantic or sexual relationship. **fling oneself into** (start to) do with great vigour.

flint *noun* **1** hard grey stone. **2** piece of this. **3** small piece of an iron alloy, used in cigarette lighters. **flinty** *adjective* **1** cruel. **2** of or like flint. **flintlock** *noun* obsolete gun in which the powder was lit by a spark from a flint.

flip ❶ *verb* **flipping, flipped 1** throw (something small or light) carelessly. **2** turn (something) over. **3** throw (a coin) so that it turns over in the air. **4** (also **flip one's lid**) *Slang* fly into an emotional state. ◆ *noun* **5** snap or tap. ◆ *adjective* **6** *Informal* flippant. **flipper** *noun* **1** limb of a sea animal adapted for

———————————— THESAURUS ————————————

flesh *noun* **1** = **meat**, tissue **2** = **fat**, brawn, weight **5** = **physical nature**, carnality, flesh and blood, human nature **one's own flesh and blood** = **family**, blood, kin, kinsfolk, kith and kin, relations, relatives

flexible *adjective* **1** = **pliable**, elastic, lithe, plastic, pliant, springy, stretchy, supple [OPPOSITE] **rigid**. **2** = **adaptable**, adjustable, discretionary, open, variable [OPPOSITE] **inflexible**

flick *verb* **1** = **strike**, dab, flip, hit, tap, touch **flick through** = **browse**, flip through, glance at, skim, skip, thumb

flicker *verb* **1** = **twinkle**, flare, flash, glimmer, gutter, shimmer, sparkle **2** = **flutter**, quiver, vibrate, waver ◆*noun* **3** = **glimmer**, flare, flash, gleam, spark **4** = **trace**, breath, glimmer, iota,

spark

flight¹ *noun* **1** = **journey**, trip, voyage **2** = **aviation**, aeronautics, flying **3** = **flock**, cloud, formation, squadron, swarm, unit

flight² *noun* = **escape**, departure, exit, exodus, fleeing, getaway, retreat, running away

flimsy *adjective* **1** = **fragile**, delicate, frail, insubstantial, makeshift, rickety, shaky [OPPOSITE] **sturdy**. **2** = **thin**, gauzy, gossamer, light, sheer, transparent **3** = **unconvincing**, feeble, implausible, inadequate, pathetic, poor, unsatisfactory, weak

flinch *verb* = **recoil**, cower, cringe, draw back, quail, shirk, shrink, shy away, wince

fling *verb* **1** = **throw**, cast, catapult, heave, hurl, propel, sling, toss ◆*noun* **2** = **binge** (*inf*), bash, good time, party, rave-up (*Brit sl*), spree

F

swimming. **2** one of a pair of paddle-like rubber devices worn on the feet to help in swimming. **flipchart** *noun* large pad of paper mounted on a stand, used in giving lectures etc. **flip-flop** *noun* rubber-soled sandal held on by a thong between the big toe and the next toe. **flip through** *verb* look at (a book or magazine) quickly or idly.

flippant ❶ *adjective* treating serious things lightly. **flippancy** *noun*

flirt ❶ *verb* **1** behave as if sexually attracted to someone. **2** consider lightly, toy (with). ◆ *noun* **3** person who flirts. **flirtation** *noun* **flirtatious** *adjective*

flit *verb* **flitting, flitted 1** move lightly and rapidly. **2** *Scot* move house. **3** *Informal* depart hurriedly and secretly. ◆ *noun* **4** act of flitting.

float ❶ *verb* **1** rest on the surface of a liquid. **2** move lightly and freely. **3** move about aimlessly. **4** launch (a company). **5** offer for sale on the stock market. **6** allow (a currency) to fluctuate against other currencies. ◆ *noun* **7** light object used to help someone or something float. **8** indicator on a fishing line that moves when a fish bites. **9** decorated lorry in a procession. **10** small delivery vehicle. **11** sum of money used for minor expenses or to provide change. **floating** *adjective* **1** moving about, changing, e.g. *floating population*. **2** (of a voter) not committed to one party.

flock¹ ❶ *noun* **1** number of animals of one kind together. **2** large group of people. **3** *Christianity* congregation. ◆ *verb* **4** gather in a crowd.

flock² *noun* **1** wool or cotton waste used as stuffing. ◆ *adjective* **2** (of wallpaper) with a velvety raised pattern.

floe *noun* sheet of floating ice.

flog ❶ *verb* **flogging, flogged 1** beat with a whip or stick. **2** *Slang* sell. **flogging** *noun*

flood ❶ *noun* **1** overflow of water onto a normally dry area. **2** large amount of water. **3** rising of the tide. ◆ *verb* **4** cover or become covered with water. **5** fill to overflowing. **6** come in large numbers or quantities. **7** supply excess petrol to (an engine) so that it does not work properly. **floodgate** *noun* gate used to control the flow of water. **floodlight** *noun* **1** lamp that casts a broad intense beam of light. ◆ *verb* **-lighting, -lit 2** illuminate by floodlight.

floor ❶ *noun* **1** lower surface of a room. **2** level of a building. **3** flat bottom surface. **4** (right to speak in) a legislative hall. ◆ *verb* **5** knock down. **6** *Informal* disconcert or defeat. **floored** *adjective* covered with a floor. **flooring** *noun* material for floors. **floorboard** *noun* long plank used for making floors. **floor show** entertainment in a nightclub.

floozy *noun, pl* **-zies** *Old-fashioned slang* disreputable woman.

flop ❶ *verb* **flopping, flopped 1** bend, fall, or collapse loosely or carelessly. **2** *Informal* fail. ◆ *noun* **3** *Informal* failure. **4** flopping movement. **floppy** *adjective* **floppier, floppiest** hanging downwards, loose. **floppy disk** *Computers* flexible magnetic disk that stores information.

——————— THESAURUS ———————

flip *verb* **1-3 = toss**, flick, spin, throw ◆*noun* **5 = snap**

flippant *adjective* **=frivolous**, cheeky, disrespectful, glib, impertinent, irreverent, offhand, superficial ⟨OPPOSITE⟩ **serious**

flirt *verb* **1 = chat up** (*inf*), lead on, make advances, make eyes at, make sheep's eyes at, philander **2 = toy with**, consider, dabble in, entertain, expose oneself to, give a thought to, play with, trifle with ◆*noun* **3 = tease**, coquette, heart-breaker, philanderer

flirtatious *adjective* **1 = teasing**, amorous, come-hither, coquettish, coy, enticing, provocative, sportive

float *verb* **1 = be buoyant**, bob, sail ⟨OPPOSITE⟩ **sink**. **2 = glide**, hang, hover, move gently, slide, slip along **3 = drift 4 = launch**, get going, promote, set up ⟨OPPOSITE⟩ **cancel**

floating *adjective* **1 = free**, fluctuating, movable, unattached, variable, wandering

flock¹ *noun* **1 = herd**, colony, drove, flight, gaggle, skein **2 = crowd**, collection, company, gathering, group, herd, host, mass **3** *Christianity* **=congregation** ◆*verb* **4 = gather**, collect, congregate, converge, crowd, herd, huddle, mass, throng

flog *verb* **1 = beat**, flagellate, flay, lash, scourge, thrash, trounce, whack, whip

flood *noun* **1 = overflow**, deluge, downpour, inundation **2 = torrent**, flow, rush, stream **3 = tide**, spate ◆*verb* **4 = immerse**, drown, engulf, inundate, overwhelm, pour over, submerge, surge, swamp **5 = overflow**, fill, saturate

floor *noun* **2 = tier**, level, stage, storey ◆*verb* **5 = knock down**, deck (*sl*), prostrate **6** *Inf* **=disconcert**, baffle, bewilder, confound, defeat, dumbfound, perplex, puzzle, stump, throw (*inf*)

flop *verb* **1 = fall**, collapse, dangle, droop, drop, sag, slump **2** *Inf* **=fail**, come unstuck, fall flat, fold (*inf*), founder, go belly-up (*sl*), misfire ⟨OPPOSITE⟩ **succeed** ◆*noun* **3** *Inf* **=failure**, debacle, disaster, fiasco, nonstarter, washout (*inf*) ⟨OPPOSITE⟩ **success**

flora *noun* plants of a given place or time.
floral ❶ *adjective* consisting of or decorated with flowers.
floret [**flaw**-ret] *noun* small flower forming part of a composite flower head.
floribunda *noun* type of rose whose flowers grow in large clusters.
florid ❶ *adjective* **1** with a red or flushed complexion. **2** ornate.
florin *noun* former British coin equivalent to ten pence.
florist *noun* seller of flowers.
floss *noun* **1** fine silky fibres. **2** see DENTAL FLOSS.
flotation *noun* launching or financing of a business enterprise.
flotilla *noun* small fleet or fleet of small ships.
flotsam ❶ *noun* floating wreckage. **flotsam and jetsam 1** odds and ends. **2** homeless or vagrant people.
flounce¹ *verb* **1** go with emphatic movements. ◆ *noun* **2** flouncing movement.
flounce² *noun* ornamental frill on a garment.
flounder¹ ❶ *verb* **1** move with difficulty, as in mud. **2** behave or speak in a bungling or hesitating manner.
flounder² *noun* edible flatfish.
flour *noun* **1** powder made by grinding grain, esp. wheat. ◆ *verb* **2** sprinkle with flour. **floury** *adjective*
flourish ❶ *verb* **1** be active, successful, or widespread. **2** be at the peak of development. **3** wave (something) dramatically. ◆ *noun* **4** dramatic waving motion. **5** ornamental curly line in writing. **flourishing** *adjective*
flout ❶ [rhymes with **out**] *verb* deliberately disobey (a rule, law, etc.).

> **LANGUAGE TIP**
>
> Be careful not to confuse this with *flaunt* meaning 'display'.

flow ❶ *verb* **1** (of liquid) move in a stream. **2** (of blood or electricity) circulate. **3** proceed smoothly. **4** hang loosely. **5** be abundant. ◆ *noun* **6** act, rate, or manner of flowing. **7** continuous stream or discharge. **flow chart** diagram showing a sequence of operations in a process.
flower ❶ *noun* **1** part of a plant that produces seeds. **2** plant grown for its colourful flowers. **3** best or finest part. ◆ *verb* **4** produce flowers, bloom. **5** reach full growth or maturity. **in flower** with flowers open. **flowered** *adjective* decorated with a floral design. **flowery** *adjective* **1** decorated with a floral design. **2** (of language or style) elaborate. **flowerbed** *noun* piece of ground for growing flowers.
flown ❶ *verb* past participle of FLY¹.
fl. oz. fluid ounce(s).
flu *noun* short for INFLUENZA.
fluctuate ❶ *verb* change frequently and erratically. **fluctuation** *noun*
flue *noun* passage or pipe for smoke or hot air.
fluent ❶ *adjective* **1** able to speak or write with ease. **2** spoken or written with ease. **fluently** *adverb* **fluency** *noun*
fluff ❶ *noun* **1** soft fibres. **2** *Informal* mistake. ◆ *verb* **3** make or become soft and puffy. **4** *Informal* make a mistake. **fluffy** *adjective*

—————— T H E S A U R U S ——————

floppy *adjective* **1** = **droopy**, baggy, flaccid, limp, loose, pendulous, sagging, soft
floral *adjective* = **flowery**, flower-patterned
florid *adjective* **1** = **flushed**, blowsy, rubicund, ruddy OPPOSITE pale. **2** = **ornate**, baroque, flamboyant, flowery, high-flown, overelaborate OPPOSITE plain
flotsam *noun* = **debris**, detritus, jetsam, junk, odds and ends, wreckage
flounder¹ *verb* **1** = **struggle**, fumble, grope, stumble, thrash, toss
flourish *verb* **1, 2** = **thrive**, bloom, blossom, boom, flower, grow, increase, prosper, succeed OPPOSITE fail. **3** = **wave**, brandish, display, flaunt, shake, wield ◆*noun* **4** = **wave 5** = **ornamentation**, curlicue, decoration, embellishment, plume, sweep
flout *verb* = **defy**, laugh in the face of, mock, scoff at, scorn, sneer at, spurn OPPOSITE respect

flow *verb* **1** = **pour**, cascade, flood, gush, rush, stream, surge, sweep **2** = **run**, circulate, course, move, roll **3** = **issue**, arise, emanate, emerge, proceed, result, spring ◆*noun* **6** = **course**, current, drift, flood, flux, outpouring, spate, tide **7** = **stream**
flower *noun* **1, 2** = **bloom**, blossom, efflorescence **3** = **elite**, best, cream, pick ◆*verb* **4** = **bloom**, blossom, flourish, open, unfold **5** = **mature**
flowery *adjective* **1** = **ornate**, baroque, embellished, fancy, florid OPPOSITE plain. **2** = **high-flown**
fluctuate *verb* = **change**, alternate, oscillate, seesaw, shift, swing, vary, veer, waver
fluency *noun* **1** = **smoothness**, articulateness **2** = **ease**, assurance, command, control, facility, readiness, slickness
fluent *adjective* **1** = **flowing**, articulate, natural, smooth, voluble, well-versed OPPOSITE

F

fluffier, fluffiest

fluid ⊕ noun 1 substance able to flow and change its shape; a liquid or a gas. ◆ adjective 2 able to flow or change shape easily. **fluidity** noun **fluid ounce** one twentieth of a pint.

fluke¹ ⊕ noun accidental stroke of luck. **fluky** adjective

fluke² noun 1 flat triangular point of an anchor. 2 lobe of a whale's tail.

fluke³ noun parasitic worm.

flume noun 1 narrow sloping channel for water. 2 enclosed water slide at a swimming pool.

flummox verb puzzle or confuse.

flung verb past of FLING.

flunk verb US, Aust & NZ informal fail.

flunky, flunkey noun, pl **flunkies, flunkeys** 1 servile person. 2 manservant who wears a livery.

fluorescence noun emission of light from a substance bombarded by particles, such as electrons, or by radiation. **fluorescent** adjective **fluorescent lamp** lamp in which ultraviolet radiation causes the chemical lining of a glass tube to glow. **fluoresce** verb exhibit fluorescence.

fluoride noun compound containing fluorine. **fluoridate** verb add fluoride to (water) as protection against tooth decay. **fluoridation** noun

fluorine noun Chem toxic yellow gas, most reactive of all the elements.

flurry ⊕ noun, pl **-ries** 1 sudden commotion. 2 gust of rain or wind or fall of snow. ◆ verb **-rying, -ried** 3 confuse.

flush¹ ⊕ verb 1 blush or cause to blush. 2 send water through (a toilet or pipe) so as to clean

it. 3 elate. ◆ noun 4 blush. 5 rush of water. 6 excitement or elation. **flushed** adjective

flush² ⊕ adjective 1 level with the surrounding surface. 2 Informal having plenty of money.

flush³ ⊕ verb drive out of a hiding place.

flush⁴ noun (in card games) hand all of one suit.

fluster ⊕ verb 1 make nervous or upset. ◆ noun 2 nervous or upset state.

flute noun 1 wind instrument consisting of a tube with sound holes and a mouth hole in the side. 2 tall narrow wineglass. **fluted** adjective having decorative grooves. **fluting** noun design of decorative grooves.

flutter ⊕ verb 1 wave rapidly. 2 flap the wings. 3 move quickly and irregularly. 4 (of the heart) beat abnormally quickly. ◆ noun 5 flapping movement. 6 nervous agitation. 7 Informal small bet. 8 abnormally fast heartbeat.

fluvial [flew-vee-al] adjective of rivers.

flux noun 1 constant change or instability. 2 flow or discharge. 3 substance mixed with metal to assist in fusion. 4 Physics strength of a field in a given area.

fly¹ ⊕ verb **flying, flew, flown** 1 move through the air on wings or in an aircraft. 2 control the flight of. 3 float, flutter, display, or be displayed in the air. 4 transport or be transported by air. 5 move quickly or suddenly. 6 (of time) pass rapidly. 7 flee. ◆ noun, pl **flies** 8 (often pl) fastening at the front of trousers. 9 flap forming the entrance to a tent. ◆ plural 10 space above a stage, used for storage. **flyer**, **flier** noun 1 small advertising leaflet. 2 aviator. **fly-by-night** adjective Informal unreliable or untrustworthy. **flyleaf** noun blank leaf at the beginning or end of a book. **flyover**

———————— T H E S A U R U S ————————

halting. 2 = **effortless**, easy

fluff noun 1 = **fuzz**, down, nap, pile ◆verb 4 Inf = **mess up** (inf), bungle, make a mess off, muddle, spoil

fluffy adjective 1 = **soft**, downy, feathery, fleecy, fuzzy

fluid noun 1 = **liquid**, liquor, solution OPPOSITE solid ◆adjective 2 = **liquid**, flowing, liquefied, melted, molten, runny, watery OPPOSITE solid

fluke¹ noun = **stroke of luck**, accident, chance, coincidence, lucky break, quirk of fate, serendipity

flurry noun 1 = **commotion**, ado, bustle, disturbance, excitement, flutter, fuss, stir 2 = **gust**, squall

flush¹ verb 1 = **blush**, colour, glow, go red, redden 2 = **rinse out**, cleanse, flood, hose down, wash out ◆noun 4 = **blush**, colour, glow,

redness, rosiness

flush² adjective 1 = **level**, even, flat, square, true 2 Inf = **wealthy**, in the money (inf), moneyed, rich, well-heeled (inf), well-off

flush³ verb = **drive out**, discover, disturb, put to flight, rouse, start, uncover

flushed adjective 1 = **blushing**, crimson, embarrassed, glowing, hot, red, rosy, ruddy

fluster verb 1 = **upset**, agitate, bother, confuse, disturb, perturb, rattle (inf), ruffle, unnerve ◆noun 2 = **turmoil**, disturbance, dither, flap (inf), flurry, flutter, furore, state (inf)

flutter verb 2 = **beat**, flap 3 = **tremble**, quiver, ripple, waver 4 = **palpitate** ◆noun 5 = **vibration**, quiver, shiver, shudder, tremble, tremor, twitching 6 = **agitation**, commotion, confusion, dither, excitement, fluster, state (inf) 8 = **palpitation**

noun road passing over another by a bridge.
fly-past *noun* ceremonial flight of aircraft.
flywheel *noun* heavy wheel regulating the speed of a machine.
fly² *noun, pl* **flies** two-winged insect.
flycatcher *noun* small insect-eating songbird.
fly-fishing *noun* fishing with an artificial fly as a lure. **flypaper** *noun* paper with a sticky poisonous coating, used to kill flies. **flyweight** *noun* boxer weighing up to 112lb (professional) or 51kg (amateur).
fly³ *adjective Slang* sharp and cunning.
flying ⊕ *adjective* hurried and brief. **flying boat** aircraft fitted with floats instead of landing wheels. **flying colours** conspicuous success, e.g. *pass with flying colours.* **flying fish** fish with winglike fins used for gliding above the water. **flying fox** large fruit-eating bat. **flying officer** junior officer in an air force. **flying phalanger** phalanger with black-striped greyish fur, which moves with gliding leaps. **flying saucer** unidentified disc-shaped flying object, supposedly from outer space. **flying squad** small group of police, soldiers, etc., ready to act quickly. **flying start** very good start.
Fm *Chem* fermium.
FM frequency modulation.
foal *noun* **1** young of a horse or related animal. ◆ *verb* **2** give birth to a foal.
foam ⊕ *noun* **1** mass of small bubbles on a liquid. **2** frothy saliva. **3** light spongelike solid used for insulation, packing, etc. ◆ *verb* **4** produce foam. **5** be very angry, e.g. *he makes me foam at the mouth.* **foamy** *adjective* **foamier, foamiest**
fob *noun* **1** short watch chain. **2** small pocket in a waistcoat.
fob off *verb* **fobbing, fobbed 1** pretend to satisfy (a person) with lies or excuses. **2** sell or pass off (inferior goods) as valuable.

fo'c's'le *noun* same as FORECASTLE.
focus ⊕ *noun, pl* **-cuses, -ci** [-sye] **1** point at which light or sound waves converge. **2** state of an optical image when it is clearly defined. **3** state of an instrument producing such an image. **4** centre of interest or activity. ◆ *verb* **-cusing, -cused** *or* **-cussing, -cussed 5** bring or come into focus. **6** concentrate (on). **focal** *adjective* of or at a focus. **focal length** distance from a lens or a mirror to its focal point. **focal point 1** point where the object seen in a lens or a mirror is in perfect focus. **2** centre of interest or attention. **focus group** group of people gathered by a market-research company to discuss and assess a product or service.
fodder *noun* feed for livestock.
foe ⊕ *noun* enemy, opponent.
foetid *adjective* same as FETID.
foetus *noun, pl* **-tuses** same as FETUS.
fog ⊕ *noun* **1** mass of condensed water vapour in the lower air, often greatly reducing visibility. **2** blurred area on a developed photograph. ◆ *verb* **fogging, fogged 3** cover with steam. **foggy** *adjective* **foggier, foggiest. fogbound** *adjective* prevented from operating by fog.
foghorn *noun* large horn sounded to warn ships in fog.
fogey, fogy *noun, pl* **-geys, -gies** old-fashioned person.
foible *noun* minor weakness or slight peculiarity.
foil¹ ⊕ *verb* ruin (someone's plan).
foil² ⊕ *noun* **1** metal in a thin sheet. **2** anything which sets off another thing to advantage.
foil³ *noun* light slender flexible sword tipped with a button.
foist ⊕ *verb* (foll. by *on* or *upon*) force or impose on.
fold¹ ⊕ *verb* **1** bend so that one part covers another. **2** interlace (the arms). **3** clasp (in the

F

——————— T H E S A U R U S ———————

fly¹ *verb* **1 = take wing**, flit, flutter, hover, sail, soar, wing **2 = pilot**, control, manoeuvre, operate **3 = display**, flap, float, flutter, show, wave **5 = rush**, career, dart, dash, hurry, race, shoot, speed, sprint, tear **6 = pass**, elapse, flit, glide, pass swiftly, roll on, run its course, slip away **7 = flee**, escape, get away, run for it, skedaddle (*inf*), take to one's heels
flying *adjective* **= hurried**, brief, fleeting, hasty, rushed, short-lived, transitory
foam *noun* **1 = froth**, bubbles, head, lather, spray, spume, suds ◆ *verb* **4 = bubble**, boil, effervesce, fizz, froth, lather
focus *noun* **4 = centre**, focal point, heart, hub,

target ◆ *verb* **6 = concentrate**, aim, centre, direct, fix, pinpoint, spotlight, zoom in
foe *noun* **= enemy**, adversary, antagonist, opponent, rival OPPOSITE **friend**
fog *noun* **1 = mist**, gloom, miasma, murk, peasouper (*inf*), smog
foggy *adjective* **1 = misty**, cloudy, dim, hazy, indistinct, murky, smoggy, vaporous OPPOSITE **clear**
foil¹ *verb* **= thwart**, balk, counter, defeat, disappoint, frustrate, nullify, stop
foil² *noun* **2 = contrast**, antithesis, complement
foist *verb* (foll. by *on* or *upon*) **= impose**, fob off, palm off, pass off, sneak in, unload

arms). **4** *Cooking* mix gently. **5** *Informal* fail or
go bankrupt. ♦ *noun* **6** folded piece or part. **7**
mark, crease, or hollow made by folding.
folder *noun* piece of folded cardboard for
holding loose papers.
fold² *noun* **1** enclosure for sheep. **2** church or
its members.
foliage *noun* leaves. **foliaceous** *adjective* of or
like leaves. **foliation** *noun* process of producing
leaves.
folio *noun, pl* **-lios 1** sheet of paper folded in
half to make two leaves of a book. **2** book
made up of such sheets. **3** page number.
folk ⊕ *noun* **1** people in general. **2** race of
people. **3** *Informal* folk music. ♦ *plural* **4**
relatives. **folksy** *adjective* simple and
unpretentious. **folk dance** traditional country
dance. **folklore** *noun* traditional beliefs and
stories of a people. **folk music 1** music handed
down from generation to generation. **2** piece
written in the style of such music. **folk song 1**
song handed down among the common
people. **2** modern song like this. **folk singer**
follicle *noun* small cavity in the body, esp. one
from which a hair grows.
follow ⊕ *verb* **1** go or come after. **2**
accompany. **3** be a logical or natural
consequence of. **4** keep to the course or track
of. **5** act in accordance with. **6** accept the ideas
or beliefs of. **7** understand. **8** have a keen
interest in. **follower** *noun* disciple or supporter.
following *adjective* **1** about to be mentioned.
2 next in time. ♦ *noun* **3** group of
supporters. ♦ *preposition* **4** as a result of.

follow-on *noun Cricket* immediate second
innings forced on a team scoring a set number
of runs fewer than its opponents in the first
innings. **follow through** *verb* **1** continue an
action or series of actions until finished. **2** *Sport*
continue a stroke, kick, etc. after striking the
ball. **follow up** *verb* **1** investigate. **2** do a
second, often similar, thing after (a first).
follow-up *noun* something done to reinforce
an initial action.
folly ⊕ *noun, pl* **-lies 1** foolishness. **2** foolish
action or idea. **3** useless extravagant building.
foment [foam-**ent**] *verb* encourage or stir up
(trouble).
fond ⊕ *adjective* **1** tender, loving. **2** unlikely to
be realized, e.g. *a fond hope*. **fond of** having a
liking for. **fondly** *adverb* **fondness** *noun*
fondant *noun* (sweet made from) flavoured
paste of sugar and water.
fondle ⊕ *verb* caress.
fondue *noun* Swiss dish of a hot melted
cheese sauce into which pieces of bread are
dipped.
font *noun* bowl in a church for baptismal
water.
fontanelle *noun* soft membranous gap
between the bones of a baby's skull.
food ⊕ *noun* what one eats, solid
nourishment. **foodie** *noun Informal* gourmet.
food chain *Ecology* series of living organisms
each member of which feeds on another in the
chain and is in turn eaten. **food poisoning**
illness caused by eating contaminated food.
food processor machine for chopping,

———————— THESAURUS ————————

fold¹ *verb* **1 = bend**, crease, double over **5** *Inf*
= go bankrupt, collapse, crash, fail, go bust
(*inf*), go to the wall, go under, shut down
♦*noun* **7 = crease**, bend, furrow, overlap, pleat,
wrinkle
folder *noun* **=file**, binder, envelope, portfolio
folk *noun* **1 = people 2 = race**, clan, tribe
♦*plural* **4 = family**, kin, kindred
follow *verb* **1 = come after**, come next,
succeed, supersede, supplant, take the place of
OPPOSITE **precede. 2 = accompany**, attend,
escort, tag along **3 = result**, arise, develop,
ensue, flow, issue, proceed, spring **4 = pursue**,
chase, dog, hound, hunt, shadow, stalk, track,
trail OPPOSITE **avoid. 5 = obey**, be guided by,
conform, heed, observe OPPOSITE **ignore. 7**
= understand, appreciate, catch on (*inf*),
comprehend, fathom, grasp, realize, take in **8**
= be interested in, cultivate, keep abreast of,
support
follower *noun* **=supporter**, adherent, apostle,

devotee, disciple, fan, pupil OPPOSITE **leader**
following *adjective* **2 = next**, consequent,
ensuing, later, subsequent, succeeding,
successive ♦*noun* **3 = supporters**, clientele,
coterie, entourage, fans, retinue, suite, train
folly *noun* **1 = foolishness**, imprudence,
indiscretion, lunacy, madness, nonsense,
rashness, stupidity OPPOSITE **wisdom**
fond *adjective* **1 = loving**, adoring,
affectionate, amorous, caring, devoted, doting,
indulgent, tender, warm OPPOSITE **indifferent.**
2 = foolish, deluded, delusive, empty, naive,
overoptimistic, vain OPPOSITE **sensible ♦ fond**
of = keen on, addicted to, attached to,
enamoured of, having a soft spot for, hooked
on, into (*inf*), partial to
fondle *verb* **=caress**, cuddle, dandle, pat, pet,
stroke
fondness *noun* **1 = liking**, affection,
attachment, devotion, fancy, love, partiality,
penchant, soft spot, taste, weakness OPPOSITE

liquidizing, or mixing food. **foodstuff** *noun* substance used as food.

fool¹ ⊙ *noun* **1** person lacking sense or judgment. **2** person made to appear ridiculous. **3** *Hist* jester, clown. ◆ *verb* **4** deceive (someone). **foolish** *adjective* unwise, silly, or absurd. **foolishly** *adverb* **foolishness** *noun* **foolery** *noun* foolish behaviour. **fool around** *verb* act or play irresponsibly or aimlessly. **foolproof** *adjective* unable to fail. **fool's paradise** state of happiness based on false hopes or beliefs.

fool² *noun* dessert of puréed fruit mixed with cream.

foolhardy ⊙ *adjective* recklessly adventurous. **foolhardiness** *noun*

foolscap *noun* size of paper, 34.3 ×43.2 centimetres.

foot ⊙ *noun, pl* **feet 1** part of the leg below the ankle. **2** unit of length of twelve inches (0.3048 metre). **3** lowest part of anything. **4** unit of poetic rhythm. **foot it** *Informal* walk. **foot the bill** pay the entire cost. **footage** *noun* amount of film used. **foot-and-mouth disease** infectious viral disease of sheep, cattle, etc. **football** *noun* game played by two teams kicking a ball in an attempt to score goals. **footbridge** *noun* bridge for pedestrians. **footfall** *noun* sound of a footstep. **foothills** *plural noun* hills at the foot of a mountain. **foothold** *noun* **1** secure position from which progress may be made. **2** small place giving a secure grip for the foot. **footlights** *plural noun* lights across the front of a stage. **footloose** *adjective* free from ties. **footman** *noun* male servant in uniform. **footnote** *noun* note printed at the foot of a page. **footpath** *noun* **1** narrow path for walkers only. **2** *Aust* raised space alongside a road, for pedestrians. **footplate**

noun platform in the cab of a locomotive for the driver. **footprint** *noun* mark left by a foot. **footstep** *noun* **1** step in walking. **2** sound made by walking. **footstool** *noun* low stool used to rest the feet on while sitting. **footwear** *noun* anything worn to cover the feet. **footwork** *noun* skilful use of the feet, as in sport or dancing.

football *noun* **1** game played by two teams of eleven players kicking a ball in an attempt to score goals, soccer. **2** any of various similar games, such as rugby. **3** ball used for this. **footballer** *noun* **football pools** form of gambling on the results of football matches. **footing ⊙** *noun* **1** basis or foundation. **2** relationship between people. **3** secure grip by or for the feet.

footle ⊙ *verb* *Informal* loiter aimlessly. **footling** *adjective* trivial.

footsie *noun* *Informal* flirtation involving the touching together of feet.

fop *noun* man excessively concerned with fashion. **foppery** *noun* **foppish** *adjective*

for ⊙ *preposition* **1** indicating a person intended to benefit from or receive something, span of time or distance, person or thingrepresented by someone, etc., e.g. *a gift for you; for five miles; playing for his country.* ◆ *conjunction* **2** because. **for it** *Informal* liable for punishment or blame.

forage ⊙ [**for**-ridge] *verb* **1** search about (for). ◆ *noun* **2** food for cattle or horses.

foray ⊙ *noun* **1** brief raid or attack. **2** first attempt or new undertaking.

forbear¹ ⊙ *verb* cease or refrain (from doing something). **forbearance** *noun* tolerance, patience.

forbear² *noun* same as FOREBEAR.

forbid ⊙ *verb* prohibit, refuse to allow.

——————— THESAURUS ———————

dislike
food *noun* =**nourishment**, cuisine, diet, fare, grub (*sl*), nutrition, rations, refreshment
fool¹ *noun* **1** =**simpleton**, blockhead, dunce, halfwit, idiot, ignoramus, imbecile (*inf*), numbskull *or* numskull, twit (*inf, chiefly Brit*) OPPOSITE⟩ **genius. 2** =**dupe**, fall guy (*inf*), laughing stock, mug (*Brit sl*), stooge (*sl*), sucker (*sl*) **3** *Hist* =**clown**, buffoon, harlequin, jester ◆*verb* **4** =**deceive**, beguile, con (*inf*), delude, dupe, hoodwink, mislead, take in, trick
foolhardy *adjective* =**rash**, hot-headed, impetuous, imprudent, irresponsible, reckless OPPOSITE⟩ **cautious**
foolish *adjective* =**unwise**, absurd, ill-judged, imprudent, injudicious, senseless, silly OPPOSITE⟩

sensible
foolishness *noun* =**stupidity**, absurdity, folly, imprudence, indiscretion, irresponsibility, silliness, weakness
foolproof *adjective* =**infallible**, certain, guaranteed, safe, sure-fire (*inf*)
footing *noun* **1** =**basis**, foundation, groundwork **2** =**relationship**, grade, position, rank, standing, status
footstep *noun* **1** =**step 2** =**footfall**, tread
forage *verb* **1** =**search**, cast about, explore, hunt, rummage, scour, seek ◆*noun* **2** =**fodder**, feed, food, provender
foray *noun* **1** =**raid**, incursion, inroad, invasion, sally, sortie, swoop
forbear¹ *verb* =**refrain**, abstain, cease, desist,

F

forbidden *adjective* **forbidden fruit** anything attractive because prohibited. **forbidding** *adjective* severe, threatening.

force ❶ *noun* **1** strength or power. **2** compulsion. **3** *Physics* influence tending to produce a change in a physical system. **4** mental or moral strength. **5** person or thing with strength or influence. **6** vehemence or intensity. **7** group of people organized for a particular task or duty. ◆ *verb* **8** compel, make (someone) do something. **9** acquire or produce through effort, strength, etc. **10** propel or drive. **11** break open. **12** impose or inflict. **13** cause to grow at an increased rate. **in force 1** having legal validity. **2** in great numbers. **forced** *adjective* **1** compulsory. **2** false or unnatural. **3** due to an emergency. **force-feed** *verb* **-feeding, -fed** compel (a person or animal) to swallow food. **forceful** *adjective* **1** emphatic and confident. **2** effective. **forcefully** *adverb* **forcible** *adjective* **1** involving physical force or violence. **2** strong and emphatic. **forcibly** *adverb*

forcemeat *noun* mixture of chopped ingredients used for stuffing.

forceps *plural noun* surgical pincers.

ford *noun* **1** shallow place where a river may be crossed. ◆ *verb* **2** cross (a river) at a ford. **fordable** *adjective*

fore *adjective* **1** in, at, or towards the front. ◆ *noun* **2** front part. ◆ *interjection* **3** golfer's shouted warning to a person in the path of a ball. **to the fore** in a conspicuous position.

fore- *prefix* **1** before in time or rank, e.g. *forefather*. **2** at the front, e.g. *forecourt*.

fore-and-aft *adjective* located at both ends of a ship.

forearm¹ *noun* arm from the wrist to the elbow.

forearm² *verb* prepare beforehand.

forebear ❶ *noun* ancestor.

foreboding ❶ *noun* feeling that something bad is about to happen.

forecast ❶ *verb* **-casting, -cast** *or* **-casted 1** predict (weather, events, etc.). ◆ *noun* **2** prediction.

forecastle [foke-sl] *noun* raised front part of a ship.

foreclose *verb* take possession of (property bought with borrowed money which has not been repaid). **foreclosure** *noun*

forecourt *noun* courtyard or open space in front of a building.

forefather ❶ *noun* ancestor.

forefinger *noun* finger next to the thumb.

forefoot *noun* either of the front feet of an animal.

forefront ❶ *noun* **1** most active or prominent position. **2** very front.

foregather *verb* meet together or assemble.

——————— T H E S A U R U S ———————

hold back, keep from, restrain oneself, stop

forbearance *noun* = **patience**, long-suffering, resignation, restraint, self-control, temperance, tolerance OPPOSITE **impatience**

forbid *verb* = **prohibit**, ban, disallow, exclude, outlaw, preclude, rule out, veto OPPOSITE **permit**

forbidden *adjective* = **prohibited**, banned, outlawed, proscribed, taboo, vetoed

forbidding *adjective* = **threatening**, daunting, frightening, hostile, menacing, ominous, sinister, unfriendly OPPOSITE **inviting**

force *noun* **1** = **power**, energy, impulse, might, momentum, pressure, strength, vigour OPPOSITE **weakness**. **2** = **compulsion**, arm-twisting (*inf*), coercion, constraint, duress, pressure, violence **6** = **intensity**, emphasis, fierceness, vehemence, vigour **7** = **army**, host, legion, patrol, regiment, squad, troop, unit ◆ *verb* **8** = **compel**, coerce, constrain, dragoon, drive, impel, make, oblige, press, pressurize OPPOSITE **coax**. **10** = **push**, propel, thrust **11** = **break open**, blast, prise, wrench, wrest **in force 1** = **valid**, binding, current, effective, in operation, operative, working **2** = **in great**

numbers, all together, in full strength

forced *adjective* **1** = **compulsory**, conscripted, enforced, involuntary, mandatory, obligatory OPPOSITE **voluntary**. **2** = **false**, affected, artificial, contrived, insincere, laboured, stiff, strained, unnatural, wooden OPPOSITE **natural**

forceful *adjective* **2** = **powerful**, cogent, compelling, convincing, dynamic, effective, persuasive OPPOSITE **weak**

forcible *adjective* **1** = **violent**, aggressive, armed, coercive **2** = **compelling**, energetic, forceful, potent, powerful, strong, weighty

forebear *noun* = **ancestor**, father, forefather, forerunner, predecessor

foreboding *noun* = **dread**, anxiety, apprehension, apprehensiveness, chill, fear, misgiving, premonition, presentiment

forecast *verb* **1** = **predict**, anticipate, augur, divine, foresee, foretell, prophesy ◆ *noun* **2** = **prediction**, conjecture, guess, prognosis, prophecy

forefather *noun* = **ancestor**, father, forebear, forerunner, predecessor

forefront *noun* **1** = **foreground**, centre, fore, prominence **2** = **lead**, front, spearhead,

forego ⊙ *verb* same as FORGO.

foregoing ⊙ *adjective* going before, preceding. **foregone conclusion** inevitable result.

foreground *noun* part of a view, esp. in a picture, nearest the observer.

forehand *noun Tennis etc.* stroke played with the palm of the hand facing forward.

forehead *noun* part of the face above the eyebrows.

foreign ⊙ *adjective* **1** not of, or in, one's own country. **2** relating to or connected with other countries. **3** unfamiliar, strange. **4** in an abnormal place or position, e.g. *foreign matter.*

foreigner *noun* **foreign minister, secretary** government minister who deals with other countries. **foreign office** ministry that deals with other countries.

foreknowledge *noun* knowledge of something before it actually happens.

foreleg *noun* either of the front legs of an animal.

forelock *noun* lock of hair over the forehead. **tug the forelock** behave servilely or obsequiously.

foreman *noun* **1** person in charge of a group of workers. **2** leader of a jury.

foremast *noun* mast nearest the bow of a ship.

foremost ⊙ *adjective, adverb* first in time, place, or importance.

forename *noun* first name.

forenoon *noun* morning.

forensic [for-**ren**-sik] *adjective* used in or connected with courts of law. **forensic medicine** use of medical knowledge for the purposes of the law.

foreordain *verb* determine events in the future.

forepaw *noun* either of the front feet of a land mammal that does not have hooves.

foreplay *noun* sexual stimulation before intercourse.

forerunner ⊙ *noun* person or thing that goes before, precursor.

foresail *noun* main sail on the foremast of a ship.

foresee ⊙ *verb* see or know beforehand.

foreseeable *adjective*

SPELLING TIP

There are 665 occurrences of the word **unforeseen** in the Bank of English. The misspelling *unforseen* occurs 50 times.

---

foreshadow ⊙ *verb* show or indicate beforehand.

foreshore *noun* part of the shore between high- and low-tide marks.

foreshorten *verb* represent (an object) in a picture as shorter than it really is, in accordance with perspective.

foresight ⊙ *noun* ability to anticipate and provide for future needs.

foreskin *noun* fold of skin covering the tip of the penis.

forest *noun* large area with a thick growth of trees. **forested** *adjective* **forestry** *noun* **1** science of planting and caring for trees. **2** management of forests. **forester** *noun* person skilled in forestry.

forestall *verb* prevent or guard against in advance.

foretaste *noun* early limited experience of something to come.

foretell ⊙ *verb* tell or indicate beforehand.

forethought ⊙ *noun* thoughtful planning for future events.

forever, for ever ⊙ *adverb* **1** without end. **2** at all times. **3** *Informal* for a long time.

———————— THESAURUS ————————

vanguard

forego see FORGO

foregoing *adjective* =**preceding**, above, antecedent, anterior, former, previous, prior

foreign *adjective* **1, 2** =**external**, exotic, imported, remote **3** =**alien**, strange, unfamiliar, unknown OPPOSITE> **native**

foreigner *noun* =**alien**, immigrant, incomer, stranger

foremost *adjective* =**leading**, chief, highest, paramount, pre-eminent, primary, prime, principal, supreme

forerunner *noun* =**precursor**, harbinger, herald, prototype

foresee *verb* =**predict**, anticipate, envisage, forecast, foretell, prophesy

foreshadow *verb* =**indicate**, augur, forebode, portend, prefigure, presage, promise, signal

foresight *noun* =**forethought**, anticipation, far-sightedness, precaution, preparedness, prescience, prudence OPPOSITE> **hindsight**

foretell *verb* =**predict**, forecast, forewarn, presage, prognosticate, prophesy

forethought *noun* =**anticipation**, far-sightedness, foresight, precaution, providence, provision, prudence

forever, for ever *adverb* **1** =**evermore**, always, endlessly, eternally, for all time, for

F

forewarn ❶ *verb* warn beforehand.
foreword *noun* introduction to a book.
forfeit ❶ [for-fit] *noun* **1** thing lost or given up as a penalty for a fault or mistake. ♦ *verb* **2** lose as a forfeit. ♦ *adjective* **3** lost as a forfeit.
forfeiture *noun*
forgather *verb* same as FOREGATHER.
forgave *verb* past tense of FORGIVE.
forge[1] ❶ *noun* **1** place where metal is worked, smithy. **2** furnace for melting metal. ♦ *verb* **3** make a fraudulent imitation of (something). **4** shape (metal) by heating and hammering it. **5** create (an alliance etc.).
forge[2] *verb* advance steadily. **forge ahead** increase speed or take the lead.
forgery ❶ *noun, pl* **-ries 1** illegal copy of something. **2** crime of making an illegal copy. **forger** *noun*
forget ❶ *verb* **-getting, -got, -gotten 1** fail to remember. **2** neglect. **3** leave behind by mistake. **forgetful** *adjective* tending to forget. **forgetfulness** *noun* **forget-me-not** *noun* plant with clusters of small blue flowers.
forgive ❶ *verb* **-giving, -gave, -given** cease to blame or hold resentment against, pardon. **forgiveness** *noun* **forgivable** *adjective* able to be forgiven. **forgiving** *adjective* willing to forgive.

forgo ❶ *verb* do without or give up.
forgot ❶ *verb* past tense of FORGET. **forgotten** *verb* past participle of FORGET.
fork ❶ *noun* **1** tool for eating food, with prongs and a handle. **2** large similarly-shaped tool for digging or lifting. **3** point where a road, river, etc. divides into branches. **4** one of the branches. ♦ *verb* **5** pick up, dig, etc. with a fork. **6** branch. **7** take one or other branch at a fork in the road. **forked** *adjective* **fork-lift truck** vehicle with a forklike device at the front which can be raised or lowered to move loads.
fork out *verb Informal* pay.
forlorn ❶ *adjective* lonely and unhappy. **forlorn hope** hopeless enterprise. **forlornly** *adverb*
form ❶ *noun* **1** shape or appearance. **2** mode in which something appears. **3** type or kind. **4** printed document with spaces for details. **5** physical or mental condition. **6** previous record of an athlete, racehorse, etc. **7** class in school. **8** procedure or etiquette. **9** bench. **10** hare's nest. ♦ *verb* **11** give a (particular) shape to or take a (particular) shape. **12** come or bring into existence. **13** make or be made. **14** train. **15** acquire or develop. **16** be an element of. **formation** *noun* structure or shape. **formless** *adjective*

———— T H E S A U R U S ————

keeps, in perpetuity **2 = constantly**, all the time, continually, incessantly, interminably, perpetually, twenty-four-seven (*inf*), unremittingly **3** *Inf* **= till the cows come home**, till Doomsday (*inf*)
forewarn *verb* **= caution**, advise, alert, apprise, give fair warning, put on guard, tip off
forfeit *noun* **1 = penalty**, damages, fine, forfeiture, loss, mulct ♦ *verb* **2 = lose**, be deprived of, be stripped of, give up, relinquish, renounce, say goodbye to, surrender
forge[1] *verb* **3 = fake**, copy, counterfeit, falsify, feign, imitate **4 = shape**, fashion, mould, work **5 = create**, construct, devise, form, frame, make
forgery *noun* **1 = fake**, counterfeit, falsification, imitation, phoney *or* phony (*inf*), sham **2 = falsification**, coining, counterfeiting, fraudulence, fraudulent imitation
forget *verb* **1 = omit**, overlook OPPOSITE> remember. **2 = neglect**, lose sight of OPPOSITE> remember. **3 = leave behind**
forgetful *adjective* **= absent-minded**, careless, inattentive, neglectful, oblivious, unmindful, vague OPPOSITE> **mindful**
forgive *verb* **= excuse**, absolve, acquit, condone, exonerate, let bygones be bygones, let off (*inf*), pardon OPPOSITE> **blame**

forgiveness *noun* **= pardon**, absolution, acquittal, amnesty, exoneration, mercy, remission
forgiving *adjective* **= lenient**, clement, compassionate, forbearing, magnanimous, merciful, soft-hearted, tolerant
forgo *verb* **= give up**, abandon, do without, relinquish, renounce, resign, surrender, waive, yield
forgotten *adjective* **= unremembered**, bygone, left behind, lost, omitted, past, past recall
fork *verb* **6 = branch**, bifurcate, diverge, divide, part, split
forked *adjective* **6 = branching**, angled, bifurcate(d), branched, divided, pronged, split, zigzag
forlorn *adjective* **= miserable**, disconsolate, down in the dumps (*inf*), helpless, hopeless, pathetic, pitiful, unhappy, woebegone, wretched OPPOSITE> **happy**
form *noun* **1 = shape**, appearance, structure **2 = formation**, configuration, pattern **3 = type**, kind, sort, style, variety **4 = document**, application, paper, sheet **5 = condition**, fettle, fitness, health, shape, trim **7 = class**, grade, rank **8 = procedure**, convention, custom,

formal ⊕ *adjective* **1** of or characterized by established conventions of ceremony and behaviour. **2** of or for formal occasions. **3** stiff in manner. **4** organized. **5** symmetrical. **formally** *adverb* **formalism** *noun* concern with outward appearances and structure at the expense of content. **formalist** *noun, adjective* **formality** *noun, pl* **-ties 1** requirement of custom or etiquette. **2** necessary procedure without real importance. **formalize** *verb* make official or formal.

formaldehyde [for-**mal**-de-hide] *noun* colourless pungent gas used to make the disinfectant and preservative formalin. **formalin** *noun* solution of formaldehyde in water, used as a disinfectant or a preservative for biological specimens.

format ⊕ *noun* **1** size and shape of a publication. **2** style in which something is arranged. ♦ *verb* **-matting, -matted 3** arrange in a format.

formation ⊕ *noun* **1** forming. **2** thing formed. **3** structure or shape. **4** arrangement of people or things acting as a unit.

formative ⊕ *adjective* **1** of or relating to development. **2** shaping.

former ⊕ *adjective* of an earlier time, previous. **the former** first mentioned of two. **formerly** *adverb*

Formica *noun* ® kind of laminated sheet used to make heat-resistant surfaces.

formic acid *noun* acid derived from ants.

formidable ⊕ *adjective* **1** frightening because difficult to overcome or manage. **2** extremely impressive. **formidably** *adverb*

formula ⊕ *noun, pl* **-las, -lae 1** group of numbers, letters, or symbols expressing a scientific or mathematical rule. **2** method or rule for doing or producing something. **3** set form of words used in religion, law, etc. **4** specific category of car in motor racing. **5** *US* powder used to produce a milky drink for babies. **formulaic** *adjective* **formulate** *verb* plan or describe precisely and clearly. **formulation** *noun*

fornicate *verb* have sexual intercourse without being married. **fornication** *noun* **fornicator** *noun*

forsake ⊕ *verb* **-saking, -sook, -saken 1** withdraw support or friendship from. **2** give up, renounce.

forsooth *adverb Obs* indeed.

forswear *verb* **-swearing, -swore, -sworn** renounce or reject.

forsythia [for-**syth**-ee-a] *noun* shrub with yellow flowers in spring.

fort ⊕ *noun* fortified building or place. **hold the fort** *Informal* keep things going during someone's absence.

forte[1] ⊕ [**for**-tay] *noun* thing at which a person excels.

forte[2] [**for**-tay] *adverb Music* loudly.

————————— THESAURUS —————————

etiquette, protocol ♦*verb* **11 = arrange**, combine, draw up, organize **12 = take shape**, appear, become visible, come into being, crystallize, grow, materialize, rise **13 = make**, build, construct, create, fashion, forge, mould, produce, shape **15 = develop**, acquire, contract, cultivate, pick up **16 = constitute**, compose, comprise, make up

formal *adjective* **1 = conventional**, correct, solemn OPPOSITE informal. **2 = official**, ceremonial, ritualistic OPPOSITE informal. **3 = stiff**, affected, precise, unbending OPPOSITE informal

formality *noun* **1 = convention**, correctness, custom, decorum, etiquette, procedure, protocol, rite **2 = ritual**, red tape

format *noun* **1 = layout**, construction, form, make-up, plan **2 = arrangement**, appearance, look, style, type

formation *noun* **1 = development**, constitution, establishment, forming, generation, genesis, manufacture, production **3, 4 = arrangement**, configuration, design, grouping, pattern, structure

formative *adjective* **1 = developmental 2 = influential**

former *adjective* **= previous**, earlier, erstwhile, one-time, prior OPPOSITE **current**

formerly *adverb* **= previously**, at one time, before, lately, once

formidable *adjective* **1 = intimidating**, daunting, dismaying, fearful, frightful, terrifying OPPOSITE **encouraging**. **2 = impressive**, awesome, great, mighty, powerful, redoubtable, terrific, tremendous

formula *noun* **2 = method**, blueprint, precept, principle, procedure, recipe, rule

formulate *verb* **a = devise**, develop, forge, invent, map out, originate, plan, work out **b = define**, detail, express, frame, give form to, set down, specify, systematize

forsake *verb* **1 = desert**, abandon, disown, leave in the lurch, strand **2 = give up**, forgo, relinquish, renounce, set aside, surrender, yield

fort *noun* **= fortress**, blockhouse, camp, castle, citadel, fortification, garrison, stronghold **hold the fort** *Inf* **= carry on**, keep things on an even keel, stand in, take over the reins

F

forth ❶ *adverb* forwards, out, or away. **and so forth** and so on.

forthcoming ❶ *adjective* **1** about to appear or happen. **2** available. **3** (of a person) communicative.

forthright ❶ *adjective* direct and outspoken.

forthwith ❶ *adverb* at once.

fortieth *adjective, noun* see FORTY.

fortify ❶ *verb* **-fying, -fied 1** make (a place) defensible, as by building walls. **2** strengthen. **3** add vitamins etc. to (food). **4** add alcohol to (wine) to make sherry or port. **fortification** *noun*

fortissimo *adverb Music* very loudly.

fortitude ❶ *noun* courage in adversity or pain.

fortnight *noun* two weeks. **fortnightly** *adverb, adjective*

FORTRAN *noun Computers* programming language for mathematical and scientific purposes.

fortress ❶ *noun* large fort or fortified town.

fortuitous [for-**tyew**-it-uss] *adjective* happening by (lucky) chance. **fortuitously** *adverb*

fortunate ❶ *adjective* **1** having good luck. **2** occurring by good luck. **fortunately** *adverb*

fortune ❶ *noun* **1** luck, esp. when favourable. **2** power regarded as influencing human destiny. **3** wealth, large sum of money. ♦ *plural* **4** person's destiny. **fortunate** *adjective* having good luck. **fortune-teller** *noun* person who claims to predict the future of others.

forty *adjective, noun, pl* **-ties** four times ten. **fortieth** *adjective, noun* **forty winks** short light sleep.

forum *noun* meeting or medium for open discussion or debate.

forward ❶ *adjective* **1** directed or moving ahead. **2** in, at, or near the front. **3** presumptuous. **4** well developed or advanced. **5** relating to the future. ♦ *noun* **6** attacking player in various team games, such as football or hockey. ♦ *adverb* **7** forwards. ♦ *verb* **8** send (a letter etc.) on to an ultimate destination. **9** advance or promote. **forwards** *adverb* **1** towards or at a place further ahead in space or time. **2** towards the front.

forwent *verb* past tense of FORGO.

fossick *verb Aust & NZ* search, esp. for gold or precious stones.

fossil *noun* **1** hardened remains of a prehistoric animal or plant preserved in rock. ♦ *adjective* **2** of, like, or being a fossil. **fossil fuel** fuel such as coal or oil that is formed from the decayed remains of prehistoric animals or plants. **fossilize** *verb* **1** turn into a fossil. **2** become out-of-date or inflexible.

foster ❶ *verb* **1** promote the growth or

———————— THESAURUS ————————

forte¹ *noun* =**speciality**, gift, long suit (*inf*), métier, strength, strong point, talent OPPOSITE> **weak point**

forth *adverb* =**forward**, ahead, away, onward, out, outward

forthcoming *adjective* **1** =**approaching**, coming, expected, future, imminent, impending, prospective, upcoming **2** =**available**, accessible, at hand, in evidence, obtainable, on tap (*inf*), ready **3** =**communicative**, chatty, expansive, free, informative, open, sociable, talkative, unreserved

forthright *adjective* =**outspoken**, blunt, candid, direct, frank, open, plain-spoken, straightforward, upfront (*inf*) OPPOSITE> **secretive**

forthwith *adverb* =**at once**, directly, immediately, instantly, quickly, right away, straightaway, without delay

fortification *noun* **1** =**defence**, bastion, fastness, fort, fortress, protection, stronghold **2** =**strengthening**, reinforcement

fortify *verb* **1** =**protect**, buttress, reinforce, shore up **2** =**strengthen**, augment, support

fortitude *noun* =**courage**, backbone, bravery, fearlessness, grit, perseverance, resolution, strength, valour

fortress *noun* =**castle**, citadel, fastness, fort, redoubt, stronghold

fortunate *adjective* **1** =**lucky**, favoured, in luck, jammy (*Brit sl*), successful, well-off OPPOSITE> **unfortunate**. **2** =**providential**, advantageous, convenient, expedient, favourable, felicitous, fortuitous, helpful, opportune, timely

fortunately *adverb* =**luckily**, by a happy chance, by good luck, happily, providentially

fortune *noun* **1** =**luck**, chance **2** =**fate**, destiny, kismet, providence **3** =**wealth**, affluence, opulence, possessions, property, prosperity, riches, treasure OPPOSITE> **poverty** ♦*plural* **4** =**destiny**, lot

forward *adjective* **1** =**leading**, advance, head **2** =**front**, first, foremost **3** =**presumptuous**, bold, brash, brazen, cheeky, familiar, impertinent, impudent, pushy (*inf*) OPPOSITE> **shy**. **4** =**well-developed**, advanced, precocious, premature ♦*adverb* **7** =**forth**, ahead, on, onward OPPOSITE> **backward(s)** ♦*verb* **8** =**send**, dispatch, post, send on **9** =**promote**, advance, assist, expedite, further,

development of. **2** bring up (a child not one's own). ♦ *adjective* **3** of or involved in fostering a child, e.g. *foster parents.* **fostering** *noun*
fought *verb* past of FIGHT.
foul **O** *adjective* **1** loathsome or offensive. **2** stinking or dirty. **3** (of language) obscene or vulgar. **4** unfair. **5** very bad-tempered. ♦ *noun* **6** *Sport* violation of the rules. ♦ *verb* **7** make dirty or polluted. **8** make or become entangled or clogged. **9** *Sport* commit a foul against (an opponent). **fall foul of** come into conflict with. **foul-mouthed** *adjective* habitually using foul language. **foul play** unfair conduct, esp. involving violence.
found¹ *verb* past of FIND.
found² **O** *verb* **1** establish or bring into being. **2** lay the foundation of. **3** (foll. by *on* or *upon*) have a basis (in). **founder** *noun* **founder member** one of the original members of a club or organization, often someone involved in setting it up.
found³ *verb* **1** cast (metal or glass) by melting and setting in a mould. **2** make (articles) by this method.
foundation **O** *noun* **1** basis or base. **2** part of a building or wall below the ground. **3** act of founding. **4** institution supported by an endowment. **5** cosmetic used as a base for make-up.
founder **O** *verb* **1** break down or fail. **2** (of a ship) sink. **3** stumble or fall.
foundling **O** *noun* abandoned baby.
foundry *noun, pl* **-ries** place where metal is melted and cast.
fount¹ *noun* **1** *Lit* fountain. **2** source.
fount² *noun* set of printing type of one style and size.

fountain **O** *noun* **1** jet of water. **2** structure from which such a jet spurts. **3** source.
fountainhead *noun* original source. **fountain pen** pen supplied with ink from a container inside it.
four *adjective, noun* **1** one more than three. ♦ *noun* **2** (crew of) four-oared rowing boat. **on all fours** on hands and knees. **four-letter word** short obscene word referring to sex or excrement. **four-poster** *noun* bed with four posts supporting a canopy. **foursome** *noun* group of four people. **foursquare** *adverb* **1** squarely or firmly. ♦ *adjective* **2** solid and strong. **3** forthright.
fourteen *adjective, noun* four and ten. **fourteenth** *adjective, noun*
fourth *adjective, noun* **1** (of) number four in a series. ♦ *noun* **2** quarter. **fourthly** *adverb* **fourth dimension** time. **fourth estate** the press.
fowl *noun* **1** domestic cock or hen. **2** any bird used for food or hunted as game.
fox *noun* **1** reddish-brown bushy-tailed animal of the dog family. **2** its fur. **3** cunning person. ♦ *verb* **4** *Informal* perplex or deceive. **foxy** *adjective* **foxier, foxiest** of or like a fox, esp. in craftiness. **foxglove** *noun* tall plant with purple or white flowers. **foxhole** *noun Mil* small pit dug for protection. **foxhound** *noun* dog bred for hunting foxes. **fox terrier** small short-haired terrier. **foxtrot** *noun* **1** ballroom dance with slow and quick steps. **2** music for this.
foyer **O** [foy-ay] *noun* entrance hall in a theatre, cinema, or hotel.
Fr 1 *Chem* francium. **2** Father.
Fr. Franc.
fracas **O** [frak-ah] *noun, pl* **-cas** noisy quarrel.

———————————— THESAURUS ————————————

hasten, hurry OPPOSITE **bar**
foster *verb* **1 = promote**, cultivate, encourage, feed, nurture, stimulate, support, uphold OPPOSITE **oppose. 2 = bring up**, mother, nurse, raise, rear, take care of
foul *adjective* **1 = offensive**, abhorrent, despicable, detestable, disgraceful, scandalous, shameful, wicked OPPOSITE **admirable. 2 = dirty**, fetid, filthy, malodorous, nauseating, putrid, repulsive, squalid, stinking, unclean OPPOSITE **clean. 3 = obscene**, abusive, blue, coarse, indecent, lewd, profane, scurrilous, vulgar **4 = unfair**, crooked, dishonest, fraudulent, shady (*inf*), underhand, unscrupulous ♦*verb* **7 = dirty**, besmirch, contaminate, defile, pollute, stain, sully, taint OPPOSITE **clear**
found¹ ² *verb* **1 = establish**, constitute, create,

inaugurate, institute, organize, originate, set up, start
foundation *noun* **1 = basis**, base, bedrock, bottom, footing, groundwork **2 = substructure**, underpinning **3 = setting up**, endowment, establishment, inauguration, institution, organization, settlement
founder *noun* **= initiator**, architect, author, beginner, father, inventor, originator ♦*verb* **1 = fail**, break down, collapse, come to grief, come unstuck, fall through, miscarry, misfire **2 = sink**, be lost, go down, go to the bottom, submerge **3 = stumble**, lurch, sprawl, stagger, trip
fountain *noun* **1 = jet**, spout, spray, spring **2 = fount**, font, well **3 = source**, cause, derivation, fount, fountainhead, origin, wellspring
foyer *noun* **= entrance hall**, antechamber,

fraction ❶ *noun* **1** numerical quantity that is not a whole number. **2** fragment, piece. **3** *Chem* substance separated by distillation.
fractional *adjective* **fractionally** *adverb*
fractious ❶ *adjective* easily upset and angered.
fracture ❶ *noun* **1** breaking, esp. of a bone. ◆ *verb* **2** break.
fragile ❶ *adjective* **1** easily broken or damaged. **2** in a weakened physical state.
fragility *noun*
fragment ❶ *noun* **1** piece broken off. **2** incomplete piece. ◆ *verb* **3** break into pieces.
fragmentary *adjective* **fragmentation** *noun*
fragrant ❶ *adjective* sweet-smelling.
fragrance *noun* **1** pleasant smell. **2** perfume, scent.
frail ❶ *adjective* **1** physically weak. **2** easily damaged. **frailty** *noun*, *pl* **-ties** physical or moral weakness.
frame ❶ *noun* **1** structure giving shape or support. **2** enclosing case or border, as round a picture. **3** person's build. **4** individual exposure on a strip of film. **5** individual game of snooker in a match. ◆ *verb* **6** put together, construct. **7** put into words. **8** put into a frame. **9** *Slang* incriminate (a person) on a false charge. **frame of mind** mood or attitude. **frame-up** *noun Slang* false incrimination. **framework** *noun*

supporting structure.
franc *noun* monetary unit of France, Switzerland, Belgium, and various African countries.
franchise *noun* **1** right to vote. **2** authorization to sell a company's goods.
Franciscan *noun, adjective* (friar or nun) of the order founded by St. Francis of Assisi.
francium *noun Chem* radioactive metallic element.
Franco- *combining form* of France or the French.
frank ❶ *adjective* **1** honest and straightforward in speech or attitude. ◆ *noun* **2** official mark on a letter permitting delivery. ◆ *verb* **3** put such a mark on (a letter). **frankly** *adverb* **frankness** *noun*
frankfurter *noun* smoked sausage.
frankincense *noun* aromatic gum resin burned as incense.
frantic ❶ *adjective* **1** distracted with rage, grief, joy, etc. **2** hurried and disorganized.
frantically *adverb*
frappé *adjective* (of drinks) chilled.
fraternal ❶ *adjective* of a brother, brotherly.
fraternally *adverb* **fraternity** *noun, pl* **-ties 1** group of people with shared interests, aims, etc. **2** brotherhood. **3** *US* male social club at

——————— THESAURUS ———————

anteroom, lobby, reception area, vestibule
fracas *noun* =**brawl**, affray (*Law*), disturbance, mêlée, riot, rumpus, scuffle, skirmish
fraction *noun* **1** =**percentage 2** =**piece**, part, portion, section, segment, share, slice
fractious *adjective* =**irritable**, captious, cross, petulant, querulous, testy, tetchy, touchy OPPOSITE affable
fracture *noun* **1** =**break**, crack ◆*verb* **2** =**break**, crack, rupture, splinter, split
fragile *adjective* **1** =**delicate**, breakable, brittle, dainty, fine, flimsy, frangible OPPOSITE durable. **2** =**weak**, frail
fragment *noun* **1** =**chip**, bit, particle, scrap, shred, sliver **2** =**piece**, portion ◆*verb* **3** =**break**, break up, come apart, come to pieces, crumble, disintegrate, shatter, splinter, split up OPPOSITE fuse
fragmentary *adjective* **1** =**broken**, bitty, disconnected, scattered, scrappy **2** =**incomplete**, incoherent, partial, piecemeal, sketchy
fragrance *noun* **1** =**smell**, aroma, bouquet, redolence, sweet odour OPPOSITE stink. **2** =**perfume**, scent
fragrant *adjective* =**aromatic**, balmy, odorous, perfumed, redolent, sweet-scented,

sweet-smelling OPPOSITE stinking
frail *adjective* **1** =**weak**, feeble, fragile, infirm, puny OPPOSITE strong. **2** =**delicate**, flimsy, insubstantial, vulnerable
frailty *noun* =**weakness**, fallibility, feebleness, frailness, infirmity, susceptibility OPPOSITE strength
frame *noun* **1** =**casing**, construction, framework, shell, structure **3** =**physique**, anatomy, body, build, carcass ◆*verb* **6** =**construct**, assemble, build, make, manufacture, put together **7** =**devise**, compose, draft, draw up, formulate, map out, sketch **8** =**mount**, case, enclose, surround
frame of mind =**mood**, attitude, disposition, humour, outlook, state, temper
framework *noun* =**structure**, foundation, frame, groundwork, plan, shell, skeleton, the bare bones
frank *adjective* **1** =**honest**, blunt, candid, direct, forthright, open, outspoken, plain-spoken, sincere, straightforward, truthful OPPOSITE secretive
frantic *adjective* **1** =**distraught**, at the end of one's tether, berserk, beside oneself, desperate, distracted, fraught (*inf*), furious, wild OPPOSITE calm. **2** =**hectic**, frenetic, frenzied OPPOSITE

college. **fraternize** *verb* associate on friendly terms. **fraternization** *noun* **fratricide** *noun* **1** crime of killing one's brother. **2** person who does this.

Frau [rhymes with **how**] *noun*, *pl* **Fraus, Frauen** German title, equivalent to *Mrs.*

Fräulein froy-*line*, *noun*, *pl* **-leins, -lein** German title, equivalent to *Miss.*

fraud ⊙ *noun* **1** (criminal) deception, swindle. **2** person who acts in a deceitful way.

fraudulent *adjective* **fraudulence** *noun*

fraught [frawt] *adjective* tense or anxious. **fraught with** involving, filled with.

fray¹ *noun* noisy quarrel or conflict.

fray² ⊙ *verb* **1** make or become ragged at the edge. **2** become strained.

frazzle *noun Informal* exhausted state.

frazzled *adjective Informal* exhausted and irritable.

freak ⊙ *noun* **1** abnormal person or thing. **2** person who is excessively enthusiastic about something. ◆ *adjective* **3** abnormal. **freakish** *adjective* **freak out** *verb Informal* (cause to) be in a heightened emotional state. **freaky** *adjective* **freakier, freakiest** *Informal* weird, peculiar.

freckle *noun* small brown spot on the skin.

freckled *adjective* marked with freckles.

free ⊙ *adjective* **freer, freest 1** able to act at will, not compelled or restrained. **2** not subject (to). **3** independent. **4** provided without charge. **5** generous, lavish. **6** not in use. **7** (of a person) not busy. **8** not fixed or joined. **9** (of a translation) not exact or literal. ◆ *verb* **freeing, freed 10** release, liberate. **11** remove (obstacles, pain, etc.) from. **12** make available or usable. **a free hand** unrestricted freedom to act. **freely** *adverb* **free-and-easy** *adjective* casual and tolerant. **freebooter** *noun* pirate. **free enterprise** economic system in which businesses compete for profit with little state

control. **free fall** part of a parachute descent before the parachute opens. **free-for-all** *noun Informal* brawl. **freehand** *adjective* drawn without guiding instruments. **freehold** *noun* tenure of land for life without restrictions. **freeholder** *noun* **free house** public house not bound to sell only one brewer's products. **freelance** *adjective, noun* (of) a self-employed person doing specific pieces of work for various employers. **freeloader** *noun Slang* habitual scrounger. **freeman** *noun* person who has been given the freedom of a city. **free-market** *adjective* denoting an economic system in which supply and demand regulate prices, wages, etc. **free-range** *adjective* kept or produced in natural conditions. **free-standing** *adjective* not attached to or supported by another object. **free-style** *noun* competition, esp. in swimming, in which each participant uses the style of his or her choice. **freethinker** *noun* person who forms his or her ideas independently of authority, esp. on religious matters. **free verse** unrhymed verse without a fixed rhythm. **freeway** *noun Chiefly US* motorway. **freewheel** *verb* travel downhill on a bicycle without pedalling. **free will 1** ability to make choices that are not externally determined. **2** ability to make a decision without outside coercion, e.g. *she left of her own free will.*

LANGUAGE TIP

Free of means 'not subject to': *free of charge. Free from* suggests a change of circumstances: *They were free from danger.*

-free *combining form* without, e.g. *a trouble-free journey.*

——————— THESAURUS ———————

together (*sl*)

fraternity *noun* **1** = **association**, brotherhood, circle, club, company, guild, league, union **2** = **companionship**, brotherhood, camaraderie, fellowship, kinship

fraternize *verb* = **associate**, consort, cooperate, hobnob, keep company, mingle, mix, socialize

fraud *noun* **1** = **deception**, chicanery, deceit, double-dealing, duplicity, sharp practice, swindling, treachery, trickery OPPOSITE honesty. **2** = **impostor**, charlatan, fake, hoaxer, phoney *or* phony (*inf*), pretender, swindler

fraudulent *adjective* = **deceitful**, crooked (*inf*),

dishonest, double-dealing, duplicitous, sham, swindling, treacherous OPPOSITE genuine

fray² *verb* **1** = **wear thin**, wear

freak *noun* **1** = **oddity**, aberration, anomaly, malformation, monstrosity, weirdo *or* weirdie (*inf*) **2** = **enthusiast**, addict, aficionado, buff (*inf*), devotee, fan, fanatic, fiend (*inf*), nut (*sl*)

◆*adjective* **3** = **abnormal**, exceptional, unparalleled, unusual

free *adjective* **1** = **allowed**, able, clear, permitted, unimpeded, unrestricted **2, 3** = **at liberty**, at large, footloose, independent, liberated, loose, on the loose, unfettered OPPOSITE confined. **4** = **complimentary**, for

freedom ❶ *noun* **1** being free. **2** exemption or immunity, e.g. *freedom from hunger*. **3** right or privilege of unlimited access, e.g. *the freedom of the city*.
Freemason *noun* member of a secret fraternity pledged to help each other.
Freemasonry *noun*
freesia *noun* plant with fragrant tubular flowers.
freeze ❶ *verb* **freezing, froze, frozen 1** change from a liquid to a solid by the reduction of temperature, as water to ice. **2** preserve (food etc.) by extreme cold. **3** (cause to) be very cold. **4** become motionless with fear, shock, etc. **5** fix (prices or wages) at a particular level. **6** ban the exchange or collection of (loans, assets, etc.). ♦ *noun* **7** period of very cold weather. **8** freezing of prices or wages.
freezer *noun* insulated cabinet for cold-storage of perishable foods. **freeze-dry** *verb* preserve (food) by rapid freezing and drying in a vacuum. **freeze-frame** *noun* single frame from a film or video recording shown as a still photograph. **freezing** *adjective Informal* very cold. **freezing point** temperature below which a liquid turns into a solid.
freight ❶ [frate] *noun* **1** commercial transport of goods. **2** cargo transported. **3** cost of this. ♦ *verb* **4** send by freight. **freighter** *noun* ship or aircraft for transporting goods.
French *noun* **1** language of France, also spoken in parts of Belgium, Canada, and Switzerland. ♦ *adjective* **2** of France, its people, or their language. **French bean** green bean whose pods are eaten. **French bread** white bread in a long thin crusty loaf. **French-Canadian** *adjective* of or from the part of Canada where French is spoken. **French dressing** salad dressing of oil and vinegar. **French fries** potato chips. **French horn** brass wind instrument with a coiled tube. **French letter** *Slang* condom. **French polish** shellac varnish for wood. **French window** window extending to floor level, used as a door.
French fries potato chips.
French horn brass wind instrument with a coiled tube.
frenetic [frin-net-ik] *adjective* uncontrolled, excited. **frenetically** *adverb*
frenzy ❶ *noun, pl* **-zies 1** violent mental derangement. **2** wild excitement. **frenzied** *adjective* **frenziedly** *adverb*
frequent ❶ *adjective* **1** happening often. **2** habitual. ♦ *verb* **3** visit habitually. **frequently** *adverb* **frequency** *noun, pl* **-cies 1** rate of occurrence. **2** *Physics* number of times a wave repeats itself in a given time.
fresco *noun, pl* **-coes, -cos** watercolour painting done on wet plaster on a wall.
fresh ❶ *adjective* **1** newly made, acquired, etc. **2** novel, original. **3** most recent. **4** further, additional. **5** (of food) not preserved. **6** (of water) not salty. **7** (of weather) brisk or invigorating. **8** not tired. **9** *Informal* impudent. **freshly** *adverb* **freshness** *noun* **freshen** *verb* **1** make or become fresh or fresher. **2** (foll. by *up*)

———————— THESAURUS ————————

free (*inf*), for nothing, free of charge, gratis, gratuitous, on the house, unpaid, without charge **5 = generous**, lavish, liberal, unsparing, unstinting OPPOSITE mean. **6 = available**, empty, spare, unoccupied, unused, vacant **7 = idle**, unemployed ♦*verb* **10 = release**, deliver, let out, liberate, loose, set free, turn loose, unchain, untie OPPOSITE confine. **11 = clear**, cut loose, disengage, disentangle, extricate, rescue
freedom *noun* **1 = liberty**, deliverance, emancipation, independence, release OPPOSITE captivity. **3 = licence**, blank cheque, carte blanche, discretion, free rein, latitude, opportunity OPPOSITE restriction
free-for-all *noun Inf* **= fight**, brawl, dust-up (*inf*), fracas, mêlée, riot, row, scrimmage
freely *adverb* **1 = willingly**, of one's own accord, of one's own free will, spontaneously, voluntarily, without prompting **5 = abundantly**, amply, copiously, extravagantly, lavishly, liberally, unstintingly

freeze *verb* **1 = ice over** *or* **up**, harden, stiffen **3 = chill 5, 6 = suspend**, fix, hold up, inhibit, stop
freezing *adjective Inf* **= icy**, arctic, biting, bitter, chill, frosty, glacial, raw, wintry
freight *noun* **1 = transportation**, carriage, conveyance, shipment **2 = cargo**, burden, consignment, goods, load, merchandise, payload
frenzied *adjective* **= uncontrolled**, distracted, feverish, frantic, frenetic, furious, rabid, wild
frenzy *noun* **1 = fury**, derangement, hysteria, paroxysm, passion, rage, seizure OPPOSITE calm
frequent *adjective* **1 = persistent**, recurrent, repeated OPPOSITE infrequent. **2 = habitual**, common, customary, everyday, familiar, usual ♦*verb* **3 = visit**, attend, hang out at (*inf*), haunt, patronize OPPOSITE avoid
frequently *adverb* **1 = often**, many times, much, not infrequently, repeatedly OPPOSITE infrequently. **2 = habitually**, commonly

refresh oneself, esp. by washing. **3** (of the wind) increase. **fresher, freshman** *noun* first-year student. **freshwater** *adjective* of or living in fresh water.

fret¹ ⊙ *verb* **fretting, fretted 1** be worried. **2** rub or wear away. ♦ *noun* **3** worried state. **fretful** *adjective* irritable.

fret² *noun* small bar on the fingerboard of a guitar etc.

fretwork *noun* decorative carving in wood. **fret saw** fine saw with a narrow blade, used for fretwork.

Freudian [froy-dee-an] *adjective* of or relating to the psychoanalyst Sigmund Freud or his theories. **Freudian slip** action or error which may reveal an unconscious wish.

Fri. Friday.

friable [fry-a-bl] *adjective* easily crumbled. **friability** *noun*

friar *noun* member of a male Roman Catholic religious order. **friary** *noun, pl* **-ries** house of friars.

fricassee *noun* stewed meat served in a thick white sauce.

fricative *noun* **1** consonant produced by friction of the breath through a partially open mouth, such as (f) or (z). ♦ *adjective* **2** relating to or being a fricative.

friction ⊙ *noun* **1** resistance met with by a body moving over another. **2** rubbing. **3** clash of wills or personalities. **frictional** *adjective*

Friday *noun* sixth day of the week. **Good**

Friday Friday before Easter.

fridge *noun* apparatus in which food and drinks are kept cool.

fried *verb* past of FRY¹.

friend ⊙ *noun* **1** person whom one knows well and likes. **2** supporter or ally. **3** (F-) Quaker. **friendly** *adjective* **-lier, -liest 1** showing or expressing liking. **2** not hostile, on the same side. ♦ *noun, pl* **-lies 3** *Sport* match played for its own sake and not as part of a competition. **-friendly** *combining form* good or easy for the person or thing specified, e.g. *user-friendly.* **friendly fire** *noun Military* firing by one's own side, esp when it harms one's own personnel. **friendly society** association of people who pay regular dues in return for pensions, sickness benefits, etc. **friendliness** *noun* **friendless** *adjective* **friendship** *noun*

fries *plural noun* see FRY¹ (sense 3).

Friesian [free-zhan] *noun* breed of black-and-white dairy cattle.

frieze [freeze] *noun* ornamental band on a wall.

frigate [frig-it] *noun* medium-sized fast warship.

fright ⊙ *noun* **1** sudden fear or alarm. **2** sudden alarming shock. **3** *Informal* grotesque person. **frighten** *verb* **1** scare or terrify. **2** force (someone) to do something from fear. **frightening** *adjective* **frighteningly** *adverb* **frightful** *adjective* **1** horrifying. **2** *Informal* very great. **frightfully** *adverb*

———————————— T H E S A U R U S ————————————

fresh *adjective* **1** = **new**, different OPPOSITE old. **2** = **novel**, original **3** = **recent**, modern, up-to-date OPPOSITE old. **4** = **additional**, added, auxiliary, extra, further, more, other, supplementary **5** = **natural**, unprocessed OPPOSITE preserved. **7** = **invigorating**, bracing, brisk, clean, cool, crisp, pure, refreshing, unpolluted OPPOSITE stale. **8** = **lively**, alert, energetic, keen, refreshed, sprightly, spry, vigorous OPPOSITE weary. **9** *Inf* = **cheeky**, disrespectful, familiar, forward, impudent, insolent, presumptuous OPPOSITE well-mannered

freshen *verb* **1, 2** = **refresh**, enliven, freshen up, liven up, restore, revitalize

fret¹ *verb* **1** = **worry**, agonize, brood, lose sleep over, obsess about, upset *or* distress oneself

fretful *adjective* = **irritable**, crotchety (*inf*), edgy, fractious, querulous, short-tempered, testy, touchy, uneasy

friction *noun* **2** = **rubbing**, abrasion, chafing, grating, rasping, resistance, scraping **3**

= **hostility**, animosity, bad blood, conflict, disagreement, discord, dissension, resentment

friend *noun* **1** = **companion**, buddy (*inf*), chum (*inf*), comrade, mate (*inf*), pal, playmate OPPOSITE foe. **2** = **supporter**, ally, associate, patron, well-wisher

friendly *adjective* **1** = **amiable**, affectionate, amicable, close, cordial, familiar, helpful, intimate, neighbourly, on good terms, pally (*inf*), sociable, sympathetic, welcoming OPPOSITE unfriendly

friendship *noun* **1** = **friendliness**, affection, amity, attachment, concord, familiarity, goodwill, harmony, intimacy OPPOSITE unfriendliness

fright *noun* **1, 2** = **fear**, alarm, consternation, dread, horror, panic, scare, shock, trepidation OPPOSITE courage

frighten *verb* **1** = **scare**, alarm, petrify, shock, startle, terrify, unnerve OPPOSITE reassure. **2** = **intimidate**, terrorize OPPOSITE reassure

frightful *adjective* **1** = **terrifying**, alarming, awful, dreadful, fearful, ghastly, horrendous,

F

frigid ⊕ [frij-id] *adjective* **1** (of a woman) sexually unresponsive. **2** very cold. **3** excessively formal. **frigidity** *noun*

frill *noun* **1** gathered strip of fabric attached at one edge. ♦ *plural* **2** superfluous decorations or details. **frilled** *adjective* **frilled lizard** large tree-living Australian lizard with an erectile fold of skin round the neck. **frilly** *adjective*

fringe ⊕ *noun* **1** hair cut short and hanging over the forehead. **2** ornamental edge of hanging threads, tassels, etc. **3** outer edge. **4** less important parts of an activity or group. ♦ *verb* **5** decorate with a fringe. ♦ *adjective* **6** (of theatre) unofficial or unconventional. **fringed** *adjective* **fringe benefit** benefit given in addition to a regular salary.

frippery *noun, pl* **-peries 1** useless ornamentation. **2** trivia.

Frisian *noun* **1** language spoken in the NW Netherlands and adjacent islands. **2** speaker of this language. ♦ *adjective* **3** of this language or its speakers.

frisk ⊕ *verb* **1** move or leap playfully. **2** *Informal* search (a person) for concealed weapons etc. ♦ *noun* **3** playful movement. **4** *Informal* instance of searching a person. **frisky** *adjective* **friskier, friskiest** lively or high-spirited. **friskily** *adverb*

frisson [frees-sonn] *noun* shiver of fear or excitement.

fritter ⊕ *noun* piece of food fried in batter.

fritter away ⊕ *verb* waste.

frivolous ⊕ *adjective* **1** not serious or sensible. **2** enjoyable but trivial. **frivolity** *noun, pl* **-ties**

frizz *verb* form (hair) into stiff wiry curls. **frizzy** *adjective* **frizzier, frizziest**

frizzle *verb* cook or heat until crisp and shrivelled.

fro *adverb* away, only in *to and fro*.

frock *noun* dress. **frock coat** man's skirted coat as worn in the 19th century.

frog *noun* smooth-skinned tailless amphibian with long back legs used for jumping. **frog in one's throat** phlegm on the vocal cords, hindering speech. **frogman** *noun* swimmer with a rubber suit and breathing equipment for working underwater. **frogmarch** *verb* force (a resisting person) to move by holding his arms. **frogspawn** *noun* jelly-like substance containing frog's eggs.

frolic ⊕ *verb* **-icking, -icked 1** run and play in a lively way. ♦ *noun* **2** lively and merry behaviour. **frolicsome** *adjective* playful.

from *preposition* indicating the point of departure, source, distance, cause, change of state, etc.

frond *noun* long leaf or leaflike part of a fern, palm, or seaweed.

front ⊕ *noun* **1** fore part. **2** position directly before or ahead. **3** seaside promenade. **4** battle line or area. **5** *Meteorol* dividing line between two different air masses. **6** outward appearance. **7** *Informal* cover for another, usu. criminal, activity. **8** group with a common goal. **9** particular field of activity, e.g. *on the economic front*. ♦ *adjective* **10** of or at the front. ♦ *verb* **11** face (onto). **12** be a front of or for. **13** be the presenter of (a television show). **frontal** *adjective* **frontage** *noun* facade of a building. **front bench** parliamentary leaders of the government or opposition. **front-bencher** *noun* **frontrunner** *noun Informal* person regarded as most likely to win a race, election, etc.

frontier ⊕ *noun* **1** area of a country bordering

———— THESAURUS ————

horrible, terrible, traumatic OPPOSITE nice

frigid *adjective* **1** = **unresponsive 2** = **cold**, arctic, frosty, frozen, glacial, icy, wintry OPPOSITE **hot. 3** = **formal**, aloof, austere, forbidding, unapproachable, unfeeling OPPOSITE **warm**

frills *plural noun* **2** = **trimmings**, additions, bells and whistles, embellishments, extras, frippery, fuss, ornamentation, ostentation

fringe *noun* **2** = **border**, edging, hem, trimming **3** = **edge**, borderline, limits, margin, outskirts, perimeter, periphery ♦ *adjective* **6** = **unofficial**, unconventional, unorthodox

frisk *verb* **1** = **frolic**, caper, cavort, gambol, jump, play, prance, skip, trip **2** *Inf* = **search**, check, inspect, run over, shake down (*US sl*)

frisky *adjective* = **lively**, coltish, frolicsome, high-spirited, kittenish, playful, sportive

OPPOSITE **sedate**

fritter away *verb* = **waste**, dissipate, idle away, misspend, run through, spend like water, squander

frivolous *adjective* **1** = **flippant**, childish, foolish, idle, juvenile, puerile, silly, superficial OPPOSITE **serious. 2** = **trivial**, footling (*inf*), minor, petty, shallow, trifling, unimportant OPPOSITE **important**

frolic *verb* **1** = **play**, caper, cavort, frisk, gambol, lark, make merry, romp, sport ♦ *noun* **2** = **revel**, antic, game, lark, romp, spree

front *noun* **1** = **foreground**, frontage **2** = **forefront**, head, lead, vanguard **4** = **front line 6** = **exterior**, facade, face **7** *Inf* = **cover**, blind, cover-up, disguise, mask, pretext ♦ *adjective* **10** = **foremost**, first, head, lead, leading, topmost OPPOSITE **back** ♦ *verb* **11**

on another. **2** edge of the settled area of a country. ♦ *plural* **3** limit of knowledge in a particular field.

frontispiece *noun* illustration facing the title page of a book.

frost ➊ *noun* **1** white frozen dew or mist. **2** atmospheric temperature below freezing point. ♦ *verb* **3** become covered with frost. **frosted** *adjective* (of glass) having a rough surface to make it opaque. **frosting** *noun Chiefly US* sugar icing. **frosty** *adjective* **frostier, frostiest 1** characterized or covered by frost. **2** unfriendly. **frostily** *adverb* **frostiness** *noun* **frostbite** *noun* destruction of tissue, esp. of the fingers or ears, by cold. **frostbitten** *adjective*

froth ➊ *noun* **1** mass of small bubbles. **2** trivial but superficially attractive ideas or entertainment. ♦ *verb* **3** foam. **frothy** *adjective* **frothier, frothiest**

frown ➊ *verb* **1** wrinkle one's brows in worry, anger, or thought. **2** look disapprovingly (on). ♦ *noun* **3** frowning expression.

frowsty *adjective* stale or musty.

frowzy, frowsy *adjective* **-zier, -ziest** or **-sier, -siest** dirty or unkempt.

froze ➊ *verb* past tense of FREEZE. **frozen** *verb* past participle of FREEZE.

FRS Fellow of the Royal Society.

fructify *verb* **-fying, -fied** (cause to) bear fruit. **fructification** *noun*

fructose *noun* crystalline sugar occurring in many fruits.

frugal ➊ [froo-gl] *adjective* **1** thrifty, sparing. **2** meagre and inexpensive. **frugally** *adverb*

frugality *noun*

fruit ➊ *noun* **1** part of a plant containing seeds, esp. if edible. **2** any plant product useful to man. **3** (often pl) result of an action or effort. ♦ *verb* **4** bear fruit. **fruiterer** *noun* person who sells fruit. **fruitful** *adjective* useful or productive. **fruitfully** *adverb* **fruitless** *adjective* useless or unproductive. **fruitlessly** *adverb* **fruity** *adjective* **fruitier, fruitiest 1** of or like fruit. **2** (of a voice) mellow. **3** *Informal* mildly bawdy. **fruitcake** *noun* cake containing dried fruit. **fruit fly 1** small fly that feeds on and lays its eggs in plant tissues. **2** similar fly that feeds on plant sap, decaying fruit, etc., and is widely used in genetics experiments. **fruit machine** coin-operated gambling machine. **fruit salad, cocktail** dish consisting of pieces of different kinds of fruit.

fruition ➊ [froo-**ish**-on] *noun* fulfilment of something worked for or desired.

frump *noun* dowdy woman. **frumpy** *adjective* **frumpier, frumpiest**

frustrate ➊ *verb* **1** upset or anger. **2** hinder or prevent. **frustrated** *adjective* **frustrating** *adjective* **frustration** *noun*

frustum *noun, pl* **-tums, -ta** *Geom* part of a cone or pyramid contained between the base and a plane parallel to the base that intersects the solid.

fry[1] *verb* **frying, fried 1** cook or be cooked in fat or oil. ♦ *noun, pl* **fries 2** (also **fry-up**) dish of fried food. ♦ *plural* **3** potato chips. **frying pan** shallow pan used for frying food. **out of the frying pan into the fire** from a bad situation

—————— THESAURUS ——————

= **face onto**, look over *or* onto, overlook **frontier** *noun* **1, 2** = **boundary**, borderline, edge, limit, perimeter, verge

frost *noun* **1** = **hoarfrost**, rime **2** = **freeze**

frosty *adjective* **1** = **cold**, chilly, frozen, icy, wintry **2** = **unfriendly**, discouraging, frigid, off-putting (*Brit inf*), standoffish, unenthusiastic, unwelcoming

froth *noun* **1** = **foam**, bubbles, effervescence, head, lather, scum, spume, suds ♦*verb* **3** = **fizz**, bubble over, come to a head, effervesce, foam, lather

frown *verb* **1** = **scowl**, glare, glower, knit one's brows, look daggers, lour *or* lower **2** = **disapprove of**, discourage, dislike, look askance at, take a dim view of

frozen *adjective* = **icy**, arctic, chilled, frigid, frosted, icebound, ice-cold, ice-covered, numb

frugal *adjective* **1** = **thrifty**, abstemious, careful, economical, niggardly, parsimonious, prudent, sparing OPPOSITE> **wasteful**

fruit *noun* **2** = **produce**, crop, harvest, product, yield **3** (often pl) = **result**, advantage, benefit, consequence, effect, end result, outcome, profit, return, reward

fruitful *adjective* = **useful**, advantageous, beneficial, effective, productive, profitable, rewarding, successful, worthwhile OPPOSITE> **useless**

fruition *noun* = **fulfilment**, attainment, completion, materialization, maturity, perfection, realization, ripeness

fruitless *adjective* = **useless**, futile, ineffectual, pointless, profitless, unavailing, unproductive, unprofitable, unsuccessful, vain OPPOSITE> **fruitful**

frustrate *verb* **2** = **thwart**, balk, block, check, counter, defeat, disappoint, foil, forestall, nullify, stymie OPPOSITE> **encourage**

frustration *noun* **1** = **annoyance**, disappointment, dissatisfaction, grievance, irritation, resentment, vexation **2** = **obstruction**, into a worse one.

fry[2] *plural noun* young fishes. **small fry** young or insignificant people.

ft. 1 foot. **2** feet.

fuchsia [fyew-sha] *noun* ornamental shrub with hanging flowers.

fuck *Taboo verb* **1** have sexual intercourse (with). ◆ *noun* **2** act of sexual intercourse. ◆ *interjection* **3** expression of strong disgust or anger. **fuck off** *verb Taboo slang* go away. **fuck up** *verb Taboo slang* make a mess of (something).

fuddle *verb* **1** cause to be intoxicated or confused. ◆ *noun* **2** confused state. **fuddled** *adjective*

fuddy-duddy ⊕ *adjective, noun, pl* **-dies** *Informal* old-fashioned (person).

fudge[1] *noun* soft caramel-like sweet.

fudge[2] ⊕ *verb* **1** make (an issue) less clear deliberately. **2** avoid making a firm statement or decision.

fuel ⊕ *noun* **1** substance burned or treated to produce heat or power. **2** something that intensifies (a feeling etc.). ◆ *verb* **fuelling, fuelled 3** provide with fuel.

fug *noun* hot stale atmosphere. **fuggy** *adjective* **fuggier, fuggiest**

fugitive ⊕ **[fyew-jit-iv]** *noun* **1** person who flees, esp. from arrest or pursuit. ◆ *adjective* **2** fleeing. **3** transient.

fugue [fyewg] *noun* musical composition in which a theme is repeated in different parts.

Führer *noun German* leader: title used by Hitler as Nazi dictator.

-ful *adj suffix* **1** full of or characterized by, e.g. *painful*; *restful*. **2** able or tending to, e.g. *useful*. ◆ *n suffix* **3** as much as will fill the thing

specified, e.g. *mouthful*.

fulcrum *noun, pl* **-crums, -cra** pivot about which a lever turns.

fulfil ⊕ *verb* **-filling, -filled 1** bring about the achievement of (a desire or promise). **2** carry out (a request or order). **3** do what is required. **fulfilment** *noun* **fulfil oneself** *verb* achieve one's potential.

full[1] ⊕ *adjective* **1** containing as much or as many as possible. **2** abundant in supply. **3** having had enough to eat. **4** plump. **5** complete, whole. **6** (of a garment) of ample cut. **7** (of a sound or flavour) rich and strong. ◆ *adverb* **8** completely. **9** directly. **10** very. **fully** *adverb* **fullness** *noun* **in full** without shortening. **full back** defensive player in various sports. **full-blooded** *adjective* vigorous or enthusiastic. **full-blown** *adjective* fully developed. **full board** provision by a hotel of a bed and all meals. **full-bodied** *adjective* having a full rich flavour or quality. **full house 1** theatre filled to capacity. **2** (in bingo) set of numbers needed to win. **full-length** *adjective* **1** (of a mirror, portrait, etc.) showing the whole human body. **2** not abridged. **full moon** phase of the moon when it is visible as a fully illuminated disc. **full-scale** *adjective* **1** (of a plan) of actual size. **2** using all resources. **full stop** punctuation mark (.) at the end of a sentence and after abbreviations. **full time** (in football, rugby, etc.) end of the game. **full-time** *adjective* for all of the normal working week. **full up** filled to capacity.

full[2] *verb* clean, shrink, and press cloth. **fuller** *noun* **fuller's earth** absorbent clay used for clarifying oils and fats, fulling cloth, etc.

fulmar *noun* Arctic sea bird.

——————— T H E S A U R U S ———————

blocking, circumvention, foiling, thwarting

fuddy-duddy *noun Inf* **=conservative,** (old) fogey, square (*inf*), stick-in-the-mud (*inf*), stuffed shirt (*inf*)

fudge[2] *verb* **1 =misrepresent,** equivocate, flannel (*Brit inf*) **2 =stall,** hedge

fuel *noun* **2 =incitement,** provocation

fugitive *noun* **1 =runaway,** deserter, escapee, refugee ◆*adjective* **3 =momentary,** brief, ephemeral, fleeting, passing, short-lived, temporary, transient, transitory

fulfil *verb* **1 =achieve,** accomplish, realise **2 =carry out,** complete, perform, satisfy OPPOSITE> **neglect. 3 =comply with,** answer, conform to, fill, meet, obey, observe

full[1] *adjective* **1 =filled,** brimming, complete, loaded, saturated, stocked OPPOSITE> **empty. 2 =extensive,** abundant, adequate, ample,

generous, plentiful OPPOSITE> **limited. 3 =satiated,** replete **4 =plump,** buxom, curvaceous, rounded, voluptuous **5 =comprehensive,** exhaustive **6 =voluminous,** baggy, capacious, large, loose, puffy OPPOSITE> **tight. 7 =rich,** clear, deep, distinct, loud, resonant, rounded OPPOSITE> **thin ◆ in full =completely,** in its entirety, in total, without exception

fullness *noun* **1 =fill,** saturation **2 =plenty,** abundance, adequateness, ampleness, copiousness, profusion, sufficiency **3 =satiety 7 =richness,** clearness, loudness, resonance, strength

full-scale *adjective* **2 =major,** all-out, comprehensive, exhaustive, in-depth, sweeping, thorough, thoroughgoing, wide-ranging

fully *adverb* **5 =totally,** altogether, completely,

fulminate *verb* (foll. by *against*) criticize or denounce angrily. **fulmination** *noun*

fulsome ❶ *adjective* distastefully excessive or insincere.

fumble ❶ *verb* **1** handle awkwardly. **2** say awkwardly. ♦ *noun* **3** act of fumbling.

fume ❶ *verb* **1** be very angry. **2** give out smoke or vapour. **3** treat with fumes. ♦ *plural noun* **4** pungent smoke or vapour.

fumigate ❶ [**fyew**-mig-gate] *verb* disinfect with fumes. **fumigation** *noun*

fun ❶ *noun* enjoyment or amusement. **make fun of** mock or tease. **funny** *adjective* **funnier, funniest 1** comical, humorous. **2** odd. **funny bone** part of the elbow where the nerve is near the surface. **funnily** *adverb*

function ❶ *noun* **1** purpose something exists for. **2** way something works. **3** large or formal social event. **4** *Maths* quantity whose value depends on the varying value of another. **5** sequence of operations performed by a computer at a key stroke. ♦ *verb* **6** operate or work. **7** (foll. by *as*) fill the role of. **functional** *adjective* **1** of or as a function. **2** practical rather than decorative. **3** in working order. **functionally** *adverb* **functionary** *noun, pl* **-aries** official.

fund ❶ *noun* **1** stock of money for a special purpose. **2** supply or store. ♦ *plural* **3** money resources. ♦ *verb* **4** provide money to. **funding** *noun*

fundamental ❶ *adjective* **1** essential or primary. **2** basic. ♦ *noun* **3** basic rule or fact.

fundamentally *adverb* **fundamentalism** *noun* literal or strict interpretation of a religion. **fundamentalist** *noun, adjective*

fundi *noun S Afr* expert or boffin.

funeral ❶ *noun* ceremony of burying or cremating a dead person. **funeral director** undertaker. **funeral parlour** place where the dead are prepared for burial or cremation.

funerary *adjective* of or for a funeral.

funereal [fyew-**neer**-ee-al] *adjective* gloomy or sombre.

funfair *noun* entertainment with machines to ride on and stalls.

fungus *noun, pl* **-gi, -guses** plant without leaves, flowers, or roots, such as a mushroom or mould. **fungal, fungous** *adjective* **fungicide** *noun* substance that destroys fungi.

funicular [fyew-**nik**-yew-lar] *noun* cable railway on a mountainside or cliff.

funk[1] *noun* style of dance music with a strong beat. **funky** *adjective* **funkier, funkiest** (of music) having a strong beat.

funk[2] *Informal noun* **1** nervous or fearful state. ♦ *verb* **2** avoid (doing something) through fear.

funnel ❶ *noun* **1** cone-shaped tube for pouring liquids into a narrow opening. **2** chimney of a ship or locomotive. ♦ *verb* **-nelling, -nelled 3** (cause to) move through or as if through a funnel. **funnel-web** *noun Aust* large poisonous black spider that builds funnel-shaped webs.

funny ❶ *adjective* see FUN.

fur *noun* **1** soft hair of a mammal. **2** animal

———————— THESAURUS ————————

entirely, in all respects, one hundred per cent, perfectly, thoroughly, utterly, wholly

fulsome *adjective* = **extravagant**, excessive, immoderate, inordinate, insincere, sycophantic, unctuous

fumble *verb* **1** = **grope**, feel around, flounder, scrabble

fume *verb* **1** (*inf*) = **rage**, rant, see red (*inf*), seethe, smoulder, storm ♦ *plural noun* **4** = **smoke**, exhaust, gas, pollution, smog, vapour

fumigate *verb* = **disinfect**, clean out *or* up, cleanse, purify, sanitize, sterilize

fun *noun* = **enjoyment**, amusement, entertainment, jollity, merriment, mirth, pleasure, recreation, sport OPPOSITE **gloom**
♦ **make fun of** = **mock**, lampoon, laugh at, parody, poke fun at, ridicule, satirize, send up (*Brit inf*)

function *noun* **1** = **purpose**, raison d'être, business, duty, job, mission, responsibility, role, task **3** = **reception**, affair, do (*inf*), gathering, social occasion ♦ *verb* **6** = **work**, go, operate,

perform, run **7** (foll. by *as*) = **act as**, behave as, do duty as

functional *adjective* **2** = **practical**, hard-wearing, serviceable, useful, utilitarian **3** = **working**, operative

fund *noun* **1** = **kitty**, pool **2** = **reserve**, stock, store, supply ♦ *verb* **4** = **finance**, pay for, subsidize, support

fundamental *adjective* **1** = **essential**, cardinal, central, key, primary, principal OPPOSITE **incidental**. **2** = **basic**, elementary, rudimentary, underlying ♦ *noun* **3** = **principle**, axiom, cornerstone, law, rudiment, rule

funds *plural noun* **3** = **money**, capital, cash, finance, ready money, resources, savings, the wherewithal

funeral *noun* = **burial**, cremation, interment, obsequies

funnel *verb* **3** = **channel**, conduct, convey, direct, filter, move, pass, pour

funny *adjective* **1** = **humorous**, amusing, comic, comical, droll, entertaining, hilarious, skin with the fur left on. **3** garment made of this. **4** whitish coating on the tongue or inside a kettle. ♦ *verb* **5** cover or become covered with fur. **furry** *adjective* **furrier, furriest. furrier** *noun* dealer in furs.

furbish *verb* smarten up.

furcate *verb* **1** divide into two parts. ♦ *adjective* **2** forked, branching.

furious ⊕ *adjective* **1** very angry. **2** violent or unrestrained. **furiously** *adverb*

furl *verb* roll up and fasten (a sail, umbrella, or flag). **furled** *adjective*

furlong *noun* eighth of a mile.

furlough [fur-loh] *noun* leave of absence from military duty.

furnace *noun* **1** enclosed chamber containing a very hot fire. **2** *Informal* very hot place.

furnish ⊕ *verb* **1** provide (a house or room) with furniture. **2** supply, provide. **furnishings** *plural noun* furniture, carpets, and fittings.

furniture *noun* large movable articles such as chairs and wardrobes.

furore ⊕ [fyew-**ror**-ee] *noun* very excited or angry reaction.

furrow ⊕ *noun* **1** trench made by a plough. **2** groove, esp. a wrinkle on the forehead. ♦ *verb* **3** make or become wrinkled. **4** make furrows in.

further ⊕ *adverb* **1** in addition. **2** to a greater distance or extent. ♦ *adjective* **3** additional. **4** more distant. ♦ *verb* **5** assist the progress of.

further education education beyond school other than at a university. **furthest** *adverb* **1** to the greatest distance or extent. ♦ *adjective* **2** most distant. **furtherance** *noun* **furthermore**

adverb besides. **furthermost** *adjective* most distant.

furtive ⊕ *adjective* sly and secretive. **furtively** *adverb*

fury ⊕ *noun, pl* -**ries 1** wild anger. **2** uncontrolled violence. **3** person with a violent temper.

furze *noun* gorse.

fuse[1] *noun* cord containing an explosive for detonating a bomb.

fuse[2] *noun* **1** safety device for electric circuits, containing a wire that melts and breaks the connection when the circuit isoverloaded. ♦ *verb* **2** (cause to) fail as a result of a blown fuse. **3** equip (a plug) with a fuse. **4** join or combine. **5** unite by melting. **6** melt with heat.

fuselage [**fyew**-zill-lahzh] *noun* body of an aircraft.

fusible *adjective* capable of being melted.

fusilier [fyew-zill-**leer**] *noun* soldier of certain regiments.

fusillade [fyew-zill-**lade**] *noun* **1** continuous discharge of firearms. **2** outburst of criticism, questions, etc.

fusion *noun* **1** melting. **2** product of fusing. **3** (also **nuclear fusion**) combination of the nucleus of two atoms with the release of energy. **4** something new created by a mixture of qualities, ideas, or things. **5** popular music blending styles, esp. jazz and funk. ♦ *adjective* **6** of a style of cooking that combines traditional Western techniques and ingredients with those used in Eastern cuisine.

fuss ⊕ *noun* **1** needless activity or worry. **2**

———————— THESAURUS ————————

riotous, side-splitting, witty OPPOSITE **serious. 2 = peculiar,** curious, mysterious, odd, queer, strange, suspicious, unusual, weird

furious *adjective* **1 = angry,** beside oneself, enraged, fuming, incensed, infuriated, livid (*inf*), raging, up in arms OPPOSITE **pleased. 2 = violent,** fierce, intense, savage, turbulent, unrestrained, vehement

furnish *verb* **1 = decorate,** equip, fit out, stock **2 = supply,** give, grant, hand out, offer, present, provide

furniture *noun* = **household goods,** appliances, fittings, furnishings, goods, possessions, things (*inf*)

furore *noun* = **commotion,** disturbance, hullabaloo, outcry, stir, to-do, uproar

furrow *noun* **1 = groove,** channel, hollow, line, rut, seam, trench **2 = wrinkle,** crease ♦ *verb* **3 = wrinkle,** corrugate, crease, draw together, knit

further *adverb* **1 = in addition,** additionally,

also, besides, furthermore, into the bargain, moreover, to boot ♦ *adjective* **3 = additional,** extra, fresh, more, new, other, supplementary ♦ *verb* **5 = promote,** advance, assist, encourage, forward, help, lend support to, work for OPPOSITE **hinder**

furthermore *adverb* = **besides,** additionally, as well, further, in addition, into the bargain, moreover, to boot, too

furthest *adjective* **2 = most distant,** extreme, farthest, furthermost, outmost, remotest, ultimate

furtive *adjective* = **sly,** clandestine, conspiratorial, secretive, sneaky, stealthy, surreptitious, underhand, under-the-table OPPOSITE **open**

fury *noun* **1 = anger,** frenzy, impetuosity, madness, passion, rage, wrath OPPOSITE **calmness. 2 = violence,** ferocity, fierceness, force, intensity, savagery, severity, vehemence OPPOSITE **peace**

complaint or objection. **3** great display of attention. ◆ *verb* **4** make a fuss. **fussy** *adjective* **fussier, fussiest 1** inclined to fuss. **2** overparticular. **3** overelaborate. **fussily** *adverb* **fussiness** *noun*

fusty ❶ *adjective* **-tier, -tiest 1** stale-smelling. **2** behind the times. **fustiness** *noun*

futile ❶ [**fyew**-tile] *adjective* unsuccessful or useless. **futility** *noun*

futon [**foo**-tonn] *noun* Japanese padded quilt, laid on the floor as a bed.

future ❶ *noun* **1** time to come. **2** what will happen. **3** prospects. ◆ *adjective* **4** yet to come or be. **5** of or relating to time to come. **6** (of a verb tense) indicating that the action specified has not yet taken place. **futuristic** *adjective* of a design appearing to belong to some future time.

fuzz¹ ❶ *noun* mass of fine or curly hairs or fibres. **fuzzy** *adjective* **fuzzier, fuzziest 1** of, like, or covered with fuzz. **2** blurred or indistinct. **3** (of hair) tightly curled. **fuzzily** *adverb* **fuzziness** *noun*

fuzz² *noun Slang* police.

fwd forward.

F

———————— T H E S A U R U S ————————

fuss *noun* **1** = **bother**, ado, commotion, excitement, hue and cry, palaver, stir, to-do **2** = **argument**, complaint, furore, objection, row, squabble, trouble ◆*verb* **4** = **worry**, fidget, flap (*inf*), fret, get worked up, take pains

fussy *adjective* **1, 2** = **difficult**, hard to please **2** = **particular**, choosy (*inf*), fastidious, finicky, nit-picking (*inf*), pernickety, picky (*inf*) **3** = **overelaborate**, busy, cluttered, overworked, rococo

fusty *adjective* **1** = **stale**, airless, damp, mildewed, mouldering, mouldy, musty, stuffy

futile *adjective* = **useless**, fruitless, ineffectual, unavailing, unprofitable, unsuccessful, vain, worthless OPPOSITE> **successful**

future *noun* **1** = **time to come**, hereafter **3** = **prospect**, expectation, outlook ◆*adjective* **4, 5** = **forthcoming**, approaching, coming, fated, impending, later, subsequent, to come OPPOSITE> **past**

fuzzy *adjective* **1** = **fluffy**, downy, woolly **2** = **indistinct**, bleary, blurred, distorted, ill-defined, out of focus, unclear, vague OPPOSITE> **clear**. **3** = **frizzy**

Gg

Ga *Chem* gallium.

GA Georgia.

gab *noun, verb* **gabbing, gabbed** *Informal* talk or chatter. **gift of the gab** eloquence.

gabby *adjective* **-bier, -biest** *Informal* talkative.

gabardine, gaberdine *noun* strong twill cloth used esp. for raincoats.

gabble ❶ *verb* **1** speak rapidly and indistinctly. ◆ *noun* **2** rapid indistinct speech.

gable *noun* triangular upper part of a wall between sloping roofs. **gabled** *adjective*

gad ❶ *verb* **gadding, gadded. gad about, around** go around in search of pleasure.

gadabout *noun* pleasure-seeker.

gadfly *noun* **1** fly that bites cattle. **2** constantly annoying person.

gadget ❶ *noun* small mechanical device or appliance. **gadgetry** *noun* gadgets.

gadoid [gay-doid] *adjective* **1** of the cod family of marine fishes. ◆ *noun* **2** gadoid fish.

gadolinium *noun Chem* silvery-white metallic element.

Gael [gayl] *noun* speaker of Gaelic. **Gaelic** [gal-lik, gay-lik] *noun* **1** any of the Celtic languages of Ireland and the Scottish Highlands. ◆ *adjective* **2** of the Gaels or their language.

gaff¹ *noun* stick with an iron hook for landing large fish.

gaff² *noun* **blow the gaff** *Slang* divulge a secret.

gaffe ❶ *noun* social blunder.

gaffer ❶ *noun* **1** *Informal* foreman or boss. **2** old man.

gag¹ ❶ *verb* **gagging, gagged 1** choke or retch. **2** stop up the mouth of (a person) with cloth etc. **3** deprive of free speech. ◆ *noun* **4** cloth etc. put into or tied across the mouth.

gag² ❶ *noun Informal* joke.

gaga [gah-gah] *adjective Slang* **1** senile. **2** foolishly doting.

gage *noun, verb US* gauge.

gaggle *noun* **1** *Informal* disorderly crowd. **2** flock of geese.

gaiety ❶ *noun* **1** cheerfulness. **2** merrymaking.

gaily *adverb* **1** merrily. **2** colourfully.

gain ❶ *verb* **1** acquire or obtain. **2** increase or improve. **3** reach. **4** (of a watch or clock) be or become too fast. ◆ *noun* **5** profit or advantage. **6** increase or improvement. **gainful** *adjective* useful or profitable. **gainfully** *adverb* **gain on, upon** *verb* get nearer to or catch up with.

THESAURUS

gabble *verb* **1** = **prattle**, babble, blabber, gibber, gush, jabber, spout ◆ *noun* **2** = **gibberish**, babble, blabber, chatter, drivel, prattle, twaddle

gadabout *noun* = **pleasure-seeker**, rambler, rover, wanderer

gadget *noun* = **device**, appliance, contraption (*inf*), contrivance, gizmo (*sl, chiefly US*), instrument, invention, thing, tool

gaffe *noun* = **blunder**, bloomer (*inf*), clanger (*inf*), faux pas, howler, indiscretion, lapse, mistake, slip, solecism

gaffer *noun* **1** *Inf* = **manager**, boss (*inf*), foreman, overseer, superintendent, supervisor **2** = **old man**, granddad, greybeard, old boy (*inf*), old fellow, old-timer (*US*)

gag¹ *verb* **1** = **retch**, heave, puke (*sl*), spew, throw up (*inf*), vomit **2** = **suppress**, curb, muffle, muzzle, quiet, silence, stifle, stop up

gag² *noun Inf* = **joke**, crack (*sl*), funny (*inf*),

hoax, jest, wisecrack (*inf*), witticism

gaiety *noun* **1** = **cheerfulness**, blitheness, exhilaration, glee, high spirits, jollity, light-heartedness, merriment, mirth **2** = **merrymaking**, conviviality, festivity, fun, jollification, revelry OPPOSITE **misery**

gaily *adverb* **1** = **cheerfully**, blithely, gleefully, happily, joyfully, light-heartedly, merrily **2** = **colourfully**, brightly, brilliantly, flamboyantly, flashily, gaudily, showily

gain *verb* **1** = **acquire**, attain, capture, collect, gather, get, land, secure OPPOSITE **lose**. **2** = **improve**, advance, increase, pick up, profit OPPOSITE **lose**. **3** = **reach**, arrive at, attain, come to, get to ◆ *noun* **5** = **profit**, advantage, benefit, dividend, return, yield OPPOSITE **loss**. **6** = **increase**, advance, growth, improvement, progress, rise

gainful *adjective* = **profitable**, advantageous, beneficial, fruitful, lucrative, productive,

gainsay ⊙ *verb* **-saying, -said** deny or contradict.
gait ⊙ *noun* manner of walking.
gaiter *noun* cloth or leather covering for the lower leg.
gal *noun Slang* girl.
gal. gallon.
gala ⊙ [gah-la] *noun* **1** festival. **2** competitive sporting event.
galaxy *noun, pl* **-axies 1** system of stars. **2** gathering of famous people. **3** (G-) Milky Way. **galactic** *adjective*
gale ⊙ *noun* **1** strong wind. **2** *Informal* loud outburst.
gall¹ ⊙ [gawl] *noun* **1** *Informal* impudence. **2** bitter feeling. **3** bile. **gall bladder** sac attached to the liver, storing bile. **gallstone** *noun* hard mass formed in the gall bladder or its ducts.
gall² ⊙ [gawl] *verb* **1** annoy. **2** make sore by rubbing. ◆ *noun* **3** sore caused by rubbing.
galling *adjective* annoying or bitterly humiliating.
gall³ [gawl] *noun* abnormal outgrowth on a tree or plant.
gallant ⊙ *adjective* **1** brave and noble. **2** (of a man) attentive to women. **gallantly** *adverb*
gallantry *noun* **1** showy, attentive treatment of women. **2** bravery.
galleon *noun* large three-masted sailing ship of the 15th-17th centuries.
gallery *noun, pl* **-ries 1** room or building for displaying works of art. **2** balcony in a church, theatre, etc. **3** passage in a mine. **4** covered walk with side openings. **5** long narrow room for a specific purpose, e.g. *shooting gallery*.

galley *noun* **1** kitchen of a ship or aircraft. **2** *Hist* ship propelled by oars, usu. rowed by slaves. **galley slave 1** slave forced to row in a galley. **2** *Informal* drudge.
Gallic *adjective* **1** French. **2** of ancient Gaul.
Gallicism *noun* French word or idiom.
gallinaceous *adjective* of an order of birds including poultry, pheasants, and grouse.
gallium *noun Chem* soft grey metallic element used in semiconductors.
gallivant ⊙ *verb* go about in search of pleasure.
gallon *noun* liquid measure of eight pints, equal to 4.55 litres.
gallop ⊙ *noun* **1** horse's fastest pace. **2** galloping. ◆ *verb* **galloping, galloped 3** go or ride at a gallop. **4** move or progress rapidly.

> **SPELLING TIP**
>
> Although **gallop** has two *l*s, remember that **galloping** and **galloped** have only one *p*.

gallows *noun* wooden structure used for hanging criminals.
Gallup poll *noun* public opinion poll carried out by questioning a cross section of the population.
galore ⊙ *adverb* in abundance, e.g. *presents galore*.
galoshes *plural noun* waterproof overshoes.
galumph *verb Informal* leap or move about clumsily.
galvanic ⊙ *adjective* **1** of or producing an

G

————————————— T H E S A U R U S —————————————

remunerative, rewarding, useful, worthwhile
gainsay *verb* =**contradict**, contravene, controvert, deny, disagree with, dispute, rebut, retract [OPPOSITE] **confirm**
gait *noun* =**walk**, bearing, carriage, pace, step, stride, tread
gala *noun* **1** =**festival**, carnival, celebration, festivity, fete, jamboree, pageant
gale *noun* **1** =**storm**, blast, cyclone, hurricane, squall, tempest, tornado, typhoon **2** *Inf* =**outburst**, burst, eruption, explosion, fit, howl, outbreak, paroxysm, peal, shout, shriek, storm
gall¹ *noun* **1** *Inf* =**impudence**, brazenness, cheek (*inf*), chutzpah (*US & Canad inf*), effrontery, impertinence, insolence, nerve (*inf*) **2** =**bitterness**, acrimony, animosity, bile, hostility, rancour
gall² *verb* **1** =**annoy**, exasperate, irk, irritate, provoke, rankle, vex **2** =**scrape**, abrade, chafe, irritate

gallant *adjective* **1** =**brave**, bold, courageous, heroic, honourable, intrepid, manly, noble, valiant [OPPOSITE] **cowardly**. **2** =**courteous**, attentive, chivalrous, gentlemanly, gracious, noble, polite [OPPOSITE] **discourteous**
gallantry *noun* **1** =**courtesy**, attentiveness, chivalry, courteousness, gentlemanliness, graciousness, nobility, politeness [OPPOSITE] **discourtesy**. **2** =**bravery**, boldness, courage, heroism, intrepidity, manliness, spirit, valour [OPPOSITE] **cowardice**
galling *adjective* =**annoying**, bitter, exasperating, irksome, irritating, provoking, vexatious
gallivant *verb* =**wander**, gad about, ramble, roam, rove
gallop *verb* **3, 4** =**run**, bolt, career, dash, hurry, race, rush, speed, sprint
galore *adverb* =**in abundance**, all over the place, aplenty, everywhere, in great quantity, in

electric current generated by chemical means. **2** *Informal* stimulating or startling. **galvanize** *verb* **1** stimulate into action. **2** coat (metal) with zinc. **galvanometer** *noun* instrument for measuring small electric currents.

gambit *noun* **1** opening line or move intended to secure an advantage. **2** *Chess* opening move involving the sacrifice of a pawn.

gamble ❶ *verb* **1** play games of chance to win money. **2** act on the expectation of something. ♦ *noun* **3** risky undertaking. **4** bet or wager. **gambler** *noun* **gambling** *noun*

gamboge [gam-**boje**] *noun* gum resin used as a yellow pigment and purgative.

gambol ❶ *verb* **-bolling, -bolled 1** jump about playfully, frolic. ♦ *noun* **2** frolic.

> **SPELLING TIP**
>
> Although the pronunciation is the same as 'gamble', both the verb and the noun **gambol** must always contain an *o*.

game¹ ❶ *noun* **1** amusement or pastime. **2** contest for amusement. **3** single period of play in a contest. **4** score needed to win a contest. **5** animals or birds hunted for sport or food. **6** their flesh. **7** scheme or trick. ♦ *plural* **8** athletic contests. ♦ *verb* **9** gamble. ♦ *adjective* **10** brave. **11** willing. **gamely** *adverb* **gaming** *noun* gambling. **gamey, gamy** *adjective* **gamier, gamiest** having the smell or flavour of game. **gamekeeper** *noun* person employed to breed game and prevent poaching. **gamer** *noun* person who plays computer games. **gamesmanship** *noun* art of winning by

cunning practices without actually cheating.

game² ❶ *adjective Brit, Aust & NZ* lame, crippled.

gamete [gam-eet] *noun Biol* reproductive cell.

gamin *noun* street urchin.

gamine [gam-een] *noun* slim boyish young woman.

gamma *noun* third letter of the Greek alphabet. **gamma ray** electromagnetic ray of shorter wavelength and higher energy than an x-ray.

gammon *noun* **1** cured or smoked ham. **2** hindquarter of a side of bacon.

gammy *adjective* **-mier, -miest** same as GAME².

gamp *noun Informal* umbrella.

gamut ❶ *noun* whole range or scale (of music, emotions, etc.).

gander *noun* **1** male goose. **2** *Informal* quick look.

gang ❶ *noun* **1** (criminal) group. **2** organized group of workmen. **gangland** *noun* criminal underworld. **gang up** *verb* form an alliance (against).

gangling ❶ *adjective* lanky and awkward.

ganglion *noun* **1** group of nerve cells. **2** small harmless tumour.

gangplank *noun* portable bridge for boarding or leaving a ship.

gangrene *noun* decay of body tissue as a result of disease or injury. **gangrenous** *adjective*

gangsta rap *noun* style of music portraying life in Black ghettos in the US.

gangster ❶ *noun* member of a criminal gang.

gangue *noun* valueless material in an ore.

gangway *noun* **1** passage between rows of seats. **2** gangplank. **3** opening in a ship's side for a gangplank.

———— THESAURUS ————

numbers, in profusion, to spare

galvanize *verb* **1** = **stimulate**, electrify, excite, inspire, invigorate, jolt, provoke, spur, stir

gamble *verb* **1** = **bet**, game, have a flutter (*inf*), play, punt, wager **2** = **risk**, chance, hazard, speculate, stick one's neck out (*inf*), take a chance ♦*noun* **3** = **risk**, chance, leap in the dark, lottery, speculation, uncertainty, venture OPPOSITE certainty. **4** = **bet**, flutter (*inf*), punt, wager

gambol *verb* **1** = **frolic**, caper, cavort, frisk, hop, jump, prance, skip ♦*noun* **2** = **frolic**, caper, hop, jump, prance, skip

game¹ *noun* **1** = **pastime**, amusement, distraction, diversion, entertainment, lark, recreation, sport OPPOSITE work. **2** = **match**, competition, contest, event, head-to-head, meeting, tournament **5** = **wild animals**, prey,

quarry **7** = **scheme**, design, plan, plot, ploy, stratagem, tactic, trick ♦*adjective* **10** = **brave**, courageous, gallant, gritty, intrepid, persistent, plucky, spirited, feisty (*US & Canad*) OPPOSITE fearful. **11** = **willing**, desirous, eager, interested, keen, prepared, ready OPPOSITE cowardly

game² *adjective* = **disabled**, bad, crippled, deformed, gammy (*Brit sl*), incapacitated, injured, lame, maimed

gamut *noun* = **range**, area, catalogue, compass, field, scale, scope, series, sweep

gang *noun* = **group**, band, clique, club, company, coterie, crowd, mob, pack, squad, team

gangling *adjective* = **tall**, angular, awkward, lanky, rangy, rawboned, spindly

gangster *noun* = **racketeer**, crook (*inf*), hood (*US sl*), hoodlum (*chiefly US*), mobster (*US sl*)

gannet noun 1 large sea bird. 2 Slang greedy person.

gantry noun, pl **-tries** structure supporting something such as a crane or rocket.

gaol [jayl] noun same as JAIL.

gap ❶ noun 1 break or opening. 2 interruption or interval. 3 divergence or difference. **gappy** adjective

gape ❶ verb 1 stare in wonder. 2 open the mouth wide. 3 be or become wide open. **gaping** adjective

garage noun 1 building used to house cars. 2 place for the refuelling, sale, and repair of cars. ◆ verb 3 put or keep a car in a garage.

garb noun 1 clothes. ◆ verb 2 clothe.

garbage ❶ noun rubbish.

garbled ❶ adjective (of a story etc.) jumbled and confused.

garden noun 1 piece of land for growing flowers, fruit, or vegetables. ◆ plural 2 ornamental park. ◆ verb 3 cultivate a garden. **gardener** noun **gardening** noun **garden centre** place selling plants and gardening equipment.

gardenia [gar-**deen**-ya] noun 1 large fragrant white waxy flower. 2 shrub bearing this.

garfish noun 1 freshwater fish with a long body and very long toothed jaws. 2 sea fish with similar characteristics.

gargantuan adjective huge.

gargle verb 1 wash the throat with (a liquid) by breathing out slowly through the liquid. ◆ noun 2 liquid used for gargling. 3 act or sound of gargling.

gargoyle noun waterspout carved in the form of a grotesque face, esp. on a church.

garish ❶ adjective crudely bright or colourful. **garishly** adverb **garishness** noun

garland ❶ noun 1 wreath of flowers worn or hung as a decoration. ◆ verb 2 decorate with garlands.

garlic noun pungent bulb of a plant of the onion family, used in cooking.

garment noun 1 article of clothing. ◆ plural 2 clothes.

garner ❶ verb collect or store.

garnet noun red semiprecious stone.

garnish ❶ verb 1 decorate (food). ◆ noun 2 decoration for food.

garret noun attic in a house.

garrison ❶ noun 1 troops stationed in a town or fort. 2 fortified place. ◆ verb 3 station troops in.

garrotte, garotte noun 1 Spanish method of execution by strangling. 2 cord or wire used for this. ◆ verb 3 kill by this method. 4 strangle.

garrulous ❶ adjective talkative. **garrulously** adverb

garter noun band worn round the leg to hold up a sock or stocking. **the Garter** highest order of British knighthood.

gas noun, pl **gases, gasses** 1 airlike substance that is not liquid or solid. 2 fossil fuel in the form of a gas, used for heating. 3 gaseous anaesthetic. 4 US & Canad petrol. 5 poisonous gas used in warfare. ◆ verb **gassing, gassed** 6 poison or render unconscious with gas. 7 Informal talk idly or boastfully. **gassy** adjective **-sier, -siest** filled with gas. **gaseous** adjective of or like gas. **gasbag** noun Informal person who talks too much. **gas chamber** airtight room which is filled with poison gas to kill

—————————— T H E S A U R U S ——————————

gap noun 1 = **opening**, break, chink, cleft, crack, hole, space 2 = **interval**, breathing space, hiatus, interlude, intermission, interruption, lacuna, lull, pause, respite 3 = **difference**, disagreement, disparity, divergence, inconsistency

gape verb 1 = **stare**, gawk, gawp (Brit sl), goggle, wonder 3 = **open**, crack, split, yawn

gaping adjective 3 = **wide**, broad, cavernous, great, open, vast, wide open, yawning

garbage noun = **waste**, refuse, rubbish, trash (chiefly US)

garbled adjective = **jumbled**, confused, distorted, double-Dutch, incomprehensible, mixed up, unintelligible

garish adjective = **gaudy**, brash, brassy, flashy, loud, showy, tacky (inf), tasteless, vulgar OPPOSITE> **dull**

garland noun 1 = **wreath**, bays, chaplet,

crown, festoon, honours, laurels ◆verb 2 = **adorn**, crown, deck, festoon, wreathe

garments plural noun = **clothes**, apparel, attire, clothing, costume, dress, garb, gear (sl), outfit, uniform

garner verb = **collect**, accumulate, amass, gather, hoard, save, stockpile, store, stow away

garnish verb 1 = **decorate**, adorn, embellish, enhance, ornament, set off, trim OPPOSITE> **strip** ◆noun 2 = **decoration**, adornment, embellishment, enhancement, ornamentation, trimming

garrison noun 1 = **troops**, armed force, command, detachment, unit 2 = **fort**, base, camp, encampment, fortification, fortress, post, station, stronghold ◆verb 3 = **station**, assign, position, post, put on duty

garrulous adjective = **talkative**, chatty, gossiping, loquacious, prattling, verbose, people or animals. **gasholder, gasometer** [gas-**som**-it-er] *noun* large tank for storing gas. **gasify** *verb* **-fying, -fied** change into a gas. **gasification** *noun* **gas mask** mask with a chemical filter to protect the wearer against poison gas. **gasworks** *noun* plant where coal gas is made.

gash ❶ *verb* **1** make a long deep cut in. ◆ *noun* **2** long deep cut.

gasket *noun* piece of rubber etc. placed between the faces of a metal joint to act as a seal.

gasoline *noun* US petrol.

gasp ❶ *verb* **1** draw in breath sharply or with difficulty. **2** utter breathlessly. **3** (foll. by *for*) crave. ◆ *noun* **4** convulsive intake of breath.

gastric *adjective* of the stomach. **gastritis** *noun* inflammation of the stomach lining. **gastroenteritis** *noun* inflammation of the stomach and intestines.

gastronomy *noun* art of good eating. **gastronomic** *adjective*

gastropod *noun* mollusc, such as a snail, with a single flattened muscular foot.

gate ❶ *noun* **1** movable barrier, usu. hinged, in a wall or fence. **2** opening with a gate. **3** any entrance or way in. **4** (entrance money paid by) those attending a sporting event. **5** exit at an airport by which passengers get to an aircraft. **gate-crash** *verb* enter (a party) uninvited. **gatehouse** *noun* building at or above a gateway. **gateway** *noun* **1** entrance with a gate. **2** means of access, e.g. *Bombay, gateway to India.*

gâteau [gat-toe] *noun, pl* **-teaux** [-toes] rich elaborate cake.

gather ❶ *verb* **1** assemble. **2** collect gradually.

3 increase gradually. **4** learn from information given. **5** pick or harvest. **6** draw (material) into small tucks or folds. **gathers** *plural noun* gathered folds in material. **gathering** *noun* assembly.

GATT General Agreement on Tariffs and Trade.

gauche ❶ [gohsh] *adjective* socially awkward. **gaucheness** *noun*

gaucho [gow-choh] *noun, pl* **-chos** S American cowboy.

gaudy ❶ *adjective* **gaudier, gaudiest** vulgarly bright or colourful. **gaudily** *adverb* **gaudiness** *noun*

gauge ❶ [gayj] *verb* **1** estimate or judge. **2** measure the amount or condition of. ◆ *noun* **3** measuring instrument. **4** scale or standard of measurement. **5** distance between the rails of a railway track. **6** capacity or extent.

SPELLING TIP

The vowels in **gauge** are often confused so that the misspelling *guage* is common in the Bank of English.

Gaul *noun* **1** native of ancient Gaul. **2** Frenchman.

gaunt ❶ *adjective* **1** lean and haggard. **2** (of a place) desolate or bleak. **gauntness** *noun*

gauntlet[1] *noun* **1** heavy glove with a long cuff. **2** medieval armoured glove. **throw down the gauntlet** offer a challenge.

gauntlet[2] *noun* **run the gauntlet** be exposed to criticism or unpleasant treatment.

gauze *noun* transparent loosely-woven fabric,

───── T H E S A U R U S ─────

voluble OPPOSITE **reserved**

gash *verb* **1** = **cut**, gouge, lacerate, slash, slit, split, tear, wound ◆*noun* **2** = **cut**, gouge, incision, laceration, slash, slit, split, tear, wound

gasp *verb* **1** = **gulp**, blow, catch one's breath, choke, pant, puff ◆*noun* **4** = **gulp**, exclamation, pant, puff, sharp intake of breath

gate *noun* **1-3** = **barrier**, door, entrance, exit, gateway, opening, passage, portal

gather *verb* **1, 2** = **assemble**, accumulate, amass, collect, garner, mass, muster, stockpile OPPOSITE **disperse**. **3** = **intensify**, deepen, expand, grow, heighten, increase, rise, swell, thicken **4** = **learn**, assume, conclude, deduce, hear, infer, surmise, understand **5** = **pick**, cull, garner, glean, harvest, pluck, reap, select **6** = **fold**, pleat, tuck

gathering *noun* = **assembly**, company,

conclave, congress, convention, crowd, group, meeting

gauche *adjective* = **awkward**, clumsy, ill-mannered, inelegant, tactless, unsophisticated OPPOSITE **sophisticated**

gaudy *adjective* = **garish**, bright, flashy, loud, showy, tacky (*inf*), tasteless, vulgar OPPOSITE **dull**

gauge *verb* **1** = **judge**, adjudge, appraise, assess, estimate, evaluate, guess, rate, reckon, value **2** = **measure**, ascertain, calculate, check, compute, count, determine, weigh ◆*noun* **3, 4** = **indicator**, criterion, guide, guideline, measure, meter, standard, test, touchstone, yardstick

gaunt *adjective* **1** = **thin**, angular, bony, haggard, lean, pinched, scrawny, skinny, spare OPPOSITE **plump**

often used for surgical dressings. **gauzy** *adjective*

gave *verb* past tense of GIVE.

gavel [**gav**-el] *noun* small hammer banged on a table by a judge, auctioneer, or chairman to call for attention.

gavotte *noun* **1** old formal dance. **2** music for this.

gawk ❶ *verb* **1** stare stupidly. ♦ *noun* **2** clumsy awkward person. **gawky** *adjective* **gawkier, gawkiest** clumsy or awkward. **gawkiness** *noun*

gawp *verb Slang* stare stupidly.

gay ❶ *adjective* **1** homosexual. **2** carefree and merry. **3** colourful. ♦ *noun* **4** homosexual. **gayness** *noun* homosexuality.

LANGUAGE TIP

The meaning 'homosexual' is now the most frequent use of *gay*, which retains the meaning 'happy' only in older books.

---

gaze ❶ *verb* **1** look fixedly. ♦ *noun* **2** fixed look.

gazebo [gaz-**zee**-boh] *noun, pl* **-bos, -boes** summerhouse with a good view.

gazelle *noun* small graceful antelope.

gazette ❶ *noun* official publication containing announcements. **gazetteer** *noun* (part of) a book that lists and describes places.

gazump *verb Brit & Aust* raise the price of a property after verbally agreeing it with (a prospective buyer).

gazunder *verb Brit* reduce an offer on a property immediately before exchanging contracts having earlier agreed a higher price with theseller.

GB Great Britain.

GBH grievous bodily harm.

GC George Cross.

GCE 1 General Certificate of Education. **2** pass in a GCE examination.

GCSE 1 General Certificate of Secondary Education. **2** pass in a GCSE examination.

Gd *Chem* gadolinium.

Ge *Chem* germanium.

gear ❶ *noun* **1** set of toothed wheels connecting with another or with a rack to change the direction or speed of transmitted motion. **2** mechanism for transmitting motion by gears. **3** setting of a gear to suit engine speed, e.g. *first gear*. **4** clothing or belongings. **5** equipment. ♦ *verb* **6** prepare or organize for something. **in, out of gear** with the gear mechanism engaged *or* disengaged. **gearbox** *noun* case enclosing a set of gears in a motor vehicle. **gear lever** lever for changing gears in a motor vehicle. **gear up** *verb* prepare for an activity.

gecko *noun, pl* **geckos, geckoes** small tropical lizard.

gee *interjection US informal* mild exclamation of surprise, admiration, etc.

geebung [**gee**-bung] *noun* **1** Australian tree or shrub with an edible but tasteless fruit. **2** fruit of this tree.

geek *noun Informal* boring, unattractive person.

geese *noun* plural of GOOSE.

geezer *noun Informal* man.

Geiger counter [**guy**-ger] *noun* instrument for detecting and measuring radiation.

geisha [**gay**-sha] *noun, pl* **-sha, -shas** (in Japan) professional female companion for men.

gel [jell] *noun* **1** jelly-like substance, esp. one used to secure a hairstyle. ♦ *verb* **gelling, gelled 2** form a gel. **3** *Informal* take on a definite form.

gelatine ❶ [**jel**-at-teen], **gelatin** *noun* **1** substance made by boiling animal bones. **2** edible jelly made of this. **gelatinous** [jel-**at**-in-uss] *adjective* of or like jelly.

geld *verb* castrate. **gelding** *noun* castrated horse.

G

————————— THESAURUS —————————

gawky *adjective* **2** = **awkward**, clumsy, gauche, loutish, lumbering, maladroit, ungainly OPPOSITE **graceful**

gay *adjective* **1** = **homosexual**, lesbian, queer (*inf, derog*) OPPOSITE **heterosexual**. **2** = **cheerful**, blithe, carefree, jovial, light-hearted, lively, merry, sparkling OPPOSITE **serious**. **3** = **colourful**, bright, brilliant, flamboyant, flashy, rich, showy, vivid OPPOSITE **drab** ♦*noun* **4** = **homosexual**, lesbian OPPOSITE **heterosexual**

gaze *verb* **1** = **stare**, gape, look, regard, view, watch, wonder ♦*noun* **2** = **stare**, fixed look,

look

gazette *noun* = **newspaper**, journal, news-sheet, paper, periodical

gear *noun* **1** = **cog**, cogwheel, gearwheel **2** = **mechanism**, cogs, machinery, works **4** = **clothing**, clothes, costume, dress, garments, outfit, togs, wear **5** = **equipment**, accoutrements, apparatus, instruments, paraphernalia, supplies, tackle, tools ♦*verb* **6** = **equip**, adapt, adjust, fit

gelatinous *adjective* = **jelly-like**, glutinous, gummy, sticky, viscous

gelignite *noun* type of dynamite used for blasting.

gem ❶ *noun* **1** precious stone or jewel. **2** highly valued person or thing. **gemfish** *noun* Australian food fish with a delicate flavour.

Gemini *noun* (the twins) third sign of the zodiac.

gen *noun Informal* information. **gen up on** *verb* **genning, genned** *Informal* make or become fully informed about.

gendarme [zhohn-darm] *noun* member of the French police force.

gender *noun* **1** state of being male or female. **2** *Grammar* classification of nouns in certain languages as masculine, feminine, or neuter.

gene [jean] *noun* part of a cell which determines inherited characteristics.

genealogy [jean-ee-al-a-gee] *noun, pl* **-gies** (study of) the history and descent of a family or families. **genealogical** *sadj* **genealogist** *noun*

genera [jen-er-a] *noun* plural of GENUS.

general ❶ *adjective* **1** common or widespread. **2** of or affecting all or most. **3** not specific. **4** including or dealing with various or miscellaneous items. **5** highest in authority or rank, e.g. *general manager.* ◆ *noun* **6** very senior army officer. **in general** mostly or usually.

generally *adverb* **generality** *noun, pl* **-ties 1** general principle. **2** state of being general.

generalize *verb* **1** draw general conclusions. **2** speak in generalities. **3** make widely known or used. **generalization** *noun* **general election** election in which representatives are chosen for every constituency. **general practitioner** nonspecialist doctor serving a local area.

generalissimo *noun, pl* **-mos** supreme commander of combined armed forces.

generate ❶ *verb* produce or bring into being.

generation *noun* all the people born about the same time. **generative** *adjective* capable of producing. **generator** *noun* machine for converting mechanical energy into electrical energy.

generation ❶ *noun* **1** all the people born about the same time. **2** successive stage in descent of people or animals. **3** average time between two generations (about 30 years). **4** generating.

generic ❶ [jin-ner-ik] *adjective* of a class, group, or genus. **generically** *adverb*

generous ❶ *adjective* **1** free in giving. **2** free from pettiness. **3** plentiful. **generously** *adverb* **generosity** *noun*

genesis ❶ [jen-iss-iss] *noun, pl* **-eses** [-iss-eez] beginning or origin.

genetic [jin-net-tik] *adjective* of genes or genetics. **genetics** *noun* study of heredity and variation in organisms. **geneticist** *noun* **genetic engineering** alteration of the genetic structure of an organism for a particular purpose. **genetic fingerprinting** use of a person's unique DNA pattern for identification. **Geneva Convention** *noun* international agreement establishing a code for wartime treatment of the sick, wounded, and prisoners of war.

genial ❶ [jean-ee-al] *adjective* cheerful and friendly. **genially** *adverb* **geniality** *noun*

genie [jean-ee] *noun* (in fairy tales) servant

——— T H E S A U R U S ———

gem *noun* **1** = **precious stone**, jewel, stone **2** = **prize**, jewel, masterpiece, pearl, treasure

general *adjective* **1** = **common**, accepted, broad, extensive, popular, prevalent, public, universal, widespread OPPOSITE **individual. 2, 4** = **universal**, across-the-board, blanket, collective, comprehensive, indiscriminate, miscellaneous, overall, overarching, sweeping, total OPPOSITE **restricted. 3** = **imprecise**, approximate, ill-defined, indefinite, inexact, loose, unspecific, vague OPPOSITE **specific**

generally *adverb* = **usually**, as a rule, by and large, commonly, customarily, extensively, normally, on the whole, ordinarily, popularly, publicly, typically, universally, widely OPPOSITE **occasionally**

generate *verb* = **produce**, breed, cause, create, engender, give rise to, make, propagate OPPOSITE **end**

generation *noun* **1** = **age group**, breed, crop **2, 3** = **age**, epoch, era, period, time **4** = **production**, creation, formation, genesis, propagation, reproduction

generic *adjective* = **collective**, blanket, common, comprehensive, general, inclusive, universal, wide OPPOSITE **specific**

generosity *noun* **1** = **unselfishness**, beneficence, bounty, charity, goodness, kindness, largesse *or* largess, liberality, munificence, open-handedness **2** = **nobleness**, high-mindedness, magnanimity

generous *adjective* **1** = **liberal**, beneficent, bountiful, charitable, hospitable, kind, lavish, open-handed, unstinting OPPOSITE **mean. 2** = **unselfish**, big-hearted, good, high-minded, lofty, magnanimous, noble **3** = **plentiful**, abundant, ample, copious, full, lavish, liberal, rich, unstinting OPPOSITE **meagre**

genesis *noun* = **beginning**, birth, creation, formation, inception, origin, start OPPOSITE who appears by magic and grants wishes.

genital *adjective* of the sexual organs or reproduction. **genitals, genitalia** [jen-it-**ail**-ya] *plural noun* external sexual organs.

genitive *noun* grammatical case indicating possession or association.

genius ❶ [**jean**-yuss] *noun* **1** (person with) exceptional ability in a particular field. **2** person considered as exerting influence of a certain sort.

genocide [**jen**-no-side] *noun* murder of a race of people.

genre ❶ [**zhohn**-ra] *noun* style of literary, musical, or artistic work.

gent *noun Informal* gentleman. **gents** *noun* men's public toilet.

genteel ❶ *adjective* affectedly proper and polite. **genteelly** *adverb* **gentility** *noun* **1** noble birth or ancestry. **2** polite and well-mannered behaviour.

gentian [**jen**-shun] *noun* mountain plant with deep blue flowers. **gentian violet** violet dye used as an antiseptic.

gentile *adjective, noun* non-Jewish (person).

gentle ❶ *adjective* **1** mild or kindly. **2** not rough or severe. **3** gradual. **4** easily controlled, tame. **gentleness** *noun* **gently** *adverb*

gentlefolk, gentlefolks *plural noun* people of good breeding. **gentleman** *noun* **1** polite well-bred man. **2** man of high social position. **3** polite name for a man. **gentlemanly** *adjective* **gentlewoman** *n fem*

gentry ❶ *noun* people just below the nobility in social rank. **gentrification** *noun* taking-over of a traditionally working-class area by middle-class incomers. **gentrify** *verb* **-fying, -fied**

genuflect *verb* bend the knee as a sign of reverence or deference. **genuflection, genuflexion** *noun*

genuine ❶ *adjective* **1** not fake, authentic. **2** sincere. **genuinely** *adverb* **genuineness** *noun*

genus [**jean**-uss] *noun, pl* **genera 1** group into which a family of animals or plants is divided. **2** kind, type.

geocentric *adjective* **1** having the earth as a centre. **2** measured as from the earth's centre.

geodesic *adjective* **1** of the geometry of curved surfaces. ◆ *noun* **2** shortest line between two points on a curve.

geodesy *noun* study of the shape and size of the earth.

geography *noun* **1** study of the earth's physical features, climate, population, etc. **2** physical features of a region. **geographer** *noun* **geographical, geographic** *adjective* **geographically** *adverb*

geology *noun* **1** study of the earth's origin, structure, and composition. **2** geological features of an area. **geological** *adjective* **geologically** *adverb* **geologist** *noun*

geometry *noun* branch of mathematics dealing with points, lines, curves, and surfaces. **geometric, geometrical** *adjective* **geometrically** *adverb* **geometrician** *noun*

Geordie *noun* **1** person from, or dialect of, Tyneside. ◆ *adjective* **2** of Tyneside or its dialect.

George Cross *noun* British award for bravery.

georgette [jor-**jet**] *noun* fine silky fabric.

Georgian *adjective* of the time of any of the kings of Britain called George, esp. 1714-1830.

geostationary *adjective* (of a satellite)

G

——————————— THESAURUS ———————————

end

genial *adjective* =**cheerful**, affable, agreeable, amiable, congenial, friendly, good-natured, jovial, pleasant, warm OPPOSITE **unfriendly**

geniality *noun* =**cheerfulness**, affability, agreeableness, amiability, conviviality, cordiality, friendliness, good cheer, joviality, warmth

genius *noun* **1** =**master**, brainbox, expert, fundi (*S Afr*), hotshot (*inf*), maestro, mastermind, virtuoso, whiz (*inf*) OPPOSITE **dunce**

genre *noun* =**type**, category, class, group, kind, sort, species, style

genteel *adjective* =**refined**, courteous, cultured, elegant, gentlemanly, ladylike, polite, respectable, urbane, well-mannered OPPOSITE **unmannerly**

gentle *adjective* **1** =**mild**, compassionate, humane, kindly, meek, placid, sweet-tempered,

tender OPPOSITE **unkind**. **2** =**moderate**, light, mild, muted, slight, soft, soothing OPPOSITE **powerful**. **3** =**gradual**, easy, imperceptible, light, mild, moderate, slight, slow OPPOSITE **sudden**. **4** =**tame**, biddable, broken, docile, manageable, placid, tractable

gentlemanly *adjective* **1** =**polite**, civil, courteous, gallant, genteel, honourable, refined, urbane, well-mannered

gentleness *noun* **1, 2** =**tenderness**, compassion, kindness, mildness, softness, sweetness

gentry *noun* =**upper class**, aristocracy, elitey, upper crust (*inf*)

genuine *adjective* **1** =**authentic**, actual, bona fide, legitimate, real, the real McCoy, true, veritable OPPOSITE **false**. **2** =**sincere**, candid, earnest, frank, heartfelt, honest, unaffected, unfeigned OPPOSITE **insincere**

orbiting so as to remain over the same point of the earth's surface.

geothermal *adjective* of or using the heat in the earth's interior.

geranium *noun* cultivated plant with red, pink, or white flowers.

gerbil [jer-bill] *noun* burrowing desert rodent of Asia and Africa.

geriatrics *noun* branch of medicine dealing with old age and its diseases. **geriatric** *adjective, noun* old (person). **geriatrician** *noun*

germ ❶ *noun* 1 microbe, esp. one causing disease. 2 beginning from which something may develop. 3 simple structure that can develop into a complete organism. **germicide** *noun* substance that kills germs.

German *noun* 1 language of Germany, Austria, and part of Switzerland. 2 person from Germany. ♦ *adjective* 3 of Germany or its language. **Germanic** *adjective* **German measles** contagious disease accompanied by a cough, sore throat, and red spots. **German shepherd dog** Alsatian.

germane ❶ *adjective* **germane to** relevant to.

germanium *noun Chem* brittle grey element that is a semiconductor.

German measles contagious disease accompanied by a cough, sore throat, and red spots.

germinate ❶ *verb* (cause to) sprout or begin to grow. **germination** *noun* **germinal** *adjective* 1 of or in the earliest stage of development. 2 of germs.

gerontology *noun* study of ageing and the problems of elderly people. **gerontologist** *noun*

gerrymandering *noun* division of voting constituencies in order to give an unfair advantage to one party.

gerund [jer-rund] *noun* noun formed from a verb, such as *living*.

Gestapo *noun* secret state police of Nazi Germany.

gestation *noun* 1 (period of) carrying of young in the womb between conception and birth. 2 developing of a plan or idea in the mind.

gesticulate ❶ *verb* make expressive movements with the hands and arms. **gesticulation** *noun*

gesture ❶ *noun* 1 movement to convey meaning. 2 thing said or done to show one's feelings. ♦ *verb* 3 gesticulate.

get ❶ *verb* **getting, got** 1 obtain or receive. 2 bring or fetch. 3 contract (an illness). 4 capture or seize. 5 (cause to) become as specified, e.g. *get wet*. 6 understand. 7 (often foll. by *to*) come (to) or arrive (at). 8 go on board (a plane, bus, etc.). 9 persuade. 10 receive a broadcast signal. 11 *Informal* annoy. 12 *Informal* have the better of. 13 be revenged on. **get across** *verb* (cause to) be understood. **get at** *verb* 1 gain access to. 2 imply or mean. 3 criticize. **getaway** *adjective, noun* (used in) escape. **get by** *verb* manage in spite of difficulties. **get off** *verb* 1 leave (a bus, train, etc.). 2 (cause to) avoid the consequences of, or punishment for, an action. **get off with** *verb Informal* start a romantic or sexual relationship with. **get on** *verb* 1 board (a bus, train, etc.). 2 be friends with. 3 (foll. by *with*) continue to do. 4 grow old. **get over** *verb* recover from. **get through** *verb* 1 (cause to) succeed. 2 use up (money or supplies). **get through to** *verb* 1 make (a person) understand. 2 contact by telephone. **get-up** *noun Informal* costume. **get up to** *verb* be involved in.

geyser [geez-er] *noun* 1 spring that

——— THESAURUS ———

germ *noun* 1 = **microbe**, bacterium, bug (*inf*), microorganism, virus 2 = **beginning**, embryo, origin, root, rudiment, seed, source, spark 3 = **embryo**, seed

germane *adjective* = **relevant**, apposite, appropriate, apropos, connected, fitting, material, pertinent, related, to the point *or* purpose

germinate *verb* = **sprout**, bud, develop, generate, grow, originate, shoot, swell, vegetate

gesticulate *verb* = **signal**, gesture, indicate, make a sign, motion, sign, wave

gesture *noun* 1 = **signal**, action, gesticulation, indication, motion, sign 2 = **signal**, indication, sign ♦ *verb* 3 = **signal**, gesticulate, indicate,

motion, sign, wave

get *verb* 1 = **obtain**, acquire, attain, gain, land, net, pick up, procure, receive, secure, win 2 = **bring**, fetch 3 = **contract**, catch, come down with, fall victim to, take 4 = **capture**, grab, lay hold of, nab (*inf*), seize, take 5 = **become**, come to be, grow, turn 6 = **understand**, catch, comprehend, fathom, follow, perceive, see, take in, work out 9 = **persuade**, convince, induce, influence, prevail upon 11 *Inf* = **annoy**, bug (*inf*), gall, irritate, upset, vex

get across *verb* = **communicate**, bring home to, convey, impart, make clear *or* understood, put over, transmit

get at *verb* 1 = **gain access to**, acquire, attain, come to grips with, get hold of, reach 2 discharges steam and hot water. **2** domestic gas water heater.

ghastly ⊕ *adjective* **-lier, -liest 1** *Informal* unpleasant. **2** deathly pale. **3** *Informal* unwell. **4** *Informal* horrible. **ghastliness** *noun*

ghat *noun* **1** (in India) steps leading down to a river. **2** (in India) place of cremation. **3** mountain pass.

ghee [gee] *noun* (in Indian cookery) clarified butter.

gherkin *noun* small pickled cucumber.

ghetto *noun, pl* **-tos, -toes** slum area inhabited by a deprived minority. **ghetto-blaster** *noun Informal* large portable cassette recorder or CD player.

ghillie *noun* same as GILLIE.

ghost ⊕ *noun* **1** disembodied spirit of a dead person. **2** faint trace. **3** faint secondary image on a television screen. ♦ *verb* **4** ghostwrite. **ghost gum** *Aust* eucalyptus with white trunk and branches. **ghostly** *adjective* **ghost town** deserted town. **ghostwrite** *verb* write (a book or article) on behalf of another person who is credited as the author. **ghostwriter** *noun*

ghoul ⊕ [gool] *noun* **1** person with morbid interests. **2** demon that eats corpses. **ghoulish** *adjective*

GHQ *Mil* General Headquarters.

GI *noun Informal* US soldier.

giant ⊕ *noun* **1** mythical being of superhuman

size. **2** very large person or thing. **3** person of exceptional ability or importance. ♦ *adjective* **4** huge. **giantess** *n fem*

gibber ⊕ [jib-ber] *verb* speak or utter rapidly and unintelligibly. **gibberish** *noun* rapid unintelligible talk.

gibbet [jib-bit] *noun* gallows for displaying executed criminals.

gibbon [gib-bon] *noun* agile tree-dwelling ape of S Asia.

gibbous *adjective* (of the moon) more than half but less than fully illuminated.

gibe ⊕ [jibe] *verb, noun* same as JIBE[1].

giblets [jib-lets] *plural noun* gizzard, liver, heart, and neck of a fowl.

gidday, g'day *interjection Aust & NZ* expression of greeting.

giddy ⊕ *adjective* **-dier, -diest 1** having or causing a feeling of dizziness. **2** happy and excited. **giddily** *adverb* **giddiness** *noun*

gift ⊕ *noun* **1** present. **2** natural talent. ♦ *verb* **3** make a present of. **gifted** *adjective* talented.

gig[1] *noun* **1** single performance by pop or jazz musicians. ♦ *verb* **gigging, gigged 2** play a gig or gigs.

gig[2] *noun* **1** light two-wheeled horse-drawn carriage. **2** long light rowing boat.

giga- *prefix* **1** denoting 10^9, e.g. *gigavolt*. **2** *Computers* denoting 2^{30}, e.g. *gigabyte*.

gigantic ⊕ *adjective* enormous.

G

———————————————— THESAURUS ————————————————

= imply, hint, intend, lead up to, mean, suggest **3 = criticize**, attack, blame, find fault with, nag, pick on

getaway *noun* **= escape**, break, break-out, flight

get by *verb* **= manage**, cope, exist, fare, get along, keep one's head above water, make both ends meet, survive

get off *verb* **1 = leave**, alight, depart, descend, disembark, dismount, escape, exit

get on *verb* **1 = board**, ascend, climb, embark, mount **2 = be friendly**, be compatible, concur, get along, hit it off (*inf*)

get over *verb* **= recover from**, come round, get better, mend, pull through, rally, revive, survive

ghastly *Inf adjective* **1, 4 = horrible**, dreadful, frightful, gruesome, hideous, horrendous, loathsome, shocking, terrible, terrifying OPPOSITE **lovely**

ghost *noun* **1 = spirit**, apparition, phantom, soul, spectre, spook (*inf*), wraith **2 = trace**, glimmer, hint, possibility, semblance, shadow, suggestion

ghostly *adjective* **1 = supernatural**, eerie,

ghostlike, phantom, spectral, spooky (*inf*), unearthly, wraithlike

ghoulish *adjective* **1 = macabre**, disgusting, grisly, gruesome, morbid, sick (*inf*), unwholesome

giant *noun* **1, 2 = ogre**, colossus, monster, titan ♦ *adjective* **4 = huge**, colossal, enormous, gargantuan, gigantic, immense, mammoth, titanic, vast OPPOSITE **tiny**

gibberish *noun* **= nonsense**, babble, drivel, gobbledegook (*inf*), mumbo jumbo, twaddle

gibe *verb, noun* see JIBE[1]

giddiness *noun* **1 = dizziness**, faintness, light-headedness, vertigo

giddy *adjective* **1 = dizzy**, dizzying, faint, light-headed, reeling, unsteady, vertiginous

gift *noun* **1 = donation**, bequest, bonus, contribution, grant, hand-out, legacy, offering, present **2 = talent**, ability, capability, capacity, flair, genius, knack, power

gifted *adjective* **= talented**, able, accomplished, brilliant, capable, clever, expert, ingenious, masterly, skilled OPPOSITE **talentless**

gigantic *adjective* **= enormous**, colossal, giant,

giggle ⊙ *verb* **1** laugh nervously or foolishly. ◆ *noun* **2** such a laugh. **3** *Informal* amusing person or thing. **giggly** *adjective*

gigolo [jig-a-lo] *noun, pl* **-los** man paid by an older woman to be her escort or lover.

gigot *noun* leg of lamb or mutton.

gild ⊙ *verb* **gilding, gilded** *or* **gilt 1** put a thin layer of gold on. **2** make falsely attractive.

gill[1] [gill] *noun* radiating structure beneath the cap of a mushroom.

gill[2] [jill] *noun* liquid measure of quarter of a pint, equal to 0.142 litres.

gillie *noun* (in Scotland) attendant for hunting or fishing.

gills [gillz] *plural noun* breathing organs in fish and other water creatures.

gillyflower *noun* fragrant flower.

gilt[1] *verb* **1** past of GILD. ◆ *adjective* **2** covered with a thin layer of gold. ◆ *noun* **3** thin layer of gold used as decoration. **gilt-edged** *adjective* denoting government stocks on which interest payments and final repayments are guaranteed.

gilt[2] *noun* young female pig.

gimbals *plural noun* set of pivoted rings which allow nautical instruments to remain horizontal at sea.

gimcrack [jim-krak] *adjective* **1** showy but cheap. **2** shoddy.

gimlet [gim-let] *noun* small tool with a screwlike tip for boring holes in wood. **gimlet-eyed** *adjective* having a piercing glance.

gimmick ⊙ *noun* something designed to attract attention or publicity. **gimmickry** *noun* **gimmicky** *adjective*

gin[1] *noun* alcoholic drink flavoured with juniper berries.

gin[2] *noun* **1** wire noose used to trap small animals. **2** machine for separating seeds from raw cotton.

ginger *noun* **1** root of a tropical plant, used as a spice. **2** light orange-brown colour. **gingery** *adjective* **ginger ale, beer** fizzy ginger-flavoured soft drink. **gingerbread** *noun* moist cake flavoured with ginger. **ginger group**

group within a larger group that agitates for a more active policy. **ginger nut, snap** crisp ginger-flavoured biscuit.

gingerly ⊙ *adverb* **1** cautiously. ◆ *adjective* **2** cautious.

gingham *noun* cotton cloth, usu. checked or striped.

gingivitis [jin-jiv-**vite**-iss] *noun* inflammation of the gums.

ginkgo [**gink**-go] *noun, pl* **-goes** ornamental Chinese tree.

ginseng [**jin**-seng] *noun* (root of) a plant believed to have tonic and energy-giving properties.

Gipsy *noun, pl* **-sies** same as GYPSY.

giraffe *noun* African ruminant mammal with a spotted yellow skin and long neck and legs.

gird ⊙ *verb* **girding, girded** *or* **girt 1** put a belt round. **2** secure with or as if with a belt. **3** surround. **gird (up) one's loins** prepare for action.

girder *noun* large metal beam.

girdle[1] ⊙ *noun* **1** woman's elastic corset. **2** belt. **3** *Anat* encircling structure or part. ◆ *verb* **4** surround or encircle.

girdle[2] *noun* Scot griddle.

girl ⊙ *noun* **1** female child. **2** young woman. **3** girlfriend. **4** *Informal* any woman. **girlhood** *noun* **girlish** *adjective* **girlie** *adjective Informal* featuring photographs of naked or scantily clad women. **girlfriend** *noun* **1** girl or woman with whom a person is romantically or sexually involved. **2** female friend. **Girl Guide** same as GUIDE.

giro [**jire**-oh] *noun, pl* **-ros 1** system of transferring money within a post office or bank directly from one account to another. **2** *Informal* social security payment by giro cheque.

girt *verb* a past of GIRD.

girth ⊙ *noun* **1** measurement round something. **2** band round a horse to hold the saddle in position.

gist ⊙ [jist] *noun* substance or main point of a

——————— T H E S A U R U S ———————

huge, immense, mammoth, stupendous, titanic, tremendous OPPOSITE **tiny**

giggle *verb* **1** ◆*noun* **2** = **laugh**, cackle, chortle, chuckle, snigger, titter, twitter

gild *verb* **2** = **embellish**, adorn, beautify, brighten, coat, dress up, embroider, enhance, ornament

gimmick *noun* = **stunt**, contrivance, device, dodge, ploy, scheme

gingerly *adverb* **1** = **cautiously**, carefully, charily, circumspectly, hesitantly, reluctantly,

suspiciously, timidly, warily OPPOSITE **boldly**

gird *verb* **3** = **surround**, encircle, enclose, encompass, enfold, hem in, ring

girdle[1] *noun* **2** = **belt**, band, cummerbund, sash, waistband ◆*verb* **4** = **surround**, bound, encircle, enclose, encompass, gird, ring

girl *noun* **1, 2** = **female child**, damsel (*arch*), daughter, lass, lassie (*inf*), maid (*arch*), maiden (*arch*), miss

girth *noun* **1** = **circumference**, bulk, measure, size matter.

give ⓸ *verb* **giving, gave, given 1** present (something) to another person. **2** transfer in exchange or payment. **3** impart. **4** attribute. **5** administer. **6** be a source of. **7** utter or emit. **8** sacrifice or devote. **9** organize or host. **10** concede. **11** yield or break under pressure. ◆ *noun* **12** resilience or elasticity. **give away** *verb* **1** donate as a gift. **2** reveal. **3** hand over (a bride) formally to her husband in a marriage ceremony. **giveaway** *noun* **1** something that reveals hidden feelings or intentions. ◆ *adjective* **2** very cheap or free. **give in** *verb* admit defeat. **give off** *verb* emit. **give out** *verb* **1** distribute. **2** emit. **3** come to an end or fail. **give over** *verb* **1** set aside for a specific purpose. **2** *Informal* cease. **give up** *verb* **1** abandon. **2** acknowledge defeat.

gizzard *noun* part of a bird's stomach.

glacé [glass-say] *adjective* preserved in a thick sugary syrup.

glacier *noun* slow-moving mass of ice formed by accumulated snow. **glacial** *adjective* **1** of ice or glaciers. **2** very cold. **3** unfriendly. **glaciated** *adjective* covered with or affected by glaciers.

glaciation *noun*

glad ⓸ *adjective* **gladder, gladdest 1** pleased and happy. **2** causing happiness. **glad to** very willing to (do something). **the glad eye** *Informal* inviting or seductive glance. **gladly** *adverb* **gladness** *noun* **gladden** *verb* make glad. **gladsome** *adjective Old-fashioned* joyous

or cheerful. **glad rags** *Informal* best clothes.

glade *noun* open space in a forest.

gladiator *noun* (in ancient Rome) man trained to fight in arenas to provide entertainment.

gladiolus *noun, pl* **-lus, -li, -luses** garden plant with sword-shaped leaves.

glamour ⓸ *noun* alluring charm or fascination. **glamorous** *adjective* alluring. **glamorize** *verb*

SPELLING TIP

People often forget to drop the *u* in **glamour** when they add *ous*. That's why there are 124 occurrences of *glamourous* in the Bank of English. But the correct spelling is **glamorous**.

---

glance ⓸ *verb* **1** look rapidly or briefly. **2** glint or gleam. ◆ *noun* **3** brief look. **glancing** *adjective* hitting at an oblique angle. **glance off** *verb* strike and be deflected off (an object) at an oblique angle.

gland *noun* **1** organ that produces and secretes substances in the body. **2** similar organ in a plant. **glandular** *adjective* **glandular fever** infectious viral disease characterized by fever and swollen lymph nodes.

glare ⓸ *verb* **1** stare angrily. **2** be unpleasantly bright. ◆ *noun* **3** angry stare. **4** unpleasant brightness. **glaring** *adjective* **1** conspicuous. **2** unpleasantly bright. **glaringly** *adverb*

--- THESAURUS ---

gist *noun* =**point**, core, essence, force, idea, meaning, sense, significance, substance

give *verb* **1** =**present**, award, contribute, deliver, donate, grant, hand over *or* out, provide, supply OPPOSITE take. **3, 7** =**announce**, communicate, issue, notify, pronounce, transmit, utter **6** =**produce**, cause, engender, make, occasion **8** =**devote**, hand over, relinquish **10** =**concede**, allow, grant **11** =**surrender**, yield

give away *verb* **2** =**reveal**, betray, disclose, divulge, expose, leak, let out, let slip, uncover

give in *verb* =**admit defeat**, capitulate, cave in (*inf*), collapse, concede, quit, submit, succumb, surrender, yield

give off *verb* =**emit**, discharge, exude, produce, release, send out, throw out

give out *verb* **2** =**emit**, discharge, exude, produce, release, send out, throw out

give up *verb* =**abandon**, call it a day *or* night, cease, desist, leave off, quit, relinquish, renounce, stop =**surrender**, cave in (*inf*)

glad *adjective* **1** =**happy**, contented,

delighted, gratified, joyful, overjoyed, pleased OPPOSITE **sad**. **2** =**pleasing**, cheerful, cheering, gratifying, pleasant

gladden *verb* =**please**, cheer, delight, gratify, hearten

gladly *adverb* =**happily**, cheerfully, freely, gleefully, readily, willingly, with pleasure OPPOSITE **reluctantly**

gladness *noun* =**happiness**, cheerfulness, delight, gaiety, glee, high spirits, joy, mirth, pleasure

glamorous *adjective* =**elegant**, attractive, dazzling, exciting, fascinating, glittering, glossy, prestigious, smart OPPOSITE **dull**

glamour *noun* =**charm**, allure, appeal, attraction, beauty, enchantment, fascination, prestige

glance *verb* **1** =**peek**, glimpse, look, peep, scan, view OPPOSITE **study**. **2** =**gleam**, flash, glimmer, glint, glisten, glitter, reflect, shimmer, shine, twinkle ◆ *noun* **3** =**peek**, dekko (*sl*), glimpse, look, peep, view OPPOSITE **good look**

glare *verb* **1** =**scowl**, frown, glower, look

glasnost *noun* policy of openness and accountability, esp., formerly, in the USSR.
glass ⊕ *noun* 1 hard brittle, usu. transparent substance consisting of metal silicates or similar compounds. 2 tumbler. 3 its contents. 4 objects made of glass. 5 mirror. 6 barometer. ♦ *plural* 7 spectacles. **glassy** *adjective* 1 like glass. 2 expressionless. **glassiness** *noun* **glasshouse** *noun* 1 greenhouse. 2 *Informal* army prison.
glaucoma *noun* eye disease.
glaze ⊕ *verb* 1 fit or cover with glass. 2 cover with a protective shiny coating. 3 cover (food) with beaten egg or milk before cooking. 4 become glassy. ♦ *noun* 5 transparent coating. 6 substance used for this. **glazier** *noun* person who fits windows with glass.
gleam ⊕ *noun* 1 small beam or glow of light. 2 brief or faint indication. ♦ *verb* 3 emit a gleam. **gleaming** *adjective*
glean *verb* 1 gather (facts etc.) bit by bit. 2 gather (the useful remnants of a crop) after harvesting. **gleaner** *noun*
glee ⊕ *noun* triumph and delight. **gleeful** *adjective* **gleefully** *adverb*
glen *noun* deep narrow valley.
glengarry *noun, pl* **-ries** brimless Scottish cap with a crease down the crown.
glib ⊕ *adjective* **glibber, glibbest** fluent but insincere or superficial. **glibly** *adverb* **glibness** *noun*
glide ⊕ *verb* 1 move easily and smoothly. 2 (of an aircraft) move without the use of engines. 3 pass gradually and imperceptibly. ♦ *noun* 4 smooth easy movement. **glider** *noun* 1 aircraft without an engine which floats on air currents. 2 flying phalanger. **gliding** *noun* sport of flying gliders.
glimmer ⊕ *verb* 1 shine faintly, flicker. ♦ *noun* 2 faint gleam. 3 faint indication.
glimpse ⊕ *noun* 1 brief or incomplete view. 2 vague indication. ♦ *verb* 3 catch a glimpse of.
glint ⊕ *verb* 1 gleam brightly. ♦ *noun* 2 bright gleam.
glissade *noun* 1 gliding step in ballet. 2 controlled slide down a snow slope. ♦ *verb* 3 perform a glissade.
glissando *noun Music* slide between two notes in which all intermediate notes are played.
glisten ⊕ *verb* gleam by reflecting light.
glitch ⊕ *noun* small problem that stops something from working properly.
glitter ⊕ *verb* 1 shine with bright flashes. 2 be showy. ♦ *noun* 3 sparkle or brilliance. 4 superficial glamour. 5 tiny pieces of shiny decorative material.

———— T H E S A U R U S ————

daggers, lour *or* lower 2 = **dazzle**, blaze, flame, flare ♦*noun* 3 = **scowl**, black look, dirty look, frown, glower, lour *or* lower 4 = **dazzle**, blaze, brilliance, flame, glow
glaring *adjective* 1 = **conspicuous**, blatant, flagrant, gross, manifest, obvious, outrageous, unconcealed OPPOSITE inconspicuous. 2 = **dazzling**, blazing, bright, garish, glowing OPPOSITE soft
glassy *adjective* 1 = **transparent**, clear, glossy, shiny, slippery, smooth 2 = **expressionless**, blank, cold, dull, empty, fixed, glazed, lifeless, vacant
glaze *verb* 2 = **coat**, enamel, gloss, lacquer, polish, varnish ♦*noun* 5, 6 = **coat**, enamel, finish, gloss, lacquer, lustre, patina, polish, shine, varnish
gleam *noun* 1 = **glow**, beam, flash, glimmer, ray, sparkle 2 = **trace**, flicker, glimmer, hint, inkling, suggestion ♦*verb* 3 = **shine**, flash, glimmer, glint, glisten, glitter, glow, shimmer, sparkle
glee *noun* = **delight**, elation, exhilaration, exuberance, exultation, joy, merriment, triumph OPPOSITE gloom
gleeful *adjective* = **delighted**, cock-a-hoop, elated, exuberant, exultant, joyful, jubilant, overjoyed, triumphant
glib *adjective* = **smooth**, easy, fluent, insincere, plausible, quick, ready, slick, suave, voluble OPPOSITE sincere
glide *verb* 1 = **slide**, coast, drift, float, flow, roll, run, sail, skate, slip 3 = **slip**, drift, slide
glimmer *verb* 1 = **flicker**, blink, gleam, glisten, glitter, glow, shimmer, shine, sparkle, twinkle ♦*noun* 2 = **gleam**, blink, flicker, glow, ray, shimmer, sparkle, twinkle 3 = **trace**, flicker, gleam, hint, inkling, suggestion
glimpse *noun* 1 = **look**, glance, peek, peep, sight, sighting ♦*verb* 3 = **catch sight of**, espy, sight, spot, spy, view
glint *verb* 1 = **gleam**, flash, glimmer, glitter, shine, sparkle, twinkle ♦*noun* 2 = **gleam**, flash, glimmer, glitter, shine, sparkle, twinkle, twinkling
glisten *verb* = **gleam**, flash, glance, glare, glimmer, glint, glitter, shimmer, shine, sparkle, twinkle
glitch *noun* = **problem**, blip, difficulty, gremlin, hitch, interruption, malfunction, snag
glitter *verb* 1 = **shine**, flash, glare, gleam, glimmer, glint, glisten, shimmer, sparkle, twinkle ♦*noun* 3 = **shine**, brightness, flash, glare, gleam, radiance, sheen, shimmer, sparkle

glitzy *adjective* **glitzier, glitziest** *Slang* showily attractive.

gloaming *noun* twilight.

gloat ⊙ *verb* (often foll. by *over*) regard one's own good fortune or the misfortune of others with smug or malicious pleasure.

glob *noun* rounded mass of thick fluid.

globe ⊙ *noun* **1** sphere with a map of the earth on it. **2** spherical object. **3** *S Afr* light bulb. **the globe** the earth. **global** *adjective* **1** worldwide. **2** total or comprehensive.

globalization *noun* process by which a company, etc., expands to operate internationally. **global warming** increase in the overall temperature worldwide believed to be caused by the greenhouse effect. **globally** *adverb* **globetrotter** *noun* habitual worldwide traveller. **globetrotting** *noun, adjective*

globule ⊙ *noun* small round drop. **globular** *adjective*

globulin *noun* simple protein found in living tissue.

glockenspiel *noun* percussion instrument consisting of small metal bars played with hammers.

gloom ⊙ *noun* **1** melancholy or depression. **2** darkness. **gloomy** *adjective* **gloomier,** gloomiest. **gloomily** *adverb*

glory ⊙ *noun, pl* **-ries 1** praise or honour. **2** splendour. **3** praiseworthy thing. **4** adoration or worship. ◆ *verb* **-rying, -ried 5** (foll. by *in*) triumph or exalt. **glorify** *verb* **-fying, -fied 1** make (something) seem more worthy than it is. **2** praise. **3** worship. **glorification** *noun* **glorious** *adjective* **1** brilliantly beautiful. **2** delightful. **3** full of or conferring glory. **gloriously** *adverb* **glory hole** *Informal* untidy cupboard or storeroom.

gloss¹ ⊙ *noun* **1** surface shine or lustre. **2** superficially attractive appearance. **3** paint or cosmetic giving a shiny finish. ◆ *verb* **4** make glossy. **glossy** *adjective* **-sier, -siest 1** smooth and shiny. **2** (of a magazine) printed on shiny paper. **3** superficially attractive or sophisticated. **glossily** *adverb* **glossiness** *noun* **gloss over** *verb* (try to) cover up or pass over (a fault or error).

gloss² ⊙ *noun* **1** explanatory comment added to the text of a book. ◆ *verb* **2** add glosses to.

glossary *noun, pl* **-ries** list of special or technical words with definitions.

glottis *noun, pl* **-tises, -tides** vocal cords and the space between them. **glottal** *adjective* **glottal stop** speech sound made by closing

G

---

4 = glamour, display, gaudiness, pageantry, show, showiness, splendour, tinsel

gloat *verb* (often foll. by *over*) **= relish**, crow, drool, exult, glory, revel in, rub it in (*inf*), triumph

global *adjective* **1 = worldwide**, international, universal, world **2 = comprehensive**, all-inclusive, exhaustive, general, total, unlimited OPPOSITE limited

globe *noun* **2 = sphere**, ball, orb **the globe = earth**, planet, world

globule *noun* **= droplet**, bead, bubble, drop, particle, pearl, pellet

gloom *noun* **1 = depression**, dejection, despondency, low spirits, melancholy, sorrow, unhappiness, woe OPPOSITE happiness. **2 = darkness**, blackness, dark, dusk, murk, obscurity, shade, shadow, twilight OPPOSITE light

gloomy *adjective* **1 = depressing**, bad, cheerless, crestfallen, dejected, disheartening, dispirited, downcast, downhearted, dreary, glum, melancholy, miserable, morose, pessimistic, sad, sombre OPPOSITE cheerful. **2 = dark**, black, dim, dismal, dreary, dull, grey, murky, sombre OPPOSITE light

glorify *verb* **1 = enhance**, aggrandize, dignify, elevate, ennoble, magnify OPPOSITE degrade.

2 = praise, celebrate, eulogize, extol, sing or sound the praises of OPPOSITE condemn. **3 = worship**, adore, bless, exalt, honour, idolize, pay homage to, revere, venerate OPPOSITE dishonour

glorious *adjective* **1 = splendid**, beautiful, brilliant, dazzling, gorgeous, shining, superb OPPOSITE dull. **2 = delightful**, excellent, fine, gorgeous, marvellous, wonderful **3 = famous**, celebrated, distinguished, eminent, honoured, illustrious, magnificent, majestic, renowned OPPOSITE ordinary

glory *noun* **1 = honour**, dignity, distinction, eminence, fame, praise, prestige, renown OPPOSITE shame. **2 = splendour**, grandeur, greatness, magnificence, majesty, nobility, pageantry, pomp ◆*verb* **5** (foll. by *in*) **= triumph**, exalt, pride oneself, relish, revel, take delight

gloss¹ *noun* **1, 2 = shine**, brightness, gleam, lustre, patina, polish, sheen, veneer

gloss² *noun* **1 = comment**, annotation, commentary, elucidation, explanation, footnote, interpretation, note, translation ◆*verb* **2 = interpret**, annotate, comment, elucidate, explain, translate

glossy *adjective* **1 = shiny**, bright, glassy, glazed, lustrous, polished, shining, silky and then opening the glottis.

glove *noun* covering for the hand with individual sheaths for each finger and the thumb. **gloved** *adjective* covered by a glove or gloves. **glove compartment** small storage area in the dashboard of a car.

glow ❶ *verb* 1 emit light and heat without flames. 2 shine. 3 have a feeling of wellbeing or satisfaction. 4 (of a colour) look warm. 5 be hot. ♦ *noun* 6 glowing light. 7 warmth of colour. 8 feeling of wellbeing. **glow-worm** *noun* insect giving out a green light.

glower ❶ [rhymes with **power**] *verb, noun* scowl.

gloxinia *noun* tropical plant with large bell-shaped flowers.

glucose *noun* kind of sugar found in fruit.

glue ❶ *noun* 1 natural or synthetic sticky substance used as an adhesive. ♦ *verb* **gluing** or **glueing, glued** 2 fasten with glue. 3 (foll. by *to*) pay full attention to, e.g. *her eyes were glued to the TV.* **gluey** *adjective* **glue-sniffing** *noun* inhaling of glue fumes for intoxicating or hallucinatory effects.

glum ❶ *adjective* **glummer, glummest** sullen or gloomy. **glumly** *adverb*

glut ❶ *noun* 1 excessive supply. ♦ *verb* **glutting, glutted** 2 oversupply. 3 feed or fill to excess.

gluten [gloo-ten] *noun* protein found in cereal grain.

glutinous [gloo-tin-uss] *adjective* sticky or gluey.

glutton ❶ *noun* 1 greedy person. 2 person with a great capacity for something.

gluttonous *adjective* **gluttony** *noun*

glycerine, glycerin [gliss-ser-in] *noun* colourless sweet liquid used widely in chemistry and industry.

glycerol [gliss-ser-ol] *noun* technical name for GLYCERINE.

gm gram.

GM 1 genetically modified. 2 grant-maintained.

G-man *noun, pl* **G-men** *US slang* FBI agent.

GMO genetically modified organism.

GMT Greenwich Mean Time.

gnarled ❶ *adjective* rough, twisted, and knobbly.

gnash *verb* grind (the teeth) together in anger or pain.

gnat *noun* small biting two-winged fly.

gnaw ❶ *verb* **gnawing, gnawed, gnawed** or **gnawn** 1 bite or chew steadily. 2 (foll. by *at*) cause constant distress (to). **gnawing** *adjective*

gneiss *noun* coarse-grained metamorphic rock.

gnome *noun* 1 imaginary creature like a little old man. 2 *Facetious* international banker or financier.

gnomic [no-mik] *adjective* of pithy sayings.

Gnosticism *noun* religious movement believing in intuitive spiritual knowledge. **Gnostic** *noun, adjective*

GNP Gross National Product.

gnu [noo] *noun* oxlike S African antelope.

go ❶ *verb* **going, went, gone** 1 move to or from a place. 2 be in regular attendance at. 3 depart. 4 function. 5 be, do, or become as specified. 6 contribute to a result, e.g. *it just goes to show.* 7 be allotted to a specific purpose or recipient. 8 be sold. 9 blend or harmonize. 10 fail or break down. 11 elapse. 12 be got rid of. 13 attend. 14 reach or exceed certain limits, e.g. *she's gone too far this time.* 15 be acceptable. 16 carry authority. ♦ *noun* 17 attempt. 18 verbal attack. 19 turn. 20 *Informal* energy or vigour. **make a go of** be successful at. **on the go** active and energetic. **go-ahead** *adjective* enterprising or ambitious. **go back on** *verb* break (a promise etc.). **go-between** *noun* intermediary. **go for** *verb* 1 *Informal* choose. 2 attack. 3 apply to equally. **go-getter** *noun*

——————— THESAURUS ———————

OPPOSITE> **dull**

glow *verb* 1 = smoulder, burn 2 = shine, brighten, burn, gleam, glimmer, redden ♦*noun* 6 = light, burning, gleam, glimmer, luminosity, phosphorescence OPPOSITE> dullness. 7 = radiance, brightness, brilliance, effulgence, splendour, vividness OPPOSITE> dullness

glower *verb* = scowl, frown, give a dirty look, glare, look daggers, lour *or* lower ♦*noun* = scowl, black look, dirty look, frown, glare, lour *or* lower

glue *noun* 1 = adhesive, cement, gum, paste

glum *adjective* = gloomy, crestfallen, dejected, doleful, low, morose, pessimistic, sullen

OPPOSITE> **cheerful**

glut *noun* 1 = surfeit, excess, oversupply, plethora, saturation, superfluity, surplus OPPOSITE> scarcity ♦*verb* 2, 3 = saturate, choke, clog, deluge, flood, inundate, overload, oversupply

glutton *noun* 1 = gourmand, gannet (*sl*), pig (*inf*)

gluttonous *adjective* = greedy, insatiable, ravenous, voracious

gluttony *noun* = greed, greediness, voracity

gnarled *adjective* = twisted, contorted, knotted, knotty, rough, rugged, weather-beaten, wrinkled

G

energetically ambitious person. **go-go dancer** scantily dressed erotic dancer. **go off** *verb* **1** stop functioning. **2** explode. **3** ring or sound. **4** occur as specified. **5** *Informal* become stale or rotten. **6** *Informal* stop liking. **go out** *verb* **1** go to entertainments or social functions. **2** be romantically involved (with). **3** be extinguished. **4** (of a broadcast) be transmitted. **go over** *verb* examine or check. **go-slow** *noun* deliberate slowing of work-rate as an industrial protest. **go through** *verb* **1** suffer or undergo. **2** examine or search.

goad ❶ *verb* **1** provoke (someone) to take some kind of action, usu. in anger. ♦ *noun* **2** spur or provocation. **3** spiked stick for driving cattle.

goal ❶ *noun* **1** *Sport* posts through which the ball or puck has to be propelled to score. **2** score made in this way. **3** aim or purpose. **goalie** *noun Informal* goalkeeper. **goalkeeper** *noun* player whose task is to stop shots entering the goal. **goalpost** *noun* one of the two posts supporting the crossbar of a goal. **move the goalposts** change the aims of an activity to ensure the desired result.

goat *noun* **1** sure-footed ruminant animal with horns. **2** foolish person. **get someone's goat** *Slang* annoy someone. **goatee** *noun* pointed tuftlike beard.

gob *noun* **1** lump of a soft substance. **2** *Slang* mouth.

gobbet *noun* lump, esp. of food.

gobble¹ ❶ *verb* eat hastily and greedily.

gobble² *noun* **1** rapid gurgling cry of the male turkey. ♦ *verb* **2** make this noise.

gobbledegook, gobbledygook ❶ *noun* unintelligible (official) language or jargon.

goblet *noun* drinking cup without handles.

goblin *noun* (in folklore) small malevolent creature.

goby *noun, pl* **-by, -bies** small spiny-finned fish.

god ❶ *noun* **1** spirit or being worshipped as having supernatural power. **2** object of worship, idol. **3** (**G-**) (in monotheistic religions) the Supreme Being, creator and ruler of the universe. **the gods** top balcony in a theatre. **goddess** *n fem* **godlike** *adjective* **godly** *adjective* devout or pious. **godliness** *noun* **god-fearing** *adjective* pious and devout. **godforsaken** *adjective* desolate or dismal. **godsend** *noun* something unexpected but welcome.

godetia *noun* plant with showy flowers.

godparent *noun* person who promises at a child's baptism to bring the child up as a Christian. **godchild** *noun* child for whom a person stands as godparent. **goddaughter** *noun* **godfather** *noun* **1** male godparent. **2** head of a criminal, esp. Mafia, organization. **godmother** *noun* **godson** *noun*

godwit *noun* shore bird with long legs and an upturned bill.

goer *noun* person who attends something regularly, e.g. *filmgoer.*

gogga *noun S Afr informal* any small insect.

goggle *verb* **1** (of the eyes) bulge. **2** stare. **goggles** *plural noun* protective spectacles. **gogglebox** *noun Slang* television set.

Goidelic *adjective, noun* (of) the group of Celtic languages consisting of Scottish Gaelic, Irish Gaelic, and Manx.

going *noun* **1** condition of the ground for walking or riding over. **2** speed or progress. **3**

G

————————————— T H E S A U R U S —————————————

gnaw *verb* **1** =**bite**, chew, munch, nibble

go *verb* **1** =**move**, advance, journey, make for, pass, proceed, set off, travel OPPOSITE **stay. 3** =**leave**, depart, make tracks, move out, slope off, withdraw **4** =**function**, move, operate, perform, run, work OPPOSITE **break (down). 6** =**contribute**, lead to, serve, tend, work towards **9** =**harmonize**, agree, blend, chime, complement, correspond, fit, match, suit **11** =**elapse**, expire, flow, lapse, pass, slip away ♦*noun* **17, 19** =**attempt**, bid, crack (*inf*), effort, shot (*inf*), try, turn **20** *Inf* =**energy**, drive, force, life, spirit, verve, vigour, vitality, vivacity

goad *verb* **1** =**provoke**, drive, egg on, exhort, incite, prod, prompt, spur ♦*noun* **2** =**provocation**, impetus, incentive, incitement, irritation, spur, stimulus, urge

goal *noun* **3** =**aim**, ambition, end, intention,

object, objective, purpose, target

gobble¹ *verb* =**devour**, bolt, cram, gorge, gulp, guzzle, stuff, swallow, wolf

gobbledegook, gobbledygook *noun* =**nonsense**, babble, cant, gabble, gibberish, hocus-pocus, jargon, mumbo jumbo, twaddle

godforsaken *adjective* =**desolate**, abandoned, bleak, deserted, dismal, dreary, forlorn, gloomy, lonely, remote, wretched

godlike *adjective* =**divine**, celestial, heavenly, superhuman, transcendent

godly *adjective* =**devout**, god-fearing, good, holy, pious, religious, righteous, saintly

godsend *noun* =**blessing**, boon, manna, stroke of luck, windfall

go for *verb* **1** *Inf* =**favour**, admire, be attracted to, be fond of, choose, like, prefer **2** =**attack**, assail, assault, launch oneself at, rush departure. ♦ *adjective* **4** thriving. **5** current or accepted. **going-over** *noun, pl* **goings-over 1** *Informal* investigation or examination. **2** scolding or thrashing. **goings-on** *plural noun* mysterious or unacceptable events.

goitre [**goy**-ter] *noun* swelling of the thyroid gland in the neck.

go-kart *noun* small low-powered racing car.

gold *noun* **1** yellow precious metal. **2** coins or articles made of this. **3** colour of gold. **4** wealth. ♦ *adjective* **5** made of gold. **6** gold-coloured. **goldcrest** *noun* small bird with a yellow crown. **gold-digger** *noun* **1** person who digs for gold. **2** *Informal* woman who uses her sexual attractions to get money from a man. **goldfinch** *noun* kind of finch, the male of which has yellow-and-black wings. **goldfish** *noun* orange fish kept in ponds or aquariums. **gold leaf** thin gold sheet used for gilding. **gold medal** medal given to the winner of a competition or race. **gold rush** migration of people to a territory where gold has been found. **goldsmith** *noun* dealer in or maker of gold articles.

golden ⊕ *adjective* **1** made of gold. **2** gold-coloured. **3** very successful or promising. **golden eagle** large mountain eagle of the N hemisphere. **golden goal** *Soccer* first goal scored in extra time, which wins the match for the side scoring it. **golden handshake** *Informal* payment to a departing employee. **golden mean** middle course between extremes. **golden rule** important principle. **golden wattle** Australian plant with yellow flowers that yields a useful gum and bark. **golden wedding** fiftieth wedding anniversary.

golf *noun* **1** outdoor game in which a ball is struck with clubs into a series of holes. ♦ *verb* **2** play golf. **golfer** *noun*

golliwog *noun* soft black-faced doll.

golly *interjection* exclamation of mild surprise.

goloshes *plural noun* same as GALOSHES.

gonad *noun* organ producing reproductive cells, such as a testicle or ovary.

gondola *noun* **1** long narrow boat used in Venice. **2** suspended cabin of a cable car, airship, etc. **gondolier** *noun* person who propels a gondola.

gone ⊕ *verb* past participle of GO. **goner** *noun* *Informal* person or thing beyond help or recovery.

gong *noun* **1** rimmed metal disc that produces a note when struck. **2** *Slang* medal.

gonorrhoea [gon-or-**ree**-a] *noun* venereal disease with a discharge from the genitals.

good ⊕ *adjective* **better, best 1** giving pleasure. **2** morally excellent. **3** beneficial. **4** kindly. **5** talented. **6** well-behaved. **7** valid. **8** reliable. **9** financially sound. **10** complete or full. ♦ *noun* **11** benefit. **12** positive moral qualities. ♦ *plural* **13** merchandise. **14** property. **as good as** virtually. **for good** permanently. **goodness** *noun* **goodly** *adjective* considerable. **goody** *noun, pl* **-dies 1** *Informal* hero in a book or film. **2** enjoyable thing. **goody-goody** *adjective, noun* smugly virtuous (person). **good-for-nothing** *adjective, noun* irresponsible or worthless (person). **Good Friday** Friday before Easter, observed by Christians as a commemoration of the Crucifixion. **good-natured** *adjective* tolerant and kindly. **Good Samaritan** person who helps another in distress. **goodwill** *noun* **1** kindly feeling. **2** value of a business in reputation etc. over and above its tangible assets.

LANGUAGE TIP

Note that *good* is an adjective. To modify a verb, use *well: She did well.*

——————— THESAURUS ———————

upon, set about *or* upon, spring upon
golden *adjective* **2 = yellow**, blond, blonde, flaxen OPPOSITE **dark**. **3 = successful**, excellent, favourable, flourishing, glorious, halcyon, happy, opportune, promising, prosperous, rich OPPOSITE **unfavourable**

good *adjective* **1 = excellent**, acceptable, admirable, fine, first-class, first-rate, great, pleasing, satisfactory, splendid, superior OPPOSITE **bad**. **2 = honourable**, admirable, ethical, honest, moral, praiseworthy, righteous, trustworthy, upright, virtuous, worthy OPPOSITE **bad**. **3 = favourable**, advantageous, beneficial, convenient, fitting, helpful, profitable, suitable,

useful, wholesome OPPOSITE **disadvantageous**. **4 = kind**, altruistic, benevolent, charitable, friendly, humane, kind-hearted, kindly, merciful, obliging OPPOSITE **unkind**. **5 = expert**, able, accomplished, adept, adroit, clever, competent, proficient, skilled, talented OPPOSITE **useless**. **6 = well-behaved**, dutiful, obedient, orderly, polite, well-mannered OPPOSITE **naughty**. **7 = valid**, authentic, bona fide, genuine, legitimate, proper, real, true OPPOSITE **invalid**. **10 = full**, adequate, ample, complete, considerable, extensive, large, substantial, sufficient OPPOSITE **scant** ♦*noun* **11 = benefit**, advantage, gain, interest, profit, use, usefulness,

goodbye ⊙ *interjection, noun* expression used on parting.

gooey *adjective* **gooier, gooiest** *Informal* **1** sticky and soft. **2** sentimental.

goof *Informal noun* **1** mistake. **2** stupid person. ♦ *verb* **3** make a mistake. **goofy** *adjective* **goofier, goofiest**

googly *noun, pl* **-lies** *Cricket* ball that spins unexpectedly from off to leg on the bounce.

goon *noun* **1** *Informal* stupid person. **2** *Chiefly US* hired thug.

goosander *noun* type of duck.

goose *noun, pl* **geese 1** web-footed bird like a large duck. **2** female of this bird. **3** silly person. **goose flesh, pimples** bumpy condition of the skin and bristling of the hair due to cold or fright. **goose step** march step in which the leg is raised rigidly.

gooseberry *noun* **1** edible yellowy-green berry. **2** *Informal* unwanted third person accompanying a couple.

gopher [**go**-fer] *noun* American burrowing rodent.

gore¹ ⊙ *noun* blood from a wound.

gore² ⊙ *verb* pierce with horns.

gore³ *noun* tapering piece of material in a garment, sail, or umbrella.

gorge ⊙ *noun* **1** deep narrow valley. ♦ *verb* **2** eat greedily. **make one's gorge rise** cause

feelings of disgust or nausea.

gorgeous ⊙ *adjective* **1** strikingly beautiful or attractive. **2** *Informal* very pleasant. **gorgeously** *adverb*

gorgon *noun* terrifying or repulsive woman.

Gorgonzola *noun* sharp-flavoured blue-veined Italian cheese.

gorilla *noun* largest of the apes, found in Africa.

gormless *adjective Informal* stupid.

gorse *noun* prickly yellow-flowered shrub.

gory ⊙ *adjective* **gorier, goriest 1** horrific or bloodthirsty. **2** involving bloodshed.

gosh *interjection* exclamation of mild surprise or wonder.

goshawk *noun* large hawk.

gosling *noun* young goose.

gospel ⊙ *noun* **1** (**G-**) any of the first four books of the New Testament. **2** doctrine held to be of great importance. **3** unquestionable truth. **4** Black religious music originating in the churches of the Southern US.

gossamer *noun* **1** very fine fabric. **2** filmy cobweb.

gossip ⊙ *noun* **1** idle talk, esp. about other people. **2** person who engages in gossip. ♦ *verb* **gossiping, gossiped 3** engage in gossip. **gossipy** *adjective*

got *verb* past of GET. **have got** possess. **have**

G

welfare, wellbeing OPPOSITE> **disadvantage. 12 = virtue**, excellence, goodness, merit, morality, rectitude, right, righteousness, worth OPPOSITE> evil ♦*plural* **13 = merchandise**, commodities, stock, stuff, wares **14 = property**, belongings, chattels, effects, gear, paraphernalia, possessions, things, trappings **for good = permanently**, finally, for ever, irrevocably, once and for all

goodbye *interjection* **=farewell**, adieu ♦*noun* **=parting**, adieu, farewell, leave-taking

good-for-nothing *adjective* **=worthless**, feckless, idle, irresponsible, useless ♦*noun* **=layabout**, black sheep, idler, ne'er-do-well, skiver (*Brit sl*), slacker (*inf*), waster, wastrel

goodly *adjective* **=considerable**, ample, large, significant, sizable *or* sizeable, substantial, tidy (*inf*)

goodness *noun* **2 = virtue**, honesty, honour, integrity, merit, morality, probity, rectitude, righteousness, uprightness OPPOSITE> **evil. 3 = benefit**, advantage, salubriousness, wholesomeness **4 = kindness**, benevolence, friendliness, generosity, goodwill, humaneness, kind-heartedness, kindliness, mercy

goodwill *noun* **1 = friendliness**, amity,

benevolence, friendship, heartiness, kindliness

gore¹ *noun* **=blood**, bloodshed, butchery, carnage, slaughter

gore² *verb* **=pierce**, impale, transfix, wound

gorge *noun* **1 = ravine**, canyon, chasm, cleft, defile, fissure, pass ♦*verb* **2 = overeat**, cram, devour, feed, glut, gobble, gulp, guzzle, stuff, wolf

gorgeous *adjective* **1 = beautiful**, dazzling, elegant, magnificent, ravishing, splendid, stunning (*inf*), sumptuous, superb OPPOSITE> **shabby. 2** *Inf* **=pleasing**, delightful, enjoyable, exquisite, fine, glorious, good, lovely OPPOSITE> awful

gory *adjective* **=bloodthirsty**, blood-soaked, bloodstained, bloody, murderous, sanguinary

gospel *noun* **2 = doctrine**, credo, creed, message, news, revelation, tidings **3 = truth**, certainty, fact, the last word

gossip *noun* **1 = idle talk**, blether, chinwag (*Brit inf*), chitchat, hearsay, scandal, small talk, tittle-tattle **2 = busybody**, chatterbox (*inf*), chatterer, gossipmonger, scandalmonger, tattler, telltale, tattletale (*chiefly US & Canad*) ♦*verb* **3 = chat**, blether, gabble, jaw (*sl*), prate, prattle, tattle

got to need or be required to.

Goth *noun* member of an East Germanic people who invaded the Roman Empire.

Gothic *adjective* **1** (of architecture) of or in the style common in Europe from the 12th-16th centuries, with pointed arches. **2** of or in an 18th-century literary style characterized by gloom and the supernatural. **3** (of print) using a heavy ornate typeface. **4** barbarous.

gotten *verb US* past participle of GET.

gouache *noun* (painting using) watercolours mixed with glue.

Gouda *noun* mild-flavoured Dutch cheese.

gouge ❶ [gowj] *verb* **1** scoop or force out. **2** cut (a hole or groove) in (something). ♦ *noun* **3** hole or groove. **4** chisel with a curved cutting edge.

goulash [goo-lash] *noun* rich stew seasoned with paprika.

gourd [goord] *noun* **1** fleshy fruit of a climbing plant. **2** its dried shell, used as a container.

gourmand [goor-mand] *noun* person who is very keen on food and drink.

gourmet ❶ [goor-may] *noun* connoisseur of food and drink.

gout [gowt] *noun* disease causing inflammation of the joints. **gouty** *adjective*

govern ❶ *verb* **1** rule, direct, or control. **2** exercise restraint over (temper etc.). **3** decide or determine. **governable** *adjective*

governance *noun* governing. **governess** *noun* woman teacher in a private household.

government *noun* **1** executive policy-making body of a state. **2** exercise of political authority over a country or state. **3** system by which a country or state is ruled. **governmental** *adjective* **governor** *noun* **1** official governing a province or state. **2** senior administrator of a

society, institution, or prison. **3** chief executive of a US state. **4** *Informal* person's father or employer. **governor general** representative of the Crown in a Commonwealth country.

> **SPELLING TIP**
>
> In the Bank of English, there are hundreds of examples of *goverment* without its middle *n*. Remember it has two *n*s: **government**.

gown ❶ *noun* **1** woman's long formal dress. **2** surgeon's overall. **3** official robe worn by judges, clergymen, etc.

goy *noun*, *pl* **goyim**, **goys** *Slang* Jewish word for a non-Jew.

GP general practitioner.

GPO General Post Office.

GPS Global Positioning System: a satellite-based navigation system.

grab ❶ *verb* **grabbing, grabbed 1** grasp suddenly, snatch. **2** take (food, drink, or rest) hurriedly. **3** seize illegally. ♦ *noun* **4** sudden snatch. **5** mechanical device for gripping.

grace ❶ *noun* **1** beauty and elegance. **2** polite, kind behaviour. **3** goodwill or favour. **4** courtesy or decency. **5** delay granted. **6** free favour of God shown towards man. **7** short prayer of thanks for a meal. **8** (**G-**) title of a duke, duchess, or archbishop. ♦ *plural* **9** (**G-**) (in Greek mythology) three sister goddesses, givers of charm and beauty. ♦ *verb* **10** honour. **11** add grace to. **graceful** *adjective* **gracefully** *adverb* **graceless** *adjective* **gracious** *adjective* **1** kind and courteous. **2** condescendingly polite. **3** elegant. **graciously** *adverb* **grace note** *Music* note ornamenting a melody.

──────── T H E S A U R U S ────────

gouge *verb* **1, 2 = scoop**, chisel, claw, cut, dig (out), hollow (out) ♦*noun* **3 = gash**, cut, furrow, groove, hollow, scoop, scratch, trench

gourmet *noun* = **connoisseur**, bon vivant, epicure, foodie (*inf*), gastronome

govern *verb* **1 = rule**, administer, command, control, direct, guide, handle, lead, manage, order **2 = restrain**, check, control, curb, discipline, hold in check, master, regulate, subdue, tame

government *noun* **1 = executive**, administration, ministry, powers-that-be, regime **2 = rule**, administration, authority, governance, mana (*NZ*), sovereignty, statecraft

governor *noun* **1, 2 = leader**, administrator, chief, commander, controller, director,

executive, head, manager, ruler

gown *noun* **1 = dress**, frock **3 = robe**, costume, garb, garment, habit

grab *verb* **1 = snatch**, capture, catch, catch *or* take hold of, clutch, grasp, grip, pluck, seize, snap up

grace *noun* **1 = elegance**, attractiveness, beauty, charm, comeliness, ease, gracefulness, poise, polish, refinement, tastefulness OPPOSITE awkwardness. **2, 4 = manners**, consideration, decency, decorum, etiquette, propriety, tact OPPOSITE **bad manners**. **3 = goodwill**, benefaction, benevolence, favour, generosity, goodness, kindliness, kindness OPPOSITE **ill will**. **5 = indulgence**, mercy, pardon, reprieve **7 = prayer**, benediction, blessing, thanks,

grade ❶ *noun* **1** place on a scale of quality, rank, or size. **2** mark or rating. **3** *US & Aust* class in school. ◆ *verb* **4** arrange in grades. **5** assign a grade to. **make the grade** succeed.
gradation *noun* **1** (stage in) a series of degrees or steps. **2** arrangement in stages.
gradient ❶ *noun* (degree of) slope.
gradual ❶ *adjective* occurring, developing, or moving in small stages. **gradually** *adverb*
graduate ❶ *verb* **1** receive a degree or diploma. **2** (often foll. by *to*) change by degrees. **3** group by type or quality. **4** mark (a container etc.) with units of measurement. ◆ *noun* **5** holder of a degree. **graduation** *noun*
graffiti [graf-**fee**-tee] *plural noun* words or drawings scribbled or sprayed on walls etc.

SPELLING TIP

People get confused about the number of *f*s and *t*s in **graffiti**. The favourite misspelling in the Bank of English is *grafitti*. The correct spelling has two *f*s and only one *t*.

---

graft[1] ❶ *noun* **1** surgical transplant of skin or tissue. **2** shoot of a plant set in the stalk of another. ◆ *verb* **3** transplant (living tissue) surgically. **4** insert (a plant shoot) in another stalk.
graft[2] *Informal noun* **1** hard work. **2** obtaining of money by misusing one's position. ◆ *verb* **3** work hard. **grafter** *noun*
grail *noun* same as HOLY GRAIL.
grain ❶ *noun* **1** seedlike fruit of a cereal plant. **2** cereal plants in general. **3** small hard particle. **4** very small amount. **5** arrangement of fibres, as in wood. **6** texture or pattern resulting from

this. ◆ *verb* **7** paint in imitation of the grain of wood or leather. **go against the grain** be contrary to one's natural inclination. **grainy** *adjective*
gram, gramme *noun* metric unit of mass equal to one thousandth of a kilogram.
gramineous, graminaceous *adjective* of or like grass.
graminivorous *adjective* (of animals) feeding on grass.
grammar *noun* **1** branch of linguistics dealing with the form, function, and order of words. **2** use of words. **3** book on the rules of grammar.
grammarian *noun* **grammatical** *adjective* according to the rules of grammar.
grammatically *adverb* **grammar school** esp. formerly, a secondary school providing an education with a strong academic bias.
gramme *noun* same as GRAM.
gramophone *noun* old-fashioned type of record player.
grampus *noun, pl* **-puses** dolphin-like mammal.
gran *noun Informal* grandmother.
granary *noun, pl* **-ries 1** storehouse for grain. **2** region that produces a large amount of grain.
grand ❶ *adjective* **1** large or impressive, imposing. **2** ambitious or important. **3** dignified or haughty. **4** *Informal* excellent. **5** (of a total) final. ◆ *noun* **6** *Slang* thousand pounds or dollars. **7** grand piano. **grandchild** *noun* child of one's child. **granddaughter** *noun* female grandchild. **grandfather** *noun* male grandparent. **grandfather clock** tall standing clock with a pendulum and wooden case.
grandmother *noun* female grandparent.
grandparent *noun* parent of one's parent.
grand piano large harp-shaped piano with the strings set horizontally. **grand slam** winning of

G

================ T H E S A U R U S ================

thanksgiving ◆*verb* **10 = honour**, dignify, favour OPPOSITE **disfavour**. **11 = enhance**, adorn, decorate, embellish, enrich, ornament, set off
graceful *adjective* **1 = elegant**, beautiful, charming, comely, easy, pleasing, tasteful OPPOSITE **ungraceful**
gracious *adjective* **1 = kind**, charitable, civil, considerate, cordial, courteous, friendly, polite, well-mannered OPPOSITE **ungracious**
grade *noun* **1-3 = level**, category (*US & Aust*), class, degree, echelon, group, rank, stage ◆*verb* **4, 5 = classify**, arrange, class, group, order, range, rank, rate, sort
gradient *noun* **= slope**, bank, declivity, grade, hill, incline, rise

gradual *adjective* **= steady**, gentle, graduated, piecemeal, progressive, regular, slow, unhurried OPPOSITE **sudden**
gradually *adverb* **= steadily**, by degrees, gently, little by little, progressively, slowly, step by step, unhurriedly
graduate *verb* **3 = classify**, arrange, grade, group, order, rank, sort **4 = mark off**, calibrate, grade, measure out, proportion, regulate
graft[1] *noun* **2 = shoot**, bud, implant, scion, splice, sprout ◆*verb* **3, 4 = transplant**, affix, implant, ingraft, insert, join, splice
grain *noun* **1 = seed**, grist, kernel **2 = cereals**, corn **4 = bit**, fragment, granule, modicum, morsel, particle, piece, scrap, speck, trace **5, 6 = texture**, fibre, nap, pattern, surface, weave

G

all the games or major tournaments in a sport in one season. **grandson** noun male grandchild. **grandstand** noun terraced block of seats giving the best view at a sports ground.

grandee noun **1** Spanish nobleman of the highest rank. **2** person of high station.

grandeur ❶ noun **1** magnificence. **2** nobility or dignity.

grandiloquent adjective using pompous language. **grandiloquence** noun

grandiose ❶ adjective **1** imposing. **2** pretentiously grand. **grandiosity** noun

Grand Prix [gron **pree**] noun international formula motor race.

grange noun country house with farm buildings.

granite [gran-nit] noun very hard igneous rock often used in building.

granivorous adjective feeding on grain or seeds.

granny, grannie noun, pl **-nies** Informal grandmother. **granny flat** flat in or added to a house, suitable for an elderly parent.

grant ❶ verb **1** consent to fulfil (a request). **2** give formally. **3** admit. ◆ noun **4** sum of money provided by a government for a specific purpose, such as education. **take for granted 1** accept as true without proof. **2** take advantage of without due appreciation.

Granth noun sacred scripture of Sikhism.

granule ❶ noun small grain. **granular** adjective of or like grains. **granulated** adjective (of sugar) in the form of coarse grains.

granulation noun

grape noun small juicy green or purple berry, eaten raw or used to produce wine, raisins, currants, or sultanas. **grapeshot** noun bullets which scatter when fired. **grapevine** noun **1** grape-bearing vine. **2** Informal unofficial way of spreading news.

grapefruit noun large round yellow citrus fruit.

graph noun drawing showing the relation of different numbers or quantities plotted against a set of axes.

graphic ❶ adjective **1** vividly descriptive. **2** of or using drawing, painting, etc. **graphics** plural noun diagrams, graphs, etc., esp. as used on a television programme or computer screen.

graphically adverb

graphite noun soft black form of carbon, used in pencil leads.

graphology noun study of handwriting.

graphologist noun

grapnel noun device with several hooks, used to grasp or secure things.

grapple ❶ verb **1** try to cope with (something difficult). **2** come to grips with (a person). ◆ noun **3** grapnel. **grappling iron** grapnel.

grasp ❶ verb **1** grip something firmly. **2** understand. **3** try to seize. ◆ noun **4** grip or clasp. **5** understanding. **6** total rule or possession. **grasping** adjective greedy or avaricious.

grass noun **1** common type of plant with jointed stems and long narrow leaves, including

---

———— THESAURUS ————

grand adjective **1** = **impressive**, grandiose, great, imposing, large, magnificent, regal, splendid, stately, sublime OPPOSITE **unimposing**. **4** Inf = **excellent**, fine, first-class, great (inf), outstanding, smashing (inf), splendid, wonderful OPPOSITE **terrible**

grandeur noun = **splendour**, dignity, magnificence, majesty, nobility, pomp, stateliness, sublimity

grandiose adjective **1** = **imposing**, grand, impressive, lofty, magnificent, majestic, monumental, stately OPPOSITE **modest**. **2** = **pretentious**, affected, bombastic, extravagant, flamboyant, high-flown, ostentatious, pompous, showy OPPOSITE **unpretentious**

grant verb **1** = **consent to**, accede to, agree to, allow, permit **2** = **give**, allocate, allot, assign, award, donate, hand out, present **3** = **admit**, acknowledge, concede ◆ noun **4** = **award**, allowance, donation, endowment, gift, hand-out, present, subsidy

granule noun = **grain**, atom, crumb, fragment, molecule, particle, scrap, speck

graphic adjective **1** = **vivid**, clear, detailed, explicit, expressive, lively, lucid, striking OPPOSITE **vague**. **2** = **pictorial**, diagrammatic, visual OPPOSITE **impressionistic**

grapple verb **1** = **deal with**, address oneself to, confront, get to grips with, tackle, take on, wrestle **2** = **grip**, clutch, grab, grasp, seize, struggle, wrestle

grasp verb **1, 3** = **grip**, catch, clasp, clinch, clutch, grab, grapple, hold, lay or take hold of, seize, snatch **2** = **understand**, catch on, catch or get the drift of, comprehend, get, realize, see, take in ◆ noun **4** = **grip**, clasp, clutches, embrace, hold, possession, tenure **5** = **understanding**, awareness, comprehension, grip, knowledge, mastery **6** = **control**, power, reach, scope

grasping adjective = **greedy**, acquisitive, avaricious, covetous, rapacious OPPOSITE **generous**

cereals and bamboo. **2** lawn. **3** pasture land. **4** *Slang* marijuana. **5** *Slang* person who informs, esp. on criminals. ◆ *verb* **6** cover with grass. **7** (often foll. by *on*) *Slang* inform on. **grassy** *adjective* **-sier, -siest**. **grasshopper** *noun* jumping insect with long hind legs. **grass roots 1** ordinary members of a group, as distinct from its leaders. **2** essentials. **grassroots** *adjective* **grass snake** harmless European snake. **grass tree** Australian plant with stiff grasslike leaves and small white flowers. **grass widow** wife whose husband is absent for a time.

grate¹ ❶ *verb* **1** rub into small bits on a rough surface. **2** scrape with a harsh rasping noise. **3** annoy. **grater** *noun* **grating** *adjective* **1** harsh or rasping. **2** annoying.

grate² *noun* framework of metal bars for holding fuel in a fireplace. **grating** *noun* framework of metal bars covering an opening.

grateful ❶ *adjective* feeling or showing gratitude. **gratefully** *adverb* **gratefulness** *noun*

gratify ❶ *verb* **-fying, -fied 1** satisfy or please. **2** indulge (a desire or whim). **gratification** *noun*

gratis *adverb, adjective* free, for nothing.

gratitude ❶ *noun* feeling of being thankful for a favour or gift.

gratuitous ❶ [grat-**tyoo**-it-uss] *adjective* **1** unjustified, e.g. *gratuitous violence*. **2** given free. **gratuitously** *adverb*

gratuity ❶ [grat-**tyoo**-it-ee] *noun, pl* **-ties** money given for services rendered, tip.

grave¹ ❶ *noun* hole for burying a corpse. **the**

grave death. **gravestone** *noun* stone marking a grave. **graveyard** *noun* cemetery.

grave² ❶ *adjective* **1** causing concern. **2** serious and solemn. **3** important. **gravely** *adverb*

grave³ [rhymes with **halve**] *noun* accent (ˋ) over a vowel to indicate a special pronunciation.

gravel *noun* **1** mixture of small stones and coarse sand. **2** small rough stones in the kidneys or bladder. ◆ *verb* **-elling, -elled 3** cover with gravel. **gravelled** *adjective* covered with gravel. **gravelly** *adjective* **1** covered with gravel. **2** rough-sounding.

graven [**grave**-en] *adjective* carved or engraved.

gravid [**grav**-id] *adjective Med* pregnant.

gravitate *verb* **1** be influenced or drawn towards. **2** *Physics* move by gravity.

gravitation *noun* **gravitational** *adjective*

gravity ❶ *noun, pl* **-ties 1** force of attraction of one object for another, esp. of objects to the earth. **2** seriousness or importance. **3** solemnity.

gravy *noun, pl* **-vies 1** juices from meat in cooking. **2** sauce made from these.

gray *adjective Chiefly US* grey.

grayling *noun* fish of the salmon family.

graze¹ ❶ *verb* feed on grass. **grazier** *noun* person who feeds cattle for market. **grazing** *noun* land on which grass for livestock is grown.

graze² ❶ *verb* **1** scratch or scrape the skin. **2** touch lightly in passing. ◆ *noun* **3** slight scratch or scrape.

grease ❶ *noun* **1** soft melted animal fat. **2** any

G

——————————— THESAURUS ———————————

grate¹ *verb* **1** = **scrape**, creak, grind, rasp, rub, scratch **3** = **annoy**, exasperate, get on one's nerves (*inf*), irritate, jar, rankle, set one's teeth on edge

grateful *adjective* = **thankful**, appreciative, beholden, indebted, obliged

gratification *noun* = **satisfaction**, delight, enjoyment, fulfilment, indulgence, pleasure, relish, reward, thrill OPPOSITE **disappointment**

gratify *verb* = **please**, delight, give pleasure, gladden, humour, requite, satisfy

grating¹ *adjective* **1** = **harsh**, discordant, jarring, raucous, strident OPPOSITE **pleasing**. **2** = **irritating**, annoying, displeasing, offensive, unpleasant OPPOSITE **pleasing**

grating² *noun* = **grille**, grate, grid, gridiron, lattice, trellis

gratitude *noun* = **thankfulness**, appreciation, gratefulness, indebtedness, obligation, recognition, thanks

gratuitous *adjective* **1** = **unjustified**, baseless,

causeless, groundless, needless, superfluous, uncalled-for, unmerited, unnecessary, unwarranted, wanton OPPOSITE **justifiable**. **2** = **voluntary**, complimentary, free, gratis, spontaneous, unasked-for, unpaid, unrewarded

grave¹ *noun* = **tomb**, burying place, crypt, mausoleum, pit, sepulchre, vault

grave² **1** *adjective* = **critical**, acute, dangerous, pressing, serious, severe, threatening OPPOSITE **trifling**. **2** = **serious**, dignified, dour, earnest, sober, solemn, sombre, unsmiling OPPOSITE **happy**. **3** = **important**, serious, urgent

graveyard *noun* = **cemetery**, burial ground, charnel house, churchyard, necropolis

gravity *noun* **2** = **importance**, acuteness, momentousness, perilousness, seriousness, severity, significance, urgency, weightiness OPPOSITE **insignificance**. **3** = **solemnity**, dignity, earnestness, seriousness, sobriety OPPOSITE **frivolity**

graze¹ *verb* = **feed**, browse, crop, pasture

thick oily substance. ◆ *verb* **3** apply grease to.
greasy *adjective* **greasier, greasiest 1**
covered with or containing grease. **2** unctuous
in manner. **greasiness** *noun* **grease gun**
appliance for injecting oil or grease into
machinery. **greasepaint** *noun* theatrical make-
up.
great ⊕ *adjective* **1** large in size or number. **2**
extreme or more than usual. **3** important. **4**
pre-eminent. **5** *Informal* excellent. **the greats**
the most successful people in a particular field.
great- *prefix* one generation older or younger
than, e.g. *great-grandfather.* **greatly** *adverb*
greatness *noun* **greatcoat** *noun* heavy
overcoat. **Great Dane** very large dog with
short smooth hair.
greave *noun* piece of armour for the shin.
grebe *noun* diving water bird.
Grecian [gree-shan] *adjective* of ancient
Greece.
greed ⊕ *noun* excessive desire for food,
wealth, etc. **greedy** *adjective* **greedier,
greediest. greedily** *adverb* **greediness** *noun*
Greek *noun* **1** language of Greece. **2** person
from Greece. ◆ *adjective* **3** of Greece, the
Greeks, or the Greek language.
green ⊕ *adjective* **1** of a colour between blue
and yellow. **2** characterized by green plants or
foliage. **3** (G-) of or concerned with
environmental issues. **4** unripe. **5** envious or
jealous. **6** immature or gullible. ◆ *noun* **7** colour
between blue and yellow. **8** area of grass kept
for a special purpose. **9** (G-) person concerned
with environmental issues. ◆ *plural* **10** green
vegetables. ◆ *verb* **11** make or become green.

greenness *noun* **greenish, greeny** *adjective*
greenery *noun* vegetation. **green belt**
protected area of open country around a town.
greenfinch *noun* European finch with dull
green plumage in the male. **green fingers** skill
in gardening. **greenfly** *noun* green aphid, a
common garden pest. **greengage** *noun* sweet
green plum. **greengrocer** *noun* shopkeeper
selling vegetables and fruit. **greenhorn** *noun*
novice. **greenhouse** *noun* glass building for
rearing plants. **greenhouse effect** rise in the
temperature of the earth caused by heat
absorbed from the sun being unable to leave
the atmosphere. **green light 1** signal to go. **2**
permission to proceed with something.
greenroom *noun* room for actors when
offstage. **greenshank** *noun* large European
sandpiper.
Greenwich Mean Time *noun* local time of
the 0° meridian passing through Greenwich,
England: the basis for calculating times
throughout the world.
greet ⊕ *verb* **1** meet with expressions of
welcome. **2** receive in a specified manner. **3** be
immediately noticeable. **greeting** *noun*
gregarious ⊕ *adjective* **1** fond of company. **2**
(of animals) living in flocks or herds.
Gregorian calendar *noun* calendar
introduced by Pope Gregory XIII and still widely
used.
Gregorian chant *noun* same as PLAINSONG.
gremlin *noun* imaginary being blamed for
mechanical malfunctions.
grenade *noun* small bomb thrown by hand or
fired from a rifle. **grenadier** *noun* soldier of a

─────── THESAURUS ───────

graze² *verb* **1** = **scratch**, abrade, chafe, scrape,
skin **2** = **touch**, brush, glance off, rub, scrape,
shave, skim ◆*noun* **3** = **scratch**, abrasion, scrape
greasy *adjective* **1** = **fatty**, oily, oleaginous,
slimy, slippery
great *adjective* **1** = **large**, big, enormous,
gigantic, huge, immense, prodigious, vast,
voluminous OPPOSITE **little**. **3** = **important**,
critical, crucial, momentous, serious, significant
OPPOSITE **trivial**. **4** = **famous**, eminent,
illustrious, noteworthy, outstanding, prominent,
remarkable, renowned OPPOSITE **insignificant**.
5 *Inf* = **excellent**, fantastic (*inf*), fine, marvellous
(*inf*), superb, terrific (*inf*), tremendous (*inf*),
wonderful OPPOSITE **unskilled**
greatly *adverb* **1, 2** = **very much**,
considerably, enormously, exceedingly, hugely,
immensely, remarkably, tremendously, vastly
greed *noun* = **gluttony**, acquisitiveness,
avarice, avidity, covetousness, craving, desire,

edacity, esurience, gormandizing, hunger,
longing, selfishness, voracity OPPOSITE
generosity
greedy *adjective* = **gluttonous**, acquisitive,
avaricious, avid, covetous, craving, desirous,
gormandizing, grasping, hungry, insatiable,
piggish, rapacious, ravenous, selfish, voracious
OPPOSITE **generous**
green *adjective* **2** = **leafy**, grassy, verdant **3**
(with cap.) = **ecological**, conservationist,
environment-friendly, non-polluting, ozone-
friendly **5** = **jealous**, covetous, envious,
grudging, resentful **6** = **inexperienced**, gullible,
immature, naive, new, raw, untrained, wet
behind the ears (*inf*) ◆*noun* **8** = **lawn**, common,
sward, turf
greet *verb* **1, 2** = **welcome**, accost, address,
compliment, hail, meet, receive, salute
gregarious *adjective* **1** = **outgoing**, affable,
companionable, convivial, cordial, friendly,

regiment formerly trained to throw grenades.
grenadine [gren-a-**deen**] *noun* syrup made
from pomegranates.
grew *verb* past tense of GROW.
grey ⊕ *adjective* **1** of a colour between black
and white. **2** (of hair) partly turned white. **3**
dismal or dark. **4** dull or boring. ♦ *noun* **5** grey
colour. **6** grey or white horse. **greying** *adjective*
(of hair) turning grey. **greyish** *adjective*
greyness *noun* **grey matter** *Informal* brains.
greyhound *noun* swift slender dog used in
racing.
greylag *noun* large grey goose.
grid *noun* **1** network of horizontal and vertical
lines, bars, etc. **2** national network of electricity
supply cables.
griddle *noun* flat iron plate for cooking.
gridiron *noun* **1** frame of metal bars for
grilling food. **2** American football pitch.
gridlock ⊕ *noun* situation where traffic is not
moving. **gridlocked** *adjective*
grief ⊕ *noun* deep sadness. **come to grief**
end unsuccessfully. **grieve** *verb* (cause to) feel
grief. **grievance** *noun* real or imaginary cause
for complaint. **grievous** *adjective* **1** very severe
or painful. **2** very serious.
griffin *noun* mythical monster with an eagle's
head and wings and a lion's body.
grill *noun* **1** device on a cooker that radiates
heat downwards. **2** grilled food. **3** gridiron. **4**
grillroom. ♦ *verb* **5** cook under a grill. **6**
question relentlessly. **grilling** *noun* relentless
questioning. **grillroom** *noun* restaurant serving
grilled foods.
grille, grill *noun* grating over an opening.

grilse [grillss] *noun* salmon on its first return
from the sea to fresh water.
grim ⊕ *adjective* **grimmer, grimmest 1** stern.
2 harsh or forbidding. **3** very unpleasant. **4**
harshly ironic or sinister. **grimly** *adverb*
grimness *noun*
grimace ⊕ *noun* **1** ugly or distorted facial
expression of pain, disgust, etc. ♦ *verb* **2** make a
grimace.
grimalkin *noun* old female cat.
grime ⊕ *noun* **1** ingrained dirt. ♦ *verb* **2** make
very dirty. **grimy** *adjective* **griminess** *noun*
grin *verb* **grinning, grinned 1** smile broadly,
showing the teeth. ♦ *noun* **2** broad smile.
grind ⊕ *verb* **grinding, ground 1** crush or rub
to a powder. **2** smooth or sharpen by friction.
3 scrape together with a harsh noise. **4**
oppress. **5** *Informal* work or study hard. ♦ *noun*
6 *Informal* hard work. **7** act or sound of
grinding. **grind out** *verb* produce in a routine
or uninspired manner. **grindstone** *noun* stone
used for grinding.
grip ⊕ *noun* **1** firm hold or grasp. **2** way in
which something is grasped. **3** mastery or
understanding. **4** *US* travelling bag. **5** handle. ♦
verb **gripping, gripped 6** grasp or hold
tightly. **7** affect strongly. **8** hold the interest or
attention of. **gripping** *adjective*
gripe *verb* **1** *Informal* complain persistently. ♦
noun **2** *Informal* complaint. **3** sudden intense
bowel pain.
grisly ⊕ *adjective* **-lier, -liest** horrifying or
ghastly.
grist *noun* grain for grinding. **grist to one's
mill** something which can be turned to

———————— T H E S A U R U S ————————

sociable, social OPPOSITE **unsociable**
grey *adjective* **3** = **dismal**, dark, depressing,
dim, drab, dreary, dull, gloomy **4**
= **characterless**, anonymous, colourless, dull
grief *noun* = **sadness**, anguish, distress,
heartache, misery, regret, remorse, sorrow,
suffering, woe OPPOSITE **joy**
grievance *noun* = **complaint**, axe to grind,
gripe (*inf*), injury, injustice
grieve *verb* = **mourn**, afflict, complain,
deplore, distress, hurt, injure, lament, pain,
regret, rue, sadden, suffer, weep, wound
OPPOSITE **gladden**
grievous *adjective* **1** = **severe**, dreadful, grave,
harmful, painful OPPOSITE **insignificant**
grim *adjective* **1, 2** = **forbidding**, formidable,
harsh, merciless, ruthless, severe, sinister, stern,
terrible OPPOSITE **easy**
grimace *noun* **1** = **scowl**, face, frown, sneer
♦*verb* **2** = **scowl**, frown, lour *or* lower, make a

face *or* faces, sneer
grime *noun* **1** = **dirt**, filth, grot (*sl*), smut, soot
grind *verb* **1** = **crush**, abrade, granulate, grate,
mill, pound, powder, pulverize, triturate **2**
= **smooth**, polish, sand, sharpen, whet **3**
= **scrape**, gnash, grate ♦*noun* **6** *Inf* = **hard
work**, chore, drudgery, labour, sweat (*inf*), toil
grip *noun* **1** = **control**, clasp, clutches,
domination, hold, influence, mana (*NZ*),
possession, power **3** = **understanding**,
command, comprehension, grasp, mastery
♦*verb* **6** = **grasp**, clasp, clutch, hold, seize, take
hold of **7** = **engross**, absorb, enthral, entrance,
fascinate, hold, mesmerize, rivet
gripping *adjective* **8** = **fascinating**,
compelling, engrossing, enthralling, entrancing,
exciting, riveting, spellbinding, thrilling
grisly *adjective* = **gruesome**, appalling, awful,
dreadful, ghastly, horrible, macabre, shocking,
terrifying OPPOSITE **pleasant**

advantage.

gristle *noun* tough stringy animal tissue found in meat. **gristly** *adjective*

grit ❶ *noun* **1** rough particles of sand. **2** courage. **3** coarse sandstone. ◆ *plural* **4** coarsely ground grain. ◆ *verb* **gritting, gritted 5** spread grit on (an icy road etc.). **6** clench or grind (the teeth). **gritty** *adjective* **-tier, -tiest. gritter** *noun* **grittiness** *noun*

grizzle *verb Informal* whine or complain.

grizzled *adjective* grey-haired.

grizzly *noun, pl* **-zlies** large American bear (also **grizzly bear**).

groan ❶ *noun* **1** deep sound of grief or pain. **2** *Informal* complaint. ◆ *verb* **3** utter a groan. **4** *Informal* complain. **5** (usu. foll. by *beneath* or *under*) be weighed down (by).

groat *noun Hist* fourpenny piece.

groats *plural noun* hulled and crushed grain of various cereals.

grocer *noun* shopkeeper selling foodstuffs.

grocery *noun, pl* **-ceries 1** business or premises of a grocer. ◆ *plural* **2** goods sold by a grocer.

grog *noun* spirit, usu. rum, and water.

groggy ❶ *adjective* **-gier, -giest** *Informal* faint, shaky, or dizzy.

groin *noun* **1** place where the legs join the abdomen. **2** edge made by the intersection of two vaults.

grommet *noun* **1** ring or eyelet. **2** *Med* tube inserted in the ear to drain fluid from the middle ear.

groom ❶ *noun* **1** person who looks after horses. **2** bridegroom. **3** officer in a royal household. ◆ *verb* **4** make or keep one's clothes and appearance neat and tidy. **5** brush or clean a horse. **6** train (someone) for a future role.

groove ❶ *noun* **1** long narrow channel in a surface. **2** spiral channel in a gramophone record. **3** routine. **grooved** *adjective* **groovy** *adjective* **groovier, grooviest** *Dated slang* attractive or exciting.

grope ❶ *verb* feel about or search uncertainly. **groping** *noun*

grosbeak *noun* finch with a large powerful bill.

grosgrain [**grow**-grain] *noun* heavy ribbed silk or rayon fabric.

gross ❶ *adjective* **1** flagrant. **2** vulgar. **3** *Slang* disgusting or repulsive. **4** repulsively fat. **5** total, without deductions. ◆ *noun* **6** twelve dozen. ◆ *verb* **7** make as total revenue before deductions. **grossly** *adverb* **grossness** *noun*

grotesque ❶ [**grow**-tesk] *adjective* **1** strangely distorted. **2** absurd. ◆ *noun* **3** grotesque person or thing. **4** artistic style mixing distorted human, animal, and plant forms. **grotesquely** *adverb*

grotto *noun, pl* **-toes, -tos 1** small picturesque cave. **2** construction imitating a cave.

grotty *adjective* **-tier, -tiest** *Informal* nasty or in bad condition.

grouch *Informal verb* **1** grumble or complain. ◆ *noun* **2** person who is always complaining. **3** persistent complaint. **grouchy** *adjective*

ground¹ ❶ *noun* **1** surface of the earth. **2** soil. **3** area used for a specific purpose, e.g. *rugby ground*. **4** position in an argument or controversy. **5** background colour of a painting. ◆ *plural* **6** enclosed land round a house. **7** reason or motive. **8** coffee dregs. ◆ *adjective* **9** on or of the ground. ◆ *verb* **10** base or establish. **11** instruct in the basics. **12** ban an aircraft or pilot from flying. **13** run (a ship)

————— T H E S A U R U S —————

grit *noun* **1** = **gravel**, dust, pebbles, sand **2** = **courage**, backbone, determination, fortitude, guts (*inf*), perseverance, resolution, spirit, tenacity ◆*verb* **6** = **grind**, clench, gnash, grate

groan *noun* **1** = **moan**, cry, sigh, whine **2** *Inf* = **complaint**, gripe (*inf*), grouse, grumble, objection, protest ◆*verb* **3** = **moan**, cry, sigh, whine **4** *Inf* = **complain**, bemoan, gripe (*inf*), grouse, grumble, lament, object

groggy *adjective Inf* = **dizzy**, confused, dazed, faint, shaky, unsteady, weak, wobbly

groom *noun* **1** = **stableman**, hostler *or* ostler (*arch*), stableboy ◆*verb* **4** = **smarten up**, clean, preen, primp, spruce up, tidy **5** = **rub down**, brush, clean, curry, tend **6** = **train**, coach, drill, educate, make ready, nurture, prepare, prime, ready

groove *noun* **1** = **indentation**, channel, cut, flute, furrow, hollow, rut, trench, trough

grope *verb* = **feel**, cast about, fish, flounder, forage, fumble, scrabble, search

gross *adjective* **1** = **blatant**, flagrant, grievous, heinous, rank, sheer, unmitigated, utter OPPOSITE▷ **qualified. 2** = **vulgar**, coarse, crude, indelicate, obscene, offensive OPPOSITE▷ **decent. 4** = **fat**, corpulent, hulking, obese, overweight OPPOSITE▷ **slim. 5** = **total**, aggregate, before deductions, before tax, entire, whole OPPOSITE▷ **net** ◆*verb* **7** = **earn**, bring in, make, rake in (*inf*), take

grotesque *adjective* **1** = **deformed**, distorted OPPOSITE▷ **natural. 2** = **unnatural**, bizarre, fantastic, freakish, outlandish, preposterous, strange OPPOSITE▷ **natural**

aground. **14** place on the ground. **groundless** *adjective* without reason. **grounding** *noun* basic knowledge of a subject. **ground-breaking** *adjective* innovative. **ground floor** floor of a building level with the ground. **groundnut** *noun* peanut. **groundsheet** *noun* waterproof sheet put on the ground under a tent. **groundsman** *noun* person employed to maintain a sports ground or park. **groundswell** *noun* rapidly developing general feeling or opinion. **groundwork** *noun* preliminary work. **ground²** *verb* past of GRIND. **ground beef** finely chopped beef used in beefburgers etc. **groundsel** [grounce-el] *noun* yellow-flowered weed.

group ① *noun* **1** number of people or things regarded as a unit. **2** small band of musicians or singers. ♦ *verb* **3** place or form into a group. **group captain** middle-ranking air force officer. **grouper** *noun* large edible sea fish. **grouse¹** *noun* **1** stocky game bird. **2** its flesh. **grouse² ①** *verb* **1** grumble or complain. ♦ *noun* **2** complaint. **grout** *noun* **1** thin mortar. ♦ *verb* **2** fill up with grout. **grove ①** *noun* small group of trees. **grovel ①** [grov-el] *verb* -**elling**, -**elled 1**

behave humbly in order to win a superior's favour. **2** crawl on the floor.

grow ① *verb* **growing, grew, grown 1** develop physically. **2** (of a plant) exist. **3** cultivate (plants). **4** increase in size or degree. **5** originate. **6** become gradually, e.g. *it was growing dark*. **growth** *noun* **1** growing. **2** increase. **3** something grown or growing. **4** tumour. **grown** *adjective* developed or advanced. **grown-up** *adjective, noun* adult. **grow on** *verb* become more acceptable to. **grow up** *verb* mature. **growl** *verb* **1** make a low rumbling sound. **2** utter with a growl. ♦ *noun* **3** growling sound. **groyne** *noun* wall built out from the shore to control erosion. **grub ①** *noun* **1** legless insect larva. **2** *Slang* food. ♦ *verb* **grubbing, grubbed 3** search carefully for something by digging or by moving things about. **4** dig up the surface of (soil). **grubby ①** *adjective* -**bier**, -**biest** dirty. **grubbiness** *noun* **grudge ①** *verb* **1** be unwilling to give or allow. ♦ *noun* **2** resentment. **grudging** *adjective* **grudgingly** *adverb* **gruel** *noun* thin porridge.

——————— THESAURUS ———————

ground¹ *noun* **1, 2** = **earth**, dry land, land, soil, terra firma, terrain, turf **3** = **stadium**, arena, field, park (*inf*), pitch ♦*plural* **6** = **land**, estate, fields, gardens, terrain, territory **7** = **reason**, basis, cause, excuse, foundation, justification, motive, occasion, pretext, rationale **8** = **dregs**, deposit, lees, sediment ♦*verb* **10** = **base**, establish, fix, found, set, settle **11** = **instruct**, acquaint with, familiarize with, initiate, teach, train, tutor **groundless** *adjective* = **unjustified**, baseless, empty, idle, uncalled-for, unfounded, unwarranted OPPOSITE **well-founded** **groundwork** *noun* = **preliminaries**, foundation, fundamentals, preparation, spadework, underpinnings **group** *noun* **1** = **set**, band, bunch, cluster, collection, crowd, gang, pack, party ♦*verb* **3** = **arrange**, bracket, class, classify, marshal, order, sort **grouse²** *verb* **1** = **complain**, bellyache (*sl*), carp, gripe (*inf*), grumble, moan, whine, whinge (*inf*) ♦*noun* **2** = **complaint**, grievance, gripe (*inf*), grouch (*inf*), grumble, moan, objection, protest **grove** *noun* = **wood**, coppice, copse, covert, plantation, spinney, thicket **grovel** *verb* **1** = **humble oneself**, abase

oneself, bow and scrape, crawl, creep, cringe, demean oneself, fawn, kowtow, toady OPPOSITE **be proud**. **2** = **crawl**, creep OPPOSITE **be proud** **grow** *verb* **1** = **increase**, develop, enlarge, expand, get bigger, multiply, spread, stretch, swell OPPOSITE **shrink**. **3** = **cultivate**, breed, farm, nurture, produce, propagate, raise **4** = **improve**, advance, flourish, progress, prosper, succeed, thrive **5** = **originate**, arise, issue, spring, stem **6** = **become**, come to be, get, turn **grown-up** *adjective* = **mature**, adult, fully-grown, of age ♦*noun* = **adult**, man, woman **growth** *noun* **1, 2** = **increase**, development, enlargement, expansion, multiplication, proliferation, stretching OPPOSITE **decrease**. **3** = **progress**, advance, expansion, improvement, prosperity, rise, success OPPOSITE **failure**. **4** = **tumour**, lump **grub** *noun* **1** = **larva**, caterpillar, maggot **2** *Sl* = **food**, nosh (*sl*), rations, sustenance, tucker (*Aust & NZ inf*), victuals ♦*verb* **3** = **search**, ferret, forage, fossick (*Aust & NZ*), hunt, rummage, scour, uncover, unearth **4** = **dig up**, burrow, pull up, root (*inf*) **grubby** *adjective* = **dirty**, filthy, grimy, messy, mucky, scruffy, scungy (*Aust & NZ inf*), seedy, shabby, sordid, squalid, unwashed

G

gruelling ⊕ *adjective* exhausting or severe.
gruesome ⊕ *adjective* causing horror and disgust.
gruff ⊕ *adjective* rough or surly in manner or voice. **gruffly** *adverb* **gruffness** *noun*
grumble ⊕ *verb* 1 complain. 2 rumble. ♦ *noun* 3 complaint. 4 rumble. **grumbler** *noun* **grumbling** *adjective, noun*
grumpy ⊕ *adjective* **grumpier, grumpiest** bad-tempered. **grumpily** *adverb* **grumpiness** *noun*
grunge *noun* 1 style of rock music with a fuzzy guitar sound. 2 deliberately untidy and uncoordinated fashion style.
grunt *verb* 1 make a low short gruff sound, like a pig. ♦ *noun* 2 pig's sound. 3 gruff noise.
Gruyère [grew-yair] *noun* hard yellow Swiss cheese with holes.
gryphon *noun* same as GRIFFIN.
G-string *noun* small strip of cloth covering the genitals and attached to a waistband.
G-suit *noun* close-fitting pressurized garment worn by the crew of high-speed aircraft.
GT gran turismo, used of a sports car.
guanaco [gwah-nah-koh] *noun, pl* -cos S American animal related to the llama.
guano [gwah-no] *noun* dried sea-bird manure, used as fertilizer.
guarantee ⊕ *noun* 1 formal assurance, esp. in writing, that a product will meet certain standards. 2 something that makes a specified condition or outcome certain. 3 guarantor. 4 guaranty. ♦ *verb* -teeing, -teed 5 give a guarantee. 6 secure against risk etc. 7 ensure.

guarantor *noun* person who gives or is bound by a guarantee. **guaranty** *noun, pl* -ties 1 pledge of responsibility for fulfilling another person's obligations in case of default. 2 thing given as security for a guaranty.
guard ⊕ *verb* 1 watch over to protect or to prevent escape. 2 protect (a right or privilege). ♦ *noun* 3 person or group that guards. 4 official in charge of a train. 5 protection. 6 screen for enclosing anything dangerous. 7 posture of defence in sports such as boxing or fencing. ♦ *plural* 8 (G-) regiment with ceremonial duties.
guarded *adjective* cautious or noncommittal. **guardedly** *adverb* **guard against** *verb* take precautions against. **guardhouse, guardroom** *noun* military police office for holding prisoners.
guardian *noun* keeper or protector.
guardsman *noun* member of the Guards.
guardian ⊕ *noun* 1 keeper or protector. 2 person legally responsible for a child, mentally ill person, etc. **guardianship** *noun*
guava [gwah-va] *noun* yellow-skinned tropical American fruit.
gubernatorial *adjective* US of or relating to a governor.
gudgeon¹ *noun* small freshwater fish.
gudgeon² *noun* socket for a hinge or rudder.
guelder-rose [geld-er-rose] *noun* shrub with clusters of white flowers.
Guernsey [gurn-zee] *noun* breed of dairy cattle.
guerrilla, guerilla ⊕ *noun* member of an unofficial armed force fighting regular forces.
guess ⊕ *verb* 1 estimate or draw a conclusion

———— THESAURUS ————

grudge *verb* 1 = **resent**, begrudge, complain, covet, envy, mind OPPOSITE welcome ♦*noun* 2 = **resentment**, animosity, antipathy, bitterness, dislike, enmity, grievance, rancour OPPOSITE goodwill
gruelling *adjective* = **exhausting**, arduous, backbreaking, demanding, laborious, punishing, severe, strenuous, taxing, tiring OPPOSITE easy
gruesome *adjective* = **horrific**, ghastly, grim, grisly, horrible, macabre, shocking, terrible OPPOSITE pleasant
gruff *adjective* a = **surly**, bad-tempered, brusque, churlish, grumpy, rough, rude, sullen, ungracious OPPOSITE polite. b = **hoarse**, croaking, guttural, harsh, husky, low, rasping, rough, throaty OPPOSITE smooth
grumble *verb* 1 = **complain**, bleat, carp, gripe (*inf*), grouch (*inf*), grouse, moan, whine, whinge (*inf*) 2 = **rumble**, growl, gurgle, murmur, mutter, roar ♦*noun* 3 = **complaint**, grievance, gripe (*inf*), grouch (*inf*), grouse, moan,

objection, protest 4 = **rumble**, growl, gurgle, murmur, muttering, roar
grumpy *adjective* = **irritable**, bad-tempered, cantankerous, crotchety (*inf*), peevish, sulky, sullen, surly, testy
guarantee *noun* 1 = **assurance**, bond, certainty, pledge, promise, security, surety, warranty, word of honour ♦*verb* 5-7 = **ensure**, assure, certify, make certain, pledge, promise, secure, vouch for, warrant
guard *verb* 1, 2 = **watch over**, defend, mind, preserve, protect, safeguard, secure, shield ♦*noun* 3 = **protector**, custodian, defender, lookout, picket, sentinel, sentry, warder, watch, watchman 5, 6 = **protection**, buffer, defence, safeguard, screen, security, shield
guarded *adjective* = **cautious**, cagey (*inf*), careful, circumspect, noncommittal, prudent, reserved, reticent, suspicious, wary
guardian *noun* 1 = **keeper**, champion, curator, custodian, defender, guard, protector,

without proper knowledge. **2** estimate correctly by guessing. **3** *US & Canad* suppose. ◆ *noun* **4** estimate or conclusion reached by guessing.
guesswork *noun* process or results of guessing.
guest ๑ *noun* **1** person entertained at another's house or at another's expense. **2** invited performer or speaker. **3** customer at a hotel or restaurant. ◆ *verb* **4** appear as a visiting player or performer. **guesthouse** *noun* boarding house.
guff *noun Slang* nonsense.
guffaw *noun* **1** crude noisy laugh. ◆ *verb* **2** laugh in this way.
guide ๑ *noun* **1** person who conducts tour expeditions. **2** person who shows the way. **3** book of instruction or information. **4** model for behaviour. **5** something used to gauge something or to help in planning one's actions. **6** (G-) member of an organization for girls equivalent to the Scouts. ◆ *verb* **7** act as a guide for. **8** control, supervise, or influence. **guidance** *noun* leadership, instruction, or advice.
guidebook *noun* handbook with information for visitors to a place. **guided missile** missile whose flight is controlled electronically. **guide dog** dog trained to lead a blind person.
guideline *noun* set principle for doing something.

guild ๑ *noun* **1** organization or club. **2** *Hist* society of men in the same trade or craft.
guilder *noun* monetary unit of the Netherlands.
guile ๑ [gile] *noun* cunning or deceit. **guileful** *adjective* **guileless** *adjective*
guillemot [gil-lee-mot] *noun* black-and-white diving sea bird.
guillotine *noun* **1** machine for beheading people. **2** device for cutting paper or sheet metal. **3** method of preventing lengthy debate in parliament by fixing a time for taking the vote. ◆ *verb* **4** behead by guillotine. **5** limit debate by the guillotine.
guilt ๑ *noun* **1** fact or state of having done wrong. **2** remorse for wrongdoing. **guiltless** *adjective* innocent. **guilty** *adjective* **guiltier, guiltiest** **1** responsible for an offence or misdeed. **2** feeling or showing guilt. **guiltily** *adverb*
guinea *noun* **1** former British monetary unit worth 21 shillings (1.05 pounds). **2** former gold coin of this value. **guinea fowl** bird related to the pheasant. **guinea pig 1** tailless S American rodent, commonly kept as a pet. **2** *Informal* person used for experimentation.
guise ๑ [rhymes with **size**] *noun* **1** false appearance. **2** external appearance.

G

———————— T H E S A U R U S ————————

warden
guerrilla, guerilla *noun* =**freedom fighter**, partisan, underground fighter
guess *verb* **1** =**estimate**, conjecture, hypothesize, predict, speculate, work out OPPOSITE **know**. **3** *Chiefly US* =**suppose**, believe, conjecture, fancy, imagine, judge, reckon, suspect, think OPPOSITE **know** ◆*noun* **4** =**supposition**, conjecture, hypothesis, prediction, shot in the dark, speculation, theory OPPOSITE **certainty**
guesswork *noun* =**speculation**, conjecture, estimation, supposition, surmise, theory
guest *noun* **1, 3** =**visitor**, boarder, caller, company, lodger, visitant
guidance *noun* =**advice**, counselling, direction, help, instruction, leadership, management, teaching
guide *noun* **1, 2** =**escort**, adviser, conductor, counsellor, guru, leader, mentor, teacher, usher **3** =**guidebook**, catalogue, directory, handbook, instructions, key, manual **4** =**model**, example, ideal, inspiration, paradigm, standard **5** =**pointer**, beacon, guiding light, landmark, lodestar, marker, sign, signpost ◆*verb* **7** =**lead**, accompany, conduct, direct, escort, shepherd, show the way, usher **8** =**supervise**,

advise, command, control, counsel, direct, handle, influence, instruct, manage, manoeuvre, oversee, steer, superintend, teach, train
guild *noun* **1** =**society**, association, brotherhood, club, company, corporation, fellowship, fraternity, league, lodge, order, organization, union
guile *noun* =**cunning**, artifice, cleverness, craft, deceit, slyness, trickery, wiliness OPPOSITE **honesty**
guilt *noun* **1** =**culpability**, blame, guiltiness, misconduct, responsibility, sinfulness, wickedness, wrongdoing OPPOSITE **innocence**. **2** =**remorse**, contrition, guilty conscience, regret, self-reproach, shame, stigma OPPOSITE **pride**
guiltless *adjective* =**innocent**, blameless, clean (*sl*), irreproachable, pure, sinless, spotless, squeaky-clean, untainted
guilty *adjective* **1** =**culpable**, at fault, blameworthy, reprehensible, responsible, sinful, to blame, wrong OPPOSITE **innocent**. **2** =**remorseful**, ashamed, conscience-stricken, contrite, regretful, rueful, shamefaced, sheepish, sorry OPPOSITE **proud**
guise *noun* **1** =**disguise**, pretence, semblance

guitar *noun* stringed instrument with a flat back and a long neck, played by plucking or strumming. **guitarist** *noun*

Gulag *noun* system or department that silences dissidents, esp. in the former Soviet Union.

gulch *noun US & Canad* a narrow ravine cut by a fast stream.

gulf ⊕ *noun* 1 large deep bay. 2 chasm. 3 large difference in opinion or understanding. **Gulf Stream** warm ocean current flowing from the Gulf of Mexico towards NW Europe.

gull[1] *noun* long-winged sea bird.

gull[2] *verb* cheat or deceive.

gullet *noun* muscular tube through which food passes from the mouth to the stomach.

gullible ⊕ *adjective* easily tricked. **gullibility** *noun*

gully ⊕ *noun, pl* **-lies** channel cut by running water.

gulp ⊕ *verb* 1 swallow hastily. 2 gasp. ♦ *noun* 3 gulping. 4 thing gulped.

gum[1] *noun* firm flesh in which the teeth are set. **gummy** *adjective* **-mier, -miest** toothless. **gumboil** *noun* abscess on the gum.

gum[2] ⊕ *noun* 1 sticky substance obtained from certain trees. 2 adhesive. 3 chewing gum. 4 gumdrop. 5 gumtree. ♦ *verb* **gumming, gummed** 6 stick with gum. **gummy** *adjective* **-mier, -miest**. **gumboots** *plural noun* Wellington boots. **gumdrop** *noun* hard jelly-like sweet. **gumtree** *noun* eucalypt tree.

gumption ⊕ *noun Informal* 1 resourcefulness. 2 courage.

gun ⊕ *noun* 1 weapon with a metal tube from which missiles are fired by explosion. 2 device from which a substance is ejected under pressure. 3 member of a shooting party. ♦ *verb*

gunning, gunned 4 cause (an engine) to run at high speed. **jump the gun** act prematurely. **gunner** *noun* artillery soldier. **gunnery** *noun* use or science of large guns. **gunboat** *noun* small warship. **guncotton** *noun* form of cellulose nitrate used as an explosive. **gun dog** dog used to retrieve game. **gun down** *verb* shoot (a person). **gun for** *verb* seek or pursue vigorously. **gunman** *noun* armed criminal. **gunmetal** *noun* 1 alloy of copper, tin, and zinc. ♦ *adjective* 2 dark grey. **gunpowder** *noun* explosive mixture of potassium nitrate, sulphur, and charcoal. **gunrunning** *noun* smuggling of guns and ammunition. **gunrunner** *noun* **gunshot** *noun* 1 shot or range of a gun. 2 sound of a gun being fired.

gunge *noun Informal* sticky unpleasant substance. **gungy** *adjective* **-gier, -giest**

gunk *noun Informal* slimy or filthy substance.

gunny *noun* strong coarse fabric used for sacks.

gunwale, gunnel [**gun**-nel] *noun* top of a ship's side.

guppy *noun, pl* **-pies** small colourful aquarium fish.

gurgle ⊕ *verb, noun* (make) a bubbling noise.

Gurkha *noun* person, esp. a soldier, belonging to a Hindu people of Nepal.

gurnard *noun* spiny armour-headed sea fish.

guru ⊕ *noun* 1 Hindu or Sikh religious teacher or leader. 2 leader or adviser.

gush ⊕ *verb* 1 flow out suddenly and profusely. 2 express admiration effusively. ♦ *noun* 3 sudden copious flow. 4 sudden surge of strong feeling. **gusher** *noun* spurting oil well. **gushing** *adjective*

gusset *noun* piece of material sewn into a garment to strengthen it.

─────── THESAURUS ───────

2 =form, appearance, aspect, demeanour, mode, shape

gulf *noun* **1 =bay**, bight, sea inlet **2 =chasm**, abyss, gap, opening, rift, separation, split, void

gullible *adjective* **=naive**, born yesterday, credulous, innocent, simple, trusting, unsuspecting, wet behind the ears (*inf*)
OPPOSITE> suspicious

gully *noun* **=channel**, ditch, gutter, watercourse

gulp *verb* **1 =swallow**, devour, gobble, guzzle, quaff, swig (*inf*), swill, wolf **2 =gasp**, choke, swallow ♦*noun* **4 =swallow**, draught, mouthful, swig (*inf*)

gum[2] *noun* **1 =resin 2 =glue**, adhesive, cement, paste ♦*verb* **6 =stick**, affix, cement, glue, paste

gumption *noun Inf* **1 =resourcefulness**, acumen, astuteness, common sense, enterprise, initiative, mother wit, savvy (*sl*), wit(s)

gun *noun* **1 =firearm**, handgun, piece (*sl*), shooter (*sl*)

gunman *noun* **=terrorist**, bandit, gunslinger (*US sl*), killer

gurgle *verb* **=murmur**, babble, bubble, lap, plash, purl, ripple, splash ♦*noun* **=murmur**, babble, purl, ripple

guru *noun* **2 =teacher**, authority, leader, mana (*NZ*), master, mentor, sage, Svengali, tutor

gush *verb* **1 =flow**, cascade, flood, pour, run, rush, spout, spurt, stream **2 =enthuse**, babble, chatter, effervesce, effuse, overstate, spout ♦*noun* **3, 4 =stream**, cascade, flood, flow, jet,

gust ❶ *noun* **1** sudden blast of wind. **2** sudden burst of rain, anger, etc. ◆ *verb* **3** blow in gusts. **gusty** *adjective*

gustation *noun* act of tasting or the faculty of taste. **gustatory** *adjective*

gusto ❶ *noun* enjoyment or zest.

gut ❶ *noun* **1** intestine. **2** *Informal* fat stomach. **3** short for CATGUT. ◆ *plural* **4** internal organs. **5** *Informal* courage. **6** *Informal* essential part. ◆ *verb* **gutting, gutted 7** remove the guts from. **8** (of a fire) destroy the inside of (a building). ◆ *adjective* **9** basic or instinctive, e.g. *a gut reaction*. **gutless** *adjective Informal* cowardly. **gutsy** *adjective* **-sier, -siest** *Informal* **1** courageous. **2** vigorous or robust, e.g. *a gutsy performance*. **3** greedy. **gutted** *adjective Informal* disappointed and upset.

gutta-percha *noun* whitish rubbery substance obtained from an Asian tree.

gutter ❶ *noun* **1** shallow channel for carrying away water from a roof or roadside. ◆ *verb* **2** (of a candle) burn unsteadily, with wax running down the sides. **the gutter** degraded or criminal environment. **guttering** *noun* material for gutters. **gutter press** newspapers that rely on sensationalism. **guttersnipe** *noun* neglected slum child.

guttural ❶ [**gut**-ter-al] *adjective* **1** (of a sound) produced at the back of the throat. **2** (of a voice) harsh-sounding.

guy[1] ❶ *noun* **1** *Informal* man or boy. **2** effigy of Guy Fawkes burnt on Nov. 5th (**Guy Fawkes Day**). ◆ *verb* **3** make fun of.

guy[2] *noun* **1** rope or chain to steady or secure something. ◆ *verb* **2** secure or guide with a guy. **guyrope** *noun*

guzzle ❶ *verb* eat or drink greedily.

gybe [jibe] *verb* **1** (of a fore-and-aft sail) swing suddenly from one side to the other. **2** (of a boat) change course by letting the sail gybe.

gym *noun* **1** gymnasium. **2** gymnastics.

gymslip *noun* tunic or pinafore formerly worn by schoolgirls.

gymkhana [jim-**kah**-na] *noun* horse-riding competition.

gymnasium *noun* large room with equipment for physical training. **gymnast** *noun* expert in gymnastics. **gymnastic** *adjective* **gymnastics** *plural noun* exercises to develop strength and agility.

gynaecology [guy-nee-**kol**-la-jee] *noun* branch of medicine dealing with diseases and conditions specific to women. **gynaecological** *adjective* **gynaecologist** *noun*

gyp *noun* **give someone gyp** *Slang* cause someone severe pain.

gypsophila *noun* garden plant with small white flowers.

gypsum *noun* chalklike mineral used to make plaster of Paris.

Gypsy ❶ *noun, pl* **-sies** member of a travelling people found throughout Europe.

gyrate [jire-**rate**] *verb* rotate or spiral about a point or axis. **gyration** *noun* **gyratory** *adjective* gyrating.

gyrfalcon [jur-**fawl**-kon] *noun* large rare falcon.

gyro *noun, pl* **-ros** short for GYROSCOPE.

gyrocompass *noun* compass using a gyroscope.

gyroscope [jire-oh-skohp] *noun* disc rotating on an axis that can turn in any direction, so the disc maintains the same position regardless of the movement of the surrounding structure. **gyroscopic** *adjective*

G

THESAURUS

rush, spout, spurt, torrent

gust *noun* **1** = **blast**, blow, breeze, puff, rush, squall **2** = **rush**, blast ◆*verb* **3** = **blow**, blast, squall

gusto *noun* = **relish**, delight, enjoyment, enthusiasm, fervour, pleasure, verve, zeal
OPPOSITE▷ apathy

gut *noun* **2** *Inf* = **paunch**, belly, potbelly, spare tyre (*Brit sl*) ◆*plural* **4** = **intestines**, belly, bowels, entrails, innards (*inf*), insides (*inf*), stomach, viscera **5** *Inf* = **courage**, audacity, backbone, bottle (*sl*), daring, mettle, nerve, pluck, spirit ◆*verb* **7** = **disembowel**, clean **8** = **ravage**, clean out, despoil, empty ◆*adjective* **9** as in **gut reaction** = **instinctive**, basic, heartfelt, intuitive,

involuntary, natural, spontaneous, unthinking, visceral

gutsy *adjective Inf* **1** = **brave**, bold, courageous, determined, gritty, indomitable, plucky, resolute, spirited, feisty (*US & Canad*)

gutter *noun* **1** = **drain**, channel, conduit, ditch, sluice, trench, trough

guttural *adjective* = **throaty**, deep, gravelly, gruff, hoarse, husky, rasping, rough, thick

guy[1] *noun* **1** *Inf* = **man**, bloke (*Brit inf*), chap, fellow, lad, person

guzzle *verb* = **devour**, bolt, cram, drink, gobble, stuff (oneself), swill, wolf

Gypsy *noun* = **traveller**, Bohemian, nomad, rambler, roamer, Romany, rover, wanderer

Hh

H *Chem* hydrogen.
habeas corpus [**hay**-bee-ass **kor**-puss] *noun* writ ordering a prisoner to be brought before a court.
haberdasher *noun Brit, Aust & NZ* dealer in small articles used for sewing. **haberdashery** *noun*
habiliments *plural noun* clothes.
habit ⊕ *noun* **1** established way of behaving. **2** addiction to a drug. **3** costume of a monk or nun. **4** woman's riding costume. **habitual** *adjective* done regularly and repeatedly.
habitable ⊕ *adjective* fit to be lived in.
habitat *noun* natural home of an animal or plant. **habitation** *noun* (occupation of) a dwelling place.
habitual ⊕ *adjective* done regularly and repeatedly. **habitually** *adverb*
habituate *verb* accustom. **habituation** *noun*
habitué [hab-**it**-yew-ay] *noun* frequent visitor to a place.
hacienda [hass-ee-**end**-a] *noun* ranch or large estate in Latin America.
hack[1] ⊕ *verb* cut or chop violently *Brit and NZ informal* tolerate. **hacking** *adjective* (of a cough) dry, painful, and harsh.
hack[2] ⊕ *noun* **1** (inferior) writer or journalist. **2** horse kept for riding. **hackwork** *noun* dull repetitive work.
hacker *noun Slang* computer enthusiast, esp. one who breaks into the computer system of a company or government.
hackles *plural noun* **make one's hackles rise** make one feel angry or hostile.
hackney *noun* taxi.
hackneyed ⊕ [**hak**-need] *adjective* (of a word or phrase) unoriginal and overused.

hacksaw *noun* small saw for cutting metal.
had *verb* past of HAVE.
haddock *noun* edible sea fish.
Hades [**hay**-deez] *noun Greek myth* underworld home of the dead.
hadj *noun* same as HAJJ.
haematite [**hee**-ma-tite] *noun* type of iron ore, reddish-brown when powdered.
haematology *noun* study of blood and its diseases. **haematologist** *noun*
haemo- *combining form* blood.
haemoglobin [hee-moh-**globe**-in] *noun* protein found in red blood cells which carries oxygen.
haemophilia [hee-moh-**fill**-lee-a] *noun* hereditary illness in which the blood does not clot. **haemophiliac** *noun*
haemorrhage [**hem**-or-ij] *noun* **1** heavy bleeding. ◆ *verb* **2** bleed heavily.

> **SPELLING TIP**
>
> The Bank of English shows that the most usual mistake in spelling **haemorrhage** is to miss out the second *h*, which is silent.

haemorrhoids [**hem**-or-oydz] *plural noun* swollen veins in the anus (also **piles**).
hafnium *noun Chem* metallic element found in zirconium ores.
haft *noun* handle of an axe, knife, or dagger.
hag ⊕ *noun* ugly old woman. **hag-ridden** *adjective* distressed or worried.
haggard ⊕ *adjective* looking tired and ill.
haggis *noun* Scottish dish made from sheep's

THESAURUS

habit *noun* **1** = **mannerism**, custom, practice, proclivity, propensity, quirk, tendency, way **2** = **addiction**, dependence
habitation *noun* **a** = **occupation**, inhabitance, occupancy, tenancy **b** = **dwelling**, abode, domicile, home, house, living quarters, lodging, quarters, residence
habitual *adjective* = **customary**, accustomed, familiar, normal, regular, routine, standard,

traditional, usual OPPOSITE **unusual**
hack[1] *verb* = **cut**, chop, hew, lacerate, mangle, mutilate, slash
hack[2] *noun* **1** = **scribbler**, literary hack **2** = **horse**, crock, nag
hackneyed *adjective* = **unoriginal**, clichéd, commonplace, overworked, stale, stereotyped, stock, threadbare, tired, trite OPPOSITE **original**
hag *noun* = **witch**, crone, harridan

offal, oatmeal, suet, and seasonings, boiled in a bag made from the sheep's stomach.

haggle ⊙ *verb* bargain or wrangle over a price.

hagiography *noun, pl* **-phies** writing about the lives of the saints. **hagiographer** *noun*

ha-ha *interjection* representation of the sound of laughter.

haiku [**hie**-koo] *noun, pl* **-ku** Japanese verse form in 17 syllables.

hail[1] ⊙ *noun* **1** (shower of) small pellets of ice. **2** large number of insults, missiles, blows, etc. ♦ *verb* **3** fall as or like hail. **hailstone** *noun*

hail[2] ⊙ *verb* **1** call out to, greet. **2** stop (a taxi) by waving. **3** acknowledge publicly, e.g. *he was hailed as a hero.* **hail from** *verb* come originally from. **Hail Mary** *RC Church* prayer to the Virgin Mary.

hair ⊙ *noun* **1** threadlike growth on the skin. **2** such growths collectively, esp. on the head.

hairy *adjective* **hairier, hairiest 1** covered with hair. **2** *Slang* dangerous or exciting. **hairiness** *noun* **hairless** *adjective* **hairdo** *noun Informal* hairstyle. **hairdresser** *noun* person who cuts and styles hair. **hairdressing** *noun* **hairgrip** *noun* small, tightly bent metal hairpin. **hairline** *noun* **1** edge of hair at the top of the forehead. ♦ *adjective* **2** very fine or narrow. **hairpiece** *noun* section of false hair added to a person's real hair. **hairpin** *noun* U-shaped wire used to hold the hair in place. **hairpin bend** very sharp bend in a road. **hair-raising** *adjective* frightening or exciting. **hair's-breadth** *noun* extremely small margin or distance. **hair shirt** shirt made of horsehair cloth worn against the skin as a penance. **hairsplitting** *noun, adjective* making petty distinctions. **hairstyle** *noun* cut and arrangement of a person's hair.

hajj *noun* pilgrimage a Muslim makes to

Mecca. **hajji** *noun* Muslim who has made a pilgrimage to Mecca.

hake *noun* **1** edible fish of the cod family. **2** *Aust* same as BARRACOUTA.

halal *noun* meat from animals slaughtered according to Muslim law.

halberd *noun* spear with an axe blade.

halcyon ⊙ [**hal**-see-on] *adjective* peaceful and happy. **halcyon days** time of peace and happiness.

hale ⊙ *adjective* healthy, robust, e.g. *hale and hearty.*

half ⊙ *noun, pl* **halves 1** either of two equal parts. **2** *Informal* half-pint of beer etc. **3** half-price ticket. ♦ *adjective* **4** denoting one of two equal parts. ♦ *adverb* **5** to the extent of half. **6** partially. **half-and-half** *adjective* half one thing and half another thing. **halfback** *noun Sport* player positioned immediately behind the forwards. **half-baked** *adjective Informal* not properly thought out. **half board** (in a hotel) bed, breakfast, and evening meal. **half-brother, half-sister** *noun* brother or sister related through one parent only. **half-caste** *noun Offens* person with parents of different races. **half-cocked** *adjective* **go off half-cocked, (at) half-cock** fail because of inadequate preparation. **half-day** *noun* day when a person works only in the morning or only in the afternoon. **half-hearted** *adjective* unenthusiastic. **half-heartedly** *adverb* **half-life** *noun* time taken for half the atoms in radioactive material to decay. **half-mast** *noun* halfway position of a flag on a mast as a sign of mourning. **half-moon** *noun* moon when half its face is illuminated. **half-nelson** *noun* wrestling hold in which one wrestler's arm is pinned behind his back by his opponent. **half-pipe** large U-shaped ramp used for skateboarding,

H

—————— THESAURUS ——————

haggard *adjective* =**gaunt**, careworn, drawn, emaciated, pinched, thin, wan [OPPOSITE⟩ robust

haggle *verb* =**bargain**, barter, beat down

hail[1] *noun* **1** = **shower**, rain, storm **2** = **barrage**, bombardment, downpour, volley ♦*verb* **3** = **shower**, batter, beat down upon, bombard, pelt, rain, rain down on

hail[2] *verb* **1** = **salute**, greet, welcome [OPPOSITE⟩ snub. **2** = **flag down**, signal to, wave down **3** = **acclaim**, acknowledge, applaud, cheer, honour [OPPOSITE⟩ condemn ♦ **hail from** = **come from**, be a native of, be born in, originate in

hair *noun* **2** = **locks**, head of hair, mane, mop, shock, tresses

hairdresser *noun* = **stylist**, barber, coiffeur *or*

coiffeuse

hair-raising *adjective* =**frightening**, alarming, bloodcurdling, horrifying, scary, shocking, spine-chilling, terrifying

hairstyle *noun* = **haircut**, coiffure, cut, hairdo, style

hairy *adjective* **1** = **shaggy**, bushy, furry, hirsute, stubbly, unshaven, woolly **2** *Sl* = **dangerous**, difficult, hazardous, perilous, risky

halcyon *adjective* = **peaceful**, calm, gentle, quiet, serene, tranquil, undisturbed **halcyon days** = **happy**, carefree, flourishing, golden, palmy, prosperous

hale *adjective* = **healthy**, able-bodied, fit, flourishing, in the pink, robust, sound, strong, vigorous, well snowboarding, etc. **half-term** *noun* holiday midway through a school term. **half-timbered** *adjective* (of a house) having an exposed wooden frame filled in with plaster. **half-time** *noun Sport* short rest period between two halves of a game. **halftone** *noun* illustration showing lights and shadows by means of very small dots. **halfway** *adverb, adjective* at or to half the distance. **halfwit** *noun* foolish or stupid person. **halfwitted** *adjective*

halfpenny [**hayp**-nee] *noun* former British coin worth half an old penny.

halibut *noun* large edible flatfish.

halitosis *noun* unpleasant-smelling breath.

hall ❶ *noun* **1** (also **hallway**) entrance passage. **2** large room or building for public meetings, dances, etc. **3** large country house.

hallelujah [hal-ee-**loo**-ya] *interjection* exclamation of praise to God.

hallmark ❶ *noun* **1** typical feature. **2** mark indicating the standard of tested gold and silver. ♦ *verb* **3** stamp with a hallmark.

hallo *interjection* same as HELLO.

halloo *interjection* shout used to call hounds at a hunt.

hallowed *adjective* regarded as holy.

Halloween, Hallowe'en *noun* October 31, celebrated by children by dressing up as ghosts, witches, etc.

hallucinate ❶ *verb* seem to see something that is not really there. **hallucination** *noun* **hallucinatory** *adjective* **hallucinogen** *noun* drug that causes hallucinations. **hallucinogenic** *adjective*

halo [**hay**-loh] *noun, pl* **-loes, -los 1** ring of light round the head of a sacred figure. **2** circle of refracted light round the sun or moon.

halogen [**hal**-oh-jen] *noun Chem* any of a group of nonmetallic elements including chlorine and iodine.

halt ❶ *verb* **1** come or bring to a stop. ♦ *noun* **2** temporary stop. **3** minor railway station without a building. **halting** *adjective* hesitant, uncertain, e.g. *in a halting voice*. **haltingly** *adverb*

halter *noun* strap round a horse's head with a rope to lead it with. **halterneck** *noun* woman's top or dress with a strap fastened at the back of the neck.

halve ❶ *verb* **1** divide in half. **2** reduce by half.

halves *noun* plural of HALF.

halyard *noun* rope for raising a ship's sail or flag.

ham¹ *noun* smoked or salted meat from a pig's thigh. **ham-fisted** *adjective* clumsy.

ham² *Informal noun* **1** amateur radio operator. **2** actor who overacts. ♦ *verb* **hamming, hammed 3 ham it up** overact.

hamburger *noun* minced beef shaped into a flat disc, cooked and usu. served in a bread roll.

hamlet *noun* small village.

hammer ❶ *noun* **1** tool with a heavy metal head and a wooden handle, used to drive in nails etc. **2** part of a gun which causes the bullet to be fired. **3** heavy metal ball on a wire, thrown as a sport. **4** auctioneer's mallet. **5** striking mechanism in a piano. ♦ *verb* **6** hit (as if) with a hammer. **7** *Informal* punish or defeat utterly. **go at it hammer and tongs** do something, esp. argue, very vigorously.

——————— THESAURUS ———————

half *noun* **1** = **equal part**, fifty per cent, hemisphere, portion, section ♦*adjective* **2** = **partial**, halved, limited, moderate ♦*adverb* **3** = **partially**, in part, partly

half-baked *adjective Inf* = **poorly planned**, ill-conceived, ill-judged, impractical, short-sighted, unformed, unthought-out *or* -through

half-hearted *adjective* = **unenthusiastic**, apathetic, indifferent, lacklustre, listless, lukewarm, perfunctory, tame OPPOSITE enthusiastic

halfway *adverb* = **midway**, to *or* in the middle ♦*adjective* = **midway**, central, equidistant, intermediate, mid, middle

halfwit *noun* = **fool**, airhead (*sl*), dunderhead, idiot, imbecile (*inf*), moron, numbskull *or* numskull, simpleton, twit (*inf, chiefly Brit*)

hall *noun* **1** = **entrance hall**, corridor, entry, foyer, lobby, passage, passageway, vestibule **2** = **meeting place**, assembly room, auditorium,

chamber, concert hall

hallmark *noun* **1** = **indication**, sure sign, telltale sign **2** = **seal**, device, endorsement, mark, sign, stamp, symbol

hallucination *noun* = **illusion**, apparition, delusion, dream, fantasy, figment of the imagination, mirage, vision

halo *noun* = **ring of light**, aura, corona, nimbus, radiance

halt *verb* **1 a** = **stop**, break off, cease, come to an end, desist, rest, stand still, wait OPPOSITE continue. **b** = **hold back**, block, bring to an end, check, curb, cut short, end, nip in the bud, terminate OPPOSITE encourage ♦*noun* **2** = **stop**, close, end, pause, standstill, stoppage OPPOSITE continuation

halting *adjective* = **faltering**, awkward, hesitant, laboured, stammering, stumbling, stuttering

halve *verb* **1** = **bisect**, cut in half, divide

hammerhead *noun* shark with a wide flattened head. **hammer out** *verb* settle (differences) with great effort. **hammertoe** *noun* condition in which a toe is permanently bent at the joint.
hammock *noun* hanging bed made of canvas or net.
hamper¹ ⊕ *verb* make it difficult for (someone or something) to move or progress.
hamper² *noun* 1 large basket with a lid. 2 selection of food and drink packed as a gift.
hamster *noun* small rodent with a short tail and cheek pouches.

> **SPELLING TIP**
>
> The word **hamster** appears 750 times in the Bank of English. The misspelling *hampster*, with a *p*, appears 13 times.

hamstring *noun* 1 tendon at the back of the knee. ◆ *verb* 2 make it difficult for (someone) to take any action. **hamstrung** *adjective*
hand ⊕ *noun* 1 part of the body at the end of the arm, consisting of a palm, four fingers, and a thumb. 2 style of handwriting. 3 round of applause. 4 manual worker. 5 pointer on a dial, esp. on a clock. 6 cards dealt to a player in a card game. 7 unit of length of four inches used to measure horses. ◆ *verb* 8 pass, give. **have a hand in** be involved in. **lend a hand** help. **out of hand** 1 beyond control. 2 definitely and finally, e.g. *the idea was rejected out of hand.* **to hand, at hand, on hand** nearby. **win hands down** win easily. **handbag** *noun* woman's small bag for carrying personal articles in.
handbill *noun* small printed notice. **handbook** *noun* small reference or instruction book.

handcuff *noun* 1 one of a linked pair of metal rings designed to be locked round a prisoner's wrists by the police. ◆ *verb* 2 put handcuffs on.
handheld *adjective* 1 (of a computer) small enough to be held in the hand. ◆ *noun* 2 computer small enough to be held in the hand.
hand-me-downs *plural noun Informal* clothes that someone has finished with and passed on to someone else. **hand-out** *noun* 1 clothing, food, or money given to a needy person. 2 written information given out at a talk etc.
hand-pick *verb* select carefully for a particular purpose. **handrail** *noun* rail alongside a stairway, to provide support. **handset** *noun* telephone mouthpiece and earpiece in a single unit. **hands-on** *adjective* involving practical experience of equipment. **handstand** *noun* act of supporting the body on the hands in an upside-down position. **hand-to-hand** *adjective* (of combat) at close quarters. **hand-to-mouth** *adjective* having barely enough food or money to live on. **handwriting** *noun* (style of) writing by hand. **handwritten** *adjective*
handful ⊕ *noun* 1 amount that can be held in the hand. 2 small number. 3 *Informal* person or animal that is difficult to control.
handicap ⊕ *noun* 1 physical or mental disability. 2 something that makes progress difficult. 3 contest in which the competitors are given advantages or disadvantages in an attempt to equalize their chances. 4 advantage or disadvantage given. ◆ *verb* 5 make it difficult for (someone) to do something. **handicapped** *adjective*
handicraft ⊕ *noun* objects made by hand.
handiwork ⊕ *noun* something that one has made or done oneself, e.g. *I looked up to admire my handiwork.*

H

——————— T H E S A U R U S ———————

equally, share equally, split in two
hammer *verb* 6 = **hit**, bang, beat, drive, knock, strike, tap 7 *Inf* = **defeat**, beat, drub, run rings around (*inf*), thrash, trounce, wipe the floor with (*inf*)
hamper¹ *verb* = **hinder**, frustrate, hamstring, handicap, impede, interfere with, obstruct, prevent, restrict OPPOSITE **help**
hand *noun* 1 = **palm**, fist, mitt (*sl*), paw (*inf*) 2 = **penmanship**, calligraphy, handwriting, script 3 = **round of applause**, clap, ovation 4 = **worker**, artisan, craftsman, employee, hired man, labourer, operative, workman ◆*verb* 8 = **give**, deliver, hand over, pass **to, at** or **on**
hand = **nearby**, at one's fingertips, available, close, handy, near, ready, within reach
handbook *noun* = **guidebook**, guide,

instruction book, manual
handcuff *noun* 1 = **shackle**, cuff (*inf*), fetter, manacle ◆*verb* 2 = **shackle**, cuff (*inf*), fetter, manacle
handful *noun* 2 = **few**, small number, smattering, sprinkling OPPOSITE **a lot**
handicap *noun* 1 = **disability**, defect, impairment 2 = **disadvantage**, barrier, drawback, hindrance, impediment, limitation, obstacle, restriction, stumbling block OPPOSITE **benefit**. 3 = **advantage**, head start ◆*verb* 5 = **hinder**, burden, encumber, hamper, hamstring, hold back, impede, limit, restrict OPPOSITE **help**
handicraft *noun* = **craftsmanship**, art, craft, handiwork, skill, workmanship
handiwork *noun* = **creation**, achievement,

handkerchief *noun* small square of fabric used to wipe the nose.

People often forget to write a *d* in **handkerchief**, probably because they don't say it or hear it either.

handle ⊕ *noun* **1** part of an object that is held so that it can be used. ◆ *verb* **2** hold, feel, or move with the hands. **3** control or deal with.
handler *noun* person who controls an animal.
handlebars *plural noun* curved metal bar used to steer a cycle.
handsome ⊕ *adjective* **1** (esp. of a man) good-looking. **2** large or generous, e.g. *a handsome profit.* **handsomely** *adverb*
handy ⊕ *adjective* **handier, handiest 1** convenient, useful. **2** good at manual work. **handily** *adverb* **handyman** *noun* man who is good at making or repairing things.
hang ⊕ *verb* **hanging, hung 1** attach or be attached at the top with the lower part free. **2** (of cloth or clothing) fall or flow in a particular way. **3** *past* **hanged** suspend or be suspended by the neck until dead. **4** fasten to a wall. **get the hang of** *Informal* begin to understand.
hanger *noun* curved piece of wood, wire, or plastic, with a hook, for hanging up clothes (also **coat hanger**). **hanger-on** *noun, pl*

hangers-on unwanted follower. **hanging** *noun* **1** execution by hanging. **2** decorative drapery hung on a wall. **hang about, around** *verb* **1** stand about idly. **2** (foll. by *with*) spend a lot of time in the company (of). **hang back** *verb* hesitate, be reluctant. **hangman** *noun* man who executes people by hanging. **hangover** *noun* headache and nausea as a result of drinking too much alcohol. **hang-up** *noun Informal* emotional or psychological problem.
hangar *noun* large shed for storing aircraft.
hangdog ⊕ *adjective* guilty, ashamed, e.g. *a hangdog look.*
hang-glider *noun* glider with a light framework from which the pilot hangs in a harness. **hang-gliding** *noun*
hank ⊕ *noun* coil, esp. of yarn.
hanker ⊕ *verb* (foll. by *after*) desire intensely. **hankering** *noun*
hanky, hankie *noun, pl* **hankies** *Informal* handkerchief.
hanky-panky *noun Informal* illicit sexual relations.
hansom cab, hansom *noun* (formerly) two-wheeled horse-drawn carriage for hire.
haphazard ⊕ *adjective* not organized or planned. **haphazardly** *adverb*
hapless *adjective* unlucky.
happen ⊕ *verb* **1** take place, occur. **2** chance (to be or do something). **happening** *noun* event, occurrence.
happy ⊕ *adjective* **-pier, -piest 1** feeling or

———— THESAURUS ————

design, invention, product, production
handle *noun* **1** = **grip**, haft, hilt, stock ◆*verb* **2** = **hold**, feel, finger, grasp, pick up, touch **3** = **control**, cope with, deal with, direct, guide, manage, manipulate, manoeuvre
hand-out *noun* **1** = **charity**, alms, dole, pogey (*Canad*) **2** = **leaflet**, bulletin, circular, literature (*inf*), mailshot, press release
handsome *adjective* **1** = **good-looking**, attractive, comely, dishy (*inf, chiefly Brit*), elegant, gorgeous, personable OPPOSITE ugly. **2** = **generous**, abundant, ample, considerable, large, liberal, plentiful, sizable *or* sizeable OPPOSITE mean
handwriting *noun* = **penmanship**, calligraphy, hand, scrawl, script
handy *adjective* **1 a** = **convenient**, accessible, at hand, at one's fingertips, available, close, nearby, on hand, within reach OPPOSITE inconvenient. **b** = **useful**, convenient, easy to use, helpful, manageable, neat, practical, serviceable, user-friendly OPPOSITE awkward. **2** = **skilful**, adept, adroit, deft, dexterous, expert,

proficient, skilled OPPOSITE unskilled
hang *verb* **1** = **suspend**, dangle, droop **3** = **execute**, lynch, string up (*inf*) **get the hang of** *Inf* = **grasp**, comprehend, understand
hang back *verb* = **be reluctant**, demur, hesitate, hold back, recoil
hangdog *adjective* = **guilty**, cowed, cringing, defeated, downcast, furtive, shamefaced, wretched
hangover *noun* = **aftereffects**, morning after (*inf*)
hang-up *noun Inf* = **preoccupation**, block, difficulty, inhibition, obsession, problem, thing (*inf*)
hank *noun* = **coil**, length, loop, piece, roll, skein
hanker *verb* (foll. by *after*) = **desire**, crave, hunger, itch, long, lust, pine, thirst, yearn
haphazard *adjective* = **unsystematic**, aimless, casual, disorganized, hit or miss (*inf*), indiscriminate, slapdash OPPOSITE systematic
happen *verb* **1** = **occur**, come about, come to pass, develop, result, take place, transpire (*inf*)

causing joy. **2** lucky, fortunate. **3** willing (to do something). **happily** *adverb* **happiness** *noun*
happy-go-lucky *adjective* carefree and cheerful.
hara-kiri *noun* (formerly, in Japan) ritual suicide by disembowelling.
harangue ❶ *verb* **1** address angrily or forcefully. ♦ *noun* **2** angry or forceful speech.
harass ❶ *verb* annoy or trouble constantly.
harassed *adjective* **harassment** *noun*

SPELLING TIP

The commonest misspelling of **harass** is *harrass*. There should be only one r, but it's obviously difficult to remember: there are 232 instances of *harrassment* in the Bank of English and 10 of *harrasment*. The correct spelling is **harassment**.

---

harbinger [har-binj-a] *noun* someone or something that announces the approach of something, e.g. *a harbinger of doom.*
harbour ❶ *noun* **1** sheltered port. ♦ *verb* **2** maintain secretly in the mind. **3** give shelter or protection to.
hard ❶ *adjective* **1** firm, solid, or rigid. **2**

difficult. **3** requiring a lot of effort. **4** unkind, unfeeling. **5** causing pain, sorrow, or hardship. **6** (of water) containing calcium salts which stop soap lathering freely. **7** (of a drug) strong and addictive. ♦ *adverb* **8** with great energy or effort. **9** with great intensity. **hard of hearing** unable to hear properly. **hard up** *Informal* short of money. **harden** *verb* **hardness** *noun*
hardship *noun* **1** suffering. **2** difficult circumstances. **hard-and-fast** *adjective* (of rules) fixed and not able to be changed. **hard-bitten** *adjective* tough and determined. **hard-boiled** *adjective* **1** (of an egg) boiled until solid. **2** *Informal* tough, unemotional. **hard cash** notes and coins, as opposed to cheques or credit cards. **hard copy** computer output printed on paper. **hard core** the members of a group who most resist change. **hard-core** *adjective* **1** (of pornography) showing sexual acts in explicit detail. **2** extremely committed, fanatical. **hard disk** *Computers* inflexible disk in a sealed container. **hard-headed** *adjective* shrewd, practical. **hardhearted** *adjective* unsympathetic, uncaring. **hard line** uncompromising policy. **hard-line** *adjective* **hard-liner** *noun* **hard sell** aggressive sales technique. **hard shoulder** surfaced verge at the edge of a motorway for emergency stops.

H

————————— THESAURUS —————————

2 = **chance**, turn out
happening *noun* = **event**, affair, episode, experience, incident, occurrence, proceeding
happily *adverb* **1** = **joyfully**, blithely, cheerfully, gaily, gleefully, joyously, merrily **2** = **luckily**, fortunately, opportunely, providentially **3** = **willingly**, freely, gladly, with pleasure
happiness *noun* **1** = **joy**, bliss, cheerfulness, contentment, delight, ecstasy, elation, jubilation, pleasure, satisfaction OPPOSITE unhappiness
happy *adjective* **1** = **joyful**, blissful, cheerful, content, delighted, ecstatic, elated, glad, jubilant, merry, overjoyed, pleased, thrilled OPPOSITE **sad**. **2** = **fortunate**, advantageous, auspicious, favourable, lucky, timely OPPOSITE unfortunate
happy-go-lucky *adjective* = **carefree**, blithe, easy-going, light-hearted, nonchalant, unconcerned, untroubled OPPOSITE **serious**
harangue *verb* **1** = **rant**, address, declaim, exhort, hold forth, lecture, spout (*inf*) ♦*noun* **2** = **speech**, address, declamation, diatribe, exhortation, tirade
harass *verb* = **annoy**, bother, harry, hassle (*inf*), hound, persecute, pester, plague, trouble,

vex
harassed *adjective* = **hassled** (*inf*), careworn, distraught, strained, tormented, troubled, under pressure, vexed, worried
harassment *noun* = **hassle** (*inf*), annoyance, bother, irritation, nuisance, persecution, pestering, trouble
harbour *noun* **1** = **port**, anchorage, haven ♦*verb* **2** = **maintain**, cling to, entertain, foster, hold, nurse, nurture, retain **3** = **shelter**, hide, protect, provide refuge, shield
hard *adjective* **1** = **tough**, firm, inflexible, rigid, rocklike, solid, stiff, strong, unyielding OPPOSITE soft. **2** = **difficult**, complicated, intricate, involved, knotty, perplexing, puzzling, thorny OPPOSITE **easy**. **3** = **strenuous**, arduous, backbreaking, exacting, exhausting, laborious, rigorous, tough OPPOSITE **easy**. **4** = **harsh**, callous, cold, cruel, hardhearted, pitiless, stern, unfeeling, unkind, unsympathetic OPPOSITE kind. **5** = **grim**, disagreeable, distressing, grievous, intolerable, painful, unpleasant ♦*adverb* **8**, **9** = **energetically**, fiercely, forcefully, forcibly, heavily, intensely, powerfully, severely, sharply, strongly, vigorously, violently, with all one's might, with might and main OPPOSITE softly

hardback *noun* book with a stiff cover.

hardboard *noun* thin stiff board made of compressed sawdust and wood chips.

hardly ⊕ *adverb* **1** scarcely or not at all. **2** with difficulty.

hardware *noun* **1** metal tools or implements. **2** machinery used in a computer system. **3** heavy military equipment, such as tanks and missiles.

hardwood *noun* wood of a deciduous tree such as oak or ash.

hardy ⊕ *adjective* **hardier, hardiest** able to stand difficult conditions. **hardiness** *noun*

hare *noun* **1** animal like a large rabbit, with longer ears and legs. ♦ *verb* **2** (usu. foll. by *off*) run (away) quickly. **harebell** *noun* blue bell-shaped flower. **harebrained** *adjective* foolish or impractical. **harelip** *noun* slight split in the upper lip.

harem *noun* (apartments of) a Muslim man's wives and concubines.

haricot bean, haricot [har-rik-oh] *noun* small pale edible bean, usu. sold dried.

hark *verb* Old-fashioned listen. **hark back** *verb* return (to an earlier subject).

harlequin *noun* **1** stock comic character with a diamond-patterned costume and mask. ♦

adjective **2** in many colours.

harlot *noun* Lit prostitute.

harm ⊕ *verb* **1** injure physically, mentally, or morally. ♦ *noun* **2** physical, mental, or moral injury. **harmful** *adjective* **harmless** *adjective*

harmonica *noun* small wind instrument played by sucking and blowing.

harmonium *noun* keyboard instrument like a small organ.

harmony ⊕ *noun, pl* **-nies 1** peaceful agreement and cooperation. **2** pleasant combination of notes sounded at the same time. **harmonious** *adjective* **1** consisting of parts that blend together well. **2** of harmony. **harmoniously** *adverb* **harmonic** *adjective* of harmony. **harmonics** *noun* science of musical sounds. **harmonize** *verb* **1** sing or play in harmony. **2** blend well together. **harmonization** *noun*

harness ⊕ *noun* **1** arrangement of straps for attaching a horse to a cart or plough. **2** set of straps fastened round someone's body to attach something, e.g. *a safety harness.* ♦ *verb* **3** put a harness on. **4** control (something) in order to make use of it.

harp *noun* large triangular stringed instrument played with the fingers. **harpist** *noun* **harp on**

——————— T H E S A U R U S ———————

hard-bitten *adjective* Inf =**tough**, cynical, hard-nosed (*inf*), matter-of-fact, practical, realistic OPPOSITE **idealistic**

hard-boiled *adjective* **2** Inf =**tough**, cynical, hard-nosed (*inf*), matter-of-fact, practical, realistic, unsentimental OPPOSITE **idealistic**

harden *verb* **1** =**solidify**, bake, cake, freeze, set, stiffen

hard-headed *adjective* =**shrewd**, level-headed, practical, pragmatic, realistic, sensible, tough, unsentimental

hardhearted *adjective* =**unsympathetic**, callous, cold, hard, heartless, insensitive, uncaring, unfeeling

hardiness *noun* =**resilience**, resolution, robustness, ruggedness, sturdiness, toughness

hardly *adverb* **1** =**barely**, just, only just, scarcely OPPOSITE **completely**. **2** =**with difficulty**

hardship *noun* =**suffering**, adversity, difficulty, misfortune, need, privation, tribulation OPPOSITE **ease**

hard up *adjective* Inf =**poor**, broke (*inf*), impecunious, impoverished, on the breadline, out of pocket, penniless, short, skint (*Brit sl*), strapped for cash (*inf*) OPPOSITE **wealthy**

hardy *adjective* =**strong**, robust, rugged, sound, stout, sturdy, tough OPPOSITE **frail**

harm *verb* **1** =**injure**, abuse, damage, hurt, ill-treat, maltreat, ruin, spoil, wound OPPOSITE **heal** ♦*noun* **2** =**injury**, abuse, damage, hurt, ill, loss, mischief, misfortune OPPOSITE **good**

harmful *adjective* =**injurious**, damaging, deleterious, destructive, detrimental, hurtful, noxious, pernicious OPPOSITE **harmless**

harmless *adjective* =**innocuous**, gentle, innocent, inoffensive, nontoxic, safe, unobjectionable OPPOSITE **dangerous**

harmonious *adjective* **1** =**compatible**, agreeable, consonant OPPOSITE **incompatible**. **2 a** =**friendly**, agreeable, amicable, compatible, congenial, cordial, sympathetic OPPOSITE **unfriendly**. **b** =**melodious**, concordant, dulcet, mellifluous, musical, sweet-sounding, tuneful OPPOSITE **discordant**

harmonize *verb* **2** =**go together**, agree, blend, coordinate, correspond, match, tally, tone in with

harmony *noun* **1** =**agreement**, accord, amicability, compatibility, concord, cooperation, friendship, peace, rapport, sympathy OPPOSITE **conflict**. **2** =**tunefulness**, euphony, melody, tune, unison OPPOSITE **discord**

harness *noun* **1** =**tack 2** =**equipment**, gear, tackle ♦*verb* **4** =**exploit**, channel, control,

about *verb* talk about continuously.
harpoon *noun* **1** barbed spear attached to a rope used for hunting whales. ◆ *verb* **2** spear with a harpoon.
harpsichord *noun* stringed keyboard instrument.
harpy *noun, pl* **-pies** nasty or bad-tempered woman.
harridan *noun* nagging or vicious woman.
harrier *noun* cross-country runner.
harrow *noun* **1** implement used to break up lumps of soil. ◆ *verb* **2** draw a harrow over.
harrowing ⊕ *adjective* very distressing.
harry ⊕ *verb* **-rying, -ried** keep asking (someone) to do something, pester.
harsh ⊕ *adjective* **1** severe and difficult to cope with. **2** unkind, unsympathetic. **3** extremely hard, bright, or rough. **harshly** *adverb* **harshness** *noun*
hart *noun* adult male deer.
hartebeest *noun* large African antelope.
harum-scarum *adjective* reckless.
harvest ⊕ *noun* **1** (season for) the gathering of crops. **2** crops gathered. ◆ *verb* **3** gather (a ripened crop). **harvester** *noun*
has *verb* third person singular of the present tense of HAVE. **has-been** *noun Informal* person who is no longer popular or successful.
hash¹ ⊕ *noun* dish of diced cooked meat and vegetables reheated. **make a hash of** *Informal* spoil, do badly.
hash² *noun Informal* hashish.
hashish [hash-eesh] *noun* drug made from the cannabis plant, smoked for its intoxicating effects.

hasp *noun* clasp that fits over a staple and is secured by a bolt or padlock, used as a fastening.
hassle ⊕ *Informal noun* **1** trouble, bother. **2** long argument. ◆ *verb* **3** bother or annoy.
hassock *noun* cushion for kneeling on in church.
haste ⊕ *noun* (excessive) quickness. **make haste** hurry, rush. **hasten** *verb* (cause to) hurry.
hasty *adjective* **hastier, hastiest** (too) quick. **hastily** *adverb*
hat *noun* covering for the head, often with a brim, usu. worn to give protection from the weather. **keep something under one's hat** keep something secret. **hat trick** any three successive achievements, esp. in sport.
hatch¹ ⊕ *verb* **1** (cause to) emerge from an egg. **2** devise (a plot).
hatch² *noun* **1** hinged door covering an opening in a floor or wall. **2** opening in the wall between a kitchen and a dining area. **3** door in an aircraft or spacecraft. **hatchback** *noun* car with a lifting door at the back.
hatchway *noun* opening in the deck of a ship.
hatchet *noun* small axe. **bury the hatchet** become reconciled. **hatchet job** malicious verbal or written attack. **hatchet man** *Informal* person carrying out unpleasant tasks for an employer.
hate ⊕ *verb* **1** dislike intensely. **2** be unwilling (to do something). ◆ *noun* **3** intense dislike. **4** person or thing hated. **hateful** *adjective* causing or deserving hate. **hater** *noun* **hatred** *noun* intense dislike.
haughty ⊕ *adjective* **-tier, -tiest** proud,

H

—————————— T H E S A U R U S ——————————

employ, mobilize, utilize
harrowing *adjective* =**distressing**, agonizing, disturbing, gut-wrenching, heart-rending, nerve-racking, painful, terrifying, tormenting, traumatic
harry *verb* =**pester**, badger, bother, chivvy, harass, hassle (*inf*), plague
harsh *adjective* **1, 2** =**severe**, austere, cruel, Draconian, drastic, hard, pitiless, punitive, ruthless, stern, tough OPPOSITE **kind. 3** =**raucous**, discordant, dissonant, grating, guttural, rasping, rough, strident OPPOSITE **soft**
harshly *adverb* **1, 2** =**severely**, brutally, cruelly, roughly, sternly, strictly
harshness *noun* **1, 2** =**severity**, asperity, brutality, rigour, roughness, sternness
harvest *noun* **1 a** =**gathering**, harvesting, harvest-time, reaping **b** =**crop**, produce, yield ◆*verb* **2** =**gather**, mow, pick, pluck, reap
hash¹ *noun* **make a hash of** *Inf* =**mess up**,

botch, bungle, make a pig's ear of (*inf*), mishandle, mismanage, muddle
hassle *Inf noun* **1** =**trouble**, bother, difficulty, grief (*inf*), inconvenience, problem **2** =**argument**, bickering, disagreement, dispute, fight, quarrel, row, squabble ◆*verb* **3** =**bother**, annoy, badger, bug (*inf*), harass, hound, pester
haste *noun* =**speed**, alacrity, hurry, impetuosity, quickness, rapidity, rush, swiftness, urgency, velocity OPPOSITE **slowness**
hasten *verb* =**rush**, dash, fly, hurry (up), make haste, race, scurry, speed OPPOSITE **dawdle**
hastily *adverb* =**quickly**, hurriedly, impetuously, precipitately, promptly, rapidly, speedily
hasty *adjective* =**speedy**, brisk, hurried, impetuous, impulsive, precipitate, prompt, rapid, swift, urgent OPPOSITE **slow**
hatch¹ *verb* **1** =**incubate**, breed, bring forth, brood **2** =**devise**, conceive, concoct, contrive,

arrogant. **haughtily** *adverb* **haughtiness** *noun*
haul ⊕ *verb* **1** pull or drag with effort. ◆ *noun* **2** hauling. **3** amount gained by effort or theft. **long haul** something that takes a lot of time and effort. **haulage** *noun* (charge for) transporting goods. **haulier** *noun* firm or person that transports goods by road.
haulm [**hawm**] *noun* stalks of beans, peas, or potatoes collectively.
haunch *noun* human hip or fleshy hindquarter of an animal.
haunt ⊕ *verb* **1** visit in the form of a ghost. **2** remain in the memory or thoughts of. ◆ *noun* **3** place visited frequently. **haunted** *adjective* **1** frequented by ghosts. **2** worried. **haunting** *adjective* memorably beautiful or sad. **hauntingly** *adverb*
haute couture [**oat** koo-**ture**] *noun French* high fashion.
hauteur [oat-**ur**] *noun* haughtiness.
Havana *noun* fine-quality cigar made in Cuba.
have ⊕ *verb* **has, having, had 1** possess, hold. **2** receive, take, or obtain. **3** experience or be affected by. **4** (foll. by *to*) be obliged, must, e.g. *I had to go.* **5** cause to be done. **6** give birth to. **7** *Slang* cheat or outwit. **8** used to form past tenses (with a past participle), e.g. *we have looked; she had done enough.* **have it out** *Informal* settle a matter by argument. **haves**

and have-nots *Informal* rich people and poor people. **have on** *verb* **1** wear. **2** *Informal* tease or trick. **have up** *verb* bring to trial.
haven ⊕ *noun* place of safety.
haver *verb Dialect* talk nonsense. **havers** *plural noun Scot* nonsense.
haversack *noun* canvas bag carried on the back or shoulder.
havoc ⊕ *noun* disorder and confusion.
haw *noun* hawthorn berry.
hawk[1] *noun* **1** bird of prey with a short hooked bill and very good eyesight. **2** *Politics* supporter or advocate of warlike policies. **hawkish, hawklike** *adjective* **hawk-eyed** *adjective* having very good eyesight.
hawk[2] *verb* offer (goods) for sale in the street or door-to-door. **hawker** *noun*
hawk[3] *verb* cough noisily.
hawser *noun* large rope used on a ship.
hawthorn *noun* thorny shrub or tree.
hay ⊕ *noun* grass cut and dried as fodder. **hay fever** allergy to pollen, causing sneezing and watery eyes. **haystack** *noun* large pile of stored hay. **haywire** *adjective* **go haywire** *Informal* not function properly.
hazard ⊕ *noun* **1** something that could be dangerous. ◆ *verb* **2** put in danger. **3** make (a guess). **hazardous** *adjective*
haze ⊕ *noun* mist, often caused by heat. **hazy**

——————— THESAURUS ———————

cook up (*inf*), design, dream up (*inf*), think up
hate *verb* **1** = **detest**, abhor, despise, dislike, loathe, recoil from OPPOSITE **love**. **2** = **be unwilling**, be loath, be reluctant, be sorry, dislike, feel disinclined, shrink from OPPOSITE **like** ◆*noun* **3** = **dislike**, animosity, antipathy, aversion, detestation, enmity, hatred, hostility, loathing OPPOSITE **love**
hateful *adjective* = **despicable**, abhorrent, detestable, horrible, loathsome, obnoxious, odious, offensive, repellent, repugnant, repulsive OPPOSITE **pleasant**
hatred *noun* = **dislike**, animosity, antipathy, aversion, detestation, enmity, hate, repugnance, revulsion OPPOSITE **love**
haughty *adjective* = **proud**, arrogant, conceited, contemptuous, disdainful, imperious, scornful, snooty (*inf*), stuck-up (*inf*), supercilious OPPOSITE **humble**
haul *verb* **1** = **drag**, draw, heave, lug, pull, tug ◆*noun* **3** = **yield**, booty, catch, gain, harvest, loot, spoils, takings
haunt *verb* **2** = **plague**, obsess, possess, prey on, recur, stay with, torment, trouble, weigh on ◆*noun* **3** = **meeting place**, rendezvous, stamping ground

haunted *adjective* **1** = **possessed**, cursed, eerie, ghostly, jinxed, spooky (*inf*) **2** = **preoccupied**, obsessed, plagued, tormented, troubled, worried
haunting *adjective* = **evocative**, nostalgic, persistent, poignant, unforgettable
have *verb* **1** = **possess**, hold, keep, obtain, own, retain **2** = **receive**, accept, acquire, gain, get, obtain, procure, secure, take **3** = **experience**, endure, enjoy, feel, meet with, suffer, sustain, undergo **4** (foll. by *to*) = **be obliged**, be bound, be compelled, be forced, have got to, must, ought, should **6** = **give birth to**, bear, beget, bring forth, deliver **7** *Sl* = **cheat**, deceive, dupe, fool, outwit, swindle, take in (*inf*), trick
haven *noun* = **sanctuary**, asylum, refuge, retreat, sanctum, shelter
have on *verb* **1** = **wear**, be clothed in, be dressed in **2** *Inf* = **tease**, deceive, kid (*inf*), pull someone's leg, take the mickey, trick, wind up (*Brit sl*)
havoc *noun* = **disorder**, chaos, confusion, disruption, mayhem, shambles
haywire *adjective* **go haywire** *Inf* = **malfunction**, break down, fail, go wrong

adjective **hazier, haziest 1** not clear, misty. **2** confused or vague.

hazel *noun* **1** small tree producing edible nuts. ♦ *adjective* **2** (of eyes) greenish-brown.

hazelnut *noun*

HB (on pencils) hard-black.

H-bomb *noun* hydrogen bomb.

h & c hot and cold (water).

he *pronoun* refers to: **1** male person or animal. **2** person or animal of unspecified sex.

He *Chem* helium.

HE His (or Her) Excellency.

head ⊙ *noun* **1** upper or front part of the body, containing the sense organs and the brain. **2** mind and mental abilities. **3** upper or most forward part of anything. **4** person in charge of a group, organization, or school. **5** pus-filled tip of a spot or boil. **6** white froth on beer. **7** *pl* **head** person or animal considered as a unit. **8** headline or heading. **9** *Informal* headache. ♦ *adjective* **10** chief, principal. ♦ *verb* **11** be at the top or front of. **12** be in charge of. **13** move (in a particular direction). **14** hit (a ball) with the head. **15** provide with a heading. **go to one's head** make one drunk or conceited. **head over heels (in love)** very much in love. **not make head nor tail of** not understand. **off one's head** *Slang* foolish or insane. **heads** *adverb Informal* with the side of a coin which has a portrait of a head on it uppermost. **header** *noun* **1** striking a ball with the head. **2** headlong fall. **heading** *noun* title written or printed at the top of a page. **heady** *adjective* **headier, headiest** intoxicating or exciting. **headache** *noun* **1** continuous pain in the head. **2** cause of worry or annoyance. **headboard** *noun* vertical board at the top end of a bed. **headdress** *noun* decorative head covering. **head-hunt** *verb* (of a company) approach and offer a job to (a person working for a rival company). **head-hunting** *noun* **head-hunter** *noun* **headland** *noun* area of land jutting out into the sea. **headlight** *noun* powerful light on the front of a vehicle. **headline** *noun* **1** title at the top of a newspaper article, esp. on the front page. ♦ *plural* **2** main points of a news broadcast. **headlong** *adverb, adjective* **1** with the head first. **2** hastily. **head-on** *adverb, adjective* **1** front foremost. **2** direct(ly) and uncompromising(ly). **headphones** *plural noun* two small loudspeakers held against the ears by a strap. **headquarters** *plural noun* centre from which operations are directed. **head start** advantage in a competition. **headstone** *noun* memorial stone on a grave. **headstrong** *adjective* self-willed, obstinate. **head teacher** person in charge of a school. **headway** *noun* progress. **headwind** *noun* wind blowing against the course of an aircraft or ship.

———————— T H E S A U R U S ————————

hazard *noun* **1** = **danger**, jeopardy, peril, pitfall, risk, threat ♦*verb* **2** = **jeopardize**, endanger, expose, imperil, risk, threaten **3** = **conjecture**, advance, offer, presume, throw out, venture, volunteer

hazardous *adjective* = **dangerous**, dicey (*inf, chiefly Brit*), difficult, insecure, perilous, precarious, risky, unsafe OPPOSITE safe

haze *noun* = **mist**, cloud, fog, obscurity, vapour

hazy *adjective* **1** = **misty**, cloudy, dim, dull, foggy, overcast OPPOSITE bright. **2** = **vague**, fuzzy, ill-defined, indefinite, indistinct, muddled, nebulous, uncertain, unclear OPPOSITE clear

head *noun* **1** = **skull**, crown, loaf (*sl*), nut (*sl*), pate **2** = **mind**, brain, brains (*inf*), intellect, intelligence, thought, understanding **3** = **top**, crest, crown, peak, pinnacle, summit, tip **4** = **leader**, boss (*inf*), captain, chief, commander, director, manager, master, principal, supervisor ♦*adjective* **10** = **chief**, arch, first, leading, main, pre-eminent, premier, prime, principal, supreme ♦*verb* **11** = **lead**, be or go first, cap, crown, lead the way, precede, top **12** = **be in charge of**, command, control, direct, govern, guide, lead, manage, run **13** = **make for**, aim, go to, make a beeline for, point, set off for, set out, start towards, steer, turn **go to one's head** = **excite**, intoxicate, make conceited, puff up

head over heels = **completely**, intensely, thoroughly, uncontrollably, utterly, wholeheartedly

headache *noun* **1** = **migraine**, head (*inf*), neuralgia **2** = **problem**, bane, bother, inconvenience, nuisance, trouble, vexation, worry

heading *noun* = **title**, caption, headline, name, rubric

headlong *adverb* **1** = **headfirst**, head-on **2** = **hastily**, heedlessly, helter-skelter, hurriedly, pell-mell, precipitately, rashly, thoughtlessly ♦*adjective* **1** = **headfirst**, head-on **2** = **hasty**, breakneck, dangerous, impetuous, impulsive, inconsiderate, precipitate, reckless, thoughtless

headstrong *adjective* = **obstinate**, foolhardy, heedless, impulsive, perverse, pig-headed, self-willed, stubborn, unruly, wilful OPPOSITE manageable

headway *noun* = **advance**, improvement, progress, progression, way

heal ⊕ *verb* make or become well. **healer** *noun* **healing** *noun, adjective*
health ⊕ *noun* normal (good) condition of someone's body. **health centre** surgery and offices of the doctors in a district. **health food** natural food, organically grown and free from additives. **health visitor** nurse who visits elderly people and mothers of newborn babies in their homes. **healthy** *adjective* **healthier, healthiest 1** having good health. **2** of or producing good health. **3** functioning well, sound. **healthily** *adverb*
heap ⊕ *noun* **1** pile of things one on top of another. **2** (also **heaps**) large number or quantity. ♦ *verb* **3** gather into a pile. **4** (foll. by on) give liberally (to), e.g. *Keegan heaped praise on his team.*
hear ⊕ *verb* **hearing, heard 1** perceive (a sound) by ear. **2** listen to. **3** learn or be informed. **4** *Law* try (a case). **hear! hear!** exclamation of approval or agreement. **hearer** *noun* **hearing** *noun* **1** ability to hear. **2** trial of a case. **within hearing** close enough to be heard.
hearken *verb Obs* listen.
hearsay ⊕ *noun* gossip, rumour.
hearse *noun* funeral car used to carry a coffin.
heart ⊕ *noun* **1** organ that pumps blood round the body. **2** centre of emotions, esp.

love. **3** courage, spirit. **4** central or most important part. **5** figure representing a heart. **6** playing card with red heart heart-shaped symbols. **break someone's heart** cause someone great grief. **by heart** from memory. **set one's heart on something** greatly desire something. **take something to heart** be upset about something. **hearten** *verb* encourage, make cheerful. **heartening** *adjective* **heartless** *adjective* cruel, unkind. **heartlessly** *adverb* **hearty** *adjective* **heartier, heartiest 1** substantial, nourishing. **2** friendly, enthusiastic. **3** strongly felt. **heartily** *adverb* **heart attack** sudden severe malfunction of the heart. **heart failure** sudden stopping of the heartbeat. **heart-rending** *adjective* causing great sorrow. **heart-throb** *noun Slang* very attractive man, esp. a film or pop star. **heart-to-heart** *adjective, noun* intimate (conversation). **heartache** ⊕ *noun* intense anguish. **heartbeat** *noun* one complete pulsation of the heart. **heartbreak** ⊕ *noun* intense grief. **heartbreaking** *adjective* **heartbroken** *adjective* **heartburn** *noun* burning sensation in the chest caused by indigestion. **heartfelt** ⊕ *adjective* felt sincerely or strongly. **hearth** *noun* floor of a fireplace. **heat** ⊕ *verb* **1** make or become hot. ♦ *noun* **2**

——————— T H E S A U R U S ———————

heady *adjective* **a =intoxicating**, inebriating, potent, strong **b =exciting**, exhilarating, stimulating, thrilling
heal *verb* =**cure**, make well, mend, regenerate, remedy, restore, treat OPPOSITE hurt
health *noun* **a =condition**, constitution, fettle, shape, state **b =wellbeing**, fitness, good condition, healthiness, robustness, soundness, strength, vigour OPPOSITE illness
healthy *adjective* **1 =well**, active, fit, hale and hearty, in fine fettle, in good shape (*inf*), in the pink, robust, strong OPPOSITE ill. **2** =**wholesome**, beneficial, hygienic, invigorating, nourishing, nutritious, salubrious, salutary OPPOSITE unwholesome
heap *noun* **1 =pile**, accumulation, collection, hoard, lot, mass, mound, stack **2** (also **heaps**) =**a lot**, great deal, load(s) (*inf*), lots (*inf*), mass, plenty, pot(s) (*inf*), stack(s), tons ♦*verb* **3 =pile**, accumulate, amass, collect, gather, hoard, stack **4** (foll. by on) =**confer**, assign, bestow, load, shower upon
hear *verb* **1 =perceive**, catch, overhear **2** =**listen to 3 =learn**, ascertain, discover, find out, gather, get wind of (*inf*), pick up **4** *Law* =**try**, examine, investigate, judge

hearing *noun* **2 =inquiry**, industrial tribunal, investigation, review, trial
hearsay *noun* =**rumour**, gossip, idle talk, report, talk, tittle-tattle, word of mouth
heart *noun* **2 =nature**, character, disposition, soul, temperament **3 =courage**, bravery, fortitude, pluck, purpose, resolution, spirit, will **4 =centre**, core, hub, middle, nucleus, quintessence **by heart =by memory**, by rote, off pat, parrot-fashion (*inf*), pat, word for word
heartache *noun* =**sorrow**, agony, anguish, despair, distress, grief, heartbreak, pain, remorse, suffering, torment, torture
heartbreak *noun* =**grief**, anguish, desolation, despair, misery, pain, sorrow, suffering
heartbreaking *adjective* =**sad**, agonizing, distressing, gut-wrenching, harrowing, heart-rending, pitiful, poignant, tragic OPPOSITE happy
heartfelt *adjective* =**sincere**, deep, devout, earnest, genuine, honest, profound, unfeigned, wholehearted OPPOSITE insincere
heartily *adverb* **2, 3 =enthusiastically**, eagerly, earnestly, resolutely, vigorously, zealously
heartless *adjective* =**cruel**, callous, cold, hard,

state of being hot. **3** energy transferred as a result of a difference in temperature. **4** hot weather. **5** intensity of feeling. **6** preliminary eliminating contest in a competition. **on, in heat** (of some female animals) ready for mating. **heated** adjective angry and excited. **heatedly** adverb **heater** noun **heating** noun **heatstroke** noun same as SUNSTROKE. **heat wave** spell of unusually hot weather.

heath noun area of open uncultivated land.

heathen ⊕ adjective, noun (of) a person who does not believe in an established religion.

heather noun low-growing plant with small purple, pinkish, or white flowers, growing on heaths and mountains.

heave ⊕ verb **1** lift with effort. **2** throw (something heavy). **3** utter (a sigh). **4** rise and fall. **5** vomit. **6** past **hove** Naut move in a specified direction. ♦ noun **7** heaving. **heave to** verb (of a ship) stop moving.

heaven ⊕ noun **1** place believed to be the home of God, where good people go when they die. **2** place or state of bliss. **the heavens** sky. **heavenly** adjective **1** of or like heaven. **2** of or occurring in space. **3** wonderful or beautiful.

heavy ⊕ adjective **heavier, heaviest 1** of great weight. **2** having a high density. **3** great

in degree or amount. **4** (of breathing) deep and loud. **5** (of food) solid and difficult to digest. **6** Informal (of a situation) serious. **heavily** adverb **heaviness** noun **heavy-duty** adjective made to withstand hard wear. **heavy industry** large-scale production of raw material or machinery. **heavy metal** very loud rock music featuring guitar riffs. **heavy water** water formed of oxygen and deuterium. **heavyweight** noun boxer weighing over 175lb (professional) or 81kg (amateur).

Hebrew noun **1** member of an ancient Semitic people. **2** ancient language of the Hebrews. **3** its modern form, used in Israel. ♦ adjective **4** of the Hebrews.

heckle ⊕ verb interrupt (a public speaker) with comments, questions, or taunts. **heckler** noun

hectare noun one hundred ares or 10 000 square metres (2.471 acres).

hectic ⊕ adjective rushed or busy.

hector verb bully. **hectoring** adjective, noun

hedge ⊕ noun **1** row of bushes forming a barrier or boundary. ♦ verb **2** be evasive or noncommittal. **3** (foll. by against) protect oneself (from). **hedgerow** noun bushes forming a hedge. **hedge sparrow** small brownish songbird.

————————— T H E S A U R U S —————————

hardhearted, merciless, pitiless, uncaring, unfeeling OPPOSITE compassionate

heart-rending adjective =moving, affecting, distressing, gut-wrenching, harrowing, heartbreaking, poignant, sad, tragic

hearty adjective **1** =substantial, ample, filling, nourishing, sizable or sizeable, solid, square **2** =friendly, back-slapping, ebullient, effusive, enthusiastic, genial, jovial, warm OPPOSITE cold

heat verb **1** =warm up, make hot, reheat OPPOSITE cool ♦noun **2** =hotness, high temperature, warmth OPPOSITE cold. **5** =passion, excitement, fervour, fury, intensity, vehemence OPPOSITE calmness

heated adjective =impassioned, angry, excited, fierce, frenzied, furious, intense, passionate, stormy, vehement OPPOSITE calm

heathen adjective =pagan, godless, idolatrous, irreligious ♦noun =pagan, infidel, unbeliever

heave verb **1** =lift, drag (up), haul (up), hoist, pull (up), raise, tug **2** =throw, cast, fling, hurl, pitch, send, sling, toss **3** =sigh, groan, puff **5** =vomit, be sick, gag, retch, spew, throw up (inf)

heaven noun **1** =paradise, bliss, Elysium or Elysian fields (Greek myth), hereafter, life everlasting, next world, nirvana (Buddhism,

Hinduism), Zion (Christianity) **2** =happiness, bliss, ecstasy, paradise, rapture, seventh heaven, utopia **the heavens** =sky, ether, firmament

heavenly adjective **1** =celestial, angelic, blessed, divine, holy, immortal OPPOSITE worldly. **3** =wonderful, beautiful, blissful, delightful, divine (inf), exquisite, lovely, ravishing, sublime OPPOSITE awful

heavily adverb **1** =ponderously, awkwardly, clumsily, weightily **2** =densely, closely, compactly, thickly **3** =considerably, a great deal, copiously, excessively, to excess, very much

heaviness noun **1** =weight, gravity, heftiness, ponderousness

heavy adjective **1** =weighty, bulky, hefty, massive, ponderous OPPOSITE light. **3** =considerable, abundant, copious, excessive, large, profuse OPPOSITE slight

heckle verb =jeer, barrack (inf), boo, disrupt, interrupt, shout down, taunt

hectic adjective =frantic, animated, chaotic, feverish, frenetic, heated, turbulent OPPOSITE peaceful

hedge noun **1** =hedgerow ♦verb **2** =dodge, duck, equivocate, evade, flannel (Brit inf), prevaricate, sidestep, temporize **3** (foll. by against) =insure, cover, guard, protect,

hedgehog *noun* small mammal with a protective covering of spines.
hedonism *noun* doctrine that pleasure is the most important thing in life. **hedonist** *noun* **hedonistic** *adjective*
heed ① *noun* **1** careful attention. ◆ *verb* **2** pay careful attention to. **heedless** *adjective* **heedless of** taking no notice of.
heel¹ ① *noun* **1** back part of the foot. **2** part of a shoe supporting the heel. **3** *Slang* contemptible person. ◆ *verb* **4** repair the heel of (a shoe). **heeler** *noun Aust & NZ* dog that herds cattle by biting at their heels.
heel² ① *verb* (foll. by *over*) lean to one side.
hefty ① *adjective* **heftier, heftiest 1** large, heavy, or strong. **2** (of a fine or bill) involving a large sum of money.
hegemony [hig-**em**-on-ee] *noun* political domination.
Hegira *noun* Mohammed's flight from Mecca to Medina in 622 AD.
heifer [**hef**-fer] *noun* young cow.
height ① *noun* **1** distance from base to top. **2** distance above sea level. **3** highest degree or topmost point. **heighten** *verb* make or become higher or more intense. **heightened** *adjective*
heinous *adjective* evil and shocking.
heir ① *noun* person entitled to inherit property or rank. **heiress** *n fem* **heir apparent** person whose right to inherit cannot be defeated.
heirloom *noun* object that has belonged to a family for generations. **heir presumptive** heir whose right may be defeated by the birth of a closer relative.

held *verb* past of HOLD¹.
helical *adjective* spiral.
helices [**hell**-iss-seez] *noun* plural of HELIX.
helicopter *noun* aircraft lifted and propelled by rotating overhead blades. **heliport** *noun* airport for helicopters.
heliograph *noun* signalling apparatus that uses a mirror to reflect the sun's rays.
heliotrope *noun* **1** plant with purple flowers. ◆ *adjective* **2** light purple.
helium [**heel**-ee-um] *noun Chem* very light colourless odourless gas.
helix [**heel**-iks] *noun, pl* **helices, helixes** spiral.
hell ① *noun* **1** place believed to be where wicked people go when they die. **2** place or state of wickedness, suffering, or punishment. **hell for leather** at great speed. **hellish** *adjective* **hellbent** *adjective* (foll. by *on*) intent.
hellebore *noun* plant with white flowers that bloom in winter.
Hellenic *adjective* of the (ancient) Greeks or their language.
hello ① *interjection* expression of greeting or surprise.
helm ① *noun* tiller or wheel for steering a ship. **at the helm** in a position of leadership or control.
helmet *noun* hard hat worn for protection.
help ① *verb* **1** make something easier, better, or quicker for (someone). **2** improve (a situation). **3** refrain from, e.g. *I can't help smiling.* ◆ *noun* **4** assistance or support. **5** person who gives assistance. **help oneself 1** take something, esp. food or drink, without

——————— T H E S A U R U S ———————

safeguard, shield
heed *noun* **1** =**care**, attention, caution, mind, notice, regard, respect, thought OPPOSITE **neglect** ◆*verb* **2** =**pay attention to**, bear in mind, consider, follow, listen to, note, obey, observe, take notice of OPPOSITE **ignore**
heedless *adjective* =**careless**, foolhardy, inattentive, oblivious, thoughtless, unmindful OPPOSITE **careful**
heel¹ *noun* **3** *Sl* =**swine**, bounder (*old-fashioned Brit sl*), cad (*Brit inf*), rotter (*sl, chiefly Brit*)
heel² (foll. by *over*) *verb* =**lean over**, keel over, list, tilt
hefty *adjective* **1** =**big**, burly, hulking, massive, muscular, robust, strapping, strong OPPOSITE **little**
height *noun* **1, 2** =**altitude**, elevation, highness, loftiness, stature, tallness OPPOSITE shortness. **3 a** =**culmination**, climax, limit, maximum, ultimate OPPOSITE **depth. b** =**peak**,

apex, crest, crown, pinnacle, summit, top, zenith OPPOSITE **base**
heighten *verb* =**intensify**, add to, amplify, enhance, improve, increase, magnify, sharpen, strengthen
heir *noun* =**successor**, beneficiary, heiress (*fem*), inheritor, next in line
hell *noun* **1** =**underworld**, abyss, fire and brimstone, Hades (*Greek myth*), hellfire, inferno, nether world **2** =**torment**, agony, anguish, misery, nightmare, ordeal, suffering, wretchedness
hellish *adjective* **1** =**devilish**, damnable, diabolical, fiendish, infernal OPPOSITE wonderful
hello *interjection* =**hi** (*inf*), gidday (*Aust & NZ*), good afternoon, good evening, good morning, greetings, how do you do?, welcome
helm *noun* =**tiller**, rudder, wheel **at the helm** =**in charge**, at the wheel, in command, in control, in the driving seat, in the saddle

being served. **2** *Informal* steal something.
helper *noun* **helpful** *adjective* **helpfully** *adverb*
helpfulness *noun* **helping** *noun* single portion
of food. **helpless** *adjective* weak or incapable.
helplessly *adverb* **helplessness** *noun* **helpline**
noun telephone line set aside for callers to
contact an organization for help with a
problem. **helpmate** *noun* companion and
helper, esp. a husband or wife.
helter-skelter ⊕ *adjective* **1** haphazard and
careless. ◆ *adverb* **2** in a haphazard and careless
manner. ◆ *noun* **3** high spiral slide at a
fairground.
hem ⊕ *noun* **1** bottom edge of a garment,
folded under and stitched down. ◆ *verb*
hemming, hemmed 2 provide with a hem.
hem in *verb* surround and prevent from
moving. **hemline** *noun* level to which the hem
of a skirt hangs.
he-man *noun Informal* strong virile man.
hemisphere *noun* half of a sphere, esp. the
earth. **hemispherical** *adjective*
hemlock *noun* poison made from a plant with
spotted stems and small white flowers.
hemp *noun* **1** (also **cannabis**) Asian plant with
tough fibres. **2** its fibre, used to make canvas
and rope. **3** narcotic drug obtained from hemp.
hen ⊕ *noun* **1** female domestic fowl. **2** female
of any bird. **hen night, party** party for women
only. **henpecked** *adjective* (of a man)
dominated by his wife.
henbane *noun* poisonous plant with sticky
hairy leaves.

hence ⊕ *conjunction* **1** for this reason. ◆ *adverb*
2 from this time. **henceforth, henceforward**
adverb from now on.
henchman ⊕ *noun* attendant or follower.
henna *noun* **1** reddish dye made from a shrub
or tree. ◆ *verb* **2** dye (the hair) with henna.
henry *noun, pl* **-ry, -ries, -rys** unit of electrical
inductance.
hepatitis *noun* inflammation of the liver.
heptagon *noun* geometric figure with seven
sides. **heptagonal** *adjective*
heptathlon *noun* athletic contest for women,
involving seven events.
her *pronoun* **1** refers to a female person or
animal or anything personified as feminine
when the object of a sentence or clause. ◆
adjective **2** belonging to her.
herald ⊕ *noun* **1** person who announces
important news. **2** forerunner. ◆ *verb* **3** signal
the approach of. **heraldry** *noun* study of coats
of arms and family trees. **heraldic** *adjective*
herb *noun* plant used for flavouring in cookery,
and in medicine. **herbal** *adjective* **herbalist**
noun person who grows or specializes in the
use of medicinal herbs. **herbaceous** *adjective*
(of a plant) soft-stemmed. **herbaceous border**
flowerbed containing perennials rather than
annuals. **herbicide** *noun* chemical used to
destroy plants, esp. weeds. **herbivore** *noun*
animal that eats only plants. **herbivorous**
[her-**biv**-or-uss] *adjective*
herculean [her-kew-**lee**-an] *adjective* requiring
great strength or effort.

H

——————————————— THESAURUS ———————————————

help *verb* **1** = **aid**, abet, assist, cooperate, lend
a hand, succour, support OPPOSITE hinder. **2**
= **improve**, alleviate, ameliorate, ease, facilitate,
mitigate, relieve OPPOSITE aggravate. **3**
= **refrain from**, avoid, keep from, prevent, resist
◆*noun* **4** = **assistance**, advice, aid, cooperation,
guidance, helping hand, support OPPOSITE
hindrance
helper *noun* **1** = **assistant**, aide, ally,
attendant, collaborator, helpmate, mate, right-
hand man, second, supporter
helpful *adjective* **a** = **useful**, advantageous,
beneficial, constructive, practical, profitable,
timely **b** = **cooperative**, accommodating,
considerate, friendly, kind, neighbourly,
supportive, sympathetic
helping *noun* = **portion**, dollop (*inf*), piece,
ration, serving
helpless *adjective* = **powerless**, disabled,
impotent, incapable, infirm, paralysed, weak
OPPOSITE powerful
helter-skelter *adjective* **1** = **haphazard**,

confused, disordered, higgledy-piggledy (*inf*),
hit-or-miss, jumbled, muddled, random, topsy-
turvy ◆*adverb* **2** = **carelessly**, anyhow, hastily,
headlong, hurriedly, pell-mell, rashly, recklessly,
wildly
hem *noun* **1** = **edge**, border, fringe, margin,
trimming
hem in *verb* = **surround**, beset, circumscribe,
confine, enclose, restrict, shut in
hence *conjunction* **1** = **therefore**, ergo, for this
reason, on that account, thus
henchman *noun* = **attendant**, associate,
bodyguard, follower, minder (*sl*), right-hand
man, sidekick (*sl*), subordinate, supporter
henpecked *adjective* = **dominated**,
browbeaten, bullied, meek, subjugated, timid
OPPOSITE domineering
herald *noun* **1** = **messenger**, crier **2**
= **forerunner**, harbinger, indication, omen,
precursor, sign, signal, token ◆*verb* **3**
= **indicate**, foretoken, portend, presage,
promise, show, usher in

herd ⓘ *noun* **1** group of animals feeding and living together. **2** large crowd of people. ◆ *verb* **3** collect into a herd. **herdsman** *noun* man who looks after a herd of animals.

here ⓘ *adverb* in, at, or to this place or point. **hereabouts** *adverb* near here. **hereafter** *adverb* after this point or time. **the hereafter** life after death. **hereby** *adverb* by means of or as a result of this. **herein** *adverb* in this place, matter, or document. **hereinafter** *adverb Law* from this point on in this document, matter, or case. **heretofore** *adverb Law* until now. **herewith** *adverb* with this.

heredity ⓘ [hir-**red**-it-ee] *noun* passing on of characteristics from one generation to another. **hereditary** *adjective* **1** passed on genetically from one generation to another. **2** passed on by inheritance.

SPELLING TIP

There are several ways to misspell **hereditary**. The problems always come after the *t*, where there should be three more letters: *-ary*.

---

heresy ⓘ [**herr**-iss-ee] *noun, pl* **-sies** opinion contrary to accepted opinion or belief. **heretic** [**herr**-it-ik] *noun* person who holds unorthodox opinions. **heretical** [hir-**ret**-ik-al] *adjective*

heritage ⓘ *noun* **1** something inherited. **2** anything from the past, considered as the inheritance of present-day society.

hermaphrodite [her-**maf**-roe-dite] *noun* animal, plant, or person with both male and female reproductive organs.

hermetic *adjective* sealed so as to be airtight. **hermetically** *adverb*

hermit ⓘ *noun* person living in solitude, esp. for religious reasons. **hermitage** *noun* home of a hermit. **hermit crab** small crab that lives in the shells of other shellfish.

hernia *noun* protrusion of an organ or part through the lining of the surrounding body cavity.

hero ⓘ *noun, pl* **heroes 1** principal character in a film, book, etc. **2** man greatly admired for his exceptional qualities or achievements. **heroine** *n fem* **heroic** *adjective* **1** courageous. **2** of or like a hero. **heroics** *plural noun* extravagant behaviour. **heroically** *adverb* **heroism** [**herr**-oh-izz-um] *noun*

heroin *noun* highly addictive drug derived from morphine.

heron *noun* long-legged wading bird.

herpes [**her**-peez] *noun* any of several inflammatory skin diseases, including shingles and cold sores.

Herr [hair] *noun, pl* **Herren** German term of address equivalent to *Mr*.

herring *noun* important food fish of northern seas. **herringbone** *noun* pattern of zigzag lines.

hers *pronoun* something belonging to her.

herself *pronoun* emphatic or reflexive form of SHE *or* HER.

hertz *noun, pl* **hertz** *Physics* unit of frequency.

hesitate ⓘ *verb* **1** be slow or uncertain in doing something. **2** be reluctant (to do something). **hesitation** *noun* **hesitant** *adjective* undecided or wavering. **hesitantly** *adverb* **hesitancy** *noun*

———————— T H E S A U R U S ————————

herd *noun* **1** = **flock**, drove **2** = **crowd**, collection, horde, mass, mob, multitude, swarm, throng ◆*verb* **3** = **congregate**, assemble, collect, flock, gather, huddle, muster, rally

hereafter *adverb* = **in future**, from now on, hence, henceforth, henceforward **the hereafter** = **afterlife**, life after death, next world

hereditary *adjective* **1** = **genetic**, inborn, inbred, inheritable, transmissible **2** = **inherited**, ancestral, traditional

heredity *noun* = **genetics**, constitution, genetic make-up, inheritance

heresy *noun* = **unorthodoxy**, apostasy, dissidence, heterodoxy, iconoclasm

heretic *noun* = **nonconformist**, apostate, dissenter, dissident, renegade, revisionist

heretical *adjective* = **unorthodox**, heterodox,

iconoclastic, idolatrous, impious, revisionist

heritage *noun* **1** = **inheritance**, bequest, birthright, endowment, legacy

hermit *noun* = **recluse**, anchorite, loner (*inf*), monk

hero *noun* **1** = **leading man**, protagonist **2** = **idol**, champion, conqueror, star, superstar, victor

heroic *adjective* **1** = **courageous**, brave, daring, fearless, gallant, intrepid, lion-hearted, valiant OPPOSITE **cowardly**

heroine *noun* **1** = **leading lady**, diva, prima donna, protagonist

heroism *noun* **1** = **bravery**, courage, courageousness, fearlessness, gallantry, intrepidity, spirit, valour

hesitant *adjective* = **uncertain**, diffident, doubtful, half-hearted, halting, irresolute, reluctant, unsure, vacillating, wavering

hessian *noun* coarse jute fabric.

hetero- *combining form* other, different, e.g. *heterosexual.*

heterodox *adjective* differing from accepted doctrines or beliefs. **heterodoxy** *noun*

heterogeneous [het-er-oh-**jean**-ee-uss] *adjective* composed of diverse elements.

heterogeneity *noun*

heterosexual *noun, adjective* (person) sexually attracted to members of the opposite sex. **heterosexuality** *noun*

het up *adjective Informal* agitated or anxious.

heuristic [**hew**-rist-ik] *adjective* involving learning by investigation.

hew ⊕ *verb* **hewing, hewed, hewed** *or* **hewn 1** cut with an axe. **2** carve from a substance.

hexagon *noun* geometrical figure with six sides. **hexagonal** *adjective*

hexagram *noun* star formed by extending the sides of a regular hexagon to meet at six points.

hey *interjection* expression of surprise or for catching attention. **hey presto!** exclamation used by conjurors at the climax of a trick.

heyday ⊕ *noun* time of greatest success, prime.

Hf *Chem* hafnium.

Hg *Chem* mercury.

HGV (formerly) heavy goods vehicle.

hi *interjection Informal* hello.

HI Hawaii.

hiatus ⊕ [hie-**ay**-tuss] *noun, pl* **-tuses, -tus** pause or interruption in continuity.

hibernate *verb* (of an animal) pass the winter as if in a deep sleep. **hibernation** *noun*

Hibernian *adjective Poetic* Irish.

hibiscus *noun, pl* **-cuses** tropical plant with large brightly coloured flowers.

hiccup, hiccough *noun* **1** spasm of the breathing organs with a sharp coughlike sound. **2** *Informal* small problem, hitch. ◆ *verb* **3** make a hiccup.

hick *noun US & Aust informal* unsophisticated country person.

hickory *noun, pl* **-ries 1** N American nut-bearing tree. **2** its wood.

hide[1] ⊕ *verb* **hiding, hid, hidden 1** put (oneself or an object) somewhere difficult to see or find. **2** keep secret. ◆ *noun* **3** place of concealment, esp. for a bird-watcher. **hiding** *noun* state of concealment, e.g. *in hiding.*

hidden agenda motives or intentions concealed from others who might object to them. **hideaway** *noun* private place. **hide-out** *noun* place to hide in.

hide[2] ⊕ *noun* skin of an animal. **hiding** *noun Slang* severe beating. **hidebound** *adjective* unwilling to accept new ideas.

hideous ⊕ [**hid**-ee-uss] *adjective* ugly, revolting. **hideously** *adverb*

hie *verb* **hying** *or* **hieing, hied** *Obs* hurry.

hierarchy ⊕ [**hire**-ark-ee] *noun, pl* **-chies** system of people or things arranged in a graded order. **hierarchical** *adjective*

hieroglyphic [hire-oh-**gliff**-ik] *adjective* **1** of a form of writing using picture symbols, as used in ancient Egypt. ◆ *noun* **2** symbol that is difficult to decipher. **3** (also **hieroglyph**) symbol representing an object, idea, or sound.

hi-fi *noun* **1** set of high-quality sound-

H

——————— T H E S A U R U S ———————

OPPOSITE⟩ confident

hesitate *verb* **1** = **waver**, delay, dither, doubt, hum and haw, pause, vacillate, wait OPPOSITE⟩ **decide. 2** = **be reluctant**, balk, be unwilling, demur, hang back, scruple, shrink from, think twice OPPOSITE⟩ **resolve**

hesitation *noun* **1** = **indecision**, delay, doubt, hesitancy, irresolution, uncertainty, vacillation **2** = **reluctance**, misgiving(s), qualm(s), scruple(s), unwillingness

hew *verb* **1** = **cut**, axe, chop, hack, lop, split **2** = **carve**, fashion, form, make, model, sculpt, sculpture, shape, smooth

heyday *noun* = **prime**, bloom, pink, prime of life, salad days

hiatus *noun* = **pause**, break, discontinuity, gap, interruption, interval, respite, space

hidden *adjective* = **concealed**, clandestine, covert, latent, secret, under wraps, unseen, veiled

hide[1] *verb* **1 a** = **go into hiding**, go to ground, go underground, hole up, lie low, take cover **b** = **conceal**, camouflage, cloak, cover, disguise, mask, obscure, secrete, shroud, stash (*inf*), veil OPPOSITE⟩ **display. 2** = **suppress**, draw a veil over, hush up, keep dark, keep secret, keep under one's hat, withhold OPPOSITE⟩ **reveal**

hide[2] *noun* = **skin**, pelt

hidebound *adjective* = **conventional**, narrow-minded, rigid, set in one's ways, strait-laced, ultraconservative OPPOSITE⟩ **broad-minded**

hideous *adjective* = **ugly**, ghastly, grim, grisly, grotesque, gruesome, monstrous, repulsive, revolting, unsightly OPPOSITE⟩ **beautiful**

hide-out *noun* = **hiding place**, den, hideaway, lair, shelter

hiding *noun* = **beating**, drubbing, licking (*inf*), spanking, thrashing, walloping (*inf*), whipping

hierarchy *noun* = **grading**, pecking order, ranking

reproducing equipment. ◆ *adjective* **2** high-fidelity.

higgledy-piggledy *adverb, adjective* in a muddle.

high ❶ *adjective* **1** of a great height. **2** far above ground or sea level. **3** being at its peak. **4** greater than usual in intensity or amount. **5** (of a sound) acute in pitch. **6** (of food) slightly decomposed. **7** of great importance, quality, or rank. **8** *Informal* under the influence of alcohol or drugs. ◆ *adverb* **9** at or to a high level. ◆ *noun* **10 on a high** *Informal* very excited and happy, (as if) intoxicated by alcohol or drugs. **highly** *adverb* **highly strung** nervous and easily upset. **Highness** *noun* title used to address or refer to a royal person. **High-Church** *adjective* belonging to a section within the Church of England stressing the importance of ceremony and ritual. **high commissioner** senior diplomatic representative sent by one Commonwealth country to another. **higher education** education at colleges and universities. **high explosive** extremely powerful chemical explosive, such as TNT. **high-fidelity** *adjective* able to reproduce sound with little or no distortion. **high-flown** *adjective* (of language) extravagant or pretentious. **high-handed** *adjective* excessively forceful. **high jump** athletic event in which competitors attempt to jump over a high bar. **high-minded** *adjective* having high moral principles. **high-powered** *adjective* dynamic and energetic. **high priest** head of a cult. **high priestess** *n fem* **high-rise** *adjective* (of a building) having many storeys. **high school** secondary school. **high-spirited** *adjective* lively, fun-loving. **high**

tea early evening meal consisting of a cooked dish, bread, cakes, and tea. **high technology** use of advanced electronic processes in industry. **high time** latest possible time.

highball *noun US* tall drink of whiskey with soda water or ginger ale and ice.

highbrow ❶ *adjective, noun* intellectual and serious (person).

highchair *noun* long-legged chair with a tray attached, used by a very young child at mealtimes.

highfalutin [hie-fa-**loot**-in] *adjective Informal* pompous or pretentious.

Highland *adjective* of the Highlands, a mountainous region of N Scotland. **Highlander** *noun*

highlands *plural noun* area of high ground.

highlight ❶ *noun* **1** outstanding part or feature. **2** light-toned area in a painting or photograph. **3** lightened streak in the hair. ◆ *verb* **4** give emphasis to.

highway *noun US & Canad* main road for fast-moving traffic. **Highway Code** regulations and recommendations applying to all road users. **highwayman** *noun* (formerly) robber, usu. on horseback, who robbed travellers at gunpoint.

hijack ❶ *verb* seize control of (an aircraft or other vehicle) while travelling. **hijacker** *noun* **hijacking** *noun*

hike ❶ *noun* **1** long walk in the country, esp. for pleasure. **2** rise in price. ◆ *verb* **3** go for a long walk. **4** (foll. by *up*) pull (up) or raise. **hiker** *noun*

hilarious ❶ *adjective* very funny. **hilariously** *adverb* **hilarity** *noun*

———————————— THESAURUS ————————————

high *adjective* **1, 2** = **tall**, elevated, lofty, soaring, steep, towering OPPOSITE **short**. **4** = **extreme**, excessive, extraordinary, great, intensified, sharp, strong OPPOSITE **low**. **5** = **high-pitched**, acute, penetrating, piercing, piping, sharp, shrill, strident OPPOSITE **deep**. **7** = **important**, arch, chief, eminent, exalted, powerful, superior, skookum (*Canad*) OPPOSITE **insignificant**. **8** *Inf* = **intoxicated**, stoned (*sl*), tripping (*inf*) ◆*adverb* **9** = **aloft**, at great height, far up, way up

highbrow *adjective* = **intellectual**, bookish, cultivated, cultured, sophisticated OPPOSITE **unintellectual** ◆*noun* = **intellectual**, aesthete, egghead (*inf*), scholar

high-flown *adjective* = **extravagant**, elaborate, exaggerated, florid, grandiose, inflated, lofty, overblown, pretentious OPPOSITE **straightforward**

high-handed *adjective* = **dictatorial**, despotic, domineering, imperious, oppressive, overbearing, tyrannical, wilful

highlight *noun* **1** = **high point**, climax, feature, focal point, focus, high spot, peak OPPOSITE **low point** ◆*verb* **4** = **emphasize**, accent, accentuate, bring to the fore, show up, spotlight, stress, underline OPPOSITE **play down**

highly *adverb* **4** = **extremely**, exceptionally, greatly, immensely, tremendously, vastly, very, very much **highly strung** = **nervous**, edgy, excitable, neurotic, sensitive, stressed, temperamental, tense, wired (*sl*)

hijack *verb* = **seize**, commandeer, expropriate, take over

hike *noun* **1** = **walk**, march, ramble, tramp, trek ◆*verb* **3** = **walk**, back-pack, ramble, tramp **4** (foll. by *up*) = **raise**, hitch up, jack up, lift, pull

hill ⊙ *noun* raised part of the earth's surface, less high than a mountain. **hilly** *adjective* **hillier, hilliest**. **hillock** *noun* small hill. **hillbilly** *noun, pl* **-billies** *US* unsophisticated country person.

hilt ⊙ *noun* handle of a sword or knife. **to the hilt, up to the hilt** to the full.

him *pronoun* refers to a male person or animal when the object of a sentence or clause.

himself *pronoun* emphatic or reflexive form of HE *or* HIM.

hind[1] ⊙ *adjective* **hinder, hindmost** situated at the back. **hindsight** *noun* ability to understand, after something has happened, what should have been done.

hind[2] *noun* female deer.

hinder ⊙ *verb* get in the way of. **hindrance** *noun*

Hinduism *noun* dominant religion of India, which involves the worship of many gods and a belief in reincarnation. **Hindu** *noun* **1** person who practises Hinduism. ◆ *adjective* **2** of Hinduism. **Hindi** *noun* language of N central India. **Hindustani** *noun* group of N Indian languages including Hindi and Urdu.

hinge ⊙ *noun* **1** device for holding together two parts so that one can swing freely. ◆ *verb* **2** (foll. by *on*) depend (on). **3** fit a hinge to.

hint ⊙ *noun* **1** indirect suggestion. **2** piece of advice. **3** small amount. ◆ *verb* **4** suggest indirectly.

hinterland *noun* land lying behind a coast or near a city, esp. a port.

hip[1] *noun* either side of the body between the waist and the thigh.

hip[2] *noun* rosehip.

hip[3] *adjective* **hipper, hippest** *Slang* aware of or following the latest trends.

hip-hop *noun* pop-culture movement of the 1980s, comprising rap music, graffiti, and break dancing.

hippie *adjective, noun* same as HIPPY.

hippo *noun, pl* **-pos** *Informal* hippopotamus.

Hippocratic oath *noun* oath taken by doctors to observe a code of medical ethics.

hippodrome *noun* music hall, variety theatre, or circus.

hippopotamus *noun, pl* **-muses, -mi** large African mammal with thick wrinkled skin, living near rivers.

hippy ⊙ *adjective, noun, pl* **-pies** (esp. in the 1960s) (of) a person whose behaviour and dress imply a rejection of conventional values.

hire ⊙ *verb* **1** pay to have temporary use of. **2** employ for wages. ◆ *noun* **3** hiring. **for hire** available to be hired. **hireling** *noun* person who works only for wages. **hire-purchase** *noun* system of purchase by which the buyer pays for goods by instalments.

hirsute [her-suit] *adjective* hairy.

his *pronoun, adjective* (something) belonging to him.

Hispanic *adjective* Spanish or Latin-American.

hiss ⊙ *noun* **1** sound like that of a long *s* (as an expression of contempt). ◆ *verb* **2** utter a hiss. **3** show derision or anger towards.

histamine [hiss-ta-meen] *noun* substance released by the body tissues in allergic reactions.

histogram *noun* statistical graph in which the frequency of values is represented by vertical bars of varying heights and widths.

——————— THESAURUS ———————

up

hilarious *adjective* =**funny**, amusing, comical, entertaining, humorous, rollicking, side-splitting, uproarious OPPOSITE **serious**

hilarity *noun* =**merriment**, amusement, exhilaration, glee, high spirits, jollity, laughter, mirth

hill *noun* =**mount**, fell, height, hillock, hilltop, knoll, mound, tor

hillock *noun* =**mound**, hummock, knoll

hilly *adjective* =**mountainous**, rolling, undulating

hilt *noun* =**handle**, grip, haft, handgrip

hinder *verb* =**obstruct**, block, check, delay, encumber, frustrate, hamper, handicap, hold up *or* back, impede, interrupt, stop OPPOSITE **help**

hinder, hindmost *adjective* =**last**, final, furthest, furthest behind, rearmost, trailing

hindrance *noun* =**obstacle**, barrier, deterrent,

difficulty, drawback, handicap, hitch, impediment, obstruction, restriction, snag, stumbling block OPPOSITE **help**

hinge *verb* **2** (foll. by *on*) =**depend on**, be contingent on, hang on, pivot on, rest on, revolve around, turn on

hint *noun* **1** =**indication**, allusion, clue, implication, innuendo, insinuation, intimation, suggestion **2** =**advice**, help, pointer, suggestion, tip **3** =**trace**, dash, suggestion, suspicion, tinge, touch, undertone ◆*verb* **4** =**suggest**, imply, indicate, insinuate, intimate

hippy *noun* =**bohemian**, beatnik, dropout

hire *verb* **1** =**rent**, charter, engage, lease, let **2** =**employ**, appoint, commission, engage, sign up, take on ◆*noun* **3** =**rental**

hiss *noun* **1 a** =**sibilation**, buzz, hissing **b** =**catcall**, boo, jeer ◆*verb* **2** =**whistle**, sibilate, wheeze, whirr, whiz **3** =**jeer**, boo, deride, hoot,

histology *noun* study of the tissues of an animal or plant. **histological** *adjective*

history ❶ *noun, pl* **-ries 1** (record or account of) past events and developments. **2** study of these. **3** record of someone's past. **historian** *noun* writer of history. **historic** *adjective* famous or significant in history. **historical** *adjective* **1** occurring in the past. **2** based on history. **historically** *adverb*

histrionic *adjective* excessively dramatic. **histrionics** *plural noun* excessively dramatic behaviour.

hit ❶ *verb* **hitting, hit 1** strike, touch forcefully. **2** come into violent contact with. **3** affect badly. **4** reach (a point or place). ♦ *noun* **5** hitting. **6** successful record, film, etc. **7** *Computers* single visit to a website. **hit it off** *Informal* get on well together. **hit the road** *Informal* start a journey. **hit-and-miss, hit-or-miss** *adjective* sometimes successful and sometimes not. **hit-and-run** *adjective* denoting a motor-vehicle accident in which a driver drives away without stopping. **hit man** hired assassin. **hit on** *verb* think of (an idea).

hitch ❶ *noun* **1** minor problem. ♦ *verb* **2** *Informal* obtain (a lift) by hitchhiking. **3** fasten with a knot or tie. **4** (foll. by *up*) pull up with a jerk. **get hitched** *Slang* get married. **hitchhike** *verb* travel by obtaining free lifts. **hitchhiker** *noun*

hi-tech *adjective* using sophisticated technology.

hither ❶ *adverb* *Old-fashioned* to or towards this place. **hitherto** *adverb* until this time.

HIV human immunodeficiency virus, the cause of AIDS.

hive *noun* same as BEEHIVE. **hive of activity** place where people are very busy. **hive off** *verb* separate from a larger group.

hives *noun* allergic reaction in which itchy red or whitish patches appear on the skin.

HM Her (or His) Majesty.

HMI Her (or His) Majesty's Inspector (of schools).

HMS Her (or His) Majesty's Ship.

HMSO Her (or His) Majesty's Stationery Office.

HNC Higher National Certificate.

HND Higher National Diploma.

Ho *Chem* holmium.

hoard ❶ *noun* **1** store hidden away for future use. ♦ *verb* **2** save or store. **hoarder** *noun*

hoarding *noun* large board for displaying advertisements.

hoarfrost *noun* white ground frost.

hoarse ❶ *adjective* **1** (of a voice) rough and unclear. **2** having a rough and unclear voice. **hoarsely** *adverb* **hoarseness** *noun*

hoary *adjective* **hoarier, hoariest 1** grey or white(-haired). **2** very old.

hoax ❶ *noun* **1** deception or trick. ♦ *verb* **2** deceive or play a trick upon. **hoaxer** *noun*

hob *noun* flat top part of a cooker, or a

———————————— T H E S A U R U S ————————————

mock

historic *adjective* =**significant**, epoch-making, extraordinary, famous, ground-breaking, momentous, notable, outstanding, remarkable OPPOSITE **unimportant**

historical *adjective* **2** =**factual**, actual, attested, authentic, documented, real OPPOSITE **contemporary**

history *noun* **1 a** =**chronicle**, account, annals, narrative, recital, record, story **b** =**the past**, antiquity, olden days, yesterday, yesteryear

hit *verb* **1** =**strike**, bang, beat, clout (*inf*), knock, slap, smack, thump, wallop (*inf*), whack **2** =**collide with**, bang into, bump, clash with, crash against, run into, smash into **3** =**affect**, damage, devastate, impact on, influence, leave a mark on, overwhelm, touch **4** =**reach**, accomplish, achieve, arrive at, attain, gain ♦*noun* **5** =**stroke**, belt (*inf*), blow, clout (*inf*), knock, rap, slap, smack, wallop (*inf*) **6** =**success**, sensation, smash (*inf*), triumph, winner **hit it off** *Inf* =**get on (well) with**, be on good terms, click (*sl*), get on like a house on fire (*inf*)

hit-and-miss, hit-or-miss *adjective* =**haphazard**, aimless, casual, disorganized, indiscriminate, random, undirected, uneven OPPOSITE **systematic**

hitch *noun* **1** =**problem**, catch, difficulty, drawback, hindrance, hold-up, impediment, obstacle, snag ♦*verb* **2** *Inf* =**hitchhike**, thumb a lift **3** =**fasten**, attach, connect, couple, harness, join, tether, tie **4** (foll. by *up*) =**pull up**, jerk, tug, yank

hitherto *adverb* =**previously**, heretofore, so far, thus far, until now

hit on *verb* =**think up**, arrive at, discover, invent, light upon, strike upon, stumble on

hoard *noun* **1** =**store**, accumulation, cache, fund, pile, reserve, stash, stockpile, supply, treasure-trove ♦*verb* **2** =**save**, accumulate, amass, collect, gather, lay up, put by, stash away (*inf*), stockpile, store

hoarse *adjective* **1** =**rough**, croaky, grating, gravelly, gruff, guttural, husky, rasping, raucous, throaty OPPOSITE **clear**

hoax *noun* **1** =**trick**, con (*inf*), deception, fraud, practical joke, prank, spoof (*inf*), swindle separate flat surface, containing gas or electric rings for cooking on.

hobble *verb* **1** walk lamely. **2** tie the legs of (a horse) together.

hobby ⊙ *noun, pl* **-bies** activity pursued in one's spare time. **hobbyhorse** *noun* **1** favourite topic. **2** toy horse.

hobgoblin *noun* mischievous goblin.

hobnail boots *plural noun* heavy boots with short nails in the soles.

hobnob ⊙ *verb* **-nobbing, -nobbed** (foll. by *with*) be on friendly terms (with).

hobo *noun, pl* **-bos** *US & Aust* tramp or vagrant.

Hobson's choice *noun* the choice of taking what is offered or nothing at all.

hock[1] *noun* joint in the back leg of an animal such as a horse that corresponds to the human ankle.

hock[2] *noun* white German wine.

hock[3] *verb Informal* pawn. **in hock** *Informal* in debt.

hockey *noun* **1** team game played on a field with a ball and curved sticks. **2** *US & Canad* ice hockey.

hocus-pocus *noun* trickery.

hod *noun* open wooden box attached to a pole, for carrying bricks or mortar.

hoe *noun* **1** long-handled tool used for loosening soil or weeding. ♦ *verb* **2** scrape or weed with a hoe.

hog *noun* **1** castrated male pig. **2** *Informal* greedy person. ♦ *verb* **hogging, hogged 3** *Informal* take more than one's share of. **go the whole hog** *Slang* do something thoroughly or unreservedly. **hogshead** *noun* large cask.

hogwash *noun Informal* nonsense.

Hogmanay *noun* (in Scotland) New Year's Eve.

ho-ho *interjection* representation of the sound of laughter.

hoick *verb* raise abruptly and sharply.

hoi polloi *noun* the ordinary people.

hoist ⊙ *verb* **1** raise or lift up. ♦ *noun* **2** device for lifting things.

hoity-toity *adjective Informal* arrogant or haughty.

hokum *noun US slang* **1** rubbish, nonsense. **2** stereotyped sentimentality in a film or play.

hold[1] ⊙ *verb* **holding, held 1** keep or support in or with the hands or arms. **2** arrange for (a meeting, party, etc.) to take place. **3** consider to be as specified, e.g. *who are you holding responsible?* **4** maintain in a specified position or state. **5** have the capacity for. **6** *Informal* wait, esp. on the telephone. **7** reserve (a room etc.). **8** restrain or keep back. **9** own, possess. **10** (cause to) remain committed to (a promise etc.). **11** believe. ♦ *noun* **12** act or way of holding. **13** controlling influence. **14** something to hold onto for support. **holder** *noun* **holding** *noun* property, such as land or stocks and shares. **holdall** *noun* large strong travelling bag. **hold forth** *verb* speak for a long time. **hold-up** *noun* **1** armed robbery. **2** delay. **hold up** *verb* **hold with** *verb* approve of, e.g. *I don't hold with this theory.*

hold[2] *noun* cargo compartment in a ship or aircraft.

hole ⊙ *noun* **1** area hollowed out in a solid. **2** opening or hollow. **3** animal's burrow. **4** *Informal* unattractive place. **5** *Informal* difficult situation. ♦ *verb* **6** make holes in. **7** hit (a golf ball) into the target hole. **holey** *adjective* **hole up** *verb Informal* go into hiding.

holiday ⊙ *noun* **1** time spent away from home

———————— T H E S A U R U S ————————

♦*verb* **2** = **deceive**, con (*sl*), dupe, fool, hoodwink, swindle, take in (*inf*), trick

hobby *noun* = **pastime**, diversion, (leisure) activity, leisure pursuit, relaxation

hobnob *verb* (foll. by *with*) = **socialize**, associate, consort, fraternize, hang about, hang out (*inf*), keep company, mingle, mix

hoist *verb* **1** = **raise**, elevate, erect, heave, lift ♦*noun* **2** = **lift**, crane, elevator, winch

hold[1] *verb* **1** = **grasp**, clasp, cling, clutch, cradle, embrace, enfold, grip **2** = **convene**, call, conduct, preside over, run ⟨OPPOSITE⟩ **cancel. 5** = **accommodate**, contain, have a capacity for, seat, take **8** = **restrain**, confine, detain, impound, imprison ⟨OPPOSITE⟩ **release. 9** = **own**, have, keep, maintain, occupy, possess, retain ⟨OPPOSITE⟩ **give. 11** = **consider**, assume, believe, deem, judge, presume, reckon, regard, think ⟨OPPOSITE⟩ **deny** ♦*noun* **12** = **grip**, clasp, grasp **13** = **control**, influence, mana (*NZ*), mastery **14** = **foothold**, footing, support

hold forth *verb* = **speak**, declaim, discourse, go on, lecture, preach, spiel (*inf*), spout (*inf*)

hold-up *noun* **1** = **robbery**, mugging (*inf*), stick-up (*sl, chiefly US*), theft **2** = **delay**, bottleneck, hitch, setback, snag, stoppage, traffic jam, wait

hold up *verb* **1** = **rob**, mug (*inf*), waylay **2** = **delay**, detain, hinder, retard, set back, slow down, stop

hold with *verb* = **approve of**, agree to or with, be in favour of, countenance, subscribe to, support

hole *noun* **1** = **cavity**, cave, cavern, chamber,

for rest or recreation. **2** day or other period of rest from work or studies.

holiness ⊕ *noun* **1** state of being holy. **2** (**H-**) title used to address or refer to the Pope.

holistic *adjective* considering the complete person, physically and mentally, in the treatment of an illness. **holism** *noun*

holler *verb, noun Informal* shout, yell.

hollow ⊕ *adjective* **1** having a hole or space inside. **2** (of a sound) as if echoing in a hollow place. **3** without any real value or worth. ♦ *noun* **4** cavity or space. **5** dip in the land. ♦ *verb* **6** form a hollow in. **hollowly** *adverb* **hollowness** *noun*

holly *noun* evergreen tree with prickly leaves and red berries.

hollyhock *noun* tall garden plant with spikes of colourful flowers.

holmium *noun Chem* silver-white metallic element, the compounds of which are highly magnetic.

holm oak *noun* evergreen oak tree with prickly leaves.

holocaust ⊕ *noun* destruction or loss of life on a massive scale.

hologram *noun* three-dimensional photographic image.

holograph *noun* document handwritten by the author.

holography *noun* science of using lasers to produce holograms. **holographic** *adjective*

holster *noun* leather case for a pistol, hung from a belt.

holt *noun* otter's lair.

holy ⊕ *adjective* **-lier, -liest 1** of God or a god. **2** devout or virtuous. **holier-than-thou** *adjective* self-righteous. **Holy Communion** *Christianity* service in which people take bread and wine in remembrance of the death and

resurrection of Jesus Christ. **Holy Grail** (in medieval legend) the bowl used by Jesus Christ at the Last Supper. **holy orders** status of an ordained Christian minister. **Holy Spirit, Ghost** *Christianity* one of the three aspects of God. **Holy Week** *Christianity* week before Easter.

homage ⊕ *noun* show of respect or honour towards someone or something.

homburg *noun* man's soft felt hat with a dented crown and a stiff upturned brim.

home ⊕ *noun* **1** place where one lives. **2** place where one was born or grew up. **3** institution for the care of the elderly, orphans, etc. ♦ *adjective* **4** of one's home, birthplace, or native country. **5** *Sport* played on one's own ground. ♦ *adverb* **5** to or at home. ♦ *verb* **7** (foll. by *in* or *in on*) direct towards (a point or target). **at home** at ease. **bring home to** make clear to. **home and dry** *Informal* safe or successful.

homeless *adjective* **1** having nowhere to live. ♦ *plural noun* **2** people who have nowhere to live. **homelessness** *noun* **homely** *adjective* **1** simple, ordinary, and comfortable. **2** *US* unattractive. **homeliness** *noun* **home page** *Computers* introductory information about a website with hyperlinks to further pages.

homeward *adjective, adverb* **homewards** *adverb* **home-brew** *noun* beer made at home.

home economics study of subjects concerned with running a home. **home help** person employed by a local authority to do housework in an elderly or disabled person's home.

home-made *adjective* made at home or on the premises. **Home Office** government department responsible for law and order, immigration, and other domestic matters. **Home Secretary** head of the Home Office. **home truths** unpleasant facts told to a person about himself or herself.

———— THESAURUS ————

hollow, pit **2** = **opening**, aperture, breach, crack, fissure, gap, orifice, perforation, puncture, tear, vent **3** = **burrow**, den, earth, lair, shelter **4** *Inf* = **hovel**, dive (*sl*), dump (*inf*), slum **5** *Inf* = **predicament**, dilemma, fix (*inf*), hot water (*inf*), jam (*inf*), mess, scrape (*inf*), spot (*inf*), tight spot

holiday *noun* **1** = **vacation**, break, leave, recess, time off **2** = **festival**, celebration, feast, fete, gala

holiness *noun* **1** = **sanctity**, divinity, godliness, piety, purity, righteousness, sacredness, saintliness, spirituality

hollow *adjective* **1** = **empty**, unfilled, vacant, void OPPOSITE> **solid. 2** = **toneless**, deep, dull, low, muted, reverberant OPPOSITE> **vibrant. 3**

= **worthless**, fruitless, futile, meaningless, pointless, useless, vain OPPOSITE> **valuable**
♦*noun* **4** = **cavity**, basin, bowl, crater, depression, hole, pit, trough OPPOSITE> **mound. 5** = **valley**, dale, dell, dingle, glen OPPOSITE> **hill**
♦*verb* **6** = **scoop**, dig, excavate, gouge

holocaust *noun* = **genocide**, annihilation, conflagration, destruction, devastation, massacre

holy *adjective* **1** = **sacred**, blessed, consecrated, hallowed, sacrosanct, sanctified, venerable OPPOSITE> **unholy. 2** = **devout**, god-fearing, godly, pious, pure, religious, righteous, saintly, virtuous OPPOSITE> **sinful**

homage *noun* = **respect**, adoration, adulation, deference, devotion, honour, reverence,

homeland ❶ *noun* country from which a person's ancestors came.

homeopathy [home-ee-**op**-ath-ee] *noun* treatment of disease by small doses of a drug that produces symptoms of the disease in healthy people. **homeopath** *noun* person who practises homeopathy. **homeopathic** [home-ee-oh-**path**-ik] *adjective*

homesick *adjective* sad because missing one's home and family. **homesickness** *noun*

homestead *noun* **1** a house or estate and the adjoining land and buildings, esp. on a farm. **2** land assigned to a N American settler.

homework *noun* school work done at home.

homicide ❶ *noun* **1** killing of a human being. **2** person who kills someone. **homicidal** *adjective*

homily ❶ *noun, pl* **-lies** speech telling people how they should behave.

homing pigeon *noun* pigeon trained to return home after travelling great distances, kept for racing.

hominid *noun* man or any extinct forerunner of man.

hominoid *adjective, noun* manlike (animal).

homo- *combining form* same, like, e.g. *homosexual.*

homogeneous ❶ [home-oh-**jean**-ee-uss] *adjective* formed of similar parts. **homogeneity** *noun* **homogenize** *verb* **1** break up fat globules in (milk or cream) to distribute them evenly. **2**

make homogeneous.

homograph *noun* word spelt the same as another, but with a different meaning.

homologous [hom-**ol**-log-uss] *adjective* having a related or similar position or structure.

homonym *noun* word spelt or pronounced the same as another, but with a different meaning.

homophobia *noun* hatred or fear of homosexuals. **homophobic** *adjective*

homophone *noun* word pronounced the same as another, but with a different meaning or spelling.

Homo sapiens [hoe-moh **sap**-ee-enz] *noun* human beings as a species.

homosexual *noun, adjective* (person) sexually attracted to members of the same sex. **homosexuality** *noun*

Hon. Honourable.

hone ❶ *verb* sharpen.

honest ❶ *adjective* **1** truthful and moral. **2** open and sincere. **honestly** *adverb* **honesty** *noun* **1** quality of being honest. **2** plant with silvery seed pods.

honey *noun* **1** sweet edible sticky substance made by bees from nectar. **2** term of endearment. **honeyed** *adjective Poetic* flattering or soothing, e.g. *honeyed words.* **honeycomb** *noun* waxy structure of six-sided cells in which honey is stored by bees in a beehive.

honeydew melon melon with a yellow skin

H

———————— THESAURUS ————————

worship OPPOSITE **contempt**

home *noun* **1** = **dwelling**, abode, domicile, habitation, house, pad (*sl*), residence **2** = **birthplace**, home town ♦*adjective* **4** = **domestic**, familiar, internal, local, native **at home** = **at ease**, comfortable, familiar, relaxed

bring home to = **make clear**, drive home, emphasize, impress upon, press home

homeland *noun* = **native land**, country of origin, fatherland, mother country, motherland

homeless *adjective* **1** = **destitute**, displaced, dispossessed, down-and-out ♦*plural noun* **2** = **vagrants**, squatters

homely *adjective* **1** = **comfortable**, cosy, friendly, homespun, modest, ordinary, plain, simple, welcoming OPPOSITE **elaborate**

homicidal *adjective* = **murderous**, deadly, lethal, maniacal, mortal

homicide *noun* **1** = **murder**, bloodshed, killing, manslaughter, slaying **2** = **murderer**, killer, slayer

homily *noun* = **sermon**, address, discourse, lecture, preaching

homogeneity *noun* = **uniformity**,

consistency, correspondence, sameness, similarity

homogeneous *adjective* = **uniform**, akin, alike, analogous, comparable, consistent, identical, similar, unvarying

homosexual *noun* = **gay**, lesbian ♦*adjective* = **gay**, lesbian

hone *verb* = **sharpen**, edge, file, grind, point, polish, whet

honest *adjective* **1** = **trustworthy**, ethical, honourable, law-abiding, reputable, scrupulous, truthful, upright, virtuous OPPOSITE **dishonest**. **2** = **open**, candid, direct, forthright, frank, plain, sincere, upfront (*inf*) OPPOSITE **false**

honestly *adverb* **1** = **ethically**, by fair means, cleanly, honourably, lawfully, legally **2** = **frankly**, candidly, in all sincerity, plainly, straight (out), to one's face, truthfully

honesty *noun* **1** = **integrity**, honour, incorruptibility, morality, probity, rectitude, scrupulousness, trustworthiness, truthfulness, uprightness, virtue **2** = **frankness**, bluntness, candour, openness, outspokenness, sincerity, straightforwardness

H

and sweet pale flesh. **honey-eater** *noun* small Australasian songbird with a brushlike tongue used for extracting nectar from flowers.
honeymoon *noun* holiday taken by a newly married couple. **honeysuckle** *noun* **1** climbing shrub with sweet-smelling flowers. **2** Australian tree or shrub with flowers in dense spikes.
honk *noun* **1** sound made by a car horn. **2** sound made by a goose. ♦ *verb* **3** (cause to) make this sound.
honour ⊕ *noun* **1** sense of honesty and fairness. **2** (award given out of) respect. **3** pleasure or privilege. ♦ *plural* **4** university degree of a higher standard than an ordinary degree. ♦ *verb* **5** give praise and attention to. **6** give an award to (someone) out of respect. **7** accept or pay (a cheque or bill). **8** keep (a promise). **do the honours** act as host or hostess by pouring drinks or giving out food.
honourable *adjective* **1** worthy of respect or esteem. **2** (H-) denoting a title of respect placed before the names of some members of the nobility, judges, etc. **honourably** *adverb*
honorary *adjective* **1** held or given only as an honour. **2** unpaid. **honorific** *adjective* showing respect.
hooch [rhymes with **smooch**] *noun US slang* alcoholic drink, esp. illicitly distilled spirits.
hood¹ *noun* **1** head covering, often attached to a coat or jacket. **2** folding roof of a convertible car or a pram. **3** *US & Aust* car bonnet. **hooded** *adjective* **1** (of a garment) having a hood. **2** (of eyes) having heavy eyelids that appear to be half-closed.
hood² *noun Slang* hoodlum.
hoodlum *noun Slang* violent criminal, gangster.

hoodoo *noun, pl* **-doos** (cause of) bad luck.
hoodwink ⊕ *verb* trick, deceive.
hooey *noun Slang* nonsense.
hoof *noun, pl* **hooves, hoofs** horny covering of the foot of a horse, deer, etc. **hoof it** *Slang* walk.
hoo-ha *noun* fuss or commotion.
hook ⊕ *noun* **1** curved piece of metal, plastic, etc., used to hang, hold, or pull something. **2** short swinging punch. ♦ *verb* **3** fasten or catch (as if) with a hook. **hooked** *adjective* **1** bent like a hook. **2** (foll. by *on*) *Slang* addicted (to) or obsessed (with). **hooker** *noun* **1** *Slang* prostitute. **2** *Rugby* player who uses his feet to get the ball in a scrum. **hook-up** *noun* linking of radio or television stations. **hookworm** *noun* blood-sucking worm with hooked mouthparts.
hookah *noun* oriental pipe in which smoke is drawn through water and a long tube.
hooligan ⊕ *noun* rowdy young person.
hooliganism *noun*
hoon *noun Aust & NZ slang* loutish youth who drives irresponsibly.
hoop ⊕ *noun* rigid circular band, used esp. as a child's toy or for animals to jump through in the circus. **hoop pine** Australian tree or shrub with flowers in dense spikes. **jump, be put through the hoops** go through an ordeal or test.
hoopla *noun* fairground game in which hoops are thrown over objects in an attempt to win them.
hoopoe [**hoop**-oo] *noun* bird with a pinkish-brown plumage and a fanlike crest.
hooray *interjection* same as HURRAH.
hoot ⊕ *noun* **1** sound of a car horn. **2** cry of an owl. **3** cry of derision. **4** *Informal* amusing

———— T H E S A U R U S ————

honorary *adjective* **1** = **nominal**, complimentary, in name *or* title only, titular, unofficial **2** = **unpaid**
honour *noun* **1** = **integrity**, decency, fairness, goodness, honesty, morality, probity, rectitude OPPOSITE dishonour. **2 a** = **tribute**, accolade, commendation, homage, praise, recognition OPPOSITE contempt. **b** = **prestige**, credit, dignity, distinction, fame, glory, renown, reputation, respect OPPOSITE disgrace. **3** = **privilege**, compliment, credit, pleasure ♦*verb* **5** = **respect**, adore, appreciate, esteem, prize, value OPPOSITE scorn. **6** = **acclaim**, commemorate, commend, decorate, praise OPPOSITE scorn. **7** = **pay**, accept, acknowledge, pass, take OPPOSITE refuse. **8** = **fulfil**, be true to, carry out, discharge, keep, live up to, observe

honourable *adjective* **1** = **respected**, creditable, estimable, reputable, respectable, virtuous
hoodwink *verb* = **deceive**, con (*inf*), delude, dupe, fool, mislead, swindle, trick
hook *noun* **1** = **fastener**, catch, clasp, link, peg ♦*verb* **3 a** = **fasten**, clasp, fix, secure **b** = **catch**, ensnare, entrap, snare, trap
hooked *adjective* **1** = **bent**, aquiline, curved, hook-shaped **2** (foll. by *on*) *Sl* = **addicted**, devoted, enamoured, obsessed, taken, turned on (*sl*)
hooligan *noun* = **delinquent**, lager lout, ruffian, vandal, yob *or* yobbo (*Brit sl*)
hooliganism *noun* = **delinquency**, disorder, loutishness, rowdiness, vandalism, violence
hoop *noun* = **ring**, band, circlet, girdle, loop, round, wheel

person or thing. ◆ *verb* **5** sound (a car horn). **6** jeer or yell contemptuously (at someone).

hooter *noun* **1** device that hoots. **2** *Slang* nose.

Hoover *noun* **1** ® vacuum cleaner. ◆ *verb* **2** (h-) clean with a vacuum cleaner.

hooves *noun* a plural of HOOF.

hop¹ ⊙ *verb* **hopping, hopped 1** jump on one foot. **2** move in short jumps. **3** *Informal* move quickly. ◆ *noun* **4** instance of hopping. **5** *Informal* dance. **6** short journey, esp. by air. **hop it** *Slang* go away. **catch someone on the hop** *Informal* catch someone unprepared.

hop² *noun* (often pl) climbing plant, the dried flowers of which are used to make beer.

hope ⊙ *verb* **1** want (something) to happen or be true. ◆ *noun* **2** expectation of something desired. **3** thing that gives cause for hope or is desired. **hopeful** *adjective* **1** having, expressing, or inspiring hope. ◆ *noun* **2** person considered to be on the brink of success. **hopefully** *adverb* **1** in a hopeful manner. **2** it is hoped. **hopefulness** *noun* **hopeless** *adjective* **hopelessly** *adverb* **hopelessness** *noun*

hopper *noun* container for storing substances such as grain or sand.

hopscotch *noun* children's game of hopping in a pattern drawn on the ground.

horde ⊙ *noun* large crowd.

horizon ⊙ *noun* **1** apparent line that divides the earth and the sky. ◆ *plural* **2** limits of scope, interest, or knowledge. **horizontal** *adjective* parallel to the horizon, level, flat.

horizontal ⊙ *adjective* parallel to the horizon, level, flat. **horizontally** *adverb*

hormone *noun* **1** substance secreted by certain glands which stimulates certain organs of the body. **2** synthetic substance with the same effect. **hormonal** *adjective*

horn *noun* **1** one of a pair of bony growths sticking out of the heads of cattle, sheep, etc. **2** substance of which horns are made. **3** musical instrument with a tube or pipe of brass fitted with a mouthpiece. **4** device on a vehicle sounded as a warning. **horned** *adjective* **horny** *adjective* **hornier, horniest 1** of or like horn. **2** *Slang* (easily) sexually aroused. **hornbeam** *noun* tree with smooth grey bark. **hornbill** *noun* bird with a bony growth on its large beak.

hornpipe *noun* (music for) a solo dance, traditionally performed by sailors.

hornblende *noun* mineral containing aluminium, calcium, sodium, magnesium, and iron.

hornet *noun* large wasp with a severe sting.

horoscope *noun* **1** prediction of a person's future based on the positions of the planets, sun, and moon at his or her birth. **2** diagram of the positions of the planets, sun, and moon at a particular time and place.

horrendous *adjective* very unpleasant and shocking. **horrendously** *adverb*

horrible ⊙ *adjective* **1** disagreeable, unpleasant. **2** causing horror. **horribly** *adverb*

horrid ⊙ *adjective* **1** disagreeable, unpleasant. **2** *Informal* nasty.

horrify ⊙ *verb* **-fying, -fied** cause to feel horror or shock. **horrifying** *adjective* **horrifyingly** *adverb* **horrific** *adjective* causing horror. **horrifically** *adverb*

horror ⊙ *noun* (thing or person causing) terror

H

—————————— THESAURUS ——————————

hoot *noun* **1** = **toot 2** = **cry**, call **3** = **catcall**, boo, hiss, jeer ◆*verb* **6** = **jeer**, boo, hiss, howl down

hop¹ *verb* **2** = **jump**, bound, caper, leap, skip, spring, trip, vault ◆*noun* **4** = **jump**, bounce, bound, leap, skip, spring, step, vault

hope *verb* **1** = **desire**, aspire, cross one's fingers, long, look forward to, set one's heart on OPPOSITE despair ◆*noun* **2** = **belief**, ambition, assumption, confidence, desire, dream, expectation, longing OPPOSITE despair

hopeful *adjective* **1 a** = **optimistic**, buoyant, confident, expectant, looking forward to, sanguine OPPOSITE despairing. **b** = **promising**, auspicious, bright, encouraging, heartening, reassuring, rosy OPPOSITE unpromising

hopefully *adverb* **1** = **optimistically**, confidently, expectantly

hopeless *adjective* = **impossible**, futile, no-win, pointless, unattainable, useless, vain

OPPOSITE **hopeful**

horde *noun* = **crowd**, band, drove, gang, host, mob, multitude, pack, swarm, throng

horizon *noun* **1** = **skyline**, vista

horizontal *adjective* = **level**, flat, parallel

horrible *adjective* **1** = **dreadful**, awful, cruel, disagreeable, horrid, mean, nasty, terrible, unpleasant OPPOSITE **wonderful**. **2** = **terrifying**, appalling, dreadful, frightful, ghastly, grim, grisly, gruesome, hideous, repulsive, revolting, shocking

horrid *adjective* **1** = **unpleasant**, awful, disagreeable, dreadful, horrible, terrible **2** *Inf* = **unkind**, beastly (inf), cruel, mean, nasty

horrific *adjective* = **horrifying**, appalling, awful, dreadful, frightful, ghastly, grisly, horrendous, shocking, terrifying

horrify *verb* = **shock**, alarm, appal, dismay, frighten, intimidate, make one's hair stand on end, outrage, petrify, scare, sicken, terrify or hatred. **horrible** *adjective* disagreeable, unpleasant.

hors d'oeuvre [or durv] *noun* appetizer served before a main meal.

horse ⊕ *noun* **1** large animal with hooves, a mane, and a tail, used for riding and pulling carts etc. **2** piece of gymnastic equipment used for vaulting over. **(straight) from the horse's mouth** from the original source. **horsey, horsy** *adjective* **horsier, horsiest 1** very keen on horses. **2** of or like a horse. **horse around** *verb Informal* play roughly or boisterously. **horsebox** *noun* trailer used for transporting horses. **horse chestnut 1** tree with broad leaves and inedible large brown shiny nuts in spiky cases. **2** the nut. **horsefly** *noun* large bloodsucking fly. **horsehair** *noun* hair from the tail or mane of a horse. **horse laugh** loud coarse laugh. **horseman, horsewoman** *noun* **1** person skilled in riding. **2** person riding a horse. **horsemanship** *noun* **horseplay** *noun* rough or rowdy play. **horsepower** *noun* unit of power (equivalent to 745.7 watts), used to measure the power of an engine. **horseradish** *noun* strong-tasting root of a plant, usu. made into a sauce. **horse sense** common sense.

horseshoe *noun* protective U-shaped piece of iron nailed to a horse's hoof, regarded as a symbol of good luck.

horticulture *noun* art or science of cultivating gardens. **horticultural** *adjective* **horticulturalist, horticulturist** *noun*

hosanna *interjection* exclamation of praise to God.

hose¹ *noun* **1** flexible pipe for conveying liquid. ♦ *verb* **2** water with a hose.

hose² *noun* stockings, socks, and tights.

hosiery *noun* stockings, socks, and tights collectively.

hoser *noun* **1** *US sl* a person who swindles or deceives others. **2** *Canad sl* an unsophisticated, esp. rural, person.

hospice [hoss-piss] *noun* nursing home for the terminally ill.

hospital *noun* place where people who are ill are looked after and treated. **hospitalize** *verb* send or admit to hospital. **hospitalization** *noun*

hospitality ⊕ *noun* kindness in welcoming strangers or guests. **hospitable** *adjective* welcoming to strangers or guests.

host¹ ⊕ *noun* **1** (*fem* **hostess**) person who entertains guests, esp. in his own home. **2** place or country providing the facilities for an event. **3** compere of a show. **4** animal or plant on which a parasite lives. **5** *Computers* computer connected to others on a network. ♦ *verb* **6** be the host of.

host² ⊕ *noun* large number.

Host *noun Christianity* bread used in Holy Communion.

hostage ⊕ *noun* person who is illegally held prisoner until certain demands are met by other people.

hostel *noun* building providing accommodation at a low cost for travellers, homeless people, etc.

hostelry *noun, pl* **-ries** *Old-fashioned or facetious* inn, pub.

hostile ⊕ *adjective* **1** unfriendly. **2** (foll. by *to*) opposed (to). **3** of an enemy. **hostility** *noun, pl* **-ties 1** unfriendly and aggressive feelings or behaviour. ♦ *plural* **2** acts of warfare.

hot ⊕ *adjective* **hotter, hottest 1** having a high temperature. **2** strong, spicy. **3** (of news)

——— T H E S A U R U S ———

OPPOSITE⟩ **comfort**

horror *noun* =**terror**, alarm, aversion, consternation, detestation, disgust, dread, fear, fright, hatred, loathing, odium, panic, repugnance, revulsion OPPOSITE⟩ **liking**

horse *noun* **1** =**nag**, colt, filly, gee-gee (*sl*), mare, mount, stallion, steed (*arch or lit*)

horseman, horsewoman *noun* =**rider**, equestrian

horseplay *noun* =**rough-and-tumble**, buffoonery, clowning, fooling around, high jinks, pranks, romping, skylarking (*inf*)

hospitable *adjective* =**welcoming**, cordial, friendly, generous, gracious, kind, liberal, sociable OPPOSITE⟩ **inhospitable**

hospitality *noun* =**welcome**, conviviality, cordiality, friendliness, neighbourliness, sociability, warmth

host¹ *noun* **1** =**master of ceremonies**, entertainer, innkeeper, landlord *or* landlady, proprietor **3** =**presenter**, anchorman *or* anchorwoman, compere (*Brit*) ♦ *verb* **6** =**present**, compere (*Brit*), front (*inf*), introduce

host² *noun* =**multitude**, army, array, drove, horde, legion, myriad, swarm, throng

hostage *noun* =**prisoner**, captive, pawn

hostile *adjective* **1** =**unfriendly**, antagonistic, belligerent, contrary, ill-disposed, opposed, rancorous OPPOSITE⟩ **friendly**. **2** (foll. by *to*) =**inhospitable**, adverse, unsympathetic, unwelcoming OPPOSITE⟩ **congenial**

hostility *noun* **1** =**unfriendliness**, animosity, antipathy, enmity, hatred, ill will, malice, opposition, resentment OPPOSITE⟩ **goodwill** ♦ *plural* **2** =**warfare**, conflict, fighting, war OPPOSITE⟩ **peace**

very recent. **4** (of a contest) fiercely fought. **5** (of a temper) quick to rouse. **6** liked very much, e.g. *a hot favourite*. **7** *Slang* stolen. **in hot water** *Informal* in trouble. **in the hot seat** *Informal* in a difficult and responsible position. **hotly** *adverb* **hotting** *noun Informal* practice of stealing fast cars and putting on a show of skilful but dangerous driving. **hotter** *noun* **hot air** *Informal* empty talk. **hot-blooded** *adjective* passionate or excitable. **hot dog** long roll split lengthways with a hot frankfurter inside. **hot-headed** *adjective* rash, having a hot temper. **hotline** *noun* direct telephone link for emergency use. **hot-water bottle** rubber container filled with hot water, used for warming a bed.

hotbed *noun* any place encouraging a particular activity, e.g. *hotbeds of unrest*.

hotchpotch ❼ *noun* jumbled mixture.

hotel *noun* commercial establishment providing lodging and meals. **hotelier** *noun* owner or manager of a hotel.

hotfoot *adverb Informal* quickly and eagerly. **hotfoot it** *Informal* go quickly and eagerly.

hothouse *noun* greenhouse.

hotplate *noun* **1** heated metal surface on an electric cooker. **2** portable device for keeping food warm.

hotpot *noun* casserole of meat and vegetables, topped with potatoes.

Hottentot *noun* (member of) a race of people of South Africa, now almost extinct.

hound ❼ *noun* **1** hunting dog. ◆ *verb* **2** pursue relentlessly.

hour *noun* **1** twenty-fourth part of a day, sixty minutes. **2** time of day. ◆ *plural* **3** period regularly appointed for work or business.

hourly *adjective, adverb* **1** (happening) every hour. **2** frequent(ly). **hourglass** *noun* device with two glass compartments, containing a quantity of sand that takes an hour to trickle from the top section tothe bottom one.

houri *noun Islam* any of the nymphs of paradise.

house ❼ *noun* **1** building used as a home. **2** building used for some specific purpose, e.g. *the opera house*. **3** business firm. **4** law-making body or the hall where it meets. **5** family or dynasty. **6** theatre or cinema audience. ◆ *verb* **7** give accommodation to. **8** contain or cover. ◆ *adjective* **9** (of wine) sold in a restaurant at a lower price than wines on the wine list. **get on like a house on fire** *Informal* get on very well together. **on the house** *Informal* provided free by the management. **housing** *noun* **1** (providing of) houses. **2** protective case or covering of a machine. **house arrest** confinement to one's home rather than in prison. **houseboat** *noun* stationary boat used as a home. **housebound** *adjective* unable to leave one's house, usu. because of illness. **housebreaker** *noun* burglar. **house-breaking** *noun* **housecoat** *noun* woman's long loose coat-shaped garment for wearing at home. **household** *noun* all the people living in a house. **household name, word** very well-known person or thing. **householder** *noun* person who owns or rents a house. **housekeeper** *noun* person employed to run someone else's household. **housekeeping** *noun* (money for) running a household. **housemaid** *noun* female servant employed to do housework. **houseman** *noun* junior hospital doctor. **house-proud** *adjective* excessively concerned with the appearance of one's house. **house-train** *verb* train (a pet) to urinate and defecate outside. **house-warming** *noun* party to celebrate moving into a new home. **housewife** *noun* woman who runs her own household and does not have a job. **housewifely** *adjective* **housework** *noun* work of running a home, such as cleaning, cooking, and shopping.

House music, House *noun* funk-based disco

H

———————— THESAURUS ————————

hot *adjective* **1** = **heated**, boiling, roasting, scalding, scorching, searing, steaming, sultry, sweltering, torrid, warm OPPOSITE cold. **2** = **spicy**, biting, peppery, piquant, pungent, sharp OPPOSITE mild. **3** = **new**, fresh, just out, latest, recent, up to the minute OPPOSITE old. **4** = **passionate**, fierce, fiery, intense, raging, stormy, violent **6** = **popular**, approved, favoured, in demand, in vogue, sought-after OPPOSITE unpopular

hot air *noun Inf* = **empty talk**, bombast, claptrap (*inf*), guff (*sl*), verbiage, wind

hot-blooded *adjective* = **passionate**, ardent,

excitable, fiery, impulsive, spirited, temperamental, wild

hotchpotch *noun* = **mixture**, farrago, jumble, medley, *melange*, mess, mishmash, potpourri

hot-headed *adjective* = **rash**, fiery, foolhardy, hasty, hot-tempered, impetuous, quick-tempered, reckless, volatile

hound *verb* **2** = **harass**, badger, goad, harry, impel, persecute, pester, provoke

house *noun* **1** = **home**, abode, domicile, dwelling, habitation, homestead, pad (*sl*), residence **3** = **firm**, business, company, organization, outfit (*inf*) **4** = **assembly**, music with fragments of other recordings edited in electronically.

hove *verb Naut* a past of HEAVE.

hovea *noun* Australian plant with purple flowers.

hovel ❶ *noun* small dirty house or hut.

hover ❶ *verb* **1** (of a bird etc.) remain suspended in one place in the air. **2** loiter. **3** be in a state of indecision. **hovercraft** *noun* vehicle which can travel over both land and sea on a cushion of air.

how ❶ *adverb* **1** in what way, by what means. **2** to what degree, e.g. *I know how hard it is.*

however *adverb* **1** nevertheless. **2** by whatever means. **3** no matter how, e.g. *however much it hurt, he could do it.*

howdah *noun* canopied seat on an elephant's back.

howitzer *noun* large gun firing shells at a steep angle.

howl ❶ *noun* **1** loud wailing cry. **2** loud burst of laughter. ◆ *verb* **3** utter a howl. **howler** *noun Informal* stupid mistake.

hoyden *noun* wild or boisterous girl.

HP, h.p. 1 hire-purchase. **2** horsepower.

HQ headquarters.

hr hour.

HRH Her (or His) Royal Highness.

HRT hormone replacement therapy.

HTML hypertext markup language: text description language used on the Internet.

hub ❶ *noun* **1** centre of a wheel, through which the axle passes. **2** central point of activity.

hubble-bubble *noun* same as HOOKAH.

hubbub *noun* confused noise of many voices.

hubby *noun, pl* -**bies** *Informal* husband.

hubris [hew-**briss**] *noun Formal* pride, arrogance.

huckster *noun* person using aggressive methods of selling.

huddle ❶ *verb* **1** hunch (oneself) through cold or fear. **2** crowd closely together. ◆ *noun* **3** small group. **4** *Informal* impromptu conference.

hue ❶ *noun* colour, shade.

hue and cry *noun* public outcry.

huff *noun* **1** passing mood of anger or resentment. ◆ *verb* **2** blow or puff heavily. **huffy** *adjective* **huffier, huffiest. huffily** *adverb*

hug ❶ *verb* **hugging, hugged 1** clasp tightly in the arms, usu. with affection. **2** keep close to (the ground, kerb, etc.). ◆ *noun* **3** tight or fond embrace.

huge ❶ *adjective* very big. **hugely** *adverb*

huh *interjection* exclamation of derision, bewilderment, or inquiry.

hula *noun* swaying Hawaiian dance. **Hula Hoop** ® plastic hoop twirled round the body by gyrating the hips.

hulk ❶ *noun* **1** body of an abandoned ship. **2** *Offens* large heavy person or thing. **hulking** *adjective* bulky, unwieldy.

hull ❶ *noun* **1** main body of a boat. **2** leaves round the stem of a strawberry, raspberry, etc. ◆ *verb* **3** remove the hulls from.

hullabaloo *noun, pl* -**loos** loud confused noise

——————— THESAURUS ———————

Commons, legislative body, parliament **5 = dynasty**, clan, family, tribe ◆*verb* **7 = accommodate**, billet, harbour, lodge, put up, quarter, take in **8 = contain**, cover, keep, protect, sheathe, shelter, store **on the house** *Inf* =**free**, for nothing, gratis

household *noun* =**family**, home, house

householder *noun* =**occupant**, homeowner, resident, tenant

housing *noun* **1 = accommodation**, dwellings, homes, houses **2 = case**, casing, container, cover, covering, enclosure, sheath

hovel *noun* =**hut**, cabin, den, hole, shack, shanty, shed

hover *verb* **1 = float**, drift, flutter, fly, hang **2 = linger**, hang about **3 = waver**, dither, fluctuate, oscillate, vacillate

however *adverb* **1 = nevertheless**, after all, anyhow, but, nonetheless, notwithstanding, still, though, yet

howl *noun* **1 = cry**, bawl, bay, clamour, groan, roar, scream, shriek, wail ◆*verb* **3 = cry**, bawl,

bellow, roar, scream, shriek, wail, weep, yell

howler *noun Inf* =**mistake**, bloomer (*Brit inf*), blunder, boob (*Brit sl*), clanger (*inf*), error, malapropism

hub *noun* **2 = centre**, core, focal point, focus, heart, middle, nerve centre

huddle *verb* **1 = curl up**, crouch, hunch up **2 = crowd**, cluster, converge, flock, gather, press, throng ◆*noun* **4** *Inf* =**conference**, confab (*inf*), discussion, meeting, powwow

hue *noun* =**colour**, dye, shade, tinge, tint, tone

hug *verb* **1 = clasp**, cuddle, embrace, enfold, hold close, squeeze, take in one's arms ◆*noun* **3 = embrace**, bear hug, clasp, clinch (*sl*), squeeze

huge *adjective* =**enormous**, colossal, gigantic, immense, large, mammoth, massive, monumental, tremendous, vast OPPOSITE▷ **tiny**

hulk *noun* **1 = wreck**, frame, hull, shell, shipwreck **2** *Offens* =**oaf**, lout, lubber, lump (*inf*)

hull *noun* **1 = frame**, body, casing, covering,

or clamour.

hullo *interjection* same as HELLO.

hum ❶ *verb* **humming, hummed 1** make a low continuous vibrating sound. **2** sing with the lips closed. **3** *Slang* (of a place) be very busy. ♦ *noun* **4** humming sound. **hummingbird** *noun* very small American bird whose powerful wings make a humming noise as they vibrate.

human ❶ *adjective* **1** of or typical of people. ♦ *noun* **2** human being. **humanly** *adverb* by human powers or means. **human being** man, woman, or child. **humane** *adjective* kind or merciful. **humanity** *noun* human race. **human nature** ordinary human behaviour, esp. when less than perfect. **human race** all men, women, and children collectively. **human rights** basic rights of people to liberty, justice, etc.

humane ❶ *adjective* kind or merciful. **humanely** *adverb*

humanism *noun* belief in human effort rather than religion. **humanist** *noun* **humanistic** *adjective*

humanitarian ❶ *noun, adjective* (person) having the interests of humankind at heart. **humanitarianism** *noun*

humanity ❶ *noun, pl* **-ties 1** human race. **2** the quality of being human. **3** kindness or mercy. ♦ *plural* **4** study of literature, philosophy, and the arts.

humanize ❶ *verb* make human or humane. **humanization** *noun*

humankind *noun* human race.

humanoid *noun, adjective* (robot or creature) resembling a human being in appearance.

humble ❶ *adjective* **1** conscious of one's failings. **2** modest, unpretentious. **3** unimportant. ♦ *verb* **4** cause to feel humble, humiliate. **humbly** *adverb*

humbug ❶ *noun* **1** hard striped peppermint sweet. **2** nonsense. **3** dishonest person.

humdinger *noun* *Slang* excellent person or thing.

humdrum ❶ *adjective* ordinary, dull.

humerus [hew-mer-uss] *noun, pl* **-meri** [-mer-rye] bone from the shoulder to the elbow.

humid ❶ *adjective* damp and hot. **humidity** *noun* **humidify** *verb* **-fying, -fied. humidifier** *noun* device for increasing the amount of water vapour in the air in a room.

humiliate ❶ *verb* lower the dignity or hurt the pride of. **humiliating** *adjective* **humiliation** *noun*

H

———————— T H E S A U R U S ————————

framework

hum *verb* **1** = **drone**, buzz, murmur, purr, throb, thrum, vibrate, whir **3** *Sl* = **be busy**, bustle, buzz, pulsate, pulse, stir

human *adjective* **1** = **mortal**, manlike OPPOSITE> nonhuman ♦*noun* **2** = **human being**, creature, individual, man *or* woman, mortal, person, soul OPPOSITE> nonhuman

humane *adjective* = **kind**, benign, compassionate, forgiving, good-natured, merciful, sympathetic, tender, understanding OPPOSITE> cruel

humanitarian *noun* = **philanthropist**, altruist, benefactor, Good Samaritan ♦*adjective* = **philanthropic**, altruistic, benevolent, charitable, compassionate, humane, public-spirited

humanity *noun* **1** = **human race**, Homo sapiens, humankind, man, mankind, people **2** = **human nature**, mortality **3** = **kindness**, charity, compassion, fellow feeling, kind-heartedness, mercy, philanthropy, sympathy

humanize *verb* = **civilize**, educate, enlighten, improve, soften, tame

humble *adjective* **1** = **modest**, meek, self-effacing, unassuming, unostentatious, unpretentious OPPOSITE> proud. **2** = **modest**, lowly, mean, obscure, ordinary, plebeian, poor, simple, undistinguished OPPOSITE>

distinguished ♦*verb* **4** = **humiliate**, chasten, crush, disgrace, put (someone) in their place, subdue, take down a peg (*inf*) OPPOSITE> exalt

humbug *noun* **2** = **nonsense**, baloney (*inf*), cant, claptrap (*inf*), hypocrisy, kak (*S Afr sl*), quackery, rubbish **3** = **fraud**, charlatan, con man (*inf*), faker, impostor, phoney *or* phony (*inf*), swindler, trickster

humdrum *adjective* = **dull**, banal, boring, dreary, monotonous, mundane, ordinary, tedious, tiresome, uneventful OPPOSITE> exciting

humid *adjective* = **damp**, clammy, dank, moist, muggy, steamy, sticky, sultry, wet OPPOSITE> dry

humidity *noun* = **damp**, clamminess, dampness, dankness, moistness, moisture, mugginess, wetness

humiliate *verb* = **embarrass**, bring low, chasten, crush, degrade, humble, mortify, put down, put (someone) in their place, shame OPPOSITE> honour

humiliating *adjective* = **embarrassing**, crushing, degrading, humbling, ignominious, mortifying, shaming

humiliation *noun* = **embarrassment**, degradation, disgrace, dishonour, humbling, ignominy, indignity, loss of face, mortification, put-down, shame

H

humility ⊙ *noun* quality of being humble.
hummock *noun* very small hill.
humour ⊙ *noun* **1** ability to say or perceive things that are amusing. **2** amusing quality in a situation, film, etc. **3** state of mind, mood. **4** *Old-fashioned* fluid in the body. ◆ *verb* **5** be kind and indulgent to. **humorous** *adjective*
humorously *adverb* **humorist** *noun* writer or entertainer who uses humour in his or her work. **humourless** *adjective*

> **SPELLING TIP**
>
> A lot of people simply add *-ous* to the noun **humour** to make *humourous*, but this is a mistake; you have to drop the second *u* when you write **humorous** or **humorist**.

hump ⊙ *noun* **1** raised piece of ground. **2** large lump on the back of an animal or person. ◆ *verb* **3** *Slang* carry or heave. **get, take the hump** *Informal* be annoyed, sulk. **humpback** *noun Offens* hunchback. **humpbacked** *adjective*
hump-back, humpbacked bridge road bridge with a sharp slope on each side.
humus [**hew**-muss] *noun* decomposing vegetable and animal mould in the soil.
Hun *noun* **1** member of the Asian people who invaded the Roman Empire in the 4th and 5th centuries AD. **2** *Informal offens* (in World War 1) German.
hunch ⊙ *noun* **1** feeling or suspicion not based on facts. ◆ *verb* **2** draw (one's shoulders) up or together. **hunchback** *noun Offens* person with

an abnormal curvature of the spine.
hunchbacked *adjective*
hundred *adjective, noun* **1** ten times ten. ◆ *noun* **2** (often pl) large but unspecified number. **hundredth** *adjective, noun* **hundredweight** *noun Brit* unit of weight of 112 pounds (50.8 kilograms).
hung *verb* **1** past of HANG. ◆ *adjective* **2** (of a parliament or jury) with no side having a clear majority. **hung over** *Informal* suffering the effects of a hangover.
Hungarian *adjective* **1** of Hungary. ◆ *noun* **2** person from Hungary. **3** language of Hungary.
hunger ⊙ *noun* **1** discomfort or weakness from lack of food. **2** lack of food that causes suffering or death, e.g. *refugees dying of hunger*. **3** desire or craving. ◆ *verb* **4** (foll. by *for*) want very much. **hunger strike** refusal of all food, as a means of protest. **hungry** *adjective* having a desire or craving (for).
hungry ⊙ *adjective* **hungrier, hungriest 1** desiring food. **2** (foll. by *for*) having a desire or craving (for). **hungrily** *adverb*
hunk ⊙ *noun* **1** large piece. **2** *Slang* sexually attractive man.
hunt ⊙ *verb* **1** seek out and kill (wild animals) for food or sport. **2** (foll. by *for*) search (for). ◆ *noun* **3** hunting. **4** (party organized for) hunting wild animals for sport. **hunter** *noun* person or animal that hunts wild animals for food or sport. **hunting** *noun* **huntsman** *noun* man who hunts wild animals, esp. foxes.
hurdle ⊙ *noun* **1** *Sport* light barrier for jumping over in some races. **2** problem or difficulty. ◆ *plural* **3** race involving hurdles. ◆ *verb* **4** jump over (something). **hurdler** *noun*

———— THESAURUS ————

humility *noun* =**modesty**, humbleness, lowliness, meekness, submissiveness, unpretentiousness OPPOSITE **pride**
humorist *noun* =**comedian**, card (*inf*), comic, funny man, jester, joker, wag, wit
humorous *adjective* **1, 2** =**funny**, amusing, comic, comical, droll, entertaining, jocular, playful, waggish, witty OPPOSITE **serious**
humour *noun* **1, 2** =**funniness**, amusement, comedy, drollery, facetiousness, fun, jocularity, ludicrousness OPPOSITE **seriousness**. **3** =**mood**, disposition, frame of mind, spirits, temper ◆*verb* **5** =**indulge**, accommodate, flatter, go along with, gratify, mollify, pander to OPPOSITE **oppose**
hump *noun* **1** =**lump**, bulge, bump, mound, projection, protrusion, protuberance, swelling ◆*verb* **3** *Sl* =**carry**, heave, hoist, lug, shoulder
hunch *noun* **1** =**feeling**, idea, impression,

inkling, intuition, premonition, presentiment, suspicion ◆*verb* **2** =**draw in**, arch, bend, curve
hunger *noun* **1** =**appetite**, emptiness, hungriness, ravenousness **2** =**starvation**, famine **3** =**desire**, ache, appetite, craving, itch, lust, thirst, yearning ◆*verb* **4** =**want**, ache, crave, desire, hanker, itch, long, thirst, wish, yearn
hungry *adjective* **1** =**empty**, famished, peckish (*inf, chiefly Brit*), ravenous, starved, starving, voracious **2** (foll. by *for*) =**eager**, athirst, avid, covetous, craving, desirous, greedy, keen, yearning
hunk *noun* **1** =**lump**, block, chunk, mass, nugget, piece, slab, wedge
hunt *verb* **1** =**stalk**, chase, hound, pursue, track, trail **2** (foll. by *for*) =**search**, ferret about, forage, fossick (*Aust & NZ*), look, scour, seek ◆*noun* **3** =**search**, chase, hunting, investigation, pursuit, quest

hurdy-gurdy *noun, pl* **-dies** mechanical musical instrument, such as a barrel organ.
hurl ❶ *verb* throw or utter forcefully.
hurling, hurley *noun* Irish game like hockey.
hurly-burly *noun* loud confusion.
hurrah, hurray *interjection* exclamation of joy or applause.
hurricane ❶ *noun* very strong, often destructive, wind or storm. **hurricane lamp** paraffin lamp with a glass covering.
hurry ❶ *verb* **-rying, -ried 1** (cause to) move or act very quickly. ♦ *noun* **2** doing something quickly or the need to do something quickly.
hurried *adjective* **hurriedly** *adverb*
hurt ❶ *verb* **hurting, hurt 1** cause physical or mental pain to. **2** be painful. **3** *Informal* feel pain. ♦ *noun* **4** physical or mental pain. **hurtful** *adjective* unkind.
hurtle ❶ *verb* move quickly or violently.
husband ❶ *noun* **1** woman's partner in marriage. ♦ *verb* **2** use economically.
husbandry *noun* **1** farming. **2** management of resources.
hush ❶ *verb* **1** make or be silent. ♦ *noun* **2** stillness or silence. **hushed** *adjective* **hush-hush** *adjective Informal* secret. **hush money** *Slang* money given to someone to ensure that something is kept secret. **hush up** *verb* suppress information about.

husk *noun* **1** outer covering of certain seeds and fruits. ♦ *verb* **2** remove the husk from.
husky[1] *adjective* **huskier, huskiest 1** slightly hoarse. **2** *Informal* big and strong.
huskily *adverb*
husky[2] *noun, pl* **huskies** Arctic sledge dog with thick hair and a curled tail.
hussar [hoo-**zar**] *noun Hist* lightly armed cavalry soldier.
hussy *noun, pl* **-sies** immodest or promiscuous woman.
hustings *plural noun* political campaigns and speeches before an election.
hustle ❶ *verb* **1** push about, jostle. ♦ *noun* **2** lively activity or bustle.
hut ❶ *noun* small house, shelter, or shed.
hutch *noun* cage for pet rabbits etc.
hyacinth *noun* sweet-smelling spring flower that grows from a bulb.
hyaena *noun* same as HYENA.
hybrid ❶ *noun* **1** offspring of two plants or animals of different species. **2** anything of mixed origin. ♦ *adjective* **3** of mixed origin.
hydra *noun* mythical many-headed water serpent.
hydrangea *noun* ornamental shrub with clusters of pink, blue, or white flowers.
hydrant *noun* outlet from a water main with a nozzle for a hose.

H

———— T H E S A U R U S ————

hurdle *noun* **1** = **fence**, barricade, barrier **2** = **obstacle**, barrier, difficulty, handicap, hazard, hindrance, impediment, obstruction, stumbling block
hurl *verb* = **throw**, cast, fling, heave, launch, let fly, pitch, propel, sling, toss
hurricane *noun* = **storm**, cyclone, gale, tempest, tornado, twister (*US inf*), typhoon
hurried *adjective* = **hasty**, brief, cursory, perfunctory, quick, rushed, short, speedy, swift
hurry *verb* **1** = **rush**, dash, fly, get a move on (*inf*), make haste, scoot, scurry, step on it (*inf*) OPPOSITE⟩ **dawdle** ♦*noun* **2** = **haste**, flurry, quickness, rush, speed, urgency OPPOSITE⟩ **slowness**
hurt *verb* **1 a** = **harm**, bruise, damage, disable, impair, injure, mar, spoil, wound OPPOSITE⟩ **heal. b** = **upset**, annoy, distress, grieve, pain, sadden, wound **2** = **ache**, be sore, be tender, burn, smart, sting, throb ♦*noun* **4** = **distress**, discomfort, pain, pang, soreness, suffering OPPOSITE⟩ **happiness** ♦*adjective* **a** = **injured**, bruised, crook (*Aust & NZ sl*), cut, damaged, harmed, scarred, wounded OPPOSITE⟩ **healed. b** = **upset**, aggrieved, crushed, offended, wounded OPPOSITE⟩ **calmed**

hurtful *adjective* = **unkind**, cruel, cutting, damaging, destructive, malicious, nasty, spiteful, upsetting, wounding
hurtle *verb* = **rush**, charge, crash, fly, plunge, race, shoot, speed, stampede, tear
husband *noun* **1** = **partner**, better half (*hum*), mate, spouse ♦*verb* **2** = **economize**, budget, conserve, hoard, save, store OPPOSITE⟩ **squander**
husbandry *noun* **1** = **farming**, agriculture, cultivation, tillage **2** = **thrift**, economy, frugality
hush *verb* **1** = **quieten**, mute, muzzle, shush, silence ♦*noun* **2** = **quiet**, calm, peace, silence, stillness, tranquillity
hush-hush *adjective Inf* = **secret**, classified, confidential, restricted, top-secret, under wraps
husky[1] *adjective* **1** = **hoarse**, croaky, gruff, guttural, harsh, raucous, rough, throaty **2** *Inf* = **muscular**, burly, hefty, powerful, rugged, stocky, strapping, thickset
hustle *verb* **1** = **jostle**, elbow, force, jog, push, shove
hut *noun* = **shed**, cabin, den, hovel, lean-to, shanty, shelter
hybrid *noun* **1** = **crossbreed**, cross, half-breed, mongrel **2** = **mixture**, amalgam, composite,

H

hydrate *noun* **1** chemical compound of water with another substance. ♦ *verb* **2** treat or impregnate with water.

hydraulic *adjective* operated by pressure forced through a pipe by a liquid such as water or oil. **hydraulics** *noun* study of the mechanical properties of fluids as they apply to practical engineering. **hydraulically** *adverb*

hydro¹ *noun, pl* **hydros** hotel offering facilities for hydropathy.

hydro² *adjective* **1** short for HYDROELECTRIC. **2** *Canad* electricity as supplied to a residence, business, institution, etc.

hydro- *combining form* **1** water, e.g. *hydroelectric.* **2** hydrogen, e.g. *hydrochloric acid.*

hydrocarbon *noun* compound of hydrogen and carbon.

hydrocephalus *noun* accumulation of fluid within the cavities of the brain, causing enlargement of the head in children.

hydrochloric acid *noun* strong colourless acid used in many industrial and laboratory processes.

hydrodynamics *noun* branch of science concerned with the mechanical properties of fluids.

hydroelectric *adjective* of the generation of electricity by water pressure.

hydrofoil *noun* fast light boat with its hull raised out of the water on one or more pairs of fins.

hydrogen *noun Chem* light flammable colourless gas that combines with oxygen to form water. **hydrogen bomb** extremely powerful bomb in which energy is released by fusion of hydrogen nuclei to give helium nuclei. **hydrogen peroxide** colourless liquid used as a hair bleach and as an antiseptic.

hydrology *noun* study of the distribution, conservation, and use of the water of the earth and its atmosphere.

hydrolysis [hie-**drol**-iss-iss] *noun* decomposition of a chemical compound reacting with water.

hydrometer [hie-**drom**-it-er] *noun* instrument for measuring the density of a liquid.

hydropathy *noun* method of treating disease by the use of large quantities of water both internally and externally. **hydropathic** *adjective*

hydrophobia *noun* **1** rabies. **2** fear of water.

hydroplane *noun* light motorboat that skims the water.

hydroponics *noun* method of growing plants in water rather than soil.

hydrotherapy *noun Med* treatment of certain diseases by exercise in water.

hyena *noun* scavenging doglike mammal of Africa and S Asia.

hygiene ⊕ *noun* **1** principles and practice of health and cleanliness. **2** study of these principles. **hygienic** *adjective* **hygienically** *adverb*

hymen *noun* membrane partly covering the opening of a girl's vagina, which breaks before puberty or at the first occurrence of sexual intercourse.

hymn ⊕ *noun* Christian song of praise sung to God or a saint. **hymnal** *noun* book of hymns (also **hymn book**).

hype ⊕ *noun* **1** intensive or exaggerated publicity or sales promotion. ♦ *verb* **2** promote (a product) using intensive or exaggerated publicity.

hyper *adjective Informal* overactive or overexcited.

hyper- *prefix* over, above, excessively, e.g. *hyperactive.*

hyperbola [hie-**per**-bol-a] *noun Geom* curve produced when a cone is cut by a plane at a steeper angle to its base than its side.

hyperbole [hie-**per**-bol-ee] *noun* deliberate exaggeration for effect. **hyperbolic** *adjective*

hyperlink *Computers noun* link from a hypertext file that gives users instant access to related material in another file.

hypermarket *noun* huge self-service store.

hypersensitive *adjective* **1** extremely sensitive to certain drugs, extremes of temperature, etc. **2** very easily upset.

hypersonic *adjective* having a speed of at least five times the speed of sound.

hypertension *noun* very high blood pressure.

hyperventilation *noun* increase in the rate of breathing, sometimes resulting in cramp and dizziness. **hyperventilate** *verb*

hyphen *noun* punctuation mark (-) indicating that two words or syllables are connected.

hyphenated *adjective* (of two words or syllables) having a hyphen between them. **hyphenation** *noun*

———————— THESAURUS ————————

compound, cross

hygiene *noun* **1** = **cleanliness**, sanitation

hygienic *adjective* = **clean**, aseptic, disinfected, germ-free, healthy, pure, sanitary, sterile

OPPOSITE > **dirty**

hymn *noun* = **song of praise**, anthem, carol, chant, paean, psalm

hype *noun* **1** = **publicity**, ballyhoo (*inf*), brouhaha, plugging (*inf*), promotion, razzmatazz (*sl*)

hypnosis ❶ *noun* artificially induced state of relaxation in which the mind is more than usually receptive to suggestion. **hypnotic** *adjective* of or (as if) producing hypnosis. **hypnotically** *adverb* **hypnotism** *noun* inducing hypnosis in someone. **hypnotist** *noun* **hypnotize** *verb*

hypo- *prefix* beneath, less than, e.g. *hypothermia*.

hypoallergenic *adjective* (of cosmetics) not likely to cause an allergic reaction.

hypochondria *noun* undue preoccupation with one's health. **hypochondriac** *noun*

hypocrisy ❶ [hip-ok-rass-ee] *noun, pl* -**sies** (instance of) pretence of having standards or beliefs that are contrary to one's real character or actual behaviour. **hypocrite** [hip-oh-krit] *noun* person who pretends to be what he or she is not. **hypocritical** *adjective* **hypocritically** *adverb*

hypodermic *adjective, noun* (denoting) a syringe or needle used to inject a drug beneath the skin.

hypotension *noun* very low blood pressure.

hypotenuse [hie-**pot**-a-news] *noun* side of a right-angled triangle opposite the right angle.

hypothermia *noun* condition in which a person's body temperature is dangerously low as a result of prolonged exposure to severe cold.

hypothesis ❶ [hie-**poth**-iss-iss] *noun, pl* -**ses** [-seez] suggested but unproved explanation of something. **hypothesize** *verb* **hypothetical** *adjective* based on assumption rather than fact or reality. **hypothetically** *adverb*

hyssop *noun* sweet-smelling herb used in folk medicine.

hysterectomy *noun, pl* -**mies** surgical removal of the womb.

hysteria ❶ *noun* state of uncontrolled excitement, anger, or panic. **hysteric** *noun* **1** hysterical person. **hysterical** *adjective* **1** in a state of hysteria. **2** *Informal* wildly funny. **hysterically** *adverb* **hysterics** *plural noun* **1** attack of hysteria. **2** *Informal* uncontrollable laughter.

Hz hertz.

————————————— THESAURUS —————————————

hypnotic *adjective* =**mesmerizing**, mesmeric, sleep-inducing, soothing, soporific, spellbinding

hypnotize *verb* =**mesmerize**, put in a trance, put to sleep

hypocrisy *noun* =**insincerity**, cant, deceitfulness, deception, duplicity, pretence OPPOSITE **sincerity**

hypocrite *noun* =**fraud**, charlatan, deceiver, impostor, phoney *or* phony (*inf*), pretender

hypocritical *adjective* =**insincere**, canting, deceitful, duplicitous, false, fraudulent, phoney *or* phony (*inf*), sanctimonious, two-faced

hypothesis *noun* =**assumption**, postulate, premise, proposition, supposition, theory, thesis

hypothetical *adjective* =**theoretical**, academic, assumed, conjectural, imaginary, putative, speculative, supposed OPPOSITE **real**

hysteria *noun* =**frenzy**, agitation, delirium, hysterics, madness, panic

hysterical *adjective* **1** =**frenzied**, crazed, distracted, distraught, frantic, overwrought, raving OPPOSITE **calm. 2** *Inf* =**hilarious**, comical, side-splitting, uproarious OPPOSITE **serious**

H

I² *Chem* iodine. **1** the Roman numeral for one.
IA Iowa.
IBA Independent Broadcasting Authority.
Iberian *adjective* of Iberia, the peninsula comprising Spain and Portugal.
ibex [**ibe**-eks] *noun* wild goat with large backward-curving horns.
ibid. (referring to a book, page, or passage already mentioned) in the same place.
ibis [**ibe**-iss] *noun* large wading bird with long legs.
ICBM intercontinental ballistic missile.
ice ⓘ *noun* **1** frozen water. **2** portion of ice cream. ♦ *verb* **3** (foll. by *up* or *over*) become covered with ice. **4** cover with icing. **break the ice** create a relaxed atmosphere, esp. between people meeting for the first time. **iced** *adjective* **1** covered with icing. **2** (of a drink) containing ice. **icy** *adjective* **icier, iciest 1** very cold. **2** covered with ice. **3** aloof and unfriendly. **icily** *adverb* **iciness** *noun* **Ice Age** period when much of the earth's surface was covered in glaciers. **iceberg** *noun* large floating mass of ice. **icebox** *noun US* refrigerator. **icebreaker** *noun* ship designed to break a channel through ice. **icecap** *noun* mass of ice permanently covering an area. **ice cream** sweet creamy frozen food. **ice cube** small square block of ice added to a drink to cool it. **ice floe** sheet of ice floating in the sea. **ice hockey** team game like hockey played on ice with a puck. **ice lolly** flavoured ice on a stick. **ice pick** pointed tool for breaking ice. **ice skate** boot with a steel blade fixed to the sole, to enable the wearer to glide over ice. **ice-skate** *verb* **ice-skater** *noun*
Icelandic *adjective* **1** of Iceland. ♦ *noun* **2** language of Iceland. **Icelander** *noun*
ichthyology [ik-thi-**ol**-a-jee] *noun* scientific study of fish. **ichthyological** *adjective* **ichthyologist** *noun*
icicle *noun* tapering spike of ice hanging where water has dripped.
icing *noun* mixture of sugar and water etc., used to cover and decorate cakes. **icing sugar** finely ground sugar for making icing.
icon *noun* **1** picture of Christ or another religious figure, regarded as holy in the Orthodox Church. **2** picture on a computer screen representing a function that can be activated by moving the cursor over it.
iconoclast *noun* person who attacks established ideas or principles. **iconoclastic** *adjective* **iconoclasm** *noun*
id *noun Psychoanalysis* the mind's instinctive unconscious energies.
ID 1 Idaho. **2** identification.
idea ⓘ *noun* **1** plan or thought formed in the mind. **2** thought of something, e.g. *the idea overwhelms me.* **3** belief or opinion. **ideal** *noun* **1** idea of perfection. **2** perfect person or thing.
ideal ⓘ *adjective* **1** most suitable. **2** perfect. ♦ *noun* **3** conception of something that is perfect. **4** perfect person or thing. **ideally** *adverb*
idealism *noun* tendency to seek perfection in everything. **idealist** *noun* **idealistic** *adjective*
idealize *verb* regard or portray as perfect or nearly perfect. **idealization** *noun*
idem *pronoun, adjective Latin* the same: used

--- THESAURUS ---

icy *adjective* **1** = **cold**, biting, bitter, chill, chilly, freezing, frosty, ice-cold, raw OPPOSITE hot. **2** = **slippery**, glassy, slippy (*inf or dial*) **3** = **unfriendly**, aloof, cold, distant, frigid, frosty, unwelcoming OPPOSITE friendly
idea *noun* **1** = **intention**, aim, object, objective, plan, purpose **2** = **thought**, concept, impression, perception **3** = **belief**, conviction, notion, opinion, teaching, view
ideal *adjective* **2** = **perfect**, archetypal, classic, complete, consummate, model, quintessential, supreme OPPOSITE flawed ♦*noun* **4** = **model**,

last word, paradigm, paragon, pattern, perfection, prototype, standard
idealist *noun* = **romantic**, dreamer, Utopian, visionary
idealistic *adjective* = **perfectionist**, impracticable, optimistic, romantic, starry-eyed, Utopian, visionary OPPOSITE realistic
idealize *verb* = **romanticize**, apotheosize, ennoble, exalt, glorify, magnify, put on a pedestal, worship
ideally *adverb* = **in a perfect world**, all things being equal, if one had one's way

to refer to an article, chapter, or book already quoted.

identical ✪ *adjective* exactly the same. **identically** *adverb*

identify ✪ *verb* **-fying, -fied 1** prove or recognize as being a certain person or thing. **2** (foll. by *with*) understand and sympathize with (a person or group that one regards as being similar or similarly situated). **3** treat as being the same. **identifiable** *adjective* **identification** *noun*

Identikit *noun* ® composite picture, assembled from descriptions given, of a person wanted by the police.

identity ✪ *noun, pl* **-ties 1** state of being a specified person or thing. **2** individuality or personality. **3** state of being the same. **identical** *adjective* very same. **identify** *verb* establish identity of.

ideology *noun, pl* **-gies** body of ideas and beliefs of a group, nation, etc. **ideological** *adjective* **ideologically** *adverb* **ideologist** *noun*

ides *noun* (in the Ancient Roman calendar) the 15th of March, May, July, or October, or the 13th of other months.

idiocy ✪ *noun* utter stupidity.

idiom ✪ *noun* **1** group of words which when used together have a different meaning from the words individually, e.g. *raining cats and dogs*. **2** way of expression natural or peculiar to a language or group. **idiomatic** *adjective* **idiomatically** *adverb*

idiosyncrasy ✪ *noun, pl* **-sies** personal peculiarity of mind, habit, or behaviour. **idiosyncratic** *adjective*

idiot ✪ *noun* **1** foolish or stupid person. **2** *Offens* mentally retarded person. **idiotic** *adjective* **idiotically** *adverb*

idle ✪ *adjective* **1** not doing anything. **2** not willing to work, lazy. **3** not being used. **4** useless or meaningless, e.g. *an idle threat.* ◆ *verb* **5** (usu. foll. by *away*) spend (time) doing very little. **6** (of an engine) run slowly with the gears disengaged. **idleness** *noun* **idler** *noun* **idly** *adverb*

idol ✪ [ide-ol] *noun* **1** object of excessive devotion. **2** image of a god as an object of worship. **idolatry** [ide-ol-a-tree] *noun* worship of idols. **idolatrous** *adjective* **idolize** *verb* love or admire excessively. **idolization** *noun*

idyll ✪ [id-ill] *noun* scene or time of great peace and happiness. **idyllic** *adjective* **idyllically** *adverb*

i.e. that is to say.

if ✪ *conjunction* **1** on the condition or supposition that. **2** whether. **3** even though. ◆

——————— T H E S A U R U S ———————

identical *adjective* =**alike**, duplicate, indistinguishable, interchangeable, matching, twin OPPOSITE **different**

identification *noun* **1** =**recognition**, naming, pinpointing **2** =**sympathy**, association, connection, empathy, fellow feeling, involvement, rapport, relationship

identify *verb* **1** =**recognize**, diagnose, make out, name, pick out, pinpoint, place, put one's finger on (*inf*), spot **2** (foll. by *with*) =**relate to**, associate with, empathize with, feel for, respond to

identity *noun* **1, 2** =**existence**, individuality, personality, self **3** =**sameness**, correspondence, unity

idiocy *noun* =**foolishness**, asininity, fatuousness, imbecility, inanity, insanity, lunacy, senselessness OPPOSITE **wisdom**

idiom *noun* **1** =**phrase**, expression, turn of phrase **2** =**language**, jargon, parlance, style, vernacular

idiosyncrasy *noun* =**peculiarity**, characteristic, eccentricity, mannerism, oddity, quirk, trick

idiot *noun* **1** =**fool**, chump, cretin, dunderhead, halfwit, imbecile, moron, nincompoop, numbskull *or* numskull,

simpleton, twit (*inf, chiefly Brit*)

idiotic *adjective* **1** =**foolish**, asinine, crazy, daft (*inf*), foolhardy, harebrained, insane, moronic, senseless, stupid OPPOSITE **wise**

idle *adjective* **1** =**inactive**, redundant, unemployed, unoccupied OPPOSITE **occupied**. **2** =**lazy**, good-for-nothing, indolent, lackadaisical, shiftless, slothful, sluggish OPPOSITE **busy**. **3** =**unused**, vacant **4** =**useless**, fruitless, futile, groundless, ineffective, pointless, unavailing, unsuccessful, vain, worthless OPPOSITE **useful** ◆*verb* **5** (usu. foll. by *away*) =**laze**, dally, dawdle, kill time, loaf, loiter, lounge, potter

idleness *noun* **1** =**inactivity**, inaction, leisure, time on one's hands, unemployment **2** =**laziness**, inertia, shiftlessness, sloth, sluggishness, torpor

idol *noun* **1** =**hero**, beloved, darling, favourite, pet, pin-up (*sl*) **2** =**graven image**, deity, god

idolatry *noun* =**adoration**, adulation, exaltation, glorification

idolize *verb* =**worship**, adore, dote upon, exalt, glorify, hero-worship, look up to, love, revere, venerate

idyllic *adjective* =**idealized**, charming, halcyon, heavenly, ideal, picturesque, unspoiled *noun* **4** uncertainty or doubt, e.g. *no ifs, ands, or buts.* **iffy** *adjective Informal* doubtful, uncertain.

igloo *noun, pl* **-loos** dome-shaped Inuit house made of snow and ice.

igneous [ig-nee-uss] *adjective* (of rock) formed as molten rock cools and hardens.

ignite ⊕ *verb* catch fire or set fire to.

ignition *noun* **1** system that ignites the fuel-and-air mixture to start an engine. **2** igniting.

ignoble *adjective* dishonourable. **ignobly** *adverb*

ignominy ⊕ [ig-nom-in-ee] *noun* humiliating disgrace. **ignominious** *adjective* **ignominiously** *adverb*

ignoramus *noun, pl* **-muses** ignorant person.

ignorant ⊕ *adjective* **1** lacking knowledge. **2** rude through lack of knowledge of good manners. **ignorance** *noun*

ignore ⊕ *verb* refuse to notice, disregard deliberately. **ignorant** *adjective* lacking knowledge.

iguana *noun* large tropical American lizard.

ikebana [eek-a-bah-na] *noun* Japanese art of flower arrangement.

ikon *noun* same as ICON.

IL Illinois.

ileum *noun* lowest part of the small intestine.

ilex *noun* any of a genus of trees or shrubs that includes holly.

ilium *noun, pl* **-ia** uppermost and widest of the three sections of the hipbone. **iliac** *adjective*

ilk *noun* type, e.g. *others of his ilk.*

ill ⊕ *adjective* **1** not in good health. **2** harmful or unpleasant, e.g. *ill effects.* ◆ *noun* **3** evil, harm. ◆ *adverb* **4** badly. **5** hardly, with difficulty, e.g. *I can ill afford to lose him.* **ill at ease** uncomfortable, unable to relax. **illness** *noun* **ill-advised** *adjective* **1** badly thought out. **2** unwise. **ill-bred** *adjective* lacking good manners, rude. **ill-disposed** *adjective* (often foll. by *towards*) unfriendly, unsympathetic. **ill-fated** *adjective* doomed to end unhappily. **ill-favoured** *adjective* ugly, unattractive. **ill-gotten** *adjective* obtained dishonestly, e.g. *ill-gotten gains.* **ill-health** *noun* condition of being unwell. **ill-mannered** *adjective* having bad manners. **ill-starred** *adjective* ill-fated, unlucky. **ill-tempered** *adjective* displaying bad temper. **ill-timed** *adjective* done or happening at an unsuitable time. **ill-treat** *verb* treat cruelly. **ill-treatment** *noun* **ill will** unkind feeling, hostility.

illegal ⊕ *adjective* against the law. **illegally** *adverb* **illegality** *noun, pl* **-ties**

illegible ⊕ *adjective* unable to be read or deciphered. **illegibility** *noun*

illegitimate ⊕ *adjective* **1** born of parents not married to each other. **2** not lawful. **illegitimacy** *noun*

——————— T H E S A U R U S ———————

if *conjunction* **1** = **provided**, assuming, on condition that, providing, supposing

ignite *verb* **a** = **catch fire**, burn, burst into flames, flare up, inflame, take fire **b** = **set fire to**, kindle, light, set alight, torch

ignominious *adjective* = **humiliating**, discreditable, disgraceful, dishonourable, indecorous, inglorious, shameful, sorry, undignified OPPOSITE **honourable**

ignominy *noun* = **disgrace**, discredit, dishonour, disrepute, humiliation, infamy, obloquy, shame, stigma OPPOSITE **honour**

ignorance *noun* **1** = **unawareness**, inexperience, innocence, unconsciousness, unfamiliarity

ignorant *adjective* **1** = **uninformed**, illiterate, inexperienced, innocent, oblivious, unaware, unconscious, uneducated, unenlightened, uninitiated, unwitting OPPOSITE **educated**. **2** = **insensitive**, crass, half-baked (*inf*), rude

ignore *verb* = **overlook**, discount, disregard, neglect, pass over, reject, take no notice of, turn a blind eye to OPPOSITE **pay attention to**

ill *adjective* **1** = **unwell**, ailing, crook (*Aust & NZ sl*), diseased, indisposed, infirm, off-colour,

poorly (*inf*), sick, under the weather (*inf*), unhealthy OPPOSITE **well**. **2** = **harmful**, bad, damaging, deleterious, detrimental, evil, foul, injurious, unfortunate OPPOSITE **favourable** ◆*noun* **3** = **harm**, affliction, hardship, hurt, injury, misery, misfortune, trouble, unpleasantness, woe OPPOSITE **good** ◆*adverb* **4** = **badly**, inauspiciously, poorly, unfavourably, unfortunately, unluckily **5** = **hardly**, barely, by no means, scantily OPPOSITE **well**

ill-advised *adjective* **1** = **misguided**, ill-considered, ill-judged, injudicious OPPOSITE **wise**. **2** = **unwise**, foolhardy, imprudent, incautious, rash, reckless, thoughtless OPPOSITE **wise**

ill-disposed *adjective* (often foll. by *towards*) = **unfriendly**, antagonistic, disobliging, hostile, inimical, uncooperative, unwelcoming

illegal *adjective* = **unlawful**, banned, criminal, felonious, forbidden, illicit, outlawed, prohibited, unauthorized, unlicensed OPPOSITE **legal**

illegality *noun* = **crime**, felony, illegitimacy, lawlessness, wrong

illegible *adjective* = **indecipherable**, obscure,

illiberal *adjective* narrow-minded, intolerant.

illicit ❶ *adjective* **1** illegal. **2** forbidden or disapproved of by society.

illiterate ❶ *noun, adjective* (person) unable to read or write. **illiteracy** *noun*

illogical ❶ *adjective* **1** unreasonable. **2** not logical. **illogicality** *noun*

illuminate ❶ *verb* **1** light up. **2** make clear, explain. **3** decorate with lights. **4** *Hist* decorate (a manuscript) with designs of gold and bright colours. **illumination** *noun* **illuminating** *adjective*

illusion ❶ *noun* deceptive appearance or belief. **illusionist** *noun* conjuror. **illusory** *adjective* seeming to be true, but actually false.

illustrate ❶ *verb* **1** explain by use of examples. **2** provide (a book or text) with pictures. **3** be an example of. **illustration** *noun*

1 picture or diagram. **2** example. **3** art of illustrating. **illustrative** *adjective* **illustrator** *noun*

illustrious ❶ *adjective* famous and distinguished.

image ❶ *noun* **1** mental picture of someone or something. **2** impression people have of a person, organization, etc. **3** representation of a person or thing in a work of art. **4** optical reproduction of someone or something, for example in a mirror. **5** person or thing that looks almost exactly like another. **6** figure of speech, esp. a metaphor or simile. **imagery** *noun* images collectively, esp. in the arts.

imagine ❶ *verb* **1** form a mental image of. **2** think, believe, or guess. **imaginable** *adjective* **imaginary** *adjective* existing only in the imagination. **imagination** *noun* **1** ability to

I

———————— THESAURUS ————————

scrawled, unreadable OPPOSITE **legible**

illegitimate *adjective* **1** = **born out of wedlock**, bastard **2** = **unlawful**, illegal, illicit, improper, unauthorized OPPOSITE **legal**

ill-fated *adjective* = **doomed**, hapless, ill-omened, ill-starred, luckless, star-crossed, unfortunate, unhappy, unlucky

illicit *adjective* **1** = **illegal**, criminal, felonious, illegitimate, prohibited, unauthorized, unlawful, unlicensed OPPOSITE **legal**. **2** = **forbidden**, clandestine, furtive, guilty, immoral, improper

illiterate *adjective* = **uneducated**, ignorant, uncultured, untaught, untutored OPPOSITE **educated**

ill-mannered *adjective* = **rude**, badly behaved, boorish, churlish, discourteous, impolite, insolent, loutish, uncouth OPPOSITE **polite**

illness *noun* **1** = **sickness**, affliction, ailment, disease, disorder, infirmity, malady

illogical *adjective* = **irrational**, absurd, inconsistent, invalid, meaningless, senseless, shonky (*Aust & NZ inf*), unreasonable, unscientific, unsound OPPOSITE **logical**

ill-treat *verb* = **abuse**, damage, harm, injure, maltreat, mishandle, misuse, oppress

illuminate *verb* **1** = **light up**, brighten OPPOSITE **darken**. **2** = **clarify**, clear up, elucidate, enlighten, explain, interpret, make clear, shed light on OPPOSITE **obscure**

illuminating *adjective* **2** = **informative**, enlightening, explanatory, helpful, instructive, revealing OPPOSITE **confusing**

illumination *noun* **1** = **light**, brightness, lighting, radiance **2** = **enlightenment**, clarification, insight, revelation

illusion *noun* **a** = **fantasy**, chimera, daydream, figment of the imagination, hallucination,

mirage, will-o'-the-wisp **b** = **misconception**, deception, delusion, error, fallacy, misapprehension OPPOSITE **reality**

illusory *adjective* = **unreal**, chimerical, deceptive, delusive, fallacious, false, hallucinatory, mistaken, sham OPPOSITE **real**

illustrate *verb* **1** = **demonstrate**, bring home, elucidate, emphasize, explain, point up, show

illustrated *adjective* **2** = **pictorial**, decorated, graphic

illustration *noun* **1** = **picture**, decoration, figure, plate, sketch **2** = **example**, case, instance, specimen

illustrious *adjective* = **famous**, celebrated, distinguished, eminent, glorious, great, notable, prominent, renowned OPPOSITE **obscure**

ill will *noun* = **hostility**, animosity, bad blood, dislike, enmity, hatred, malice, rancour, resentment, venom OPPOSITE **goodwill**

image *noun* **1, 2** = **concept**, idea, impression, mental picture, perception **3** = **representation**, effigy, figure, icon, idol, likeness, picture, portrait, statue **5** = **replica**, counterpart, (dead) ringer (*sl*), doppelgänger, double, facsimile, spitting image (*inf*)

imaginable *adjective* = **possible**, believable, comprehensible, conceivable, credible, likely, plausible OPPOSITE **unimaginable**

imaginary *adjective* = **fictional**, fictitious, hypothetical, illusory, imagined, invented, made-up, nonexistent, unreal OPPOSITE **real**

imagination *noun* **2** = **creativity**, enterprise, ingenuity, invention, inventiveness, originality, resourcefulness, vision

imaginative *adjective* = **creative**, clever, enterprising, ingenious, inspired, inventive, original OPPOSITE **unimaginative**

make mental images of things that may not exist in real life. **2** creative mental ability. **imaginative** *adjective* having or showing a lot of creative mental ability. **imaginatively** *adverb*

> **SPELLING TIP**
>
> Remembering that an *e* changes to an *a* to form **imagination** is a good way of getting **imaginary** right, because it has an *a* instead of an *e* too.

imago [im-**may**-go] *noun, pl* **imagoes, imagines** [im-**maj**-in-ees] sexually mature adult insect.

imam *noun* **1** leader of prayers in a mosque. **2** title of some Islamic leaders.

IMAX ® [**eye**-max] *noun* film projection process which produces an image ten times larger than standard.

imbalance *noun* lack of balance or proportion.

imbecile ❶ [**imb**-ess-eel] *noun* **1** stupid person. **2** *Offens* mentally retarded person. ♦ *adjective* **3** (also **imbecilic**) stupid or senseless. **imbecility** *noun*

imbed *verb* same as EMBED.

imbibe ❶ *verb* **1** drink (alcoholic drinks). **2** *Lit*

absorb (ideas etc.).

imbroglio ❶ [imb-**role**-ee-oh] *noun, pl* **-ios** confusing and complicated situation.

imbue *verb* **-buing, -bued** (usu. foll. by *with*) fill or inspire with (ideals or principles).

IMF International Monetary Fund.

imitate ❶ *verb* **1** take as a model. **2** copy the voice and mannerisms of, esp. for entertainment. **imitation** *noun* **1** copy of an original. **2** imitating. ♦ *adjective* **3** made to look like a material of superior quality, e.g. *imitation leather*. **imitative** *adjective* **imitator** *noun*

immaculate ❶ *adjective* **1** completely clean or tidy. **2** completely flawless. **immaculately** *adverb*

immanent *adjective* present within and throughout something. **immanence** *noun*

immaterial ❶ *adjective* not important, not relevant.

immature ❶ *adjective* **1** not fully developed. **2** lacking wisdom or stability because of youth. **immaturity** *noun*

immeasurable *adjective* too great to be measured. **immeasurably** *adverb*

immediate ❶ *adjective* **1** occurring at once. **2** next or nearest in time, space, or relationship. **immediately** *adverb* **immediacy** *noun*

immemorial *adjective* **since, from time**

———— THESAURUS ————

imagine *verb* **1** = **envisage**, conceive, conceptualize, conjure up, picture, plan, think of, think up, visualize **2** = **believe**, assume, conjecture, fancy, guess (*inf, chiefly US & Canad*), infer, suppose, surmise, suspect, take it, think

imbecile *noun* **1** = **idiot**, chump, cretin, fool, halfwit, moron, numbskull *or* numskull, thickhead, twit (*inf, chiefly Brit*) ♦*adjective* **3** (also **imbecilic**) = **stupid**, asinine, fatuous, feeble-minded, foolish, idiotic, moronic, thick, witless

imbibe *verb* **1** = **drink**, consume, knock back (*inf*), quaff, sink (*inf*), swallow, swig (*inf*) **2** *Lit* = **absorb**, acquire, assimilate, gain, gather, ingest, receive, take in

imbroglio *noun* = **complication**, embarrassment, entanglement, involvement, misunderstanding, quandary

imitate *verb* **1** = **follow**, emulate, mirror, simulate **2** = **copy**, ape, echo, mimic, repeat

imitation *noun* **1** = **replica**, fake, forgery, impersonation, impression, reproduction, sham, substitution **2** = **mimicry**, counterfeiting, duplication, likeness, resemblance, simulation ♦*adjective* **3** = **artificial**, dummy, ersatz, man-made, mock, phoney *or* phony (*inf*),

reproduction, sham, simulated, synthetic OPPOSITE> **real**

imitative *adjective* **1** = **derivative**, second-hand, simulated, unoriginal **2** = **parrot-like**, copycat (*inf*), mimetic

imitator *noun* **2** = **impersonator**, copier, copycat (*inf*), impressionist, mimic, parrot

immaculate *adjective* **1** = **clean**, neat, spick-and-span, spotless, spruce, squeaky-clean OPPOSITE> **dirty**. **2** = **pure**, above reproach, faultless, flawless, impeccable, perfect, unblemished, unexceptionable, untarnished OPPOSITE> **corrupt**

immaterial *adjective* = **irrelevant**, extraneous, inconsequential, inessential, insignificant, of no importance, trivial, unimportant OPPOSITE> **important**

immature *adjective* **1** = **young**, adolescent, undeveloped, unformed, unripe OPPOSITE> **adult**. **2** = **childish**, callow, inexperienced, infantile, juvenile, puerile OPPOSITE> **adult**

immaturity *noun* **1** = **unripeness**, greenness, imperfection, rawness, unpreparedness **2** = **childishness**, callowness, inexperience, puerility

immediate *adjective* **1** = **instant**, instantaneous OPPOSITE> **later**. **2** = **nearest**,

immemorial longer than anyone can remember.

immense ❶ *adjective* extremely large.

immensely *adverb* to a very great degree.

immensity *noun*

immerse ❶ *verb* 1 involve deeply, engross, e.g. *immersed in his work*. 2 plunge (something or someone) into liquid. **immersion** *noun*

immersion heater electrical device in a domestic hot-water tank for heating water.

immigration ❶ *noun* coming to a foreign country in order to settle there. **immigrate** *verb* **immigrant** *noun* person who comes to a foreign country in order to settle there.

imminent ❶ *adjective* about to happen. **imminently** *adverb* **imminence** *noun*

immobile ❶ *adjective* 1 not moving. 2 unable to move. **immobility** *noun* **immobilize** *verb* make unable to move or work.

immoderate ❶ *adjective* excessive or unreasonable.

immodest *adjective* 1 behaving in an indecent or improper manner. 2 behaving in a boastful or conceited manner. **immodesty** *noun*

immolate *verb* kill as a sacrifice. **immolation** *noun*

immoral ❶ *adjective* 1 morally wrong, corrupt. 2 sexually depraved or promiscuous. **immorality** *noun*

LANGUAGE TIP

Do not confuse *immoral* with *amoral*, which means 'having no moral standards'.

---

immortal ❶ *adjective* 1 living forever. 2 famous for all time. ◆ *noun* 3 person whose fame will last for all time. 4 immortal being. **immortality** *noun* **immortalize** *verb*

immovable, immoveable ❶ *adjective* 1 unable to be moved. 2 unwilling to change one's opinions or beliefs. 3 not affected by feeling, emotionless. **immovability, immoveability** *noun* **immovably, immoveably** *adverb*

immune ❶ *adjective* 1 protected against a specific disease. 2 (foll. by *to*) secure (against). 3 (foll. by *from*) exempt (from). **immunity** *noun, pl* **-ties** 1 ability to resist disease. 2 freedom from prosecution, tax, etc. **immunize** *verb* make immune to a disease. **immunization**

——————— T H E S A U R U S ———————

close, direct, near, next OPPOSITE **far**

immediately *adverb* 1 = **at once**, directly, forthwith, instantly, now, promptly, right away, straight away, this instant, without delay

immense *adjective* = **huge**, colossal, enormous, extensive, gigantic, great, massive, monumental, stupendous, tremendous, vast OPPOSITE **tiny**

immensity *noun* = **size**, bulk, enormity, expanse, extent, greatness, hugeness, magnitude, vastness

immerse *verb* 1 = **engross**, absorb, busy, engage, involve, occupy, take up 2 = **plunge**, bathe, dip, douse, duck, dunk, sink, submerge

immersion *noun* 1 = **involvement**, absorption, concentration, preoccupation 2 = **dipping**, dousing, ducking, dunking, plunging, submerging

immigrant *noun* = **settler**, incomer, newcomer

imminent *adjective* = **near**, at hand, close, coming, forthcoming, gathering, impending, in the pipeline, looming OPPOSITE **remote**

immobile *adjective* = **stationary**, at a standstill, at rest, fixed, immovable, motionless, rigid, rooted, static, still, stock-still, unmoving OPPOSITE **mobile**

immobility *noun* = **stillness**, fixity, inertness, motionlessness, stability, steadiness

immobilize *verb* = **paralyse**, bring to a standstill, cripple, disable, freeze, halt, stop, transfix

immoderate *adjective* = **excessive**, exaggerated, exorbitant, extravagant, extreme, inordinate, over the top (*sl*), undue, unjustified, unreasonable

immoral *adjective* 1 = **wicked**, bad, corrupt, sinful, unethical, unprincipled, wrong OPPOSITE **moral**. 2 = **depraved**, debauched, dissolute, indecent OPPOSITE **moral**

immorality *noun* 1 = **wickedness**, corruption, sin, wrong 2 = **depravity**, debauchery, dissoluteness, vice OPPOSITE **morality**

immortal *adjective* 1 = **eternal**, deathless, enduring, everlasting, imperishable, lasting, perennial, undying OPPOSITE **passing** ◆*noun* 3 = **great**, genius, hero 4 = **god**, goddess OPPOSITE **mortal**

immortality *noun* 1 = **eternity**, everlasting life, perpetuity 2 = **fame**, celebrity, glory, greatness, renown

immortalize *verb* 2 = **commemorate**, celebrate, exalt, glorify

immovable, immoveable *adjective* 1 = **fixed**, firm, immutable, jammed, secure, set, stable, stationary, stuck 2 = **inflexible**, adamant, obdurate, resolute, steadfast, unshakable, unwavering, unyielding OPPOSITE **flexible**

noun

immunodeficiency *noun* deficiency in or breakdown of a person's ability to fight diseases.

immunology *noun* branch of medicine concerned with the study of immunity. **immunological** *adjective* **immunologist** *noun*

immure *verb Lit* imprison.

immutable [im-mute-a-bl] *adjective* unchangeable. **immutability** *noun*

imp ① *noun* 1 (in folklore) mischievous small creature with magical powers. 2 mischievous child.

impact ① *noun* 1 strong effect. 2 (force of) a collision. ◆ *verb* 3 have a strong effect on. 4 press firmly into something.

impair ① *verb* weaken or damage. **impairment** *noun*

impala [imp-ah-la] *noun* southern African antelope.

impale *verb* pierce with a sharp object.

impalpable *adjective* difficult to define or understand.

impart ① *verb* 1 communicate (information). 2 give, e.g. *butter imparts a full rich taste to a cake.*

impartial ① *adjective* not favouring one side or the other. **impartially** *adverb* **impartiality** *noun*

impassable ① *adjective* (of a road etc.) impossible to travel through or over.

impasse ① [am-pass] *noun* situation in which progress is impossible.

impassible *adjective* impassive or unmoved.

impassioned ① *adjective* full of emotion.

impassive *adjective* showing no emotion, calm. **impassively** *adverb*

impasto 1 paint applied thickly, so that brush marks are evident. 2 technique of painting in this way.

impatient ① *adjective* 1 irritable at any delay or difficulty. 2 restless (to have or do something). **impatiently** *adverb* **impatience** *noun*

impeach ① *verb* charge with a serious crime against the state. **impeachment** *noun*

impeccable ① *adjective* without fault, excellent. **impeccably** *adverb*

impecunious ① *adjective* penniless, poor.

impedance [imp-eed-anss] *noun Electricity* measure of the opposition to the flow of an alternating current.

———————————— THESAURUS ————————————

immune *adjective* 1 = **protected**, clear, free, resistant 2 = **invulnerable**, proof (against), safe, unaffected 3 = **exempt**

immunity *noun* 1 = **resistance**, immunization, protection OPPOSITE susceptibility. 3 = **exemption**, amnesty, freedom, indemnity, invulnerability, licence, release

immunize *verb* = **vaccinate**, inoculate, protect, safeguard

imp *noun* 1 = **demon**, devil, sprite 2 = **rascal**, brat, minx, rogue, scamp

impact *noun* 1 = **effect**, consequences, impression, influence, repercussions, significance 2 = **collision**, blow, bump, contact, crash, jolt, knock, smash, stroke, thump

impair *verb* = **worsen**, blunt, damage, decrease, diminish, harm, hinder, injure, lessen, reduce, undermine, weaken OPPOSITE improve

impaired *adjective* = **damaged**, defective, faulty, flawed, imperfect, shonky (*Aust & NZ inf*), unsound

impart *verb* 1 = **communicate**, convey, disclose, divulge, make known, pass on, relate, reveal, tell 2 = **give**, accord, afford, bestow, confer, grant, lend, yield

impartial *adjective* = **neutral**, detached, disinterested, equitable, even-handed, fair, just, objective, open-minded, unbiased, unprejudiced OPPOSITE unfair

impartiality *noun* = **neutrality**, detachment, disinterestedness, dispassion, equity, even-handedness, fairness, objectivity, open-mindedness OPPOSITE unfairness

impassable *adjective* = **blocked**, closed, impenetrable, obstructed

impasse *noun* = **deadlock**, dead end, stalemate, standoff, standstill

impassioned *adjective* = **intense**, animated, fervent, fiery, heated, inspired, passionate, rousing, stirring OPPOSITE cool

impatience *noun* 1 = **irritability**, intolerance, quick temper, shortness, snappiness OPPOSITE patience. 2 = **restlessness**, agitation, anxiety, eagerness, edginess, fretfulness, nervousness, uneasiness OPPOSITE calm

impatient *adjective* 1 = **irritable**, demanding, hot-tempered, intolerant, quick-tempered, snappy, testy OPPOSITE easy-going. 2 = **restless**, eager, edgy, fretful, straining at the leash OPPOSITE calm

impeach *verb* = **charge**, accuse, arraign, indict

impeccable *adjective* = **faultless**, blameless, flawless, immaculate, irreproachable, perfect, squeaky-clean, unblemished, unimpeachable OPPOSITE flawed

impecunious *adjective* = **poor**, broke (*inf*), destitute, down and out, indigent, insolvent, penniless, poverty-stricken

impede ❶ *verb* hinder in action or progress.
impediment *noun* something that makes action, speech, or progress difficult.
impedimenta *plural noun* objects impeding progress, esp. baggage or equipment.
impel ❶ *verb* **-pelling, -pelled** push or force (someone) to do something.
impending ❶ *adjective* (esp. of something bad) about to happen.
impenetrable ❶ *adjective* **1** impossible to get through. **2** impossible to understand.
imperative ❶ *adjective* **1** extremely urgent, vital. **2** *Grammar* denoting a mood of verbs used in commands. ♦ *noun* **3** *Grammar* imperative mood.
imperceptible ❶ *adjective* too slight or gradual to be noticed. **imperceptibly** *adverb*
imperfect ❶ *adjective* **1** having faults or mistakes. **2** not complete. **3** *Grammar* denoting a tense of verbs describing continuous, incomplete, or repeated past actions. ♦ *noun* **4** *Grammar* imperfect tense. **imperfection** *noun*
imperial ❶ *adjective* **1** of or like an empire or emperor. **2** denoting a system of weights and measures formerly used in Britain. **imperialism**

noun rule by one country over many others.
imperialist *adjective, noun*
imperil ❶ *verb* **-illing, -illed** put in danger.
imperious *adjective* proud and domineering.
impersonal ❶ *adjective* **1** not relating to any particular person, objective. **2** lacking human warmth or sympathy. **3** *Grammar* (of a verb) without a personal subject, e.g. *it is snowing.* **impersonality** *noun*
impersonate ❶ *verb* **1** pretend to be (another person). **2** copy the voice and mannerisms of, esp. for entertainment. **impersonation** *noun* **impersonator** *noun*
impertinent ❶ *adjective* disrespectful or rude. **impertinently** *adverb* **impertinence** *noun*
imperturbable ❶ *adjective* calm, not excitable.
impervious ❶ *adjective* (foll. by *to*) **1** not letting (water etc.) through. **2** not influenced by (a feeling, argument, etc.).
impetigo [imp-it-**tie**-go] *noun* contagious skin disease.
impetuous ❶ *adjective* done or acting without thought, rash. **impetuously** *adverb* **impetuosity** *noun*

——————— THESAURUS ———————

impede *verb* =**hinder**, block, check, disrupt, hamper, hold up, obstruct, slow (down), thwart
impediment *noun* =**obstacle**, barrier, difficulty, encumbrance, hindrance, obstruction, snag, stumbling block OPPOSITE aid
impel *verb* =**force**, compel, constrain, drive, induce, oblige, push, require OPPOSITE discourage
impending *adjective* =**looming**, approaching, coming, forthcoming, gathering, imminent, in the pipeline, near, upcoming
impenetrable *adjective* **1** =**impassable**, dense, impermeable, impervious, inviolable, solid, thick OPPOSITE accessible. **2** =**incomprehensible**, arcane, enigmatic, inscrutable, mysterious, obscure, unfathomable, unintelligible OPPOSITE clear
imperative *adjective* **1** =**urgent**, crucial, essential, pressing, vital OPPOSITE unnecessary
imperceptible *adjective* =**undetectable**, faint, indiscernible, invisible, microscopic, minute, slight, small, subtle, tiny OPPOSITE perceptible
imperfect *adjective* =**flawed**, damaged, defective, faulty, impaired, incomplete, limited, unfinished OPPOSITE perfect
imperfection *noun* **1** =**fault**, blemish, defect, deficiency, failing, flaw, frailty, shortcoming, taint, weakness OPPOSITE perfection
imperial *adjective* **2** =**royal**, kingly, majestic,

princely, queenly, regal, sovereign OPPOSITE protect
imperil *verb* =**endanger**, expose, jeopardize, risk
impersonal *adjective* **2** =**detached**, aloof, cold, dispassionate, formal, inhuman, neutral, remote OPPOSITE personal
impersonate *verb* **1** =**pretend to be**, masquerade as, pass oneself off as, pose as (*inf*) **2** =**imitate**, ape, do (*inf*), mimic, take off (*inf*)
impersonation *noun* **2** =**imitation**, caricature, impression, mimicry, parody, takeoff (*inf*)
impertinence *noun* =**rudeness**, brazenness, cheek (*inf*), disrespect, effrontery, front, impudence, insolence, nerve (*inf*), presumption
impertinent *adjective* =**rude**, brazen, cheeky (*inf*), disrespectful, impolite, impudent, insolent, presumptuous OPPOSITE polite
imperturbable *adjective* =**calm**, collected, composed, cool, nerveless, self-possessed, serene, unexcitable, unflappable (*inf*), unruffled OPPOSITE agitated
impervious *adjective* **1** (foll. by *to*) =**sealed**, impassable, impenetrable, impermeable, resistant **2** =**unaffected**, immune, invulnerable, proof against, unmoved, untouched
impetuosity *noun* =**haste**, impulsiveness, precipitateness, rashness
impetuous *adjective* =**rash**, hasty, impulsive,

impetus ❶ [imp-it-uss] *noun, pl* **-tuses 1** incentive, impulse. **2** force that starts a body moving.

impinge ❶ *verb* (foll. by *on*) affect or restrict.

impious ❶ [imp-ee-uss] *adjective* showing a lack of respect or reverence.

impish ❶ *adjective* mischievous.

implacable ❶ *adjective* not prepared to be appeased, unyielding. **implacably** *adverb* **implacability** *noun*

implant ❶ *noun* **1** *Med* something put into someone's body, usu. by surgical operation, e.g. *silicone implants.* ◆ *verb* **2** put (something) into someone's body, usu. by surgical operation. **3** fix firmly in someone's mind. **implantation** *noun*

implement ❶ *verb* **1** carry out (instructions etc.). ◆ *noun* **2** tool, instrument. **implementation** *noun*

implicate ❶ *verb* show to be involved, esp. in a crime. **implication** *noun* something implied.

implicit ❶ *adjective* **1** expressed indirectly. **2** absolute and unquestioning, e.g. *implicit*

support. **implicitly** *adverb*

implode *verb* collapse inwards.

implore ❶ *verb* beg earnestly.

imply ❶ *verb* **-plying, -plied 1** indicate by hinting, suggest. **2** involve as a necessary consequence.

impolite ❶ *adjective* showing bad manners.

impolitic *adjective* unwise or inadvisable.

imponderable *noun, adjective* (something) impossible to assess.

import ❶ *verb* **1** bring in (goods) from another country. ◆ *noun* **2** something imported. **3** importance. **4** meaning. **importation** *noun* **importer** *noun*

important ❶ *adjective* **1** of great significance or value. **2** having influence or power. **importance** *noun*

importunate ❶ *adjective* persistent or demanding. **importune** *verb* harass with persistent requests. **importunity** *noun, pl* **-ties**

impose ❶ *verb* **1** force the acceptance of. **2** (foll. by *on*) take unfair advantage (of). **imposing** *adjective* grand, impressive.

——————————————— THESAURUS ———————————————

precipitate, unthinking OPPOSITE **cautious**
impetus *noun* **1** = **incentive**, catalyst, goad, impulse, motivation, push, spur, stimulus **2** = **force**, energy, momentum, power

impinge *verb* (foll. by *on*) = **affect**, bear upon, have a bearing on, impact, influence, relate to, touch

impious *adjective* = **sacrilegious**, blasphemous, godless, irreligious, irreverent, profane, sinful, ungodly, unholy, wicked

impish *adjective* = **mischievous**, devilish, puckish, rascally, roguish, sportive, waggish

implacable *adjective* = **unyielding**, inflexible, intractable, merciless, pitiless, unbending, uncompromising, unforgiving OPPOSITE **merciful**

implant *verb* **1** = **insert**, fix, graft **2** = **instil**, inculcate, infuse

implement *verb* **1** = **carry out**, bring about, complete, effect, enforce, execute, fulfil, perform, realize OPPOSITE **hinder** ◆*noun* **2** = **tool**, apparatus, appliance, device, gadget, instrument, utensil

implicate *verb* = **incriminate**, associate, embroil, entangle, include, inculpate, involve OPPOSITE **dissociate**

implication *noun* = **suggestion**, inference, innuendo, meaning, overtone, presumption, significance

implicit *adjective* **1** = **implied**, inferred, latent, tacit, taken for granted, undeclared, understood, unspoken OPPOSITE **explicit**. **2**

= **absolute**, constant, firm, fixed, full, steadfast, unqualified, unreserved, wholehearted

implied *adjective* **1** = **unspoken**, hinted at, implicit, indirect, suggested, tacit, undeclared, unexpressed, unstated

implore *verb* = **beg**, beseech, entreat, importune, plead with, pray

imply *verb* **1** = **hint**, insinuate, intimate, signify, suggest **2** = **entail**, indicate, involve, mean, point to, presuppose

impolite *adjective* = **bad-mannered**, discourteous, disrespectful, ill-mannered, insolent, loutish, rude, uncouth OPPOSITE **polite**

import *verb* **1** = **bring in**, introduce ◆*noun* **3** = **importance**, consequence, magnitude, moment, significance, substance, weight **4** = **meaning**, drift, gist, implication, intention, sense, significance, thrust

importance *noun* **1** = **significance**, concern, consequence, import, interest, moment, substance, usefulness, value, weight **2** = **prestige**, distinction, eminence, esteem, influence, mana (*NZ*), prominence, standing, status

important *adjective* **1** = **significant**, far-reaching, momentous, seminal, serious, substantial, urgent, weighty OPPOSITE **unimportant**. **2** = **powerful**, eminent, high-ranking, influential, noteworthy, pre-eminent, prominent, skookum (*Canad*)

importunate *adjective Formal* = **persistent**,

imposition *noun* **1** imposing. **2** unreasonable demand.

impossible ⊕ *adjective* **1** not able to be done or to happen. **2** absurd or unreasonable. **impossibly** *adverb* **impossibility** *noun, pl* **-ties**

imposter, impostor *noun* person who cheats or swindles by pretending to be someone else.

imposture *noun* deception, esp. by pretending to be someone else.

impotent ⊕ [imp-a-tent] *adjective* **1** powerless. **2** (of a man) incapable of sexual intercourse. **impotence** *noun* **impotently** *adverb*

impound *verb* take legal possession of, confiscate.

impoverish ⊕ *verb* make poor or weak. **impoverishment** *noun*

impracticable ⊕ *adjective* incapable of being put into practice.

impractical ⊕ *adjective* not sensible.

imprecation *noun* curse.

impregnable ⊕ *adjective* impossible to break into. **impregnability** *noun*

impregnate ⊕ *verb* **1** saturate, spread all through. **2** make pregnant. **impregnation** *noun*

impresario *noun, pl* **-ios** person who runs theatre performances, concerts, etc.

SPELLING TIP

Don't be fooled into spelling **impresario** as *impressario*, which occurs 33 times in the Bank of English. The correct spelling has only one *s*.

---

impress ⊕ *verb* **1** affect strongly, usu. favourably. **2** stress, emphasize. **3** imprint, stamp. **impression** *noun* **1** effect, esp. a strong or favourable one. **2** vague idea. **3** impersonation for entertainment. **4** mark made by pressing. **impressionable** *adjective* easily impressed or influenced. **impressionist** *noun* person who impersonates other people for entertainment. **impressive** *adjective* making a strong impression, esp. through size, importance, or quality.

Impressionism *noun* art style that gives a

—————————— T H E S A U R U S ——————————

demanding, dogged, insistent, pressing, urgent

impose *verb* **1** =**establish**, decree, fix, institute, introduce, levy, ordain **2** (foll. by *on*) =**inflict**, saddle (someone) with, take advantage of

imposing *adjective* =**impressive**, commanding, dignified, grand, majestic, stately, striking OPPOSITE **unimposing**

imposition *noun* **1** =**application**, introduction, levying **2** =**intrusion**, liberty, presumption

impossibility *noun* **1** =**hopelessness**, impracticability, inability

impossible *adjective* **1** =**inconceivable**, impracticable, out of the question, unachievable, unattainable, unobtainable, unthinkable OPPOSITE **possible**. **2** =**absurd**, ludicrous, outrageous, preposterous, unreasonable

imposter, impostor *noun* =**impersonator**, charlatan, deceiver, fake, fraud, phoney *or* phony (*inf*), pretender, sham, trickster

impotence *noun* **1** =**powerlessness**, feebleness, frailty, helplessness, inability, incapacity, incompetence, ineffectiveness, paralysis, uselessness, weakness OPPOSITE **powerfulness**

impotent *adjective* **1** =**powerless**, feeble, frail, helpless, incapable, incapacitated, incompetent, ineffective, paralysed, weak

OPPOSITE **powerful**

impoverish *verb* =**bankrupt**, beggar, break, ruin

impoverished *adjective* =**poor**, bankrupt, destitute, impecunious, needy, on one's uppers, penurious, poverty-stricken OPPOSITE **rich**

impracticable *adjective* =**unfeasible**, impossible, out of the question, unachievable, unattainable, unworkable OPPOSITE **practicable**

impractical *adjective* =**unworkable**, impossible, impracticable, inoperable, nonviable, unrealistic, wild OPPOSITE **practical**

impregnable *adjective* =**invulnerable**, impenetrable, indestructible, invincible, secure, unassailable, unbeatable, unconquerable OPPOSITE **vulnerable**

impregnate *verb* **1** =**saturate**, infuse, permeate, soak, steep, suffuse **2** =**fertilize**, inseminate, make pregnant

impress *verb* **1** =**excite**, affect, inspire, make an impression, move, stir, strike, touch **2** =**stress**, bring home to, emphasize, fix, inculcate, instil into **3** =**imprint**, emboss, engrave, indent, mark, print, stamp

impression *noun* **1** =**effect**, feeling, impact, influence, reaction **2** =**idea**, belief, conviction, feeling, hunch, notion, sense, suspicion **3** =**imitation**, impersonation, parody, send-up (*Brit inf*), takeoff (*inf*) **4** =**mark**, dent, hollow, general effect or mood rather than form or structure. **Impressionist** noun **Impressionistic** adjective

impressive ❶ adjective making a strong impression, esp. through size, importance, or quality.

imprimatur [imp-rim-**ah**-ter] noun official approval to print a book.

imprint ❶ noun **1** mark made by printing or stamping. **2** publisher's name and address on a book. ◆ verb **3** produce (a mark) by printing or stamping. **4** fix firmly in someone's mind.

imprison ❶ verb put in prison. **imprisonment** noun

improbable ❶ adjective not likely to be true or to happen. **improbability** noun, pl **-ties**

improbity noun dishonesty or wickedness.

impromptu ❶ adjective without planning or preparation.

improper ❶ adjective **1** indecent. **2** incorrect or irregular. **improper fraction** fraction in which the numerator is larger than the denominator, as in 5/3.

impropriety ❶ [imp-roe-**pry**-a-tee] noun, pl **-ties** unsuitable or slightly improper behaviour.

improve ❶ verb make or become better. **improvement** noun

improvident ❶ adjective not planning for future needs. **improvidence** noun

improvise ❶ verb **1** make use of whatever materials are available. **2** make up (a piece of music, speech, etc.) as one goes along. **improvisation** noun

imprudent ❶ adjective not sensible or wise. **imprudence** noun

impudent ❶ adjective cheeky, disrespectful. **impudently** adverb **impudence** noun

impugn [imp-**yoon**] verb challenge the truth or validity of.

impulse ❶ noun **1** sudden urge to do something. **2** short electrical signal passing along a wire or nerve or through the air. **on impulse** suddenly and without planning.

impulsive adjective acting or done without

——————— THESAURUS ———————

imprint, indentation, outline, stamp

impressionable adjective = **suggestible**, gullible, ingenuous, open, receptive, responsive, sensitive, susceptible, vulnerable OPPOSITE **blasé**

impressive adjective = **grand**, awesome, dramatic, exciting, moving, powerful, stirring, striking OPPOSITE **unimpressive**

imprint noun **1** = **mark**, impression, indentation, sign, stamp ◆verb **3** = **fix**, engrave, etch, impress, print, stamp

imprison verb = **jail**, confine, detain, incarcerate, intern, lock up, put away, send down (inf) OPPOSITE **free**

imprisoned adjective = **jailed**, behind bars, captive, confined, incarcerated, in jail, inside (sl), locked up, under lock and key

imprisonment noun = **custody**, confinement, detention, incarceration, porridge (sl)

improbability noun = **doubt**, dubiety, uncertainty, unlikelihood

improbable adjective = **doubtful**, dubious, fanciful, far-fetched, implausible, questionable, unconvincing, unlikely, weak OPPOSITE **probable**

impromptu adjective = **unprepared**, ad-lib, extemporaneous, improvised, offhand, off the cuff (inf), spontaneous, unrehearsed, unscripted OPPOSITE **planned**

improper adjective **1** = **indecent**, risqué, smutty, suggestive, unbecoming, unseemly, untoward, vulgar OPPOSITE **decent**. **2** = **inappropriate**, out of place, uncalled-for, unfit, unsuitable, unwarranted OPPOSITE **appropriate**

impropriety noun = **indecency**, bad taste, incongruity, vulgarity OPPOSITE **decency** OPPOSITE **propriety**

improve verb **a** = **enhance**, ameliorate, better, correct, help, rectify, touch up, upgrade OPPOSITE **worsen**. **b** = **progress**, advance, develop, make strides, pick up, rally, rise

improvement noun **a** = **enhancement**, advancement, betterment **b** = **progress**, advance, development, rally, recovery, upswing

improvident adjective = **imprudent**, careless, negligent, prodigal, profligate, reckless, short-sighted, spendthrift, thoughtless, wasteful

improvisation noun **1** = **makeshift**, ad-lib, expedient **2** = **spontaneity**, ad-libbing, extemporizing, invention

improvise verb **1** = **concoct**, contrive, devise, throw together **2** = **extemporize**, ad-lib, busk, invent, play it by ear (inf), speak off the cuff (inf), wing it (inf)

imprudent adjective = **unwise**, careless, foolhardy, ill-advised, ill-considered, ill-judged, injudicious, irresponsible, rash, reckless OPPOSITE **prudent**

impudence noun = **boldness**, audacity, brazenness, cheek (inf), effrontery, impertinence, insolence, nerve (inf), presumption, shamelessness

impudent adjective = **bold**, audacious, brazen, cheeky (inf), impertinent, insolent, presumptuous, rude, shameless OPPOSITE

careful consideration. **impulsively** *adverb*
impunity ● [imp-yoon-it-ee] *noun* **with impunity** without punishment.
impure ● *adjective* **1** having dirty or unwanted substances mixed in. **2** immoral, obscene. **impurity** *noun, pl* **-ties**
impute ● *verb* attribute responsibility to. **imputation** *noun*
in *preposition* **1** indicating position inside, state or situation, etc., e.g. *in the net; in tears.* ◆ *adverb* **2** indicating position inside, entry into, etc., e.g. *she stayed in; come in.* ◆ *adjective* **3** fashionable. **inward** *adjective* **1** directed towards the middle. **2** situated within. **3** spiritual or mental. ◆ *adverb* **4** (also **inwards**) towards the inside or middle. **inwardly** *adverb*
In *Chem* indium.
IN Indiana.
in. inch.
in-¹ *prefix* **1** not, non-, e.g. *incredible.* **2** lack of, e.g. *inexperience.*
in-² *prefix* in, into, towards, within, on, e.g. *infiltrate.*
inability *noun* lack of means or skill to do something.
inaccessible ● *adjective* **1** impossible or very difficult to reach. **2** difficult to understand or

appreciate. **inaccessibility** *noun*
inaccurate ● *adjective* not correct.
inaccuracy *noun, pl* **-cies**
inaction *noun* doing nothing. **inactive** *adjective* **inactivity** *noun*
inadequate ● *adjective* **1** not enough. **2** not good enough. **inadequacy** *noun, pl* **-cies**
inadmissible *adjective* not allowable or acceptable.
inadvertent *adjective* unintentional.
inadvertently *adverb*
inalienable *adjective* not able to be taken away, e.g. *an inalienable right.*
inamorata, *(masc)* **inamorato** *noun, pl* **-s** *Lit* lover.
inane ● *adjective* senseless, silly. **inanity** *noun, pl* **-ties**
inanimate ● *adjective* not living.
inapplicable *adjective* not suitable or relevant.
inappropriate *adjective* not suitable.
inapt *adjective* not apt or fitting.
inarticulate *adjective* unable to express oneself clearly or well.
inasmuch as *conjunction* because or in so far as.
inattentive *adjective* not paying attention.
inattention *noun*

———————— T H E S A U R U S ————————

polite
impulse *noun* **1** = **urge**, caprice, feeling, inclination, notion, whim, wish
impulsive *adjective* = **instinctive**, devil-may-care, hasty, impetuous, intuitive, passionate, precipitate, rash, spontaneous OPPOSITE cautious
impunity *noun* **with impunity** = **without punishment**, at liberty, with freedom, with immunity, with licence, with permission
impure *adjective* **1 a** = **unclean**, contaminated, defiled, dirty, infected, polluted, tainted OPPOSITE clean. **b** = **unrefined**, adulterated, debased, mixed **2** = **immoral**, corrupt, indecent, lascivious, lewd, licentious, obscene, unchaste OPPOSITE moral
impurity *noun* **1** = **contamination**, defilement, dirtiness, infection, pollution, taint
imputation *noun* = **blame**, accusation, aspersion, censure, insinuation, reproach, slander, slur
inaccessible *adjective* **1** = **out of reach**, impassable, out of the way, remote, unapproachable, unattainable, unreachable OPPOSITE accessible
inaccuracy *noun* = **error**, defect, erratum, fault, lapse, mistake
inaccurate *adjective* = **incorrect**, defective,

erroneous, faulty, imprecise, mistaken, out, shonky *(Aust & NZ inf)*, unreliable, unsound, wrong OPPOSITE accurate
inactive *adjective* = **unused**, dormant, idle, inoperative, unemployed, unoccupied OPPOSITE used
inactivity *noun* = **immobility**, dormancy, hibernation, inaction, passivity, unemployment OPPOSITE mobility
inadequacy *noun* **1** = **shortage**, dearth, insufficiency, meagreness, paucity, poverty, scantiness **2** = **deficiency**, defect, failing, imperfection, inability, incapacity, incompetence, ineffectiveness, shortcoming, weakness
inadequate *adjective* **1** = **insufficient**, meagre, scant, sketchy, sparse OPPOSITE sufficient. **2** = **deficient**, faulty, found wanting, incapable, incompetent, not up to scratch *(inf)*, unqualified OPPOSITE fit
inadvertently *adverb* = **unintentionally**, accidentally, by accident, by mistake, involuntarily, mistakenly, unwittingly OPPOSITE deliberately
inane *adjective* = **senseless**, empty, fatuous, frivolous, futile, idiotic, mindless, silly, stupid, vacuous OPPOSITE sensible
inanimate *adjective* = **lifeless**, cold, dead,

inaudible *adjective* not loud enough to be heard. **inaudibly** *adverb*

inaugurate ❶ *verb* **1** open or begin the use of, esp. with ceremony. **2** formally establish (a new leader) in office. **inaugural** *adjective* **inauguration** *noun*

inauspicious *adjective* unlucky, likely to have an unfavourable outcome.

inboard *adjective* (of a boat's engine) inside the hull.

inborn ❶ *adjective* existing from birth, natural.

inbred ❶ *adjective* **1** produced as a result of inbreeding. **2** inborn or ingrained.

inbreeding *noun* breeding of animals or people that are closely related.

inbuilt *adjective* present from the start.

Inc. *US & Aust* (of a company) incorporated.

incalculable ❶ *adjective* too great to be estimated.

in camera *adverb* see CAMERA.

incandescent *adjective* glowing with heat. **incandescence** *noun*

incantation ❶ *noun* ritual chanting of magic words or sounds.

incapable *adjective* **1** (foll. by *of*) unable (to do something). **2** incompetent.

incapacitate ❶ *verb* deprive of strength or ability. **incapacity** *noun*

incarcerate ❶ *verb* imprison. **incarceration** *noun*

incarnate ❶ *adjective* in human form, e.g. *she is evil incarnate*. **incarnation** *noun* **Incarnation** *noun Christianity* God's coming to earth in human form as Jesus Christ.

incendiary [in-**send**-ya-ree] *adjective* **1** (of a bomb, attack, etc.) designed to cause fires. ♦ *noun, pl* **-aries 2** bomb designed to cause fires.

incense¹ ❶ *verb* make very angry.

incense² *noun* substance that gives off a sweet perfume when burned.

incentive ❶ *noun* something that encourages effort or action.

inception ❶ *noun* beginning.

incessant ❶ *adjective* never stopping. **incessantly** *adverb*

incest *noun* sexual intercourse between two people too closely related to marry. **incestuous** *adjective*

inch *noun* **1** unit of length equal to one twelfth of a foot or 2.54 centimetres. ♦ *verb* **2** move slowly and gradually.

inchoate [in-**koe**-ate] *adjective* just begun and

———— THESAURUS ————

defunct, extinct, inert OPPOSITE animate

inaugural *adjective* **1** = **first**, initial, introductory, maiden, opening

inaugurate *verb* **1** = **launch**, begin, commence, get under way, initiate, institute, introduce, set in motion **2** = **invest**, induct, install

inauguration *noun* **1** = **launch**, initiation, institution, opening, setting up **2** = **investiture**, induction, installation

inborn *adjective* = **natural**, congenital, hereditary, inbred, ingrained, inherent, innate, instinctive, intuitive, native

inbred *adjective* **2** = **innate**, constitutional, deep-seated, ingrained, inherent, native, natural

incalculable *adjective* = **countless**, boundless, infinite, innumerable, limitless, numberless, untold, vast

incantation *noun* = **chant**, charm, formula, invocation, spell

incapacitate *verb* = **disable**, cripple, immobilize, lay up (*inf*), paralyse, put out of action (*inf*)

incapacitated *adjective* = **indisposed**, hors de combat, immobilized, laid up (*inf*), out of action (*inf*), unfit

incapacity *noun* = **inability**, impotence, inadequacy, incapability, incompetency, ineffectiveness, powerlessness, unfitness,

weakness

incarcerate *verb* = **imprison**, confine, detain, impound, intern, jail *or* gaol, lock up, throw in jail

incarceration *noun* = **imprisonment**, captivity, confinement, detention, internment

incarnate *adjective* = **personified**, embodied, typified

incarnation *noun* = **embodiment**, epitome, manifestation, personification, type

incense¹ *verb* = **anger**, enrage, inflame, infuriate, irritate, madden, make one's hackles rise, rile (*inf*)

incensed *adjective* = **angry**, enraged, fuming, furious, indignant, infuriated, irate, maddened, steamed up (*sl*), up in arms

incentive *noun* = **encouragement**, bait, carrot (*inf*), enticement, inducement, lure, motivation, spur, stimulus OPPOSITE **disincentive**

inception *noun* = **beginning**, birth, commencement, dawn, initiation, origin, outset, start OPPOSITE **end**

incessant *adjective* = **endless**, ceaseless, constant, continual, eternal, interminable, never-ending, nonstop, perpetual, unceasing, unending OPPOSITE **intermittent**

incessantly *adverb* = **endlessly**, ceaselessly, constantly, continually, eternally, interminably, nonstop, perpetually, persistently, twenty-fournot yet properly developed.

incidence noun extent or frequency of occurrence.

incident ❶ noun **1** something that happens. **2** event involving violence. **incidental** adjective occurring in connection with or resulting from something more important.

incidental ❶ adjective occurring in connection with or resulting from something more important. **incidentally** adverb **incidental music** background music for a film or play.

incinerate ❶ verb burn to ashes. **incineration** noun **incinerator** noun furnace for burning rubbish.

incipient ❶ adjective just starting to appear or happen.

incise ❶ verb cut into with a sharp tool. **incision** noun **incisive** adjective direct and forceful. **incisor** noun front tooth, used for biting into food.

incite ❶ verb stir up, provoke. **incitement** noun

incivility ❶ noun, pl **-ties** rudeness or a rude remark.

inclement ❶ adjective (of weather) stormy or severe. **inclemency** noun

incline ❶ verb **1** lean, slope. **2** (cause to) have a certain disposition or tendency. ◆ noun **3** slope. **inclination** noun **1** liking, tendency, or preference. **2** slope.

include ❶ verb **1** have as part of the whole. **2** put in as part of a set or group. **inclusion** noun **inclusive** adjective including everything (specified). **inclusively** adverb

incognito ❶ [in-kog-nee-toe] adjective, adverb **1** having adopted a false identity. ◆ noun, pl **-tos 2** false identity.

incoherent ❶ adjective unclear and impossible to understand. **incoherence** noun **incoherently** adverb

income ❶ noun amount of money earned from work, investments, etc. **income support** (formerly, in Britain) allowance paid by the government to people with a very low income. **income tax** personal tax levied on annual income.

——————— THESAURUS ———————

seven (inf)

incident noun **1** = **happening**, adventure, episode, event, fact, matter, occasion, occurrence **2** = **disturbance**, clash, commotion, confrontation, contretemps, scene

incidental adjective = **secondary**, ancillary, minor, nonessential, occasional, subordinate, subsidiary OPPOSITE **important**

incidentally adverb = **parenthetically**, by the bye, by the way, in passing

incinerate verb = **burn up**, carbonize, char, cremate, reduce to ashes

incipient adjective = **beginning**, commencing, developing, embryonic, inchoate, nascent, starting

incision noun = **cut**, gash, notch, opening, slash, slit

incisive adjective = **penetrating**, acute, keen, perspicacious, piercing, trenchant OPPOSITE **dull**

incite verb = **provoke**, encourage, foment, inflame, instigate, spur, stimulate, stir up, urge, whip up OPPOSITE **discourage**

incitement noun = **provocation**, agitation, encouragement, impetus, instigation, prompting, spur, stimulus

incivility noun = **rudeness**, bad manners, boorishness, discourteousness, discourtesy, disrespect, ill-breeding, impoliteness

inclement adjective = **stormy**, foul, harsh, intemperate, rough, severe, tempestuous OPPOSITE **fine**

inclination noun **1** = **tendency**, disposition, liking, partiality, penchant, predilection, predisposition, proclivity, proneness, propensity OPPOSITE **dislike**. **2** = **slope**, angle, gradient, incline, pitch, slant, tilt

incline verb **1** = **slope**, lean, slant, tilt, tip, veer **2** = **predispose**, influence, persuade, prejudice, sway ◆noun **3** = **slope**, ascent, descent, dip, grade, gradient, rise

inclined adjective **2** = **disposed**, apt, given, liable, likely, minded, predisposed, prone, willing

include verb **1** = **contain**, comprise, cover, embrace, encompass, incorporate, involve, subsume, take in OPPOSITE **exclude**. **2** = **introduce**, add, enter, insert

inclusion noun **2** = **addition**, incorporation, insertion OPPOSITE **exclusion**

inclusive adjective = **comprehensive**, across-the-board, all-embracing, blanket, general, global, overarching, sweeping, umbrella OPPOSITE **limited**

incognito adjective **1** = **in disguise**, disguised, under an assumed name, unknown, unrecognized

incoherence noun = **unintelligibility**, disjointedness, inarticulateness

incoherent adjective = **unintelligible**, confused, disjointed, disordered, inarticulate, inconsistent, jumbled, muddled, rambling, stammering, stuttering OPPOSITE **coherent**

income noun = **revenue**, earnings, pay,

incoming ⊕ *adjective* 1 coming in. 2 about to come into office.

incommode *verb* cause inconvenience to.

incommunicado *adjective, adverb* deprived of communication with other people.

incomparable ⊕ *adjective* beyond comparison, unequalled. **incomparably** *adverb*

incompatible ⊕ *adjective* inconsistent or conflicting. **incompatibility** *noun*

incompetent ⊕ *adjective* 1 not having the necessary ability or skill to do something. ◆ *noun* 2 incompetent person. **incompetence** *noun*

inconceivable ⊕ *adjective* extremely unlikely, unimaginable.

inconclusive ⊕ *adjective* not giving a final decision or result.

incongruous ⊕ *adjective* inappropriate or out of place. **incongruously** *adverb* **incongruity** *noun, pl* **-ties**

inconsequential *adjective* unimportant, insignificant.

inconsiderable ⊕ *adjective* **not inconsiderable** fairly large.

inconsiderate ⊕ *adjective* not considering other people.

inconsistent ⊕ *adjective* 1 changeable in behaviour or mood. 2 containing contradictory elements, e.g. *witnesses told inconsistent stories.* 3 not in accordance, e.g. *the outburst was inconsistent with his image.* **inconsistency** *noun, pl* **-cies**

inconsolable ⊕ *adjective* very distressed. **inconsolably** *adverb*

inconspicuous ⊕ *adjective* not easily noticed or seen. **inconspicuously** *adverb*

inconstant *adjective* liable to change one's loyalties or opinions.

incontestable *adjective* impossible to deny or argue with.

incontinent *adjective* unable to control one's bladder or bowels. **incontinence** *noun*

incontrovertible ⊕ *adjective* impossible to deny or disprove.

inconvenience ⊕ *noun* 1 trouble or difficulty. ◆ *verb* 2 cause trouble or difficulty to. **inconvenient** *adjective*

incorporate ⊕ *verb* include or be included as

——— THESAURUS ———

proceeds, profits, receipts, salary, takings, wages

incoming *adjective* 1 = **arriving**, approaching, entering, homeward, landing, returning OPPOSITE **leaving**. 2 = **new**

incomparable *adjective* = **unequalled**, beyond compare, inimitable, matchless, peerless, superlative, supreme, transcendent, unmatched, unparalleled, unrivalled

incompatible *adjective* = **inconsistent**, conflicting, contradictory, incongruous, mismatched, unsuited OPPOSITE **compatible**

incompetence *noun* = **ineptitude**, inability, inadequacy, incapability, incapacity, ineffectiveness, unfitness, uselessness

incompetent *adjective* 1 = **inept**, bungling, floundering, incapable, ineffectual, inexpert, unfit, useless OPPOSITE **competent**

inconceivable *adjective* = **unimaginable**, beyond belief, incomprehensible, incredible, mind-boggling (*inf*), out of the question, unbelievable, unheard-of, unthinkable

inconclusive *adjective* = **indecisive**, ambiguous, indeterminate, open, unconvincing, undecided, up in the air (*inf*), vague OPPOSITE **conceivable**

incongruity *noun* = **inappropriateness**, conflict, discrepancy, disparity, incompatibility, inconsistency, unsuitability

incongruous *adjective* = **inappropriate**, discordant, improper, incompatible, out of

keeping, out of place, unbecoming, unsuitable OPPOSITE **appropriate**

inconsiderable *adjective* **not inconsiderable** = **large**, appreciable, goodly, great, marked, noticeable, plentiful, sizable *or* sizeable, substantial

inconsiderate *adjective* = **selfish**, indelicate, insensitive, rude, tactless, thoughtless, unkind, unthinking OPPOSITE **considerate**

inconsistency *noun* 1 = **unreliability**, fickleness, instability, unpredictability, unsteadiness 2, 3 = **incompatibility**, disagreement, discrepancy, disparity, divergence, incongruity, variance

inconsistent *adjective* 1 = **changeable**, capricious, erratic, fickle, inconstant, unpredictable, unstable, unsteady, variable OPPOSITE **consistent**. 2, 3 = **incompatible**, at odds, conflicting, contradictory, discordant, incongruous, irreconcilable, out of step OPPOSITE **compatible**

inconsolable *adjective* = **heartbroken**, brokenhearted, desolate, despairing

inconspicuous *adjective* = **unobtrusive**, camouflaged, hidden, insignificant, ordinary, plain, unassuming, unnoticeable, unostentatious OPPOSITE **obvious**

incontrovertible *adjective* = **indisputable**, certain, established, incontestable, indubitable, irrefutable, positive, sure, undeniable, unquestionable

part of a larger unit. **incorporation** *noun*
incorporeal *adjective* without material form.
incorrigible ❶ *adjective* beyond correction or
reform. **incorrigibly** *adverb*
incorruptible ❶ *adjective* **1** too honest to be
bribed or corrupted. **2** not subject to decay.
increase ❶ *verb* **1** make or become greater in
size, number, etc. ♦ *noun* **2** rise in number, size,
etc. **3** amount by which something increases.
on the increase becoming more common.
increasingly *adverb*
incredible ❶ *adjective* **1** hard to believe or
imagine. **2** *Informal* marvellous, amazing.
incredibly *adverb*
incredulous ❶ *adjective* not willing to believe
something. **incredulity** *noun*
increment ❶ *noun* increase in money or
value, esp. a regular salary increase.
incremental *adjective*
incriminate ❶ *verb* make (someone) seem
guilty of a crime. **incriminating** *adjective*
incubate [in-cube-ate] *verb* **1** (of a bird) hatch
(eggs) by sitting on them. **2** grow (bacteria). **3**
(of bacteria) remain inactive in an animal or
person before causing disease. **incubation** *noun*
incubator *noun* **1** heated enclosed apparatus
for rearing premature babies. **2** apparatus for

artificially hatching birds' eggs.
incubus [in-cube-uss] *noun, pl* **-bi, -buses 1**
(in folklore) demon believed to have sex with
sleeping women. **2** nightmarish burden or
worry.
inculcate *verb* fix in someone's mind by
constant repetition. **inculcation** *noun*
inculpate *verb* cause (someone) to be blamed
for a crime.
incumbent *noun* **1** person holding a
particular office or position. ♦ *adjective* **2**
holding a particular office or position, e.g. *the
incumbent president.* **3 it is incumbent on** it is
the duty of. **incumbency** *noun, pl* **-cies**
incur ❶ *verb* **-curring, -curred** cause
(something unpleasant) to happen.
incurable ❶ *adjective* **1** not able to be cured.
2 not willing or able to change, e.g. *an
incurable romantic.* **incurably** *adverb*
incurious *adjective* showing no curiosity or
interest.
incursion *noun* sudden brief invasion.
indebted ❶ *adjective* **1** owing gratitude for
help or favours. **2** owing money.
indebtedness *noun*
indecent ❶ *adjective* **1** morally or sexually
offensive. **2** unsuitable or unseemly, e.g.

——————— THESAURUS ———————

inconvenience *noun* **1** = **trouble**,
awkwardness, bother, difficulty, disadvantage,
disruption, disturbance, fuss, hindrance,
nuisance ♦ *verb* **2** = **trouble**, bother,
discommode, disrupt, disturb, put out, upset
inconvenient *adjective* = **troublesome**,
awkward, bothersome, disadvantageous,
disturbing, inopportune, unsuitable, untimely
OPPOSITE〉 **convenient**
incorporate *verb* = **include**, absorb,
assimilate, blend, combine, integrate, merge,
subsume
incorrigible *adjective* = **incurable**, hardened,
hopeless, intractable, inveterate, irredeemable,
unreformed
incorruptible *adjective* **1** = **honest**, above
suspicion, straight, trustworthy, upright **2**
= **imperishable**, everlasting, undecaying
increase *verb* **1** = **grow**, advance, boost,
develop, enlarge, escalate, expand, extend,
multiply, raise, spread, swell OPPOSITE〉
decrease ♦ *noun* **2** = **growth**, development,
enlargement, escalation, expansion, extension,
gain, increment, rise, upturn OPPOSITE〉
decrease
increasingly *adverb* = **progressively**, more
and more
incredible *adjective* **1** = **implausible**, beyond

belief, far-fetched, improbable, inconceivable,
preposterous, unbelievable, unimaginable,
unthinkable **2** *Inf* = **amazing**, astonishing,
astounding, extraordinary, prodigious,
sensational (*inf*), wonderful
incredulity *noun* = **disbelief**, distrust, doubt,
scepticism
incredulous *adjective* = **disbelieving**,
distrustful, doubtful, dubious, sceptical,
suspicious, unbelieving, unconvinced OPPOSITE〉
credulous
increment *noun* = **increase**, accrual, addition,
advancement, augmentation, enlargement,
gain, step up, supplement
incriminate *verb* = **implicate**, accuse, blame,
charge, impeach, inculpate, involve
incur *verb* = **earn**, arouse, bring (upon oneself),
draw, expose oneself to, gain, meet with,
provoke
incurable *adjective* **1** = **fatal**, inoperable,
irremediable, terminal
indebted *adjective* **1** = **grateful**, beholden,
obligated, obliged, under an obligation **2** = **in
debt**, owing money
indecency *noun* **1** = **obscenity**, immodesty,
impropriety, impurity, indelicacy, lewdness,
licentiousness, pornography, vulgarity OPPOSITE〉
decency

indecent haste. **indecently** adverb **indecency** noun **indecent assault** sexual attack which does not include rape. **indecent exposure** showing of one's genitals in public.

indecipherable adjective impossible to read.

indecisive ⊙ adjective unable to make decisions. **indecision** noun

indeed ⊙ adverb **1** really, certainly. ◆ interjection **2** expression of indignation or surprise.

indefatigable adjective never getting tired. **indefatigably** adverb

indefensible ⊙ adjective **1** unable to be justified. **2** impossible to defend.

indefinable adjective difficult to describe or explain.

indefinite ⊙ adjective **1** without exact limits, e.g. for an indefinite period. **2** vague, unclear. **indefinite article** Grammar the word a or an. **indefinitely** adverb

indelible ⊙ adjective **1** impossible to erase or remove. **2** making indelible marks. **indelibly** adverb

indelicate ⊙ adjective offensive or embarrassing.

indemnify ⊙ verb **-ifying, -ified 1** secure against loss, damage, or liability. **2** compensate for loss or damage.

indemnity ⊙ noun, pl **-ties 1** insurance against loss or damage. **2** compensation for loss

or damage.

indent verb **1** start (a line of writing) further from the margin than the other lines. **2** order (goods) using a special order form. **indented** adjective having indentations along the edge.

indentation noun dent in a surface or edge.

indenture noun **1** contract, esp. one binding an apprentice to his or her employer. ◆ verb **2** bind (an apprentice) by indenture.

independent ⊙ adjective **1** free from the control or influence of others. **2** separate. **3** financially self-reliant. **4** capable of acting for oneself or on one's own. ◆ noun **5** politician who does represent any political party.

independently adverb **independence** noun

SPELLING TIP

People often get confused about how to spell **independent**. It is spelt independant 44 times in the Bank of English. It should be spelt with an e at the end in the same way as the noun it is related to: **independent** and **independence**.

---

in-depth adjective detailed, thorough.

indescribable ⊙ adjective too intense or extreme for words. **indescribably** adverb

———————— T H E S A U R U S ————————

indecent adjective **1 = lewd**, crude, dirty, filthy, immodest, improper, impure, licentious, pornographic, salacious, scungy (Aust & NZ inf) OPPOSITE decent. **2 = unbecoming**, in bad taste, indecorous, unseemly, vulgar OPPOSITE proper

indecision noun **= hesitation**, dithering, doubt, indecisiveness, shillyshallying (inf), uncertainty, vacillation, wavering

indecisive adjective **= hesitating**, dithering, faltering, in two minds (inf), tentative, uncertain, undecided, vacillating, wavering OPPOSITE decisive

indeed adverb **1 = really**, actually, certainly, in truth, truly, undoubtedly

indefensible adjective **1 = unforgivable**, inexcusable, unjustifiable, unpardonable, untenable, unwarrantable, wrong OPPOSITE defensible

indefinite adjective **= unclear**, doubtful, equivocal, ill-defined, imprecise, indeterminate, inexact, uncertain, unfixed, vague OPPOSITE clear

indefinitely adverb **= endlessly**, ad infinitum, continually, for ever

indelible adjective **1 = permanent**, enduring, indestructible, ineradicable, ingrained, lasting OPPOSITE temporary

indelicate adjective **= offensive**, coarse, crude, embarrassing, immodest, risqué, rude, suggestive, tasteless, vulgar

indemnify verb **1 = insure**, guarantee, protect, secure, underwrite **2 = compensate**, reimburse, remunerate, repair, repay

indemnity noun **1 = insurance**, guarantee, protection, security **2 = compensation**, redress, reimbursement, remuneration, reparation, restitution

independence noun **1 = freedom**, autonomy, liberty, self-reliance, self-rule, self-sufficiency, sovereignty OPPOSITE dependence

independent adjective **1 = free**, autonomous, liberated, self-determining, self-governing, separate, sovereign, unconstrained, uncontrolled OPPOSITE controlled. **3 = self-sufficient**, liberated, self-contained, self-reliant, self-supporting

independently adverb **= separately**, alone, autonomously, by oneself, individually, on one's own, solo, unaided

indestructible ⓘ *adjective* not able to be destroyed.

indeterminate ⓘ *adjective* uncertain in extent, amount, or nature. **indeterminacy** *noun*

index *noun, pl* **indices** [in-diss-eez] **1** alphabetical list of names or subjects dealt with in a book. **2** file or catalogue used to find things. **3** system by which changes in the value of something can be measured. ♦ *verb* **4** provide (a book) with an index. **5** enter in an index. **6** make index-linked. **index finger** finger next to the thumb. **index-linked** *adjective* (of pensions, wages, etc.) rising or falling in line with the cost of living.

Indian *noun, adjective* **1** (person) from India. **2** Native American. **Indian summer** period of warm sunny weather in autumn.

indicate ⓘ *verb* **1** be a sign or symptom of. **2** point out. **3** state briefly. **4** use the indicators in a car to show that it is going to turn left or right. **5** (of a measuring instrument) show a reading of. **indication** *noun* **indicative** [in-dik-a-tiv] *adjective* **1** (foll. by *of*) suggesting, e.g. *outer mess is indicative of inner confusion.* **2** *Grammar* denoting a mood of verbs used to make a statement. ♦ *noun* **3** *Grammar* indicative mood. **indicator** *noun* **1** something acting as a sign or indication. **2** flashing light on a vehicle showing the driver's intention to turn. **3** dial or gauge.

indices *noun* plural of INDEX.

indict ⓘ [in-**dite**] *verb* formally charge with a crime. **indictable** *adjective* **indictment** *noun* **1** indication of how bad something is, e.g. *that's a pretty sad indictment of the UN.* **2** formal charge.

indie *adjective Informal* (of rock music) released by an independent record company.

indifferent ⓘ *adjective* **1** showing no interest or concern. **2** of poor quality. **indifference** *noun* **indifferently** *adverb*

indigenous [in-dij-in-uss] *adjective* born in or natural to a country.

indigent *adjective* extremely poor. **indigence** *noun*

indigestion ⓘ *noun* (discomfort or pain caused by) difficulty in digesting food. **indigestible** *adjective*

indignation ⓘ *noun* anger at something unfair or wrong. **indignant** *adjective* feeling or showing indignation. **indignantly** *adverb*

indignity ⓘ *noun, pl* **-ties** embarrassing or humiliating treatment.

indigo *adjective* **1** deep violet-blue. ♦ *noun* **2** dye of this colour.

indirect ⓘ *adjective* **1** done or caused by someone or something else. **2** not by a straight route. **indirectly** *adverb* **indirect object** *Grammar* person or thing indirectly affected by the action of a verb, e.g. *Amy* in *I bought Amy a bag.* **indirect speech** same as REPORTED SPEECH.

———————— THESAURUS ————————

indescribable *adjective* =**unutterable**, beyond description, beyond words, indefinable, inexpressible

indestructible *adjective* =**permanent**, enduring, everlasting, immortal, imperishable, incorruptible, indelible, indissoluble, lasting, unbreakable OPPOSITE **breakable**

indeterminate *adjective* =**uncertain**, imprecise, indefinite, inexact, undefined, unfixed, unspecified, unstipulated, vague OPPOSITE **fixed**

indicate *verb* **1** =**signify**, betoken, denote, imply, manifest, point to, reveal, suggest **2** =**point out**, designate, specify **5** =**show**, display, express, read, record, register

indication *noun* **1** =**sign**, clue, evidence, hint, inkling, intimation, manifestation, mark, suggestion, symptom

indicative *adjective* **1** (foll. by *of*) =**suggestive**, pointing to, significant, symptomatic

indicator *noun* **1** =**sign**, guide, mark, pointer, signal, symbol **3** =**gauge**, dial, meter

indict *verb* =**charge**, accuse, arraign, impeach,

prosecute, summon

indictment *noun* **2** =**charge**, accusation, allegation, impeachment, prosecution, summons

indifference *noun* **1** =**disregard**, aloofness, apathy, coldness, coolness, detachment, inattention, negligence, nonchalance, unconcern OPPOSITE **interest**

indifferent *adjective* **1** =**unconcerned**, aloof, callous, cold, cool, detached, impervious, inattentive, uninterested, unmoved, unsympathetic OPPOSITE **interested.** **2** =**mediocre**, moderate, no great shakes (*inf*), ordinary, passable, so-so (*inf*), undistinguished OPPOSITE **excellent**

indigestion *noun* =**heartburn**, dyspepsia, upset stomach

indignant *adjective* =**resentful**, angry, disgruntled, exasperated, incensed, irate, peeved (*inf*), riled, scornful, up in arms (*inf*)

indignation *noun* =**resentment**, anger, exasperation, pique, rage, scorn, umbrage

indignity *noun* =**humiliation**, affront, dishonour, disrespect, injury, insult,

indirect tax tax, such as VAT, added to the price of something.
indiscernible *adjective* not able to be seen clearly.
indiscreet ⓘ *adjective* incautious or tactless in revealing secrets. **indiscreetly** *adverb* **indiscretion** *noun*
indiscriminate ⓘ *adjective* showing lack of careful thought.
indispensable ⓘ *adjective* absolutely essential.

SPELLING TIP

For every twenty examples of the word **indispensable** in the Bank of English, there is one example of the misspelling *indispensible*. So remember that it ends in *-able*.

---

indisposed ⓘ *adjective* unwell, ill.
indisposition *noun*
indisputable ⓘ *adjective* beyond doubt.
indisputably *adverb*
indissoluble *adjective* permanent.

indistinct ⓘ *adjective* unable to be seen or heard clearly.
indium *noun Chem* soft silvery-white metallic element.
individual ⓘ *adjective* 1 characteristic of or meant for a single person or thing. 2 separate, distinct. 3 distinctive, unusual. ♦ *noun* 4 single person or thing. **individually** *adverb* **individuality** *noun* **individualism** *noun* principle of living one's life in one's own way. **individualist** *noun* **individualistic** *adjective*
indoctrinate ⓘ *verb* teach (someone) to accept a doctrine or belief uncritically.
indoctrination *noun*
Indo-European *adjective, noun* (of) a family of languages spoken in most of Europe and much of Asia, including English, Russian, and Hindi.
indolent ⓘ *adjective* lazy. **indolence** *noun*
indomitable ⓘ *adjective* too strong to be defeated or discouraged. **indomitably** *adverb*
indoor *adjective* inside a building. **indoors** *adverb*
indubitable ⓘ [in-**dew**-bit-a-bl] *adjective* beyond doubt, certain. **indubitably** *adverb*
induce ⓘ *verb* 1 persuade or influence. 2

—————— T H E S A U R U S ——————

opprobrium, slight, snub
indirect *adjective* 1 = **incidental**, secondary, subsidiary, unintended 2 = **circuitous**, long-drawn-out, meandering, oblique, rambling, roundabout, tortuous, wandering OPPOSITE **direct**
indiscreet *adjective* = **tactless**, impolitic, imprudent, incautious, injudicious, naive, rash, reckless, unwise OPPOSITE **discreet**
indiscretion *noun* = **mistake**, error, faux pas, folly, foolishness, gaffe, lapse, slip
indiscriminate *adjective* = **random**, careless, desultory, general, uncritical, undiscriminating, unsystematic, wholesale OPPOSITE **systematic**
indispensable *adjective* = **essential**, crucial, imperative, key, necessary, needed, requisite, vital OPPOSITE **dispensable**
indisposed *adjective* = **ill**, ailing, crook (*Aust & NZ sl*), poorly (*inf*), sick, under the weather, unwell OPPOSITE **well**
indisposition *noun* = **illness**, ailment, ill health, sickness
indisputable *adjective* = **undeniable**, beyond doubt, certain, incontestable, incontrovertible, indubitable, irrefutable, unquestionable
indistinct *adjective* = **unclear**, blurred, faint, fuzzy, hazy, ill-defined, indeterminate, shadowy, undefined, vague OPPOSITE **clear**
individual *adjective* 1 = **personal**,

characteristic, exclusive, own, special, specific OPPOSITE **general**. 3 = **distinctive**, idiosyncratic, munted (*NZ sl*), particular, peculiar, singular, unique OPPOSITE **ordinary** ♦*noun* 4 = **person**, being, character, creature, soul, unit
individualist *noun* = **maverick**, freethinker, independent, loner, lone wolf, nonconformist, original
individuality *noun* 3 = **distinctiveness**, character, originality, personality, separateness, singularity, uniqueness
individually *adverb* 2 = **separately**, apart, independently, one at a time, one by one, singly
indoctrinate *verb* = **train**, brainwash, drill, ground, imbue, initiate, instruct, school, teach
indoctrination *noun* = **training**, brainwashing, drilling, grounding, inculcation, instruction, schooling
indolent *adjective* = **lazy**, idle, inactive, inert, languid, lethargic, listless, slothful, sluggish, workshy
indomitable *adjective* = **invincible**, bold, resolute, staunch, steadfast, unbeatable, unconquerable, unflinching, unyielding OPPOSITE **weak**
indubitable *adjective* = **certain**, incontestable, incontrovertible, indisputable, irrefutable,

cause. **3** *Med* cause (a woman) to go into labour or bring on (labour) by the use of drugs etc. **inducement** *noun* something used to persuade someone to do something.

induct *verb* formally install (someone, esp. a clergyman) in office.

inductance *noun* property of an electric circuit creating voltage by a change of current.

induction *noun* **1** reasoning process by which general conclusions are drawn from particular instances. **2** *Med* process of inducing labour. **3** process by which electrical or magnetic properties are produced by the proximity of an electrified or magneticobject. **4** formal introduction into an office or position.

inductive *adjective* **induction coil** transformer for producing a high voltage from a low voltage. **induction course** training course to help familiarize someone with a new job.

indulge ⊕ *verb* **1** allow oneself pleasure, e.g. *indulging in rich foods.* **2** allow (someone) to have or do everything he or she wants.

indulgence *noun* **1** something allowed because it gives pleasure. **2** act of indulging oneself or someone else. **3** liberal or tolerant treatment.

indulgent *adjective* **indulgently** *adverb*

industrial ⊕ *adjective* of, used in, or employed in industry. **industrialize** *verb* develop large-scale industry in (a country or region).

industrialization *noun* **industrialism** *noun* social organization based on large-scale manufacturing industry rather than trade or farming. **industrialist** *noun* person who owns or controls large amounts of money or property in industry. **industrial action** ways in which workers can protest about their conditions, e.g. by striking or working to rule. **industrial estate** area of land set aside for factories and warehouses. **industrial relations** relations between management and workers.

industry ⊕ *noun, pl* **-tries 1** manufacture of goods. **2** branch of this, e.g. *the music industry.* **3** quality of working hard. **industrial** *adjective* of, used in, or employed in industry.

industrious *adjective* hard-working.

inebriate ⊕ *noun, adjective* (person who is) habitually drunk. **inebriated** *adjective* drunk. **inebriation** *noun*

inedible *adjective* not fit to be eaten.

ineducable [in-ed-yuke-a-bl] *adjective* incapable of being educated, esp. through mental retardation.

ineffable *adjective* too great for words. **ineffably** *adverb*

ineffectual ⊕ *adjective* having very little effect.

inefficient ⊕ *adjective* unable to perform a task or function to the best advantage. **inefficiency** *noun*

inelegant *adjective* lacking elegance or refinement.

ineligible ⊕ *adjective* not qualified for or entitled to something.

ineluctable *adjective* impossible to avoid.

—————— T H E S A U R U S ——————

obvious, sure, undeniable, unquestionable

induce *verb* **1** = **persuade**, convince, encourage, incite, influence, instigate, prevail upon, prompt, talk into [OPPOSITE] stop. **2** = **cause**, bring about, effect, engender, generate, give rise to, lead to, occasion, produce [OPPOSITE] stop

inducement *noun* = **incentive**, attraction, bait, carrot (*inf*), encouragement, incitement, lure, reward

indulge *verb* **1** = **gratify**, feed, give way to, pander to, satisfy, yield to **2** = **spoil**, cosset, give in to, go along with, humour, mollycoddle, pamper

indulgence *noun* **1** = **luxury**, extravagance, favour, privilege, treat **2** = **gratification**, appeasement, fulfilment, satiation, satisfaction [OPPOSITE] **temperance**. **3** = **tolerance**, forbearance, patience, understanding

indulgent *adjective* **3** = **lenient**, compliant, easy-going, forbearing, kindly, liberal, permissive, tolerant, understanding [OPPOSITE] strict

industrialist *noun* = **capitalist**, big businessman, captain of industry, magnate, manufacturer, tycoon

industrious *adjective* = **hard-working**, busy, conscientious, diligent, energetic, persistent, purposeful, tireless, zealous [OPPOSITE] **lazy**

industry *noun* **1, 2** = **business**, commerce, manufacturing, production, trade **3** = **effort**, activity, application, diligence, labour, tirelessness, toil, zeal

inebriated *adjective* = **drunk**, half-cut (*inf*), intoxicated, legless (*inf*), merry (*Brit inf*), paralytic (*inf*), plastered (*sl*), tight (*inf*), tipsy, under the influence (*inf*)

ineffectual *adjective* = **weak**, feeble, impotent, inadequate, incompetent, ineffective, inept

inefficiency *noun* = **incompetence**, carelessness, disorganization, muddle, slackness, sloppiness

inefficient *adjective* = **incompetent**, disorganized, ineffectual, inept, wasteful, weak [OPPOSITE] **efficient**

ineligible *adjective* = **unqualified**, disqualified,

inept ❶ *adjective* clumsy, lacking skill.
ineptitude *noun*
inequality ❶ *noun, pl* **-ties 1** state or quality of being unequal. **2** instance of this.
inequitable *adjective* unfair. **inequity** *noun, pl* **-ties**
ineradicable *adjective* impossible to remove.
inert ❶ *adjective* **1** without the power of motion or resistance. **2** chemically unreactive. **inertly** *adverb* **inertness** *noun*
inertia ❶ *noun* **1** feeling of unwillingness to do anything. **2** *Physics* tendency of a body to remain still or continue moving unless a force is applied to it. **inertia reel seat belt** car seat belt in which the belt is free to unwind from a metal drum except when the drum locks because of suddenbraking. **inertia selling** practice of sending householders unrequested goods followed by a bill if the goods are not returned.
inescapable ❶ *adjective* unavoidable.
inestimable ❶ *adjective* too great to be estimated. **inestimably** *adverb*
inevitable ❶ *adjective* unavoidable, sure to happen. **the inevitable** something that cannot be prevented. **inevitably** *adverb* **inevitability** *noun*
inexorable ❶ *adjective* unable to be

prevented from continuing or progressing.
inexorably *adverb*
inexperienced ❶ *adjective* having no knowledge or experience of a particular situation, activity, etc. **inexperience** *noun*
inexpert *adjective* lacking skill.
inexplicable ❶ *adjective* impossible to explain.
inexplicably *adverb*
in extremis *adverb Latin* **1** in great difficulty. **2** on the point of death.
inextricable *adjective* **1** impossible to escape from. **2** impossible to disentangle or separate.
inextricably *adverb*
infallible ❶ *adjective* never wrong. **infallibly** *adverb* **infallibility** *noun*
infamous ❶ [in-fam-uss] *adjective* well-known for something bad. **infamously** *adverb* **infamy** *noun*
infant ❶ *noun* very young child. **infancy** *noun* **1** early childhood. **2** early stage of development. **infantile** *adjective* childish.
infanta *noun* **1** (formerly) daughter of a king of Spain or Portugal. **2** wife of an infante.
infante *noun* (formerly) any son of a king of Spain or Portugal, except the heir to the throne.
infanticide *noun* **1** murder of an infant. **2** person guilty of this.

———— T H E S A U R U S ————

ruled out, unacceptable, unfit, unsuitable
inept *adjective* =**incompetent**, bumbling, bungling, clumsy, inexpert, maladroit OPPOSITE **able**
ineptitude *noun* =**incompetence**, clumsiness, inexpertness, unfitness
inequality *noun* **1** =**disparity**, bias, difference, disproportion, diversity, irregularity, prejudice, unevenness
inert *adjective* **1** =**inactive**, dead, dormant, immobile, lifeless, motionless, static, still, unresponsive OPPOSITE **moving. 2** =**unreactive**
inertia *noun* **1** =**inactivity**, apathy, immobility, lethargy, listlessness, passivity, sloth, unresponsiveness OPPOSITE **activity**
inescapable *adjective* =**unavoidable**, certain, destined, fated, ineluctable, inevitable, inexorable, sure
inestimable *adjective* =**incalculable**, immeasurable, invaluable, precious, priceless, prodigious
inevitable *adjective* =**unavoidable**, assured, certain, destined, fixed, ineluctable, inescapable, inexorable, sure OPPOSITE **avoidable**
inevitably *adverb* =**unavoidably**, as a result, automatically, certainly, necessarily, of necessity,

perforce, surely, willy-nilly
inexorable *adjective* =**unrelenting**, inescapable, relentless, remorseless, unbending, unyielding OPPOSITE **relenting**
inexperience *noun* =**unfamiliarity**, callowness, greenness, ignorance, newness, rawness
inexperienced *adjective* =**immature**, callow, green, new, raw, unpractised, untried, unversed OPPOSITE **experienced**
inexplicable *adjective* =**unaccountable**, baffling, enigmatic, incomprehensible, insoluble, mysterious, mystifying, strange, unfathomable, unintelligible OPPOSITE **explicable**
inextricably *adverb* **2** =**inseparably**, indistinguishably, intricately
infallibility *noun* =**perfection**, impeccability, omniscience, supremacy, unerringness
infallible *adjective* =**sure**, certain, dependable, foolproof, reliable, sure-fire (*inf*), trustworthy, unbeatable, unfailing OPPOSITE **unreliable**
infamous *adjective* =**notorious**, disreputable, ignominious, ill-famed OPPOSITE **esteemed**
infancy *noun* **2** =**beginnings**, cradle, dawn, inception, origins, outset, start OPPOSITE **end**
infant *noun* =**baby**, babe, bairn (*Scot*), child,

infantry *noun* soldiers who fight on foot.
infatuate ❶ *verb* inspire with intense unreasoning passion. **infatuated** *adjective* **infatuation** *noun*
infect ❶ *verb* **1** affect with a disease. **2** affect with a feeling. **infection** *noun* **infectious** *adjective* **1** (of a disease) spreading without actual contact. **2** spreading from person to person, e.g. *infectious enthusiasm*.
infer ❶ *verb* **-ferring, -ferred** work out from evidence. **inference** *noun*
inferior ❶ *adjective* **1** lower in quality, position, or status. ♦ *noun* **2** person of lower position or status. **inferiority** *noun* **inferiority complex** *Psychiatry* disorder arising from a feeling of inferiority to others, characterized by aggressiveness or extreme shyness.
infernal ❶ *adjective* **1** of hell. **2** *Informal* irritating. **infernally** *adverb*
inferno *noun, pl* **-nos** intense raging fire.
infertile ❶ *adjective* **1** unable to produce offspring. **2** (of soil) barren, not productive. **infertility** *noun*
infest ❶ *verb* inhabit or overrun in unpleasantly large numbers. **infestation** *noun*
infidel *noun* **1** person with no religion. **2**

person who rejects a particular religion, esp. Christianity or Islam.
infidelity *noun, pl* **-ties** (act of) sexual unfaithfulness to one's husband, wife, or lover.
infield *noun* **1** *Cricket* area of the field near the pitch. **2** *Baseball* area of the playing field enclosed by the base lines.
infighting *noun* quarrelling within a group.
infiltrate ❶ *verb* enter gradually and secretly. **infiltration** *noun* **infiltrator** *noun*
infinite ❶ [in-fin-it] *adjective* without any limit or end. **infinitely** *adverb* **infinity** *noun* endless space, time, or number.
infinitesimal ❶ *adjective* extremely small.
infinitive [in-**fin**-it-iv] *noun* *Grammar* form of a verb not showing tense, person, or number, e.g. *to sleep*.
infinity ❶ *noun* endless space, time, or number.
infirm ❶ *adjective* physically or mentally weak. **infirmity** *noun, pl* **-ties**
infirmary *noun, pl* **-ries** hospital.
in flagrante delicto [in flag-**grant**-ee dee-**lick**-toe] *adverb* while committing the offence.
inflame ❶ *verb* make angry or excited.
inflamed *adjective* (of part of the body) red,

——————————— T H E S A U R U S ———————————

toddler, tot
infantile *adjective* =**childish**, babyish, immature, puerile OPPOSITE **mature**
infatuate *verb* =**obsess**, bewitch, captivate, enchant, enrapture, fascinate
infatuated *adjective* =**obsessed**, besotted, bewitched, captivated, carried away, enamoured, enraptured, fascinated, possessed, smitten (*inf*), spellbound
infatuation *noun* =**obsession**, crush (*inf*), fixation, madness, passion, thing (*inf*)
infect *verb* **1** = **contaminate**, affect, blight, corrupt, defile, poison, pollute, taint
infection *noun* **1** = **contamination**, contagion, corruption, defilement, poison, pollution, virus
infectious *adjective* **1** = **catching**, communicable, contagious, spreading, transmittable, virulent
infer *verb* =**deduce**, conclude, derive, gather, presume, surmise, understand
inference *noun* =**deduction**, assumption, conclusion, presumption, reading, surmise
inferior *adjective* **1** = **lower**, lesser, menial, minor, secondary, subordinate, subsidiary OPPOSITE **superior** ♦*noun* **2** = **underling**, junior, menial, subordinate OPPOSITE **superior**
inferiority *noun* **a** = **inadequacy**, deficiency, imperfection, insignificance, mediocrity, shoddiness, worthlessness **b** = **subservience**,

abasement, lowliness, subordination OPPOSITE **superiority**
infernal *adjective* **1** = **devilish**, accursed, damnable, damned, diabolical, fiendish, hellish, satanic OPPOSITE **heavenly**
infertile *adjective* =**barren**, sterile, unfruitful, unproductive OPPOSITE **productive**
infertility *noun* =**sterility**, barrenness, infecundity, unproductiveness
infest *verb* =**overrun**, beset, invade, penetrate, permeate, ravage, swarm, throng
infested *adjective* =**overrun**, alive, crawling, ravaged, ridden, swarming, teeming
infiltrate *verb* =**penetrate**, filter through, insinuate oneself, make inroads (into), percolate, permeate, pervade, sneak in (*inf*)
infinite *adjective* =**never-ending**, boundless, eternal, everlasting, illimitable, immeasurable, inexhaustible, limitless, measureless, unbounded OPPOSITE **finite**
infinitesimal *adjective* =**microscopic**, insignificant, minuscule, minute, negligible, teeny, tiny, unnoticeable
infinity *noun* =**eternity**, boundlessness, endlessness, immensity, vastness
infirm *adjective* =**frail**, ailing, debilitated, decrepit, doddering, enfeebled, failing, feeble, weak OPPOSITE **strong**
infirmity *noun* =**frailty**, decrepitude, ill health,

swollen, and painful because of infection.
inflammation noun
inflammable ⊕ adjective easily set on fire.
inflammatory ⊕ adjective likely to provoke
anger.
inflate ⊕ verb 1 expand by filling with air or
gas. 2 cause economic inflation in. **inflatable**
adjective 1 able to be inflated. ◆ noun 2 plastic
or rubber object which can be inflated.
inflation ⊕ noun 1 inflating. 2 increase in
prices and fall in the value of money.
inflationary adjective
inflection, inflexion noun 1 change in the
pitch of the voice. 2 Grammar change in the
form of a word to show grammatical use.
inflexible ⊕ adjective 1 unwilling to be
persuaded, obstinate. 2 (of a policy etc.) firmly
fixed, unalterable. 3 incapable of being bent.
inflexibly adverb **inflexibility** noun
inflict ⊕ verb impose (something unpleasant)
on. **infliction** noun
inflorescence noun Botany arrangement of
flowers on a stem.
inflow noun 1 something, such as liquid or
gas, that flows in. 2 flowing in, influx.

influence ⊕ noun 1 effect of one person or
thing on another. 2 (person with) the power to
have such an effect. ◆ verb 3 have an effect on.
influential adjective
influenza noun contagious viral disease
causing headaches, muscle pains, and fever.
influx ⊕ noun arrival or entry of many people
or things.
info noun Informal information.
inform ⊕ verb 1 tell. 2 give incriminating
information to the police. **informant** noun
person who gives information. **information**
noun knowledge or facts. **informative** adjective
giving useful information. **information
superhighway** worldwide network of
computers transferring information at high
speed. **information technology** use of
computers and electronic technology to store
and communicate information. **informer** noun
person who informs to the police.
informal ⊕ adjective 1 relaxed and friendly. 2
appropriate for everyday life or use. **informally**
adverb **informality** noun
infra dig adjective Informal beneath one's
dignity.

———————— T H E S A U R U S ————————

sickliness, vulnerability OPPOSITE **health**
inflame verb = **enrage**, anger, arouse, excite,
incense, infuriate, madden, provoke, rouse,
stimulate OPPOSITE **calm**
inflamed adjective = **sore**, fevered, hot,
infected, red, swollen
inflammable adjective = **flammable**,
combustible, incendiary
inflammation noun = **soreness**, painfulness,
rash, redness, tenderness
inflammatory adjective = **provocative**,
explosive, fiery, intemperate, like a red rag to a
bull, rabble-rousing
inflate verb 1 = **expand**, bloat, blow up,
dilate, distend, enlarge, increase, puff up or out,
pump up, swell OPPOSITE **deflate**
inflation noun 1 = **expansion**, enlargement,
escalation, extension, increase, rise, spread,
swelling
inflexibility noun 1 = **obstinacy**,
intransigence, obduracy
inflexible adjective 1 = **obstinate**, implacable,
intractable, obdurate, resolute, set in one's
ways, steadfast, stubborn, unbending,
uncompromising OPPOSITE **flexible**. 3
= **inelastic**, hard, rigid, stiff, taut OPPOSITE
flexible
inflict verb = **impose**, administer, apply,
deliver, levy, mete or deal out, visit, wreak
infliction noun = **imposition**, administration,

perpetration, wreaking
influence noun 1 = **effect**, hold, magnetism,
power, spell, sway, weight 2 = **power**,
ascendancy, authority, clout (inf), control,
domination, importance, leverage, mana (NZ),
mastery, prestige, pull (inf) ◆verb 3 = **affect**,
control, direct, guide, manipulate, sway
influential adjective = **important**,
authoritative, instrumental, leading, potent,
powerful, significant, telling, weighty OPPOSITE
powerless
influx noun = **arrival**, incursion, inrush,
inundation, invasion, rush
inform verb 1 = **tell**, advise, communicate,
enlighten, instruct, notify, teach, tip off 2
= **betray**, blow the whistle on (inf), denounce,
grass (Brit sl), incriminate, inculpate, shop (sl,
chiefly Brit), squeal (sl)
informal adjective 1 = **relaxed**, casual,
colloquial, cosy, easy, familiar, natural, simple,
unofficial OPPOSITE **formal**
informality noun 1 = **familiarity**, casualness,
ease, naturalness, relaxation, simplicity
information noun = **facts**, data, intelligence,
knowledge, message, news, notice, report
informative adjective = **instructive**, chatty,
communicative, edifying, educational,
enlightening, forthcoming, illuminating,
revealing
informer noun = **betrayer**, accuser, Judas,

infrared *adjective* of or using rays below the red end of the visible spectrum.

infrastructure *noun* basic facilities, services, and equipment needed for a country or organization to function properly.

infrequent ❶ *adjective* not happening often. **infrequently** *adverb*

infringe ❶ *verb* **1** break (a law or agreement). **2** (foll. by *on*) interfere (with), encroach (on).

infringement *noun*

infuriate ❶ *verb* make very angry.

infuse *verb* **1** fill (with an emotion or quality). **2** soak to extract flavour. **infusion** *noun* **1** infusing. **2** liquid obtained by infusing.

ingenious ❶ [in-**jean**-ee-uss] *adjective* showing cleverness and originality. **ingeniously** *adverb*

ingenuity [in-jen-**new**-it-ee] *noun*

ingénue [**an**-jay-new] *noun* naive young woman, esp. as a role played by an actress.

ingenuous ❶ [in-**jen**-new-uss] *adjective* unsophisticated and trusting. **ingenuously** *adverb*

ingest *verb* take (food or liquid) into the body. **ingestion** *noun*

inglenook *noun* corner by a fireplace.

inglorious *adjective* dishonourable, shameful.

ingot *noun* oblong block of cast metal.

ingrained *adjective* firmly fixed.

ingratiate ❶ *verb* try to make (oneself) popular with someone. **ingratiating** *adjective* **ingratiatingly** *adverb*

ingratitude *noun* lack of gratitude or thanks.

ingredient ❶ *noun* component of a mixture or compound.

ingress *noun* act or right of entering.

ingrowing *adjective* (of a toenail) growing abnormally into the flesh.

inhabit ❶ *verb* **-habiting, -habited** live in.

inhabitable *adjective* **inhabitant** *noun*

inhale ❶ *verb* breathe in (air, smoke, etc.).

inhalation *noun* **inhalant** [in-**hale**-ant] *noun* medical preparation inhaled to help breathing problems. **inhaler** *noun* container for an inhalant.

inherent ❶ *adjective* existing as an inseparable part. **inherently** *adverb*

inherit ❶ *verb* **-heriting, -herited 1** receive (money etc.) from someone who has died. **2** receive (a characteristic) from an earlier generation. **3** receive from a predecessor.

inheritance *noun* **inheritance tax** tax paid on property left at death. **inheritor** *noun*

inhibit ❶ *verb* **-hibiting, -hibited 1** restrain (an impulse or desire). **2** hinder or prevent (action). **inhibited** *adjective* **inhibition** *noun* feeling of fear or embarrassment that stops one from behaving naturally.

inhospitable ❶ *adjective* **1** not welcoming,

——————————— THESAURUS ———————————

sneak, stool pigeon

infrequent *adjective* = **occasional**, few and far between, once in a blue moon, rare, sporadic, uncommon, unusual OPPOSITE **frequent**

infringe *verb* **1** = **break**, contravene, disobey, transgress, violate

infringement *noun* **1** = **contravention**, breach, infraction, transgression, trespass, violation

infuriate *verb* = **enrage**, anger, exasperate, incense, irritate, madden, provoke, rile OPPOSITE **soothe**

infuriating *adjective* = **annoying**, exasperating, galling, irritating, maddening, mortifying, provoking, vexatious

ingenious *adjective* = **creative**, bright, brilliant, clever, crafty, inventive, original, resourceful, shrewd OPPOSITE **unimaginative**

ingenuity *noun* = **originality**, cleverness, flair, genius, gift, inventiveness, resourcefulness, sharpness, shrewdness OPPOSITE **dullness**

ingenuous *adjective* = **naive**, artless, guileless, honest, innocent, open, plain, simple, sincere, trusting, unsophisticated

ingratiate *verb* = **pander to**, crawl, curry favour, fawn, flatter, grovel, insinuate oneself,

toady

ingratiating *adjective* = **sycophantic**, crawling, fawning, flattering, humble, obsequious, servile, toadying, unctuous

ingredient *noun* = **component**, constituent, element, part

inhabit *verb* = **live**, abide, dwell, occupy, populate, reside

inhabitant *noun* = **dweller**, citizen, denizen, inmate, native, occupant, occupier, resident, tenant

inhabited *adjective* = **populated**, colonized, developed, occupied, peopled, settled, tenanted

inhale *verb* = **breathe in**, draw in, gasp, respire, suck in OPPOSITE **exhale**

inherent *adjective* = **innate**, essential, hereditary, inborn, inbred, ingrained, inherited, intrinsic, native, natural OPPOSITE **extraneous**

inherit *verb* **1** = **be left**, come into, fall heir to, succeed to

inheritance *noun* **1** = **legacy**, bequest, birthright, heritage, patrimony

inhibit *verb* **1** = **restrain**, check, constrain, curb, discourage, hold back *or* in OPPOSITE **further**. **2** = **hinder**, check, frustrate, hold back,

unfriendly. **2** difficult to live in, harsh.
inhuman ❶ *adjective* **1** cruel or brutal. **2** not
human.
inhumane ❶ *adjective* cruel or brutal.
inhumanity *noun*
inimical ❶ *adjective* unfavourable or hostile.
inimitable ❶ *adjective* impossible to imitate,
unique.
iniquity ❶ *noun, pl* **-ties 1** injustice or
wickedness. **2** wicked act. **iniquitous** *adjective*
initial ❶ *adjective* **1** first, at the beginning. ◆
noun **2** first letter, esp. of a person's name. ◆
verb **-tialling, -tialled 3** sign with one's initials.
initially *adverb*
initiate ❶ *verb* **1** begin or set going. **2** admit
(someone) into a closed group. **3** instruct in the
basics of something. ◆ *noun* **4** recently initiated
person. **initiation** *noun* **initiator** *noun*
initiative ❶ *noun* **1** first step, commencing
move. **2** ability to act independently.

inject ❶ *verb* **1** put (a fluid) into the body with
a syringe. **2** introduce (a new element), e.g. *try
to inject a bit of humour*. **injection** *noun*
injudicious *adjective* showing poor judgment,
unwise.
injunction ❶ *noun* court order not to do
something.
injure ❶ *verb* hurt physically or mentally.
injury *noun, pl* **-ries**. **injury time** *Sport* playing
time added at the end of a match to
compensate for time spent treating injured
players. **injurious** *adjective*
injustice ❶ *noun* **1** unfairness. **2** unfair action.
ink *noun* **1** coloured liquid used for writing or
printing. ◆ *verb* **2** (foll. by *in*) mark in ink
(something already marked in pencil). **inky**
adjective **inkier, inkiest 1** dark or black. **2**
covered in ink.
inkling ❶ *noun* slight idea or suspicion.
inlaid *adjective* **1** set in another material so

——————— T H E S A U R U S ———————

impede, obstruct, prevent OPPOSITE ▷ allow
inhibited *adjective* **1 =shy**, constrained,
guarded, repressed, reserved, reticent, self-
conscious, subdued OPPOSITE ▷ uninhibited
inhibition *noun* **=shyness**, block, hang-up
(*inf*), reserve, restraint, reticence, self-
consciousness
inhospitable *adjective* **1 =unfriendly**, cool,
uncongenial, unreceptive, unsociable,
unwelcoming, xenophobic OPPOSITE ▷
welcoming. **2 =bleak**, barren, desolate,
forbidding, godforsaken, hostile
inhuman *adjective* **1 =cruel**, barbaric, brutal,
cold-blooded, heartless, merciless, pitiless,
ruthless, savage, unfeeling OPPOSITE ▷ humane
inhumane *adjective* **=cruel**, brutal, heartless,
pitiless, unfeeling, unkind, unsympathetic
inhumanity *noun* **=cruelty**, atrocity,
barbarism, brutality, heartlessness, pitilessness,
ruthlessness, unkindness
inimical *adjective* **=hostile**, adverse,
antagonistic, ill-disposed, opposed,
unfavourable, unfriendly, unwelcoming
OPPOSITE ▷ helpful
inimitable *adjective* **=unique**, consummate,
incomparable, matchless, peerless, unparalleled,
unrivalled
iniquitous *adjective* **=wicked**, criminal, evil,
immoral, reprehensible, sinful, unjust
iniquity *noun* **=wickedness**, abomination, evil,
injustice, sin, wrong OPPOSITE ▷ goodness
initial *adjective* **1 =first**, beginning, incipient,
introductory, opening, primary OPPOSITE ▷ last
initially *adverb* **1 =at first**, at *or* in the
beginning, first, firstly, originally, primarily

initiate *verb* **1 =begin**, commence, get under
way, kick off (*inf*), launch, open, originate, set
in motion, start **2 =induct**, indoctrinate,
introduce, invest **3 =instruct**, acquaint with,
coach, familiarize with, teach, train ◆*noun* **4**
=novice, beginner, convert, entrant, learner,
member, probationer
initiation *noun* **2 =introduction**, debut,
enrolment, entrance, inauguration, induction,
installation, investiture
initiative *noun* **1 =first step**, advantage, first
move, lead **2 =resourcefulness**, ambition,
drive, dynamism, enterprise, get-up-and-go
(*inf*), leadership
inject *verb* **1 =vaccinate**, inoculate **2**
=introduce, bring in, infuse, insert, instil
injection *noun* **1 =vaccination**, inoculation,
jab (*inf*), shot (*inf*) **2 =introduction**, dose,
infusion, insertion
injunction *noun* **=order**, command,
exhortation, instruction, mandate, precept,
ruling
injure *verb* **=hurt**, damage, harm, impair, ruin,
spoil, undermine, wound
injured *adjective* **=hurt**, broken, crook (*Aust &
NZ sl*), damaged, disabled, undermined,
weakened, wounded
injury *noun* **=harm**, damage, detriment,
disservice, hurt, ill, trauma (*Path*), wound,
wrong
injustice *noun* **1 =unfairness**, bias,
discrimination, inequality, inequity, iniquity,
oppression, partisanship, prejudice, wrong
OPPOSITE ▷ justice
inkling *noun* **=suspicion**, clue, conception,

that the surface is smooth. **2** made like this, e.g. *an inlaid table.*

inland ❶ *adjective, adverb* in or towards the interior of a country, away from the sea. **Inland Revenue** government department that collects taxes.

in-laws *plural noun* one's husband's or wife's family.

inlay *noun* inlaid substance or pattern.

inlet ❶ *noun* **1** narrow strip of water extending from the sea into the land. **2** valve etc. through which liquid or gas enters.

inmate *noun* person living in an institution such as a prison.

inmost ❶ *adjective* innermost.

inn ❶ *noun* pub or small hotel, esp. in the country. **innkeeper** *noun*

innards *plural noun Informal* **1** internal organs. **2** working parts of a machine.

innate ❶ *adjective* being part of someone's nature, inborn.

inner ❶ *adjective* **1** happening or located inside. **2** relating to private feelings, e.g. *the inner self.* **3** of a group with most power within a larger organization, e.g. *the inner circle.*

innermost *adjective* furthest inside. **inner city** parts of a city near the centre, esp. having social and economic problems.

innings *noun* **1** *Sport* player's or side's turn of batting. **2** period of opportunity.

innocent ❶ *adjective* **1** not guilty of a crime. **2** without experience of evil. **3** without malicious intent. ✦ *noun* **4** innocent person, esp. a child. **innocently** *adverb* **innocence** *noun*

innocuous *adjective* not harmful. **innocuously** *adverb*

SPELLING TIP

Always make sure there are two *n*s in **innocuous**. It is more common to miss out an *n* than to double the *c* by mistake.

---

innovation ❶ *noun* **1** new idea or method. **2** introduction of new ideas or methods. **innovate** *verb* **innovative** *adjective* **innovator** *noun*

innuendo ❶ *noun, pl* **-does** (remark making) an indirect reference to something rude or unpleasant.

innumerable ❶ *adjective* too many to be counted.

innumerate *adjective* having no understanding of mathematics or science. **innumeracy** *noun*

inoculate *verb* protect against disease by injecting with a vaccine. **inoculation** *noun*

SPELLING TIP

The verb **inoculate** has only one *n* and one *c*. There are 235 occurrences of the correct spelling of the noun **inoculation** in the Bank of English, with lots of different misspellings. The most popular one, *innoculation*, occurs 31 times.

---

inoffensive *adjective* causing no harm or

THESAURUS

hint, idea, indication, intimation, notion, suggestion, whisper

inland *adjective* =**interior**, domestic, internal, upcountry

inlet *noun* **1** =**bay**, bight, creek, firth *or* frith (*Scot*), fjord, passage

inmost *adjective* =**deepest**, basic, central, essential, innermost, intimate, personal, private, secret

innate *adjective* =**inborn**, congenital, constitutional, essential, inbred, ingrained, inherent, instinctive, intuitive, native, natural OPPOSITE> **acquired**

inner *adjective* **1** =**inside**, central, interior, internal, inward, middle OPPOSITE> **outer**. **2** =**hidden**, intimate, personal, private, repressed, secret, unrevealed OPPOSITE> **revealed**

innkeeper *noun* =**publican**, host *or* hostess, hotelier, landlord *or* landlady, mine host

innocence *noun* **1** =**guiltlessness**, blamelessness, clean hands, incorruptibility, probity, purity, uprightness, virtue OPPOSITE> **guilt**. **2** =**naivety**, artlessness, credulousness, gullibility, inexperience, ingenuousness, simplicity, unworldliness OPPOSITE> **cunning**. **3** =**harmlessness**, innocuousness, inoffensiveness

innocent *adjective* **1** =**not guilty**, blameless, guiltless, honest, in the clear, uninvolved OPPOSITE> **guilty**. **2** =**naive**, artless, childlike, credulous, gullible, ingenuous, open, simple, unworldly OPPOSITE> **worldly**. **3** =**harmless**, innocuous, inoffensive, unobjectionable, well-intentioned, well-meant OPPOSITE> **malicious**

innovation *noun* **1** =**modernization**, alteration, change, departure, newness, novelty, variation

innuendo *noun* =**insinuation**, aspersion, hint, implication, imputation, intimation, overtone, annoyance.

inoperable *adjective* (of a tumour or cancer) unable to be surgically removed.

inoperative *adjective* not working or functioning.

inopportune *adjective* badly timed, unsuitable.

inordinate ❶ *adjective* excessive. **inordinately** *adverb*

inorganic ❶ *adjective* 1 not having the characteristics of living organisms. 2 of chemical substances that do not contain carbon.

inpatient *noun* patient who stays in a hospital for treatment.

input *noun* 1 resources put into a project etc. 2 data fed into a computer. ◆ *verb* **-putting, -put** 3 enter (data) in a computer.

inquest ❶ *noun* 1 official inquiry into a sudden death. 2 *Inf* investigation or discussion.

inquietude *noun* restlessness or anxiety.

inquire ❶ *verb* seek information or ask (about). **inquirer** *noun* **inquiry** *noun, pl* **-ries** 1 question. 2 investigation.

inquisition ❶ *noun* 1 thorough investigation. 2 (I-) *Hist* organization within the Catholic Church for suppressing heresy. **inquisitor** *noun*

inquisitorial *adjective*

inquisitive ❶ *adjective* 1 excessively curious about other people's affairs. 2 eager to learn. **inquisitively** *adverb*

inquorate *adjective* without enough people present to make a quorum.

inroads *plural noun* **make inroads into** start affecting or reducing, e.g. *Italy could make inroads into its interest burden.*

ins. inches.

insalubrious *adjective* unpleasant, unhealthy, or sordid.

insane ❶ *adjective* 1 mentally ill. 2 stupidly irresponsible. **insanely** *adverb* **insanity** *noun*

insanitary ❶ *adjective* dirty or unhealthy.

insatiable ❶ [in-**saysh**-a-bl] *adjective* unable to be satisfied.

inscribe ❶ *verb* write or carve words on. **inscription** *noun* words inscribed.

inscrutable ❶ *adjective* mysterious, enigmatic. **inscrutably** *adverb* **inscrutability** *noun*

insect *noun* small animal with six legs and usu. wings, such as an ant or fly. **insecticide** *noun* substance for killing insects. **insectivorous** *adjective* insect-eating.

insecure ❶ *adjective* 1 anxious, not confident. 2 not safe or well-protected.

——————— T H E S A U R U S ———————

suggestion, whisper

innumerable *adjective* =**countless**, beyond number, incalculable, infinite, multitudinous, myriad, numberless, numerous, unnumbered, untold OPPOSITE **limited**

inordinate *adjective* =**excessive**, disproportionate, extravagant, immoderate, intemperate, preposterous, unconscionable, undue, unreasonable, unwarranted OPPOSITE **moderate**

inorganic *adjective* 1 = **artificial**, chemical, man-made

inquest *noun* =**inquiry**, inquisition, investigation, probe

inquire *verb* =**investigate**, ask, examine, explore, look into, make inquiries, probe, query, question, research

inquiry *noun* 1 =**question**, query 2 =**investigation**, examination, exploration, inquest, interrogation, probe, research, study, survey

inquisition *noun* 1 =**investigation**, cross-examination, examination, grilling (*inf*), inquest, inquiry, questioning, third degree (*inf*)

inquisitive *adjective* 1 = **prying**, curious, nosy (*inf*), probing OPPOSITE **uninterested**. 2 =**inquiring**, curious, questioning OPPOSITE

uninterested

insane *adjective* 1 = **mad**, crazed, crazy, demented, deranged, mentally ill, out of one's mind OPPOSITE **sane**. 2 = **stupid**, daft (*inf*), foolish, idiotic, impractical, irrational, irresponsible, preposterous, senseless OPPOSITE **sensible**

insanitary *adjective* =**unhealthy**, dirty, disease-ridden, filthy, infested, insalubrious, polluted, unclean, unhygienic

insanity *noun* 1 = **madness**, delirium, dementia, mental disorder, mental illness OPPOSITE **sanity**. 2 = **stupidity**, folly, irresponsibility, lunacy, senselessness OPPOSITE **sense**

insatiable *adjective* =**unquenchable**, greedy, intemperate, rapacious, ravenous, voracious

inscribe *verb* =**carve**, cut, engrave, etch, impress, imprint

inscription *noun* =**engraving**, dedication, legend, words

inscrutable *adjective* a = **mysterious**, hidden, incomprehensible, inexplicable, unexplainable, unfathomable, unintelligible OPPOSITE **clear**. b = **enigmatic**, blank, deadpan, impenetrable, poker-faced (*inf*), unreadable OPPOSITE **open**

insecure *adjective* 1 = **anxious**, afraid,

insemination *noun* putting semen into a woman's or female animal's body to try to make her pregnant. **inseminate** *verb*

insensate *adjective* **1** without sensation, unconscious. **2** unfeeling.

insensible ✪ *adjective* **1** unconscious, without feeling. **2** (foll. by *to* or *of*) not aware (of) or affected (by). **insensibility** *noun*

insensitive ✪ *adjective* unaware of or ignoring other people's feelings. **insensitivity** *noun*

inseparable ✪ *adjective* **1** (of two people) spending most of the time together. **2** (of two things) impossible to separate.

> **SPELLING TIP**
>
> The word **inseparable** occurs in the Bank of English 914 times. The misspelling *inseperable*, with an *e* instead of an *a* in the middle, appears 6 times.

insert ✪ *verb* **1** put inside or include. ◆ *noun* **2** something inserted. **insertion** *noun*

inset *noun* small picture inserted within a larger one.

inshore *adjective* **1** close to the shore. ◆ *adjective, adverb* **2** towards the shore.

inside ✪ *preposition* **1** in or to the interior of. ◆ *adjective* **2** on or of the inside. **3** by or from someone within an organization, e.g. *inside information.* ◆ *adverb* **4** on, in, or to the inside, indoors. **5** *Slang* in(to) prison. ◆ *noun* **6** inner side, surface, or part. ◆ *plural* **7** *Informal* stomach and bowels. **inside out** with the inside facing outwards. **know inside out** know thoroughly. **insider** *noun* member of a group who has privileged knowledge about it.

insidious ✪ *adjective* subtle or unseen but dangerous. **insidiously** *adverb*

insight ✪ *noun* deep understanding.

insignia ✪ [in-**sig**-nee-a] *noun, pl* **-nias, -nia** badge or emblem of honour or office.

insignificant ✪ *adjective* not important. **insignificance** *noun*

insincere ✪ *adjective* showing false feelings, not genuine. **insincerely** *adverb* **insincerity** *noun, pl* **-ties**

insinuate ✪ *verb* **1** suggest indirectly. **2** work (oneself) into a position by gradual manoeuvres. **insinuation** *noun*

insipid ✪ *adjective* lacking interest, spirit, or flavour. **insipidity** *noun*

insist ✪ *verb* demand or state firmly. **insistent**

——————— THESAURUS ———————

uncertain, unsure OPPOSITE **confident. 2** = **unsafe,** defenceless, exposed, unguarded, unprotected, vulnerable, wide-open OPPOSITE **protected**

insensible *adjective* **2** (foll. by *to* or *of*) = **unaware,** impervious, oblivious, unaffected, unconscious, unmindful

insensitive *adjective* = **unfeeling,** callous, hardened, indifferent, thick-skinned, tough, uncaring, unconcerned OPPOSITE **sensitive**

inseparable *adjective* **1** = **devoted,** bosom, close, intimate **2** = **indivisible,** indissoluble

insert *verb* **1** = **enter,** embed, implant, introduce, place, put, stick in OPPOSITE **remove**

insertion *noun* = **inclusion,** addition, implant, interpolation, introduction, supplement

inside *adjective* **2** = **inner,** interior, internal, inward OPPOSITE **outside. 3** = **confidential,** classified, exclusive, internal, private, restricted, secret ◆*adverb* **4** = **indoors,** under cover, within ◆*noun* **6** = **interior,** contents ◆*plural* **7** *Inf* = **stomach,** belly, bowels, entrails, guts, innards (*inf*), viscera, vitals

insidious *adjective* = **stealthy,** deceptive, sly, smooth, sneaking, subtle, surreptitious OPPOSITE **straightforward**

insight *noun* = **understanding,** awareness,

comprehension, discernment, judgment, observation, penetration, perception, perspicacity, vision

insignia *noun* = **badge,** crest, emblem, symbol

insignificance *noun* = **unimportance,** inconsequence, irrelevance, meaninglessness, pettiness, triviality, worthlessness OPPOSITE **importance**

insignificant *adjective* = **unimportant,** inconsequential, irrelevant, meaningless, minor, nondescript, paltry, petty, trifling, trivial OPPOSITE **important**

insincere *adjective* = **deceitful,** dishonest, disingenuous, duplicitous, false, hollow, hypocritical, lying, two-faced, untruthful OPPOSITE **sincere**

insincerity *noun* = **deceitfulness,** dishonesty, dissimulation, duplicity, hypocrisy, pretence, untruthfulness

insinuate *verb* **1** = **imply,** allude, hint, indicate, intimate, suggest **2** = **ingratiate,** curry favour, get in with, worm *or* work one's way in

insinuation *noun* **1** = **implication,** allusion, aspersion, hint, innuendo, slur, suggestion

insipid *adjective* **a** = **bland,** anaemic, characterless, colourless, prosaic, uninteresting, vapid, wishy-washy (*inf*) OPPOSITE **interesting. b** = **tasteless,** bland, flavourless, unappetizing,

I

adjective **1** making persistent demands. **2** demanding attention. **insistently** *adverb*
insistence *noun*
in situ *adverb, adjective Latin* in its original position.
in so far as, insofar as *preposition* to the extent that.
insole *noun* inner sole of a shoe or boot.
insolent ⊕ *adjective* rude and disrespectful.
insolence *noun* **insolently** *adverb*
insoluble ⊕ *adjective* **1** incapable of being solved. **2** incapable of being dissolved.
insolvent ⊕ *adjective* unable to pay one's debts. **insolvency** *noun*
insomnia ⊕ *noun* inability to sleep. **insomniac** *noun*
insomuch *adverb* (foll. by *as* or *that*) to such an extent.
insouciant *adjective* carefree and unconcerned. **insouciance** *noun*
inspect ⊕ *verb* check closely or officially. **inspection** *noun* **inspector** *noun* **1** person who inspects. **2** high-ranking police officer.

inspire ⊕ *verb* **1** fill with enthusiasm, stimulate. **2** arouse (an emotion). **inspiration** *noun* **1** creative influence or stimulus. **2** brilliant idea. **inspirational** *adjective*
inst. instant (this month).
instability ⊕ *noun* lack of steadiness or reliability.
install ⊕ *verb* **1** put in and prepare (equipment) for use. **2** place (a person) formally in a position or rank. **installation** *noun* **1** installing. **2** equipment installed. **3** place containing equipment for a particular purpose, e.g. *oil installations.*
instalment ⊕ *noun* any of the portions of a thing presented or a debt paid in successive parts.
instance ⊕ *noun* **1** particular example. ♦ *verb* **2** mention as an example. **for instance** as an example.
instant ⊕ *noun* **1** very brief time. **2** particular moment. ♦ *adjective* **3** happening at once. **4** (of foods) requiring little preparation. **instantly** *adverb*

——————— T H E S A U R U S ———————

watery OPPOSITE⟩ tasty
insist *verb* **a** = **demand**, lay down the law, put one's foot down (*inf*), require **b** = **state**, assert, aver, claim, maintain, reiterate, repeat, swear, vow
insistence *noun* = **persistence**, emphasis, importunity, stress
insistent *adjective* = **persistent**, dogged, emphatic, importunate, incessant, persevering, unrelenting, urgent
insolence *noun* = **rudeness**, boldness, cheek (*inf*), disrespect, effrontery, impertinence, impudence OPPOSITE⟩ **politeness**
insolent *adjective* = **rude**, bold, contemptuous, impertinent, impudent, insubordinate, insulting OPPOSITE⟩ **polite**
insoluble *adjective* **1** = **inexplicable**, baffling, impenetrable, indecipherable, mysterious, unaccountable, unfathomable, unsolvable OPPOSITE⟩ **explicable**
insolvency *noun* = **bankruptcy**, failure, liquidation, ruin
insolvent *adjective* = **bankrupt**, broke (*inf*), failed, gone bust (*inf*), gone to the wall, in receivership, munted (*NZ sl*), ruined
insomnia *noun* = **sleeplessness**, wakefulness
inspect *verb* = **examine**, check, go over *or* through, investigate, look over, scrutinize, survey, vet
inspection *noun* = **examination**, check, checkup, investigation, once-over (*inf*), review, scrutiny, search, survey

inspector *noun* **1** = **examiner**, auditor, censor, investigator, overseer, scrutinizer, superintendent, supervisor
inspiration *noun* **1** = **influence**, muse, spur, stimulus OPPOSITE⟩ **deterrent**. **2** = **revelation**, creativity, illumination, insight
inspire *verb* **1** = **stimulate**, animate, encourage, enliven, galvanize, gee up, influence, spur OPPOSITE⟩ **discourage**. **2** = **arouse**, enkindle, excite, give rise to, produce
inspired *adjective* **1** = **uplifted**, elated, enthused, exhilarated, stimulated
inspiring *adjective* **1, 2** = **uplifting**, exciting, exhilarating, heartening, moving, rousing, stimulating, stirring OPPOSITE⟩ **uninspiring**
instability *noun* = **unpredictability**, changeableness, fickleness, fluctuation, impermanence, inconstancy, insecurity, unsteadiness, variability, volatility OPPOSITE⟩ **stability**
install *verb* **1** = **set up**, fix, lay, lodge, place, position, put in, station **2** = **induct**, establish, inaugurate, institute, introduce, invest
installation *noun* **1 a** = **setting up**, establishment, fitting, instalment, placing, positioning **b** = **induction**, inauguration, investiture **2** = **equipment**, machinery, plant, system
instalment *noun* = **portion**, chapter, division, episode, part, repayment, section
instance *noun* **1** = **example**, case, illustration, occasion, occurrence, situation ♦ *verb* **2** = **quote**,

instantaneous ❶ *adjective* happening at once. **instantaneously** *adverb*
instead ❶ *adverb* as a replacement or substitute. **instead of** in place of, as an alternative to.
instep *noun* 1 part of the foot forming the arch between the ankle and toes. 2 part of a shoe etc. covering this.
instigate ❶ *verb* cause to happen. **instigation** *noun* **instigator** *noun*
instil ❶ *verb* **-stilling, -stilled** introduce (an idea etc.) gradually into someone's mind.
instinct ❶ *noun* inborn tendency to behave in a certain way. **instinctive** *adjective* **instinctively** *adverb*
institute ❶ *noun* 1 organization set up for a specific purpose, esp. research or teaching. ◆ *verb* 2 start or establish. **institution** *noun* large important organization such as a university or bank.
institution ❶ *noun* 1 large important organization such as a university or bank. 2 hospital etc. for people with special needs. 3 long-established custom. **institutional** *adjective* **institutionalize** *verb*
instruct ❶ *verb* 1 order to do something. 2 teach (someone) how to do something.
instruction *noun* 1 order to do something. 2 teaching. ◆ *plural* 3 information on how to do or use something. **instructive** *adjective* informative or helpful. **instructor** *noun*
instrument ❶ *noun* 1 tool used for particular work. 2 object played to produce a musical sound. 3 measuring device to show height, speed, etc. 4 *Informal* someone or something used to achieve an aim. **instrumental** *adjective* 1 (foll. by *in*) having an important function (in). 2 played by or composed for musical instruments. **instrumentalist** *noun* player of a musical instrument. **instrumentation** *noun* 1 set of instruments in a car etc. 2 arrangement of music for instruments.

I

——————— THESAURUS ———————

adduce, cite, mention, name, specify
instant *noun* 1 = **second**, flash, jiffy (*inf*), moment, split second, trice, twinkling of an eye (*inf*) 2 = **juncture**, moment, occasion, point, time ◆*adjective* 3 = **immediate**, direct, instantaneous, on-the-spot, prompt, quick, split-second 4 = **precooked**, convenience, fast, ready-mixed
instantaneous *adjective* = **immediate**, direct, instant, on-the-spot, prompt
instantaneously *adverb* = **immediately**, at once, instantly, in the twinkling of an eye (*inf*), on the spot, promptly, straight away
instantly *adverb* 3 = **immediately**, at once, directly, instantaneously, now, right away, straight away, this minute
instead *adverb* = **rather**, alternatively, in lieu, in preference, on second thoughts, preferably
instead of = **in place of**, in lieu of, rather than
instigate *verb* = **provoke**, bring about, incite, influence, initiate, prompt, set off, start OPPOSITE> **suppress**
instigation *noun* = **prompting**, behest, bidding, encouragement, incitement, urging
instigator *noun* = **ringleader**, agitator, leader, motivator, prime mover, troublemaker
instil *verb* = **introduce**, engender, imbue, implant, inculcate, infuse, insinuate
instinct *noun* = **intuition**, faculty, gift, impulse, knack, predisposition, proclivity, talent, tendency
instinctive *adjective* = **inborn**, automatic, inherent, innate, intuitive, involuntary, natural, reflex, spontaneous, unpremeditated, visceral

OPPOSITE> **acquired**
instinctively *adverb* = **intuitively**, automatically, by instinct, involuntarily, naturally, without thinking
institute *noun* 1 = **society**, academy, association, college, foundation, guild, institution, school ◆*verb* 2 = **establish**, fix, found, initiate, introduce, launch, organize, originate, pioneer, set up, start OPPOSITE> **end**
institution *noun* 1 = **establishment**, academy, college, foundation, institute, school, society 3 = **custom**, convention, law, practice, ritual, rule, tradition
institutional *adjective* 3 = **conventional**, accepted, established, formal, orthodox
instruct *verb* 1 = **order**, bid, charge, command, direct, enjoin, tell 2 = **teach**, coach, drill, educate, ground, school, train, tutor
instruction *noun* 1 = **order**, command, demand, directive, injunction, mandate, ruling 2 = **teaching**, coaching, education, grounding, guidance, lesson(s), schooling, training, tuition ◆*plural* 3 = **orders**, advice, directions, guidance, information, key, recommendations, rules
instructive *adjective* = **informative**, edifying, educational, enlightening, helpful, illuminating, revealing, useful
instructor *noun* 2 = **teacher**, adviser, coach, demonstrator, guide, mentor, trainer, tutor
instrument *noun* 1 = **tool**, apparatus, appliance, contraption (*inf*), device, gadget, implement, mechanism 4 *Inf* = **means**, agency, agent, mechanism, medium, organ, vehicle

insubordinate ✪ *adjective* not submissive to authority. **insubordination** *noun*
insubstantial ✪ *adjective* flimsy, fine, or slight.
insufferable ✪ *adjective* unbearable.
insular ✪ *adjective* not open to new ideas, narrow-minded. **insularity** *noun*
insulate ✪ *verb* **1** prevent or reduce the transfer of electricity, heat, or sound by surrounding or lining with a nonconducting material. **2** isolate or set apart. **insulation** *noun* **insulator** *noun*
insulin [in-syoo-lin] *noun* hormone produced in the pancreas that controls the amount of sugar in the blood.
insult ✪ *verb* **1** behave rudely to, offend. ◆ *noun* **2** insulting remark or action. **insulting** *adjective*
insuperable ✪ *adjective* impossible to overcome.
insupportable ✪ *adjective* **1** impossible to tolerate. **2** impossible to justify.
insurance ✪ *noun* **1** agreement by which one makes regular payments to a company who pay an agreed sum if damage, loss, or death occurs.

2 money paid to or by an insurance company. **3** means of protection. **insure** *verb* protect by insurance. **insurance policy** contract of insurance.
insurgent ✪ *noun, adjective* (person) in revolt against an established authority. **insurgency** *noun*
insurmountable ✪ *adjective* impossible to overcome, e.g. *an insurmountable problem.*
insurrection ✪ *noun* rebellion.
intact ✪ *adjective* not changed or damaged in any way.
intaglio [in-**tah**-lee-oh] *noun, pl* -**lios** (gem carved with) an engraved design.
intake *noun* amount or number taken in.
intangible *adjective* not clear or definite enough to be seen or felt easily, e.g. *an intangible quality.*
integer *noun* positive or negative whole number or zero.
integral ✪ *adjective* **1** being an essential part of a whole. ◆ *noun* **2** *Maths* sum of a large number of very small quantities.
integrate ✪ *verb* **1** combine into a whole. **2** amalgamate (a religious or racial group) into a

——— T H E S A U R U S ———

instrumental *adjective* **1** (foll. by *in*) = **active**, contributory, helpful, influential, involved, useful
insubordinate *adjective* = **disobedient**, defiant, disorderly, mutinous, rebellious, recalcitrant, refractory, undisciplined, ungovernable, unruly
insubordination *noun* = **disobedience**, defiance, indiscipline, insurrection, mutiny, rebellion, recalcitrance, revolt
insubstantial *adjective* = **flimsy**, feeble, frail, poor, slight, tenuous, thin, weak OPPOSITE substantial
insufferable *adjective* = **unbearable**, detestable, dreadful, impossible, insupportable, intolerable, unendurable
insular *adjective* = **narrow-minded**, blinkered, circumscribed, inward-looking, limited, narrow, parochial, petty, provincial OPPOSITE **broad-minded**
insulate *verb* **2** = **isolate**, close off, cocoon, cushion, cut off, protect, sequester, shield
insult *verb* **1** = **offend**, abuse, affront, call names, put down, slander, slight, snub OPPOSITE **praise** ◆*noun* **2** = **abuse**, affront, aspersion, insolence, offence, put-down, slap in the face (*inf*), slight, snub
insulting *adjective* = **offensive**, abusive, contemptuous, degrading, disparaging, insolent, rude, scurrilous OPPOSITE

complimentary
insuperable *adjective* = **insurmountable**, impassable, invincible, unconquerable OPPOSITE surmountable
insupportable *adjective* **1** = **intolerable**, insufferable, unbearable, unendurable **2** = **unjustifiable**, indefensible, untenable
insurance *noun* = **protection**, assurance, cover, guarantee, indemnity, safeguard, security, warranty
insure *verb* = **protect**, assure, cover, guarantee, indemnify, underwrite, warrant
insurgent *noun* = **rebel**, insurrectionist, mutineer, revolutionary, rioter ◆*adjective* = **rebellious**, disobedient, insubordinate, mutinous, revolting, revolutionary, riotous, seditious
insurmountable *adjective* = **insuperable**, hopeless, impassable, impossible, invincible, overwhelming, unconquerable
insurrection *noun* = **rebellion**, coup, insurgency, mutiny, revolt, revolution, riot, uprising
intact *adjective* = **undamaged**, complete, entire, perfect, sound, unbroken, unharmed, unimpaired, unscathed, whole OPPOSITE damaged
integral *adjective* **1** = **essential**, basic, component, constituent, fundamental, indispensable, intrinsic, necessary OPPOSITE

community. **integration** *noun* **integrated circuit** tiny electronic circuit on a silicon chip.
integrity ⊕ *noun* **1** quality of having high moral principles. **2** quality of being united.
intellect ⊕ *noun* power of thinking and reasoning. **intellectual** *adjective* **1** of or appealing to the intellect. **2** clever, intelligent. ◆ *noun* **3** intellectual person. **intellectually** *adverb* **intellectualism** *noun*
intelligent ⊕ *adjective* **1** able to understand, learn, and think things out quickly. **2** (of a computerized device) able to initiate or modify action in the light of ongoing events.
intelligence *noun* **1** quality of being intelligent. **2** secret government or military information. **3** people or department collecting such information. **intelligently** *adverb* **intelligence quotient** a measure of the intelligence of a person calculated by dividing the person's mental age by his or her actual age andmultiplying the result by 100.
intelligentsia ⊕ *noun* intellectual or cultured people in a society.
intelligible ⊕ *adjective* able to be understood.

intelligibility *noun*
intemperate ⊕ *adjective* **1** unrestrained, uncontrolled, e.g. *intemperate language.* **2** drinking alcohol to excess. **intemperance** *noun*
intend ⊕ *verb* **1** propose or plan (to do something). **2** have as one's purpose. **intended** *adjective* **1** planned or future. ◆ *noun* **2** *Informal* person whom one is to marry.
intense ⊕ *adjective* **1** of great strength or degree. **2** deeply emotional. **intensity** *noun*
intensify *verb* **-fying, -fied** make or become more intense. **intensification** *noun*
intensive ⊕ *adjective* using or needing concentrated effort or resources. **intensively** *adverb* **intensive care** thorough supervised treatment of an acutely ill patient in a hospital.
intent ⊕ *noun* **1** intention. **2** intention to commit a crime. ◆ *adjective* **3** paying close attention. **intently** *adverb* **intentness** *noun* **intent on doing something** determined to do something. **to all intents and purposes** in almost every respect.
intention ⊕ *noun* something intended.
intentional *adjective* planned in advance,

——————— THESAURUS ———————

unnecessary
integrate *verb* **1** =**combine**, amalgamate, assimilate, blend, fuse, incorporate, join, merge, unite OPPOSITE **separate**. **2** =**unite**, amalgamate, incorporate
integration *noun* **1** =**combining**, amalgamation, assimilation, blending, fusing, incorporation, mixing **2** =**unification**, amalgamation, incorporation
integrity *noun* **1** =**honesty**, goodness, honour, incorruptibility, principle, probity, purity, rectitude, uprightness, virtue OPPOSITE **dishonesty**. **2** =**soundness**, coherence, cohesion, completeness, unity, wholeness OPPOSITE **fragility**
intellect *noun* =**intelligence**, brains (*inf*), judgment, mind, reason, sense, understanding
intellectual *adjective* **2** =**scholarly**, bookish, cerebral, highbrow, intelligent, studious, thoughtful OPPOSITE **stupid** ◆*noun* **3** =**academic**, egghead (*inf*), highbrow, thinker OPPOSITE **idiot**
intelligence *noun* **1** =**understanding**, acumen, brain power, brains (*inf*), cleverness, comprehension, intellect, perception, sense OPPOSITE **ignorance**. **2** =**information**, data, facts, findings, knowledge, news, notification, report OPPOSITE **misinformation**
intelligent *adjective* **1** =**clever**, brainy (*inf*), bright, enlightened, perspicacious, quick-witted, sharp, smart, well-informed OPPOSITE **stupid**

intelligentsia *noun* =**intellectuals**, highbrows, literati
intelligible *adjective* =**understandable**, clear, comprehensible, distinct, lucid, open, plain OPPOSITE **unintelligible**
intemperate *adjective* **1** =**excessive**, extreme, immoderate, profligate, self-indulgent, unbridled, unrestrained, wild OPPOSITE **temperate**
intend *verb* =**plan**, aim, have in mind *or* view, mean, propose, purpose
intense *adjective* **1** =**extreme**, acute, deep, excessive, fierce, great, powerful, profound, severe OPPOSITE **moderate**. **2** =**passionate**, ardent, fanatical, fervent, fierce, heightened, impassioned, vehement OPPOSITE **indifferent**
intensify *verb* =**increase**, add to, aggravate, deepen, escalate, heighten, magnify, redouble, reinforce, sharpen, strengthen OPPOSITE **decrease**
intensity *noun* **2** =**force**, ardour, emotion, fanaticism, fervour, fierceness, passion, strength, vehemence
intensive *adjective* =**concentrated**, comprehensive, demanding, exhaustive, in-depth, thorough, thoroughgoing
intent *noun* **1** =**intention**, aim, design, end, goal, meaning, object, objective, plan, purpose OPPOSITE **chance** ◆*adjective* **3** =**intense**, absorbed, attentive, engrossed, preoccupied, rapt, steadfast, watchful OPPOSITE **casual**

deliberate. **intentionally** *adverb*
inter ❶ [in-ter] *verb* **-terring, -terred** bury (a corpse). **interment** *noun*
inter- *prefix* between or among, e.g. *international.*
interact *verb* act on or in close relation with each other. **interaction** *noun* **interactive** *adjective*
interbreed *verb* breed within a related group.
intercede ❶ *verb* try to end a dispute between two people or groups. **intercession** *noun*
intercept ❶ *verb* seize or stop in transit. **interception** *noun* **interceptor** *noun*
interchange ❶ *verb* **1** (cause to) exchange places. ♦ *noun* **2** motorway junction.
interchangeable *adjective*
Intercity *adjective* ® denoting a fast train (service) travelling between cities.
intercom *noun* internal communication system with loudspeakers.
intercommunion *noun* association between Churches, involving mutual reception of Holy Communion.
intercontinental *adjective* travelling between or linking continents.
intercourse ❶ *noun* **1** sexual intercourse. **2** communication or dealings between people or groups.
interdenominational *adjective* among or involving more than one denomination of the Christian Church.
interdiction, interdict *noun* formal order forbidding something.
interdisciplinary *adjective* involving more than one branch of learning.
interest ❶ *noun* **1** desire to know or hear more about something. **2** something in which one is interested. **3** (often pl) advantage, benefit, e.g. *acting in the interests of the oil company.* **4** sum paid for the use of borrowed money. **5** (often pl) right or share. ♦ *verb* **6** arouse the interest of. **interested** *adjective* **1** feeling or showing interest. **2** involved in or affected by something. **interesting** *adjective* **interestingly** *adverb*
interface ❶ *noun* **1** area where two things interact or link. **2** circuit linking a computer and another device.
interfere ❶ *verb* **1** try to influence other people's affairs where one is not involved or wanted. **2** (foll. by *with*) clash (with). **3** (foll. by *with*) *Euphemistic* abuse (a child) sexually. **interfering** *adjective* **interference** *noun* **1** interfering. **2** *Radio* interruption of reception by atmospherics or unwanted signals.
interferon *noun* protein that stops the development of an invading virus.
interim ❶ *adjective* **1** temporary or provisional. ♦ *noun* **2 in the interim** in the intervening time.
interior ❶ *noun* **1** inside. **2** inland region. ♦

———————— THESAURUS ————————

intention *noun* =**purpose**, aim, design, end, goal, idea, object, objective, point, target
intentional *adjective* =**deliberate**, calculated, intended, meant, planned, premeditated, wilful OPPOSITE unintentional
intentionally *adverb* =**deliberately**, designedly, on purpose, wilfully
inter *verb* =**bury**, entomb, lay to rest
intercede *verb* =**mediate**, arbitrate, intervene, plead
intercept *verb* =**seize**, block, catch, cut off, head off, interrupt, obstruct, stop
interchange *verb* **1** =**switch**, alternate, exchange, reciprocate, swap ♦*noun* **2** =**junction**, intersection
interchangeable *adjective* **1** =**identical**, equivalent, exchangeable, reciprocal, synonymous
intercourse *noun* **1** =**sexual intercourse**, carnal knowledge, coitus, copulation, sex (*inf*) **2** =**communication**, commerce, contact, dealings
interest *noun* **1** =**curiosity**, attention, concern, notice, regard OPPOSITE disregard. **2** =**hobby**, activity, diversion, pastime,
preoccupation, pursuit **3** (often pl) =**advantage**, benefit, good, profit **5** (often pl) =**stake**, claim, investment, right, share ♦*verb* **6** =**arouse one's curiosity**, attract, catch one's eye, divert, engross, fascinate, intrigue OPPOSITE bore
interested *adjective* **1** =**curious**, attracted, drawn, excited, fascinated, keen OPPOSITE bored. **2** =**involved**, concerned, implicated
interesting *adjective* **6** =**intriguing**, absorbing, appealing, attractive, compelling, engaging, engrossing, gripping, stimulating, thought-provoking OPPOSITE uninteresting
interface *noun* **1** =**connection**, border, boundary, frontier, link
interfere *verb* **1** =**intrude**, butt in, intervene, meddle, stick one's oar in (*inf*), tamper **2** (foll. by *with*) =**conflict**, clash, hamper, handicap, hinder, impede, inhibit, obstruct
interference *noun* **1 a** =**intrusion**, intervention, meddling, prying **b** =**conflict**, clashing, collision, obstruction, opposition
interim *adjective* **1** =**temporary**, acting, caretaker, improvised, makeshift, provisional,

adjective **3** inside, inner. **4** mental or spiritual.
interject *verb* make (a remark) suddenly or as an interruption. **interjection** *noun*
interlace *verb* join together as if by weaving.
interleave *verb* insert between other leaves, for example blank leaves in a book.
interlink *verb* connect together.
interlock *verb* join firmly together.
interlocutor [in-ter-**lok**-yew-ter] *noun* person who takes part in a conversation.
interloper ❶ [in-ter-lope-er] *noun* person in a place or situation where he or she has no right to be.
interlude ❶ *noun* short rest or break in an activity or event.
intermarry *verb* (of families, races, or religions) become linked by marriage.
intermarriage *noun*
intermediary ❶ *noun, pl* **-ries** person trying to create agreement between others.
intermediate ❶ *adjective* coming between two points or extremes.
intermezzo [in-ter-**met**-so] *noun, pl* **-zos** short piece of music, esp. one performed between the acts of an opera.
interminable ❶ *adjective* seemingly endless because boring. **interminably** *adverb*
intermingle *verb* mix together.
intermission ❶ *noun* interval between parts of a play, film, etc.
intermittent ❶ *adjective* occurring at intervals. **intermittently** *adverb*

intern ❶ *verb* **1** imprison, esp. during a war. ◆ *noun* **2** *Chiefly US* trainee doctor in a hospital.
internment *noun* **internee** *noun* person who is interned.
internal ❶ *adjective* **1** of or on the inside. **2** within a country or organization. **3** spiritual or mental. **internally** *adverb* **internal-combustion engine** engine powered by the explosion of a fuel-and-air mixture within the cylinders.
international ❶ *adjective* **1** of or involving two or more countries. ◆ *noun* **2** game or match between teams of different countries. **3** player in such a match. **internationally** *adverb*
internecine *adjective* mutually destructive.
Internet, internet ❶ *noun* large international computer network.
interplanetary *adjective* of or linking planets.
interplay *noun* action and reaction of two things upon each other.
Interpol International Criminal Police Organization.
interpolate [in-ter-**pole**-ate] *verb* insert (a comment or passage) into (a conversation or text). **interpolation** *noun*
interpose ❶ *verb* **1** insert between or among things. **2** say as an interruption.
interpret ❶ *verb* **1** explain the meaning of. **2** translate orally from one language into another. **3** convey the meaning of (a poem, song, etc.) in performance. **interpretation** *noun*
interpreter *noun*

I

─────────── THESAURUS ───────────

stopgap
interior *noun* **1** =**inside**, centre, core, heart OPPOSITE exterior ◆*adjective* **3** =**inside**, inner, internal, inward **4** =**mental**, hidden, inner, intimate, personal, private, secret, spiritual
interloper *noun* =**trespasser**, gate-crasher (*inf*), intruder, meddler
interlude *noun* =**interval**, break, breathing space, delay, hiatus, intermission, pause, respite, rest, spell, stoppage
intermediary *noun* =**mediator**, agent, broker, go-between, middleman
intermediate *adjective* =**middle**, halfway, in-between (*inf*), intervening, mid, midway, transitional
interment *noun* =**burial**, funeral
interminable *adjective* =**endless**, ceaseless, everlasting, infinite, long-drawn-out, long-winded, never-ending, perpetual, protracted OPPOSITE limited
intermission *noun* =**interval**, break, interlude, pause, recess, respite, rest, stoppage
intermittent *adjective* =**periodic**, broken,

fitful, irregular, occasional, spasmodic, sporadic OPPOSITE continuous
intern *verb* **1** =**imprison**, confine, detain, hold, hold in custody
internal *adjective* **1** =**inner**, inside, interior OPPOSITE external. **2** =**domestic**, civic, home, in-house, intramural
international *adjective* **1** =**universal**, cosmopolitan, global, intercontinental, worldwide
Internet *noun* =**information superhighway**, cyberspace, the net (*inf*), the web (*inf*), World Wide Web
interpose *verb* **1** =**insert 2** =**interrupt**, interject, put one's oar in
interpret *verb* **1** =**explain**, decipher, decode, elucidate, make sense of **2** =**translate**, construe **3** =**render**
interpretation *noun* **1** =**explanation**, analysis, clarification, elucidation, exposition **2** =**translation 3** =**version**, portrayal, rendition
interpreter *noun* **1** =**commentator 2** =**translator**

interregnum *noun, pl* **-nums, -na** interval between reigns.

interrelate *verb* connect (two or more things) to each other. **interrelation** *noun*

interrogate ❶ *verb* question closely. **interrogation** *noun* **interrogative** *adjective* **1** questioning. ♦ *noun* **2** word used in asking a question, such as *how* or *why*. **interrogator** *noun*

interrupt ❶ *verb* **1** break into (a conversation etc.). **2** stop (a process or activity) temporarily. **interruption** *noun*

intersect ❶ *verb* **1** (of roads) meet and cross. **2** divide by passing across or through. **intersection** *noun*

interspersed *adjective* scattered (among, between, or on).

interstellar *adjective* between or among stars.

interstice [in-ter-stiss] *noun* small crack or gap between things.

intertwine *verb* twist together.

interval ❶ *noun* **1** time between two particular moments or events. **2** break between parts of a play, concert, etc. **3** difference in pitch between musical notes. **at intervals 1** repeatedly. **2** with spaces left between.

intervene ❶ *verb* **1** involve oneself in a situation, esp. to prevent conflict. **2** happen so as to stop something. **intervention** *noun*

interview ❶ *noun* **1** formal discussion, esp. between a job-seeker and an employer. **2** questioning of a well-known person about his or her career, views, etc., by a reporter. ♦ *verb* **3** conduct an interview with. **interviewee** *noun* **interviewer** *noun*

interweave *verb* weave together.

intestate *adjective* not having made a will. **intestacy** *noun*

intestine *noun* (often pl) lower part of the alimentary canal between the stomach and the anus. **intestinal** *adjective*

intimate[1] ❶ *adjective* **1** having a close personal relationship. **2** personal or private. **3** (of knowledge) extensive and detailed. **4** (foll. by *with*) *Euphemistic* having a sexual relationship (with). **5** having a friendly quiet atmosphere. ♦ *noun* **6** close friend. **intimately** *adverb* **intimacy** *noun, pl* **-cies**

intimate[2] ❶ *verb* **1** hint at or suggest. **2** announce. **intimation** *noun*

intimidate ❶ *verb* subdue or influence by fear. **intimidating** *adjective* **intimidation** *noun*

——————— T H E S A U R U S ———————

interrogate *verb* =**question**, cross-examine, examine, grill (*inf*), investigate, pump, quiz

interrogation *noun* =**questioning**, cross-examination, examination, grilling (*inf*), inquiry, inquisition, third degree (*inf*)

interrupt *verb* **1** =**intrude**, barge in (*inf*), break in, butt in, disturb, heckle, interfere (with) **2** =**suspend**, break off, cut short, delay, discontinue, hold up, lay aside, stop

interruption *noun* **2** =**stoppage**, break, disruption, disturbance, hitch, intrusion, pause, suspension

intersection *noun* **1** =**junction**, crossing, crossroads, interchange

interval *noun* **1** =**break**, delay, gap, pause, respite, rest, space, spell **2** =**interlude**, intermission

intervene *verb* **1** =**step in** (*inf*), arbitrate, intercede, interfere, intrude, involve oneself, mediate, take a hand (*inf*) **2** =**happen**, befall, come to pass, ensue, occur, take place

intervention *noun* **1** =**mediation**, agency, interference, intrusion

interview *noun* **2** =**meeting**, audience, conference, consultation, dialogue, press conference, talk ♦*verb* **3** =**question**, examine, interrogate, talk to

interviewer *noun* **3** =**questioner**, examiner, interrogator, investigator, reporter

intestine *noun* (often pl) =**guts**, bowels, entrails, innards (*inf*), insides (*inf*), viscera

intimacy *noun* **1** =**familiarity**, closeness OPPOSITE aloofness. **2** =**confidentiality**

intimate[1] *adjective* **1** =**close**, bosom, confidential, dear, near, thick (*inf*) OPPOSITE distant. **2** =**private**, confidential, personal, secret OPPOSITE public. **3** =**detailed**, deep, exhaustive, first-hand, immediate, in-depth, profound, thorough **5** =**snug**, comfy (*inf*), cosy, friendly, warm ♦*noun* **6** =**friend**, close friend, cobber (*Aust or old-fashioned NZ inf*), confidant *or* confidante, (constant) companion, crony OPPOSITE stranger

intimate[2] *verb* **1** =**suggest**, hint, imply, indicate, insinuate **2** =**announce**, communicate, declare, make known, state

intimately *adverb* **1** =**confidingly**, affectionately, confidentially, familiarly, personally, tenderly, warmly **3** =**in detail**, fully, inside out, thoroughly, very well

intimation *noun* **1** =**hint**, allusion, indication, inkling, insinuation, reminder, suggestion, warning **2** =**announcement**, communication, declaration, notice

intimidate *verb* =**frighten**, browbeat, bully, coerce, daunt, overawe, scare, subdue, terrorize, threaten

intimidation *noun* =**bullying**, arm-twisting

into *preposition* **1** indicating motion towards the centre, result of a change, division, etc., e.g. *into the valley; turned into a madman; cut into pieces.* **2** *Informal* interested in.

intolerable *adjective* more than can be endured. **intolerably** *adverb*

intolerant *adjective* refusing to accept practices and beliefs different from one's own. **intolerance** *noun*

intonation *noun* sound pattern produced by variations in the voice.

intone ❶ *verb* speak or recite in an unvarying tone of voice.

in toto *adverb Latin* totally, entirely.

intoxicate ❶ *verb* **1** make drunk. **2** excite to excess. **intoxicant** *noun* intoxicating drink. **intoxication** *noun*

intractable *adjective* **1** (of a person) difficult to control. **2** (of a problem or issue) difficult to deal with.

intranet *noun Computers* internal network that makes use of Internet technology.

intransigent ❶ *adjective* refusing to change one's attitude. **intransigence** *noun*

intransitive *adjective* (of a verb) not taking a direct object.

intrauterine *adjective* within the womb.

intravenous [in-tra-**vee**-nuss] *adjective* into a vein. **intravenously** *adverb*

intrepid ❶ *adjective* fearless, bold. **intrepidity** *noun*

intricate ❶ *adjective* **1** involved or complicated. **2** full of fine detail. **intricately** *adverb* **intricacy** *noun, pl* **-cies**

intrigue ❶ *verb* **1** make interested or curious. **2** plot secretly. ◆ *noun* **3** secret plotting. **4** secret love affair. **intriguing** *adjective*

intrinsic ❶ *adjective* essential to the basic nature of something. **intrinsically** *adverb*

introduce ❶ *verb* **1** present (someone) by name (to another person). **2** present (a radio or television programme). **3** bring forward for discussion. **4** bring into use. **5** insert.

introduction *noun* **1** presentation of one person to another. **2** preliminary part or treatment. **introductory** *adjective*

introspection ❶ *noun* examination of one's own thoughts and feelings. **introspective** *adjective*

introvert ❶ *noun* person concerned more with his or her thoughts and feelings than with the outside world. **introverted** *adjective* **introversion** *noun*

intrude ❶ *verb* come in or join in without

—————— T H E S A U R U S ——————

(*inf*), browbeating, coercion, menaces, pressure, terrorization, threat(s)
intone *verb* =**recite**, chant
intoxicated *adjective* **1** =**drunk**, drunken, inebriated, legless (*inf*), paralytic (*inf*), plastered (*sl*), tipsy, under the influence **2** =**euphoric**, dizzy, ecstatic, elated, enraptured, excited, exhilarated, high (*inf*)
intoxicating *adjective* **1** =**alcoholic**, strong **2** =**exciting**, exhilarating, heady, thrilling
intoxication *noun* **1** =**drunkenness**, inebriation, insobriety, tipsiness **2** =**excitement**, delirium, elation, euphoria, exhilaration
intransigent *adjective* =**uncompromising**, hard-line, intractable, obdurate, obstinate, stiff-necked, stubborn, unbending, unyielding OPPOSITE> **compliant**
intrepid *adjective* =**fearless**, audacious, bold, brave, courageous, daring, gallant, plucky, stouthearted, valiant OPPOSITE> **fearful**
intricacy *noun* **1** =**complexity**, complication, convolutions **2** =**elaborateness**
intricate *adjective* **1** =**complicated**, complex, convoluted, involved, labyrinthine, tangled, tortuous OPPOSITE> **simple**. **2** =**elaborate**, fancy OPPOSITE> **simple**
intrigue *verb* **1** =**interest**, attract, fascinate,

rivet, titillate **2** =**plot**, connive, conspire, machinate, manoeuvre, scheme ◆*noun* **3** =**plot**, chicanery, collusion, conspiracy, machination, manoeuvre, scheme, stratagem, wile **4** =**affair**, amour, intimacy, liaison, romance
intriguing *adjective* **1** =**interesting**, beguiling, compelling, diverting, exciting, fascinating, tantalizing, titillating
intrinsic *adjective* =**inborn**, basic, built-in, congenital, constitutional, essential, fundamental, inbred, inherent, native, natural OPPOSITE> **extrinsic**
introduce *verb* **1** =**present**, acquaint, familiarize, make known **3** =**bring up**, advance, air, broach, moot, put forward, submit **4** =**bring in**, establish, found, initiate, institute, launch, pioneer, set up, start **5** =**insert**, add, inject, put in, throw in (*inf*)
introduction *noun* **2** =**opening**, foreword, intro (*inf*), lead-in, preamble, preface, prelude, prologue OPPOSITE> **conclusion**
introductory *adjective* **4** =**preliminary**, first, inaugural, initial, opening, preparatory OPPOSITE> **concluding**
introspective *adjective* =**inward-looking**, brooding, contemplative, introverted, meditative, pensive
introverted *adjective* =**introspective**, inner-

being invited. **intruder** *noun* **intrusion** *noun*
intrusive *adjective*
intuition ① *noun* instinctive knowledge or
insight without conscious reasoning. **intuitive**
adjective **intuitively** *adverb*
Inuit *noun* Eskimo of North America or
Greenland.
Inuk *noun* a member of any Inuit people.
Inuktitut *noun Canad* the language of the
Inuit.
inundate ① *verb* **1** flood. **2** overwhelm.
inundation *noun*
inured *adjective* accustomed, esp. to hardship
or danger.
invade ① *verb* **1** enter (a country) by military
force. **2** enter in large numbers. **3** disturb
(someone's privacy). **invader** *noun*
invalid[1] ① *adjective, noun* **1** disabled or
chronically ill (person). ♦ *verb* **2** (often foll. by
out) dismiss from active service because of
illness or injury. **invalidity** *noun*
invalid[2] ① *adjective* **1** having no legal force. **2**
(of an argument etc.) not valid because based

on a mistake. **invalidate** *verb* make or show to
be invalid.
invaluable ① *adjective* of very great value or
worth.
invasion ① *noun* **1** invading. **2** intrusion, e.g.
an invasion of privacy.
invective ① *noun* abusive speech or writing.
inveigh [in-**vay**] *verb* (foll. by *against*) criticize
strongly.
inveigle *verb* coax by cunning or trickery.
invent ① *verb* **1** think up or create (something
new). **2** make up (a story, excuse, etc.).
invention *noun* **1** something invented. **2** ability
to invent. **inventive** *adjective* creative and
resourceful. **inventiveness** *noun* **inventor**
noun
inventory ① [in-ven-tree] *noun, pl* -**tories**
detailed list of goods or furnishings.
inverse ① *adjective* **1** reversed in effect,
sequence, direction, etc. **2** *Maths* linking two
variables in such a way that one increases as
the other decreases. **inversely** *adverb*
invert ① *verb* turn upside down or inside out.

——————— THESAURUS ———————

directed, inward-looking, self-contained,
withdrawn
intrude *verb* =**interfere**, butt in, encroach,
infringe, interrupt, meddle, push in, trespass
intruder *noun* =**trespasser**, gate-crasher (*inf*),
infiltrator, interloper, invader, prowler
intrusion *noun* =**invasion**, encroachment,
infringement, interference, interruption, trespass
intrusive *adjective* =**interfering**, impertinent,
importunate, meddlesome, nosy (*inf*),
presumptuous, pushy (*inf*), uncalled-for,
unwanted
intuition *noun* =**instinct**, hunch, insight,
perception, presentiment, sixth sense
intuitive *adjective* =**instinctive**, innate,
spontaneous, untaught
inundate *verb* **1** =**flood**, drown, engulf,
immerse, overflow, submerge, swamp **2**
=**overwhelm**, overrun
invade *verb* **1** =**attack**, assault, burst in,
descend upon, encroach, infringe, make
inroads, occupy, raid, violate **2** =**infest**,
overrun, permeate, pervade, swarm over
invader *noun* **1** =**attacker**, aggressor,
plunderer, raider, trespasser
invalid[1] *adjective* =**disabled**, ailing, bedridden,
frail, ill, infirm, sick ♦*noun* =**patient**,
convalescent, valetudinarian
invalid[2] *adjective* **1** =**null and void**,
inoperative, void OPPOSITE valid. **2** =**unsound**,
fallacious, false, illogical, irrational, shonky (*Aust
& NZ inf*), unfounded, worthless OPPOSITE

valid
invalidate *verb* **1** =**nullify**, annul, cancel,
overthrow, undermine OPPOSITE validate
invaluable *adjective* =**precious**, inestimable,
priceless, valuable, worth one's or its weight in
gold OPPOSITE worthless
invasion *noun* **1** =**attack**, assault, campaign,
foray, incursion, inroad, offensive, onslaught,
raid **2** =**intrusion**, breach, encroachment,
infraction, infringement, usurpation, violation
invective *noun* =**abuse**, censure,
denunciation, diatribe, tirade, tongue-lashing,
vilification, vituperation
invent *verb* **1** =**create**, coin, conceive, design,
devise, discover, formulate, improvise, originate,
think up **2** =**make up**, concoct, cook up (*inf*),
fabricate, feign, forge, manufacture, trump up
invention *noun* **1 a** =**creation**, brainchild
(*inf*), contraption, contrivance, design, device,
discovery, gadget, instrument **b** =**fiction**,
fabrication, falsehood, fantasy, forgery, lie,
untruth, yarn **2** =**creativity**, genius,
imagination, ingenuity, inventiveness,
originality, resourcefulness
inventive *adjective* =**creative**, fertile,
imaginative, ingenious, innovative, inspired,
original, resourceful OPPOSITE uninspired
inventor *noun* =**creator**, architect, author,
coiner, designer, maker, originator
inventory *noun* =**list**, account, catalogue, file,
record, register, roll, roster
inverse *adjective* **1** =**opposite**, contrary,

inversion *noun* **inverted commas** quotation marks.
invertebrate *noun* animal with no backbone.
invest ❶ *verb* **1** spend (money, time, etc.) on something with the expectation of profit. **2** (foll. by *with*) give (power or rights) to, e.g. *invested with the powers of government*.
investment *noun* **1** money invested. **2** something invested in. **investor** *noun* **invest in** *verb* buy.
investigate ❶ *verb* inquire into, examine.
investigation *noun* **investigative** *adjective*
investigator *noun*
investiture ❶ *noun* formal installation of a person in an office or rank.
inveterate ❶ *adjective* firmly established in a habit or condition, e.g. *an inveterate gambler*.
invidious *adjective* likely to cause resentment.
invigilate ❶ [in-**vij**-il-late] *verb* supervise people sitting an examination. **invigilator** *noun*
invigorate ❶ *verb* give energy to, refresh.
invincible ❶ *adjective* impossible to defeat.
invincibility *noun*
inviolable ❶ *adjective* unable to be broken or

violated.
inviolate ❶ *adjective* unharmed, unaffected.
invisible ❶ *adjective* not able to be seen.
invisibly *adverb* **invisibility** *noun*
invite ❶ *verb* **1** request the company of. **2** ask politely for. **3** encourage or provoke, e.g. *the two works inevitably invite comparison.* ◆ *noun* **4** *Informal* invitation. **inviting** *adjective* tempting, attractive. **invitation** *noun*
in-vitro *adjective* happening outside the body in an artificial environment, e.g. *in-vitro fertilization*.
invoice *verb, noun* (present with) a bill for goods or services supplied.
invoke ❶ *verb* **1** put (a law or penalty) into operation. **2** prompt or cause (a certain feeling). **3** call on (a god or spirit) for help, inspiration, etc. **invocation** *noun*
involuntary ❶ *adjective* not done consciously, unintentional. **involuntarily** *adverb*
involve ❶ *verb* **1** include as a necessary part. **2** affect, concern. **3** implicate (a person).
involved *adjective* **1** complicated. **2** concerned, taking part. **involvement** *noun*

———————— THESAURUS ————————

converse, reverse, reversed, transposed
invert *verb* =**overturn**, reverse, transpose, upset, upturn
invest *verb* **1** =**spend**, advance, devote, lay out, put in, sink **2** (foll. by *with*) =**empower**, authorize, charge, license, sanction, vest
investigate *verb* =**examine**, explore, go into, inquire into, inspect, look into, probe, research, study
investigation *noun* =**examination**, exploration, inquest, inquiry, inspection, probe, review, search, study, survey
investigator *noun* =**examiner**, inquirer, (private) detective, private eye (*inf*), researcher, sleuth
investiture *noun* =**installation**, enthronement, inauguration, induction, ordination
investment *noun* **1** =**stake**, ante (*inf*), contribution **2** =**transaction**, speculation, venture
inveterate *adjective* =**long-standing**, chronic, confirmed, deep-seated, dyed-in-the-wool, entrenched, habitual, hardened, incorrigible, incurable
invigilate *verb* =**watch over**, conduct, keep an eye on, oversee, preside over, run, superintend, supervise
invigorate *verb* =**refresh**, energize, enliven, exhilarate, fortify, galvanize, liven up, revitalize, stimulate

invincible *adjective* =**unbeatable**, impregnable, indestructible, indomitable, insuperable, invulnerable, unassailable, unconquerable OPPOSITE **vulnerable**
inviolable *adjective* =**sacrosanct**, hallowed, holy, inalienable, sacred, unalterable
inviolate *adjective* =**intact**, entire, pure, unbroken, undefiled, unhurt, unpolluted, unsullied, untouched, whole
invisible *adjective* =**unseen**, imperceptible, indiscernible OPPOSITE **visible**
invitation *noun* **1** =**request**, call, invite (*inf*), summons
invite *verb* **1** =**request**, ask, beg, bid, summon **2** =**ask for** (*inf*) **3** =**encourage**, attract, court, entice, provoke, tempt
inviting *adjective* =**tempting**, alluring, appealing, attractive, enticing, lekker (*S Afr sl*), mouthwatering, seductive, welcoming OPPOSITE **uninviting**
invocation *noun* **3** =**appeal**, entreaty, petition, prayer, supplication
invoke *verb* **1** =**apply**, implement, initiate, put into effect, resort to, use **3** =**call upon**, appeal to, beg, beseech, entreat, implore, petition, pray, supplicate
involuntary *adjective* =**unintentional**, automatic, instinctive, reflex, spontaneous, unconscious, uncontrolled, unthinking OPPOSITE **voluntary**
involve *verb* **1** =**entail**, imply, mean,

invulnerable ❶ *adjective* not able to be wounded or harmed.

inward *adjective, adverb* see IN.

iodine *noun Chem* bluish-black element used in medicine and photography. **iodize** *verb* treat with iodine.

ion *noun* electrically charged atom. **ionic** *adjective* **ionize** *verb* change into ions.

ionization *noun* **ionosphere** *noun* region of ionized air in the upper atmosphere that reflects radio waves.

iota [eye-oh-ta] *noun* **1** ninth letter in the Greek alphabet. **2** very small amount.

IOU *noun* signed paper acknowledging debt.

IPA International Phonetic Alphabet.

ipecacuanha [ip-pee-kak-yoo-an-na], **ipecac** [ip-pee-kak] *noun* drug made from the dried roots of a S American plant, used to cause vomiting.

ipso facto *adverb Latin* by that very fact.

IQ intelligence quotient.

Ir *Chem* iridium.

IRA Irish Republican Army.

Iranian *noun, adjective* (person) from Iran.

Iraqi *noun, adjective* (person) from Iraq.

irascible *adjective* easily angered. **irascibility** *noun*

irate ❶ *adjective* very angry.

ire *noun Lit* anger.

iridescent *adjective* having shimmering changing colours like a rainbow. **iridescence** *noun*

iridium *noun Chem* very hard corrosion-resistant metal.

iris *noun* **1** coloured circular membrane of the eye containing the pupil. **2** tall plant with purple, yellow, or white flowers.

Irish *adjective* of Ireland. **Irish coffee** hot coffee mixed with whiskey and topped with cream.

irk *verb* irritate, annoy. **irksome** *adjective* irritating, annoying.

iron ❶ *noun* **1** strong silvery-white metallic element, widely used for structural and engineering purposes. **2** appliance used, when heated, to press clothes. **3** metal-headed golf club. ◆ *plural* **4** chains, restraints. ◆ *adjective* **5** made of iron. **6** strong, inflexible, e.g. *iron will.* ◆ *verb* **7** smooth (clothes or fabric) with an iron. **ironbark** *noun* Australian eucalyptus with hard rough bark. **ironing** *noun* clothes to be ironed. **ironing board** long cloth-covered board with folding legs, for ironing clothes on. **Iron Age** era when iron tools were used. **iron out** *verb* settle (a problem) through discussion.

ironic, ironical ❶ *adjective* **1** using irony. **2** odd or amusing because the opposite of what one would expect. **ironically** *adverb*

ironmonger *noun* shopkeeper or shop dealing in hardware. **ironmongery** *noun*

ironstone *noun* rock consisting mainly of iron ore.

irony ❶ *noun, pl* **-nies** **1** mildly sarcastic use of words to imply the opposite of what is said. **2** aspect of a situation that is odd or amusing because the opposite of what one would expect.

irradiate *verb* subject to or treat with radiation. **irradiation** *noun*

irrational ❶ *adjective* not based on or not using logical reasoning. **irrational number** *Maths* any real number that cannot be expressed as the ratio of two integers, such as π.

irreconcilable *adjective* not able to be resolved or settled, e.g. *irreconcilable differences.* **irreconcilability** *noun*

irredeemable *adjective* not able to be

———————————— T H E S A U R U S ————————————

necessitate, presuppose, require **2 =concern**, affect, draw in, implicate, touch

involved *adjective* **1 =complicated**, complex, confusing, convoluted, elaborate, intricate, labyrinthine, tangled, tortuous OPPOSITE straightforward. **2 =concerned**, caught (up), implicated, mixed up in *or* with, participating, taking part

involvement *noun* **2, 3 =connection**, association, commitment, interest, participation

invulnerable *adjective* **=safe**, impenetrable, indestructible, insusceptible, invincible, proof against, secure, unassailable OPPOSITE vulnerable

irate *adjective* **=angry**, annoyed, cross, enraged, furious, incensed, indignant, infuriated, livid

iron *adjective* **5 =ferrous**, ferric **6 =inflexible**, adamant, hard, implacable, indomitable, steely, strong, tough, unbending OPPOSITE flexible

ironic, ironical *adjective* **1 =sarcastic**, double-edged, mocking, sardonic, satirical, with tongue in cheek, wry **2 =paradoxical**, incongruous

iron out *verb* **=settle**, clear up, get rid of, put right, reconcile, resolve, smooth over, sort out, straighten out

irony *noun* **1 =sarcasm**, mockery, satire **2 =paradox**, incongruity

irrational *adjective* **=illogical**, absurd, crazy, nonsensical, preposterous, unreasonable OPPOSITE rational reformed or corrected.

irreducible *adjective* impossible to put in a simpler form.

irrefutable ❶ *adjective* impossible to deny or disprove.

irregular ❶ *adjective* **1** not regular or even. **2** not conforming to accepted practice. **3** (of a word) not following the typical pattern of formation in a language. **irregularly** *adverb* **irregularity** *noun, pl* **-ties**

irrelevant ❶ *adjective* not connected with the matter in hand. **irrelevantly** *adverb* **irrelevance** *noun*

irreparable ❶ *adjective* not able to be repaired or put right. **irreparably** *adverb*

irreplaceable *adjective* impossible to replace.

irrepressible ❶ *adjective* lively and jolly. **irrepressibly** *adverb*

irreproachable ❶ *adjective* blameless, faultless. **irreproachably** *adverb*

irresistible ❶ *adjective* too attractive or strong to resist. **irresistibly** *adverb*

irresolute *adjective* unable to make decisions. **irresolution** *noun*

irrespective of *preposition* without taking

account of.

irresponsible ❶ *adjective* **1** not showing or not done with due care for the consequences of one's actions or attitudes. **2** not capable of accepting responsibility. **irresponsibility** *noun*

irretrievable *adjective* impossible to put right or make good. **irretrievably** *adverb*

irreverent ❶ *adjective* not showing due respect. **irreverence** *noun*

irreversible ❶ *adjective* not able to be reversed or put right again, e.g. *irreversible change*. **irreversibly** *adverb*

irrevocable ❶ *adjective* not possible to change or undo. **irrevocably** *adverb*

irrigate ❶ *verb* supply (land) with water by artificial channels or pipes. **irrigation** *noun*

irritate ❶ *verb* **1** annoy, anger. **2** cause (a body part) to itch or become inflamed. **irritable** *adjective* easily annoyed. **irritability** *noun* **irritably** *adverb* **irritant** *noun, adjective* (person or thing) causing irritation. **irritation** *noun*

is *verb* third person singular present tense of BE.

ISA Individual Savings Account.

isinglass [ize-ing-glass] *noun* kind of gelatine

——————— T H E S A U R U S ———————

irrefutable *adjective* =**undeniable**, certain, incontestable, incontrovertible, indisputable, indubitable, sure, unquestionable

irregular *adjective* **1 a** = **variable**, erratic, fitful, haphazard, occasional, random, spasmodic, sporadic, unsystematic OPPOSITE steady. **b** = **uneven**, asymmetrical, bumpy, crooked, jagged, lopsided, ragged, rough OPPOSITE even. **2** = **unconventional**, abnormal, exceptional, extraordinary, munted (*NZ sl*), peculiar, unofficial, unorthodox, unusual OPPOSITE standard

irregularity *noun* **1 a** = **uncertainty**, desultoriness, disorganization, haphazardness **b** = **unevenness**, asymmetry, bumpiness, jaggedness, lopsidedness, raggedness, roughness **2** = **abnormality**, anomaly, oddity, peculiarity, unorthodoxy

irrelevant *adjective* = **unconnected**, beside the point, extraneous, immaterial, impertinent, inapplicable, inappropriate, neither here nor there, unrelated OPPOSITE relevant

irreparable *adjective* = **beyond repair**, incurable, irremediable, irretrievable, irreversible

irrepressible *adjective* = **ebullient**, boisterous, buoyant, effervescent, unstoppable

irreproachable *adjective* = **blameless**, beyond reproach, faultless, impeccable, innocent, perfect, pure, unimpeachable

irresistible *adjective* = **overwhelming**,

compelling, compulsive, overpowering, urgent

irresponsible *adjective* **1** = **thoughtless**, careless, immature, reckless, scatterbrained, shiftless, shonky (*Aust & NZ inf*), unreliable, untrustworthy OPPOSITE responsible

irreverent *adjective* = **disrespectful**, cheeky (*inf*), flippant, iconoclastic, impertinent, impudent, mocking, tongue-in-cheek OPPOSITE reverent

irreversible *adjective* = **irrevocable**, final, incurable, irreparable, unalterable

irrevocable *adjective* = **fixed**, fated, immutable, irreversible, predestined, predetermined, settled, unalterable

irrigate *verb* = **water**, flood, inundate, moisten, wet

irritable *adjective* = **bad-tempered**, cantankerous, crotchety (*inf*), ill-tempered, irascible, oversensitive, prickly, testy, tetchy, touchy OPPOSITE even-tempered

irritate *verb* **1** = **annoy**, anger, bother, exasperate, get on one's nerves (*inf*), infuriate, needle (*inf*), nettle, rankle with, try one's patience OPPOSITE calm. **2** = **rub**, chafe, inflame, pain

irritation *noun* **1** = **annoyance**, anger, displeasure, exasperation, indignation, resentment, testiness, vexation OPPOSITE pleasure. **2** = **nuisance**, drag (*inf*), pain in the neck (*inf*), thorn in one's flesh obtained from some freshwater fish.

Islam *noun* **1** Muslim religion teaching that there is one God and that Mohammed is his prophet. **2** Muslim countries and civilization. **Islamic** *adjective*

island ⊕ *noun* piece of land surrounded by water. **islander** *noun* person who lives on an island.

isle *noun Poetic* island. **islet** *noun* small island.

-ism *n suffix* indicating: **1** political or religious belief, e.g. *Communism*; *Buddhism*. **2** characteristic quality, e.g. *cynicism*. **3** an action, e.g. *criticism*. **4** prejudice on the basis specified, e.g. *racism*.

isobar [ice-oh-bar] *noun* line on a map connecting places of equal atmospheric pressure.

isolate ⊕ *verb* **1** place apart or alone. **2** *Chem* obtain (a substance) in uncombined form.

isolation *noun* **isolationism** *noun* policy of not participating in international affairs. **isolationist** *noun, adjective*

isomer [ice-oh-mer] *noun* substance whose molecules contain the same atoms as another but in a different arrangement.

isometric *adjective* relating to muscular contraction without shortening of the muscle. **isometrics** *plural noun* isometric exercises.

isosceles triangle [ice-soss-ill-eez] *noun* triangle with two sides of equal length.

isotherm [ice-oh-therm] *noun* line on a map connecting points of equal temperature.

isotope [ice-oh-tope] *noun* one of two or more atoms with the same number of protons in the nucleus but a different number of neutrons.

ISP Internet service provider.

Israeli *noun, pl* **-lis, -li,** *adjective* (person) from Israel.

issue ⊕ *noun* **1** topic of interest or discussion. **2** reason for quarrelling. **3** particular edition of a magazine or newspaper. **4** outcome or result. **5** *Law* child or children. ♦ *verb* **6** make (a

statement etc.) publicly. **7** supply officially (with). **8** produce and make available. **9** (foll. by *from*) come out of. **take issue with** disagree with.

-ist *n suffix* indicating: **1** person who performs a particular action, e.g. *exorcist*. **2** person who does a particular type of work, e.g. *physicist*. ♦ *adj suffix, n suffix* indicating: **3** (of) a person who holds a particular political or religious belief, e.g. *Communist*; *Buddhist*. **4** (of) a person who is prejudiced on the basis specified, e.g. *racist*.

isthmus [iss-muss] *noun, pl* **-muses** narrow strip of land connecting two areas of land.

it *pronoun* **1** refers to a nonhuman, animal, plant, or inanimate object. **2** refers to a thing mentioned or being discussed. **3** used as the subject of impersonal verbs, e.g. *it's windy*. **4** *Informal* crucial or ultimate point. **its** *adjective, pronoun* belonging to it. **it's 1** it is. **2** it has.

itself *pronoun* emphatic form of IT.

SPELLING TIP

Many people find **its** and **it's** confusing. But it's quite simple really. **It's** only needs an apostrophe when it is used as the informal short form of 'it is' or 'it has'.

IT information technology.

Italian *noun* **1** language of Italy and one of the languages of Switzerland. **2** person from Italy. ♦ *adjective* **3** of Italy.

italic *adjective* (of printing type) sloping to the right. **italics** *plural noun* this type, used for emphasis. **italicize** *verb* put in italics.

itch ⊕ *noun* **1** skin irritation causing a desire to scratch. **2** restless desire. ♦ *verb* **3** have an itch. **itchy** *adjective* **itchier, itchiest**

item ⊕ *noun* **1** single thing in a list or collection. **2** piece of information. **itemize** *verb*

——————— T H E S A U R U S ———————

island *noun* =isle, ait or eyot (*dial*), atoll, cay or key, islet

isolate *verb* **1** =**separate**, cut off, detach, disconnect, insulate, segregate, set apart

isolated *adjective* **1** =**remote**, hidden, lonely, off the beaten track, out-of-the-way, secluded

isolation *noun* **1** =**separation**, detachment, remoteness, seclusion, segregation, solitude

issue *noun* **1** =**topic**, matter, point, question, subject **2** =**problem**, bone of contention **3** =**edition**, copy, number, printing **4** =**outcome**, consequence, effect, end result,

result, upshot **5** *Law* =**children**, descendants, heirs, offspring, progeny OPPOSITE> parent ♦*verb* **6** =**announce**, broadcast **8** =**give out**, circulate, deliver, distribute, publish, put out, release OPPOSITE> withdraw ♦ **take issue with** =**disagree with**, challenge, dispute, object to, oppose, raise an objection to, take exception to

itch *noun* **1** =**irritation**, itchiness, prickling, tingling **2** =**desire**, craving, hankering, hunger, longing, lust, passion, yearning, yen (*inf*) ♦*verb* **3 a** =**prickle**, irritate, tickle, tingle **b** =**long**, ache, crave, hanker, hunger, lust, pine, yearn make a list of.

iterate *verb* repeat. **iteration** *noun*

itinerant ➊ *adjective* travelling from place to place. **itinerary** *noun* detailed plan of a journey.

itinerary ➊ *noun, pl* **-aries** detailed plan of a journey.

ITV Independent Television.

IUD intrauterine device: a coil-shaped contraceptive fitted into the womb.

IVF in-vitro fertilization.

ivory *noun* **1** hard white bony substance forming the tusks of elephants. ◆ *adjective* **2** yellowish-white. **ivory tower** remoteness from the realities of everyday life.

ivy *noun, pl* **ivies** evergreen climbing plant.

———————— THESAURUS ————————

item *noun* **1** = **detail**, article, component, entry, matter, particular, point, thing **2** = **report**, account, article, bulletin, dispatch, feature, note, notice, paragraph, piece

itinerant *adjective* = **wandering**, migratory, nomadic, peripatetic, roaming, roving, travelling, vagrant OPPOSITE settled

itinerary *noun* = **schedule**, programme, route, timetable

I

Jj

J joule(s).

jab ⓸ _verb_ **jabbing, jabbed 1** poke sharply. ◆ _noun_ **2** quick punch or poke. **3** _Informal_ injection.

jabber ⓸ _verb_ **1** talk rapidly or incoherently. ◆ _noun_ **2** rapid or incoherent talk.

jabot [zhab-oh] _noun_ frill or ruffle on the front of a blouse or shirt.

jacaranda _noun_ tropical tree with sweet-smelling wood.

jack ⓸ _noun_ **1** device for raising a motor vehicle or other heavy object. **2** playing card with a picture of a pageboy. **3** _Bowls_ small white bowl aimed at by the players. **4** socket in electrical equipment into which a plug fits. **5** flag flown at the bow of a ship, showing nationality. **6** piece used in the game of jacks. ◆ _plural_ **7** game in which pieces are thrown and picked up between bounces of a ball. **jack in** _verb Slang_ abandon. **jack-in-the-box** _noun_ toy consisting of a figure on a spring in a box. **jack of all trades** person who can do many kinds of work. **jack up** _verb_ raise with a jack.

jackal _noun_ doglike wild animal of Africa and Asia.

jackass _noun_ **1** fool. **2** male of the ass. **laughing jackass** same as KOOKABURRA.

jackboot _noun_ **1** high military boot. **2** oppressive military rule.

jackdaw _noun_ black-and-grey bird of the crow family.

jacket ⓸ _noun_ **1** short coat. **2** skin of a baked potato. **3** outer paper cover on a hardback book. **jacket potato** potato baked in its skin.

jackknife _verb_ **1** (of an articulated lorry) go out of control so that the trailer swings round at a sharp angle to the cab. ◆ _noun_ **2** large clasp knife. **3** dive with a sharp bend at the waist in mid-air.

jackpot ⓸ _noun_ largest prize that may be won in a game. **hit the jackpot** be very successful through luck.

jack rabbit _noun_ American hare with long hind legs and large ears.

Jacobean [jak-a-**bee**-an] _adjective_ of the reign of James I of England.

Jacobite _noun_ supporter of James II of England and his descendants.

Jacquard [jak-ard] _noun_ fabric in which the design is incorporated into the weave.

Jacuzzi [jak-oo-zee] _noun_ ® circular bath with a device that swirls the water.

jade _noun_ **1** ornamental semiprecious stone, usu. dark green. ◆ _adjective_ **2** bluish-green.

jaded ⓸ _adjective_ tired and unenthusiastic.

Jaffa _noun_ large orange with a thick skin.

jagged [jag-gid] _adjective_ having an uneven edge with sharp points.

jaguar _noun_ large S American spotted cat.

jail ⓸ _noun_ **1** prison. ◆ _verb_ **2** send to prison.

jailer _noun_ **jailbird** _noun Informal_ person who has often been in prison.

jalopy [jal-**lop**-ee] _noun, pl_ **-lopies** _Informal_ old car.

jam¹ ⓸ _verb_ **jamming, jammed 1** pack tightly into a place. **2** crowd or congest. **3** make or become stuck. **4** _Radio_ block (another station) with impulses of equal wavelength. **5** play a jam session. ◆ _noun_ **6** hold-up of traffic. **7** _Informal_ awkward situation. **jam on the brakes** apply brakes fiercely. **jam-packed** _adjective_ filled to capacity. **jam session** informal rock or

---

THESAURUS

jab _verb_ **1** = **poke**, dig, lunge, nudge, prod, punch, stab, thrust ◆_noun_ **2** = **poke**, dig, lunge, nudge, prod, punch, stab, thrust

jabber _verb_ **1** = **chatter**, babble, blether, gabble, mumble, prate, rabbit (on) (_Brit inf_), ramble, yap (_inf_)

jacket _noun_ **3** = **cover**, wrapper

jackpot _noun_ = **prize**, award, bonanza, reward, winnings

jack up _verb_ = **lift**, elevate, hoist, lift up, raise

jaded _adjective_ = **tired**, exhausted, fatigued, spent, weary OPPOSITE fresh

jagged _adjective_ = **uneven**, barbed, craggy, indented, ragged, serrated, spiked, toothed OPPOSITE rounded

jail _noun_ **1** = **prison**, nick (_Brit sl_), penitentiary (_US_), reformatory, slammer (_sl_) ◆_verb_ **2** = **imprison**, confine, detain, incarcerate, lock up, send down

jailer _noun_ = **guard**, keeper, warden, warder

jazz performance.

jam² *noun* food made from fruit boiled with sugar.

jamb *noun* side post of a door or window frame.

jamboree ❶ *noun* large gathering or celebration.

jammy *adjective* **-mier, -miest** *Slang* lucky.

Jan. January.

jangle ❶ *verb* **1** (cause to) make a harsh ringing noise. **2** (of nerves) be upset or irritated. ◆ *noun* **3** harsh ringing noise.

janitor ❶ *noun* caretaker of a school or other building.

January *noun* first month of the year.

japan *noun* **1** very hard varnish, usu. black. ◆ *verb* **-panning, -panned 2** cover with this varnish.

Japanese *noun, adjective* (native or language) of Japan.

jape *noun* *Old-fashioned* joke or prank.

japonica *noun* shrub with red flowers.

jar¹ ❶ *noun* **1** wide-mouthed container, usu. round and made of glass. **2** *Informal* glass of beer.

jar² ❶ *verb* **jarring, jarred 1** have a disturbing or unpleasant effect. **2** be in conflict. **3** jolt or bump. ◆ *noun* **4** jolt or shock.

jardiniere *noun* ornamental plant pot.

jargon ❶ *noun* **1** specialized technical language of a particular subject. **2** pretentious language.

jasmine *noun* shrub with sweet-smelling yellow or white flowers.

jasper *noun* red, yellow, dark green, or brown variety of quartz.

jaundice ❶ *noun* disease marked by yellowness of the skin. **jaundiced** *adjective* **1** (of an attitude or opinion) bitter or cynical. **2** having jaundice.

jaunt ❶ *noun* **1** short journey for pleasure. ◆ *verb* **2** make such a journey.

jaunty ❶ *adjective* **-tier, -tiest 1** sprightly and cheerful. **2** smart. **jauntily** *adverb*

javelin *noun* light spear thrown in sports competitions.

jaw ❶ *noun* **1** one of the bones in which the teeth are set. **2** lower part of the face. ◆ *plural* **3** mouth. **4** gripping part of a tool. **5** narrow opening of a gorge or valley. ◆ *verb* **6** *Slang* talk lengthily. **jawbone** *noun* lower jaw of a person or animal.

jay *noun* bird with a pinkish body and blue-and-black wings.

jaywalking *noun* crossing the road in a careless or dangerous manner. **jaywalker** *noun*

jazz ❶ *noun* kind of music with an exciting rhythm, usu. involving improvisation. **and all that jazz** *Slang* and other related things. **jazzy** *adjective* **-zier, -ziest 1** flashy or showy. **2** of or like jazz. **jazz up** *verb* make more lively.

JCB *noun* ® construction machine with a shovel at the front and an excavator at the rear.

jealous ❶ *adjective* **1** fearful of losing a partner or possession to a rival. **2** envious. **3** suspiciously watchful. **jealously** *adverb*

jealousy *noun, pl* **-sies**

jeans ❶ *plural noun* casual denim trousers.

——————— THESAURUS ———————

jam¹ *verb* **1 = pack**, cram, force, press, ram, squeeze, stuff, wedge **2 = crowd**, congest, crush, throng **3 = stick**, block, clog, obstruct, stall ◆*noun* **7** *Inf* **= predicament**, deep water, fix (*inf*), hole (*sl*), hot water, pickle (*inf*), tight spot, trouble

jamboree *noun* **= festival**, carnival, celebration, festivity, fete, revelry

jangle *verb* **1 = rattle**, chime, clank, clash, clatter, jingle, vibrate

janitor *noun* **= caretaker**, concierge, custodian, doorkeeper, porter

jar¹ *noun* **1 = pot**, container, crock, jug, pitcher, urn, vase

jar² *verb* **1 = irritate**, annoy, get on one's nerves (*inf*), grate, irk, nettle, offend **3 = jolt**, bump, convulse, rattle, rock, shake, vibrate ◆*noun* **4 = jolt**, bump, convulsion, shock, vibration

jargon *noun* **1 = parlance**, argot, idiom, usage

jaundiced *adjective* **1 a = bitter**, envious,

hostile, jealous, resentful, spiteful, suspicious **b = cynical**, sceptical OPPOSITE **optimistic**

jaunt *noun* **1 = outing**, airing, excursion, expedition, ramble, stroll, tour, trip

jaunty *adjective* **1 = sprightly**, buoyant, carefree, high-spirited, lively, perky, self-confident, sparky OPPOSITE **serious**

jaw *verb* **6** *Sl* **= talk**, chat, chatter, gossip, spout

jazz up *verb* **= enliven**, animate, enhance, improve

jazzy *adjective* **1 = flashy**, fancy, gaudy, snazzy (*inf*)

jealous *adjective* **1 = possessive**, mistrustful, protective OPPOSITE **trusting**. **2 = envious**, covetous, desirous, green, grudging, resentful OPPOSITE **satisfied**. **3 = suspicious**, vigilant, wary, watchful OPPOSITE **trusting**

jealousy *noun* **1 = possessiveness**, mistrust **2 = envy**, covetousness, resentment, spite **3 = suspicion**

jeans *plural noun* **= denims**

J

Jeep *noun* ® four-wheel-drive motor vehicle.
jeer ❶ *verb* **1** scoff or deride. ◆ *noun* **2** cry of derision.
Jehovah *noun* God. **Jehovah's Witness** member of a Christian sect believing that the end of the world is near.
jejune *adjective* **1** simple or naive. **2** dull or boring.
jell ❶ *verb* **1** form into a jelly-like substance. **2** take on a definite form.
jelly *noun, pl* **-lies 1** soft food made of liquid set with gelatine. **2** jam made from fruit juice and sugar. **jellied** *adjective* prepared in a jelly.
jellyfish *noun* small jelly-like sea animal.
jemmy *noun, pl* **-mies** short steel crowbar used by burglars.
jenny *noun, pl* **-nies** female ass or wren.
jeopardy ❶ *noun* danger. **jeopardize** *verb* place in danger.
jerboa *noun* small mouselike rodent with long hind legs.
jerk ❶ *verb* **1** move or throw abruptly. ◆ *noun* **2** sharp or abruptly stopped movement. **3** *Slang* contemptible person. **jerky** *adjective* **jerkier, jerkiest** sudden or abrupt. **jerkily** *adverb* **jerkiness** *noun*
jerkin *noun* sleeveless jacket.
Jerry *noun Brit slang* German or Germans collectively.
jerry-built ❶ *adjective* built badly using flimsy materials.
jerry can *noun* flat-sided can for carrying petrol etc.
jersey *noun* **1** knitted jumper. **2** machine-knitted fabric. **3** (J-) breed of cow.
Jerusalem artichoke *noun* small yellowish-white root vegetable.

jest ❶ *noun, verb* joke. **jester** *noun Hist* professional clown at court.
Jesuit [jezz-yoo-it] *noun* member of the Society of Jesus, a Roman Catholic order.
Jesus *noun* **1** (also **Jesus Christ, Jesus of Nazareth**) ?4 AD-?29 AD, founder of Christianity, believed by Christians to be the Son of God. ◆ *interjection* **2** *Taboo slang* oath used to express intense surprise, dismay, etc.
jet¹ ❶ *noun* **1** aircraft driven by jet propulsion. **2** stream of liquid or gas, esp. one forced from a small hole. **3** nozzle from which gas or liquid is forced. ◆ *verb* **jetting, jetted 4** fly by jet aircraft. **jet lag** fatigue caused by crossing time zones in an aircraft. **jet propulsion** propulsion by thrust provided by a jet of gas or liquid. **jet-propelled** *adjective* **jet set** rich and fashionable people who travel the world for pleasure.
jet² *noun* hard black mineral. **jet-black** *adjective* glossy black.
jetsam *noun* goods thrown overboard to lighten a ship.
jettison ❶ *verb* **-soning, -soned 1** abandon. **2** throw overboard.
jetty ❶ *noun, pl* **-ties 1** small pier. **2** structure built from a shore to protect a harbour.
Jew *noun* **1** person whose religion is Judaism. **2** descendant of the ancient Hebrews. **Jewess** *n fem now often offens* **Jewish** *adjective* **Jewry** *noun* Jews collectively. **jew's-harp** *noun* musical instrument held between the teeth and played by plucking a metal strip with one's finger.
jewel ❶ *noun* **1** precious stone. **2** special person or thing. **jeweller** *noun* dealer in jewels. **jewellery** *noun* objects decorated with precious stones.

———— T H E S A U R U S ————

jeer *verb* **1** = **mock**, barrack, deride, gibe, heckle, ridicule, scoff, taunt OPPOSITE **cheer** ◆*noun* **2** = **mockery**, abuse, boo, catcall, derision, gibe, ridicule, taunt OPPOSITE **applause**
jell *verb* **1** = **solidify**, congeal, harden, set, thicken **2** = **take shape**, come together, crystallize, materialize
jeopardize *verb* = **endanger**, chance, expose, gamble, imperil, risk, stake, venture
jeopardy *noun* = **danger**, insecurity, peril, risk, vulnerability
jerk *verb* **1** = **tug**, jolt, lurch, pull, thrust, twitch, wrench, yank ◆*noun* **2** = **tug**, jolt, lurch, pull, thrust, twitch, wrench, yank
jerky *adjective* **2** = **bumpy**, convulsive, jolting, jumpy, shaky, spasmodic OPPOSITE **smooth**
jerry-built *adjective* = **ramshackle**, cheap, defective, flimsy, rickety, shabby, slipshod,

thrown together
jest *noun* = **joke**, bon mot, crack (*sl*), jape, pleasantry, prank, quip, wisecrack (*inf*), witticism ◆*verb* = **joke**, kid (*inf*), mock, quip, tease
jester *noun Hist* = **clown**, buffoon, fool, harlequin
jet¹ *noun* **2** = **stream**, flow, fountain, gush, spout, spray, spring **3** = **nozzle**, atomizer, sprayer, sprinkler ◆*verb* **4** = **fly**, soar, zoom
jet-black *adjective* = **black**, coal-black, ebony, inky, pitch-black, raven, sable
jettison *verb* **1** = **abandon**, discard, dump, scrap **2** = **throw overboard**, eject, expel, unload
jetty *noun* **1** = **pier**, dock, quay, wharf **2** = **breakwater**, groyne, mole
jewel *noun* **1** = **gemstone**, ornament, rock (*sl*),

jewfish *noun Aust* freshwater catfish.
Jezebel *noun* shameless or scheming woman.
jib[1] *noun* triangular sail set in front of a mast.
jib[2] ⊕ *verb* **jibbing, jibbed** (of a horse, person, etc.) stop and refuse to go on. **jib at** *verb* object to (a proposal etc.).
jib[3] *noun* projecting arm of a crane or derrick.
jibe[1] ⊕ *noun, verb* taunt or jeer.
jibe[2] *verb* same as GYBE.
jiffy *noun, pl* **-fies** *Informal* very short period of time.
jig ⊕ *noun* **1** type of lively dance. **2** music for it. **3** device that holds a component in place for cutting etc. ◆ *verb* **jigging, jigged 4** dance a jig. **5** make jerky up-and-down movements.
jiggery-pokery *noun Informal* trickery or mischief.
jiggle *verb* move up and down with short jerky movements.
jigsaw *noun* **1** (also **jigsaw puzzle**) picture cut into interlocking pieces, which the user tries to fit together again. **2** mechanical saw for cutting along curved lines.
jihad *noun* Islamic holy war against unbelievers.
jilt *verb* leave or reject (one's lover).
jingle ⊕ *noun* **1** catchy verse or song used in a radio or television advert. **2** gentle ringing noise. ◆ *verb* **3** (cause to) make a gentle ringing sound.
jingoism *noun* aggressive nationalism. **jingoistic** *adjective*
jinks *plural noun* **high jinks** boisterous merrymaking.
jinni *noun, pl* **jinn** spirit in Muslim mythology.
jinx ⊕ *noun* **1** person or thing bringing bad luck. ◆ *verb* **2** be or put a jinx on.

jitters ⊕ *plural noun* worried nervousness.
jittery *adjective* nervous.
jive *noun* **1** lively dance of the 1940s and '50s. ◆ *verb* **2** dance the jive.
job ⊕ *noun* **1** occupation or paid employment. **2** task to be done. **3** performance of a task. **4** *Informal* difficult task. **5** *Informal* crime, esp. robbery. **jobbing** *adjective* doing individual jobs for payment. **jobless** *adjective, plural noun* unemployed (people). **Jobcentre, job centre** *noun* government office displaying information about available jobs. **job lot** assortment sold together. **job sharing** splitting of one post between two people working part-time.
Job's comforter *noun* person who adds to distress while pretending to give sympathy.
jockey *noun* **1** (professional) rider of racehorses. ◆ *verb* **2 jockey for position** manoeuvre to obtain an advantage.
jockstrap *noun* belt with a pouch to support the genitals, worn by male athletes.
jocose [joke-**kohss**] *adjective* playful or humorous. **jocosely** *adverb*
jocular ⊕ *adjective* **1** fond of joking. **2** meant as a joke. **jocularity** *noun* **jocularly** *adverb*
jocund [**jok**-kund] *adjective Lit* merry or cheerful.
jodhpurs *plural noun* riding trousers, loose-fitting above the knee but tight below.
jog ⊕ *verb* **jogging, jogged 1** run at a gentle pace, esp. for exercise. **2** nudge slightly. ◆ *noun* **3** slow run. **jog someone's memory** remind someone of something. **jogger** *noun* **jogging** *noun*
joggle *verb* shake or move jerkily.
john *noun US slang* toilet.
John Dory *noun* European dory with a deep

J

——————— THESAURUS ———————

sparkler (*inf*) **2 = rarity**, collector's item, find, gem, humdinger (*sl*), pearl, treasure, wonder
jewellery *noun* **= jewels**, finery, gems, ornaments, regalia, treasure, trinkets
jib[2] *verb* **= refuse**, balk, recoil, retreat, shrink, stop short
jibe[1] *noun* **= taunt**, jeering, mockery, ridicule, scoffing, scorn, sneering ◆*verb* **= taunt**, jeer, make fun of, mock, poke fun at, ridicule, scoff, scorn, sneer
jig *verb* **4 = skip**, bob, bounce, caper, prance, wiggle
jingle *noun* **1 = song**, chorus, ditty, melody, tune **2 = rattle**, clink, reverberation, ringing, tinkle ◆*verb* **3 = ring**, chime, clink, jangle, rattle, tinkle
jinx *noun* **1 = curse**, hex (*US & Canad inf*), hoodoo (*inf*), nemesis ◆*verb* **2 = curse**, bewitch,

hex (*US & Canad inf*)
jitters *plural noun* **= nerves**, anxiety, butterflies (in one's stomach) (*inf*), cold feet (*inf*), fidgets, nervousness, the shakes (*inf*)
jittery *adjective* **= nervous**, agitated, anxious, fidgety, jumpy, shaky, trembling, wired (*sl*)
OPPOSITE **calm**
job *noun* **1 = occupation**, business, calling, career, employment, livelihood, profession, vocation **2 = task**, assignment, chore, duty, enterprise, errand, undertaking, venture, work
jobless *adjective* **= unemployed**, idle, inactive, out of work, unoccupied
jocular *adjective* **= humorous**, amusing, droll, facetious, funny, joking, jovial, playful, sportive, teasing, waggish
jog *verb* **1 = run**, canter, lope, trot **2 = nudge**, prod, push, shake, stir

compressed body, spiny dorsal fins, and massive jaws.

Johnny Canuck *noun Canad* **1** an informal name for a Canadian. **2** a personification of Canada.

joie de vivre ⊕ [jwah de **veev**-ra] *noun French* enjoyment of life.

join ⊕ *verb* **1** become a member (of). **2** become part of. **3** come into someone's company. **4** take part (in). **5** come or bring together. **6** connect (two points). ◆ *noun* **7** place where two things are joined. **join in** *verb* take part in. **join up** *verb* enlist in the armed services. **joined-up** *adjective* integrated by an overall strategy, e.g. *joined-up government*. **joiner** *noun* maker of finished woodwork. **joinery** *noun* joiner's work.

joint ⊕ *adjective* **1** shared by two or more. ◆ *noun* **2** place where bones meet but can move. **3** junction of two or more parts or objects. **4** piece of meat for roasting. **5** *Slang* house or place, esp. a disreputable bar or nightclub. **6** *Slang* marijuana cigarette. ◆ *verb* **7** divide meat into joints. **8** provide with a joint. **out of joint 1** disorganized. **2** dislocated. **jointed** *adjective* **jointly** *adverb* **joint-stock company** firm whose capital is jointly owned by shareholders.

joist *noun* horizontal beam that helps support a floor or ceiling.

jojoba [hoe-**hoe**-ba] *noun* shrub whose seeds yield oil used in cosmetics.

joke ⊕ *noun* **1** thing said or done to cause laughter. **2** amusing or ridiculous person or thing. ◆ *verb* **3** make jokes. **jokey** *adjective* **jokingly** *adverb* **joker** *noun* **1** person who

jokes. **2** *Slang* fellow. **3** extra card in a pack, counted as any other in some games.

jolly ⊕ *adjective* **-lier, -liest 1** (of a person) happy and cheerful. **2** (of an occasion) merry and festive. ◆ *adverb* **3** *Informal* extremely. ◆ *verb* **-lying, -lied 4 jolly along** try to keep (someone) cheerful by flattery or coaxing.

jollity *noun* **jollification** *noun* merrymaking.

jolt ⊕ *noun* **1** unpleasant surprise or shock. **2** sudden jerk or bump. ◆ *verb* **3** surprise or shock. **4** move or shake with a jerk.

Jonah *noun* person believed to bring bad luck to those around him or her.

jonquil *noun* fragrant narcissus.

josh *verb Chiefly US slang* tease.

joss stick *noun* stick of incense giving off a sweet smell when burnt.

jostle ⊕ *verb* **1** knock or push against. **2** compete with someone.

jot ⊕ *verb* **jotting, jotted 1** write briefly. ◆ *noun* **2** very small amount. **jotter** *noun* notebook. **jottings** *plural noun* notes jotted down.

joual *noun* nonstandard Canadian French dialect, esp. as associated with ill-educated speakers.

joule [jool] *noun Physics* unit of work or energy.

journal ⊕ *noun* **1** daily newspaper or magazine. **2** daily record of events. **journalese** *noun* superficial style of writing, found in some newspapers. **journalism** *noun* writing in or editing of newspapers and magazines. **journalist** *noun* **journalistic** *adjective*

journey ⊕ *noun* **1** act or process of travelling

——— THESAURUS ———

joie de vivre *noun French* =**enthusiasm**, ebullience, enjoyment, gusto, relish, zest

join *verb* **1** =**enrol**, enlist, enter, sign up **5, 6** =**connect**, add, append, attach, combine, couple, fasten, link, unite OPPOSITE **separate**

joint *adjective* **1** =**shared**, collective, combined, communal, cooperative, joined, mutual, united ◆*noun* **3** =**junction**, connection, hinge, intersection, nexus, node ◆*verb* **7** =**divide**, carve, cut up, dissect, segment, sever

jointly *adverb* **1** =**collectively**, as one, in common, in conjunction, in league, in partnership, mutually, together OPPOSITE **separately**

joke *noun* **1** =**jest**, gag (*inf*), jape, prank, pun, quip, wisecrack (*inf*), witticism **2** =**laughing stock**, buffoon, clown ◆*verb* **3** =**jest**, banter, kid (*inf*), mock, play the fool, quip, taunt, tease

joker *noun* **1** =**comedian**, buffoon, clown, comic, humorist, jester, prankster, trickster,

wag, wit

jolly *adjective* **1** =**happy**, cheerful, chirpy (*inf*), genial, jovial, merry, playful, sprightly, upbeat (*inf*) OPPOSITE **miserable**

jolt *noun* **1** =**surprise**, blow, bolt from the blue, bombshell, setback, shock **2** =**jerk**, bump, jar, jog, jump, lurch, shake, start ◆*verb* **3** =**surprise**, discompose, disturb, perturb, stagger, startle, stun **4** =**jerk**, jar, jog, jostle, knock, push, shake, shove

jostle *verb* **1** =**push**, bump, elbow, hustle, jog, jolt, shake, shove

jot *verb* **1** =**note down**, list, record, scribble ◆*noun* **2** =**bit**, fraction, grain, morsel, scrap, speck

journal *noun* **1** =**newspaper**, daily, gazette, magazine, monthly, periodical, weekly **2** =**diary**, chronicle, log, record

journalist *noun* **1** =**reporter**, broadcaster, columnist, commentator, correspondent, hack,

from one place to another. **2** time taken or distance travelled in a journey. ♦ verb **3** travel.
journeyman noun qualified craftsman employed by another.
joust Hist noun **1** combat with lances between two mounted knights. ♦ verb **2** fight on horseback using lances.
jovial ⊕ adjective happy and cheerful. **jovially** adverb **joviality** noun
jowl[1] noun **1** lower jaw. ♦ plural **2** cheeks.
jowl[2] noun fatty flesh hanging from the lower jaw.
joy ⊕ noun **1** feeling of great delight or pleasure. **2** cause of this feeling. **joyful** adjective **joyless** adjective **joyous** adjective extremely happy and enthusiastic. **joyriding** noun driving for pleasure, esp. in a stolen car. **joyride** noun **joyrider** noun **joystick** noun control device for an aircraft or computer.
JP Justice of the Peace.
JPEG [jay-peg] Computing **1** standard compressed file format used for pictures. **2** picture held in this file format.
Jr Junior.
JSA jobseeker's allowance: in Britain, a payment made to unemployed people.
jubilant ⊕ adjective feeling or expressing great joy. **jubilantly** adverb **jubilation** noun
jubilee ⊕ noun special anniversary, esp. 25th (**silver jubilee**) or 50th (**golden jubilee**).
Judaism noun religion of the Jews, based on the Old Testament and the Talmud. **Judaic** adjective
Judas noun person who betrays a friend.
judder verb **1** vibrate violently. ♦ noun **2** violent vibration.
judge ⊕ noun **1** public official who tries cases and passes sentence in a court of law. **2** person who decides the outcome of a contest. **3** person of reliable opinion on a subject. ♦ verb **4** act as a judge. **5** appraise critically. **6** consider something to be the case. **judgment, judgement** noun **1** opinion reached after careful thought. **2** verdict of a judge. **3** ability to appraise critically. **Judgment Day** occasion of the Last Judgment by God at the end of the world. **judgmental, judgemental** adjective
judicial ⊕ adjective **1** of or by a court or judge. **2** showing or using judgment. **judicially** adverb
judiciary noun system of courts and judges.
judicious ⊕ adjective well-judged and sensible. **judiciously** adverb
judo noun sport in which two opponents try to throw each other to the ground.
jug ⊕ noun container for liquids, with a handle and small spout. **jugged hare** hare stewed in an earthenware pot.
juggernaut noun **1** large heavy lorry. **2** any irresistible destructive force.
juggle ⊕ verb **1** throw and catch (several objects) so that most are in the air at the same time. **2** manipulate (figures, situations, etc.) to

J

——————————— THESAURUS ———————————

journo (sl), pressman
journey noun **1** = **trip**, excursion, expedition, odyssey, pilgrimage, tour, trek, voyage ♦verb **3** = **travel**, go, proceed, roam, rove, tour, traverse, trek, voyage, wander
jovial adjective = **cheerful**, animated, cheery, convivial, happy, jolly, merry, mirthful OPPOSITE> solemn
joy noun **1** = **delight**, bliss, ecstasy, elation, gaiety, glee, pleasure, rapture, satisfaction OPPOSITE> sorrow
joyful adjective **1** = **delighted**, elated, enraptured, glad, gratified, happy, jubilant, merry, pleased
joyless adjective **1** = **unhappy**, cheerless, depressed, dismal, dreary, gloomy, miserable, sad
joyous adjective = **joyful**, festive, merry, rapturous
jubilant adjective = **overjoyed**, elated, enraptured, euphoric, exuberant, exultant, thrilled, triumphant OPPOSITE> downcast
jubilation noun = **joy**, celebration, ecstasy, elation, excitement, exultation, festivity,
triumph
jubilee noun = **celebration**, festival, festivity, holiday
judge noun **1** = **magistrate**, beak (Brit sl), justice **2** = **referee**, adjudicator, arbiter, arbitrator, moderator, umpire **3** = **critic**, arbiter, assessor, authority, connoisseur, expert ♦verb **4** = **adjudicate**, arbitrate, decide, mediate, referee, umpire **5** = **consider**, appraise, assess, esteem, estimate, evaluate, rate, value
judgment, judgement noun **1** = **opinion**, appraisal, assessment, belief, diagnosis, estimate, finding, valuation, view **2** = **verdict**, arbitration, decision, decree, finding, ruling, sentence **3** = **sense**, acumen, discernment, discrimination, prudence, shrewdness, understanding, wisdom
judicial adjective **1** = **legal**, official
judicious adjective = **sensible**, astute, careful, discriminating, enlightened, prudent, shrewd, thoughtful, well-judged, wise OPPOSITE> injudicious
jug noun = **container**, carafe, crock, ewer, jar, pitcher, urn, vessel

suit one's purposes. **juggler** *noun*
jugular, jugular vein *noun* one of three
large veins of the neck that return blood from
the head to the heart.
juice ⊕ *noun* **1** liquid part of vegetables, fruit,
or meat. **2** *Informal* petrol. ◆ *plural* **3** fluids
secreted by an organ of the body. **juicy**
adjective **juicier, juiciest 1** full of juice. **2**
interesting.
jujitsu *noun* Japanese art of wrestling and self-
defence.
juju *noun* W African magic charm or fetish.
jukebox *noun* coin-operated machine on
which records, CDs, or videos can be played.
Jul. July.
julep *noun* sweet alcoholic drink.
Julian calendar *noun* calendar introduced by
Julius Caesar, in which leap years occurred
every fourth year.
julienne *adjective* **1** (of vegetables or meat)
cut into thin shreds. ◆ *noun* **2** clear soup
containing thinly shredded vegetables.
July *noun* seventh month of the year.
jumble ⊕ *noun* **1** confused heap or state. **2**
articles for a jumble sale. ◆ *verb* **3** mix in a
disordered way. **jumble sale** sale of
miscellaneous second-hand items.
jumbo ⊕ *adjective* **1** *Informal* very large. ◆ *noun*
2 (also **jumbo jet**) large jet airliner.
jump ⊕ *verb* **1** leap or spring into the air using
the leg muscles. **2** move quickly and suddenly.
3 jerk with surprise. **4** increase suddenly. **5**
change the subject abruptly. **6** *Informal* attack
without warning. **7** pass over or miss out
(intervening material). ◆ *noun* **8** act of jumping.
9 sudden rise. **10** break in continuity. **11** step
or degree. **jump the gun** act prematurely.

jump the queue not wait one's turn. **jumpy**
adjective **jumpier, jumpiest** nervous. **jump at**
verb accept (a chance etc.) gladly. **jumped-up**
adjective arrogant because of recent promotion.
jump jet fixed-wing jet that can take off and
land vertically. **jump leads** electric cables to
connect a flat car battery to an external battery
to aid starting an engine. **jump on** *verb* attack
suddenly and forcefully. **jump suit** one-piece
garment of trousers and top.
jumper[1] ⊕ *noun* sweater or pullover.
jumper[2] *noun* person or animal that jumps.
Jun. 1 June. **2** Junior.
junction ⊕ *noun* place where routes, railway
lines, or roads meet.
juncture ⊕ *noun* point in time, esp. a critical
one.
June *noun* sixth month of the year.
jungle *noun* **1** tropical forest of dense tangled
vegetation. **2** confusion or mess. **3** place of
intense struggle for survival.
junior ⊕ *adjective* **1** of lower standing. **2**
younger. ◆ *noun* **3** junior person. **junior school**
school for children between seven and eleven.
juniper *noun* evergreen shrub with purple
berries.
junk[1] ⊕ *noun* **1** discarded or useless objects. **2**
Informal rubbish. **3** *Slang* narcotic drug, esp.
heroin. **junkie, junky** *noun, pl* **junkies** *Slang*
drug addict. **junk food** snack food of low
nutritional value. **junk mail** unwanted mail
advertising goods or services.
junk[2] *noun* flat-bottomed Chinese sailing boat.
junket *noun* **1** excursion by public officials
paid for from public funds. **2** sweetened milk
set with rennet. **3** feast. **junketing** *noun*
junta *noun* group of military officers holding

———— THESAURUS ————

juggle *verb* **2** =**manipulate**, alter, change,
manoeuvre, modify
juice *noun* **1** =**liquid**, extract, fluid, liquor,
nectar, sap
juicy *adjective* **1** =**moist**, lush, succulent **2**
=**interesting**, colourful, provocative, racy,
risqué, sensational, spicy (*inf*), suggestive, vivid
jumble *noun* **1** =**muddle**, clutter, confusion,
disarray, disorder, mess, mishmash, mixture
◆*verb* **3** =**mix**, confuse, disorder, disorganize,
mistake, muddle, shuffle
jumbo *adjective* **1** *Inf* =**giant**, gigantic, huge,
immense, large, oversized OPPOSITE> **tiny**
jump *verb* **1** =**leap**, bounce, bound, hop,
hurdle, skip, spring, vault **3** =**recoil**, flinch, jerk,
start, wince **4** =**increase**, advance, ascend,
escalate, rise, surge **7** =**miss**, avoid, evade,
omit, skip ◆*noun* **8** =**leap**, bound, hop, skip,

spring, vault **9** =**rise**, advance, increase,
increment, upsurge, upturn **10** =**interruption**,
break, gap, hiatus, lacuna, space
jumped-up *adjective* =**conceited**, arrogant,
insolent, overbearing, pompous, presumptuous
jumper[1] *noun* =**sweater**, jersey, pullover,
woolly
jumpy *adjective* =**nervous**, agitated, anxious,
apprehensive, fidgety, jittery (*inf*), on edge,
restless, tense, wired (*sl*) OPPOSITE> **calm**
junction *noun* =**connection**, coupling, linking,
union
juncture *noun* =**moment**, occasion, point,
time
junior *adjective* **1** =**lower**, inferior, lesser,
minor, secondary, subordinate OPPOSITE>
senior. **2** =**younger** OPPOSITE> **senior**
junk[1] *noun* **1, 2** =**rubbish**, clutter, debris,

power in a country, esp. after a coup.
Jupiter *noun* **1** king of the Roman gods. **2** largest of the planets.
juridical *adjective* of law or the administration of justice.
jurisdiction ⊕ *noun* **1** right or power to administer justice and apply laws. **2** extent of this right or power. **3** authority in general.
jurisprudence *noun* science or philosophy of law.
jurist *noun* expert in law.
jury *noun, pl* **-ries 1** group of people sworn to deliver a verdict in a court of law. **2** judges of a competition. **juror** *noun* member of a jury.
just ⊕ *adverb* **1** very recently. **2** at this instant. **3** merely, only. **4** exactly. **5** barely. **6** really. ◆ *adjective* **7** fair or impartial in action or judgment. **8** proper or right. **justice** *noun* **1** quality of being just. **2** judicial proceedings. **3** magistrate. **justify** *verb* prove right or

reasonable. **justly** *adverb* **justness** *noun*
justice ⊕ *noun* **1** quality of being just. **2** judicial proceedings. **3** judge or magistrate.
justice of the peace person who is authorized to act as a judge in a local court of law.
justify ⊕ *verb* **-fying, -fied 1** prove right or reasonable. **2** explain the reasons for an action. **3** align (text) so the margins are straight.
justifiable *adjective* **justifiably** *adverb* **justification** *noun*
jut ⊕ *verb* **jutting, jutted** project or stick out.
jute *noun* plant fibre, used for rope, canvas, etc.
juvenile ⊕ *adjective* **1** young. **2** of or suitable for young people. **3** immature and rather silly. ◆ *noun* **4** young person or child. **juvenilia** *plural noun* works produced in an author's youth.
juvenile delinquent young person guilty of a crime.
juxtapose ⊕ *verb* put side by side.
juxtaposition *noun*

——————— T H E S A U R U S ———————

litter, odds and ends, refuse, scrap, trash, waste
jurisdiction *noun* **1, 3 = authority**, command, control, influence, power, rule **2 = range**, area, bounds, compass, field, province, scope, sphere
just *adverb* **1 = recently**, hardly, lately, only now, scarcely **3 = merely**, by the skin of one's teeth, only, simply, solely **4 = exactly**, absolutely, completely, entirely, perfectly, precisely ◆*adjective* **7 = fair**, conscientious, equitable, fair-minded, good, honest, upright, virtuous OPPOSITE **unfair. 8 = fitting**, appropriate, apt, deserved, due, justified, merited, proper, rightful OPPOSITE **inappropriate**
justice *noun* **1 = fairness**, equity, honesty, integrity, law, legality, legitimacy, right OPPOSITE **injustice. 3 = judge**, magistrate
justifiable *adjective* **1, 2 = reasonable**, acceptable, defensible, excusable, legitimate,

sensible, understandable, valid, warrantable OPPOSITE **indefensible**
justification *noun* **1, 2 = reason**, basis, defence, excuse, explanation, grounds, rationalization, vindication, warrant
justify *verb* **1, 2 = explain**, defend, exculpate, excuse, exonerate, support, uphold, vindicate, warrant
justly *adverb* **8 = properly**, correctly, equitably, fairly, lawfully
jut *verb* **= stick out**, bulge, extend, overhang, poke, project, protrude
juvenile *adjective* **1 = young**, youthful OPPOSITE **adult. 3 = immature**, babyish, callow, childish, inexperienced, infantile, puerile ◆*noun* **4 = child**, adolescent, boy, girl, infant, minor, youth OPPOSITE **adult**
juxtaposition *noun* **= proximity**, closeness, contact, nearness, propinquity, vicinity

J

Kabloona *noun* (in Canada) a person who is not of Inuit ancestry, esp. a White person.
Kaffir [**kaf**-fer] *noun S Afr offens obs* Black African.
kaftan *noun* **1** long loose Eastern garment. **2** woman's dress resembling this.
kai *noun NZ informal* food.
kaiser [**kize**-er] *noun Hist* German or Austro-Hungarian emperor.
kak *noun S Afr slang* **1** faeces. **2** rubbish.
Kalashnikov *noun* Russian-made automatic rifle.
kale *noun* cabbage with crinkled leaves.
kaleidoscope *noun* **1** tube-shaped toy containing loose coloured pieces reflected by mirrors so that intricate patterns form when the tube istwisted. **2** complicated or rapidly changing set of colours, circumstances, etc. **kaleidoscopic** *adjective*
kalends *plural noun* same as CALENDS.
kamik *noun Canad* a traditional Inuit boot made of caribou hide or sealskin.
kamikaze ❶ [kam-mee-**kah**-zee] *noun* **1** (in World War II) Japanese pilot who performed a suicide mission. ♦ *adjective* **2** (of an action) undertaken in the knowledge that it will kill or injure the person performing it.
kangaroo *noun, pl* **-roos** Australian marsupial which moves by jumping with its powerful hind legs. **kangaroo court** unofficial court set up by a group to discipline its members. **kangaroo paw** Australian plant with green-and-red flowers.
kaolin *noun* fine white clay used to make porcelain and in some medicines.
kapok *noun* fluffy fibre from a tropical tree, used to stuff cushions etc.
kaput [kap-**poot**] *adjective Informal* ruined or broken.
karaoke *noun* form of entertainment in which people sing over a prerecorded backing tape.

karate *noun* Japanese system of unarmed combat using blows with the feet, hands, elbows, and legs.
karma *noun Buddhism, Hinduism* person's actions affecting his or her fate in the next reincarnation.
karoo *noun S Afr* high arid plateau.
kart *noun* same as GO-KART.
kasbah *noun* same as CASBAH.
katydid *noun* large green grasshopper of N America.
kauri *noun* large NZ conifer that yields valuable timber and resin.
kayak *noun* **1** Inuit canoe made of sealskins stretched over a frame. **2** fibreglass or canvas-covered canoe of this design.
kazoo *noun, pl* **-zoos** cigar-shaped metal musical instrument that produces a buzzing sound when the player hums into it.
KBE Knight Commander of the Order of the British Empire.
kbyte *Computers* kilobyte.
kcal kilocalorie.
kea *noun* large brownish-green parrot of NZ.
kebab *noun* **1** dish of small pieces of meat grilled on skewers. **2** (also **doner kebab**) grilled minced lamb served in a split slice of unleavened bread.
kedgeree *noun* dish of fish with rice and eggs.
keel ❶ *noun* main lengthways timber or steel support along the base of a ship. **keel over** *verb* **1** turn upside down. **2** *Informal* collapse suddenly. **on an even keel** working or progressing smoothly.
keen[1] ❶ *adjective* **1** eager or enthusiastic. **2** intense or strong. **3** intellectually acute. **4** (of the senses) capable of recognizing small distinctions. **5** sharp. **6** cold and penetrating. **7** competitive. **keenly** *adverb* **keenness** *noun*
keen[2] ❶ *verb* wail over the dead.

THESAURUS

kamikaze *adjective* **2** = **self-destructive**, foolhardy, suicidal
keel over *verb* **2** *Inf* = **collapse**, black out (*inf*), faint, pass out
keen[1] *adjective* **1** = **eager**, ardent, avid,

enthusiastic, impassioned, zealous **2** = **intense 3** = **astute**, canny, clever, perceptive, quick, shrewd, wise OPPOSITE **indifferent. 5** = **sharp**, cutting, incisive, razor-like OPPOSITE **dull**
keen[2] *verb* = **lament**, bewail, grieve, mourn,

keep ❶ *verb* **keeping, kept 1** have or retain possession of. **2** take temporary charge of. **3** store. **4** stay or cause to stay (in, on, or at a place or position). **5** continue or persist. **6** support financially. **7** detain (someone). **8** look after or maintain. **9** (of food) remain good. ◆ *noun* **10** cost of food and everyday expenses. **11** central tower of a castle. **keeper** *noun* **1** person who looks after animals in a zoo. **2** person in charge of a museum or collection. **3** short for GOALKEEPER. **keeping** *noun* care or charge. **in, out of keeping with** appropriate *or* inappropriate for. **keep fit** exercises designed to promote physical fitness. **keepsake** *noun* gift treasured for the sake of the giver. **keep up** *verb* maintain at the current level. **keep up with** *verb* maintain a pace set by (someone). **keep up with the Joneses** *Informal* compete with friends or neighbours in material possessions.

keg ❶ *noun* small metal beer barrel.

kelp *noun* large brown seaweed.

kelvin *noun* SI unit of temperature. **Kelvin scale** temperature scale starting at absolute zero (-273.15° Celsius).

ken *verb* **kenning, kenned** *or* **kent** *Scot* know. **beyond one's ken** beyond one's range of knowledge.

kendo *noun* Japanese sport of fencing using wooden staves.

kennel *noun* **1** hutlike shelter for a dog. ◆ *plural* **2** place for breeding, boarding, or training dogs.

kept *verb* past of KEEP.

keratin *noun* fibrous protein found in the hair and nails.

kerb *noun* stone edging to a footpath. **kerb crawling** act of driving slowly beside a pavement to pick up a prostitute.

kerchief *noun* piece of cloth worn over the head or round the neck.

kerfuffle *noun* *Informal* commotion or disorder.

kernel ❶ *noun* **1** seed of a nut, cereal, or fruit stone. **2** central and essential part of something.

kerosene *noun* *US & Canad* another name for PARAFFIN.

kestrel *noun* type of small falcon.

ketch *noun* two-masted sailing ship.

ketchup *noun* thick cold sauce, usu. made of tomatoes.

kettle *noun* container with a spout and handle used for boiling water. **a different kettle of fish** something entirely different. **kettledrum** *noun* large bowl-shaped metal drum.

key[1] ❶ *noun* **1** device for operating a lock by moving a bolt. **2** device turned to wind a clock, operate a machine, etc. **3** any of a set of levers or buttons pressed to operate a typewriter, computer, or musical keyboard instrument. **4** *Music* set of related notes. **5** something crucial in providing an explanation or interpretation. **6** means of achieving a desired end. **7** list of explanations of codes, symbols, etc. ◆ *adjective* **8** of great importance. ◆ *verb* **9** (also **key in**) enter (text) using a keyboard. **keyed up** very excited or nervous.

key[2] *noun* same as CAY.

keyboard *noun* **1** set of keys on a piano, computer, etc. **2** musical instrument played using a keyboard. ◆ *verb* **3** enter (text) using a keyboard.

keyhole *noun* opening for inserting a key into

K

——————— T H E S A U R U S ———————

wail, weep

keenness *noun* **1** = **eagerness**, ardour, enthusiasm, fervour, passion, zeal, zest **2** = **intensity**

keep *verb* **1** = **retain**, conserve, control, hold, maintain, possess, preserve OPPOSITE lose. **2** = **look after**, care for, guard, maintain, manage, mind, protect, tend, watch over **3** = **store**, carry, deposit, hold, place, stack, stock **6** = **support**, maintain, provide for, subsidize, sustain **7** = **detain**, delay, hinder, hold back, keep back, obstruct, prevent, restrain OPPOSITE release ◆*noun* **10** = **board**, food, living, maintenance **11** = **tower**, castle

keeper *noun* **2** = **guardian**, attendant, caretaker, curator, custodian, guard, preserver, steward, warden

keeping *noun* = **care**, charge, custody, guardianship, possession, protection, safekeeping **in keeping with** = **in agreement with**, complying with, conforming to, corresponding to, in accord with, in balance with, in harmony with, in proportion with

keepsake *noun* = **souvenir**, memento, relic, reminder, symbol, token

keep up *verb* = **maintain**, continue, keep pace, preserve, sustain

keg *noun* = **barrel**, cask, drum, vat

kernel *noun* **2** = **essence**, core, germ, gist, nub, pith, substance

key[1] *noun* **1** = **opener**, latchkey **5** = **answer**, explanation, solution ◆*adjective* **8** = **essential**, crucial, decisive, fundamental, important, leading, main, major, pivotal, principal OPPOSITE minor ◆*verb* **9** (also **key in**) = **type**, enter, input, keyboard a lock. **keyhole surgery** surgery performed through a narrow hole cut in the body.

keynote ⊙ *adjective* **1** central or dominating. ◆ *noun* **2** dominant idea of a speech etc. **3** basic note of a musical key.

keyring *noun* decorative metal ring for keeping keys on.

keystone *noun* **1** most important part of a process, organization, etc. **2** central stone of an arch which locks the others in position.

kg kilogram(s).

KG Knight of the Order of the Garter.

KGB *noun* (formerly) Soviet secret police.

khaki *adjective* **1** dull yellowish-brown. ◆ *noun* **2** hard-wearing fabric of this colour used for military uniforms.

khan *noun* title of respect in Afghanistan and central Asia.

kHz kilohertz.

kibbutz *noun, pl* **kibbutzim** communal farm or factory in Israel.

kibosh *noun* **put the kibosh on** *Slang* put a stop to.

kick ⊙ *verb* **1** drive, push, or strike with the foot. **2** (of a gun) recoil when fired. **3** *Informal* object or resist. **4** *Informal* free oneself of (an addiction). **5** *Rugby* score with a kick. ◆ *noun* **6** thrust or blow with the foot. **7** recoil of a gun. **8** *Informal* excitement or thrill. **kickback** *noun* money paid illegally for favours done. **kick off** *verb* **1** start a game of football. **2** *Informal* begin. **kickoff** *noun* **kick out** *verb* dismiss or expel forcibly. **kick-start** *verb* **1** start (a motorcycle) by kicking a pedal. **2** do something bold or drastic in order to begin or improve the performance of something. ◆ *noun* **3** (also **kick-starter**) pedal on a motorcycle that is kicked downwards to start the engine. **kick up** *verb Informal* create (a fuss).

kid¹ ⊙ *noun* **1** (also **kiddie**) *Informal* child. **2**

young goat. **3** leather made from the skin of a young goat. **treat, handle someone with kid gloves** treat someone with great tact in order not to upset them.

kid² ⊙ *verb* **kidding, kidded** *Informal* tease or deceive (someone).

kidnap ⊙ *verb* **-napping, -napped** seize and hold (a person) to ransom. **kidnapper** *noun* **kidnapping** *noun*

kidney *noun* **1** either of the pair of organs that filter waste products from the blood to produce urine. **2** animal kidney used as food. **kidney bean** reddish-brown kidney-shaped bean, edible when cooked.

kill ⊙ *verb* **1** cause the death of. **2** *Informal* cause (someone) pain or discomfort. **3** put an end to. **4** pass (time). ◆ *noun* **5** act of killing. **6** animals or birds killed in a hunt. **killer** *noun*

killing *Informal adjective* **1** very tiring. **2** very funny. ◆ *noun* **3** sudden financial success.

killjoy *noun* person who spoils others' pleasure.

kiln *noun* oven for baking, drying, or processing pottery, bricks, etc.

kilo *noun* short for KILOGRAM.

kilo- *combining form* one thousand, e.g. *kilometre.*

kilobyte *noun Computers* 1024 units of information.

kilocalorie *noun* one thousand calories.

kilogram, kilogramme *noun* one thousand grams.

kilohertz *noun* one thousand hertz.

kilojoule *noun* one thousand joules.

kilometre *noun* one thousand metres.

kilowatt *noun Electricity* one thousand watts.

kilowatt-hour *noun* unit of energy equal to the work done by a power of one thousand watts in an hour.

kilt *noun* knee-length pleated tartan skirt worn orig. by Scottish Highlanders. **kilted** *adjective*

——————— THESAURUS ———————

keynote *noun* **1** = **heart**, centre, core, essence, gist, substance, theme

kick *verb* **1** = **boot**, punt **4** *Inf* = **give up**, abandon, desist from, leave off, quit, stop ◆*noun* **8** *Inf* = **thrill**, buzz (*sl*), pleasure, stimulation

kick off *verb* **2** *Inf* = **begin**, commence, get the show on the road, initiate, open, start

kick out *verb Inf* = **dismiss**, eject, evict, expel, get rid of, remove, sack (*inf*)

kid¹ *noun* **1** (also **kiddie**) *Inf* = **child**, baby, bairn, infant, teenager, tot, youngster, youth

kid² *verb Inf* = **tease**, delude, fool, hoax, jest, joke, pretend, trick, wind up (*Brit sl*)

kidnap *verb* = **abduct**, capture, hijack, hold to

ransom, seize

kill *verb* **1** = **slay**, assassinate, butcher, destroy, execute, exterminate, liquidate, massacre, murder, slaughter **3** = **suppress**, extinguish, halt, quash, quell, scotch, smother, stifle, stop

killer *noun* **1** = **assassin**, butcher, cut-throat, executioner, exterminator, gunman, hit man (*sl*), murderer, slayer

killing *Inf adjective* **1** = **tiring**, debilitating, exhausting, fatiguing, punishing **2** = **hilarious**, comical, ludicrous, uproarious ◆*noun* **3** = **bonanza**, bomb (*sl*), cleanup (*inf*), coup, gain, profit, success, windfall

killjoy *noun* = **spoilsport**, dampener, wet blanket (*inf*)

kimono [kim-**moan**-no] *noun, pl* **-nos 1** loose wide-sleeved Japanese robe, fastened with a sash. **2** European dressing gown resembling this.

kin, kinsfolk ⊕ *noun* person's relatives collectively. **kinship** *noun* **1** blood relationship. **2** state of having common characteristics. **kinsman, kinswoman** *noun* relative.

kind¹ ⊕ *adjective* considerate, friendly, and helpful. **kindness** *noun* **kindly** *adjective* **-lier, -liest 1** having a warm-hearted nature. **2** pleasant or agreeable. ♦ *adverb* **3** in a considerate way. **4** please, e.g. *will you kindly be quiet!* **kindliness** *noun* **kind-hearted** *adjective*

kind² ⊕ *noun* **1** class or group with common characteristics. **2** essential nature or character. **in kind 1** (of payment) in goods rather than money. **2** with something similar. **kind of** to a certain extent.

> **LANGUAGE TIP**
>
> Note the singular/plural usage: *this* (or *that*) *kind of dog; these* (or *those*) *kinds of dog*. In the second, plural example, you can also say *these kinds of dogs*.

kindergarten *noun* class or school for children of about four to six years old.
kindle ⊕ *verb* **1** set (a fire) alight. **2** (of a fire) start to burn. **3** arouse or be aroused. **kindling**

noun dry wood or straw for starting fires.
kindred ⊕ *adjective* **1** having similar qualities. **2** related by blood or marriage. ♦ *noun* **3** same as KIN.

kindy, kindie *noun, pl* **-dies** *Aust & NZ informal* kindergarten.
kine *plural noun Obs* cows or cattle.
kinetic [kin-**net**-ik] *adjective* relating to or caused by motion.

king ⊕ *noun* **1** male ruler of a monarchy. **2** ruler or chief. **3** best or most important of its kind. **4** piece in chess that must be defended. **5** playing card with a picture of a king on it. **kingship** *noun* **kingdom** *noun* **1** state ruled by a king or queen. **2** division of the natural world.
king prawn large prawn, fished commercially in Australian waters. **king-size, king-sized** *adjective* larger than standard size.
kingfisher *noun* small bird with a bright greenish-blue and orange plumage, that dives for fish.
kingpin *noun* most important person in an organization.

kink ⊕ *noun* **1** twist or bend in rope, wire, hair, etc. **2** *Informal* quirk in someone's personality. **kinky** *adjective* **kinkier, kinkiest 1** *Slang* given to unusual sexual practices. **2** full of kinks.
kiosk ⊕ *noun* **1** small booth selling drinks, cigarettes, newspapers, etc. **2** public telephone box.
kip *noun, verb* **kipping, kipped** *Informal* sleep.

K

—————— THESAURUS ——————

kin, kinsfolk *noun* =**family**, kindred, relations, relatives
kind¹ *adjective* =**considerate**, benign, charitable, compassionate, courteous, friendly, generous, humane, kindly, obliging, philanthropic, tender-hearted OPPOSITE **unkind**
kind² *noun* **1** =**class**, brand, breed, family, set, sort, species, variety
kind-hearted *adjective* =**sympathetic**, altruistic, compassionate, considerate, generous, good-natured, helpful, humane, kind, tender-hearted
kindle *verb* **1** =**set fire to**, ignite, inflame, light OPPOSITE **extinguish**. **3** =**arouse**, awaken, induce, inspire, provoke, rouse, stimulate, stir
kindliness *noun* **1** =**kindness**, amiability, benevolence, charity, compassion, friendliness, gentleness, humanity, kind-heartedness
kindly *adjective* **1** =**benevolent**, benign, compassionate, good-natured, helpful, kind, pleasant, sympathetic, warm OPPOSITE **cruel**
♦*adverb* **3** =**benevolently**, agreeably, cordially,

graciously, politely, tenderly, thoughtfully OPPOSITE **cruelly**
kindness *noun* =**goodwill**, benevolence, charity, compassion, generosity, humanity, kindliness, philanthropy, understanding OPPOSITE **cruelty**
kindred *adjective* **1** =**similar**, akin, corresponding, like, matching, related ♦*noun* **2** =**family**, kin, kinsfolk, relations, relatives
king *noun* **1** =**ruler**, emperor, monarch, sovereign
kingdom *noun* **1** =**country**, nation, realm, state, territory
kink *noun* **1** =**twist**, bend, coil, wrinkle **2** *Inf* =**quirk**, eccentricity, fetish, foible, idiosyncrasy, vagary, whim
kinky *adjective* **1** *Sl* =**perverted**, depraved, deviant, unnatural, warped **2** =**twisted**, coiled, curled, tangled
kinship *noun* **1** =**relation**, consanguinity, kin, ties of blood **2** =**similarity**, affinity, association, connection, correspondence, relationship
kiosk *noun* **1** =**booth**, bookstall, counter,

kipper *noun* cleaned, salted, and smoked herring.
kirk *noun Scot* church.
Kirsch *noun* brandy made from cherries.
kismet *noun* fate or destiny.
kiss ⊕ *verb* **1** touch with the lips in affection or greeting. **2** join lips with a person in love or desire. ♦ *noun* **3** touch with the lips. **kisser** *noun Slang* mouth or face. **kissagram** *noun* greetings service in which a messenger kisses the person celebrating. **kiss of life** mouth-to-mouth resuscitation.
kist *noun S Afr* large wooden chest.
kit ⊕ *noun* **1** outfit or equipment for a specific purpose. **2** set of pieces of equipment sold ready to be assembled. **kitbag** *noun* bag for a soldier's or traveller's belongings. **kit out** *verb* **kitting, kitted** provide with clothes or equipment needed for a particular activity.
kitchen *noun* room used for cooking.
kitchenette *noun* small kitchen. **kitchen garden** garden for growing vegetables, herbs, etc.
kite *noun* **1** light frame covered with a thin material flown on a string in the wind. **2** large hawk with a forked tail. **Kite mark** official mark on articles approved by the British Standards Institution.
kith *noun* **kith and kin** friends and relatives.
kitsch *noun* art or literature with popular sentimental appeal.
kitten *noun* young cat. **kittenish** *adjective* lively and flirtatious.
kittiwake *noun* type of seagull.
kitty *noun, pl* **-ties 1** communal fund. **2** total amount wagered in certain gambling games.
kiwi *noun* **1** NZ flightless bird with a long beak and no tail. **2** *Informal* New Zealander. **kiwi fruit** edible fruit with a fuzzy brownish skin and green flesh.
kJ kilojoule(s).
klaxon *noun* loud horn used on emergency vehicles as a warning signal.

kleptomania *noun* compulsive tendency to steal. **kleptomaniac** *noun*
kloof *noun S Afr* mountain pass or gorge.
km kilometre(s).
knack ⊕ *noun* **1** skilful way of doing something. **2** innate ability.
knacker *noun* buyer of old horses for killing.
knackered *adjective Slang* **1** extremely tired. **2** no longer functioning.
knapsack *noun* soldier's or traveller's bag worn strapped on the back.
knave ⊕ *noun* **1** jack at cards. **2** *Obs* dishonest man.
knead ⊕ *verb* **1** work (dough) into a smooth mixture with the hands. **2** squeeze or press with the hands.
knee *noun* **1** joint between thigh and lower leg. **2** lap. **3** part of a garment covering the knee. ♦ *verb* **kneeing, kneed 4** strike or push with the knee. **kneecap** *noun* **1** bone in front of the knee. ♦ *verb* **2** shoot in the kneecap.
kneejerk *adjective* (of a reply or reaction) automatic and predictable. **knees-up** *noun Informal* party.
kneel ⊕ *verb* **kneeling, kneeled** *or* **knelt** fall or rest on one's knees.
knell ⊕ *noun* **1** sound of a bell, esp. at a funeral or death. **2** portent of doom.
knew *verb* past tense of KNOW.
knickerbockers *plural noun* loose-fitting short trousers gathered in at the knee.
knickers ⊕ *plural noun* woman's or girl's undergarment covering the lower trunk and having legs or legholes.
knick-knack ⊕ *noun* trifle or trinket.
knife ⊕ *noun, pl* **knives 1** cutting tool or weapon consisting of a sharp-edged blade with a handle. ♦ *verb* **2** cut or stab with a knife. **knife edge** critical point in the development of a situation.
knight *noun* **1** man who has been given a knighthood. **2** *Hist* man who served his lord as a mounted armoured soldier. **3** chess piece

——— THESAURUS ———

newsstand, stall, stand
kiss *verb* **1, 2 = osculate**, neck (*inf*), peck (*inf*) ♦*noun* **3 = osculation**, peck (*inf*), smacker (*sl*)
kit *noun* **1 = equipment**, apparatus, gear, paraphernalia, tackle, tools
kit out *verb* **= equip**, accoutre, arm, deck out, fit out, fix up, furnish, provide with, supply
knack *noun* **1 = skill**, trick **2 = gift**, ability, aptitude, capacity, expertise, facility, propensity, skill, talent [OPPOSITE] **ineptitude**
knave *noun* **2** *Obs* **= rogue**, blackguard, bounder (*old-fashioned Brit sl*), rascal, rotter (*sl*,

chiefly *Brit*), scoundrel, villain
knead *verb* **2 = squeeze**, form, manipulate, massage, mould, press, rub, shape, work
kneel *verb* **= genuflect**, stoop
knell *noun* **1 = ringing**, chime, peal, sound, toll
knickers *plural noun* **= underwear**, bloomers, briefs, broekies (*S Afr inf*), drawers, panties, smalls
knick-knack *noun* **= trinket**, bagatelle, bauble, bric-a-brac, plaything, trifle
knife *noun* **1 = blade**, cutter ♦*verb* **2 = cut**,

shaped like a horse's head. ◆ *verb* **4** award a knighthood to. **knighthood** *noun* honorary title given to a man by the British sovereign. **knightly** *adjective*

knit ① *verb* **knitting, knitted** *or* **knit 1** make (a garment) by interlocking a series of loops in wool or other yarn. **2** join closely together. **3** draw (one's eyebrows) together. **knitting** *noun* **knitwear** *noun* knitted clothes, such as sweaters.

knives *noun* plural of KNIFE.

knob ① *noun* **1** rounded projection, such as a switch on a radio. **2** rounded handle on a door or drawer. **3** small amount of butter. **knobbly** *adjective* covered with small bumps.

knock ① *verb* **1** give a blow or push to. **2** rap audibly with the knuckles. **3** make or drive by striking. **4** *Informal* criticize adversely. **5** (of an engine) make a regular banging noise as a result of a fault. ◆ *noun* **6** blow or rap. **7** knocking sound. **8** misfortune, rejection, or setback. **knocker** *noun* metal fitting for knocking on a door. **knock about, around** *verb* **1** wander or spend time aimlessly. **2** hit or kick brutally. **knockabout** *adjective* (of comedy) boisterous. **knock back** *verb Informal* **1** drink quickly. **2** cost. **3** reject or refuse. **knock down** *verb* **1** demolish. **2** reduce the price of. **knockdown** *adjective* (of a price) very low. **knock-knees** *plural noun* legs that curve in at the knees. **knock-kneed** *adjective* **knock off** *verb* **1** *Informal* cease work. **2** *Informal* make or do (something) hurriedly or easily. **3** take (a specified amount) off a price. **4** *Informal* steal. **knock-on effect** indirect result of an action or decision. **knock out** *verb* **1** render (someone) unconscious. **2** *Informal* overwhelm or amaze. **3** defeat in a knockout competition. **knockout** *noun* **1** blow that renders an opponent unconscious. **2** competition from which competitors are progressively eliminated. **3** *Informal* overwhelmingly attractive person or thing. **knock up** *verb* **1** *Informal* assemble (something) quickly. **2** *Informal* waken. **3** *Slang* make pregnant. **knock-up** *noun* practice session at tennis, squash, or badminton.

knoll *noun* small rounded hill.

knot ① *noun* **1** fastening made by looping and pulling tight strands of string, cord, or rope. **2** tangle (of hair). **3** small cluster or huddled group. **4** round lump or spot in timber. **5** feeling of tightness, caused by tension or nervousness. **6** unit of speed used by ships, equal to one nautical mile per hour. ◆ *verb* **knotting, knotted 7** tie with or into a knot. **knotty** *adjective* **-tier, -tiest 1** full of knots. **2** puzzling or difficult.

know ① *verb* **knowing, knew, known 1** be or feel certain of the truth of (information etc.). **2** be acquainted with. **3** have a grasp of or understand (a skill or language). **4** be aware of. **in the know** *Informal* informed or aware. **knowable** *adjective* **knowing** *adjective* suggesting secret knowledge. **knowingly** *adverb* **1** deliberately. **2** in a way that suggests secret knowledge. **knowledge** *noun* facts or experiences known by a person. **know-all** *noun Offens* person who acts as if knowing more than other people. **know-how** *noun Informal* ingenuity, aptitude, or skill.

K

——————————— THESAURUS ———————————

lacerate, pierce, slash, stab, wound

knit *verb* **2** = **join**, bind, fasten, intertwine, link, tie, unite, weave **3** = **wrinkle**, crease, furrow, knot, pucker

knob *noun* **1** = **lump**, bump, hump, knot, projection, protrusion, stud

knock *verb* **1** = **hit**, belt (*inf*), cuff, punch, smack, strike, thump **2** = **rap 4** *Inf* = **criticize**, abuse, belittle, censure, condemn, denigrate, deprecate, disparage, find fault, run down ◆*noun* **6** = **blow**, clip, clout (*inf*), cuff, rap, slap, smack, thump **8** = **setback**, defeat, failure, rebuff, rejection, reversal

knockabout *adjective* = **boisterous**, farcical, riotous, rollicking, slapstick

knock about, around *verb* **1** = **wander**, ramble, range, roam, rove, travel **2** = **hit**, abuse, batter, beat up (*inf*), maltreat, manhandle, maul, mistreat, strike

knock down *verb* **1** = **demolish**, destroy, fell, level, raze

knock off *verb* **1** *Inf* = **stop work**, clock off, clock out, finish **4** *Inf* = **steal**, nick (*sl, chiefly Brit*), pinch, rob, thieve

knockout *noun* **1** = **killer blow**, coup de grâce, KO *or* K.O. (*sl*) **3** *Inf* = **success**, hit, sensation, smash, smash hit, triumph, winner OPPOSITE **failure**

knot *noun* **1** = **connection**, bond, joint, ligature, loop, tie **3** = **cluster**, bunch, clump, collection ◆*verb* **7** = **tie**, bind, loop, secure, tether

know *verb* **1** = **understand**, comprehend, feel certain, notice, perceive, realize, recognize, see **2** = **be acquainted with**, be familiar with, have dealings with, have knowledge of, recognize OPPOSITE **be ignorant of**

know-how *noun Inf* = **capability**, ability, aptitude, expertise, ingenuity, knack, knowledge, savoir-faire, skill, talent

knowledge ❶ *noun* **1** facts or experiences known by a person. **2** state of knowing. **3** specific information on a subject.
knowledgeable, knowledgable *adjective* intelligent or well-informed. **knowledgeably, knowledgably** *adverb*
knuckle *noun* **1** bone at the finger joint. **2** knee joint of a calf or pig. **near the knuckle** *Informal* rather rude or offensive. **knuckle-duster** *noun* metal appliance worn on the knuckles to add force to a blow. **knuckle under** *verb* yield or submit.
KO knockout.
koala *noun* tree-dwelling Australian marsupial with dense grey fur (also **native bear**).
kohl *noun* cosmetic powder used to darken the edges of the eyelids.
kook *noun US informal* eccentric person.
kooky *adjective* **kookier, kookiest**
kookaburra *noun* large Australian kingfisher with a cackling cry.
kopeck *noun* former Russian monetary unit, one hundredth of a rouble.
kopje, koppie *noun S Afr* small hill.
Koran *noun* sacred book of Islam.
Korean *adjective* **1** of North or South Korea or their language. ◆ *noun* **2** person from North or South Korea. **3** language of North and South Korea.
kosher [koh-sher] *adjective* **1** conforming to Jewish religious law, esp. (of food) to Jewish dietary law. **2** *Informal* legitimate or authentic. ◆ *noun* **3** kosher food.

kowtow *verb* be servile (towards).
kph kilometres per hour.
Kr *Chem* krypton.
kraal *noun S* African village surrounded by a strong fence.
Kremlin *noun* central government of Russia and, formerly, the Soviet Union.
krill *noun, pl* **krill** small shrimplike sea creature.
krona *noun, pl* **kronor** standard monetary unit of Sweden.
krone [kroh-na] *noun, pl* **-ner** [-ner] standard monetary unit of Norway and Denmark.
krypton *noun Chem* colourless gas present in the atmosphere and used in fluorescent lights.
KS Kansas.
kudos [kyoo-doss] *noun* fame or credit.
kudu *noun* African antelope with spiral horns.
kugel [koog-el] *noun S Afr* rich, fashion-conscious, materialistic young woman.
Ku Klux Klan *noun* secret organization of White Protestant Americans who use violence against African-Americans and Jews.
kumara *noun NZ* tropical root vegetable with yellow flesh.
kumquat [kumm-kwott] *noun* citrus fruit resembling a tiny orange.
kung fu *noun* Chinese martial art combining hand, foot, and weapon techniques.
kurrajong *noun* Australian tree or shrub with tough fibrous bark.
kW kilowatt.
kWh kilowatt-hour.
KY Kentucky.

——————— T H E S A U R U S ———————

knowing *adjective* =**meaningful**, expressive, significant
knowingly *adverb* **1** =**deliberately**, consciously, intentionally, on purpose, purposely, wilfully, wittingly
knowledge *noun* **1** =**learning**, education, enlightenment, erudition, instruction, intelligence, scholarship, wisdom OPPOSITE ignorance. **2** =**acquaintance**, familiarity,

intimacy OPPOSITE **unfamiliarity**
knowledgeable *adjective* **a** =**intelligent**, educated, erudite, learned, scholarly **b** =**well-informed**, *au fait*, aware, clued-up (*inf*), cognizant, conversant, experienced, familiar, in the know (*inf*), in the loop
known *adjective* **2** =**famous**, acknowledged, avowed, celebrated, noted, recognized, well-known OPPOSITE **unknown**

l litre.
L 1 large. **2** learner (driver). **3** the Roman numeral for fifty.
L. lake.
la *noun Music* same as LAH.
La *Chem* lanthanum.
LA Louisiana.
lab *noun Informal* short for LABORATORY.
Lab. Labour.
label ⊕ *noun* **1** piece of card or other material fixed to an object to show its ownership, destination, etc. **2** brief descriptive term. ♦ *verb* **-elling, -elled 3** give a label to. **4** describe in a phrase.
labia *plural noun, sing* **labium** four liplike folds of skin forming part of the female genitals.
labial *[lay-bee-al] adjective* of the lips.
laboratory *noun, pl* **-ries** building or room designed for scientific research or for the teaching of practical science.
laborious ⊕ *adjective* involving great prolonged effort. **laboriously** *adverb*
labour ⊕ *noun* **1** physical work or exertion. **2** workers in industry. **3** final stage of pregnancy, leading to childbirth. ♦ *verb* **4** work hard. **5** make one's way with difficulty. **6** stress to excess or too persistently. **7** be at a disadvantage because of a mistake or false belief. **laboured** *adjective* uttered or done with difficulty. **labourer** *noun* person who labours, esp. someone doing manual work for wages.
Labour Party major British political party advocating social equality.
labrador *noun* large retriever dog with a usu. gold or black coat.
laburnum *noun* ornamental tree with yellow hanging flowers.
labyrinth ⊕ *[lab-er-inth] noun* **1** complicated network of passages. **2** any complex system. **3** interconnecting cavities in the internal ear. **labyrinthine** *adjective*
lace ⊕ *noun* **1** delicate decorative fabric made from threads woven into an open weblike pattern. **2** cord drawn through eyelets and tied. ♦ *verb* **3** fasten with laces. **4** thread a cord or string through holes in something. **5** add a small amount of alcohol, a drug, etc. to (food or drink). **lacy** *adjective* fine, like lace. **lace-ups** *plural noun* shoes which fasten with laces.
lacerate ⊕ *[lass-er-rate] verb* tear (flesh). **laceration** *noun*
lachrymose *adjective* **1** tearful. **2** sad.
lack ⊕ *noun* **1** shortage or absence of something needed or wanted. ♦ *verb* **2** need or be short of (something).
lackadaisical ⊕ *adjective* **1** lacking vitality and purpose. **2** lazy and careless in a dreamy way.
lackey ⊕ *noun* **1** servile follower. **2** uniformed

THESAURUS

label *noun* **1 = tag**, marker, sticker, ticket ♦*verb* **3 = tag**, mark, stamp
laborious *adjective* **=hard**, arduous, backbreaking, exhausting, onerous, strenuous, tiring, tough, wearisome OPPOSITE **easy**
labour *noun* **1 = work**, industry, toil, yakka (*Aust & NZ inf*) OPPOSITE **leisure. 2 = workers**, employees, hands, labourers, workforce **3 = childbirth**, delivery, parturition ♦*verb* **4 = work**, endeavour, slave, strive, struggle, sweat (*inf*), toil OPPOSITE **rest. 6 = overemphasize**, dwell on, elaborate, go on about, overdo, strain **7 = be disadvantaged**, be a victim of, be burdened by, suffer
laboured *adjective* **=difficult**, awkward, forced, heavy, stiff, strained
labourer *noun* **=worker**, blue-collar worker, drudge, hand, manual worker, navvy (*Brit inf*)
labyrinth *noun* **1, 2 = maze**, intricacy, jungle, tangle
lace *noun* **1 = netting**, filigree, openwork **2 = cord**, bootlace, shoelace, string, tie ♦*verb* **3 = fasten**, bind, do up, thread, tie **4 = intertwine**, interweave, twine **5 = mix in**, add to, fortify, spike
lacerate *verb* **=tear**, claw, cut, gash, mangle, rip, slash, wound
laceration *noun* **=cut**, gash, rent, rip, slash, tear, wound
lack *noun* **1 = shortage**, absence, dearth, deficiency, need, scarcity, want OPPOSITE **abundance** ♦*verb* **2 = need**, be deficient in, be short of, be without, miss, require, want OPPOSITE **have**

male servant.
lacklustre ⊕ *adjective* lacking brilliance or vitality.
laconic ⊕ *adjective* using only a few words, terse. **laconically** *adverb*
lacquer *noun* 1 hard varnish for wood or metal. 2 clear sticky substance sprayed onto the hair to hold it in place. **lacquered** *adjective*
lacrimal [lack-rim-al] *adjective* of tears or the glands which produce them.
lacrosse *noun* sport in which teams catch and throw a ball using long sticks with a pouched net at the end, in an attempt to score goals.
lactation *noun* secretion of milk by female mammals to feed young. **lactic** *adjective* of or derived from milk. **lactose** *noun* white crystalline sugar found in milk.
lacuna [lak-**kew**-na] *noun, pl* **-nae** gap or missing part, esp. in a document or series.
lad ⊕ *noun* boy or young man. **laddish** *adjective Informal* behaving in a macho or immature manner.
ladder *noun* 1 frame of two poles connected by horizontal steps used for climbing. 2 system with ascending stages, e.g. *the social ladder*. 3 line of stitches that have come undone in tights or stockings. ♦ *verb* 4 have or cause to have such a line of undone stitches.
laden ⊕ *adjective* 1 loaded. 2 burdened.
la-di-da, lah-di-dah *adjective Informal* affected or pretentious.
ladle *noun* 1 spoon with a long handle and a large bowl, used for serving soup etc. ♦ *verb* 2 serve out.
lady ⊕ *noun, pl* **-dies** 1 woman regarded as having characteristics of good breeding or high rank. 2 polite term of address for a woman. 3 (**L-**) title of some female members of the

nobility. **Our Lady** the Virgin Mary. **Lady Day** Feast of the Annunciation, March 25. **ladies**, **ladies' room** *noun* women's public toilet.
lady-in-waiting *noun, pl* **ladies-in-waiting** female servant of a queen or princess.
ladykiller *noun Informal* man who is or thinks he is irresistible to women. **ladylike** *adjective* polite and dignified. **Ladyship** *noun* title used to address a Lady.
ladybird *noun* small red beetle with black spots.
lag¹ ⊕ *verb* **lagging, lagged** 1 go too slowly, fall behind. ♦ *noun* 2 delay between events.
laggard *noun* person who lags behind.
lag² *verb* **lagging, lagged** wrap (a boiler, pipes, etc.) with insulating material. **lagging** *noun* insulating material.
lag³ *noun* **old lag** *Slang* convict.
lager *noun* light-bodied beer.
lagoon *noun* body of water cut off from the open sea by coral reefs or sand bars.
lah *noun Music* (in tonic sol-fa) sixth degree of any major scale.
laid ⊕ *verb* past of LAY¹. **laid-back** *adjective Informal* relaxed.
lain *verb* past participle of LIE².
lair ⊕ *noun* 1 resting place of an animal. 2 *Informal* hiding place.
laird *noun* Scottish landowner.
laissez-faire [less-ay-**fair**] *noun* principle of nonintervention, esp. by a government in commercial affairs.
laity [**lay**-it-ee] *noun* people who are not members of the clergy.
lake¹ ⊕ *noun* expanse of water entirely surrounded by land. **lakeside** *noun*
lake² *noun* red pigment.
lama *noun* Buddhist priest in Tibet or

────────── T H E S A U R U S ──────────

lackadaisical *adjective* 1 =**lethargic**, apathetic, dull, half-hearted, indifferent, languid, listless 2 =**lazy**, abstracted, dreamy, idle, indolent, inert
lackey *noun* 1 =**hanger-on**, flatterer, minion, sycophant, toady, yes man 2 =**manservant**, attendant, flunky, footman, valet
lacklustre *adjective* =**flat**, drab, dull, leaden, lifeless, muted, prosaic, uninspired, vapid
laconic *adjective* =**terse**, brief, concise, curt, monosyllabic, pithy, short, succinct long-winded
lad *noun* =**boy**, fellow, guy (*inf*), juvenile, kid (*inf*), youngster, youth
laden *adjective* =**loaded**, burdened, charged, encumbered, full, weighed down
lady *noun* 1 =**gentlewoman**, dame 2

=**woman**, female
ladykiller *noun Inf* =**womanizer**, Casanova, Don Juan, heartbreaker, ladies' man, libertine, philanderer, rake, roué
ladylike *adjective* =**refined**, elegant, genteel, modest, polite, proper, respectable, sophisticated, well-bred OPPOSITE> **unladylike**
lag¹ *verb* 1 =**hang back**, dawdle, delay, linger, loiter, straggle, tarry, trail
laggard *noun* =**straggler**, dawdler, idler, loiterer, slowcoach (*Brit inf*), sluggard, snail
laid-back *adjective Inf* =**relaxed**, casual, easy-going, free and easy, unflappable (*inf*), unhurried OPPOSITE> **tense**
lair *noun* 1 =**nest**, burrow, den, earth, hole
laissez-faire *noun* =**nonintervention**, free enterprise, free trade

Mongolia.

lamb *noun* **1** young sheep. **2** its meat. ♦ *verb* **3** (of sheep) give birth to a lamb or lambs. **lambskin** *noun* **lambswool** *noun*

lambast, lambaste *verb* **1** beat or thrash. **2** reprimand severely.

lambent *adjective Lit* (of a flame) flickering softly.

lame ⊕ *adjective* **1** having an injured or disabled leg or foot. **2** (of an excuse) unconvincing. ♦ *verb* **3** make lame. **lamely** *adverb* **lameness** *noun* **lame duck** person or thing unable to cope without help.

lamé [lah-may] *noun, adjective* (fabric) interwoven with gold or silver thread.

lament ⊕ *verb* **1** feel or express sorrow (for). ♦ *noun* **2** passionate expression of grief. **3** song of grief. **lamentable** *adjective* very disappointing. **lamentation** *noun* **lamented** *adjective* grieved for.

laminate *verb* **1** make (a sheet of material) by sticking together thin sheets. **2** cover with a thin sheet of material. **3** split or beat into thin sheets. ♦ *noun* **4** laminated sheet. **laminated** *adjective*

lamington *noun Aust & NZ* sponge cake coated with a sweet frosting.

Lammas *noun* August 1, formerly a harvest festival.

lamp *noun* device which produces light from electricity, oil, or gas. **lamppost** *noun* post supporting a lamp in the street. **lampshade** *noun*

lampoon ⊕ *noun* **1** humorous satire ridiculing someone. ♦ *verb* **2** satirize or ridicule.

lamprey *noun* eel-like fish with a round sucking mouth.

lance *noun* **1** long spear used by a mounted soldier. ♦ *verb* **2** pierce (a boil or abscess) with a lancet. **lancer** *noun* formerly, cavalry soldier armed with a lance. **lance corporal**

noncommissioned army officer of the lowest rank.

lanceolate *adjective* narrow and tapering to a point at each end.

lancet *noun* **1** pointed two-edged surgical knife. **2** narrow window in the shape of a pointed arch.

land ⊕ *noun* **1** solid part of the earth's surface. **2** ground, esp. with reference to its type or use. **3** rural or agricultural area. **4** property consisting of land. **5** country or region. ♦ *verb* **6** come or bring to earth after a flight, jump, or fall. **7** go or take from a ship at the end of a voyage. **8** come to or touch shore. **9** come or bring to some point or condition. **10** *Informal* obtain. **11** take (a hooked fish) from the water. **12** *Informal* deliver (a punch). **landed** *adjective* possessing or consisting of lands. **landless** *adjective* **landward** *adjective* **1** nearest to or facing the land. ♦ *adverb* **2** (also **landwards**) towards land. **landfall** *noun* ship's first landing after a voyage. **landfill** *noun* disposing of rubbish by covering it with earth. **landlocked** *adjective* completely surrounded by land. **landlord** *noun* person who rents out land, houses, etc. **landmark** *noun* prominent object in or feature of a landscape. **land mine** explosive device laid in the ground. **landscape** *noun* extensive piece of inland scenery seen from one place. **land up** *verb* arrive at a final point or condition.

landau [lan-daw] *noun* four-wheeled carriage with two folding hoods.

landing *noun* **1** floor area at the top of a flight of stairs. **2** bringing or coming to land. **3** (also **landing stage**) place where people or goods go onto or come off a boat. **landing gear** undercarriage of an aircraft.

landlord, landlady ⊕ *noun* **1** person who rents out land, houses, etc. **2** owner or manager of a pub or boarding house.

L

——————— THESAURUS ———————

lake[1] *noun* = **pond**, lagoon, loch (*Scot*), lough (*Irish*), mere, reservoir, tarn

lame *adjective* **1** = **disabled**, crippled, game, handicapped, hobbling, limping **2** = **unconvincing**, feeble, flimsy, inadequate, pathetic, poor, thin, unsatisfactory, weak

lament *verb* **1** = **bemoan**, bewail, complain, deplore, grieve, mourn, regret, sorrow, wail, weep ♦ *noun* **2** = **complaint**, lamentation, moan, wailing **3** = **dirge**, elegy, requiem, threnody

lamentable *adjective* = **regrettable**, deplorable, distressing, grievous, mournful, tragic, unfortunate, woeful

lampoon *noun* **1** = **satire**, burlesque, caricature, parody, send-up (*Brit inf*), skit, takeoff (*inf*) ♦ *verb* **2** = **ridicule**, caricature, make fun of, mock, parody, satirize, send up (*Brit inf*), take off (*inf*)

land *noun* **1** = **ground**, dry land, earth, terra firma **2** = **soil**, dirt, ground, loam **3** = **countryside**, farmland **4** = **property**, estate, grounds, realty, homestead (*US & Canad*) **5** = **country**, district, nation, province, region, territory, tract ♦ *verb* **6** = **alight**, arrive, come to rest, touch down **7** = **disembark 8** = **dock 10** *Inf* = **obtain**, acquire, gain, get, secure, win

landlord *noun* **1** = **owner**, freeholder, lessor,

landlubber *noun* person who is not experienced at sea.

landmark ❶ *noun* **1** prominent object in or feature of a landscape. **2** event, decision, etc. considered as an important development.

landscape ❶ *noun* **1** extensive piece of inland scenery seen from one place. **2** picture of it. ◆ *verb* **3** improve natural features of (a piece of land). **landscape gardener** person who designs gardens or parks so that they look attractive.

landslide ❶ *noun* **1** (also **landslip**) falling of soil, rock, etc. down the side of a mountain. **2** overwhelming electoral victory.

lane ❶ *noun* **1** narrow road. **2** area of road for one stream of traffic. **3** specified route followed by ships or aircraft. **4** strip of a running track or swimming pool for use by one competitor.

language ❶ *noun* **1** system of sounds, symbols, etc. for communicating thought. **2** particular system used by a nation or people. **3** style or method of expression. **4** specialized words used by a particular group. **5** (also **programming language**) system of words and symbols for computer programming.

languid ❶ *adjective* lacking energy or enthusiasm. **languidly** *adverb*

languish ❶ *verb* **1** suffer neglect or hardship. **2** lose or diminish in strength or vigour. **3** pine (for). **languishing** *adjective*

languor [lang-ger] *noun* **1** state of dreamy relaxation. **2** laziness or weariness. **languorous** *adjective*

lank ❶ *adjective* **1** (of hair) straight and limp. **2** thin or gaunt. **lanky** *adjective* ungracefully tall and thin. **lankiness** *noun*

lanolin *noun* grease from sheep's wool used in ointments etc.

lantern *noun* **1** light in a transparent protective case. **2** structure on top of a dome which lets in light. **3** upper part of a lighthouse that houses the light. **lantern jaw** long thin jaw. **lantern-jawed** *adjective*

lanthanum *noun Chem* silvery-white metallic element. **lanthanide series** class of 15 elements chemically related to lanthanum.

lanyard *noun* **1** cord worn round the neck to hold a knife or whistle. **2** *Naut* short rope.

lap¹ *noun* part between the waist and knees of a person when sitting. **in the lap of luxury** in conditions of great comfort and wealth. **laptop** *adjective* (of a computer) small enough to fit on a user's lap.

lap² ❶ *noun* **1** single circuit of a racecourse or track. **2** stage of a journey. ◆ *verb* **lapping, lapped 3** overtake an opponent so as to be one or more circuits ahead.

lap³ ❶ *verb* **lapping, lapped** (of waves) beat softly against (a shore etc.). **lap up** *verb* **1** drink by scooping up with the tongue. **2** accept (information or attention) eagerly.

lapel [lap-**pel**] *noun* part of the front of a coat or jacket folded back towards the shoulders.

lapidary *adjective* of or relating to stones.

lapis lazuli [lap-iss **lazz**-yoo-lie] *noun* bright blue gemstone.

Lapp *noun, adjective* (member or language) of a people living chiefly in N Scandinavia.

lapse ❶ *noun* **1** temporary drop in a standard, esp. through forgetfulness or carelessness. **2** instance of bad behaviour by someone usually well-behaved. **3** break in occurrence or usage. ◆ *verb* **4** drop in standard. **5** end or become invalid, esp. through disuse. **6** drift (into a condition or habit). **7** abandon religious faith. **8** (of time) slip away. **lapsed** *adjective*

———————————— T H E S A U R U S ————————————

proprietor **2 = innkeeper**, host, hotelier

landmark *noun* **1 = feature**, monument **2 = milestone**, turning point, watershed

landscape *noun* **1 = scenery**, countryside, outlook, panorama, prospect, scene, view, vista

landslide *noun* **1 = landslip**, avalanche, rockfall

land up *verb* **= end up**, turn up, wind up

lane *noun* **1 = road**, alley, footpath, passageway, path, pathway, street, way

language *noun* **1 = speech**, communication, discourse, expression, parlance, talk **2 = tongue**, dialect, patois, vernacular

languid *adjective* **a = lethargic**, dull, heavy, sluggish, torpid OPPOSITE> **energetic**. **b = lazy**, indifferent, lackadaisical, languorous, listless, unenthusiastic OPPOSITE> **energetic**

languish *verb* **1 = waste away**, be abandoned, be neglected, rot, suffer OPPOSITE> **thrive**. **2 = decline**, droop, fade, fail, faint, flag, weaken, wilt, wither OPPOSITE> **thrive**. **3 = pine**, desire, hanker, hunger, long, yearn

lank *adjective* **1 = limp**, lifeless, straggling **2 = thin**, emaciated, gaunt, lean, scrawny, skinny, slender, slim, spare

lanky *adjective* **= gangling**, angular, bony, gaunt, rangy, spare, tall OPPOSITE> **chubby**

lap² *noun* **1 = circuit**, circle, loop, orbit, tour

lap³ *verb* **= ripple**, gurgle, plash, purl, splash, swish, wash **lap up 1 = drink**, lick, sip, sup

lapse *noun* **1 = mistake**, error, failing, fault, negligence, omission, oversight, slip **2 = indescretion 3 = interval**, break, breathing space, gap, intermission, interruption, lull,

lapwing *noun* plover with a tuft of feathers on the head.

larboard *adjective, noun Old-fashioned* port (side of a ship).

larceny *noun, pl* **-nies** *Law* theft.

larch *noun* deciduous coniferous tree.

lard *noun* **1** soft white fat obtained from a pig. ◆ *verb* **2** insert strips of bacon in (meat) before cooking. **3** decorate (speech or writing) with strange words unnecessarily.

larder *noun* storeroom for food.

large ⊕ *adjective* **1** great in size, number, or extent. **2** comprehensive. **at large 1** in general. **2** free, not confined. **3** fully. **largely** *adverb* **largish** *adjective* **large-scale** *adjective* wide-ranging or extensive.

largesse, largess [lar-**jess**] *noun* generous giving, esp. of money.

largo *noun, pl* **-gos**, *adverb Music* (piece to be played) in a slow and dignified manner.

lariat *noun* **1** *US & Canad* another word for LASSO. **2** rope for tethering animals.

lark¹ *noun* small brown songbird, skylark.

lark² ⊕ *noun Informal* **1** harmless piece of mischief or fun. **2** unnecessary activity or job. **lark about** *verb* play pranks.

larkspur *noun* plant with spikes of blue, pink, or white flowers with spurs.

larrikin *noun Aust or NZ old-fashioned slang* mischievous or unruly person.

larva *noun, pl* **-vae** insect in an immature stage, often resembling a worm. **larval** *adjective*

larynx *noun, pl* **larynges** part of the throat containing the vocal cords. **laryngeal** *adjective* **laryngitis** *noun* inflammation of the larynx.

lasagne, lasagna [laz-**zan**-ya] *noun* **1** pasta in wide flat sheets. **2** dish made from layers of lasagne, meat, and cheese.

lascivious [lass-**iv**-ee-uss] *adjective* showing or producing sexual desire. **lasciviously** *adverb*

laser [**lay**-zer] *noun* device that produces a very narrow intense beam of light, used for cutting very hard materials and in surgery etc.

lash¹ ⊕ *noun* **1** eyelash. **2** sharp blow with a whip. **3** flexible end of a whip. ◆ *verb* **4** hit with a whip. **5** (of rain or waves) beat forcefully against. **6** attack verbally, scold. **7** flick or wave sharply to and fro. **8** urge as with a whip. **lash out** *verb* **1** make a sudden physical or verbal attack. **2** *Informal* spend (money) extravagantly.

lash² ⊕ *verb* fasten or bind tightly with cord etc.

lashings *plural noun Old-fashioned* large amounts.

lass, lassie ⊕ *noun* girl.

Lassa fever *noun* serious African disease with high fever and muscular pains.

lassitude *noun* physical or mental weariness.

lasso [lass-**oo**] *noun, pl* **-sos, -soes 1** rope with a noose for catching cattle and horses. ◆ *verb* **-soing, -soed 2** catch with a lasso.

last¹ ⊕ *adjective, adverb* **1** coming at the end or after all others. **2** most recent(ly). ◆ *adjective* **3** only remaining. ◆ *noun* **4** last person or thing. **lastly** *adverb* **last-ditch** *adjective* done as a final resort. **Last Judgment** God's verdict on the destinies of all humans at the end of the world. **last post** army bugle-call played at sunset or funerals. **last straw** small irritation or setback that, coming after others, is too much to bear. **last word 1** final comment in an argument. **2** most recent or best example of something.

last² ⊕ *verb* **1** continue. **2** be sufficient for (a specified amount of time). **3** remain fresh, uninjured, or unaltered. **lasting** *adjective*

last³ *noun* model of a foot on which shoes and boots are made or repaired.

L

——————————— THESAURUS ———————————

pause ◆*verb* **4 = drop**, decline, degenerate, deteriorate, fall, sink, slide, slip **5 = end**, expire, run out, stop, terminate

lapsed *adjective* **5 = expired**, discontinued, ended, finished, invalid, out of date, run out

large *adjective* **1 = big**, considerable, enormous, gigantic, great, huge, immense, massive, monumental, sizable *or* sizeable, substantial, vast OPPOSITE little ◆ **at large 1 = in general**, as a whole, chiefly, generally, in the main, mainly **2 = free**, at liberty, on the loose, on the run, unconfined **3 = fully**, at length, exhaustively, greatly, in full detail

largely *adverb* **= mainly**, as a rule, by and large, chiefly, generally, mostly, predominantly, primarily, principally, to a great extent

large-scale *adjective* **= wide-ranging**, broad, extensive, far-reaching, global, sweeping, vast, wholesale, wide

lark² *Inf noun* **1 = prank**, caper, escapade, fun, game, jape, mischief **lark about** ◆*verb* **= play**, caper, cavort, have fun, make mischief

lash¹ *noun* **2 = blow**, hit, stripe, stroke, swipe (*inf*) ◆*verb* **4 = whip**, beat, birch, flog, scourge, thrash **5 = pound**, beat, buffet, dash, drum, hammer, smack, strike **6 = censure**, attack, blast, criticize, put down, rouse on (*Aust*), scold, slate (*inf, chiefly Brit*), tear into (*inf*), upbraid

lash² *verb* **= fasten**, bind, make fast, secure, strap, tie

lass, lassie *noun* **= girl**, damsel, maid, maiden, young woman

lat. latitude.

latch ❶ *noun* **1** fastening for a door with a bar and lever. **2** lock which can only be opened from the outside with a key. ◆ *verb* **3** fasten with a latch. **latch onto** *verb* become attached to (a person or idea).

late ❶ *adjective* **1** after the normal or expected time. **2** towards the end of a period. **3** being at an advanced time. **4** recently dead. **5** recent. **6** former. ◆ *adverb* **7** after the normal or expected time. **8** at a relatively advanced age. **9** recently. **lately** *adverb* in recent times. **lateness** *noun* **latish** *adjective, adverb* **latecomer** *noun*

latent ❶ *adjective* hidden and not yet developed. **latency** *noun*

lateral ❶ [lat-ter-al] *adjective* of or relating to the side or sides. **laterally** *adverb* **lateral thinking** way of solving problems by apparently illogical methods.

latex *noun* milky fluid found in some plants, esp. the rubber tree, used in making rubber.

lath *noun* thin strip of wood used to support plaster, tiles, etc.

lathe *noun* machine for turning wood or metal while it is being shaped.

lather ❶ *noun* **1** froth of soap and water. **2** frothy sweat. **3** *Informal* state of agitation. ◆ *verb* **4** make frothy. **5** rub with soap until lather appears.

Latin *noun* **1** language of the ancient Romans. ◆ *adjective* **2** of or in Latin. **3** of a people whose language derives from Latin. **4** of the Roman Catholic Church. **Latin America** parts of South and Central America whose official language is Spanish or Portuguese. **Latin American** *noun, adjective*

latitude ❶ *noun* **1** angular distance measured in degrees N or S of the equator. **2** scope for freedom of action or thought. ◆ *plural* **3** regions considered in relation to their distance from the equator. **latitudinal** *adjective*

latrine *noun* toilet in a barracks or camp.

latter ❶ *adjective* **1** second of two. **2** later. **3** recent. **latterly** *adverb* **latter-day** *adjective* modern.

> **LANGUAGE TIP**
>
> *Latter* is used for the last mentioned of two items. When there are more, use *last-named*.

lattice ❶ [lat-iss] *noun* **1** framework of intersecting strips of wood, metal, etc. **2** gate, screen, etc. formed of such a framework. **latticed** *adjective*

laud ❶ *verb* praise or glorify. **laudable** *adjective* praiseworthy. **laudably** *adverb* **laudatory** *adjective* praising or glorifying.

laudanum [lawd-a-num] *noun* opium-based

——————— T H E S A U R U S ———————

last¹ *adjective* **1 = final**, at the end, closing, concluding, hindmost, rearmost, terminal, ultimate OPPOSITE **first**. **2 = most recent**, latest

last² *verb* **1 = continue**, abide, carry on, endure, keep on, persist, remain OPPOSITE **end**. **3 = survive**, stand up

lasting *adjective* **1, 3 = continuing**, abiding, durable, enduring, long-standing, long-term, perennial, permanent OPPOSITE **passing**

latch *noun* **1 = fastening**, bar, bolt, catch, hasp, hook, lock ◆*verb* **3 = fasten**, bar, bolt, make fast, secure

late *adjective* **1 = overdue**, behind, behindhand, belated, delayed, last-minute, tardy OPPOSITE **early**. **4 = dead**, deceased, defunct, departed, former, past OPPOSITE **alive**. **5 = recent**, advanced, fresh, modern, new OPPOSITE **old** ◆*adverb* **7 = belatedly**, at the last minute, behindhand, behind time, dilatorily, tardily OPPOSITE **early**

lately *adverb* **= recently**, in recent times, just now, latterly, not long ago, of late

lateness *noun* **1 = delay**, belatedness, tardiness

latent *adjective* **= hidden**, concealed, dormant,

invisible, potential, undeveloped, unrealized OPPOSITE **obvious**

later *adverb* **7 = afterwards**, after, by and by, in a while, in time, later on, subsequently, thereafter

lateral *adjective* **= sideways**, edgeways, flanking

latest *adjective* **5 = up-to-date**, current, fashionable, modern, most recent, newest, up-to-the-minute

lather *noun* **1 = froth**, bubbles, foam, soapsuds, suds **3** *Inf* **= fluster**, dither, flap (*inf*), fuss, state (*inf*), sweat, tizzy (*inf*) ◆*verb* **4 = froth**, foam **5 = soap**

latitude *noun* **2 = scope**, elbowroom, freedom, laxity, leeway, liberty, licence, play, space

latter *adjective* **1 = second 2 = later**, closing, concluding, last, last-mentioned OPPOSITE **earlier**

latterly *adverb* **3 = recently**, lately, of late

lattice *noun* **= grid**, grating, grille, trellis

laudable *adjective* **= praiseworthy**, admirable, commendable, creditable, excellent, meritorious, of note, worthy OPPOSITE sedative.

laugh ❶ *verb* **1** make inarticulate sounds with the voice expressing amusement, merriment, or scorn. **2** utter or express with laughter. ◆ *noun* **3** act or instance of laughing. **4** *Informal* person or thing causing amusement. **laughable** *adjective* ridiculously inadequate. **laughter** *noun* sound or action of laughing. **laughing gas** nitrous oxide as an anaesthetic. **laughing stock** object of general derision. **laugh off** *verb* treat (something serious or difficult) lightly.

launch[1] ❶ *verb* **1** put (a ship or boat) into the water, esp. for the first time. **2** begin (a campaign, project, etc.). **3** put a new product on the market. **4** send (a missile or spacecraft) into space or the air. ◆ *noun* **5** launching. **launcher** *noun* **launch into** *verb* start doing something enthusiastically. **launch out** *verb* start doing something new.

launch[2] *noun* open motorboat.

launder *verb* **1** wash and iron (clothes and linen). **2** make (illegally obtained money) seem legal by passing it through foreign banks or legitimate businesses. **laundry** *noun, pl* **-dries 1** clothes etc. for washing or which have recently been washed. **2** place for washing clothes and linen. **Launderette** *noun* ® shop with coin-operated washing and drying machines.

laureate [lor-ee-at] *adjective* see POET LAUREATE.

laurel *noun* **1** glossy-leaved shrub, bay tree. ◆ *plural* **2** wreath of laurel, an emblem of victory or merit.

lava *noun* molten rock thrown out by volcanoes, which hardens as it cools.

lavatory ❶ *noun, pl* **-ries** toilet.

lavender *noun* **1** shrub with fragrant flowers. ◆ *adjective* **2** bluish-purple. **lavender water** light perfume made from lavender.

lavish ❶ *adjective* **1** great in quantity or richness. **2** giving or spending generously. **3** extravagant. ◆ *verb* **4** give or spend generously. **lavishly** *adverb*

law ❶ *noun* **1** rule binding on a community. **2** system of such rules. **3** *Informal* police. **4** invariable sequence of events in nature. **5** general principle deduced from facts. **lawful** *adjective* allowed by law. **lawfully** *adverb* **lawless** *adjective* breaking the law, esp. in a violent way. **lawlessness** *noun* **law-abiding** *adjective* obeying the laws. **law-breaker** *noun* **Law Lords** members of the House of Lords who sit as the highest court of appeal. **lawsuit** *noun* court case brought by one person or group against another.

lawn[1] *noun* area of tended and mown grass. **lawn mower** machine for cutting grass. **lawn tennis** tennis, esp. when played on a grass court.

——————— T H E S A U R U S ———————

blameworthy

laugh *verb* **1** = **chuckle**, be in stitches, chortle, giggle, guffaw, snigger, split one's sides, titter ◆*noun* **3** = **chuckle**, chortle, giggle, guffaw, snigger, titter **4** *Inf* **a** = **clown**, card (*inf*), entertainer, hoot (*inf*), scream (*inf*) **b** = **joke**, hoot (*inf*), lark

laughable *adjective* = **ridiculous**, absurd, derisory, farcical, ludicrous, nonsensical, preposterous, risible

laughing stock *noun* = **figure of fun**, Aunt Sally (*Brit*), butt, target, victim

laugh off *verb* = **disregard**, brush aside, dismiss, ignore, minimize, pooh-pooh, shrug off

laughter *noun* = **amusement**, glee, hilarity, merriment, mirth

launch[1] *verb* **2** = **begin**, commence, embark upon, inaugurate, initiate, instigate, introduce, open, start **4** = **propel**, discharge, dispatch, fire, project, send off, set in motion

laurels *plural noun* **2** = **glory**, credit, distinction, fame, honour, praise, prestige, recognition, renown

lavatory *noun* = **toilet**, bathroom, cloakroom (*Brit*), latrine, loo (*Brit inf*), powder room, privy, (public) convenience, washroom, water closet,

W.C.

lavish *adjective* **1** = **plentiful**, abundant, copious, profuse, prolific OPPOSITE meagre. **2** = **generous**, bountiful, free, liberal, munificent, open-handed, unstinting OPPOSITE stingy. **3** = **extravagant**, exaggerated, excessive, immoderate, prodigal, unrestrained, wasteful, wild OPPOSITE sparing ◆*verb* **4** = **spend**, deluge, dissipate, expend, heap, pour, shower, squander, waste OPPOSITE stint/lawful

law *noun* **1** = **rule**, act, command, commandment, decree, edict, order, ordinance, regulation, statute **2** = **constitution**, charter, code **5** = **principle**, axiom, canon, precept

law-abiding *adjective* = **obedient**, compliant, dutiful, good, honest, honourable, lawful, orderly, peaceable

law-breaker *noun* = **criminal**, convict, crook (*inf*), culprit, delinquent, felon (*formerly criminal law*), miscreant, offender, villain, wrongdoer

lawful *adjective* = **legal**, authorized, constitutional, legalized, legitimate, licit, permissible, rightful, valid, warranted OPPOSITE unlawful

lawless *adjective* = **disorderly**, anarchic, chaotic, rebellious, riotous, unruly, wild

lawn² *noun* fine linen or cotton fabric.
lawrencium *noun Chem* element artificially produced from californium.
lawyer **⊕** *noun* professionally qualified legal expert.
lax **⊕** *adjective* not strict. **laxity** *noun*
laxative *noun, adjective* (medicine) inducing the emptying of the bowels.
lay¹ **⊕** *verb* **laying, laid 1** cause to lie, e.g. *Mary laid a clean towel carefully on the grass.* **2** devise or prepare, e.g. *she would lay her plans.* **3** set in a particular place or position, e.g. *he laid a wreath at the graveside.* **4** attribute (blame). **5** put forward (a plan, argument, etc.). **6** (of a bird or reptile) produce eggs. **7** place (a bet), e.g. *I'll lay money he's already gone home.* **8** arrange (a table) for a meal. **lay aside** *verb* **1** abandon or reject. **2** put aside (one thing) in order to take up another. **3** store for future use. **lay bare** reveal or explain: *a century of neurophysiology has laid bare the structure of the brain.* **lay-by** *noun* stopping place for traffic beside a road. **lay down** *verb* **1** set down. **2** sacrifice. **3** formulate (a rule). **4** store (wine). **lay hold of** seize or grasp. **lay in** *verb* accumulate and store. **lay into** *verb Informal* attack or scold severely. **lay off** *verb* dismiss staff during a slack period. **lay-off** *noun* **lay on** *verb* provide or supply. **lay oneself open** make oneself vulnerable (to criticism or attack). **lay open** reveal or disclose. **lay out** *verb* **1** arrange or spread out. **2** prepare (a corpse) for burial. **3** *Informal* spend money, esp. lavishly. **4** *Informal* knock unconscious. **layout** *noun* arrangement, esp. of matter for printing or of a building.
lay up *verb* **1** *Informal* confine through illness. **2** store for future use. **lay waste** devastate.
lay² **⊕** *verb* past tense of LIE². **layabout** *noun* lazy person.
lay³ **⊕** *adjective* **1** of or involving people who are not clergymen. **2** nonspecialist. **layman, laywoman** *noun* **1** person who is not a member of the clergy. **2** person without specialist knowledge.
lay⁴ **⊕** *noun* short narrative poem designed to be sung.
layer **⊕** *noun* **1** single thickness of some substance, as a cover or coating on a surface. **2** laying hen. **3** shoot of a plant pegged down or partly covered with earth to encourage root growth. ◆ *verb* **4** form a layer. **5** propagate plants by layers. **layered** *adjective*
layette *noun* clothes for a newborn baby.
laze *verb* **1** be idle or lazy. ◆ *noun* **2** time spent lazing.
lazy **⊕** *adjective* **lazier, laziest 1** not inclined to work or exert oneself. **2** done in a relaxed manner without much effort. **3** (of movement) slow and gentle. **lazily** *adverb* **laziness** *noun* **lazybones** *noun Informal* lazy person.
lb pound (weight).

———————— T H E S A U R U S ————————

OPPOSITE> **law-abiding**
lawsuit *noun* =**case**, action, dispute, industrial tribunal, litigation, proceedings, prosecution, suit, trial
lawyer *noun* =**legal adviser**, advocate, attorney, barrister, counsel, counsellor, solicitor
lax *adjective* =**slack**, careless, casual, lenient, negligent, overindulgent, remiss, slapdash, slipshod OPPOSITE> **severe**
lay¹ *verb* **1, 3** =**place**, deposit, leave, plant, position, put, set, set down, spread **2** =**devise**, concoct, contrive, design, hatch, plan, plot, prepare, work out **4** =**attribute**, allocate, allot, ascribe, assign, impute **5** =**put forward**, advance, bring forward, lodge, offer, present, submit **6** =**produce**, bear, deposit **7** =**bet**, gamble, give odds, hazard, risk, stake, wager **8** =**arrange**, organize, set out
lay³ *adjective* **1** =**nonclerical**, secular **2** =**nonspecialist**, amateur, inexpert, nonprofessional
lay⁴ *noun* =**poem**, ballad, lyric, ode, song
layabout *noun* =**idler**, couch potato (*sl*), good-for-nothing, loafer, lounger, ne'er-do-well,
skiver (*Brit sl*), wastrel
layer *noun* **1** =**tier**, row, seam, stratum, thickness
layman, laywoman *noun* **2** =**nonprofessional**, amateur, lay person, outsider
lay off *verb* =**dismiss**, discharge, let go, make redundant, pay off
lay-off *noun* =**unemployment**, discharge, dismissal
lay on *verb* =**provide**, cater (for), furnish, give, purvey, supply
layout *noun* =**arrangement**, design, format, formation, outline, plan
lay out *verb* **1** =**arrange**, design, display, exhibit, plan, spread out **3** *Inf* =**spend**, disburse, expend, fork out (*sl*), invest, pay, shell out (*inf*) **4** *Inf* =**knock out**, knock for six (*inf*), knock unconscious, KO *or* K.O. (*sl*)
lazy *adjective* **1** =**idle**, inactive, indolent, inert, slack, slothful, slow, workshy OPPOSITE> **industrious**. **3** =**lethargic**, drowsy, languid, languorous, sleepy, slow-moving, sluggish, somnolent, torpid OPPOSITE> **quick**

lbw *Cricket* leg before wicket.
lea *noun Poetic* meadow.
leach ⊙ *verb* remove or be removed from a substance by a liquid passing through it.
lead¹ ⊙ *verb* **leading, led 1** guide or conduct. **2** cause to feel, think, or behave in a certain way. **3** be the most important person or thing in. **4** be, go, or play first. **5** (of a road, path, etc.) go towards. **6** control or direct. **7** (foll. by *to*) result in. **8** pass or spend (one's life). ◆ *noun* **9** first or most prominent place. **10** example or leadership. **11** amount by which a person or group is ahead of another. **12** clue. **13** length of leather or chain attached to a dog's collar to control it. **14** principal role or actor in a film, play, etc. **15** most important news story in a newspaper. **16** cable bringing current to an electrical device. ◆ *adjective* **17** acting as a leader or lead. **leader** *noun* person who leads. **leading** *adjective* **1** principal. **2** in the first position. **leading light** important person in an organization. **leading question** question worded to prompt the answer desired. **lead-in** *noun* introduction to a subject. **lead on** *verb* lure or entice, esp. into wrongdoing. **lead up to** *verb* act as a preliminary to.
lead² *noun* **1** soft heavy grey metal. **2** (in a pencil) graphite. **3** lead weight on a line, used for sounding depths of water. ◆ *plural* **4** strips of lead used as a roof covering. ◆ *verb* **5** cover or secure with lead. **leaded** *adjective* (of windows) made from many small panes of glass held together by lead strips. **leaden** *adjective* **1** heavy or sluggish. **2** dull grey. **3** made from lead.
leader ⊙ *noun* **1** person who leads. **2** (also **leading article**) article in a newspaper expressing editorial views. **3** principal first violinist of an orchestra. **leadership** *noun*
leaf ⊙ *noun, pl* **leaves 1** flat usu. green blade attached to the stem of a plant. **2** single sheet of paper in a book. **3** very thin sheet of metal. **4** extending flap on a table. **leafy** *adjective* **leafless** *adjective* **leaf mould** rich soil composed of decayed leaves. **leaf through** *verb* turn pages without reading them.
leaflet ⊙ *noun* **1** sheet of printed matter for distribution. **2** small leaf.
league¹ ⊙ *noun* **1** association promoting the interests of its members. **2** association of sports clubs organizing competitions between its members. **3** *Informal* class or level.
league² *noun Obs* measure of distance, about three miles.
leak ⊙ *noun* **1** hole or defect that allows the escape or entrance of liquid, gas, radiation, etc. **2** liquid etc. that escapes or enters. **3** disclosure of secrets. ◆ *verb* **4** let liquid etc. in or out. **5** (of liquid etc.) find its way through a leak. **6** disclose secret information. **leakage** *noun* act or instance of leaking. **leaky** *adjective*
lean¹ ⊙ *verb* **leaning, leaned** *or* **leant 1** rest

leach *verb* =**extract**, drain, filter, percolate, seep, strain
lead¹ *verb* **1** =**guide**, conduct, escort, pilot, precede, show the way, steer, usher **2** =**cause**, dispose, draw, incline, induce, influence, persuade, prevail, prompt **3** =**command**, direct, govern, head, manage, preside over, supervise **4** =**be ahead (of)**, blaze a trail, come first, exceed, excel, outdo, outstrip, surpass, transcend **7** (foll. by *to*) =**result in**, bring on, cause, contribute to, produce **8** =**live**, experience, have, pass, spend, undergo ◆*noun* **9** =**first place**, precedence, primacy, priority, supremacy, vanguard **10** =**example**, direction, guidance, leadership, model **11** =**advantage**, edge, margin, start **12** =**clue**, hint, indication, suggestion **14** =**leading role**, principal, protagonist, title role ◆*adjective* **17** =**main**, chief, first, foremost, head, leading, premier, primary, prime, principal
leader *noun* **1** =**principal**, boss (*inf*), captain, chief, chieftain, commander, director, guide, head, ringleader, ruler OPPOSITE **follower**
leadership *noun* **1** =**authority**, command, control, direction, domination, guidance, influence, initiative, mana (*NZ*), management, pre-eminence, running, superintendency, supremacy
leading *adjective* **1** =**principal**, chief, dominant, first, foremost, greatest, highest, main, primary OPPOSITE **minor**
lead on *verb* =**entice**, beguile, deceive, draw on, lure, seduce, string along (*inf*), tempt
lead up to *verb* =**introduce**, pave the way, prepare for
leaf *noun* **1** =**frond**, blade **2** =**page**, folio, sheet **leaf through** ◆*verb* =**skim**, browse, flip, glance, riffle, thumb (through)
leaflet *noun* **1** =**booklet**, brochure, circular, pamphlet
league¹ *noun* **1** =**association**, alliance, coalition, confederation, consortium, federation, fraternity, group, guild, partnership, union **3** *Inf* =**class**, category, level
leak *noun* **1** =**hole**, aperture, chink, crack, crevice, fissure, opening, puncture **2** =**leakage**, drip, percolation, seepage **3** =**disclosure**, divulgence ◆*verb* **5** =**escape**, drip, exude, ooze,

against. **2** bend or slope from an upright position. **3** tend (towards). **leaning** *noun* tendency. **lean on** *verb* **1** *Informal* threaten or intimidate. **2** depend on for help or advice. **lean-to** *noun* shed built against an existing wall.

lean² ❶ *adjective* **1** thin but healthy-looking. **2** (of meat) lacking fat. **3** unproductive. ◆ *noun* **4** lean part of meat. **leanness** *noun*

leap ❶ *verb* **leaping, leapt** *or* **leaped 1** make a sudden powerful jump. ◆ *noun* **2** sudden powerful jump. **3** abrupt increase, as in costs or prices. **leapfrog** *noun* game in which a player vaults over another bending down. **leap year** year with February 29th as an extra day.

learn ❶ *verb* **learning, learned** *or* **learnt 1** gain skill or knowledge by study, practice, or teaching. **2** memorize (something). **3** find out or discover. **learned** *adjective* **1** erudite, deeply read. **2** showing much learning. **learner** *noun* **learning** *noun* knowledge got by study.

lease ❶ *noun* **1** contract by which land or property is rented for a stated time by the owner to a tenant. ◆ *verb* **2** let or rent by lease. **new lease of life** prospect of renewed energy, health, or happiness. **leasehold** *noun, adjective* (land or property) held on lease. **leaseholder**

noun

leash ❶ *noun* lead for a dog.

least ❶ *adjective* **1** superlative of LITTLE. **2** smallest. ◆ *noun* **3** smallest one. ◆ *adverb* **4** in the smallest degree.

leather ❶ *noun* **1** material made from specially treated animal skins. ◆ *adjective* **2** made of leather. ◆ *verb* **3** beat or thrash. **leathery** *adjective* like leather, tough.

leave¹ ❶ *verb* **leaving, left 1** go away from. **2** allow to remain, accidentally or deliberately. **3** cause to be or remain in a specified state. **4** discontinue membership of. **5** permit. **6** entrust. **7** bequeath. **leavings** *plural noun* something remaining, such as refuse. **leave out** *verb* exclude or omit.

leave² ❶ *noun* **1** permission to be absent from work or duty. **2** period of such absence. **3** permission to do something. **4** formal parting. **leaven** [lev-ven] *noun* **1** substance that causes dough to rise. **2** influence that produces a gradual change. ◆ *verb* **3** raise with leaven. **4** spread through and influence (something).

lecherous ❶ [letch-er-uss] *adjective* (of a man) having or showing excessive sexual desire. **lecher** *noun* **lechery** *noun*

lectern *noun* sloping reading desk, esp. in a

pass, percolate, seep, spill, trickle **6 = disclose**, divulge, give away, let slip, make known, make public, pass on, reveal, tell

leaky *adjective* **1 = leaking**, cracked, holey, perforated, porous, punctured, split

lean¹ *verb* **1 = rest**, be supported, prop, recline, repose **2 = bend**, heel, incline, slant, slope, tilt, tip **3 = tend**, be disposed to, be prone to, favour, prefer **lean on 2 = depend on**, count on, have faith in, rely on, trust

lean² *adjective* **1 = trim**, angular, bony, rangy, skinny, slender, slim, spare, thin, wiry OPPOSITE fat. **3 = poor**, barren, meagre, scanty, unfruitful, unproductive OPPOSITE rich

leaning *noun* **= tendency**, bent, bias, disposition, inclination, partiality, penchant, predilection, proclivity, propensity

leap *verb* **1 = jump**, bounce, bound, hop, skip, spring ◆*noun* **2 = jump**, bound, spring, vault **3 = rise**, change, escalation, increase, surge, upsurge, upswing

learn *verb* **1 = master**, grasp, pick up **2 = memorize**, commit to memory, get off pat, learn by heart **3 = discover**, ascertain, detect, discern, find out, gather, hear, understand

learned *adjective* **= scholarly**, academic, erudite, highbrow, intellectual, versed, well-informed, well-read OPPOSITE **uneducated**

learner *noun* **1 = beginner**, apprentice, neophyte, novice, tyro OPPOSITE **expert**

learning *noun* **= knowledge**, culture, education, erudition, information, lore, scholarship, study, wisdom

lease *verb* **2 = hire**, charter, let, loan, rent

leash *noun* **= lead**, rein, tether

least *adjective* **1, 2 = smallest**, fewest, lowest, meanest, minimum, poorest, slightest, tiniest

leathery *adjective* **= tough**, hard, rough

leave¹ *verb* **1 = depart**, decamp, disappear, exit, go, go away, make tracks, move, pull out, quit, retire, slope off, withdraw OPPOSITE arrive. **2 = forget**, leave behind, mislay **3 = cause**, deposit, generate, produce, result in **4 = give up**, abandon, drop, relinquish, renounce, surrender OPPOSITE **stay with**. **6 = entrust**, allot, assign, cede, commit, consign, give over, refer **7 = bequeath**, hand down, will

leave² *noun* **1, 2 = holiday**, furlough, leave of absence, sabbatical, time off, vacation **3 = permission**, allowance, authorization, concession, consent, dispensation, freedom, liberty, sanction OPPOSITE **refusal**. **4 = departure**, adieu, farewell, goodbye, leave-taking, parting, retirement, withdrawal OPPOSITE **arrival**

leave out *verb* **= omit**, cast aside, disregard,

church.

lecture ⊕ *noun* **1** informative talk to an audience on a subject. **2** lengthy rebuke or scolding. ♦ *verb* **3** give a talk. **4** scold. **lecturer** *noun* **lectureship** *noun* appointment as a lecturer.

led *verb* past of LEAD¹.

LED light-emitting diode.

ledge ⊕ *noun* **1** narrow shelf sticking out from a wall. **2** shelflike projection from a cliff etc.

ledger *noun* book of debit and credit accounts of a firm. **ledger line** *Music* short line above or below the staff for notes outside the range of the staff.

lee ⊕ *noun* **1** sheltered part or side. ♦ *adjective* **2** away from the wind. **leeward** *adjective, noun* **1** (on) the lee side. ♦ *adverb* **2** towards this side. **leeway** *noun* **1** room for free movement within limits. **2** sideways drift of a boat or plane.

leech *noun* **1** species of bloodsucking worm. **2** person who lives off others.

leek *noun* vegetable of the onion family with a long bulb and thick stem.

leer ⊕ *verb* **1** look or grin at in a sneering or suggestive manner. ♦ *noun* **2** sneering or suggestive look or grin.

leery *adjective Informal* suspicious or wary (of).

lees ⊕ *plural noun* sediment of wine.

left¹ ⊕ *adjective* **1** of the side that faces west when the front faces north. ♦ *adverb* **2** on or towards the left. ♦ *noun* **3** left hand or part. **4** *Politics* people supporting socialism rather than capitalism. **leftist** *noun, adjective* (person) of the political left. **left-handed** *adjective* **1** more

adept with the left hand than with the right. **2** done with the left hand. **3** designed for use by the left hand. **left-wing** *adjective* **1** socialist. **2** belonging to the more radical part of a political party. **left-winger** *noun*

left² *verb* past of LEAVE¹.

leftover ⊕ *noun* unused portion of food or material.

leg ⊕ *noun* **1** one of the limbs on which a person or animal walks, runs, or stands. **2** part of a garment covering the leg. **3** structure that supports, such as one of the legs of a table. **4** stage of a journey. **5** *Sport* (part of) one game or race in a series. **6** *Cricket* part of the field to the left of a right-handed batsman. **pull someone's leg** tease someone. **leggy** *adjective* having long legs. **legless** *adjective* **1** without legs. **2** *Slang* very drunk. **leggings** *plural noun* **1** covering of leather or other material for the legs. **2** close-fitting trousers for women or children.

legacy ⊕ *noun, pl* **-cies 1** thing left in a will. **2** thing handed down to a successor.

legal ⊕ *adjective* **1** established or permitted by law. **2** relating to law or lawyers. **legally** *adverb* **legalistic** *adjective* showing strict adherence to the letter of the law. **legality** *noun* **legalize** *verb* make legal. **legalization** *noun*

legate *noun* messenger or representative, esp. from the Pope. **legation** *noun* **1** diplomatic minister and his staff. **2** official residence of a diplomatic minister.

legatee *noun* recipient of a legacy.

legato [leg-**ah**-toe] *noun, pl* **-tos**, *adverb Music*

L

--- THESAURUS ---

exclude, ignore, neglect, overlook, reject

lecherous *adjective* =**lustful**, lascivious, lewd, libidinous, licentious, prurient, randy (*inf, chiefly Brit*), salacious OPPOSITE **puritanical**

lecture *noun* **1** =**talk**, address, discourse, instruction, lesson, speech **2** =**telling off**, dressing-down (*inf*), rebuke, reprimand, reproof, scolding, talking-to (*inf*) (*inf*) ♦*verb* **3** =**talk**, address, discourse, expound, hold forth, speak, spout, teach **4** =**tell off**, admonish, berate, castigate, censure, reprimand, reprove, rouse on (*Aust*), scold (*inf*)

ledge *noun* **1** =**shelf**, mantle, projection, sill **2** =**ridge**, step

leer *noun, verb* =**grin**, gloat, goggle, ogle, smirk, squint, stare

lees *plural noun* =**sediment**, deposit, dregs, grounds

leeway *noun* **1** =**room**, elbowroom, latitude, margin, play, scope, space

left¹ *adjective* **1** =**left-hand**, larboard (*Naut*),

port

leftover *noun* =**remnant**, oddment, scrap

left-wing *adjective* **1** =**socialist**, communist, left, leftist, radical, red (*inf*)

leg *noun* **1** =**limb**, lower limb, member, pin (*inf*), stump (*inf*) **3** =**support**, brace, prop, upright **4** =**stage**, lap, part, portion, section, segment, stretch **pull someone's leg** =**tease**, fool, kid (*inf*), make fun of, trick, wind up (*Brit sl*)

legacy *noun* =**bequest**, estate, gift, heirloom, inheritance

legal *adjective* **1** =**lawful**, allowed, authorized, constitutional, legitimate, licit, permissible, sanctioned, valid **2** =**judicial**, forensic, judiciary, juridical

legality *noun* =**lawfulness**, legitimacy, rightfulness, validity

legalize *verb* =**permit**, allow, approve, authorize, decriminalize, legitimate, legitimize, license, sanction, validate (piece to be played) smoothly.

legend ⊕ *noun* **1** traditional story or myth. **2** traditional literature. **3** famous person or event. **4** stories about such a person or event. **5** inscription. **6** explanation of symbols on a map etc. **legendary** *adjective* **1** famous. **2** of or in legend.

legerdemain [lej-er-de-**main**] *noun* **1** sleight of hand. **2** cunning deception.

legible ⊕ *adjective* easily read. **legibility** *noun* **legibly** *adverb*

legion ⊕ *noun* **1** large military force. **2** large number. **3** association of veterans. **4** infantry unit in the Roman army. **legionary** *adjective*, *noun* **legionnaire** *noun* member of a legion. **legionnaire's disease** serious bacterial disease similar to pneumonia.

legislate ⊕ *verb* make laws. **legislation** *noun* **1** legislating. **2** laws made. **legislative** *adjective* **legislator** *noun* maker of laws. **legislature** *noun* body of people that makes, amends, or repeals laws.

legitimate ⊕ *adjective* **1** authorized by or in accordance with law. **2** fairly deduced. **3** born to parents married to each other. ◆ *verb* **4** make legitimate. **legitimacy** *noun* **legitimately** *adverb* **legitimize** *verb* make legitimate, legalize. **legitimization** *noun*

Lego *noun* ® construction toy of plastic bricks fitted together by studs.

leguaan *noun* large S African lizard.

legume *noun* **1** pod of a plant of the pea or bean family. ◆ *plural* **2** peas or beans. **leguminous** *adjective* (of plants) pod-bearing.

lei *noun* (in Hawaii) garland of flowers.

leisure ⊕ *noun* time for relaxation or hobbies. **at one's leisure** when one has time. **leisurely** *adjective* **1** deliberate, unhurried. ◆ *adverb* **2** slowly. **leisured** *adjective* with plenty of spare time. **leisure centre** building with facilities such as a swimming pool, gymnasium, and café.

leitmotif [**lite**-mote-eef] *noun Music* recurring theme associated with a person, situation, or thought.

lekker *adjective S Afr slang* **1** attractive or nice. **2** tasty.

lemming *noun* rodent of arctic regions, reputed to run into the sea and drown during mass migrations.

lemon *noun* **1** yellow oval fruit that grows on trees. **2** *Slang* useless or defective person or thing. ◆ *adjective* **3** pale-yellow. **lemonade** *noun* lemon-flavoured soft drink, often fizzy. **lemon curd** creamy spread made of lemons, butter, etc. **lemon sole** edible flatfish.

lemur *noun* nocturnal animal like a small monkey, found in Madagascar.

lend ⊕ *verb* **lending, lent 1** give the temporary use of. **2** provide (money) temporarily, often for interest. **3** add (a quality or effect), e.g. *her presence lent beauty to the scene*. **lend itself to** be suitable for. **lender** *noun*

length ⊕ *noun* **1** extent or measurement from end to end. **2** period of time for which something happens. **3** quality of being long. **4** piece of something narrow and long. **at length 1** at last. **2** in full detail. **lengthy** *adjective* very long or tiresome. **lengthily** *adverb* **lengthen**

———— THESAURUS ————

legend *noun* **1** =**myth**, fable, fiction, folk tale, saga, story, tale **3** =**celebrity**, luminary, megastar (*inf*), phenomenon, prodigy **5** =**inscription**, caption, motto

legendary *adjective* **1** =**famous**, celebrated, famed, illustrious, immortal, renowned, well-known OPPOSITE **unknown**. **2** =**mythical**, apocryphal, fabled, fabulous, fictitious, romantic, traditional OPPOSITE **factual**

legible *adjective* =**readable**, clear, decipherable, distinct, easy to read, neat

legion *noun* **1** =**army**, brigade, company, division, force, troop **2** =**multitude**, drove, horde, host, mass, myriad, number, throng

legislation *noun* **1** =**lawmaking**, enactment, prescription, regulation **2** =**law**, act, bill, charter, measure, regulation, ruling, statute

legislative *adjective* =**law-making**, judicial, law-giving

legislator *noun* =**lawmaker**, lawgiver

legislature *noun* =**parliament**, assembly, chamber, congress, senate

legitimate *adjective* **1** =**lawful**, authentic, authorized, genuine, kosher (*inf*), legal, licit, rightful OPPOSITE **illegal**. **2** =**reasonable**, admissible, correct, justifiable, logical, sensible, valid, warranted, well-founded OPPOSITE **unreasonable** ◆*verb* **4** =**legitimize**, authorize, legalize, permit, pronounce lawful, sanction

legitimize *verb* =**legalize**, authorize, permit, sanction

leisure *noun* =**spare time**, ease, freedom, free time, liberty, recreation, relaxation, rest OPPOSITE **work**

leisurely *adjective* **1** =**unhurried**, comfortable, easy, gentle, lazy, relaxed, slow OPPOSITE **rushed**

lend *verb* **2** =**loan**, advance **3** =**give**, add, bestow, confer, grant, impart, provide, supply **lend itself to** =**be appropriate**, be

verb make or become longer. **lengthways, lengthwise** *adjective, adverb*
lenient ⊕ [lee-nee-ent] *adjective* tolerant, not strict or severe. **leniency** *noun* **leniently** *adverb*
lens *noun, pl* **lenses 1** piece of glass or similar material with one or both sides curved, used to bring together or spread light rays incameras, spectacles, telescopes, etc. **2** transparent structure in the eye that focuses light.
lent *verb* past of LEND.
Lent *noun* period from Ash Wednesday to Easter Saturday. **Lenten** *adjective* of, in, or suitable to Lent.
lentil *noun* edible seed of a leguminous Asian plant.
lento *noun, pl* **-tos,** *adverb Music* (piece to be played) slowly.
Leo *noun* (the lion) fifth sign of the zodiac.
leonine *adjective* like a lion.
leopard *noun* large spotted carnivorous animal of the cat family. **leopardess** *n fem*
leotard *noun* tight-fitting garment covering most of the body, worn for dancing or exercise.
leper *noun* **1** person suffering from leprosy. **2** ignored or despised person.
lepidoptera *plural noun* order of insects with four wings covered with fine gossamer scales, as moths and butterflies. **lepidopterous** *adjective* **lepidopterist** *noun* person who studies or collects butterflies or moths.
leprechaun *noun* mischievous elf of Irish folklore.
leprosy *noun* disease attacking the nerves and skin, resulting in loss of feeling in the affected parts. **leprous** *adjective*
lesbian ⊕ *noun* **1** homosexual woman. ◆ *adjective* **2** of homosexual women. **lesbianism** *noun*
lese-majesty [lezz-maj-est-ee] *noun* **1** treason. **2** taking of liberties against people in

authority.
lesion *noun* **1** structural change in an organ of the body caused by illness or injury. **2** injury or wound.
less ⊕ *adjective* **1** smaller in extent, degree, or duration. **2** not so much. **3** comparative of LITTLE. ◆ *pronoun* **4** smaller part or quantity. ◆ *adverb* **5** to a smaller extent or degree. ◆ *preposition* **6** after deducting, minus. **lessen** *verb* make or become smaller or not as much.
lesser *adjective* not as great in quantity, size, or worth.

LANGUAGE TIP

Avoid confusion with *few(er)*. *Less* is used with amounts that cannot be counted: *less time; less fuss. Few(er)* is used of things that can be counted.

lessee *noun* person to whom a lease is granted.
lesson ⊕ *noun* **1** single period of instruction in a subject. **2** content of this. **3** experience that teaches. **4** portion of Scripture read in church.
lest *conjunction* **1** so as to prevent any possibility that. **2** for fear that.
let¹ ⊕ *verb* **letting, let 1** allow, enable, or cause. **2** used as an auxiliary to express a proposal, command, threat, or assumption. **3** grant use of for rent, lease. **4** allow to escape. ◆ *noun* **5** act of letting property. **let alone** not to mention. **let down** *verb* **1** disappoint. **2** lower. **3** deflate. **letdown** *noun* disappointment. **let off** *verb* **1** excuse from (a duty or punishment). **2** fire or explode (a weapon). **3** emit (gas, steam, etc.). **let on** *verb Informal* reveal (a secret). **let out** *verb* **1** emit. **2** release. **3** rent out. **let up** *verb* diminish or stop. **let-up** *noun*

——————— THESAURUS ———————

serviceable, suit
length *noun* **1** = **distance**, extent, longitude, measure, reach, span **2** = **duration**, period, space, span, stretch, term **4** = **piece**, measure, portion, section, segment **at length 1** = **at last**, at long last, eventually, finally, in the end **2** = **in detail**, completely, fully, in depth, thoroughly, to the full
lengthen *verb* = **extend**, continue, draw out, elongate, expand, increase, prolong, protract, spin out, stretch OPPOSITE **shorten**
lengthy *adjective* = **long**, drawn-out, extended, interminable, long-drawn-out, long-winded, prolonged, protracted, tedious OPPOSITE **brief**

lenient *adjective* = **merciful**, compassionate, forbearing, forgiving, indulgent, kind, sparing, tolerant OPPOSITE **severe**
lesbian *adjective* **2** = **homosexual**, gay
less *adjective* **1** = **smaller**, shorter ◆*preposition* **6** = **minus**, excepting, lacking, subtracting, without
lessen *verb* = **reduce**, contract, decrease, diminish, ease, lower, minimize, narrow, shrink OPPOSITE **increase**
lesser *adjective* = **lower**, inferior, less important, minor, secondary OPPOSITE **greater**
lesson *noun* **1** = **class**, coaching, instruction, period, schooling, teaching, tutoring **3** = **example**, deterrent, message, moral

lessening.

let² *noun* **1** *Tennis* minor infringement or obstruction of the ball requiring a replay of the point. **2** hindrance.

lethal ⓘ *adjective* deadly.

lethargy ⓘ *noun* **1** sluggishness or dullness. **2** abnormal lack of energy. **lethargic** *adjective* **lethargically** *adverb*

letter ⓘ *noun* **1** written message, usu. sent by post. **2** alphabetical symbol. **3** strict meaning (of a law etc.). ◆ *plural* **4** literary knowledge or ability. **lettered** *adjective* learned. **lettering** *noun* **letter bomb** explosive device in a parcel or letter that explodes on opening. **letter box 1** slot in a door through which letters are delivered. **2** box in a street or post office where letters are posted. **letterhead** *noun* printed heading on stationery giving the sender's name and address.

lettuce *noun* plant with large green leaves used in salads.

leucocyte [**loo**-koh-site] *noun* white blood cell.

leukaemia [loo-**kee**-mee-a] *noun* disease caused by uncontrolled overproduction of white blood cells.

levee *noun US* natural or artificial river embankment.

level ⓘ *adjective* **1** horizontal. **2** having an even surface. **3** of the same height as something else. **4** equal to or even with (someone or something else). **5** not going above the top edge of (a spoon etc.). **6** not irregular. ◆ *verb* **-elling, -elled 7** make even or horizontal. **8** make equal in position or status. **9** direct (a gun, accusation, etc.) at. **10** raze to the ground. ◆ *noun* **11** horizontal line or surface. **12** device for showing or testing if something is horizontal. **13** position on a scale. **14** standard or grade. **15** flat area of land. **on the level** *Informal* honest or trustworthy. **level crossing** point where a railway line and road cross. **level-headed** *adjective* not apt to be carried away by emotion.

lever ⓘ *noun* **1** handle used to operate machinery. **2** bar used to move a heavy object or to open something. **3** rigid bar pivoted about a fulcrum to transfer a force to a load. **4** means of exerting pressure to achieve an aim. ◆ *verb* **5** prise or move with a lever. **leverage** *noun* **1** action or power of a lever. **2** influence or strategic advantage. **leveraged buyout** *noun* takeover bid in which a small company uses its assets, and those of the target company, to raise the loans required to finance the takeover.

─────── THESAURUS ───────

let¹ *verb* **1** = **allow**, authorize, entitle, give permission, give the go-ahead, permit, sanction, tolerate **3** = **lease**, hire, rent

let² *noun* **2** = **hindrance**, constraint, impediment, interference, obstacle, obstruction, prohibition, restriction

let down *verb* **1** = **disappoint**, disenchant, disillusion, dissatisfy, fail, fall short, leave in the lurch, leave stranded

letdown *noun* = **disappointment**, anticlimax, blow, comedown (*inf*), setback, washout (*inf*)

lethal *adjective* = **deadly**, dangerous, destructive, devastating, fatal, mortal, murderous, virulent OPPOSITE **harmless**

lethargic *adjective* = **sluggish**, apathetic, drowsy, dull, languid, listless, sleepy, slothful OPPOSITE **energetic**

lethargy *noun* = **sluggishness**, apathy, drowsiness, inertia, languor, lassitude, listlessness, sleepiness, sloth OPPOSITE **energy**

let off *verb* **1** = **excuse**, absolve, discharge, exempt, exonerate, forgive, pardon, release, spare **2** = **fire**, detonate, discharge, explode **3** = **emit**, exude, give off, leak, release

let on *verb Inf* = **reveal**, admit, disclose, divulge, give away, let the cat out of the bag (*inf*), make known, say

let out *verb* **1** = **emit**, give vent to, produce **2** = **release**, discharge, free, let go, liberate

letter *noun* **1** = **message**, communication, dispatch, epistle, line, missive, note **2** = **character**, sign, symbol

let up *verb* = **stop**, abate, decrease, diminish, ease (up), moderate, outspan (*S Afr*), relax, slacken, subside

let-up *noun* = **lessening**, break, breathing space, interval, lull, pause, remission, respite, slackening

level *adjective* **1** = **horizontal**, flat OPPOSITE **slanted**. **2** = **even**, consistent, plain, smooth, uniform **4** = **equal**, balanced, commensurate, comparable, equivalent, even, neck and neck, on a par, proportionate ◆*verb* **7** = **flatten**, even off *or* out, plane, smooth **8** = **equalize**, balance, even up **9** = **direct**, aim, focus, point, train **10** = **destroy**, bulldoze, demolish, devastate, flatten, knock down, pull down, raze, tear down OPPOSITE **build** ◆*noun* **14** = **position**, achievement, degree, grade, rank, stage, standard, standing, status **on the level** *Inf* = **honest**, above board, fair, genuine, square, straight

level-headed *adjective* = **calm**, balanced, collected, composed, cool, sensible, steady,

leveret [**lev**-ver-it] *noun* young hare.
leviathan [lev-**vie**-ath-an] *noun* **1** sea monster.
2 anything huge or formidable.
Levis *plural noun* ® denim jeans.
levitation *noun* raising of a solid body into the air supernaturally. **levitate** *verb* rise or cause to rise into the air.
levity ● *noun, pl* **-ties** inclination to make a joke of serious matters.
levy ● [**lev**-vee] *verb* **levying, levied 1** impose and collect (a tax). **2** raise (troops). ♦ *noun, pl* **levies 3** imposition or collection of taxes. **4** money levied. **5** troops conscripted for service.
lewd ● *adjective* lustful or indecent. **lewdly** *adverb* **lewdness** *noun*
lexicon *noun* **1** dictionary. **2** vocabulary of a language. **lexical** *adjective* relating to the vocabulary of a language. **lexicographer** *noun* writer of dictionaries. **lexicography** *noun*
LGV large goods vehicle.
Li *Chem* lithium.
liable ● *adjective* **1** legally obliged or responsible. **2** given to or at risk from a condition. **liability** *noun* **1** hindrance or disadvantage. **2** state of being liable. **3** financial obligation.
liaise ● *verb* establish and maintain communication (with). **liaison** *noun* **1** communication and contact between groups. **2** secret or adulterous relationship.

> **SPELLING TIP**
>
> A lot of people forget to include a second *i* in **liaise**. They make the same mistake when they write *liason*, which occurs 58 times in the Bank of English and which should, of course, be **liaison**.

liar ● *noun* person who tells lies.
lib *noun Informal* short for LIBERATION.
libation [lie-**bay**-shun] *noun* drink poured as an offering to the gods.
libel ● *noun* **1** published statement falsely damaging a person's reputation. ♦ *verb* **-belling, -belled 2** falsely damage the reputation of (someone). **libellous** *adjective*
liberal ● *adjective* **1** having social and political views that favour progress and reform. **2** generous. **3** tolerant. **4** abundant. **5** (of education) designed to develop general cultural interests. ♦ *noun* **6** person who has liberal ideas or opinions. **liberally** *adverb* **liberalism** *noun* belief in democratic reforms and individual freedom. **liberality** *noun* generosity. **liberalize** *verb* make (laws, a country, etc.) less restrictive. **liberalization** *noun* **Liberal Democrat** member of the Liberal Democrats, a British political party favouring a regulated market or mixed economy.
liberate ● *verb* set free. **liberation** *noun*

——————— THESAURUS ———————

unflappable (*inf*)
lever *noun* **1, 2** = **handle**, bar ♦ *verb* **5** = **prise**, force
leverage *noun* **2** = **influence**, authority, clout (*inf*), mana (*NZ*), pull (*inf*), weight
levity *noun* = **light-heartedness**, facetiousness, flippancy, frivolity, silliness, skittishness, triviality
levy *verb* **1** = **impose**, charge, collect, demand, exact **2** = **conscript**, call up, mobilize, muster, raise ♦ *noun* **3** = **imposition**, assessment, collection, exaction, gathering **4** = **tax**, duty, excise, fee, tariff, toll
lewd *adjective* = **indecent**, bawdy, lascivious, libidinous, licentious, lustful, obscene, pornographic, smutty, wanton
liability *noun* **1** = **disadvantage**, burden, drawback, encumbrance, handicap, hindrance, inconvenience, millstone, nuisance **2** = **responsibility**, accountability, answerability, culpability **3** = **debt**, debit, obligation
liable *adjective* **1** = **responsible**, accountable, answerable, obligated **2** = **vulnerable**, exposed, open, subject, susceptible

liaise *verb* = **communicate**, keep contact, link, mediate
liaison *noun* **1** = **communication**, connection, contact, hook-up, interchange **2** = **affair**, amour, entanglement, fling, intrigue, love affair, romance
liar *noun* = **falsifier**, fabricator, fibber, perjurer
libel *noun* **1** = **defamation**, aspersion, calumny, denigration, smear ♦ *verb* **2** = **defame**, blacken, malign, revile, slur, smear, vilify
libellous *adjective* = **defamatory**, derogatory, false, injurious, malicious, scurrilous, untrue
liberal *adjective* **1** = **progressive**, libertarian, radical, reformist OPPOSITE> **conservative. 2** = **generous**, beneficent, bountiful, charitable, kind, open-handed, open-hearted, unstinting OPPOSITE> **stingy. 3** = **tolerant**, broad-minded, indulgent, permissive OPPOSITE> **intolerant. 4** = **abundant**, ample, bountiful, copious, handsome, lavish, munificent, plentiful, profuse, rich OPPOSITE> **small**
liberality *noun* **1** = **generosity**, beneficence, benevolence, bounty, charity, kindness, largesse

L

liberator *noun*

libertarian *noun* **1** believer in freedom of thought and action. ◆ *adjective* **2** having such a belief.

libertine ❶ [lib-er-teen] *noun* morally dissolute person.

liberty ❶ *noun, pl* **-ties 1** freedom. **2** act or comment regarded as forward or socially unacceptable. **at liberty 1** free. **2** having the right. **take liberties** be presumptuous.

libido ❶ [lib-ee-doe] *noun, pl* **-dos 1** psychic energy. **2** emotional drive, esp. of sexual origin. **libidinal** *adjective* **libidinous** *adjective* lustful.

Libra *noun* (the scales) seventh sign of the zodiac.

library *noun, pl* **-braries 1** room or building where books are kept. **2** collection of books, records, etc. for consultation or borrowing. **3** set of books published in a series. **librarian** *noun* keeper of or worker in a library. **librarianship** *noun*

libretto *noun, pl* **-tos, -ti** words of an opera. **librettist** *noun*

lice *noun* a plural of LOUSE.

licence ❶ *noun* **1** document giving official permission to do something. **2** formal permission. **3** disregard of conventions for effect, e.g. *poetic licence.* **4** excessive liberty.

license *verb* grant a licence to. **licensed** *adjective* **licensee** *noun* holder of a licence, esp. to sell alcohol.

license plate *noun* the US and Canadian term for NUMBERPLATE.

licentiate *noun* person licensed as competent

to practise a profession.

licentious ❶ *adjective* sexually unrestrained or promiscuous. **licentiousness** *noun*

lichen *noun* small flowerless plant forming a crust on rocks, trees, etc.

licit *adjective* lawful, permitted.

lick ❶ *verb* **1** pass the tongue over. **2** touch lightly or flicker round. **3** *Slang* defeat. **4** *Slang* thrash. ◆ *noun* **5** licking. **6** small amount (of paint etc.). **7** *Informal* blow. **8** *Informal* fast pace.

licorice *noun* same as LIQUORICE.

lid *noun* **1** movable cover. **2** short for EYELID.

lido [lee-doe] *noun, pl* **-dos** open-air centre for swimming and water sports.

lie¹ ❶ *verb* **lying, lied 1** make a deliberately false statement. **2** give a false impression. ◆ *noun* **3** deliberate falsehood. **white lie** see WHITE.

lie² ❶ *verb* **lying, lay, lain 1** place oneself or be in a horizontal position. **2** be situated. **3** be or remain in a certain state or position. **4** exist or be found. ◆ *noun* **5** way something lies. **lie-down** *noun* rest. **lie in** *verb* remain in bed late into the morning. **lie-in** *noun* long stay in bed in the morning.

> **LANGUAGE TIP**
>
> Note that the past of *lie* is *lay*: *She lay on the beach all day.* Do not confuse with the main verb *lay* meaning 'put'.

or largess, munificence, philanthropy **2** = **broad-mindedness**, latitude, liberalism, libertarianism, permissiveness, toleration

liberate *verb* =**free**, deliver, emancipate, let loose, let out, release, rescue, set free OPPOSITE imprison

liberation *noun* =**freeing**, deliverance, emancipation, freedom, liberty, release

liberator *noun* =**deliverer**, emancipator, freer, redeemer, rescuer, saviour

libertine *noun* =**reprobate**, debauchee, lecher, profligate, rake, roué, sensualist, voluptuary, womanizer

liberty *noun* **1** =**freedom**, autonomy, emancipation, immunity, independence, liberation, release, self-determination, sovereignty OPPOSITE restraint. **2** = **impertinence**, impropriety, impudence, insolence, presumption **at liberty 1** =**free**, on the loose **2** =**unrestricted**

libidinous *adjective* **2** =**lustful**, carnal,

debauched, lascivious, lecherous, randy (*inf, chiefly Brit*), sensual, wanton

licence *noun* **1** =**certificate**, charter, permit, warrant **2** =**permission**, authority, authorization, blank cheque, carte blanche, dispensation, entitlement, exemption, immunity, leave, liberty, right OPPOSITE restriction. **3** =**freedom**, independence, latitude, leeway, liberty OPPOSITE restraint. **4** =**laxity**, excess, immoderation, indulgence, irresponsibility OPPOSITE moderation

license *verb* =**permit**, accredit, allow, authorize, certify, empower, sanction, warrant OPPOSITE forbid

licentious *adjective* =**promiscuous**, abandoned, debauched, dissolute, immoral, lascivious, lustful, sensual, wanton

lick *verb* **1** =**taste**, lap, tongue **2** =**flicker**, dart, flick, play over, ripple, touch **3** *Inf* =**beat**, defeat, master, outdo, outstrip, overcome, rout, trounce, vanquish ◆*noun* **6** =**dab**, bit, stroke,

lied [leed] *noun, pl* **lieder** *Music* setting for voice and piano of a romantic poem.
liege [leej] *adjective* **1** bound to give or receive feudal service. ♦ *noun* **2** lord.
lien *noun* right to hold another's property until a debt is paid.
lieu [lyew] *noun* **in lieu of** instead of.
lieutenant [lef-**ten**-ant] *noun* **1** junior officer in the army or navy. **2** main assistant.
life ⊕ *noun, pl* **lives 1** state of living beings, characterized by growth, reproduction, and response to stimuli. **2** period between birth and death or between birth and the present time. **3** living person. **4** way of living. **5** sentence of imprisonment for life. **6** amount of time something is active or functions. **7** biography. **8** liveliness or high spirits. **9** living beings collectively. **lifeless** *adjective* **1** dead. **2** not lively or exciting. **3** unconscious. **lifelike** *adjective* **lifelong** *adjective* lasting all of a person's life. **lifer** *noun Informal* prisoner sentenced to imprisonment for life. **life belt, jacket** buoyant device to keep afloat a person in danger of drowning. **lifeblood** *noun* **1** blood vital to life. **2** vital thing for success or development. **lifeboat** *noun* boat used for rescuing people at sea. **life cycle** series of changes undergone by each generation of an animal or plant. **lifeguard** *noun* person who saves people from drowning. **lifeline** *noun* **1** means of contact or support. **2** rope used in rescuing a person in danger. **life science** any science concerned with living organisms, such as biology, botany, or zoology. **life-size, life-sized** *adjective* representing actual size. **lifestyle** *noun* particular attitudes, habits, etc. **life-support** *adjective* (of equipment or treatment) necessary to keep a person alive.
lifetime *noun* length of time a person is alive.
lift ⊕ *verb* **1** move upwards in position, status, volume, etc. **2** revoke or cancel. **3** take (plants) out of the ground for harvesting. **4** disappear. **5** make or become more cheerful. **6** *Informal* plagiarize (music or writing). ♦ *noun* **7** cage raised and lowered in a vertical shaft to transport people or goods. **8** ride in a car etc. as a passenger. **9** *Informal* feeling of cheerfulness. **10** lifting. **liftoff** *noun* moment a rocket leaves the ground.
ligament *noun* band of tissue joining bones.
ligature *noun* **1** link, bond, or tie. **2** *Printing* two or more joined letters.
light[1] ⊕ *noun* **1** electromagnetic radiation by which things are visible. **2** source of this, lamp. **3** anything that lets in light, such as a window. **4** aspect or view. **5** mental vision. **6** brightness of countenance. **7** means of setting fire to. ♦ *plural* **8** traffic lights. ♦ *adjective* **9** bright. **10** (of a colour) pale. ♦ *verb* **lighting, lighted** *or* **lit 11** ignite. **12** illuminate or cause to illuminate. **13** guide by a light. **lighten** *verb* make less dark. **lighting** *noun* apparatus for and use of artificial light in theatres, films, etc. **light bulb** glass part of an electric lamp. **lighthouse** *noun* tower with a light to guide ships. **lightship** *noun* moored ship used as a lighthouse. **light up** *verb* **1** illuminate. **2** make or become cheerful. **3** light a cigarette or pipe. **light year** *Astronomy* distance light travels in one year, about six million million miles.
light[2] ⊕ *adjective* **1** not heavy, weighing relatively little. **2** relatively low in strength, amount, density, etc. **3** lacking sufficient weight. **4** not clumsy. **5** not serious or

L

touch **8** *Sl* =**pace**, clip (*inf*), rate, speed
lie[1] *verb* **1** =**fib**, dissimulate, equivocate, fabricate, falsify, prevaricate, tell untruths ♦*noun* **3** =**falsehood**, deceit, fabrication, fib, fiction, invention, prevarication, untruth
lie[2] *verb* **1** =**recline**, loll, lounge, repose, rest, sprawl, stretch out **2** =**be situated**, be, be placed, exist **3** =**be**, remain **4** =**exist**
life *noun* **1** =**being**, sentience, vitality **2** =**existence**, being, lifetime, span, time **4** =**behaviour**, conduct, life style, way of life **7** =**biography**, autobiography, confessions, history, life story, memoirs, story **8** =**liveliness**, animation, energy, high spirits, spirit, verve, vigour, vitality, vivacity, zest
lifeless *adjective* **1** =**dead**, deceased, defunct, extinct, inanimate OPPOSITE> **living**. **2** =**dull**, colourless, flat, lacklustre, lethargic, listless, sluggish, wooden OPPOSITE> **spirited**. **3** =**unconscious**, comatose, dead to the world (*inf*), insensible
lifelike *adjective* =**realistic**, authentic, exact, faithful, natural, true-to-life, vivid
lifelong *adjective* =**long-lasting**, enduring, lasting, long-standing, perennial, persistent
lifetime *noun* =**existence**, career, day(s), span, time
lift *verb* **1** =**raise**, draw up, elevate, hoist, pick up, uplift, upraise OPPOSITE> **drop**. **2** =**revoke**, annul, cancel, countermand, end, remove, rescind, stop, terminate OPPOSITE> **establish**. **4** =**disappear**, be dispelled, disperse, dissipate, vanish ♦*noun* **7** =**elevator** (*chiefly US*) **8** =**ride**, drive, run **9** *Inf* =**boost**, encouragement, fillip, gee-up, pick-me-up, shot in the arm (*inf*) OPPOSITE> **blow**

profound. **6** easily digested. **7** free from care, cheerful. ◆ *adverb* **8** with little equipment or luggage. ◆ *verb* **lighting, lighted, lit 9** (esp. of birds) settle after flight. **10** come (upon) by chance. **lightly** *adverb* **lightness** *noun* **lighten** *verb* **1** make less heavy or burdensome. **2** make more cheerful or lively. **light-fingered** *adjective* skilful at stealing. **light-headed** *adjective* feeling faint, dizzy. **light-hearted** *adjective* carefree. **light heavyweight** boxer weighing up to 175lb (professional) or 81kg (amateur). **lightweight** *noun, adjective* **1** (person) of little importance. ◆ *noun* **2** boxer weighing up to 135lb (professional) or 60kg (amateur).

lighter[1] *noun* device for lighting cigarettes etc.

lighter[2] *noun* flat-bottomed boat for unloading ships.

lightning *noun* **1** visible discharge of electricity in the atmosphere. ◆ *adjective* **2** fast and sudden. **lightning conductor** metal rod attached to the top of a building to divert lightning safely to earth.

SPELLING TIP

Do not confuse this noun with the verb 'lighten', which has the form 'lightening'. The Bank of English shows that people often make the mistake of writing *lightening*, when they mean the noun **lightning**, which doesn't have an *e* in the middle.

lights *plural noun* lungs of animals as animal food.

ligneous *adjective* of or like wood.

lignite [lig-nite] *noun* woody textured rock used as fuel.

like[1] **❶** *preposition, conjunction, adjective, pronoun* indicating similarity, comparison, etc. **liken** *verb* compare. **likeness** *noun* **1** resemblance. **2** portrait. **likewise** *adverb* similarly.

like[2] **❶** *verb* **1** find enjoyable. **2** be fond of. **3** prefer, choose, or wish. **likeable, likable** *adjective* **likely** *adjective* probable. **liking** *noun* **1** fondness. **2** preference.

——————— THESAURUS ———————

light[1] *noun* **1** = **brightness**, brilliance, glare, gleam, glint, glow, illumination, luminosity, radiance, shine OPPOSITE **dark**. **2** = **lamp**, beacon, candle, flare, lantern, taper, torch **4** = **aspect**, angle, context, interpretation, point of view, slant, vantage point, viewpoint **7** = **match**, flame, lighter ◆*adjective* **9** = **bright**, brilliant, illuminated, luminous, lustrous, shining, well-lit OPPOSITE **dark**. **10** = **pale**, bleached, blond, blonde, faded, fair, pastel OPPOSITE **deep** ◆*verb* **11** = **ignite**, inflame, kindle OPPOSITE **put out**. **12** = **illuminate**, brighten, light up OPPOSITE **cloud**

light[2] *adjective* **1** = **insubstantial**, airy, buoyant, flimsy, portable, slight OPPOSITE **heavy**. **2** = **weak**, faint, gentle, indistinct, mild, moderate, slight, soft OPPOSITE **strong**. **3** = **underweight 4** = **nimble**, agile, graceful, lithe, sprightly, sylphlike OPPOSITE **clumsy**. **5** = **insignificant**, inconsequential, inconsiderable, scanty, slight, small, trifling, trivial OPPOSITE **serious**. **6** = **digestible**, frugal, modest OPPOSITE **rich**. **7** = **light-hearted**, frivolous OPPOSITE **serious** ◆*verb* **9** = **settle**, alight, land, perch **10** = **come across**, chance upon, discover, encounter, find, happen upon, hit upon, stumble on

lighten[1] *verb* = **brighten**, become light, illuminate, irradiate, light up

lighten[2] *verb* **1** = **ease**, allay, alleviate, ameliorate, assuage, lessen, mitigate, reduce, relieve OPPOSITE **intensify**. **2** = **cheer**, brighten, buoy up, lift, perk up, revive OPPOSITE **depress**

light-headed *adjective* = **faint**, dizzy, giddy, hazy, vertiginous, woozy (*inf*) OPPOSITE **gloomy**

light-hearted *adjective* = **carefree**, blithe, cheerful, happy-go-lucky, jolly, jovial, playful, upbeat (*inf*)

lightly *adverb* **2 a** = **gently**, delicately, faintly, slightly, softly OPPOSITE **forcefully**. **b** = **moderately**, sparingly, sparsely, heavily **7** = **carelessly**, breezily, flippantly, frivolously, heedlessly, thoughtlessly OPPOSITE **seriously**

lightweight *adjective* **1** = **unimportant**, inconsequential, insignificant, paltry, petty, slight, trifling, trivial, worthless OPPOSITE **important**

like[1] *adjective* = **similar**, akin, alike, analogous, corresponding, equivalent, identical, parallel, same OPPOSITE **different**

like[2] *verb* **1** = **enjoy**, be fond of, be keen on, be partial to, delight in, go for, love, relish, revel in OPPOSITE **hate**. **2** = **admire**, appreciate, approve, cherish, esteem, hold dear, prize, take to OPPOSITE **hate**. **3** = **wish**, care to, choose, desire, fancy, feel inclined, prefer, want

likeable, likable *adjective* = **attractive**, agreeable, amiable, appealing, charming,

L

likely ⊕ *adjective* **1** tending or inclined. **2** probable. **3** hopeful, promising. ◆ *adverb* **4** probably. **not likely** *Informal* definitely not.
likelihood *noun* probability.
lilac *noun* **1** shrub with pale mauve or white flowers. ◆ *adjective* **2** light-purple.
Lilliputian [lil-lip-**pew**-shun] *adjective* tiny.
Lilo *noun, pl* **-los** ® inflatable rubber mattress.
lilt *noun* **1** pleasing musical quality in speaking. **2** jaunty rhythm. **3** graceful rhythmic motion. ◆ *verb* **4** speak with a lilt. **lilting** *adjective*
lily *noun, pl* **lilies** plant which grows from a bulb and has large, often white, flowers. **lily of the valley** small plant with fragrant white flowers.
limb ⊕ *noun* **1** arm, leg, or wing. **2** main branch of a tree. **out on a limb** in a dangerous or isolated position.
limber *adjective* pliant or supple. **limber up** *verb* loosen stiff muscles by exercising.
limbo[1] *noun, pl* **-bos** supposed region intermediate between Heaven and Hell for the unbaptized. **in limbo** not knowing the result or next stage of something and powerless to influence it.
limbo[2] *noun, pl* **-bos** West Indian dance in which dancers lean backwards to pass under a bar.
lime[1] ⊕ *noun* calcium compound used as a fertilizer or in making cement. **limelight** *noun* glare of publicity. **limestone** *noun* sedimentary rock used in building.
lime[2] *noun* small green citrus fruit. **lime-green** *adjective* greenish-yellow.

lime[3] *noun* deciduous tree with heart-shaped leaves and fragrant flowers.
limerick [**lim**-mer-ik] *noun* humorous verse of five lines.
limey *noun US slang* British person.
limit ⊕ *noun* **1** ultimate extent, degree, or amount of something. **2** boundary or edge. ◆ *verb* **-iting, -ited 3** restrict or confine.
limitation *noun* **limitless** *adjective* **limited company** company whose shareholders' liability for debts is restricted. **limited edition** edition of a book, record, etc. which has been restricted to a particular number of copies.
limn *verb* represent in drawing or painting.
limousine *noun* large luxurious car.
limp[1] ⊕ *verb* **1** walk with an uneven step. **2** proceed with difficulty. ◆ *noun* **3** limping walk.
limp[2] ⊕ *adjective* **1** without firmness or stiffness. **2** lacking strength or energy. **limply** *adverb*
limpet *noun* shellfish which sticks tightly to rocks.
limpid *adjective* **1** clear or transparent. **2** easy to understand. **limpidity** *noun*
linchpin, lynchpin *noun* **1** pin to hold a wheel on its axle. **2** essential person or thing.
linctus *noun, pl* **-tuses** syrupy cough medicine.
linden *noun* same as LIME[3].
line[1] ⊕ *noun* **1** long narrow mark. **2** indented mark or wrinkle. **3** continuous length without breadth. **4** boundary or limit. **5** mark on a sports ground showing divisions of a pitch or track. **6** edge or contour of a shape. **7** string or

L

THESAURUS

engaging, lekker *S Afr sl* nice, pleasant, sympathetic
likelihood *noun* =**probability**, chance, possibility, prospect
likely *adjective* **1** =**inclined**, apt, disposed, liable, prone, tending **2** =**probable**, anticipated, expected, odds-on, on the cards, to be expected **3** =**promising**, hopeful, up-and-coming
liken *verb* =**compare**, equate, match, parallel, relate, set beside
likeness *noun* **1** =**resemblance**, affinity, correspondence, similarity **2** =**portrait**, depiction, effigy, image, picture, representation
likewise *adverb* =**similarly**, in like manner, in the same way
liking *noun* **1** =**fondness**, affection, love, soft spot, weakness OPPOSITE dislike. **2** =**preference**, inclination, partiality, penchant, taste OPPOSITE **dislike**
limb *noun* **1** =**part**, appendage, arm,

extremity, leg, member, wing **2** =**branch**, bough, offshoot, projection, spur
limelight *noun* =**publicity**, attention, celebrity, fame, prominence, public eye, recognition, stardom, the spotlight
limit *noun* **1** =**end**, breaking point, deadline, ultimate **2** =**boundary**, border, edge, frontier, perimeter ◆*verb* **3** =**restrict**, bound, check, circumscribe, confine, curb, ration, restrain
limitation *noun* **3** =**restriction**, check, condition, constraint, control, curb, qualification, reservation, restraint
limited *adjective* **3** =**restricted**, bounded, checked, circumscribed, confined, constrained, controlled, curbed, finite OPPOSITE **unlimited**
limitless *adjective* **2** =**infinite**, boundless, countless, endless, inexhaustible, unbounded, unlimited, untold, vast
limp[1] *verb* **1, 2** =**hobble**, falter, hop, shamble, shuffle ◆*noun* **3** =**lameness**, hobble
limp[2] *adjective* **1** =**floppy**, drooping, flabby,

wire for a particular use. **8** telephone connection. **9** wire or cable for transmitting electricity. **10** shipping company. **11** railway track. **12** course or direction of movement. **13** course or method of action. **14** prescribed way of thinking. **15** field of interest or activity. **16** row or queue of people. **17** class of goods. **18** row of words. **19** unit of verse. **20** military formation. ♦ *plural* **21** words of a theatrical part. **22** school punishment of writing out a sentence a specified number of times. ♦ *verb* **23** mark with lines. **24** be or form a border or edge. **in line for** likely to receive. **in line with** in accordance with. **line dancing** form of dancing performed by rows of people to country and western music. **line-up** *noun* people or things assembled for a particular purpose. **line up** *verb* form or organize a line-up.

line² ⊕ *verb* **1** give a lining to. **2** cover the inside of.

lineage [lin-ee-ij] *noun* descent from an ancestor. **lineal** *adjective* in direct line of descent.

lineament *noun* facial feature.

linear [lin-ee-er] *adjective* of or in lines.

linen *noun* **1** cloth or thread made from flax. **2** sheets, tablecloths, etc.

liner¹ *noun* large passenger ship or aircraft.

liner² *noun* something used as a lining.

linesman *noun* **1** (in some sports) an official who helps the referee or umpire. **2** person who maintains railway, electricity, or telephone lines.

ling¹ *noun* slender food fish.

ling² *noun* heather.

linger ⊕ *verb* **1** delay or prolong departure. **2** continue in a weakened state for a long time before dying or disappearing. **3** spend a long time doing something. **lingering** *adjective*

lingerie [lan-zher-ee] *noun* women's underwear or nightwear.

lingo *noun, pl* **-goes** *Informal* foreign or

unfamiliar language or jargon.

lingua franca *noun, pl* **lingua francas, linguae francae** language used for communication between people of different mother tongues.

lingual *adjective* **1** of the tongue. **2** (of a sound) made by the tongue.

linguist *noun* **1** person skilled in foreign languages. **2** person who studies linguistics.

linguistic *adjective* of languages. **linguistics** *noun* scientific study of language.

liniment *noun* medicated liquid rubbed on the skin to relieve pain or stiffness.

lining *noun* **1** layer of cloth attached to the inside of a garment etc. **2** inner covering of anything.

link ⊕ *noun* **1** any of the rings forming a chain. **2** person or thing forming a connection. ♦ *verb* **3** connect with or as if with links. **4** connect by association. **linkage** *noun* **link-up** *noun* joining together of two systems or groups.

links *plural noun* golf course, esp. one by the sea.

linnet *noun* songbird of the finch family.

lino *noun* short for LINOLEUM.

linoleum *noun* floor covering of hessian or jute with a smooth decorative coating of powdered cork.

Linotype *noun* ® typesetting machine which casts lines of words in one piece.

linseed *noun* seed of the flax plant.

lint *noun* soft material for dressing a wound.

lintel *noun* horizontal beam at the top of a door or window.

lion *noun* **1** large animal of the cat family, the male of which has a shaggy mane. **2** courageous person. **lioness** *n fem* **the lion's share** the biggest part. **lionize** *verb* treat as a celebrity. **lion-hearted** *adjective* brave.

lip ⊕ *noun* **1** either of the fleshy edges of the mouth. **2** rim of a jug etc. **3** *Slang* impudence.

——————— THESAURUS ———————

flaccid, pliable, slack, soft OPPOSITE **stiff**

line¹ *noun* **1** = **stroke**, band, groove, mark, score, scratch, streak, stripe **2** = **wrinkle**, crease, crow's foot, furrow, mark **4** = **boundary**, border, borderline, edge, frontier, limit **7** = **string**, cable, cord, rope, thread, wire **12** = **trajectory**, course, direction, path, route, track **15** = **occupation**, area, business, calling, employment, field, job, profession, specialization, trade **16** = **row**, column, file, procession, queue, rank ♦*plural noun* **21** = **words**, part, script ♦*verb* **23** = **mark**, crease, furrow, rule, score **24** = **border**, bound, edge, fringe **in line for** = **due for**, in the running for

line² *verb* = **fill**, ceil, cover, face, interline

lined *adjective* **1** = **ruled**, feint **2** = **wrinkled**, furrowed, wizened, worn

line-up *noun* = **arrangement**, array, row, selection, team

linger *verb* **1** = **stay**, hang around, loiter, remain, stop, tarry, wait **3** = **delay**, dally, dawdle, drag one's feet *or* heels, idle, take one's time

link *noun* **2** = **connection**, affinity, association, attachment, bond, relationship, tie-up ♦*verb* **3** = **connect**, attach, bind, couple, fasten, join, tie, unite OPPOSITE **separate**. **4** = **associate**, bracket, connect, identify, relate

lip-reading *noun* method of understanding speech by interpreting lip movements. **lip-read** *verb* **lip service** insincere tribute or respect.
lipstick *noun* cosmetic in stick form, for colouring the lips.
liquefy *verb* **-fying, -fied** make or become liquid. **liquefaction** *noun*
liqueur [lik-**cure**] *noun* flavoured and sweetened alcoholic spirit.
liquid ❶ *noun* **1** substance in a physical state which can change shape but not size. ◆ *adjective* **2** of or being a liquid. **3** transparent and shining. **4** flowing smoothly. **5** (of assets) in the form of money or easily converted into money. **liquidize** *verb* make or become liquid. **liquidizer** *noun* kitchen appliance that liquidizes food. **liquidity** *noun* state of being able to meet financial obligations.
liquidate ❶ *verb* **1** pay (a debt). **2** dissolve a company and share its assets among creditors. **3** wipe out or kill. **liquidation** *noun* **liquidator** *noun* official appointed to liquidate a business.
liquor ❶ *noun* **1** alcoholic drink, esp. spirits. **2** liquid in which food has been cooked.
liquorice [lik-ker-iss] *noun* black substance used in medicine and as a sweet.
lira *noun, pl* **-re, -ras** monetary unit of Italy and Turkey.
lisle [rhymes with **mile**] *noun* strong fine cotton thread or fabric.
lisp *noun* **1** speech defect in which *s* and *z* are pronounced *th*. ◆ *verb* **2** speak or utter with a lisp.
lissom, lissome *adjective* supple, agile.
list¹ ❶ *noun* **1** item-by-item record of names or things, usu. written one below another. ◆ *verb* **2** make a list of. **3** include in a list. **listed**

building building protected from demolition or alteration because of its historical or architectural interest.
list² ❶ *verb* **1** (of a ship) lean to one side. ◆ *noun* **2** leaning to one side.
listen ❶ *verb* **1** concentrate on hearing something. **2** heed or pay attention to. **listener** *noun* **listen in** *verb* listen secretly, eavesdrop.
listeriosis *noun* dangerous form of food poisoning.
listing *noun* **1** list or an entry in a list. ◆ *plural* **2** lists of films, concerts, etc. printed in newspapers and magazines.
listless ❶ *adjective* lacking interest or energy. **listlessly** *adverb*
lists *plural noun* field of combat in a tournament. **enter the lists** engage in a conflict.
lit *verb* past of LIGHT¹ *or* LIGHT².
litany *noun, pl* **-nies 1** prayer with responses from the congregation. **2** any tedious recital.
literacy ❶ *noun* ability to read and write.
literal ❶ *adjective* **1** according to the explicit meaning of a word or text, not figurative. **2** (of a translation) word for word. **3** dull or unimaginative. **4** actual, true. **literally** *adverb*
literary ❶ *adjective* **1** of or knowledgeable about literature. **2** (of a word) formal, not colloquial. **literariness** *noun*
literate ❶ *adjective* **1** able to read and write. **2** educated. **literati** *plural noun* literary people.
literature ❶ *noun* **1** written works such as novels, plays, and poetry. **2** books and writings of a country, period, or subject. **3** printed matter on a subject.
lithe ❶ *adjective* flexible or supple, pliant.
lithium *noun Chem* chemical element, the

L

———————— T H E S A U R U S ————————

lip *noun* **2** =**edge**, brim, brink, margin, rim **3** *Sl* =**impudence**, backchat (*inf*), cheek (*inf*), effrontery, impertinence, insolence
liquid *noun* **1** =**fluid**, juice, solution ◆*adjective* **2** =**fluid**, aqueous, flowing, melted, molten, runny **5** *Of assets* =**convertible**, negotiable
liquidate *verb* **1** =**pay**, clear, discharge, honour, pay off, settle, square **2** =**dissolve**, abolish, annul, cancel, terminate **3** =**kill**, destroy, dispatch, eliminate, exterminate, get rid of, murder, wipe out (*inf*)
liquor *noun* **1** =**alcohol**, booze (*inf*), drink, hard stuff (*inf*), spirits, strong drink **2** =**juice**, broth, extract, liquid, stock
list¹ *noun* **1** =**inventory**, catalogue, directory, index, record, register, roll, series, tally ◆*verb* **2, 3** =**itemize**, catalogue, enter, enumerate, record, register, tabulate

list² *verb* **1** =**lean**, careen, heel over, incline, tilt, tip ◆*noun* **2** =**tilt**, cant, leaning, slant
listen *verb* **1** =**hear**, attend, lend an ear, prick up one's ears **2** =**pay attention**, heed, mind, obey, observe, take notice
listless *adjective* =**languid**, apathetic, indifferent, indolent, lethargic, sluggish
OPPOSITE **energetic**
literacy *noun* =**education**, knowledge, learning
literal *adjective* **1** =**explicit**, precise, strict **2** =**exact**, accurate, close, faithful, verbatim, word for word **4** =**actual**, bona fide, genuine, plain, real, simple, true, unvarnished
literary *adjective* **1** =**well-read**, bookish, erudite, formal, learned, scholarly
literate *adjective* **2** =**educated**, informed, knowledgeable

lightest known metal.

litho *noun, pl* **-thos 1** short for LITHOGRAPH. ♦ *adjective* **2** short for LITHOGRAPHIC.

lithography [lith-**og**-ra-fee] *noun* method of printing from a metal or stone surface in which the printing areas are made receptive to ink. **lithograph** *noun* **1** print made by lithography. ♦ *verb* **2** reproduce by lithography. **lithographer** *noun* **lithographic** *adjective*

litigate ⊕ *verb* **1** bring or contest a law suit. **2** engage in legal action. **litigant** *noun* person involved in a lawsuit. **litigation** *noun* legal action. **litigious** [lit-**ij**-uss] *adjective* frequently going to law.

litmus *noun* blue dye turned red by acids and restored to blue by alkalis. **litmus paper** paper impregnated with litmus. **litmus test** something which is regarded as a simple and accurate test of a particular thing.

litotes [lie-**toe**-teez] *noun* ironical understatement used for effect.

litre *noun* unit of liquid measure equal to 1.76 pints.

litter ⊕ *noun* **1** untidy rubbish dropped in public places. **2** group of young animals produced at one birth. **3** straw etc. as bedding for an animal. **4** dry material to absorb a cat's excrement. **5** bed or seat on parallel sticks for carrying people. ♦ *verb* **6** strew with litter. **7** scatter or be scattered about untidily. **8** give birth to young.

little ⊕ *adjective* **1** small or smaller than average. **2** young. ♦ *adverb* **3** not a lot. **4** hardly. **5** not much or often. ♦ *noun* **6** small amount, extent, or duration. **little by little** by small degrees.

littoral *adjective* **1** of or by the seashore. ♦ *noun* **2** coastal district.

liturgy *noun, pl* **-gies** prescribed form of public worship. **liturgical** *adjective*

live¹ ⊕ *verb* **1** be alive. **2** remain in life or existence. **3** exist in a specified way, e.g. *we live well.* **4** reside. **5** continue or last. **6** subsist. **7** enjoy life to the full. **liver** *noun* person who lives in a specified way. **live down** *verb* wait till people forget a past mistake or misdeed. **live-in** *adjective* resident. **live together** *verb* (of an unmarried couple) share a house and have a sexual relationship. **live up to** *verb* meet (expectations). **live with** *verb* tolerate.

live² ⊕ *adjective* **1** living, alive. **2** (of a broadcast) transmitted during the actual performance. **3** (of a performance) done in front of an audience. **4** (of a wire, circuit, etc.) carrying an electric current. **5** causing interest or controversy. **6** capable of exploding. **7** glowing or burning. ♦ *adverb* **8** in the form of a live performance. **lively** *adjective* **1** full of life or vigour. **2** animated. **3** vivid. **liveliness** *noun* **liven up** *verb* make (more) lively. **live wire 1** *Informal* energetic person. **2** wire carrying an electric current.

livelihood ⊕ *noun* occupation or employment.

liver *noun* **1** organ secreting bile. **2** animal liver as food. **liverish** *adjective* **1** having a disorder of the liver. **2** touchy or irritable.

liverwort *noun* plant resembling seaweed or

——— T H E S A U R U S ———

literature *noun* =**writings**, lore
lithe *adjective* =**supple**, flexible, limber, lissom(e), loose-limbed, pliable
litigant *noun* =**claimant**, party, plaintiff
litigate *verb* =**sue**, go to court, press charges, prosecute
litigation *noun* =**lawsuit**, action, case, prosecution
litter *noun* **1** =**rubbish**, debris, detritus, garbage (*chiefly US*), muck, refuse, trash **2** =**brood**, offspring, progeny, young ♦*verb* **6** =**clutter**, derange, disarrange, disorder, mess up, muss (*US & Canad*) **7** =**scatter**, strew
little *adjective* **1** =**small**, diminutive, miniature, minute, petite, short, tiny, wee OPPOSITE big. **2** =**young**, babyish, immature, infant, undeveloped ♦*adverb* **4** =**hardly**, barely OPPOSITE much. **5** =**rarely**, hardly ever, not often, scarcely, seldom OPPOSITE much ♦*noun* **6** =**bit**, fragment, hint, particle, speck, spot, touch, trace OPPOSITE lot

live¹ *verb* **1** =**exist**, be, be alive, breathe **4** =**dwell**, abide, inhabit, lodge, occupy, reside, settle **5** =**persist**, last, prevail **6** =**survive**, endure, get along, make ends meet, subsist, support oneself **7** =**thrive**, flourish, prosper
live² *adjective* **1** =**living**, alive, animate, breathing **5** =**topical**, burning, controversial, current, hot, pertinent, pressing, prevalent **7** =**burning**, active, alight, blazing, glowing, hot, ignited, smouldering
livelihood *noun* =**occupation**, bread and butter (*inf*), employment, job, living, work, yakka (*Aust & NZ inf*)
lively *adjective* **1** =**vigorous**, active, agile, alert, brisk, energetic, keen, perky, quick, sprightly OPPOSITE slow. **2** =**animated**, cheerful, chirpy (*inf*), sparky, spirited, upbeat (*inf*), vivacious OPPOSITE slow. **3** =**vivid**, bright, colourful, exciting, forceful, invigorating, refreshing, stimulating OPPOSITE dull
liven up *verb* =**stir**, animate, brighten, buck

leafy moss.

livery ❶ *noun, pl* **-eries 1** distinctive dress, esp. of a servant or servants. **2** distinctive design or colours of a company. **liveried** *adjective* **livery stable** stable where horses are kept at a charge or hired out.

lives *noun* plural of LIFE.

livestock *noun* farm animals.

livid ❶ *adjective* **1** *Informal* angry or furious. **2** bluish-grey.

living ❶ *adjective* **1** possessing life, not dead or inanimate. **2** currently in use or existing. **3** of everyday life, e.g. *living conditions.* ◆ *noun* **4** condition of being alive. **5** manner of life. **6** financial means. **7** church office yielding annual income. **living room** room in a house used for relaxation and entertainment. **living wage** wage adequate for a worker to live on in reasonable comfort.

lizard *noun* four-footed reptile with a long body and tail.

llama *noun* woolly animal of the camel family used as a beast of burden in S America.

LLB Bachelor of Laws.

lo *interjection* Old-fashioned look!

loach *noun* carplike freshwater fish.

load ❶ *noun* **1** burden or weight. **2** amount carried. **3** source of worry. **4** amount of electrical energy drawn from a source. ◆ *plural* **5** *Informal* lots. ◆ *verb* **6** put a load on or into. **7** burden or oppress. **8** supply in abundance. **9** cause to be biased. **10** put ammunition into (a weapon). **11** put film into (a camera). **12** transfer (a program) into computer memory. **a**

load of *Informal* a quantity of. **loaded** *adjective* **1** (of a question) containing a hidden trap or implication. **2** (of dice) dishonestly weighted. **3** *Slang* wealthy. **4** *Slang* drunk.

loaf[1] ❶ *noun, pl* **loaves 1** shaped mass of baked bread. **2** shaped mass of food. **3** *Slang* head, esp. as the source of common sense, e.g. *use your loaf.*

loaf[2] ❶ *verb* idle, loiter. **loafer** *noun*

loam *noun* fertile soil.

loan ❶ *noun* **1** money lent at interest. **2** lending. **3** thing lent. ◆ *verb* **4** lend. **loan shark** person who lends money at an extremely high interest rate.

loath, loth ❶ [rhymes with **both**] *adjective* unwilling or reluctant (to).

LANGUAGE TIP

Distinguish between *loath* 'reluctant' and *loathe* 'be disgusted by'.

---

loathe ❶ *verb* hate, be disgusted by. **loathing** *noun* **loathsome** *adjective*

loaves *noun* plural of LOAF[1].

lob *Sport noun* **1** ball struck or thrown in a high arc. ◆ *verb* **lobbing, lobbed 2** strike or throw (a ball) in a high arc.

lobby ❶ *noun, pl* **-bies 1** corridor into which rooms open. **2** group which tries to influence legislators. **3** hall in a legislative building to which the public has access. ◆ *verb* **-bying, -bied 4** try to influence (legislators) in the

L

THESAURUS

up (*inf*), enliven, perk up, rouse

livery *noun* **1** = **costume**, attire, clothing, dress, garb, regalia, suit, uniform

livid *adjective* **1** *Inf* = **angry**, beside oneself, enraged, fuming, furious, incensed, indignant, infuriated, outraged OPPOSITE **happy. 2** = **discoloured**, black-and-blue, bruised, contused, purple

living *adjective* **1** = **alive**, active, breathing, existing OPPOSITE **dead. 2** = **current**, active, contemporary, extant, in use OPPOSITE obsolete ◆*noun* **4** = **existence**, being, existing, life, subsistence **5** = **lifestyle**, way of life

load *noun* **1** = **cargo**, consignment, freight, shipment **3** = **burden**, albatross, encumbrance, millstone, onus, trouble, weight, worry ◆*verb* **6** = **fill**, cram, freight, heap, pack, pile, stack, stuff **7** = **burden**, encumber, oppress, saddle with, weigh down, worry **10** *Firearms* = **make ready**, charge, prime

loaded *adjective* **1** = **tricky**, artful, insidious,

manipulative, prejudicial **3** *Sl* = **rich**, affluent, flush (*inf*), moneyed, wealthy, well-heeled (*inf*), well off, well-to-do

loaf[1] *noun* **2** = **lump**, block, cake, cube, slab **3** *Sl* = **head**, gumption (*Brit inf*), nous (*Brit sl*), sense

loaf[2] *verb* = **idle**, laze, lie around, loiter, lounge around, take it easy

loan *noun* **1-3** = **advance**, credit ◆*verb* **4** = **lend**, advance, let out

loath, loth *adjective* = **unwilling**, averse, disinclined, opposed, reluctant OPPOSITE willing

loathe *verb* = **hate**, abhor, abominate, despise, detest, dislike

loathing *noun* = **hatred**, abhorrence, antipathy, aversion, detestation, disgust, repugnance, repulsion, revulsion

loathsome *adjective* = **hateful**, abhorrent, detestable, disgusting, nauseating, obnoxious, odious, offensive, repugnant, repulsive,

formulation of policy. **lobbyist** *noun*
lobe *noun* **1** rounded projection. **2** soft
hanging part of the ear. **3** subdivision of a body
organ. **lobed** *adjective*
lobelia *noun* garden plant with blue, red, or
white flowers.
lobotomy *noun, pl* **-mies** surgical incision into
a lobe of the brain to treat mental disorders.
lobster *noun* shellfish with a long tail and
claws, which turns red when boiled. **lobster
pot** basket-like trap for catching lobsters.
local ✿ *adjective* **1** of or existing in a particular
place. **2** confined to a particular place. ◆ *noun* **3**
person belonging to a particular district. **4**
Informal pub close to one's home. **locally**
adverb **locality** *noun* **1** neighbourhood or area.
2 site. **localize** *verb* restrict to a particular
place. **locale** [loh-**kahl**] *noun* scene of an event.
local anaesthetic anaesthetic which produces
loss of feeling in one part of the body. **local
authority** governing body of a county or
district. **local government** government of
towns, counties, and districts by locally elected
political bodies.
locate ✿ *verb* **1** discover the whereabouts of.
2 situate or place. **location** *noun* **1** site or
position. **2** act of discovering where something
is. **3** site of a film production away from the
studio. **4** *S Afr* Black African or coloured
township.
loch *noun Scot* **1** lake. **2** long narrow bay.
loci *noun* plural of LOCUS.
lock[1] ✿ *noun* **1** appliance for fastening a door,
case, etc. **2** section of a canal shut off by gates
between which the water level can be altered
to aid boats moving from one level to another.
3 extent to which a vehicle's front wheels will
turn. **4** interlocking of parts. **5** mechanism for
firing a gun. **6** wrestling hold. ◆ *verb* **7** fasten or
become fastened securely. **8** become or cause

to become fixed or united. **9** become or cause
to become immovable. **10** embrace closely.
lockout *noun* closing of a workplace by an
employer to force workers to accept terms.
locksmith *noun* person who makes and mends
locks. **lockup** *noun* **1** prison. **2** garage or
storage place away from the main premises.
lock up *verb* **1** imprison. **2** secure (a building)
by locking.
lock[2] ✿ *noun* strand of hair.
locker *noun* small cupboard with a lock.
locket *noun* small hinged pendant for a
portrait etc.
lockjaw *noun* tetanus.
locomotive *noun* **1** self-propelled engine for
pulling trains. ◆ *adjective* **2** of locomotion.
locomotion *noun* action or power of moving.
locum *noun* temporary stand-in for a doctor or
clergyman.
locus [loh-kuss] *noun, pl* **loci** [loh-sigh] **1** area
or place where something happens. **2** *Maths* set
of points or lines satisfying one or more
specified conditions.
locust *noun* **1** destructive African insect that
flies in swarms and eats crops. **2** N American
tree with prickly branches.
lode *noun* vein of ore. **lodestar** *noun* star used
in navigation or astronomy as a point of
reference. **lodestone** *noun* magnetic iron ore.
lodge ✿ *noun* **1** gatekeeper's house. **2** house
or cabin used occasionally by hunters, skiers,
etc. **3** porters' room in a university or college. **4**
local branch of some societies. **5** beaver's
home. ◆ *verb* **6** live in another's house at a fixed
charge. **7** stick or become stuck (in a place). **8**
leave for safety or storage. **9** make (a complaint
etc.) formally. **lodger** *noun* **lodging** *noun* **1**
temporary residence. ◆ *plural* **2** rented room or
rooms in another person's house.
loft *noun* **1** space between the top storey and

———————— T H E S A U R U S ————————

revolting, vile OPPOSITE **delightful**
lobby *noun* **1** = **corridor**, entrance hall, foyer,
hallway, passage, porch, vestibule **2** = **pressure
group** ◆*verb* **4** = **campaign**, influence,
persuade, press, pressure, promote, push, urge
local *adjective* **1** = **regional**, provincial **2**
= **restricted**, confined, limited ◆*noun* **3**
= **resident**, inhabitant, native
locality *noun* **1** = **neighbourhood**, area,
district, neck of the woods (*inf*), region, vicinity
2 = **site**, locale, location, place, position, scene,
setting, spot
localize *verb* = **restrict**, circumscribe, confine,
contain, delimit, limit
locate *verb* **1** = **find**, come across, detect,

discover, pin down, pinpoint, track down,
unearth **2** = **place**, establish, fix, put, seat, set,
settle, situate
location *noun* **1** = **site**, locale, place, point,
position, situation, spot, venue
lock[1] *noun* **1** = **fastening**, bolt, clasp, padlock
◆*verb* **7** = **fasten**, bolt, close, seal, secure, shut
8 = **unite**, engage, entangle, entwine, join, link
9 = **clench**, freeze **10** = **embrace**, clasp, clutch,
encircle, enclose, grasp, hug, press
lock[2] *noun* = **strand**, curl, ringlet, tress, tuft
lockup *noun* **1** = **prison**, cell, jail *or* gaol
lock up *verb* **1** = **imprison**, cage, confine,
detain, incarcerate, jail, put behind bars, shut
up

roof of a building. **2** gallery in a church etc. **3** room over a stable used to store hay. ♦ *verb* **4** *Sport* strike, throw, or kick (a ball) high into the air.

lofty ⊕ *adjective* **loftier, loftiest 1** of great height. **2** exalted or noble. **3** haughty. **loftily** *adverb* haughtily. **loftiness** *noun*

log¹ ⊕ *noun* **1** portion of a felled tree stripped of branches. **2** detailed record of a journey of a ship, aircraft, etc. ♦ *verb* **logging, logged 3** saw logs from a tree. **4** record in a log. **logging** *noun* work of cutting and transporting logs. **logbook** *noun* book recording the details about a car or a ship's journeys. **log in, out** *verb* gain entrance to or leave a computer system by keying in a special command.

log² *noun* short for LOGARITHM.

loganberry *noun* purplish-red fruit, similar to a raspberry.

logarithm *noun* one of a series of arithmetical functions used to make certain calculations easier. **logarithmic** *adjective*

loggerheads ⊕ *plural noun* **at loggerheads** quarrelling, disputing.

loggia [loj-ya] *noun* covered gallery at the side of a building.

logic ⊕ *noun* **1** philosophy of reasoning. **2** particular system of reasoning. **3** reasoned thought or argument. **logical** *adjective* **1** of logic. **2** capable of or using clear valid

reasoning. **3** reasonable. **logically** *adverb*

logician *noun*

logistics *noun* detailed planning and organization of a large, esp. military, operation. **logistical, logistic** *adjective* **logistically** *adverb*

logo [loh-go] *noun, pl* **-os** company emblem or similar device.

loin *noun* **1** part of the body between the ribs and the hips. **2** cut of meat from this part of an animal. ♦ *plural* **3** hips and inner thighs. **4** *Euphemistic* genitals. **loincloth** *noun* piece of cloth covering the loins only.

loiter ⊕ *verb* stand or wait aimlessly or idly.

loll ⊕ *verb* **1** lounge lazily. **2** hang loosely.

lollipop *noun* **1** boiled sweet on a small wooden stick. **2** ice lolly. **lollipop man, lady** *Informal* person holding a circular sign on a pole, who controls traffic so that children may cross the road safely.

lollop *verb* move clumsily.

lolly *noun, pl* **-ies 1** *Informal* lollipop or ice lolly. **2** *Aust & NZ informal* sweet. **3** *Slang* money.

lone ⊕ *adjective* **1** solitary. **2** isolated. **lonely** *adjective* **1** sad because alone. **2** resulting from being alone. **3** unfrequented. **loneliness** *noun*

loner *noun Informal* person who prefers to be alone.

lonesome ⊕ *adjective Chiefly US & Canad* another word for LONELY.

L

——————————————— T H E S A U R U S ———————————————

lodge *noun* **1** = **gatehouse 2** = **cabin**, chalet, cottage, hut, shelter **4** = **society**, branch, chapter, club, group ♦*verb* **6** = **stay**, board, room **7** = **stick**, come to rest, imbed, implant **9** = **register**, file, put on record, submit

lodger *noun* **6** = **tenant**, boarder, paying guest, resident

lodging *noun* **1** = **accommodation**, residence, shelter **2** ♦*plural* = **rooms**, abode, apartments, digs (*Brit inf*), quarters

lofty *adjective* **1** = **high**, elevated, raised, soaring, towering OPPOSITE **low. 2** = **noble**, dignified, distinguished, elevated, exalted, grand, illustrious, renowned OPPOSITE **mean. 3** = **haughty**, arrogant, condescending, disdainful, patronizing, proud, supercilious OPPOSITE **warm**

log¹ *noun* **1** = **stump**, block, chunk, trunk **2** = **record**, account, journal, logbook ♦*verb* **3** = **chop**, cut, fell, hew **4** = **record**, chart, note, register, set down

loggerheads *plural noun* **at loggerheads** = **quarrelling**, at daggers drawn, at each other's throats, at odds, feuding, in dispute, opposed

logic *noun* **3** = **reason**, good sense, sense

logical *adjective* **2** = **rational**, clear, cogent, coherent, consistent, sound, valid, well-organized OPPOSITE **unreasonable. 3** = **reasonable**, plausible, sensible, wise OPPOSITE **unlikely**

loiter *verb* = **linger**, dally, dawdle, dilly-dally (*inf*), hang about or around, idle, loaf, skulk

loll *verb* **1** = **lounge**, loaf, outspan (*S Afr*), recline, relax, slouch, slump, sprawl **2** = **droop**, dangle, drop, flap, flop, hang, sag

lone *adjective* **1** = **solitary**, one, only, single, sole, unaccompanied

loneliness *noun* = **solitude**, desolation, isolation, seclusion

lonely *adjective* **1** = **alone**, abandoned, companionless, destitute, forlorn, forsaken, friendless, isolated, lone, lonesome (*chiefly US & Canad*), single, solitary, withdrawn **3** = **desolate**, deserted, godforsaken, isolated, out-of-the-way, remote, secluded, unfrequented, uninhabited OPPOSITE **crowded**

loner *noun Inf* = **individualist**, lone wolf, maverick, outsider, recluse

lonesome *adjective* (*chiefly US & Canad*) = **lonely**, companionless, desolate, dreary,

long¹ ⊕ *adjective* **1** having length, esp. great length, in space or time. ✦ *adverb* **2** for a certain time. **3** for an extensive period. **4** a considerable amount of time, e.g. *long ago*. **longways, longwise** *adverb* lengthways. **longboat** *noun* largest boat carried on a ship. **longbow** *noun* large powerful bow. **long-distance** *adjective* going between places far apart. **long face** glum expression. **longhand** *noun* ordinary writing, not shorthand or typing. **long johns** *Informal* long underpants. **long jump** contest of jumping the farthest distance from a fixed mark. **long-life** *adjective* (of milk, batteries, etc.) lasting longer than the regular kind. **long-lived** *adjective* living or lasting for a long time. **long-range** *adjective* **1** extending into the future. **2** (of vehicles, weapons, etc.) designed to cover great distances. **long shot** competitor, undertaking, or bet with little chance of success. **long-sighted** *adjective* able to see distant objects in focus but not nearby ones. **long-standing** *adjective* existing for a long time. **long-suffering** *adjective* enduring trouble or unhappiness without complaint. **long-term** *adjective* lasting or effective for a long time. **long wave** radio wave with a wavelength of over 1000 metres. **long-winded** *adjective* speaking or writing at tedious length. **long² ⊕** *verb* have a strong desire (for). **longing** *noun* yearning. **longingly** *adverb*

long. longitude.
longevity [lon-**jev**-it-ee] *noun* long life.
longitude *noun* distance east or west from a standard meridian. **longitudinal** *adjective* **1** of length or longitude. **2** lengthways.
longshoreman *noun* a man employed in the loading or unloading of ships.
loo *noun Informal* toilet.
loofah *noun* sponge made from the dried pod of a gourd.
look ⊕ *verb* **1** direct the eyes or attention (towards). **2** have the appearance of being. **3** face in a particular direction. **4** search (for). **5** hope (for). ✦ *noun* **6** instance of looking. **7** view or sight. **8** (often pl) appearance. **look after** *verb* take care of. **lookalike** *noun* person who is the double of another. **look down on** *verb* treat as inferior or unimportant. **look forward to** *verb* anticipate with pleasure. **look-in** *noun Informal* chance to participate. **look in** *verb Informal* pay a short visit. **looking glass** mirror. **look on** *verb* **1** be a spectator. **2** consider or regard. **lookout** *noun* **1** act of watching for danger or for an opportunity. **2** guard. **3** place for watching. **4** *Informal* worry or concern. **5** chances or prospect. **look out** *verb* be careful. **look up** *verb* **1** discover or confirm by checking in a book. **2** improve. **3** visit. **look up to** *verb* respect.
loom¹ *noun* machine for weaving cloth.

——————— THESAURUS ———————

forlorn, friendless, gloomy
long¹ *adjective* **1 a** =**elongated**, expanded, extended, extensive, far-reaching, lengthy, spread out, stretched ⎡OPPOSITE⎤ **short. b** =**prolonged**, interminable, lengthy, lingering, long-drawn-out, protracted, sustained ⎡OPPOSITE⎤ **short**
long² *verb* =**desire**, crave, hanker, itch, lust, pine, want, wish, yearn
longing *noun* =**desire**, ambition, aspiration, craving, hope, itch, thirst, urge, wish, yearning, yen (*inf*) ⎡OPPOSITE⎤ **disgust**
long-lived *adjective* =**long-lasting**, enduring
long-standing *adjective* =**established**, abiding, enduring, fixed, long-established, long-lasting, time-honoured
long-suffering *adjective* =**uncomplaining**, easy-going, forbearing, forgiving, patient, resigned, stoical, tolerant
long-winded *adjective* =**rambling**, lengthy, long-drawn-out, prolix, prolonged, repetitious, tedious, tiresome, verbose, wordy ⎡OPPOSITE⎤ **brief**
look *verb* **1** =**see**, behold (*arch*), consider, contemplate, examine, eye, gaze, glance,

observe, scan, study, survey, view, watch **2** =**seem**, appear, look like, strike one as **3** =**face**, front, overlook **4** =**search**, forage, fossick (*Aust & NZ*), hunt, seek **5** =**hope**, anticipate, await, expect, reckon on ✦*noun* **7** =**glimpse**, examination, gaze, glance, inspection, observation, peek, sight, view **8** (often pl) =**appearance**, air, aspect, bearing, countenance, demeanour, expression, manner, semblance
look after *verb* =**take care of**, attend to, care for, guard, keep an eye on, mind, nurse, protect, supervise, take charge of, tend
look down on *verb* =**disdain**, contemn, despise, scorn, sneer, spurn
look forward to *verb* =**anticipate**, await, expect, hope for, long for, look for, wait for
lookout *noun* **1** =**watch**, guard, readiness, vigil **2** =**watchman**, guard, sentinel, sentry **3** =**watchtower**, observation post, observatory, post **4** *Inf* =**concern**, business, worry
look out *verb* =**be careful**, beware, keep an eye out, pay attention, watch out
look up *verb* **1** =**research**, find, hunt for, search for, seek out, track down **2** =**improve**,

loom² ⊕ *verb* **1** appear dimly. **2** seem ominously close.

loon *noun* diving bird.

loonie *noun Canad sl* **1** a Canadian dollar coin with a loon bird on one of its faces. **2** the Canadian currency.

loony *Slang adjective* **loonier, looniest 1** foolish or insane. ◆ *noun, pl* **loonies 2** foolish or insane person.

loop ⊕ *noun* **1** rounded shape made by a curved line or rope crossing itself. **2** closed circuit through which an electronic signal can circulate. **3** continuous strip of film or tape. **4** set of instructions to be repeatedly performed in a computer program. ◆ *verb* **5** form or fasten with a loop. **loop the loop** fly or be flown in a complete vertical circle. **loophole** *noun* means of evading a rule without breaking it.

loose ⊕ *adjective* **1** not tight, fastened, fixed, or tense. **2** vague. **3** dissolute or promiscuous. ◆ *adverb* **4** in a loose manner. ◆ *verb* **5** free. **6** unfasten. **7** slacken. **8** let fly (an arrow, bullet, etc.). **at a loose end** bored, with nothing to do. **on the loose** free from confinement. **loosely** *adverb* **looseness** *noun* **loosen** *verb* make loose. **loosen up** *verb* relax, stop worrying. **loose-leaf** *adjective* allowing the addition or removal of pages.

loot ⊕ *noun, verb* **1** plunder. ◆ *noun* **2** *Informal* money. **looter** *noun* **looting** *noun*

lop *verb* **lopping, lopped 1** cut away twigs and branches. **2** chop off.

lope *verb* **1** run with long easy strides. ◆ *noun* **2** loping stride.

lop-eared *adjective* having drooping ears.

lopsided ⊕ *adjective* greater in height, weight, or size on one side.

loquacious *adjective* talkative. **loquacity** *noun*

lord ⊕ *noun* **1** person with power over others, such as a monarch or master. **2** male member of the nobility. **3** *Hist* feudal superior. **4** (**L-**) God or Jesus. **5** (**L-**) title given to certain male officials and peers. **House of Lords** unelected upper chamber of the British parliament. **lord it over** act in a superior manner towards. **the Lord's Prayer** prayer taught by Christ to his disciples. **lordly** *adjective* imperious, proud. **Lordship** *noun* title of some male officials and peers.

lore ⊕ *noun* body of traditions on a subject.

lorgnette [lor-**nyet**] *noun* pair of spectacles mounted on a long handle.

lorry *noun, pl* **-ries** large vehicle for transporting loads by road.

lose ⊕ *verb* **losing, lost 1** come to be without, esp. by accident or carelessness. **2** fail to keep or maintain. **3** be deprived of. **4** get rid of. **5** fail to get or make use of. **6** be defeated in a competition etc. **7** fail to perceive or understand. **8** go astray or allow to go astray. **9** be or become engrossed, e.g. *lost in thought.* **10** die or be destroyed. **11** (of a clock etc.) run slow (by a specified amount). **loser** *noun* **1** person or thing that loses. **2** *Informal* person

L

get better, perk up, pick up, progress, shape up (*inf*) **3** =**visit**, call on, drop in on (*inf*), look in on **look up to** =**respect**, admire, defer to, esteem, honour, revere

loom² *verb* **1** =**appear**, bulk, emerge, hover, take shape **2** =**threaten**, impend, menace

loop *noun* **1** =**curve**, circle, coil, curl, ring, spiral, twirl, twist, whorl ◆*verb* **5** =**twist**, coil, curl, knot, roll, spiral, turn, wind round

loophole *noun* =**let-out**, escape, excuse

loose *adjective* **1 a** =**slack**, easy, relaxed, sloppy OPPOSITE> **tight. b** =**free**, insecure, unattached, unbound, unfastened, unfettered, unrestricted, untied OPPOSITE> **bind. 2** =**vague**, ill-defined, imprecise, inaccurate, indistinct, inexact, rambling, random OPPOSITE> **clear. 3** =**promiscuous**, abandoned, debauched, dissipated, dissolute, fast, immoral, profligate OPPOSITE> **moral** ◆*verb* **5, 6** =**free**, detach, disconnect, liberate, release, set free, unfasten, unleash, untie

loosen *verb* **a** =**free**, liberate, release, set free **b** =**untie**, detach, separate, undo, unloose

loosen up *verb* =**relax**, ease up *or* off, go easy (*inf*), let up, outspan (*S Afr*), soften

loot *noun* **1** =**plunder**, booty, goods, haul, prize, spoils, swag (*sl*) ◆*verb* **1** =**plunder**, despoil, pillage, raid, ransack, ravage, rifle, rob, sack

lopsided *adjective* =**crooked**, askew, asymmetrical, awry, cockeyed, disproportionate, skewwhiff (*Brit inf*), squint, unbalanced, uneven, warped

lord *noun* **1** =**master**, commander, governor, leader, liege, overlord, ruler, superior **2** =**nobleman**, earl, noble, peer, viscount **4** (with cap.) =**Jesus Christ**, Christ, God, Jehovah, the Almighty **lord it over** =**order around**, boss around (*inf*), domineer, pull rank, put on airs, swagger

lordly *adjective* =**proud**, arrogant, condescending, disdainful, domineering, haughty, high-handed, imperious, lofty, overbearing

lore *noun* =**traditions**, beliefs, doctrine, sayings, teaching, wisdom who seems destined to fail. **loss** *noun* **1** losing. **2** that which is lost. **lost** *adjective* unable to find one's way.

SPELLING TIP

The verb **lose** (*I don't want to lose my hair*) should not be confused with **loose**, which, although existing as a verb, is more often used as an adjective (*a loose tooth*) or adverb (*to work loose*).

---

loss ⊕ *noun* **1** losing. **2** that which is lost. **3** damage resulting from losing. **at a loss 1** confused or bewildered. **2** not earning enough to cover costs. **loss leader** item sold at a loss to attract customers.

lost ⊕ *verb* **1** past of LOSE. ♦ *adjective* **2** unable to find one's way. **3** unable to be found. **4** bewildered or confused. **5** (foll. by *on*) not used, noticed, or understood by. **6** no longer possessed or existing.

lot ⊕ *pronoun* **1** great number. ♦ *noun* **2** collection of people or things. **3** fate or destiny. **4** one of a set of objects drawn at random to make a selection or choice. **5** item at auction. **6** *US* area of land. ♦ *plural* **7** *Informal* great numbers or quantities. **a lot** *Informal* a great deal. **bad lot** disreputable person. **the lot** entire amount or number.

loth ⊕ *adjective* same as LOATH.

lotion ⊕ *noun* medical or cosmetic liquid for use on the skin.

lottery ⊕ *noun, pl* **-teries 1** method of raising money by selling tickets that win prizes by chance. **2** gamble.

lotto *noun* game of chance like bingo.

lotus *noun* **1** legendary plant whose fruit induces forgetfulness. **2** Egyptian water lily.

loud ⊕ *adjective* **1** relatively great in volume. **2** capable of making much noise. **3** insistent and emphatic. **4** unpleasantly patterned or colourful. **loudly** *adverb* **loudness** *noun* **loudspeaker** *noun* instrument for converting electrical signals into sound.

lough *noun Irish* loch.

lounge ⊕ *noun* **1** living room in a private house. **2** (also **lounge bar**) more expensive bar in a pub. **3** area for waiting in an airport. ♦ *verb* **4** sit, lie, or stand in a relaxed manner. **lounge suit** man's suit for daytime wear.

lour *verb* same as LOWER².

louse *noun* **1** *pl* **lice** wingless parasitic insect. **2** *pl* **louses** unpleasant person. **lousy** *adjective* **lousier, lousiest 1** *Slang* mean or unpleasant. **2** bad, inferior. **3** unwell. **4** infested with lice.

lout ⊕ *noun* crude, oafish, or aggressive person. **loutish** *adjective*

louvre [loo-ver] *noun* one of a set of parallel slats slanted to admit air but not rain. **louvred** *adjective*

lovage *noun* European plant used for flavouring food.

love ⊕ *verb* **1** have a great affection for. **2** feel sexual passion for. **3** enjoy (something) very much. ♦ *noun* **4** great affection. **5** sexual

---
THESAURUS
---

lose *verb* **1** = **mislay**, drop, forget, misplace **2, 5** = **forfeit**, miss, pass up (*inf*), yield **3** = **be deprived of 6** = **be defeated**, come to grief, lose out

loser *noun* = **failure**, also-ran, dud (*inf*), flop (*inf*)

loss *noun* **1** = **losing**, defeat, failure, forfeiture, mislaying, squandering, waste OPPOSITE finding. **2** = **deficit**, debit, debt, deficiency, depletion OPPOSITE gain. **3** = **damage**, cost, destruction, harm, hurt, injury, ruin OPPOSITE advantage ♦ **at a loss 1** = **confused**, at one's wits' end, baffled, bewildered, helpless, nonplussed, perplexed, puzzled, stumped

lost *adjective* **2, 4** = **off-course**, adrift, astray, at sea, disoriented, off-track **3** = **missing**, disappeared, mislaid, misplaced, vanished

lot *noun* **2** = **collection**, assortment, batch, bunch (*inf*), consignment, crowd, group, quantity, set **3** = **destiny**, accident, chance, doom, fate, fortune **a lot** *Inf* = **plenty**, abundance, a great deal, heap(s), load(s) (*inf*), masses (*inf*), piles (*inf*), scores, stack(s)

loth see LOATH

lotion *noun* = **cream**, balm, embrocation, liniment, salve, solution

lottery *noun* **1** = **raffle**, draw, sweepstake **2** = **gamble**, chance, hazard, risk, toss-up (*inf*)

loud *adjective* **1** = **noisy**, blaring, booming, clamorous, deafening, ear-splitting, forte (*Music*), resounding, thundering, tumultuous, vociferous OPPOSITE quiet. **4** = **garish**, brash, flamboyant, flashy, gaudy, glaring, lurid, showy OPPOSITE conservative

lounge *verb* **4** = **relax**, laze, lie about, loaf, loiter, loll, outspan (*S Afr*), sprawl, take it easy

lout *noun* = **oaf**, boor, dolt, yob *or* yobbo (*Brit sl*)

lovable, loveable *adjective* = **endearing**, adorable, amiable, charming, cute, delightful, enchanting, likable *or* likeable, lovely, sweet OPPOSITE detestable passion. **6** wholehearted liking for something. **7** beloved person. **8** *Tennis, squash, etc.* score of nothing. **fall in love** become in love. **in love (with)** feeling a strong emotional (and sexual) attraction (for). **make love (to)** have sexual intercourse (with). **lovable, loveable** *adjective* **loveless** *adjective* **lovely** *adjective* **-lier, -liest 1** very attractive. **2** highly enjoyable. **lover** *noun* **1** person having a sexual relationship outside marriage. **2** person in love. **3** someone who loves a specified person or thing. **loving** *adjective* affectionate, tender. **lovingly** *adverb* **love affair** romantic or sexual relationship between two people who are not married to each other. **lovebird** *noun* small parrot. **love child** *Euphemistic* child of an unmarried couple. **love life** person's romantic or sexual relationships. **lovelorn** *adjective* miserable because of unhappiness in love. **lovemaking** *noun*

low[1] **ⓘ** *adjective* **1** not tall, high, or elevated. **2** of little or less than the usual amount, degree, quality, or cost. **3** coarse or vulgar. **4** dejected. **5** ill. **6** not loud. **7** deep in pitch. **8** (of a gear) providing a relatively low speed. ◆ *adverb* **9** in or to a low position, level, or degree. ◆ *noun* **10** low position, level, or degree. **11** area of low atmospheric pressure, depression. **lowly** *adjective* modest, humble. **lowliness** *noun* **lowbrow** *noun, adjective* (person) with nonintellectual tastes and interests. **Low Church** section of the Anglican Church stressing evangelical beliefs and practices. **lowdown** *noun Informal* inside information. **low-down** *adjective Informal* mean, underhand, or dishonest. **low-key** *adjective* subdued, restrained, not intense. **lowland** *noun* **1** low-lying country. ◆ *plural* **2** (L-) less mountainous parts of Scotland. **low profile** position or attitude avoiding prominence or publicity. **low-spirited** *adjective* depressed.

low[2] *noun* **1** cry of cattle, moo. ◆ *verb* **2** moo.

lower[1] **ⓘ** *adjective* **1** below one or more other things. **2** smaller or reduced in amount or value. ◆ *verb* **3** cause or allow to move down. **4** behave in a way that damages one's respect. **5** lessen. **lower case** small, as distinct from capital, letters.

lower[2], **lour ⓘ** *verb* (of the sky or weather) look gloomy or threatening. **lowering** *adjective*

loyal ⓘ *adjective* faithful to one's friends, country, or government. **loyally** *adverb* **loyalty**

L

THESAURUS

---

love *verb* **1** = **adore**, cherish, dote on, hold dear, idolize, prize, treasure, worship OPPOSITE> hate. **3** = **enjoy**, appreciate, delight in, like, relish, savour, take pleasure in OPPOSITE> **hate** ◆*noun* **4** = **affection**, adoration, attachment, devotion, infatuation, tenderness, warmth **5** = **passion**, ardour OPPOSITE> hate. **6** = **liking**, devotion, enjoyment, fondness, inclination, partiality, relish, soft spot, taste, weakness **7** = **beloved**, darling, dear, dearest, lover, sweetheart, truelove OPPOSITE> enemy ◆ **in love (with)** = **enamoured**, besotted, charmed, enraptured, infatuated, smitten

love affair *noun* = **romance**, affair, amour, intrigue, liaison, relationship

lovely *adjective* **1** = **beautiful**, adorable, attractive, charming, comely, exquisite, graceful, handsome, lekker (*S Afr sl*), pretty OPPOSITE> ugly. **2** = **enjoyable**, agreeable, delightful, engaging, lekker (*S Afr sl*), nice, pleasant, pleasing OPPOSITE> revolting

lover *noun* **1, 2** = **sweetheart**, admirer, beloved, boyfriend *or* girlfriend, flame (*inf*), mistress, suitor

loving *adjective* = **affectionate**, amorous, dear, devoted, doting, fond, tender, warm-hearted OPPOSITE> cruel

low[1] *adjective* **1** = **small**, little, short, squat, stunted OPPOSITE> towering. **2** = **inferior**,

deficient, inadequate, poor, second-rate, shoddy **3** = **coarse**, common, crude, disreputable, rough, rude, undignified, vulgar **4** = **dejected**, depressed, despondent, disheartened, downcast, down in the dumps (*inf*), fed up, gloomy, glum, miserable OPPOSITE> high. **5** = **ill**, debilitated, frail, stricken, weak OPPOSITE> strong. **6** = **quiet**, gentle, hushed, muffled, muted, soft, subdued, whispered OPPOSITE> loud

lowdown *noun Inf* = **information**, gen (*Brit inf*), info (*inf*), inside story, intelligence

lower[1] *adjective* **1** = **under**, inferior, junior, lesser, minor, secondary, second-class, smaller, subordinate **2** = **reduced**, curtailed, decreased, diminished, lessened OPPOSITE> higher ◆*verb* **3** = **drop**, depress, fall, let down, sink, submerge, take down OPPOSITE> raise. **5** = **lessen**, cut, decrease, diminish, minimize, prune, reduce, slash OPPOSITE> increase

lower[2], **lour** *verb* = **darken**, be brewing, blacken, cloud up *or* over, loom, menace, threaten

low-key *adjective* = **subdued**, muted, quiet, restrained, toned down, understated

lowly *adjective* = **humble**, meek, mild, modest, unassuming

low-spirited *adjective* = **depressed**, dejected, despondent, dismal, down, down-hearted, fed noun **loyalty card** swipe card issued by a supermarket or chain store to a customer, used to record credit points awarded for money spent in the store. **loyalist** noun

lozenge noun **1** medicated tablet held in the mouth until it dissolves. **2** four-sided diamond-shaped figure.

LP noun record playing approximately 20-25 minutes each side.

L-plate noun sign on a car being driven by a learner driver.

Lr Chem lawrencium.

LSD lysergic acid diethylamide, a hallucinogenic drug.

Lt Lieutenant.

Ltd Limited (Liability).

Lu Chem lutetium.

lubricate ❶ [loo-brik-ate] verb oil or grease to lessen friction. **lubricant** noun lubricating substance, such as oil. **lubrication** noun

lubricious [loo-**brish**-uss] adjective Lit lewd.

lucerne noun fodder plant like clover, alfalfa.

lucid ❶ adjective **1** clear and easily understood. **2** able to think clearly. **3** bright and clear. **lucidly** adverb **lucidity** noun

Lucifer noun Satan.

luck ❶ noun **1** fortune, good or bad. **2** good fortune. **lucky** adjective having or bringing good luck. **lucky dip** game in which prizes are picked from a tub at random. **luckily** adverb fortunately. **luckless** adjective having bad luck.

lucrative ❶ adjective very profitable.

lucre ❶ [loo-ker] noun **filthy lucre** Facetious

money.

Luddite noun person opposed to change in industrial methods.

luderick noun Australian fish, usu. black or dark brown in colour.

ludicrous ❶ adjective absurd or ridiculous. **ludicrously** adverb

ludo noun game played with dice and counters on a board.

luff verb sail (a ship) towards the wind.

lug¹ verb **lugging, lugged** carry or drag with great effort.

lug² noun **1** projection serving as a handle. **2** Informal ear.

luggage ❶ noun traveller's cases, bags, etc.

lugubrious ❶ [loo-goo-bree-uss] adjective mournful, gloomy. **lugubriously** adverb

lugworm noun large worm used as bait.

lukewarm ❶ adjective **1** moderately warm, tepid. **2** indifferent or half-hearted.

lull ❶ verb **1** soothe (someone) by soft sounds or motions. **2** calm (fears or suspicions) by deception. ◆ noun **3** brief time of quiet in a storm etc.

lullaby noun, pl **-bies** quiet song to send a child to sleep.

lumbago [lum-**bay**-go] noun pain in the lower back. **lumbar** adjective relating to the lower back.

lumber¹ ❶ noun **1** unwanted disused household articles. **2** Chiefly US sawn timber. ◆ verb **3** Informal burden with something unpleasant. **lumberjack** noun US man who fells

up, low, miserable, sad

loyal adjective =**faithful**, constant, dependable, devoted, dutiful, staunch, steadfast, true, trustworthy, trusty, unwavering OPPOSITE **disloyal**

loyalty noun =**faithfulness**, allegiance, constancy, dependability, devotion, fidelity, staunchness, steadfastness, trustworthiness

lubricate verb =**oil**, grease, smear

lucid adjective **1** =**clear**, comprehensible, explicit, intelligible, transparent OPPOSITE **confused**. **2** =**clear-headed**, compos mentis, all there, in one's right mind, rational, sane OPPOSITE **confused**. **3** =**translucent**, clear, crystalline, diaphanous, glassy, limpid, pellucid, transparent

luck noun **1** =**fortune**, accident, chance, destiny, fate **2** =**good fortune**, advantage, blessing, godsend, prosperity, serendipity, success, windfall

luckily adverb =**fortunately**, favourably, happily, opportunely, propitiously,

providentially

lucky adjective =**fortunate**, advantageous, blessed, charmed, favoured, jammy (Brit sl), successful OPPOSITE **unlucky**

lucrative adjective =**profitable**, advantageous, fruitful, productive, remunerative, well-paid

lucre noun **filthy lucre** Facetious =**money**, gain, lolly (Aust & NZ sl), mammon, pelf, profit, riches, spoils, wealth

ludicrous adjective =**ridiculous**, absurd, crazy, farcical, laughable, nonsensical, outlandish, preposterous, silly

luggage noun =**baggage**, bags, cases, gear, impedimenta, paraphernalia, suitcases, things

lugubrious adjective =**gloomy**, doleful, melancholy, mournful, sad, serious, sombre, sorrowful, woebegone

lukewarm adjective **1** =**tepid**, warm **2** =**half-hearted**, apathetic, cool, indifferent, unenthusiastic, unresponsive

lull verb **1** =**calm**, allay, pacify, quell, soothe, subdue, tranquillize ◆noun **3** =**respite**, calm,

trees and prepares logs for transport.
lumber² ⊕ *verb* move heavily and awkwardly.
lumbering *adjective*
luminous ⊕ *adjective* reflecting or giving off
light. **luminosity** *noun* **luminary** *noun* **1**
famous person. **2** *Lit* heavenly body giving off
light. **luminescence** *noun* emission of light at
low temperatures by any process other than
burning. **luminescent** *adjective*
lump¹ ⊕ *noun* **1** shapeless piece or mass. **2**
swelling. **3** *Informal* awkward or stupid person.
♦ *verb* **4** consider as a single group. **lump in
one's throat** tight dry feeling in one's throat,
usu. caused by great emotion. **lumpish**
adjective stupid or clumsy. **lumpy** *adjective*
lump sum relatively large sum of money paid
at one time.
lump² *verb* **lump it** *Informal* tolerate or put up
with it.
lunar *adjective* relating to the moon.
lunatic ⊕ *adjective* **1** foolish and irresponsible.
♦ *noun* **2** foolish or annoying person. **3** *Old-
fashioned* insane person. **lunacy** *noun*
lunch *noun* **1** meal taken in the middle of the
day. ♦ *verb* **2** eat lunch. **luncheon** *noun* formal
lunch. **luncheon meat** tinned ground mixture
of meat and cereal. **luncheon voucher** voucher
for a certain amount, given to an employee and
accepted by some restaurants as payment for a
meal.
lung *noun* organ that allows an animal or bird

to breathe air: humans have two lungs in the
chest. **lungfish** *noun* freshwater bony fish with
an air-breathing lung of South America and
Australia.
lunge ⊕ *noun* **1** sudden forward motion. **2**
thrust with a sword. ♦ *verb* **3** move with or
make a lunge.
lupin *noun* garden plant with tall spikes of
flowers.
lupine *adjective* like a wolf.
lupus *noun* ulcerous skin disease.
lurch¹ ⊕ *verb* **1** tilt or lean suddenly to one
side. **2** stagger. ♦ *noun* **3** lurching movement.
lurch² *noun* **leave someone in the lurch**
abandon someone in difficulties.
lurcher *noun* crossbred dog trained to hunt
silently.
lure ⊕ *verb* **1** tempt or attract by the promise
of reward. ♦ *noun* **2** person or thing that lures.
3 brightly-coloured artificial angling bait. **4**
feathered decoy for attracting a falcon.
lurid ⊕ *adjective* **1** vivid in shocking detail,
sensational. **2** glaring in colour. **luridly** *adverb*
lurk ⊕ *verb* **1** lie hidden or move stealthily,
esp. for sinister purposes. **2** be latent.
luscious ⊕ [lush-uss] *adjective* **1** extremely
pleasurable to taste or smell. **2** very attractive.
lush¹ ⊕ *adjective* **1** (of grass etc.) growing
thickly and healthily. **2** opulent.
lush² *noun* *Slang* alcoholic.
lust ⊕ *noun* **1** strong sexual desire. **2** any

L

——————————————— T H E S A U R U S ———————————————

hush, let-up (*inf*), pause, quiet, silence
lumber¹ *noun* **1** =**junk**, clutter, jumble, refuse,
rubbish, trash ♦*verb* **3** *Inf* =**burden**, encumber,
land, load, saddle
lumber² *verb* =**plod**, shamble, shuffle, stump,
trudge, trundle, waddle
lumbering *adjective* =**awkward**, clumsy,
heavy, hulking, ponderous, ungainly
luminous *adjective* =**bright**, glowing,
illuminated, luminescent, lustrous, radiant,
shining
lump¹ *noun* **1** =**piece**, ball, chunk, hunk,
mass, nugget **2** =**swelling**, bulge, bump,
growth, hump, protrusion, tumour ♦*verb* **4**
=**group**, collect, combine, conglomerate,
consolidate, mass, pool
lumpy *adjective* =**bumpy**, knobbly, uneven
lunacy *noun* **1** =**foolishness**, absurdity,
craziness, folly, foolhardiness, madness,
stupidity OPPOSITE **reason**. **3** *Old-fashioned*
=**insanity**, dementia, derangement, madness,
mania, psychosis OPPOSITE **reason**
lunatic *adjective* **1** =**irrational**, crackbrained,
crackpot (*inf*), crazy, daft, deranged, insane,

mad ♦*noun* **3** *Old-fashioned* =**madman**, maniac,
nutcase (*sl*), psychopath
lunge *noun* **1** =**pounce**, charge, spring, swing
2 =**thrust**, jab ♦*verb* **3 a** =**pounce**, charge,
dive, leap **b** =**thrust**, jab
lurch¹ *verb* **1** =**tilt**, heave, heel, lean, list,
pitch, rock, roll **2** =**stagger**, reel, stumble,
sway, totter, weave
lure *verb* **1** =**tempt**, allure, attract, draw,
ensnare, entice, invite, seduce ♦*noun* **2**
=**temptation**, allurement, attraction, bait,
carrot (*inf*), enticement, incentive, inducement
lurid *adjective* **1** =**sensational**, graphic,
melodramatic, shocking, vivid OPPOSITE
controlled. **2** =**glaring**, intense OPPOSITE **pale**
lurk *verb* **1** =**hide**, conceal oneself, lie in wait,
prowl, skulk, slink, sneak
luscious *adjective* **1** =**delicious**, appetizing,
juicy, mouth-watering, palatable, succulent,
sweet, toothsome
lush¹ *adjective* **1** =**abundant**, dense,
flourishing, green, rank, verdant **2** =**luxurious**,
elaborate, extravagant, grand, lavish, opulent,
ornate, palatial, plush (*inf*), sumptuous

L

strong desire. ◆ *verb* **3** have passionate desire (for). **lustful** *adjective* **lusty** *adjective* vigorous, healthy. **lustily** *adverb*

lustre ❶ *noun* **1** gloss, sheen. **2** splendour or glory. **3** metallic pottery glaze. **lustrous** *adjective* shining, luminous.

lute *noun* ancient guitar-like musical instrument with a body shaped like a half pear.

lutetium [loo-**tee**-shee-um] *noun Chem* silvery-white metallic element.

Lutheran *adjective* of Martin Luther (1483-1546), German Reformation leader, his doctrines, or a Church following these doctrines.

lux *noun, pl* **lux** unit of illumination.

luxuriant *adjective* **1** rich and abundant. **2** very elaborate. **luxuriance** *noun* **luxuriantly** *adverb*

luxuriate *verb* **1** take self-indulgent pleasure (in). **2** flourish.

luxury ❶ *noun, pl* **-ries 1** enjoyment of rich, very comfortable living. **2** enjoyable but not essential thing. ◆ *adjective* **3** of or providing luxury. **luxurious** *adjective* full of luxury, sumptuous. **luxuriously** *adverb*

LV luncheon voucher.

lychee [lie-**chee**] *noun* Chinese fruit with a whitish juicy pulp.

lych gate *noun* roofed gate to a churchyard.

Lycra *noun* ® elastic fabric used for tight-fitting garments, such as swimsuits.

lye *noun* caustic solution made from wood ash.

lying ❶ *verb* present participle of LIE¹ *or* LIE².

lying-in *noun Old-fashioned* period of confinement during childbirth.

lymph *noun* colourless bodily fluid consisting mainly of white blood cells. **lymphatic** *adjective*

lymph node mass of tissue that helps to fight infection in the body.

lymphocyte *noun* type of white blood cell.

lynch *verb* put to death without a trial.

lynx *noun* animal of the cat family with tufted ears and a short tail.

lyre *noun* ancient musical instrument like a U-shaped harp. **lyrebird** *noun* pheasant-like Australian bird the male of which spreads its tail out into the shape of a lyre.

lyric ❶ *adjective* **1** (of poetry) expressing personal emotion in songlike style. **2** like a song. ◆ *noun* **3** short poem in a songlike style. ◆ *plural* **4** words of a popular song. **lyrical** *adjective* **1** lyric. **2** enthusiastic. **lyricism** *noun* **lyricist** *noun* person who writes the words of songs or musicals.

——————— THESAURUS ———————

lust *noun* **1** = **lechery**, lasciviousness, lewdness, sensuality **2** = **desire**, appetite, craving, greed, longing, passion, thirst ◆*verb* **3** = **desire**, covet, crave, hunger for or after, want, yearn

lustre *noun* **1** = **sparkle**, gleam, glint, glitter, gloss, glow, sheen, shimmer, shine **2** = **glory**, distinction, fame, honour, prestige, renown

lusty *adjective* = **vigorous**, energetic, healthy, hearty, powerful, robust, strong, sturdy, virile

luxurious *adjective* = **sumptuous**, comfortable, expensive, lavish, magnificent, opulent, plush (*inf*), rich, splendid

luxury *noun* **1** = **opulence**, affluence, hedonism, richness, splendour, sumptuousness [OPPOSITE] **want**. **2** = **extravagance**, extra, frill, indulgence, treat [OPPOSITE] **necessity**

lying *noun* **1** = **dishonesty**, deceit, mendacity, perjury, untruthfulness ◆*adjective* **2** = **deceitful**, dishonest, false, mendacious, perfidious, treacherous, two-faced, untruthful [OPPOSITE] **straight**

lyrical *adjective* **2** = **enthusiastic**, carried away, ecstatic, effusive, impassioned, inspired, poetic, rapturous, rhapsodic

Mm

m 1 metre(s). 2 mile(s). 3 minute(s).
M 1 Motorway. 2 *pl* **MM** Monsieur. 3 mega-.
4 the Roman numeral for 1000.
m 1 male. 2 married. 3 masculine. 4 meridian.
5 month.
ma *noun Informal* mother.
MA 1 Master of Arts. 2 Massachusetts.
ma'am *noun* madam.
mac *noun Informal* mackintosh.
macabre ❶ [mak-**kahb**-ra] *adjective* strange and horrible, gruesome.
macadam *noun* road surface of pressed layers of small broken stones. **macadamize** *verb* pave (a road) with macadam.
macaque [mac-**kahk**] *noun* monkey of Asia and Africa with cheek pouches and either a short tail or no tail.
macaroni *noun* pasta in short tube shapes.
macaroon *noun* small biscuit or cake made with ground almonds.
macaw *noun* large tropical American parrot.
mace[1] *noun* 1 ceremonial staff of office. 2 medieval weapon with a spiked metal head.
mace[2] *noun* spice made from the dried husk of the nutmeg.
macerate [**mass**-er-ate] *verb* soften by soaking. **maceration** *noun*
Mach [mak] *noun* short for MACH NUMBER.
machete [mash-**ett**-ee] *noun* broad heavy knife used for cutting or as a weapon.
Machiavellian ❶ [mak-ee-a-**vel**-yan] *adjective* unprincipled, crafty, and opportunist.
machinations [mak-in-**nay**-shunz] *plural noun* cunning plots and ploys.
machine ❶ *noun* 1 apparatus, usu. powered by electricity, designed to perform a particular task. 2 vehicle, such as a car or aircraft. 3 controlling system of an organization. ♦ *verb* 4 make or produce by machine. **machinery** *noun*

1 machines or machine parts collectively. 2 standard procedures of an organization.
machinist *noun* person who operates a machine. **machine gun** automatic gun that fires rapidly and continuously. **machine-gun** *verb* fire at with such a gun. **machine language** instructions for a computer in binary code that require no conversion or translation by the computer. **machine-readable** *adjective* (of data) in a form suitable for processing by a computer.
machismo [mak-**izz**-moh] *noun* exaggerated or strong masculinity.
Mach number [mak] *noun* 1
macho ❶ [**match**-oh] *adjective* strongly or exaggeratedly masculine.
mack *noun Informal* mackintosh.
mackerel *noun* edible sea fish with blue and silver stripes.
mackintosh, macintosh *noun* 1 waterproof raincoat of rubberized cloth. 2 any raincoat.
macramé [mak-**rah**-mee] *noun* ornamental work of knotted cord.
macro- *combining form* large, long, or great, e.g. *macroscopic*.
macrobiotics *noun* dietary system advocating whole grains and vegetables grown without chemical additives. **macrobiotic** *adjective*
macrocosm *noun* 1 the universe. 2 any large complete system.
mad ❶ *adjective* **madder, maddest** 1 mentally deranged, insane. 2 very foolish. 3 *Informal* angry. 4 frantic. 5 (foll. by *about* or *on*) very enthusiastic (about). **like mad** *Informal* with great energy, enthusiasm, or haste. **madly** *adverb* 1 with great speed and energy. 2 *Informal* extremely or excessively. **madness** *noun* **madden** *verb* infuriate or irritate. **maddening** *adjective* **maddeningly** *adverb*

M

THESAURUS

macabre *adjective* =**gruesome**, dreadful, eerie, frightening, ghastly, ghostly, ghoulish, grim, grisly, morbid OPPOSITE delightful
Machiavellian *adjective* =**scheming**, astute, crafty, cunning, cynical, double-dealing, opportunist, sly, underhand, unscrupulous
machine *noun* 1 =**appliance**, apparatus,

contraption, contrivance, device, engine, instrument, mechanism, tool 3 =**system**, machinery, organization, setup (*inf*), structure
machinery *noun* 1 =**equipment**, apparatus, gear, instruments, tackle, tools
macho *adjective* =**manly**, chauvinist, masculine, virile

madman, madwoman *noun*

madam *noun* **1** polite form of address to a woman. **2** *Informal* precocious or conceited girl.

madame [mad-**dam**] *noun, pl* **mesdames** [may-**dam**] French title equivalent to *Mrs.*

madcap ❶ *adjective* foolish or reckless.

madder *noun* **1** climbing plant. **2** red dye made from its root.

made *verb* past of MAKE. **have (got) it made** *Informal* be assured of success.

Madeira [mad-**deer**-a] *noun* fortified white wine. **Madeira cake** rich sponge cake.

mademoiselle [mad-mwah-**zel**] *noun, pl* **mesdemoiselles** [maid-mwah-**zel**] French title equivalent to *Miss.*

madhouse *noun* **1** *Informal* place filled with uproar or confusion. **2** *Old-fashioned* mental hospital.

Madonna *noun* **1** the Virgin Mary. **2** picture or statue of her.

madrigal *noun* 16th-17th-century part song for unaccompanied voices.

maelstrom ❶ [**male**-strom] *noun* **1** great whirlpool. **2** turmoil.

maestro ❶ [**my**-stroh] *noun, pl* **-tri, -tros 1** outstanding musician or conductor. **2** any

master of an art.

mae west *noun* inflatable life jacket.

Mafia *noun* international secret criminal organization founded in Sicily. **mafioso** *noun, pl* **-sos, -si** member of the Mafia.

magazine ❶ *noun* **1** periodical publication with articles by different writers. **2** television or radio programme made up of short nonfictional items. **3** appliance for automatically supplying cartridges to a gun or slides to a projector. **4** storehouse for explosives or arms.

magenta [maj-**jen**-ta] *adjective* deep purplish-red.

maggot *noun* larva of an insect. **maggoty** *adjective*

Magi [**maje**-eye] *plural noun* wise men from the East who came to worship the infant Jesus.

magic ❶ *noun* **1** supposed art of invoking supernatural powers to influence events. **2** conjuring tricks done to entertain. **3** mysterious quality or power. ◆ *adjective* **4** (also **magical**) of, using, or like magic. **5** *Informal* wonderful, marvellous. **magically** *adverb* **magician** *noun* **1** conjuror. **2** person with magic powers.

magistrate ❶ *noun* **1** public officer administering the law. **2** justice of the peace.

M

———————— T H E S A U R U S ————————

mad *adjective* **1** = **insane**, *non compos mentis*, crazy (*inf*), demented, deranged, nuts (*sl*), of unsound mind, out of one's mind, psychotic, raving, unhinged, unstable OPPOSITE **rational. 2** = **foolish**, absurd, asinine, daft (*inf*), foolhardy, irrational, nonsensical, preposterous, senseless, wild OPPOSITE **sound. 3** *Inf* = **angry**, berserk, enraged, furious, incensed, livid (*inf*), pissed (*taboo sl*), pissed off (*taboo sl*), wild OPPOSITE **calm. 4** = **frenzied**, excited, frenetic, uncontrolled, unrestrained, wild **5** = **enthusiastic**, ardent, avid, crazy (*inf*), fanatical, impassioned, infatuated, wild OPPOSITE **uncaring ◆ like mad** *Inf* = **energetically**, enthusiastically, excitedly, furiously, rapidly, speedily, violently, wildly

madcap *adjective* = **reckless**, crazy, foolhardy, hare-brained, imprudent, impulsive, rash, thoughtless

madden *verb* = **infuriate**, annoy, derange, drive one crazy, enrage, incense, inflame, irritate, upset OPPOSITE **calm**

madly *adverb* **1** = **energetically**, excitedly, furiously, like mad (*inf*), recklessly, speedily, wildly **2** *Inf* = **passionately**, desperately, devotedly, intensely, to distraction

madman, madwoman *noun* = **lunatic**, maniac, nutcase (*sl*), psycho (*sl*), psychopath

madness *noun* **1** = **insanity**, aberration,

craziness, delusion, dementia, derangement, distraction, lunacy, mania, mental illness, psychopathy, psychosis, wildness **2** = **foolishness**, absurdity, daftness (*inf*), folly, foolhardiness, idiocy, nonsense, preposterousness

maelstrom *noun* **1** = **whirlpool**, vortex **2** = **turmoil**, chaos, confusion, disorder, tumult, upheaval

maestro *noun* **1** = **virtuoso 2** = **master**, expert, fundi (*S Afr*), genius

magazine *noun* **1** = **journal**, pamphlet, periodical **4** = **storehouse**, arsenal, depot, store, warehouse

magic *noun* **1** = **sorcery**, black art, enchantment, necromancy, witchcraft, wizardry **2** = **conjuring**, illusion, legerdemain, prestidigitation, sleight of hand, trickery **3** = **charm**, allurement, enchantment, fascination, glamour, magnetism, power ◆*adjective* **4** (also **magical**) = **miraculous**, bewitching, charming, enchanting, entrancing, fascinating, spellbinding **5** *Inf* = **marvellous**

magician *noun* **1** = **conjuror** *or* **conjuror**, illusionist **2** = **sorcerer**, enchanter *or* enchantress, necromancer, warlock, witch, wizard

magisterial *adjective* **1** = **authoritative**, commanding, lordly, masterful OPPOSITE

magisterial *adjective* **1** commanding or authoritative. **2** of a magistrate.

magma *noun* molten rock inside the earth's crust.

magnanimous ❶ *adjective* noble and generous. **magnanimously** *adverb* **magnanimity** *noun*

magnate ❶ *noun* influential or wealthy person, esp. in industry.

magnesia *noun* white tasteless substance used as an antacid and a laxative; magnesium oxide.

magnesium *noun Chem* silvery-white metallic element.

magnet ❶ *noun* **1** piece of iron or steel capable of attracting iron and pointing north when suspended. **2** person or thing that exerts a great attraction. **magnetic** *adjective* **1** having the properties of a magnet. **2** powerfully attractive. **magnetically** *adverb* **magnetism** *noun* **1** magnetic property. **2** powerful personal charm. **3** science of magnetic properties. **magnetize** *verb* **1** make into a magnet. **2** attract strongly. **magnetic field** area around a magnet in which its power of attraction is felt. **magnetic north** direction in which a compass needle points. **magnetic tape** plastic strip coated with a magnetic substance for recording sound or video signals.

magneto [mag-**nee**-toe] *noun, pl* **-tos** apparatus for ignition in an internal-combustion engine.

magnificent ❶ *adjective* **1** splendid or impressive. **2** excellent. **magnificently** *adverb* **magnificence** *noun*

magnify ❶ *verb* **-fying, -fied 1** increase in apparent size, as with a lens. **2** exaggerate.

magnification *noun* **magnifying glass** convex lens used to produce an enlarged image of an object.

magnitude ❶ *noun* relative importance or size.

magnolia *noun* shrub or tree with showy white or pink flowers.

magnum *noun* large wine bottle holding about 1.5 litres.

magnum opus *noun* greatest single work of art or literature of a particular artist.

magpie *noun* **1** black-and-white bird. **2** any of various similar Australian birds, e.g. the butcherbird.

Magyar *noun* **1** member of the main ethnic group in Hungary. **2** Hungarian language. ♦ *adjective* **3** of the Magyars.

maharajah *noun* former title of some Indian princes. **maharani, maharanee** *n fem*

maharishi *noun* Hindu religious teacher or mystic.

mahatma *noun Hinduism* person revered for holiness and wisdom.

mah jong, mah-jongg *noun* Chinese table game for four, played with tiles bearing different designs.

mahogany *noun* hard reddish-brown wood of several tropical trees.

mahout [ma-**howt**] *noun* (in India and the East Indies) elephant driver or keeper.

maid ❶ *noun* **1** (also **maidservant**) female servant. **2** *Lit* young unmarried woman.

M

——————————— THESAURUS ———————————

subservient

magistrate *noun* **1** = judge **2** = justice of the peace, J.P., justice

magnanimity *noun* = generosity, benevolence, big-heartedness, largesse *or* largess, nobility, selflessness, unselfishness

magnanimous *adjective* = generous, big-hearted, bountiful, charitable, kind, noble, selfless, unselfish OPPOSITE petty

magnate *noun* = tycoon, baron, big hitter (*inf*), captain of industry, heavy hitter (*inf*), mogul, plutocrat

magnetic *adjective* **2** = attractive, captivating, charismatic, charming, fascinating, hypnotic, irresistible, lekker (*S Afr sl*), mesmerizing, seductive OPPOSITE repulsive

magnetism *noun* **2** = charm, allure, appeal, attraction, charisma, drawing power, magic, pull, seductiveness

magnification *noun* **1** = increase, amplification, enlargement, expansion,

heightening **2** = intensification, enhancement

magnificence *noun* = splendour, brilliance, glory, grandeur, majesty, nobility, opulence, stateliness, sumptuousness

magnificent *adjective* **1** = splendid, glorious, gorgeous, imposing, impressive, majestic, regal, sublime, sumptuous OPPOSITE ordinary. **2** = excellent, brilliant, fine, outstanding, splendid, superb OPPOSITE ordinary

magnify *verb* **1** = enlarge, amplify, blow up (*inf*), boost, dilate, expand, heighten, increase OPPOSITE reduce. **2** = exaggerate, inflate, intensify, overemphasize, overplay, overstate OPPOSITE understate

magnitude *noun* **a** = importance, consequence, greatness, moment, note, significance, weight OPPOSITE insignificance. **b** = size, amount, amplitude, extent, mass, quantity, volume

maid *noun* **1** (also **maidservant**) = servant, housemaid, maidservant, serving-maid **2** *Lit*

maiden ❶ *noun* **1** *Lit* young unmarried woman. ♦ *adjective* **2** unmarried. **3** first, e.g. *maiden voyage.* **maid** *noun* female servant. **maidenly** *adjective* modest. **maidenhair** *noun* fern with delicate fronds. **maidenhead** *noun* virginity. **maiden name** woman's surname before marriage. **maiden over** *Cricket* over in which no runs are scored.

mail[1] *noun* **1** letters and packages transported and delivered by the post office. **2** postal system. **3** single collection or delivery of mail. **4** train, ship, or aircraft carrying mail. **5** same as E-MAIL. ♦ *verb* **6** send by mail. **mailing list** *noun* register of names and addresses to which information and advertising material is sent by post or electronic mail. **mail order** system of buying goods by post. **mailshot** *noun* posting of advertising material to many selected people at once.

mail[2] *noun* flexible armour of interlaced rings or links.

mailbox *noun US & Canad* **1** public box into which letters are put for collection and delivery. **2** private box outside house where occupant's mail is delivered.

mailman *noun* person who collects or delivers mail.

maim ❶ *verb* cripple or mutilate.

main ❶ *adjective* **1** chief or principal. ♦ *noun* **2** principal pipe or line carrying water, gas, or electricity. ♦ *plural* **3** main distribution network for water, gas, or electricity. **in the main** on the whole. **mainly** *adverb* for the most part,

chiefly. **mainframe** *noun, adjective Computers* (denoting) a high-speed general-purpose computer. **mainland** *noun* stretch of land which forms the main part of a country.

mainmast *noun* chief mast of a ship. **mainsail** *noun* largest sail on a mainmast. **mainspring** *noun* **1** chief cause or motive. **2** chief spring of a watch or clock. **mainstay** *noun* **1** chief support. **2** rope securing a mainmast.

mainstream *adjective* (of) a prevailing cultural trend.

maintain ❶ *verb* **1** continue or keep in existence. **2** keep up or preserve. **3** support financially. **4** assert. **maintenance** *noun* **1** maintaining. **2** upkeep of a building, car, etc. **3** provision of money for a separated or divorced spouse.

maisonette *noun* flat with more than one floor.

maize *noun* type of corn with spikes of yellow grains.

Maj. Major.

majesty ❶ *noun, pl* **-ties 1** stateliness or grandeur. **2** supreme power. **majestic** *adjective* **majestically** *adverb*

majolica *noun* type of ornamented Italian pottery.

major ❶ *adjective* **1** greater in number, quality, or extent. **2** significant or serious. ♦ *noun* **3** middle-ranking army officer. **4** scale in music. **5** *US & Canad* principal field of study at a university etc. ♦ *verb* **6** (foll. by *in*) *US, Canad, Aust & NZ* do one's principal study in

M

——————— T H E S A U R U S ———————

=**girl**, damsel, lass, lassie (*inf*), maiden, wench
maiden *noun* **1** *Lit* =**girl**, damsel, lass, lassie (*inf*), maid, virgin, wench ♦*adjective* **2** =**unmarried**, unwed **3** =**first**, inaugural, initial, introductory
maidenly *adjective* =**modest**, chaste, decent, decorous, demure, pure, virginal
mail[1] *noun* **1** =**letters**, correspondence **1-3** =**post** ♦*verb* **6** =**post**, dispatch, forward, send
maim *verb* =**cripple**, disable, hurt, injure, mutilate, wound
main *adjective* **1** =**chief**, central, essential, foremost, head, leading, pre-eminent, primary, principal OPPOSITE least ♦*noun* **2** =**conduit**, cable, channel, duct, line, pipe **in the main** =**on the whole**, for the most part, generally, in general, mainly, mostly
mainly *adverb* =**chiefly**, for the most part, in the main, largely, mostly, on the whole, predominantly, primarily, principally
mainstay *noun* **1** =**pillar**, anchor, backbone, bulwark, buttress, prop

mainstream *adjective* **2** =**conventional**, accepted, current, established, general, orthodox, prevailing, received OPPOSITE unconventional
maintain *verb* **1** =**continue**, carry on, perpetuate, prolong, retain, sustain OPPOSITE end. **2** =**keep up**, care for, preserve **3** =**look after**, provide for, support, take care of **4** =**assert**, avow, claim, contend, declare, insist, profess, state OPPOSITE disavow
maintenance *noun* **1** =**continuation**, carrying-on, perpetuation, prolongation **2** =**upkeep**, care, conservation, keeping, nurture, preservation, repairs **3** =**allowance**, alimony, keep, support
majestic *adjective* **1** =**grand**, grandiose, impressive, magnificent, monumental, regal, splendid, stately, sublime, superb OPPOSITE modest
majesty *noun* **1** =**grandeur**, glory, magnificence, nobility, pomp, splendour, stateliness OPPOSITE triviality

(a particular subject). **majorette** *noun* one of a group of girls who practise formation marching and baton twirling. **major-domo** *noun, pl* **-domos** chief steward of a great household. **major-general** *noun* senior military officer. **majority** *noun* greater number.

majority ⊕ *noun, pl* **-ties 1** greater number. **2** number by which the votes on one side exceed those on the other. **3** largest party voting together. **4** state of being legally an adult.

make ⊕ *verb* **making, made 1** create, construct, or establish. **2** cause to do or be. **3** bring about or produce. **4** perform (an action). **5** appoint. **6** serve as or become. **7** amount to. **8** earn. ♦ *noun* **9** brand, type, or style. **make do** manage with an inferior alternative. **make it** *Informal* be successful. **on the make** *Informal* out for profit or conquest. **maker** *noun* **1** person or company that makes something. **2** (**M-**) title given to God. **making** *noun* **1** creation or production. ♦ *plural* **2** necessary requirements or qualities. **make-believe** *noun* fantasy or pretence. **make for** *verb* head towards. **make off with** *verb* steal or abduct.

make out *verb* **1** manage to see or hear (something), perceive. **2** understand. **3** write out (a cheque). **4** pretend. **5** attempt to establish or prove. **6** *Informal* manage or fare, e.g. *how did you make out in the competition?* **makeshift** *adjective* serving as a temporary substitute. **make up** *verb* **1** form or constitute. **2** prepare. **3** invent. **4** supply what is lacking, complete. **5** (foll. by *for*) compensate (for). **6** settle a quarrel. **7** apply cosmetics. **make-up** *noun* **1** cosmetics. **2** way something is made. **3** mental or physical constitution. **makeweight** *noun* something unimportant added to make up a lack.

mako *noun, pl* **makos** powerful shark of the Atlantic and Pacific Oceans.

mal- *combining form* bad or badly, e.g. *malformation.*

malachite [mal-a-kite] *noun* green mineral.

maladjusted ⊕ *adjective Psychol* unable to meet the demands of society. **maladjustment** *noun*

maladministration ⊕ *noun* inefficient or dishonest administration.

THESAURUS

---

major *adjective* **1** = **main**, bigger, chief, greater, higher, leading, senior, supreme OPPOSITE **minor**. **2** = **important**, critical, crucial, great, notable, outstanding, serious, significant OPPOSITE **trivial**

majority *noun* **1** = **most**, best part, bulk, greater number, mass, preponderance **4** = **adulthood**, manhood *or* womanhood, maturity, seniority

make *verb* **1** = **create**, assemble, build, construct, fashion, form, manufacture, produce, put together, synthesize **2** = **force**, cause, compel, constrain, drive, impel, induce, oblige, prevail upon, require **3** = **produce**, accomplish, bring about, cause, create, effect, generate, give rise to, lead to **4** = **perform**, carry out, do, effect, execute **7** = **amount to**, add up to, compose, constitute, form **8** = **earn**, clear, gain, get, net, obtain, win ♦*noun* **9** = **brand**, kind, model, sort, style, type, variety

make for *verb* = **head for**, aim for, be bound for, head towards

make it *verb Inf* = **succeed**, arrive (*inf*), crack it (*inf*), get on, prosper

make off with *verb* = **steal**, abduct, carry off, filch, kidnap, nick (*sl, chiefly Brit*), pinch (*inf*), run away *or* off with

make out *verb* **1** = **see**, detect, discern, discover, distinguish, perceive, recognize **2** = **understand**, comprehend, decipher, fathom, follow, grasp, work out **3** = **write out**, complete, draw up, fill in *or* out **4** = **pretend**, let on, make as if *or* though **5** = **claim**, assert **6** *Inf* = **fare**, get on, manage

maker *noun* **1** = **manufacturer**, builder, constructor, producer

makeshift *adjective* = **temporary**, expedient, provisional, stopgap, substitute

make up *verb* **1** = **form**, compose, comprise, constitute **3** = **invent**, coin, compose, concoct, construct, create, devise, dream up, formulate, frame, originate **4** = **complete**, fill, supply **5** (foll. by *for*) = **compensate for**, atone for, make amends for **6** = **settle**, bury the hatchet, call it quits, reconcile

make-up *noun* **1** = **cosmetics**, face (*inf*), greasepaint (*Theatre*), paint (*inf*), powder **2** = **structure**, arrangement, assembly, composition, configuration, constitution, construction, format, organization **3** = **nature**, character, constitution, disposition, temperament

making *noun* **1** = **creation**, assembly, building, composition, construction, fabrication, manufacture, production

makings *plural noun* **2** = **beginnings**, capacity, ingredients, potential

maladjusted *adjective Psychol* = **disturbed**, alienated, neurotic, unstable

maladministration *noun* = **mismanagement**, corruption, dishonesty, incompetence, inefficiency, malpractice, misrule

M

maladroit [mal-a-**droyt**] *adjective* clumsy or awkward.

malady [**mal**-a-dee] *noun, pl* **-dies** disease or illness.

malaise [mal-**laze**] *noun* **1** something wrong which affects a section of society or area of activity. **2** vague feeling of unease, illness, or depression.

malapropism *noun* comical misuse of a word by confusion with one which sounds similar.

malaria *noun* infectious disease caused by the bite of some mosquitoes. **malarial** *adjective*

Malay *noun* **1** member of a people of Malaysia or Indonesia. **2** language of this people. ◆ *adjective* **3** of the Malays or their language. **Malayan** *adjective, noun*

malcontent *noun* discontented person.

male *adjective* **1** of the sex which can fertilize female reproductive cells. ◆ *noun* **2** male person or animal. **maleness** *noun* **male chauvinism** belief, held by some men, that men are superior to women. **male chauvinist** (characteristic of) a man who believes that men are superior to women.

malediction [mal-lid-**dik**-shun] *noun* curse.

malefactor [**mal**-if-act-or] *noun* criminal or wrongdoer.

malevolent [mal-**lev**-a-lent] *adjective* wishing evil to others. **malevolently** *adverb* **malevolence** *noun*

malfeasance [mal-**fee**-zanss] *noun* misconduct, esp. by a public official.

malformed *adjective* misshapen or deformed. **malformation** *noun*

malfunction *verb* **1** function imperfectly or fail to function. ◆ *noun* **2** defective functioning or failure to function.

malice [**mal**-iss] *noun* desire to cause harm to others. **malice aforethought** *Law* deliberate intention to do something unlawful. **malicious** *adjective* **maliciously** *adverb*

malign [mal-**line**] *verb* **1** slander or defame. ◆ *adjective* **2** evil in influence or effect. **malignity** [mal-**lig**-nit-tee] *noun* evil disposition.

malignant [mal-**lig**-nant] *adjective* **1** seeking to harm others. **2** (of a tumour) harmful and uncontrollable. **malignancy** *noun*

malinger [mal-**ling**-ger] *verb* feign illness to avoid work. **malingerer** *noun*

mall [**mawl**] *noun* street or shopping area closed to vehicles.

mallard *noun* wild duck.

malleable [**mal**-lee-a-bl] *adjective* **1** capable of being hammered or pressed into shape. **2** easily influenced. **malleability** *noun*

mallet *noun* **1** (wooden) hammer. **2** stick with a head like a hammer, used in croquet or polo.

mallow *noun* plant with pink or purple flowers.

malnutrition *noun* inadequate nutrition.

malodorous [mal-**lode**-or-uss] *adjective* bad-smelling.

M

————————— T H E S A U R U S —————————

maladroit *adjective* = **clumsy**, awkward, cack-handed (*inf*), ham-fisted *or* ham-handed (*inf*), inept, inexpert, unskilful

malady *noun* = **disease**, affliction, ailment, complaint, disorder, illness, infirmity, sickness

malaise *noun* **2** = **unease**, anxiety, depression, disquiet, melancholy

malcontent *noun* = **troublemaker**, agitator, mischief-maker, rebel, stirrer (*inf*)

male *adjective* **1** = **masculine**, manly, virile OPPOSITE **female**

malefactor *noun* = **wrongdoer**, criminal, delinquent, evildoer, miscreant, offender, villain

malevolence *noun* = **malice**, hate, hatred, ill will, nastiness, rancour, spite, vindictiveness

malevolent *adjective* = **spiteful**, hostile, ill-natured, malicious, malign, vengeful, vindictive OPPOSITE **benevolent**

malformation *noun* = **deformity**, distortion, misshapenness

malformed *adjective* = **misshapen**, abnormal, crooked, deformed, distorted, irregular, twisted

malfunction *verb* **1** = **break down**, fail, go wrong ◆*noun* **2** = **fault**, breakdown, defect, failure, flaw, glitch

malice *noun* = **spite**, animosity, enmity, evil intent, hate, hatred, ill will, malevolence, vindictiveness

malicious *adjective* = **spiteful**, ill-disposed, ill-natured, malevolent, rancorous, resentful, vengeful OPPOSITE **benevolent**

malign *verb* **1** = **disparage**, abuse, defame, denigrate, libel, run down, slander, smear, vilify OPPOSITE **praise** ◆*adjective* **2** = **evil**, bad, destructive, harmful, hostile, injurious, malevolent, malignant, pernicious, wicked OPPOSITE **good**

malignant *adjective* **1** = **hostile**, destructive, harmful, hurtful, malevolent, malign, pernicious, spiteful OPPOSITE **kind**. **2** = **uncontrollable**, cancerous, dangerous, deadly, fatal, irremediable OPPOSITE **benign**

malleable *adjective* **1** = **workable**, ductile, plastic, soft, tensile **2** = **manageable**, adaptable, biddable, compliant, impressionable, pliable, tractable

malodorous *adjective* = **smelly**, fetid, mephitic, nauseating, noisome, offensive,

malpractice ❶ *noun* immoral, illegal, or unethical professional conduct.

malt *noun* **1** grain, such as barley, prepared for use in making beer or whisky. **2** malt whisky. ♦ *verb* **3** make into or make with malt. **malty** *adjective* **malted milk** drink made from powdered milk with malted cereals. **malt whisky** whisky made from malted barley.

Maltese *adjective* **1** of Malta or its language. ♦ *noun* **2** *pl* **-tese** person from Malta. **3** language of Malta. **Maltese cross** cross with triangular arms that taper towards the centre.

maltreat ❶ *verb* treat badly. **maltreatment** *noun*

mama [mam-ma] *noun Old-fashioned* mother.

mamba *noun* deadly S African snake.

mamma *noun* same as MAMA.

mammal *noun* animal of the type that suckles its young. **mammalian** *adjective*

mammary *adjective* of the breasts or milk-producing glands.

mammon *noun* wealth regarded as a source of evil.

mammoth ❶ *noun* **1** extinct elephant-like mammal. ♦ *adjective* **2** colossal.

man ❶ *noun, pl* **men 1** adult male. **2** human being or person. **3** mankind. **4** manservant. **5** (usu. pl) member of the armed forces who is not an officer. **6** piece used in chess etc. ♦ *verb* **manning, manned 7** supply with sufficient people for operation or defence. **man in the street** average person. **manhood** *noun* **mankind** *noun* human beings collectively. **manly** *adjective* **-lier, -liest** (possessing qualities) appropriate to a man. **manliness**

noun **manned** *adjective* having a human personnel or crew. **mannish** *adjective* like a man. **man-hour** *noun* work done by one person in one hour. **man-made** *adjective* made artificially.

mana *noun NZ* authority, influence.

manacle ❶ [man-a-kl] *noun, verb* handcuff or fetter.

manage ❶ *verb* **1** succeed in doing. **2** be in charge of, administer. **3** handle or control. **4** cope with (financial) difficulties. **manageable** *adjective* **management** *noun* **1** managers collectively. **2** administration or organization.

manager, manageress *noun* person in charge of a business, institution, actor, sports team, etc. **managerial** *adjective*

mañana [man-**yah**-na] *adverb, noun Spanish* **1** tomorrow. **2** some later (unspecified) time.

manatee *noun* large tropical plant-eating aquatic mammal.

mandarin *noun* **1** high-ranking government official. **2** kind of small orange.

Mandarin Chinese, Mandarin *noun* official language of China.

mandate ❶ *noun* **1** official or authoritative command. **2** authorization or instruction from an electorate to its representative or government. ♦ *verb* **3** give authority to.

mandatory *adjective* compulsory.

mandible *noun* lower jawbone or jawlike part.

mandolin *noun* musical instrument with four pairs of strings.

mandrake *noun* plant with a forked root, formerly used as a narcotic.

mandrel *noun* shaft on which work is held in a

M

————————— THESAURUS —————————

putrid, reeking, stinking

malpractice *noun* =**misconduct**, abuse, dereliction, mismanagement, negligence

maltreat *verb* =**abuse**, bully, harm, hurt, ill-treat, injure, mistreat

mammoth *adjective* **2** =**colossal**, enormous, giant, gigantic, huge, immense, massive, monumental, mountainous, prodigious OPPOSITE> **tiny**

man *noun* **1** =**male**, bloke (*Brit inf*), chap (*inf*), gentleman, guy (*inf*) **2** =**human**, human being, individual, person, soul **3** =**mankind**, Homo sapiens, humanity, humankind, human race, people **4** =**manservant**, attendant, retainer, servant, valet ♦*verb* **7** =**staff**, crew, garrison, occupy, people

manacle *noun* =**handcuff**, bond, chain, fetter, iron, shackle ♦*verb* =**handcuff**, bind, chain, fetter, put in chains, shackle

manage *verb* **1** =**succeed**, accomplish,

arrange, contrive, effect, engineer **2** =**administer**, be in charge (of), command, conduct, direct, handle, run, supervise **3** =**handle**, control, manipulate, operate, use **4** =**cope**, carry on, get by (*inf*), make do, muddle through, survive

manageable *adjective* **3 a** =**docile**, amenable, compliant, submissive **b** =**easy**, handy, user-friendly OPPOSITE> **hard**

management *noun* **1** =**directors**, administration, board, employers, executive(s) **2** =**administration**, command, control, direction, handling, operation, running, supervision

manager *noun* =**supervisor**, administrator, boss (*inf*), director, executive, governor, head, organizer

mandate *noun* **1** =**command**, commission, decree, directive, edict, instruction, order

mandatory *adjective* =**compulsory**, binding, obligatory, required, requisite OPPOSITE>

lathe.

mandrill *noun* large blue-faced baboon.

mane *noun* **1** long hair on the neck of a horse, lion, etc. **2** long thick human hair.

manful ⊕ *adjective* determined and brave. **manfully** *adverb*

manfully ⊕ *adverb* bravely and determinedly.

manganese *noun Chem* brittle greyish-white metallic element.

mange *noun* skin disease of domestic animals.

mangelwurzel *noun* variety of beet used as cattle food.

manger *noun* eating trough in a stable or barn.

mangetout [mawnzh-too] *noun* variety of pea with an edible pod.

mangle¹ ⊕ *verb* **1** destroy by crushing and twisting. **2** spoil.

mangle² *noun* **1** machine with rollers for squeezing water from washed clothes. ◆ *verb* **2** put through a mangle.

mango *noun, pl* **-goes, -gos** tropical fruit with sweet juicy yellow flesh.

mangrove *noun* tropical tree with exposed roots, which grows beside water.

mangy ⊕ *adjective* **mangier, mangiest 1** having mange. **2** scruffy or shabby.

manhandle ⊕ *verb* treat roughly.

manhole *noun* hole with a cover, through which a person can enter a drain or sewer.

manhunt *noun* organized search, usu. by police, for a wanted man or a fugitive.

mania ⊕ *noun* **1** extreme enthusiasm. **2** madness. **maniac** *noun* **1** mad person. **2** *Informal* person who has an extreme enthusiasm for something. **maniacal** [man-**eye**-a-kl] *adjective*

manic *adjective* **1** extremely excited or energetic. **2** affected by mania. **manic-depressive** *adjective, noun Psychiatry* (person afflicted with) a mental disorder that causes mood swings from extreme euphoria to deep depression.

manicure *noun* **1** cosmetic care of the fingernails and hands. ◆ *verb* **2** care for (the fingernails and hands) in this way. **manicurist** *noun*

manifest ⊕ *adjective* **1** easily noticed, obvious. ◆ *verb* **2** show plainly. **3** be evidence of. ◆ *noun* **4** list of cargo or passengers for customs. **manifestly** *adverb* **manifestation** *noun*

manifesto *noun, pl* **-tos, -toes** declaration of policy as issued by a political party.

manifold ⊕ *adjective* **1** numerous and varied. ◆ *noun* **2** pipe with several outlets, esp. in an internal-combustion engine.

manikin, mannikin *noun* **1** little man or dwarf. **2** model of the human body.

manila, manilla *noun* strong brown paper used for envelopes.

manipulate ⊕ *verb* **1** handle skilfully. **2** control cleverly or deviously. **manipulation** *noun* **manipulative** *adjective* **manipulator** *noun*

manna *noun* **1** *Bible* miraculous food which

———————— THESAURUS ————————

optional

manfully *adverb* =**bravely**, boldly, courageously, determinedly, gallantly, hard, resolutely, stoutly, valiantly

mangle *verb* **1** =**crush**, deform, destroy, disfigure, distort, mutilate, tear **2** =**spoil**, ruin, wreck

mangy *adjective* **2** =**scruffy**, dirty, moth-eaten, scungy (*Aust & NZ inf*), seedy, shabby, shoddy, squalid

manhandle *verb* =**rough up**, knock about *or* around, maul, paw (*inf*)

manhood *noun* =**manliness**, masculinity, virility

mania *noun* **1** =**obsession**, craze, fad (*inf*), fetish, fixation, passion, preoccupation, thing (*inf*) **2** =**madness**, delirium, dementia, derangement, insanity, lunacy

maniac *noun* **1** =**madman** *or* **madwoman**, lunatic, psycho (*sl*), psychopath **2** *Inf* =**fanatic**, enthusiast, fan, fiend (*inf*), freak (*inf*)

manifest *adjective* **1** =**obvious**, apparent, blatant, clear, conspicuous, evident, glaring,

noticeable, palpable, patent OPPOSITE concealed ◆*verb* **2** =**display**, demonstrate, exhibit, expose, express, reveal, show OPPOSITE hide

manifestation *noun* =**display**, demonstration, exhibition, expression, indication, mark, show, sign, symptom

manifold *adjective* **1** =**numerous**, assorted, copious, diverse, many, multifarious, multiple, varied, various

manipulate *verb* **1** =**work**, handle, operate, use **2** =**influence**, control, direct, engineer, manoeuvre

mankind *noun* =**people**, Homo sapiens, humanity, humankind, human race, man

manliness *noun* =**virility**, boldness, bravery, courage, fearlessness, masculinity, valour, vigour

manly *adjective* =**virile**, bold, brave, courageous, fearless, manful, masculine, strapping, strong, vigorous OPPOSITE effeminate

man-made *adjective* =**artificial**, ersatz, manufactured, mock, synthetic sustained the Israelites in the wilderness. **2** windfall.

mannequin *noun* **1** woman who models clothes at a fashion show. **2** life-size dummy of the human body used to fit or display clothes.

manner ⊙ *noun* **1** way a thing happens or is done. **2** person's bearing or behaviour. **3** type or kind. **4** custom or style. ◆ *plural* **5** (polite) social behaviour. **mannered** *adjective* affected.

mannerism *noun* person's distinctive habit or trait. **mannerly** *adjective* having good manners, polite.

mannikin *noun* same as MANIKIN.

manoeuvre ⊙ [man-**noo**-ver] *noun* **1** skilful movement. **2** contrived, complicated, and possibly deceptive plan or action. ◆ *plural* **3** military or naval exercises. ◆ *verb* **4** manipulate or contrive skilfully or cunningly. **5** perform manoeuvres. **manoeuvrable** *adjective*

manor *noun* large country house and its lands. **manorial** *adjective*

manpower *noun* available number of workers.

manqué [**mong**-kay] *adjective* would-be, e.g. *an actor manqué.*

mansard roof *noun* roof with a break in its slope, the lower part being steeper than the upper.

manse *noun* house provided for a minister in some religious denominations.

manservant *noun, pl* **menservants** male servant, esp. a valet.

mansion ⊙ *noun* large house.

manslaughter *noun* unlawful but unintentional killing of a person.

mantel *noun* structure round a fireplace.

mantelpiece, mantel shelf *noun* shelf above a fireplace.

mantilla *noun* (in Spain) a lace scarf covering a woman's head and shoulders.

mantis *noun, pl* **-tises, -tes** carnivorous insect like a grasshopper.

mantle ⊙ *noun* **1** loose cloak. **2** covering. **3** responsibilities and duties which go with a particular job or position. **4** incandescent gauze round a gas jet.

mantra *noun Hinduism, Buddhism* any sacred word or syllable used as an object of concentration.

manual ⊙ *adjective* **1** of or done with the hands. **2** by human labour rather than automatic means. ◆ *noun* **3** handbook. **4** organ keyboard. **manually** *adverb*

manufacture ⊙ *verb* **1** process or make (goods) on a large scale using machinery. **2** invent or concoct (an excuse etc.). ◆ *noun* **3** process of manufacturing goods. **manufacturer** *noun*

manure ⊙ *noun* **1** animal excrement used as a fertilizer. ◆ *verb* **2** fertilize (land) with this.

manuscript *noun* **1** book or document, orig. one written by hand. **2** copy for printing.

Manx *adjective* **1** of the Isle of Man or its inhabitants. ◆ *noun* **2** almost extinct language of the Isle of Man. **Manx cat** tailless breed of cat.

many ⊙ *adjective* **more, most 1** numerous. ◆ *noun* **2** large number.

Maoism *noun* form of Marxism advanced by Mao Tse-tung in China. **Maoist** *noun, adjective*

Maori *noun* **1** member of the indigenous race of New Zealand. **2** language of the Maoris. ◆ *adjective* **3** of the Maoris or their language.

——————— T H E S A U R U S ———————

manner *noun* **1** = **way**, method, mode **2** = **behaviour**, air, aspect, bearing, conduct, demeanour **3** = **type**, brand, category, form, kind, sort, variety **4** = **style**, custom, fashion

mannered *adjective* = **affected**, artificial, pretentious, stilted OPPOSITE▷ **natural**

mannerism *noun* = **habit**, characteristic, foible, idiosyncrasy, peculiarity, quirk, trait, trick

manners *plural noun* **5** = **behaviour**, conduct, courtesy, decorum, demeanour, etiquette, politeness, p's and q's, refinement

manoeuvre *noun* **1** = **movement**, exercise, operation **2** = **stratagem**, dodge, intrigue, machination, ploy, ruse, scheme, subterfuge, tactic, trick ◆*verb* **4** = **manipulate**, contrive, engineer, machinate, pull strings, scheme, wangle (*inf*) **5** = **move**, deploy, exercise

mansion *noun* = **residence**, hall, manor, seat, villa

mantle *noun* **1** = **cloak**, cape, hood, shawl, wrap **2** = **covering**, blanket, canopy, curtain, pall, screen, shroud, veil

manual *adjective* **1** = **hand-operated 2** = **human**, physical ◆*noun* **3** = **handbook**, bible, guide, instructions

manufacture *verb* **1** = **make**, assemble, build, construct, create, mass-produce, produce, put together, turn out **2** = **concoct**, cook up (*inf*), devise, fabricate, invent, make up, think up, trump up ◆*noun* **3** = **making**, assembly, construction, creation, production

manufacturer *noun* = **maker**, builder, constructor, creator, industrialist, producer

manure *noun* **1** = **compost**, droppings, dung, excrement, fertilizer, kak (*S Afr sl*), muck, ordure

many *adjective* **1** = **numerous**, abundant, countless, innumerable, manifold, myriad, umpteen (*inf*), various ◆*noun* **2** = **a lot**, heaps

M

map *noun* **1** representation of the earth's surface or some part of it, showing geographical features. **2** *Maths* (also **mapping**) same as FUNCTION (sense 4) ◆ *verb* **mapping, mapped 3** make a map of. **4** *Maths* represent or transform (a function, figure, or set). **map out** *verb* plan.

maple *noun* tree with broad leaves, a variety of which (**sugar maple**) **yields sugar. maple syrup** very sweet syrup made from the sap of the sugar maple.

maple sugar *noun US & Canad* sugar made from the sap of the sugar maple.

mar ⊕ *verb* **marring, marred** spoil or impair.

Mar. March.

marabou *noun* **1** large black-and-white African stork. **2** its soft white down, used to trim hats etc.

maraca [mar-**rak**-a] *noun* shaken percussion instrument made from a gourd containing dried seeds etc.

maraschino cherry [mar-rass-**kee**-no] *noun* cherry preserved in a cherry liqueur with a taste like bitter almonds.

marathon *noun* **1** long-distance race of 26 miles 385 yards (42.195 kilometres). **2** long or arduous task.

marauding ⊕ *adjective* wandering or raiding in search of plunder. **marauder** *noun*

marble *noun* **1** kind of limestone with a mottled appearance, which can be highly polished. **2** slab of or sculpture in this. **3** small glass ball used in playing marbles. ◆ *plural* **4** game of rolling these at one another. **marbled** *adjective* having a mottled appearance like marble. **marbling** *noun*

marcasite *noun* crystals of iron pyrites, used in jewellery.

march¹ ⊕ *verb* **1** walk with a military step. **2** make (a person or group) proceed. **3** progress steadily. ◆ *noun* **4** action of marching. **5** steady progress. **6** distance covered by marching. **7** piece of music, as for a march. **marcher** *noun*

march² *noun* border or frontier.

March *noun* third month of the year.

marchioness [marsh-on-**ness**] *noun* **1** woman holding the rank of marquis. **2** wife or widow of a marquis.

Mardi Gras [**mar**-dee **grah**] *noun* festival of Shrove Tuesday, celebrated in some cities with great revelry.

mare *noun* female horse or zebra. **mare's nest** discovery which proves worthless.

margarine *noun* butter substitute made from animal or vegetable fats.

marge *noun Informal* margarine.

margin ⊕ *noun* **1** edge or border. **2** blank space round a printed page. **3** additional amount or one greater than necessary. **4** limit.

marginal *adjective* **1** insignificant, unimportant. **2** near a limit. **3** *Politics* (of a constituency) won by only a small margin. ◆ *noun* **4** *Politics* marginal constituency. **marginally** *adverb*

marguerite *noun* large daisy.

marigold *noun* plant with yellow or orange flowers.

marijuana ⊕ [mar-ree-**wah**-na] *noun* dried flowers and leaves of the cannabis plant, used as a drug, esp. in cigarettes.

marimba *noun* Latin American percussion instrument resembling a xylophone.

marina *noun* harbour for yachts and other pleasure boats.

marinade *noun* **1** seasoned liquid in which fish or meat is soaked before cooking. ◆ *verb* **2** same as MARINATE. **marinate** *verb* soak in marinade.

marine ⊕ *adjective* **1** of the sea or shipping. **2** used at or found in the sea. ◆ *noun* **3** soldier trained for land and sea combat. **4** country's shipping or fleet. **mariner** [**mar**-in-er] *noun* sailor.

marionette *noun* puppet worked with strings.

marital ⊕ *adjective* relating to marriage.

maritime ⊕ *adjective* **1** relating to shipping. **2** of, near, or living in the sea.

———————— THESAURUS ————————

(*inf*), lots (*inf*), plenty, scores

mar *verb* = **spoil**, blemish, damage, detract from, disfigure, hurt, impair, ruin, scar, stain, taint, tarnish OPPOSITE **improve**

marauder *noun* = **raider**, bandit, brigand, buccaneer, outlaw, plunderer

march¹ *verb* **1** = **walk**, pace, parade, stride, strut **3** = **file** ◆ *noun* **4** = **walk**, routemarch, trek **5** = **progress**, advance, development, evolution, progression

margin *noun* **1** = **edge**, border, boundary, brink, perimeter, periphery, rim, side, verge

marginal *adjective* **1** = **insignificant**, minimal, minor, negligible, slight, small **2** = **borderline**, bordering, on the edge, peripheral

marijuana *noun* = **cannabis**, dope (*sl*), grass (*sl*), hemp, pot (*sl*)

marine *adjective* **1** = **nautical**, maritime, naval, seafaring, seagoing

mariner *noun* = **sailor**, salt, sea dog, seafarer, seaman

marital *adjective* = **matrimonial**, conjugal, connubial, nuptial

maritime *adjective* **1** = **nautical**, marine, naval,

marjoram *noun* aromatic herb used for seasoning food and in salads.

mark[1] 🛈 *noun* **1** line, dot, scar, etc. visible on a surface. **2** distinguishing sign or symbol. **3** written or printed symbol. **4** letter or number used to grade academic work. **5** indication of position. **6** indication of some quality. **7** target or goal. ♦ *verb* **8** make a mark on. **9** characterize or distinguish. **10** indicate. **11** pay attention to. **12** notice or watch. **13** grade (academic work). **14** stay close to (a sporting opponent) to hamper his or her play. **mark time 1** move the feet up and down as if marching, without moving forward. **2** wait for something more interesting to happen. **marked** *adjective* noticeable. **markedly** [mark-id-lee] *adverb* **marker** *noun* **1** object used to show the position of something. **2** (also **marker pen**) thick felt-tipped pen for drawing and colouring. **marking** *noun*

mark[2] *noun* same as DEUTSCHMARK.

market 🛈 *noun* **1** assembly or place for buying and selling. **2** demand for goods. ♦ *verb* **-keting, -keted 3** offer or produce for sale. **on the market** for sale. **marketable** *adjective* **marketing** *noun* part of a business that controls the way that goods or services are sold. **market garden** place where fruit and vegetables are grown for sale. **market maker** *Stock Exchange* person who uses a firm's money to create a market for a stock. **marketplace** *noun* **1** market. **2** commercial world. **market research** research into consumers' needs and purchases.

marksman 🛈 *noun* person skilled at shooting. **marksmanship** *noun*

marl *noun* soil formed of clay and lime, used as fertilizer.

marlin *noun* large food and game fish of warm and tropical seas, with a very long upper jaw.

marlinespike, marlinspike [mar-lin-spike] *noun* pointed hook used to separate strands of rope.

marmalade *noun* jam made from citrus fruits.

marmoreal [mar-more-ee-al] *adjective* of or like marble.

marmoset *noun* small bushy-tailed monkey.

marmot *noun* burrowing rodent.

maroon[1] *adjective* reddish-purple.

maroon[2] 🛈 *verb* **1** abandon ashore, esp. on an island. **2** isolate without resources.

marquee *noun* large tent used for a party or exhibition.

marquess [mar-kwiss] *noun Brit* nobleman of the rank below a duke.

marquetry *noun* ornamental inlaid work of wood.

marquis *noun* (in various countries) nobleman of the rank above a count.

marquise [mar-keez] *noun* same as MARCHIONESS.

marram grass *noun* grass that grows on sandy shores.

marrow *noun* **1** fatty substance inside bones. **2** long thick striped green vegetable with whitish flesh.

marry 🛈 *verb* **-rying, -ried 1** take as a husband or wife. **2** join or give in marriage. **3** unite closely. **marriage** *noun* **1** state of being married. **2** wedding. **3** close union or relationship. **marriageable** *adjective*

Mars *noun* **1** Roman god of war. **2** fourth planet from the sun.

Marsala [mar-sah-la] *noun* dark sweet wine.

Marseillaise [mar-say-yaze] *noun* French national anthem.

marsh 🛈 *noun* low-lying wet land. **marshy** *adjective* **marshier, marshiest**

M

———————— THESAURUS ————————

oceanic, seafaring **2 = coastal**, littoral, seaside

mark[1] *noun* **1 = spot**, blemish, blot, line, scar, scratch, smudge, stain, streak **2 = sign**, badge, device, emblem, flag, hallmark, label, token **3 = symbol 6 = criterion**, measure, norm, standard, yardstick **7 = target**, aim, goal, object, objective, purpose ♦*verb* **8 = scar**, blemish, blot, scratch, smudge, stain, streak **9 = distinguish**, brand, characterize, denote, exemplify, flag, identify, illustrate, label, show, stamp **11 = pay attention**, attend, mind, pay heed **12 = observe**, note, notice, watch **13 = grade**, appraise, assess, correct, evaluate

marked *adjective* **= noticeable**, blatant, clear, conspicuous, decided, distinct, obvious, patent, prominent, pronounced, striking OPPOSITE imperceptible

markedly *adverb* **= noticeably**, clearly, considerably, conspicuously, decidedly, distinctly, obviously, strikingly

market *noun* **1 = fair**, bazaar, mart ♦*verb* **3 = sell**, retail, vend

marketable *adjective* **2 = sought after**, in demand, saleable, wanted

marksman *noun* **= sharpshooter**, crack shot (*inf*), good shot

maroon[2] *verb* **1 = abandon**, desert, leave **2 = strand**, leave high and dry (*inf*)

marriage *noun* **1 = matrimony**, wedlock **2 = wedding**, nuptials **3 = match**

marry *verb* **1 = wed**, get hitched (*sl*), tie the knot (*inf*) **3 = unite**, ally, bond, join, knit, link,

marshal ❶ *noun* **1** officer of the highest rank. **2** official who organizes ceremonies or events. **3** *US* law officer. ◆ *verb* **-shalling, -shalled 4** arrange in order. **5** assemble. **6** conduct with ceremony. **marshalling yard** railway depot for goods trains.

marshmallow *noun* spongy pink or white sweet.

marsupial [mar-**soop**-ee-al] *noun* animal that carries its young in a pouch, such as a kangaroo.

mart *noun* market.

Martello tower *noun* round tower for coastal defence.

marten *noun* **1** weasel-like animal. **2** its fur.

martial ❶ *adjective* of war, warlike. **martial art** any of various philosophies and techniques of self-defence, orig. Eastern, such as karate.

martial law law enforced by military authorities in times of danger or emergency.

Martian [**marsh**-an] *adjective* **1** of Mars. ◆ *noun* **2** supposed inhabitant of Mars.

martin *noun* bird with a slightly forked tail.

martinet ❶ *noun* person who maintains strict discipline.

martingale *noun* strap from the reins to the girth of a horse, preventing it from throwing up its head.

martini *noun* cocktail of vermouth and gin.

martyr ❶ *noun* **1** person who dies or suffers for his or her beliefs. ◆ *verb* **2** make a martyr of. **be a martyr to** be constantly suffering from.

martyrdom *noun*

marvel ❶ *verb* **-velling, -velled 1** be filled with wonder. ◆ *noun* **2** wonderful thing.

marvellous *adjective* **1** amazing. **2** wonderful.

marvellously *adverb*

Marxism *noun* political philosophy of Karl Marx. **Marxist** *noun, adjective*

marzipan *noun* paste of ground almonds, sugar, and egg whites.

masc. masculine.

mascara *noun* cosmetic for darkening the eyelashes.

mascot *noun* person, animal, or thing supposed to bring good luck.

masculine ❶ *adjective* **1** relating to males. **2** manly. **3** *Grammar* of the gender of nouns that includes some male animate things.

masculinity *noun*

maser *noun* device for amplifying microwaves.

mash *noun* **1** a soft pulpy mass. **2** *Informal* mashed potatoes. **3** bran or meal mixed with warm water as food for horses etc. ◆ *verb* **4** crush into a soft mass.

mask ❶ *noun* **1** covering for the face, as a disguise or protection. **2** behaviour that hides one's true feelings. ◆ *verb* **3** cover with a mask. **4** hide or disguise. **masking tape** adhesive tape used to protect surfaces surrounding an area to be painted.

masochism [**mass**-oh-kiz-zum] *noun* condition in which (sexual) pleasure is obtained from feeling pain or from being humiliated. **masochist** *noun* **masochistic** *adjective* **masochistically** *adverb*

mason *noun* **1** person who works with stone. **2** (**M-**) Freemason. **Masonic** *adjective* of Freemasonry. **masonry** *noun* **1** stonework. **2** (**M-**) Freemasonry.

masque [mask] *noun Hist* 16th-17th-century form of dramatic entertainment.

masquerade ❶ [mask-er-**aid**] *noun* **1** deceptive show or pretence. **2** party at which masks and costumes are worn. ◆ *verb* **3** pretend to be someone or something else.

—————— T H E S A U R U S ——————

merge, unify, yoke

marsh *noun* =**swamp**, bog, fen, morass, quagmire, slough, muskeg (*Canad*)

marshal *verb* **4** = **arrange**, align, array, draw up, line up, order, organize **5** = **group**, deploy **6** = **conduct**, escort, guide, lead, shepherd, usher

marshy *adjective* =**swampy**, boggy, quaggy, waterlogged, wet

martial *adjective* =**military**, bellicose, belligerent, warlike

martinet *noun* =**disciplinarian**, stickler

martyrdom *noun* **1** = **persecution**, ordeal, suffering

marvel *verb* **1** = **wonder**, be amazed, be awed, gape ◆*noun* **2** = **wonder**, miracle, phenomenon, portent, prodigy

marvellous *adjective* **1** = **amazing**, astonishing, astounding, breathtaking, brilliant, extraordinary, jaw-dropping, miraculous, phenomenal, prodigious, spectacular, stupendous **2** = **excellent**, fabulous (*inf*), fantastic (*inf*), great (*inf*), splendid, superb, terrific (*inf*), wonderful OPPOSITE **terrible**

masculine *adjective* **1** = **male**, manlike, mannish **2** = **manly**, virile

mask *noun* **1** = **disguise**, camouflage, cover, veil **2** = **front**, facade, guise, screen ◆*verb* **4** = **disguise**, camouflage, cloak, conceal, cover, hide, obscure, screen, veil

masquerade *noun* **1** = **pretence**, cloak, cover-up, deception, disguise, mask, pose, screen, subterfuge **2** = **masked ball**, fancy dress party, revel ◆*verb* **3** = **pose**, disguise, dissemble,

mass ⊕ *noun* **1** coherent body of matter. **2** large quantity or number. **3** *Physics* amount of matter in a body. ◆ *adjective* **4** large-scale. **5** involving many people. ◆ *verb* **6** form into a mass. **massed** *adjective* **the masses** ordinary people. **massive** *adjective* large and heavy. **massively** *adverb* **mass-market** *adjective* for or appealing to a large number of people. **mass media** means of communication to many people, such as television and newspapers. **mass-produce** *verb* manufacture (standardized goods) in large quantities. **mass production** manufacturing of standardized goods in large quantities. **Mass** *noun* service of the Eucharist, esp. in the RC Church. **massacre** ⊕ [**mass**-a-ker] *noun* **1** indiscriminate killing of large numbers of people. ◆ *verb* **2** kill in large numbers. **massage** ⊕ [**mass**-ahzh] *noun* **1** rubbing and kneading of parts of the body to reduce pain or stiffness. ◆ *verb* **2** give a massage to. **masseur** [mass-**ur**], (*fem*) **masseuse** [mass-**uz**] *noun* person who gives massages. **massif** [**mass**-seef] *noun* connected group of mountains. **mast**[1] *noun* tall pole for supporting something, esp. a ship's sails. **masthead** *noun* **1** *Naut* head of a mast. **2** name of a newspaper printed at

the top of the front page. **mast**[2] *noun* fruit of the beech, oak, etc., used as pig fodder. **mastectomy** [mass-**tek**-tom-ee] *noun, pl* **-mies** surgical removal of a breast. **master** ⊕ *noun* **1** person in control, such as an employer or an owner of slaves or animals. **2** expert. **3** great artist. **4** original thing from which copies are made. **5** male teacher. **6** (**M-**) title of a boy. ◆ *adjective* **7** overall or controlling. **8** main or principal. ◆ *verb* **9** acquire knowledge of or skill in. **10** overcome. **masterful** *adjective* **1** domineering. **2** showing great skill. **masterly** *adjective* showing great skill. **mastery** *noun* **1** expertise. **2** control or command. **master key** key that opens all the locks of a set. **mastermind** *verb* **1** plan and direct (a complex task). ◆ *noun* **2** person who plans and directs a complex task. **master of ceremonies** person who presides over a public ceremony, formal dinner, or entertainment, introducing the events and performers. **masterpiece** *noun* outstanding work of art. **masterstroke** *noun* outstanding piece of strategy, skill, or talent. **mastic** *noun* **1** gum obtained from certain trees. **2** putty-like substance used as a filler, adhesive, or seal. **masticate** *verb* chew. **mastication** *noun*

M

———— THESAURUS ————

dissimulate, impersonate, pass oneself off, pretend (to be)
mass *noun* **1** = **piece**, block, chunk, hunk, lump **2** = **lot**, bunch, collection, heap, load, pile, quantity, stack **3** = **size**, bulk, greatness, magnitude ◆*adjective* **4** = **large-scale**, extensive, general, indiscriminate, wholesale, widespread ◆*verb* **6** = **gather**, accumulate, assemble, collect, congregate, rally, swarm, throng
massacre *noun* **1** = **slaughter**, annihilation, blood bath, butchery, carnage, extermination, holocaust, murder ◆*verb* **2** = **slaughter**, butcher, cut to pieces, exterminate, kill, mow down, murder, wipe out
massage *noun* **1** = **rub-down**, manipulation ◆*verb* **2** = **rub down**, knead, manipulate
massive *adjective* = **huge**, big, colossal, enormous, gigantic, hefty, immense, mammoth, monumental, whopping (*inf*) OPPOSITE **tiny**
master *noun* **1** = **head**, boss (*inf*), chief, commander, controller, director, governor, lord, manager, ruler OPPOSITE **subject**. **2** = **expert**, ace (*inf*), doyen, fundi (*S Afr*), genius, maestro, past master, virtuoso, wizard OPPOSITE **novice**.

5 = **teacher**, guide, guru, instructor, tutor OPPOSITE **student** ◆*adjective* **8** = **main**, chief, foremost, leading, predominant, prime, principal OPPOSITE **minor** ◆*verb* **9** = **learn**, get the hang of (*inf*), grasp **10** = **overcome**, conquer, defeat, tame, triumph over, vanquish OPPOSITE **yield to**
masterful *adjective* **1** = **domineering**, arrogant, bossy (*inf*), high-handed, imperious, overbearing, overweening OPPOSITE **weak**. **2** = **skilful**, adroit, consummate, expert, fine, first-rate, masterly, superlative, supreme, world-class OPPOSITE **incompetent**
masterly *adjective* = **skilful**, adroit, consummate, crack (*inf*), expert, first-rate, masterful, supreme, world-class
mastermind *verb* **1** = **plan**, conceive, devise, direct, manage, organize ◆*noun* **2** = **organizer**, architect, brain(s) (*inf*), director, engineer, manager, planner
masterpiece *noun* = **classic**, jewel, magnum opus, pièce de résistance, tour de force
mastery *noun* **1** = **expertise**, finesse, know-how (*inf*), proficiency, prowess, skill, virtuosity **2** = **control**, ascendancy, command, domination, superiority, supremacy, upper hand, whip hand

mastiff *noun* large dog.
mastitis *noun* inflammation of a breast or udder.
mastodon *noun* extinct elephant-like mammal.
mastoid *noun* projection of the bone behind the ear. **mastoiditis** *noun* inflammation of this area.
masturbate *verb* fondle the genitals (of). **masturbation** *noun*
mat¹ *noun* **1** piece of fabric used as a floor covering or to protect a surface. **2** thick tangled mass. ◆ *verb* **matting, matted 3** tangle or become tangled into a dense mass. **on the mat** *Informal* summoned for a reprimand. **matted** *adjective*
mat² *adjective* same as MATT.
matador *noun* man who kills the bull in bullfights.
match¹ ❶ *noun* **1** contest in a game or sport. **2** person or thing exactly like, equal to, or in harmony with another. **3** marriage. ◆ *verb* **4** be exactly like, equal to, or in harmony with. **5** put in competition (with). **6** find a match for. **7** join (in marriage). **matchless** *adjective* unequalled.
matchmaker *noun* person who schemes to bring about a marriage. **matchmaking** *noun, adjective*
match² *noun* small stick with a tip which ignites when scraped on a rough surface.
matchbox *noun* **matchstick** *noun* **1** wooden part of a match. ◆ *adjective* **2** (of drawn figures) thin and straight. **matchwood** *noun* small splinters.
mate¹ ❶ *noun* **1** *Informal* friend. **2** *Informal* common British and Australian term of address between males. **3** associate or colleague, e.g. *running mate; team-mate.* **4** sexual partner of an animal. **5** officer in a merchant ship. **6**

tradesman's assistant. ◆ *verb* **7** pair (animals) or (of animals) be paired for reproduction.
mate² *noun, verb* *Chess* checkmate.
material ❶ *noun* **1** substance of which a thing is made. **2** cloth. **3** information on which a piece of work may be based. ◆ *plural* **4** things needed for an activity. ◆ *adjective* **5** of matter or substance. **6** not spiritual. **7** affecting physical wellbeing. **8** relevant. **materially** *adverb* considerably. **materialism** *noun* **1** excessive interest in or desire for money and possessions. **2** belief that only the material world exists. **materialist** *adjective, noun* **materialistic** *adjective* **materialize** *verb* **1** actually happen. **2** come into existence or view. **materialization** *noun*
maternal ❶ *adjective* **1** of a mother. **2** related through one's mother. **maternity** *noun* **1** motherhood. ◆ *adjective* **2** of or for pregnant women, e.g. *maternity leave.*
matey ❶ *adjective* *Informal* friendly or intimate.
math *noun* *US & Canad* mathematics.
mathematics *noun* science of number, quantity, shape, and space. **mathematical** *adjective* **mathematically** *adverb* **mathematician** *noun*
maths *noun* *Informal* mathematics.
matinée [mat-in-nay] *noun* afternoon performance in a theatre or cinema.
matins *plural noun* early morning service in various Christian Churches.
maître d'hôtel [met-ra dote-tell] *noun* French head waiter.
matriarch [mate-ree-ark] *noun* female head of a tribe or family. **matriarchal** *adjective*
matriarchy *noun, pl* **-archies** society governed by a female, in which descent is traced through the female line.
matrices [may-triss-eez] *noun* plural of MATRIX.

———————— T H E S A U R U S ————————

match¹ *noun* **1** = **game**, bout, competition, contest, head-to-head, test, trial **2** = **equal**, counterpart, peer, rival **3** = **marriage**, alliance, pairing, partnership ◆*verb* **4** = **correspond**, accord, agree, fit, go with, harmonize, tally **5** = **rival**, compare, compete, emulate, equal, measure up to
matchless *adjective* = **unequalled**, incomparable, inimitable, superlative, supreme, unmatched, unparalleled, unrivalled, unsurpassed OPPOSITE **average**
mate¹ *noun* **1** *Inf* = **friend**, buddy *(inf)*, chum *(inf)*, comrade, crony, pal *(inf)* **3** = **colleague**, associate, companion **6** = **assistant**, helper, subordinate ◆*verb* **7** = **pair**, breed, couple
material *noun* **1** = **substance**, matter, stuff **2**

= **cloth**, fabric **3** = **information**, data, evidence, facts, notes ◆*adjective* **5** = **tangible**, concrete, palpable, substantial **6** = **physical**, bodily, corporeal **8** = **relevant**, applicable, apposite, apropos, germane, pertinent
materialize *verb* **1** = **occur**, come about, come to pass, happen **2** = **appear**, take shape, turn up
materially *adverb* = **significantly**, essentially, gravely, greatly, much, seriously, substantially
maternal *adjective* **1** = **motherly**
maternity *noun* **1** = **motherhood**, motherliness
matey *adjective* *Inf* = **friendly**, chummy *(inf)*, hail-fellow-well-met, intimate, pally *(inf)*, sociable, thick *(inf)*

matricide noun **1** crime of killing one's mother. **2** person who does this.
matriculate verb enrol or be enrolled in a college or university. **matriculation** noun
matrimony ⊕ noun marriage. **matrimonial** adjective
matrix [**may**-trix] noun, pl **matrices 1** substance or situation in which something originates, takes form, or is enclosed. **2** mould for casting. **3** Maths rectangular array of numbers or elements.
matron noun **1** staid or dignified married woman. **2** woman who supervises the domestic or medical arrangements of an institution. **3** former name for NURSING OFFICER. **matronly** adjective (of a woman) middle-aged and plump.
matt adjective dull, not shiny.
matter ⊕ noun **1** substance of which something is made. **2** physical substance. **3** event, situation, or subject. **4** written material in general. **5** pus. ♦ verb **6** be of importance. **what's the matter?** what is wrong? **matter-of-fact** adjective unimaginative or emotionless. **matter-of-factly** adverb **matter-of-factness** noun
matting noun coarsely woven fabric used as a floor-covering and packing material.
mattock noun large pick with one of its blade ends flattened for loosening soil.
mattress noun large stuffed flat case, often with springs, used on or as a bed.
mature ⊕ adjective **1** fully developed or grown-up. **2** ripe. ♦ verb **3** make or become

mature. **4** (of a bill or bond) become due for payment. **maturity** noun state of being mature.
maturation noun process of becoming mature.
maudlin ⊕ adjective foolishly or tearfully sentimental.
maul ⊕ verb **1** handle roughly. **2** beat or tear.
maunder verb talk or act aimlessly or idly.
mausoleum [maw-so-**lee**-um] noun stately tomb.
mauve adjective pale purple.
maverick ⊕ noun, adjective independent and unorthodox (person).
maw noun animal's mouth, throat, or stomach.
mawkish ⊕ adjective foolishly sentimental.
mawkishness noun
max. maximum.
maxim ⊕ noun general truth or principle.
maximum ⊕ adjective, noun, pl **-mums, -ma** greatest possible (amount or number).
maximal adjective maximum. **maximize** verb increase to a maximum. **maximization** noun
may ⊕ verb, past tense **might** used as an auxiliary to express possibility, permission, opportunity, etc. **maybe** adverb perhaps, possibly.

> **LANGUAGE TIP**
>
> In very careful usage may is used in preference to can for asking permission. Might is used to express a more tentative request: May/might I ask a favour?

M

—————————— THESAURUS ——————————

matrimonial adjective = **marital**, conjugal, connubial, nuptial
matrimony noun = **marriage**, nuptials, wedding ceremony, wedlock
matted adjective **3** = **tangled**, knotted, tousled, uncombed
matter noun **1** = **substance**, material, stuff **2** = **body 3** = **situation**, affair, business, concern, event, incident, proceeding, question, subject, topic ♦ verb **6** = **be important**, carry weight, count, make a difference, signify **what's the matter?** = **problem**, complication, difficulty, distress, trouble, worry
matter-of-fact adjective = **unsentimental**, deadpan, down-to-earth, emotionless, mundane, plain, prosaic, sober, unimaginative
mature adjective **1** = **grown-up**, adult, full-grown, fully fledged, of age OPPOSITE immature. **2** = **ripe**, mellow, ready, seasoned ♦ verb **3** = **develop**, age, bloom, blossom, come of age, grow up, mellow, ripen
maturity noun = **adulthood**, experience, manhood or womanhood, ripeness, wisdom

OPPOSITE immaturity
maudlin adjective = **sentimental**, mawkish, overemotional, slushy (inf), soppy (Brit inf), tearful, weepy (inf)
maul verb **1** = **ill-treat**, abuse, batter, manhandle, molest **2** = **tear**, claw, lacerate, mangle
maverick noun = **rebel**, dissenter, eccentric, heretic, iconoclast, individualist, nonconformist, protester, radical OPPOSITE traditionalist ♦ adjective = **rebel**, dissenting, eccentric, heretical, iconoclastic, individualistic, nonconformist, radical
mawkish adjective = **sentimental**, emotional, maudlin, schmaltzy (sl), slushy (inf), soppy (Brit inf)
maxim noun = **saying**, adage, aphorism, axiom, dictum, motto, proverb, rule
maximum adjective = **greatest**, highest, most, paramount, supreme, topmost, utmost OPPOSITE lowest ♦ noun = **top**, ceiling, height, peak, pinnacle, summit, upper limit, utmost, zenith OPPOSITE bottom

May *noun* **1** fifth month of the year. **2** (**m-**) same as HAWTHORN. **mayfly** *noun* short-lived aquatic insect. **maypole** *noun* pole set up for dancing round on the first day of May to celebrate spring.

maybe ❶ *adverb* perhaps, possibly.

Mayday *noun* international radio distress signal.

mayhem ❶ *noun* violent destruction or confusion.

mayonnaise *noun* creamy sauce of egg yolks, oil, and vinegar.

> **SPELLING TIP**
>
> There are two *ns* to remember in the middle of **mayonnaise** - possibly a good reason for the increasing use of the abbreviation 'mayo'.

mayor *noun* head of a municipality. **mayoress** *noun* **1** mayor's wife. **2** female mayor.

mayoralty *noun, pl* **-ties** (term of) office of a mayor.

maze ❶ *noun* **1** complex network of paths or lines designed to puzzle. **2** any confusing network or system.

mazurka *noun* **1** lively Polish dance. **2** music for this.

MB 1 Bachelor of Medicine. **2** Manitoba.

MBE Member of the Order of the British Empire.

MC Master of Ceremonies.

MCC Marylebone Cricket Club.

Md *Chem* mendelevium.

MD 1 Doctor of Medicine. **2** Managing Director. **3** Maryland.

MDMA *noun* same as ECSTASY (sense 2).

MDT (in the US and Canada) Mountain Daylight Time.

me[1] *pronoun* objective form of I[1].

me[2] *noun Music* (in tonic sol-fa) third degree of any major scale.

ME 1 myalgic encephalomyelitis: painful muscles and general weakness sometimes persisting long after a viral illness. **2** Maine.

mead *noun* alcoholic drink made from honey.

meadow ❶ *noun* piece of grassland.

meadowsweet *noun* plant with dense heads of small fragrant flowers.

meagre ❶ *adjective* scanty or insufficient.

meal[1] *noun* **1** occasion when food is served and eaten. **2** the food itself. **make a meal of** *Informal* perform (a task) with an unnecessary amount of effort. **meals-on-wheels** *noun* service taking hot meals to elderly or infirm people in their own homes. **meal ticket** *Slang* person or situation providing a source of livelihood or income.

meal[2] *noun* grain ground to powder. **mealy** *adjective* **mealier, mealiest**. **mealy-mouthed** *adjective* not outspoken enough.

mealie *noun S Afr* maize.

mean[1] ❶ *verb* **meaning, meant 1** intend to convey or express. **2** signify, denote, or portend. **3** intend. **4** have importance as specified. **meaning** *noun* sense, significance. **meaningful** *adjective* important or significant. **meaningfully** *adverb* **meaningfulness** *noun* **meaningless** *adjective* **meaninglessly** *adverb* **meaninglessness** *noun*

mean[2] ❶ *adjective* **1** miserly, ungenerous, or petty. **2** despicable or callous. **3** *Chiefly US informal* bad-tempered. **meanly** *adverb* **meanness** *noun* **meanie** *noun Informal* unkind or miserly person.

mean[3] ❶ *noun* **1** middle point between two extremes. **2** average. ◆ *plural* **3** method by which something is done. **4** money. ◆ *adjective* **5** intermediate in size or quantity. **6** average. **by all means** certainly. **by no means** in no way. **means test** inquiry into a person's means to decide on eligibility for financial aid.

—————— T H E S A U R U S ——————

maybe *adverb* =**perhaps**, perchance (*arch*), possibly

mayhem *noun* =**chaos**, commotion, confusion, destruction, disorder, fracas, havoc, trouble, violence

maze *noun* **1** =**labyrinth 2** =**web**, confusion, imbroglio, tangle

meadow *noun* =**field**, grassland, lea (*poet*), pasture

meagre *adjective* =**insubstantial**, inadequate, measly, paltry, poor, puny, scanty, slight, small

mean[1] *verb* **1** =**express**, convey, imply, indicate **2** =**signify**, denote, represent, spell, stand for, symbolize **3** =**intend**, aim, aspire, design, desire, plan, set out, want, wish

mean[2] *adjective* **1** =**miserly**, mercenary, niggardly, parsimonious, penny-pinching, stingy, tight-fisted, ungenerous OPPOSITE **generous. 2** =**dishonourable**, callous, contemptible, despicable, hard-hearted, petty, shabby, shameful, sordid, vile OPPOSITE **good**

meander ❶ [mee-**and**-er] *verb* **1** follow a winding course. **2** wander aimlessly. ◆ *noun* **3** winding course.

meant *verb* past of MEAN¹.

meantime ❶ *noun* **1** intervening period. ◆ *adverb* **2** meanwhile.

meanwhile *adverb* **1** during the intervening period. **2** at the same time.

measles ❶ *noun* infectious disease producing red spots. **measly** *adjective* **-lier, -liest** *Informal* meagre.

measure ❶ *noun* **1** size or quantity. **2** graduated scale etc. for measuring size or quantity. **3** unit of size or quantity. **4** extent. **5** action taken. **6** law. **7** poetical rhythm. ◆ *verb* **8** determine the size or quantity of. **9** be (a specified amount) in size or quantity. **measurable** *adjective* **measured** *adjective* **1** slow and steady. **2** carefully considered. **measurement** *noun* **1** measuring. **2** size. **measure up to** *verb* fulfil (expectations or

requirements).

meat ❶ *noun* animal flesh as food. **meaty** *adjective* **meatier, meatiest 1** (tasting) of or like meat. **2** brawny. **3** full of significance or interest.

Mecca *noun* **1** holy city of Islam. **2** place that attracts visitors.

mechanic ❶ *noun* person skilled in repairing or operating machinery. **mechanics** *noun* scientific study of motion and force. **mechanical** *adjective* **1** of or done by machines. **2** (of an action) without thought or feeling. **mechanically** *adverb*

mechanism ❶ *noun* **1** way a machine works. **2** piece of machinery. **3** process or technique, e.g. *defence mechanism*. **mechanistic** *adjective* **mechanize** *verb* **1** equip with machinery. **2** make mechanical or automatic. **3** *Mil* equip (an army) with armoured vehicles. **mechanization** *noun*

med. 1 medical. **2** medicine. **3** medieval. **4**

——————————— THESAURUS ———————————

mean³ *noun* **1** = **middle**, balance, compromise, happy medium, midpoint ◆*adjective* **6** = **average**, norm, standard

meander *verb* **1** = **wind**, snake, turn, zigzag **2** = **wander**, ramble, stroll ◆*noun* **3** = **curve**, bend, coil, loop, turn, twist, zigzag

meaning *noun* = **sense**, connotation, drift, gist, message, significance, substance

meaningful *adjective* = **significant**, important, material, purposeful, relevant, useful, valid, worthwhile OPPOSITE useless

meaningless *adjective* = **pointless**, empty, futile, inane, inconsequential, insignificant, senseless, useless, vain, worthless OPPOSITE deep

meanness *noun* **1** = **miserliness**, niggardliness, parsimony, selfishness, stinginess **2** = **pettiness**, disgracefulness, ignobility, narrow-mindedness, shabbiness, shamefulness

means *plural noun* **3** = **method**, agency, instrument, medium, mode, process, way **4** = **money**, affluence, capital, fortune, funds, income, lolly (*Aust & NZ sl*), resources, wealth, wherewithal **by all means** = **certainly**, definitely, doubtlessly, of course, surely **by no means** = **in no way**, definitely not, not in the least, on no account

meantime *adverb* **2** = **at the same time**, concurrently, in the interim, simultaneously

measly *adjective Inf* = **meagre**, miserable, paltry, pathetic, pitiful, poor, puny, scanty, skimpy

measurable *adjective* = **quantifiable**,

assessable, perceptible, significant

measure *noun* **1** = **quantity**, allotment, allowance, amount, portion, quota, ration, share **2** = **gauge**, metre, rule, scale, yardstick **5** = **action**, act, deed, expedient, manoeuvre, means, procedure, step **6** = **law**, act, bill, resolution, statute **7** = **rhythm**, beat, cadence, metre, verse ◆*verb* **8** = **quantify**, assess, calculate, calibrate, compute, determine, evaluate, gauge, weigh

measured *adjective* **1** = **steady**, dignified, even, leisurely, regular, sedate, slow, solemn, stately, unhurried **2** = **considered**, calculated, deliberate, reasoned, sober, studied, well-thought-out

measurement *noun* **1** = **calculation**, assessment, calibration, computation, evaluation, mensuration, valuation

measure up to *verb* = **fulfil the expectations**, be equal to, be suitable, come up to scratch (*inf*), fit *or* fill the bill, make the grade (*inf*)

meat *noun* = **food**, flesh, tucker (*Aust & NZ inf*)

meaty *adjective* **2** = **brawny**, beefy (*inf*), burly, heavily built, heavy, muscular, solid, strapping, sturdy **3** = **interesting**, meaningful, profound, rich, significant, substantial

mechanical *adjective* **1** = **automatic**, automated OPPOSITE manual. **2** = **unthinking**, automatic, cursory, impersonal, instinctive, involuntary, perfunctory, routine, unfeeling OPPOSITE thinking

mechanism *noun* **2** = **machine**, apparatus, appliance, contrivance, device, instrument, tool

M

medium.
medal *noun* piece of metal with an inscription etc., given as a reward or memento. **medallion** *noun* **1** disc-shaped ornament worn on a chain round the neck. **2** large medal. **3** circular decorative device in architecture. **medallist** *noun* winner of a medal.
meddle ⊕ *verb* interfere annoyingly. **meddler** *noun* **meddlesome** *adjective*
media *noun* **1** a plural of MEDIUM. **2** the mass media collectively. **media event** event that is staged for or exploited by the mass media.

> **LANGUAGE TIP**
>
> Although *media* is a plural noun, there is an increasing tendency to use it as a singular noun, as in *the use of this media* and *the media is obsessed with celebrities*. This is probably because a lot of people do not realize the '-a' ending is a plural one.

mediaeval [med-ee-**eve**-al] *adjective* same as MEDIEVAL.
medial [**mee**-dee-al] *adjective* of or in the middle.
median *adjective, noun* middle (point or line).
mediate ⊕ [**mee**-dee-ate] *verb* intervene in a dispute to bring about agreement. **mediation** *noun* **mediator** *noun*
medic *noun Informal* doctor or medical student.
medical *adjective* **1** of the science of medicine.

♦ *noun* **2** *Informal* medical examination.
medically *adverb* **medicament** [mid-**dik**-a-ment] *noun* a medicine. **medicate** *verb* treat with a medicinal substance. **medication** *noun* (treatment with) a medicinal substance.
medicine ⊕ *noun* **1** substance used to treat disease. **2** science of preventing, diagnosing, or curing disease. **medicinal** [med-**diss**-in-al] *adjective* having therapeutic properties. **medical** *adjective* **medicinally** *adverb* **medicine man** witch doctor.
medieval [med-ee-**eve**-al] *adjective* of the Middle Ages.
mediocre ⊕ [mee-dee-**oak**-er] *adjective* **1** average in quality. **2** second-rate. **mediocrity** [mee-dee-**ok**-rit-ee] *noun* **1** state of being mediocre. **2** *pl* **-rities** mediocre person.
meditate ⊕ *verb* **1** reflect deeply, esp. on spiritual matters. **2** think about or plan. **meditation** *noun* **meditative** *adjective* **meditatively** *adverb* **meditator** *noun*
Mediterranean *adjective* of (the area around) the Mediterranean Sea, between S Europe, N Africa, and SW Asia.
medium ⊕ *adjective* **1** midway between extremes, average. ♦ *noun, pl* **-dia, -diums 2** middle state, degree, or condition. **3** intervening substance producing an effect. **4** means of communicating news or information to the public, such as radio or newspapers. **5** person who can supposedly communicate with the dead. **6** surroundings or environment. **7** category of art according to the material used. **medium wave** radio wave with a wavelength between 100 and 1000 metres.
medlar *noun* apple-like fruit of a small tree,

3 = process, agency, means, method, methodology, operation, procedure, system, technique, way
meddle *verb* **=interfere**, butt in, intervene, intrude, pry, tamper
meddlesome *adjective* **=interfering**, intrusive, meddling, mischievous, officious, prying
mediate *verb* **=intervene**, arbitrate, conciliate, intercede, reconcile, referee, step in (*inf*), umpire
mediation *noun* **=arbitration**, conciliation, intercession, intervention, reconciliation
mediator *noun* **=negotiator**, arbiter, arbitrator, go-between, honest broker, intermediary, middleman, peacemaker, referee, umpire
medicinal *adjective* **=therapeutic**, curative, healing, medical, remedial, restorative

medicine *noun* **1 =remedy**, cure, drug, medicament, medication, nostrum
mediocre *adjective* **1 =average**, indifferent, middling, ordinary, passable, pedestrian, run-of-the-mill, so-so (*inf*), undistinguished **2 =second-rate**, inferior OPPOSITE> **excellent**
mediocrity *noun* **1 a =insignificance**, indifference, ordinariness, unimportance **b =inferiority**
meditate *verb* **1 =reflect**, cogitate, consider, contemplate, deliberate, muse, ponder, ruminate, think **2 =plan**, have in mind, intend, purpose, scheme
meditation *noun* **=reflection**, cogitation, contemplation, musing, pondering, rumination, study, thought
medium *adjective* **1 =average**, fair, intermediate, mean, median, mediocre, middle, middling, midway OPPOSITE> **unique** ♦*noun* **2**

eaten when it begins to decay.

medley ❶ *noun* **1** miscellaneous mixture. **2** musical sequence of different tunes.

medulla [mid-**dull**-la] *noun, pl* **-las, -lae** marrow, pith, or inner tissue.

meek ❶ *adjective* submissive or humble. **meekly** *adverb* **meekness** *noun*

meerkat *noun* S African mongoose.

meerschaum [**meer**-shum] *noun* **1** white substance like clay. **2** tobacco pipe with a bowl made of this.

meet¹ ❶ *verb* **meeting, met 1** come together (with). **2** come into contact (with). **3** be at the place of arrival of. **4** make the acquaintance of. **5** satisfy (a need etc.). **6** experience. ◆ *noun* **7** sports meeting. **8** assembly of a hunt. **meeting** *noun* **1** coming together. **2** assembly.

LANGUAGE TIP

Meet is only followed by *with* in the context of misfortune: *I met his son; I met with an accident.*

---

meet² *adjective Obs* fit or suitable.

mega *adjective Slang* extremely good, great, or successful.

mega- *combining form* **1** denoting one million, e.g. *megawatt.* **2** very great, e.g. *megastar.*

megabyte *noun Computers* 220 or 1 048 576 bytes.

megahertz *noun, pl* **-hertz** one million hertz.

megalith *noun* great stone, esp. as part of a prehistoric monument. **megalithic** *adjective*

megalomania *noun* craving for or mental delusions of power. **megalomaniac** *adjective, noun*

megaphone *noun* cone-shaped instrument used to amplify the voice.

megapode *noun* bird of Australia, New Guinea, and adjacent islands.

megaton *noun* explosive power equal to that of one million tons of TNT.

meiosis [my-**oh**-siss] *noun* type of cell division in which reproductive cells are produced, each containing half the chromosome number of theparent nucleus.

melamine *noun* colourless crystalline compound used in making synthetic resins.

melancholy ❶ [**mel**-an-kol-lee] *noun* **1** sadness or gloom. ◆ *adjective* **2** sad or gloomy.

melancholia [mel-an-**kole**-lee-a] *noun* state of depression. **melancholic** *adjective, noun*

melange [may-**lahnzh**] *noun* mixture.

melanin *noun* dark pigment found in the hair, skin, and eyes of humans and animals.

Melba toast *noun* very thin crisp toast.

mêlée [**mel**-lay] *noun* noisy confused fight or crowd.

mellifluous ❶ [mel-**lif**-flew-uss] *adjective* (of sound) smooth and sweet.

mellow ❶ *adjective* **1** soft, not harsh. **2** kind-hearted, esp. through maturity. **3** (of fruit) ripe. ◆ *verb* **4** make or become mellow.

M

———————— THESAURUS ————————

= **middle**, average, centre, compromise, mean, midpoint **3** = **means**, agency, channel, instrument, mode, organ, vehicle, way **5** = **spiritualist**, channeller **6** = **environment**, atmosphere, conditions, milieu, setting, surroundings

medley *noun* **1** = **mixture**, assortment, farrago, hotchpotch, jumble, *melange*, miscellany, mishmash, mixed bag (*inf*), potpourri

meek *adjective* = **submissive**, acquiescent, compliant, deferential, docile, gentle, humble, mild, modest, timid, unassuming, unpretentious OPPOSITE **overbearing**

meekness *noun* = **submissiveness**, acquiescence, compliance, deference, docility, gentleness, humility, mildness, modesty, timidity

meet¹ *verb* **1** = **gather**, assemble, collect, come together, congregate, convene, muster OPPOSITE **scatter**. **2 a** = **encounter**, bump into, chance on, come across, confront, contact, find, happen on, run across, run into

OPPOSITE **miss. b** = **converge**, come together, connect, cross, intersect, join, link up, touch OPPOSITE **diverge. 5** = **fulfil**, answer, come up to, comply with, discharge, match, measure up to, satisfy OPPOSITE **fail. 6** = **experience**, bear, encounter, endure, face, go through, suffer, undergo

meeting *noun* **1** = **encounter**, assignation, confrontation, engagement, introduction, rendezvous, tryst **2** = **conference**, assembly, conclave, congress, convention, gathering, get-together (*inf*), reunion, session

melancholy *noun* **1** = **sadness**, dejection, depression, despondency, gloom, low spirits, misery, sorrow, unhappiness OPPOSITE **delight** ◆ *adjective* **2** = **sad**, depressed, despondent, dispirited, downhearted, gloomy, glum, miserable, mournful, sorrowful OPPOSITE **happy**

mêlée *noun* = **fight**, brawl, fracas, free-for-all (*inf*), rumpus, scrimmage, scuffle, set-to (*inf*), skirmish, tussle

mellifluous *adjective* = **sweet**, dulcet, euphonious, honeyed, silvery, smooth, soft,

melodrama ❶ *noun* **1** play full of extravagant action and emotion. **2** overdramatic behaviour or emotion. **melodramatic** *adjective*

melody ❶ *noun, pl* **-dies 1** series of musical notes which make a tune. **2** sweet sound. **melodic** [mel-**lod**-ik] *adjective* **1** of melody. **2** melodious. **melodious** [mel-**lode**-ee-uss] *adjective* **1** pleasing to the ear. **2** tuneful.

melon *noun* large round juicy fruit with a hard rind.

melt ❶ *verb* **1** (cause to) become liquid by heat. **2** dissolve. **3** disappear. **4** blend (into). **5** soften through emotion. **meltdown** *noun* (in a nuclear reactor) melting of the fuel rods, with the possible release of radiation. **melting pot** place or situation in which many races, ideas, etc., are mixed.

member ❶ *noun* **1** individual making up a body or society. **2** limb. **membership** *noun* **Member of Parliament** person elected to parliament.

membrane *noun* thin flexible tissue in a plant or animal body. **membranous** *adjective*

memento ❶ *noun, pl* **-tos, -toes** thing serving to remind, souvenir.

memo *noun, pl* **memos** short for MEMORANDUM.

memoir ❶ [**mem**-wahr] *noun* **1** biography or historical account based on personal knowledge. ♦ *plural* **2** collection of these. **3** autobiography.

memorable ❶ *adjective* worth remembering, noteworthy. **memorably** *adverb* **memorabilia** *plural noun* objects connected with famous people or events.

memorandum ❶ *noun, pl* **-dums, -da 1** written record or communication within a business. **2** note of things to be remembered.

memory ❶ *noun, pl* **-ries 1** ability to remember. **2** sum of things remembered. **3** particular recollection. **4** length of time one can remember. **5** commemoration. **6** part of a computer which stores information. **memorable** *adjective* **memorize** *verb* commit to memory. **memorial** *noun* **1** something serving to commemorate a person or thing. ♦ *adjective* **2** serving as a memorial.

memsahib *noun* (formerly, in India) term of respect used for a European married woman.

men *noun* plural of MAN.

menace ❶ *noun* **1** threat. **2** *Informal* nuisance. ♦ *verb* **3** threaten, endanger. **menacing** *adjective* **menacingly** *adverb*

ménage [may-**nahzh**] *noun* household.

menagerie [min-**naj**-er-ee] *noun* collection of wild animals for exhibition.

mend ❶ *verb* **1** repair or patch. **2** recover or

M

———— THESAURUS ————

soothing, sweet-sounding

mellow *adjective* **1 = soft**, delicate **3 = ripe**, full-flavoured, mature, rich, sweet OPPOSITE unripe ♦ *verb* **4 = mature**, develop, improve, ripen, season, soften, sweeten

melodious *adjective* **1 = sweet-sounding**, dulcet, euphonious **2 = musical**, harmonious, melodic, tuneful

melodramatic *adjective* **2 = theatrical**, blood-and-thunder, extravagant, histrionic, overdramatic, overemotional, sensational

melody *noun* **1 = tune**, air, music, song, strain, theme **2 = tunefulness**, euphony, harmony, melodiousness, musicality

melt *verb* **1, 2 = dissolve**, fuse, liquefy, soften, thaw **3 = disappear**, disperse, dissolve, evanesce, evaporate, fade, vanish **5 = soften**, disarm, mollify, outspan (*S Afr*), relax

member *noun* **1 = representative**, associate, fellow **2 = limb**, appendage, arm, extremity, leg, part

membership *noun* **1 = members**, associates, body, fellows

memento *noun* **= souvenir**, keepsake, memorial, relic, remembrance, reminder, token, trophy

memoir *noun* **1 = account**, biography, essay, journal, life, monograph, narrative, record

memoirs *plural noun* **3 = autobiography**, diary, experiences, journals, life story, memories, recollections, reminiscences

memorable *adjective* **= noteworthy**, celebrated, famous, historic, momentous, notable, remarkable, significant, striking, unforgettable

memorandum *noun* **1 = note**, communication, jotting, memo, message, minute **2 = reminder**

memorial *noun* **1 = monument**, memento, plaque, record, remembrance, souvenir ♦ *adjective* **2 = commemorative**, monumental

memorize *verb* **= remember**, commit to memory, learn, learn by heart, learn by rote

memory *noun* **1 = recall**, retention **3 = recollection**, remembrance, reminiscence **5 = commemoration**, honour, remembrance

menace *noun* **1 = threat**, intimidation, warning **2** *Inf* **= nuisance**, annoyance, pest, plague, troublemaker ♦ *verb* **3 = threaten**, bully, frighten, intimidate, loom, lour *or* lower, terrorize

menacing *adjective* **= threatening**, forbidding, frightening, intimidating, looming, louring *or* lowering, ominous heal. **3** make or become better. ♦ *noun* **4** mended area. **on the mend** regaining health.

mendacity ⊙ *noun* (tendency to) untruthfulness. **mendacious** *adjective*

mendelevium *noun Chem* artificially produced radioactive element.

mendicant *adjective* **1** begging. ♦ *noun* **2** beggar.

menfolk *plural noun* men collectively, esp. the men of a particular family.

menhir [men-hear] *noun* single upright prehistoric stone.

menial ⊙ [mean-nee-al] *adjective* **1** involving boring work of low status. ♦ *noun* **2** domestic servant.

meningitis [men-in-**jite**-iss] *noun* inflammation of the membranes of the brain.

meniscus *noun* **1** curved surface of a liquid. **2** crescent-shaped lens.

menopause *noun* time when a woman's menstrual cycle ceases. **menopausal** *adjective*

menstruation *noun* approximately monthly discharge of blood and cellular debris from the womb of a nonpregnant woman. **menstruate** *verb* **menstrual** *adjective*

mensuration *noun* measuring, esp. in geometry.

mental ⊙ *adjective* **1** of, in, or done by the mind. **2** of or for mental illness. **3** *Informal*

insane. **mentally** *adverb* **mentality** *noun, pl* **-ties** way of thinking.

menthol *noun* organic compound found in peppermint, used medicinally.

mention ⊙ *verb* **1** refer to briefly. **2** acknowledge. ♦ *noun* **3** brief reference to a person or thing. **4** acknowledgment.

mentor ⊙ *noun* adviser or guide.

menu ⊙ *noun* **1** list of dishes to be served, or from which to order. **2** *Computers* list of options displayed on a screen.

MEP Member of the European Parliament.

mercantile ⊙ *adjective* of trade or traders.

Mercator projection [mer-**kate**-er] *noun* method of map-making in which latitude and longitude form a rectangular grid.

mercenary ⊙ *adjective* **1** influenced by greed. **2** working merely for reward. ♦ *noun, pl* **-aries 3** hired soldier.

mercerized *adjective* (of cotton) given lustre by treating with chemicals.

merchandise ⊙ *noun* commodities.

merchant ⊙ *noun* person engaged in trade, wholesale trader. **merchandise** *noun* commodities. **merchant bank** bank dealing mainly with businesses and investment. **merchantman** *noun* trading ship. **merchant navy** ships or crew engaged in a nation's commercial shipping.

M

—————————— THESAURUS ——————————

mend *verb* **1** = **repair**, darn, fix, patch, refit, renew, renovate, restore, retouch **2** = **heal**, convalesce, get better, recover, recuperate **3** = **improve**, ameliorate, amend, correct, emend, rectify, reform, revise ♦*noun* **4** = **repair**, darn, patch, stitch **on the mend** = **convalescent**, getting better, improving, recovering, recuperating

mendacious *adjective* = **lying**, deceitful, deceptive, dishonest, duplicitous, fallacious, false, fraudulent, insincere, untruthful

menial *adjective* **1** = **unskilled**, boring, dull, humdrum, low-status, routine OPPOSITE> **high** ♦*noun* **2** = **servant**, attendant, dogsbody (*inf*), drudge, flunky, lackey, skivvy (*chiefly Brit*), underling OPPOSITE> **lord**

mental *adjective* **1** = **intellectual**, cerebral **3** *Inf* = **insane**, deranged, disturbed, mad, mentally ill, psychotic, unbalanced, unstable

mentality *noun* = **attitude**, cast of mind, character, disposition, make-up, outlook, personality, psychology

mentally *adverb* **1** = **in the mind**, in one's head, intellectually, inwardly, psychologically

mention *verb* **1** = **refer to**, bring up, declare, disclose, divulge, intimate, point out, reveal,

state, touch upon ♦*noun* **3** = **reference**, allusion, indication, observation, remark **4** = **acknowledgment**, citation, recognition, tribute

mentor *noun* = **guide**, adviser, coach, counsellor, guru, instructor, teacher, tutor

menu *noun* **1** = **bill of fare**, *carte du jour*, tariff (*chiefly Brit*)

mercantile *adjective* = **commercial**, trading

mercenary *adjective* **1** = **greedy**, acquisitive, avaricious, grasping, money-grubbing (*inf*), sordid, venal OPPOSITE> **liberal** ♦*noun* **3** = **hireling**, soldier of fortune

merchandise *noun* = **goods**, commodities, produce, products, stock, wares

merchant *noun* = **tradesman**, broker, dealer, purveyor, retailer, salesman, seller, shopkeeper, supplier, trader, trafficker, vendor, wholesaler

merciful *adjective* **1** = **compassionate**, clement, forgiving, generous, gracious, humane, kind, lenient, sparing, sympathetic, tender-hearted OPPOSITE> **cruel**

merciless *adjective* = **cruel**, barbarous, callous, hard-hearted, harsh, heartless, pitiless, ruthless, unforgiving

mercurial *adjective* = **lively**, active, capricious,

mercury ❶ *noun* **1** *Chem* silvery liquid metal. **2** (**M-**) *Roman myth* messenger of the gods. **3** (**M-**) planet nearest the sun. **mercurial** [mer-**cure**-ee-al] *adjective* lively, changeable.
mercy ❶ *noun, pl* **-cies 1** compassionate treatment of an offender or enemy who is in one's power. **2** merciful act. **merciful** *adjective* **1** compassionate. **2** giving relief. **mercifully** *adverb* **merciless** *adjective* **mercilessly** *adverb*
mere¹ ❶ *adjective* nothing more than, e.g. *mere chance.* **merely** *adverb*
mere² *noun Obs* lake.
meretricious ❶ *adjective* superficially or garishly attractive but of no real value.
merganser [mer-**gan**-ser] *noun* large crested diving duck.
merge ❶ *verb* combine or blend. **merger** *noun* combination of business firms into one.
meridian *noun* imaginary circle of the earth passing through both poles.
meringue [mer-**rang**] *noun* **1** baked mixture of egg whites and sugar. **2** small cake of this.
merino *noun, pl* **-nos 1** breed of sheep with fine soft wool. **2** this wool.
merit ❶ *noun* **1** excellence or worth. ◆ *plural* **2** admirable qualities. ◆ *verb* **-iting, -ited 3** deserve. **meritorious** *adjective* deserving praise. **meritocracy** [mer-it-**tok**-rass-ee] *noun* rule by people of superior talent or intellect.
merlin *noun* small falcon.
mermaid *noun* imaginary sea creature with

the upper part of a woman and the lower part of a fish.
merry ❶ *adjective* **-rier, -riest 1** cheerful or jolly. **2** *Informal* slightly drunk. **merrily** *adverb* **merriment** *noun* **merry-go-round** *noun* roundabout. **merrymaking** *noun* noisy, cheerful celebrations or fun.
mescaline *noun* hallucinogenic drug obtained from the tops of mescals. **mescal** [mess-**kal**] *noun* spineless globe-shaped cactus of Mexico and the SW of the USA.
mesdames *noun* plural of MADAME.
mesdemoiselles *noun* plural of MADEMOISELLE.
mesembryanthemum *noun* low-growing plant with bright daisy-like flowers.
mesh ❶ *noun* **1** network or net. **2** (open space between) strands forming a network. ◆ *verb* **3** (of gear teeth) engage.
mesmerize ❶ *verb* **1** hold spellbound. **2** *Obs* hypnotize. **mesmerizing** *adjective*
meso- *combining form* middle or intermediate, e.g. *mesosphere.*
meson [**mee**-zon] *noun* elementary atomic particle.
mess ❶ *noun* **1** untidy or dirty confusion. **2** trouble or difficulty. **3** place where servicemen eat. **4** group of servicemen who regularly eat together. ◆ *verb* **5** muddle or dirty. **6** (foll. by *about*) potter about. **7** (foll. by *with*) interfere with. **8** (of servicemen) eat in a group.
message ❶ *noun* **1** communication sent. **2**

──────── THESAURUS ────────

changeable, impulsive, irrepressible, mobile, quicksilver, spirited, sprightly, unpredictable, volatile
mercy *noun* **1** = **compassion**, clemency, forbearance, forgiveness, grace, kindness, leniency, pity OPPOSITE cruelty. **2** = **blessing**, boon, godsend
mere¹ *adjective* = **simple**, bare, common, nothing more than, plain, pure, sheer
meretricious *adjective* = **trashy**, flashy, garish, gaudy, gimcrack, showy, tawdry, tinsel
merge *verb* = **combine**, amalgamate, blend, coalesce, converge, fuse, join, meet, mingle, mix, unite OPPOSITE part
merger *noun* = **union**, amalgamation, coalition, combination, consolidation, fusion, incorporation
merit *noun* **1** = **worth**, advantage, asset, excellence, goodness, integrity, quality, strong point, talent, value, virtue ◆ *verb* **3** = **deserve**, be entitled to, be worthy of, earn, have a right to, rate, warrant
meritorious *adjective* = **praiseworthy**, admirable, commendable, creditable, deserving,

excellent, good, laudable, virtuous, worthy
merriment *noun* **1** = **fun**, amusement, festivity, glee, hilarity, jollity, joviality, laughter, mirth, revelry
merry *adjective* **1** = **cheerful**, blithe, carefree, convivial, festive, happy, jolly, joyous OPPOSITE sad. **2** *Inf* = **tipsy**, happy, mellow, squiffy (*Brit inf*), tiddly (*sl, chiefly Brit*)
mesh *noun* **1** = **net**, netting, network, tracery, web ◆ *verb* **3** = **engage**, combine, connect, coordinate, dovetail, harmonize, interlock, knit
mesmerize *verb* **1** = **entrance**, captivate, enthral, fascinate, grip, hold spellbound, hypnotize
mess *noun* **1** = **disorder**, chaos, clutter, confusion, disarray, disorganization, hotchpotch, jumble, litter, shambles, untidiness **2** = **difficulty**, deep water, dilemma, fix (*inf*), hole (*inf*), jam (*inf*), muddle, pickle (*inf*), plight, predicament, tight spot ◆ *verb* **5** = **dirty**, clutter, disarrange, dishevel, muck up (*Brit sl*), muddle, pollute, scramble, muss (*US & Canad*) **6** (foll. by *about*) = **potter**, amuse oneself, dabble, fool (about or around), muck about (*inf*), play about

meaning or moral. **messenger** noun bearer of a message. **get the message** Informal understand.

Messiah noun 1 Jews' promised deliverer. 2 Christ. **Messianic** adjective

messieurs noun plural of MONSIEUR.

Messrs [mess-erz] noun plural of MR.

messy ⊕ adjective **messier, messiest** dirty, confused, or untidy. **messily** adverb

met verb past of MEET[1].

Met adjective, noun Informal Meteorological (Office).

metabolism [met-tab-oh-liz-zum] noun chemical processes of a living body. **metabolic** adjective **metabolize** verb produce or be produced by metabolism.

metal noun 1 chemical element, such as iron or copper, that is malleable and capable of conducting heat and electricity. 2 short for ROAD METAL. 3 Informal short for HEAVY METAL. ◆ adjective 4 made of metal. **metallic** adjective **metallurgy** noun scientific study of the structure, properties, extraction, and refining of metals.

metallurgical adjective **metallurgist** noun

metalwork noun 1 craft of making objects from metal. 2 metal part of something.

metamorphosis ⊕ [met-a-more-foss-is] noun, pl **-phoses** [-foss-eez] change of form or character. **metamorphic** adjective (of rocks) changed in texture or structure by heat and pressure. **metamorphose** verb transform.

metaphor ⊕ noun figure of speech in which a term is applied to something it does not literally denote in order to imply a resemblance, e.g. he is a lion in battle. **metaphorical** adjective **metaphorically** adverb

metaphysics noun branch of philosophy concerned with being and knowing. **metaphysical** adjective

mete ⊕ verb (usu. with out) deal out as punishment.

meteor ⊕ noun small fast-moving heavenly body, visible as a streak of incandescence if it enters the earth's atmosphere. **meteoric** [meet-ee-or-rik] adjective 1 of a meteor. 2 brilliant and very rapid, e.g. his meteoric rise to power. **meteorite** noun meteor that has fallen to earth.

meteorology noun study of the earth's atmosphere, esp. for weather forecasting. **meteorological** adjective **meteorologist** noun

meter noun 1 instrument for measuring and recording something, such as the consumption of gas or electricity. ◆ verb 2 measure by meter.

methane noun colourless inflammable gas.

methanol noun colourless poisonous liquid used as a solvent and fuel (also **methyl alcohol**).

methinks verb, past tense **methought** Obs it seems to me.

method ⊕ noun 1 way or manner. 2 technique. 3 orderliness. **methodical** adjective orderly. **methodically** adverb **methodology** noun, pl **-gies** particular method or procedure.

Methodist noun 1 member of any of the Protestant churches originated by John Wesley and his followers. ◆ adjective 2 of Methodists or their Church. **Methodism** noun

meths noun Informal methylated spirits.

methyl noun (compound containing) a saturated hydrocarbon group of atoms.

methylated spirits alcohol with methanol added, used as a solvent and for heating.

methylated spirits noun alcohol with methanol added, used as a solvent and for heating.

meticulous ⊕ adjective very careful about details. **meticulously** adverb

M

—————————— THESAURUS ——————————

or around, trifle 7 (foll. by with) = **interfere**, fiddle (inf), meddle, play, tamper, tinker

message noun 1 = **communication**, bulletin, communiqué, dispatch, letter, memorandum, note, tidings, word 2 = **point**, idea, import, meaning, moral, purport, theme

messenger noun = **courier**, carrier, delivery boy, emissary, envoy, errand-boy, go-between, herald, runner

messy adjective = **untidy**, chaotic, cluttered, confused, dirty, dishevelled, disordered, disorganized, muddled, shambolic, sloppy (inf) OPPOSITE▷ ordered

metamorphosis noun = **transformation**, alteration, change, conversion, mutation, transmutation

metaphor noun = **figure of speech**, allegory, analogy, image, symbol, trope

metaphorical adjective = **figurative**, allegorical, emblematic, symbolic

mete verb = **distribute**, administer, apportion, assign, deal, dispense, dole, portion

meteoric adjective 2 = **spectacular**, brilliant, dazzling, fast, overnight, rapid, speedy, sudden, swift

method noun 1 = **manner**, approach, mode, modus operandi, procedure, process, routine, style, system, way 2 = **technique** 3 = **orderliness**, order, organization, pattern, planning, purpose, regularity, system

methodical adjective = **orderly**, businesslike, deliberate, disciplined, meticulous, organized,

métier [met-ee-ay] *noun* **1** profession or trade. **2** one's strong point.

metonymy [mit-**on**-im-ee] *noun* figure of speech in which one thing is replaced by another associated with it, such as 'the Crown' for 'the queen'.

metre *noun* **1** basic unit of length equal to about 1.094 yards (100 centimetres). **2** rhythm of poetry. **metric** *adjective* of the decimal system of weights and measures based on the metre. **metric ton** same as TONNE. **metrical** *adjective* **1** of measurement. **2** of poetic metre.

metrication *noun* conversion to the metric system.

metro *noun, pl* **metros** underground railway system, esp. in Paris.

metronome *noun* instrument which marks musical time by means of a ticking pendulum.

metropolis [mit-**trop**-oh-liss] *noun* chief city of a country or region. **metropolitan** *adjective* of a metropolis.

mettle ❼ *noun* courage or spirit. **on one's mettle** roused to making one's best efforts.

mew *noun* **1** cry of a cat. ◆ *verb* **2** utter this cry.

mews *noun* yard or street orig. of stables, now often converted into houses.

Mexican *adjective* **1** of Mexico. ◆ *noun* **2** person from Mexico.

mezzanine [**mez**-zan-een] *noun* intermediate storey, esp. between the ground and first floor.

mezzo-soprano [met-so-] *noun* voice or singer between a soprano and contralto (also **mezzo**).

mezzotint [**met**-so-tint] *noun* **1** method of engraving by scraping the roughened surface of a metal plate. **2** print so made.

mg milligram(s).

Mg *Chem* magnesium.

Mgr 1 manager. **2** Monseigneur. **3** Monsignor.

MHz megahertz.

mi *noun Music* same as ME².

MI 1 Military Intelligence. **2** Michigan.

MI5 Military Intelligence, section five: British Government counterintelligence agency.

MI6 Military Intelligence, section six: British Government intelligence and espionage agency.

miaow [mee-**ow**] *noun, verb* same as MEW.

miasma [mee-**azz**-ma] *noun* unwholesome or foreboding atmosphere.

mica [**my**-ka] *noun* glasslike mineral used as an electrical insulator.

mice *noun* plural of MOUSE.

Michaelmas [**mik**-kl-mass] *noun* Sept. 29th, feast of St Michael the archangel. **Michaelmas daisy** garden plant with small daisy-shaped flowers.

mickey *noun* **take the mickey (out of)** *Informal* tease.

micro *noun, pl* **-cros** short for MICROCOMPUTER or MICROPROCESSOR.

micro- *combining form* **1** small or minute, e.g. *microcopy*. **2** denoting a millionth part, e.g. *microsecond*.

microbe ❼ *noun* minute organism, esp. one causing disease. **microbial** *adjective*

microbiology *noun* branch of biology involving the study of microorganisms. **microbiological** *adjective* **microbiologist** *noun*

microchip *noun* small wafer of silicon containing electronic circuits.

microcircuit *noun* miniature electronic circuit, esp. an integrated circuit.

microcomputer *noun* computer with a central processing unit contained in one or more silicon chips.

microcosm *noun* **1** miniature representation of something. **2** man regarded as epitomizing the universe.

microdot *noun* photographic copy of a document reduced to pinhead size.

microelectronics *noun* branch of electronics concerned with microcircuits. **microelectronic** *adjective*

microfiche [**my**-kroh-feesh] *noun* microfilm in sheet form.

microfilm *noun* miniaturized recording of books or documents on a roll of film.

microlight, microlite *noun* very small light private aircraft with large wings.

micrometer [my-**krom**-it-er] *noun* instrument for measuring very small distances or angles.

micron [**my**-kron] *noun* one millionth of a metre.

microorganism *noun* organism of microscopic size.

microphone *noun* instrument for amplifying or transmitting sounds.

microprocessor *noun* integrated circuit

——— THESAURUS ———

precise, regular, structured, systematic

meticulous *adjective* =**thorough**, exact, fastidious, fussy, painstaking, particular, precise, punctilious, scrupulous, strict OPPOSITE **haphazard**

mettle *noun* =**courage**, bravery, fortitude, gallantry, life, nerve, pluck, resolution, spirit, valour, vigour

microbe *noun* =**microorganism**, bacillus, bacterium, bug (*inf*), germ, virus acting as the central processing unit in a small computer.

microscope ❶ *noun* instrument with lens(es) which produces a magnified image of a very small object. **microscopic** *adjective* **1** too small to be seen except with a microscope. **2** very small. **3** of a microscope. **microscopically** *adverb* **microscopy** *noun* use of a microscope.

microstructure *noun* structure on a microscopic scale, esp. of a metal or a cell.

microsurgery *noun* intricate surgery using a special microscope and miniature precision instruments.

microwave *noun* **1** electromagnetic wave with a wavelength of a few centimetres, used in radar and cooking. **2** microwave oven. ◆ *verb* **3** cook in a microwave oven. **microwave oven** oven using microwaves to cook food quickly.

micturate *verb* urinate. **micturition** *noun*

mid *adjective* intermediate, middle. **midnight** *noun* twelve o'clock at night. **mid-off** *noun* Cricket fielding position on the off side closest to the bowler. **mid-on** *noun* Cricket fielding position on the on side closest to the bowler.

midway *adjective, adverb* halfway.

midair *noun* some point above ground level, in the air.

midday ❶ *noun* noon.

midden *noun* dunghill or rubbish heap.

middle ❶ *adjective* **1** equidistant from two extremes. **2** medium, intermediate. ◆ *noun* **3** middle point or part. **middle age** period of life between youth and old age. **middle-aged** *adjective* **Middle Ages** period from about 1000 AD to the 15th century. **middle class** social class of business and professional people. **middle-class** *adjective* **middle ear** sound-conducting part of the ear immediately inside the eardrum. **Middle East** area around the eastern Mediterranean up to and including Iran. **middleman** *noun* trader who buys from the producer and sells to the consumer. **middle-of-the-road** *adjective* **1** politically moderate. **2**

(of music) generally popular. **middleweight** *noun* boxer weighing up to 160lb (professional) or 75kg (amateur).

middling ❶ *adjective* **1** mediocre. **2** moderate. ◆ *adverb* **3** moderately.

midfield *noun* Soccer area between the two opposing defences.

midge *noun* small mosquito-like insect.

midget ❶ *noun* very small person or thing.

midland *noun* **1** middle part of a country. ◆ *plural* **2** (M-) central England.

midnight ❶ *noun* twelve o'clock at night.

midriff *noun* middle part of the body.

midshipman *noun* naval officer of the lowest commissioned rank.

midst ❶ *noun* **in the midst of 1** surrounded by. **2** at a point during.

midsummer *noun* **1** middle of summer. **2** summer solstice. **Midsummer's Day, Midsummer Day** June 24th.

midtown *noun* US & Canad the centre of a town.

midway ❶ *adjective, adverb* halfway.

midwife *noun* trained person who assists at childbirth. **midwifery** [mid-**wiff**-fer-ree] *noun*

midwinter *noun* **1** middle or depth of winter. **2** winter solstice.

mien [mean] *noun* Lit person's bearing, demeanour, or appearance.

miffed *adjective* Informal offended or upset.

might[1] *verb* past tense of MAY.

> **LANGUAGE TIP**
>
> Both *might* and *may* can be used to express a tentative request: *Might/may I ask a favour?*

might[2] ❶ *noun* power or strength. **with might and main** energetically or forcefully. **mighty** *adjective* **mightier, mightiest 1** powerful. **2** important. ◆ *adverb* **3** US & Aust informal very.

——————— THESAURUS ———————

microscopic *adjective* **1, 2** = **tiny**, imperceptible, infinitesimal, invisible, minuscule, minute, negligible

midday *noun* = **noon**, noonday, twelve o'clock

middle *adjective* **1** = **central**, halfway, intermediate, intervening, mean, median, mid **2** = **medium** ◆ *noun* **3** = **centre**, focus, halfway point, heart, midpoint, midsection, midst

middle-class *adjective* = **bourgeois**, conventional, traditional

middling *adjective* **1** = **mediocre**, indifferent, run-of-the-mill, so-so (*inf*), tolerable,

unexceptional, unremarkable **2** = **moderate**, adequate, all right, average, fair, medium, modest, O.K. or okay (*inf*), ordinary, passable, serviceable

midget *noun* = **dwarf**, pygmy or pigmy, shrimp (*inf*), Tom Thumb

midnight *noun* = **twelve o'clock**, dead of night, middle of the night, the witching hour

midst *noun* **in the midst of 1** = **among**, amidst, in the middle of, in the thick of, surrounded by **2** = **during**

midway *adjective, adverb* = **halfway**, betwixt

mightily adverb

mignonette [min-yon-**net**] noun grey-green plant with sweet-smelling flowers.

migraine [**mee**-grain] noun severe headache, often with nausea and visual disturbances.

migrate ⊕ verb 1 move from one place to settle in another. 2 (of animals) journey between different habitats at specific seasons. **migration** noun **migrant** noun 1 person or animal that moves from one place to another. ◆ adjective 2 moving from one place to another, e.g. migrant workers. **migratory** adjective (of an animal) migrating every year.

mikado noun, pl -**dos** Old-fashioned Japanese emperor.

mike noun Informal microphone.

milch [**miltch**] adjective (of a cow) giving milk.

mild ⊕ adjective 1 not strongly flavoured. 2 gentle. 3 calm or temperate. **mildly** adverb **mildness** noun

mildew noun destructive fungus on plants or things exposed to damp. **mildewed** adjective

mile noun unit of length equal to 1760 yards or 1.609 kilometres. **mileage** noun 1 distance travelled in miles. 2 miles travelled by a motor vehicle per gallon of petrol. 3 Informal usefulness of something. **mileometer** [mile-om-it-er] noun device that records the number of miles a vehicle has travelled. **milestone** noun 1 significant event. 2 stone marker showing the distance to a certain place.

milieu ⊕ [meal-**yer**] noun, pl **milieux, milieus** [meal-**yerz**] environment or surroundings.

militant ⊕ adjective aggressive or vigorous in support of a cause. **militancy** noun **militantly**

adverb

military ⊕ adjective 1 of or for soldiers, armies, or war. ◆ noun 2 armed services. **militarily** adverb **militarism** noun belief in the use of military force and methods. **militarist** noun **militaristic** adjective **militarized** adjective

militate ⊕ verb (usu. with against or for) have a strong influence or effect.

militia [mill-**ish**-a] noun military force of trained citizens for use in emergency only. **militiaman** noun

milk ⊕ noun 1 white fluid produced by female mammals to feed their young. 2 milk of cows, goats, etc., used by humans as food. 3 fluid in some plants. ◆ verb 4 draw milk from. 5 exploit (a person or situation). **milking** noun **milky** adjective **milkier, milkiest. Milky Way** luminous band of stars stretching across the night sky. **milk float** small electrically powered vehicle used to deliver milk to houses.

milkmaid noun (esp. in former times) woman who milks cows. **milkman** noun man who delivers milk to people's houses. **milk round 1** route along which a milkman regularly delivers milk. 2 regular series of visits to colleges made by recruitment officers from industry.

milkshake noun frothy flavoured cold milk drink. **milksop** noun feeble man. **milk teeth** first set of teeth in young children.

mill ⊕ noun 1 factory. 2 machine for grinding, processing, or rolling. ◆ verb 3 grind, press, or process in or as if in a mill. 4 cut fine grooves across the edges of (coins). 5 move in a confused manner. **miller** noun person who works in a mill.

———————— THESAURUS ————————

and between, in the middle

might[2] noun =**power**, energy, force, strength, vigour **with might and main** = **forcefully**, lustily, manfully, mightily, vigorously

mightily adverb =**powerfully**, energetically, forcefully, lustily, manfully, strongly, vigorously

mighty adjective 1 =**powerful**, forceful, lusty, robust, strapping, strong, sturdy, vigorous

migrant noun 1 =**wanderer**, drifter, emigrant, immigrant, itinerant, nomad, rover, traveller ◆adjective 2 = **travelling**, drifting, immigrant, itinerant, migratory, nomadic, roving, shifting, transient, vagrant, wandering

migrate verb 1 = **move**, emigrate, journey, roam, rove, travel, trek, voyage, wander

migration noun =**wandering**, emigration, journey, movement, roving, travel, trek, voyage

migratory adjective = **nomadic**, itinerant, migrant, peripatetic, roving, transient

mild adjective 1 = **bland**, smooth 2 = **gentle**,

calm, docile, easy-going, equable, meek, peaceable, placid OPPOSITE strong. 3 = **temperate**, balmy, calm, moderate, tranquil, warm OPPOSITE cold

mildness noun = **gentleness**, calmness, clemency, docility, moderation, placidity, tranquillity, warmth

milieu noun = **surroundings**, background, element, environment, locale, location, scene, setting

militant adjective = **aggressive**, active, assertive, combative, vigorous OPPOSITE peaceful

military adjective 1 = **warlike**, armed, martial, soldierly ◆noun 2 = **armed forces**, army, forces, services

militate verb **militate against** = **counteract**, be detrimental to, conflict with, counter, oppose, resist, tell against, weigh against

milk verb 5 = **exploit**, extract, pump, take

millennium [mill-en-nee-um] *noun, pl* **-nia** [-nee-a] **-niums 1** period of a thousand years. **2** future period of peace and happiness.
millennium bug computer problem caused by the date change at the beginning of the 21st century.

> **SPELLING TIP**
>
> If you spell **millennium** with only one *n*, you are not alone: there are 338 occurrences of this in the Bank of English. The correct spelling has two *l*s and two *n*s.

millet *noun* a cereal grass.
milli- *combining form* denoting a thousandth part, e.g. *millisecond*.
milliard *noun Brit* one thousand millions.
millibar *noun* unit of atmospheric pressure.
milligram, milligramme *noun* thousandth part of a gram.
millilitre *noun* thousandth part of a litre.
millimetre *noun* thousandth part of a metre.
milliner *noun* maker or seller of women's hats. **millinery** *noun*
million *noun* one thousand thousands. **millionth** *adjective, noun* **millionaire** *noun* person who owns at least a million pounds, dollars, etc.

> **SPELLING TIP**
>
> Lots of people find it difficult to decide how many *l*s and *n*s to put in **millionaire**. They usually get the double *l* right, but remembering the single *n* is trickier.

millipede *noun* small animal with a jointed body and many pairs of legs.

millstone ⊕ *noun* flat circular stone for grinding corn. **millstone round one's neck** heavy burden of responsibility or obligation.
millwheel *noun* waterwheel that drives a mill.
milometer [mile-om-it-er] *noun* same as MILEOMETER.
milt *noun* sperm of fish.
mime ⊕ *noun* **1** acting without the use of words. **2** performer who does this. ◆ *verb* **3** act in mime. **4** perform as if singing or playing music that is prerecorded.
mimic ⊕ *verb* **-icking, -icked 1** imitate (a person or manner), esp. for satirical effect. ◆ *noun* **2** person or animal that is good at mimicking. **mimicry** *noun*
mimosa *noun* shrub with fluffy yellow flowers and sensitive leaves.
min. 1 minimum. **2** minute(s).
Min. 1 Minister. **2** Ministry.
minaret *noun* tall slender tower of a mosque.
minatory *adjective* threatening or menacing.
mince ⊕ *verb* **1** cut or grind into very small pieces. **2** walk or speak in an affected manner. **3** soften or moderate (one's words). ◆ *noun* **4** minced meat. **mincer** *noun* machine for mincing meat. **mincing** *adjective* affected in manner. **mincemeat** *noun* sweet mixture of dried fruit and spices. **mince pie** pie containing mincemeat.
mind ⊕ *noun* **1** thinking faculties. **2** memory or attention. **3** intention. **4** sanity. ◆ *verb* **5** take offence at. **6** pay attention to. **7** take care of. **8** be cautious or careful about (something). **change one's mind** alter one's decision or opinion. **in one's mind's eye** in one's imagination. **make up one's mind** reach a decision. **minded** *adjective* having an inclination as specified, e.g. *politically minded*.
minder *noun Informal* aide or bodyguard.
mindful *adjective* **1** heedful. **2** keeping aware.
mindless *adjective* **1** stupid. **2** requiring no thought. **3** careless.
mine¹ *pronoun* belonging to me.

M

———————— THESAURUS ————————

advantage of
mill *noun* **1** = **factory**, foundry, plant, works **2** = **grinder**, crusher ◆ *verb* **3** = **grind**, crush, grate, pound, powder **5** = **swarm**, crowd, throng
millstone *noun* **1** = **grindstone**, quernstone
millstone round one's neck = **burden**, affliction, albatross, encumbrance, load, weight
mime *verb* **3** = **act out**, gesture, represent, simulate
mimic *verb* **1** = **imitate**, ape, caricature, do (*inf*), impersonate, parody, take off (*inf*) ◆ *noun* **2**

= **imitator**, caricaturist, copycat (*inf*), impersonator, impressionist
mimicry *noun* = **imitation**, burlesque, caricature, impersonation, mimicking, mockery, parody, take-off (*inf*)
mince *verb* **1** = **cut**, chop, crumble, grind, hash **3** = **tone down**, moderate, soften, spare, weaken
mincing *adjective* = **affected**, camp (*inf*), dainty, effeminate, foppish, precious, pretentious, sissy
mind *noun* **1** = **intelligence**, brain(s) (*inf*), grey

mine² ⊕ *noun* **1** deep hole for digging out coal, ores, etc. **2** bomb placed under the ground or in water. **3** profitable source, e.g. *a mine of information.* ◆ *verb* **4** dig for minerals. **5** dig (minerals) from a mine. **6** place explosive mines in or on. **miner** *noun* person who works in a mine. **mining** *noun* **minefield** *noun* area of land or water containing mines. **minesweeper** *noun* ship for clearing away mines.
mineral *noun* **1** naturally occurring inorganic substance, such as metal. ◆ *adjective* **2** of, containing, or like minerals. **mineralogy** [min-er-**al**-a-jee] *noun* study of minerals. **mineralogist** *noun* **mineral water** water containing dissolved mineral salts or gases.
minestrone [min-ness-**strone**-ee] *noun* soup containing vegetables and pasta.
mingle ⊕ *verb* **1** mix or blend. **2** come into association (with).
mingy *adjective* **-gier, -giest** *Informal* miserly.
mini *noun, adjective* **1** (something) small or miniature. **2** short (skirt).
mini- *combining form* smaller or shorter than usual, e.g. *mini-budget; minidress.*
miniature ⊕ *noun* **1** small portrait, model, or copy. ◆ *adjective* **2** small-scale. **miniaturist** *noun* **miniaturize** *verb* make to a very small scale. **miniaturization** *noun*

minibar *noun* selection of drinks and confectionery provided in a hotel room.
minibus *noun* small bus.
minicab *noun* ordinary car used as a taxi.
minicomputer *noun* computer smaller than a mainframe but more powerful than a microcomputer.
minidisc *noun* small recordable compact disc.
minim *noun Music* note half the length of a semibreve.
minimum ⊕ *adjective, noun, pl* **-mums, -ma** least possible (amount or number). **minimal** *adjective* minimum. **minimally** *adverb* **minimize** *verb* **1** reduce to a minimum. **2** belittle. **minimization** *noun*
minion ⊕ *noun* servile assistant.
miniseries *noun* TV programme shown in several parts, often on consecutive days.
miniskirt *noun* very short skirt.
minister ⊕ *noun* **1** head of a government department. **2** diplomatic representative. **3** clergyman. ◆ *verb* **4** (foll. by *to*) attend to the needs of. **ministerial** *adjective* **ministration** *noun* giving of help. **ministry** *noun, pl* **-tries 1** profession or duties of a clergyman. **2** ministers collectively. **3** government department.
mink *noun* **1** stoatlike animal. **2** its highly valued fur.

——————— T H E S A U R U S ———————

matter (*inf*), intellect, reason, sense, understanding, wits **2 = memory,** recollection, remembrance **3 = intention,** desire, disposition, fancy, inclination, leaning, notion, urge, wish **4 = sanity,** judgment, marbles (*inf*), mental balance, rationality, reason, senses, wits ◆*verb* **5 = take offence,** be affronted, be bothered, care, disapprove, dislike, object, resent **6 = pay attention,** heed, listen to, mark, note, obey, observe, pay heed to, take heed **7 = guard,** attend to, keep an eye on, look after, take care of, tend, watch **8 = be careful,** be cautious, be on (one's) guard, be wary, take care, watch **make up one's mind = decide,** choose, determine, resolve
mindful *adjective* **1 = conscious,** heedful **2 = aware,** alert, alive to, careful, wary, watchful
mindless *adjective* **1 = unthinking,** foolish, idiotic, inane, moronic, stupid, thoughtless, witless
mine² *noun* **1 = pit,** colliery, deposit, excavation, shaft **3 = source,** abundance, fund, hoard, reserve, stock, store, supply, treasury, wealth ◆*verb* **4, 5 = dig up,** dig for, excavate, extract, hew, quarry, unearth
miner *noun* **= coalminer,** collier (*Brit*), pitman (*Brit*)

mingle *verb* **1 = mix,** blend, combine, intermingle, interweave, join, merge, unite OPPOSITE **part. 2 = associate,** consort, fraternize, hang about *or* around, hobnob, rub shoulders (*inf*), socialize OPPOSITE **avoid**
miniature *adjective* **2 = small,** diminutive, little, minuscule, minute, scaled-down, tiny, toy OPPOSITE **giant**
minimal *adjective* **= minimum,** least, least possible, nominal, slightest, smallest, token
minimize *verb* **1 = reduce,** curtail, decrease, diminish, miniaturize, prune, shrink OPPOSITE **increase. 2 = play down,** belittle, decry, deprecate, discount, disparage, make light *or* little of, underrate OPPOSITE **praise**
minimum *adjective* **= least,** least possible, lowest, minimal, slightest, smallest OPPOSITE ◆*noun* **= least,** lowest, nadir OPPOSITE **maximum**
minion *noun* **= follower,** flunky, hanger-on, henchman, hireling, lackey, underling, yes man
minister *noun* **3 = clergyman,** cleric, parson, pastor, preacher, priest, rector, vicar ◆*verb* **4 = attend to,** administer, cater to, pander to, serve, take care of, tend
ministry *noun* **1 = holy orders 2 = the priesthood,** the church **3 = department,**

minnow *noun* small freshwater fish.
minor **ᴑ** *adjective* **1** lesser. **2** *Music* (of a scale) having a semitone between the second and third notes. ◆ *noun* **3** person regarded legally as a child. **4** *Music* minor scale. **minority** *noun, pl* **-ties** **1** lesser number. **2** smaller party voting together. **3** group in a minority in any state.
minster *noun* cathedral or large church.
minstrel **ᴑ** *noun* medieval singer or musician.
mint¹ *noun* **1** plant with aromatic leaves used for seasoning and flavouring. **2** sweet flavoured with this.
mint² **ᴑ** *noun* **1** place where money is coined. ◆ *verb* **2** make (coins).
minuet [min-new-**wet**] *noun* **1** stately dance. **2** music for this.
minus *preposition, adjective* **1** indicating subtraction. ◆ *adjective* **2** less than zero. ◆ *noun* **3** sign (-) denoting subtraction or a number less than zero.
minuscule **ᴑ** [min-niss-skyool] *adjective* very small.

SPELLING TIP

The pronunciation of **minuscule** often influences the way people spell it. It's spelt *miniscule* 121 times in the Bank of English, but it should only one *i* and two *us*.

---

minute¹ **ᴑ** [**min**-it] *noun* **1** 60th part of an hour or degree. **2** moment. ◆ *plural* **3** record of the proceedings of a meeting. ◆ *verb* **4** record in the minutes.
minute² **ᴑ** [my-**newt**] *adjective* **1** very small. **2** precise. **minutely** *adverb* **minutiae** [my-**new**-shee-eye] *plural noun* trifling or precise details.
minx **ᴑ** *noun* bold or flirtatious girl.
miracle **ᴑ** *noun* **1** wonderful supernatural event. **2** marvel. **miraculous** *adjective* **miraculously** *adverb* **miracle play** medieval play based on a sacred subject.
mirage **ᴑ** [mir-**rahzh**] *noun* optical illusion, esp. one caused by hot air.
mire **ᴑ** *noun* **1** swampy ground. **2** mud.
mirror **ᴑ** *noun* **1** coated glass surface for reflecting images. ◆ *verb* **2** reflect in or as if in a mirror. **mirror image** image or object that has left and right reversed as if seen in a mirror.
mirth **ᴑ** *noun* laughter, merriment, or gaiety.
mirthful *adjective* **mirthless** *adjective* **mirthlessly** *adverb*
mis- *prefix* wrong(ly), bad(ly).
misadventure **ᴑ** *noun* unlucky chance.
misanthrope **ᴑ** [**miz**-zan-thrope] *noun* person who dislikes people in general. **misanthropic** [miz-zan-**throp**-ik] *adjective* **misanthropy** [miz-**zan**-throp-ee] *noun*
misapplication *noun* use of something for the wrong purpose.
misapprehend **ᴑ** *verb* misunderstand.

M

———— THESAURUS ————

bureau, council, office, quango
minor *adjective* **1** = **small**, inconsequential, insignificant, lesser, petty, slight, trivial, unimportant OPPOSITE **major**
minstrel *noun* = **musician**, bard, singer, songstress, troubadour
mint² *verb* **2** = **make**, cast, coin, produce, punch, stamp, strike
minuscule *adjective* = **tiny**, diminutive, infinitesimal, little, microscopic, miniature, minute
minute¹ *noun* **2** = **moment**, flash, instant, jiffy (*inf*), second, tick (*Brit inf*), trice ◆*plural* **3** = **record**, memorandum, notes, proceedings, transactions, transcript
minute² *adjective* **1** = **small**, diminutive, infinitesimal, little, microscopic, miniature, minuscule, tiny OPPOSITE **huge**. **2** = **precise**, close, critical, detailed, exact, exhaustive, meticulous, painstaking, punctilious OPPOSITE **rough**
minutiae *plural noun* = **details**, finer points, niceties, particulars, subtleties, trifles, trivia
minx *noun* = **flirt**, coquette, hussy

miracle *noun* **2** = **wonder**, marvel, phenomenon, prodigy
miraculous *adjective* **2** = **wonderful**, amazing, astonishing, astounding, extraordinary, incredible, phenomenal, prodigious, unaccountable, unbelievable OPPOSITE **common**
mirage *noun* = **illusion**, hallucination, optical illusion
mire *noun* **1** = **swamp**, bog, marsh, morass, quagmire, muskeg (*Canad*) **2** = **mud**, dirt, muck, ooze, slime
mirror *noun* **1** = **looking-glass**, glass, reflector ◆*verb* **2** = **reflect**, copy, echo, emulate, follow
mirth *noun* = **merriment**, amusement, cheerfulness, fun, gaiety, glee, hilarity, jollity, joviality, laughter, revelry
mirthful *adjective* = **merry**, blithe, cheerful, cheery, festive, happy, jolly, jovial, light-hearted, playful, sportive
misadventure *noun* = **misfortune**, accident, bad luck, calamity, catastrophe, debacle, disaster, mishap, reverse, setback
misanthropic *adjective* = **antisocial**, cynical,

misapprehension *noun*
misapprehension ❶ *noun* misunderstanding.
misappropriate ❶ *verb* take and use
(money) dishonestly. **misappropriation** *noun*
misbehave *verb* behave badly. **misbehaviour**
noun
miscalculate ❶ *verb* calculate or judge
wrongly. **miscalculation** *noun*
miscarriage ❶ *noun* **1** spontaneous
premature expulsion of a fetus from the womb.
2 failure, e.g. *a miscarriage of justice.* **miscarry**
verb **1** have a miscarriage. **2** fail.
miscast *verb* **-casting, -cast** cast (a role or
actor) in (a play or film) inappropriately.
miscegenation [miss-ij-in-**nay**-shun] *noun*
interbreeding of races.
miscellaneous ❶ [miss-sell-**lane**-ee-uss]
adjective mixed or assorted. **miscellany** [miss-
sell-a-nee] *noun* mixed assortment.
mischance ❶ *noun* unlucky event.
mischief ❶ *noun* **1** annoying but not
malicious behaviour. **2** inclination to tease. **3**
harm. **mischievous** [miss-chiv-uss] *adjective* **1**
full of mischief. **2** intended to cause harm.

mischievously *adverb*
miscible [**miss**-sib-bl] *adjective* able to be
mixed.
misconception ❶ *noun* wrong idea or belief.
misconceived *adjective*
misconduct ❶ *noun* immoral or unethical
behaviour.
misconstrue *verb* interpret wrongly.
misconstruction *noun*
miscreant ❶ [**miss**-kree-ant] *noun* wrongdoer.
misdeed ❶ *noun* wrongful act.
misdemeanour ❶ *noun* minor wrongdoing.
misdirect *verb* give (someone) wrong
directions or instructions. **misdirection** *noun*
miser ❶ *noun* person who hoards money and
hates spending it. **miserly** *adjective*
miserable ❶ *adjective* **1** very unhappy,
wretched. **2** causing misery. **3** squalid. **4** mean.
miserably *adverb* **misery** *noun, pl* **-eries 1**
great unhappiness. **2** *Informal* complaining
person.
misfire ❶ *verb* **1** (of a firearm or engine) fail to
fire correctly. **2** (of a plan) fail to turn out as
intended.

—————————— T H E S A U R U S ——————————

malevolent, unfriendly
misapprehend *verb* =**misunderstand,**
misconstrue, misinterpret, misread, mistake
misapprehension *noun*
=**misunderstanding,** delusion, error, fallacy,
misconception, misinterpretation, mistake
misappropriate *verb* =**steal,** embezzle,
misspend, misuse, peculate, pocket
miscalculate *verb* =**misjudge,** blunder, err,
overestimate, overrate, slip up, underestimate,
underrate
miscarriage *noun* **2** =**failure,** breakdown,
error, mishap, perversion
miscarry *verb* **2** =**fail,** come to grief, fall
through, go awry, go pear-shaped (*inf*), go
wrong, misfire
miscellaneous *adjective* =**mixed,** assorted,
diverse, jumbled, motley, sundry, varied,
various
miscellany *noun* =**assortment,** anthology,
collection, hotchpotch, jumble, medley,
mélange, mixed bag, mixture, potpourri, variety
mischance *noun* =**misfortune,** accident,
calamity, disaster, misadventure, mishap
mischief *noun* **1** =**misbehaviour,** impishness,
monkey business (*inf*), naughtiness, shenanigans
(*inf*), trouble, waywardness **3** =**harm,** damage,
evil, hurt, injury, misfortune, trouble
mischievous *adjective* **1** =**naughty,** impish,
playful, puckish, rascally, roguish, sportive,
troublesome, wayward **2** =**malicious,**

damaging, destructive, evil, harmful, hurtful,
spiteful, vicious, wicked
misconception *noun* =**delusion,** error,
fallacy, misapprehension, misunderstanding
misconduct *noun* =**immorality,** impropriety,
malpractice, mismanagement, wrongdoing
miscreant *noun* =**wrongdoer,** blackguard,
criminal, rascal, reprobate, rogue, scoundrel,
sinner, vagabond, villain
misdeed *noun* =**offence,** crime, fault,
misconduct, misdemeanour, sin, transgression,
wrong
misdemeanour *noun* =**offence,** fault,
infringement, misdeed, peccadillo, transgression
miser *noun* =**hoarder,** cheapskate (*inf*),
niggard, penny-pincher (*inf*), Scrooge, skinflint
miserable *adjective* **1** =**unhappy,** dejected,
depressed, despondent, disconsolate, forlorn,
gloomy, sorrowful, woebegone, wretched
OPPOSITE **happy. 2** =**despicable,** deplorable,
lamentable, shameful, sordid, sorry **3** =**squalid,**
wretched
miserly *adjective* =**mean,** avaricious, grasping,
niggardly, parsimonious, penny-pinching (*inf*),
stingy, tightfisted, ungenerous
misery *noun* **1** =**unhappiness,** anguish,
depression, desolation, despair, distress, gloom,
grief, sorrow, suffering, torment, woe OPPOSITE
ease. **2** *Inf* =**moaner,** killjoy, pessimist, prophet
of doom, sourpuss (*inf*), spoilsport, wet blanket
(*inf*)

misfit ⊕ *noun* person not suited to his or her social environment.

misfortune ⊕ *noun* (piece of) bad luck.

misgiving ⊕ *noun* feeling of fear or doubt.

misguided ⊕ *adjective* mistaken or unwise.

mishandle ⊕ *verb* handle badly or inefficiently.

mishap ⊕ *noun* minor accident.

mishear *verb* hear (what someone says) wrongly.

mishmash *noun* confused collection or mixture.

misinform ⊕ *verb* give incorrect information to. **misinformation** *noun*

misinterpret ⊕ *verb* understand or represent (something) wrongly. **misinterpretation** *noun*

misjudge ⊕ *verb* judge wrongly or unfairly. **misjudgment, misjudgement** *noun*

mislay ⊕ *verb* lose (something) temporarily.

mislead ⊕ *verb* give false or confusing information to. **misleading** *adjective* **misleadingly** *adverb*

mismanage *verb* organize or run (something) badly. **mismanagement** *noun*

misnomer [miss-no-mer] *noun* **1** incorrect or unsuitable name. **2** use of this.

misogyny [miss-oj-in-ee] *noun* hatred of women. **misogynist** *noun*

misplace ⊕ *verb* **1** mislay. **2** put in the wrong place. **3** give (trust or affection) inappropriately.

misprint ⊕ *noun* printing error.

mispronounce *verb* pronounce (a word) wrongly. **mispronunciation** *noun*

misquote ⊕ *verb* quote inaccurately. **misquotation** *noun*

misread *verb* **1** misinterpret (a situation etc.). **2** read incorrectly.

misrepresent ⊕ *verb* represent wrongly or inaccurately. **misrepresentation** *noun*

misrule ⊕ *verb* **1** govern inefficiently or unjustly. ♦ *noun* **2** inefficient or unjust government.

miss ⊕ *verb* **1** fail to notice, hear, hit, reach, find, or catch. **2** not be in time for. **3** notice or regret the absence of. **4** avoid. **5** (of an engine) misfire. ♦ *noun* **6** fact or instance of missing.

missing *adjective* lost or absent. **miss out** *verb* **1** leave out or overlook. **2** (foll. by *on*) fail to take part in (something enjoyable or beneficial).

Miss *noun* title of a girl or unmarried woman.

missal *noun* book containing the prayers and rites of the Mass.

misshapen ⊕ *adjective* badly shaped, deformed.

missile ⊕ *noun* **1** rocket with an exploding warhead, used as a weapon. **2** object or weapon thrown, shot, or launched at a target.

mission ⊕ *noun* **1** specific task or duty. **2** task or duty that a person believes he or she must achieve. **3** group of people sent on a mission. **4**

M

——————————— T H E S A U R U S ———————————

misfire *verb* **2** = **fail**, fall through, go pear-shaped (*inf*), go wrong, miscarry

misfit *noun* = **nonconformist**, eccentric, fish out of water (*inf*), oddball (*inf*), square peg (in a round hole) (*inf*)

misfortune *noun* = **bad luck**, adversity, hard luck, ill luck, infelicity OPPOSITE **good luck**

misgiving *noun* = **unease**, anxiety, apprehension, distrust, doubt, qualm, reservation, suspicion, trepidation, uncertainty, worry

misguided *adjective* = **unwise**, deluded, erroneous, ill-advised, imprudent, injudicious, misplaced, mistaken, unwarranted

mishandle *verb* = **mismanage**, botch, bungle, make a mess of, mess up (*inf*), muff

mishap *noun* = **accident**, calamity, misadventure, mischance, misfortune

misinform *verb* = **mislead**, deceive, misdirect, misguide

misinterpret *verb* = **misunderstand**, distort, misapprehend, misconceive, misconstrue, misjudge, misread, misrepresent, mistake

misjudge *verb* = **miscalculate**, overestimate, overrate, underestimate, underrate

mislay *verb* = **lose**, lose track of, misplace

mislead *verb* = **deceive**, delude, fool, hoodwink, misdirect, misguide, misinform, take in (*inf*)

misleading *adjective* = **confusing**, ambiguous, deceptive, disingenuous, evasive, false

misplace *verb* **1** = **lose**, lose track of, mislay

misprint *noun* = **mistake**, corrigendum, erratum, literal, typo (*inf*)

misquote *verb* = **misrepresent**, falsify, twist

misrepresent *verb* = **distort**, disguise, falsify, misinterpret

misrule *noun* **2** = **disorder**, anarchy, chaos, confusion, lawlessness, turmoil

miss *verb* **1** = **omit**, leave out, let go, overlook, pass over, skip **3** = **long for**, pine for, yearn for **4** = **avoid**, escape, evade ♦ *noun* **6** = **mistake**, blunder, error, failure, omission, oversight

misshapen *adjective* = **deformed**, contorted, crooked, distorted, grotesque, malformed, twisted, warped

missile *noun* = **rocket**, projectile, weapon

missing *adjective* = **absent**, astray, lacking, left out, lost, mislaid, misplaced, unaccounted-for OPPOSITE **present**

building in which missionaries work. **5** *S Afr*
long and difficult process. **missionary** *noun, pl*
-aries person sent abroad to do religious and
social work.

missive ⊕ *noun* letter.

misspell *verb* spell (a word) wrongly.

misspent ⊕ *adjective* wasted or misused.

missus, missis *noun Informal* one's wife or
the wife of the person addressed or referred to.

mist ⊕ *noun* **1** thin fog. **2** fine spray of liquid.
misty *adjective* **mistier, mistiest 1** full of mist.
2 dim or obscure. **mist over** *verb* **1** (also **mist
up**) (of glass) become covered with small drops
of moisture causing a misty effect. **2** (of eyes)
fill up with tears.

mistake ⊕ *noun* **1** error or blunder. ◆ *verb*
-taking, -took, -taken 2 misunderstand. **3**
confuse (a person or thing) with another.
mistaken *adjective* wrong in judgment or
opinion. **mistakenly** *adverb*

Mister *noun* polite form of address to a man.

mistime *verb* do (something) at the wrong
time.

mistletoe *noun* evergreen plant with white
berries growing as a parasite on trees.

mistral *noun* strong dry northerly wind of S
France.

mistreat ⊕ *verb* treat (a person or animal)
badly.

mistress ⊕ *noun* **1** woman who has a
continuing sexual relationship with a married
man. **2** woman in control of people or animals.
3 female teacher.

mistrial *noun Law* trial made void because of
some error.

mistrust ⊕ *verb* **1** have doubts or suspicions
about. ◆ *noun* **2** lack of trust. **mistrustful**
adjective

misunderstand ⊕ *verb* fail to understand
properly. **misunderstanding** *noun*

misuse ⊕ *noun* **1** incorrect, improper, or
careless use. ◆ *verb* **2** use wrongly. **3** treat
badly.

mite *noun* **1** very small spider-like animal. **2**
very small thing or amount. **a mite** somewhat.

mitigate ⊕ *verb* make less severe. **mitigating**
adjective **mitigation** *noun*

mitosis *noun* type of cell division in which the
nucleus divides into two nuclei which each
contain the same number of chromosomes
asthe original nucleus.

mitre [**my**-ter] *noun* **1** bishop's pointed
headdress. **2** joint between two pieces of wood
bevelled to meet at right angles. ◆ *verb* **3** join

M

──────── THESAURUS ────────

mission *noun* **1 = task**, assignment,
commission, duty, errand, job, quest,
undertaking **2 = vocation**

missionary *noun* **= evangelist**, apostle,
preacher

missive *noun* **= letter**, communication,
dispatch, epistle, memorandum, message, note,
report

misspent *adjective* **= wasted**, dissipated,
imprudent, profitless, squandered

mist *noun* **1 = fog**, cloud, film, haze, smog,
spray, steam, vapour

mistake *noun* **1 = error**, blunder, erratum,
fault, faux pas, gaffe, howler (*inf*),
miscalculation, oversight, slip ◆*verb* **2**
= misunderstand, misapprehend, misconstrue,
misinterpret, misjudge, misread **3 = confuse**
with, mix up with, take for

mistaken *adjective* **= wrong**, erroneous, false,
faulty, inaccurate, incorrect, misguided,
unsound, wide of the mark OPPOSITE▷ **right**

mistakenly *adverb* **= incorrectly**, by mistake,
erroneously, fallaciously, falsely, inaccurately,
misguidedly, wrongly

mistimed *adjective* **= inopportune**, badly
timed, ill-timed, untimely

mistreat *verb* **= abuse**, harm, ill-treat, injure,
knock about *or* around, maltreat, manhandle,

misuse, molest

mistress *noun* **1 = lover**, concubine,
girlfriend, kept woman, paramour

mistrust *verb* **1 = doubt**, be wary of, distrust,
fear, suspect ◆*noun* **2 = suspicion**, distrust,
doubt, misgiving, scepticism, uncertainty,
wariness

mistrustful *adjective* **= suspicious**, chary,
cynical, distrustful, doubtful, fearful, hesitant,
sceptical, uncertain, wary

misty *adjective* **1 = foggy**, blurred, cloudy,
dim, hazy, indistinct, murky, obscure, opaque,
overcast

misunderstand *verb* **= misinterpret**, be at
cross-purposes, get the wrong end of the stick,
misapprehend, misconstrue, misjudge, misread,
mistake

misunderstanding *noun* **= mistake**, error,
misconception, misinterpretation, misjudgment,
mix-up

misuse *noun* **1 = waste**, abuse, desecration,
misapplication, squandering ◆*verb* **3 = waste**,
abuse, desecrate, misapply, prostitute, squander

mitigate *verb* **= ease**, extenuate, lessen,
lighten, moderate, soften, subdue, temper
OPPOSITE▷ **intensify**

mitigation *noun* **= relief**, alleviation,
diminution, extenuation, moderation, remission

mitt *noun* **1** short for MITTEN. **2** *Slang* hand. **3** baseball catcher's glove.

mitten *noun* glove with one section for the thumb and one for the four fingers together.

mix ❶ *verb* **1** combine or blend into one mass. **2** form (something) by mixing. **3** be sociable. ◆ *noun* **4** mixture. **mixed** *adjective* **mixed blessing** something that has advantages as well as disadvantages. **mixed grill** dish of several kinds of grilled meat, tomatoes, and mushrooms. **mix up** *verb* **1** confuse. **2** make into a mixture. **mixed up** *adjective* **mix-up** *noun* **mixer** *noun* **1** kitchen appliance used for mixing foods. **2** *Informal* person considered in relation to his or her ability to mix socially, e.g. *a good mixer*. **3** nonalcoholic drink, e.g. tonic water, that is mixed with an alcoholic drink.

mixture *noun* **1** something mixed. **2** combination.

mizzenmast *noun* (on a vessel with three or more masts) third mast from the bow.

mks units *plural noun* metric system of units based on the metre, kilogram, and second.

ml millilitre(s).

Mlle *pl* **Mlles** Mademoiselle.

mm millimetre(s).

MM plural of M (sense 1).

Mme *pl* **Mmes** Madame.

Mn *Chem* manganese.

MN Minnesota.

mnemonic [nim-on-ik] *noun, adjective* (something, such as a rhyme) intended to help the memory.

mo *noun, pl* **mos** *Informal* short for MOMENT.

Mo *Chem* molybdenum.

MO 1 Medical Officer. **2** Missouri.

moan ❶ *noun* **1** low cry of pain. **2** *Informal* grumble. ◆ *verb* **3** make or utter with a moan. **4** *Informal* grumble. **moaner** *noun*

moat *noun* deep wide ditch, esp. round a castle.

mob ❶ *noun* **1** disorderly crowd. **2** *Slang* gang. ◆ *verb* **mobbing, mobbed 3** surround in a mob to acclaim or attack.

mobile ❶ *adjective* **1** able to move. ◆ *noun* **2** same as MOBILE PHONE. **3** hanging structure designed to move in air currents. **mobile phone** cordless phone powered by batteries. **mobility** *noun*

mobilize ❶ *verb* **1** (of the armed services) prepare for active service. **2** organize for a purpose. **mobilization** *noun*

moccasin *noun* soft leather shoe.

> **SPELLING TIP**
>
> One **moccasin** has a double *c*, but only one *s*. The plural, **moccasins**, has two *ss*, but they are not together.

mocha [mock-a] *noun* **1** kind of strong dark coffee. **2** flavouring made from coffee and chocolate.

mock ❶ *verb* **1** make fun of. **2** mimic. ◆ *adjective* **3** sham or imitation. **mocks** *plural noun Informal* (in England and Wales) practice exams taken before public exams. **put the mockers on** *Informal* ruin the chances of success of. **mockery** *noun* **1** derision. **2** inadequate or worthless attempt. **mocking**

M

————————————— T H E S A U R U S —————————————

mix *verb* **1, 2** = **combine**, blend, cross, fuse, intermingle, interweave, join, jumble, merge, mingle **3** = **socialize**, associate, consort, fraternize, hang out (*inf*), hobnob, mingle ◆*noun* **4** = **mixture**, alloy, amalgam, assortment, blend, combination, compound, fusion, medley

mixed *adjective* **1, 2** = **combined**, amalgamated, blended, composite, compound, joint, mingled, united OPPOSITE **pure**. **4** = **varied**, assorted, cosmopolitan, diverse, heterogeneous, miscellaneous, motley OPPOSITE **homogeneous**

mixed up *adjective* = **confused**, at sea, bewildered, distraught, disturbed, maladjusted, muddled, perplexed, puzzled, upset

mixture *noun* **1** = **assortment**, jumble, medley, mix, potpourri, variety **2** = **blend**, amalgam, brew, compound, fusion

mix up *verb* **1** = **confuse**, confound, muddle **2**

= **combine**, blend, mix

mix-up *noun* = **confusion**, mess, mistake, misunderstanding, muddle, tangle

moan *noun* **1** = **groan**, lament, sigh, sob, wail, whine **2** *Inf* = **grumble**, complaint, gripe (*inf*), grouch (*inf*), grouse, protest, whine ◆*verb* **3** = **groan**, lament, sigh, sob, whine **4** *Inf* = **grumble**, bleat, carp, complain, groan, grouse, whine, whinge (*inf*)

mob *noun* **1** = **crowd**, drove, flock, horde, host, mass, multitude, pack, swarm, throng **2** *Sl* = **gang**, crew (*inf*), group, lot, set ◆*verb* **3** = **surround**, crowd around, jostle, set upon, swarm around

mobile *adjective* **1** = **movable**, itinerant, moving, peripatetic, portable, travelling, wandering

mobilize *verb* **1** = **call to arms**, activate, call up, marshal **2** = **prepare**, get *or* make ready, adjective **mockingbird** noun N American bird which imitates other birds' songs. **mockingly** adverb **mock orange** shrub with white fragrant flowers. **mock-up** noun full-scale model for test or study.

mod[1] noun member of a group of young people, orig. in the mid-1960s, who were very clothes-conscious and rode motor scooters.

mod[2] noun annual Highland Gaelic meeting with musical and literary competitions.

MOD Ministry of Defence.

mod. 1 moderate. 2 modern.

mod cons plural noun Informal modern conveniences, such as heating and hot water.

mode ❶ noun 1 method or manner. 2 current fashion.

model ❶ noun 1 (miniature) representation. 2 pattern. 3 person or thing worthy of imitation. 4 person who poses for an artist or photographer. 5 person who wears clothes to display them to prospective buyers. ◆ adjective 6 excellent or perfect, e.g. a model husband. ◆ verb **-elling, -elled** 7 make a model of. 8 mould. 9 plan or create according to a model or models. 10 display (clothing) as a model.

modelling noun

modem [mode-em] noun device for connecting two computers by a telephone line.

moderate ❶ adjective 1 not extreme. 2 self-restrained. 3 average. ◆ noun 4 person of moderate views. ◆ verb 5 make or become less violent or extreme. **moderately** adverb **moderation** noun **moderator** noun 1 (Presbyterian Church) minister appointed to preside over a Church court, general assembly, etc. 2 person who presides over a public or legislative assembly.

modern ❶ adjective 1 of present or recent times. 2 up-to-date. **modern languages** languages spoken in present-day Europe, with the exception of English. **modern pentathlon** athletic contest consisting of five different events. **modernity** noun **modernism** noun (support of) modern tendencies, thoughts, or styles. **modernist** adjective, noun **modernize** verb bring up to date. **modernization** noun

modest ❶ adjective 1 not vain or boastful. 2 not excessive. 3 not showy. 4 shy. **modestly** adverb **modesty** noun

modicum ❶ noun small quantity.

———————— T H E S A U R U S ————————

organize, rally, ready

mock verb 1 = **laugh at**, deride, jeer, make fun of, poke fun at, ridicule, scoff, scorn, sneer, taunt, tease OPPOSITE respect. 2 = **mimic**, ape, caricature, imitate, lampoon, parody, satirize, send up (Brit inf) ◆adjective 3 = **imitation**, artificial, dummy, fake, false, feigned, phoney or phony (inf), pretended, sham, spurious OPPOSITE real

mockery noun 1 = **derision**, contempt, disdain, disrespect, insults, jeering, ridicule, scoffing, scorn 2 = **farce**, apology (inf), disappointment, joke, letdown

mocking adjective 1 = **scornful**, contemptuous, derisive, disdainful, disrespectful, sarcastic, sardonic, satirical, scoffing

mode noun 1 = **method**, form, manner, procedure, process, style, system, technique, way 2 = **fashion**, craze, look, rage, style, trend, vogue

model noun 1 = **representation**, copy, dummy, facsimile, image, imitation, miniature, mock-up, replica 2 = **pattern**, example, original, paradigm, prototype, standard 3 = **ideal**, archetype, paragon 4 = **sitter**, poser, subject ◆verb 8 = **shape**, carve, design, fashion, form, mould, sculpt 10 = **show off**, display, sport (inf), wear

moderate adjective 1 = **middle-of-the-road**,

limited 2 = **restrained**, controlled, gentle, mild, modest, reasonable, steady OPPOSITE extreme. 3 = **average**, fair, indifferent, mediocre, middling, ordinary, passable, so-so (inf), unexceptional OPPOSITE unusual ◆verb 5 = **lessen**, control, curb, ease, modulate, regulate, restrain, soften, subdue, temper, tone down OPPOSITE increase

moderation noun 2 = **restraint**, fairness, reasonableness, temperance

modern adjective 1 = **current**, contemporary, present-day, recent 2 = **up-to-date**, fresh, new, newfangled, novel OPPOSITE old

modernity noun 2 = **novelty**, currency, freshness, innovation, newness

modernize verb 2 = **update**, make over, rejuvenate, remake, remodel, renew, renovate, revamp

modest adjective 1, 4 = **shy**, bashful, coy, demure, diffident, reserved, reticent, retiring, self-effacing 2 = **moderate**, fair, limited, middling, small 3 = **unpretentious**, ordinary, unexceptional

modesty noun 1, 4 = **reserve**, bashfulness, coyness, demureness, diffidence, humility, reticence, shyness, timidity OPPOSITE confidence

modicum noun = **little**, bit, crumb, drop, fragment, scrap, shred, touch

modification noun 1 = **change**, adjustment,

modify ❶ *verb* **-fying, -fied 1** change slightly. **2** tone down. **3** (of a word) qualify (another word). **modifier** *noun* word that qualifies the sense of another. **modification** *noun*
modish ❶ [mode-ish] *adjective* in fashion.
modulate ❶ *verb* **1** vary in tone. **2** adjust. **3** change the key of (music). **modulation** *noun* **modulator** *noun*
module *noun* **1** self-contained unit, section, or component with a specific function. **2** short study course that together with other such courses counts towards a qualification. **modular** *adjective*
modus operandi [mode-uss op-er-**an**-die] *noun Latin* method of operating.
modus vivendi [mode-uss viv-**venn**-die] *noun Latin* working arrangement between conflicting interests.
moggy, moggie *noun, pl* **-gies** *Slang* cat.
mogul ❶ [moh-gl] *noun* important or powerful person.
MOH Medical Officer of Health.
mohair *noun* **1** fine hair of the Angora goat. **2** yarn or fabric made from this.
mohican *noun* punk hairstyle with shaved sides and a stiff central strip of hair, often brightly coloured.
moiety [moy-it-ee] *noun, pl* **-ties** half.
moiré [mwahr-ray] *adjective* **1** having a watered or wavelike pattern. ◆ *noun* **2** any fabric that has such a pattern.
moist ❶ *adjective* slightly wet. **moisten** *verb* make or become moist. **moisture** *noun* liquid diffused as vapour or condensed in drops.
moisturize *verb* add moisture to (the skin etc.). **moisturizer** *noun*
moke *noun* **1** *Slang* donkey. **2** *Aust & NZ* horse of inferior quality.
molar *noun* large back tooth used for grinding.
molasses *noun* dark syrup, a by-product of sugar refining.

mole¹ *noun* small dark raised spot on the skin.
mole² *noun* **1** small burrowing mammal. **2** *Informal* spy who has infiltrated and become a trusted member of an organization. **molehill** *noun* small mound of earth thrown up by a burrowing mole. **make a mountain out of a molehill** exaggerate an unimportant matter out of all proportion.
mole³ *noun* unit of amount of substance.
mole⁴ ³ *noun* **1** breakwater. **2** harbour protected by this.
molecule ❶ [mol-lik-kyool] *noun* **1** simplest freely existing chemical unit, composed of two or more atoms. **2** very small particle. **molecular** [mol-**lek**-yew-lar] *adjective*
molest ❶ *verb* **1** interfere with sexually. **2** annoy or injure. **molester** *noun* **molestation** *noun*
moll *noun Slang* gangster's female accomplice.
mollify ❶ *verb* **-fying, -fied** pacify or soothe. **mollification** *noun*
mollusc *noun* soft-bodied, usu. hard-shelled, animal, such as a snail or oyster.
mollycoddle ❶ *verb* pamper.
Molotov cocktail *noun* petrol bomb.
molten *adjective* liquefied or melted.
molybdenum [mol-**lib**-din-um] *noun Chem* hard silvery-white metallic element.
mom *noun Chiefly US & Canad* an informal word for MOTHER.
moment ❶ *noun* **1** short space of time. **2** (present) point in time. **momentary** *adjective* lasting only a moment. **momentarily** *adverb*

LANGUAGE TIP

Note that some American speakers use *momentarily* to mean 'soon' rather than 'for a moment'.

M

———————— THESAURUS ————————

alteration, qualification, refinement, revision, variation
modify *verb* **1** = **change**, adapt, adjust, alter, convert, reform, remodel, revise, rework **2** = **tone down**, ease, lessen, lower, moderate, qualify, restrain, soften, temper
modish *adjective* = **fashionable**, contemporary, current, in, smart, stylish, trendy (*Brit inf*), up-to-the-minute, voguish
modulate *verb* **1** = **vary 2** = **adjust**, attune, balance, regulate **3** = **tune**
mogul *noun* = **tycoon**, baron, big hitter (*inf*), big noise (*inf*), big shot (*inf*), heavy hitter (*inf*), magnate, V.I.P.

moist *adjective* = **damp**, clammy, dewy, humid, soggy, wet
moisten *verb* = **dampen**, damp, moisturize, soak, water, wet
moisture *noun* = **damp**, dew, liquid, water, wetness
molecule *noun* **2** = **particle**, jot, speck
molest *verb* **1** = **abuse**, ill-treat, interfere with, maltreat **2** = **annoy**, attack, badger, beset, bother, disturb, harass, harm, hurt, persecute, pester, plague, torment, worry
mollify *verb* = **pacify**, appease, calm, conciliate, placate, quiet, soothe, sweeten
mollycoddle *verb* = **pamper**, baby, cosset,

momentous ๋ [moh-**men**-tuss] *adjective* of great significance.

momentum ๋ [moh-**men**-tum] *noun* **1** impetus to go forward, develop, or get stronger. **2** impetus of a moving body. **3** product of a body's mass and velocity.

Mon. Monday.

monarch ๋ *noun* sovereign ruler of a state.
monarchical *adjective* **monarchist** *noun* supporter of monarchy. **monarchy** *noun, pl* **-chies** government by or a state ruled by a sovereign.

monastery ๋ *noun, pl* **-teries** residence of a community of monks. **monastic** *adjective* **1** of monks, nuns, or monasteries. **2** simple and austere. **monasticism** *noun*

monatomic *adjective* consisting of single atoms.

Monday *noun* second day of the week.

monetary ๋ *adjective* of money or currency.
monetarism *noun* **1** theory that inflation is caused by an increase in the money supply. **2** economic policy based on this theory.
monetarist *noun, adjective*

money ๋ *noun* medium of exchange, coins or banknotes. **moneyed, monied** *adjective* rich.
moneylender *noun* person who lends money at a high rate of interest as a living.

Mongolian *noun* **1** person from Mongolia. **2** language of Mongolia. ✦ *adjective* **3** of Mongolia or its language.

mongolism *noun Offens* Down's syndrome.
mongol *noun, adjective Offens* (person) affected by this.

mongoose *noun, pl* **-gooses** stoatlike mammal of Asia and Africa that kills snakes.

mongrel ๋ *noun* **1** animal, esp. a dog, of mixed breed. **2** something arising from a variety of sources. ✦ *adjective* **3** of mixed breed or origin.

monitor ๋ *noun* **1** person or device that checks, controls, warns, or keeps a record of something. **2** pupil assisting a teacher with duties. **3** television set used in a studio to check what is being transmitted. **4** type of large lizard. ✦ *verb* **5** watch and check on.

monk ๋ *noun* member of an all-male religious community bound by vows. **monkish** *adjective*
monkshood *noun* poisonous plant with hooded flowers.

monkey ๋ *noun* **1** long-tailed primate. **2** mischievous child. ✦ *verb* **3** (usu. foll. by *about* or *around*) meddle or fool. **monkey nut** peanut. **monkey puzzle** coniferous tree with sharp stiff leaves. **monkey wrench** wrench with adjustable jaws.

mono *adjective* **1** short for MONOPHONIC. ✦ *noun* **2** monophonic sound.

mono- *combining form* single, e.g. *monosyllable.*

monochrome *adjective* **1** *Photog* black-and-white. **2** in only one colour.

monocle [**mon**-a-kl] *noun* eyeglass for one eye only.

monocotyledon [mon-no-kot-ill-**leed**-on] *noun* flowering plant with a single embryonic seed leaf.

monocular *adjective* having or for one eye

———————————— THESAURUS ————————————

indulge, spoil

moment *noun* **1** = **instant**, flash, jiffy (*inf*), second, split second, trice, twinkling **2** = **time**, juncture, point, stage

momentarily *adverb* **1** = **briefly**, for a moment, temporarily

momentary *adjective* = **short-lived**, brief, fleeting, passing, short, temporary, transitory

momentous *adjective* = **significant**, critical, crucial, fateful, historic, important, pivotal, vital, weighty OPPOSITE **unimportant**

momentum *noun* **1, 2** = **impetus**, drive, energy, force, power, propulsion, push, strength, thrust

monarch *noun* = **ruler**, emperor *or* empress, king, potentate, prince *or* princess, queen, sovereign

monarchy *noun* **a** = **sovereignty**, autocracy, kingship, monocracy **b** = **kingdom**, empire, principality, realm

monastery *noun* = **abbey**, cloister, convent,

friary, nunnery, priory

monastic *adjective* **1** = **monkish**, cloistered, contemplative, hermit-like, reclusive, secluded, sequestered, withdrawn **2** = **ascetic**

monetary *adjective* = **financial**, budgetary, capital, cash, fiscal, pecuniary

money *noun* = **cash**, capital, coin, currency, hard cash, legal tender, lolly (*Aust & NZ sl*), readies (*inf*), riches, silver, wealth

mongrel *noun* **1** = **crossbreed**, cross, half-breed **2** = **hybrid** ✦*adjective* **3** = **hybrid**, crossbred

monitor *noun* **1** = **watchdog**, guide, invigilator, supervisor **2** = **prefect** (*Brit*) ✦*verb* **5** = **check**, follow, keep an eye on, keep tabs on, keep track of, observe, survey, watch

monk *noun* = **friar**, brother (*loosely*)

monkey *noun* **1** = **simian**, primate **2** = **rascal**, devil, imp, rogue, scamp ✦*verb* **3** (usu. foll. by *about* or *around*) = **fool**, meddle, mess, play, tinker only.

monogamy *noun* custom of being married to one person at a time. **monogamous** *adjective*

monogram *noun* design of combined letters, esp. a person's initials. **monogrammed** *adjective* marked with such a design.

monograph *noun* book or paper on a single subject.

monolith ๑ *noun* large upright block of stone. **monolithic** *adjective*

monologue ๑ *noun* **1** long speech by one person. **2** dramatic piece for one performer.

monomania *noun* obsession with one thing. **monomaniac** *noun, adjective*

monophonic *adjective* (of a system of broadcasting, recording, or reproducing sound) using only one channel between source and loudspeaker.

monoplane *noun* aeroplane with one pair of wings.

monopoly ๑ *noun* **1** *pl* **-lies** exclusive possession of or right to do something. **2 (M-)** ® board game for four to six players who deal in 'property' as they move around the board. **monopolist** *noun* **monopolistic** *adjective* **monopolize** *verb* have or take exclusive possession of.

monorail *noun* single-rail railway.

monosodium glutamate *noun* white crystalline substance used as a food additive to enhance protein flavours.

monosyllable *noun* word of one syllable. **monosyllabic** *adjective*

monotheism *noun* belief in only one God. **monotheistic** *adjective*

monotone ๑ *noun* unvaried pitch in speech or sound. **monotonous** *adjective* tedious due to lack of variety. **monotonously** *adverb*

monotony *noun* wearisome routine, dullness.

monoxide *noun* oxide that contains one oxygen atom per molecule.

Monseigneur [mon-sen-**nyur**] *noun, pl* **Messeigneurs** [may-sen-**nyur**] title of French prelates.

monsieur [muss-**syur**] *noun, pl* **messieurs** [may-**syur**] French title of address equivalent to *sir* or *Mr.*

Monsignor *noun* RC Church title attached to certain offices.

monsoon *noun* **1** seasonal wind of SE Asia. **2** rainy season accompanying this.

monster ๑ *noun* **1** imaginary, usu. frightening, beast. **2** huge person, animal, or thing. **3** very wicked person. ♦ *adjective* **4** huge. **monstrosity** *noun, pl* **-ities** large ugly thing. **monstrous** *adjective* **1** unnatural or ugly. **2** outrageous or shocking. **3** huge. **monstrously** *adverb*

monstrance *noun* RC Church container in which the consecrated Host is exposed for adoration.

montage [mon-**tahzh**] *noun* **1** (making of) a picture composed from pieces of others. **2** method of film editing incorporating several shots to form a single image.

month *noun* **1** one of the twelve divisions of the calendar year. **2** period of four weeks.

monthly *adjective* **1** happening or payable once a month. ♦ *adverb* **2** once a month. ♦ *noun, pl* **-lies 3** monthly magazine.

monument ๑ *noun* something, esp. a building or statue, that commemorates something. **monumental** *adjective* **1** large, impressive, or lasting. **2** of or being a monument. **3** *Informal* extreme.

monumentally *adverb Informal* extremely.

—————— T H E S A U R U S ——————

monolithic *adjective* =**huge**, colossal, impenetrable, intractable, massive, monumental, solid

monologue *noun* **1** =**speech**, harangue, lecture, sermon **2** =**soliloquy**

monopolize *verb* =**control**, corner the market in, dominate, hog (*sl*), keep to oneself, take over

monotonous *adjective* =**tedious**, boring, dull, humdrum, mind-numbing, repetitive, tiresome, unchanging, wearisome OPPOSITE⟩ **interesting**

monotony *noun* =**tedium**, boredom, monotonousness, repetitiveness, routine, sameness, tediousness

monster *noun* **1** =**freak**, monstrosity, mutant **2** =**giant**, colossus, mammoth, titan **3** =**brute**, beast, demon, devil, fiend, villain ♦*adjective* **4**

=**huge**, colossal, enormous, gigantic, immense, mammoth, massive, stupendous, tremendous

monstrosity *noun* =**eyesore**, freak, horror, monster

monstrous *adjective* **1** =**unnatural**, fiendish, freakish, frightful, grotesque, gruesome, hideous, horrible OPPOSITE⟩ **appealing. 2** =**outrageous**, diabolical, disgraceful, foul, inhuman, intolerable, scandalous, shocking OPPOSITE⟩ **good. 3** =**huge**, colossal, enormous, immense, mammoth, massive, prodigious, stupendous, tremendous OPPOSITE⟩ **little**

monument *noun* =**memorial**, cairn, cenotaph, commemoration, gravestone, headstone, marker, mausoleum, shrine, tombstone

monumental *adjective* **1** =**important**,

moo *noun* **1** long deep cry of a cow. ♦ *verb* **2** make this noise.

mooch *verb Slang* loiter about aimlessly.

mood[1] ⊕ *noun* temporary (gloomy) state of mind. **moody** *adjective* **moodier, moodiest 1** sullen or gloomy. **2** changeable in mood. **moodily** *adverb* **moodiness** *noun*

mood[2] *noun Grammar* form of a verb indicating whether it expresses a fact, wish, supposition, or command.

moon ⊕ *noun* **1** natural satellite of the earth. **2** natural satellite of any planet. ♦ *verb* **3** (foll. by *about* or *around*) be idle in a listless or dreamy way. **moonless** *adjective* **moony** *adjective Informal* dreamy or listless. **moonbeam** *noun* ray of moonlight. **moonlight** *noun* **1** light from the moon. ♦ *adjective* **2** illuminated by the moon, e.g. *a moonlight drive.* ♦ *verb* **3** *Informal* work at a secondary job, esp. illegally. **moonlit** *adjective* **moonshine** *noun* **1** illicitly distilled whisky. **2** nonsense. **moonstone** *noun* translucent semiprecious stone. **moonstruck** *adjective* slightly mad or odd.

moor[1] ⊕ *noun* tract of open uncultivated ground covered with grass and heather. **moorhen** *noun* small black water bird. **moorland** *noun*

moor[2] ⊕ *verb* secure (a ship) with ropes etc. **mooring** *noun* **1** place for mooring a ship. ♦ *plural* **2** ropes etc. used in mooring a ship.

Moor *noun* member of a Muslim people of NW Africa who ruled Spain between the 8th and 15th centuries. **Moorish** *adjective*

moose *noun* large N American deer.

moot ⊕ *adjective* **1** debatable, e.g. *a moot point.* ♦ *verb* **2** bring up for discussion.

mop ⊕ *noun* **1** long stick with twists of cotton or a sponge on the end, used for cleaning. **2** thick mass of hair. ♦ *verb* **mopping, mopped 3** clean or soak up with or as if with a mop.

mope ⊕ *verb* be gloomy and apathetic.

moped *noun* light motorized cycle.

mopoke *noun* small spotted owl of Australia and New Zealand.

moraine *noun* accumulated mass of debris deposited by a glacier.

moral ⊕ *adjective* **1** concerned with right and wrong conduct. **2** based on a sense of right and wrong. **3** (of support or a victory) psychological rather than practical. ♦ *noun* **4** lesson to be obtained from a story or event. ♦ *plural* **5** principles of behaviour with respect to right and wrong. **morally** *adverb* **moralist** *noun* person with a strong sense of right and wrong. **moralistic** *adjective* **morality** *noun* **1** good moral conduct. **2** moral goodness or badness. **morality play** medieval play with a moral lesson. **moralize** *verb* make moral pronouncements.

morale ⊕ [mor-**rahl**] *noun* degree of confidence or hope of a person or group.

morass ⊕ *noun* **1** marsh. **2** mess.

moratorium ⊕ *noun, pl* **-ria, -riums** legally authorized ban or delay.

—————— THESAURUS ——————

awesome, enormous, epoch-making, historic, majestic, memorable, significant, unforgettable OPPOSITE> ordinary. **3** *Inf* =**immense**, colossal, great, massive, staggering OPPOSITE> **small**

mood[1] *noun* =**state of mind**, disposition, frame of mind, humour, spirit, temper

moody *adjective* **1** =**sulky**, gloomy, glum, ill-tempered, irritable, morose, pissed (*taboo sl*), pissed off (*taboo sl*), sad, sullen, temperamental, touchy OPPOSITE> **happy**. **2** =**changeable**, capricious, erratic, fickle, flighty, impulsive, mercurial, temperamental, unpredictable, volatile OPPOSITE> **stable**

moon *noun* **1, 2** =**satellite** ♦*verb* **3** =**idle**, daydream, languish, mope, waste time

moor[1] *noun* =**moorland**, fell (*Brit*), heath

moor[2] *verb* =**tie up**, anchor, berth, dock, lash, make fast, secure

moot *adjective* **1** =**debatable**, arguable, contestable, controversial, disputable, doubtful, undecided, unresolved, unsettled ♦*verb* **2** =**bring up**, broach, propose, put forward, suggest

mop *noun* **1** =**squeegee**, sponge, swab **2** =**mane**, shock, tangle, thatch

mop *verb* **1** =**clean up**, soak up, sponge, swab, wash, wipe

mope *verb* =**brood**, fret, languish, moon, pine, pout, sulk

moral *adjective* **1, 2** =**good**, decent, ethical, high-minded, honourable, just, noble, principled, right, virtuous OPPOSITE> **immoral** ♦*noun* **4** =**lesson**, meaning, message, point, significance

morale *noun* =**confidence**, esprit de corps, heart, self-esteem, spirit

morality *noun* **1** =**integrity**, decency, goodness, honesty, justice, righteousness, virtue **2** =**standards**, conduct, ethics, manners, morals, mores, philosophy, principles

morals *plural noun* **5** =**morality**, behaviour, conduct, ethics, habits, integrity, manners, mores, principles, scruples, standards

morass *noun* **1** =**marsh**, bog, fen, quagmire, slough, swamp, muskeg (*Canad*) **2** =**mess**, confusion, mix-up, muddle, tangle

moray *noun* large voracious eel.

morbid ❶ *adjective* **1** unduly interested in death or unpleasant events. **2** gruesome. **morbidly** *adverb*

mordant ❶ *adjective* **1** sarcastic or scathing. ◆ *noun* **2** substance used to fix dyes.

more ❶ *adjective* **1** greater in amount or degree. **2** comparative of MUCH *or* MANY. **3** additional or further. ◆ *adverb* **4** to a greater extent. **5** in addition. ◆ *pronoun* **6** greater or additional amount or number. **moreover** *adverb* in addition to what has already been said.

morel *noun* edible mushroom with a pitted cap.

mores [more-rayz] *plural noun* customs and conventions embodying the fundamental values of a community.

Moreton Bay bug *noun* Australian flattish edible shellfish.

morganatic marriage *noun* marriage of a person of high rank to a lower-ranking person whose status remains unchanged.

morgue ❶ *noun* mortuary.

moribund ❶ *adjective* without force or vitality.

Mormon *noun* member of a religious sect founded in the USA.

morn *noun* Poetic morning.

mornay *adjective* served with a cheese sauce, e.g. *sole mornay.*

morning ❶ *noun* part of the day before noon. **the morning after** *Informal* the aftereffects of overindulgence, hangover. **morning coat** frock coat. **morning dress** formal day dress for men, comprising a morning coat, grey trousers, and a top hat. **morning-glory** plant with

trumpet-shaped flowers which close in the late afternoon. **morning sickness** nausea shortly after rising, often experienced in early pregnancy.

Moroccan *adjective* **1** of Morocco. ◆ *noun* **2** person from Morocco.

morocco *noun* goatskin leather.

moron ❶ *noun* **1** Informal foolish or stupid person. **2** (formerly) person with a low intelligence quotient. **moronic** *adjective*

morose ❶ [mor-rohss] *adjective* sullen or moody. **morosely** *adverb*

morphine, morphia *noun* drug extracted from opium, used as an anaesthetic and sedative.

morphology *noun* science of forms and structures of organisms or words. **morphological** *adjective*

morris dance *noun* traditional English folk dance performed by men.

morrow *noun* Poetic next day.

Morse *noun* former system of signalling in which letters of the alphabet are represented by combinations of short and long signals.

morsel ❶ *noun* small piece, esp. of food.

mortal ❶ *adjective* **1** subject to death. **2** causing death. ◆ *noun* **3** human being. **mortally** *adverb* **mortality** *noun* **1** state of being mortal. **2** great loss of life. **3** death rate. **mortal sin** RC Church sin meriting damnation.

mortar *noun* **1** small cannon with a short range. **2** mixture of lime, sand, and water for holding bricks and stones together. **3** bowl in which substances are pounded. **mortarboard** *noun* square academic cap.

mortgage *noun* **1** conditional pledging of

—————— T H E S A U R U S ——————

moratorium *noun* =**postponement**, freeze, halt, standstill, suspension

morbid *adjective* **1** =**unwholesome**, ghoulish, gloomy, melancholy, sick, sombre, unhealthy OPPOSITE happy. **2** =**gruesome**, dreadful, ghastly, grisly, hideous, horrid, macabre

mordant *adjective* **1** =**sarcastic**, biting, caustic, cutting, incisive, pungent, scathing, stinging, trenchant

more *adjective* **1** =**extra**, added, additional, further, new, new-found, other, supplementary ◆*adverb* **4** =**to a greater extent**, better, further, longer

moreover *adverb* =**furthermore**, additionally, also, as well, besides, further, in addition, too

morgue *noun* =**mortuary**

moribund *adjective* =**declining**, on its last legs, stagnant, waning, weak

morning *noun* =**dawn**, a.m., break of day,

daybreak, forenoon, morn (*poet*), sunrise

moron *noun* **1** *Inf* =**fool**, blockhead, cretin, dunce, dunderhead, halfwit, idiot, imbecile, oaf

moronic *adjective* **1** =**idiotic**, cretinous, foolish, halfwitted, imbecilic, mindless, stupid, unintelligent

morose *adjective* =**sullen**, depressed, dour, gloomy, glum, ill-tempered, moody, sour, sulky, surly, taciturn OPPOSITE cheerful

morsel *noun* =**piece**, bit, bite, crumb, mouthful, part, scrap, soupçon, taste, titbit

mortal *adjective* **1** =**human**, ephemeral, impermanent, passing, temporal, transient, worldly **2** =**fatal**, deadly, death-dealing, destructive, killing, lethal, murderous, terminal ◆*noun* **3** =**human being**, being, earthling, human, individual, man, person, woman

mortality *noun* **1** =**humanity**, impermanence, transience **2** =**killing**, property, esp. a house, as security for the repayment of a loan. **2** the loan itself. ◆ *verb* **3** pledge (property) as security thus. **mortgagee** *noun* creditor in a mortgage. **mortgagor, mortgager** *noun* debtor in a mortgage.

mortice, mortise [more-tiss] *noun* hole in a piece of wood or stone shaped to receive a matching projection on another piece. **mortice lock** lock set into a door.

mortify ❶ *verb* **-fying, -fied 1** humiliate. **2** subdue by self-denial. **3** (of flesh) become gangrenous. **mortification** *noun*

mortuary ❶ *noun, pl* **-aries** building where corpses are kept before burial or cremation.

mosaic [mow-zay-ik] *noun* design or decoration using small pieces of coloured stone or glass.

Mosaic *adjective* of Moses.

Moselle *noun* light white German wine.

Moslem *noun, adjective* same as MUSLIM.

mosque *noun* Muslim temple.

mosquito *noun, pl* **-toes, -tos** blood-sucking flying insect.

moss *noun* small flowerless plant growing in masses on moist surfaces. **mossy** *adjective* **mossier, mossiest**

most ❶ *noun* **1** greatest number or degree. ◆ *adjective* **2** greatest in number or degree. **3** superlative of MUCH *or* MANY. ◆ *adverb* **4** in the greatest degree. **mostly** *adverb* for the most part, generally.

MOT, MOT test *noun* compulsory annual test of the roadworthiness of vehicles over a certain age.

mote *noun* tiny speck.

motel *noun* roadside hotel for motorists.

motet [moh-tet] *noun* short sacred choral song.

moth ❶ *noun* nocturnal insect like a butterfly.

mothball *noun* **1** small ball of camphor or naphthalene used to repel moths from stored clothes. ◆ *verb* **2** store (something operational) for future use. **3** postpone (a project etc.).

moth-eaten *adjective* **1** decayed or scruffy. **2** eaten or damaged by moth larvae.

mother ❶ *noun* **1** female parent. **2** head of a female religious community. ◆ *adjective* **3** native or inborn, e.g. *mother wit.* ◆ *verb* **4** look after as a mother. **motherhood** *noun* **motherly** *adjective* **motherless** *adjective* **mother country, motherland** country where one was born. **mother-in-law** *noun, pl* **mothers-in-law** mother of one's husband or wife. **mother of pearl** iridescent lining of certain shells. **mother tongue** one's native language.

motif ❶ [moh-teef] *noun* (recurring) theme or design.

motion ❶ *noun* **1** process, action, or way of moving. **2** proposal in a meeting. **3** evacuation of the bowels. ◆ *verb* **4** direct (someone) by gesture. **motionless** *adjective* not moving. **motion picture** cinema film.

motive ❶ *noun* **1** reason for a course of action. ◆ *adjective* **2** causing motion. **motivate** *verb* give incentive to. **motivation** *noun*

motley ❶ *adjective* **1** miscellaneous. **2**

——————— THESAURUS ———————

bloodshed, carnage, death, destruction, fatality
mortification *noun* **1 = humiliation,** annoyance, chagrin, discomfiture, embarrassment, shame, vexation **2 = discipline,** abasement, chastening, control, denial, subjugation **3 = gangrene,** corruption, festering
mortified *adjective* **1 = humiliated,** ashamed, chagrined, chastened, crushed, deflated, embarrassed, humbled, shamed
mortify *verb* **1 = humiliate,** chagrin, chasten, crush, deflate, embarrass, humble, shame **2 = discipline,** abase, chasten, control, deny, subdue **3** *Of flesh* **= putrefy,** cark (*Aust & NZ sl*), deaden, die, fester
mortuary *noun* **= morgue,** funeral parlour
mostly *adverb* **= generally,** as a rule, chiefly, largely, mainly, on the whole, predominantly, primarily, principally, usually
moth-eaten *adjective* **1 = decayed,** decrepit, dilapidated, ragged, shabby, tattered, threadbare, worn-out
mother *noun* **1 = parent,** dam, ma (*inf*),

mater, mum (*Brit inf*), mummy (*Brit inf*), mom (*US & Canad*) ◆*adjective* **3 = native,** inborn, innate, natural ◆*verb* **4 = nurture,** care for, cherish, nurse, protect, raise, rear, tend
motherly *adjective* **4 = maternal,** affectionate, caring, comforting, loving, protective, sheltering
motif *noun* **a = theme,** concept, idea, leitmotif, subject **b = design,** decoration, ornament, shape
motion *noun* **1 = movement,** flow, locomotion, mobility, move, progress, travel **2 = proposal,** proposition, recommendation, submission, suggestion ◆*verb* **4 = gesture,** beckon, direct, gesticulate, nod, signal, wave
motionless *adjective* **= still,** fixed, frozen, immobile, paralysed, standing, static, stationary, stock-still, transfixed, unmoving
motivate *verb* **= inspire,** arouse, cause, drive, induce, move, persuade, prompt, stimulate, stir
motivation *noun* **1 = incentive,** incitement, inducement, inspiration, motive, reason, spur,

M

multicoloured.

motocross *noun* motorcycle race over a rough course.

motor *noun* **1** engine, esp. of a vehicle. **2** machine that converts electrical energy into mechanical energy. **3** car. ♦ *verb* **4** travel by car. **motorist** *noun* driver of a car. **motorized** *adjective* equipped with a motor or motor transport. **motorbike** *noun* **motorboat** *noun* **motorcade** *noun* procession of cars carrying important people. **motorcar** *noun* **motorcycle** *noun* **motorcyclist** *noun* **motor scooter** light motorcycle with small wheels and an enclosed engine. **motorway** *noun* main road for fast-moving traffic.

mottled ⊕ *adjective* marked with blotches.

motto ⊕ *noun, pl* **-toes, -tos 1** saying expressing an ideal or rule of conduct. **2** verse or maxim in a paper cracker.

mould¹ ⊕ *noun* **1** hollow container in which metal etc. is cast. **2** shape, form, or pattern. **3** nature or character. ♦ *verb* **4** shape. **5** influence or direct. **moulding** *noun* moulded ornamental edging.

mould² ⊕ *noun* fungal growth caused by dampness. **mouldy** *adjective* **mouldier, mouldiest 1** stale or musty. **2** dull or boring.

mould³ ⊕ *noun* loose soil. **moulder** *verb* decay

into dust.

moult *verb* **1** shed feathers, hair, or skin to make way for new growth. ♦ *noun* **2** process of moulting.

mound ⊕ *noun* **1** heap, esp. of earth or stones. **2** small hill.

mount ⊕ *verb* **1** climb or ascend. **2** get up on (a horse etc.). **3** increase or accumulate. **4** fix on a support or backing. **5** organize, e.g. *mount a campaign.* ♦ *noun* **6** backing or support on which something is fixed. **7** horse for riding. **8** hill.

mountain ⊕ *noun* **1** hill of great size. **2** large heap. **mountainous** *adjective* **1** full of mountains. **2** huge. **mountaineer** *noun* person who climbs mountains. **mountaineering** *noun* **mountain bike** bicycle with straight handlebars and heavy-duty tyres, for cycling over rough terrain. **mountain lion** same as PUMA.

mountebank *noun* charlatan or fake.

Mountie *noun Informal* member of the Royal Canadian Mounted Police.

mourn ⊕ *verb* feel or express sorrow for (a dead person or lost thing). **mourner** *noun* **mournful** *adjective* sad or dismal. **mournfully** *adverb* **mourning** *noun* **1** grieving. **2** conventional symbols of grief for death, such as the wearing of black.

M

——————— T H E S A U R U S ———————

stimulus

motive *noun* **1** = **reason**, ground(s), incentive, inducement, inspiration, object, purpose, rationale, stimulus

motley *adjective* **1** = **miscellaneous**, assorted, disparate, heterogeneous, mixed, varied OPPOSITE **homogeneous. 2** = **multicoloured**, chequered, variegated

mottled *adjective* = **blotchy**, dappled, flecked, piebald, speckled, spotted, stippled, streaked

motto *noun* **1** = **saying**, adage, dictum, maxim, precept, proverb, rule, slogan, tag-line, watchword

mould¹ *noun* **1** = **cast**, pattern, shape **2** = **design**, build, construction, fashion, form, format, kind, pattern, shape, style **3** = **nature**, calibre, character, kind, quality, sort, stamp, type ♦*verb* **4** = **shape**, construct, create, fashion, forge, form, make, model, sculpt, work **5** = **influence**, affect, control, direct, form, make, shape

mould² *noun* = **fungus**, blight, mildew

mould³ *noun* = **soil**, dirt, earth, humus, loam

mouldy *adjective* **1** = **stale**, bad, blighted, decaying, fusty, mildewed, musty, rotten

mound *noun* **1** = **heap**, drift, pile, rick, stack **2** = **hill**, bank, dune, embankment, hillock, knoll,

rise

mount *verb* **1** = **ascend**, clamber up, climb, go up, scale OPPOSITE **descend. 2** = **get (up) on**, bestride, climb onto, jump on OPPOSITE **get off. 3** = **increase**, accumulate, build, escalate, grow, intensify, multiply, pile up, swell OPPOSITE **reduce** ♦*noun* **6** = **backing**, base, frame, setting, stand, support **7** = **horse**, steed (*lit*)

mountain *noun* **1** = **peak**, alp, berg (*S Afr*), fell (*Brit*), mount **2** = **heap**, abundance, mass, mound, pile, stack, ton

mountainous *adjective* **1** = **high**, alpine, highland, rocky, soaring, steep, towering, upland **2** = **huge**, daunting, enormous, gigantic, great, immense, mammoth, mighty, monumental OPPOSITE **little**

mourn *verb* = **grieve**, bemoan, bewail, deplore, lament, rue, wail, weep

mournful *adjective* **a** = **sad**, melancholy, piteous, plaintive, sorrowful, tragic, unhappy, woeful OPPOSITE **happy. b** = **dismal**, disconsolate, downcast, gloomy, grieving, heavy-hearted, lugubrious, miserable, rueful, sombre OPPOSITE **happy**

mourning *noun* **1** = **grieving**, bereavement, grief, lamentation, weeping, woe **2** = **black**,

M

mouse *noun, pl* **mice 1** small long-tailed rodent. **2** timid person. **3** *Computers* hand-held device for moving the cursor without keying. **mouser** *noun* cat used to catch mice. **mousy** *adjective* **mousier, mousiest 1** like a mouse, esp. in hair colour. **2** meek and shy.

moussaka *noun* dish made with meat, aubergines, and tomatoes, topped with cheese sauce.

mousse *noun* **1** dish of flavoured cream whipped and set. **2** foamy substance applied to the hair before styling to hold the style.

moustache *noun* hair on the upper lip.

mouth ❶ *noun* **1** opening in the head for eating and issuing sounds. **2** lips. **3** entrance. **4** point where a river enters the sea. **5** opening. ◆ *verb* **6** form (words) with the lips without speaking. **7** speak or utter insincerely, esp. in public. **mouthful** *noun* **1** amount of food or drink put into the mouth at any one time when eating or drinking. **2** word, phrase, or name that is difficult to say. **mouth organ** same as HARMONICA. **mouthpiece** *noun* **1** part of a telephone into which a person speaks. **2** part of a wind instrument into which the player blows. **3** spokesperson. **mouthwash** *noun* medicated liquid for gargling and cleansing the mouth.

move ❶ *verb* **1** change in place or position. **2** change (one's house etc.). **3** take action. **4** stir the emotions of. **5** incite. **6** suggest (a proposal) formally. ◆ *noun* **7** moving. **8** action towards some goal. **movable, moveable** *adjective* **movement** *noun* **1** action or process of moving. **2** group with a common aim. **3**

division of a piece of music. **4** moving parts of a machine. **moving** *adjective* arousing or touching the emotions. **movingly** *adverb*

movie ❶ *noun Informal* cinema film.

mow ❶ *verb* **mowing, mowed** or **mown** cut (grass or crops). **mower** *noun* **mow down** *verb* kill in large numbers.

mozzarella [mot-sa-**rel**-la] *noun* moist white cheese originally made in Italy from buffalo milk.

MP 1 Member of Parliament. **2** Military Police(man).

MP3 *Computing* Motion Picture Expert Group-1, Audio Layer-3: a digital compression format used to compress audio files to a fraction of their original size without loss of sound quality.

MPEG [**em**-peg] *Computing* Motion Picture Expert Group: standard compressed file format used for audio and video files.

mpg miles per gallon.

mph miles per hour.

Mr Mister.

Mrs *noun* title of a married woman.

Ms [mizz] *noun* title used instead of Miss or Mrs.

MS 1 *pl* **MSS** manuscript. **2** multiple sclerosis. **3** Mississippi.

MSc Master of Science.

MSS manuscripts.

Mt Mount.

MT Montana.

much ❶ *adjective* **more, most 1** large amount or degree of. ◆ *noun* **2** large amount or degree. ◆ *adverb* **more, most 3** to a great degree. **4** nearly. **much of a muchness** very similar.

——————— THESAURUS ———————

sackcloth and ashes, widow's weeds

mouth *noun* **1** = **maw**, gob (*sl, esp. Brit*), jaws **2** = **lips 3** = **door**, entrance, gateway, inlet **5** = **opening**, aperture, orifice

mouthful *noun* **1** = **taste**, bit, bite, little, morsel, sample, spoonful, swallow

mouthpiece *noun* **3** = **spokesperson**, agent, delegate, representative, spokesman *or* spokeswoman

movable *adjective* **1** = **portable**, detachable, mobile, transferable, transportable

move *verb* **1** = **change**, advance, budge, go, proceed, progress, shift, stir, switch, transfer, transpose **2** = **relocate**, leave, migrate, pack one's bags (*inf*), quit, remove **3** = **drive**, activate, operate, propel, shift, start, turn **4** = **touch**, affect, excite, impress, inspire, rouse **5** = **prompt**, cause, incite, induce, influence, motivate, persuade OPPOSITE discourage. **6** = **propose**, advocate, put forward, recommend,

suggest, urge ◆*noun* **7** = **transfer**, relocation, removal, shift **8** = **action**, manoeuvre, measure, ploy, step, stratagem, stroke, turn

movement *noun* **1** = **motion**, action, activity, change, development, flow, manoeuvre, progress, stirring **2** = **group**, campaign, crusade, drive, faction, front, grouping, organization, party **3** *Music* = **section**, division, part, passage **4** = **workings**, action, machinery, mechanism, works

movie *noun Inf* = **film**, feature, flick (*sl*), picture

moving *adjective* = **emotional**, affecting, inspiring, pathetic, persuasive, poignant, stirring, touching OPPOSITE **uninspiring**

mow *verb* = **cut**, crop, scythe, shear, trim

mow down *verb* = **massacre**, butcher, cut down, cut to pieces, shoot down, slaughter

much *adjective* **1** = **great**, abundant, a lot of, ample, considerable, copious, plenty of, sizable *or* sizeable, substantial ◆*noun* **2** = **a lot**, a good

mucilage [mew-sill-ij] *noun* gum or glue.
muck ➊ *noun* **1** dirt, filth. **2** manure. **3** *Slang* something of poor quality, rubbish. **mucky** *adjective* **muckier, muckiest**. **muck about** *verb* *Slang* waste time or misbehave. **muck in** *verb* *Slang* share a task with other people. **muck out** *verb* clean (a byre, stable, etc.). **muckraking** *noun* seeking out and exposing scandal relating to well-known people. **muckraker** *noun* **muck up** *verb* *Slang* ruin or spoil.
mucus [mew-kuss] *noun* slimy secretion of the mucous membranes. **mucous** *adjective* **mucous membrane** tissue lining body cavities or passages.
mud ➊ *noun* wet soft earth. **muddy** *adjective* **-dier, -diest 1** covered or filled with mud. **2** not clear or bright, e.g. *muddy brown.* ◆ *verb* **-dying, -dies 3** make muddy. **4** make (a situation or issue) less clear. **mud flat** area of low muddy land that is covered by the sea only at high tide. **mudguard** *noun* cover over a wheel to prevent mud or water being thrown up by it. **mudpack** *noun* **cosmetic paste to improve the complexion**
muddle ➊ *verb* **1** (often foll. by *up*) confuse. **2** mix up. ◆ *noun* **3** state of confusion.
muesli [mewz-lee] *noun* mixture of grain, nuts, and dried fruit, eaten with milk.
muezzin [moo-ezz-in] *noun* official who summons Muslims to prayer.
muff¹ *noun* tube-shaped covering to keep the hands warm.
muff² *verb* bungle (an action).
muffin *noun* **1** light round flat yeast cake. **2** small cup-shaped sweet bread roll.

muffle ➊ *verb* wrap up for warmth or to deaden sound. **muffler** *noun* scarf.
mufti *noun* civilian clothes worn by a person who usually wears a uniform.
mug¹ ➊ *noun* large drinking cup.
mug² ➊ *noun* **1** *Slang* face. **2** *Slang* gullible person. ◆ *verb* **mugging, mugged 3** *Informal* attack in order to rob. **mugger** *noun* **mugging** *noun* **mug shot** *Informal* photograph of the face of a suspect or criminal, held in a police file.
mug³ ➊ *verb* **mugging, mugged** (foll. by *up*) *Informal* study hard.
muggins *noun* *Informal* stupid or gullible person.
muggy ➊ *adjective* **-gier, -giest** (of weather) damp and stifling.
mujaheddin, mujahedeen [moo-ja-hed-deen] *plural noun* fundamentalist Muslim guerrillas.
mulatto [mew-lat-toe] *noun, pl* **-tos, -toes** child of one Black and one White parent.
mulberry *noun* **1** tree whose leaves are used to feed silkworms. **2** purple fruit of this tree.
mulch *noun* **1** mixture of wet straw, leaves, etc., used to protect the roots of plants. ◆ *verb* **2** cover (land) with mulch.
mule¹ *noun* offspring of a horse and a donkey. **mulish** *adjective* obstinate. **muleteer** *noun* mule driver.
mule² *noun* backless shoe or slipper.
mull ➊ *verb* think (over) or ponder. **mulled** *adjective* (of wine or ale) flavoured with sugar and spices and served hot.
mullah *noun* Muslim scholar, teacher, or

M

———————— THESAURUS ————————

deal, a great deal, heaps (*inf*), loads (*inf*), lots (*inf*), plenty OPPOSITE little ◆*adverb* **3** =**greatly**, a great deal, a lot, considerably, decidedly, exceedingly
muck *noun* **1** =**dirt**, filth, gunge (*inf*), mire, mud, ooze, slime, sludge **2** =**manure**, dung, kak (*S Afr sl*), ordure
muck up *verb* *Sl* =**ruin**, blow (*sl*), botch, bungle, make a mess of, make a pig's ear of (*inf*), mess up, muff, spoil
mucky *adjective* **1** =**dirty**, begrimed, filthy, grimy, messy, muddy
mud *noun* =**dirt**, clay, mire, ooze, silt, slime, sludge
muddle *verb* **1** =**confuse**, befuddle, bewilder, confound, daze, disorient, perplex, stupefy **2** =**jumble**, disarrange, disorder, disorganize, mess, mix up, scramble, spoil, tangle ◆*noun* **3** =**confusion**, chaos, disarray, disorder, disorganization, jumble, mess, mix-up,

predicament, tangle
muddy *adjective* **1** =**dirty**, bespattered, boggy, grimy, marshy, mucky, mud-caked, quaggy, soiled, swampy
muffle *verb* **a** =**wrap up**, cloak, cover, envelop, shroud, swaddle, swathe **b** =**deaden**, muzzle, quieten, silence, soften, stifle, suppress
mug¹ *noun* =**cup**, beaker, pot, tankard
mug² *noun* **1** *Sl* =**face**, countenance, features, visage **2** *Sl* =**fool**, chump (*inf*), easy or soft touch (*sl*), simpleton, sucker (*sl*) ◆*verb* **3** *Inf* =**attack**, assault, beat up, rob, set about *or* upon
mug³ *verb* (foll. by *up*) *Inf* =**study**, bone up on (*inf*), burn the midnight oil (*inf*), cram (*inf*), swot (*Brit inf*)
muggy *adjective* =**humid**, clammy, close, moist, oppressive, sticky, stuffy, sultry
mull *verb* =**ponder**, consider, contemplate, deliberate, meditate, reflect on, ruminate, think

religious leader.

mullet *noun* edible sea fish.

mulligatawny *noun* soup made with curry powder.

mullion *noun* vertical dividing bar in a window. **mullioned** *adjective* having mullions.

mulloway *noun* large Australian sea fish, valued for sport and food.

multi- *combining form* many, e.g. *multicultural; multistorey.*

multicoloured *adjective* having many different colours.

multifarious ⊕ [mull-tee-**fare**-ee-uss] *adjective* having many various parts.

multilateral *adjective* of or involving more than two nations or parties.

multilingual *adjective* speaking or written in more than two languages.

multimillionaire *noun* person who owns several million pounds, dollars, etc.

multinational *adjective* **1** operating in several countries. **2** involving people from several countries. ♦ *noun* **3** large company operating in several countries.

multiple ⊕ *adjective* **1** having many parts. ♦ *noun* **2** quantity which contains another an exact number of times. **multiply** *verb* **1** increase in number, quantity, or degree. **2** add (a number) to itself a given number of times. **3** increase in number by reproduction. **multiple-choice** *adjective* having a number of possible given answers out of which the correct one must be chosen. **multiple sclerosis** chronic progressive disease of the nervous system, resulting in speech and visual disorders, tremor, and partial paralysis.

multiplex *noun* **1** purpose-built complex containing several cinemas and usu. restaurants and bars. ♦ *adjective* **2** having many elements, complex.

multiplicity *noun, pl* **-ties** large number or great variety.

multiply ⊕ *verb* **-plying, -plied 1** (cause to) increase in number, quantity, or degree. **2** add

(a number or quantity) to itself a given number of times. **3** increase in number by reproduction.

multiplication *noun* **multiplicand** *noun Maths* number to be multiplied. **multiplier** *noun Maths* number by which another number is multiplied.

multipurpose *adjective* having many uses, e.g. *a multipurpose vehicle.*

multiracial *adjective* made up of people from many races, e.g. *a multiracial society.*

multitude ⊕ *noun* **1** great number. **2** great crowd. **multitudinous** *adjective* very numerous.

mum[1] *noun Informal* mother.

mum[2] *adjective* **keep mum** remain silent.

mumble *verb* **1** speak indistinctly, mutter. ♦ *noun* **2** indistinct utterance.

mumbo jumbo *noun* **1** meaningless language. **2** foolish religious ritual or incantation.

mummer *noun* actor in a folk play or mime.

mummy[1] *noun, pl* **-mies** body embalmed and wrapped for burial in ancient Egypt.

mummified *adjective* (of a body) preserved as a mummy.

mummy[2] *noun, pl* **-mies** child's word for MOTHER.

mumps *noun* infectious disease with swelling in the glands of the neck.

munch ⊕ *verb* chew noisily and steadily.

mundane ⊕ *adjective* **1** everyday. **2** earthly.

municipal ⊕ *adjective* relating to a city or town. **municipality** *noun, pl* **-ities 1** city or town with local self-government. **2** governing body of this.

munificent [mew-**niff**-fiss-sent] *adjective* very generous. **munificence** *noun*

muniments [**mew**-nim-ments] *plural noun* title deeds or similar documents.

munitions [mew-**nish**-unz] *plural noun* military stores.

munted *adjective NZ slang* **1** destroyed or ruined. **2** abnormal or peculiar.

mural [**myoor**-al] *noun* painting on a wall.

murder ⊕ *noun* **1** unlawful intentional killing

——————— T H E S A U R U S ———————

over, weigh

multifarious *adjective* =**diverse**, different, legion, manifold, many, miscellaneous, multiple, numerous, sundry, varied

multiple *adjective* **1** = **many**, manifold, multitudinous, numerous, several, sundry, various

multiply *verb* **1** =**increase**, build up, expand, extend, proliferate, spread OPPOSITE> **reduce**. **3** =**reproduce**, breed, propagate

multitude *noun* **2** =**mass**, army, crowd,

horde, host, mob, myriad, swarm, throng

munch *verb* =**chew**, champ, chomp, crunch

mundane *adjective* **1** = **ordinary**, banal, commonplace, day-to-day, everyday, humdrum, prosaic, routine, workaday OPPOSITE> **interesting**. **2** = **earthly**, mortal, secular, temporal, terrestrial, worldly OPPOSITE> **heavenly**

municipal *adjective* =**civic**, public, urban

municipality *noun* **1** = **town**, borough, city, district, dorp (*S Afr*), township

of a human being. ♦ *verb* **2** kill in this way.
murderer, murderess *noun* **murderous**
adjective
murk ⊕ *noun* thick darkness. **murky** *adjective*
murkier, murkiest 1 dark or gloomy. **2**
suspicious or shady.
murmur ⊕ *verb* **-muring, -mured 1** speak or
say in a quiet indistinct way. **2** complain. ♦
noun **3** continuous low indistinct sound. **4**
complaint, e.g. *she went without a murmur.* **5**
abnormal soft blowing sound heard made by
the heart.
murrain [murr-rin] *noun* cattle plague.
muscle ⊕ *noun* **1** tissue in the body which
produces movement by contracting. **2** strength
or power. **muscular** *adjective* **1** with well-
developed muscles. **2** of muscles. **muscular
dystrophy** disease with wasting of the muscles.
muscle in *verb Informal* force one's way in.
muse ⊕ *verb* ponder quietly.
Muse *noun* **1** *Greek myth* one of nine
goddesses, each of whom inspired an art or
science. **2 (m-)** force that inspires a creative
artist.
museum *noun* building where natural, artistic,
historical, or scientific objects are exhibited and
preserved. **museum piece** *Informal* very old
object or building.
mush¹ ⊕ *noun* **1** soft pulpy mass. **2** *Informal*
cloying sentimentality. **mushy** *adjective*
mushier, mushiest
mush² *interjection* order to dogs in sled team
to advance.
mushroom *noun* **1** edible fungus with a stem

and cap. ♦ *verb* **2** grow rapidly. **mushroom
cloud** large mushroom-shaped cloud produced
by a nuclear explosion.
music ⊕ *noun* **1** art form using a melodious
and harmonious combination of notes. **2**
written or printed form of this. **musical**
adjective **1** of or like music. **2** talented in or
fond of music. **3** pleasant-sounding. ♦ *noun* **4**
play or film with songs and dancing. **musically**
adverb **musician** *noun* **musicianship** *noun*
musicology *noun* scientific study of music.
musicologist *noun* **music centre** combined
record or CD player, radio, and cassette player.
music hall variety theatre.
musk *noun* scent obtained from a gland of the
musk deer or produced synthetically. **musky**
adjective **muskier, muskiest. muskrat** *noun* **1**
N American beaver-like rodent. **2** its fur.
muskeg ⊕ *noun Canad* bog or swamp.
musket *noun Hist* long-barrelled gun.
musketeer *noun* **musketry** *noun* (use of)
muskets.
Muslim *noun* **1** follower of the religion of
Islam. ♦ *adjective* **2** of or relating to Islam.
muslin *noun* fine cotton fabric.
musquash *noun* muskrat fur.
muss ⊕ *verb US & Canad inf* to make untidy.
mussel *noun* edible shellfish with a dark
hinged shell.
must¹ ⊕ *verb* **1** used as an auxiliary to express
obligation, certainty, or resolution. ♦ *noun* **2**
essential or necessary thing.
must² *noun* newly pressed grape juice.
mustang *noun* wild horse of SW USA.

M

——————— T H E S A U R U S ———————

murder *noun* **1 = killing**, assassination,
bloodshed, butchery, carnage, homicide,
manslaughter, massacre, slaying ♦*verb* **2 = kill**,
assassinate, bump off (*sl*), butcher, eliminate
(*sl*), massacre, slaughter, slay
murderer *noun* **= killer**, assassin, butcher,
cut-throat, hit man (*sl*), homicide, slaughterer,
slayer
murderous *adjective* **2 = deadly**, bloodthirsty,
brutal, cruel, cut-throat, ferocious, lethal,
savage
murky *adjective* **1 = dark**, cloudy, dim, dull,
gloomy, grey, misty, overcast
murmur *verb* **1 = mumble**, mutter, whisper **2
= grumble**, complain, moan (*inf*) ♦*noun* **3
= drone**, buzzing, humming, purr, whisper
muscle *noun* **1 = tendon**, sinew **2 = strength**,
brawn, clout (*inf*), forcefulness, might, power,
stamina, weight **muscle in** ♦*verb Inf* **= impose**
oneself, butt in, force one's way in
muscular *adjective* **1 = strong**, athletic,

powerful, robust, sinewy, strapping, sturdy,
vigorous
muse *verb* **= ponder**, brood, cogitate,
consider, contemplate, deliberate, meditate,
mull over, reflect, ruminate
mushy *adjective* **1 = soft**, pulpy, semi-solid,
slushy, squashy, squelchy, squidgy (*inf*) **2** *Inf*
= sentimental, maudlin, mawkish, saccharine,
schmaltzy (*sl*), sloppy (*inf*), slushy (*inf*)
musical *adjective* **1 = melodious**, dulcet,
euphonious, harmonious, lyrical, melodic,
sweet-sounding, tuneful
muskeg *noun Canad* **= swamp**, bog, marsh,
quagmire, moss (*Scot*) (*Northern English dialect*),
slough, fen, mire, morass, everglade(s) (*US*),
pakihi (*NZ*)
muss *US & Canad verb* **= mess (up)**,
disarrange, dishevel, ruffle, rumple, make
untidy, tumble
must¹ *noun* **= necessity**, essential,
fundamental, imperative, prerequisite,

mustard *noun* **1** paste made from the powdered seeds of a plant, used as a condiment. **2** the plant. **mustard gas** poisonous gas causing blistering burns and blindness.

muster ❶ *verb* **1** summon up (strength, energy, or support). **2** assemble. ◆ *noun* **3** assembly of military personnel. **pass muster** be acceptable.

musty ❶ *adjective* **mustier, mustiest** smelling mouldy and stale. **mustiness** *noun*

mutable ❶ [mew-tab-bl] *adjective* liable to change. **mutability** *noun*

mutation ❶ [mew-tay-shun] *noun* (genetic) change. **mutate** [mew-**tate**] *verb* (cause to) undergo mutation. **mutant** [mew-tant] *noun* mutated animal, plant, etc.

mute ❶ *adjective* **1** silent. **2** unable to speak. ◆ *noun* **3** person who is unable to speak. **4** *Music* device to soften the tone of an instrument. **muted** *adjective* **1** (of sound or colour) softened. **2** (of a reaction) subdued. **mutely** *adverb*

mutilate ❶ [mew-till-ate] *verb* **1** deprive of a limb or other part. **2** damage (a book or text). **mutilated** *adjective* **mutilation** *noun*

mutiny ❶ [mew-tin-ee] *noun, pl* **-nies 1** rebellion against authority, esp. by soldiers or sailors. ◆ *verb* **-nying, -nied 2** commit mutiny. **mutineer** *noun* **mutinous** *adjective*

mutt *noun Slang* **1** stupid person. **2** mongrel dog.

mutter ❶ *verb* **1** utter or speak indistinctly. **2** grumble. ◆ *noun* **3** muttered sound or grumble. **muttering** *noun*

mutton *noun* flesh of sheep, used as food.

mutual ❶ [mew-chew-al] *adjective* **1** felt or expressed by each of two people about the other. **2** common to both or all. **mutually** *adverb*

Muzak *noun* ® recorded light music played in shops etc.

muzzle ❶ *noun* **1** animal's mouth and nose. **2** cover for these to prevent biting. **3** open end of a gun. ◆ *verb* **4** prevent from being heard or noticed. **5** put a muzzle on.

muzzy *adjective* **-zier, -ziest 1** confused or muddled. **2** blurred or hazy.

mW milliwatt(s).

MW 1 megawatt(s). **2** medium wave.

my *adjective* belonging to me.

myall *noun* Australian acacia with hard scented wood.

mycology *noun* study of fungi.

mynah *noun* Asian bird which can mimic human speech.

myopia [my-oh-pee-a] *noun* short-sightedness. **myopic** [my-**op**-ik] *adjective* **myopically** *adverb*

myriad ❶ [mir-ree-ad] *adjective* **1** innumerable. ◆ *noun* **2** large indefinite number.

myrrh [mur] *noun* aromatic gum used in perfume, incense, and medicine.

myrtle [mur-tl] *noun* flowering evergreen shrub.

myself *pronoun* emphatic or reflexive form of I[1] or ME[1].

mystery ❶ *noun, pl* **-teries 1** strange or inexplicable event or phenomenon. **2** obscure or secret thing. **3** story or film that arouses suspense. **mysterious** *adjective* **mysteriously**

—————— THESAURUS ——————

requirement, requisite, *sine qua non*

muster *verb* **2 = assemble**, call together, convene, gather, marshal, mobilize, rally, summon ◆*noun* **3 = assembly**, collection, congregation, convention, gathering, meeting, rally, roundup

musty *adjective* **= stale**, airless, dank, fusty, mildewed, mouldy, old, smelly, stuffy

mutable *adjective* **= changeable**, adaptable, alterable, fickle, inconsistent, inconstant, unsettled, unstable, variable, volatile

mutation *noun* **= change**, alteration, evolution, metamorphosis, modification, transfiguration, transformation, variation

mute *adjective* **1, 2 = silent**, dumb, mum, speechless, unspoken, voiceless, wordless

mutilate *verb* **1 = maim**, amputate, cut up, damage, disfigure, dismember, injure, lacerate, mangle **2 = distort**, adulterate, bowdlerize, censor, cut, damage, expurgate

mutiny *noun* **1 = rebellion**, disobedience, insubordination, insurrection, revolt, revolution, riot, uprising ◆*verb* **2 = rebel**, disobey, resist, revolt, rise up

mutter *verb* **2 = grumble**, complain, grouse, mumble, murmur, rumble

mutual *adjective* **1 = reciprocal**, requited, returned **2 = shared**, common, interchangeable, joint

muzzle *noun* **1 = jaws**, mouth, nose, snout **2 = gag**, guard ◆*verb* **4 = suppress**, censor, curb, gag, restrain, silence, stifle

myriad *adjective* **1 = innumerable**, countless, immeasurable, incalculable, multitudinous, untold ◆*noun* **2 = multitude**, army, horde, host, swarm

mysterious *adjective* **1 = strange**, arcane, enigmatic, inexplicable, inscrutable, mystifying, perplexing, puzzling, secret, uncanny, unfathomable, weird OPPOSITE clear. **2**

adverb
mystic ❶ *noun* **1** person who seeks spiritual knowledge. ♦ *adjective* **2** mystical. **mystical** *adjective* having a spiritual or religious significance beyond human understanding. **mysticism** *noun*
mystify ❶ *verb* **-fying, -fied** bewilder or puzzle. **mystification** *noun*
mystique ❶ [miss-**steek**] *noun* aura of mystery or power.

myth ❶ *noun* **1** tale with supernatural characters, usu. of how the world and mankind began. **2** untrue idea or explanation. **3** imaginary person or object. **mythical, mythic** *adjective* **mythology** *noun* **1** myths collectively. **2** study of myths. **mythological** *adjective*
myxomatosis [mix-a-mat-**oh**-siss] *noun* contagious fatal viral disease of rabbits.

——————— THESAURUS ———————

= secretive, cloak-and-dagger, covert, furtive
mystery *noun* **1** = puzzle, conundrum, enigma, problem, question, riddle, secret, teaser
mystic *adjective* **2** = supernatural, inscrutable, metaphysical, mysterious, occult, otherworldly, paranormal, preternatural, transcendental
mystify *verb* = puzzle, baffle, bewilder, confound, confuse, flummox, nonplus, perplex, stump
mystique *noun* = fascination, awe, charisma,

charm, glamour, magic, spell
myth *noun* **1** = legend, allegory, fable, fairy story, fiction, folk tale, saga, story **2** = illusion, delusion, fancy, fantasy, figment, imagination, superstition, tall story
mythical *adjective* **2** = imaginary, fictitious, invented, made-up, make-believe, nonexistent, pretended, unreal, untrue **3** = legendary, fabled, fabulous, fairy-tale, mythological
mythology *noun* **1** = legend, folklore, lore, tradition

M

n *adjective* **1** indefinite number (of), e.g. *there are n ways of doing this.* ♦ *noun* **2** *Maths* number whose value is not stated, e.g. *two to the power n.* **nth** *adjective*

N 1 *Chem* nitrogen. **2** *Physics* newton(s). **3** North(ern). **4** nuclear, e.g. *N test.*

n. 1 neuter. **2** noun. **3** number.

Na *Chem* sodium.

n/a, N.A. not applicable: used to indicate that a question on a form is not relevant to the person filling it in.

Naafi *noun* canteen or shop for military personnel.

naan *noun* same as NAN BREAD.

nab ⊕ *verb* **nabbing, nabbed** *Informal* **1** arrest (someone). **2** catch (someone) in wrongdoing.

nabob [**nay**-bob] *noun Informal* rich or important person.

nacelle [nah-**sell**] *noun* streamlined enclosure on an aircraft, esp. one housing an engine.

nacre [**nay**-ker] *noun* mother of pearl.

nacreous *adjective*

nadir ⊕ *noun* **1** point in the sky opposite the zenith. **2** lowest point.

naevus ⊕ [**nee**-vuss] *noun, pl* **-vi** birthmark or mole.

naff ⊕ *adjective Slang* lacking quality or taste, e.g. *one of the naffest songs ever.*

nag¹ ⊕ *verb* **nagging, nagged 1** scold or find fault constantly. **2** be a constant source of discomfort or worry to. ♦ *noun* **3** person who nags. **nagging** *adjective, noun*

nag² ⊕ *noun Informal* old horse.

naiad [**nye**-ad] *noun, pl* **naiads, naiades** [**nye**-ad-deez] *Greek myth* water nymph.

nail ⊕ *noun* **1** pointed piece of metal with a head, hit with a hammer to join two objects together. **2** hard covering of the upper tips of the fingers and toes. ♦ *verb* **3** attach (something) with nails. **4** *Informal* catch or arrest. **hit the nail on the head** say something exactly correct. **on the nail** at once, esp. in *pay on the nail.* **nailfile** *noun* small metal file used to smooth or shape the finger or toe nails. **nail varnish, polish** cosmetic lacquer applied to the finger or toe nails.

naive ⊕ [nye-**eev**] *adjective* **1** innocent and gullible. **2** simple and lacking sophistication. **naively** *adverb* **naivety, naïveté** [nye-**eev**-tee] *noun*

naked ⊕ *adjective* **1** without clothes. **2** not concealed, e.g. *naked hostility.* **3** without any covering, e.g. *naked flame.* **the naked eye** the eye unassisted by any optical instrument. **nakedly** *adverb* **nakedness** *noun*

namby-pamby ⊕ *adjective* sentimental or insipid.

name ⊕ *noun* **1** word by which a person or

THESAURUS

nab *verb Inf* **1 = apprehend**, arrest, capture, catch, collar (*inf*) **2 = catch**, apprehend, arrest, capture, collar (*inf*), grab, seize

nadir *noun* **2 = bottom**, depths, lowest point, minimum, rock bottom OPPOSITE height

naevus *noun* **= birthmark**, mole

naff *adjective Sl* **= bad**, duff (*Brit inf*), inferior, low-grade, poor, rubbishy, second-rate, shabby, shoddy, worthless OPPOSITE **excellent**

nag¹ *verb* **1 = scold**, badger (*inf*), henpeck, upbraid **2 = worry**, annoy, harass, hassle, irritate, pester, plague ♦*noun* **3 = scold**, harpy, shrew, tartar, virago

nag² *noun Inf* **= horse**, hack

nagging *adjective* **1 = irritating**, scolding, shrewish **2 = worrying**, persistent

nail *verb* **3 = fasten**, attach, fix, hammer, join, pin, secure, tack

naive *adjective* **1 = gullible**, callow, credulous, green, innocent, trusting, unsuspicious, wet behind the ears (*inf*) **2 = unsophisticated**, artless, guileless, ingenuous, innocent, simple, unworldly OPPOSITE **worldly**

naivety, naïveté *noun* **1 = gullibility**, callowness, credulity, innocence **2 = simplicity**, artlessness, guilelessness, inexperience, ingenuousness, innocence, naturalness

naked *adjective* **1 = nude**, bare, exposed, starkers (*inf*), stripped, unclothed, undressed, without a stitch on (*inf*) OPPOSITE **covered**

nakedness *noun* **1 = nudity**, bareness, undress

namby-pamby *adjective* **= feeble**, insipid, sentimental, spineless, vapid, weak, weedy (*inf*), thing is known. **2** reputation, esp. a good one. **3** famous person, e.g. *a big name in the music business.* ♦ *verb* **4** give a name to. **5** refer to by name. **6** fix or specify. **call someone names, a name** insult someone by using rude words to describe him or her. **in name only** not possessing the powers implied by his, her, or its title, e.g. *ruler in name only.* **nameless** *adjective* **1** without a name. **2** unspecified. **3** too horrible to be mentioned. **namely** *adverb* that is to say. **name day** *RC Church* feast day of a saint whose name one bears. **name-dropping** *noun* referring to famous people as if they were friends, in order to impress others. **name-dropper** *noun* **nameplate** *noun* small sign on or by a door giving the occupant's name and, sometimes, profession. **namesake** *noun* person with the same name as another.

nan bread *noun* slightly leavened Indian bread in a large flat leaf shape.

nancy, nancy boy *noun* effeminate or homosexual boy or man.

nanny *noun, pl* **-nies 1** woman whose job is looking after young children. ♦ *verb* **2** be too protective towards. **nanny goat** female goat.

nano- *combining form* denoting one thousand millionth, e.g. *nanosecond.*

nap¹ ❶ *noun* **1** short sleep. ♦ *verb* **napping, napped 2** have a short sleep.

nap² ❶ *noun* raised fibres of velvet or similar cloth.

nap³ *noun* **1** card game similar to whist. **2** *Horse racing* tipster's choice for a certain winner. ♦ *verb* **napping, napped 3** name (a horse) as a certain winner.

napalm *noun* **1** highly inflammable jellied petrol, used in bombs. ♦ *verb* **2** attack (people or places) with napalm.

nape *noun* back of the neck.

naphtha *noun* liquid mixture distilled from coal tar or petroleum, used as a solvent and in petrol. **naphthalene** *noun* white crystalline product distilled from coal tar or petroleum, used in disinfectants, mothballs, and explosives.

napkin ❶ *noun* piece of cloth or paper for wiping the mouth or protecting the clothes while eating.

nappy *noun, pl* **-pies** piece of absorbent material fastened round a baby's lower torso to absorb urine and faeces.

narcissism ❶ *noun* exceptional interest in or admiration for oneself. **narcissistic** *adjective*

narcissus *noun, pl* **-cissi** yellow, orange, or white flower related to the daffodil.

narcotic ❶ *noun, adjective* (of) a drug, such as morphine or opium, which produces numbness and drowsiness, used medicinally but addictive. **narcosis** *noun* effect of a narcotic.

nark ❶ *Slang verb* **1** annoy. ♦ *noun* **2** informer or spy. **3** someone who complains in an irritating manner. **narky** *adjective* **narkier, narkiest** *Slang* irritable or complaining.

narrate ❶ *verb* **1** tell (a story). **2** speak the words accompanying and telling what is happening in a film or TV programme. **narration** *noun* **narrator** *noun* **narrative** *noun* **1** account, story. ♦ *adjective* **2** telling a story, e.g. *a narrative poem.*

narrow ❶ *adjective* **1** small in breadth in comparison to length. **2** limited in range, extent, or outlook. **3** with little margin, e.g. *a narrow escape.* ♦ *verb* **4** make or become

N

———————— T H E S A U R U S ————————

wimpish *or* wimpy (*inf*), wishy-washy (*inf*)

name *noun* **1** = **title**, designation, epithet, handle (*sl*), nickname, sobriquet, term **2** = **fame**, distinction, eminence, esteem, honour, note, praise, renown, repute ♦ *verb* **4** = **call**, baptize, christen, dub, entitle, label, style, term **6** = **nominate**, appoint, choose, designate, select, specify

named *adjective* = **called**, baptized, christened, dubbed, entitled, known as, labelled, styled, termed

nameless *adjective* **1** = **anonymous**, unnamed, untitled **2** = **unknown**, incognito, obscure, undistinguished, unheard-of, unsung **3** = **horrible**, abominable, indescribable, unmentionable, unspeakable, unutterable

namely *adverb* = **specifically**, to wit, viz.

nap¹ *noun* **1** = **sleep**, catnap, forty winks (*inf*), kip (*Brit sl*), rest, siesta ♦ *verb* **2** = **sleep**, catnap,

doze, drop off (*inf*), kip (*Brit sl*), nod off (*inf*), rest, snooze

nap² *noun* = **weave**, down, fibre, grain, pile

napkin *noun* = **serviette**, cloth

narcissism *noun* = **egotism**, self-love, vanity

narcotic *noun* = **drug**, anaesthetic, analgesic, anodyne, opiate, painkiller, sedative, tranquillizer ♦ *adjective* = **sedative**, analgesic, calming, hypnotic, painkilling, soporific

nark *Sl verb* **1** = **annoy**, bother, exasperate, get on one's nerves (*inf*), irritate, nettle

narrate *verb* **1** = **tell**, chronicle, describe, detail, recite, recount, relate, report

narration *noun* **1** = **telling**, description, explanation, reading, recital, relation

narrative *noun* **1** = **story**, account, chronicle, history, report, statement, tale

narrator *noun* **1** = **storyteller**, author, chronicler, commentator, reporter, writer

narrow. **5** (often foll. by *down*) limit or restrict.
narrows *plural noun* narrow part of a strait,
river, or current. **narrowly** *adverb* **narrowness**
noun **narrow boat** long bargelike canal boat.
narrow-gauge *adjective* (of a railway) having
less than the standard distance of 56½ inches
between the rails. **narrow-minded** *adjective*
intolerant or bigoted. **narrow-mindedness**
noun

narwhal *noun* arctic whale with a long spiral
tusk.

NASA *US* National Aeronautics and Space
Administration.

nasal *adjective* **1** of the nose. **2** (of a sound)
pronounced with air passing through the nose.
3 (of a voice) characterized by nasal sounds.
nasally *adverb*

nascent *adjective* starting to grow or develop.

nasturtium *noun* plant with yellow, red, or
orange trumpet-shaped flowers.

nasty ⊕ *adjective* **-tier, -tiest 1** unpleasant. **2**
(of an injury) dangerous or painful. **3** spiteful or
unkind. ◆ *noun, pl* **-ties 4** something
unpleasant. **nastily** *adverb* **nastiness** *noun*

nat. 1 national. **2** nationalist.

natal [nay-tal] *adjective* of or relating to birth.

nation ⊕ *noun* people of one or more cultures
or races organized as a single state. **national**
adjective **1** of or serving a national as a whole.
2 characteristic of a particular nation.
nationality *noun* fact of being a citizen of a
particular nation. **nationwide** *adjective* covering
all of a nation.

national ⊕ *adjective* **1** of or serving a nation as
a whole. **2** characteristic of a particular nation.
◆ *noun* **3** citizen of a nation. **nationally** *adverb*
national anthem official patriotic song of a

nation. **National Curriculum** curriculum of
subjects taught in state schools in England and
Wales since 1989. **national debt** total
outstanding debt of a country's government.
national grid network of high-voltage power
lines linking power stations. **National Health
Service** system of national medical services
financed mainly by taxation. **national
insurance** state insurance scheme providing
payments to the unemployed, sick, and retired.
national park area of countryside protected by
a government for its natural or environmental
importance. **national service** compulsory
military service.

nationalism ⊕ *noun* **1** policy of national
independence. **2** patriotism, sometimes to an
excessive degree. **nationalist** *noun, adjective*
nationalistic *adjective* fiercely or excessively
patriotic.

nationality ⊕ *noun, pl* **-ities 1** fact of being a
citizen of a particular nation. **2** group of people
of the same race, e.g. *young men of all
nationalities.*

nationalize *verb* put (an industry or a
company) under state control. **nationalization**
noun

native ⊕ *adjective* **1** relating to a place where
a person was born. **2** born in a specified place.
3 (foll. by *to*) originating (in). **4** inborn. ◆ *noun*
5 person born in a specified place. **6**
indigenous animal or plant. **7** member of the
original race of a country. **Native American**
(person) descended from the original
inhabitants of the American continent. **native
bear** *Aust* same as KOALA. **native companion**
Aust same as BROLGA. **native dog** *Aust* dingo.
Nativity *noun Christianity* birth of Jesus Christ.

——————— T H E S A U R U S ———————

narrow *adjective* **1 = thin**, attenuated, fine,
slender, slim, spare, tapering OPPOSITE **wide. 2**
= insular, dogmatic, illiberal, intolerant,
narrow-minded, partial, prejudiced, small-
minded **3 = limited**, close, confined,
constricted, contracted, meagre, restricted,
tight OPPOSITE **big** ◆*verb* **4 = tighten**, constrict,
limit, reduce

narrowly *adverb* **3 = just**, barely, by the skin
of one's teeth, only just, scarcely

narrow-minded *adjective* **= intolerant**,
bigoted, hidebound, illiberal, opinionated,
parochial, prejudiced, provincial, small-minded

nastiness *noun* **3 = unpleasantness**, malice,
meanness, spitefulness

nasty *adjective* **1 = objectionable**,
disagreeable, loathsome, obnoxious, offensive,
unpleasant, vile OPPOSITE **nice. 2 = painful**,

bad, critical, dangerous, serious, severe **3**
= spiteful, despicable, disagreeable, distasteful,
malicious, mean, unpleasant, vicious, vile
OPPOSITE **kind**

nation *noun* **= country**, people, race, realm,
society, state, tribe

national *adjective* **1 = nationwide**,
countrywide, public, widespread ◆*noun* **3**
= citizen, inhabitant, native, resident, subject

nationalism *noun* **2 = patriotism**, allegiance,
chauvinism, jingoism, loyalty

nationality *noun* **1 = nation**, birth, race **2**
= race, birth

nationwide *adjective* **= national**, countrywide,
general, widespread

native *adjective* **1, 2 = local**, domestic, home,
indigenous **3** (foll. by *to*) **= indigenous 4**
= inborn, congenital, hereditary, inbred,

N

NATO North Atlantic Treaty Organization.

natter ⊙ *Informal verb* **1** talk idly or chatter. ◆ *noun* **2** long idle chat.

natty ⊙ *adjective* **-tier, -tiest** *Informal* smart and spruce.

natural ⊙ *adjective* **1** normal or to be expected. **2** genuine or spontaneous. **3** of, according to, existing in, or produced by nature. **4** not created by human beings. **5** not synthetic. **6** (of a parent) not adoptive. **7** (of a child) illegitimate. **8** *Music* not sharp or flat, e.g. B natural. ◆ *noun* **9** person with an inborn talent or skill. **10** *Music* symbol cancelling the effect of a previous sharp or flat. **naturally** *adverb* **1** of course. **2** in a natural or normal way. **3** instinctively. **naturalness** *noun* **natural gas** gas found below the ground, used mainly as a fuel. **natural history** study of animals and plants in the wild. **natural number** positive integer, such as 1, 2, 3, etc. **natural philosophy** *Old-fashioned* physics. **natural science** science dealing with the physical world, such as physics, biology or geology. **natural selection** process by which only creatures and plants well adapted to their environment survive.

naturalism ⊙ *noun* movement in art and literature advocating detailed realism. **naturalistic** *adjective*

naturalist ⊙ *noun* student of natural history.

naturalize *verb* give citizenship to (a person born in another country). **naturalization** *noun*

nature ⊙ *noun* **1** whole system of the existence, forces, and events of the physical world that are not controlled by human beings. **2** fundamental or essential qualities. **3** kind or sort. **natural** *adjective* normal or to be expected.

naturism *noun* nudism. **naturist** *noun*

naught *noun* *Lit* nothing.

naughty ⊙ *adjective* **-tier, -tiest 1** disobedient or mischievous. **2** mildly indecent. **naughtily** *adverb* **naughtiness** *noun*

nausea ⊙ [naw-zee-a] *noun* feeling of being about to vomit. **nauseate** *verb* **1** make (someone) feel sick. **2** disgust. **nauseous** *adjective* **1** as if about to vomit. **2** sickening.

nautical ⊙ *adjective* of the sea or ships. **nautical mile** 1852 metres (6076.12 feet).

nautilus *noun, pl* **-luses, -li** shellfish with many tentacles.

naval ⊙ *adjective* see NAVY.

nave *noun* long central part of a church.

navel *noun* hollow in the middle of the abdomen where the umbilical cord was attached. **navel orange** sweet orange with a navel-like hollow at the top.

navigate ⊙ *verb* **1** direct or plot the path or position of a ship, aircraft, or car. **2** travel over or through. **navigation** *noun* **navigational** *adjective* **navigator** *noun* **navigable** *adjective* **1**

N

———————— T H E S A U R U S ————————

ingrained, innate, instinctive, intrinsic, natural ◆*noun* **5 = inhabitant**, citizen, countryman, dweller, national, resident **7 = aborigine**

natter *Inf verb* **1 = gossip**, blether, chatter, gabble, jaw (*sl*), prattle, rabbit (on) (*Brit inf*), talk ◆*noun* **2 = gossip**, chat, chinwag (*Brit inf*), chitchat, conversation, gab (*inf*), jaw (*sl*), prattle, talk

natty *Inf adjective* **= smart**, dapper, elegant, fashionable, neat, snazzy (*inf*), spruce, stylish, trim

natural *adjective* **1 = normal**, common, everyday, legitimate, logical, ordinary, regular, typical, usual OPPOSITE **strange**. **2 = unaffected**, genuine, ingenuous, open, real, simple, spontaneous, unpretentious, unsophisticated OPPOSITE **affected**. **3 = innate**, characteristic, essential, inborn, inherent, instinctive, intuitive, native **5 = pure**, organic, plain, unrefined, whole OPPOSITE **processed**

naturalist *noun* **= biologist**, botanist, ecologist, zoologist

naturalistic *adjective* **= realistic**, lifelike, true-to-life

naturally *adverb* **1 = of course**, certainly **2**

= genuinely, normally, simply, spontaneously, typically, unaffectedly, unpretentiously **3 = spontaneously**

nature *noun* **1 = creation**, cosmos, earth, environment, universe, world **2 = make-up**, character, complexion, constitution, essence **3 = kind**, category, description, sort, species, style, type, variety

naughty *adjective* **1 = disobedient**, bad, impish, misbehaved, mischievous, refractory, wayward, wicked, worthless OPPOSITE **good**. **2 = obscene**, improper, lewd, ribald, risqué, smutty, vulgar OPPOSITE **proper**

nausea *noun* **= sickness**, biliousness, queasiness, retching, squeamishness, vomiting

nauseate *verb* **1, 2 = sicken**, disgust, offend, repel, repulse, revolt, turn one's stomach

nauseous *adjective* **2 = sickening**, abhorrent, disgusting, distasteful, nauseating, offensive, repugnant, repulsive, revolting

nautical *adjective* **= maritime**, marine, naval

naval *adjective* **= nautical**, marine, maritime

navigable *adjective* **1 = passable**, clear, negotiable, unobstructed **2 = sailable**, controllable, dirigible wide, deep, or safe enough to be sailed through. **2** able to be steered.

navvy ⊕ *noun, pl* **-vies** labourer employed on a road or a building site.

navy ⊕ *noun, pl* **-vies 1** branch of a country's armed services comprising warships with their crews and organization. **2** warships of a nation. ◆ *adjective* **3** navy-blue. **naval** *adjective* of or relating to a navy or ships. **navy-blue** *adjective* very dark blue.

nay *interjection Obs* no.

Nazi *noun* **1** member of the fascist National Socialist Party, which came to power in Germany in 1933 under Adolf Hitler. ◆ *adjective* **2** of or relating to the Nazis. **Nazism** *noun*

Nb *Chem* niobium.

NB 1 New Brunswick. **2** note well.

NC North Carolina.

NCO noncommissioned officer.

Nd *Chem* neodymium.

ND North Dakota.

Ne *Chem* neon.

NE 1 Nebraska. **2** northeast(ern).

Neanderthal [nee-ann-der-tahl] *adjective* of a type of primitive man that lived in Europe before 12 000ᴀᴅ.

neap tide *noun* tide at the first and last quarters of the moon when there is the smallest rise and fall in tidal level.

near ⊕ *preposition, adverb, adjective* **1** indicating a place or time not far away. ◆ *adjective* **2** almost being the thing specified, e.g. *a near disaster*. ◆ *verb* **3** draw close (to).

nearly *adverb* almost. **nearness** *noun* **nearby** *adjective* not far away. **Near East** same as

MIDDLE EAST. **nearside** *noun* side of a vehicle that is nearer the kerb. **near-sighted** *adjective* (of a person) short-sighted.

neat ⊕ *adjective* **1** tidy and clean. **2** smoothly or competently done. **3** undiluted. **4** *US & Canad* good or pleasing. **neatly** *adverb* **neatness** *noun* **neaten** *verb* make neat.

nebula [neb-yew-la] *noun, pl* **-lae** [-lee] *Astronomy* hazy cloud of particles and gases. **nebular** *adjective* **nebulous** *adjective* vague, indistinct.

nebulous ⊕ *adjective* vague, indistinct.

NEC National Executive Committee.

necessary ⊕ *adjective* **1** needed to obtain the desired result, e.g. *the necessary skills*. **2** certain or unavoidable, e.g. *the necessary consequences*. **necessaries** *plural noun* essential items, e.g. *the necessaries of life*. **necessarily** *adverb*

necessitate *verb* compel or require.

necessitous *adjective* very needy. **necessity** *noun, pl* **-ties 1** circumstances that inevitably require a certain result. **2** something needed. **3** great poverty.

> **SPELLING TIP**
>
> There are 41 examples of the misspelling *neccessary* in the Bank of English; single letters throughout (*necesary*) are also popular. The correct spelling, **necessary**, has one c and two ss. When you add *un-* at the beginning, you end up with a double *n* too: **unnecessary**.

———— THESAURUS ————

navigate *verb* **1** = **sail**, drive, guide, handle, manoeuvre, pilot, steer **2** = **voyage**

navigation *noun* = **sailing**, seamanship, voyaging

navigator *noun* = **pilot**, mariner, seaman

navvy *noun* = **labourer**, worker, workman

navy *noun* **2** = **fleet**, armada, flotilla

near *adjective* **1** = **close**, adjacent, adjoining, nearby, neighbouring OPPOSITE far. **2** = **forthcoming**, approaching, imminent, impending, in the offing, looming, nigh, upcoming OPPOSITE remote

nearby *adjective* = **neighbouring**, adjacent, adjoining, convenient, handy

nearly *adverb* = **almost**, approximately, as good as, just about, practically, roughly, virtually, well-nigh

nearness *noun* **1** = **closeness**, accessibility, availability, handiness, proximity, vicinity

near-sighted *adjective* = **short-sighted**, myopic

neat *adjective* **1** = **tidy**, orderly, shipshape, smart, spick-and-span, spruce, systematic, trim OPPOSITE disorderly. **2** = **elegant**, adept, adroit, deft, dexterous, efficient, graceful, nimble, skilful, stylish OPPOSITE clumsy. **3** = **undiluted**, pure, straight, unmixed

neatly *adverb* **1** = **tidily**, daintily, fastidiously, methodically, smartly, sprucely, systematically **2** = **elegantly**, adeptly, adroitly, deftly, dexterously, efficiently, expertly, gracefully, nimbly, skilfully

neatness *noun* **1** = **tidiness**, daintiness, orderliness, smartness, spruceness, trimness **2** = **elegance**, adroitness, deftness, dexterity, efficiency, grace, nimbleness, skill, style

nebulous *adjective* = **vague**, confused, dim, hazy, imprecise, indefinite, indistinct, shadowy,

neck *noun* **1** part of the body joining the head to the shoulders. **2** part of a garment round the neck. **3** long narrow part of a bottle or violin. ◆ *verb* **4** *Slang* kiss and cuddle. **neck and neck** absolutely level in a race or competition. **stick one's neck out** *Informal* risk criticism or ridicule by speaking one's mind. **neckerchief** *noun* piece of cloth worn tied round the neck. **necklace** *noun* decorative piece of jewellery worn around the neck. **neckline** *noun* shape or position of the upper edge of a dress or top. **neck of the woods** *Informal* particular area. **necktie** *noun US* same as TIE (sense 5).

necromancy ❶ [neck-rome-man-see] *noun* **1** communication with the dead. **2** sorcery. **necromancer** *noun*

necrophilia *noun* sexual attraction for or intercourse with dead bodies.

necropolis ❶ [neck-**rop**-pol-liss] *noun* cemetery.

necrosis *noun Biol, Med* death of cells in the body.

nectar *noun* **1** sweet liquid collected from flowers by bees. **2** drink of the gods. **3** any delicious drink.

nectarine *noun* smooth-skinned peach.

née [nay] *preposition* indicating the maiden name of a married woman.

need ❶ *verb* **1** require or be in want of. **2** be obliged (to do something). ◆ *noun* **3** condition of lacking something. **4** requirement or necessity. **5** poverty. **needs** *adverb* (preceded or foll. by *must*) necessarily. **needy** *adjective* **needier, neediest** poor, in need of financial support. **needful** *adjective* necessary or required. **needless** *adjective* unnecessary. **needlessly** *adverb*

needle ❶ *noun* **1** thin pointed piece of metal with an eye through which thread is passed for sewing. **2** long pointed rod used in knitting. **3** pointed part of a hypodermic syringe. **4** small pointed part in a record player that touches the record and picks up the sound signals, stylus. **5** pointer on a measuring instrument or compass. **6** long narrow stiff leaf. **7** *Informal* intense rivalry or ill-feeling, esp. in a sports match. ◆ *verb* **8** *Informal* goad or provoke. **needlecord** *noun* finely-ribbed corduroy. **needlepoint** *noun* embroidery done on canvas. **needlework** *noun* sewing and embroidery.

ne'er ❶ *adverb Lit* never. **ne'er-do-well** *noun* useless or lazy person.

ne'er-do-well ❶ *noun* useless or lazy person.

nefarious ❶ [nif-**fair**-ee-uss] *adjective* wicked.

negate ❶ *verb* **1** invalidate. **2** deny the existence of. **negation** *noun*

uncertain, unclear
necessarily *adverb* **2** = **certainly**, automatically, compulsorily, incontrovertibly, inevitably, inexorably, naturally, of necessity, undoubtedly
necessary *adjective* **1** = **needed**, compulsory, essential, imperative, indispensable, mandatory, obligatory, required, requisite, vital OPPOSITE〉 **unnecessary**. **2** = **certain**, fated, inescapable, inevitable, inexorable, unavoidable OPPOSITE〉 **unnecessary**
necessitate *verb* = **compel**, call for, coerce, constrain, demand, force, impel, oblige, require
necessities *plural noun* = **essentials**, exigencies, fundamentals, needs, requirements
necessity *noun* **1** = **inevitability**, compulsion, inexorableness, obligation **2** = **essential**, desideratum, fundamental, need, prerequisite, requirement, requisite, *sine qua non*
necromancy *noun* **2** = **magic**, black magic, divination, enchantment, sorcery, witchcraft, wizardry
necropolis *noun* = **cemetery**, burial ground, churchyard, graveyard
need *verb* **1** = **require**, call for, demand, entail, lack, miss, necessitate, want ◆*noun* **3** = **lack**, inadequacy, insufficiency, paucity,

shortage **4** = **requirement**, demand, desideratum, essential, necessity, requisite **5** = **poverty**, deprivation, destitution, penury
needed *adjective* **1** = **necessary**, called for, desired, lacked, required, wanted
needful *adjective* = **necessary**, essential, indispensable, needed, required, requisite, stipulated, vital
needle *verb* **8** *Inf* = **irritate**, annoy, get on one's nerves (*inf*), goad, harass, nag, pester, provoke, rile, taunt
needless *adjective* = **unnecessary**, gratuitous, groundless, pointless, redundant, superfluous, uncalled-for, unwanted, useless
needlework *noun* = **embroidery**, needlecraft, sewing, stitching, tailoring
needy *adjective* **5** = **poor**, deprived, destitute, disadvantaged, impoverished, penniless, poverty-stricken, underprivileged
ne'er-do-well *noun* = **layabout**, black sheep, good-for-nothing, idler, loafer, loser, skiver (*Brit sl*), wastrel
nefarious *adjective* = **wicked**, criminal, depraved, evil, foul, heinous, infernal, villainous
negate *verb* **1** = **invalidate**, annul, cancel, countermand, neutralize, nullify, obviate, reverse, wipe out **2** = **deny**, contradict,

negative ① *adjective* **1** expressing a denial or refusal. **2** lacking positive qualities. **3** (of an electrical charge) having the same electrical charge as an electron. **4** *Med* indicating the absence of a condition for which a test was made. ◆ *noun* **5** negative word or statement. **6** *Photog* image with a reversal of tones or colours from which positive prints are made.

neglect ① *verb* **1** take no care of. **2** fail (to do something) through carelessness. **3** disregard. ◆ *noun* **4** neglecting or being neglected. **neglectful** *adjective*

negligee, négligée [neg-lee-zhay] *noun* woman's lightweight usu. lace-trimmed dressing gown.

negligence ① *noun* neglect or carelessness. **negligent** *adjective* **negligently** *adverb*

negligible ① *adjective* so small or unimportant as to be not worth considering.

negotiate ① *verb* **1** discuss in order to reach (an agreement). **2** succeed in passing round or over (a place or problem). **negotiation** *noun* **negotiator** *noun* **negotiable** *adjective*

Negro *noun, pl* **-groes** *Old-fashioned* member of any of the Black peoples originating in Africa. **Negroid** *adjective* of or relating to the Negro race.

neigh *noun* **1** loud high-pitched sound made

by a horse. ◆ *verb* **2** make this sound.

neighbour ① *noun* person who lives or is situated near another. **neighbouring** *adjective* situated nearby. **neighbourhood** *noun* **1** district. **2** surroundings. **3** people of a district. **neighbourhood watch** scheme in which the residents of an area keep an eye on each other's property as a means of preventing crime. **neighbourly** *adjective* kind, friendly, and helpful.

neither *adjective, pronoun* **1** not one nor the other. ◆ *conjunction* **2** not.

LANGUAGE TIP

When *neither* is followed by a plural noun it is acceptable to make the verb plural too: *Neither of these books are useful.*

---

nelson *noun* wrestling hold in which a wrestler places his arm(s) under his opponent's arm(s) from behind and exerts pressure with hispalms on the back of his opponent's neck.

nematode, nematode worm *noun* slender cylindrical unsegmented worm.

nemesis ① [nem-miss-iss] *noun, pl* **-ses**

N

———— T H E S A U R U S ————

disallow, disprove, gainsay (*arch or lit*), oppose, rebut, refute OPPOSITE **maintain**

negation *noun* **1** = **cancellation**, neutralization, nullification **2** = **denial**, contradiction, converse, disavowal, inverse, opposite, rejection, renunciation, reverse

negative *adjective* **1** = **contradictory**, contrary, denying, dissenting, opposing, refusing, rejecting, resisting OPPOSITE **positive**. **2** = **pessimistic**, cynical, gloomy, jaundiced, uncooperative, unenthusiastic, unwilling OPPOSITE **positive** ◆*noun* **5** = **contradiction**, denial, refusal

neglect *verb* **2** = **forget**, be remiss, evade, omit, pass over, shirk, skimp **3** = **disregard**, disdain, ignore, overlook, rebuff, scorn, slight, spurn OPPOSITE **look after** ◆*noun* **4** = **negligence**, carelessness, dereliction, failure, laxity, oversight, slackness OPPOSITE **care**

neglected *adjective* **1** = **abandoned**, derelict, overgrown **3** = **disregarded**, unappreciated, underestimated, undervalued

neglectful *adjective* **2** = **careless**, heedless, inattentive, indifferent, lax, negligent, remiss, thoughtless, uncaring

negligence *noun* = **carelessness**, dereliction, disregard, inattention, indifference, laxity,

neglect, slackness, thoughtlessness

negligent *adjective* = **careless**, forgetful, heedless, inattentive, neglectful, remiss, slack, slapdash, thoughtless, unthinking OPPOSITE **careful**

negligible *adjective* = **insignificant**, imperceptible, inconsequential, minor, minute, small, trifling, trivial, unimportant

negotiable *adjective* **1** = **debatable**, variable

negotiate *verb* **1** = **deal**, arrange, bargain, conciliate, cut a deal, debate, discuss, mediate, transact, work out **2** = **get round**, clear, cross, get over, get past, pass, surmount

negotiation *noun* **1** = **bargaining**, arbitration, debate, diplomacy, discussion, mediation, transaction, wheeling and dealing (*inf*)

negotiator *noun* **1** = **mediator**, ambassador, delegate, diplomat, honest broker, intermediary, moderator

neighbourhood *noun* **1, 2** = **district**, community, environs, locale, locality, quarter, region, vicinity

neighbouring *adjective* = **nearby**, adjacent, adjoining, bordering, connecting, near, next, surrounding

neighbourly *adjective* = **helpful**, considerate, friendly, harmonious, hospitable, kind, obliging, retribution or vengeance.

neo- *combining form* new, recent, or a modern form of, e.g. *neoclassicism.*

neoclassicism *noun* late 18th- and early 19th-century style of art and architecture, based on ancient Roman and Greek models. **neoclassical** *adjective*

neocolonialism *noun* political control yielded by one country over another through control of its economy. **neocolonial** *adjective*

neodymium *noun Chem* silvery-white metallic element of lanthanide series.

Neolithic *adjective* of the later Stone Age.

neologism [nee-**ol**-a-jiz-zum] *noun* newly-coined word or an established word used in a new sense.

neon *noun Chem* colourless odourless gaseous element used in illuminated signs and lights.

neonatal *adjective* relating to the first few weeks of a baby's life.

neophyte *noun* **1** beginner or novice. **2** new convert.

nephew *noun* son of one's sister or brother.

nephritis [nif-**frite**-tiss] *noun* inflammation of a kidney.

nepotism ⊕ [**nep**-a-tiz-zum] *noun* favouritism in business shown to relatives and friends.

Neptune *noun* **1** Roman god of the sea. **2** eighth planet from the sun.

neptunium *noun Chem* synthetic radioactive metallic element.

nerd, nurd ⊕ *noun Slang* **1** boring person obsessed with a particular subject. **2** stupid and feeble person.

nerve ⊕ *noun* **1** cordlike bundle of fibres that conducts impulses between the brain and other parts of the body. **2** bravery and determination. **3** impudence. ♦ *plural* **4** anxiety or tension. **5** ability or inability to remain calm in a difficult situation. **get on someone's nerves** irritate someone. **nerve oneself** prepare oneself (to do something difficult or unpleasant).

nerveless *adjective* **1** numb, without feeling. **2** fearless. **nervy** *adjective* **nervier, nerviest** excitable or nervous. **nerve centre** place from which a system or organization is controlled.

nerve gas poisonous gas which affects the nervous system. **nerve-racking** *adjective* very distressing or harrowing.

nervous ⊕ *adjective* **1** apprehensive or worried. **2** of or relating to the nerves. **nervously** *adverb* **nervousness** *noun* **nervous breakdown** mental illness in which the sufferer ceases to function properly. **nervous system** brain, spinal column and nerves, which together control thought, feeling and movement.

ness *noun* headland, cape.

nest ⊕ *noun* **1** place or structure in which birds or certain animals lay eggs or give birth to young. **2** secluded place. **3** set of things of graduated sizes designed to fit together. ♦ *verb* **4** make or inhabit a nest. **5** (of a set of objects) fit one inside another. **nest egg** fund of money kept in reserve.

nestle ⊕ *verb* **1** snuggle. **2** be in a sheltered position.

nestling ⊕ *noun* bird too young to leave the nest.

net[1] ⊕ *noun* **1** fabric of meshes of string, thread, or wire with many openings. **2** piece of net used to protect or hold things or to trap

—————— THESAURUS ——————

sociable

nemesis *noun* =**retribution**, destiny, destruction, fate, vengeance

nepotism *noun* =**favouritism**, bias, partiality, patronage, preferential treatment

nerd, nurd *noun Sl* **1** =**bore**, anorak (*inf*), dork (*sl*), geek (*inf*), obsessive, train spotter (*inf*)

nerve *noun* **2** =**bravery**, bottle (*Brit sl*), courage, daring, fearlessness, grit, guts (*inf*), pluck, resolution, will **3** *Inf* =**impudence**, audacity, boldness, brazenness, cheek (*inf*), impertinence, insolence, temerity **nerve oneself** =**brace oneself**, fortify oneself, gee oneself up, steel oneself

nerveless *adjective* **1** =**calm**, composed, controlled, cool, impassive, imperturbable, self-possessed, unemotional **2** =**fearless**, brave, courageous, daring, gutsy (*sl*), plucky, unafraid

nerve-racking *adjective* =**tense**, difficult,

distressing, frightening, gut-wrenching, harrowing, stressful, trying, worrying

nerves *plural* =**tension**, anxiety, butterflies (in one's stomach) (*inf*), cold feet (*inf*), fretfulness, nervousness, strain, stress, worry

nervous *adjective* **1** =**apprehensive**, anxious, edgy, fearful, jumpy, on edge, tense, uneasy, uptight (*inf*), wired (*sl*), worried OPPOSITE⟩ **calm**

nervousness *noun* **1** =**anxiety**, agitation, disquiet, excitability, fluster, tension, touchiness, worry

nervy *adjective* =**anxious**, agitated, fidgety, jittery (*inf*), jumpy, nervous, on edge, tense, wired (*sl*)

nest *noun* **2** =**refuge**, den, haunt, hideaway, retreat **nest egg** =**reserve**, cache, deposit, fall-back, fund(s), savings, store

nestle *verb* **1** =**snuggle**, cuddle, curl up, huddle, nuzzle

N

animals. **3** (in certain sports) piece of net over which the ball or shuttlecock must be hit. **4** goal in soccer or hockey. **5** strategy intended to trap people, e.g. *he had slipped through a police net.* ◆ *verb* **netting, netted 6** catch (a fish or animal) in a net. **the Net** short for INTERNET. **netting** *noun* material made of net. **netball** *noun* team game in which a ball has to be thrown through a net hanging from a ring at the top of a pole.

net², **nett** ⊕ *adjective* **1** left after all deductions. **2** (of weight) excluding the wrapping or container. **3** final or conclusive, e.g. *the net result.* ◆ *verb* **netting, netted 4** yield or earn as a clear profit.

nether ⊕ *adjective* lower. **nethermost** *adjective* lowest.

nettle ⊕ *noun* plant with stinging hairs on the leaves. **nettled** *adjective* irritated or annoyed. **nettle rash** skin condition in which itchy red or white raised patches appear.

network ⊕ *noun* **1** system of intersecting lines, roads, etc. **2** interconnecting group or system. **3** (in broadcasting) group of stations that all transmit the same programmes simultaneously. **4** *Computers* system of interconnected circuits. ◆ *verb* **5** broadcast (a programme) over a network.

neural *adjective* of a nerve or the nervous system.

neuralgia *noun* severe pain along a nerve.

neuritis [nyoor-**rite**-tiss] *noun* inflammation of a nerve or nerves.

neurology *noun* scientific study of the nervous system. **neurological** *adjective* **neurologist** *noun*

neuron, neurone *noun* cell specialized to conduct nerve impulses.

neurosis ⊕ *noun, pl* **-ses** mental disorder producing hysteria, anxiety, depression, or obsessive behaviour. **neurotic** *adjective* **1** emotionally unstable. **2** suffering from neurosis. ◆ *noun* **3** neurotic person.

neurosurgery *noun* branch of surgery concerned with the nervous system. **neurosurgical** *adjective* **neurosurgeon** *noun*

neuter ⊕ *adjective* **1** belonging to a particular class of grammatical inflections in some languages. **2** (of an animal) sexually underdeveloped. ◆ *verb* **3** castrate (an animal).

neutral ⊕ *adjective* **1** taking neither side in a war or dispute. **2** of or belonging to a neutral party or country. **3** not displaying emotions or opinions. **4** (of a colour) not definite or striking. ◆ *noun* **5** neutral person or nation. **6** neutral gear. **neutrality** *noun* **neutralize** *verb* make ineffective or neutral. **neutral gear** position of the controls of a gearbox that leaves the gears unconnected to the engine.

neutrino [new-**tree**-no] *noun, pl* **-nos** elementary particle with no mass or electrical charge.

neutron *noun* electrically neutral elementary particle of about the same mass as a proton. **neutron bomb** nuclear bomb designed to kill people and animals while leaving buildings virtually undamaged.

never ⊕ *adverb* at no time. **never-ending** *adjective* long and boring. **nevermore** *adverb* *Lit* never again. **nevertheless** *adverb* in spite of that.

never-never *noun Informal* hire-purchase.

———————— THESAURUS ————————

nestling *noun* =**chick**, fledgling

net¹ *noun* **1** =**mesh**, lattice, netting, network, openwork, tracery, web ◆*verb* **6** =**catch**, bag, capture, enmesh, ensnare, entangle, trap

net², **nett** *adjective* **1** =**take-home**, after taxes, clear, final ◆*verb* **4** =**earn**, accumulate, bring in, clear, gain, make, realize, reap

nether *adjective* =**lower**, below, beneath, bottom, inferior, under, underground

nettled *adjective* =**irritated**, annoyed, exasperated, galled, harassed, incensed, peeved, put out, riled, vexed

network *noun* **1, 2** =**system**, arrangement, complex, grid, labyrinth, lattice, maze, organization, structure, web **4** *Computers* =**web**, system

neurosis *noun* =**obsession**, abnormality, affliction, derangement, instability, maladjustment, mental illness, phobia

neurotic *adjective* **1** =**unstable**, abnormal, compulsive, disturbed, maladjusted, manic, nervous, obsessive, unhealthy

neuter *verb* **3** =**castrate**, doctor (*inf*), emasculate, fix (*inf*), geld, spay

neutral *adjective* **1** =**unbiased**, even-handed, impartial, nonaligned, nonpartisan, uncommitted, uninvolved, unprejudiced OPPOSITE active. **4** =**indeterminate**, dull, indistinct, intermediate, undefined

neutrality *noun* **1** =**impartiality**, detachment, nonalignment, noninterference, noninvolvement, nonpartisanship

neutralize *verb* =**counteract**, cancel, compensate for, counterbalance, frustrate, negate, nullify, offset, undo

never *adverb* =**at no time**, not at all, on no account, under no circumstances OPPOSITE always

never-never land imaginary idyllic place.
new ❶ *adjective* **1** not existing before. **2** recently acquired. **3** having lately come into some state. **4** additional. **5** (foll. by *to*) unfamiliar. ♦ *adverb* **6** recently. **newness** *noun*
New Age late 1980s philosophy characterized by a belief in alternative medicine and spiritualism. **newbie** *Informal noun* person new to a job, club, etc. **newborn** *adjective* recently or just born. **newcomer** *noun* recent arrival or participant. **newfangled** *adjective* objectionably or unnecessarily modern. **new-found** *adjective* newly or recently discovered. **newly** *adverb*
newlyweds *plural noun* recently married couple. **new moon** moon when it appears as a narrow crescent at the beginning of its cycle.
New Testament part of the Christian Bible dealing with life and teachings of Christ and his followers. **new town** town planned and built as a complete unit. **New World** the Americas; the western hemisphere. **New Year** (holiday marking) the first day or days of the year.
newel *noun* post at the top or bottom of a flight of stairs that supports the handrail.
news ❶ *noun* **1** important or interesting new happenings. **2** information about such events reported in the mass media. **3** television or radio programme presenting such information. **newsy** *adjective* full of news. **newsagent** *noun* shopkeeper who sells newspapers and magazines. **newsflash** *noun* brief important news item, which interrupts a radio or television programme. **newsletter** *noun* bulletin issued periodically to members of a group. **newspaper** *noun* weekly or daily publication containing news. **newsprint** *noun* inexpensive paper used for newspapers. **newsreader**, **newscaster** *noun* person who reads the news

on the television or radio. **newsreel** *noun* short film giving news. **newsroom** *noun* room where news is received and prepared for publication or broadcasting. **newsworthy** *adjective* sufficiently interesting to be reported as news.
newt *noun* small amphibious creature with a long slender body and tail.
newton *noun* unit of force.
next ❶ *adjective, adverb* **1** immediately following. **2** nearest. **next door** *adjective, adverb* (often hyphenated) in, at, or to the adjacent house or flat. **next-of-kin** *noun* closest relative.
nexus *noun, pl* **nexus** connection or link.
NF Newfoundland.
NH New Hampshire.
NHS National Health Service.
Ni *Chem* nickel.
NI 1 *Brit* National Insurance. **2** Northern Ireland.
nib *noun* writing point of a pen.
nibble ❶ *verb* **1** take little bites (of). ♦ *noun* **2** little bite. **3** light meal.
nibs *noun* **his, her nibs** *Slang* mock title of respect.
nice ❶ *adjective* **1** pleasant. **2** kind, e.g. *a nice gesture*. **3** good or satisfactory, e.g. *they made a nice job of it*. **4** subtle, e.g. *a nice distinction*.
nicely *adverb* **niceness** *noun*

LANGUAGE TIP

The adjective *nice* has been so overused that ithas lost a lot of its effectiveness. It is therefore better to use a more interesting or descriptive word in its place wherever possible.

N

——————— THESAURUS ———————

nevertheless *adverb* =**nonetheless**, but, even so, (even) though, however, notwithstanding, regardless, still, yet
new *adjective* **1** =**modern**, contemporary, current, fresh, ground-breaking, latest, novel, original, recent, state-of-the-art, unfamiliar, up-to-date OPPOSITE> old. **3** =**changed**, altered, improved, modernized, redesigned, renewed, restored **4** =**extra**, added, more, new-found, supplementary
newcomer *noun* =**novice**, arrival, beginner, Johnny-come-lately (*inf*), parvenu
newfangled *adjective* =**new**, contemporary, fashionable, gimmicky, modern, novel, recent, state-of-the-art
newly *adverb* =**recently**, anew, freshly, just, lately, latterly

newness *noun* **1** =**novelty**, freshness, innovation, oddity, originality, strangeness, unfamiliarity, uniqueness
news *noun* **1, 2** =**information**, bulletin, communiqué, exposé, gossip, hearsay, intelligence, latest (*inf*), report, revelation, rumour, story
newsworthy *adjective* =**interesting**, important, notable, noteworthy, remarkable, significant, stimulating
next *adjective* **1** =**following**, consequent, ensuing, later, subsequent, succeeding **2** =**nearest**, adjacent, adjoining, closest, neighbouring ♦*adverb* **1** =**afterwards**, following, later, subsequently, thereafter
nibble *verb* **1** =**bite**, eat, gnaw, munch, nip, peck, pick at ♦*noun* **2** =**taste**, crumb, morsel,

nicety ⊕ *noun, pl* **-ties 1** subtle point. **2** refinement or delicacy.

niche ⊕ [neesh] *noun* **1** hollow area in a wall. **2** suitable position for a particular person.

nick ⊕ *verb* **1** make a small cut in. **2** *Slang* steal. **3** *Slang* arrest. ◆ *noun* **4** small cut. **5** *Slang* prison or police station. **in good nick** *Informal* in good condition. **in the nick of time** just in time.

nickel *noun* **1** *Chem* silvery-white metal often used in alloys. **2** US coin worth five cents.

nickelodeon *noun US* early type of jukebox.

nicker *noun, pl* **nicker** *Brit slang* pound sterling.

nickname ⊕ *noun* **1** familiar name given to a person or place. ◆ *verb* **2** call by a nickname.

nicotine *noun* poisonous substance found in tobacco.

nictitate *verb* blink. **nictitating membrane** (in reptiles, birds, and some mammals) thin fold of skin that can be drawn across the eye beneath the eyelid.

niece *noun* daughter of one's sister or brother.

nifty ⊕ *adjective* **-tier, -tiest** *Informal* neat or smart.

niggard ⊕ *noun* stingy person. **niggardly** *adjective*

nigger *noun Offens* Black person.

niggle ⊕ *verb* **1** worry slightly. **2** continually find fault (with). ◆ *noun* **3** small worry or doubt.

nigh *adverb, preposition Lit* near.

night ⊕ *noun* **1** time of darkness between sunset and sunrise. **2** evening. **3** period between going to bed and morning. **4** nightfall or dusk. **5** an evening designated for a specified activity, e.g. *parents' night*. ◆ *adjective* **6** of, occurring, or working at night, e.g. *the night shift*. **nightly** *adjective, adverb* (happening) each night. **nightcap** *noun* **1** drink taken just before bedtime. **2** soft cap formerly worn in bed. **nightclub** *noun* establishment for dancing, music, etc., open late at night. **nightdress** *noun* woman's loose dress worn in bed. **nightfall** *noun* approach of darkness. **nightgown** *noun* loose garment worn in bed; nightdress or nightshirt. **nightie** *noun Informal* nightdress. **nightingale** *noun* small bird with a musical song usu. heard at night. **nightjar** *noun* nocturnal bird with a harsh cry. **nightlife** *noun* entertainment and social activities available at night in a town or city. **night-light** *noun* dim light left on overnight. **nightmare** *noun* **1** very bad dream. **2** very unpleasant experience. **nightmarish** *adjective* **night safe** safe built into the outside wall of a bank, which customers can deposit money in when the bank is closed. **night school** place where adults can attend educational courses in the evenings. **nightshade** *noun* plant with bell-shaped flowers which are often poisonous. **nightshirt** *noun* long loose shirt worn in bed. **night-time** *noun* time from sunset to sunrise.

nihilism [nye-ill-liz-zum] *noun* rejection of all

——————— T H E S A U R U S ———————

peck, *soupçon*, titbit **3** = **snack**, bite

nice *adjective* **1** = **pleasant**, agreeable, attractive, charming, delightful, good, pleasurable OPPOSITE **awful. 2** = **kind**, courteous, friendly, likable *or* likeable, polite, well-mannered OPPOSITE **mean. 3** = **neat**, dainty, fine, tidy, trim **4** = **subtle**, careful, delicate, fastidious, fine, meticulous, precise, strict

nicely *adverb* **1** = **pleasantly**, acceptably, agreeably, attractively, charmingly, delightfully, pleasurably, well OPPOSITE **unpleasantly. 2** = **kindly**, amiably, commendably, courteously, politely **3** = **neatly**, daintily, finely, tidily, trimly

nicety *noun* = **subtlety**, daintiness, delicacy, discrimination, distinction, nuance, refinement

niche *noun* **1** = **alcove**, corner, hollow, nook, opening, recess **2** = **position**, calling, pigeonhole (*inf*), place, slot (*inf*), vocation

nick *verb* **1** = **cut**, chip, dent, mark, notch, scar, score, scratch, snick **2** *Sl* = **steal**, pilfer, pinch (*inf*), swipe (*sl*) ◆ *noun* **4** = **cut**, chip, dent, mark, notch, scar, scratch

nickname *noun* **1** = **pet name**, diminutive, epithet, label, sobriquet

nifty *adjective Inf* = **neat**, attractive, chic, deft, pleasing, smart, stylish

niggard *noun* = **miser**, cheapskate (*inf*), Scrooge, skinflint

niggardly *adjective* = **stingy**, avaricious, frugal, grudging, mean, miserly, parsimonious, tightfisted, ungenerous OPPOSITE **liberal**

niggle *verb* **1** = **worry**, annoy, irritate, rankle **2** = **criticize**, carp, cavil, find fault, fuss

niggling *adjective* **1** = **persistent**, gnawing, irritating, troubling, worrying **2** = **petty**, finicky, fussy, nit-picking (*inf*), pettifogging, picky (*inf*), quibbling

night *noun* **1** = **darkness**, dark, night-time **3** = **night-time**

nightfall *noun* = **evening**, dusk, sundown, sunset, twilight

nightly *adjective* = **nocturnal**, night-time ◆ *adverb* = **every night**, each night, night after night, nights (*inf*)

nightmare *noun* **1** = **bad dream**, hallucination

N

established authority and institutions. **nihilist** noun **nihilistic** adjective

nil ❶ noun nothing, zero.

nimble ❶ adjective **1** agile and quick. **2** mentally alert or acute. **nimbly** adverb

nimbus noun, pl **-bi, -buses 1** dark grey rain cloud. **2** halo.

nincompoop ❶ noun Informal stupid person.

nine adjective, noun one more than eight. **ninth** adjective, noun (of) number nine in a series. **ninepins** noun game of skittles. **nineteen** adjective, noun ten and nine. **talk nineteen to the dozen** talk very fast. **nineteenth** adjective, noun **nineteenth hole** Slang bar in a golf clubhouse.

ninety adjective, noun ten times nine. **ninetieth** adjective, noun

niobium noun Chem white superconductive metallic element.

nip¹ ❶ verb **nipping, nipped 1** Informal hurry. **2** pinch or squeeze. **3** bite lightly. **4** (of the cold) cause pain. ◆ noun **5** pinch or light bite. **6** sharp coldness, e.g. *a nip in the air.* **nippy** adjective **-pier, -piest 1** frosty or chilly. **2** Informal quick or nimble. **nipper** noun Informal small child.

nip² ❶ noun small alcoholic drink.

nipple noun **1** projection in the centre of a breast. **2** small projection through which oil or grease can be put into a machine or component.

nirvana ❶ [near-**vah**-na] noun Buddhism, Hinduism absolute spiritual enlightenment and bliss.

nisi [**nye**-sigh] adjective see DECREE NISI.

Nissen hut noun tunnel-shaped military hut made of corrugated steel.

nit ❶ noun **1** egg or larva of a louse. **2** Informal short for NITWIT. **nit-picking** adjective Informal overconcerned with insignificant detail, esp. to find fault. **nitwit** noun Informal stupid person.

nitrogen [**nite**-roj-jen] noun Chem colourless odourless gas that forms four fifths of the air. **nitric, nitrous, nitrogenous** adjective of or containing nitrogen. **nitrate** noun compound of nitric acid, used as a fertilizer. **nitroglycerine, nitroglycerin** noun explosive liquid. **nitric acid** corrosive liquid widely used in industry. **nitrous oxide** anaesthetic gas.

nitty-gritty ❶ noun Informal basic facts.

NJ New Jersey.

NM New Mexico.

NNE north-northeast.

NNW north-northwest.

no ❶ interjection **1** expresses denial, disagreement, or refusal. ◆ adjective **2** not any, not a. ◆ adverb **3** not at all. ◆ noun, pl **noes, nos 4** answer or vote of 'no'. **5** person who answers or votes 'no'. **no-ball** noun (in cricket or rounders) improperly bowled ball. **no-claims bonus, no-claim bonus** reduction in the cost of an insurance policy made if no claims have been made in a specified period. **no-go area** district barricaded off so that the police or army can enter only by force. **no-man's-land** noun land between boundaries, esp. contested land between two opposing forces. **no-one, no one** pronoun nobody.

LANGUAGE TIP

When *no-one* refers to 'people in general' it may be followed by a plural: *No-one finished their drink.*

---

no. number.

No¹, **Noh** noun, pl **No, Noh** Japanese classical drama, using music and dancing.

No² Chem nobelium.

n.o. Cricket not out.

nob ❶ noun Slang person of wealth or social

N

——————— THESAURUS ———————

2 = ordeal, horror, torment, trial, tribulation

nil noun **= nothing**, love, naught, none, zero

nimble adjective **1 = agile**, brisk, deft, dexterous, lively, quick, sprightly, spry, swift
OPPOSITE **clumsy**

nimbly adverb **1 = quickly**, briskly, deftly, dexterously, easily, readily, smartly, spryly, swiftly

nincompoop noun Inf **= idiot**, blockhead, chump, fool, nitwit (inf), numbskull or numbskull, twit (inf, chiefly Brit)

nip¹ verb **2 = pinch**, squeeze, tweak **3 = bite**

nip² noun **= dram**, draught, drop, mouthful, shot (inf), sip, snifter (inf)

nipper noun Inf **= child**, baby, boy, girl, infant, kid (inf), tot

nippy adjective **1 = chilly**, biting, sharp **2** Inf **= quick**, active, agile, fast, nimble, spry

nirvana noun Buddhism, Hinduism **= paradise**, bliss, joy, peace, serenity, tranquillity

nit-picking adjective Inf **= fussy**, captious, carping, finicky, hairsplitting, pedantic, pettifogging, quibbling

nitty-gritty noun Inf **= basics**, brass tacks (inf), core, crux, essentials, fundamentals, gist, substance

nitwit noun Inf **= fool**, dimwit (inf), dummy (sl), halfwit, nincompoop, oaf, simpleton distinction.

nobble ❶ verb Slang **1** attract the attention of (someone) in order to talk to him or her. **2** bribe or threaten.

nobelium noun Chem artificially-produced radioactive element.

Nobel Prize [no-**bell**] noun prize awarded annually for outstanding achievement in various fields.

noble ❶ adjective **1** showing or having high moral qualities. **2** of the nobility. **3** impressive and magnificent. ◆ noun **4** member of the nobility. **nobility** noun **1** quality of being noble. **2** class of people holding titles and high social rank. **nobly** adverb **nobleman**, **noblewoman** noun **noble gas** Chem any of a group of very unreactive gases, including helium and neon.

noblesse oblige [no-**bless** oh-**bleezh**] noun Often ironic supposed obligation of the nobility to be honourable and generous.

nobody ❶ pronoun **1** no person. ◆ noun, pl **-bodies 2** person of no importance.

nock noun notch on an arrow or a bow for the bowstring.

nocturnal ❶ adjective **1** of the night. **2** active at night.

nocturne noun short dreamy piece of music.

nod ❶ verb **nodding, nodded 1** lower and raise (one's head) briefly in agreement or

greeting. **2** let one's head fall forward with sleep. ◆ noun **3** act of nodding. **nod off** verb Informal fall asleep.

noddle noun Informal the head.

node noun **1** point on a plant stem from which leaves grow. **2** point at which a curve crosses itself. **nodal** adjective

nodule noun **1** small knot or lump. **2** rounded mineral growth on the root of a plant. **nodular** adjective

Noel, Noël noun Christmas.

nog noun alcoholic drink containing beaten egg.

noggin ❶ noun **1** Informal head. **2** small quantity of an alcoholic drink.

noise ❶ noun sound, usu. a loud or disturbing one. **be noised abroad** be rumoured. **noisy** adjective **noisier, noisiest 1** making a lot of noise. **2** full of noise. **noisily** adverb **noiseless** adjective **noiselessly** adverb

noisome ❶ adjective **1** (of smells) offensive. **2** harmful or poisonous.

nomad ❶ noun member of a tribe with no fixed dwelling place, wanderer. **nomadic** adjective

nom de plume ❶ noun, pl **noms de plume** pen name.

nomenclature ❶ [no-**men**-klatch-er] noun system of names used in a particular subject.

———— THESAURUS ————

no interjection **1 = never**, nay, not at all, no way OPPOSITE yes ◆noun **4 = refusal**, denial, negation, rejection OPPOSITE acceptance

nob noun Sl **= aristocrat**, big hitter (inf), bigwig (inf), heavy hitter (inf), toff (Brit sl), V.I.P.

nobble verb Sl **2 = bribe**, get at, influence, intimidate, win over

nobility noun **1 = integrity**, honour, incorruptibility, uprightness, virtue **2 = aristocracy**, elite, lords, nobles, patricians, peerage, upper class

noble adjective **1 = worthy**, generous, honourable, magnanimous, upright, virtuous OPPOSITE selfish. **2 = aristocratic**, blue-blooded, highborn, lordly, patrician, titled OPPOSITE base. **3 = impressive**, dignified, distinguished, grand, great, imposing, lofty, splendid, stately OPPOSITE mean ◆noun **4 = lord**, aristocrat, nobleman, peer

nobody pronoun **1 = no-one** ◆noun **2 = nonentity**, cipher, lightweight (inf), menial OPPOSITE celebrity

nocturnal adjective **= nightly**, night-time

nod verb **1 = acknowledge**, bow, gesture, indicate, signal **2 = sleep**, doze, drowse, nap ◆noun **3 = gesture**, acknowledgment, greeting,

indication, sign, signal

noggin noun Inf **1 = head**, block (inf), nut (sl) **2 = cup**, dram, mug, nip, tot

noise noun **1 = sound**, clamour, commotion, din, hubbub, racket, row, uproar OPPOSITE silence

noiseless adjective **= silent**, hushed, inaudible, mute, quiet, soundless, still

noisome adjective **1 = offensive**, disgusting, fetid, foul, malodorous, noxious, putrid, smelly, stinking **2 = poisonous**, bad, harmful, pernicious, pestilential, unhealthy, unwholesome

noisy adjective **= loud**, boisterous, cacophonous, clamorous, deafening, ear-splitting, strident, tumultuous, uproarious, vociferous OPPOSITE quiet

nomad noun **= wanderer**, drifter, itinerant, migrant, rambler, rover, vagabond

nomadic adjective **= wandering**, itinerant, migrant, peripatetic, roaming, roving, travelling, vagrant

nom de plume noun **= pseudonym**, alias, assumed name, nom de guerre, pen name

nomenclature noun **= terminology**, classification, codification, phraseology,

nominal ❶ *adjective* **1** in name only. **2** very small in comparison with real worth. **nominally** *adverb*

nominate ❶ *verb* **1** suggest as a candidate. **2** appoint to an office or position. **nomination** *noun* **nominee** *noun* candidate. **nominative** *noun* form of a noun indicating the subject of a verb.

non- *prefix* indicating: **1** negation, e.g. *nonexistent*. **2** refusal or failure, e.g. *noncooperation*. **3** exclusion from a specified class, e.g. *nonfiction*. **4** lack or absence, e.g. *nonevent*.

nonage *noun* **1** *Law* state of being under full legal age for various actions. **2** any period of immaturity.

nonagenarian *noun* person aged between ninety and ninety-nine.

nonaggression *noun* policy of not attacking other countries.

nonagon *noun* geometric figure with nine sides.

nonalcoholic *adjective* containing no alcohol.

nonaligned ❶ *adjective* (of a country) not part of a major alliance or power bloc.

nonalignment *noun*

nonbelligerent *adjective* (of a country) not taking part in a war.

nonce *noun* **for the nonce** for the present.

nonce word word coined for a single occasion.

nonchalant ❶ [non-shall-ant] *adjective* casually unconcerned or indifferent.

nonchalantly *adverb* **nonchalance** *noun*

noncombatant ❶ *noun* member of the armed forces whose duties do not include fighting.

noncommissioned officer *noun* (in the armed forces) a subordinate officer, risen from the ranks.

noncommittal ❶ *adjective* not committing oneself to any particular opinion.

non compos mentis ❶ *adjective* of unsound mind.

nonconductor *noun* substance that is a poor conductor of heat, electricity, or sound.

nonconformist ❶ *noun* **1** person who does not conform to generally accepted patterns of behaviour or thought. **2 (N-)** member of a Protestant group separated from the Church of England. ◆ *adjective* **3** (of behaviour or ideas) not conforming to accepted patterns.

nonconformity *noun*

noncontributory *adjective* denoting a pension scheme for employees, the premiums of which are paid entirely by the employer.

non-cooperation *noun* refusal to do more than is legally or contractually required of one.

nondescript ❶ *adjective* lacking outstanding features.

none ❶ *pronoun* **1** not any. **2** no-one.

nonetheless *adverb* despite that, however.

LANGUAGE TIP

Although *none* means 'not one', and can take a singular verb, it more often takes a plural: *None of them are mine.*

N

nonentity ❶ [non-enn-tit-tee] *noun, pl* **-ties**

————————— T H E S A U R U S —————————

taxonomy, vocabulary

nominal *adjective* **1 = so-called**, formal, ostensible, professed, puppet, purported, supposed, theoretical, titular **2 = small**, inconsiderable, insignificant, minimal, symbolic, token, trifling, trivial

nominate *verb* **1 = suggest**, propose, recommend **2 = name**, appoint, assign, choose, designate, elect, select

nomination *noun* **1 = suggestion**, proposal, recommendation **2 = choice**, appointment, designation, election, selection

nominee *noun* **= candidate**, aspirant, contestant, entrant, protégé, runner

nonaligned *adjective* **= neutral**, impartial, uncommitted, undecided

nonchalance *noun* **= indifference**, calm, composure, equanimity, imperturbability, sang-froid, self-possession, unconcern

nonchalant *adjective* **= casual**, blasé, calm, careless, indifferent, insouciant, laid-back (*inf*), offhand, unconcerned, unperturbed OPPOSITE concerned

noncombatant *noun* **= civilian**, neutral, nonbelligerent

noncommittal *adjective* **= evasive**, cautious, circumspect, equivocal, guarded, neutral, politic, temporizing, tentative, vague, wary

non compos mentis *adjective* **= insane**, crazy, deranged, mentally ill, unbalanced, unhinged

nonconformist *noun* **1 = maverick**, dissenter, eccentric, heretic, iconoclast, individualist, protester, radical, rebel OPPOSITE **traditionalist**

nonconformity *noun* **1 = dissent**, eccentricity, heresy, heterodoxy

nondescript *adjective* **= ordinary**, commonplace, dull, featureless, run-of-the-mill, undistinguished, unexceptional, unremarkable OPPOSITE **distinctive**

insignificant person or thing.
nonessential *adjective* not absolutely
necessary.
nonevent ⊙ *noun* disappointing or
insignificant occurrence.
nonexistent ⊙ *adjective* not existing,
imaginary. **nonexistence** *noun*
nonferrous *adjective* **1** denoting metal other
than iron. **2** not containing iron.
nonflammable *adjective* not easily set on fire.
nonintervention *noun* refusal to intervene in
the affairs of others.
noniron *adjective* not requiring ironing.
non-nuclear *adjective* not involving or using
nuclear power or weapons.
nonpareil [non-par-**rail**] *noun* person or thing
that is unsurpassed.
nonpartisan *adjective* not supporting any
single political party.
nonpayment *noun* failure to pay money
owed.
nonplussed *adjective* perplexed.
non-profit-making *adjective* not run with the
intention of making a profit.
nonproliferation *noun* limitation of the
production or spread of something, such as
nuclear weapons.
nonrepresentational *adjective* Art abstract.
nonresident *noun* person who does not live
in a particular country or place.
nonsectarian *adjective* not confined to any
specific religion.
nonsense ⊙ *noun* **1** something that has or
makes no sense. **2** absurd language. **3** foolish
behaviour. **nonsensical** *adjective*
non sequitur [**sek**-wit-tur] *noun* statement
with little or no relation to what preceded it.
nonsmoker *noun* **1** person who does not
smoke. **2** train carriage or compartment in

which smoking is forbidden. **nonsmoking, no-
smoking** *adjective* denoting an area in which
smoking is forbidden.
nonstandard *adjective* denoting language
that is not regarded as correct by educated
native speakers.
nonstarter ⊙ *noun* person or idea that has
little chance of success.
nonstick *adjective* coated with a substance
that food will not stick to when cooked.
nonstop ⊙ *adjective, adverb* without a stop.
nontoxic *adjective* not poisonous.
nonunion *adjective* **1** (of a company) not
employing trade union members. **2** (of a
person) not belonging to a trade union.
nonviolent *adjective* using peaceful methods
to bring about change. **nonviolence** *noun*
nonvoting *adjective* (of shares in a company)
not entitling the owner to vote at company
meetings.
noodles *plural noun* long thin strips of pasta.
nook ⊙ *noun* **1** corner or recess. **2** sheltered
place.
noon ⊙ *noun* twelve o'clock midday. **noonday**
adjective happening at noon.
noose *noun* loop in the end of a rope, tied
with a slipknot.
nor *conjunction* and not.
Nordic *adjective* of Scandinavia or its typically
tall blond and blue-eyed people.
norm ⊙ *noun* standard that is regarded as
usual. **normal** *adjective* usual, regular, or
typical.
normal ⊙ *adjective* **1** usual, regular, or typical.
2 free from mental or physical disorder. ♦ *noun*
3 usual or regular state, degree or form.
normally *adverb* **normality** *noun* **normalize**
verb **1** make or become normal. **2** make
comply with a standard. **normalization** *noun*

———— THESAURUS ————

none *pronoun* =**not any**, nil, nobody, no-one,
nothing, not one, zero
nonentity *noun* =**nobody**, cipher, lightweight
(*inf*), mediocrity, small fry
nonetheless *adverb* =**nevertheless**, despite
that, even so, however, in spite of that, yet
nonevent *noun* =**flop** (*inf*), disappointment,
dud (*inf*), failure, fiasco, washout
nonexistent *adjective* =**imaginary**,
chimerical, fictional, hypothetical, illusory,
legendary, mythical, unreal
nonsense *noun* **1, 2** =**rubbish**, balderdash,
claptrap (*inf*), double Dutch (*Brit inf*), drivel,
gibberish, hot air (*inf*), stupidity, tripe (*inf*),
twaddle OPPOSITE sense
nonsensical *adjective* =**senseless**, absurd,

crazy, foolish, inane, incomprehensible,
irrational, meaningless, ridiculous, silly
nonstarter *noun* =**dead loss**, dud (*inf*),
lemon (*inf*), loser, no-hoper (*inf*), turkey (*inf*),
washout (*inf*)
nonstop *adjective* =**continuous**, constant,
endless, incessant, interminable, relentless,
unbroken, uninterrupted OPPOSITE **broken**
♦*adverb* =**continuously**, ceaselessly, constantly,
endlessly, incessantly, interminably, perpetually,
relentlessly, twenty-four-seven (*inf*)
nook *noun* =**niche**, alcove, corner, cubbyhole,
hide-out, opening, recess, retreat
noon *noun* =**midday**, high noon, noonday,
noontide, twelve noon
norm *noun* =**standard**, average, benchmark,

normative *adjective* of or setting a norm or standard.

Norman *noun* **1** person from Normandy in N France, esp. one of the people who conquered England in 1066. **2** (also **Norman French**) medieval Norman and English dialect of French. ◆ *adjective* **3** of the Normans or their dialect of French. **4** of Normandy. **5** of a style of architecture used in Britain from the Norman Conquest until the 12th century, with massive masonry wallsand rounded arches.

Norse *noun, adjective* (language) of ancient and medieval Norway. **Norseman** *noun* Viking.

north ❶ *noun* **1** direction towards the North Pole, opposite south. **2** area lying in or towards the north. ◆ *adjective* **3** to or in the north. **4** (of a wind) from the north. ◆ *adverb* **5** in, to, or towards the north. **northerly** *adjective* **northern** *adjective* **northerner** *noun* person from the north of a country or area.

northward *adjective, adverb* **northwards** *adverb* **northeast** *noun, adjective, adverb* (in or to) direction between north and east.

northwest *noun, adjective, adverb* (in or to) direction between north and west. **North Pole** northernmost point on the earth's axis.

Norwegian *adjective* **1** of Norway, its language, or its people. ◆ *noun* **2** language of Norway. **3** person from Norway.

nos. numbers.

nose ❶ *noun* **1** organ of smell, used also in breathing. **2** sense of smell. **3** front part of a vehicle. **4** distinctive smell of a wine, perfume, etc. **5** instinctive skill in finding something, e.g.

a nose for a bargain. ◆ *verb* **6** move forward slowly and carefully. **7** pry or snoop. **nosebag** *noun* bag containing feed fastened round a horse's head. **nosebleed** *noun* bleeding from the nose. **nose dive** sudden drop. **nosegay** *noun* small bunch of flowers. **nose out** *verb* discover by searching or prying. **nosey, nosy** *adjective* **nosier, nosiest** *Informal* prying or inquisitive. **nosiness** *noun*

nosh *Slang noun* **1** food. ◆ *verb* **2** eat. **nosh-up** *noun Slang* large meal.

nostalgia ❶ *noun* sentimental longing for the past. **nostalgic** *adjective*

nostril *noun* one of the two openings at the end of the nose.

nostrum ❶ *noun* **1** quack medicine. **2** favourite remedy.

not *adverb* expressing negation, refusal, or denial.

nota bene [**note**-a **ben**-nay] note well, take note.

notable ❶ [**note**-a-bl] *adjective* **1** worthy of being noted, remarkable. ◆ *noun* **2** person of distinction. **notably** *adverb* **notability** [note-a-**bill**-lit-tee] *noun*

notary, notary public [note-a-ree] *noun, pl* **-ries** person authorized to witness the signing of legal documents.

notation ❶ [no-**tay**-shun] *noun* **1** representation of numbers or quantities in a system by a series of symbols. **2** set of such symbols.

notch ❶ *noun* **1** V-shaped cut. **2** *Informal* step or level. ◆ *verb* **3** make a notch in. **4** (foll. by

N

——————— T H E S A U R U S ———————

criterion, par, pattern, rule, yardstick
normal *adjective* **1** =**usual**, average, common, conventional, natural, ordinary, regular, routine, standard, typical OPPOSITE **rare**. **2** =**sane**, rational, reasonable, well-adjusted

normality *noun* **1** =**regularity**, conventionality, naturalness **2** =**sanity**, balance, rationality, reason

normally *adverb* **1** =**usually**, as a rule, commonly, generally, habitually, ordinarily, regularly, typically

north *adjective* **3** =**northern**, Arctic, boreal, northerly, polar ◆*adverb* **5** =**northward(s)**, northerly

nose *noun* **1** =**snout**, beak, bill, hooter (*sl*), proboscis ◆*verb* **6** =**ease forward**, nudge, nuzzle, push, shove **7** =**pry**, meddle, snoop (*inf*)

nosegay *noun* =**posy**, bouquet

nosey, nosy *adjective* =**inquisitive**, curious, eavesdropping, interfering, intrusive,

meddlesome, prying, snooping (*inf*)

nostalgia *noun* =**reminiscence**, homesickness, longing, pining, regretfulness, remembrance, wistfulness, yearning

nostalgic *adjective* =**sentimental**, emotional, homesick, longing, maudlin, regretful, wistful

nostrum *noun* **1** =**panacea**, elixir **2** =**medicine**, cure, drug, potion, remedy, treatment

notability *noun* **2** =**fame**, celebrity, distinction, eminence, esteem, renown

notable *adjective* **1** =**remarkable**, conspicuous, extraordinary, memorable, noteworthy, outstanding, rare, striking, uncommon, unusual OPPOSITE **hidden** ◆*noun* **2** =**celebrity**, big name, dignitary, luminary, personage, V.I.P. OPPOSITE **unknown**

notably *adverb* **1** =**particularly**, especially, outstandingly, strikingly

notation *noun* **2** =**signs**, characters, code, script, symbols, system up) score or achieve.

note ❶ *noun* **1** short letter. **2** brief comment or record. **3** banknote. **4** (symbol for) a musical sound. **5** hint or mood. ♦ *verb* **6** notice, pay attention to. **7** record in writing. **8** remark upon. **noted** *adjective* well-known. **notebook** *noun* book for writing in. **notelet** *noun* small folded card with a design on the front, used for writing informal letters. **notepaper** *noun* paper used for writing letters. **noteworthy** *adjective* worth noting, remarkable.

nothing ❶ *pronoun* **1** not anything. **2** matter of no importance. **3** figure 0. ♦ *adverb* **4** not at all. **nothingness** *noun* **1** nonexistence. **2** insignificance.

notice ❶ *noun* **1** observation or attention. **2** sign giving warning or an announcement. **3** advance notification of intention to end a contract of employment. **4** review in a newspaper of a book or play. ♦ *verb* **5** observe, become aware of. **6** point out or remark upon. **noticeable** *adjective* easily seen or detected, appreciable. **noticeably** *adverb* **notice board** board on which notices are displayed.

noticeable ❶ *adjective* easily seen or detected, appreciable.

notify ❶ *verb* **-fying, -fied** inform. **notification** *noun* **notifiable** *adjective* having to be reported to the authorities.

notion ❶ *noun* **1** idea or opinion. **2** whim. **notional** *adjective* speculative, imaginary, or unreal.

notorious ❶ *adjective* well known for something bad. **notoriously** *adverb* **notoriety** *noun*

notwithstanding ❶ *preposition* **1** in spite of. ♦ *adverb* **2** nevertheless.

nougat *noun* chewy sweet containing nuts and fruit.

nought ❶ *noun* **1** figure 0. **2** nothing.

noughties *Informal plural noun* decade from 2000 to 2009.

noun *noun* word that refers to a person, place, or thing.

nourish ❶ *verb* **1** feed. **2** encourage or foster (an idea or feeling). **nourishment** *noun* **nourishing** *adjective* providing the food necessary for life and growth.

———————— THESAURUS ————————

notch *noun* **1** = **cut**, cleft, incision, indentation, mark, nick, score **2** *Inf* = **level**, degree, grade, step ♦*verb* **3** = **cut**, indent, mark, nick, score, scratch

notch up *verb* = **register**, achieve, gain, make, score

note *noun* **1, 2** = **message**, comment, communication, epistle, jotting, letter, memo, memorandum, minute, remark, reminder ♦*verb* **6** = **see**, notice, observe, perceive **7** = **mark**, denote, designate, indicate, record, register **8** = **mention**, remark

notebook *noun* = **jotter**, diary, exercise book, journal

noted *adjective* = **famous**, acclaimed, celebrated, distinguished, eminent, illustrious, notable, prominent, renowned, well-known

noteworthy *adjective* = **remarkable**, exceptional, extraordinary, important, notable, outstanding, significant, unusual

nothing *pronoun* **1** = **nothingness**, emptiness, nullity, void **3** = **nought**, nil, zero

nothingness *noun* **1** = **oblivion**, nonbeing, nonexistence, nullity **2** = **insignificance**, unimportance, worthlessness

notice *noun* **1** = **interest**, cognizance, consideration, heed, note, observation, regard OPPOSITE **neglect**. **2** = **announcement**, advice, communication, instruction, intimation, news, notification, order, warning ♦*verb* **5** = **observe**, detect, discern, distinguish, mark, note,

perceive, see, spot OPPOSITE **ignore**

noticeable *adjective* = **obvious**, appreciable, clear, conspicuous, evident, manifest, perceptible, plain, striking

notification *noun* = **announcement**, advice, declaration, information, intelligence, message, notice, statement, warning

notify *verb* = **inform**, advise, alert, announce, declare, make known, publish, tell, warn

notion *noun* **1** = **idea**, belief, concept, impression, inkling, opinion, sentiment, view **2** = **whim**, caprice, desire, fancy, impulse, inclination, wish

notional *adjective* = **speculative**, abstract, conceptual, hypothetical, imaginary, theoretical, unreal OPPOSITE **actual**

notoriety *noun* = **scandal**, dishonour, disrepute, infamy, obloquy, opprobrium

notorious *adjective* = **infamous**, dishonourable, disreputable, opprobrious, scandalous

notoriously *adverb* = **infamously**, dishonourably, disreputably, opprobriously, scandalously

notwithstanding *preposition* **1** = **despite**, in spite of

nought *noun* **1** = **zero**, nil **2** = **nothing**, nil, zero

nourish *verb* **1** = **feed**, nurse, nurture, supply, sustain, tend **2** = **encourage**, comfort, cultivate, foster, maintain, promote, support

nous *noun Old-fashioned slang* common sense.
nouveau riche [noo-voh **reesh**] *noun, pl*
nouveaux riches [noo-voh **reesh**] person who
has recently become rich and is regarded as
vulgar.
nouvelle cuisine [noo-**vell** kwee-**zeen**] *noun*
style of preparing and presenting food with
light sauces and unusual combinations of
flavours.
Nov. November.
nova *noun, pl* **-vae, -vas** star that suddenly
becomes brighter and then gradually decreases
to its original brightness.
novel[1] ❶ *noun* long fictitious story in book
form. **novelist** *noun* writer of novels.
novelette *noun* short novel, esp. one regarded
as trivial or sentimental. **novella** *noun, pl* **-las,
-lae** short novel.
novel[2] ❶ *adjective* fresh, new, or original.
novelty *noun* **1** newness. **2** something new or
unusual. **3** cheap toy or trinket.
November *noun* eleventh month of the year.
novena [no-**vee**-na] *noun, pl* **-nas** *RC Church*
set of prayers or services on nine consecutive
days.
novice ❶ [**nov**-viss] *noun* **1** beginner. **2** person
who has entered a religious order but has not
yet taken vows.
novitiate, noviciate *noun* **1** period of being
a novice. **2** part of a monastery or convent
where the novices live.
now ❶ *adverb* **1** at or for the present time. **2**
immediately. ♦ *conjunction* **3** seeing that, since.
just now very recently. **now and again, then**
occasionally. **nowadays** *adverb* in these times.
Nowell *noun* same as NOEL.
nowhere *adverb* not anywhere.
noxious ❶ *adjective* **1** poisonous or harmful. **2**
extremely unpleasant.
nozzle *noun* projecting spout through which

fluid is discharged.
Np *Chem* neptunium.
nr near.
NS Nova Scotia.
NSPCC National Society for the Prevention of
Cruelty to Children.
NSW New South Wales.
NT 1 National Trust New Testament Northern
Territory.
nuance ❶ [**new**-ahnss] *noun* subtle difference
in colour, meaning, or tone.
nub *noun* point or gist (of a story etc.).
nubile ❶ [**new**-bile] *adjective* (of a young
woman) **1** sexually attractive. **2** old enough to
get married.
nuclear *adjective* **1** of nuclear weapons or
energy. **2** of a nucleus, esp. the nucleus of an
atom. **nuclear energy** energy released as a
result of nuclear fission or fusion. **nuclear
family** family consisting only of parents and
their offspring. **nuclear fission** splitting of an
atomic nucleus. **nuclear fusion** combination of
two nuclei to form a heavier nucleus with the
release of energy. **nuclear power** power
produced by a nuclear reactor. **nuclear
reaction** change in structure and energy
content of an atomic nucleus by interaction
with another nucleus or particle. **nuclear
reactor** device in which a nuclear reaction is
maintained and controlled to produce nuclear
energy. **nuclear weapon** weapon whose force
is due to uncontrolled nuclear fusion or fission.
nuclear winter theoretical period of low
temperatures and little light after a nuclear war.
nucleic acid *noun* complex compound, such
as DNA or RNA, found in all living cells.
nucleonics *noun* branch of physics dealing
with the applications of nuclear energy.
nucleus ❶ *noun, pl* **-clei 1** centre, esp. of an
atom or cell. **2** central thing around which

N

———————— T H E S A U R U S ————————

nourishing *adjective* = **nutritious**, beneficial,
nutritive, wholesome
nourishment *noun* = **food**, nutriment,
nutrition, sustenance
novel[1] *noun* = **story**, fiction, narrative,
romance, tale
novel[2] *adjective* = **new**, different, fresh,
innovative, original, strange, uncommon,
unfamiliar, unusual OPPOSITE **ordinary**
novelty *noun* **1** = **newness**, freshness,
innovation, oddity, originality, strangeness,
surprise, unfamiliarity, uniqueness **2** = **gimmick**,
curiosity, gadget **3** = **knick-knack**, bauble,
memento, souvenir, trifle, trinket
novice *noun* **1** = **beginner**, amateur,

apprentice, learner, newcomer, probationer,
pupil, trainee OPPOSITE **expert**
now *adverb* **1** = **nowadays**, any more, at the
moment **2** = **immediately**, at once, instantly,
promptly, straightaway **now and again** *or*
then = **occasionally**, from time to time,
infrequently, intermittently, on and off,
sometimes, sporadically
nowadays *adverb* = **now**, any more, at the
moment, in this day and age, today
noxious *adjective* **1** = **harmful**, deadly,
destructive, foul, hurtful, injurious, poisonous,
unhealthy, unwholesome
nuance *noun* = **subtlety**, degree, distinction,
gradation, nicety, refinement, shade, tinge

others are grouped.

nude ❶ *adjective* 1 naked. ✦ *noun* 2 naked figure in painting, sculpture, or photography. **nudity** *noun* **nudism** *noun* practice of not wearing clothes. **nudist** *noun*

nudge ❶ *verb* 1 push gently, esp. with the elbow. ✦ *noun* 2 gentle push or touch.

nugatory [new-gat-tree] *adjective* 1 of little value. 2 not valid.

nugget ❶ *noun* 1 small lump of gold in its natural state. 2 something small but valuable. ✦ *verb* 3 *NZ & S Afr* polish footwear.

nuisance ❶ *noun* something or someone that causes annoyance or bother.

nuke *Slang verb* 1 attack with nuclear weapons. ✦ *noun* 2 nuclear weapon.

null ❶ *adjective* **null and void** not legally valid. **nullity** *noun* **nullify** *verb* **-fying, -fied** 1 make ineffective. 2 cancel.

numb ❶ *adjective* 1 without feeling, as through cold, shock, or fear. ✦ *verb* 2 make numb. **numbly** *adverb* **numbness** *noun*

numbskull *noun* stupid person.

number ❶ *noun* 1 sum or quantity. 2 word or symbol used to express a sum or quantity, numeral. 3 numeral or string of numerals used to identify a person or thing. 4 one of a series, such as a copy of a magazine. 5 song or piece of music. 6 group of people. 7 *Grammar* classification of words depending on how many persons or things are referred to. ✦ *verb* 8

count. 9 give a number to. 10 amount to. 11 include in a group. **numberless** *adjective* too many to be counted. **number crunching** *Computers* large-scale processing of numerical data. **number one** *noun Informal* 1 oneself. 2 bestselling pop record in any one week. ✦ *adjective* 3 first in importance or quality.

numberplate *noun* plate on a car showing the registration number.

numeral ❶ *noun* word or symbol used to express a sum or quantity.

numerate *adjective* able to do basic arithmetic. **numeracy** *noun*

numeration *noun* act or process of numbering or counting.

numerator *noun Maths* number above the line in a fraction.

numerical *adjective* measured or expressed in numbers. **numerically** *adverb*

numerology *noun* study of numbers and their supposed influence on human affairs.

numerous ❶ *adjective* existing or happening in large numbers.

numinous *adjective* 1 arousing religious or spiritual emotions. 2 mysterious or awe-inspiring.

numismatist *noun* coin collector.

numismatics *noun* study or collection of coins. **numismatic** *adjective*

numskull *noun* same as NUMBSKULL.

nun ❶ *noun* female member of a religious

———————————— T H E S A U R U S ————————————

nubile *adjective* 2 **= marriageable**, ripe (*inf*)

nucleus *noun* 2 **= centre**, basis, core, focus, heart, kernel, nub, pivot

nude *adjective* 1 **= naked**, bare, disrobed, stark-naked, stripped, unclad, unclothed, undressed, without a stitch on (*inf*) OPPOSITE dressed

nudge *verb, noun* **= push**, bump, dig, elbow, jog, poke, prod, shove, touch

nudity *noun* **= nakedness**, bareness, deshabille, nudism, undress

nugget *noun* **= lump**, chunk, clump, hunk, mass, piece

nuisance *noun* **= problem**, annoyance, bother, drag (*inf*), hassle (*inf*), inconvenience, irritation, pain in the neck, pest, trouble OPPOSITE benefit

null *adjective* **null and void = invalid**, inoperative, useless, valueless, void, worthless

nullify *verb* **= invalidate**, counteract, negate, neutralize, obviate, render null and void OPPOSITE authorize **= cancel**, veto

nullity *noun* **= nonexistence**, invalidity, powerlessness, uselessness, worthlessness

numb *adjective* 1 **= unfeeling**, benumbed, dead, deadened, frozen, immobilized, insensitive, paralysed, torpid OPPOSITE feeling ✦*verb* 2 **= deaden**, benumb, dull, freeze, immobilize, paralyse

number *noun* 1 **= quantity**, aggregate, amount, collection OPPOSITE want. 2 **= numeral**, character, digit, figure, integer 4 **= issue**, copy, edition, imprint, printing 6 **= throng**, collection, crowd, horde, multitude ✦*verb* 8 **= calculate**, account, add, compute, count, enumerate, include, reckon, total OPPOSITE guess

numberless *adjective* **= infinite**, countless, endless, innumerable, multitudinous, myriad, unnumbered, untold

numbness *noun* **= deadness**, dullness, insensitivity, paralysis, torpor

numbskull *noun* **= fool**, blockhead, clot (*Brit inf*), dolt, dummy (*sl*), dunce, oaf, twit (*inf*)

numeral *noun* **= number**, digit, figure, integer

numerous *adjective* **= many**, abundant, copious, plentiful, profuse, several, thick on the ground

N

order. **nunnery** *noun, pl* **-neries** convent.
nuncio ❶ *noun, pl* **-cios** *RC Church* pope's
ambassador.
nuptial ❶ *adjective* relating to marriage.
nuptials *plural noun* wedding.
nurse ❶ *noun* **1** person employed to look after
sick people, usu. in a hospital. **2** (also
nursemaid, nursery nurse) woman employed
to look after children. ◆ *verb* **3** look after (a sick
person). **4** breast-feed (a baby). **5** try to cure
(an ailment). **6** harbour or foster (a feeling).
nursing home private hospital or home for old
people. **nursing officer** administrative head of
the nursing staff of a hospital.
nursery ❶ *noun, pl* **-ries 1** room where
children sleep or play. **2** place where children
are taken care of while their parents are at
work. **3** place where plants are grown for sale.
nurseryman *noun* person who raises plants for
sale. **nursery rhyme** short traditional verse or
song for children. **nursery school** school for
children from 3 to 5 years old. **nursery slopes**
gentle ski slopes for beginners.
nurture ❶ *noun* **1** act or process of promoting
the development of a child or young plant. ◆
verb **2** promote or encourage the development
of.
nut ❶ *noun* **1** fruit consisting of a hard shell
and a kernel. **2** small piece of metal that screws
onto a bolt. **3** (also **nutcase**) *Slang* insane or
eccentric person. **4** *Slang* head. **nuts** *adjective*
Slang insane or eccentric. **nuts and bolts**
Informal essential or practical details. **nutshell**
noun **in a nutshell** in essence, briefly. **nutty**
adjective **-tier, -tiest 1** containing or

resembling nuts. **2** *Slang* insane or eccentric.
nutter *noun Slang* insane person. **nutcracker**
noun device for cracking the shells of nuts.
nuthatch *noun* small songbird. **nutmeg** *noun*
spice made from the seed of a tropical tree.
nutria [new-tree-a] *noun* fur of the coypu.
nutrient [new-tree-ent] *noun* substance that
provides nourishment.
nutriment [new-tree-ment] *noun* food or
nourishment required by all living things to
grow and stay healthy.
nutrition ❶ [new-trish-shun] *noun* **1** process
of taking in and absorbing nutrients. **2** process
of being nourished. **3** study of nutrition.
nutritional *adjective* **nutritious, nutritive**
adjective nourishing.
nuzzle ❶ *verb* push or rub gently with the
nose or snout.
NV Nevada.
NW northwest(ern).
NWT Northwest Territories.
NY New York.
nylon *noun* **1** synthetic material used for
clothing etc. ◆ *plural* **2** stockings made of
nylon.
nymph ❶ *noun* **1** mythical spirit of nature,
represented as a beautiful young woman. **2**
larva of certain insects, resembling the adult
form.
nymphet *noun* sexually precocious young girl.
nymphomaniac *noun* woman with an
abnormally intense sexual desire.
nymphomania *noun* abnormally intense sexual
desire in women.
NZ New Zealand.

—————————————— THESAURUS ——————————————

nuncio *noun RC Church* =**ambassador**, envoy,
legate, messenger
nunnery *noun* =**convent**, abbey, cloister, house
nuptial *adjective* =**marital**, bridal, conjugal,
connubial, matrimonial
nuptials *plural noun* =**wedding**, marriage,
matrimony
nurse *verb* **3** = **look after**, care for, minister to,
tend, treat **4** = **breast-feed**, feed, nourish,
nurture, suckle, wet-nurse **6** = **foster**, cherish,
cultivate, encourage, harbour, preserve,
promote, succour, support
nursery *noun* **2** = **crèche**, kindergarten,
playgroup
nurture *noun* **1** = **development**, discipline,

education, instruction, rearing, training,
upbringing ◆*verb* **2** = **develop**, bring up,
discipline, educate, instruct, rear, school, train
OPPOSITE ignore
nut *noun* **3** (also **nutcase**) *Sl* = **madman**, crank
(*inf*), lunatic, maniac, nutcase (*sl*), psycho (*sl*) **4**
Sl = **head**, brain, mind, reason, senses
nutrition *noun* **1, 2** = **food**, nourishment,
nutriment, sustenance
nutritious *adjective* = **nourishing**, beneficial,
health-giving, invigorating, nutritive,
strengthening, wholesome
nuzzle *verb* = **snuggle**, burrow, cuddle, fondle,
nestle, pet
nymph *noun* **1** = **sylph**, dryad, naiad

N

Oo

O¹ 1 *Chem* oxygen. **2** Old. **3** same as NOUGHT (sense 1).

O² *interjection* same as OH.

o' *preposition Informal* of, e.g. *a cup o' tea.*

oaf ⊙ *noun* stupid or clumsy person. **oafish** *adjective*

oak *noun* **1** deciduous forest tree. **2** its wood, used for furniture. **oaken** *adjective* **oak apple** brownish lump found on oak trees.

oakum *noun* fibre obtained by unravelling old rope.

OAP old-age pensioner.

oar *noun* pole with a broad blade, used for rowing a boat. **oarsman, oarswoman** *noun*

oasis *noun, pl* **-ses** fertile area in a desert.

oast *noun* oven for drying hops. **oast house** building containing oasts.

oat *noun* **1** hard cereal grown as food. ♦ *plural* **2** grain of this cereal. **sow one's wild oats** have many sexual relationships when young. **oaten** *adjective* **oatcake** *noun* thin flat biscuit of oatmeal. **oatmeal** *noun* **1** coarse flour made from oats. ♦ *adjective* **2** pale brownish-cream.

oath ⊙ *noun* **1** solemn promise, esp. to be truthful in court. **2** swearword.

obbligato [ob-lig-**gah**-toe] *noun, pl* **-tos** *Music* essential part or accompaniment.

obdurate ⊙ *adjective* hardhearted or stubborn. **obduracy** *noun*

OBE Officer of the Order of the British Empire.

obedient ⊙ *adjective* obeying or willing to obey. **obedience** *noun* **obediently** *adverb*

obeisance [oh-**bay**-sanss] *noun* **1** attitude of respect. **2** bow or curtsy.

obelisk ⊙ [**ob**-bill-isk] *noun* four-sided stone column tapering to a pyramid at the top.

obese ⊙ [oh-**beess**] *adjective* very fat. **obesity** *noun*

obey ⊙ *verb* carry out instructions or orders.

obfuscate ⊙ *verb* make (something) confusing. **obfuscation** *noun*

obituary *noun, pl* **-aries** announcement of someone's death, esp. in a newspaper. **obituarist** *noun*

object¹ ⊙ *noun* **1** physical thing. **2** focus of thoughts or action. **3** aim or purpose. **4** *Grammar* word that a verb or preposition affects. **no object** not a hindrance.

object² ⊙ *verb* express disapproval. **objection** *noun* **objectionable** *adjective* unpleasant. **objector** *noun*

objective ⊙ *noun* **1** aim or purpose. ♦

THESAURUS

oaf *noun* =**dolt**, blockhead, clod, dunce, fool, goon, idiot, lout, moron, numbskull *or* numskull

oafish *adjective* =**stupid**, dense, dim-witted (*inf*), doltish, dumb (*inf*), loutish, moronic, thick

oath *noun* **1** =**promise**, affirmation, avowal, bond, pledge, vow, word **2** =**swearword**, blasphemy, curse, expletive, profanity

obdurate *adjective* =**stubborn**, dogged, hard-hearted, immovable, implacable, inflexible, obstinate, pig-headed, unyielding

obedience *noun* =**submissiveness**, acquiescence, compliance, docility, observance, respect, reverence, subservience

obedient *adjective* =**submissive**, acquiescent, biddable, compliant, deferential, docile, dutiful, respectful, subservient, well-trained

obelisk *noun* =**column**, monolith, monument, needle, pillar, shaft

obese *adjective* =**fat**, corpulent, gross, heavy, overweight, paunchy, plump, portly, rotund, stout, tubby OPPOSITE **thin**

obesity *noun* =**fatness**, bulk, corpulence, grossness, portliness, stoutness, tubbiness

obey *verb* =**carry out**, abide by, act upon, adhere to, comply, conform, follow, heed, keep, observe OPPOSITE **disobey**

obfuscate *verb* =**confuse**, befog, cloud, darken, muddy the waters, obscure, perplex

object¹ *noun* **1** =**thing**, article, body, entity, item, phenomenon **2** =**target**, focus, recipient, victim **3** =**purpose**, aim, design, end, goal, idea, intention, objective, point

object² *verb* =**protest**, argue against, demur, draw the line (at something), expostulate, oppose, take exception OPPOSITE **accept**

objection *noun* =**protest**, counter-argument, demur, doubt, opposition, remonstrance, scruple

objectionable *adjective* =**unpleasant**, deplorable, disagreeable, intolerable,

adjective **2** not biased. **3** existing in the real world outside the human mind. **objectively** *adverb* **objectivity** *noun*
objet d'art [ob-zhay **dahr**] *noun, pl* **objets d'art** small object of artistic value.
oblation *noun* religious offering.
oblige ⊕ *verb* **1** compel (someone) morally or by law to do something. **2** do a favour for (someone). **obliging** *adjective* ready to help other people. **obligingly** *adverb* **obligated** *adjective* obliged to do something. **obligation** *noun* **1** duty. **2** indebtedness for a favour.
obligatory *adjective* required by a rule or law.
oblique ⊕ [oh-**bleak**] *adjective* **1** slanting. **2** indirect. ◆ *noun* **3** the symbol (/). **obliquely** *adverb* **oblique angle** angle that is not a right angle.
obliterate ⊕ *verb* wipe out, destroy.

obliteration *noun*
oblivious ⊕ *adjective* unaware. **oblivion** *noun* **1** state of being forgotten. **2** state of being unaware or unconscious.
oblong *adjective* **1** having two long sides, two short sides, and four right angles. ◆ *noun* **2** oblong figure.
obloquy ⊕ [ob-**lock**-wee] *noun, pl* **-quies 1** verbal abuse. **2** discredit.
obnoxious ⊕ *adjective* offensive.
obnoxiousness *noun*
oboe *noun* double-reeded woodwind instrument. **oboist** *noun*
obscene ⊕ *adjective* **1** portraying sex offensively. **2** disgusting. **obscenity** *noun*
obscure ⊕ *adjective* **1** not well known. **2** hard to understand. **3** indistinct. ◆ *verb* **4** make (something) obscure. **obscurity** *noun*

—————— T H E S A U R U S ——————

obnoxious, offensive, regrettable, repugnant, unseemly
objective *noun* **1 = purpose,** aim, ambition, end, goal, intention, mark, object, target
◆*adjective* **2 = unbiased,** detached, disinterested, dispassionate, even-handed, fair, impartial, impersonal, open-minded, unprejudiced OPPOSITE **prejudiced**
objectively *adverb* **2 = impartially,** disinterestedly, dispassionately, even-handedly, with an open mind
objectivity *noun* **2 = impartiality,** detachment, disinterestedness, dispassion
obligation *noun* **1 = duty,** accountability, burden, charge, compulsion, liability, requirement, responsibility
obligatory *adjective* **= compulsory,** de rigueur, binding, essential, imperative, mandatory, necessary, required, requisite, unavoidable OPPOSITE **voluntary**
oblige *verb* **1 = compel,** bind, constrain, force, impel, make, necessitate, require **2 = do (someone) a favour** *or* **a kindness,** accommodate, benefit, gratify, indulge, please OPPOSITE **trouble**
obliging *adjective* **= cooperative,** accommodating, agreeable, considerate, good-natured, helpful, kind, polite, willing
oblique *adjective* **1 = slanting,** angled, aslant, sloping, tilted **2 = indirect,** backhanded, circuitous, implied, roundabout, sidelong OPPOSITE **open**
obliterate *verb* **= destroy,** annihilate, blot out, efface, eradicate, erase, expunge, extirpate, root out, wipe out OPPOSITE **make**
obliteration *noun* **= annihilation,** elimination, eradication, extirpation, wiping out OPPOSITE

construction
oblivion *noun* **1 = neglect,** abeyance, disregard, forgetfulness **2 = unconsciousness,** insensibility, obliviousness, unawareness OPPOSITE **perception**
oblivious *adjective* **= unaware,** forgetful, heedless, ignorant, insensible, neglectful, negligent, regardless, unconcerned, unconscious, unmindful
obloquy *noun* **1 = abuse,** aspersion, attack, blame, censure, criticism, invective, reproach, slander, vilification **2 = disgrace,** discredit, dishonour, humiliation, ignominy, infamy, shame, stigma
obnoxious *adjective* **= offensive,** disagreeable, insufferable, loathsome, nasty, nauseating, objectionable, odious, repulsive, revolting, unpleasant OPPOSITE **seemly**
obscene *adjective* **1 = indecent,** dirty, filthy, immoral, improper, lewd, offensive, pornographic, salacious, scungy (*Aust & NZ inf*) **2 = disgusting,** atrocious, evil, heinous, loathsome, outrageous, shocking, sickening, vile, wicked OPPOSITE **seemly**
obscenity *noun* **1 = indecency,** coarseness, dirtiness, impropriety, lewdness, licentiousness, pornography, smut OPPOSITE **innocence. 2 = atrocity,** abomination, affront, blight, evil, offence, outrage, wrong
obscure *adjective* **1 = little-known,** humble, lowly, out-of-the-way, remote, undistinguished, unheard-of, unknown OPPOSITE **major. 2 = vague,** ambiguous, arcane, confusing, cryptic, enigmatic, esoteric, mysterious, opaque, recondite, unclear OPPOSITE **clear. 3 = dark,** blurred, cloudy, dim, faint, gloomy, indistinct, murky, shadowy OPPOSITE **distinct** ◆*verb* **4**

O

obsequies [ob-sick-weez] *plural noun* funeral rites.
obsequious ❶ [ob-**seek**-wee-uss] *adjective* overattentive in order to gain favour. **obsequiousness** *noun*
observe ❶ *verb* 1 see or notice. 2 watch (someone or something) carefully. 3 remark. 4 act according to (a law or custom).
observation *noun* 1 action or habit of observing. 2 remark. 3 detailed examination of something before diagnosis, or interpretation, e.g. *you may be admitted to hospital for observation.* 4 facts learned from observing. 5 ability to notice things e.g. *she has good powers of observation.* **observer** *noun* **observable** *adjective* **observance** *noun* 1 observing of a custom. 2 ritual or ceremony. **observant** *adjective* quick to notice things. **observatory** *noun* building equipped for studying the weather and the stars.
obsess ❶ *verb* preoccupy (someone)

compulsively. **obsessed** *adjective* **obsessive** *adjective* **obsession** *noun* **obsessional** *adjective*
obsidian *noun* dark glassy volcanic rock.
obsolete ❶ *adjective* no longer in use.
obsolescent *adjective* becoming obsolete. **obsolescence** *noun*
obstacle ❶ *noun* something that makes progress difficult.
obstetrics *noun* branch of medicine concerned with pregnancy and childbirth. **obstetric** *adjective* **obstetrician** *noun* doctor who specializes in obstetrics.
obstinate ❶ *adjective* 1 stubborn. 2 difficult to remove or change. **obstinately** *adverb* **obstinacy** *noun*
obstreperous ❶ *adjective* unruly, noisy.
obstruct ❶ *verb* 1 block with an obstacle. 2 make (progress) difficult. **obstruction** *noun* **obstructive** *adjective*
obtain ❶ *verb* 1 acquire intentionally. 2 be

=conceal, cover, disguise, hide, obfuscate, screen, veil OPPOSITE **show**
obscurity *noun* 1 **=insignificance**, lowliness, unimportance 3 **=darkness**, dimness, dusk, gloom, haze, shadows
obsequious *adjective* **=sycophantic**, cringing, deferential, fawning, flattering, grovelling, ingratiating, servile, submissive, unctuous
observable *adjective* 1 **=noticeable**, apparent, detectable, discernible, evident, obvious, perceptible, recognizable, visible
observance *noun* 1 **=carrying out**, compliance, fulfilment, honouring, performance OPPOSITE **neglect of**
observant *adjective* **=attentive**, alert, eagle-eyed, perceptive, quick, sharp-eyed, vigilant, watchful, wide-awake OPPOSITE **unobservant**
observation *noun* 1 **=study**, examination, inspection, monitoring, review, scrutiny, surveillance, watching 2 **=comment**, note, opinion, pronouncement, reflection, remark, thought, utterance
observe *verb* 1 **=see**, detect, discern, discover, note, notice, perceive, spot, witness 2 **=watch**, check, keep an eye on (*inf*), keep track of, look at, monitor, scrutinize, study, survey, view 3 **=remark**, comment, mention, note, opine, say, state 4 **=carry out**, abide by, adhere to, comply, conform to, follow, heed, honour, keep, obey, respect OPPOSITE **ignore**
observer *noun* 1, 2 **=spectator**, beholder, bystander, eyewitness, fly on the wall, looker-on, onlooker, viewer, watcher, witness
obsessed *adjective* **=preoccupied**,

dominated, gripped, haunted, hung up on (*sl*), infatuated, troubled
obsession *noun* **=preoccupation**, complex, fetish, fixation, hang-up (*inf*), infatuation, mania, phobia, thing (*inf*)
obsessive *adjective* **=compulsive**, besetting, consuming, gripping, haunting
obsolescent *adjective* **=becoming obsolete**, ageing, declining, dying out, on the wane, on the way out, past its prime, waning
obsolete *adjective* **=out of date**, antiquated, archaic, discarded, disused, extinct, old, old-fashioned, outmoded, passé OPPOSITE **up-to-date**
obstacle *noun* **=difficulty**, bar, barrier, block, hindrance, hitch, hurdle, impediment, obstruction, snag, stumbling block OPPOSITE **help**
obstinacy *noun* 1 **=stubbornness**, doggedness, inflexibility, intransigence, obduracy, persistence, pig-headedness, tenacity, wilfulness
obstinate *adjective* 1 **=stubborn**, determined, dogged, inflexible, intractable, intransigent, pig-headed, refractory, self-willed, strong-minded, wilful OPPOSITE **flexible**
obstreperous *adjective* **=unruly**, disorderly, loud, noisy, riotous, rowdy, turbulent, unmanageable, wild
obstruct *verb* 1 **=block**, bar, barricade 2 **=impede**, check, hamper, hinder, restrict, stop, thwart OPPOSITE **help**
obstruction *noun* 1 **=obstacle**, bar, barricade, barrier, blockage OPPOSITE **aid**. 2

customary. **obtainable** *adjective*
obtrude 𝟶 *verb* push oneself or one's ideas on others. **obtrusive** *adjective* unpleasantly noticeable. **obtrusively** *adverb*
obtuse 𝟶 *adjective* **1** mentally slow. **2** *Maths* (of an angle) between 90° and 180°. **3** not pointed. **obtuseness** *noun*
obverse *noun* **1** opposite way of looking at an idea. **2** main side of a coin or medal.
obviate 𝟶 *verb* make unnecessary.
obvious 𝟶 *adjective* easy to see or understand, evident. **obviously** *adverb*
ocarina *noun* small oval wind instrument.
occasion 𝟶 *noun* **1** time at which a particular thing happens. **2** reason, e.g. *no occasion for complaint*. **3** special event. ♦ *verb* **4** cause.
occasional *adjective* happening sometimes.
occasionally *adverb*

SPELLING TIP

The commonest misspelling of **occasion** is *occassion*, with 44 occurrences in the Bank of English. As you might expect, there are also examples of *ocasion* and *ocassion*. The correct spelling has two *c*s and one *s*.

Occident *noun Lit* the West. **Occidental** *adjective*
occiput [**ox**-sip-put] *noun Anat* back of the head or skull.
occlude *verb* **1** obstruct. **2** close off.
occlusion *noun* **occluded front** *Meteorol* front formed when a cold front overtakes a warm front and warm air rises.
occult 𝟶 *adjective* **1** relating to the supernatural. **2** beyond ordinary human understanding. **3** secret or mysterious. **the occult** knowledge or study of the supernatural.
occupant 𝟶 *noun* person occupying a specified place. **occupancy** *noun* (length of) a person's stay in a specified place.
occupation 𝟶 *noun* **1** profession. **2** activity that occupies one's time. **3** control of a country by a foreign military power. **4** being occupied.
occupational *adjective* **occupational hazard** unpleasant thing that occurs due to one's job. **occupational therapy** purposeful activities, designed to aid recovery from illness etc.
occupy 𝟶 *verb* **-pying, -pied 1** live or work in (a building). **2** take up the attention of (someone). **3** take up (space or time). **4** take possession of (a place) by force. **5** hold (an office or position). **occupant** *noun* **occupation**

——————— T H E S A U R U S ———————

= **difficulty**, hindrance, impediment
obstructive *adjective* **1** = **blocking 2**
= **unhelpful**, awkward, delaying, difficult, hindering, restrictive, stalling, uncooperative
obtain *verb* **1** = **get**, achieve, acquire, attain, earn, gain, land, procure, secure OPPOSITE lose. **2** = **exist**, be in force, be prevalent, be the case, hold, prevail
obtainable *adjective* **1** = **available**, achievable, attainable, on tap (*inf*), to be had
obtrusive *adjective* **2** = **noticeable**, blatant, obvious, prominent, protruding, protuberant, sticking out OPPOSITE hidden
obtuse *adjective* **1** = **stupid**, dense, dull, dumb (*inf*), slow, stolid, thick, uncomprehending OPPOSITE clever
obviate *verb* = **preclude**, avert, prevent, remove
obvious *adjective* = **evident**, apparent, clear, conspicuous, distinct, indisputable, manifest, noticeable, plain, self-evident, undeniable, unmistakable OPPOSITE unclear
obviously *adverb* = **clearly**, manifestly, of course, palpably, patently, plainly, undeniably, unmistakably, unquestionably, without doubt
occasion *noun* **1** = **time**, moment **2** = **reason**, call, cause, excuse, ground(s), justification,

motive, prompting, provocation **3**
= **opportunity**, chance, opening, window **4**
= **event**, affair, celebration, experience, happening, occurrence ♦ *verb* **5** = **cause**, bring about, engender, generate, give rise to, induce, inspire, lead to, produce, prompt, provoke
occasional *adjective* = **infrequent**, incidental, intermittent, irregular, odd, rare, sporadic, uncommon
occasionally *adverb* = **sometimes**, at times, from time to time, irregularly, now and again, once in a while, periodically
occult *adjective* = **supernatural**, arcane, esoteric, magical, mysterious, mystical
occupancy *noun* = **tenancy**, possession, residence, tenure, use
occupant *noun* = **inhabitant**, incumbent, indweller, inmate, lessee, occupier, resident, tenant
occupation *noun* **1** = **profession**, business, calling, employment, job, line (of work), pursuit, trade, vocation, walk of life **3**
= **invasion**, conquest, seizure, subjugation
occupied *adjective* **1** = **inhabited**, lived-in, peopled, settled, tenanted OPPOSITE empty. **2**
= **busy**, employed, engaged, working **3** = **in use**, engaged, full, taken, unavailable

O

noun profession. **occupier** noun
occur ⊙ verb **-curring, -curred 1** happen. **2** exist. **occur to** come to the mind of.
occurrence noun **1** something that occurs. **2** fact of occurring.

> **SPELLING TIP**
>
> Rather surprisingly, there are no examples in the Bank of English where **occurrence** has been spelt with only one c. However, there are 85 examples of occurence, with only one r, as opposed to 2013 instances where the word is spelt correctly: **occurrence**.

ocean noun **1** vast area of sea between continents. **2** large quantity or expanse.
oceanic adjective **oceanography** noun scientific study of the oceans. **oceanographer** noun **ocean-going** adjective able to sail on the open sea.
ocelot [**oss**-ill-lot] noun American wild cat with a spotted coat.
oche [**ok**-kee] noun Darts mark on the floor behind which a player must stand.
ochre [**oak**-er] adjective, noun brownish-yellow (earth).
o'clock adverb used after a number to specify an hour.
Oct. October.
octagon noun geometric figure with eight sides. **octagonal** adjective

octahedron [ok-ta-**heed**-ron] noun, pl **-drons, -dra** three-dimensional geometric figure with eight faces.
octane noun hydrocarbon found in petrol.
octane rating measure of petrol quality.
octave noun Music (interval between the first and) eighth note of a scale.
octavo noun, pl **-vos** book size in which the sheets are folded into eight leaves.
octet noun **1** group of eight performers. **2** music for such a group.
October noun tenth month of the year.
octogenarian noun person aged between eighty and eighty-nine.
octopus noun, pl **-puses** sea creature with a soft body and eight tentacles.
ocular adjective relating to the eyes or sight.
OD Informal noun **1** overdose. ♦ verb **OD'ing, OD'd 2** take an overdose.
odd ⊙ adjective **1** unusual. **2** occasional. **3** leftover or additional. **4** not divisible by two. **5** not part of a set. **odds** plural noun **1** (ratio showing) the probability of something happening. **2** likelihood. **at odds** in conflict.
odds and ends small miscellaneous items.
oddity noun odd person or thing. **oddly** adverb **oddness** noun quality of being odd.
oddball noun Informal eccentric person.
oddments plural noun things left over.
ode noun lyric poem, usu. addressed to a particular subject.
odium ⊙ [**oh**-dee-um] noun widespread dislike. **odious** adjective offensive.
odour ⊙ noun particular smell. **odorous** adjective **odourless** adjective

O

——————— THESAURUS ———————

occupy verb **1 = live in,** dwell in, inhabit, own, possess, reside in OPPOSITE **abandon. 2 = take up,** divert, employ, engage, engross, involve, monopolize, preoccupy, tie up **3 = fill,** cover, permeate, pervade, take up **4 = invade,** capture, overrun, seize, take over OPPOSITE **withdraw**
occur verb **1 = happen,** befall, come about, crop up (inf), take place, turn up (inf) **2 = exist,** appear, be found, be present, develop, manifest itself, show itself **occur to = come to mind,** cross one's mind, dawn on, enter one's head, spring to mind, strike one, suggest itself
occurrence noun **1 = incident,** adventure, affair, circumstance, episode, event, happening, instance **2 = existence,** appearance, development, manifestation, materialization
odd adjective **1 = unusual,** bizarre, extraordinary, freakish, irregular, munted (NZ sl), peculiar, rare, remarkable, singular, strange

2 = occasional, casual, incidental, irregular, periodic, random, sundry, various OPPOSITE **regular. 3 = spare,** leftover, remaining, solitary, surplus OPPOSITE **matched. 5 = unmatched,** unpaired
oddity noun **a = misfit,** crank (inf), maverick, oddball (inf) **b = irregularity,** abnormality, anomaly, eccentricity, freak, idiosyncrasy, peculiarity, quirk
oddments plural noun **= leftovers,** bits, fag ends, fragments, offcuts, remnants, scraps, snippets
odds plural noun **1 = probability 2 = chances,** likelihood **at odds = in conflict,** at daggers drawn, at loggerheads, at sixes and sevens, at variance, out of line
odds and ends plural noun **= scraps,** bits, bits and pieces, debris, oddments, remnants
odious adjective **= offensive,** detestable, horrid, loathsome, obnoxious, repulsive,

odyssey [**odd**-iss-ee] *noun* long eventful journey.

OECD Organization for Economic Cooperation and Development.

oedema [id-**deem**-a] *noun, pl* -**mata** *Med* abnormal swelling.

o'er *preposition, adverb Poetic* over.

oesophagus [ee-**soff**-a-guss] *noun, pl* -**gi** passage between the mouth and stomach.

oestrogen [**ee**-stra-jen] *noun* female hormone that controls the reproductive cycle.

of *preposition* **1** belonging to. **2** consisting of. **3** connected with. **4** characteristic of.

off ❶ *preposition* **1** away from. ◆ *adverb* **2** away. **3** so as to stop or disengage. ◆ *adjective* **4** not operating. **5** cancelled. **6** not up to the usual standard. **7** (of food) gone bad. ◆ *noun* **8** *Cricket* side of the field to which the batsman's feet point. **offbeat** *adjective* unusual or eccentric. **off chance** slight possibility. **off colour** slightly ill. **off-line** *adjective* (of a computer) not directly controlled by a central processor. **off-message** *adjective* (esp. of a politician) not following the official Party line. **off-putting** *adjective* rather unpleasant or disturbing.

offal *noun* edible organs of an animal, such as liver or kidneys.

offcut *noun* piece remaining after the required parts have been cut out.

offend ❶ *verb* **1** hurt the feelings of, insult. **2** disgust. **3** commit a crime. **offender** *noun*

offence *noun* **1** (cause of) hurt feelings or annoyance. **2** illegal act. **offensive** *adjective* **1** disagreeable. **2** insulting. **3** aggressive. ◆ *noun* **4** position or action of attack.

offer ❶ *verb* **1** present (something) for acceptance or rejection. **2** provide. **3** be willing (to do something). **4** present for sale. **5** propose as payment. ◆ *noun* **6** something offered. **7** instance of offering something.

offering *noun* thing offered. **offertory** *noun* *Christianity* **1** offering of the bread and wine for Communion. **2** collection of money at Communion.

offhand ❶ *adjective* **1** (also **offhanded**) casual, curt. ◆ *adverb* **2** without preparation.

office ❶ *noun* **1** room or building where people work at desks. **2** department of a commercial organization. **3** formal position of responsibility. **4** place where tickets or information can be obtained. **5** religious ceremony. **officer** *noun* **1** person in authority in the armed services. **2** member of the police force. **3** person with special responsibility in an organization.

——————— THESAURUS ———————

revolting, unpleasant

odour *noun* =**smell**, aroma, bouquet, essence, fragrance, perfume, redolence, scent, stench, stink

odyssey *noun* =**journey**, crusade, pilgrimage, quest, trek, voyage

off *adverb* **2** =**away**, apart, aside, elsewhere, out ◆*adjective* **5** =**cancelled**, finished, gone, postponed, unavailable **7** =**bad**, mouldy, rancid, rotten, sour, turned

offbeat *adjective* =**unusual**, eccentric, left-field (*inf*), novel, outré, strange, unconventional, unorthodox, way-out (*inf*)

off colour *adjective* =**ill**, crook (*Aust & NZ sl*), out of sorts, peaky, poorly (*inf*), queasy, run down, sick, under the weather (*inf*), unwell

offence *noun* **1 a** =**insult**, affront, hurt, indignity, injustice, outrage, slight, snub **b** =**annoyance**, anger, displeasure, indignation, pique, resentment, umbrage, wrath **2** =**crime**, fault, misdeed, misdemeanour, sin, transgression, trespass, wrongdoing

offend *verb* **1** =**insult**, affront, annoy, displease, hurt (someone's) feelings, outrage, slight, snub, upset, wound OPPOSITE **please**

offended *adjective* **1** =**resentful**, affronted, disgruntled, displeased, outraged, piqued, put

out (*inf*), smarting, stung, upset

offender *noun* **3** =**criminal**, crook, culprit, delinquent, lawbreaker, miscreant, sinner, transgressor, villain, wrongdoer

offensive *adjective* **1** =**disgusting**, disagreeable, nauseating, obnoxious, odious, repellent, revolting, unpleasant, vile OPPOSITE **attractive**. **2** =**insulting**, abusive, discourteous, disrespectful, impertinent, insolent, objectionable, rude OPPOSITE **civil**. **3** =**attacking**, aggressive, invading OPPOSITE **defensive** ◆*noun* **4** =**attack**, campaign, drive, onslaught, push (*inf*)

offer *verb* **1** =**propose**, advance, submit, suggest **2** =**provide**, afford, furnish, present OPPOSITE **refuse**. **3** =**volunteer**, come forward, offer one's services **5** =**proffer**, bid, tender ◆*noun* **6** =**proposal**, bid, tender **7** =**suggestion**, proposition, submission

offering *noun* =**contribution**, donation, gift, hand-out, present, sacrifice, subscription

offhand *adjective* **1** (also **offhanded**) =**casual**, aloof, brusque, careless, curt, glib OPPOSITE **serious** ◆*adverb* **2** =**impromptu**, ad lib, extempore, off the cuff (*inf*)

office *noun* **3** =**post**, function, occupation, place, responsibility, role, situation

O

official ⓐ *adjective* **1** of a position of authority. **2** approved or arranged by someone in authority. **3** formal. ◆ *noun* **4** person who holds a position of authority. **officially** *adverb*
officialdom *noun* officials collectively. **Official Receiver** person who deals with the affairs of a bankrupt company.
officiate ⓐ *verb* act in an official role.
officious ⓐ *adjective* interfering unnecessarily.
offing ⓐ *noun* area of the sea visible from the shore. **in the offing** likely to happen soon.
off-licence *noun* shop licensed to sell alcohol for drinking elsewhere.
off-load *verb* get rid of (something).
offset ⓐ *verb* cancel out, compensate for.
offshoot ⓐ *noun* **1** something developed from something else. **2** shoot growing on the main stem of a plant.
offside *adjective, adverb Sport* (positioned) illegally ahead of the ball.
offspring ⓐ *noun, pl* **offspring** child.
often ⓐ *adverb* frequently, much of the time.
oft *adverb Poetic* often.
ogle ⓐ *verb* stare at (someone) lustfully.
ogre ⓐ *noun* **1** giant that eats human flesh. **2** monstrous or cruel person.
oh *interjection* exclamation of surprise, pain, etc.
OH Ohio.
ohm *noun* unit of electrical resistance.
OHMS On Her *or* His Majesty's Service.

oil ⓐ *noun* **1** viscous liquid, insoluble in water and usu. flammable. **2** same as PETROLEUM. **3** petroleum derivative, used as a fuel or lubricant. ◆ *plural* **4** oil-based paints used in art. ◆ *verb* **5** lubricate (a machine) with oil. **oily** *adjective* **oilcloth** *noun* waterproof material. **oilfield** *noun* area containing oil reserves. **oil rig** platform constructed for drilling oil wells. **oilskin** *noun* (garment made from) waterproof material. **oil well** well bored into the earth or sea bed to a supply of oil.
ointment ⓐ *noun* greasy substance used for healing skin or as a cosmetic.
OK Oklahoma.
O.K., okay *Informal interjection* **1** expression of approval. ◆ *adjective, adverb* **2** in satisfactory condition. ◆ *verb* **3** approve (something). ◆ *noun* **4** approval.
okapi [ok-**kah**-pee] *noun* African animal related to the giraffe but with a shorter neck.
okra *noun* tropical plant with edible green pods.
old ⓐ *adjective* **1** having lived or existed for a long time. **2** of a specified age, e.g. *two years old*. **3** former. **olden** *adjective* old, e.g. *in the olden days*. **oldie** *noun Informal* old but popular song or film. **old age pensioner** retired person receiving an allowance from the government. **old boy, girl** former pupil of a school. **old-fashioned** *adjective* no longer commonly used or valued. **old guard** group of people in an

O

—————————— THESAURUS ——————————

officer *noun* **3** = **official**, agent, appointee, executive, functionary, office-holder, representative
official *adjective* **2** = **authorized**, accredited, authentic, certified, legitimate, licensed, sanctioned OPPOSITE **unofficial**. **3** = **formal**, proper ◆*noun* **4** = **officer**, agent, bureaucrat, executive, functionary, office bearer, representative
officiate *verb* = **preside**, chair, conduct, manage, oversee, serve, superintend
officious *adjective* = **interfering**, dictatorial, intrusive, meddlesome, obtrusive, overzealous, pushy (*inf*), self-important
offing *noun* **in the offing** = **imminent**, in prospect, on the horizon, upcoming
off-putting *adjective* = **discouraging**, daunting, disconcerting, dispiriting, disturbing, formidable, intimidating, unnerving, unsettling
offset *verb* = **cancel out**, balance out, compensate for, counteract, counterbalance, make up for, neutralize
offshoot *noun* **1** = **by-product**, adjunct, appendage, development, spin-off

offspring *noun* **a** = **child**, descendant, heir, scion, successor OPPOSITE **parent** ◆*plural noun* **b** = **children**, brood, descendants, family, heirs, issue, progeny, young
often *adverb* = **frequently**, generally, repeatedly, time and again OPPOSITE **never**
ogle *verb* = **leer**, eye up (*inf*)
ogre *noun* **1** = **giant** **2** = **monster**, bogeyman, bugbear, demon, devil, spectre
oil *verb* **5** = **lubricate**, grease
oily *adjective* = **greasy**, fatty, oleaginous
ointment *noun* = **lotion**, balm, cream, embrocation, emollient, liniment, salve, unguent
O.K., okay *Inf interjection* **1** = **all right**, agreed, right, roger, very good, very well, ya (*S Afr*), yebo (*S Afr inf*), yes ◆*adjective, adverb* **2** = **fine**, acceptable, adequate, all right, good, in order, permitted, satisfactory, up to scratch (*inf*) OPPOSITE **unacceptable** ◆*verb* **3** = **approve**, agree to, authorize, endorse, give the green light, rubber-stamp (*inf*), sanction ◆*noun* **4** = **approval**, agreement, assent, authorization, consent, go-ahead (*inf*), green light, permission,

organization who have traditional values. **old hand** skilled and experienced person. **old hat** boring because so familiar. **old maid** elderly unmarried woman. **old master** European painter or painting from the period 1500-1800. **Old Nick** *Informal* the Devil. **old school tie** system of mutual help between former pupils of public schools. **Old Testament** part of the Bible recording Hebrew history. **Old World** world as it was known before the discovery of the Americas.

oleaginous [ol-lee-**aj**-in-uss] *adjective* oily, producing oil.

oleander [ol-lee-**ann**-der] *noun* Mediterranean flowering evergreen shrub.

olfactory *adjective* relating to the sense of smell.

oligarchy [**ol**-lee-gark-ee] *noun, pl* **-chies 1** government by a small group of people. **2** state governed this way. **oligarchic, oligarchical** *adjective*

olive *noun* **1** small green or black fruit used as food or pressed for its oil. **2** tree on which this fruit grows. ◆ *adjective* **3** greyish-green. **olive branch** peace offering.

Olympic Games *plural noun* four-yearly international sports competition. **Olympic** *adjective*

OM Order of Merit.

ombudsman *noun* official who investigates complaints against government organizations.

omega *noun* last letter in the Greek alphabet.

omelette *noun* dish of eggs beaten and fried.

> **SPELLING TIP**
>
> You don't hear it in the pronunciation, but there is an *e* after the *m* in **omelette**.

omen ① *noun* happening or object thought to foretell success or misfortune. **ominous**

adjective worrying, seeming to foretell misfortune.

omit ① *verb* **omitting, omitted 1** leave out. **2** neglect (to do something). **omission** *noun* **1** something that has been left out or passed over. **2** an act of missing out or failing to do something, e.g. *we regret the omission of these and the names of other fine artists.*

omnibus *noun* **1** several books or TV or radio programmes made into one. **2** *Old-fashioned* bus.

omnipotent ① [om-**nip**-a-tent] *adjective* having unlimited power. **omnipotence** *noun*

omnipresent *adjective* present everywhere. **omnipresence** *noun*

omniscient ① [om-**niss**-ee-ent] *adjective* knowing or seeming to know everything. **omniscience** *noun*

omnivorous [om-**niv**-vor-uss] *adjective* **1** eating food obtained from both animals and plants. **2** taking in everything indiscriminately. **omnivore** *noun* animal that eats any type of food.

on *preposition* **1** indicating position above, attachment, closeness, etc., e.g. *lying on the ground; a puppet on a string; on the coast.* ◆ *adverb* **2** in operation. **3** attached to or in contact with. **4** continuing. **5** forwards. ◆ *adjective* **6** operating. **7** taking place. ◆ *noun* **8** *Cricket* side of the field on which the batsman stands. **on line, online** *adjective* **1** (of a computer) directly controlled by a central processor. **2** relating to the Internet, e.g. *online shopping.* **on-message** *adjective* (esp. of a politician) following the official Party line.

ON Ontario.

ONC Ordinary National Certificate.

once ① *adverb* **1** on one occasion. **2** formerly. ◆ *conjunction* **3** as soon as. ◆ *noun* **4** one occasion. **at once 1** immediately. **2** simultaneously. **once-over** *noun Informal* quick examination.

O

————————————————— THESAURUS —————————————————

sanction, say-so (*inf*), seal of approval

old *adjective* **1** = **aged**, ancient, antediluvian, antiquated, antique, decrepit, elderly, mature, senile, timeworn, venerable OPPOSITE young. **3** = **former**, earlier, erstwhile, one-time, previous

old-fashioned *adjective* = **out of date**, behind the times, dated, obsolescent, obsolete, old hat, outdated, outmoded, passé, unfashionable OPPOSITE current

omen *noun* = **sign**, foreboding, indication, portent, premonition, presage, warning

ominous *adjective* = **threatening**, fateful, foreboding, inauspicious, portentous, sinister,

unpromising, unpropitious

omission *noun* = **exclusion**, failure, lack, neglect, oversight

omit *verb* **1** = **leave out**, drop, eliminate, exclude, pass over, skip OPPOSITE include. **2** = **forget**, neglect, overlook

omnipotence *noun* = **supremacy**, invincibility, mastery

omnipotent *adjective* = **almighty**, all-powerful, supreme OPPOSITE powerless

omniscient *adjective* = **all-knowing**, all-wise

once *adverb* **2** = **at one time**, formerly, long ago, once upon a time, previously **at once 1**

oncogene [on-koh-jean] *noun* gene that can cause cancer when abnormally activated.
oncoming ❶ *adjective* approaching from the front.
OND Ordinary National Diploma.
one ❶ *adjective* **1** single, lone. **2** only. ◆ *noun* **3** number or figure 1. **4** single unit. ◆ *pronoun* **5** any person. **oneness** *noun* unity. **oneself** *pronoun* reflexive form of ONE. **one-armed bandit** fruit machine operated by a lever on one side. **one-liner** *noun* witty remark. **one-night stand** sexual encounter lasting one night. **one-sided** *adjective* considering only one point of view. **one-way** *adjective* allowing movement in one direction only.
onerous ❶ [own-er-uss] *adjective* (of a task) difficult to carry out.
ongoing ❶ *adjective* in progress, continuing.
onion *noun* strongly flavoured edible bulb.
onlooker ❶ *noun* person who watches without taking part.
only ❶ *adjective* **1** alone of its kind. ◆ *adverb* **2** exclusively. **3** merely. **4** no more than. ◆ *conjunction* **5** but.

> **LANGUAGE TIP**
>
> The use of *only* to connect sentences is rather informal: *I would come only I'm busy.* In formal use *only* is placed directly before the words it modifies: *The club opens only on Thursdays* but in everyday use this becomes: *The club only opens on Thursdays.*

o.n.o. or near(est) offer.
onomatopoeia [on-a-mat-a-pee-a] *noun* use of a word which imitates the sound it represents, such as *hiss*. **onomatopoeic** *adjective*
onset ❶ *noun* beginning.
onslaught ❶ *noun* violent attack.
onto *preposition* **1** to a position on. **2** aware of, e.g. *she's onto us.*
ontology *noun* branch of philosophy concerned with existence. **ontological** *adjective*
onus ❶ [own-uss] *noun, pl* **onuses** responsibility or burden.
onward ❶ *adjective* **1** directed or moving forward. ◆ *adverb* **2** (also **onwards**) ahead, forward.
onyx *noun* type of quartz with coloured layers.
oodles *plural noun Informal* great quantities.
oolite [oh-a-lite] *n* limestone made up of tiny grains of calcium carbonate.
oops *interjection* exclamation of surprise or apology.
ooze[1] ❶ *verb* **1** flow slowly. **2** overflow with (a quality). ◆ *noun* **3** sluggish flow. **oozy** *adjective*
ooze[2] ❶ *noun* soft mud at the bottom of a lake or river.
op *noun Informal* operation.
op. opus.
opal *noun* iridescent precious stone.
opalescent *adjective* iridescent like an opal.
opaque ❶ *adjective* **1** not able to be seen through, not transparent. **2** hard to understand. **opacity** *noun*
op. cit. [op sit] in the work cited.
OPEC Organization of Petroleum-Exporting Countries.
open ❶ *adjective* **1** not closed. **2** not covered.

———— THESAURUS ————

=immediately, directly, forthwith, instantly, now, right away, straight away, this (very) minute **2 =simultaneously**, at the same time, together
oncoming *adjective* **=approaching**, advancing, forthcoming, looming
onerous *adjective* **=difficult**, burdensome, demanding, exacting, hard, heavy, laborious, oppressive, taxing OPPOSITE **easy**
one-sided *adjective* **=biased**, lopsided, partial, partisan, prejudiced, unfair, unjust OPPOSITE **impartial**
ongoing *adjective* **=in progress**, continuous, developing, evolving, progressing, unfinished, unfolding
onlooker *noun* **=observer**, bystander, eyewitness, looker-on, spectator, viewer, watcher, witness

only *adjective* **1 =sole**, exclusive, individual, lone, single, solitary, unique ◆*adverb* **3** **=merely**, barely, just, purely, simply
onset *noun* **=beginning**, inception, outbreak, start OPPOSITE **ending**
onslaught *noun* **=attack**, assault, blitz, charge, offensive, onrush, onset OPPOSITE **retreat**
onus *noun* **=burden**, liability, load, obligation, responsibility, task
onward *adverb* **2** (also **onwards**) **=ahead**, beyond, forth, forward, in front, on
ooze[1] *verb* **1 =seep**, drain, dribble, drip, escape, filter, leak
ooze[2] *noun* **=mud**, alluvium, mire, silt, slime, sludge
opaque *adjective* **1 =cloudy**, dim, dull, filmy, hazy, impenetrable, murky OPPOSITE **clear**

3 unfolded. **4** ready for business. **5** free from obstruction, accessible. **6** unrestricted. **7** not finalized. **8** frank. ✦ *verb* **9** (cause to) become open. **10** begin. ✦ *noun* **11** *Sport* competition which all may enter. **in the open** outdoors. **opener** *noun* tool for opening cans and bottles. **openly** *adverb* without concealment. **opening** *noun* **1** beginning. **2** opportunity. **3** hole. ✦ *adjective* **4** first. **open air** outdoors. **open-and-shut case** problem that is easily solved. **opencast mining** mining at the surface and not underground. **open day** day on which a school or college is open to the public. **open-ended** *adjective* without definite limits. **open-handed** *adjective* generous. **open-hearted** *adjective* **1** generous. **2** frank. **open-heart surgery** surgery on the heart during which the blood circulation is maintained by machine. **open house** hospitality to visitors at any time. **open letter** letter to an individual that the writer makes public in a newspaper or magazine. **open-minded** *adjective* receptive to new ideas. **open-plan** *adjective* (of a house or office) having few interior walls. **open prison** prison with minimal security. **open verdict** coroner's verdict not stating the cause of death. **opera**¹ *noun* drama in which the text is sung to an orchestral accompaniment. **operatic** *adjective* **operetta** *noun* light-hearted comic

opera. **opera glasses** small binoculars used by theatre audiences.
opera² *noun* a plural of OPUS.
operate ⊕ *verb* **1** (cause to) work. **2** direct. **3** perform an operation. **operator** *noun*
operation *noun* **1** method or procedure of working. **2** action or series of actions. **3** medical procedure in which the body is worked on to repair a damaged part. **4** military campaign.
operational *adjective* **1** in working order. **2** relating to an operation. **operative** [op-rat-tiv] *adjective* **1** working. **2** having particular significance. ✦ *noun* **3** worker with a special skill.
ophthalmic *adjective* relating to the eye.
ophthalmia *noun* inflammation of the eye.
ophthalmology *noun* study of the eye and its diseases. **ophthalmologist** *noun*
ophthalmoscope *noun* instrument for examining the interior of the eye. **ophthalmic optician** see OPTICIAN.
opiate [oh-pee-ate] *noun* **1** narcotic drug containing opium. **2** thing producing a stupefying effect.
opinion ⊕ *noun* **1** personal belief or judgment. **2** judgment given by an expert. **opinionated** *adjective* having strong opinions. **opine** *verb* *Old-fashioned* express an opinion. **opinion poll** see POLL (sense 1).

—————— THESAURUS ——————

open *adjective* **1** = **unclosed**, agape, ajar, gaping, uncovered, unfastened, unlocked, yawning OPPOSITE **closed**. **3** = **extended**, unfolded, unfurled OPPOSITE **shut**. **5** = **accessible**, available, free, public, unoccupied, vacant **6** = **unrestricted 7** = **unresolved**, arguable, debatable, moot, undecided, unsettled **8** = **frank**, candid, guileless, honest, sincere, transparent OPPOSITE **reserved** ✦*verb* **9** = **unfasten**, expand, spread (out), unblock, uncork, uncover, undo, unfold, unfurl, unlock, unroll, untie, unwrap OPPOSITE **close**. **10** = **start**, begin, commence, inaugurate, initiate, kick off (*inf*), launch, set in motion
open-handed *adjective* = **generous**, bountiful, free, lavish, liberal, munificent, unstinting
opening *noun* **1** = **beginning**, commencement, dawn, inception, initiation, launch, outset, start OPPOSITE **ending**. **2** = **opportunity**, chance, look-in (*inf*), occasion, vacancy **3** = **hole**, aperture, chink, cleft, crack, fissure, gap, orifice, perforation, slot, space OPPOSITE **seal** ✦*adjective* **4** = **first**, beginning, inaugural, initial, introductory, maiden, primary
openly *adverb* = **candidly**, forthrightly, frankly, overtly, plainly, unhesitatingly, unreservedly

OPPOSITE **privately**
open-minded *adjective* = **unprejudiced**, broad-minded, impartial, liberal, reasonable, receptive, tolerant, unbiased, undogmatic
operate *verb* **1** = **handle**, be in charge of, manage, use, work **2** = **manoeuvre 3** = **work**, act, function, go, perform, run OPPOSITE **stop**
operation *noun* **1** = **procedure**, process **2** = **action**, course, exercise, motion, movement, performance
operational *adjective* **1** = **working**, functional, going, operative, prepared, ready, up and running, usable, viable, workable
operative *adjective* **1** = **in force**, active, effective, functioning, in operation, operational OPPOSITE **powerless** ✦*noun* **3** = **worker**, artisan, employee, labourer
operator *noun* **1, 2** = **worker**, conductor, driver, handler, mechanic, operative, practitioner, technician
opinion *noun* **1** = **belief**, assessment, feeling, idea, impression, judgment, point of view, sentiment, theory, view
opinionated *adjective* = **dogmatic**, bigoted, cocksure, doctrinaire, overbearing, pig-headed, prejudiced, single-minded

O

opium [oh-pee-um] *noun* addictive narcotic drug made from poppy seeds.

opossum *noun* small marsupial of America or Australia.

opponent ❶ *noun* person one is working against in a contest, battle, or argument.

opportunity ❶ *noun, pl* **-ties 1** favourable time or condition. **2** good chance.

opportunity shop *Aust & NZ* shop selling second-hand clothes, sometimes for charity (also **op-shop**). **opportune** *adjective* happening at a suitable time. **opportunist** *noun, adjective* (person) doing whatever is advantageous without regard for principles. **opportunism** *noun*

> **SPELLING TIP**
>
> Lots of people forget that
> **opportunity**, which is a very
> common word, has two *ps*.

oppose ❶ *verb* **1** work against. **2** contrast. **be opposed to** disagree with or disapprove of.

opposite *adjective* situated on the other side.

opposition *noun* **1** obstruction or hostility. **2** group opposing another. **3** political party not in power.

opposite ❶ *adjective* **1** situated on the other side. **2** facing. **3** completely different. ♦ *noun* **4** person or thing that is opposite. ♦ *preposition* **5**

facing. ♦ *adverb* **6** on the other side.

oppress ❶ *verb* **1** control by cruelty or force. **2** depress. **oppression** *noun* **oppressor** *noun*

oppressive *adjective* **1** tyrannical. **2** depressing. **3** (of weather) hot and humid. **oppressively** *adverb*

opprobrium [op-**probe**-ree-um] *noun* state of being criticized severely for wrong one has done. **opprobrious** *adjective*

opt ❶ *verb* show a preference, choose. **opt out** *verb* choose not to be part (of).

optic *adjective* relating to the eyes or sight.

optics *noun* science of sight and light. **optical** *adjective* **optical character reader** device that electronically reads and stores text. **optical fibre** fine glass-fibre tube used to transmit information.

optician *noun* **1** (also **ophthalmic optician**) person qualified to prescribe glasses. **2** (also **dispensing optician**) person who supplies and fits glasses.

optician *noun* person who supplies and fits glasses.

optimism ❶ *noun* tendency to take the most hopeful view. **optimist** *noun* **optimistic** *adjective* **optimistically** *adverb*

optimum ❶ *noun, pl* **-ma, -mums 1** best possible conditions. ♦ *adjective* **2** most favourable. **optimal** *adjective* **optimize** *verb* make the most of.

option ❶ *noun* **1** choice. **2** thing chosen. **3**

O

———— THESAURUS ————

opponent *noun* =**adversary**, antagonist, challenger, competitor, contestant, enemy, foe, rival OPPOSITE **ally**

opportune *adjective* =**timely**, advantageous, appropriate, apt, auspicious, convenient, favourable, fitting, suitable, well-timed

opportunism *noun* =**expediency**, exploitation, pragmatism, unscrupulousness

opportunity *noun* =**chance**, moment, occasion, opening, scope, time

oppose *verb* **1** =**fight**, block, combat, counter, defy, resist, take issue with, take on, thwart, withstand OPPOSITE **support**

opposed *adjective* **1** =**against**, antagonistic, averse, clashing, conflicting, contrary, dissentient, hostile

opposing *adjective* **1** =**conflicting**, contrary, enemy, hostile, incompatible, opposite, rival

opposite *adjective* **2** =**facing**, fronting **3** =**different**, antithetical, conflicting, contrary, contrasted, reverse, unlike OPPOSITE **like** ♦*noun* **4** =**reverse**, antithesis, contradiction, contrary, converse, inverse

opposition *noun* **1** =**hostility**, antagonism,

competition, disapproval, obstruction, prevention, resistance, unfriendliness OPPOSITE **agreement. 2** =**opponent**, antagonist, competition, foe, other side, rival

oppress *verb* **1** =**subjugate**, abuse, maltreat, persecute, subdue, suppress, wrong OPPOSITE **free. 2** =**depress**, afflict, burden, dispirit, harass, sadden, torment, vex

oppressed *adjective* **1** =**downtrodden**, abused, browbeaten, disadvantaged, harassed, maltreated, tyrannized, underprivileged

oppression *noun* **1** =**subjugation**, abuse, brutality, cruelty, injury, injustice, maltreatment, persecution, subjection, tyranny

oppressive *adjective* **1** =**tyrannical**, brutal, cruel, despotic, harsh, inhuman, repressive, severe, unjust OPPOSITE **just. 3** =**stifling**, airless, close, muggy, stuffy, sultry

oppressor *noun* =**persecutor**, autocrat, bully, despot, scourge, slave-driver, tormentor, tyrant

opt *verb* =**choose**, decide (on), elect, go for, plump for, prefer OPPOSITE **reject**

optimistic *adjective* =**hopeful**, buoyant, cheerful, confident, encouraged, expectant, right to buy or sell something at a specified price within a given time. **optional** *adjective* possible but not compulsory.

optometrist [op-**tom**-met-trist] *noun* person qualified to prescribe glasses. **optometry** *noun*

opulent ❶ [**op**-pew-lent] *adjective* **1** having or indicating wealth. **2** abundant. **opulence** *noun*

opus ❶ [**oh**-puss] *noun, pl* **opuses, opera** artistic creation, esp. a musical work.

or *conjunction* used to join alternatives, e.g. *tea or coffee.*

OR Oregon.

oracle ❶ *noun* **1** shrine of an ancient god. **2** prophecy, often obscure, revealed at a shrine. **3** person believed to make infallible predictions. **4** (**O-**) ® ITV teletext service. **oracular** *adjective*

oral ❶ *adjective* **1** spoken. **2** of or for the mouth. **3** (of a drug) to be taken by mouth. ◆ *noun* **4** spoken examination. **orally** *adverb*

orange *noun* **1** reddish-yellow citrus fruit. ◆ *adjective* **2** reddish-yellow. **orangeade** *noun* orange-flavoured, usu. fizzy drink. **orangery** *noun* greenhouse for growing orange trees. **Orangeman** *noun* member of a society in Ireland for the upholding of Protestantism.

orang-utan, orang-utang *noun* large reddish-brown ape with long arms.

orator ❶ [**or**-rat-tor] *noun* skilful public speaker. **oration** *noun* formal speech.

oratorio [or-rat-**tor**-ee-oh] *noun, pl* **-rios**

musical composition for choir and orchestra, usu. with a religious theme.

oratory¹ ❶ [**or**-rat-tree] *noun* art of making speeches. **oratorical** *adjective*

oratory² *noun, pl* **-ries** small private chapel.

orb ❶ *noun* **1** ceremonial decorated sphere with a cross on top, carried by a monarch. **2** globe.

orbit ❶ *noun* **1** curved path of a planet, satellite, or spacecraft around another body. **2** sphere of influence. ◆ *verb* **orbiting, orbited 3** move in an orbit around. **4** put (a satellite or spacecraft) into orbit. **orbital** *adjective*

Orcadian *noun* **1** person from the Orkneys. ◆ *adjective* **2** of the Orkneys.

orchard *noun* area where fruit trees are grown.

orchestra ❶ *noun* **1** large group of musicians, esp. playing a variety of instruments. **2** (also **orchestra pit**) area of a theatre in front of the stage, reserved for the musicians. **orchestral** *adjective* **orchestrate** *verb* **1** arrange (music) for orchestra. **2** organize (something) to produce a particular result. **orchestration** *noun*

orchid *noun* plant with flowers that have unusual lip-shaped petals.

ordain ❶ *verb* **1** make (someone) a member of the clergy. **2** order or establish with authority.

ordeal ❶ *noun* painful or difficult experience.

order ❶ *noun* **1** instruction to be carried out.

———————— THESAURUS ————————

positive, rosy, sanguine OPPOSITE **pessimistic**

optimum *adjective* **2** = **ideal**, best, highest, optimal, peak, perfect, superlative OPPOSITE **worst**

option *noun* **1** = **choice**, alternative, preference, selection

optional *adjective* = **voluntary**, discretionary, elective, extra, open, possible

opulence *noun* **1** = **wealth**, affluence, luxuriance, luxury, plenty, prosperity, riches OPPOSITE **want**. **2** = **abundance**, copiousness, cornucopia, fullness, profusion, richness, superabundance

opulent *adjective* **1** = **rich**, affluent, lavish, luxurious, moneyed, prosperous, sumptuous, wealthy, well-off, well-to-do OPPOSITE **poor**. **2** = **abundant**, copious, lavish, luxuriant, plentiful, profuse, prolific

opus *noun* = **work**, brainchild, composition, creation, oeuvre, piece, production

oracle *noun* **2** = **prophecy**, divination, prediction, prognostication, revelation **3** = **authority**, adviser, guru, mana (*NZ*), mastermind, mentor, pundit, wizard

oral *adjective* **1** = **spoken**, verbal, vocal

oration *noun* = **speech**, address, discourse, harangue, homily, lecture

orator *noun* = **public speaker**, declaimer, lecturer, rhetorician, speaker

oratorical *adjective* = **rhetorical**, bombastic, declamatory, eloquent, grandiloquent, high-flown, sonorous

oratory¹ *noun* = **eloquence**, declamation, elocution, grandiloquence, public speaking, rhetoric, speech-making

orb *noun* **2** = **sphere**, ball, circle, globe, ring

orbit *noun* **1** = **path**, circle, course, cycle, revolution, rotation, trajectory **2** = **sphere of influence**, ambit, compass, domain, influence, range, reach, scope, sweep ◆*verb* **3** = **circle**, circumnavigate, encircle, revolve around

orchestrate *verb* **1** = **score**, arrange **2** = **organize**, arrange, coordinate, put together, set up, stage-manage

ordain *verb* **1** = **appoint**, anoint, consecrate, invest, nominate **2** = **order**, decree, demand, dictate, fix, lay down, legislate, prescribe, rule, will

ordeal *noun* = **hardship**, agony, anguish, baptism of fire, nightmare, suffering, test,

2 methodical arrangement or sequence. **3** established social system. **4** condition of a law-abiding society. **5** request for goods to be supplied. **6** goods so supplied. **7** written instruction to pay money. **8** social class. **9** group of similar plants or animals. **10** kind, sort. **11** religious society of monks or nuns. **12** group of people who have been awarded an honour. ♦ *verb* **13** give an instruction to. **14** request (something) to be supplied. **15** arrange methodically. **in order 1** appropriate or fitting. **2** so that it is possible. **orderly** *adjective* **1** well-organized. **2** well-behaved. ♦ *noun, pl* **-lies 3** male hospital attendant. **4** soldier attending an officer. **orderliness** *noun*
ordinal number *noun* number showing a position in a series, e.g. *first; second*.
ordinance *noun* official rule or order.
ordinary ❶ *adjective* **1** usual or normal. **2** dull or commonplace. **ordinarily** *adverb* **ordinary seaman** navy rank equivalent to an army private.
ordination *noun* act of making someone a member of the clergy.
ordnance *noun* weapons and military supplies. **Ordnance Survey** official organization making maps of Britain.
ordure *noun* excrement.

ore *noun* (rock containing) a mineral which yields metal.
oregano [or-rig-**gah**-no] *noun* sweet-smelling herb used in cooking.
organ ❶ *noun* **1** part of an animal or plant that has a particular function, such as the heart or lungs. **2** musical keyboard instrument in which notes are produced by forcing air through pipes. **3** means of conveying information, esp. a newspaper. **organist** *noun* organ player. **organ-grinder** *noun* formerly, a person who played a barrel organ in the streets.
organdie *noun* fine cotton fabric.
organic ❶ *adjective* **1** of or produced from animals or plants. **2** grown without artificial fertilizers or pesticides. **3** *Chem* relating to compounds of carbon. **4** (of change or development) gradual and natural. **5** organized systematically. **organically** *adverb* **organism** *noun* **1** any living animal or plant. **2** organized body or system.
organism ❶ *noun* any living animal or plant.
organize ❶ *verb* **1** make arrangements for. **2** arrange systematically. **organization** *noun* **1** group of people working together. **2** act of organizing. **3** method of arrangement. **organizational** *adjective* **organized** *adjective* **organizer** *noun*

——— T H E S A U R U S ———

torture, trial, tribulation(s) OPPOSITE **pleasure**
order *noun* **1** = **instruction**, command, decree, dictate, direction, directive, injunction, law, mandate, regulation, rule **2 a** = **sequence**, arrangement, array, grouping, layout, line-up, method, organization, pattern, progression, series, structure, system **b** = **tidiness**, neatness, orderliness, regularity, symmetry OPPOSITE **mess**. **4** = **peace**, calm, control, discipline, law, law and order, quiet, tranquillity **5** = **request**, application, booking, commission, requisition, reservation **8** = **class**, caste, grade, position, rank, status **10** = **kind**, class, family, genre, ilk, sort, type **11** = **community**, association, brotherhood, company, fraternity ♦*verb* **13** = **command**, bid, charge, decree, demand, direct, instruct, require OPPOSITE **forbid**. **14** = **request**, apply for, book, reserve, send away for **15** = **arrange**, catalogue, classify, group, marshal, organize, sort out, systematize OPPOSITE **confuse**
orderly *adjective* **1** = **well-organized**, businesslike, in order, methodical, neat, regular, scientific, shipshape, systematic, tidy OPPOSITE **disorderly**. **2** = **well-behaved**, controlled, disciplined, law-abiding, peaceable, quiet, restrained OPPOSITE **disorderly**

ordinarily *adverb* = **usually**, as a rule, commonly, customarily, generally, habitually, in general, normally
ordinary *adjective* **1** = **usual**, common, conventional, everyday, normal, regular, routine, standard, stock, typical **2** = **commonplace**, banal, humble, humdrum, modest, mundane, plain, run-of-the-mill, unremarkable, workaday OPPOSITE **special**
organ *noun* **1** = **part**, element, structure, unit **3** = **medium**, forum, mouthpiece, vehicle, voice
organic *adjective* **1** = **natural**, animate, biological, live, living **5** = **systematic**, integrated, methodical, ordered, organized, structured
organism *noun* **1** = **creature**, animal, being, body, entity **2** = **structure**
organization *noun* **1** = **group**, association, body, company, confederation, corporation, institution, outfit (*inf*), syndicate **2** = **management**, construction, coordination, direction, organizing, planning, running, structuring **3** = **structure**, arrangement, chemistry, composition, format, make-up, pattern, unity
organize *verb* **1** = **plan**, arrange, coordinate, marshal, put together, run, set up, take care of

orgasm *noun* most intense point of sexual pleasure. **orgasmic** *adjective*

orgy ❂ *noun, pl* **-gies 1** party involving promiscuous sexual activity. **2** unrestrained indulgence, e.g. *an orgy of destruction*. **orgiastic** *adjective*

oriel window *noun* upper window built out from a wall.

orient, orientate ❂ *verb* **1** position (oneself) according to one's surroundings. **2** position (a map) in relation to the points of the compass. **orientation** *noun* **orienteering** *noun* sport in which competitors hike over a course using a compass and map.

Orient *noun* **the Orient** *Lit* East Asia. **Oriental** *adjective* **1** of the Orient. **2** (**o-**) eastern. ◆ *noun* **3** person from the Orient. **Orientalist** *noun* specialist in the languages and history of the Far East.

orifice ❂ [or-rif-fiss] *noun* opening or hole.

origami [or-rig-**gah**-mee] *noun* Japanese decorative art of paper folding.

origin ❂ *noun* **1** point from which something develops. **2** ancestry. **original** *adjective* **1** first or earliest. **2** new, not copied or based on something else. **3** able to think up new ideas. ◆ *noun* **4** first version, from which others are copied. **original sin** human imperfection and mortality as a result of Adam's disobedience. **originality** *noun* **originally** *adverb* **originate** *verb* come or bring into existence. **origination** *noun* **originator** *noun*

oriole *noun* tropical or American songbird.

ormolu *noun* gold-coloured alloy used for decoration.

ornament ❂ *noun* **1** decorative object. **2** decorations collectively. **3** person regarded as an asset to a group. ◆ *verb* **4** decorate. **ornamental** *adjective* **ornamentation** *noun*

ornate ❂ *adjective* highly decorated, elaborate.

ornithology *noun* study of birds. **ornithological** *adjective* **ornithologist** *noun*

orphan *noun* **1** child whose parents are dead. ◆ *verb* **2** deprive of parents. **orphanage** *noun* children's home for orphans. **orphaned** *adjective* having no living parents.

orrery *noun, pl* **-ries** mechanical model of the solar system.

orris *noun* **1** kind of iris. **2** (also **orris root**) fragrant root used for perfume.

orthodontics *noun* branch of dentistry concerned with correcting irregular teeth. **orthodontist** *noun*

orthodox ❂ *adjective* conforming to

———————— T H E S A U R U S ————————

OPPOSITE upset. **2 = put in order**, arrange, classify, group, systematize OPPOSITE **scramble**

orgy *noun* **1 = revel**, bacchanalia, carousal, debauch, revelry, Saturnalia **2 = spree**, binge (*inf*), bout, excess, indulgence, overindulgence, splurge, surfeit

orient, orientate *verb* **1 = adjust**, acclimatize, adapt, align, familiarize **2 = get one's bearings**

orientation *noun* **1 = adjustment**, acclimatization, adaptation, assimilation, familiarization, introduction, settling in **2 = position**, bearings, direction, location

orifice *noun* **= opening**, aperture, cleft, hole, mouth, pore, rent, vent

origin *noun* **1 = root**, base, basis, derivation, foundation, fount, fountainhead, inception, launch, source, start, wellspring **2 = beginning**, birth, creation, emergence, genesis OPPOSITE **end**

original *adjective* **1 = first**, earliest, initial, introductory, opening, primary, starting OPPOSITE **last**. **2 = new**, fresh, ground-breaking, innovative, novel, seminal, unprecedented, unusual OPPOSITE **old**. **3 = creative**, fertile, imaginative, ingenious, inventive, resourceful ◆*noun* **4 = prototype**, archetype, master, model, paradigm, pattern,

precedent, standard OPPOSITE **copy**

originality *noun* **2, 3 = novelty**, creativity, freshness, imagination, ingenuity, innovation, inventiveness, newness, unorthodoxy

originally *adverb* **1 = initially**, at first, first, in the beginning, to begin with

originate *verb* **a = begin**, arise, come, derive, emerge, result, rise, spring, start, stem OPPOSITE **end**. **b = introduce**, bring about, create, formulate, generate, institute, launch, pioneer

originator *noun* **= creator**, architect, author, father *or* mother, founder, inventor, maker, pioneer

ornament *noun* **1 = decoration**, accessory, bauble, knick-knack, trinket **2 = trimming**, adornment, embellishment, festoon ◆*verb* **4 = decorate**, adorn, beautify, embellish, festoon, grace, prettify

ornamental *adjective* **1 = decorative**, attractive, beautifying, embellishing, for show, showy

ornamentation *noun* **1 = decoration**, adornment, elaboration, embellishment, embroidery, frills, ornateness

ornate *adjective* **= elaborate**, baroque, busy, decorated, fancy, florid, fussy, ornamented, overelaborate, rococo OPPOSITE **plain**

O

established views. **orthodoxy** noun **Orthodox Church** dominant Christian Church in Eastern Europe.

orthography noun correct spelling. **orthographic** adjective

orthopaedics noun branch of medicine concerned with disorders of the bones or joints. **orthopaedic** adjective

oryx noun large African antelope.

Os Chem osmium.

OS 1 Ordnance Survey. **2** outsize(d).

Oscar noun award in the form of a statuette given for achievements in films.

oscillate ⊕ [oss-ill-late] verb **1** swing back and forth. **2** waver. **3** (of an electric current) vary between values. **oscillation** noun **oscillator** noun **oscilloscope** [oss-**sill**-oh-scope] noun instrument that shows the shape of a wave on a cathode-ray tube.

osier [oh-zee-er] noun **1** willow tree. **2** willow branch used in basketwork.

osmium noun Chem heaviest known metallic element.

osmosis noun **1** movement of a liquid through a membrane from a lower to a higher concentration. **2** process of subtle influence. **osmotic** adjective

osprey noun large fish-eating bird of prey.

ossify ⊕ verb **-fying, -fied 1** (cause to) become bone, harden. **2** become inflexible. **ossification** noun

ostensible ⊕ adjective apparent, seeming. **ostensibly** adverb

ostentation ⊕ noun pretentious display. **ostentatious** adjective **ostentatiously** adverb

osteopathy noun medical treatment involving manipulation of the joints. **osteopath** noun

osteoporosis noun brittleness of the bones, caused by lack of calcium.

ostler noun Hist stableman at an inn.

ostracize ⊕ verb exclude (a person) from a group. **ostracism** noun

ostrich noun large African bird that runs fast but cannot fly.

OT Old Testament.

OTC Officers' Training Corps.

other ⊕ adjective **1** remaining in a group of which one or some have been specified. **2** different from the ones specified or understood. **3** additional. ♦ noun **4** other person or thing.

otherwise conjunction **1** or else, if not. ♦ adverb **2** differently, in another way. **3** in other respects. **otherworldly** adjective concerned with spiritual rather than practical matters.

otiose [oh-tee-oze] adjective not useful, e.g. otiose language.

otter noun small brown freshwater mammal that eats fish.

ottoman noun, pl **-mans** storage chest with a padded lid for use as a seat. **Ottoman** noun, adjective Hist (member) of the former Turkish empire.

oubliette [oo-blee-ett] noun dungeon entered only by a trapdoor.

ouch interjection exclamation of sudden pain.

ought verb used to express: **1** obligation, e.g. you ought to pay. **2** advisability, e.g. you ought to diet. **3** probability, e.g. you ought to know by then.

Ouija board noun ® lettered board on which supposed messages from the dead are spelt out.

orthodox adjective =**established**, accepted, approved, conventional, customary, official, received, traditional, well-established OPPOSITE unorthodox

orthodoxy noun =**conformity**, authority, conventionality, received wisdom, traditionalism OPPOSITE flexibility

oscillate verb **1** =**swing**, seesaw, sway, vibrate **2** =**waver**, fluctuate, vacillate, vary OPPOSITE settle

oscillation noun **1** =**swing**, variation **2** =**wavering**, fluctuation, instability, vacillation

ossify verb **2** =**harden**, solidify, stiffen

ostensible adjective =**apparent**, outward, pretended, professed, purported, seeming, so-called, superficial, supposed

ostensibly adverb =**apparently**, on the face of it, professedly, seemingly, supposedly

ostentation noun =**display**, affectation,

exhibitionism, flamboyance, flashiness, flaunting, parade, pomp, pretentiousness, show, showing off (inf)

ostentatious adjective =**pretentious**, brash, conspicuous, flamboyant, flashy, gaudy, loud, obtrusive, showy

ostracism noun =**exclusion**, banishment, exile, isolation, rejection

ostracize verb =**exclude**, banish, cast out, cold-shoulder, exile, give (someone) the cold shoulder, reject, send to Coventry, shun

other adjective **1** =**spare 2** =**different**, alternative, contrasting, dissimilar, distinct, diverse, separate, unrelated, variant **3** =**additional**, added, auxiliary, extra, further, more, supplementary

otherwise conjunction **1** =**or else**, if not, or then ♦adverb **2** =**differently**, any other way, contrarily

ounce ❶ *noun* **1** unit of weight equal to one sixteenth of a pound (28.4 grams). **2** a small amount.

our *adjective* belonging to us. **ours** *pronoun* thing(s) belonging to us. **ourselves** *pronoun* emphatic and reflexive form of WE *or* US.

ousel *noun* see DIPPER.

oust ❶ *verb* force (someone) out, expel.

out ❶ *adverb, adjective* **1** denoting movement or distance away from, a state of being used up or extinguished, public availability, etc., e.g. *oil was pouring out; turn the light out; her new book is out.* ♦ *verb* **2** *Informal* name (a public figure) as being homosexual. **out of** at or to a point outside. **out-of-date** *adjective* old-fashioned. **out-of-the-way** *adjective* remote. **outer** *adjective* **1** on the outside. **2** further from the middle. **outermost** *adjective* furthest out.

outer space space beyond the earth's atmosphere. **outing** *noun* leisure trip. **outward** *adjective* **1** apparent. **2** of the outside. **3** away from a place. ♦ *adverb* **4** (also **outwards**) away from somewhere. **outwardly** *adverb*

out- *prefix* **1** surpassing, e.g. *outlive; outdistance.* **2** outside, away, e.g. *outpatient; outgrowth.*

outback *noun* remote bush country of Australia.

outbid *verb* offer a higher price than.

outboard motor *noun* engine externally attached to the stern of a boat.

outbreak ❶ *noun* sudden occurrence (of something unpleasant).

outbuilding *noun* outhouse.

outburst ❶ *noun* **1** sudden expression of emotion. **2** sudden period of violent activity.

outcast ❶ *noun* person rejected by a particular group.

outclass ❶ *verb* surpass in quality.

outcome ❶ *noun* result.

outcrop *noun* part of a rock formation that sticks out of the earth.

outcry ❶ *noun, pl* **-cries** vehement or widespread protest.

outdated ❶ *adjective* old-fashioned.

outdo ❶ *verb* surpass in performance.

outdoors ❶ *adverb* **1** in(to) the open air. ♦ *noun* **2** the open air. **outdoor** *adjective*

outface *verb* subdue or disconcert (someone) by staring.

outfall *noun* mouth of a river or drain.

outfield *noun* Cricket area far from the pitch.

outfit ❶ *noun* **1** matching set of clothes. **2** *Informal* group of people working together. **3** kit for a job. **outfitter** *noun* Old-fashioned supplier of men's clothes.

outflank *verb* **1** get round the side of (an enemy army). **2** outdo (someone).

outgoing ❶ *adjective* **1** leaving. **2** sociable.

outgoings *plural noun* expenses.

outgrow *verb* become too large or too old for. **outgrowth** *noun* **1** natural development. **2**

ounce *noun* **2** = **shred**, atom, crumb, drop, grain, scrap, speck, trace

oust *verb* = **expel**, depose, dislodge, displace, dispossess, eject, throw out, topple, turn out, unseat

out *adjective* **1 a** = **away**, abroad, absent, elsewhere, gone, not at home, outside **b** = **extinguished**, at an end, dead, ended, exhausted, expired, finished, used up OPPOSITE **burning**

outbreak *noun* = **eruption**, burst, epidemic, explosion, flare-up, outburst, rash, upsurge

outburst *noun* **1** = **outpouring**, paroxysm, spasm, surge **2** = **outbreak**, eruption, explosion, flare-up

outcast *noun* = **pariah**, persona non grata, castaway, exile, leper, refugee, vagabond, wretch

outclass *verb* = **surpass**, eclipse, excel, leave standing (*inf*), outdo, outshine, outstrip, overshadow, run rings around (*inf*)

outcome *noun* = **result**, conclusion, consequence, end, issue, payoff (*inf*), upshot

outcry *noun* = **protest**, clamour, commotion,

complaint, hue and cry, hullaballoo, outburst, uproar

outdated *adjective* = **old-fashioned**, antiquated, archaic, obsolete, outmoded, out of date, passé, unfashionable

outdo *verb* = **surpass**, beat, best, eclipse, exceed, get the better of, outclass, outmanoeuvre, overcome, top, transcend

outdoor *adjective* = **open-air**, alfresco, out-of-door(s), outside

outer *adjective* **1** = **external**, exposed, exterior, outside, outward, surface OPPOSITE **central**. **2** = **peripheral**, outlying

outfit *noun* **1** = **costume**, clothes, ensemble, garb, get-up (*inf*), kit, suit **2** *Inf* = **group**, company, crew, organization, setup (*inf*), squad, team, unit

outgoing *adjective* **1** = **leaving**, departing, former, retiring, withdrawing OPPOSITE **arriving**. **2** = **sociable**, approachable, communicative, expansive, extrovert, friendly, gregarious, open, warm OPPOSITE **cold**

outgoings *plural noun* = **expenses**, costs, expenditure, outlay, overheads thing growing out from a main body.

outhouse *noun* building near a main building.

outlandish ⊕ *adjective* extremely unconventional.

outlast *verb* last longer than.

outlaw ⊕ *noun* **1** *Hist* criminal deprived of legal protection, bandit. ◆ *verb* **2** make illegal. **3** *Hist* make (someone) an outlaw. **outlawed** *adjective*

outlay ⊕ *noun* expenditure.

outlet ⊕ *noun* **1** means of expressing emotion. **2** market for a product. **3** place where a product is sold. **4** opening or way out.

outline ⊕ *noun* **1** short general explanation. **2** line defining the shape of something. ◆ *verb* **3** summarize. **4** show the general shape of.

outlive ⊕ *verb* **1** live longer than. **2** live through (an unpleasant experience).

outlook ⊕ *noun* **1** attitude. **2** probable outcome. **3** view.

outlying ⊕ *adjective* distant from the main area.

outmanoeuvre *verb* get an advantage over.

outmoded ⊕ *adjective* no longer fashionable or accepted.

outnumber *verb* exceed in number.

outpatient *noun* patient who does not stay in hospital overnight.

outport *noun* *Canad* isolated fishing village, esp. in Newfoundland.

outpost *noun* outlying settlement.

outpouring ⊕ *noun* **1** great amount produced very rapidly. **2** passionate outburst.

output ⊕ *noun* **1** amount produced. **2** power, voltage, or current delivered by an electrical circuit. **3** *Computers* data produced. ◆ *verb* **4** *Computers* produce (data) at the end of a process.

outrage ⊕ *noun* **1** great moral indignation. **2** gross violation of morality. ◆ *verb* **3** offend morally. **outrageous** *adjective* **1** shocking. **2** offensive. **outrageously** *adverb*

outré [oo-tray] *adjective* shockingly eccentric.

outrider *noun* motorcyclist acting as an escort.

outrigger *noun* stabilizing frame projecting from a boat.

outright ⊕ *adjective, adverb* **1** absolute(ly). **2** open(ly) and direct(ly).

outrun *verb* **1** run faster than. **2** exceed.

——————— T H E S A U R U S ———————

outing *noun* = **trip**, excursion, expedition, jaunt, spin (*inf*)

outlandish *adjective* = **strange**, bizarre, exotic, fantastic, far-out (*sl*), freakish, outré, preposterous, unheard-of, weird OPPOSITE> **normal**

outlaw *noun* **1** *Hist* = **bandit**, brigand, desperado, fugitive, highwayman, marauder, outcast, robber ◆*verb* **2** = **forbid**, ban, bar, disallow, exclude, prohibit, proscribe OPPOSITE> **legalise. 3** *Hist* = **put a price on (someone's) head**

outlay *noun* = **expenditure**, cost, expenses, investment, outgoings, spending

outlet *noun* **1** = **release**, vent **3** = **shop**, market, store **4** = **opening**, avenue, channel, duct, exit, release

outline *noun* **1** = **summary**, recapitulation, résumé, rundown, synopsis, thumbnail sketch **2** = **shape**, configuration, contour, delineation, figure, form, profile, silhouette ◆*verb* **3** = **summarize**, adumbrate **4** = **draft**, delineate, plan, rough out, sketch (in), trace

outlive *verb* **1** = **survive**, outlast

outlook *noun* **1** = **attitude**, angle, frame of mind, perspective, point of view, slant, standpoint, viewpoint **2** = **prospect**, expectations, forecast, future

outlying *adjective* = **remote**, distant, far-flung, out-of-the-way, peripheral, provincial

outmoded *adjective* = **old-fashioned**, anachronistic, antiquated, archaic, obsolete, out-of-date, outworn, passé, unfashionable OPPOSITE> **modern**

out-of-date *adjective* = **old-fashioned**, antiquated, dated, expired, invalid, lapsed, obsolete, outmoded, outworn, passé OPPOSITE> **modern**

outpouring *noun* **1** = **stream**, cascade, effusion, flow, spate, spurt, torrent

output *noun* **1** = **production**, achievement, manufacture, productivity, yield

outrage *noun* **1** = **indignation**, anger, fury, hurt, resentment, shock, wrath **2** = **violation**, abuse, affront, desecration, indignity, insult, offence, sacrilege, violence ◆*verb* **3** = **offend**, affront, incense, infuriate, madden, scandalize, shock

outrageous *adjective* **1** = **unreasonable**, exorbitant, extravagant, immoderate, preposterous, scandalous, shocking, steep (*inf*) OPPOSITE> **fair. 2** = **atrocious**, disgraceful, flagrant, heinous, iniquitous, nefarious, offensive, shocking, unspeakable, villainous, wicked OPPOSITE> **minor**

outré *adjective* = **eccentric**, bizarre, fantastic, freakish, odd, off-the-wall (*sl*), outlandish, unconventional, weird

outright *adjective* **1** = **absolute**, complete, out-and-out, perfect, thorough, thoroughgoing,

outsell verb be sold in greater quantities than.
outset ❶ noun beginning.
outshine verb surpass (someone) in excellence.
outside ❶ preposition, adjective, adverb **1** indicating movement to or position on the exterior. ◆ adjective **2** unlikely, e.g. an outside chance. **3** coming from outside. ◆ noun **4** external area or surface. **outsider** noun **1** person outside a specific group. **2** contestant thought unlikely to win.
outsize, outsized ❶ adjective larger than normal.
outskirts ❶ plural noun outer areas, esp. of a town.
outsmart verb Informal outwit.
outspan verb S Afr relax.
outspoken ❶ adjective **1** tending to say what one thinks. **2** said openly.
outstanding ❶ adjective **1** excellent. **2** still to be dealt with or paid.
outstay verb overstay.
outstretched adjective stretched out as far as possible.
outstrip ❶ verb **1** surpass. **2** go faster than.
outtake noun unreleased take from a recording session, film, or TV programme.
outvote verb defeat by getting more votes than.

outweigh ❶ verb **1** be more important, significant, or influential than. **2** be heavier than.
outwit ❶ verb **-witting, -witted** get the better of (someone) by cunning.
outworn ❶ adjective no longer in use.
ouzel [ooze-el] noun see DIPPER.
ouzo [ooze-oh] noun strong aniseed-flavoured spirit from Greece.
ova noun plural of OVUM.
oval ❶ adjective **1** egg-shaped. ◆ noun **2** anything that is oval in shape.
ovary noun, pl **-ries 1** female egg-producing organ. **2** part of a plant containing the ovules. **ovarian** adjective
ovation ❶ noun enthusiastic round of applause.
oven noun heated compartment or container for cooking or for drying or firing ceramics.
over ❶ preposition, adverb **1** indicating position on the top of, movement to the other side of, amount greater than, etc., e.g. a room over the garage; climbing over the fence; over fifty pounds. ◆ adjective **2** finished. ◆ noun **3** Cricket series of six balls bowled from one end. **overly** adverb excessively.
over- prefix **1** too much, e.g. overeat. **2** above, e.g. overlord. **3** on top, e.g. overshoe.
overact verb act in an exaggerated way.

——————— THESAURUS ———————

total, unconditional, unmitigated, unqualified **2** = **direct**, definite, flat, straightforward, unequivocal, unqualified ◆adverb **1** = **absolutely**, completely, straightforwardly, thoroughly, to the full **2** = **openly**, overtly
outset noun = **beginning**, commencement, inauguration, inception, kickoff (inf), onset, opening, start OPPOSITE finish
outside adjective **1** = **external**, exterior, extraneous, outer, outward OPPOSITE inside. **2** as in **an outside chance** = **remote**, distant, faint, marginal, slight, slim, small, unlikely ◆noun **4** = **exterior**, facade, face, front, skin, surface, topside
outsider noun **1** = **interloper**, incomer, intruder, newcomer, odd one out, stranger
outsize, outsized adjective = **extra-large**, giant, gigantic, huge, jumbo (inf), mammoth, monster, oversized OPPOSITE tiny
outskirts plural noun = **edge**, boundary, environs, periphery, suburbia, suburbs
outspoken adjective **1** = **forthright**, abrupt, blunt, explicit, frank, open, unceremonious OPPOSITE reserved. **2** = **plain-spoken**, unequivocal
outstanding adjective **1** = **excellent**,

exceptional, great, important, impressive, special, superior, superlative OPPOSITE ordinary. **2** = **unpaid**, due, payable, pending, remaining, uncollected, unsettled
outstrip verb **1** = **surpass**, better, eclipse, exceed, excel, outdo, transcend **2** = **overtake**
outweigh verb **1** = **override**, cancel (out), compensate for, eclipse, prevail over, take precedence over, tip the scales
outwit verb = **outsmart** (inf), cheat, dupe, get the better of, outfox, outmanoeuvre, outthink, put one over on (inf), swindle, take in (inf)
outworn adjective = **outdated**, antiquated, discredited, disused, hackneyed, obsolete, outmoded, out-of-date, worn-out
oval adjective **1** = **elliptical**, egg-shaped, ovoid
ovation noun = **applause**, acclaim, acclamation, big hand, cheers, clapping, plaudits, tribute OPPOSITE derision
over preposition **1 a** = **on top of**, above, on, upon **b** = **more than**, above, exceeding, in excess of ◆adverb **1 a** = **above**, aloft, on high, overhead **b** = **extra**, beyond, in addition, in excess, left over ◆adjective **2** = **finished**, bygone, closed, completed, concluded, done (with), ended, gone, past

O

overall ⊕ *adjective, adverb* **1** in total. ◆ *noun* **2** coat-shaped protective garment. ◆ *plural* **3** protective garment consisting of trousers with a jacket or bib and braces attached.
overarm *adjective, adverb* (thrown) with the arm above the shoulder.
overawe ⊕ *verb* affect (someone) with an overpowering sense of awe.
overbalance ⊕ *verb* lose balance.
overbearing ⊕ *adjective* unpleasantly forceful.
overblown ⊕ *adjective* excessive.
overboard *adverb* from a boat into the water. **go overboard** go to extremes, esp. in enthusiasm.
overcast ⊕ *adjective* (of the sky) covered by clouds.
overcharge ⊕ *verb* charge too much.
overcoat *noun* heavy coat.
overcome ⊕ *verb* **1** gain control over after an effort. **2** (of an emotion) affect strongly. **3** defeat (someone) in a conflict.
overcrowded *adjective* containing more people or things than is desirable.
overcrowding *noun*
overdo ⊕ *verb* **1** do to excess. **2** exaggerate (something). **3** cook too long. **overdo it** do something to a greater degree than is advisable.

overdose *noun* **1** excessive dose of a drug. ◆ *verb* **2** take an overdose.
overdraft *noun* **1** overdrawing. **2** amount overdrawn.
overdraw *verb* withdraw more money than is in (one's bank account). **overdrawn** *adjective* **1** having overdrawn one's account. **2** (of an account) in debit.
overdressed *adjective* dressed too elaborately or formally.
overdrive *noun* **1** very high gear in a motor vehicle. **2** state of great activity or excitement.
overdue ⊕ *adjective* still due after the time allowed.
overestimate *verb* estimate too highly.
overflow ⊕ *verb* **1** flow over. **2** be filled beyond capacity. ◆ *noun* **3** something that overflows. **4** outlet for excess liquid. **5** excess amount.
overgrown *adjective* thickly covered with plants and weeds.
overhang ⊕ *verb* **1** project beyond something. ◆ *noun* **2** overhanging part.
overhaul ⊕ *verb* **1** examine and repair. **2** overtake. ◆ *noun* **3** examination and repair.
overhead ⊕ *adverb, adjective* above one's head. **overheads** *plural noun* general cost of maintaining a business.

——————— T H E S A U R U S ———————

overall *adjective* **1** = **total**, all-embracing, blanket, complete, comprehensive, general, global, inclusive, overarching ◆*adverb* **1** = **in general**, on the whole
overawe *verb* = **intimidate**, abash, alarm, daunt, frighten, scare, terrify
overbalance *verb* = **topple over**, capsize, keel over, overturn, slip, tip over, tumble, turn turtle
overbearing *adjective* = **dictatorial**, arrogant, bossy (*inf*), domineering, haughty, high-handed, imperious, supercilious, superior OPPOSITE▷ **submissive**
overblown *adjective* = **excessive**, disproportionate, immoderate, inflated, overdone, over the top, undue
overcast *adjective* = **cloudy**, dismal, dreary, dull, grey, leaden, louring *or* lowering, murky OPPOSITE▷ **bright**
overcharge *verb* = **cheat**, diddle (*inf*), fleece, rip off (*sl*), short-change, sting (*inf*), surcharge
overcome *verb* **1** = **surmount**, master, overpower, overwhelm, prevail, subdue, subjugate, triumph over **3** = **conquer**, beat, defeat, vanquish ◆*adjective* **2** = **affected**, at a loss for words, bowled over (*inf*), overwhelmed, speechless, swept off one's feet
overdo *verb* **1** = **go overboard** (*inf*), belabour,

overindulge, overreach **2** = **exaggerate**, gild the lily, overstate OPPOSITE▷ **play down**
◆ **overdo it** = **overwork**, bite off more than one can chew, burn the candle at both ends (*inf*), overload oneself, strain *or* overstrain oneself, wear oneself out
overdone *adjective* **2** = **excessive**, exaggerated, fulsome, immoderate, inordinate, overelaborate, too much, undue, unnecessary OPPOSITE▷ **moderated**. **3** = **overcooked**, burnt, charred, dried up, spoiled
overdue *adjective* = **late**, behindhand, behind schedule, belated, owing, tardy, unpunctual OPPOSITE▷ **early**
overflow *verb* **1** = **spill**, brim over, bubble over, pour over, run over, well over ◆*noun* **5** = **surplus**, overabundance, spilling over
overhang *verb* **1** = **project**, extend, jut, loom, protrude, stick out
overhaul *verb* **1** = **check**, do up (*inf*), examine, inspect, recondition, repair, restore, service **2** = **overtake**, catch up with, get ahead of, pass ◆*noun* **3** = **checkup**, check, examination, going-over (*inf*), inspection, reconditioning, service
overhead *adverb* = **above**, aloft, in the sky, on high, skyward, up above, upward OPPOSITE▷

overhear *verb* hear (a speaker or remark) unintentionally or without the speaker's knowledge.

overjoyed ❶ *adjective* extremely pleased.

overkill *noun* treatment that is greater than required.

overland *adjective, adverb* by land.

overlap *verb* **1** share part of the same space or period of time (as). ◆ *noun* **2** area overlapping.

overlay *verb* cover with a thin layer.

overleaf *adverb* on the back of the current page.

overload *verb* **1** put too large a load on or in. ◆ *noun* **2** excessive load.

overlook ❶ *verb* **1** fail to notice. **2** ignore. **3** look at from above.

overman *verb* provide with too many staff.

overmuch *adverb, adjective* too much.

overnight *adjective, adverb* **1** (taking place) during one night. **2** (happening) very quickly.

overpower ❶ *verb* **1** subdue or overcome (someone). **2** make helpless or ineffective.

overpowering *adjective*

overrate ❶ *verb* have too high an opinion of.

overreach *verb* **overreach oneself** fail by trying to be too clever.

overreact *verb* react more strongly than is necessary.

override ❶ *verb* **1** overrule. **2** replace.

overrule ❶ *verb* **1** reverse the decision of (a person with less power). **2** reverse (someone else's decision).

overrun ❶ *verb* **1** conquer rapidly. **2** spread over (a place) rapidly. **3** extend beyond a set limit.

overseas *adverb, adjective* to, of, or from a distant country.

oversee ❶ *verb* watch over from a position of authority. **overseer** *noun*

overshadow ❶ *verb* **1** reduce the significance of (a person or thing) by comparison. **2** sadden the atmosphere of.

overshoe *noun* protective shoe worn over an ordinary shoe.

overshoot *verb* go beyond (a mark or target).

oversight ❶ *noun* mistake caused by not noticing something.

oversleep *verb* sleep beyond the intended time.

overspill *noun* rehousing of people from crowded cities in smaller towns.

overstate *verb* state too strongly. **overstatement** *noun*

overstay *verb* **overstay one's welcome** stay longer than one's host or hostess would like.

overstep *verb* go beyond (a certain limit).

overt ❶ *adjective* open, not hidden. **overtly** *adverb*

overtake ❶ *verb* **1** move past (a vehicle or person) travelling in the same direction. **2** come upon suddenly or unexpectedly.

overtax *verb* **1** put too great a strain on. **2** tax too heavily.

overthrow ❶ *verb* **1** defeat and replace. ◆ *noun* **2** downfall, destruction.

O

—————— THESAURUS ——————

below ◆*adjective* =**aerial**, overhanging, upper

overheads *plural noun* =**running costs**, operating costs

overjoyed *adjective* =**delighted**, cock-a-hoop, elated, euphoric, jubilant, on cloud nine (*inf*), over the moon (*inf*), thrilled

overlook *verb* **1** =**miss**, disregard, forget, neglect, omit, pass OPPOSITE notice. **2** =**ignore**, condone, disregard, excuse, forgive, make allowances for, pardon, turn a blind eye to, wink at **3** =**have a view of**, look over *or* out on

overpower *verb* =**overwhelm**, conquer, crush, defeat, master, overcome, overthrow, vanquish **2** =**subdue**, quell, subjugate

overpowering *adjective* =**overwhelming**, forceful, invincible, irrefutable, irresistible, powerful, strong

overrate *verb* =**overestimate**, exaggerate, overvalue

override *verb* **1** =**overrule**, annul, cancel, countermand, nullify, outweigh **2** =**supersede**

overrule *verb* =**reverse**, alter, annul, cancel, countermand, override, overturn, repeal, rescind, veto OPPOSITE allow

overrun *verb* **1** =**overwhelm**, invade, occupy, rout **2** =**spread over**, choke, infest, inundate, permeate, ravage, swarm over **3** =**exceed**, go beyond, overshoot, run over *or* on

overseer *noun* =**supervisor**, boss (*inf*), chief, foreman, master, superintendent

overshadow *verb* **1** =**outshine**, dominate, dwarf, eclipse, leave *or* put in the shade, surpass, tower above **2** =**spoil**, blight, mar, put a damper on, ruin, temper

oversight *noun* =**mistake**, blunder, carelessness, error, fault, lapse, neglect, omission, slip

overt *adjective* =**open**, blatant, manifest, observable, obvious, plain, public, unconcealed, undisguised OPPOSITE hidden

overtake *verb* **1** =**pass**, catch up with, get past, leave behind, outdistance, outdo, outstrip, overhaul **2** =**befall**, engulf, happen, hit,

overtime *noun, adverb* **1** (paid work done) in addition to one's normal working hours. ◆ *noun* **2** period of extra time in a contest or game.

overtone ❶ *noun* additional meaning.

overture ❶ *noun* **1** *Music* orchestral introduction. ◆ *plural* **2** opening moves in a new relationship.

overturn ❶ *verb* **1** turn upside down. **2** overrule (a legal decision). **3** overthrow (a government).

overview *noun* general survey.

overweening *adjective* excessive or immoderate.

overweight ❶ *adjective* weighing more than is healthy.

overwhelm ❶ *verb* **1** overpower, esp. emotionally. **2** defeat by force. **overwhelming** *adjective* **overwhelmingly** *adverb*

overwork ❶ *verb* **1** work too much. **2** use too much. ◆ *noun* **3** excessive work.

overwrought ❶ *adjective* nervous and agitated.

oviduct *noun* tube through which eggs are conveyed from the ovary.

ovine *adjective* of or like a sheep.

ovoid [oh-void] *adjective* egg-shaped.

ovulate [ov-yew-late] *verb* release an egg cell from an ovary. **ovulation** *noun*

ovule *noun* plant part that contains the egg

cell and becomes the seed after fertilization.

ovum [oh-vum] *noun, pl* **ova** unfertilized egg cell.

owe ❶ *verb* **1** be obliged to pay (a sum of money) to (a person). **2** feel an obligation to do. **owe to** have as a result of. **owing to** as a result of.

owl *noun* night bird of prey. **owlish** *adjective*

own ❶ *adjective* **1** used to emphasize possession, e.g. *my own idea.* ◆ *pronoun* **2** thing(s) belonging to a particular person. ◆ *verb* **3** possess. **4** acknowledge. **hold one's own** be able to deal successfully with a situation. **on one's own 1** without help. **2** alone. **owner** *noun* **ownership** *noun* **own up** *verb* confess.

ox *noun, pl* **oxen** castrated bull.

oxalic acid *noun* poisonous acid found in many plants.

Oxbridge *noun* universities of Oxford and Cambridge.

Oxfam Oxford Committee for Famine Relief.

oxide *noun* compound of oxygen and one other element. **oxidize** *verb* combine chemically with oxygen, as in burning or rusting. **oxidation** *noun* oxidizing.

oxygen *noun Chem* gaseous element essential to life and combustion. **oxygenate** *verb* add oxygen to.

oxymoron [ox-see-**more**-on] *noun* figure of

——————— T H E S A U R U S ———————

overwhelm, strike

overthrow *verb* **1** =**defeat**, bring down, conquer, depose, dethrone, oust, overcome, overpower, topple, unseat, vanquish OPPOSITE support ◆*noun* **2** =**downfall**, defeat, destruction, dethronement, fall, ousting, undoing, unseating OPPOSITE **defence**

overtone *noun* =**hint**, connotation, implication, innuendo, intimation, nuance, sense, suggestion, undercurrent

overture *noun* **1** *Music* =**introduction**, opening, prelude OPPOSITE finale ◆*plural* **2** =**approach**, advance, invitation, offer, proposal, proposition OPPOSITE **withdrawal**

overturn *verb* **1** =**tip over**, capsize, keel over, overbalance, topple, upend, upturn **3** =**overthrow**, bring down, depose, destroy, unseat

overweight *adjective* =**fat**, bulky, chubby, chunky, corpulent, heavy, hefty, obese, plump, portly, stout, tubby (*inf*)

overwhelm *verb* **1** =**overcome**, bowl over (*inf*), devastate, knock (someone) for six (*inf*), stagger, sweep (someone) off his *or* her feet, take (someone's) breath away **2** =**destroy**, crush, cut to pieces, massacre, overpower,

overrun, rout

overwhelming *adjective* **1** =**overpowering**, breathtaking, crushing, devastating, irresistible, shattering, stunning, towering OPPOSITE trivial

overwork *verb* **1** =**strain oneself**, burn the midnight oil, sweat (*inf*), work one's fingers to the bone **2** =**overuse**, exhaust, exploit, fatigue, oppress, wear out, weary

overwrought *adjective* =**agitated**, distracted, excited, frantic, keyed up, on edge, overexcited, tense, uptight (*inf*), wired (*sl*) OPPOSITE **calm**

owe *verb* **1** =**be in debt**, be in arrears **2** =**be obligated** *or* **indebted**

owing to *preposition* =**because of**, as a result of, on account of

own *adjective* **1** =**personal**, individual, particular, private ◆*verb* **3** =**possess**, be in possession of, enjoy, have, hold, keep, retain **4** =**acknowledge**, admit, allow, concede, confess, grant, recognize **hold one's own** =**keep going**, compete, keep one's end up, keep one's head above water **on one's own 1** =**unaided**, unassisted, under one's own steam **2** =**alone**, by oneself, independently, singly **own up** =**confess**, admit, come clean, tell the truth

O

speech that combines two apparently contradictory ideas, e.g. *cruel kindness*.
oyez *interjection Hist* shouted three times by a public crier, listen.
oyster *noun* edible shellfish. **oystercatcher** *noun* wading bird with black-and-white feathers.

oz. ounce.
Oz *noun Slang* Australia.
ozone *noun* **1** strong-smelling form of oxygen. **2** bracing seaside air. **ozone layer** layer of ozone in the upper atmosphere that filters out ultraviolet radiation.

———————————————— T H E S A U R U S ————————————————

owner *noun* **3** = **possessor**, holder, landlord *or* landlady, proprietor

ownership *noun* **3** = **possession**, dominion, title

O

Pp

p penny or pence.
P 1 *Chem* phosphorus. **2** parking.
p. *pl* **pp.** page.
Pa *Chem* protactinium.
PA 1 Pennsylvania. **2** personal assistant. **3** public-address system.
p.a. each year.
pace[1] **⊕** *noun* **1** single step in walking. **2** length of a step. **3** rate of progress. ♦ *verb* **4** walk up and down, esp. in anxiety. **5** (foll. by *out*) cross or measure with steps. **keep pace with** advance at the same rate as. **pace oneself** do something at a steady rate.
pacemaker *noun* **1** electronic device surgically implanted in a person with heart disease to regulate the heartbeat. **2** person who, by taking the lead early in a race, sets the pace for the rest of the competitors.
pace[2] *preposition* with due respect to: used to express polite disagreement.
pachyderm [pak-ee-durm] *noun* thick-skinned animal such as an elephant.
pacifier *noun US & Canad* a baby's dummy or teething ring.
pacifist ⊕ *noun* person who refuses on principle to take part in war. **pacifism** *noun*
pacify ⊕ *verb* **-fying, -fied** soothe, calm. **pacification** *noun*
pack ⊕ *verb* **1** put (clothes etc.) together in a suitcase or bag. **2** put (goods) into containers or parcels. **3** fill with people or things. ♦ *noun* **4** bag carried on a person's or animal's back. **5** *Chiefly US* same as PACKET. **6** set of playing cards. **7** group of dogs or wolves that hunt together. **8** group of people who do things together. **packing** *noun* material, such as paper or plastic, used to protect packed goods. **pack ice** mass of floating ice in the sea. **pack in** *verb Informal* stop doing, e.g. *I packed in the job.* **pack off** *verb* send away. **pack up** *verb* **1** put (one's belongings) in a case, bag, etc. **2** *Informal* stop (doing something), e.g. *I'd packed up smoking.* **3** *Informal* (of a machine) break down.
package ⊕ *noun* **1** small parcel. **2** (also **package deal**) deal in which separate items are presented together as a unit. ♦ *verb* **3** put into a package. **packaging** *noun* **package holiday** holiday in which everything is arranged by one company for a fixed price.
packet ⊕ *noun* **1** small container (and contents). **2** small parcel. **3** *Slang* large sum of money. **packet boat** (formerly) boat carrying mail, goods, or passengers on a fixed short route.
packhorse *noun* horse used for carrying goods.
packsack *noun* a US and Canadian word for HAVERSACK.
pact ⊕ *noun* formal agreement.

THESAURUS

pace[1] *noun* **1** = **step**, gait, stride, tread, walk **3** = **speed**, rate, tempo, velocity ♦*verb* **4** = **stride**, march, patrol, pound **5** (foll. by *out*) = **measure**, count, mark out, step
pacifist *noun* = **peace lover**, conscientious objector, dove
pacify *verb* = **calm**, allay, appease, assuage, mollify, placate, propitiate, soothe
pack *verb* **1** = **package**, bundle, load, store, stow **2, 3** = **cram**, compress, crowd, fill, jam, press, ram, stuff ♦*noun* **4** = **bundle**, back pack, burden, kitbag, knapsack, load, parcel, rucksack **5** *Chiefly US* = **packet**, package **8** = **group**, band, bunch, company, crowd, flock, gang, herd, mob, troop **pack in** ♦*verb Inf* = **stop**, cease, chuck (*inf*), give up or over, kick (*inf*)

pack off = **send away**, dismiss, send packing (*inf*)
package *noun* **1** = **parcel**, box, carton, container, packet **2** (also **package deal**) = **unit**, combination, whole ♦*verb* **3** = **pack**, box, parcel (up), wrap
packet *noun* **1** = **container**, bag, carton **2** = **package**, parcel **3** *Sl* = **fortune**, bomb (*Brit sl*), king's ransom (*inf*), pile (*inf*), small fortune, tidy sum (*inf*)
pack in *verb Inf* = **stop**, cease, chuck (*inf*), give up, kick, over
pack off *verb* = **send away**, dismiss, send packing (*inf*)
pack up *verb* **1** = **put away**, store **2** *Inf* = **stop**, finish, give up, pack in (*Brit inf*) **3** *Inf*

pad ✪ *noun* **1** piece of soft material used for protection, support, absorption of liquid, etc. **2** number of sheets of paper fastened at the edge. **3** fleshy underpart of an animal's paw. **4** place for launching rockets. **5** *Slang* home. ◆ *verb* **padding, padded 6** protect or fill with soft material. **7** walk with soft steps. **padding** *noun* **1** soft material used to pad something. **2** unnecessary words put into a speech or written work to make it longer. **pad out** *verb* add unnecessary words to (a speech or written work) to make it longer.

paddle¹ ✪ *noun* **1** short oar with a broad blade at one or each end. ◆ *verb* **2** move (a canoe etc.) with a paddle. **paddle steamer** ship propelled by paddle wheels. **paddle wheel** wheel with crosswise blades that strike the water successively to propel a ship.

paddle² ✪ *verb* walk barefoot in shallow water.

paddock *noun* small field or enclosure for horses.

paddy *noun Informal* fit of temper.

paddy field *noun* field where rice is grown (also **paddy**).

pademelon, paddymelon [pad-ee-mel-an] *noun* small Australian wallaby.

padlock *noun* **1** detachable lock with a hinged hoop fastened over a ring on the object to be secured. ◆ *verb* **2** fasten (something) with a padlock.

padre [**pah**-dray] *noun* chaplain to the armed forces.

paean [**pee**-an] *noun* song of triumph or thanksgiving.

paediatrics *noun* branch of medicine concerned with diseases of children. **paediatrician** *noun*

paedophile *noun* person who is sexually attracted to children

paedophilia *noun* condition of being sexually attracted to children. **paedophile** *noun* person who is sexually attracted to children.

paedophilia *noun*

paella [pie-**ell**-a] *noun* Spanish dish of rice, chicken, shellfish, and vegetables.

pagan ✪ *noun, adjective* (person) not belonging to one of the world's main religions. **paganism** *noun*

page¹ ✪ *noun* **1** (one side of) a sheet of paper forming a book etc. **2** screenful of information from a website or teletext service.

page² ✪ *noun* **1** (also **pageboy**) small boy who attends a bride at her wedding. **2** *Hist* boy in training for knighthood. ◆ *verb* **3** summon (someone) by bleeper or loudspeaker, in order to pass on a message.

pageant ✪ *noun* parade or display of people in costume, usu. illustrating a scene from history. **pageantry** *noun*

paginate *verb* number the pages of (a book etc.). **pagination** *noun*

pagoda *noun* pyramid-shaped Asian temple or tower.

paid *verb* past of PAY. **put paid to** *Informal* end or destroy, e.g. *the recession put paid to most of our long-term plans.*

pail *noun* (contents of) a bucket.

pain ✪ *noun* **1** physical or mental suffering. ◆ *plural* **2** trouble, effort, e.g. *Taylor was at pains to reassure Wright.* ◆ *verb* **3** cause (someone) mental or physical suffering. **on pain of** subject to the penalty of. **painful** *adjective* **painfully** *adverb* **painless** *adjective* **painlessly** *adverb* **painkiller** *noun* drug that relieves pain.

painstaking ✪ *adjective* extremely thorough

P

———————— THESAURUS ————————

=**break down**, conk out (*inf*), fail

pact *noun* =**agreement**, alliance, bargain, covenant, deal, treaty, understanding

pad *noun* **1** =**cushion**, buffer, protection, stuffing, wad **2** =**writing pad**, block, jotter **3** =**paw**, foot, sole **5** *Sl* =**home**, apartment, flat, place ◆*verb* **6** =**pack**, cushion, fill, protect, stuff **7** =**sneak**, creep, go barefoot, steal

padding *noun* **1** =**filling**, packing, stuffing, wadding **2** =**waffle** (*inf, chiefly Brit*), hot air (*inf*), verbiage, verbosity, wordiness

paddle¹ *noun* **1** =**oar**, scull ◆*verb* **2** =**row**, propel, pull, scull

paddle² *verb* =**wade**, slop, splash (about)

pad out *verb* =**lengthen**, elaborate, fill out, flesh out, protract, spin out, stretch

pagan *noun* =**heathen**, idolater, infidel,

polytheist ◆*adjective* =**heathen**, idolatrous, infidel, polytheistic

page¹ *noun* **1** =**folio**, leaf, sheet, side

page² *noun* **1** =**attendant**, bellboy (US) pageboy **2** *Hist* =**squire** ◆*verb* **3** =**call**, send for, summon

pageant *noun* =**show**, display, parade, procession, spectacle, tableau

pageantry *noun* =**spectacle**, display, grandeur, parade, pomp, show, splendour, theatricality

pain *noun* **1 a** =**hurt**, ache, discomfort, irritation, pang, soreness, tenderness, throb, twinge **b** =**suffering**, agony, anguish, distress, heartache, misery, torment, torture ◆*plural* **2** =**trouble**, bother, care, diligence, effort ◆*verb* **3 a** =**hurt**, smart, sting, throb **b** =**distress**, and careful.

paint ❶ *noun* **1** coloured substance, spread on a surface with a brush or roller. ◆ *verb* **2** colour or coat with paint. **3** use paint to make a picture of. **painter** *noun* **painting** *noun*

painter *noun* rope at the front of a boat, for tying it up.

pair ❶ *noun* **1** set of two things matched for use together. **2** two people, animals, or things used or grouped together. ◆ *verb* **3** group or be grouped in twos.

> **LANGUAGE TIP**
>
> *Pair* is followed by a singular verb if it refers to a unit: *A pair of shoes was on the floor,* and by a plural verb if it refers to two individuals: *That pair are good friends.*

paisley pattern *noun* pattern of small curving shapes, used in fabric.

pajamas *plural noun US* pyjamas.

Pakistani *noun, adjective* (person) from Pakistan.

pal ❶ *noun Informal* friend.

palace *noun* **1** residence of a king, bishop, etc. **2** large grand building.

paladin *noun Hist* knight who did battle for a monarch.

palaeography [pal-ee-**og**-ra-fee] *noun* study of ancient manuscripts.

Palaeolithic [pal-ee-oh-**lith**-ik] *adjective* of the Old Stone Age.

palaeontology [pal-ee-on-**tol**-a-jee] *noun* study of past geological periods and fossils. **palaeontologist** *noun*

palatable ❶ *adjective* **1** pleasant to taste. **2** acceptable or satisfactory, e.g. *that option is not very palatable.*

palate ❶ *noun* **1** roof of the mouth. **2** sense of taste.

palatial ❶ *adjective* like a palace, magnificent.

palaver ❶ [pal-**lah**-ver] *noun* time-wasting fuss.

pale¹ ❶ *adjective* **1** light, whitish. **2** whitish in the face, esp. through illness or shock. ◆ *verb* **3** become pale. **pale in, by comparison with** appear inferior when compared with.

pale² ❶ *noun* wooden or metal post used in fences. **beyond the pale** outside the limits of social convention.

palette *noun* artist's flat board for mixing colours on. **palette knife** spatula with a broad flat flexible blade, used in painting or cookery.

palindrome *noun* word or phrase that reads the same backwards as forwards.

paling *noun* wooden or metal post used in fences.

palisade *noun* fence made of wooden posts driven into the ground.

——————— THESAURUS ———————

P

agonize, cut to the quick, grieve, hurt, sadden, torment, torture

painful *adjective* **1** = **sore**, aching, agonizing, smarting, tender OPPOSITE **painless**. **2** = **difficult**, arduous, hard, laborious, troublesome, trying OPPOSITE **easy**. **3** = **distressing**, disagreeable, distasteful, grievous, unpleasant OPPOSITE **satisfying**

painfully *adverb* **3** = **distressingly**, clearly, dreadfully, sadly, unfortunately

painkiller *noun* = **analgesic**, anaesthetic, anodyne, drug

painless *adjective* = **simple**, easy, effortless, fast, quick

painstaking *adjective* = **thorough**, assiduous, careful, conscientious, diligent, meticulous, scrupulous

paint *noun* **1** = **colouring**, colour, dye, pigment, stain, tint ◆*verb* **2** = **coat**, apply, colour, cover, daub **3** = **depict**, draw, picture, portray, represent, sketch

pair *noun* **2** = **couple**, brace, duo, twins ◆*verb* **3** = **couple**, bracket, join, match (up), team, twin

pal *noun Inf* = **friend**, buddy (*inf*), chum (*inf*), cobber (*Aust or old-fashioned NZ inf*), companion, comrade, crony, mate (*inf*)

palatable *adjective* **1** = **delicious**, appetizing, lekker (*S Afr sl*), luscious, mouthwatering, tasty OPPOSITE **bland**

palate *noun* **2** = **taste**, appetite, stomach

palatial *adjective* = **magnificent**, grand, imposing, majestic, opulent, regal, splendid, stately

palaver *noun* = **fuss**, business (*inf*), carry-on (*inf, chiefly Brit*), pantomime (*inf, chiefly Brit*), performance (*inf*), rigmarole, song and dance (*Brit inf*), to-do

pale¹ *adjective* **1** = **white**, ashen, bleached, colourless, faded, light **2** = **ashen**, pallid, pasty, wan, white OPPOSITE **glowing** ◆*verb* **3** = **become pale**, blanch, go white, lose colour, whiten

pale² *noun* = **post**, paling, palisade, picket, slat, stake, upright **beyond the pale** = **unacceptable**, barbaric, forbidden, improper, inadmissible, indecent, irregular, not done, out of line, unseemly, unspeakable, unsuitable

pall[1] **O** *noun* **1** cloth spread over a coffin. **2** dark cloud (of smoke). **3** depressing oppressive atmosphere. **pallbearer** *noun* person who helps to carry the coffin at a funeral.

pall[2] **O** *verb* become boring.

palladium *noun Chem* silvery-white element of the platinum metal group.

pallet[1] *noun* portable platform for storing and moving goods.

pallet[2] *noun* straw-filled mattress or bed.

palliasse *noun* straw-filled mattress.

palliate *verb* lessen the severity of (something) without curing it. **palliative** *adjective* **1** giving temporary or partial relief. ♦ *noun* **2** something, for example a drug, that palliates.

pallid O *adjective* pale, esp. because ill or weak. **pallor** *noun*

pally *adjective* **-lier, -liest** *Informal* on friendly terms.

palm[1] **O** *noun* inner surface of the hand. **palm off** *verb* get rid of (an unwanted thing or person), esp. by deceit. **palmtop** *noun* computer small enough to be held in the hand.

palm[2] *noun* tropical tree with long pointed leaves growing out of the top of a straight trunk. **Palm Sunday** Sunday before Easter.

palmistry *noun* fortune-telling from lines on the palm of the hand. **palmist** *noun*

palomino *noun, pl* **-nos** gold-coloured horse with a white mane and tail.

palpable O *adjective* **1** obvious, e.g. *a palpable hit*. **2** so intense as to seem capable of being touched, e.g. *the tension is almost palpable*. **palpably** *adverb*

palpate *verb Med* examine (an area of the body) by touching.

palpitate O *verb* **1** (of the heart) beat rapidly. **2** flutter or tremble. **palpitation** *noun*

palsy [pawl-zee] *noun* paralysis. **palsied** *adjective* affected with palsy.

paltry O *adjective* **-trier, -triest** insignificant.

pampas *plural noun* vast grassy plains in S America. **pampas grass** tall grass with feathery ornamental flower branches.

pamper O *verb* treat (someone) with great indulgence, spoil.

pamphlet O *noun* thin paper-covered booklet. **pamphleteer** *noun* writer of pamphlets.

pan[1] **O** *noun* **1** wide long-handled metal container used in cooking. **2** bowl of a toilet. ♦ *verb* **panning, panned 3** sift gravel from (a river) in a pan to search for gold. **4** *Informal* criticize harshly. **pan out** *verb* result.

pan[2] **O** *verb* **panning, panned** (of a film camera) be moved slowly so as to cover a whole scene or follow a moving object.

pan- *combining form* all, e.g. *pan-American*.

panacea O [pan-a-see-a] *noun* remedy for all diseases or problems.

panache O [pan-ash] *noun* confident elegant style.

panama hat, panama *noun* man's straw hat.

panatella *noun* long slender cigar.

pancake *noun* thin flat circle of fried batter. **Pancake Day** Shrove Tuesday, when people traditionally eat pancakes. **pancake landing** landing in which an aircraft comes down to a height of a few feet and then drops flat onto the ground. **pancake roll** small pancake filled with Chinese-style vegetables and rolled up.

panchromatic *adjective Photog* sensitive to light of all colours.

pancreas [pang-kree-ass] *noun* large gland behind the stomach that produces insulin and helps digestion. **pancreatic** *adjective*

panda *noun* large black-and-white bearlike mammal from China. **panda car** police patrol car.

pandemic *adjective* (of a disease) occurring over a wide area.

pandemonium O *noun* wild confusion,

P

———————————— THESAURUS ————————————

pall[1] *noun* **2** = **cloud**, mantle, shadow, shroud, veil **3** = **gloom**, check, damp, damper

pall[2] *verb* = **become boring**, become dull, become tedious, cloy, jade, sicken, tire, weary

pallid *adjective* = **pale**, anaemic, ashen, colourless, pasty, wan

palm off *verb* = **fob off**, foist off, pass off

palpable *adjective* **1** = **obvious**, clear, conspicuous, evident, manifest, plain, unmistakable, visible

palpitate *verb* = **beat**, flutter, pound, pulsate, throb, tremble

paltry *adjective* = **insignificant**, contemptible, despicable, inconsiderable, meagre, mean,

measly, minor, miserable, petty, poor, puny, slight, small, trifling, trivial, unimportant, worthless OPPOSITE **important**

pamper *verb* = **spoil**, coddle, cosset, indulge, mollycoddle, pet

pamphlet *noun* = **booklet**, brochure, circular, leaflet, tract

pan[1] *noun* **1** = **pot**, container, saucepan ♦ *verb* **3** = **sift out**, look for, search for **4** *Inf* = **criticize**, censure, knock (*inf*), slam (*sl*), tear into (*inf*)

pan[2] *verb* = **move**, follow, sweep, track

panacea *noun* = **cure-all**, nostrum, universal cure

panache *noun* = **style**, dash, élan,

uproar.

pander ❶ *noun* person who procures a sexual partner for someone. **pander to** *verb* indulge (a person or his or her desires).

pane *noun* sheet of glass in a window or door.

panegyric [pan-ee-**jire**-ik] *noun* formal speech or piece of writing in praise of someone or something.

panel *noun* 1 flat distinct section of a larger surface, for example in a door. 2 group of people as a team in a quiz etc. 3 list of jurors, doctors, etc. 4 board or surface containing switches and controls to operate equipment. ◆ *verb* **-elling, -elled** 5 cover or decorate with panels. **panelling** *noun* panels collectively, esp. on a wall. **panellist** *noun* member of a panel. **panel beater** person who repairs damage to car bodies.

pang ❶ *noun* sudden sharp feeling of pain or sadness.

pangolin *noun* animal of tropical countries with a scaly body and a long snout for eating ants and termites (also **scaly anteater**).

panic ❶ *noun* 1 sudden overwhelming fear, often affecting a whole group of people. ◆ *verb* **-icking, -icked** 2 feel or cause to feel panic. **panicky** *adjective* **panic-stricken** *adjective*

panicle *noun* loose, irregularly branched cluster of flowers.

pannier *noun* 1 bag fixed on the back of a cycle. 2 basket carried by a beast of burden.

panoply ❶ [**pan**-a-plee] *noun* magnificent array.

panorama ❶ *noun* 1 wide unbroken view of a scene. 2 picture of a scene unrolled so as to appear continuous. **panoramic** *adjective*

pansy *noun, pl* **-sies** 1 small garden flower with velvety purple, yellow, or white petals. 2 *Offens* effeminate or homosexual man.

pant ❶ *verb* breathe quickly and noisily after exertion.

pantaloons *plural noun* baggy trousers

gathered at the ankles.

pantechnicon *noun* large van for furniture removals.

pantheism *noun* 1 belief that God is present in everything. 2 willingness to worship all gods. **pantheist** *noun* **pantheistic** *adjective*

pantheon *noun* (in ancient Greece and Rome) temple built to honour all the gods.

panther *noun* leopard, esp. a black one.

panties *plural noun* women's underpants.

pantile *noun* roofing tile with an S-shaped cross section.

pantomime *noun* 1 play based on a fairy tale, performed at Christmas time. 2 same as MIME (sense 1). 3 confused or farcical situation.

pantry *noun, pl* **-tries** small room or cupboard for storing food.

pants ❶ *plural noun* 1 undergarment for the lower part of the body. 2 *US & Canad* trousers

pap *noun* 1 soft food for babies or invalids. 2 worthless entertainment or information.

papacy [**pay**-pa-see] *noun, pl* **-cies** position or term of office of a pope. **papal** *adjective* of the pope.

paparazzo [pap-a-**rat**-so] *noun, pl* **-razzi** photographer specializing in candid photographs of famous people.

papaya [pa-**pie**-ya] *noun* large sweet West Indian fruit.

paper ❶ *noun* 1 material made in sheets from wood pulp or other fibres. 2 printed sheet of this. 3 newspaper. 4 set of examination questions. 5 article or essay. ◆ *plural* 6 personal documents. ◆ *verb* 7 cover (walls) with wallpaper. **on paper** in theory, as opposed to fact, e.g. *this system looks good on paper but it is expensive.* **paperback** *noun* book with covers made of flexible card. **paper money** banknotes, rather than coins. **paperweight** *noun* heavy decorative object placed on top of loose papers. **paperwork** *noun* clerical work, such as writing reports and letters.

———— THESAURUS ————

flamboyance

pandemonium *noun* =uproar, bedlam, chaos, confusion, din, hullabaloo, racket, rumpus, turmoil

pander to *verb* =indulge, cater to, gratify, play up to (*inf*), please, satisfy

pang *noun* =twinge, ache, pain, prick, spasm, stab, sting

panic *noun* 1 =fear, alarm, fright, hysteria, scare, terror ◆*verb* 2 =go to pieces, alarm, become hysterical, lose one's nerve, scare, unnerve

panic-stricken *adjective* =frightened,

frightened out of one's wits, hysterical, in a cold sweat (*inf*), panicky, scared, scared stiff, terrified

panoply *noun* =array, attire, dress, garb, regalia, trappings

panorama *noun* 1 =view, prospect, vista

panoramic *adjective* 1 =wide, comprehensive, extensive, overall, sweeping

pant *verb* =puff, blow, breathe, gasp, heave, wheeze

pants *plural noun* 1 =underpants, boxer shorts, briefs, broekies (*S Afr inf*), drawers, knickers, panties 2 *US, Canad, Aust & NZ* =trousers, slacks

papier-mâché [pap-yay **mash**-ay] *noun* material made from paper mixed with paste and moulded when moist.

papist *noun, adjective Offens* Roman Catholic.

papoose *noun* Native American child.

paprika *noun* mild powdered seasoning made from red peppers.

Pap smear, test *noun* same as SMEAR TEST.

papyrus [pap-**ire**-uss] *noun, pl* **-ri, -ruses 1** tall water plant. **2** (manuscript written on) a kind of paper made from this plant.

par ❶ *noun* **1** usual or average condition, e.g. *feeling under par.* **2** *Golf* expected standard score. **3** face value of stocks and shares. **on a par with** equal to.

para- *combining form* beside, beyond, e.g. *parameter; parapsychology.*

parable ❶ *noun* story that illustrates a religious teaching.

parabola [par-**ab**-bol-a] *noun* regular curve resembling the course of an object thrown forward and up. **parabolic** *adjective*

paracetamol *noun* mild pain-relieving drug.

parachute *noun* **1** large fabric canopy that slows the descent of a person or object from an aircraft. ♦ *verb* **2** land or drop by parachute. **parachutist** *noun*

parade ❶ *noun* **1** procession or march. **2** street or promenade. ♦ *verb* **3** display or flaunt. **4** march in procession. **parade ground** place where soldiers assemble regularly for inspection or display.

paradigm ❶ [**par**-a-dime] *noun* example or model.

paradise ❶ *noun* **1** heaven. **2** place or situation that is near-perfect.

paradox ❶ *noun* **1** person or thing made up of contradictory elements. **2** statement that

seems self-contradictory but may be true.

paradoxical *adjective* **paradoxically** *adverb*

paraffin *noun* liquid mixture distilled from petroleum and used as a fuel or solvent.

SPELLING TIP

People have trouble remembering whether the *r* or the *f* is doubled in **paraffin**, but according to the Bank of English, the most popular mistake is to decide on neither, as in *parafin*.

---

paragliding *noun* cross-country gliding wearing a parachute shaped like wings.

paragon ❶ *noun* model of perfection.

paragraph ❶ *noun* section of a piece of writing starting on a new line.

parakeet *noun* small long-tailed parrot.

parallax *noun* apparent change in an object's position due to a change in the observer's position.

parallel ❶ *adjective* **1** separated by an equal distance at every point. **2** exactly corresponding. ♦ *noun* **3** line separated from another by an equal distance at every point. **4** thing with similar features to another. **5** line of latitude. ♦ *verb* **6** correspond to.

parallelogram *noun* four-sided geometric figure with opposite sides parallel.

paralysis ❶ *noun* inability to move or feel, because of damage to the nervous system.

paralyse *verb* **1** affect with paralysis. **2** make temporarily unable to move or take action.

paralytic *noun, adjective* **1** (person) affected with paralysis. ♦ *adjective* **2** *Informal* very drunk.

P

=================== THESAURUS ===================

paper *noun* **3** = **newspaper**, daily, gazette, journal **5** = **essay**, article, dissertation, report, treatise ♦*plural* **6** = **documents**, archive, certificates, deeds, diaries, dossier, file, letters, records ♦*verb* **7** = **wallpaper**, hang

par *noun* **1** = **average**, level, mean, norm, standard, usual

parable *noun* = **lesson**, allegory, fable, moral tale, story

parade *noun* **1** = **procession**, array, cavalcade, march, pageant ♦*verb* **3** = **flaunt**, display, exhibit, show off (*inf*) **4** = **march**, process

paradigm *noun* = **model**, example, ideal, pattern

paradise *noun* **1** = **heaven**, Elysian fields, Happy Valley (*Islam*), Promised Land **2** = **bliss**, delight, felicity, heaven, utopia

paradox *noun* **2** = **contradiction**, anomaly, enigma, oddity, puzzle

paradoxical *adjective* **2** = **contradictory**, baffling, confounding, enigmatic, puzzling

paragon *noun* = **model**, epitome, exemplar, ideal, nonpareil, pattern, quintessence

paragraph *noun* = **section**, clause, item, part, passage, subdivision

parallel *adjective* **1** = **equidistant**, alongside, side by side OPPOSITE> divergent. **2** = **matching**, analogous, corresponding, like, resembling, similar ♦*noun* **4** = **similarity**, analogy, comparison, likeness, resemblance OPPOSITE> difference

paralyse *verb* **1** = **disable**, cripple, incapacitate, lame **2** = **immobilize**, freeze, halt, numb, petrify, stun

paramedic *noun* person working in support of the medical profession. **paramedical** *adjective*

parameter ❶ [par-**am**-it-er] *noun* limiting factor, boundary.

paramilitary *adjective* organized on military lines.

paramount ❶ *adjective* of the greatest importance.

paramour *noun Old-fashioned* lover, esp. of a person married to someone else.

paranoia ❶ *noun* **1** mental illness causing delusions of grandeur or persecution. **2** *Informal* intense fear or suspicion. **paranoid, paranoiac** *adjective, noun*

paranormal *adjective* beyond scientific explanation. **the paranormal** paranormal events or matters.

parapet *noun* low wall or railing along the edge of a balcony or roof.

paraphernalia ❶ *noun* personal belongings or bits of equipment.

paraphrase ❶ *verb* **1** put (a statement or text) into other words. ✦ *noun* **2** expression of a statement or text in other words.

paraplegia [par-a-**pleej**-ya] *noun* paralysis of the lower half of the body. **paraplegic** *adjective, noun*

parapsychology *noun* study of mental phenomena such as telepathy.

Paraquat *noun* ® extremely poisonous weedkiller.

parasite ❶ *noun* **1** animal or plant living in or on another. **2** person who lives at the expense of others. **parasitic** *adjective*

parasol *noun* umbrella-like sunshade.

paratroops *plural noun* troops trained to be dropped by parachute into a battle area.

paratrooper *noun* member of the paratroops.

parboil *verb* boil until partly cooked.

parcel ❶ *noun* **1** something wrapped up, package. ✦ *verb* **-celling, -celled 2** (often foll. by *up*) wrap up. **parcel out** *verb* divide into parts.

parch ❶ *verb* **1** make very hot and dry. **2** make thirsty.

parchment *noun* thick smooth writing material made from animal skin.

pardon ❶ *verb* **1** forgive, excuse. ✦ *noun* **2** forgiveness. **3** official release from punishment for a crime. **pardonable** *adjective*

pare ❶ *verb* **1** cut off the skin or top layer of. **2** (often foll. by *down*) reduce in size or amount. **paring** *noun* piece pared off.

parent ❶ *noun* father or mother. **parental** *adjective* **parenthood** *noun* **parentage** *noun* ancestry or family. **parenting** *noun* activity of bringing up children.

parenthesis [par-**en**-thiss-iss] *noun, pl* **-ses 1** word or sentence inserted into a passage, marked off by brackets or dashes. ✦ *plural* **2** round brackets, ( ). **parenthetical** *adjective*

par excellence *adverb* beyond comparison, e.g. *he is a travel writer par excellence.*

pariah ❶ [par-**rye**-a] *noun* social outcast.

parietal [par-**rye**-it-al] *adjective* of the walls of a body cavity such as the skull.

parish ❶ *noun* area that has its own church and clergyman. **parishioner** *noun* inhabitant of

P

———————— T H E S A U R U S ————————

paralysis *noun* = **immobility**, palsy

paralytic *adjective* **1** = **paralysed**, crippled, disabled, incapacitated, lame, palsied

parameter *noun* = **limit**, framework, limitation, restriction, specification

paramount *adjective* = **principal**, cardinal, chief, first, foremost, main, primary, prime, supreme OPPOSITE **secondary**

paranoid *adjective* **1** = **mentally ill**, deluded, disturbed, manic, neurotic, paranoiac, psychotic **2** *Inf* = **suspicious**, fearful, nervous, worried

paraphernalia *noun* = **equipment**, apparatus, baggage, belongings, effects, gear, stuff, tackle, things, trappings

paraphrase *verb* **1** = **reword**, express in other words *or* one's own words, rephrase, restate ✦ *noun* **2** = **rewording**, rephrasing, restatement

parasite *noun* **2** = **sponger**, bloodsucker (*inf*), hanger-on, leech, scrounger (*inf*) (*inf*)

parasitic *adjective* **2** = **scrounging** (*inf*), bloodsucking (*inf*), sponging (*inf*)

parcel *noun* **1** = **package**, bundle, pack ✦ *verb* **2** (often foll. by *up*) = **wrap**, do up, pack, package, tie up

parch *verb* **1** = **dry up**, dehydrate, desiccate, evaporate, shrivel, wither

pardon *verb* **1** = **forgive**, absolve, acquit, excuse, exonerate, let off (*inf*), overlook OPPOSITE **condemn** ✦ *noun* **2** = **forgiveness**, absolution, exoneration OPPOSITE **penalty**. **3** = **acquittal**, amnesty

pardonable *adjective* = **forgivable**, excusable, minor, understandable, venial

pare *verb* **1** = **peel**, clip, cut, shave, skin, trim **2** (often foll. by *down*) = **cut back**, crop, cut, decrease, dock, reduce

parent *noun* = **father** *or* **mother**, procreator, progenitor, sire

parentage *noun* = **family**, ancestry, birth, descent, lineage, pedigree, stock

pariah *noun* = **outcast**, exile, undesirable, untouchable a parish.

parity ⊕ *noun* equality or equivalence.

park ⊕ *noun* **1** area of open land for recreational use by the public. **2** area containing a number of related enterprises, e.g. *a business park.* **3** area of private land around a large country house. ◆ *verb* **4** stop and leave (a vehicle) temporarily. **parking meter** coin-operated device beside a parking space that indicates how long a vehicle may be parked there. **parking ticket** notice of a fine served on a motorist for a parking offence.

parka *noun* long jacket with a quilted lining and a fur-trimmed hood.

parkade *noun Canad* a building used as a car park.

parkette *noun Canadian* a small public park.

parking lot *noun US & Canad* area or building where vehicles may be left for a time.

Parkinson's disease *noun* progressive disorder of the central nervous system which causes impaired muscular coordination and tremor (also **Parkinsonism**).

parky *adjective* **parkier, parkiest** *Informal* (of the weather) chilly.

parlance ⊕ *noun* particular way of speaking, idiom.

parley *noun* **1** meeting between leaders or representatives of opposing forces to discuss terms. ◆ *verb* **2** have a parley.

parliament ⊕ *noun* law-making assembly of a country. **parliamentary** *adjective*

parliamentarian *noun* expert in parliamentary procedures.

parlour ⊕ *noun Old-fashioned* living room for receiving visitors.

parlous ⊕ *adjective Old-fashioned* dangerous.

Parmesan *noun* hard strong-flavoured Italian cheese, used grated on pasta dishes and soups.

parochial ⊕ *adjective* **1** narrow in outlook. **2** of a parish. **parochialism** *noun*

parody ⊕ *noun, pl* **-dies 1** exaggerated and amusing imitation of someone else's style. ◆ *verb* **-dying, -died 2** make a parody of.

parole *noun* **1** early freeing of a prisoner on condition that he or she behaves well. ◆ *verb* **2** put on parole. **on parole** (of a prisoner) released on condition that he or she behaves well.

paroxysm ⊕ *noun* **1** uncontrollable outburst of rage, delight, etc. **2** spasm or convulsion of coughing, pain, etc.

parquet [par-kay] *noun* **1** floor covering made of wooden blocks arranged in a geometric pattern. ◆ *verb* **2** cover with parquet. **parquetry** *noun*

parricide *noun* **1** crime of killing either of one's parents. **2** person who does this.

parrot ⊕ *noun* **1** tropical bird with a short hooked beak and an ability to imitate human speech. ◆ *verb* **-roting, -roted 2** repeat (someone else's words) without thinking.

parry ⊕ *verb* **-rying, -ried 1** ward off (an attack). **2** cleverly avoid (an awkward question). ◆ *noun* **3** parrying.

parse [parz] *verb* analyse (a sentence) in terms of grammar.

parsimony ⊕ *noun* extreme caution in spending money. **parsimonious** *adjective*

parsley *noun* herb used for seasoning and decorating food.

parsnip *noun* long tapering cream-coloured root vegetable.

parson ⊕ *noun* parish priest in the Church of England. **parsonage** *noun* parson's house. **parson's nose** rump of a cooked fowl.

P

———————— THESAURUS ————————

parish *noun* =**community**, church, congregation, flock

parity *noun* =**equality**, consistency, equivalence, uniformity, unity

park *noun* **3** =**parkland**, estate, garden, grounds, woodland

parlance *noun* =**language**, idiom, jargon, phraseology, speech, talk, tongue

parliament *noun* =**assembly**, congress, convention, council, legislature, senate

parliamentary *adjective* =**governmental**, law-making, legislative

parlour *noun Old-fashioned* =**sitting room**, drawing room, front room, living room, lounge

parlous *adjective Old-fashioned* =**dangerous**, hazardous, risky

parochial *adjective* **1** =**provincial**, insular, limited, narrow, narrow-minded, petty, small-minded OPPOSITE cosmopolitan

parody *noun* **1** =**takeoff**, burlesque, caricature, satire, send-up (*Brit inf*), skit, spoof (*inf*) (*inf*) ◆*verb* **2** =**take off**, burlesque, caricature, do a takeoff of (*inf*), satirize, send up (*Brit inf*) (*inf*)

paroxysm *noun* **2** =**outburst**, attack, convulsion, fit, seizure, spasm

parrot *verb* **2** =**repeat**, copy, echo, imitate, mimic

parry *verb* **1** =**ward off**, block, deflect, rebuff, repel, repulse **2** =**evade**, avoid, dodge, sidestep

parsimonious *adjective* =**mean**, close, frugal, miserly, niggardly, penny-pinching (*inf*), stingy, tightfisted

parson *noun* =**clergyman**, churchman, cleric,

part ❶ *noun* **1** one of the pieces that make up a whole. **2** one of several equal divisions. **3** actor's role. **4** (often pl) region, area. **5** component of a vehicle or machine. ◆ *verb* **6** divide or separate. **7** (of people) leave each other. **part and parcel of** necessary part of. **take someone's part** support someone in an argument etc. **take (something) in good part** respond to (teasing or criticism) with good humour. **parting** *noun* **1** occasion when one person leaves another. **2** line of scalp between sections of hair combed in opposite directions. **3** dividing or separating. **partly** *adverb* not completely. **part of speech** particular grammatical class of words, such as noun or verb. **part time** for less than the full working week. **part-time** *adjective* occupying or working less than the full working week. **part with** *verb* give away, hand over.

partake ❶ *verb* **-taking, -took, -taken 1** (foll. by *of*) take (food or drink). **2** (foll. by *in*) take part in.

partial ❶ *adjective* **1** not complete. **2** prejudiced. **partial to** having a liking for. **partiality** *noun* **partially** *adverb*

participate ❶ *verb* become actively involved.

participant *noun* **participation** *noun*

participle *noun* form of a verb used in compound tenses or as an adjective, e.g. *worried; worrying.*

particle ❶ *noun* **1** extremely small piece or amount. **2** *Physics* minute piece of matter, such as a proton or electron.

particular ❶ *adjective* **1** relating to one person or thing, not general. **2** exceptional or special. **3** very exact. **4** difficult to please, fastidious. ◆ *noun* **5** item of information, detail. **6** separate distinct item as opposed to a generalization, e.g. *to go from the general to the particular.* **particularly** *adverb* **particularize** *verb* give details about.

partisan ❶ *noun* **1** strong supporter of a party or group. **2** guerrilla, member of a resistance movement. ◆ *adjective* **3** prejudiced or one-sided.

partition ❶ *noun* **1** screen or thin wall that divides a room. **2** division of a country into independent parts. ◆ *verb* **3** divide with a partition.

partner ❶ *noun* **1** either member of a couple in a relationship or activity. **2** member of a business partnership. ◆ *verb* **3** be the partner of.

——————— THESAURUS ———————

minister, pastor, preacher, priest, vicar
part *noun* **1 = piece**, bit, fraction, fragment, portion, scrap, section, share OPPOSITE entirety. **2 = division**, branch, component, constituent, member, unit **3 = role**, character, lines **4** (often pl) **= region**, area, district, neighbourhood, quarter, vicinity ◆*verb* **6 = divide**, break, come apart, detach, rend, separate, sever, split, tear OPPOSITE unite. **7 = leave**, depart, go, go away, separate, split up, withdraw OPPOSITE gather
partake *verb* **1** (foll. by *of*) **= consume**, eat, take **2** (foll. by *in*) **= participate in**, engage in, share in, take part in
partial *adjective* **1 = incomplete**, imperfect, uncompleted, unfinished OPPOSITE complete. **2 = biased**, discriminatory, one-sided, partisan, prejudiced, unfair, unjust OPPOSITE objective
partiality *noun* **2 = bias**, favouritism, preference, prejudice OPPOSITE equity
partially *adverb* **1 = partly**, fractionally, incompletely, in part, not wholly, somewhat
participant *noun* **= participator**, contributor, member, player
participate *verb* **= take part**, be involved in, join in, partake, perform, share OPPOSITE refrain from
participation *noun* **= taking part**, contribution, involvement, joining in, partaking,

sharing in
particle *noun* **1 = bit**, grain, iota, jot, mite, piece, scrap, shred, speck
particular *adjective* **1 = specific**, distinct, exact, peculiar, precise, special OPPOSITE general. **2 = special**, especial, exceptional, marked, notable, noteworthy, remarkable, singular, uncommon, unusual **4 = fussy**, choosy (*inf*), demanding, fastidious, finicky, pernickety (*inf*), picky (*inf*) OPPOSITE easy ◆*noun* **5 = detail**, circumstance, fact, feature, item, specification
particularly *adverb* **1 = specifically**, distinctly, especially, explicitly, expressly, in particular **2 = especially**, exceptionally, notably, singularly, uncommonly, unusually
parting *noun* **1 = going**, farewell, goodbye **3 = division**, breaking, rift, rupture, separation, split
partisan *noun* **1 = supporter**, adherent, devotee, upholder OPPOSITE leader. **2 = underground fighter**, guerrilla, resistance fighter ◆*adjective* **3 = prejudiced**, biased, interested, one-sided, partial, sectarian OPPOSITE impartial
partition *noun* **1 = screen**, barrier, wall **2 = division**, segregation, separation ◆*verb* **3 = separate**, divide, screen
partly *adverb* **= partially**, slightly, somewhat

P

partnership *noun* joint business venture between two or more people.
partridge *noun* game bird of the grouse family.
parturition *noun* act of giving birth.
party ❶ *noun, pl* **-ties 1** social gathering for pleasure. **2** group of people travelling or working together. **3** group of people with a common political aim. **4** person or people forming one side in a lawsuit or dispute. ◆ *verb* **5** celebrate, have fun. **party line 1** official view of a political party. **2** telephone line shared by two or more subscribers. **party wall** common wall separating adjoining buildings.
parvenu [**par**-ven-new] *noun* person newly risen to a position of power or wealth.
pascal *noun* unit of pressure.
paschal [**pass**-kal] *adjective* of the Passover or Easter.
pass ❶ *verb* **1** go by, past, or through. **2** move or extend in a particular direction. **3** be successful in (a test or examination). **4** spend (time) or (of time) go by. **5** give, hand. **6** be inherited by. **7** *Sport* hit, kick, or throw (the ball) to another player. **8** (of a law-making body) agree to (a law). **9** announce (a sentence or verdict) officially. **10** exceed. **11** choose not to answer a question or not to take one's turn in a game. **12** discharge (urine etc.) from the body. **13** come to an end. ◆ *noun* **14** successful result in a test or examination. **15** *Sport* transfer of a ball. **16** narrow gap through mountains.

17 permit or licence. **make a pass at** *Informal* make sexual advances to. **pass for** be accepted as. **passable** *adjective* **1** (just) acceptable. **2** (of a road) capable of being travelled along.
passing *adjective* **1** brief or transitory. **2** cursory or casual. **pass away** *verb* die. **pass out** *verb Informal* faint. **pass over** *verb* take no notice of, disregard. **pass up** *verb Informal* fail to take advantage of (something).
passage ❶ *noun* **1** channel or opening providing a way through. **2** hall or corridor. **3** section of a book etc. **4** journey by sea. **5** act of passing from one place or condition to another. **6** right or freedom to pass. **passageway** *noun* passage or corridor.
passbook *noun* book issued by a bank or building society for keeping a record of deposits and withdrawals.
passé [**pas**-say] *adjective* out-of-date.
passenger ❶ *noun* **1** person travelling in a vehicle driven by someone else. **2** member of a team who does not pull his or her weight.
passer-by ❶ *noun, pl* **passers-by** person who is walking past something or someone.
passerine *adjective* belonging to the order of perching birds.
passim *adverb Latin* everywhere, throughout.
passion ❶ *noun* **1** intense sexual love. **2** any strong emotion. **3** great enthusiasm. **4** (P-) *Christianity* the suffering of Christ. **passionate** *adjective* **passionately** *adverb* **passionflower** *noun* tropical American plant. **passion fruit**

—————— THESAURUS ——————

partner *noun* **1** = **spouse**, consort, husband *or* wife, mate, significant other (*US inf*) **2** = **associate**, colleague
partnership *noun* = **company**, alliance, cooperative, firm, house, society, union
party *noun* **1** = **get-together** (*inf*), celebration, do (*inf*), festivity, function, gathering, reception, social gathering **2** = **group**, band, company, crew, gang, squad, team, unit **3** = **faction**, camp, clique, coterie, league, set, side
pass *verb* **1** = **go by** *or* **past**, elapse, go, lapse, move, proceed, run OPPOSITE **stop**. **3** = **qualify**, do, get through, graduate, succeed OPPOSITE **fail**. **4** = **spend**, fill, occupy, while away **5** = **give**, convey, deliver, hand, send, transfer **8** = **approve**, accept, decree, enact, legislate, ordain, ratify OPPOSITE **refuse**. **10** = **exceed**, beat, go beyond, outdo, outstrip, overtake, surpass **13** = **end**, blow over, cease, go ◆ *noun* **16** = **gap**, canyon, gorge, ravine, route **17** = **licence**, authorization, passport, permit, ticket, warrant
passable *adjective* **1** = **adequate**, acceptable,

all right, average, fair, mediocre, so-so (*inf*), tolerable OPPOSITE **extraordinary**
passage *noun* **1** = **way**, alley, avenue, channel, course, path, road, route **2** = **corridor**, hall, lobby, vestibule **3** = **extract**, excerpt, piece, quotation, reading, section, text **4** = **journey**, crossing, trek, trip, voyage **6** = **safe-conduct**, freedom, permission, right
passageway *noun* = **corridor**, aisle, alley, hall, hallway, lane, passage
pass away *verb* = **die**, cark (*Aust & NZ sl*), expire, kick the bucket (*sl*), pass on, pass over, shuffle off this mortal coil, snuff it (*inf*)
passé *adjective* = **out-of-date**, dated, obsolete, old-fashioned, old hat, outdated, outmoded, unfashionable
passenger *noun* **1** = **traveller**, fare, rider
passer-by *noun* = **bystander**, onlooker, witness
passing *adjective* **1** = **momentary**, brief, ephemeral, fleeting, short-lived, temporary, transient, transitory **2** = **superficial**, casual, cursory, glancing, quick, short

edible fruit of the passionflower. **Passion play** play about Christ's suffering.

passive ⊕ *adjective* **1** not playing an active part. **2** submissive and receptive to outside forces. **3** *Grammar* (of a verb) in a form indicating that the subject receives the action, e.g. *was jeered* in *he was jeered by the crowd.* **passively** *adverb* **passivity** *noun* **passive resistance** resistance to a government, law, etc. by nonviolent acts. **passive smoking** inhalation of smoke from others' cigarettes by a nonsmoker.

Passover *noun* Jewish festival commemorating the sparing of the Jews in Egypt.

passport *noun* official document granting permission to travel abroad.

password ⊕ *noun* secret word or phrase that ensures admission.

past ⊕ *adjective* **1** of the time before the present. **2** ended, gone by. **3** *Grammar* (of a verb tense) indicating that the action specified took place earlier. ♦ *noun* **4** period of time before the present. **5** person's earlier life, esp. a disreputable period. **6** *Grammar* past tense. ♦ *adverb* **7** ago. **8** by, along. ♦ *preposition* **9** beyond. **past it** *Informal* unable to do the things one could do when younger. **past master** person with great talent or experience in a particular subject.

pasta *noun* type of food, such as spaghetti, that is made in different shapes from flour and water.

paste ⊕ *noun* **1** moist soft mixture, such as toothpaste. **2** adhesive, esp. for paper. **3** smooth preparation of fish etc. for spreading on bread. **4** pastry dough. **5** shiny glass used to make imitation jewellery. ♦ *verb* **6** fasten with paste. **pasting** *noun Informal* **1** heavy defeat. **2** strong criticism. **pasteboard** *noun* stiff thick paper.

pastel ⊕ *noun* **1** coloured chalk crayon for drawing. **2** picture drawn in pastels. **3** pale delicate colour. ♦ *adjective* **4** pale and delicate in colour.

pasteurize *verb* sterilize by heating. **pasteurization** *noun*

pastiche ⊕ [pass-**teesh**] *noun* work of art that mixes styles or copies the style of another artist.

pastille *noun* small fruit-flavoured and sometimes medicated sweet.

pastime ⊕ *noun* activity that makes time pass pleasantly.

pastor ⊕ *noun* clergyman in charge of a congregation. **pastoral** *adjective* **1** of or depicting country life. **2** of a clergyman or his duties. ♦ *noun* **3** poem or picture portraying country life.

pastrami *noun* highly seasoned smoked beef.

pastry *noun, pl* **-ries 1** baking dough made of flour, fat, and water. **2** cake or pie.

pasture ⊕ *noun* grassy land for farm animals to graze on.

pasty¹ ⊕ [**pay**-stee] *adjective* **pastier, pastiest** (of a complexion) pale and unhealthy.

——————— THESAURUS ———————

passion *noun* **1** = **love**, ardour, desire, infatuation, lust **2** = **emotion**, ardour, excitement, feeling, fervour, fire, heat, intensity, warmth, zeal OPPOSITE **indifference**. **3** = **mania**, bug (*inf*), craving, craze, enthusiasm, fascination, obsession

passionate *adjective* **1** = **loving**, amorous, ardent, erotic, hot, lustful OPPOSITE **cold**. **2** = **emotional**, ardent, eager, fervent, fierce, heartfelt, impassioned, intense, strong OPPOSITE **calm**

passive *adjective* **1, 2** = **submissive**, compliant, docile, inactive, quiescent, receptive OPPOSITE **spirited**

pass out *verb Inf* = **faint**, become unconscious, black out (*inf*), lose consciousness

pass over *verb* = **disregard**, ignore, overlook, take no notice of

pass up *verb Inf* = **miss**, abstain, decline, forgo, give (something) a miss (*inf*), let slip, neglect

password *noun* = **signal**, key word, watchword

past *adjective* **1** = **former**, ancient, bygone, early, olden, previous OPPOSITE **future**. **2** = **over**, done, ended, finished, gone ♦*noun* **4** = **former times**, days gone by, long ago, olden days OPPOSITE **now**. **5** = **background**, history, life, past life ♦*preposition* **9** = **beyond**, across, by, over

paste *noun* **2** = **adhesive**, cement, glue, gum ♦*verb* **6** = **stick**, cement, glue, gum

pastel *adjective* **4** = **pale**, delicate, light, muted, soft OPPOSITE **bright**

pastiche *noun* = **medley**, *melange*, blend, hotchpotch, miscellany, mixture

pastime *noun* = **activity**, amusement, diversion, entertainment, game, hobby, recreation

pastor *noun* = **clergyman**, churchman, ecclesiastic, minister, parson, priest, rector, vicar

pastoral *adjective* **1** = **rustic**, bucolic, country, rural **2** = **ecclesiastical**, clerical, ministerial, priestly

pasture *noun* = **grassland**, grass, grazing, meadow

pasty² [**pass**-tee] *noun, pl* **pasties** round of pastry folded over a savoury filling.
pat¹ ❶ *verb* **patting, patted 1** tap lightly. ◆ *noun* **2** gentle tap or stroke. **3** small shaped mass of butter etc.
pat² ❶ *adjective* quick, ready, or glib. **off pat** learned thoroughly.
patch ❶ *noun* **1** piece of material sewn on a garment. **2** small contrasting section. **3** plot of ground. **4** protective pad for the eye. ◆ *verb* **5** mend with a patch. **patchy** *adjective* **patchier, patchiest** of uneven quality or intensity. **patch up** *verb* **1** repair clumsily. **2** make up (a quarrel). **patchwork** *noun* needlework made of pieces of different materials sewn together.
pate *noun Old-fashioned* head.
pâté [**pat**-ay] *noun* spread of finely minced liver etc.
patella *noun, pl* **-lae** kneecap.
patent ❶ *noun* **1** document giving the exclusive right to make or sell an invention. ◆ *adjective* **2** open to public inspection, e.g. *letters patent.* **3** obvious. **4** protected by a patent. ◆ *verb* **5** obtain a patent for. **patently** *adverb* obviously. **patent leather** leather processed to give a hard glossy surface.
paternal ❶ *adjective* **1** fatherly. **2** related through one's father. **paternity** *noun* fact or state of being a father. **paternalism** *noun* authority exercised in a way that limits individual responsibility. **paternalistic** *adjective*
path ❶ *noun* **1** surfaced walk or track. **2** course or direction. **3** course of action.
pathetic ❶ *adjective* **1** causing feelings of pity or sadness. **2** distressingly inadequate.

pathetically *adverb*
pathogen *noun* thing that causes disease. **pathogenic** *adjective*
pathology *noun* scientific study of diseases. **pathological** *adjective* **1** of pathology. **2** *Informal* compulsively motivated. **pathologist** *noun*
pathos ❶ *noun* power of arousing pity or sadness.
patient ❶ *adjective* **1** enduring difficulties or delays calmly. ◆ *noun* **2** person receiving medical treatment. **patience** *noun* **1** quality of being patient. **2** card game for one.
patina *noun* **1** fine layer on a surface. **2** sheen of age on woodwork.
patio *noun, pl* **-tios** paved area adjoining a house.
patois [**pat**-wah] *noun, pl* **patois** [**pat**-wahz] regional dialect.
patriarch *noun* **1** male head of a family or tribe. **2** highest-ranking bishop in Orthodox Churches. **patriarchal** *adjective* **patriarchy** *noun, pl* **-chies** society in which men have most of the power.
patrician *noun* **1** member of the nobility. ◆ *adjective* **2** of noble birth.
patricide *noun* **1** crime of killing one's father. **2** person who does this.
patrimony *noun, pl* **-nies** property inherited from ancestors.
patriot ❶ *noun* person who loves his or her country and supports its interests. **patriotic** *adjective* **patriotism** *noun*
patrol ❶ *noun* **1** regular circuit by a guard. **2** person or small group patrolling. **3** unit of

P

———————————— THESAURUS ————————————

pasty¹ *adjective* =**pale**, anaemic, pallid, sickly, wan
pat¹ *verb* **1** =**stroke**, caress, fondle, pet, tap, touch ◆*noun* **2** =**stroke**, clap, tap
pat² *adjective* =**glib**, automatic, easy, facile, ready, simplistic, slick, smooth **off pat** =**perfectly**, exactly, faultlessly, flawlessly, precisely
patch *noun* **1** =**reinforcement**, piece of material **2** =**spot**, bit, scrap, shred, small piece **3** =**plot**, area, ground, land, tract ◆*verb* **5** =**mend**, cover, reinforce, repair, sew up
patchy *adjective* =**uneven**, erratic, fitful, irregular, sketchy, spotty, variable OPPOSITE constant
patent *noun* **1** =**copyright**, licence ◆*adjective* **3** =**obvious**, apparent, clear, evident, glaring, manifest
paternal *adjective* **1** =**fatherly**, concerned, protective, solicitous

paternity *noun* =**fatherhood**
path *noun* **1** =**way**, footpath, road, track, trail **2** =**course**, direction, road, route, way
pathetic *adjective* **1** =**sad**, affecting, distressing, gut-wrenching, heart-rending, moving, pitiable, plaintive, poignant, tender, touching OPPOSITE funny
pathos *noun* =**sadness**, pitifulness, plaintiveness, poignancy
patience *noun* **1** =**forbearance**, calmness, restraint, serenity, sufferance, tolerance OPPOSITE passion
patient *adjective* **1** =**long-suffering**, calm, enduring, persevering, philosophical, resigned, stoical, submissive, uncomplaining OPPOSITE impatient ◆*noun* **2** =**sick person**, case, invalid, sufferer
patriot *noun* =**nationalist**, chauvinist, loyalist
patriotic *adjective* =**nationalistic**, chauvinistic, jingoistic, loyal

Scouts or Guides. ♦ *verb* **-trolling, -trolled 4** go round on guard, or reconnoitring. **patrol car** police car used for patrolling streets.
patron ❶ *noun* **1** person who gives financial support to charities, artists, etc. **2** regular customer of a shop, pub, etc. **patronage** *noun* support given by a patron. **patronize** *verb* **1** treat in a condescending way. **2** be a patron of. **patronizing** *adjective* **patron saint** saint regarded as the guardian of a country or group.
patronymic *noun* name derived from one's father or a male ancestor.
patter¹ ❶ *verb* **1** make repeated soft tapping sounds. ♦ *noun* **2** quick succession of taps.
patter² ❶ *noun* glib rapid speech.
pattern ❶ *noun* **1** arrangement of repeated parts or decorative designs. **2** regular way that something is done. **3** diagram or shape used as a guide to make something. **patterned** *adjective* decorated with a pattern.
patty *noun, pl* **-ties** small round meat pie.
paucity ❶ *noun* **1** scarcity. **2** smallness of amount or number.
paunch ❶ *noun* protruding belly.
pauper ❶ *noun* very poor person.
pause ❶ *verb* **1** stop for a time. **2** hesitate. ♦ *noun* **3** stop or rest in speech or action. **4** *Music* continuation of a note or rest beyond its normal length.
pave ❶ *verb* form (a surface) with stone or

brick. **pavement** *noun* paved path for pedestrians.
pavilion *noun* **1** building on a playing field etc. **2** building for housing an exhibition etc.
pavlova *noun* meringue cake topped with whipped cream and fruit.
paw ❶ *noun* **1** animal's foot with claws and pads. ♦ *verb* **2** scrape with the paw or hoof. **3** *Informal* touch in a rough or overfamiliar way.
pawl *noun* pivoted lever shaped to engage with a ratchet to prevent motion in a particular direction.
pawn¹ ❶ *verb* deposit (an article) as security for money borrowed. **in pawn** deposited as security with a pawnbroker. **pawnbroker** *noun* lender of money on goods deposited.
pawn² ❶ *noun* **1** chessman of the lowest value. **2** person manipulated by someone else.
pawpaw *noun* same as PAPAYA.
pay ❶ *verb* **paying, paid 1** give money etc. in return for goods or services. **2** settle a debt or obligation. **3** compensate (for). **4** give. **5** be profitable to. ♦ *noun* **6** wages or salary.
payment *noun* **1** act of paying. **2** money paid. **payable** *adjective* due to be paid. **payee** *noun* person to whom money is paid or due. **paying guest** lodger. **pay off** *verb* **1** pay (debt) in full. **2** turn out successfully. **pay out** *verb* **1** spend. **2** release (a rope) bit by bit.
PAYE pay as you earn: system by which

———————————— THESAURUS ————————————

patriotism *noun* =**nationalism**, jingoism
patrol *noun* **1** =**policing**, guarding, protecting, vigilance, watching **2** =**guard**, patrolman, sentinel, watch, watchman ♦*verb* **4** =**police**, guard, inspect, keep guard, keep watch, safeguard
patron *noun* **1** =**supporter**, backer, benefactor, champion, friend, helper, philanthropist, sponsor **2** =**customer**, buyer, client, frequenter, habitué, shopper
patronage *noun* =**support**, aid, assistance, backing, help, promotion, sponsorship
patronize *verb* **1** =**talk down to**, look down on **2 a** =**support**, back, fund, help, maintain, promote, sponsor **b** =**be a customer** *or* **client of**, do business with, frequent, shop at
patronizing *adjective* **1** =**condescending**, disdainful, gracious, haughty, snobbish, supercilious, superior
patter¹ *verb* **1** =**tap**, beat, pat, pitter-patter ♦*noun* **2** =**tapping**, pattering, pitter-patter
patter² *noun* =**spiel**, line, pitch (*inf*)
pattern *noun* **1** =**design**, arrangement, decoration, device, figure, motif **2** =**order**, method, plan, sequence, system **3** =**plan**,

design, diagram, guide, original, stencil, template
paucity *noun* =**scarcity**, dearth, deficiency, lack, rarity, scantiness, shortage, sparseness
paunch *noun* =**belly**, pot, potbelly, spare tyre (*Brit sl*)
pauper *noun* =**down-and-out**, bankrupt, beggar, mendicant, poor person
pause *verb* **1** =**stop briefly**, break, cease, delay, halt, have a breather (*inf*), interrupt, rest, take a break, wait OPPOSITE **continue** ♦*noun* **2** =**stop**, break, breather (*inf*), cessation, gap, halt, interlude, intermission, interval, lull, respite, rest, stoppage OPPOSITE **advancement**
pave *verb* =**cover**, concrete, floor, surface, tile
paw *verb* **3** *Inf* =**manhandle**, grab, handle roughly, maul, molest
pawn¹ *verb* =**hock** (*inf, chiefly US*), deposit, mortgage, pledge
pawn² *noun* **2** =**tool**, cat's-paw, instrument, plaything, puppet, stooge (*sl*)
pay *verb* **1, 2** =**reimburse**, give, remit, remunerate, requite, reward, settle **3** =**compensate**, recompense **4** =**give**, bestow, extend, grant, hand out, present **5** =**be**

income tax is paid by an employer straight to the government.

payload noun **1** passengers or cargo of an aircraft. **2** explosive power of a missile etc.

payola noun Informal bribe to get special treatment, esp. to promote a commercial product.

payroll noun list of employees who receive regular pay.

Pb Chem lead.

pc per cent.

PC 1 personal computer. **2** Police Constable. **3** politically correct. **4** Privy Councillor.

Pd Chem palladium.

PDA personal digital assistant.

PE 1 physical education. **2** Prince Edward Island.

pea noun **1** climbing plant with seeds growing in pods. **2** its seed, eaten as a vegetable.

peasouper noun Informal thick fog.

peace ⊕ noun **1** calm, quietness. **2** absence of anxiety. **3** freedom from war. **4** harmony between people. **peaceable** adjective inclined towards peace. **peaceably** adverb **peaceful** adjective **peacefully** adverb **peacemaker** noun person who brings about peace, esp. between others.

peach noun **1** soft juicy fruit with a stone and a downy skin. **2** Informal very pleasing person or thing. ♦ adjective **3** pinkish-orange.

peacock noun large male bird with a brilliantly coloured fanlike tail. **peahen** n fem **peafowl** noun peacock or peahen.

peak ⊕ noun **1** pointed top, esp. of a mountain. **2** point of greatest development etc.

3 projecting piece on the front of a cap. ♦ verb **4** form or reach a peak. ♦ adjective **5** of or at the point of greatest demand. **peaked** adjective **peaky** adjective **peakier, peakiest** pale and sickly.

peal ⊕ noun **1** long loud echoing sound, esp. of bells or thunder. ♦ verb **2** sound with a peal or peals.

peanut noun **1** pea-shaped nut that ripens underground. ♦ plural **2** Informal trifling amount of money.

pear noun sweet juicy fruit with a narrow top and rounded base.

pearl noun hard round shiny object found inside some oyster shells and used as a jewel. **pearly** adjective **pearlier, pearliest**. **pearl barley** barley ground into small round grains.

peasant ⊕ noun farmer or farmworker of a low social class. **peasantry** noun peasants collectively.

pease pudding noun dish of boiled split peas.

peat noun decayed vegetable material found in bogs, used as fertilizer or fuel.

pebble noun small roundish stone. **pebbly** adjective **pebblier, pebbliest**. **pebble dash** coating for exterior walls consisting of small stones set in plaster.

pecan [pee-kan] noun edible nut of a N American tree.

peccadillo ⊕ noun, pl **-loes, -los** trivial misdeed.

peck[1] ⊕ verb **1** strike or pick up with the beak. **2** Informal kiss quickly. ♦ noun **3** pecking movement. **peckish** adjective Informal slightly

P

profitable, benefit, be worthwhile, make a return, make money, repay ♦noun **6** =**wages**, allowance, earnings, fee, income, payment, recompense, reimbursement, remuneration, reward, salary, stipend

payable adjective =**due**, outstanding, owed, owing

payment noun **1** =**paying**, discharge, remittance, settlement **2** =**wage**, advance, deposit, fee, hire, instalment, premium, remittance, remuneration, reward

pay off verb **1** =**settle**, clear, discharge, pay in full, square **2** =**succeed**, be effective, work

pay out verb **1** =**spend**, disburse, expend, fork out or over or up (sl), shell out (inf)

peace noun **1** =**stillness**, calm, calmness, hush, quiet, repose, rest, silence, tranquillity **2** =**serenity**, calm, composure, contentment, repose **3** =**truce**, armistice, treaty OPPOSITE war. **4** =**harmony**, accord, agreement, concord

peaceable adjective =**peace-loving**, conciliatory, friendly, gentle, mild, peaceful, unwarlike

peaceful adjective **1** =**calm**, placid, quiet, restful, serene, still, tranquil, undisturbed OPPOSITE disturbed. **3** =**peace-loving**, conciliatory, peaceable, unwarlike OPPOSITE belligerent. **4** =**at peace**, amicable, friendly, harmonious, nonviolent OPPOSITE warring

peacemaker noun =**mediator**, arbitrator, conciliator, pacifier

peak noun **1** =**point**, apex, brow, crest, pinnacle, summit, tip, top **2** =**high point**, acme, climax, crown, culmination, zenith ♦verb **4** =**culminate**, climax, come to a head

peal noun **1** =**ring**, blast, chime, clang, clap, crash, reverberation, roar, rumble ♦verb **2** =**ring**, chime, crash, resound, roar, rumble

peasant noun =**rustic**, countryman

peccadillo noun =**misdeed**, error,

hungry. **peck at** verb nibble, eat reluctantly.
pecking order order of seniority or power in a group.
peck² noun fourth part of a bushel, 2 gallons.
pectin noun substance in fruit that makes jam set.
pectoral adjective **1** of the chest or thorax. ◆ noun **2** pectoral muscle or fin.
peculiar ⊕ adjective **1** strange. **2** distinct, special. **3** belonging exclusively to. **peculiarity** noun, pl **-ties 1** oddity, eccentricity. **2** distinguishing trait.
pecuniary adjective relating to, or consisting of, money.
pedagogue ⊕ noun schoolteacher, esp. a pedantic one.
pedal noun **1** foot-operated lever used to control a vehicle or machine, or to modify the tone of a musical instrument. ◆ verb **-alling, -alled 2** propel (a bicycle) by using its pedals.
pedant ⊕ noun person who is excessively concerned with details and rules, esp. in academic work. **pedantic** adjective **pedantry** noun
peddle ⊕ verb sell (goods) from door to door.
peddler noun person who sells illegal drugs.
pederast noun man who has homosexual relations with boys. **pederasty** noun
pedestal ⊕ noun base supporting a column, statue, etc.
pedestrian ⊕ noun **1** person who walks. ◆

adjective **2** dull, uninspiring. **pedestrian crossing** place marked where pedestrians may cross a road. **pedestrian precinct** (shopping) area for pedestrians only.
pedicure noun medical or cosmetic treatment of the feet.
pedigree ⊕ noun register of ancestors, esp. of a purebred animal.
pediment noun triangular part over a door etc.
pedlar ⊕ noun person who sells goods from door to door.
pedometer [pid-**dom**-it-er] noun instrument which measures the distance walked.
pee Informal verb **peeing, peed 1** urinate. ◆ noun **2** urine. **3** act of urinating.
peek ⊕ verb, noun peep or glance.
peel ⊕ verb **1** remove the skin or rind of (a vegetable or fruit). **2** (of skin or a surface) come off in flakes. ◆ noun **3** rind or skin. **peelings** plural noun
peep¹ ⊕ verb **1** look slyly or quickly. ◆ noun **2** peeping look. **Peeping Tom** man who furtively watches women undressing.
peep² ⊕ verb **1** make a small shrill noise. ◆ noun **2** small shrill noise.
peer¹ ⊕ noun **1** (fem (**peeress**) member of the nobility. **2** person of the same status, age, etc. **peerage** noun **1** whole body of peers. **2** rank of a peer. **peerless** adjective unequalled, unsurpassed. **peer group** group of people of

—————————— THESAURUS ——————————

indiscretion, lapse, misdemeanour, slip
peck¹ verb **1** =**pick**, dig, hit, jab, poke, prick, strike, tap
peculiar adjective **1** =**odd**, abnormal, bizarre, curious, eccentric, extraordinary, freakish, funny, munted (NZ sl), offbeat, outlandish, outré, quaint, queer, singular, strange, uncommon, unconventional, unusual, weird OPPOSITE> **ordinary. 2** =**specific**, characteristic, distinctive, particular, special, unique OPPOSITE> **general**
peculiarity noun **1** =**eccentricity**, abnormality, foible, idiosyncrasy, mannerism, oddity, quirk **2** =**characteristic**, attribute, feature, mark, particularity, property, quality, trait
pedagogue noun =**teacher**, instructor, master or mistress, schoolmaster or schoolmistress
pedant noun =**hairsplitter**, nit-picker (inf), quibbler
pedantic adjective =**hairsplitting**, academic, bookish, donnish, formal, fussy, nit-picking (inf), particular, precise, punctilious

pedantry noun =**hairsplitting**, punctiliousness, quibbling
peddle verb =**sell**, flog (sl), hawk, market, push (inf), trade
pedestal noun =**support**, base, foot, mounting, plinth, stand
pedestrian noun **1** =**walker**, foot-traveller OPPOSITE> **driver** ◆adjective **2** =**dull**, banal, boring, commonplace, humdrum, mediocre, mundane, ordinary, prosaic, run-of-the-mill, uninspired OPPOSITE> **interesting**
pedigree noun =**lineage**, ancestry, blood, breed, descent, extraction, family, family tree, genealogy, line, race, stock
pedlar noun =**seller**, door-to-door salesman, hawker, huckster, vendor
peek verb =**glance**, eyeball (sl), look, peep ◆noun =**glance**, glimpse, look, look-see (sl), peep
peel verb **1** =**skin**, pare, strip off **2** =**flake off**, scale ◆noun **3** =**skin**, peeling, rind
peep¹ verb **1** =**peek**, eyeball (sl), look, sneak a look, steal a look ◆noun **2** =**look**, glimpse, look-see (sl), peek
peep² verb **1** =**tweet**, cheep, chirp, squeak

similar age, status, etc.
peer² ❶ *verb* look closely and intently.
peeved *adjective Informal* annoyed.
peevish ❶ *adjective* fretful or irritable.
peevishly *adverb*
peewit *noun* same as LAPWING.
peg ❶ *noun* **1** pin or clip for joining, fastening, marking, etc. **2** hook or knob for hanging things on. ♦ *verb* **pegging, pegged 3** fasten with pegs. **4** stabilize (prices). **off the peg** (of clothes) ready-to-wear, not tailor-made.
peignoir [**pay**-nwahr] *noun* woman's light dressing gown.
pejorative ❶ [pij-**jor**-a-tiv] *adjective* (of words etc.) with an insulting or critical meaning.
Pekingese, Pekinese *noun, pl* **-ese** small dog with a short wrinkled muzzle.
pelargonium *noun* plant with red, white, or pink flowers.
pelican *noun* large water bird with a pouch beneath its bill for storing fish. **pelican crossing** road crossing with pedestrian-operated traffic lights.
pellagra *noun* disease caused by lack of vitamin B.
pellet *noun* small ball of something.
pell-mell *adverb* in utter confusion, headlong.
pellucid *adjective* very clear.
pelmet *noun* ornamental drapery or board, concealing a curtain rail.
pelt¹ ❶ *verb* **1** throw missiles at. **2** run fast, rush. **3** rain heavily. **at full pelt** at top speed.
pelt² ❶ *noun* skin of a fur-bearing animal.
pelvis *noun* framework of bones at the base of

the spine, to which the hips are attached.
pelvic *adjective*
pen¹ ❶ *noun* **1** instrument for writing in ink. ♦ *verb* **penning, penned 2** write or compose.
pen friend friend with whom a person corresponds without meeting. **penknife** *noun* small knife with blade(s) that fold into the handle. **pen name** name used by a writer instead of his or her real name.
pen² ❶ *noun* **1** small enclosure for domestic animals. ♦ *verb* **penning, penned 2** put or keep in a pen. **penned in** trapped or confined.
pen³ *noun* female swan.
penal ❶ [**pee**-nal] *adjective* of or used in punishment. **penalize** *verb* **1** impose a penalty on. **2** handicap, hinder. **penalty** *noun, pl* **-ties 1** punishment for a crime or offence. **2** *Sport* handicap or disadvantage imposed for breaking a rule.
penance ❶ *noun* voluntary self-punishment to make amends for wrongdoing.
pence *noun* a plural of PENNY.
penchant ❶ [**pon**-shon] *noun* inclination or liking.
pencil *noun* **1** thin cylindrical instrument containing graphite, for writing or drawing. ♦ *verb* **-cilling, -cilled 2** draw, write, or mark with a pencil.
pendant *noun* ornament worn on a chain round the neck.
pendent *adjective* hanging.
pending ❶ *preposition* **1** while waiting for. ♦ *adjective* **2** not yet decided or settled.
pendulous *adjective* hanging, swinging.

P

——————— T H E S A U R U S ———————

♦*noun* **2** = **tweet**, cheep, chirp, squeak
peer¹ *noun* **1** = **noble**, aristocrat, lord, nobleman **2** = **equal**, compeer, fellow, like
peer² *verb* = **squint**, gaze, inspect, peep, scan, snoop, spy
peerage *noun* **1** = **aristocracy**, lords and ladies, nobility, peers
peerless *adjective* = **unequalled**, beyond compare, excellent, incomparable, matchless, outstanding, unmatched, unparalleled, unrivalled
peevish *adjective* = **irritable**, cantankerous, childish, churlish, cross, crotchety (*inf*), fractious, fretful, grumpy, petulant, querulous, snappy, sulky, sullen, surly
peg *verb* **3** = **fasten**, attach, fix, join, secure
pejorative *adjective* = **derogatory**, deprecatory, depreciatory, disparaging, negative, uncomplimentary, unpleasant
pelt¹ *verb* **1** = **throw**, batter, bombard, cast, hurl, pepper, shower, sling, strike **2** = **rush**, belt

(*sl*), charge, dash, hurry, run fast, shoot, speed, tear **3** = **pour**, bucket down (*inf*), rain cats and dogs (*inf*), rain hard, teem
pelt² *noun* = **coat**, fell, hide, skin
pen¹ *verb* **2** = **write**, compose, draft, draw up, jot down **pen name** = **pseudonym**, nom de plume
pen² *noun* **1** = **enclosure**, cage, coop, fold, hutch, pound, sty ♦*verb* **2** = **enclose**, cage, confine, coop up, fence in, hedge, shut up *or* in
penal *adjective* = **disciplinary**, corrective, punitive
penalize *verb* **1** = **punish**, discipline, impose a penalty on **2** = **handicap**
penalty *noun* **1** = **punishment**, fine, forfeit, price **2** *Sport* = **handicap**
penance *noun* = **atonement**, penalty, reparation, sackcloth and ashes
penchant *noun* = **liking**, bent, bias, fondness, inclination, leaning, partiality, predilection, proclivity, propensity, taste, tendency

pendulum *noun* suspended weight swinging to and fro, esp. as a regulator for a clock.
penetrate ⊙ *verb* **1** find or force a way into or through. **2** arrive at the meaning of.
penetrable *adjective* capable of being penetrated. **penetrating** *adjective* **1** (of a sound) loud and unpleasant. **2** quick to understand. **penetration** *noun*
penguin *noun* flightless black-and-white Antarctic sea bird.
penicillin *noun* antibiotic drug effective against a wide range of diseases and infections.
peninsula *noun* strip of land nearly surrounded by water. **peninsular** *adjective*
penis *noun* organ of copulation and urination in male mammals.
penitent ⊙ *adjective* **1** feeling sorry for having done wrong. ◆ *noun* **2** someone who is penitent. **penitence** *noun* **penitentiary** *noun*, *pl* **-ries 1** US prison. ◆ *adjective* **2** (also **penitential**) relating to penance.
pennant ⊙ *noun* long narrow flag.
pennon *noun* triangular or tapering flag.
penny ⊙ *noun*, *pl* **pence, pennies 1** British bronze coin worth one hundredth of a pound. **2** former British coin worth one twelfth of a shilling. **penniless** *adjective* very poor. **penny-pinching** *adjective* excessively careful with money.
penology [pee-**nol**-a-jee] *noun* study of punishment and prison management.
pension¹ ⊙ *noun* regular payment to people above a certain age, retired employees, widows, etc. **pensionable** *adjective* **pensioner** *noun*

person receiving a pension. **pension off** *verb* force (someone) to retire from a job and pay him or her a pension.
pension² [**pon**-syon] *noun* boarding house in Europe.
pensive ⊙ *adjective* deeply thoughtful, often with a tinge of sadness.
pentagon *noun* **1** geometric figure with five sides. **2** (P-) headquarters of the US military. **pentagonal** *adjective*
pentagram, pentacle *noun* five-pointed star.
pentameter [pen-**tam**-it-er] *noun* line of poetry with five metrical feet.
Pentateuch [**pent**-a-tyuke] *noun* first five books of the Old Testament.
Pentecost *noun* Christian festival celebrating the descent of the Holy Spirit to the apostles, Whitsuntide. **Pentecostal** *adjective* of a Christian group that has a charismatic and fundamentalist approach to Christianity.
penthouse *noun* flat built on the roof or top floor of a building.
pent-up ⊙ *adjective* (of an emotion) not released, repressed.
penultimate *adjective* second last.
penumbra *noun*, *pl* **-brae, -bras 1** (in an eclipse) the partially shadowed region which surrounds the full shadow. **2** partial shadow. **penumbral** *adjective*
penury ⊙ *noun* extreme poverty. **penurious** *adjective*
peony *noun*, *pl* **-nies** garden plant with showy red, pink, or white flowers.

P

———— T H E S A U R U S ————

pending *adjective* **2 = undecided**, awaiting, imminent, impending, in the balance, undetermined, unsettled
penetrate *verb* **1 = pierce**, bore, enter, go through, prick, stab **2 = grasp**, comprehend, decipher, fathom, figure out (*inf*), get to the bottom of, suss (out) (*sl*), work out
penetrating *adjective* **1 = sharp**, carrying, harsh, piercing, shrill OPPOSITE **sweet**. **2 = perceptive**, acute, astute, incisive, intelligent, keen, perspicacious, quick, sharp, sharp-witted, shrewd OPPOSITE **stupid**
penetration *noun* **1 = piercing**, entrance, entry, incision, puncturing **2 = perception**, acuteness, astuteness, insight, keenness, sharpness, shrewdness
penitence *noun* **1 = repentance**, compunction, contrition, regret, remorse, shame, sorrow
penitent *adjective* **1 = repentant**, abject, apologetic, conscience-stricken, contrite,

regretful, remorseful, sorry
pennant *noun* **= flag**, banner, ensign, pennon, streamer
penniless *adjective* **= poor**, broke (*inf*), destitute, dirt-poor (*inf*), down and out, flat broke (*inf*), impecunious, impoverished, indigent, penurious, poverty-stricken, skint (*Brit sl*), stony-broke (*Brit sl*) OPPOSITE **rich**
pension¹ *noun* **= allowance**, annuity, benefit, superannuation
pensioner *noun* **= senior citizen**, O.A.P., retired person
pensive *adjective* **= thoughtful**, contemplative, dreamy, meditative, musing, preoccupied, reflective, sad, serious, solemn, wistful OPPOSITE **carefree**
pent-up *adjective* **= suppressed**, bottled up, curbed, held back, inhibited, repressed, smothered, stifled
penury *noun* **= poverty**, beggary, destitution, indigence, need, privation, want

people ❶ *plural noun* **1** persons generally. **2** the community. **3** one's family. ◆ *noun* **4** race or nation. ◆ *verb* **5** provide with inhabitants.
pep *noun Informal* high spirits, energy, or enthusiasm. **pep pill** *Informal* tablet containing a stimulant drug. **pep talk** *Informal* talk designed to increase confidence and enthusiasm. **pep up** *verb* **pepping, pepped** stimulate, invigorate.
pepper ❶ *noun* **1** sharp hot condiment made from the fruit of an East Indian climbing plant. **2** colourful tropical fruit used as a vegetable, capsicum. ◆ *verb* **3** season with pepper. **4** sprinkle, dot. **5** pelt with missiles. **peppery** *adjective* **1** tasting of pepper. **2** irritable.
peppercorn *noun* dried berry of the pepper plant. **peppercorn rent** low or nominal rent.
pepper mill small hand mill used to grind peppercorns.
peppermint *noun* **1** plant that yields an oil with a strong sharp flavour. **2** sweet flavoured with this.
peptic *adjective* relating to digestion or the digestive juices. **peptic ulcer** ulcer in the stomach or duodenum.
per *preposition* for each. **as per** in accordance with.
perambulate *verb* walk through or about (a place). **perambulation** *noun* **perambulator** *noun* pram.
per annum *adverb Latin* in each year.
per capita *adjective, adverb Latin* of or for each person.
perceive ❶ *verb* **1** become aware of (something) through the senses. **2** understand. **perception** *noun*
percentage *noun* proportion or rate per hundred. **per cent** in each hundred.

perceptible ❶ *adjective* discernible, recognizable. **perceptibly** *adverb*
perception ❶ *noun* **1** act of perceiving. **2** intuitive judgment. **perceptive** *adjective*
perch[1] ❶ *noun* **1** resting place for a bird. ◆ *verb* **2** alight, rest, or place on or as if on a perch.
perch[2] *noun* edible freshwater fish.
perchance *adverb Old-fashioned* perhaps.
percipient *adjective* quick to notice things, observant.
percolate *verb* **1** pass or filter through small holes. **2** spread gradually. **3** make (coffee) or (of coffee) be made in a percolator.
percolation *noun* **percolator** *noun* coffeepot in which boiling water is forced through a tube and filters down through coffee.
percussion ❶ *noun* **1** striking of one thing against another. **2** *Music* percussion instruments collectively. **percussionist** *noun* **percussion instrument** musical instrument played by being struck, such as drums or cymbals.
perdition *noun* spiritual ruin.
peregrination *noun* travels, roaming.
peregrine falcon *noun* falcon with dark upper parts and a light underside.
peremptory ❶ *adjective* authoritative, imperious.
perennial ❶ *adjective* **1** lasting through many years. ◆ *noun* **2** plant lasting more than two years. **perennially** *adverb*
perestroika *noun* (formerly, in the USSR) policy of restructuring the economy and political system.
perfect ❶ *adjective* **1** having all the essential elements. **2** faultless. **3** correct, precise. **4** utter or absolute. **5** excellent. **6** *Grammar* denoting a tense of verbs describing completed actions. ◆

P

——————— THESAURUS ———————

people *plural noun* **1** = **persons**, humanity, mankind, men and women, mortals **2** = **nation**, citizens, community, folk, inhabitants, population, public **3** = **family**, clan, race, tribe ◆*verb* **5** = **inhabit**, colonize, occupy, populate, settle
pepper *noun* **1** = **seasoning**, flavour, spice ◆*verb* **4** = **sprinkle**, dot, fleck, spatter, speck **5** = **pelt**, bombard, shower
perceive *verb* **1** = **see**, behold, discern, discover, espy, make out, note, notice, observe, recognize, spot **2** = **understand**, comprehend, gather, grasp, learn, realize, see, suss (out) (*sl*)
perceptible *adjective* = **visible**, apparent, appreciable, clear, detectable, discernible, evident, noticeable, observable, obvious, recognizable, tangible

perception *noun* **1** = **understanding**, awareness, conception, consciousness, feeling, grasp, idea, impression, notion, sensation, sense
perceptive *adjective* **2** = **observant**, acute, alert, astute, aware, percipient, perspicacious, quick, sharp
perch[1] *noun* **1** = **resting place**, branch, pole, post ◆*verb* **2** = **sit**, alight, balance, land, rest, roost, settle
percussion *noun* **1** = **impact**, blow, bump, clash, collision, crash, knock, smash, thump
peremptory *adjective* = **imperious**, authoritative, bossy (*inf*), dictatorial, dogmatic, domineering, overbearing
perennial *adjective* **1** = **lasting**, abiding, constant, continual, enduring, incessant, persistent, recurrent

noun **7** *Grammar* perfect tense. ♦ *verb* **8** improve. **9** make fully correct. **perfectly** *adverb*
perfection *noun* state of being perfect.
perfectionist *noun* person who demands the highest standards of excellence. **perfectionism** *noun*
perfidious ❶ *adjective* treacherous, disloyal. **perfidy** *noun*
perforate ❶ *verb* make holes in. **perforation** *noun*
perforce *adverb* of necessity.
perform ❶ *verb* **1** carry out (an action). **2** act, sing, or present a play before an audience. **3** fulfil (a request etc.). **performance** *noun* **performer** *noun*
perfume ❶ *noun* **1** liquid cosmetic worn for its pleasant smell. **2** fragrance. ♦ *verb* **3** give a pleasant smell to. **perfumed** *adjective*
perfumer *noun* person who makes or sells perfume. **perfumery** *noun* perfumes in general.
perfunctory ❶ *adjective* done only as a matter of routine, superficial. **perfunctorily** *adverb*
pergola *noun* arch or framework of trellis supporting climbing plants.
perhaps ❶ *adverb* **1** possibly, maybe. **2** approximately.
pericardium *noun, pl* **-dia** membrane enclosing the heart.
perigee *noun* point in the orbit of the moon or a satellite that is nearest the earth.
perihelion *noun, pl* **-lia** point in the orbit of a planet or comet that is nearest to the sun.
peril ❶ *noun* great danger. **perilous** *adjective* **perilously** *adverb*
perimeter ❶ [per-**rim**-it-er] *noun* (length of) the outer edge of an area.
perinatal *adjective* of or in the weeks shortly before or after birth.
period ❶ *noun* **1** particular portion of time. **2** single occurrence of menstruation. **3** division of time at school etc. when a particular subject is taught. **4** *US* full stop. ♦ *adjective* **5** (of furniture, dress, a play, etc.) dating from or in the style of an earlier time. **periodic** *adjective* recurring at intervals. **periodic table** *Chem* chart of the elements, arranged to show their relationship to each other. **periodical** *noun* **1** magazine issued at regular intervals. ♦ *adjective* **2** periodic.
peripatetic [per-rip-a-**tet**-ik] *adjective* travelling about from place to place.

——————— T H E S A U R U S ———————

perfect *adjective* **1** = **complete**, absolute, consummate, entire, finished, full, sheer, unmitigated, utter, whole **2** = **faultless**, flawless, immaculate, impeccable, pure, spotless, unblemished OPPOSITE **flawed**. **3** = **exact**, accurate, correct, faithful, precise, true, unerring **5** = **excellent**, ideal, splendid, sublime, superb, superlative, supreme OPPOSITE **bad** ♦ *verb* **8** = **improve**, develop, polish, refine OPPOSITE **mar**
perfection *noun* = **completeness**, exactness, excellence, exquisiteness, faultlessness, integrity, maturity, perfectness, precision, purity, sublimity, superiority, wholeness
perfectionist *noun* = **stickler**, precisionist, purist
perfectly *adverb* **2** = **flawlessly**, faultlessly, ideally, impeccably, superbly, supremely, wonderfully OPPOSITE **badly**. **4** = **completely**, absolutely, altogether, fully, quite, thoroughly, totally, utterly, wholly
perfidious *adjective* = **treacherous**, disloyal, double-dealing, traitorous, two-faced, unfaithful
perforate *verb* = **pierce**, bore, drill, penetrate, punch, puncture
perform *verb* **1, 3** = **carry out**, accomplish, achieve, complete, discharge, do, execute, fulfil, pull off, work **2** = **present**, act, enact, play, produce, put on, represent, stage

performance *noun* **1, 3** = **carrying out**, accomplishment, achievement, act, completion, execution, fulfilment, work, yakka (*Aust & NZ inf*) **2** = **presentation**, acting, appearance, exhibition, gig (*inf*), play, portrayal, production, show
performer *noun* **2** = **artiste**, actor *or* actress, player, Thespian, trouper
perfume *noun* **2** = **fragrance**, aroma, bouquet, odour, scent, smell
perfunctory *adjective* = **offhand**, cursory, heedless, indifferent, mechanical, routine, sketchy, superficial OPPOSITE **thorough**
perhaps *adverb* **1** = **maybe**, conceivably, feasibly, it may be, perchance (*arch*), possibly
peril *noun* = **danger**, hazard, jeopardy, menace, risk, uncertainty OPPOSITE **security**
perilous *adjective* = **dangerous**, hazardous, precarious, risky, threatening, unsafe
perimeter *noun* = **boundary**, ambit, border, bounds, circumference, confines, edge, limit, margin, periphery OPPOSITE **centre**
period *noun* **1** = **time**, interval, season, space, span, spell, stretch, term, while
periodic *adjective* = **recurrent**, cyclical, intermittent, occasional, regular, repeated, sporadic
periodical *noun* **1** = **publication**, journal, magazine, monthly, paper, quarterly, weekly

periphery ❶ [per-**if**-er-ee] *noun, pl* -**eries 1** boundary or edge. **2** fringes of a field of activity. **peripheral** [per-**if**-er-al] *adjective* **1** unimportant, not central. **2** of or on the periphery. ◆ *noun* **3** any extra device that can be attached to or put in a computer.

periscope *noun* instrument used, esp. in submarines, to give a view of objects on a different level.

perish ❶ *verb* **1** be destroyed or die. **2** decay, rot. **perishable** *adjective* liable to rot quickly. **perishing** *adjective Informal* very cold.

peritoneum [per-rit-toe-**nee**-um] *noun, pl* -**nea, -neums** membrane lining the internal surface of the abdomen. **peritonitis** [per-rit-tone-**ite**-iss] *noun* inflammation of the peritoneum.

periwinkle¹ *noun* small edible shellfish, the winkle.

periwinkle² *noun* plant with trailing stems and blue flowers.

perjury ❶ [per-jer-ee] *noun, pl* -**juries** act or crime of lying while under oath in a court. **perjure oneself** commit perjury.

perk ❶ *noun Informal* incidental benefit gained from a job, such as a company car.

perk up *verb* cheer up. **perky** *adjective* **perkier, perkiest** lively or cheerful.

perm *noun* **1** long-lasting curly hairstyle produced by treating the hair with chemicals. ◆

verb **2** give (hair) a perm.

permafrost *noun* permanently frozen ground.

permanent ❶ *adjective* lasting forever. **permanence** *noun* **permanently** *adverb*

permanganate *noun* a salt of an acid of manganese.

permeate ❶ *verb* pervade or pass through the whole of (something). **permeable** *adjective* able to be permeated, esp. by liquid.

permit ❶ *verb* -**mitting, -mitted 1** give permission, allow. ◆ *noun* **2** document giving permission to do something. **permission** *noun* authorization to do something. **permissible** *adjective* **permissive** *adjective* (excessively) tolerant, esp. in sexual matters.

permissiveness *noun*

permutation *noun* **1** any of the ways a number of things can be arranged or combined. **2** *Maths* arrangement of a number of quantities in every possible order. **3** fixed combination for selections of results on football pools.

pernicious ❶ *adjective* **1** wicked. **2** extremely harmful, deadly.

pernickety ❶ *adjective Informal* (excessively) fussy about details.

peroration *noun* concluding part of a speech, usu. summing up the main points.

peroxide *noun* **1** hydrogen peroxide used as a hair bleach. **2** oxide containing a high

———————————— THESAURUS ————————————

peripheral *adjective* **1** = **incidental**, inessential, irrelevant, marginal, minor, secondary, unimportant **2** = **outermost**, exterior, external, outer, outside

perish *verb* **1 a** = **be destroyed**, cark (*Aust & NZ sl*), collapse, decline, disappear, fall, vanish **b** = **die**, be killed, expire, lose one's life, pass away **2** = **rot**, decay, decompose, disintegrate, moulder, waste

perishable *adjective* = **short-lived**, decaying, decomposable

perjury *noun* = **lying under oath**, bearing false witness, false statement, forswearing, giving false testimony **perjure oneself** = **commit perjury**, bear false witness, forswear, give false testimony, lie under oath, swear falsely

perk *noun Inf* = **bonus**, benefit, extra, fringe benefit, perquisite, plus

permanence *noun* = **continuity**, constancy, continuance, durability, endurance, finality, indestructibility, perpetuity, stability

permanent *adjective* = **lasting**, abiding, constant, enduring, eternal, everlasting, immutable, perpetual, persistent, stable,

steadfast, unchanging OPPOSITE **temporary**

permeate *verb* = **pervade**, charge, fill, imbue, impregnate, infiltrate, penetrate, saturate, spread through

permissible *adjective* = **permitted**, acceptable, allowable, all right, authorized, lawful, legal, legitimate, O.K. *or* okay (*inf*)

permission *noun* = **authorization**, allowance, approval, assent, consent, dispensation, go-ahead (*inf*), green light, leave, liberty, licence, sanction

permissive *adjective* = **tolerant**, easy-going, forbearing, free, indulgent, lax, lenient, liberal

permit *verb* **1** = **allow**, authorize, consent, enable, entitle, give leave *or* permission, give the green light to, grant, let, license, sanction OPPOSITE **ban** ◆*noun* **2** = **licence**, authorization, pass, passport, permission, warrant OPPOSITE **ban**

pernicious *adjective* **1** = **wicked**, bad, evil **2** = **deadly**, damaging, dangerous, destructive, detrimental, fatal, harmful, hurtful, malign, poisonous

pernickety *adjective Inf* = **fussy**, exacting, fastidious, finicky, overprecise, particular, picky

P

proportion of oxygen.

perpendicular ⊙ *adjective* **1** at right angles to a line or surface. **2** upright or vertical. ◆ *noun* **3** line or plane at right angles to another.

perpetrate ⊙ *verb* commit or be responsible for (a wrongdoing). **perpetration** *noun* **perpetrator** *noun*

perpetual ⊙ *adjective* **1** lasting forever. **2** continually repeated. **perpetually** *adverb* **perpetuate** *verb* cause to continue or be remembered. **perpetuation** *noun* **perpetuity** *noun* eternity. **in perpetuity** forever.

perplex ⊙ *verb* puzzle, bewilder. **perplexity** *noun, pl* **-ties**

perquisite ⊙ *noun Formal* same as PERK.

perry *noun, pl* **-ries** alcoholic drink made from fermented pears.

per se [per **say**] *adverb Latin* in itself.

persecute ⊙ *verb* **1** treat cruelly because of race, religion, etc. **2** subject to persistent harassment. **persecution** *noun* **persecutor** *noun*

persevere ⊙ *verb* keep making an effort despite difficulties. **perseverance** *noun*

Persian *adjective* **1** of ancient Persia or modern Iran, their people, or their languages. ◆ *noun* **2** person from modern Iran, Iranian. **Persian carpet, rug** hand-made carpet *or* rug

with flowing or geometric designs in rich colours. **Persian cat** long-haired domestic cat.

persiflage [per-sif-**flahzh**] *noun* light frivolous talk or writing.

persimmon *noun* sweet red tropical fruit.

persist ⊙ *verb* **1** continue to be or happen, last. **2** continue in spite of obstacles or objections. **persistent** *adjective* **persistently** *adverb* **persistence** *noun*

person ⊙ *noun* **1** human being. **2** body of a human being. **3** *Grammar* form of pronouns and verbs that shows if a person is speaking, spoken to, or spoken of. **personal** *adjective* individual, private. **personality** *noun* distinctive character. **in person** actually present.

LANGUAGE TIP

Person is generally used in the singular and *people* is used to indicate more than one. The plural *persons* is restricted to formal notices.

---

persona [per-**soh**-na] *noun, pl* **-nae** [-nee] someone's personality as presented to others.

personable ⊙ *adjective* pleasant in appearance and personality.

———————— T H E S A U R U S ————————

(*inf*) OPPOSITE slack

perpendicular *adjective* **1, 2** = **upright**, at right angles to, on end, plumb, straight, vertical

perpetrate *verb* = **commit**, carry out, do, enact, execute, perform, wreak

perpetual *adjective* **1** = **everlasting**, endless, eternal, infinite, lasting, never-ending, perennial, permanent, unchanging, unending OPPOSITE passing. **2** = **continual**, constant, continuous, endless, incessant, interminable, never-ending, persistent, recurrent, repeated OPPOSITE temporary

perpetuate *verb* = **maintain**, immortalize, keep going, preserve

perplex *verb* = **puzzle**, baffle, bewilder, confound, confuse, mystify, stump

perplexing *adjective* = **puzzling**, baffling, bewildering, complex, complicated, confusing, difficult, enigmatic, hard, inexplicable, mystifying

perplexity *noun* = **puzzlement**, bafflement, bewilderment, confusion, difficulty, fix (*inf*), incomprehension, mystery, mystification, paradox

perquisite same as PERK

persecute *verb* **1** = **victimize**, afflict, ill-treat, maltreat, oppress, pick on, torment, torture

OPPOSITE back. **2** = **harass**, annoy, badger, bother, hassle (*inf*), pester, tease OPPOSITE let alone

perseverance *noun* = **persistence**, determination, diligence, doggedness, endurance, pertinacity, resolution, tenacity

persevere *verb* = **keep going**, carry on, continue, go on, hang on, persist, remain, stick at *or* to OPPOSITE give up

persist *verb* **1** = **continue**, carry on, keep up, last, linger, remain **2** = **persevere**, continue, insist, stand firm

persistence *noun* **2** = **determination**, doggedness, endurance, grit, perseverance, pertinacity, resolution, tenacity, tirelessness

persistent *adjective* **1** = **continuous**, constant, continual, endless, incessant, never-ending, perpetual, repeated OPPOSITE occasional. **2** = **determined**, dogged, obdurate, obstinate, persevering, pertinacious, steadfast, steady, stubborn, tenacious, tireless, unflagging OPPOSITE yielding

person *noun* **1** = **individual**, being, body, human, soul **in person** = **personally**, bodily, in the flesh, oneself

personable *adjective* = **pleasant**, agreeable, amiable, attractive, charming, good-looking,

personage ❶ *noun* important person.
personal ❶ *adjective* **1** individual or private. **2** of the body, e.g. *personal hygiene*. **3** (of a remark etc.) offensive. **personalize** *verb* **personalized** *adjective* **personally** *adverb* **1** directly, not by delegation to others. **2** in one's own opinion. **personal assistant** person employed to help someone, esp. with secretarial and administrative work. **personal column** newspaper column containing personal messages and advertisements. **personal computer** small computer used for word processing or computer games. **personal pronoun** pronoun like *I* or *she* that stands for a definite person. **personal stereo** very small portable cassette player with headphones.
personality ❶ *noun, pl* **-ties 1** person's distinctive characteristics. **2** celebrity. ♦ *plural* **3** personal remarks, e.g. *the discussion degenerated into personalities*.
personify ❶ *verb* **-fying, -fied 1** give human characteristics to. **2** be an example of, typify. **personification** *noun*
personnel ❶ *noun* people employed in an organization.

perspective ❶ *noun* **1** view of the relative importance of situations or facts. **2** method of drawing that gives the effect of solidity and relative distances and sizes. **3** appearance of objects or buildings relative to each other.
Perspex *noun* ® transparent acrylic substitute for glass.
perspicacious ❶ *adjective* having quick mental insight. **perspicacity** *noun*
perspire ❶ *verb* sweat. **perspiration** *noun*
persuade ❶ *verb* **1** make (someone) do something by argument, charm, etc. **2** convince. **persuasion** *noun* **1** act of persuading. **2** way of thinking or belief. **persuasive** *adjective*
pert ❶ *adjective* saucy and cheeky.
pertain ❶ *verb* belong or be relevant (to).
pertinacious *adjective* very persistent and determined. **pertinacity** *noun*
pertinent ❶ *adjective* relevant. **pertinence** *noun*
perturb ❶ *verb* disturb greatly. **perturbation** *noun*
peruse ❶ *verb* read in a careful or leisurely manner. **perusal** *noun*

————————— T H E S A U R U S —————————

handsome, lekker (*S Afr sl*), likable *or* likeable, nice
personage *noun* =**personality**, big shot (*inf*), celebrity, dignitary, luminary, megastar (*inf*), notable, public figure, somebody, V.I.P.
personal *adjective* **1** =**private**, exclusive, individual, intimate, own, particular, peculiar, special **3** =**offensive**, derogatory, disparaging, insulting, nasty
personality *noun* **1** =**nature**, character, disposition, identity, individuality, make-up, temperament **2** =**celebrity**, famous name, household name, megastar (*inf*), notable, personage, star
personally *adverb* **1** =**by oneself**, alone, independently, on one's own, solely **2** =**in one's opinion**, for one's part, from one's own viewpoint, in one's books, in one's own view
personification *noun* **2** =**embodiment**, epitome, image, incarnation, portrayal, representation
personify *verb* **2** =**embody**, epitomize, exemplify, represent, symbolize, typify
personnel *noun* =**employees**, helpers, human resources, people, staff, workers, workforce
perspective *noun* **1** =**objectivity**, proportion, relation, relative importance, relativity
perspicacious *adjective* =**perceptive**, acute, alert, astute, discerning, keen, percipient, sharp, shrewd

perspiration *noun* =**sweat**, moisture, wetness
perspire *verb* =**sweat**, exude, glow, pour with sweat, secrete, swelter
persuade *verb* **1** =**talk into**, bring round (*inf*), coax, entice, impel, incite, induce, influence, sway, urge, win over OPPOSITE forbid. **2** =**convince**, cause to believe, satisfy
persuasion *noun* **1** =**urging**, cajolery, enticement, inducement, wheedling **2** =**creed**, belief, conviction, credo, faith, opinion, tenet, views
persuasive *adjective* =**convincing**, cogent, compelling, credible, effective, eloquent, forceful, influential, plausible, sound, telling, valid, weighty
pert *adjective* =**impudent**, bold, cheeky, forward, impertinent, insolent, sassy (*US inf*), saucy
pertain *verb* =**relate**, apply, befit, belong, be relevant, concern, refer, regard
pertinent *adjective* =**relevant**, applicable, apposite, appropriate, apt, fit, fitting, germane, material, proper, to the point OPPOSITE irrelevant
perturb *verb* =**disturb**, agitate, bother, disconcert, faze, fluster, ruffle, trouble, unsettle, vex, worry
perturbed *adjective* =**disturbed**, agitated, anxious, disconcerted, flustered, shaken, troubled, uncomfortable, uneasy, worried

P

pervade ๏ *verb* spread right through (something). **pervasive** *adjective*

perverse ๏ *adjective* deliberately doing something different from what is thought normal or proper. **perversely** *adverb* **perversity** *noun*

pervert ๏ *verb* **1** use or alter for a wrong purpose. **2** lead into abnormal (sexual) behaviour. ◆ *noun* **3** person who practises sexual perversion. **perversion** *noun* **1** sexual act or desire considered abnormal. **2** act of perverting.

pervious *adjective* able to be penetrated, permeable.

peseta [pa-**say**-ta] *noun* monetary unit of Spain.

peso [**pay**-so] *noun, pl* **pesos** monetary unit of Argentina, Mexico, etc.

pessary *noun, pl* **-ries 1** appliance worn in the vagina, either to prevent conception or to support the womb. **2** vaginal suppository.

pessimism ๏ *noun* tendency to expect the worst in all things. **pessimist** *noun* **pessimistic** *adjective* **pessimistically** *adverb*

pest ๏ *noun* **1** annoying person. **2** insect or animal that damages crops. **pesticide** *noun* chemical for killing insect pests.

pester ๏ *verb* annoy or nag continually.

pestilence ๏ *noun* deadly epidemic disease.

pestilent *adjective* **1** annoying, troublesome. **2** deadly. **pestilential** *adjective*

pestle *noun* club-shaped implement for grinding things to powder in a mortar.

pet ๏ *noun* **1** animal kept for pleasure and companionship. **2** person favoured or indulged. ◆ *adjective* **3** kept as a pet. **4** particularly cherished. ◆ *verb* **petting, petted 5** treat as a pet. **6** pat or stroke affectionately. **7** *Informal* kiss and caress erotically.

petal *noun* one of the brightly coloured outer parts of a flower. **petalled** *adjective*

petard *noun* hoist with one's own petard being the victim of one's own schemes.

peter out ๏ *verb* gradually come to an end.

petite ๏ *adjective* (of a woman) small and dainty.

petition ๏ *noun* **1** formal request, esp. one signed by many people and presented to parliament. ◆ *verb* **2** present a petition to. **petitioner** *noun*

——————— T H E S A U R U S ———————

peruse *verb* =**read**, browse, check, examine, eyeball (*sl*), inspect, scan, scrutinize, study

pervade *verb* =**spread through**, charge, fill, imbue, infuse, penetrate, permeate, suffuse

pervasive *adjective* =**widespread**, common, extensive, general, omnipresent, prevalent, rife, ubiquitous, universal

perverse *adjective* =**stubborn**, contrary, cussed (*inf*), disobedient, dogged, headstrong, intractable, intransigent, obdurate, obstinate, pig-headed, rebellious, refractory, stiff-necked, troublesome, wayward, wilful OPPOSITE cooperative

perversion *noun* **1** =**deviation**, aberration, abnormality, debauchery, depravity, immorality, kink (*Brit inf*), kinkiness (*sl*), unnaturalness, vice **2** =**distortion**, corruption, falsification, misinterpretation, misrepresentation, twisting

perversity *noun* =**contrariness**, contradictoriness, intransigence, obduracy, refractoriness, waywardness, wrong-headedness

pervert *verb* **1** =**distort**, abuse, falsify, garble, misrepresent, misuse, twist, warp **2** =**corrupt**, debase, debauch, degrade, deprave, lead astray ◆*noun* **3** =**deviant**, degenerate, weirdo *or* weirdie (*inf*)

pessimism *noun* =**gloominess**, dejection, depression, despair, despondency, distrust, gloom, hopelessness, melancholy

pessimist *noun* =**wet blanket** (*inf*), cynic, defeatist, killjoy, prophet of doom, worrier

pessimistic *adjective* =**gloomy**, bleak, cynical, dark, dejected, depressed, despairing, despondent, glum, hopeless, morose OPPOSITE optimistic

pest *noun* **1** =**nuisance**, annoyance, bane, bother, drag (*inf*), irritation, pain (*inf*), thorn in one's flesh, trial, vexation **2** =**infection**, blight, bug, epidemic, pestilence, plague, scourge

pester *verb* =**annoy**, badger, bedevil, be on one's back (*sl*), bother, bug (*inf*), harass, harry, hassle (*inf*), nag, plague, torment

pestilence *noun* =**plague**, epidemic, visitation

pestilent *adjective* **1** =**annoying**, bothersome, irksome, irritating, tiresome, vexing **2** =**harmful**, detrimental, evil, injurious, pernicious

pestilential *adjective* **2** =**deadly**, dangerous, destructive, detrimental, harmful, hazardous, injurious, pernicious

pet *noun* **2** =**favourite**, darling, idol, jewel, treasure ◆*adjective* **4** =**favourite**, cherished, dearest, dear to one's heart, favoured ◆*verb* **5** =**pamper**, baby, coddle, cosset, mollycoddle, spoil **6** =**fondle**, caress, pat, stroke **7** *Inf* =**cuddle**, canoodle (*sl*), kiss, neck (*inf*), smooch (*inf*), snog (*Brit sl*)

peter out *verb* =**die out**, dwindle, ebb, fade, fail, run out, stop, taper off, wane

petite *adjective* =**small**, dainty, delicate, elfin,

petrel *noun* sea bird with a hooked bill and tubular nostrils.

petrify ⊙ *verb* **-fying, -fied 1** frighten severely. **2** turn to stone. **petrification** *noun*

petrochemical *noun* substance, such as acetone, obtained from petroleum.

petrodollar *noun* money earned by a country by exporting petroleum.

petrol *noun* flammable liquid obtained from petroleum, used as fuel in internal-combustion engines. **petrol bomb** home-made incendiary device consisting of a bottle filled with petrol. **petrol station** place selling petrol, oil, etc.

petroleum *noun* thick dark oil found underground.

petticoat *noun* woman's skirt-shaped undergarment.

pettifogging *adjective* excessively concerned with unimportant detail.

petty ⊙ *adjective* **-tier, -tiest 1** unimportant, trivial. **2** small-minded. **3** on a small scale, e.g. *petty crime.* **pettiness** *noun* **petty cash** cash kept by a firm to pay minor expenses. **petty officer** noncommissioned officer in the navy.

petulant ⊙ *adjective* childishly irritable or peevish. **petulance** *noun* **petulantly** *adverb*

petunia *noun* garden plant with funnel-shaped flowers.

pew *noun* **1** fixed benchlike seat in a church. **2** *Informal* chair, seat.

pewter *noun* greyish metal made of tin and lead.

pH *Chem* measure of the acidity of a solution.

phalanger *noun* long-tailed Australian tree-dwelling marsupial.

phalanx *noun, pl* **phalanxes, phalanges** closely grouped mass of people.

phallus *noun, pl* **-luses, -li** penis, esp. as a symbol of reproductive power in primitive rites. **phallic** *adjective*

phantasm *noun* unreal vision, illusion.

phantasmal *adj.*

phantasmagoria *noun* shifting medley of dreamlike figures.

phantasy *noun, pl* **-sies** same as FANTASY.

phantom ⊙ *noun* **1** ghost. **2** unreal vision.

Pharaoh [**fare**-oh] *noun* title of the ancient Egyptian kings.

Pharisee *noun* **1** member of an ancient Jewish sect teaching strict observance of Jewish traditions. **2** self-righteous hypocrite.

pharmaceutical *adjective* of pharmacy.

pharmacology *noun* study of drugs. **pharmacological** *adjective* **pharmacologist** *noun*

pharmacopoeia [far-ma-koh-**pee**-a] *noun* book with a list of and directions for the use of drugs.

pharmacy *noun, pl* **-cies 1** preparation and dispensing of drugs and medicines. **2** pharmacist's shop. **pharmacist** *noun* person qualified to prepare and sell drugs and medicines.

pharynx [**far**-rinks] *noun, pl* **pharynges, pharynxes** cavity forming the back part of the mouth. **pharyngeal** *adjective* **pharyngitis** [far-rin-**jite**-iss] *noun* inflammation of the pharynx.

phase ⊙ *noun* **1** any distinct or characteristic stage in a development or chain of events. ♦ *verb* **2** arrange or carry out in stages or to coincide with something else. **phase in, out** *verb* introduce or discontinue gradually.

PhD Doctor of Philosophy.

pheasant *noun* game bird with bright plumage.

phenobarbitone *noun* drug inducing sleep or relaxation.

phenol *noun* chemical used in disinfectants and antiseptics.

phenomenon ⊙ *noun, pl* **-ena 1** anything appearing or observed. **2** remarkable person or thing. **phenomenal** *adjective* extraordinary,

P

——————— THESAURUS ———————

little, slight

petition *noun* **1** = **appeal**, entreaty, plea, prayer, request, solicitation, suit, supplication ♦*verb* **2** = **appeal**, adjure, ask, beg, beseech, entreat, plead, pray, solicit, supplicate

petrify *verb* **1** = **terrify**, horrify, immobilize, paralyse, stun, stupefy, transfix **2** = **fossilize**, calcify, harden, turn to stone

petty *adjective* **1** = **trivial**, contemptible, inconsiderable, insignificant, little, measly (*inf*), negligible, paltry, slight, small, trifling, unimportant OPPOSITE important. **2** = **small-minded**, mean, mean-minded, shabby, spiteful, ungenerous OPPOSITE liberal

petulance *noun* = **sulkiness**, bad temper, ill humour, irritability, peevishness, pique, sullenness

petulant *adjective* = **sulky**, bad-tempered, huffy, ill-humoured, moody, peevish, sullen OPPOSITE good-natured

phantom *noun* **1** = **spectre**, apparition, ghost, phantasm, shade (*lit*), spirit, spook (*inf*), wraith **2** = **illusion**, figment of the imagination, hallucination, vision

phase *noun* **1** = **stage**, chapter, development, juncture, period, point, position, step, time

phase out *verb* = **wind down**, close, ease off, eliminate, pull out, remove, run down,

outstanding. **phenomenally** *adverb*
phew *interjection* exclamation of relief,
surprise, etc.
phial *noun* small bottle for medicine etc.
philadelphus *noun* shrub with sweet-scented
flowers.
philanderer ❶ *noun* man who flirts or has
many casual love affairs. **philandering**
adjective, noun
philanthropy ❶ *noun* practice of helping
people less well-off than oneself. **philanthropic**
adjective **philanthropist** *noun*
philately [fill-**lat**-a-lee] *noun* stamp collecting.
philatelist *noun*
philharmonic *adjective* (in names of
orchestras etc.) music-loving.
philippic *noun* bitter or impassioned speech of
denunciation, invective.
philistine *adjective, noun* boorishly
uncultivated (person). **philistinism** *noun*
philology *noun* science of the structure and
development of languages. **philological**
adjective **philologist** *noun*
philosophy ❶ *noun, pl* **-phies 1** study of the
meaning of life, knowledge, thought, etc. **2**
theory or set of ideas held by a particular
philosopher. **3** person's outlook on life.
philosopher *noun* person who studies
philosophy. **philosophical, philosophic**
adjective **1** of philosophy. **2** calm in the face of

difficulties or disappointments. **philosophically**
adverb **philosophize** *verb* discuss in a
philosophical manner.
philtre *noun* magic drink supposed to arouse
love in the person who drinks it.
phlebitis [fleb-**bite**-iss] *noun* inflammation of a
vein.
phlegm [**flem**] *noun* thick yellowish substance
formed in the nose and throat during a cold.
phlegmatic ❶ [fleg-**mat**-ik] *adjective* not easily
excited, unemotional. **phlegmatically** *adverb*
phlox *noun, pl* **phlox, phloxes** flowering
garden plant.
phobia ❶ *noun* intense and unreasoning fear
or dislike. **phobic** *adjective*
phoenix *noun* legendary bird said to set fire to
itself and rise anew from its ashes.
phone ❶ *noun, verb Informal* telephone.
phonecard *noun* card used to operate certain
public telephones. **phone-in** *noun* broadcast in
which telephone comments or questions from
the public are transmitted live.
phonetic *adjective* **1** of speech sounds. **2** (of
spelling) written as it is sounded. **phonetics**
noun science of speech sounds. **phonetically**
adverb
phoney, phony ❶ *Informal adjective*
phonier, phoniest 1 not genuine. **2** insincere.
♦ *noun, pl* **phoneys, phonies 3** phoney person
or thing.

—————— THESAURUS ——————

terminate, wind up, withdraw
phenomenon *noun* **1** = **occurrence**,
circumstance, episode, event, fact, happening,
incident **2** = **wonder**, exception, marvel,
miracle, prodigy, rarity, sensation
phenominal *adjective* **2** = **extraordinary**,
exceptional, fantastic, marvellous, miraculous,
outstanding, prodigious, remarkable, unusual
philanderer *noun* = **womanizer**, Casanova,
Don Juan, flirt, ladies' man, lady-killer (*inf*),
Lothario, playboy, stud (*sl*), wolf (*inf*) (*inf*)
philanthropic *adjective* = **humanitarian**,
beneficent, benevolent, charitable, generous,
humane, kind, kind-hearted, munificent,
public-spirited
philanthropist *noun* = **humanitarian**,
benefactor, contributor, donor, giver, patron
philanthropy *noun* = **humanitarianism**,
beneficence, benevolence, brotherly love,
charitableness, charity, generosity, kind-
heartedness
philistine *adjective* = **uncultured**, boorish,
ignorant, lowbrow, tasteless, uncultivated,
uneducated, unrefined ♦*noun* = **boor**,
barbarian, ignoramus, lout, lowbrow, vulgarian,

yahoo
philosopher *noun* = **thinker**, logician,
metaphysician, sage, theorist, wise man
philosophical, philosophic *adjective* **1**
= **rational**, abstract, logical, sagacious,
theoretical, thoughtful, wise OPPOSITE
scientific. **2** = **stoical**, calm, collected,
composed, cool, serene, tranquil, unruffled
OPPOSITE emotional
philosophy *noun* **1** = **thought**, knowledge,
logic, metaphysics, rationalism, reasoning,
thinking, wisdom **2, 3** = **outlook**, beliefs,
convictions, doctrine, ideology, principles,
tenets, thinking, values, viewpoint, world view
phlegmatic *adjective* = **unemotional**,
apathetic, impassive, indifferent, placid, stoical,
stolid, undemonstrative, unfeeling
phobia *noun* = **terror**, aversion, detestation,
dread, fear, hatred, horror, loathing, repulsion,
revulsion, thing (*inf*) OPPOSITE mania
phone *noun Inf* = **telephone**, blower (*inf*) ♦*verb*
Inf = **call**, get on the blower (*inf*), give someone
a call, give someone a ring (*inf, chiefly Brit*), give
someone a tinkle (*Brit inf*), make a call, ring
(up) (*inf, chiefly Brit*), telephone

phonograph *noun US old-fashioned* record player.
phonology *noun* study of the speech sounds in a language.
phosgene [foz-jean] *noun* poisonous gas used in warfare.
phosphorescence *noun* faint glow in the dark. **phosphorescent** *adjective*
phosphorus *noun Chem* toxic flammable nonmetallic element which appears luminous in the dark. **phosphate** *noun* **1** compound of phosphorus. **2** fertilizer containing phosphorus.
photo *noun, pl* **photos** short for PHOTOGRAPH.
photo finish finish of a race in which the contestants are so close that a photograph is needed to decide the result.
photo- *combining form* light, e.g. *photometer.*
photocell *noun* cell which produces a current or voltage when exposed to light or other electromagnetic radiation.
photocopy *noun, pl* **-copies 1** photographic reproduction. ♦ *verb* **-copying, -copied 2** make a photocopy of. **photocopier** *noun*
photoelectric *adjective* using or worked by electricity produced by the action of light.
Photofit *noun* ® picture made by combining photographs of different facial features.
photogenic *adjective* always looking attractive in photographs.
photograph ✪ *noun* **1** picture made by the chemical action of light on sensitive film. ♦ *verb* **2** take a photograph of. **photographer** *noun*
photographic *adjective* **photography** *noun* art of taking photographs.
photogravure *noun* process in which an etched metal plate for printing is produced by photography.
photometer [foe-**tom**-it-er] *noun* instrument for measuring the intensity of light.
photon *noun* quantum of electromagnetic radiation energy, such as light, having both particle and wave behaviour.
photostat *noun* copy made by photocopying machine.

photosynthesis *noun* process by which a green plant uses sunlight to build up carbohydrate reserves. **photosynthesize** *verb*
phrase ✪ *noun* **1** group of words forming a unit of meaning, esp. within a sentence. **2** short effective expression. ♦ *verb* **3** express in words.
phrasal verb phrase consisting of a verb and an adverb or preposition, with a meaning different from the parts, such as *take in* meaning *deceive.* **phrase book** book containing frequently used expressions and their equivalent in a foreign language.
phraseology ✪ *noun, pl* **-gies** way in which words are used.
phrenology *noun* formerly, the study of the shape and size of the skull as a means of finding out a person's character and mental ability. **phrenologist** *noun*
phut *adverb* **go phut** *Informal* (of a machine) break down.
phylactery *noun, pl* **-teries** leather case containing religious texts, worn by Jewish men.
phylum *noun, pl* **-la** major taxonomic division of animals and plants that contains one or more classes.
physical ✪ *adjective* **1** of the body, as contrasted with the mind or spirit. **2** of material things or nature. **3** of physics. **physically** *adverb* **physical education** training and practice in sports and gymnastics. **physical geography** branch of geography dealing with the features of the earth's surface.
physician ✪ *noun* doctor of medicine.
physics *noun* science of the properties of matter and energy. **physicist** *noun* person skilled in or studying physics.
physio *noun* **1** short for PHYSIOTHERAPY. **2** *pl* **physios** short for PHYSIOTHERAPIST.
physiognomy [fiz-ee-**on**-om-ee] *noun* face.
physiology *noun* science of the normal function of living things. **physiological** *adjective* **physiologist** *noun*
physiotherapy *noun* treatment of disease or injury by physical means such as massage,

P

———————————— T H E S A U R U S ————————————

phoney, phony *Inf adjective* **1** = **fake**, bogus, counterfeit, ersatz, false, imitation, pseudo (*inf*), sham OPPOSITE **real** ♦ *noun* **3** = **fake**, counterfeit, forgery, fraud, impostor, pseud (*inf*), sham OPPOSITE **genuine**
photograph *noun* **1** = **picture**, photo (*inf*), print, shot, snap (*inf*), snapshot, transparency ♦ *verb* **2** = **take a picture of**, film, record, shoot, snap (*inf*), take (someone's) picture
phrase *noun* **1** = **expression**, group of words, idiom, remark, saying ♦ *verb* **3** = **express**, put,

put into words, say, voice, word
phraseology *noun* = **wording**, choice of words, expression, idiom, language, parlance, phrase, phrasing, speech, style, syntax
physical *adjective* **1** = **bodily**, corporal, corporeal, earthly, fleshly, incarnate, mortal **2** = **material**, natural, palpable, real, solid, substantial, tangible
physician *noun* = **doctor**, doc (*inf*), doctor of medicine, general practitioner, G.P., M.D., medic (*inf*), medical practitioner

rather than by drugs. **physiotherapist** *noun*
physique ❶ *noun* person's bodily build and
muscular development.
pi *noun* **1** sixteenth letter in the Greek
alphabet. **2** *Maths* ratio of the circumference of
a circle to its diameter.
pianissimo *adverb Music* very quietly.
piano[1] *noun, pl* **pianos** musical instrument
with strings which are struck by hammers
worked by a keyboard (also **pianoforte**).
pianist *noun* **Pianola** *noun* ® mechanically
played piano.
piano[2] *adverb Music* quietly.
piazza *noun* square or marketplace, esp. in
Italy.
pibroch [**pee**-brok] *noun* form of bagpipe
music.
pic *noun, pl* **pics, pix** *Informal* photograph or
illustration.
picador *noun* mounted bullfighter with a
lance.
picaresque *adjective* denoting a type of
fiction in which the hero, a rogue, has a series
of adventures.
piccalilli *noun* pickle of vegetables in mustard
sauce.
piccolo *noun, pl* **-los** small flute.
pick[1] ❶ *verb* **1** choose. **2** remove (flowers or
fruit) from a plant. **3** take hold of and move
with the fingers. **4** provoke (a fight etc.)
deliberately. **5** steal from (someone's pocket). **6**
open (a lock) by means other than a key. ◆
noun **7** choice, e.g. *take your pick.* **8** best part.
pick-me-up *noun Informal* stimulating drink,
tonic. **pick on** *verb* continually treat unfairly.
pick out *verb* recognize, distinguish. **pick up**
verb **1** raise, lift. **2** collect. **3** improve, get
better. **4** learn as one goes along. **5** become

acquainted with for a sexual purpose. **pick-up**
noun **1** small truck. **2** casual acquaintance made
for a sexual purpose. **3** device for conversion of
vibrations into electrical signals, as in a record
player.
pick[2] *noun* tool with a curved iron crossbar
and wooden shaft, for breaking up hard ground
or rocks.
pickaxe *noun* large pick.
picket ❶ *noun* **1** person or group standing
outside a workplace to deter would-be workers
during a strike. **2** sentry or sentries posted to
give warning of an attack. **3** pointed stick used
as part of a fence. ◆ *verb* **4** form a picket
outside (a workplace). **picket line** line of
people acting as pickets.
pickings *plural noun* money easily acquired.
pickle ❶ *noun* **1** food preserved in vinegar or
salt water. **2** *Informal* awkward situation. ◆ *verb*
3 preserve in vinegar or salt water. **pickled**
adjective **1** preserved in vinegar or salt water. **2**
Informal drunk.
pickpocket *noun* thief who steals from
someone's pocket.
picnic ❶ *noun* **1** informal meal out of doors. **2**
Informal easy task. ◆ *verb* **-nicking, -nicked 3**
have a picnic.
picot [**peek**-oh] *noun* any of pattern of small
loops, as on lace.
Pict *noun* member of an ancient race of N
Britain. **Pictish** *adjective*
pictograph *noun* picture or symbol standing
for word or group of words, as in written
Chinese.
pictorial ❶ *adjective* **1** of or in painting or
pictures. ◆ *noun* **2** newspaper etc. with many
pictures.
picture ❶ *noun* **1** drawing or painting. **2**

——————— T H E S A U R U S ———————

physique *noun* =**build**, body, constitution,
figure, form, frame, shape, structure
pick[1] *verb* **1** =**select**, choose, decide upon,
elect, fix upon, hand-pick, opt for, settle upon,
single out OPPOSITE> **reject. 2** =**gather**, collect,
harvest, pluck, pull **4** =**provoke**, incite,
instigate, start **6** =**open**, break into, break
open, crack, force ◆*noun* **7** =**choice**, decision,
option, preference, selection **8** =**the best**,
elect, elite, the cream
picket *noun* **1** =**protester**, demonstrator,
picketer **2** =**lookout**, guard, patrol, sentinel,
sentry, watch **3** =**stake**, pale, paling, post,
stanchion, upright ◆*verb* **4** =**blockade**, boycott,
demonstrate
pickle *noun* **2** *Inf* =**predicament**, bind (*inf*),
difficulty, dilemma, fix (*inf*), hot water (*inf*), jam

(*inf*), quandary, scrape (*inf*), tight spot ◆*verb* **3**
=**preserve**, marinade, steep
pick-me-up *noun Inf* =**tonic**, bracer (*inf*),
refreshment, restorative, shot in the arm (*inf*),
stimulant
pick on *verb* =**torment**, badger, bait, bully,
goad, hector, tease
pick out *verb* =**identify**, discriminate,
distinguish, make out, perceive, recognize, tell
apart
pick up *verb* **1** =**lift**, gather, grasp, raise, take
up, uplift **2** =**collect**, call for, get **3** =**recover**,
be on the mend, get better, improve, mend,
rally, take a turn for the better, turn the corner
4 =**learn**, acquire, get the hang of (*inf*), master
picnic *noun* **1** =**excursion**, outdoor meal,
outing

photograph. **3** mental image. **4** description or account of a situation. **5** beautiful or picturesque object. **6** image on a TV screen. ◆ *plural* **7** cinema. ◆ *verb* **8** visualize, imagine. **9** represent in a picture. **picturesque** *adjective* **1** (of a place or view) pleasant to look at. **2** (of language) forceful, vivid. **picture rail** narrow piece of wood near the top of a wall from which pictures are hung. **picture window** large window made of a single sheet of glass.
piddle *verb Informal* urinate.
piddling *adjective Informal* small or unimportant.
pidgin *noun* language, not a mother tongue, made up of elements of two or more other languages.
pie *noun* dish of meat, fruit, etc. baked in pastry. **pie chart** circular diagram with sectors representing quantities.
piebald ❶ *noun, adjective* (horse) with irregular black-and-white markings.
piece ❶ *noun* **1** separate bit or part. **2** instance, e.g. *a piece of luck.* **3** example, specimen. **4** literary or musical composition. **5** coin. **6** small object used in draughts, chess, etc. **piece together** *verb* make or assemble bit by bit.
pièce de résistance [pyess de ray-**ziss**-tonss] *noun French* most impressive item.
piecemeal ❶ *adverb* a bit at a time.
piecework *noun* work paid for according to the quantity produced.
pied *adjective* having markings of two or more colours.

pied-à-terre [pyay da **tair**] *noun, pl* **pieds-à-terre** [pyay da **tair**] small flat or house for occasional use.
pie-eyed *adjective Slang* drunk.
pier ❶ *noun* **1** platform on stilts sticking out into the sea. **2** pillar, esp. one supporting a bridge.
pierce ❶ *verb* **1** make a hole in or through with a sharp instrument. **2** make a way through. **piercing** *adjective* **1** (of a sound) shrill and high-pitched. **2** (of wind or cold) fierce, penetrating.
Pierrot [**pier**-roe] *noun* pantomime clown with a whitened face.
piety ❶ *noun, pl* **-ties** deep devotion to God and religion.
piffle *noun Informal* nonsense.
pig ❶ *noun* **1** animal kept and killed for pork, ham, and bacon. **2** *Informal* greedy, dirty, or rude person. **piglet** *noun* young pig. **piggish**, **piggy** *adjective* **1** *Informal* dirty. **2** greedy. **3** stubborn. **piggery** *noun, pl* **-geries** place for keeping and breeding pigs. **piggy bank** child's bank shaped like a pig with a slot for coins.
pig-headed *adjective* obstinate. **pig iron** crude iron produced in a blast furnace.
pigeon¹ ❶ *noun* bird with a heavy body and short legs, sometimes trained to carry messages. **pigeonhole** *noun* **1** compartment for papers in a desk etc. ◆ *verb* **2** classify. **3** put aside and do nothing about. **pigeon-toed** *adjective* with the feet or toes turned inwards.
pigeon² *noun Informal* concern or responsibility.

P

——————— T H E S A U R U S ———————

pictorial *adjective* **1** = **graphic**, illustrated, sque, representational, scenic
picture *noun* **1** = **representation**, drawing, engraving, illustration, image, likeness, painting, portrait, print, sketch **2** = **photograph 4** = **description**, account, depiction, image, impression, report ◆*plural* **7** = **flicks** (*sl*), movies (*US inf*) ◆*verb* **8** = **imagine**, conceive of, envision, see, visualize **9** = **represent**, depict, draw, illustrate, paint, photograph, show, sketch
picturesque *adjective* **1** = **interesting**, attractive, beautiful, charming, pretty, quaint, scenic, striking OPPOSITE everyday. **2** = **vivid**, colourful, graphic OPPOSITE dull
piebald *adjective* = **pied**, black and white, brindled, dappled, flecked, mottled, speckled, spotted
piece *noun* **1** = **bit**, chunk, fragment, morsel, part, portion, quantity, segment, slice **4** = **work**, article, composition, creation, item,

study, work of art
piecemeal *adverb* = **bit by bit**, by degrees, gradually, little by little
pier *noun* **1** = **jetty**, landing place, promenade, quay, wharf **2** = **pillar**, buttress, column, pile, post, support, upright
pierce *verb* **1** = **penetrate**, bore, drill, enter, perforate, prick, puncture, spike, stab, stick into
piercing *adjective* **1** = **penetrating**, ear-splitting, high-pitched, loud, sharp, shrill OPPOSITE low. **2** = **cold**, arctic, biting, bitter, freezing, nippy, wintry
piety *noun* = **holiness**, faith, godliness, piousness, religion, reverence
pig *noun* **1** = **hog**, boar, porker, sow, swine **2** *Inf* = **slob** (*sl*), boor, brute, glutton, swine
pigeonhole *noun* **1** = **compartment**, cubbyhole, locker, niche, place, section ◆*verb* **2** = **classify**, categorize, characterize, compartmentalize, ghettoize, label, slot (*inf*) **3** = **put off**, defer, postpone, shelve

piggyback *noun* **1** ride on someone's shoulders. ◆ *adverb* **2** carried on someone's shoulders.

pigment ❶ *noun* colouring matter, paint or dye. **pigmentation** *noun*

Pigmy *noun, pl* **-mies** same as PYGMY.

pigsty *noun, pl* **-sties 1** pen for pigs. **2** untidy place.

pigtail *noun* plait of hair hanging from the back or either side of the head.

pike[1] *noun* large predatory freshwater fish.

pike[2] *noun Hist* long-handled spear.

pikelet *noun Aust & NZ* small thick pancake.

piker *noun Aust & NZ slang* shirker.

pilaster *noun* square column, usu. set in a wall.

pilau, pilaf, pilaff *noun* Middle Eastern dish of meat, fish, or poultry boiled with rice, spices, etc.

pilchard *noun* small edible sea fish of the herring family.

pile[1] **❶** *noun* **1** number of things lying on top of each other. **2** *Informal* large amount. **3** large building. ◆ *verb* **4** collect into a pile. **5** (foll. by *in* or *out*) move in a group. **pile-up** *noun Informal* traffic accident involving several vehicles.

pile[2] **❶** *noun* beam driven into the ground, esp. as a foundation for building.

pile[3] **❶** *noun* fibres of a carpet or a fabric, esp. velvet, that stand up from the weave.

piles *plural noun* swollen veins in the rectum, haemorrhoids.

pilfer ❶ *verb* steal in small quantities.

pilgrim ❶ *noun* person who journeys to a holy place. **pilgrimage** *noun*

pill ❶ *noun* small ball of medicine swallowed whole. **the pill** pill taken by a woman to prevent pregnancy. **pillbox** *noun* **1** small box for pills. **2** small concrete fort.

pillage ❶ *verb* **1** steal property by violence in war. ◆ *noun* **2** violent seizure of goods, esp. in war.

pillar ❶ *noun* **1** upright post, usu. supporting a roof. **2** strong supporter. **pillar box** red pillar-shaped letter box in the street.

pillion *noun* seat for a passenger behind the rider of a motorcycle.

pillory ❶ *noun, pl* **-ries 1** *Hist* frame with holes for the head and hands in which an offender was locked and exposed to public abuse. ◆ *verb* **-rying, -ried 2** ridicule publicly.

pillow *noun* **1** stuffed cloth bag for supporting the head in bed. ◆ *verb* **2** rest as if on a pillow.

pillowcase, pillowslip *noun* removable cover for a pillow.

pilot ❶ *noun* **1** person qualified to fly an aircraft or spacecraft. **2** person employed to steer a ship entering or leaving a harbour. ◆ *adjective* **3** experimental and preliminary. ◆ *verb* **4** act as the pilot of. **5** guide, steer. **pilot light** small flame lighting the main one in a gas appliance. **pilot officer** most junior commissioned rank in certain air forces.

pimento *noun, pl* **-tos** mild-tasting red pepper.

pimp *noun* **1** man who gets customers for a prostitute in return for a share of his or her earnings. ◆ *verb* **2** act as a pimp.

pimpernel *noun* wild plant with small star-

——————— T H E S A U R U S ———————

pig-headed *adjective* =**stubborn**, contrary, inflexible, mulish, obstinate, self-willed, stiff-necked, unyielding

pigment *noun* =**colour**, colouring, dye, paint, stain, tincture, tint

pile[1] *noun* **1** =**heap**, accumulation, berg (*S Afr*), collection, hoard, mass, mound, mountain, stack **2** *Inf* =**a lot**, great deal, ocean, quantity, stacks **3** =**building**, edifice, erection, structure ◆*verb* **4** =**collect**, accumulate, amass, assemble, gather, heap, hoard, stack **5** (foll. by *in* or *out*) =**crowd**, crush, flock, flood, jam, pack, rush, stream

pile[2] *noun* =**foundation**, beam, column, pillar, post, support, upright

pile[3] *noun* =**nap**, down, fibre, fur, hair, plush

pile-up *noun Inf* =**collision**, accident, crash, multiple collision, smash, smash-up (*inf*)

pilfer *verb* =**steal**, appropriate, embezzle, filch, knock off (*sl*), lift (*inf*), nick (*sl, chiefly Brit*),

pinch (*inf*), purloin, snaffle (*Brit inf*), swipe (*sl*), take

pilgrim *noun* =**traveller**, wanderer, wayfarer

pilgrimage *noun* =**journey**, excursion, expedition, mission, tour, trip

pill *noun* =**tablet**, capsule, pellet **the pill** =**oral contraceptive**

pillage *verb* **1** =**plunder**, despoil, loot, maraud, raid, ransack, ravage, sack ◆*noun* **2** =**plunder**, marauding, robbery, sack, spoliation

pillar *noun* **1** =**support**, column, pier, post, prop, shaft, stanchion, upright **2** =**supporter**, leader, leading light (*inf*), mainstay, upholder

pillory *verb* **2** =**ridicule**, brand, denounce, stigmatize

pilot *noun* **1** =**airman**, aviator, flyer **2** =**helmsman**, navigator, steersman ◆*adjective* **3** =**trial**, experimental, model, test ◆*verb* **4, 5** =**fly**, conduct, direct, drive, guide, handle, navigate, operate, steer shaped flowers.

pimple ❶ *noun* small pus-filled spot on the skin. **pimply** *adjective*

pin ❶ *noun* **1** short thin piece of stiff wire with a point and head, for fastening things. **2** wooden or metal peg or stake. ♦ *verb* **pinning, pinned 3** fasten with a pin. **4** seize and hold fast. **pin down** *verb* **1** force (someone) to make a decision, take action, etc. **2** define clearly. **pin money** small amount earned to buy small luxuries. **pins and needles** *Informal* tingling sensation in a part of the body. **pin tuck** narrow ornamental fold in shirt etc. **pin-up** *noun* picture of a sexually attractive person, esp. (partly) naked.

pinafore *noun* **1** apron. **2** dress with a bib top.

pinball *noun* electrically operated table game in which a small ball is shot through various hazards.

pince-nez [panss-**nay**] *noun, pl* **pince-nez** glasses kept in place only by a clip on the bridge of the nose.

pincers *plural noun* **1** tool consisting of two hinged arms, for gripping. **2** claws of a lobster etc.

pinch ❶ *verb* **1** squeeze between finger and thumb. **2** cause pain by being too tight. **3** *Informal* steal. **4** *Informal* arrest. ♦ *noun* **5** act of pinching. **6** as much as can be taken up between the finger and thumb. **at a pinch** if absolutely necessary. **feel the pinch** have to economize.

pinchbeck *noun* alloy of zinc and copper, used as imitation gold.

pincushion *noun* small cushion in which pins are stuck ready for use.

pine¹ *noun* **1** evergreen coniferous tree. **2** its wood. **pine cone** woody seed case of the pine tree. **pine marten** wild mammal of the coniferous forests of Europe and Asia.

pine² ❶ *verb* **1** (foll. by *for*) feel great longing

(for). **2** become thin and ill through grief etc.

pineal gland [pin-ee-al] *noun* small cone-shaped gland at the base of the brain.

pineapple *noun* large tropical fruit with juicy yellow flesh and a hard skin.

ping *verb, noun* (make) a short high-pitched sound. **pinger** *noun* device, esp. a timer, that makes a pinging sound.

Ping-Pong *noun* ® table tennis.

pinion¹ ❶ *noun* **1** bird's wing. ♦ *verb* **2** immobilize (someone) by tying or holding his or her arms.

pinion² ❶ *noun* small cogwheel.

pink ❶ *noun* **1** pale reddish colour. **2** fragrant garden plant. ♦ *adjective* **3** of the colour pink. ♦ *verb* **4** (of an engine) make a metallic noise because not working properly, knock. **in the pink** in good health.

pinking shears *plural noun* scissors with a serrated edge that give a wavy edge to material to prevent fraying.

pinnace *noun* ship's boat.

pinnacle ❶ *noun* **1** highest point of success etc. **2** mountain peak. **3** small slender spire.

pinnate *adjective* (of compound leaves) having leaflets growing opposite each other in pairs.

pinpoint ❶ *verb* **1** locate or identify exactly. ♦ *adjective* **2** exact.

pinprick *noun* small irritation or annoyance.

pinstripe *noun* **1** very narrow stripe in fabric. **2** the fabric itself.

pint *noun* liquid measure, 1/8 gallon (.568 litre).

pintail *noun* greyish-brown duck with a pointed tail.

Pinyin *noun* system for representing Chinese in Roman letters.

pioneer ❶ *noun* **1** explorer or early settler of a new country. **2** originator or developer of something new. ♦ *verb* **3** be the pioneer or leader of.

pious ❶ *adjective* deeply religious, devout.

P

——————— THESAURUS ———————

pimple *noun* = **spot**, boil, plook (*Scot*), pustule, zit (*sl*)

pin *verb* **3** = **fasten**, affix, attach, fix, join, secure **4** = **hold fast**, fix, hold down, immobilize, pinion

pinch *verb* **1** = **squeeze**, compress, grasp, nip, press **2** = **hurt**, cramp, crush, pain **3** *Inf* = **steal**, filch, knock off (*sl*), lift (*inf*), nick (*sl, chiefly Brit*), pilfer, purloin, snaffle (*Brit inf*), swipe (*sl*) ♦ *noun* **5** = **squeeze**, nip

pin down *verb* **1** = **force**, compel, constrain, make, press, pressurize **2** = **determine**, identify, locate, name, pinpoint, specify

pine² *verb* **1** (foll. by *for*) = **long**, ache, crave, desire, eat one's heart out over, hanker, hunger for, thirst for, wish for, yearn for **2** = **waste**, decline, fade, languish, sicken

pinion¹ *verb* **2** = **immobilize**, bind, chain, fasten, fetter, manacle, shackle, tie

pink *adjective* **3** = **rosy**, flushed, reddish, rose, roseate, salmon

pinnacle *noun* **2** = **peak**, apex, crest, crown, height, summit, top, vertex, zenith

pinpoint **1** *verb* = **identify**, define, distinguish, locate

pioneer *noun* **1** = **settler**, colonist, explorer **2**

pip[1] *noun* small seed in a fruit.

pip[2] *noun* **1** high-pitched sound used as a time signal on radio. **2** spot on a playing card, dice, etc. **3** *Informal* star on a junior army officer's shoulder showing rank.

pip[3] *noun* **give someone the pip** *Brit, NZ & S Afr slang* annoy.

pipe ❶ *noun* **1** tube for conveying liquid or gas. **2** tube with a small bowl at the end for smoking tobacco. **3** tubular musical instrument. ♦ *plural* **4** bagpipes. ♦ *verb* **5** play on a pipe. **6** utter in a shrill tone. **7** convey by pipe. **8** decorate with piping. **piper** *noun* player on a pipe or bagpipes. **piping** *noun* **1** system of pipes. **2** decoration of icing on a cake etc. **3** fancy edging on clothes etc. **piping hot** extremely hot. **pipe cleaner** piece of wire coated with tiny tufts of yarn for cleaning the stem of a tobacco pipe. **piped music** recorded music played as background music in public places. **pipe down** *verb Informal* stop talking. **pipe dream** fanciful impossible plan. **pipeline** *noun* **1** long pipe for transporting oil, water, etc. **2** means of communication. **in the pipeline** in preparation. **pipe up** *verb* speak suddenly or shrilly.

pipette *noun* slender glass tube used to transfer or measure fluids.

pipit *noun* small brownish songbird.

pippin *noun* type of eating apple.

piquant ❶ [pee-kant] *adjective* **1** having a pleasant spicy taste. **2** mentally stimulating. **piquancy** *noun*

pique ❶ [peek] *noun* **1** feeling of hurt pride, baffled curiosity, or resentment. ♦ *verb* **2** hurt the pride of. **3** arouse (curiosity).

piqué [pee-kay] *noun* stiff ribbed cotton fabric.

piquet [pik-**ket**] *noun* card game for two.

piranha *noun* small fierce freshwater fish of tropical America.

pirate ❶ *noun* **1** sea robber. **2** person who illegally publishes or sells work owned by someone else. **3** person or company that broadcasts illegally. ♦ *verb* **4** sell or reproduce (artistic work etc.) illegally. **piracy** *noun* **piratical** *adjective*

pirouette *verb, noun* (make) a spinning turn balanced on the toes of one foot.

piscatorial *adjective* of fishing or fishes.

Pisces *plural noun* (the fishes) twelfth sign of the zodiac.

piss *Taboo verb* **1** urinate. ♦ *noun* **2** act of urinating. **3** urine.

pistachio *noun, pl* **-chios** edible nut of a Mediterranean tree.

piste [peest] *noun* ski slope.

pistil *noun* seed-bearing part of a flower.

pistol *noun* short-barrelled handgun.

piston *noun* cylindrical part in an engine that slides to and fro in a cylinder.

pit ❶ *noun* **1** deep hole in the ground. **2** coal mine. **3** dent or depression. **4** servicing and refuelling area on a motor-racing track. **5** same as ORCHESTRA PIT. ♦ *verb* **pitting, pitted 6** mark with small dents or scars. **pit one's wits against** compete against in a test or contest. **pit bull terrier** strong muscular terrier with a short coat.

pitapat *adverb* **1** with quick light taps. ♦ *noun* **2** such taps.

pitch[1] ❶ *verb* **1** throw, hurl. **2** set up (a tent). **3** fall headlong. **4** (of a ship or plane) move with the front and back going up and down alternately. **5** set the level or tone of. ♦ *noun* **6**

——————— THESAURUS ———————

= **founder**, developer, innovator, leader, trailblazer ♦*verb* **3** = **develop**, create, discover, establish, initiate, instigate, institute, invent, originate, show the way, start

pious *adjective* = **religious**, devout, God-fearing, godly, holy, reverent, righteous, saintly OPPOSITE> **irreverent**

pipe *noun* **1** = **tube**, conduit, duct, hose, line, main, passage, pipeline ♦*verb* **5** = **play**, sound **6** = **whistle**, cheep, peep, sing, warble **7** = **convey**, channel, conduct

pipe down *verb Inf* = **be quiet**, hold one's tongue, hush, quieten down, shush, shut one's mouth, shut up (*inf*)

pipeline *noun* **1** = **tube**, conduit, duct, passage, pipe

piquant *adjective* **1** = **spicy**, biting, pungent, savoury, sharp, tangy, tart OPPOSITE>

mild. **2** = **interesting**, lively, provocative, scintillating, sparkling, stimulating OPPOSITE> **boring**

pique *noun* **1** = **resentment**, annoyance, displeasure, huff, hurt feelings, irritation, offence, umbrage, wounded pride ♦*verb* **2** = **displease**, affront, annoy, get (*inf*), irk, irritate, nettle, offend, rile, sting **3** = **arouse**, excite, rouse, spur, stimulate, stir, whet

piracy *noun* **1** = **robbery**, buccaneering, freebooting, stealing, theft

pirate *noun* **1** = **buccaneer**, corsair, freebooter, marauder, raider **2** = **plagiarist**, cribber (*inf*), infringer, plagiarizer ♦*verb* **4** = **copy**, appropriate, crib (*inf*), plagiarize, poach, reproduce, steal

pit *noun* **1** = **hole**, abyss, cavity, chasm, crater, dent, depression, hollow ♦*verb* **6** = **scar**, dent,

P

area marked out for playing sport. **7** degree or angle of slope. **8** degree of highness or lowness of a (musical) sound. **9** act or manner of throwing a ball. **10** place where a street or market trader regularly sells. **11** *Informal* persuasive sales talk. **pitched battle** fierce fight. **pitch in** *verb* join in enthusiastically. **pitch into** *verb Informal* attack.

pitch² ❶ *noun* dark sticky substance obtained from tar. **pitch-black, pitch-dark** *adjective* very dark.

pitchblende *noun* mineral composed largely of uranium oxide, yielding radium.

pitcher *noun* large jug with a narrow neck.

pitchfork *noun* **1** large long-handled fork for lifting hay. ◆ *verb* **2** thrust abruptly or violently.

pitfall ❶ *noun* hidden difficulty or danger.

pith ❶ *noun* **1** soft white lining of the rind of oranges etc. **2** essential part. **3** soft tissue in the stems of certain plants. **pithy** *adjective* **pithier, pithiest** short and full of meaning.

pithead *noun* top of a mine shaft and the buildings and hoisting gear around it.

piton [**peet**-on] *noun* metal spike used in climbing to secure a rope.

pitta bread, pitta *noun* flat slightly leavened bread, orig. from the Middle East.

pittance ❶ *noun* very small amount of money.

pitter-patter *noun* **1** sound of light rapid taps or pats, as of raindrops. ◆ *verb* **2** make such a sound.

pituitary *noun, pl* **-taries** gland at the base of the brain, that helps to control growth (also **pituitary gland**).

pity ❶ *noun, pl* **pities 1** sympathy or sorrow for others' suffering. **2** regrettable fact. ◆ *verb* **pitying, pitied 3** feel pity for. **piteous, pitiable** *adjective* arousing pity. **pitiful** *adjective* **1** arousing pity. **2** woeful, contemptible. **pitifully** *adverb* **pitiless** *adjective* feeling no pity or mercy.

pivot ❶ *noun* **1** central shaft on which something turns. ◆ *verb* **2** provide with or turn on a pivot. **pivotal** *adjective* of crucial importance.

pix *noun Informal* a plural of PIC.

pixie ❶ *noun* (in folklore) fairy.

pizza *noun* flat disc of dough covered with a wide variety of savoury toppings and baked.

pizzazz *noun Informal* attractive combination of energy and style.

pizzicato [pit-see-**kah**-toe] *adjective Music* played by plucking the string of a violin etc. with the finger.

pl. 1 place. **2** plural.

placard ❶ *noun* notice that is carried or

——————— T H E S A U R U S ———————

indent, mark, pockmark
pitch¹ *verb* **1 = throw**, cast, chuck (*inf*), fling, heave, hurl, lob (*inf*), sling, toss **2 = set up**, erect, put up, raise, settle **3 = fall**, dive, drop, topple, tumble **4 = toss**, lurch, plunge, roll ◆*noun* **6 = sports field**, field of play, ground, park (*US & Canad*) **7 = slope**, angle, degree, dip, gradient, height, highest point, incline, level, point, summit, tilt **8 = tone**, modulation, sound, timbre **11** *Inf* **= sales talk**, patter, spiel (*inf*)
pitch-black *adjective* **= jet-black**, dark, inky, pitch-dark, unlit
pitch in *verb* **= help**, chip in (*inf*), contribute, cooperate, do one's bit, join in, lend a hand, participate
pitch into *verb Inf* **= attack**, assail, assault, get stuck into (*inf*), tear into (*inf*)
piteous *adjective* **= pathetic**, affecting, distressing, gut-wrenching, harrowing, heartbreaking, heart-rending, moving, pitiable, pitiful, plaintive, poignant, sad
pitfall *noun* **= danger**, catch, difficulty, drawback, hazard, peril, snag, trap
pith *noun* **2 = essence**, core, crux, gist, heart, kernel, nub, point, quintessence, salient point
pithy *adjective* **= succinct**, brief, cogent,

concise, epigrammatic, laconic, pointed, short, terse, to the point, trenchant
pitiful *adjective* **1 = pathetic**, distressing, grievous, gut-wrenching, harrowing, heartbreaking, heart-rending, piteous, pitiable, sad, wretched OPPOSITE> **happy**. **2** **= contemptible**, abject, base, low, mean, miserable, paltry, shabby, sorry OPPOSITE> **significant**
pitiless *adjective* **= merciless**, callous, cold-blooded, cold-hearted, cruel, hardhearted, heartless, implacable, relentless, ruthless, unmerciful
pittance *noun* **= peanuts** (*sl*), chicken feed (*sl*), drop, mite, slave wages, trifle
pity *noun* **1 = compassion**, charity, clemency, fellow feeling, forbearance, kindness, mercy, sympathy OPPOSITE> **anger**. **2 = shame**, bummer (*sl*), crying shame, misfortune, sin ◆*verb* **3 = feel sorry for**, bleed for, feel for, grieve for, have compassion for, sympathize with, weep for
pivot *noun* **1 = axis**, axle, centre, fulcrum, heart, hinge, hub, kingpin, spindle, swivel ◆*verb* **2 = turn**, revolve, rotate, spin, swivel, twirl
pivotal *adjective* **= crucial**, central, critical, decisive, vital

P

displayed in public.

placate ⊕ *verb* make (someone) stop feeling angry or upset. **placatory** *adjective*

place ⊕ *noun* **1** particular part of an area or space. **2** particular town, building, etc. **3** position or point reached. **4** open square lined with houses. **5** seat or space. **6** duty or right. **7** position of employment. **8** usual position. ◆ *verb* **9** put in a particular place. **10** identify, put in context. **11** make (an order, bet, etc.). **be placed** (of a competitor in a race) be among the first three. **take place** happen, occur.

placement *noun* **1** arrangement. **2** temporary employment. **3** process of finding someone a job or a home. **place setting** cutlery, crockery, and glassware laid for one person at a meal.

placebo [plas-see-bo] *noun, pl* **-bos, -boes** sugar pill etc. given to an unsuspecting patient instead of an active drug.

placenta [plass-ent-a] *noun, pl* **-tas, -tae** organ formed in the womb during pregnancy, providing nutrients for the fetus. **placental** *adjective*

placid ⊕ *adjective* not easily excited or upset, calm. **placidity** *noun*

plagiarize ⊕ [play-jer-ize] *verb* steal ideas, passages, etc. from (someone else's work) and present them as one's own. **plagiarism** *noun* **plagiarist** *noun*

plague ⊕ *noun* **1** fast-spreading fatal disease. **2** *Hist* bubonic plague. **3** widespread infestation. ◆ *verb* **plaguing, plagued 4** trouble or annoy continually.

plaice *noun* edible European flatfish.

plaid *noun* **1** long piece of tartan cloth worn as part of Highland dress. **2** tartan cloth or pattern.

plain ⊕ *adjective* **1** easy to see or understand. **2** expressed honestly and clearly. **3** without decoration or pattern. **4** not beautiful. **5** simple, ordinary. ◆ *noun* **6** large stretch of level country. **plainly** *adverb* **plainness** *noun* **plain clothes** ordinary clothes, as opposed to uniform. **plain sailing** easy progress. **plain speaking** saying exactly what one thinks.

plainsong *noun* unaccompanied singing, esp. in a medieval church.

plaintiff *noun* person who sues in a court of law.

plaintive ⊕ *adjective* sad, mournful. **plaintively** *adverb*

plait [platt] *noun* **1** intertwined length of hair. ◆ *verb* **2** intertwine separate strands in a pattern.

plan ⊕ *noun* **1** way thought out to do or achieve something. **2** diagram showing the layout or design of something. ◆ *verb* **planning, planned 3** arrange beforehand. **4** make a diagram of. **planner** *noun*

———— THESAURUS ————

pixie *noun* =**elf**, brownie, fairy, sprite

placard *noun* =**notice**, advertisement, bill, poster

placate *verb* =**calm**, appease, assuage, conciliate, humour, mollify, pacify, propitiate, soothe

place *noun* **1** =**spot**, area, location, point, position, site, venue, whereabouts **3** =**position**, grade, rank, station, status **6** =**duty**, affair, charge, concern, function, prerogative, responsibility, right, role **7** =**job**, appointment, employment, position, post ◆*verb* **9** =**put**, deposit, install, lay, locate, position, rest, set, situate, stand, station, stick (*inf*) **10** =**identify**, know, put one's finger on, recognize, remember **take place** =**happen**, come about, go on, occur, transpire (*inf*)

placid *adjective* =**calm**, collected, composed, equable, even-tempered, imperturbable, serene, tranquil, unexcitable, unruffled, untroubled [OPPOSITE] **emotional**

plagiarism *noun* =**copying**, borrowing, cribbing (*inf*), infringement, piracy, theft

plagiarize *verb* =**copy**, borrow, crib (*inf*), lift (*inf*), pirate, steal

plague *noun* **1** =**disease**, epidemic, infection, pestilence **3** =**affliction**, bane, blight, curse, evil, scourge, torment ◆*verb* **4** =**pester**, annoy, badger, bother, harass, harry, hassle (*inf*), tease, torment, torture, trouble, vex

plain *adjective* **1** =**clear**, comprehensible, distinct, evident, manifest, obvious, overt, patent, unambiguous, understandable, unmistakable, visible [OPPOSITE] **hidden**. **2** =**straightforward**, blunt, candid, direct, downright, forthright, frank, honest, open, outspoken, upfront (*inf*) [OPPOSITE] **indirect**. **3** =**unadorned**, austere, bare, basic, severe, simple, Spartan, stark, unembellished, unfussy, unornamented [OPPOSITE] **adorned**. **4** =**ugly**, ill-favoured, no oil painting (*inf*), not beautiful, unattractive, unlovely, unprepossessing [OPPOSITE] **beautiful**. **5** =**ordinary**, common, commonplace, everyday, simple, unaffected, unpretentious [OPPOSITE] **worldly** ◆*noun* **6** =**flatland**, grassland, plateau, prairie, steppe, veld

plaintive *adjective* =**sorrowful**, heart-rending, mournful, pathetic, piteous, pitiful, sad

plan *noun* **1** =**scheme**, design, method, plot,

plane[1] ❶ *noun* **1** an aircraft. **2** *Maths* flat surface. **3** level of attainment etc. ♦ *adjective* **4** perfectly flat or level. ♦ *verb* **5** glide or skim.
plane[2] *noun* **1** tool for smoothing wood. ♦ *verb* **2** smooth (wood) with a plane.
plane[3] *noun* tree with broad leaves.
planet *noun* large body in space that revolves round the sun or another star. **planetary** *adjective*
planetarium *noun, pl* **-iums, -ia** building where the movements of the stars, planets, etc. are shown by projecting lights on the inside of a dome.
plangent [plan-jent] *adjective* (of sounds) mournful and resounding.
plank *noun* long flat piece of sawn timber.
plankton *noun* minute animals and plants floating in the surface water of a sea or lake.
plant ❶ *noun* **1** living organism that grows in the ground and has no power to move. **2** equipment or machinery used in industrial processes. **3** factory or other industrial premises. ♦ *verb* **4** put in the ground to grow. **5** place firmly in position. **6** *Informal* put (a person) secretly in an organization to spy. **7** *Informal* hide (stolen goods etc.) on a person to make him or her seem guilty. **planter** *noun* **1** owner of a plantation. **2** ornamental pot for house plants.
plantain[1] *noun* low-growing wild plant with broad leaves.
plantain[2] *noun* tropical fruit like a green banana.
plantation *noun* **1** estate for the cultivation of tea, tobacco, etc. **2** wood of cultivated trees.
plaque *noun* **1** inscribed commemorative stone or metal plate. **2** filmy deposit on teeth that causes decay.
plasma *noun* **1** clear liquid part of blood. **2** *Physics* hot ionized gas containing positive ions and free electrons.

plaster ❶ *noun* **1** mixture of lime, sand, etc. for coating walls. **2** adhesive strip of material for dressing cuts etc. ♦ *verb* **3** cover with plaster. **4** coat thickly. **plastered** *adjective Slang* drunk. **plasterboard** *noun* thin rectangular sheets of cardboard held together with plaster, used to cover interior walls etc. **plaster of Paris** white powder which dries to form a hard solid when mixed with water, used for sculptures and casts for broken limbs.
plastic ❶ *noun* **1** synthetic material that can be moulded when soft but sets in a hard long-lasting shape. **2** credit cards etc. as opposed to cash. ♦ *adjective* **3** made of plastic. **4** easily moulded, pliant. **plasticity** *noun* ability to be moulded. **plastic bullet** solid PVC cylinder fired by police in riot control. **plastic explosive** jelly-like explosive substance. **plastic surgery** repair or reconstruction of missing or malformed parts of the body.
Plasticine *noun* ® soft coloured modelling material used esp. by children.
plate ❶ *noun* **1** shallow dish for holding food. **2** flat thin sheet of metal, glass, etc. **3** thin coating of metal on another metal. **4** dishes or cutlery made of gold or silver. **5** illustration, usu. on fine quality paper, in a book. **6** *Informal* set of false teeth. ♦ *verb* **7** cover with a thin coating of gold, silver, or other metal. **plateful** *noun* **plate glass** glass in thin sheets, used for mirrors and windows. **plate tectonics** study of the structure of the earth's crust, esp. the movement of layers of rocks.
plateau ❶ *noun, pl* **-teaus, -teaux 1** area of level high land. **2** stage when there is no change or development.
platelet *noun* minute particle occurring in blood of vertebrates and involved in clotting of blood.
platen *noun* **1** roller of a typewriter, against which the paper is held. **2** plate in a printing

——————— THESAURUS ———————

programme, proposal, strategy, suggestion, system **2 = diagram**, blueprint, chart, drawing, layout, map, representation, sketch ♦*verb* **3 = devise**, arrange, contrive, design, draft, formulate, organize, outline, plot, scheme, think out
plane[1] *noun* **1 = aeroplane**, aircraft, jet **2** *Maths* **= flat surface**, level surface **3 = level**, condition, degree, position ♦*adjective* **4 = level**, even, flat, horizontal, regular, smooth ♦*verb* **5 = skim**, glide, sail, skate
plant *noun* **1 = vegetable**, bush, flower, herb, shrub, weed **2 = machinery**, apparatus, equipment, gear **3 = factory**, foundry, mill,

shop, works, yard ♦*verb* **4 = sow**, put in the ground, scatter, seed, transplant **5 = place**, establish, fix, found, insert, put, set
plaster *noun* **1 = mortar**, gypsum, plaster of Paris, stucco **2 = bandage**, adhesive plaster, dressing, Elastoplast, sticking plaster ♦*verb* **4 = cover**, coat, daub, overlay, smear, spread
plastic *adjective* **4 = pliant**, ductile, flexible, mouldable, pliable, soft, supple OPPOSITE hard
plate *noun* **1 = platter**, dish, trencher (*arch*) **2 = layer**, panel, sheet, slab **5 = illustration**, lithograph, print ♦*verb* **7 = coat**, cover, gild, laminate, overlay
plateau *noun* **1 = upland**, highland, table,

P

press by which the paper is pressed against the type.

platform ❶ *noun* **1** raised floor. **2** raised area in a station from which passengers board trains. **3** structure in the sea which holds machinery, stores, etc. for drilling an oil well. **4** programme of a political party.

platinum *noun Chem* valuable silvery-white metal. **platinum blonde** woman with silvery-blonde hair.

platitude ❶ *noun* remark that is true but not interesting or original. **platitudinous** *adjective*

platonic *adjective* friendly or affectionate but not sexual.

platoon ❶ *noun* smaller unit within a company of soldiers.

platteland *noun S Afr* rural district.

platter ❶ *noun* large dish.

platypus *noun* Australian egg-laying amphibious mammal, with dense fur, webbed feet, and a ducklike bill (also **duck-billed platypus, duckbill**).

plaudits ❶ *plural noun* expressions of approval.

plausible ❶ *adjective* **1** apparently true or reasonable. **2** persuasive but insincere. **plausibly** *adverb* **plausibility** *noun*

play ❶ *verb* **1** occupy oneself in (a game or recreation). **2** compete against in a game or sport. **3** behave carelessly. **4** act (a part) on the stage. **5** perform on (a musical instrument). **6**

cause (a radio, record player, etc.) to give out sound. **7** move lightly or irregularly, flicker. ♦ *noun* **8** story performed on stage or broadcast. **9** activities children take part in for amusement. **10** playing of a game. **11** conduct, e.g. *fair play*. **12** (scope for) freedom of movement. **player** *noun* **playful** *adjective* lively. **play back** *verb* listen to or watch (something recorded). **play down** *verb* minimize the importance of. **playground** *noun* outdoor area for children to play on, esp. one with swings etc. or adjoining a school. **playgroup** *noun* regular meeting of very young children for supervised play. **playhouse** *noun* theatre. **playing card** one of a set of 52 cards used in card games. **playing field** extensive piece of ground for sport. **play-lunch** *noun Aust & NZ* child's mid-morning snack at school. **play off** *verb* set (two people) against each other for one's own ends. **play on** *verb* exploit or encourage (someone's sympathy or weakness). **playpen** *noun* small portable enclosure in which a young child can safely be left to play. **playschool** *noun* nursery group for young children. **plaything** *noun* **1** toy. **2** person regarded or treated as a toy. **play up** *verb* **1** give prominence to. **2** cause trouble. **playwright** *noun* author of plays. **playboy** ❶ *noun* rich man who lives only for pleasure. **plaza** *noun* **1** open space or square. **2** modern shopping complex.

———————— THESAURUS ————————

P

tableland **2** = **levelling off**, level, stability, stage **platform** *noun* **1** = **stage**, dais, podium, rostrum, stand **4** = **policy**, manifesto, objective(s), party line, principle, programme **platitude** *noun* = **cliché**, banality, commonplace, truism **platoon** *noun* = **squad**, company, group, outfit (*inf*), patrol, squadron, team **platter** *noun* = **plate**, dish, salver, tray, trencher (*arch*) **plaudits** *plural noun* = **approval**, acclaim, acclamation, applause, approbation, praise **plausible** *adjective* **1** = **believable**, conceivable, credible, likely, persuasive, possible, probable, reasonable, tenable OPPOSITE **impossible**. **2** = **glib**, smooth, smooth-talking, smooth-tongued, specious **play** *verb* **1** = **amuse oneself**, entertain oneself, fool, have fun, revel, romp, sport, trifle **2** = **compete**, challenge, contend against, participate, take on, take part **4** = **act**, act the part of, perform, portray, represent ♦*noun* **8** = **drama**, comedy, dramatic piece, farce, pantomime, piece, show, stage show, tragedy **9**

= **amusement**, diversion, entertainment, fun, game, pastime, recreation, sport **12** = **space**, elbowroom, latitude, leeway, margin, room, scope **playboy** *noun* = **womanizer**, ladies' man, lady-killer (*inf*), philanderer, rake, roué **play down** *verb* = **minimize**, gloss over, make light of, make little of, soft-pedal (*inf*), underplay, underrate **player** *noun* **2** = **sportsman** *or* **sportswoman**, competitor, contestant, participant **4** = **performer**, actor *or* actress, entertainer, Thespian, trouper **5** = **musician**, artist, instrumentalist, performer, virtuoso **playful** *adjective* = **lively**, frisky, impish, merry, mischievous, spirited, sportive, sprightly, vivacious OPPOSITE **serious** **play on** *verb* = **take advantage of**, abuse, capitalize on, exploit, impose on, trade on **plaything** *noun* **1** = **toy**, amusement, game, pastime, trifle **play up** *verb* **1** = **emphasize**, accentuate, highlight, stress, underline **2** = **be awkward**, be disobedient, be stroppy (*Brit sl*), give trouble,

PLC, plc Public Limited Company.
plea ❶ *noun* **1** serious or urgent request, entreaty. **2** statement of a prisoner or defendant. **3** excuse.
plead ❶ *verb* **1** ask urgently or with deep feeling. **2** give as an excuse. **3** *Law* declare oneself to be guilty or innocent of a charge made against one.
pleasant ❶ *adjective* pleasing, enjoyable.
pleasantly *adverb* **pleasantry** *noun, pl* **-tries** polite or joking remark.
please ❶ *verb* **1** give pleasure or satisfaction to. ◆ *adverb* **2** polite word of request. **pleasant** *adjective* pleasing, enjoyable. **please oneself** do as one likes. **pleased** *adjective* **pleasing** *adjective* giving pleasure or satisfaction.
pleasure *noun* **1** feeling of happiness and satisfaction. **2** something that causes this.
pleasure ❶ *noun* **1** feeling of happiness and satisfaction. **2** something that causes this.
pleasurable *adjective* giving pleasure.
pleasurably *adverb*
pleat *noun* **1** fold made by doubling material back on itself. ◆ *verb* **2** arrange (material) in pleats.
plebeian ❶ [pleb-**ee**-an] *adjective* **1** of the lower social classes. **2** vulgar or rough. ◆ *noun* **3** (also **pleb**) member of the lower social classes.

plebiscite [pleb-iss-ite] *noun* decision by direct voting of the people of a country.
plectrum *noun, pl* **-trums, -tra** small implement for plucking the strings of a guitar etc.
pledge ❶ *noun* **1** solemn promise. **2** something valuable given as a guarantee that a promise will be kept or a debt paid. ◆ *verb* **3** promise solemnly. **4** bind by or as if by a pledge, e.g. *pledge to secrecy.*
plenary *adjective* (of a meeting) attended by all members.
plenipotentiary *adjective* **1** having full powers. ◆ *noun, pl* **-aries 2** diplomat or representative having full powers.
plenitude *noun* completeness, abundance.
plenteous *adjective* plentiful.
plenty ❶ *noun* **1** large amount or number. **2** quite enough. **plentiful** *adjective* existing in large amounts or numbers. **plentifully** *adverb*
pleonasm *noun* use of more words than necessary.
plethora ❶ *noun* excess.
pleurisy *noun* inflammation of the membrane covering the lungs.
pliable ❶ *adjective* **1** easily bent. **2** easily influenced. **pliability** *noun*
pliant ❶ *adjective* pliable. **pliancy** *noun*

——————— THESAURUS ———————

misbehave
plea *noun* **1** = **appeal**, entreaty, intercession, petition, prayer, request, suit, supplication **3** = **excuse**, defence, explanation, justification
plead *verb* **1, 2** = **appeal**, ask, beg, beseech, entreat, implore, petition, request
pleasant *adjective* = **pleasing**, affable, agreeable, amiable, amusing, charming, congenial, delightful, engaging, enjoyable, fine, friendly, genial, lekker (*S Afr sl*), likable *or* likeable, lovely, nice, pleasurable OPPOSITE awful
pleasantry *noun* = **joke**, badinage, banter, jest, quip, witticism
please *verb* **1** = **delight**, amuse, entertain, gladden, gratify, humour, indulge, satisfy, suit OPPOSITE anger
pleased *adjective* **1** = **happy**, chuffed (*Brit sl*), contented, delighted, euphoric, glad, gratified, over the moon (*inf*), satisfied, thrilled
pleasing *adjective* = **enjoyable**, agreeable, charming, delightful, engaging, gratifying, likable *or* likeable, pleasurable, satisfying OPPOSITE boring
pleasurable *adjective* = **enjoyable**, agreeable, delightful, fun, good, lekker (*S Afr sl*), lovely, nice, pleasant

pleasure *noun* **1, 2** = **happiness**, amusement, bliss, delectation, delight, enjoyment, gladness, gratification, joy, satisfaction OPPOSITE suffering
plebian *adjective* **1, 2** = **common**, base, coarse, low, lower-class, proletarian, uncultivated, unrefined, vulgar, working-class OPPOSITE upper-class ◆ *noun* **3** (also **pleb**) = **commoner**, common man, man in the street, pleb, prole (*Offens*), proletarian
pledge *noun* **1** = **promise**, assurance, covenant, oath, undertaking, vow, warrant, word **2** = **guarantee**, bail, collateral, deposit, pawn, security, surety ◆ *verb* **3** = **promise**, contract, engage, give one's oath, give one's word, swear, vow
plentiful *adjective* = **abundant**, ample, bountiful, copious, generous, lavish, liberal, overflowing, plenteous, profuse OPPOSITE sparing
plenty *noun* **1** = **lots** (*inf*), abundance, enough, great deal, heap(s) (*inf*), masses, pile(s) (*inf*), plethora, quantity, stack(s)
plethora *noun* = **excess**, glut, overabundance, profusion, superabundance, surfeit, surplus OPPOSITE shortage
pliable *adjective* **1** = **flexible**, bendable, bendy,

P

pliers *plural noun* tool with hinged arms and jaws for gripping.

plight[1] ⊙ *noun* difficult or dangerous situation.

plight[2] *verb* **plight one's troth** *Old-fashioned* promise to marry.

Plimsoll line *noun* mark on a ship showing the level water should reach when the ship is fully loaded.

plimsolls *plural noun* rubber-soled canvas shoes.

plinth *noun* slab forming the base of a statue, column, etc.

PLO Palestine Liberation Organization.

plod ⊙ *verb* **plodding, plodded 1** walk with slow heavy steps. **2** work slowly but determinedly. **plodder** *noun*

plonk[1] *verb* put (something) down heavily and carelessly.

plonk[2] *noun Informal* cheap inferior wine.

plop *noun* **1** sound of an object falling into water without a splash. ◆ *verb* **plopping, plopped 2** make this sound.

plot[1] ⊙ *noun* **1** secret plan to do something illegal or wrong. **2** story of a film, novel, etc. ◆ *verb* **plotting, plotted 3** plan secretly, conspire. **4** mark the position or course of (a ship or aircraft) on a map. **5** mark and join up (points on a graph).

plot[2] ⊙ *noun* small piece of land.

plough ⊙ *noun* **1** agricultural tool for turning over soil. ◆ *verb* **2** turn over (earth) with a plough. **3** (usu with *through*) move or work through slowly and laboriously. **ploughman**

noun **ploughman's lunch** snack lunch of bread and cheese with pickle. **ploughshare** *noun* blade of a plough.

plover *noun* shore bird with a straight bill and long pointed wings.

ploy ⊙ *noun* manoeuvre designed to gain an advantage.

pluck ⊙ *verb* **1** pull or pick off. **2** pull out the feathers of (a bird for cooking). **3** sound the strings of (a guitar etc.) with the fingers or a plectrum. ◆ *noun* **4** courage. **plucky** *adjective* **pluckier, pluckiest** brave. **pluckily** *adverb* **pluck up** *verb* summon up (courage).

plug ⊙ *noun* **1** thing fitting into and filling a hole. **2** device connecting an appliance to an electricity supply. **3** *Informal* favourable mention of a product etc., to encourage people to buy it. ◆ *verb* **plugging, plugged 4** block or seal (a hole or gap) with a plug. **5** *Informal* advertise (a product etc.) by constant repetition. **plug away** *verb Informal* work steadily. **plug in** *verb* connect (an electrical appliance) to a power source by pushing a plug into a socket.

plum ⊙ *noun* **1** oval usu. dark red fruit with a stone in the middle. ◆ *adjective* **2** dark purplish-red. **3** very desirable.

plumage *noun* bird's feathers.

plumb ⊙ *verb* **1** understand (something obscure). **2** test with a plumb line. ◆ *adverb* **3** exactly. **plumb the depths of** experience the worst extremes of (an unpleasant quality or emotion). **plumber** *noun* person who fits and repairs pipes and fixtures for water and

malleable, plastic, pliant, supple OPPOSITE stiff. **2 = compliant**, adaptable, docile, easily led, impressionable, pliant, receptive, responsive, susceptible, tractable OPPOSITE stubborn

pliant *adjective* **a = flexible**, bendable, bendy, plastic, pliable, supple **b = impressionable**, biddable, compliant, easily led, pliable, susceptible, tractable

plight[1] *noun* **= difficulty**, condition, jam (*inf*), predicament, scrape (*inf*), situation, spot (*inf*), state, trouble

plod *verb* **1 = trudge**, clump, drag, lumber, tramp, tread **2 = slog**, grind (*inf*), labour, persevere, plough through, plug away (*inf*), soldier on, toil

plot[1] *noun* **1 = plan**, cabal, conspiracy, intrigue, machination, scheme, stratagem **2 = story**, action, narrative, outline, scenario, story line, subject, theme ◆ *verb* **3 = devise**, collude, conceive, concoct, conspire, contrive, cook up, design, hatch, intrigue, lay (*inf*), machinate, manoeuvre, plan, scheme **4 = chart**, calculate,

locate, map, mark, outline

plot[2] *noun* **= patch**, allotment, area, ground, lot, parcel, tract

plough *verb* **2 = turn over**, cultivate, dig, till **3** (usu. with *through*) **= forge**, cut, drive, plunge, press, push, wade

ploy *noun* **= tactic**, device, dodge, manoeuvre, move, ruse, scheme, stratagem, trick, wile

pluck *verb* **1 = pull out** *or* off, collect, draw, gather, harvest, pick **3 = strum**, finger, pick, twang ◆ *noun* **4 = courage**, backbone, boldness, bottle (*Brit sl*), bravery, grit, guts (*inf*), nerve

plucky *adjective* **4 = courageous**, bold, brave, daring, game, gutsy (*sl*), have-a-go (*inf*), intrepid, feisty (*US & Canad*)

plug *noun* **1 = stopper**, bung, cork, spigot **3** *Inf* **= mention**, advert (*Brit inf*), advertisement, hype, publicity, push ◆ *verb* **4 = seal**, block, bung, close, cork, fill, pack, stop, stopper, stop up, stuff **5** *Inf* **= mention**, advertise, build up, hype, promote, publicize, push **plug away** *Inf* **= slog**, grind (*inf*), labour, peg away, plod, toil drainage systems. **plumbing** noun pipes and fixtures used in water and drainage systems.

plumb in verb connect (an appliance such as a washing machine) to a water supply. **plumb line** string with a weight at the end, used to test the depth of water or to test whether something is vertical.

plume ⊕ noun feather, esp. one worn as an ornament.

plummet ⊕ verb -meting, -meted plunge downward.

plump¹ ⊕ adjective moderately or attractively fat. **plumpness** noun **plump up** verb make (a pillow) fuller or rounded.

plump² ⊕ verb sit or fall heavily and suddenly. **plump for** verb choose, vote for.

plunder ⊕ verb 1 take by force, esp. in time of war. ♦ noun 2 things plundered, spoils.

plunge ⊕ verb 1 put or throw forcibly or suddenly (into). 2 descend steeply. ♦ noun 3 plunging, dive. **take the plunge** Informal embark on a risky enterprise. **plunger** noun rubber suction cup used to clear blocked pipes. **plunge into** verb become deeply involved in.

plunk verb pluck the strings of (a banjo etc.) to produce a twanging sound.

pluperfect noun, adjective Grammar (tense) expressing an action completed before a past time, e.g. had gone in his wife had gone already.

plural adjective 1 of or consisting of more than one. ♦ noun 2 word indicating more than one.

pluralism noun existence and toleration of a variety of peoples, opinions, etc. in a society. **pluralist** noun **pluralistic** adjective

plus ⊕ preposition, adjective 1 indicating addition. ♦ adjective 2 more than zero. 3 positive. 4 advantageous. ♦ noun 5 sign (+)

denoting addition. 6 advantage.

plus fours plural noun trousers gathered in at the knee.

plush ⊕ noun 1 fabric with long velvety pile. ♦ adjective 2 (also **plushy**) luxurious.

Pluto noun 1 Greek god of the underworld. 2 farthest planet from the sun.

plutocrat noun person who is powerful because of being very rich. **plutocracy** noun **plutocratic** adjective

plutonium noun Chem radioactive metallic element used esp. in nuclear reactors and weapons.

pluvial adjective of or caused by the action of rain.

ply¹ ⊕ verb **plying, plied** 1 work at (a job or trade). 2 use (a tool). 3 (of a ship) travel regularly along or between. **ply with** verb supply with or subject to persistently.

ply² ⊕ noun thickness of wool, fabric, etc.

plywood noun board made of thin layers of wood glued together.

Pm Chem promethium.

PM prime minister.

p.m. 1 after noon. 2 postmortem.

PMS premenstrual syndrome.

PMT premenstrual tension.

pneumatic adjective worked by or inflated with wind or air.

pneumonia noun inflammation of the lungs.

Po Chem polonium.

PO 1 postal order. 2 Post Office.

poach¹ ⊕ verb 1 catch (animals) illegally on someone else's land. 2 encroach on or steal something belonging to someone else. **poacher** noun

poach² verb simmer (food) gently in liquid.

pocket ⊕ noun 1 small bag sewn into clothing

P

──────────── T H E S A U R U S ────────────

plum adjective 3 = **choice**, best, first-class, prize

plumb verb 1 = **delve**, explore, fathom, gauge, go into, penetrate, probe, unravel ♦adverb 3 = **exactly**, bang, precisely, slap, spot-on (Brit inf) **plumb line** = **weight**, lead, plumb bob, plummet

plume noun = **feather**, crest, pinion, quill

plummet verb = **plunge**, crash, descend, dive, drop down, fall, nose-dive, tumble

plump¹ adjective = **chubby**, corpulent, dumpy, fat, podgy, roly-poly, rotund, round, stout, tubby OPPOSITE> scrawny

plump² verb = **flop**, drop, dump, fall, sink, slump **plump for** = **choose**, back, come down in favour of, favour, opt for, side with, support

plunder verb 1 = **loot**, pillage, raid, ransack, rifle, rob, sack, strip ♦noun 2 = **loot**, booty, ill-

gotten gains, pillage, prize, spoils, swag (sl)

plunge verb 1 = **throw**, career, cast, charge, dash, hurtle, jump, pitch, rush, tear 2 = **descend**, dip, dive, drop, fall, nose-dive, plummet, sink, tumble ♦noun 3 = **dive**, descent, drop, fall, jump

plus preposition 1 = **and**, added to, coupled with, with ♦noun 6 = **advantage**, asset, benefit, bonus, extra, gain, good point

plush adjective 2 = **luxurious**, de luxe, lavish, luxury, opulent, rich, sumptuous OPPOSITE> cheap

ply¹ verb 1 = **work at**, carry on, exercise, follow, practise, pursue 2 = **use**, employ, handle, manipulate, wield

ply² noun = **thickness**, fold, layer, leaf, sheet, strand

for carrying things. **2** pouchlike container, esp. for catching balls at the edge of a snooker table. **3** isolated or distinct group or area. ◆ *verb* **pocketing, pocketed 4** put into one's pocket. **5** take secretly or dishonestly. ◆ *adjective* **6** small. **out of pocket** having made a loss.
pocket money 1 small regular allowance given to children by parents. **2** money for small personal expenses.

pockmarked *adjective* (of the skin) marked with hollow scars where diseased spots have been.

pod ❶ *noun* long narrow seed case of peas, beans, etc.

podgy ❶ *adjective* **podgier, podgiest** short and fat.

podium ❶ *noun, pl* **-diums, -dia** small raised platform for a conductor or speaker.

poem ❶ *noun* imaginative piece of writing in rhythmic lines.

poep *noun Aust & NZ slang* emission of gas from the anus.

poesy *noun Obs* poetry.

poet ❶ *noun* writer of poems. **poetry** *noun* **1** poems. **2** art of writing poems. **3** beautiful or pleasing quality. **poetic, poetical** *adjective* of or like poetry. **poetically** *adverb* **poetic justice** suitable reward or punishment for someone's past actions. **poetic licence** freedom from the normal rules of language and truth, as in poetry. **poet laureate** poet appointed by the British sovereign to write poems on important occasions.

po-faced *adjective* wearing a disapproving stern expression.

pogey ❶ *noun Canad sl* money received from the state while out of work.

pogo stick *noun* pole with steps for the feet and a spring at the bottom, so that the user

can bounce up, down, and along on it.

pogrom *noun* organized persecution and massacre.

poignant ❶ *adjective* sharply painful to the feelings. **poignancy** *noun*

poinsettia *noun* Central American shrub widely grown for its clusters of scarlet leaves, which resemble petals.

point ❶ *noun* **1** main idea in a discussion, argument, etc. **2** aim or purpose. **3** detail or item. **4** characteristic. **5** particular position, stage, or time. **6** dot indicating decimals. **7** full stop. **8** sharp end. **9** headland. **10** unit for recording a value or score. **11** one of the direction marks of a compass. **12** movable rail used to change a train to other rails. **13** electrical socket. ◆ *plural* **14** electrical contacts in the distributor of an engine. ◆ *verb* **15** show the direction or position of something or draw attention to it by extending a finger or other pointed object towards it. **16** direct or face towards. **17** finish or repair the joints in brickwork with mortar. **18** (of a gun dog) show where game is by standing rigidly with the muzzle towards it. **on the point of** very shortly going to. **pointed** *adjective* **1** having a sharp end. **2** (of a remark) obviously directed at a particular person. **pointedly** *adverb* **pointer** *noun* **1** helpful hint. **2** indicator on a measuring instrument. **3** breed of gun dog. **pointless** *adjective* meaningless, irrelevant. **point-blank** *adjective* **1** fired at a very close target. **2** (of a remark or question) direct, blunt. ◆ *adverb* **3** directly or bluntly. **point duty** control of traffic by a policeman at a road junction. **point of view** way of considering something. **point-to-point** *noun* horse race across open country.

poise ❶ *noun* calm dignified manner. **poised**

——— THESAURUS ———

poach¹ *verb* **2** = **encroach**, appropriate, infringe, intrude, trespass
pocket *noun* **2** = **pouch**, bag, compartment, receptacle, sack ◆*verb* **5** = **steal**, appropriate, filch, lift (*inf*), pilfer, purloin, take ◆*adjective* **6** = **small**, abridged, compact, concise, little, miniature, portable
pod *noun* = **shell**, hull, husk, shuck
podgy *adjective* = **tubby**, chubby, dumpy, fat, plump, roly-poly, rotund, stout
podium *noun* = **platform**, dais, rostrum, stage
poem *noun* = **verse**, lyric, ode, rhyme, song, sonnet
poet *noun* = **bard**, lyricist, rhymer, versifier
poetic, poetical *adjective* = **lyrical**, elegiac, lyric, metrical

poetry *noun* **1** = **verse**, poems, rhyme, rhyming
pogey *Canad* = **benefits**, the dole (*Brit & Austral*), welfare, social security, unemployment benefit, state benefit, allowance
poignancy *noun* = **sharpness**, bitterness, intensity, keenness, pathos, sadness
poignant *adjective* = **moving**, bitter, distressing, gut-wrenching, heart-rending, intense, painful, pathetic, sad, touching
point *noun* **1** = **essence**, crux, drift, gist, heart, import, meaning, nub, pith, question, subject, thrust **2** = **aim**, end, goal, intent, intention, motive, object, objective, purpose, reason **3** = **item**, aspect, detail, feature, particular **4** = **characteristic**, aspect, attribute, quality,

adjective **1** absolutely ready. **2** behaving with or showing poise.

poison ❶ *noun* **1** substance that kills or injures when swallowed or absorbed. ♦ *verb* **2** give poison to. **3** have a harmful or evil effect on, spoil. **poisoner** *noun* **poisonous** *adjective*

poison-pen letter malicious anonymous letter.

poke ❶ *verb* **1** jab or prod with one's finger, a stick, etc. **2** thrust forward or out. ♦ *noun* **3** poking. **poky** *adjective* **pokier, pokiest** small and cramped.

poker¹ *noun* metal rod for stirring a fire.

poker² *noun* card game in which players bet on the hands dealt. **poker-faced** *adjective* expressionless.

polar *adjective* of or near either of the earth's poles. **polar bear** white bear that lives in the regions around the North Pole.

polarize *verb* **1** form or cause to form into groups with directly opposite views. **2** *Physics* restrict (light waves) to certain directions of vibration. **polarization** *noun*

Polaroid *noun* ® **1** plastic which polarizes light and so reduces glare. **2** camera that develops a print very quickly inside itself.

polder *noun* land reclaimed from the sea.

pole¹ ❶ *noun* long rounded piece of wood etc. **pole vault** event in which competitors try to clear a high bar with the aid of a flexible long pole.

pole² ❶ *noun* **1** point furthest north or south on the earth's axis of rotation. **2** either of the opposite ends of a magnet or electric cell. **pole position** advantageous starting position. **Pole Star** star nearest to the North Pole in the northern hemisphere.

poleaxe *verb* hit or stun with a heavy blow.

polecat *noun* small animal of the weasel family.

polemic [pol-**em**-ik] *noun* fierce attack on or defence of a particular opinion, belief, etc. **polemical** *adjective*

police ❶ *noun* **1** organized force in a state which keeps law and order. ♦ *verb* **2** control or watch over with police or a similar body. **policeman, policewoman** *noun* member of a police force. **police dog** dog trained to help the police. **police state** state or country in which the government controls people's freedom by means of esp. secret police. **police station** office of the police force of a district.

policy¹ ❶ *noun, pl* **-cies** plan of action adopted by a person, group, or state.

policy² *noun, pl* **-cies** document containing an insurance contract.

polio *noun* disease affecting the spinal cord,

———————— THESAURUS ————————

respect, trait **5** = **place**, instant, juncture, location, moment, position, site, spot, stage, time, very minute **7** = **full stop**, dot, mark, period, stop **8** = **end**, apex, prong, sharp end, spike, spur, summit, tip, top **9** = **headland**, cape, head, promontory **10** = **unit**, score, tally ♦*verb* **15** = **indicate**, call attention to, denote, designate, direct, show, signify **16** = **aim**, direct, level, train

point-blank *adjective* **2** = **direct**, blunt, downright, explicit, express, plain ♦*adverb* **3** = **directly**, bluntly, candidly, explicitly, forthrightly, frankly, openly, plainly, straight

pointed *adjective* **1** = **sharp**, acute, barbed, edged **2** = **cutting**, acute, biting, incisive, keen, penetrating, pertinent, sharp, telling

pointer *noun* **1** = **hint**, advice, caution, information, recommendation, suggestion, tip **2** = **indicator**, guide, hand, needle

pointless *adjective* = **senseless**, absurd, aimless, fruitless, futile, inane, irrelevant, meaningless, silly, stupid, useless

poise *noun* = **composure**, aplomb, assurance, calmness, cool (*sl*), dignity, presence, sang-froid, self-possession

poised *adjective* **1** = **ready**, all set, prepared, standing by, waiting **2** = **composed**, calm, collected, dignified, self-confident, self-possessed, together (*inf*) OPPOSITE **excited**

poison *noun* **1** = **toxin**, bane, venom ♦*verb* **2** = **murder**, give (someone) poison, kill **3** = **corrupt**, contaminate, defile, deprave, infect, pervert, pollute, subvert, taint, undermine, warp

poisonous *adjective* **1** = **toxic**, deadly, fatal, lethal, mortal, noxious, venomous, virulent **3** = **evil**, baleful, corrupting, malicious, noxious, pernicious

poke *verb* **1** = **jab**, dig, nudge, prod, push, shove, stab, stick, thrust ♦*noun* **3** = **jab**, dig, nudge, prod, thrust

poky *adjective* = **small**, confined, cramped, narrow, tiny

pole¹ *noun* = **rod**, bar, mast, post, shaft, spar, staff, stick

pole² *noun* **1** = **extremity**, antipode, limit, terminus

police *noun* **1** = **the law** (*inf*), boys in blue (*inf*), constabulary, fuzz (*sl*), police force, the Old Bill (*sl*) ♦*verb* **2** = **control**, guard, patrol, protect, regulate, watch

policeman, policewoman *noun* = **cop** (*sl*), bobby (*inf*), constable, copper (*sl*), fuzz (*sl*), officer

P

which often causes paralysis (also **poliomyelitis**).

polish ⊕ verb 1 make smooth and shiny by rubbing. 2 make more nearly perfect. ◆ noun 3 substance used for polishing. 4 shine or gloss. 5 pleasing elegant style. **polished** adjective 1 accomplished. 2 done or performed well or professionally. **polish off** verb finish completely, dispose of.

Polish adjective 1 of Poland, its people, or their language. ◆ noun 2 official language of Poland.

polite ⊕ adjective 1 showing consideration for others in one's manners, speech, etc. 2 socially correct or refined. **politely** adverb **politeness** noun

politic ⊕ adjective wise and likely to prove advantageous.

politics ⊕ noun 1 winning and using of power to govern society. 2 (study of) the art of government. 3 person's beliefs about how a country should be governed. **political** adjective of the state, government, or public administration. **politically** adverb **politically correct** (of language) intended to avoid any implied prejudice. **political prisoner** person imprisoned because of his or her political beliefs. **politician** noun person actively engaged in politics, esp. a member of parliament.

polka noun 1 lively 19th-century dance. 2 music for this. **polka dots** pattern of bold spots on fabric.

poll ⊕ noun 1 (also **opinion poll**) questioning of a random sample of people to find out general opinion. 2 voting. 3 number of votes recorded. ◆ verb 4 receive (votes). 5 question in an opinion poll. **pollster** noun person who conducts opinion polls. **polling booth** compartment in which a voter can mark his or her ballot paper in private. **polling station** building where people vote in an election. **poll tax** tax levied on every adult person.

pollarded adjective (of a tree) growing very bushy because its top branches have been cut short.

pollen noun fine dust produced by flowers to fertilize other flowers. **pollinate** verb fertilize with pollen. **pollen count** measure of the amount of pollen in the air, esp. as a warning to people with hay fever.

pollute ⊕ verb contaminate with something poisonous or harmful. **pollution** noun

pollutant noun something that pollutes.

polo noun game like hockey played by teams of players on horseback. **polo neck** sweater with tight turned-over collar. **polo shirt** cotton short-sleeved shirt with a collar and three-button opening at the neck.

polonaise noun 1 old stately dance. 2 music for this.

polonium noun Chem radioactive element that occurs in trace amounts in uranium ores.

poltergeist noun spirit believed to move furniture and throw objects around.

poltroon noun Obs utter coward.

poly- combining form many, much.

polyandry noun practice of having more than one husband at the same time.

polyanthus noun garden primrose.

polychromatic adjective many-coloured.

———— THESAURUS ————

policy[1] noun = **procedure**, action, approach, code, course, custom, plan, practice, rule, scheme

polish verb 1 = **shine**, brighten, buff, burnish, rub, smooth, wax 2 = **perfect**, brush up, enhance, finish, improve, refine, touch up ◆noun 3 = **varnish**, wax 4 = **sheen**, brightness, finish, glaze, gloss, lustre 5 = **style**, breeding, class (inf), elegance, finesse, finish, grace, refinement

polished adjective 1 = **accomplished**, adept 2 = **professional**, expert, fine, masterly, skilful, superlative OPPOSITE **inept**

polite adjective 1 = **mannerly**, civil, complaisant, courteous, gracious, respectful, well-behaved, well-mannered OPPOSITE **rude**. 2 = **refined**, civilized, cultured, elegant, genteel, polished, sophisticated, well-bred OPPOSITE **unrefined**

politeness noun 1 = **courtesy**, civility, courteousness, decency, etiquette, mannerliness

politic adjective = **wise**, advisable, diplomatic, expedient, judicious, prudent, sensible

political adjective = **governmental**, parliamentary, policy-making

politician noun = **statesman**, legislator, Member of Parliament, M.P., office bearer, public servant

politics noun 2 = **statesmanship**, affairs of state, civics, government, political science

poll noun 1 (also **opinion poll**) = **canvass**, census, sampling, survey 2 = **vote**, ballot, count, voting 3 = **figures**, returns, tally ◆verb 4 = **tally**, register 5 = **question**, ballot, canvass, interview, sample, survey

pollute verb = **contaminate**, dirty, foul, infect, poison, soil, spoil, stain, taint OPPOSITE **clean**

pollution noun = **contamination**, corruption, defilement, dirtying, foulness, impurity, taint, uncleanness

polyester *noun* synthetic material used to make plastics and textile fibres.

polygamy [pol-**ig**-a-mee] *noun* practice of having more than one husband or wife at the same time. **polygamous** *adjective* **polygamist** *noun*

polyglot *noun, adjective* (person) able to speak or write several languages.

polygon *noun* geometrical figure with three or more angles and sides. **polygonal** *adjective*

polygraph *noun* instrument for recording pulse rate and perspiration, used esp. as a lie detector.

polyhedron *noun, pl* **-drons, -dra** solid figure with four or more sides.

polymath *noun* person of great and varied learning.

polymer *noun* chemical compound with large molecules made of simple molecules of the same kind. **polymerize** *verb* form into polymers. **polymerization** *noun*

polynomial *adjective* **1** of two or more names or terms. ♦ *noun* **2** mathematical expression consisting of the sum of a number of terms.

polyp *noun* **1** small simple sea creature with a hollow cylindrical body. **2** small growth on a mucous membrane.

polyphonic *adjective Music* consisting of several melodies played simultaneously.

polystyrene *noun* synthetic material used esp. as white rigid foam for packing and insulation.

polytechnic *noun* formerly, college offering courses in many subjects at and below degree level.

polytheism *noun* belief in many gods. **polytheist** *noun* **polytheistic** *adjective*

polythene *noun* light plastic used for bags etc.

polyunsaturated *adjective* of a group of fats that do not form cholesterol in the blood.

polyurethane *noun* synthetic material used esp. in paints.

pom *noun Aust & NZ slang* person from England (also **pommy**).

pomade *noun* perfumed oil put on the hair to make it smooth and shiny.

pomander *noun* (container for) a mixture of sweet-smelling petals, herbs, etc.

pomegranate *noun* round tropical fruit with a thick rind containing many seeds in a red pulp.

Pomeranian *noun* small dog with long straight hair.

pommel *noun* **1** raised part on the front of a saddle. **2** knob at the top of a sword hilt.

pommy *noun, pl* **-mies** *Aust & NZ slang* person from Britain (also **pom**).

pomp ❶ *noun* stately display or ceremony.

pompom *noun* decorative ball of tufted wool, silk, etc.

pompous ❶ *adjective* foolishly serious and grand, self-important. **pompously** *adverb* **pomposity** *noun*

ponce *noun Offens* **1** effeminate man. **2** pimp.

ponce around *verb* act stupidly, waste time.

poncho *noun, pl* **-chos** loose circular cloak with a hole for the head.

pond ❶ *noun* small area of still water.

pondweed *noun* plant that grows in ponds.

ponder ❶ *verb* think thoroughly or deeply (about).

ponderous ❶ *adjective* **1** serious and dull. **2** heavy and unwieldy. **3** (of movement) slow and clumsy. **ponderously** *adverb*

pong *verb, noun Informal* (give off) a strong unpleasant smell.

pontiff ❶ *noun* the Pope. **pontificate** *verb* **1** state one's opinions as if they were the only possible correct ones. ♦ *noun* **2** period of office of a Pope.

pontoon[1] *noun* floating platform supporting a temporary bridge.

pontoon[2] *noun* gambling card game.

pony *noun, pl* **ponies** small horse. **ponytail** *noun* long hair tied in one bunch at the back of

P

—————— THESAURUS ——————

pomp *noun* **a** = **show**, display, grandiosity, ostentation **b** = **ceremony**, flourish, grandeur, magnificence, pageant, pageantry, splendour, state

pomposity *noun* = **self-importance**, affectation, airs, grandiosity, pompousness, portentousness, pretension, pretentiousness

pompous *adjective* **a** = **grandiloquent**, boastful, bombastic, high-flown, inflated OPPOSITE direct. **b** = **self-important**, arrogant, grandiose, ostentatious, pretentious, puffed up, showy OPPOSITE simple

pond *noun* = **pool**, duck pond, fish pond, millpond, small lake, tarn

ponder *verb* = **think**, brood, cogitate, consider, contemplate, deliberate, meditate, mull over, muse, reflect, ruminate

ponderous *adjective* **1** = **dull**, heavy, long-winded, pedantic, tedious **2** = **unwieldy**, bulky, cumbersome, heavy, huge, massive, weighty **3** = **clumsy**, awkward, heavy-footed, lumbering OPPOSITE graceful

pontificate *verb* **1** = **expound**, hold forth, lay down the law, preach, pronounce, sound off the head. **pony trekking** pastime of riding ponies cross-country.

poodle noun dog with curly hair often clipped fancifully.

poof noun Offens homosexual man.

pooh interjection exclamation of disdain, contempt, or disgust. **pooh-pooh** verb express disdain or scorn for.

pool¹ ❶ noun 1 small body of still water. 2 puddle of spilt liquid. 3 swimming pool.

pool² ❶ noun 1 shared fund or group of workers or resources. 2 game like snooker. ◆ plural 3 short for FOOTBALL POOLS. ◆ verb 4 put in a common fund.

poop noun raised part at the back of a sailing ship.

poor ❶ adjective 1 having little money and few possessions. 2 less, smaller, or weaker than is needed or expected. 3 inferior. 4 unlucky, pitiable. **poorly** adverb 1 in a poor manner. ◆ adjective 2 not in good health.

pop¹ ❶ verb popping, popped 1 make or cause to make a small explosive sound. 2 Informal go, put, or come unexpectedly or suddenly. ◆ noun 3 small explosive sound. 4 nonalcoholic fizzy drink. **popcorn** noun grains of maize heated until they puff up and burst.

pop² noun 1 music of general appeal, esp. to young people. ◆ adjective 2 popular. **pop art** movement in modern art that uses the methods, styles, and themes of popular culture and mass media.

pop³ noun Informal father.

Pope noun head of the Roman Catholic Church. **popish** adjective Offens Roman Catholic.

popeyed adjective staring in astonishment.

popinjay noun conceited or talkative person.

poplar noun tall slender tree.

poplin noun ribbed cotton material.

poppadom noun thin round crisp Indian bread.

poppet noun term of affection for a small child or sweetheart.

poppy noun, pl **-pies 1** plant with a large red flower. **2** artificial red poppy worn to mark Remembrance Sunday.

poppycock noun Informal nonsense.

Popsicle noun US & Canad an ice lolly.

populace ❶ noun the ordinary people.

popular ❶ adjective 1 widely liked and admired. 2 of or for the public in general. **popularly** adverb **popularity** noun **popularize** verb 1 make popular. 2 make (something technical or specialist) easily understood.

populate ❶ verb 1 live in, inhabit. 2 fill with inhabitants. **population** noun 1 all the people who live in a particular place. 2 the number of people living in a particular place. **populous** adjective densely populated.

——————— T H E S A U R U S ———————

P

pool¹ noun 1 = **pond**, lake, mere, puddle, tarn 3 = **swimming pool**, swimming bath

pool² noun 1 a = **kitty**, bank, funds, jackpot, pot b = **syndicate**, collective, consortium, group, team, trust ◆verb 4 = **combine**, amalgamate, join forces, league, merge, put together, share

poor adjective 1 = **impoverished**, broke (inf), destitute, down and out, hard up (inf), impecunious, indigent, needy, on the breadline, penniless, penurious, poverty-stricken, short, skint (Brit sl), stony-broke (Brit sl) OPPOSITE rich. 2 = **meagre**, deficient, inadequate, incomplete, insufficient, lacking, measly, scant, scanty, skimpy OPPOSITE complete. 3 = **inferior**, below par, low-grade, mediocre, no great shakes (inf), rotten (inf), rubbishy, second-rate, substandard, unsatisfactory 4 = **unfortunate**, hapless, ill-fated, pitiable, unlucky, wretched OPPOSITE successful

poorly adverb 1 = **badly**, inadequately, incompetently, inexpertly, insufficiently, unsatisfactorily, unsuccessfully ◆adjective 2 = **ill**, below par, crook (Aust & NZ sl), off colour, rotten (inf), seedy (inf), sick, under the weather

(inf), unwell OPPOSITE well

pop¹ verb 1 = **burst**, bang, crack, explode, go off, snap ◆noun 3 = **bang**, burst, crack, explosion, noise, report

Pope noun = **Holy Father**, Bishop of Rome, pontiff, Vicar of Christ

populace noun = **people**, general public, hoi polloi, masses, mob, multitude

popular adjective 1 = **well-liked**, accepted, approved, fashionable, favourite, in, in demand, in favour, liked, sought-after OPPOSITE unpopular. 2 = **common**, conventional, current, general, prevailing, prevalent, universal OPPOSITE rare

popularity noun 1 = **favour**, acceptance, acclaim, approval, currency, esteem, regard, vogue

popularize verb 1 = **make popular**, disseminate, give currency to, give mass appeal, make available to all, spread, universalize

populate verb 1 = **inhabit**, colonize, live in, occupy, settle

population noun 1 = **inhabitants**, community, denizens, folk, natives, people, residents, society

populist *noun, adjective* (person) appealing to the interests or prejudices of ordinary people. **populism** *noun*

porbeagle *noun* kind of shark.

porcelain *noun* **1** fine china. **2** objects made of it.

porch *noun* covered approach to the entrance of a building.

porcine *adjective* of or like a pig.

porcupine *noun* animal covered with long pointed quills.

pore ⊕ *noun* tiny opening in the skin or in the surface of a plant.

pore over *verb* make a careful study or examination of (a book, map, etc.).

pork *noun* pig meat. **porker** *noun* pig raised for food.

porn, porno *noun, adjective Informal* short for PORNOGRAPHY *or* PORNOGRAPHIC.

pornography ⊕ *noun* writing, films, or pictures designed to be sexually exciting. **pornographer** *noun* producer of pornography. **pornographic** *adjective*

porous ⊕ *adjective* allowing liquid to pass through gradually. **porosity** *noun*

porphyry [por-fir-ee] *noun* reddish rock with large crystals in it.

porpoise *noun* fishlike sea mammal.

porridge *noun* **1** breakfast food made of oatmeal cooked in water or milk. **2** *Slang* term in prison.

port¹ ⊕ *noun* (town with) a harbour.

port² *noun* left side of a ship or aircraft when facing the front of it.

port³ *noun* strong sweet wine, usu. red.

port⁴ *noun* **1** opening in the side of a ship. **2** porthole.

portable ⊕ *adjective* easily carried. **portability** *noun*

portage *noun* (route for) transporting boats and supplies overland between navigable waterways.

portal *noun* large imposing doorway or gate.

portcullis *noun* grating suspended above a castle gateway, that can be lowered to block the entrance.

portend ⊕ *verb* be a sign of.

portent ⊕ *noun* sign of a future event.

portentous *adjective* **1** of great or ominous significance. **2** pompous, self-important.

porter¹ ⊕ *noun* **1** man who carries luggage. **2** hospital worker who transfers patients between rooms etc.

porter² ⊕ *noun* doorman or gatekeeper of a building.

portfolio *noun, pl* **-os 1** (flat case for carrying) examples of an artist's work. **2** area of responsibility of a government minister. **3** list of investments held by an investor.

porthole *noun* small round window in a ship or aircraft.

portico *noun, pl* **-coes, -cos** porch or covered walkway with columns supporting the roof.

portion ⊕ *noun* **1** part or share. **2** helping of food for one person. **3** destiny or fate. **portion out** *verb* divide into shares.

portly ⊕ *adjective* **-lier, -liest** rather fat.

portmanteau *noun, pl* **-teaus, -teaux 1** *Old-fashioned* large suitcase that opens into two compartments. ♦ *adjective* **2** combining aspects

P

———— THESAURUS ————

populous *adjective* =**populated**, crowded, heavily populated, overpopulated, packed, swarming, teeming

pore *noun* =**opening**, hole, orifice, outlet

pore over *verb* =**study**, examine, peruse, ponder, read, scrutinize

pornographic *adjective* =**obscene**, blue, dirty, filthy, indecent, lewd, salacious, scungy (*Aust & NZ inf*), smutty

pornography *noun* =**obscenity**, dirt, filth, indecency, porn (*inf*), smut

porous *adjective* =**permeable**, absorbent, absorptive, penetrable, spongy

port¹ *noun* =**harbour**, anchorage, haven, seaport

portable *adjective* =**light**, compact, convenient, easily carried, handy, manageable, movable

portend *verb* =**foretell**, augur, betoken, bode, foreshadow, herald, indicate, predict,

prognosticate, promise, warn of

portent *noun* =**omen**, augury, forewarning, indication, prognostication, sign, warning

portentous *adjective* **1** = **significant**, crucial, fateful, important, menacing, momentous, ominous **2** = **pompous**, ponderous, self-important, solemn

porter¹ *noun* **1** =**baggage attendant**, bearer, carrier

porter² *noun* =**doorman**, caretaker, concierge, gatekeeper, janitor

portion *noun* **1 a** =**part**, bit, fragment, morsel, piece, scrap, section, segment **b** = **share**, allocation, allotment, allowance, lot, measure, quantity, quota, ration **2** =**helping**, piece, serving **3** = **destiny**, fate, fortune, lot, luck **portion out** ♦*verb* =**divide**, allocate, allot, apportion, deal, distribute, dole out, share out

portly *adjective* =**stout**, burly, corpulent, fat, fleshy, heavy, large, plump

of different things.
portrait ● *noun* **1** picture of a person. **2** lifelike description.
portray ● *verb* describe or represent by artistic means, as in writing or film. **portrait** *noun* picture of a person. **portrayal** *noun*
Portuguese *adjective* **1** of Portugal, its people, or their language. ◆ *noun* **2** person from Portugal. **3** language of Portugal and Brazil. **Portuguese man-of-war** sea creature resembling a jellyfish, with stinging tentacles.
pose ● *verb* **1** place in or take up a particular position to be photographed or drawn. **2** behave in an affected way. **3** raise (a problem). **4** ask (a question). ◆ *noun* **5** position while posing. **6** behaviour adopted for effect. **pose as** pretend to be. **poser** *noun* **1** puzzling question. **2** *Informal* person who likes to be seen in trendy clothes in fashionable places. **3** poseur. **poseur** *noun* person who behaves in an affected way to impress others.
posh ● *adjective Informal* **1** smart, luxurious. **2** affectedly upper-class.
posit ● [pozz-it] *verb* lay down as a basis for argument.
position ● *noun* **1** place. **2** usual or expected place. **3** way in which something is placed or arranged. **4** attitude, point of view. **5** social standing. **6** job. ◆ *verb* **7** place. **positional**

adjective
positive ● *adjective* **1** feeling no doubts, certain. **2** confident, hopeful. **3** helpful, providing encouragement. **4** absolute, downright. **5** *Maths* greater than zero. **6** (of an electrical charge) having a deficiency of electrons. **7** *Med* indicating the presence of a condition for which a test was made. **positively** *adverb* **positive discrimination** provision of special opportunities for a disadvantaged group.
positivism *noun* philosophical system which accepts only things that can be seen or proved. **positivist** *noun, adjective*
positron *noun Physics* particle with same mass as electron but positive charge.
posse [poss-ee] *noun* **1** *US* group of men organized to maintain law and order. **2** *Informal* group or gang.
possess ● *verb* **1** have as one's property. **2** (of a feeling, belief, etc.) have complete control of, dominate. **possessed** *adjective* **possessor** *noun* **possession** *noun* **1** state of possessing, ownership. ◆ *plural* **2** things a person possesses.
possessive *adjective* **1** wanting all the attention or love of another person. **2** (of a word) indicating the person or thing that something belongs to. **possessiveness** *noun*
possible ● *adjective* **1** able to exist, happen,

──────── T H E S A U R U S ────────

portrait *noun* **1** = **picture**, image, likeness, painting, photograph, representation **2** = **description**, characterization, depiction, portrayal, profile, thumbnail sketch
portray *verb* **a** = **represent**, depict, draw, figure, illustrate, paint, picture, sketch **b** = **describe**, characterize, depict, put in words **c** = **play**, act the part of, represent
pose *verb* **1** = **position**, model, sit **2** = **put on airs**, posture, show off (*inf*) ◆ *noun* **5** = **posture**, attitude, bearing, position, stance **6** = **act**, affectation, air, facade, front, mannerism, posturing, pretence **pose as** ◆ *verb* = **impersonate**, masquerade as, pass oneself off as, pretend to be, profess to be
posh *adjective Inf* **1** = **smart**, classy (*sl*), grand, luxurious, ritzy (*sl*), stylish, swanky (*inf*), swish (*inf, chiefly Brit*) **2** = **upper-class**, high-class, up-market
posit *verb* = **put forward**, advance, assume, postulate, presume, propound, state
position *noun* **1** = **place**, area, bearings, locale, location, point, post, situation, spot, station, whereabouts **3** = **posture**, arrangement, attitude, pose, stance **4** = **attitude**, belief, opinion, outlook, point of view, slant, stance,

view, viewpoint **5** = **status**, importance, place, prestige, rank, reputation, standing, station, stature **6** = **job**, duty, employment, occupation, office, place, post, role, situation ◆ *verb* **7** = **place**, arrange, lay out, locate, put, set, stand
positive *adjective* **1, 2** = **certain**, assured, confident, convinced, sure OPPOSITE **uncertain**. **3** = **helpful**, beneficial, constructive, practical, productive, progressive, useful OPPOSITE **useless**. **4 a** = **definite**, absolute, categorical, certain, clear, conclusive, decisive, explicit, express, firm, real **b** = **absolute**, complete, consummate, downright, out-and-out, perfect, thorough, utter OPPOSITE **uncertain**
positively *adverb* **1, 4** = **definitely**, absolutely, assuredly, categorically, certainly, emphatically, firmly, surely, unequivocally, unquestionably
possess *verb* **1** = **have**, enjoy, hold, own **2** = **dominate**, control, seize, take over
possessed *adjective* **2** = **crazed**, berserk, demented, frenzied, obsessed, raving
possession *noun* **1** = **ownership**, control, custody, hold, occupation, tenure, title ◆ *plural* **2** = **property**, assets, belongings, chattels, effects, estate, things
possessive *adjective* **1** = **jealous**, controlling,

or be done. **2** worthy of consideration. ◆ *noun* **3** person or thing that might be suitable or chosen. **possibility** *noun*, *pl* **-ties**. **possibly** *adverb* perhaps, not necessarily.

possum *noun* **1** same as OPOSSUM. **2** *Aust & NZ* same as PHALANGER. **play possum** pretend to be dead or asleep to deceive an opponent.

post¹ ❶ *noun* **1** official system of delivering letters and parcels. **2** (single collection or delivery of) letters and parcels sent by this system. ◆ *verb* **3** send by post. **keep someone posted** supply someone regularly with the latest information. **postage** *noun* charge for sending a letter or parcel by post. **postal** *adjective* **postal order** written money order sent by post and cashed at a post office by the person who receives it. **postbag** *noun* **1** postman's bag. **2** post received by a magazine, famous person, etc. **postbox** *noun* same as LETTER BOX (sense 2). **postcode** *noun* system of letters and numbers used to aid the sorting of mail. **postie** *Aust, NZ & Scot informal* postman. **postman, postwoman** *noun* person who collects and delivers post. **postmark** *noun* official mark stamped on letters showing place and date of posting. **postmaster, postmistress** *noun* official in charge of a post office. **post office** place where postal business is conducted. **post shop** *NZ* shop providing postal services.

post² ❶ *noun* **1** length of wood, concrete, etc. fixed upright to support or mark something. ◆ *verb* **2** put up (a notice) in a public place.

post³ ❶ *noun* **1** job. **2** position to which someone, esp. a soldier, is assigned for duty. **3** military establishment. ◆ *verb* **4** send (a person) to a new place to work. **5** put (a guard etc.) on duty.

post- *prefix* after, later than, e.g. *postwar*.

postcard *noun* card for sending a message by post without an envelope.

postdate *verb* write a date on (a cheque) that is later than the actual date.

poster ❶ *noun* large picture or notice stuck on a wall.

poste restante *noun French* post-office department where a traveller's letters are kept until called for.

posterior *noun* **1** buttocks. ◆ *adjective* **2** behind, at the back of.

posterity ❶ *noun* future generations, descendants.

postern *noun* small back door or gate.

postgraduate *noun* person with a degree who is studying for a more advanced qualification.

posthaste *adverb* with great speed.

posthumous [poss-tume-uss] *adjective* **1** occurring after one's death. **2** published after the author's death. **posthumously** *adverb*

postilion, postillion *noun Hist* person riding one of a pair of horses drawing a carriage.

postmortem *noun* medical examination of a body to establish the cause of death.

postnatal *adjective* occurring after childbirth.

postpone ❶ *verb* put off to a later time. **postponement** *noun*

postscript ❶ *noun* passage added at the end of a letter.

postulant *noun* candidate for admission to a religious order.

postulate ❶ *verb* assume to be true as the

P

—————————————— THESAURUS ——————————————

covetous, dominating, domineering, overprotective, selfish

possibility *noun* **1 a** = **likelihood**, chance, hope, liability, odds, probability, prospect, risk **b** = **feasibility**, likelihood, potentiality, practicability, workableness **2** (often pl) = **potential**, capabilities, potentiality, promise, prospects, talent

possible *adjective* **1 a** = **conceivable**, credible, hypothetical, imaginable, likely, potential **b** = **likely**, hopeful, potential, probable, promising OPPOSITE impossible. **c** = **feasible**, attainable, doable, practicable, realizable, viable, workable OPPOSITE impossible

possibly *adverb* = **perhaps**, maybe, perchance (*arch*)

post¹ *noun* **1** = **mail**, collection, delivery, postal service ◆ *verb* **3** = **send**, dispatch, mail, transmit **keep someone posted** = **notify**,

advise, brief, fill in on (*inf*), inform, report to

post² *noun* **1** = **support**, column, picket, pillar, pole, shaft, stake, upright ◆ *verb* **2** = **put up**, affix, display, pin up

post³ *noun* **1** = **job**, appointment, assignment, employment, office, place, position, situation **2** = **station**, beat, place, position ◆ *verb* **4** = **station**, assign, place, position, put, situate

poster *noun* = **notice**, advertisement, announcement, bill, placard, public notice, sticker

posterity *noun* **a** = **future**, succeeding generations **b** = **descendants**, children, family, heirs, issue, offspring, progeny

postpone *verb* = **put off**, adjourn, defer, delay, put back, put on the back burner (*inf*), shelve, suspend OPPOSITE go ahead with

postscript *noun* = **P.S.**, addition, afterthought, supplement

basis of an argument or theory. **postulation**
noun

posture ● *noun* **1** position or way in which
someone stands, walks, etc. ♦ *verb* **2** behave in
an exaggerated way to get attention.

posy *noun, pl* **-sies** small bunch of flowers.

pot¹ ● *noun* **1** round deep container. **2**
teapot. ♦ *plural* **3** *Informal* a lot. ♦ *verb* **potting,
potted 4** plant in a pot. **5** *Snooker* hit (a ball)
into a pocket. **potted** *adjective* **1** grown in a
pot. **2** (of meat or fish) cooked or preserved in
a pot. **3** *Informal* abridged. **potbelly** *noun*
bulging belly. **potsherd** *noun* broken fragment
of pottery. **pot shot** shot taken without aiming
carefully. **potting shed** shed where plants are
potted.

pot² *noun Slang* cannabis.

potable [**pote**-a-bl] *adjective* drinkable.

potash *noun* white powdery substance
obtained from ashes and used as fertilizer.

potassium *noun Chem* silvery metallic
element.

potato *noun, pl* **-toes** roundish starchy
vegetable that grows underground.

potato chip *noun* the US and Canadian term
for CRISP.

poteen *noun* (in Ireland) illegally made
alcoholic drink.

potent ● *adjective* **1** having great power or
influence. **2** (of a male) capable of having
sexual intercourse. **potency** *noun*

potentate *noun* ruler or monarch.

potential ● *adjective* **1** possible but not yet
actual. ♦ *noun* **2** ability or talent not yet fully
used. **3** *Electricity* level of electric pressure.
potentially *adverb* **potentiality** *noun, pl* **-ties**

pothole *noun* **1** hole in the surface of a road.
2 deep hole in a limestone area. **potholing**
noun sport of exploring underground caves.

potholer *noun*

potion ● *noun* dose of medicine or poison.

potluck *noun* **take potluck** accept whatever
happens to be available.

potoroo *noun, pl* **-roos** Australian leaping
rodent.

potpourri [po-**poor**-ee] *noun* **1** fragrant
mixture of dried flower petals. **2** assortment or
medley.

pottage *noun* thick soup or stew.

potter¹ *noun* person who makes pottery.

potter² ● *verb* be busy in a pleasant but
aimless way.

pottery ● *noun, pl* **-ries 1** articles made from
baked clay. **2** place where they are made. **3**
craft of making such articles.

potty¹ *adjective* **-tier, -tiest** *Informal* crazy or
silly.

potty² *noun, pl* **-ties** bowl used by a small
child as a toilet.

pouch ● *noun* **1** small bag. **2** baglike pocket
of skin on an animal.

pouf, pouffe [poof] *noun* large solid cushion
used as a seat.

poulterer *noun* person who sells poultry.

poultice [**pole**-tiss] *noun* moist dressing, often
heated, applied to inflamed skin.

poultry *noun* domestic fowls.

pounce ● *verb* **1** spring upon suddenly to
attack or capture. ♦ *noun* **2** pouncing.

pound¹ *noun* **1** monetary unit of Britain and
some other countries. **2** unit of weight equal to
0.454 kg.

pound² ● *verb* **1** hit heavily and repeatedly. **2**
crush to pieces or powder. **3** (of the heart)
throb heavily. **4** run heavily.

pound³ ● *noun* enclosure for stray animals or
officially removed vehicles.

poundage *noun* charge of so much per

———— THESAURUS ————

postulate *verb* =**presuppose**, assume,
hypothesize, posit, propose, suppose, take for
granted, theorize

posture *noun* **1** =**bearing**, attitude, carriage,
disposition, set, stance ♦*verb* **2** =**show off**,
affect, pose, put on airs (*inf*)

pot¹ *noun* **1** =**container**, bowl, pan, vessel

potency *noun* =**power**, effectiveness, force,
influence, mana (*NZ*), might, strength

potent *adjective* =**powerful**, authoritative,
commanding, dominant, dynamic, forceful,
influential, mighty, strong, vigorous OPPOSITE
ineffective

potential *adjective* **1** =**possible**, dormant,
future, hidden, inherent, latent, likely,
promising ♦*noun* **2** =**ability**, aptitude,

capability, capacity, possibility, potentiality,
power, wherewithal

potion *noun* =**concoction**, brew, dose,
draught, elixir, mixture, philtre

potter² *verb* =**mess about**, dabble, footle
(*inf*), tinker

pottery *noun* **1** =**ceramics**, earthenware,
stoneware, terracotta

pouch *noun* **1** =**bag**, container, pocket, purse,
sack

pounce *verb* **1** =**spring**, attack, fall upon,
jump, leap at, strike, swoop ♦*noun* **2** =**spring**,
assault, attack, bound, jump, leap, swoop

pound² *verb* **1** =**beat**, batter, belabour,
clobber (*sl*), hammer, pummel, strike, thrash,
thump **2** =**crush**, powder, pulverize **3**

pound of weight or sterling.

pour ❶ *verb* **1** flow or cause to flow out in a stream. **2** rain heavily. **3** come or go in large numbers.

pout ❶ *verb* **1** thrust out one's lips, look sulky. ♦ *noun* **2** pouting look.

pouter *noun* pigeon that can puff out its crop.

poverty ❶ *noun* **1** state of being without enough food or money. **2** lack of, scarcity.

poverty-stricken *adjective* very poor. **poverty trap** situation of being unable to raise one's living standard because any extra income would result in state benefits beingreduced.

POW prisoner of war.

powder ❶ *noun* **1** substance in the form of tiny loose particles. **2** medicine or cosmetic in this form. ♦ *verb* **3** apply powder to.

powdered *adjective* in the form of a powder, e.g. *powdered milk*. **powdery** *adjective* **powder puff** soft pad used to apply cosmetic powder to the skin. **powder room** ladies' toilet.

power ❶ *noun* **1** ability to do or act. **2** strength. **3** position of authority or control. **4** person or thing having authority. **5** *Maths* product from continuous multiplication of a number by itself. **6** *Physics* rate at which work is done. **7** electricity supply. **8** particular form of energy, e.g. *nuclear power*. **powered** *adjective* having or operated by mechanical or electrical power. **powerful** *adjective* **powerless** *adjective*

power cut temporary interruption in the supply of electricity. **power point** socket on a wall for plugging in electrical appliances.

power station installation for generating and distributing electric power. **power steering** type of steering on vehicles in which the turning of the steering wheel is assisted by power from the engine.

powwow *noun* talk, conference.

pox *noun* **1** disease in which skin pustules form. **2** *Informal* syphilis.

p & p postage and packing.

pp 1 past participle. **2** (in signing a document) for and on behalf of. **3** *Music* pianissimo.

pp. pages.

PQ Quebec.

Pr *Chem* praseodymium.

PR 1 proportional representation. **2** public relations.

practicable ❶ *adjective* capable of being done successfully. **practicability** *noun*

practical ❶ *adjective* **1** involving experience or actual use rather than theory. **2** concerned with everyday matters. **3** sensible, useful, and effective. **4** good at making or doing things. **5** in effect though not in name. ♦ *noun* **6** examination in which something has to be done or made. **practically** *adverb* **practicality** *noun, pl* **-ties**. **practical joke** trick intended to make someone look foolish.

——————— T H E S A U R U S ———————

= pulsate, beat, palpitate, pulse, throb **4** = stomp (*inf*), march, thunder, tramp

pound³ *noun* = enclosure, compound, pen, yard

pour *verb* **1** = flow, course, decant, emit, gush, let flow, run, rush, spew, spill, splash, spout, stream **2** = rain, bucket down (*inf*), pelt (down), teem **3** = stream, crowd, swarm, teem, throng

pout *verb* **1** = sulk, glower, look petulant, pull a long face ♦ *noun* **2** = sullen look, glower, long face

poverty *noun* **1** = pennilessness, beggary, destitution, hardship, indigence, insolvency, need, penury, privation, want OPPOSITE wealth. **2** = scarcity, dearth, deficiency, insufficiency, lack, paucity, shortage OPPOSITE abundance

poverty-stricken *adjective* = penniless, broke (*inf*), destitute, down and out, flat broke (*inf*), impecunious, impoverished, indigent, poor

powder *noun* **1** = dust, fine grains, loose particles, talc ♦ *verb* **3** = dust, cover, dredge, scatter, sprinkle, strew

powdery *adjective* = fine, crumbly, dry, dusty, grainy, granular

power *noun* **1** = ability, capability, capacity, competence, competency, faculty, potential OPPOSITE inability. **2** = strength, brawn, energy, force, forcefulness, intensity, might, muscle, potency, vigour OPPOSITE weakness. **3** = control, ascendancy, authority, command, dominance, domination, dominion, influence, mana (*NZ*), mastery, prerogative, privilege, rule

powerful *adjective* **2** = strong, energetic, mighty, potent, strapping, sturdy, vigorous OPPOSITE feeble. **3 a** = controlling, authoritative, commanding, dominant, influential, prevailing, skookum (*Canad*) OPPOSITE weak. **b** = persuasive, cogent, compelling, convincing, effectual, forceful, impressive, storming, striking, telling, weighty

powerless *adjective* **1** = defenceless, dependent, ineffective, subject, tied, unarmed, vulnerable **2** = weak, debilitated, disabled, feeble, frail, helpless, impotent, incapable, incapacitated, ineffectual OPPOSITE strong

practicability *noun* = feasibility, advantage, possibility, practicality, use, usefulness, viability

practicable *adjective* = feasible, achievable, attainable, doable, possible, viable

P

practice ❶ noun 1 something done regularly or habitually. 2 repetition of something so as to gain skill. 3 doctor's or lawyer's place of work. **in practice** what actually happens as distinct from what is supposed to happen. **put into practice** carry out, do.

> **SPELLING TIP**
>
> It is extremely common for people to confuse the noun, **practice**, which has a c at the end, and the verb **practise**, which has an s.

practise ❶ verb 1 do repeatedly so as to gain skill. 2 take part in, follow (a religion etc.). 3 work at, e.g. *practise medicine*. 4 do habitually. **practice** noun something done regularly or habitually.

practitioner noun person who practises a profession.

pragmatic ❶ adjective concerned with practical consequences rather than theory. **pragmatism** noun **pragmatist** noun

prairie noun a treeless grassy plain of the central US and S Canada. **prairie dog** rodent that lives in burrows in the N American prairies.

praise ❶ verb 1 express approval or admiration of (someone or something). 2 express honour and thanks to (one's God). ♦ noun 3 something said or written to show approval or admiration. **sing someone's praises** praise someone highly. **praiseworthy** adjective

praline [prah-leen] noun sweet made of nuts and caramelized sugar.

pram noun four-wheeled carriage for a baby, pushed by hand.

prance ❶ verb walk with exaggerated bouncing steps.

prang verb, noun Old-fashioned slang (have) a crash in a car or aircraft.

prank ❶ noun mischievous trick.

praseodymium [pray-zee-oh-**dim**-ee-um] noun Chem silvery-white metallic element of the lanthanide series.

prat noun Offens stupid person.

prattle ❶ verb 1 chatter in a childish or foolish way. ♦ noun 2 childish or foolish talk.

prawn noun edible shellfish like a large shrimp.

praxis noun practice as opposed to theory.

pray ❶ verb 1 say prayers. 2 ask earnestly, entreat. **prayer** noun 1 thanks or appeal addressed to one's God. 2 set form of words used in praying. 3 earnest request.

——————— T H E S A U R U S ———————

practical adjective 1 = **functional**, applied, empirical, experimental, factual, pragmatic, realistic, utilitarian OPPOSITE **unrealistic**. 2 = **ordinary**, businesslike, down-to-earth, hard-headed, matter-of-fact, realistic OPPOSITE **unrealistic**. 3 = **sensible**, doable, feasible, practicable, serviceable, useful, workable OPPOSITE **impossible**. 4 = **skilled**, accomplished, efficient, experienced, proficient OPPOSITE **inexperienced**

practically adverb 2 = **realistically**, matter-of-factly 3 = **sensibly**, clearly, rationally, reasonably 5 = **almost**, all but, basically, essentially, fundamentally, in effect, just about, nearly, very nearly, virtually, well-nigh

practice noun 1 = **custom**, habit, method, mode, routine, rule, system, tradition, usage, way, wont 2 = **rehearsal**, drill, exercise, preparation, repetition, study, training 3 = **profession**, business, career, vocation, work, yakka (*Aust & NZ inf*)

practise verb 1 = **rehearse**, drill, exercise, go over, go through, prepare, repeat, study, train 2 = **follow**, observe, perform 3 = **work at**, carry on, engage in, pursue

pragmatic adjective = **practical**, businesslike, down-to-earth, hard-headed, realistic, sensible,

utilitarian OPPOSITE **idealistic**

praise verb 1 = **approve**, acclaim, admire, applaud, cheer, compliment, congratulate, eulogize, extol, honour, laud OPPOSITE **criticize**. 2 = **give thanks to**, adore, bless, exalt, glorify, worship ♦noun 3 a = **approval**, acclaim, acclamation, approbation, commendation, compliment, congratulation, eulogy, plaudit, tribute OPPOSITE **criticism**. b = **thanks**, adoration, glory, homage, worship

praiseworthy adjective 1 = **creditable**, admirable, commendable, laudable, meritorious, worthy

prance verb = **dance**, caper, cavort, frisk, gambol, parade, romp, show off (*inf*), skip, stalk, strut, swagger, swank (*inf*)

prank noun = **trick**, escapade, jape, lark (*inf*), practical joke

prattle verb 1 = **chatter**, babble, blather, blether, gabble, jabber, rabbit (on) (*Brit inf*), waffle (*inf, chiefly Brit*), witter (*inf*)

pray verb 1 = **say one's prayers**, offer a prayer, recite the rosary 2 = **beg**, adjure, ask, beseech, entreat, implore, petition, plead, request, solicit

prayer noun 1 = **orison**, devotion, invocation, supplication 2 = **litany** 3 = **plea**, appeal, entreaty, petition, request, supplication

P

pre- *prefix* before, beforehand, e.g. *prenatal*; *prerecorded; preshrunk*.
preach ❶ *verb* **1** give a talk on a religious theme as part of a church service. **2** speak in support of (an idea, principle, etc.). **preacher** *noun*
preamble ❶ *noun* introductory part to something said or written.
prearranged *adjective* arranged beforehand.
prebendary *noun, pl* **-daries** clergyman who is a member of the chapter of a cathedral.
precarious ❶ *adjective* insecure, unsafe, likely to fall or collapse. **precariously** *adverb*
precaution ❶ *noun* action taken in advance to prevent something bad happening.
precautionary *adjective*
precede ❶ *verb* go or be before. **precedence** [**press**-ee-denss] *noun* formal order of rank or position. **take precedence over** be more important than. **precedent** *noun* previous case or occurrence regarded as an example to be followed.
precentor *noun* person who leads the singing in a church.
precept ❶ *noun* rule of behaviour.

precinct ❶ *noun* **1** area in a town closed to traffic. **2** enclosed area round a building, e.g. *cathedral precinct*. **3** *US* administrative area of a city. ♦ *plural* **4** surrounding region.
precious ❶ *adjective* **1** of great value and importance. **2** loved and treasured. **3** (of behaviour) affected, unnatural. **precious metal** gold, silver, or platinum. **precious stone** rare mineral, such as a ruby, valued as a gem.
precipice ❶ *noun* very steep cliff or rockface.
precipitous *adjective* sheer.
precipitate ❶ *verb* **1** cause to happen suddenly. **2** condense and fall as snow or rain. **3** *Chem* cause to be deposited in solid form from a solution. **4** throw headlong. ♦ *adjective* **5** done rashly or hastily. ♦ *noun* **6** *Chem* substance precipitated from a solution. **precipitately** *adverb* **precipitation** *noun* **1** precipitating. **2** rain, snow, etc.
précis ❶ [**pray**-see] *noun, pl* **précis 1** short written summary of a longer piece. ♦ *verb* **2** make a précis of.
precise ❶ *adjective* **1** exact, accurate in every detail. **2** strict in observing rules or standards. **precisely** *adverb* **precision** *noun*

——————— T H E S A U R U S ———————

preach *verb* **1** = **deliver a sermon**, address, evangelize **2** = **lecture**, advocate, exhort, moralize, sermonize
preacher *noun* **1** = **clergyman**, evangelist, minister, missionary, parson
preamble *noun* = **introduction**, foreword, opening statement *or* remarks, preface, prelude
precarious *adjective* = **dangerous**, dodgy (*Brit, Aust & NZ inf*), hazardous, insecure, perilous, risky, shaky, shonky (*Aust & NZ inf*), tricky, unreliable, unsafe, unsure OPPOSITE **safe**
precaution *noun* = **safeguard**, care, caution, forethought, protection, safety measure, wariness
precede *verb* = **go before**, antedate, come first, head, introduce, lead, preface
precedence *noun* = **priority**, antecedence, pre-eminence, primacy, rank, seniority, superiority, supremacy
precedent *noun* = **instance**, antecedent, example, model, paradigm, pattern, prototype, standard
preceding *adjective* = **previous**, above, aforementioned, aforesaid, earlier, foregoing, former, past, prior
precept *noun* = **rule**, canon, command, commandment, decree, instruction, law, order, principle, regulation, statute
precinct *noun* **1** = **area**, district, quarter, section, sector, zone **2** = **enclosure**, confine,

limit
precious *adjective* **1** = **valuable**, costly, dear, expensive, fine, invaluable, priceless, prized OPPOSITE **cheap**. **2** = **loved**, adored, beloved, cherished, darling, dear, prized, treasured **3** = **affected**, artificial, overnice, overrefined, twee (*Brit inf*)
precipice *noun* = **cliff**, bluff, crag, height, rock face
precipitate *verb* **1** = **quicken**, accelerate, advance, bring on, expedite, hasten, hurry, speed up, trigger **4** = **throw**, cast, fling, hurl, launch, let fly ♦*adjective* **5** = **hasty**, abrupt, breakneck, brief, headlong, heedless, impetuous, impulsive, precipitous, quick, rapid, rash, reckless, rushing, sudden, swift, unexpected, without warning
precipitous *adjective* = **sheer**, abrupt, dizzy, high, perpendicular, steep
précis *noun* **1** = **summary**, abridgment, outline, résumé, synopsis ♦*verb* **2** = **summarize**, abridge, outline, shorten, sum up
precise *adjective* **1** = **exact**, absolute, accurate, correct, definite, explicit, express, particular, specific, strict OPPOSITE **vague**. **2** = **strict**, careful, exact, fastidious, finicky, formal, meticulous, particular, punctilious, rigid, scrupulous, stiff OPPOSITE **relaxed**
precisely *adverb* **1** = **exactly**, absolutely, accurately, correctly, just so, plumb (*inf*), smack

P

preclude ❶ *verb* make impossible to happen.

precocious ❶ *adjective* having developed or matured early or too soon. **precocity** *noun*

precognition *noun* alleged ability to foretell the future.

preconceived ❶ *adjective* (of an idea) formed without real experience or reliable information. **preconception** *noun*

precondition *noun* something that must happen or exist before something else can.

precursor ❶ *noun* something that precedes and is a signal of something else, forerunner.

predate *verb* **1** occur at an earlier date than. **2** write a date on (a document) that is earlier than the actual date.

predatory ❶ [pred-a-tree] *adjective* habitually hunting and killing other animals for food.

predator *noun* predatory animal.

predecease *verb* die before (someone else).

predecessor ❶ *noun* **1** person who precedes another in an office or position. **2** ancestor.

predestination ❶ *noun* belief that future events have already been decided by God or fate. **predestined** *adjective*

predetermined ❶ *adjective* decided in advance.

predicament ❶ *noun* embarrassing or difficult situation.

predicate *noun* **1** *Grammar* part of a sentence in which something is said about the subject, e.g. *went home* in *I went home.* ◆ *verb* **2** declare or assert. **predicated on** based on.

predicative *adjective* of or in the predicate of a sentence.

predict ❶ *verb* tell about in advance, prophesy. **predictable** *adjective* **predictive** *adjective* (of a word processer or cell phone) able to complete words after only part of a word has been keyed. **prediction** *noun*

predilection ❶ *noun* preference or liking.

predispose ❶ *verb* **1** influence (someone) in favour of something. **2** make (someone) susceptible to something. **predisposition** *noun*

predominate ❶ *verb* be the main or controlling element. **predominance** *noun*

predominant *adjective* **predominantly** *adverb*

pre-eminent ❶ *adjective* excelling all others, outstanding. **pre-eminence** *noun*

pre-empt ❶ *verb* prevent an action by doing something which makes it pointless or impossible. **pre-emption** *noun* **pre-emptive** *adjective*

preen ❶ *verb* (of a bird) clean or trim (feathers) with the beak. **preen oneself 1**

THESAURUS

(*inf*), square, squarely, strictly

precision *noun* **1** = **exactness**, accuracy, care, meticulousness, particularity, preciseness

preclude *verb* = **prevent**, check, debar, exclude, forestall, inhibit, obviate, prohibit, rule out, stop

precocious *adjective* = **advanced**, ahead, bright, developed, forward, quick, smart OPPOSITE> **backward**

preconceived *adjective* = **presumed**, forejudged, prejudged, presupposed

preconception *noun* = **preconceived idea** *or* **notion**, bias, notion, predisposition, prejudice, presupposition

precursor *noun* **a** = **herald**, forerunner, harbinger, vanguard **b** = **forerunner**, antecedent, forebear, predecessor

predatory *adjective* = **hunting**, carnivorous, predacious, raptorial

predecessor *noun* **1** = **previous job holder**, antecedent, forerunner, precursor **2** = **ancestor**, antecedent, forebear, forefather

predestination *noun* = **fate**, destiny, foreordainment, foreordination, predetermination

predestined *adjective* = **fated**, doomed, meant, preordained

predetermined *adjective* = **prearranged**,

agreed, fixed, preplanned, set

predicament *noun* = **fix** (*inf*), dilemma, hole (*sl*), jam (*inf*), mess, pinch, plight, quandary, scrape (*inf*), situation, spot (*inf*)

predict *verb* = **foretell**, augur, divine, forecast, portend, prophesy

predictable *adjective* = **likely**, anticipated, certain, expected, foreseeable, reliable, sure

prediction *noun* = **prophecy**, augury, divination, forecast, prognosis, prognostication

predilection *noun* = **liking**, bias, fondness, inclination, leaning, love, partiality, penchant, preference, propensity, taste, weakness

predispose *verb* **1** = **incline**, affect, bias, dispose, influence, lead, prejudice, prompt

predominant *adjective* = **main**, ascendant, chief, dominant, leading, paramount, prevailing, prevalent, prime, principal OPPOSITE> **minor**

predominate *verb* = **prevail**, be most noticeable, carry weight, hold sway, outweigh, overrule, overshadow

pre-eminent *adjective* = **outstanding**, chief, distinguished, excellent, foremost, incomparable, matchless, predominant, renowned, superior, supreme

pre-empt *verb* = **anticipate**, appropriate, assume, usurp

smarten oneself. **2** show self-satisfaction.
prefab noun prefabricated house.
prefabricated adjective (of a building) manufactured in shaped sections for rapid assembly on site.
preface ⓘ [**pref**-iss] noun **1** introduction to a book. ♦ verb **2** serve as an introduction to (a book, speech, etc.). **prefatory** adjective
prefect noun **1** senior pupil in a school, with limited power over others. **2** senior administrative officer in some countries.
prefecture noun office or area of authority of a prefect.
prefer ⓘ verb **-ferring, -ferred 1** like better. **2** Law bring (charges) before a court.
preferable adjective more desirable.
preferably adverb **preference** noun
preferential adjective showing preference.
preferment noun promotion or advancement.
prefigure verb represent or suggest in advance.
prefix noun **1** letter or group of letters put at the beginning of a word to make a new word, such as un- in unhappy. ♦ verb **2** put as an introduction or prefix (to).
pregnant ⓘ adjective **1** carrying a fetus in the womb. **2** full of meaning or significance, e.g. a pregnant pause. **pregnancy** noun, pl **-cies**
prehensile adjective capable of grasping.

prehistoric ⓘ adjective of the period before written history begins. **prehistory** noun
prejudge ⓘ verb judge beforehand without sufficient evidence.
prejudice ⓘ noun **1** unreasonable or unfair dislike or preference. ♦ verb **2** cause (someone) to have a prejudice. **3** harm, cause disadvantage to. **prejudicial** adjective harmful, disadvantageous.

SPELLING TIP

There are examples in the Bank of English of **prejudice** being misspelt as predjudice, with an extra d. Although d often combines with g in English, it is not necessary before j.

---

prelate [**prel**-it] noun bishop or other churchman of high rank.
preliminary ⓘ adjective **1** happening before and in preparation, introductory. ♦ noun, pl **-naries 2** preliminary remark, contest, etc.
prelude ⓘ [**prel**-yewd] noun **1** introductory movement in music. **2** event preceding and introducing something else.
premarital adjective occurring before marriage.

——————— T H E S A U R U S ———————

preen verb =**clean**, plume **preen oneself 1** =**smarten**, dress up, spruce up, titivate **2** =**pride oneself**, congratulate oneself
preface noun **1** =**introduction**, foreword, preamble, preliminary, prelude, prologue ♦verb **2** =**introduce**, begin, open, prefix
prefer verb **1** =**like better**, be partial to, choose, desire, fancy, favour, go for, incline towards, opt for, pick
preferable adjective =**better**, best, chosen, favoured, more desirable, superior
preferably adverb **1** =**rather**, by choice, first, in or for preference, sooner
preference noun **1** =**first choice**, choice, desire, favourite, option, partiality, pick, predilection, selection
preferential adjective =**privileged**, advantageous, better, favoured, special
preferment noun =**promotion**, advancement, elevation, exaltation, rise, upgrading
pregnant adjective **1** =**expectant**, big or heavy with child, expecting (inf), in the club (Brit sl), with child **2** =**meaningful**, charged, eloquent, expressive, loaded, pointed, significant, telling, weighty

prehistoric adjective =**earliest**, early, primeval, primitive, primordial
prejudge verb =**jump to conclusions**, anticipate, presume, presuppose
prejudice noun **1 a** =**discrimination**, bigotry, chauvinism, injustice, intolerance, narrow-mindedness, unfairness **b** =**bias**, partiality, preconceived notion, preconception, prejudgment ♦verb **2** =**bias**, colour, distort, influence, poison, predispose, slant **3** =**harm**, damage, hinder, hurt, impair, injure, mar, spoil, undermine
prejudiced 1 adjective =**biased**, bigoted, influenced, intolerant, narrow-minded, one-sided, opinionated, unfair
prejudicial adjective =**harmful**, damaging, deleterious, detrimental, disadvantageous, hurtful, injurious, unfavourable
preliminary adjective **1** =**first**, initial, introductory, opening, pilot, prefatory, preparatory, prior, test, trial ♦noun **2** =**introduction**, beginning, opening, overture, preamble, preface, prelude, start
prelude noun **1** =**overture 2** =**introduction**, beginning, foreword, preamble, preface, prologue, start

P

premature ❶ *adjective* **1** happening or done before the normal or expected time. **2** (of a baby) born before the end of the normal period of pregnancy. **prematurely** *adverb*
premedication *noun* drugs given to prepare a patient for a general anaesthetic.
premeditated ❶ *adjective* planned in advance. **premeditation** *noun*
premenstrual *adjective* occurring or experienced before a menstrual period, e.g. *premenstrual tension.*
premier ❶ *noun* **1** prime minister. ◆ *adjective* **2** chief, leading. **premiership** *noun*
première *noun* first performance of a play, film, etc.
premise, premiss ❶ *noun* statement assumed to be true and used as the basis of reasoning.
premises ❶ *plural noun* house or other building and its land.
premium ❶ *noun* **1** additional sum of money, as on a wage or charge. **2** (regular) sum paid for insurance. **at a premium** in great demand because scarce. **premium bonds** savings certificates issued by the government, on which no interest is paid but cash prizes can be won.
premonition ❶ *noun* feeling that something unpleasant is going to happen; foreboding. **premonitory** *adjective*
prenatal *adjective* before birth, during pregnancy.
preoccupy ❶ *verb* **-pying, -pied** fill the thoughts or attention of (someone) to the exclusion of other things. **preoccupation** *noun*
preordained *adjective* decreed or determined

in advance.
prep. 1 preparatory. **2** preposition.
prepacked *adjective* sold already wrapped.
prepaid *adjective* paid for in advance.
prepare ❶ *verb* make or get ready. **prepared** *adjective* **1** willing. **2** ready. **preparation** *noun* **1** preparing. **2** something done in readiness for something else. **3** mixture prepared for use as a cosmetic, medicine, etc. **preparatory** [prip-**par**-a-tree] *adjective* preparing for. **preparatory school** private school for children going on to public school.
preponderance ❶ *noun* greater force, amount, or influence. **preponderant** *adjective*
preposition *noun* word used before a noun or pronoun to show its relationship with other words, such as *by* in *go by bus.* **prepositional** *adjective*

LANGUAGE TIP

It used to be considered incorrect to end a sentence with a preposition, as in *New York is a place I'd love to go to.* However, this practice is now widely accepted, and in many cases, where it gives a more natural-sounding sentence, it may even be the preferred form: *New York is a place to which I'd love to go* would sound very awkward.

---

prepossessing ❶ *adjective* making a

---

premature *adjective* **1 a** =**hasty**, ill-timed, overhasty, previous (*inf*), rash, too soon, untimely **b** =**early**
premeditated *adjective* =**planned**, calculated, conscious, considered, deliberate, intentional, wilful OPPOSITE **unplanned**
premier *noun* **1** =**head of government**, chancellor, chief minister, P.M., prime minister ◆ *adjective* **2** =**chief**, first, foremost, head, highest, leading, main, primary, prime, principal
première *noun* =**first night**, debut, opening
premise, premiss *noun* =**assumption**, argument, assertion, hypothesis, postulation, presupposition, proposition, supposition
premises *plural noun* =**building**, establishment, place, property, site
premium *noun* **1** =**bonus**, bounty, fee, perk (*Brit inf*), perquisite, prize, reward **at a premium** =**in great demand**, hard to come

by, in short supply, rare, scarce
premonition *noun* =**feeling**, foreboding, hunch, idea, intuition, presentiment, suspicion
preoccupation *noun* **a** =**obsession**, bee in one's bonnet, fixation **b** =**absorption**, absent-mindedness, abstraction, daydreaming, immersion, reverie, woolgathering
preoccupied *adjective* =**absorbed**, absent-minded, distracted, engrossed, immersed, lost in, oblivious, rapt, wrapped up
preparation *noun* **1** =**groundwork**, getting ready, preparing **2** =**arrangement**, measure, plan, provision **3** =**mixture**, compound, concoction, medicine
preparatory *adjective* =**introductory**, opening, prefatory, preliminary, primary
prepare *verb* =**make** *or* **get ready**, adapt, adjust, arrange, practise, prime, train, warm up
prepared *adjective* **1** =**willing**, disposed, inclined **2** =**ready**, arranged, in order, in

favourable impression, attractive.
preposterous ❶ *adjective* utterly absurd.
prep school *noun* short for PREPARATORY
SCHOOL.
prepuce [**pree**-pyewss] *noun* retractable fold
of skin covering the tip of the penis, foreskin.
prerecorded *adjective* recorded in advance to
be played or broadcast later.
prerequisite ❶ *noun, adjective* (something)
required before something else is possible.
prerogative ❶ *noun* special power or
privilege.

SPELLING TIP

The way **prerogative** is often
pronounced is presumably the
reason why *perogative* is a
common way of misspelling it.

---

pres. 1 present (time). **2** presidential.
Pres. president.
presage [**press**-ij] *verb* be a sign or warning
of.
Presbyterian *noun, adjective* (member) of a
Protestant church governed by lay elders.
Presbyterianism *noun*
presbytery *noun, pl* **-teries 1** *Presbyterian
Church* local church court. **2** *RC Church* priest's

house.
prescience ❶ [**press**-ee-enss] *noun*
knowledge of events before they happen.
prescient *adjective*
prescribe ❶ *verb* **1** recommend the use of (a
medicine). **2** lay down as a rule. **prescription**
noun written instructions from a doctor for the
making up and use of a medicine. **prescriptive**
adjective laying down rules.
presence ❶ *noun* **1** fact of being in a
specified place. **2** impressive dignified
appearance. **presence of mind** ability to act
sensibly in a crisis.
present¹ ❶ *adjective* **1** being in a specified
place. **2** existing or happening now. **3**
Grammar (of a verb tense) indicating that the
action specified is taking place now. ♦ *noun* **4**
present time or tense. **presence** *noun* **1** fact of
being in a specified place. **2** impressive
dignified appearance. **presently** *adverb* **1** soon.
2 *US & Scot* now.
present² ❶ *noun* **1** something given to bring
pleasure to another person. ♦ *verb* **2** introduce
formally or publicly. **3** introduce and compère
(a TV or radio show). **4** cause, e.g. *present a
difficulty*. **5** give, award. **presentation** *noun*
presentable *adjective* attractive, neat, fit for
people to see. **presenter** *noun* person
introducing a TV or radio show.

———————————— THESAURUS ————————————

readiness, primed, set
preponderance *noun* =**predominance**,
dominance, domination, extensiveness, greater
numbers, greater part, lion's share, mass,
prevalence, supremacy
prepossessing *adjective* =**attractive**,
appealing, charming, engaging, fetching,
good-looking, handsome, likable *or* likeable,
pleasing
preposterous *adjective* =**ridiculous**, absurd,
crazy, incredible, insane, laughable, ludicrous,
nonsensical, out of the question, outrageous,
unthinkable
prerequisite *noun* =**requirement**, condition,
essential, must, necessity, precondition,
qualification, requisite, *sine qua non* ♦*adjective*
=**required**, essential, indispensable, mandatory,
necessary, obligatory, requisite, vital
prerogative *noun* =**right**, advantage, due,
exemption, immunity, liberty, privilege
prescribe *verb* **2** =**order**, decree, dictate,
direct, lay down, ordain, recommend, rule, set,
specify, stipulate
prescription *noun* =**instruction**, direction,
formula, recipe
presence *noun* **1** =**being**, attendance,

existence, inhabitance, occupancy, residence **2**
=**personality**, air, appearance, aspect, aura,
bearing, carriage, demeanour, poise, self-
assurance
presence of mind *noun* =**level-headedness**,
calmness, composure, cool (*sl*), coolness, self-
possession, wits
present¹ *adjective* **1** =**here**, at hand, near,
nearby, ready, there OPPOSITE⟩ **absent. 2**
=**current**, contemporary, existent, existing,
immediate, present-day ♦*noun* **4** =**now**, here
and now, the present moment, the time being,
today
present² *noun* **1** =**gift**, boon, donation,
endowment, grant, gratuity, hand-out, offering,
prezzie (*inf*) ♦*verb* **2** =**introduce**, acquaint with,
make known **3** =**put on**, display, exhibit, give,
show, stage **5** =**give**, award, bestow, confer,
grant, hand out, hand over
presentable *adjective* =**decent**, acceptable,
becoming, fit to be seen, O.K. *or* okay (*inf*),
passable, respectable, satisfactory, suitable
OPPOSITE⟩ **unpresentable**
presentation *noun* **1** =**giving**, award,
bestowal, conferral, donation, offering **3**
=**performance**, demonstration, display,

P

presentiment [priz-**zen**-tim-ent] *noun* sense of something unpleasant about to happen.

preserve ⊕ *verb* **1** keep from being damaged, changed, or ended. **2** treat (food) to prevent it decaying. ◆ *noun* **3** area of interest restricted to a particular person or group. **4** fruit preserved by cooking in sugar. **5** area where game is kept for private hunting or fishing. **preservation** *noun* **preservative** *noun* chemical that prevents decay.

preshrunk *adjective* (of fabric or a garment) having been shrunk during manufacture so that further shrinkage will not occur when washed.

preside ⊕ *verb* be in charge, esp. of a meeting. **president** *noun* **1** head of state in countries without a king or queen. **2** head of a society, institution, etc.

president *noun* **1** head of state in countries without a king or queen. **2** head of a society, institution, etc. **presidential** *adjective* **presidency** *noun, pl* **-cies**

press¹ ⊕ *verb* **1** apply force or weight to. **2** squeeze. **3** smooth by applying pressure or heat. **4** urge insistently. **5** crowd, push. ◆ *noun* **6** printing machine. **pressed for** short of, e.g. *pressed for time*. **the press 1** news media collectively, esp. newspapers. **2** reporters, journalists. **pressing** *adjective* urgent. **press box** room at a sports ground reserved for reporters. **press conference** interview for reporters given by a celebrity. **press release** official announcement or account of a news item supplied to the press. **press stud** fastener in which one part with a projecting knob snaps

into a hole on another part.

press² *verb* **press into service** force to be involved or used. **press gang** *Hist* group of men used to capture men and boys and force them to join the navy.

press-up *noun* exercise in which the body is raised from and lowered to the floor by straightening and bending the arms.

pressure ⊕ *noun* **1** force produced by pressing. **2** urgent claims or demands, e.g. *working under pressure*. **3** *Physics* force applied to a surface per unit of area. ◆ *verb* **4** persuade forcefully. **bring pressure to bear on** use influence or authority to persuade. **pressurize** *verb* **pressure cooker** airtight pot which cooks food quickly by steam under pressure.

pressure group group that tries to influence policies, public opinion, etc.

prestidigitation *noun* skilful quickness with the hands, conjuring.

prestige ⊕ *noun* high status or respect resulting from success or achievements. **prestigious** *adjective*

presto *adverb* *Music* very quickly.

prestressed *adjective* (of concrete) containing stretched steel wires to strengthen it.

presume ⊕ *verb* **1** suppose to be the case. **2** dare (to). **presumably** *adverb* one supposes (that). **presumption** *noun* **1** basis on which an assumption is made. **2** bold insolent behaviour. **3** strong probability. **presumptuous** *adjective* doing things one has no right or authority to do. **presumptive** *adjective* assumed to be true

P

———— THESAURUS ————

exhibition, production, show

presently *adverb* **1** = **soon**, anon (*arch*), before long, by and by, shortly

preservation *noun* **1** = **protection**, conservation, maintenance, safeguarding, safekeeping, safety, salvation, support

preserve *verb* **1 a** = **protect**, care for, conserve, defend, keep, safeguard, save, shelter, shield OPPOSITE▷ **attack**. **b** = **maintain**, continue, keep, keep up, perpetuate, sustain, uphold OPPOSITE▷ **end** ◆*noun* **3** = **area**, domain, field, realm, sphere

preside *verb* = **run**, administer, chair, conduct, control, direct, govern, head, lead, manage, officiate

press¹ *verb* **1** = **compress**, crush, depress, force down, jam, mash, push, squeeze **2** = **hug**, clasp, crush, embrace, fold in one's arms, hold close, squeeze **3** = **smooth**, flatten, iron **4** = **urge**, beg, entreat, exhort, implore, petition, plead, pressurize **5** = **crowd**, flock, gather,

herd, push, seethe, surge, swarm, throng **the press 1** = **newspapers**, Fleet Street, fourth estate, news media, the papers **2** = **journalists**, columnists, correspondents, reporters

pressing *adjective* = **urgent**, crucial, high-priority, imperative, important, importunate, serious, vital

pressure *noun* **1** = **force**, compressing, compression, crushing, squeezing, weight **2 a** = **power**, coercion, compulsion, constraint, force, influence, mana (*NZ*), sway **b** = **stress**, burden, demands, hassle (*inf*), heat, load, strain, urgency

prestige *noun* = **status**, credit, distinction, eminence, fame, honour, importance, kudos, renown, reputation, standing

prestigious *adjective* = **celebrated**, eminent, esteemed, great, illustrious, important, notable, prominent, renowned, respected

presumably *adverb* = **it would seem**, apparently, in all likelihood, in all probability, or valid until the contrary is proved.

presuppose ❶ *verb* need as a previous condition in order to be true. **presupposition** *noun*

pretend ❶ *verb* claim or give the appearance of (something untrue) to deceive or in play.

pretender *noun* person who makes a false or disputed claim to a position of power.

pretence *noun* behaviour intended to deceive, pretending. **pretentious** *adjective* making (unjustified) claims to special merit or importance. **pretension** *noun*

preternatural *adjective* beyond what is natural, supernatural.

pretext ❶ *noun* false reason given to hide the real one.

pretty ❶ *adjective* **-tier, -tiest 1** pleasing to look at. ♦ *adverb* **2** fairly, moderately, e.g. *I'm*

pretty certain. **prettily** *adverb* **prettiness** *noun*

sitting pretty in a favourable state.

pretzel *noun* brittle salted biscuit.

prevail ❶ *verb* **1** gain mastery. **2** be generally established. **prevailing** *adjective* **1** widespread. **2** predominant. **prevalence** *noun* **prevalent** *adjective* widespread, common.

prevaricate ❶ *verb* avoid giving a direct or truthful answer. **prevarication** *noun*

prevent ❶ *verb* keep from happening or doing. **preventable** *adjective* **prevention** *noun* **preventive** *adjective, noun*

preview ❶ *noun* **1** advance showing of a film or exhibition before it is shown to the public. ♦ *verb* **2** view in advance.

previous ❶ *adjective* coming or happening before. **previously** *adverb*

prey ❶ *noun* **1** animal hunted and killed for

——————— THESAURUS ———————

on the face of it, probably, seemingly

presume *verb* **1** =**believe**, assume, conjecture, guess (*inf, chiefly US & Canad*), infer, postulate, suppose, surmise, take for granted, think **2** =**dare**, go so far, make so bold, take the liberty, venture

presumption *noun* **1** =**basis 2** =**cheek** (*inf*), audacity, boldness, effrontery, gall (*inf*), impudence, insolence, nerve (*inf*) **3** =**probability**, chance, likelihood

presumptuous *adjective* =**pushy** (*inf*), audacious, bold, forward, insolent, overconfident, too big for one's boots, uppish (*Brit inf*)

presuppose *verb* =**presume**, assume, imply, posit, postulate, take as read, take for granted

presupposition *noun* =**assumption**, belief, preconception, premise, presumption, supposition

pretence *noun* **a** =**deception**, acting, charade, deceit, falsehood, feigning, sham, simulation, trickery OPPOSITE **honesty**. **b** =**show**, affectation, artifice, display, façade, veneer OPPOSITE **fact**

pretend *verb* **a** =**feign**, affect, allege, assume, fake, falsify, impersonate, profess, sham, simulate **b** =**make believe**, act, imagine, make up, suppose

pretension *noun* **a** =**claim**, aspiration, assumption, demand, pretence, profession **b** =**affectation**, airs, conceit, ostentation, pretentiousness, self-importance, show, snobbery

pretentious *adjective* =**affected**, conceited, grandiloquent, grandiose, high-flown, inflated, mannered, ostentatious, pompous, puffed up, showy, snobbish

pretext *noun* =**guise**, cloak, cover, excuse, ploy, pretence, ruse, show

pretty *adjective* **1** =**attractive**, beautiful, bonny, charming, comely, fair, good-looking, lekker (*S Afr sl*), lovely OPPOSITE **unattractive** ♦*adverb* **2** =**fairly**, kind of (*inf*), moderately, quite, rather, reasonably, somewhat

prevail *verb* **1** =**win**, be victorious, overcome, overrule, succeed, triumph **2** =**be widespread**, abound, be current, be prevalent, exist generally, predominate

prevailing *adjective* **1** =**widespread**, common, current, customary, established, fashionable, general, in vogue, ordinary, popular, prevalent, usual **2** =**predominating**, dominant, main, principal, ruling

prevalent *adjective* =**common**, current, customary, established, frequent, general, popular, universal, usual, widespread OPPOSITE **rare**

prevaricate *verb* =**evade**, beat about the bush, cavil, deceive, dodge, equivocate, flannel (*Brit inf*), hedge

prevent *verb* =**stop**, avert, avoid, foil, forestall, frustrate, hamper, hinder, impede, inhibit, obstruct, obviate, preclude, thwart OPPOSITE **help**

prevention *noun* =**elimination**, avoidance, deterrence, precaution, safeguard, thwarting

preventive *adjective* **a** =**protective**, counteractive, deterrent, precautionary **b** =**hindering**, hampering, impeding, obstructive ♦*noun* **a** =**protection**, deterrent, prevention, remedy, safeguard, shield **b** =**hindrance**, block, impediment, obstacle, obstruction

preview *noun* **1** =**sample**, advance showing, foretaste, sneak preview, taster, trailer

P

food by another animal. **2** victim. **bird of prey** bird that kills and eats other birds or animals. **prey on** *verb* **1** hunt and kill for food. **2** worry, obsess.

price ⊕ *noun* **1** amount of money for which a thing is bought or sold. **2** unpleasant thing that must be endured to get something desirable. ◆ *verb* **3** fix or ask the price of. **priceless** *adjective* **1** very valuable. **2** *Informal* very funny. **pricey** *adjective* **pricier, priciest** *Informal* expensive.

prick ⊕ *verb* **1** pierce lightly with a sharp point. **2** cause to feel mental pain. **3** (of an animal) make (the ears) stand erect. ◆ *noun* **4** sudden sharp pain caused by pricking. **5** mark made by pricking. **6** remorse. **7** *Taboo slang* penis. **prick up one's ears** listen intently.

prickle ⊕ *noun* **1** thorn or spike on a plant. ◆ *verb* **2** have a tingling or pricking sensation. **prickly** *adjective* **prickly heat** itchy rash occurring in hot moist weather.

pride ⊕ *noun* **1** feeling of pleasure and satisfaction when one has done well. **2** too high an opinion of oneself. **3** sense of dignity and self-respect. **4** something that causes one to feel pride. **5** group of lions. **pride of place** most important position. **pride oneself on** feel pride about.

priest ⊕ *noun* **1** (in the Christian church) a person who can administer the sacraments and preach. **2** (in some other religions) an official who performs religious ceremonies. **priestess** *n fem* **priesthood** *noun* **priestly** *adjective*

prig ⊕ *noun* self-righteous person who acts as if superior to others. **priggish** *adjective* **priggishness** *noun*

prim ⊕ *adjective* **primmer, primmest** formal, proper, and rather prudish. **primly** *adverb*

prima ballerina *noun* leading female ballet dancer.

primacy *noun, pl* **-cies 1** state of being first in rank, grade, etc. **2** office of an archbishop.

prima donna *noun* **1** leading female opera singer. **2** *Informal* temperamental person.

primaeval *adjective* same as PRIMEVAL.

prima facie [prime-a fay-shee] *adverb Latin* as it seems at first.

primal *adjective* of basic causes or origins.

primary ⊕ *adjective* **1** chief, most important. **2** being the first stage, elementary. **primarily** *adverb* **primary colours** (in physics) red, green, and blue or (in art) red, yellow, and blue, from which all other colours can be produced by mixing. **primary school** school for children from five to eleven years.

primate[1] *noun* member of an order of mammals including monkeys and humans.

primate[2] *noun* archbishop.

prime ⊕ *adjective* **1** main, most important. **2**

——————— T H E S A U R U S ———————

previous *adjective* =**earlier**, erstwhile, foregoing, former, past, preceding, prior OPPOSITE **later**

previously *adverb* =**before**, beforehand, earlier, formerly, hitherto, in the past, once

prey *noun* **1** =**quarry**, game, kill **2** =**victim**, dupe, fall guy (*inf*), mug (*Brit sl*), target

price *noun* **1** =**cost**, amount, charge, damage (*inf*), estimate, expense, fee, figure, rate, value, worth **2** =**consequences**, cost, penalty, toll ◆*verb* **3** =**evaluate**, assess, cost, estimate, rate, value

priceless *adjective* **1** =**valuable**, costly, dear, expensive, invaluable, precious OPPOSITE **common**. **2** *Inf* =**hilarious**, amusing, comic, droll, funny, rib-tickling, side-splitting

pricey *adjective Inf* **1** =**expensive**, costly, dear, high-priced, steep (*inf*)

prick *verb* **1** =**pierce**, jab, lance, perforate, punch, puncture, stab ◆*noun* **5** =**puncture**, hole, perforation, pinhole, wound

prickle *noun* **1** =**spike**, barb, needle, point, spine, spur, thorn ◆*verb* **2** =**tingle**, itch, smart, sting

prickly *adjective* **1** =**spiny**, barbed, bristly, thorny **2** =**itchy**, crawling, scratchy, sharp, smarting, stinging, tingling

pride *noun* **1** =**satisfaction**, delight, gratification, joy, pleasure **2** =**conceit**, arrogance, egotism, hubris, self-importance, vanity OPPOSITE **modesty**. **3** =**self-respect**, dignity, honour, self-esteem, self-worth **4** =**gem**, jewel, pride and joy, treasure

priest *noun* **1** =**clergyman**, cleric, curate, divine, ecclesiastic, father, minister, pastor, vicar

prig *noun* =**goody-goody** (*inf*), prude, puritan, stuffed shirt (*inf*)

priggish *adjective* =**self-righteous**, goody-goody (*inf*), holier-than-thou, prim, prudish, puritanical

prim *adjective* =**prudish**, demure, fastidious, fussy, priggish, prissy (*inf*), proper, puritanical, strait-laced OPPOSITE **liberal**

primarily *adverb* **1** =**chiefly**, above all, essentially, fundamentally, generally, largely, mainly, mostly, principally **2** =**at first**, at or from the start, first and foremost, initially, in the beginning, in the first place, originally

primary *adjective* **1** =**chief**, cardinal, first, greatest, highest, main, paramount, prime, principal OPPOSITE **secondary**. **2** =**elementary**, introductory, rudimentary, simple of the highest quality. ♦ *noun* **3** time when someone is at his or her best or most vigorous. ♦ *verb* **4** give (someone) information in advance to prepare them for something. **5** prepare (a surface) for painting. **6** prepare (a gun, pump, etc.) for use. **primer** *noun* special paint applied to bare wood etc. before the main paint. **Prime Minister** leader of a government. **prime number** number that can be divided exactly only by itself and one. **prime time** peak viewing time on television.

primer *noun* beginners' school book or manual.

primeval ❶ [prime-**ee**-val] *adjective* of the earliest age of the world.

primitive ❶ *adjective* **1** of an early simple stage of development. **2** basic, crude, e.g. *a primitive hut.*

primogeniture *noun* system under which the eldest son inherits all his parents' property.

primordial *adjective* existing at or from the beginning.

primrose *noun* pale yellow spring flower.

primula *noun* type of primrose with brightly coloured flowers.

Primus *noun* ® portable cooking stove used esp. by campers.

prince ❶ *noun* **1** male member of a royal family, esp. the son of the king or queen. **2** male ruler of a small country. **princely** *adjective* **1** of or like a prince. **2** generous, lavish, or magnificent. **prince consort** husband of a reigning queen. **Prince of Wales** eldest son of the British sovereign. **princess** *noun* female member of a royal family, esp. the daughter of the king or queen. **Princess Royal** title sometimes given to the eldest daughter of the British sovereign.

principal ❶ *adjective* **1** main, most important. ♦ *noun* **2** head of a school or college. **3** person taking a leading part in something. **4** sum of money lent on which interest is paid.

principally *adverb* **principal boy** leading male role in pantomime, played by a woman.

> **LANGUAGE TIP**
>
> Distinguish the spellings of *principal* and *principle*. These are different words but often confused.

principality *noun, pl* **-ties** territory ruled by a prince.

principle ❶ *noun* **1** moral rule guiding behaviour. **2** general or basic truth, e.g. *the principle of equality.* **3** scientific law concerning the working of something. **in principle** in theory but not always in practice. **on principle** because of one's beliefs.

> **LANGUAGE TIP**
>
> Distinguish the spellings of *principle* and *principal*. These are different words but often confused.

print ❶ *verb* **1** reproduce (a newspaper, book, etc.) in large quantities by mechanical or electronic means. **2** reproduce (text or pictures) by pressing ink onto paper etc. **3** write in letters that are not joined up. **4** stamp (fabric) with a design. **5** *Photog* produce (pictures) from negatives. ♦ *noun* **6** printed words etc. **7** printed copy of a painting. **8** printed lettering.

P

————————— THESAURUS —————————

prime *adjective* **1** = **main**, chief, leading, predominant, pre-eminent, primary, principal **2** = **best**, choice, excellent, first-class, first-rate, highest, quality, select, top ♦*noun* **3** = **peak**, bloom, flower, height, heyday, zenith ♦*verb* **4** = **inform**, brief, clue in (*inf*), coach, fill in (*inf*), get ready, make ready, notify, prepare, tell, train

primeval *adjective* = **earliest**, ancient, early, first, old, prehistoric, primal, primitive, primordial

primitive *adjective* **1** = **early**, elementary, first, original, primary, primeval, primordial [OPPOSITE⟩ **advanced**. **2** = **crude**, rough, rudimentary, simple, unrefined [OPPOSITE⟩ **elaborate**

prince *noun* **2** = **ruler**, lord, monarch,

sovereign

princely *adjective* **1** = **regal**, imperial, majestic, noble, royal, sovereign **2** = **generous**, bounteous, gracious, lavish, liberal, munificent, open-handed, rich

principal *adjective* **1** = **main**, cardinal, chief, essential, first, foremost, key, leading, paramount, pre-eminent, primary, prime [OPPOSITE⟩ **minor** ♦*noun* **2** = **headmaster** *or* **headmistress**, dean, head (*inf*), head teacher, master *or* mistress, rector **3** = **star**, lead, leader **4** = **capital**, assets, money

principle *noun* **1** = **morals**, conscience, integrity, probity, scruples, sense of honour **2** = **rule**, canon, criterion, doctrine, dogma, fundamental, law, maxim, precept, standard, truth **in principle** = **in theory**, ideally,

9 photograph. **10** printed fabric. **11** mark left on a surface by something that has pressed against it. **out of print** no longer available from a publisher. **printer** noun **1** person or company engaged in printing. **2** machine that prints. **3** machine connected to a computer that prints out results on paper. **printing** noun
printed circuit electronic circuit with wiring printed on an insulating base. **print-out** noun printed information from a computer.
prior¹ ❶ adjective earlier. **prior to** before.
prior² noun head monk in a priory. **prioress** noun deputy head nun in a convent. **priory** noun, pl **-ries** place where certain orders of monks or nuns live.
priority ❶ noun, pl **-ties 1** most important thing that must be dealt with first. **2** right to be or go before others.
prise verb force open by levering.
prism noun transparent block usu. with triangular ends and rectangular sides, used to disperse light into a spectrum or refract it in optical instruments. **prismatic** adjective **1** of or shaped like a prism. **2** (of colour) as if produced by refraction through a prism, rainbow-like.
prison ❶ noun building where criminals and accused people are held. **prisoner** noun person held captive. **prisoner of war** serviceman captured by an enemy in wartime.
prissy ❶ adjective **-sier, -siest** prim, correct, and easily shocked. **prissily** adverb
pristine ❶ adjective clean, new, and unused.
private ❶ adjective **1** for the use of one person or group only. **2** secret. **3** personal, unconnected with one's work. **4** owned or paid for by individuals rather than by the government. **5** quiet, not likely to be disturbed. ◆ noun **6** soldier of the lowest rank. **privately** adverb **privacy** noun **private company** limited

company that does not issue shares for public subscription. **private detective** person hired by a client to do detective work. **private member's bill** law proposed by a Member of Parliament who is not a government minister. **private parts** Euphemistic genitals. **private school** school controlled by a private body, accepting mostly fee-paying pupils. **private sector** part of a country's economy not controlled or financially supported by the government.
privateer noun **1** Hist privately owned armed vessel authorized by the government to take part in a war. **2** captain of such a ship.
privation noun loss or lack of the necessities of life.
privatize verb sell (a publicly owned company) to individuals or a private company. **privatization** noun
privet noun bushy evergreen shrub used for hedges.
privilege ❶ noun **1** advantage or favour that only some people have. **2** rare opportunity to do something which gives great satisfaction.
privileged adjective enjoying a special right or immunity.

> **SPELLING TIP**
>
> Although the Bank of English shows that people find it difficult to decide whether to use is or es when spelling **privilege**, the commonest mistake is to insert an extra d to make priviledge. The adjective, **privileged**, should not have a d in the middle either.

——————— T H E S A U R U S ———————

theoretically
print verb **1** = **publish 2** = **imprint**, impress, issue, mark, stamp ◆noun **6** = **publication**, book, magazine, newspaper, newsprint, periodical, printed matter **7** = **reproduction**, copy **9** = **photograph**, photo (inf), picture
prior¹ adjective = **earlier**, foregoing, former, preceding, pre-existing, previous **prior to** = **before**, earlier than, preceding, previous to
priority noun **2** = **precedence**, pre-eminence, preference, rank, right of way, seniority
priory noun = **monastery**, abbey, convent, nunnery, religious house
prison noun = **jail**, clink (sl), confinement, cooler (sl), dungeon, jug (sl), lockup, nick (Brit sl), penitentiary (US), slammer (sl)

prisoner noun = **captive**, con (sl), convict, detainee, hostage, internee, jailbird, lag (sl)
pristine adjective = **new**, immaculate, pure, uncorrupted, undefiled, unspoiled, unsullied, untouched, virginal
privacy noun **5** = **seclusion**, isolation, retirement, retreat, solitude
private adjective **1** = **exclusive**, individual, intimate, own, personal, reserved, special [OPPOSITE] **public**. **2** = **secret**, clandestine, confidential, covert, hush-hush (inf), off the record, unofficial [OPPOSITE] **public**. **5** = **separate**, isolated, secluded, secret, sequestered, solitary, withdrawn [OPPOSITE] **busy**
privilege noun **1** = **right**, advantage, claim,

privy ❶ *adjective* **1** sharing knowledge of something secret. ♦ *noun, pl* **privies 2** *Obs* toilet, esp. an outside one. **Privy Council** private council of the British monarch.

prize¹ ❶ *noun* **1** reward given for success in a competition etc. ♦ *adjective* **2** winning or likely to win a prize. **prizefighter** *noun* boxer who fights for money. **prizefight** *noun*

prize² ❶ *verb* value highly.

prize³ *verb* same as PRISE.

pro¹ *adverb, preposition* in favour of. **pros and cons** arguments for and against.

pro² *noun, pl* **pros** *Informal* **1** professional. **2** prostitute.

pro- *prefix* **1** in favour of, e.g. *pro-Russian.* **2** instead of, e.g. *pronoun.*

proactive *adjective* tending to initiate change rather than reacting to events.

probable ❶ *adjective* likely to happen or be true. **probably** *adverb* **probability** *noun, pl* **-ties**

probate *noun* **1** process of proving the validity of a will. **2** certificate stating that a will is genuine.

probation ❶ *noun* **1** system of dealing with law-breakers, esp. juvenile ones, by placing them under supervision. **2** period when someone is assessed for suitability for a job etc. **probationer** *noun* person on probation. **probationary** *adjective* **probation officer** person who supervises offenders placed on

probation.

probe ❶ *verb* **1** search into or examine closely. ♦ *noun* **2** surgical instrument used to examine a wound, cavity, etc. **3** thorough inquiry.

probiotic *noun* **1** bacterium that protects the body from harmful bacteria. ♦ *adjective* **2** relating to probiotics *probiotic yogurts.*

probity *noun* honesty, integrity.

problem ❶ *noun* **1** something difficult to deal with or solve. **2** question or puzzle set for solution. **problematic, problematical** *adjective*

proboscis [pro-**boss**-iss] *noun* **1** long trunk or snout. **2** elongated mouth of some insects.

procedure ❶ *noun* way of doing something, esp. the correct or usual one. **procedural** *adjective*

proceed ❶ *verb* **1** start or continue doing. **2** *Formal* walk, go. **3** start a legal action. **4** arise from. **proceeds** *plural noun* money obtained from an event or activity. **proceedings** *plural noun* **1** organized or related series of events. **2** minutes of a meeting. **3** legal action.

procedure *noun* way of doing something, esp. the correct or usual one.

process ❶ *noun* **1** series of actions or changes. **2** method of doing or producing something. ♦ *verb* **3** handle or prepare by a special method of manufacture. **processed** *adjective* (of food) treated to prevent it decaying. **processor** *noun* *Computers* same as CENTRAL PROCESSING UNIT.

procession ❶ *noun* line of people or vehicles

——————— T H E S A U R U S ———————

concession, due, entitlement, freedom, liberty, prerogative
privileged *adjective* =**special**, advantaged, elite, entitled, favoured, honoured
privy *adjective* **1** =**secret**, confidential, private ♦*noun* **2** *Obs* =**lavatory**, latrine, outside toilet
prize¹ *noun* **1** =**reward**, accolade, award, haul, honour, jackpot, purse, stakes, trophy, winnings ♦*adjective* **2** =**champion**, award-winning, best, first-rate, outstanding, top, winning
prize² *verb* =**value**, cherish, esteem, hold dear, treasure
probability *noun* =**likelihood**, chance(s), expectation, liability, likeliness, odds, prospect
probable *adjective* =**likely**, apparent, credible, feasible, plausible, possible, presumable, reasonable OPPOSITE **unlikely**
probably *adverb* =**likely**, doubtless, maybe, most likely, perchance (*arch*), perhaps, possibly, presumably
probation *noun* **2** =**trial period**, apprenticeship, trial
probe *verb* **1 a** =**examine**, explore, go into,

investigate, look into, scrutinize, search **b** =**explore**, feel around, poke, prod ♦*noun* **3** =**examination**, detection, exploration, inquiry, investigation, scrutiny, study
problem *noun* **1** =**difficulty**, complication, dilemma, dispute, predicament, quandary, trouble **2** =**puzzle**, conundrum, enigma, poser, question, riddle
procedure *noun* =**method**, action, conduct, course, custom, modus operandi, policy, practice, process, routine, strategy, system
proceed *verb* **1** =**go on**, carry on, continue, go ahead, move on, press on, progress OPPOSITE **stop. 4** =**arise**, come, derive, emanate, flow, issue, originate, result, spring, stem
proceedings *plural noun* **2** =**business**, account, affairs, archives, doings, minutes, records, report, transactions
proceeds *plural noun* =**income**, earnings, gain, products, profit, returns, revenue, takings, yield
process *noun* **1** =**development**, advance, evolution, growth, movement, progress,

P

moving forward together in order.

proclaim ❶ verb declare publicly. **proclamation** noun

proclivity noun, pl -ties inclination, tendency.

procrastinate ❶ verb put off taking action, delay. **procrastination** noun **procrastinator** noun

procreate verb Formal produce offspring. **procreation** noun

procurator fiscal noun (in Scotland) law officer who acts as public prosecutor and coroner.

procure ❶ verb 1 get, provide. 2 obtain (people) to act as prostitutes. **procurement** noun **procurer, procuress** noun person who obtains people to act as prostitutes.

prod ❶ verb **prodding, prodded** 1 poke with something pointed. 2 goad (someone) to take action. ◆ noun 3 prodding.

prodigal ❶ adjective recklessly extravagant, wasteful. **prodigality** noun

prodigy ❶ noun, pl -gies 1 person with some marvellous talent. 2 wonderful thing.

prodigious adjective 1 very large, immense. 2 wonderful. **prodigiously** adverb

produce ❶ verb 1 bring into existence. 2 present to view, show. 3 make, manufacture. 4 present on stage, film, or television. ◆ noun 5 food grown for sale. **producer** noun 1 person with control over the making of a film, record, etc. 2 person or company that produces something.

product ❶ noun 1 something produced. 2 number resulting from multiplication.

production noun 1 producing. 2 things produced. 3 presentation of a play, opera, etc.

productive adjective 1 producing large quantities. 2 useful, profitable. **productivity** noun

profane ❶ adjective 1 showing disrespect for religion or holy things. 2 (of language) coarse, blasphemous. ◆ verb 3 treat (something sacred) irreverently, desecrate. **profanation** noun act of profaning. **profanity** noun, pl -ties profane talk or behaviour, blasphemy.

profess ❶ verb 1 state or claim (something as

——————— THESAURUS ———————

progression 2 = **procedure**, action, course, manner, means, measure, method, operation, performance, practice, system ◆verb 3 = **handle**

procession noun = **parade**, cavalcade, cortege, file, march, train

proclaim verb = **declare**, advertise, announce, circulate, herald, indicate, make known, profess, publish OPPOSITE conceal

procrastinate verb = **delay**, dally, drag one's feet (inf), gain time, play for time, postpone, put off, stall, temporize OPPOSITE hurry (up)

procure verb 1 = **obtain**, acquire, buy, come by, find, gain, get, pick up, purchase, score (sl), secure, win

prod verb 1 = **poke**, dig, drive, jab, nudge, push, shove 2 = **prompt**, egg on, goad, impel, incite, motivate, move, rouse, spur, stimulate, urge ◆noun 3 a = **poke**, dig, jab, nudge, push, shove b = **prompt**, cue, reminder, signal, stimulus

prodigal adjective = **extravagant**, excessive, immoderate, improvident, profligate, reckless, spendthrift, wasteful OPPOSITE economical

prodigious adjective 1 = **huge**, colossal, enormous, giant, gigantic, immense, massive, vast OPPOSITE small. 2 = **wonderful**, amazing, exceptional, extraordinary, fabulous, fantastic (inf), marvellous, phenomenal, remarkable, staggering OPPOSITE normal

prodigy noun 1 = **genius**, mastermind, talent, whizz (inf), wizard 2 = **wonder**, marvel, miracle, phenomenon, sensation

produce verb 1 = **bring forth**, bear, beget, breed, bring about, cause, deliver, effect, generate, give rise to 2 = **show**, advance, demonstrate, exhibit, offer, present 3 = **make**, compose, construct, create, develop, fabricate, invent, manufacture 4 = **present**, direct, do, exhibit, mount, put on, show, stage ◆noun 5 = **fruit and vegetables**, crop, greengrocery, harvest, product, yield

producer noun 1 = **director**, impresario 2 = **maker**, cockie (Aust & NZ inf), farmer, grower, manufacturer

product noun 1 a = **goods**, artefact, commodity, creation, invention, merchandise, produce, work b = **result**, consequence, effect, outcome, upshot

production noun 1 = **producing**, construction, creation, fabrication, formation, making, manufacture, manufacturing 3 = **presentation**, direction, management, staging

productive adjective 1 = **fertile**, creative, fecund, fruitful, inventive, plentiful, prolific, rich OPPOSITE poor. 2 = **useful**, advantageous, beneficial, constructive, effective, profitable, rewarding, valuable, worthwhile OPPOSITE useless

productivity noun = **output**, production, work rate, yield

profane adjective 1 = **sacrilegious**, disrespectful, godless, impious, impure, irreligious, irreverent, sinful, ungodly, wicked

true), sometimes falsely. **2** have as one's belief or religion. **professed** *adjective* supposed.
profession ❶ *noun* **1** type of work, such as being a doctor, that needs special training. **2** all the people employed in a profession, e.g. *the legal profession*. **3** declaration of a belief or feeling. **professional** *adjective* **1** working in a profession. **2** taking part in an activity, such as sport or music, for money. **3** very competent. ◆ *noun* **4** person who works in a profession. **5** person paid to take part in sport, music, etc. **professionally** *adverb* **professionalism** *noun*
professor ❶ *noun* teacher of the highest rank in a university. **professorial** *adjective* **professorship** *noun*
proffer *verb* offer.
proficient ❶ *adjective* skilled, expert. **proficiency** *noun*
profile ❶ *noun* **1** outline, esp. of the face, as seen from the side. **2** brief biographical sketch.
profit ❶ *noun* **1** money gained. **2** benefit obtained. ◆ *verb* **3** gain or benefit. **profitable**

adjective making profit. **profitably** *adverb* **profitability** *noun* **profiteer** *noun* person who makes excessive profits at the expense of the public. **profiteering** *noun*
profligate ❶ *adjective* **1** recklessly extravagant. **2** shamelessly immoral. ◆ *noun* **3** profligate person. **profligacy** *noun*
pro forma *adjective Latin* prescribing a set form.
profound ❶ *adjective* **1** showing or needing great knowledge. **2** strongly felt, intense.
profoundly *adverb* **profundity** *noun, pl* **-ties**
profuse ❶ *adjective* plentiful. **profusion** *noun*
progeny ❶ [proj-in-ee] *noun, pl* **-nies** children. **progenitor** [pro-**jen**-it-er] *noun* ancestor.
progesterone *noun* hormone which prepares the womb for pregnancy and prevents further ovulation.
prognosis ❶ *noun, pl* **-noses 1** doctor's forecast about the progress of an illness. **2** any forecast.

————————————— T H E S A U R U S —————————————

OPPOSITE religious. **2 = crude**, blasphemous, coarse, filthy, foul, obscene, vulgar ◆*verb* **3 = desecrate**, commit sacrilege, debase, defile, violate
profanity *noun* **a = swearing**, curse, cursing, irreverence, obscenity **b = sacrilege**, blasphemy, impiety, profaneness
profess *verb* **1 a = state**, admit, affirm, announce, assert, avow, confess, declare, proclaim, vouch **b = claim**, allege, fake, feign, make out, pretend, purport
professed *adjective* **= supposed**, alleged, ostensible, pretended, purported, self-styled, so-called, would-be
profession *noun* **1 = occupation**, business, calling, career, employment, office, position, sphere, vocation **3 = declaration**, affirmation, assertion, avowal, claim, statement
professional *adjective* **3 = expert**, adept, competent, efficient, experienced, masterly, proficient, qualified, skilled OPPOSITE **incapable** ◆*noun* **4, 5 = expert**, adept, fundi (*S Afr*), guru, maestro, master, past master, pro (*inf*), specialist, virtuoso
professor *noun* **= don** (*Brit*), fellow (*Brit*), prof (*inf*)
proficient *adjective* **= skilled**, able, accomplished, adept, capable, competent, efficient, expert, gifted, masterly, skilful OPPOSITE **amateurish**
profile *noun* **1 = outline**, contour, drawing, figure, form, side view, silhouette, sketch **2 = biography**, characterization, sketch,

thumbnail sketch, vignette
profit *noun* **1 = earnings**, gain, proceeds, receipts, return, revenue, takings, yield OPPOSITE **loss**. **2 = benefit**, advancement, advantage, gain, good, use, value OPPOSITE **cost** ◆*verb* **3 a = make money**, earn, gain **b = benefit**, be of advantage to, gain, help, improve, promote, serve
profitable *adjective* **a = money-making**, commercial, cost-effective, fruitful, lucrative, paying, remunerative, worthwhile **b = beneficial**, advantageous, fruitful, productive, rewarding, useful, valuable, worthwhile OPPOSITE **useless**
profiteer *noun* **= racketeer**, exploiter
profligate *adjective* **1 = extravagant**, immoderate, improvident, prodigal, reckless, spendthrift, wasteful **2 = depraved**, debauched, degenerate, dissolute, immoral, licentious, shameless, wanton, wicked, wild OPPOSITE **principled** ◆*noun* **3 a = spendthrift**, squanderer, waster, wastrel **b = degenerate**, debauchee, libertine, rake, reprobate, roué
profound *adjective* **1 = wise**, abstruse, deep, learned, penetrating, philosophical, sagacious, sage OPPOSITE **stupid**. **2 = sincere**, acute, deeply felt, extreme, great, heartfelt, intense, keen OPPOSITE **shallow**
profuse *adjective* **= plentiful**, abundant, ample, bountiful, copious, luxuriant, overflowing, prolific OPPOSITE **inadequate**
progeny *noun* **= children**, descendants, family, issue, lineage, offspring, race, stock,

P

prognostication *noun* forecast or prediction.
program *noun* **1** sequence of coded
instructions for a computer. ◆ *verb* **-gramming,
-grammed 2** arrange (data) so that it can be
processed by a computer. **3** feed a program
into (a computer). **programmer** *noun*
programmable *adjective*
programme ❼ *noun* **1** planned series of
events. **2** broadcast on radio or television. **3** list
of items or performers in an entertainment.
progress ❼ *noun* **1** improvement,
development. **2** movement forward. ◆ *verb* **3**
become more advanced or skilful. **4** move
forward. **in progress** taking place.
progression *noun* **1** act of progressing,
advance. **2** sequence of numbers in which each
differs from the next by a fixed ratio.
progressive *adjective* **1** favouring political or
social reform. **2** happening gradually.
progressively *adverb*
prohibit ❼ *verb* forbid or prevent from
happening. **prohibition** *noun* **1** act of
forbidding. **2** ban on the sale or drinking of
alcohol. **prohibitive** *adjective* (of prices) too

high to be affordable. **prohibitively** *adverb*
project ❼ *noun* **1** planned scheme to do or
examine something over a period. ◆ *verb* **2**
make a forecast based on known data. **3** make
(a film or slide) appear on a screen. **4**
communicate (an impression). **5** stick out
beyond a surface or edge. **projector** *noun*
apparatus for projecting photographic images,
films, or slides on a screen. **projection** *noun*
projectionist *noun* person who operates a
projector.
projectile ❼ *noun* object thrown as a weapon
or fired from a gun.
prolapse *noun* slipping down of an internal
organ of the body from its normal position.
prolapsed *adjective*
prole *adjective, noun Offens* proletarian.
proletariat ❼ [pro-lit-**air**-ee-at] *noun* working
class. **proletarian** *adjective, noun*
proliferate ❼ *verb* grow or reproduce rapidly.
proliferation *noun*
prolific ❼ *adjective* very productive.
prolifically *adverb*
prolix *adjective* (of speech or a piece of

———————————— T H E S A U R U S ————————————

young
prognosis *noun* **1** = **diagnosis 2** = **forecast,**
prediction, prognostication, projection
programme *noun* **1** = **schedule,** agenda,
curriculum, line-up, list, listing, order of events,
plan, syllabus, timetable **2** = **show,** broadcast,
performance, presentation, production
progress *noun* **1** = **development,** advance,
breakthrough, gain, growth, headway,
improvement OPPOSITE decline. **2**
= **movement,** advance, course, headway,
passage OPPOSITE regression ◆ *verb* **3**
= **develop,** advance, gain, grow, improve
OPPOSITE regress. **4** = **move on,** advance,
continue, go forward, make headway, proceed,
travel OPPOSITE recede ◆ **in progress** = **going
on,** being done, happening, occurring,
proceeding, taking place, under way
progression *noun* **1** = **progress,** advance,
advancement, furtherance, gain, headway,
movement forward
progressive *adjective* **1** = **enlightened,**
advanced, avant-garde, forward-looking, liberal,
modern, radical, reformist, revolutionary **2**
= **growing,** advancing, continuing, developing,
increasing, ongoing
prohibit *verb* **a** = **forbid,** ban, debar, disallow,
outlaw, proscribe, veto OPPOSITE allow. **b**
= **prevent,** hamper, hinder, impede, restrict,
stop OPPOSITE let
prohibition *noun* **1** = **prevention,** ban, bar,

boycott, constraint, embargo, exclusion,
injunction, interdict, obstruction, proscription,
restriction, veto
prohibitive *adjective* = **exorbitant,** excessive,
extortionate, steep (*inf*)
project *noun* **1** = **scheme,** activity,
assignment, enterprise, job, occupation, plan,
task, undertaking, venture, work ◆ *verb* **2**
= **forecast,** calculate, estimate, extrapolate,
gauge, predict, reckon **5** = **stick out,** bulge,
extend, jut, overhang, protrude, stand out
projectile *noun* = **missile,** bullet, rocket, shell
projection *noun* **2** = **forecast,** calculation,
computation, estimate, estimation,
extrapolation, reckoning **5** = **protrusion,** bulge,
ledge, overhang, protuberance, ridge, shelf
proletarian *adjective* = **working-class,**
common, plebeian ◆ *noun* = **worker,** commoner,
man of the people, pleb, plebeian, prole
(*offens*)
proletariat *noun* = **working class,**
commoners, hoi polloi, labouring classes, lower
classes, plebs, proles (*offens*), the common
people, the masses OPPOSITE ruling class
proliferate *verb* = **increase,** breed, expand,
grow rapidly, multiply
proliferation *noun* = **multiplication,**
expansion, increase, spread
prolific *adjective* = **productive,** abundant,
copious, fecund, fertile, fruitful, luxuriant,
profuse OPPOSITE barren

writing) overlong and boring. **prolixity** *noun*
prologue ⊕ *noun* introduction to a play or book.
prolong ⊕ *verb* make (something) last longer. **prolongation** *noun*
prom *noun* short for PROMENADE *or* PROMENADE CONCERT.
promenade ⊕ *noun* **1** paved walkway along the seafront at a holiday resort. ♦ *verb, noun* **2** *Old-fashioned* (take) a leisurely walk.
promenade concert concert at which part of the audience stands rather than sits.
promethium [pro-**meeth**-ee-um] *noun Chem* artificial radioactive element of the lanthanide series.
prominent ⊕ *adjective* **1** very noticeable. **2** famous, widely known. **prominently** *adverb* **prominence** *noun*
promiscuous ⊕ *adjective* having many casual sexual relationships. **promiscuity** *noun*
promise ⊕ *verb* **1** say that one will definitely do or not do something. **2** show signs of, seem likely. ♦ *noun* **3** undertaking to do or not to do something. **4** indication of future success. **show promise** seem likely to succeed. **promising** *adjective* likely to succeed or turn out well.

promissory note written promise to pay a sum of money to a particular person on a certain date or on demand.
promo *noun, pl* -**mos** *Informal* short video film made to promote a pop record.
promontory ⊕ *noun, pl* -**ries** point of high land jutting out into the sea.
promote ⊕ *verb* **1** help to make (something) happen or increase. **2** raise to a higher rank or position. **3** encourage the sale of by advertising. **promoter** *noun* person who organizes or finances an event etc. **promotion** *noun* **promotional** *adjective*
prompt ⊕ *verb* **1** cause (an action). **2** remind (an actor or speaker) of words that he or she has forgotten. ♦ *adjective* **3** done without delay. ♦ *adverb* **4** exactly, e.g. *six o'clock prompt*. **promptly** *adverb* immediately, without delay. **promptness** *noun* **prompter** *noun* person offstage who prompts actors.
promulgate ⊕ *verb* **1** put (a law etc.) into effect by announcing it officially. **2** make widely known. **promulgation** *noun* **promulgator** *noun*
prone ⊕ *adjective* **1** (foll. by *to*) likely to do or be affected by (something). **2** lying face

————— THESAURUS —————

prologue *noun* =**introduction**, foreword, preamble, preface, prelude
prolong *verb* =**lengthen**, continue, delay, drag out, draw out, extend, perpetuate, protract, spin out, stretch OPPOSITE> **shorten**
promenade *noun* **1** =**walkway**, esplanade, parade, prom ♦*verb, noun* **2** *Old-fashioned* =**stroll**, saunter, walk
prominence *noun* **1** =**conspicuousness**, markedness **2** =**fame**, celebrity, distinction, eminence, importance, name, prestige, reputation
prominent *adjective* **1** =**noticeable**, conspicuous, eye-catching, obtrusive, obvious, outstanding, pronounced OPPOSITE> **insignificant**. **2** =**famous**, distinguished, eminent, foremost, important, leading, main, notable, renowned, top, well-known OPPOSITE> **minor**
promiscuous *adjective* =**licentious**, abandoned, debauched, fast, immoral, libertine, loose, wanton, wild OPPOSITE> **chaste**
promise *verb* **1** =**guarantee**, assure, contract, give one's word, pledge, swear, take an oath, undertake, vow, warrant **2** =**seem likely**, augur, betoken, indicate, look like, show signs of, suggest ♦*noun* **3** =**guarantee**, assurance, bond, oath, pledge, undertaking, vow, word **4** =**potential**, ability, aptitude,

capability, capacity, talent
promising *adjective* **a** =**encouraging**, auspicious, bright, favourable, hopeful, likely, propitious, reassuring, rosy OPPOSITE> **discouraging**. **b** =**talented**, able, gifted, rising
promontory *noun* =**point**, cape, foreland, head, headland
promote *verb* **1** =**help**, advance, aid, assist, back, boost, encourage, forward, foster, gee up, support OPPOSITE> **prevent**. **2** =**raise**, elevate, exalt, upgrade OPPOSITE> **downgrade**. **3** =**advertise**, hype, plug (*inf*), publicize, push, sell
promotion *noun* **1** =**encouragement**, advancement, boosting, furtherance, support **2** =**rise**, advancement, elevation, exaltation, honour, move up, preferment, upgrading **3** =**publicity**, advertising, plugging (*inf*)
prompt *verb* **1** =**cause**, elicit, give rise to, occasion, provoke OPPOSITE> **discourage**. **2** =**remind**, assist, cue, help out ♦*adjective* **3** =**immediate**, early, instant, quick, rapid, speedy, swift, timely OPPOSITE> **late** ♦*adverb* **4** =**exactly**, on the dot, promptly, punctually, sharp
promulgate *verb* **2** =**make known**, broadcast, circulate, communicate, disseminate, make public, proclaim, promote, publish, spread

P

downwards.
prong ⊙ *noun* one spike of a fork or similar
instrument. **pronged** *adjective*
pronoun *noun* word, such as *she* or *it*, used to
replace a noun. **pronominal** *adjective*
pronounce ⊙ *verb* **1** form the sounds of
(words or letters), esp. clearly or in a particular
way. **2** declare formally or officially.
pronounceable *adjective* **pronounced**
adjective very noticeable. **pronouncement**
noun formal announcement. **pronunciation**
noun way in which a word or language is
pronounced.

> **SPELLING TIP**
>
> The noun **pronunciation**, which
> appears in the Bank of English
> 823 times, is spelt
> *pronounciation* 21 times,
> probably because of the way
> **pronounce** is spelt. Remember,
> there is no *o* between the *n* and
> the *u*.

pronto *adverb Informal* at once.
proof ⊙ *noun* **1** evidence that shows that
something is true or has happened. **2** copy of
something printed, such as the pages of a
book, for checking before final production. **3**
Photog trial print from a negative. ◆ *adjective* **4**
able to withstand, e.g. *proof against criticism*. **5**
denoting the strength of an alcoholic drink, e.g.

seventy proof. **proofread** *verb* read and correct
(printer's proofs). **proofreader** *noun*
prop[1] ⊙ *verb* **propping, propped 1** support
(something) so that it stays upright or in place.
◆ *noun* **2** pole, beam, etc. used as a support.
prop[2] *noun* movable object used on the set of
a film or play.
prop[3] *noun Informal* propeller.
propaganda ⊙ *noun* (organized promotion
of) information to assist or damage the cause of
a government or movement. **propagandist**
noun
propagate ⊙ *verb* **1** spread (information and
ideas). **2** reproduce, breed, or grow.
propagation *noun*
propane *noun* flammable gas found in
petroleum and used as a fuel.
propel ⊙ *verb* **-pelling, -pelled** cause to
move forward. **propellant** *noun* **1** something
that provides or causes propulsion. **2** gas used
in an aerosol spray. **propeller** *noun* revolving
shaft with blades for driving a ship or aircraft.
propulsion *noun* **1** method by which
something is propelled. **2** act of propelling or
state of being propelled.
propensity ⊙ *noun, pl* **-ties** natural tendency.
proper ⊙ *adjective* **1** real or genuine. **2**
appropriate. **3** suited to a particular purpose. **4**
correct in behaviour. **5** excessively moral. **6**
Informal complete. **properly** *adverb* **proper
noun** name of a person or place, as in *David* or
Iceland.
property ⊙ *noun, pl* **-ties 1** something

P

—————— T H E S A U R U S ——————

prone *adjective* **1** (foll. by *to*) = **liable**, apt,
bent, disposed, given, inclined, likely,
predisposed, subject, susceptible, tending
OPPOSITE **disinclined**. **2 = face down**, flat,
horizontal, prostrate, recumbent OPPOSITE
erect
prong *noun* = **point**, spike, tine
pronounce *verb* **1 = say**, accent, articulate,
enunciate, sound, speak **2 = declare**, affirm,
announce, decree, deliver, proclaim
pronounced *adjective* = **noticeable**,
conspicuous, decided, definite, distinct, evident,
marked, obvious, striking
pronouncement *noun* = **announcement**,
declaration, decree, dictum, edict, judgment,
proclamation, statement
pronunciation *noun* = **intonation**, accent,
articulation, diction, enunciation, inflection,
speech, stress
proof *noun* **1 = evidence**, authentication,
confirmation, corroboration, demonstration,
substantiation, testimony, verification ◆*adjective*

4 = impervious, impenetrable, repellent,
resistant, strong
prop[1] *verb* **1 = support**, bolster, brace,
buttress, hold up, stay, sustain, uphold ◆*noun* **2
= support**, brace, buttress, mainstay, stanchion,
stay
propaganda *noun* = **information**, advertising,
disinformation, hype, promotion, publicity
propagate *verb* **1 = spread**, broadcast,
circulate, disseminate, promote, promulgate,
publish, transmit OPPOSITE **suppress**. **2
= reproduce**, beget, breed, engender,
generate, increase, multiply, procreate, produce
propel *verb* = **drive**, force, impel, launch,
push, send, shoot, shove, thrust OPPOSITE **stop**
propensity *noun* = **tendency**, bent,
inclination, liability, penchant, predisposition,
proclivity
proper *adjective* **2, 3 = suitable**, appropriate,
apt, becoming, befitting, fit, fitting, right
OPPOSITE **inappropriate**. **4 = correct**,
accepted, conventional, established, formal,

owned. **2** possessions collectively. **3** land or buildings owned by somebody. **4** quality or attribute.

prophet ⊙ *noun* **1** person supposedly chosen by God to spread His word. **2** person who predicts the future. **prophetic** *adjective* **prophetically** *adverb* **prophecy** *noun, pl* **-cies** **1** prediction. **2** message revealing God's will.

prophesy *verb* **-sying, -sied** foretell.

prophylactic *noun, adjective* (drug) used to prevent disease.

propitiate ⊙ *verb* appease, win the favour of. **propitiation** *noun* **propitious** *adjective* favourable or auspicious.

proponent *noun* person who argues in favour of something.

proportion ⊙ *noun* **1** relative size or extent. **2** correct relation between connected parts. **3** part considered with respect to the whole. ♦ *plural* **4** dimensions or size. ♦ *verb* **5** adjust in relative amount or size. **in proportion 1** comparable in size, rate of increase, etc. **2** without exaggerating. **proportional, proportionate** *adjective* being in proportion. **proportionally, proportionately** *adverb* **proportional representation** representation of political parties in parliament in proportion to the votes they win.

propose ⊙ *verb* **1** put forward for consideration. **2** nominate. **3** intend or plan (to do). **4** make an offer of marriage. **proposal** *noun* **proposition** *noun* **1** offer. **2** statement or assertion. **3** *Maths* theorem. **4** *Informal* thing to be dealt with. ♦ *verb* **5** *Informal* ask (someone) to have sexual intercourse.

propound *verb* put forward for consideration.

proprietor ⊙ *noun* owner of a business establishment. **proprietress** *n fem* **proprietary** *adjective* **1** made and distributed under a trade name. **2** denoting or suggesting ownership.

propriety ⊙ *noun, pl* **-ties 1** quality of being appropriate or fitting. **2** correct conduct.

propulsion ⊙ *noun* see PROPEL.

pro rata *adverb, adjective Latin* in proportion.

prorogue *verb* suspend (parliament) without dissolving it. **prorogation** *noun*

prosaic ⊙ [pro-**zay**-ik] *adjective* lacking imagination, dull. **prosaically** *adverb*

proscenium *noun, pl* **-nia, -niums** arch in a theatre separating the stage from the auditorium.

proscribe ⊙ *verb* prohibit, outlaw. **proscription** *noun* **proscriptive** *adjective*

prose *noun* ordinary speech or writing in

——————————— THESAURUS ———————————

orthodox, precise, right **5 = polite**, decent, decorous, genteel, gentlemanly, ladylike, mannerly, respectable, seemly

property *noun* **2 = possessions**, assets, belongings, capital, effects, estate, goods, holdings, riches, wealth **3 = land**, estate, freehold, holding, real estate **4 = quality**, attribute, characteristic, feature, hallmark, trait

prophecy *noun* **= prediction**, augury, divination, forecast, prognostication, second sight, soothsaying

prophesy *verb* **= predict**, augur, divine, forecast, foresee, foretell, prognosticate

prophet *noun* **2 = soothsayer**, diviner, forecaster, oracle, prophesier, seer, sibyl

propitious *adjective* **= favourable**, auspicious, bright, encouraging, fortunate, happy, lucky, promising

proportion *noun* **1 = relative amount**, ratio, relationship **2 = balance**, congruity, correspondence, harmony, symmetry **3 = part**, amount, division, fraction, percentage, quota, segment, share ♦*plural noun* **4 = dimensions**, capacity, expanse, extent, size, volume

proportional, proportionate *adjective* **= balanced**, commensurate, compatible, consistent, corresponding, equitable, even, in

proportion

proposal *noun* **1 = suggestion**, bid, offer, plan, presentation, programme, project, recommendation, scheme

propose *verb* **1 = put forward**, advance, present, submit, suggest **2 = nominate**, name, present, recommend **3 = intend**, aim, design, have in mind, mean, plan, scheme **4 = offer marriage**, ask for someone's hand (in marriage), pop the question (*inf*)

proposition *noun* **1 = proposal**, plan, recommendation, scheme, suggestion ♦*verb* **5** *Inf* **= make a pass at**, accost, make an improper suggestion, solicit

propriety *noun* **1 = correctness**, aptness, fitness, rightness, seemliness **2 = decorum**, courtesy, decency, etiquette, manners, politeness, respectability, seemliness OPPOSITE indecency

propulsion *noun* **= drive**, impetus, impulse, propelling force, push, thrust

prosaic *adjective* **= dull**, boring, everyday, humdrum, matter-of-fact, mundane, ordinary, pedestrian, routine, trite, unimaginative OPPOSITE exciting

proscribe *verb* **a = prohibit**, ban, embargo, forbid, interdict OPPOSITE allow. **b = outlaw**, contrast to poetry.

prosecute ❶ *verb* **1** bring a criminal charge against. **2** continue to do. **prosecution** *noun* **prosecutor** *noun*

proselyte [**pross**-ill-ite] *noun* recent convert.

proselytize [**pross**-ill-it-ize] *verb* attempt to convert.

prosody [**pross**-a-dee] *noun* study of poetic metre and techniques.

prospect ❶ *noun* **1** something anticipated, e.g. *the prospect of defeat.* **2** *Old-fashioned* view from a place. ◆ *plural* **3** probability of future success. ◆ *verb* **4** explore, esp. for gold.

prospective *adjective* **1** future. **2** expected.

prospector *noun* **prospectus** *noun* booklet giving details of a university, company, etc.

prosper ❶ *verb* be successful. **prosperity** *noun* success and wealth. **prosperous** *adjective*

prostate *noun* gland in male mammals that surrounds the neck of the bladder.

prosthesis [pross-**theess**-iss] *noun, pl* **-ses** [-seez] artificial body part, such as a limb or breast. **prosthetic** *adjective*

prostitute ❶ *noun* **1** person who offers sexual intercourse in return for payment. ◆ *verb* **2** make a prostitute of. **3** offer (oneself or one's talents) for unworthy purposes. **prostitution** *noun*

prostrate ❶ *adjective* **1** lying face downwards. **2** physically or emotionally exhausted. ◆ *verb* **3**

lie face downwards. **4** exhaust physically or emotionally. **prostration** *noun*

protactinium *noun Chem* toxic radioactive metallic element.

protagonist ❶ *noun* **1** supporter of a cause. **2** leading character in a play or a story.

protea [pro-tee-a] *noun* African shrub with showy flowers.

protean [pro-tee-an] *adjective* constantly changing.

protect ❶ *verb* defend from trouble, harm, or loss. **protection** *noun* **protectionism** *noun* policy of protecting industries by taxing competing imports. **protectionist** *noun, adjective* **protective** *adjective* **1** giving protection, e.g. *protective clothing.* **2** tending or wishing to protect someone. **protector** *noun* **1** person or thing that protects. **2** regent.

protectorate *noun* **1** territory largely controlled by a stronger state. **2** (period of) rule of a regent.

protégé, *(fem)* **protégée** [pro-ti-zhay] *noun* person who is protected and helped by another.

protein *noun* any of a group of complex organic compounds that are essential for life.

pro tempore *adverb, adjective* for the time being (also **pro tem**).

protest ❶ *noun* **1** declaration or demonstration of objection. ◆ *verb* **2** object,

——————— THESAURUS ———————

banish, deport, exclude, exile, expatriate, expel, ostracize

prosecute *verb* **1** = **put on trial**, arraign, bring to trial, indict, litigate, sue, take to court, try

prospect *noun* **1** = **expectation**, anticipation, future, hope, odds, outlook, probability, promise **2** *Old-fashioned* = **view**, landscape, outlook, scene, sight, spectacle, vista ◆*plural noun* **3** = **likelihood**, chance, possibility ◆*verb* **4** = **look for**, fossick (*Aust & NZ*), search for, seek

prospective *adjective* **1** = **future 2** = **expected**, anticipated, coming, destined, forthcoming, imminent, intended, likely, possible, potential

prospectus *noun* = **catalogue**, list, outline, programme, syllabus, synopsis

prosper *verb* = **succeed**, advance, do well, flourish, get on, progress, thrive

prosperity *noun* **a** = **success**, good fortune **b** = **wealth**, affluence, fortune, luxury, plenty, prosperousness, riches

prosperous *adjective* **a** = **successful**, booming, doing well, flourishing, fortunate, lucky, thriving **b** = **wealthy**, affluent, moneyed,

rich, well-heeled (*inf*), well-off, well-to-do
⟨OPPOSITE⟩ **poor**

prostitute *noun* **1** = **whore**, call girl, fallen woman, harlot, hooker (*US sl*), loose woman, pro (*sl*), scrubber (*Brit & Aust sl*), streetwalker, strumpet, tart (*inf*), trollop ◆*verb* **3** = **cheapen**, debase, degrade, demean, devalue, misapply, pervert, profane

prostrate *adjective* **1** = **prone**, flat, horizontal **2** = **exhausted**, dejected, depressed, desolate, drained, inconsolable, overcome, spent, worn out ◆*verb* **4** = **exhaust**, drain, fatigue, sap, tire, wear out, weary

protagonist *noun* **1** = **supporter**, advocate, champion, exponent **2** = **leading character**, central character, hero or heroine, principal

protect *verb* = **keep safe**, defend, guard, look after, preserve, safeguard, save, screen, shelter, shield, stick up for (*inf*), support, watch over
⟨OPPOSITE⟩ **endanger**

protection *noun* **a** = **safety**, aegis, care, custody, defence, protecting, safeguard, safekeeping, security **b** = **safeguard**, barrier, buffer, cover, guard, screen, shelter, shield

protector *noun* **1** = **defender**, bodyguard,

disagree. **3** assert formally. **protester** *noun*
protestation *noun* strong declaration.
Protestant *noun* **1** follower of any of the
Christian churches that split from the Roman
Catholic Church in the sixteenth century. ◆
adjective **2** of or relating to such a church.
Protestantism *noun*
protium *noun* most common isotope of
hydrogen.
proto- *combining form* first, e.g. *protohuman*.
protocol ❶ *noun* rules of behaviour for formal
occasions.
proton *noun* positively charged particle in the
nucleus of an atom.
protoplasm *noun* substance forming the
living contents of a cell.
prototype ❶ *noun* original or model to be
copied or developed.
protozoan [pro-toe-**zoe**-an] *noun, pl* **-zoa**
microscopic one-celled creature.
protract ❶ *verb* lengthen or extend.
protracted *adjective* **protractor** *noun*
instrument for measuring angles.
protrude ❶ *verb* stick out, project.

protrusion *noun*
protuberant ❶ *adjective* swelling out,
bulging. **protuberance** *noun*
proud ❶ *adjective* **1** feeling pleasure and
satisfaction. **2** feeling honoured. **3** thinking
oneself superior to other people. **4** dignified.
proudly *adverb*
prove ❶ *verb* **proving, proved, proved** or
proven 1 establish the validity of. **2**
demonstrate, test. **3** be found to be. **proven**
adjective known from experience to work.
provenance [**prov**-in-anss] *noun* place of
origin.
provender *noun Old-fashioned* fodder.
proverb ❶ *noun* short saying that expresses a
truth or gives a warning. **proverbial** *adjective*
provide ❶ *verb* make available. **provider**
noun **provided that, providing** on condition
that. **provide for** *verb* **1** take precautions
(against). **2** support financially.
providence ❶ *noun* God or nature seen as a
protective force that arranges people's lives.
provident *adjective* **1** thrifty. **2** showing
foresight. **providential** *adjective* lucky.

——————————————— THESAURUS ———————————————

champion, guard, guardian, patron
protest *noun* **1 =objection,** complaint,
dissent, outcry, protestation, remonstrance
◆*verb* **2 =object,** complain, cry out,
demonstrate, demur, disagree, disapprove,
express disapproval, oppose, remonstrate **3
=assert,** affirm, attest, avow, declare, insist,
maintain, profess
protestation *noun* **=declaration,** affirmation,
avowal, profession, vow
protester *noun* **=demonstrator,** agitator,
rebel
protocol *noun* **=code of behaviour,**
conventions, customs, decorum, etiquette,
manners, propriety
prototype *noun* **=original,** example, first,
model, pattern, standard, type
protracted *adjective* **=extended,** dragged
out, drawn-out, long-drawn-out, prolonged
protrude *verb* **=stick out,** bulge, come
through, extend, jut, obtrude, project, stand
out
protrusion *noun* **=projection,** bulge, bump,
lump, outgrowth, protuberance
protuberance *noun* **=bulge,** bump,
excrescence, hump, knob, lump, outgrowth,
process, prominence, protrusion, swelling
proud *adjective* **1 =satisfied,** content, glad,
gratified, pleased, well-pleased [OPPOSITE]
discontented. 3 =conceited, arrogant,
boastful, disdainful, haughty, imperious, lordly,

overbearing, self-satisfied, snobbish, supercilious
[OPPOSITE] **modest**
prove *verb* **1 =verify,** authenticate, confirm,
demonstrate, determine, establish, justify, show,
substantiate [OPPOSITE] **rule out. 2 =test,**
analyse, assay, check, examine, try **3 =turn
out,** come out, end up, result
proven *adjective* **=established,** attested,
confirmed, definite, proved, reliable, tested,
verified
proverb *noun* **=saying,** adage, dictum,
maxim, saw
proverbial *adjective* **=conventional,**
acknowledged, axiomatic, current, famed,
famous, legendary, notorious, traditional,
typical, well-known
provide *verb* **1 =supply,** add, afford, bring,
cater, equip, furnish, give, impart, lend, outfit,
present, produce, purvey, render, serve, stock
up, yield [OPPOSITE] **refuse ◆ provide for 1
=take precautions,** anticipate, forearm, plan
ahead, plan for, prepare for **2 =support,** care
for, keep, maintain, sustain, take care of
provided that, providing *conjunction* **=on
condition that,** as long as, given
providence *noun* **=fate,** destiny, fortune
provident *adjective* **1 =thrifty,** economical,
frugal, prudent **2 =foresighted,** careful,
cautious, discreet, far-seeing, forearmed,
shrewd, vigilant, well-prepared, wise
providential *adjective* **=lucky,** fortuitous,

P

province ⊕ *noun* **1** area governed as a unit of a country or empire. **2** area of learning, activity, etc. ♦ *plural* **3** parts of a country outside the capital. **provincial** *adjective* **1** of a province or the provinces. **2** unsophisticated and narrow-minded. ♦ *noun* **3** unsophisticated person. **4** person from a province or the provinces. **provincialism** *noun* narrow-mindedness and lack of sophistication.

provision ⊕ *noun* **1** act of supplying something. **2** something supplied. **3** *Law* condition incorporated in a document. ♦ *plural* **4** food. ♦ *verb* **5** supply with food. **provisional** *adjective* temporary or conditional. **provisionally** *adverb*

proviso ⊕ [pro-**vize**-oh] *noun, pl* **-sos, -soes** condition, stipulation.

provoke ⊕ *verb* **1** deliberately anger. **2** cause (an adverse reaction). **provocation** *noun* **provocative** *adjective*

provost *noun* **1** head of certain university colleges. **2** chief councillor of a Scottish town. **provost marshal** head of military police.

prow *noun* bow of a vessel.

prowess ⊕ *noun* **1** superior skill or ability. **2** bravery, fearlessness.

prowl ⊕ *verb* **1** move stealthily around a place as if in search of prey or plunder. ♦ *noun* **2** prowling. **prowler** *noun*

proximity ⊕ *noun* **1** nearness in space or time. **2** nearness or closeness in a series. **proximate** *adjective*

proxy ⊕ *noun, pl* **proxies 1** person authorized to act on behalf of someone else. **2** authority to act on behalf of someone else.

prude ⊕ *noun* person who is excessively modest, prim, or proper. **prudish** *adjective* **prudery** *noun*

prudent ⊕ *adjective* cautious, discreet, and sensible. **prudence** *noun* **prudential** *adjective Old-fashioned* prudent.

prune[1] *noun* dried plum.

prune[2] ⊕ *verb* **1** cut off dead parts or excessive branches from (a tree or plant). **2** shorten, reduce.

prurient *adjective* excessively interested in

——————— T H E S A U R U S ———————

fortunate, happy, heaven-sent, opportune, timely

province *noun* **1** = **region**, colony, department, district, division, domain, patch, section, zone **2** = **area**, business, capacity, concern, duty, field, function, line, responsibility, role, sphere

provincial *adjective* **1** = **rural**, country, homespun, local, rustic OPPOSITE **urban**. **2** = **parochial**, hick (*inf, chiefly US & Canad*), insular, limited, narrow, narrow-minded, small-minded, small-town (*chiefly US*), unsophisticated OPPOSITE **sophisticated** ♦*noun* **3** = **yokel**, country cousin, hayseed (*US & Canad inf*), hick (*inf, chiefly US & Canad*), rustic

provision *noun* **1** = **supplying**, catering, equipping, furnishing, providing **3** *Law* = **condition**, clause, demand, proviso, requirement, rider, stipulation, term ♦*plural* **4** = **food**, comestibles, eatables, edibles, fare, foodstuffs, rations, stores, supplies, tucker (*Aust & NZ inf*), victuals

provisional *adjective* **a** = **temporary**, interim OPPOSITE **permanent**. **b** = **conditional**, contingent, limited, qualified, tentative OPPOSITE **definite**

proviso *noun* = **condition**, clause, qualification, requirement, rider, stipulation

provocation *noun* **1** = **offence**, affront, annoyance, challenge, dare, grievance, indignity, injury, insult, taunt **2** = **cause**, grounds, incitement, motivation, reason,

stimulus

provocative *adjective* **1** = **offensive**, annoying, galling, goading, insulting, provoking

provoke *verb* **1** = **anger**, aggravate (*inf*), annoy, enrage, hassle (*inf*), incense, infuriate, irk, irritate, madden, rile OPPOSITE **calm**. **2** = **rouse**, bring about, cause, elicit, evoke, incite, induce, occasion, produce, promote, prompt, stir OPPOSITE **ease**

prowess *noun* **1** = **skill**, ability, accomplishment, adeptness, aptitude, excellence, expertise, genius, mastery, talent OPPOSITE **inability**. **2** = **bravery**, courage, daring, fearlessness, heroism, mettle, valiance, valour OPPOSITE **fear**

prowl *verb* **1** = **move stealthily**, skulk, slink, sneak, stalk, steal

proximity *noun* = **nearness**, closeness

proxy *noun* **1** = **representative**, agent, delegate, deputy, factor, substitute

prudence *noun* **a** = **care**, caution, vigilance, wariness **b** = **discretion c** = **common sense**, good sense, judgment, wisdom

prudent *adjective* **a** = **careful**, canny, cautious, discerning, judicious, shrewd, vigilant, wary OPPOSITE **rash**. **b** = **discreet**, politic **c** = **sensible**, wise OPPOSITE **irrational**

prudish *adjective* = **prim**, old-maidish (*inf*), priggish, prissy (*inf*), proper, puritanical, starchy (*inf*), strait-laced, stuffy, Victorian

prune[2] *verb* **1** = **cut**, clip, dock, shape, snip, trim **2** = **reduce**, shorten

sexual matters. **prurience** *noun*
pry ❶ *verb* **prying, pried** make an impertinent
or uninvited inquiry into a private matter.
PS postscript.
psalm ❶ *noun* sacred song. **psalmist** *noun*
writer of psalms.
Psalter *noun* book containing (a version of)
psalms from the Bible. **psaltery** *noun, pl* **-ries**
ancient instrument played by plucking strings.
PSBR public sector borrowing requirement.
psephology [sef-**fol**-a-jee] *noun* statistical
study of elections.
pseud *noun Informal* pretentious person.
pseudo- *combining form* false, pretending, or
unauthentic, e.g. *pseudoclassical.*
pseudonym ❶ *noun* fictitious name adopted
esp. by an author. **pseudonymous** *adjective*
psittacosis *noun* disease of parrots that can
be transmitted to humans.
psoriasis [so-**rye**-a-siss] *noun* skin disease with
reddish spots and patches covered with silvery
scales.
psyche ❶ [**sye**-kee] *noun* human mind or soul.
psychedelic *adjective* **1** denoting a drug that
causes hallucinations. **2** having vivid colours
and complex patterns similar to those
experienced during hallucinations.

> **SPELLING TIP**
>
> The main problem with
> **psychedelic** is which vowel
> follows the *ch*; it should be *e* of
> course.

psychiatry ❶ *noun* branch of medicine
concerned with mental disorders. **psychiatric**
adjective **psychiatrist** *noun*
psychic ❶ *adjective* (also **psychical**) **1** having
mental powers which cannot be explained by

natural laws. **2** relating to the mind. ◆ *noun* **3**
person with psychic powers.
psycho *noun, pl* **-chos** *Informal* psychopath.
psycho- *combining form* mind, mental
processes, e.g. *psychology; psychosomatic.*
psychoanalysis *noun* method of treating
mental and emotional disorders by discussion
and analysis of one's thoughts and feelings.
psychoanalyse *verb* **psychoanalyst** *noun*
psychology ❶ *noun, pl* **-gies 1** study of
human and animal behaviour. **2** *Informal*
person's mental make-up. **psychologist** *noun*
psychological *adjective* **1** of or affecting the
mind. **2** of psychology. **psychological
moment** most appropriate time for producing
a desired effect. **psychological warfare**
military application of psychology, esp. to
influence morale in time of war.
psychologically *adverb*
psychopath ❶ *noun* person afflicted with a
personality disorder causing him or her to
commit antisocial or violent acts. **psychopathic**
adjective
psychosis ❶ *noun, pl* **-ses** severe mental
disorder in which the sufferer's contact with
reality becomes distorted. **psychotic** *adjective*
psychosomatic *adjective* (of a physical
disorder) thought to have psychological causes.
psychotherapy *noun* treatment of nervous
disorders by psychological methods.
psychotherapeutic *adjective* **psychotherapist**
noun
psych up *verb* prepare (oneself) mentally for a
contest or task.
pt 1 part. **2** point.
Pt *Chem* platinum.
PT *Old-fashioned* physical training.
pt. pint.
PTA Parent-Teacher Association.
ptarmigan [**tar**-mig-an] *noun* bird of the

P

——————— THESAURUS ———————

pry *verb* =**be inquisitive**, be nosy (*inf*),
interfere, intrude, meddle, poke, snoop (*inf*)
psalm *noun* =**hymn**, chant
pseudo- *combining form* =**false**, artificial, fake,
imitation, mock, phoney *or* phony (*inf*),
pretended, sham, spurious
pseudonym *noun* =**false name**, alias,
assumed name, incognito, nom de plume, pen
name
psyche *noun* =**soul**, anima, individuality,
mind, personality, self, spirit
psychiatrist *noun* =**psychotherapist**, analyst,
headshrinker (*sl*), psychoanalyst, psychologist,
shrink (*sl*), therapist
psychic *adjective* (also **psychical**) **1**

=**supernatural**, mystic, occult **2** =**mental**,
psychological, spiritual
psychological *adjective* **1** =**mental**, cerebral,
cognitive, intellectual
psychology *noun* **1** =**behaviourism**, science
of mind, study of personality **2** *Inf* =**way of
thinking**, attitude, mental make-up, mental
processes, thought processes, what makes one
tick
psychopath *noun* =**madman**, lunatic,
maniac, nutcase (*sl*), nutter (*Brit sl*), psychotic,
sociopath
psychotic *adjective* =**mad**, certifiable,
demented, deranged, insane, lunatic, mental
(*sl*), *non compos mentis*, unbalanced

grouse family which turns white in winter.
pterodactyl [terr-roe-**dak**-til] *noun* extinct
flying reptile with batlike wings.
PTO please turn over.
ptomaine [**toe**-main] *noun* any of a group of
poisonous alkaloids found in decaying matter.
Pu *Chem* plutonium.
pub ❶ *noun* building with a bar licensed to sell
alcoholic drinks.
puberty ❶ [**pew**-ber-tee] *noun* beginning of
sexual maturity. **pubertal** *adjective*
pubescent *adjective* **1** reaching or having
reached puberty. **2** covered with fine short hairs
or down, as some plants and animals.
pubescence *noun*
pubic [**pew**-bik] *adjective* of the lower
abdomen, e.g. *pubic hair*.
pubis *noun, pl* **-bes** one of the three sections
of the hipbone that forms part of the pelvis.
public ❶ *adjective* **1** of or concerning the
people as a whole. **2** for use by everyone. **3**
well-known. **4** performed or made openly. ◆
noun **5** the community, people in general.
publicly *adverb* **public company** limited
company whose shares may be purchased by
the public. **public house** pub. **public
relations** promotion of a favourable opinion
towards an organization among the public.
public school private fee-paying school in
Britain. **public sector** part of a country's
economy controlled and financially supported
by the government. **public-spirited** *adjective*
having or showing an active interest in the
good of the community.
publican *noun* person who owns or runs a

pub.
publicity ❶ *noun* **1** process or information
used to arouse public attention. **2** public
interest so aroused. **publicize** *verb* advertise.
publicist *noun* person, esp. a press agent or
journalist, who publicizes something.
publish ❶ *verb* **1** produce and issue (printed
matter) for sale. **2** announce formally or in
public. **publication** *noun* **publisher** *noun*
puce *adjective* purplish-brown.
puck¹ *noun* small rubber disc used in ice
hockey.
puck² *noun* mischievous or evil spirit. **puckish**
adjective
pucker ❶ *verb* **1** gather into wrinkles. ◆ *noun* **2**
wrinkle or crease.
pudding ❶ *noun* **1** dessert, esp. a cooked one
served hot. **2** savoury dish with pastry or batter,
e.g. *steak-and-kidney pudding*. **3** sausage-like
mass of meat, e.g. *black pudding*.
puddle *noun* small pool of water, esp. of rain.
pudenda *plural noun* human external genital
organs, esp. of a female.
puerile ❶ *adjective* silly and childish.
puerperal [pew-**er**-per-al] *adjective*
concerning the period following childbirth.
puff ❶ *noun* **1** (sound of) a short blast of
breath, wind, etc. **2** act of inhaling cigarette
smoke. ◆ *verb* **3** blow or breathe in short quick
draughts. **4** take draws at (a cigarette). **5** send
out in small clouds. **6** swell. **out of puff** out of
breath. **puffy** *adjective* **puff adder** large
venomous African viper. **puffball** *noun* ball-
shaped fungus. **puff pastry** light flaky pastry.
puffin *noun* black-and-white sea bird with a

P

————— T H E S A U R U S —————

pub *noun* =**tavern**, bar, inn, beer parlour
(*Canad*), beverage room (*Canad*)
puberty *noun* =**adolescence**, pubescence,
teens
public *adjective* **1** = **general**, civic, common,
national, popular, social, state, universal,
widespread **2** = **open**, accessible, communal,
unrestricted OPPOSITE **private. 3** = **well-
known**, important, prominent, respected **4**
= **known**, acknowledged, obvious, open, overt,
patent, plain OPPOSITE **secret** ◆*noun* **5**
= **people**, citizens, community, electorate,
everyone, nation, populace, society
publication *noun* **1** = **pamphlet**, brochure,
issue, leaflet, magazine, newspaper, periodical,
title **2** = **announcement**, broadcasting,
declaration, disclosure, notification,
proclamation, publishing, reporting
publicity *noun* **1** = **advertising**, attention,
boost, hype, plug (*inf*), press, promotion

publicize *verb* =**advertise**, hype, make
known, play up, plug (*inf*), promote, push
OPPOSITE **conceal**
public-spirited *adjective* =**altruistic**,
charitable, humanitarian, philanthropic,
unselfish
publish *verb* **1** = **put out**, issue, print, produce
2 = **announce**, advertise, broadcast, circulate,
disclose, divulge, proclaim, publicize, reveal,
spread
pucker *verb* **1** = **wrinkle**, contract, crease,
draw together, gather, knit, purse, screw up,
tighten ◆*noun* **2** = **wrinkle**, crease, fold
pudding *noun* **1** = **dessert**, afters (*Brit inf*),
pud (*inf*), sweet
puerile *adjective* =**childish**, babyish, foolish,
immature, juvenile, silly, trivial OPPOSITE
mature
puff *noun* **1** = **blast**, breath, draught, gust,
whiff **2** = **smoke**, drag (*sl*), pull ◆*verb* **3** = **blow**,

brightly-coloured beak.

pug noun small snub-nosed dog. **pug nose** short stubby upturned nose.

pugilist ⊕ [pew-jil-ist] noun boxer. **pugilism** noun **pugilistic** adjective

pugnacious adjective ready and eager to fight. **pugnacity** noun

puissance noun showjumping competition that tests a horse's ability to jump large obstacles.

puke Slang verb **1** vomit. ◆ noun **2** act of vomiting. **3** vomited matter.

pukka adjective Anglo-Indian **1** properly done, constructed, etc. **2** genuine, real.

pulchritude noun Lit beauty.

pull ⊕ verb **1** exert force on (an object) to move it towards the source of the force. **2** strain or stretch. **3** remove or extract. **4** attract. ◆ noun **5** act of pulling. **6** force used in pulling. **7** act of taking in drink or smoke. **8** Informal power, influence. **pull oneself together** Informal regain one's self-control. **pull in** verb **1** (of a vehicle or driver) draw in to the side of the road or stop. **2** reach a destination. **3** attract in large numbers. **4** Slang arrest. **pull off** verb Informal succeed in performing. **pull out** verb **1** (of a vehicle or driver) move away from the side of the road or move out to overtake. **2** (of a train) depart. **3** withdraw. **4** remove by pulling. **pull through** verb survive or recover, esp. after a serious illness. **pull up** verb **1** (of a vehicle or driver) stop. **2** remove by the roots. **3** reprimand.

pullet noun young hen.

pulley noun wheel with a grooved rim in which a belt, chain, or piece of rope runs in order to lift weights by a downward pull.

Pullman noun, pl **-mans** luxurious railway coach.

pullover noun sweater that is pulled on over the head.

pulmonary adjective of the lungs.

pulp ⊕ noun **1** soft wet substance made from crushed or beaten matter. **2** flesh of a fruit. **3** poor-quality books and magazines. ◆ verb **4** reduce to pulp.

pulpit noun raised platform for a preacher.

pulsar noun small dense star which emits regular bursts of radio waves.

pulse¹ ⊕ noun **1** regular beating of blood through the arteries at each heartbeat. **2** any regular beat or vibration. **pulsate** verb throb, quiver. **pulsation** noun

pulse² noun edible seed of a pod-bearing plant such as a bean or pea.

pulverize ⊕ verb **1** reduce to fine pieces. **2** destroy completely. **pulverization** noun

puma noun large American wild cat with a greyish-brown coat.

pumice [pumm-iss] noun light porous stone used for scouring.

pummel ⊕ verb **-melling, -melled** strike repeatedly with or as if with the fists.

pump¹ ⊕ noun **1** machine used to force a liquid or gas to move in a particular direction. ◆ verb **2** raise or drive with a pump. **3** supply in large amounts. **4** operate or work in the manner of a pump. **5** extract information from.

pump² noun light flat-soled shoe.

pumpernickel noun sour black bread made

P

breathe, exhale, gasp, gulp, pant, wheeze **4** = **smoke**, drag (sl), draw, inhale, pull at or on, suck **6** = **swell**, bloat, dilate, distend, expand, inflate

pugilist noun = **boxer**, fighter, prizefighter

pull verb **1** = **draw**, drag, haul, jerk, tow, trail, tug, yank OPPOSITE drive. **2** = **strain**, dislocate, rip, sprain, stretch, tear, wrench **3** = **extract**, draw out, gather, pick, pluck, remove, take out, uproot OPPOSITE plant. **4** = **attract**, draw, entice, lure, magnetize OPPOSITE discourage ◆noun **5** = **tug**, jerk, twitch, yank OPPOSITE push. **7** = **puff**, drag (sl), inhalation **8** Inf = **influence**, clout (inf), mana (NZ), muscle, power, weight

pull off verb Inf = **succeed**, accomplish, carry out, do the trick, manage

pull out verb **2** = **depart**, leave, quit **3** = **withdraw**, evacuate, retreat

pull through verb = **survive**, get better, rally, recover

pull up verb **1** = **stop**, brake, halt **3** = **reprimand**, admonish, bawl out (inf), rap over the knuckles, read the riot act, rebuke, reprove, rouse on (Aust), slap on the wrist, tear (someone) off a strip (Brit inf), tell off (inf)

pulp noun **1** = **paste**, mash, mush **2** = **flesh**, soft part ◆verb **4** = **crush**, mash, pulverize, squash

pulsate verb = **throb**, beat, palpitate, pound, pulse, quiver, thump

pulse¹ noun **1** = **beat**, beating, pulsation, throb, throbbing **2** = **vibration**, rhythm

pulverize verb **1** = **crush**, granulate, grind, mill, pound **2** = **defeat**, annihilate, crush, demolish, destroy, flatten, smash, wreck

pummel verb = **beat**, batter, hammer, pound, punch, strike, thump

pump verb **2** = **drive**, force, inject, push **3** = **supply**, pour, send **5** = **interrogate**, cross-examine, probe, quiz of coarse rye flour.

pumpkin *noun* large round fruit with an orange rind, soft flesh, and many seeds.

pun ❶ *noun* 1 use of words to exploit double meanings for humorous effect. ♦ *verb* **punning, punned** 2 make puns.

punch¹ ❶ *verb* 1 strike at with a clenched fist. ♦ *noun* 2 blow with a clenched fist. 3 *Informal* effectiveness or vigour. **punchy** *adjective* **punchier, punchiest** forceful. **punch-drunk** *adjective* dazed by or as if by repeated blows to the head. **punch line** line of a joke or funny story that gives it its point. **punch-up** *noun Informal* fight or brawl.

punch² ❶ *noun* 1 tool or machine for shaping, piercing, or engraving. ♦ *verb* 2 pierce, cut, stamp, shape, or drive with a punch.

punch³ *noun* drink made from a mixture of wine, spirits, fruit, sugar, and spices.

punctilious ❶ *adjective* 1 paying great attention to correctness in etiquette. 2 careful about small details.

punctual ❶ *adjective* arriving or taking place at the correct time. **punctuality** *noun* **punctually** *adverb*

punctuate ❶ *verb* 1 put punctuation marks in. 2 interrupt at frequent intervals.

punctuation *noun* (use of) marks such as commas, colons, etc. in writing, to assist in making the sense clear. **punctuation mark** any of the signs used in punctuation, such as a comma.

puncture ❶ *noun* 1 small hole made by a sharp object, esp. in a tyre. ♦ *verb* 2 pierce a hole in.

pundit *noun* expert who speaks publicly on a subject.

pungent ❶ *adjective* having a strong sharp bitter flavour. **pungency** *noun*

punish ❶ *verb* cause (someone) to suffer or undergo a penalty for some wrongdoing. **punishing** *adjective* harsh or difficult.

punishment *noun* **punitive** [pew-nit-tiv] *adjective* relating to punishment.

punitive [pew-nit-tiv] *adjective* relating to punishment.

punk *noun* 1 anti-Establishment youth movement and style of rock music of the late 1970s. 2 follower of this music. 3 worthless person.

punkah *noun* fan made of palm leaves.

punnet *noun* small basket for fruit.

punt¹ *noun* 1 open flat-bottomed boat propelled by a pole. ♦ *verb* 2 travel in a punt.

punt² *Sport noun* 1 kick of a ball before it touches the ground when dropped from the hands. ♦ *verb* 2 kick (a ball) in this way.

punt³ *noun* monetary unit of the Irish Republic.

punter ❶ *noun* 1 person who bets. 2 any member of the public.

puny ❶ *adjective* **-nier, -niest** small and feeble.

pup *noun* young of certain animals, such as dogs and seals.

pupa [pew-pa] *noun, pl* **-pae, -pas** insect at the stage of development between a larva and an adult. **pupal** *adjective*

pupil¹ ❶ *noun* person who is taught by a teacher.

pupil² *noun* round dark opening in the centre of the eye.

puppet ❶ *noun* 1 small doll or figure moved

pun *noun* 1 = **play on words**, double entendre, quip, witticism

punch¹ *verb* 1 = **hit**, belt (*inf*), bop (*inf*), box, pummel, smash, sock (*sl*), strike, swipe (*inf*) ♦*noun* 2 = **blow**, bop (*inf*), hit, jab, sock (*sl*), swipe (*inf*), wallop (*inf*) 3 *Inf* = **effectiveness**, bite, drive, forcefulness, impact, verve, vigour

punch² *verb* 2 = **pierce**, bore, cut, drill, perforate, prick, puncture, stamp

punctilious *adjective* 1 = **formal**, proper 2 = **particular**, exact, finicky, fussy, meticulous, nice, precise, strict

punctual *adjective* = **on time**, exact, on the dot, precise, prompt, timely OPPOSITE **late**

punctuate *verb* 2 = **interrupt**, break, intersperse, pepper, sprinkle

puncture *noun* 1 a = **hole**, break, cut, damage, leak, nick, opening, slit **b** = **flat tyre**, flat ♦*verb* 2 = **pierce**, bore, cut, nick, penetrate, perforate, prick, rupture

pungent *adjective* = **strong**, acrid, bitter, hot, peppery, piquant, sharp, sour, spicy, tart OPPOSITE **weak**

punish *verb* = **discipline**, castigate, chasten, chastise, correct, penalize, sentence

punishing *adjective* = **hard**, arduous, backbreaking, exhausting, gruelling, strenuous, taxing, tiring, wearing

punishment *noun* = **penalty**, chastening, chastisement, correction, discipline, penance, retribution

punitive *adjective* = **retaliatory**, in reprisal, retaliative

punter *noun* 1 = **gambler**, backer, better 2 = **person**, man in the street

puny *adjective* = **feeble**, frail, little, sickly, stunted, tiny, weak OPPOSITE **strong**

pupil¹ *noun* = **learner**, beginner, disciple,

by strings or by the operator's hand. **2** person or country controlled by another. **puppeteer** *noun*

puppy *noun, pl* **-pies** young dog. **puppy fat** fatty tissue in a child or adolescent, usu. disappearing with maturity.

purchase ❶ *verb* **1** obtain by payment. ♦ *noun* **2** thing that is bought. **3** act of buying. **4** leverage, grip. **purchaser** *noun*

purdah *noun* Muslim and Hindu custom of keeping women in seclusion, with clothing that conceals them completely when they go out.

pure ❶ *adjective* **1** unmixed, untainted. **2** innocent. **3** complete, e.g. *pure delight.* **4** concerned with theory only, e.g. *pure mathematics.* **purely** *adverb* **purity** *noun* **purify** *verb* **-fying, -fied** make or become pure. **purification** *noun* **purist** *noun* person obsessed with strict obedience to the traditions of a subject.

purée [**pure**-ray] *noun* **1** pulp of cooked food. ♦ *verb* **-réeing, -réed 2** make into a purée.

purgatory *noun* **1** place or state of temporary suffering. **2** (**P-**) *RC Church* place where souls of the dead undergo punishment for their sins before being admitted to Heaven. **purgatorial** *adjective*

purge ❶ *verb* **1** rid (a thing or place) of (unwanted things or people). ♦ *noun* **2** purging.

purgative *noun, adjective* (medicine) designed to cause defecation.

Puritan ❶ *noun* **1** *Hist* member of the English Protestant group who wanted simpler church ceremonies. **2** (**p-**) person with strict moral and religious principles. **puritanical** *adjective* **puritanism** *noun*

purl *noun* **1** stitch made by knitting a plain stitch backwards. ♦ *verb* **2** knit in purl.

purlieus [**per**-lyooz] *plural noun Lit* outskirts.

purloin ❶ *verb* steal.

purple *adjective, noun* (of) a colour between red and blue.

purport ❶ *verb* **1** claim (to be or do something). ♦ *noun* **2** apparent meaning, significance.

purpose ❶ *noun* **1** reason for which something is done or exists. **2** determination. **3** practical advantage or use, e.g. *use the time to good purpose.* **purposeful** *adjective* with a definite purpose, determined. **purposely** *adverb* intentionally (also **on purpose**).

purr *verb* **1** (of cats) make low vibrant sound, usu. when pleased. ♦ *noun* **2** this sound.

purse ❶ *noun* **1** small bag for money. **2** *US & Canad* handbag. **3** financial resources. **4** prize money. ♦ *verb* **5** draw (one's lips) together into a small round shape. **purser** *noun* ship's officer who keeps the accounts.

———————— THESAURUS ————————

novice, schoolboy *or* schoolgirl, student OPPOSITE⟩ **teacher**

puppet *noun* **1** = **marionette**, doll **2** = **pawn**, cat's-paw, instrument, mouthpiece, stooge, tool

purchase *verb* **1** = **buy**, acquire, come by, gain, get, obtain, pay for, pick up, score (*sl*) OPPOSITE⟩ **sell** ♦*noun* **2** = **buy**, acquisition, asset, gain, investment, possession, property **4** = **grip**, foothold, hold, leverage, support

pure *adjective* **1 a** = **unmixed**, authentic, flawless, genuine, natural, real, simple, straight, unalloyed OPPOSITE⟩ **mixed**. **b** = **clean**, germ-free, neat, sanitary, spotless, squeaky-clean, sterilized, uncontaminated, unpolluted, untainted, wholesome OPPOSITE⟩ **dirty**. **2** = **innocent**, blameless, chaste, impeccable, modest, squeaky-clean, uncorrupted, unsullied, virginal, virtuous OPPOSITE⟩ **corrupt**. **3** = **complete**, absolute, outright, sheer, thorough, unmitigated, unqualified, utter OPPOSITE⟩ **qualified**

purge *verb* **1** = **get rid of**, do away with, eradicate, expel, exterminate, remove, wipe out ♦*noun* **2** = **removal**, ejection, elimination, eradication, expulsion

purify *verb* **a** = **clean**, clarify, cleanse,

decontaminate, disinfect, refine, sanitize, wash OPPOSITE⟩ **contaminate**. **b** = **absolve**, cleanse, redeem, sanctify OPPOSITE⟩ **taint**

puritan *noun* **2** = **moralist**, fanatic, prude, rigorist, zealot

puritanical *adjective* **2** = **strict**, ascetic, austere, moralistic, narrow-minded, prudish, severe, strait-laced

purity *noun* **1** = **cleanness**, cleanliness, immaculateness, pureness, wholesomeness OPPOSITE⟩ **contamination**. **2** = **innocence**, chastity, decency, honesty, integrity, virginity, virtue OPPOSITE⟩ **impurity**

purloin *verb* = **steal**, appropriate, filch, nick (*sl, chiefly Brit*), pilfer, pinch (*inf*), swipe (*sl*), thieve

purport *verb* **1** = **claim**, allege, assert, profess ♦*noun* **2** = **significance**, drift, gist, idea, implication, import, meaning

purpose *noun* **1 a** = **aim**, ambition, desire, end, goal, hope, intention, object, plan, wish **b** = **reason**, aim, idea, intention, object, point **2** = **determination**, firmness, persistence, resolution, resolve, single-mindedness, tenacity, will

purposely *adverb* (also **on purpose**) = **deliberately**, consciously, expressly,

pursue ● *verb* **1** chase. **2** follow (a goal). **3** engage in. **4** continue to discuss or ask about (something). **pursuer** *noun* **pursuit** *noun* **1** pursuing. **2** occupation or pastime.

SPELLING TIP

The misspelling *persue* is very common, occurring in the Bank of English 52 times. It should, of course, be spelt with a *u* in each half of the word, as in **pursuing** and **pursued**.

---

purulent [**pure**-yoo-lent] *adjective* of or containing pus.

purvey ● *verb* supply (provisions). **purveyor** *noun*

purview *noun* scope or range of activity or outlook.

pus *noun* yellowish matter produced by infected tissue.

push ● *verb* **1** move or try to move by steady force. **2** drive or spur (oneself or another person) to do something. **3** *Informal* sell (drugs) illegally. ◆ *noun* **4** act of pushing. **5** drive or determination. **6** special effort. **the push** *Slang* dismissal from a job or relationship. **pusher** *noun* person who sells illegal drugs. **pushy** *adjective* **pushier, pushiest** too assertive or

ambitious. **push-bike** *noun Informal* bicycle. **pushchair** *noun* folding chair on wheels for a baby. **pushover** *noun Informal* **1** something easily achieved. **2** person or team easily taken advantage of or defeated.

pusillanimous *adjective* timid and cowardly. **pusillanimity** *noun*

puss, pussy *noun, pl* **pusses, pussies** *Informal* cat.

pussyfoot ● *verb Informal* **1** move about stealthily. **2** behave too cautiously.

pustule *noun* pimple containing pus.

put ● *verb* **putting, put** **1** cause to be (in a position, state, or place). **2** estimate or judge. **3** express. **4** throw (the shot) in the shot put. ◆ *noun* **5** throw in putting the shot. **put about** *verb* make widely known. **put across** *verb* express successfully. **put down** *verb* **1** make a written record of. **2** repress (a rebellion). **3** put (an animal) to death. **4** *Slang* belittle or humiliate. **put-down** *noun* cruelly crushing remark. **put off** *verb* **1** postpone. **2** evade (a person) by delay. **3** disconcert. **4** repel. **put out** *verb* annoy or anger. **put over** *verb Informal* communicate (facts or information). **put up** *verb* **1** erect. **3** offer. **4** nominate. **put up with** *verb* tolerate. **put-upon** *adjective* taken advantage of.

putative [**pew**-tat-iv] *adjective* reputed, supposed.

——————— THESAURUS ———————

P

intentionally, knowingly, with intent

purse *noun* **1** = **pouch**, money-bag, wallet **3** = **money**, exchequer, funds, lolly (*Aust & NZ inf*), means, resources, treasury, wealth ◆*verb* **5** = **pucker**, contract, pout, press together, tighten

pursue *verb* **1** = **follow**, chase, dog, hound, hunt, hunt down, run after, shadow, stalk, tail (*inf*), track OPPOSITE▷ **avoid**. **2** = **try for**, aim for, desire, seek, strive for, work towards OPPOSITE▷ **eschew**. **3** = **engage in**, carry on, conduct, perform, practise **4** = **continue**, carry on, keep on, maintain, persevere in, persist in, proceed

pursuit *noun* **1** = **pursuing**, chase, hunt, quest, search, seeking, trailing **2** = **occupation**, activity, hobby, interest, line, pastime, pleasure

purvey *verb* = **supply**, cater, deal in, furnish, provide, sell, trade in

push *verb* **1** = **shove**, depress, drive, press, propel, ram, thrust OPPOSITE▷ **pull**. **2** = **urge**, encourage, gee up, hurry, impel, incite, persuade, press, spur OPPOSITE▷ **discourage** ◆*noun* **4** = **shove**, butt, nudge, thrust OPPOSITE▷ **pull**. **5** = **drive**, ambition, dynamism, energy,

enterprise, go (*inf*), initiative, vigour, vitality **the push** *Sl* = **dismissal**, discharge, one's cards (*inf*), the boot (*sl*), the sack (*inf*)

pushover *noun Inf* **1** = **piece of cake** (*Brit inf*), breeze (*US & Canad inf*), child's play (*inf*), cinch (*sl*), doddle (*Brit sl*), picnic (*inf*), plain sailing, walkover (*inf*) OPPOSITE▷ **challenge**. **2** = **sucker** (*sl*), easy game (*inf*), easy *or* soft mark (*inf*), mug (*Brit sl*), soft touch (*sl*), walkover (*inf*)

pushy *adjective* **2** = **forceful**, ambitious, assertive, bold, brash, bumptious, obtrusive, presumptuous, self-assertive

pussyfoot *verb Inf* **2** = **hedge**, beat about the bush, be noncommittal, equivocate, flannel (*Brit inf*), hum and haw, prevaricate, sit on the fence

put *verb* **1** = **place**, deposit, lay, position, rest, set, settle, situate **3** = **express**, phrase, state, utter, word **4** = **throw**, cast, fling, heave, hurl, lob, pitch, toss

put down *verb* **1** = **record**, enter, set down, take down, write down **2** = **repress**, crush, quash, quell, stamp out, suppress **3** = **put to sleep**, destroy, do away with, put out of its misery **4** *Sl* = **humiliate**, disparage, mortify, shame, slight, snub

putrid ❶ *adjective* rotten and foul-smelling.
putrefy *verb* **-fying, -fied** rot and produce an offensive smell. **putrefaction** *noun* **putrescent** *adjective* rotting.
putsch *noun* sudden violent attempt to remove a government from power.
putt *Golf noun* **1** stroke on the putting green to roll the ball into or near the hole. ◆ *verb* **2** strike (the ball) in this way. **putter** *noun* golf club for putting. **putting green** *Golf* area of closely mown grass around the hole.
putty *noun* paste used to fix glass into frames and fill cracks in woodwork.
puzzle ❶ *verb* **1** perplex and confuse or be perplexed or confused. ◆ *noun* **2** problem that cannot be easily solved. **3** toy, game, or question that requires skill or ingenuity to solve. **puzzlement** *noun* **puzzled** *adjective* **puzzling** *adjective*
PVC polyvinyl chloride: plastic material used in clothes etc.
Pygmy *noun, pl* **-mies 1** member of one of the very short peoples of Equatorial Africa. **2** (**p-**) very small person or thing. ◆ *adjective* **3** (**p-**) very small.

pygmy *adjective* **1** very small. ◆ *noun, pl* **-mies** very small person or thing.
pyjamas *plural noun* loose-fitting trousers and top worn in bed.
pylon *noun* steel tower-like structure supporting electrical cables.
pyorrhoea [pire-**ree**-a] *noun* disease of the gums and tooth sockets which causes bleeding of the gums and the formation of pus.
pyramid *noun* **1** solid figure with a flat base and triangular sides sloping upwards to a point. **2** building of this shape, esp. an ancient Egyptian one. **pyramidal** *adjective*
pyre *noun* pile of wood for burning a corpse on.
Pyrex *noun* ® heat-resistant glassware.
pyromania *noun* uncontrollable urge to set things on fire. **pyromaniac** *noun*
pyrotechnics *noun* **1** art of making fireworks. **2** firework display. **pyrotechnic** *adjective*
Pyrrhic victory [**pir**-ik] *noun* victory in which the victor's losses are as great as those of the defeated.
python *noun* large nonpoisonous snake that crushes its prey.

——————— T H E S A U R U S ———————

put off *verb* **1** = **postpone**, defer, delay, hold over, put on the back burner (*inf*), take a rain check on (*US & Canad inf*) **3** = **disconcert**, confuse, discomfit, dismay, faze, nonplus, perturb, throw (*inf*), unsettle **4** = **discourage**, dishearten, dissuade
putrid *adjective* = **rotten**, bad, decayed, decomposed, off, putrefied, rancid, rotting, spoiled
put up *verb* **1** = **build**, construct, erect, fabricate, raise **2** = **accommodate**, board,

house, lodge, take in **3** = **submit**, offer, present **4** = **nominate**, propose, put forward, recommend **put up with** = **stand**, abide, bear, endure, stand for, swallow, take, tolerate
puzzle *verb* **1** = **perplex**, baffle, bewilder, confound, confuse, mystify, stump ◆*noun* **2, 3** = **problem**, conundrum, enigma, mystery, paradox, poser, question, riddle
puzzling *adjective* = **perplexing**, abstruse, baffling, bewildering, enigmatic, incomprehensible, involved, mystifying

P

Qq

QC Queen's Counsel.
QED which was to be shown or proved.
QLD Queensland.
QM Quartermaster.
qr. 1 quarter. **2** quire.
qt. quart.
q.t. *noun* **on the q.t.** *Informal* secretly.
qua [kwah] *preposition* in the capacity of.
quack¹ *verb* **1** (of a duck) utter a harsh
guttural sound. **2** make a noise like a duck. ◆
noun **3** sound made by a duck.
quack² ⊕ *noun* **1** unqualified person who
claims medical knowledge. **2** *Informal* doctor.
quad *noun* **1** see QUADRANGLE (sense 1). **2**
Informal quadruplet. ◆ *adjective* **3** short for
QUADRAPHONIC. **quad bike** vehicle like a small
motorcycle with four large wheels, designed for
agricultural and sporting uses.
quadrangle *noun* **1** (also **quad**) rectangular
courtyard with buildings on all four sides. **2**
geometric figure consisting of four points
connected by four lines. **quadrangular**
adjective
quadrant *noun* **1** quarter of a circle. **2** quarter
of a circle's circumference. **3** instrument for
measuring the altitude of the stars.
quadraphonic *adjective* using four
independent channels to reproduce or record
sound.
quadratic *Maths noun* **1** equation in which
the variable is raised to the power of two, but
nowhere raised to a higher power. ◆ *adjective* **2**
of the second power.

quadrennial *adjective* **1** occurring every four
years. **2** lasting four years.
quadri- *combining form* four, e.g. *quadrilateral*.
quadrilateral *adjective* **1** having four sides. ◆
noun **2** polygon with four sides.
quadrille *noun* square dance for four couples.
quadriplegia *noun* paralysis of all four limbs.
quadriplegic *adjective*
quadruped [kwod-roo-ped] *noun* any animal
with four legs.
quadruple *verb* **1** multiply by four. ◆ *adjective*
2 four times as much or as many. **3** consisting
of four parts.
quadruplet *noun* one of four offspring born
at one birth.
quaff ⊕ [kwoff] *verb* drink heartily or in one
draught.
quagga *noun, pl* **-ga, -gas** recently extinct
zebra, striped only on the head and shoulders.
quagmire ⊕ [kwog-mire] *noun* soft wet area
of land.
quail¹ *noun, pl* **quail, quails** small game bird
of the partridge family.
quail² ⊕ *verb* shrink back with fear.
quaint ⊕ *adjective* attractively unusual, esp. in
an old-fashioned style. **quaintly** *adverb*
quake ⊕ *verb* **1** shake or tremble with or as if
with fear. ◆ *noun* **2** *Informal* earthquake.
Quaker *noun* member of a Christian sect, the
Society of Friends. **Quakerism** *noun*
qualify ⊕ *verb* **-fying, -fied 1** provide or be
provided with the abilities necessary for a task,
office, or duty. **2** moderate or restrict (a

THESAURUS

quack² *noun* **1 = charlatan**, fake, fraud,
humbug, impostor, mountebank, phoney *or*
phony (*inf*)
quaff *verb* **= drink**, down, gulp, imbibe,
swallow, swig (*inf*)
quagmire *noun* **= bog**, fen, marsh, mire,
morass, quicksand, slough, swamp, muskeg
(*Canad*)
quail² *verb* **= shrink**, blanch, blench, cower,
cringe, falter, flinch, have cold feet (*inf*), recoil,
shudder
quaint *adjective* **= old-fashioned**, antiquated,
old-world, picturesque OPPOSITE **new**

quake *verb* **1 = shake**, move, quiver, rock,
shiver, shudder, tremble, vibrate
qualification *noun* **2 = attribute**, ability,
aptitude, capability, eligibility, fitness, quality,
skill, suitability **3 = condition**, caveat, limitation,
modification, proviso, requirement, reservation,
rider, stipulation
qualified *adjective* **1 = capable**, able, adept,
competent, efficient, experienced, expert, fit,
practised, proficient, skilful, trained OPPOSITE
amateur. 2 = restricted, bounded, conditional,
confined, contingent, limited, modified,
provisional, reserved OPPOSITE **outright**

statement). **3** be classified as, e.g. *their romance hardly qualifies as news.* **4** reach the later stages of a competition, as by being successful in earlier rounds. **5** *Grammar* modify the sense of a word. **qualified** *adjective* **qualifier** *noun* **qualification** *noun* **1** official record of achievement in a course or examination. **2** quality or skill needed for a particular activity. **3** condition that modifies or limits. **4** act of qualifying.

quality ⊕ *noun, pl* **-ties 1** degree or standard of excellence. **2** distinguishing characteristic or attribute. **3** basic character or nature of something. ♦ *adjective* **4** excellent or superior. **5** (of a newspaper) concentrating on detailed and serious accounts of the news, business affairs and the arts. **qualitative** *adjective* of or relating to quality. **quality control** checking of the relative quality of products, usu. by testing samples.

qualm ⊕ [kwahm] *noun* **1** pang of conscience. **2** sudden sensation of misgiving.

quandary ⊕ *noun, pl* **-ries** difficult situation or dilemma.

quandong [kwon-dong] *noun* **1** small Australian tree with edible fruit and nuts used in preserves. **2** Australian tree with pale timber.

quango *noun, pl* **-gos** quasi-autonomous nongovernmental organization: any partly independent official body set up by a government.

quanta *noun* plural of QUANTUM.

quantify *verb* **-fying, -fied** discover or express the quantity of. **quantifiable** *adjective* **quantification** *noun*

quantity ⊕ *noun, pl* **-ties 1** specified or definite amount or number. **2** aspect of anything that can be measured, weighed, or counted. **3** large amount. **quantitative** *adjective* of or relating to quantity. **quantity**

surveyor person who estimates the cost of the materials and labour necessary for a construction job.

quantum *noun, pl* **-ta 1** desired or required amount, esp. a very small one. **2** *Physics* smallest amount of some physical property, such as energy, that a system can possess. **quantum leap, jump** *Informal* sudden large change, increase, or advance. **quantum theory** physics theory based on the idea that energy of electrons is discharged in discrete quanta.

quarantine *noun* **1** period of isolation of people or animals to prevent the spread of disease. ♦ *verb* **2** isolate in or as if in quarantine.

quark *noun Physics* subatomic particle thought to be the fundamental unit of matter.

quarrel ⊕ *noun* **1** angry disagreement. **2** cause of dispute. ♦ *verb* **-relling, -relled 3** have a disagreement or dispute. **quarrelsome** *adjective*

quarry[1] *noun, pl* **-ries 1** place where stone is dug from the surface of the earth. ♦ *verb* **-rying, -ried 2** extract (stone) from a quarry.

quarry[2] ⊕ *noun, pl* **-ries** person or animal that is being hunted.

quart *noun* unit of liquid measure equal to two pints.

quarter ⊕ *noun* **1** one of four equal parts of something. **2** fourth part of a year. **3** *Informal* unit of weight equal to 4 ounces. **4** region or district of a town or city. **5** *US* 25-cent piece. **6** mercy or pity, as shown towards a defeated opponent. **7** either of two phases of the moon when it appears as a semicircle. **8** (sometimes pl) unspecified people or group of people, e.g. *the highest quarters.* ♦ *plural* **9** lodgings. ♦ *verb* **10** divide into four equal parts. **11** billet or be billeted in lodgings. **quarterly** *adjective* **1** occurring, due, or issued at intervals of three months. ♦ *noun, pl* **-lies 2** magazine issued

—————— THESAURUS ——————

qualify *verb* **1** = **certify**, empower, equip, fit, permit, prepare, ready, train OPPOSITE> prevent. **2** = **moderate**, diminish, ease, lessen, limit, reduce, regulate, restrain, restrict, soften, temper

quality *noun* **1** = **excellence**, calibre, distinction, grade, merit, position, rank, standing, status **2** = **characteristic**, aspect, attribute, condition, feature, mark, property, trait **3** = **nature**, character, kind, make, sort

qualm *noun* **1** = **compunction**, scruple, twinge or pang of conscience **2** = **misgiving**, anxiety, apprehension, disquiet, doubt, hesitation, uneasiness

quandary *noun* = **difficulty**, cleft stick,

dilemma, impasse, plight, predicament, puzzle, strait

quantity *noun* **1** = **amount**, lot, number, part, sum, total **2** = **size**, bulk, capacity, extent, length, magnitude, mass, measure, volume

quarrel *noun* **1** = **disagreement**, argument, brawl, breach, contention, controversy, dispute, dissension, feud, fight, row, squabble, tiff OPPOSITE> agreement ♦*verb* **3** = **disagree**, argue, bicker, brawl, clash, differ, dispute, fall out (*inf*), fight, row, squabble OPPOSITE> agree

quarrelsome *adjective* = **argumentative**, belligerent, combative, contentious, disputatious, pugnacious

quarry[2] *noun* = **prey**, aim, game, goal,

Q

every three months. ◆ *adverb* **3** once every three months. **quarterback** *noun* player in American football who directs attacking play. **quarter day** any of the four days in the year when certain payments become due. **quarterdeck** *noun Naut* rear part of the upper deck of a ship. **quarterfinal** *noun* round before the semifinal in a competition. **quarterlight** *noun* small triangular window in the door of a car. **quartermaster** *noun* military officer responsible for accommodation, food, and equipment.

quartet *noun* **1** group of four performers. **2** music for such a group. **3** any group of four people or things.

quarto *noun, pl* **-tos** book size in which the sheets are folded into four leaves.

quartz *noun* hard glossy mineral. **quartz clock, watch** very accurate clock or watch operated by a vibrating crystal of quartz.

quasar [**kway**-zar] *noun* extremely distant starlike object that emits powerful radio waves.

quash ⊕ *verb* **1** annul or make void. **2** subdue forcefully and completely.

quasi- [**kway**-zie] *combining form* almost but not really, e.g. *quasi-religious; a quasi-scholar*.

quassia [**kwosh**-a] *noun* tropical American tree, the wood of which yields a substance used in insecticides.

quaternary *adjective* having four parts.

quatrain *noun* stanza or poem of four lines.

quatrefoil *noun* **1** leaf composed of four leaflets. **2** *Archit* carved ornament having four arcs arranged about a common centre.

quaver ⊕ *verb* **1** (of a voice) quiver or tremble. ◆ *noun* **2** *Music* note half the length of

a crotchet. **3** tremulous sound or note.

quay [**kee**] *noun* wharf built parallel to the shore.

queasy ⊕ *adjective* **-sier, -siest 1** having the feeling that one is about to vomit. **2** feeling or causing uneasiness. **queasily** *adverb* **queasiness** *noun*

queen ⊕ *noun* **1** female sovereign who is the official ruler or head of state. **2** wife of a king. **3** woman, place, or thing considered to be the best of her or its kind. **4** *Slang* effeminate male homosexual. **5** only fertile female in a colony of bees, wasps, or ants. **6** the most powerful piece in chess. **queen it** *Informal* behave in an overbearing manner. **queenly** *adjective* **Queen Mother** widow of a former king who is also the mother of the current monarch. **Queen's Counsel** barrister or advocate appointed Counsel to the Crown.

Queensberry rules *plural noun* **1** code of rules followed in modern boxing. **2** *Informal* gentlemanly conduct, esp. in a dispute.

queer ⊕ *adjective* **1** not normal or usual. **2** dubious or suspicious. **3** faint, giddy, or queasy. **4** *Offens* homosexual. ◆ *noun* **5** *Offens* homosexual. **queer someone's pitch** *Informal* spoil someone's chances of something. **in queer street** *Informal* in debt or facing bankruptcy.

quell ⊕ *verb* **1** suppress. **2** overcome.

quench ⊕ *verb* **1** satisfy (one's thirst). **2** put out or extinguish.

quern *noun* stone hand mill for grinding corn.

querulous ⊕ [**kwer**-yoo-luss] *adjective* complaining or whining. **querulously** *adverb*

query ⊕ *noun, pl* **-ries 1** question, esp. one

Q

——————— THESAURUS ———————

objective, prize, victim

quarter *noun* **4** = **district**, area, locality, neighbourhood, part, place, province, region, side, zone **6** = **mercy**, clemency, compassion, forgiveness, leniency, pity ◆*plural* **9** = **lodgings**, abode, barracks, billet, chambers, dwelling, habitation, residence, rooms ◆*verb* **11** = **accommodate**, billet, board, house, lodge, place, post, station

quash *verb* **1** = **annul**, cancel, invalidate, overrule, overthrow, rescind, reverse, revoke **2** = **suppress**, beat, crush, overthrow, put down, quell, repress, squash, subdue

quasi- *combining form* = **pseudo-**, apparent, seeming, semi-, so-called, would-be

quaver *verb* **1** = **tremble**, flicker, flutter, quake, quiver, shake, vibrate, waver ◆*noun* **3** = **trembling**, quiver, shake, tremble, tremor, vibration

queasy *adjective* **1** = **sick**, bilious, green around the gills (*inf*), ill, nauseated, off colour, squeamish, upset **2** = **uneasy**, anxious, fidgety, ill at ease, restless, troubled, uncertain, worried

queen *noun* **1** = **sovereign**, consort, monarch, ruler **3** = **ideal**, model, star

queer *adjective* **1** = **strange**, abnormal, curious, droll, extraordinary, funny, munted (*NZ sl*), odd, peculiar, uncommon, unusual, weird OPPOSITE normal. **3** = **faint**, dizzy, giddy, light-headed, queasy

quell *verb* **1, 2** = **suppress**, conquer, crush, defeat, overcome, overpower, put down, quash, subdue, vanquish

quench *verb* **1** = **satisfy**, allay, appease, sate, satiate, slake **2** = **put out**, crush, douse, extinguish, smother, stifle, suppress

querulous *adjective* = **complaining**, captious, carping, critical, discontented, dissatisfied,

DICTIONARY

raising doubt. **2** question mark. ♦ *verb* **-rying, -ried 3** express uncertainty, doubt, or an objection concerning (something).
quest ⊕ *noun* **1** long and difficult search. ♦ *verb* **2** (foll. by *for* or *after*) go in search of.
question ⊕ *noun* **1** form of words addressed to a person in order to obtain an answer. **2** point at issue. **3** difficulty or uncertainty. ♦ *verb* **4** put a question or questions to (a person). **5** express uncertainty about. **in question** under discussion. **out of the question** impossible. **questionable** *adjective* of disputable value or authority. **questionably** *adverb* **questionnaire** *noun* set of questions on a form, used to collect information from people. **question mark 1** punctuation mark (?) written at the end of questions. **2** a doubt or uncertainty, e.g. *a question mark still hangs over their success.* **question master** chairman of a radio or television quiz or panel game. **question time** (in a parliament) period when MPs can question government ministers.

SPELLING TIP

There are 28 occurrences of the misspelling *questionaire* (with only one *n*), in the Bank of English. The correct spelling, **questionnaire**, has two *ns*, and appears in the Bank of English over 3000 times.

---

queue ⊕ *noun* **1** line of people or vehicles

waiting for something. ♦ *verb* **queuing** or **queueing, queued 2** (often foll. by *up*) form or remain in a line while waiting.
quibble ⊕ *verb* **1** make trivial objections. ♦ *noun* **2** trivial objection.
quiche [keesh] *noun* savoury flan with an egg custard filling to which vegetables etc. are added.
quick ⊕ *adjective* **1** speedy, fast. **2** lasting or taking a short time. **3** alert and responsive. **4** easily excited or aroused. ♦ *noun* **5** area of sensitive flesh under a nail. ♦ *adverb* **6** *Informal* in a rapid manner. **cut someone to the quick** hurt someone's feelings deeply. **quickly** *adverb* **quicken** *verb* **1** make or become faster. **2** make or become more lively. **3** (of a fetus) reach the stage of development where its movements can be felt. **quickie** *noun Informal* anything done or made hurriedly. **quicklime** *noun* white solid used in the manufacture of glass and steel.
quicksand *noun* deep mass of loose wet sand that sucks anything on top of it into it.
quicksilver *noun* mercury. **quickstep** *noun* fast modern ballroom dance.
quid[1] *noun, pl* **quid** *Brit slang* pound (sterling).
quid[2] *noun* piece of tobacco for chewing.
quid pro quo *noun, pl* **quid pro quos** one thing, esp. an advantage or object, given in exchange for another.
quiescent [kwee-**ess**-ent] *adjective* quiet, inactive, or dormant. **quiescence** *noun*
quiet ⊕ *adjective* **1** with little noise. **2** calm or tranquil. **3** untroubled. **4** private or low-key. ♦ *noun* **5** quietness. ♦ *verb* **6** make or become

---

THESAURUS

fault-finding, grumbling, peevish, whining
query *noun* **1** = **question**, doubt, inquiry, objection, problem, suspicion ♦*verb* **3** = **doubt**, challenge, disbelieve, dispute, distrust, mistrust, question, suspect
quest *noun* **1** = **search**, adventure, crusade, enterprise, expedition, fossick (*Aust & NZ*), hunt, journey, mission
question *noun* **2** = **issue**, motion, point, point at issue, proposal, proposition, subject, theme, topic **3** = **difficulty**, argument, contention, controversy, dispute, doubt, problem, query ♦*verb* **4** = **ask**, cross-examine, examine, inquire, interrogate, interview, probe, quiz OPPOSITE answer. **5** = **dispute**, challenge, disbelieve, doubt, mistrust, oppose, query, suspect OPPOSITE accept ♦ **in question** = **under discussion**, at issue, in doubt, open to debate **out of the question** = **impossible**, inconceivable, unthinkable
questionable *adjective* = **dubious**,

controversial, debatable, dodgy (*Brit, Aust & NZ inf*), doubtful, iffy (*inf*), moot, suspect, suspicious
queue *noun* **1** = **line**, chain, file, sequence, series, string, train
quibble *verb* **1** = **split hairs**, carp, cavil ♦*noun* **2** = **objection**, cavil, complaint, criticism, nicety, niggle
quick *adjective* **1** = **fast**, brisk, express, fleet, hasty, rapid, speedy, swift OPPOSITE **slow. 2** = **brief**, cursory, hasty, hurried, perfunctory **3** = **intelligent**, acute, alert, astute, bright (*inf*), clever, perceptive, quick-witted, sharp, shrewd, smart **4** = **excitable**, irascible, irritable, passionate, testy, touchy
quicken *verb* **1** = **speed**, accelerate, expedite, hasten, hurry, impel, precipitate **2** = **invigorate**, arouse, energize, excite, incite, inspire, revive, stimulate, vitalize
quickly *adverb* **1** = **swiftly**, abruptly, apace, briskly, fast, hastily, hurriedly, promptly, pronto

quiet. **on the quiet** without other people knowing, secretly. **quietly** *adverb* **quietness** *noun* **quieten** *verb* (often foll. by *down*) make or become quiet. **quietude** *noun* quietness, peace, or tranquillity.

quietism *noun* passivity and calmness of mind towards external events. **quietist** *noun, adjective*

quietus *noun* **1** release from life; death. **2** discharge or settlement of debts or duties.

quiff *noun* tuft of hair brushed up above the forehead.

quill *noun* **1** pen made from the feather of a bird's wing or tail. **2** stiff hollow spine of a hedgehog or porcupine. **3** large stiff feather in a bird's wing or tail.

quilt ❶ *noun* padded covering for a bed.

quilted *adjective* consisting of two layers of fabric with a layer of soft material between them.

quin *noun* short for QUINTUPLET.

quince *noun* acid-tasting pear-shaped fruit.

quinine *noun* bitter drug used as a tonic and formerly to treat malaria.

quinquennial *adjective* **1** occurring every five years. **2** lasting five years.

quinquereme *noun* ancient Roman galley with five banks of oars.

quinsy *noun* inflammation of the throat or tonsils.

quintessence ❶ *noun* most perfect representation of a quality or state. **quintessential** *adjective*

quintet *noun* **1** group of five performers. **2** music for such a group.

quintuple *verb* **1** multiply by five. ◆ *adjective* **2** five times as much or as many. **3** consisting of five parts. ◆ *noun* **4** quantity or number five times as great as another.

quintuplet *noun* one of five offspring born at one birth.

quip ❶ *noun* **1** witty saying. ◆ *verb* **quipping, quipped 2** make a quip.

quire *noun* set of 24 or 25 sheets of paper.

quirk ❶ *noun* **1** peculiarity of character. **2** unexpected twist or turn, e.g. *a quirk of fate*.

quirky *adjective* **quirkier, quirkiest**

quisling *noun* traitor who aids an occupying enemy force.

quit ❶ *verb* **quitting, quit 1** stop (doing something). **2** give up (a job). **3** depart from.

quitter *noun* person who lacks perseverance.

quits *adjective Informal* on an equal footing.

quite ❶ *adverb* **1** somewhat, e.g. *she's quite pretty*. **2** absolutely, e.g. *you're quite right*. **3** in actuality, truly. ◆ *interjection* **4** expression of agreement.

quiver¹ ❶ *verb* **1** shake with a tremulous movement. ◆ *noun* **2** shaking or trembling.

quiver² *noun* case for arrows.

quixotic ❶ [kwik-**sot**-ik] *adjective* romantic and unrealistic. **quixotically** *adverb*

quiz ❶ *noun, pl* **quizzes 1** entertainment in which the knowledge of the players is tested by a series of questions. ◆ *verb* **quizzing, quizzed 2** investigate by close questioning. **quizzical**

—————— T H E S A U R U S ——————

Q

(*inf*), rapidly, soon, speedily

quiet *adjective* **1 = silent**, hushed, inaudible, low, noiseless, peaceful, soft, soundless OPPOSITE **loud**. **2, 3 = calm**, mild, peaceful, placid, restful, serene, smooth, tranquil OPPOSITE **noisy**. **4 = undisturbed**, isolated, private, secluded, sequestered, unfrequented ◆*noun* **5 = peace**, calmness, ease, quietness, repose, rest, serenity, silence, stillness, tranquillity

quieten *verb* (often foll. by *down*) **= silence**, compose, hush, muffle, mute, quell, quiet, stifle, still, stop, subdue OPPOSITE **upset**

quietly *adverb* **1 = silently**, in an undertone, inaudibly, in silence, mutely, noiselessly, softly **2 = calmly**, mildly, patiently, placidly, serenely

quilt *noun* **= bedspread**, continental quilt, counterpane, coverlet, duvet, eiderdown

quintessence *noun* **= essence**, distillation, soul, spirit

quintessential *adjective* **= ultimate**, archetypal, definitive, typical

quip *noun* **1 = joke**, gibe, jest, pleasantry, retort, riposte, sally, wisecrack (*inf*), witticism

quirk *noun* **1 = peculiarity**, aberration, characteristic, eccentricity, foible, habit, idiosyncrasy, kink, mannerism, oddity, trait

quirky *adjective* **1 = odd**, eccentric, idiosyncratic, offbeat, peculiar, unusual

quit *verb* **1 = stop**, abandon, cease, discontinue, drop, end, give up, halt OPPOSITE **continue**. **2 = resign**, abdicate, go, leave, pull out, retire, step down (*inf*) **3 = depart**, go, leave, pull out

quite *adverb* **1 = somewhat**, fairly, moderately, rather, reasonably, relatively **2 = absolutely**, completely, entirely, fully, perfectly, totally, wholly **3 = truly**, in fact, in reality, in truth, really

quiver¹ *verb* **1 = shake**, oscillate, quake, quaver, shiver, shudder, tremble, vibrate ◆*noun* **2 = shake**, oscillation, shiver, shudder, tremble, tremor, vibration

quixotic *adjective* **= unrealistic**, dreamy,

adjective questioning and mocking, e.g. *a quizzical look.* **quizzically** *adverb*

quod *noun Brit slang* jail.

quoin *noun* **1** external corner of a building. **2** small wedge.

quoit *noun* **1** large ring used in the game of quoits. ◆ *plural* **2** game in which quoits are tossed at a stake in the ground in attempts to encircle it.

quondam *adjective Formal* of an earlier time; former.

quorum *noun* minimum number of people required to be present at a meeting before any transactions can take place. **quorate** *adjective* having or being a quorum.

quota ❶ *noun* **1** share that is due from, due to, or allocated to a group or person. **2** prescribed number or quantity allowed, required, or admitted.

quote ❶ *verb* **1** repeat (words) exactly from (an earlier work, speech, or conversation). **2** state (a price) for goods or a job of work. ◆ *noun* **3** *Informal* quotation. **quotable** *adjective*

quotation *noun* **1** written or spoken passage repeated exactly in a later work, speech, or conversation. **2** act of quoting. **3** estimate of costs submitted by a contractor to a prospective client. **quotation marks** raised commas used in writing to mark the beginning and end of a quotation or passage of speech.

quoth *verb Obs* said.

quotidian *adjective* **1** daily. **2** commonplace.

quotient *noun* result of the division of one number or quantity by another.

Quran *noun* same as KORAN.

q.v. which see: used to refer a reader to another item in the same book.

qwerty, QWERTY keyboard *noun* standard English language typewriter or computer keyboard.

———————— THESAURUS ————————

fanciful, idealistic, impractical, romantic

quiz *noun* **1** = **examination**, investigation, questioning, test ◆*verb* **2** = **question**, ask, examine, interrogate, investigate

quizzical *adjective* = **mocking**, arch, questioning, sardonic, teasing

quota *noun* **1** = **share**, allowance, assignment, part, portion, ration, slice, whack (*inf*)

quotation *noun* **1** = **passage**, citation, excerpt, extract, quote (*inf*), reference **3** = **estimate**, charge, cost, figure, price, quote (*inf*), rate, tender

quote *verb* **1** = **repeat**, cite, detail, instance, name, recall, recite, recollect, refer to

Q

Rr

r 1 radius. **2** ratio. **3** right.

R 1 Queen. **2** King. **3** River.

Ra *Chem* radium.

RA 1 Royal Academy. **2** Royal Artillery.

rabbi [rab-bye] *noun, pl* **-bis** Jewish spiritual leader. **rabbinical** *adjective*

rabbit *noun* small burrowing mammal with long ears. **rabbit on** *verb* **rabbiting, rabbited** *Informal* talk too much.

rabble ⊕ *noun* disorderly crowd of noisy people. **rabble-rouser** *noun* person who stirs up the feelings of the mob.

Rabelaisian *adjective* characterized by broad, often bawdy humour and sharp satire.

rabid ⊕ *adjective* **1** fanatical. **2** having rabies. **rabidly** *adverb*

rabies [ray-beez] *noun* usu. fatal viral disease transmitted by dogs and certain other animals.

RAC Royal Automobile Club.

raccoon *noun* small N American mammal with a long striped tail.

race¹ ⊕ *noun* **1** contest of speed. **2** any competition or rivalry, e.g. *the arms race*. **3** rapid current or channel. ♦ *plural* **4** meeting for horse racing. ♦ *verb* **5** compete with in a race. **6** run swiftly. **7** (of an engine) run faster than normal. **racer** *noun* **racecourse** *noun* **racehorse** *noun* **racetrack** *noun*

race² ⊕ *noun* group of people of common ancestry with distinguishing physical features, such as skin colour. **racial** *adjective* **racism, racialism** *noun* hostile attitude or behaviour to members of other races, based on a belief in the innate superiority of one's own race. **racist, racialist** *adjective, noun*

raceme [rass-**eem**] *noun* cluster of flowers along a central stem, as in the foxglove.

rack¹ ⊕ *noun* **1** framework for holding particular articles, such as coats or luggage. **2** straight bar with teeth on its edge, to work with a cogwheel. **3** *Hist* instrument of torture that stretched the victim's body. ♦ *verb* **4** cause great suffering to. **rack one's brains** try very hard to remember.

rack² *noun* **go to rack and ruin** be destroyed.

racket¹ ⊕ *noun* **1** noisy disturbance. **2** occupation by which money is made illegally. **3** *Slang* business or occupation. ♦ *verb* **-eting, -eted 4** (often foll. by *about* or *around*) make a commotion.

racket², racquet *noun* bat with strings stretched in an oval frame, used in tennis etc.

rackets *noun* ball game played in a paved walled court.

racketeer *noun* person making illegal profits. **racketeering** *noun*

raconteur [rak-on-**tur**] *noun* skilled storyteller.

racoon *noun* same as RACCOON.

racy ⊕ *adjective* **racier, raciest 1** slightly shocking. **2** spirited or lively. **racily** *adverb*

radar *noun* device for tracking distant objects by bouncing high-frequency radio pulses off them.

raddled *adjective* (of a person) unkempt or run-down in appearance.

radial *adjective* **1** spreading out from a common central point. **2** of a radius. **3** (also **radial-ply**) (of a tyre) having flexible sides strengthened with radial cords.

radian *noun* unit for measuring angles, equal

THESAURUS

rabble *noun* =**mob**, canaille, crowd, herd, horde, swarm, throng OPPOSITE **upper classes**

rabid *adjective* **1** =**fanatical**, extreme, fervent, irrational, narrow-minded, zealous OPPOSITE **moderate. 2** =**mad**, hydrophobic

race¹ *noun* **1, 2** =**contest**, chase, competition, dash, pursuit, rivalry ♦*verb* **5** =**compete**, contest, run **6** =**run**, career, dart, dash, fly, gallop, hurry, speed, tear, zoom

race² *noun* =**people**, blood, folk, nation, stock, tribe, type

racial *adjective* =**ethnic**, ethnological, folk, genealogical, genetic, national, tribal

rack¹ *noun* **1** =**frame**, framework, stand, structure ♦*verb* **4** =**torture**, afflict, agonize, crucify, harrow, oppress, pain, torment

racket¹ *noun* **1** =**noise**, clamour, din, disturbance, fuss, outcry, pandemonium, row **2** =**fraud**, scheme

racy *adjective* **1** =**risqué**, bawdy, blue, naughty, near the knuckle (*inf*), smutty, suggestive **2** =**lively**, animated, energetic, to 57.296°.

radiant ⊕ *adjective* **1** looking happy. **2** shining. **3** emitted as radiation, e.g. *radiant heat*. **4** emitting radiation. **radiantly** *adverb* **radiance** *noun*

radiate ⊕ *verb* **1** spread out from a centre. **2** show (an emotion or quality) to a great degree. **3** emit or be emitted as radiation. **radiator** *noun* **1** arrangement of pipes containing hot water or steam to heat a room. **2** tubes containing water as cooling apparatus for a car engine.

radiation *noun* **1** transmission of energy from one body to another. **2** particles or waves emitted in nuclear decay. **3** process of radiating. **radiation sickness** illness caused by overexposure to radioactive material or x-rays.

radical ⊕ *adjective* **1** fundamental. **2** thorough. **3** advocating fundamental change. ◆ *noun* **4** person advocating fundamental (political) change. **5** number expressed as the root of another. **6** group of atoms which acts as a unit during chemical reactions. **radically** *adverb* **radicalism** *noun*

radicle *noun* small or developing root.

radii *noun* a plural of RADIUS.

radio *noun*, *pl* **-dios** **1** use of electromagnetic waves for broadcasting, communication, etc. **2** device for receiving and amplifying radio signals. **3** communications device for sending and receiving messages using radio waves. **4** sound broadcasting. ◆ *verb* **5** transmit (a message) by radio. ◆ *adjective* **6** of, relating to, or using radio, e.g. *radio drama*. **radiocontrolled** *adjective* controlled by signals sent by radio. **radio telephone** telephone which sends and receives messages using radio waves rather than wires. **radio telescope** instrument which picks up and analyses radio signals from space.

radio- *combining form* of radio, radiation, or radioactivity.

radioactive *adjective* emitting radiation as a result of nuclear decay. **radioactivity** *noun*

radiocarbon *noun* radioactive form of carbon used in calculating the age of very old objects.

radiography [ray-dee-og-ra-fee] *noun* production of an image on a film or plate by radiation. **radiographer** *noun*

radioisotope *noun* radioactive isotope.

radiology [ray-dee-ol-a-jee] *noun* science of using x-rays in medicine. **radiologist** *noun*

radiotherapy *noun* treatment of disease, esp. cancer, by radiation. **radiotherapist** *noun*

radish *noun* small hot-flavoured root vegetable eaten raw in salads.

radium *noun Chem* radioactive metallic element.

radius *noun*, *pl* **radii, radiuses** **1** (length of) a straight line from the centre to the circumference of a circle. **2** outer of two bones in the forearm. **3** circular area of a specified size round a central point, e.g. *everyone within a two-mile radius*.

radon [ray-don] *noun Chem* radioactive gaseous element.

RAF Royal Air Force.

raffia *noun* prepared palm fibre for weaving mats etc.

raffish *adjective* slightly disreputable.

raffle ⊕ *noun* **1** lottery with goods as prizes. ◆ *verb* **2** offer as a prize in a raffle.

raft *noun* floating platform of logs, planks, etc.

rafter *noun* one of the main beams of a roof.

rag[1] *noun* **1** fragment of cloth. **2** *Informal* newspaper. ◆ *plural* **3** tattered clothing. **from rags to riches** from being extremely poor to being extremely wealthy. **ragged** [rag-gid] *adjective* **1** dressed in shabby or torn clothes. **2** torn. **3** lacking smoothness. **ragbag** *noun* confused assortment, jumble.

rag[2] *verb* **ragging, ragged** **1** tease. **2** play practical jokes on. ◆ *adjective*, *noun* **3** (of) events organized by students to raise money for charities.

ragamuffin ⊕ *noun* ragged dirty child.

rage ⊕ *noun* **1** violent anger or passion. **2** aggressive behaviour associated with a certain

———————— THESAURUS ————————

entertaining, exciting, sparkling, spirited

radiance *noun* **1** =**happiness**, delight, gaiety, joy, pleasure, rapture, warmth **2** =**brightness**, brilliance, glare, gleam, glow, light, lustre, shine

radiant *adjective* **1** = **happy**, blissful, delighted, ecstatic, glowing, joyful, joyous, on cloud nine (*inf*), rapturous OPPOSITE> **miserable**. **2** =**bright**, brilliant, gleaming, glittering, glowing, luminous, lustrous, shining OPPOSITE> **dark**

radiate *verb* **1** =**spread out**, branch out, diverge, issue **3** = **emit**, diffuse, give off *or* out,

pour, scatter, send out, shed, spread

radical *adjective* **1** =**fundamental**, basic, deep-seated, innate, natural, profound OPPOSITE> **minor**. **2** =**extreme**, complete, drastic, entire, severe, sweeping, thorough **3** =**revolutionary**, extremist, fanatical ◆*noun* **4** =**extremist**, fanatic, militant, revolutionary OPPOSITE> **conservative**

raffle *noun* **1** =**draw**, lottery, sweep, sweepstake

ragamuffin *noun* =**urchin**, guttersnipe

activity, e.g. *traffic rage.* ◆ *verb* **3** speak or act with fury. **4** proceed violently and without check, e.g. *a storm was raging.* **all the rage** very popular.

raglan *adjective* (of a sleeve) joined to a garment by diagonal seams from the neck to the underarm.

ragout [rag-**goo**] *noun* richly seasoned stew of meat and vegetables.

ragtime *noun* style of jazz piano music.

raid ❶ *noun* **1** sudden surprise attack or search. ◆ *verb* **2** make a raid on. **3** sneak into (a place) in order to steal. **raider** *noun*

rail¹ ❶ *noun* **1** horizontal bar, esp. as part of a fence or track. **2** railway. **go off the rails** start behaving eccentrically or improperly. **railing** *noun* fence made of rails supported by posts.

railcard *noun* card which pensioners, young people, etc. can buy, entitling them to cheaper rail travel. **railroad** *noun* **1** *US* railway. ◆ *verb* **2** *Informal* force (a person) into an action with haste or by unfair means. **railway** *noun* **1** track of iron rails on which trains run. **2** company operating a railway.

rail² *verb* (foll. by *at* or *against*) complain bitterly or loudly. **raillery** *noun* teasing or joking.

rail³ *noun* small marsh bird.

raiment *noun Obs* clothing.

rain ❶ *noun* **1** water falling in drops from the clouds. **2** large quantity of anything falling rapidly. ◆ *verb* **3** fall or pour down as rain. **4** fall rapidly and in large quantities. **the rains** season in the tropics when there is a lot of rain. **rainy** *adjective* **rainy day** future time of need, esp. financial need. **rainbow** *noun* arch of colours in the sky. **rainbow trout** freshwater trout with black spots and two red stripes. **raincoat** *noun* water-resistant overcoat. **rainfall** *noun* amount of rain. **rainforest** *noun* dense forest in the tropics.

raise ❶ *verb* **1** lift up. **2** set upright. **3** increase in amount or intensity. **4** collect or levy. **5** bring up (a family). **6** grow (a crop). **7** put forward for consideration. **8** build. **9** end, e.g. *raise a siege.* ◆ *noun* **10** *US & Canad* pay rise. **raised** *adjective* higher than the surrounding area.

raisin *noun* dried grape.

raison d'être [ray-zon **det**-ra] *noun, pl* **raisons d'être** [ray-zon **det**-ra] *French* reason or justification for existence.

raita [**rye**-ta] *noun* Indian dish of chopped cucumber, mint, etc., in yogurt, served with curries.

Raj *noun* **the Raj** former British rule in India.

raja, rajah *noun Hist* Indian prince or ruler.

rake¹ ❶ *noun* **1** tool with a long handle and a crosspiece with teeth, used for smoothing earth or gathering leaves, hay, etc. ◆ *verb* **2** gather or smooth with a rake. **3** search (through). **4** sweep (with gunfire). **rake it in** *Informal* make a large amount of money. **rake-off** *noun Slang* share of profits, esp. illegal. **rake up** *verb* revive memories of (a forgotten unpleasant event).

rake² ❶ *noun* dissolute or immoral man. **rakish** *adjective*

rake³ *noun* **1** slope, esp. backwards, of an object. ◆ *verb* **2** slope from the vertical. **raked** *adjective* (of a surface) sloping so that it is higher at the back than the front.

rakish ❶ [**ray**-kish] *adjective* dashing or jaunty.

——————— T H E S A U R U S ———————

R

rage *noun* **1** =**fury**, anger, frenzy, ire, madness, passion, rampage, wrath OPPOSITE calmness ◆*verb* **3** =**be furious**, blow one's top, blow up (*inf*), fly off the handle (*inf*), fume, go ballistic (*sl, chiefly US*), go up the wall (*sl*), lose it (*inf*), lose one's temper, lose the plot (*inf*), seethe, storm OPPOSITE stay calm

ragged *adjective* **1** =**shabby**, in rags, in tatters, tattered, tatty, threadbare, unkempt OPPOSITE smart. **2** =**torn 3** =**rough**, jagged, rugged, serrated, uneven, unfinished

raid *noun* **1** =**attack**, foray, incursion, inroad, invasion, sally, sortie ◆*verb* **2** =**attack**, assault, foray, invade, pillage, plunder, sack

raider *noun* =**attacker**, invader, marauder, plunderer, robber, thief

railing *noun* =**fence**, balustrade, barrier, paling, rails

rain *noun* **1** =**rainfall**, cloudburst, deluge, downpour, drizzle, fall, raindrops, showers **2** =**shower**, deluge ◆*verb* **3** =**pour**, bucket down (*inf*), come down in buckets (*inf*), drizzle, pelt (down), teem **4** =**fall**, deposit, drop, shower, sprinkle

rainy 1, 3 *adjective* =**wet**, damp, drizzly, showery

raise *verb* **1** =**lift**, elevate, heave, hoist, rear, uplift **3** =**increase**, advance, amplify, boost, enhance, enlarge, heighten, inflate, intensify, magnify, strengthen OPPOSITE drop. **4** =**collect**, assemble, form, gather, mass, obtain, rally, recruit **5** =**bring up**, develop, nurture, rear **6** =**grow**, produce **7** =**put forward**, advance, broach, introduce, moot, suggest **8** =**build**, construct, erect, put up OPPOSITE level

rake¹ *verb* **2** =**gather**, collect, remove **3** =**search**, comb, scour, scrutinize

rally ❶ *noun, pl* **-lies 1** large gathering of people for a meeting. **2** marked recovery of strength. **3** *Tennis etc.* lively exchange of strokes. **4** car-driving competition on public roads. ♦ *verb* **-lying, -lied 5** bring or come together after dispersal or for a common cause. **6** regain health or strength, revive. **rally round** *verb* group together to help someone.
ram ❶ *noun* **1** male sheep. **2** hydraulic machine. ♦ *verb* **ramming, rammed 3** strike against with force. **4** force or drive. **5** cram or stuff. **ram (something) down someone's throat** put forward or emphasize (an idea or argument) with excessive force. **ram raid** *Informal* raid on a shop in which a stolen car is driven into the window. **ram raider**
RAM *Computers* random access memory.
Ramadan *noun* **1** 9th Muslim month. **2** strict fasting from dawn to dusk observed during this time.
ramble ❶ *verb* **1** walk without a definite route. **2** talk incoherently. ♦ *noun* **3** walk, esp. in the country. **rambler** *noun* **1** person who rambles. **2** climbing rose. **rambling** *adjective* **1** large and irregularly shaped. **2** (of speech or writing) confused and long-winded. ♦ *noun* **3** activity of going for long walks in the country.
ramekin [**ram**-ik-in] *noun* small ovenproof dish for a single serving of food.
ramifications *plural noun* consequences

resulting from an action.
ramp ❶ *noun* **1** slope joining two level surfaces. **2** place where the level of a road surface changes because of road works. **3** mobile stairs by which passengers enter or leave an aircraft.
rampage ❶ *verb* dash about violently. **on the rampage** behaving violently or destructively.
rampant ❶ *adjective* **1** growing or spreading uncontrollably. **2** (of a heraldic beast) on its hind legs.
rampart ❶ *noun* mound or wall for defence.
ramrod *noun* **1** long thin rod used for cleaning the barrel of a gun or forcing gunpowder into an old-fashioned gun. ♦ *adjective* **2** (of someone's posture) very straight and upright.
ramshackle ❶ *adjective* tumbledown, rickety, or makeshift.
ran *verb* past tense of RUN.
ranch *noun* large cattle farm in the American West. **rancher** *noun*
rancid ❶ *adjective* (of butter, bacon, etc.) stale and having an offensive smell. **rancidity** *noun*
rancour ❶ *noun* deep bitter hate. **rancorous** *adjective*
rand *noun* monetary unit of S Africa.
random ❶ *adjective* made or done by chance or without plan. **at random** haphazard(ly). **randomly** *adverb*

———————— THESAURUS ————————

rake² *noun* =**libertine**, debauchee, lecher, playboy, roué, swinger (*sl*) OPPOSITE **puritan**
rakish *adjective* =**dashing**, dapper, debonair, devil-may-care, jaunty, natty (*inf*), raffish, smart
rally *noun* **1** =**gathering**, assembly, congress, convention, meeting **2** =**recovery**, improvement, recuperation, revival OPPOSITE **collapse** ♦*verb* **5** =**reassemble**, regroup, reorganize, unite **6** =**recover**, get better, improve, recuperate, revive OPPOSITE **deteriorate**
ram *verb* **3** =**hit**, butt, crash, dash, drive, force, impact, smash **4, 5** =**cram**, crowd, force, jam, stuff, thrust
ramble *verb* **1** =**walk**, range, roam, rove, saunter, stray, stroll, wander **2** =**babble**, rabbit (on) (*Brit inf*), waffle (*inf, chiefly Brit*), witter on (*inf*) ♦*noun* **3** =**walk**, hike, roaming, roving, saunter, stroll, tour
rambler *noun* **1** =**walker**, hiker, rover, wanderer, wayfarer
rambling *adjective* **2** =**long-winded**, circuitous, digressive, disconnected, discursive, disjointed, incoherent, wordy OPPOSITE **direct**
ramifications *plural noun* =**consequences**,

developments, results, sequel, upshot
ramp *noun* **1** =**slope**, gradient, incline, rise
rampage *verb* =**go berserk**, rage, run amok, run riot, storm ♦*noun* **on the rampage** =**berserk**, amok, out of control, raging, riotous, violent, wild
rampant *adjective* **1** =**widespread**, prevalent, profuse, rife, spreading like wildfire, unchecked, uncontrolled, unrestrained **2** =**upright**, erect, rearing, standing
rampart *noun* =**defence**, bastion, bulwark, fence, fortification, wall
ramshackle *adjective* =**rickety**, crumbling, decrepit, derelict, flimsy, shaky, tumbledown, unsafe, unsteady
rancid *adjective* =**rotten**, bad, fetid, foul, off, putrid, rank, sour, stale, strong-smelling, tainted OPPOSITE **fresh**
rancour *noun* =**hatred**, animosity, bad blood, bitterness, hate, ill feeling, ill will
random *adjective* =**chance**, accidental, adventitious, casual, fortuitous, haphazard, hit or miss, incidental OPPOSITE **planned** ♦ **at random** =**haphazardly**, arbitrarily, by chance, randomly, unsystematically, willy-nilly

R

randy ❶ *adjective* **randier, randiest** *Informal* sexually aroused. **randiness** *noun*

ranee *noun* same as RANI.

rang *verb* past tense of RING¹.

range ❶ *noun* **1** limits of effectiveness or variation. **2** distance that a missile or plane can travel. **3** distance of a mark shot at. **4** difference in pitch between the highest and lowest note a voice or instrument can make. **5** whole set of related things. **6** chain of mountains. **7** place for shooting practice or rocket testing. **8** kitchen stove. ◆ *verb* **9** vary between one point and another. **10** cover or extend over. **11** roam. **ranger** *noun* **1** official in charge of a nature reserve etc. **2** (R-) member of the senior branch of Guides. **rangefinder** *noun* instrument for finding how far away an object is.

rangy ❶ [rain-jee] *adjective* **rangier, rangiest** having long slender limbs.

rani *noun* wife or widow of a rajah.

rank¹ ❶ *noun* **1** relative place or position. **2** status. **3** social class. **4** row or line. **5** *Brit* place where taxis wait to be hired. ◆ *verb* **6** have a specific rank or position. **7** arrange in rows or lines. **rank and file** ordinary people or members. **the ranks** common soldiers.

rank² ❶ *adjective* **1** complete or absolute, e.g. *rank favouritism*. **2** smelling offensively strong. **3** growing too thickly.

rankle ❶ *verb* continue to cause resentment or bitterness.

ransack ❶ *verb* **1** search thoroughly. **2** pillage, plunder.

ransom ❶ *noun* **1** money demanded in return for the release of someone who has been kidnapped. ◆ *verb* **2** pay money to obtain the release of a captive. **3** release a captive in return for money.

rant ❶ *verb* talk in a loud and excited way. **ranter** *noun* **ranting** *noun, adjective*

ranunculus *noun, pl* **-luses, -li** genus of plants including the buttercup.

rap ❶ *verb* **rapping, rapped 1** hit with a sharp quick blow. **2** utter (a command) abruptly. **3** perform a rhythmic monologue with musical backing. ◆ *noun* **4** quick sharp blow. **5** rhythmic monologue performed to music. **take the rap** *Slang* suffer punishment for something whether guilty or not. **rapper** *noun*

rapacious ❶ *adjective* greedy or grasping. **rapacity** *noun*

rape¹ ❶ *verb* **1** force to submit to sexual intercourse. ◆ *noun* **2** act of raping. **3** any violation or abuse. **rapist** *noun*

rape² *noun* plant with oil-yielding seeds, also used as fodder.

rapid ❶ *adjective* quick, swift. **rapids** *plural noun* part of a river with a fast turbulent current. **rapidly** *adverb* **rapidity** *noun*

rapier [ray-pyer] *noun* fine-bladed sword.

rapine [rap-pine] *noun* pillage or plundering.

rapport ❶ [rap-pore] *noun* harmony or agreement.

rapprochement [rap-**prosh**-mong] *noun*

——————— THESAURUS ———————

R

randy *adjective* Inf =**lustful**, amorous, aroused, horny (*sl*), hot, lascivious, turned-on (*sl*)

range *noun* **1** =**limits**, area, bounds, orbit, province, radius, reach, scope, sphere **5** =**series**, assortment, collection, gamut, lot, selection, variety ◆*verb* **9** =**vary 10** =**extend**, reach, run, stretch **11** =**roam**, ramble, rove, traverse, wander

rangy *adjective* =**long-limbed**, gangling, lanky, leggy, long-legged

rank¹ *noun* **1, 2** =**status**, caste, class, degree, division, grade, level, order, position, sort, type **3** =**class**, caste **4** =**row**, column, file, group, line, range, series, tier ◆*verb* **7** =**arrange**, align, array, dispose, line up, order, sort **rank and file** =**general public**, majority, mass, masses

rank² *adjective* **1** =**absolute**, arrant, blatant, complete, downright, flagrant, gross, sheer, thorough, total, utter **2** =**foul**, bad, disgusting, noisome, noxious, offensive, rancid, revolting, stinking **3** =**abundant**, dense, lush, luxuriant, profuse

rankle *verb* =**annoy**, anger, gall, get on one's nerves (*inf*), irk, irritate, rile

ransack *verb* **1** =**search**, comb, explore, go through, rummage, scour, turn inside out **2** =**plunder**, loot, pillage, raid, strip

ransom *noun* **1** =**payment**, money, payoff, price

rant *verb* =**shout**, cry, declaim, rave, roar, yell

rap *verb* **1** =**hit**, crack, knock, strike, tap ◆*noun* **4** =**blow**, clout (*inf*), crack, knock, tap **take the rap** *Sl* =**rebuke**, blame, punishment, responsibility

rapacious *adjective* =**greedy**, avaricious, grasping, insatiable, predatory, preying, voracious

rape¹ *verb* **1** =**sexually assault**, abuse, force, outrage, ravish, violate ◆*noun* **2** =**sexual assault**, outrage, ravishment, violation **3** =**desecration**, abuse, defilement, violation

rapid *adjective* =**quick**, brisk, express, fast, hasty, hurried, prompt, speedy, swift OPPOSITE **gradual**

re-establishment of friendly relations, esp. between nations.

rapscallion *noun Old-fashioned* rascal or rogue.

rapt ❶ *adjective* engrossed or spellbound.

rapture *noun* ecstasy. **rapturous** *adjective*

raptor *noun* any bird of prey. **raptorial** *adjective*

rare¹ ❶ *adjective* **1** uncommon. **2** infrequent. **3** of uncommonly high quality. **4** (of air at high altitudes) having low density, thin. **rarely** *adverb* seldom. **rarity** *noun, pl* **-ities**

rare² ❶ *adjective* (of meat) lightly cooked.

rarebit *noun* see WELSH RAREBIT.

rarefied ❶ [rare-if-ide] *adjective* **1** highly specialized, exalted. **2** (of air) thin.

raring ❶ *adjective* **raring to** enthusiastic, willing, or ready to.

rascal ❶ *noun* **1** rogue. **2** naughty (young) person. **rascally** *adjective*

rase *verb* same as RAZE.

rash¹ ❶ *adjective* hasty, reckless, or incautious. **rashly** *adverb*

rash² ❶ *noun* **1** eruption of spots or patches on the skin. **2** outbreak of (unpleasant) occurrences.

rasher *noun* thin slice of bacon.

rasp *noun* **1** harsh grating noise. **2** coarse file. ◆ *verb* **3** speak in a grating voice. **4** make a scraping noise.

raspberry *noun* **1** red juicy edible berry. **2** *Informal* spluttering noise made with the tongue and lips, to show contempt.

Rastafarian *noun, adjective* (member) of a religion originating in Jamaica and regarding Haile Selassie as God (also **Rasta**).

rat *noun* **1** small rodent. **2** *Informal* contemptible person, esp. a deserter or informer. ◆ *verb* **ratting, ratted 3** *Informal* inform (on). **4** hunt rats. **smell a rat** detect something suspicious. **ratty** *adjective* **-tier, -tiest** *Informal* bad-tempered, irritable. **rat race** continual hectic competitive activity.

ratafia [rat-a-**fee**-a] *noun* **1** liqueur made from fruit. **2** almond-flavoured biscuit.

ratatouille [rat-a-**twee**] *noun* vegetable casserole of tomatoes, aubergines, etc.

ratchet *noun* set of teeth on a bar or wheel allowing motion in one direction only.

rate¹ ❶ *noun* **1** degree of speed or progress. **2** proportion between two things. **3** charge. ◆ *plural* **4** local tax on business. **5** (in Australia and formerly in Britain) local tax on domestic property. ◆ *verb* **6** consider or value. **7** estimate the value of. **8** be worthy of, deserve. **at any rate** in any case. **rateable** *adjective* **1** able to be rated. **2** (of property) liable to payment of rates. **ratepayer** *noun*

rate² ❶ *verb* scold or criticize severely.

rather ❶ *adverb* **1** to some extent. **2** more

——————— THESAURUS ———————

rapport *noun* =**bond**, affinity, empathy, harmony, link, relationship, sympathy, tie, understanding

rapt *adjective* =**spellbound**, absorbed, engrossed, enthralled, entranced, fascinated, gripped OPPOSITE **bored**

rapture *noun* =**ecstasy**, bliss, delight, euphoria, joy, rhapsody, seventh heaven, transport

rapturous *adjective* =**ecstatic**, blissful, euphoric, in seventh heaven, joyful, overjoyed, over the moon (*inf*), transported

rare¹ *adjective* **1** =**uncommon**, few, infrequent, scarce, singular, sparse, strange, unusual OPPOSITE **common. 2** =**infrequent**, few, uncommon, unusual **3** =**superb**, choice, excellent, fine, great, peerless, superlative

rare² *adjective* =**underdone**, bloody, half-cooked, half-raw, undercooked

rarefied *adjective* **1** =**exalted**, elevated, high, lofty, noble, spiritual, sublime

rarely *adverb* =**seldom**, hardly, hardly ever, infrequently OPPOSITE **often**

raring *adjective* as in **raring to** =**eager**, desperate, enthusiastic, impatient, keen,

longing, ready

rarity *noun* **1, 2** =**uncommonness**, infrequency, scarcity, shortage, sparseness, strangeness, unusualness

rascal *noun* **1** =**rogue**, blackguard, devil, good-for-nothing, ne'er-do-well, scoundrel, villain **2** =**imp**, scamp

rash¹ *adjective* =**reckless**, careless, foolhardy, hasty, heedless, ill-advised, impetuous, imprudent, impulsive, incautious OPPOSITE **cautious**

rash² *noun* **1** =**outbreak**, eruption **2** =**spate**, flood, outbreak, plague, series, wave

rate¹ *noun* **1** =**speed**, pace, tempo, velocity **2** =**degree**, proportion, ratio, scale, standard **3** =**charge**, cost, fee, figure, price ◆*verb* **6** =**evaluate**, consider, count, estimate, grade, measure, rank, reckon, value **7** =**estimate**, evaluate, value **8** =**deserve**, be entitled to, be worthy of, merit **at any rate** =**in any case**, anyhow, anyway, at all events

rate² *verb* =**scold**, bawl out (*inf*), berate, blame, carpet (*inf*), castigate, censure, chew out (*US & Canad inf*), chide, criticize severely, give a rocket (*Brit & NZ inf*), haul over the coals (*inf*),

truly or appropriately. **3** more willingly.
ratify ⊕ *verb* **-fying, -fied** give formal
approval to. **ratification** *noun*
rating ⊕ *noun* **1** valuation or assessment. **2**
classification. **3** noncommissioned sailor. ◆ *plural*
4 size of the audience for a TV programme.
ratio ⊕ *noun, pl* **-tios** relationship between
two numbers or amounts expressed as a
proportion.
ration ⊕ *noun* **1** fixed allowance of food etc. ◆
verb **2** limit to a certain amount per person. **3**
(often foll. by *out*) distribute a fixed amount of
food etc. to each person in a group.
rational ⊕ *adjective* **1** reasonable, sensible. **2**
capable of reasoning. **3** *Maths* (of a number)
able to be expressed as a ratio of two integers.
rationally *adverb* **rationality** *noun* **rationale**
[rash-a-**nahl**] *noun* reason for an action or
decision. **rationalism** *noun* philosophy that
regards reason as the only basis for beliefs or
actions. **rationalist** *noun, adjective* **rationalistic**
adjective **rationalize** *verb* **1** justify by plausible
reasoning. **2** reorganize to improve efficiency or
profitability. **rationalization** *noun*
rattan *noun* climbing palm with jointed stems
used for canes.
rattle ⊕ *verb* **1** give out a succession of short
sharp sounds. **2** send, move or drive with such
a sound. **3** shake briskly causing sharp sounds.
4 *Informal* confuse or fluster. **5** (often foll. by *off*
or *out*) recite perfunctorily or rapidly. **6** (often
foll. by *on* or *away*) talk quickly and at length

about something unimportant. ◆ *noun* **7** short
sharp sound. **8** instrument for making such a
sound. **rattling** *adverb* **1** *Informal old-fashioned*
exceptionally, very. ◆ *noun* **2** succession of short
sharp sounds. **rattlesnake** *noun* poisonous
snake with loose horny segments on the tail
that make a rattling sound. **rattle through**
verb do very quickly.
raucous ⊕ *adjective* hoarse or harsh.
raunchy ⊕ *adjective* **-chier, -chiest** *Slang*
earthy, sexy.
ravage ⊕ *verb* cause extensive damage to.
ravages *plural noun* damaging effects.
rave ⊕ *verb* **1** talk wildly or with enthusiasm. ◆
noun **2** *Informal* enthusiastically good review. **3**
Slang large-scale party with electronic dance
music. **raving** *adjective* **1** delirious. **2** *Informal*
exceptional, e.g. *a raving beauty*.
ravel *verb* **-elling, -elled** tangle or become
entangled.
raven *noun* **1** black bird like a large crow. ◆
adjective **2** (of hair) shiny black.
ravening *adjective* (of animals) hungrily
searching for prey.
ravenous ⊕ *adjective* very hungry.
ravine ⊕ [rav-**veen**] *noun* narrow steep-sided
valley worn by a stream.
ravioli *plural noun* small squares of pasta with
a savoury filling.
ravish ⊕ *verb* **1** enrapture. **2** *Lit* rape.
ravishing *adjective* lovely or entrancing.
raw ⊕ *adjective* **1** uncooked. **2** not

———————— THESAURUS ————————

read the riot act, rebuke, reprimand, reprove,
roast (*inf*), rouse on (*Aust*), take to task, tear
into (*inf*), tear (someone) off a strip (*inf*), tell off
(*inf*), tongue-lash, upbraid
rather *adverb* **1** = **to some extent**, a little,
fairly, moderately, quite, relatively, somewhat,
to some degree **3** = **preferably**, more readily,
more willingly, sooner
ratify *verb* = **approve**, affirm, authorize,
confirm, endorse, establish, sanction, uphold
OPPOSITE **annul**
rating *noun* **2** = **position**, class, degree, grade,
order, placing, rank, rate, status
ratio *noun* = **proportion**, fraction, percentage,
rate, relation
ration *noun* **1** = **allowance**, allotment,
helping, measure, part, portion, quota, share
◆*verb* **2** = **limit**, budget, control, restrict
rational *adjective* **1, 2** = **sensible**, intelligent,
logical, lucid, realistic, reasonable, sane, sound,
wise OPPOSITE **irrational**
rationale *noun* = **reason**, grounds, logic,
motivation, philosophy, principle, *raison d'être*,

theory
rationalize *verb* **1** = **justify**, account for,
excuse, vindicate
rattle *verb* **1** = **clatter**, bang, jangle **2, 3**
= **shake**, bounce, jar, jolt, vibrate **4** *Inf* = **fluster**,
disconcert, disturb, faze, perturb, shake, upset
raucous *adjective* = **harsh**, grating, hoarse,
loud, noisy, rough, strident OPPOSITE **quiet**
raunchy *adjective* *Sl* = **sexy**, coarse, earthy,
lusty, sexual, steamy (*inf*)
ravage *verb* = **destroy**, demolish, despoil,
devastate, lay waste, ransack, ruin, spoil
ravages *plural noun* = **damage**, destruction,
devastation, havoc, ruin, ruination, spoliation
rave *verb* **1 a** = **rant**, babble, be delirious,
rage, roar **b** = **enthuse**, be mad about (*inf*), be
wild about (*inf*), gush, praise
ravenous *adjective* = **starving**, famished,
starved OPPOSITE **full**
ravine *noun* = **canyon**, defile, gorge, gulch (*US
& Canad*), gully, pass
raving *adjective* **1** = **mad**, crazed, crazy,
delirious, hysterical, insane, irrational, wild

R

manufactured or refined. **3** (of the skin or a wound) painful, with the surface scraped away. **4** inexperienced, e.g. *raw recruits*. **5** chilly. **raw deal** unfair or dishonest treatment. **rawhide** *noun* untanned hide.

ray¹ ❶ *noun* **1** single line or narrow beam of light. **2** any of a set of radiating lines. **3** slight indication of something desirable, e.g. *a ray of hope*.

ray² *noun* large sea fish with a flat body and a whiplike tail.

ray³ *noun Music* (in tonic sol-fa) second note of any major scale.

rayon *noun* (fabric made of) a synthetic fibre.

raze ❶ *verb* destroy (buildings or a town) completely.

razor *noun* sharp instrument for shaving.

razorbill *noun* sea bird with a stout sideways flattened bill. **razor shell** (burrowing shellfish with) a long narrow shell. **razor wire** strong wire with pieces of sharp metal set across it at intervals.

razzle-dazzle, razzmatazz *noun Slang* showy activity.

R & B rhythm and blues.

Rb *Chem* rubidium.

RC 1 Roman Catholic. **2** Red Cross.

R & D research and development.

Rd Road.

re¹ ❶ *preposition* with reference to, concerning.

re² *noun* same as RAY³.

Re *Chem* rhenium.

RE religious education.

re- *prefix* again, e.g. *re-enter; retrial*.

reach ❶ *verb* **1** arrive at. **2** make a movement in order to grasp or touch. **3** succeed in touching. **4** make contact or communication with. **5** extend as far as. ◆ *noun* **6** distance that one can reach. **7** range of influence. ◆ *plural* **8** stretch of a river. **reachable** *adjective*

react ❶ *verb* **1** act in response (to). **2** (foll. by *against*) act in an opposing or contrary manner. **3** undergo a chemical reaction. **reaction** *noun* **1** physical or emotional response to a stimulus. **2** any action resisting another. **3** opposition to change. **4** chemical or nuclear change, combination, or decomposition. **reactionary** *noun, pl* **-aries,** *adjective* (person) opposed to change, esp. in politics. **reactance** *noun Electricity* resistance to the flow of an alternating current caused by the inductance or capacitance of the circuit. **reactive** *adjective* chemically active. **reactor** *noun* apparatus in which a nuclear reaction is maintained and controlled to produce nuclear energy.

read ❶ *verb* **reading, read 1** look at and understand or take in (written or printed matter). **2** look at and say aloud. **3** have a certain wording, e.g. *the statement reads as follows*. **4** interpret the significance or meaning of. **5** (of an instrument) register. **6** make out the true mood of. **7** study. ◆ *noun* **8** matter suitable for reading, e.g. *a good read*. **9** spell of reading. **readable** *adjective* **1** enjoyable to read. **2** legible. **reader** *noun* **1** person who reads. **2** textbook. **3** senior university lecturer. **readership** *noun* readers of a publication collectively. **reading** *noun*

THESAURUS

ravish *verb* **1** = **enchant**, captivate, charm, delight, enrapture, entrance, fascinate, spellbind **2** *Lit* = **rape**, abuse, force, sexually assault, violate

ravishing *adjective* = **enchanting**, beautiful, bewitching, charming, entrancing, gorgeous, lovely

raw *adjective* **1** = **uncooked**, fresh, natural OPPOSITE> **cooked**. **2** = **unrefined**, basic, coarse, crude, natural, rough, unfinished, unprocessed OPPOSITE> **prepared**. **4** = **inexperienced**, callow, green, immature, new OPPOSITE> **experienced**. **5** = **chilly**, biting, bitter, cold, freezing, parky (*Brit inf*), piercing

ray¹ *noun* **1** = **beam**, bar, flash, gleam, shaft

raze *verb* = **destroy**, demolish, flatten, knock down, level, pull down, ruin

re¹ *preposition* = **concerning**, about, apropos, regarding, with reference to, with regard to

reach *verb* **1** = **arrive at**, attain, get to, make **3, 5** = **touch**, contact, extend to, grasp, stretch to **4** = **contact**, communicate with, get hold of, get in touch with, get through to ◆*noun* **6** = **range**, distance, extension, extent, grasp, stretch **7** = **power**, capacity, influence, mana (*NZ*), scope

react *verb* **1** = **respond**, answer, reply

reaction *noun* **1** = **response**, answer, reply **2** = **counteraction**, backlash, recoil **3** = **conservatism**, the right

reactionary *noun* = **conservative**, die-hard, right-winger ◆*adjective* = **conservative**, right-wing

read *verb* **1** = **look at**, comprehend, construe, decipher, discover, interpret, peruse, pore over, scan, see, study, understand **5** = **register**, display, indicate, record, show **7** = **study**, pore over

readable *adjective* **1** = **enjoyable**, entertaining, enthralling, gripping, interesting OPPOSITE> **heavy**. **2** = **legible**, clear, comprehensible, decipherable OPPOSITE>

R

readjust *verb* adapt to a new situation.
readjustment *noun*
readmit *verb* **-mitting, -mitted** let (a person, country, etc.) back in to a place or organization.
ready ⊕ *adjective* **readier, readiest 1** prepared for use or action. **2** willing, prompt. **readily** *adverb* **readiness** *noun* **ready-made** *adjective* for immediate use by any customer. **ready money, the ready, the readies** *Informal* cash for immediate use.
reaffirm *verb* state again, confirm.
reaffirmation *noun*
reafforest *verb* plant new trees in (an area that was formerly forested). **reafforestation** *noun*
reagent [ree-**age**-ent] *noun* chemical substance that reacts with another, used to detect the presence of the other.
real ⊕ *adjective* **1** existing in fact. **2** actual. **3** genuine. **really** *adverb* **1** very. **2** truly. ◆ *interjection* **3** exclamation of dismay, doubt, or surprise. **reality** *noun* state of things as they are. **reality TV** television programmes focusing on members of the public living in conditions created especially by the programme makers. **real ale** beer allowed to ferment in the barrel. **real estate** property consisting of land and houses. **real number** any rational or irrational number. **real tennis** old form of tennis played in a four-walled indoor court. **real-time** *adjective* (of a computer system) processing data as it is received.
realistic ⊕ *adjective* seeing and accepting things as they really are, practical. **realistically**
adverb **realism** *noun* **1** awareness or acceptance of things as they are. **2** style in art or literature that attempts to portray the world as it really is. **realist** *noun*
realize ⊕ *verb* **1** become aware or grasp the significance of. **2** achieve (a plan, hopes, etc.). **3** convert into money. **realization** *noun*
realm ⊕ *noun* **1** kingdom. **2** sphere of interest.
realtor *noun US & Canad* agent, esp. accredited one who sells houses, etc. for others.
ream *noun* **1** twenty quires of paper, generally 500 sheets. ◆ *plural* **2** *Informal* large quantity (of written matter).
reap ⊕ *verb* **1** cut and gather (a harvest). **2** receive as the result of a previous activity. **reaper** *noun*
reappear *verb* appear again. **reappearance** *noun*
reappraise *verb* consider or review to see if changes are needed. **reappraisal** *noun*
rear¹ ⊕ *noun* **1** back part. **2** part of an army, procession, etc. behind the others. **bring up the rear** come last. **rearmost** *adjective* **rearward** *adjective, adverb* **rear admiral** high-ranking naval officer. **rearguard** *noun* troops protecting the rear of an army. **rear-view mirror** mirror inside a vehicle which allows the driver to see out of the rear window.
rear² ⊕ *verb* **1** care for and educate (children). **2** breed (animals). **3** (of a horse) rise on its hind feet.
rearm *verb* **1** arm again. **2** equip with better weapons. **rearmament** *noun*
rearrange *verb* organize differently, alter.
rearrangement *noun*

———— THESAURUS ————

incomprehensible
reading *noun* **2** = **recital**, lesson, performance, sermon **4** = **interpretation**, grasp, impression, version **7** = **perusal**, examination, inspection, scrutiny, study
ready *adjective* **1** = **prepared**, accessible, arranged, available, convenient, fit, handy, near, organized, present, primed, ripe, set OPPOSITE unprepared. **2** = **willing**, agreeable, alert, bright, clever, disposed, eager, glad, happy, inclined, keen, prompt, prone, quick OPPOSITE reluctant
real *adjective* = **genuine**, actual, authentic, factual, rightful, sincere, true, unfeigned, valid
realistic *adjective* = **practical**, common-sense, down-to-earth, level-headed, matter-of-fact, real, sensible OPPOSITE unrealistic
reality *noun* = **truth**, actuality, fact, realism, validity, verity
realization *noun* **1** = **awareness**, cognizance,
comprehension, conception, grasp, perception, recognition, understanding **2** = **achievement**, accomplishment, fulfilment
realize *verb* **1** = **become aware of**, comprehend, get the message, grasp, take in, understand **2** = **achieve**, accomplish, carry out or through, complete, do, effect, fulfil, perform
really *adverb* **2** = **truly**, actually, certainly, genuinely, in actuality, indeed, in fact, positively, surely
realm *noun* **1** = **kingdom**, country, domain, dominion, empire, land **2** = **field**, area, branch, department, province, sphere, territory, world
reap *verb* **1** = **collect**, bring in, cut, garner, gather, harvest **2** = **get**, acquire, derive, gain, obtain
rear¹ *noun* **1** = **back**, end, rearguard, stern, tail, tail end OPPOSITE front
rear² *verb* **1** = **bring up**, educate, foster, nurture, raise, train **2** = **breed 3** = **rise**

reason ❶ *noun* **1** cause or motive. **2** faculty of rational thought. **3** sanity. ◆ *verb* **4** think logically in forming conclusions. **reason with** persuade by logical argument into doing something. **reasonable** *adjective* **1** sensible. **2** not excessive. **3** logical. **reasonably** *adverb*

reassess *verb* reconsider the value or importance of.

reassure ❶ *verb* restore confidence to. **reassurance** *noun* **reassuring** *adjective*

rebate ❶ *noun* discount or refund.

rebel ❶ *verb* **-belling, -belled 1** revolt against the ruling power. **2** reject accepted conventions. ◆ *noun* **3** person who rebels. **rebellion** *noun* **1** organized open resistance to authority. **2** rejection of conventions. **rebellious** *adjective*

rebirth *noun* revival or renaissance. **reborn** *adjective* active again after a period of inactivity.

rebore, reboring *noun* boring of a cylinder to restore its true shape.

rebound ❶ *verb* **1** spring back. **2** misfire so as to hurt the perpetrator of a plan or deed. ◆ *noun* **3** act of rebounding. **on the rebound** *Informal* while recovering from rejection.

rebuff ❶ *verb* **1** reject or snub. ◆ *noun* **2** blunt refusal, snub.

rebuke ❶ *verb* **1** scold sternly. ◆ *noun* **2** stern scolding.

rebus [ree-buss] *noun, pl* **-buses** puzzle consisting of pictures and symbols representing words or syllables.

rebut ❶ *verb* **-butting, -butted** prove that (a claim) is untrue. **rebuttal** *noun*

recalcitrant *adjective* wilfully disobedient. **recalcitrance** *noun*

recall ❶ *verb* **1** recollect or remember. **2** order to return. **3** annul or cancel. ◆ *noun* **4** ability to remember. **5** order to return.

recant ❶ *verb* withdraw (a statement or belief) publicly. **recantation** *noun*

recap *Informal verb* **-capping, -capped 1** recapitulate. ◆ *noun* **2** recapitulation.

recapitulate ❶ *verb* state again briefly, repeat. **recapitulation** *noun*

recapture *verb* **1** experience again. **2** capture again.

recast *verb* **-casting, -cast 1** organize or set out in a different way. **2** assign a part in a play or film to an actor other than the one originally intended.

recce *Slang verb* **-ceing, -ced** *or* **-ceed 1** reconnoitre. ◆ *noun* **2** reconnaissance.

recede ❶ *verb* **1** move to a more distant

——————— THESAURUS ———————

reason *noun* **1 =cause**, aim, goal, grounds, incentive, intention, motive, object, purpose **2 =sense**, intellect, judgment, logic, understanding OPPOSITE **emotion**. **3 =sanity**, mind, rationality, soundness ◆*verb* **4 =deduce**, conclude, infer, make out, think, work out **reason with =persuade**, bring round (*inf*), prevail upon, talk into or out of, urge, win over **reasonable** *adjective* **1, 3 =sensible**, logical, plausible, practical, sane, sober, sound, tenable, wise OPPOSITE **unreasonable**. **2 =fair**, equitable, fit, just, moderate, proper, right OPPOSITE **unfair**

reassure *verb* **=encourage**, comfort, gee up, hearten, put or set one's mind at rest, restore confidence to

rebate *noun* **=refund**, allowance, bonus, deduction, discount, reduction

rebel *verb* **1 =revolt**, mutiny, resist, rise up **2 =defy** ◆*noun* **3 =revolutionary**, insurgent, revolutionist, secessionist

rebellion *noun* **1 =resistance**, mutiny, revolt, revolution, rising, uprising **2 =nonconformity**, defiance, heresy, schism

rebellious *adjective* **1 =revolutionary**, disloyal, disobedient, disorderly, insurgent, mutinous, rebel, seditious, unruly OPPOSITE **loyal**. **2 =defiant**

rebound *verb* **1 =bounce**, recoil, ricochet **2 =misfire**, backfire, boomerang, recoil

rebuff *verb* **1 =reject**, cold-shoulder, cut, knock back (*sl*), refuse, repulse, slight, snub, spurn, turn down OPPOSITE **encourage** ◆*noun* **2 =rejection**, cold shoulder, kick in the teeth (*sl*), knock-back (*sl*), refusal, repulse, slap in the face (*inf*), slight, snub

rebuke *verb* **1 =scold**, admonish, castigate, censure, chide, dress down (*inf*), give a rocket (*Brit & NZ inf*), haul (someone) over the coals (*inf*), reprimand, reprove, rouse on (*Aust*), tear (someone) off a strip (*inf*), tell off (*inf*) OPPOSITE **praise** ◆*noun* **2 =scolding**, admonition, censure, dressing down (*inf*), reprimand, row, telling-off (*inf*)

rebut *verb* **=disprove**, confute, invalidate, negate, overturn, prove wrong, refute

recall *verb* **1 =recollect**, bring or call to mind, evoke, remember **3 =annul**, cancel, countermand, repeal, retract, revoke, withdraw ◆*noun* **4 =recollection**, memory, remembrance **5 =repeal**, rescindment, retraction, withdrawal

recant *verb* **=withdraw**, disclaim, forswear, renege, repudiate, retract, revoke, take back OPPOSITE **maintain**

recapitulate *verb* **=restate**, outline, recap

R

place. **2** (of the hair) stop growing at the front.
receipt ❶ *noun* **1** written acknowledgment of money or goods received. **2** receiving or being received.
receive ❶ *verb* **1** take, accept, or get. **2** experience. **3** greet (guests). **4** have (an honour) bestowed. **5** admit (a person) to a society or condition. **6** convert radio or television signals into sound or vision. **7** support or sustain (the weight of something). **received** *adjective* generally accepted. **receiver** *noun* **1** part of telephone that is held to the ear. **2** equipment in a telephone, radio, or television that converts electrical signals into sound. **3** person appointed by a court to manage the property of a bankrupt. **4** person who handles stolen goods knowing they have been stolen. **receivership** *noun* state of being administered by a receiver.
recent ❶ *adjective* **1** having happened lately. **2** new. **recently** *adverb*
receptacle ❶ *noun* object used to contain something.
reception ❶ *noun* **1** area for receiving guests, clients, etc. **2** formal party. **3** manner of receiving. **4** welcome. **5** (in broadcasting) quality of signals received. **receptionist** *noun* person who receives guests, clients, etc.
reception room room in a house suitable for entertaining guests.
receptive ❶ *adjective* willing to accept new ideas, suggestions, etc. **receptivity**, **receptiveness** *noun*

recess ❶ *noun* **1** niche or alcove. **2** holiday between sessions of work. **3** secret hidden place. **recessed** *adjective* hidden or placed in a recess.
recession ❶ *noun* **1** period of economic difficulty when little is being bought or sold. **2** act of receding. **recessive** *adjective* receding.
recharge *verb* cause (a battery etc.) to take in and store electricity again. **rechargeable** *adjective*
recherché [rish-**air**-shay] *adjective* **1** refined or elegant. **2** known only to experts.
recidivism *noun* habitual relapse into crime. **recidivist** *noun*
recipe ❶ *noun* **1** directions for cooking a dish. **2** method for achieving something.
recipient *noun* person who receives something.
reciprocal ❶ [ris-**sip**-pro-kl] *adjective* **1** mutual. **2** given or done in return. ♦ *noun* **3** *Maths* number or quantity that gives a product of one when multiplied by a given number or quantity, e.g. *0.25 is the reciprocal of 4.*
reciprocally *adverb* **reciprocate** *verb* **1** give or feel in return. **2** (of a machine part) move backwards and forwards. **reciprocation** *noun* **reciprocity** *noun*
recite ❶ *verb* **1** repeat (a poem etc.) aloud to an audience. **2** give a detailed account of.
recital [ris-**site**-al] *noun* **1** musical performance by a soloist or soloists. **2** act of reciting.
recitation *noun* recital, usu. from memory, of poetry or prose. **recitative** [ress-it-a-**teev**] *noun*

——————— THESAURUS ———————

(*inf*), recount, repeat, summarize
recede *verb* **1** = **fall back**, abate, ebb, regress, retire, retreat, return, subside, withdraw
receipt *noun* **1** = **sales slip**, counterfoil, proof of purchase **2** = **receiving**, acceptance, delivery, reception
receive *verb* **1** = **get**, accept, acquire, be given, collect, obtain, pick up, take **2** = **experience**, bear, encounter, suffer, sustain, undergo **3** = **greet**, accommodate, admit, entertain, meet, welcome **5** = **admit**, welcome
recent *adjective* **1** = **late 2** = **new**, current, fresh, modern, novel, present-day, up-to-date OPPOSITE **old**
recently *adverb* **1** = **lately**, latterly, not long ago, of late **2** = **newly**, currently, freshly
receptacle *noun* = **container**, holder, repository
reception *noun* **2** = **party**, function, soiree **3** = **response**, acknowledgment, greeting, reaction, treatment, welcome **4** = **welcome**, greeting

receptive *adjective* = **open**, amenable, interested, open-minded, open to suggestions, susceptible, sympathetic OPPOSITE **unreceptive**
recess *noun* **1** = **alcove**, bay, corner, hollow, niche, nook **2** = **break**, holiday, intermission, interval, respite, rest, vacation
recession *noun* = **depression**, decline, drop, slump OPPOSITE **boom**
recipe *noun* **1** = **directions**, ingredients, instructions **2** = **method**, formula, prescription, procedure, process, technique
reciprocal *adjective* **1, 2** = **mutual**, alternate, complementary, correlative, corresponding, equivalent, exchanged, interchangeable OPPOSITE **unilateral**
reciprocate *verb* **1** = **return**, exchange, reply, requite, respond, swap, trade
recital *noun* **1** = **performance**, rehearsal, rendering **2** = **recitation**, account, narrative, reading, relation, statement, telling
recitation *noun* = **recital**, lecture, passage,

R

speechlike style of singing, used esp. for narrative passages in opera.

reckless ⊕ *adjective* heedless of danger. **recklessly** *adverb* **recklessness** *noun*

reckon ⊕ *verb* **1** consider or think. **2** make calculations, count. **3** expect. **4** (foll. by *with* or *without*) take into account *or* fail to take into account. **5** (foll. by *on* or *upon*) rely on. **reckoning** *noun*

reclaim ⊕ *verb* **1** regain possession of. **2** make fit for cultivation. **3** recover (useful substances) from waste. **reclamation** *noun*

recline ⊕ *verb* rest in a leaning position. **reclining** *adjective*

recluse ⊕ *noun* person who avoids other people. **reclusive** *adjective*

recognize ⊕ *verb* **1** identify as (a person or thing) already known. **2** accept as true or existing. **3** treat as valid. **4** notice, show appreciation of. **recognition** *noun* **recognizable** *adjective* **recognizance** [rik-og-nizz-anss] *noun* undertaking before a court to observe some condition.

recoil ⊕ *verb* **1** jerk or spring back. **2** draw back in horror. **3** (of an action) go wrong so as to hurt the doer. ◆ *noun* **4** backward jerk. **5**

recoiling.

recollect ⊕ *verb* call back to mind, remember. **recollection** *noun*

recommend ⊕ *verb* **1** advise or counsel. **2** praise or commend. **3** make acceptable. **recommendation** *noun*

SPELLING TIP

If you wonder how many *c*s and *m*s to put in **recommend**, you are not alone. Most people who make the wrong decision go for single letters throughout (*recomend* and *recomendation*); they should, of course, double the *m*, as in **recommendation**.

---

recompense ⊕ *verb* **1** pay or reward. **2** compensate or make up for. ◆ *noun* **3** compensation. **4** reward or remuneration.

reconcile ⊕ *verb* **1** harmonize (conflicting beliefs etc.). **2** bring back into friendship. **3** accept or cause to accept (an unpleasant situation). **reconciliation** *noun*

recondite ⊕ *adjective* difficult to understand.

——————— THESAURUS ———————

performance, piece, reading

recite *verb* **1** = **repeat**, declaim, deliver, narrate, perform, speak

reckless *adjective* = **careless**, hasty, headlong, heedless, imprudent, mindless, precipitate, rash, thoughtless, wild OPPOSITE **cautious**

reckon *verb* **1** = **consider**, account, assume, believe, count, deem, esteem, guess (*inf, chiefly US & Canad*), imagine, judge, rate, regard, suppose, think **2** = **count**, add up, calculate, compute, figure, number, tally, total

reckoning *noun* **2** = **count**, addition, calculation, estimate

reclaim *verb* **1** = **regain**, recapture, recover, redeem, retrieve **3** = **salvage**

recline *verb* = **lean**, lie (down), loll, lounge, repose, rest, sprawl OPPOSITE **stand up**

recluse *noun* = **hermit**, anchoress, anchorite, monk, solitary

reclusive *adjective* = **solitary**, hermit-like, isolated, retiring, withdrawn

recognition *noun* **1** = **identification**, discovery, recollection, remembrance **2** = **acceptance**, admission, allowance, confession **4** = **appreciation**, notice, respect

recognize *verb* **1** = **identify**, know, notice, place, recall, recollect, remember, spot **2** = **acknowledge**, accept, admit, allow, concede, grant OPPOSITE **forget**. **4** = **appreciate**, notice,

respect

recoil *verb* **1** = **jerk back**, kick, react, rebound, spring back **2** = **draw back**, falter, quail, shrink **3** = **backfire**, boomerang, go pear-shaped (*inf*), misfire, rebound ◆*noun* **4** = **reaction**, backlash, kick, rebound, repercussion

recollect *verb* = **remember**, place, recall, summon up

recollection *noun* = **memory**, impression, recall, remembrance, reminiscence

recommend *verb* **1** = **advise**, advance, advocate, counsel, prescribe, propose, put forward, suggest OPPOSITE **reject**. **2** = **commend**, approve, endorse, praise

recompense *verb* **1** = **reward**, pay, remunerate **2** = **compensate**, make up for, pay for, reimburse, repay, requite, ress ◆*noun* **3** = **compensation**, amends, damages, payment, remuneration, reparation, repayment, requital, restitution **4** = **reward**, payment, return, wages

reconcile *verb* **1** = **resolve**, adjust, compose, put to rights, rectify, settle, square **2** = **make peace between**, appease, conciliate, propitiate, reunite **3** = **accept**, put up with (*inf*), resign oneself, submit, yield

reconciliation *noun* **2** = **pacification**, conciliation, reconcilement, reunion OPPOSITE **estrangement**

recondite *adjective* = **obscure**, arcane,

R

recondition ⊕ *verb* restore to good condition or working order.
reconnaissance ⊕ [rik-**kon**-iss-anss] *noun* survey for military or engineering purposes.

SPELLING TIP

The Bank of English shows that the most common way to misspell **reconnaissance** is to miss out an *s*, although there are examples where an *n* has been missed out instead. Remember, there are two *n*s in the middle and two *s*s.

reconnoitre ⊕ [rek-a-**noy**-ter] *verb* make a reconnaissance of.
reconsider ⊕ *verb* think about again, consider changing.
reconstitute *verb* **1** reorganize. **2** restore (dried food) to its former state by adding water. **reconstitution** *noun*
reconstruct ⊕ *verb* **1** rebuild. **2** use evidence to re-create. **reconstruction** *noun*
record ⊕ *noun* [**rek**-ord] **1** document or other thing that preserves information. **2** disc with indentations which a record player transforms into sound. **3** best recorded achievement. **4** known facts about a person's past. ◆ *verb* [rik-**kord**] **5** put in writing. **6** preserve (sound, TV programmes, etc.) on plastic disc, magnetic tape, etc., for reproduction on a playback device. **7** show or register. **off the record** not for publication. **recorder** *noun* **1** person or machine that records, esp. a video, cassette, or tape recorder. **2** type of flute, held vertically. **3** judge in certain courts. **recording** *noun*
recorded delivery postal service by which an official receipt is obtained for the posting and delivery of a letter or parcel. **record player** instrument for reproducing sound on records.
recount ⊕ *verb* tell in detail.
re-count *verb* **1** count again. ◆ *noun* **2** second or further count, esp. of votes.
recoup ⊕ [rik-**koop**] *verb* **1** regain or make good (a loss). **2** recompense or compensate.
recourse ⊕ *noun* source of help. **have recourse to** turn to a source of help or course of action.
recover ⊕ *verb* **1** become healthy again. **2** regain a former condition. **3** find again. **4** get back (a loss or expense). **5** obtain (useful substances) from waste. **recovery** *noun* **recoverable** *adjective*
re-create *verb* make happen or exist again. **re-creation** *noun*
recreation ⊕ *noun* agreeable or refreshing occupation, relaxation, or amusement.
recreational *adjective* **recreational vehicle** *noun chiefly US* a large vanlike vehicle equipped to be lived in.

——— T H E S A U R U S ———

concealed, dark, deep, difficult, hidden, mysterious, occult, profound, secret
recondition *verb* = **restore**, do up (*inf*), overhaul, remodel, renew, renovate, repair, revamp
reconnaissance *noun* = **inspection**, exploration, investigation, observation, recce (*sl*), scan, survey
reconnoitre *verb* = **inspect**, case (*sl*), explore, investigate, observe, scan, spy out, survey
reconsider *verb* = **rethink**, reassess, review, revise, think again
reconstruct *verb* **1** = **rebuild**, recreate, regenerate, remake, remodel, renovate, restore **2** = **deduce**, build up, piece together
record *noun* **1** = **document**, account, chronicle, diary, entry, file, journal, log, register, report **2** = **disc**, album, LP, single, vinyl **4** = **background**, career, history, performance ◆*verb* **5** = **set down**, chronicle, document, enter, log, minute, note, register, take down, write down **6** = **make a recording of**, tape, tape-record, video, video-tape **7** = **register**, give evidence of, indicate, say, show **off the**

record = **not for publication**, confidential, private, unofficial
recorder *noun* **1** = **chronicler**, archivist, clerk, diarist, historian, scribe
recording *noun* **6** = **record**, disc, tape, video
recount *verb* = **tell**, depict, describe, narrate, recite, relate, repeat, report
recoup *verb* **1** = **regain**, recover, retrieve, win back **2** = **compensate**, make up for, refund, reimburse, repay, requite
recourse *noun* = **option**, alternative, choice, expedient, remedy, resort, resource, way out
recover *verb* **1** = **get better**, convalesce, get well, heal, improve, mend, rally, recuperate, revive [OPPOSITE] **weaken**. **2-4** = **regain**, get back, recapture, reclaim, repossess, restore, retrieve [OPPOSITE] **lose**
recovery *noun* **1** = **improvement**, convalescence, healing, mending, recuperation, revival **2-4** = **retrieval**, reclamation, repossession, restoration
recreation *noun* = **pastime**, amusement, diversion, enjoyment, entertainment, fun, hobby, leisure activity, play, relaxation, sport

DICTIONARY

recrimination ⊙ *noun* mutual blame.
recriminatory *adjective*
recrudescence *noun* outbreak of trouble or a disease after a period of quiet.
recruit ⊙ *verb* **1** enlist (new soldiers, members, etc.). ◆ *noun* **2** newly enlisted soldier. **3** new member or supporter. **recruitment** *noun*
rectal *adjective* see RECTUM.
rectangle *noun* oblong four-sided figure with four right angles. **rectangular** *adjective*
rectify ⊙ *verb* **-fying, -fied 1** put right, correct. **2** *Chem* purify by distillation. **3** *Electricity* convert (alternating current) into direct current. **rectification** *noun* **rectifier** *noun*
rectilinear [rek-tee-**lin**-ee-er] *adjective* **1** in a straight line. **2** characterized by straight lines.
rectitude ⊙ *noun* moral correctness.
recto *noun, pl* **-tos 1** right-hand page of a book. **2** front of a sheet of paper.
rector *noun* **1** clergyman in charge of a parish. **2** head of certain academic institutions. **rectory** *noun, pl* **-ories** rector's house.
rectum *noun, pl* **-tums, -ta** final section of the large intestine. **rectal** *adjective*
recumbent *adjective* lying down.
recuperate ⊙ *verb* recover from illness. **recuperation** *noun* **recuperative** *adjective*
recur ⊙ *verb* **-curring, -curred** happen again. **recurrence** *noun* repetition. **recurrent** *adjective* **recurring decimal** number in which a pattern of digits is repeated indefinitely after the decimal point.
recycle ⊙ *verb* reprocess (used materials) for further use. **recyclable** *adjective*
red ⊙ *adjective* **redder, reddest 1** of a colour varying from crimson to orange and seen in blood, fire, etc. **2** flushed in the face from anger, shame, etc. ◆ *noun* **3** red colour. **4** (**R-**) *Informal* communist. **in the red** *Informal* in debt. **see red** *Informal* be angry. **redness** *noun* **redden** *verb* make or become red. **reddish**

adjective **redback spider** small venomous Australian spider with a red stripe on the back of the abdomen. **red blood cell** same as ERYTHROCYTE. **red-blooded** *adjective Informal* vigorous or virile. **redbrick** *adjective* (of a university) founded in the late 19th or early 20th century. **red card** *Soccer* piece of red pasteboard shown by a referee to indicate that a player has been sent off. **red carpet** very special welcome for an important guest.
redcoat *noun* **1** *Hist* British soldier. **2** *Canad informal* Mountie. **Red Crescent** name and symbol used by the Red Cross in Muslim countries. **Red Cross** international organization providing help for victims of war or natural disasters. **redcurrant** *noun* small round edible red berry. **red flag 1** symbol of revolution. **2** danger signal. **red-handed** *adjective Informal* (caught) in the act of doing something wrong or illegal. **redhead** *noun* person with reddish hair. **redheaded** *adjective* **red herring** something which diverts attention from the main issue. **red-hot** *adjective* **1** glowing red. **2** extremely hot. **3** very keen. **Red Indian** *Offens* Native American. **red-letter day** memorably happy or important occasion. **red light 1** traffic signal to stop. **2** danger signal. **red-light district** area where prostitutes work. **red meat** dark meat, esp. beef or lamb. **red rag** something that infuriates or provokes.
redshank *noun* large sandpiper with red legs. **red shift** appearance of lines in the spectra of distant stars nearer the red end of the spectrum than on earth: used to calculate the velocity of objects in relation to the earth. **redskin** *noun* *Informal offens* Native American. **redstart** *noun* European bird of the thrush family, the male of which has an orange-brown tail and breast. **red tape** excessive adherence to official rules.
redwood *noun* giant Californian conifer with reddish bark.
redeem ⊙ *verb* **1** make up for. **2** reinstate

R

THESAURUS

recrimination *noun* =**bickering**, counterattack, mutual accusation, quarrel, squabbling
recruit *verb* **1** = **enlist**, draft, enrol, levy, mobilize, muster, raise OPPOSITE **dismiss** ◆*noun* **3** = **beginner**, apprentice, convert, helper, initiate, learner, novice, trainee
rectify *verb* **1** = **correct**, adjust, emend, fix, improve, redress, remedy, repair, right
rectitude *noun* =**morality**, decency, goodness, honesty, honour, integrity, principle, probity, virtue OPPOSITE **corruption**
recuperate *verb* =**recover**, convalesce, get

better, improve, mend
recur *verb* =**happen again**, come again, persist, reappear, repeat, return, revert
recurrent *adjective* =**periodic**, continued, frequent, habitual, recurring
recycle *verb* =**reprocess**, reclaim, reuse, salvage, save
red *adjective* **1** = **crimson**, carmine, cherry, coral, ruby, scarlet, vermilion **2** = **flushed**, blushing, embarrassed, florid, shamefaced **in the red** *Inf* =**in debt**, in arrears, insolvent, overdrawn **see red** *Inf* =**lose one's temper**, be or get pissed (off) (*taboo sl*), blow one's top,

(oneself) in someone's good opinion. **3** free from sin. **4** buy back. **5** pay off (a loan or debt). **the Redeemer** Jesus Christ. **redeeming** *adjective* **redeemable** *adjective* **redemption** *noun* **redemptive** *adjective*

redeploy *verb* assign to a new position or task. **redeployment** *noun*

redevelop *verb* rebuild or renovate (an area or building). **redevelopment** *noun*

redirect *verb* **1** send in a new direction or course. **2** send (mail) to a different address.

redolent *adjective* **1** reminiscent (of). **2** smelling strongly (of). **redolence** *noun*

redouble *verb* increase, multiply, or intensify.

redoubt *noun* small fort defending a hilltop or pass.

redoubtable ❶ *adjective* formidable.

redound *verb* cause advantage or disadvantage (to).

redox *noun* chemical reaction in which one substance is reduced and the other is oxidized.

redress ❶ *verb* **1** make amends for. ♦ *noun* **2** compensation or amends.

reduce ❶ *verb* **1** bring down, lower. **2** lessen, weaken. **3** bring by force or necessity to some state or action. **4** slim. **5** simplify. **6** make (a sauce) more concentrated. **7** lose oxygen atoms in a chemical reaction. **reducible** *adjective* **reduction** *noun*

redundant ❶ *adjective* **1** (of a worker) no longer needed. **2** superfluous. **redundancy** *noun, pl* **-cies**

reduplicate *verb* make double, repeat.

re-echo *verb* **-echoing, -echoed** echo over and over again, resound.

reed *noun* **1** tall grass that grows in swamps and shallow water. **2** tall straight stem of this

plant. **3** *Music* vibrating cane or metal strip in certain wind instruments. **reedy** *adjective* **reedier, reediest 1** harsh and thin in tone. **2** full of reeds.

reef¹ *noun* **1** ridge of rock or coral near the surface of the sea. **2** vein of ore.

reef² *noun* **1** part of a sail which can be rolled up to reduce its area. ♦ *verb* **2** take in a reef of.

reefer *noun* **1** short thick jacket worn esp. by sailors. **2** *Old-fashioned slang* hand-rolled cigarette containing cannabis. **reef knot** two simple knots turned opposite ways.

reek ❶ *verb* **1** smell strongly. ♦ *noun* **2** strong unpleasant smell. **reek of** give a strong suggestion of.

reel¹ *noun* **1** cylindrical object on which film, tape, thread, or wire is wound. **2** winding apparatus, as of a fishing rod. **3** roll of film. **reel in** *verb* draw in by means of a reel. **reel off** *verb* recite or write fluently or quickly.

reel² ❶ *verb* stagger, sway, or whirl.

reel³ *noun* lively Scottish dance.

re-enter *verb* **1** come back into a place, esp. a country. **2** (of a spacecraft) return into the earth's atmosphere. **re-entry** *noun*

ref *noun Informal* referee in sport.

refectory *noun, pl* **-tories** room for meals in a college etc. **refectory table** long narrow dining table supported by two trestles.

refer ❶ *verb* **-ferring, -ferred** (foll. by *to*) **1** allude (to). **2** be relevant (to). **3** send (to) for information. **4** direct (a patient) to another doctor. **5** submit (to) for decision. **referable, referrable** *adjective* **referral** *noun* **reference** *noun* **1** act of referring. **2** citation or direction in a book. **3** written testimonial regarding character or capabilities. **with reference to**

———————— T H E S A U R U S ————————

R

crack up (*inf*), fly off the handle (*inf*), go ballistic (*sl, chiefly US*), go mad (*inf*), lose it (*inf*)

red-blooded *adjective Inf* =**vigorous**, lusty, robust, strong, virile

redeem *verb* **1** =**make up for**, atone for, compensate for, make amends for **2** =**reinstate**, absolve, restore to favour **3** =**save**, deliver, free **4** =**buy back**, reclaim, recover, regain, repurchase, retrieve

redemption *noun* **1** =**compensation**, amends, atonement, reparation **3** =**salvation**, deliverance **4** =**repurchase**, reclamation, recovery, repossession, retrieval

red-handed *adjective Inf* =**in the act**, bang to rights (*sl*), (in) flagrante delicto

redoubtable *adjective* =**formidable**, fearful, fearsome, mighty, powerful, strong

redress *verb* **1** =**make amends for**,

compensate for, make up for ♦*noun* **2** =**amends**, atonement, compensation, payment, recompense, reparation

reduce *verb* **1, 2** =**lessen**, abate, curtail, cut, cut down, decrease, diminish, lower, moderate, shorten, weaken [OPPOSITE] **increase**. **3** =**degrade**, break, bring low, downgrade, humble [OPPOSITE] **promote**

redundancy *noun* **1** =**unemployment**, joblessness, lay-off, the axe (*inf*), the sack (*inf*)

redundant *adjective* **1** =**unemployed**, jobless, out of work **2** =**superfluous**, extra, inessential, supernumerary, surplus, unnecessary, unwanted [OPPOSITE] **needed**

reek *verb* **1** =**stink**, pong (*Brit inf*), smell ♦*noun* **2** =**stink**, fetor, odour, pong (*Brit inf*), smell, stench

reel² *verb* =**stagger**, lurch, pitch, revolve, rock,

concerning. **reference book** book, such as an encyclopedia or dictionary, containing information or facts. **reference library** library in which books may be consulted but not borrowed.

> **LANGUAGE TIP**
>
> Do not confuse a *reference* with a *testimonial*, which is an open letter of recommendation about someone.

referee ❶ *noun* **1** umpire in sports, esp. football or boxing. **2** person willing to testify to someone's character etc. **3** arbitrator. ♦ *verb* **-eeing, -eed 4** act as referee of.
referendum ❶ *noun, pl* **-dums, -da** direct vote of the electorate on an important question.
refill *verb* **1** fill again. ♦ *noun* **2** second or subsequent filling. **3** replacement supply of something in a permanent container.
refine ❶ *verb* **1** purify. **2** improve. **3** separate (a mixture) into its components. **refined** *adjective* **1** cultured or polite. **2** purified.
refinement *noun* **1** improvement or elaboration. **2** fineness of taste or manners. **3** subtlety. **refinery** *noun, pl* **-eries** place where sugar, oil, etc. is refined.
refit *verb* **1** make ready for use again by repairing or re-equipping. ♦ *noun* **2** repair or re-equipping for further use.
reflation *noun* increase in the supply of money and credit designed to encourage economic activity. **reflate** *verb* **reflationary** *adjective*

reflect ❶ *verb* **1** throw back, esp. rays of light, heat, etc. **2** form an image of. **3** show. **4** consider at length. **5** bring credit or discredit upon. **reflecting telescope** telescope in which the initial image is formed by a concave mirror. **reflection** *noun* **1** act of reflecting. **2** return of rays of heat, light, etc. from a surface. **3** image of an object given back by a mirror etc. **4** conscious thought or meditation. **5** attribution of discredit or blame. **reflective** *adjective* **1** quiet, contemplative. **2** capable of reflecting images. **reflector** *noun* **1** polished surface for reflecting light etc. **2** reflecting telescope.
reflex *noun* **1** involuntary response to a stimulus or situation. ♦ *adjective* **2** (of a muscular action) involuntary. **3** reflected. **4** (of an angle) more than 180°. **reflexive** *adjective Grammar* **1** denoting a pronoun that refers back to the subject of a sentence or clause. **2** denoting a verb whose subject is the same as its object, e.g. *dress oneself*. **reflex camera** camera which uses a mirror to channel light from a lens to the viewfinder, so that the image seen is the same as the imagephotographed.
reflexology *noun* foot massage as a therapy in alternative medicine.
reform ❶ *noun* **1** improvement. ♦ *verb* **2** improve. **3** abandon evil practices. **reformer** *noun* **reformation** [ref-fer-**may**-shun] *noun* **1** a reforming. **2** (**R**-) religious movement in 16th-century Europe that resulted in the establishment of the Protestant Churches.
reformatory *noun, pl* **-ries** (formerly) institution for reforming young offenders.
reformist *noun, adjective* (person) seeking the reform of something rather than its abolition or overthrow.

——————————————— THESAURUS ———————————————

roll, spin, sway, swirl, whirl
refer *verb* (foll. by *to*) **1** = **allude**, bring up, cite, mention, speak of **2** = **relate**, apply, belong, be relevant to, concern, pertain **3** = **consult**, apply, go, look up, turn to **4** = **direct**, guide, point, send
referee *noun* **1** = **umpire**, adjudicator, judge, ref (*inf*) **3** = **arbitrator**, arbiter ♦ *verb* **5 a** = **umpire**, adjudicate, judge **b** = **arbitrate**, mediate
reference *noun* **2** = **citation**, allusion, mention, note, quotation **3** = **testimonial**, character, credentials, endorsement, recommendation
referendum *noun* = **public vote**, plebiscite
refine *verb* **1** = **purify**, clarify, cleanse, distil, filter, process **2** = **improve**, hone, perfect, polish
refined *adjective* **1** = **cultured**, civilized,

cultivated, elegant, polished, polite, well-bred
OPPOSITE **common**. **2** = **purified**, clarified, clean, distilled, filtered, processed, pure
OPPOSITE **coarse**
refinement *noun* **2** = **sophistication**, breeding, civility, courtesy, cultivation, culture, discrimination, gentility, good breeding, polish, taste **3** = **subtlety**, fine point, nicety, nuance
reflect *verb* **1** = **throw back**, echo, return **2** = **mirror**, reproduce **3** = **show**, demonstrate, display, indicate, manifest, reveal **4** = **consider**, cogitate, meditate, muse, ponder, ruminate, think, wonder
reflection *noun* **2** = **echo 3** = **image**, mirror image **4** = **consideration**, cogitation, contemplation, idea, meditation, musing, observation, opinion, thinking, thought
reflective *adjective* **1** = **thoughtful**,

refract *verb* change the course of (light etc.) passing from one medium to another.
refraction *noun* **refractive** *adjective* **refractor** *noun* **refracting telescope** telescope in which the image is formed by a series of lenses (also **refractor**).
refractory *adjective* **1** unmanageable or rebellious. **2** *Med* resistant to treatment. **3** resistant to heat.
refrain¹ ๏ *verb* **refrain from** keep oneself from doing.
refrain² ๏ *noun* frequently repeated part of a song.
refresh ๏ *verb* **1** revive or reinvigorate, as through food, drink, or rest. **2** stimulate (the memory). **refresher** *noun* **refreshing** *adjective* **1** having a reviving effect. **2** pleasantly different or new. **refreshment** *noun* something that refreshes, esp. food or drink.
refrigerate ๏ *verb* cool or freeze in order to preserve. **refrigeration** *noun* **refrigerator** *noun* full name for FRIDGE. **refrigerant** *noun* **1** fluid capable of vaporizing at low temperatures, used in refrigerators. ◆ *adjective* **2** refrigerating.
refuel *verb* **-elling, -elled** supply or be supplied with fresh fuel.
refuge ๏ *noun* (source of) shelter or protection. **refugee** *noun* person who seeks refuge, esp. in a foreign country.
refulgent *adjective* shining, radiant.
refund ๏ *verb* **1** pay back. ◆ *noun* **2** return of money. **3** amount returned.
refurbish ๏ *verb* renovate and brighten up.
refurbishment *noun*
refuse¹ ๏ *verb* **1** decline, deny, or reject. **2** (of a horse) be unwilling to jump a fence. **refusal** *noun* denial of anything demanded or offered.
refusenik *noun* person who refuses to obey a law or cooperate with the government because of strong beliefs.
refuse² ๏ *noun* rubbish or useless matter.
refute ๏ *verb* disprove. **refutation** *noun*
regain ๏ *verb* **1** get back or recover. **2** reach again.
regal ๏ *adjective* of or like a king or queen. **regally** *adverb* **regalia** *plural noun* ceremonial emblems of royalty or high office.
regale ๏ *verb* entertain (someone) with stories etc.
regard ๏ *verb* **1** consider. **2** look at. **3** heed. ◆ *noun* **4** respect or esteem. **5** attention. **6** look. ◆ *plural* **7** expression of goodwill. **as regards**, **regarding** in respect of, concerning.
regardless *adjective* **1** heedless. ◆ *adverb* **2** in spite of everything.
regatta *noun* meeting for yacht or boat races.

——————— THESAURUS ———————

contemplative, meditative, pensive
reform *noun* **1** = **improvement**, amendment, betterment, rehabilitation ◆ *verb* **2** = **improve**, amend, correct, mend, rectify, restore **3** = **mend one's ways**, clean up one's act (*inf*), go straight (*inf*), pull one's socks up (*Brit inf*), shape up (*inf*), turn over a new leaf
refrain¹ *verb* = **stop**, abstain, avoid, cease, desist, forbear, leave off, renounce
refrain² *noun* = **chorus**, melody, tune
refresh *verb* **1** = **revive**, brace, enliven, freshen, invigorate, revitalize, stimulate **2** = **stimulate**, jog, prompt, renew
refreshing *adjective* **1** = **stimulating**, bracing, fresh, invigorating OPPOSITE tiring. **2** = **new**, novel, original
refreshment *noun* = **food and drink**, drink, snack, titbit
refrigerate *verb* = **cool**, chill, freeze, keep cold
refuge *noun* = **shelter**, asylum, haven, hide-out, protection, retreat, sanctuary
refugee *noun* = **exile**, displaced person, émigré, escapee
refund *verb* **1** = **repay**, pay back, reimburse, restore, return ◆ *noun* **2, 3** = **repayment**, reimbursement, return

refurbish *verb* = **renovate**, clean up, do up (*inf*), mend, overhaul, repair, restore, revamp
refusal *noun* = **rejection**, denial, knock-back (*sl*), rebuff
refuse¹ *verb* **1** = **reject**, decline, deny, say no, spurn, turn down, withhold OPPOSITE allow
refuse² *noun* = **rubbish**, garbage, junk (*inf*), litter, trash, waste
refute *verb* = **disprove**, discredit, negate, overthrow, prove false, rebut OPPOSITE prove
regain *verb* **1** = **recover**, get back, recapture, recoup, retrieve, take back, win back **2** = **get back to**, reach again, return to
regal *adjective* = **royal**, kingly *or* queenly, magnificent, majestic, noble, princely
regale *verb* = **entertain**, amuse, delight, divert
regalia *plural noun* = **trappings**, accoutrements, decorations, emblems, finery, paraphernalia
regard *verb* **1** = **consider**, believe, deem, esteem, judge, rate, see, suppose, think, view **2** = **look at**, behold, check out (*inf*), clock (*Brit sl*), eye, eyeball (*US sl*), gaze at, observe, scrutinize, view, watch **3** = **heed**, attend, listen to, mind, pay attention to, take notice of ◆ *noun* **4** = **respect**, care, concern, consideration, esteem, thought **5** = **heed**, attention, interest, mind,

regenerate ⊕ *verb* [ri-**jen**-er-ate] **1** (cause to) undergo spiritual, moral, or physical renewal. **2** reproduce or re-create. ◆ *adjective* [ri-**jen**-er-it] **3** spiritually, morally, or physically renewed.
regeneration *noun* **regenerative** *adjective*
regent *noun* **1** ruler of a kingdom during the absence, childhood, or illness of its monarch. ◆ *adjective* **2** ruling as a regent, e.g. *prince regent*.
regency *noun, pl* **-cies** status or period of office of a regent.
reggae *noun* style of Jamaican popular music with a strong beat.
regicide *noun* **1** killing of a king. **2** person who kills a king.
regime ⊕ [ray-**zheem**] *noun* **1** system of government. **2** particular administration. **3** *Med* regimen.
regimen *noun* prescribed system of diet etc.
regiment *noun* **1** organized body of troops as a unit of the army. **2** large number or group.
regimental *adjective* **regimentals** *plural noun* military uniform. **regimentation** *noun*
regimented *adjective* very strictly controlled.
region ⊕ *noun* **1** administrative division of a country. **2** area considered as a unit but with no definite boundaries. **3** part of the body. **in the region of** approximately. **regional** *adjective* **regionalism** *noun* **1** division of a country or organization into geographical regions each having some autonomy. **2** loyalty to one's home region.
register ⊕ *noun* **1** (book containing) an official list or record of things. **2** range of a voice or instrument. ◆ *verb* **3** enter in a register

or set down in writing. **4** show or be shown on a meter or the face. **5** *Informal* have an effect or make an impression. **registered** *adjective* (of mail) insured against loss by the Post Office, e.g. *a registered letter.* **registration** *noun*
registration document document giving identification details of a vehicle, including its owner's name. **registration number** numbers and letters displayed on a vehicle to identify it.
registrar *noun* **1** keeper of official records. **2** senior hospital doctor, junior to a consultant.
registry *noun, pl* **-tries 1** place where official records are kept. **2** registration of a ship's place of origin, e.g. *a tanker of Liberian registry.*
register office, registry office place where births, marriages, and deaths are recorded.
Regius professor [**reej**-yuss] *noun* professor appointed by the Crown to a university chair founded by a royal patron.
regress ⊕ *verb* revert to a former worse condition. **regression** *noun* **1** act of regressing. **2** *Psychol* use of an earlier (inappropriate) mode of behaviour. **regressive** *adjective*
regret ⊕ *verb* **-gretting, -gretted 1** feel sorry about. **2** express apology or distress. ◆ *noun* **3** feeling of repentance, guilt, or sorrow.
regretful *adjective* **regrettable** *adjective*
regrettably *adverb*
regular ⊕ *adjective* **1** normal, customary, or usual. **2** symmetrical or even. **3** done or occurring according to a rule. **4** periodical. **5** employed continuously in the armed forces. ◆ *noun* **6** regular soldier. **7** *Informal* frequent customer. **regularity** *noun* **regularize** *verb*

———— T H E S A U R U S ————

notice **6 = look**, gaze, glance, scrutiny, stare ◆*plural* **7 = good wishes**, best wishes, compliments, greetings, respects **as regards, regarding = concerning**, about, in *or* with regard to, on the subject of, pertaining to, re, relating to, respecting, with reference to
regardless *adjective* **1 = heedless**, inconsiderate, indifferent, neglectful, negligent, rash, reckless, unmindful ◆*adverb* **2 = in spite of everything**, anyway, in any case, nevertheless
regenerate *verb* **1 = renew**, breathe new life into, invigorate, reawaken, reinvigorate, rejuvenate, restore, revive OPPOSITE degenerate
regime *noun* **1, 2 = government**, leadership, management, reign, rule, system
region *noun* **1 = area**, district, locality, part, place, quarter, section, sector, territory, tract, zone
regional *adjective* **1 = local**, district, parochial,

provincial, zonal
register *noun* **1 = list**, archives, catalogue, chronicle, diary, file, log, record, roll, roster ◆*verb* **3 = record**, catalogue, chronicle, enlist, enrol, enter, list, note **4 = show**, display, exhibit, express, indicate, manifest, mark, reveal
regress *verb* **= revert**, backslide, degenerate, deteriorate, fall away *or* off, go back, lapse, relapse, return OPPOSITE progress
regret *verb* **1 = feel sorry about**, bewail, deplore, lament OPPOSITE be satisfied with. **2 = grieve**, bemoan, miss, mourn, repent, rue ◆*noun* **3 = sorrow**, bitterness, compunction, contrition, penitence, remorse, repentance, ruefulness
regretful *adjective* **3 = sorry**, apologetic, contrite, penitent, remorseful, repentant, rueful, sad, sorrowful
regrettable *adjective* **= unfortunate**, disappointing, distressing, lamentable, sad, shameful

R

regularly *adverb*
regulate ⊕ *verb* **1** control, esp. by rules. **2** adjust slightly. **regulation** *noun* **1** rule. **2** regulating. ◆ *adjective* **3** in accordance with rules or conventions. **regulator** *noun* device that automatically controls pressure, temperature, etc. **regulatory** *adjective*
regurgitate ⊕ *verb* **1** vomit. **2** (of some birds and animals) bring back (partly digested food) into the mouth. **3** reproduce (ideas, facts, etc.) without understanding them. **regurgitation** *noun*
rehabilitate ⊕ *verb* **1** help (a person) to readjust to society after illness, imprisonment, etc. **2** restore to a former position or rank. **3** restore the good reputation of. **rehabilitation** *noun*
rehash ⊕ *verb* **1** rework or reuse. ◆ *noun* **2** old ideas presented in a new form.
rehearse ⊕ *verb* **1** practise (a play, concert, etc.). **2** repeat aloud. **rehearsal** *noun*
rehouse *verb* provide with a new (and better) home.
Reich [**rike**] *noun German* kingdom or regime. **Third Reich** Nazi dictatorship in Germany from 1933-45.
reign ⊕ *noun* **1** period of a sovereign's rule. **2** period when a person or thing is dominant, e.g. *reign of terror*. ◆ *verb* **3** rule (a country). **4**

be supreme.
reimburse ⊕ *verb* refund, pay back.
reimbursement *noun*
rein ⊕ *verb* **1** check or manage with reins. **2** control or limit. **reins** *plural noun* **1** narrow straps attached to a bit to guide a horse. **2** narrow straps attached to a harness to control a young child. **3** means of control. **give (a) free rein** allow a considerable amount of freedom.
reincarnation *noun* **1** rebirth of a soul in successive bodies. **2** one of a series of such transmigrations. **reincarnate** *verb*
reindeer *noun, pl* **-deer, -deers** deer of arctic regions with large branched antlers.
reinforce ⊕ *verb* **1** give added emphasis to. **2** strengthen with new support, material, or force. **3** strengthen with additional troops, ships, etc.
reinforcement *noun* **reinforced concrete** concrete strengthened by having steel mesh or bars embedded in it.
reinstate ⊕ *verb* restore to a former position.
reinstatement *noun*
reiterate ⊕ *verb* repeat again and again.
reiteration *noun*
reject ⊕ *verb* **1** refuse to accept or believe. **2** rebuff (a person). **3** discard as useless. **4** fail to accept (a tissue graft or organ transplant). ◆ *noun* **5** person or thing rejected as not up to standard. **rejection** *noun*

——————————— T H E S A U R U S ———————————

regular *adjective* **1** = **normal**, common, customary, habitual, ordinary, routine, typical, usual OPPOSITE **rare**. **2** = **even**, balanced, flat, level, smooth, straight, symmetrical, uniform OPPOSITE **irregular**. **3** = **systematic**, consistent, constant, even, fixed, ordered, set, stated, steady, uniform OPPOSITE **varied**
regulate *verb* **1** = **control**, direct, govern, guide, handle, manage, rule, run, supervise **2** = **adjust**, balance, fit, moderate, modulate, tune
regulation *noun* **1** = **rule**, decree, dictate, edict, law, order, precept, statute **2** = **control**, direction, government, management, supervision
regurgitate *verb* **1** = **vomit**, disgorge, puke (*sl*), sick up (*inf*), spew (out *or* up), throw up (*inf*)
rehabilitate *verb* **1** = **reintegrate**, adjust **3** = **redeem**, clear, reform, restore, save
rehash *verb* **1** = **rework**, refashion, rejig (*inf*), reuse, rewrite ◆*noun* **2** = **reworking**, new version, rearrangement, rewrite
rehearsal *noun* **1** = **practice**, drill, preparation, rehearsing, run-through
rehearse *verb* **1** = **practise**, drill, go over, prepare, run through, train **2** = **repeat**, recite

reign *noun* **1** = **rule**, command, control, dominion, monarchy, power ◆*verb* **3** = **rule**, be in power, command, govern, influence **4** = **be supreme**, hold sway, predominate, prevail
reimburse *verb* = **pay back**, compensate, recompense, refund, remunerate, repay, return
rein *verb* **2** = **control**, check, curb, halt, hold back, limit, restrain, restrict ◆*plural noun* **3** = **control**, brake, bridle, check, curb, harness, hold, restraint
reinforce *verb* **1** = **emphasize**, stress **2** = **support**, bolster, fortify, prop, strengthen, supplement, toughen
reinforcement *noun* **2** = **support**, augmentation, brace, buttress, fortification, prop, stay, strengthening
reinstate *verb* = **restore**, recall, re-establish, replace, return
reiterate *verb* = **repeat**, do again, restate, say again
reject *verb* **1** = **deny**, decline, disallow, exclude, renounce, repudiate, veto OPPOSITE **allow**. **2** = **rebuff**, jilt, refuse, repulse, say no to, spurn, turn down OPPOSITE **accept**. **3** = **discard**, eliminate, jettison, scrap, throw away *or* out OPPOSITE **accept** ◆*noun* **5** = **castoff**,

rejig ❶ *verb* **-jigging, -jigged 1** re-equip (a factory or plant). **2** rearrange.
rejoice ❶ *verb* feel or express great happiness. **rejoicing** *noun*
rejoin[1] *verb* join again.
rejoin[2] ❶ *verb* reply. **rejoinder** *noun* answer, retort.
rejuvenate ❶ *verb* restore youth or vitality to. **rejuvenation** *noun*
rekindle *verb* arouse former emotions or interests.
relapse ❶ *verb* **1** fall back into bad habits, illness, etc. ◆ *noun* **2** return of bad habits, illness, etc.
relate ❶ *verb* **1** establish a relation between. **2** have reference or relation to. **3** have an understanding (of people or ideas). **4** tell (a story) or describe (an event). **related** *adjective*
relation ❶ *noun* **1** connection between things. **2** relative. **3** connection by blood or marriage. **4** act of relating (a story). ◆ *plural* **5** social or political dealings. **6** family. **7** *Euphemistic* sexual intercourse. **relationship** *noun* **1** dealings and feelings between people or countries. **2**

emotional or sexual affair. **3** connection between two things. **4** association by blood or marriage, kinship. **relative** *adjective* true to a certain degree or extent.
relative ❶ *adjective* **1** true to a certain degree or extent. **2** dependent on relation to something else, not absolute. **3** having reference or relation (to). **4** *Grammar* referring to a word or clause earlier in the sentence. ◆ *noun* **5** person connected by blood or marriage.
relatively *adverb* **relativity** *noun* **1** subject of two theories of Albert Einstein, dealing with relationships of space, time, and motion, and acceleration andgravity. **2** state of being relative.
relax ❶ *verb* **1** make or become looser, less tense, or less rigid. **2** ease up from effort or attention, rest. **3** be less strict about. **4** become more friendly. **relaxed** *adjective* **relaxing** *adjective* **relaxation** *noun*
relay ❶ *noun* **1** fresh set of people or animals relieving others. **2** *Electricity* device for making or breaking a local circuit. **3** broadcasting station receiving and retransmitting

——————— THESAURUS ———————

discard, failure, second OPPOSITE **prize**
rejig *verb* **2** = **rearrange**, alter, juggle, manipulate, reorganize, tweak
rejoice *verb* = **be glad**, be happy, be overjoyed, celebrate, exult, glory OPPOSITE **lament**
rejoicing *noun* = **happiness**, celebration, elation, exultation, gladness, joy, jubilation, merrymaking
rejoin[2] *verb* = **reply**, answer, respond, retort, riposte
rejoinder *noun* = **reply**, answer, comeback (*inf*), response, retort, riposte
rejuvenate *verb* = **revitalize**, breathe new life into, refresh, regenerate, renew, restore
relapse *verb* **1 a** = **lapse**, backslide, degenerate, fail, regress, revert, slip back **b** = **worsen**, deteriorate, fade, fail, sicken, sink, weaken OPPOSITE **improve** ◆*noun* **2 a** = **lapse**, backsliding, regression, retrogression **b** = **worsening**, deterioration, turn for the worse, weakening OPPOSITE **improvement**
relate *verb* **1** = **connect**, associate, correlate, couple, join, link **2** = **concern**, apply, be relevant to, have to do with, pertain, refer **4** = **tell**, describe, detail, narrate, recite, recount, report
related *adjective* **1** = **akin**, kindred **2** = **associated**, affiliated, akin, connected, interconnected, joint, linked OPPOSITE **unrelated**

relation *noun* **1** = **connection**, bearing, bond, comparison, correlation, link **2** = **relative**, kin, kinsman *or* kinswoman **3** = **kinship**, affinity, kindred ◆*plural* **5** = **dealings**, affairs, connections, contact, interaction, intercourse, relationship **6** = **family**, clan, kin, kindred, kinsfolk, kinsmen, relatives, tribe
relationship *noun* **2** = **affair**, liaison **3** = **connection**, correlation, link, parallel, similarity, tie-up
relative *adjective* **1 2** = **dependent**, allied, associated, comparative, contingent, corresponding, proportionate, related **3** = **relevant**, applicable, apposite, appropriate, apropos, germane, pertinent ◆*noun* **5** = **relation**, kinsman *or* kinswoman, member of one's *or* one's family
relatively *adverb* **1** = **comparatively**, rather, somewhat
relax *verb* **1** = **lessen**, abate, ease, ebb, let up, loosen, lower, moderate, reduce, relieve, slacken, weaken OPPOSITE **tighten**. **2** = **be** *or* feel at ease, calm, chill out (*sl, chiefly US*), outspan (*S Afr*), rest, take it easy, unwind **3** = **lighten up** (*sl*), chill out (*sl, chiefly US*), take it easy
relaxation *noun* **2** = **leisure**, enjoyment, fun, pleasure, recreation, rest
relaxed *adjective* **2** = **easy-going**, casual, comfortable, easy, free and easy, informal, laid-back (*inf*), leisurely

R

release

programmes. ♦ verb **-laying, -layed 4** pass on (a message). **relay race** race between teams in which each runner races part of the distance.
release ❶ verb **1** set free. **2** let go or fall. **3** issue (a record, film, etc.) for sale or public showing. **4** emit heat, energy, etc. ♦ noun **5** setting free. **6** statement to the press. **7** act of issuing for sale or publication. **8** newly issued film, record, etc.
relegate ❶ verb **1** put in a less important position. **2** demote (a sports team) to a lower league. **relegation** noun
relent ❶ verb give up a harsh intention, become less severe. **relentless** adjective **1** unremitting. **2** merciless.
relevant ❶ adjective to do with the matter in hand. **relevance** noun

> **SPELLING TIP**
>
> A common word in English, **relevant** is not always spelt correctly. The final syllable is the problem and sometimes appears incorrectly in the Bank of English as -ent.

reliable ❶ adjective able to be trusted, dependable. **reliably** adverb **reliability** noun
reliance ❶ noun dependence, confidence, or trust. **reliant** adjective
relic ❶ noun **1** something that has survived from the past. **2** body or possession of a saint, regarded as holy. ♦ plural **3** remains or traces.
relict noun Obs **1** relic. **2** widow.
relief ❶ noun **1** gladness at the end or removal of pain, distress, etc. **2** release from monotony or duty. **3** money or food given to victims of disaster, poverty, etc. **4** freeing of a besieged city etc. **5** person who replaces another. **6** projection of a carved design from the surface. **7** any vivid effect resulting from contrast, e.g. comic relief. **relieve** verb bring relief to. **relieve oneself** urinate or defecate. **relief map** map showing the shape and height of land by shading.
religion ❶ noun system of belief in and worship of a supernatural power or god.
religious adjective **1** of religion. **2** pious or devout. **3** scrupulous or conscientious. **religiously** adverb
relinquish ❶ verb give up or abandon. **relinquishment** noun
reliquary [rel-lik-wer-ee] noun, pl **-quaries** case or shrine for holy relics.
relish ❶ verb **1** enjoy, like very much. **2** anticipate eagerly. ♦ noun **3** liking or enjoyment. **4** pleasurable anticipation. **5** appetizing savoury food, such as pickle. **6** zestful quality or flavour.

——————— THESAURUS ———————

relay noun **1 = shift**, relief, turn ♦verb **4 = pass on**, broadcast, carry, communicate, send, spread, transmit
release verb **1 = set free**, discharge, drop, extricate, free, liberate, loose, unbridle, undo, unfasten OPPOSITE **keep**. **3 = issue**, circulate, distribute, launch, make known, make public, publish, put out OPPOSITE **suppress** ♦noun **5 = liberation**, deliverance, discharge, emancipation, freedom, liberty OPPOSITE **detention**. **6 = proclamation 7 = issue**, publication
relegate verb **= demote**, downgrade
relent verb **= be merciful**, capitulate, change one's mind, come round, have pity, show mercy, soften, yield OPPOSITE **remain firm**
relentless adjective **1 = unremitting**, incessant, nonstop, persistent, unrelenting, unrelieved **2 = merciless**, cruel, fierce, implacable, pitiless, remorseless, ruthless, unrelenting OPPOSITE **yielding**
relevant adjective **= significant**, apposite, appropriate, apt, fitting, germane, pertinent, related, to the point OPPOSITE **irrelevant**
reliable adjective **= dependable**, faithful, safe, sound, staunch, sure, true, trustworthy OPPOSITE **irresponsible**
reliance noun **= trust**, belief, confidence, dependence, faith
relic noun **1 = remnant**, fragment, keepsake, memento, souvenir, trace, vestige
relief noun **1 = ease**, comfort, cure, deliverance, mitigation, release, remedy, solace **2 = rest**, break, breather (inf), relaxation, respite **3 = aid**, assistance, help, succour, support
relieve verb **a = ease**, alleviate, assuage, calm, comfort, console, cure, mitigate, outspan (S Afr), relax, soften, soothe OPPOSITE **aggravate**. **b = help**, aid, assist, succour, support, sustain
religious adjective **2 = devout**, devotional, faithful, godly, holy, pious, sacred, spiritual OPPOSITE **secular**. **3 = conscientious**, faithful, meticulous, punctilious, rigid, scrupulous
relinquish verb **= give up**, abandon, abdicate, cede, drop, forsake, leave, let go, renounce, surrender
relish verb **1 = enjoy**, delight in, fancy, like, revel in, savour OPPOSITE **dislike** ♦noun **3 = enjoyment**, fancy, fondness, gusto, liking, love, partiality, penchant, predilection, taste

relive *verb* experience (a sensation etc.) again, esp. in the imagination.
relocate *verb* move to a new place to live or work. **relocation** *noun*
reluctant ❶ *adjective* unwilling or disinclined. **reluctantly** *adverb* **reluctance** *noun*
rely ❶ *verb* **-lying, -lied 1** depend (on). **2** trust. **reliable** *adjective* able to be trusted.
remain ❶ *verb* **1** continue. **2** stay, be left behind. **3** be left (over). **4** be left to be done, said, etc. **remains** *plural noun* **1** relics, esp. of ancient buildings. **2** dead body. **remainder** *noun* **1** part which is left. **2** amount left over after subtraction or division. **3** copy of a book sold cheaply because it has been impossible to sell at full price. ♦ *verb* **4** offer (copies of a poorly selling book) at reduced prices.
remand *verb* send back into custody or put on bail before trial. **on remand** in custody or on bail before trial. **remand centre** place where accused people are detained awaiting trial.
remark ❶ *verb* **1** make a casual comment (on). **2** say. **3** observe or notice. ♦ *noun* **4** observation or comment. **remarkable** *adjective* **1** worthy of note or attention. **2** striking or unusual. **remarkably** *adverb*
remarry *verb* **-rying, -ried** marry again following a divorce or the death of one's previous husband or wife.
rematch *noun Sport* second or return game or contest between two players.

remedy ❶ *noun, pl* **-edies 1** means of curing pain or disease. **2** means of solving a problem. ♦ *verb* **-edying, -edied 3** put right.
remediable *adjective* able to be put right.
remedial *adjective* intended to correct a specific disability, handicap, etc.
remember ❶ *verb* **1** retain in or recall to one's memory. **2** keep in mind. **3** give money to, as in a tip or through a will. **remember to** pass on someone's greeting to, e.g. *remember me to your mother*. **remembrance** *noun* **1** memory. **2** token or souvenir. **3** honouring of the memory of a person or event.
Remembrance Day, Remembrance Sunday Sunday closest to November 11th, on which the dead of both World Wars are commemorated.
remind ❶ *verb* **1** cause to remember. **2** put in mind (of). **reminder** *noun* **1** something that recalls the past. **2** note to remind a person of something not done.
reminisce ❶ *verb* talk or write of past times, experiences, etc. **reminiscence** *noun* **1** remembering. **2** thing recollected. ♦ *plural* **3** memoirs. **reminiscent** *adjective* reminding or suggestive (of).
remiss ❶ *adjective* negligent or careless.
remission ❶ *noun* **1** reduction in the length of a prison term. **2** pardon or forgiveness. **3** easing of intensity, as of an illness.
remit ❶ *verb* [rim-**mitt**] **-mitting, -mitted 1**

——————— THESAURUS ———————

OPPOSITE dislike. **5 = condiment**, sauce, seasoning **6 = flavour**, piquancy, smack, spice, tang, taste, trace
reluctant *adjective* **= unwilling**, disinclined, hesitant, loath, unenthusiastic OPPOSITE **willing**
rely *verb* **1 = depend**, bank, bet, count ♦*noun* **2 = trust**
remain *verb* **1 = continue**, abide, dwell, endure, go on, last, persist, stand, stay, survive OPPOSITE **go**. **2 = stay behind**, be left, delay, linger, wait
remainder *noun* **1 = rest**, balance, excess, leavings, remains, remnant, residue, surplus
remaining *adjective* **3 = left-over**, lingering, outstanding, persisting, surviving, unfinished
remains *plural noun* **1 = remnants**, debris, dregs, leavings, leftovers, relics, residue, rest **2 = corpse**, body, cadaver, carcass
remark *verb* **1, 2 = comment**, declare, mention, observe, pass comment, reflect, say, state **3 = notice**, espy, make out, mark, note, observe, perceive, see ♦*noun* **4 = comment**, observation, reflection, statement, utterance
remarkable *adjective* **1 = notable**,

outstanding **2 = extraordinary**, rare, singular, striking, surprising, uncommon, unusual, wonderful
remedy *noun* **1 = cure**, medicine, nostrum, treatment ♦*verb* **3 = put right**, correct, fix, rectify
remember *verb* **1 = recall**, call to mind, commemorate, look back (on), recollect, reminisce, think back OPPOSITE **forget**. **2 = bear in mind**, keep in mind
remembrance *noun* **1 = memory**, recall, recollection, reminiscence, thought **2 = souvenir**, commemoration, keepsake, memento, memorial, monument, reminder, token
remind *verb* **= call to mind**, jog one's memory, make (someone) remember, prompt
reminisce *verb* **= recall**, hark back, look back, recollect, remember, think back
reminiscence *noun* **= recollection**, anecdote, memoir, memory, recall, remembrance
reminiscent *adjective* **= suggestive**, evocative, similar
remiss *adjective* **= careless**, forgetful, heedless,

R

send (money) for goods, services, etc., esp. by post. **2** cancel (a punishment or debt). **3** refer (a decision) to a higher authority or later date. ◆ *noun* [**ree**-mitt] **4** area of competence or authority. **remittance** *noun* money sent as payment.

remix *verb* **1** change the relative prominence of each performer's part of (a recording). ◆ *noun* **2** remixed version of a recording.

remnant ⊕ *noun* **1** small piece, esp. of fabric, left over. **2** surviving trace.

remonstrate ⊕ *verb* argue in protest. **remonstrance, remonstration** *noun*

remorse ⊕ *noun* feeling of sorrow and regret for something one did. **remorseful** *adjective* **remorseless** *adjective* **1** pitiless. **2** persistent. **remorselessly** *adverb*

remote ⊕ *adjective* **1** far away, distant. **2** aloof. **3** slight or faint. **remotely** *adverb* **remote control** control of an apparatus from a distance by an electrical device.

remould *verb* **1** change completely. **2** renovate (a worn tyre). ◆ *noun* **3** renovated tyre.

remove ⊕ *verb* **1** take away or off. **2** get rid

of. **3** dismiss from office. ◆ *noun* **4** degree of difference. **removable** *adjective* **removal** *noun* removing, esp. changing residence.

remunerate ⊕ *verb* reward or pay. **remuneration** *noun* **remunerative** *adjective*

renaissance ⊕ *noun* **1** revival or rebirth. **2** (**R-**) revival of learning in the 14th-16th centuries. ◆ *adjective* **3** (**R-**) of the Renaissance.

renal [**ree**-nal] *adjective* of the kidneys.

renascent *adjective* becoming active or vigorous again.

rend ⊕ *verb* **rending, rent 1** tear or wrench apart. **2** (of a sound) break (the silence) violently.

render ⊕ *verb* **1** cause to become. **2** give or provide (aid, a service, etc.). **3** submit or present (a bill). **4** portray or represent. **5** cover with plaster. **6** melt down (fat).

rendezvous ⊕ [**ron**-day-voo] *noun, pl* **-vous 1** appointment. **2** meeting place. ◆ *verb* **3** meet as arranged.

rendition ⊕ *noun* **1** performance. **2** translation.

renegade ⊕ *noun* person who deserts a cause.

——————— T H E S A U R U S ———————

lax, neglectful, negligent, thoughtless

remission *noun* **2** = **pardon**, absolution, amnesty, discharge, exemption, release, reprieve **3** = **lessening**, abatement, alleviation, ebb, lull, relaxation, respite

remit *verb* **1** = **send**, dispatch, forward, mail, post, transmit **2** = **cancel**, halt, repeal, rescind, stop **3** = **postpone**, defer, delay, put off, shelve, suspend

remittance *noun* = **payment**, allowance, fee

remnant *noun* = **remainder**, end, fragment, leftovers, remains, residue, rest, trace, vestige

remonstrate *verb* = **protest**, argue, dispute, dissent, object, take issue

remorse *noun* = **regret**, anguish, compunction, contrition, grief, guilt, penitence, repentance, shame, sorrow

remorseless *adjective* **1** = **pitiless**, callous, cruel, inhumane, merciless, ruthless **2** = **relentless**, inexorable, persistent

remote *adjective* **1** = **distant**, far, inaccessible, in the middle of nowhere, isolated, out-of-the-way, secluded OPPOSITE near. **2** = **aloof**, abstracted, cold, detached, distant, reserved, standoffish, uncommunicative, withdrawn OPPOSITE interested. **3** = **slight**, doubtful, dubious, faint, outside, slender, slim, small, unlikely OPPOSITE good

removal *noun* **a** = **taking away** or **off** or **out**, dislodgment, ejection, elimination, eradication,

extraction, uprooting, withdrawal **b** = **dismissal**, expulsion **c** = **move**, departure, flitting (*Scot & N Eng dial*), relocation, transfer

remove *verb* **1, 2** = **take away** or **off** or **out**, abolish, delete, detach, displace, eject, eliminate, erase, excise, extract, get rid of, wipe from the face of the earth, withdraw OPPOSITE **replace. 3** = **dismiss**, depose, dethrone, discharge, expel, oust, throw out OPPOSITE install

remunerate *verb* = **pay**, compensate, recompense, reimburse, repay, requite, reward

renaissance *noun* **1** = **rebirth**, reappearance, reawakening, renewal, restoration, resurgence, revival

rend *verb* **1** = **tear**, rip, rupture, separate, wrench

render *verb* **1** = **make**, cause to become, leave **2** = **provide**, furnish, give, hand out, pay, present, submit, supply, tender **4** = **represent**, act, depict, do, give, perform, play, portray

rendezvous *noun* **1** = **appointment**, assignation, date, engagement, meeting, tryst (*arch*) **2** = **meeting place**, gathering point, venue ◆*verb* **3** = **meet**, assemble, come together, gather, join up

rendition *noun* **1** = **performance**, arrangement, interpretation, portrayal, presentation, reading, rendering, version **2** = **translation**, interpretation, reading,

renege ❶ [rin-**nayg**] *verb* go back (on a promise etc.).
renew ❶ *verb* **1** begin again. **2** make valid again. **3** grow again. **4** restore to a former state. **5** replace (a worn part). **6** restate or reaffirm. **renewable** *adjective* **renewal** *noun*
rennet *noun* substance for curdling milk to make cheese.
renounce ❶ *verb* **1** give up (a belief, habit, etc.) voluntarily. **2** give up (a title or claim) formally. **renunciation** *noun*
renovate ❶ *verb* restore to good condition. **renovation** *noun*
renown ❶ *noun* widespread good reputation. **renowned** *adjective* famous.
rent¹ ❶ *verb* **1** give or have use of in return for regular payments. ◆ *noun* **2** regular payment for use of land, a building, machine, etc. **rental** *noun* **1** sum payable as rent. ◆ *adjective* **2** of or relating to rent.
rent² ❶ *noun* **1** tear or fissure. ◆ *verb* **2** past of REND.
rentier [ron-tee-ay] *noun French* person who lives off unearned income such as rents or interest.
renunciation ❶ *noun* see RENOUNCE.
reorganize *verb* organize in a new and more efficient way. **reorganization** *noun*

rep¹ *noun* short for REPERTORY COMPANY.
rep² *noun* short for REPRESENTATIVE.
repaid *verb* past of REPAY.
repair¹ ❶ *verb* **1** restore to good condition, mend. ◆ *noun* **2** act of repairing. **3** repaired part. **4** state or condition, e.g. *in good repair*. **repairable** *adjective* **reparation** *noun* something done or given as compensation.
repair² ❶ *verb* go (to).
repartee ❶ *noun* **1** interchange of witty retorts. **2** witty retort.
repast *noun* meal.
repatriate *verb* send (someone) back to his or her own country. **repatriation** *noun*
repay ❶ *verb* **repaying, repaid 1** pay back, refund. **2** do something in return for, e.g. *repay hospitality*. **repayable** *adjective* **repayment** *noun*
repeal ❶ *verb* **1** cancel (a law) officially. ◆ *noun* **2** act of repealing.
repeat ❶ *verb* **1** say or do again. **2** happen again, recur. ◆ *noun* **3** act or instance of repeating. **4** programme broadcast again. **5** *Music* passage that is identical to the one before it. **repeated** *adjective* **repeatedly** *adverb*
repeater *noun* firearm that may be discharged many times without reloading. **repetition** *noun* act of repeating.

——————— THESAURUS ———————

transcription, version
renegade *noun* =**deserter**, apostate, defector, traitor, turncoat
renege *verb* =**break one's word**, back out, break a promise, default, go back
renew *verb* =**recommence**, continue, extend, recreate, reopen, repeat, resume **4** =**restore**, mend, modernize, overhaul, refit, refurbish, renovate, repair **5** =**replace**, refresh, replenish, restock **6** =**reaffirm**
renounce *verb* =**give up**, abjure, deny, disown, forsake, forswear, quit, recant, relinquish, waive ⟨OPPOSITE⟩ **claim**
renovate *verb* =**restore**, do up (*inf*), modernize, overhaul, recondition, refit, refurbish, renew, repair
renown *noun* =**fame**, distinction, eminence, note, reputation, repute
renowned *adjective* =**famous**, celebrated, distinguished, eminent, esteemed, notable, noted, well-known
rent¹ *verb* **1** =**hire**, charter, lease, let ◆*noun* **2** =**hire**, fee, lease, payment, rental
rent² *noun* **1** =**tear**, gash, hole, opening, rip, slash, slit, split
renunciation *noun* =**giving up**, abandonment, abdication, abjuration, denial,

disavowal, forswearing, rejection, relinquishment, repudiation
repair¹ *verb* **1** =**mend**, fix, heal, patch, patch up, renovate, restore ⟨OPPOSITE⟩ **damage** ◆*noun* **2, 3** =**mend**, darn, overhaul, patch, restoration **4** =**condition**, form, shape (*inf*), state
repair² *verb* =**go**, betake oneself, head for, leave for, move, remove, retire, set off for, withdraw
reparation *noun* =**compensation**, atonement, damages, recompense, restitution, satisfaction
repartee *noun* **1** =**wit**, badinage, banter, wittiness, wordplay **2** =**riposte**
repay *verb* **1** =**pay back**, compensate, recompense, refund, reimburse, requite, return, square **2** =**reciprocate**, avenge, get even with (*inf*), get one's own back on (*inf*), hit back, retaliate, revenge
repeal *verb* **1** =**abolish**, annul, cancel, invalidate, nullify, recall, reverse, revoke ⟨OPPOSITE⟩ **pass** ◆*noun* **2** =**abolition**, annulment, cancellation, invalidation, rescindment ⟨OPPOSITE⟩ **introduction**
repeat *verb* **1** =**reiterate**, echo, replay, reproduce, rerun, restate, retell ◆*noun* **3** =**repetition**, echo, reiteration, replay, rerun

R

repel ❶ *verb* **-pelling, -pelled 1** be disgusting to. **2** drive back, ward off. **3** resist. **repellent** *adjective* **1** distasteful. **2** resisting water etc. ◆ *noun* **3** something that repels, esp. a chemical to repel insects.

repent ❶ *verb* feel regret for (a deed or omission). **repentance** *noun* **repentant** *adjective*

repercussions *plural noun* indirect effects, often unpleasant.

repertoire ❶ *noun* **1** stock of plays, songs, etc. that a player or company can give. **2** range of things someone or something is capable of doing.

repertory *noun, pl* **-ries** repertoire.

repertory company permanent theatre company producing a succession of plays.

repetition ❶ *noun* **1** act of repeating. **2** thing repeated. **repetitive, repetitious** *adjective* full of repetition.

rephrase *verb* express in different words.

repine *verb* fret or complain.

replace ❶ *verb* **1** substitute for. **2** put back. **replacement** *noun*

replay *noun* **1** (also **action replay**) immediate reshowing on TV of an incident in sport, esp. in slow motion. **2** second sports match, esp. one following an earlier draw. ◆ *verb* **3** play (a match, recording, etc.) again.

replenish ❶ *verb* fill up again, resupply. **replenishment** *noun*

replete ❶ *adjective* filled or gorged. **repletion** *noun*

replica ❶ *noun* exact copy. **replicate** *verb* make or be a copy of. **replication** *noun*

reply ❶ *verb* **-plying, -plied 1** answer or respond. ◆ *noun, pl* **-plies 2** answer or response.

report ❶ *verb* **1** give an account of. **2** make a report (on). **3** make a formal complaint about. **4** present oneself (to). **5** be responsible (to). ◆ *noun* **6** account or statement. **7** rumour. **8** written statement of a child's progress at school. **9** bang. **reportedly** *adverb* according to rumour. **reporter** *noun* person who gathers news for a newspaper, TV, etc. **reported speech** report that gives the content of what someone said but not the actual words.

repose¹ ❶ *noun* **1** peace. **2** composure. **3** sleep. ◆ *verb* **4** lie or lay at rest. **5** lie when

———————— THESAURUS ————————

repeatedly *adverb* **2** = over and over, frequently, many times, often

repel *verb* **1** = disgust, gross out (*US sl*), nauseate, offend, revolt, sicken OPPOSITE attract. **2, 3** = drive off, fight, hold off, parry, rebuff, repulse, resist, ward off OPPOSITE submit to

repellent *adjective* **1** = disgusting, abhorrent, hateful, horrid, loathsome, nauseating, noxious, offensive, repugnant, repulsive, revolting, sickening **3** = proof, impermeable, repelling, resistant

repent *verb* = regret, be sorry, feel remorse, rue

repentance *noun* = regret, compunction, contrition, grief, guilt, penitence, remorse

repentant *adjective* = regretful, contrite, penitent, remorseful, rueful, sorry

repercussions *plural noun* = consequences, backlash, result, sequel, side effects

repertoire *noun* **1** = range, collection, list, repertory, stock, store, supply

repetition *noun* = repeating, echo, recurrence, reiteration, renewal, replication, restatement, tautology

repetitive, repetitous *adjective* = monotonous, boring, dull, mechanical, recurrent, tedious, unchanging, unvaried

replace *verb* **1** = take the place of, follow, oust, substitute, succeed, supersede, supplant,

take over from **2** = put back, re-establish, reinstate, restore

replacement *noun* **1** = successor, double, proxy, stand-in, substitute, surrogate, understudy

replenish *verb* = refill, fill, provide, reload, replace, restore, top up OPPOSITE empty

replete *adjective* = filled, crammed, full, full up, glutted, gorged, sated, stuffed OPPOSITE empty

replica *noun* = duplicate, carbon copy (*inf*), copy, facsimile, imitation, model, reproduction OPPOSITE original

replicate *verb* = copy, duplicate, mimic, recreate, reduplicate, reproduce

reply *verb* **1** = answer, counter, reciprocate, rejoin, respond, retaliate, retort ◆*noun* **2** = answer, counter, counterattack, reaction, rejoinder, response, retaliation, retort

report *verb* **1, 2** = communicate, broadcast, cover, describe, detail, inform of, narrate, pass on, recount, relate, state, tell **4** = present oneself, appear, arrive, come, turn up ◆*noun* **6** = account, communication, description, narrative, news, record, statement, word **7** = rumour, buzz, gossip, hearsay, talk **9** = bang, blast, boom, crack, detonation, discharge, explosion, noise, sound

reporter *noun* = journalist, correspondent, hack (*derog*), journo (*sl*), pressman, writer

dead.
repose² *verb* place one's trust (in).
repository ❶ *noun, pl* **-ries** place where valuables are deposited for safekeeping, store.
repossess *verb* (of a lender) take back property from a customer who is behind with payments. **repossession** *noun*
reprehend ❶ *verb* find fault with.
reprehensible *adjective* open to criticism, unworthy.
reprehensible ❶ *adjective* open to criticism, unworthy.
represent ❶ *verb* **1** act as a delegate or substitute for. **2** stand for. **3** symbolize. **4** make out to be. **5** portray, as in art. **representation** *noun* **representational** *adjective* (of art) portraying people or things, not abstract.
representative *noun* **1** person chosen to stand for a group. **2** (travelling) salesperson. ◆ *adjective* **3** typical.
repress ❶ *verb* **1** keep (feelings) in check. **2** restrict the freedom of. **repression** *noun* **repressive** *adjective*

reprieve ❶ *verb* **1** postpone the execution of (a condemned person). **2** give temporary relief to. ◆ *noun* **3** (document granting) postponement or cancellation of a punishment. **4** temporary relief.
reprimand ❶ *verb* **1** blame (someone) officially for a fault. ◆ *noun* **2** official blame.
reprint *verb* **1** print further copies of (a book). ◆ *noun* **2** reprinted copy.
reprisal ❶ *noun* retaliation.
reproach ❶ *noun, verb* blame, rebuke.
reproachful *adjective* **reproachfully** *adverb*
reprobate [rep-roh-bate] *adjective, noun* depraved or disreputable (person).
reprobation *noun* disapproval or blame.
reproduce ❶ *verb* **1** produce a copy of. **2** bring new individuals into existence. **3** re-create. **reproducible** *adjective* **reproduction** *noun* **1** process of reproducing. **2** facsimile, as of a painting etc. **3** quality of sound from an audio system. ◆ *adjective* **4** made in imitation of an earlier style, e.g. *reproduction furniture*.
reproductive *adjective*

—————————— T H E S A U R U S ——————————

repose¹ *noun* **1** = **peace**, ease, quietness, relaxation, respite, rest, stillness, tranquillity **2** = **composure**, calmness, poise, self-possession **3** = **sleep**, slumber ◆*verb* **4** = **rest**, lie, lie down, recline, rest upon
repository *noun* = **store**, depository, storehouse, treasury, vault
reprehensible *adjective* = **blameworthy**, bad, culpable, disgraceful, objectionable, shameful, unworthy OPPOSITE **praiseworthy**
represent *verb* **1, 2** = **stand for**, act for, betoken, mean, serve as, speak for, symbolize **3** = **exemplify**, embody, epitomize, personify, symbolize, typify **5** = **depict**, denote, describe, illustrate, outline, picture, portray, show
representation *noun* **5 a** = **picture**, illustration, image, likeness, model, portrait **b** = **portrayal**, account, depiction, description
representative *noun* **1** = **delegate**, agent, deputy, member, proxy, spokesman *or* spokeswoman **2** = **salesman**, agent, commercial traveller, rep ◆*adjective* **3** = **typical**, archetypal, characteristic, exemplary, symbolic OPPOSITE **extraordinary**
repress *verb* **1** = **control**, bottle up, check, curb, hold back, inhibit, restrain, stifle, suppress OPPOSITE **release**. **2** = **subdue**, quell, subjugate OPPOSITE **free**
repression *noun* **2** = **subjugation**, constraint, control, despotism, domination, restraint, suppression, tyranny
repressive *adjective* **2** = **oppressive**, absolute,

authoritarian, despotic, dictatorial, tyrannical
reprieve *verb* **1** = **grant a stay of execution to**, let off the hook (*sl*), pardon **2** = **relieve**, abate, allay, alleviate, mitigate, palliate ◆*noun* **3** = **stay of execution**, amnesty, deferment, pardon, postponement, remission **4** = **relief**, alleviation, mitigation, palliation, respite
reprimand *verb* **1** = **blame**, censure, dress down (*inf*), haul over the coals (*inf*), rap over the knuckles, rebuke, rouse on (*Aust*), scold, tear (someone) off a strip (*Brit inf*) OPPOSITE **praise** ◆*noun* **2** = **blame**, censure, dressing-down (*inf*), rebuke, reproach, reproof, talking-to (*inf*) OPPOSITE **praise**
reprisal *noun* = **retaliation**, retribution, revenge, vengeance
reproach *noun* = **blame**, censure, condemnation, disapproval, opprobrium, rebuke ◆*verb* = **blame**, censure, condemn, criticize, lambast(e), read the riot act, rebuke, reprimand, rouse on (*Aust*), scold, upbraid
reproduce *verb* **1** = **copy**, duplicate, echo, imitate, match, mirror, recreate, repeat, replicate **2** = **breed**, multiply, procreate, propagate, spawn
reproduction *noun* **1** = **breeding**, generation, increase, multiplication **2** = **copy**, duplicate, facsimile, imitation, picture, print, replica OPPOSITE **original**
reproof *noun* = **rebuke**, blame, censure, condemnation, criticism, reprimand, scolding OPPOSITE **praise**

R

reprove ⊕ *verb* speak severely to (someone) about a fault. **reproof** *noun* severe blaming of someone for a fault.

reptile *noun* cold-blooded egg-laying vertebrate with horny scales or plates, such as a snake or tortoise. **reptilian** *adjective*

republic *noun* **1** form of government in which the people or their elected representatives possess the supreme power. **2** country in which a president is the head of state. **republican** *adjective* **1** of or supporting a republic. ♦ *noun* **2** person who supports or advocates a republic. **republicanism** *noun* **Republican** *noun*, *adjective* **1** (member or supporter) of the Republican Party, the more conservative of the two main political parties in the US. **2** (member or supporter) of the Irish Republican Army. **Republicanism** *noun*

repudiate ⊕ [rip-**pew**-dee-ate] *verb* **1** reject the authority or validity of. **2** disown. **repudiation** *noun*

repugnant ⊕ *adjective* offensive or distasteful. **repugnance** *noun*

repulse ⊕ *verb* **1** be disgusting to. **2** drive (an army) back. **3** rebuff or reject. ♦ *noun* **4** driving back. **5** rejection or rebuff. **repulsion** *noun* **1** distaste or aversion. **2** *Physics* force separating two objects. **repulsive** *adjective* loathsome,

disgusting.

reputation ⊕ *noun* estimation in which a person is held. **reputable** [**rep**-pew-tab-bl] *adjective* of good reputation, respectable. **repute** *noun* reputation. **reputed** *adjective* supposed. **reputedly** *adverb*

request ⊕ *verb* **1** ask. ♦ *noun* **2** asking. **3** thing asked for.

Requiem [**rek**-wee-em] *noun* **1** Mass for the dead. **2** music for this.

require ⊕ *verb* **1** want or need. **2** demand. **requirement** *noun* **1** essential condition. **2** specific need or want.

requisite ⊕ [**rek**-wizz-it] *adjective* **1** necessary, essential. ♦ *noun* **2** essential thing.

requisition ⊕ *verb* **1** demand (supplies). ♦ *noun* **2** formal demand, such as for materials or supplies.

requite ⊕ *verb* return to someone (the same treatment or feeling as received). **requital** *noun*

reredos [**rear**-doss] *noun* ornamental screen behind an altar.

rerun *noun* **1** film or programme that is broadcast again, repeat. **2** race that is run again. ♦ *verb* **3** put on (a film or programme) again. **4** run (a race) again.

resale *noun* selling of something purchased earlier.

——————— T H E S A U R U S ———————

reprove *verb* =**rebuke**, berate, blame, censure, condemn, read the riot act, reprimand, rouse on (*Aust*), scold, tear into (*inf*), tear (someone) off a strip (*Brit inf*), tell off (*inf*)

repudiate *verb* **1** =**reject**, deny, disavow, disclaim, renounce OPPOSITE own. **2** =**disown**

repugnance *noun* =**distaste**, abhorrence, aversion, disgust, dislike, hatred, loathing

repugnant *adjective* =**distasteful**, abhorrent, disgusting, loathsome, nauseating, offensive, repellent, revolting, sickening, vile OPPOSITE attractive

repulse *verb* **1** =**disgust**, nauseate, offend, put off, repel, revolt, sicken, turn one's stomach **2** =**drive back**, beat off, fight off, rebuff, repel, ward off **3** =**reject**, rebuff, refuse, snub, spurn, turn down

repulsion *noun* **1** =**disgust**, abhorrence, aversion, detestation, distaste, hatred, loathing, repugnance, revulsion

repulsive *adjective* =**disgusting**, abhorrent, foul, loathsome, nauseating, repellent, revolting, sickening, vile

reputable *adjective* =**respectable**, creditable, excellent, good, honourable, reliable, trustworthy, well-thought-of, worthy

reputation *noun* =**name**, character, esteem,

estimation, renown, repute, standing, stature

repute *noun* =**reputation**, celebrity, distinction, eminence, fame, name, renown, standing, stature

reputed *adjective* =**supposed**, alleged, believed, considered, deemed, estimated, held, reckoned, regarded

request *verb* **1** =**ask (for)**, appeal for, demand, desire, entreat, invite, seek, solicit ♦*noun* **2** =**asking**, appeal, call, demand, desire, entreaty, suit

require *verb* **1** =**need**, crave, desire, lack, miss, want, wish **2** =**order**, ask, bid, call upon, command, compel, demand, exact, insist upon

requirement *noun* **1** =**necessity**, demand, essential, must, prerequisite, stipulation **2** =**need**, lack, want

requisite *adjective* **1** =**necessary**, called for, essential, indispensable, needed, needful, obligatory, required ♦*noun* **2** =**necessity**, condition, essential, must, need, prerequisite, requirement

requisition *verb* **1** =**demand**, call for, request ♦*noun* **2** =**demand**, call, request, summons

requital *noun* =**return**, repayment

requite *verb* =**return**, get even, give in return, pay (someone) back in his *or* her own coin,

rescind ❼ *verb* annul or repeal.
rescue ❼ *verb* **-cuing, -cued 1** deliver from danger or trouble, save. ✦ *noun* **2** rescuing.
rescuer *noun*
research ❼ *noun* **1** systematic investigation to discover facts or collect information. ✦ *verb* **2** carry out investigations. **researcher** *noun*
resemble ❼ *verb* be or look like.
resemblance *noun*
resent ❼ *verb* feel indignant or bitter about.
resentful *adjective* **resentment** *noun*
reservation ❼ *noun* **1** doubt. **2** exception or limitation. **3** seat, room, etc. that has been reserved. **4** area of land reserved for use by a particular group. **5** (also **central reservation**) strip of ground separating the two carriageways of a dual carriageway or motorway.
reserve ❼ *verb* **1** set aside, keep for future use. **2** obtain by arranging beforehand, book. **3** retain. ✦ *noun* **4** something, esp. money or troops, kept for emergencies. **5** area of land reserved for a particular purpose. **6** *Sport* substitute. **7** concealment of feelings or friendliness. **reservation** *noun* **1** doubt. **2** exception or limitation. **3** seat, room, etc. that has been reserved. **reserved** *adjective* **1** not

showing one's feelings, lacking friendliness. **2** set aside for use by a particular person.
reservist *noun* member of a military reserve.
reserve price minimum price acceptable to the owner of property being auctioned.
reservoir ❼ *noun* **1** natural or artificial lake storing water for community supplies. **2** store or supply of something.
reshuffle *noun* **1** reorganization. ✦ *verb* **2** reorganize.
reside ❼ *verb* dwell permanently. **residence** *noun* **1** home or house. **2** (period of) living in a place. **in residence** (of an artist) working for a set period at a college, gallery, etc., e.g. *writer in residence*. **resident** *noun* **1** person who lives in a place. **2** bird or animal that does not migrate. ✦ *adjective* **3** living in a place. **4** (of a bird or animal) not migrating. **residential** *adjective* **1** (of part of a town) consisting mainly of houses. **2** providing living accommodation.
residue ❼ *noun* **1** what is left, remainder. **2** *Law* what is left of an estate after debts have been paid and specific gifts made. **residual** *adjective* **residuum** *noun, pl* **-ua** residue.
resign ❼ *verb* **1** give up office, a job, etc. **2** reconcile (oneself) to. **3** give up a right, claim,

——————— T H E S A U R U S ———————

reciprocate, repay, respond, retaliate
rescind *verb* =**annul**, cancel, countermand, declare null and void, invalidate, repeal, set aside confirm
rescue *verb* **1** =**save**, deliver, get out, liberate, recover, redeem, release, salvage OPPOSITE **abandon** ✦*noun* **2** =**liberation**, deliverance, recovery, redemption, release, salvage, salvation, saving
research *noun* **1** =**investigation**, analysis, examination, exploration, probe, study ✦*verb* **2** =**investigate**, analyse, examine, explore, probe, study
resemblance *noun* =**similarity**, correspondence, kinship, likeness, parallel, sameness, similitude
resemble *verb* =**be like**, bear a resemblance to, be similar to, look like, mirror, parallel
resent *verb* =**be bitter about**, begrudge, be pissed (off) about (*taboo sl*), grudge, object to, take exception to, take offence at OPPOSITE **be content with**
resentful *adjective* =**bitter**, angry, embittered, grudging, indignant, miffed (*inf*), offended, piqued, pissed (off) (*taboo sl*)
resentment *noun* =**bitterness**, animosity, bad blood, grudge, ill feeling, ill will, indignation, pique, rancour, umbrage
reservation *noun* **1** =**doubt**, hesitancy,

scruple **2** =**condition**, proviso, qualification, rider, stipulation **4** =**reserve**, p, sanctuary, territory
reserve *verb* **1** =**keep**, hoard, hold, put by, retain, save, set aside, stockpile, store **2** =**book**, engage, prearrange, secure ✦*noun* **4** =**store**, cache, fund, hoard, reservoir, savings, stock, supply **5** =**reservation**, park, preserve, sanctuary, tract **6** *Sport* =**substitute 7** =**shyness**, constraint, reservation, restraint, reticence, secretiveness, silence, taciturnity
reserved *adjective* **1** =**uncommunicative**, restrained, reticent, retiring, secretive, shy, silent, standoffish, taciturn, undemonstrative OPPOSITE **open**. **2** =**set aside**, booked, engaged, held, kept, restricted, retained, spoken for, taken
reservoir *noun* **1** =**lake**, basin, pond, tank **2** =**store**, pool, reserves, source, stock, supply
reside *verb* =**live**, abide, dwell, inhabit, lodge, stay OPPOSITE **visit**
residence *noun* **1** =**home**, abode, domicile, dwelling, flat, habitation, house, lodging, place
resident *noun* **1** =**inhabitant**, citizen, local, lodger, occupant, tenant OPPOSITE **visitor**
residual *adjective* **1** =**remaining**, leftover, unconsumed, unused, vestigial
residue *noun* **1** =**remainder**, dregs, excess, extra, leftovers, remains, remnant, rest, surplus

R

etc. **resigned** *adjective* content to endure.
resignation *noun* 1 resigning. 2 passive
endurance of difficulties.
resilient ❶ *adjective* 1 (of a person) recovering
quickly from a shock etc. 2 able to return to
normal shape after stretching etc. **resilience**
noun
resin [rezz-in] *noun* 1 sticky substance from
plants, esp. pines. 2 similar synthetic substance.
resinous *adjective*
resist ❶ *verb* 1 withstand or oppose. 2 refrain
from despite temptation. 3 be proof against.
resistance *noun* 1 act of resisting. 2 capacity
to withstand something. 3 *Electricity* opposition
offered by a circuit to the passage of a current
through it. 4 any force that slows or hampers
movement, e.g. *wind resistance*. 5 (R-) illegal
organization fighting for national liberty in a
country under enemy occupation. **resistant**
adjective **resistible** *adjective* **resistor** *noun*
component of an electrical circuit producing
resistance.
resit *verb* -sitting, -sat 1 take (an exam)
again. ♦ *noun* 2 exam that has to be taken
again.
resolute ❶ *adjective* firm in purpose.
resolutely *adverb* **resolution** *noun* 1 firmness

of conduct or character. 2 thing resolved upon.
3 decision of a court or vote of an assembly. 4
act of resolving. 5 ability of a television,
microscope, etc. to show fine detail.
resolve ❶ *verb* 1 decide with an effort of will.
2 form (a resolution) by a vote. 3 separate the
component parts of. 4 make clear, settle. ♦
noun 5 absolute determination. **resolved**
adjective determined.
resonance ❶ *noun* 1 echoing, esp. with a
deep sound. 2 sound produced in one object
by sound waves coming from another object.
resonant *adjective* **resonate** *verb* **resonator**
noun
resort ❶ *verb* 1 have recourse (to) for help
etc. ♦ *noun* 2 place for holidays. 3 recourse.
resound ❶ [riz-**zownd**] *verb* 1 echo or ring
with sound. 2 (of sounds) echo or ring. 3 be
widely known, e.g. *his fame resounded through
the land*. **resounding** *adjective* 1 echoing. 2
clear and emphatic.
resource ❶ *noun* 1 thing resorted to for
support. 2 ingenuity. 3 means of achieving
something. ♦ *plural* 4 sources of economic
wealth. 5 stock that can be drawn on, funds.
resourceful *adjective* **resourcefulness** *noun*
respect ❶ *noun* 1 consideration. 2 deference

——————— T H E S A U R U S ———————

resign *verb* 1 = **quit**, abdicate, give in one's
notice, leave, step down (*inf*), vacate 2
= **accept**, acquiesce, give in, resign oneself,
submit, succumb, yield 3 = **give up**, abandon,
forgo, forsake, relinquish, renounce, surrender,
yield
resignation *noun* 1 = **leaving**, abandonment,
abdication, departure 2 = **acceptance**,
acquiescence, compliance, endurance,
nonresistance, passivity, patience, submission,
sufferance OPPOSITE **resistance**
resigned *adjective* = **stoical**, compliant, long-
suffering, patient, subdued, unresisting
resilient *adjective* 1 = **tough**, buoyant, hardy,
irrepressible, strong OPPOSITE **weak**. 2
= **flexible**, elastic, plastic, pliable, rubbery,
springy, supple OPPOSITE **stiff**
resist *verb* 1 = **oppose**, battle, combat, defy,
hinder, stand up to OPPOSITE **accept**. 2
= **refrain from**, abstain from, avoid, forbear,
forgo, keep from OPPOSITE **enjoy**. 3
= **withstand**, be proof against
resistance *noun* 1 = **fighting**, battle,
defiance, fight, hindrance, impediment,
obstruction, opposition, struggle
resistant *adjective* 1 = **opposed**, antagonistic,
hostile, intractable, intransigent, unwilling 3
= **impervious**, hard, proof against, strong,

tough, unaffected by
resolute *adjective* = **determined**, dogged,
firm, fixed, immovable, inflexible, set, steadfast,
strong-willed, tenacious, unshakable,
unwavering OPPOSITE **irresolute**
resolution *noun* 1 = **determination**,
doggedness, firmness, perseverance, purpose,
resoluteness, resolve, steadfastness, tenacity,
willpower 2 = **decision**, aim, declaration,
determination, intent, intention, purpose,
resolve
resolve *verb* 1 = **decide**, agree, conclude,
determine, fix, intend, purpose 3 = **break
down**, analyse, reduce, separate 4 = **work out**,
answer, clear up, crack, fathom ♦*noun* 5
= **determination**, firmness, resoluteness,
resolution, steadfastness, willpower OPPOSITE
indecision
resonant *adjective* 1 = **echoing**, booming,
resounding, reverberating, ringing, sonorous
resort *verb* 1 = **have recourse to**, employ, fall
back on, turn to, use, utilize ♦*noun* 2 = **holiday
centre**, haunt, retreat, spot, tourist centre 3
= **recourse**, reference
resound *verb* 1, 2 = **echo**, re-echo, resonate,
reverberate, ring
resounding *adjective* 1 = **echoing**, booming,
full, powerful, resonant, ringing, sonorous

or esteem. **3** point or aspect. **4** reference or relation, e.g. *with respect to.* ♦ *plural* **5** polite greetings. ♦ *verb* **6** treat with esteem. **7** show consideration for. **respecter** *noun* **respectful** *adjective* **respectfully** *adverb* **respecting** *preposition* concerning.
respectable ❶ *adjective* **1** worthy of respect. **2** having good social standing and reputation. **3** fairly good. **respectably** *adverb* **respectability** *noun*
respective ❶ *adjective* relating separately to each of those in question. **respectively** *adverb*
respiration [ress-per-ray-shun] *noun* **1** breathing. **2** process in plants and animals of taking in oxygen and giving out carbon dioxide. **3** breakdown of complex organic substances by living cells to produce energy and carbon dioxide. **respirator** *noun* apparatus worn over the mouth and breathed through as protection against dust, poison gas, etc., or to provideartificial respiration. **respiratory** *adjective* **respire** *verb* breathe.
respite ❶ *noun* **1** pause, interval of rest. **2** delay.
resplendent ❶ *adjective* **1** brilliant or splendid. **2** shining. **resplendence** *noun*
respond ❶ *verb* **1** answer. **2** act in answer to

any stimulus. **3** react favourably. **respondent** *noun Law* defendant. **response** *noun* **1** answer. **2** reaction to a stimulus. **3** (in some Christian churches) words sung or recited in reply to a priest during a service. **responsive** *adjective* readily reacting to some influence. **responsiveness** *noun*
responsible ❶ *adjective* **1** having control and authority. **2** being the cause (of some action). **3** reporting or accountable (to). **4** sensible and dependable. **5** involving responsibility. **responsibly** *adverb* **responsibility** *noun, pl* **-ties 1** state of being responsible. **2** person or thing for which one is responsible.
respray *noun* new coat of paint applied to a car, van, etc.
rest[1] ❶ *noun* **1** freedom from exertion etc. **2** repose. **3** pause, esp. in music. **4** object used for support. ♦ *verb* **5** take a rest. **6** give a rest (to). **7** be supported. **8** place on a support. **9** depend or rely, e.g. *their hopes rested on an early end to the dispute.* **10** (of someone's gaze) direct at or settle on, e.g. *her eyes rested on the dog.* **restful** *adjective* **restless** *adjective*
rest[2] ❶ *noun* **1** what is left. **2** others. ♦ *verb* **3** remain, continue to be.
restaurant ❶ *noun* commercial establishment

——————————— T H E S A U R U S ———————————

resource *noun* **2** =**ingenuity**, ability, capability, cleverness, initiative, inventiveness **3** =**means**, course, device, expedient, resort ♦*plural* **4** =**assets**, capital, holdings, lolly (*Aust & NZ sl*), money, riches, wealth **5** =**funds**, reserves, supplies
resourceful *adjective* **2** =**ingenious**, able, bright, capable, clever, creative, inventive
respect *noun* **1** =**consideration 2** =**regard**, admiration, deference, esteem, estimation, honour, recognition OPPOSITE> contempt. **3** =**particular**, aspect, characteristic, detail, feature, matter, point, sense, way **4** *as in* **with respect to** =**relation**, bearing, connection, reference, regard ♦*verb* **6** =**think highly of**, admire, defer to, esteem, have a good *or* high opinion of, honour, look up to, value **7** =**abide by**, adhere to, comply with, follow, heed, honour, obey, observe, show consideration for OPPOSITE> ignore
respectable *adjective* **1, 2** =**honourable**, decent, estimable, good, honest, reputable, upright, worthy OPPOSITE> indecent. **3** =**reasonable**, ample, appreciable, considerable, decent, fair, sizable *or* sizeable, substantial OPPOSITE> small
respectful *adjective* **2** =**polite**, civil, courteous, deferential, mannerly, reverent,

well-mannered
respective *adjective* =**specific**, individual, own, particular, relevant
respite *noun* **1** =**pause**, break, cessation, halt, interval, lull, recess, relief, rest
resplendent *adjective* =**brilliant**, bright, dazzling, glorious, radiant, shining, splendid
respond *verb* **1** =**answer**, counter, reciprocate, rejoin, reply, retort, return OPPOSITE> ignore. **2** =**react**
response *noun* **1** =**answer**, feedback, rejoinder, reply, retort, return **2** =**reaction**
responsibility *noun* **1** =**accountability**, answerability, blame, culpability, fault, guilt, liability **2** =**duty**, care, charge, liability, obligation, onus
responsible *adjective* **1** =**in charge**, in authority, in control **2** =**to blame**, at fault, culpable, guilty **3** =**accountable**, answerable, liable OPPOSITE> unaccountable. **4** =**sensible**, dependable, level-headed, rational, reliable, trustworthy OPPOSITE> irresponsible
responsive *adjective* =**sensitive**, alive, impressionable, open, reactive, receptive, susceptible
rest[1] *noun* **1** =**inactivity 2** =**relaxation**, leisure, repose **3** =**pause**, break, cessation, halt, interlude, intermission, interval, lull, respite,

R

serving meals. **restaurateur** [rest-er-a-**tur**] *noun* person who owns or runs a restaurant.

restaurant car railway coach where meals are served.

restitution ❶ *noun* **1** giving back. **2** reparation or compensation.

restive ❶ *adjective* restless or impatient.

restore ❶ *verb* **1** return (a building, painting, etc.) to its original condition. **2** cause to recover health or spirits. **3** give back, return. **4** re-establish. **restoration** *noun* **restorative** [rest-or-a-tiv] *adjective* **1** restoring. ◆ *noun* **2** food or medicine to strengthen etc. **restorer** *noun*

restrain ❶ *verb* **1** hold (someone) back from action. **2** control or restrict. **restraint** *noun* **1** something that restrains. **2** control, esp. self-control. **3** restraining. **restrained** *adjective* not displaying emotion.

restrict ❶ *verb* confine to certain limits. **restriction** *noun* **restrictive** *adjective*

restrictive practice trading or industrial agreement which is against the interests of the public or other business interests.

restructure *verb* reorganize.

result ❶ *noun* **1** outcome or consequence. **2** score. **3** number obtained from a calculation. **4** exam mark or grade. ◆ *verb* **5** (foll. by *from*) be the outcome or consequence (of). **6** (foll. by *in*) end (in). **resultant** *adjective* **1** arising as a result. ◆ *noun* **2** *Maths, physics* sum of two or more vectors, such as the force resulting from two or more forces acting on a single point.

resume ❶ *verb* **1** begin again. **2** occupy or take again. **resumption** *noun*

résumé [**rezz**-yew-may] *noun* summary.

resurgence ❶ *noun* rising again to vigour. **resurgent** *adjective*

resurrect ❶ *verb* **1** restore to life. **2** use once more (something discarded etc.), revive. **resurrection** *noun* **1** rising again (esp. from the dead). **2** revival.

resuscitate ❶ [ris-**suss**-it-tate] *verb* restore to consciousness. **resuscitation** *noun*

——————— THESAURUS ———————

stop **4** = **support**, base, holder, prop, stand ◆*verb* **5 a** = **relax**, be at ease, put one's feet up, sit down, take it easy OPPOSITE **work**. **b** = **stop**, break off, cease, halt, have a break, take a breather (*inf*) OPPOSITE **work**. **7** = **be supported**, lean, lie, recline, repose, sit **8** = **place**, lean, lie, prop, sit

rest[2] *noun* **1** = **remainder**, balance, excess, remains, remnants, residue, surplus **2** = **others**

restaurant *noun* = **café**, bistro, cafeteria, diner (*chiefly US & Canad*), tearoom

restful *adjective* **1**, **2** = **relaxing**, calm, calming, peaceful, quiet, relaxed, serene, soothing, tranquil

restitution *noun* **1** = **return**, restoration **2** = **compensation**, amends, recompense, reparation, requital

restive *adjective* = **restless**, edgy, fidgety, impatient, jumpy, nervous, on edge, wired (*sl*)

restless *adjective* **a** = **moving**, nomadic, roving, transient, unsettled, unstable, wandering OPPOSITE **settled**. **b** = **unsettled**, edgy, fidgeting, fidgety, jumpy, nervous, on edge, restive, wired (*sl*)

restore *verb* **1** = **repair**, fix, mend, rebuild, recondition, reconstruct, refurbish, renew, renovate OPPOSITE **wreck**. **2** = **revive**, build up, refresh, revitalize, strengthen OPPOSITE **weaken**. **3** = **return**, bring back, give back, recover, reinstate, replace OPPOSITE **abolish**. **4** = **reinstate**, re-establish, reintroduce

restrain *verb* **1**, **2** = **hold back**, check, constrain, contain, control, curb, curtail, hamper, hinder, inhibit, restrict OPPOSITE **help**

restrained *adjective* = **controlled**, calm, mild, moderate, self-controlled, undemonstrative OPPOSITE **wild**

restraint *noun* **1** = **limitation**, ban, check, curb, embargo, interdict, limit, rein OPPOSITE **freedom**. **2** = **self-control**, control, inhibition, moderation, self-discipline, self-possession, self-restraint OPPOSITE **licence**

restrict *verb* = **limit**, bound, confine, contain, hamper, handicap, inhibit, regulate, restrain OPPOSITE **widen**

result *noun* **1** = **consequence**, effect, end, end result, outcome, product, sequel, upshot OPPOSITE **beginning** ◆*verb* **5** (foll. by *from*) = **arise**, appear, derive, develop, ensue, follow, happen, issue, spring **6** (foll. by *in*) = **end**, culminate

resume *verb* **1** = **begin again**, carry on, continue, go on, proceed, reopen, restart OPPOSITE **stop**

résumé *noun* = **summary**, précis, recapitulation, rundown, synopsis

resurgence *noun* = **revival**, rebirth, re-emergence, renaissance, resumption, resurrection, return

resurrect *verb* **1** = **restore to life**, raise from the dead **2** = **revive**, bring back, reintroduce, renew

resurrection *noun* **1** = **raising** *or* **rising from the dead**, return from the dead **2** = **revival**, reappearance, rebirth, renaissance, renewal, restoration, resurgence, return OPPOSITE **killing**

DICTIONARY

> **SPELLING TIP**
>
> There is a silent c in
> **resuscitate**, but only one: it
> comes after the second s, not
> after the first one.

retail noun **1** selling of goods individually or in small amounts to the public. ♦ adjective **2** of or engaged in such selling. ♦ adverb **3** by retail. ♦ verb **4** sell or be sold retail. **5** recount in detail. **retailer** noun

retain ⊕ verb **1** keep in one's possession. **2** be able to hold or contain. **3** engage the services of. **retainer** noun **1** fee to retain someone's services. **2** payment to reserve a room or flat for future use. **3** old-established servant of a family.

retake verb **-taking, -took, -taken 1** recapture. **2** take something, such as an examination, again. ♦ noun **3** Films act of rephotographing a scene.

retaliate ⊕ verb repay an injury or wrong in kind. **retaliation** noun **retaliatory** adjective

retard ⊕ verb delay or slow (progress or development). **retarded** adjective underdeveloped, esp. mentally. **retardation** noun

retch ⊕ verb try to vomit.

retention noun **1** retaining. **2** ability to remember. **3** abnormal holding of something, esp. fluid, in the body. **retentive** adjective

capable of retaining or remembering.

rethink verb consider again, esp. with a view to changing one's tactics.

reticent ⊕ adjective uncommunicative, reserved. **reticence** noun

retina noun, pl **-nas, -nae** light-sensitive membrane at the back of the eye.

retinue ⊕ noun band of attendants.

retire ⊕ verb **1** (cause to) give up office or work, esp. through age. **2** go away or withdraw. **3** go to bed. **retired** adjective having retired from work etc. **retirement** noun **retirement pension** weekly pension paid by the government to retired people over a specified age. **retiring** adjective shy.

retort[1] ⊕ verb **1** reply quickly, wittily, or angrily. ♦ noun **2** quick, witty, or angry reply.

retort[2] noun glass container with a bent neck used for distilling.

retouch verb restore or improve by new touches, esp. of paint.

retrace verb go back over (a route etc.) again.

retract ⊕ verb **1** withdraw (a statement etc.). **2** draw in or back. **retractable, retractile** adjective able to be retracted. **retraction** noun

retread verb, noun same as REMOULD.

retreat ⊕ verb **1** move back from a position, withdraw. ♦ noun **2** act of or military signal for retiring or withdrawal. **3** place to which anyone retires, refuge. **4** period of seclusion, esp. for religious contemplation.

THESAURUS

off

resuscitate verb =**revive**, bring round, resurrect, revitalize, save

retain verb **1** =**keep**, hold, maintain, preserve, reserve, save OPPOSITE **lose**. **2** =**hold 3** =**hire**, commission, employ, engage, pay, reserve

retainer noun **1, 2** =**fee**, advance, deposit **3** =**servant**, attendant, domestic

retaliate verb =**pay (someone) back**, get even with (inf), get one's own back (inf), hit back, reciprocate, strike back, take revenge OPPOSITE **turn the other cheek**

retaliation noun =**revenge**, an eye for an eye, repayment, reprisal, requital, vengeance

retard verb =**slow down**, arrest, check, delay, handicap, hinder, hold back or up, impede, set back OPPOSITE **speed up**

retch verb =**gag**, be sick, heave, puke (sl), regurgitate, spew, throw up (inf), vomit

reticent adjective =**uncommunicative**, close-lipped, quiet, reserved, silent, taciturn, tight-lipped, unforthcoming OPPOSITE **communicative**

retinue noun =**attendants**, aides, entourage,

escort, followers, servants

retire verb **1** =**stop working**, give up work **2** =**withdraw**, depart, exit, go away, leave **3** =**go to bed**, hit the hay (sl), hit the sack (sl), turn in (inf)

retirement noun **2** =**withdrawal**, privacy, retreat, seclusion, solitude

retiring adjective =**shy**, bashful, quiet, reserved, self-effacing, timid, unassertive, unassuming

retort[1] verb **1** =**reply**, answer, come back with, counter, respond, return, riposte ♦noun **2** =**reply**, answer, comeback (inf), rejoinder, response, riposte

retract verb **1** =**withdraw**, deny, disavow, disclaim, eat one's words, recant, renege, renounce, revoke, take back **2** =**draw in**, pull back, pull in, sheathe

retreat verb **1** =**withdraw**, back away, back off, depart, draw back, fall back, go back, leave, pull back OPPOSITE **advance** ♦noun **2** =**withdrawal**, departure, evacuation, flight, retirement **3** =**refuge**, haven, hideaway, sanctuary, seclusion, shelter

R

retrench *verb* reduce expenditure, cut back.
retrenchment *noun*

retrial *noun* second trial of a case or defendant in a court of law.

retribution ❶ *noun* punishment or vengeance for evil deeds. **retributive** *adjective*

retrieve ❶ *verb* 1 fetch back again. 2 restore to a better state. 3 rescue or save. 4 recover (information) from a computer. **retrievable** *adjective* **retrieval** *noun* **retriever** *noun* dog trained to retrieve shot game.

retro *adjective* associated with or revived from the past, e.g. *retro fashion.*

retro- *prefix* back or backwards, e.g. *retroactive.*

retroactive *adjective* effective from a date in the past.

retrograde ❶ *adjective* 1 tending towards an earlier worse condition. 2 moving or bending backwards.

retrogress ❶ *verb* go back to an earlier worse condition. **retrogression** *noun* **retrogressive** *adjective*

retrorocket *noun* small rocket engine used to slow a spacecraft.

retrospect *noun* **in retrospect** when looking back on the past. **retrospective** *adjective* 1 looking back in time. 2 applying from a date in the past. ♦ *noun* 3 exhibition of an artist's life's work.

retroussé [rit-**troo**-say] *adjective* (of a nose) turned upwards.

retsina *noun* Greek wine flavoured with resin.

return ❶ *verb* 1 go or come back. 2 give, put, or send back. 3 repay with something of equivalent value, e.g. *return the compliment.* 4 *Sport* hit, throw, or play (a ball) back. 5 reply. 6 elect. ♦ *noun* 7 returning. 8 (thing) being returned. 9 profit. 10 official report, as of taxable income. 11 return ticket. ♦ *adjective* 12 of or being a return, e.g. *a return visit.*

returnable *adjective* **returning officer** person in charge of an election **return ticket** ticket allowing a passenger to travel to a place and back.

reunify *verb* bring together again something previously divided. **reunification** *noun*

reunion *noun* meeting of people who have been apart. **reunite** *verb* bring or come together again after a separation.

reuse *verb* use again. **reusable** *adjective*

rev *Informal noun* 1 revolution (of an engine). ♦ *verb* **revving, revved** 2 (foll. by *up*) increase the speed of revolution of (an engine).

Rev., Revd. Reverend.

revalue *verb* adjust the exchange value of (a currency) upwards. **revaluation** *noun*

revamp ❶ *verb* renovate or restore.

reveal ❶ *verb* 1 make known. 2 expose or show. **revealing** *adjective* **revelation** *noun*

reveille [riv-**val**-ee] *noun* morning bugle call to waken soldiers.

revel ❶ *verb* **-elling, -elled** 1 take pleasure (in). 2 make merry. **revels** *plural noun* merrymaking. **reveller** *noun* **revelry** *noun* festivity.

revenge ❶ *noun* 1 retaliation for wrong done. ♦ *verb* 2 make retaliation for. 3 avenge (oneself or another). **revengeful** *adjective*

revenue ❶ *noun* income, esp. of a state.

——————— THESAURUS ———————

R

retribution *noun* = **punishment**, justice, Nemesis, reckoning, reprisal, retaliation, revenge, vengeance

retrieve *verb* = **get back**, recapture, recoup, recover, redeem, regain, restore, save, win back

retrograde *adjective* 1 = **deteriorating**, backward, declining, degenerative, downward, regressive, retrogressive, worsening

retrogress *verb* = **deteriorate**, backslide, decline, go back, go downhill (*inf*), regress, relapse, worsen

return *verb* 1 = **come back**, go back, reappear, rebound, recur, retreat, revert, turn back OPPOSITE leave. 2 = **put back**, re-establish, reinstate, replace, restore OPPOSITE leave. 3 = **give back**, pay back, recompense, refund, reimburse, repay OPPOSITE keep. 5 = **reply**, answer, respond, retort 6 = **elect**, choose, vote in ♦ *noun* 9 = **profit**, gain, income, interest, proceeds, revenue, takings, yield

OPPOSITE loss. 10 = **statement**, account, form, list, report, summary

revamp *verb* = **renovate**, do up (*inf*), overhaul, recondition, refurbish, restore

reveal *verb* 1 = **make known**, announce, disclose, divulge, give away, impart, let out, let slip, make public, proclaim, tell OPPOSITE hide. 2 = **show**, display, exhibit, manifest, uncover, unearth, unmask, unveil OPPOSITE conceal

revel *verb* 1 **revel in** = **enjoy**, delight in, indulge in, lap up, luxuriate in, relish, take pleasure in, thrive on 2 = **celebrate**, carouse, live it up (*inf*), make merry **revels** ♦ *plural noun* = **merrymaking**, carousal, celebration, festivity, party, spree

revelation *noun* = **disclosure**, exhibition, exposé, exposure, news, proclamation, publication, uncovering, unearthing, unveiling

revelry *noun* 2 = **merrymaking**, carousal, celebration, festivity, fun, jollity, party, spree

Inland Revenue see INLAND.
reverberate ⊕ *verb* echo or resound.
reverberation *noun*
revere ⊕ *verb* be in awe of and respect greatly. **reverence** *noun* awe mingled with respect and esteem. **Reverend** *adjective* title of respect for a clergyman. **reverent** *adjective* showing reverence. **reverently** *adverb* **reverential** *adjective* marked by reverence.
reverie ⊕ *noun* absent-minded daydream.
revers [riv-**veer**] *noun* turned back part of a garment, such as the lapel.
reverse ⊕ *verb* **1** turn upside down or the other way round. **2** change completely. **3** move (a vehicle) backwards. ◆ *noun* **4** opposite. **5** back side. **6** change for the worse. **7** reverse gear. ◆ *adjective* **8** opposite or contrary. **reverse the charges** make a telephone call at the recipient's expense. **reversal** *noun* **reversible** *adjective* **reverse gear** mechanism enabling a vehicle to move backwards. **reversing lights** lights on the back of a motor vehicle that go on when the vehicle is moving backwards.
revert ⊕ *verb* **1** return to a former state. **2**

come back to a subject. **3** (of property) return to its former owner. **reversion** *noun* **1** return to a former state, practice, or belief. **2** (of property) rightful passing to the owner, designated heir, etc.
review ⊕ *noun* **1** critical assessment of a book, concert, etc. **2** publication with critical articles. **3** general survey. **4** formal inspection. ◆ *verb* **5** hold or write a review of. **6** examine, reconsider, or look back on. **7** inspect formally. **reviewer** *noun* writer of reviews.
revile ⊕ *verb* be abusively scornful of.
revise ⊕ *verb* **1** change or alter. **2** prepare a new edition of (a book etc.). **3** restudy (work) in preparation for an examination. **revision** *noun*
revive ⊕ *verb* bring or come back to life, vigour, use, etc. **revival** *noun* **1** reviving or renewal. **2** movement seeking to restore religious faith. **3** new production of a play that has not been recently performed. **revivalism** *noun* **revivalist** *noun*
revoke ⊕ *verb* cancel (a will, agreement, etc.). **revocation** *noun*
revolt ⊕ *noun* **1** uprising against authority. ◆

——————————————— T H E S A U R U S ———————————————

revenge *noun* **1** =**retaliation**, an eye for an eye, reprisal, retribution, vengeance ◆*verb* **2, 3** =**avenge**, get even, get one's own back for (*inf*), repay, retaliate, take revenge for
revenue *noun* =**income**, gain, proceeds, profits, receipts, returns, takings, yield OPPOSITE> **expenditure**
reverberate *verb* =**echo**, re-echo, resound, ring, vibrate
revere *verb* =**be in awe of**, exalt, honour, look up to, respect, reverence, venerate, worship
reverence *noun* =**respect**, admiration, awe, high esteem, honour, veneration, worship OPPOSITE> **contempt**
reverent *adjective* =**respectful**, awed, deferential, humble, reverential
reverie *noun* =**daydream**, abstraction, brown study, woolgathering
reverse *verb* **1** =**turn round**, invert, transpose, turn back, turn over, turn upside down, upend **2** =**change**, overthrow, overturn OPPOSITE> **carry out**. **3** =**go backwards**, back, back up, move backwards, retreat OPPOSITE> **advance** ◆*noun* **4** =**opposite**, contrary, converse, inverse **5** =**back**, other side, rear, underside, wrong side OPPOSITE> **front**. **6** =**misfortune**, adversity, affliction, blow, disappointment, failure, hardship, misadventure, mishap, reversal, setback

◆*adjective* **8** =**opposite**, contrary, converse
revert *verb* **1, 2** =**return**, come back, go back, resume
review *noun* **1** =**critique**, commentary, criticism, evaluation, judgment, notice **2** =**magazine**, journal, periodical **3** =**survey**, analysis, examination, scrutiny, study **4** =**inspection**, march past, parade ◆*verb* **5** =**assess**, criticize, evaluate, judge, study **6** =**look back on**, examine, inspect, reassess, recall, recollect, reconsider, re-evaluate, re-examine, reflect on, remember, rethink, revise, think over
reviewer *noun* =**critic**, commentator, judge
revile *verb* =**malign**, abuse, bad-mouth (*sl, chiefly US & Canad*), denigrate, knock (*inf*), reproach, run down, slag (off) (*sl*), vilify
revise *verb* **1** =**change**, alter, amend, correct, edit, emend, redo, review, rework, update **3** =**study**, cram (*inf*), go over, run through, swot up (*Brit inf*)
revision *noun* **1** =**change**, amendment, correction, emendation, updating **3** =**studying**, cramming (*inf*), homework, swotting (*Brit inf*)
revival *noun* **1** =**renewal**, reawakening, rebirth, renaissance, resurgence, resurrection, revitalization
revive *verb* =**revitalize**, awaken, bring round, come round, invigorate, reanimate, recover, refresh, rekindle, renew, restore OPPOSITE>

R

verb **2** rise in rebellion. **3** cause to feel disgust.
revolting adjective disgusting, horrible.
revolution ❶ noun **1** overthrow of a
government by the governed. **2** great change.
3 spinning round. **4** complete rotation.
revolutionary adjective **1** advocating or
engaged in revolution. **2** radically new or
different. ◆ noun, pl **-aries 3** person advocating
or engaged in revolution. **revolutionize** verb
change considerably.
revolve ❶ verb turn round, rotate. **revolve
around** be centred on. **revolver** noun
repeating pistol.
revue noun theatrical entertainment with
topical sketches and songs.
revulsion ❶ noun strong disgust.
reward ❶ noun **1** something given in return
for a service. **2** sum of money offered for
finding a criminal or missing property. ◆ verb **3**
pay or give something to (someone) for a
service, information, etc. **rewarding** adjective
giving personal satisfaction, worthwhile.
rewind verb run (a tape or film) back to an
earlier point in order to replay.
rewire verb provide (a house, engine, etc.)
with new wiring.
rewrite verb **1** write again in a different way.
◆ noun **2** something rewritten.
Rh 1 Chem rhodium. **2** rhesus.
rhapsody ❶ noun, pl **-dies 1** freely structured
emotional piece of music. **2** expression of
ecstatic enthusiasm. **rhapsodic** adjective

rhapsodize verb speak or write with
extravagant enthusiasm.
rhea [ree-a] noun S American three-toed
ostrich.
rhenium noun Chem silvery-white metallic
element with a high melting point.
rheostat noun instrument for varying the
resistance of an electrical circuit.
rhesus [ree-suss] noun small long-tailed
monkey of S Asia. **rhesus factor, Rh factor**
antigen commonly found in human blood: the
terms **Rh positive** and **Rh negative** are used
to indicate its presence or absence.
rhetoric ❶ [ret-a-rik] noun **1** art of effective
speaking or writing. **2** artificial or exaggerated
language. **rhetorical** [rit-**tor**-ik-kal] adjective **1**
(of a question) not requiring an answer. **2** of,
like, or using rhetoric. **rhetorically** adverb
rheum [room] noun watery discharge from the
eyes or nose. **rheumy** adjective
rheumatism noun painful inflammation of
joints or muscles. **rheumatic** noun, adjective
(person) affected by rheumatism. **rheumatoid**
adjective of or like rheumatism. **rheumatoid
arthritis** chronic disease characterized by
inflammation and swelling of the joints.
Rh factor noun see RHESUS.
rhinestone noun imitation diamond.
rhino noun, pl **rhinos** short for RHINOCEROS.
rhinoceros noun, pl **-oses, -os** large thick-
skinned animal with one or two horns on its
nose.

——————— THESAURUS ———————

exhaust
revoke verb =**cancel**, annul, countermand,
disclaim, invalidate, negate, nullify, obviate,
quash, repeal, rescind, retract, reverse, set
aside, withdraw OPPOSITE **endorse**
revolt noun **1** =**uprising**, insurgency,
insurrection, mutiny, rebellion, revolution, rising
◆verb **2** =**rebel**, mutiny, resist, rise **3** =**disgust**,
gross out (US sl), make one's flesh creep,
nauseate, repel, repulse, sicken, turn one's
stomach
revolting adjective =**disgusting**, foul, horrible,
horrid, nauseating, repellent, repugnant,
repulsive, sickening, yucky or yukky (sl)
revolution noun **1** =**revolt**, coup, insurgency,
mutiny, rebellion, rising, uprising **2**
=**transformation**, innovation, reformation, sea
change, shift, upheaval **4** =**rotation**, circle,
circuit, cycle, lap, orbit, spin, turn
revolutionary adjective **1** =**rebel**, extremist,
insurgent, radical, subversive OPPOSITE **loyalist**.
2 =**innovative**, different, drastic, ground-
breaking, new, novel, progressive, radical

OPPOSITE **conservative**
revolutionize verb =**transform**, modernize,
reform
revolve verb =**go round**, circle, orbit, rotate,
spin, turn, twist, wheel, whirl
revulsion noun =**disgust**, abhorrence,
detestation, loathing, repugnance, repulsion
OPPOSITE **liking**
reward noun **1** =**payment**, bonus, bounty,
compensation, premium, prize, recompense,
repayment, return, wages OPPOSITE **fine** ◆verb
3 =**compensate**, pay, recompense,
remunerate, repay OPPOSITE **penalize**
rewarding adjective =**satisfying**, beneficial,
enriching, fruitful, fulfilling, productive,
profitable, valuable, worthwhile
rhapsodize verb =**enthuse**, go into ecstasies,
gush, rave (inf)
rhetoric noun **1** =**oratory**, eloquence **2**
=**hyperbole**, bombast, grandiloquence,
magniloquence, verbosity, wordiness
rhetorical adjective **2** =**high-flown**,
bombastic, grandiloquent, oratorical, verbose

R

rhizome *noun* thick underground stem
producing new plants.

rhodium *noun Chem* hard metallic element.

rhododendron *noun* evergreen flowering
shrub.

rhombus *noun, pl* **-buses, -bi** parallelogram
with sides of equal length but no right angles,
diamond-shaped figure. **rhomboid** *noun*
parallelogram with adjacent sides of unequal
length.

rhubarb *noun* garden plant of which the
fleshy stalks are cooked as fruit.

rhyme ❶ *noun* **1** sameness of the final sounds
at the ends of lines of verse, or in words. **2**
word identical in sound to another in its final
sounds. **3** verse marked by rhyme. ◆ *verb* **4**
make a rhyme.

rhythm ❶ *noun* **1** any regular movement or
beat. **2** arrangement of the durations of and
stress on the notes of a piece of music, usu.
grouped into a regular pattern. **3** (in poetry)
arrangement of words to form a regular pattern
of stresses. **rhythmic, rhythmical** *adjective*
rhythmically *adverb* **rhythm and blues**
popular music, orig. Black American, influenced
by the blues.

RI Rhode Island.

rib[1] *noun* **1** one of the curved bones forming
the framework of the upper part of the body. **2**
cut of meat including the rib(s). **3** curved
supporting part, as in the hull of a boat. **4**
raised series of rows in knitting. ◆ *verb* **ribbing,
ribbed 5** provide or mark with ribs. **6** knit to
form a rib pattern. **ribbed** *adjective* **ribbing**
noun **ribcage** *noun* bony structure of ribs
enclosing the lungs.

rib[2] *verb* **ribbing, ribbed** *Informal* tease or
ridicule. **ribbing** *noun*

ribald ❶ *adjective* humorously or mockingly
rude or obscene. **ribaldry** *noun*

RIBA Royal Institute of British Architects.

ribbon *noun* **1** narrow band of fabric used for
trimming, tying, etc. **2** any long strip, for
example of inked tape in a typewriter. **3** (also
riband, ribband) small strip of coloured cloth
worn as a badge or as the symbol of an award.
◆ *plural* **4** ragged strips or shreds. **ribbon
development** *Brit & Aust* building of houses
along a main road.

riboflavin [rye-boe-**flay**-vin] *noun* form of
vitamin B.

ribonucleic acid *noun see* RNA.

rice *noun* **1** cereal plant grown on wet ground
in warm countries. **2** its seeds as food. **rice
paper** thin edible paper.

rich ❶ *adjective* **1** owning a lot of money or
property, wealthy. **2** abounding. **3** fertile. **4** (of
food) containing much fat or sugar. **5** mellow.
6 intense or vivid. **7** amusing. **riches** *plural
noun* wealth. **richly** *adverb* **1** elaborately. **2**
fully. **richness** *noun*

Richter scale *noun* scale for measuring the
intensity of earthquakes.

rick[1] *noun* stack of hay etc.

rick[2] *verb, noun* sprain or wrench.

rickets *noun* disease of children marked by
softening of the bones, bow legs, etc., caused
by vitamin D deficiency.

rickety ❶ *adjective* shaky or unstable.

R

——————— THESAURUS ———————

rhyme *noun* **3** = **poetry**, ode, poem, song,
verse ◆ *verb* **4** = **sound like**, harmonize

rhythm *noun* **1** = **beat**, accent, cadence, lilt,
metre, pulse, swing, tempo, time

ribald *adjective* = **coarse**, bawdy, blue, broad,
earthy, naughty, near the knuckle (*inf*),
obscene, racy, rude, smutty, vulgar

rich *adjective* **1** = **wealthy**, affluent, loaded (*sl*),
moneyed, prosperous, well-heeled (*inf*), well-off,
well-to-do OPPOSITE> **poor. 2** = **well-stocked**,
full, productive, well-supplied OPPOSITE>
wanting. 3 = **fruitful**, abounding, abundant,
ample, copious, fertile, lush, luxurious, plentiful,

productive, prolific OPPOSITE> **barren. 4** = **full-
bodied**, creamy, fatty, luscious, succulent,
sweet, tasty OPPOSITE> **dull**

riches *plural noun* = **wealth**, affluence, assets,
fortune, plenty, resources, substance, treasure
OPPOSITE> **want**

richly *adverb* **1** = **elaborately**, elegantly,
expensively, exquisitely, gorgeously, lavishly,
luxuriously, opulently, splendidly, sumptuously
2 = **fully**, amply, appropriately, properly,
suitably, thoroughly, well

rickety *adjective* = **shaky**, insecure, precarious,
ramshackle, shonky (*Aust & NZ inf*), tottering,

rickshaw *noun* light two-wheeled man-drawn Asian vehicle.

ricochet [rik-osh-ay] *verb* **1** (of a bullet) rebound from a solid surface. ◆ *noun* **2** such a rebound.

rid ⊕ *verb* **ridding, rid** clear or relieve (of). **get rid of** free oneself of (something undesirable). **good riddance** relief at getting rid of something or someone.

ridden *verb* **1** past participle of RIDE. ◆ *adjective* **2** afflicted or affected by the thing specified, e.g. *disease-ridden*.

riddle[1] ⊕ *noun* **1** question made puzzling to test one's ingenuity. **2** puzzling person or thing. ◆ *verb* **3** speak in riddles.

riddle[2] ⊕ *verb* **1** pierce with many holes. ◆ *noun* **2** coarse sieve for gravel etc. **riddled with** full of.

ride ⊕ *verb* **riding, rode, ridden 1** sit on and control or propel (a horse, bicycle, etc.). **2** go on horseback or in a vehicle. **3** travel over. **4** be carried on or across. **5** lie at anchor. ◆ *noun* **6** journey on a horse etc., or in a vehicle. **7** type of movement experienced in a vehicle. **rider** *noun* **1** person who rides. **2** supplementary clause added to a document. **riding** *noun* art or practice of horsemanship. **ride out** *verb* survive (a period of difficulty or danger) successfully. **ride up** *verb* (of a garment) move up from the proper position.

ridge *noun* **1** long narrow hill. **2** long narrow raised part on a surface. **3** line where two sloping surfaces meet. **4** *Meteorol* elongated area of high pressure. **ridged** *adjective*

ridiculous ⊕ *adjective* deserving to be laughed at, absurd. **ridicule** *noun* **1** treatment of a person or thing as ridiculous. ◆ *verb* **2** laugh at, make fun of.

Riding *noun* former administrative district of Yorkshire.

riesling *noun* type of white wine.

rife ⊕ *adjective* widespread or common. **rife with** full of.

riff *noun* *Jazz, rock* short repeated melodic figure.

riffle *verb* flick through (pages etc.) quickly.

riffraff ⊕ *noun* rabble, disreputable people.

rifle[1] *noun* **1** firearm with a long barrel. ◆ *verb* **2** cut spiral grooves inside the barrel of a gun.

rifle[2] ⊕ *verb* **1** search and rob. **2** steal.

rift ⊕ *noun* **1** break in friendly relations. **2** crack, split, or cleft. **rift valley** long narrow valley resulting from subsidence between faults.

rig ⊕ *verb* **rigging, rigged 1** arrange in a dishonest way. **2** equip, esp. a ship. ◆ *noun* **3** apparatus for drilling for oil and gas. **4** way a ship's masts and sails are arranged. **5** (also **rigout**) *Informal* outfit of clothes. **rigging** *noun* ship's spars and ropes. **rig up** *verb* set up or build temporarily.

right ⊕ *adjective* **1** just. **2** true or correct. **3** proper. **4** most favourable or convenient. **5** in a satisfactory condition. **6** of the side that faces east when the front is turned to the north. **7** of the outer side of a fabric. ◆ *adverb* **8** correctly. **9** properly. **10** straight or directly. **11** on or to the right side. **12** all the way. **13** exactly or precisely. ◆ *noun* **14** claim, title, etc. allowed or due. **15** what is just or due. **16** (R-) conservative political party or group. ◆ *verb* **17** bring or come back to a normal or correct state. **18** bring or come back to a vertical

———————— THESAURUS ————————

unsound, unsteady, wobbly

rid *verb* =**free**, clear, deliver, disburden, disencumber, make free, purge, relieve, unburden **get rid of** = **dispose of**, dump, eject, eliminate, expel, remove, throw away *or* out

riddle[1] *noun* **1, 2** = **puzzle**, conundrum, enigma, mystery, poser, problem

riddle[2] *verb* **1** = **pierce**, honeycomb, pepper, perforate, puncture ◆*noun* **2** = **sieve**, filter, screen, strainer

ride *verb* **1** = **control**, handle, manage **2** = **travel**, be carried, go, move ◆*noun* **6** = **journey**, drive, jaunt, lift, outing, trip

ridicule *noun* **1** = **mockery**, chaff, derision, gibe, jeer, laughter, raillery, scorn ◆*verb* **2** = **laugh at**, chaff, deride, jeer, make fun of, mock, poke fun at, sneer

ridiculous *adjective* = **laughable**, absurd, comical, farcical, funny, ludicrous, risible, silly,

stupid OPPOSITE **sensible**

rife *adjective* = **widespread**, common, frequent, general, prevalent, rampant, ubiquitous, universal

riffraff *noun* = **rabble**, hoi polloi, ragtag and bobtail

rifle[2] *verb* = **ransack**, burgle, go through, loot, pillage, plunder, rob, sack, strip

rift *noun* **1** = **breach**, disagreement, division, falling out (*inf*), quarrel, separation, split **2** = **split**, break, cleft, crack, crevice, fault, fissure, flaw, gap, opening

rig *verb* **1** = **fix** (*inf*), arrange, engineer, gerrymander, manipulate, tamper with **2** = **equip**, fit out, furnish, kit out, outfit, supply ◆*noun* **3** = **apparatus**, equipment, fittings, fixtures, gear, tackle **5** (also **rigout**) *Inf* = **outfit**, costume, dress, garb, gear (*inf*), get-up (*inf*), togs position. **19** compensate for. **in the right** morally or legally correct. **right away** immediately. **rightly** *adverb* **rightful** *adjective* **rightfully** *adverb* **rightist** *noun, adjective* (person) on the political right. **right angle** angle of 90°. **right-handed** *adjective* using or for the right hand. **right-hand man** person's most valuable assistant. **right-minded, right-thinking** *adjective* having opinions or principles deemed acceptable by the speaker. **right of way 1** right of one vehicle to go before another. **2** legal right to pass over someone's land. **right-wing** *adjective* **1** conservative or reactionary. **2** belonging to the more conservative part of a political party. **right-winger** *noun*

righteous ⊕ [rye-chuss] *adjective* **1** upright, godly, or virtuous. **2** morally justified. **righteousness** *noun*

rigid ⊕ *adjective* **1** inflexible or strict. **2** unyielding or stiff. **rigidly** *adverb* **rigidity** *noun*

rigmarole ⊕ *noun* **1** long complicated procedure. **2** meaningless string of words.

rigor mortis *noun* stiffening of the body after death.

rigour ⊕ *noun* **1** harshness, severity, or strictness. **2** hardship. **rigorous** *adjective* harsh, severe, or stern.

rile ⊕ *verb* anger or annoy.

rill *noun* small stream.

rim ⊕ *noun* **1** edge or border. **2** outer ring of a wheel. **rimmed** *adjective*

rime *noun Lit* hoarfrost.

rind ⊕ *noun* tough outer coating of fruits, cheese, or bacon.

ring¹ ⊕ *verb* **ringing, rang, rung 1** give out a clear resonant sound, as a bell. **2** cause (a bell) to sound. **3** telephone. **4** resound. ◆ *noun* **5** ringing. **6** telephone call. **7** inherent quality, e.g. *the ring of truth.* **ring off** *verb* end a telephone call. **ringtone** *noun* tune played by a cell phone when it receives a call. **ring up** *verb* **1** telephone. **2** record on a cash register.

ring² ⊕ *noun* **1** circle of gold etc., esp. for a finger. **2** any circular band, coil, or rim. **3** circle of people. **4** circular course. **5** enclosed area, esp. a circle for a circus or a roped-in square for boxing. **6** group operating (illegal) control of a market. ◆ *verb* **7** put a ring round. **8** mark (a bird) with a ring. **9** kill (a tree) by cutting the bark round the trunk. **ringer** *noun Slang* person or thing apparently identical to another (also **dead ringer**). **ringlet** *noun* curly lock of hair. **ring binder** binder with metal rings that can be opened to insert perforated paper. **ringdove** *noun* large pigeon with white patches on the wings and neck. **ring finger** third finger, esp. of the left hand, on which the wedding ring is worn. **ringleader** *noun* instigator of a mutiny, riot, etc. **ringmaster** *noun* master of ceremonies in a circus. **ring road** main road that bypasses a town (centre). **ringside** *noun* row of seats nearest a boxing or circus ring. **ringtail** *noun Aust* possum with a

—————————— T H E S A U R U S ——————————

right *adjective* **1** = **just**, equitable, ethical, fair, good, honest, lawful, moral, proper OPPOSITE **evil**. **2** = **correct**, accurate, exact, factual, genuine, precise, true, valid **3** = **proper**, appropriate, becoming, desirable, done, fit, fitting, seemly, suitable OPPOSITE **wrong** ◆*adverb* **8** = **correctly**, accurately, exactly, genuinely, precisely, truly **9** = **suitably**, appropriately, aptly, fittingly, properly OPPOSITE **improperly**. **10** = **straight**, directly, promptly, quickly, straightaway OPPOSITE slowly. **13** = **exactly**, precisely, squarely ◆*noun* **14** = **prerogative**, authority, business, claim, due, freedom, liberty, licence, mana (*NZ*), permission, power, privilege **15** = **justice**, fairness, lawfulness, legality, righteousness, truth ◆*verb* **17** = **rectify**, correct, fix, put right, redress, settle, sort out, straighten **right away** = **immediately**, at once, directly, forthwith, instantly, now, pronto (*inf*), straightaway

righteous¹ *adjective* = **virtuous**, ethical, fair, good, honest, honourable, just, moral, pure, upright OPPOSITE **bad**

rightful *adjective* **1** = **lawful**, due, just, legal, legitimate, proper, real **2** = **true**, valid

rigid *adjective* **1** = **strict**, exact, fixed, inflexible, rigorous, set, stringent, unbending, uncompromising OPPOSITE **soft**. **2** = **stiff**, inflexible, unyielding OPPOSITE **flexible**

rigmarole *noun* **1** = **procedure**, bother, carry-on (*inf, chiefly Brit*), fuss, hassle (*inf*), nonsense, palaver, pantomime (*inf*), performance (*inf*) **2** = **twaddle**, gibberish

rigorous *adjective* = **strict**, demanding, exacting, hard, harsh, inflexible, severe, stern, stringent, tough OPPOSITE **kind**

rigour *noun* **1** = **strictness**, harshness, inflexibility, rigidity, sternness, stringency **2** = **hardship**, ordeal, privation, suffering, trial

rig up *verb* = **set up**, arrange, assemble, build, construct, erect, fix up, improvise, put together, put up

rile *verb* = **anger**, aggravate (*inf*), annoy, get *or* put one's back up, irk, irritate

rim *noun* **1** = **edge**, border, brim, brink, lip, margin, verge

R

curling tail used to grip branches while climbing. **ringworm** *noun* fungal skin disease in circular patches.

rink *noun* 1 sheet of ice for skating or curling. 2 floor for roller-skating. 3 building for ice-skating or roller-skating.

rinkhals *noun* S African cobra that can spit venom.

rinse ❶ *verb* 1 remove soap from (washed clothes, hair, etc.) by applying clean water. 2 wash lightly. ♦ *noun* 3 rinsing. 4 liquid to tint hair.

riot ❶ *noun* 1 disorderly unruly disturbance. 2 loud revelry. 3 profusion. 4 *Slang* very amusing person or thing. ♦ *verb* 5 take part in a riot. **read the riot act** reprimand severely. **run riot** 1 behave without restraint. 2 grow profusely. **rioter** *noun* **riotous** *adjective* 1 unrestrained. 2 unruly or rebellious.

rip ❶ *verb* **ripping, ripped** 1 tear violently. 2 tear away. 3 *Informal* rush. ♦ *noun* 4 split or tear. **let rip** act or speak without restraint.

ripcord *noun* cord pulled to open a parachute.

rip off *verb Slang* cheat by overcharging. **rip-off** *noun Slang* 1 overpriced article. 2 cheat or swindle. **rip-roaring** *adjective Informal* boisterous and exciting.

RIP rest in peace.

riparian [rip-**pair**-ee-an] *adjective* of or on the banks of a river.

ripe ❶ *adjective* 1 ready to be reaped, eaten, etc. 2 matured. 3 ready or suitable. **ripen** *verb* 1 grow ripe. 2 mature.

riposte ❶ [rip-**posst**] *noun* 1 verbal retort. 2 counterattack, esp. in fencing. ♦ *verb* 3 make a riposte.

ripple *noun* 1 slight wave or ruffling of a surface. 2 sound like ripples of water. ♦ *verb* 3 flow or form into little waves (on). 4 (of sounds) rise and fall gently.

rise ❶ *verb* **rising, rose, risen** 1 get up from a lying, sitting, or kneeling position. 2 get out of bed. 3 move upwards. 4 (of the sun or moon) appear above the horizon. 5 reach a higher level. 6 (of an amount or price) increase. 7 rebel. 8 (of a court) adjourn. 9 have its source. ♦ *noun* 10 rising. 11 upward slope. 12 increase, esp. of wages. **take a rise out of** *Slang* provoke an angry reaction from. **give rise to** cause. **riser** *noun* 1 person who rises, esp. from bed. 2 vertical part of a step. **rising** *noun* 1 revolt. ♦ *adjective* 2 increasing in rank or maturity.

risible [**riz**-zib-bl] *adjective* causing laughter, ridiculous.

risk ❶ *noun* 1 chance of disaster or loss. 2

———————— T H E S A U R U S ————————

rind *noun* = skin, crust, husk, outer layer, peel

ring¹ *verb* 1, 2 = **chime**, clang, peal, reverberate, sound, toll 3 = **phone**, buzz (*inf, chiefly Brit*), call, telephone ♦*noun* 5 = **chime**, knell, peal 6 = **call**, buzz (*inf, chiefly Brit*), phone call

ring² *noun* 1, 2 = **circle**, band, circuit, halo, hoop, loop, round 5 = **arena**, circus, enclosure, rink 6 = **gang**, association, band, cartel, circle, group, mob, syndicate ♦*verb* 7 = **encircle**, enclose, gird, girdle, surround

rinse *verb* 1, 2 = **wash**, bathe, clean, cleanse, dip, splash ♦*noun* 3 = **wash**, bath, dip, splash

riot *noun* 1 = **disturbance**, anarchy, confusion, disorder, lawlessness, strife, tumult, turbulence, turmoil, upheaval 2 = **merrymaking**, carousal, festivity, frolic, high jinks, revelry 3 = **display**, extravaganza, profusion, show, splash ♦*verb* 5 = **rampage**, go on the rampage **run riot** 1 = **rampage**, be out of control, go wild 2 = **grow profusely**, spread like wildfire

riotous *adjective* 1 = **unrestrained**, boisterous, loud, noisy, uproarious, wild 2 = **unruly**, anarchic, disorderly, lawless, rebellious, rowdy, ungovernable, violent OPPOSITE **quiet**

rip *verb* 1 = **tear**, burst, claw, cut, gash, lacerate, rend, slash, slit, split ♦*noun* 4 = **tear**,

cut, gash, hole, laceration, rent, slash, slit, split

ripe *adjective* 1, 2 = **mature**, mellow, ready, ripened, seasoned OPPOSITE **unripe**. 3 = **suitable**, auspicious, favourable, ideal, opportune, right, timely OPPOSITE **inappropriate**

ripen *verb* = **mature**, burgeon, develop, grow ripe, season

rip off *verb Sl* = **cheat**, con (*inf*), defraud, fleece, rob, skin (*sl*), swindle

rip-off *noun Sl* 2 = **cheat**, con (*inf*), con trick (*inf*), fraud, scam (*sl*), swindle, theft

riposte *noun* 1 = **retort**, answer, comeback (*inf*), rejoinder, reply, response, sally ♦*verb* 3 = **retort**, answer, come back, reply, respond

rise *verb* 1 = **get up**, arise, get to one's feet, stand up 3 = **go up**, ascend, climb OPPOSITE **fall**. 5 = **advance**, get on, progress, prosper 6 = **increase**, go up, grow, intensify, mount OPPOSITE **drop**. 7 = **rebel**, mutiny, revolt 9 = **originate**, happen, issue, occur, spring ♦*noun* 10 = **advancement**, climb, progress, promotion 11 = **upward slope**, ascent, elevation, incline 12 = **increase**, increment, pay increase, raise (*US*), upsurge, upswing, upturn OPPOSITE **fall** ♦ **give rise to** = **cause**, bring about, effect, produce, result in

R

person or thing considered as a potential hazard. ◆ *verb* **3** act in spite of the possibility of (injury or loss). **4** expose to danger or loss.
risky *adjective* **riskier, riskiest** full of risk, dangerous.
risotto *noun, pl* **-tos** dish of rice cooked in stock with vegetables, meat, etc.
risqué [risk-ay] *adjective* bordering on indecency.
rissole *noun* cake of minced meat, coated with breadcrumbs and fried.
rite ⊙ *noun* formal practice or custom, esp. religious. **rite of passage** event that marks an important change in a person's life.
ritual ⊙ *noun* **1** prescribed order of rites. **2** regular repeated action or behaviour. ◆ *adjective* **3** concerning rites. **ritually** *adverb* **ritualistic** *adjective* like a ritual.
ritzy *adjective* **ritzier, ritziest** *Slang* luxurious or elegant.
rival ⊙ *noun* **1** person or thing that competes with or equals another for favour, success, etc. ◆ *adjective* **2** in the position of a rival. ◆ *verb* **-valling, -valled 3** (try to) equal. **rivalry** *noun* keen competition.
riven *adjective* **1** split apart. **2** torn to shreds.
river ⊙ *noun* **1** large natural stream of water. **2** plentiful flow.
rivet ⊙ [riv-vit] *noun* **1** bolt for fastening metal plates, the end being put through holes and then beaten flat. ◆ *verb* **riveting, riveted 2** fasten with rivets. **3** cause to be fixed, as in fascination. **riveting** *adjective* very interesting and exciting.
rivulet *noun* small stream.
Rn *Chem* radon.
RN Royal Navy.
RNA ribonucleic acid: substance in living cells

essential for the synthesis of protein.
roach¹ *noun* freshwater fish.
roach² *noun US* same as COCKROACH.
road ⊙ *noun* **1** way prepared for passengers, vehicles, etc. **2** route in a town or city with houses along it. **3** way or course, e.g. *the road to fame.* **4** roadstead. **on the road** travelling.
roadie *noun Informal* person who transports and sets up equipment for a band. **roadblock** *noun* barricade across a road to stop traffic for inspection etc. **road hog** *Informal* selfish aggressive driver. **roadholding** *noun* extent to which a vehicle does not skid on bends or wet surfaces. **roadhouse** *noun* pub or restaurant on a country road. **road metal** broken stones used in building roads. **road rage** aggressive behaviour by a motorist in response to another motorist's driving. **road show** *Radio* live broadcast from a radio van taking a particular programme on a tour of the country. **roadside** *noun, adjective* **roadstead** *noun Naut* partly sheltered anchorage. **road test** test of a vehicle etc. in actual use. **road-test** *verb* test (a vehicle etc.) in actual use. **roadway** *noun* the part of a road used by vehicles. **roadworks** *plural noun* repairs to a road, esp. blocking part of the road. **roadworthy** *adjective* (of a vehicle) mechanically sound.
roam ⊙ *verb* wander about.
roan *adjective* **1** (of a horse) having a brown or black coat sprinkled with white hairs. ◆ *noun* **2** roan horse.
roar ⊙ *verb* **1** make or utter a loud deep hoarse sound like that of a lion. **2** shout (something) as in anger. **3** laugh loudly. ◆ *noun* **4** such a sound. **a roaring trade** *Informal* brisk and profitable business. **roaring drunk** noisily drunk.

———————— T H E S A U R U S ————————

risk *noun* **1** = **danger**, chance, gamble, hazard, jeopardy, peril, pitfall, possibility ◆ *verb* **3, 4** = **dare**, chance, endanger, gamble, hazard, imperil, jeopardize, venture
risky *adjective* = **dangerous**, chancy (*inf*), dicey (*inf, chiefly Brit*), dodgy (*Brit, Aust & NZ inf*), hazardous, perilous, uncertain, unsafe
risqué *adjective* = **suggestive**, bawdy, blue, improper, indelicate, naughty, near the knuckle (*inf*), racy, ribald
rite *noun* = **ceremony**, custom, observance, practice, procedure, ritual
ritual *noun* **1** = **ceremony**, observance, rite **2** = **custom**, convention, habit, practice, procedure, protocol, routine, tradition ◆ *adjective* **3** = **ceremonial**, conventional, customary, habitual, routine

rival *noun* **1** = **opponent**, adversary, competitor, contender, contestant OPPOSITE friend ◆ *adjective* **2** = **competing**, conflicting, opposing ◆ *verb* **3** = **compete**, be a match for, compare with, equal, match
rivalry *noun* = **competition**, conflict, contention, contest, opposition
river *noun* **1** = **stream**, brook, burn (*Scot*), creek, tributary, waterway **2** = **flow**, flood, rush, spate, torrent
riveting *adjective* = **enthralling**, absorbing, captivating, engrossing, fascinating, gripping, hypnotic, spellbinding
road *noun* **1** = **way**, course, highway, lane, motorway, path, pathway, roadway, route, track
roam *verb* = **wander**, prowl, ramble, range,

R

roast *verb* **1** cook by dry heat, as in an oven. **2** make or be very hot. ♦ *noun* **3** roasted joint of meat. ♦ *adjective* **4** roasted. **roasting** *Informal adjective* **1** extremely hot. ♦ *noun* **2** severe criticism or scolding.

rob ⊕ *verb* **robbing, robbed 1** steal from. **2** deprive. **robber** *noun* **robbery** *noun, pl* **-beries**

robe ⊕ *noun* **1** long loose outer garment. ♦ *verb* **2** put a robe on.

robin *noun* small brown bird with a red breast.

robot ⊕ *noun* **1** automated machine, esp. one performing functions in a human manner. **2** person of machine-like efficiency. **3** *S Afr* set of coloured lights at a junction to control the traffic flow. **robotic** *adjective* **robotics** *noun* science of designing and using robots.

robust ⊕ *adjective* **1** very strong and healthy. **2** sturdily built. **3** requiring physical strength. **robustly** *adverb* **robustness** *noun*

roc *noun* monstrous bird of Arabian mythology.

rock¹ ⊕ *noun* **1** hard mineral substance that makes up part of the earth's crust, stone. **2** large rugged mass of stone. **3** *US & Aust* a stone. **4** hard sweet in sticks. **on the rocks 1** (of a marriage) about to end. **2** (of an alcoholic drink) served with ice. **rocky** *adjective* **rockier, rockiest** having many rocks. **rockery** *noun, pl* **-eries** mound of stones in a garden for rock plants. **rock bottom** lowest possible level. **rock cake** small fruit cake with a rough surface. **rock plant** any plant which grows on rocky ground. **rock salt** common salt as a naturally occurring mineral.

rock² ⊕ *verb* **1** (cause to) sway to and fro. **2** (cause to) feel shock, e.g. *the scandal rocked the government.* ♦ *noun* **3** (also **rock music**) style of pop music with a heavy beat. ♦ *adjective* **4** of or relating to rock music. **rocky** *adjective* **rockier,**

rockiest shaky or unstable. **rock and roll, rock'n'roll** style of pop music blending rhythm and blues and country music. **rocking chair** chair allowing the sitter to rock backwards and forwards. **rocking horse** toy horse on which a child can rock to and fro.

rocker *noun* **1** rocking chair. **2** curved piece of wood etc. on which something may rock. **3** rock music performer, fan, or song. **off one's rocker** *Informal* insane.

rocket *noun* **1** self-propelling device powered by the burning of explosive contents (used as a firework, weapon, etc.). **2** vehicle propelled by a rocket engine, as a weapon or carrying a spacecraft. **3** *Informal* severe reprimand. ♦ *verb* **-eting, -eted 4** move fast, esp. upwards, like a rocket.

rock melon *noun Aust, NZ & US* type of melon with sweet orange flesh.

rococo [rok-koe-koe] *adjective* (of furniture, architecture, etc.) having much elaborate decoration in an early 18th-century style.

rod ⊕ *noun* **1** slender straight bar, stick. **2** cane.

rode *verb* past tense of RIDE.

rodent *noun* animal with teeth specialized for gnawing, such as a rat, mouse, or squirrel.

rodeo *noun, pl* **-deos** display of skill by cowboys, such as bareback riding.

roe¹ *noun* mass of eggs in a fish, sometimes eaten as food.

roe² *noun* small species of deer.

roentgen [ront-gan] *noun* unit measuring a radiation dose.

roger *interjection* (used in signalling) message received and understood.

rogue ⊕ *noun* **1** dishonest or unprincipled person. **2** mischief-loving person. **3** inferior or defective specimen, esp. of a plant. ♦ *adjective* **4** (of a wild beast) having a savage temper and

——————— THESAURUS ———————

rove, stray, travel, walk

roar *verb* **2** = **cry**, bawl, bellow, howl, shout, yell **3** = **guffaw**, hoot, laugh heartily, split one's sides (*inf*) ♦ *noun* **4** = **cry**, bellow, hoot, howl, outcry, shout, yell

rob *verb* **1** = **steal from**, burgle, cheat, con (*inf*), defraud, dispossess, do out of (*inf*), hold up, loot, mug (*inf*), pillage, plunder, raid **2** = **deprive**, do out of

robbery *noun* **1** = **theft**, burglary, hold-up, larceny, mugging (*inf*), pillage, plunder, raid, rip-off (*sl*), stealing, stick-up (*sl, chiefly US*), swindle

robe *noun* **1** = **gown**, costume, habit ♦ *verb* **2** = **clothe**, dress, garb

robot *noun* **1** = **machine**, android, automaton, mechanical man

robust *adjective* **1, 2** = **strong**, fit, hale, hardy, healthy, muscular, powerful, stout, strapping, sturdy, tough, vigorous OPPOSITE> weak

rock¹ *noun* **2** = **stone**, boulder

rock² *verb* **1** = **sway**, lurch, pitch, reel, roll, swing, toss **2** = **shock**, astonish, astound, shake, stagger, stun, surprise

rocky¹ *adjective* **2** = **rough**, craggy, rugged, stony

rocky *adjective* **1** = **unstable**, rickety, shaky, unsteady, wobbly

rod *noun* = **stick**, bar, baton, cane, pole, shaft, staff, wand

living apart from the herd. **roguery** *noun*
roguish *adjective*
roister *verb* make merry noisily or
boisterously.
role, rôle ⊕ *noun* **1** task or function. **2** actor's
part. **role model** person regarded by others,
esp. younger people, as a good example to
follow.
roll ⊕ *verb* **1** move by turning over and over. **2**
move or sweep along. **3** wind round. **4**
undulate. **5** smooth out with a roller. **6** (of a
ship or aircraft) turn from side to side about a
line from nose to tail. **7** (of machinery) (begin
to) operate. **8** (of a drum, thunder, etc.) make
a continuous deep loud noise. **9** walk with a
swaying gait. ◆ *noun* **10** act of rolling over or
from side to side. **11** piece of paper etc. rolled
up. **12** small round individually baked piece of
bread. **13** list or register. **14** complete rotation
of an aircraft about a line from nose to tail. **15**
continuous sound, as of drums, thunder, etc.
16 swaying unsteady movement or gait.
rolling *adjective* **1** (of hills) gently sloping,
undulating. **2** (of a gait) slow and swaying. **roll
call** calling out of a list of names, as in a school
or the army, to check who is present. **rolled
gold** metal coated with a thin layer of gold.
rolling pin cylindrical roller for flattening
pastry. **rolling stock** locomotives and coaches
of a railway. **rolling stone** restless wandering
person. **rollmop** *noun* herring fillet rolled round
onion slices and pickled. **roll-on/roll-off**
adjective denoting a ship allowing vehicles to be
driven straight on and off. **roll-top** *adjective* (of
a desk) having a flexible lid sliding in grooves.
roll up *verb Informal* appear or arrive. **roll-up**
noun Informal cigarette made by the smoker
from loose tobacco and cigarette paper.
roller *noun* **1** rotating cylinder used for
smoothing or supporting a thing to be moved,
spreading paint, etc. **2** small tube around
which hair is wound to make it curly. **3** long

wave of the sea. **Rollerblade** *noun* ® roller
skate with the wheels set in one straight line.
roller coaster (at a funfair) narrow railway
with steep slopes. **roller skate** skate with
wheels.
rollicking *adjective* boisterously carefree.
roly-poly ⊕ *adjective* round or plump.
ROM *Computers* read only memory.
Roman *adjective* of Rome or the Roman
Catholic Church. **Roman alphabet** alphabet
used for writing W European languages,
including English. **Roman candle** firework that
emits a steady stream of coloured sparks.
Roman Catholic (member) of that section of
the Christian Church that acknowledges the
supremacy of the Pope. **Roman nose** nose
with a high prominent bridge. **Roman
numerals** the letters I, V, X, L, C, D, M, used to
represent numbers. **roman type** plain upright
letters in printing.
romance ⊕ *noun* **1** love affair. **2** love idealized
for its purity or beauty. **3** mysterious or exciting
quality. **4** novel or film dealing with love, esp.
sentimentally. **5** story with scenes remote from
ordinary life. ◆ *verb* **6** exaggerate or fantasize.
romantic *adjective*
Romance *adjective* (of a language) developed
from Latin, such as French or Spanish.
Romanesque *adjective, noun* (in) a style of
architecture of the 9th-12th centuries,
characterized by round arches.
romantic ⊕ *adjective* **1** of or dealing with love.
2 idealistic but impractical. **3** (of literature,
music, etc.) displaying passion and imagination
rather than order and form. ◆ *noun* **4** romantic
person or artist. **romantically** *adverb*
romanticism *noun* **romanticize** *verb* describe
or regard in an idealized and unrealistic way.
Romany *noun, pl* **-nies,** *adjective* Gypsy.
Romeo *noun, pl* **Romeos** ardent male lover.
romp ⊕ *verb* **1** play wildly and joyfully. ◆ *noun*
2 boisterous activity. **romp home** win easily.

R

——————— THESAURUS ———————

rogue *noun* **1** = **scoundrel**, blackguard, crook
(*inf*), fraud, rascal, scally (*NW Eng dial*), villain **2**
= **scamp**, rascal
role, rôle *noun* **1** = **job**, capacity, duty,
function, part, position, post, task **2** = **part**,
character, portrayal, representation
roll *verb* **1** = **turn**, go round, revolve, rotate,
spin, swivel, trundle, twirl, wheel, whirl **3**
= **wind**, bind, enfold, envelop, furl, swathe,
wrap **4** = **flow**, run, undulate **5** = **level**, even,
flatten, press, smooth **6** = **toss**, lurch, reel, rock,
sway, tumble ◆*noun* **10** = **turn**, cycle, reel,
revolution, rotation, spin, twirl, wheel, whirl **13**

= **register**, census, index, list, record **15**
= **rumble**, boom, reverberation, roar, thunder
roly-poly *adjective* = **plump**, buxom, chubby,
fat, podgy, rounded, tubby
romance *noun* **1** = **love affair**, affair, amour,
attachment, liaison, relationship **3**
= **excitement**, charm, colour, fascination,
glamour, mystery **4, 5** = **story**, fairy tale,
fantasy, legend, love story, melodrama, tale
romantic *adjective* **1** = **loving**, amorous, fond,
passionate, sentimental, tender OPPOSITE
insensitive. **2** = **idealistic**, dreamy, impractical,
starry-eyed, unrealistic OPPOSITE **practical**

rompers *plural noun* child's overalls.

rondavel *noun S Afr* circular building, often thatched.

rondo *noun, pl* **-dos** piece of music with a leading theme continually returned to.

roo *noun Aust informal* kangaroo.

rood *noun* **1** *Christianity* the Cross. **2** crucifix.

rood screen (in a church) screen separating the nave from the choir.

roof *noun, pl* **roofs 1** outside upper covering of a building, car, etc. ◆ *verb* **2** put a roof on.

roof rack rack for carrying luggage attached to the roof of a car.

rooibos *noun S Afr* tea prepared from the dried leaves of an African plant.

rook¹ *noun* **1** bird of the crow family. ◆ *verb* **2** *Old-fashioned slang* swindle. **rookery** *noun, pl* **-eries** colony of rooks, penguins, or seals.

rook² *noun* chess piece shaped like a castle.

rookie *noun Informal* new recruit.

room ⊕ *noun* **1** enclosed area in a building. **2** unoccupied space. **3** scope or opportunity. ◆ *plural* **4** lodgings. ◆ *verb* **5** *US* occupy or share a room. **roomy** *adjective* **roomier, roomiest** spacious.

roost *noun* **1** perch for fowls. ◆ *verb* **2** perch.

rooster *noun US & Canad* domestic cock.

root¹ ⊕ *noun* **1** part of a plant that grows down into the earth obtaining nourishment. **2** plant with an edible root, such as a carrot. **3** part of a tooth, hair, etc. below the skin. **4** source or origin. **5** form of a word from which other words and forms are derived. **6** *Maths* factor of a quantity which, when multiplied by itself the number of times indicated, gives the quantity. ◆ *plural* **7** person's sense of belonging. ◆ *verb* **8** establish a root and start to grow. **rootless** *adjective* having no sense of

belonging. **root for** *verb Informal* cheer on.

root out *verb* get rid of completely. **rootstock** *noun* rhizome.

root², rootle ⊕ *verb* **1** dig or burrow. **2** *Informal* search vigorously but unsystematically.

rope ⊕ *noun* thick cord. **know the ropes** be thoroughly familiar with an activity. **rope in** *verb* persuade to join in. **rope off** *verb* enclose or divide with a rope.

ropey, ropy ⊕ *adjective* **ropier, ropiest** *Informal* **1** inferior or inadequate. **2** not well.

Roquefort *noun* strong blue-veined cheese made from ewes' or goats' milk.

rorqual *noun* toothless whale with a dorsal fin.

rort *noun Aust informal* dishonest scheme.

rosary *noun, pl* **-saries 1** series of prayers. **2** string of beads for counting these prayers.

rose¹ *noun* **1** shrub or climbing plant with prickly stems and fragrant flowers. **2** flower of this plant. **3** perforated flat nozzle for a hose. **4** pink colour. ◆ *adjective* **5** pink. **roseate** [roe-zee-ate] *adjective* rose-coloured. **rose window** circular window with spokes branching from the centre. **rosewood** *noun* fragrant wood used to make furniture.

rose² *verb* past tense of RISE.

rosé [roe-zay] *noun* pink wine.

rosehip *noun* berry-like fruit of a rose plant.

rosemary *noun* **1** fragrant flowering shrub. **2** its leaves as a herb.

rosette *noun* rose-shaped ornament, esp. a circular bunch of ribbons.

Rosh Hashanah, Rosh Hashana *noun Hebrew* Jewish New Year festival.

rosin [rozz-in] *noun* **1** resin used for treating the bows of violins etc. ◆ *verb* **2** apply rosin to.

roster ⊕ *noun* list of people and their turns of duty.

R

——————— T H E S A U R U S ———————

◆*noun* **4** = **idealist**, dreamer, sentimentalist

romp *verb* **1** = **frolic**, caper, cavort, frisk, gambol, have fun, sport ◆*noun* **2** = **frolic**, caper, lark (*inf*) **romp home** = **win easily**, walk it (*inf*), win by a mile (*inf*), win hands down

room *noun* **1** = **chamber**, apartment, office **2** = **space**, area, capacity, expanse, extent, leeway, margin, range, scope **3** = **opportunity**, chance, occasion, scope

roomy *adjective* = **spacious**, ample, broad, capacious, commodious, extensive, generous, large, sizable *or* sizeable, wide

root¹ *noun* **1** = **stem**, rhizome, tuber **4** = **source**, base, bottom, cause, core, foundation, heart, nucleus, origin, seat, seed ◆*plural* **7** = **sense of belonging**, heritage, origins ◆*verb* **8** = **become established**, anchor,

establish, fasten, fix, ground, implant, moor, set, stick

root², rootle *verb* **1** = **dig**, burrow, ferret

root out *verb* = **get rid of**, abolish, do away with, eliminate, eradicate, exterminate, extirpate, remove, weed out

rope *noun* = **cord**, cable, hawser, line, strand **know the ropes** = **be experienced**, be an old hand, be knowledgeable

rope in *verb* = **persuade**, engage, enlist, inveigle, involve, talk into

ropey, ropy *adjective Inf* **1** = **inferior**, deficient, inadequate, of poor quality, poor, substandard **2** = **unwell**, below par, crook (*Aust & NZ sl*), off colour, under the weather (*inf*)

roster *noun* = **rota**, agenda, catalogue, list, register, roll, schedule, table

rostrum ❶ *noun, pl* **-trums, -tra** platform or stage.
rosy ❶ *adjective* **rosier, rosiest 1** pink-coloured. **2** hopeful or promising.
rot ❶ *verb* **rotting, rotted 1** decompose or decay. **2** slowly deteriorate physically or mentally. ◆ *noun* **3** decay. **4** *Informal* nonsense. **rotten** *adjective*
rota *noun* list of people who take it in turn to do a particular task.
rotary ❶ *adjective* **1** revolving. **2** operated by rotation.
rotate ❶ *verb* **1** (cause to) move round a centre or on a pivot. **2** (cause to) follow a set sequence. **3** plant different crops from one year to the next to maintain the fertility of the soil. **rotation** *noun*
rote *noun* mechanical repetition. **by rote** by memory.
rotisserie *noun* rotating spit for cooking meat.
rotor *noun* **1** revolving portion of a dynamo, motor, or turbine. **2** rotating device with long blades that provides thrust to lift a helicopter.
rotten ❶ *adjective* **1** decaying. **2** *Informal* very bad. **3** corrupt. **rottenness** *noun*
rotter ❶ *noun Slang* despicable person.
Rottweiler [rot-vile-er] *noun* large sturdy dog with a smooth black and tan coat and usu. a docked tail.
rotund ❶ [roe-**tund**] *adjective* **1** round and plump. **2** sonorous. **rotundity** *noun*
rotunda *noun* circular building or room, esp. with a dome.
rouble [roo-bl] *noun* monetary unit of Russia, Belarus, and Tajikistan.
roué [roo-ay] *noun* man given to immoral living.
rouge *noun* **1** red cosmetic used to colour the cheeks. ◆ *verb* **2** apply rouge to.
rough ❶ *adjective* **1** uneven or irregular. **2** not careful or gentle. **3** difficult or unpleasant. **4** approximate. **5** violent, stormy, or boisterous. **6** in preliminary form. **7** lacking refinement. ◆ *verb* **8** make rough. ◆ *noun* **9** rough state or area. **10** sketch. **rough it** live without the usual comforts etc. **roughen** *verb* **roughly** *adverb* **roughness** *noun* **roughage** *noun* indigestible constituents of food which aid digestion.
rough-and-ready *adjective* hastily prepared but adequate. **rough-and-tumble** *noun* playful fight. **rough-hewn** *adjective* roughly shaped. **roughhouse** *noun Slang* fight. **roughneck** *noun Slang* **1** violent person. **2** worker on an oil rig. **rough out** *verb* prepare (a sketch or report) in preliminary form.
roughcast *noun* **1** mixture of plaster and small stones for outside walls. ◆ *verb* **2** coat

——————— T H E S A U R U S ———————

rostrum *noun* = **stage**, dais, platform, podium, stand
rosy *adjective* **1** = **pink**, red **2** = **promising**, auspicious, bright, cheerful, encouraging, favourable, hopeful, optimistic OPPOSITE **depressing**
rot *verb* **1** = **decay**, crumble, decompose, go bad, moulder, perish, putrefy, spoil **2** = **deteriorate**, decline, waste away ◆*noun* **3** = **decay**, blight, canker, corruption, decomposition, mould, putrefaction **4** *Inf* = **nonsense**, claptrap (*inf*), codswallop (*Brit sl*), drivel, garbage (*chiefly US*), hogwash, kak (*S Afr sl*), poppycock (*inf*), rubbish, trash, tripe (*inf*), twaddle
rotary *adjective* = **revolving**, rotating, spinning, turning
rotate *verb* **1** = **revolve**, go round, gyrate, pivot, reel, spin, swivel, turn, wheel **2** = **follow in sequence**, alternate, switch, take turns
rotten *adjective* **1** = **decaying**, bad, corrupt, crumbling, decomposing, festering, mouldy, perished, putrescent, rank, sour, stinking OPPOSITE **good**. **2** *Inf* = **despicable**, base, contemptible, dirty, mean, nasty **3** = **corrupt**, crooked (*inf*), dishonest, dishonourable, immoral, perfidious OPPOSITE **moral**
rotter *noun Sl* = **scoundrel**, blackguard, bounder (*old-fashioned Brit sl*), cad (*Brit inf*), rat (*inf*)
rotund *adjective* **1** = **plump**, chubby, corpulent, fat, fleshy, globular, podgy, portly, rounded, spherical, stout, tubby OPPOSITE **thin**
rough *adjective* **1** = **uneven**, broken, bumpy, craggy, irregular, jagged, rocky, stony OPPOSITE **even**. **2** = **harsh**, cruel, hard, nasty, tough, unfeeling, unpleasant, violent OPPOSITE **civil**. **3** = **unpleasant**, arduous, difficult, hard, tough, uncomfortable OPPOSITE **easy**. **4** = **approximate**, estimated, general, imprecise, inexact, sketchy, vague OPPOSITE **exact**. **5** = **stormy**, choppy, squally, turbulent, wild **6** = **basic**, crude, imperfect, incomplete, rudimentary, sketchy, unfinished, unpolished, unrefined OPPOSITE **finished**. **7** = **ungracious**, blunt, brusque, coarse, impolite, rude, unceremonious, uncivil, uncouth, unmannerly ◆*noun* **10** = **outline**, draft, mock-up, preliminary sketch
rough-and-ready *adjective* = **makeshift**, crude, improvised, provisional, sketchy, stopgap, unpolished, unrefined

R

with this.

roughshod *adverb* **ride roughshod over** act with total disregard for.

roulette *noun* gambling game played with a revolving wheel and a ball.

round ❶ *adjective* **1** spherical, cylindrical, circular, or curved. **2** complete or whole, e.g. *round numbers.* ◆ *adverb, preposition* **3** indicating an encircling movement, presence on all sides, etc., e.g. *tied round the waist; books scattered round the room.* ◆ *verb* **4** move round. ◆ *noun* **5** round shape. **6** recurrent duties. **7** customary course, as of a milkman. **8** game (of golf). **9** stage in a competition. **10** one of several periods in a boxing match etc. **11** number of drinks bought at one time. **12** bullet or shell for a gun. **13** part song in which singers join at equal intervals. **14** circular movement. **15** set of sandwiches. **roundly** *adverb* thoroughly. **rounders** *noun* bat-and-ball team game. **round on** *verb* attack angrily. **round robin** petition signed with names in a circle to conceal the order. **round table** meeting of people on equal terms for discussion. **round-the-clock** *adjective* throughout the day and night. **round trip** journey out and back again. **round up** *verb* gather (people or animals) together. **roundup** *noun*

roundabout ❶ *noun* **1** road junction at which traffic passes round a central island. **2** revolving circular platform on which people ride for amusement. ◆ *adjective* **3** not straightforward.

roundel *noun* small disc. **roundelay** *noun*

simple song with a refrain.

Roundhead *noun Hist* supporter of Parliament against Charles I in the English Civil War.

rouse¹ ❶ *verb* **1** wake up. **2** provoke or excite.

rousing *adjective* lively, vigorous.

rouse² [rhymes with **mouse**] *verb* (foll. by *on*) *Aust* scold or rebuke.

roustabout *noun* labourer on an oil rig.

rout ❶ *noun* **1** overwhelming defeat. **2** disorderly retreat. ◆ *verb* **3** defeat and put to flight.

route ❶ *noun* **1** roads taken to reach a destination. **2** chosen way. ◆ *verb* **3** send by a particular route. **routemarch** *noun* long military training march.

routine ❶ *noun* **1** usual or regular method of procedure. **2** set sequence. ◆ *adjective* **3** ordinary or regular.

roux [roo] *noun* fat and flour cooked together as a basis for sauces.

rove ❶ *verb* wander. **rover** *noun*

row¹ ❶ [rhymes with **go**] *noun* straight line of people or things. **in a row** in succession.

row² [rhymes with **go**] *verb* **1** propel (a boat) by oars. ◆ *noun* **2** spell of rowing. **rowing boat** boat propelled by oars.

row³ ❶ [rhymes with **now**] *Informal noun* **1** dispute. **2** disturbance. **3** reprimand. ◆ *verb* **4** quarrel noisily.

rowan *noun* tree producing bright red berries, mountain ash.

rowdy ❶ *adjective* **-dier, -diest 1** disorderly, noisy, and rough. ◆ *noun, pl* **-dies 2** person like this.

——— T H E S A U R U S ———

rough out *verb* =**outline**, draft, plan, sketch
round *adjective* **1** =**spherical**, circular, curved, cylindrical, globular, rotund, rounded ◆*verb* **4** =**go round**, bypass, circle, encircle, flank, skirt, turn ◆*noun* **5** =**sphere**, ball, band, circle, disc, globe, orb, ring **7** =**course**, beat, circuit, routine, schedule, series, tour **9** =**stage**, division, lap, level, period, session, turn
roundabout *adjective* **3** =**indirect**, circuitous, devious, discursive, evasive, oblique, tortuous
OPPOSITE **direct**
round up *verb* =**gather**, collect, drive, group, herd, marshal, muster, rally
roundup *noun* =**gathering**, assembly, collection, herding, marshalling, muster, rally
rouse¹ *verb* **1** =**wake up**, awaken, call, rise, wake **2** =**excite**, agitate, anger, animate, incite, inflame, move, provoke, stimulate, stir
rousing *adjective* =**lively**, exciting, inspiring, moving, spirited, stimulating, stirring
rout *noun* **1** =**defeat**, beating, debacle,

drubbing, overthrow, pasting (*sl*), thrashing
◆*verb* **3** =**defeat**, beat, conquer, crush, destroy, drub, overthrow, thrash, wipe the floor with (*inf*)
route *noun* **2** =**way**, beat, circuit, course, direction, itinerary, journey, path, road
routine *noun* **1** =**procedure**, custom, method, order, pattern, practice, programme
◆*adjective* **3** =**usual**, customary, everyday, habitual, normal, ordinary, standard, typical
OPPOSITE **different**
rove *verb* =**wander**, drift, ramble, range, roam, stray, traipse (*inf*)
row¹ *noun* =**line**, bank, column, file, range, series, string **in a row** =**consecutively**, one after the other, successively
row³ *Inf noun* **1** =**quarrel**, brawl, dispute, squabble, tiff, trouble **2** =**disturbance**, commotion, noise, racket, rumpus, tumult, uproar ◆*verb* **4** =**quarrel**, argue, dispute, fight, squabble, wrangle

rowel [rhymes with **towel**] *noun* small spiked wheel on a spur.
rowlock [**rol**-luk] *noun* device on a boat that holds an oar in place.
royal ❶ *adjective* **1** of, befitting, or supported by a king or queen. **2** splendid. ♦ *noun* **3** *Informal* member of a royal family. **royally** *adverb* **royalist** *noun* supporter of monarchy.
royalty *noun* **1** royal people. **2** rank or power of a monarch. **3** *pl* **-ties** payment to an author, musician, inventor, etc. **royal blue** deep blue.
RPI retail price index: measure of change in the average level of prices.
rpm revolutions per minute.
RR Right Reverend.
RSI repetitive strain injury.
RSPCA Royal Society for the Prevention of Cruelty to Animals.
RSVP please reply.
Rt Hon. Right Honourable.
Ru *Chem* ruthenium.
rub ❶ *verb* **rubbing, rubbed 1** apply pressure and friction to (something) with a circular or backwards-and-forwards movement. **2** clean, polish, or dry by rubbing. **3** chafe or fray through rubbing. ♦ *noun* **4** act of rubbing. **5** difficulty. **rub it in** emphasize an unpleasant fact. **rub along** *verb* have a friendly relationship. **rub off** *verb* affect through close association. **rub out** *verb* remove with a rubber.
rubato *adverb, noun Music* (with) expressive flexibility of tempo.
rubber[1] *noun* **1** strong waterproof elastic material, orig. made from the dried sap of a tropical tree, now usu. synthetic. **2** piece of rubber used for erasing writing. ♦ *adjective* **3** made of or producing rubber. **rubberize** *verb* coat or treat with rubber. **rubbery** *adjective* **rubberneck** *verb US* stare with unthinking curiosity. **rubber plant** house plant with glossy leaves. **rubber stamp 1** device for imprinting the date, a name, etc. **2** automatic authorization.
rubber[2] *noun* **1** match consisting of three games of bridge, whist, etc. **2** series of matches.
rubbish ❶ *noun* **1** waste matter. **2** anything worthless. **3** nonsense. ♦ *verb* **4** *Informal* criticize. **rubbishy** *adjective*
rubble *noun* fragments of broken stone, brick, etc.
rubella [roo-**bell**-a] *noun* same as GERMAN MEASLES.
rubicund [roo-**bik**-kund] *adjective* ruddy.
rubidium [roo-**bid**-ee-um] *noun Chem* soft highly reactive radioactive element.
rubric [**roo**-brik] *noun* **1** set of rules for behaviour. **2** heading or explanation inserted in a text.
ruby *noun, pl* **-bies 1** red precious gemstone. ♦ *adjective* **2** deep red. **ruby wedding** fortieth wedding anniversary.
ruche *noun* pleat or frill of lace etc. as a decoration.
ruck[1] *noun* **1** rough crowd of common people. **2** *Rugby* loose scrummage.
ruck[2] *noun, verb* wrinkle or crease.
rucksack *noun* large pack carried on the back.
ructions ❶ *plural noun Informal* noisy uproar.
rudder *noun* vertical hinged piece at the stern of a boat or at the rear of an aircraft, for steering.
ruddy ❶ *adjective* **-dier, -diest 1** of a fresh healthy red colour. ♦ *adverb, adjective* **2** *Slang* bloody.
rude ❶ *adjective* **1** impolite or insulting. **2** coarse, vulgar, or obscene. **3** unexpected and unpleasant. **4** roughly made. **5** robust. **rudely** *adverb* **rudeness** *noun*
rudiments ❶ *plural noun* simplest and most

R

──────── THESAURUS ────────

rowdy *adjective* **1** = **disorderly**, loud, noisy, rough, unruly, wild OPPOSITE **mannerly** ♦*noun* **2** = **hooligan**, lout, ruffian, tearaway (*Brit*), yob or yobbo (*Brit sl*)
royal *adjective* **1** = **regal**, imperial, kingly, princely, queenly, sovereign **2** = **splendid**, grand, impressive, magnificent, majestic, stately
rub *verb* **1** = **stroke**, caress, massage **2** = **polish**, clean, scour, shine, wipe **3** = **chafe**, abrade, fray, grate, scrape ♦*noun* **4** = **massage**, caress, kneading, polish, shine, stroke, wipe
rubbish *noun* **1, 2** = **waste**, garbage (*chiefly US*), junk (*inf*), litter, lumber, refuse, scrap, trash **3** = **nonsense**, claptrap (*inf*), codswallop (*Brit sl*), garbage (*chiefly US*), hogwash, hot air (*inf*), kak (*S Afr sl*), rot, tommyrot, trash, tripe (*inf*), twaddle
rub out *verb* = **erase**, cancel, delete, efface, obliterate, remove, wipe out
ructions *plural noun Inf* = **row**, commotion, disturbance, fracas, fuss, hue and cry, trouble, uproar
ruddy *adjective* **1** = **rosy**, blooming, fresh, glowing, healthy, radiant, red, reddish, rosy-cheeked OPPOSITE **white**
rude *adjective* **1** = **impolite**, abusive, cheeky, discourteous, disrespectful, ill-mannered, impertinent, impudent, insolent, insulting, uncivil, unmannerly OPPOSITE **civil**. **2** = **vulgar**, boorish, brutish, coarse, graceless, loutish,

basic stages of a subject. **rudimentary** *adjective* basic, elementary.

rue¹ ❶ *verb* **ruing, rued** feel regret for. **rueful** *adjective* regretful or sorry. **ruefully** *adverb*

rue² *noun* plant with evergreen bitter leaves.

ruff¹ *noun* **1** starched and frilled collar. **2** natural collar of feathers, fur, etc. on certain birds and animals. **3** kind of sandpiper.

ruff² *noun, verb Cards* same as TRUMP¹.

ruffian ❶ *noun* violent lawless person.

ruffle ❶ *verb* **1** disturb the calm of. **2** annoy, irritate. ◆ *noun* **3** frill or pleat.

rufous *adjective* reddish-brown.

rug *noun* **1** small carpet. **2** thick woollen blanket.

rugby *noun* form of football played with an oval ball which may be handled by the players.

rugged ❶ [rug-gid] *adjective* **1** rocky or steep. **2** uneven and jagged. **3** strong-featured. **4** tough and sturdy.

rugger *noun Informal* rugby.

ruin ❶ *verb* **1** destroy or spoil completely. **2** impoverish. ◆ *noun* **3** destruction or decay. **4** loss of wealth, position, etc. **5** broken-down

unused building. **ruination** *noun* **1** act of ruining. **2** state of being ruined. **3** cause of ruin. **ruinous** *adjective* **1** causing ruin. **2** more expensive than can be afforded. **ruinously** *adverb*

rule ❶ *noun* **1** statement of what is allowed, for example in a game or procedure. **2** what is usual. **3** government, authority, or control. **4** measuring device with a straight edge. ◆ *verb* **5** govern. **6** be pre-eminent. **7** give a formal decision. **8** mark with straight line(s). **9** restrain. **as a rule** usually. **ruler** *noun* **1** person who governs. **2** measuring device with a straight edge. **ruling** *noun* formal decision. **rule of thumb** practical but imprecise approach. **rule out** *verb* exclude.

rum¹ *noun* alcoholic drink distilled from sugar cane.

rum² *adjective Informal* odd, strange.

rumba *noun* lively ballroom dance of Cuban origin.

rumble *verb* **1** make a low continuous noise. **2** *Informal* discover the (disreputable) truth about. ◆ *noun* **3** deep resonant sound.

oafish, rough, uncivilized, uncouth, uncultured OPPOSITE **learned**. **3** =**unpleasant**, abrupt, harsh, sharp, startling, sudden **4** =**roughly-made**, artless, crude, inartistic, inelegant, makeshift, primitive, raw, rough, simple OPPOSITE **finished**

rudimentary *adjective* =**basic**, early, elementary, fundamental, initial, primitive, undeveloped OPPOSITE **advanced**

rudiments *plural noun* =**basics**, beginnings, elements, essentials, foundation, fundamentals

rue¹ *verb* =**regret**, be sorry for, kick oneself for, lament, mourn, repent

rueful *adjective* =**regretful**, contrite, mournful, penitent, remorseful, repentant, sorrowful, sorry

ruffian *noun* =**thug**, brute, bully, heavy (*sl*), hoodlum, hooligan, rough (*inf*), tough

ruffle *verb* **1** =**disarrange**, dishevel, disorder, mess up, rumple, tousle, muss (*US & Canad*) **2** =**annoy**, agitate, fluster, irritate, nettle, peeve (*inf*), upset OPPOSITE **ease**

rugged *adjective* **1** =**rocky**, craggy **2** =**uneven**, broken, bumpy, craggy, difficult, irregular, jagged, ragged, rough OPPOSITE **even**. **3** =**strong-featured**, rough-hewn, weather-beaten **4** =**tough**, brawny, burly, husky (*inf*), muscular, robust, strong, sturdy, well-built OPPOSITE **soft**

ruin *verb* **1** =**destroy**, blow (*sl*), botch, crush, damage, defeat, demolish, devastate, lay waste, make a mess of, mess up, screw up (*inf*), smash,

spoil, wreck OPPOSITE **preserve**. **2** =**bankrupt**, impoverish, pauperize ◆*noun* **3** =**disrepair**, decay, disintegration, ruination, wreckage **4 a** =**destruction**, breakdown, collapse, defeat, devastation, downfall, fall, undoing, wreck OPPOSITE **success**. **b** =**bankruptcy**, destitution, insolvency

ruinous *adjective* **1** =**destructive**, calamitous, catastrophic, devastating, dire, disastrous, shattering **2** =**extravagant**, crippling, immoderate, wasteful

rule *noun* **1** =**regulation**, axiom, canon, decree, direction, guideline, law, maxim, precept, principle, tenet **2** =**custom**, convention, habit, practice, procedure, routine, tradition **3** =**government**, authority, command, control, dominion, jurisdiction, mana (*NZ*), mastery, power, regime, reign ◆*verb* **5** =**govern**, be in authority, be in power, command, control, direct, reign **7** =**decree**, decide, judge, pronounce, settle **as a rule** =**usually**, generally, mainly, normally, on the whole, ordinarily

rule out *verb* =**exclude**, ban, debar, dismiss, disqualify, eliminate, leave out, preclude, prohibit, reject

ruler *noun* **1** =**governor**, commander, controller, head of state, king *or* queen, leader, lord, monarch, potentate, sovereign **2** =**measure**, rule, yardstick

ruling *noun* =**decision**, adjudication, decree,

rumbustious *adjective* boisterous or unruly.
ruminate ⊕ *verb* **1** chew the cud. **2** ponder or meditate. **ruminant** *adjective, noun* cud-chewing (animal, such as a cow, sheep, or deer). **rumination** *noun* quiet meditation and reflection. **ruminative** *adjective*
rummage ⊕ *verb* **1** search untidily and at length. ◆ *noun* **2** untidy search through a collection of things.
rummy *noun* card game in which players try to collect sets or sequences.
rumour ⊕ *noun* **1** unproved statement. **2** gossip or common talk. **rumoured** *adjective* suggested by rumour.
rump ⊕ *noun* **1** buttocks. **2** rear of an animal.
rumple *verb* make untidy, crumpled, or dishevelled.
rumpus ⊕ *noun, pl* **-puses** noisy commotion.
run ⊕ *verb* **running, ran, run 1** move with a more rapid gait than walking. **2** go quickly (across). **3** compete in a race, election, etc. **4** operate a vehicle. **5** travel according to schedule. **6** function. **7** manage. **8** continue in a particular direction or for a specified period. **9** expose oneself to (a risk). **10** flow. **11** spread. **12** (of stitches) unravel. **13** (of a newspaper) publish (a story). **14** smuggle (goods, esp. arms). ◆ *noun* **15** act or spell of running. **16** ride in a car. **17** unrestricted access. **18** continuous period. **19** sequence. **20** heavy demand. **21** series of unravelled stitches,

ladder. **22** steep snow-covered course for skiing. **23** enclosure for domestic fowls. **24** migration of fish upstream to spawn. **25** score of one at cricket. **run across** *verb* meet by chance. **run away** *verb* make one's escape, flee. **runaway** *noun* person or animal that runs away. **run down** *verb* **1** be rude about. **2** reduce in number or size. **3** stop working. **rundown** *noun* **run-down** *adjective* **1** exhausted. **2** dilapidated. **run in** *verb* **1** run (an engine) gently. **2** *Informal* arrest. **run-in** *noun Informal* argument. **run into** *verb* meet. **run-of-the-mill** *adjective* ordinary. **run out** *verb* be completely used up. **run over** *verb* knock down (a person) with a moving vehicle. **run up** *verb* incur (a debt). **run-up** *noun* time just before an event.
rune *noun* **1** any character of the earliest Germanic alphabet. **2** obscure piece of writing using mysterious symbols. **runic** *adjective*
rung[1] *noun* crossbar on a ladder.
rung[2] *verb* past participle of RING[1].
runnel *noun* small brook.
runner ⊕ *noun* **1** competitor in a race. **2** messenger. **3** smuggler. **4** part underneath an ice skate etc., on which it slides. **5** slender horizontal stem of a plant, such as a strawberry, running along the ground and forming new roots at intervals. **6** long strip of carpet or decorative cloth. **runner bean** seeds and pod of a climbing bean plant. **runner-up** *noun*

———————————— THESAURUS ————————————

ruminate *verb* **2** = **ponder**, cogitate, consider, contemplate, deliberate, mull over, muse, reflect, think, turn over in one's mind
rummage *verb* **1** = **search**, delve, forage, hunt, ransack, root
rumour *noun* **2** = **story**, buzz, dirt (*US sl*), gossip, hearsay, news, report, talk, whisper, word
rump *noun* = **buttocks**, backside (*inf*), bottom, bum (*Brit sl*), butt (*US & Canad inf*), hindquarters, posterior, rear, rear end, seat
rumpus *noun* = **commotion**, disturbance, furore, fuss, hue and cry, noise, row, uproar
run *verb* **1** = **race**, bolt, dash, gallop, hare (*Brit inf*), hurry, jog, leg it (*inf*), lope, rush, scurry, sprint OPPOSITE⟩ **walk**. **2** = **move**, course, glide, go, pass, roll, skim **3** = **compete**, be a candidate, contend, put oneself up for, stand, take part **6** = **work**, function, go, operate, perform **7** = **manage**, administer, be in charge of, control, direct, handle, head, lead, operate **8** = **continue**, extend, go, proceed, reach, stretch OPPOSITE⟩ **stop**. **10** = **flow**, discharge, go, gush,

leak, pour, spill, spout, stream **11** = **melt**, dissolve, go soft, liquefy **13** = **publish**, display, feature, print **14** = **smuggle**, bootleg, traffic in ◆*noun* **15** = **race**, dash, gallop, jog, rush, sprint, spurt **16** = **ride**, drive, excursion, jaunt, outing, spin (*inf*), trip **19** = **sequence**, course, period, season, series, spell, stretch, string **23** = **enclosure**, coop, pen
run away *verb* = **flee**, abscond, bolt, do a runner (*sl*), escape, fly the coop (*US & Canad inf*), make a run for it, scram (*inf*), take to one's heels OPPOSITE⟩ **remain**
runaway *noun* = **fugitive**, deserter, escapee, refugee, truant
run down *verb* **1** = **criticize**, bad-mouth (*sl, chiefly US & Canad*), belittle, decry, denigrate, disparage, knock (*inf*), rubbish (*inf*), slag (off) (*sl*) **2** = **reduce**, curtail, cut, cut back, decrease, trim
run-down *adjective* **1** = **exhausted**, below par, debilitated, drained, enervated, unhealthy, weak, weary, worn-out OPPOSITE⟩ **well**. **2** = **dilapidated**, broken-down, decrepit, ramshackle, seedy, shabby, worn-out

R

person who comes second in a competition.
running ❶ *adjective* **1** continuous. **2**
consecutive. **3** (of water) flowing. ◆ *noun* **4** act
of moving or flowing quickly. **5** management of
a business etc. **in, out of the running** having
or not having a good chance in a competition.
runny ❶ *adjective* **-nier, -niest 1** tending to
flow. **2** exuding moisture.
runt *noun* **1** smallest animal in a litter. **2**
undersized person.
runway *noun* hard level roadway where
aircraft take off and land.
rupee *noun* monetary unit of India and
Pakistan.
rupture ❶ *noun* **1** breaking, breach. **2** hernia.
◆ *verb* **3** break, burst, or sever.
rural ❶ *adjective* in or of the countryside.
ruse ❶ [rooz] *noun* stratagem or trick.
rush[1] ❶ *verb* **1** move or do very quickly. **2**
force (someone) to act hastily. **3** make a
sudden attack upon (a person or place). ◆ *noun*
4 sudden quick or violent movement. **5** sudden
demand. ◆ *plural* **6** first unedited prints of a
scene for a film. ◆ *adjective* **7** done with speed,
hasty. **rush hour** period at the beginning and
end of the working day, when many people are
travelling to or from work.
rush[2] *noun* marsh plant with a slender pithy
stem. **rushy** *adjective* full of rushes.
rusk *noun* hard brown crisp biscuit, used esp.
for feeding babies.

russet *adjective* **1** reddish-brown. ◆ *noun* **2**
apple with rough reddish-brown skin.
Russian *adjective* **1** of Russia. ◆ *noun* **2** person
from Russia. **3** official language of Russia and,
formerly, of the Soviet Union. **Russian roulette**
act of bravado in which a person spins the
cylinder of a revolver loaded with only one
cartridge and presses thetrigger with the barrel
against his or her own head.
rust ❶ *noun* **1** reddish-brown coating formed
on iron etc. that has been exposed to moisture.
2 disease of plants which produces rust-
coloured spots. ◆ *adjective* **3** reddish-brown. ◆
verb **4** become coated with rust. **5** deteriorate
through lack of use. **rusty** *adjective* **rustier,
rustiest 1** coated with rust. **2** of a rust colour.
3 out of practice.
rustic ❶ *adjective* **1** of or resembling country
people. **2** rural. **3** crude, awkward, or uncouth.
4 (of furniture) made of untrimmed branches. ◆
noun **5** person from the country. **rusticity** *noun*
rusticate *verb* **1** banish temporarily from
university as a punishment. **2** retire to the
country.
rustle[1] ❶ *verb, noun* (make) a low whispering
sound.
rustle[2] *verb* US steal (cattle). **rustler** *noun* US
cattle thief. **rustle up** *verb* prepare at short
notice.
rut[1] ❶ *noun* **1** furrow made by wheels. **2** dull
settled habits or way of living.

——————— THESAURUS ———————

runner *noun* **1 = athlete**, jogger, sprinter **2**
= messenger, courier, dispatch bearer, errand
boy
running *adjective* **1, 2 = continuous**, constant,
incessant, perpetual, unbroken, uninterrupted **3**
= flowing, moving, streaming ◆*noun* **5**
= management, administration, control,
direction, leadership, organization, supervision
runny *adjective* **1 = flowing**, fluid, liquefied,
liquid, melted, watery
run-of-the-mill *adjective* **= ordinary**, average,
bog-standard (*Brit & Irish sl*), mediocre,
middling, passable, tolerable, undistinguished,
unexceptional
run out *verb* **a = be used up**, be exhausted,
dry up, fail, finish, give out **b = expire**, end,
terminate
run over *verb* **= knock down**, hit, knock over,
run down
rupture *noun* **1 = break**, breach, burst, crack,
fissure, rent, split, tear ◆*verb* **3 = break**, burst,
crack, separate, sever, split, tear
rural *adjective* **= rustic**, agricultural, country,
pastoral, sylvan OPPOSITE> **urban**

ruse *noun* **= trick**, device, dodge, hoax,
manoeuvre, ploy, stratagem, subterfuge
rush[1] *verb* **1 = hurry**, bolt, career, dash, fly,
hasten, race, run, shoot, speed, tear OPPOSITE>
wait. **2 = push**, hurry, hustle, press **3 = attack**,
charge, storm ◆*noun* **4 a = hurry**, charge, dash,
haste, race, scramble, stampede, surge **b**
= attack, assault, charge, onslaught ◆*adjective* **7**
= hasty, fast, hurried, quick, rapid, swift, urgent
OPPOSITE> **slow**
rust *noun* **1 = corrosion**, oxidation **2**
= mildew, blight, mould, must, rot ◆*verb* **4**
= corrode, oxidize
rustic *adjective* **1, 2 = rural**, country, pastoral,
sylvan OPPOSITE> **urban**. **3 = uncouth**, awkward,
coarse, crude, rough ◆*noun* **5 = yokel**, boor,
bumpkin, clod, clodhopper (*inf*), hick (*inf, chiefly
US & Canad*), peasant OPPOSITE> **sophisticate**
rustle[1] *verb* **= crackle**, crinkle, whisper ◆*noun*
= crackle, crinkling, rustling, whisper
rusty *adjective* **1 = corroded**, oxidized, rust-
covered, rusted **2 = reddish-brown**, chestnut,
coppery, reddish, russet, rust-coloured **3 = out
of practice**, stale, unpractised, weak

R

rut² *noun* **1** recurrent period of sexual excitability in male deer. ♦ *verb* **rutting, rutted 2** be in a period of sexual excitability.
rutabaga *noun* the US and Canadian name for SWEDE.
ruthenium *noun Chem* rare hard brittle white element.

ruthless ❶ *adjective* pitiless, merciless.
ruthlessly *adverb* **ruthlessness** *noun*
rye *noun* **1** kind of grain used for fodder and bread. **2** *US* whiskey made from rye.
rye-grass *noun* any of several grasses cultivated for fodder.

————————————— T H E S A U R U S —————————————

rut¹ *noun* **1 = groove**, furrow, indentation, track, trough, wheel mark **2 = habit**, dead end, pattern, routine, system

ruthless *adjective* **=merciless**, brutal, callous, cruel, harsh, heartless, pitiless, relentless, remorseless OPPOSITE **merciful**

R

Ss

s second(s).

S 1 South(ern). **2** *Chem* sulphur.

SA 1 Salvation Army. **2** South Africa South Australia.

Sabbath *noun* day of worship and rest: Saturday for Jews, Sunday for Christians.

sabbatical *adjective, noun* (denoting) leave for study.

sable *noun* **1** dark fur from a small weasel-like Arctic animal. ♦ *adjective* **2** black.

sabot [sab-oh] *noun* wooden shoe, clog.

sabotage ❶ *noun* **1** intentional damage done to machinery, systems, etc. ♦ *verb* **2** damage intentionally. **saboteur** *noun* person who commits sabotage.

sabre *noun* **1** curved cavalry sword. **2** light fencing sword.

sac *noun* pouchlike structure in an animal or plant.

saccharin ❶ *noun* artificial sweetener.

saccharine *adjective* **1** excessively sweet. **2** of or like sugar.

sacerdotal *adjective* of priests.

sachet *noun* **1** small envelope or bag containing a single portion. **2** small bag of perfumed powder for scenting clothing.

sack¹ ❶ *noun* **1** large bag made of coarse material. **2** *Informal* dismissal. **3** *Slang* bed. ♦ *verb* **4** *Informal* dismiss. **sacking** *noun* rough woven material used for sacks. **sackcloth** *noun* coarse fabric used for sacks, formerly worn as a penance.

sack² ❶ *noun* **1** plundering of a captured town. ♦ *verb* **2** plunder (a captured town).

sacrament *noun* ceremony of the Christian Church, esp. Communion. **sacramental** *adjective*

sacred ❶ *adjective* **1** holy. **2** connected with religion. **3** set apart, reserved. **sacred cow** person, custom, etc. regarded as being beyond criticism.

sacrifice ❶ *noun* **1** giving something up. **2** thing given up. **3** making of an offering to a god. **4** thing offered. ♦ *verb* **5** offer as a sacrifice. **6** give (something) up. **sacrificial** *adjective*

sacrilege ❶ *noun* misuse or desecration of something sacred. **sacrilegious** *adjective*

SPELLING TIP

It may sound as if **sacrilegious** has something to do with the word 'religious', which might explain why the most common misspelling of the word in the Bank of English is *sacreligious*. But it should be spelt **sacrilegious**.

---

sacristan *noun* person in charge of the contents of a church. **sacristy** *noun, pl* **-ties** room in a church where sacred objects are kept.

THESAURUS

sabotage *noun* **1** = **damage**, destruction, disruption, subversion, wrecking ♦*verb* **2** = **damage**, destroy, disable, disrupt, incapacitate, subvert, vandalize, wreck

saccharine *adjective* **1** = **oversweet**, cloying, honeyed, nauseating, sickly

sack¹ *noun* **2** *Inf* = **dismissal**, discharge, the axe (*inf*), the boot (*sl*), the push (*sl*) ♦*verb* **4** *Inf* = **dismiss**, axe (*inf*), discharge, fire (*inf*), give (someone) the push (*inf*)

sack² *noun* **1** = **plundering**, looting, pillage ♦*verb* **2** = **plunder**, loot, pillage, raid, rob, ruin, strip

sacred *adjective* **1** = **holy**, blessed, divine,

hallowed, revered, sanctified OPPOSITE **worldly**. **2** = **religious**, ecclesiastical, holy OPPOSITE **unconsecrated**. **3** = **inviolable**, protected, sacrosanct

sacrifice *noun* **1** = **surrender**, loss, renunciation **3, 4** = **offering**, oblation ♦*verb* **5** = **offer**, immolate, offer up **6** = **give up**, forego, forfeit, let go, lose, say goodbye to, surrender

sacrilege *noun* = **desecration**, blasphemy, heresy, impiety, irreverence, profanation, violation OPPOSITE **respect**

sacrilegious *adjective* = **profane**, blasphemous, desecrating, impious, irreligious, irreverent

sacristy *noun, pl* **-ties** room in a church where sacred objects are kept.
sacrosanct ❶ *adjective* regarded as sacred, inviolable.
sacrum [**say**-krum] *noun, pl* **-cra** wedge-shaped bone at the base of the spine.
sad ❶ *adjective* **sadder, saddest 1** sorrowful, unhappy. **2** causing or expressing sorrow. **3** deplorably bad. **sadden** *verb* make sad. **sadly** *adverb* **sadness** *noun*
saddle ❶ *noun* **1** rider's seat on a horse or bicycle. **2** joint of meat. ◆ *verb* **3** put a saddle on (a horse). **4** burden (with a responsibility). **saddler** *noun* maker or seller of saddles. **saddlery** *noun*
sadism ❶ [**say**-dizz-um] *noun* gaining of (sexual) pleasure from inflicting pain. **sadist** *noun* **sadistic** *adjective* **sadistically** *adverb*
sadomasochism *noun* combination of sadism and masochism. **sadomasochist** *noun*
s.a.e. stamped addressed envelope.
safari *noun, pl* **-ris** expedition to hunt or observe wild animals, esp. in Africa. **safari park** park where lions, elephants, etc. are kept uncaged so that people can see them from cars.
safe ❶ *adjective* **1** secure, protected. **2** uninjured, out of danger. **3** not involving risk. **4** not dangerous, e.g. *the beef is safe to eat.* ◆ *noun* **5** strong lockable container. **safely** *adverb*
safe-conduct *noun* permit allowing travel through a dangerous area. **safe deposit** place where valuables can be stored safely.
safekeeping *noun* protection. **safety** *noun*

safeguard ❶ *verb* **1** protect. ◆ *noun* **2** protection.
safety ❶ *noun, pl* **-ties** state of being safe. **safety belt** same as SEAT BELT. **safety lamp** miner's lamp designed to prevent it from igniting gas. **safety net** net to catch performers on a trapeze or high wire if they fall. **safety pin** pin with a spring fastening and a guard over the point when closed. **safety valve 1** valve that allows steam etc. to escape if pressure becomes excessive. **2** harmless outlet for emotion.
safflower *noun* thistle-like plant with flowers used for dye and oil.
saffron *noun* **1** orange-coloured flavouring obtained from a crocus. ◆ *adjective* **2** orange.
sag ❶ *verb* **sagging, sagged 1** sink in the middle. **2** tire. **3** (of clothes) hang loosely. ◆ *noun* **4** droop.
saga ❶ [**sah**-ga] *noun* **1** legend of Norse heroes. **2** any long story.
sagacious *adjective* wise. **sagacity** *noun*
sage[1] ❶ *noun* **1** very wise man. ◆ *adjective* **2** *Lit* wise. **sagely** *adverb*
sage[2] *noun* aromatic herb with grey-green leaves.
sagebrush *noun* aromatic plant of West N America.
Sagittarius *noun* (the archer) ninth sign of the zodiac.
sago *noun* starchy cereal from the powdered pith of the sago palm tree.
sahib *noun* Indian term of address placed after a man's name as a mark of respect.

———————— THESAURUS ————————

sacrosanct *adjective* =**inviolable**, hallowed, inviolate, sacred, sanctified, set apart, untouchable
sad *adjective* **1** =**unhappy**, blue, dejected, depressed, doleful, down, low, low-spirited, melancholy, mournful, woebegone OPPOSITE **happy. 2** =**tragic**, depressing, dismal, grievous, harrowing, heart-rending, moving, pathetic, pitiful, poignant, upsetting **3** =**deplorable**, bad, lamentable, sorry, wretched OPPOSITE **good**
sadden *verb* =**upset**, deject, depress, distress, grieve, make sad
saddle *verb* **4** =**burden**, encumber, load, lumber (*Brit inf*)
sadistic *adjective* =**cruel**, barbarous, brutal, ruthless, vicious
sadness *noun* **1** =**unhappiness**, dejection, depression, despondency, grief, melancholy, misery, poignancy, sorrow, the blues
safe *adjective* **1** =**secure**, impregnable, in safe

hands, out of danger, out of harm's way, protected, safe and sound OPPOSITE **threatened. 2** =**unharmed**, all right, intact, O.K. *or* okay (*inf*), undamaged, unhurt, unscathed **3** =**risk-free**, certain, impregnable, secure, sound **5** =**strongbox**, coffer, deposit box, repository, safe-deposit box, vault
safeguard *verb* **1** =**protect**, defend, guard, look after, preserve ◆*noun* **2** =**protection**, defence, guard, security
safely *adverb* =**in safety**, in one piece, safe and sound, with impunity, without risk
safety *noun* =**security**, impregnability, protection OPPOSITE **risk**
sag *verb* **1** =**sink**, bag, dip, droop, fall, give way, hang loosely, slump **2** =**tire**, droop, flag, wane, weaken, wilt
saga *noun* **2** =**tale**, epic, narrative, story, yarn
sage[1] *noun* **1** =**wise man**, elder, guru, master, philosopher ◆*adjective* **2** *Lit* =**wise**, judicious, sagacious, sapient, sensible

S

said *verb* past of SAY.

sail ● *noun* **1** sheet of fabric stretched to catch the wind for propelling a sailing boat. **2** journey by boat. **3** arm of a windmill. ◆ *verb* **4** travel by water. **5** begin a voyage. **6** navigate a vessel. **7** move smoothly. **sailor** *noun* **1** member of a ship's crew. **2** person considered as liable or not liable to seasickness, e.g. *a bad sailor; a good sailor.* **sailboard** *noun* board with a mast and single sail, used for windsurfing. **sailcloth** *noun* **1** fabric for making sails. **2** light canvas for making clothes.

saint ● *noun* **1** *Christianity* person venerated after death as specially holy. **2** exceptionally good person. **saintly** *adjective* **saintliness** *noun* **sainthood** *noun*

saithe *noun* dark-coloured edible sea fish.

sake[1] ● *noun* **1** benefit. **2** purpose. **for the sake of 1** for the purpose of. **2** to please or benefit (someone).

sake[2], **saki** [sah-kee] *noun* Japanese alcoholic drink made from fermented rice.

salaam [sal-ahm] *noun* **1** low bow of greeting among Muslims. ◆ *verb* **2** make a salaam.

salacious ● *adjective* excessively concerned with sex.

salad *noun* dish of raw vegetables, eaten as a meal or part of a meal. **salad days** period of youth and inexperience. **salad dressing** sauce of oil and vinegar or mayonnaise.

salamander *noun* amphibian which looks like a lizard.

salami *noun* highly spiced sausage.

salary ● *noun, pl* **-ries** fixed regular payment, usu. monthly, to an employee. **salaried** *adjective*

sale ● *noun* **1** exchange of goods for money. **2** amount sold. **3** selling of goods at unusually low prices. **4** auction. ◆ *plural* **5** department that sells its company's products. **saleable** *adjective* fit or likely to be sold. **saleroom** *noun* place where goods are sold by auction. **salesman, saleswoman, salesperson** *noun* person who sells goods. **salesmanship** *noun*

skill in selling.

salient ● [say-lee-ent] *adjective* **1** prominent, noticeable. ◆ *noun* **2** *Mil* projecting part of a front line.

saline [say-line] *adjective* containing salt. **salinity** *noun*

saliva [sal-lie-va] *noun* liquid that forms in the mouth, spittle. **salivary** *adjective* **salivate** *verb* produce saliva.

sallee *noun Aust* (also **snow gum**) **1** SE Australian eucalyptus with a pale grey bark. **2** acacia tree.

sallow ● *adjective* of an unhealthy pale or yellowish colour.

sally *noun, pl* **-lies 1** witty remark. **2** sudden brief attack by troops. ◆ *verb* **-lying, -lied** (foll. by *forth*) **3** rush out. **4** go out.

salmon *noun* **1** large fish with orange-pink flesh valued as food. **2** any of several unrelated fish. ◆ *adjective* **3** orange-pink.

salmonella *noun, pl* **-lae** bacterium causing food poisoning.

salon *noun* **1** commercial premises of a hairdresser, beautician, etc. **2** elegant reception room for guests. **3** informal gathering of important people.

saloon *noun* **1** car with a fixed roof. **2** large public room, as on a ship. **3** *US* bar serving alcoholic drinks. **saloon bar** more expensive bar in a pub.

salt ● *noun* **1** white crystalline substance used to season food. **2** chemical compound of acid and metal. **3** liveliness, wit. ◆ *plural* **4** mineral salts used as a medicine. ◆ *verb* **5** season or preserve with salt. **6** scatter salt over (an icy road) to melt the ice. **old salt** experienced sailor. **with a pinch of salt** allowing for exaggeration. **worth one's salt** efficient. **salty** *adjective* **salt away** *verb* hoard or save. **saltbush** *noun* shrub that grows in alkaline desert regions. **saltcellar** *noun* small container for salt at table. **saltwater** *adjective* living in the sea.

saltpetre *noun* compound used in

——————— THESAURUS ———————

sail *verb* **5** = **embark**, set sail **6** = **pilot**, steer **7** = **glide**, drift, float, fly, skim, soar, sweep, wing

sailor *noun* **1** = **mariner**, marine, sea dog, seafarer, seaman

saintly *adjective* = **virtuous**, godly, holy, pious, religious, righteous, saintlike

sake[1] *noun* **1** = **benefit**, account, behalf, good, interest, welfare **1** = **purpose**, aim, end, motive, objective, reason

salacious *adjective* = **lascivious**, carnal, erotic, lecherous, lewd, libidinous, lustful

salary *noun* = **pay**, earnings, income, wage, wages

sale *noun* **1** = **selling**, deal, disposal, marketing, transaction

salient *adjective* **1** = **prominent**, conspicuous, important, noticeable, outstanding, pronounced, striking

sallow *adjective* = **wan**, anaemic, pale, pallid, pasty, sickly, unhealthy, yellowish OPPOSITE rosy

salt *noun* **1** = **seasoning**, flavour, relish,

gunpowder and as a preservative.

salubrious ⊙ *adjective* favourable to health.

Saluki *noun* tall hound with a silky coat.

salutary ⊙ *adjective* producing a beneficial result.

salute ⊙ *noun* **1** motion of the arm as a formal military sign of respect. **2** firing of guns as a military greeting of honour. ◆ *verb* **3** greet with a salute. **4** make a salute. **5** acknowledge with praise. **salutation** *noun* greeting by words or actions.

salvage ⊙ *noun* **1** saving of a ship or other property from destruction. **2** property so saved. ◆ *verb* **3** save from destruction or waste. **4** gain (something beneficial) from a failure.

salvation ⊙ *noun* **1** fact or state of being saved from harm or the consequences of sin. **2** person or thing that preserves from harm.

salve ⊙ *noun* **1** healing or soothing ointment. ◆ *verb* **2** soothe or appease, e.g. *salve one's conscience.*

salver *noun* (silver) tray on which something is presented.

salvia *noun* plant with blue or red flowers.

salvo *noun, pl* **-vos, -voes 1** simultaneous discharge of guns etc. **2** burst of applause or questions.

sal volatile [sal vol-**at**-ill-ee] *noun* preparation of ammonia, used to revive a person who feels faint.

SAM surface-to-air missile.

Samaritan *noun* person who helps people in distress.

samarium *noun Chem* silvery metallic element.

samba *noun* lively Brazilian dance.

same ⊙ *adjective* **1** identical, not different, unchanged. **2** just mentioned. **all the same, just the same** nevertheless. **sameness** *noun*

samovar *noun* Russian tea urn.

Samoyed *noun* dog with a thick white coat and tightly curled tail.

sampan *noun* small boat with oars used in China.

samphire *noun* plant found on rocks by the seashore.

sample ⊙ *noun* **1** part taken as representative of a whole. ◆ *noun* **2** *Music* short extract from an existing recording mixed into a backing track to produce a new recording. ◆ *verb* **3** take and test a sample of. **sampler** *noun* piece of embroidery showing the embroiderer's skill. **sampling** *noun*

samurai *noun, pl* **-rai** member of an ancient Japanese warrior caste.

sanatorium *noun, pl* **-riums, -ria 1** institution for invalids or convalescents. **2** room for sick pupils at a boarding school.

sanctify ⊙ *verb* **-fying, -fied 1** make holy. **2** approve as religiously binding.

sanctimonious ⊙ *adjective* pretending to be religious and virtuous.

sanction ⊙ *noun* **1** permission, authorization. **2** coercive measure or penalty. ◆ *verb* **3** allow, authorize.

sanctity ⊙ *noun* sacredness, inviolability.

sanctuary ⊙ *noun, pl* **-aries 1** holy place. **2** part of a church nearest the altar. **3** place of safety for a fugitive. **4** place where animals or birds can live undisturbed.

sanctum *noun, pl* **-tums, -ta 1** sacred place. **2**

—————————— THESAURUS ——————————

savour, taste **with a pinch of salt = sceptically**, cynically, disbelievingly, suspiciously, with reservations

salty *adjective* **1 = salt**, brackish, briny, saline

salubrious *adjective* **= health-giving**, beneficial, good for one, healthy, wholesome

salutary *adjective* **= beneficial**, advantageous, good for one, profitable, useful, valuable

salute *noun* **1 = salutation** ◆*verb* **3 = greet**, acknowledge, address, hail, welcome **5 = honour**, acknowledge, pay tribute *or* homage to, recognize

salvage *verb* **3 = save**, recover, rescue, retrieve **4 = redeem**

salvation *noun* **1 = saving**, deliverance, escape, preservation, redemption, rescue ⬡OPPOSITE⬡ **loss**

salve *noun* **1 = ointment**, balm, cream, lotion

same *adjective* **1 a = identical**, alike, corresponding, duplicate, equal, twin ⬡OPPOSITE⬡

different. **b = unchanged**, changeless, consistent, constant, invariable, unaltered, unvarying ⬡OPPOSITE⬡ **altered**. **2 = aforementioned**, aforesaid

sample *noun* **1 = specimen**, example, instance, model, pattern ◆*verb* **2 = test**, experience, inspect, taste, try

sanctify *verb* **1 = consecrate**, cleanse, hallow

sanctimonious *adjective* **= holier-than-thou**, hypocritical, pious, self-righteous, smug

sanction *noun* **1 = permission**, approval, authority, authorization, backing (*inf*), mana (*NZ*), O.K. *or* okay, stamp *or* seal of approval ⬡OPPOSITE⬡ **ban**. **2 = ban**, boycott, coercive measures, embargo, penalty ⬡OPPOSITE⬡ **authority** ◆*verb* **3 = permit**, allow, approve, authorize, endorse ⬡OPPOSITE⬡ **refuse**

sanctity *noun* **= holiness**, godliness, goodness, grace, inviolability, piety, sacredness

sanctuary *noun* **1 = church**, temple **2**

S

person's private room.

sand noun **1** substance consisting of small grains of rock, esp. on a beach or in a desert. ◆ plural **2** stretches of sand forming a beach or desert. ◆ verb **3** smooth with sandpaper. **4** fill with sand. **sander** noun power tool for smoothing surfaces. **sandy** adjective **1** covered with sand. **2** (of hair) reddish-fair. **sandbag** noun **1** bag filled with sand, used as protection against gunfire or flood water. ◆ verb **2** protect with sandbags. **sandbank** noun bank of sand below the surface of a river or sea. **sandblast** verb, noun (clean with) a jet of sand blown from a nozzle under pressure. **sand castle** model of a castle made from sand. **sandpaper** noun **1** paper coated with sand for smoothing a surface. ◆ verb **2** smooth with sandpaper. **sandpiper** noun shore bird with a long bill and slender legs. **sandstone** noun rock composed of sand. **sandstorm** noun desert wind that whips up clouds of sand.

sandal noun light shoe consisting of a sole attached by straps.

sandalwood noun sweet-scented wood.

sandwich noun **1** two slices of bread with a layer of food between. ◆ verb **2** insert between two other things. **sandwich board** pair of boards hung over a person's shoulders to display advertisements in front and behind. **sandwich course** course consisting of alternate periods of study and work.

sane ⊕ adjective **1** of sound mind. **2** sensible, rational. **sanity** noun

sang verb past tense of SING.

sang-froid [shahng-**frwah**] noun composure and calmness.

sangria noun Spanish drink of wine and fruit juice.

sanguinary adjective **1** accompanied by bloodshed. **2** bloodthirsty.

sanguine ⊕ adjective **1** cheerful, optimistic. **2** ruddy.

Sanhedrin [san-id-rin] noun Judaism highest court of the ancient Jewish nation.

sanitary ⊕ adjective **1** promoting health by getting rid of dirt and germs. **2** hygienic. **sanitation** noun sanitary measures, esp. drainage or sewerage. **sanitary towel** absorbent pad worn externally during menstruation.

sank verb past tense of SINK.

Sanskrit noun ancient language of India.

Santa Claus noun legendary patron saint of children, who brings presents at Christmas.

sap¹ ⊕ noun **1** moisture that circulates in plants. **2** Informal gullible person. **sappy** adjective

sap² ⊕ verb **sapping, sapped 1** undermine. **2** weaken. ◆ noun **3** trench dug to undermine an enemy position. **sapper** noun soldier in an engineering unit.

sapient [**say**-pee-ent] adjective Lit wise, shrewd. **sapience** noun

sapling noun young tree.

sapphire noun **1** blue precious stone. ◆ adjective **2** deep blue.

saprophyte noun plant that lives on dead organic matter.

sarabande, saraband noun slow stately Spanish dance.

Saracen noun Hist Arab or Muslim who opposed the Crusades.

sarcasm ⊕ noun (use of) bitter or wounding ironic language. **sarcastic** adjective **sarcastically** adverb

sarcoma noun, pl **-mata, -mas** malignant tumour beginning in connective tissue.

sarcophagus noun, pl **-gi, -guses** stone coffin.

sardine noun small fish of the herring family, usu. preserved in tightly packed tins.

sardonic ⊕ adjective mocking or scornful. **sardonically** adverb

sardonyx noun brown-and-white gemstone.

S

——————— THESAURUS ———————

= shrine, altar **3** = **protection**, asylum, haven, refuge, retreat, shelter **4** = **reserve**, conservation area, national park, nature reserve

sane adjective **1** = **of sound mind**, all there (inf), compos mentis, in one's right mind, mentally sound OPPOSITE **mad**. **2** = **sensible**, balanced, judicious, level-headed, rational, reasonable, sound OPPOSITE **foolish**

sanguine adjective **1** = **cheerful**, buoyant, confident, hopeful, optimistic OPPOSITE **down**

sanitary adjective **2** = **hygienic**, clean, germ-free, healthy, wholesome

sanity noun **1** = **mental health**, normality,

rationality, reason, saneness OPPOSITE **madness**. **2** = **good sense**, common sense, level-headedness, rationality, sense OPPOSITE **folly**

sap¹ noun **1** = **vital fluid**, essence, lifeblood **2** Inf = **fool**, idiot, jerk (sl, chiefly US & Canad), ninny, simpleton, twit (inf), wally (sl)

sap² verb **1** = **undermine 2** = **weaken**, deplete, drain, exhaust

sarcasm noun = **irony**, bitterness, cynicism, derision, mockery, ridicule, satire

sarcastic adjective = **ironical**, acid, biting, caustic, cutting, cynical, mocking, sardonic,

sargassum, sargasso *noun* type of floating seaweed.

sari, saree *noun* long piece of cloth draped around the body and over one shoulder, worn by Hindu women.

sarmie *noun S Afr slang* sandwich.

sarong *noun* long piece of cloth tucked around the waist or under the armpits, worn esp. in Malaysia.

sarsaparilla *noun* soft drink, orig. made from the root of a tropical American plant.

sartorial *adjective* of men's clothes or tailoring.

SAS Special Air Service.

sash[1] *noun* decorative strip of cloth worn round the waist or over one shoulder.

sash[2] *noun* wooden frame containing the panes of a window. **sash window** window consisting of two sashes that can be opened by sliding one over the other.

sassafras *noun* American tree with aromatic bark used medicinally.

Sassenach *noun Scot* English person.

sat *verb* past of SIT.

Sat. Saturday.

Satan ⊙ *noun* the Devil. **satanic** *adjective* 1 of Satan. 2 supremely evil. **Satanism** *noun* worship of Satan.

satay, saté [sat-ay] *noun* Indonesian and Malaysian dish consisting of pieces of chicken, pork, etc., grilled on skewers and served with peanut sauce.

satchel *noun* bag, usu. with a shoulder strap, for carrying school books.

sate *verb* satisfy (a desire or appetite) fully.

satellite *noun* 1 man-made device orbiting in space. 2 heavenly body that orbits another. 3 country that is dependent on a more powerful one. ♦ *adjective* 4 of or used in the transmission of television signals from a satellite to the home.

satiate ⊙ [say-she-ate] *verb* provide with more than enough, so as to disgust. **satiable** *adjective* **satiety** [sat-**tie**-a-tee] *noun* feeling of having had too much.

satin *noun* silky fabric with a glossy surface on one side. **satiny** *adjective* of or like satin.

satinwood *noun* tropical tree yielding hard wood.

satire ⊙ *noun* 1 use of ridicule to expose vice or folly. 2 poem or other work that does this. **satirical** *adjective* **satirist** *noun* **satirize** *verb* ridicule by means of satire.

satisfy ⊙ *verb* -fying, -fied 1 please, content. 2 provide amply for (a need or desire). 3 convince, persuade. 4 fulfil the requirements of. **satisfaction** *noun* **satisfactory** *adjective*

satnav *noun Motoring Informal* satellite navigation.

satsuma *noun* kind of small orange.

saturate ⊙ *verb* 1 soak thoroughly. 2 cause to absorb the maximum amount of something. **saturation** *noun* **saturation point** point at which some capacity is at its fullest.

Saturday *noun* seventh day of the week.

Saturn *noun* 1 Roman god of agriculture. 2 sixth planet from the sun. **saturnine** *adjective* gloomy in temperament or appearance.

saturnalia *noun* wild party or orgy.

saturnine ⊙ *adjective* gloomy in temperament or appearance.

satyr *noun* 1 woodland god, part man, part goat. 2 lustful man.

sauce ⊙ *noun* 1 liquid added to food to enhance flavour. 2 *Informal* impudence. **saucy** *adjective* 1 impudent. 2 pert, jaunty. **saucily**

---

sarky (*Brit inf*), satirical

sardonic *adjective* =**mocking**, cynical, derisive, dry, ironical, sarcastic, sneering, wry

Satan *noun* =**The Devil**, Beelzebub, Lord of the Flies, Lucifer, Mephistopheles, Old Nick (*inf*), Prince of Darkness, The Evil One

satanic *adjective* =**evil**, black, demonic, devilish, diabolic, fiendish, hellish, infernal, wicked

satiate *verb* =**glut**, cloy, gorge, jade, nauseate, overfill, stuff, surfeit

satire *noun* 1 =**mockery**, irony, ridicule 2 =**parody**, burlesque, caricature, lampoon

satirical *adjective* 1 =**mocking**, biting, caustic, cutting, incisive, ironical

satirize *verb* =**ridicule**, burlesque, deride, lampoon, parody, pillory

satisfaction *noun* 1 =**contentment**, comfort, content, enjoyment, happiness, pleasure, pride OPPOSITE> pain. 2 =**assuaging**, gratification, repletion, satiety 4 =**fulfilment**, achievement

satisfactory *adjective* =**adequate**, acceptable, all right, average, fair, good enough, passable, sufficient

satisfy *verb* 1 =**content**, assuage, gratify, indulge, pacify, pander to, please, quench, sate, slake OPPOSITE> frustrate. 2 =**be sufficient**, answer, be enough, do, fulfil, meet, serve, suffice 3 =**convince**, assure, persuade, reassure OPPOSITE> dissuade

saturate *verb* =**soak**, drench, imbue, souse, steep, suffuse, waterlog, wet through

saturnine *adjective* =**gloomy**, dour, glum, grave, morose, sombre *adverb* **saucepan** *noun* cooking pot with a long handle.

saucer *noun* small round dish put under a cup.

sauerkraut *noun* shredded cabbage fermented in brine.

sauna *noun* Finnish-style steam bath.

saunter ❶ *verb* **1** walk in a leisurely manner, stroll. ♦ *noun* **2** leisurely walk.

saurian *adjective* of or like a lizard.

sausage *noun* minced meat in an edible tube-shaped skin. **sausage roll** skinless sausage covered in pastry.

sauté [so-tay] *verb* **-téing** *or* **-téeing, -téed** fry quickly in a little fat.

savage ❶ *adjective* **1** wild, untamed. **2** cruel and violent. **3** uncivilized, primitive. ♦ *noun* **4** uncivilized person. ♦ *verb* **5** attack ferociously. **6** criticize violently. **savagely** *adverb* **savagery** *noun*

savannah, savanna *noun* extensive open grassy plain in Africa.

savant *noun* learned person.

save ❶ *verb* **1** rescue or preserve from harm, protect. **2** avoid the waste or loss of. **3** keep for the future. **4** set aside (money). **5** prevent the necessity for. **6** *Sport* prevent the scoring of (a goal). ♦ *noun* **7** *Sport* act of preventing a goal. ♦ *preposition* **8** *Old-fashioned* except. **saver** *noun* **saving** *noun* **1** economy. ♦ *plural* **2** money put by for future use. ♦ *preposition* **3** except. **saving grace** good quality that prevents a person from being worthless.

saveloy *noun* spicy smoked sausage.

saviour ❶ *noun* **1** person who rescues another. **2** (S-) Christ.

savoir-faire ❶ [sav-wahr-**fair**] *noun French* ability to do and say the right thing in any situation.

savory *noun* aromatic herb used in cooking.

savour ❶ *verb* **1** enjoy, relish. **2** (foll. by *of*) have a flavour or suggestion of. ♦ *noun* **3** characteristic taste or odour. **4** slight but distinctive quality. **savoury** *adjective* **1** salty or spicy. **2** pleasant or acceptable. ♦ *noun, pl* **-vouries 3** savoury dish served before or after a meal.

savoy *noun* variety of cabbage.

savvy *Slang verb* **-vying, -vied 1** understand. ♦ *noun* **2** understanding, intelligence.

saw[1] *noun* **1** cutting tool with a toothed metal blade. ♦ *verb* **sawing, sawed, sawed** *or* **sawn 2** cut with a saw. **3** move (something) back and forth. **sawyer** *noun* person who saws timber for a living. **sawdust** *noun* fine wood fragments made in sawing. **sawfish** *noun* fish with a long toothed snout. **sawmill** *noun* mill where timber is sawn into planks.

saw[2] *verb* past tense of SEE[1].

saw[3] *noun* wise saying, proverb.

sax *noun Informal* short for SAXOPHONE.

saxifrage *noun* alpine rock plant with small flowers.

Saxon *noun* **1** member of the W Germanic people who settled widely in Europe in the early Middle Ages. ♦ *adjective* **2** of the Saxons.

———— THESAURUS ————

saucy *adjective* **1 = impudent**, cheeky (*inf*), forward, impertinent, insolent, pert, presumptuous, rude **2 = jaunty**, dashing, gay, natty (*inf*), perky

saunter *verb* **1 = stroll**, amble, meander, mosey (*inf*), ramble, roam, wander ♦*noun* **2 = stroll**, airing, amble, ramble, turn, walk

savage *adjective* **1 = wild**, feral, rough, rugged, uncultivated, undomesticated, untamed OPPOSITE tame. **2 = cruel**, barbarous, bestial, bloodthirsty, brutal, ferocious, fierce, harsh, ruthless, sadistic, vicious OPPOSITE kind. **3 = primitive**, rude, uncivilized, unspoilt OPPOSITE civilized ♦*noun* **4 = lout**, boor, yahoo, yob (*Brit sl*) ♦*verb* **5 = attack**, lacerate, mangle, maul

savagery *noun* **2 = cruelty**, barbarity, brutality, ferocity, ruthlessness, viciousness

save *verb* **1 a = rescue**, deliver, free, liberate, recover, redeem, salvage OPPOSITE risk. **b = protect**, conserve, guard, keep safe, look after, preserve, safeguard **3, 4 = keep**, collect,

gather, hoard, hold, husband, lay by, put by, reserve, set aside, store

saving *noun* **1 = economy**, bargain, discount, reduction

savings *plural noun* **2 = nest egg**, fund, reserves, resources, store

saviour *noun* **1 = rescuer**, defender, deliverer, liberator, preserver, protector, redeemer

Saviour *noun* **2 = Christ**, Jesus, Messiah, Redeemer

savoir-faire *noun French* **= social know-how** (*inf*), diplomacy, discretion, finesse, poise, social graces, tact, urbanity

savour *verb* **1 = enjoy**, appreciate, delight in, luxuriate in, relish, revel in **2** (foll. by *of*) **= suggest**, be suggestive of, show signs of, smack of ♦*noun* **3 = flavour**, piquancy, relish, smack, smell, tang, taste **4 = trace**, distinctive quality

savoury *adjective* **1 = spicy**, full-flavoured, piquant, rich OPPOSITE tasteless. **2 = palatable**, appetizing, lekker (*S Afr sl*),

saxophone *noun* brass wind instrument with keys and a curved body. **saxophonist** *noun*
say ❶ *verb* **saying, said 1** speak or utter. **2** express (an idea) in words. **3** give as one's opinion. **4** indicate or show. **5** suppose as an example or possibility. ◆ *noun* **6** right or chance to speak. **7** share in a decision. **saying** *noun* maxim, proverb. **say-so** *noun Informal* permission.
SAYE save as you earn: system by which regular payments are made into a savings account from a salary.
Sb *Chem* antimony.
Sc *Chem* scandium.
SC South Carolina.
scab *noun* **1** crust formed over a wound. **2** *Offens* blackleg. **3** disease of plants and animals. **scabby** *adjective* **1** covered with scabs. **2** *Informal* despicable.
scabbard *noun* sheath for a sword or dagger.
scabies [**skay**-beez] *noun* itchy skin disease.
scabrous [**skay**-bruss] *adjective* **1** rough and scaly. **2** indecent.
scaffold *noun* **1** temporary platform for workmen. **2** gallows. **scaffolding** *noun* (materials for building) scaffolds.
scalar *noun, adjective* (variable quantity) having magnitude but no direction.
scald *verb* **1** burn with hot liquid or steam. **2** sterilize with boiling water. **3** heat (liquid) almost to boiling point. ◆ *noun* **4** injury by scalding.
scale¹ ❶ *noun* **1** one of the thin overlapping plates covering fishes and reptiles. **2** thin flake. **3** coating which forms in kettles etc. due to hard water. **4** tartar formed on the teeth. ◆ *verb* **5** remove scales from. **6** come off in scales. **scaly** *adjective*
scale² *noun* (often pl) weighing instrument.

scale³ ❶ *noun* **1** graduated table or sequence of marks at regular intervals, used as a reference in making measurements. **2** ratio of size between a thing and a representation of it. **3** graded system, e.g. *a wage scale*. **4** relative degree or extent. **5** fixed series of notes in music. **6** notation of a number system. ◆ *verb* **7** climb. **scale up, down** *verb* increase or decrease proportionately in size.
scalene *adjective* (of a triangle) with three unequal sides.
scallion *noun* spring onion.
scallop *noun* **1** edible shellfish with two fan-shaped shells. **2** one of a series of small curves along an edge. **scalloped** *adjective* decorated with small curves along the edge.
scallywag *noun Informal* scamp, rascal.
scalp *noun* **1** skin and hair on top of the head. **2** part of this taken as a trophy from a slain person by a Native American. ◆ *verb* **3** cut off the scalp of.
scalpel *noun* small surgical knife.
scamp ❶ *noun* mischievous child.
scamper ❶ *verb* **1** run about hurriedly or in play. ◆ *noun* **2** scampering.
scampi *plural noun* large prawns.
scan ❶ *verb* **scanning, scanned 1** scrutinize carefully. **2** glance over quickly. **3** examine or search (an area) by passing a radar or sonar beam over it. **4** (of verse) conform to metrical rules. ◆ *noun* **5** scanning. **scanner** *noun* electronic device used for scanning. **scansion** *noun* metrical scanning of verse.
scandal ❶ *noun* **1** disgraceful action or event. **2** shame or outrage. **3** malicious gossip.
scandalize *verb* shock by scandal.
scandalmonger *noun* person who spreads gossip. **scandalous** *adjective*
Scandinavian *noun, adjective* (inhabitant or

luscious, mouthwatering, tasty
say *verb* **1 =speak**, announce, express, mention, pronounce, remark, state, utter, voice **2 =express**, communicate, convey, imply **3 =declare**, affirm, assert, maintain **5 =suppose**, assume, conjecture, estimate, guess, imagine, presume, surmise ◆*noun* **6 =chance to speak**, voice, vote **7 =influence**, authority, clout (*inf*), mana (*NZ*), power, weight
saying *noun* **=proverb**, adage, aphorism, axiom, dictum, maxim
scale¹ *noun* **=flake**, lamina, layer, plate
scale³ *noun* **1, 3 =graduation**, gradation, hierarchy, ladder, progression, ranking, sequence, series, steps **2 =ratio**, proportion **4 =degree**, extent, range, reach, scope ◆*verb* **7**

=climb, ascend, clamber, escalade, mount, surmount **scale up, down =adjust**, proportion, regulate
scamp *noun* **=rascal**, devil, imp, monkey, rogue, scallywag (*inf*)
scamper *verb* **1 =run**, dart, dash, hasten, hurry, romp, scoot, scurry, scuttle
scan *verb* **1 =scrutinize**, check, check out (*inf*), examine, eye, eyeball (*sl*), investigate **2 =glance over**, look through, run one's eye over, run over, skim **3 =survey**, scour, search, sweep
scandal *noun* **1 =crime**, disgrace, embarrassment, offence, sin, wrongdoing **2 =shame**, defamation, discredit, disgrace, dishonour, ignominy, infamy, opprobrium,

language) of Scandinavia (Norway, Denmark, Sweden, Finland, and Iceland).

scandium *noun Chem* rare silvery-white metallic element.

scant ⊕ *adjective* barely sufficient, meagre.

scanty ⊕ *adjective* **scantier, scantiest** barely sufficient or not sufficient. **scantily** *adverb* **scantiness** *noun*

scapegoat ⊕ *noun* person made to bear the blame for others.

scapula *noun, pl* **-lae, -las** shoulder blade. **scapular** *adjective* of the scapula.

scar¹ ⊕ *noun* **1** mark left by a healed wound. **2** permanent emotional damage left by an unpleasant experience. ♦ *verb* **scarring, scarred 3** mark or become marked with a scar.

scar² *noun* bare craggy rock formation.

scarab *noun* sacred beetle of ancient Egypt.

scarce ⊕ *adjective* **1** insufficient to meet demand. **2** not common, rarely found. **make oneself scarce** *Informal* go away. **scarcely** *adverb* **1** hardly at all. **2** definitely or probably not. **scarcity** *noun*

scare ⊕ *verb* **1** frighten or be frightened. **2** (foll. by *away* or *off*) drive away by frightening. ♦ *noun* **3** fright, sudden panic. **4** period of general alarm. **scary** *adjective Informal* frightening. **scarecrow** *noun* **1** figure dressed in old clothes, set up to scare birds away from crops. **2** raggedly dressed person.

scaremonger *noun* person who spreads alarming rumours.

scarf¹ *noun, pl* **scarves, scarfs** piece of material worn round the neck, head, or shoulders.

scarf² *noun* **1** joint between two pieces of timber made by notching the ends and fastening them together. ♦ *verb* **2** join in this way.

scarify *verb* **-fying, -fied 1** scratch or cut slightly all over. **2** break up and loosen (topsoil). **3** criticize mercilessly. **scarification** *noun*

scarlatina *noun* scarlet fever.

scarlet *adjective, noun* brilliant red. **scarlet fever** infectious fever with a scarlet rash.

scarp *noun* steep slope.

scarper ⊕ *verb Slang* run away.

scat¹ *verb* **scatting, scatted** *Informal* go away.

scat² *noun* jazz singing using improvised vocal sounds instead of words.

scathing ⊕ *adjective* harshly critical.

scatological *adjective* preoccupied with obscenity, esp. with references to excrement. **scatology** *noun*

scatter ⊕ *verb* **1** throw about in various directions. **2** disperse. ♦ *noun* **3** scattering.

scatterbrain *noun* empty-headed person.

scatty *adjective* **-tier, -tiest** *Informal* empty-headed.

scavenge *verb* search for (anything usable) among discarded material. **scavenger** *noun* **1** person who scavenges. **2** animal that feeds on decaying matter.

SCE Scottish Certificate of Education.

————————————— THESAURUS —————————————

stigma **3** = **gossip**, aspersion, dirt, rumours, slander, talk, tattle

scandalize *verb* = **shock**, affront, appal, horrify, offend, outrage

scandalous *adjective* **1** = **shocking**, disgraceful, disreputable, infamous, outrageous, shameful, unseemly OPPOSITE> **proper. 3** = **slanderous**, defamatory, libellous, scurrilous, untrue

scant *adjective* = **meagre**, barely sufficient, little, minimal, sparse OPPOSITE> **full**

scanty *adjective* = **meagre**, bare, deficient, inadequate, insufficient, poor, scant, short, skimpy, sparse, thin

scapegoat *noun* = **whipping boy**, fall guy (*inf*)

scar¹ *noun* **1** = **mark**, blemish, injury, wound ♦ *verb* **3** = **mark**, damage, disfigure

scarce *adjective* **1** = **in short supply**, few, few and far between, infrequent, insufficient OPPOSITE> **sufficient. 2** = **rare**, uncommon OPPOSITE> **common**

scarcely *adverb* **1** = **hardly**, barely **2** = **definitely not**, hardly

scarcity *noun* **1** = **shortage**, dearth, deficiency, insufficiency, lack, paucity, rareness, want

scare *verb* **1** = **frighten**, alarm, dismay, intimidate, panic, shock, startle, terrify ♦ *noun* **3** = **fright**, panic, shock, start, terror

scarper *verb Sl* = **run away**, abscond, beat it (*sl*), clear off (*inf*), disappear, flee, run for it, scram (*inf*), take to one's heels

scary *adjective Inf* = **frightening**, alarming, chilling, creepy (*inf*), horrifying, spine-chilling, spooky (*inf*), terrifying

scathing *adjective* = **critical**, biting, caustic, cutting, harsh, sarcastic, scornful, trenchant, withering

scatter *verb* **1** = **throw about**, diffuse, disseminate, fling, shower, spread, sprinkle, strew OPPOSITE> **collect. 2** = **disperse**, disband, dispel, dissipate OPPOSITE> **assemble**

scatterbrain *noun* = **featherbrain**, butterfly,

scenario ❶ *noun, pl* **-rios 1** summary of the plot of a play or film. **2** imagined sequence of future events.

scene ❶ *noun* **1** place of action of a real or imaginary event. **2** subdivision of a play or film in which the action is continuous. **3** scenery. **4** view of a place. **5** display of emotion. **6** *Informal* specific activity or interest, e.g. *the fashion scene*. **behind the scenes 1** backstage. **2** in secret. **scenery** *noun* **1** natural features of a landscape. **2** painted backcloths or screens used on stage to represent the scene of action. **scenic** *adjective* **1** picturesque. **2** of stage scenery.

scent ❶ *noun* **1** pleasant smell. **2** smell left in passing, by which an animal can be traced. **3** series of clues. **4** perfume. ♦ *verb* **5** detect by smell. **6** suspect. **7** fill with fragrance.

sceptic ❶ [skep-tik] *noun* person who habitually doubts generally accepted beliefs. **sceptical** *adjective* **sceptically** *adverb* **scepticism** *noun*

sceptre *noun* ornamental rod symbolizing royal power.

schedule ❶ *noun* **1** plan of procedure for a project. **2** list. **3** timetable. ♦ *verb* **4** plan to occur at a certain time. **5** make or place in a schedule.

schema *noun, pl* **-mata** overall plan or diagram. **schematic** *adjective* presented as a plan or diagram. **schematize** *verb* arrange in a scheme.

schematic *adjective* presented as a plan or diagram.

scheme ❶ *noun* **1** systematic plan. **2** systematic arrangement. **3** secret plot. ♦ *verb* **4** plan in an underhand manner. **schemer** *noun* **scheming** *adjective, noun*

scherzo [skairt-so] *noun, pl* **-zos, -zi** brisk lively piece of music.

schilling *noun* standard monetary unit of Austria.

schism ❶ [skizz-um] *noun* (group resulting from) division in an organization. **schismatic** *adjective, noun*

schist [skist] *noun* crystalline rock which splits into layers.

schizo [skit-so] *adjective, noun, pl* **-os** *Offens* schizophrenic (person).

schizoid *adjective* **1** abnormally introverted. **2** *Informal* contradictory. ♦ *noun* **3** schizoid person.

schizophrenia *noun* **1** mental disorder involving deterioration of or confusion about the personality. **2** *Informal* contradictory behaviour or attitudes. **schizophrenic** *adjective, noun*

schmaltz *noun* excessive sentimentality. **schmaltzy** *adjective*

schnapps *noun* strong alcoholic spirit.

schnitzel *noun* thin slice of meat, esp. veal.

scholar ❶ *noun* **1** learned person. **2** student receiving a scholarship. **3** pupil. **scholarly** *adjective* learned. **scholarship** *noun* **1** learning. **2** financial aid given to a student because of academic merit. **scholastic** *adjective* of schools or scholars.

school[1] ❶ *noun* **1** place where children are

———————— THESAURUS ————————

flibbertigibbet

scenario *noun* **1** = **story line**, outline, résumé, summary, synopsis

scene *noun* **1** = **site**, area, locality, location, place, position, setting, spot **2** = **act**, division, episode, part **3** = **setting**, backdrop, background, set **4** = **view**, landscape, panorama, prospect, vista **5** = **fuss**, carry-on (*inf, chiefly Brit*), commotion, exhibition, performance, row, tantrum, to-do **6** *Inf* = **world**, arena, business, environment

scenery *noun* **1** = **landscape**, surroundings, terrain, view, vista **2** = **set**, backdrop, flats, setting, stage set

scenic *adjective* **1** = **picturesque**, beautiful, panoramic, spectacular, striking

scent *noun* **1** = **aroma**, bouquet, odour, smell **2** = **trail**, spoor, track **4** = **fragrance**, perfume ♦ *verb* **5** = **detect**, discern, nose out, sense, smell, sniff

sceptic *noun* = **doubter**, cynic, disbeliever,

doubting Thomas

sceptical *adjective* = **doubtful**, cynical, disbelieving, dubious, incredulous, mistrustful, unconvinced

scepticism *noun* = **doubt**, cynicism, disbelief, incredulity, unbelief

schedule *noun* **1** = **plan**, agenda **2** = **list**, calendar, catalogue, inventory **3** = **timetable**, programme ♦ *verb* **4** = **plan**, appoint, arrange, book, organize, programme

scheme *noun* **1** = **plan**, programme, project, proposal, strategy, system, tactics **2** = **diagram**, blueprint, chart, draft, layout, outline, pattern **3** = **plot**, conspiracy, intrigue, manoeuvre, ploy, ruse, stratagem, subterfuge ♦ *verb* **4** = **plot**, collude, conspire, intrigue, machinate, manoeuvre

scheming *adjective* **4** = **calculating**, artful, conniving, cunning, sly, tricky, underhand, wily

schism *noun* = **division**, breach, break, rift, rupture, separation, split

S

taught or instruction is given in a subject. **2** staff and pupils of a school. **3** department specializing in a subject. **4** group of artists, thinkers, etc. with shared principles or methods. ◆ *verb* **5** educate or train. **scholar** *noun* **1** learned person. **2** student receiving a scholarship. **3** pupil. **schooling** *noun* education.

schoolboy, schoolgirl *noun* child attending school. **schoolteacher, schoolmaster, schoolmistress** *noun* person who teaches in a school.

school² *noun* shoal of fish, whales, etc.

schooner *noun* **1** sailing ship rigged fore-and-aft. **2** large glass.

schottische *noun* type of slow polka.

sciatica *noun* severe pain in the large nerve in the back of the leg. **sciatic** *adjective* **1** of the hip. **2** of or afflicted with sciatica.

science ❶ *noun* **1** systematic study and knowledge of natural or physical phenomena. **2** branch of this knowledge. **3** skill or technique. **scientific** *adjective* **1** of science. **2** systematic. **scientifically** *adverb* **scientist** *noun* person who studies or practises a science. **science fiction** stories making imaginative use of scientific knowledge. **science park** area where scientific research and commercial development are carried on in cooperation.

sci-fi *noun* short for SCIENCE FICTION.

scimitar *noun* curved oriental sword.

scintillate ❶ *verb* give off sparks. **scintillating** *adjective* very lively and amusing. **scintillation** *noun*

scintillating ❶ *adjective* very lively and amusing.

scion [sy-on] *noun* **1** descendant or heir. **2** shoot of a plant for grafting.

scissors *plural noun* cutting instrument with two crossed pivoted blades.

sclerosis *noun, pl* **-ses** abnormal hardening of body tissues.

scoff¹ ❶ *verb* **1** express derision. ◆ *noun* **2** mocking expression.

scoff² ❶ *verb Informal* eat rapidly.

scold ❶ *verb* **1** find fault with, reprimand. ◆ *noun* **2** person who scolds. **scolding** *noun*

scollop *noun* same as SCALLOP.

sconce *noun* bracket on a wall for holding candles or lights.

scone *noun* small plain cake baked in an oven or on a griddle.

scoop ❶ *noun* **1** shovel-like tool for ladling or hollowing out. **2** news story reported in one newspaper before all its rivals. ◆ *verb* **3** take up or hollow out with or as if with a scoop. **4** beat (rival newspapers) in reporting a news item.

scoot *verb Slang* leave or move quickly.

scooter *noun* **1** child's vehicle propelled by pushing on the ground with one foot. **2** light motorcycle.

scope ❶ *noun* **1** opportunity for using abilities. **2** range of activity.

scorch ❶ *verb* **1** burn on the surface. **2** parch or shrivel from heat. ◆ *noun* **3** slight burn.

——————— THESAURUS ———————

scholar *noun* **1** = **intellectual**, academic, savant **3** = **student**, disciple, learner, pupil, schoolboy *or* schoolgirl

scholarly *adjective* = **learned**, academic, bookish, erudite, intellectual, lettered, scholastic

scholarship *noun* **1** = **learning**, book-learning, education, erudition, knowledge **2** = **bursary**, fellowship

scholastic *adjective* = **learned**, academic, lettered, scholarly

school¹ *noun* **1** = **academy**, college, faculty, institute, institution, seminary **4** = **group**, adherents, circle, denomination, devotees, disciples, faction, followers, set ◆ *verb* **5** = **train**, coach, discipline, drill, educate, instruct, tutor

schooling *noun* = **teaching**, coaching, drill, education, instruction, training, tuition

science *noun* **2** = **discipline**, body of knowledge, branch of knowledge **3** = **skill**, art, technique

scientific *adjective* **2** = **systematic**, accurate, controlled, exact, mathematical, precise

scientist *noun* = **inventor**, boffin (*inf*)

scintillating *adjective* = **brilliant**, animated, bright, dazzling, exciting, glittering, lively, sparkling, stimulating

scoff¹ *verb* **1** = **scorn**, belittle, deride, despise, jeer, knock (*inf*), laugh at, mock, pooh-pooh, ridicule, sneer

scoff² *verb Inf* = **gobble (up)**, bolt, devour, gorge oneself on, gulp down, guzzle, wolf

scold *verb* **1** = **reprimand**, berate, castigate, censure, find fault with, give (someone) a dressing-down, lecture, rebuke, reproach, reprove, rouse on (*Aust*), tell off (*inf*), tick off (*inf*), upbraid OPPOSITE praise ◆ *noun* **2** = **nag**, shrew, termagant (*rare*)

scolding *noun* = **rebuke**, dressing-down (*inf*), lecture, row, telling-off (*inf*), ticking-off (*inf*)

scoop *noun* **1** = **ladle**, dipper, spoon **2** = **exclusive**, exposé, revelation, sensation ◆ *verb* **3 a** = **lift**, gather up, pick up, take up **b** = **hollow**, bail, dig, empty, excavate, gouge, shovel

scope *noun* **1** = **opportunity**, freedom, latitude, liberty, room, space **2** = **range**, area,

S

scorcher noun Informal very hot day.
score ❶ noun 1 points gained in a game or competition. 2 twenty. 3 written version of a piece of music showing parts for each musician. 4 mark or cut. 5 record of amounts due. 6 reason. 7 grievance, e.g. *settle old scores*. ◆ *plural* 8 lots. ◆ *verb* 9 gain (points) in a game. 10 keep a record of points. 11 mark or cut. 12 (foll. by *out*) cross out. 13 arrange music (for). 14 achieve a success. **score off** *verb* gain an advantage at someone else's expense.
scorn ❶ noun 1 open contempt. ◆ *verb* 2 despise. 3 reject with contempt. **scornful** *adjective* **scornfully** *adverb*
Scorpio noun (the scorpion) eighth sign of the zodiac.
scorpion noun small lobster-shaped animal with a sting at the end of a jointed tail.
Scot noun person from Scotland. **Scottish** *adjective* of Scotland, its people, or their languages. **Scots** *adjective* 1 Scottish. ◆ *noun* 2 English dialect spoken in Scotland. **Scotsman, Scotswoman** *noun*

> **LANGUAGE TIP**
>
> *Scotch* is used only in certain fixed expressions like *Scotch egg*. The use of *Scotch* for *Scots* or *Scottish* is otherwise felt to be incorrect, esp. when applied to people.

Scotch noun whisky distilled in Scotland.

Scotch broth thick soup of beef or lamb and vegetables. **Scotch egg** hard-boiled egg encased in sausage meat and breadcrumbs.
scotch *verb* 1 put an end to. 2 wound without killing.
scot-free *adjective* without harm or punishment.
Scotland Yard noun headquarters of the police force of metropolitan London.
scoundrel ❶ noun Old-fashioned cheat or deceiver.
scour¹ ❶ *verb* 1 clean or polish by rubbing with something rough. 2 clear or flush out. ◆ *noun* 3 scouring. **scourer** noun small rough nylon pad used for cleaning pots and pans.
scour² ❶ *verb* 1 search thoroughly and energetically. 2 move swiftly over.
scourge ❶ noun 1 person or thing causing severe suffering. 2 whip. ◆ *verb* 3 cause severe suffering to. 4 whip.
Scouse Informal noun 1 (also **Scouser**) person from Liverpool. 2 dialect of Liverpool. ◆ *adjective* 3 of Liverpool, its people, or their dialect.
scout ❶ noun 1 person sent out to reconnoitre. 2 (**S-**) member of the Scout Association, an organization for boys which aims to develop character and promotes outdooractivities. ◆ *verb* 3 act as a scout. 4 reconnoitre. **Scouter** noun leader of a troop of Scouts.
scow noun unpowered barge.
scowl ❶ *verb, noun* (have) an angry or sullen expression.

———————— THESAURUS ————————

capacity, orbit, outlook, reach, span, sphere
scorch *verb* 1 = **burn**, roast, sear, singe 2 = **shrivel**, parch, wither
score noun 1 = **points**, grade, mark, outcome, record, result, total 6 = **grounds**, basis, cause, ground, reason 7 = **grievance**, grudge, injury, injustice, wrong ◆*plural* 8 = **lots**, hundreds, masses, millions, multitudes, myriads, swarms ◆*verb* 9 = **gain**, achieve, chalk up (*inf*), make, notch up (*inf*), win 10 = **keep count**, count, record, register, tally 11 = **cut**, deface, gouge, graze, mark, scrape, scratch, slash 12 (foll. by *out*) = **cross out**, cancel out, delete, obliterate, strike out 13 = **arrange**, adapt, orchestrate, set
scorn noun 1 = **contempt**, derision, disdain, disparagement, mockery, sarcasm OPPOSITE respect ◆*verb* 2 = **despise**, be above, deride, disdain, scoff at 3 = **reject**, flout, slight, spurn OPPOSITE esteem
scornful *adjective* = **contemptuous**, derisive, disdainful, haughty, jeering, mocking, sarcastic,

sardonic, scathing, scoffing, sneering
scoundrel noun Old-fashioned = **rogue**, bastard (*offens*), blackguard, good-for-nothing, heel (*sl*), miscreant, ne'er-do-well, rascal, reprobate, rotter (*sl, chiefly Brit*), scally (*NW Eng dial*), scamp, swine, villain
scour¹ *verb* 1 = **rub**, abrade, buff, clean, polish, scrub 2 = **wash**, cleanse
scour² *verb* 1 = **search**, beat, comb, hunt, ransack
scourge noun 1 = **affliction**, bane, curse, infliction, misfortune, pest, plague, terror, torment OPPOSITE benefit. 2 = **whip**, cat, lash, strap, switch, thong ◆*verb* 3 = **afflict**, curse, plague, terrorize, torment 4 = **whip**, beat, cane, flog, horsewhip, lash, thrash
scout noun 1 = **vanguard**, advance guard, lookout, outrider, precursor, reconnoitrer ◆*verb* 3, 4 = **reconnoitre**, investigate, observe, probe, recce (*sl*), spy, survey, watch
scowl *verb* = **glower**, frown, lour *or* lower

S

scrabble ⊙ *verb* **1** scrape at with the hands, feet, or claws. ♦ *noun* **2** (**S-**) ® board game in which words are formed by letter tiles.

scrag ⊙ *noun* **1** thin end of a neck of mutton. **2** scrawny person or animal. **scraggy** *adjective* thin, bony.

scram¹ ⊙ *verb* **scramming, scrammed** *Informal* go away quickly.

scram² *noun* **1** emergency shutdown of a nuclear reactor. ♦ *verb* **scramming, scrammed** **2** (of a nuclear reactor) shut or be shut down in an emergency.

scramble ⊙ *verb* **1** climb or crawl hastily or awkwardly. **2** struggle with others (for). **3** mix up. **4** cook (eggs beaten up with milk). **5** (of an aircraft or aircrew) take off hurriedly in an emergency. **6** make (transmitted speech) unintelligible by the use of an electronic device. ♦ *noun* **7** scrambling. **8** rough climb. **9** disorderly struggle. **10** motorcycle race over rough ground. **scrambler** *noun* electronic device that makes transmitted speech unintelligible.

scrap¹ ⊙ *noun* **1** small piece. **2** waste metal collected for reprocessing. ♦ *plural* **3** leftover food. ♦ *verb* **scrapping, scrapped** **4** discard as useless. **scrappy** *adjective* fragmentary, disjointed. **scrapbook** *noun* book with blank pages in which newspaper cuttings or pictures are stuck.

scrap² ⊙ *noun, verb* **scrapping, scrapped** *Informal* fight or quarrel.

scrape ⊙ *verb* **1** rub with something rough or sharp. **2** clean or smooth thus. **3** rub with a harsh noise. **4** economize. ♦ *noun* **5** act or sound of scraping. **6** mark or wound caused by scraping. **7** *Informal* awkward situation. **scraper** *noun* **scrape through** *verb* succeed in or obtain with difficulty.

scratch ⊙ *verb* **1** mark or cut with claws, nails, or anything rough or sharp. **2** scrape (skin) with nails or claws to relieve itching. **3** cross out. **4** withdraw from a race or competition. ♦ *noun* **5** wound, mark, or sound made by scratching. ♦ *adjective* **6** put together at short notice. **7** *Sport* with no handicap allowed. **from scratch** from the very beginning. **up to scratch** up to standard. **scratchy** *adjective* **scratchcard** *noun* ticket that reveals whether or not the holder has won a prize when the surface is removed by scratching.

scrawl ⊙ *verb* **1** write carelessly or hastily. ♦ *noun* **2** scribbled writing.

scrawny ⊙ *adjective* **scrawnier, scrawniest** thin and bony.

scream ⊙ *verb* **1** utter a piercing cry, esp. of fear or pain. **2** utter with a scream. ♦ *noun* **3** shrill piercing cry. **4** *Informal* very funny person or thing.

scree *noun* slope of loose shifting stones.

———— THESAURUS ————

♦*noun* = **glower**, black look, dirty look, frown
scrabble *verb* **1** = **scrape**, claw, scramble, scratch

scraggy *adjective* = **scrawny**, angular, bony, lean, skinny

scram¹ *verb Inf* = **go away**, abscond, beat it (*sl*), clear off (*inf*), get lost (*inf*), leave, make oneself scarce (*inf*), make tracks, scarper (*Brit sl*), vamoose (*sl, chiefly US*)

scramble *verb* **1** = **struggle**, climb, crawl, scrabble, swarm **2** = **strive**, contend, jostle, push, run, rush, vie ♦*noun* **8** = **climb**, trek **9** = **struggle**, commotion, competition, confusion, mêlée, race, rush, tussle

scrap¹ *noun* **1** = **piece**, bit, crumb, fragment, grain, morsel, part, particle, portion, sliver, snippet **2** = **waste**, junk, offcuts ♦*plural* **3** = **leftovers**, bits, leavings, remains ♦*verb* **4** = **get rid of**, abandon, discard, ditch (*sl*), drop, jettison, throw away *or* out, write off OPPOSITE▷ bring back

scrap² *noun Inf* = **fight**, argument, battle, disagreement, dispute, quarrel, row, squabble, wrangle ♦*verb Inf* = **fight**, argue, row, squabble, wrangle

scrape *verb* **1** = **rub**, bark, graze, scratch, scuff **2** = **scour**, clean, erase, remove, rub, skin **3** = **grate**, grind, rasp, scratch, squeak **4** = **scrimp**, pinch, save, skimp, stint ♦*noun* **7** *Inf* = **predicament**, awkward situation, difficulty, dilemma, fix (*inf*), mess, plight, tight spot
scrape through ♦*verb* = **get by** (*inf*), just make it, struggle

scrappy *adjective* = **incomplete**, bitty, disjointed, fragmentary, piecemeal, sketchy, thrown together

scratch *verb* **1** = **mark**, claw, cut, damage, etch, grate, graze, lacerate, score, scrape **3** = **erase**, cancel, cross out, delete, eliminate **4** = **withdraw**, pull out ♦*noun* **5** = **mark**, blemish, claw mark, gash, graze, laceration, scrape ♦*adjective* **6** = **improvised**, impromptu, rough-and-ready **up to scratch** = **adequate**, acceptable, satisfactory, sufficient, up to standard

scrawl *verb, noun* **1** = **scribble**, doodle, squiggle

scrawny *adjective* = **thin**, bony, gaunt, lean, scraggy, skin-and-bones (*inf*), skinny, undernourished

screech ❶ *verb, noun* (utter) a shrill cry.
screech owl barn owl.
screed *noun* long tedious piece of writing.
screen ❶ *noun* **1** surface of a television set, VDU, etc., on which an image is formed. **2** white surface on which films or slides are projected. **3** movable structure used to shelter, divide, or conceal something. ♦ *verb* **4** shelter or conceal with or as if with a screen. **5** examine (a person or group) to determine suitability for a task or to detect the presence of disease or weapons. **6** show (a film). **the screen** cinema generally. **screenplay** *noun* script for a film. **screen saver** *Computers* a changing image on a monitor when the computer is operative but idle.
screw ❶ *noun* **1** metal pin with a spiral ridge along its length, twisted into materials to fasten them together. **2** *Slang* prison guard. ♦ *verb* **3** turn (a screw). **4** twist. **5** fasten with screw(s). **6** *Informal* extort. **screwy** *adjective Informal* crazy or eccentric. **screwdriver** *noun* tool for turning screws. **screw up** *verb* **1** *Informal* bungle. **2** distort. **3** summon up (courage).
scribble ❶ *verb* **1** write hastily or illegibly. **2** make meaningless or illegible marks. ♦ *noun* **3** something scribbled.
scribe ❶ *noun* **1** person who copied manuscripts before the invention of printing. **2** Bible scholar of the Jewish Law.
scrimmage *noun* **1** rough or disorderly struggle. ♦ *verb* **2** engage in a scrimmage.
scrimp ❶ *verb* be very economical.
scrip *noun* certificate representing a claim to

stocks or shares.
script ❶ *noun* **1** text of a film, play, or TV programme. **2** particular system of writing, e.g. *Arabic script.* **3** candidate's answer paper in an exam. **4** handwriting. ♦ *verb* **5** write a script for.
scripture *noun* **1** sacred writings of a religion. **2** (**S-**) Old and New Testaments. **scriptural** *adjective*
scrofula *noun* tuberculosis of the lymphatic glands. **scrofulous** *adjective*
scroll *noun* **1** roll of parchment or paper. **2** ancient book in scroll form. **3** ornamental carving shaped like a scroll. ♦ *verb* **4** move (text) up or down on a VDU screen.
Scrooge *noun* miserly person.
scrotum *noun, pl* **-ta, -tums** pouch of skin containing the testicles.
scrounge ❶ *verb Informal* get by cadging or begging. **scrounger** *noun*
scrub[1] ❶ *verb* **scrubbing, scrubbed 1** clean by rubbing, often with a hard brush and water. **2** *Informal* delete or cancel. ♦ *noun* **3** scrubbing.
scrub[2] *noun* **1** stunted trees. **2** area of land covered with scrub. **scrubby** *adjective* **1** covered with scrub. **2** stunted. **3** *Informal* shabby. **scrub turkey** same as MEGAPODE.
scruff[1] *noun* nape (of the neck).
scruff[2] ❶ *noun Informal* untidy person. **scruffy** *adjective* unkempt or shabby.
scrum, scrummage *noun* **1** *Rugby* restarting of play in which opposing packs of forwards push against each other to gain possession of the ball. **2** disorderly struggle.
scrump *verb Brit dialect* steal (apples) from an

———————— T H E S A U R U S ————————

scream *verb* **1, 2** = **cry**, bawl, screech, shriek, yell ♦*noun* **3** = **cry**, howl, screech, shriek, yell, yelp
screech *verb, noun* = **cry**, scream, shriek
screen *noun* **3 a** = **cover**, awning, canopy, guard, mesh, net, shade, shelter, shield **b** = **partition**, room divider **c** = **cloak** ♦*verb* **4 a** = **protect**, defend, guard, shelter, shield **b** = **cover**, cloak, conceal, hide, mask, shade, veil **5** = **vet**, evaluate, examine, filter, gauge, scan, sift, sort **6** = **broadcast**, present, put on, show
screw *verb* **3** = **turn**, tighten **4** = **twist 6** *Inf* = **extort**, extract, wrest, wring
screw up *verb* **1** *Inf* = **bungle**, botch, make a hash of (*inf*), make a mess of (*sl*), mess up, mishandle, spoil **2** = **contort**, distort, pucker, wrinkle
screwy *adjective Inf* = **crazy**, crackpot (*inf*), eccentric, loopy (*inf*), nutty (*sl*), odd, off-the-wall (*sl*), out to lunch (*inf*), round the bend (*Brit sl*), weird

scribble *verb* **1** = **scrawl**, dash off, jot, write
scribe *noun* **1** = **copyist**, amanuensis, writer
scrimp *verb* = **economize**, be frugal, save, scrape, skimp, stint, tighten one's belt
script *noun* **1** = **text**, book, copy, dialogue, libretto, lines, words **4** = **handwriting**, calligraphy, penmanship, writing
Scripture *noun* **2** = **The Bible**, Holy Bible, Holy Scripture, Holy Writ, The Good Book, The Gospels, The Scriptures
scrounge *verb Inf* = **cadge**, beg, blag (*sl*), bludge (*Aust & NZ*), bum (*inf*), freeload (*sl*), sponge (*inf*)
scrounger *adjective Inf* = **cadger**, freeloader (*sl*), parasite, sponger (*inf*)
scrub[1] *verb* **1** = **scour**, clean, cleanse, rub **2** *Inf* = **cancel**, abolish, call off, delete, drop, forget about, give up
scruffy *adjective* = **tatty**, ill-groomed, mangy, messy, ragged, run-down, seedy, shabby, unkempt, untidy OPPOSITE> neat

S

orchard or garden.

scrumptious ⊕ *adjective Informal* delicious.

scrumpy *noun* rough dry cider.

scrunch *verb* **1** crumple or crunch or be crumpled or crunched. ◆ *noun* **2** act or sound of scrunching.

scrunchie *noun* loop of elastic covered loosely with fabric, used to hold the hair in a ponytail.

scruple ⊕ *noun* **1** doubt produced by one's conscience or morals. ◆ *verb* **2** have doubts on moral grounds. **scrupulous** *adjective* **1** very conscientious. **2** very careful or precise. **scrupulously** *adverb*

scrutiny ⊕ *noun, pl* **-nies 1** close examination. **2** searching look. **scrutinize** *verb* examine closely.

scuba diving *noun* sport of swimming under water using cylinders containing compressed air attached to breathing apparatus.

scud *verb* **scudding, scudded 1** move along swiftly. **2** run before a gale.

scuff *verb* **1** drag (the feet) while walking. **2** scrape (one's shoes) by doing so. ◆ *noun* **3** mark caused by scuffing.

scuffle ⊕ *verb* **1** fight in a disorderly manner. ◆ *noun* **2** disorderly struggle. **3** scuffling sound.

scull *noun* **1** small oar. ◆ *verb* **2** row (a boat) using sculls.

scullery *noun, pl* **-leries** small room where washing-up and other kitchen work is done.

sculpture ⊕ *noun* **1** art of making figures or designs in wood, stone, etc. **2** product of this art. ◆ *verb* **3** (also **sculpt**) represent in sculpture. **sculptor, sculptress** *noun* **sculptural** *adjective*

scum ⊕ *noun* **1** impure or waste matter on the surface of a liquid. **2** worthless people.

scummy *adjective*

scungy *adjective* **-ier, -iest** *Aust & NZ informal* sordid or dirty.

scupper¹ ⊕ *verb Informal* defeat or ruin.

scupper² *noun* drain in the side of a ship.

scurf *noun* flaky skin on the scalp. **scurfy** *adjective*

scurrilous ⊕ *adjective* untrue and defamatory.

scurry ⊕ *verb* **-rying, -ried 1** move hastily. ◆ *noun* **2** act or sound of scurrying.

scurvy *noun* **1** disease caused by lack of vitamin C. ◆ *adjective* **2** mean and despicable.

scut *noun* short tail of the hare, rabbit, or deer.

scuttle¹ *noun* fireside container for coal.

scuttle² ⊕ *verb* **1** run with short quick steps. ◆ *noun* **2** hurried run.

scuttle³ *verb* make a hole in (a ship) to sink it.

scythe *noun* **1** long-handled tool with a curved blade for cutting grass. ◆ *verb* **2** cut with a scythe.

SD South Dakota.

Se *Chem* selenium.

SE southeast(ern).

sea ⊕ *noun* **1** mass of salt water covering three quarters of the earth's surface. **2** particular area of this. **3** vast expanse. **at sea 1** in a ship on the ocean. **2** confused or bewildered. **sea anemone** sea animal with suckers like petals. **seaboard** *noun* coast. **sea dog** experienced sailor. **seafaring** *adjective* working or travelling by sea. **seafood** *noun* edible saltwater fish or shellfish. **seagoing** *adjective* built for travelling on the sea. **seagull** *noun* gull. **sea horse** small sea fish with a plated body and horselike head. **sea legs** ability to keep one's balance at sea and resist seasickness. **sea level** average level of the sea's surface in relation to the land. **sea**

———— THESAURUS ————

scrumptious *adjective Inf* **= delicious,** appetizing, delectable, luscious, mouthwatering, succulent, yummy (*sl*)

scruple *noun* **1 = misgiving,** compunction, doubt, hesitation, qualm, reluctance, second thoughts, uneasiness ◆*verb* **2 = have misgivings about,** demur, doubt, have qualms about, hesitate, think twice about

scrupulous *adjective* **1 = moral,** conscientious, honourable, principled, upright OPPOSITE dishonest. **2 = careful,** exact, fastidious, meticulous, precise, punctilious, rigorous, strict OPPOSITE reckless

scrutinize *verb* **= examine,** explore, inspect, investigate, peruse, pore over, probe, scan, search, study

scrutiny *noun* **1 = examination,** analysis, exploration, inspection, investigation, perusal,

search, study

scuffle *verb* **1 = fight,** clash, grapple, jostle, struggle, tussle ◆*noun* **2 = fight,** brawl, commotion, disturbance, fray, scrimmage, skirmish, tussle

sculpture *verb* **3** (also **sculpt**) **= sculpt,** carve, chisel, fashion, form, hew, model, mould, shape

scum *noun* **1 = impurities,** dross, film, froth **2 = rabble,** dregs of society, riffraff, trash (*chiefly US & Canad*)

scupper¹ *verb Inf* **= destroy,** defeat, demolish, put paid to, ruin, torpedo, wreck

scurrilous *adjective* **= slanderous,** abusive, defamatory, insulting, scandalous, vituperative

scurry *verb* **1 = hurry,** dart, dash, race, scamper, scoot, scuttle, sprint OPPOSITE wander ◆*noun* **2 = flurry,** scampering, whirl

scuttle² *verb* **1 = run,** bustle, hasten, hurry,

lion kind of large seal. **seaman** noun sailor.
seaplane noun aircraft designed to take off
from and land on water. **seascape** noun
picture of a scene at sea. **seashell** noun empty
shell of a mollusc. **seasick** adjective suffering
from nausea caused by the motion of a ship.
seasickness noun **seaside** noun area, esp. a
holiday resort, on the coast. **sea urchin** sea
animal with a round spiky shell. **seaweed** noun
plant growing in the sea. **seaworthy** adjective
(of a ship) in fit condition for a sea voyage.
seal¹ ⊕ noun 1 piece of wax, lead, etc. with a
special design impressed upon it, attached to a
letter or document as a mark of authentication.
2 device for making such an impression. 3
device or material used to close an opening
tightly. ◆ verb 4 close with or as if with a seal. 5
make airtight or watertight. 6 affix a seal to or
stamp with a seal. 7 decide (one's fate)
irrevocably. **sealant** noun any substance used
for sealing. **sealing wax** hard material which
softens when heated, used to make a seal. **seal
off** verb enclose or isolate (a place) completely.
seal² noun 1 amphibious mammal with
flippers as limbs. ◆ verb 2 hunt seals. **sealskin**
noun
seam ⊕ noun 1 line where two edges are
joined, as by stitching. 2 thin layer of coal or
ore. ◆ verb 3 mark with furrows or wrinkles.
seamless adjective **seamy** adjective sordid.
seamstress noun woman who sews.
seance [say-anss] noun meeting at which
spiritualists attempt to communicate with the
dead.
sear ⊕ verb scorch, burn the surface of.
searing adjective 1 (of pain) very sharp. 2
highly critical.

search ⊕ verb 1 examine closely in order to
find something. 2 make a search. ◆ noun 3
searching. **searching** adjective keen or
thorough, e.g. a searching look. **search engine**
Computers Internet service enabling users to
search for items of interest. **searchlight** noun
powerful light with a beam that can be shone
in any direction. **search warrant** document
permitting the entry and search of premises.
season ⊕ noun 1 one of four divisions of the
year, each of which has characteristic weather
conditions. 2 period during which a thing
happens or is plentiful. 3 any definite or
indefinite period, e.g. the busy season. 4 fitting
or proper time. ◆ verb 5 flavour with salt, herbs,
etc. 6 dry (timber) till ready for use.
seasonable adjective 1 appropriate for the
season. 2 timely or opportune. **seasonal**
adjective depending on or varying with the
seasons. **seasoned** adjective experienced.
seasoning noun salt, herbs, etc. added to food
to enhance flavour. **season ticket** ticket for a
series of journeys or events within a specified
period.
seat ⊕ noun 1 thing designed or used for
sitting on. 2 part of a chair on which one sits. 3
place to sit in a theatre, esp. one that requires a
ticket. 4 buttocks. 5 part of a garment covering
the buttocks. 6 place in which something is
based. 7 country house. 8 membership of a
legislative or administrative body. ◆ verb 9 cause
to sit. 10 provide seating for. **seating** noun
supply or arrangement of seats. **seat belt** belt
worn in a car or aircraft to prevent a person
being thrown forward in a crash.

—————————— THESAURUS ——————————

rush, scamper, scoot, scurry
sea noun 1 = **ocean**, main, the deep, the
waves 3 = **expanse**, abundance, mass,
multitude, plethora, profusion **at sea 2**
= **bewildered**, baffled, confused, lost, mystified,
puzzled
seafaring adjective = **nautical**, marine,
maritime, naval
seal¹ noun 1 = **authentication**, confirmation,
imprimatur, insignia, ratification, stamp ◆verb 5
= **close**, bung, enclose, fasten, plug, shut, stop,
stopper, stop up 6 = **authenticate**, confirm,
ratify, stamp, validate 7 = **settle**, clinch,
conclude, consummate, finalize **seal off**
= **isolate**, put out of bounds, quarantine,
segregate
seam noun 1 = **joint**, closure 2 = **layer**, lode,
stratum, vein
sear verb = **scorch**, burn, sizzle

search verb 1, 2 = **look**, comb, examine,
explore, fossick (Aust & NZ), hunt, inspect,
investigate, ransack, scour, scrutinize ◆noun 3
= **look**, examination, exploration, hunt,
inspection, investigation, pursuit, quest
searching adjective = **keen**, close, intent,
penetrating, piercing, probing, quizzical, sharp
season noun 3 = **period**, spell, term, time
◆verb 5 = **flavour**, enliven, pep up, salt, spice
seasonable adjective 2 = **appropriate**,
convenient, fit, opportune, providential,
suitable, timely, well-timed
seasoned adjective = **experienced**, hardened,
practised, time-served, veteran
seasoning noun = **flavouring**, condiment,
dressing, relish, salt and pepper, sauce, spice
seat noun 1 = **chair**, bench, pew, settle, stall,
stool 6 = **centre**, capital, heart, hub, place, site,
situation, source 7 = **mansion**, abode, ancestral

S

sebaceous *adjective* of, like, or secreting fat or oil.
sec¹ *adjective* (of wines) dry.
sec² *noun Informal* second (of time).
sec. 1 second (of time). 2 secondary. 3 secretary.
secateurs *plural noun* small pruning shears.
secede 🟊 *verb* withdraw formally from a political alliance or federation. **secession** *noun* **secessionist** *noun*
seclude 🟊 *verb* keep (a person) from contact with others. **secluded** *adjective* private, sheltered. **seclusion** *noun*
second¹ 🟊 *adjective* 1 coming directly after the first. 2 alternate, additional. 3 inferior. ♦ *noun* 4 person or thing coming second. 5 attendant in a duel or boxing match. ♦ *plural* 6 inferior goods. ♦ *verb* 7 express formal support for (a motion proposed in a meeting). **secondly** *adverb* **second-best** *adjective* next to the best. **second-class** *adjective* 1 inferior. 2 cheaper, slower, or less comfortable than first-class. **second-hand** *adjective* 1 bought after use by another. 2 not from an original source. **second nature** something so habitual that it seems part of one's character. **second-rate** *adjective* not of the highest quality. **second sight** supposed ability to predict events. **second thoughts** revised opinion on a matter already considered. **second wind** renewed ability to continue effort.

second² 🟊 *noun* 1 sixtieth part of a minute of an angle or time. 2 moment.
second³ [si-**kawnd**] *verb* transfer (a person) temporarily to another job. **secondment** *noun*
secondary 🟊 *adjective* 1 of less importance. 2 coming after or derived from what is primary or first. 3 relating to the education of people between the ages of 11 and 18.
secret 🟊 *adjective* 1 kept from the knowledge of others. 2 secretive. ♦ *noun* 3 something kept secret. 4 mystery. 5 underlying explanation, e.g. *the secret of my success.* **in secret** without other people knowing. **secretly** *adverb*
secrecy *noun* **secretive** *adjective* inclined to keep things secret. **secretiveness** *noun* **secret agent** spy. **secret service** government department concerned with spying.
secretariat *noun* administrative office or staff of a legislative body.
secretary *noun, pl* **-ries** 1 person who deals with correspondence and general clerical work. 2 (S-) head of a state department, e.g. *Home Secretary.* 3 person who keeps records for a company. **secretarial** *adjective* **Secretary of State** head of a major government department.
secrete¹ 🟊 *verb* (of an organ, gland, etc.) produce and release (a substance). **secretion** *noun* **secretory** [sek-**reet**-or-ee] *adjective*
secrete² 🟊 *verb* hide or conceal.
sect 🟊 *noun* subdivision of a religious or

———— T H E S A U R U S ————

hall, house, residence 8 = **membership**, chair, constituency, incumbency, place ♦*verb* 9 = **sit**, fix, install, locate, place, set, settle 10 = **hold**, accommodate, cater for, contain, sit, take
seating *noun* = **accommodation**, chairs, places, room, seats
secede *verb* = **withdraw**, break with, leave, pull out, quit, resign, split from
secluded *adjective* = **private**, cloistered, cut off, isolated, lonely, out-of-the-way, sheltered, solitary
seclusion *noun* = **privacy**, isolation, shelter, solitude
second¹ *adjective* 1 = **next**, following, subsequent, succeeding 2 = **additional**, alternative, extra, further, other 3 = **inferior**, lesser, lower, secondary, subordinate ♦*noun* 5 = **supporter**, assistant, backer, helper ♦*verb* 7 = **support**, approve, assist, back, endorse, go along with
second² *noun* 2 = **moment**, flash, instant, jiffy (*inf*), minute, sec (*inf*), trice
secondary *adjective* 1 = **subordinate**, inferior, lesser, lower, minor, unimportant [OPPOSITE]

main. 2 = **resultant**, contingent, derived, indirect [OPPOSITE] **original**
second-class *adjective* 1 = **inferior**, indifferent, mediocre, second-best, second-rate, undistinguished, uninspiring
second-hand *adjective* 1 = **used**, hand-me-down (*inf*), nearly new
secondly *adverb* 1 = **next**, in the second place, second
second-rate *adjective* = **inferior**, low-grade, low-quality, mediocre, poor, rubbishy, shoddy, substandard, tacky (*inf*), tawdry, two-bit (*US & Canad sl*)
secrecy *noun* 1 = **mystery**, concealment, confidentiality, privacy, silence 2 = **secretiveness**, clandestineness, covertness, furtiveness, stealth
secret *adjective* 1 = **concealed**, close, confidential, disguised, furtive, hidden, undercover, underground, undisclosed, unknown, unrevealed [OPPOSITE] **unconcealed**. 2 = **stealthy**, secretive, sly, underhand [OPPOSITE] **unconcealed** ♦*noun* 3 = **enigma**, code, key 4 = **mystery in secret** = **secretly**,

political group, esp. one with extreme beliefs.
sectarian *adjective* **1** of a sect. **2** narrow-minded. **sectarianism** *noun*
section ❶ *noun* **1** part cut off. **2** part or subdivision of something. **3** distinct part of a country or community. **4** cutting. **5** drawing of something as if cut through. ♦ *verb* **6** cut or divide into sections. **sectional** *adjective*
sector ❶ *noun* **1** part or subdivision. **2** part of a circle enclosed by two radii and the arc which they cut off. **3** portion of an area for military operations.
secular ❶ *adjective* **1** worldly, as opposed to sacred. **2** not connected with religion or the church. **secularism** *noun* belief that religion should have no place in education. **secularize** *verb* remove from the influence of the Church.
secure ❶ *adjective* **1** free from danger. **2** free from anxiety. **3** firmly fixed. **4** reliable. ♦ *verb* **5** obtain. **6** make safe. **7** make firm. **8** guarantee payment of (a loan) by giving something as security. **securely** *adverb* **security** *noun, pl* **-ties 1** precautions against theft, espionage, or other danger. **2** state of being secure. **3** certificate of ownership of a share, stock, or bond. **4** something given or pledged to guarantee payment of a loan.
sedan *noun US & Aust* saloon car. **sedan chair** *Hist* enclosed chair for one person, carried on poles by two bearers.
sedate[1] ❶ *adjective* **1** calm and dignified. **2** slow or unhurried. **sedately** *adverb*
sedate[2] ❶ *verb* give a sedative drug to.
sedation *noun* **sedative** *adjective* **1** having a soothing or calming effect. ♦ *noun* **2** sedative drug.
sedentary ❶ [sed-en-tree] *adjective* done sitting down, involving little exercise.
sedge *noun* coarse grasslike plant growing on wet ground. **sedgy** *adjective*
sediment ❶ *noun* **1** matter which settles to the bottom of a liquid. **2** material deposited by water, ice, or wind. **sedimentary** *adjective*
sedition ❶ *noun* speech or action encouraging rebellion against the government. **seditious** *adjective*
seduce ❶ *verb* **1** persuade into sexual intercourse. **2** tempt into wrongdoing. **seducer, seductress** *noun* **seduction** *noun* **seductive** *adjective*

——————————————— T H E S A U R U S ———————————————

slyly, surreptitiously
secrete[1] *verb* =**give off**, emanate, emit, exude
secrete[2] *verb* =**hide**, cache, conceal, harbour, stash (*inf*), stow OPPOSITE **display**
secretive *adjective* =**reticent**, close, deep, reserved, tight-lipped, uncommunicative
secretly *adverb* =**in secret**, clandestinely, covertly, furtively, privately, quietly, stealthily, surreptitiously
sect *noun* =**group**, camp, denomination, division, faction, party, schism
sectarian *adjective* **2** =**narrow-minded**, bigoted, doctrinaire, dogmatic, factional, fanatical, limited, parochial, partisan OPPOSITE **liberal**
section *noun* **1** =**slice 2** =**part**, division, fraction, instalment, passage, piece, portion, segment **3** =**district**, area, region, sector, zone
sector *noun* **1** =**part**, division **3** =**zone**, area
secular *adjective* **1** =**worldly**, earthly, nonspiritual, temporal OPPOSITE **religious. 2** =**lay**, civil OPPOSITE **religious**
secure *adjective* **1** =**safe**, immune, protected, unassailable OPPOSITE **endangered. 2** =**sure**, assured, certain, confident, easy, reassured OPPOSITE **uncertain. 3** =**fixed**, fast, fastened, firm, immovable, stable, steady OPPOSITE **loose** ♦*verb* **5** =**obtain**, acquire, gain, get, procure, score (*sl*) OPPOSITE **lose. 7** =**fasten**, attach,
bolt, chain, fix, lock, make fast, tie up OPPOSITE **loose**
security *noun* **1** =**precautions**, defence, protection, safeguards, safety measures **2 a** =**safety**, care, custody, refuge, safekeeping, sanctuary **b** =**assurance**, certainty, confidence, conviction, positiveness, reliance, sureness OPPOSITE **uncertainty. 4** =**pledge**, collateral, gage, guarantee, hostage, insurance, pawn, surety
sedate[1] *adjective* **1** =**calm**, collected, composed, cool, dignified, serene, tranquil OPPOSITE **wild. 2** =**unhurried**, deliberate, slow-moving
sedative *adjective* **1** =**calming**, anodyne, relaxing, soothing, tranquillizing ♦*noun* **2** =**tranquillizer**, anodyne, downer or down (*sl*)
sedentary *adjective* =**inactive**, desk, desk-bound, seated, sitting
sediment *noun* **1** =**dregs**, deposit, grounds, lees, residue
sedition *noun* =**rabble-rousing**, agitation, incitement to riot, subversion
seditious *adjective* =**revolutionary**, dissident, mutinous, rebellious, refractory, subversive
seduce *verb* **1** =**corrupt**, debauch, deflower, deprave, dishonour **2** =**tempt**, beguile, deceive, entice, inveigle, lead astray, lure, mislead
seduction *noun* **1** =**corruption 2**

S

sedulous *adjective* diligent or persevering.
sedulously *adverb*
sedum *noun* rock plant.
see[1] **𝗧** *verb* **seeing, saw, seen 1** perceive with the eyes or mind. **2** understand. **3** watch. **4** find out. **5** make sure (of something). **6** consider or decide. **7** have experience of. **8** meet or visit. **9** interview. **10** frequent the company of. **11** accompany. **seeing** *noun* **1** use of the eyes. ♦ *conjunction* **2** in view of the fact that. **see about** *verb* attend to. **see off** *verb* be present at the departure of. **see through** *verb* **1** perceive the true nature of. **2** remain with until the end. **see-through** *adjective* transparent.
see[2] **𝗧** *noun* diocese of a bishop.
seed 𝗧 *noun* **1** mature fertilized grain of a plant. **2** such grains used for sowing. **3** origin. **4** *Obs* offspring. **5** *Sport* player ranked according to his or her ability. ♦ *verb* **6** sow with seed. **7** produce seeds. **8** remove seeds from. **9** arrange (the draw of a sports tournament) so that the outstanding competitors will not meet in the early rounds. **go, run to seed 1** (of plants) produce or shed seeds after flowering. **2** lose vigour or usefulness. **seedling** *noun* young plant raised from a seed. **seedy** *adjective* **1** shabby. **2** *Informal* unwell. **3** full of seeds.
seek 𝗧 *verb* **seeking, sought 1** try to find or obtain. **2** try (to do something).
seem 𝗧 *verb* **1** appear to be. **2** have the impression. **seeming** *adjective* apparent but not real. **seemingly** *adverb*
seemly 𝗧 *adjective* **-lier, -liest** proper or fitting.
seen *verb* past participle of SEE[1].
seep 𝗧 *verb* trickle through slowly, ooze. **seepage** *noun*
seer 𝗧 *noun* prophet.
seersucker *noun* light cotton fabric with a slightly crinkled surface.
seesaw 𝗧 *noun* **1** plank balanced in the middle so that two people seated on either end ride up and down alternately. ♦ *verb* **2** move up and down.
seethe 𝗧 *verb* **seething, seethed 1** be very agitated. **2** (of a liquid) boil or foam.
segment 𝗧 *noun* **1** one of several sections into which something may be divided. **2** part of a circle cut off by an intersecting line. ♦ *verb* **3** divide into segments. **segmentation** *noun*
segregate 𝗧 *verb* **1** set apart. **2** keep (a racial or minority group) apart from the rest of the

—————— THESAURUS ——————

= **temptation**, enticement, lure, snare
seductive *adjective* = **alluring**, attractive, bewitching, enticing, inviting, provocative, tempting
seductress *noun* **1** = **temptress**, enchantress, *femme fatale*, siren, vamp (*inf*)
see[1] *verb* **1** = **perceive**, behold, catch sight of, discern, distinguish, espy, eyeball (*sl*), glimpse, look, make out, notice, sight, spot, witness **2** = **understand**, appreciate, comprehend, fathom, feel, follow, get, grasp, realize **3** = **observe 4** = **find out**, ascertain, determine, discover, learn **5** = **make sure**, ensure, guarantee, make certain, see to it **6** = **consider**, decide, deliberate, reflect, think over **8** = **visit**, receive **9** = **speak to**, confer with, consult, interview **10** = **go out with**, court, date (*inf, chiefly US*), go steady with (*inf*) **11** = **accompany**, escort, lead, show, usher, walk
see[2] *noun* = **diocese**, bishopric
seed *noun* **1, 2** = **grain**, germ, kernel, pip, spore **3** = **origin**, beginning, germ, nucleus, source, start **4** *Obs* = **offspring**, children, descendants, issue, progeny **go, run to seed 2** = **decline**, decay, degenerate, deteriorate, go downhill (*inf*), go to pot, let oneself go
seedy *adjective* **1** = **shabby**, dilapidated, grotty (*sl*), grubby, mangy, run-down, scruffy, sleazy, squalid, tatty OPPOSITE smart. **2** *Inf* = **unwell**, crook (*Aust & NZ sl*), ill, off colour, out of sorts, poorly (*inf*), under the weather (*inf*)
seeing *conjunction* **2** = **since**, as, inasmuch as, in view of the fact that
seek *verb* **1** = **look for**, be after, follow, hunt, pursue, search for **2** = **try**, aim, aspire to, attempt, endeavour, essay, strive
seem *verb* **1** = **appear**, assume, give the impression, look
seemly *adjective* = **fitting**, appropriate, becoming, decent, decorous, fit, proper, suitable
seep *verb* = **ooze**, exude, leak, permeate, soak, trickle, well
seer *noun* = **prophet**, sibyl, soothsayer
seesaw *verb* **2** = **alternate**, fluctuate, oscillate, swing
seethe *verb* **1** = **be furious**, be livid, be pissed (off) (*taboo sl*), fume, go ballistic (*sl, chiefly US*), rage, see red (*inf*), simmer **2** = **boil**, bubble, fizz, foam, froth
see through *verb* **1** = **be undeceived by**, be wise to (*inf*), fathom, not fall for, penetrate **2 a** = **persevere (with)**, keep at, persist, stick out (*inf*) **b** = **help out**, stick by, support
segment *noun* **1** = **section**, bit, division, part, piece, portion, slice, wedge

community. **segregation** *noun*
seigneur *noun* feudal lord.
seine [sane] *noun* large fishing net that hangs vertically from floats.
seismic *adjective* relating to earthquakes.
seismology *noun* study of earthquakes.
seismological *adjective* **seismologist** *noun*
seismograph, seismometer *noun* instrument that records the strength of earthquakes.
seize ❶ *verb* **1** take hold of forcibly or quickly. **2** take immediate advantage of. **3** take legal possession of. **4** understand quickly. **5** (usu. foll. by *up*) (of mechanical parts) stick tightly through overheating. **seizure** *noun* **1** sudden violent attack of an illness. **2** seizing or being seized.
seldom ❶ *adverb* not often, rarely.
select ❶ *verb* **1** pick out or choose. ◆ *adjective* **2** chosen in preference to others. **3** restricted to a particular group, exclusive. **selection** *noun* **1** selecting. **2** things that have been selected. **3** range from which something may be selected.
selective *adjective* chosen or choosing carefully. **selectively** *adverb* **selectivity** *noun* **selector** *noun*
selenium *noun Chem* nonmetallic element with photoelectric properties.
self ❶ *noun, pl* **selves 1** distinct individuality or identity of a person or thing. **2** one's basic nature. **3** one's own welfare or interests. **selfish** *adjective* caring too much about oneself and not enough about others. **selfishly** *adverb* **selfishness** *noun* **selfless** *adjective* unselfish.
self- *prefix* used with many main words to mean: **1** of oneself or itself. **2** by, to, in, due to, for, or from the self. **3** automatic(ally). **self-addressed** *adjective* addressed to the sender. **self-assertion** *noun* putting forward one's opinions, esp. aggressively. **self-assertive** *adjective* **self-assured** *adjective* confident. **self-catering** *adjective* (of accommodation) for people who provide their own food. **self-centred** *adjective* totally preoccupied with

one's own concerns. **self-coloured** *adjective* having only a single colour. **self-confessed** *adjective* according to one's own admission. **self-confidence** *noun* belief in one's own abilities. **self-confident** *adjective* **self-conscious** *adjective* embarrassed at being the object of others' attention. **self-contained** *adjective* **1** containing everything needed, complete. **2** (of a flat) having its own facilities. **self-control** *noun* ability to control one's feelings and reactions. **self-defence** *noun* defending of oneself or one's property. **self-determination** *noun* the right of a nation to decide its own form of government. **self-effacing** *adjective* unwilling to draw attention to oneself. **self-employed** *adjective* earning a living from one's own business. **self-esteem** *noun* favourable opinion of oneself. **self-evident** *adjective* obvious without proof. **self-government** *noun* government of a nation or community by its own people. **self-help** *noun* **1** use of one's own abilities to solve problems. **2** practice of solving one's problems within a group of people with similar problems. **self-important** *adjective* having an unduly high opinion of one's importance. **self-importance** *noun* **self-indulgent** *adjective* tending to indulge one's desires. **self-interest** *noun* one's own advantage. **self-made** *adjective* having achieved wealth or status by one's own efforts. **self-opinionated** *adjective* clinging stubbornly to one's own opinions. **self-possessed** *adjective* having control of one's emotions, calm. **self-raising** *adjective* (of flour) containing a raising agent. **self-respect** *noun* sense of one's dignity and integrity. **self-righteous** *adjective* thinking oneself more virtuous than others. **selfsame** *adjective* the very same. **self-satisfied** *adjective* conceited. **self-seeking** *adjective, noun* seeking to promote only one's own interests. **self-service** *adjective* denoting a shop, café, or garage where customers serve themselves and then pay a cashier. **self-styled**

S

——————— T H E S A U R U S ———————

segregate *verb* **1** = **set apart**, dissociate, isolate, separate OPPOSITE **unite**. **2** = **discriminate against**
segregation *noun* **1** = **separation**, isolation **2** = **apartheid**, discrimination
seize *verb* **1** = **grab**, catch up, clutch, grasp, grip, lay hands on, snatch, take OPPOSITE **let go**. **3** = **confiscate**, impound, take possession of OPPOSITE **relinquish**
seizure *noun* **1** = **attack**, convulsion, fit, paroxysm, spasm **2** = **taking**, annexation, commandeering, confiscation, grabbing

seldom *adverb* = **rarely**, hardly ever, infrequently, not often OPPOSITE **often**
select *verb* **1** = **choose**, opt for, pick, single out OPPOSITE **reject** ◆*adjective* **2** = **choice**, excellent, first-class, hand-picked, special, superior, top-notch (*inf*) OPPOSITE **ordinary**. **3** = **exclusive**, cliquish, elite, privileged OPPOSITE **indiscriminate**
selection *noun* **1** = **choice**, choosing, option, pick, preference **3** = **range**, assortment, choice, collection, medley, variety
selective *adjective* = **particular**, careful,

adjective using a title or name that one has taken without right. **self-sufficient** *adjective* able to provide for oneself without help. **self-willed** *adjective* stubbornly determined to get one's own way.

sell ⊕ *verb* **selling, sold 1** exchange (something) for money. **2** stock, deal in. **3** (of goods) be sold. **4** (foll. by *for*) have a specified price. **5** promote. **6** be in demand. **7** *Informal* persuade (someone) to accept (something). **8** give up for a price or reward. ♦ *noun* **9** manner of selling. **seller** *noun* **sell-by date** date printed on packaged food specifying the date after which the food should not be sold. **past one's sell-by date** *Informal* beyond one's prime. **sell out** *verb* **1** dispose of (something) completely by selling. **2** *Informal* betray. **sellout** *noun* **1** performance of a show etc. for which all the tickets are sold. **2** *Informal* betrayal. **sell up** *verb* sell all one's goods.

Sellotape *noun* **1** ® type of adhesive tape. ♦ *verb* **2** stick with Sellotape.

selvage, selvedge *noun* edge of cloth, woven so as to prevent unravelling.

selves *noun* plural of SELF.

semantic *adjective* relating to the meaning of words. **semantics** *noun* study of linguistic meaning.

semaphore *noun* system of signalling by holding two flags in different positions to represent letters of the alphabet.

semblance ⊕ *noun* outward or superficial appearance.

semen *noun* sperm-carrying fluid produced by male animals.

semester *noun* either of two divisions of the academic year.

semi *noun Informal* semidetached house.

semi- *prefix* used with many main words to mean: **1** half, e.g. *semicircle*. **2** partly or almost, e.g. *semiprofessional*. **3** occurring twice in a specified period, e.g. *semiweekly*.

semibreve *noun* musical note four beats long.

semicircle *noun* half of a circle. **semicircular** *adjective*

semicolon *noun* the punctuation mark (;).

semiconductor *noun* substance with an electrical conductivity that increases with temperature.

semidetached *adjective* (of a house) joined to another on one side.

semifinal *noun* match or round before the final. **semifinalist** *noun*

seminal ⊕ *adjective* **1** original and influential. **2** capable of developing. **3** of semen or seed.

seminar *noun* meeting of a group of students for discussion.

seminary *noun, pl* **-ries** college for priests.

semiotics *noun* study of human communications, esp. signs and symbols.

———————————— T H E S A U R U S ————————————

discerning, discriminating

self-centred *adjective* = selfish, egotistic, narcissistic, self-seeking

self-confidence *noun* = self-assurance, aplomb, confidence, nerve, poise

self-confident *adjective* = self-assured, assured, confident, poised, sure of oneself

self-conscious *adjective* = embarrassed, awkward, bashful, diffident, ill at ease, insecure, nervous, uncomfortable

self-control *noun* = willpower, restraint, self-discipline, self-restraint

self-esteem *noun* = self-respect, confidence, faith in oneself, pride, self-assurance, self-regard

self-evident *adjective* = obvious, clear, incontrovertible, inescapable, undeniable

self-important *adjective* = conceited, bigheaded, cocky, full of oneself, pompous, swollen-headed

selfish *adjective* = self-centred, egoistic, egoistical, egotistic, egotistical, greedy, self-interested, ungenerous

selfless *adjective* = unselfish, altruistic, generous, self-denying, self-sacrificing

self-possessed *adjective* = self-assured,

collected, confident, cool, poised, unruffled

self-respect *noun* = pride, dignity, morale, self-esteem

self-righteous *adjective* = sanctimonious, complacent, holier-than-thou, priggish, self-satisfied, smug, superior

self-satisfied *adjective* = smug, complacent, pleased with oneself, self-congratulatory

self-seeking *adjective* = selfish, careerist, looking out for number one (*inf*), out for what one can get, self-interested, self-serving

sell *verb* **1** = trade, barter, exchange OPPOSITE buy. **2** = deal in, handle, market, peddle, retail, stock, trade in, traffic in OPPOSITE buy

seller *noun* = dealer, agent, merchant, purveyor, retailer, salesman *or* saleswoman, supplier, vendor

sell out *verb* **1** = dispose of, be out of stock of, get rid of, run out of **2** *Inf* = betray, double-cross (*inf*), sell down the river (*inf*), stab in the back

semblance *noun* = appearance, aspect, facade, mask, pretence, resemblance, show, veneer

seminal *adjective* **1** = influential, formative,

S

semiprecious *adjective* (of gemstones) having less value than precious stones.

semiquaver *noun* musical note half the length of a quaver.

semiskilled *adjective* partly trained but not for specialized work.

Semite *noun* member of the group of peoples including Jews and Arabs. **Semitic** *adjective*

semitone *noun* smallest interval between two notes in Western music.

semolina *noun* hard grains of wheat left after the milling of flour, used to make puddings and pasta.

Senate *noun* **1** upper house of some parliaments. **2** governing body of some universities. **senator** *noun* member of a Senate. **senatorial** *adjective*

send ❶ *verb* **sending, sent 1** cause (a person or thing) to go to or be taken or transmitted to a place. **2** (foll. by *for*) issue a request for. **3** bring into a specified state or condition. **sender** *noun* **send down** *verb* **1** expel from university. **2** *Informal* send to jail. **sendoff** *noun* demonstration of good wishes at a person's departure. **send up** *verb Informal* make fun of by imitating. **send-up** *noun Informal* imitation.

senescent *adjective* growing old. **senescence** *noun*

senile ❶ *adjective* mentally or physically weak because of old age. **senility** *noun*

senior ❶ *adjective* **1** superior in rank or standing. **2** older. **3** of or for older pupils. ◆ *noun* **4** senior person. **seniority** *noun* **senior citizen** old person, esp. a pensioner.

senna *noun* **1** tropical plant. **2** its dried leaves or pods used as a laxative.

señor [sen-**nyor**] *noun, pl* **-ores** Spanish term of address equivalent to *sir* or *Mr.* **señora** [sen-**nyor**-a] *noun* Spanish term of address equivalent to *madam* or *Mrs.* **señorita** [sen-nyor-**ee**-ta] *noun* Spanish term of address equivalent to *madam* or *Miss.*

sensation ❶ *noun* **1** ability to feel things physically. **2** physical feeling. **3** general feeling or awareness. **4** state of excitement. **5** exciting person or thing. **sensational** *adjective* **1** causing intense shock, anger, or excitement. **2** *Informal* very good. **sensationalism** *noun* deliberate use of sensational language or subject matter. **sensationalist** *adjective, noun*

sense ❶ *noun* **1** any of the faculties of perception or feeling (sight, hearing, touch, taste, or smell). **2** ability to perceive. **3** feeling perceived through one of the senses. **4** awareness. **5** moral discernment. **6** (sometimes *pl*) sound practical judgment or intelligence. **7** reason or purpose. **8** specific meaning. ◆ *verb* **9** perceive. **senseless** *adjective* **1** foolish. **2** unconscious.

sensible ❶ *adjective* **1** having or showing

———————— THESAURUS ————————

ground-breaking, important, innovative, original

send *verb* **1** = **dispatch**, convey, direct, forward, remit, transmit **2** (foll. by *for*) = **summon**, call for, order, request

sendoff *noun* = **farewell**, departure, leave-taking, start, valediction

send up *verb Inf* = **imitate**, burlesque, lampoon, make fun of, mimic, mock, parody, satirize, spoof (*inf*), take off (*inf*)

send-up *noun Inf* = **imitation**, parody, satire, skit, spoof (*inf*), take-off (*inf*)

senile *adjective* = **doddering**, decrepit, doting, in one's dotage

senility *noun* = **dotage**, decrepitude, infirmity, loss of one's faculties, senile dementia

senior *adjective* **1** = **higher ranking**, superior OPPOSITE▷ lower. **2** = **older**, elder, major (*Brit*) OPPOSITE▷ younger

senior citizen *noun* = **pensioner**, O.A.P., old age pensioner, old *or* elderly person, retired person

seniority *noun* **1** = **superiority**, precedence, priority, rank

sensation *noun* **3** = **feeling**, awareness, consciousness, impression, perception, sense **4**

= **excitement**, commotion, furore, stir, thrill

sensational *adjective* **1** = **exciting**, amazing, astounding, dramatic, melodramatic, shock-horror (*facetious*), shocking, thrilling OPPOSITE▷ boring. **2** *Inf* = **excellent**, fabulous (*inf*), impressive, marvellous, mean (*sl*), mind-blowing (*inf*), out of this world (*inf*), smashing (*inf*), superb OPPOSITE▷ ordinary

sense *noun* **1** = **faculty 3** = **feeling**, sensation **4** = **feeling**, atmosphere, aura, awareness, consciousness, impression, perception **6** (sometimes *pl*) = **intelligence**, brains (*inf*), cleverness, common sense, judgment, reason, sagacity, sanity, sharpness, understanding, wisdom, wit(s) OPPOSITE▷ stupidity. **8** = **meaning**, drift, gist, implication, import, significance ◆*verb* **9** = **perceive**, be aware of, discern, feel, get the impression, pick up, realize, understand OPPOSITE▷ miss

senseless *adjective* **1** = **stupid**, asinine, crazy, daft (*inf*), foolish, idiotic, illogical, inane, irrational, mad, mindless, nonsensical, pointless, ridiculous, silly **2** = **unconscious**, insensible, out, out cold, stunned OPPOSITE▷ conscious

sensibility *noun* **1** = **sensitivity**,

S

good sense. **2** practical, e.g. *sensible shoes*. **3** capable of being perceived by the senses. **4** (foll. by *of*) aware. **sensibly** *adverb* **sensibility** *noun* **1** ability to experience deep feelings. **2** (usu. pl) tendency to be influenced or offended. **sensitive ❶** *adjective* **1** easily hurt or offended. **2** responsive to external stimuli. **3** (of a subject) liable to arouse controversy or strong feelings. **4** (of an instrument) responsive to slight changes. **sensitively** *adverb* **sensitivity** *noun* **sensitize** *verb* make sensitive.

sensor *noun* device that detects or measures the presence of something, such as radiation.
sensory *adjective* of the senses or sensation.
sensual ❶ *adjective* **1** giving pleasure to the body and senses rather than the mind. **2** having a strong liking for physical pleasures. **sensually** *adverb* **sensuality** *noun* **sensualist** *noun*
sensuous ❶ *adjective* pleasing to the senses. **sensuously** *adverb*
sent *verb* past of SEND.
sentence ❶ *noun* **1** sequence of words capable of standing alone as a statement, question, or command. **2** punishment passed on a criminal. ◆ *verb* **3** pass sentence on (a convicted person).
sentencious ❶ *adjective* **1** trying to sound wise. **2** pompously moralizing. **sententiously** *adverb*

sentient ❶ [sen-tee-ent] *adjective* capable of feeling. **sentience** *noun*
sentiment ❶ *noun* **1** thought, opinion, or attitude. **2** feeling expressed in words. **3** exaggerated or mawkish emotion. **sentimental** *adjective* excessively romantic or nostalgic. **sentimentalism** *noun* **sentimentality** *noun* **sentimentalize** *verb* make sentimental.
sentinel ❶ *noun* sentry.
sentry *noun, pl* **-tries** soldier on watch.
sepal *noun* leaflike division of the calyx of a flower.
separate ❶ *verb* **1** act as a barrier between. **2** distinguish between. **3** divide up into parts. **4** sever or be severed. **5** (of a couple) stop living together. ◆ *adjective* **6** not the same, different. **7** set apart. **8** not shared, individual.
separately *adverb* **separation** *noun* **1** separating or being separated. **2** *Law* living apart of a married couple without divorce.
separable *adjective* **separatist** *noun* person who advocates the separation of a group from an organization or country. **separatism** *noun*

SPELLING TIP

There are 101 examples of *seperate* in the Bank of English, which makes it the most popular misspelling of **separate**.

─────────────── THESAURUS ───────────────

responsiveness, sensitiveness, susceptibility **2** (usu. pl) = **feelings**, emotions, moral sense, sentiments, susceptibilities
sensible *adjective* **1** = **wise**, canny, down-to-earth, intelligent, judicious, prudent, rational, realistic, sage, sane, shrewd, sound OPPOSITE ignorant. **2** = **practical 4** (foll. by *of*) = **aware of**, conscious of, mindful of, sensitive to
sensitive *adjective* **1** = **easily hurt**, delicate, easily offended, easily upset, tender, thin-skinned, touchy OPPOSITE tough. **2** = **susceptible**, easily affected, impressionable, responsive **4** = **precise**, acute, fine, keen, responsive OPPOSITE imprecise
sensitivity *noun* **1** = **delicacy 2** = **sensitiveness**, receptiveness, responsiveness, susceptibility
sensual *adjective* **1** = **physical**, animal, bodily, carnal, fleshly, luxurious, voluptuous **2** = **erotic**, lascivious, lecherous, lewd, lustful, raunchy (*sl*), sexual
sensuality *noun* **2** = **eroticism**, carnality, lasciviousness, lecherousness, lewdness, sexiness (*inf*), voluptuousness
sensuous *adjective* = **pleasurable**, gratifying,

hedonistic, sybaritic
sentence *noun* **2** = **punishment**, condemnation, decision, decree, judgment, order, ruling, verdict ◆ *verb* **3** = **condemn**, doom, penalize
sentencious *adjective* **2** = **pompous**, canting, judgmental, moralistic, preachifying (*inf*), sanctimonious
sentient *adjective* = **feeling**, conscious, living, sensitive
sentiment *noun* **1** = **opinion**, attitude, belief, feeling, idea, judgment, view **3** = **sentimentality**, emotionalism, mawkishness, romanticism
sentimental *adjective* = **romantic**, emotional, maudlin, nostalgic, overemotional, schmaltzy (*sl*), slushy (*inf*), soft-hearted, touching, weepy (*inf*)
sentimentality *noun* **3** = **romanticism**, corniness (*sl*), emotionalism, mawkishness, nostalgia, schmaltz (*sl*)
sentinel *noun* = **guard**, lookout, sentry, watch, watchman
separable *adjective* = **distinguishable**, detachable, divisible

sepia *adjective, noun* reddish-brown (pigment).
sepoy *noun* (formerly) Indian soldier in the service of the British.
sepsis *noun* poisoning caused by pus-forming bacteria.
sept *n* clan, esp. in Ireland or Scotland.
Sept. September.
September *noun* ninth month of the year.
septet *noun* **1** group of seven performers. **2** music for such a group.
septic ❶ *adjective* **1** (of a wound) infected. **2** of or caused by harmful bacteria. **septic tank** tank in which sewage is decomposed by the action of bacteria.
septicaemia [sep-tis-**see**-mee-a] *noun* infection of the blood.
septuagenarian *noun* person aged between seventy and seventy-nine.
septum *noun, pl* **-ta** dividing partition between two tissues or cavities in the body, such as in the nose.
sepulchre ❶ [sep-pull-ker] *noun* tomb or burial vault. **sepulchral** [sip-**pulk**-ral] *adjective* gloomy.
sequel ❶ *noun* **1** novel, play, or film that continues the story of an earlier one. **2** thing that follows something else. **3** consequence.
sequence ❶ *noun* **1** arrangement of two or more things in successive order. **2** the successive order of two or more things. **3** section of a film showing a single uninterrupted episode. **sequential** *adjective*
sequester *verb* **1** seclude. **2** sequestrate.
sequestrate *verb* confiscate (property) until its owner's debts are paid or a court order is complied with. **sequestration** *noun*
sequin *noun* small ornamental metal disc on a garment. **sequined** *adjective*
sequoia *noun* giant Californian coniferous tree.

seraglio [sir-ah-lee-oh] *noun, pl* **-raglios 1** harem of a Muslim palace. **2** Turkish sultan's palace.
seraph *noun, pl* **-aphs, -aphim** member of the highest order of angels. **seraphic** *adjective*
Serbian, Serb *adjective* **1** of Serbia. ◆ *noun* **2** person from Serbia. **3** dialect of Serbo-Croat spoken in Serbia. **Serbo-Croat, Serbo-Croatian** *adjective, noun* (of) the chief official language of Serbia and Croatia.
serenade *noun* **1** music played or sung to a woman by a lover. **2** piece of music for a small orchestra. ◆ *verb* **3** sing or play a serenade to (someone).
serendipity *noun* gift of making fortunate discoveries by accident.
serene ❶ *adjective* **1** calm, peaceful. **2** (of the sky) clear. **serenely** *adverb* **serenity** *noun*
serf *noun* medieval farm labourer who could not leave the land he worked on. **serfdom** *noun*
serge *noun* strong woollen fabric.
sergeant *noun* **1** noncommissioned officer in the army. **2** police officer ranking between constable and inspector. **sergeant at arms** parliamentary or court officer with ceremonial duties. **sergeant major** highest rank of noncommissioned officer in the army.
serial *noun* **1** story or play produced in successive instalments. ◆ *adjective* **2** of or forming a series. **3** published or presented as a serial. **serialize** *verb* publish or present as a serial. **serial killer** person who commits a series of murders.
series ❶ *noun, pl* **-ries 1** group or succession of related things, usu. arranged in order. **2** set of radio or TV programmes about the same subject or characters.

——————————— T H E S A U R U S ———————————

separate *verb* **2** = **single out**, isolate, segregate **3** = **divide 4** = **sever**, come apart, come away, detach, disconnect, disjoin, remove, split, sunder OPPOSITE **unite. 5** = **part**, break up, disunite, diverge, divorce, estrange, part company, split up OPPOSITE **join** ◆*adjective* **7** = **unconnected**, detached, disconnected, divided, divorced, isolated, unattached OPPOSITE **united. 8** = **individual**, alone, apart, distinct, particular, single, solitary
separately *adverb* **8** = **individually**, alone, apart, severally, singly OPPOSITE **together**
separation *noun* **1** = **division**, break, disconnection, dissociation, disunion, gap **2** *Law* = **split-up**, break-up, parting, rift, split

septic *adjective* **1** = **infected**, festering, poisoned, putrefying, putrid, suppurating
sepulchre *noun* = **tomb**, burial place, grave, mausoleum, vault
sequel *noun* **2** = **follow-up**, continuation, development **3** = **consequence**, conclusion, end, outcome, result, upshot
sequence *noun* **1, 2** = **succession**, arrangement, chain, course, cycle, order, progression, series
serene *adjective* **1** = **calm**, composed, peaceful, tranquil, unruffled, untroubled
serenity *noun* **1** = **calmness**, calm, composure, peace, peacefulness, quietness, stillness, tranquillity

serious ❶ *adjective* **1** giving cause for concern. **2** concerned with important matters. **3** not cheerful, grave. **4** sincere, not joking. **5** *Informal* impressive, e.g. *serious money*. **seriously** *adverb* **seriousness** *noun*

sermon ❶ *noun* **1** speech on a religious or moral subject by a clergyman in a church service. **2** long moralizing speech. **sermonize** *verb* make a long moralizing speech.

serpent *noun* snake. **serpentine** *adjective* twisting like a snake.

serrated *adjective* having a notched or sawlike edge. **serration** *noun*

serried *adjective* in close formation.

serum [seer-um] *noun* **1** watery fluid left after blood has clotted. **2** this fluid from the blood of immunized animals used for inoculation or vaccination.

serval *noun* feline African mammal.

servant ❶ *noun* person employed to do household work for another.

serve ❶ *verb* **1** work for (a person, community, or cause). **2** perform official duties. **3** attend to (customers). **4** provide with food or drink. **5** present (food or drink). **6** provide with a service. **7** be a member of the armed forces. **8** spend (time) in prison. **9** be useful or suitable. **10** *Tennis etc.* put (the ball) into play. **11** deliver (a legal document) to (a person). ◆ *noun* **12** *Tennis etc.* act of serving the ball.

servant *noun* person employed to do household work for another. **serve someone right** *Informal* be what someone deserves for doing something wrong. **serving** *noun* portion of food.

service ❶ *noun* **1** serving. **2** system that provides something needed by the public. **3** department of public employment and its employees. **4** maintenance of goods provided by a dealer after sale. **5** availability for use. **6** overhaul of a machine or vehicle. **7** set of dishes etc. for serving a meal. **8** formal religious ceremony. **9** *Tennis etc.* act, manner, or right of serving the ball. ◆ *plural* **10** armed forces. ◆ *adjective* **11** serving the public rather than producing goods, e.g. *service industry*. ◆ *verb* **12** provide a service or services to. **13** overhaul (a machine or vehicle). **serviceable** *adjective* **1** useful or helpful. **2** able or ready to be used.

service area area beside a motorway with garage, restaurant, and toilet facilities. **service charge** additional cost on a restaurant bill to pay for service. **service flat** flat where domestic services are provided. **serviceman, servicewoman** *noun* member of the armed forces. **service road** narrow road giving access to houses and shops. **service station** garage selling fuel for motor vehicles.

serviette *noun* table napkin.

servile ❶ *adjective* **1** too eager to obey people, fawning. **2** suitable for a slave. **servility** *noun*

servitude *noun* bondage or slavery.

sesame [sess-am-ee] *noun* plant cultivated for its seeds and oil, which are used in cooking.

session ❶ *noun* **1** period spent in an activity. **2** meeting of a court, parliament, or council. **3** series or period of such meetings. **4** academic term or year.

set¹ ❶ *verb* **setting, set 1** put in a specified

——————————————— THESAURUS ———————————————

series *noun* **1** = **sequence**, chain, course, order, progression, run, set, string, succession, train

serious *adjective* **1** = **grave**, acute, critical, dangerous, severe **2** = **important**, crucial, fateful, grim, momentous, no laughing matter, pressing, significant, urgent, worrying OPPOSITE insignificant. **3** = **solemn**, grave, humourless, sober, unsmiling OPPOSITE frivolous. **4** = **sincere**, earnest, genuine, honest, in earnest

seriously *adverb* **1** = **badly**, acutely, critically, dangerously, gravely, severely **3** = **gravely 4** = **sincerely**, in earnest

seriousness *noun* **2** = **importance**, gravity, significance, urgency **4** = **solemnity**, earnestness, gravity

sermon *noun* = **homily**, address

servant *noun* = **attendant**, domestic, help, maid, retainer, skivvy (*chiefly Brit*), slave

serve *verb* **1** = **work for**, aid, assist, help **2** = **perform**, act, complete, discharge, do, fulfil **3** = **attend to**, minister to, wait on **4, 6** = **provide**, supply **5** = **present**, deliver, dish up, set out **9** = **be adequate**, answer the purpose, be acceptable, do, function as, satisfy, suffice, suit

service *noun* **1** = **help**, assistance, avail, benefit, use, usefulness **3** = **work**, business, duty, employment, labour, office, yakka (*Aust & NZ inf*) **6** = **overhaul**, check, maintenance **8** = **ceremony**, observance, rite, worship ◆*verb* **13** = **overhaul**, check, fine tune, go over, maintain, tune (up)

serviceable *adjective* **1** = **useful**, beneficial, helpful, practical, profitable, utilitarian **2** = **usable**, functional, operative

servile *adjective* **1** = **subservient**, abject, fawning, grovelling, obsequious, sycophantic, toadying

session *noun* **1** = **period 2** = **meeting**,

position or state. **2** make ready. **3** make or become firm or rigid. **4** put (a broken bone) or (of a broken bone) be put into a normal position for healing. **5** adjust (a clock) to a particular position. **6** establish, arrange. **7** prescribe, assign. **8** arrange (hair) while wet, so that it dries in position. **9** place (a jewel) in a setting. **10** put to music. **11** arrange (type) for printing. **12** (of the sun) go down. **13** (of plants) produce (fruit or seeds). **14** (of a gun dog) face game. ♦ *noun* **15** setting or being set. **16** bearing or posture. **17** scenery used in a play or film. ♦ *adjective* **18** fixed or established beforehand. **19** rigid or inflexible. **20** conventional or stereotyped. **21** determined (to do something). **22** ready. **set back** *verb* **1** hinder. **2** cost. **setback** *noun* anything that delays progress. **set off** *verb* **1** embark on a journey. **2** cause to begin. **3** cause to explode. **4** act as a contrast to. **set square** flat right-angled triangular instrument used for drawing angles. **set to** *verb* begin working. **set-to** *noun* brief fight. **set up** *verb* arrange or establish. **setup** *noun* way in which anything is organized or arranged.

set² ❶ *noun* **1** number of things or people grouped or belonging together. **2** *Maths* group of numbers or objects that satisfy a given condition or share a property. **3** television or radio receiver. **4** *Sport* group of games in a match. **5** series of songs performed by a musician or group. **set theory** branch of mathematics concerned with the properties of sets.

sett, set *noun* **1** badger's burrow. **2** small paving stone.

settee *noun* couch.

setter *noun* long-haired gun dog.

setting ❶ *noun* **1** background or surroundings. **2** time and place where a film, book, etc. is supposed to have taken place. **3** music written for the words of a text. **4** decorative metalwork in which a gem is set. **5** plates and cutlery for a single place at table. **6** position or level to which the controls of a machine can be adjusted.

settle¹ ❶ *verb* **1** arrange or put in order. **2** come to rest. **3** establish or become established as a resident. **4** colonize. **5** make quiet, calm, or stable. **6** pay (a bill). **7** dispose of, conclude. **8** bestow (property) legally. **9** end (a dispute). **settlement** *noun* **1** act of settling. **2** place newly colonized. **3** subsidence (of a building). **4** property bestowed legally. **settler** *noun* colonist. **settle down** *verb* **1** make or become calm. **2** (foll. by *to*) concentrate on. **3** adopt a routine way of life. **settle for** *verb* accept in spite of dissatisfaction.

settle² *noun* long wooden bench with high back and arms.

─────────────── T H E S A U R U S ───────────────

discussion, hearing, sitting **3** = **congress**, assembly, conference

set¹ *verb* **1** = **put**, deposit, lay, locate, place, plant, position, rest, seat, situate, station, stick **2** = **prepare**, arrange, lay, make ready, spread **3** = **harden**, cake, congeal, crystallize, solidify, stiffen, thicken **6** = **arrange**, appoint, decide (upon), determine, establish, fix, fix up, resolve, schedule, settle, specify **7** = **assign**, allot, decree, impose, ordain, prescribe, specify **12** = **go down**, decline, dip, disappear, sink, subside, vanish ♦*noun* **16** = **position**, attitude, bearing, carriage, posture **17** = **scenery**, scene, setting, stage set ♦*adjective* **18** = **fixed**, agreed, appointed, arranged, decided, definite, established, prearranged, predetermined, scheduled, settled **19** = **inflexible**, hard and fast, immovable, rigid, stubborn OPPOSITE⟩ open. **20** = **conventional**, stereotyped, traditional, unspontaneous

set² *noun* **1 a** = **series**, assortment, batch, collection, compendium **b** = **group**, band, circle, clique, company, coterie, crowd, faction, gang

set back *verb* **1** = **hold up**, delay, hinder,

impede, retard, slow

setback *noun* = **hold-up**, blow, check, defeat, disappointment, hitch, misfortune, reverse

set off *verb* **1** = **leave**, depart, embark, start out **3** = **detonate**, explode, ignite

setting *noun* **1** = **surroundings**, backdrop, background, location, scene, scenery, set, site **2** = **context**

settle¹ *verb* **1** = **put in order**, adjust, order, regulate, straighten out, work out **2** = **land**, alight, come to rest, descend, light **3** = **move to**, dwell, inhabit, live, make one's home, put down roots, reside, set up home, take up residence **4** = **colonize**, people, pioneer, populate **5** = **calm**, lull, outspan (*S Afr*), pacify, quell, quiet, quieten, reassure, relax, relieve, soothe OPPOSITE⟩ **trouble**. **6** = **pay**, clear, discharge, square (up) **7** = **decide**, agree, confirm, determine, establish, fix **9** = **resolve**, clear up, decide, put an end to, reconcile

settlement *noun* **1** = **agreement**, arrangement, conclusion, confirmation, establishment, working out **2** = **colony**, community, encampment, outpost

settler *noun* = **colonist**, frontiersman,

S

seven *adjective, noun* one more than six.
seventh *adjective, noun* (of) number seven in a
series. **seventeen** *adjective, noun* ten and
seven. **seventeenth** *adjective, noun* **seventy**
adjective, noun ten times seven. **seventieth**
adjective, noun
sever ⊕ *verb* **1** cut through or off. **2** break off
(a relationship). **severance** *noun* **severance
pay** compensation paid by a firm to an
employee who leaves because the job he or she
was appointed to do no longer exists.
several ⊕ *adjective* **1** some, a few. **2** various,
separate. **3** distinct or different. **severally**
adverb separately.
severe ⊕ *adjective* **1** strict or harsh. **2** very
intense or unpleasant. **3** strictly restrained in
appearance. **severely** *adverb* **severity** *noun*
sew *verb* **sewing, sewed, sewn** or **sewed 1**
join with thread repeatedly passed through with
a needle. **2** make or fasten by sewing.
sewage *noun* waste matter or excrement
carried away in sewers. **sewer** *noun* drain to
remove waste water and sewage. **sewerage**
noun system of sewers.
sewn *verb* a past participle of SEW.
sex ⊕ *noun* **1** state of being male or female. **2**
male or female category. **3** sexual intercourse.
4 sexual feelings or behaviour. ♦ *verb* **5** find out
the sex of. **sexy** *adjective* **1** sexually exciting or
attractive. **2** *Informal* exciting or trendy. **sexism**
noun discrimination on the basis of a person's

sex. **sexist** *adjective, noun* **sexual** *adjective*
sexually *adverb* **sexuality** *noun* **sexual
intercourse** sexual act in which the male's
penis is inserted into the female's vagina. **sex
up** *verb Informal* make (something) more
exciting.
sexagenarian *noun* person aged between
sixty and sixty-nine.
sextant *noun* navigator's instrument for
measuring angles, as between the sun and
horizon, to calculate one's position.
sextet *noun* **1** group of six performers. **2**
music for such a group.
sexton *noun* official in charge of a church and
churchyard.
sextuplet *noun* one of six children born at
one birth.
SF science fiction.
SFA Scottish Football Association.
Sgt. Sergeant.
sh *interjection* be quiet!
shabby ⊕ *adjective* **-bier, -biest 1** worn or
dilapidated in appearance. **2** mean or
unworthy, e.g. *shabby treatment.* **shabbily**
adverb **shabbiness** *noun*
shack ⊕ *noun* rough hut. **shack up with** *verb
Slang* live with (one's lover).
shackle ⊕ *noun* **1** one of a pair of metal rings
joined by a chain, for securing a person's wrists
or ankles. **2** anything that restricts freedom. ♦
verb **3** fasten with shackles. **4** hinder.

———————— THESAURUS ————————

immigrant, pioneer
set up *verb* **a** = **build**, assemble, construct,
erect, put together, put up, raise **b** = **establish**,
arrange, begin, found, initiate, institute,
organize, prearrange, prepare
setup *noun* = **arrangement**, conditions,
organization, regime, structure, system
sever *verb* **1** = **cut**, cut in two, detach,
disconnect, disjoin, divide, part, separate, split
OPPOSITE unite. **2** = **discontinue**, break off,
dissociate, put an end to, terminate OPPOSITE
continue
several *adjective* **1** = **some**, many **2** = **various**,
sundry **3** = **different**, diverse, manifold
severe *adjective* **1** = **strict**, austere, cruel,
drastic, hard, harsh, oppressive, rigid,
unbending OPPOSITE easy. **2** = **intense**, acute,
extreme, fierce **3 a** = **grim**, forbidding, grave,
serious, stern, tight-lipped, unsmiling OPPOSITE
genial. **b** = **plain**, austere, classic, restrained,
simple, Spartan, unadorned, unembellished,
unfussy OPPOSITE fancy
severely *adverb* **1** = **strictly**, harshly, sharply,
sternly **2** = **seriously**, acutely, badly, extremely,

gravely
severity *noun* **1** = **strictness**, hardness,
harshness, severeness, sternness, toughness
sex *noun* **1, 2** = **gender 3** = (sexual)
intercourse, coition, coitus, copulation,
fornication, lovemaking, sexual relations
sexual *adjective* **3** = **reproductive**, genital,
procreative, sex **4** = **carnal**, erotic, intimate,
sensual, sexy
sexual intercourse *noun* = **copulation**,
bonking (*inf*), carnal knowledge, coition, coitus,
sex (*inf*), union
sexuality *noun* **4** = **desire**, carnality, eroticism,
lust, sensuality, sexiness (*inf*)
sexy *adjective* **1** = **erotic**, arousing, naughty,
provocative, seductive, sensual, sensuous,
suggestive, titillating
shabby *adjective* **1** = **tatty**, dilapidated, mean,
ragged, run-down, scruffy, seedy, tattered,
threadbare, worn OPPOSITE smart. **2** = **mean**,
cheap, contemptible, despicable, dirty,
dishonourable, low, rotten (*inf*), scurvy
OPPOSITE fair
shack *noun* = **hut**, cabin, shanty

shad *noun* herring-like fish.

shade ❶ *noun* 1 relative darkness. 2 place sheltered from sun. 3 screen or cover used to protect from a direct source of light. 4 depth of colour. 5 slight amount. 6 *Lit* ghost. ◆ *plural* 7 *Slang* sunglasses. ◆ *verb* 8 screen from light. 9 darken. 10 represent (darker areas) in drawing. 11 change slightly or by degrees. **shady** *adjective* 1 situated in or giving shade. 2 of doubtful honesty or legality. **in the shade** in a position of relative obscurity.

shadow ❶ *noun* 1 dark shape cast on a surface when something stands between a light and the surface. 2 patch of shade. 3 slight trace. 4 threatening influence. 5 inseparable companion. 6 person who secretly trails another. ◆ *verb* 7 cast a shadow over. 8 follow secretly. **shadowy** *adjective* **shadow-boxing** *noun* boxing against an imaginary opponent for practice. **Shadow Cabinet** members of the main opposition party in Parliament who would be ministers if their party were in power.

shaft ❶ *noun* 1 long narrow straight handle of a tool or weapon. 2 ray of light. 3 revolving rod that transmits power in a machine. 4 vertical passageway, as for a lift or a mine. 5 one of the bars between which an animal is harnessed to a vehicle. 6 something directed like a missile, e.g. *shafts of wit.* 7 middle part of a column.

shag¹ ❶ *noun* 1 coarse shredded tobacco. 2 tangled hair or wool. ◆ *adjective* 3 (of a carpet) having a long pile. **shaggy** *adjective* 1 covered with rough hair or wool. 2 tousled, unkempt. **shaggy-dog story** long anecdote with a humorous twist at the end.

shag² *noun* kind of cormorant.

shagreen *noun* 1 sharkskin. 2 rough grainy untanned leather.

shah *noun* formerly, ruler of Iran.

shake ❶ *verb* **shaking, shook, shaken** 1 move quickly up and down or back and forth. 2 make unsteady. 3 tremble. 4 grasp (someone's hand) in greeting or agreement. 5 shock or upset. 6 undermine or weaken. ◆ *noun* 7 shaking. 9 vibration. 9 *Informal* short period of time. **shaker** *noun* container in which drinks are mixed or from which powder is shaken. **shaky** *adjective* 1 unsteady. 2 uncertain or questionable. **shakily** *adverb* **shake off** *verb* 1 remove. 2 escape from. **shake up** *verb* 1 mix by shaking. 2 reorganize drastically. 3 shock.

shale *noun* flaky sedimentary rock.

shall *verb, past tense* **should** used as an auxiliary to make the future tense or to indicate intention, obligation, or inevitability.

LANGUAGE TIP

The use of *shall* with *I* and *we* is a matter of preference, not rule. *Shall* is commonly used for questions in southern England but less often in the north and Scotland.

————————————— T H E S A U R U S —————————————

shackle *noun* 1 **=fetter**, bond, chain, iron, leg-iron, manacle ◆*verb* 3 **=fetter**, bind, chain, manacle, put in irons

shade *noun* 1 **=dimness**, dusk, gloom, gloominess, semidarkness, shadow 3 **=screen**, blind, canopy, cover, covering, curtain, shield, veil 4 **=hue**, colour, tinge, tint, tone 5 **=dash**, hint, suggestion, trace 6 *Lit* **=ghost**, apparition, phantom, spectre, spirit ◆*verb* 8 **=cover**, conceal, hide, obscure, protect, screen, shield, veil 9 **=darken**, cloud, dim, shadow

shadow *noun* 2 **=dimness**, cover, darkness, dusk, gloom, shade 3 **=trace**, hint, suggestion, suspicion 4 **=cloud**, blight, gloom, sadness ◆*verb* 7 **=shade**, darken, overhang, screen, shield 8 **=follow**, stalk, tail (*inf*), trail

shadowy *adjective* 2 **=dark**, dim, dusky, gloomy, murky, shaded, shady 3 **=vague**, dim, dreamlike, faint, ghostly, nebulous, phantom, spectral, unsubstantial

shady *adjective* 1 **=shaded**, cool, dim [OPPOSITE] **bright**. 2 **=crooked**, disreputable, dodgy (*Brit, Aust & NZ inf*), dubious, questionable, shifty, suspect, suspicious, unethical [OPPOSITE] **straight**

shaft *noun* 1 **=handle**, pole, rod, shank, stem 2 **=ray**, beam, gleam

shaggy *adjective* 1 **=hairy**, hirsute, long-haired 2 **=unkempt**, rough, tousled, unshorn

shake *verb* 1 **=wave**, brandish, flourish 2 **=jolt**, bump, jar, rock 3 **=tremble**, quake, quiver, shiver, totter, vibrate 5 **=upset**, distress, disturb, frighten, rattle (*inf*), shock, unnerve ◆*noun* 7 **=quaking**, agitation, convulsion, jerk, jolt, shiver, shudder, trembling 8 **=vibration**, tremor

shake up *verb* 1 **=stir (up)**, agitate, churn (up), mix 2 **=reorganize**, overturn, turn upside down 3 **=upset**, disturb, shock, unsettle

shaky *adjective* 1 **=unsteady**, faltering, precarious, quivery, rickety, trembling, unstable, weak [OPPOSITE] **strong**. 2 **=uncertain**, dubious, iffy (*inf*), questionable, suspect [OPPOSITE] **dependable**

S

shallot [shal-**lot**] *noun* kind of small onion.
shallow ❶ *adjective* **1** not deep. **2** lacking
depth of character or intellect. **3** (of breathing)
consisting of short breaths. **shallows** *plural
noun* area of shallow water. **shallowness** *noun*
sham ❶ *noun* **1** thing or person that is not
genuine. ◆ *adjective* **2** not genuine. ◆ *verb*
shamming, shammed 3 fake, feign.
shamble *verb* walk in a shuffling awkward
way.
shambles ❶ *noun* **1** disorderly event or place.
2 slaughterhouse. **shambolic** *adjective Informal*
completely disorganized.
shame ❶ *noun* **1** painful emotion caused by
awareness of having done something
dishonourable or foolish. **2** capacity to feel
shame. **3** disgrace. **4** cause of shame. **5** cause
for regret. ◆ *verb* **6** cause to feel shame. **7**
disgrace. **8** compel by shame, e.g. *she was
shamed into helping.* **shameful** *adjective* causing
or deserving shame. **shamefully** *adverb*
shameless *adjective* with no sense of shame.
shamefaced *adjective* looking ashamed. **put to
shame** *verb* show up as being inferior by
comparison.
shammy *noun, pl* **-mies** *Informal* piece of
chamois leather.
shampoo *noun* **1** liquid soap for washing hair,
carpets, or upholstery. **2** process of
shampooing. ◆ *verb* **3** wash with shampoo.
shamrock *noun* clover leaf, esp. as the Irish

emblem.
shandy *noun, pl* **-dies** drink made of beer and
lemonade.
shanghai *verb* **-haiing, -haied** force or trick
(someone) into doing something. ◆ *noun Aust &
NZ* catapult.
shank *noun* **1** lower leg. **2** shaft or stem.
shan't shall not.
shantung *noun* soft Chinese silk with a
knobbly surface.
shanty¹ ❶ *noun, pl* **-ties** shack or crude
dwelling. **shantytown** *noun* slum consisting of
shanties.
shanty² *noun, pl* **-ties** sailor's traditional song.
shape ❶ *noun* **1** outward form of an object. **2**
way in which something is organized. **3** pattern
or mould. **4** condition or state. ◆ *verb* **5** form or
mould. **6** devise or develop. **shapeless**
adjective **shapely** *adjective* having an attractive
shape. **shape up** *verb Informal* develop
satisfactorily.
shard *noun* broken piece of pottery or
glass.
share¹ ❶ *noun* **1** part of something that
belongs to or is contributed by a person. **2** one
of the equal parts into which the capital stock
of a public company is divided. ◆ *verb* **3** give or
take a share of (something). **4** join with others
in doing or using (something). **5** divide and
distribute. **shareholder** *noun*
share² *noun* blade of a plough.

——————— T H E S A U R U S ———————

shallow *adjective* **1** = **superficial**, empty,
slight, surface, trivial OPPOSITE **deep. 2**
= **unintelligent**, foolish, frivolous, ignorant,
puerile, simple
sham *noun* **1** = **phoney** *or* **phony** (*inf*),
counterfeit, forgery, fraud, hoax, humbug,
imitation, impostor, pretence OPPOSITE
original ◆*adjective* **2** = **false**, artificial, bogus,
counterfeit, feigned, imitation, mock, phoney *or*
phony (*inf*), pretended, simulated OPPOSITE
real ◆*verb* **3** = **fake**, affect, assume, feign,
pretend, put on, simulate
shambles *noun* **1** = **chaos**, confusion,
disarray, disorder, havoc, madhouse, mess,
muddle
shame *noun* **1** = **embarrassment**, abashment,
humiliation, ignominy, mortification OPPOSITE
boldness. 3 = **disgrace**, blot, discredit, dishonour,
disrepute, infamy, reproach, scandal, smear
OPPOSITE **credit** ◆*verb* **6** = **embarrass**, abash,
disgrace, humble, humiliate, mortify OPPOSITE
make proud. 7 = **dishonour**, blot, debase,
defile, degrade, smear, stain OPPOSITE **credit**
shamefaced *adjective* = **embarrassed**,

abashed, ashamed, humiliated, mortified, red-
faced, sheepish
shameful *adjective* **a** = **embarrassing**, cringe-
making (*Brit inf*), humiliating, mortifying **b**
= **disgraceful**, base, dishonourable, low, mean,
outrageous, scandalous, wicked
shameless *adjective* = **brazen**, audacious,
barefaced, flagrant, hardened, insolent,
unabashed, unashamed
shanty¹ *noun* = **shack**, cabin, hut, shed
shape *noun* **1** = **form**, build, contours, figure,
lines, outline, profile, silhouette **2**
= **configuration 3** = **pattern**, frame, model,
mould **4** = **condition**, fettle, health, state, trim
◆*verb* **5** = **form**, create, fashion, make, model,
mould, produce **6** = **develop**, adapt, devise,
frame, modify, plan
shapeless *adjective* **1** = **formless**, amorphous,
irregular, misshapen, unstructured
shapely *adjective* = **well-formed**, curvaceous,
elegant, graceful, neat, trim, well-proportioned
share¹ *noun* **1** = **part**, allotment, allowance,
contribution, due, lot, portion, quota, ration,
whack (*inf*) ◆*verb* **3** = **divide**, assign, distribute,

S

shark *noun* **1** large usu. predatory sea fish. **2** person who cheats others.

sharkskin *noun* stiff glossy fabric.

sharp ⊕ *adjective* **1** having a keen cutting edge or fine point. **2** not gradual. **3** clearly defined. **4** mentally acute. **5** clever but underhand. **6** shrill. **7** bitter or sour in taste. **8** *Music* above the true pitch. ◆ *adverb* **9** promptly. **10** *Music* too high in pitch. ◆ *noun* **11** *Music* symbol raising a note one semitone above natural pitch. **sharply** *adverb* **sharpness** *noun* **sharpen** *verb* make or become sharp or sharper. **sharpener** *noun* **sharper** *noun* person who cheats. **sharpshooter** *noun* marksman.

shatter ⊕ *verb* **1** break into pieces. **2** destroy completely. **shattered** *adjective Informal* **1** completely exhausted. **2** badly upset.

shave ⊕ *verb* **shaving, shaved, shaved** or **shaven 1** remove (hair) from (the face, head, or body) with a razor or shaver. **2** pare away. **3** touch lightly in passing. ◆ *noun* **4** shaving. **close shave** *Informal* narrow escape. **shaver** *noun* electric razor. **shavings** *plural noun* parings.

shawl *noun* piece of cloth worn over a woman's head or shoulders or wrapped around a baby.

she *pronoun* refers to: **1** female person or animal previously mentioned. **2** something regarded as female, such as a car, ship, or nation.

sheaf *noun, pl* **sheaves 1** bundle of papers. **2** tied bundle of reaped corn. ◆ *verb* **3** tie into a sheaf.

shear *verb* **shearing, sheared, sheared** or **shorn 1** clip hair or wool from. **2** cut through. **3** cause (a part) to break or (of a part) break

through strain or twisting. **shears** *plural noun* large scissors or a cutting tool shaped like these. **shearer** *noun*

sheath *noun* **1** close-fitting cover, esp. for a knife or sword. **2** condom. **sheathe** *verb* **1** put into a sheath. **2** cover with a sheath.

sheaves *noun* plural of SHEAF.

shebeen *noun Irish, S Afr & Scot* place where alcohol is sold illegally.

shed[1] ⊕ *noun* building used for storage or shelter or as a workshop.

shed[2] ⊕ *verb* **shedding, shed 1** get rid off. **2** pour forth (tears). **3** cast off (skin, hair, or leaves).

sheen ⊕ *noun* glistening brightness on the surface of something.

sheep *noun, pl* **sheep 1** ruminant animal bred for wool and meat. **2** timid person. **sheep-dip** *noun* liquid disinfectant in which sheep are immersed. **sheepdog** *noun* dog used for herding sheep. **sheepskin** *noun* skin of a sheep with the fleece still on, used for clothing or rugs.

sheepish ⊕ *adjective* embarrassed because of feeling foolish. **sheepishly** *adverb*

sheer[1] ⊕ *adjective* **1** absolute, complete, e.g. *sheer folly.* **2** perpendicular, steep. **3** (of material) so fine as to be transparent. ◆ *adverb* **4** steeply.

sheer[2] *verb* **1** change course suddenly. **2** avoid an unpleasant person or thing.

sheet[1] ⊕ *noun* **1** large piece of cloth used as an inner bed cover. **2** broad thin piece of any material. **3** large expanse. **sheeting** *noun* material from which sheets are made. **sheet lightning** lightning that appears to flash across a large part of the sky at once.

split 4 = **partake**, participate, receive **5** = **go halves**, go fifty-fifty (*inf*)

sharp *adjective* **1** = **keen**, acute, jagged, pointed, serrated, spiky OPPOSITE **dull. 2** = **sudden**, abrupt, distinct, extreme, marked OPPOSITE **slow. 3** = **clear**, crisp, distinct, well-defined OPPOSITE **blurred. 4** = **quick-witted**, alert, astute, bright, clever, discerning, knowing, penetrating, perceptive, quick OPPOSITE **slow. 5** = **cunning**, artful, crafty, dishonest, sly, unscrupulous, wily **7** = **sour**, acid, acrid, hot, piquant, pungent, tart ◆*adverb* **9** = **promptly**, exactly, on the dot, on time, precisely, punctually OPPOSITE **roughly**

sharpen *verb* **1** = **whet**, edge, grind, hone

shatter *verb* **1** = **smash**, break, burst, crack, crush, pulverize **2** = **destroy**, demolish, ruin, torpedo, wreck

shattered *adjective Inf* **1** = **exhausted**, all in (*sl*), dead beat (*inf*), done in (*inf*), drained, knackered (*sl*), ready to drop, tired out, worn out **2** = **devastated**, crushed, gutted (*sl*)

shave *verb* **1, 2** = **trim**, crop, pare, shear

shed[1] *noun* = **hut**, outhouse, shack

shed[2] *verb* **1** = **cast**, drop **2** = **spill**, emit, give, give out, radiate, scatter, shower **3** = **cast off**, discard, moult, slough

sheen *noun* = **shine**, brightness, gleam, gloss, lustre, polish

sheepish *adjective* = **embarrassed**, abashed, ashamed, mortified, self-conscious, shamefaced

sheer[1] *adjective* **1** = **total**, absolute, complete, downright, out-and-out, pure, unmitigated, utter OPPOSITE **moderate. 2** = **steep**, abrupt, precipitous OPPOSITE **gentle. 3** = **fine**, diaphanous, gauzy, gossamer, see-through,

sheet² *noun* rope for controlling the position of a sail. **sheet anchor 1** strong anchor for use in an emergency. **2** person or thing relied on.

sheikh, sheik [shake] *noun* Arab chief. **sheikhdom, sheikdom** *noun*

sheila *noun Aust slang* girl or woman.

shekel *noun* **1** monetary unit of Israel. ◆ *plural* **2** *Informal* money.

shelf *noun, pl* **shelves 1** board fixed horizontally for holding things. **2** ledge. **on the shelf** past the age where marriage is likely. **shelf life** time a packaged product will remain fresh.

shell ⊕ *noun* **1** hard outer covering of an egg, nut, or certain animals. **2** external frame of something. **3** explosive projectile fired from a large gun. **4** light rowing boat. ◆ *verb* **5** take the shell from. **6** fire at with artillery shells. **shellfish** *noun* sea-living animal, esp. one that can be eaten, with a shell. **shell out** *verb Informal* pay out or hand over (money). **shell shock** nervous disorder caused by exposure to battle conditions. **shell suit** lightweight tracksuit made of a waterproof nylon layer over a cotton layer.

shellac *noun* **1** resin used in varnishes. ◆ *verb* **-lacking, -lacked 2** coat with shellac.

shelter ⊕ *noun* **1** structure providing protection from danger or the weather. **2** protection. ◆ *verb* **3** give shelter to. **4** take shelter.

shelve¹ ⊕ *verb* **1** put aside or postpone. **2** provide with shelves. **shelving** *noun* (material for) shelves.

shelve² *verb* slope.

shelves *noun* plural of SHELF.

shenanigans *plural noun Informal* **1** mischief or nonsense. **2** trickery.

shepherd ⊕ *noun* **1** person who tends sheep. ◆ *verb* **2** guide or watch over (people). **shepherdess** *n fem* **shepherd's pie** baked dish of mince covered with mashed potato.

sherbet *noun* fruit-flavoured fizzy powder.

sheriff *noun* **1** (in the US) chief law enforcement officer of a county. **2** (in England and Wales) chief executive officer of the Crown in a county. **3** (in Scotland) chief judge of a district.

Sherpa *noun* member of a people of Tibet and Nepal.

sherry *noun, pl* **-ries** pale or dark brown fortified wine.

Shetland pony *noun* very small sturdy breed of pony.

shibboleth *noun* slogan or principle, usu. considered outworn, characteristic of a particular group.

shied *verb* past of SHY.

shield ⊕ *noun* **1** piece of armour carried on the arm to protect the body from blows or missiles. **2** anything that protects. **3** sports trophy in the shape of a shield. ◆ *verb* **4** protect.

shift ⊕ *verb* **1** move. **2** transfer (blame or responsibility). **3** remove or be removed. ◆ *noun* **4** shifting. **5** group of workers who work during a specified period. **6** period of time during which they work. **7** loose-fitting straight underskirt or dress. **shiftless** *adjective* lacking in ambition or initiative. **shifty** *adjective* evasive or untrustworthy. **shiftiness** *noun*

shillelagh [shil-lay-lee] *noun* (in Ireland) a cudgel.

shilling *noun* **1** former British coin, replaced by the 5p piece. **2** monetary unit in some E African countries.

———— THESAURUS ————

S

thin, transparent [OPPOSITE] **heavy**

sheet¹ *noun* **2** = **coat**, film, lamina, layer, overlay, panel, plate, slab, stratum, surface, veneer **3** = **expanse**, area, blanket, covering, stretch, sweep

shell *noun* **1** = **case**, husk, pod **2** = **frame**, framework, hull, structure ◆*verb* **6** = **bomb**, attack, blitz, bombard, strafe

shell out *verb Inf* = **pay out**, fork out (*sl*), give, hand over

shelter *noun* **1** = **cover**, screen **2** = **protection**, asylum, defence, guard, haven, refuge, retreat, safety, sanctuary, security ◆*verb* **3** = **protect**, cover, defend, guard, harbour, hide, safeguard, shield [OPPOSITE] **expose**. **4** = **take shelter**, hide, seek refuge

shelve¹ *verb* **1** = **postpone**, defer, freeze, put

aside, put on ice, put on the back burner (*inf*), suspend, take a rain check on (*US & Canad inf*)

shepherd *noun* **1** = **herdsman**, drover, grazier, stockman ◆*verb* **2** = **guide**, conduct, herd, steer, usher

shield *noun* **2** = **protection**, cover, defence, guard, safeguard, screen, shelter ◆*verb* **4** = **protect**, cover, defend, guard, safeguard, screen, shelter

shift *verb* **1** = **move**, budge, displace, move around, rearrange, relocate, reposition ◆*noun* **4** = **move**, displacement, rearrangement, shifting

shiftless *adjective* = **lazy**, aimless, good-for-nothing, idle, lackadaisical, slothful, unambitious, unenterprising

shifty *adjective* = **untrustworthy**, deceitful, devious, evasive, furtive, slippery, sly, tricky,

shillyshally *verb* **-lying, -lied** *Informal* be indecisive.

shimmer ❶ *verb, noun* (shine with) a faint unsteady light.

shin *noun* **1** front of the lower leg. ◆ *verb* **shinning, shinned 2** climb by using the hands or arms and legs. **shinbone** *noun* tibia.

shindig *noun Informal* **1** noisy party. **2** brawl.

shine ❶ *verb* **shining, shone 1** give out or reflect light. **2** aim (a light). **3** polish. **4** excel. ◆ *noun* **5** brightness or lustre. **take a shine to** *Informal* take a liking to (someone). **shiny** *adjective* **shiner** *noun Informal* black eye.

shingle[1] *noun* **1** wooden roof tile. ◆ *verb* **2** cover (a roof) with shingles.

shingle[2] *noun* coarse gravel found on beaches.

shingles *noun* disease causing a rash of small blisters along a nerve.

Shinto *noun* Japanese religion in which ancestors and nature spirits are worshipped. **Shintoism** *noun*

shinty *noun* game like hockey.

ship ❶ *noun* **1** large seagoing vessel. **2** airship or spaceship. ◆ *verb* **shipping, shipped 3** send or transport by carrier, esp. a ship. **4** bring or go aboard a ship. **5** *Informal* send away. **6** be hired to work on a ship. **shipment** *noun* **1** act of shipping cargo. **2** consignment of goods shipped. **shipping** *noun* **1** freight transport business. **2** ships collectively. **shipmate** *noun* sailor serving on the same ship as another. **shipshape** *adjective* orderly or neat. **shipwreck** *noun* **1** destruction of a ship through storm or collision. **2** ruin or destruction. ◆ *verb* **3** cause to undergo shipwreck. **shipyard** *noun* place where ships are built.

shire *noun* county.

shire horse *noun* large powerful breed of horse.

shirk ❶ *verb* avoid (duty or work). **shirker** *noun*

shirt *noun* garment for the upper part of the body. **shirtsleeves** *plural noun* **in one's shirtsleeves** not wearing a jacket.

shirty *adjective* **-tier, -tiest** *Slang* bad-tempered or annoyed.

shish kebab *noun* meat and vegetable dish cooked on a skewer.

shit *Taboo verb* **shitting, shitted, shit** or **shat 1** defecate. ◆ *noun* **2** excrement. **3** *Slang* nonsense. **4** *Slang* worthless person. ◆ *interjection* **5** *Slang* exclamation of anger or disgust. **shitty** *adjective*

shiver[1] ❶ *verb* **1** tremble, as from cold or fear. ◆ *noun* **2** shivering. **shivery** *adjective*

shiver[2] ❶ *verb* **1** splinter into pieces. ◆ *noun* **2** splintered piece.

shoal[1] *noun* **1** large number of fish swimming together. **2** large group of people.

shoal[2] *noun* **1** stretch of shallow water. **2** sandbank.

shock[1] ❶ *verb* **1** horrify, disgust, or astonish. ◆ *noun* **2** sudden violent emotional disturbance. **3** sudden violent blow or impact. **4** something causing this. **5** state of bodily collapse caused by physical or mental shock. **6** pain and muscular spasm caused by an electric current passing through the body. **shocker** *noun* **shocking** *adjective* **1** causing horror, disgust, or astonishment. **2** *Informal* very bad. **shock absorber** device on a car for reducing the effects of travelling over bumps. **shock therapy** electroconvulsive therapy.

shock[2] *noun* bushy mass (of hair).

——————————— T H E S A U R U S ———————————

underhand

shimmer *verb* =**gleam**, glisten, scintillate, twinkle ◆*noun* =**gleam**, iridescence

shine *verb* **1** =**gleam**, beam, flash, glare, glisten, glitter, glow, radiate, sparkle, twinkle **3** =**polish**, brush, buff, burnish **4** =**be outstanding**, be conspicuous, excel, stand out ◆*noun* **5** =**brightness**, glare, gleam, gloss, light, lustre, polish, radiance, sheen, shimmer, sparkle

shiny *adjective* **5** =**bright**, gleaming, glistening, glossy, lustrous, polished

ship *noun* **1** =**vessel**, boat, craft

shipshape *adjective* =**tidy**, neat, orderly, spick-and-span, trim, well-ordered, well-organized

shirk *verb* =**dodge**, avoid, evade, get out of, skive (*Brit sl*), slack

shirker *noun* =**slacker**, clock-watcher, dodger, idler, piker (*Aust & NZ sl*), skiver (*Brit sl*)

shiver[1] *verb* **1** =**tremble**, quake, quiver, shake, shudder ◆*noun* **2** =**trembling**, flutter, quiver, shudder, tremor

shiver[2] *verb* **1** =**splinter**, break, crack, fragment, shatter, smash, smash to smithereens

shivery *adjective* =**shaking**, chilled, chilly, cold, quaking, quivery

shock *verb* **1 a** =**horrify**, appal, disgust, nauseate, revolt, scandalize, sicken **b** =**astound**, jolt, shake, stagger, stun, stupefy ◆*noun* **2** =**upset**, blow, bombshell, distress, disturbance, stupefaction, stupor, trauma, turn (*inf*) **3** =**impact**, blow, clash, collision

shocking *adjective* **1** =**dreadful**, appalling, atrocious, disgraceful, disgusting, ghastly, horrifying, nauseating, outrageous, revolting,

shod verb past of SHOE.

shoddy ❶ adjective **-dier, -diest** made or done badly.

shoe noun **1** outer covering for the foot, ending below the ankle. **2** horseshoe. ◆ verb **shoeing, shod 3** fit with a shoe or shoes. **shoehorn** noun smooth curved implement inserted at the heel of a shoe to ease the foot into it. **shoelace** noun cord for fastening shoes. **shoestring** noun **on a shoestring** using a very small amount of money. **shoetree** noun piece of metal, wood, or plastic inserted in a shoe to keep its shape.

shone verb past of SHINE.

shonky adjective **-kier, -kiest** Aust & NZ informal unreliable or unsound.

shoo interjection **1** go away! ◆ verb **2** drive away as by saying 'shoo'.

shook verb past tense of SHAKE.

shoot ❶ verb **shooting, shot 1** hit, wound, or kill with a missile fired from a weapon. **2** fire (a missile from) a weapon. **3** hunt. **4** send out or move rapidly. **5** (of a plant) sprout. **6** photograph or film. **7** Sport take a shot at goal. ◆ noun **8** new branch or sprout of a plant. **9** hunting expedition. **10** Informal photographic assignment. **shooting star** meteor. **shooting stick** stick with a spike at one end and a folding seat at the other.

shop ❶ noun **1** place for sale of goods and services. **2** workshop. ◆ verb **shopping, shopped 3** visit a shop or shops to buy goods. **4** Slang inform against (someone). **talk shop** discuss one's work, esp. on a social occasion.

shopper noun **shopping** noun **1** act of going to shops and buying things. **2** things bought. **shopping centre** area or building with many shops. **shop around** verb visit various shops to compare goods and prices. **shop assistant** person serving in a shop. **shop floor 1** production area of a factory. **2** workers in a factory. **shoplifter** noun person who steals

from a shop. **shopsoiled** adjective soiled or faded from being displayed in a shop. **shop steward** trade-union official elected to represent his or her fellow workers.

shore¹ ❶ noun **1** edge of a sea or lake. **2** land.

shore² ❶ verb **1** (foll. by up) prop or support. ◆ noun **2** prop set under or against something as a support.

shorn verb a past participle of SHEAR.

short ❶ adjective **1** not long. **2** not tall. **3** not lasting long, brief. **4** deficient, e.g. short of cash. **5** abrupt, rude. **6** (of a drink) consisting chiefly of a spirit. **7** (of pastry) crumbly. ◆ adverb **8** abruptly. ◆ noun **9** drink of spirits. **10** short film. **11** Informal short circuit. ◆ plural **12** short trousers. ◆ verb **13** short-circuit. **shortage** noun deficiency. **shorten** verb make or become shorter. **shortly** adverb **1** soon. **2** rudely. **shortbread, shortcake** noun crumbly biscuit made with butter. **short-change** verb **1** give (someone) less than the correct amount of change. **2** Slang swindle. **short circuit** faulty or accidental connection in a circuit, which deflects current through a path of low resistance. **short-circuit** verb **1** develop a short circuit. **2** bypass. **shortcoming** noun failing or defect. **short cut** quicker route or method. **shortfall** noun deficit. **shorthand** noun system of rapid writing using symbols to represent words. **short-handed** adjective not having enough workers. **short list** selected list of candidates for a job or prize, from which the final choice will be made. **short-list** verb put on a short list. **short-lived** adjective lasting a short time. **short shrift** brief and unsympathetic treatment. **short-sighted** adjective **1** unable to see distant things clearly. **2** lacking in foresight. **short-tailed shearwater** same as MEGAPODE. **short-tempered** adjective easily angered. **short-term** adjective of or lasting a short time. **short wave** radio wave with a wavelength of less than 60 metres.

———— T H E S A U R U S ————

scandalous, sickening OPPOSITE fine

shoddy adjective =**inferior**, cheap, poor, rubbishy, second-rate, slipshod, tawdry, trashy OPPOSITE **excellent**

shoot verb **1** = **hit**, blast (sl), bring down, kill, open fire, plug (sl) **2** = **fire**, discharge, emit, fling, hurl, launch, project, propel **4** = **speed**, bolt, charge, dart, dash, fly, hurtle, race, rush, streak, tear ◆noun **8** = **sprout**, branch, bud, offshoot, sprig

shop noun **1** = **store**, boutique, emporium, hypermarket, supermarket

shore¹ noun **1** = **beach**, coast, sands,

seashore, strand (poet)

shore² verb **1** (foll. by up) = **support**, brace, buttress, hold, prop, reinforce, strengthen, underpin

short adjective **1** = **concise**, brief, compressed, laconic, pithy, succinct, summary, terse OPPOSITE **long**. **2** = **small**, diminutive, dumpy, little, petite, squat OPPOSITE **tall**. **3** = **brief**, fleeting, momentary **4** = **lacking**, deficient, limited, low (on), scant, scarce, wanting OPPOSITE **sufficient**. **5** = **abrupt**, brusque, curt, discourteous, impolite, sharp, terse, uncivil ◆adverb **8** = **abruptly**, suddenly, without warning

shot¹ ❶ noun **1** shooting. **2** small lead pellets used in a shotgun. **3** person with specified skill in shooting. **4** Slang attempt. **5** Sport act or instance of hitting, kicking, or throwing the ball. **6** photograph. **7** uninterrupted film sequence. **8** Informal injection. **9** Informal drink of spirits. **shotgun** noun gun for firing a charge of shot at short range. **shotgun wedding** wedding enforced because the bride is pregnant.

shot² ❶ verb **1** past of SHOOT. ◆ adjective **2** woven to show changing colours, e.g. shot silk. **3** streaked with colour.

shot put noun athletic event in which contestants hurl a heavy metal ball as far as possible. **shot-putter** noun

should verb past tense of **shall** used as an auxiliary to make the subjunctive mood or to indicate obligation or possibility.

shoulder ❶ noun **1** part of the body to which an arm, foreleg, or wing is attached. **2** cut of meat including the upper foreleg. **3** part of a garment which covers the shoulder. **4** side of a road. ◆ verb **5** bear (a burden or responsibility). **6** push with one's shoulder. **7** put on one's shoulder. **shoulder blade** large flat triangular bone at the shoulder.

shouldn't should not.

shout ❶ noun **1** loud cry. ◆ verb **2** cry out loudly. **3** Aust & NZ informal treat (someone) to (something, such as a drink). **shout down** verb silence (someone) by shouting.

shove ❶ verb **1** push roughly. **2** Informal put. ◆ noun **3** rough push. **shove off** verb Informal

go away.

shovel ❶ noun **1** tool for lifting or moving loose material. ◆ verb **-elling, -elled 2** lift or move as with a shovel.

show ❶ verb **showing, showed, shown** or **showed 1** make, be, or become noticeable or visible. **2** exhibit or display. **3** indicate. **4** instruct by demonstration. **5** prove. **6** guide. **7** reveal or display (an emotion). ◆ noun **8** public exhibition. **9** theatrical or other entertainment. **10** mere display or pretence. **11** Slang thing or affair. **showy** adjective **1** gaudy. **2** ostentatious. **showily** adverb **showing** noun **1** exhibition. **2** manner of presentation. **show business** the entertainment industry.

showcase noun **1** situation in which something is displayed to best advantage. **2** glass case used to display objects. **showdown** noun confrontation that settles a dispute.

showjumping noun competitive sport of riding horses to demonstrate skill in jumping.

showman noun man skilled at presenting anything spectacularly. **showmanship** noun

show off verb **1** exhibit to invite admiration. **2** Informal behave flamboyantly in order to attract attention. **show-off** noun Informal person who shows off. **showpiece** noun excellent specimen shown for display or as an example. **showroom** noun room in which goods for sale are on display. **show up** verb **1** reveal or be revealed clearly. **2** expose the faults or defects of. **3** Informal embarrass. **4** Informal arrive.

shower ❶ noun **1** kind of bath in which a

———————— T H E S A U R U S ————————

shortage noun = **deficiency**, dearth, insufficiency, lack, paucity, scarcity, want

shortcoming noun = **failing**, defect, fault, flaw, imperfection, weakness

shorten verb = **cut**, abbreviate, abridge, curtail, decrease, diminish, lessen, reduce OPPOSITE> increase

shortly adverb **1** = **soon**, before long, in a little while, presently

short-sighted adjective **1** = **near-sighted**, myopic **2** = **unthinking**, ill-advised, ill-considered, impolitic, impractical, improvident, imprudent, injudicious

short-tempered adjective = **quick-tempered**, hot-tempered, impatient, irascible, ratty (Brit & NZ inf), testy

shot¹ noun **1** = **throw**, discharge, lob, pot shot **2** = **pellet**, ball, bullet, lead, projectile, slug **3** = **marksman**, shooter **4** Sl = **attempt**, effort, endeavour, go (inf), stab (inf), try, turn

shot² adjective **2** = **iridescent**, moiré,

opalescent, watered

shoulder verb **5** = **bear**, accept, assume, be responsible for, carry, take on **6** = **push**, elbow, jostle, press, shove

shout noun **1** = **cry**, bellow, call, roar, scream, yell ◆verb **2** = **cry (out)**, bawl, bellow, call (out), holler (inf), roar, scream, yell

shout down verb = **silence**, drown, drown out, overwhelm

shove verb **1** = **push**, drive, elbow, impel, jostle, press, propel, thrust

shovel verb **2** = **move**, dredge, heap, ladle, load, scoop, toss

shove off verb Inf = **go away**, clear off (inf), depart, leave, push off (inf), scram (inf)

show verb **1** = **be visible**, appear OPPOSITE> be invisible. **2** = **present**, display, exhibit OPPOSITE> hide. **3** = **indicate**, demonstrate, display, manifest, register, reveal OPPOSITE> refute. **4** = **instruct**, demonstrate, explain, teach **5** = **prove**, clarify, demonstrate, elucidate,

S

person stands while being sprayed with water. **2** wash in this. **3** short period of rain, hail, or snow. **4** sudden abundant fall of objects, e.g. *shower of sparks.* ◆ *verb* **5** wash in a shower. **6** sprinkle with or as if with a shower. **7** bestow (things) or present (someone) with things liberally. **showery** *adjective*

shown *verb* a past participle of SHOW.

shrank *verb* a past tense of SHRINK.

shrapnel *noun* **1** artillery shell filled with pellets which scatter on explosion. **2** fragments from this.

shred ⊕ *noun* **1** long narrow strip torn from something. **2** small amount. ◆ *verb* **shredding, shredded** or **shred 3** tear to shreds.

shrew ⊕ *noun* **1** small mouselike animal. **2** bad-tempered nagging woman. **shrewish** *adjective*

shrewd ⊕ *adjective* clever and perceptive. **shrewdly** *adverb* **shrewdness** *noun*

shriek ⊕ *noun* **1** shrill cry. ◆ *verb* **2** utter (with) a shriek.

shrike *noun* songbird with a heavy hooked bill.

shrill ⊕ *adjective* **1** (of a sound) sharp and high-pitched. ◆ *verb* **2** utter shrilly. **shrillness** *noun* **shrilly** *adverb*

shrimp *noun* **1** small edible shellfish. **2** *Informal* small person. **shrimping** *noun* fishing

for shrimps.

shrine *noun* **1** place of worship associated with a sacred person or object. **2** container for holy relics.

shrink ⊕ *verb* **shrinking, shrank** or **shrunk, shrunk** or **shrunken 1** become or make smaller. **2** recoil or withdraw. ◆ *noun* **3** *Slang* psychiatrist. **shrinkage** *noun* decrease in size, value, or weight.

shrivel ⊕ *verb* **-elling, -elled** shrink and wither.

shroud ⊕ *noun* **1** piece of cloth used to wrap a dead body. **2** anything which conceals. ◆ *verb* **3** conceal.

Shrove Tuesday *noun* day before Ash Wednesday.

shrub *noun* woody plant smaller than a tree. **shrubbery** *noun, pl* **-beries** area planted with shrubs.

shrug *verb* **shrugging, shrugged 1** raise and then drop (the shoulders) as a sign of indifference, ignorance, or doubt. ◆ *noun* **2** shrugging. **shrug off** *verb* dismiss as unimportant.

shrunk *verb* a past of SHRINK.

shrunken *verb* a past participle of SHRINK.

shudder ⊕ *verb* **1** shake or tremble violently, esp. with horror. ◆ *noun* **2** shaking or trembling.

shuffle ⊕ *verb* **1** walk without lifting the feet.

—————— THESAURUS ——————

point out **6 = guide,** accompany, attend, conduct, escort, lead ◆*noun* **8 = exhibition,** array, display, fair, parade, sight, spectacle **9 = entertainment,** pageant, presentation, production **10 = pretence,** affectation, air, appearance, display, illusion, parade, pose
showdown *noun* **=confrontation,** clash, face-off (*sl*)
shower *noun* **3, 4 = deluge,** barrage, stream, torrent, volley ◆*verb* **7 = inundate,** deluge, heap, lavish, pour, rain
showman *noun* **=performer,** entertainer
show off *verb* **1 = exhibit,** demonstrate, display, flaunt, parade **2** *Inf* **=boast,** blow one's own trumpet, brag, skite (*Aust & NZ*), swagger
show-off *noun Inf* **=exhibitionist,** boaster, braggart, poseur
show up *verb* **1 = stand out,** appear, be conspicuous, be visible **2** *Inf* **= reveal,** expose, highlight, lay bare **3** *Inf* **=embarrass,** let down, mortify, put to shame **4** *Inf* **=arrive,** appear, come, turn up
showy *adjective* **1 = gaudy,** garish, loud **2 = ostentatious,** brash, flamboyant, flash (*inf*), flashy, over the top (*inf*)
shred *noun* **1 = strip,** bit, fragment, piece,

scrap, sliver, tatter **2 = particle,** atom, grain, iota, jot, scrap, trace
shrew *noun* **2 = nag,** harpy, harridan, scold, spitfire, vixen
shrewd *adjective* **=clever,** astute, calculating, canny, crafty, cunning, intelligent, keen, perceptive, perspicacious, sharp, smart
OPPOSITE> naive
shrewdness *noun* **=cleverness,** astuteness, canniness, discernment, judgment, perspicacity, quick wits, sharpness, smartness
shriek *verb, noun,* **=cry,** scream, screech, squeal, yell
shrill *adjective* **1 = piercing,** high, penetrating, sharp OPPOSITE> deep
shrink *verb* **1 = decrease,** contract, diminish, dwindle, grow smaller, lessen, narrow, shorten OPPOSITE> increase. **2 = recoil,** cower, cringe, draw back, flinch, quail
shrivel *verb* **= wither,** dehydrate, desiccate, shrink, wilt, wizen
shroud *noun* **1 = winding sheet,** grave clothes **2 = covering,** mantle, pall, screen, veil ◆*verb* **3 = conceal,** blanket, cloak, cover, envelop, hide, screen, veil
shudder *verb* **1 = shiver,** convulse, quake,

2 jumble together. **3** rearrange. ◆ *noun* **4** shuffling. **5** rearrangement.

shun ❶ *verb* **shunning, shunned** avoid.

shunt *verb* **1** move (objects or people) to a different position. **2** move (a train) from one track to another. ◆ *noun* **3** shunting. **4** railway point.

shush *interjection* **1** be quiet! ◆ *verb* **2** quiet by saying 'shush'.

shut ❶ *verb* **shutting, shut 1** bring together or fold, close. **2** prevent access to. **3** (of a shop etc.) stop operating for the day. **shutter** *noun* **1** hinged doorlike cover for closing off a window. **2** device in a camera letting in the light required to expose a film. ◆ *verb* **3** close or equip with a shutter. **shut down** *verb* close or stop (a factory, machine, or business). **shutdown** *noun* **shuteye** *noun Slang* sleep. **shut up** *verb* **1** *Informal* stop talking. **2** confine.

shuttle ❶ *noun* **1** vehicle going to and fro over a short distance. **2** instrument which passes the weft thread between the warp threads in weaving. **3** small thread-holding device in a sewing machine. ◆ *verb* **4** travel by or as if by shuttle.

shuttlecock *noun* small light cone with feathers stuck in one end, struck to and fro in badminton.

shy¹ ❶ *adjective* **1** not at ease in company. **2** timid. **3** (foll. by *of*) cautious or wary. **4** reluctant, e.g. workshy. ◆ *verb* **shying, shied 5** start back in fear. **6** (foll. by *away from*) avoid (doing something) through fear or lack of confidence. **shyly** *adverb* **shyness** *noun*

shy² ❶ *verb* **shying, shied 1** throw. ◆ *noun, pl* **shies 2** throw.

Si *Chem* silicon.

SI *French* Système International (d'Unités), international metric system of units of measurement.

Siamese *adjective* of Siam, former name of Thailand. **Siamese cat** breed of cat with cream fur, dark ears and face, and blue eyes. **Siamese twins** twins born joined to each other at some part of the body.

sibilant *adjective* **1** hissing. ◆ *noun* **2** consonant pronounced with a hissing sound.

sibling *noun* brother or sister.

sibyl *noun* (in ancient Greece and Rome) prophetess.

sic *Latin* thus: used to indicate that an odd spelling or reading is in fact accurate.

sick ❶ *adjective* **1** vomiting or likely to vomit. **2** physically or mentally unwell. **3** *Informal* amused by something sadistic or morbid. **4** (foll. by *of*) *Informal* disgusted (by) or weary (of). ◆ *noun* **5** *Informal* vomit. **sickness** *noun* **sicken** *verb* **1** make nauseated or disgusted. **2** become ill. **sickly** *adjective* **1** unhealthy, weak. **2** looking pale and ill. **3** causing revulsion or nausea. **sickbay** *noun* place for sick people, such as that on a ship.

sickle *noun* tool with a curved blade for cutting grass or grain.

side ❶ *noun* **1** line or surface that borders anything. **2** either of two halves into which something can be divided. **3** either surface of a flat object. **4** slope of a hill. **5** right or left part

———————— T H E S A U R U S ————————

quiver, shake, tremble ◆*noun* **2** = **shiver**, quiver, spasm, tremor

shuffle *verb* **1** = **scuffle**, drag, scrape, shamble **2** = **jumble**, disarrange, disorder, mix **3** = **rearrange**

shun *verb* = **avoid**, keep away from, steer clear of

shut *verb* **1** = **close**, fasten, seal, secure, slam OPPOSITE **open**

shut down *verb* **a** = **close**, shut up **b** = **stop**, halt, switch off

shuttle *verb* **4** = **go back and forth**, alternate, commute, go to and fro

shut up *verb* **1** *Inf* = **be quiet**, fall silent, gag, hold one's tongue, hush, silence **2** = **confine**, cage, coop up, immure, imprison, incarcerate

shy¹ *adjective* **1, 2** = **timid**, bashful, coy, diffident, retiring, self-conscious, self-effacing, shrinking OPPOSITE **forward**. **3** (foll. by *of*) = **cautious of**, chary of, distrustful of, hesitant about, suspicious of, wary of OPPOSITE **rash**

◆*verb* **5** (foll. by *away from*) = **recoil**, balk, draw back, flinch, start

shy² *verb* **1** = **throw**, cast, fling, hurl, pitch, sling, toss

shyness *noun* **1, 2** = **timidness**, bashfulness, diffidence, lack of confidence, self-consciousness, timidity, timorousness

sick *adjective* **1** = **nauseous**, ill, nauseated, queasy **2** = **unwell**, ailing, crook (*Aust & NZ sl*), diseased, indisposed, poorly (*inf*), under the weather OPPOSITE **well**. **3** *Inf* = **morbid**, black, ghoulish, macabre, sadistic **4** (foll. by *of*) *Inf* = **tired**, bored, fed up, jaded, weary

sicken *verb* **1** = **disgust**, gross out (*US sl*), nauseate, repel, revolt, turn one's stomach **2** = **fall ill**, ail, take sick

sickly *adjective* **1** = **unhealthy**, ailing, delicate, faint, feeble, infirm, weak **2** = **pallid**, peaky, wan **3** = **nauseating**, cloying, mawkish

sickness *noun* **1** = **nausea**, queasiness, vomiting **2** = **illness**, affliction, ailment, bug

S

of the body. **6** area immediately next to a person or thing. **7** region. **8** aspect or part. **9** one of two opposing groups or teams. **10** line of descent through one parent. **11** *Slang* conceit. ♦ *adjective* **12** at or on the side. **13** subordinate. **on the side 1** as an extra. **2** unofficially. **siding** *noun* short stretch of railway track on which trains or wagons are shunted from the main line. **sideboard** *noun* piece of furniture for holding plates, cutlery, etc. in a dining room. **sideburns, sideboards** *plural noun* man's side whiskers. **sidecar** *noun* small passenger car on the side of a motorcycle. **side effect** additional undesirable effect. **sidekick** *noun Informal* close friend or associate. **sidelight** *noun* either of two small lights on the front of a vehicle. **sideline** *noun* **1** subsidiary interest or source of income. **2** *Sport* line marking the boundary of a playing area. **sidelong** *adjective* **1** sideways. ♦ *adverb* **2** obliquely. **side-saddle** *noun* saddle designed to allow a woman rider to sit with both legs on the same side of the horse. **sideshow** *noun* entertainment offered along with the main show. **sidestep** *verb* **1** dodge (an issue). **2** avoid by stepping sideways. **sidetrack** *verb* divert from the main topic. **sideways** *adverb* **1** to or from the side. **2** obliquely. **side with** *verb* support (one side in a dispute).

sidereal [side-**eer**-ee-al] *adjective* of or determined with reference to the stars.

sidewalk *noun US & Canad* paved path for pedestrians.

sidle **⊕** *verb* move in a furtive manner.

SIDS sudden infant death syndrome, cot death.

siege *noun* surrounding and blockading of a place.

siemens *noun* SI unit of electrical conductance.

sienna *noun* reddish- or yellowish-brown pigment made from natural earth.

sierra *noun* range of mountains in Spain or America with jagged peaks.

siesta **⊕** *noun* afternoon nap, taken in hot countries.

sieve **⊕** [siv] *noun* **1** utensil with mesh through which a substance is sifted or strained. ♦ *verb* **2** sift or strain through a sieve.

sift **⊕** *verb* **1** remove the coarser particles from a substance with a sieve. **2** examine (information or evidence) to select what is important.

sigh *noun* **1** long audible breath expressing sadness, tiredness, relief, or longing. ♦ *verb* **2** utter a sigh. **sigh for** *verb* long for.

sight **⊕** *noun* **1** ability to see. **2** instance of seeing. **3** range of vision. **4** thing seen. **5** *Informal* unsightly thing. **6** device for guiding the eye while using a gun or optical instrument. **7** thing worth seeing. **8** *Informal* a lot. ♦ *verb* **9** catch sight of. **10** aim (a weapon) using a sight. **sightless** *adjective* blind. **sight-read** *verb* play or sing printed music without previous preparation. **sightseeing** *noun* visiting places of interest. **sightseer** *noun*

sign **⊕** *noun* **1** indication of something not immediately or outwardly observable. **2** gesture, mark, or symbol conveying a meaning. **3** notice displayed to advertise, inform, or warn. **4** visible indication. **5** omen. ♦ *verb* **6** write (one's name) on (a document or letter) to show its authenticity or one's agreement. **7** communicate using sign language. **8** make a sign or gesture. **9** engage by signing a contract. **sign language** system of communication by

——————— T H E S A U R U S ———————

(*inf*), complaint, disease, disorder, malady
side *noun* **1** =**border**, boundary, division, edge, limit, margin, perimeter, rim, sector, verge **3** =**surface**, facet **8** =**part**, aspect, face, flank, hand, view **9** =**party**, camp, cause, faction, sect, team **11** *Sl* =**conceit**, airs, arrogance ♦*adjective* **13** =**subordinate**, ancillary, incidental, lesser, marginal, minor, secondary, subsidiary OPPOSITE **main** ♦ **side with** ♦*verb* =**support**, ally with, favour, go along with, take the part of
sidelong *adjective* **1** =**sideways**, covert, indirect, oblique
sidestep *verb* **1** =**avoid**, circumvent, dodge, duck (*inf*), evade, skirt
sidetrack *verb* =**distract**, deflect, divert
sideways *adverb* **1** =**obliquely**, edgeways,

laterally, sidelong, to the side
sidle *verb* =**edge**, creep, inch, slink, sneak, steal
siesta *noun* =**nap**, catnap, doze, forty winks (*inf*), sleep, snooze (*inf*)
sieve *noun* **1** =**strainer**, colander ♦*verb* **2** =**sift**, separate, strain
sift *verb* **1** =**sieve**, filter, separate **2** =**examine**, analyse, go through, investigate, research, scrutinize, work over
sight *noun* **1** =**vision**, eye, eyes, eyesight, seeing **3** =**view**, range of vision, visibility **4** =**spectacle**, display, exhibition, pageant, scene, show, vista **5** *Inf* =**eyesore**, mess, monstrosity ♦*verb* **9** =**spot**, behold, catch sight of, discern, distinguish, espy, glimpse, make out, observe, perceive, see

gestures, as used by deaf people (also **signing**).
sign on *verb* **1** register as unemployed. **2** sign a document committing oneself to a job, course, etc. **signpost** *noun* **1** post bearing a sign that shows the way. ◆ *verb* **2** mark with signposts.
signal ⊕ *noun* **1** sign or gesture to convey information. **2** sequence of electrical impulses or radio waves transmitted or received. ◆ *adjective* **3** *Formal* very important. ◆ *verb* **-nalling, -nalled 4** convey (information) by signal. **signally** *adverb* **signal box** building from which railway signals are operated. **signalman** *noun* railwayman in charge of signals and points.
signatory [sig-na-tree] *noun, pl* **-ries** one of the parties who sign a document.
signature *noun* **1** person's name written by himself or herself in signing something. **2** identifying characteristic. **3** sign at the start of a piece of music to show the key or tempo.
signature tune tune used to introduce a particular television or radio programme.
signet *noun* small seal used to authenticate documents. **signet ring** finger ring bearing a signet.
significant ⊕ *adjective* **1** important. **2** having or expressing a meaning. **significantly** *adverb* **significance** *noun*
signify ⊕ *verb* **-fying, -fied 1** indicate or suggest. **2** be a symbol or sign for. **3** be important. **signification** *noun* meaning.
signor [see-nyor] *noun* Italian term of address equivalent to *sir* or *Mr*. **signora** [see-**nyor**-a] *noun* Italian term of address equivalent to

madam or *Mrs*. **signorina** [see-nyor-**ee**-na] *noun* Italian term of address equivalent to *madam* or *Miss*.
Sikh [seek] *noun* member of an Indian religion having only one God. **Sikhism** *noun*
silage [**sile**-ij] *noun* fodder crop harvested while green and partially fermented in a silo.
silence ⊕ *noun* **1** absence of noise or speech. **2** refusal or failure to speak or communicate. ◆ *verb* **3** make silent. **4** put a stop to. **silent** *adjective* **silently** *adverb* **silencer** *noun* device to reduce the noise of an engine exhaust or gun.
silhouette ⊕ *noun* **1** outline of a dark shape seen against a light background. **2** outline drawing of a profile. ◆ *verb* **3** show in silhouette.
silica *noun* hard glossy mineral found as quartz and in sandstone. **silicosis** *noun* lung disease caused by inhaling silica dust.
silicate *noun* compound of silicon, oxygen, and a metal.
silicon *noun Chem* brittle nonmetallic element widely used in chemistry and industry. **silicone** *noun* tough synthetic substance made from silicon and used in lubricants, paints, and resins.
silicon chip tiny wafer of silicon processed to form an integrated circuit.
silk ⊕ *noun* **1** fibre made by the larva (**silkworm**) of a certain moth. **2** thread or fabric made from this. **take silk** become a Queen's (or King's) Counsel. **silky, silken** *adjective* of or like silk.
sill *noun* ledge at the bottom of a window or door.

——————————— T H E S A U R U S ———————————

sign *noun* **1** = **indication**, clue, evidence, gesture, hint, mark, proof, signal, symptom, token **2** = **symbol**, badge, device, emblem, logo, mark **3** = **notice**, board, placard, warning **5** = **omen**, augury, auspice, foreboding, portent, warning ◆*verb* **6** = **autograph**, endorse, initial, inscribe **8** = **gesture**, beckon, gesticulate, indicate, signal
signal *noun* **1** = **sign**, beacon, cue, gesture, indication, mark, token ◆*verb* **4** = **gesture**, beckon, gesticulate, indicate, motion, sign, wave
significance *noun* **1** = **importance**, consequence, moment, relevance, weight **2** = **meaning**, force, implication(s), import, message, point, purport, sense
significant *adjective* **1** = **important**, critical, material, momentous, noteworthy, serious, vital, weighty OPPOSITE insignificant. **2** = **meaningful**, eloquent, expressive, indicative,

suggestive OPPOSITE meaningless
signify *verb* **1, 2** = **indicate**, be a sign of, betoken, connote, denote, imply, intimate, mean, portend, suggest **3** = **matter**, be important, carry weight, count
silence *noun* **1** = **quiet**, calm, hush, lull, peace, stillness OPPOSITE noise. **2** = **muteness**, dumbness, reticence, taciturnity OPPOSITE speech ◆*verb* **3** = **quieten**, deaden, gag, muffle, quiet, stifle, still, suppress OPPOSITE support. **4** = **cut off**, cut short
silent *adjective* **1** = **quiet**, hushed, muted, noiseless, soundless, still OPPOSITE noisy. **2** = **mute**, dumb, speechless, taciturn, voiceless, wordless OPPOSITE loud
silently *adjective* **1** = **quietly**, inaudibly, in silence, mutely, noiselessly, soundlessly, without a sound, wordlessly
silhouette *noun* **1** = **outline**, form, profile, shape ◆*verb* **3** = **outline**, etch, stand out

S

silly ❶ *adjective* **-lier, -liest** foolish. **silliness**
noun

silo *noun, pl* **-los 1** pit or airtight tower for
storing silage. **2** underground structure in
which nuclear missiles are kept ready for
launching.

silt ❶ *noun* **1** mud deposited by moving water.
♦ *verb* **2** (foll. by *up*) fill or be choked with silt.

silvan *adjective* same as SYLVAN.

silver *noun* **1** white precious metal. **2** coins or
articles made of silver. ♦ *adjective* **3** made of or
of the colour of silver. ♦ *verb* **4** coat with silver.
silvery *adjective* **1** like silver. **2** having a clear
ringing sound. **silverbeet** *noun Aust & NZ* leafy
green vegetable with white stalks. **silver birch**
tree with silvery-white bark. **silverfish** *noun*
small wingless silver-coloured insect. **silver
medal** medal given to the runner-up in a
competition or race. **silver-plated** *adjective*
covered with a thin layer of silver. **silverside**
noun cut of beef from below the rump and
above the leg. **silversmith** *noun* person who
makes articles of silver. **silver wedding**
twenty-fifth wedding anniversary.

silviculture *noun* cultivation of forest trees.

sim *noun* computer game that simulates an
activity such as flying or playing a sport.

simian *adjective, noun* (of or like) a monkey or
ape.

similar ❶ *adjective* alike but not identical.
similarity *noun* **similarly** *adverb*

simile [sim-ill-ee] *noun* figure of speech
comparing one thing to another, using 'as' or
'like', e.g. *as blind as a bat.*

similitude *noun* similarity, likeness.

simmer ❶ *verb* **1** cook gently at just below
boiling point. **2** be in a state of suppressed
rage. **simmer down** *verb Informal* calm down.

simnel cake *noun* fruit cake covered with
marzipan.

simper ❶ *verb* **1** smile in a silly or affected
way. **2** utter (something) with a simper. ♦ *noun*
3 simpering smile.

simple ❶ *adjective* **1** easy to understand or do.
2 plain or unpretentious. **3** not combined or
complex. **4** sincere or frank. **5** feeble-minded.
simply *adverb* **1** in a simple manner. **2** merely.
3 absolutely. **simplicity** *noun* **simplify** *verb*
-fying, -fied make less complicated.
simplification *noun* **simplistic** *adjective* too
simple or naive. **simple fraction** fraction in
which the numerator and denominator are
whole numbers. **simple-minded** *adjective*
unsophisticated. **simpleton** *noun* foolish or
half-witted person.

simulate ❶ *verb* **1** make a pretence of. **2**

——————————— T H E S A U R U S ———————————

silky, silken *adjective* =**smooth**, sleek, velvety

silly *adjective* =**foolish**, absurd, asinine, daft,
fatuous, idiotic, inane, ridiculous, senseless,
stupid, unwise OPPOSITE> **wise**

silt *noun* **1** =**sediment**, alluvium, deposit,
ooze, sludge ♦*verb* **2** (foll. by *up*) =**clog up**,
choke up, congest

similar *adjective* =**alike**, analogous, close,
comparable, like, resembling OPPOSITE>
different

similarity *noun* =**resemblance**, affinity,
agreement, analogy, closeness, comparability,
correspondence, likeness, sameness

simmer *verb* **2** =**fume**, be angry, be pissed
(off) (*taboo sl*), rage, seethe, smoulder

simmer down *verb Inf* =**calm down**, control
oneself, cool off *or* down

simper *verb* **1** =**smile coyly**, smile affectedly,
smirk

simple *adjective* **1** =**uncomplicated**, clear,
easy, intelligible, lucid, plain, straightforward,
understandable, uninvolved OPPOSITE>
involved. **2** =**plain**, classic, homely, humble,

modest, naked, natural, stark, unembellished,
unfussy, unpretentious, unsophisticated
OPPOSITE> **elaborate**. **3** =**pure**, elementary,
unalloyed, uncombined, unmixed **4** =**sincere**,
artless, bald, childlike, direct, frank, guileless,
honest, ingenuous, innocent, naive, natural,
plain, unaffected OPPOSITE> **worldly**. **5**
=**feeble-minded**, dumb (*inf*), foolish, half-
witted, moronic, slow, stupid

simple-minded *adjective* =**feeble-minded**,
backward, dim-witted, foolish, idiot, idiotic,
moronic, retarded, simple, stupid

simpleton *noun* =**halfwit**, dullard, fool, idiot,
imbecile (*inf*), moron, numskull *or* numbskull

simplicity *noun* **1** =**ease**, clarity, clearness,
straightforwardness OPPOSITE> **difficulty**. **2**
=**plainness**, lack of adornment, purity, restraint
OPPOSITE> **decoration**. **4** =**artlessness**, candour,
directness, innocence, naivety, openness

simplify *verb* =**make simpler**, abridge,
disentangle, dumb down, reduce to essentials,
streamline

simply *adverb* **1** =**plainly**, clearly, directly,

S

imitate the conditions of (a particular situation). **3** have the appearance of. **simulation** *noun* **simulator** *noun*

simultaneous ⊕ *adjective* occurring at the same time. **simultaneity** *noun* **simultaneously** *adverb*

sin¹ ⊕ *noun* **1** breaking of a religious or moral law. **2** offence against a principle or standard. ◆ *verb* **sinning, sinned 3** commit a sin. **sinful** *adjective* **1** guilty of sin. **2** being a sin. **sinfully** *adverb* **sinner** *noun*

sin² *Maths* sine.

since *preposition* **1** during the period of time after. ◆ *conjunction* **2** from the time when. **3** for the reason that. ◆ *adverb* **4** from that time.

sincere ⊕ *adjective* without pretence or deceit. **sincerely** *adverb* **sincerity** *noun*

sine *noun* (in trigonometry) ratio of the length of the opposite side to that of the hypotenuse in a right-angled triangle.

sinecure ⊕ [**sin**-ee-cure] *noun* paid job with minimal duties.

sine die [**sin**-ay **dee**-ay] *adverb Latin* with no date fixed for future action.

sine qua non [**sin**-ay kwah **non**] *noun Latin* essential requirement.

sinew *noun* **1** tough fibrous tissue joining muscle to bone. **2** muscles or strength. **sinewy** *adjective*

sing ⊕ *verb* **singing, sang, sung 1** make musical sounds with the voice. **2** perform (a song). **3** make a humming or whistling sound. **singer** *noun* **singing telegram** service in which a messenger presents greetings to a person by singing. **singsong** *noun* **1** informal singing session. ◆ *adjective* **2** (of the voice) repeatedly rising and falling in pitch.

singe ⊕ *verb* **singeing, singed 1** burn the surface of. ◆ *noun* **2** superficial burn.

single ⊕ *adjective* **1** one only. **2** distinct from others of the same kind. **3** unmarried. **4** designed for one user. **5** formed of only one part. **6** (of a ticket) valid for an outward journey only. ◆ *noun* **7** single thing. **8** thing intended for one person. **9** record with one short song or tune on each side. **10** single ticket. ◆ *plural* **11** game between two players. ◆ *verb* **12** (foll. by *out*) pick out from others. **singly** *adverb*

single-breasted *adjective* (of a garment) having only slightly overlapping fronts and one row of buttons. **single file** (of people or things) arranged in one line. **single-handed** *adjective* without assistance. **single-minded** *adjective* having one aim only.

singlet *noun* sleeveless vest.

singular ⊕ *adjective* **1** (of a word or form) denoting one person or thing. **2** remarkable, unusual. ◆ *noun* **3** singular form of a word. **singularity** *noun* **singularly** *adverb*

Sinhalese, Singhalese *noun, adjective*

————————————— THESAURUS —————————————

easily, intelligibly, naturally, straightforwardly, unpretentiously **2 = just**, merely, only, purely, solely **3 = totally**, absolutely, completely, really, utterly, wholly

simulate *verb* **1, 2 = pretend**, act, affect, feign, put on, sham

simultaneous *adjective* **= coinciding**, at the same time, coincident, concurrent, contemporaneous, synchronous

simultaneously *adverb* **= at the same time**, concurrently, together

sin¹ *noun* **1, 2 = wrongdoing**, crime, error, evil, guilt, iniquity, misdeed, offence, transgression ◆*verb* **3 = transgress**, err, fall, go astray, lapse, offend

sincere *adjective* **= honest**, candid, earnest, frank, genuine, guileless, heartfelt, real, serious, true, unaffected

sincerely *adverb* **= honestly**, earnestly, genuinely, in earnest, seriously, truly, wholeheartedly

sincerity *noun* **= honesty**, candour, frankness, genuineness, seriousness, truth

sinecure *noun* **= cushy number** (*inf*), gravy train (*sl*), money for jam *or* old rope (*inf*), soft

job (*inf*), soft option

sinful *adjective* **1 = wicked**, bad, corrupt, criminal, erring, guilty, immoral, iniquitous

sing *verb* **1, 2 = warble**, carol, chant, chirp, croon, pipe, trill, yodel **3 = hum**, buzz, purr, whine

singe *verb* **1 = burn**, char, scorch, sear

singer *noun* **2 = vocalist**, balladeer, chorister, crooner, minstrel, soloist

single *adjective* **1 = one**, individual, lone, only, separate, sole, solitary **2 = individual**, distinct, exclusive, separate, undivided, unshared **3 = unmarried**, free, unattached, unwed **5 = simple**, unblended, unmixed ◆*verb* **12** (foll. by *out*) **= pick**, choose, distinguish, fix on, pick on *or* out, select, separate, set apart

single-minded *adjective* **= determined**, dedicated, dogged, fixed, unswerving

singly *adverb* **1 = one by one**, individually, one at a time, separately

singular *adjective* **1 = single**, individual, separate, sole **2 a = remarkable**, eminent, exceptional, notable, noteworthy, outstanding OPPOSITE⟩ **common. b = unusual**, curious, eccentric, extraordinary, munted (*NZ sl*), odd,

S

(member or language) of a people living mainly in Sri Lanka.

sinister ❶ *adjective* threatening or suggesting evil or harm.

sink ❶ *verb* **sinking, sank, sunk** or **sunken 1** submerge (in liquid). **2** descend or cause to descend. **3** decline in value or amount. **4** become weaker in health. **5** seep or penetrate. **6** dig or drill (a hole or shaft). **7** invest (money). **8** *Golf, snooker* hit (a ball) into a hole or pocket. ◆ *noun* **9** fixed basin with a water supply and drainage pipe. **sinker** *noun* weight for a fishing line. **sink in** *verb* penetrate the mind. **sinking fund** money set aside regularly to repay a long-term debt.

Sino- *combining form* Chinese.

sinuous *adjective* **1** curving. **2** lithe. **sinuously** *adverb*

sinus [**sine**-uss] *noun* hollow space in a bone, esp. an air passage opening into the nose.

sinusitis *noun* inflammation of a sinus membrane.

sip ❶ *verb* **sipping, sipped 1** drink in small mouthfuls. ◆ *noun* **2** amount sipped.

siphon *noun* **1** bent tube which uses air pressure to draw liquid from a container. ◆ *verb* **2** draw off thus. **3** redirect (resources).

sir *noun* **1** polite term of address for a man. **2** (**S-**) title of a knight or baronet.

sire *noun* **1** male parent of a horse or other domestic animal. **2** respectful term of address to a king. ◆ *verb* **3** father.

siren *noun* **1** device making a loud wailing noise as a warning. **2** dangerously alluring woman.

sirloin *noun* prime cut of loin of beef.

sirocco *noun*, *pl* **-cos** hot wind blowing from N Africa into S Europe.

sis *interjection S Afr informal* exclamation of disgust.

sisal [**size**-al] *noun* (fibre of) plant used in making ropes.

siskin *noun* yellow-and-black finch.

sissy ❶ *adjective, noun, pl* **-sies** weak or cowardly (person).

sister *noun* **1** girl or woman with the same parents as another person. **2** female fellow-member of a group. **3** senior nurse. **4** nun. ◆ *adjective* **5** closely related, similar. **sisterhood** *noun* **1** state of being a sister. **2** group of women united by common aims or beliefs. **sisterly** *adjective* **sister-in-law** *noun*, *pl* **sisters-in-law 1** sister of one's husband or wife. **2** one's brother's wife.

sit ❶ *verb* **sitting, sat 1** rest one's body upright on the buttocks. **2** cause to sit. **3** perch. **4** (of a bird) incubate (eggs) by sitting on them. **5** be situated. **6** pose for a portrait. **7** occupy an official position. **8** (of an official body) hold a session. **9** fit or hang as specified. **10** take (an examination). **sit tight** *Informal* wait patiently without taking action. **sitter** *noun* **1** baby-sitter. **2** person posing for a picture. **sitting** *noun* **1** time when a meal is served. **2** meeting of an official body. ◆ *adjective* **3** current. **4** seated. **sitting room** room in a house where people sit and relax. **sit down** *verb* (cause to) adopt a sitting posture. **sit-in** *noun* protest in which demonstrators occupy a place and refuse to move. **sit on** *verb* *Informal* delay action on. **sit out** *verb* endure to the end.

sitar *noun* Indian stringed musical instrument.

sitcom *noun Informal* situation comedy.

site ❶ *noun* **1** place where something is, was, or is intended to be located. ◆ *noun* **2** same as WEBSITE. ◆ *verb* **3** provide with a site.

situate ❶ *verb* place. **situation** *noun* **1** state of affairs. **2** location and surroundings. **3** position of employment. **situation comedy** radio or

——————— T H E S A U R U S ———————

peculiar, queer, strange OPPOSITE normal
singularly *adverb* **2 a =remarkably**, especially, exceptionally, notably, outstandingly, particularly **b =unusually**, uncommonly
sinister *adjective* **=threatening**, dire, disquieting, evil, malign, menacing, ominous OPPOSITE reassuring
sink *verb* **1 =submerge**, founder, go under **2 =descend**, dip, drop, fall, go down, lower, plunge, subside OPPOSITE arise. **3 =fall**, abate, collapse, drop, lapse, slip, subside **4 =decline**, decay, decrease, deteriorate, diminish, dwindle, fade, fail, flag, lessen, weaken, worsen OPPOSITE rise. **6 =dig**, bore, drill, drive, excavate

sink in *verb* **=be understood**, get through to, penetrate, register (*inf*)
sip *verb* **1 =drink**, sample, sup, taste ◆*noun* **2 =swallow**, drop, taste, thimbleful
sissy *adjective* **=wimpish** or **wimpy**, cowardly, effeminate, feeble, namby-pamby, soft (*inf*), unmanly, weak, wet (*Brit inf*) (*inf*) ◆*noun* **=wimp**, coward, milksop, mummy's boy, namby-pamby, softie (*inf*), weakling, wet (*Brit inf*) (*inf*)
sit *verb* **1-3, 5 =rest**, perch, settle **7 =officiate**, preside **8 =convene**, assemble, deliberate, meet
site *noun* **1 =location**, place, plot, position, setting, spot ◆*verb* **2 =locate**, install, place,

television series involving the same characters in various situations.

six *adjective, noun* one more than five. **sixth** *adjective, noun* (of) number six in a series. **sixteen** *adjective, noun* six and ten. **sixteenth** *adjective, noun* **sixty** *adjective, noun* six times ten. **sixtieth** *adjective, noun* **sixpence** *noun* former British coin worth six pennies. **sixth sense** perception beyond the five senses.

size¹ ⊕ *noun* **1** dimensions, bigness. **2** one of a series of standard measurements of goods. ◆ *verb* **3** arrange according to size. **sizeable, sizable** *adjective* quite large. **size up** *verb Informal* assess.

size² *noun* **1** gluey substance used as a protective coating. ◆ *verb* **2** treat with size.

sizzle ⊕ *verb* **1** make a hissing sound like frying fat. ◆ *noun* **2** hissing sound.

SK Saskatchewan.

skanky *adjective Slang* dirty or unattractive.

skate¹ *noun* **1** boot with a steel blade or sets of wheels attached to the sole for gliding over ice or a hard surface. ◆ *verb* **2** glide on or as if on skates. **skateboard** *noun* board mounted on small wheels for riding on while standing up. **skate over, round** *verb* avoid discussing or dealing with (a matter) fully.

skate² *noun* large marine flatfish.

skean-dhu *noun* dagger worn in the stocking as part of the Highland dress.

skedaddle *verb Informal* run off.

skein *noun* **1** yarn wound in a loose coil. **2** flock of geese in flight.

skeleton ⊕ *noun* **1** framework of bones inside a person's or animal's body. **2** essential framework of a structure. **3** skinny person or animal. **4** outline of bare essentials. ◆ *adjective* **5** reduced to a minimum. **skeletal** *adjective* **skeleton key** key which can open many different locks.

skerry *noun, pl* **-ries** rocky island or reef.

sketch ⊕ *noun* **1** rough drawing. **2** brief description. **3** short humorous play. ◆ *verb* **4** make a sketch (of). **sketchy** *adjective* incomplete or inadequate. **sketch out** *verb* make a brief description of.

skew *verb* **1** make slanting or crooked. ◆ *adjective* **2** slanting or crooked. **skewed** *adjective* distorted or biased because of lack of information. **skewwhiff** *adjective Informal* slanting or crooked.

skewbald *noun, adjective* (horse) marked with patches of white and another colour.

skewer *noun* **1** pin to hold meat together during cooking. ◆ *verb* **2** fasten with a skewer.

ski *noun* **1** one of a pair of long runners fastened to boots for gliding over snow or water. ◆ *verb* **skiing, skied** or **ski'd 2** travel on skis. **skier** *noun*

skid *verb* **skidding, skidded 1** (of a moving vehicle) slide sideways uncontrollably. ◆ *noun* **2** skidding. **skid row** *US slang* dilapidated part of a city frequented by down-and-outs.

skiff *noun* small boat.

skill ⊕ *noun* **1** special ability or expertise. **2** something requiring special training or expertise. **skilful** *adjective* having or showing skill. **skilfully** *adverb* **skilled** *adjective*

SPELLING TIP

When you make an adjective from **skill**, you should drop an *l* to make **skilful**. This is not the case in American English, and th is is probably why there are over 100 examples of *skillful* in the Bank of English.

---

skillet *noun* small frying pan or shallow

THESAURUS

position, set, situate
situation *noun* **1 = state of affairs**, case, circumstances, condition, equation, plight, state **2 = location**, place, position, setting, site, spot **3 = job**, employment, office, place, position, post
size¹ *noun* **1 = dimensions**, amount, bulk, extent, immensity, magnitude, mass, proportions, range, volume
sizeable, sizable *adjective* **= large**, considerable, decent, goodly, largish, respectable, substantial
size up *verb Inf* **= assess**, appraise, evaluate, take stock of
sizzle *verb* **1 = hiss**, crackle, frizzle, fry, spit

skeleton *noun* **2 = framework**, frame, outline, structure **4 = bare bones**, draft, sketch
sketch *noun* **1 = drawing**, delineation, design, draft, outline, plan ◆*verb* **4 = draw**, delineate, depict, draft, outline, represent, rough out
sketchy *adjective* **= incomplete**, cursory, inadequate, perfunctory, rough, scrappy, skimpy, superficial
skilful *adjective* **= expert**, able, adept, adroit, clever, competent, dexterous, masterly, practised, professional, proficient, skilled
skill *noun* **1 = expertise**, ability, art, cleverness, competence, craft, dexterity, facility, knack, proficiency, skilfulness, talent, technique
OPPOSITE **clumsiness**

cooking pot.

skim ⊕ *verb* **skimming, skimmed 1** remove floating matter from the surface of (a liquid). **2** glide smoothly over. **3** throw across a surface. **4** read quickly. **skimmed, skim milk** milk from which the cream has been removed.

skimp ⊕ *verb* not invest enough time, money, material, etc. **skimpy** *adjective* scanty or insufficient.

skin ⊕ *noun* **1** outer covering of the body. **2** complexion. **3** outer layer or covering. **4** film on a liquid. **5** animal skin used as a material or container. ♦ *verb* **skinning, skinned 6** remove the skin of. **7** graze. **8** *Slang* swindle. **skinless** *adjective* **skinny** *adjective* thin. **skin-deep** *adjective* superficial. **skin diving** underwater swimming using flippers and light breathing apparatus. **skin-diver** *noun* **skinflint** *noun* miser. **skinhead** *noun* youth with very short hair. **skintight** *adjective* fitting tightly over the body.

skint *adjective Slang* having no money.

skip¹ ⊕ *verb* **skipping, skipped 1** leap lightly from one foot to the other. **2** jump over a rope as it is swung under one. **3** *Informal* pass over, omit. **4** change quickly from one subject to another. ♦ *noun* **5** skipping.

skip² *noun* **1** large open container for builders' rubbish. **2** cage used as a lift in mines.

skipper *noun, verb* captain.

skirl *noun* sound of bagpipes.

skirmish ⊕ *noun* **1** brief or minor fight or argument. ♦ *verb* **2** take part in a skirmish.

skirt ⊕ *noun* **1** woman's garment hanging from the waist. **2** part of a dress or coat below the waist. **3** circular hanging part. **4** cut of beef from the flank. ♦ *verb* **5** border. **6** go round. **7** avoid dealing with (an issue). **skirting board** narrow board round the bottom of an interior wall.

skit ⊕ *noun* brief satirical sketch.

skite *verb, noun Aust & NZ* boast.

skittish ⊕ *adjective* **1** playful or lively. **2** (of a horse) easily frightened.

skittle *noun* **1** bottle-shaped object used as a target in some games. ♦ *plural* **2** game in which players try to knock over skittles by rolling a ball at them.

skive ⊕ *verb Informal* evade work or responsibility.

skivvy *noun, pl* **-vies** female servant who does menial work.

skookum ⊕ *adjective Canad* powerful or big.

skua *noun* large predatory gull.

skulduggery ⊕ *noun Informal* trickery.

skulk ⊕ *verb* **1** move stealthily. **2** lurk.

skull *noun* **1** bony framework of the head. **2** *Informal* brain or mind. **skullcap** *noun* close-fitting brimless cap.

skunk *noun* **1** small black-and-white N American mammal which emits a foul-smelling fluid when attacked. **2** *Slang* despicable person.

sky ⊕ *noun, pl* **skies 1** upper atmosphere as seen from the earth. ♦ *verb* **skying, skied 2** *Informal* hit high in the air. **skydiving** *noun* sport of jumping from an aircraft and performing manoeuvres before opening one's parachute. **skylark** *noun* lark that sings while soaring at a great height. **skylight** *noun* window in a roof or ceiling. **skyline** *noun* outline of buildings, trees, etc. against the sky. **skyscraper** *noun* very tall building.

——————— T H E S A U R U S ———————

skim *verb* **1** = separate, cream **2** = glide, coast, float, fly, sail, soar **4** = scan, glance, run one's eye over

skimp *verb* = stint, be mean with, be sparing with, cut corners, scamp, scrimp OPPOSITE be extravagant

skin *noun* **3** = coating, casing, crust, film, husk, outside, peel, rind **5** = hide, fell, pelt ♦ *verb* **6** = peel, flay, scrape

skinflint *noun* = miser, meanie *or* meany (*inf, chiefly Brit*), niggard, penny-pincher (*inf*), Scrooge

skinny *adjective* = thin, emaciated, lean, scrawny, undernourished

skip¹ *verb* **1** = hop, bob, bounce, caper, dance, flit, frisk, gambol, prance, trip **3** *Inf* = pass over, eschew, give (something) a miss, leave out, miss out, omit

skirmish *noun* **1** = fight, battle, brush, clash, conflict, encounter, fracas, scrap (*inf*) ♦ *verb* **2** = fight, clash, collide

skirt *verb* **5** = border, edge, flank **6, 7** = avoid, circumvent, evade, steer clear of

skit *noun* = parody, burlesque, sketch, spoof (*inf*), takeoff (*inf*)

skittish *adjective* **1** = lively, wired (*sl*) **2** = nervous, excitable, fidgety, highly strung, jumpy, restive OPPOSITE relaxed

skive *verb Inf* = slack, idle, malinger, shirk, swing the lead

skookum *adjective Canad* = powerful, influential, big, dominant, controlling, commanding, supreme, prevailing, authoritative

skulduggery *noun Inf* = trickery, double-dealing, duplicity, machinations, underhandedness

skulk *verb* **1** = sneak, creep, prowl, slink **2** = lurk, lie in wait, loiter

slab ❶ *noun* broad flat piece.
slack¹ ❶ *adjective* **1** not tight. **2** negligent. **3** (of water) moving slowly. **4** not busy. ♦ *noun* **5** slack part. **6** slack period. ♦ *plural* **7** *informal* trousers. ♦ *verb* **8** neglect one's work or duty. **9** loosen or slacken. **slackness** *noun* **slacken** *verb* make or become slack. **slacker** *noun*
slack² *noun* coal dust or small pieces of coal.
slag ❶ *noun* **1** waste left after metal is smelted. **2** *Brit slang* a sexually immoral woman. ♦ *verb* **slagging, slagged 3** (foll. by *off*) *Slang* criticize. **slag heap** pile of waste from smelting or mining.
slain *verb* past participle of SLAY.
slake ❶ *verb* **1** satisfy (thirst or desire). **2** combine (quicklime) with water.
slalom *noun* skiing or canoeing race over a winding course.
slam ❶ *verb* **slamming, slammed 1** shut, put down, or hit violently and noisily. **2** *Informal* criticize harshly. ♦ *noun* **3** act or sound of slamming. **grand slam** see GRAND.
slander ❶ *noun* **1** false and malicious statement about a person. **2** crime of making such a statement. ♦ *verb* **3** utter slander about.
slanderous *adjective*
slang *noun* very informal language. **slangy** *adjective* **slanging match** abusive argument.
slant ❶ *verb* **1** lean at an angle, slope. **2** present (information) in a biased way. ♦ *noun* **3** slope. **4** point of view, esp. a biased one.
slanting *adjective*
slap ❶ *noun* **1** blow with the open hand or a flat object. ♦ *verb* **slapping, slapped 2** strike with the open hand or a flat object. **3** *Informal* place forcefully or carelessly. **slapdash** *adjective* careless and hasty. **slap-happy** *adjective Informal* cheerfully careless. **slapstick** *noun* boisterous knockabout comedy. **slap-up** *adjective* (of a meal) large and luxurious.
slash ❶ *verb* **1** cut with a sweeping stroke. **2** gash. **3** reduce drastically. **4** criticize harshly. ♦ *noun* **5** sweeping stroke. **6** gash.
slat *noun* narrow strip of wood or metal.
slate¹ *noun* **1** rock which splits easily into thin layers. **2** piece of this for covering a roof or, formerly, for writing on. ♦ *verb* **3** cover with slates. **4** *US* plan or arrange. ♦ *adjective* **5** dark grey.
slate² ❶ *verb Informal* criticize harshly. **slating** *noun*
slattern *noun Old-fashioned* slovenly woman. **slatternly** *adjective*
slaughter ❶ *verb* **1** kill (animals) for food. **2** kill (people) savagely or indiscriminately. ♦ *noun* **3** slaughtering. **slaughterhouse** *noun* place where animals are killed for food.
Slav *noun* member of any of the peoples of E Europe or the former Soviet Union who speak a Slavonic language. **Slavonic** *noun* **1** language

——————— T H E S A U R U S ———————

sky *noun* **1** = **heavens**, firmament
slab *noun* = **piece**, chunk, lump, portion, slice, wedge
slack¹ *adjective* **1** = **loose**, baggy, lax, limp, relaxed OPPOSITE stretched. **2** = **negligent**, lax, neglectful, remiss, slapdash, slipshod OPPOSITE strict. **3** = **slow**, quiet, slow-moving, sluggish OPPOSITE active. **4** = **inactive**, idle, lazy ♦*noun* **5** = **room**, excess, give (*inf*), leeway ♦*verb* **8** = **shirk**, dodge, idle, skive (*Brit sl*)
slacken *verb* = **lessen**, abate, decrease, diminish, drop off, moderate, reduce, relax
slacker *noun* **8** = **layabout**, dodger, idler, loafer, piker (*Aust & NZ sl*), shirker, skiver (*Brit sl*)
slag *verb* **3** (foll. by *off*) *Sl* = **criticize**, abuse, deride, insult, malign, mock, slander, slate
slake *verb* **1** = **satisfy**, assuage, quench, sate
slam *verb* **1 a** = **bang**, crash, smash **b** = **throw**, dash, fling, hurl
slander *noun* **1** = **defamation**, calumny, libel, scandal, smear OPPOSITE praise ♦*verb* **3** = **defame**, blacken (someone's) name, libel, malign, smear OPPOSITE acclaim
slanderous *adjective* = **defamatory**, damaging, libellous, malicious
slant *verb* **1** = **slope**, bend, bevel, cant, heel, incline, lean, list, tilt **2** = **bias**, angle, colour, distort, twist ♦*noun* **3** = **slope**, camber, gradient, incline, tilt **4** = **bias**, angle, emphasis, one-sidedness, point of view, prejudice
slanting *adjective* **1** = **sloping**, angled, at an angle, bent, diagonal, inclined, oblique, tilted, tilting
slap *noun* **1** = **smack**, blow, cuff, spank, swipe ♦*verb* **2** = **smack**, clap, cuff, spank, swipe
slapdash *adjective* = **careless**, clumsy, hasty, hurried, messy, slipshod, sloppy (*inf*), untidy
slap-up *adjective* = **luxurious**, lavish, magnificent, splendid, sumptuous, superb
slash *verb* **1, 2** = **cut**, gash, hack, lacerate, rend, rip, score, slit **3** = **reduce**, cut, drop, lower ♦*noun* **6** = **cut**, gash, incision, laceration, rent, rip, slit
slate² *verb Inf* = **criticize**, censure, rebuke, rouse on (*Aust*), scold, tear into (*inf*)
slaughter *verb* **2** = **slay**, butcher, kill, massacre, murder ♦*noun* **3** = **slaying**, bloodshed, butchery, carnage, killing, massacre, murder

S

group including Russian, Polish, and Czech. ◆
adjective **2** of this language group.
slave ❶ *noun* **1** person owned by another for
whom he or she has to work. **2** person
dominated by another or by a habit. **3** drudge.
◆ *verb* **4** work like a slave. **slaver** *noun* person
or ship engaged in the slave trade. **slavery**
noun **1** state or condition of being a slave. **2**
practice of owning slaves. **slavish** *adjective* **1** of
or like a slave. **2** imitative. **slave-driver** *noun*
person who makes others work very hard.
slaver [slav-ver] *verb* **1** dribble saliva from the
mouth. ◆ *noun* **2** saliva dribbling from the
mouth.
slay ❶ *verb* **slaying, slew, slain** kill.
sleazy ❶ *adjective* **-zier, -ziest** run-down or
sordid. **sleaze** *noun*
sledge[1], **sled** *noun* **1** carriage on runners for
sliding on snow. **2** light wooden frame for
sliding over snow. ◆ *verb* **3** travel by sledge.
sledge[2], **sledgehammer** *noun* heavy
hammer with a long handle.
sleek ❶ *adjective* **1** glossy, smooth, and shiny.
2 elegantly dressed.
sleep ❶ *noun* **1** state of rest characterized by
unconsciousness. **2** period of this. ◆ *verb*
sleeping, slept 3 be in or as if in a state of
sleep. **4** have sleeping accommodation for (a
specified number). **sleeper** *noun* **1** railway car
fitted for sleeping in. **2** beam supporting the
rails of a railway. **3** ring worn in a pierced ear
to stop the hole from closing up. **4** person who
sleeps. **sleepy** *adjective* **1** needing sleep. **2**
without activity or bustle. **sleepily** *adverb*

sleepiness *noun* **sleepless** *adjective* **sleep in**
verb sleep longer than usual. **sleeping bag**
padded bag for sleeping in. **sleeping partner**
business partner who does not play an active
role. **sleeping sickness** African disease spread
by the tsetse fly. **sleepout** *noun NZ* small
building for sleeping in. **sleepover** *noun chiefly
US* occasion when a person stays overnight at a
friend's house. **sleepwalk** *verb* walk while
asleep. **sleepwalker** *noun* **sleep with,
together** *verb* have sexual intercourse (with).
sleet *noun* **1** rain and snow or hail falling
together. ◆ *verb* **2** fall as sleet.
sleeve *noun* **1** part of a garment which covers
the arm. **2** tubelike cover. **3** gramophone
record cover. **up one's sleeve** secretly ready.
sleeveless *adjective*
sleigh *noun, verb* sledge.
sleight of hand [slite] *noun* skilful use of the
hands when performing conjuring tricks.
slender ❶ *adjective* **1** slim. **2** small in amount.
slept *verb* past of SLEEP.
sleuth ❶ [slooth] *noun* detective.
slew[1] *verb* past tense of SLAY.
slew[2] *verb* twist or swing round.
slice ❶ *noun* **1** thin flat piece cut from
something. **2** share. **3** kitchen tool with a broad
flat blade. **4** *Sport* hitting of a ball so that it
travels obliquely. ◆ *verb* **5** cut into slices. **6** cut
(through). **7** *Sport* hit (a ball) with a slice.
slick ❶ *adjective* **1** persuasive and glib. **2**
skilfully devised or carried out. **3** well-made and
attractive, but superficial. ◆ *noun* **4** patch of oil
on water. ◆ *verb* **5** make smooth or sleek.

——————— THESAURUS ———————

slaughterhouse *noun* =**abattoir**, butchery
slave *noun* **1** =**servant**, serf, vassal **3**
=**drudge**, skivvy (*chiefly Brit*) ◆*verb* **4** =**toil**,
drudge, slog
slavery *noun* **1** =**servitude**, bondage,
captivity **2** =**enslavement**, subjugation
slavish *adjective* **1** =**servile**, abject, base,
cringing, fawning, grovelling, obsequious,
submissive, sycophantic OPPOSITE assertive. **2**
=**imitative**, second-hand, unimaginative,
unoriginal OPPOSITE independent
slay *verb* =**kill**, butcher, massacre, mow down,
murder, slaughter
sleaze *noun* =**corruption**, bribery, dishonesty,
extortion, fraud, unscrupulousness, venality
sleazy *adjective* =**sordid**, disreputable, low,
run-down, scungy (*Aust & NZ sl*), seedy, squalid
sleek *adjective* **1** =**glossy**, lustrous, shiny,
smooth OPPOSITE rough
sleep *noun* **1, 2** =**slumber(s)**, doze, forty
winks (*inf*), hibernation, nap, siesta, snooze

(*inf*), zizz (*Brit inf*) ◆*verb* **3** =**slumber**, catnap,
doze, drowse, hibernate, snooze (*inf*), take a
nap
sleepless *adjective* =**wakeful**, insomniac,
restless
sleepy *adjective* **1** =**drowsy**, dull, heavy
OPPOSITE alert. **2** =**inactive**, lethargic, sluggish
OPPOSITE active
slender *adjective* **1** =**slim**, lean, narrow, slight,
willowy OPPOSITE fat. **2** =**meagre**, little, scant,
scanty, small OPPOSITE large
sleuth *noun* =**detective**, private eye (*inf*),
(private) investigator
slice *noun* **1, 2** =**piece**, cut, helping, portion,
segment, share, sliver, wedge ◆*verb* **5, 6** =**cut**,
carve, divide, sever
slick *adjective* **1** =**glib**, plausible, polished,
smooth, specious **2** =**skilful**, adroit, deft,
dexterous, polished, professional OPPOSITE
amateur ◆*verb* **5** =**smooth**, plaster down,
sleek

slide ⊙ *verb* **sliding, slid 1** slip smoothly along (a surface). **2** pass unobtrusively. **3** go into or become (something) by degrees, e.g. *the states slid into barbarism.* ♦ *noun* **4** sliding. **5** piece of glass holding an object to be viewed under a microscope. **6** photographic transparency. **7** surface or structure for sliding on or down. **8** ornamental hair clip. **9** sliding curved part of a trombone. **slide rule** mathematical instrument formerly used for rapid calculations. **sliding scale** variable scale according to which things such as wages alter in response to changes in other factors.

slight ⊙ *adjective* **1** small in quantity or extent. **2** not important. **3** slim and delicate. ♦ *verb, noun* **4** snub. **slightly** *adverb*

slim ⊙ *adjective* **slimmer, slimmest 1** not heavy or stout, thin. **2** slight. ♦ *verb* **slimming, slimmed 3** make or become slim by diet and exercise. **slimmer** *noun*

slime ⊙ *noun* unpleasant thick slippery substance. **slimy** *adjective* **slimier, slimiest 1** of, like, or covered with slime. **2** ingratiating.

sling¹ ⊙ *noun* **1** bandage hung from the neck to support an injured hand or arm. **2** rope or strap for lifting something. **3** strap with a string at each end for throwing a stone. ♦ *verb* **slinging, slung 4** throw. **5** carry, hang, or throw with or as if with a sling. **slingback** shoe with a strap that goes around the back of the heel.

sling² *noun* sweetened drink with a spirit base, e.g. *gin sling.*

slink ⊙ *verb* **slinking, slunk** move furtively or guiltily. **slinky** *adjective* **slinkier, slinkiest** (of clothes) figure-hugging.

slip¹ ⊙ *verb* **slipping, slipped 1** lose balance by sliding. **2** move smoothly, easily, or quietly. **3** place quickly or stealthily. **4** (foll. by *on* or *off*) put on or take off easily or quickly. **5** pass out of (the mind). **6** become worse. **7** dislocate (a bone). ♦ *noun* **8** slipping. **9** mistake. **10** petticoat. **11** *Cricket* fielding position behind and to the offside of the wicketkeeper. **give someone the slip** escape from someone. **slippy** *adjective Informal* slippery. **slipknot** *noun* knot tied so that it will slip along the rope round which it is made. **slip-on** *adjective* (of a garment or shoe) made to be put on easily. **slipped disc** painful condition in which one of the discs connecting the bones of the spine becomes displaced. **slip road** narrow road giving access to a motorway. **slipshod** *adjective* (of an action) careless. **slipstream** *noun* stream of air forced backwards by a fast-moving object. **slip up** *verb* make a mistake. **slipway** *noun* launching slope on which ships are built or repaired.

slip² ⊙ *noun* **1** small piece (of paper). **2** cutting from a plant. **3** slender person.

slip³ *noun* clay mixed with water used for decorating pottery.

slipper *noun* light shoe for indoor wear.

slippery ⊙ *adjective* **1** so smooth or wet as to cause slipping or be difficult to hold. **2** (of a person) untrustworthy.

slit ⊙ *noun* **1** long narrow cut or opening. ♦ *verb* **slitting, slit 2** make a long straight cut in.

——————— THESAURUS ———————

slide *verb* **1** = **slip**, coast, glide, skim, slither

slight *adjective* **2** = **small**, feeble, insignificant, meagre, measly, minor, paltry, scanty, trifling, trivial, unimportant OPPOSITE great. **3** = **slim**, delicate, feeble, fragile, lightly-built, small, spare OPPOSITE solid ♦*verb, noun* **4** = **snub**, affront, disdain, ignore, insult, rebuff, scorn, slap in the face (*inf*) OPPOSITE praise

slightly *adverb* **1** = **a little**, somewhat

slim *adjective* **1** = **slender**, lean, narrow, slight, svelte, thin, trim OPPOSITE wide. **2** = **slight**, faint, poor, remote, slender OPPOSITE good ♦*verb* **3** = **lose weight**, diet, reduce OPPOSITE put on weight

slimy *adjective* **1** = **viscous**, clammy, glutinous, oozy **2** = **obsequious**, creeping, grovelling, oily, servile, smarmy (*Brit inf*), unctuous

sling¹ *verb* **4** = **throw**, cast, chuck (*inf*), fling, heave, hurl, lob (*inf*), shy, toss **5** = **hang**, dangle, suspend

slink *verb* = **creep**, prowl, skulk, slip, sneak, steal

slinky *adjective* = **figure-hugging**, clinging, close-fitting, skintight

slip¹ *verb* **1** = **fall**, skid **2** = **slide**, glide, skate, slither **3** = **sneak**, conceal, creep, hide, steal ♦*noun* **9** = **mistake**, blunder, error, failure, fault, lapse, omission, oversight **give someone the slip** = **escape from**, dodge, elude, evade, get away from, lose (someone) **slip up** ♦*verb* = **make a mistake**, blunder, err, miscalculate

slip² *noun* **1** = **strip**, piece, sliver **2** = **cutting**, offshoot, runner, scion, shoot, sprig, sprout

slippery *adjective* **1** = **smooth**, glassy, greasy, icy, slippy (*inf*), unsafe **2** = **untrustworthy**, crafty, cunning, devious, dishonest, evasive, shifty, tricky

slipshod *adjective* = **careless**, casual, slapdash, sloppy (*inf*), slovenly, untidy

slit *noun* **1** = **cut**, gash, incision, opening, rent, split, tear ♦*verb* **2** = **cut (open)**, gash, knife, lance, pierce, rip, slash

S

slither ⊕ *verb* **1** slide unsteadily. **2** move in a twisting way.

sliver ⊕ [**sliv**-ver] *noun* **1** small thin piece. ◆ *verb* **2** cut into slivers.

slob ⊕ *noun Informal* lazy and untidy person. **slobbish** *adjective*

slobber ⊕ *verb* **1** dribble or drool. **2** behave in a gushy way. **slobbery** *adjective*

sloe *noun* sour blue-black fruit.

slog ⊕ *verb* **slogging, slogged 1** work hard and steadily. **2** make one's way with difficulty. **3** hit hard. ◆ *noun* **4** long and exhausting work or walk.

slogan ⊕ *noun* catchword or phrase used in politics or advertising.

sloop *noun* small single-masted ship.

slop ⊕ *verb* **slopping, slopped 1** splash or spill. ◆ *noun* **2** spilt liquid. **3** liquid food. ◆ *plural* **4** liquid refuse and waste food used to feed animals. **sloppy** *adjective* **-pier, -piest 1** careless or untidy. **2** gushingly sentimental.

slope ⊕ *verb* **1** slant. ◆ *noun* **2** sloping surface. **3** degree of inclination. ◆ *plural* **4** hills. **slope off** *verb Informal* go furtively.

slosh *verb* **1** pour carelessly. **2** splash carelessly. **3** *Slang* hit hard. ◆ *noun* **4** splashing sound. **sloshed** *adjective Slang* drunk.

slot ⊕ *noun* **1** narrow opening for inserting something. **2** *Informal* place in a series or scheme. ◆ *verb* **slotting, slotted 3** make a slot or slots in. **4** fit into a slot. **slot machine** automatic machine worked by placing a coin in a slot.

sloth ⊕ [rhymes with **both**] *noun* **1** slow-moving animal of tropical America. **2** laziness. **slothful** *adjective* lazy or idle.

slouch ⊕ *verb* **1** sit, stand, or move with a drooping posture. ◆ *noun* **2** drooping posture. **be no slouch** *Informal* be very good or talented.

slough¹ [rhymes with **now**] *noun* bog.

slough² [**sluff**] *verb* **1** (of a snake) shed (its skin) or (of a skin) be shed. ◆ *noun* **2** outer covering that has been shed. **slough off** *verb* get rid of (something unwanted or unnecessary).

Slovak *adjective, noun* **1** (person) from Slovakia. ◆ *noun* **2** language of Slovakia.

sloven ⊕ *noun* habitually dirty or untidy person. **slovenly** *adjective* **1** dirty or untidy. **2** careless.

Slovene *adjective, noun* **1** (also **Slovenian**) (person) from Slovenia. ◆ *noun* **2** language of Slovenia.

slovenly ⊕ *adjective* **1** dirty or untidy. **2** careless.

slow ⊕ *adjective* **1** taking a longer time than is usual or expected. **2** not fast. **3** (of a clock or watch) showing a time earlier than the correct one. **4** stupid. **5** dull or uninteresting. ◆ *adverb* **6** slowly. ◆ *verb* **7** reduce the speed (of). **slowly** *adverb* **slowness** *noun* **slowcoach** *noun Informal* person who moves or works slowly. **slow motion** movement on film made to appear much slower than it actually is.

slowworm *noun* small legless lizard.

——————— T H E S A U R U S ———————

slither *verb* **1 = slide**, glide, slink, slip **2 = undulate**, snake

sliver *noun* **1 = shred**, fragment, paring, shaving, splinter

slob *noun Inf =* **layabout**, couch potato (*sl*), good-for-nothing, idler, loafer, lounger

slobber *verb* **1 = drool**, dribble, drivel, salivate, slaver

slobbish *adjective Inf =* **messy**, slovenly, unclean, unkempt, untidy

slog *verb* **1 = work**, labour, plod, plough through, slave, toil **2 = trudge**, tramp, trek **3 = hit**, punch, slug, sock (*sl*), strike, thump, wallop (*inf*) ◆*noun* **4 a = labour**, effort, exertion, struggle **b = trudge**, hike, tramp, trek

slogan *noun =* **catch phrase**, catchword, motto, tag-line

slop *verb* **1 = spill**, overflow, slosh (*inf*), splash

slope *verb* **1 = slant**, drop away, fall, incline, lean, rise, tilt ◆*noun* **2 = incline**, ramp, rise, slant, tilt **3 = inclination**, gradient **slope off** ◆*verb Inf =* **slink away**, creep away, slip away

sloppy *adjective* **1** *Inf =* **careless**, messy, slipshod, slovenly, untidy **2 = sentimental**, gushing, icky (*inf*), mawkish, slushy (*inf*), soppy (*Brit inf*)

slot *noun* **1 = opening**, aperture, groove, hole, slit, vent **2** *Inf =* **place**, opening, position, space, time, vacancy ◆*verb* **4 = fit in**, fit, insert

sloth *noun* **2 = laziness**, idleness, inactivity, inertia, slackness, sluggishness, torpor

slothful *adjective =* **lazy**, idle, inactive, indolent, skiving (*Brit sl*), workshy

slouch *verb* **1 = slump**, droop, loll, stoop

slovenly *adjective* **1 = untidy**, disorderly **2 = careless**, negligent, slack, slapdash, slipshod, sloppy (*inf*) OPPOSITE careful

slow *adjective* **1 = late**, backward, behind, delayed, lingering, long-drawn-out, prolonged, protracted, tardy **2 = unhurried**, dawdling, gradual, lackadaisical, laggard, lazy, leisurely, ponderous, sluggish OPPOSITE quick. **4 = stupid**, braindead (*inf*), dense, dim, dozy (*Brit inf*), dull-witted, obtuse, retarded, thick

S

sludge ⊙ *noun* **1** thick mud. **2** sewage.
slug[1] ⊙ *noun* land snail with no shell. **sluggish**
adjective slow-moving, lacking energy.
sluggishly *adverb* **sluggishness** *noun*
sluggard *noun* lazy person.
slug[2] *noun* **1** bullet. **2** *Informal* mouthful of an
alcoholic drink.
slug[3] *verb* **slugging, slugged 1** hit hard. ♦
noun **2** heavy blow.
sluice *noun* **1** channel carrying off water. **2**
sliding gate used to control the flow of water in
this. **3** water controlled by a sluice. ♦ *verb* **4**
pour a stream of water over or through.
slum ⊙ *noun* **1** squalid overcrowded house or
area. ♦ *verb* **slumming, slummed 2** temporarily
and deliberately experience poorer places or
conditions than usual. **slummy** *adjective*
slumber ⊙ *verb, noun Lit* sleep.
slump ⊙ *verb* **1** (of prices or demand) decline
suddenly. **2** sink or fall heavily. ♦ *noun* **3** sudden
decline in prices or demand. **4** time of
substantial unemployment.
slung *verb* past of SLING[1].
slunk *verb* past of SLINK.
slur ⊙ *verb* **slurring, slurred 1** pronounce or
utter (words) indistinctly. **2** disparage. **3** *Music*
sing or play (notes) smoothly without a break.
4 treat carelessly. ♦ *noun* **5** slurring of words. **6**
remark intended to discredit someone. **7** *Music*
slurring of notes. **8** curved line indicating notes
to be slurred.
slurp *Informal verb* **1** eat or drink noisily. ♦
noun **2** slurping sound.
slurry *noun, pl* **-ries** muddy liquid mixture.
slush *noun* **1** watery muddy substance. **2**

sloppy sentimental talk or writing. **slushy**
adjective **slush fund** fund for financing bribery
or corruption.
slut ⊙ *noun Offens* dirty or immoral woman.
sluttish *adjective*
sly ⊙ *adjective* **slyer, slyest** or **slier, sliest 1**
crafty. **2** secretive and cunning. **3** roguish. **on
the sly** secretly. **slyly** *adverb* **slyness** *noun*
Sm *Chem* samarium.
smack[1] ⊙ *verb* **1** slap sharply. **2** open and
close (the lips) loudly in enjoyment or
anticipation. ♦ *noun* **3** sharp slap. **4** loud kiss. **5**
slapping sound. ♦ *adverb* **6** *Informal* squarely or
directly, e.g. *smack in the middle*. **smacker**
noun Slang **1** loud kiss. **2** pound note or dollar
bill.
smack[2] *noun* **1** slight flavour or trace. **2** *Slang*
heroin. ♦ *verb* **3** have a slight flavour or trace
(of).
smack[3] *noun* small single-masted fishing boat.
small ⊙ *adjective* **1** not large in size, number,
or amount. **2** unimportant. **3** mean or petty. ♦
noun **4** narrow part of the lower back. ♦ *plural* **5**
Informal underwear. ♦ *adverb* **6** into small
pieces. **smallness** *noun* **small change** coins of
low value. **smallholding** *noun* small area of
farming land. **small hours** hours just after
midnight. **small-minded** *adjective* intolerant,
petty. **smallpox** *noun* contagious disease with
blisters that leave scars. **small talk** light social
conversation. **small-time** *adjective* insignificant
or minor.
smarmy ⊙ *adjective* **smarmier, smarmiest**
Informal unpleasantly suave or flattering.
smart ⊙ *adjective* **1** well-kept and neat. **2**

———————— THESAURUS ————————

OPPOSITE⟩ **bright** ♦*verb* **7 = reduce speed**,
brake, decelerate, handicap, hold up, retard,
slacken (off) OPPOSITE⟩ **accelerate**
slowly *adverb* **2 = gradually**, leisurely,
unhurriedly
sludge *noun* **1 = sediment**, mire, muck, mud,
ooze, residue, silt, slime
sluggish *adjective* **= inactive**, dull, heavy,
indolent, inert, lethargic, slothful, slow, torpid
slum *noun* **1 = hovel**, ghetto
slumber *verb Lit* **= sleep**, doze, drowse, nap,
snooze (*inf*), zizz (*Brit inf*)
slump *verb* **1 = fall**, collapse, crash, plunge,
sink, slip OPPOSITE⟩ **increase. 2 = sag**, droop,
hunch, loll, slouch ♦*noun* **3 = fall**, collapse,
crash, decline, downturn, drop, reverse, trough
OPPOSITE⟩ **increase. 4 = recession**, depression
slur *noun* **6 = insult**, affront, aspersion,
calumny, innuendo, insinuation, smear, stain
slut *noun Offens* **= tart**, scrubber (*Brit & Aust*

sl), slag (*Brit sl*), slapper (*Brit sl*), trollop
sly *adjective* **1, 2 = cunning**, artful, clever,
crafty, devious, scheming, secret, shifty,
stealthy, subtle, underhand, wily OPPOSITE⟩
open. 3 = roguish, arch, impish, knowing,
mischievous **on the sly = secretly**, covertly, on
the quiet, privately, surreptitiously
smack[1] *verb* **1 = slap**, clap, cuff, hit, spank,
strike, swipe ♦*noun* **3 = slap**, blow, swipe
♦*adverb* **6** *Inf* **= directly**, exactly, precisely, right,
slap (*inf*), squarely, straight
small *adjective* **1 = little**, diminutive, mini,
miniature, minute, petite, pygmy or pigmy,
teeny, teeny-weeny, tiny, undersized, wee
OPPOSITE⟩ **great. 2 = unimportant**, insignificant,
minor, negligible, paltry, petty, trifling, trivial
OPPOSITE⟩ **major. 3 = petty**, base, mean, narrow
small-minded *adjective* **= petty**, bigoted,
intolerant, mean, narrow-minded, ungenerous
small-time *adjective* **= minor**, insignificant, of

S

astute. **3** witty. **4** fashionable. **5** brisk. **6** causing a stinging pain. ◆ *verb* **7** feel or cause stinging pain. ◆ *noun* **8** stinging pain. **smartly** *adverb* **smartness** *noun* **smart aleck** *Informal* irritatingly clever person. **smart card** plastic card used for storing and processing computer data. **smarten** *verb* make or become smart. **smash** ❶ *verb* **1** break violently and noisily. **2** throw (against) violently. **3** collide forcefully. **4** destroy. ◆ *noun* **5** act or sound of smashing. **6** violent collision of vehicles. **7** *Informal* popular success. **8** *Sport* powerful overhead shot. ◆ *adverb* **9** with a smash. **smasher** *noun Informal* attractive person or thing. **smashing** *adjective Informal* excellent.

smattering ❶ *noun* slight knowledge.

smear ❶ *verb* **1** spread with a greasy or sticky substance. **2** rub so as to produce a dirty mark or smudge. **3** slander. ◆ *noun* **4** dirty mark or smudge. **5** slander. **6** *Med* sample of a secretion smeared on to a slide for examination under a microscope. **smear test** *Med* examination of stained cells in a specimen taken from the neck or lining of the womb for detection of cancer.

smell ❶ *verb* **smelling, smelt** or **smelled 1** perceive (a scent or odour) by means of the nose. **2** have or give off a smell. **3** have an unpleasant smell. **4** detect by instinct. **5** (foll. by *of*) indicate, suggest. ◆ *noun* **6** ability to perceive odours by the nose. **7** odour or scent. **8** smelling. **smelly** *adjective* having a nasty smell. **smelling salts** preparation of ammonia used to revive a person who feels faint.

smelt¹ *verb* extract (a metal) from (an ore) by heating. **smelter** *noun*

smelt² *noun* small fish of the salmon family.

smelt³ *verb* a past of SMELL.

smile *noun* **1** turning up of the corners of the mouth to show pleasure, amusement, or friendliness. ◆ *verb* **2** give a smile. **3** express by a smile. **smile on, upon** *verb* regard favourably.

smirch *verb, noun* disgrace.

smirk ❶ *noun* **1** smug smile. ◆ *verb* **2** give a smirk.

smite ❶ *verb* **smiting, smote, smitten 1** *Old-fashioned* strike hard. **2** affect severely.

smith *noun* worker in metal. **smithy** *noun* blacksmith's workshop.

smithereens *plural noun* shattered fragments.

smitten ❶ *verb* **1** past participle of SMITE. ◆ *adjective* **2** affected by love.

smock *noun* **1** loose overall. **2** woman's loose blouselike garment. ◆ *verb* **3** gather (material) by sewing in a honeycomb pattern. **smocking** *noun*

smog *noun* mixture of smoke and fog.

smoke *noun* **1** cloudy mass that rises from something burning. **2** act of smoking tobacco. **3** *Informal* cigarette or cigar. ◆ *verb* **4** give off smoke. **5** inhale and expel smoke of (a cigar, cigarette, or pipe). **6** do this habitually. **7** cure (meat, fish, or cheese) by treating with smoke. **smokeless** *adjective* **smoker** *noun* **smoky** *adjective* **smoke out** *verb* drive out of hiding, esp. by using smoke. **smoke screen** something said or done to hide the truth. **smokestack** *noun* tall chimney of a factory.

smolt *noun* young salmon at the stage when it migrates to the sea.

smooch *Informal verb* **1** kiss and cuddle. ◆

——————— THESAURUS ———————

no account, petty, unimportant

smarmy *adjective Inf* =**obsequious**, crawling, ingratiating, servile, smooth, suave, sycophantic, toadying, unctuous

smart *adjective* **1** =**neat**, spruce, trim **2** =**astute**, acute, bright, canny, clever, ingenious, intelligent, keen, shrewd OPPOSITE thick. **3** =**sharp**, quick **4** =**chic**, elegant, natty (*inf*), snappy, stylish OPPOSITE scruffy. **5** =**brisk**, lively, quick, vigorous ◆*verb* **7** =**sting**, burn, hurt ◆*noun* **8** =**sting**, pain, soreness

smart aleck *noun Inf* =**know-all** (*inf*), clever-clogs (*inf*), smarty pants (*inf*), wise guy (*inf*)

smarten *verb* =**tidy**, groom, put in order, put to rights, spruce up

smash *verb* **1** =**break**, crush, demolish, pulverize, shatter **3** =**collide**, crash **4** =**destroy**, lay waste, ruin, trash (*sl*), wreck ◆*noun* **5** =**destruction**, collapse, downfall, failure, ruin **6** =**collision**, accident, crash

smashing *adjective Inf* =**excellent**, awesome (*sl*), brilliant (*inf*), cracking (*Brit inf*), fabulous (*inf*), fantastic (*inf*), great (*inf*), magnificent, marvellous, mean (*sl*), sensational (*inf*), super (*inf*), superb, terrific (*inf*), wonderful

smattering *noun* =**modicum**, bit, rudiments

smear *verb* **1** =**spread over**, bedaub, coat, cover, daub, rub on **2** =**dirty**, smudge, soil, stain, sully **3** =**slander**, besmirch, blacken, malign ◆*noun* **4** =**smudge**, blot, blotch, daub, splotch, streak **5** =**slander**, calumny, defamation, libel

smell *verb* **1** =**sniff**, scent **3** =**stink**, pong (*Brit inf*), reek ◆*noun* **7** =**odour**, aroma, bouquet, fragrance, perfume, scent

smelly *adjective* =**stinking**, fetid, foul, foul-smelling, malodorous, noisome, reeking

smirk *noun* **1** =**smug look**, simper

smitten *adjective* **2** =**infatuated**, beguiled, bewitched, captivated, charmed, enamoured noun **2** smooching.

smooth ❶ *adjective* **1** even in surface, texture, or consistency. **2** without obstructions or difficulties. **3** charming and polite but possibly insincere. **4** free from jolts. **5** not harsh in taste. ◆ *verb* **6** make smooth. **7** calm. **smoothly** *adverb*

smorgasbord *noun* buffet meal of assorted dishes.

smote *verb* past tense of SMITE.

smother ❶ *verb* **1** suffocate or stifle. **2** surround or overwhelm (with). **3** suppress. **4** cover thickly.

smoulder ❶ *verb* **1** burn slowly with smoke but no flame. **2** (of feelings) exist in a suppressed state.

SMS short message system: used for sending data to mobile phones.

smudge ❶ *verb* **1** make or become smeared or soiled. ◆ *noun* **2** dirty mark. **3** blurred form. **smudgy** *adjective*

smug ❶ *adjective* **smugger, smuggest** self-satisfied. **smugly** *adverb* **smugness** *noun*

smuggle ❶ *verb* **1** import or export (goods) secretly and illegally. **2** take somewhere secretly. **smuggler** *noun*

smut ❶ *noun* **1** obscene jokes, pictures, etc. **2** speck of soot or dark mark left by soot. **3** fungal disease of cereals. **smutty** *adjective*

Sn *Chem* tin.

snack ❶ *noun* light quick meal. **snack bar** place where snacks are sold.

snaffle *noun* **1** jointed bit for a horse. ◆ *verb* **2** *Slang* steal.

snag ❶ *noun* **1** difficulty or disadvantage. **2** sharp projecting point. **3** hole in fabric caused by a sharp object. ◆ *verb* **snagging, snagged 4** catch or tear on a point.

snail *noun* slow-moving mollusc with a spiral shell. **snail mail** *Informal* conventional post, as opposed to e-mail. **snail's pace** very slow speed.

snake *noun* **1** long thin scaly limbless reptile. ◆ *verb* **2** move in a winding course like a snake. **snake in the grass** treacherous person. **snaky** *adjective* twisted or winding.

snap ❶ *verb* **snapping, snapped 1** break suddenly. **2** (cause to) make a sharp cracking sound. **3** move suddenly. **4** bite (at) suddenly. **5** speak sharply and angrily. **6** take a snapshot of. ◆ *noun* **7** act or sound of snapping. **8** fastener that closes with a snapping sound. **9** *Informal* snapshot. **10** thin crisp biscuit. **11** sudden brief spell of cold weather. **12** card game in which the word 'snap' is called when two similar cards are put down. ◆ *adjective* **13** made on the spur of the moment. ◆ *adverb* **14** with a snap. **snappy** *adjective* **1** (also **snappish**) irritable. **2** *Slang* quick. **3** *Slang* smart and fashionable. **snapdragon** *noun* plant with flowers that can open and shut like a mouth. **snapper** *noun* food fish of Australia and New Zealand with a pinkish body covered with blue spots. **snapshot** *noun* informal photograph. **snap up** *verb* take eagerly and quickly.

snare¹ ❶ *noun* **1** trap with a noose. ◆ *verb* **2** catch in or as if in a snare.

snare² *noun Music* set of gut strings wound with wire fitted across the bottom of a drum to

——————————— T H E S A U R U S ———————————

smooth *adjective* **1** = **even**, flat, flush, horizontal, level, plane OPPOSITE **rough. 2** = **easy**, effortless, well-ordered **3** = **suave**, facile, glib, persuasive, slick, smarmy (*Brit inf*), unctuous, urbane **4** = **flowing**, regular, rhythmic, steady, uniform **5** = **mellow**, agreeable, mild, pleasant ◆*verb* **6** = **flatten**, iron, level, plane, press **7** = **ease**, appease, assuage, calm, mitigate, mollify, soften, soothe OPPOSITE **aggravate**

smother *verb* **1 a** = **suffocate**, choke, strangle **b** = **extinguish**, snuff, stifle **3** = **suppress**, conceal, hide, muffle, repress, stifle

smoulder *verb* **2** = **seethe**, boil, fume, rage, simmer

smudge *verb* **1** = **smear**, daub, dirty, mark, smirch ◆*noun* **2** = **smear**, blemish, blot

smug *adjective* = **self-satisfied**, complacent, conceited, superior

smuggler *noun* **1** = **trafficker**, bootlegger, runner

smutty *adjective* **1** = **obscene**, bawdy, blue, coarse, crude, dirty, indecent, indelicate, scungy (*Aust & NZ sl*), suggestive, vulgar

snack *noun* = **light meal**, bite, refreshment(s)

snag *noun* **1** = **difficulty**, catch, complication, disadvantage, downside, drawback, hitch, obstacle, problem ◆*verb* **4** = **catch**, rip, tear

snap *verb* **1** = **break**, crack, separate **2** = **crackle**, click, pop **4** = **bite at**, bite, nip, snatch **5** = **speak sharply**, bark, jump down (someone's) throat (*inf*), lash out at ◆*noun* **7** = **crackle**, pop ◆*adjective* **13** = **instant**, immediate, spur-of-the-moment, sudden

snappy *adjective* **1** (also **snappish**) = **irritable**, cross, edgy, pissed (*taboo sl*), pissed off (*taboo sl*), ratty (*Brit & NZ inf*), testy, tetchy, touchy **3** *Sl* = **smart**, chic, dapper, fashionable, natty (*inf*), stylish

snap up *verb* = **take advantage of**, grab,

increase vibration. **snare drum** cylindrical double-headed drum with snares.

snarl[1] verb **1** (of an animal) growl with bared teeth. **2** speak or utter fiercely. ♦ noun **3** act or sound of snarling.

snarl[2] ⊕ noun **1** tangled mess. ♦ verb **2** make tangled. **snarl-up** noun Informal confused situation such as a traffic jam.

snatch ⊕ verb **1** seize or try to seize suddenly. **2** take (food, rest, etc.) hurriedly. **3** remove suddenly. ♦ noun **4** snatching. **5** fragment.

snazzy adjective **-zier, -ziest** Informal stylish and flashy.

sneak ⊕ verb **1** move furtively. **2** bring, take, or put furtively. **3** Informal tell tales. ♦ noun **4** cowardly or underhand person. **sneaking** adjective **1** slight but persistent. **2** secret. **sneaky** adjective

sneakers plural noun US & Canad canvas shoes with rubber soles.

sneer ⊕ noun **1** contemptuous expression or remark. ♦ verb **2** show contempt by a sneer.

sneeze verb **1** expel air from the nose suddenly, involuntarily, and noisily. ♦ noun **2** act or sound of sneezing. **sneeze at** verb Informal dismiss lightly.

snib noun Scot catch of a door or window.

snick verb, noun (make) a small cut or notch.

snicker noun, verb same as SNIGGER.

snide ⊕ adjective critical in an unfair and nasty way.

sniff ⊕ verb **1** inhale through the nose in short audible breaths. **2** smell by sniffing. ♦ noun **3**

act or sound of sniffing. **sniffle** verb **1** sniff repeatedly, as when suffering from a cold. ♦ noun **2** slight cold. **sniff at** verb express contempt for. **sniffer dog** police dog trained to detect drugs or explosives by smell.

snifter noun Informal small quantity of alcoholic drink.

snigger ⊕ noun **1** sly disrespectful laugh, esp. one partly stifled. ♦ verb **2** utter a snigger.

snip ⊕ verb **snipping, snipped 1** cut in small quick strokes with scissors or shears. ♦ noun **2** Informal bargain. **3** act or sound of snipping. **4** piece snipped off. **snippet** noun small piece.

snipe ⊕ noun **1** wading bird with a long straight bill. ♦ verb **2** (foll. by at) shoot at (a person) from cover. **3** make critical remarks about. **sniper** noun

snitch Informal verb **1** act as an informer. **2** steal. ♦ noun **3** informer.

snivel ⊕ verb **-elling, -elled 1** cry in a whining way. **2** have a runny nose.

snob ⊕ noun **1** person who judges others by social rank. **2** person who feels smugly superior in his or her tastes or interests. **snobbery** noun **snobbish** adjective

snog verb **snogging, snogged** Informal kiss and cuddle.

snood noun pouch, often of net, loosely holding a woman's hair at the back.

snook noun **cock a snook at** show contempt for.

snooker noun **1** game played on a billiard table. ♦ verb **2** leave (a snooker opponent) in a

pounce upon, seize

snare[1] noun **1** = **trap**, gin, net, noose, wire ♦ verb **2** = **trap**, catch, entrap, net, seize, wire

snarl[2] verb **2** = **tangle**, entangle, entwine, muddle, ravel

snarl-up noun Inf = **tangle**, confusion, entanglement, muddle

snatch verb **1** = **seize**, clutch, grab, grasp, grip **2** = **grab** ♦ noun **5** = **bit**, fragment, part, piece, snippet

sneak verb **1** = **slink**, lurk, pad, skulk, slip, steal **2** = **slip**, smuggle, spirit **3** Inf = **inform on**, grass on (Brit sl), shop (sl, chiefly Brit), tell on (inf), tell tales ♦ noun **4** = **informer**, telltale

sneaking adjective **1** = **nagging**, persistent, uncomfortable, worrying **2** = **secret**, hidden, private, undivulged, unexpressed, unvoiced

sneaky adjective = **sly**, deceitful, devious, dishonest, double-dealing, furtive, low, mean, shifty, untrustworthy

sneer noun **1** = **scorn**, derision, gibe, jeer, mockery, ridicule ♦ verb **2** = **scorn**, deride,

disdain, jeer, laugh, mock, ridicule

snide adjective = **nasty**, cynical, disparaging, hurtful, ill-natured, malicious, sarcastic, scornful, sneering, spiteful

sniff verb **1, 2** = **inhale**, breathe, smell

snigger noun, verb = **laugh**, giggle, snicker, titter

snip verb **1** = **cut**, clip, crop, dock, shave, trim ♦ noun **2** Inf = **bargain**, giveaway, good buy, steal (inf) **4** = **bit**, clipping, fragment, piece, scrap, shred

snipe verb **3** = **criticize**, carp, denigrate, disparage, jeer, knock (inf), put down

snippet noun = **piece**, fragment, part, scrap, shred

snivel verb **1** = **whine**, cry, grizzle (inf, chiefly Brit), moan, whimper, whinge (inf) **2** = **sniffle**

snob noun = **elitist**, highbrow, prig

snobbery noun = **arrogance**, airs, pretension, pride, snobbishness

snobbish adjective = **superior**, arrogant, patronizing, pretentious, snooty (inf), stuck-up position such that another ball blocks the target ball. **3** *Informal* put (someone) in a position where he or she can do nothing.

snoop ⊙ *Informal verb* **1** pry. ◆ *noun* **2** snooping. **snooper** *noun*

snooty *adjective* **snootier, snootiest** *Informal* haughty.

snooze ⊙ *Informal verb* **1** take a brief light sleep. ◆ *noun* **2** brief light sleep.

snore *verb* **1** make snorting sounds while sleeping. ◆ *noun* **2** sound of snoring.

snorkel *noun* **1** tube allowing a swimmer to breathe while face down on the surface of the water. **2** device supplying air to a submarine when under water. ◆ *verb* **-kelling, -kelled 3** swim using a snorkel.

snort *verb* **1** exhale noisily through the nostrils. **2** express contempt or anger by snorting. **3** say with a snort. ◆ *noun* **4** act or sound of snorting. **5** *Informal* small drink of alcohol.

snot *noun Slang* mucus from the nose. **snotty** *adjective Slang* **1** covered with mucus from the nose. **2** haughty.

snout *noun* animal's projecting nose and jaws.

snow *noun* **1** frozen vapour falling from the sky in flakes. **2** *Slang* cocaine. ◆ *verb* **3** fall as or like snow. **be snowed under** be overwhelmed, esp. with paperwork. **snowy** *adjective*

snowball *noun* **1** snow pressed into a ball for throwing. ◆ *verb* **2** increase rapidly. **snow-blind** *adjective* temporarily blinded by the brightness of the sun on snow. **snowboard** *noun* board on which a person stands to slide across the snow. **snowboarding** *noun* **snowbound** *adjective* shut in by snow. **snowdrift** *noun* bank of deep snow. **snowdrop** *noun* small white bell-shaped spring flower. **snowflake** *noun* single crystal of snow. **snow gum** same as SALLEE. **snow line** (on a mountain) height above which there is permanent snow. **snowman** *noun* figure shaped out of snow. **snowplough** *noun* vehicle for clearing away snow.

snowshoes *plural noun* racket-shaped shoes for travelling on snow.

SNP Scottish National Party.

snub ⊙ *verb* **snubbing, snubbed 1** insult deliberately. ◆ *noun* **2** deliberate insult. ◆ *adjective* **3** (of a nose) short and blunt. **snub-nosed** *adjective*

snuff[1] *noun* powdered tobacco for sniffing up the nostrils.

snuff[2] *verb* extinguish (a candle). **snuff it** *Informal* die. **snuff out** *verb Informal* put an end to.

snuff[3] *verb* take in air through the nose.

snuffle *verb* **1** breathe noisily or with difficulty. **2** speak through the nose.

snug ⊙ *adjective* **snugger, snuggest 1** warm and comfortable. **2** comfortably close-fitting. ◆ *noun* **3** small room in a pub. **snugly** *adverb*

snuggle ⊙ *verb* nestle into a person or thing for warmth or from affection.

so[1] *adverb* **1** to such an extent. **2** in such a manner. **3** very. **4** also. **5** thereupon. ◆ *conjunction* **6** in order that. **7** with the result that. **8** therefore. ◆ *interjection* **9** exclamation of surprise, triumph, or realization. **or so** approximately. **so-and-so** *noun* **1** *Informal* person whose name is not specified. **2** unpleasant person or thing. **so-called** *adjective* called (in the speaker's opinion, wrongly) by that name. **so long** goodbye. **so that** in order that.

so[2] *noun Music* same as SOH.

soak ⊙ *verb* **1** make wet. **2** put or lie in liquid so as to become thoroughly wet. **3** (of liquid) penetrate. ◆ *noun* **4** soaking. **5** *Slang* drunkard. **soaking** *noun, adjective* **soak up** *verb* absorb.

soap *noun* **1** compound of alkali and fat, used with water as a cleaning agent. **2** *Informal* soap opera. ◆ *verb* **3** apply soap to. **soapy** *adjective* **soapbox** *noun* crate used as a platform for speech-making. **soap opera** radio or television serial dealing with domestic themes.

soapstone *noun* soft mineral used for making table tops and ornaments.

soar ⊙ *verb* **1** rise or fly upwards. **2** increase suddenly.

sob ⊙ *verb* **sobbing, sobbed 1** weep with

S

——————————————— THESAURUS ———————————————

(*inf*)

snoop *Inf verb* **1** = **pry**, interfere, poke one's nose in (*inf*), spy

snooper *noun* = **nosy parker** (*inf*), busybody, meddler, snoop (*inf*)

snooze *Inf verb* **1** = **doze**, catnap, nap, take forty winks (*inf*) ◆*noun* **2** = **doze**, catnap, forty winks (*inf*), nap, siesta

snub *verb* **1** = **insult**, cold-shoulder, cut (*inf*), humiliate, put down, rebuff, slight ◆*noun* **2**

= **insult**, affront, put-down, slap in the face

snug *adjective* **1** = **cosy**, comfortable, comfy (*inf*), warm

snuggle *verb* = **nestle**, cuddle, nuzzle

soak *verb* **1, 2** = **wet**, bathe, damp, drench, immerse, moisten, saturate, steep **3** = **penetrate**, permeate, seep **soak up** = **absorb**, assimilate

soaking *adjective* = **soaked**, drenched, dripping, saturated, sodden, sopping, convulsive gasps. **2** utter with sobs. ♦ *noun* **3** act or sound of sobbing. **sob story** tale of personal distress told to arouse sympathy.

sober ⓘ *adjective* **1** not drunk. **2** temperate. **3** serious. **4** (of colours) plain and dull. ♦ *verb* **5** make or become sober. **soberly** *adverb*

sobriety *noun* state of being sober.

sobriquet [so-brik-ay] *noun* nickname.

Soc. Society.

soccer *noun* football played by two teams of eleven kicking a spherical ball.

sociable ⓘ *adjective* **1** friendly or companionable. **2** (of an occasion) providing companionship. **sociability** *noun* **sociably** *adverb*

social ⓘ *adjective* **1** living in a community. **2** of society or its organization. **3** of the behaviour of people living in groups. **4** sociable. ♦ *noun* **5** informal gathering. **socially** *adverb* **socialize** *verb* **1** meet others socially. **2** prepare for life in society. **socialite** *noun* member of fashionable society. **social democrat** socialist who believes in the gradual transformation of capitalism into democratic socialism. **social science** scientific study of society and its relationships. **social security** state provision for the unemployed, aged, or sick. **social services** welfare services provided by the local authorities. **social work** work which involves helping people with serious financial or family problems.

socialism *noun* political system which advocates public ownership of industries, resources, and transport. **socialist** *noun*, *adjective*

society ⓘ *noun, pl* **-ties 1** human beings considered as a group. **2** organized community. **3** structure and institutions of such a community. **4** organized group with common aims and interests. **5** upper-class or fashionable people collectively. **6** companionship.

sociology *noun* study of human societies. **sociological** *adjective* **sociologist** *noun*

sock[1] *noun* cloth covering for the foot.

sock[2] *Slang verb* **1** hit hard. ♦ *noun* **2** hard blow.

socket *noun* hole or recess into which something fits.

sod[1] *noun* (piece of) turf.

sod[2] *noun Slang* obnoxious person.

soda *noun* **1** compound of sodium. **2** soda water. **soda water** fizzy drink made from water charged with carbon dioxide.

sodden ⓘ *adjective* **1** soaked. **2** dulled, esp. by drink.

sodium *noun Chem* silvery-white metallic element. **sodium bicarbonate** white soluble compound used in baking powder. **sodium hydroxide** white alkaline substance used in making paper and soap.

sodomy *noun* anal intercourse. **sodomite** *noun* person who practises sodomy.

sofa ⓘ *noun* couch.

soft ⓘ *adjective* **1** easy to shape or cut. **2** not hard, rough, or harsh. **3** (of a breeze or climate) mild. **4** (too) lenient. **5** easily influenced or imposed upon. **6** feeble or silly. **7** not robust. **8** (of drugs) not liable to cause addiction. **9** *Informal* easy. **10** (of water) containing few mineral salts. ♦ *adverb* **11** softly. **softly** *adverb* **soften** *verb* **1** make or become soft or softer. **2** make or become more gentle. **softie, softy** *noun Informal* person who is easily upset. **soft drink** nonalcoholic drink. **soft furnishings** curtains, rugs, lampshades, and

S

streaming, wet through, wringing wet

soar *verb* **1** = **ascend**, fly, mount, rise, wing OPPOSITE **fall. 2** = **rise**, climb, escalate, rocket, shoot up

sob *verb* **1** = **cry**, howl, shed tears, weep

sober *adjective* **2** = **abstinent**, abstemious, moderate, temperate OPPOSITE **drunk. 3** = **serious**, composed, cool, grave, level-headed, rational, reasonable, sedate, solemn, staid, steady OPPOSITE **unrealistic. 4** = **plain**, dark, drab, quiet, sombre, subdued OPPOSITE **bright**

sobriety *noun* **2** = **abstinence**, abstemiousness, moderation, nonindulgence, soberness, temperance **3** = **seriousness**, gravity, level-headedness, solemnity, staidness, steadiness

so-called *adjective* = **alleged**, pretended, professed, self-styled, supposed

sociable *adjective* **1** = **friendly**, affable, companionable, convivial, cordial, genial, gregarious, outgoing, social, warm OPPOSITE **unsociable**

social *adjective* **2** = **communal**, collective, common, community, general, group, public ♦*noun* **5** = **get-together** (*inf*), gathering, party

socialize *verb* **1** = **mix**, fraternize, get about *or* around, go out

society *noun* **1** = **civilization**, humanity, mankind, people, the community, the public **4** = **organization**, association, circle, club, fellowship, group, guild, institute, league, order, union **5** = **upper classes**, beau monde, elite, gentry, high society **6** = **companionship**, company, fellowship, friendship

sodden *adjective* **1** = **soaked**, drenched, saturated, soggy, sopping, waterlogged furniture covers. **soft option** easiest alternative. **soft-pedal** verb deliberately avoid emphasizing something. **soft-soap** verb Informal flatter. **soft touch** Informal person easily persuaded, esp. to lend money. **software** noun computer programs. **softwood** noun wood of a coniferous tree.

soggy ❶ adjective -gier, -giest 1 soaked. 2 moist and heavy. **sogginess** noun

soh noun Music (in tonic sol-fa) fifth degree of any major scale.

soigné, (fem) **soignée** [swah-nyay] adjective well-groomed, elegant.

soil[1] ❶ noun 1 top layer of earth. 2 country or territory.

soil[2] ❶ verb 1 make or become dirty. 2 disgrace. ♦ noun 3 soiled spot. 4 refuse.

soiree [swah-ray] noun evening party or gathering.

sojourn [soj-urn] noun 1 temporary stay. ♦ verb 2 stay temporarily.

sol noun Music same as SOH.

solace ❶ [sol-iss] noun, verb comfort in distress.

solar adjective 1 of the sun. 2 using the energy of the sun. **solar plexus 1** network of nerves at the pit of the stomach. **2** this part of the stomach. **solar system** the sun and the heavenly bodies that go round it.

solarium noun, pl **-lariums, -laria** place with beds and ultraviolet lights used for acquiring an artificial suntan.

sold verb past of SELL.

solder noun 1 soft alloy used to join two metal surfaces. ♦ verb 2 join with solder.

soldering iron tool for melting and applying solder.

soldier ❶ noun 1 member of an army. ♦ verb 2 serve in an army. **soldierly** adjective **soldier on** verb persist doggedly.

sole[1] ❶ adjective 1 one and only. 2 not shared, exclusive. **solely** adverb 1 only, completely. 2 alone.

sole[2] noun 1 underside of the foot. 2 underside of a shoe. 3 lower surface of something. ♦ verb 4 provide (a shoe) with a sole.

sole[3] noun small edible flatfish.

solecism [sol-iss-izz-um] noun 1 minor grammatical mistake. 2 breach of etiquette.

solemn ❶ adjective 1 serious, deeply sincere. 2 formal. 3 glum. **solemnly** adverb **solemnity** noun **solemnize** verb 1 celebrate or perform (a ceremony). 2 make solemn.

solenoid [sole-in-oid] noun coil of wire magnetized by passing a current through it.

sol-fa noun system of syllables used as names for the notes of a scale.

solicit verb **-iting, -ited** 1 request. 2 (of a prostitute) offer (a person) sex for money. **solicitation** noun

solicitor noun lawyer who advises clients and prepares documents and cases.

solicitous ❶ adjective 1 anxious about someone's welfare. 2 eager. **solicitude** noun

solid ❶ adjective 1 (of a substance) keeping its shape. 2 not liquid or gas. 3 not hollow. 4 of the same substance throughout. 5 strong or substantial. 6 sound or reliable. 7 having three dimensions. ♦ noun 8 three-dimensional shape.

—————— THESAURUS ——————

sofa noun = **couch**, chaise longue, divan, settee

soft adjective **1** = **pliable**, bendable, elastic, flexible, gelatinous, malleable, mouldable, plastic, pulpy, spongy, squashy, supple, yielding OPPOSITE **hard**. **3** = **mild**, balmy, temperate **4** = **lenient**, easy-going, indulgent, lax, overindulgent, permissive, spineless OPPOSITE **strict**. **7** = **out of condition**, effeminate, flabby, flaccid, limp, weak **9** Inf = **easy**, comfortable, cushy (inf), undemanding

soften verb = **lessen**, allay, appease, cushion, ease, mitigate, moderate, mollify, still, subdue, temper

soggy adjective = **sodden**, dripping, moist, saturated, soaked, sopping, waterlogged

soil[1] noun **1** = **earth**, clay, dirt, dust, ground **2** = **land**, country

soil[2] verb **1, 2** = **dirty**, befoul, besmirch, defile, foul, pollute, spot, stain, sully, tarnish OPPOSITE **clean**

solace noun = **comfort**, consolation, relief ♦verb = **comfort**, console

soldier noun **1** = **fighter**, man-at-arms, serviceman, squaddie or squaddy (Brit sl), trooper, warrior

sole adjective **1** = **only**, individual, one, single, solitary **2** = **alone**, exclusive

solely adverb **1** = **only**, completely, entirely, merely **2** = **alone**, exclusively

solemn adjective **1** = **serious**, earnest, grave, sedate, sober, staid OPPOSITE **bright**. **2** = **formal**, ceremonial, dignified, grand, grave, momentous, stately OPPOSITE **informal**

solemnity noun **1** = **seriousness**, earnestness, gravity **2** = **formality**, grandeur, impressiveness, momentousness

solicitous adjective **1** = **concerned**, anxious, attentive, careful

solicitude noun **1** = **concern**, anxiety, attentiveness, care, consideration, regard

S

9 solid substance. **solidly** adverb **solidify** verb make or become solid or firm. **solidity** noun
solidarity ❶ noun agreement in aims or interests, total unity.
solidus noun, pl **-di** short oblique stroke (/) used to separate items in text.
soliloquy noun, pl **-quies** speech made by a person while alone, esp. in a play. **soliloquize** verb utter a soliloquy.
solipsism noun doctrine that the self is the only thing known to exist. **solipsist** noun
solitaire noun **1** game for one person played with pegs set in a board. **2** gem set by itself. **3** US card game for one person.
solitary ❶ adjective **1** alone, single. **2** (of a place) lonely. ◆ noun, pl **-aries 3** hermit.
solitude noun state of being alone. **solitary confinement** isolation of a prisoner in a special cell.
solo noun, pl **-los 1** music for one performer. **2** any act done without assistance. ◆ adjective **3** done alone. ◆ adverb **4** by oneself, alone.
soloist noun
solstice noun either the shortest (in winter) or longest (in summer) day of the year.
soluble adjective **1** able to be dissolved. **2** able to be solved. **solubility** noun
solution ❶ noun **1** answer to a problem. **2** act of solving a problem. **3** liquid with something dissolved in it. **4** process of dissolving.
solve ❶ verb find the answer to (a problem). **solvable** adjective
solvent adjective **1** having enough money to pay one's debts. ◆ noun **2** liquid capable of dissolving other substances. **solvency** noun
solvent abuse deliberate inhaling of intoxicating fumes from certain solvents.
somatic adjective of the body, as distinct from

the mind.
sombre ❶ adjective dark, gloomy.
sombrero noun, pl **-ros** wide-brimmed Mexican hat.
some ❶ adjective **1** unknown or unspecified. **2** unknown or unspecified quantity or number of. **3** considerable number or amount of. **4** a little. **5** Informal remarkable. ◆ pronoun **6** certain unknown or unspecified people or things. **7** unknown or unspecified number or quantity. ◆ adverb **8** approximately. **somebody** pronoun **1** some person. ◆ noun **2** important person.
somehow adverb in some unspecified way.
someone pronoun somebody. **something** pronoun **1** unknown or unspecified thing or amount. **2** impressive or important thing.
sometime adverb **1** at some unspecified time. ◆ adjective **2** former. **sometimes** adverb from time to time, now and then. **somewhat** adverb to some extent, rather. **somewhere** adverb in, to, or at some unspecified or unknown place.
somersault noun **1** leap or roll in which the trunk and legs are turned over the head. ◆ verb **2** perform a somersault.
somnambulist noun person who walks in his or her sleep. **somnambulism** noun
somnolent adjective drowsy. **somnolence** noun
son noun **1** male offspring. **2** man who comes from a certain place or is connected with a certain thing. **son-in-law** noun, pl **sons-in-law** daughter's husband.
sonar noun device for detecting underwater objects by the reflection of sound waves.
sonata noun piece of music in several movements for one instrument with or without piano. **sonatina** noun short sonata.
son et lumière [sawn eh loo-mee-er] noun

———— T H E S A U R U S ————

S

solid adjective **1 = firm**, compact, concrete, dense, hard OPPOSITE **unsubstantial**. **5 = strong**, stable, sturdy, substantial, unshakable OPPOSITE **unstable**. **6 = reliable**, dependable, genuine, good, pure, real, sound, trusty, upright, upstanding, worthy OPPOSITE **unreliable**
solidarity noun **= unity**, accord, cohesion, concordance, like-mindedness, team spirit, unanimity, unification
solidify verb **= harden**, cake, coagulate, cohere, congeal, jell, set
solitary adjective **1 = single**, alone, lone, sole **2 = isolated**, hidden, lonely, out-of-the-way, remote, unfrequented OPPOSITE **public**
solitude noun **= isolation**, loneliness, privacy, retirement, seclusion

solution noun **1 = answer**, explanation, key, result **3 = mixture**, blend, compound, mix, solvent
solve verb **= answer**, clear up, crack, decipher, disentangle, get to the bottom of, resolve, suss (out) (sl), unravel, work out
sombre adjective **= gloomy**, dark, dim, dismal, doleful, drab, dull, grave, joyless, lugubrious, mournful, sad, sober OPPOSITE **happy**
somebody noun **2 = celebrity**, dignitary, household name, luminary, megastar (inf), name, notable, personage, star
somehow adverb **= one way or another**, by fair means or foul, by hook or (by) crook, by some means or other, come hell or high water (inf), come what may
sometimes adverb **= occasionally**, at times,

French night-time entertainment with lighting and sound effects, telling the story of the place where it is staged.

song ❶ *noun* **1** music for the voice. **2** tuneful sound made by certain birds. **3** singing. **for a song** very cheaply. **songster, songstress** *noun* singer. **songbird** *noun* any bird with a musical call.

sonic *adjective* of or producing sound. **sonic boom** loud bang caused by an aircraft flying faster than sound.

sonnet *noun* fourteen-line poem with a fixed rhyme scheme.

sonny *noun Informal* term of address to a boy.

sonorous *adjective* **1** (of sound) deep or resonant. **2** (of speech) pompous. **sonorously** *adverb* **sonority** *noun*

soon ❶ *adverb* in a short time. **as soon as** at the very moment that. **sooner** *adverb* rather, e.g. *I'd sooner go alone.* **sooner or later** eventually.

soot *noun* black powder formed by the incomplete burning of an organic substance. **sooty** *adjective*

soothe ❶ *verb* **1** make calm. **2** relieve (pain etc.).

soothsayer ❶ *noun* seer or prophet.

sop ❶ *noun* **1** concession to pacify someone. ♦ *plural* **2** food soaked in liquid. ♦ *verb* **sopping, sopped 3** mop up or absorb (liquid). **sopping** *adjective* completely soaked. **soppy** *adjective Informal* oversentimental.

sophist *noun* person who uses clever but

invalid arguments. **sophistry, sophism** *noun* clever but invalid argument.

sophisticate ❶ *verb* **1** make less natural or innocent. **2** make more complex or refined. ♦ *noun* **3** sophisticated person. **sophisticated** *adjective* **1** having or appealing to refined or cultured tastes and habits. **2** complex and refined. **sophistication** *noun*

sophistry, sophism *noun* clever but invalid argument.

sophomore *noun US* student in second year at college.

soporific ❶ *adjective* **1** causing sleep. ♦ *noun* **2** drug that causes sleep.

soprano *noun, pl* **-pranos 1** (singer with) the highest female or boy's voice. **2** highest pitched of a family of instruments.

sorbet *noun* flavoured water ice.

sorcerer ❶ *noun* magician. **sorceress** *n fem* **sorcery** *noun* witchcraft or magic.

sordid ❶ *adjective* **1** dirty, squalid. **2** base, vile. **3** selfish and grasping. **sordidly** *adverb* **sordidness** *noun*

sore ❶ *adjective* **1** painful. **2** causing annoyance. **3** resentful. **4** (of need) urgent. ♦ *noun* **5** painful area on the body. ♦ *adverb* **6** *Obs* greatly. **sorely** *adverb* greatly. **soreness** *noun*

sorghum *noun* kind of grass cultivated for grain.

sorority *noun, pl* **-ties** *US* society for female students.

sorrel *noun* bitter-tasting plant.

———————— THESAURUS ————————

now and then

song *noun* **1** = **ballad**, air, anthem, carol, chant, chorus, ditty, hymn, number, psalm, tune

soon *adverb* = **before long**, in the near future, shortly

soothe *verb* **1** = **calm**, allay, appease, hush, lull, mollify, pacify, quiet, still OPPOSITE worry. **2** = **relieve**, alleviate, assuage, ease OPPOSITE irritate

soothsayer *noun* = **prophet**, diviner, fortune-teller, seer, sibyl

sophisticated *adjective* **1** = **cultured**, cosmopolitan, cultivated, refined, urbane, worldly OPPOSITE unsophisticated. **2** = **complex**, advanced, complicated, delicate, elaborate, intricate, refined, subtle OPPOSITE simple

sophistication *noun* **1** = **savoir-faire**, finesse, poise, urbanity, worldliness, worldly wisdom

soporific *adjective* **1** = **sleep-inducing**, sedative, somnolent, tranquillizing ♦*noun* **2**

= **sedative**, narcotic, opiate, tranquillizer

soppy *adjective Inf* = **sentimental**, icky (*inf*), overemotional, schmaltzy (*sl*), slushy (*inf*), weepy (*inf*)

sorcerer, sorceress *noun* = **magician**, enchanter, necromancer, warlock, witch, wizard

sorcery *noun* = **black magic**, black art, enchantment, magic, necromancy, witchcraft, wizardry

sordid *adjective* **1** = **dirty**, filthy, foul, mean, scungy (*Aust & NZ sl*), seedy, sleazy, squalid, unclean OPPOSITE clean. **2** = **base**, debauched, degenerate, low, shabby, shameful, vicious, vile OPPOSITE honourable. **3** = **mercenary**, avaricious, covetous, grasping, selfish

sore *adjective* **1** = **painful**, angry, burning, inflamed, irritated, raw, sensitive, smarting, tender **2** = **annoying**, severe, sharp, troublesome **3** = **annoyed**, aggrieved, angry, cross, hurt, irked, irritated, pained, pissed (*taboo sl*), pissed (off) (*taboo sl*), resentful, stung, upset **4** = **urgent**, acute, critical,

S

sorrow ⊕ *noun* **1** grief or sadness. **2** cause of sorrow. ♦ *verb* **3** grieve. **sorrowful** *adjective* **sorrowfully** *adverb*

sorry ⊕ *adjective* **-rier, -riest 1** feeling pity or regret. **2** pitiful or wretched. **3** of poor quality.

sort ⊕ *noun* **1** group all sharing certain qualities or characteristics. **2** *Informal* type of character. ♦ *verb* **3** arrange according to kind. **4** mend or fix. **out of sorts** slightly unwell or bad-tempered. **sort out** *verb* **1** find a solution. **2** put in order. **3** *Informal* scold or punish.

sortie *noun* **1** relatively short return trip. **2** raid into enemy territory. **3** operational flight made by military aircraft.

SOS *noun* **1** international code signal of distress. **2** call for help.

so-so *adjective* **1** *Informal* mediocre. ♦ *adverb* **2** in an average way.

sot *noun* habitual drunkard.

sotto voce [sot-toe **voe**-chay] *adverb* in an undertone.

sou *noun* **1** former French coin. **2** small amount of money.

soubriquet [so-**brik**-ay] *noun* same as SOBRIQUET.

soufflé [**soo**-flay] *noun* light fluffy dish made with beaten egg whites and other ingredients.

sough [rhymes with **now**] *verb* (of the wind) make a sighing sound.

sought [sawt] *verb* past of SEEK.

souk [sook] *noun* marketplace in Muslim countries, often open-air.

soul ⊕ *noun* **1** spiritual and immortal part of a human being. **2** essential part or fundamental nature. **3** deep and sincere feelings. **4** person regarded as typifying some quality. **5** person. **6** (also **soul music**) type of Black music combining blues, pop, and gospel. **soulful** *adjective* full of emotion. **soulless** *adjective* **1** lacking human qualities, mechanical. **2** (of a person) lacking sensitivity. **soul-destroying** *adjective* extremely monotonous. **soul-searching** *noun* deep examination of one's actions and feelings.

sound[1] ⊕ *noun* **1** something heard, noise. **2** vibrations travelling in waves through air, water, etc. ♦ *verb* **3** make or cause to make a sound. **4** seem to be as specified. **5** announce by a sound. **6** pronounce. **sound barrier** *Informal* sudden increase in air resistance against an object as it approaches the speed of sound. **soundproof** *adjective* **1** not penetrable by sound. ♦ *verb* **2** make soundproof. **soundtrack** *noun* recorded sound accompaniment to a film.

sound[2] ⊕ *adjective* **1** in good condition. **2** firm, substantial. **3** financially reliable. **4** showing good judgment. **5** ethically correct. **6** (of sleep) deep. **7** thorough. **soundly** *adverb*

sound[3] ⊕ *verb* **1** find the depth of (water etc.). **2** examine (the body) by tapping or with a stethoscope. **3** ascertain the views of. **soundings** *plural noun* measurements of depth taken by sounding. **sounding board** person or group used to test a new idea.

sound[4] ⊕ *noun* channel or strait.

soup *noun* liquid food made from meat, vegetables, etc. **soupy** *adjective* **soup kitchen** place where food and drink is served to needy

——————— T H E S A U R U S ———————

desperate, dire, extreme, pressing

sorrow *noun* **1** = **grief**, anguish, distress, heartache, heartbreak, misery, mourning, regret, sadness, unhappiness, woe OPPOSITE joy. **2** = **affliction**, hardship, misfortune, trial, tribulation, trouble, woe OPPOSITE **good fortune** ♦*verb* **3** = **grieve**, agonize, bemoan, be sad, bewail, lament, mourn OPPOSITE **celebrate**

sorrowful *adjective* = **sad**, dejected, dismal, doleful, grieving, miserable, mournful, sorry, unhappy, woebegone, woeful, wretched

sorry *adjective* **1** = **regretful**, apologetic, conscience-stricken, contrite, penitent, remorseful, repentant, shamefaced OPPOSITE **unrepentant. 2** = **wretched**, mean, miserable, pathetic, pitiful, poor, sad **3** = **deplorable**

sort *noun* **1** = **kind**, brand, category, class, ilk, make, nature, order, quality, style, type, variety ♦*verb* **3** = **arrange**, categorize, classify, divide, grade, group, order, put in order, rank

sort out *verb* **1** = **resolve**, clarify, clear up **2** = **organize**, tidy up

soul *noun* **1** = **spirit**, essence, life, vital force **2** = **essence**, embodiment, epitome, personification, quintessence, type **5** = **person**, being, body, creature, individual, man *or* woman

sound[1] *noun* **1** = **noise**, din, report, reverberation, tone ♦*verb* **3** = **resound**, echo, reverberate **4** = **seem**, appear, look **5, 6** = **pronounce**, announce, articulate, declare, express, utter

sound[2] *adjective* **1** = **perfect**, fit, healthy, intact, solid, unhurt, unimpaired, uninjured, whole OPPOSITE **weak. 4** = **sensible**, correct, logical, proper, prudent, rational, reasonable, right, trustworthy, valid, well-founded, wise OPPOSITE **irresponsible. 6** = **deep**, unbroken, undisturbed, untroubled OPPOSITE **broken**

sound[3] *verb* **1** = **fathom**, plumb, probe

sound[4] *noun* = **channel**, arm of the sea, fjord,

people. **souped-up** *adjective* (of an engine) adjusted so as to be more powerful than normal.

soupçon [soop-sonn] *noun* small amount.

sour ❶ *adjective* **1** sharp-tasting. **2** (of milk) gone bad. **3** (of a person's temperament) sullen. ◆ *verb* **4** make or become sour. **sourly** *adverb* **sourness** *noun* **sour cream** cream soured by bacteria for use in cooking. **sour grapes** attitude of claiming to despise something when one cannot have it oneself.

source ❶ *noun* **1** origin or starting point. **2** person, book, etc. providing information. **3** spring where a river or stream begins.

souse *verb* **1** plunge (something) into liquid. **2** drench. **3** pickle. **soused** *adjective Slang* drunk.

soutane [soo-**tan**] *noun* Roman Catholic priest's cassock.

south *noun* **1** direction towards the South Pole, opposite north. **2** area lying in or towards the south. ◆ *adjective* **3** to or in the south. **4** (of a wind) from the south. ◆ *adverb* **5** in, to, or towards the south. **southerly** *adjective* **southern** *adjective* **southerner** *noun* person from the south of a country or area. **southward** *adjective, adverb* **southwards** *adverb* **southeast** *noun, adjective, adverb* (in or to) direction between south and east. **southwest** *noun, adjective, adverb* (in or to) direction between south and west. **southpaw** *noun Informal* left-handed person, esp. a boxer. **South Pole** southernmost point on the earth's axis.

souvenir ❶ *noun* keepsake, memento.

sou'wester *noun* seaman's waterproof hat covering the head and back of the neck.

sovereign ❶ *noun* **1** king or queen. **2** former British gold coin worth one pound. ◆ *adjective* **3** (of a state) independent. **4** supreme in rank or authority. **5** excellent. **sovereignty** *noun*

soviet *noun* **1** formerly, elected council at various levels of government in the USSR. ◆ *adjective* **2** (**S-**) of the former USSR.

sow[1] ❶ [rhymes with **know**] *verb* **sowing, sowed, sown** *or* **sowed 1** scatter or plant (seed) in or on (the ground). **2** implant or introduce.

sow[2] [rhymes with **cow**] *noun* female adult pig.

soya *noun* plant whose edible bean (**soya bean**) is used for food and as a source of oil.

soy sauce sauce made from fermented soya beans, used in Chinese and Japanese cookery.

sozzled *adjective Slang* drunk.

spa *noun* resort with a mineral-water spring.

space ❶ *noun* **1** unlimited expanse in which all objects exist and move. **2** interval. **3** blank portion. **4** unoccupied area. **5** the universe beyond the earth's atmosphere. ◆ *verb* **6** place at intervals. **spacious** *adjective* having a large capacity or area. **spacecraft**, **spaceship** *noun* vehicle for travel beyond the earth's atmosphere. **space shuttle** manned reusable vehicle for repeated space flights. **space station** artificial satellite used as a base for people travelling and researching in space.

spacesuit *noun* sealed pressurized suit worn by an astronaut.

spacious ❶ *adjective* having a large capacity or area.

spade[1] ❶ *noun* tool for digging. **spadework** *noun* hard preparatory work.

spade[2] *noun* playing card of the suit marked with black leaf-shaped symbols.

spaghetti *noun* pasta in the form of long strings.

span ❶ *noun* **1** space between two points. **2** complete extent. **3** distance from thumb to little finger of the expanded hand. ◆ *verb* **spanning, spanned 4** stretch or extend across.

S

——————— THESAURUS ———————

inlet, passage, strait, voe

sour *adjective* **1** = **sharp**, acetic, acid, bitter, pungent, tart OPPOSITE **sweet**. **2** = **gone off**, curdled, gone bad, turned OPPOSITE **fresh**. **3** = **ill-natured**, acrimonious, disagreeable, embittered, ill-tempered, peevish, tart, ungenerous, waspish OPPOSITE **pleasant**

source *noun* **1** = **origin**, author, beginning, cause, derivation, fount, originator **2** = **informant**, authority

souvenir *noun* = **keepsake**, memento, reminder

sovereign *noun* **1** = **monarch**, chief, emperor *or* empress, king *or* queen, potentate, prince *or* princess, ruler ◆*adjective* **4** = **supreme**, absolute,

imperial, kingly *or* queenly, principal, royal, ruling **5** = **excellent**, effectual, efficacious, efficient

sovereignty *noun* **4** = **supreme power**, domination, kingship, primacy, supremacy

sow[1] *verb* **1** = **scatter**, plant, seed **2** = **implant**

space *noun* **1** = **expanse**, extent **2** = **interval**, capacity, duration, elbowroom, leeway, margin, period, play, room, scope, span, time, while **3** = **gap**, blank, distance, interval, omission

spacious *adjective* = **roomy**, ample, broad, capacious, commodious, expansive, extensive, huge, large, sizable *or* sizeable

spadework *noun* = **preparation**, donkey-work, groundwork, labour

spangle *noun* **1** small shiny metallic ornament. ◆ *verb* **2** decorate with spangles.
Spaniard *noun* person from Spain.
spaniel *noun* dog with long ears and silky hair.
Spanish *noun* **1** official language of Spain and most countries of S and Central America. ◆ *adjective* **2** of Spain or its language or people.
spank ⊙ *verb* **1** slap with the open hand, on the buttocks or legs. ◆ *noun* **2** such a slap. **spanking** *noun*
spanking *adjective* **1** *Informal* outstandingly fine or smart. **2** quick.
spanner *noun* tool for gripping and turning a nut or bolt.
spar[1] *noun* pole used as a ship's mast, boom, or yard.
spar[2] ⊙ *verb* **sparring, sparred 1** box or fight using light blows for practice. **2** argue (with someone). ◆ *noun* **3** argument.
spare ⊙ *adjective* **1** extra. **2** in reserve. **3** (of a person) thin. **4** very plain or simple. **5** *Slang* upset or angry. ◆ *noun* **6** duplicate kept in case of damage or loss. ◆ *verb* **7** refrain from punishing or harming. **8** protect (someone) from (something unpleasant). **9** afford to give. **to spare** in addition to what is needed.
sparing *adjective* economical. **spare ribs** pork ribs with most of the meat trimmed off. **spare tyre** *Informal* roll of fat at the waist.
spark ⊙ *noun* **1** fiery particle thrown out from a fire or caused by friction. **2** flash of light produced by an electrical discharge. **3** trace or hint (of a particular quality). **4** liveliness or humour. ◆ *verb* **5** give off sparks. **6** initiate.
sparkie *noun NZ informal* electrician. **spark**

plug device in an engine that ignites the fuel by producing an electric spark.
sparkle ⊙ *verb* **1** glitter with many points of light. **2** be vivacious or witty. ◆ *noun* **3** sparkling points of light. **4** vivacity or wit. **sparkler** *noun* hand-held firework that emits sparks. **sparkling** *adjective* (of wine or mineral water) slightly fizzy.
sparrow *noun* small brownish bird.
sparrowhawk *noun* small hawk.
sparse ⊙ *adjective* thinly scattered. **sparsely** *adverb* **sparseness** *noun*
spartan *adjective* strict and austere.
spasm ⊙ *noun* **1** involuntary muscular contraction. **2** sudden burst of activity or feeling. **spasmodic** *adjective* occurring in spasms. **spasmodically** *adverb*
spastic *noun* **1** person with cerebral palsy. ◆ *adjective* **2** suffering from cerebral palsy. **3** affected by spasms.
spat[1] *noun* slight quarrel.
spat[2] *verb* past of SPIT[1].
spate ⊙ *noun* **1** large number of things happening within a period of time. **2** sudden outpouring or flood.
spathe *noun* large sheathlike leaf enclosing a flower cluster.
spatial *adjective* of or in space.
spats *plural noun* coverings formerly worn over the ankle and instep.
spatter *verb* **1** scatter or be scattered in drops over (something). ◆ *noun* **2** spattering sound. **3** something spattered.
spatula *noun* utensil with a broad flat blade for spreading or stirring.

——————— THESAURUS ———————

span *noun* **1** = **period**, duration, spell, term **2** = **extent**, amount, distance, length, reach, spread, stretch ◆*verb* **4** = **extend across**, bridge, cover, cross, link, traverse
spank *verb* **1** = **smack**, cuff, slap
spar[2] *verb* **2** = **argue**, bicker, row, scrap (*inf*), squabble, wrangle
spare *adjective* **1** = **extra**, additional, free, leftover, odd, over, superfluous, surplus, unoccupied, unused, unwanted OPPOSITE needed. **3** = **thin**, gaunt, lean, meagre, wiry OPPOSITE heavy ◆*verb* **7** = **have mercy on**, be merciful to, go easy on (*inf*), leave, let off (*inf*), pardon, save from OPPOSITE condemn. **9** = **afford**, do without, give, grant, let (someone) have, manage without, part with
sparing *adjective* = **economical**, careful, frugal, prudent, saving, thrifty
spark *noun* **1** = **flicker**, flare, flash, gleam, glint **3** = **trace**, atom, hint, jot, scrap, vestige

◆*verb* **6** = **start**, inspire, precipitate, provoke, set off, stimulate, trigger (off)
sparkle *verb* **1** = **glitter**, dance, flash, gleam, glint, glisten, scintillate, shimmer, shine, twinkle ◆*noun* **3** = **glitter**, brilliance, flash, flicker, gleam, glint, twinkle **4** = **vivacity**, dash, élan, life, liveliness, spirit, vitality
sparse *adjective* = **scattered**, few and far between, meagre, scanty, scarce OPPOSITE thick
Spartan *adjective* = **austere**, ascetic, disciplined, frugal, plain, rigorous, self-denying, severe, strict
spasm *noun* **1** = **convulsion**, contraction, paroxysm, twitch **2** = **burst**, eruption, fit, frenzy, outburst, seizure
spasmodic *adjective* = **sporadic**, convulsive, erratic, fitful, intermittent, irregular, jerky
spate *noun* **2** = **flood**, deluge, flow, outpouring, rush, torrent

S

spawn *noun* **1** jelly-like mass of eggs of fish, frogs, or molluscs. ♦ *verb* **2** (of fish, frogs, or molluscs) lay eggs. **3** generate.

spay *verb* remove the ovaries from (a female animal).

speak ⓞ *verb* **speaking, spoke, spoken 1** say words, talk. **2** communicate or express in words. **3** give a speech or lecture. **4** know how to talk in (a specified language). **speaker** *noun* **1** person who speaks, esp. at a formal occasion. **2** loudspeaker. **3** (S-) official chairman of a body. **speak out, speak up 1** state one's beliefs firmly. **2** speak more loudly.

spear[1] ⓞ *noun* **1** weapon consisting of a long shaft with a sharp point. ♦ *verb* **2** pierce with or as if with a spear. **spearhead** *verb* **1** lead (an attack or campaign). ♦ *noun* **2** leading force in an attack or campaign.

spear[2] *noun* slender shoot.

spearmint *noun* type of mint.

spec *noun* **on spec** *Informal* as a risk or gamble.

special ⓞ *adjective* **1** distinguished from others of its kind. **2** for a specific purpose. **3** exceptional. **4** particular. ♦ *noun* **5** product, programme, etc. which is only available at a certain time. **specially** *adverb* **specialist** *noun* expert in a particular activity or subject.

speciality *noun* **1** special interest or skill. **2** product specialized in. **specialize** *verb* be a specialist. **specialization** *noun* **Special Branch** British police department concerned with political security.

specie *noun* coins as distinct from paper money.

species ⓞ *noun, pl* **-cies** group of plants or animals that are related closely enough to interbreed naturally.

specific ⓞ *adjective* **1** particular, definite. **2** relating to a particular thing. ♦ *noun* **3** drug used to treat a particular disease. ♦ *plural* **4** particular details. **specifically** *adverb* **specification** *noun* detailed description of something to be made or done. **specify** *verb* **1** refer to or state specifically. **2** state as a condition. **specific gravity** ratio of the density of a substance to that of water.

specimen ⓞ *noun* **1** individual or part typifying a whole. **2** sample of blood etc. taken for analysis. **3** *Informal* person.

specious [spee-shuss] *adjective* apparently true, but actually false.

speck ⓞ *noun* small spot or particle. **speckle** *noun* **1** small spot. ♦ *verb* **2** mark with speckles.

specs *plural noun Informal* short for SPECTACLES.

spectacle ⓞ *noun* **1** strange, interesting, or ridiculous sight. **2** impressive public show. ♦ *plural* **3** pair of glasses for correcting faulty vision. **spectacular** *adjective* **1** impressive. ♦ *noun* **2** spectacular public show. **spectacularly** *adverb*

spectate ⓞ *verb* watch. **spectator** *noun* person viewing anything, onlooker.

spectre ⓞ *noun* **1** ghost. **2** menacing mental

——————————— T H E S A U R U S ———————————

speak *verb* **1, 2** =**talk**, articulate, converse, express, pronounce, say, state, tell, utter **3** =**lecture**, address, declaim, discourse, hold forth

speaker *noun* **1** =**orator**, lecturer, public speaker, spokesman *or* spokeswoman, spokesperson

speak out, speak up *verb* **1** =**speak one's mind**, have one's say, make one's position plain

spearhead *verb* **1** =**lead**, head, initiate, launch, pioneer, set in motion, set off

special *adjective* **1, 2, 4** =**specific**, appropriate, distinctive, individual, particular, precise OPPOSITE **general**. **3** =**exceptional**, extraordinary, important, memorable, significant, uncommon, unique, unusual OPPOSITE **common**

specialist *noun* =**expert**, authority, buff (*inf*), connoisseur, consultant, fundi (*S Afr*), guru, mana (*NZ*), master, professional

speciality *noun* **1** =**forte**, bag (*sl*), métier, pièce de résistance, specialty

species *noun* =**kind**, breed, category, class, group, sort, type, variety

specific *adjective* **1** =**particular**, characteristic, distinguishing, special OPPOSITE **general**

specification *noun* =**requirement**, condition, detail, particular, qualification, stipulation

specify *verb* **1** =**state**, define, designate, detail, indicate, mention, name **2** =**stipulate**

specimen *noun* **1** =**example**, exemplification, instance, model, pattern, representative, sample, type **2** =**sample**

speck *noun* =**particle**, atom, bit, blemish, dot, fleck, grain, iota, jot, mark, mite, mote, shred, speckle, spot, stain

spectacle *noun* **1** =**sight**, curiosity, marvel, phenomenon, scene, wonder **2** =**show**, display, event, exhibition, extravaganza, pageant, performance

spectacular *adjective* **1** =**impressive**, dazzling, dramatic, grand, magnificent, sensational, splendid, striking, stunning (*inf*) OPPOSITE **ordinary** ♦*noun* **2** =**show**, display, spectacle

spectator *noun* =**onlooker**, bystander,

S

image. **spectral** *adjective*
spectrum *noun, pl* **-tra 1** range of different colours, radio waves, etc. in order of their wavelengths. **2** entire range of anything.
spectroscope *noun* instrument for producing or examining spectra.
speculate ⊕ *verb* **1** guess, conjecture. **2** buy property, shares, etc. in the hope of selling them at a profit. **speculation** *noun*
speculative *adjective* **speculator** *noun*
speculum *noun, pl* **-la, -lums** medical instrument for examining body cavities.
sped *verb* a past of SPEED.
speech ⊕ *noun* **1** act, power, or manner of speaking. **2** utterance. **3** talk given to an audience. **4** language or dialect. **speechify** *verb* make speeches, esp. boringly. **speechless** *adjective* unable to speak because of great emotion. **speech therapy** treatment of people with speech problems.
speed ⊕ *noun* **1** swiftness. **2** rate at which something moves or acts. **3** measure of the light sensitivity of photographic film. **4** *Slang* amphetamine. ♦ *verb* **speeding, sped** or **speeded 5** go quickly. **6** drive faster than the legal limit. **speedy** *adjective* **1** prompt. **2** rapid. **speedily** *adverb* **speedboat** *noun* light fast motorboat. **speed limit** maximum legal speed for travelling on a particular road.
speedometer *noun* instrument to show the speed of a vehicle. **speed up** *verb* accelerate.
speedway *noun* track for motorcycle racing.

speedwell *noun* plant with small blue flowers.
speleology *noun* study and exploration of caves. **speleologist** *noun*
spell[1] ⊕ *verb* **spelling, spelt** or **spelled 1** give in correct order the letters that form (a word). **2** (of letters) make up (a word). **3** indicate. **spelling** *noun* **1** way a word is spelt. **2** person's ability to spell. **spell out** *verb* make explicit.
spell[2] ⊕ *noun* **1** formula of words supposed to have magic power. **2** effect of a spell. **3** fascination. **spellbound** *adjective* entranced.
spell[3] ⊕ *noun* period of time of weather or activity.
spelt *verb* a past of SPELL[1].
spend ⊕ *verb* **spending, spent 1** pay out (money). **2** use or pass (time). **3** use up completely. **spendthrift** *noun* person who spends money wastefully.
sperm *noun* **sperms** or **sperm 1** male reproductive cell. **2** semen. **spermicide** *noun* substance that kills sperm. **sperm whale** large toothed whale.
spermaceti [sper-ma-**set**-ee] *noun* waxy solid obtained from the sperm whale.
spermatozoon [sper-ma-toe-**zoe**-on] *noun, pl* **-zoa** sperm.
spew ⊕ *verb* **1** vomit. **2** send out in a stream.
sphagnum *noun* moss found in bogs.
sphere ⊕ *noun* **1** perfectly round solid object. **2** field of activity. **3** social class. **spherical** *adjective*

———————— T H E S A U R U S ————————

looker-on, observer, viewer, watcher
spectre *noun* **1** = **ghost**, apparition, phantom, spirit, vision, wraith
speculate *verb* **1** = **conjecture**, consider, guess, hypothesize, suppose, surmise, theorize, wonder **2** = **gamble**, hazard, risk, venture
speech *noun* **1** = **communication**, conversation, dialogue, discussion, talk **3** = **talk**, address, discourse, homily, lecture, oration, spiel (*inf*) **4** = **language**, articulation, dialect, diction, enunciation, idiom, jargon, parlance, tongue
speechless *adjective* = **astounded**, aghast, amazed, dazed, shocked
speed *noun* **1** = **swiftness**, haste, hurry, pace, quickness, rapidity, rush, velocity OPPOSITE slowness ♦ *verb* **5** = **race**, career, gallop, hasten, hurry, make haste, rush, tear, zoom OPPOSITE creep
speed up *verb* = **accelerate**, gather momentum, increase the tempo
speedy *adjective* **1** = **prompt**, immediate, precipitate **2** = **quick**, express, fast, hasty,

headlong, hurried, rapid, swift
spell[1] *verb* **3** = **indicate**, augur, imply, mean, point to, portend, signify
spell[2] *noun* **1** = **incantation**, charm **2, 3** = **enchantment**, allure, bewitchment, fascination, glamour, magic
spell[3] *noun* = **period**, bout, course, interval, season, stretch, term, time
spellbound *adjective* = **entranced**, bewitched, captivated, charmed, enthralled, fascinated, gripped, mesmerized, rapt
spend *verb* **1** = **pay out**, disburse, expend, fork out (*sl*) OPPOSITE save. **2** = **pass**, fill, occupy, while away **3** = **use up**, consume, dissipate, drain, empty, exhaust, run through, squander, waste OPPOSITE keep
spendthrift *noun* = **squanderer**, big spender, profligate, spender, waster OPPOSITE penny-pincher
spew *verb* **1** = **vomit**, disgorge, puke (*sl*), regurgitate, throw up (*inf*)
sphere *noun* **1** = **ball**, circle, globe, globule, orb **2** = **field**, capacity, department, domain,

sphincter *noun* ring of muscle which controls the opening and closing of a hollow organ.
Sphinx *noun* **1** statue in Egypt with a lion's body and human head. **2** (**s-**) enigmatic person.
spice ❶ *noun* **1** aromatic substance used as flavouring. **2** something that adds zest or interest. ♦ *verb* **3** flavour with spices. **4** add zest or interest to. **spicy** *adjective* **1** flavoured with spices. **2** *Informal* slightly scandalous.
spick-and-span *adjective* neat and clean.
spider *noun* small eight-legged creature which spins a web to catch insects for food. **spidery** *adjective*
spiel *noun* speech made to persuade someone to do something.
spigot *noun* stopper for, or tap fitted to, a cask.
spike¹ ❶ *noun* **1** sharp point. **2** sharp pointed metal object. ♦ *plural* **3** sports shoes with spikes for greater grip. ♦ *verb* **4** put spikes on. **5** pierce or fasten with a spike. **6** add alcohol to (a drink). **spike someone's guns** thwart someone. **spiky** *adjective*
spike² *noun* **1** long pointed flower cluster. **2** ear of corn.
spill¹ ❶ *verb* **spilling, spilt** or **spilled 1** pour from or as if from a container. **2** come out of a place. **3** shed (blood). ♦ *noun* **4** fall. **5** amount spilt. **spill the beans** *Informal* give away a secret. **spillage** *noun*
spill² *noun* thin strip of wood or paper for lighting pipes or fires.
spin ❶ *verb* **spinning, spun 1** revolve or cause to revolve rapidly. **2** draw out and twist (fibres) into thread. **3** (of a spider) form (a web) from a silky fibre from the body. **4** grow dizzy. ♦ *noun* **5** revolving motion. **6** continuous spiral descent of an aircraft. **7** spinning motion given to a ball in sport. **8** *Informal* short drive for pleasure. **9** *Informal* presenting of information in a way that

creates a favourable impression. **spin a yarn** tell an improbable story. **spinner** *noun* **spin doctor** *Informal* person who provides a favourable slant to a news item or policy on behalf of a politician or a political party. **spin-dry** *verb* dry (clothes) in a spin-dryer. **spin-dryer** *noun* machine in which washed clothes are spun in a perforated drum to remove excess water. **spinning wheel** wheel-like machine for spinning, worked by hand or foot. **spin-off** *noun* incidental benefit. **spin out** *verb* prolong.
spina bifida *noun* condition in which part of the spinal cord protrudes through a gap in the backbone, often causing paralysis.
spinach *noun* dark green leafy vegetable.
spindle *noun* **1** rotating rod that acts as an axle. **2** weighted rod rotated for spinning thread by hand. **spindly** *adjective* long, slender, and frail.
spindrift *noun* spray blown up from the sea.
spine ❶ *noun* **1** backbone. **2** edge of a book on which the title is printed. **3** sharp point on an animal or plant. **spinal** *adjective* of the spine. **spinal cord** cord of nerves inside the spine, which connects the brain to the nerves in the body. **spineless** *adjective* lacking courage. **spiny** *adjective* covered with spines. **spine-chiller** *noun* terrifying film or story.
spinet *noun* small harpsichord.
spinnaker *noun* large sail on a racing yacht.
spinneret *noun* organ through which silk threads come out of a spider.
spinney *noun* small wood.
spinster *noun* unmarried woman.
spiral ❶ *noun* **1** continuous curve formed by a point winding about a central axis at an ever-increasing distance from it. **2** steadily accelerating increase or decrease. ♦ *verb* **-ralling, -ralled 3** move in a spiral. **4** increase or decrease with steady acceleration. ♦ *adjective* **5** having the form of a spiral.

——————————— T H E S A U R U S ———————————

function, patch, province, realm, scope, territory, turf (*US sl*)
spherical *adjective* **1** = **round**, globe-shaped, globular, rotund
spice *noun* **1** = **seasoning**, relish, savour **2** = **excitement**, colour, pep, piquancy, zest, zing (*inf*)
spicy *adjective* **1** = **hot**, aromatic, piquant, savoury, seasoned **2** *Inf* = **scandalous**, hot (*inf*), indelicate, racy, ribald, risqué, suggestive, titillating
spike¹ *noun* **1** = **point**, barb, prong, spine ♦*verb* **5** = **impale**, spear, spit, stick
spill¹ *verb* **1** = **pour**, discharge, disgorge,

overflow, slop over ♦*noun* **4** = **fall**, tumble
spin *verb* **1** = **revolve**, gyrate, pirouette, reel, rotate, turn, twirl, whirl **4** = **reel**, swim, whirl ♦*noun* **5** = **revolution**, gyration, roll, whirl **8** *Inf* = **drive**, joy ride (*inf*), ride
spine *noun* **1** = **backbone**, spinal column, vertebrae, vertebral column **3** = **barb**, needle, quill, ray, spike, spur
spineless *adjective* = **weak**, cowardly, faint-hearted, feeble, gutless (*inf*), lily-livered, soft, weak-kneed (*inf*)
spin out *verb* = **prolong**, amplify, delay, drag out, draw out, extend, lengthen
spiral *noun* **1** = **coil**, corkscrew, helix, whorl

spire *noun* pointed part of a steeple.
spirit¹ ⊕ *noun* **1** nonphysical aspect of a person concerned with profound thoughts. **2** nonphysical part of a person believed to live on after death. **3** prevailing feeling. **4** mood or attitude. **5** temperament or disposition. **6** liveliness. **7** courage. **8** essential meaning as opposed to literal interpretation. **9** ghost. ◆ *plural* **10** emotional state. ◆ *verb* **-iting, -ited** **11** carry away mysteriously. **spirited** *adjective* **1** lively. **2** characterized by the mood specified, e.g. *low-spirited*.
spirit² *noun* liquid obtained by distillation.
spirit level glass tube containing a bubble in liquid, used to check whether a surface is level.
spiritual ⊕ *adjective* **1** relating to the spirit. **2** relating to sacred things. ◆ *noun* **3** type of religious folk song originating among Black slaves in America. **spiritually** *adverb*
spirituality *noun* **spiritualism** *noun* belief that the spirits of the dead can communicate with the living. **spiritualist** *noun*
spit¹ ⊕ *verb* **spitting, spat 1** eject (saliva or food) from the mouth. **2** throw out particles explosively. **3** rain slightly. **4** utter (words) in a violent manner. ◆ *noun* **5** saliva. **spitting image** *Informal* person who looks very like another. **spittle** *noun* fluid produced in the mouth, saliva. **spittoon** *noun* bowl to spit into.
spit² *noun* **1** sharp rod on which meat is skewered for roasting. **2** long strip of land projecting into the sea.
spite ⊕ *noun* **1** deliberate nastiness. ◆ *verb* **2** annoy or hurt from spite. **in spite of** in

defiance of. **spiteful** *adjective* **spitefully** *adverb*
spitfire *noun* person with a fiery temper.
spiv *noun* *Slang* smartly dressed man who makes a living by shady dealings.
splash ⊕ *verb* **1** scatter liquid on (something). **2** scatter (liquid) or (of liquid) be scattered in drops. **3** print (a story or photograph) prominently in a newspaper. ◆ *noun* **4** splashing sound. **5** amount splashed. **6** patch (of colour or light). **7** extravagant display. **8** small amount of liquid added to a drink. **splashdown** *noun* landing of a spacecraft on water. **splash out** *verb Informal* spend extravagantly.
splatter *verb, noun* splash.
splay *verb* spread out, with ends spreading in different directions.
spleen *noun* **1** abdominal organ which filters bacteria from the blood. **2** bad temper.
splenetic *adjective* spiteful or irritable.
splendid ⊕ *adjective* **1** excellent. **2** brilliant in appearance. **splendidly** *adverb* **splendour** *noun*
splice *verb* join by interweaving or overlapping ends. **get spliced** *Slang* get married.
splint *noun* rigid support for a broken bone.
splinter ⊕ *noun* **1** thin sharp piece broken off, esp. from wood. ◆ *verb* **2** break into fragments.
splinter group group that has broken away from an organization.
split ⊕ *verb* **splitting, split 1** break into separate pieces. **2** separate. **3** separate because of disagreement. **4** share. **5** (foll. by *on*) *Slang* inform. ◆ *noun* **6** splitting. **7** crack or division caused by splitting. **8** dessert of sliced fruit, ice

◆*adjective* **5 = coiled**, helical, whorled, winding
spirit¹ *noun* **2 = life force**, life, soul, vital spark **3 = feeling**, atmosphere, gist, tenor, tone **4, 5** **= temperament**, attitude, character, disposition, outlook, temper **6 = liveliness**, animation, brio, energy, enthusiasm, fire, force, life, mettle, vigour, zest **7 = courage**, backbone, gameness, grit, guts (*inf*), spunk (*inf*) **8 = intention**, essence, meaning, purport, purpose, sense, substance **9 = ghost**, apparition, phantom, spectre ◆*plural* **10** **= mood**, feelings, frame of mind, morale ◆*verb* **11 = remove**, abduct, abstract, carry away, purloin, seize, steal, whisk away
spirited *adjective* **1 = lively**, active, animated, energetic, feisty (*inf, chiefly US & Canad*), mettlesome, vivacious
spiritual *adjective* **1 = nonmaterial**, immaterial, incorporeal OPPOSITE **material.** **2 = sacred**, devotional, divine, holy, religious
spit¹ *verb* **1 = eject**, expectorate, splutter **2**

= throw out ◆*noun* **5 = saliva**, dribble, drool, slaver, spittle
spite *noun* **1 = malice**, animosity, hatred, ill will, malevolence, spitefulness, spleen, venom OPPOSITE **kindness** ◆*verb* **2 = annoy**, harm, hurt, injure, vex OPPOSITE **help** ◆ **in spite of** **= despite**, (even) though, notwithstanding, regardless of
splash *verb* **1, 2 = scatter**, shower, slop, spatter, spray, sprinkle, wet **3 = publicize**, broadcast, tout, trumpet ◆*noun* **6 = dash**, burst, patch, spattering, touch **7 = display**, effect, impact, sensation, stir
splendid *adjective* **1 = excellent**, cracking (*Brit inf*), fantastic (*inf*), first-class, glorious, great (*inf*), marvellous, wonderful OPPOSITE **poor. 2** **= magnificent**, costly, gorgeous, grand, impressive, lavish, luxurious, ornate, resplendent, rich, sumptuous, superb OPPOSITE **drab**
splinter *noun* **1 = sliver**, chip, flake, fragment

S

cream, and cream. ◆ *plural* **9** act of sitting with the legs outstretched in opposite directions.
splitting *adjective* (of a headache) very painful.
split-level *adjective* (of a house or room) having the ground floor on different levels.
split personality 1 tendency to change mood rapidly. **2** *Informal* schizophrenia. **split second** very short period of time.
splotch, splodge *noun, verb* splash, daub.
splurge *verb* **1** spend money extravagantly. ◆ *noun* **2** bout of extravagance.
splutter *verb* **1** utter with spitting or choking sounds. **2** make hissing spitting sounds. ◆ *noun* **3** spluttering.
spoil ❶ *verb* **spoiling, spoilt** *or* **spoiled 1** damage. **2** harm the character of (a child) by giving it all it wants. **3** rot, go bad. **spoils** *plural noun* **1** booty. **2** benefits of public office. **spoiling for** eager for. **spoiler** *noun* device on an aircraft or car to increase drag. **spoilsport** *noun* person who spoils the enjoyment of others.
spoke¹ *verb* past tense of SPEAK.
spoke² *noun* bar joining the hub of a wheel to the rim.
spoken *verb* past participle of SPEAK.
spokesman, spokeswoman, spokesperson *noun* person chosen to speak on behalf of a group.
spoliation *noun* plundering.
sponge ❶ *noun* **1** sea animal with a porous absorbent skeleton. **2** skeleton of a sponge, or a substance like it, used for cleaning. **3** type of light cake. **4** rub with a wet sponge. ◆ *verb* **5** wipe with a sponge. **6** live at the expense of others. **sponger** *noun Slang* person who sponges on others. **spongy** *adjective* **sponge**

bag small bag for holding toiletries.
sponsor ❶ *noun* **1** person who promotes something. **2** person who agrees to give money to a charity on completion of a specified activity by another. **3** godparent. **4** person who pays the costs of a programme in return for advertising. ◆ *verb* **5** act as a sponsor for.
sponsorship *noun*
spontaneous ❶ *adjective* **1** not planned or arranged. **2** occurring through natural processes without outside influence.
spontaneously *adverb* **spontaneity** *noun*
spoof ❶ *noun* **1** mildly satirical parody. **2** trick.
spook ❶ *noun Informal* ghost. **spooky** *adjective*
spool *noun* cylinder round which something can be wound.
spoon *noun* **1** shallow bowl attached to a handle for eating, stirring, or serving food. ◆ *verb* **2** lift with a spoon. **spoonful** *noun*
spoon-feed *verb* **1** feed with a spoon. **2** give (someone) too much help. **spoonbill** *noun* wading bird of warm regions with a long flat bill.
spoonerism *noun* accidental changing over of the initial sounds of a pair of words, such as *half-warmed fish* for *half-formed wish*.
spoor *noun* trail of an animal.
sporadic ❶ *adjective* intermittent, scattered.
sporadically *adverb*
spore *noun* minute reproductive body of some plants.
sporran *noun* pouch worn in front of a kilt.
sport ❶ *noun* **1** activity for pleasure, competition, or exercise. **2** such activities collectively. **3** enjoyment. **4** playful joking. **5** person who reacts cheerfully. ◆ *verb* **6** wear

———————— THESAURUS ————————

◆*verb* **2** = **shatter**, disintegrate, fracture, split
split *verb* **1** = **break**, burst, come apart, come undone, crack, give way, open, rend, rip **2** = **separate**, branch, cleave, disband, disunite, diverge, fork, part **3** = **separate**, break up, divorce, part **4** = **share out**, allocate, allot, apportion, distribute, divide, halve, partition ◆*noun* **6** = **division**, breach, break-up, discord, dissension, estrangement, rift, rupture, schism **7** = **crack**, breach, division, fissure, gap, rent, rip, separation, slit, tear
spoil *verb* **1** = **ruin**, damage, destroy, disfigure, harm, impair, injure, mar, mess up, trash (*sl*), wreck [OPPOSITE] save. **2** = **overindulge**, coddle, cosset, indulge, mollycoddle, pamper [OPPOSITE] deprive. **3** = **go bad**, addle, curdle, decay, decompose, go off (*Brit inf*), rot, turn
spoils *plural noun* **1** = **booty**, loot, plunder,

prey, swag (*sl*)
spoilsport *noun Inf* = **killjoy**, damper, dog in the manger, misery (*Brit inf*), wet blanket (*inf*)
spongy *adjective* **2** = **porous**, absorbent
sponsor *noun* **1** = **backer**, patron, promoter ◆*verb* **5** = **back**, finance, fund, patronize, promote, subsidize
spontaneous *adjective* **1** = **unplanned**, impromptu, impulsive, instinctive, natural, unprompted, voluntary, willing [OPPOSITE] planned
spoof *noun Inf* **1** = **parody**, burlesque, caricature, mockery, satire, send-up (*Brit inf*), take-off (*inf*)
spooky *adjective* = **eerie**, chilling, creepy (*inf*), frightening, scary (*inf*), spine-chilling, uncanny, unearthly, weird
sporadic *adjective* = **intermittent**, irregular,

proudly. **sporting** *adjective* **1** of sport. **2** behaving in a fair and decent way. **sporting chance** reasonable chance of success. **sporty** *adjective* **sportive** *adjective* playful. **sports car** fast low-built car, usu. open-topped. **sports jacket** man's casual jacket. **sportsman, sportswoman** *noun* **1** person who plays sports. **2** person who plays fair and is good-humoured when losing. **sportsmanlike** *adjective* **sportsmanship** *noun* **sport utility vehicle** *noun chiefly US* powerful four-wheel drive vehicle for rough terrain.

spot ✪ *noun* **1** small mark on a surface. **2** pimple. **3** location. **4** *Informal* small quantity. **5** *Informal* awkward situation. **6** part of a show assigned to a performer. ✦ *verb* **spotting, spotted 7** notice. **8** mark with spots. **9** watch for and take note of. **10** rain lightly. **on the spot 1** at the place in question. **2** immediately. **3** in an awkward predicament. **spotless** *adjective* absolutely clean. **spotlessly** *adverb* **spotted** *adjective* **spotty** *adjective* **1** with spots. **2** inconsistent. **spot check** random examination. **spotlight** *noun* **1** powerful light illuminating a small area. **2** centre of attention. ✦ *verb* **3** draw attention to. **spot-on** *adjective* *Informal* absolutely accurate.

spouse ✪ *noun* husband or wife.

spout ✪ *verb* **1** pour out in a stream or jet. **2** *Slang* utter (a stream of words) lengthily. ✦ *noun* **3** projecting tube or lip for pouring liquids. **4** stream or jet of liquid. **up the spout** *Slang* ruined or lost.

sprain *verb* **1** injure (a joint) by a sudden twist. ✦ *noun* **2** such an injury.

sprang *verb* a past tense of SPRING.

sprat *noun* small sea fish.

sprawl ✪ *verb* **1** lie or sit with the limbs spread out. **2** spread out in a straggling manner. ✦ *noun* **3** part of a city that has spread untidily over a large area.

spray¹ ✪ *noun* **1** (device for producing) fine drops of liquid. **2** number of small objects flying through the air. ✦ *verb* **3** scatter in fine drops. **4** cover with a spray. **spray gun** device for spraying paint etc.

spray² ✪ *noun* **1** branch with buds, leaves, flowers, or berries. **2** ornament like this.

spread ✪ *verb* **spreading, spread 1** open out or be displayed to the fullest extent. **2** extend over a larger expanse. **3** apply as a coating. **4** send or be sent in all directions. ✦ *noun* **5** spreading. **6** extent. **7** *Informal* large meal. **8** soft food which can be spread. **9** two facing pages in a magazine or book. **spread-eagled** *adjective* with arms and legs outstretched. **spreadsheet** *noun* computer program for manipulating figures.

spree ✪ *noun* session of overindulgence, usu. in drinking or spending money.

sprig *noun* **1** twig or shoot. **2** design like this. **sprigged** *adjective*

——————— THESAURUS ———————

occasional, scattered, spasmodic

sport *noun* **1, 2 = game**, amusement, diversion, exercise, pastime, play, recreation **4 = fun**, badinage, banter, jest, joking, teasing ✦*verb* **6 = wear**, display, exhibit, show off

sporting *adjective* **2 = fair**, game (*inf*), sportsmanlike

sporty *adjective* **1 = athletic**, energetic, outdoor

spot *noun* **1 = mark**, blemish, blot, blotch, scar, smudge, speck, speckle, stain **2 = pimple**, pustule, zit (*sl*) **3 = place**, location, point, position, scene, site **5** *Inf* **= predicament**, difficulty, hot water (*inf*), mess, plight, quandary, tight spot, trouble ✦*verb* **7 = see**, catch sight of, detect, discern, espy, make out, observe, recognize, sight **8 = mark**, dirty, fleck, mottle, smirch, soil, spatter, speckle, splodge, splotch, stain

spotless *adjective* **= clean**, flawless, gleaming, immaculate, impeccable, pure, shining, unblemished, unstained, unsullied, untarnished OPPOSITE▷ **soiled**

spotlight *noun* **2 = attention**, fame, limelight, public eye ✦*verb* **3 = highlight**, accentuate, draw attention to

spotted *adjective* **1 = speckled**, dappled, dotted, flecked, mottled

spouse *noun* **= partner**, consort, husband *or* wife, mate, significant other (*US inf*)

spout *verb* **1 = stream**, discharge, gush, shoot, spray, spurt, surge

sprawl *verb* **1 = loll**, flop, lounge, slouch, slump **2 = spread**, ramble, straggle, trail

spray¹ *noun* **1 = aerosol**, atomizer, sprinkler **2 = droplets**, drizzle, fine mist ✦*verb* **3 = scatter**, diffuse, shower, sprinkle

spray² *noun* **1 = sprig**, branch **2 = corsage**, floral arrangement

spread *verb* **1 = open (out)**, broaden, dilate, expand, extend, sprawl, stretch, unfold, unroll, widen **4 = circulate**, broadcast, disseminate, make known, propagate OPPOSITE▷ **repress** ✦*noun* **5 = increase**, advance, development, dispersal, dissemination, expansion, proliferation **6 = extent**, span, stretch, sweep

spree *noun* **= binge** (*inf*), bacchanalia, bender (*inf*), carousal, fling, orgy, revel

sprightly ❶ *adjective* **-lier, -liest** lively and brisk. **sprightliness** *noun*

spring ❶ *verb* **springing, sprang** *or* **sprung, sprung 1** move suddenly upwards or forwards in a single motion, jump. **2** cause to happen unexpectedly. **3** develop unexpectedly. **4** originate (from). **5** provide with springs. **6** *Informal* arrange the escape of (someone) from prison. ♦ *noun* **7** season between winter and summer. **8** jump. **9** coil which can be compressed, stretched, or bent and returns to its original shape when released. **10** natural pool forming the source of a stream. **11** elasticity. **springy** *adjective* elastic.

springboard *noun* **1** flexible board used to gain height or momentum in diving or gymnastics. **2** thing acting as an impetus.

spring-clean *verb* clean (a house) thoroughly.

spring onion onion with a tiny bulb and long green leaves. **spring tide** high tide at new or full moon. **springtime** *noun* season of spring.

springbok *noun* S African antelope.

springer *noun* small spaniel.

sprinkle ❶ *verb* **1** scatter (liquid or powder) in tiny drops or particles over (something). **2** distribute over. **sprinkler** *noun* **sprinkling** *noun* small quantity or number.

sprint ❶ *noun* **1** short race run at top speed. **2** fast run. ♦ *verb* **3** run a short distance at top speed. **sprinter** *noun*

sprit *noun* small spar set diagonally across a sail to extend it. **spritsail** *noun* sail extended by a sprit.

sprite ❶ *noun* elf.

sprocket *noun* wheel with teeth on the rim,

that drives or is driven by a chain.

sprout ❶ *verb* **1** put forth shoots. **2** begin to grow or develop. ♦ *noun* **3** shoot. **4** short for BRUSSELS SPROUT.

spruce[1] *noun* kind of fir.

spruce[2] ❶ *adjective* neat and smart. **spruce up** *verb* make neat and smart.

sprung *verb* a past of SPRING.

spry ❶ *adjective* **spryer, spryest** *or* **sprier, spriest** active or nimble.

spud *noun Informal* potato.

spume *noun, verb* froth.

spun *verb* past of SPIN.

spunk *noun Informal* courage, spirit. **spunky** *adjective*

spur ❶ *noun* **1** stimulus or incentive. **2** spiked wheel on the heel of a rider's boot used to urge on a horse. **3** projection. ♦ *verb* **spurring, spurred 4** urge on, incite (someone). **on the spur of the moment** on impulse.

spurge *noun* plant with milky sap.

spurious ❶ *adjective* not genuine.

spurn ❶ *verb* reject with scorn.

spurt ❶ *verb* **1** gush or cause to gush out in a jet. ♦ *noun* **2** short sudden burst of activity or speed. **3** sudden gush.

sputnik *noun* early Soviet artificial satellite.

sputter *verb, noun* splutter.

sputum *noun, pl* **-ta** spittle, usu. mixed with mucus.

spy ❶ *noun, pl* **spies 1** person employed to obtain secret information. **2** person who secretly watches others. ♦ *verb* **spying, spied 3** act as a spy. **4** catch sight of. **spyglass** *noun* small telescope.

———————— THESAURUS ————————

sprightly *adjective* =**lively**, active, agile, brisk, energetic, nimble, spirited, spry, vivacious

spring *verb* **1** =**jump**, bounce, bound, leap, vault **2, 3** =**appear**, develop, mushroom, shoot up **4** =**originate**, arise, come, derive, descend, issue, proceed, start, stem ♦*noun* **8** =**jump**, bound, leap, vault **11** =**elasticity**, bounce, buoyancy, flexibility, resilience

springy *adjective* =**elastic**, bouncy, buoyant, flexible, resilient

sprinkle *verb* **1** =**scatter**, dredge, dust, pepper, powder, shower, spray, strew

sprinkling *noun* **1** =**scattering**, dash, dusting, few, handful, sprinkle

sprint *verb* **3** =**race**, dart, dash, hare (*Brit inf*), shoot, tear

sprout *verb* **1, 2** =**grow**, bud, develop, shoot, spring

spruce[2] *adjective* =**smart**, dapper, natty (*inf*), neat, trim, well-groomed, well turned out

spruce up *verb* =**smarten up**, tidy, titivate

spry *adjective* =**active**, agile, nimble, sprightly, supple

spur *noun* **1** =**stimulus**, impetus, impulse, incentive, incitement, inducement, motive **2** =**goad**, prick ♦*verb* **4** =**incite**, animate, drive, goad, impel, prick, prod, prompt, stimulate, urge **on the spur of the moment** =**on impulse**, impromptu, impulsively, on the spot, without planning

spurious *adjective* =**false**, artificial, bogus, fake, phoney *or* phony (*inf*), pretended, sham, specious, unauthentic

spurn *verb* =**reject**, despise, disdain, rebuff, repulse, scorn, slight, snub

spurt *verb* **1** =**gush**, burst, erupt, shoot, squirt, surge ♦*noun* **2** =**burst**, fit, rush, spate, surge

spy *noun* **1** =**undercover agent**, mole, nark (*Brit, Aust & NZ sl*) ♦*verb* **4** =**catch sight of**,

S

Sq. Square.

squab *noun* young bird yet to leave the nest.

squabble ❶ *verb, noun* (engage in) a petty or noisy quarrel.

squad ❶ *noun* small group of people working or training together.

squadron *noun* division of an air force, fleet, or cavalry regiment.

squalid ❶ *adjective* **1** dirty and unpleasant. **2** morally sordid. **squalor** *noun* disgusting dirt and filth.

squall[1] *noun* sudden strong wind.

squall[2] *verb* **1** cry noisily, yell. ◆ *noun* **2** harsh cry.

squander ❶ *verb* waste (money or resources).

square ❶ *noun* **1** geometric figure with four equal sides and four right angles. **2** open area in a town in this shape. **3** product of a number multiplied by itself. ◆ *adjective* **4** square in shape. **5** denoting a measure of area. **6** straight or level. **7** fair and honest. **8** with all accounts or debts settled. **9** *Informal* old-fashioned. ◆ *verb* **10** multiply (a number) by itself. **11** make square. **12** settle (a debt). **13** level the score. **14** be or cause to be consistent. ◆ *adverb* **15** squarely, directly. **squarely** *adverb* **1** in a direct way. **2** in an honest and frank manner. **square dance** formation dance in which the couples form squares. **square meal** substantial meal. **square root** number of which a given number is the square. **square up to** *verb* prepare to confront (a person or problem).

squash[1] ❶ *verb* **1** crush flat. **2** suppress. **3** push into a confined space. **4** humiliate with a crushing retort. ◆ *noun* **5** sweet fruit drink diluted with water. **6** crowd of people in a confined space. **7** (also **squash rackets**) game played in an enclosed court with a rubber ball and long-handled rackets. **squashy** *adjective*

squash[2] *noun* marrow-like vegetable.

squat *verb* **squatting, squatted** **1** crouch with the knees bent and the weight on the feet. **2** occupy unused premises to which one has no legal right. ◆ *noun* **3** place where squatters live. ◆ *adjective* **4** short and broad. **squatter** *noun* illegal occupier of unused premises.

squaw *noun* Offens Native American woman.

squawk ❶ *noun* **1** loud harsh cry. **2** loud complaint. ◆ *verb* **3** utter a squawk.

squeak ❶ *noun* **1** short shrill cry or sound. ◆ *verb* **2** make or utter a squeak. **narrow squeak** *Informal* narrow escape. **squeaky** *adjective*

squeal ❶ *noun* **1** long shrill cry or sound. ◆ *verb* **2** make or utter a squeal. **3** *Slang* inform on someone to the police.

squeamish ❶ *adjective* easily sickened or shocked.

squeegee *noun* tool with a rubber blade for clearing water from a surface.

squeeze ❶ *verb* **1** grip or press firmly. **2** crush or press to extract liquid. **3** push into a confined space. **4** hug. **5** obtain (something) by force or great effort. ◆ *noun* **6** squeezing. **7** amount extracted by squeezing. **8** hug. **9** crush of people in a confined space. **10** restriction on borrowing.

squelch *verb* **1** make a wet sucking sound, as by walking through mud. ◆ *noun* **2** squelching sound.

squib *noun* small firework that hisses before exploding.

squid *noun* sea creature with a long soft body

———————— T H E S A U R U S ————————

espy, glimpse, notice, observe, spot

squabble *verb* =**quarrel**, argue, bicker, dispute, fight, row, wrangle ◆*noun* =**quarrel**, argument, disagreement, dispute, fight, row, tiff

squad *noun* =**team**, band, company, crew, force, gang, group, troop

squalid *adjective* =**dirty**, filthy, scungy (*Aust & NZ sl*), seedy, sleazy, slummy, sordid, unclean OPPOSITE clean

squalor *noun* =**filth**, foulness, sleaziness, squalidness

squander *verb* =**waste**, blow (*sl*), expend, fritter away, misspend, misuse, spend

square *adjective* **7** =**honest**, above board, ethical, fair, genuine, kosher (*inf*), on the level (*inf*), straight ◆*verb* **12** =**pay off**, settle **13** =**even up**, level **14** =**match**, agree, correspond, fit, reconcile, tally

squash[1] *verb* **1** =**crush**, compress, distort, flatten, mash, press, pulp, smash **4** =**suppress**, annihilate, crush, humiliate, quell, silence

squashy *adjective* =**soft**, mushy, pulpy, spongy, yielding

squawk *verb* **3** =**cry**, hoot, screech

squeak *verb* **2** =**peep**, pipe, squeal

squeal *noun* **1** =**scream**, screech, shriek, wail, yell ◆*verb* **2** =**scream**, screech, shriek, wail, yell

squeamish *adjective* =**fastidious**, delicate, nauseous, prudish, queasy, sick, strait-laced OPPOSITE tough

squeeze *verb* **1** =**press**, clutch, compress, crush, grip, pinch, squash, wring **3** =**cram**, crowd, force, jam, pack, press, ram, stuff **4** =**hug**, clasp, cuddle, embrace, enfold **5** =**extort**, milk, pressurize, wrest ◆*noun* **8** =**hug**, clasp, embrace **9** =**crush**, congestion, crowd, jam, press, squash and ten tentacles.

squiffy *adjective Informal* slightly drunk.

squiggle *noun* wavy line. **squiggly** *adjective*

squint ❶ *verb* **1** have eyes which face in different directions. **2** glance sideways. ◆ *noun* **3** squinting condition of the eye. **4** *Informal* glance. ◆ *adjective* **5** crooked.

squire *noun* **1** country gentleman, usu. the main landowner in a community. **2** *Hist* knight's apprentice. ◆ *verb* **3** (of a man) escort (a woman).

squirm ❶ *verb* **1** wriggle, writhe. **2** feel embarrassed. ◆ *noun* **3** wriggling movement.

squirrel *noun* small bushy-tailed tree-living animal.

squirt *verb* **1** force (a liquid) or (of a liquid) be forced out of a narrow opening. **2** squirt liquid at. ◆ *noun* **3** jet of liquid. **4** *Informal* small or insignificant person.

squish *verb, noun* (make) a soft squelching sound. **squishy** *adjective*

Sr 1 Senior. **2** Señor. **3** *Chem* strontium.

SRN State Registered Nurse.

SS 1 Schutzstaffel: Nazi paramilitary security force. **2** steamship.

SSE south-southeast.

SSW south-southwest.

St 1 Saint. **2** Street.

st. stone (weight).

stab ❶ *verb* **stabbing, stabbed 1** pierce with something pointed. **2** jab (at). ◆ *noun* **3** stabbing. **4** sudden unpleasant sensation. **5** *Informal* attempt.

stabilize *verb* make or become stable. **stabilization** *noun* **stabilizer** *noun* device for stabilizing a child's bicycle, an aircraft, or a ship.

stable¹ ❶ *noun* **1** building in which horses are kept. **2** establishment that breeds and trains racehorses. **3** establishment that manages or trains several entertainers or athletes. ◆ *verb* **4** put or keep (a horse) in a stable.

stable² ❶ *adjective* **1** firmly fixed or

established. **2** firm in character. **3** *Science* not subject to decay or decomposition. **stability** *noun*

staccato [stak-**ah**-toe] *adjective, adverb* **1** *Music* with the notes sharply separated. ◆ *adjective* **2** consisting of short abrupt sounds.

stack ❶ *noun* **1** ordered pile. **2** large amount. **3** chimney. ◆ *verb* **4** pile in a stack. **5** control (aircraft waiting to land) so that they fly at different altitudes.

stadium *noun, pl* **-diums, -dia** sports arena with tiered seats for spectators.

staff¹ ❶ *noun* **1** people employed in an organization. **2** stick used as a weapon, support, etc. ◆ *verb* **3** supply with personnel. **staff nurse** qualified nurse of the rank below a sister.

staff² *noun, pl* **staves** set of five horizontal lines on which music is written.

stag *noun* adult male deer. **stag beetle** beetle with large branched jaws. **stag night, party** party for men only.

stage ❶ *noun* **1** step or period of development. **2** platform in a theatre where actors perform. **3** scene of action. **4** portion of a journey. ◆ *verb* **5** put (a play) on stage. **6** organize and carry out (an event). **the stage** theatre as a profession. **stagey** *adjective* overtheatrical. **stagecoach** *noun* large horse-drawn vehicle formerly used to carry passengers and mail. **stage door** theatre door leading backstage. **stage fright** nervousness felt by a person about to face an audience. **stagehand** *noun* person who moves props and scenery on a stage. **stage-manage** *verb* arrange from behind the scenes. **stage-manager** *noun* **stage whisper** loud whisper intended to be heard by an audience.

stagger ❶ *verb* **1** walk unsteadily. **2** astound. **3** set apart to avoid congestion. ◆ *noun* **4** staggering. **staggering** *adjective*

stagnant ❶ *adjective* **1** (of water or air) stale from not moving. **2** not growing or developing.

S

—————————— T H E S A U R U S ——————————

squint *adjective* **5** = **crooked**, askew, aslant, awry, cockeyed, skew-whiff (*inf*)

squirm *verb* **1** = **wriggle**, twist, writhe

stab *verb* **1** = **pierce**, impale, jab, knife, spear, stick, thrust, transfix, wound ◆*noun* **3** = **wound**, gash, incision, jab, puncture, thrust **4** = **twinge**, ache, pang, prick **5** *Inf* = **attempt**, endeavour, go, try

stable² *adjective* **1** = **firm**, constant, established, fast, fixed, immovable, lasting, permanent, secure, sound, strong OPPOSITE> **uncertain. 2** = **steady**, reliable, staunch,

steadfast, sure OPPOSITE> **unstable**

stack *noun* **1, 2** = **pile**, berg (*S Afr*), heap, load, mass, mound, mountain ◆*verb* **4** = **pile**, accumulate, amass, assemble, heap up, load

staff¹ *noun* **1** = **workers**, employees, personnel, team, workforce **2** = **stick**, cane, crook, pole, rod, sceptre, stave, wand

stage *noun* **1** = **step**, division, juncture, lap, leg, level, period, phase, point

stagger *verb* **1** = **totter**, lurch, reel, sway, wobble **2** = **astound**, amaze, astonish, confound, overwhelm, shake, shock, stun,

stagnate verb be stagnant. **stagnation** noun
staid ⊕ adjective sedate, serious, and rather dull.
stain ⊕ verb 1 discolour, mark. 2 colour with a penetrating pigment. ♦ noun 3 discoloration or mark. 4 moral blemish or slur. 5 penetrating liquid used to colour things. **stainless** adjective **stainless steel** steel alloy that does not rust.
stairs plural noun flight of steps between floors, usu. indoors. **stair** noun one step in a flight of stairs. **staircase**, **stairway** noun flight of stairs with a handrail or banisters.
stake¹ ⊕ noun 1 pointed stick or post driven into the ground as a support or marker. ♦ verb 2 support or mark out with stakes. **stake a claim to** claim a right to. **stake out** verb Slang (of police) keep (a place) under surveillance.
stake² ⊕ noun 1 money wagered. 2 interest, usu. financial, held in something. ♦ plural 3 prize in a race or contest. ♦ verb 4 wager, risk. 5 support financially. **at stake** being risked.
stakeholder noun person who has a concern or interest in something, esp. a business.
stalactite noun lime deposit hanging from the roof of a cave.
stalagmite noun lime deposit sticking up from the floor of a cave.
stale ⊕ adjective 1 not fresh. 2 lacking energy or ideas through overwork or monotony. 3 uninteresting from overuse. **staleness** noun
stalemate noun 1 Chess position in which any of a player's moves would put his king in check, resulting in a draw. 2 deadlock, impasse.
stalk¹ noun plant's stem.
stalk² ⊕ verb 1 follow or approach stealthily. 2 pursue persistently and, sometimes, attack (a

person with whom one is obsessed). 3 walk in a stiff or haughty manner. **stalking-horse** noun pretext.
stall¹ noun 1 small stand for the display and sale of goods. 2 compartment in a stable. 3 small room or compartment. ♦ plural 4 ground-floor seats in a theatre or cinema. 5 row of seats in a church for the choir or clergy. ♦ verb 6 stop (a motor vehicle or engine) or (of a motor vehicle or engine) stop accidentally.
stall² ⊕ verb employ delaying tactics.
stallion noun uncastrated male horse.
stalwart ⊕ [stawl-wart] adjective 1 strong and sturdy. 2 dependable. ♦ noun 3 stalwart person.
stamen noun pollen-producing part of a flower.
stamina ⊕ noun enduring energy and strength.
stammer ⊕ verb 1 speak or say with involuntary pauses or repetition of syllables. ♦ noun 2 tendency to stammer.
stamp ⊕ noun 1 (also **postage stamp**) piece of gummed paper stuck to an envelope or parcel to show that the postage has been paid. 2 act of stamping. 3 instrument for stamping a pattern or mark. 4 pattern or mark stamped. 5 characteristic feature. ♦ verb 6 bring (one's foot) down forcefully. 7 walk with heavy footsteps. 8 characterize. 9 impress (a pattern or mark) on. 10 stick a postage stamp on. **stamping ground** favourite meeting place. **stamp out** verb suppress by force.
stampede ⊕ noun 1 sudden rush of frightened animals or of a crowd. ♦ verb 2 (cause to) take part in a stampede.
stance ⊕ noun 1 attitude. 2 manner of

──────── T H E S A U R U S ────────

stupefy **3 =** alternate, overlap, step
stagnant adjective **=** stale, quiet, sluggish, still OPPOSITE moving
stagnate verb **=** vegetate, decay, decline, idle, languish, rot, rust
staid adjective **=** sedate, calm, composed, grave, serious, sober, solemn, steady
stain verb **1 =** mark, blemish, blot, dirty, discolour, smirch, soil, spot, tinge **2 =** dye, colour, tint ♦noun **3 =** mark, blemish, blot, discoloration, smirch, spot **4 =** stigma, disgrace, dishonour, shame, slur **5 =** dye, colour, tint
stake¹ noun **1 =** pole, pale, paling, palisade, picket, post, stick
stake² noun **1 =** bet, ante, pledge, wager **2 =** interest, concern, investment, involvement, share ♦verb **4 =** bet, chance, gamble, hazard, risk, venture, wager
stale adjective **1 =** old, decayed, dry, flat,

fusty, hard, musty, sour OPPOSITE fresh. **2, 3 =** unoriginal, banal, hackneyed, overused, stereotyped, threadbare, trite, worn-out OPPOSITE new
stalk² verb **1, 2 =** pursue, follow, haunt, hunt, shadow, track
stall verb **=** play for time, hedge, temporize
stalwart adjective **1 =** strong, stout, strapping, sturdy OPPOSITE feeble. **2 =** loyal, dependable, reliable, staunch
stamina noun **=** staying power, endurance, energy, force, power, resilience, strength
stammer verb **1 =** stutter, falter, hesitate, pause, stumble
stamp noun **3 =** imprint, brand, earmark, hallmark, mark, signature ♦verb **6 =** trample, crush **8 =** identify, brand, categorize, label, mark, reveal, show to be **9 =** imprint, impress, mark, print

standing.
stanch ❶ [stahnch] *verb* same as STAUNCH².
stanchion *noun* upright bar used as a support.
stand ❶ *verb* **standing, stood 1** be in, rise to, or place in an upright position. **2** be situated. **3** be in a specified state or position. **4** remain unchanged or valid. **5** tolerate. **6** survive. **7** offer oneself as a candidate. **8** *Informal* treat to. ♦ *noun* **9** stall for the sale of goods. **10** structure for spectators at a sports ground. **11** firmly held opinion. **12** *US & Aust* witness box. **13** rack or piece of furniture on which things may be placed. **14** act of standing. **15** halt to counter-attack. **standing** *adjective* **1** permanent, lasting. **2** used to stand in. ♦ *noun* **3** reputation or status. **4** duration. **stand by** *verb* **1** be available and ready. **2** watch without taking any action. **3** be faithful to. **stand-by** *noun* person or thing ready to be used in an emergency. **stand down** *verb* resign or withdraw. **stand for** *verb* **1** represent or mean. **2** *Informal* tolerate. **stand in** *verb* act as a substitute. **stand-in** *noun* substitute. **standing order** instruction to a bank to pay a stated sum at regular intervals. **standoffish** *adjective* reserved or haughty. **stand out** *verb* be distinctive. **stand up** *verb* **1** rise to one's feet. **2** *Informal* fail to keep an appointment. **3** withstand examination. **stand up for** *verb*

support or defend. **stand up to** *verb* **1** confront and resist. **2** withstand and endure.
standard ❶ *noun* **1** level of quality. **2** example against which others are judged or measured. **3** moral principle. **4** distinctive flag. **5** upright pole. ♦ *adjective* **6** usual, regular, or average. **7** of recognized authority. **8** accepted as correct.
standardize *verb* cause to conform to a standard. **standardization** *noun* **standard-bearer** *noun* leader of a movement. **standard lamp** lamp attached to an upright pole on a base.
standpipe *noun* tap attached to a water main to provide a public water supply.
standpoint ❶ *noun* point of view.
standstill *noun* complete halt.
stank *verb* a past tense of STINK.
stanza *noun* verse of a poem.
staple¹ *noun* **1** U-shaped piece of metal used to fasten papers or secure things. ♦ *verb* **2** fasten with staples. **stapler** *noun* small device for fastening papers together.
staple² ❶ *adjective* **1** of prime importance, principal. ♦ *noun* **2** main constituent of anything.
star ❶ *noun* **1** hot gaseous mass in space, visible in the night sky as a point of light. **2** star-shaped mark used to indicate excellence. **3** asterisk. **4** celebrity in the entertainment or

——————— T H E S A U R U S ———————

stampede *noun* **1** = **rush**, charge, flight, rout
stamp out *verb* = **eliminate**, crush, destroy, eradicate, put down, quell, scotch, suppress
stance *noun* **1** = **attitude**, position, stand, standpoint, viewpoint **2** = **posture**, bearing, carriage, deportment
stanch see STAUNCH²
stand *verb* **1 a** = **be upright**, be erect, be vertical, rise **b** = **put**, mount, place, position, set **4** = **exist**, be valid, continue, hold, obtain, prevail, remain **5** = **tolerate**, abide, allow, bear, brook, countenance, endure, handle, put up with (*inf*), stomach, take ♦ *noun* **9** = **stall**, booth, table **11** = **position**, attitude, determination, opinion, stance **13** = **support**, base, bracket, dais, platform, rack, stage, tripod
standard *noun* **1** = **level**, gauge, grade, measure **2** = **criterion**, average, benchmark, example, guideline, model, norm, yardstick **3** = **principles**, ethics, ideals, morals **4** = **flag**, banner, ensign ♦ *adjective* **6** = **usual**, average, basic, customary, normal, orthodox, regular, typical OPPOSITE strange. **7, 8** = **accepted**, approved, authoritative, definitive, established, official, recognized OPPOSITE **unofficial**
standardize *verb* = **bring into line**,

institutionalize, regiment
stand by *verb* **1** = **be prepared**, wait **3** = **support**, back, be loyal to, champion, take (someone's) part
stand for *verb* **1** = **represent**, betoken, denote, indicate, mean, signify, symbolize **2** *Inf* = **tolerate**, bear, brook, endure, put up with
stand in *verb* = **be a substitute for**, cover for, deputize for, represent, take the place of
stand-in *noun* = **substitute**, deputy, locum, replacement, reserve, stopgap, surrogate, understudy
standing *adjective* **1** = **permanent**, fixed, lasting, regular ♦ *noun* **3** = **status**, eminence, footing, position, rank, reputation, repute **4** = **duration**, continuance, existence
standoffish *adjective* = **reserved**, aloof, cold, distant, haughty, remote, unapproachable, unsociable
stand out *verb* = **be conspicuous**, be distinct, be obvious, be prominent
standpoint *noun* = **point of view**, angle, position, stance, viewpoint
stand up for *verb* = **support**, champion, defend, stick up for (*inf*), uphold
staple² *adjective* **1** = **principal**, basic, chief,

S

sports world. ♦ *plural* **5** astrological forecast, horoscope. ♦ *verb* **starring, starred 6** feature or be featured as a star. **7** mark with a star or stars. ♦ *adjective* **8** leading, famous. **stardom** *noun* status of a star in the entertainment or sports world. **starlet** *noun* young actress presented as a future star. **starry** *adjective* full of or like stars. **starry-eyed** *adjective* full of naive optimism. **starfish** *noun* star-shaped sea creature. **Stars and Stripes** national flag of America. **star sign** sign of the zodiac under which a person was born.

starboard *noun* **1** right-hand side of a ship, when facing forward. ♦ *adjective* **2** of or on this side.

starch *noun* **1** carbohydrate forming the main food element in bread, potatoes, etc., and used mixed with water for stiffening fabric. ♦ *verb* **2** stiffen (fabric) with starch. **starchy** *adjective* **1** containing starch. **2** stiff and formal.

stare ① *verb* **1** look or gaze fixedly (at). ♦ *noun* **2** fixed gaze.

stark ① *adjective* **1** harsh, unpleasant, and plain. **2** desolate, bare. **3** absolute. ♦ *adverb* **4** completely. **stark-naked** *adjective* completely naked.

starling *noun* songbird with glossy black speckled feathers.

start ① *verb* **1** take the first step, begin. **2** set or be set in motion. **3** make a sudden involuntary movement from fright. **4** establish or set up. ♦ *noun* **5** first part of something. **6** place or time of starting. **7** advantage or lead in

a competitive activity. **8** sudden movement made from fright. **starter** *noun* **1** first course of a meal. **2** device for starting a car's engine. **3** person who signals the start of a race. **start-up** *noun* recently launched project or business enterprise.

startle ① *verb* slightly surprise or frighten.

starve *verb* **1** die or suffer or cause to die or suffer from hunger. **2** deprive of something needed. **starvation** *noun*

stash *Informal verb* **1** store in a secret place. ♦ *noun* **2** secret store.

state ① *noun* **1** condition of a person or thing. **2** sovereign political power or its territory. **3** (S-) the government. **4** *Informal* excited or agitated condition. **5** pomp. ♦ *adjective* **6** of or concerning the State. **7** involving ceremony. ♦ *verb* **8** express in words. **the States** United States of America. **stately** *adjective* dignified or grand. **statehouse** *noun* NZ publicly-owned house rented to a low-income tenant.

statement *noun* **1** something stated. **2** printed financial account. **stateroom** *noun* **1** private cabin on a ship. **2** large room in a palace, used for ceremonial occasions.

statesman, stateswoman *noun* experienced and respected political leader. **statesmanship** *noun*

static ① *adjective* **1** stationary or inactive. **2** (of a force) acting but producing no movement. ♦ *noun* **3** crackling sound or speckled picture caused by interference in radio or television reception. **4** (also **static electricity**) electric

———————— T H E S A U R U S ————————

fundamental, key, main, predominant
star *noun* **1** = **heavenly body 4** = **celebrity**, big name, luminary, main attraction, megastar (*inf*), name ♦*adjective* **8** = **leading**, brilliant, celebrated, major, prominent, well-known
stare *verb* **1** = **gaze**, eyeball (*sl*), gape, gawk, gawp (*Brit sl*), goggle, look, watch
stark *adjective* **1, 2** = **harsh**, austere, bare, barren, bleak, grim, hard, plain, severe **3** = **absolute**, blunt, downright, out-and-out, pure, sheer, unmitigated, utter ♦*adverb* **4** = **absolutely**, altogether, completely, entirely, quite, utterly, wholly
start *verb* **1** = **begin**, appear, arise, commence, embark upon, issue, make a beginning, originate, set about, take the first step OPPOSITE **stop**. **2** = **set in motion**, activate, get going, initiate, instigate, kick-start, open, originate, trigger OPPOSITE **end**. **3** = **jump**, flinch, jerk, recoil, shy **4** = **establish**, begin, create, found, inaugurate, initiate, institute, launch, pioneer, set up OPPOSITE **stop**

♦*noun* **5, 6** = **beginning**, birth, dawn, foundation, inception, initiation, onset, opening, outset **7** = **advantage**, edge, head start, lead **8** = **jump**, convulsion, spasm
startle *verb* = **surprise**, frighten, make (someone) jump, scare, shock
starving *adjective* **1** = **hungry**, famished, ravenous, starved
state *noun* **1** = **condition**, attitude, circumstances, equation, frame of mind, humour, mood, position, predicament, shape, situation, spirits **2** = **country**, commonwealth, federation, kingdom, land, nation, republic, territory **5** = **ceremony**, display, glory, grandeur, majesty, pomp, splendour, style ♦*verb* **8** = **express**, affirm, articulate, assert, declare, expound, present, say, specify, utter, voice
stately *adjective* = **grand**, august, dignified, lofty, majestic, noble, regal, royal
statement *noun* **1** = **account**, announcement, communication, communiqué, declaration,

sparks produced by friction. **statics** *noun* branch of mechanics dealing with the forces producing a state of equilibrium.

station ⊙ *noun* **1** place where trains stop for passengers. **2** headquarters or local offices of the police or a fire brigade. **3** building with special equipment for a particular purpose, e.g. *power station*. **4** television or radio channel. **5** place or position assigned to a person. **6** position in society. **7** large Australian sheep or cattle ranch. ◆ *verb* **8** assign (someone) to a particular place. **stationmaster** *noun* official in charge of a railway station.

stationary ⊙ *adjective* not moving.

> **SPELLING TIP**
>
> The words **stationary** and **stationery** are completely different in meaning and should not be confused.

stationery *noun* writing materials such as paper and pens. **stationer** *noun* dealer in stationery.

station wagon *noun US & Canad* automobile with a rear door and luggage space behind the rear seats.

statistic *noun* numerical fact collected and classified systematically. **statistics** *noun* science of classifying and interpreting numerical information. **statistical** *adjective* **statistically** *adverb* **statistician** *noun* person who compiles and studies statistics.

statue ⊙ *noun* large sculpture of a human or animal figure. **statuary** *noun* statues collectively. **statuesque** [stat-yoo-**esk**] *adjective* (of a woman) tall and well-proportioned.

statuette *noun* small statue.

stature ⊙ *noun* **1** person's height. **2** reputation of a person or their achievements.

status ⊙ *noun* **1** social position. **2** prestige. **3** person's legal standing. **status quo** existing state of affairs. **status symbol** possession regarded as a sign of position or wealth.

statute *noun* written law. **statutory** *adjective* required or authorized by law.

staunch[1] ⊙ *adjective* loyal, firm.

staunch[2], **stanch** ⊙ *verb* stop (a flow of blood).

stave *noun* **1** one of the strips of wood forming a barrel. **2** *Music* same as STAFF[2] **3** thick stick. **4** stanza. **stave in** *verb* **staving, stove** burst a hole in. **stave off** *verb* **staving, staved** ward off.

staves *noun* plural of STAFF[2] *or* STAVE.

stay[1] ⊙ *verb* **1** remain in a place or condition. **2** reside temporarily. **3** endure. ◆ *noun* **4** period of staying in a place. **5** postponement. **staying power** stamina.

stay[2] ⊙ *noun* **1** prop or buttress. ◆ *plural* **2** corset.

stay[3] *noun* rope or wire supporting a ship's mast.

STD 1 sexually transmitted disease. **2** subscriber trunk dialling.

stead *noun* **in someone's stead** in someone's place. **stand someone in good stead** be useful to someone.

steadfast ⊙ *adjective* firm, determined. **steadfastly** *adverb*

steady ⊙ *adjective* **steadier, steadiest 1** not shaky or wavering. **2** regular or continuous. **3** sensible and dependable. ◆ *verb* **steadying, steadied 4** make steady. ◆ *adverb* **5** in a steady manner. **steadily** *adverb* **steadiness** *noun*

──────────── THESAURUS ────────────

proclamation, report
static *adjective* **1** = **stationary**, fixed, immobile, motionless, still, unmoving
station *noun* **2** = **headquarters**, base, depot **5** = **place**, location, position, post, seat, situation **6** = **position**, post, rank, situation, standing, status ◆*verb* **8** = **assign**, establish, install, locate, post, set
stationary *adjective* = **motionless**, fixed, parked, standing, static, stock-still, unmoving
statuesque *adjective* = **well-proportioned**, imposing, Junoesque
stature *noun* **2** = **importance**, eminence, prestige, prominence, rank, standing
status *noun* **1, 2** = **position**, condition, consequence, eminence, grade, prestige, rank, standing

staunch[1] *adjective* = **loyal**, faithful, firm, sound, stalwart, steadfast, true, trusty
staunch[2], **stanch** *verb* = **stop**, check, dam, halt, stay, stem
stay[1] *verb* **1** = **remain**, abide, continue, halt, linger, loiter, pause, stop, tarry, wait OPPOSITE go ◆*noun* **4** = **visit**, holiday, sojourn, stop, stopover **5** = **postponement**, deferment, delay, halt, stopping, suspension
stay[2] *noun* **1** = **support**, brace, buttress, prop, reinforcement, shoring, stanchion
steadfast *adjective* = **firm**, faithful, fast, fixed, intent, loyal, resolute, stalwart, staunch, steady, unswerving, unwavering OPPOSITE **faltering**
steady *adjective* **1** = **firm**, fixed, safe, secure, stable OPPOSITE **unstable**. **2** = **continuous**, ceaseless, consistent, constant, incessant,

steak *noun* **1** thick slice of meat, esp. beef. **2** slice of fish.

steal ⊕ *verb* **stealing, stole, stolen 1** take unlawfully or without permission. **2** move stealthily.

stealth ⊕ *noun* **1** moving carefully and quietly. **2** secret or underhand behaviour. ◆ *adjective* **3** (of technology) able to render an aircraft almost invisible to radar. **4** disguised or hidden, *stealth taxes.* **stealthy** *adjective* **stealthily** *adverb*

steam *noun* **1** vapour into which water changes when boiled. **2** power, energy, or speed. ◆ *verb* **3** give off steam. **4** (of a vehicle) move by steam power. **5** cook or treat with steam. **steamer** *noun* **1** steam-propelled ship. **2** container used to cook food in steam. **steamy** *adjective* **steamier, steamiest 1** full of steam. **2** *Informal* erotic. **steam engine** engine worked by steam. **steamroller** *noun* **1** steam-powered vehicle with heavy rollers, used to level road surfaces. ◆ *verb* **2** use overpowering force to make (someone) do what one wants.

steatite [stee-a-tite] *noun* same as SOAPSTONE.

steed *noun Lit* horse.

steel *noun* **1** hard malleable alloy of iron and carbon. **2** steel rod used for sharpening knives. **3** hardness of character or attitude. ◆ *verb* **4** prepare (oneself) for something unpleasant. **steely** *adjective* **steel band** band of people playing on metal drums, popular in the West Indies.

steep[1] ⊕ *adjective* **1** sloping sharply. **2** *Informal* (of a price) unreasonably high. **steeply** *adverb* **steepness** *noun*

steep[2] ⊕ *verb* soak or be soaked in liquid.

steeped in filled with, e.g. *steeped in history.*

steeple *noun* church tower with a spire.

steeplejack *noun* person who repairs steeples

and chimneys.

steeplechase *noun* **1** horse race with obstacles to jump. **2** track race with hurdles and a water jump.

steer[1] ⊕ *verb* **1** direct the course of (a vehicle or ship). **2** direct (one's course). **steerage** *noun* cheapest accommodation on a passenger ship. **steering wheel** wheel turned by the driver of a vehicle in order to steer it.

steer[2] *noun* castrated male ox.

stein [stine] *noun* earthenware beer mug.

stellar *adjective* of stars.

stem[1] ⊕ *noun* **1** long thin central part of a plant. **2** long slender part, as of a wineglass. **3** part of a word to which inflections are added. ◆ *verb* **stemming, stemmed 4 stem from** originate from.

stem[2] ⊕ *verb* **stemming, stemmed** stop (the flow of something).

stench ⊕ *noun* foul smell.

stencil *noun* **1** thin sheet with cut-out pattern through which ink or paint passes to form the pattern on the surface below. **2** pattern made thus. ◆ *verb* **-cilling, -cilled 3** make (a pattern) with a stencil.

stenographer *noun* shorthand typist.

stentorian *adjective* (of a voice) very loud.

step ⊕ *verb* **stepping, stepped 1** move and set down the foot, as when walking. **2** walk a short distance. ◆ *noun* **3** stepping. **4** distance covered by a step. **5** sound made by stepping. **6** foot movement in a dance. **7** one of a sequence of actions taken in order to achieve a goal. **8** degree in a series or scale. **9** flat surface for placing the foot on when going up or down. ◆ *plural* **10** stepladder. **11** flight of stairs. **step in** *verb* intervene. **stepladder** *noun* folding portable ladder with supporting frame. **stepping stone 1** one of a series of stones for

S

nonstop, persistent, regular, unbroken, uninterrupted OPPOSITE occasional. **3** **= dependable,** balanced, calm, equable, level-headed, reliable, sensible, sober OPPOSITE unpredictable ◆*verb* **4 = stabilize,** brace, secure, support OPPOSITE shake

steal *verb* **1 = take,** appropriate, embezzle, filch, lift (*inf*), misappropriate, nick (*sl, chiefly Brit*), pilfer, pinch (*inf*), purloin, thieve **2** **= sneak,** creep, slink, slip, tiptoe

stealth *noun* **= secrecy,** furtiveness, slyness, sneakiness, stealthiness, surreptitiousness, unobtrusiveness

stealthy *adjective* **= secret,** furtive, secretive, sneaking, surreptitious

steep[1] *adjective* **1 = sheer,** abrupt, precipitous

OPPOSITE **gentle. 2** *Inf* **= high,** exorbitant, extortionate, extreme, overpriced, unreasonable OPPOSITE **fair**

steep[2] *verb* **= soak,** drench, immerse, marinate (*Cookery*), moisten, souse, submerge **steeped in = saturated,** filled with, imbued, infused, permeated, pervaded, suffused

steer[1] *verb* **1 = drive,** control, direct, guide, handle, pilot

stem[1] *noun* **1 = stalk,** axis, branch, shoot, trunk ◆*verb* **4 stem from = originate from,** arise from, be caused by, derive from

stem[2] *verb* **= stop,** check, curb, dam, hold back, staunch

stench *noun* **= stink,** foul smell, pong (*Brit inf*), reek, whiff (*Brit sl*) stepping on in crossing a stream. **2** means of progress towards a goal. **step up** *verb* increase (something) by stages.

step- *prefix* denoting a relationship created by the remarriage of a parent, e.g. *stepmother*.

steppes *plural noun* wide grassy treeless plains.

stereo *adjective* **1** short for STEREOPHONIC. ◆ *noun* **2** stereophonic record player. **3** stereophonic sound.

stereophonic *adjective* using two separate loudspeakers to give the effect of naturally distributed sound.

stereoscopic *adjective* having a three-dimensional effect.

stereotype ✿ *noun* **1** standardized idea of a type of person or thing. **2** monotonously familiar idea. ◆ *verb* **3** form a stereotype of.

sterile ✿ *adjective* **1** free from germs. **2** unable to produce offspring or seeds. **3** lacking inspiration or vitality. **sterility** *noun* **sterilize** *verb* make sterile. **sterilization** *noun*

sterling ✿ *noun* **1** British money system. ◆ *adjective* **2** genuine and reliable. **sterling silver** alloy with 92.5 per cent silver.

stern[1] ✿ *adjective* severe, strict. **sternly** *adverb* **sternness** *noun*

stern[2] *noun* rear part of a ship.

sternum *noun, pl* **-na, -nums** same as BREASTBONE.

steroid *noun* organic compound containing a carbon ring system, such as many hormones.

stertorous *adjective* (of breathing) laboured and noisy.

stet *interjection* instruction to ignore an alteration previously made by a proofreader.

stethoscope *noun* medical instrument for listening to sounds made inside the body.

Stetson *noun* ® tall broad-brimmed hat, worn mainly by cowboys.

stevedore *noun* person who loads and unloads ships.

stew *noun* **1** food cooked slowly in a closed pot. **2** *Informal* troubled or worried state. ◆ *verb* **3** cook slowly in a closed pot.

steward *noun* **1** person who looks after passengers on a ship or aircraft. **2** official who helps at a public event such as a race. **3** person who administers another's property.

stewardess *n fem*

stick[1] ✿ *noun* **1** long thin piece of wood. **2** such a piece of wood shaped for a special purpose, e.g. *hockey stick*. **3** something like a stick, e.g. *stick of celery*. **4** *Slang* verbal abuse, criticism. **the sticks** *Informal* remote country area. **stick insect** tropical insect resembling a twig.

stick[2] ✿ *verb* **sticking, stuck 1** push (a pointed object) into (something). **2** fasten or be fastened by or as if by pins or glue. **3** (foll. by *out*) extend beyond something else, protrude. **4** *Informal* put. **5** jam. **6** come to a standstill. **7** remain for a long time. **8** *Slang* tolerate, abide. **sticker** *noun* adhesive label or sign. **sticky** *adjective* **1** covered with an adhesive substance. **2** *Informal* difficult, unpleasant. **3** (of weather) warm and humid. **stick around** *verb Informal* remain in a place. **stick-in-the-mud** *noun* person who does not like anything new. **stick-up** *noun Slang* robbery at gunpoint. **stick up for** *verb Informal* support or defend.

stickleback *noun* small fish with sharp spines on its back.

stickler ✿ *noun* person who insists on something, e.g. *stickler for detail*.

stiff ✿ *adjective* **1** not easily bent or moved. **2**

step *verb* **1** = **walk**, move, pace, tread ◆ *noun* **3** = **footstep**, footfall, footprint, pace, print, stride, track **7** = **action**, act, deed, expedient, means, measure, move **8** = **degree**, level, rank

step in *verb Inf* = **intervene**, become involved, take action

step up *verb Inf* = **increase**, intensify, raise

stereotype *noun* **1** = **formula**, pattern ◆ *verb* **3** = **categorize**, pigeonhole, standardize, typecast

sterile *adjective* **1** = **germ-free**, aseptic, disinfected, sterilized OPPOSITE **dirty**. **2** = **barren**, bare, dry, empty, fruitless, unfruitful, unproductive OPPOSITE **productive**

sterilize *verb* **1** = **disinfect**, fumigate, purify

sterling *adjective* **2** = **excellent**, fine, genuine, sound, superlative, true

stern[1] *adjective* = **severe**, austere, forbidding, grim, hard, harsh, inflexible, rigid, serious, strict OPPOSITE **warm**

stick[1] *noun* **1, 2** = **cane**, baton, crook, pole, rod, staff, twig **4** *Sl* = **abuse**, criticism, flak (*inf*)

stick[2] *verb* **1** = **poke**, dig, jab, penetrate, pierce, prod, puncture, spear, stab, thrust, transfix **2** = **fasten**, adhere, affix, attach, bind, bond, cling, fix, glue, hold, join, paste, weld **3** (foll. by *out*) = **protrude**, bulge, extend, jut, obtrude, poke, project, show **4** *Inf* = **put**, deposit, lay, place, set **7** = **stay**, linger, persist, remain **8** *Sl* = **tolerate**, abide, stand, stomach, take

stickler *noun* = **fanatic**, fusspot (*Brit inf*), perfectionist, purist

stick up for *verb Inf* = **defend**, champion,

S

moving with pain. **3** difficult. **4** severe, e.g. *stiff punishment*. **5** unrelaxed or awkward. **6** firm in consistency. **7** strong, e.g. *a stiff drink*. ◆ *noun* **8** *Slang* corpse. **stiffly** *adverb* **stiffness** *noun* **stiffen** *verb* make or become stiff. **stiff-necked** *adjective* haughtily stubborn.

stifle ⊕ *verb* **1** suppress. **2** feel difficulty in breathing. **3** suffocate. **stifling** *adjective* uncomfortably hot and stuffy.

stigma ⊕ *noun, pl* **-mas, -mata 1** mark of social disgrace. **2** part of a plant that receives pollen. **stigmata** *plural noun* marks resembling the wounds of the crucified Christ. **stigmatize** *verb* mark as being shameful.

stile *noun* set of steps allowing people to climb a fence.

stiletto *noun, pl* **-tos 1** (also **stiletto heel**) high narrow heel on a woman's shoe. **2** small slender dagger.

still¹ ⊕ *adverb* **1** now or in the future as before. **2** up to this or that time. **3** even or yet, e.g. *still more insults*. **4** nevertheless. **5** quietly or without movement. ◆ *adjective* **6** motionless. **7** silent and calm, undisturbed. **8** (of a drink) not fizzy. ◆ *noun* **9** calmness. **10** photograph from a film scene. ◆ *verb* **11** make still. **12** relieve or end. **stillness** *noun* **stillborn** *adjective* born dead. **still life** painting of inanimate objects.

still² *noun* apparatus for distilling alcoholic drinks.

stilted ⊕ *adjective* stiff and formal in manner.
Stilton *noun* ® strong-flavoured cheese.
stilts *plural noun* **1** pair of poles with footrests for walking raised from the ground. **2** long posts supporting a building above ground level.
stimulus ⊕ *noun, pl* **-li** something that rouses a person or thing to activity. **stimulant** *noun* something, such as a drug, that acts as a stimulus. **stimulate** *verb* act as a stimulus (on). **stimulation** *noun*
sting ⊕ *verb* **stinging, stung 1** (of certain animals or plants) wound by injecting with poison. **2** feel or cause to feel sharp physical or mental pain. **3** incite. **4** *Slang* cheat (someone) by overcharging. ◆ *noun* **5** wound or pain caused by or as if by stinging. **6** mental pain. **7** sharp pointed organ of certain animals or plants by which poison can be injected. **stingray** *noun* flatfish capable of inflicting painful wounds.
stingy ⊕ *adjective* **-gier, -giest** mean or miserly. **stinginess** *noun*
stink ⊕ *noun* **1** strong unpleasant smell. **2** *Slang* unpleasant fuss. ◆ *verb* **stinking, stank** or **stunk, stunk 3** give off a strong unpleasant smell. **4** *Slang* be very unpleasant. **stinker** *noun* *Informal* difficult or unpleasant person or thing.
stinking *Informal adjective* **1** unpleasant. ◆ *adverb* **2** extremely.
stint ⊕ *verb* **1** (foll. by *on*) be miserly with (something). ◆ *noun* **2** allotted amount of work.

———————— THESAURUS ————————

stand up for, support
sticky *adjective* **1** = **tacky**, adhesive, clinging, gluey, glutinous, gooey (*inf*), gummy, icky (*inf*), viscid, viscous **2** *Inf* = **difficult**, awkward, delicate, embarrassing, nasty, tricky, unpleasant **3** = **humid**, clammy, close, muggy, oppressive, sultry, sweltering
stiff *adjective* **1** = **inflexible**, firm, hard, inelastic, rigid, solid, taut, tense, tight, unbending, unyielding OPPOSITE **flexible**. **3** = **difficult**, arduous, exacting, hard, tough **4** = **severe**, drastic, extreme, hard, harsh, heavy, strict **5** = **awkward**, clumsy, constrained, forced, formal, graceless, inelegant, jerky (*inf*), stilted, ungainly, ungraceful, unnatural, unrelaxed OPPOSITE **easy**
stiffen *verb* **1** = **brace**, reinforce, tauten, tense
stifle *verb* **1** = **suppress**, check, hush, repress, restrain, silence, smother, stop **2** = **choke 3** = **suffocate**, asphyxiate, choke, smother, strangle
stigma *noun* **1** = **disgrace**, dishonour, shame, slur, smirch, stain
still¹ *adjective* **6** = **motionless**, calm, peaceful,

restful, serene, stationary, tranquil, undisturbed OPPOSITE **moving**. **7** = **silent**, hushed, quiet OPPOSITE **noisy** ◆ *verb* **11** = **quieten**, allay, calm, hush, lull, pacify, quiet, settle, silence, soothe
stilted *adjective* = **stiff**, constrained, forced, unnatural, wooden
stimulant *noun* = **pick-me-up** (*inf*), restorative, tonic, upper (*sl*)
stimulate *verb* = **encourage**, arouse, fire, gee up, impel, incite, inspire, prompt, provoke, rouse, spur
stimulus *noun* = **incentive**, encouragement, fillip, geeing-up, goad, impetus, incitement, inducement, spur
sting *verb* **2** = **hurt**, burn, pain, smart, tingle, wound **4** *Sl* = **cheat**, defraud, do (*sl*), fleece, overcharge, rip off (*sl*), swindle
stingy *adjective* = **mean**, miserly, niggardly, parsimonious, penny-pinching (*inf*), tightfisted, ungenerous
stink *noun* **1** = **stench**, fetor, foul smell, pong (*Brit inf*) ◆ *verb* **3** = **reek**, pong (*Brit inf*)
stint *verb* **1** (foll. by *on*) = **be mean**, be frugal,

stipend [sty-pend] *noun* regular allowance or salary, esp. that paid to a clergyman. **stipendiary** *adjective* receiving a stipend.

stipple *verb* paint, draw, or engrave using dots.

stipulate ❶ *verb* specify as a condition of an agreement. **stipulation** *noun*

stir ❶ *verb* **stirring, stirred 1** mix up (a liquid) by moving a spoon etc. around in it. **2** move. **3** excite or stimulate (a person) emotionally. ◆ *noun* **4** a stirring. **5** strong reaction, usu. of excitement. **stir up** *verb* instigate.

stirrup *noun* metal loop attached to a saddle for supporting a rider's foot.

stitch *noun* **1** link made by drawing thread through material with a needle. **2** loop of yarn formed round a needle or hook in knitting or crochet. **3** sharp pain in the side. ◆ *verb* **4** sew. **in stitches** *Informal* laughing uncontrollably. **not a stitch** *Informal* no clothes at all.

stoat *noun* small mammal of the weasel family, with brown fur that turns white in winter.

stock ❶ *noun* **1** total amount of goods available for sale in a shop. **2** supply stored for future use. **3** financial shares in, or capital of, a company. **4** livestock. **5** lineage. **6** handle of a rifle. **7** liquid produced by boiling meat, fish, bones, or vegetables. **8** fragrant flowering plant. **9** standing or status. ◆ *plural* **10** *Hist* instrument of punishment consisting of a wooden frame with holes into which the hands and feet of the victim were locked. ◆ *adjective* **11** kept in stock, standard. **12** hackneyed. ◆ *verb* **13** keep for sale or future use. **14** supply (a farm) with livestock or (a lake etc.) with fish.

stockist *noun* dealer who stocks a particular product. **stocky** *adjective* (of a person) broad and sturdy. **stockbroker** *noun* person who buys and sells stocks and shares for customers. **stock car** car modified for a form of racing in which the cars often collide. **stock exchange, market** institution for the buying and selling of shares. **stock in trade** thing constantly used as part of a profession. **stockpile** *verb* **1** store a large quantity of (something) for future use. ◆ *noun* **2** accumulated store. **stock-still** *adjective* motionless. **stocktaking** *noun* counting and valuing of the goods in a shop. **stockyard** *noun* yard where farm animals are sold.

stockade *noun* enclosure or barrier made of stakes.

stockinette *noun* machine-knitted elastic fabric.

stocking *noun* close-fitting covering for the foot and leg. **stocking stitch** alternate rows of plain and purl in knitting.

stodgy ❶ *adjective* **stodgier, stodgiest 1** (of food) heavy and starchy. **2** (of a person) serious and boring. **stodge** *noun* heavy starchy food.

stoep [stoop] *noun S Afr* verandah.

stoic ❶ [stow-ik] *noun* **1** person who suffers hardship without showing his or her feelings. ◆ *adjective* **2** (also **stoical**) suffering hardship without showing one's feelings. **stoically** *adverb* **stoicism** [stow-iss-izz-um] *noun*

stoke *verb* feed and tend (a fire or furnace). **stoker** *noun*

stole¹ *verb* past tense of STEAL.

stole² *noun* long scarf or shawl.

stolen *verb* past participle of STEAL.

stolid ❶ *adjective* showing little emotion or interest. **stolidity** *noun* **stolidly** *adverb*

stomach ❶ *noun* **1** organ in the body which digests food. **2** front of the body around the

———————— T H E S A U R U S ————————

be sparing, hold back, skimp on ◆*noun* **2** = **share**, period, quota, shift, spell, stretch, term, time, turn

stipulate *verb* = **specify**, agree, contract, covenant, insist upon, require, settle

stipulation *noun* = **condition**, agreement, clause, precondition, proviso, qualification, requirement, specification

stir *verb* **1** = **mix**, agitate, beat, shake **3** = **stimulate**, arouse, awaken, excite, incite, move, provoke, rouse, spur OPPOSITE **curb** ◆*noun* **5** = **commotion**, activity, bustle, disorder, disturbance, excitement, flurry, fuss

stock *noun* **1** = **goods**, array, choice, commodities, merchandise, range, selection, variety, wares **2** = **supply**, fund, hoard, reserve, stockpile, store **3** = **property**, assets, capital,

funds, investment **4** = **livestock**, beasts, cattle, domestic animals ◆*adjective* **11** = **standard**, conventional, customary, ordinary, regular, routine, usual **12** = **hackneyed**, banal, overused, trite ◆*verb* **13** = **sell**, deal in, handle, keep, supply, trade in **14** = **provide with**, equip, fit out, furnish, supply

stocky *adjective* = **thickset**, chunky, dumpy, solid, stubby, sturdy

stodgy *adjective* **1** = **heavy**, filling, leaden, starchy OPPOSITE **light**. **2** = **dull**, boring, fuddy-duddy (*inf*), heavy going, staid, stuffy, tedious, unexciting OPPOSITE **interesting**

stoic *adjective* **2** (also **stoical**) = **resigned**, dispassionate, impassive, long-suffering, philosophic, phlegmatic, stolid

stolid *adjective* = **apathetic**, dull, lumpish,

waist. **3** desire or inclination. ◆ *verb* **4** put up with.

stomp *verb Informal* tread heavily.

stone ❶ *noun* **1** material of which rocks are made. **2** piece of this. **3** gem. **4** piece of rock for a specific purpose. **5** hard central part of a fruit. **6** unit of weight equal to 14 pounds or 6.350 kilograms. **7** hard deposit formed in the kidney or bladder. ◆ *verb* **8** throw stones at. **9** remove stones from (a fruit). **stoned** *adjective Slang* under the influence of alcohol or drugs. **stony** *adjective* **1** of or like stone. **2** unfeeling or hard. **stony-broke** *adjective Slang* completely penniless. **stonily** *adverb* **Stone Age** prehistoric period when tools were made of stone. **stone-cold** *adjective* completely cold. **stone-deaf** *adjective* completely deaf.

stonewall *verb* obstruct or hinder discussion.

stoneware *noun* hard kind of pottery fired at a very high temperature. **stonework** *noun* part of a building made of stone.

stood *verb* past of STAND.

stooge *noun* **1** actor who feeds lines to a comedian or acts as the butt of his jokes. **2** *Slang* person taken advantage of by a superior.

stool *noun* **1** chair without arms or back. **2** piece of excrement.

stool pigeon *noun* informer for the police.

stoop ❶ *verb* **1** bend (the body) forward and downward. **2** carry oneself habitually in this way. **3** degrade oneself. ◆ *noun* **4** stooping posture.

stop ❶ *verb* **stopping, stopped 1** cease or cause to cease from doing (something). **2** bring to or come to a halt. **3** prevent or restrain. **4** withhold. **5** block or plug. **6** stay or rest. **7** instruct a bank not to honour (a cheque). ◆

noun **8** stopping or being stopped. **9** place where something stops. **10** device that prevents, limits, or ends the motion of a mechanism. **11** full stop. **12** knob on an organ that is pulled out to allow a set of pipes to sound. **stoppage** *noun* **stoppage time** same as INJURY TIME. **stopper** *noun* plug for closing a bottle etc. **stopcock** *noun* valve to control or stop the flow of fluid in a pipe. **stopgap** *noun* temporary substitute. **stopover** *noun* short break in a journey. **stop press** news item put into a newspaper after printing has been started. **stopwatch** *noun* watch which can be stopped instantly for exact timing of a sporting event.

store ❶ *verb* **1** collect and keep (things) for future use. **2** put (furniture etc.) in a warehouse for safekeeping. **3** stock (goods). **4** *Computers* enter or retain (data). ◆ *noun* **5** shop. **6** supply kept for future use. **7** storage place, such as a warehouse. ◆ *plural* **8** stock of provisions. **in store** about to happen. **set great store by** value greatly. **storage** *noun* **1** storing. **2** space for storing. **storage heater** electric device that can accumulate and radiate heat generated by off-peak electricity.

storey *noun* floor or level of a building.

stork *noun* large wading bird.

storm ❶ *noun* **1** violent weather with wind, rain, or snow. **2** strongly expressed reaction. **3** heavy shower of missiles. ◆ *verb* **4** attack or capture (a place) suddenly. **5** shout angrily. **6** rush violently or angrily. **stormy** *adjective* **1** characterized by storms. **2** involving violent emotions. **storm trooper** member of the Nazi militia.

story ❶ *noun, pl* **-ries 1** description of a series

——————— THESAURUS ———————

unemotional, wooden

stomach *noun* **2** = **belly**, abdomen, gut (*inf*), pot, tummy (*inf*) **3** = **inclination**, appetite, desire, relish, taste ◆*verb* **4** = **bear**, abide, endure, swallow, take, tolerate

stony *adjective* **2** = **cold**, blank, chilly, expressionless, hard, hostile, icy, unresponsive

stoop *verb* **1** = **bend**, bow, crouch, duck, hunch, lean **3** = **lower oneself by**, descend to, resort to, sink to ◆*noun* **4** = **slouch**, bad posture

stop *verb* **1, 2** = **halt**, cease, conclude, cut short, desist, discontinue, end, finish, pause, put an end to, quit, refrain, shut down, terminate [OPPOSITE] start. **3** = **prevent**, arrest, forestall, hinder, hold back, impede, repress, restrain [OPPOSITE] further. **5** = **plug**, block, obstruct, seal, staunch, stem **6** = **stay**, lodge, rest ◆*noun* **8** = **end**, cessation, finish, halt,

standstill **9** = **station**, depot, terminus

stopgap *noun* = **makeshift**, improvisation, resort, substitute

stoppage *noun* **1, 2** = **stopping**, arrest, close, closure, cutoff, halt, shutdown, standstill

store *verb* **1, 2** = **put by**, deposit, garner, hoard, keep, put aside, reserve, save, stockpile ◆*noun* **5** = **shop**, market, mart, outlet **6** = **supply**, accumulation, cache, fund, hoard, quantity, reserve, stock, stockpile **7** = **repository**, depository, storeroom, warehouse

storm *noun* **1** = **tempest**, blizzard, gale, hurricane, squall **2** = **outburst**, agitation, commotion, disturbance, furore, outbreak, outcry, row, rumpus, strife, tumult, turmoil ◆*verb* **4** = **attack**, assail, assault, charge, rush **5** = **rage**, bluster, rant, rave, thunder **6** = **rush**, flounce, fly, stamp of events told or written for entertainment. **2** plot of a book or film. **3** news report. **4** *Informal* lie.

stoup [stoop] *noun* small basin for holy water.

stout ● *adjective* **1** fat. **2** thick and strong. **3** brave and resolute. ◆ *noun* **4** strong dark beer. **stoutly** *adverb*

stove¹ *noun* apparatus for cooking or heating.

stove² *verb* a past of STAVE.

stow ● *verb* pack or store. **stowage** *noun* space or charge for stowing goods. **stowaway** *noun* person who hides on a ship or aircraft in order to travel free. **stow away** *verb* hide as a stowaway.

straddle *verb* have one leg or part on each side of (something).

strafe *verb* attack (an enemy) with machine guns from the air.

straggle *verb* **1** go or spread in a rambling or irregular way. **2** linger behind. **straggler** *noun* **straggly** *adjective*

straight ● *adjective* **1** not curved or crooked. **2** level or upright. **3** orderly. **4** honest or frank. **5** in continuous succession. **6** (of spirits) undiluted. **7** *Theatre* serious. **8** *Slang* heterosexual. **9** *Slang* conventional. ◆ *adverb* **10** in a straight line. **11** immediately. **12** in a level

or upright position. **13** uninterruptedly. ◆ *noun* **14** straight part, esp. of a racetrack. **go straight** *Informal* reform after being a criminal. **straighten** *verb* **straightaway** *adverb* immediately. **straight face** serious facial expression concealing a desire to laugh.

straightforward *adjective* **1** honest, frank. **2** (of a task) easy.

strain¹ ● *verb* **1** subject to mental tension. **2** cause (something) to be used or tested beyond its limits. **3** make an intense effort. **4** injure by overexertion. **5** sieve. **6** draw or be drawn taut. ◆ *noun* **7** tension or tiredness. **8** force exerted by straining. **9** injury from overexertion. **10** great demand on strength or resources. **11** melody or theme. **strained** *adjective* **1** not natural, forced. **2** not relaxed, tense. **strainer** *noun* sieve.

strain² ● *noun* **1** breed or race. **2** trace or streak.

strait ● *noun* **1** narrow channel connecting two areas of sea. ◆ *plural* **2** position of acute difficulty. **straitjacket** *noun* strong jacket with long sleeves used to bind the arms of a violent person. **strait-laced**, **straight-laced** *adjective* prudish or puritanical.

straitened *adjective* **in straitened**

—————————— T H E S A U R U S ——————————

stormy *adjective* **1** = **wild**, blustery, inclement, raging, rough, squally, turbulent, windy

story *noun* **1** = **tale**, account, anecdote, history, legend, narrative, romance, yarn **3** = **report**, article, feature, news, news item, scoop

stout *adjective* **1** = **fat**, big, bulky, burly, corpulent, fleshy, heavy, overweight, plump, portly, rotund, tubby OPPOSITE lean. **2** = **strong**, able-bodied, brawny, muscular, robust, stalwart, strapping, sturdy OPPOSITE frail. **3** = **brave**, bold, courageous, fearless, gallant, intrepid, plucky, resolute, valiant OPPOSITE fearful

stow *verb* = **pack**, bundle, load, put away, stash (*inf*), store

straight *adjective* **1** = **direct**, near, short **2 a** = **level**, aligned, even, horizontal, right, smooth, square, true **b** = **upright**, erect, plumb, vertical **3** = **orderly**, arranged, in order, neat, organized, shipshape, tidy **4 a** = **honest**, above board, fair, honourable, just, law-abiding, reliable, respectable, trustworthy, upright **b** = **frank**, blunt, bold, candid, forthright, honest, outright, plain, straightforward OPPOSITE vague. **5** = **successive**, consecutive, continuous, nonstop, running, solid OPPOSITE interrupted. **6** = **undiluted**, neat, pure, unadulterated,

unmixed **9** *Sl* = **conventional**, bourgeois, conservative ◆*adverb* **11** = **directly**, at once, immediately, instantly

straightaway *adverb* = **immediately**, at once, directly, instantly, now, right away

straighten *verb* **3** = **neaten**, arrange, order, put in order, tidy (up)

straightforward *adjective* **1** = **honest**, candid, direct, forthright, genuine, open, sincere, truthful, upfront (*inf*) OPPOSITE sharp. **2** = **simple**, easy, elementary, routine, uncomplicated OPPOSITE complex

strain¹ *verb* **3** = **strive**, bend over backwards (*inf*), endeavour, give it one's best shot (*inf*), go for it (*inf*), knock oneself out (*inf*), labour, struggle OPPOSITE rest. **4** = **overexert**, injure, overtax, overwork, pull, sprain, tax, tear, twist, wrench **5** = **sieve**, filter, purify, sift **6** = **stretch**, distend, draw tight, tauten, tighten ◆*noun* **7** = **stress**, anxiety, burden, pressure, tension **8** = **exertion**, effort, force, struggle OPPOSITE ease. **9** = **injury**, pull, sprain, wrench

strain² *noun* **1** = **breed**, ancestry, blood, descent, extraction, family, lineage, race **2** = **trace**, streak, suggestion, tendency

strained *adjective* **1** = **forced**, artificial, false, put on, unnatural OPPOSITE natural. **2** = **tense**, awkward, difficult, embarrassed, stiff, uneasy

S

circumstances not having much money.
strand¹ ❶ *verb* **1** run aground. **2** leave in difficulties. ◆ *noun* **3** *Poetic* shore.
strand² ❶ *noun* **1** single thread of string, wire, etc. **2** element of something.
strange ❶ *adjective* **1** odd or unusual. **2** not familiar. **3** inexperienced (in) or unaccustomed (to). **strangely** *adverb* **strangeness** *noun*
stranger *noun* person who is not known or is new to a place or experience.
strangle ❶ *verb* **1** kill by squeezing the throat. **2** prevent the development of. **strangler** *noun* **strangulation** *noun* strangling. **stranglehold** *noun* **1** strangling grip in wrestling. **2** powerful control.
strap ❶ *noun* **1** strip of flexible material for lifting, fastening, or holding in place. ◆ *verb* **strapping, strapped 2** fasten with a strap or straps. **strapping** *adjective* tall and sturdy.
strata *noun* plural of STRATUM.
stratagem ❶ *noun* clever plan, trick.
strategy ❶ *noun, pl* **-gies 1** overall plan. **2** art of planning in war. **strategic** [strat-ee-jik] *adjective* **1** advantageous. **2** (of weapons) aimed at an enemy's homeland. **strategically** *adverb* **strategist** *noun*
strathspey *noun* Scottish dance with gliding steps.
stratosphere *noun* atmospheric layer between about 15 and 50 kilometres above the earth.
stratum [strah-tum] *noun, pl* **strata 1** layer,

esp. of rock. **2** social class. **stratified** *adjective* divided into strata. **stratification** *noun*
straw *noun* **1** dried stalks of grain. **2** single stalk of straw. **3** long thin tube used to suck up liquid into the mouth. **straw-coloured** *adjective* pale yellow. **straw poll** unofficial poll taken to determine general opinion.
strawberry *noun* sweet fleshy red fruit with small seeds on the outside. **strawberry mark** red birthmark.
stray ❶ *verb* **1** wander. **2** digress. **3** deviate from certain moral standards. ◆ *adjective* **4** having strayed. **5** scattered, random. ◆ *noun* **6** stray animal.
streak ❶ *noun* **1** long band of contrasting colour or substance. **2** sudden flash. **3** quality or characteristic. **4** short stretch (of good or bad luck). ◆ *verb* **5** mark with streaks. **6** move rapidly. **7** *Informal* run naked in public. **streaker** *noun* **streaky** *adjective*
stream ❶ *noun* **1** small river. **2** steady flow, as of liquid, speech, or people. **3** schoolchildren grouped together because of similar ability. ◆ *verb* **4** flow steadily. **5** move in unbroken succession. **6** float in the air. **7** group (pupils) in streams. **streamer** *noun* **1** strip of coloured paper that unrolls when tossed. **2** long narrow flag.
streamline *verb* **1** make more efficient by simplifying. **2** give (a car, plane, etc.) a smooth even shape to offer least resistance to the flow of air or water.

——————— THESAURUS ———————

OPPOSITE⟩ relaxed
strait *noun* **1** = **channel**, narrows, sound ◆*plural* **2** = **difficulty**, dilemma, extremity, hardship, plight, predicament
strait-laced, straight-laced *adjective* = **puritanical**, moralistic, narrow-minded, prim, proper, prudish, strict
strand² ** *noun* **1 = **filament**, fibre, string, thread
stranded *adjective* **1** = **beached**, aground, ashore, grounded, marooned, shipwrecked **2** = **helpless**, abandoned, high and dry
strange *adjective* **1** = **odd**, abnormal, bizarre, curious, extraordinary, munted (*NZ sl*), peculiar, queer, uncommon, weird, wonderful OPPOSITE⟩ usual. **2** = **unfamiliar**, alien, exotic, foreign, new, novel, unknown, untried OPPOSITE⟩ familiar
stranger *noun* = **newcomer**, alien, foreigner, guest, incomer, outlander, visitor
strangle *verb* **1** = **throttle**, asphyxiate, choke, strangulate **2** = **suppress**, inhibit, repress, stifle
strap *noun* **1** = **belt**, thong, tie ◆*verb* **2** = **fasten**, bind, buckle, lash, secure, tie

strapping *adjective* = **well-built**, big, brawny, husky (*inf*), powerful, robust, sturdy
stratagem *noun* = **trick**, device, dodge, manoeuvre, plan, ploy, ruse, scheme, subterfuge
strategy *noun* **1** = **plan**, approach, policy, procedure, scheme
stray *verb* **1** = **wander**, drift, err, go astray **2** = **digress**, deviate, diverge, get off the point ◆*adjective* **4** = **lost**, abandoned, homeless, roaming, vagrant **5** = **random**, accidental, chance
streak *noun* **1** = **band**, layer, line, slash, strip, stripe, stroke, vein **3** = **trace**, dash, element, strain, touch, vein ◆*verb* **6** = **speed**, dart, flash, fly, hurtle, sprint, tear, whizz (*inf*), zoom
stream *noun* **1** = **river**, bayou, beck, brook, burn (*Scot*), rivulet, tributary **2** = **flow**, course, current, drift, run, rush, surge, tide, torrent ◆*verb* **4, 5** = **flow**, cascade, flood, gush, issue, pour, run, spill, spout
streamlined *adjective* **1** = **efficient**, organized, rationalized, slick, smooth-running

street ⊕ *noun* public road, usu. lined with buildings. **streetwalker** *noun* prostitute.
streetwise *adjective* knowing how to survive in big cities.
streetcar *noun US & Canad* public transport vehicle powered by an overhead wire and running on rails laid in the road.
strength ⊕ *noun* 1 quality of being strong. 2 quality or ability considered an advantage. 3 degree of intensity. 4 total number of people in a group. **on the strength of** on the basis of.
strengthen *verb*
strenuous ⊕ *adjective* requiring great energy or effort. **strenuously** *adverb*
streptococcus [strep-toe-**kok**-uss] *noun, pl* **-cocci** bacterium occurring in chains, many species of which cause disease.
streptomycin *noun* antibiotic drug.
stress ⊕ *noun* 1 tension or strain. 2 emphasis. 3 stronger sound in saying a word or syllable. 4 *Physics* force producing strain. ♦ *verb* 5 emphasize. 6 put stress on (a word or syllable). **stressed-out** *adjective Informal* suffering from tension. **stressful** *adjective*
stretch ⊕ *verb* 1 extend or be extended. 2 be able to be stretched. 3 extend the limbs or body. 4 pull tight. 5 strain (resources or abilities) to the utmost. ♦ *noun* 6 stretching. 7 continuous expanse. 8 period. 9 *Informal* term of imprisonment. **stretchy** *adjective* **stretcher** *noun* frame covered with canvas, on which an injured person is carried.
strew *verb* **strewing, strewed, strewed** *or* **strewn** scatter (things) over a surface.

striation *noun* 1 scratch or groove. 2 pattern of scratches or grooves. **striated** *adjective*
stricken *adjective* seriously affected by disease, grief, pain, etc.
strict ⊕ *adjective* 1 stern or severe. 2 adhering closely to specified rules. 3 complete, absolute. **strictly** *adverb* **strictness** *noun*
stricture *noun* severe criticism.
stride *verb* **striding, strode, stridden** 1 walk with long steps. ♦ *noun* 2 long step. 3 regular pace. ♦ *plural* 4 progress.
strident ⊕ *adjective* loud and harsh. **stridently** *adverb* **stridency** *noun*
strife ⊕ *noun* conflict, quarrelling.
strike ⊕ *verb* **striking, struck** 1 cease work as a protest. 2 hit. 3 attack suddenly. 4 ignite (a match) by friction. 5 sound (a note) on a musical instrument. 6 (of a clock) indicate (a time) by sounding a bell. 7 affect in a particular way. 8 enter the mind of. 9 render. 10 afflict. 11 discover (gold, oil, etc.). 12 agree (a bargain). 13 take up (a posture). 14 make (a coin) by stamping it. ♦ *noun* 15 stoppage of work as a protest. 16 striking. 17 military attack. 18 discovery of gold, oil, etc. **strike camp** dismantle and pack up tents. **strike home** have the desired effect. **striker** *noun* 1 striking worker. 2 attacking footballer.
striking *adjective* 1 impressive. 2 noteworthy. **strikebreaker** *noun* person who works while others are on strike. **strike off, out** cross out. **strike up** *verb* 1 begin (a conversation or friendship). 2 begin to play music.

———————— T H E S A U R U S ————————

street *noun* =**road**, avenue, lane, roadway, row, terrace
strength *noun* 1 =**might**, brawn, courage, fortitude, muscle, robustness, stamina, sturdiness, toughness OPPOSITE **weakness**. 2 =**strong point**, advantage, asset OPPOSITE **failing**. 3 =**power**, effectiveness, efficacy, force, intensity, potency, vigour OPPOSITE **feebleness**
strengthen *verb* 1 =**fortify**, augment, bolster, brace, brace up, build up, buttress, consolidate, gee up, harden, intensify, invigorate, reinforce, restore, stiffen, support, toughen OPPOSITE **undermine**
strenuous *adjective* =**demanding**, arduous, hard, laborious, taxing, tough, uphill OPPOSITE **easy**
stress *noun* 1 =**strain**, anxiety, burden, pressure, tension, trauma, worry 2 =**emphasis**, force, significance, weight 3 =**accent**, accentuation, beat, emphasis ♦*verb* 5

=**emphasize**, accentuate, dwell on, underline
stretch *verb* 1 =**extend**, cover, put forth, reach, spread, unroll 2 =**distend**, draw out, elongate, expand, strain, tighten 4 =**tighten**, pull 5 =**strain** ♦*noun* 7 =**expanse**, area, distance, extent, spread, tract 8 =**period**, space, spell, stint, term, time
strict *adjective* 1 =**severe**, authoritarian, firm, harsh, stern, stringent 2 =**exact**, accurate, close, faithful, meticulous, precise, scrupulous, true 3 =**absolute**, total, utter
strident *adjective* =**harsh**, discordant, grating, jarring, raucous, screeching, shrill OPPOSITE **soft**
strife *noun* =**conflict**, battle, clash, discord, dissension, friction, quarrel
strike *verb* 1 =**walk out**, down tools, mutiny, revolt 2 =**hit**, beat, clobber (*sl*), clout (*inf*), cuff, hammer, knock, punch, slap, smack, swipe, thump, wallop (*inf*) 3 =**attack**, assail, assault, hit 7 =**affect**, hit, register (*inf*) 8 =**occur to**,

S

string ❶ *noun* **1** thin cord used for tying. **2** set of objects threaded on a string. **3** series of things or events. **4** stretched wire or cord on a musical instrument that produces sound when vibrated. ♦ *plural* **5** restrictions or conditions. **6** section of an orchestra consisting of stringed instruments. ♦ *verb* **stringing, strung 7** provide with a string or strings. **8** thread on a string. **9** extend in a line. **pull strings** use one's influence. **stringed** *adjective* (of a musical instrument) having strings that are plucked or played with a bow. **stringy** *adjective* **1** like string. **2** (of meat) fibrous. **stringy-bark** *noun* Aust eucalyptus with a fibrous bark. **string along** *verb* **1** *Informal* accompany. **2** deceive over a period of time. **string up** *verb Informal* kill by hanging.

stringent ❶ [strin-jent] *adjective* strictly controlled or enforced. **stringently** *adverb* **stringency** *noun*

strip¹ ❶ *verb* **stripping, stripped 1** take (the covering or clothes) off. **2** take a title or possession away from (someone). **3** remove (paint) from (a surface). **4** dismantle (an engine). ♦ *noun* **5** act of stripping. **stripper** *noun* person who performs a striptease. **striptease** *noun* entertainment in which a performer undresses to music.

strip² ❶ *noun* **1** long narrow piece. **2** clothes a football team plays in. **strip cartoon** sequence of drawings telling a story.

stripe *noun* **1** long narrow band of contrasting colour or substance. **2** chevron on a uniform to indicate rank. **striped, stripy, stripey** *adjective* **stripling** *noun* youth.

strive ❶ *verb* **striving, strove, striven** make

a great effort.

strobe *noun* short for STROBOSCOPE.

stroboscope *noun* instrument producing a very bright flashing light.

strode *verb* past tense of STRIDE.

stroke ❶ *verb* **1** touch or caress lightly with the hand. ♦ *noun* **2** light touch or caress with the hand. **3** rupture of a blood vessel in the brain. **4** blow. **5** action or occurrence of the kind specified, e.g. *a stroke of luck*. **6** chime of a clock. **7** mark made by a pen or paintbrush. **8** hitting of the ball in some sports. **9** style or method of swimming. **10** single pull on the oars in rowing.

stroll ❶ *verb* **1** walk in a leisurely manner. ♦ *noun* **2** leisurely walk.

stroller *noun US & Canad* chair-shaped carriage for a baby.

strong ❶ *adjective* **1** having physical power. **2** not easily broken. **3** great in degree or intensity. **4** having moral force. **5** having a powerful taste or smell. **6** having a specified number, e.g. *twenty strong*. **going strong** *Informal* thriving. **strongly** *adverb* **strong-arm** *adjective* involving violence. **stronghold** *noun* **1** area of predominance of a particular belief. **2** fortress. **strong point** thing at which one excels. **strongroom** *noun* room designed for the safekeeping of valuables.

strontium *noun Chem* silvery-white metallic element. **strontium-90** *noun* radioactive isotope present in the fallout of nuclear explosions.

strop *noun* leather strap for sharpening razors.

stroppy *adjective* **-pier, -piest** *Slang* angry or awkward.

THESAURUS

---

come to, dawn on *or* upon, hit, register (*inf*)
striking *adjective* =**impressive**, conspicuous, dramatic, jaw-dropping, noticeable, outstanding OPPOSITE **average**
string *noun* **1** =**cord**, fibre, twine **3** =**series**, chain, file, line, procession, row, sequence, succession
stringent *adjective* =**strict**, inflexible, rigid, rigorous, severe, tight, tough
stringy *adjective* **2** =**fibrous**, gristly, sinewy, tough
strip¹ *verb* **1** =**undress**, disrobe, unclothe **2** =**divest**, rob
strip² *noun* **1** =**piece**, band, belt, shred
strive *verb* =**try**, attempt, bend over backwards (*inf*), break one's neck (*inf*), do one's best, give it one's best shot (*inf*), go all out (*inf*), knock oneself out (*inf*), labour, make an all-out effort (*inf*), struggle, toil

stroke *verb* **1** =**caress**, fondle, pet, rub ♦*noun* **3** =**apoplexy**, attack, collapse, fit, seizure **4** =**blow**, hit, knock, pat, rap, swipe, thump
stroll *verb* **1** =**walk**, amble, promenade, ramble, saunter ♦*noun* **2** =**walk**, breath of air, constitutional, promenade, ramble
strong *adjective* **1** =**powerful**, athletic, brawny, burly, hardy, lusty, muscular, robust, strapping, sturdy, tough OPPOSITE **weak**. **2** =**durable**, hard-wearing, heavy-duty, sturdy, substantial, well-built OPPOSITE **fragile**. **3** =**intense**, acute, deep, fervent, fervid, fierce, firm, keen, vehement, violent, zealous **4** =**persuasive**, compelling, convincing, effective, potent, sound, telling, weighty, well-founded **5** =**distinct**, clear, marked, overpowering, unmistakable
stronghold *noun* **2** =**fortress**, bastion, bulwark, castle, citadel, fort

strove *verb* past tense of STRIVE.
struck *verb* past of STRIKE.
structure ❶ *noun* **1** complex construction. **2** manner or basis of construction or organization. ◆ *verb* **3** give a structure to. **structural** *adjective*
structuralism *noun* approach to literature, social sciences, etc., which sees changes in the subject as caused and organized by a hidden set of universal rules. **structuralist** *noun, adjective*
strudel *noun* thin sheet of filled dough rolled up and baked, usu. with an apple filling.
struggle ❶ *verb* **1** work, strive, or make one's way with difficulty. **2** move about violently in an attempt to get free. **3** fight (with someone). ◆ *noun* **4** striving. **5** fight.
strum *verb* **strumming, strummed** play (a guitar or banjo) by sweeping the thumb or a plectrum across the strings.
strumpet *noun* Old-fashioned prostitute.
strung *verb* past of STRING.
strut ❶ *verb* **strutting, strutted 1** walk pompously, swagger. ◆ *noun* **2** bar supporting a structure.
strychnine [strik-neen] *noun* very poisonous drug used in small quantities as a stimulant.
stub ❶ *noun* **1** short piece left after use. **2** counterfoil of a cheque or ticket. ◆ *verb* **stubbing, stubbed 3** strike (the toe) painfully against an object. **4** put out (a cigarette) by pressing the end against a surface. **stubby** *adjective* short and broad.
stubble *noun* **1** short stalks of grain left in a field after reaping. **2** short growth of hair on the chin of a man who has not shaved recently. **stubbly** *adjective*

stubborn ❶ *adjective* **1** refusing to agree or give in. **2** difficult to deal with. **stubbornly** *adverb* **stubbornness** *noun*
stucco *noun* plaster used for coating or decorating walls. **stuccoed** *adjective*
stuck ❶ *verb* past of STICK². **stuck-up** *adjective Informal* conceited or snobbish.
stud¹ ❶ *noun* **1** small piece of metal attached to a surface for decoration. **2** disc-like removable fastener for clothes. **3** one of several small round objects fixed to the sole of a football boot to give better grip. ◆ *verb* **studding, studded 4** set with studs.
stud² *noun* **1** male animal, esp. a stallion, kept for breeding. **2** (also **stud farm**) place where horses are bred. **3** *Slang* virile or sexually active man.
student ❶ *noun* person who studies a subject, esp. at university.
studio ❶ *noun, pl* **-dios 1** workroom of an artist or photographer. **2** room or building in which television or radio programmes, records, or films are made. **studio flat** one-room flat with a small kitchen and bathroom.
study ❶ *verb* **studying, studied 1** be engaged in learning (a subject). **2** investigate by observation and research. **3** scrutinize. ◆ *noun, pl* **studies 4** act or process of studying. **5** room for studying in. **6** book or paper produced as a result of study. **7** sketch done as practice or preparation. **8** musical composition designed to improve playing technique.
student *noun* person who studies a subject, esp. at university. **studied** *adjective* carefully practised or planned. **studious** [styoo-dee-uss] *adjective* **1** fond of study. **2** careful and

——————— T H E S A U R U S ———————

structure *noun* **1** = **building**, construction, edifice, erection **2** = **arrangement**, configuration, construction, design, form, formation, make-up, organization ◆*verb* **3** = **arrange**, assemble, build up, design, organize, shape
struggle *verb* **1** = **strive**, exert oneself, give it one's best shot (*inf*), go all out (*inf*), knock oneself out (*inf*), labour, make an all-out effort (*inf*), strain, toil, work **3** = **fight**, battle, compete, contend, grapple, wrestle ◆*noun* **4** = **effort**, exertion, labour, pains, scramble, toil, work, yakka (*Aust & NZ inf*) **5** = **fight**, battle, brush, clash, combat, conflict, contest, tussle
strut *verb* **1** = **swagger**, parade, peacock, prance
stub *noun* **1** = **butt**, dog-end (*inf*), end, remnant, stump, tail, tail end **2** = **counterfoil**
stubborn *adjective* = **obstinate**, dogged,

headstrong, inflexible, intractable, obdurate, pig-headed, recalcitrant, tenacious, unyielding OPPOSITE **yielding**
stubby *adjective* = **stocky**, chunky, dumpy, short, squat, thickset
stuck *adjective* = **fastened**, cemented, fast, fixed, glued, joined
stuck-up *adjective Inf* = **snobbish**, arrogant, bigheaded (*inf*), conceited, haughty, proud, snooty (*inf*), toffee-nosed (*sl, chiefly Brit*)
stud¹ *verb* **4** = **ornament**, dot, spangle, spot
student *noun* = **learner**, apprentice, disciple, pupil, scholar, trainee, undergraduate
studied *adjective* = **planned**, conscious, deliberate, intentional, premeditated
studio *noun* **1** = **workshop**, atelier
studious *adjective* **1** = **scholarly**, academic, assiduous, bookish, diligent, hard-working, intellectual OPPOSITE **lazy**

S

deliberate. **studiously** adverb
stuff ⊕ noun **1** substance or material. **2** collection of unnamed things. **3** raw material of something. **4** subject matter. **5** woollen fabric. ◆ verb **6** pack, cram, or fill completely. **7** fill (food) with a seasoned mixture. **8** fill (an animal's skin) with material to restore the shape of the live animal. **stuff oneself** Informal eat large quantities. **stuffing** noun **1** seasoned mixture with which food is stuffed. **2** padding.
stuffy ⊕ adjective **stuffier, stuffiest 1** lacking fresh air. **2** Informal dull or conventional.
stultifying adjective very boring and repetitive.
stumble ⊕ verb **1** trip and nearly fall. **2** walk in an unsure way. **3** make frequent mistakes in speech. ◆ noun **4** stumbling. **stumble across** verb discover accidentally. **stumbling block** obstacle or difficulty.
stump ⊕ noun **1** base of a tree left when the main trunk has been cut away. **2** part of a thing left after a larger part has been removed. **3** Cricket one of the three upright sticks forming the wicket. ◆ verb **4** baffle. **5** Cricket dismiss (a

batsman) by breaking his wicket with the ball. **6** walk with heavy steps. **stumpy** adjective short and thick. **stump up** verb Informal give (the money required).
stun ⊕ verb **stunning, stunned 1** shock or overwhelm. **2** knock senseless. **stunner** noun Informal beautiful person or thing. **stunning** adjective very attractive or impressive.
stung verb past of STING.
stunk verb a past of STINK.
stunt¹ ⊕ verb prevent or impede the growth of. **stunted** adjective
stunt² ⊕ noun **1** acrobatic or dangerous action. **2** anything spectacular done to gain publicity.
stupefy ⊕ verb **-fying, -fied 1** make insensitive or lethargic. **2** astound.
stupefaction noun
stupendous ⊕ adjective very large or impressive. **stupendously** adverb
stupid ⊕ adjective **1** lacking intelligence. **2** silly. **3** in a stupor. **stupidity** noun **stupidly** adverb
stupor ⊕ noun dazed or unconscious state.

——————— T H E S A U R U S ———————

study verb **1 = learn**, cram (inf), mug up (Brit sl), read up, swot (up) (Brit inf) **2 = contemplate**, consider, examine, go into, ponder, pore over, read **3 = examine**, analyse, investigate, look into, research, scrutinize, survey ◆noun **4 a = learning**, application, lessons, reading, research, school work, swotting (Brit inf) **b = examination**, analysis, consideration, contemplation, inquiry, inspection, investigation, review, scrutiny, survey
stuff noun **1 = substance**, essence, matter **2 = things**, belongings, effects, equipment, gear, kit, objects, paraphernalia, possessions, tackle **5 = material**, cloth, fabric, textile ◆verb **6 = cram**, crowd, fill, force, jam, pack, push, ram, shove, squeeze
stuffing noun **2 = filling**, packing, wadding
stuffy adjective **1 = airless**, close, frowsty, heavy, muggy, oppressive, stale, stifling, sultry, unventilated OPPOSITE **fresh. 2** Inf **= staid**, dreary, dull, pompous, priggish, prim, stodgy
stumble verb **1 = trip**, fall, falter, lurch, reel, slip, stagger **stumble across = discover**, chance upon, come across, find
stump verb **4 = baffle**, bewilder, confuse, flummox, mystify, nonplus, perplex, puzzle
stumpy adjective **= stocky**, dumpy, short, squat, stubby, thickset
stun verb **1 = overcome**, astonish, astound, bewilder, confound, confuse, overpower, shock,

stagger, stupefy **2 = knock out**, daze
stunning adjective **=wonderful**, beautiful, dazzling, gorgeous, impressive, jaw-dropping, lovely, marvellous, sensational (inf), spectacular, striking OPPOSITE **average**
stunt² noun **=feat**, act, deed, exploit, trick
stunted adjective **=undersized**, diminutive, little, small, tiny
stupefy verb **2 = astound**, amaze, daze, dumbfound, shock, stagger, stun
stupendous adjective **a =wonderful**, amazing, astounding, breathtaking, jaw-dropping, marvellous, overwhelming, sensational (inf), staggering, superb OPPOSITE **average. b =huge**, colossal, enormous, gigantic, mega (sl), vast OPPOSITE **tiny**
stupid adjective **1 =unintelligent**, brainless, dense, dim, half-witted, moronic, obtuse, simple, simple-minded, slow, slow-witted, thick OPPOSITE **bright. 2 = silly**, asinine, daft (inf), foolish, idiotic, imbecilic, inane, nonsensical, pointless, rash, senseless, unintelligent OPPOSITE **wise. 3 = dazed**, groggy, insensate, semiconscious, stunned, stupefied
stupidity noun **1 = lack of intelligence**, brainlessness, denseness, dimness, dullness, imbecility, obtuseness, slowness, thickness **2 = silliness**, absurdity, fatuousness, folly, foolishness, idiocy, inanity, lunacy, madness
stupor noun **=daze**, coma, insensibility, stupefaction, unconsciousness

S

sturdy ❶ *adjective* **-dier, -diest 1** healthy and robust. **2** strongly built. **sturdily** *adverb*

sturgeon *noun* fish from which caviar is obtained.

stutter ❶ *verb* **1** speak with repetition of initial consonants. ♦ *noun* **2** tendency to stutter.

sty *noun, pl* **sties** pen for pigs.

stye, sty *noun, pl* **styes, sties** inflammation at the base of an eyelash.

Stygian [stij-jee-an] *adjective Lit* gloomy.

style ❶ *noun* **1** shape or design. **2** manner of writing, speaking, or doing something. **3** elegance, refinement. **4** prevailing fashion. **5** part of a flower that bears the stigma. ♦ *verb* **6** shape or design. **7** name or call. **stylish** *adjective* smart, elegant, and fashionable. **stylishly** *adverb* **stylist** *noun* **1** hairdresser. **2** person who writes or performs with great attention to style. **stylistic** *adjective* of literary or artistic style. **stylize** *verb* cause to conform to an established stylistic form.

stylus *noun* needle-like device on a record player that rests in the groove of the record and picks up the sound signals.

stymie *verb* **-mieing, -mied** hinder or thwart.

styptic *noun, adjective* (drug) used to stop bleeding.

suave ❶ [swahv] *adjective* smooth and sophisticated in manner. **suavely** *adverb*

sub *noun* **1** subeditor. **2** submarine. **3** subscription. **4** substitute. **5** *Informal* advance payment of wages or salary. ♦ *verb* **subbing, subbed 6** act as a substitute. **7** grant advance payment to.

sub- *prefix* used with many main words to mean: **1** under or beneath, e.g. *submarine*. **2** subordinate, e.g. *sublieutenant*. **3** falling short of, e.g. *subnormal*. **4** forming a subdivision, e.g. *subheading*.

subaltern *noun* army officer below the rank of captain.

subatomic *adjective* of or being one of the particles which make up an atom.

subcommittee *noun* small committee formed from some members of a larger committee.

subconscious ❶ *adjective* **1** happening or existing without one's awareness. ♦ *noun* **2** *Psychoanalysis* that part of the mind of which one is not aware but which can influence one's behaviour. **subconsciously** *adverb*

subcontinent *noun* large land mass that is a distinct part of a continent.

subcontract *noun* **1** secondary contract by which the main contractor for a job puts work out to others. ♦ *verb* **2** put out (work) on a subcontract. **subcontractor** *noun*

subcutaneous [sub-cute-**ayn**-ee-uss] *adjective* under the skin.

subdivide *verb* divide (a part of something) into smaller parts. **subdivision** *noun*

subdue ❶ *verb* **-duing, -dued 1** overcome. **2** make less intense.

subeditor *noun* person who checks and edits text for a newspaper or magazine.

subhuman *adjective* less than human.

subject ❶ *noun* **1** person or thing being dealt with or studied. **2** figure, scene, etc. portrayed by an artist or photographer. **3** *Grammar* word or phrase that represents the person or thing performing the action of the verb in a sentence. **4** person under the rule of a monarch or government. ♦ *adjective* **5** being under the rule of a monarch or government. ♦ *verb* (foll. by *to*) **6** cause to undergo. **7** bring under the control (of). **subject to 1** liable to. **2** conditional upon. **subjection** *noun* **subjective** *adjective* based on personal feelings or prejudices. **subjectively** *adverb*

sturdy *adjective* **1** = **robust**, athletic, brawny, hardy, lusty, muscular, powerful OPPOSITE weak. **2** = **substantial**, durable, solid, well-built, well-made OPPOSITE **frail**

stutter *verb* **1** = **stammer**, falter, hesitate, stumble

style *noun* **1** = **design**, cut, form, manner **2** = **manner**, approach, method, mode, technique, way **3** = **elegance**, affluence, chic, comfort, ease, élan, flair, grandeur, luxury, panache, polish, smartness, sophistication, taste **4** = **fashion**, mode, rage, trend, vogue ♦*verb* **6** = **design**, adapt, arrange, cut, fashion, shape, tailor **7** = **call**, designate, dub, entitle, label, name, term

stylish *adjective* = **smart**, chic, dressy (*inf*),

fashionable, modish, trendy (*Brit inf*), voguish

suave *adjective* = **smooth**, charming, courteous, debonair, polite, sophisticated, urbane

subconscious *adjective* **1** = **hidden**, inner, intuitive, latent, repressed, subliminal OPPOSITE **knowing**

subdue *verb* **1** = **overcome**, break, conquer, control, crush, defeat, master, overpower, quell, tame, vanquish **2** = **moderate**, mellow, quieten down, soften, suppress, tone down OPPOSITE **provoke**

subdued *adjective* **1** = **quiet**, chastened, crestfallen, dejected, downcast, down in the mouth, sad, serious OPPOSITE **happy**. **2** = **soft**, dim, hushed, muted, quiet, subtle, toned

S

sub judice [sub joo-diss-ee] *adjective Latin* before a court of law.

subjugate ⊕ *verb* bring (a group of people) under one's control. **subjugation** *noun*

subjunctive *Grammar noun* 1 mood of verbs used when the content of the clause is doubted, supposed, or wished. ♦ *adjective* 2 in or of that mood.

sublet *verb* **-letting, -let** rent out (property rented from someone else).

sublieutenant *noun* naval officer of the lowest rank.

sublimate *verb Psychol* direct the energy of (a strong desire, esp. a sexual one) into socially acceptable activities. **sublimation** *noun*

sublime ⊕ *adjective* 1 of high moral, intellectual, or spiritual value. 2 unparalleled, supreme. ♦ *verb* 3 *Chem* change from a solid to a vapour without first melting. **sublimely** *adverb*

subliminal *adjective* relating to mental processes of which the individual is not aware.

sub-machine-gun *noun* portable machine gun with a short barrel.

submarine *noun* 1 vessel which can operate below the surface of the sea. ♦ *adjective* 2 below the surface of the sea.

submerge ⊕ *verb* 1 put or go below the surface of water or other liquid. 2 involve totally. **submersion** *noun* **submersible** *noun, adjective* (vehicle) able to work under water.

submit ⊕ *verb* **-mitting, -mitted** 1 surrender. 2 put forward for consideration. 3 be (voluntarily) subjected to a process or treatment. **submission** *noun* 1 submitting. 2 something submitted for consideration. 3 state of being submissive. **submissive** *adjective* meek and obedient.

subnormal *adjective* less than normal, esp. in intelligence.

subordinate ⊕ *adjective* 1 of lesser rank or importance. ♦ *noun* 2 subordinate person or thing. ♦ *verb* 3 make or treat as subordinate. **subordination** *noun*

suborn *verb Formal* bribe or incite (a person) to commit a wrongful act.

subpoena [sub-pee-na] *noun* 1 writ requiring a person to appear before a lawcourt. ♦ *verb* 2 summon (someone) with a subpoena.

sub rosa [sub rose-a] *adverb Latin* in secret.

subscribe ⊕ *verb* 1 pay (a subscription). 2 give support or approval (to). **subscriber** *noun*

subscription *noun* 1 payment for issues of a publication over a period. 2 money contributed to a charity etc. 3 membership fees paid to a society.

subscript *noun, adjective* (character) printed below the line.

subsection *noun* division of a section.

subsequent ⊕ *adjective* occurring after, succeeding. **subsequently** *adverb*

subservient ⊕ *adjective* submissive, servile.

——————— THESAURUS ———————

down, unobtrusive OPPOSITE **bright**

subject *noun* 1 = **topic**, affair, business, issue, matter, object, point, question, substance, theme 4 = **citizen**, national, subordinate ♦*adjective* 5 = **subordinate**, dependent, inferior, obedient, satellite ♦*verb* (foll. by *to*) 6 = **put through**, expose, lay open, submit, treat

subject to 1 = **liable to**, prone to 2 = **conditional on**, contingent on, dependent on

subjective *adjective* = **personal**, biased, nonobjective, prejudiced

subjugate *verb* = **conquer**, enslave, master, overcome, overpower, quell, subdue, suppress, vanquish

sublime *adjective* 1 = **noble**, elevated, exalted, glorious, grand, great, high, lofty OPPOSITE **ordinary**

submerge *verb* 1 = **immerse**, deluge, dip, duck, engulf, flood, inundate, overflow, overwhelm, plunge, sink, swamp

submission *noun* 1 = **surrender**, assent, capitulation, cave-in (*inf*), giving in, yielding 2 = **presentation**, entry, handing in, tendering 3 = **meekness**, compliance, deference, docility,

obedience, passivity, resignation

submissive *adjective* = **meek**, accommodating, acquiescent, amenable, compliant, docile, obedient, passive, pliant, tractable, unresisting, yielding

submit *verb* 1 = **surrender**, accede, agree, capitulate, cave in (*inf*), comply, endure, give in, succumb, tolerate, yield 2 = **present**, hand in, proffer, put forward, table, tender

subordinate *adjective* 1 = **lesser**, dependent, inferior, junior, lower, minor, secondary, subject OPPOSITE **senior** ♦*noun* 2 = **inferior**, aide, assistant, attendant, junior, second OPPOSITE **head**

subordination *noun* 3 = **inferiority**, inferior or secondary status, servitude, subjection

subscribe *verb* 1 = **contribute**, donate, give 2 = **support**, advocate, endorse

subscription *noun* 2 = **contribution**, donation, gift 3 = **membership fee**, annual payment, dues

subsequent *adjective* = **following**, after, ensuing, later, succeeding, successive

subsequently *adverb* = **later**, afterwards

S

subservience *noun*
subside ⊙ *verb* **1** become less intense. **2** sink to a lower level. **subsidence** *noun* act or process of subsiding.
subsidiarity *noun* principle of taking political decisions at the lowest practical level.
subsidiary ⊙ *adjective* **1** of lesser importance. ♦ *noun, pl* **-aries 2** subsidiary person or thing.
subsidize ⊙ *verb* help financially. **subsidy** *noun, pl* **-dies** any financial aid, grant, or contribution.
subsist *verb* manage to live. **subsistence** *noun*
subsoil *noun* earth just below the surface soil.
subsonic *adjective* moving at a speed less than that of sound.
substance ⊙ *noun* **1** physical composition of something. **2** solid, powder, liquid, or paste. **3** essential meaning of something. **4** solid or meaningful quality. **5** wealth. **substantial** *adjective* **1** of considerable size or value. **2** (of food or a meal) sufficient and nourishing. **3** solid or strong. **4** real. **substantially** *adverb*
substantiate *verb* support (a story) with evidence. **substantiation** *noun* **substantive** *noun* **1** noun. ♦ *adjective* **2** of or being the essential element of a thing.
substitute ⊙ *verb* **1** take the place of or put in place of another. ♦ *noun* **2** person or thing taking the place of (another). **substitution** *noun*
subsume *verb* include (an idea, case, etc.) under a larger classification or group.
subterfuge ⊙ *noun* trick used to achieve an objective.

subterranean *adjective* underground.
subtitle *noun* **1** secondary title of a book. ♦ *plural* **2** printed translation at the bottom of the picture in a film with foreign dialogue. ♦ *verb* **3** provide with a subtitle or subtitles.
subtle ⊙ *adjective* **1** not immediately obvious. **2** delicate. **3** having or requiring ingenuity. **subtly** *adverb* **subtlety** *noun*
subtract ⊙ *verb* take (one number or quantity) from another. **subtraction** *noun*
subtropical *adjective* of the regions bordering on the tropics.
suburb *noun* residential area on the outskirts of a city. **suburban** *adjective* **1** of or inhabiting a suburb. **2** narrow or unadventurous in outlook. **suburbanite** *noun* **suburbia** *noun* suburbs and their inhabitants.
subvention *noun Formal* subsidy.
subvert ⊙ *verb* overthrow the authority of. **subversion** *noun* **subversive** *adjective, noun*
subway *noun* **1** passage under a road or railway. **2** *US & Canad* underground railway.
succeed ⊙ *verb* **1** accomplish an aim. **2** turn out satisfactorily. **3** come next in order after (something). **4** take over a position from (someone). **success** *noun* **1** achievement of something attempted. **2** attainment of wealth, fame, or position. **3** successful person or thing. **successful** *adjective* having success.
successfully *adverb* **succession** *noun* **1** series of people or things following one another in order. **2** act or right by which one person succeeds another in a position. **successive** *adjective* consecutive. **successively** *adverb* **successor** *noun* person who succeeds someone

——————— T H E S A U R U S ———————

subservient *adjective* =**servile**, abject, deferential, obsequious, slavish, submissive, sycophantic OPPOSITE **bossy**
subside *verb* **1** =**decrease**, abate, diminish, ease, ebb, lessen, quieten, slacken, wane OPPOSITE **rise**. **2** =**collapse**, cave in, drop, lower, settle, sink
subsidiary *adjective* **1** =**lesser**, ancillary, auxiliary, minor, secondary, subordinate, supplementary OPPOSITE **leading**
subsidize *verb* =**fund**, finance, promote, sponsor, support
subsidy *noun* =**aid**, allowance, assistance, grant, help, support
substance *noun* **1** =**material**, body, fabric, stuff **3** =**meaning**, essence, gist, import, main point, significance **4** =**reality**, actuality, concreteness **5** =**wealth**, assets, estate, means, property, resources
substantial *adjective* **1** =**big**, ample,

considerable, large, significant, sizable or sizeable OPPOSITE **small**
substantiate *verb* =**support**, authenticate, confirm, establish, prove, verify
substitute *verb* **1** =**replace**, change, exchange, interchange, swap, switch ♦*noun* **2** =**replacement**, agent, deputy, locum, proxy, reserve, sub, surrogate
subterfuge *noun* =**trick**, deception, dodge, manoeuvre, ploy, ruse, stratagem
subtle *adjective* **1** =**faint**, delicate, implied, slight, understated OPPOSITE **blatant**. **2** =**sophisticated**, delicate, refined **3** =**crafty**, artful, cunning, devious, ingenious, shrewd, sly, wily OPPOSITE **straightforward**
subtract *verb* =**take away**, deduct, diminish, remove, take from, take off
subversive *adjective* =**seditious**, riotous, treasonous ♦*noun* =**dissident**, fifth columnist, saboteur, terrorist, traitor

S

in a position.

SPELLING TIP

The Bank of English evidence shows that people are able to remember the double s at the end of **success** more easily than the double c in the middle.

succinct ❶ *adjective* brief and clear. **succinctly** *adverb*

succour ❶ *verb, noun* help in distress.

succulent ❶ *adjective* **1** juicy and delicious. **2** (of a plant) having thick fleshy leaves. ♦ *noun* **3** succulent plant. **succulence** *noun*

succumb ❶ *verb* **1** (foll. by *to*) give way (to something overpowering). **2** die of (an illness).

such *adjective* **1** of the kind specified. **2** so great, so much. ♦ *pronoun* **3** such things. **such-and-such** *adjective* specific, but not known or named. **suchlike** *pronoun* such or similar things.

suck ❶ *verb* **1** draw (liquid or air) into the mouth. **2** take (something) into the mouth and moisten, dissolve, or roll it around with the tongue. **3** (foll. by *in*) draw in by irresistible force. ♦ *noun* **4** sucking. **sucker** *noun* **1** *Slang* person who is easily deceived or swindled. **2** organ or device which adheres by suction. **3** shoot coming from a plant's root or the base of its main stem. **suck up to** *verb Informal* flatter

(someone) for one's own profit.

suckle *verb* feed at the breast. **suckling** *noun* unweaned baby or young animal.

sucrose [soo-kroze] *noun* chemical name for sugar.

suction *noun* **1** sucking. **2** force produced by drawing air out of a space to make a vacuum that will suck in a substance from another space.

sudden ❶ *adjective* done or occurring quickly and unexpectedly. **all of a sudden** quickly and unexpectedly. **suddenly** *adverb* **suddenness** *noun* **sudden death** *Sport* period of extra time in which the first competitor to score wins.

sudorific [syoo-dor-**if**-ik] *noun, adjective* (drug) causing sweating.

suds *plural noun* froth of soap and water.

sue ❶ *verb* **suing, sued** start legal proceedings against.

suede *noun* leather with a velvety finish on one side.

suet *noun* hard fat obtained from sheep and cattle, used in cooking.

suffer ❶ *verb* **1** undergo or be subjected to. **2** tolerate. **sufferer** *noun* **suffering** *noun* **sufferance** *noun* **on sufferance** tolerated with reluctance.

suffice ❶ [suf-**fice**] *verb* be enough for a purpose. **sufficiency** *noun* adequate amount. **sufficient** *adjective* enough, adequate. **sufficiently** *adverb*

suffix *noun* letter or letters added to the end

subvert *verb* = **overturn**, sabotage, undermine

succeed *verb* **1, 2** = **make it** (*inf*), be successful, crack it (*inf*), do well, flourish, make good, make the grade (*inf*), prosper, thrive, triumph, work OPPOSITE **fail**. **3** = **follow**, come next, ensue, result OPPOSITE **precede**. **4** = **take over**, accede, assume the office of, come into, come into possession of, inherit

success *noun* **1, 2** = **favourable outcome**, fame, fortune, happiness, luck, prosperity, triumph OPPOSITE **failure**. **3** = **hit** (*inf*), celebrity, megastar (*inf*), sensation, smash (*inf*), star, winner OPPOSITE **flop**

successful *adjective* = **thriving**, booming, flourishing, fortunate, fruitful, lucky, profitable, rewarding, top, victorious OPPOSITE **failed**

succession *noun* **1** = **series**, chain, course, cycle, order, progression, run, sequence, train **2** = **taking over**, accession, assumption, inheritance

successive *adjective* = **consecutive**, following, in succession

succinct *adjective* = **brief**, compact, concise,

laconic, pithy, terse

succour *verb* = **help**, aid, assist ♦*noun* = **help**, aid, assistance

succulent *adjective* **1** = **juicy**, luscious, lush, moist

succumb *verb* **1** (foll. by *to*) = **surrender**, capitulate, cave in (*inf*), give in, submit, yield OPPOSITE **beat**. **2** = **die**, cark (*Aust & NZ sl*), fall

sucker *noun* **1** *Sl* = **fool**, dupe, mug (*Brit sl*), pushover (*sl*), victim

sudden *adjective* = **quick**, abrupt, hasty, hurried, rapid, rash, swift, unexpected

sue *verb* = **take (someone) to court**, charge, indict, prosecute, summon

suffer *verb* **1** = **undergo**, bear, endure, experience, go through, sustain **2** = **tolerate**, put up with (*inf*)

suffering *noun* **1** = **pain**, agony, anguish, discomfort, distress, hardship, misery, ordeal, torment

suffice *verb* = **be enough**, be adequate, be sufficient, do, meet requirements, serve

sufficient *adjective* = **adequate**, enough,

of a word to form another word.

suffocate ⊙ *verb* **1** kill or be killed by deprivation of oxygen. **2** feel uncomfortable from heat and lack of air. **suffocation** *noun*

suffragan *noun* bishop appointed to assist an archbishop.

suffrage *noun* right to vote in public elections. **suffragette** *noun* (in Britain in the early 20th century) a woman who campaigned militantly for the right to vote.

suffuse *verb* spread through or over (something). **suffusion** *noun*

sugar *noun* **1** sweet crystalline carbohydrate found in many plants and used to sweeten food and drinks. ◆ *verb* **2** sweeten or cover with sugar. **sugary** *adjective* **sugar beet** beet grown for the sugar obtained from its roots. **sugar cane** tropical grass grown for the sugar obtained from its canes. **sugar daddy** *Slang* elderly man who gives a young woman money and gifts in return for sexual favours. **sugar glider** common Australian phalanger that glides from tree to tree feeding on insects and nectar.

suggest ⊙ *verb* **1** put forward (an idea) for consideration. **2** bring to mind by the association of ideas. **3** give a hint of.

suggestible *adjective* easily influenced.

suggestion *noun* **1** thing suggested. **2** hint or indication. **suggestive** *adjective* **1** suggesting something indecent. **2** conveying a hint (of). **suggestively** *adverb*

suicide *noun* **1** killing oneself intentionally. **2** person who kills himself intentionally. **3** self-inflicted ruin of one's own prospects or interests. **suicidal** *adjective* liable to commit suicide. **suicidally** *adverb*

suit ⊙ *noun* **1** set of clothes designed to be worn together. **2** outfit worn for a specific purpose. **3** one of the four sets into which a pack of cards is divided. **4** lawsuit. ◆ *verb* **5** be appropriate for. **6** be acceptable to. **suitable** *adjective* appropriate or proper. **suitably** *adverb* **suitability** *noun* **suitcase** *noun* portable travelling case for clothing.

suite ⊙ *noun* **1** set of connected rooms in a hotel. **2** matching set of furniture. **3** set of musical pieces in the same key.

suitor ⊙ *noun Old-fashioned* man who is courting a woman.

sulk ⊙ *verb* **1** be silent and sullen because of resentment or bad temper. ◆ *noun* **2** resentful or sullen mood. **sulky** *adjective* **sulkily** *adverb* **sulkiness** *noun*

sullen ⊙ *adjective* unwilling to talk or be sociable. **sullenly** *adverb* **sullenness** *noun*

sully ⊙ *verb* **-lying, -lied 1** ruin (someone's reputation). **2** make dirty.

sulphate *noun* salt or ester of sulphuric acid.

sulphide *noun* compound of sulphur with another element.

sulphite *noun* salt or ester of sulphurous acid.

sulphonamide [sulf-**on**-a-mide] *noun* any of a class of drugs that prevent the growth of bacteria.

sulphur *noun Chem* pale yellow nonmetallic element. **sulphuric, sulphurous** *adjective* of or containing sulphur. **sulphuric acid** colourless corrosive liquid used for making explosives.

sulphurous acid acid used for bleaching and as a preservative.

sultan *noun* sovereign of a Muslim country. **sultana** *noun* **1** kind of raisin. **2** sultan's wife, mother, or daughter. **sultanate** *noun* territory of a sultan.

sultry ⊙ *adjective* **-trier, -triest 1** (of weather or climate) hot and humid. **2** passionate, sensual.

——————— T H E S A U R U S ———————

satisfactory

suffocate *verb* **1** = **choke**, asphyxiate, smother, stifle **2** = **stifle**, choke

suggest *verb* **1** = **recommend**, advise, advocate, prescribe, propose **2** = **bring to mind**, evoke **3** = **hint**, imply, indicate, intimate

suggestion *noun* **1** = **recommendation**, motion, plan, proposal, proposition **2** = **hint**, breath, indication, intimation, trace, whisper

suggestive *adjective* **1** = **smutty**, bawdy, blue, indelicate, racy, ribald, risqué, rude

suit *noun* **2** = **outfit**, clothing, costume, dress, ensemble, habit **4** = **lawsuit**, action, case, cause, proceeding, prosecution, trial ◆*verb* **5** = **befit**, agree, become, go with, harmonize, match, tally **6** = **be acceptable to**, do, gratify,

please, satisfy

suitable *adjective* = **appropriate**, apt, becoming, befitting, fit, fitting, proper, right, satisfactory OPPOSITE inappropriate

suite *noun* **1** = **rooms**, apartment

suitor *noun Old-fashioned* = **admirer**, beau, young man

sulky *adjective* **1** = **huffy**, cross, disgruntled, in the sulks, moody, petulant, querulous, resentful, sullen

sullen *adjective* = **morose**, cross, dour, glowering, moody, sour, sulky, surly, unsociable

sully *verb* **1** = **dishonour**, besmirch, disgrace, ruin, smirch **2** = **defile**, stain, tarnish

sultry *adjective* **1** = **humid**, close, hot, muggy, oppressive, sticky, stifling OPPOSITE fresh. **2**

sum ❶ *noun* **1** result of addition, total. **2** problem in arithmetic. **3** quantity of money. **4** gist of a matter. **sum total** complete or final total. **sum up** *verb* **summing, summed 1** summarize. **2** form a quick opinion of.

summary ❶ *noun, pl* **-ries 1** brief account giving the main points of something. ◆ *adjective* **2** done quickly, without formalities. **summarily** *adverb* **summarize** *verb* make or be a summary of (something). **summation** *noun* **1** summary. **2** adding up.

summer *noun* warmest season of the year, between spring and autumn. **summery** *adjective* **summerhouse** *noun* small building in a garden. **summer school** academic course held during the summer. **summertime** *noun* period or season of summer.

summit ❶ *noun* **1** top of a mountain or hill. **2** highest point. **3** conference between heads of state.

summon ❶ *verb* **1** order (someone) to come. **2** send for (someone) to appear in court. **3** call upon (someone) to do something. **4** gather (one's courage, strength, etc.). **summons** *noun* **1** command summoning someone. **2** order requiring someone to appear in court. ◆ *verb* **3** order (someone) to appear in court.

sumo *noun* Japanese style of wrestling.

sump *noun* **1** container in an internal-combustion engine into which oil can drain. **2** hollow into which liquid drains.

sumptuous ❶ *adjective* lavish, magnificent. **sumptuously** *adverb*

sun ❶ *noun* **1** star around which the earth and other planets revolve. **2** any star around which planets revolve. **3** heat and light from the sun. ◆ *verb* **sunning, sunned 4** expose (oneself) to the sun's rays. **sunless** *adjective* **sunny** *adjective* **1** full of or exposed to sunlight. **2** cheerful. **sunbathe** *verb* lie in the sunshine in order to get a suntan. **sunbeam** *noun* ray of sun. **sunburn** *noun* painful reddening of the skin

caused by overexposure to the sun. **sunburnt, sunburned** *adjective* **sundial** *noun* device showing the time by means of a pointer that casts a shadow on a marked dial. **sundown** *noun* sunset. **sunflower** *noun* tall plant with large golden flowers. **sunglasses** *plural noun* dark glasses to protect the eyes from the sun. **sun lamp** lamp that gives off ultraviolet rays. **sunrise** *noun* **1** daily appearance of the sun above the horizon. **2** time of this. **sunroof** *noun* panel in the roof of a car that opens to let in air. **sunset** *noun* **1** daily disappearance of the sun below the horizon. **2** time of this. **sunshine** *noun* light and warmth from the sun. **sunspot** *noun* **1** dark patch appearing temporarily on the sun's surface. **2** *Aust* small area of skin damage caused by exposure to the sun. **sunstroke** *noun* illness caused by prolonged exposure to intensely hot sunlight. **suntan** *noun* browning of the skin caused by exposure to the sun. **sun-up** *noun* US sunrise.

Sun. Sunday.

sundae *noun* ice cream topped with fruit etc.

Sunday *noun* first day of the week and the Christian day of worship. **Sunday school** school for teaching children about Christianity.

sundry ❶ *adjective* several, various. **sundries** *plural noun* several things of various sorts. **all and sundry** everybody.

sung *verb* past participle of SING.

sunk *verb* a past participle of SINK.

sunken ❶ *verb* **1** a past participle of SINK. ◆ *adjective* **2** unhealthily hollow. **3** situated at a low level. **4** underwater.

sup *verb* **supping, supped 1** take (liquid) by sips. ◆ *noun* **2** sip.

super ❶ *adjective* Informal excellent.

super- *prefix* used with many main words to mean: **1** above or over, e.g. *superimpose*. **2** outstanding, e.g. *superstar*. **3** of greater size or extent, e.g. *supermarket*.

superannuation *noun* **1** regular payment by

——————— T H E S A U R U S ———————

= seductive, provocative, sensual, sexy (*inf*)

sum *noun* **1** = **total**, aggregate, amount, tally, whole

summarize *verb* = **sum up**, abridge, condense, encapsulate, epitomize, précis

summary *noun* **1** = **synopsis**, abridgment, outline, précis, résumé, review, rundown

summit *noun* **1, 2** = **peak**, acme, apex, head, height, pinnacle, top, zenith OPPOSITE **base**

summon *verb* **1** = **send for**, bid, call, invite **4** = **gather**, draw on, muster

sumptuous *adjective* = **luxurious**, gorgeous, grand, lavish, opulent, splendid, superb

sum up *verb* **1** = **summarize**, put in a nutshell, recapitulate, review

sundry *adjective* = **various**, assorted, different, miscellaneous, several, some

sunken *adjective* **2** = **hollow**, drawn, haggard **3** = **lower**, buried, recessed **4** = **submerged**

sunny *adjective* **1** = **bright**, clear, fine, radiant, summery, sunlit, unclouded OPPOSITE **overcast**. **2** = **cheerful**, buoyant, cheery, happy, joyful, light-hearted OPPOSITE **miserable**

sunrise *noun* = **dawn**, break of day, cockcrow, daybreak

sunset *noun* = **nightfall**, close of (the) day,

an employee into a pension fund. **2** pension paid from this. **superannuated** *adjective* discharged with a pension, owing to old age or illness.

superb ❶ *adjective* excellent, impressive, or splendid. **superbly** *adverb*

superbug *noun Informal* bacterium resistant to antibiotics.

supercharged *adjective* (of an engine) having a supercharger. **supercharger** *noun* device that increases the power of an internal-combustion engine by forcing extra air into it.

supercilious ❶ *adjective* showing arrogant pride or scorn.

superconductor *noun* substance which has almost no electrical resistance at very low temperatures. **superconductivity** *noun*

superficial ❶ *adjective* **1** not careful or thorough. **2** (of a person) without depth of character, shallow. **3** of or on the surface. **superficially** *adverb* **superficiality** *noun*

superfluous ❶ [soo-per-flew-uss] *adjective* more than is needed. **superfluity** *noun*

supergrass *noun* person who acts as a police informer on a large scale.

superhuman ❶ *adjective* beyond normal human ability or experience.

superimpose *verb* place (something) on or over something else.

superintend ❶ *verb* supervise (a person or activity). **superintendent** *noun* **1** senior police officer. **2** supervisor.

superior ❶ *adjective* **1** greater in quality, quantity, or merit. **2** higher in position or rank.

3 believing oneself to be better than others. ◆ *noun* **4** person of greater rank or status. **superiority** *noun*

superlative ❶ [soo-per-lat-iv] *adjective* **1** of outstanding quality. **2** *Grammar* denoting the form of an adjective or adverb indicating *most*. ◆ *noun* **3** *Grammar* superlative form of a word.

superman *noun* man with great physical or mental powers.

supermarket *noun* large self-service store selling food and household goods.

supermodel *noun* famous and highly-paid fashion model.

supernatural ❶ *adjective* of or relating to things beyond the laws of nature. **the supernatural** supernatural forces, occurrences, and beings collectively.

supernova *noun, pl* **-vae, -vas** star that explodes and briefly becomes exceptionally bright.

supernumerary *adjective* **1** exceeding the required or regular number. ◆ *noun, pl* **-ries 2** supernumerary person or thing.

superpower *noun* extremely powerful nation.

superscript *noun, adjective* (character) printed above the line.

supersede ❶ *verb* replace, supplant.

SPELLING TIP

Although there is a word 'cede', spelt with a *c*, the word **supersede** must have an *s* in the middle.

THESAURUS

---

dusk, eventide

super *adjective Inf* =**excellent**, cracking (*Brit inf*), glorious, magnificent, marvellous, outstanding, sensational (*inf*), smashing (*inf*), superb, terrific (*inf*), wonderful

superb *adjective* =**splendid**, excellent, exquisite, fine, first-rate, grand, magnificent, marvellous, superior, superlative, world-class OPPOSITE **bad**

supercilious *adjective* =**scornful**, arrogant, contemptuous, disdainful, haughty, lofty, snooty (*inf*), stuck-up (*inf*)

superficial *adjective* **1** =**hasty**, casual, cursory, desultory, hurried, perfunctory, sketchy, slapdash OPPOSITE **comprehensive. 2** =**shallow**, empty-headed, frivolous, silly, trivial OPPOSITE **serious. 3** =**surface**, exterior, external, on the surface, slight

superfluous *adjective* =**excess**, extra, left over, redundant, remaining, spare, supernumerary, surplus

superhuman *adjective* =**heroic**, paranormal, phenomenal, prodigious, supernatural

superintendent *noun* **2** =**supervisor**, chief, controller, director, governor, inspector, manager, overseer

superior *adjective* **1 a** =**better**, grander, greater, higher, surpassing, unrivalled OPPOSITE **worse. b** =**first-class**, choice, de luxe, excellent, exceptional, exclusive, first-rate OPPOSITE **average. 3** =**supercilious**, condescending, disdainful, haughty, lofty, lordly, patronizing, pretentious, snobbish ◆*noun* **4** =**boss** (*inf*), chief, director, manager, principal, senior, supervisor OPPOSITE **subordinate**

superiority *noun* **1, 2** =**supremacy**, advantage, ascendancy, excellence, lead, predominance

superlative *adjective* **1** =**supreme**, excellent, outstanding, unparalleled, unrivalled, unsurpassed

S

supersonic *adjective* of or travelling at a speed greater than the speed of sound.

superstar *noun* very famous entertainer or sportsperson.

superstition *noun* **1** belief in omens, ghosts, etc. **2** idea or practice based on this. **superstitious** *adjective*

superstore *noun* large supermarket.

superstructure *noun* **1** structure erected on something else. **2** part of a ship above the main deck.

supertanker *noun* large fast tanker.

supertax *noun* extra tax on incomes above a certain level.

supervene *verb* occur as an unexpected development. **supervention** *noun*

supervise ➊ *verb* watch over to direct or check. **supervision** *noun* **supervisor** *noun* **supervisory** *adjective*

supine [soo-pine] *adjective* lying flat on one's back.

supper *noun* light evening meal.

supplant ➊ *verb* take the place of, oust.

supple ➊ *adjective* **1** (of a person) moving and bending easily and gracefully. **2** bending easily without damage. **suppleness** *noun*

supplement ➊ *noun* **1** thing added to complete something or make up for a lack. **2** magazine inserted into a newspaper. **3** section added to a publication to supply further information. ◆ *verb* **4** provide or be a supplement to (something). **supplementary**

adjective

supplication ➊ *noun* humble request.

supplicant *noun* person who makes a humble request.

supply ➊ *verb* **-plying, -plied 1** provide with something required. ◆ *noun, pl* **-plies 2** supplying. **3** amount available. **4** *Economics* willingness and ability to provide goods and services. ◆ *plural* **5** food or equipment. ◆ *adjective* **6** acting as a temporary substitute. **supplier** *noun*

support ➊ *verb* **1** bear the weight of. **2** provide the necessities of life for. **3** give practical or emotional help to. **4** take an active interest in (a sports team, political principle, etc.). **5** help to prove (a theory etc.). **6** speak in favour of. **7** play a subordinate part. ◆ *noun* **8** supporting. **9** means of support. **supporter** *noun* person who supports a team, principle, etc. **supportive** *adjective*

suppose ➊ *verb* **1** presume to be true. **2** consider as a proposal for the sake of discussion. **3** presuppose. **supposed** *adjective* presumed to be true without proof, doubtful. **supposed to 1** expected or required to, e.g. *you were supposed to phone me.* **2** permitted to, e.g. *we're not supposed to swim here.* **supposedly** *adverb* **supposition** *noun* **1** supposing. **2** something supposed.

suppositious *adjective* deduced from an idea or statement believed or assumed to be true.

suppository *noun, pl* **-ries** solid medication

———— THESAURUS ————

supernatural *adjective* =**paranormal**, ghostly, miraculous, mystic, occult, psychic, spectral, uncanny, unearthly

supersede *verb* =**replace**, displace, oust, supplant, take the place of, usurp

supervise *verb* =**oversee**, control, direct, handle, look after, manage, run, superintend

supervision *noun* =**superintendence**, care, charge, control, direction, guidance, management

supervisor *noun* =**boss** (*inf*), administrator, chief, foreman, inspector, manager, overseer

supplant *verb* =**replace**, displace, oust, supersede, take the place of

supple *adjective* **1** =**flexible**, limber, lissom(e), lithe OPPOSITE> **stiff**. **2** =**pliant**, pliable OPPOSITE> **firm**

supplement *noun* **1** =**addition**, add-on, extra **2** =**pull-out**, insert **3** =**appendix**, postscript ◆*verb* **4** =**add**, augment, extend, reinforce

supplementary *adjective* **1** =**additional**, add-on, ancillary, auxiliary, extra, secondary

supplication *noun* Formal =**plea**, appeal, entreaty, petition, prayer, request

supply *verb* **1** =**provide**, contribute, endow, equip, furnish, give, grant, produce, stock, yield ◆*noun* **3** =**store**, cache, fund, hoard, quantity, reserve, source, stock ◆*plural* **5** =**provisions**, equipment, food, materials, necessities, rations, stores, tucker (*Aust & NZ inf*)

support *verb* **1** =**bear**, brace, buttress, carry, hold, prop, reinforce, sustain **2** =**provide for**, finance, fund, keep, look after, maintain, sustain OPPOSITE> **live off. 3** =**help**, aid, assist, back, champion, defend, second, side with **5** =**bear out**, confirm, corroborate, substantiate, verify OPPOSITE> **deny** ◆*noun* **8** =**help**, aid, assistance, backing, encouragement, loyalty **9** =**prop**, brace, foundation, pillar, post OPPOSITE> **antagonist**

supporter *noun* =**follower**, adherent, advocate, champion, cobber (*Aust or old-fashioned NZ inf*), fan, friend, helper, patron, sponsor, well-wisher

suppose *verb* **1** =**presume**, assume,

S

inserted into the rectum or vagina and left to melt.
suppress ⊕ *verb* **1** put an end to. **2** prevent publication of (information). **3** restrain (an emotion or response). **suppression** *noun*
suppurate *verb* (of a wound etc.) produce pus.
supreme ⊕ *adjective* highest in authority, rank, or degree. **supremely** *adverb* extremely. **supremacy** *noun* **1** supreme power. **2** state of being supreme. **supremo** *noun Informal* person in overall authority.
surcharge *noun* additional charge.
surd *noun Maths* number that cannot be expressed in whole numbers.
sure ⊕ *adjective* **1** free from uncertainty or doubt. **2** reliable. **3** inevitable. **4** physically secure. ♦ *adverb, interjection* **5** *Informal* certainly. **for sure** without a doubt. **surely** *adverb* it must be true that. **sure-fire** *adjective Informal* certain to succeed. **sure-footed** *adjective* unlikely to slip or stumble.
surety *noun, pl* **-ties** person who takes responsibility, or thing given as a guarantee, for the fulfilment of another's obligation.
surf *noun* **1** foam caused by waves breaking on the shore. ♦ *verb* **2** take part in surfing. **3** move quickly through a medium such as the

Internet. **surfing** *noun* sport of riding towards the shore on a surfboard on the crest of a wave. **surfer** *noun* **surfboard** *noun* long smooth board used in surfing.
surface ⊕ *noun* **1** outside or top of an object. **2** material covering the surface of an object. **3** superficial appearance. **4** top level of the land or sea. ♦ *verb* **5** become apparent. **6** rise to the surface. **7** put a surface on.
surfeit ⊕ *noun* excessive amount.
surge ⊕ *noun* **1** sudden powerful increase. **2** strong rolling movement, esp. of the sea. ♦ *verb* **3** increase suddenly. **4** move forward strongly.
surgeon *noun* doctor who specializes in surgery. **surgery** *noun* **1** treatment in which the patient's body is cut open in order to treat the affected part. **2** *pl* **-geries** place where, or time when, a doctor, dentist, MP, etc. can be consulted. **surgical** *adjective* **surgically** *adverb* **surgical spirit** spirit used for sterilizing and cleaning.
surly ⊕ *adjective* **-lier, -liest** ill-tempered and rude. **surliness** *noun*
surmise ⊕ *verb, noun* guess, conjecture.
surmount *verb* **1** overcome (a problem). **2** be on top of (something). **surmountable** *adjective*
surname *noun* family name.
surpass ⊕ *verb* be greater than or superior to.

———————— THESAURUS ————————

conjecture, expect, guess (*inf, chiefly US & Canad*), imagine, think **2** = **imagine**, conjecture, consider, hypothesize, postulate, pretend
supposed *adjective* = **presumed**, accepted, alleged, assumed, professed **supposed to 1** = **meant**, expected, obliged, required
supposedly *adverb* = **presumably**, allegedly, hypothetically, ostensibly, theoretically
supposition *noun* = **guess**, conjecture, hypothesis, presumption, speculation, surmise, theory
suppress *verb* **1** = **stop**, check, conquer, crush, overpower, put an end to, quash, quell, subdue **3** = **restrain**, conceal, contain, curb, hold in *or* back, repress, silence, smother, stifle
supremacy *noun* = **domination**, mastery, predominance, primacy, sovereignty, supreme power, sway
supreme *adjective* = **highest**, chief, foremost, greatest, head, leading, paramount, pre-eminent, prime, principal, top, ultimate [OPPOSITE] **lowest**
supremo *noun Inf* = **head**, boss (*inf*), commander, director, governor, leader, master, principal, ruler
sure *adjective* **1** = **certain**, assured, confident,

convinced, decided, definite, positive [OPPOSITE] **uncertain**. **2** = **reliable**, accurate, dependable, foolproof, infallible, undeniable, undoubted, unerring, unfailing [OPPOSITE] **unreliable**. **3** = **inevitable**, assured, bound, guaranteed, inescapable [OPPOSITE] **unsure**
surely *adverb* = **undoubtedly**, certainly, definitely, doubtlessly, indubitably, unquestionably, without doubt
surface *noun* **1** = **outside**, exterior, face, side, top **2** = **covering**, veneer **3** = **veneer** ♦*verb* **5** = **appear**, arise, come to light, come up, crop up (*inf*), emerge, materialize, transpire
surfeit *noun* = **excess**, glut, plethora, superfluity
surge *noun* **1** = **rush**, flood, flow, gush, outpouring **2** = **wave**, billow, roller, swell ♦*verb* **3** = **rush**, gush, rise **4** = **roll**, heave
surly *adjective* = **ill-tempered**, churlish, cross, grouchy (*inf*), morose, sulky, sullen, uncivil, ungracious
surmise *verb* = **guess**, conjecture, imagine, presume, speculate, suppose ♦*noun* = **guess**, assumption, conjecture, presumption, speculation, supposition
surpass *verb* = **outdo**, beat, eclipse, exceed, excel, outshine, outstrip, transcend

S

surplice *noun* loose white robe worn by clergymen and choristers.

surplus ⊙ *noun* **1** amount left over in excess of what is required. ◆ *adjective* **2** extra.

surprise ⊙ *noun* **1** unexpected event. **2** amazement and wonder. **3** act of taking someone unawares. ◆ *verb* **4** cause to feel amazement or wonder. **5** come upon, attack, or catch suddenly and unexpectedly. **take someone by surprise** catch someone unprepared.

surrealism *noun* movement in art and literature involving the combination of incongruous images, as in a dream. **surreal** *adjective* bizarre. **surrealist** *noun, adjective* **surrealistic** *adjective*

surrender ⊙ *verb* **1** give oneself up. **2** give (something) up to another. **3** yield (to a temptation or influence). ◆ *noun* **4** surrendering.

surreptitious ⊙ *adjective* done secretly or stealthily. **surreptitiously** *adverb*

surrogate ⊙ *noun* substitute. **surrogate mother** woman who gives birth to a child on behalf of a couple who cannot have children.

surround ⊙ *verb* **1** be, come, or place all around (a person or thing). ◆ *noun* **2** border or edging. **surroundings** *plural noun* area or environment around a person, place, or thing.

surtax *noun* extra tax on incomes above a certain level.

surveillance ⊙ *noun* close observation.

survey ⊙ *verb* **1** view or consider in a general way. **2** make a map of (an area). **3** inspect (a building) to assess its condition and value. **4** find out the incomes, opinions, etc. of (a group of people). ◆ *noun* **5** surveying. **6** report produced by a survey. **surveyor** *noun*

survive ⊙ *verb* **1** continue to live or exist after (a difficult experience). **2** live after the death of (another). **survival** *noun* **1** condition of having survived. **2** thing that has survived from an earlier time. **survivor** *noun*

susceptible ⊙ *adjective* liable to be influenced or affected by. **susceptibility** *noun*

suspect ⊙ *verb* **1** believe (someone) to be guilty without having any proof. **2** think (something) to be false or questionable. **3** believe (something) to be the case. ◆ *adjective* **4** not to be trusted. ◆ *noun* **5** person who is suspected.

suspend ⊙ *verb* **1** hang from a high place. **2** cause to remain floating or hanging. **3** cause to cease temporarily. **4** remove (someone) temporarily from a job or team. **suspenders** *plural noun* **1** straps for holding up stockings. **2** US braces. **suspended sentence** prison sentence that is not served unless the offender commits another crime during a specified period.

suspense ⊙ *noun* state of uncertainty while awaiting news, an event, etc.

———— THESAURUS ————

surplus *noun* **1** = **excess**, balance, remainder, residue, surfeit ◆*adjective* **2** = **extra**, excess, odd, remaining, spare, superfluous OPPOSITE insufficient

surprise *noun* **1** = **shock**, bombshell, eye-opener (*inf*), jolt, revelation **2** = **amazement**, astonishment, incredulity, wonder ◆*verb* **4** = **amaze**, astonish, stagger, stun, take aback **5** = **catch unawares** or **off-guard**, discover, spring upon, startle

surrender *verb* **1** = **give in**, capitulate, cave in (*inf*), give way, submit, succumb, yield OPPOSITE **resist**. **2** = **give up**, abandon, cede, concede, part with, relinquish, renounce, waive, yield **3** = **yield**, give in ◆*noun* **4** = **submission**, capitulation, cave-in (*inf*), relinquishment, renunciation, resignation

surreptitious *adjective* = **secret**, covert, furtive, sly, stealthy, underhand

surrogate *noun* = **substitute**, proxy, representative, stand-in

surround *verb* **1** = **enclose**, encircle, encompass, envelop, hem in, ring

surroundings *plural noun* = **environment**, background, location, milieu, setting

surveillance *noun* = **observation**, inspection, scrutiny, supervision, watch

survey *verb* **1** = **look over**, contemplate, examine, inspect, observe, scrutinize, view **2** = **plot**, measure, plan, size up **3** = **estimate**, appraise, assess ◆*noun* **5** = **examination**, inspection, scrutiny **6** = **study**, report, review

survive *verb* = **remain alive**, endure, last, live on, outlast, outlive

susceptible *adjective* = **liable**, disposed, given, impressionable, inclined, prone, receptive, responsive, sensitive, subject, suggestible, vulnerable OPPOSITE **unresponsive**

suspect *verb* **1** = **believe**, consider, feel, guess, speculate, suppose OPPOSITE **be certain.** **2** = **distrust**, doubt, mistrust OPPOSITE **trust** ◆*adjective* **4** = **dubious**, doubtful, iffy (*inf*), questionable OPPOSITE **innocent**

suspend *verb* **1** = **hang**, attach, dangle **3** = **postpone**, cease, cut short, defer, discontinue, interrupt, put off, shelve OPPOSITE **continue**

suspense *noun* = **uncertainty**, anxiety,

suspension ❶ noun **1** suspending or being suspended. **2** system of springs and shock absorbers supporting the body of a vehicle. **3** mixture of fine particles of a solid in a fluid.
suspension bridge bridge hanging from cables attached to towers at each end.
suspicion ❶ noun **1** feeling of not trusting a person or thing. **2** belief that something is true without definite proof. **3** slight trace.
suspicious adjective feeling or causing suspicion. **suspiciously** adverb
suss out verb Slang work out using one's intuition.
sustain ❶ verb **1** maintain or prolong. **2** keep up the vitality or strength of. **3** suffer (an injury or loss). **4** support. **5** confirm. **sustenance** noun food.
suture [soo-cher] noun stitch joining the edges of a wound.
SUV sport utility vehicle.
suzerain noun **1** state or sovereign with limited authority over another self-governing state. **2** feudal lord. **suzerainty** noun
svelte adjective attractively or gracefully slim.
SW southwest(ern).
swab noun **1** small piece of cotton wool used to apply medication, clean a wound, etc. ◆ verb **swabbing, swabbed 2** clean (a wound) with a swab. **3** clean (the deck of a ship) with a mop.
swaddle verb wrap (a baby) in swaddling clothes. **swaddling clothes** long strips of cloth formerly wrapped round a newborn baby.
swag noun Slang stolen property. **swagman** noun Aust tramp who carries his belongings in a bundle on his back.

swagger ❶ verb **1** walk or behave arrogantly. ◆ noun **2** arrogant walk or manner.
swain noun Poetic **1** suitor. **2** country youth.
swallow¹ ❶ verb **1** cause to pass down one's throat. **2** make a gulping movement in the throat, as when nervous. **3** Informal believe (something) gullibly. **4** refrain from showing (a feeling). **5** engulf or absorb. ◆ noun **6** swallowing. **7** amount swallowed.
swallow² noun small migratory bird with long pointed wings and a forked tail.
swam verb past tense of SWIM.
swamp ❶ noun **1** watery area of land, bog. ◆ verb **2** cause (a boat) to fill with water and sink. **3** overwhelm. **swampy** adjective
swan noun **1** large usu. white water bird with a long graceful neck. ◆ verb **swanning, swanned 2** Informal wander about idly. **swan song** person's last performance before retirement or death.
swank Slang verb **1** show off or boast. ◆ noun **2** showing off or boasting. **swanky** adjective Slang expensive and showy, stylish.
swap ❶ verb **swapping, swapped 1** exchange (something) for something else. ◆ noun **2** exchange.
sward noun stretch of short grass.
swarm¹ ❶ noun **1** large group of bees or other insects. **2** large crowd. ◆ verb **3** move in a swarm. **4** (of a place) be crowded or overrun.
swarm² verb (foll. by up) climb (a ladder or rope) by gripping with the hands and feet.
swarthy ❶ adjective **-thier, -thiest** dark-complexioned.
swashbuckling ❶ adjective having the

——————— T H E S A U R U S ———————

apprehension, doubt, expectation, insecurity, irresolution, tension
suspension noun **1** = **postponement**, abeyance, break, breaking off, deferment, discontinuation, interruption
suspicion noun **1** = **distrust**, doubt, dubiety, misgiving, mistrust, qualm, scepticism, wariness **2** = **idea**, guess, hunch, impression, notion **3** = **trace**, hint, shade, soupçon, streak, suggestion, tinge, touch
suspicious adjective **a** = **distrustful**, doubtful, sceptical, unbelieving, wary OPPOSITE **trusting**. **b** = **suspect**, dodgy (Brit, Aust & NZ inf), doubtful, dubious, fishy (inf), questionable OPPOSITE **straight**
sustain verb **1** = **maintain**, continue, keep up, prolong, protract **2** = **keep alive**, aid, assist, help, nourish **3** = **suffer**, bear, endure, experience, feel, undergo, withstand **4** = **support**, bear, uphold

sustained adjective **1** = **continuous**, constant, nonstop, perpetual, prolonged, steady, unremitting
swagger verb **1** = **show off** (inf), boast, brag, parade, skite (Aust & NZ)
swallow¹ verb **1** = **gulp**, consume, devour, drink, eat, swig (inf)
swamp noun **1** = **bog**, fen, marsh, mire, morass, quagmire, slough, muskeg (Canad) ◆verb **2** = **flood**, capsize, engulf, inundate, sink, submerge **3** = **overwhelm**, engulf, flood, inundate, overload, submerge
swap verb **1** = **exchange**, barter, interchange, switch, trade
swarm¹ noun **2** = **multitude**, army, crowd, flock, herd, horde, host, mass, throng ◆verb **3** = **crowd**, flock, mass, stream, throng **4** = **teem**, abound, bristle, crawl
swarthy adjective = **dark-skinned**, black, brown, dark, dark-complexioned, dusky

S

exciting behaviour of pirates, esp. those depicted in films. **swashbuckler** noun

swastika noun symbol in the shape of a cross with the arms bent at right angles, used as the emblem of Nazi Germany.

swat verb **swatting, swatted 1** hit sharply. ◆ noun **2** sharp blow.

swatch noun sample of cloth.

swath [swawth] noun see SWATHE.

swathe ⊕ verb **1** wrap in bandages or layers of cloth. ◆ noun **2** long strip of cloth wrapped around something. **3** (also **swath**) the width of one sweep of a scythe or mower. **4** strip cut in one sweep.

sway ⊕ verb **1** swing to and fro or from side to side. **2** waver or cause to waver in opinion. ◆ noun **3** power or influence. **4** swaying motion.

swear ⊕ verb **swearing, swore, sworn 1** use obscene or blasphemous language. **2** state or promise on oath. **3** state earnestly. **swear by** verb have complete confidence in. **swear in** verb cause to take an oath. **swearword** noun word considered obscene or blasphemous.

sweat ⊕ noun **1** salty liquid given off through the pores of the skin. **2** Slang drudgery or hard labour. **3** Informal state of anxiety. ◆ verb **4** have sweat coming through the pores. **5** be anxious. **sweaty** adjective **sweatband** noun strip of cloth tied around the forehead or wrist to absorb sweat. **sweatshirt** noun long-sleeved cotton jersey. **sweatshop** noun place where employees work long hours in poor conditions for low pay.

sweater noun (woollen) garment for the upper part of the body.

swede noun **1** kind of turnip. **2** (**S-**) person from Sweden. **Swedish** noun, adjective (language) of Sweden.

sweep ⊕ verb **sweeping, swept 1** remove dirt from (a floor) with a broom. **2** move smoothly and quickly. **3** spread rapidly. **4** move majestically. **5** carry away suddenly or forcefully. **6** stretch in a long wide curve. ◆ noun **7** sweeping. **8** sweeping motion. **9** wide expanse. **10** curving line. **11** sweepstake. **12** chimney sweep. **sweeping** adjective **1** wide-ranging. **2** indiscriminate. **sweepstake** noun lottery in which the stakes of the participants make up the prize.

sweet ⊕ adjective **1** tasting of or like sugar. **2** kind and charming. **3** agreeable to the senses or mind. **4** (of wine) with a high sugar content. ◆ noun **5** shaped piece of food consisting mainly of sugar. **6** dessert. **sweetly** adverb **sweetness** noun **sweeten** verb **sweetener** noun **1** sweetening agent that does not contain sugar. **2** Slang bribe. **sweetie** noun Informal **1** lovable person. **2** sweet. **sweetbread** noun animal's pancreas used as food. **sweet corn** type of maize with sweet yellow kernels, eaten as a vegetable. **sweetheart** noun lover. **sweetmeat** noun Old-fashioned sweet delicacy such as a small cake. **sweet pea** climbing plant with bright fragrant flowers. **sweet potato** tropical root vegetable with yellow flesh. **sweet-talk** verb Informal coax or flatter. **sweet tooth** strong liking for sweet foods. **sweet william** garden plant with clusters of scented flowers.

swell ⊕ verb **swelling, swelled, swollen** or

———— T H E S A U R U S ————

swashbuckling adjective = **dashing**, bold, daredevil, flamboyant

swathe verb **1** = **wrap**, bundle up, cloak, drape, envelop, shroud

sway verb **1** = **bend**, lean, rock, roll, swing **2** = **influence**, affect, guide, induce, persuade ◆noun **3** = **power**, authority, clout (inf), control, influence, mana (NZ)

swear verb **1** = **curse**, be foul-mouthed, blaspheme **2** = **vow**, attest, promise, testify **3** = **declare**, affirm, assert

swearing noun **1** = **bad language**, blasphemy, cursing, foul language, profanity

swearword noun = **oath**, curse, expletive, four-letter word, obscenity, profanity

sweat noun **1** = **perspiration 2** Sl = **labour**, chore, drudgery, toil **3** Inf = **worry**, agitation, anxiety, distress, panic, strain ◆verb **4** = **perspire**, glow **5** = **worry**, agonize, fret, suffer, torture oneself

sweaty adjective **1** = **perspiring**, clammy, sticky

sweep verb **1** = **clear**, brush, clean, remove **2** = **sail**, fly, glide, pass, skim, tear, zoom ◆noun **8** = **stroke**, move, swing **9** = **extent**, range, scope, stretch **10** = **arc**, bend, curve

sweeping adjective **1** = **wide-ranging**, all-embracing, all-inclusive, broad, comprehensive, extensive, global, overarching, wide OPPOSITE limited. **2** = **indiscriminate**, blanket, exaggerated, overstated, unqualified, wholesale

sweet adjective **1** = **sugary**, cloying, icky (inf), saccharine OPPOSITE sour. **2** = **charming**, appealing, engaging, kind, likable or likeable, lovable, winning OPPOSITE nasty. **3** = **fragrant**, agreeable, aromatic, clean, fresh, pure OPPOSITE rank ◆noun **5** = **confectionery**, bonbon, candy (US), lolly (Aust & NZ inf) **6** = **dessert**, pudding

sweeten verb **1** = **sugar**

swelled 1 expand or increase. **2** (of an emotion) become more intense. **3** (of a sound) become gradually louder. ◆ *noun* **4** swelling or being swollen. **5** movement of waves in the sea. **6** *Old-fashioned slang* fashionable person. ◆ *adjective* **7** *US slang* excellent or fine. **swelling** *noun* enlargement of part of the body, caused by injury or infection.

sweltering ⊕ *adjective* uncomfortably hot. **swelter** *verb*

swept *verb* past of SWEEP.

swerve ⊕ *verb* **1** turn aside from a course sharply or suddenly. ◆ *noun* **2** swerving.

swift ⊕ *adjective* **1** moving or able to move quickly. **2** performed or happening quickly. ◆ *noun* **3** fast-flying bird with pointed wings. **swiftly** *adverb* **swiftness** *noun*

swig *noun* **1** large mouthful of drink. ◆ *verb* **swigging, swigged 2** drink in large mouthfuls.

swill *verb* **1** drink greedily. **2** rinse (something) in large amounts of water. ◆ *noun* **3** sloppy mixture containing waste food, fed to pigs. **4** deep drink.

swim *verb* **swimming, swam, swum 1** move along in water by movements of the limbs. **2** be covered or flooded with liquid. **3** float on a liquid. **4** reel, e.g. *her head was swimming.* ◆ *noun* **5** act or period of swimming. **swimmer** *noun* **swimmingly** *adverb* successfully and effortlessly. **swimming costume, swimsuit** *noun* swimming garment that leaves the arms and legs bare. **swimming pool** (building containing) an artificial pond for swimming in.

swindle ⊕ *verb* **1** cheat (someone) out of money. ◆ *noun* **2** instance of swindling. **swindler** *noun*

swine *noun* **1** contemptible person. **2** pig.

swing ⊕ *verb* **swinging, swung 1** move to and fro, sway. **2** turn, as on a hinge. **3** move in a curve. **4** (of an opinion or mood) change sharply. **5** hit out with a sweeping motion. **6** *Slang* be hanged. **7** *Informal* manipulate or influence. ◆ *noun* **8** swinging. **9** suspended seat on which a child can swing to and fro. **10** style of popular dance music played by big bands in the 1930s. **11** sudden or extreme change.

swingeing ⊕ [swin-jing] *adjective* punishing, severe.

swipe ⊕ *verb* **1** strike (at) with a sweeping blow. **2** *Slang* steal. **3** pass (a credit card) through a machine which electronically reads information stored in the card. ◆ *noun* **4** hard blow.

swirl ⊕ *verb* **1** turn with a whirling motion. ◆ *noun* **2** whirling motion. **3** twisting shape.

swish *verb* **1** move with a whistling or hissing sound. ◆ *noun* **2** whistling or hissing sound. ◆ *adjective* **3** *Informal* fashionable, smart.

Swiss *adjective* **1** of Switzerland or its people. ◆ *noun, pl* **Swiss 2** person from Switzerland. **swiss roll** sponge cake spread with jam or cream and rolled up.

switch ⊕ *noun* **1** device for opening and closing an electric circuit. **2** abrupt change. **3** exchange or swap. **4** flexible rod or twig. ◆ *verb* **5** change abruptly. **6** exchange or swap. **switchback** *noun* road or railway with many sharp hills or bends. **switchboard** *noun* installation in a telephone exchange or office where telephone calls are connected. **switch on, off** *verb* turn (a device) on *or* off by means of a switch.

———————————— T H E S A U R U S ————————————

sweetheart *noun* =**love**, beloved, boyfriend *or* girlfriend, darling, dear, lover

swell *verb* **1** =**expand**, balloon, bloat, bulge, dilate, distend, enlarge, grow, increase, rise OPPOSITE **fall**. **2** =**increase**, heighten, intensify, mount, surge OPPOSITE **contract** ◆*noun* **5** =**wave**, billow, surge

swelling *noun* =**enlargement**, bulge, bump, distension, inflammation, lump, protuberance

sweltering *adjective* =**hot**, boiling, burning, oppressive, scorching, stifling

swerve *verb* **1** =**veer**, bend, deflect, deviate, diverge, stray, swing, turn, turn aside

swift *adjective* **1, 2** =**quick**, fast, hurried, prompt, rapid, speedy OPPOSITE **slow**

swiftly *adverb* **1** =**quickly**, fast, hurriedly, promptly, rapidly, speedily

swiftness *noun* **1** =**speed**, promptness, quickness, rapidity, speediness, velocity

swindle *verb* **1** =**cheat**, con, defraud, do (*sl*), fleece, rip (someone) off (*sl*), skin (*sl*), sting (*inf*), trick ◆*noun* **2** =**fraud**, con trick (*inf*), deception, fiddle (*Brit inf*), racket, rip-off (*sl*), scam (*sl*)

swindler *noun* =**cheat**, con man (*inf*), fraud, rogue, shark, trickster

swing *verb* **1** =**sway**, oscillate, rock, veer, wave **2** =**turn**, pivot, rotate, swivel **3** =**curve 6** *Sl* =**hang** ◆*noun* **8** =**swaying**, oscillation

swingeing *adjective* =**severe**, drastic, excessive, harsh, heavy, punishing, stringent

swipe *verb* **1** =**hit**, lash out at, slap, strike, wallop (*inf*) **2** *Sl* =**steal**, appropriate, filch, lift (*inf*), nick (*sl, chiefly Brit*), pinch (*inf*), purloin ◆*noun* **4** =**blow**, clout (*inf*), cuff, slap, smack, thump, wallop (*inf*)

swirl *verb* **1** =**whirl**, churn, eddy, spin, twist

switch *noun* **2** =**change**, reversal, shift **3**

swivel ⊙ *verb* **-elling, -elled 1** turn on a central point. ◆ *noun* **2** coupling device that allows an attached object to turn freely.

swizz, swiz *noun Brit informal* swindle or disappointment.

swizzle stick *noun* small stick used to stir cocktails.

swollen ⊙ *verb* a past participle of SWELL.

swoon *verb, noun* faint.

swoop ⊙ *verb* **1** sweep down or pounce on suddenly. ◆ *noun* **2** swooping.

swop ⊙ *verb* **swopping, swopped,** *noun* same as SWAP.

sword *noun* weapon with a long sharp blade.

sword dance Highland dance performed over swords on the ground. **swordfish** *noun* large fish with a very long upper jaw. **swordsman** *noun* person skilled in the use of a sword.

swore *verb* past tense of SWEAR.

sworn *verb* **1** past participle of SWEAR. ◆ *adjective* **2** bound by or as if by an oath, e.g. *sworn enemies.*

swot ⊙ *Informal verb* **swotting, swotted 1** study hard. ◆ *noun* **2** person who studies hard.

swum *verb* past participle of SWIM.

swung *verb* past of SWING.

sybarite [sib-bar-ite] *noun* lover of luxury. **sybaritic** *adjective*

sycamore *noun* tree with five-pointed leaves and two-winged fruits.

sycophant ⊙ *noun* person who uses flattery to win favour from people with power or influence. **sycophantic** *adjective* **sycophancy** *noun*

syllable *noun* part of a word pronounced as a unit. **syllabic** *adjective*

syllabub *noun* dessert of beaten cream, sugar, and wine.

syllabus ⊙ *noun, pl* **-buses, -bi** list of subjects for a course of study.

syllogism *noun* form of logical reasoning consisting of two premises and a conclusion. **syllogistic** *adjective*

sylph *noun* **1** slender graceful girl or woman. **2** imaginary being supposed to inhabit the air. **sylphlike** *adjective*

sylvan *adjective Lit* relating to woods and trees.

symbiosis *noun* close association of two species living together to their mutual benefit. **symbiotic** *adjective*

symbol ⊙ *noun* sign or thing that stands for something else. **symbolic** *adjective* **symbolically** *adverb* **symbolism** *noun* **1** representation of something by symbols. **2** movement in art and literature using symbols to express abstract and mystical ideas. **symbolist** *noun, adjective* **symbolize** *verb* **1** be a symbol of. **2** represent with a symbol.

symmetry ⊙ *noun* **1** state of having two halves that are mirror images of each other. **2** beauty resulting from a balanced arrangement of parts. **symmetrical** *adjective* **symmetrically** *adverb*

sympathy ⊙ *noun, pl* **-thies 1** compassion for someone's pain or distress. **2** agreement with someone's feelings or interests. **3** feelings of loyalty and support for an idea. **sympathetic** *adjective* **1** feeling or showing sympathy. **2** likeable or appealing. **sympathetically** *adverb* **sympathize** *verb* **1** feel or express sympathy. **2** agree with. **sympathizer** *noun*

———————— THESAURUS ————————

= exchange, substitution, swap ◆ *verb* **5** = change, deflect, deviate, divert, shift **6** = exchange, substitute, swap

swivel *verb* **1** = **turn**, pivot, revolve, rotate, spin

swollen *adjective* = **enlarged**, bloated, distended, inflamed, puffed up

swoop *verb* **1** = **pounce**, descend, dive, rush, stoop, sweep ◆ *noun* **2** = **pounce**, descent, drop, lunge, plunge, rush, stoop, sweep

swop see SWAP

swot *verb Inf* **1** = **study**, cram (*inf*), mug up (*Brit sl*), revise

sycophant *noun* = **crawler**, bootlicker (*inf*), fawner, flatterer, toady, yes man

sycophantic *adjective* = **obsequious**, crawling, fawning, flattering, grovelling, ingratiating, servile, smarmy (*Brit inf*), toadying, unctuous

syllabus *noun* = **course of study**, curriculum

symbol *noun* = **sign**, badge, emblem, figure, image, logo, mark, representation, token

symbolic *adjective* = **representative**, allegorical, emblematic, figurative

symbolize *verb* **2** = **represent**, denote, mean, personify, signify, stand for, typify

symmetrical *adjective* = **balanced**, in proportion, regular

symmetry *noun* = **balance**, evenness, order, proportion, regularity

sympathetic *adjective* **1** = **caring**, compassionate, concerned, interested, kind, pitying, supportive, understanding, warm OPPOSITE indifferent. **2** = **like-minded**, agreeable, companionable, compatible, congenial, friendly OPPOSITE unresponsive

sympathize *verb* **1** = **feel for**, commiserate, condole, pity OPPOSITE mock. **2** = **agree**, side with, understand OPPOSITE reject

symphony *noun, pl* **-nies 1** composition for orchestra, with several movements. **2** visually pleasing arrangement. **symphonic** *adjective*
symposium *noun, pl* **-siums, -sia 1** conference for discussion of a particular topic. **2** collection of essays on a topic.
symptom ⊕ *noun* **1** sign indicating the presence of an illness. **2** sign that something is wrong. **symptomatic** *adjective*
synagogue *noun* Jewish place of worship and religious instruction.
sync, synch *Informal noun* **1** synchronization. ♦ *verb* **2** synchronize.
synchromesh *adjective* (of a gearbox) having a device that synchronizes the speeds of gears before they engage.
synchronize *verb* **1** (of two or more people) perform (an action) at the same time. **2** set (watches) to show the same time. **3** match (the soundtrack and action of a film) precisely. **synchronization** *noun* **synchronous** *adjective* happening or existing at the same time.
syncopate *verb Music* stress the weak beats in (a rhythm) instead of the strong ones. **syncopation** *noun*
syncope [**sing**-kop-ee] *noun Med* a faint.
syndicate *noun* **1** group of people or firms undertaking a joint business project. **2** agency that sells material to several newspapers. ♦ *verb* **3** publish (material) in several newspapers. **4** form a syndicate. **syndication** *noun*
syndrome *noun* **1** combination of symptoms indicating a particular disease. **2** set of characteristics indicating a particular problem.
synergy *noun* potential ability for people or groups to be more successful working together than on their own.
synod *noun* church council.
synonym *noun* word with the same meaning as another. **synonymous** *adjective*

synopsis *noun, pl* **-ses** summary or outline.
syntax *noun Grammar* way in which words are arranged to form phrases and sentences. **syntactic** *adjective*
synthesis ⊕ *noun, pl* **-ses 1** combination of objects or ideas into a whole. **2** artificial production of a substance. **synthesize** *verb* produce by synthesis. **synthesizer** *noun* electronic musical instrument producing a range of sounds. **synthetic** *adjective* **1** (of a substance) made artificially. **2** not genuine, insincere. **synthetically** *adverb*
syphilis *noun* serious sexually transmitted disease. **syphilitic** *adjective*
syphon *noun, verb* same as SIPHON.
Syrian *adjective* **1** of Syria, its people, or their dialect of Arabic. ♦ *noun* **2** person from Syria.
syringe *noun* **1** device for withdrawing or injecting fluids, consisting of a hollow cylinder, a piston, and a hollow needle. ♦ *verb* **2** wash out or inject with a syringe.
syrup *noun* **1** solution of sugar in water. **2** thick sweet liquid. **3** sugar solution containing medicine. **syrupy** *adjective* **1** thick and sweet. **2** excessively sentimental.
system ⊕ *noun* **1** method or set of methods. **2** orderliness. **3** scheme of classification or arrangement. **4** network or assembly of parts that form a whole. **5** body considered as a whole. **the system** society or government regarded as oppressive and exploitative.
systematic *adjective* **systematically** *adverb*
systematize *verb* organize using a system. **systematization** *noun* **systemic** *adjective* affecting the entire animal or body. **systemically** *adverb*
systole [**siss**-tol-ee] *noun* regular contraction of the heart as it pumps blood. **systolic** *adjective*

——————— THESAURUS ———————

sympathy *noun* **1** = **compassion**, commiseration, pity, understanding OPPOSITE **indifference. 2** = **affinity**, agreement, fellow feeling, rapport OPPOSITE **opposition**
symptom *noun* **2** = **sign**, expression, indication, mark, token, warning

synthetic *adjective* **1** = **artificial**, fake, man-made **2** = **fake**, artificial
system *noun* **1** = **method**, practice, procedure, routine, technique **3** = **arrangement**, classification, organization, scheme, structure

S

Tt

t tonne.

T *noun* **to a T 1** in every detail. **2** perfectly.

t. ton.

ta *interjection Informal* thank you.

Ta *Chem* tantalum.

TA Territorial Army.

tab *noun* small flap or projecting label. **keep tabs on** *Informal* watch closely.

tabard *noun* short sleeveless tunic decorated with a coat of arms, worn in medieval times.

Tabasco *noun* ® very hot red pepper sauce.

tabby *noun, pl* **-bies**, *adjective* (cat) with dark stripes on a lighter background.

tabernacle *noun* **1** portable shrine of the Israelites. **2** Christian place of worship not called a church. **3** *RC Church* receptacle for the consecrated Host.

tabla *noun, pl* **-bla, -blas** one of a pair of Indian drums played with the hands.

table ⊙ *noun* **1** piece of furniture with a flat top supported by legs. **2** arrangement of information in columns. ◆ *verb* **3** submit (a motion) for discussion by a meeting. **4** *US* suspend discussion of (a proposal). **tablecloth** *noun* cloth for covering the top of a table, esp. during meals. **tableland** *noun* high plateau.

tablespoon *noun* large spoon for serving food.

table tennis game like tennis played on a table with small bats and a light ball.

tableau ⊙ [tab-loh] *noun, pl* **-leaux** silent motionless group arranged to represent some scene.

table d'hôte [tah-bla dote] *noun, pl* **tables d'hôte,** *adjective* (meal) having a set number of dishes at a fixed price.

tablet *noun* **1** pill of compressed medicinal substance. **2** flattish cake of soap etc. **3** inscribed slab of stone etc.

tabloid *noun* small-sized newspaper with many photographs and a concise, usu. sensational style.

taboo ⊙ *noun, pl* **-boos 1** prohibition resulting from religious or social conventions. ◆ *adjective* **2** forbidden by a taboo.

tabor *noun* small drum, used esp. in the Middle Ages.

tabular *adjective* arranged in a table. **tabulate** *verb* arrange (information) in a table.

tabulation *noun*

tachograph *noun* device for recording the speed and distance travelled by a motor vehicle.

tachometer *noun* device for measuring speed, esp. that of a revolving shaft.

tacit ⊙ [tass-it] *adjective* implied but not spoken. **tacitly** *adverb*

taciturn ⊙ [tass-it-turn] *adjective* habitually uncommunicative. **taciturnity** *noun*

tack¹ ⊙ *noun* **1** short nail with a large head. **2** long loose stitch. ◆ *verb* **3** fasten with tacks. **4** stitch with tacks. **tack on** *verb* append.

tack² ⊙ *noun* **1** course of a ship sailing obliquely into the wind. **2** course of action. ◆ *verb* **3** sail into the wind on a zigzag course.

tack³ *noun* riding harness for horses.

tackies, takkies *plural noun, sing* **tacky** *S Afr informal* tennis shoes or plimsolls.

tackle ⊙ *verb* **1** deal with (a task). **2** confront

T

THESAURUS

table *noun* **1** = **counter**, bench, board, stand **2** = **list**, catalogue, chart, diagram, record, register, roll, schedule, tabulation ◆*verb* **3** = **submit**, enter, move, propose, put forward, suggest

tableau *noun* = **picture**, representation, scene, spectacle

taboo *noun* **1** = **prohibition**, anathema, ban, interdict, proscription, restriction ◆*adjective* **2** = **forbidden**, anathema, banned, outlawed, prohibited, proscribed, unacceptable, unmentionable OPPOSITE⟩ **allowed**

tacit *adjective* = **implied**, implicit, inferred, undeclared, understood, unexpressed, unspoken, unstated OPPOSITE⟩ **stated**

taciturn *adjective* = **uncommunicative**, quiet, reserved, reticent, silent, tight-lipped, unforthcoming, withdrawn OPPOSITE⟩ **communicative**

tack¹ *noun* **1** = **nail**, drawing pin, pin ◆*verb* **3** = **fasten**, affix, attach, fix, nail, pin **4** = **stitch**, baste, sew **tack on** = **append**, add, attach, tag

tack² *noun* **2** = **course**, approach, direction, heading, line, method, path, plan, procedure, (an opponent). **3** *Sport* attempt to get the ball from (an opposing player). ♦ *noun* **4** *Sport* act of tackling an opposing player. **5** equipment for a particular activity. **6** set of ropes and pulleys for lifting heavy weights.

tacky¹ **❶** *adjective* **tackier, tackiest** slightly sticky. **tackiness** *noun*

tacky² **❶** *adjective* **tackier, tackiest 1** *Informal* vulgar and tasteless. **2** shabby. **tackiness** *noun*

taco [tah-koh] *noun, pl* **tacos** *Mexican cookery* tortilla fried until crisp, served with a filling.

tact ❶ *noun* skill in avoiding giving offence. **tactful** *adjective* **tactfully** *adverb* **tactless** *adjective* **tactlessly** *adverb* **tactlessness** *noun*

tactics ❶ *noun* art of directing military forces in battle. **tactic** *noun* method or plan to achieve an end. **tactical** *adjective* **tactically** *adverb* **tactician** *noun*

tactile *adjective* of or having the sense of touch.

tadpole *noun* limbless tailed larva of a frog or toad.

taffeta *noun* shiny silk or rayon fabric.

tag¹ **❶** *noun* **1** label bearing information. **2** pointed end of a cord or lace. **3** trite quotation. ♦ *verb* **tagging, tagged 4** attach a tag to. **tag along** *verb* accompany someone, esp. if uninvited.

tag² *noun* **1** children's game where the person being chased becomes the chaser upon being touched. ♦ *verb* **tagging, tagged 2** touch and catch in this game.

tagliatelle *noun* pasta in long narrow strips.

tail ❶ *noun* **1** rear part of an animal's body, usu. forming a flexible appendage. **2** rear or last part or parts of something. **3** *Informal* person employed to follow and spy on another. ♦ *plural* **4** *Informal* tail coat. ♦ *adjective* **5** at the rear. ♦ *verb* **6** *Informal* follow (someone) secretly. **turn tail** run away. **tailless** *adjective* **tails** *adverb* with the side of a coin uppermost that does not have a portrait of a head on it. **tailback** *noun* queue of traffic stretching back from an obstruction. **tailboard** *noun* removable or hinged rear board on a lorry etc. **tail coat** man's coat with a long back split into two below the waist. **tail off, away** *verb* diminish gradually. **tailplane** *noun* small stabilizing wing at the rear of an aircraft. **tailspin** *noun* uncontrolled spinning dive of an aircraft. **tailwind** *noun* wind coming from the rear.

tailor ❶ *noun* **1** person who makes men's clothes. ♦ *verb* **2** cut or style (a garment) to specific requirements. **3** adapt to suit a purpose. **tailored** *adjective* made to fit close to a particular person's body. **tailor-made** *adjective* **1** made by a tailor. **2** perfect for a purpose.

taint ❶ *verb* **1** spoil with a small amount of decay, contamination, or other bad quality. ♦ *noun* **2** something that taints.

take ❶ *verb* **taking, took, taken 1** remove

——————— THESAURUS ———————

way

tackle *verb* **1** = **deal with**, attempt, come *or* get to grips with, embark upon, get stuck into (*inf*), have a go *or* stab at (*inf*), set about, undertake **2** = **confront**, challenge, grab, grasp, halt, intercept, seize, stop ♦*noun* **4** *Sport* = **challenge**, block **5** = **equipment**, accoutrements, apparatus, gear, paraphernalia, tools, trappings

tacky¹ *adjective* = **sticky**, adhesive, gluey, gummy, wet

tacky² *adjective* **1** *Inf* = **vulgar**, cheap, naff (*Brit sl*), sleazy, tasteless **2** = **shabby**, seedy, shoddy, tatty

tact *noun* = **diplomacy**, consideration, delicacy, discretion, sensitivity, thoughtfulness, understanding OPPOSITE **tactlessness**

tactful *adjective* = **diplomatic**, considerate, delicate, discreet, polite, politic, sensitive, thoughtful, understanding

tactic *noun* = **policy**, approach, manoeuvre, method, move, ploy, scheme, stratagem ♦*plural noun* = **strategy**, campaigning, manoeuvres, plans

tactical *adjective* = **strategic**, cunning, diplomatic, shrewd, smart

tactician *noun* = **strategist**, general, mastermind, planner, schemer

tactless *adjective* = **insensitive**, impolite, impolitic, inconsiderate, indelicate, indiscreet, thoughtless, undiplomatic, unsubtle

tag¹ *noun* **1** = **label**, flap, identification, mark, marker, note, slip, tab, ticket ♦*verb* **4** = **label**, mark **tag along** = **accompany**, attend, follow, shadow, tail (*inf*), trail

tail *noun* **1, 2** = **extremity**, appendage, end, rear end, tailpiece ♦*verb* **6** *Inf* = **follow**, shadow, stalk, track, trail **turn tail** = **run away**, cut and run, flee, retreat, run off, take to one's heels

tailor *noun* **1** = **outfitter**, clothier, costumier, couturier, dressmaker, seamstress ♦*verb* **2** = **style**, alter **3** = **adapt**, adjust, customize, fashion, modify, mould, shape

taint *verb* **1** = **spoil**, blemish, contaminate, corrupt, damage, defile, pollute, ruin, stain, sully, tarnish OPPOSITE **clean** ♦*noun* **2** = **stain**, black mark, blemish, blot, defect, demerit, fault, flaw, spot

T

from a place. **2** carry or accompany. **3** use. **4** get possession of, esp. dishonestly. **5** capture. **6** select. **7** require (time, resources, or ability). **8** assume. **9** accept. **10** perform, do, or make. **11** write down. **12** subtract or deduct. ◆ *noun* **13** one of a series of recordings from which the best will be used. **take place** happen. **taking** *adjective* charming. **takings** *plural noun* money received by a shop. **take after** *verb* look or behave like (a parent etc.). **take against** *verb* start to dislike. **take away** *verb* remove or subtract. **takeaway** *adjective* **1** (of food) sold for consumption away from the premises. ◆ *noun* **2** shop or restaurant selling meals for eating elsewhere. **3** meal bought at a takeaway. **take in** *verb* **1** understand. **2** deceive or swindle. **3** make (clothing) smaller. **take off** *verb* **1** (of an aircraft) leave the ground. **2** *Informal* depart. **3** *Informal* become successful. **4** *Informal* parody. **takeoff** *noun* **takeover** *noun* act of taking control of a company by buying a large number of its shares. **take up** *verb* **1** occupy or fill (space or time). **2** adopt the study or activity of. **3** shorten (a garment). **4** accept (an offer).

talc *noun* **1** talcum powder. **2** soft mineral of

magnesium silicate. **talcum powder** powder, usu. scented, used to dry or perfume the body.
tale ❶ *noun* **1** story. **2** malicious piece of gossip.
talent ❶ *noun* **1** natural ability. **2** *Informal* attractive members of the opposite sex. **3** ancient unit of weight or money. **talented** *adjective*
talisman ❶ *noun, pl* **-mans** object believed to have magic power. **talismanic** *adjective*
talk ❶ *verb* **1** express ideas or feelings by means of speech. **2** utter. **3** discuss, e.g. *let's talk business.* **4** reveal information. **5** (be able to) speak in a specified language. ◆ *noun* **6** speech or lecture. **7** conversation. **talker** *noun*
talkative *adjective* fond of talking. **talk back** *verb* answer impudently. **talkback** *noun NZ* broadcast in which telephone comments or questions from the public are transmitted live.
talking-to *noun Informal* telling-off. **talk into** *verb* persuade (someone) to do something by talking. **talk out of** *verb* dissuade (someone) from doing something by talking.
tall ❶ *adjective* **1** higher than average. **2** of a specified height. **tall order** difficult task. **tall story** unlikely and probably untrue tale.

————————— THESAURUS —————————

take *verb* **2** = **carry**, accompany, bear, bring, conduct, convey, convoy, escort, ferry, fetch, guide, haul, lead, transport, usher OPPOSITE **send**. **4** = **obtain**, acquire, appropriate, catch, get, grasp, grip, misappropriate, pinch (*inf*), pocket, purloin, secure, seize, steal OPPOSITE **give**. **5** = **capture**, seize OPPOSITE **free**. **7** = **require**, call for, demand, necessitate, need **8** = **assume**, believe, consider, perceive, presume, regard, understand **9** = **accept**, accommodate, contain, have room for, hold **12** = **subtract**, deduct, eliminate, remove
take in *verb* **1** = **understand**, absorb, assimilate, comprehend, digest, get the hang of (*inf*), grasp **2** = **deceive**, cheat, con (*inf*), dupe, fool, hoodwink, mislead, swindle, trick
takeoff *noun* **1** = **departure**, launch, liftoff **4** *Inf* = **parody**, caricature, imitation, lampoon, satire, send-up (*Brit inf*), spoof (*inf*)
take off *verb* **1** = **lift off**, take to the air **2** *Inf* = **depart**, abscond, decamp, disappear, go, leave, slope off **4** *Inf* = **parody**, caricature, imitate, lampoon, mimic, mock, satirize, send up (*Brit inf*)
takeover *noun* = **merger**, coup, incorporation
take up *verb* **1** = **occupy**, absorb, consume, cover, extend over, fill, use up **2** = **start**, adopt, become involved in, engage in
taking *adjective* = **charming**, attractive,

beguiling, captivating, enchanting, engaging, fetching (*inf*), lekker (*S Afr sl*), likable *or* likeable, prepossessing
takings *plural noun* = **revenue**, earnings, income, proceeds, profits, receipts, returns, take
tale *noun* **1** = **story**, account, anecdote, fable, legend, narrative, saga, yarn (*inf*)
talent *noun* **1** = **ability**, aptitude, capacity, flair, genius, gift, knack
talented *adjective* **1** = **gifted**, able, brilliant
talisman *noun* = **charm**, amulet, fetish, lucky charm, mascot
talk *verb* **1, 2** = **speak**, chat, chatter, communicate, converse, gossip, natter, utter **3** = **discuss**, confabulate, confer, negotiate, parley **4** = **inform**, blab, give the game away, grass (*Brit sl*), let the cat out of the bag, tell all ◆*noun* **6** = **speech**, address, discourse, disquisition, lecture, oration, sermon
talkative *adjective* = **loquacious**, chatty, effusive, garrulous, gossipy, long-winded, mouthy, verbose, voluble, wordy
talker *noun* = **speaker**, chatterbox, conversationalist, lecturer, orator
talking-to *noun Inf* = **reprimand**, criticism, dressing-down (*inf*), lecture, rebuke, reproach, reproof, scolding, telling-off (*inf*), ticking-off (*inf*)
tall *adjective* **1** = **high**, big, elevated, giant,

tallboy *noun* high chest of drawers.

tallow *noun* hard animal fat used to make candles.

tally ⊕ *verb* **-lying, -lied 1** (of two things) correspond. ◆ *noun, pl* **-lies 2** record of a debt or score.

tally-ho *interjection* huntsman's cry when the quarry is sighted.

Talmud *noun* body of Jewish law. **Talmudic** *adjective*

talon *noun* bird's hooked claw.

tamarind *noun* **1** tropical tree. **2** its acid fruit.

tamarisk *noun* evergreen shrub with slender branches and feathery flower clusters.

tambourine *noun* percussion instrument like a small drum with jingling metal discs attached.

tame ⊕ *adjective* **1** (of animals) brought under human control. **2** (of animals) not afraid of people. **3** meek or submissive. **4** uninteresting. ◆ *verb* **5** make tame. **tamely** *adverb* **tamer** *noun*

Tamil *noun* **1** member of a people of Sri Lanka and S India. **2** their language.

tam-o'-shanter *noun* brimless wool cap with a bobble in the centre.

tamp *verb* pack down by repeated taps.

tamper ⊕ *verb* (foll. by *with*) interfere.

tampon *noun* absorbent plug of cotton wool inserted into the vagina during menstruation.

tan *noun* **1** brown coloration of the skin from exposure to sunlight. ◆ *verb* **tanning, tanned 2** (of skin) go brown from exposure to sunlight. **3** convert (a hide) into leather. ◆ *adjective* **4** yellowish-brown. **tannery** *noun, pl* **-eries** place where hides are tanned.

tandem *noun* bicycle for two riders, one behind the other. **in tandem** together.

tandoori *adjective* (of food) cooked in an Indian clay oven.

tang ⊕ *noun* **1** strong taste or smell. **2** trace or hint. **tangy** *adjective* **tangier, tangiest**

tangent *noun* **1** line that touches a curve without intersecting it. **2** (in trigonometry) ratio of the length of the opposite side to that of the adjacent side of a right-angled triangle. **go off at a tangent** suddenly take a completely different line of thought or action. **tangential** *adjective* **1** of superficial relevance only. **2** of a tangent. **tangentially** *adverb*

tangerine *noun* small orange-like fruit of an Asian citrus tree.

tangible ⊕ *adjective* **1** able to be touched. **2** clear and definite. **tangibly** *adverb* **tangibility** *noun*

tangle ⊕ *noun* **1** confused mass or situation. ◆ *verb* **2** twist together in a tangle. **3** (often foll. by *with*) come into conflict.

tango *noun, pl* **-gos 1** S American dance. ◆ *verb* **2** dance a tango.

tank *noun* **1** container for liquids or gases. **2** armoured fighting vehicle moving on tracks.

tanker *noun* ship or lorry for carrying liquid in bulk.

tankard *noun* large beer-mug, often with a hinged lid.

tannin, tannic acid *noun* vegetable substance used in tanning.

Tannoy *noun* ® type of public-address system.

tansy *noun, pl* **-sies** yellow-flowered plant.

tantalize ⊕ *verb* torment by showing but withholding something desired. **tantalizing**

---

lanky, lofty, soaring, towering OPPOSITE **small** ◆ **tall order** =**difficult**, demanding, hard, unreasonable, well-nigh impossible **tall story** =**implausible**, absurd, cock-and-bull (*inf*), exaggerated, far-fetched, incredible, preposterous, unbelievable OPPOSITE **true**

tally *verb* **1** =**agree**, accord, coincide, concur, conform, correspond, fit, harmonize, match, square OPPOSITE **conflict** ◆*noun* **2** =**record**, count, mark, reckoning, running total, score, total

tame *adjective* **1** =**broken**, amenable, disciplined, docile, gentle, obedient, tractable OPPOSITE **wild**. **2** =**domesticated 3** =**submissive**, compliant, docile, manageable, meek, obedient, subdued, unresisting OPPOSITE **aggressive**. **4** =**unexciting**, bland, boring, dull, humdrum, insipid, uninspiring, uninteresting, vapid OPPOSITE **interesting** ◆*verb* **5** a

=**domesticate**, house-train, train **b** =**subdue**, break in, master OPPOSITE **arouse**

tamper *verb* (foll. by *with*) =**interfere with**, alter, fiddle with (*inf*), fool about with (*inf*), meddle with, mess about with, tinker with

tangible *adjective* **1** =**palpable**, actual, concrete, material, real OPPOSITE **intangible**. **2** =**definite**, perceptible, positive OPPOSITE **intangible**

tangle *noun* **1 a** =**knot**, coil, entanglement, jungle, twist, web **b** =**confusion**, complication, entanglement, fix (*inf*), imbroglio, jam, mess, mix-up ◆*verb* **2** =**twist**, coil, entangle, interweave, knot, mat, mesh, ravel OPPOSITE **unravel**. **3** (often foll. by *with*) =**come into conflict with**, come up against, contend with, contest, cross swords with, dispute with, lock horns with

tangy *adjective* **1** =**sharp**, piquant, pungent,

T

adjective **tantalizingly** *adverb*

tantalum *noun Chem* hard greyish-white metallic element.

tantamount ⊕ *adjective* **tantamount to** equivalent in effect to.

tantrum ⊕ *noun* childish outburst of temper.

Taoism [**tow**-iz-zum] *noun* system of religion and philosophy advocating a simple, honest life and noninterference with the course of natural events. **Taoist** *noun, adjective*

tap¹ ⊕ *verb* **tapping, tapped 1** knock lightly and usu. repeatedly. ♦ *noun* **2** light knock. **tap dancing** style of dancing in which the feet beat out an elaborate rhythm.

tap² ⊕ *noun* **1** valve to control the flow of liquid from a pipe or cask. ♦ *verb* **tapping, tapped 2** listen in on (a telephone call) secretly by making an illegal connection. **3** obtain something useful or desirable from (something). **4** draw off with or as if with a tap. **on tap 1** *Informal* readily available. **2** (of beer etc.) drawn from a cask.

tape ⊕ *noun* **1** narrow long strip of material. **2** (recording made on) a cassette containing magnetic tape. **3** string stretched across a race track to mark the finish. ♦ *verb* **4** record on magnetic tape. **5** bind or fasten with tape. **have a person, situation taped** *Informal* have full understanding and control of a person *or* situation. **tape measure** tape marked off in centimetres or inches for measuring. **tape recorder** device for recording and reproducing sound on magnetic tape. **tapeworm** *noun* long flat parasitic worm living in the intestines of vertebrates.

taper ⊕ *verb* **1** become narrower towards one end. ♦ *noun* **2** long thin candle. **3** narrowing. **taper off** become gradually less.

tapestry *noun, pl* **-tries** fabric decorated with coloured woven designs.

tapioca *noun* beadlike starch made from cassava root, used in puddings.

tapir [**tape**-er] *noun* piglike mammal of tropical America and SE Asia, with a long snout.

tappet *noun* short steel rod in an engine, transferring motion from one part to another.

taproot *noun* main root of a plant, growing straight down.

tar *noun* **1** thick black liquid distilled from coal etc. ♦ *verb* **tarring, tarred 2** coat with tar.

taramasalata *noun* creamy pink pâté made from fish roe.

tarantella *noun* **1** lively Italian dance. **2** music for this.

tarantula *noun* large hairy spider with a poisonous bite.

tardy *adjective* **tardier, tardiest** slow or late. **tardily** *adverb* **tardiness** *noun*

tare¹ *noun* **1** weight of the wrapping or container of goods. **2** unladen weight of a vehicle.

tare² *noun* **1** type of vetch plant. **2** *Bible* weed.

target ⊕ *noun* **1** object or person a missile is aimed at. **2** goal or objective. **3** object of criticism. ♦ *verb* **-geting, -geted 4** aim or direct.

SPELLING TIP

Lots of people put an extra *t* into *targetting* and *targetted*, but they are wrong: the words are **targeting** and **targeted**.

---

tariff ⊕ *noun* **1** tax levied on imports. **2** list of fixed prices.

Tarmac *noun* **1** ® mixture of tar, bitumen, and crushed stones used for roads etc. **2** (**t-**) airport runway.

tarn *noun* small mountain lake.

tarnish ⊕ *verb* **1** make or become stained or less bright. **2** damage or taint. ♦ *noun* **3** discoloration or blemish.

tarot [**tarr**-oh] *noun* special pack of cards used

T

——————— THESAURUS ———————

spicy, tart

tantalize *verb* =**torment**, frustrate, lead on, taunt, tease, torture

tantamount *adjective* **tantamount to** =**equivalent to**, commensurate with, equal to, synonymous with

tantrum *noun* =**outburst**, fit, flare-up, hysterics, temper

tap¹ *verb* **1** =**knock**, beat, drum, pat, rap, strike, touch ♦*noun* **2** =**knock**, pat, rap, touch

tap² *noun* **1** =**valve**, stopcock, faucet (*US & Canad*) ♦*verb* **2** =**listen in on**, bug (*inf*), eavesdrop on **4** =**draw off**, bleed, drain,

siphon off **on tap 1** *Inf* =**available**, at hand, in reserve, on hand, ready **2** =**on draught**

tape *noun* **1** =**strip**, band, ribbon ♦*verb* **4** =**record**, tape-record, video **5** =**bind**, seal, secure, stick, wrap

taper *verb* **1** =**narrow**, come to a point, thin
OPPOSITE▷ **widen** ♦ **taper off** =**decrease**, die away, dwindle, fade, lessen, reduce, subside, wane, wind down

target *noun* **2** =**goal**, aim, ambition, end, intention, mark, object, objective **3** =**victim**, butt, scapegoat

tariff *noun* **1** =**tax**, duty, excise, levy, toll **2**

mainly in fortune-telling. **tarot card** card in a tarot pack.

tarpaulin *noun* (sheet of) heavy waterproof fabric.

tarragon *noun* aromatic herb.

tarry *verb* **-rying, -ried** *Old-fashioned* **1** linger or delay. **2** stay briefly.

tarsus *noun, pl* **-si** bones of the heel and ankle collectively.

tart[1] **⊕** *noun* pie or flan with a sweet filling.

tart[2] **⊕** *adjective* sharp or bitter. **tartly** *adverb* **tartness** *noun*

tart[3] **⊕** *noun Informal* sexually provocative or promiscuous woman. **tart up** *verb Informal* dress or decorate in a smart or flashy way.

tartan *noun* **1** design of straight lines crossing at right angles, esp. one associated with a Scottish clan. **2** cloth with such a pattern.

tartar[1] *noun* **1** hard deposit on the teeth. **2** deposit formed during the fermentation of wine.

tartar[2] *noun* fearsome or formidable person.

Tartar, Tatar *noun* **1** member of a Mongoloid people who established a powerful state in central Asia in the 13th century. **2** descendant of this people. ♦ *adjective* **3** of the Tartars.

tartare sauce *noun* mayonnaise sauce mixed with chopped herbs and capers, served with seafood.

tartrazine [tar-traz-zeen] *noun* artificial yellow dye used in food etc.

TAS Tasmania.

task **⊕** *noun* (difficult or unpleasant) piece of work to be done. **take to task** criticize or scold. **task force** (military) group formed to carry out a specific task. **taskmaster** *noun* person who enforces hard work.

Tasmanian devil *noun* small carnivorous marsupial found in Tasmania.

Tasmanian tiger same as THYLACINE.

tassel *noun* decorative fringed knot of threads.

taste **⊕** *noun* **1** sense by which the flavour of a substance is distinguished in the mouth. **2** distinctive flavour. **3** small amount tasted. **4** brief experience of something. **5** liking. **6** ability to appreciate what is beautiful or excellent. ♦ *verb* **7** distinguish the taste of (a substance). **8** take a small amount of (something) into the mouth. **9** have a specific taste. **10** experience briefly. **tasteful** *adjective* having or showing good taste. **tastefully** *adverb* **tasteless** *adjective* **1** bland or insipid. **2** showing bad taste. **tastelessly** *adverb* **tasty** *adjective* pleasantly flavoured. **taste bud** small organ on the tongue which perceives flavours.

tat *noun* tatty or tasteless article(s).

Tatar *noun, adjective* same as TARTAR.

tattered *adjective* ragged or torn. **in tatters** in ragged pieces.

tattle *verb, noun* gossip or chatter.

tattletale **⊕** *Chiefly US & Canad noun* a scandalmonger or gossip.

tattoo[1] *noun* **1** pattern made on the body by

—————— T H E S A U R U S ——————

= **price list**, menu, schedule

tarnish *verb* **1** = **stain**, blemish, blot, darken, discolour OPPOSITE **brighten**. **2** = **damage**, blacken, smirch, sully, taint OPPOSITE **enhance** ♦*noun* **3** = **stain**, blemish, blot, discoloration, spot, taint

tart[1] *noun* = **pie**, pastry, tartlet

tart[2] *adjective* = **sharp**, acid, bitter, piquant, pungent, sour, tangy, vinegary OPPOSITE **sweet**

tart[3] *noun Inf* = **slut**, call girl, floozy (*sl*), prostitute, trollop, whore

task *noun* = **job**, assignment, chore, duty, enterprise, exercise, mission, undertaking **take to task** = **criticize**, blame, censure, rebuke, reprimand, reproach, reprove, rouse on (*Aust*), scold, tell off (*inf*), upbraid

taste *noun* **2** = **flavour**, relish, savour, smack, tang OPPOSITE **blandness**. **3** = **bit**, bite, dash, morsel, mouthful, sample, soupçon, spoonful, titbit **5** = **liking**, appetite, fancy, fondness, inclination, partiality, penchant, predilection, preference OPPOSITE **dislike**. **6** = **refinement**,

appreciation, discernment, discrimination, elegance, judgment, sophistication, style OPPOSITE **tackiness** ♦*verb* **7** = **distinguish**, differentiate, discern, perceive OPPOSITE **fail to discern**. **8** = **sample**, savour, sip, test, try **9** = **have a flavour of**, savour of, smack of **10** = **experience**, encounter, know, meet with, partake of, undergo OPPOSITE **miss**

tasteful *adjective* = **refined**, artistic, cultivated, cultured, discriminating, elegant, exquisite, in good taste, polished, stylish

tasteless *adjective* **1** = **insipid**, bland, boring, dull, flat, flavourless, mild, thin, weak OPPOSITE **delicious**. **2** = **vulgar**, crass, crude, gaudy, gross, inelegant, naff (*Brit sl*), tacky (*inf*), tawdry OPPOSITE **elegant**

tasty *adjective* = **delicious**, appetizing, delectable, full-flavoured, lekker (*S Afr sl*), luscious, palatable, savoury, scrumptious (*inf*), toothsome

tattletale *noun chiefly US & Canad* = **gossip**, busybody, babbler, bigmouth (*slang*), scandalmonger, gossipmonger

T

pricking the skin and staining it with indelible inks. ◆ *verb* **-tooing, -tooed 2** make such a pattern on the skin. **tattooist** *noun*

tattoo² *noun* **1** military display or pageant. **2** drumming or tapping.

tatty ⊕ *adjective* **-tier, -tiest** shabby or worn out.

taught *verb* past of TEACH.

taunt ⊕ *verb* **1** tease with jeers. ◆ *noun* **2** jeering remark.

taupe *adjective* brownish-grey.

Taurus *noun* (the bull) second sign of the zodiac.

taut ⊕ *adjective* **1** drawn tight. **2** showing nervous strain. **tauten** *verb* make or become taut.

tautology *noun, pl* **-gies** use of words which merely repeat something already stated. **tautological** *adjective*

tavern ⊕ *noun* Old-fashioned pub.

tawdry ⊕ *adjective* **-drier, -driest** cheap, showy, and of poor quality.

tawny *adjective* **-nier, -niest** yellowish-brown.

tax ⊕ *noun* **1** compulsory payment levied by a government on income, property, etc. to raise revenue. ◆ *verb* **2** levy a tax on. **3** make heavy demands on. **taxable** *adjective* **taxation** *noun* levying of taxes. **taxing** *adjective* demanding, onerous. **tax-free** *adjective* (of goods and services) not taxed. **taxpayer** *noun* **tax relief** reduction in the amount of tax a person or company has to pay. **tax return** statement of personal income for tax purposes.

taxi *noun* **1** (also **taxicab**) car with a driver that may be hired to take people to any specified destination. ◆ *verb* **taxiing, taxied 2** (of an aircraft) run along the ground before taking off or after landing. **taximeter** *noun* meter in a taxi that registers the fare. **taxi rank** place where taxis wait to be hired.

taxidermy *noun* art of stuffing and mounting

animal skins to give them a lifelike appearance. **taxidermist** *noun*

taxonomy *noun* classification of plants and animals into groups. **taxonomic** *adjective* **taxonomist** *noun*

Tb *Chem* terbium.

TB tuberculosis.

T-bone steak *noun* steak cut from the sirloin of beef, containing a T-shaped bone.

tbs., tbsp. tablespoon(ful).

Tc *Chem* technetium.

te *noun Music* (in tonic sol-fa) seventh degree of any major scale.

Te *Chem* tellurium.

tea *noun* **1** drink made from infusing the dried leaves of an Asian bush in boiling water. **2** leaves used to make this drink. **3** main evening meal. **4** light afternoon meal of tea, cakes, etc. **5** drink like tea, made from other plants. **tea bag** small porous bag of tea leaves. **tea cosy** covering for a teapot to keep the tea warm. **teapot** *noun* container with a lid, spout, and handle for making and serving tea. **teaspoon** *noun* small spoon for stirring tea. **tea towel**, **tea cloth** towel for drying dishes. **tea tree** tree of Australia and New Zealand that yields an oil used as an antiseptic.

teach ⊕ *verb* **teaching, taught 1** tell or show (someone) how to do something. **2** give lessons in (a subject). **3** cause to learn or understand. **teacher** *noun* **teaching** *noun*

teak *noun* very hard wood of an E Indian tree.

teal *noun* kind of small duck.

team ⊕ *noun* **1** group of people forming one side in a game. **2** group of people or animals working together. **teamster** *noun US* lorry driver. **team spirit** willingness to cooperate as part of a team. **team up** *verb* make or join a team. **teamwork** *noun* cooperative work by a team.

tear¹, teardrop ⊕ *noun* drop of fluid

———————— THESAURUS ————————

tatty *adjective* = **shabby**, bedraggled, dilapidated, down at heel, neglected, ragged, run-down, scruffy, threadbare, worn

taunt *verb* **1** = **jeer**, deride, insult, mock, provoke, ridicule, tease, torment ◆*noun* **2** = **jeer**, derision, dig, gibe, insult, provocation, ridicule, sarcasm, teasing

taut *adjective* **1** = **tight**, flexed, rigid, strained, stressed, stretched, tense OPPOSITE relaxed

tavern *noun Old-fashioned* = **inn**, alehouse (*arch*), bar, hostelry, pub (*inf, chiefly Brit*), public house, beer parlour (*Canad*), beverage room (*Canad*)

tawdry *adjective* = **vulgar**, cheap, gaudy,

gimcrack, naff (*Brit sl*), tacky (*inf*), tasteless, tatty OPPOSITE stylish

tax *noun* **1** = **charge**, duty, excise, levy, tariff, tithe, toll ◆*verb* **2** = **charge**, assess, rate **3** = **strain**, burden, exhaust, load, stretch, test, try, weaken, weary

taxing *adjective* = **demanding**, exacting, onerous, punishing, sapping, stressful, tiring, tough, trying

teach *verb* = **instruct**, coach, drill, educate, enlighten, guide, inform, show, train, tutor

teacher *noun* = **instructor**, coach, educator, guide, lecturer, master *or* mistress, mentor, schoolteacher, trainer, tutor appearing in and falling from the eye. **in tears** weeping. **tearful** *adjective* weeping or about to weep. **tear gas** gas that stings the eyes and causes temporary blindness. **tear-jerker** *noun Informal* excessively sentimental film or book.

tear² ❶ *verb* **tearing, tore, torn 1** rip a hole in. **2** rip apart. **3** rush. **4** remove by force. ◆ *noun* **5** hole or split. **tearaway** *noun* wild or unruly person.

tease ❶ *verb* **1** make fun of (someone) in a provoking or playful way. ◆ *noun* **2** person who teases. **teaser** *noun* annoying or difficult problem. **teasing** *adjective, noun* **tease out** *verb* remove tangles from (hair etc.) by combing.

teasel, teazel, teazle *noun* plant with prickly leaves and flowers.

teat *noun* **1** nipple of a breast or udder. **2** rubber nipple of a feeding bottle.

tech *noun Informal* technical college.

techie *Informal noun* **1** person who is skilled in the use of technology. ◆ *adjective* **2** relating to or skilled in the use of technology.

technetium [tek-**neesh**-ee-um] *noun Chem* artificially produced silvery-grey metallic element.

technical ❶ *adjective* **1** of or specializing in industrial, practical, or mechanical arts and applied sciences. **2** skilled in technical subjects. **3** relating to a particular field. **4** according to the letter of the law. **5** showing technique, e.g. *technical brilliance.* **technically** *adverb* **technicality** *noun, pl* **-ties** petty point based on a strict application of rules. **technician** *noun* person skilled in a particular technical field. **technical college** higher educational institution with courses in art and technical

subjects. **technique** *noun* **1** method or skill used for a particular task. **2** technical proficiency.

Technicolor *noun* ⓡ system of colour photography used for the cinema.

technique ❶ *noun* **1** method or skill used for a particular task. **2** technical proficiency.

techno *noun* type of electronic dance music with a very fast beat.

technocracy *noun, pl* **-cies** government by technical experts. **technocrat** *noun*

technology *noun* **1** application of practical or mechanical sciences to industry or commerce. **2** scientific methods used in a particular field. **technological** *adjective* **technologist** *noun*

tectonics *noun* study of the earth's crust and the forces affecting it.

teddy *noun, pl* **-dies 1** teddy bear. **2** combined camisole and knickers. **teddy bear** soft toy bear.

teddy boy *noun* youth who wore mock Edwardian fashions in Britain esp. in the mid-1950s.

Te Deum [tee **dee**-um] *noun* ancient Latin hymn of praise.

tedious ❶ *adjective* causing fatigue or boredom. **tediously** *adverb* **tedium** *noun* monotony.

tee *noun* **1** small peg from which a golf ball can be played at the start of each hole. **2** area of a golf course from which the first stroke of a hole is made. **tee off** *verb* make the first stroke of a hole in golf.

teem¹ *verb* be full of.

teem² *verb* rain heavily.

teenage ❶ *adjective* of the period of life between the ages of 13 and 19. **teenager**

team *noun* **1** = **side**, line-up, squad **2** = **group**, band, body, bunch, company, gang, set **team up** = **join**, band together, cooperate, couple, get together, link, unite, work together

teamwork *noun* = **cooperation**, collaboration, coordination, esprit de corps, fellowship, harmony, unity

tear¹ *noun* **in tears** = **weeping**, blubbering, crying, distressed, sobbing

tear² *verb* **1** = **rip**, rend, rupture, scratch, shred, split **2** = **pull apart**, claw, lacerate, mangle, mutilate **3** = **rush**, bolt, charge, dash, fly, hurry, race, run, speed, sprint, zoom ◆*noun* **5** = **hole**, laceration, rent, rip, rupture, scratch, split

tearaway *noun* = **hooligan**, delinquent, good-for-nothing, rowdy, ruffian

tearful *adjective* = **weeping**, blubbering,

crying, in tears, lachrymose, sobbing, weepy (*inf*), whimpering

tease *verb* **1** = **mock**, goad, provoke, pull someone's leg (*inf*), taunt, torment

technical *adjective* **1, 2** = **scientific**, hi-tech *or* high-tech, skilled, specialist, specialized, technological

technique *noun* **1** = **method**, approach, manner, means, mode, procedure, style, system, way **2** = **skill**, artistry, craft, craftsmanship, execution, performance, proficiency, touch

tedious *adjective* = **boring**, drab, dreary, dull, humdrum, irksome, laborious, mind-numbing, monotonous, tiresome, wearisome OPPOSITE▷ exciting

tedium *noun* = **boredom**, drabness, dreariness, dullness, monotony, routine, sameness,

T

noun person aged between 13 and 19.

teens *plural noun* period of being a teenager.

teeny *adjective* **-nier, -niest** *Informal* extremely small.

teepee *noun* same as TEPEE.

tee-shirt *noun* same as T-SHIRT.

teeter ❶ *verb* wobble or move unsteadily.

teeth *noun* plural of TOOTH.

teethe *verb* (of a baby) grow his or her first teeth. **teething troubles** problems during the early stages of something.

teetotal ❶ *adjective* drinking no alcohol. **teetotaller** *noun*

TEFL Teaching of English as a Foreign Language.

Teflon *noun* ® substance used for nonstick coatings on saucepans etc.

telecommunications *noun* communications using telephone, radio, television, etc.

telegram *noun* formerly, a message sent by telegraph.

telegraph *noun* 1 formerly, a system for sending messages over a distance along a cable. ♦ *verb* 2 communicate by telegraph. **telegraphic** *adjective* **telegraphist** *noun*

telegraphy *noun* science or use of a telegraph.

telekinesis *noun* movement of objects by thought or willpower.

Telemessage *noun* ® message sent by telephone or telex and delivered in printed form.

telemetry *noun* use of electronic devices to record or measure a distant event and transmit the data to a receiver.

teleology *noun* belief that all things have a predetermined purpose. **teleological** *adjective*

telepathy ❶ *noun* direct communication between minds. **telepathic** *adjective* **telepathically** *adverb*

telephone ❶ *noun* 1 device for transmitting sound over a distance along wires. ♦ *verb* 2 call or talk to (a person) by telephone. **telephony**

noun **telephonic** *adjective* **telephonist** *noun* person operating a telephone switchboard.

telephoto lens *noun* camera lens producing a magnified image of a distant object.

teleprinter *noun* apparatus like a typewriter for sending and receiving typed messages by wire.

Teleprompter *noun* ® device under a television camera enabling a speaker to read the script while appearing to look at the camera.

telesales *noun* selling of a product or service by telephone.

telescope ❶ *noun* 1 optical instrument for magnifying distant objects. ♦ *verb* 2 shorten. **telescopic** *adjective*

Teletext *noun* ® system which shows information and news on television screens.

television ❶ *noun* 1 system of producing a moving image and accompanying sound on a distant screen. 2 device for receiving broadcast signals and converting them into sound and pictures. 3 content of television programmes. **televise** *verb* broadcast on television. **televisual** *adjective*

teleworking *noun* use of home computers, telephones, etc., to enable a person to work from home while maintaining contact with colleagues or customers. **teleworker** *noun*

telex *noun* 1 international communication service using teleprinters. 2 machine used in such a service. 3 message sent by telex. ♦ *verb* 4 transmit by telex.

tell ❶ *verb* **telling, told** 1 make known in words. 2 order or instruct. 3 give an account of. 4 discern or distinguish. 5 have an effect. 6 *Informal* reveal secrets. **teller** *noun* 1 narrator. 2 bank cashier. 3 person who counts votes. **telling** *adjective* having a marked effect. **tell off** *verb* reprimand. **telling-off** *noun* **telltale** *noun* 1 person who reveals secrets. ♦ *adjective* 2 revealing.

———————— T H E S A U R U S ————————

tediousness

teenager *noun* =youth, adolescent, boy, girl, juvenile, minor

teeter *verb* =wobble, rock, seesaw, stagger, sway, totter, waver

teetotaller *noun* =abstainer, nondrinker

telepathy *noun* =mind-reading, sixth sense

telephone *noun* 1 =phone, dog and bone (*sl*), handset, line, mobile (phone) ♦*verb* 2 =call, dial, phone, ring (*chiefly Brit*)

telescope *noun* 1 =glass, spyglass ♦*verb* 2 =shorten, abbreviate, abridge, compress, condense, contract, shrink OPPOSITE extend

television *noun* 2 =TV, small screen (*inf*), telly (*Brit inf*), the box (*Brit inf*), the tube (*sl*)

tell *verb* 1 =inform, announce, communicate, disclose, divulge, express, make known, notify, proclaim, reveal, state 2 =instruct, bid, call upon, command, direct, order, require, summon 3 =describe, chronicle, depict, narrate, portray, recount, relate, report 4 =distinguish, differentiate, discern, discriminate, identify 5 =have or take effect, carry weight, count, make its presence felt, register, take its toll, weigh

telling *adjective* =effective, considerable,

tellurium *noun Chem* brittle silvery-white nonmetallic element.

telly *noun, pl* **-lies** *Informal* television.

temerity ⊕ [tim-**merr**-it-tee] *noun* boldness or audacity.

temp *Informal noun* **1** temporary employee, esp. a secretary. ♦ *verb* **2** work as a temp.

temp. **1** temperature. **2** temporary.

temper ⊕ *noun* **1** outburst of anger. **2** tendency to become angry. **3** calm mental condition, e.g. *I lost my temper.* **4** frame of mind. ♦ *verb* **5** make less extreme. **6** strengthen or toughen (metal).

tempera *noun* painting medium for powdered pigments.

temperament ⊕ *noun* person's character or disposition. **temperamental** *adjective* **1** having changeable moods. **2** *Informal* erratic and unreliable. **temperamentally** *adverb*

temperate ⊕ *adjective* **1** (of climate) not extreme. **2** self-restrained or moderate.

temperance *noun* **1** moderation. **2** abstinence from alcohol.

temperature *noun* **1** degree of heat or cold.

2 *Informal* abnormally high body temperature.

tempest ⊕ *noun* violent storm. **tempestuous** *adjective* **1** violent or stormy. **2** extremely emotional or passionate. **tempestuously** *adverb*

template *noun* pattern used to cut out shapes accurately.

temple[1] **⊕** *noun* building for worship.

temple[2] *noun* region on either side of the forehead. **temporal** *adjective*

tempo *noun, pl* **-pi, -pos** **1** rate or pace. **2** speed of a piece of music.

temporal *adjective* **1** of time. **2** worldly rather than spiritual.

temporary ⊕ *adjective* lasting only for a short time. **temporarily** *adverb*

temporize *verb* **1** gain time by negotiation or evasiveness. **2** adapt to circumstances.

tempt ⊕ *verb* entice (a person) to do something wrong. **tempt fate** take foolish or unnecessary risks. **tempter, temptress** *noun* **temptation** *noun* **1** tempting. **2** tempting thing. **tempting** *adjective* attractive or inviting.

ten *adjective, noun* one more than nine. **tenth**

———————— THESAURUS ————————

decisive, forceful, impressive, influential, marked, powerful, significant, striking

telling-off *noun* =**reprimand**, criticism, dressing-down (*inf*), lecture, rebuke, reproach, reproof, scolding, talking-to, ticking-off (*inf*)

tell off *verb* =**reprimand**, berate, censure, chide, haul over the coals (*inf*), lecture, read the riot act, rebuke, reproach, rouse on (*Aust*), scold

temerity *noun* =**audacity**, boldness, cheek, chutzpah (*US & Canad inf*), effrontery, front, impudence, nerve (*inf*), rashness, recklessness

temper *noun* **1** =**rage**, bad mood, fury, passion, tantrum **2** =**irritability**, hot-headedness, irascibility, passion, petulance, resentment, surliness OPPOSITE> **goodwill**. **3** =**self-control**, calmness, composure, cool (*sl*), equanimity OPPOSITE> **anger**. **4** =**frame of mind**, constitution, disposition, humour, mind, mood, nature, temperament ♦*verb* **5** =**moderate**, assuage, lessen, mitigate, mollify, restrain, soften, soothe, tone down OPPOSITE> **intensify**. **6** =**strengthen**, anneal, harden, toughen OPPOSITE> **soften**

temperament *noun* **a** =**nature**, bent, character, constitution, disposition, humour, make-up, outlook, personality, temper **b** =**excitability**, anger, hot-headedness, moodiness, petulance, volatility

temperamental *adjective* **1** =**moody**, capricious, emotional, excitable, highly strung, hypersensitive, irritable, sensitive, touchy,

volatile OPPOSITE> **calm**. **2** *Inf* =**unreliable**, erratic, inconsistent, inconstant, unpredictable OPPOSITE> **reliable**

temperance *noun* **1** =**moderation**, continence, discretion, forbearance, restraint, self-control, self-discipline, self-restraint OPPOSITE> **excess**. **2** =**teetotalism**, abstemiousness, abstinence, sobriety

temperate *adjective* **1** =**mild**, calm, cool, fair, gentle, moderate, pleasant OPPOSITE> **severe**. **2** =**moderate**, calm, composed, dispassionate, even-tempered, mild, reasonable, self-controlled, self-restrained, sensible OPPOSITE> **wild**

tempest *noun* =**storm**, cyclone, gale, hurricane, squall, tornado, typhoon OPPOSITE> **peace**

tempestuous *adjective* **1** =**stormy**, blustery, gusty, inclement, raging, squally, turbulent, windy **2** =**passionate**, boisterous, emotional, furious, heated, intense, stormy, turbulent, violent, wild OPPOSITE> **serene**

temple[1] *noun* =**shrine**, church, sanctuary

temporarily *adverb* =**briefly**, fleetingly, for the time being, momentarily, pro tem

temporary *adjective* =**impermanent**, brief, ephemeral, fleeting, interim, momentary, provisional, short-lived, transitory OPPOSITE> **permanent**

tempt *verb* **1** =**entice**, coax, invite, lead on, lure, seduce, tantalize OPPOSITE> **discourage**

T

adjective, noun (of) number ten in a series.
tenable ⊕ *adjective* able to be upheld or maintained.
tenacious ⊕ *adjective* **1** holding fast. **2** stubborn. **tenaciously** *adverb* **tenacity** *noun*
tenant ⊕ *noun* person who rents land or a building. **tenancy** *noun*
tench *noun, pl* **tench** freshwater game fish of the carp family.
tend¹ ⊕ *verb* **1** be inclined. **2** go in the direction of. **tendency** *noun* inclination to act in a certain way. **tendentious** *adjective* biased, not impartial.
tend² ⊕ *verb* take care of.
tender¹ ⊕ *adjective* **1** not tough. **2** gentle and affectionate. **3** vulnerable or sensitive. **tenderly** *adverb* **tenderness** *noun* **tenderize** *verb* soften (meat) by pounding or treatment with a special substance. **tenderizer** *noun* **tenderloin** *noun* tender cut of pork from between the sirloin and the ribs.
tender² ⊕ *verb* **1** offer. **2** make a formal offer to supply goods or services at a stated cost. ♦ *noun* **3** such an offer. **legal tender** currency that must, by law, be accepted as payment.
tender³ *noun* **1** small boat that brings supplies to a larger ship in a port. **2** carriage for fuel and water attached to a steam locomotive.
tendon *noun* strong tissue attaching a muscle

to a bone.
tendril *noun* slender stem by which a climbing plant clings.
tenement *noun* building divided into several flats.
tenet [ten-nit] *noun* doctrine or belief.
tenner *noun Informal* ten-pound note.
tennis *noun* game in which players use rackets to hit a ball back and forth over a net.
tenon *noun* projecting end on a piece of wood fitting into a slot in another.
tenor *noun* **1** (singer with) the second highest male voice. **2** general meaning. ♦ *adjective* **3** (of a voice or instrument) between alto and baritone.
tenpin bowling *noun* game in which players try to knock over ten skittles by rolling a ball at them.
tense¹ ⊕ *adjective* **1** emotionally strained. **2** stretched tight. ♦ *verb* **3** make or become tense.
tension *noun* **1** hostility or suspense. **2** emotional strain. **3** degree of stretching.
tense² *noun Grammar* form of a verb showing the time of action.
tensile *adjective* of tension. **tensile strength** measure of the ability of a material to withstand lengthways stress.
tension ⊕ *noun* **1** hostility or suspense. **2** emotional strain. **3** degree of stretching.

——————— T H E S A U R U S ———————

temptation *noun* **1** = **enticement**, allurement, inducement, lure, pull, seduction, tantalization **2** = **appeal**, attraction
tempting *adjective* = **inviting**, alluring, appetizing, attractive, enticing, lekker (*S Afr sl*), mouthwatering, seductive, tantalizing
tenable *adjective* = **sound**, arguable, believable, defensible, justifiable, plausible, rational, reasonable, viable
tenacious *adjective* **1** = **firm**, clinging, forceful, immovable, iron, strong, tight, unshakable **2** = **stubborn**, adamant, determined, dogged, obdurate, obstinate, persistent, resolute, steadfast, unswerving, unyielding OPPOSITE **wavering**
tenacity *noun* **2** = **perseverance**, application, determination, doggedness, obduracy, persistence, resolve, steadfastness, stubbornness
tenancy *noun* = **lease**, occupancy, possession, renting, residence
tenant *noun* = **leaseholder**, inhabitant, lessee, occupant, occupier, renter, resident
tend¹ *verb* **1** = **be inclined**, be apt, be liable, gravitate, have a tendency, incline, lean **2** = **go**, aim, bear, head, lead, make for, move, point
tend² *verb* = **take care of**, attend, cultivate,

keep, look after, maintain, manage, nurture, watch over OPPOSITE **ignore**
tendency *noun* = **inclination**, disposition, leaning, liability, proclivity, proneness, propensity, susceptibility
tender¹ *adjective* **2** = **gentle**, affectionate, caring, compassionate, considerate, kind, loving, sympathetic, tenderhearted, warm-hearted OPPOSITE **hard**. **3** = **sensitive**, bruised, inflamed, painful, raw, sore, vulnerable
tender² *verb* **1** = **offer**, give, hand in, present, proffer, propose, put forward, submit, volunteer ♦ *noun* **3** = **offer**, bid, estimate, proposal, submission
tenderness *noun* **2** = **gentleness**, affection, care, compassion, consideration, kindness, love, sentimentality, sympathy, warmth OPPOSITE **cruelty**. **3** = **soreness**, inflammation, pain, sensitivity
tense¹ *adjective* **1** = **nervous**, anxious, apprehensive, edgy, jumpy, keyed up, on edge, on tenterhooks, strained, uptight (*inf*), wired (*sl*) OPPOSITE **collected**. **2** = **tight**, rigid, strained, stretched, taut OPPOSITE **relaxed** ♦ *verb* **3** = **tighten**, brace, flex, strain, stretch OPPOSITE **relax**

tent *noun* portable canvas shelter.
tentacle *noun* flexible organ of many invertebrates, used for grasping, feeding, etc.
tentative ❶ *adjective* **1** provisional or experimental. **2** cautious or hesitant.
tentatively *adverb*
tenterhooks *plural noun* **on tenterhooks** in anxious suspense.
tenuous ❶ *adjective* slight or flimsy.
tenuously *adverb*
tenure *noun* **1** (period of) the holding of an office or position. **2** legal right to live in a building or use land for a period of time.
tenuto *adjective, adverb Music* (of a note) to be held for or beyond its full time value.
tepee [tee-pee] *noun* cone-shaped tent, formerly used by Native Americans.
tepid ❶ *adjective* **1** slightly warm. **2** half-hearted.
tequila *noun* Mexican alcoholic drink.
terbium *noun Chem* rare metallic element.
tercentenary *adjective, noun, pl* **-naries** (of a) three hundredth anniversary.
term ❶ *noun* **1** word or expression. **2** fixed period. **3** period of the year when a school etc. is open or a lawcourt holds sessions. ◆ *plural* **4** conditions. **5** mutual relationship. ◆ *verb* **6** name or designate.
termagant *noun* unpleasant and bad-tempered woman.
terminal ❶ *adjective* **1** (of an illness) ending in death. **2** at or being an end. ◆ *noun* **3** place where people or vehicles begin or end a journey. **4** point where current enters or leaves

an electrical device. **5** keyboard and VDU having input and output links with a computer.
terminally *adverb* **terminal velocity** *Physics* maximum velocity reached by a body falling under gravity.
terminate ❶ *verb* bring or come to an end.
termination *noun* **terminable** *adjective* capable of being terminated.
terminology ❶ *noun* technical terms relating to a subject. **terminological** *adjective*
terminus ❶ *noun, pl* **-ni, -nuses** railway or bus station at the end of a line.
termite *noun* white antlike insect that destroys timber.
tern *noun* gull-like sea bird with a forked tail and pointed wings.
ternary *adjective* **1** consisting of three parts. **2** *Maths* (of a number system) to the base three.
Terpsichorean *adjective* of dancing.
terrace *noun* **1** row of houses built as one block. **2** paved area next to a building. **3** level tier cut out of a hill. ◆ *plural* **4** (also **terracing**) tiered area in a stadium where spectators stand. ◆ *verb* **5** form into or provide with a terrace.
terracotta *adjective, noun* **1** (made of) brownish-red unglazed pottery. ◆ *adjective* **2** brownish-red.
terra firma *noun Latin* dry land or solid ground.
terrain ❶ *noun* area of ground, esp. with reference to its physical character.
terrapin *noun* small turtle-like reptile.
terrarium *noun, pl* **-raria, -rariums** enclosed container for small plants or animals.

——————————— T H E S A U R U S ———————————

tension *noun* **1** = **hostility**, apprehension, suspense **2** = **strain**, anxiety, nervousness, pressure, stress, unease OPPOSITE relaxation. **3** = **tightness**, pressure, rigidity, stiffness, stress, stretching, tautness
tentative *adjective* **1** = **unconfirmed**, conjectural, experimental, indefinite, provisional, speculative, unsettled OPPOSITE final. **2** = **hesitant**, cautious, diffident, doubtful, faltering, timid, uncertain, undecided, unsure OPPOSITE confident
tenuous *adjective* = **slight**, doubtful, dubious, flimsy, insubstantial, nebulous, shaky, sketchy, weak OPPOSITE strong
tepid *adjective* **1** = **lukewarm**, warmish **2** = **half-hearted**, apathetic, cool, indifferent, lukewarm, unenthusiastic OPPOSITE keen
term *noun* **1** = **word**, expression, name, phrase, title **2** = **period**, duration, interval, season, span, spell, time, while ◆ *verb* **6** = **call**, designate, dub, entitle, label, name, style

terminal *adjective* **1** = **fatal**, deadly, incurable, killing, lethal, mortal **2** = **final**, concluding, extreme, last, ultimate, utmost OPPOSITE first ◆ *noun* **3** = **terminus**, depot, end of the line, station
terminate *verb* = **end**, abort, cease, close, complete, conclude, discontinue, finish, stop OPPOSITE start
termination *noun* = **ending**, abortion, cessation, completion, conclusion, discontinuation, end, finish OPPOSITE start
terminology *noun* = **language**, jargon, nomenclature, phraseology, terms, vocabulary
terminus *noun* = **end of the line**, depot, garage, last stop, station
terms *plural noun* **4** = **conditions**, particulars, provisions, provisos, qualifications, specifications, stipulations **5** = **relationship**, footing, relations, standing, status
terrain *noun* = **ground**, country, going, land, landscape, topography

T

terrazzo *noun, pl* **-zos** floor of marble chips set in mortar and polished.
terrestrial ❶ *adjective* **1** of the earth. **2** of or living on land.
terrible ❶ *adjective* **1** very serious. **2** *Informal* very bad. **3** causing fear. **terribly** *adverb*
terrier *noun* any of various breeds of small active dog.
terrific ❶ *adjective* **1** great or intense. **2** *Informal* excellent.
terrify ❶ *verb* **-fying, -fied** fill with fear. **terrified** *adjective* **terrifying** *adjective* **terrifyingly** *adverb*
terrine [terr-**reen**] *noun* **1** earthenware dish with a lid. **2** pâté or similar food.
territory ❶ *noun, pl* **-ries 1** district. **2** area under the control of a particular government. **3** area inhabited and defended by an animal. **4** area of knowledge. **5** (T-) region of a country, esp. of a federal state, that does not enjoy full rights. **territorial** *adjective* **Territorial Army** reserve army. **territorial waters** parts of the sea over which a country exercises control, esp. with regard to fishing rights.
terror ❶ *noun* **1** great fear. **2** terrifying person or thing. **3** *Informal* troublesome person or thing. **terrorism** *noun* use of violence and intimidation to achieve political ends. **terrorist** *noun, adjective* **terrorize** *verb* force or oppress by fear or violence.
terry *noun* fabric with small loops covering both sides, used esp. for making towels.

terse ❶ *adjective* **1** neat and concise. **2** curt. **tersely** *adverb*
tertiary [**tur**-shar-ee] *adjective* third in degree, order, etc.
Terylene *noun* ® synthetic polyester yarn or fabric.
tessellated *adjective* paved or inlaid with a mosaic of small tiles. **tessera** *noun, pl* **-serae** small square tile used in mosaics.
test ❶ *verb* **1** try out to ascertain the worth, capability, or endurance of. **2** carry out an examination on. ◆ *noun* **3** critical examination. **4** Test match. **testing** *adjective* **test case** lawsuit that establishes a precedent. **Test match** one of a series of international cricket or rugby matches. **test pilot** pilot who tests the performance of new aircraft. **test tube** narrow round-bottomed glass tube used in scientific experiments. **test-tube baby** baby conceived outside the mother's body.
testament ❶ *noun* **1** proof or tribute. **2** *Law* will. **3** (T-) one of the two main divisions of the Bible.
testate *adjective* having left a valid will. **testacy** *noun* **testator** [test-**tay**-tor], (*fem*) **testatrix** [test-**tay**-triks] *noun* maker of a will.
testicle *noun* either of the two male reproductive glands.
testify ❶ *verb* **-fying, -fied** give evidence under oath. **testify to** be evidence of.
testimony ❶ *noun, pl* **-nies 1** declaration of truth or fact. **2** evidence given under oath.

———————— THESAURUS ————————

terrestrial *adjective* **1** = **earthly**, global, worldly
terrible *adjective* **1** = **serious**, dangerous, desperate, extreme, severe OPPOSITE **mild**. **2** *Inf* = **bad**, abysmal, awful, dire, dreadful, poor, rotten (*inf*) OPPOSITE **great**. **3** = **fearful**, dreadful, frightful, horrendous, horrible, horrifying, monstrous, shocking, terrifying
terribly *adverb* **1** = **extremely**, awfully (*inf*), decidedly, desperately, exceedingly, seriously, thoroughly, very
terrific *adjective* **1** = **great**, enormous, fearful, gigantic, huge, intense, tremendous OPPOSITE **moderate**. **2** *Inf* = **excellent**, amazing, brilliant, fantastic (*inf*), magnificent, marvellous, outstanding, sensational (*inf*), stupendous, superb, wonderful OPPOSITE **bad**
terrified *adjective* = **frightened**, alarmed, appalled, horrified, horror-struck, panic-stricken, petrified, scared
terrify *verb* = **frighten**, alarm, appal, horrify, make one's hair stand on end, scare, shock, terrorize

territory *noun* **1** = **district**, area, country, domain, land, patch, province, region, zone
terror *noun* **1** = **fear**, alarm, anxiety, dread, fright, horror, panic, shock **2** = **scourge**, bogeyman, bugbear, devil, fiend, monster
terrorize *verb* = **oppress**, browbeat, bully, coerce, intimidate, menace, threaten
terse *adjective* **1** = **concise**, brief, condensed, laconic, monosyllabic, pithy, short, succinct OPPOSITE **lengthy**. **2** = **curt**, abrupt, brusque, short, snappy OPPOSITE **polite**
test *verb* **1** = **try out**, experiment, put to the test **2** = **check**, analyse, assess, examine, investigate, research ◆ *noun* **3** = **examination**, acid test, analysis, assessment, check, evaluation, investigation, research, trial
testament *noun* **1** = **proof**, demonstration, evidence, testimony, tribute, witness **2** *Law* = **will**, last wishes
testify *verb* = **bear witness**, affirm, assert, attest, certify, corroborate, state, swear, vouch OPPOSITE **dispute**
testimonial *noun* = **tribute**, commendation,

testimonial *noun* **1** recommendation of the worth of a person or thing. **2** tribute for services or achievement.

> **LANGUAGE TIP**
>
> A *testimonial* is an open letter of recommendation about someone. A *reference* is a confidential report that is not read by the person who is the subject.

testis *noun, pl* **-tes** testicle.
testosterone *noun* male sex hormone secreted by the testes.
testy *adjective* **-tier, -tiest** irritable or touchy. **testily** *adverb* **testiness** *noun*
tetanus *noun* acute infectious disease producing muscular spasms and convulsions.
tetchy *adjective* **tetchier, tetchiest** cross and irritable.
tête-à-tête *noun, pl* **-têtes, -tête** private conversation.
tether ⊕ *noun* **1** rope or chain for tying an animal to a spot. ◆ *verb* **2** tie up with rope. **at the end of one's tether** at the limit of one's endurance.
tetragon *noun* figure with four angles and four sides. **tetragonal** *adjective*
tetrahedron [tet-ra-**heed**-ron] *noun, pl* **-drons, -dra** solid figure with four faces.
tetralogy *noun, pl* **-gies** series of four related works.
tetrameter [tet-**tram**-it-er] *noun* **1** line of poetry with four metrical feet. **2** verse composed of such lines.
Teutonic [tew-**tonn**-ik] *adjective* of or like the (ancient) Germans.
text ⊕ *noun* **1** main body of a book as distinct from illustrations etc. **2** any written material. **3** passage of the Bible as the subject of a sermon. **4** novel or play studied for a course. **5** text message. ◆ *verb* **6** send a text message to (someone). **textual** *adjective* **textbook** *noun* **1** standard book on a particular subject. ◆ *adjective* **2** perfect, e.g. *a textbook landing*. **text message** message sent in text form, esp. by means of a cell phone.
textile *noun* **1** fabric or cloth, esp. woven. ◆ *adjective* **2** of (the making of) fabrics.
texture ⊕ *noun* structure, feel, or consistency. **textured** *adjective* **textural** *adjective*
Th *Chem* thorium.
Thai *adjective* **1** of Thailand. ◆ *noun* **2** *pl* **Thais, Thai** person from Thailand. **3** language of Thailand.
thalidomide [thal-**lid**-oh-mide] *noun* drug formerly used as a sedative, but found to cause abnormalities in developing fetuses.
thallium *noun Chem* highly toxic metallic element.
than *conjunction, preposition* used to introduce the second element of a comparison.
thane *noun Hist* Anglo-Saxon or medieval Scottish nobleman.
thank ⊕ *verb* **1** express gratitude to. **2** hold responsible. **thanks** *plural noun* **1** words of gratitude. ◆ *interjection* **2** (also **thank you**) polite expression of gratitude. **thanks to** because of. **thankful** *adjective* grateful. **thankless** *adjective* unrewarding or unappreciated. **Thanksgiving Day** autumn public holiday in Canada and the US.
that *adjective, pronoun* **1** used to refer to something already mentioned or familiar, or further away. ◆ *conjunction* **2** used to introduce a clause. ◆ *pronoun* **3** used to introduce a relative clause.
thatch *noun* **1** roofing material of reeds or straw. ◆ *verb* **2** roof (a house) with reeds or straw. **thatched** *adjective*

——————— T H E S A U R U S ———————

endorsement, recommendation, reference
testimony *noun* **1** = **proof**, corroboration, demonstration, evidence, indication, manifestation, support, verification **2** = **evidence**, affidavit, deposition, statement, submission
testing *adjective* = **difficult**, arduous, challenging, demanding, exacting, rigorous, searching, strenuous, taxing, tough
tether *noun* **1** = **rope**, chain, fetter, halter, lead, leash ◆ *verb* **2** = **tie**, bind, chain, fasten, fetter, secure **at the end of one's tether** = **exasperated**, at one's wits' end, exhausted
text *noun* **1** = **contents**, body **2** = **words**, wording
texture *noun* = **feel**, consistency, grain, structure, surface, tissue
thank *verb* **1** = **say thank you**, show one's appreciation
thankful *adjective* = **grateful**, appreciative, beholden, indebted, in (someone's) debt, obliged, pleased, relieved OPPOSITE ungrateful
thankless *adjective* = **unrewarding**, fruitless, unappreciated, unprofitable, unrequited
thanks *plural noun* **1** = **gratitude**, acknowledgment, appreciation, credit, gratefulness, recognition **thanks to** = **because of**, as a result of, due to, owing to, through

thaw ❶ *verb* **1** make or become unfrozen. **2** become more relaxed or friendly. ✦ *noun* **3** thawing. **4** weather causing snow or ice to melt.

the *adjective* the definite article, used before a noun.

theatre ❶ *noun* **1** place where plays etc. are performed. **2** hospital operating room. **3** drama and acting in general. **4** region in which a war takes place. **theatrical** *adjective* **1** of the theatre. **2** exaggerated or affected. **theatricals** *plural noun* (amateur) dramatic performances. **theatrically** *adverb* **theatricality** *noun*

thee *pronoun Obs* objective form of THOU.

theft ❶ *noun* act or an instance of stealing.

their *adjective* of or associated with them.

theirs *pronoun* (thing or person) belonging to them.

SPELLING TIP

Do not confuse **their** and **theirs**, which do not have apostrophes, with **they're** and **there's**, which do because letters have been missed out where two words have been joined together.

---

theism [**thee**-iz-zum] *noun* belief in a God or gods. **theist** *noun, adjective* **theistic** *adjective*

them *pronoun* refers to people or things other than the speaker or those addressed.

themselves *pronoun* emphatic and reflexive form of THEY *or* THEM.

theme ❶ *noun* **1** main idea or subject being discussed. **2** recurring idea in literature, art, etc. **3** recurring melodic figure in music. **thematic** *adjective* **thematically** *adverb* **theme park** leisure area in which all the activities and displays are based on a single theme. **theme tune, song** tune *or* song used to introduce a television or radio programme.

then *adverb* **1** at that time. **2** after that. **3** that being so.

thence *adverb* **1** from that place or time. **2** therefore.

theocracy *noun, pl* **-cies** government by a god or priests. **theocratic** *adjective*

theodolite [thee-**odd**-oh-lite] *noun* surveying instrument for measuring angles.

theology ❶ *noun, pl* **-gies** study of religions and religious beliefs. **theologian** *noun* **theological** *adjective* **theologically** *adverb*

theorem *noun* proposition that can be proved by reasoning.

theory ❶ *noun, pl* **-ries 1** set of ideas to explain something. **2** abstract knowledge or reasoning. **3** idea or opinion. **in theory** in an ideal or hypothetical situation. **theoretical** *adjective* based on theory rather than practice or fact. **theoretically** *adverb* **theorist** *noun* **theorize** *verb* form theories, speculate.

theosophy *noun* religious or philosophical system claiming to be based on intuitive insight into the divine nature. **theosophical** *adjective*

therapy ❶ *noun, pl* **-pies** curing treatment. **therapist** *noun* **therapeutic** [ther-rap-**pew**-tik] *adjective* curing. **therapeutics** *noun* art of curing.

there ❶ *adverb* **1** in or to that place. **2** in that respect. **thereby** *adverb* by that means.

therefore *adverb* consequently, that being so.

thereupon *adverb* immediately after that.

SPELLING TIP

Do not confuse **there**, which is closely connected in meaning and in spelling with 'here', and **their**, which means 'belonging to them'.

---

therm *noun* unit of measurement of heat.

——— THESAURUS ———

thaw *verb* **1** = **melt**, defrost, dissolve, liquefy, soften, unfreeze, warm OPPOSITE **freeze**

theatrical *adjective* **1** = **dramatic**, Thespian **2** = **exaggerated**, affected, dramatic, histrionic, mannered, melodramatic, ostentatious, showy, stagy OPPOSITE **natural**

theft *noun* = **stealing**, embezzlement, fraud, larceny, pilfering, purloining, robbery, thieving

theme *noun* **1** = **subject**, idea, keynote, subject matter, topic **2, 3** = **motif**, leitmotif

theological *adjective* = **religious**, doctrinal, ecclesiastical

theoretical *adjective* = **abstract**, academic, conjectural, hypothetical, notional, speculative OPPOSITE **applied**

theorize *verb* = **speculate**, conjecture, formulate, guess, hypothesize, project, propound, suppose

theory *noun* **3** = **hypothesis**, assumption, conjecture, presumption, speculation, supposition, surmise, thesis OPPOSITE **fact**

therapeutic *adjective* = **beneficial**, corrective, curative, good, healing, remedial, restorative, salutary

therapist *noun* = **healer**, physician

therapy *noun* = **remedy**, cure, healing,

thermal *adjective* **1** of heat. **2** hot or warm. **3** (of clothing) retaining heat. ♦ *noun* **4** rising current of warm air.

thermionic valve *noun* electronic valve in which electrons are emitted from a heated rather than a cold cathode.

thermodynamics *noun* scientific study of the relationship between heat and other forms of energy.

thermoelectric *adjective* of or relating to the conversion of heat energy to electrical energy.

thermometer *noun* instrument for measuring temperature.

thermonuclear *adjective* **1** involving nuclear fusion. **2** involving atomic weapons.

thermoplastic *adjective* (of a plastic) softening when heated and resetting on cooling.

Thermos *noun* ® vacuum flask.

thermosetting *adjective* (of a plastic) remaining hard when heated.

thermostat *noun* device for automatically regulating temperature. **thermostatic** *adjective* **thermostatically** *adverb*

thesaurus [thiss-**sore**-uss] *noun, pl* **-ruses** book containing lists of synonyms and related words.

these *adjective, pronoun* plural of THIS.

thesis ❶ *noun, pl* **theses 1** written work submitted for a degree. **2** opinion supported by reasoned argument.

thespian *noun* **1** actor or actress. ♦ *adjective* **2** of the theatre.

they *pronoun* refers to: **1** people or things other than the speaker or people addressed. **2**

people in general. **3** *Informal* he or she.

thiamine *noun* vitamin found in the outer coat of rice and other grains.

thick ❶ *adjective* **1** of great or specified extent from one side to the other. **2** having a dense consistency. **3** *Informal* stupid or insensitive. **4** (of an accent) very noticeable. **5** *Informal* friendly. **a bit thick** *Informal* unfair or unreasonable. **the thick** busiest or most intense part. **thick with** full of. **thicken** *verb* make or become thick or thicker. **thickener** *noun* substance used to thicken liquids. **thickly** *adverb* **thickness** *noun* **1** state of being thick. **2** dimension through an object. **3** layer. **thickset** *adjective* **1** stocky in build. **2** set closely together. **thick-skinned** *adjective* insensitive to criticism or hints.

thicket ❶ *noun* dense growth of small trees.

thief ❶ *noun, pl* **thieves** person who steals.

thieve *verb* steal. **thieving** *adjective*

thigh *noun* upper part of the human leg.

thimble *noun* cap protecting the end of the finger when sewing.

thin ❶ *adjective* **thinner, thinnest 1** not thick. **2** slim or lean. **3** sparse or meagre. **4** of low density. **5** poor or unconvincing. ♦ *verb* **thinning, thinned 6** make or become thin. **thinly** *adverb* **thinness** *noun* **thin-skinned** *adjective* sensitive to criticism or hints.

thine *pronoun, adjective Obs* (something) of or associated with you (thou).

thing ❶ *noun* **1** material object. **2** object, fact, or idea considered as a separate entity. **3** *Informal* obsession. ♦ *plural* **4** possessions, clothes, etc.

think ❶ *verb* **thinking, thought 1** consider,

——————— T H E S A U R U S ———————

treatment

therefore *adverb* =**consequently**, accordingly, as a result, ergo, hence, so, then, thence, thus

thesis *noun* **1** =**dissertation**, essay, monograph, paper, treatise **2** =**proposition**, contention, hypothesis, idea, opinion, proposal, theory, view

thick *adjective* **1** =**wide**, broad, bulky, fat, solid, substantial OPPOSITE **thin**. **2** =**dense**, close, compact, concentrated, condensed, heavy, impenetrable, opaque OPPOSITE **clear**. **3** *Inf* =**stupid**, brainless, dense, dopey (*inf*), moronic, obtuse, slow, thickheaded OPPOSITE **bright**. **5** *Inf* =**friendly**, close, devoted, familiar, inseparable, intimate, pally (*inf*) OPPOSITE **distant** ♦ **a bit thick** *Inf* =**unreasonable**, unfair, unjust

thicken *verb* =**set**, clot, coagulate, condense,

congeal, jell OPPOSITE **thin**

thicket *noun* =**wood**, brake, coppice, copse, covert, grove

thickset *adjective* **1** =**stocky**, bulky, burly, heavy, muscular, strong, sturdy, well-built OPPOSITE **gaunt**

thief *noun* =**robber**, burglar, embezzler, housebreaker, pickpocket, pilferer, plunderer, shoplifter, stealer

thieve *verb* =**steal**, filch, nick (*sl, chiefly Brit*), pilfer, pinch (*inf*), purloin, rob, swipe (*sl*)

thin *adjective* **1** =**narrow**, attenuated, fine OPPOSITE **thick**. **2** =**slim**, bony, emaciated, lean, scrawny, skeletal, skinny, slender, slight, spare, spindly OPPOSITE **heavy**. **3** =**meagre**, deficient, scanty, scarce, scattered, skimpy, sparse, wispy **4** =**fine**, delicate, diaphanous, filmy, flimsy, gossamer, sheer, unsubstantial **5** =**unconvincing**, feeble, flimsy, inadequate,

T

judge, or believe. **2** make use of the mind. **3** be considerate enough or remember to do something. **thinker** noun **thinking** adjective, noun **think-tank** noun group of experts studying specific problems. **think up** verb invent or devise.

third adjective **1** of number three in a series. **2** rated or graded below the second level. ♦ noun **3** one of three equal parts. **third degree** violent interrogation. **third party** (applying to) a person involved by chance or only incidentally in legal proceedings, an accident, etc. **Third World** developing countries of Africa, Asia, and Latin America.

thirst ⓞ noun **1** desire to drink. **2** craving or yearning. ♦ verb **3** feel thirst. **thirsty** adjective **thirstier, thirstiest. thirstily** adverb

thirteen adjective, noun three plus ten. **thirteenth** adjective, noun

thirty adjective, noun three times ten. **thirtieth** adjective, noun

this adjective, pronoun **1** used to refer to a thing or person nearby, just mentioned, or about to be mentioned. ♦ adjective **2** used to refer to the present time, e.g. this morning.

thistle noun prickly plant with dense flower heads. **thistledown** noun mass of feathery plumed seeds produced by thistles.

thither adverb Obs to or towards that place.

tho', tho conjunction, adverb short for THOUGH.

thole, tholepin noun wooden pin set in the side of a rowing boat to serve as a fulcrum for rowing.

thong noun **1** thin strip of leather etc. **2** skimpy article of underwear or beachwear that leaves the buttocks bare.

thorax noun, pl **thoraxes, thoraces** part of the body between the neck and the abdomen. **thoracic** adjective

thorium noun Chem radioactive metallic element.

thorn ⓞ noun **1** prickle on a plant. **2** bush with thorns. **thorn in one's side, flesh** source of irritation. **thorny** adjective **1** covered with thorns. **2** (of a problem, subject) difficult or unpleasant.

thorough ⓞ adjective **1** complete. **2** careful or methodical. **thoroughly** adverb **thoroughness** noun **thoroughbred** noun, adjective (animal) of pure breed. **thoroughfare** noun way through from one place to another. **thoroughgoing** adjective extremely thorough.

those adjective, pronoun plural of THAT.

thou pronoun Obs singular form of YOU.

though ⓞ conjunction **1** despite the fact that. ♦ adverb **2** nevertheless.

thought ⓞ verb **1** past of THINK. ♦ noun **2** thinking. **3** concept or idea. **4** ideas typical of a time or place. **5** consideration. **6** intention or expectation. **thoughtful** adjective **1**

——————— THESAURUS ———————

lame, poor, superficial, weak OPPOSITE **strong**

thing noun **1, 2** = **object**, article, being, body, entity, something, substance **3** Inf = **obsession**, bee in one's bonnet, fetish, fixation, hang-up (inf), mania, phobia, preoccupation ♦plural noun **4** = **possessions**, belongings, clobber (Brit sl), effects, equipment, gear, luggage, stuff

think verb **1** = **believe**, consider, deem, estimate, imagine, judge, reckon, regard, suppose **2** = **ponder**, cerebrate, cogitate, contemplate, deliberate, meditate, muse, obsess, reason, reflect, ruminate

thinking adjective = **thoughtful**, contemplative, intelligent, meditative, philosophical, rational, reasoning, reflective ♦noun = **reasoning**, conjecture, idea, judgment, opinion, position, theory, view

think up verb = **devise**, come up with, concoct, contrive, create, dream up, invent, visualize

thirst noun **1** = **thirstiness**, drought, dryness **2** = **craving**, appetite, desire, hankering, keenness, longing, passion, yearning OPPOSITE **dislike**

thirsty adjective **1** = **parched**, arid, dehydrated, dry **2** = **eager**, avid, craving, desirous, greedy, hungry, itching, longing, yearning

thorn noun **1** = **prickle**, barb, spike, spine

thorny adjective **1** = **prickly**, barbed, bristly, pointed, sharp, spiky, spiny

thorough adjective **1** = **complete**, absolute, out-and-out, outright, perfect, total, unmitigated, unqualified, utter OPPOSITE **partial**. **2** = **careful**, assiduous, conscientious, efficient, exhaustive, full, in-depth, intensive, meticulous, painstaking OPPOSITE **cursory**

thoroughbred adjective = **purebred**, pedigree

thoroughfare noun = **road**, avenue, highway, passage, passageway, street, way

thoroughly adverb **1** = **completely**, absolutely, downright, perfectly, quite, totally, to the hilt, utterly OPPOSITE **partly**. **2** = **carefully**, assiduously, conscientiously, efficiently, exhaustively, from top to bottom, fully, intensively, meticulously, painstakingly, scrupulously OPPOSITE **carelessly**

though conjunction **1** = **although**, even if, even though, notwithstanding, while ♦adverb **2** = **nevertheless**, for all that, however,

considerate. **2** showing careful thought. **3** pensive or reflective. **thoughtfully** *adverb* **thoughtless** *adjective* inconsiderate. **thoughtlessly** *adverb*
thousand *adjective, noun* **1** ten hundred. **2** large but unspecified number. **thousandth** *adjective, noun* (of) number one thousand in a series.
thrall *noun* state of being in the power of another person.
thrash ⊕ *verb* **1** beat, esp. with a stick or whip. **2** defeat soundly. **3** move about wildly. **4** thresh. **thrashing** *noun* severe beating. **thrash out** *verb* solve by thorough argument.
thread ⊕ *noun* **1** fine strand or yarn. **2** unifying theme. **3** spiral ridge on a screw, nut, or bolt. ◆ *verb* **4** pass thread through. **5** pick (one's way etc.). **threadbare** *adjective* **1** (of fabric) with the nap worn off. **2** hackneyed. **3** shabby.
threat ⊕ *noun* **1** declaration of intent to harm. **2** strong possibility of something dangerous happening. **3** dangerous person or thing.
threaten *verb* **1** make or be a threat to. **2** be a

menacing indication of. **threatening** *adjective* **threateningly** *adverb*
three *adjective, noun* one more than two. **threefold** *adjective, adverb* (having) three times as many or as much. **threesome** *noun* group of three. **three-dimensional, 3-D** *adjective* having three dimensions. **three-ply** *adjective* having three layers or strands. **three-point turn** complete turn of a motor vehicle using forward and reverse gears. **three-quarter** *adjective* being three quarters of something.
threnody *noun, pl* **-dies** lament for the dead.
thresh *verb* beat (wheat etc.) to separate the grain from the husks and straw. **thresh about** move about wildly.
threshold ⊕ *noun* **1** bar forming the bottom of a doorway. **2** entrance. **3** starting point. **4** point at which something begins to take effect.
threw *verb* past tense of THROW.
thrice *adverb Lit* three times.
thrift ⊕ *noun* **1** wisdom and caution with money. **2** low-growing plant with pink flowers. **thrifty** *adjective* **thriftier, thriftiest**
thrill ⊕ *noun* **1** sudden feeling of excitement. ◆

——————— T H E S A U R U S ———————

nonetheless, notwithstanding, still, yet
thought *noun* **2** = **thinking**, cogitation, consideration, deliberation, meditation, musing, reflection, rumination **3** = **idea**, concept, judgment, notion, opinion, view **5** = **consideration**, attention, heed, regard, scrutiny, study **6 a** = **intention**, aim, design, idea, notion, object, plan, purpose **b** = **expectation**, anticipation, aspiration, hope, prospect
thoughtful *adjective* **1** = **considerate**, attentive, caring, helpful, kind, kindly, solicitous, unselfish OPPOSITE selfish. **2** = **well-thought-out**, astute, canny, prudent **3** = **reflective**, contemplative, deliberative, meditative, pensive, ruminative, serious, studious OPPOSITE shallow
thoughtless *adjective* = **inconsiderate**, impolite, insensitive, rude, selfish, tactless, uncaring, undiplomatic, unkind OPPOSITE thoughtful
thrash *verb* **1** = **beat**, belt (*inf*), cane, flog, give (someone) a (good) hiding (*inf*), scourge, spank, whip **2** = **defeat**, beat, crush, drub, rout, run rings around (*inf*), slaughter (*inf*), trounce, wipe the floor with (*inf*) **3** = **thresh**, flail, jerk, toss and turn, writhe
thrashing *noun* = **beating**, belting (*inf*), flogging, hiding (*inf*), punishment, whipping
thrash out *verb* = **settle**, argue out, debate, discuss, have out, resolve, solve, talk over
thread *noun* **1** = **strand**, fibre, filament, line,

string, yarn **2** = **theme**, direction, drift, plot, story line, train of thought ◆*verb* **4** = **string 5** = **pass**, ease, pick (one's way), squeeze through
threadbare *adjective* **2** = **hackneyed**, commonplace, conventional, familiar, overused, stale, stereotyped, tired, trite, well-worn OPPOSITE fresh. **3** = **shabby**, down at heel, frayed, old, ragged, scruffy, tattered, tatty, worn OPPOSITE new
threat *noun* **1** = **menace**, threatening remark **2** = **warning**, foreboding, foreshadowing, omen, portent, presage, writing on the wall **3** = **danger**, hazard, menace, peril, risk
threaten *verb* **1 a** = **intimidate**, browbeat, bully, lean on (*sl*), menace, pressurize, terrorize OPPOSITE protect. **b** = **endanger**, imperil, jeopardize, put at risk, put in jeopardy, put on the line OPPOSITE guard. **2** = **foreshadow**, forebode, portend, presage
threatening *adjective* **1** = **menacing**, bullying, intimidating **2** = **ominous**, forbidding, grim, inauspicious, sinister OPPOSITE promising
threshold *noun* **2** = **entrance**, door, doorstep, doorway **3** = **start**, beginning, brink, dawn, inception, opening, outset, verge OPPOSITE end. **4** = **minimum**, lower limit
thrift *noun* **1** = **economy**, carefulness, frugality, parsimony, prudence, saving, thriftiness OPPOSITE extravagance
thrifty *adjective* **1** = **economical**, careful, frugal, parsimonious, provident, prudent,

verb **2** (cause to) feel a thrill. **thrilling** adjective

thriller noun book, film, etc. with an atmosphere of mystery or suspense.

thrive ❶ verb **thriving, thrived** or **throve, thrived** or **thriven 1** flourish or prosper. **2** grow well.

throat noun **1** passage from the mouth and nose to the stomach and lungs. **2** front of the neck. **throaty** adjective (of the voice) hoarse.

throb ❶ verb **throbbing, throbbed 1** pulsate repeatedly. **2** vibrate rhythmically. ◆ noun **3** throbbing.

throes plural noun violent pangs or pains. **in the throes of** struggling to cope with.

thrombosis noun, pl **-ses** forming of a clot in a blood vessel or the heart.

throne noun **1** ceremonial seat of a monarch or bishop. **2** sovereign power.

throng ❶ noun, verb crowd.

throstle noun song thrush.

throttle ❶ noun **1** device controlling the amount of fuel entering an engine. ◆ verb **2** strangle.

through ❶ preposition **1** from end to end or side to side of. **2** because of. **3** during. ◆ adjective **4** finished. **5** (of transport) going directly to a place. **through and through** completely. **throughout** preposition, adverb in every part (of). **throughput** noun amount of material processed.

throve verb a past tense of THRIVE.

throw ❶ verb **throwing, threw, thrown 1**

hurl through the air. **2** move or put suddenly or carelessly. **3** bring into a specified state, esp. suddenly. **4** move (a switch, lever, etc.). **5** shape (pottery) on a wheel. **6** give (a party). **7** Informal baffle or disconcert. **8** direct (a look, light, etc.). **9** project (the voice) so that it seems to come from elsewhere. ◆ noun **10** throwing. **11** distance thrown. **throwaway** adjective **1** done or said casually. **2** designed to be discarded after use. **throwback** noun person or thing that reverts to an earlier type. **throw up** verb vomit.

thrum verb **thrumming, thrummed 1** strum rhythmically but without expression on (a musical instrument). **2** make a low beating or humming sound.

thrush[1] noun brown songbird.

thrush[2] noun fungal disease of the mouth or vagina.

thrust ❶ verb **thrusting, thrust 1** push forcefully. ◆ noun **2** forceful stab. **3** force or power. **4** essential part. **5** intellectual or emotional drive.

thud ❶ noun **1** dull heavy sound. ◆ verb **thudding, thudded 2** make such a sound.

thug ❶ noun violent man, esp. a criminal. **thuggery** noun **thuggish** adjective

thulium noun Chem malleable ductile silvery-grey element.

thumb noun **1** short thick finger set apart from the others. ◆ verb **2** touch or handle with the thumb. **3** signal with the thumb for a lift in a

———— T H E S A U R U S ————

saving, sparing

thrill noun **1 =pleasure**, buzz (sl), kick (inf), stimulation, tingle, titillation OPPOSITE **boredom** ◆verb **2 =excite**, arouse, electrify, move, stimulate, stir, titillate

thrilling adjective **1 =exciting**, electrifying, gripping, riveting, rousing, sensational, stimulating, stirring OPPOSITE **boring**

thrive verb **1 =prosper**, boom, develop, do well, flourish, get on, increase, succeed OPPOSITE **decline**. **2 =grow**

throb verb **1 =pulsate**, beat, palpitate, pound, pulse, thump **2 =vibrate** ◆noun **3 =pulse**, beat, palpitation, pounding, pulsating, thump, thumping, vibration

throng noun **=crowd**, crush, horde, host, mass, mob, multitude, pack, swarm ◆verb **=crowd**, congregate, converge, flock, mill around, pack, swarm around OPPOSITE **separate**

throttle verb **2 =strangle**, choke, garrotte, strangulate

through preposition **1 =from one side to the**

other of, between, by, past **2 =because of**, by means of, by way of, using, via **3 =during**, in, throughout ◆adjective **4 =completed**, done, ended, finished **through and through =completely**, altogether, entirely, fully, thoroughly, totally, utterly, wholly

throughout preposition **=through the whole of**, all over, everywhere in, right through ◆adverb **=from start to finish**, right through

throw verb **1, 2 =hurl**, cast, chuck (inf), fling, launch, lob (inf), pitch, send, sling, toss **7** Inf **=confuse**, astonish, baffle, confound, disconcert, dumbfound, faze ◆noun **10 =toss**, fling, heave, lob (inf), pitch, sling

throwaway adjective **1 =casual**, careless, offhand, passing, understated

thrust verb **1 =push**, drive, force, jam, plunge, propel, ram, shove ◆noun **2 =push**, drive, lunge, poke, prod, shove, stab **3 =momentum**, impetus

thud noun, verb **1, 2 =thump**, crash, knock, smack

thug noun **=ruffian**, bruiser (inf), bully boy,

vehicle. **thumb through** flick through (a book or magazine). **thumb index** series of notches cut into the edge of a book to allow quick reference.

thumbtack *noun* the US and Canadian name for DRAWING PIN.

thump ⊕ *noun* 1 (sound of) a dull heavy blow. ♦ *verb* 2 strike heavily. **thumping** *adjective Informal* huge or excessive.

thunder ⊕ *noun* 1 loud noise accompanying lightning. 2 any loud sound. ♦ *verb* 3 rumble with thunder. 4 shout. 5 move fast, heavily, and noisily. **thunderous** *adjective* **thundery** *adjective* **thunderbolt** *noun* 1 lightning flash. 2 something sudden and unexpected.

thunderclap *noun* peal of thunder.

thunderstorm *noun* storm with lightning and thunder. **thunderstruck** *adjective* amazed.

Thurs. Thursday.

Thursday *noun* fifth day of the week.

thus ⊕ *adverb* 1 therefore. 2 in this way.

thwack *verb, noun* whack.

thwart ⊕ *verb* 1 foil or frustrate. ♦ *noun* 2 seat across a boat.

thy *adjective Obs* of or associated with you (thou). **thyself** *pronoun Obs* emphatic form of THOU.

thylacine *noun* extinct doglike Tasmanian marsupial.

thyme [time] *noun* aromatic herb.

thymol *noun* substance obtained from thyme, used as an antiseptic.

thymus *noun, pl* **-muses, -mi** small gland at the base of the neck.

thyroid *adjective, noun* (of) a gland in the neck controlling body growth.

ti *noun Music* same as TE.

Ti *Chem* titanium.

tiara *noun* semicircular jewelled headdress.

tibia *noun, pl* **tibiae, tibias** inner bone of the lower leg. **tibial** *adjective*

tic *noun* spasmodic muscular twitch.

tick¹ ⊕ *noun* 1 mark (✓) used to check off or indicate the correctness of something. 2 recurrent tapping sound, as of a clock. 3 *Informal* moment. ♦ *verb* 4 mark with a tick. 5 make a ticking sound. **tick off** *verb* 1 mark with a tick. 2 reprimand. **tick over** *verb* 1 (of an engine) idle. 2 function smoothly. **ticktack** *noun* bookmakers' sign language.

tick² *noun* tiny bloodsucking parasitic animal.

tick³ ⊕ *noun Informal* credit or account.

ticket ⊕ *noun* 1 card or paper entitling the holder to admission, travel, etc. 2 label, esp. showing price. 3 official notification of a parking or traffic offence. 4 declared policy of a political party. ♦ *verb* **-eting, -eted** 5 attach or issue a ticket to.

ticking *noun* strong material for mattress covers.

tickle *verb* 1 touch or stroke (a person) to produce laughter. 2 itch or tingle. 3 please or amuse. ♦ *noun* 4 tickling. **ticklish** *adjective* 1 sensitive to tickling. 2 requiring care or tact.

tiddly¹ *adjective* **-dlier, -dliest** tiny. **tiddler** *noun Informal* very small fish.

tiddly² *adjective* **-dlier, -dliest** *Informal* slightly drunk.

tiddlywinks *noun* game in which players try to flip small plastic discs into a cup.

tide ⊕ *noun* 1 rise and fall of the sea caused by the gravitational pull of the sun and moon. 2 current caused by this. 3 widespread feeling or tendency. **tidal** *adjective* **tidal wave** large destructive wave. **tideline** *noun* mark left by the highest or lowest point of the tide. **tide**

——————— THESAURUS ———————

gangster, heavy (*sl*), hooligan, tough

thump *noun* 1 **a = thud**, bang, clunk, crash, thwack **b = blow**, clout (*inf*), knock, punch, rap, smack, swipe, wallop (*inf*), whack ♦*verb* 2 **= strike**, beat, clobber (*sl*), clout (*inf*), hit, knock, pound, punch, smack, swipe, wallop (*inf*), whack

thunder *noun* 2 **= rumble**, boom, crash, explosion ♦*verb* 3 **= rumble**, boom, crash, peal, resound, reverberate, roar 4 **= shout**, bark, bellow, roar, yell

thunderous *adjective* 2 **= loud**, booming, deafening, ear-splitting, noisy, resounding, roaring, tumultuous

thunderstruck *adjective* **= amazed**, astonished, astounded, dumbfounded, flabbergasted (*inf*), open-mouthed, shocked,

staggered, stunned, taken aback

thus *adverb* 1 **= therefore**, accordingly, consequently, ergo, for this reason, hence, on that account, so, then 2 **= in this way**, as follows, like this, so

thwart *verb* 1 **= frustrate**, foil, hinder, obstruct, outwit, prevent, snooker, stymie
OPPOSITE⟩ assist

tick¹ *noun* 1 **= mark**, dash, stroke 2 **= tapping**, clicking, ticktock 3 *Inf* **= moment**, flash, instant, minute, second, split second, trice, twinkling ♦*verb* 4 **= mark**, check off, indicate 5 **= tap**, click, ticktock

tick³ *noun Inf* **= credit**, account, the slate (*Brit inf*)

ticket *noun* 1 **= voucher**, card, certificate, coupon, pass, slip, token 2 **= label**, card,

T

over *verb* help (someone) temporarily.

tidings *plural noun* news.

tidy ⊕ *adjective* **-dier, -diest 1** neat and orderly. **2** *Informal* considerable. ♦ *verb* **-dying, -died 3** put in order. **tidily** *adverb* **tidiness** *noun*

tie ⊕ *verb* **tying, tied 1** fasten or be fastened with string, rope, etc. **2** make (a knot or bow) in (something). **3** restrict or limit. **4** score the same as another competitor. ♦ *noun* **5** long narrow piece of material worn knotted round the neck. **6** bond or fastening. **7** match in an eliminating competition. **8** drawn game or contest. **tie-break, tie-breaker** *noun* extra game or question that decides the result of a contest ending in a draw. **tied** *adjective* **1** (of a pub) allowed to sell only the beer of a particular brewery. **2** (of a cottage etc.) rented to the tenant only as long as he or she is employed by the owner.

tier ⊕ *noun* one of a set of rows placed one above and behind the other.

tiff *noun* petty quarrel.

tiger *noun* large yellow-and-black striped Asian cat. **tigress** *noun* **1** female tiger. **2** *Informal* fierce woman. **tiger snake** *noun* highly venomous brown-and-yellow Australian snake.

tight ⊕ *adjective* **1** stretched or drawn taut. **2** closely fitting. **3** secure or firm. **4** cramped. **5** (of a situation) difficult or dangerous. **6** *Informal* not generous. **7** (of a match or game) very close. **8** *Informal* drunk. **tights** *plural noun* one-piece clinging garment covering the body from the waist to the feet. **tightly** *adverb* **tighten**

verb make or become tight or tighter. **tight-fisted** *adjective* very mean. **tight-lipped** *adjective* **1** secretive. **2** with lips pressed tightly together, as through anger. **tightrope** *noun* rope stretched taut on which acrobats perform.

tikka *adjective Indian cookery* marinated in spices and dry-roasted, e.g. *chicken tikka*.

tilde *noun* mark (˜) used in Spanish to indicate that the letter 'n' is to be pronounced in a particular way.

tile *noun* **1** flat piece of ceramic, plastic, etc. used to cover a roof, floor, or wall. ♦ *verb* **2** cover with tiles. **tiled** *adjective* **tiling** *noun* tiles collectively.

till¹ *conjunction, preposition* until.

till² ⊕ *verb* cultivate (land). **tillage** *noun*

till³ ⊕ *noun* drawer for money, usu. in a cash register.

tiller *noun* lever to move a rudder of a boat.

tilt ⊕ *verb* **1** slant at an angle. **2** *Hist* compete against in a jousting contest. ♦ *noun* **3** slope. **4** *Hist* jousting contest. **5** attempt. **at full tilt** at full speed or force.

tilth *noun* (condition of) land that has been tilled.

timber ⊕ *noun* **1** wood as a building material. **2** trees collectively. **3** wooden beam in the frame of a house, boat, etc. **timbered** *adjective* **timber line** limit beyond which trees will not grow.

timbre ⊕ [**tam**-bra] *noun* distinctive quality of sound of a voice or instrument.

time ⊕ *noun* **1** past, present, and future as a continuous whole. **2** specific point in time. **3**

docket, marker, slip, sticker, tab, tag

tide *noun* **2** = **current**, ebb, flow, stream, tideway, undertow **3** = **tendency**, direction, drift, movement, trend

tidy *adjective* **1** = **neat**, clean, methodical, orderly, shipshape, spruce, well-kept, well-ordered OPPOSITE **untidy**. **2** *Inf* = **considerable**, ample, generous, goodly, handsome, healthy, large, sizable *or* sizeable, substantial OPPOSITE **little** ♦*verb* **3** = **neaten**, clean, groom, order, spruce up, straighten OPPOSITE **mess up**

tie *verb* **1** = **fasten**, attach, bind, connect, join, knot, link, secure, tether OPPOSITE **loose**. **3** = **restrict**, bind, confine, hamper, hinder, limit, restrain OPPOSITE **free**. **4** = **draw**, equal, match ♦*noun* **6 a** = **bond**, affiliation, allegiance, commitment, connection, liaison, relationship **b** = **fastening**, bond, cord, fetter, knot, ligature, link **8** = **draw**, dead heat, deadlock, stalemate

tier *noun* = **row**, bank, layer, level, line, rank, storey, stratum

tight *adjective* **1** = **taut**, rigid, stretched OPPOSITE **relaxed**. **2** = **close-fitting**, close **3** = **secure**, fast, firm, fixed **4** = **cramped**, constricted, narrow, snug OPPOSITE **loose**. **6** *Inf* = **miserly**, grasping, mean, niggardly, parsimonious, stingy, tightfisted OPPOSITE **generous**. **7** = **close**, even, evenly-balanced, well-matched **8** *Inf* = **drunk**, inebriated, intoxicated, paralytic (*inf*), plastered (*sl*), tipsy, under the influence (*inf*) OPPOSITE **sober**

tighten *verb* = **squeeze**, close, constrict, narrow OPPOSITE **slacken**

till² *verb* = **cultivate**, dig, plough, work

till³ *noun* = **cash register**, cash box

tilt *verb* **1** = **slant**, heel, incline, lean, list, slope, tip ♦*noun* **3** = **slope**, angle, inclination, incline, list, pitch, slant **4** *Hist* = **joust**, combat, duel, fight, lists, tournament **(at) full tilt** = **full speed**, for dear life, headlong

timber *noun* **1** = **wood**, boards, logs, planks **2** = **trees**, forest **3** = **beams**

unspecified interval. **4** instance or occasion. **5** period with specific features. **6** musical tempo. **7** *Slang* imprisonment. ♦ *verb* **8** note the time taken by. **9** choose a time for. **timeless** *adjective* **1** unaffected by time. **2** eternal. **timely** *adjective* at the appropriate time. **times** *preposition* multiplied by. **timing** *noun* ability to judge when to do or say something so as to make the best effect. **time-honoured** *adjective* sanctioned by custom. **time-lag** *noun* period between cause and effect. **timepiece** *noun* watch or clock. **timeserver** *noun* person who changes his or her views to gain support or favour. **time sharing 1** system of part ownership of a holiday property for a specified period each year. **2** system enabling users at different terminals of a computer to use it at the same time. **time signature** *Music* sign that indicates the number and length of beats in the bar. **timetable** *noun* plan showing the times when something takes place, the departure and arrival times of trains or buses, etc. **time zone** region throughout which the same standard time is used.

timid ❶ *adjective* **1** easily frightened. **2** shy, not bold. **timidly** *adverb* **timidity** *noun*

timorous [tim-mor-uss] *adjective* timid.

timpani [tim-pan-ee] *plural noun* set of kettledrums. **timpanist** *noun*

tin *noun* **1** soft metallic element. **2** (airtight) metal container. **tinned** *adjective* (of food) preserved by being sealed in a tin. **tinny** *adjective* (of sound) thin and metallic. **tinpot** *adjective Informal* worthless or unimportant.

tincture *noun* medicinal extract in a solution

of alcohol.

tinder *noun* dry easily-burning material used to start a fire. **tinderbox** *noun* formerly, small box for tinder, esp. one fitted with a flint and steel.

tine *noun* prong of a fork or antler.

ting *noun* high metallic sound, as of a small bell.

tinge ❶ *noun* **1** slight tint. **2** trace. ♦ *verb* **tingeing, tinged 3** give a slight tint or trace to.

tingle ❶ *verb, noun* (feel) a prickling or stinging sensation.

tinker ❶ *noun* **1** travelling mender of pots and pans. **2** *Scot & Irish* Gypsy. ♦ *verb* **3** fiddle with (an engine etc.) in an attempt to repair it.

tinkle *verb* **1** ring with a high tinny sound like a small bell. ♦ *noun* **2** this sound or action.

tinsel *noun* **1** decorative metallic strips or threads. **2** anything cheap and gaudy.

tint ❶ *noun* **1** (pale) shade of a colour. **2** dye for the hair. ♦ *verb* **3** give a tint to.

tintinnabulation *noun* ringing or pealing of bells.

tiny ❶ *adjective* **tinier, tiniest** very small.

tip¹ ❶ *noun* **1** narrow or pointed end of anything. **2** small piece forming an end. ♦ *verb* **tipping, tipped 3** put a tip on.

tip² ❶ *noun* **1** money given in return for service. **2** helpful hint or warning. **3** piece of inside information. ♦ *verb* **tipping, tipped 4** give a tip to. **tipster** *noun* person who sells tips about races.

tip³ ❶ *verb* **tipping, tipped 1** tilt or overturn. **2** dump (rubbish). ♦ *noun* **3** rubbish dump.

——————— T H E S A U R U S ———————

timbre *noun* = **tone**, colour, resonance, ring

time *noun* **3** = **period**, duration, interval, season, space, span, spell, stretch, term **4** = **occasion**, instance, juncture, point, stage **6** = **tempo**, beat, measure, rhythm ♦ *verb* **9** = **schedule**, set

timeless *adjective* **1** = **changeless**, ageless **2** = **eternal**, enduring, everlasting, immortal, lasting, permanent

timely *adjective* = **opportune**, appropriate, convenient, judicious, propitious, seasonable, suitable, well-timed

timetable *noun* = **schedule**, agenda, calendar, curriculum, diary, list, programme

timid *adjective* **1** = **fearful**, apprehensive, faint-hearted, shrinking, timorous OPPOSITE⟩ **bold**. **2** = **shy**, bashful, coy, diffident OPPOSITE⟩ **bold**

timorous *adjective* = **timid**, apprehensive, bashful, coy, diffident, faint-hearted, fearful,

shrinking, shy

tinge *noun* **1** = **tint**, colour, shade **2** = **bit**, dash, drop, smattering, sprinkling, suggestion, touch, trace ♦ *verb* **3** = **tint**, colour, imbue, suffuse

tingle *verb* = **prickle**, have goose pimples, itch, sting, tickle ♦ *noun* = **quiver**, goose pimples, itch, pins and needles (*inf*), prickling, shiver, thrill

tinker *verb* **3** = **meddle**, dabble, fiddle (*inf*), mess about, play, potter

tint *noun* **1** = **shade**, colour, hue, tone **2** = **dye**, rinse, tincture, tinge, wash ♦ *verb* **3** = **dye**, colour

tiny *adjective* = **small**, diminutive, infinitesimal, little, microscopic, miniature, minute, negligible, petite, slight OPPOSITE⟩ **huge**

tip¹ *noun* **1** = **end**, extremity, head, peak, pinnacle, point, summit, top ♦ *verb* **3** = **cap**, crown, finish, surmount, top

T

tipple ❶ *verb* **1** drink alcohol habitually, esp. in small quantities. ♦ *noun* **2** alcoholic drink. **tippler** *noun*

tipsy *adjective* **-sier, -siest** slightly drunk.

tiptoe *verb* **-toeing, -toed** walk quietly with the heels off the ground.

tiptop *adjective* of the highest quality or condition.

tirade ❶ *noun* long angry speech.

tire ❶ *verb* **1** reduce the energy of, as by exertion. **2** weary or bore. **tired** *adjective* **1** exhausted. **2** bored. **3** hackneyed or stale. **tiring** *adjective* **tireless** *adjective* energetic and determined. **tirelessly** *adverb* **tiresome** *adjective* boring and irritating.

tissue *noun* **1** substance of an animal body or plant. **2** piece of thin soft paper used as a handkerchief etc. **3** interwoven series, e.g. *a tissue of lies.*

tit[1] *noun* any of various small songbirds.

tit[2] *noun Slang* female breast.

titanic *adjective* huge or very important. **titan** *noun* person who is huge, strong, or very important.

titanium *noun Chem* strong light metallic element used to make alloys.

titbit ❶ *noun* **1** tasty piece of food. **2** pleasing scrap of scandal.

tit-for-tat *adjective* done in retaliation.

tithe *noun* **1** esp. formerly, one tenth of one's income or produce paid to the church as a tax. ♦ *verb* **2** charge or pay a tithe.

Titian [tish-an] *adjective* (of hair) reddish-gold.

titillate ❶ *verb* excite or stimulate pleasurably. **titillating** *adjective* **titillation** *noun*

titivate *verb* smarten up. **titivation** *noun*

title ❶ *noun* **1** name of a book, film, etc. **2** book or periodical. **3** name signifying rank or position. **4** formal designation, such as Mrs. **5** *Sport* championship. **6** *Law* legal right of possession. **titled** *adjective* aristocratic. **title deed** legal document of ownership. **titleholder** *noun* person who holds a title, esp. a sporting championship. **title role** role of the character after whom a film or play is named.

titration *noun Chem* operation in which a measured amount of one solution is added to a known quantity of another solution until the reaction between the two is complete.

titter ❶ *verb* **1** laugh in a suppressed way. ♦ *noun* **2** suppressed laugh.

tittle-tattle *noun, verb* gossip.

titular *adjective* **1** in name only. **2** of a title.

tizzy *noun, pl* **-zies** *Informal* confused or agitated state.

Tl *Chem* thallium.

Tm *Chem* thulium.

TN Tennessee.

TNT *noun* trinitrotoluene, a powerful explosive.

to *preposition* **1** indicating movement towards, equality or comparison, etc., e.g. *walking to school; forty miles to the gallon.* **2** used to mark the indirect object or infinitive of a verb. ♦ *adverb* **3** to a closed position, e.g. *pull the door to.* **to and fro** back and forth.

toad *noun* animal like a large frog.

toad-in-the-hole *noun* sausages baked in batter.

toadstool *noun* poisonous fungus like a mushroom.

toady ❶ *noun, pl* **toadies 1** ingratiating person. ♦ *verb* **toadying, toadied 2** be

———————— T H E S A U R U S ————————

tip[2] *noun* **1** = **gratuity**, gift **2** = **hint**, pointer, suggestion ♦*verb* **4 a** = **reward**, remunerate **b** = **advise**, suggest

tip[3] *verb* **1** = **tilt**, incline, lean, list, slant **2** = **dump**, empty, pour out, unload ♦*noun* **3** = **dump**, refuse heap, rubbish heap

tipple *verb* **1** = **drink**, imbibe, indulge (*inf*), quaff, swig, tope ♦*noun* **2** = **alcohol**, booze (*inf*), drink, liquor

tirade *noun* = **outburst**, diatribe, fulmination, harangue, invective, lecture

tire *verb* **1** = **exhaust**, drain, fatigue, wear out, weary OPPOSITE restore. **2** = **bore**, exasperate, irk, irritate, weary

tired *adjective* **1** = **exhausted**, drained, drowsy, fatigued, flagging, sleepy, weary, worn out OPPOSITE refreshed. **2** = **bored**, fed up, sick, weary OPPOSITE keen on. **3** = **hackneyed**, clichéd, corny (*sl*), old, outworn, stale,

threadbare, trite, well-worn OPPOSITE original

tireless *adjective* = **energetic**, indefatigable, industrious, resolute, unflagging, untiring, vigorous

tiresome *adjective* = **boring**, dull, irksome, irritating, tedious, trying, vexatious, wearing, wearisome

tiring *adjective* **1** = **exhausting**, arduous, demanding, exacting, laborious, strenuous, tough, wearing

titbit *noun* **1** = **delicacy**, dainty, morsel, snack, treat

titillate *verb* = **excite**, arouse, interest, stimulate, tantalize, tease, thrill

title *noun* **1** = **name**, designation, handle (*sl*), term **5** *Sport* = **championship**, crown **6** *Law* = **ownership**, claim, entitlement, prerogative, privilege, right

titter *verb* **1** = **snigger**, chortle (*inf*), chuckle,

DICTIONARY

ingratiating.

toast[1] ⊕ *noun* **1** sliced bread browned by heat. ◆ *verb* **2** brown (bread) by heat. **3** warm or be warmed. **toaster** *noun* electrical device for toasting bread.

toast[2] ⊕ *noun* **1** tribute or proposal of health or success marked by people raising glasses and drinking together. **2** person or thing so honoured. ◆ *verb* **3** drink a toast to.

tobacco *noun, pl* **-cos, -coes** plant with large leaves dried for smoking. **tobacconist** *noun* person or shop selling tobacco, cigarettes, etc.

toboggan *noun* **1** narrow sledge for sliding over snow. ◆ *verb* **-ganing, -ganed 2** ride a toboggan.

toby jug *noun* mug in the form of a stout seated man.

toccata [tok-**kah**-ta] *noun* rapid piece of music for a keyboard instrument.

today *noun* **1** this day. **2** the present age. ◆ *adverb* **3** on this day. **4** nowadays.

toddle *verb* walk with short unsteady steps. **toddler** *noun* child beginning to walk.

toddy *noun, pl* **-dies** sweetened drink of spirits and hot water.

to-do *noun, pl* **-dos** fuss or commotion.

toe *noun* **1** digit of the foot. **2** part of a shoe or sock covering the toes. ◆ *verb* **toeing, toed 3** touch or kick with the toe. **toecap** *noun* strengthened covering for the toe of a shoe. **toehold** *noun* **1** small space on a mountain for supporting the toe of the foot in climbing. **2** means of gaining access or advantage. **toerag** *noun Slang* contemptible person. **toe the line** conform.

toff *noun Slang* well-dressed or upper-class person.

toffee *noun* chewy sweet made of boiled sugar. **toffee-apple** *noun* apple fixed on a stick and coated with toffee. **toffee-nosed** *adjective Informal* snobbish.

tofu *noun* soft food made from soya-bean curd.

tog *noun* **1** unit for measuring the insulating power of duvets. ◆ *plural* **2** *Informal* clothes.

toga [**toe**-ga] *noun* garment worn by citizens of ancient Rome.

together ⊕ *adverb* **1** in company. **2** simultaneously. ◆ *adjective* **3** *Informal* organized.

toggle *noun* **1** small bar-shaped button inserted through a loop for fastening. **2** switch used to turn a machine or computer function on or off.

toil ⊕ *noun* **1** hard work. ◆ *verb* **2** work hard. **3** progress with difficulty.

toilet ⊕ *noun* **1** (room with) a bowl connected to a drain for receiving and disposing of urine and faeces. **2** washing and dressing. **toiletry** *noun, pl* **-ries** object or cosmetic used to clean or groom oneself. **toilet paper** thin absorbent paper used for cleaning oneself after defecation. **toilet water** light perfume.

token ⊕ *noun* **1** sign or symbol. **2** voucher exchangeable for goods of a specified value. **3** disc used as money in a slot machine. ◆ *adjective* **4** nominal or slight. **tokenism** *noun* policy of making only a token effort, esp. to comply with a law.

told *verb* past of TELL.

tolerate ⊕ *verb* **1** allow to exist or happen. **2**

THESAURUS

giggle, laugh

toady *noun* **1** = **sycophant**, bootlicker (*inf*), crawler (*sl*), creep (*sl*), flatterer, flunkey, hanger-on, lackey, minion, yes man ◆*verb* **2** = **fawn on**, crawl, creep, cringe, flatter, grovel, kowtow to, pander to, suck up to (*inf*) OPPOSITE **oppose**

toast[1] *verb* **2** = **brown**, grill, roast **3** = **warm**, heat

toast[2] *noun* **1** = **tribute**, compliment, health, pledge, salutation, salute **2** = **favourite**, darling, hero *or* heroine ◆*verb* **3** = **drink to**, drink (to) the health of, salute

together *adverb* **1** = **collectively**, as one, hand in glove, in concert, in unison, jointly, mutually, shoulder to shoulder, side by side OPPOSITE **individually**. **2** = **at the same time**, at one fell swoop, concurrently, contemporaneously, simultaneously ◆*adjective* **3** *Inf* = **self-possessed**, composed, well-adjusted,

well-balanced

toil *noun* **1** = **hard work**, application, drudgery, effort, elbow grease (*inf*), exertion, graft (*inf*), slog, sweat OPPOSITE **inertia** ◆*verb* **2** = **labour**, drudge, graft (*inf*), slave, slog, strive, struggle, sweat (*inf*), work, work one's fingers to the bone

toilet *noun* **1** = **lavatory**, bathroom, convenience, gents *or* ladies (*Brit inf*), ladies' room, latrine, loo (*Brit inf*), privy, urinal, water closet, W.C.

token *noun* **1** = **symbol**, badge, expression, indication, mark, note, representation, sign ◆*adjective* **4** = **nominal**, hollow, minimal, perfunctory, superficial, symbolic

tolerable *adjective* **1** = **bearable**, acceptable, allowable, endurable, sufferable, supportable OPPOSITE **unacceptable**. **2** *Inf* = **fair**, acceptable, adequate, all right, average, O.K. *or* okay (*inf*), passable OPPOSITE **bad**

T

endure patiently. **tolerable** *adjective* **1**
bearable. **2** *Informal* quite good. **tolerably**
adverb **tolerance** *noun* **1** acceptance of other
people's rights to their own opinions or actions.
2 ability to endure something. **tolerant**
adjective **tolerantly** *adverb* **toleration** *noun*
toll¹ ❶ *verb* **1** ring (a bell) slowly and regularly,
esp. to announce a death. ◆ *noun* **2** tolling.
toll² ❶ *noun* **1** charge for the use of a bridge
or road. **2** total loss or damage from a disaster.
toluene *noun* colourless volatile flammable
liquid obtained from petroleum and coal tar.
tom *noun* male cat.
tomahawk *noun* fighting axe of the Native
Americans.
tomato *noun, pl* **-toes** red fruit used in salads
and as a vegetable.
tomb ❶ *noun* **1** grave. **2** monument over a
grave. **tombstone** *noun* gravestone.
tombola *noun* lottery with tickets drawn from
a revolving drum.
tomboy *noun* girl who acts or dresses like a
boy.
tome *noun* large heavy book.
tomfoolery ❶ *noun* foolish behaviour.
Tommy *noun, pl* **-mies** *Brit informal* private
soldier in the British army.
Tommy gun *noun* light sub-machine-gun.
tomorrow *adverb, noun* **1** (on) the day after
today. **2** (in) the future.
tom-tom *noun* drum beaten with the hands.
ton *noun* unit of weight equal to 2240 pounds
or 1016 kilograms (**long ton**) or, in the US,
2000 pounds or 907kilograms (**short ton**).
tonnage *noun* weight capacity of a ship.
tone ❶ *noun* **1** sound with reference to its

pitch, volume, etc. **2** *US* musical note. **3** *Music*
(also **whole tone**) interval of two semitones. **4**
quality of a sound or colour. **5** general
character. **6** healthy bodily condition. ◆ *verb* **7**
harmonize (with). **8** give tone to. **tonal**
adjective Music written in a key. **tonality** *noun*
toneless *adjective* **tone-deaf** *adjective* unable
to perceive subtle differences in pitch. **tone
down** *verb* make or become more moderate.
tone up *verb* make or become more healthy.
tongs *plural noun* large pincers for grasping
and lifting.
tongue ❶ *noun* **1** muscular organ in the
mouth, used in speaking and tasting. **2**
language. **3** animal tongue as food. **4** thin
projecting strip. **5** flap of leather on a shoe.
tonguing *noun* technique of playing a wind
instrument by obstructing and uncovering the
air passage through the lips with the tongue.
tongue-tied *adjective* speechless, esp. with
shyness or embarrassment. **tongue twister**
sentence or phrase that is difficult to say
quickly.
tonic ❶ *noun* **1** medicine to improve body
tone. **2** anything that is strengthening or
cheering. **3** tonic water. **4** *Music* first note of a
scale. ◆ *adjective* **5** invigorating. **tonic water**
mineral water containing quinine.
tonight *adverb, noun* (in or during) the night
or evening of this day.
toning table *noun* exercise table with
mechanically moving parts, which is
programmed to repeat certain movements for a
set time, inorder to exercise specific parts of the
body of the personlying on it.
tonne [tunn] *noun* unit of weight equal to

——————— T H E S A U R U S ———————

tolerance *noun* **1** = **broad-mindedness**,
forbearance, indulgence, open-mindedness,
permissiveness OPPOSITE discrimination. **2**
= **endurance**, fortitude, hardiness, resilience,
resistance, stamina, staying power, toughness
tolerant *adjective* **1** = **broad-minded**,
catholic, forbearing, liberal, long-suffering,
open-minded, understanding, unprejudiced
OPPOSITE **authoritarian**
tolerate *verb* **1** = **allow**, accept, brook,
condone, permit, put up with (*inf*), take
OPPOSITE **ban**. **2** = **endure**, put up with (*inf*),
stand, stomach, take
toll¹ *verb* **1** = **ring**, chime, clang, knell, peal,
sound, strike ◆*noun* **2** = **ringing**, chime, clang,
knell, peal
toll² *noun* **1** = **charge**, duty, fee, levy,
payment, tariff, tax **2** = **damage**, cost, loss,
penalty

tomb *noun* = **grave**, catacomb, crypt,
mausoleum, sarcophagus, sepulchre, vault
tombstone *noun* = **gravestone**, headstone,
marker, memorial, monument
tomfoolery *noun* = **foolishness**, buffoonery,
clowning, fooling around (*inf*), horseplay,
shenanigans (*inf*), silliness, skylarking (*inf*)
OPPOSITE **seriousness**
tone *noun* **1** = **pitch**, inflection, intonation,
modulation, timbre **4** = **colour**, hue, shade,
tinge, tint **5** = **character**, air, attitude, feel,
manner, mood, spirit, style, temper ◆*verb* **7**
= **harmonize**, blend, go well with, match, suit
tone down *verb* = **moderate**, play down,
reduce, restrain, soften, subdue, temper
tongue *noun* **2** = **language**, dialect, parlance,
speech
tonic *noun* **2** = **stimulant**, boost, fillip, pick-
me-up (*inf*), restorative, shot in the arm (*inf*)

1000 kilograms.

tonsil *noun* small gland in the throat.

tonsillectomy *noun* surgical removal of the tonsils. **tonsillitis** *noun* inflammation of the tonsils.

tonsure *noun* **1** shaving of all or the top of the head as a religious or monastic practice. **2** shaved part of the head. **tonsured** *adjective*

too ❶ *adverb* **1** also, as well. **2** to excess. **3** extremely.

took *verb* past tense of TAKE.

tool ❶ *noun* **1** implement used by hand. **2** person used by another to perform unpleasant or dishonourable tasks. ◆ *verb* **3** work on with a tool.

toonie, twonie *noun Inf* Canadian two-dollar coin.

toot *noun* **1** short hooting sound. ◆ *verb* **2** (cause to) make such a sound.

tooth *noun, pl* **teeth 1** bonelike projection in the jaws of most vertebrates for biting and chewing. **2** toothlike prong or point. **sweet tooth** strong liking for sweet food. **toothless** *adjective* **1** lacking teeth. **2** (of an official body) lacking power or influence. **toothpaste** *noun* paste used to clean the teeth. **toothpick** *noun* small stick for removing scraps of food from between the teeth.

top¹ ❶ *noun* **1** highest point or part. **2** lid or cap. **3** highest rank. **4** garment for the upper part of the body. ◆ *adjective* **5** at or of the top. ◆ *verb* **topping, topped 6** form a top on. **7** be at the top of. **8** exceed or surpass. **topping** *noun* sauce or garnish for food. **topless** *adjective* (of a costume or woman) with no covering for the breasts. **topmost** *adjective* highest or best. **top brass** most important officers or leaders. **top-dress** *verb* spread fertilizer on the surface of the land. **top dressing** layer of fertilizer spread on the surface of land. **top hat** man's tall cylindrical hat. **top-heavy** *adjective* unstable through being overloaded at the top. **top-notch** *adjective* excellent, first-class. **top-secret** *adjective* (of military or government information) classified as needing the highest level of secrecy and security. **topsoil** *noun* surface layer of soil.

top² *noun* toy which spins on a pointed base.

topaz [toe-pazz] *noun* semiprecious stone in various colours.

tope¹ *verb* drink alcohol regularly.

tope² *noun* small European shark.

topee, topi [toe-pee] *noun* lightweight hat worn in tropical countries.

topiary [tope-yar-ee] *noun* art of trimming trees and bushes into decorative shapes. **topiarist** *noun*

topic ❶ *noun* subject of a conversation, book, etc. **topical** *adjective* relating to current events. **topicality** *noun*

topography *noun, pl* **-phies** (science of describing) the surface features of a place. **topographer** *noun* **topographical** *adjective*

topology *noun* geometry of the properties of a shape which are unaffected by continuous distortion. **topological** *adjective*

topple ❶ *verb* **1** (cause to) fall over. **2** overthrow (a government etc.).

topsy-turvy ❶ *adjective* **1** upside down. **2** in confusion.

toque [toke] *noun* small round hat.

tor *noun* high rocky hill.

Torah *noun* body of traditional Jewish teaching.

torch *noun* **1** small portable battery-powered lamp. **2** wooden shaft dipped in wax and set alight. ◆ *verb* **3** *Informal* deliberately set (a building) on fire. **carry a torch for** be in love

——— THESAURUS ———

too *adverb* **1** = **also**, as well, besides, further, in addition, likewise, moreover, to boot **2, 3** = **excessively**, extremely, immoderately, inordinately, overly, unduly, unreasonably, very

tool *noun* **1** = **implement**, appliance, contraption, contrivance, device, gadget, instrument, machine, utensil **2** = **puppet**, cat's-paw, hireling, lackey, minion, pawn, stooge (*sl*)

top¹ *noun* **1** = **peak**, apex, crest, crown, culmination, head, height, pinnacle, summit, zenith OPPOSITE **base**. **2** = **lid**, cap, cover, stopper **3** = **first place**, head, lead ◆*adjective* **5** = **leading**, best, chief, elite, finest, first, foremost, head, highest, pre-eminent, principal, uppermost OPPOSITE **worst** ◆*verb* **6** = **cover**, cap, crown, finish, garnish **7** = **lead**, be first,

head **8** = **surpass**, beat, better, eclipse, exceed, excel, outstrip, transcend OPPOSITE **fall short of**

topic *noun* = **subject**, issue, matter, point, question, subject matter, theme

topical *adjective* = **current**, contemporary, newsworthy, up-to-date, up-to-the-minute

topmost *adjective* = **highest**, dominant, foremost, leading, paramount, principal, supreme, top, uppermost

topple *verb* **1** = **fall over**, collapse, fall, keel over, overbalance, overturn, totter, tumble **2** = **overthrow**, bring down, bring low, oust, overturn, unseat

topsy-turvy *adjective* **1** = **upside-down 2** = **disorganized**, chaotic, confused, disorderly, with (someone).

tore *verb* past tense of TEAR².

toreador [torr-ee-a-dor] *noun* bullfighter.

torment ❶ *verb* **1** cause (someone) great suffering. **2** tease cruelly. ◆ *noun* **3** great suffering. **4** source of suffering. **tormentor** *noun*

torn ❶ *verb* past participle of TEAR².

tornado ❶ *noun, pl* **-dos, -does** violent whirlwind.

torpedo *noun, pl* **-does 1** self-propelled underwater missile. ◆ *verb* **-doing, -doed 2** attack or destroy with or as if with torpedoes.

torpid ❶ *adjective* sluggish and inactive.

torpor *noun* torpid state.

torque [tork] *noun* **1** force causing rotation. **2** Celtic necklace or armband of twisted metal.

torrent ❶ *noun* **1** rushing stream. **2** rapid flow of questions, abuse, etc. **torrential** *adjective* (of rain) very heavy.

torrid ❶ *adjective* **1** very hot and dry. **2** highly emotional.

torsion *noun* twisting of a part by equal forces being applied at both ends but in opposite directions.

torso *noun, pl* **-sos 1** trunk of the human body. **2** statue of a nude human trunk.

tort *noun Law* civil wrong or injury for which damages may be claimed.

tortilla *noun* thin Mexican pancake.

tortoise *noun* slow-moving land reptile with a dome-shaped shell. **tortoiseshell** *noun* **1** mottled brown shell of a turtle, used for making ornaments. ◆ *adjective* **2** having brown, orange, and black markings.

tortuous ❶ *adjective* **1** winding or twisting. **2** not straightforward.

torture ❶ *verb* **1** cause (someone) severe pain or mental anguish. ◆ *noun* **2** severe physical or mental pain. **3** torturing. **torturer** *noun*

Tory *noun, pl* **Tories 1** member of the Conservative Party in Great Britain or Canada. ◆ *adjective* **2** of Tories. **Toryism** *noun*

toss ❶ *verb* **1** throw lightly. **2** fling or be flung about. **3** coat (food) by gentle stirring or mixing. **4** (of a horse) throw (its rider). **5** move (one's head) suddenly backwards. **6** throw up (a coin) to decide between alternatives by guessing which side will land uppermost. ◆ *noun* **7** tossing. **toss up** *verb* toss a coin. **toss-up** *noun* even chance or risk.

tot¹ ❶ *noun* **1** small child. **2** small drink of spirits.

tot² ❶ *verb* **totting, totted. tot up** add (numbers) together.

total ❶ *noun* **1** whole, esp. a sum of parts. ◆ *adjective* **3** complete. **3** of being a total. ◆ *verb* **-talling, -talled 4** amount to. **5** add up. **totally** *adverb* **totality** *noun* **totalizator** *noun* machine operating a betting system in which money is paid out to the winners in proportion to their stakes.

totalitarian ❶ *adjective* of a dictatorial one-party government. **totalitarianism** *noun*

——————— T H E S A U R U S ———————

inside-out, jumbled, messy, mixed-up

torment *verb* **1 = torture**, crucify, distress, rack OPPOSITE soothe. **2 = tease**, annoy, bother, harass, hassle (*inf*), irritate, nag, pester, vex ◆*noun* **3 = suffering**, agony, anguish, distress, hell, misery, pain, torture OPPOSITE joy

torn *adjective* **2 = cut**, lacerated, ragged, rent, ripped, slit, split

tornado *noun* **= whirlwind**, cyclone, gale, hurricane, squall, storm, tempest, typhoon

torpor *noun* **= inactivity**, apathy, drowsiness, indolence, laziness, lethargy, listlessness, sloth, sluggishness

torrent *noun* **1 = stream**, cascade, deluge, downpour, flood, flow, rush, spate, tide

torrid *adjective* **1 = arid**, dried, parched, scorched **2 = passionate**, ardent, fervent, intense, steamy (*inf*)

tortuous *adjective* **1 = winding**, circuitous, convoluted, indirect, mazy, meandering, serpentine, sinuous, twisting **2 = complicated**, ambiguous, convoluted, devious, indirect, involved, roundabout, tricky OPPOSITE direct

torture *verb* **1 = torment**, afflict, crucify, distress, persecute, put on the rack, rack OPPOSITE comfort ◆*noun* **2 = agony**, anguish, distress, pain, persecution, suffering, torment OPPOSITE delight

toss *verb* **1 = throw**, cast, fling, flip, hurl, launch, lob (*inf*), pitch, sling **2 = thrash**, rock, roll, shake, wriggle, writhe ◆*noun* **7 = throw**, lob (*inf*), pitch

tot¹ *noun* **1 = infant**, baby, child, mite, toddler **2 = measure**, dram, finger, nip, shot (*inf*), slug, snifter (*inf*)

tot² *verb* **tot up = add up**, calculate, count up, reckon, tally, total

total *noun* **1 = whole**, aggregate, entirety, full amount, sum, totality OPPOSITE part ◆*adjective* **2, 3 = complete**, absolute, comprehensive, entire, full, gross, overarching, thoroughgoing, undivided, utter, whole OPPOSITE part ◆*verb* **4 = amount to**, come to, mount up to, reach **5 = add up**, reckon, tot up OPPOSITE deduct

totalitarian *adjective* **= dictatorial**, authoritarian, despotic, oppressive, tyrannous,

tote[1] *verb* carry (a gun etc.).

tote[2] *noun* short for TOTALIZATOR.

totem *noun* tribal badge or emblem. **totem pole** post carved or painted with totems by Native Americans.

totter ⊙ *verb* **1** move unsteadily. **2** be about to fall.

toucan *noun* tropical American bird with a large bill.

touch ⊙ *verb* **1** come into contact with. **2** tap, feel, or stroke. **3** affect. **4** move emotionally. **5** eat or drink. **6** equal or match. **7** *Slang* ask for money. ◆ *noun* **8** sense by which an object's qualities are perceived when they come into contact with part of the body. **9** contact with the body. **10** gentle tap, push, or caress. **11** small amount. **12** characteristic style. **13** detail. **touch and go** risky or critical. **touched** *adjective* **1** emotionally moved. **2** slightly mad. **touching** *adjective* emotionally moving. **touchy** *adjective* easily offended. **touch base** make contact, renew communication. **touch down** *verb* (of an aircraft) land. **touchline** *noun* side line of the pitch in some games. **touch on** *verb* refer to in passing. **touch-type** *verb* type without looking at the keyboard. **touchy-feely** *adjective Informal, sometimes offens.* sensitive and caring.

touché [**too**-shay] *interjection*

acknowledgment of the striking home of a remark or witty reply.

touchstone ⊙ *noun* standard by which a judgment is made.

tough ⊙ *adjective* **1** strong or resilient. **2** difficult to chew or cut. **3** firm and determined. **4** rough and violent. **5** difficult. **6** *Informal* unlucky or unfair. ◆ *noun* **7** *Informal* rough violent person. **toughness** *noun* **toughen** *verb* make or become tough or tougher.

toupee [**too**-pay] *noun* small wig.

tour ⊙ *noun* **1** journey visiting places of interest along the way. **2** trip to perform or play in different places. ◆ *verb* **3** make a tour (of). **tourism** *noun* tourist travel as an industry. **tourist** *noun* person travelling for pleasure. **touristy** *adjective Informal often derogatory* full of tourists or tourist attractions.

tour de force *noun, pl* **tours de force** *French* brilliant stroke or achievement.

tourmaline *noun* crystalline mineral used for optical instruments and as a gem.

tournament ⊙ *noun* **1** sporting competition with several stages to decide the overall winner. **2** *Hist* contest between knights on horseback.

tourniquet [**tour**-nick-kay] *noun* something twisted round a limb to stop bleeding.

tousled *adjective* ruffled and untidy.

tout [rhymes with **shout**] *verb* **1** seek business

———————————— THESAURUS ————————————

undemocratic OPPOSITE **democratic**

totality *noun* **1** = **whole**, aggregate, entirety, sum, total

totally *adverb* **2** = **completely**, absolutely, comprehensively, entirely, fully, one hundred per cent, thoroughly, utterly, wholly

totter *verb* **1** = **falter 2** = **stagger**, lurch, reel, stumble, sway, wobble

touch *verb* **1** = **come into contact**, abut, adjoin, be in contact, border, contact, graze, impinge upon, meet **2** = **handle**, brush, caress, contact, feel, finger, fondle, stroke, tap **3** = **affect**, impress, influence, inspire **4** = **move**, disturb, stir **5** = **consume**, drink, eat, partake of **6** = **match**, compare with, equal, hold a candle to (*inf*), parallel, rival ◆*noun* **8** = **feeling**, handling, physical contact **9** = **contact**, brush, caress, stroke **10** = **tap**, pat **11** = **bit**, dash, drop, jot, small amount, smattering, *soupçon*, spot, trace **12** = **style**, manner, method, technique, trademark, way **touch on** = **refer to**, allude to, bring in, cover, deal with, mention, speak of

touch and go *adjective* = **risky**, close, critical, near, nerve-racking, precarious

touching *adjective* = **moving**, affecting,

emotive, pathetic, pitiable, poignant, sad, stirring

touchstone *noun* = **standard**, criterion, gauge, measure, norm, par, yardstick

touchy *adjective* = **oversensitive**, irascible, irritable, querulous, quick-tempered, testy, tetchy, thin-skinned OPPOSITE **easy-going**

tough *adjective* **1** = **resilient**, durable, hard, inflexible, leathery, resistant, rugged, solid, strong, sturdy OPPOSITE **delicate**. **3** = **firm**, hard, hardy, resolute, seasoned, stern, stout, strapping, strong, sturdy, unbending, vigorous **4** = **rough**, hard-bitten, merciless, pugnacious, ruthless, violent OPPOSITE **soft**. **5** = **difficult**, arduous, exacting, hard, laborious, strenuous, troublesome, uphill **6** *Inf* = **unlucky**, lamentable, regrettable, unfortunate ◆*noun* **7** *Inf* = **ruffian**, bruiser (*inf*), bully, hooligan, roughneck (*sl*), thug

tour *noun* **1** = **journey**, excursion, expedition, jaunt, outing, trip ◆*verb* **3** = **visit**, explore, go round, journey, sightsee, travel through

tourist *noun* = **traveller**, excursionist, globetrotter, holiday-maker, sightseer, tripper, voyager

tournament *noun* **1** = **competition**, contest,

in a persistent manner. **2** recommend (a person or thing). ♦ *noun* **3** person who sells tickets for a popular event at inflated prices.

tow¹ ❶ *verb* **1** drag, esp. by means of a rope. ♦ *noun* **2** towing. **in tow** following closely behind. **on tow** being towed. **towbar** *noun* metal bar on a car for towing vehicles.

towpath *noun* path beside a canal or river, originally for horses towing boats. **towrope** *noun* rope or cable used for towing a vehicle or vessel.

tow² *noun* fibre of hemp or flax.

towards, toward ❶ *preposition* **1** in the direction of. **2** with regard to. **3** as a contribution to.

towel *noun* **1** cloth for drying things. ♦ *verb* **-elling, -elled 2** dry or wipe with a towel. **throw in the towel** give up completely. **towelling** *noun* material used for making towels.

tower ❶ *noun* tall structure, often forming part of a larger building. **towering** *adjective* very tall or impressive. **tower block** tall building divided into flats or offices. **tower of strength** person who supports or comforts. **tower over** *verb* be much taller than.

town *noun* **1** group of buildings larger than a village. **2** central part of this. **3** people of a town. **township** *noun* **1** small town. **2** (in S Africa) urban settlement of Black or Coloured people. **town hall** large building used for council meetings, concerts, etc. **town planning** comprehensive planning of the physical and social development of a town.

toxaemia [tox-**seem**-ya] *noun* **1** blood poisoning. **2** high blood pressure in pregnancy.

toxic ❶ *adjective* **1** poisonous. **2** caused by poison. **toxicity** *noun* **toxicology** *noun* study of poisons. **toxin** *noun* poison of bacterial

origin.

toy ❶ *noun* **1** something designed to be played with. ♦ *adjective* **2** designed to be played with. **3** (of a dog) of a variety much smaller than is normal for that breed. **toy with** *verb* play or fiddle with.

toy-toy *S Afr noun* **1** dance of political protest. ♦ *verb* **2** perform this dance.

trace ❶ *verb* **1** locate or work out (the cause of something). **2** track down and find. **3** follow the course of. **4** copy exactly by drawing on a thin sheet of transparent paper set on top of the original. ♦ *noun* **5** track left by something. **6** minute quantity. **7** indication. **traceable** *adjective* **tracer** *noun* projectile which leaves a visible trail. **tracery** *noun* pattern of interlacing lines. **tracing** *noun* traced copy. **trace element** chemical element occurring in very small amounts in soil etc.

traces *plural noun* strap by which a horse pulls a vehicle. **kick over the traces** escape or defy control.

trachea [track-**kee**-a] *noun, pl* **tracheae** windpipe. **tracheotomy** [track-ee-**ot**-a-mee] *noun* surgical incision into the trachea.

track ❶ *noun* **1** rough road or path. **2** mark or trail left by the passage of anything. **3** railway line. **4** course for racing. **5** separate section on a record, tape, or CD. **6** course of action or thought. **7** endless band round the wheels of a tank, bulldozer, etc. ♦ *verb* **8** follow the trail or path of. **track down** *verb* hunt for and find. **track event** athletic sport held on a running track. **track record** past accomplishments of a person or organization. **track shoe** light running shoe fitted with spikes for better grip. **tracksuit** *noun* warm loose-fitting suit worn by athletes etc., esp. during training.

tract¹ ❶ *noun* **1** wide area. **2** *Anat* system of

————— T H E S A U R U S —————

event, meeting, series

tow¹ *verb* **1** = **drag**, draw, haul, lug, pull, tug, yank

towards *preposition* **1** = **in the direction of**, en route for, for, on the way to, to **2** = **regarding**, about, concerning, for, with regard to, with respect to

tower *noun* = **column**, belfry, obelisk, pillar, skyscraper, steeple, turret

towering *adjective* **a** = **tall**, colossal, elevated, high, lofty, soaring **b** = **impressive**, imposing, magnificent

toxic *adjective* **1** = **poisonous**, deadly, harmful, lethal, noxious, pernicious, pestilential, septic

OPPOSITE> **harmless**

toy *noun* **1** = **plaything**, doll, game ♦*verb* (with

with) = **play**, amuse oneself with, dally with, fool (about *or* around) with, trifle

trace *verb* **2** = **find**, detect, discover, ferret out, hunt down, track, unearth **3** = **outline**, draw, sketch **4** = **copy** ♦*noun* **5** = **track**, footmark, footprint, footstep, path, spoor, trail **6** = **bit**, drop, hint, shadow, suggestion, suspicion, tinge, touch, whiff **7** = **remnant**, evidence, indication, mark, record, sign, survival, vestige

track *noun* **1** = **path**, course, line, orbit, pathway, road, trajectory, way **2** = **trail**, footmark, footprint, footstep, mark, path, spoor, trace, wake **3** = **line**, permanent way, rails ♦*verb* **8** = **follow**, chase, hunt down, pursue, shadow, stalk, tail (*inf*), trace, trail

track down *verb* = **find**, dig up, discover,

organs with a particular function.
tract² ❶ *noun* pamphlet, esp. a religious one.
tractable *adjective* easy to manage or
control.
traction ❶ *noun* **1** pulling, esp. by engine
power. **2** *Med* application of a steady pull on an
injured limb by weights and pulleys. **3** grip of
the wheels of a vehicle on the ground. **traction
engine** old-fashioned steam-powered vehicle
for pulling heavy loads.
tractor *noun* motor vehicle with large rear
wheels for pulling farm machinery.
trade ❶ *noun* **1** buying, selling, or exchange
of goods. **2** person's job or craft. **3** (people
engaged in) a particular industry or business. ◆
verb **4** buy and sell. **5** exchange. **6** engage in
trade. **trader** *noun* **trading** *noun* **trade-in**
noun used article given in part payment for a
new one. **trademark** *noun* (legally registered)
name or symbol used by a firm to distinguish
its goods. **trade-off** *noun* exchange made as a
compromise. **trade secret** secret formula,
technique, or process known and used to
advantage by only one manufacturer.
tradesman *noun* **1** skilled worker. **2**
shopkeeper. **trade union** society of workers
formed to protect their interests. **trade wind**
wind blowing steadily towards the equator.
tradescantia [trad-dess-**kan**-shee-a] *noun*
widely cultivated plant with striped variegated
leaves.
tradition ❶ *noun* **1** handing down from
generation to generation of customs and

beliefs. **2** body of beliefs, customs, etc. handed
down from generation to generation. **3** custom
or practice of long standing. **traditional**
adjective **traditionally** *adverb* **traditionalist**
noun person who supports established customs
or beliefs. **traditionalism** *noun*
traduce *verb* slander.
traffic ❶ *noun* **1** vehicles coming and going
on a road. **2** (illicit) trade. ◆ *verb* **-ficking,
-ficked 3** trade, usu. illicitly. **trafficker** *noun*
traffic lights set of coloured lights at a
junction to control the traffic flow. **traffic
warden** person employed to control the
movement and parking of traffic.
tragedy ❶ *noun, pl* **-dies 1** shocking or sad
event. **2** serious play, film, etc. in which the
hero is destroyed by a personal failing in
adverse circumstances. **tragedian** [traj-**jee**-
dee-an], **tragedienne** [traj-jee-dee-**enn**] *noun*
person who acts in or writes tragedies. **tragic**
adjective of or like a tragedy. **tragically** *adverb*
tragicomedy *noun* play with both tragic and
comic elements.
trail ❶ *noun* **1** path, track, or road. **2** tracks left
by a person, animal, or object. ◆ *verb* **3** drag
along the ground. **4** lag behind. **5** follow the
tracks of. **trailer** *noun* **1** vehicle designed to be
towed by another vehicle. **2** extract from a film
or programme used to advertise it. **trailer park**
noun US site for parking mobile homes.
train ❶ *verb* **1** instruct in a skill. **2** learn the
skills needed to do a particular job or activity. **3**
prepare for a sports event etc. **4** aim (a gun

——————— THESAURUS ———————

hunt down, run to earth *or* ground, sniff out,
trace, unearth
tract¹ *noun* **1** = **area**, district, expanse, extent,
plot, region, stretch, territory
tract² *noun* = **treatise**, booklet, dissertation,
essay, homily, monograph, pamphlet
traction *noun* **1** = **pulling**, pull **3** = **grip**,
friction, purchase, resistance
trade *noun* **1** = **commerce**, barter, business,
dealing, exchange, traffic, transactions, truck **2**
= **job**, business, craft, employment, line of
work, métier, occupation, profession ◆*verb* **4**
= **deal**, bargain, cut a deal, do business, have
dealings, peddle, traffic, transact, truck **5**
= **exchange**, barter, swap, switch
trader *noun* = **dealer**, merchant, purveyor,
seller, supplier
tradesman *noun* **1** = **craftsman**, artisan,
journeyman, workman **2** = **shopkeeper**, dealer,
merchant, purveyor, retailer, seller, supplier,
vendor
tradition *noun* **2** = **lore**, folklore **3** = **custom**,

convention, habit, institution, ritual
traditional *adjective* **3** = **customary**,
accustomed, conventional, established, old,
time-honoured, usual OPPOSITE **new**
traffic *noun* **1** = **transport**, freight,
transportation, vehicles **2** = **trade**, business,
commerce, dealings, exchange, peddling, truck
◆*verb* **3** = **trade**, bargain, cut a deal, deal, do
business, exchange, have dealings, peddle
tragedy *noun* **1** = **disaster**, adversity, calamity,
catastrophe, misfortune OPPOSITE **success**
tragic *adjective* = **distressing**, appalling,
calamitous, catastrophic, deadly, dire,
disastrous, dreadful, miserable, mournful,
pathetic, sad, unfortunate OPPOSITE **lucky**
trail *noun* **1** = **path**, footpath, road, route,
track, way **2** = **tracks**, footprints, marks, path,
scent, spoor, trace, wake ◆*verb* **3** = **drag**,
dangle, draw, haul, pull, tow **4** = **lag**, dawdle,
follow, hang back, linger, loiter, straggle,
traipse (*inf*) **5** = **follow**, chase, hunt, pursue,
shadow, stalk, tail (*inf*), trace, track

T

etc.). **5** cause (an animal) to perform or (a plant) to grow in a particular way. ◆ *noun* **6** line of railway coaches or wagons drawn by an engine. **7** sequence or series. **8** long trailing back section of a dress. **trainer** *noun* **1** person who trains an athlete or sportsman. **2** person who trains racehorses. **3** piece of equipment employed in training, such as a simulated aircraft cockpit. **4** sports shoe. **trainee** *noun* person being trained. **train spotter** person who collects the numbers of railway trains.

traipse ➊ *verb Informal* walk wearily.

trait ➊ *noun* characteristic feature.

traitor ➊ *noun* person guilty of treason or treachery. **traitorous** *adjective*

trajectory ➊ *noun, pl* **-ries** line of flight, esp. of a projectile.

tram *noun* public transport vehicle powered by an overhead wire and running on rails laid in the road. **tramlines** *plural noun* track for trams.

tramp ➊ *verb* **1** travel on foot, hike. **2** walk heavily. ◆ *noun* **3** homeless person who travels on foot. **4** hike. **5** sound of tramping. **6** cargo ship available for hire. **7** *US & Aust slang* promiscuous woman.

trample ➊ *verb* tread on and crush.

trampoline *noun* **1** tough canvas sheet attached to a frame by springs, used by acrobats etc. ◆ *verb* **2** bounce on a trampoline.

trance ➊ *noun* unconscious or dazed state.

tranche *noun* portion of something large, esp. a sum of money.

tranquil ➊ *adjective* calm and quiet.

tranquilly *adverb* **tranquillity** *noun*

tranquillize *verb* make calm. **tranquillizer** *noun* drug which reduces anxiety or tension.

trans- *prefix* across, through, or beyond.

transact ➊ *verb* conduct or negotiate (a business deal). **transaction** *noun* business deal transacted.

transatlantic *adjective* on, from, or to the other side of the Atlantic.

transceiver *noun* transmitter and receiver of radio or electronic signals.

transcend ➊ *verb* **1** rise above. **2** be superior to. **transcendence** *noun* **transcendent** *adjective* **transcendental** *adjective* **1** based on intuition rather than experience. **2** supernatural or mystical. **transcendentalism** *noun*

transcribe ➊ *verb* **1** write down (something said). **2** record for a later broadcast. **3** arrange (music) for a different instrument. **transcript** *noun* copy.

transducer *noun* device that converts one form of energy to another.

transept *noun* either of the two shorter wings of a cross-shaped church.

transfer ➊ *verb* **-ferring, -ferred** **1** move or send from one person or place to another. ◆ *noun* **2** transferring. **3** design which can be transferred from one surface to another. **transferable** *adjective* **transference** *noun* transferring.

transfigure *verb* change in appearance.

——————— THESAURUS ———————

train *verb* **1** = **instruct**, coach, drill, educate, guide, prepare, school, teach, tutor **3** = **exercise**, prepare, work out **4** = **aim**, direct, focus, level, point ◆*noun* **7** = **sequence**, chain, progression, series, set, string, succession

trainer *noun* **1** = **coach**

traipse *verb Inf* = **trudge**, drag oneself, slouch, trail, tramp

trait *noun* = **characteristic**, attribute, feature, idiosyncrasy, mannerism, peculiarity, quality, quirk

traitor *noun* = **betrayer**, apostate, backstabber, defector, deserter, Judas, quisling, rebel, renegade, turncoat

trajectory *noun* = **path**, course, flight path, line, route, track

tramp *verb* **1** = **hike**, march, ramble, roam, rove, slog, trek, walk **2** = **trudge**, plod, stump, toil, traipse (*inf*) ◆*noun* **3** = **vagrant**, derelict, down-and-out, drifter **4** = **hike**, march, ramble, slog, trek **5** = **tread**, footfall, footstep

trample *verb* = **crush**, flatten, run over, squash, stamp, tread, walk over

trance *noun* = **daze**, abstraction, dream, rapture, reverie, stupor, unconsciousness

tranquil *adjective* = **calm**, peaceful, placid, quiet, restful, sedate, serene, still, undisturbed
OPPOSITE▷ **troubled**

tranquillize *verb* = **calm**, lull, outspan (*S Afr*), pacify, quell, quiet, relax, sedate, settle one's nerves, soothe

tranquillizer *noun* = **sedative**, barbiturate, bromide, downer (*sl*), opiate

transaction *noun* = **deal**, bargain, business, enterprise, negotiation, undertaking

transcend *verb* **1** = **rise above** **2** = **surpass**, eclipse, exceed, excel, go beyond, outdo, outstrip

transcendent *adjective* **2** = **unparalleled**, consummate, incomparable, matchless, preeminent, sublime, unequalled, unrivalled

transcribe *verb* **1** = **write out**, copy out, reproduce, take down, transfer

transcript *noun* = **copy**, duplicate, manuscript, record, reproduction, transcription

transfer *verb* **1** = **move**, change, convey,

transfiguration *noun*
transfix ⊙ *verb* **1** astound or stun. **2** pierce through.
transform ⊙ *verb* change the shape or character of. **transformation** *noun*
transformer *noun* device for changing the voltage of an alternating current.
transfusion *noun* injection of blood into the blood vessels of a patient. **transfuse** *verb* **1** give a transfusion to. **2** permeate or infuse.
transgress ⊙ *verb* break (a moral law). **transgression** *noun* **transgressor** *noun*
transient ⊙ *adjective* lasting only for a short time. **transience** *noun*
transistor *noun* **1** semiconducting device used to amplify electric currents. **2** portable radio using transistors. **transistorized** *adjective*
transit ⊙ *noun* movement from one place to another. **transition** *noun* change from one state to another. **transitional** *adjective* **transitive** *adjective Grammar* (of a verb) requiring a direct object. **transitory** *adjective* not lasting long.
translate ⊙ *verb* turn from one language into another. **translatable** *adjective* **translation** *noun* **1** piece of writing or speech translated into another language. **2** *Maths* transformation in which the origin of a coordinate system is moved to another position so that each axis retains the samedirection. **translator** *noun*
transliterate *verb* convert to the letters of a

different alphabet. **transliteration** *noun*
translucent *adjective* letting light pass through, but not transparent. **translucency**, **translucence** *noun*
transmigrate *verb* (of a soul) pass into another body. **transmigration** *noun*
transmit ⊙ *verb* **-mitting, -mitted 1** pass (something) from one person or place to another. **2** send out (signals) by radio waves. **3** broadcast (a radio or television programme). **transmission** *noun* **1** transmitting. **2** shafts and gears through which power passes from a vehicle's engine to its wheels. **transmittable** *adjective* **transmitter** *noun* **1** piece of equipment used for broadcasting radio or television programmes. **2** person or thing that transmits.
transmogrify *verb* **-fying, -fied** *Informal* change completely.
transmute *verb* change the form or nature of. **transmutation** *noun*
transom *noun* **1** horizontal bar across a window. **2** bar separating a door from the window over it.
transparent ⊙ *adjective* **1** able to be seen through, clear. **2** easily understood or recognized. **transparently** *adverb*
transparency *noun* **1** transparent quality. **2** *pl* **-cies** colour photograph on transparent film that can be viewed by means of a projector.
transpire ⊙ *verb* **1** become known. **2** *Informal*

——————————————— THESAURUS ———————————————

hand over, pass on, relocate, shift, transplant, transport, transpose ♦*noun* **2 = move**, change, handover, relocation, shift, transference, translation, transmission, transposition
transfix *verb* **1 = stun**, engross, fascinate, hold, hypnotize, mesmerize, paralyse OPPOSITE **bore. 2 = pierce**, impale, puncture, run through, skewer, spear
transform *verb* **=change**, alter, convert, remodel, revolutionize, transmute
transformation *noun* **=change**, alteration, conversion, metamorphosis, revolution, sea change, transmutation
transgress *verb* **=break**, break the law, contravene, disobey, exceed, go beyond, infringe, offend, overstep, sin, trespass, violate
transgression *noun* **=crime**, contravention, infraction, infringement, misdeed, misdemeanour, offence, sin, trespass, violation
transient *adjective* **=brief**, ephemeral, fleeting, impermanent, momentary, passing, short-lived, temporary, transitory
transit *noun* **=movement**, carriage, conveyance, crossing, passage, transfer,

transport, transportation
transition *noun* **=change**, alteration, conversion, development, metamorphosis, passing, progression, shift, transmutation
transitory *adjective* **=short-lived**, brief, ephemeral, fleeting, impermanent, momentary, passing, short, temporary, transient
translate *verb* **=interpret**, construe, convert, decipher, decode, paraphrase, render
translation *noun* **1 = interpretation**, decoding, paraphrase, rendering, rendition, version
transmission *noun* **1 a = transfer**, conveyance, dissemination, sending, shipment, spread, transference **b = broadcasting**, dissemination, putting out, relaying, sending, showing
transmit *verb* **1 = pass on**, bear, carry, convey, disseminate, hand on, impart, send, spread, transfer **3 = broadcast**, disseminate, radio, relay, send out
transparency *noun* **1 = clarity**, clearness, limpidity, pellucidness, translucence OPPOSITE **opacity. 2 = photograph**, slide

T

happen. **3** give off water vapour through pores. **transpiration** *noun*

transplant ⊙ *verb* **1** transfer (an organ or tissue) surgically from one part or body to another. **2** remove and transfer (a plant) to another place. ◆ *noun* **3** surgical transplanting. **4** thing transplanted. **transplantation** *noun*

transport ⊙ *verb* **1** convey from one place to another. **2** *Hist* exile (a criminal) to a penal colony. **3** enrapture. ◆ *noun* **4** business or system of transporting. **5** vehicle used in transport. **6** ecstasy or rapture. **transportation** *noun* **transporter** *noun* large goods vehicle.

transpose ⊙ *verb* **1** interchange two things. **2** put (music) into a different key. **3** *Maths* move (a term) from one side of an equation to the other with a corresponding reversal in sign. **transposition** *noun*

transsexual, transexual *noun* **1** person of one sex who believes his or her true identity is of the opposite sex. **2** person who has had a sex-change operation.

transubstantiation *noun* Christianity doctrine that the bread and wine consecrated in Communion changes into the substance of Christ's body and blood.

transuranic [tranz-yoor-**ran**-ik] *adjective* (of an element) having an atomic number greater than that of uranium.

transverse *adjective* crossing from side to side.

transvestite *noun* person who seeks sexual pleasure by wearing the clothes of the opposite sex. **transvestism** *noun*

trap ⊙ *noun* **1** device for catching animals. **2** plan for tricking or catching a person. **3** situation from which it is difficult to escape. **4** bend in a pipe containing liquid to prevent the escape of gas. **5** stall in which greyhounds are enclosed before a race. **6** two-wheeled carriage. **7** *Slang* mouth. ◆ *verb* **trapping, trapped 8** catch. **9** trick. **trapper** *noun* person who traps animals for their fur. **trapdoor** *noun* door in floor or roof. **trap-door spider** spider that builds a silk-lined hole in the ground closed by a hinged door of earth and silk.

trapeze *noun* horizontal bar suspended from two ropes, used by circus acrobats.

trapezium *noun, pl* **-ziums, -zia** quadrilateral with two parallel sides of unequal length.

trapezoid [**trap**-piz-zoid] *noun* **1** quadrilateral with no sides parallel. **2** *Chiefly US* trapezium.

trappings ⊙ *plural noun* accessories that symbolize an office or position.

Trappist *noun* member of an order of Christian monks who observe strict silence.

trash ⊙ *noun* **1** anything worthless. **2** *US & Canad* rubbish. **trashy** *adjective*

trauma ⊙ [**traw**-ma] *noun* **1** emotional shock. **2** injury or wound. **traumatic** *adjective* **traumatically** *adverb* **traumatize** *verb*

travail *noun Lit* labour or toil.

travel ⊙ *verb* **-elling, -elled 1** go from one place to another, through an area, or for a

——————— THESAURUS ———————

transparent *adjective* **1** = **clear**, crystalline, diaphanous, limpid, lucid, see-through, sheer, translucent OPPOSITE **thick**. **2** = **obvious**, evident, explicit, manifest, patent, plain, recognizable, unambiguous, undisguised OPPOSITE **hidden**

transpire *verb* **1** = **become known**, come out, come to light, emerge **2** *Inf* = **happen**, arise, befall, chance, come about, occur, take place

transplant *verb* **2** = **transfer**, displace, relocate, remove, resettle, shift, uproot

transport *verb* **1** = **convey**, bear, bring, carry, haul, move, take, transfer **2** *Hist* = **exile**, banish, deport **3** = **enrapture**, captivate, delight, enchant, entrance, move, ravish ◆*noun* **4** = **vehicle**, conveyance, transportation **5** = **transference**, conveyance, shipment, transportation **6** = **ecstasy**, bliss, delight, enchantment, euphoria, heaven, rapture, ravishment

transpose *verb* **1** = **interchange**, alter, change, exchange, move, reorder, shift, substitute, swap, switch, transfer

trap *noun* **1** = **snare**, ambush, gin, net, noose, pitfall **2** = **trick**, ambush, deception, ruse, stratagem, subterfuge, wile ◆*verb* **8** = **catch**, corner, enmesh, ensnare, entrap, snare, take **9** = **trick**, ambush, beguile, deceive, dupe, ensnare, inveigle

trappings *plural noun* = **accessories**, accoutrements, equipment, finery, furnishings, gear, panoply, paraphernalia, things, trimmings

trash *noun* **1** = **nonsense**, drivel, hogwash, kak (*S Afr sl*), moonshine, poppycock (*inf*), rot, rubbish, tripe (*inf*), twaddle OPPOSITE **reason**. **2** *US* = **litter**, dross, garbage, junk (*inf*), refuse, rubbish, waste

trashy *adjective* **1** = **worthless**, cheap, inferior, rubbishy, shabby, shoddy, tawdry

trauma *noun* **1** = **shock**, anguish, ordeal, pain, suffering, torture **2** = **injury**, agony, damage, hurt, wound

traumatic *adjective* **1** = **shocking**, disturbing, painful, scarring, upsetting OPPOSITE **relaxing**. **2** = **wounding**, agonizing, damaging, hurtful, injurious

T

specified distance. ♦ *noun* **2** travelling, esp. as a tourist. ♦ *plural* **3** (account of) travelling.
traveller *noun* person who makes a journey or travels a lot. **travelogue** *noun* film or talk about someone's travels. **travel agency** agency that arranges holidays. **traveller's cheque** cheque sold by a bank to the bearer, who signs it on purchase and cashes it abroad by signing it again.
traverse ❶ *verb* move over or back and forth over.
travesty ❶ *noun, pl* **-ties 1** grotesque imitation or mockery. ♦ *verb* **-tying, -tied 2** make or be a travesty of.
trawl *noun* **1** net dragged at deep levels behind a fishing boat. ♦ *verb* **2** fish with such a net. **trawler** *noun* trawling boat.
tray *noun* **1** flat board, usu. with a rim, for carrying things. **2** open receptacle for office correspondence.
treachery ❶ *noun, pl* **-eries** wilful betrayal. **treacherous** *adjective* **1** disloyal. **2** unreliable or dangerous. **treacherously** *adverb*
treacle *noun* thick dark syrup produced when sugar is refined. **treacly** *adjective*
tread ❶ *verb* **treading, trod, trodden** or **trod 1** set one's foot on. **2** crush by walking on. ♦ *noun* **3** way of walking or dancing. **4**

upper surface of a step. **5** part of a tyre or shoe that touches the ground. **tread water** stay afloat in an upright position by moving the legs in a walking motion. **treadmill** *noun* **1** *Hist* cylinder turned by treading on steps projecting from it. **2** dreary routine.
treadle [**tred**-dl] *noun* lever worked by the foot to turn a wheel.
treason ❶ *noun* **1** betrayal of one's sovereign or country. **2** treachery or disloyalty. **treasonable, treasonous** *adjective*
treasure ❶ *noun* **1** collection of wealth, esp. gold or jewels. **2** valued person or thing. ♦ *verb* **3** prize or cherish. **treasurer** *noun* official in charge of funds. **treasury** *noun* **1** storage place for treasure. **2** (T-) government department in charge of finance. **treasure-trove** *noun* treasure found with no evidence of ownership.
treat ❶ *verb* **1** deal with or regard in a certain manner. **2** give medical treatment to. **3** subject to a chemical or industrial process. **4** provide (someone) with (something) as a treat. ♦ *noun* **5** pleasure, entertainment, etc. given or paid for by someone else. **treatment** *noun* **1** medical care. **2** way of treating a person or thing.
treatise ❶ [**treat**-izz] *noun* formal piece of writing on a particular subject.
treaty ❶ *noun, pl* **-ties** signed contract

——————— T H E S A U R U S ———————

travel *verb* **1** = **go**, journey, move, progress, roam, tour, trek, voyage, wander ♦*plural noun* **3** = **journey**, excursion, expedition, globetrotting, tour, trip, voyage, wandering
traveller *noun* = **voyager**, explorer, globetrotter, gypsy, holiday-maker, tourist, wanderer, wayfarer
traverse *verb* = **cross**, go over, span, travel over
travesty *noun* **1** = **mockery**, burlesque, caricature, distortion, lampoon, parody, perversion ♦*verb* **2** = **mock**, burlesque, caricature, lampoon, make a mockery of, parody, ridicule
treacherous *adjective* **1** = **disloyal**, deceitful, double-dealing, duplicitous, faithless, false, perfidious, traitorous, unfaithful, untrustworthy OPPOSITE **true**. **2** = **dangerous**, deceptive, hazardous, icy, perilous, precarious, risky, slippery, unreliable, unsafe, unstable OPPOSITE **safe**
treachery *noun* = **betrayal**, disloyalty, double-dealing, duplicity, faithlessness, infidelity, perfidy, treason
tread *verb* **1** = **step**, hike, march, pace, stamp, stride, walk **2** = **crush underfoot**, squash, trample ♦*noun* **3** = **step**, footfall, footstep, gait,

pace, stride, walk
treason *noun* = **disloyalty**, duplicity, lese-majesty, mutiny, perfidy, sedition, traitorousness, treachery
treasure *noun* **1** = **riches**, cash, fortune, gold, jewels, money, valuables, wealth **2** = **darling**, apple of one's eye, gem, jewel, nonpareil, paragon, pride and joy ♦*verb* **3** = **prize**, adore, cherish, esteem, hold dear, idolize, love, revere, value
treasury *noun* **1** = **storehouse**, bank, cache, hoard, repository, store, vault
treat *verb* **1** = **behave towards**, act towards, consider, deal with, handle, look upon, manage, regard, use **2** = **take care of**, attend to, care for, nurse **4** = **provide**, entertain, lay on, regale, stand (*inf*) ♦*noun* **5 a** = **pleasure**, delight, enjoyment, fun, joy, satisfaction, surprise, thrill **b** = **entertainment**, banquet, celebration, feast, gift, party, refreshment
treatise *noun* = **paper**, dissertation, essay, monograph, pamphlet, study, thesis, tract, work
treatment *noun* **1** = **care**, cure, healing, medication, medicine, remedy, surgery, therapy **2** = **handling**, action, behaviour, conduct, dealing, management, manipulation

T

between states.

treble *adjective* **1** triple. **2** *Music* high-pitched. ♦ *noun* **3** (singer with or part for) a soprano voice. ♦ *verb* **4** increase three times. **trebly** *adverb*

tree *noun* large perennial plant with a woody trunk. **treeless** *adjective* **tree kangaroo** tree-living kangaroo of New Guinea and N Australia. **tree surgery** repair of damaged trees. **tree surgeon**

trefoil [tref-foil] *noun* **1** plant, such as clover, with a three-lobed leaf. **2** carved ornament like this.

trek ⊙ *noun* **1** long difficult journey, esp. on foot. **2** *S Afr* migration by ox wagon. ♦ *verb* **trekking, trekked 3** make such a journey.

trellis *noun* framework of horizontal and vertical strips of wood.

tremble ⊙ *verb* **1** shake or quiver. **2** feel fear or anxiety. ♦ *noun* **3** trembling. **trembling** *adjective*

tremendous ⊙ *adjective* **1** huge. **2** *Informal* great in quality or amount. **tremendously** *adverb*

tremolo *noun*, *pl* **-los** *Music* quivering effect in singing or playing.

tremor ⊙ *noun* **1** involuntary shaking. **2** minor earthquake.

tremulous *adjective* trembling, as from fear or excitement. **tremulously** *adverb*

trench ⊙ *noun* long narrow ditch, esp. one used as a shelter in war. **trench coat** double-breasted waterproof coat.

trenchant *adjective* **1** incisive. **2** effective.

trencher *noun Hist* wooden plate for serving food. **trencherman** *noun* hearty eater.

trend ⊙ *noun* **1** general tendency or direction. **2** fashion. **trendy** *adjective, noun Informal* consciously fashionable (person). **trendiness** *noun* **trendsetter** *noun* person or thing that creates, or may create, a new fashion. **trendsetting** *adjective*

trepidation ⊙ *noun* fear or anxiety.

trespass ⊙ *verb* **1** go onto another's property without permission. ♦ *noun* **2** trespassing. **3** *Old-fashioned* sin or wrongdoing. **trespasser** *noun* **trespass on** *verb* take unfair advantage of (someone's friendship, patience, etc.).

tresses *plural noun* long flowing hair.

trestle *noun* board fixed on pairs of spreading legs, used as a support.

trevally *noun*, *pl* **-lies** *Aust & NZ* any of various food and game fishes.

trews *plural noun* close-fitting tartan trousers.

tri- *combining form* three.

triad *noun* **1** group of three. **2** (**T-**) Chinese criminal secret society.

trial ⊙ *noun* **1** *Law* investigation of a case before a judge. **2** trying or testing. **3** thing or person straining endurance or patience. ♦ *plural* **4** sporting competition for individuals. **trial and error** method of discovery based on practical experience and experiment rather than theory.

triangle *noun* **1** geometric figure with three sides. **2** triangular percussion instrument. **3** situation involving three people. **triangular** *adjective*

tribe ⊙ *noun* group of clans or families believed to have a common ancestor. **tribal**

———————————— THESAURUS ————————————

treaty *noun* =**agreement**, alliance, compact, concordat, contract, entente, pact

trek *noun* **1** =**journey**, expedition, hike, march, odyssey, safari, slog, tramp ♦*verb* **3** =**journey**, hike, march, slog, traipse (*inf*), tramp, trudge

tremble *verb* **1** =**shake**, quake, quiver, shiver, shudder, totter, vibrate, wobble ♦*noun* **3** =**shake**, quake, quiver, shiver, shudder, tremor, vibration, wobble

tremendous *adjective* **1** =**huge**, colossal, enormous, formidable, gigantic, great, immense, stupendous, terrific [OPPOSITE] little. **2** *Inf* =**excellent**, amazing, brilliant, exceptional, extraordinary, fantastic (*inf*), great, marvellous, sensational (*inf*), wonderful [OPPOSITE] average

tremor *noun* **1** =**shake**, quaking, quaver, quiver, shiver, trembling, wobble **2** =**earthquake**, quake (*inf*), shock

trench *noun* =**ditch**, channel, drain,

excavation, furrow, gutter, trough

trend *noun* **1** =**tendency**, bias, current, direction, drift, flow, inclination, leaning **2** =**fashion**, craze, fad (*inf*), mode, rage, style, thing, vogue

trendy *adjective Inf* =**fashionable**, in fashion, in vogue, modish, stylish, voguish, with it (*inf*)

trepidation *noun* =**anxiety**, alarm, apprehension, consternation, disquiet, dread, fear, nervousness, uneasiness, worry

trespass *verb* **1** =**intrude**, encroach, infringe, invade, obtrude ♦*noun* **2** =**intrusion**, encroachment, infringement, invasion, unlawful entry

trespasser *noun* =**intruder**, interloper, invader, poacher

trial *noun* **1** *Law* =**hearing**, litigation, tribunal **2** =**test**, audition, dry run (*inf*), experiment, probation, test-run **3** =**hardship**, adversity, affliction, distress, ordeal, suffering, tribulation,

adjective **tribalism** *noun* loyalty to a tribe.
tribulation *noun* great distress.
tribunal ❶ *noun* **1** board appointed to inquire into a specific matter. **2** lawcourt.
tribune *noun* people's representative, esp. in ancient Rome.
tributary *noun, pl* -**taries 1** stream or river flowing into a larger one. ♦ *adjective* **2** (of a stream or river) flowing into a larger one.
tribute ❶ *noun* **1** sign of respect or admiration. **2** tax paid by one state to another.
trice *noun* **in a trice** instantly.
triceps *noun* muscle at the back of the upper arm.
trichology [trick-ol-a-jee] *noun* study and treatment of hair and its diseases. **trichologist** *noun*
trick ❶ *noun* **1** deceitful or cunning action or plan. **2** joke or prank. **3** feat of skill or cunning. **4** deceptive illusion. **5** mannerism. **6** cards played in one round. ♦ *verb* **7** cheat or deceive.
trickery *noun* **trickster** *noun* **tricky** *adjective* **1** difficult, needing careful handling. **2** crafty.
trickle ❶ *verb* **1** (cause to) flow in a thin stream or drops. **2** move gradually. ♦ *noun* **3** gradual flow.
tricolour [trick-kol-lor] *noun* three-coloured striped flag.
tricycle *noun* three-wheeled cycle.
trident *noun* three-pronged spear.
triennial *adjective* happening every three years.
trifle ❶ *noun* **1** insignificant thing or amount. **2** dessert of sponge cake, fruit, custard, and

cream. **trifling** *adjective* insignificant. **trifle with** *verb* toy with.
trigger ❶ *noun* **1** small lever releasing a catch on a gun or machine. **2** action that sets off a course of events. ♦ *verb* **3** (usu. foll. by *off*) set (an action or process) in motion. **trigger-happy** *adjective* too quick to use guns.
trigonometry *noun* branch of mathematics dealing with relations of the sides and angles of triangles.
trike *noun Informal* tricycle.
trilateral *adjective* having three sides.
trilby *noun, pl* -**bies** man's soft felt hat.
trill *noun* **1** *Music* rapid alternation between two notes. **2** shrill warbling sound made by some birds. ♦ *verb* **3** play or sing a trill.
trillion *noun* **1** one million million, 10^{12}. **2** *Brit* (formerly) one million million million, 10^{18}.
trilobite [trile-oh-bite] *noun* small prehistoric sea animal.
trilogy [trill-a-jee] *noun, pl* -**gies** series of three related books, plays, etc.
trim ❶ *adjective* **trimmer, trimmest 1** neat and smart. **2** slender. ♦ *verb* **trimming, trimmed 3** cut or prune into good shape. **4** decorate with lace, ribbons, etc. **5** adjust the balance of (a ship or aircraft) by shifting the cargo etc. **6** adjust the sails of a ship to take advantage of the wind. ♦ *noun* **7** decoration. **8** upholstery and decorative facings in a car. **9** trim state. **10** haircut that neatens the existing style. **trimming** *noun* **1** decoration. ♦ *plural* **2** usual accompaniments, e.g. *turkey with all the trimmings*.

——————— T H E S A U R U S ———————

trouble
tribe *noun* =**race**, clan, family, people
tribunal *noun* **2** =**hearing**, court, trial
tribute *noun* **1** =**accolade**, commendation, compliment, eulogy, panegyric, recognition, testimonial OPPOSITE **blame. 2** =**tax**, charge, homage, payment, ransom
trick *noun* **1** =**deception**, fraud, hoax, manoeuvre, ploy, ruse, stratagem, subterfuge, swindle, trap, wile **2** =**joke**, antic, jape, leg-pull (*Brit inf*), practical joke, prank, stunt **3** =**secret**, hang (*inf*), knack, know-how (*inf*), skill, technique **4** =**sleight of hand**, legerdemain **5** =**mannerism**, characteristic, foible, habit, idiosyncrasy, peculiarity, practice, quirk, trait ♦*verb* **7** =**deceive**, cheat, con (*inf*), dupe, fool, hoodwink, kid (*inf*), mislead, swindle, take in (*inf*), trap
trickery *noun* **1** =**deception**, cheating, chicanery, deceit, dishonesty, guile, jiggery-pokery (*inf, chiefly Brit*), monkey business (*inf*)

trickle *verb* **1** =**dribble**, drip, drop, exude, ooze, run, seep, stream ♦*noun* **3** =**dribble**, drip, seepage
tricky *adjective* **1** =**difficult**, complicated, delicate, knotty, problematic, risky, thorny, ticklish OPPOSITE **clear. 2** =**crafty**, artful, cunning, deceitful, devious, scheming, slippery, sly, wily OPPOSITE **open**
trifle *noun* **1** =**knick-knack**, bagatelle, bauble, plaything, toy **trifle with** ♦*verb* =**toy with**, dally with, mess about, play with
trifling *adjective* =**insignificant**, measly, negligible, paltry, trivial, unimportant, worthless
trigger *verb* **3** =**set off**, activate, cause, generate, produce, prompt, provoke, spark off, start OPPOSITE **stop**
trim *adjective* **1** =**neat**, dapper, natty (*inf*), shipshape, smart, spruce, tidy, well-groomed OPPOSITE **disorderly. 2** =**slender**, fit, shapely, sleek, slim, streamlined, svelte, willowy ♦*verb* **3** =**cut**, clip, crop, even up, pare, prune, shave,

T

trimaran [trime-a-ran] *noun* three-hulled boat.

trinitrotoluene *noun* full name for TNT.

trinity *noun, pl* **-ties 1** group of three. **2** (**T-**) *Christianity* union of three persons, Father, Son, and Holy Spirit, in one God.

trinket ✪ *noun* small or worthless ornament or piece of jewellery.

trio ✪ *noun, pl* **trios 1** group of three. **2** piece of music for three performers.

trip ✪ *noun* **1** journey to a place and back, esp. for pleasure. **2** stumble. **3** act of causing someone to stumble. **4** *Informal* hallucinogenic drug experience. **5** switch on a mechanism. ◆ *verb* **tripping, tripped 6** (cause to) stumble. **7** (often foll. by *up*) catch (someone) in a mistake. **8** move or tread lightly. **9** *Informal* experience the hallucinogenic effects of a drug. **tripper** *noun* tourist.

tripartite *adjective* involving or composed of three people or parts.

tripe *noun* **1** stomach of a cow used as food. **2** *Informal* nonsense.

triple ✪ *adjective* **1** having three parts. **2** (of musical time or rhythm) having three beats in each bar. **3** three times as great or as many. ◆ *verb* **4** increase three times. **triplet** *noun* one of three babies born at one birth. **triple jump** athletic event in which competitors make a hop, a step, and a jump as a continuous movement.

triplicate *adjective* triple. **in triplicate** in three copies.

tripod [tripe-pod] *noun* three-legged stand, stool, etc.

tripos [tripe-poss] *noun* final examinations for an honours degree at Cambridge University.

triptych [trip-tick] *noun* painting or carving on three hinged panels, often forming an altarpiece.

trite ✪ *adjective* (of a remark or idea) commonplace and unoriginal.

tritium *noun* radioactive isotope of hydrogen.

triumph ✪ *noun* **1** (happiness caused by) victory or success. ◆ *verb* **2** be victorious or successful. **3** rejoice over a victory. **triumphal** *adjective* celebrating a triumph. **triumphant** *adjective* feeling or showing triumph. **triumphantly** *adverb*

triumvirate [try-umm-vir-rit] *noun* group of three people in joint control.

trivalent *adjective Chem* **1** having a valency of three. **2** having three valencies. **trivalency** *noun*

trivet [triv-vit] *noun* metal stand for a pot or kettle.

trivial ✪ *adjective* of little importance. **trivially** *adverb* **trivia** *plural noun* trivial things or details. **triviality** *noun* **trivialize** *verb* make (something) seem less important or complex than it is.

trod *verb* past tense and a past participle of TREAD.

trodden *verb* a past participle of TREAD.

troglodyte *noun* cave dweller.

———————— THESAURUS ————————

tidy **4** = **decorate**, adorn, array, beautify, deck out, dress, embellish, ornament ◆*noun* **7** = **decoration**, adornment, border, edging, embellishment, frill, ornamentation, piping, trimming **9** = **condition**, fettle, fitness, health, shape (*inf*), state, wellness **10** = **cut**, clipping, crop, shave, tidying up

trimming *noun* **1** = **decoration**, adornment, border, edging, embellishment, frill, ornamentation, piping ◆*plural noun* **2** = **extras**, accessories, accompaniments, frills, ornaments, paraphernalia, trappings

trinket *noun* = **ornament**, bagatelle, bauble, knick-knack, toy, trifle

trio *noun* **1** = **threesome**, triad, trilogy, trinity, triumvirate

trip *noun* **1** = **journey**, errand, excursion, expedition, foray, jaunt, outing, run, tour, voyage **2** = **stumble**, fall, misstep, slip ◆*verb* **6** = **stumble**, fall, lose one's footing, misstep, slip, tumble **7** = **catch out**, trap **8** = **skip**, dance, gambol, hop

triple *adjective* **1** = **threefold**, three-way,

tripartite ◆*verb* **4** = **treble**, increase threefold

trite *adjective* = **unoriginal**, banal, clichéd, commonplace, hackneyed, stale, stereotyped, threadbare, tired

triumph *noun* **1 a** = **joy**, elation, exultation, happiness, jubilation, pride, rejoicing **b** = **success**, accomplishment, achievement, attainment, conquest, coup, feat, victory OPPOSITE **defeat** ◆*verb* **2** = **succeed**, overcome, prevail, prosper, vanquish, win OPPOSITE **lose**. **3** = **rejoice**, celebrate, crow, exult, gloat, glory, revel

triumphant *adjective* **a** = **victorious**, cock-a-hoop, conquering, elated, exultant, proud, successful, winning OPPOSITE **beaten**. **b** = **celebratory**, jubilant

trivia *plural noun* = **minutiae**, details, trifles, trivialities

trivial *adjective* = **unimportant**, incidental, inconsequential, insignificant, meaningless, minor, petty, small, trifling, worthless

trivialize *verb* = **undervalue**, belittle, laugh off, make light of, minimize, play down, scoff

troika noun 1 Russian vehicle drawn by three horses abreast. 2 group of three people in authority.

Trojan adjective 1 of Ancient Troy. ◆ noun 2 person from ancient Troy. 3 hard-working person. **Trojan Horse** trap intended to undermine an enemy.

troll[1] noun giant or dwarf in Scandinavian folklore.

troll[2] verb fish by dragging a baited hook through the water.

trolley noun 1 small wheeled table for food and drink. 2 wheeled cart for moving goods. **trolley bus** bus powered by electricity from an overhead wire but not running on rails.

trollop noun promiscuous or slovenly woman.

trombone noun brass musical instrument with a sliding tube. **trombonist** noun

troop ⊕ noun 1 large group. 2 artillery or cavalry unit. 3 Scout company. ◆ plural 4 soldiers. ◆ verb 5 move in a crowd. 6 Brit mil parade (the colour or flag of a regiment) ceremonially. **trooper** noun cavalry soldier.

trope noun figure of speech.

trophy ⊕ noun, pl **-phies** 1 cup, shield, etc. given as a prize. 2 memento of success.

tropic ⊕ noun 1 either of two lines of latitude at 23½°N **(tropic of Cancer)** or 23½°S **(tropic of Capricorn)**. ◆ plural 2 part of the earth's surface between these lines. **tropical** adjective 1 of or in the tropics. 2 (of climate) very hot.

tropism noun tendency of a plant or animal to turn or curve in response to an external stimulus.

troposphere noun lowest layer of the earth's atmosphere.

trot ⊕ verb **trotting, trotted** 1 (of a horse) move at a medium pace, lifting the feet in diagonal pairs. 2 (of a person) move at a steady brisk pace. ◆ noun 3 trotting. **trotter** noun pig's foot. **trot out** verb repeat (old ideas etc.) without fresh thought.

troth [rhymes with **growth**] noun Obs pledge of devotion, esp. a betrothal.

Trotskyist, Trotskyite noun, adjective (supporter) of the theories of Leon Trotsky, Russian communist writer.

troubadour [troo-bad-oor] noun medieval travelling poet and singer.

trouble ⊕ noun 1 (cause of) distress or anxiety. 2 disease or malfunctioning. 3 state of disorder or unrest. 4 care or effort. ◆ verb 5 (cause to) worry. 6 exert oneself. 7 cause inconvenience to. **troubled** adjective **troublesome** adjective **troublemaker** noun person who causes trouble, esp. between people. **troubleshooter** noun person employed to locate and deal with faults or problems. **trouble spot** place where there is frequent fighting or violence.

trough ⊕ [troff] noun 1 long open container, esp. for animals' food or water. 2 narrow channel between two waves or ridges. 3 low point in a cycle. 4 Meteorol area of low pressure.

trounce ⊕ verb defeat utterly.

troupe ⊕ [troop] noun company of performers. **trouper** noun

———————— THESAURUS ————————

at, underestimate, underplay

troop noun 1 = **group**, band, body, crowd, horde, multitude, team, unit 2 = **company**, squad ◆plural 4 = **soldiers**, armed forces, army, men, servicemen, soldiery ◆verb 5 = **flock**, march, stream, swarm, throng, traipse (inf)

trophy noun 1 = **prize**, award, booty, cup 2 = **memento**, laurels, souvenir, spoils

tropical adjective 2 = **hot**, steamy, stifling, sultry, sweltering, torrid

trot verb 1, 2 = **run**, canter, jog, lope, scamper ◆noun 3 = **run**, canter, jog, lope

trouble noun 1 = **distress**, anxiety, disquiet, grief, misfortune, pain, sorrow, torment, woe, worry [OPPOSITE] pleasure. 2 = **ailment**, complaint, defect, disease, disorder, failure, illness, malfunction 3 = **disorder**, agitation, bother (inf), commotion, discord, disturbance, strife, tumult, unrest [OPPOSITE] peace. 4 = **effort**, care, exertion, inconvenience, labour, pains, thought, work [OPPOSITE] facility ◆verb 5

= **bother**, disconcert, distress, disturb, pain, perturb, plague, sadden, upset, worry [OPPOSITE] please. 6 = **take pains**, exert oneself, make an effort, take the time [OPPOSITE] avoid. 7 = **inconvenience**, bother, burden, disturb, impose upon, incommode, put out [OPPOSITE] relieve

troublesome adjective 1 = **bothersome**, annoying, demanding, difficult, inconvenient, irksome, taxing, tricky, trying, vexatious, worrying [OPPOSITE] easy. 3 = **disorderly**, rebellious, rowdy, turbulent, uncooperative, undisciplined, unruly, violent [OPPOSITE] disciplined

trough noun 1 = **manger**, water trough 2 = **channel**, canal, depression, ditch, duct, furrow, gully, gutter, trench

trounce verb = **defeat utterly**, beat, crush, drub, give a hiding (inf), hammer (inf), rout, slaughter (inf), thrash, wipe the floor with (inf)

troupe noun = **company**, band, cast

T

trousers *plural noun* two-legged outer garment with legs reaching usu. to the ankles. **trouser** *adjective* of trousers.

trousseau [troo-so] *noun, pl* **-seaux, -seaus** bride's collection of clothing etc. for her marriage.

trout *noun* game fish related to the salmon.

trowel *noun* hand tool with a wide blade for spreading mortar, lifting plants, etc.

troy weight, troy *noun* system of weights used for gold, silver, and jewels.

truant ❶ *noun* pupil who stays away from school without permission. **play truant** stay away from school without permission. **truancy** *noun*

truce ❶ *noun* temporary agreement to stop fighting.

truck[1] *noun* **1** railway goods wagon. **2** lorry.

truck[2] *noun* **have no truck with** refuse to be involved in.

trucker *noun US & Canad* truck driver.

truckle bed *noun* low bed on wheels, stored under a larger bed.

truculent [truck-yew-lent] *adjective* aggressively defiant. **truculence** *noun*

trudge ❶ *verb* **1** walk heavily or wearily. ♦ *noun* **2** long tiring walk.

true ❶ *adjective* **truer, truest 1** in accordance with facts. **2** genuine. **3** faithful. **4** exact. **truly** *adverb* **1** in a true manner. **2** really. **truism** *noun* self-evident truth. **truth** *noun* **1** state of being true. **2** something true. **truthful** *adjective* **1** honest. **2** exact. **truthfully** *adverb* **true-blue** *adjective* fiercely loyal. **true blue** *Brit* staunch Royalist or Conservative.

truffle *noun* **1** edible underground fungus. **2** sweet flavoured with chocolate.

trug *noun* long shallow basket used by gardeners.

trump[1] *noun, adjective* **1** (card) of the suit outranking the others. ♦ *verb* **2** play a trump card on (another card). ♦ *plural noun* **3** suit outranking the others. **turn up trumps** achieve an unexpected success. **trumped up** invented or concocted.

trump[2] *noun Lit* (sound of) a trumpet.

trumpery *noun, pl* **-eries 1** something useless or worthless. ♦ *adjective* **2** useless or worthless.

trumpet *noun* **1** valved brass instrument with a flared tube. ♦ *verb* **-peting, -peted 2** proclaim loudly. **3** (of an elephant) cry loudly. **trumpeter** *noun*

truncate ❶ *verb* cut short.

truncheon *noun* small club carried by a policeman.

trundle *verb* move heavily on wheels.

trunk ❶ *noun* **1** main stem of a tree. **2** large case or box for clothes etc. **3** person's body excluding the head and limbs. **4** elephant's long nose. **5** *US* car boot. ♦ *plural* **6** man's swimming shorts. **trunk call** long-distance telephone call. **trunk road** main road.

truss ❶ *verb* **1** tie or bind up. ♦ *noun* **2** device for holding a hernia in place. **3** framework supporting a roof, bridge, etc.

trust ❶ *verb* **1** believe in and rely on. **2** consign to someone's care. **3** expect or hope. ♦ *noun* **4** confidence in the truth, reliability, etc. of a person or thing. **5** obligation arising from responsibility. **6** arrangement in which one person administers property, money, etc. on another's behalf. **7** property held for another. **8** *Brit* self-governing hospital or group of hospitals within the National Health Service. **9** group of companies joined to control a market. **trustee** *noun* person holding property on another's behalf. **trustful, trusting** *adjective* inclined to trust others. **trustworthy** *adjective* reliable or honest. **trusty** *adjective* faithful or reliable. **trust fund** money or securities held in trust.

————————— T H E S A U R U S —————————

truancy *noun* =**absence**, absence without leave, malingering, shirking, skiving (*Brit sl*)

truant *noun* =**absentee**, malingerer, piker (*Aust & NZ sl*), runaway, shirker, skiver (*Brit sl*)

truce *noun* =**ceasefire**, armistice, cessation, let-up (*inf*), lull, moratorium, peace, respite

trudge *verb* **1** =**plod**, lumber, slog, stump, traipse (*inf*), tramp, trek ♦*noun* **2** =**tramp**, hike, march, slog, traipse (*inf*), trek

true *adjective* **1** =**correct**, accurate, factual, precise, right, truthful, veracious [OPPOSITE] **false**. **2** =**genuine**, authentic, real **3** =**faithful**, dedicated, devoted, dutiful, loyal, reliable, staunch, steady, trustworthy [OPPOSITE] **untrue**. **4** =**exact**, accurate, on target, perfect, precise,

spot-on (*Brit inf*), unerring [OPPOSITE] **incorrect**

truism *noun* =**cliché**, axiom, bromide, commonplace, platitude

truncate *verb* =**shorten**, abbreviate, curtail, cut short, dock, lop, pare, prune, trim

trunk *noun* **1** =**stem**, bole, stalk **2** =**chest**, box, case, casket, coffer, crate **3** =**body**, torso

truss *verb* **1** =**tie**, bind, fasten, make fast, secure, strap, tether ♦*noun* **2** =**support**, bandage **3** =**joist**, beam, brace, buttress, prop, stanchion, stay, strut, support

trust *verb* **1** =**believe in**, bank on, count on, depend on, have faith in, rely upon [OPPOSITE] **doubt**. **2** =**entrust**, assign, commit, confide, consign, delegate, give **3** =**expect**, assume,

truth ❶ *noun* see TRUE.

try ❶ *verb* **trying, tried 1** make an effort or attempt. **2** test or sample. **3** put strain on, e.g. *he tries my patience.* **4** investigate (a case). **5** examine (a person) in a lawcourt. ◆ *noun, pl* **tries 6** attempt or effort. **7** *Rugby* score gained by touching the ball down over the opponent's goal line. **try it on** *Informal* try to deceive or fool someone. **trying** *adjective Informal* difficult or annoying.

tryst *noun* arrangement to meet.

tsar, czar [zahr] *noun Hist* Russian emperor.

tsetse fly [tset-see] *noun* bloodsucking African fly whose bite transmits disease, esp. sleeping sickness.

T-shirt *noun* short-sleeved casual shirt or top.

tsp. teaspoon.

T-square *noun* T-shaped ruler.

tsunami *noun, pl* **-mis, -mi** tidal wave, usu. caused by an earthquake under the sea.

TT teetotal.

tub ❶ *noun* **1** open, usu. round container. **2** bath. **tubby** *adjective* (of a person) short and fat.

tuba [tube-a] *noun* valved low-pitched brass instrument.

tube *noun* **1** hollow cylinder. **2** flexible cylinder with a cap to hold pastes. **the tube** underground railway, esp. the one in London. **tubing** *noun* **1** length of tube. **2** system of tubes. **tubular** [tube-yew-lar] *adjective* of or shaped like a tube.

tuber [tube-er] *noun* fleshy underground root of a plant such as a potato. **tuberous** *adjective*

tubercle [tube-er-kl] *noun* small rounded swelling.

tuberculosis [tube-berk-yew-**lohss**-iss] *noun* infectious disease causing tubercles, esp. in the lungs. **tubercular** *adjective* **tuberculin** *noun* extract from a bacillus used to test for tuberculosis.

TUC Trades Union Congress.

tuck ❶ *verb* **1** push or fold into a small space. **2** thrust the loose ends or sides of (a shirt etc.) into a space. **3** stitch in folds. ◆ *noun* **4** stitched fold. **5** *Informal* food. **tuck away** *verb* **1** eat (a large amount of food). **2** store in a safe place.

tucker *noun Aust & NZ informal* food.

Tudor *adjective* **1** of the English royal house ruling from 1485-1603. **2** in an architectural style characterized by half-timbered buildings.

Tues. Tuesday.

Tuesday *noun* third day of the week.

tufa [tew-fa] *noun* porous rock formed as a deposit from springs.

tuffet *noun* small mound or seat.

tuft ❶ *noun* bunch of feathers, grass, hair, etc. held or growing together at the base. **tufted** *adjective*

tug ❶ *verb* **tugging, tugged 1** pull hard. ◆ *noun* **2** hard pull. **3** (also **tugboat**) small ship used to tow other vessels. **tug of war** contest in which two teams pull against one another on a rope.

tuition ❶ *noun* instruction, esp. received individually or in a small group.

tulip *noun* plant with bright cup-shaped flowers.

tulle [tewl] *noun* fine net fabric of silk etc.

tumble ❶ *verb* **1** (cause to) fall, esp. awkwardly or violently. **2** roll or twist, esp. in play. **3** rumple. ◆ *noun* **4** fall. **5** somersault.

———————— THESAURUS ————————

hope, presume, suppose, surmise ◆*noun* **4** =**confidence**, assurance, belief, certainty, conviction, credence, credit, expectation, faith, reliance

trustful, trusting *adjective* =**unsuspecting**, credulous, gullible, naive, unsuspicious, unwary

trustworthy *adjective* =**dependable**, honest, honourable, principled, reliable, reputable, responsible, staunch, steadfast, trusty

trusty *adjective* =**reliable**, dependable, faithful, solid, staunch, steady, strong, trustworthy

truth *noun* =**truthfulness**, accuracy, exactness, fact, genuineness, legitimacy, precision, reality, validity, veracity OPPOSITE> error

truthful *adjective* **1** =**honest**, candid, frank, sincere, straight, true, trustworthy OPPOSITE> lying. **2** =**true**, accurate, correct, precise OPPOSITE> made-up

try *verb* **1** =**attempt**, aim, endeavour, have a go, make an effort, seek, strive, struggle **2** =**test**, appraise, check out, evaluate, examine, investigate, put to the test, sample, taste ◆*noun* **6** =**attempt**, crack (*inf*), effort, go (*inf*), shot (*inf*), stab (*inf*), whack (*inf*)

trying *adjective Inf* =**annoying**, bothersome, difficult, exasperating, hard, stressful, taxing, tiresome, tough, wearisome

tubby *adjective* =**fat**, chubby, corpulent, obese, overweight, plump, portly, stout

tuck *verb* **1** =**push**, fold, gather, insert ◆*noun* **4** =**fold**, gather, pinch, pleat **5** *Inf* =**food**, grub (*sl*), nosh (*sl*)

tuft *noun* =**clump**, bunch, cluster, collection, knot, tussock

tug *verb* **1** =**pull**, jerk, wrench, yank ◆*noun* **2** =**pull**, jerk, yank

tuition *noun* =**training**, education, instruction,

T

tumbler *noun* **1** stemless drinking glass. **2** acrobat. **3** spring catch in a lock. **tumbledown** *adjective* dilapidated. **tumble dryer, drier** machine that dries laundry by rotating it in warm air. **tumble to** *verb Informal* realize, understand.

tumbril, tumbrel *noun* farm cart used during the French Revolution to take prisoners to the guillotine.

tumescent [tew-**mess**-ent] *adjective* swollen or becoming swollen.

tummy *noun, pl* -**mies** *Informal* stomach.

tumour ⊕ [**tew**-mer] *noun* abnormal growth in or on the body.

tumult ⊕ [**tew**-mult] *noun* uproar or commotion. **tumultuous** [tew-**mull**-tew-uss] *adjective*

tumulus [**tew**-mew-luss] *noun, pl* -**li** [-lie] burial mound.

tun *noun* large beer cask.

tuna [**tune**-a] *noun* large marine food fish.

tundra *noun* vast treeless Arctic region with permanently frozen subsoil.

tune ⊕ *noun* **1** (pleasing) sequence of musical notes. **2** correct musical pitch, e.g. *she sang out of tune*. ◆ *verb* **3** adjust (a musical instrument) so that it is in tune. **4** adjust (a machine) to obtain the desired performance. **tuneful** *adjective* **tunefully** *adverb* **tuneless** *adjective*

tuner *noun* part of a radio or television receiver for selecting channels. **tune in** *verb* adjust (a radio or television) to receive (a station or programme). **tuning fork** small steel instrument which produces a note of a fixed musical pitch when struck.

tungsten *noun Chem* greyish-white metal.

tunic *noun* **1** close-fitting jacket forming part of some uniforms. **2** loose knee-length garment.

tunnel ⊕ *noun* **1** underground passage. ◆ *verb* -**nelling, -nelled 2** make a tunnel (through).

tunnel vision 1 condition in which a person is unable to see things that are not straight in front of him or her. **2** narrowness of viewpoint caused by concentration on a single idea or opinion.

tunny *noun, pl* -**nies, -ny** same as TUNA.

tup *noun* male sheep.

tupik, tupek *noun Canad* (esp. in the Arctic) a tent of animal skins, a traditional type of Inuit dwelling.

turban *noun* Muslim, Hindu, or Sikh man's head covering, made by winding cloth round the head.

turbid *adjective* muddy, not clear.

turbine *noun* machine or generator driven by gas, water, etc. turning blades.

turbocharger *noun* device that increases the power of an internal-combustion engine by using the exhaust gases to drive a turbine.

turbofan *noun* engine in which a large fan driven by a turbine forces air rearwards to increase the thrust.

turboprop *noun* gas turbine for driving an aircraft propeller.

turbot *noun* large European edible flatfish.

turbulence ⊕ *noun* **1** confusion, movement, or agitation. **2** atmospheric instability causing gusty air currents. **turbulent** *adjective*

tureen *noun* serving dish for soup.

turf ⊕ *noun, pl* **turfs, turves 1** short thick even grass. **2** square of this with roots and soil attached. ◆ *verb* **3** cover with turf. **the turf 1** racecourse. **2** horse racing. **turf accountant** bookmaker. **turf out** *verb Informal* throw out.

turgid [**tur**-jid] *adjective* **1** (of language) pompous. **2** swollen and thick. **turgidity** *noun*

turkey *noun* large bird bred for food.

Turkish *adjective* **1** of Turkey, its people, or their language. ◆ *noun* **2** Turkish language. **Turkish bath** steam bath. **Turkish delight** jelly-like sweet coated with icing sugar.

turmeric *noun* yellow spice obtained from the root of an Asian plant.

lessons, schooling, teaching, tutelage, tutoring

tumble *verb* **1 = fall,** drop, flop, plummet, stumble, topple ◆*noun* **4 = fall,** drop, plunge, spill, stumble, trip

tumbledown *adjective* **= dilapidated,** crumbling, decrepit, munted (*NZ sl*), ramshackle, rickety, ruined

tumour *noun* **= growth,** cancer, carcinoma (*Path*), lump, sarcoma (*Med*), swelling

tumult *noun* **= commotion,** clamour, din, hubbub, pandemonium, riot, row, turmoil, upheaval, uproar OPPOSITE **peace**

tune *noun* **1 = melody,** air, song, strain, theme

2 = concord, consonance, euphony, harmony, pitch ◆*verb* **3 = adjust,** adapt, attune, harmonize, pitch, regulate

tunnel *noun* **1 = passage,** burrow, channel, hole, passageway, shaft, subway, underpass ◆*verb* **2 = dig,** burrow, excavate, mine, scoop out

turbulence *noun* **1 = confusion,** agitation, commotion, disorder, instability, tumult, turmoil, unrest, upheaval

turbulent *adjective* **1 = agitated,** foaming, furious, raging, tumultuous OPPOSITE **still. 2 = blustery,** choppy, rough, tempestuous

turf *noun* **1, 2 = grass,** sod, sward **the turf 2**

turmoil ❶ *noun* agitation or confusion.
turn ❶ *verb* 1 change the position or direction (of). 2 move around an axis, rotate. 3 (usu. foll. by *into*) change in nature or character. 4 reach or pass in age, time, etc., e.g. *she has just turned twenty*. 5 shape on a lathe. 6 become sour. ◆ *noun* 7 turning. 8 opportunity to do something as part of an agreed succession. 9 direction or drift. 10 period or spell. 11 short excursion. 12 slight attack of an illness. 13 short theatrical performance. **good, bad turn** helpful *or* unhelpful act. **turner** *noun* **turning** *noun* road or path leading off a main route. **turncoat** *noun* person who deserts one party or cause to join another. **turn down** *verb* 1 reduce the volume or brightness (of). 2 refuse or reject. **turn in** *verb* 1 go to bed. 2 hand in. **turning circle** smallest circle in which a vehicle can turn. **turning point** moment when a decisive change occurs. **turn off** *verb* stop (something) working by using a knob etc. **turn on** *verb* 1 start (something) working by using a knob etc. 2 become aggressive towards. 3 *Informal* excite, esp. sexually. **turnout** *noun* number of people appearing at a gathering. **turn out** *verb* 1 produce or create. 2 be discovered. 3 end up or result. **turnover** *noun* 1 total sales made by a business over a certain period. 2 small pastry. 3 rate at which staff leave and are replaced. **turnpike** *noun* road where a toll is collected at barriers. **turnstile**

noun revolving gate for admitting one person at a time. **turntable** *noun* revolving platform.
turn up *verb* 1 arrive or appear. 2 find or be found. 3 increase the volume or brightness (of).
turn-up *noun* 1 turned-up fold at the bottom of a trouser leg. 2 *Informal* unexpected event.
turnip *noun* root vegetable with orange or white flesh.
turpentine *noun* (oil made from) the resin of certain trees. **turps** *noun* turpentine oil.
turpitude *noun* wickedness.
turquoise *adjective* 1 blue-green. ◆ *noun* 2 blue-green precious stone.
turret *noun* 1 small tower. 2 revolving gun tower on a warship or tank. **turreted** *adjective*
turtle *noun* sea tortoise. **turn turtle** capsize.
turtledove *noun* small wild dove. **turtleneck** *noun* (sweater with) a round high close-fitting neck.
tusk *noun* long pointed tooth of an elephant, walrus, etc.
tussle ❶ *noun, verb* fight or scuffle.
tussock *noun* tuft of grass.
tutelage [tew-till-lij] *noun* 1 instruction or guidance, esp. by a tutor. 2 state of being supervised by a guardian or tutor. **tutelary** [tew-till-lar-ee] *adjective*
tutor ❶ *noun* 1 person teaching individuals or small groups. ◆ *verb* 2 act as a tutor to. **tutorial** *noun* period of instruction with a tutor.
tutti *adjective, adverb Music* to be performed

——————— T H E S A U R U S ———————

=horse-racing, racing, the flat
turmoil *noun* =**confusion**, agitation, chaos, commotion, disarray, disorder, tumult, upheaval
turn *verb* 1 =**change course**, move, shift, swerve, switch, veer, wheel 2 =**rotate**, circle, go round, gyrate, pivot, revolve, roll, spin, twist, whirl 3 (usu. foll. by *into*) =**change into**, alter, convert, mould, mutate into, remodel, shape, transform into 5 =**shape**, fashion, frame, make, mould 6 =**go bad**, curdle, go off (*Brit inf*), sour, spoil, taint ◆*noun* 7 =**rotation**, circle, cycle, gyration, revolution, spin, twist, whirl 8 =**opportunity**, chance, crack (*inf*), go, stint, time, try 9 =**direction**, drift, heading, tendency, trend
turncoat *noun* =**traitor**, apostate, backslider, defector, deserter, renegade
turn down *verb* 1 =**lower**, lessen, muffle, mute, quieten, soften 2 =**refuse**, decline, rebuff, reject, repudiate, spurn
turn in *verb* 1 =**go to bed**, go to sleep, hit the sack (*sl*) 2 =**hand in**, deliver, give up, hand over, return, submit, surrender, tender
turning *noun* =**turn-off**, bend, crossroads,

curve, junction, side road, turn
turning point *noun* =**crossroads**, change, crisis, crux, moment of truth
turn off *verb* =**stop**, cut out, put out, shut down, switch off, turn out, unplug
turn on *verb* 1 =**start**, activate, ignite, kick-start, start up, switch on 2 =**attack**, assail, assault, fall on, round on 3 *Inf* =**arouse**, attract, excite, please, stimulate, thrill, titillate
turnout *noun* =**attendance**, assembly, audience, congregation, crowd, gate, number, throng
turnover *noun* 1 =**output**, business, productivity 3 =**movement**, change, coming and going
turn up *verb* 1 =**arrive**, appear, attend, come, put in an appearance, show one's face, show up (*inf*) 2 a =**find**, dig up, disclose, discover, expose, reveal, unearth b =**come to light**, crop up (*inf*), pop up 3 =**increase**, amplify, boost, enhance, intensify, raise
tussle *noun* =**fight**, battle, brawl, conflict, contest, scrap (*inf*), scuffle, struggle ◆*verb* =**fight**, battle, grapple, scrap (*inf*), scuffle,

by the whole orchestra or choir.

tutti-frutti *noun* ice cream or other sweet food containing small pieces of candied or fresh fruits.

tutu *noun* short stiff skirt worn by ballerinas.

tuxedo *noun, pl* **-dos** *US & Canad* dinner jacket.

TV television.

twaddle ⊕ *noun* silly or pretentious talk or writing.

twain *noun Obs* two.

twang *noun* **1** sharp ringing sound. **2** nasal speech. ♦ *verb* **3** (cause to) make a twang. **twangy** *adjective*

tweak ⊕ *verb* **1** pinch or twist sharply. ♦ *noun* **2** tweaking.

twee *adjective Informal* too sentimental, sweet, or pretty.

tweed *noun* **1** thick woollen cloth. ♦ *plural* **2** suit of tweed. **tweedy** *adjective* **1** of or made of tweed. **2** showing a fondness for country life, often associated with wearers of tweed.

tweet *noun, verb* chirp. **tweeter** *noun* loudspeaker reproducing high-frequency sounds.

tweezers *plural noun* small pincer-like tool.

twelve *adjective, noun* two more than ten. **twelfth** *adjective, noun* (of) number twelve in a series.

twenty *adjective, noun* two times ten. **twentieth** *adjective, noun* **twenty-four-seven, 24/7** *adverb Informal* all the time.

twerp *noun Informal* silly person.

twice *adverb* two times.

twiddle *verb* fiddle or twirl in an idle way.

twiddle one's thumbs be bored, have nothing to do.

twig[1] *noun* small branch or shoot.

twig[2] ⊕ *verb* **twigging, twigged** *Informal* realize or understand.

twilight ⊕ *noun* **1** soft dim light just after sunset. **2** period in which strength or importance is gradually declining. **twilit** *adjective*

twill *noun* fabric woven to produce parallel ridges.

twin ⊕ *noun* **1** one of a pair, esp. of two children born at one birth. ♦ *verb* **twinning, twinned** **2** pair or be paired. **twin town** *Brit* town that has cultural and social links with a foreign town.

twine ⊕ *noun* **1** string or cord. ♦ *verb* **2** twist or coil round.

twinge ⊕ *noun* sudden sharp pain or emotional pang.

twinkle ⊕ *verb* **1** shine brightly but intermittently. ♦ *noun* **2** flickering brightness. **in the twinkling of an eye** in a very short time.

twirl ⊕ *verb* **1** turn or spin around quickly. **2** twist or wind, esp. idly.

twist ⊕ *verb* **1** turn out of the natural position. **2** distort or pervert. **3** wind or twine. ♦ *noun* **4** twisting. **5** twisted thing. **6** unexpected development in the plot of a film, book, etc. **7** bend or curve. **8** distortion. **twisted** *adjective* (of a person) cruel or perverted. **twister** *noun Informal* swindler.

twit[1] *verb* **twitting, twitted** poke fun at (someone).

twit[2] ⊕ *noun Informal* foolish person.

————— T H E S A U R U S —————

tutor *noun* **1** = **teacher**, coach, educator, guardian, guide, guru, instructor, lecturer, mentor ♦*verb* **2** = **teach**, coach, drill, educate, guide, instruct, school, train

twaddle *noun* = **nonsense**, claptrap (*inf*), drivel, garbage (*inf*), gobbledegook (*inf*), kak (*S Afr sl*), poppycock (*inf*), rubbish, waffle (*inf, chiefly Brit*)

tweak *verb, noun* **1, 2** = **twist**, jerk, pinch, pull, squeeze

twig[1] *noun* = **branch**, shoot, spray, sprig, stick

twig[2] *verb Inf* = **understand**, catch on (*inf*), comprehend, fathom, find out, get, grasp, make out, rumble (*Brit inf*), see, tumble to (*inf*)

twilight *noun* **1** = **dusk**, dimness, evening, gloaming (*Scot or poet*), gloom, half-light, sundown, sunset OPPOSITE morning

twin *noun* **1** = **double**, clone, counterpart, duplicate, fellow, likeness, lookalike, match, mate ♦*verb* **2** = **pair**, couple, join, link, match,

yoke

twine *noun* **1** = **string**, cord, yarn ♦*verb* **2** = **coil**, bend, curl, encircle, loop, spiral, twist, wind

twinge *noun* = **pain**, pang, prick, spasm, stab, stitch

twinkle *verb* **1** = **sparkle**, blink, flash, flicker, gleam, glint, glisten, glitter, shimmer, shine ♦*noun* **2** = **sparkle**, flash, flicker, gleam, glimmer, shimmer, spark

twirl *verb* **1** = **turn**, pirouette, pivot, revolve, rotate, spin, wheel, whirl **2** = **twist**, wind

twist *verb* **1** = **screw**, curl, spin, swivel, wrap, wring OPPOSITE untwist. **2** = **distort**, contort, screw up OPPOSITE straighten. **3** = **wind**, coil ♦*noun* **4** = **wind**, coil, curl, spin, swivel **6** = **development**, change, revelation, slant, surprise, turn, variation **7** = **curve**, arc, bend, meander, turn, undulation, zigzag **8** = **distortion**, defect, deformation, flaw,

twitch ❶ *verb* **1** move spasmodically. **2** pull sharply. ◆ *noun* **3** nervous muscular spasm. **4** sharp pull.

twitter *verb* **1** (of birds) utter chirping sounds. **2** talk nervously. ◆ *noun* **3** act or sound of twittering.

two ❶ *adjective, noun* one more than one. **two-edged** *adjective* (of a remark) having both a favourable and an unfavourable interpretation. **two-faced** *adjective* deceitful, hypocritical. **two-ply** *adjective* having two layers or strands. **two-stroke** *adjective* (of an internal-combustion engine) making one explosion to every two strokes of the piston. **two-time** *verb Informal* deceive (a lover) by having an affair with someone else. **two-way** *adjective* **1** moving in, or allowing movement in, two opposite directions. **2** involving mutual involvement or cooperation. **3** (of a radio or transmitter) capable of both transmission and reception of messages.

TX Texas.

tycoon ❶ *noun* powerful wealthy businessman.

tyke *noun Informal* small cheeky child.

tympanum *noun, pl* **-nums, -na 1** cavity of the middle ear. **2** tympanic membrane. **3** *Archit* space between the arch and the lintel above a door. **tympanic** *adjective* **tympanic membrane** thin membrane separating the external ear from the middle ear.

type ❶ *noun* **1** class or category. **2** *Informal* person, esp. of a specified kind. **3** block with a

raised character used for printing. **4** printed text. ◆ *verb* **5** print with a typewriter or word processor. **6** typify. **7** classify. **typist** *noun* person who types with a typewriter or word processor. **typecast** *verb* continually cast (an actor or actress) in similar roles. **typeface** *noun Printing* style of the type. **typescript** *noun* typewritten document. **typewriter** *noun* machine which prints a character when the appropriate key is pressed.

typhoid fever *noun* acute infectious feverish disease.

typhoon ❶ *noun* violent tropical storm.

typhus *noun* infectious feverish disease.

typical ❶ *adjective* true to type, characteristic. **typically** *adverb* **typify** *verb* **-fying, -fied** be typical of.

typography *noun* art or style of printing. **typographical** *adjective* **typographer** *noun*

tyrannosaurus [tirr-ran-oh-**sore**-uss] *noun* large two-footed flesh-eating dinosaur.

tyrant ❶ *noun* **1** oppressive or cruel ruler. **2** person who exercises authority oppressively. **tyrannical** *adjective* like a tyrant, oppressive. **tyrannize** *verb* exert power (over) oppressively or cruelly. **tyrannous** *adjective* **tyranny** *noun* tyrannical rule.

tyre *noun* rubber ring, usu. inflated, over the rim of a vehicle's wheel to grip the road.

tyro *noun, pl* **-ros** novice or beginner.

tzar *noun* same as TSAR.

tzetze fly *noun* same as TSETSE FLY.

——————— THESAURUS ———————

imperfection, kink, warp

twit[2] *noun Inf* =**fool**, ass, chump (*inf*), halfwit, idiot, nincompoop, numbskull *or* numskull, prat (*sl*), twerp *or* twirp (*inf*)

twitch *verb* **1** = **jerk**, flutter, jump, squirm **2** = **pull**, pluck, tug, yank ◆*noun* **3** = **jerk**, flutter, jump, spasm, tic

two-faced *adjective* = **hypocritical**, deceitful, dissembling, duplicitous, false, insincere, treacherous, untrustworthy

tycoon *noun* = **magnate**, baron, capitalist, fat cat (*sl, chiefly US*), financier, industrialist, mogul, plutocrat

type *noun* **1** = **kind**, category, class, genre, group, order, sort, species, style, variety

typhoon *noun* = **storm**, cyclone, squall, tempest, tornado

typical *adjective* = **characteristic**, archetypal, average, model, normal, orthodox, representative, standard, stock, usual OPPOSITE unique

typify *verb* = **represent**, characterize, embody, epitomize, exemplify, illustrate, personify, sum up, symbolize

tyrannical *adjective* = **oppressive**, authoritarian, autocratic, cruel, despotic, dictatorial, domineering, high-handed, imperious, overbearing, tyrannous

tyranny *noun* = **oppression**, absolutism, authoritarianism, autocracy, cruelty, despotism, dictatorship, high-handedness, imperiousness

tyrant *noun* = **dictator**, absolutist, authoritarian, autocrat, bully, despot, martinet, oppressor, slave-driver

T

Uu

U *Chem* uranium.

UB40 *noun Brit* registration card issued to an unemployed person.

ubiquitous ❶ [yew-**bik**-wit-uss] *adjective* being or seeming to be everywhere at once. **ubiquity** *noun*

U-boat *noun* German submarine.

udder *noun* large baglike milk-producing gland of cows, sheep, or goats.

UDI Unilateral Declaration of Independence.

UEFA Union of European Football Associations.

UFO unidentified flying object.

ugh [uhh] *interjection* exclamation of disgust.

ugly ❶ *adjective* **uglier, ugliest 1** of unpleasant appearance. **2** ominous or menacing. **ugliness** *noun*

UHF ultrahigh frequency.

UHT (of milk or cream) ultra-heat-treated.

UK United Kingdom.

ukulele, ukelele [yew-kal-**lay**-lee] *noun* small guitar with four strings.

ulcer ❶ *noun* open sore on the surface of the skin or mucous membrane. **ulcerated** *adjective* made or becoming ulcerous. **ulceration** *noun* **ulcerous** *adjective* of, like, or characterized by ulcers.

ulna *noun, pl* **-nae, -nas** inner and longer of the two bones of the human forearm.

ulster *noun* man's heavy double-breasted overcoat.

ulterior ❶ [ult-**ear**-ee-or] *adjective* (of an aim, reason, etc.) concealed or hidden, e.g. *ulterior motives.*

ultimate ❶ *adjective* **1** final in a series or process. **2** highest or supreme. **3** most extreme. **ultimately** *adverb*

ultimatum [ult-im-**may**-tum] *noun* final warning stating that action will be taken unless certain conditions are met.

ultra- *prefix* **1** beyond a specified extent, range, or limit, e.g. *ultrasonic.* **2** extremely, e.g. *ultramodern.*

ultrahigh frequency *noun* radio frequency between 3000 and 300 megahertz.

ultramarine *adjective* vivid blue.

ultrasonic *adjective* of or producing sound waves with a higher frequency than the human ear can hear.

ultrasound *noun* ultrasonic waves, used in medical diagnosis and therapy and in echo sounding.

ultraviolet *adjective, noun* (of) light beyond the limit of visibility at the violet end of the spectrum.

ululate [**yewl**-yew-late] *verb* howl or wail. **ululation** *noun*

umbel *noun* umbrella-like flower cluster with the stalks springing from the central point.

umbelliferous *adjective* denoting a plant with flowers in umbels.

umber *adjective* dark brown to reddish-brown.

umbilical [um-**bill**-ik-al] *adjective* of the navel.

umbilical cord long flexible tube of blood vessels that connects a fetus with the placenta.

umbra *noun, pl* **-brae, -bras** shadow, esp. the shadow cast by the moon onto the earth during a solar eclipse.

umbrage *noun* **take umbrage** feel offended or upset.

umbrella *noun* **1** portable device used for protection against rain, consisting of a folding frame covered in material attached to a centralrod. **2** single organization, idea, etc. that

U

THESAURUS

ubiquitous *adjective* = **everywhere**, ever-present, omnipresent, pervasive, universal

ugly *adjective* **1** = **unattractive**, distasteful, homely (*chiefly US*), horrid, ill-favoured, plain, unlovely, unpleasant, unprepossessing, unsightly OPPOSITE pretty. **2** = **ominous**, baleful, dangerous, menacing, sinister OPPOSITE friendly

ulcer *noun* = **sore**, abscess, boil, gumboil,

peptic ulcer, pustule

ulterior *adjective* = **hidden**, concealed, covert, secret, undisclosed

ultimate *adjective* **1** = **final**, end, last **2, 3** = **supreme**, extreme, greatest, highest, paramount, superlative, utmost

ultimately *adverb* **1** = **finally**, after all, at last, eventually, in due time, in the end, sooner or later contains or covers many different organizations, ideas, etc.

umiak [oo-mee-ak] *noun* Inuit boat made of skins.

umlaut [oom-lowt] *noun* mark (¨) placed over a vowel, esp. in German, to indicate a change in its sound.

umpire ⊕ *noun* 1 official who rules on the playing of a game. ◆ *verb* 2 act as umpire in (a game).

umpteen *adjective Informal* very many.

umpteenth *noun, adjective*

UN United Nations.

un- *prefix* 1 not, e.g. *unidentified*. 2 denoting reversal of an action, e.g. *untie*. 3 denoting removal from, e.g. *unthrone*.

unabated *adverb* without any reduction in force, e.g. *the storm continued unabated*.

unable ⊕ *adjective* **unable to** lacking the necessary power, ability, or authority to (do something).

unaccountable ⊕ *adjective* 1 unable to be explained. 2 (foll. by *to*) not answerable to. **unaccountably** *adverb*

unadulterated *adjective* with nothing added, pure.

unaffected ⊕ *adjective* 1 unpretentious, natural, sincere. 2 not influenced or moved by

something.

unanimous ⊕ [yew-**nan**-im-uss] *adjective* 1 in complete agreement. 2 agreed by all. **unanimously** *adverb* **unanimity** *noun*

unannounced *adverb* without warning, e.g. *he turned up unannounced*.

unapproachable ⊕ *adjective* discouraging friendliness, aloof.

unarmed ⊕ *adjective* without weapons.

unassailable ⊕ *adjective* unable to be attacked or disputed.

unassuming ⊕ *adjective* modest or unpretentious.

unattached ⊕ *adjective* 1 not connected with any specific group or organization. 2 not married or involved in a steady relationship.

unavailing *adjective* useless or futile.

unavoidable ⊕ *adjective* unable to be avoided or prevented. **unavoidably** *adverb*

unaware ⊕ *adjective* not aware or conscious, e.g. *unaware of the danger*. **unawares** *adverb* 1 by surprise, e.g. *caught unawares*. 2 without knowing.

unbalanced ⊕ *adjective* 1 biased or one-sided. 2 mentally deranged.

unbearable ⊕ *adjective* not able to be endured. **unbearably** *adverb*

unbecoming ⊕ *adjective* unattractive or

—————— THESAURUS ——————

umpire *noun* 1 = **referee**, arbiter, arbitrator, judge ◆*verb* 2 = **referee**, adjudicate, arbitrate, judge

unable *adjective* **unable to** = **incapable**, impotent, ineffectual, powerless, unfit, unqualified

unaccountable *adjective* 1 = **inexplicable**, baffling, mysterious, odd, puzzling, unexplainable, unfathomable OPPOSITE understandable. 2 (foll. by *to*) = **not answerable to**, exempt, not responsible to

unaffected *adjective* 1 = **natural**, artless, genuine, plain, simple, sincere, unpretentious 2 = **impervious**, proof, unmoved, unresponsive, untouched

unanimity *noun* 1 = **agreement**, accord, assent, concord, concurrence, consensus, harmony, like-mindedness, unison

unanimous *adjective* 1 = **agreed**, common, concerted, harmonious, in agreement, like-minded, united OPPOSITE split

unanimously *adverb* 2 = **without exception**, nem. con., with one accord

unapproachable *adjective* = **unfriendly**, aloof, chilly, cool, distant, remote, reserved, standoffish

unarmed *adjective* = **defenceless**, exposed,

helpless, open, unprotected, weak

unassailable *adjective* = **impregnable**, invincible, invulnerable, secure OPPOSITE uncertain

unassuming *adjective* = **modest**, humble, quiet, reserved, retiring, self-effacing, unassertive, unobtrusive, unpretentious OPPOSITE pretentious

unattached *adjective* 1 = **free**, independent OPPOSITE attached. 2 = **single**, available, not spoken for, unengaged, unmarried

unavoidable *adjective* = **inevitable**, certain, fated, inescapable

unaware *adjective* = **ignorant**, not in the loop (*inf*), oblivious, unconscious, uninformed, unknowing OPPOSITE aware

unawares *adverb* 1 = **by surprise**, off guard, suddenly, unexpectedly OPPOSITE prepared. 2 = **unknowingly**, accidentally, by accident, inadvertently, unwittingly OPPOSITE knowingly

unbalanced *adjective* 1 = **biased**, one-sided, partial, partisan, prejudiced, unfair 2 = **deranged**, crazy, demented, disturbed, eccentric, insane, irrational, mad, *non compos mentis*, not all there, unhinged, unstable

unbearable *adjective* = **intolerable**, insufferable, too much (*inf*), unacceptable

U

unsuitable.

unbeknown *adverb* **unbeknown to** without the knowledge of (a person).

unbelievable ⊙ *adjective* **1** too unlikely to be believed. **2** *Informal* marvellous, amazing. **3** *Informal* terrible, shocking. **unbelievably** *adverb*

unbend ⊙ *verb Informal* become less strict or more informal in one's attitudes or behaviour.

unbending *adjective* rigid or inflexible.

unbending ⊙ *adjective* rigid or inflexible.

unbidden *adjective* not ordered or asked.

unborn ⊙ *adjective* not yet born.

unbosom *verb* relieve (oneself) of (secrets or feelings) by telling someone.

unbridled ⊙ *adjective* (of feelings or behaviour) not controlled in any way.

unburden ⊙ *verb* relieve (one's mind or oneself) of a worry by confiding in someone.

uncalled-for ⊙ *adjective* not fair or justified.

uncanny ⊙ *adjective* weird or mysterious. **uncannily** *adverb*

unceremonious *adjective* **1** relaxed and informal. **2** abrupt or rude. **unceremoniously** *adverb*

uncertain ⊙ *adjective* **1** not able to be accurately known or predicted. **2** not able to be depended upon. **3** changeable. **uncertainty** *noun*

uncharacteristic *adjective* not typical. **uncharacteristically** *adverb*

uncharitable *adjective* unkind or harsh. **uncharitably** *adverb*

un-Christian *adjective* not in accordance with Christian principles.

uncivilized ⊙ *adjective* **1** (of a tribe or people) not yet civilized. **2** lacking culture or sophistication.

uncle *noun* **1** brother of one's father or mother. **2** husband of one's aunt.

unclean ⊙ *adjective* lacking moral, spiritual, or physical cleanliness.

uncomfortable ⊙ *adjective* **1** not physically relaxed. **2** anxious or uneasy. **uncomfortably** *adverb*

uncommon ⊙ *adjective* **1** not happening or encountered often. **2** in excess of what is normal. **uncommonly** *adverb*

uncompromising ⊙ *adjective* not prepared to compromise. **uncompromisingly** *adverb*

unconcerned ⊙ *adjective* lacking in concern or involvement. **unconcernedly** [un-kon-**sern**-id-lee] *adverb*

unconditional ⊙ *adjective* without conditions

——————— T H E S A U R U S ———————

unbecoming *adjective* = **unattractive**, unbefitting, unflattering, unsightly, unsuitable OPPOSITE seemly

unbelievable *adjective* **1** = **incredible**, astonishing, far-fetched, implausible, impossible, improbable, inconceivable, jaw-dropping, preposterous, unconvincing OPPOSITE possible. **2** *Inf* = **wonderful**, excellent, fabulous (*inf*), fantastic (*inf*), great (*inf*), splendid, superb, terrific (*inf*) OPPOSITE bad

unbending *adjective* = **inflexible**, firm, intractable, resolute, rigid, severe, strict, stubborn, tough, uncompromising

unborn *adjective* = **expected**, awaited, embryonic

unbridled *adjective* = **unrestrained**, excessive, intemperate, licentious, riotous, unchecked, unruly, wanton

unburden *verb* = **confess**, confide, disclose, get (something) off one's chest (*inf*), reveal

uncalled-for *adjective* = **unnecessary**, gratuitous, needless, undeserved, unjustified, unwarranted

uncanny *adjective* = **weird**, mysterious, strange, supernatural, unearthly, unnatural

uncertain *adjective* **1** = **unpredictable**, doubtful, indefinite, questionable, risky, speculative OPPOSITE decided. **2** = **unsure**, dubious, hazy, irresolute, unclear, unconfirmed, undecided, vague OPPOSITE sure

uncertainty *noun* **1** = **unpredictability**, ambiguity OPPOSITE predictability. **2** = **doubt**, confusion, dubiety, hesitancy, indecision OPPOSITE confidence

uncivilized *adjective* **1** = **primitive**, barbarian, savage, wild **2** = **uncouth**, boorish, coarse, philistine, uncultivated, uneducated

unclean *adjective* = **dirty**, corrupt, defiled, evil, filthy, foul, impure, polluted, soiled, stained OPPOSITE clean

uncomfortable *adjective* **1** = **painful**, awkward, cramped, rough **2** = **uneasy**, awkward, discomfited, disturbed, embarrassed, troubled OPPOSITE relaxed

uncommon *adjective* **1** = **rare**, infrequent, munted (*NZ sl*), novel, odd, peculiar, queer, scarce, strange, unusual OPPOSITE common. **2** = **extraordinary**, distinctive, exceptional, notable, outstanding, remarkable, special OPPOSITE average

uncommonly *adverb* **1** = **rarely**, hardly ever, infrequently, occasionally, seldom **2** = **exceptionally**, particularly, very

uncompromising *adjective* = **inflexible**, firm, inexorable, intransigent, rigid, strict, tough, unbending

U

or limitations. **unconditionally** adverb

unconscionable adjective **1** having no principles, unscrupulous. **2** excessive in amount or degree.

unconscious ❶ adjective **1** lacking normal awareness through the senses. **2** not aware of one's actions or behaviour. ◆ noun **3** part of the mind containing instincts and ideas that exist without one's awareness. **unconsciously** adverb **unconsciousness** noun

unconventional ❶ adjective not conforming to accepted rules or standards.

uncooperative adjective not willing to help other people with what they are doing.

uncouth ❶ adjective lacking in good manners, refinement, or grace.

uncover ❶ verb **1** reveal or disclose. **2** remove the cover, top, etc., from.

unction noun act of anointing with oil in sacramental ceremonies.

unctuous adjective pretending to be kind and concerned.

undecided ❶ adjective **1** not having made up one's mind. **2** (of an issue or problem) not agreed or decided upon.

undeniable ❶ adjective unquestionably true. **undeniably** adverb

under ❶ preposition, adverb **1** indicating movement to or position beneath the underside or base. ◆ preposition **2** less than. **3** subject to.

under- prefix **1** below, e.g. underground. **2** insufficient or insufficiently, e.g. underrate.

underachieve verb fail to achieve a performance appropriate to one's age or talents. **underachiever** noun

underage adjective below the required or standard age.

underarm adjective **1** Sport denoting a style of throwing, bowling, or serving in which the hand is swung below shoulder level. **2** of or denoting the armpit. ◆ adverb **3** Sport in an underarm style.

undercarriage noun **1** landing gear of an aircraft. **2** framework supporting the body of a vehicle.

underclass noun class consisting of the most disadvantaged people, such as the long-term unemployed.

undercoat noun coat of paint applied before the final coat.

undercover ❶ adjective done or acting in secret.

undercurrent ❶ noun **1** current that is not apparent at the surface. **2** underlying opinion or emotion.

undercut verb charge less than (a competitor) to obtain trade.

underdeveloped adjective **1** immature or undersized. **2** (of a country) lacking the finance, industries, and organization necessary to advance.

underdog ❶ noun person or team in a weak or underprivileged position.

underdone adjective not cooked enough.

underestimate ❶ verb **1** make too low an estimate of. **2** not realize the full potential of.

——————— THESAURUS ———————

unconcerned adjective =**indifferent**, aloof, apathetic, cool, detached, dispassionate, distant, uninterested, unmoved OPPOSITE **concerned**

unconditional adjective =**absolute**, complete, entire, full, outright, positive, total, unlimited, unqualified, unreserved

unconscious adjective **1** =**senseless**, insensible, knocked out, out, out cold, stunned OPPOSITE **conscious**. **2 a** =**unintentional**, accidental, inadvertent, unwitting OPPOSITE **planned**. **b** =**unaware**, ignorant, oblivious, unknowing OPPOSITE **aware**

unconventional adjective =**unusual**, eccentric, individual, irregular, nonconformist, odd, offbeat, original, outré, unorthodox OPPOSITE **normal**

uncouth adjective =**coarse**, barbaric, boorish, crude, graceless, ill-mannered, loutish, oafish, rough, rude, vulgar

uncover verb **1** =**reveal**, disclose, divulge, expose, make known **2** =**open**, bare, show, strip, unwrap

undecided adjective **1** =**unsure**, dithering, hesitant, in two minds, irresolute, torn, uncertain OPPOSITE **decided**. **2** =**unsettled**, debatable, iffy (inf), indefinite, moot, open, unconcluded, undetermined OPPOSITE **definite**

undeniable adjective =**certain**, clear, incontrovertible, indisputable, obvious, sure, unquestionable

under preposition **1** =**below**, beneath, underneath OPPOSITE **over**. **3** =**subject to**, governed by, secondary to, subordinate to ◆adverb **1** =**below**, beneath, down, lower OPPOSITE **over**

undercover adjective =**secret**, concealed, covert, hidden, private

undercurrent noun **1** =**undertow**, riptide **2** =**undertone**, atmosphere, feeling, hint, overtone, sense, suggestion, tendency, tinge, vibes (sl)

underdog noun =**weaker party**, little fellow (inf), outsider

U

underfelt *noun* thick felt laid under a carpet to increase insulation.

underfoot *adverb* under the feet.

undergarment *noun* any piece of underwear.

undergo ❶ *verb* experience, endure, or sustain.

undergraduate *noun* person studying in a university for a first degree.

underground ❶ *adjective* **1** occurring, situated, used, or going below ground level. **2** secret. ◆ *noun* **3** electric passenger railway operated in underground tunnels. **4** movement dedicated to overthrowing a government or occupation forces.

undergrowth ❶ *noun* small trees and bushes growing beneath taller trees in a wood or forest.

underhand ❶ *adjective* sly, deceitful, and secretive.

underlay *noun* felt or rubber laid beneath a carpet to increase insulation and resilience.

underlie ❶ *verb* **1** lie or be placed under. **2** be the foundation, cause, or basis of. **underlying** *adjective* fundamental or basic.

underline ❶ *verb* **1** draw a line under. **2** state forcibly, emphasize.

underling *noun* subordinate.

undermine ❶ *verb* **1** weaken gradually. **2** (of the sea or wind) wear away the base of (cliffs).

underneath *preposition, adverb* **1** under or beneath. ◆ *adjective, noun* **2** lower (part or surface).

underpants *plural noun* man's undergarment for the lower part of the body.

underpass *noun* section of a road that passes under another road or a railway line.

underpin *verb* give strength or support to.

underprivileged ❶ *adjective* lacking the rights and advantages of other members of society.

underrate ❶ *verb* not realize the full potential of. **underrated** *adjective*

underseal *noun* coating of tar etc. applied to the underside of a motor vehicle to prevent corrosion.

undersecretary *noun* senior civil servant or junior minister in a government department.

underside *noun* bottom or lower surface.

undersized ❶ *adjective* smaller than normal.

underskirt *noun* skirtlike garment worn under a skirt or dress, petticoat.

understand ❶ *verb* **1** know and comprehend the nature or meaning of. **2** realize or grasp (something). **3** assume, infer, or believe.

understandable *adjective* **understandably** *adverb* **understanding** *noun* **1** ability to learn, judge, or make decisions. **2** personal interpretation of a subject. **3** mutual agreement, usu. an informal or private one. ◆ *adjective* **4** kind and sympathetic.

understate *verb* **1** describe or represent (something) in restrained terms. **2** state that (something, such as a number) is less than it is. **understatement** *noun*

understudy ❶ *noun* **1** actor who studies a part in order to be able to replace the usual actor if necessary. ◆ *verb* **2** act as an understudy for.

———— T H E S A U R U S ————

underestimate *verb* **2** =**underrate**, belittle, minimize, miscalculate, undervalue OPPOSITE> overestimate

undergo *verb* =**experience**, bear, endure, go through, stand, suffer, sustain

underground *adjective* **1** =**subterranean**, buried, covered **2** =**secret**, clandestine, covert, hidden ◆*noun* **3** =**the tube**, the metro, the subway (*Brit*) **4** =**the Resistance**, partisans

undergrowth *noun* =**scrub**, bracken, briars, brush, underbrush

underhand *adjective* =**sly**, crafty, deceitful, devious, dishonest, furtive, secret, sneaky, stealthy OPPOSITE> honest

underline *verb* **1** =**underscore**, mark **2** =**emphasize**, accentuate, highlight, stress OPPOSITE> play down

underlying *adjective* **2** =**fundamental**, basic, elementary, intrinsic, primary, prime

undermine *verb* **1** =**weaken**, disable, sabotage, sap, subvert OPPOSITE> promote

underprivileged *adjective* =**disadvantaged**, deprived, destitute, impoverished, needy, poor

underrate *verb* =**underestimate**, belittle, discount, undervalue

undersized *adjective* =**stunted**, dwarfish, miniature, pygmy or pigmy, small

understand *verb* **2** =**comprehend**, conceive, fathom, follow, get, grasp, perceive, realize, see, take in **3** =**believe**, assume, gather, presume, suppose, think

understandable *adjective* **2** =**reasonable**, justifiable, legitimate, natural, to be expected

understanding *noun* **1** =**perception**, appreciation, awareness, comprehension, discernment, grasp, insight, judgment, knowledge, sense OPPOSITE> ignorance. **2** =**interpretation**, belief, idea, judgment, notion, opinion, perception, view **3** =**agreement**, accord, pact ◆*adjective* **4** =**sympathetic**, compassionate, considerate, kind, patient, sensitive, tolerant OPPOSITE> insensitive

U

undertake ⊕ *verb* **1** agree or commit oneself to (something) or to do (something). **2** promise. **undertaking** *noun* **1** task or enterprise. **2** agreement to do something.
undertaker *noun* person whose job is to prepare corpses for burial or cremation and organize funerals.
undertone ⊕ *noun* **1** quiet tone of voice. **2** underlying quality or feeling.
undertow *noun* strong undercurrent flowing in a different direction from the surface current.
underwater ⊕ *adjective, adverb* (situated, occurring, or for use) below the surface of the sea, a lake, or a river.
underwear ⊕ *noun* clothing worn under the outer garments and next to the skin.
underworld ⊕ *noun* **1** criminals and their associates. **2** *Greek & Roman myth* regions below the earth's surface regarded as the abode of the dead.
underwrite ⊕ *verb* **1** accept financial responsibility for (a commercial project). **2** sign and issue (an insurance policy), thus accepting liability. **underwriter** *noun*
undesirable ⊕ *adjective* **1** not desirable or pleasant, objectionable. ♦ *noun* **2** objectionable

person.
undies *plural noun Informal* underwear, esp. women's.
undistinguished *adjective* not particularly good or bad, mediocre.
undo ⊕ *verb* **1** open, unwrap. **2** reverse the effects of. **3** cause the downfall of. **undone** *adjective* **undoing** *noun* cause of someone's downfall.
undoubted ⊕ *adjective* certain or indisputable. **undoubtedly** *adverb*
undress ⊕ *verb* **1** take off the clothes of (oneself or another person). ♦ *noun* **2 in a state of undress** naked or nearly naked.
undue ⊕ *adjective* greater than is reasonable, excessive. **unduly** *adverb*
undulate *verb* move in waves. **undulation** *noun*
undying ⊕ *adjective* never ending, eternal.
unearned income *noun* income from property or investments rather than work.
unearth ⊕ *verb* **1** reveal or discover by searching. **2** dig up out of the earth.
unearthly ⊕ *adjective* **1** ghostly or eerie. **2** ridiculous or unreasonable, e.g. *an unearthly hour.*

——————— T H E S A U R U S ———————

understudy *noun* **1 = stand-in**, replacement, reserve, substitute
undertake *verb* **1 = agree**, bargain, contract, engage **2 = promise**, guarantee, pledge
undertaking *noun* **1 = task**, affair, attempt, business, effort, endeavour, enterprise, operation, project, venture **2 = promise**, assurance, commitment, pledge, vow, word
undertone *noun* **1 = murmur**, whisper **2 = undercurrent**, hint, suggestion, tinge, touch, trace
underwater *adjective* **= submerged**, submarine, sunken
underwear *noun* **= underclothes**, lingerie, undergarments, underthings, undies (*inf*)
underworld *noun* **1 = criminals**, gangland (*inf*), gangsters, organized crime **2** *Greek & Roman myth* **= nether world**, Hades, nether regions
underwrite *verb* **1 = finance**, back, fund, guarantee, insure, sponsor, subsidize **2 = sign**, endorse, initial
undesirable *adjective* **1 = objectionable**, disagreeable, distasteful, unacceptable, unattractive, unsuitable, unwanted, unwelcome
undo *verb* **1 = open**, disentangle, loose, unbutton, unfasten, untie **2 = reverse**, annul, cancel, invalidate, neutralize, offset **3 = ruin**, defeat, destroy, overturn, quash, shatter,

subvert, undermine, upset, wreck
undoing *noun* **= ruin**, collapse, defeat, disgrace, downfall, overthrow, reversal, shame
undone *adjective* **3 = ruined**, betrayed, destroyed, forlorn, hapless, munted (*NZ sl*), overcome, prostrate, wretched
undoubted *adjective* **= certain**, acknowledged, definite, indisputable, indubitable, sure, undisputed, unquestioned
undoubtedly *adverb* **= certainly**, assuredly, definitely, doubtless, surely, without doubt
undress *verb* **1 = strip**, disrobe, shed, take off one's clothes ♦*noun* **2 in a state of undress = naked**, nude
undue *adjective* **= excessive**, extreme, improper, inappropriate, needless, uncalled-for, unnecessary, unwarranted
unduly *adverb* **= excessively**, overly, unnecessarily, unreasonably
undying *adjective* **= eternal**, constant, deathless, everlasting, infinite, permanent, perpetual, unending
unearth *verb* **1 = discover**, expose, find, reveal, uncover **2 = dig up**, dredge up, excavate, exhume
unearthly *adjective* **1 = eerie**, ghostly, phantom, spectral, spooky (*inf*), strange, supernatural, uncanny, weird
uneasiness *noun* **1 = anxiety**, disquiet,

U

uneasy ⊕ *adjective* **1** (of a person) anxious or apprehensive. **2** (of a condition) precarious or uncomfortable. **uneasily** *adverb* **uneasiness** *noun* **unease** *noun* **1** feeling of anxiety. **2** state of dissatisfaction.

unemployed ⊕ *adjective* **1** out of work. ♦ *plural noun* **2 the unemployed** people who are out of work. **unemployment** *noun*

unequivocal ⊕ *adjective* completely clear in meaning. **unequivocally** *adverb*

unerring ⊕ *adjective* never mistaken, consistently accurate.

UNESCO United Nations Educational, Scientific, and Cultural Organization.

uneven ⊕ *adjective* **1** not level or flat. **2** not consistent in quality, e.g. *an uneven performance*. **3** not fairly matched, e.g. *an uneven race*.

unexceptionable *adjective* beyond criticism or objection.

unexceptional ⊕ *adjective* ordinary or normal.

unexpected ⊕ *adjective* surprising or unforeseen. **unexpectedly** *adverb*

unfailing ⊕ *adjective* continuous or reliable. **unfailingly** *adverb*

unfair ⊕ *adjective* not right, fair, or just. **unfairly** *adverb* **unfairness** *noun*

unfaithful ⊕ *adjective* **1** having sex with someone other than one's regular partner. **2** not true to a promise or vow. **unfaithfulness** *noun*

unfathomable ⊕ *adjective* too strange or too complicated to be understood.

unfavourable ⊕ *adjective* **1** unlikely to produce the desired outcome, inauspicious, e.g. *unfavourable weather conditions*. **2** disapproving, e.g. *an unfavourable opinion*. **unfavourably** *adverb*

unfeeling ⊕ *adjective* without sympathy.

unfit ⊕ *adjective* **1** unqualified or unsuitable. **2** in poor physical condition.

unflappable ⊕ *adjective Informal* not easily upset. **unflappability** *noun*

unfold ⊕ *verb* **1** open or spread out from a folded state. **2** reveal or be revealed.

unforeseen *adjective* surprising because not expected.

unforgettable *adjective* impossible to forget, memorable. **unforgettably** *adverb*

unfortunate ⊕ *adjective* **1** unlucky, unsuccessful, or unhappy. **2** regrettable or

——————— THESAURUS ———————

doubt, misgiving, qualms, trepidation, worry
uneasy *adjective* **1 =anxious**, disturbed, edgy, nervous, on edge, perturbed, troubled, uncomfortable, worried OPPOSITE **relaxed**. **2 =precarious**, awkward, insecure, shaky, strained, tense, uncomfortable

unemployed *adjective* **1 =out of work**, idle, jobless, laid off, redundant OPPOSITE **working**

unequivocal *adjective* **=clear**, absolute, certain, definite, explicit, incontrovertible, indubitable, manifest, plain, unambiguous

unerring *adjective* **=accurate**, exact, infallible, perfect, sure, unfailing

uneven *adjective* **1 =rough**, bumpy, lopsided OPPOSITE **even**. **2 =variable**, broken, fitful, irregular, jerky, patchy, spasmodic **3 =unequal**, ill-matched, unfair

unexceptional *adjective* **=ordinary**, commonplace, conventional, mediocre, normal, pedestrian, run-of-the-mill, undistinguished, unremarkable

unexpected *adjective* **=unforeseen**, abrupt, chance, fortuitous, sudden, surprising, unanticipated, unlooked-for, unpredictable

unfailing *adjective* **a =continuous**, boundless, endless, persistent, unflagging **b =reliable**, certain, dependable, faithful, loyal, staunch, sure, true OPPOSITE **unreliable**

unfair *adjective* **a =unscrupulous**, dishonest,

unethical, unsporting, wrongful OPPOSITE **just**. **b =biased**, bigoted, one-sided, partial, partisan, prejudiced, unjust

unfaithful *adjective* **1 =faithless**, adulterous, inconstant, two-timing (*inf*), untrue OPPOSITE **faithful**. **2 =disloyal**, deceitful, faithless, false, traitorous, treacherous, untrustworthy OPPOSITE **true**

unfathomable *adjective* **=baffling**, deep, impenetrable, incomprehensible, indecipherable, inexplicable, profound

unfavourable *adjective* **1 =adverse**, contrary, inauspicious, unfortunate, unlucky, unpropitious **2 =hostile**, inimical, negative, unfriendly

unfeeling *adjective* **=callous**, apathetic, cold, cruel, hardhearted, heartless, insensitive, pitiless, uncaring

unfit *adjective* **1 a =incapable**, inadequate, incompetent, ineffective, no good, useless **b =unsuitable**, unqualified, unsuited **2 =out of shape**, feeble, flabby, in poor condition, unhealthy

unflappable *adjective Inf* **=imperturbable**, calm, collected, composed, cool, impassive, level-headed, self-possessed

unfold *verb* **1 =open**, expand, spread out, undo, unfurl, unravel, unroll, unwrap **2 =reveal**, disclose, divulge, make known, present, show, uncover

unsuitable. ♦ *noun* **3** unlucky person.
unfortunately *adverb*
unfounded ❶ *adjective* not based on facts or evidence.
unfrock *verb* deprive (a priest in holy orders) of his priesthood.
unfurl *verb* unroll or unfold.
ungainly ❶ *adjective* **-lier, -liest** lacking grace when moving. **ungainliness** *noun*
ungodly ❶ *adjective* **1** *Informal* unreasonable or outrageous, e.g. *an ungodly hour.* **2** wicked or sinful. **ungodliness** *noun*
ungovernable *adjective* not able to be disciplined or restrained.
ungrateful *adjective* not grateful or thankful.
unguarded ❶ *adjective* **1** not protected. **2** incautious or careless.
unguent [ung-gwent] *noun Lit* ointment.
unhand *verb Old-fashioned or lit* release from one's grasp.
unhappy ❶ *adjective* **1** sad or depressed. **2** unfortunate or wretched. **unhappily** *adverb* **unhappiness** *noun*
unhealthy ❶ *adjective* **1** likely to cause poor health. **2** not fit or well. **3** morbid, unnatural.
unheard-of ❶ *adjective* **1** without precedent. **2** highly offensive or shocking.
unhinge *verb* derange or unbalance (a person

or his or her mind).
unholy ❶ *adjective* **1** immoral or wicked. **2** *Informal* unnatural or outrageous, e.g. *an unholy mess.*
uni- *combining form* of, consisting of, or having only one, e.g. *unicellular.*
UNICEF *noun* agency of United Nations that funds education and children's health.
unicorn *noun* imaginary horselike creature with one horn growing from its forehead.
uniform ❶ *noun* **1** special identifying set of clothes for the members of an organization, such as soldiers. ♦ *adjective* **2** regular and even throughout, unvarying. **3** alike or like.
uniformly *adverb* **uniformity** *noun*
unify ❶ *verb* **-fying, -fied** make or become one. **unification** *noun*
unilateral *adjective* made or done by only one person or group. **unilaterally** *adverb*
unimpeachable *adjective* completely honest and reliable.
uninterested ❶ *adjective* having or showing no interest in someone or something.
union ❶ *noun* **1** uniting or being united. **2** short for TRADE UNION. **3** association or confederation of individuals or groups for a common purpose. **unionist** *noun* member or supporter of a trade union. **unionism** *noun*

——————— THESAURUS ———————

unfortunate *adjective* **1 a** =**unlucky**, cursed, doomed, hapless, ill-fated, unhappy, wretched OPPOSITE **lucky**. **b** = **disastrous**, adverse, calamitous, unsuccessful OPPOSITE **fortunate**. **c** = **deplorable**, lamentable **2** = **regrettable**, unsuitable OPPOSITE **appropriate**
unfounded *adjective* = **groundless**, baseless, false, idle, spurious, unjustified
ungainly *adjective* = **awkward**, clumsy, inelegant, lumbering, ungraceful OPPOSITE **graceful**
ungodly *adjective* **1** *Inf* = **unreasonable**, dreadful, intolerable, outrageous, unearthly **2** = **wicked**, corrupt, depraved, godless, immoral, impious, irreligious, profane, sinful
unguarded *adjective* **1** = **unprotected**, defenceless, undefended, vulnerable **2** = **careless**, heedless, ill-considered, imprudent, incautious, rash, thoughtless, unthinking, unwary
unhappiness *noun* = **sadness**, blues, dejection, depression, despondency, gloom, heartache, low spirits, melancholy, misery, sorrow, wretchedness
unhappy *adjective* **1** = **sad**, blue, dejected, depressed, despondent, downcast, melancholy, miserable, mournful, sorrowful OPPOSITE

happy. **2** = **unlucky**, cursed, hapless, ill-fated, unfortunate, wretched OPPOSITE **lucky**
unhealthy *adjective* **1** = **harmful**, detrimental, insalubrious, insanitary, unwholesome OPPOSITE **healthy**. **2** = **sick**, ailing, crook (*Aust & NZ sl*), delicate, feeble, frail, infirm, invalid, sickly, unwell OPPOSITE **well**
unheard-of *adjective* **1** = **unprecedented**, inconceivable, new, novel, obscure, singular, unfamiliar, unique, unknown **2** = **shocking**, disgraceful, outrageous, preposterous
unholy *adjective* **1** = **evil**, corrupt, profane, sinful, ungodly, wicked OPPOSITE **godly**
unification *noun* = **union**, alliance, amalgamation, coalescence, coalition, confederation, federation, uniting
uniform *noun* **1** = **outfit**, costume, dress, garb, habit, livery, regalia, suit ♦ *adjective* **2** = **unvarying**, consistent, constant, even, regular, smooth, unchanging OPPOSITE **varying**. **3** = **alike**, equal, like, same, similar
uniformity *noun* **2, 3** = **regularity**, constancy, evenness, invariability, sameness, similarity
unify *verb* = **unite**, amalgamate, combine, confederate, consolidate, join, merge OPPOSITE **divide**
uninterested *adjective* = **indifferent**,

U

unionize *verb* organize (workers) into a trade union. **unionization** *noun* **Union Jack, Flag** national flag of the United Kingdom.

unique ❶ [yoo-**neek**] *adjective* **1** being the only one of a particular type. **2** without equal or like. **unique to** concerning or belonging to a particular person, thing, or group. **uniquely** *adverb*

unisex *adjective* designed for use by both sexes.

unison ❶ *noun* **1** complete agreement. **2** *Music* singing or playing of the same notes together at the same time. **in unison** at the same time as another person or other people.

UNISON *noun* British trade union consisting mainly of council and hospital workers.

unit ❶ *noun* **1** single undivided entity or whole. **2** group or individual regarded as a basic element of a larger whole. **3** fixed quantity etc., used as a standard of measurement. **4** piece of furniture designed to be fitted with other similar pieces, e.g. *kitchen units*. **unit trust** investment trust that issues units for public sale and invests the money in many different businesses.

Unitarian *noun* person who believes that God is one being and rejects the Trinity. **Unitarianism** *noun*

unitary *adjective* **1** consisting of a single undivided whole. **2** of a unit or units.

unite ❶ *verb* **1** make or become an integrated whole. **2** (cause to) enter into an association or alliance.

unity ❶ *noun* **1** state of being one. **2** mutual agreement.

universe ❶ *noun* **1** whole of all existing matter, energy, and space. **2** the world.

universal *adjective* **1** of or typical of the whole of mankind or of nature. **2** existing everywhere. **universally** *adverb* **universality** *noun*

university *noun, pl* **-ties** institution of higher education with the authority to award degrees.

unkempt ❶ *adjective* **1** (of the hair) not combed. **2** slovenly or untidy.

unkind ❶ *adjective* unsympathetic or cruel. **unkindly** *adverb* **unkindness** *noun*

unknown ❶ *adjective* **1** not known. **2** not famous. ◆ *noun* **3** unknown person, quantity, or thing.

unleaded *adjective* (of petrol) containing less tetraethyl lead, in order to reduce environmental pollution.

unleash ❶ *verb* set loose or cause (something bad).

unleavened [un-**lev**-vend] *adjective* (of bread) made without yeast.

unless *conjunction* except under the circumstances that.

unlike ❶ *adjective* **1** dissimilar or different. ◆ *preposition* **2** not like or typical of.

——————— T H E S A U R U S ———————

apathetic, blasé, bored, listless, unconcerned

union *noun* **1** = **uniting**, accord, agreement, amalgamation, blend, combination, concord, conjunction, fusion, harmony, joining, mixture, unanimity, unison, unity **3** = **alliance**, association, coalition, confederacy, federation, league

unique *adjective* **1** = **single**, lone, only, solitary **2** = **unparalleled**, matchless, unequalled, unmatched, without equal

unison *noun* **1** = **agreement**, accord, concert, concord, harmony, unity

unit *noun* **1** = **item**, entity, whole **2** = **part**, component, constituent, element, member, section, segment **3** = **measure**, measurement, quantity

unite *verb* **1** = **join**, amalgamate, blend, combine, couple, fuse, link, merge, unify OPPOSITE⟩ **part. 2** = **cooperate**, ally, band, collaborate, join forces, pool OPPOSITE⟩ **separate**

unity *noun* **1** = **wholeness**, entity, integrity, oneness, singleness, union OPPOSITE⟩ **division. 2** = **agreement**, accord, assent, concord, consensus, harmony, solidarity, unison

OPPOSITE⟩ **disagreement**

universal *adjective* **1** = **widespread**, common, general, overarching, total, unlimited, whole, worldwide

universally *adverb* **2** = **everywhere**, always, invariably, without exception

universe *noun* **1** = **cosmos**, creation, macrocosm, nature

unkempt *adjective* **1** = **uncombed**, shaggy, tousled **2** = **untidy**, dishevelled, disordered, messy, scruffy, slovenly, ungroomed OPPOSITE⟩ **neat**

unkind *adjective* = **cruel**, hardhearted, harsh, malicious, mean, nasty, spiteful, uncharitable, unfeeling, unfriendly, unsympathetic

unknown *adjective* **1 a** = **unidentified**, anonymous, nameless, uncharted, undiscovered, unexplored, unnamed **b** = **hidden**, concealed, dark, mysterious, secret, unrevealed **c** = **strange**, alien, new **2** = **obscure**, humble, unfamiliar OPPOSITE⟩ **famous**

unleash *verb* = **release**, free, let go, let loose

unlike *adjective* **1** = **different**, dissimilar, distinct, diverse, not alike, opposite, unequal OPPOSITE⟩ **similar to**

U

unlikely ⊙ *adjective* improbable.
unload ⊙ *verb* **1** remove (cargo) from (a ship, lorry, or plane). **2** tell someone your problems or worries. **3** remove the ammunition from (a firearm).
unlooked-for ⊙ *adjective* unexpected or unforeseen.
unlucky ⊙ *adjective* **1** having bad luck, unfortunate. **2** ill-omened or inauspicious.
unman *verb* cause to lose courage or nerve.
unmanned *adjective* having no personnel or crew.
unmask ⊙ *verb* **1** remove the mask or disguise from. **2** (cause to) appear in true character.
unmentionable ⊙ *adjective* unsuitable as a topic of conversation.
unmistakable, unmistakeable ⊙ *adjective* not ambiguous, clear. **unmistakably, unmistakeably** *adverb*
unmitigated ⊙ *adjective* **1** not reduced or lessened in severity etc. **2** total and complete.
unmoved *adjective* not affected by emotion, indifferent.
unnatural ⊙ *adjective* **1** strange and frightening because not usual. **2** not in accordance with accepted standards of behaviour. **unnaturally** *adverb* **not unnaturally** as one would expect.
unnecessary ⊙ *adjective* not essential, or more than is essential. **unnecessarily** *adverb*
unnerve ⊙ *verb* cause to lose courage,

confidence, or self-control. **unnerving** *adjective*
unnumbered *adjective* **1** countless. **2** not counted or given a number.
UNO United Nations Organization.
unobtrusive *adjective* not drawing attention to oneself or itself, inconspicuous. **unobtrusively** *adverb*
unorthodox *adjective* **1** (of ideas, methods, etc.) unconventional and not generally accepted. **2** (of a person) having unusual opinions or methods.
unpack *verb* **1** remove the contents of (a suitcase, trunk, etc.). **2** take (something) out of a packed container.
unpalatable *adjective* **1** (of food) unpleasant to taste. **2** (of a fact, idea, etc.) unpleasant and hard to accept.
unparalleled ⊙ *adjective* not equalled, supreme.
unpick *verb* undo (the stitches) of (a piece of sewing).
unpleasant ⊙ *adjective* not pleasant or agreeable. **unpleasantly** *adverb* **unpleasantness** *noun*
unpopular ⊙ *adjective* generally disliked or disapproved of. **unpopularity** *noun*
unprecedented ⊙ *adjective* never having happened before, unparalleled.
unprepossessing *adjective* unattractive in appearance.
unpretentious *adjective* modest, unassuming,

——————————— T H E S A U R U S ———————————

unlikely *adjective* =**improbable**, doubtful, faint, implausible, incredible, questionable, remote, slight, unbelievable OPPOSITE> **expected**
unload *verb* **1** =**empty**, discharge, dump, lighten, relieve, unpack
unlooked-for *adjective* =**unexpected**, chance, fortuitous, surprising, unanticipated, unforeseen, unpredicted
unlucky *adjective* **1** =**unfortunate**, cursed, hapless, luckless, miserable, unhappy, wretched OPPOSITE> **fortunate**. **2** =**ill-fated**, doomed, inauspicious, ominous, unfavourable
unmask *verb* =**reveal**, disclose, discover, expose, lay bare, uncover
unmentionable *adjective* =**taboo**, forbidden, indecent, obscene, scandalous, shameful, shocking, unspeakable
unmistakable, unmistakeable *adjective* =**clear**, certain, distinct, evident, manifest, obvious, plain, sure, unambiguous
unmitigated *adjective* **1** =**unrelieved**, intense, persistent, unalleviated, unbroken, undiminished **2** =**complete**, absolute, arrant,

downright, outright, sheer, thorough, utter
unnatural *adjective* **1** =**strange**, extraordinary, freakish, outlandish, queer OPPOSITE> **normal**. **2** =**false**, affected, artificial, feigned, forced, insincere, phoney *or* phony (*inf*), stiff, stilted OPPOSITE> **genuine**
unnecessary *adjective* =**needless**, expendable, inessential, redundant, superfluous, unneeded, unrequired
unnerve *verb* =**intimidate**, demoralize, discourage, dishearten, dismay, faze, fluster, frighten, psych out (*inf*), rattle (*inf*), shake, upset
unparalleled *adjective* =**unequalled**, incomparable, matchless, superlative, unique, unmatched, unprecedented, unsurpassed
unpleasant *adjective* =**nasty**, bad, disagreeable, displeasing, distasteful, horrid, objectionable OPPOSITE> **nice**
unpopular *adjective* =**disliked**, rejected, shunned, unwanted, unwelcome
unprecedented *adjective* =**extraordinary**, abnormal, munted (*NZ sl*), new, novel, original, remarkable, singular, unheard-of

U

and down-to-earth.

unprincipled ⊕ *adjective* lacking moral principles, unscrupulous.

unprintable *adjective* unsuitable for printing for reasons of obscenity or libel.

unprofessional ⊕ *adjective* contrary to the accepted code of a profession. **unprofessionally** *adverb*

unprofitable *adjective* **1** not making a profit. **2** not helpful or beneficial.

unqualified ⊕ *adjective* **1** lacking the necessary qualifications. **2** total or complete.

unquestionable ⊕ *adjective* not to be doubted, indisputable. **unquestionably** *adverb*

unquote *interjection* expression used to indicate the end of a quotation that was introduced with the word 'quote'.

unravel ⊕ *verb* **-elling, -elled 1** reduce (something knitted or woven) to separate strands. **2** become unravelled. **3** explain or solve.

unreadable *adjective* **1** unable to be read or deciphered. **2** too difficult or dull to read.

unreal ⊕ *adjective* **1** (as if) existing only in the imagination. **2** insincere or artificial. **unreality** *noun*

unreasonable ⊕ *adjective* **1** immoderate or excessive. **2** refusing to listen to reason. **unreasonably** *adverb*

unremitting *adjective* never slackening or stopping. **unremittingly** *adverb*

unrequited *adjective* not returned, e.g. *unrequited love.*

unreserved ⊕ *adjective* completely, without reservation. **unreservedly** [un-re-**zerv**-id-lee] *adverb*

unrest ⊕ *noun* rebellious state of discontent.

unrivalled ⊕ *adjective* having no equal.

unroll *verb* open out or unwind (something rolled or coiled) or (of something rolled or coiled) become opened out or unwound.

unruffled *adjective* **1** calm and unperturbed. **2** smooth and still.

unruly ⊕ *adjective* **-lier, -liest** difficult to control or organize.

unsaturated *adjective* **1** (of an organic compound) containing a double or triple bond and therefore capable of combining with other substances. **2** (of a fat, esp. a vegetable fat) containing a high proportion of fatty acids with double bonds.

unsavoury ⊕ *adjective* distasteful or objectionable.

unscathed ⊕ *adjective* not harmed or injured.

unscrupulous ⊕ *adjective* prepared to act dishonestly, unprincipled.

unseasonable *adjective* inappropriate or unusual for the time of year. **unseasonably** *adverb*

unseat ⊕ *verb* **1** throw or displace from a seat or saddle. **2** depose from an office or position.

unseemly ⊕ *adjective* not according to

——— T H E S A U R U S ———

unprincipled *adjective* =**dishonest**, amoral, crooked, devious, dishonourable, immoral, underhand, unethical, unscrupulous

unprofessional *adjective* **a** =**unethical**, improper, lax, negligent, unprincipled **b** =**amateurish**, cowboy (*inf*), incompetent, inefficient, inexpert OPPOSITE **expert**

unqualified *adjective* **1** =**unfit**, ill-equipped, incapable, incompetent, ineligible, unprepared **2** =**total**, absolute, complete, downright, outright, thorough, utter

unquestionable *adjective* =**certain**, absolute, clear, conclusive, definite, incontrovertible, indisputable, sure, undeniable, unequivocal, unmistakable

unravel *verb* **1** =**undo**, disentangle, free, separate, untangle, unwind **3** =**solve**, explain, figure out (*inf*), resolve, work out

unreal *adjective* **1** =**imaginary**, dreamlike, fabulous, fanciful, illusory, make-believe, visionary **2** =**fake**, artificial, false, insincere, mock, pretended, sham

unreasonable *adjective* **1** =**excessive**, extortionate, immoderate, undue, unfair,

unjust, unwarranted OPPOSITE **fair. 2** =**biased**, blinkered, opinionated OPPOSITE **flexible**

unreserved *adjective* =**total**, absolute, complete, entire, full, unlimited, wholehearted

unrest *noun* =**discontent**, agitation, discord, dissension, protest, rebellion, sedition, strife OPPOSITE **peace**

unrivalled *adjective* =**unparalleled**, beyond compare, incomparable, matchless, supreme, unequalled, unmatched, unsurpassed

unruly *adjective* =**uncontrollable**, disobedient, mutinous, rebellious, wayward, wild, wilful OPPOSITE **manageable**

unsavoury *adjective* =**distasteful**, nasty, nauseating, obnoxious, offensive, repellent, repulsive, revolting, sickening, unpleasant OPPOSITE **appetizing**

unscathed *adjective* =**unharmed**, safe, unhurt, uninjured, unmarked, whole

unscrupulous *adjective* =**unprincipled**, corrupt, dishonest, dishonourable, immoral, improper, unethical

unseat *verb* **1** =**throw**, unhorse, unsaddle **2** =**depose**, dethrone, displace, oust, overthrow, expected standards of behaviour.

unsettled ᴓ *adjective* **1** lacking order or stability. **2** disturbed and restless. **3** constantly changing or moving from place to place.

unshakable, unshakeable *adjective* (of beliefs) completely firm, not wavering. **unshakably, unshakeably** *adverb*

unsightly ᴓ *adjective* unpleasant to look at.

unsocial *adjective* **1** (also **unsociable**) avoiding the company of other people. **2** falling outside the normal working day, e.g. *unsocial hours*.

unsound ᴓ *adjective* **1** unhealthy or unstable. **2** not based on truth or fact.

unspeakable ᴓ *adjective* indescribably bad or evil. **unspeakably** *adverb*

unstable ᴓ *adjective* **1** lacking stability or firmness. **2** having abrupt changes of mood or behaviour.

unsteady ᴓ *adjective* **1** not securely fixed. **2** shaky or staggering. **unsteadily** *adverb*

unstinting *adjective* generous, gladly given, e.g. *unstinting praise*.

unstructured *adjective* without formal or systematic organization.

unstuck *adjective* **come unstuck** *Informal* fail badly.

unstudied *adjective* natural or spontaneous.

unsuccessful *adjective* not achieving success. **unsuccessfully** *adverb*

unsuitable *adjective* not right or appropriate for a particular purpose. **unsuitably** *adverb*

unsuited *adjective* **1** not appropriate for a particular task or situation. **2** (of a couple) having different personalities or tastes and unlikely to form a lasting relationship.

unsung *adjective* not acclaimed or honoured, e.g. *unsung heroes*.

unswerving ᴓ *adjective* firm, constant, not changing.

unsympathetic *adjective* **1** not feeling or showing sympathy. **2** unpleasant, not likeable. **3** (foll. by *to*) opposed to.

untapped *adjective* not yet used, e.g. *untapped resources*.

untenable ᴓ *adjective* (of a theory, idea, etc.) incapable of being defended.

unthinkable ᴓ *adjective* out of the question, inconceivable.

untidy ᴓ *adjective* messy and disordered. **untidily** *adverb* **untidiness** *noun*

untie ᴓ *verb* **1** open or free (something that is tied). **2** free from constraint.

until *conjunction* **1** up to the time that. ♦ *preposition* **2** in or throughout the period before. **not until** not before (a time or event).

untimely ᴓ *adjective* **1** occurring before the expected or normal time. **2** inappropriate to the occasion or time. **untimeliness** *noun*

unto *preposition* Old-fashioned to.

——————— THESAURUS ———————

remove

unseemly *adjective* =**improper**, inappropriate, indecorous, unbecoming, undignified, unsuitable

unsettled *adjective* **1** =**unstable**, disorderly, insecure, shaky, unsteady **2** =**restless**, agitated, anxious, confused, disturbed, flustered, restive, shaken, tense **3** =**inconstant**, changing, uncertain, variable

unsightly *adjective* =**ugly**, disagreeable, hideous, horrid, repulsive, unattractive OPPOSITE attractive

unsocial *adjective* **1** (also **unsociable**) =**unfriendly**, chilly, cold, distant, hostile, retiring, unforthcoming, withdrawn

unsound *adjective* **1** =**unhealthy**, ailing, crook (*Aust & NZ sl*), defective, diseased, ill, unbalanced, unstable, unwell, weak OPPOSITE solid. **2** =**invalid**, defective, fallacious, false, flawed, illogical, shaky, specious, unreliable, weak

unspeakable *adjective* **a** =**indescribable**, inconceivable, unbelievable, unimaginable **b** =**dreadful**, abominable, appalling, awful, heinous, horrible, monstrous, shocking

unstable *adjective* **1** =**insecure**, precarious, shaky, tottering, unsettled, unsteady, wobbly **2** =**changeable**, capricious, erratic, fitful, fluctuating, inconsistent, inconstant, irrational, temperamental, unpredictable, variable, volatile OPPOSITE steady

unsteady *adjective* **1** =**unstable**, infirm, insecure, precarious, unsafe **2** =**shaky**, wobbly

unswerving *adjective* =**constant**, firm, resolute, single-minded, staunch, steadfast, steady, true, unwavering

untenable *adjective* =**unsustainable**, groundless, illogical, indefensible, insupportable, shaky, unsound, weak

unthinkable *adjective* **a** =**impossible**, absurd, out of the question, unreasonable **b** =**inconceivable**, implausible, incredible, unimaginable

untidy *adjective* =**messy**, chaotic, cluttered, disarrayed, disordered, jumbled, littered, muddled, shambolic, unkempt OPPOSITE neat

untie *verb* **1** =**undo**, free, loosen, release, unbind, unfasten, unlace

untimely *adjective* **1** =**early**, premature, unseasonable OPPOSITE timely. **2** =**ill-timed**,

U

untold ❶ *adjective* **1** incapable of description. **2** incalculably great in number or quantity.

untouchable *adjective* **1** above reproach or suspicion. **2** unable to be touched. ◆ *noun* **3** member of the lowest Hindu caste in India.

untoward ❶ *adjective* causing misfortune or annoyance.

untrue ❶ *adjective* **1** incorrect or false. **2** disloyal or unfaithful. **untruth** *noun* statement that is not true, lie. **untruthful** *adjective* **untruthfully** *adverb*

unusual ❶ *adjective* uncommon or extraordinary. **unusually** *adverb*

unutterable *adjective* incapable of being expressed in words. **unutterably** *adverb*

unvarnished *adjective* not elaborated upon, e.g. *the unvarnished truth*.

unveil ❶ *verb* **1** ceremonially remove the cover from (a new picture, plaque, etc.). **2** make public (a secret). **unveiling** *noun*

unwarranted ❶ *adjective* not justified, not necessary.

unwell ❶ *adjective* not healthy, ill.

unwieldy ❶ *adjective* too heavy, large, or awkward to be easily handled.

unwind ❶ *verb* **1** relax after a busy or tense time. **2** slacken, undo, or unravel.

unwitting ❶ *adjective* **1** not intentional. **2** not knowing or conscious. **unwittingly** *adverb*

unwonted *adjective* out of the ordinary.

unworthy ❶ *adjective* **1** not deserving or worthy. **2** lacking merit or value. **unworthy of** beneath the level considered befitting (to).

unwrap *verb* remove the wrapping from (something).

unwritten ❶ *adjective* **1** not printed or in writing. **2** operating only through custom, e.g. *an unwritten rule*.

up *preposition, adverb* **1** indicating movement to or position at a higher place. ◆ *adverb* **2** indicating readiness, intensity or completeness, etc., e.g. *warm up*; *drink up.* ◆ *adjective* **3** of a high or higher position. **4** out of bed. ◆ *verb* **upping, upped 5** increase or raise. **up against** having to cope with. **up and** *Informal* do something suddenly, e.g. *he upped and left.* **ups and downs** alternating periods of good and bad luck. **up to 1** engaged in (usu. something shady, secretive, or mischievous). **2** the responsibility of, e.g. *it's up to you to lock the doors.* **3** equal to or capable of (doing something). **what's up?** *Informal* what is wrong? **upward** *adjective* **1** directed or moving towards a higher place or level. ◆ *adverb* **2** (also **upwards**) from a lower to a higher place, level, or condition.

——————— T H E S A U R U S ———————

awkward, inappropriate, inconvenient, inopportune, mistimed OPPOSITE appropriate

untold *adjective* **1** = **indescribable**, inexpressible, undreamed of, unimaginable, unthinkable, unutterable **2** = **countless**, incalculable, innumerable, myriad, numberless, uncountable

untoward *adjective* **a** = **unfavourable**, adverse, inauspicious, inopportune, unlucky **b** = **troublesome**, annoying, awkward, inconvenient, irritating, unfortunate

untrue *adjective* **1** = **incorrect**, erroneous, false, inaccurate, mistaken, wrong OPPOSITE **right**. **2** = **unfaithful**, deceitful, deceptive, dishonest, disloyal, faithless, false, inconstant, lying, treacherous, untrustworthy OPPOSITE **loyal**

untruth *noun* = **lie**, deceit, falsehood, fib, pork pie (*Brit sl*), porky (*Brit sl*), story

untruthful *adjective* = **dishonest**, deceitful, deceptive, false, lying, mendacious

unusual *adjective* = **extraordinary**, curious, different, exceptional, odd, queer, rare, remarkable, singular, strange, uncommon, unconventional OPPOSITE **common**

unveil *verb* **2** = **reveal**, disclose, divulge, expose, make known, uncover

unwarranted *adjective* = **unnecessary**, gratuitous, groundless, indefensible, inexcusable, uncalled-for, unjustified, unprovoked

unwell *adjective* = **ill**, ailing, crook (*Aust & NZ sl*), sick, sickly, under the weather (*inf*), unhealthy OPPOSITE **well**

unwieldy *adjective* **a** = **bulky**, clumsy, hefty, massive, ponderous **b** = **awkward**, cumbersome, inconvenient, unmanageable

unwind *verb* **1** = **relax**, loosen up, take it easy, wind down **2** = **unravel**, slacken, uncoil, undo, unroll, untwine, untwist

unwitting *adjective* **1** = **unintentional**, accidental, chance, inadvertent, involuntary, unplanned OPPOSITE **intended**. **2** = **unknowing**, ignorant, innocent, unaware, unconscious, unsuspecting OPPOSITE **knowing**

unworthy *adjective* **1** = **undeserving**, not fit for, not good enough OPPOSITE **deserving**. **2** = **dishonourable**, base, contemptible, degrading, discreditable, disgraceful, disreputable, ignoble, shameful OPPOSITE **honourable** ◆ **unworthy of** = **unbefitting**, beneath, inappropriate, unbecoming, unfitting, unseemly, unsuitable

unwritten *adjective* **1** = **oral**, vocal **2**

up-and-coming *adjective* likely to be successful in the future.

upbeat ❶ *adjective* **1** *Informal* cheerful and optimistic. ◆ *noun* **2** *Music* unaccented beat.

upbraid ❶ *verb* scold or reproach.

upbringing ❶ *noun* education of a person during the formative years.

update ❶ *verb* bring up to date.

upend *verb* turn or set (something) on its end.

upfront *adjective* **1** open and frank. ◆ *adverb*, *adjective* **2** (of money) paid out at the beginning of a business arrangement.

upgrade ❶ *verb* promote (a person or job) to a higher rank. **upgrading** *noun*

upheaval ❶ *noun* strong, sudden, or violent disturbance.

uphill ❶ *adjective* **1** sloping or leading upwards. **2** requiring a great deal of effort. ◆ *adverb* **3** up a slope. ◆ *noun* S Afr difficulty.

uphold ❶ *verb* **1** maintain or defend against opposition. **2** give moral support to. **upholder** *noun*

upholster *verb* fit (a chair or sofa) with padding, springs, and covering. **upholstered** *adjective* **upholsterer** *noun* **upholstery** *noun* soft covering on a chair or sofa.

upkeep ❶ *noun* act, process, or cost of keeping something in good repair.

upland *adjective* of or in an area of high or relatively high ground. **uplands** *plural noun*

area of high or relatively high ground.

uplift ❶ *verb* **1** raise or lift up. **2** raise morally or spiritually. ◆ *noun* **3** act or process of improving moral, social, or cultural conditions. **uplifting** *adjective*

up-market *adjective* expensive and of superior quality.

upon *preposition* **1** on. **2** up and on.

upper ❶ *adjective* **1** higher or highest in physical position, wealth, rank, or status. ◆ *noun* **2** part of a shoe above the sole. **on one's uppers** destitute. **uppermost** *adjective* **1** highest in position, power, or importance. ◆ *adverb* **2** in or into the highest place or position. **upper case** capital letters. **upper class** highest social class. **upper-class** *adjective* **upper crust** *Informal* upper class. **uppercut** *noun* short swinging upward punch delivered to the chin. **upper hand** position of control.

uppish, uppity *adjective Informal* snobbish, arrogant, or presumptuous.

upright ❶ *adjective* **1** vertical or erect. **2** honest or just. ◆ *adverb* **3** vertically or in an erect position. ◆ *noun* **4** vertical support, such as a post. **uprightness** *noun*

uprising ❶ *noun* rebellion or revolt.

uproar ❶ *noun* disturbance characterized by loud noise and confusion. **uproarious** *adjective* **1** very funny. **2** (of laughter) loud and boisterous. **uproariously** *adverb*

——————— THESAURUS ———————

= **customary**, accepted, tacit, understood
upbeat *adjective* **1** *Inf* = **cheerful**, cheery, encouraging, hopeful, optimistic, positive
upbraid *verb* = **scold**, admonish, berate, rebuke, reprimand, reproach, reprove
upbringing *noun* = **education**, breeding, raising, rearing, training
update *verb* = **bring up to date**, amend, modernize, renew, revise
upgrade *verb* = **promote**, advance, better, elevate, enhance, improve, raise OPPOSITE⟩ degrade
upheaval *noun* = **disturbance**, disorder, disruption, revolution, turmoil
uphill *adjective* **1** = **ascending**, climbing, mounting, rising OPPOSITE⟩ descending. **2** = **arduous**, difficult, exhausting, gruelling, hard, laborious, strenuous, taxing, tough
uphold *verb* **1** = **defend**, maintain, sustain **2** = **support**, advocate, aid, back, champion, endorse, promote
upkeep *noun* **a** = **maintenance**, keep, repair, running, subsistence **b** = **running costs**, expenditure, expenses, overheads
uplift *verb* **1** = **raise**, elevate, hoist, lift up **2**

= **improve**, advance, better, edify, inspire, raise, refine ◆*noun* **3** = **improvement**, advancement, edification, enhancement, enlightenment, enrichment, refinement
upper *adjective* **1 a** = **higher**, high, loftier, top, topmost OPPOSITE⟩ lower. **b** = **superior**, eminent, greater, important OPPOSITE⟩ lower
upper-class *adjective* = **aristocratic**, blue-blooded, highborn, high-class, noble, patrician
upper hand *noun* = **control**, advantage, ascendancy, edge, mastery, supremacy
uppermost *adjective* **1 a** = **top**, highest, loftiest, topmost OPPOSITE⟩ lowest. **b** = **supreme**, chief, dominant, foremost, greatest, leading, main, principal OPPOSITE⟩ least
uppish, uppity *adjective Inf* = **conceited**, bumptious, cocky, full of oneself, impertinent, self-important
upright *adjective* **1** = **vertical**, erect, perpendicular, straight OPPOSITE⟩ flat. **2** = **honest**, conscientious, ethical, good, honourable, just, principled, righteous, virtuous OPPOSITE⟩ corrupt
uprising *noun* = **rebellion**, disturbance, insurgence, insurrection, mutiny, revolt,

U

uproot ❶ *verb* **1** pull up by or as if by the roots. **2** displace (a person or people) from their native or usual surroundings.

upset ❶ *adjective* **1** emotionally or physically disturbed or distressed. ♦ *verb* **2** tip over. **3** disturb the normal state or stability of. **4** disturb mentally or emotionally. **5** make physically ill. ♦ *noun* **6** unexpected defeat or reversal. **7** disturbance or disorder of the emotions, mind, or body. **upsetting** *adjective*

upshot ❶ *noun* final result or conclusion.

upside down ❶ *adjective* **1** turned over completely. **2** *Informal* confused or jumbled. ♦ *adverb* **3** in an inverted fashion. **4** in a chaotic manner.

upstage *adjective* **1** at the back half of the stage. ♦ *verb* **2** *Informal* draw attention to oneself from (someone else).

upstairs *adverb* **1** to or on an upper floor of a building. ♦ *noun* **2** upper floor. ♦ *adjective* **3** situated on an upper floor.

upstanding ❶ *adjective* of good character.

upstart ❶ *noun* person who has risen suddenly to a position of power and behaves arrogantly.

upstream *adverb, adjective* in or towards the higher part of a stream.

upsurge *noun* rapid rise or swell.

uptake *noun* **quick, slow on the uptake** *Informal* quick or slow to understand or learn.

uptight ❶ *adjective Informal* nervously tense, irritable, or angry.

up-to-date ❶ *adjective* modern or fashionable.

uptown *adjective, adverb US & Canad* towards, in, or relating to some part of a town that is away from the centre. ♦ *noun* such a part of a town, esp. a residential part.

upturn ❶ *noun* upward trend or improvement.

upturned *adjective* facing upwards.

uranium [yew-**rain**-ee-um] *noun Chem* radioactive silvery-white metallic element, used chiefly as a source of nuclear energy.

Uranus *noun* **1** *Greek myth* god of the sky. **2** seventh planet from the sun.

urban ❶ *adjective* **1** of or living in a city or town. **2** denoting modern pop music of African-American origin, such as hip-hop.

urbanize *verb* make (a rural area) more industrialized and urban. **urbanization** *noun*

urbane ❶ *adjective* characterized by courtesy, elegance, and sophistication. **urbanity** *noun*

urchin ❶ *noun* mischievous child.

Urdu [**oor**-doo] *noun* language of Pakistan.

ureter [yew-**reet**-er] *noun* tube that conveys urine from the kidney to the bladder.

urethra [yew-**reeth**-ra] *noun* canal that carries urine from the bladder out of the body.

urge ❶ *noun* **1** strong impulse, inner drive, or yearning. ♦ *verb* **2** plead with or press (a person to do something). **3** advocate earnestly. **4** force or drive onwards. **urgent** *adjective* needing attention at once.

——————— THESAURUS ———————

revolution, rising

uproar *noun* =**commotion**, din, furore, mayhem, noise, outcry, pandemonium, racket, riot, turmoil

uproarious *adjective* **1** =**hilarious**, hysterical, killing (*inf*), rib-tickling, rip-roaring (*inf*), side-splitting, very funny OPPOSITE> **serious. 2** =**boisterous**, loud, rollicking, unrestrained OPPOSITE> **quiet**

uproot *verb* **1** =**pull up**, dig up, rip up, root out, weed out **2** =**displace**, exile

upset *adjective* **1 a** =**distressed**, agitated, bothered, dismayed, disturbed, grieved, hurt, put out, troubled, worried **b** =**sick**, ill, queasy ♦*verb* **2** =**tip over**, capsize, knock over, overturn, spill **3** =**mess up**, change, disorder, disorganize, disturb, spoil **4** =**distress**, agitate, bother, disconcert, disturb, faze, fluster, grieve, perturb, ruffle, trouble ♦*noun* **6** =**reversal**, defeat, shake-up (*inf*) **7 a** =**distress**, agitation, bother, disturbance, shock, trouble, worry **b** =**illness**, bug (*inf*), complaint, disorder, malady, sickness

upshot *noun* =**result**, culmination, end, end result, finale, outcome, sequel

upside down *adjective* **1** =**inverted**, overturned, upturned **2** *Inf* =**confused**, chaotic, disordered, higgledy-piggledy (*inf*), muddled, topsy-turvy

upstanding *adjective* =**honest**, ethical, good, honourable, incorruptible, moral, principled, upright OPPOSITE> **bad**

upstart *noun* =**social climber**, arriviste, nouveau riche, parvenu

uptight *adjective Inf* =**tense**, anxious, edgy, on edge, uneasy, wired (*sl*)

up-to-date *adjective* =**modern**, current, fashionable, in vogue, stylish, trendy (*Brit inf*), up-to-the-minute OPPOSITE> **old fashioned**

upturn *noun* =**rise**, advancement, improvement, increase, recovery, revival, upsurge, upswing

urban *adjective* =**civic**, city, dorp (*S Afr*), metropolitan, municipal, town

urbane *adjective* =**sophisticated**, cultivated, cultured, debonair, polished, refined, smooth, suave, well-bred

urchin *noun* =**ragamuffin**, brat, gamin, waif

urge *noun* **1** =**impulse**, compulsion, desire,

U

urgent ⊕ *adjective* requiring speedy action or attention. **urgency** *noun* **urgently** *adverb*
uric acid *noun* white odourless crystalline acid present in the blood and urine.
urine *noun* pale yellow fluid excreted by the kidneys to the bladder and passed as waste from the body. **urinary** *adjective* **urinate** *verb* discharge urine. **urination** *noun* **urinal** *noun* sanitary fitting used by men for urination.
URL uniform resource locator: the address of a location on the Internet.
urn *noun* **1** vase used as a container for the ashes of the dead. **2** large metal container with a tap, used for making and holding tea or coffee.
ursine *adjective* of or like a bear.
us *pronoun* objective case of WE.
US, USA United States (of America).
use ⊕ *verb* **1** put into service or action. **2** take advantage of, exploit. **3** consume or expend. ◆ *noun* **4** using or being used. **5** ability or permission to use. **6** usefulness or advantage. **7** purpose for which something is used. **user** *noun* **user-friendly** *adjective* easy to familiarize oneself with, understand, and use. **usable** *adjective* able to be used. **usage** *noun* **1** regular or constant use. **2** way in which a word is used in a language. **use-by date** *Aust, NZ, S Afr & US* date on packaged food after which it should not be sold. **used** *adjective* second-hand. **used**

to *adjective* **1** accustomed to. ◆ *verb* **2** used as an auxiliary to express past habitual or accustomed actions, e.g. *I used to live there.*
useful *adjective* **1** able to be used advantageously or for several different purposes. **2** *Informal* commendable or capable, e.g. *a useful day's work.* **usefully** *adverb* **usefulness** *noun* **useless** *adjective* **1** having no practical use. **2** *Informal* ineffectual, weak, or stupid, e.g. *useless at maths.* **uselessly** *adverb* **uselessness** *noun*

> **SPELLING TIP**
>
> The Bank of English shows that it's very common to write *usualy*, forgetting the double *l* of **usually**.

usher ⊕ *noun* **1** official who shows people to their seats, as in a church. ◆ *verb* **2** conduct or escort. **usherette** *noun* female assistant in a cinema who shows people to their seats.
USSR (formerly) Union of Soviet Socialist Republics.
usual ⊕ *adjective* of the most normal, frequent, or regular type. **as usual** as happens normally. **usually** *adverb* most often, in most cases.
usurp ⊕ [yewz-**zurp**] *verb* seize (a position or power) without authority. **usurpation** *noun*

——————— THESAURUS ———————

drive, itch, longing, thirst, wish, yearning OPPOSITE reluctance ◆*verb* **2** = **beg**, beseech, entreat, exhort, implore, plead **3** = **advocate**, advise, counsel, recommend, support OPPOSITE discourage. **4** = **drive**, compel, encourage, force, gee up, goad, impel, incite, induce, press, push, spur
urgency *noun* = **importance**, extremity, gravity, hurry, necessity, need, pressure, seriousness
urgent *adjective* = **crucial**, compelling, critical, immediate, imperative, important, pressing, top-priority OPPOSITE minor
usable *adjective* = **serviceable**, available, current, functional, practical, utilizable, valid, working
usage *noun* **1** = **practice**, convention, custom, habit, method, mode, procedure, regime, routine
use *verb* **1** = **employ**, apply, exercise, exert, operate, practise, utilize, work **2** = **take advantage of**, exploit, manipulate **3** = **consume**, exhaust, expend, run through, spend ◆*noun* **4** = **usage**, application, employment, exercise, handling, operation,

practice, service **6** = **good**, advantage, avail, benefit, help, point, profit, service, usefulness, value **7** = **purpose**, end, object, reason
used *adjective* = **second-hand**, cast-off, nearly new, shopsoiled
used to *adjective* **1** = **accustomed to**, familiar with
useful *adjective* **1** = **helpful**, advantageous, beneficial, effective, fruitful, practical, profitable, serviceable, valuable, worthwhile
usefulness *noun* **1** = **helpfulness**, benefit, convenience, effectiveness, efficacy, practicality, use, utility, value, worth
useless *adjective* **1** = **worthless**, fruitless, futile, impractical, ineffectual, pointless, unproductive, vain, valueless OPPOSITE useful. **2** *Inf* = **inept**, hopeless, incompetent, ineffectual, no good
usher *noun* **1** = **attendant**, doorkeeper, doorman, escort, guide ◆*verb* **2** = **escort**, conduct, direct, guide, lead
usual *adjective* = **normal**, common, customary, everyday, general, habitual, ordinary, regular, routine, standard, typical
usually *adverb* = **normally**, as a rule, commonly, generally, habitually, mainly,

U

usurper *noun*
usury *noun* practice of lending money at an extremely high rate of interest. **usurer** [yewz-yoor-er] *noun*
UT Utah.
utensil *noun* tool or container for practical use.
uterus [yew-ter-russ] *noun* womb. **uterine** *adjective*
utilitarian *adjective* 1 useful rather than beautiful. 2 of utilitarianism. **utilitarianism** *noun* doctrine that the right action is the one that brings about the greatest good for the greatest number of people.
utility ① *noun* 1 usefulness. 2 *pl* **-ties** public service, such as electricity. ◆ *adjective* 3 designed for use rather than beauty. **utility room** room used for large domestic appliances and equipment. **utility truck** *Aust & NZ* small truck with an open body and low sides.
utilize ① *verb* make practical use of.

utilization *noun*
utmost ① *adjective, noun* (of) the greatest possible degree or amount.
Utopia ① [yew-**tope**-ee-a] *noun* any real or imaginary society, place, or state considered to be perfect or ideal. **Utopian** *adjective*
utter¹ ① *verb* express (something) in sounds or words. **utterance** *noun* 1 something uttered. 2 act or power of uttering.
utter² ① *adjective* total or absolute. **utterly** *adverb*
uttermost *adjective, noun* same as UTMOST.
U-turn *noun* 1 turn, made by a vehicle, in the shape of a U, resulting in a reversal of direction. 2 complete change in policy.
UV ultraviolet.
uvula [yew-view-la] *noun* small fleshy part of the soft palate that hangs in the back of the throat.
uxorious [ux-or-ee-uss] *adjective* excessively fond of or dependent on one's wife.

──────────── T H E S A U R U S ────────────

mostly, on the whole
usurp *verb* = **seize**, appropriate, assume, commandeer, take, take over, wrest
utility *noun* 1 = **usefulness**, benefit, convenience, efficacy, practicality, serviceableness
utilize *verb* = **use**, avail oneself of, employ, make use of, put to use, take advantage of, turn to account
utmost *adjective* **a** = **greatest**, chief, highest, maximum, paramount, pre-eminent, supreme **b** = **farthest**, extreme, final, last ◆*noun* = **greatest**, best, hardest, highest
Utopia *noun* = **paradise**, bliss, Eden, Garden

of Eden, heaven, Shangri-la
Utopian *adjective* = **perfect**, dream, fantasy, ideal, idealistic, imaginary, romantic, visionary
utter¹ *verb* = **express**, articulate, pronounce, say, speak, voice
utter² *adjective* = **absolute**, complete, downright, outright, sheer, thorough, total, unmitigated
utterance *noun* 1 = **speech**, announcement, declaration, expression, remark, statement, words
utterly *adverb* = **totally**, absolutely, completely, entirely, extremely, fully, perfectly, thoroughly

U

V 1 *Chem* vanadium. **2** volt. **3** the Roman numeral for five.

v. 1 verb. **2** versus. **3** very.

VA Virginia.

vacant ❶ *adjective* **1** (of a toilet, room, etc.) unoccupied. **2** without interest or understanding. **vacantly** *adverb* **vacancy** *noun, pl* **-cies 1** unfilled job. **2** unoccupied room in a guesthouse. **3** state of being unoccupied.

vacate ❶ *verb* **1** cause (something) to be empty by leaving. **2** give up (a job or position).

vacation *noun* **1** time when universities and law courts are closed. **2** *US & Canad* holiday.

vaccinate *verb* inject with a vaccine.

vaccination *noun* **vaccine** *noun* substance designed to cause a mild form of a disease to make a person immune to the disease itself.

vacillate [**vass**-ill-late] *verb* keep changing one's mind or opinions. **vacillation** *noun*

vacuous ❶ *adjective* not expressing intelligent thought. **vacuity** *noun*

vacuum ❶ *noun, pl* **vacuums, vacua 1** empty space from which all or most air or gas has been removed. **2** same as VACUUM CLEANER. ◆ *verb* **3** clean with a vacuum cleaner. **vacuum cleaner** electrical appliance which sucks up dust and dirt from carpets and upholstery. **vacuum flask** double-walled flask with a vacuum between the walls that keeps drinks hot or cold. **vacuum-packed** *adjective* contained in packaging from which the air has been removed.

vagabond ❶ *noun* person with no fixed home, esp. a beggar.

vagary [**vaig**-a-ree] *noun, pl* **-garies 1** unpredictable change. **2** whim.

vagina [vaj-**jine**-a] *noun, pl* **-nas, -nae** (in female mammals) passage from the womb to the external genitals. **vaginal** *adjective*

vagrant ❶ [**vaig**-rant] *noun* **1** person with no settled home. ◆ *adjective* **2** wandering. **vagrancy** *noun*

vague ❶ *adjective* **1** not clearly explained. **2** deliberately withholding information. **3** unable to be seen or heard clearly. **4** absent-minded. **vaguely** *adverb*

vain ❶ *adjective* **1** excessively proud, esp. of one's appearance. **2** bound to fail, futile. **in vain** unsuccessfully.

vainglorious *adjective Lit* boastful.

valance [**val**-lenss] *noun* piece of drapery round the edge of a bed.

vale *noun Lit* valley.

valedictory [val-lid-**dik**-tree] *adjective* (of a speech, performance, etc.) intended as a farewell. **valediction** *noun* farewell speech.

valence [**vale**-ence] *noun* molecular bonding between atoms.

valency *noun, pl* **-cies** power of an atom to make molecular bonds.

valentine *noun* (person to whom one sends) a romantic card on Saint Valentine's Day, 14th

---

THESAURUS

vacancy *noun* **1** = **job**, opening, opportunity, position, post, situation

vacant *adjective* **1** = **unoccupied**, available, empty, free, idle, unfilled, untenanted, void OPPOSITE **taken**. **2** = **blank**, absent-minded, abstracted, dreamy, idle, inane, vacuous, vague OPPOSITE **lively**

vacate *verb* **1** = **leave**, evacuate, quit

vacuous *adjective* = **unintelligent**, blank, inane, stupid, uncomprehending, vacant

vacuum *noun* **1** = **emptiness**, gap, nothingness, space, vacuity, void

vagabond *noun* = **vagrant**, beggar, down-and-out, itinerant, rover, tramp

vagrant *noun* **1** = **tramp**, drifter, hobo (*US*), itinerant, rolling stone, wanderer ◆*adjective* **2** = **itinerant**, nomadic, roaming, rootless, roving, unsettled, vagabond OPPOSITE **settled**

vague *adjective* **1** = **unclear**, hazy, imprecise, indefinite, loose, uncertain, unspecified, woolly OPPOSITE **clear**. **3** = **indistinct**, hazy, ill-defined, indeterminate, nebulous, unclear OPPOSITE **distinct**

vain *adjective* **1** = **proud**, arrogant, conceited, egotistical, narcissistic, self-important, swaggering OPPOSITE **modest**. **2** = **futile**, abortive, fruitless, idle, pointless, senseless, unavailing, unprofitable, useless, worthless OPPOSITE **successful** ◆ **in vain** = **to no avail**, fruitless(ly), ineffectual(ly), unsuccessful(ly),

February.

valerian *noun* herb used as a sedative.

valet *noun* man's personal male servant.

valetudinarian [val-lit-yew-din-**air**-ee-an] *noun* **1** person with a long-term illness. **2** person overconcerned about his or her health.

valiant ⊙ *adjective* brave or courageous. **valiantly** *adverb*

valid ⊙ *adjective* **1** soundly reasoned. **2** having legal force. **validate** *verb* make valid. **validation** *noun* **validity** *noun*

valise [val-**leez**] *noun Old-fashioned* small suitcase.

Valium *noun* ® drug used as a tranquillizer.

valley ⊙ *noun* low area between hills, often with a river running through it.

valour ⊙ *noun Lit* bravery.

value ⊙ *noun* **1** importance, usefulness. **2** monetary worth. **3** satisfaction, e.g. *value for money*. **4** *Maths* particular number represented by a figure or symbol. ◆ *plural* **5** moral principles. ◆ *verb* **valuing, valued 6** assess the worth or desirability of. **7** have a high regard for. **valuable** *adjective* having great worth. **valuables** *plural noun* valuable personal property. **valuation** *noun* assessment of worth. **valueless** *adjective* **valuer** *noun* **value-added tax** *Brit* see VAT. **value judgment** opinion based on personal belief.

valve *noun* **1** device to control the movement of fluid through a pipe. **2** *Anat* flap in a part of the body allowing blood to flow in one direction only. **3** *Physics* tube containing a vacuum, allowing current to flow from a cathode to an anode. **4** *Zool* one of the hinged shells of an oyster or clam. **5** *Music* device on brass instruments to lengthen the tube.

valvular *adjective* **1** of or having valves. **2** like valves.

vamp¹ *noun Informal* sexually attractive woman who seduces men.

vamp² *verb* **vamp up** make (a story, piece of music, etc.) seem new by inventing additional parts.

vampire *noun* (in folklore) corpse that rises at night to drink the blood of the living. **vampire bat** tropical bat that feeds on blood.

van¹ *noun* **1** motor vehicle for transporting goods. **2** *Brit & Aust* railway carriage for goods, luggage, or mail.

van² *noun* short for VANGUARD.

vanadium *noun Chem* metallic element, used in steel.

vandal ⊙ *noun* person who deliberately damages property. **vandalism** *noun* **vandalize** *verb*

vane *noun* flat blade on a rotary device such as a weathercock or propeller.

vanguard ⊙ *noun* **1** unit of soldiers leading an army. **2** most advanced group or position in a movement or activity.

vanilla *noun* seed pod of a tropical climbing orchid, used for flavouring.

vanish ⊙ *verb* **1** disappear suddenly or mysteriously. **2** cease to exist.

vanity ⊙ *noun, pl* **-ties** (display of) excessive pride. **vanity case** small bag for carrying cosmetics.

———————— T H E S A U R U S ————————

useless(ly), vain(ly)

valiant *adjective* =**brave**, bold, courageous, fearless, gallant, heroic, intrepid, lion-hearted OPPOSITE> **cowardly**

valid *adjective* **1** =**sound**, cogent, convincing, good, logical, telling, well-founded, well-grounded OPPOSITE> **weak. 2** =**legal**, authentic, bona fide, genuine, lawful, legitimate, official OPPOSITE> **illegal**

validate *verb* =**confirm**, authenticate, authorize, certify, corroborate, endorse, prove, ratify, substantiate

validity *noun* **1** =**soundness**, cogency, force, power, strength, weight **2** =**legality**, authority, lawfulness, legitimacy, mana (*NZ*), right

valley *noun* =**hollow**, dale, dell, depression, glen, vale

valour *noun Lit* =**bravery**, boldness, courage, fearlessness, gallantry, heroism, intrepidity, spirit OPPOSITE> **cowardice**

valuable *adjective* **a** =**useful**, beneficial, helpful, important, prized, profitable, worthwhile OPPOSITE> **useless. b** =**precious**, costly, dear, expensive, high-priced OPPOSITE> **cheap** ◆*plural noun* =**treasures**, heirlooms

value *noun* **1** =**importance**, advantage, benefit, desirability, merit, profit, usefulness, utility, worth OPPOSITE> **insignificance. 2** =**cost**, market price, rate ◆*plural* **5** =**principles**, ethics, (moral) standards ◆*verb* **6** =**evaluate**, appraise, assess, estimate, price, rate, set at **7** =**regard highly**, appreciate, cherish, esteem, hold dear, prize, respect, treasure OPPOSITE> **underestimate**

vandal *noun* =**hooligan**, delinquent, rowdy, yob *or* yobbo (*Brit sl*)

vanguard *noun* **2** =**forefront**, cutting edge, forerunners, front line, leaders, spearhead, trailblazers, trendsetters, van OPPOSITE> **rearguard**

vanish *verb* =**disappear**, dissolve, evanesce, evaporate, fade (away), melt (away) OPPOSITE>

vanquish ⊕ *verb Lit* defeat (someone) utterly.
vantage *noun* **vantage point** position that gives one an overall view.
vapid ⊕ *adjective* lacking character, dull.
vapidity *noun*
vapour ⊕ *noun* **1** moisture suspended in air as steam or mist. **2** gaseous form of something that is liquid or solid at room temperature.
vaporize *verb* change into a vapour. **vaporizer** *noun* **vaporous** *adjective*
variable ⊕ *adjective* **1** not always the same, changeable. ◆ *noun* **2** something that is subject to variation. **3** *Maths* expression with a range of values. **variability** *noun*
variant ⊕ *adjective* **1** differing from a standard or type. ◆ *noun* **2** something that differs from a standard or type. **at variance** in disagreement.
variation ⊕ *noun* **1** something presented in a slightly different form. **2** difference in level, amount, or quantity. **3** *Music* repetition in different forms of a basic theme.
varicose veins *plural noun* knotted and swollen veins, esp. in the legs.
variegated *adjective* having patches or streaks of different colours. **variegation** *noun*
variety ⊕ *noun, pl* **-ties** **1** state of being diverse or various. **2** different things of the same kind. **3** particular sort or kind. **4** light entertainment composed of unrelated acts.
various ⊕ *adjective* of several kinds. **variously** *adverb*
varnish ⊕ *noun* **1** solution of oil and resin, put on a surface to make it hard and glossy. ◆ *verb*

2 apply varnish to.
varsity *noun Brit informal* university.
vary ⊕ *verb* **varying, varied 1** change. **2** cause differences in. **varied** *adjective*
vascular *adjective Biol* relating to vessels.
vas deferens *noun, pl* **vasa deferentia** *Anat* sperm-carrying duct in each testicle.
vase *noun* ornamental jar, esp. for flowers.
vasectomy *noun, pl* **-mies** surgical removal of part of the vas deferens, as a contraceptive method.
Vaseline *noun* ® thick oily cream made from petroleum, used in skin care.
vassal *noun* **1** *Hist* man given land by a lord in return for military service. **2** subordinate person or nation. **vassalage** *noun*
vast ⊕ *adjective* extremely large. **vastly** *adverb* **vastness** *noun*
vat *noun* large container for liquids.
VAT *Brit* value-added tax: tax on the difference between the cost of materials and the selling price.
Vatican *noun* **1** the Pope's palace. **2** authority of the Pope.
vaudeville *noun* variety entertainment of songs and comic turns.
vault[1] ⊕ *noun* **1** secure room for storing valuables. **2** underground burial chamber.
vaulted *adjective* having an arched roof.
vault[2] ⊕ *verb* **1** jump over (something) by resting one's hand(s) on it. ◆ *noun* **2** such a jump.
vaunt *verb* describe or display (success or

——————— T H E S A U R U S ———————

appear
vanity *noun* =pride, arrogance, conceit, conceitedness, egotism, narcissism OPPOSITE modesty
vanquish *verb Lit* =defeat, beat, conquer, crush, master, overcome, overpower, overwhelm, triumph over
vapid *adjective* =dull, bland, boring, flat, insipid, tame, uninspiring, uninteresting, weak, wishy-washy (*inf*)
vapour *noun* **1** = mist, exhalation, fog, haze, steam
variable *adjective* **1** = changeable, flexible, fluctuating, inconstant, mutable, shifting, temperamental, uneven, unstable, unsteady OPPOSITE constant
variant *adjective* **1** = different, alternative, divergent, modified ◆*noun* **2** = variation, alternative, development, modification **at variance** = in disagreement, at loggerheads, at odds, at sixes and sevens (*inf*), conflicting, out of line

variation *noun* **1** = difference, change, departure, deviation, diversity, innovation, modification, novelty, variety OPPOSITE uniformity
variety *noun* **1** = diversity, change, difference, discrepancy, diversification, multifariousness, variation OPPOSITE similarity. **2** = range, array, assortment, collection, cross section, medley, miscellany, mixture **3** = type, brand, breed, category, class, kind, sort, species, strain
various *adjective* = different, assorted, disparate, distinct, diverse, miscellaneous, several, sundry, varied OPPOSITE same
varnish *noun, verb* **1, 2** = lacquer, glaze, gloss, polish
vary *verb* **1** = change, alter, fluctuate **2** = alternate
vast *adjective* = huge, boundless, colossal, enormous, gigantic, great, immense, massive, monumental, wide OPPOSITE tiny
vault[1] *noun* **1** = strongroom, depository, repository **2** = crypt, catacomb, cellar, charnel

V

possessions) boastfully. **vaunted** adjective
VC 1 Vice Chancellor. **2** Victoria Cross.
VCR video cassette recorder.
VD venereal disease.
VDU visual display unit.
veal noun calf meat.
vector noun **1** Maths quantity that has size
and direction, such as force. **2** animal, usu. an
insect, that carries disease.
veer ⊕ verb change direction suddenly.
vegan [**vee**-gan] noun **1** person who eats no
meat, fish, eggs, or dairy products. ◆ adjective **2**
suitable for a vegan. **veganism** noun
vegetable noun **1** edible plant. **2** Informal
severely brain-damaged person. ◆ adjective **3** of
or like plants or vegetables.
vegetarian noun **1** person who eats no meat
or fish. ◆ adjective **2** suitable for a vegetarian.
vegetarianism noun
vegetate ⊕ verb live a dull boring life with no
mental stimulation.
vegetation noun plant life of a given place.
vegetative adjective of plant life or growth.
vehement ⊕ adjective expressing strong
feelings. **vehemence** noun **vehemently** adverb
vehicle ⊕ noun **1** machine, esp. with an
engine and wheels, for carrying people or
objects. **2** something used to achieve a
particular purpose or as a means of expression.
vehicular adjective
veil ⊕ noun **1** piece of thin cloth covering the
head or face. **2** something that masks the truth,
e.g. a veil of secrecy. ◆ verb **3** cover with or as if
with a veil. **take the veil** become a nun.
veiled adjective disguised.
vein ⊕ noun **1** tube that takes blood to the

heart. **2** line in a leaf or an insect's wing. **3**
layer of ore or mineral in rock. **4** streak in
marble, wood, or cheese. **5** feature of
someone's writing or speech, e.g. a vein of
humour. **6** mood or style, e.g. in a lighter vein.
veined adjective
Velcro noun ® fastening consisting of one
piece of fabric with tiny hooked threads and
another with a coarse surface that sticks to it.
veld, veldt noun high grassland in southern
Africa.
vellum noun **1** fine calfskin parchment. **2** type
of strong good-quality paper.
velocity ⊕ [vel-**loss**-it-ee] noun, pl **-ties** speed
of movement in a given direction.
velour, velours [vel-**loor**] noun fabric similar
to velvet.
velvet ⊕ noun fabric with a thick soft pile.
velvety adjective soft and smooth. **velveteen**
noun cotton velvet.
venal [**vee**-nal] adjective **1** easily bribed. **2**
characterized by bribery. **venally** adverb
vend verb sell. **vendor** noun **vending
machine** machine that dispenses goods when
coins are inserted.
vendetta ⊕ noun **1** long-lasting quarrel
between people or organizations in which they
attempt to harm each other. **2** prolonged
quarrel between families, esp. one involving
revenge killings.
veneer ⊕ noun **1** thin layer of wood etc.
covering a cheaper material. **2** superficial
appearance, e.g. a veneer of sophistication.
venerable ⊕ adjective worthy of deep respect.
venerate verb hold (a person) in deep respect.
veneration noun

———————— THESAURUS ————————

house, mausoleum, tomb, undercroft
vault² verb **1** = **jump**, bound, clear, hurdle,
leap, spring
veer verb = **change direction**, change course,
sheer, shift, swerve, turn
vegetate verb = **stagnate**, deteriorate, go to
seed, idle, languish, loaf OPPOSITE> **grow**
vehemence noun = **forcefulness**, ardour,
emphasis, energy, fervour, force, intensity,
passion, vigour
vehement adjective = **strong**, ardent,
emphatic, fervent, fierce, forceful, impassioned,
intense, passionate, powerful OPPOSITE> **half-
hearted**
vehicle noun **1** = **transport**, conveyance,
transportation **2** = **medium**, apparatus,
channel, means, mechanism, organ
veil noun **1** = **cover**, blind, cloak, curtain,
disguise, film, mask, screen, shroud ◆verb **3**

= **cover**, cloak, conceal, disguise, hide, mask,
obscure, screen, shield OPPOSITE> **reveal**
veiled adjective = **disguised**, concealed, covert,
hinted at, implied, masked, suppressed
vein noun **1** = **blood vessel 3** = **seam**, lode,
stratum **4** = **streak**, stripe **6** = **mood**, mode,
note, style, temper, tenor, tone
velocity noun = **speed**, pace, quickness,
rapidity, swiftness
velvety adjective = **soft**, delicate, downy,
smooth
vendetta noun **2** = **feud**, bad blood, quarrel
veneer noun **1** = **layer**, finish, gloss **2** = **mask**,
appearance, facade, front, guise, pretence,
semblance, show
venerable adjective = **respected**, august,
esteemed, honoured, revered, sage, wise,
worshipped
venerate verb = **respect**, adore, esteem,

V

venereal disease [ven-**ear**-ee-al] *noun* disease transmitted sexually.

Venetian *adjective* **1** of Venice, port in NE Italy. ♦ *noun* **2** native or inhabitant of Venice.

Venetian blind window blind made of thin horizontal slats that turn to let in more or less light.

vengeance ❶ *noun* revenge. **with a vengeance** to an excessive degree. **vengeful** *adjective* wanting revenge.

venial [**veen**-ee-al] *adjective* (of a sin or fault) easily forgiven.

venison *noun* deer meat.

venom ❶ *noun* **1** malice or spite. **2** poison produced by snakes etc. **venomous** *adjective* **venomously** *adverb*

venous [**vee**-nuss] *adjective Anat* of veins.

vent[1] ❶ *noun* **1** outlet releasing fumes or fluid. ♦ *verb* **2** express (an emotion) freely. **give vent to** release (an emotion) in an outburst.

vent[2] *noun* vertical slit in a jacket.

ventilate *verb* **1** let fresh air into. **2** discuss (ideas or feelings) openly. **ventilation** *noun* **ventilator** *noun* device to let fresh air into a room or building.

ventral *adjective* relating to the front of the body.

ventricle *noun Anat* one of the four cavities of the heart or brain.

ventriloquist *noun* entertainer who can speak without moving his or her lips, so that a voice seems to come from elsewhere. **ventriloquism** *noun*

venture ❶ *noun* **1** risky undertaking, esp. in business. ♦ *verb* **2** do something risky. **3** dare to express (an opinion). **4** go to an unknown place. **venturesome** *adjective* daring.

venue *noun* place where an organized gathering is held.

Venus *noun* **1** planet second nearest to the sun. **2** Roman goddess of love. **Venus flytrap, Venus's flytrap** plant that traps and digests insects between hinged leaves.

veracious *adjective* habitually truthful. **veracity** *noun*

verandah, veranda *noun* open porch attached to a house.

verb ❶ *noun* word that expresses the idea of action, happening, or being. **verbal** *adjective* **1** spoken. **2** of a verb. **verbally** *adverb* **verbalize** *verb* express (something) in words.

verbatim ❶ [verb-**bait**-im] *adverb, adjective* word for word.

verbena *noun* plant with sweet-smelling flowers.

verbiage *noun* excessive use of words.

verbose ❶ [verb-**bohss**] *adjective* speaking at tedious length. **verbosity** *noun*

verdant ❶ *adjective Lit* covered in green vegetation.

verdict ❶ *noun* **1** decision of a jury. **2** opinion formed after examining the facts.

verdigris [**ver**-dig-riss] *noun* green film on copper, brass, or bronze.

verdure *noun Lit* flourishing green vegetation.

verge ❶ *noun* grass border along a road. **on the verge of** having almost reached (a point or condition). **verge on** *verb* be near to (a condition).

verger *noun C of E* church caretaker.

——————— T H E S A U R U S ———————

vengeance *noun* =**revenge**, reprisal, requital, retaliation, retribution OPPOSITE **pardon**

venom *noun* **1** =**malice**, acrimony, bitterness, hate, rancour, spite, spleen, virulence OPPOSITE **love**. **2** =**poison**, bane, toxin

venomous *adjective* **1** =**malicious**, hostile, malignant, rancorous, savage, spiteful, vicious, vindictive OPPOSITE **loving**. **2** =**poisonous**, mephitic, noxious, toxic, virulent OPPOSITE **harmless**

vent[1] *noun* **1** =**outlet**, aperture, duct, opening, orifice ♦*verb* **2** =**express**, air, discharge, emit, give vent to, pour out, release, utter, voice OPPOSITE **repress**

venture *noun* **1** =**undertaking**, adventure, endeavour, enterprise, gamble, hazard, project, risk ♦*verb* **2** =**risk**, chance, hazard, speculate, stake, wager **3** =**dare**, hazard, make bold, presume, take the liberty, volunteer **4** =**go**, embark on, plunge into, set out

verbal *adjective* **1** =**spoken**, oral, unwritten, word-of-mouth

verbatim *adverb* =**word for word**, exactly, precisely, to the letter

verbose *adjective* =**long-winded**, circumlocutory, diffuse, periphrastic, prolix, tautological, windy, wordy

verbosity *noun* =**long-windedness**, loquaciousness, prolixity, verboseness, wordiness

verdant *adjective Lit* =**green**, flourishing, fresh, grassy, leafy, lush

verdict *noun* =**decision**, adjudication, conclusion, finding, judgment, opinion, sentence

verge *noun* =**border**, boundary, brim, brink, edge, limit, margin, threshold **verge on** ♦*verb* =**come near to**, approach, border

verification *noun* =**proof**, authentication,

V

verify ❶ *verb* **-ifying, -ified** check the truth or accuracy of. **verifiable** *adjective* **verification** *noun*

verily *adverb Obs* in truth.

verisimilitude *noun* appearance of being real or true.

veritable *adjective* rightly called, without exaggeration, e.g. *a veritable feast.* **veritably** *adverb*

verity *noun, pl* **-ties** true statement or principle.

vermicelli [ver-me-**chell**-ee] *noun* **1** fine strands of pasta. **2** tiny strands of chocolate.

vermiform *adjective* shaped like a worm.

vermiform appendix *Anat* same as APPENDIX.

vermilion *adjective* orange-red.

vermin *plural noun* **1** animals, esp. insects and rodents, that spread disease or cause damage. **2** people who are considered dangerous or harmful to others. **verminous** *adjective*

vermouth [**ver**-muth] *noun* wine flavoured with herbs.

vernacular ❶ [ver-**nak**-yew-lar] *noun* **1** most widely spoken language of a particular people or place. ◆ *adjective* **2** in or using the vernacular.

vernal *adjective* occurring in spring.

vernier [**ver**-nee-er] *noun* movable scale on a graduated measuring instrument for taking readings in fractions.

veronica *noun* plant with small blue, pink, or white flowers.

verruca [ver-**roo**-ka] *noun* wart, usu. on the foot.

versatile ❶ *adjective* having many skills or uses. **versatility** *noun*

verse *noun* **1** group of lines forming part of a song or poem. **2** poetry as distinct from prose. **3** subdivision of a chapter of the Bible. **versed in** knowledgeable about. **versify** *verb* **-fying, -fied** write in verse. **versification** *noun*

version ❶ *noun* **1** form of something, such as a piece of writing, with some differences from other forms. **2** account of an incident from a particular point of view.

verso *noun, pl* **-sos 1** left-hand page of a book. **2** back of a sheet of printed paper.

versus *preposition* **1** in opposition to or in contrast with. **2** *Sport, Law* against.

vertebra [**ver**-tib-ra] *noun, pl* **vertebrae** [**ver**-tib-ree] one of the bones that form the spine. **vertebral** *adjective* **vertebrate** *noun, adjective* (animal) having a spine.

vertex *noun, pl* **-texes, -tices 1** *Maths* point on a geometric figure where the sides form an angle. **2** highest point of a triangle.

vertical ❶ *adjective* **1** straight up and down. ◆ *noun* **2** vertical direction. **vertically** *adverb*

vertigo ❶ *noun* dizziness, usu. when looking down from a high place. **vertiginous** *adjective*

vervain *noun* plant with spikes of blue, purple, or white flowers.

verve ❶ *noun* enthusiasm or liveliness.

very ❶ *adverb* **1** more than usually, extremely. ◆ *adjective* **2** absolute, exact, e.g. *the very top; the very man.*

vesicle *noun Biol* sac or small cavity, esp. one containing fluid.

vespers *plural noun RC Church* (service of) evening prayer.

vessel ❶ *noun* **1** ship. **2** *Lit* container, esp. for liquids. **3** *Biol* tubular structure in animals and plants that carries body fluids, such as blood or sap.

vest ❶ *noun* **1** undergarment worn on the top half of the body. **2** *US & Aust* waistcoat. ◆ *verb* **3** (foll. by *in* or *with*) give (authority) to (someone). **vested interest** interest someone has in a matter because he or she might benefit from it.

——————— THESAURUS ———————

confirmation, corroboration, substantiation, validation

verify *verb* =**check**, authenticate, bear out, confirm, corroborate, prove, substantiate, support, validate OPPOSITE **deny**

vernacular *noun* **1** =**dialect**, idiom, parlance, patois, speech

versatile *adjective* =**adaptable**, adjustable, all-purpose, all-round, flexible, multifaceted, resourceful, variable OPPOSITE **limited**

versed in *adjective* =**knowledgeable about**, acquainted with, conversant with, experienced in, familiar with, practised in, proficient in, seasoned in, well informed about

version *noun* **1 a** =**form**, design, model, style, variant **1 b** =**adaptation**, portrayal, rendering **2** =**account**, interpretation

vertical *adjective* **1** =**upright**, erect, on end, perpendicular OPPOSITE **horizontal**

vertigo *noun* =**dizziness**, giddiness, light-headedness

verve *noun* =**enthusiasm**, animation, energy, gusto, liveliness, sparkle, spirit, vitality OPPOSITE **indifference**

very *adverb* **1** =**extremely**, acutely, decidedly, deeply, exceedingly, greatly, highly, profoundly, really, uncommonly, unusually ◆*adjective* **2** =**exact**, precise, selfsame

vessel *noun* **1** =**ship**, boat, craft **2** *Lit* =**container**, pot, receptacle, utensil

vestal *adjective* pure, chaste. **vestal virgin** (in ancient Rome) one of the virgin priestesses dedicated to the goddess Vesta and to maintaining the sacred fire in hertemple.

vestibule ⊕ *noun* small entrance hall.

vestige ⊕ [**vest**-ij] *noun* small amount or trace. **vestigial** [vest-**ij**-ee-al] *adjective*

vestments *plural noun* priest's robes.

vestry *noun, pl* **-tries** room in a church used as an office by the priest or minister.

vet[1] ⊕ *noun* **1** short for VETERINARY SURGEON. ♦ *verb* **vetting, vetted 2** check the suitability of.

vet[2] *noun US & Aust* military veteran.

vetch *noun* climbing plant with a beanlike fruit used as fodder.

veteran ⊕ *noun* **1** person with long experience in a particular activity, esp. military service. ♦ *adjective* **2** long-serving. **veteran car** car built before 1919, esp. before 1905.

veterinarian *noun US* veterinary surgeon.

veterinary *adjective* concerning animal health. **veterinary surgeon** medical specialist who treats sick animals.

veto ⊕ [**vee**-toe] *noun, pl* **-toes 1** official power to cancel a proposal. ♦ *verb* **-toing, -toed 2** enforce a veto against.

vex ⊕ *verb* frustrate, annoy. **vexation** *noun* **1** something annoying. **2** being annoyed. **vexatious** *adjective* **vexed question** much debated subject.

VHF very high frequency: radio frequency band between 30 and 300 MHz.

VHS ® Video Home System: format for recording on video.

VI Vancouver Island.

via *preposition* by way of.

viable ⊕ *adjective* **1** able to be put into practice. **2** *Biol* able to live and grow independently. **viability** *noun*

viaduct *noun* bridge over a valley.

Viagra *noun* ® drug used to treat impotence in men.

vial *noun* same as PHIAL.

viands *plural noun Obs* food.

viaticum *noun, pl* **-ca, -cums** Holy Communion given to a person who is dying or in danger of death.

vibes *plural noun Informal* **1** emotional reactions between people. **2** atmosphere of a place. **3** short for VIBRAPHONE.

vibrant ⊕ [**vibe**-rant] *adjective* **1** vigorous in appearance, energetic. **2** (of a voice) resonant. **3** (of a colour) strong and bright. **vibrancy** *noun*

vibraphone *noun* musical instrument with metal bars that resonate electronically when hit.

vibrate ⊕ *verb* **1** move back and forth rapidly. **2** (cause to) resonate. **vibration** *noun* **vibrator** *noun* device that produces vibratory motion, used for massage or as a sex aid. **vibratory** *adjective*

vibrato *noun, pl* **-tos** *Music* rapid fluctuation in the pitch of a note.

viburnum [vie-**burn**-um] *noun* subtropical shrub with white flowers and berry-like fruits.

VIC Victoria (Australian state).

vicar *noun C of E* clergyman in charge of a parish. **vicarage** *noun* vicar's house.

vicarious ⊕ [vick-**air**-ee-uss] *adjective* **1** felt indirectly by imagining what another person experiences. **2** delegated. **vicariously** *adverb*

vice[1] ⊕ *noun* **1** immoral or evil habit or action.

—————————————— THESAURUS ——————————————

vest *verb* **3** (foll. by *in* or *with*) = **place in**, bestow upon, confer on, consign to, endow with, entrust with, invest with, settle on

vestibule *noun* = **hall**, anteroom, foyer, lobby, porch, portico

vestige *noun* = **trace**, glimmer, indication, remnant, scrap, suspicion

vet[1] *verb* **2** = **check**, appraise, examine, investigate, review, scrutinize

veteran *noun* **1** = **old hand**, old stager, past master, warhorse (*inf*) OPPOSITE> **novice** ♦*adjective* **2** = **long-serving**, battle-scarred, old, seasoned

veto *noun* **1** = **ban**, boycott, embargo, interdict, prohibition OPPOSITE> **approval** ♦*verb* **2** = **ban**, boycott, disallow, forbid, prohibit, reject, rule out, turn down OPPOSITE> **pass**

vex *verb* = **annoy**, bother, distress, exasperate, irritate, plague, trouble, upset, worry OPPOSITE>

soothe

vexation *noun* **1** = **problem**, bother, difficulty, hassle (*inf*), headache (*inf*), nuisance, trouble, worry **2** = **annoyance**, chagrin, displeasure, dissatisfaction, exasperation, frustration, irritation, pique

viable *adjective* **1** = **workable**, applicable, feasible, operable, practicable, usable OPPOSITE> **unworkable**

vibrant *adjective* **1** = **energetic**, alive, animated, dynamic, sparkling, spirited, storming, vigorous, vivacious, vivid

vibrate *verb* **1** = **shake**, fluctuate, judder (*inf*), oscillate, pulsate, quiver, sway, throb, tremble **2** = **reverberate**

vibration *noun* **1** = **shake**, judder (*inf*), oscillation, pulsation, quiver, throbbing, trembling, tremor **2** = **reverberation**

vicarious *adjective* **1** = **indirect**, at one

V

2 habit regarded as a weakness in someone's character. **3** criminal immorality, esp. involving sex.

vice² noun tool with a pair of jaws for holding an object while working on it.

vice³ adjective serving in place of.

vice chancellor noun chief executive of a university.

vice president noun officer ranking immediately below the president and serving as his or her deputy. **vice-presidency** noun

viceroy noun governor of a colony who represents the monarch. **viceregal** adjective

vice versa ❶ [vie-see ver-sa] adverb Latin conversely, the other way round.

Vichy water [vee-shee waw-ter] noun mineral water from Vichy in France, reputed to be good for the health.

vicinity ❶ [viss-in-it-ee] noun surrounding area.

vicious ❶ adjective cruel and violent. **viciously** adverb **vicious circle, cycle** situation in which an attempt to resolve one problem creates new problems that recreate the original one.

vicissitudes [viss-iss-it-yewds] plural noun changes in fortune.

victim ❶ noun **1** person or thing harmed or killed. **2** person who has suffered because of misfortune or other people's actions. **victimize** verb **1** punish unfairly. **2** discriminate against. **victimization** noun

victor ❶ noun person who has defeated an opponent, esp. in war or in sport. **victorious** adjective **victory** noun, pl **-tories** winning of a battle or contest.

victoria noun large sweet plum, red and yellow in colour.

Victoria Cross noun Brit highest award for bravery.

Victorian adjective **1** of or in the reign of Queen Victoria (1837-1901). **2** characterized by

prudery or hypocrisy. ♦ noun **3** person who lived during Victoria's reign.

victuals [vit-tals] plural noun Old-fashioned food and drink. **victual** verb **victualling, victualled** Old-fashioned supply with or obtain victuals. **victualler** noun

vicuña [vik-koo-nya] noun **1** S American animal like the llama. **2** fine cloth made from its wool.

vide [vie-dee] Latin see.

videlicet [vid-deal-ee-set] Latin namely.

video noun, pl **-os 1** short for VIDEO CASSETTE (RECORDER). ♦ verb **videoing, videoed 2** record (a TV programme or event) on video. ♦ adjective **3** relating to or used in producing television images. **video nasty** horrific or pornographic film, usu. made for video. **videotext** noun means of representing on a TV screen information that is held in a computer.

video cassette noun cassette containing video tape. **video cassette recorder** tape recorder for recording and playing back TV programmes and films.

video tape noun **1** magnetic tape used to record video-frequency signals in TV production. **2** magnetic tape used to record programmes when they are broadcast. **videotape** verb record (a TV programme) on video tape. **video tape recorder** tape recorder for vision signals, used in TV production.

Videotex noun ® same as VIEWDATA.

vie ❶ verb **vying, vied** compete (with someone).

Vietnamese adjective **1** of Vietnam, in SE Asia. ♦ noun **2** pl **-ese** native of Vietnam. **3** language of Vietnam.

view ❶ noun **1** opinion or belief. **2** understanding of or outlook on something. **3** everything that can be seen from a given place. **4** picture of this. ♦ verb **5** think of (something) in a particular way. **6** see or watch. **in view of**

———————————— T H E S A U R U S ————————————

remove, substituted, surrogate **2 = delegated,** deputed

vice¹ noun **1 = wickedness,** corruption, depravity, evil, immorality, iniquity, sin, turpitude OPPOSITE virtue. **2 = fault,** blemish, defect, failing, imperfection, shortcoming, weakness

vice versa adverb Latin **=conversely,** contrariwise, in reverse, the other way round

vicinity noun **=neighbourhood,** area, district, environs, locality, neck of the woods (inf), proximity

vicious adjective **a =malicious,** cruel, mean, spiteful, venomous, vindictive **b = savage,**

barbarous, cruel, ferocious, violent OPPOSITE kind

victim noun **1 =casualty,** fatality, sufferer OPPOSITE survivor. **2 =sacrifice,** martyr, scapegoat

victimize verb **2 =persecute,** discriminate against, have it in for (someone) (inf), pick on

victor noun **=winner,** champion, conqueror, prizewinner, vanquisher OPPOSITE loser

victorious adjective **=winning,** champion, conquering, first, prizewinning, successful, triumphant, vanquishing

victory noun **=win,** conquest, success, triumph

V

taking into consideration. **on view** exhibited to the public. **viewer** *noun* **1** person who watches television. **2** hand-held device for looking at photographic slides. **viewfinder** *noun* window on a camera showing what will appear in a photograph.

Viewdata *noun* ® videotext service linking users to a computer by telephone.

vigil ⊕ [**vij**-ill] *noun* night-time period of staying awake to look after a sick person, pray, etc. **vigilant** *adjective* watchful in case of danger. **vigilance** *noun*

vigilante [vij-ill-**ant**-ee] *noun* person, esp. as one of a group, who takes it upon himself or herself to enforce the law.

vignette [vin-**yet**] *noun* **1** concise description of the typical features of something. **2** small decorative illustration in a book.

vigour ⊕ *noun* physical or mental energy. **vigorous** *adjective* **vigorously** *adverb*

Viking *noun Hist* seafaring raider and settler from Scandinavia.

vile ⊕ *adjective* **1** very wicked. **2** disgusting. **vilely** *adverb* **vileness** *noun*

vilify ⊕ [**vill**-if-fie] *verb* **-ifying, -ified** attack the character of. **vilification** *noun*

villa *noun* **1** large house with gardens. **2** holiday home, usu. in the Mediterranean.

village *noun* **1** small group of houses in a country area. **2** rural community. **villager** *noun*

villain ⊕ *noun* **1** wicked person. **2** main wicked character in a play. **villainous** *adjective* **villainy** *noun*

villein [**vill**-an] *noun Hist* peasant bound in service to his lord.

vim *noun Informal* force, energy.

vinaigrette *noun* salad dressing of oil and vinegar.

vindicate ⊕ *verb* **1** clear (someone) of guilt. **2** provide justification for. **vindication** *noun*

vindictive ⊕ *adjective* maliciously seeking revenge. **vindictiveness** *noun* **vindictively** *adverb*

vine *noun* climbing plant, esp. one producing grapes. **vineyard** [**vinn**-yard] *noun* plantation of grape vines, esp. for making wine.

vinegar *noun* acid liquid made from wine, beer, or cider. **vinegary** *adjective*

viniculture *noun* process or business of growing grapes and making wine.

vino [**vee**-noh] *noun Informal* wine.

vintage ⊕ *noun* **1** wine from a particular harvest of grapes. ♦ *adjective* **2** best and most typical. **vintage car** car built between 1919 and 1930.

vintner *noun* dealer in wine.

vinyl [**vine**-ill] *noun* type of plastic, used in mock leather and records.

viol [**vie**-oll] *noun* early stringed instrument preceding the violin.

viola[1] [vee-**oh**-la] *noun* stringed instrument lower in pitch than a violin.

—————————— THESAURUS ——————————

vie *verb* = **compete**, contend, strive, struggle

view *noun* **1** = **opinion**, attitude, belief, conviction, feeling, point of view, sentiment **2** = **impression** **3** = **scene**, landscape, outlook, panorama, perspective, picture, prospect, spectacle, vista ♦*verb* **5** = **regard**, consider, deem, look on

viewer *noun* **1** = **watcher**, observer, onlooker, spectator

vigilance *noun* = **watchfulness**, alertness, attentiveness, carefulness, caution, circumspection, observance

vigilant *adjective* = **watchful**, alert, attentive, careful, cautious, circumspect, on one's guard, on the lookout, wakeful

vigorous *adjective* = **energetic**, active, dynamic, forceful, lively, lusty, powerful, spirited, strenuous, strong OPPOSITE **feeble**

vigorously *adverb* = **energetically**, forcefully, hard, lustily, strenuously, strongly

vigour *noun* = **energy**, animation, dynamism, forcefulness, gusto, liveliness, power, spirit, strength, verve, vitality OPPOSITE **weakness**

vile *adjective* **1** = **wicked**, corrupt, degenerate, depraved, evil, nefarious, perverted OPPOSITE **pure**. **2** = **disgusting**, foul, horrid, nasty, nauseating, offensive, repugnant, repulsive, revolting, sickening OPPOSITE **lovely**

vilify *verb* = **malign**, abuse, berate, denigrate, disparage, revile, slander, smear OPPOSITE **praise**

villain *noun* **1** = **evildoer**, blackguard, criminal, miscreant, reprobate, rogue, scoundrel, wretch OPPOSITE **hero**. **2** = **antihero**, baddy (*inf*)

villainous *adjective* **1** = **wicked**, bad, cruel, degenerate, depraved, evil, fiendish, nefarious, vicious, vile

villainy *noun* **1** = **wickedness**, delinquency, depravity, devilry, iniquity, turpitude, vice

vindicate *verb* **1** = **clear**, absolve, acquit, exculpate, exonerate, rehabilitate OPPOSITE **accuse**. **2** = **justify**, defend, excuse

vindication *noun* **1** = **exoneration**, exculpation **2** = **justification**, defence, excuse

vindictive *adjective* = **vengeful**, implacable, malicious, resentful, revengeful, spiteful, unforgiving, unrelenting

vintage *adjective* **2** = **best**, choice, classic,

V

viola² [**vie**-ol-la] *noun* variety of pansy.
violate ⊙ *verb* **1** break (a law or agreement).
2 disturb (someone's privacy). **3** treat (a sacred place) disrespectfully. **4** rape. **violation** *noun*
violator *noun*
violence ⊙ *noun* **1** use of physical force, usu. intended to cause injury or destruction. **2** great force or strength in action, feeling, or expression. **violent** *adjective* **violently** *adverb*
violet *noun* **1** plant with bluish-purple flowers.
♦ *adjective* **2** bluish-purple.
violin *noun* small four-stringed musical instrument played with a bow. **violinist** *noun*
violoncello [vie-oll-on-**chell**-oh] *noun, pl* **-los** same as CELLO.
VIP ⊙ very important person.
viper *noun* poisonous snake.
virago [vir-**rah**-go] *noun, pl* **-goes, -gos** aggressive woman.
viral [**vie**-ral] *adjective* of or caused by a virus.
virgin ⊙ *noun* **1** person, esp. a woman, who has not had sexual intercourse. ♦ *adjective* **2** not having had sexual intercourse. **3** not yet exploited or explored. **virginal** *adjective* **1** like a virgin. **2** extremely pure or fresh. ♦ *noun* **3** early keyboard instrument like a small harpsichord.
virginity *noun* **the Virgin, the Virgin Mary** *Christianity* Mary, the mother of Christ.
Virginia creeper *noun* climbing plant that turns red in autumn.

Virgo *noun* (the virgin) sixth sign of the zodiac.
virile ⊙ *adjective* having the traditional male characteristics of physical strength and a high sex drive. **virility** *noun*
virology *noun* study of viruses.
virtual ⊙ *adjective* **1** having the effect but not the form of. **2** of or relating to virtual reality.
virtual reality computer-generated environment that seems real to the user.
virtually *adverb* practically, almost.
virtue ⊙ *noun* **1** moral goodness. **2** positive moral quality. **3** merit. **by virtue of** by reason of. **virtuous** *adjective* morally good. **virtuously** *adverb*
virtuoso ⊙ *noun, pl* **-sos, -si** person with impressive esp. musical skill. **virtuosity** *noun*
virulent ⊙ [**vir**-yew-lent] *adjective* **1** extremely bitter or hostile. **2** very infectious. **3** violently harmful. **virulently** *adverb* **virulence** *noun*
virus *noun* **1** microorganism that causes disease in humans, animals, and plants. **2** *Computers* program that propagates itself, via disks and electronic networks, to cause disruption.
visa *noun* permission to enter a country, granted by its government and shown by a stamp on one's passport.
visage [**viz**-zij] *noun Lit* face.
vis-à-vis [veez-ah-**vee**] *preposition* in relation

——————— T H E S A U R U S ———————

violate *verb* **1 = break**, contravene, disobey, disregard, infringe, transgress OPPOSITE respect. **2 = encroach upon 3 = desecrate**, abuse, befoul, defile, dishonour, pollute, profane OPPOSITE honour. **4 = rape**, abuse, assault, debauch, ravish
violation *noun* **1 = infringement**, abuse, breach, contravention, infraction, transgression **2 = trespass**, encroachment **3 = desecration**, defilement, profanation, sacrilege, spoliation
violence *noun* **1 = force**, bloodshed, brutality, cruelty, ferocity, fighting, savagery, terrorism **2 = intensity**, abandon, fervour, force, severity, vehemence
violent *adjective* **1 = destructive**, brutal, cruel, hot-headed, murderous, riotous, savage, uncontrollable, unrestrained, vicious OPPOSITE gentle
VIP *noun* **= celebrity**, big hitter (*inf*), big name, heavy hitter (*inf*), luminary, somebody, star
virgin *noun* **1 = maiden**, girl (*arch*) ♦*adjective* **2 = pure**, chaste, immaculate, uncorrupted, undefiled, vestal, virginal OPPOSITE corrupted
virginity *noun* **= chastity**, maidenhood

virile *adjective* **= manly**, lusty, macho, manlike, masculine, red-blooded, strong, vigorous OPPOSITE effeminate
virility *noun* **= masculinity**, machismo, manhood, vigour
virtual *adjective* **1 = practical**, essential, in all but name
virtually *adverb* **= practically**, almost, as good as, in all but name, in effect, in essence, nearly
virtue *noun* **1, 2 = goodness**, incorruptibility, integrity, morality, probity, rectitude, righteousness, uprightness, worth OPPOSITE vice. **3 = merit**, advantage, asset, attribute, credit, good point, plus (*inf*), strength OPPOSITE failing
virtuosity *noun* **= mastery**, brilliance, craft, expertise, flair, panache, polish, skill
virtuoso *noun* **= master**, artist, genius, maestro, magician
virtuous *adjective* **= good**, ethical, honourable, incorruptible, moral, praiseworthy, righteous, upright, worthy OPPOSITE evil
virulent *adjective* **2 = deadly**, lethal, pernicious, poisonous, toxic, venomous OPPOSITE harmless

V

to, regarding.

viscera [**viss**-er-a] *plural noun* large abdominal organs. **visceral** *adjective* 1 instinctive. 2 of or relating to the viscera.

viscid [**viss**-id] *adjective* sticky.

viscose *noun* synthetic fabric made from cellulose.

viscount [**vie**-count] *noun* British nobleman ranking between an earl and a baron. **viscountcy** *noun, pl* **-cies**

viscountess [**vie**-count-iss] *noun* 1 woman holding the rank of viscount in her own right. 2 wife or widow of a viscount.

viscous ❶ *adjective* thick and sticky. **viscosity** *noun*

visible ❶ *adjective* 1 able to be seen. 2 able to be perceived by the mind. **visibly** *adverb* **visibility** *noun* range or clarity of vision.

vision ❶ *noun* 1 ability to see. 2 mental image of something. 3 foresight. 4 hallucination. **visionary** *adjective* 1 showing foresight. 2 idealistic but impractical. ◆ *noun, pl* **-aries** 3 visionary person.

visit ❶ *verb* **-iting, -ited** 1 go or come to see. 2 stay temporarily with. 3 (foll. by *upon*) *Lit* afflict. ◆ *noun* 4 instance of visiting. 5 official call. **visitor** *noun* **visitation** *noun* 1 formal visit or inspection. 2 catastrophe seen as divine punishment.

visor [**vize**-or] *noun* 1 transparent part of a helmet that pulls down over the face. 2 eyeshade, esp. in a car. 3 peak on a cap.

vista ❶ *noun* (beautiful) extensive view.

visual ❶ *adjective* 1 done by or used in seeing. 2 designed to be looked at. **visualize** *verb* form a mental image of. **visualization** *noun* **visual display unit** device with a screen for displaying data held in a computer.

vital ❶ *adjective* 1 essential or highly important. 2 lively. 3 necessary to maintain life. **vitals** *plural noun* bodily organs necessary to maintain life. **vitally** *adverb* **vitality** *noun* physical or mental energy. **vital statistics** 1 statistics of births, deaths, and marriages. 2 *Informal* woman's bust, waist, and hip measurements.

vitamin *noun* one of a group of substances that are essential in the diet for specific body processes.

vitiate [**vish**-ee-ate] *verb* spoil the effectiveness of. **vitiation** *noun*

viticulture *noun* cultivation of grapevines.

vitreous *adjective* like or made from glass. **vitreous humour** gelatinous substance that fills the eyeball.

vitrify *verb* **-ifying, -ified** change or be changed into glass or a glassy substance. **vitrification** *noun*

vitriol ❶ *noun* 1 language expressing bitterness and hatred. 2 sulphuric acid. **vitriolic** *adjective*

vituperative [vite-**tyew**-pra-tiv] *adjective* bitterly abusive. **vituperation** *noun*

viva[1] *interjection* long live (a person or thing).

—————— THESAURUS ——————

viscous *adjective* =**thick**, gelatinous, sticky, syrupy

visible *adjective* 1 =**apparent**, clear, discernible, evident, in view, manifest, observable, perceptible, unconcealed OPPOSITE **invisible**

vision *noun* 1 =**sight**, eyesight, perception, seeing, view 2 =**image**, concept, conception, daydream, dream, fantasy, idea, ideal 3 =**foresight**, discernment, farsightedness, imagination, insight, intuition, penetration, prescience 4 =**hallucination**, apparition, chimera, delusion, illusion, mirage, revelation

visionary *adjective* 1 =**prophetic**, mystical 2 =**idealistic**, impractical, quixotic, romantic, speculative, starry-eyed, unrealistic, unworkable, utopian OPPOSITE **realistic** ◆*noun* 3 =**idealist**, daydreamer, dreamer, mystic, prophet, seer OPPOSITE **cynic**

visit *verb* 1 =**call on**, drop in on (*inf*), look (someone) up, stop by 2 =**stay with** ◆*noun* 4 =**call**, sojourn, stay, stop

visitation *noun* 1 =**inspection**, examination,

visit 2 =**catastrophe**, blight, calamity, cataclysm, disaster, ordeal, punishment, scourge

visitor *noun* 1 =**caller**, company 2 =**guest**

vista *noun* =**view**, panorama, perspective, prospect

visual *adjective* 1 =**optical**, ocular, optic 2 =**observable**, discernible, perceptible, visible OPPOSITE **imperceptible**

visualize *verb* =**picture**, conceive of, envisage, imagine

vital *adjective* 1 =**essential**, basic, fundamental, imperative, indispensable, necessary, requisite OPPOSITE **unnecessary**. 2 =**lively**, animated, dynamic, energetic, spirited, vibrant, vigorous, vivacious, zestful OPPOSITE **lethargic**. 3 =**important**, critical, crucial, decisive, key, life-or-death, significant, urgent

vitality *noun* =**energy**, animation, exuberance, life, liveliness, strength, vigour, vivacity

vitriolic *adjective* 1 =**bitter**, acerbic, caustic, envenomed, sardonic, scathing, venomous,

V

viva² *noun* examination in the form of an interview.

vivace [viv-**vah**-chee] *adverb Music* in a lively manner.

vivacious ⊕ *adjective* full of energy and enthusiasm. **vivacity** *noun*

vivarium *noun, pl* **-iums**, **-ia** place where animals are kept in natural conditions.

viva voce [**vive**-a **voh**-chee] *adverb* **1** by word of mouth. ◆ *noun* **2** same as VIVA².

vivid ⊕ *adjective* **1** very bright. **2** conveying images that are true to life. **vividly** *adverb* **vividness** *noun*

vivify *verb* **-ifying**, **-ified** animate, inspire.

viviparous [viv-**vip**-a-russ] *adjective* producing live offspring.

vivisection *noun* performing surgical experiments on living animals. **vivisectionist** *noun*

vixen *noun* **1** female fox. **2** *Informal* spiteful woman.

viz. (introducing specified items) namely.

vizier [viz-**zeer**] *noun* high official in certain Muslim countries.

vizor *noun* same as VISOR.

VLF, vlf *Radio* very low frequency.

V neck *noun* neck on a garment shaped like the letter 'V'. **V-neck, V-necked** *adjective*

vocabulary ⊕ *noun, pl* **-aries 1** all the words that a person knows. **2** all the words in a language. **3** specialist terms used in a given subject. **4** list of words in another language with their translation.

vocal ⊕ *adjective* **1** relating to the voice. **2** outspoken. **vocals** *plural noun* singing part of a piece of pop music. **vocally** *adverb* **vocalist** *noun* singer. **vocalize** *verb* express with or use the voice. **vocalization** *noun* **vocal cords** membranes in the larynx that vibrate to produce sound.

vocation ⊕ *noun* **1** profession or trade. **2** occupation that someone feels called to.

vocational *adjective* directed towards a particular profession or trade.

vocative *noun* (in some languages) case of nouns used when addressing a person.

vociferate *verb* exclaim, cry out.

vociferation *noun*

vociferous ⊕ *adjective* shouting, noisy. **vociferously** *adverb*

vodka *noun* (Russian) spirit distilled from potatoes or grain.

vogue ⊕ *noun* **1** popular style. **2** period of popularity. **in vogue** fashionable.

voice ⊕ *noun* **1** (quality of) sound made when speaking or singing. **2** expression of opinion by a person or group. **3** property of verbs that makes them active or passive. ◆ *verb* **4** express verbally. **voiceless** *adjective* **voice mail** electronic system for the storage of telephone messages. **voice-over** *noun* film commentary spoken by someone off-camera.

void ⊕ *adjective* **1** not legally binding. **2** empty. ◆ *noun* **3** feeling of deprivation. **4** empty space. ◆ *verb* **5** make invalid. **6** empty.

voile [voyl] *noun* light semitransparent fabric.

vol. volume.

volatile ⊕ [**voll**-a-tile] *adjective* **1** liable to sudden change, esp. in behaviour. **2** evaporating quickly. **volatility** *noun*

---

virulent, withering

vivacious *adjective* =**lively**, bubbling, ebullient, high-spirited, sparkling, spirited, sprightly, upbeat (*inf*), vital OPPOSITE **lethargic**

vivacity *noun* =**liveliness**, animation, ebullience, energy, gaiety, high spirits, sparkle, spirit, sprightliness

vivid *adjective* **1** =**bright**, brilliant, clear, colourful, glowing, intense, rich OPPOSITE **dull**. **2** =**clear**, dramatic, graphic, lifelike, memorable, powerful, realistic, stirring, telling, true to life OPPOSITE **vague**

vocabulary *noun* **2** =**words**, dictionary, glossary, language, lexicon

vocal *adjective* **1** =**spoken**, oral, said, uttered, voiced **2** =**outspoken**, articulate, eloquent, expressive, forthright, frank, plain-spoken, strident, vociferous OPPOSITE **reserved**

vocation *noun* **1** =**profession**, career, job, pursuit, trade **2** =**calling**, mission

vociferous *adjective* =**noisy**, clamorous, loud, outspoken, strident, uproarious, vehement, vocal OPPOSITE **quiet**

vogue *noun* **1** =**fashion**, craze, custom, mode, style, trend, way **in vogue** =**popular**, accepted, current, in favour, in use, prevalent

voice *noun* **1** =**sound**, articulation, tone, utterance **2** =**say**, view, vote, will, wish ◆*verb* **4** =**express**, air, articulate, declare, enunciate, utter

void *adjective* **1** =**invalid**, ineffective, inoperative, null and void, useless, vain, worthless **2** =**empty**, bare, free, tenantless, unfilled, unoccupied, vacant ◆*noun* **4** =**emptiness**, blankness, gap, lack, space, vacuity, vacuum ◆*verb* **5** =**invalidate**, cancel, nullify, rescind **6** =**empty**, drain, evacuate

volatile *adjective* **1** a =**changeable**, erratic, explosive, inconstant, unsettled, unstable, unsteady, up and down (*inf*), variable OPPOSITE

vol-au-vent [**voll**-oh-von] *noun* small puff-pastry case with a savoury filling.
volcano *noun, pl* **-noes, -nos** mountain with a vent through which lava is ejected. **volcanic** *adjective*
vole *noun* small rodent.
volition ❶ *noun* ability to decide things for oneself. **of one's own volition** through one's own choice.
volley ❶ *noun* **1** simultaneous discharge of ammunition. **2** burst of questions or critical comments. **3** *Sport* stroke or kick at a moving ball before it hits the ground. ◆ *verb* **4** discharge (ammunition) in a volley. **5** hit or kick (a ball) in a volley. **volleyball** *noun* team game where a ball is hit with the hands over a high net.
volt *noun* unit of electric potential. **voltaic** *adjective* same as GALVANIC (sense 1). **voltage** *noun* electric potential difference expressed in volts. **voltmeter** *noun* instrument for measuring voltage.
volte-face [volt-**fass**] *noun* reversal of opinion.
voluble ❶ *adjective* talking easily and at length. **volubility** *noun* **volubly** *adverb*
volume ❶ *noun* **1** size of the space occupied by something. **2** amount. **3** loudness of sound. **4** control on a radio or TV for adjusting this. **5** book, esp. one of a series. **voluminous** *adjective* **1** (of clothes) large and roomy. **2** (of writings) extensive. **volumetric** *adjective* relating to measurement by volume.
voluntary ❶ *adjective* **1** done by choice. **2** done or maintained without payment. **3** (of muscles) controlled by the will. ◆ *noun, pl*

-taries 4 organ solo in a church service.
voluntarily *adverb*
volunteer ❶ *noun* **1** person who offers voluntarily to do something. **2** person who voluntarily undertakes military service. ◆ *verb* **3** offer one's services. **4** give (information) willingly. **5** offer the services of (another person).
voluptuous ❶ *adjective* **1** (of a woman) sexually alluring through fullness of figure. **2** sensually pleasurable. **voluptuary** *noun, pl* **-aries** person devoted to sensual pleasures.
volute *noun* spiral or twisting turn, form, or object.
vomit ❶ *verb* **-iting, -ited 1** eject (the contents of the stomach) through the mouth. ◆ *noun* **2** matter vomited.
voodoo *noun* religion involving ancestor worship and witchcraft, practised by Black people in the West Indies, esp. in Haiti.
voracious ❶ *adjective* **1** craving great quantities of food. **2** insatiably eager. **voraciously** *adverb* **voracity** *noun*
vortex ❶ *noun, pl* **-texes, -tices 1** whirlpool. **2** situation which people are drawn into against their will.
votary *noun, pl* **-ries** person dedicated to religion or to a cause.
vote ❶ *noun* **1** choice made by a participant in a shared decision, esp. in electing a candidate. **2** right to this choice. **3** total number of votes cast. **4** collective voting power of a given group, e.g. *the Black vote.* ◆ *verb* **5** make a choice by a vote. **6** authorize (something) by vote. **voter** *noun*
votive *adjective* done or given to fulfil a vow.

—————— T H E S A U R U S ——————

stable. **b = temperamental**, fickle, mercurial OPPOSITE **calm**
volition *noun* **= free will**, choice, choosing, discretion, preference, will
volley *noun* **1 = barrage**, blast, bombardment, burst, cannonade, fusillade, hail, salvo, shower
voluble *adjective* **= talkative**, articulate, fluent, forthcoming, glib, loquacious OPPOSITE **reticent**
volume *noun* **1 = capacity**, compass, dimensions **2 = amount**, aggregate, body, bulk, mass, quantity, total **5 = book**, publication, title, tome, treatise
voluminous *adjective* **1 = large**, ample, capacious, cavernous, roomy, vast OPPOSITE **small**
voluntarily *adverb* **1 = willingly**, by choice, freely, off one's own bat, of one's own accord
voluntary *adjective* **1 = unforced**, optional,

spontaneous, willing OPPOSITE **forced**. **2** **= discretionary**, free
volunteer *verb* **3 = offer**, step forward OPPOSITE **refuse**
voluptuous *adjective* **1 = buxom**, ample, curvaceous (*inf*), enticing, seductive, shapely **2 = sensual**, epicurean, hedonistic, licentious, luxurious, self-indulgent, sybaritic OPPOSITE **Spartan**
vomit *verb* **1 = be sick**, disgorge, emit, heave, regurgitate, retch, spew out *or* up, throw up (*inf*)
voracious *adjective* **1 = gluttonous**, greedy, hungry, insatiable, omnivorous, ravenous **2 = avid**, hungry, insatiable, rapacious, uncontrolled, unquenchable OPPOSITE **moderate**
vortex *noun* **1 = whirlpool**, eddy, maelstrom
vote *noun* **1 = poll**, ballot, franchise,

V

vouch ❶ *verb* **vouch for 1** give one's personal assurance about. **2** provide evidence for.

voucher ❶ *noun* **1** ticket used instead of money to buy specified goods. **2** record of a financial transaction, receipt.

vouchsafe *verb* **1** *Old-fashioned* give, entrust. **2** offer assurances about.

vow ❶ *noun* **1** solemn and binding promise. ◆ *plural* **2** formal promises made when marrying or entering a religious order. ◆ *verb* **3** promise solemnly.

vowel *noun* **1** speech sound made without obstructing the flow of breath. **2** letter representing this.

vox pop *noun* interviews with members of the public on TV or radio.

vox populi *noun* public opinion.

voyage ❶ *noun* **1** long journey by sea or in space. ◆ *verb* **2** make a voyage. **voyager** *noun*

voyeur *noun* person who obtains pleasure from watching people undressing or having sex. **voyeurism** *noun* **voyeuristic** *adjective*

vs versus.

V-sign *noun* **1** offensive gesture made by sticking up the index and middle fingers with the palm inwards. **2** similar gesture, with the palm outwards, meaning victory or peace.

VSO Voluntary Service Overseas.

VSOP (of brandy or port) very superior old pale.

VT Vermont.

VTOL vertical takeoff and landing.

VTR video tape recorder.

vulcanize *verb* strengthen (rubber) by treating it with sulphur. **vulcanization** *noun* **vulcanite** *noun* vulcanized rubber.

vulgar ❶ *adjective* showing lack of good taste, decency, or refinement. **vulgarly** *adverb* **vulgarity** *noun* **vulgarian** *noun* vulgar (rich) person. **vulgarism** *noun* coarse word or phrase. **vulgarize** *verb* make vulgar or too common. **vulgarization** *noun* **vulgar fraction** simple fraction.

Vulgate *noun* fourth-century Latin version of the Bible.

vulnerable ❶ *adjective* **1** liable to be physically or emotionally hurt. **2** exposed to attack. **3** financially weak and likely to fail. **vulnerability** *noun*

vulpine *adjective* of or like a fox.

vulture *noun* large bird that feeds on the flesh of dead animals.

vulva *noun* woman's external genitals.

vying *verb* present participle of VIE.

———————— THESAURUS ————————

plebiscite, referendum, show of hands ◆*verb* **5** = **cast one's vote**, elect, opt

voucher *noun* **1** = **ticket**, coupon, token

vouch for *verb* **1** = **guarantee**, answer for, certify, give assurance of, stand witness, swear to **2** = **confirm**, affirm, assert, attest to, support, uphold

vow *noun* **1** = **promise**, oath, pledge ◆*verb* **3** = **promise**, affirm, pledge, swear

voyage *noun* **1** = **journey**, crossing, cruise, passage, trip

vulgar *adjective* = **crude**, coarse, common, impolite, indecent, ribald, risqué, rude, tasteless, uncouth, unrefined

vulgarity *noun* = **crudeness**, bad taste, coarseness, indelicacy, ribaldry, rudeness, tastelessness OPPOSITE **good taste**

vulnerable *adjective* **1** = **susceptible**, sensitive, tender, thin-skinned, weak OPPOSITE **immune**. **2** = **exposed**, accessible, assailable, defenceless, unprotected, wide open OPPOSITE **guarded**

V

Ww

W 1 *Chem* tungsten. **2** watt. **3** West(ern).
WA 1 Washington. **2** Western Australia.
wacky *adjective* **wackier, wackiest** *Informal*
eccentric or funny. **wackiness** *noun*
wad ❶ *noun* **1** small mass of soft material. **2**
roll or bundle, esp. of banknotes. **wadded**
adjective **wadding** *noun* soft material used for
padding or stuffing.
waddle ❶ *verb* **1** walk with short swaying
steps. ◆ *noun* **2** swaying walk.
wade ❶ *verb* **1** walk with difficulty through
water or mud. **2** proceed with difficulty. **wader**
noun **1** long-legged water bird. ◆ *plural* **2**
angler's long waterproof boots.
wadi [**wod**-dee] *noun, pl* **-dies** (in N Africa
and Arabia) river which is dry except in the wet
season.
wafer *noun* **1** thin crisp biscuit. **2** thin disc of
unleavened bread used at Communion. **3** thin
slice. **wafer-thin** *adjective* extremely thin.
waffle¹ ❶ *Informal verb* **1** speak or write in a
vague wordy way. ◆ *noun* **2** vague wordy talk
or writing.
waffle² *noun* square crisp pancake with a
gridlike pattern.
waft ❶ *verb* **1** drift or carry gently through the
air. ◆ *noun* **2** something wafted.
wag ❶ *verb* **wagging, wagged 1** move
rapidly from side to side. ◆ *noun* **2** wagging
movement. **3** *Old-fashioned* humorous witty

person. **waggish** *adjective* **wagtail** *noun* small
long-tailed bird.
wage ❶ *noun* **1** (often pl) payment for work
done, esp. when paid weekly. ◆ *verb* **2** engage
in (an activity).
wager ❶ *noun, verb* bet on the outcome of
something.
waggle ❶ *verb* move with a rapid shaking or
wobbling motion. **waggly** *adjective*
wagon, waggon *noun* **1** four-wheeled
vehicle for heavy loads. **2** railway freight truck.
wahoo *noun* food and game fish of tropical
seas.
waif ❶ *noun* young person who is, or seems,
homeless or neglected.
wail ❶ *verb* **1** cry out in pain or misery. ◆ *noun*
2 mournful cry.
wain *noun Poetic* farm wagon.
wainscot, wainscoting *noun* wooden lining
of the lower part of the walls of a room.
waist *noun* **1** part of the body between the
ribs and hips. **2** narrow middle part.
waistband *noun* band of material sewn on to
the waist of a garment to strengthen it.
waistcoat *noun* sleeveless garment which
buttons up the front, usu. worn over a shirt and
under a jacket. **waistline** *noun* (size of) the
waist of a person or garment.
wait ❶ *verb* **1** remain inactive in expectation
(of something). **2** be ready (for something). **3**

THESAURUS

wad *noun* **1** =**mass**, hunk **2** =**roll**, bundle
waddle *verb* **1** =**shuffle**, sway, toddle, totter,
wobble
wade *verb* **1** =**walk through**, ford, paddle,
splash **2** =**plough through**, drudge at, labour
at, peg away at, toil at, work one's way
through
waffle¹ *verb* **1** *Inf* =**prattle**, blather, jabber,
prate, rabbit (on) (*Brit inf*), witter on (*inf*) ◆*noun*
2 =**verbosity**, padding, prolixity, verbiage,
wordiness
waft *verb* **1** =**carry**, bear, convey, drift, float,
transport
wag *verb* **1** =**wave**, bob, nod, quiver, shake,
stir, vibrate, waggle, wiggle ◆*noun* **2** =**wave**,
bob, nod, quiver, shake, vibration, waggle,

wiggle **3** *Old-fashioned* =**joker**, card (*inf*),
clown, comedian, comic, humorist, jester, wit
wage *noun* **1** (often pl) =**payment**, allowance,
emolument, fee, pay, recompense,
remuneration, reward, stipend ◆*verb* **2**
=**engage in**, carry on, conduct, practise,
proceed with, prosecute, pursue, undertake
wager *noun* =**bet**, flutter (*Brit inf*), gamble,
punt (*chiefly Brit*) ◆*verb* =**bet**, chance, gamble,
lay, risk, speculate, stake, venture
waggle *verb* =**wag**, flutter, oscillate, shake,
wave, wiggle, wobble
waif *noun* =**stray**, foundling, orphan
wail *verb* **1** =**cry**, bawl, grieve, howl, lament,
weep, yowl ◆*noun* **2** =**cry**, complaint, howl,
lament, moan, weeping, yowl

delay or be delayed. **4** serve in a restaurant etc. ◆ *noun* **5** act or period of waiting. **waiter** *noun* man who serves in a restaurant etc. **waitress** *n fem* **waiting list** list of people who have applied for something that is not immediately available. **waiting-room** *noun* room for waiting in, as at a station or surgery.

waive ⊕ *verb* refrain from enforcing (a law, right, etc.). **waiver** *noun* (written statement of) this act.

wake¹ ⊕ *verb* **waking, woke, woken 1** rouse from sleep or inactivity. ◆ *noun* **2** vigil beside a corpse the night before the funeral. **wake up to** become aware of. **waken** *verb* wake. **wakeful** *adjective* **wakefulness** *noun*

wake² ⊕ *noun* track left by a moving ship. **in the wake of** following, often as a result.

walk ⊕ *verb* **1** move on foot with at least one foot always on the ground. **2** pass through or over on foot. **3** escort or accompany on foot. ◆ *noun* **4** short journey on foot, usu. for pleasure. **5** act or instance of walking. **6** distance walked. **7** manner of walking. **8** place or route for walking. **walk of life** social position or profession. **walker** *noun* **walkabout** *noun* informal walk among the public by royalty etc. **walkie-talkie** *noun* portable radio transmitter and receiver. **walking stick** stick used as a support when walking. **walk into** *verb* meet with unwittingly. **Walkman** *noun* ® small portable cassette player with headphones. **walk-on** *adjective* (of a part in a film or play) small and not involving speaking. **walkout** *noun* **1** strike. **2** act of leaving as a protest.

walkover *noun* easy victory.

wall ⊕ *noun* **1** structure of brick, stone, etc. used to enclose, divide, or support. **2** something having the function or effect of a wall. ◆ *verb* **3** enclose or seal with a wall or walls. **go to the wall** be ruined, esp. financially. **wall-to-wall** *adjective* (of carpeting) completely covering a floor. **wallflower** *noun* **1** fragrant garden plant. **2** (at a dance) woman who remains seated because she has no partner. **wallpaper** *noun* decorative paper to cover interior walls.

wallaby *noun, pl* **-bies** marsupial like a small kangaroo.

wallaroo *noun* large stocky Australian kangaroo of rocky regions.

wallet ⊕ *noun* small folding case for paper money, documents, etc.

walleye *noun* fish with large staring eyes (also **dory**).

walleyed *adjective* having eyes with an abnormal amount of white showing due to a squint.

wallop ⊕ *Informal verb* **-loping, -loped 1** hit hard. ◆ *noun* **2** hard blow. **walloping** *Informal noun* **1** thrashing. ◆ *adjective* **2** large or great.

wallow ⊕ *verb* **1** revel in an emotion. **2** roll in liquid or mud. ◆ *noun* **3** act or instance of wallowing. **4** muddy place where animals wallow.

wally *noun, pl* **-lies** *Slang* stupid person.

walnut *noun* **1** edible nut with a wrinkled shell. **2** tree it grows on. **3** its wood, used for making furniture.

——————— T H E S A U R U S ———————

wait *verb* **1** = **remain**, hang fire, hold back, linger, pause, rest, stay, tarry OPPOSITE> go ◆*noun* **3** = **delay**, halt, hold-up, interval, pause, rest, stay

waive *verb* = **set aside**, abandon, dispense with, forgo, give up, relinquish, remit, renounce OPPOSITE> claim

wake¹ *verb* **1 a** = **awaken**, arise, awake, bestir, come to, get up, rouse, stir OPPOSITE> sleep. **b** = **activate**, animate, arouse, excite, fire, galvanize, kindle, provoke, stimulate, stir up ◆*noun* **2** = **vigil**, deathwatch, funeral, watch

wake² *noun* = **slipstream**, aftermath, backwash, path, track, trail, train, wash, waves

waken *verb* = **awaken**, activate, arouse, awake, rouse, stir OPPOSITE> sleep

walk *verb* **1, 2** = **go**, amble, hike, march, move, pace, step, stride, stroll **3** = **escort**, accompany, convoy, take ◆*noun* **4** = **stroll**, hike, march, promenade, ramble, saunter, trek, trudge **7** = **gait**, carriage, step **8** = **path**, alley,

avenue, esplanade, footpath, lane, promenade, trail **walk of life** = **profession**, calling, career, field, line, trade, vocation

walker *noun* = **pedestrian**, hiker, rambler, wayfarer

walkout *noun* **1** = **strike**, industrial action, protest, stoppage

walkover *noun* = **pushover**, breeze (*US & Canad inf*), cakewalk (*inf*), child's play (*inf*), doddle (*Brit sl*), picnic (*inf*), piece of cake (*inf*) (*sl*)

wall *noun* **1** = **partition**, enclosure, screen **2** = **barrier**, fence, hedge, impediment, obstacle, obstruction

wallet *noun* = **holder**, case, pouch, purse

wallop *Inf verb* **1** = **hit**, batter, beat, clobber (*sl*), pound, pummel, strike, swipe, thrash, thump, whack ◆*noun* **2** = **blow**, bash, punch, slug, smack, swipe, thump, thwack, whack

wallow *verb* **1** = **revel**, bask, delight, glory, luxuriate, relish, take pleasure OPPOSITE> avoid.

W

walrus *noun, pl* **-ruses, -rus** large sea mammal with long tusks.

waltz *noun* **1** ballroom dance. **2** music for this. ◆ *verb* **3** dance a waltz. **4** *Informal* move in a relaxed confident way.

wampum *noun US & Canad* shells woven together, formerly used by N American Indians for money and ornament.

wan ❶ [rhymes with **swan**] *adjective* **wanner, wannest** pale and sickly looking.

wand ❶ *noun* thin rod, esp. one used in performing magic tricks.

wander ❶ *verb* **1** move about without a definite destination or aim. **2** go astray, deviate. **3** (of the mind) lose concentration. ◆ *noun* **4** act or instance of wandering. **wanderer** *noun* **wanderlust** *noun* great desire to travel.

wane ❶ *verb* **1** decrease gradually in size or strength. **2** (of the moon) decrease in size. **on the wane** decreasing in size, strength, or power.

wangle ❶ *verb Informal* get by devious methods.

want ❶ *verb* **1** need or long for. **2** desire or wish. ◆ *noun* **3** act or instance of wanting. **4** thing wanted. **5** lack or absence, e.g. *a want of foresight.* **6** state of being in need, poverty. **wanted** *adjective* sought by the police. **wanting** *adjective* **1** lacking. **2** not good enough.

wanton ❶ *adjective* **1** without motive, provocation, or justification. **2** maliciously and

unnecessarily cruel. **3** *Old-fashioned* (of a woman) sexually unrestrained or immodest. **wantonly** *adverb*

WAP Wireless Application Protocol.

wapiti [**wop**-pit-tee] *noun, pl* **-tis** large N American and NZ deer.

war ❶ *noun* **1** fighting between nations. **2** conflict or contest. ◆ *adjective* **3** of, like, or caused by war. ◆ *verb* **warring, warred 4** conduct a war. **warring** *adjective* **warlike** *adjective* **1** of or relating to war. **2** hostile and eager to have a war. **on the warpath** *Informal* angry and prepared for conflict. **war crime** crime, such as killing, committed during a war in violation of accepted conventions. **war criminal** person who has committed war crimes. **war cry 1** shout used in battle. **2** slogan for rallying support for a cause. **warfare** *noun* fighting or hostilities. **warhead** *noun* explosive front part of a missile. **warmonger** *noun* person who encourages war. **warmongering** *noun, adjective* **warship** *noun* ship designed and equipped for naval combat.

warble ❶ *verb* sing in a trilling voice. **warbler** *noun* any of various small songbirds.

ward ❶ *noun* **1** room in a hospital for patients needing a similar kind of care. **2** electoral division of a town. **3** child under the care of a guardian or court. **warder** *noun* prison officer. **wardress** *n fem* **wardship** *noun* state of being a ward. **ward off** *verb* avert or repel. **wardroom** *noun* officers' quarters on a

———————— T H E S A U R U S ————————

2 = roll about, splash around

wan *adjective* =**pale**, anaemic, ashen, pallid, pasty, sickly, washed out, white OPPOSITE glowing

wand *noun* =**stick**, baton, rod

wander *verb* **1 = roam**, drift, meander, ramble, range, rove, stray, stroll **2 = deviate**, depart, digress, diverge, err, go astray, swerve, veer ◆*noun* **4 = excursion**, cruise, meander, ramble

wane *verb* **1 = decline**, decrease, diminish, dwindle, ebb, fade, fail, lessen, subside, taper off, weaken OPPOSITE **grow** ◆ **on the wane** =**declining**, dwindling, ebbing, fading, obsolescent, on the decline, tapering off, weakening

wangle *verb Inf* =**contrive**, arrange, engineer, fiddle (*inf*), fix (*inf*), manipulate, manoeuvre, pull off

want *verb* **1 = need**, call for, demand, lack, miss, require **2 = desire**, covet, crave, hanker after, hope for, hunger for, long for, thirst for, wish, yearn for OPPOSITE **have** ◆*noun* **3 = wish**,

appetite, craving, desire, longing, need, requirement, yearning **5 = lack**, absence, dearth, deficiency, famine, insufficiency, paucity, scarcity, shortage OPPOSITE **plenty. 6 = poverty**, destitution, neediness, penury, privation OPPOSITE **ease**

wanting *adjective* **1 = lacking**, absent, incomplete, missing, short, shy OPPOSITE **full. 2 = inadequate**, defective, deficient, faulty, imperfect, poor, substandard, unsound OPPOSITE **good**

wanton *adjective* **1 = unprovoked**, arbitrary, gratuitous, groundless, motiveless, needless, senseless, uncalled-for, unjustifiable, wilful OPPOSITE **justified. 3** *Old-fashioned* =**promiscuous**, dissipated, dissolute, immoral, lecherous, libidinous, loose, lustful, shameless, unchaste OPPOSITE **prudish**

war *noun* **1, 2 = fighting**, battle, combat, conflict, enmity, hostilities, struggle, warfare OPPOSITE **peace** ◆*verb* **4 = fight**, battle, campaign against, clash, combat, take up arms, wage war OPPOSITE **co-operate**

W

warship.

warden ❶ *noun* **1** person in charge of a building and its occupants. **2** official responsible for the enforcement of regulations.

wardrobe ❶ *noun* **1** cupboard for hanging clothes in. **2** person's collection of clothes. **3** costumes of a theatrical company.

ware ❶ *noun* **1** articles of a specified type or material, e.g. *silverware*. ♦ *plural* **2** goods for sale. **warehouse** *noun* building for storing goods prior to sale or distribution.

warlock *noun* man who practises black magic.

warm ❶ *adjective* **1** moderately hot. **2** providing warmth. **3** (of a colour) predominantly yellow or red. **4** affectionate. **5** enthusiastic. ♦ *verb* **6** make or become warm. **warmly** *adverb* **warmth** *noun* **1** mild heat. **2** cordiality. **3** intensity of emotion. **warm-blooded** *adjective* **1** *Zool* (of mammals and birds) having a constant body temperature, usu. higher than the surroundings. **2** passionate. **warm up** *verb* **1** make or become warmer. **2** do preliminary exercises before a race or more strenuous exercise. **3** make or become more lively. **warm-up** *noun*

warn ❶ *verb* **1** make aware of possible danger or harm. **2** caution or scold. **3** inform (someone) in advance. **warning** *noun* **1**

something that warns. **2** scolding or caution. **warn off** *verb* advise (someone) not to become involved with.

warp ❶ *verb* **1** twist out of shape. **2** pervert. ♦ *noun* **3** state of being warped. **4** lengthwise threads on a loom.

warrant ❶ *noun* **1** (document giving) official authorization. ♦ *verb* **2** make necessary. **3** guarantee. **warranty** *noun*, *pl* **-ties** (document giving) a guarantee. **warrant officer** officer in certain armed services with a rank between a commissioned and noncommissioned officer.

warren *noun* **1** series of burrows in which rabbits live. **2** overcrowded building or part of a town.

warrigal *Aust noun* **1** dingo. ♦ *adjective* **2** wild.

warrior ❶ *noun* person who fights in a war.

wart *noun* small hard growth on the skin. **warty** *adjective* **wart hog** kind of African wild pig.

wary ❶ [ware-ree] *adjective* **warier, wariest** watchful or cautious. **warily** *adverb* **wariness** *noun*

was *verb* first and third person singular past tense of BE.

wash ❶ *verb* **1** clean (oneself, clothes, etc.) with water and usu. soap. **2** be washable. **3** flow or sweep over or against. **4** *Informal* be believable or acceptable, e.g. *that excuse won't*

——————— T H E S A U R U S ———————

warble *verb* = **sing**, chirp, trill, twitter

ward *noun* **1** = **room**, apartment, cubicle **2** = **district**, area, division, precinct, quarter, zone **3** = **dependant**, charge, minor

warden *noun* **1** = **keeper**, administrator, caretaker, curator, custodian, guardian, ranger, superintendent

warder, wardress *noun* = **jailer**, custodian, guard, prison officer, screw (*sl*)

ward off *verb* = **repel**, avert, avoid, deflect, fend off, parry, stave off

wardrobe *noun* **1** = **clothes cupboard**, closet **2** = **clothes**, apparel, attire

warehouse *noun* = **store**, depository, depot, stockroom, storehouse

wares *plural noun* = **goods**, commodities, merchandise, produce, products, stock, stuff

warfare *noun* = **war**, arms, battle, combat, conflict, fighting, hostilities

warlike *adjective* **2** = **belligerent**, aggressive, bellicose, bloodthirsty, hawkish, hostile, martial, warmongering

warm *adjective* **1** = **heated**, balmy, lukewarm, pleasant, sunny, tepid, thermal [OPPOSITE] **cool**. **4** = **affectionate**, amorous, cordial, friendly, hospitable, kindly, loving, tender [OPPOSITE]

cold ♦*verb* **6** = **heat**, heat up, melt, thaw, warm up

warmth *noun* **1** = **heat**, hotness, warmness [OPPOSITE] **cold**. **2** = **affection**, amorousness, cordiality, heartiness, kindliness, love, tenderness [OPPOSITE] **hostility**

warn *verb* **1** = **alert**, tip off **2** = **caution 3** = **forewarn**, advise, apprise, give notice, inform, make (someone) aware, notify

warning *noun* **1** = **caution**, advice, alarm, alert, notification, omen, sign, tip-off

warp *verb* **1** = **twist**, bend, contort, deform, distort ♦*noun* **3** = **twist**, bend, contortion, distortion, kink

warrant *noun* **1** = **authorization**, authority, licence, mana (*NZ*), permission, permit, sanction ♦*verb* **2** = **call for**, demand, deserve, excuse, justify, license, necessitate, permit, require, sanction **3** = **guarantee**, affirm, attest, certify, declare, pledge, vouch for

warranty *noun* = **guarantee**, assurance, bond, certificate, contract, covenant, pledge

warrior *noun* = **soldier**, combatant, fighter, gladiator, man-at-arms

wary *adjective* = **cautious**, alert, careful, chary, circumspect, distrustful, guarded, suspicious,

W

wash. ♦ noun **5** act or process of washing. **6** clothes washed at one time. **7** thin coat of paint. **8** disturbance in the water after a ship has passed by. **washable** adjective **washer** noun ring put under a nut or bolt or in a tap as a seal. **washing** noun clothes to be washed. **washing machine** electric machine for washing clothes and linen. **washing-up** noun (washing of) dishes and cutlery needing to be cleaned after a meal. **wash away** verb carry or be carried off by moving water. **washbasin** noun basin for washing the face and hands. **washout** noun Informal complete failure. **washed-out** adjective **1** exhausted. **2** faded. **wash up** verb wash dishes and cutlery after a meal.

wasp noun stinging insect with a slender black-and-yellow striped body. **waspish** adjective bad-tempered.

Wasp, WASP noun US derogatory White Anglo-Saxon Protestant.

wassail noun **1** formerly, festivity when much drinking took place. ♦ verb **2** drink health of (a person) at a wassail.

waste ❶ verb **1** use pointlessly or thoughtlessly. **2** fail to take advantage of. ♦ noun **3** act of wasting or state of being wasted. **4** anything wasted. **5** rubbish. ♦ plural **6** desert. ♦ adjective **7** rejected as worthless or surplus to requirements. **8** not cultivated or inhabited. **waste away** (cause to) decline in health or strength. **wastage** noun **1** loss by wear or

waste. **2** reduction in size of a workforce by not filling vacancies. **wasted** adjective **1** unnecessary or unfruitful. **2** pale, thin, and unhealthy. **wasteful** adjective extravagant. **wastefully** adverb **waster, wastrel** noun layabout. **wasteland** noun barren or desolate area of land. **wastepaper basket** container for discarded paper.

watch ❶ verb **1** look at closely. **2** look after. **3** maintain a careful interest in. **4** guard or supervise. ♦ noun **5** portable timepiece for the wrist or pocket. **6** (period of) watching. **7** sailor's spell of duty. **watchable** adjective **watcher** noun **watchful** adjective vigilant or alert. **watchfully** adverb **watchfulness** noun **watchdog** noun **1** dog kept to guard property. **2** person or group guarding against inefficiency or illegality. **watch for** verb be keenly alert to or cautious about. **watchman** noun man employed to guard a building or property. **watchword** noun word or phrase that sums up the attitude of a particular group.

water ❶ noun **1** clear colourless tasteless liquid that falls as rain and forms rivers etc. **2** body of water, such as a sea or lake. **3** level of the tide. **4** urine. ♦ verb **5** put water on or into. **6** (of the eyes) fill with tears. **7** (of the mouth) salivate. **watery** adjective **water buffalo** oxlike Asian animal. **water closet** Old-fashioned (room containing) a toilet flushed by water. **watercolour** noun **1** paint thinned with water.

——————— THESAURUS ———————

vigilant, watchful OPPOSITE rash
wash verb **1** = **clean**, bathe, cleanse, launder, rinse, scrub **3** = **sweep away**, bear away, carry off, move **4** Inf = **be plausible**, bear scrutiny, be convincing, carry weight, hold up, hold water, stand up, stick ♦noun **5** = **cleaning**, cleansing, laundering, rinse, scrub **7** = **coat**, coating, film, layer, overlay **8** = **swell**, surge, wave
washout noun Inf = **failure**, disappointment, disaster, dud (inf), fiasco, flop (inf) OPPOSITE success
waste verb **1** = **squander**, blow (sl), dissipate, fritter away, lavish, misuse, throw away OPPOSITE save ♦noun **3** = **squandering**, dissipation, extravagance, frittering away, misuse, prodigality, wastefulness OPPOSITE saving. **5** = **rubbish**, debris, dross, garbage, leftovers, litter, refuse, scrap, trash ♦plural **6** = **desert**, wasteland, wilderness ♦adjective **7** = **unwanted**, leftover, superfluous, supernumerary, unused, useless, worthless OPPOSITE needed. **8** = **uncultivated**, bare, barren, desolate, empty, uninhabited, unproductive, wild OPPOSITE developed

♦ **waste away** = **decline**, atrophy, crumble, decay, dwindle, fade, wane, wear out, wither
wasteful adjective = **extravagant**, lavish, prodigal, profligate, spendthrift, thriftless, uneconomical
waster, wastrel noun = **layabout**, good-for-nothing, idler, loafer, ne'er-do-well, piker (Aust & NZ sl), shirker, skiver (Brit sl)
watch verb **1** = **look at**, contemplate, eye, eyeball (sl), observe, regard, see, view **2, 4** = **guard**, keep, look after, mind, protect, superintend, take care of, tend ♦noun **5** = **wristwatch**, chronometer, timepiece **6** = **lookout**, observation, surveillance, vigil
watchdog noun **1** = **guard dog 2** = **guardian**, custodian, monitor, protector, scrutineer
watchful adjective = **alert**, attentive, observant, on the lookout, suspicious, vigilant, wary, wide awake
watchman noun = **guard**, caretaker, custodian, security guard
watchword noun = **motto**, battle cry, byword, catch phrase, catchword, maxim, rallying cry, slogan, tag-line

W

2 painting done in this. **watercourse** noun bed of a stream or river. **watercress** noun edible plant growing in clear ponds and streams. **water down** verb dilute, make less strong. **waterfall** noun place where the waters of a river drop vertically. **waterfront** noun part of a town alongside a body of water. **waterhole** noun pond or pool in a dry area where animals drink. **water ice** ice cream made from frozen fruit-flavoured syrup. **watering place 1** place where drinking water may be obtained for people or animals. **2** resort or spa. **water lily** water plant with large floating leaves. **waterline** noun level to which a ship's hull will be immersed when afloat. **waterlogged** adjective saturated with water. **watermark** noun faint translucent design in a sheet of paper. **watermelon** noun melon with green skin and red flesh. **water polo** team game played by swimmers with a ball. **waterproof** adjective **1** not letting water through. ◆ noun **2** waterproof garment. ◆ verb **3** make waterproof. **watershed** noun **1** important period or factor serving as a dividing line. **2** line separating two river systems. **water-skiing** noun sport of riding over water on skis towed by a speedboat. **watertight** adjective **1** not letting water through. **2** with no loopholes or weak points. **water wheel** large wheel which is turned by flowing water to drive machinery. **watt** [wott] noun unit of power. **wattage** noun electrical power expressed in watts. **wattle** [wott-tl] noun **1** branches woven over sticks to make a fence. **2** Australian acacia with flexible branches formerly used for making fences. **3** fold of skin hanging from the neck of certain birds. **wave ⊕** verb **1** move the hand to and fro as a

greeting or signal. **2** direct (someone) to move in a particular direction by waving. **3** move or flap to and fro. ◆ noun **4** moving ridge on water. **5** curve(s) in the hair. **6** prolonged spell of something, e.g. the recent wave of violence. **7** gesture of waving. **8** vibration carrying energy through a medium. **wavy** adjective **wavier, waviest. wavelength** noun distance between the same points of two successive waves. **waver ⊕** verb **1** hesitate or be irresolute. **2** be or become unsteady. **waverer** noun **wavering** adjective
wax¹ noun **1** solid shiny fatty or oily substance used for sealing, making candles, etc. **2** similar substance made by bees. **3** waxy secretion of the ear. ◆ verb **4** coat or polish with wax. **waxed** adjective **waxen** adjective made of or like wax. **waxy** adjective **waxier, waxiest. waxwork** noun **1** lifelike wax model of a (famous) person. ◆ plural **2** place exhibiting these.
wax² ⊕ verb **1** increase in size or strength. **2** (of the moon) get gradually larger.
way ⊕ noun **1** manner or method. **2** characteristic manner. **3** route or direction. **4** track or path. **5** distance. **6** room for movement or activity, e.g. you're in the way. **7** passage or journey. **8** Informal state or condition, e.g in a bad way. ◆ plural **9** habits or customs. **wayfarer** noun traveller. **waylay** verb lie in wait for and accost or attack. **way-out** adjective Informal extremely unconventional. **wayside** adjective, noun (situated by) the side of a road.
wayward ⊕ adjective erratic, selfish, or stubborn. **waywardness** noun
Wb Physics weber.
WC water closet.

——————————— T H E S A U R U S ———————————

water noun **1** = liquid, H₂O ◆ verb **5** = moisten, dampen, douse, drench, hose, irrigate, soak, spray
water down verb = dilute, thin, water, weaken
waterfall noun = cascade, cataract, fall
waterlogged adjective = soaked, drenched, dripping, saturated, sodden, sopping, streaming, wet through, wringing wet
watertight adjective **1** = waterproof, sound OPPOSITE leaky. **2** = foolproof, airtight, flawless, impregnable, sound, unassailable OPPOSITE weak
wave verb **1** = signal, gesticulate, gesture, sign **2** = direct, beckon, indicate **3** = flap, brandish, flourish, flutter, oscillate, shake, stir, swing, wag ◆ noun **4** = ripple, billow, breaker, ridge, roller,

swell, undulation **6** = outbreak, flood, rash, rush, stream, surge, upsurge
waver verb **1** = hesitate, dither, falter, fluctuate, hum and haw, seesaw, vacillate OPPOSITE resolve. **2** = tremble, flicker, quiver, shake, totter, wobble
wax² verb **1** = increase, develop, enlarge, expand, grow, magnify, swell OPPOSITE wanr
way noun **1** = method, fashion, manner, means, mode, procedure, process, system, technique **2** = style, custom, habit, manner, nature, personality, practice, wont **3** = route, channel, course, direction **4** = track, path, pathway, road, trail **5** = distance, length, stretch **7** = journey, approach, march, passage
wayward adjective **a** = erratic, capricious, inconstant, unpredictable **b** = unmanageable,

we *pronoun* (used as the subject of a verb) **1** the speaker or writer and one or more others. **2** people in general. **3** formal word for 'I' used by editors and monarchs.

weak *adjective* **1** lacking strength. **2** liable to give way. **3** unconvincing. **4** lacking flavour. **weaken** *verb* make or become weak. **weakling** *noun* feeble person or animal. **weakly** *adverb* **1** feebly. ♦ *adjective* **2** weak or sickly. **weakness** *noun* **1** being weak. **2** failing. **3** self-indulgent liking. **weak-kneed** *adjective Informal* lacking determination.

weal¹ *noun* raised mark left on the skin by a blow.

weal² *noun Obs* prosperity or wellbeing, esp. in *the common weal*.

wealth ⊕ *noun* **1** state of being rich. **2** large amount of money and valuables. **3** great amount or number. **wealthy** *adjective* **wealthier, wealthiest**

wean *verb* **1** accustom (a baby or young mammal) to food other than mother's milk. **2** coax (someone) away from former habits.

weapon *noun* **1** object used in fighting. **2** anything used to get the better of an opponent. **weaponry** *noun* weapons collectively.

wear ⊕ *verb* **wearing, wore, worn 1** have on the body as clothing or ornament. **2** show as one's expression. **3** have (the hair) in a particular style. **4** (cause to) deteriorate by constant use or action. **5** *Informal* tolerate. **6** endure constant use. ♦ *noun* **7** clothes suitable for a particular time or purpose, e.g. *beach wear*. **8** damage caused by use. **9** ability to endure constant use. **wearable** *adjective* **wearer** *noun* **wearing** *adjective* tiring and sometimes trying. **wear and tear** damage or loss from ordinary use. **wear off** *verb* gradually decrease in intensity. **wear on** *verb* (of time) pass slowly. **wear out** *verb* **1** make or become useless through wear. **2** exhaust or tire.

weary ⊕ *adjective* **-rier, -riest 1** tired or exhausted. **2** tiring. ♦ *verb* **-rying, -ried 3** make or become weary. **wearily** *adverb* **weariness** *noun* **wearisome** *adjective* tedious. **wearying** *adjective*

weasel *noun* small carnivorous mammal with a long body and short legs.

weather ⊕ *noun* **1** day-to-day atmospheric conditions of a place. ♦ *verb* **2** (cause to) be affected by the weather. **3** come safely

——————————— THESAURUS ———————————

ungovernable, unruly
weak *adjective* **1** =**feeble**, debilitated, effete, fragile, frail, infirm, puny, sickly, unsteady OPPOSITE **strong**. **2** =**unsafe**, defenceless, exposed, helpless, unguarded, unprotected, vulnerable **3** =**unconvincing**, feeble, flimsy, hollow, lame, pathetic, unsatisfactory OPPOSITE **powerful**. **4** =**tasteless**, diluted, insipid, runny, thin, watery OPPOSITE **potent**
weaken *verb* **a** =**lessen**, diminish, dwindle, fade, flag, lower, moderate, reduce, sap, undermine, wane OPPOSITE **increase**. **b** =**dilute**, thin out, water down
weakling *noun* =**sissy**, drip (*inf*), wet (*Brit inf*), wimp (*inf*)
weakness *noun* **1** =**frailty**, decrepitude, feebleness, fragility, infirmity, powerlessness, vulnerability OPPOSITE **power**. **2** =**failing**, blemish, defect, deficiency, fault, flaw, imperfection, lack, shortcoming OPPOSITE **advantage**. **3** =**liking**, fondness, inclination, partiality, passion, penchant, soft spot OPPOSITE **dislike**
wealth *noun* **2** =**riches**, affluence, capital, fortune, lolly (*Aust & NZ sl*), money, opulence, prosperity OPPOSITE **poverty**. **3** =**plenty**, abundance, copiousness, cornucopia, fullness, profusion, richness
wealthy *adjective* **1** =**rich**, affluent, flush (*inf*), moneyed, opulent, prosperous, well-heeled (*inf*), well-off, well-to-do OPPOSITE **poor**
wear *verb* **1** =**be dressed in**, don, have on, put on, sport (*inf*) **2** =**show**, display, exhibit **4** =**deteriorate**, abrade, corrode, erode, fray, grind, rub ♦*noun* **7** =**clothes**, apparel, attire, costume, dress, garb, garments, gear (*inf*), things **8** =**damage**, abrasion, attrition, corrosion, deterioration, erosion, wear and tear OPPOSITE **repair**
weariness *noun* **1** =**tiredness**, drowsiness, exhaustion, fatigue, languor, lassitude, lethargy, listlessness
wearing *adjective* =**tiresome**, exasperating, fatiguing, irksome, oppressive, trying, wearisome
wearisome *adjective* =**tedious**, annoying, boring, exhausting, fatiguing, irksome, oppressive, tiresome, troublesome, trying, wearing
wear off *verb* =**subside**, decrease, diminish, disappear, dwindle, fade, peter out, wane
weary *adjective* **1** =**tired**, done in (*inf*), drained, drowsy, exhausted, fatigued, flagging, jaded, sleepy, worn out OPPOSITE **fresh**. **2** =**tiring**, arduous, laborious, tiresome, wearisome OPPOSITE **exciting** ♦*verb* **3** =**tire**, drain, enervate, fatigue, sap, take it out of (*inf*), tax, tire out, wear out

W

through. **under the weather** *Informal* slightly ill. **weather-beaten** *adjective* worn, damaged, or (of skin) tanned by exposure to the weather. **weathercock, weathervane** *noun* device that revolves to show the direction of the wind. **weatherman** *Informal* person who forecasts the weather on television or radio. **weave ❶** *verb* **weaving, wove** *or* **weaved, woven** *or* **weaved 1** make (fabric) by interlacing (yarn) on a loom. **2** compose (a story). **3** move from side to side while going forwards. **weaver** *noun* **weaving** *noun* **web ❶** *noun* **1** net spun by a spider. **2** anything intricate or complex, e.g. *web of deceit*. **3** skin between the toes of a duck, frog, etc. **the Web** short for WORLD WIDE WEB. **webbed** *adjective* **webbing** *noun* strong fabric woven in strips. **webcam** *noun* camera that transmits images over the Internet. **webcast** *noun* broadcast of an event over the Internet. **weblog** *noun* person's online journal (also **blog**). **website** *noun* group of connected pages on the World Wide Web. **weber** [**vay-**ber] *noun* SI unit of magnetic flux. **wed ❶** *verb* **wedding, wedded** *or* **wed 1** marry. **2** unite closely. **wedded** *adjective* **1** of marriage. **2** firmly in support of an idea or institution. **wedding** *noun* act or ceremony of marriage. **wedlock** *noun* marriage. **Wed.** Wednesday. **wedge ❶** *noun* **1** piece of material thick at one end and thin at the other. ◆ *verb* **2** fasten or split with a wedge. **3** squeeze into a narrow space. **wedge-tailed eagle** large brown Australian eagle with a wedge-shaped tail. **Wednesday** *noun* fourth day of the week. **wee** *adjective* small. **weed ❶** *noun* **1** plant growing where undesired. **2** *Informal* thin ineffectual person. ◆

verb **3** clear of weeds. **weedy** *adjective* **weedier, weediest 1** *Informal* (of a person) thin and weak. **2** full of or like weeds. **weed out** *verb* remove or eliminate (what is unwanted). **weeds** *plural noun Obs* widow's mourning clothes. **week** *noun* **1** period of seven days, esp. one beginning on a Sunday. **2** hours or days of work in a week. **weekly** *adjective, adverb* **1** happening, done, etc. once a week. ◆ *noun, pl* **-lies 2** newspaper or magazine published once a week. **weekday** *noun* any day of the week except Saturday or Sunday. **weekend** *noun* Saturday and Sunday. **weep ❶** *verb* **weeping, wept 1** shed tears. **2** ooze liquid. ◆ *noun* **3** spell of weeping. **weepy** *adjective* **weepier, weepiest** liable to cry. **weeping willow** willow with drooping branches. **weevil** *noun* small beetle which eats grain etc. **weft** *noun* cross threads in weaving. **weigh ❶** *verb* **1** have a specified weight. **2** measure the weight of. **3** consider carefully. **4** be influential. **5** be burdensome. **weigh anchor** raise a ship's anchor or (of a ship) have its anchor raised. **weighbridge** *noun* machine for weighing vehicles by means of a metal plate set into the road. **weight ❶** *noun* **1** heaviness of an object. **2** unit of measurement of weight. **3** object of known mass used for weighing. **4** heavy object. **5** importance or influence. ◆ *verb* **6** add weight to. **7** slant (a system) so that it favours one side rather than another. **weightless** *adjective* **weightlessness** *noun* **weightlifting** *noun* sport of lifting heavy weights. **weightlifter** *noun* **weight training** physical exercise using weights to improve muscles.

———————— T H E S A U R U S ————————

weather *noun* **1** = **climate**, conditions ◆*verb* **3** = **withstand**, brave, come through, endure, overcome, resist, ride out, stand, survive ⌐OPPOSITE⌐ **yield to**
weave *verb* **1** = **knit**, braid, entwine, interlace, intertwine, plait **2** = **create**, build, construct, contrive, fabricate, make up, put together, spin **3** = **zigzag**, crisscross, wind
web *noun* **1** = **spider's web**, cobweb **2** = **network**, lattice, tangle
wed *verb* **1** = **marry**, get married, take the plunge (*inf*), tie the knot (*inf*) ⌐OPPOSITE⌐ **divorce. 2** = **unite**, ally, blend, combine, interweave, join, link, merge ⌐OPPOSITE⌐ **divide**
wedding *noun* = **marriage**, nuptials, wedlock
wedge *noun* **1** = **block**, chunk, lump ◆*verb* **3**

= **squeeze**, cram, crowd, force, jam, lodge, pack, ram, stuff, thrust
wedlock *noun* = **marriage**, matrimony
weed out *verb* = **eliminate**, dispense with, eradicate, get rid of, remove, root out, uproot
weedy *adjective* **1** *Inf* = **weak**, feeble, frail, ineffectual, namby-pamby, puny, skinny, thin
weep *verb* **1** = **cry**, blubber, lament, mourn, shed tears, snivel, sob, whimper ⌐OPPOSITE⌐ **rejoice**
weigh *verb* **1** = **have a weight of**, tip the scales at (*inf*) **3** = **consider**, contemplate, deliberate upon, evaluate, examine, meditate upon, ponder, reflect upon, think over **4** = **matter**, carry weight, count
weight *noun* **1** = **heaviness**, load, mass,

weighting *noun* extra allowance paid in special circumstances.
weighty ❶ *adjective* **weightier, weightiest 1** important or serious. **2** very heavy. **weightily** *adverb*
weir *noun* river dam.
weird ❶ *adjective* **1** strange or bizarre. **2** unearthly or eerie. **weirdly** *adverb*

SPELLING TIP

The pronunciation of **weird** possibly leads people to spell it with the vowels the wrong way round. The Bank of English shows that *wierd* is a common misspelling.

---

weirdo *noun, pl* **-dos** *Informal* peculiar person.
welch *verb* same as WELSH.
welcome ❶ *verb* **-coming, -comed 1** greet with pleasure. **2** receive gladly. ♦ *noun* **3** kindly greeting. ♦ *adjective* **4** received gladly. **5** freely permitted.
weld ❶ *verb* **1** join (pieces of metal or plastic) by softening with heat. **2** unite closely. ♦ *noun* **3** welded joint. **welder** *noun*
welfare ❶ *noun* **1** wellbeing. **2** help given to people in need. **welfare state** system in which the government takes responsibility for the wellbeing of its citizens.

well¹ ❶ *adverb* **better, best 1** satisfactorily. **2** skilfully. **3** completely. **4** prosperously. **5** suitably. **6** intimately. **7** favourably. **8** considerably. **9** very likely. ♦ *adjective* **10** in good health. **11** satisfactory. ♦ *interjection* **12** exclamation of surprise, interrogation, etc.
well² ❶ *noun* **1** hole sunk into the earth to reach water, oil, or gas. **2** deep open shaft. ♦ *verb* **3** flow upwards or outwards.
wellbeing *noun* state of being well, happy, or prosperous.
well-built *adjective* strong and muscular.
well-disposed *adjective* inclined to be friendly or sympathetic.
well-done *adjective* **1** accomplished satisfactorily. **2** (of food, esp. meat) thoroughly cooked.
well-heeled *adjective Informal* wealthy.
wellies *plural noun Informal* wellingtons.
wellingtons *plural noun* high waterproof rubber boots.
well-known ❶ *adjective* famous.
well-meaning *adjective* having good intentions.
well-nigh *adverb* almost.
well-off ❶ *adjective* **1** moderately wealthy. **2** in a fortunate position.
well-spoken *adjective* speaking in a polite or articulate way.
well-to-do ❶ *adjective* moderately wealthy.
well-worn ❶ *adjective* **1** (of a word or phrase)

——————————— T H E S A U R U S ———————————

poundage, tonnage **5 = importance**, authority, consequence, impact, import, influence, mana (*NZ*), power, value ♦*verb* **6 = load**, freight **7 = bias**, load, slant, unbalance
weighty *adjective* **1 = important**, consequential, crucial, grave, momentous, portentous, serious, significant, solemn OPPOSITE minor. **2 = heavy**, burdensome, cumbersome, hefty (*inf*), massive, ponderous
weird *adjective* **1 = strange**, bizarre, freakish, odd, queer, unnatural OPPOSITE natural. **2 = eerie**, creepy (*inf*), mysterious, spooky (*inf*)
welcome *verb* **1 = greet**, embrace, hail, meet OPPOSITE refuse. **2 = receive** ♦*noun* **3 = greeting**, acceptance, hospitality, reception, salutation OPPOSITE slight ♦*adjective* **4 = acceptable**, agreeable, appreciated, delightful, desirable, gratifying, pleasant, refreshing OPPOSITE unacceptable. **5 = free**, under no obligation
weld *verb* **1 = solder**, fuse **2 = unite**, bind, bond, connect, join, link
welfare *noun* **1 = wellbeing**, advantage, benefit, good, happiness, health, interest,

prosperity
well¹ *adverb* **1 = satisfactorily**, agreeably, nicely, pleasantly, smoothly, splendidly, successfully OPPOSITE wrongly. **2 = skilfully**, ably, adeptly, adequately, admirably, correctly, efficiently, expertly, proficiently, properly OPPOSITE badly. **3 = fully**, thoroughly **4 = prosperously**, comfortably **5 = suitably**, fairly, fittingly, justly, properly, rightly **6 = intimately**, deeply, profoundly OPPOSITE somewhat. **7 = favourably**, approvingly, glowingly, highly, kindly, warmly **8 = considerably**, abundantly, amply, fully, greatly, heartily, highly, substantially, thoroughly, very much ♦*adjective* **10 = healthy**, fit, in fine fettle, sound **11 = satisfactory**, agreeable, fine, pleasing, proper, right
well² *noun* **1, 2 = hole**, bore, pit, shaft ♦*verb* **3 = flow**, gush, jet, pour, spout, spring, spurt, surge
well-known *adjective* **= famous**, celebrated, familiar, noted, popular, renowned
well-off *adjective* **1 = rich**, affluent, comfortable, moneyed, prosperous, wealthy,

W

stale from overuse. **2** so much used as to be affected by wear.

welsh *verb* fail to pay a debt or fulfil an obligation.

Welsh *adjective* **1** of Wales. ♦ *noun* **2** language or people of Wales. **Welsh rarebit, rabbit** dish of melted cheese on toast.

welt ⊕ *noun* **1** raised mark on the skin produced by a blow. **2** raised or strengthened seam.

welter *noun* jumbled mass.

welterweight *noun* boxer weighing up to 147lb (professional) or 67kg (amateur).

wen *noun* cyst on the scalp.

wench *noun Facetious* young woman.

wend *verb* go or travel.

wensleydale *noun* type of white cheese of flaky texture.

went *verb* past tense of GO.

wept *verb* past of WEEP.

were *verb* **1** form of the past tense of **be** used after *we, you, they, or a plural noun.* **2** subjunctive of BE.

we're we are.

weren't were not.

werewolf *noun* (in folklore) person who can turn into a wolf.

west *noun* **1** (direction towards) the part of the horizon where the sun sets. **2** region lying in this direction. **3** (**W-**) western Europe and the US. ♦ *adjective* **4** to or in the west. **5** (of a wind) from the west. ♦ *adverb* **6** in, to, or towards the west. **westerly** *adjective* **western** *adjective* **1** of or in the west. ♦ *noun* **2** film or story about cowboys in the western US. **westerner** *noun* person from the west of a country or area. **westernize** *verb* adapt to the customs and culture of the West. **westward** *adjective, adverb* **westwards** *adverb*

wet ⊕ *adjective* **wetter, wettest 1** covered or

soaked with water or another liquid. **2** not yet dry, e.g. *wet paint.* **3** rainy. **4** *Informal* (of a person) feeble or foolish. ♦ *noun* **5** moisture or rain. **6** *Informal* feeble or foolish person. **7** *Brit* moderate Conservative politician. ♦ *verb* **wetting, wet** *or* **wetted 8** make wet. **wetly** *adverb* **wetness** *noun* **wet blanket** *Informal* person who has a depressing effect on others. **wetland** *noun* area of marshy land. **wet nurse** woman employed to breast-feed another's child. **wet suit** close-fitting rubber suit worn by divers etc.

whack ⊕ *verb* **1** strike with a resounding blow. ♦ *noun* **2** such a blow. **3** *Informal* share. **4** *Informal* attempt. **whacked** *adjective* exhausted. **whacking** *adjective Informal* huge.

whale *noun* large fish-shaped sea mammal. **a whale of a time** *Informal* a very enjoyable time. **whaling** *noun* hunting of whales. **whaler** *noun* ship or person involved in whaling.

whalebone *noun* horny substance hanging from the upper jaw of toothless whales.

wham *interjection* expression indicating suddenness or forcefulness.

wharf ⊕ *noun, pl* **wharves, wharfs** platform at a harbour for loading and unloading ships.

wharfie *noun Aust* person employed to load and unload ships.

what *pronoun* **1** which thing. **2** that which. **3** request for a statement to be repeated. ♦ *interjection* **4** exclamation of anger, surprise, etc. ♦ *adverb* **5** in which way, how much, e.g. *what do you care?* **what for?** why? **whatever** *pronoun* **1** everything or anything that. **2** no matter what. **whatnot** *noun Informal* similar unspecified things. **whatsoever** *adjective* at all.

wheat *noun* **1** grain used in making flour, bread, and pasta. **2** plant producing this. **wheaten** *adjective* made of the grain or flour of wheat. **wheatear** *noun* small songbird.

——————— T H E S A U R U S ———————

well-heeled (*inf*), well-to-do OPPOSITE **broke**

well-to-do *adjective* =**rich**, affluent, comfortable, moneyed, prosperous, wealthy, well-heeled (*inf*), well-off

well-worn *adjective* **1** =**stale**, banal, commonplace, hackneyed, overused, stereotyped, trite

welt *noun* **1** =**mark**, contusion, streak, stripe, wale, weal

wet *adjective* **1** =**damp**, dank, moist, saturated, soaking, sodden, soggy, sopping, waterlogged, watery OPPOSITE **dry. 3** =**rainy**, drizzling, pouring, raining, showery, teeming OPPOSITE **sunny. 4** *Inf* =**feeble**, effete, ineffectual, namby-pamby, soft, spineless,

timorous, weak, weedy (*inf*) ♦*noun* **5** =**moisture**, condensation, damp, dampness, drizzle, humidity, liquid, rain, water, wetness **6** *Inf* =**weakling**, drip (*inf*), weed (*inf*), wimp (*inf*) ♦*verb* **8** =**moisten**, dampen, douse, irrigate, saturate, soak, spray, water

whack *verb* **1** =**strike**, bang, belt (*inf*), clobber (*sl*), hit, smack, swipe, thrash, thump, thwack, wallop (*inf*) ♦*noun* **2** =**blow**, bang, belt (*inf*), hit, smack, stroke, swipe, thump, thwack, wallop (*inf*) **3** *Inf* =**share**, bit, cut (*inf*), part, portion, quota **4** *Inf* =**attempt**, bash (*inf*), crack (*inf*), go (*inf*), shot (*inf*), stab (*inf*), try, turn

wharf *noun* =**dock**, jetty, landing stage, pier, quay

W

wheatgerm *noun* vitamin-rich embryo of the wheat kernel. **wheatmeal** *adjective, noun* (made with) brown, but not wholemeal, flour.

wheedle ⊙ *verb* coax or cajole.

wheel ⊙ *noun* **1** disc that revolves on an axle. **2** something repeated in cycles, e.g *wheel of life*. **3** pivoting movement. ◆ *verb* **4** push or pull (something with wheels). **5** turn as if on an axis. **6** turn round suddenly. **wheeling and dealing** use of shrewd and sometimes unscrupulous methods to achieve success. **wheeler-dealer** *noun* **wheelie** *noun* manoeuvre on a bike in which the front wheel is raised off the ground. **wheelie bin** large container for household rubbish, mounted on wheels for easy movement. **wheelbarrow** *noun* shallow box for carrying loads, with a wheel at the front and two handles. **wheelbase** *noun* distance between a vehicle's front and back axles. **wheelchair** *noun* chair mounted on wheels for use by people who cannot walk. **wheel clamp** immobilizing device fixed to one wheel of an illegally parked car. **wheelwright** *noun* person who makes or mends wheels as a trade.

wheeze ⊙ *verb* **1** breathe with a hoarse whistling noise. ◆ *noun* **2** wheezing sound. **3** *Informal* trick or plan. **wheezy** *adjective* **wheezier, wheeziest**

whelk *noun* edible snail-like shellfish.

whelp *noun* **1** pup or cub. **2** *Offens* youth. ◆ *verb* **3** (of an animal) give birth.

when *adverb* **1** at what time? ◆ *conjunction* **2** at the time that. **3** although. **4** considering the fact that. ◆ *pronoun* **5** at which time.

whenever *adverb, conjunction* at whatever time.

whence *adverb, conjunction Obs* from what place or source.

where ⊙ *adverb* **1** in, at, or to what place? ◆ *pronoun* **2** in, at, or to which place. ◆

conjunction **3** in the place at which.

whereabouts *noun* **1** present position. ◆ *adverb* **2** at what place. **whereas** *conjunction* but on the other hand. **whereby** *pronoun* by which. **wherefore** *Obs adverb* **1** why. ◆ *conjunction* **2** consequently. **whereupon** *conjunction* at which point. **wherever** *conjunction, adverb* at whatever place. **wherewithal** *noun* necessary funds, resources, etc.

whet ⊙ *verb* **whetting, whetted** sharpen (a tool). **whet someone's appetite** increase someone's desire. **whetstone** *noun* stone for sharpening tools.

whether *conjunction* used to introduce an indirect question or a clause expressing doubt or choice.

whew *interjection* exclamation expressing relief, delight, etc.

whey [way] *noun* watery liquid that separates from the curd when milk is clotted.

which *adjective, pronoun* **1** used to request or refer to a choice from different possibilities. ◆ *pronoun* **2** used to refer to a thing already mentioned. **whichever** *adjective, pronoun* **1** any out of several. **2** no matter which.

whiff ⊙ *noun* **1** puff of air or odour. **2** trace or hint.

Whig *noun* member of a British political party of the 18th-19th centuries that sought limited reform.

while *conjunction* **1** at the same time that. **2** during the time that. **3** whereas. ◆ *noun* **4** period of time. **whilst** *conjunction* while. **while away** *verb* pass (time) idly but pleasantly.

whim ⊙ *noun* sudden fancy. **whimsy** *noun, pl* **-sies 1** capricious idea. **2** light or fanciful humour. **whimsical** *adjective* unusual, playful, and fanciful.

whimper ⊙ *verb* **1** cry in a soft whining way. ◆ *noun* **2** soft plaintive whine.

— THESAURUS —

wheedle *verb* = **coax**, cajole, entice, inveigle, persuade

wheel *noun* **3** = **circle**, gyration, pivot, revolution, rotation, spin, turn ◆*verb* **5, 6** = **turn**, gyrate, pirouette, revolve, rotate, spin, swing, swivel, twirl, whirl

wheeze *verb* **1** = **gasp**, cough, hiss, rasp, whistle ◆*noun* **2** = **gasp**, cough, hiss, rasp, whistle **3** *Inf* = **trick**, idea, plan, ploy, ruse, scheme, stunt

whereabouts *noun* **1** = **position**, location, site, situation

wherewithal *noun* = **resources**, capital, funds, lolly (*Aust & NZ sl*), means, money, supplies

whet *verb* **1** = **sharpen**, hone [OPPOSITE] suppress ◆ **whet someone's appetite** = **stimulate**, arouse, awaken, enhance, excite, kindle, quicken, rouse, stir

whiff *noun* **1** = **smell**, aroma, hint, odour, scent, sniff

whim *noun* = **impulse**, caprice, fancy, notion, urge

whimper *verb* **1** = **cry**, moan, snivel, sob, weep, whine, whinge (*inf*) ◆*noun* **2** = **sob**, moan, snivel, whine

whimsical *adjective* = **fanciful**, curious, eccentric, freakish, funny, odd, playful, quaint, unusual

W

whin *noun* gorse.

whine ❶ *noun* **1** high-pitched plaintive cry. **2** peevish complaint. ◆ *verb* **3** make such a sound. **whining** *noun, adjective*

whinge ❶ *Informal verb* **1** complain. ◆ *noun* **2** complaint.

whinny *verb* **-nying, -nied 1** neigh softly. ◆ *noun, pl* **-nies 2** soft neigh.

whip ❶ *noun* **1** cord attached to a handle, used for beating animals or people. **2** politician responsible for organizing and disciplining fellow party members. **3** call made on members of Parliament to attend for important votes. **4** dessert made from beaten cream or egg whites. ◆ *verb* **whipping, whipped 5** strike with a whip, strap, or cane. **6** *Informal* pull, remove, or move quickly. **7** beat (esp. eggs or cream) to a froth. **8** rouse into a particular condition. **9** *Informal* steal. **whip bird** *Aust* bird with a whistle ending in a whipcrack note. **whip hand** advantage. **whiplash injury** neck injury caused by a sudden jerk to the head, as in a car crash. **whipping boy** scapegoat. **whip-round** *noun Informal* collection of money.

whippet *noun* racing dog like a small greyhound.

whirl ❶ *verb* **1** spin or revolve. **2** be dizzy or confused. ◆ *noun* **3** whirling movement. **4** bustling activity. **5** confusion or giddiness. **whirlpool** *noun* strong circular current of water. **whirlwind** *noun* **1** column of air whirling violently upwards in a spiral. ◆ *adjective* **2** much quicker than normal.

whirr, whir *noun* **1** prolonged soft buzz. ◆ *verb* **whirring, whirred 2** (cause to) make a whirr.

whisk ❶ *verb* **1** move or remove quickly. **2** beat (esp. eggs or cream) to a froth. ◆ *noun* **3** quick movement. **4** egg-beating utensil.

whisker *noun* **1** any of the long stiff hairs on the face of a cat or other mammal. ◆ *plural* **2** hair growing on a man's face. **by a whisker** *Informal* only just. **whiskered, whiskery** *adjective*

whisky *noun, pl* **-kies** spirit distilled from fermented cereals. **whiskey** *noun, pl* **-keys** Irish or American whisky.

whisper ❶ *verb* **1** speak softly, without vibration of the vocal cords. **2** rustle. ◆ *noun* **3** soft voice. **4** *Informal* rumour. **5** rustling sound.

whist *noun* card game in which one pair of players tries to win more tricks than another pair. **whist drive** social event at which whist is played.

whistle *verb* **1** produce a shrill sound, esp. by forcing the breath through pursed lips. **2** signal by a whistle. ◆ *noun* **3** whistling sound. **4** instrument blown to make a whistling sound. **blow the whistle on** *Informal* inform on or put a stop to. **whistling** *noun, adjective*

whit *noun* **not a whit** not the slightest amount.

white ❶ *adjective* **1** of the colour of snow. **2** pale. **3** light in colour. **4** (of coffee) served with milk. ◆ *noun* **5** colour of snow. **6** clear fluid round the yolk of an egg. **7** white part, esp. of the eyeball. **8** (W-) member of the race of people with light-coloured skin. **whiten** *verb* make or become white or whiter. **whiteness** *noun* **whitish** *adjective* **white ant** same as TERMITE. **white blood cell** same as LEUCOCYTE. **white-collar** *adjective* denoting professional and clerical workers. **white elephant** useless or unwanted possession. **white fish** any sea fish with white flesh used as food. **white flag** signal of surrender or truce. **white goods** large household appliances such as cookers and fridges. **white-hot** *adjective* very hot. **White House 1** official residence of the US president. **2** US presidency. **white lie** minor unimportant

———————— T H E S A U R U S ————————

whine *noun* **1** = **cry**, moan, sob, wail, whimper **2** = **complaint**, gripe (*inf*), grouch (*inf*), grouse, grumble, moan, whinge (*inf*) ◆*verb* **3** = **cry**, moan, sniffle, snivel, sob, wail, whimper

whinge *Inf verb* **1** = **complain**, bleat, carp, gripe (*inf*), grouse, grumble, moan ◆*noun* **2** = **complaint**, gripe (*inf*), grouch, grouse, grumble, moan, whine

whip *noun* **1** = **lash**, birch, cane, cat-o'-nine-tails, crop, scourge ◆*verb* **5** = **lash**, beat, birch, cane, flagellate, flog, scourge, spank, strap, thrash **6** *Inf* = **dash**, dart, dive, fly, rush, shoot, tear, whisk **7** = **whisk**, beat **8** = **incite**, agitate, drive, foment, goad, spur, stir, work up

whirl *verb* **1** = **spin**, pirouette, revolve, roll,

rotate, swirl, turn, twirl, twist **2** = **feel dizzy**, reel, spin ◆*noun* **3** = **revolution**, pirouette, roll, rotation, spin, swirl, turn, twirl, twist **4** = **bustle**, flurry, merry-go-round, round, series, succession **5** = **confusion**, daze, dither, giddiness, spin

whirlwind *noun* **1** = **tornado**, waterspout ◆*adjective* **2** = **rapid**, hasty, quick, short, speedy, swift OPPOSITE⟩ **considered**

whisk *verb* **1** = **flick**, brush, sweep, whip **2** = **beat**, fluff up, whip ◆*noun* **3** = **flick**, brush, sweep, whip **4** = **beater**

whisper *verb* **1** = **murmur**, breathe OPPOSITE⟩ **shout**. **2** = **rustle**, hiss, sigh, swish ◆*noun* **3** = **murmur**, undertone **4** *Inf* = **rumour**, gossip, innuendo, insinuation, report **5** = **rustle**, hiss, lie. **white paper** report by the government, outlining its policy on a matter. **white sauce** thick sauce made from butter, flour, and milk or stock.

whitebait *noun* small edible fish.

whitewash ❶ *noun* **1** substance for whitening walls. **2** attempt to conceal unpleasant facts. ♦ *verb* **3** cover with whitewash. **4** conceal or gloss over unpleasant facts.

whither *adverb Obs* to what place.

whiting [white-ing] *noun* edible sea fish.

whitlow *noun* inflamed sore on a finger or toe, esp. round a nail.

Whitsun, Whitsuntide *noun* Christian festival celebrating the descent of the Holy Spirit to the apostles.

whittle ❶ *verb* cut or carve (wood) with a knife. **whittle down, away** *verb* reduce or wear away gradually.

whizz, whiz *verb* **whizzing, whizzed 1** make a loud buzzing sound. **2** *Informal* move quickly. ♦ *noun, pl* **whizzes 3** loud buzzing sound. **4** *Informal* person skilful at something. **whizz kid, whiz kid** *Informal* person who is outstandingly able for his or her age.

who *pronoun* **1** which person. **2** used to refer to a person or people already mentioned.

whoever *pronoun* **1** any person who. **2** no matter who.

WHO World Health Organization.

whoa *interjection* command used, esp. to horses, to stop or slow down.

whodunnit, whodunit [hoo-**dun**-nit] *noun Informal* detective story, play, or film.

whole ❶ *adjective* **1** containing all the elements or parts. **2** uninjured or undamaged. ♦ *noun* **3** complete thing or system. **on the whole** taking everything into consideration. **wholly** *adverb* **wholefood** *noun* food that has been processed as little as possible.

wholehearted *adjective* sincere or enthusiastic.

wholemeal *adjective* **1** (of flour) made from the whole wheat grain. **2** made from wholemeal flour. **whole number** number that does not contain a fraction.

wholesale ❶ *adjective, adverb* **1** dealing by selling goods in large quantities to retailers. **2** on a large scale. **wholesaler** *noun*

wholesome ❶ *adjective* physically or morally beneficial.

whom *pronoun* objective form of WHO.

whoop *verb, noun* shout or cry to express excitement.

whoopee *interjection Informal* cry of joy.

whooping cough *noun* infectious disease marked by convulsive coughing and noisy breathing.

whoops *interjection* exclamation of surprise or of apology.

whopper ❶ *noun Informal* **1** anything unusually large. **2** huge lie. **whopping** *adjective*

whore ❶ [hore] *noun* prostitute.

whorl *noun* **1** ring of leaves or petals. **2** one turn of a spiral. **3** something coiled.

whose *pronoun* of whom or of which.

why *adverb* **1** for what reason. ♦ *pronoun* **2** because of which.

WI 1 Wisconsin. **2** *Brit* Women's Institute.

wick *noun* cord through a lamp or candle which carries fuel to the flame.

—————————— THESAURUS ——————————

sigh, swish

white *adjective* **2** = **pale**, ashen, pallid, pasty, wan

white-collar *adjective* = **clerical**, nonmanual, professional, salaried

whiten *verb* = **pale**, blanch, bleach, fade OPPOSITE colour

whitewash *noun* **2** = **cover-up**, camouflage, concealment, deception ♦ *verb* **4** = **cover up**, camouflage, conceal, gloss over, suppress OPPOSITE reveal

whittle *verb* = **carve**, cut, hew, pare, shape, shave, trim

whittle down, away *verb* = **reduce**, consume, eat away, erode, wear away

whole *adjective* **1** = **complete**, entire, full, total, unabridged, uncut, undivided OPPOSITE cut. **2** = **undamaged**, in one piece, intact, unbroken, unharmed, unscathed, untouched OPPOSITE broken ♦ *noun* **3** = **totality**,

ensemble, entirety OPPOSITE part ♦ **on the whole** = **all in all**, all things considered, by and large

wholehearted *adjective* = **sincere**, committed, dedicated, determined, devoted, enthusiastic, unstinting, zealous

wholesale *adjective* = **extensive**, broad, comprehensive, far-reaching, indiscriminate, mass, sweeping, wide-ranging OPPOSITE limited ♦ *adverb* = **extensively**, comprehensively, indiscriminately

wholesome *adjective* **a** = **healthy**, beneficial, good, nourishing, nutritious, salubrious OPPOSITE unhealthy. **b** = **moral**, decent, edifying, improving OPPOSITE corrupt

whopper *noun Inf* **1** = **giant**, colossus, crackerjack (*inf*), jumbo (*inf*), leviathan, mammoth, monster **2** = **big lie**, fabrication, falsehood, tall story (*inf*), untruth

whore *noun* = **prostitute**, call girl,

W

wicked ⊕ *adjective* **1** morally bad. **2** mischievous. **3** dangerous. **4** *Slang* very good. **wickedly** *adverb* **wickedness** *noun*

wicker *adjective* made of woven cane. **wickerwork** *noun*

wicket *noun* **1** set of three cricket stumps and two bails. **2** ground between the two wickets on a cricket pitch. **wicketkeeper** *noun* fielder positioned directly behind the wicket.

wide ⊕ *adjective* **1** large from side to side. **2** having a specified width. **3** spacious or extensive. **4** far from the target. **5** opened fully. ♦ *adverb* **6** to the full extent. **7** over an extensive area. **8** far from the target. **widely** *adverb* **widen** *verb* make or become wider. **wide-awake** *adjective* fully awake. **wide-eyed** *adjective* **1** naive or innocent. **2** surprised or frightened. **widespread** *adjective* affecting a wide area or a large number of people.

widgeon *noun* same as WIGEON.

widow *noun* woman whose husband is dead and who has not remarried. **widowed** *adjective* **widowhood** *noun* **widower** *noun* man whose wife is dead and who has not remarried.

width ⊕ *noun* **1** distance from side to side. **2** quality of being wide.

wield ⊕ *verb* **1** hold and use (a weapon). **2** have and use (power).

wife ⊕ *noun, pl* **wives** woman to whom a man is married. **wifely** *adjective*

wig *noun* artificial head of hair.

wigeon *noun* duck found in marshland.

wigging *noun* Brit slang reprimand.

wiggle ⊕ *verb* **1** move jerkily from side to side. ♦ *noun* **2** wiggling movement. **wiggly** *adjective* **wigglier, wiggliest**

wigwam *noun* Native American's tent.

wilco *interjection* expression in telecommunications etc., indicating that the message just received will be complied with.

wild ⊕ *adjective* **1** (of animals) not tamed or domesticated. **2** (of plants) not cultivated. **3** not civilized. **4** lacking restraint or control. **5** violent or stormy. **6** *Informal* excited. **7** *Informal* furious. **8** random. **wilds** *plural noun* desolate or uninhabited place. **wildly** *adverb* **wildness** *noun* **wild-goose chase** search that has little chance of success. **Wild West** western US, which was lawless during settlement.

wildcat *noun* European wild animal like a large domestic cat. **wildcat strike** sudden unofficial strike.

wildebeest *noun* gnu.

wilderness ⊕ *noun* **1** uninhabited uncultivated region. **2** state of no longer being in a prominent position.

wildfire *noun* **spread like wildfire** spread quickly and uncontrollably.

wildlife *noun* wild animals and plants collectively.

wiles ⊕ *plural noun* tricks or ploys. **wily** *adjective* **wilier, wiliest** crafty or sly.

———————— T H E S A U R U S ————————

streetwalker, tart (*inf*)

wicked *adjective* **1** = **bad**, corrupt, depraved, devilish, evil, fiendish, immoral, sinful, vicious, villainous OPPOSITE good. **2** = **mischievous**, impish, incorrigible, naughty, rascally, roguish OPPOSITE **obedient**

wide *adjective* **1** = **broad**, expansive, extensive, far-reaching, immense, large, overarching, sweeping, vast OPPOSITE **narrow**. **3** = **spacious**, baggy, capacious, commodious, full, loose, roomy OPPOSITE **tight**. **4** = **distant**, off course, off target, remote **5** = **expanded**, dilated, distended, outspread, outstretched OPPOSITE **closed** ♦*adverb* **6** = **fully**, completely OPPOSITE **partly**. **8** = **off target**, astray, off course, off the mark, out

widen *verb* = **broaden**, dilate, enlarge, expand, extend, spread, stretch OPPOSITE **reduce**

widespread *adjective* = **common**, broad, extensive, far-reaching, general, pervasive, popular, universal

width *noun* **1** = **breadth**, compass, diameter, extent, girth, scope, span, thickness

wield *verb* **1** = **brandish**, employ, flourish, handle, manage, manipulate, ply, swing, use **2** = **exert**, exercise, have, maintain, possess

wife *noun* = **spouse**, better half (*hum*), bride, mate, partner

wiggle *verb, noun* **1, 2** = **jerk**, jiggle, shake, shimmy, squirm, twitch, wag, waggle, writhe

wild *adjective* **1** = **untamed**, feral, ferocious, fierce, savage, unbroken, undomesticated OPPOSITE **broken**. **2** = **uncultivated**, natural OPPOSITE **planted**. **3** = **uncivilized**, barbaric, barbarous, brutish, ferocious, fierce, primitive, savage **4** = **uncontrolled**, disorderly, riotous, rowdy, turbulent, undisciplined, unmanageable, unrestrained, unruly, wayward OPPOSITE **controlled**. **5** = **stormy**, blustery, choppy, raging, rough, tempestuous, violent **6** *Inf* = **excited**, crazy (*inf*), enthusiastic, hysterical, raving ♦*plural noun* **wilds** = **wilderness**, back of beyond, desert, middle of nowhere (*inf*), wasteland

wilderness *noun* **1** = **desert**, jungle, wasteland, wilds

wiles *plural noun* = **trickery**, artfulness,

W

wilful ① *adjective* **1** headstrong or obstinate. **2** intentional. **wilfully** *adverb* **wilfulness** *noun*

will¹ ① *verb, past* **would** used as an auxiliary to form the future tense or to indicate intention, ability, or expectation.

> **LANGUAGE TIP**
>
> *Will* is normal for discussing the future. The use of *shall* with *I* and *we* is a matter of preference, not of rule. *Shall* is commonly used for questions in Southern England but less often in the North and Scotland.

will² ① *noun* **1** strong determination. **2** desire or wish. **3** directions written for disposal of one's property after death. ♦ *verb* **4** use one's will in an attempt to do (something). **5** wish or desire. **6** leave (property) by a will. **willing** *adjective* **1** ready or inclined (to do something). **2** keen and obliging. **willingly** *adverb* **willingness** *noun* **willpower** *noun* ability to control oneself and one's actions.

willies *plural noun* **give someone the willies** *Slang* cause nervousness or fright.

will-o'-the-wisp *noun* **1** elusive person or thing. **2** pale light sometimes seen over marshes at night.

willow *noun* **1** tree with thin flexible branches. **2** its wood, used for making cricket bats. **willowy** *adjective* slender and graceful.

willy-nilly *adverb* whether desired or not.

wilt ① *verb* (cause to) become limp or lose strength.

wimp ① *noun Informal* feeble ineffectual person.

wimple *noun* garment framing the face, worn by medieval women and now by nuns.

win ① *verb* **winning, won 1** come first in (a competition, fight, etc.). **2** gain (a prize) in a competition. **3** get by effort. ♦ *noun* **4** victory, esp. in a game. **winner** *noun* **winning** *adjective* **1** gaining victory. **2** charming. **winnings** *plural noun* sum won, esp. in gambling. **win over** *verb* gain the support or consent of (someone).

wince ① *verb* **1** draw back, as if in pain. ♦ *noun* **2** wincing.

winch *noun* **1** machine for lifting or hauling using a cable wound round a drum. ♦ *verb* **2** lift or haul using a winch.

wind¹ ① *noun* **1** current of air. **2** hint or suggestion. **3** breath. **4** flatulence. **5** idle talk. ♦ *verb* **6** render short of breath. **windy** *adjective* **windier, windiest. windward** *adjective, noun* (of or in) the direction from which the wind is blowing. **windbag** *noun Slang* person who talks much but uninterestingly. **windbreak** *noun* fence or line of trees providing shelter from the wind. **windfall** *noun* **1** unexpected good luck. **2** fallen fruit. **wind instrument** musical instrument played by blowing. **windmill** *noun* machine for grinding or pumping driven by sails turned by the wind. **windpipe** *noun* tube linking the throat and the lungs. **windscreen** *noun* front window of a motor vehicle. **windscreen wiper** device that wipes rain etc. from a windscreen. **windsock** *noun* cloth cone on a mast at an airfield to indicate wind direction. **windsurfing** *noun* sport of riding on water using a surfboard propelled and steered by a sail. **windswept** *adjective* exposed to the wind.

wind² ① *verb* **winding, wound 1** coil or wrap around. **2** tighten the spring of (a clock or

——————— THESAURUS ———————

chicanery, craftiness, cunning, guile, slyness
wilful *adjective* **1** = **obstinate**, determined, headstrong, inflexible, intransigent, obdurate, perverse, pig-headed, stubborn, uncompromising OPPOSITE **yielding. 2** = **intentional**, conscious, deliberate, intended, purposeful, voluntary OPPOSITE **unconscious**
will² *noun* **1** = **determination**, purpose, resolution, resolve, willpower **2** = **wish**, desire, fancy, inclination, mind, preference, volition **3** = **testament**, last wishes ♦*verb* **5** = **wish**, desire, prefer, see fit, want **6** = **bequeath**, confer, give, leave, pass on, transfer
willing *adjective* **1** = **ready**, agreeable, amenable, compliant, consenting, game (*inf*), inclined, prepared OPPOSITE **reluctant**
willpower *noun* = **self-control**, determination,

drive, grit, resolution, resolve, self-discipline, single-mindedness
wilt *verb* **a** = **droop**, sag, shrivel, wither **b** = **weaken**, fade, flag, languish, wane
wily *adjective* = **cunning**, artful, astute, crafty, guileful, sharp, shrewd, sly, tricky
wimp *noun Inf* = **weakling**, coward, drip (*inf*), mouse, sissy, softy *or* softie
win *verb* **1** = **triumph**, come first, conquer, overcome, prevail, succeed, sweep the board OPPOSITE **lose. 3** = **gain**, achieve, acquire, attain, earn, get, land, obtain, procure, secure OPPOSITE **lose** ♦*noun* **4** = **victory**, conquest, success, triumph OPPOSITE **loss**
wince *verb* **1** = **flinch**, blench, cower, cringe, draw back, quail, recoil, shrink, start ♦*noun* **2** = **flinch**, cringe, start

W

watch). **3** move in a twisting course. **wind up** verb **1** bring to or reach an end. **2** tighten the spring of (a clock or watch). **3** *Informal* make tense or agitated. **4** *Slang* tease.

windlass noun winch worked by a crank.

window noun **1** opening in a wall to let in light or air. **2** glass pane or panes fitted in such an opening. **3** display area behind the window of a shop. **4** area on a computer screen that can be manipulated separately from the rest of the display area. **5** period of unbooked time in a diary or schedule. **window-dressing** noun **1** arrangement of goods in a shop window. **2** attempt to make something more attractive than it really is. **window-shopping** noun looking at goods in shop windows without intending to buy. **windowsill** noun ledge below a window.

windshield noun the US and Canadian name for WINDSCREEN.

wine noun **1** alcoholic drink made from fermented grapes. **2** similar drink made from other fruits. ◆ adjective **3** of a dark purplish-red colour. **wine and dine** entertain or be entertained with fine food and drink.

wing ⊙ noun **1** one of the limbs or organs of a bird, insect, or bat that are used for flying. **2** one of the winglike supporting parts of an aircraft. **3** projecting side part of a building. **4** faction of a political party. **5** part of a car body surrounding the wheels. **6** *Sport* (player on) either side of the pitch. ◆ plural **7** sides of a stage. ◆ verb **8** fly. **9** wound slightly in the wing or arm. **winged** adjective **winger** noun Sport

player positioned on a wing. **wing commander** middle-ranking commissioned air-force officer. **wingspan** noun distance between the wing tips of an aircraft, bird, or insect.

wink ⊙ verb **1** close and open (an eye) quickly as a signal. **2** twinkle. ◆ noun **3** winking. **4** smallest amount of sleep.

winkle noun shellfish with a spiral shell.

winkle out verb Informal extract or prise out.

winnow verb **1** separate (chaff) from (grain). **2** examine to select desirable elements.

winsome adjective charming or winning.

winter ⊙ noun **1** coldest season. ◆ verb **2** spend the winter. **wintry** adjective **wintrier, wintriest 1** of or like winter. **2** cold or unfriendly. **winter sports** open-air sports held on snow or ice.

wipe ⊙ verb **1** clean or dry by rubbing. **2** erase (a tape). ◆ noun **3** wiping. **wipe out** verb destroy completely.

wire ⊙ noun **1** thin flexible strand of metal. **2** length of this used to carry electric current. **3** wire or cable connecting points in a telephone or telegraph system. **4** Obs telegram. ◆ verb **5** fasten with wire. **6** equip with wires. **wired** adjective Slang **1** excited or nervous. **2** using computers and the Internet to send and receive information. **wiring** noun system of wires. **wiry** adjective **wirier, wiriest 1** lean and tough. **2** like wire. **wire-haired** adjective (of a dog) having a stiff wiry coat. **wire netting** net made of wire, used for fences.

wireless noun Old-fashioned same as RADIO.

————— THESAURUS —————

wind¹ noun **1** = **air**, blast, breeze, draught, gust, zephyr **2** = **hint**, inkling, notice, report, rumour, suggestion, warning, whisper **3** = **breath**, puff, respiration **4** = **flatulence**, gas **5** = **talk**, babble, bluster, boasting, hot air

wind² verb **1** = **coil**, curl, encircle, loop, reel, roll, spiral, twist **3** = **meander**, bend, curve, ramble, snake, turn, twist, zigzag

windfall noun **1** = **godsend**, bonanza, find, jackpot, manna from heaven

wind up verb **1** = **end**, close, conclude, finalize, finish, settle, terminate, wrap up **3** Inf = **excite**, put on edge, work up

windy adjective **1** = **breezy**, blowy, blustery, gusty, squally, stormy, wild, windswept OPPOSITE> still

wing noun **4** = **faction**, arm, branch, group, section ◆ verb **8** = **fly**, glide, soar **9** = **wound**, clip, hit

wink verb **1** = **blink**, bat, flutter **2** = **twinkle**, flash, gleam, glimmer, sparkle ◆noun **3** = **blink**, flutter

winner noun **1** = **victor**, champ (inf), champion, conqueror, master OPPOSITE> loser

winning adjective **1** = **victorious**, conquering, successful, triumphant **2** = **charming**, alluring, attractive, cute, disarming, enchanting, endearing, engaging, lekker (S Afr sl), likable or likeable OPPOSITE> offensive

winnings plural noun = **spoils**, gains, prize, proceeds, profits, takings

win over verb = **convince**, bring or talk round, convert, influence, persuade, prevail upon, sway

wintry adjective **1** = **cold**, chilly, freezing, frosty, frozen, icy, snowy

wipe verb **1** = **clean**, brush, mop, rub, sponge, swab **2** = **erase**, remove ◆noun **3** = **rub**, brush

wipe out verb = **destroy**, annihilate, eradicate, erase, expunge, exterminate, massacre, obliterate

wiry adjective **1** = **lean**, sinewy, strong, tough OPPOSITE> fat

wisdom ⊕ *noun* **1** good sense and judgment. **2** accumulated knowledge. **wisdom tooth** any of the four large molar teeth that come through usu. after the age of twenty.

wise¹ ⊕ *adjective* having intelligence and knowledge. **wisely** *adverb* **wiseacre** *noun* person who wishes to seem wise.

wise² *noun Obs* manner.

-wise *adv suffix* **1** indicating direction or manner, e.g. *clockwise; likewise.* **2** with reference to, e.g. *businesswise.*

wisecrack ⊕ *Informal noun* **1** clever, sometimes unkind, remark. ♦ *verb* **2** make a wisecrack.

wish ⊕ *verb* **1** want or desire. **2** feel or express a hope about someone's wellbeing, success, etc. ♦ *noun* **3** expression of a desire. **4** thing desired. **wishful** *adjective* too optimistic. **wishful thinking** interpretation of the facts as one would like them to be, rather than as they are. **wishbone** *noun* V-shaped bone above the breastbone of a fowl. **wish list** list of things a person wants.

wishy-washy *adjective Informal* insipid or bland.

wisp *noun* **1** light delicate streak. **2** twisted bundle or tuft. **wispy** *adjective* **wispier, wispiest**

wisteria *noun* climbing shrub with blue or purple flowers.

wistful ⊕ *adjective* sadly longing. **wistfully** *adverb* **wistfulness** *noun*

wit¹ ⊕ *noun* **1** ability to use words or ideas in a clever and amusing way. **2** person with this ability. **3** (sometimes pl) practical intelligence. **witless** *adjective* foolish.

wit² *verb* **to wit** that is to say; namely.

witch ⊕ *noun* **1** person, usu. female, who practises (black) magic. **2** ugly or wicked woman. **witchcraft** *noun* use of magic. **witch doctor** (in certain societies) a man appearing to cure or cause injury or disease by magic. **witch-hunt** *noun* campaign against people with unpopular views.

with *preposition* indicating presence alongside, possession, means of performance, characteristic manner, etc., e.g. *walking with his dog; a man with two cars; hit with a hammer; playing with skill.* **within** *preposition, adverb* in or inside. **without** *preposition* not accompanied by, using, or having.

withdraw ⊕ *verb* **-drawing, -drew, -drawn** take or move out or away. **withdrawal** *noun* **withdrawn** *adjective* unsociable.

wither ⊕ *verb* **1** wilt or dry up. **2** fade or waste. **withering** *adjective* (of a look or remark) scornful.

withers *plural noun* ridge between a horse's shoulder blades.

withhold ⊕ *verb* **-holding, -held** refrain from giving.

withstand ⊕ *verb* **-standing, -stood** oppose or resist successfully.

witness ⊕ *noun* **1** person who has seen something happen. **2** person giving evidence in court. **3** person who confirms that a document is genuine by signing it. **4** evidence or testimony. ♦ *verb* **5** see at first hand. **6** be the

──────────────── T H E S A U R U S ────────────────

wisdom *noun* **1** = **understanding,** discernment, enlightenment, erudition, insight, intelligence, judgment, sense OPPOSITE **stupidity. 2** = **knowledge,** learning

wise¹ *adjective* = **sensible,** clever, discerning, enlightened, erudite, intelligent, judicious, perceptive, prudent, sage OPPOSITE **stupid**

wisecrack *Inf noun* **1** = **joke,** jest, jibe, quip, witticism ♦*verb* **2** = **joke,** jest, jibe, quip

wish *verb* **1** = **want,** aspire, crave, desire, hanker, hope, long, yearn ♦*noun* **3** = **desire,** aspiration, hope, intention, urge, want, whim, will OPPOSITE **dislike**

wistful *adjective* = **melancholy,** contemplative, dreamy, longing, meditative, pensive, reflective, thoughtful

wit¹ *noun* **1** = **humour,** badinage, banter, drollery, jocularity, raillery, repartee, wordplay OPPOSITE **gravity. 2** = **humorist,** card (*inf*), comedian, joker, wag **3** (sometimes *pl*) = **cleverness,** acumen, brains, common sense,

ingenuity, intellect, sense, wisdom OPPOSITE **ignorance**

witch *noun* = **enchantress,** crone, hag, magician, sorceress

witchcraft *noun* = **magic,** black magic, enchantment, necromancy, occultism, sorcery, the black art, voodoo, wizardry

withdraw *verb* = **remove,** draw back, extract, pull out, take away, take off OPPOSITE **go on**

withdrawal *noun* = **removal,** extraction

wither *verb* **1** = **wilt,** decline, perish, shrivel OPPOSITE **develop. 2** = **fade,** decay, disintegrate, waste

withering *adjective* = **scornful,** devastating, humiliating, hurtful, mortifying, snubbing

withhold *verb* = **keep back,** conceal, hide, hold back, refuse, reserve, retain, suppress OPPOSITE **give**

withstand *verb* = **resist,** bear, cope with, endure, hold off, oppose, stand up to, suffer, tolerate

W

scene of. **7** sign (a document) to certify that it is genuine. **witness box** place in a court where a witness stands to give evidence.

witter verb chatter pointlessly or at unnecessary length.

wittingly adverb intentionally.

witty ⊕ adjective **wittier, wittiest** clever and amusing. **wittily** adverb **witticism** noun witty remark.

wives noun plural of WIFE.

wizard ⊕ noun **1** magician. **2** person with outstanding skill in a particular field. **wizardry** noun

wizened ⊕ [wiz-zend] adjective shrivelled or wrinkled.

WMD weapon(s) of mass destruction.

woad noun blue dye obtained from a plant.

wobble ⊕ verb **1** move unsteadily. **2** shake. ♦ noun **3** wobbling movement or sound. **wobbly** adjective **wobblier, wobbliest**

wodge noun Informal thick lump or chunk.

woe ⊕ noun grief. **woeful** adjective **1** extremely sad. **2** pitiful. **woefully** adverb **woebegone** adjective looking miserable.

wok noun bowl-shaped Chinese cooking pan, used for stir-frying.

woke verb past tense of WAKE¹. **woken** verb past participle of WAKE¹.

wold noun high open country.

wolf noun, pl **wolves 1** wild predatory canine

mammal. ♦ verb **2** eat ravenously. **cry wolf** raise a false alarm. **wolfhound** noun very large breed of dog. **wolf whistle** whistle by a man indicating that he thinks a woman is attractive.

wolverine noun carnivorous mammal of Arctic regions.

woman ⊕ noun, pl **women 1** adult human female. **2** women collectively. **womanhood** noun **womanish** adjective effeminate. **womanly** adjective having qualities traditionally associated with a woman. **womanizing** noun practice of indulging in casual affairs with women.

womanizer noun **Women's Liberation** movement for the removal of inequalities between women and men (also **women's lib**).

womb noun hollow organ in female mammals where babies are conceived and develop.

wombat noun small heavily-built burrowing Australian marsupial.

won verb past of WIN.

wonder ⊕ verb **1** be curious about. **2** be amazed. ♦ noun **3** wonderful thing. **4** emotion caused by an amazing or unusual thing. ♦ adjective **5** spectacularly successful, e.g. *a wonder drug*. **wonderful** adjective **1** very fine. **2** remarkable. **wonderfully** adverb **wonderment** noun **wondrous** adjective Old-fashioned wonderful. **wonderland** noun real or imaginary place full of wonders.

wonky ⊕ adjective **-kier, -kiest** Informal **1**

———— THESAURUS ————

witness noun **1** = **observer**, beholder, bystander, eyewitness, looker-on, onlooker, spectator, viewer, watcher **2** = **testifier**, corroborator ♦verb **5** = **see**, note, notice, observe, perceive, view, watch **7** = **sign**, countersign, endorse

witter verb = **chatter**, babble, blather, chat, gabble, jabber, prate, prattle, waffle (*inf, chiefly Brit*)

witticism noun = **quip**, bon mot, one-liner (*sl*), pun, riposte

witty adjective = **humorous**, amusing, clever, droll, funny, piquant, sparkling, whimsical

wizard noun **1** = **magician**, conjuror, magus, necromancer, occultist, shaman, sorcerer, warlock, witch

wizened adjective = **wrinkled**, dried up, gnarled, lined, shrivelled, shrunken, withered

wobble verb **1** = **sway**, rock, teeter, totter **2** = **shake**, tremble ♦noun **3** = **unsteadiness**, shake, tremble, tremor

wobbly adjective = **unsteady**, rickety, shaky, teetering, tottering, uneven

woe noun = **grief**, agony, anguish, distress, gloom, misery, sadness, sorrow, unhappiness,

wretchedness OPPOSITE> **pleasure**

woeful adjective **1** = **sad**, deplorable, dismal, distressing, grievous, lamentable, miserable, pathetic, tragic, wretched OPPOSITE> **happy**. **2** = **pitiful**, abysmal, appalling, bad, deplorable, dreadful, feeble, pathetic, poor, sorry

woman noun **1** = **lady**, female, girl OPPOSITE> **man**

womanizer noun = **philanderer**, Casanova, Don Juan, lady-killer, lecher, seducer

womanly adjective = **feminine**, female, ladylike, matronly, motherly, tender, warm

wonder verb **1** = **think**, conjecture, meditate, ponder, puzzle, query, question, speculate **2** = **be amazed**, be astonished, gape, marvel, stare ♦noun **3** = **phenomenon**, curiosity, marvel, miracle, prodigy, rarity, sight, spectacle **4** = **amazement**, admiration, astonishment, awe, bewilderment, fascination, surprise, wonderment

wonderful adjective **1** = **excellent**, brilliant, fabulous (*inf*), fantastic (*inf*), great (*inf*), magnificent, marvellous, outstanding, superb, terrific, tremendous OPPOSITE> **bad**. **2** = **remarkable**, amazing, astonishing,

W

shaky or unsteady. **2** insecure or unreliable.
wont [rhymes with **don't**] *adjective* **1**
accustomed. ♦ *noun* **2** custom.
won't will not.
woo ❶ *verb* **1** try to persuade. **2** *Old-fashioned*
try to gain the love of.
wood ❶ *noun* **1** substance trees are made of,
used in carpentry and as fuel. **2** area where
trees grow. **3** long-shafted golf club, usu. with
wooden head. ♦ *adjective* **4** made of or using
wood. **wooded** *adjective* covered with trees.
wooden *adjective* **1** made of wood. **2** without
expression. **woody** *adjective* **woodier,**
woodiest. woodbine *noun* honeysuckle.
woodcock *noun* game bird. **woodcut** *noun*
(print made from) an engraved block of wood.
woodland *noun* forest. **woodlouse** *noun* small
insect-like creature with many legs.
woodpecker *noun* bird which searches tree
trunks for insects. **woodwind** *adjective, noun*
(of) a type of wind instrument made of wood.
woodwork *noun* **1** parts of a room or building
made of wood. **2** skill of making things in
wood. **woodworm** *noun* insect larva that bores
into wood.
woof[1] *noun* cross threads in weaving.
woof[2] *noun* barking noise made by a dog.
woofer *noun* loudspeaker reproducing low-
frequency sounds.
wool ❶ *noun* **1** soft hair of sheep, goats, etc. **2**
yarn spun from this. **woollen** *adjective* **woolly**
adjective **woollier, woolliest 1** of or like wool.
2 vague or muddled. ♦ *noun, pl* **-lies 3** knitted
woollen garment. **woolgathering** *noun*
daydreaming.
woozy *adjective* **woozier, wooziest** *Informal*
weak, dizzy, and confused.
wop-wops *plural noun NZ informal* remote
rural areas.
word ❶ *noun* **1** smallest single meaningful unit
of speech or writing. **2** chat or discussion. **3**

brief remark. **4** message. **5** promise. **6**
command. ♦ *verb* **7** express in words. **wordless**
adjective **wordy** *adjective* **wordier, wordiest**
using too many words. **wording** *noun* choice
and arrangement of words. **word-perfect**
adjective (of a speaker or actor) knowing one's
speech or role perfectly. **word processor**
keyboard, microprocessor, and VDU for
electronic organization and storage of text.
word processing
wore *verb* past tense of WEAR.
work ❶ *noun* **1** physical or mental effort
directed to making or doing something. **2** paid
employment. **3** duty or task. **4** something
made or done. ♦ *plural* **5** factory. **6** total of a
writer's or artist's achievements. **7** *Informal* full
treatment. **8** mechanism of a machine. ♦
adjective **9** of or for work. ♦ *verb* **10** (cause to)
do work. **11** be employed. **12** (cause to)
operate. **13** (of a plan etc.) be successful. **14**
cultivate (land). **15** manipulate, shape, or
process. **16** (cause to) reach a specified
condition. **work-to-rule** *noun* protest in which
workers keep strictly to all regulations to reduce
the rate of work. **workable** *adjective* **worker**
noun **workaday** *adjective* ordinary. **workaholic**
noun person obsessed with work. **workforce**
noun total number of workers. **workhorse**
noun person or thing that does a lot of dull or
routine work. **workhouse** *noun Hist* institution
where the poor were given food and lodgings
in return for work. **working class** social class
consisting of wage earners, esp. manual
workers. **working-class** *adjective* **working
party** committee investigating a specific
problem. **workman** *noun* manual worker.
workmanship *noun* skill with which an object
is made. **work out** *verb* **1** solve by reasoning or
calculation. **2** happen in a particular way. **3**
take part in physical exercise. **workout** *noun*
session of physical exercise for training or

———— T H E S A U R U S ————

extraordinary, incredible, jaw-dropping,
miraculous, phenomenal, staggering, startling,
unheard-of OPPOSITE **common**
wonky *Inf adjective* **1 = shaky,** unsteady,
wobbly
woo *verb* **1 = court,** cultivate, pursue
wood *noun* **1 = timber,** planks **2 = woodland,**
coppice, copse, forest, grove, thicket
wooden *adjective* **1 = woody,** ligneous,
timber **2 = expressionless,** deadpan, lifeless,
unresponsive
wool *noun* **1 = fleece,** hair **2 = yarn**
woolly *adjective* **1 = fleecy,** hairy, shaggy,
woollen **2 = vague,** confused, hazy, ill-defined,

indefinite, indistinct, muddled, unclear
OPPOSITE **clear**
word *noun* **1 = term,** expression, name **2**
= chat, confab (*inf*), consultation, discussion,
talk, tête-à-tête **3 = remark,** comment,
utterance **4 = message,** communiqué, dispatch,
information, intelligence, news, notice, report **5**
= promise, assurance, guarantee, oath, pledge,
vow **6 = command,** bidding, decree, mandate,
order ♦ *verb* **7 = express,** couch, phrase, put,
say, state, utter
wording *noun* **= phraseology,** language,
phrasing, terminology, words
wordy *adjective* **= long-winded,** diffuse, prolix,

W

fitness. **workshop** noun **1** room or building for a manufacturing process. **2** session of group study or practice of a subject. **work station** area in an office where one person works. **worktop** noun surface in a kitchen, used for food preparation. **work up** verb **1** make angry or excited. **2** build up.

world ❶ noun **1** the planet earth. **2** mankind. **3** society of a particular area or period. **4** sphere of existence. ◆ adjective **5** of the whole world. **worldly** adjective **1** not spiritual. **2** concerned with material things. **3** wise in the ways of the world. **world-weary** adjective no longer finding pleasure in life. **worldwide** adjective applying or extending throughout the world. **World Wide Web** global network of linked computer files.

worm noun **1** small limbless invertebrate animal. **2** Informal wretched or spineless person. **3** shaft with a spiral thread forming part of a gear system. ◆ noun **4** Computers type of virus. ◆ plural **5** illness caused by parasitic worms in the intestines. ◆ verb **6** rid of worms. **worm one's**

way **1** crawl. **2** insinuate (oneself). **wormy** adjective **wormier, wormiest. wormcast** noun coil of earth excreted by a burrowing worm. **worm-eaten** adjective eaten into by worms. **worm out** verb extract (information) craftily. **wormwood** noun bitter plant.

worn ❶ verb past participle of WEAR. **worn-out** adjective **1** threadbare, valueless, or useless. **2** completely exhausted.

worry ❶ verb **-rying, -ried 1** (cause to) be anxious or uneasy. **2** annoy or bother. **3** (of a dog) chase and try to bite (sheep etc.). ◆ noun, pl **-ries 4** (cause of) anxiety or concern. **worried** adjective **worrying** adjective, noun

worse ❶ adjective, adverb comparative of BAD or BADLY. **worst** adjective, adverb **1** superlative of BAD or BADLY. ◆ noun **2** worst thing. **worsen** verb make or grow worse.

worship ❶ verb **-shipping, -shipped 1** show religious devotion to. **2** love and admire. ◆ noun **3** act or instance of worshipping. **4** (W-) title for a mayor or magistrate. **worshipper** noun **worshipful** adjective worshipping.

———————— THESAURUS ————————

rambling, verbose, windy

work noun **1** = **effort**, drudgery, elbow grease (facetious), exertion, industry, labour, sweat, toil OPPOSITE **rest. 2** = **employment**, business, duty, job, livelihood, occupation, profession, trade OPPOSITE **play. 3** = **task**, assignment, chore, commission, duty, job, stint, undertaking **4** = **creation**, achievement, composition, handiwork, opus, piece, production ◆verb **10** = **labour**, drudge, exert oneself, peg away, slave, slog (away), sweat, toil OPPOSITE **play. 11** = **be employed**, be in work **12** = **operate**, control, drive, handle, manage, manipulate, move, run, use **14** = **cultivate**, dig, farm, till **15** = **manipulate**, fashion, form, knead, mould, shape

worker noun **2** = **employee**, artisan, craftsman, hand, labourer, tradesman, workman

workman noun = **labourer**, artisan, craftsman, employee, hand, journeyman, mechanic, operative, tradesman, worker

workmanship noun = **skill**, artistry, craftsmanship, expertise, handiwork, technique

work out verb **1** = **solve**, calculate, figure out, find out **2** = **happen**, develop, evolve, result, turn out **3** = **exercise**, practise, train, warm up

works plural noun **5** = **factory**, mill, plant, workshop **6** = **writings**, canon, oeuvre, output **8** = **mechanism**, action, machinery, movement, parts, workings

workshop noun **1** = **studio**, factory, mill, plant, workroom

world noun **1** = **earth**, globe **2** = **mankind**, everybody, everyone, humanity, humankind, man, the public **4** = **sphere**, area, domain, environment, field, realm

worldly adjective **1** = **earthly**, physical, profane, secular, temporal, terrestrial OPPOSITE **heavenly. 2** = **materialistic**, grasping, greedy, selfish OPPOSITE **moral. 3** = **worldly-wise**, blasé, cosmopolitan, experienced, knowing, sophisticated, urbane OPPOSITE **naive**

worldwide adjective = **global**, general, international, omnipresent, pandemic, ubiquitous, universal

worn adjective = **ragged**, frayed, shabby, tattered, tatty, the worse for wear, threadbare

worn-out adjective **1** = **run-down**, on its last legs, ragged, shabby, threadbare, used-up, useless, worn **2** = **exhausted**, all in (sl), done in (inf), fatigued, fit to drop, spent, tired out, weary OPPOSITE **rested**

worry verb **1** = **be anxious**, agonize, brood, fret, obsess **2** = **trouble**, annoy, bother, disturb, perturb, pester, unsettle, upset, vex OPPOSITE **comfort** ◆noun **4 a** = **problem**, bother, care, hassle (inf), trouble **b** = **anxiety**, apprehension, concern, fear, misgiving, trepidation, trouble, unease

worsen verb **a** = **aggravate**, damage, exacerbate **b** = **deteriorate**, decay, decline, degenerate, get worse, go downhill (inf), sink OPPOSITE **improve**

worship verb **1** = **praise**, adore, exalt, glorify,

W

worsted [**wooss**-tid] *noun* type of woollen yarn or fabric.

worth **ⓘ** *preposition* **1** having a value of. **2** meriting or justifying. ◆ *noun* **3** value or price. **4** excellence. **5** amount to be had for a given sum. **worthless** *adjective* **worthy** *adjective* **-thier, -thiest** **1** deserving admiration or respect. ◆ *noun, pl* **-thies** **2** *Informal* notable person. **worthy of** deserving of. **worthily** *adverb* **worthiness** *noun* **worthwhile** *adjective* worth the time or effort involved.

would **ⓘ** *verb* used as an auxiliary to express a request, describe a habitual past action, or form the past tense or subjunctive mood of WILL[1]. **would-be** *adjective* wishing or pretending to be.

wouldn't would not.

wound[1] **ⓘ** *noun* **1** injury caused by violence. **2** injury to the feelings. ◆ *verb* **3** inflict a wound on.

wound[2] *verb* past of WIND[2].

wove *verb* a past tense of WEAVE. **woven** *verb* a past participle of WEAVE.

wow *interjection* **1** exclamation of astonishment. ◆ *noun* **2** *Informal* astonishing person or thing. ◆ *verb* **3** *Informal* be a great success with.

wowser *noun Aust & NZ slang* **1** puritanical person. **2** teetotaller.

wpm words per minute.

WRAC Women's Royal Army Corps.

wrack *noun* seaweed.

WRAF Women's Royal Air Force.

wraith *noun* ghost.

wrangle **ⓘ** *verb* **1** argue noisily. ◆ *noun* **2** noisy argument.

wrap **ⓘ** *verb* **wrapping, wrapped** **1** fold (something) round (a person or thing) so as to cover. ◆ *noun* **2** garment wrapped round the shoulders. **3** sandwich made by wrapping a filling in a tortilla. **wrapper** *noun* cover for a product. **wrapping** *noun* material used to wrap. **wrap up** *verb* **1** fold paper round. **2** put warm clothes on. **3** *Informal* finish or settle (a matter).

wrasse *noun* colourful sea fish.

wrath **ⓘ** [roth] *noun* intense anger. **wrathful** *adjective*

wreak *verb* **wreak havoc** cause chaos. **wreak vengeance on** take revenge on.

wreath **ⓘ** *noun* twisted ring or band of flowers or leaves used as a memorial or tribute. **wreathed** *adjective* surrounded or encircled.

wreck **ⓘ** *verb* **1** destroy. ◆ *noun* **2** remains of something that has been destroyed or badly damaged, esp. a ship. **3** person in very poor condition. **wrecker** *noun* formerly, person who lured ships onto the rocks in order to plunder them. **wreckage** *noun* wrecked remains.

wren *noun* **1** small brown songbird. **2**

———————— THESAURUS ————————

honour, pray to, revere, venerate OPPOSITE mock. **2 = love**, adore, idolize, put on a pedestal OPPOSITE **despise** ◆*noun* **3 = praise**, adoration, adulation, devotion, glory, honour, regard, respect, reverence

worth *noun* **3 = value**, cost, price, rate, valuation OPPOSITE **worthlessness**. **4 = importance**, excellence, goodness, merit, quality, usefulness, value, worthiness OPPOSITE **wretchedness**

worthless *adjective* **a = useless**, ineffectual, rubbishy, unimportant, valueless OPPOSITE **valuable**. **b = good-for-nothing**, contemptible, despicable, vile OPPOSITE **decent**

worthwhile *adjective* **= useful**, beneficial, constructive, expedient, helpful, productive, profitable, valuable

worthy *adjective* **1 = praiseworthy**, admirable, creditable, deserving, laudable, meritorious, valuable, virtuous, worthwhile OPPOSITE **useless**

would-be *adjective* **= budding**, self-appointed, self-styled, unfulfilled, wannabe (*inf*)

wound[1] *noun* **1 = injury**, cut, gash, hurt, laceration, lesion, trauma (*Path*) **2 = insult**,

offence, slight ◆*verb* **3 a = injure**, cut, gash, hurt, lacerate, pierce, wing **b = offend**, annoy, cut (someone) to the quick, hurt, mortify, sting

wrangle *verb* **1 = argue**, bicker, contend, disagree, dispute, fight, quarrel, row, squabble ◆*noun* **2 = argument**, altercation, bickering, dispute, quarrel, row, squabble, tiff

wrap *verb* **1 = cover**, bind, bundle up, encase, enclose, enfold, pack, package, shroud, swathe OPPOSITE **open** ◆*noun* **2 = cloak**, cape, mantle, shawl, stole

wrapper *noun* **= cover**, case, envelope, jacket, packaging, wrapping

wrap up *verb* **1 = giftwrap**, bundle up, pack, package **3** *Inf* **= end**, conclude, finish off, polish off, round off, terminate, wind up

wrath *noun* **= anger**, displeasure, fury, indignation, ire, rage, resentment, temper

wreath *noun* **= garland**, band, chaplet, crown, festoon, ring

wreck *verb* **1 = destroy**, break, demolish, devastate, ruin, shatter, smash, spoil OPPOSITE **build** ◆*noun* **2 = shipwreck**, hulk

wreckage *noun* **= remains**, debris, fragments, pieces, rubble, ruin

W

Australian warbler.

Wren *noun Informal* member of the Women's Royal Naval Service.

wrench ● *verb* **1** twist or pull violently. **2** sprain (a joint). ◆ *noun* **3** violent twist or pull. **4** sprain. **5** difficult or painful parting. **6** adjustable spanner.

wrest ● *verb* **1** twist violently. **2** take by force.

wrestle ● *verb* **1** fight, esp. as a sport, by grappling with and trying to throw down an opponent. **2** struggle hard with. **wrestler** *noun* **wrestling** *noun*

wretch ● *noun* **1** despicable person. **2** pitiful person. **wretched** [retch-id] *adjective* **1** miserable or unhappy. **2** worthless. **wretchedly** *adverb* **wretchedness** *noun*

wrier *adjective* a comparative of WRY. **wriest** *adjective* a superlative of WRY.

wriggle ● *verb* **1** move with a twisting action. **2** manoeuvre oneself by devious means. ◆ *noun* **3** wriggling movement.

wright *noun* maker, e.g. *wheelwright*.

wring ● *verb* **wringing, wrung 1** twist, esp. to squeeze liquid out of. **2** clasp and twist (the hands). **3** obtain by forceful means.

wrinkle ● *noun* **1** slight crease, esp. one in the skin due to age. ◆ *verb* **2** make or become slightly creased. **wrinkled** *adjective* **wrinkly** *adjective*

wrist *noun* joint between the hand and the arm. **wristwatch** *noun* watch worn on the wrist.

writ ● *noun* written legal command.

write ● *verb* **writing, wrote, written 1** mark paper etc. with symbols or words. **2** set down in words. **3** communicate by letter. **4** be the author or composer of. **writing** *noun* **writer** *noun* **1** author. **2** person who has written something specified. **write-off** *noun Informal* something damaged beyond repair. **write-up** *noun* published account of something.

writhe ● *verb* twist or squirm in or as if in pain.

WRNS Women's Royal Naval Service.

wrong ● *adjective* **1** incorrect or mistaken. **2** immoral or bad. **3** not intended or suitable. **4** not working properly. ◆ *adverb* **5** in a wrong manner. ◆ *noun* **6** something immoral or unjust. ◆ *verb* **7** treat unjustly. **8** malign. **wrongly** *adverb* **wrongful** *adjective* **wrongfully** *adverb* **wrongdoing** *noun* immoral or illegal behaviour. **wrongdoer** *noun*

wrote *verb* past tense of WRITE.

wrought [rawt] *verb* **1** *Lit* past of WORK. ◆ *adjective* **2** (of metals) shaped by hammering or beating. **wrought iron** pure form of iron used for decorative work.

wrung *verb* past of WRING.

WRVS Women's Royal Voluntary Service.

wry ● *adjective* **wrier, wriest** or **wryer, wryest 1** drily humorous. **2** (of a facial expression) contorted. **wryly** *adverb*

——————— T H E S A U R U S ———————

wrench *verb* **1 = twist**, force, jerk, pull, rip, tear, tug, yank **2 = sprain**, rick, strain ◆*noun* **3 = twist**, jerk, pull, rip, tug, yank **4 = sprain**, strain, twist **5 = blow**, pang, shock, upheaval **6 = spanner**, adjustable spanner

wrest *verb* **2 = seize**, extract, force, take, win, wrench

wrestle *verb* **= fight**, battle, combat, grapple, scuffle, struggle, tussle

wretch *noun* **1 = scoundrel**, good-for-nothing, miscreant, rascal, rogue, swine, worm

wretched *adjective* **1 = unhappy**, dejected, depressed, disconsolate, downcast, forlorn, hapless, miserable, woebegone OPPOSITE happy. **2 = worthless**, inferior, miserable, paltry, pathetic, poor, sorry OPPOSITE great

wriggle *verb* **1 = crawl**, jerk, jiggle, slink, snake, squirm, turn, twist, waggle, wiggle, worm, writhe, zigzag **2 = manoeuvre**, dodge, extricate oneself ◆*noun* **3 = twist**, jerk, jiggle, squirm, turn, waggle, wiggle

wring *verb* **1 = twist**, squeeze **3 = force**, extract, screw

wrinkle *noun* **1 = crease**, corrugation, crinkle, crow's-foot, crumple, fold, furrow, line ◆*verb* **2 = crease**, corrugate, crumple, fold, furrow, gather, pucker, rumple OPPOSITE level

writ *noun* **= summons**, court order, decree, document

write *verb* **1, 2 = record**, draft, draw up, inscribe, jot down, pen, scribble, set down

writer *noun* **1 = author**, hack, novelist, penpusher, scribbler, scribe, wordsmith

writhe *verb* **= squirm**, jerk, struggle, thrash, thresh, toss, twist, wiggle, wriggle

writing *noun* **1 = script**, calligraphy, hand, handwriting, penmanship, scrawl, scribble **4 = document**, book, composition, opus, publication, work

wrong *adjective* **1 = incorrect**, erroneous, fallacious, false, inaccurate, mistaken, untrue, wide of the mark **2 = bad**, criminal, dishonest, evil, illegal, immoral, sinful, unjust, unlawful, wicked, wrongful OPPOSITE just. **3 = inappropriate**, incongruous, incorrect, unacceptable, unbecoming, undesirable, unseemly, unsuitable OPPOSITE correct. **4 = defective**, amiss, askew, awry, faulty ◆*adverb*

W

wt. weight.
wuss *noun slang chiefly US* feeble person.
WV West Virginia.
WWI World War One.

WWII World War Two.
WWW World Wide Web.
WY Wyoming.
wych-elm *noun* elm with large rough leaves.

———————————— T H E S A U R U S ————————————

5 = **incorrectly**, badly, erroneously, inaccurately, mistakenly, wrongly OPPOSITE **correctly** ♦*noun* **6** = **offence**, crime, error, injury, injustice, misdeed, sin, transgression ♦*verb* **7** = **mistreat**, cheat, oppress, take

advantage of **8** = **malign**, abuse, dishonour, harm, hurt
wry *adjective* **1** = **ironic**, droll, dry, mocking, sarcastic, sardonic **2** = **contorted**, crooked, twisted, uneven OPPOSITE **even**

W

Xx

X 1 indicating an error, a choice, or a kiss. **2** indicating an unknown, unspecified, or variable factor, number, person, or thing. **3** the Roman numeral for ten.

X-chromosome *noun* sex chromosome that occurs in pairs in the females of many animals, and as one of a pair with the Y-chromosome in males.

Xe *Chem* xenon.

xenon *noun Chem* colourless odourless gas found in very small quantities in the air.

xenophobia [zen-oh-**fobe**-ee-a] *noun* fear or hatred of people from other countries.

xenophobic *adjective*

Xerox [**zeer**-ox] *noun* **1** ® machine for copying printed material. **2** ® copy made by a Xerox machine. ♦ *verb* **3** copy (a document) using such a machine.

Xmas ❼ [**eks**-mass] *noun Informal* Christmas.

X-ray, x-ray *noun* **1** stream of radiation that can pass through some solid materials. **2** picture made by sending X-rays through someone's body to examine internal organs. ♦ *verb* **3** photograph, treat, or examine using X-rays.

xylem [**zy**-lem] *noun* plant tissue that conducts water and minerals from the roots to all other parts.

xylophone [**zile**-oh-fone] *noun* musical instrument made of a row of wooden bars played with hammers.

─────────── THESAURUS ───────────

Xmas *noun Inf* = **Christmas**, Noel, Yule (*arch*)

X

Yy

Y *Chem* yttrium.

ya *interjection S Afr* yes.

yacht [yott] *noun* **1** large boat with sails or an engine, used for racing or pleasure cruising. ◆ *verb* **2** sail in a yacht. **yachting** *noun* **yachtsman, yachtswoman** *noun*

yahoo *noun* crude coarse person.

yak¹ *noun* Tibetan ox with long shaggy hair.

yak² *verb* **yakking, yakked** *Slang* talk continuously about unimportant matters.

yakka *noun Aust & NZ informal* work.

Yale lock *noun* ® cylinder lock using a flat serrated key.

yam *noun* tropical root vegetable.

yank ⊕ *verb* **1** pull or jerk suddenly. ◆ *noun* **2** sudden pull or jerk.

Yankee, Yank *noun Slang* **1** person from the United States. **2** *US* person from the Northern United States.

yap *verb* **yapping, yapped 1** bark with a high-pitched sound. **2** *Informal* talk continuously. ◆ *noun* **3** high-pitched bark.

yard¹ ⊕ *noun* **1** unit of length equal to 36 inches or about 91.4 centimetres. **2** spar slung across a ship's mast to extend the sail.

yardarm *noun* outer end of a ship's yard.

yardstick *noun* standard against which to judge other people or things.

yard² *noun* **1** enclosed area, usu. next to a building and often used for a particular purpose, e.g. *builder's yard*. **2** *US* garden of a house.

yarmulke [yar-mull-ka] *noun* skullcap worn by Jewish men.

yarn ⊕ *noun* **1** thread used for knitting or making cloth. **2** *Informal* long involved story.

yashmak *noun* veil worn by a Muslim woman to cover her face in public.

yaw *verb* (of an aircraft or ship) turn to one side or from side to side while moving.

yawl *noun* two-masted sailing boat.

yawn ⊕ *verb* **1** open the mouth wide and take in air deeply, often when sleepy or bored. **2** (of an opening) be large and wide. ◆ *noun* **3** act of yawning. **yawning** *adjective*

yaws *noun* infectious tropical skin disease.

Yb *Chem* ytterbium.

Y-chromosome *noun* sex chromosome that occurs as one of a pair with the X-chromosome in the males of many animals.

yd yard.

ye [yee] *pronoun Obs* you.

yea *interjection Old-fashioned* yes.

yeah *interjection Informal* yes.

year ⊕ *noun* **1** time taken for the earth to make one revolution around the sun, about 365 days. **2** twelve months from January 1 to December 31. **3** any period of twelve months. **4** group of people who have started a course at the same time. ◆ *plural* **5** a long time. **6** age.

yearly *adjective, adverb* (happening) every year or once a year. **yearling** *noun* animal between one and two years old. **yearbook** *noun* reference book published annually containing details of the previous year's events.

yearn ⊕ *verb* **1** want (something) very much. **2** feel tenderness. **yearning** *noun, adjective*

yeast *noun* fungus used to make bread rise and to ferment alcoholic drinks. **yeasty** *adjective*

yebo *interjection S Afr informal* yes.

yell ⊕ *verb* **1** shout or scream in a loud or piercing way. ◆ *noun* **2** loud cry of pain, anger, or fear.

yellow *noun* **1** the colour of gold, a lemon, etc. ◆ *adjective* **2** of this colour. **3** *Informal*

THESAURUS

yank *verb, noun* =**pull**, hitch, jerk, snatch, tug, wrench

yardstick *noun* =**standard**, benchmark, criterion, gauge, measure, par, touchstone

yarn *noun* **1** =**thread**, fibre **2** *Inf* =**story**, anecdote, cock-and-bull story (*inf*), fable, tale, tall story, urban legend, urban myth

yawning *adjective* **2** =**gaping**, cavernous,

vast, wide

yearly *adjective* =**annual** ◆*adverb* =**annually**, every year, once a year, per annum

yearn *verb* **1** =**long**, ache, covet, crave, desire, hanker, hunger, itch

yell *verb* **1** =**scream**, bawl, holler (*inf*), howl, screech, shout, shriek, squeal OPPOSITE▷ whisper ◆*noun* **2** =**scream**, cry, howl, screech,

Y

cowardly. ♦ *verb* **4** make or become yellow.
yellow belly *Aust* freshwater food fish with
yellow underparts. **yellow card** *Soccer* piece of
yellow pasteboard shown by a referee to
indicate that a player has been booked. **yellow
fever** serious infectious tropical disease.
yellowhammer *noun* European songbird with a
yellow head and body. **Yellow Pages** ®
telephone directory which lists businesses under
the headings of the type of service they
provide.
yelp ❶ *verb, noun* (give) a short sudden cry.
yen[1] *noun, pl* **yen** main unit of currency in
Japan.
yen[2] ❶ *noun Informal* longing or desire.
yeoman [yo-man] *noun, pl* **-men** *Hist* farmer
owning and farming his own land. **yeomanry**
noun **1** yeomen. **2** (in Britain) former volunteer
cavalry force. **yeoman of the guard** member
of the ceremonial bodyguard of the British
monarchy.
yes ❶ *interjection* **1** expresses consent,
agreement, or approval. **2** used to answer
when one is addressed. ♦ *noun* **3** answer or
vote of yes. **yes man** person who always agrees
with their superior.
yesterday *adverb, noun* **1** (on) the day before
today. **2** (in) the recent past.
yet ❶ *conjunction* **1** nevertheless, still. ♦ *adverb*
2 up until then or now. **3** still. **4** now. **5**
eventually.
yeti *noun* same as ABOMINABLE SNOWMAN.
yew *noun* evergreen tree with needle-like
leaves and red berries.
YHA Youth Hostels Association.
Yiddish *adjective, noun* (of or in) a language of
German origin spoken by many Jews in Europe
and elsewhere.
yield ❶ *verb* **1** produce or bear. **2** give up
control of, surrender. **3** give in. **4** agree (to). **5**

grant or allow. ♦ *noun* **6** amount produced.
yielding *adjective* **1** submissive. **2** soft or
flexible.
yippee *interjection* exclamation of joy or
pleasure.
Y2K *noun Informal* name for the year 2000 AD
(esp. referring to the millennium bug).
YMCA Young Men's Christian Association.
yob, yobbo ❶ *noun Slang* bad-mannered
aggressive person.
yodel *verb* **-delling, -delled** sing with abrupt
changes between a normal and a falsetto voice.
yodelling *noun*
yoga *noun* Hindu method of exercise and
discipline aiming at spiritual, mental, and
physical wellbeing. **yogi** *noun* person who
practises yoga.
yogurt, yoghurt *noun* slightly sour custard-
like food made from milk that has had bacteria
added to it, often sweetened and flavoured
with fruit.
yoke *noun* **1** wooden bar put across the necks
of two animals to hold them together. **2** frame
fitting over a person's shoulders for carrying
buckets. **3** *Lit* oppressive force, e.g. *the yoke of
the tyrant.* **4** fitted part of a garment to which a
fuller part is attached. ♦ *verb* **5** put a yoke on. **6**
unite or link.
yokel ❶ *noun Offens* person who lives in the
country and is usu. simple and old-fashioned.
yolk *noun* yellow part of an egg that provides
food for the developing embryo.
Yom Kippur *noun* annual Jewish religious
holiday.
yon *adjective Old-fashioned or dialect* that or
those over there.
yonder *adjective, adverb* (situated) over there.
yonks *plural noun Informal* very long time.
yoo-hoo *interjection* call to attract attention.
yore *noun Lit* **of yore** a long time ago.

—————————— THESAURUS ——————————

shriek, whoop
yelp *verb* =**cry**, yap, yowl
yen[2] *noun Inf* =**longing**, ache, craving, desire,
hankering, hunger, itch, passion, thirst,
yearning
yes man *noun* =**sycophant**, bootlicker (*inf*),
crawler (*sl*), minion, timeserver, toady
yet *conjunction* **1** =**nevertheless**, however,
notwithstanding, still ♦*adverb* **2** =**so far**, as yet,
thus far, until now, up to now **3** =**still**, besides,
in addition, into the bargain, to boot **4** =**now**,
just now, right now, so soon
yield *verb* **1** =**produce**, bear, bring forth,
earn, generate, give, net, provide, return,
supply OPPOSITE **use**. **2, 3** =**surrender**, bow,

capitulate, cave in (*inf*), give in, relinquish,
resign, submit, succumb OPPOSITE **keep** ♦*noun*
6 =**profit**, crop, earnings, harvest, income,
output, produce, return, revenue, takings
OPPOSITE **loss**
yielding *adjective* **1** =**submissive**,
accommodating, acquiescent, biddable,
compliant, docile, flexible, obedient, pliant
OPPOSITE **stubborn**. **2** =**soft**, elastic, pliable,
spongy, springy, supple, unresisting
yob, yobbo *noun Inf* =**thug**, hooligan, lout,
roughneck (*sl*), ruffian
yokel *noun Offens* =**peasant**, (country)
bumpkin, countryman, hick (*inf, chiefly US &
Canad*), hillbilly, rustic

yorker noun Cricket ball that pitches just under the bat.

Yorkshire pudding noun baked batter made from flour, milk, and eggs.

you pronoun refers to: **1** the person or people addressed. **2** an unspecified person or people in general.

young ⊙ adjective **1** in an early stage of life or growth. ◆ plural noun **2** young people in general. **3** offspring, esp. young animals. **youngish** adjective **youngster** noun young person.

your adjective **1** of, belonging to, or associated with you. **2** of, belonging to, or associated with an unspecified person or people in general.

yours pronoun something belonging to you.

yourself pronoun

youth ⊙ noun **1** time of being young. **2** state of being young. **3** boy or young man. **4** young people as a group. **youthful** adjective **youthfulness** noun **youth club** club that provides leisure activities for young people.

youth hostel inexpensive lodging place for young people travelling cheaply.

yowl verb, noun (produce) a loud mournful cry.

yo-yo noun, pl **-yos** toy consisting of a spool attached to a string, by which it is repeatedly spun out and reeled in.

YT Yukon Territory.

ytterbium [it-**terb**-ee-um] noun Chem soft silvery element.

yttrium [**it**-ree-um] noun Chem silvery metallic element used in various alloys.

yucca noun tropical plant with spikes of white leaves.

yucky adjective **yuckier, yuckiest** Slang disgusting, nasty.

Yugoslav noun **1** person from the former Yugoslavia. ◆ adjective **2** of the former Yugoslavia.

Yule noun Lit Christmas (season).

yummy adjective **-mier, -miest** Informal delicious.

yuppie noun **1** young highly-paid professional person, esp. one who has a fashionable way of life. ◆ adjective **2** typical of or reflecting the values of yuppies.

YWCA Young Women's Christian Association.

———————— THESAURUS ————————

young adjective **1** = **immature**, adolescent, callow, early, fledgling, green, infant, junior, juvenile, little, new, recent, undeveloped, youthful OPPOSITE **adult** ◆ plural noun **3** = **offspring**, babies, brood, family, issue, litter, progeny OPPOSITE **parents**

youngster noun = **youth**, boy, girl, juvenile, kid (inf), lad, lass, teenager

youth noun **1** = **immaturity**, adolescence, boyhood or girlhood, girlhood, salad days OPPOSITE **age. 3** = **boy**, adolescent, kid (inf), lad, stripling, teenager, young man, youngster

youthful adjective **2** = **young**, boyish, childish, girlish, immature, inexperienced, juvenile OPPOSITE **old**

Y

Zz

Z *Chem* atomic number.

zany ⊕ [**zane**-ee] *adjective* **zanier, zaniest** comical in an endearing way.

zap *verb* **zapping, zapped 1** *Slang* kill (by shooting). **2** change TV channels rapidly by remote control. **3** move quickly.

zeal ⊕ *noun* great enthusiasm or eagerness.

zealot [**zel**-lot] *noun* fanatic or extreme enthusiast. **zealous** [**zel**-luss] *adjective* extremely eager or enthusiastic. **zealously** *adverb*

zebra *noun* black-and-white striped African animal of the horse family. **zebra crossing** pedestrian crossing marked by black and white stripes on the road.

zebu [**zee**-boo] *noun* Asian ox with a humped back and long horns.

Zen *noun* Japanese form of Buddhism that concentrates on learning through meditation and intuition.

zenith ⊕ *noun* **1** highest point of success or power. **2** point in the sky directly above an observer.

zephyr [**zef**-fer] *noun* soft gentle breeze.

zeppelin *noun* *Hist* large cylindrical airship.

zero ⊕ *noun*, *pl* **-ros, -roes 1** (symbol representing) the number 0. **2** point on a scale of measurement from which the graduations commence. **3** lowest point. **4** nothing, nil. ♦ *adjective* **5** having no measurable quantity or size. **zero hour** time at which something is set to happen. **zero in on** *verb* **1** aim at. **2** *Informal* concentrate on.

zest ⊕ *noun* **1** enjoyment or excitement. **2** interest, flavour, or charm. **3** peel of an orange or lemon.

zigzag *noun* **1** line or course having sharp turns in alternating directions. ♦ *verb* **-zagging, -zagged 2** move in a zigzag. ♦ *adjective* **3** formed in or proceeding in a zigzag. ♦ *adverb* **4** in a zigzag manner.

zilch *noun* *Slang* nothing.

zinc *noun* *Chem* bluish-white metallic element used in alloys and to coat metal.

zing *noun* *Informal* quality in something that makes it lively or interesting.

Zionism *noun* movement to found and support a Jewish homeland in Israel. **Zionist** *noun, adjective*

zip ⊕ *noun* **1** fastener with two rows of teeth that are closed or opened by a small clip pulled between them. **2** *Informal* energy, vigour. **3** short whizzing sound. ♦ *verb* **zipping, zipped 4** fasten with a zip. **5** move with a sharp whizzing sound. **6** rush.

zircon *noun* mineral used as a gemstone and in industry.

zirconium *noun* *Chem* greyish-white metallic element that is resistant to corrosion.

zither *noun* musical instrument consisting of strings stretched over a flat box and plucked to produce musical notes.

zloty *noun*, *pl* **-tys, -ty** monetary unit of Poland.

Zn *Chem* zinc.

zodiac *noun* imaginary belt in the sky within which the sun, moon, and planets appear to move, divided into twelve equal areas, called

---

THESAURUS

zany *adjective* = **comical**, clownish, crazy, eccentric, goofy (*inf*), madcap, wacky (*sl*)

zeal *noun* = **enthusiasm**, ardour, eagerness, fanaticism, fervour, gusto, keenness, passion, spirit, verve, zest

zealot *noun* = **fanatic**, bigot, enthusiast, extremist, militant

zealous *adjective* = **enthusiastic**, ardent, devoted, eager, fanatical, fervent, impassioned, keen, passionate

zenith *noun* **1** = **height**, acme, apex, apogee, climax, crest, high point, peak, pinnacle, summit, top

zero *noun* **1** = **nothing**, nil, nought **2** = **nought 3** = **bottom**, nadir, rock bottom **4** = **nil**, nothing

zest *noun* **1** = **enjoyment**, appetite, gusto, keenness, relish, zeal OPPOSITE loathing. **2** = **flavour**, charm, interest, piquancy, pungency, relish, spice, tang, taste

zip *noun* **2** *Inf* = **energy**, drive, gusto, liveliness, verve, vigour, zest OPPOSITE apathy ♦*verb* **6** = **speed**, flash, fly, shoot, whizz (*inf*), zoom signs of the zodiac, each named after a constellation.

zombie, zombi *noun* **1** person who appears to be lifeless, apathetic, or totally lacking in independent judgment. **2** corpse brought back to life by witchcraft.

zone ⊙ *noun* **1** area with particular features or properties. **2** one of the divisions of the earth's surface according to temperature. ◆ *verb* **3** divide into zones. **zonal** *adjective*

zoo *noun, pl* **zoos** place where live animals are kept for show.

zoology *noun* study of animals. **zoologist** *noun* **zoological** *adjective* **zoological garden** zoo.

zoom ⊙ *verb* **1** move or rise very rapidly. **2** make or move with a buzzing or humming sound. **zoom lens** lens that can make the details of a picture larger or smaller while keeping the picture in focus.

Zr *Chem* zirconium.

zucchini [zoo-**keen**-ee] *noun, pl* **-ni, -nis** the US and Canadian name for COURGETTE.

Zulu *noun* **1** member of a tall Black people of southern Africa. **2** language of this people.

zygote *noun* fertilized egg cell.

————————— THESAURUS —————————

zone *noun* **1** = **area**, belt, district, region, section, sector, sphere

zoom *verb* **1** = **speed**, dash, flash, fly, hurtle, pelt, rush, shoot, whizz (*inf*)

Z

LANGUAGE IN ACTION

Supplement

TABLE OF CONTENTS

LANGUAGE IN ACTION

Throughout life you often need to communicate your thoughts and feelings in writing. Writing concise and effective letters, speeches, and emails is easy, once you know exactly what you want to say. This supplement covers the basic rules of style and form to follow, whether you are writing a business letter or a text message to a friend. Whatever you need to write, however, the two most important rules for expressing yourself through language are simple, but often ignored:

✔ Be clear

Choose words that occur to you naturally and convey exactly what you mean. If you have a choice between a basic word and a showy one, choose the basic one. Do not repeat yourself, exaggerate, or stray from your main topic. To find the best words to express your thoughts, particularly on difficult or complex subjects, refer to this dictionary and a good thesaurus. Check that each sentence flows easily, and sends a clear message.

✔ Think of your audience

When writing to or for someone, think of that specific person's position, interests, and relationship to you. What information does he or she need from you? How can you persuade him or her to do what you ask? What language would this person best understand? When writing to strangers or business contacts, write in a polite and formal style. When writing to close friends, you are free to use more casual and personal language, including slang. People always respond better to letters that show regard for who they are and what matters to them.

This guide outlines everything you should need to know to communicate effectively and clearly through writing in all areas of life. It shows examples of good letters for work, school, money matters, and social situations. It covers basic rules of etiquette for emails, and text messaging language. It also includes advice for writing and delivering confident and memorable speeches.

Every section of this supplement provides practical answers to frequently asked questions (FAQs) about the format and words required for a particular situation. This guide also suggests useful phrases that you might include in your writing. For each topic and situation, it gives useful tips and examples, and advice regarding how and when to approach a particular subject.

Think through what you want to say. Then use this supplement to write it down in a style that will smoothly communicate your message to your audience.

JOB APPLICATIONS

Useful phrases

First of all, identify the job you are applying for:

- I would like to inquire as to whether there are any openings for junior telesales operators in your company.
- I am writing to apply for the post of senior marketing manager.
- I would like to apply for the position of online learning co-ordinator, as advertised on your website.
- I am writing to apply for the above post, as advertised in *the Guardian* of 8 August 2003.

Next, give some examples of personal achievements:

- I have gained experience in several major aspects of publishing.
- I co-ordinated the change-over from one accounting system to another.
- I developed designs for a new range of knitwear.
- I have supervised a team of telesales operators on several projects.
- I contributed to the development of our new database software.

Then outline your personal qualities:

- I see myself as systematic and meticulous in my approach to work.
- I am a fair and broad-minded person, with an ability to get on well with people from all walks of life.
- I am hardworking and business minded, and I tend to thrive under pressure.

Explain why you want this job:

- I am now keen to find a post with more responsibility.
- I now wish to find a more permanent full-time position.
- I would like to further my career in the field of production.
- I feel that your company's activities most closely match my own values and interests.

Express your willingness to attend an interview.

LANGUAGE IN ACTION

● Application for an advertised post

✓ When applying for an advertised post, ensure that you head the letter
with the exact name of the post, quoting any reference number given.

LANGUAGE IN ACTION

45 Fairways
Little Fordnam
Northumberland
N21 3RS

30 June 2003

Mrs F Reid
Recruitment Officer
Affinity Development Projects
3 Albion Court
Newcastle
N4 7JS

Dear Mrs Reid

**application for post of Community Development Officer:
post no: 513/6**

I am writing in response to your advertisement in the June
edition of *Community Now*, and am enclosing my CV for your
review.

As you will see, I have gained valuable experience in
working with Black and Asian communities, and have a
strong understanding of community development. I am self-
motivating, and can work as an effective leader of a team.

In my current position at the Northumberland Renewal
Programme, I have initiated a strategic framework for
obtaining funding and attaining targets.

I am at present completing a distance-learning course on
Equality and Diversity Policy Development, and am now
looking for a post which gives me an opportunity to use my
new skills.

I look forward to having the opportunity to discuss this
further with you.

Yours sincerely

Brian Hanlan

Brian Hanlan

● A speculative job application

✓ When applying for a job on a speculative basis, try to speak to the person responsible for recruitment in the appropriate department beforehand. This way, you will have a specific person to write to, as well as having established a relationship with them.

34 St Dunstan's Way
Hove
BN13 5HY

19 July 2003

Ms D Wallis
Youngs Accountancy and Finance
19 Lockwood Road
Brighton
BN2 6HM

Dear Ms Wallis

post of software development co-ordinator

Thank you very much for taking the time to speak to me yesterday about the possibility of a position as software development co-ordinator with your company.

Please find attached a CV which highlights my prior professional experience, and the qualities which I feel make me suited to this position. You will see that I have a strong interest in, and knowledge of, staff management, and have gained extensive experience in handling large development projects and meeting deadlines.

I see myself as being well-organized and self-motivated, and have excellent communication skills. I am keen to develop my career with Youngs Accountancy and Finance, and so would very much appreciate the opportunity to discuss further my suitability for the post.

Please feel free to contact me, either by email: smitchell@netserve.com, or by leaving a message on 01783 639012. I look forward to speaking to you soon.

Yours sincerely

D Gorman

Deborah Gorman

LANGUAGE IN ACTION

FAQ

Q. *How should a CV be presented?*

A. It should be constructed on a word-processor, well laid out and printed on a good quality printer. Do not use too many different font types and sizes. Use bullets or similar to start sub-sections or lists.

Q. *I usually send the same CV out to all potential employers. But should I be tailoring it to different jobs?*

A. Yes, you should. Consider carefully how your skills, education, and experience compare with the skills that the job requires. Ask for more detail if needed. Spend time researching the employer - their structure, products and approach.

Q. *What details do I need to include in my CV?*

A. You should include the following:

personal details: name, home address, phone number, email address, URL of your own web page if you have one, date of birth.

education: Give places of education where you have studied, with most recent first.

work experience: List your most recent experience first. Give the name of your employer, job title, and what you actually did and achieved in that job. Make sure all time periods are accounted for.

interests: If you are just entering the work force, and have little employment experience, an employer will be particularly interested in activities where you have leadership or responsibility, or which involve you in relating to others in a team.

skills: Ability in other languages, computing experience, or possession of a driving licence should be included.

references: Usually give two names. Make sure that referees are willing to give you a reference. If you do not wish to name them on your CV, it is perfectly acceptable to write 'on request'.

Q. *How long should my CV be?*

A. Keep it as short and relevant as possible. One page is ideal. It should not normally be longer than three pages.

Q. *I've heard people talk about writing a 'personal objective statement' at the top of a CV. Is this expected/appropriate?*

A. It can be a good idea to start with a personal objective statement. This is a short overview of your skills, qualities, hopes and plans. If you are replying to a specific job advertisement, review what key words and tasks were used. Which of these words apply to you? Use these words in your statement. But if you do not feel confident about doing this, there is no obligation to include one.

● **Basic graduate CV**

CV
Kate Maxwell

Date of birth	29.02.75
Address	19, The Poplars Bristol B10 2JU
Telephone	0117 123 4567
Email	katemaxwell@atlantic.net
Nationality	British

Education

1994–1998	**BA Hons in Modern Languages, University of Exeter** (final grade 2.1)
1992–1994	**Clifton Road Secondary School**: 3 'A' levels - French (A) German (A) History (B)
1987–1992	**Clifton Road Secondary School**: 8 GCSEs including Maths and English

Employment history

1994–1995	**Sales Assistant, Langs Bookshop, Bristol** I was responsible for training and supervising weekend and holiday staff.
1995–1996	**English Assistant, Lycée Benoit, Lyons** I taught conversational English to pupils aged 12-18, preparing the older students for both technical and more academic qualifications. I organized an educational trip to the UK for fourth-year pupils.

Positions of responsibility held

1995–1996	**Entertainments Officer for University Student Social Society** I organized and budgeted for entertainment for a student society with over 1000 members.
1994 – present	**Captain of the university women's netball team** I was in charge of training, organizing and motivating the women's team from 1995 to date.

Other skills

Fluent French and German
Extensive knowledge of Microsoft Word, Excel and Access
I hold a clean driving licence

References
on request

● CV for experienced candidate

CV

Andrew Baird
134 Newton Road, Lincoln, LI5 6HB
tel: 01453 678234
email: abaird@coms.net
date of birth: 8 September 1965

Work experience

1995 to present
Coogan and Kidd Web Design Ltd, Lincoln – Website Developer
- Development of company website
- Responsible for team of 8 staff
- Project management: have led several projects providing web design and support for a number of leading insurance companies
- Training: overseeing development of technical training programmes
- Customer support: following up and advising customers on website management
- Quality assurance
- Information architecture

1990–1995
Centaur Software Development, Cambridge – Computer Programmer
- programming
- database design: set up database for network of travel companies
- software design: assisted in the design of financial management application for use by financial advisers

Programming languages

C, C++, Java, Perl, Visual Basic, VBScript, JavaScript

Applications

Visual Interdev, Dreamweaver

Servers

Apache, IIS

Other skills

clean driving licence held

Education

1999 – Microsoft Certified Systems Engineer+Internet
1990 – MSc Multimedia Design
1988 – BSc Computer Science (2.1)

References

on request

WRITING FOR BUSINESS

● Writing business letters

Tips

- Keep letters short and to the point.
- The subject heading indicates the subject of the letter for quick reference and should only be two or three words.
- Make sure you open with a statement of intent and close with a request or promise of action.
- Avoid using ambiguous words or phrases. If there is any chance of a misunderstanding, find an alternative way to say it.
- Think out your letter before you start to compose it. Make notes if it helps to organize the information in a logical order.
- Remember that the standard method of closing before the signature depends on the opening at the start of the letter. If you opened with 'Dear Sir', you should close with 'Yours faithfully', if you opened with 'Dear Mr….' you should close with 'Yours sincerely'.
- All parts of a letter are designed to give important information. If your letters give accurate information, you will increase efficiency.
- If you can amend a standard or similar letter to say what you need to say, do so. It will save you time.
- If the sender is not available to sign, the letter can be signed *per procurationem* ('for and on behalf of') by another person (the signatory). This is indicated by the abbreviation 'pp' written or typed before the signatory.
- Always proofread your letters for spelling errors and other details. Don't rely on your computer spell-check facility.
- If the letter has been marked 'Personal', 'Private' or 'Confidential', ensure that the envelope has been marked in the same way. Private means personal, confidential means sensitive.

LANGUAGE IN ACTION

Useful phrases

- Thank you for your letter/email …
- With regard to … I am writing to …
- Further to our recent telephone conversation …
- Further to your recent email …
- If you require further information please don't hesitate to get in touch.

Ms R. Aitchison
124, Raven Road
HARROGATE
HG2 8OP

27th January, 2003

Dear Ms Aitchison

I am writing to thank you for coming down to Oxford yesterday so that we could discuss the possibility of our company taking over responsibility for publishing *The Big Book of Yo-Yos*. This is an exciting opportunity for us and I hope that we are able to reach a mutually beneficial agreement.

I will present this title to my sales and marketing team at our regular meeting midweek, and will then take the proposal to the more formal acquisitions meeting early next week. I have sounded my marketing director out already and he is as enthusiastic as I am to publish your book, so I am not anticipating too many problems getting a positive response from the sales team.

I will also look at the financial side of the project, and you are kindly going to send me a copy of your current contract, detailing royalty rates. I have requested a copy of our standard author contract from the legal department and will forward this to you as soon as it arrives.

I enjoyed meeting you on Friday and hope that this is the start of a fruitful relationship. I will of course keep you up to date with progress.

Yours sincerely

James Nichols

James Nichols
Publishing Manager

● Writing memoranda

FAQ

Q. *What is a memorandum?*

A. A memorandum (or memo) is a short letter or note sent to a particular in-house member of staff or circulated to groups of people.

Q. *Can I send a memo to someone in another company?*

A. Memos are not usually sent out of house.

Q. *What information does a memo usually contain?*

A. A memo usually contains: the sender's name and department; the addressee's name and department; date; and the subject.

Q. *Can memos be used for confidential information and do they need a signature?*

A. They are not normally used for confidential information, but if they are they should be placed in a sealed envelope marked 'Confidential'. Memos are not usually signed, but if they contain financial information it may be usual for the sender to add initials as confirmation.

Q. *Do I need to keep a copy?*

A. Always keep and file copies of all memoranda, as with other forms of correspondence.

To: Amy Wall
Publishing Production

From: Lorna Gilmour
Editorial Department

23/01/03

THE BIG BOOK OF YO-YOS
TEXT PRINTING COPY

Amy,

With regard to passing the book for press, I enclose the text printing copy:

– complete set of text pages, with book pages marked and margins ruled up for all prelims.
– pagination and margins list.
– sheet showing book pages and their content.

Please pass this and request a full set of proofs from the printer for checking.

Cover copy for this edition already passed.

Thanks,
Lorna

LANGUAGE IN ACTION

● Writing business reports

FAQ

Q. *How do I start?*

A. You will find it much easier to write if you have a clear idea in your mind of the line of argument you want to take before you begin to write. Begin by making a note of all the evidence you have amassed and decide on a line of argument. Group together the evidence under various headings and gradually the argument will begin to take shape.

Q. *What should a report contain?*

A. Reports should include: a heading; a reason for the report; an argument; and a conclusion or recommendation.

Q. *How do I persuade the reader to accept my proposal?*

A. The golden rule is to find out what the priorities of your reader are, and then write the report from that point of view.

 Tips

- Aim to be accurate, concise and brief.
- Never use words that you don't understand. Keep jargon to a minimum, but use technical words accurately.
- Reports on meetings should be written in the third person: 'It was decided', 'A proposal was put forward'. Individual reports can be written in the first person: 'I looked into the cost of …'
- Think about whether or not you need to include graphics or illustrations (such as pie charts, bar graphs, line graphs or flow charts) in your report and choose the ones that are best suited to your purpose.
- Decide whether you want to use paragraph numbering or headings. Paragraph numbering is often much clearer than using headings and allows you to refer back and forward to specific paragraphs by number. It also reduces the need for page numbering. If you do decide to use headings, make sure that the hierarchy is consistent.
- Also think about the general layout. Do you want the text to be justified or unjustified? Where are you going to position the page numbers, if you use them? Are you going to include footnotes and a bibliography?
- To make sure you've included everything, ask yourself four questions:
  - Have I included all the information that may be needed for the reader to make a decision?

- Have I covered all the possible options and made a convincing case for the alternative that I am recommending?
- Have I explained my proposal adequately and proved that it is better than alternatives?
- Have I successfully put myself in the reader's shoes, and presented the problem and the solutions with his or her priorities in mind?

● Always pay attention to:
- consistency in headings or numbering.
- accuracy of information in graphics, tables, footnotes, etc.
- spelling, punctuation and grammar.
- overall order of the argument.
- length: is the report too long?

● Asking for increased salary

FAQ

Q. *Isn't this usually done verbally?*
A. Yes, but you may be asked to follow up in writing. The advantage of putting your request in writing is that it enables you to set down your thoughts clearly, and gives your supervisor something concrete to use when negotiating with upper management on your behalf.

Q. *Is it a good idea to threaten to leave as a way of getting a pay increase?*
A. Generally not. Your boss is likely to call your bluff, and you may have problems further down the line if you need to ask him or her for a reference. However, if you have genuinely been offered another job with a higher salary, but are reluctant to leave your current job, it may be worth mentioning this.

Q. *Whom should I address my letter to?*
A. Check with your supervisor, but it is a good idea to address it to your supervisor, and to copy in his or her manager and the human resource manager if there is one.

 Tips

- Open by telling your recipient how much you enjoy being a part of the team at your company, mentioning specific skills that you have.
- Let your recipient know how valuable you are to them, by listing some accomplishments, especially in terms of revenue you have brought in to the company or money saved.
- Finish off by saying that you would like to continue being a valuable asset to the firm and that you appreciate their serious

consideration of your request for an increase.
- Be realistic in the amount that you ask for: find out how much others make in comparable jobs.
- You could also attach an updated copy of your CV, which should show all of your accomplishments in your current position as well as those for your previous jobs.

Useful phrases

- I am writing to ask if you could consider the question of my salary.
- I enjoy my work with … very much.
- Since joining PGL, I have greatly enjoyed being a member of the I.T. department.
- During my time with PGL I have made several valuable contributions to the company's success: …
- Many responsibilities have been added to my work over the last year.
- I am therefore requesting a salary increase of £… per annum.
- I would like to continue being a valuable asset to the firm and I appreciate your serious consideration of my request.
- Please find attached an updated copy of my CV, which details my skills and accomplishments.
- I should appreciate the opportunity to discuss this with you further.
- If you would like to discuss this matter further, please do not hesitate to contact me to arrange a meeting at your convenience.

LANGUAGE IN ACTION

48 Ashgate Drive
Preston
Lancs
PR3 6NZ

14 April 2003

Mr A Williamson
Head of I.T.
Planet Insurance Ltd
Henderson Way
Preston
Lancs
PR1 4TG

Dear Mr Williamson

request for increased salary

In the three years that I have been working for Planet Insurance, I have greatly enjoyed being a member of the I.T. department, combining my programming knowledge with my communication and people skills.

I feel that during this time, I have not only benefitted greatly from the experience, but that I have also made certain accomplishments that have been of benefit to the company. In 2001, for example, I wrote a computer program which greatly reduced the time spent on certain backup procedures, and in July 2002 I was responsible for the successful introduction of the online account management system.

With these points in mind, I would like to request a salary increase of £2000 per annum.

I am very keen to continue being a valuable asset to the firm and I appreciate your serious consideration of my request.

Please find attached an updated copy of my CV, which details my skills and accomplishments, both in my current work at Planet Insurance and in my previous jobs.

If you would like to discuss this matter further, please do not hesitate to arrange a meeting at your convenience.

Yours sincerely

Patrick Evans

Patrick Evans

LANGUAGE IN ACTION

WRITING FOR BUSINESS

● Giving notification of maternity leave

✓ You are required by law to give your employer 21 days' notice in writing of your intention to take maternity leave. You must tell them the date you intend to stop work, the week the baby is due, and whether you intend to return to your job. This protects your right to maternity pay and return to work. **You must give at least 21 days' notice, in writing, of the date on which you intend to return to work.**

6 Dudley Avenue
Livingston
Edinburgh EH14 5TY

15 July 2003

Mr C McLeod
Cardrona Housing Association
3 Victoria Road
Edinburgh EH3 5WD

Dear Mr McLeod

maternity leave notification

I am writing to notify you that I am pregnant, the expected date of delivery being 24 September 2003. Please find attached a copy of form MAT B1, which confirms this date. I plan to begin my maternity leave on 27 August 2003.

I intend to return to work in April 2004, and will give you at least 21 days' notice of the exact date of my return.

Yours sincerely

Linda Allen

Linda Allen

> 6 Dudley Avenue
> Livingston
> Edinburgh EH14 5TY
>
> 15 July 2003
>
> Mr C McLeod
> Cardrona Housing Association
> 3 Victoria Road
> Edinburgh EH3 5WD
>
> Dear Mr McLeod
>
> **notification of return to work**
>
> I am writing to notify you that I intend to return to work on 4 April 2004.
>
> I am looking forward to taking up my post with you again after maternity leave.
>
> Yours sincerely
>
> *Linda Allen*
>
> Linda Allen

● Asking for holiday entitlement

✓ It may not be necessary to write a letter when asking for holiday entitlement. An email is often considered satisfactory.

> Dear George
> I would like to take two weeks of my holiday entitlement from 25 April 2003–7 March 2003.
>
> I have checked schedules, and feel confident that my work on the first stage of the current web project will be completed by then.
>
> I hope these dates will be convenient.
>
> Kind regards
> Jack Lyons

LANGUAGE IN ACTION

● Asking for unpaid leave

> Dear George
> I would like to request permission to be absent from work from
> 6–10 June 2004. My mother will be undergoing an operation on
> 3 June, and she will be requiring assistance with daily chores on
> her return home.
> I hope you will give my request consideration. I realize that I
> would not be paid for this week's leave.
> Kind regards
> *Sandra Greene*
> Sandra Greene

● Writing a letter of resignation

 ### *Tips*

- Keep it simple.
- If giving your reason for leaving, try to avoid indirectly criticizing the company or your co-workers: you may wish to use your employer as a reference at a later date.
- Thank the recipient for any help or support you feel they have given you during your time at the company.
- Show that you are willing to make the transfer as easy as possible.

Useful phrases

- I have decided that it is time to move on and I have accepted a position elsewhere.
- This is to inform you that an opportunity has presented itself that will enable me to work in the area of …
- Please accept this letter as my formal resignation as Systems Administrator for DAL publishing, to become effective as of …
- I am tendering my resignation from your company and wish to advise you that … will be my last day of employment.
- As required by my contract of employment, I hereby give you 4 weeks' notice of my intention to leave my position as …
- I am confident that my new role will help me to move towards some of the goals I have for my career.
- I believe this position will offer me more opportunity for advancement, and allow me to broaden my own experience and knowledge.
- I want to take this opportunity to thank you for your time and

LANGUAGE IN ACTION

efforts in my training and advancement during the past three years.

- The support shown by you and the rest of the management team has been greatly appreciated.
- My experience with FTL has been very rewarding.
- Thank you for your time and consideration, and I wish you all the best in the future.
- Please be assured that I will do all I can to assist in the smooth transfer of my responsibilities before leaving.

16 Lonsdale Crescent
Betchworth
Surrey
RH10 7KM

4 April 2003

Mr K Robertson
Managing Director
Geode Publishing
3-5 Guildford Road
Dorking
Surrey
RH7 4GL

Dear Keith

resignation

I am writing to inform you that I have decided it is time to move on, and I have accepted a position at Topline Publishing in Croydon, starting on 5 April 2003. I believe this position will offer me more opportunity for advancement, and allow me to broaden my own experience and knowledge.

I want to take this opportunity to thank you for your time and effort in my training during the past three years, and wish you all the best for continued success in the future.

Please be assured that I will do all I can to assist in the smooth transfer of my responsibilities before leaving.

Yours sincerely

James Payne

James Payne

FAQ

Q. *Whom should I address my letter to?*

A. For straightforward matters such as homework and absences, write to your child's class teacher. For more serious issues or complaints, address your letter to the headteacher. If you are not satisfied with the response, you local education authority will be able to tell you whom to contact next.

Q. *How can I find out about legal issues regarding bullying, truancy, exclusion, etc?*

A. The Advisory Centre for Education (ACE) publishes booklets outlining your rights on these matters. The material can also be read on their website.

● Explaining a child's absence from school

> 16 Newstead Road
> Bournemouth
> BO3 6HM
>
> 12 Jan 2003
>
> Dear Mr Dobson
> Stephen was unable to attend school yesterday as he was suffering from a 24-hour stomach bug. He seems to be well enough to come in today.
> Please advise us of any work he should be doing to make up for lost time.
>
> Thank you.
> Yours
> Lesley Allen

● Excusing a child from school

✓ Your letter is more likely to receive a positive response if you phrase it as a request rather than as a *fait accompli*. Ensure that the educational value of the arrangement is stressed. Express willingness to make up for any missed work.

39 Kayside Cottages
Perth
PE2 5GK
16 Jan 2003

Mrs H Ross
Headteacher
St Mary's High School
Perth
PE3 5RA

Dear Mrs Ross

request for absence from school

On 1 Feb 2003, my employer, the NHS, will be observing 'Take your child to work day'. The purpose of this event is to introduce children aged 8 to 16 to the world of work, and to encourage them to consider a career in medicine. The programme will include many educational activities, including workshops, tours and demonstrations. I feel sure that the experience will prove to be rewarding for all children concerned.

I am therefore writing to request that my daughter, Isobel, be excused from school that day. She will, of course, make every effort to catch up on any vital school or homework that she will be forced to miss.

I look forward to hearing from you. If you wish to discuss the matter further, please do not hesitate to call me on 01252 568356.

Yours sincerely

Irene Marchant

Irene Marchant

● Notifying school of bullying

✓ Attach a report giving details of exactly where and when the incident(s) took place, who was responsible, what happened, and how your child was affected by this. Be sure to ask for details of the school's anti-bullying strategy. (The headteacher must by law have measures in place to deal with bullying among pupils.)

Useful phrases

- I wish to inform you of a serious situation involving …
- I am writing to express my deep concern about …
- My daughter has recently been experiencing …
- I have spoken to … but the situation has not improved.
- He has spoken to his class teacher, who has reprimanded those concerned. However, …
- My daughter is usually able to look after herself, but …
- As you can imagine, this problem is causing him great anxiety.
- I am anxious to resolve this problem as soon as possible.
- Please find attached a report of the series of incidents in question.
- I would like to request a meeting to discuss a resolution to this problem.

LANGUAGE IN ACTION

19 Fairfield Drive
Hornslea
Bucks.
RD15 6YS

25 March 2003

Mr D Fitzgerald
Headteacher
Hornslea Primary School
Hornslea
Bucks
RD15 7JA

Dear Mr Fitzgerald

For the last three days my daughter, Hannah Moore, has been arriving home in tears, due to continual name-calling from a small group of girls in her class. I have mentioned it to her class teacher, who has spoken to those concerned, but it has only made the problem worse. As you can imagine, this problem is causing Helen great anxiety, and now she is becoming fearful of going to school.

I understand that the school and the LEA have a duty of care towards my child, and so I would like to request a meeting at your earliest convenience to discuss this.

I look forward to hearing from you.

Yours sincerely,

Katherine Moore

Katherine Moore (Mrs)

56 Holmes Drive
Reigate
Surrey
RH2 5GD

25 February 2003

Mr R Thomson
Headteacher
Croydon High School
Selsdon Road
Croydon
SE14 6YE

Dear Mr Thomson

change of school

I would like to inform you that my daughter, Emma Dixon, will be leaving Croydon High School at the end of this term.

My husband has taken a new job in Scotland, and we will therefore be moving to Edinburgh at the end of April. Emma has a place at James Gillespie's School in Marchmont, which I am told has an excellent academic record.

I would like to take this opportunity to thank you for all the help and encouragement you and your staff have given Emma over the last three years.

Yours sincerely

Pauline Dixon

Pauline Dixon

LANGUAGE IN ACTION

SCHOOL-RELATED CORRESPONDENCE

● Excusing a child from religious instruction

67 Langley Avenue
Crawley
W. Sussex
RH8 3FX

12 July 2003

Mrs J Wilson
Langley Green Secondary School
Langley Drive
Crawley
RH8 4WA

Dear Mrs Wilson

religious instruction

My son, Aashir, will be attending your school from the beginning of next term, and I am writing to ask that he be excused from religious education classes.

He is being raised in the Muslim faith, and receives his religious instruction outside school.

Thank you very much for your understanding.

Yours sincerely

Mahira Pandit

Mahira Pandit (Mrs)

● Non-completion of homework

Dear Mr Mitchell

John was unable to finish his essay that was due to be handed in today, as he was suffering from a severe migraine for most of yesterday evening.
He will make every effort to complete it tonight and hand it in tomorrow.
Thank you for your understanding.
Yours sincerely

Helen Maxwell

LANGUAGE IN ACTION

● To a landlord concerning outstanding repairs

✓ In the first instance, simply list the repairs required, and ask the landlord to contact you so that a time may be arranged for them to be carried out.

56 Kayside Close
Redditch
Worcs.
RD14 7NX

4 April 2003

Dear Mr Fairchild

I am writing to notify you that the following repairs to 56 Kayside Close require attention:

There are several loose tiles on the roof.
The kitchen tap is leaking.
The sealant round the bath needs replacing.

I would appreciate it if you would contact me as soon as possible to arrange a time to have these problems taken care of. Thank you very much.

Yours sincerely

Matthew Chalmers

Matthew Chalmers

✓ If repairs are not forthcoming within a reasonable amount of time, write again, once more itemizing the repairs, and reminding the recipient how long you have been waiting. This time you might want to give the landlord a deadline, and show that you are aware of your rights in law.

LANGUAGE IN ACTION

Useful phrases

- Further to my previous correspondence, the following repairs to the above address remain outstanding: ...
- I have been waiting for a considerable amount of time to have these repairs completed.
- By law, a landlord is responsible for providing and maintaining residence in a good state of repair.
- Please contact me immediately so that we may resolve this problem.
- I would be glad if you could see that the matter is resolved as soon as possible.

LANGUAGE IN ACTION

56 Kayside Close
Redditch
Worcs.
RD14 7NX

1 May 2003

Dear Mr Fairchild

In my previous correspondence to you I requested repairs to be completed to 56 Kayside Close. The following items remain outstanding:

There are several loose tiles on the roof.
The kitchen tap is leaking.
The sealant round the bath needs replacing.

I have been waiting for a considerable amount of time to have these repairs completed. I would ask you to take care of this matter within one week of receipt of this letter.

I remind you that by law, a landlord is responsible for providing and maintaining residence in a good state of repair, and for complying with housing and maintenance standards.

Please contact me immediately so that we may resolve this problem.

Yours sincerely

Matthew Chalmers

Matthew Chalmers

● Letter to a housing advice centre regarding unfair rent

✓ If your landlord/landlady is trying to put the rent up and you don't agree to the increase, it may be worth negotiating with them. They may agree to a lower rent increase in return rather than having to relet the property. Alternatively, they may agree to increase the rent in stages over a period of time.

> 45 Victoria Street
> Headley
> Northants.
> NO3 7FS
>
> 16 April 2003

The Rents Adviser
Headley Housing Advice
4 The Row
Headley
Northants.
NO2 4TY

Dear Sir/Madam

unfair rent query

I am writing to request your advice on an issue regarding what I consider to be an unfair increase in rent.

My landlord has recently increased my rent from £300 a month to £360 a month. Not only do I find this amount unreasonable, but I am also having difficulty sustaining the payments. Furthermore, there are several outstanding repairs to be attended to in the house.

I would be grateful if you could inform me of my rights, and let me know what, if anything, I can do to challenge this increase. I look forward to hearing from you.

Yours faithfully

Katherine Gulliver

Katherine Gulliver

LANGUAGE IN ACTION

● Letter to a housing advice centre regarding eviction

✓ Most private tenants can only be evicted if their landlord gets a possession order from the court. If your landlord has evicted you without following the correct procedure this may be illegal.

34 Tadworth Court
Ducksbury
Berkshire
RD7 4GN

3 June 2003

Dear Sir/Madam

eviction query

I am writing to request advice from you regarding a matter of urgency.

My landlord has just issued me with an eviction notice, due to come into force on 4 July 2003. His justification for this action is that I have not paid my rent for the last two months.

I am a single mother with two young children, and I have been unable to pay the rent due to the fact that my ex-husband has not kept up regular maintenance payments over the last four months.

Could you please inform me of my rights, and advise me on how I should proceed?

I look forward to hearing from you. If you wish to speak to me directly, please call me on 01456 783219.

Thank you in advance.

Yours faithfully

Sally Nettles

Sally Nettles

● letter to planning authority inquiring as to whether planning permission is needed

✓ Some minor developments (such as certain extensions to domestic property, or changes in the way a building is used) may not need express planning permission. With buildings that are listed for preservation, it is generally best to consult with the local planning authority before any changes are made. If you are unsure as to whether or not your development requires planning permission, you should contact your local planning authority.

19 Limes Avenue
Cambridge
CB12 4LA
tel: 01356 721673

17 June 2003

The Planning Department
Cambridge District Council
University Road
Cambridge
CB2 7KS

Dear Sir/Madam

inquiry re. necessity of planning permission

I am writing to inquire as to whether I will need to apply for planning permission for a proposed development I wish to undertake at the above address.

The specifications of the development are as follows:

description:
garage
location:
side of property
use:
car storage
dimensions:
floor surface area: 6m x 3.5m
height: 2.5m

If you require any further information, please do not hesitate to contact me at the telephone number above. I look forward to hearing from you.

Yours faithfully
Harriet Yates
Harriet Yates (Mrs)

LANGUAGE IN ACTION

● Objecting to a planning permission application

FAQ

Q. *What sort of objection is considered valid, and what is not?*
A. Objections should be confined to such issues as:

> design, appearance and general impact
> significant overlooking or overshadowing
> traffic impact
> noise, smell or other pollutants
> harm to local landmarks or public views

Objections which cannot normally be considered include:

> loss of a personal view from a particular property
> loss of property value

Tips

- Write to the Director of Planning at your local district council.
- Refer to the application number and the site address.
- Clearly outline the reasons why you wish to object to the proposal.

Useful phrases

- I wish to object to the above planning permission application for …
- I am writing to register my objection to the planning application detailed above.
- I am seriously concerned that the noise and the smell from the plant would be detrimental to my health.
- The increase in traffic caused by the development would significantly affect the character of the area.
- This building would significantly affect my family's quality of life.
- I request that you take this into account when considering this application.
- I urge you to give my objection serious consideration.
- I urge you to reject this application.

7 Fallowfield Terrace
Fordham
Hants
SO12 5AZ

19 May 2003

The Director of Planning and Technical Services
Fordham District Council
Riverside House
Fordham
Hants
SO13 5HB

Dear Sir/Madam

Planning application no: 00006721 45793

I wish to object to the above planning permission application for 5 Fallowfield Terrace.

This extension, if constructed, would significantly affect the amount of light reaching the back rooms of my house, as well as compromising my family's privacy and quality of life.

I request that you take this into account when considering this application and urge you to reject it.

Yours faithfully

Malcolm Skinner

Malcolm Skinner

• Objecting to the proposed erection of a mobile phone mast

FAQ

Q. *To whom should I address my letter?*
A. Write to the council's planning department and copy it to your local councillor and the landowner. You could also write to your MP about the application and contact the local press.

Q. *How should I formulate my objection?*
A. Some ideas for formulating your objection are:
Have the regulations been followed? To find out the details of

regulations affecting mobile phone masts, visit your local library, or find an appropriate site on the World Wide Web.

Is it necessary?

Are there alternative sites, and if so, is the application accompanied by evidence that they were considered?

 Tips

- Identify the deadline date for objections.
- Different regions have different policies on the erection of mobile phone masts.
- Find out what your council's policy is before writing your letter.

45 Hopetoun Gardens
Hopetoun, West Lothian
LV4 7NX

3 April 2003

Mr R. McKinnon
Chief Planning Officer
Hopetoun District Council
Hopetoun, West Lothian
LV2 4GY

Dear Mr McKinnon

Re: planning application no. 39100921/000128

I am writing in objection to the proposed erection of a telecommunication mast on land situated at Hopetoun Park, West Lothian. My objection is based on the following grounds:

As you will be aware, there are a large number of conflicting academic reports on the dangers of irradiation emitted from base stations. The proposed mast would be situated only 30 metres away from a residential area. With no clear evidence showing that such masts are safe, particularly with regard to children's health, I feel that this is proximity is unacceptable.

The mast is unnecessary, since the signal for the network concerned is adequate in this area.

With these points in mind, I urge you to reject this application.

Yours sincerely

Roger Hall

Roger Hall

LANGUAGE IN ACTION

MONEY-RELATED CORRESPONDENCE

● letter to a lender advising of difficulty in mortgage payment

 Tips

- Identify the deadline date for objections.
- If you are having trouble with your mortgage payments, or if you can see that you are going to have problems, contact your lender as soon as possible.
- In your letter, show that you are willing to negotiate with the lender. Most will help you explore your options.
- Make it clear to your lender that you are keen to keep paying as much as you can afford.

Useful phrases

- I am writing to inform you that I am anticipating having some difficulty in continuing to meet my mortgage payments.
- I am currently finding it hard to meet all my financial commitments.
- My employers went into liquidation two months ago.
- I have recently been made redundant.
- I am suffering from a long-term illness, and am no longer entitled to sickness pay.
- I was wondering if it would be possible to reduce my monthly payments.
- I would like to request that my mortgage payments be reduced from July.
- I am keen to continue paying as much as possible.
- I would be pleased to come into your office and discuss this matter further with you.
- Would it be possible to arrange an interview with you, so that we may come to some sort of arrangement?
- I do hope that you will give sympathetic consideration to my situation, and look forward to hearing from you.

LANGUAGE IN ACTION

92 Lockwood Avenue
Leadingham
Bucks
GR2 9TN

15 May 2003

Mr J McVee
Senior Credit Controller
Castle Building Society
2 York Road
Leeds
N. Yorks
LE3 3RA

Dear Mr McVee

request for reduction in mortgage payments

I am writing to inform you that, due to my recent redundancy, I am anticipating having some difficulty in continuing to meet my mortgage payments.

I am making every attempt to find work elsewhere, but if I am unsuccessful, I would like to request that my mortgage payments be temporarily reduced from July, and the terms of my mortgage extended accordingly.

I am keen to continue paying as much as possible, and am currently in consultation with my financial adviser to calculate how much money I can reasonably afford each month.

Would it be possible to arrange an interview with you, so that we may come to some sort of arrangement?

I do hope that you will give sympathetic consideration to my situation, and look forward to hearing from you.

Yours sincerely

Jack Everett

Jack Everett

LANGUAGE IN ACTION

MONEY-RELATED CORRESPONDENCE

- **letter to an insurance company advising of an accident**

Ken Howland
2 Rowlands Ave
Birmingham
B6 7PL

25 July 2003

The Claims Officer
Hotline Insurance
3 Castle Court
London
W1 5HT

Dear Sir/Madam
Policy No: 0000931 45621

I am writing to notify you that I wish to make a claim under the provisions of the insurance policy detailed above.

The loss came about on 12 July 2003 as a result of an accident between the insured vehicle and another vehicle at the intersection of Channel Street and Caddonfoot Road in Pitlochry, Perthshire. As a result, the insured vehicle suffered damage to the rear bumper and the lights.

Please contact me at the address shown above, so that a formal claim according to your company's procedures may be made. Thank you for your attention to this matter.

Yours faithfully

Kenneth Howland

Kenneth Howland

37

● letter to an insurance company advising of a home burglary

Patrick Norton
23 Lucas Rd
Kingston-Upon-Thames
Surrey
KT6 2PL

25 July 2003

The Claims Officer
UK Assured Ltd
6 West Gorton Rd
Lincoln
LI4 9TZ

Dear Sir/Madam

Policy No: 12409745 000002

I am writing to inform you that I have suffered a loss to the above-named property, insured with you, and I would like to make a claim under the provisions of the insurance policy named above.

The loss came about on 23 July 2003, as a result of a burglary. I sustained losses of jewellery believed to have a value of £2000, a television with a value of £350, and damage to the home which will cost £500 to repair.

I would be grateful if you could contact me at the address shown above, so that a formal claim according to your company's procedures may be made.

Thank you for your attention to this matter.

Yours faithfully

Patrick Norton

Patrick Norton

LANGUAGE IN ACTION

LETTERS OF COMPLAINT

FAQ

Q. *Is it OK to send a complaint by email?*

A. On the whole, it is advisable to send your complaint in the form of a letter, rather than an email.

Q. *To whom should I address the letter?*

A. For a large company, direct your letter in the first instance to the Customer Relations Manager.
For a small company, you should write directly to the Managing Director.

Q. *What is the best way to ensure a speedy reply and get the desired result?*

A. Collect together all the relevant facts, then calmly set them down in a logical sequence. If you have a reference number that will help to identify the purchase or invoice in question, quote this in the subject heading of the letter. Show that you are a reasonable person by making reference to positive aspects of your contact with the company. Finally, specify a time limit (usually 14 days) within which you expect to hear from the company, stating the action you wish to be taken.

Q. *What sort of tone should I use? Is an angry tone more likely to get results?*

A. A letter that is polite and firm, and that sticks to the facts is far more effective than one written in a fit of temper.

Q. *What do I need to know about my legal rights?*

A. It often helps if you know the basics of the Sale of Goods Act, and to make this fact known to your recipient. Unless you are really sure about particular laws, though, it is best just to suggest that you know your legal rights and will use them if reasonable action is not taken.

Q. *How should I respond if I just get a bland, non-committal reply?*

A. Contact the managing director of the company, explaining your problem again. If you still do not get results, try contacting a Citizens' Advice Bureau to get legal help.

LANGUAGE IN ACTION

Useful phrases

- I am writing to express my dissatisfaction with the service I received from your ...
- At the time of booking it was agreed that ...
- However, on our arrival, we discovered that ...
- I recently bought ...(include colour, model and price) in your shop in ...
- When I tried to use this item, I discovered that ...
- I have contacted you by telephone three times and each time you have promised to visit and put the faults right.
- To date these problems have not been resolved.

LETTERS OF COMPLAINT

- Under the terms of your guarantee, I would like to request a full reimbursement of the amount paid.
- I am withholding payment of the above invoice until I have heard your response to the points outlined above.
- Under the Goods and Services Act 1982, I am entitled to expect work to be carried out using due care and skill.
- If I do not hear from you within 14 days, I will have no choice but to take the matter further.
- Because of these faults I now consider you to be in breach of contract.

● letter of complaint regarding unsatisfactory holiday accommodation

16 Hopeside Crescent
East Sussex
EG13 6HJ

24 August 2002

The Customer Relations Manager
Sunkiss Holidays
58-60 East Preston Street
Manchester
M2 9LP

Dear Sir

Re. booking reference number 610004367

I am writing to express my dissatisfaction at the standard of holiday accommodation my family and I were forced to accept at the above holiday apartment in Ibiza last week.

At the time of booking, I requested a three-bedroomed apartment with living room and fully-equipped kitchen. However, on our arrival, we discovered that the third 'bedroom' consisted of a sofa-bed in the living area, and the kitchen was small, dirty and in a very bad state of repair. I enclose photos.

Under the Supply of Goods and Services Act 1982, I am entitled to expect the accommodation provided to be of a satisfactory standard, and for it to be as described in your brochure. I look forward to an offer of compensation within 14 days.

Yours faithfully

Charles MacLennan

Charles MacLennan (Mr)

LANGUAGE IN ACTION

LETTERS OF COMPLAINT

● letter of complaint regarding a faulty appliance

41 Selwood Avenue
Kingston-upon-Hull
East Yorks
HU7 4DS

4 May 2003

Ms Jane Andrews
Customer Relations Officer
Stewarts Electrics
Electra House
Foxton High Road
London
SW3 6BZ

Dear Ms Andrews

Re: faulty appliance: Giolaggio Express A261

I recently bought a chrome 'Giolaggio Express' A261 espresso machine (£129.99) from your store in Middleham. When I tried to use it, I discovered that the element was faulty, and that the resulting coffee was lukewarm.

I have returned to your store in Middleham on several occasions, firstly requesting a replacement appliance, and subsequently, due to an extended delay, requesting a refund. The latter has not been forthcoming, and I have been advised by the shop manager to take my complaint to you.

Under the Sale of Goods Act 1979, purchased items should be of satisfactory quality and fit for their purpose. Since neither of these criteria are met, I would like to request a full reimbursement of the amount paid.

I look forward to your reply within 14 days, and hope this matter can be resolved quickly.

Yours sincerely,

A. Fraser

Anne Fraser (Mrs)

LETTERS OF COMPLAINT

● Complaining about public transport

☑ If your letter of complaint is triggered by a series of problems that have been experienced in relation to a particular service, it is important that your letter should not become a long and verbose essay. It can be easy to get carried away with all the negative implications of each error, in the misguided belief that you will arouse your recipient's sympathy. Instead, list your complaint clearly and succinctly. If you are using a computer, you could separate the items with bullet points.

35 Fairways Drive
Penicuik
Midlothian
EH17 4KC

4 October 2002

The Customer Relations Manager
Scotbus
Burns House
McGowan Road
Glasgow
G4 7JY

Dear Sir/Madam

Re: Route 95, Penicuik to Edinburgh, 2 October 2002

I am writing to complain about the bus journey I undertook yesterday on the number 95 bus from Penicuik to Edinburgh. I had scheduled a meeting for lunchtime, and gave myself ample time, choosing to take the 11.15 service. I was dissatisfied with the service in the following ways:

The bus arrived 20 minutes late.

The bus finally left the bus station 30 minutes late.

The temperature inside the bus was about 35 degrees Centigrade. I asked the driver if he could turn the heating off, but he explained that it had to be switched on, as it formed part of the bus's cooling system.

Being nearly 7 months' pregnant, I found this journey very uncomfortable, and by the end, quite distressing.

I would be interested to hear your comments on this, and any offer of compensation you may consider appropriate.

Yours faithfully

P. Holmes

Patricia Holmes

LETTERS OF COMPLAINT

● Shoddy workmanship

 Tips

- Discuss the problem with the tradesperson first, and give them a chance to put it right. If this doesn't work, put your complaint in writing giving a deadline. Send it to the head office if there is one.
- Keep copies of all letters sent and received and make a note of conversations.
- If you chose a contractor that belongs to a trade association, they may offer a conciliation or arbitration service to settle your dispute.

77 Bishop Road
Newport
Gwent
NP3 5NQ

31 October 2002

The Customer Services Manager
L. Smart & Co. Contractors
17 Trevellyan Road
Cardiff
CA4 5GT

Dear Sir/Madam

Re: estimate 700003412

I am writing to express my dissatisfaction with the service I received from one of your builders recently.

Before accepting your estimate for the job, I was assured that the work would be completed by 10 October. Three weeks later, the work is still incomplete. Moreover, the work that has been done is defective. The new door that was fitted is not flush with the frame, and the lock is consequently very stiff.

If the work is not completed and the defect rectified within 14 days, I shall consider our contract to be at an end. I shall then instruct another firm to complete the work, and deduct the cost from your original price.

Yours faithfully

Douglas Fairburn

Douglas Fairburn

LETTERS OF COMPLAINT

● Complaining to a health authority

 Tips

- Address your letter to the Complaints Manager of the Local Health Authority
- Give name of doctor, GP or practitioner concerned.
- Give a brief background to case.
- State the problem. If your complaint consists of a catalogue of errors, itemize them clearly and succinctly.
- Note that it is one of the NHS's officially stated core principles that it is committed to shaping its services around the needs and preferences of individual patients, their families and carers.

7 Oaklands
Horley RH6 2QT

17 November 2002

The Complaints Manager
East Surrey Local Health Authority
5 Market Street
Redhill
RH1 4GA

Dear Sir

I am writing to express my concern about the treatment that my elderly mother, Mrs Grace Harding, is currently undergoing. Her GP is Dr Middleton at the Longwood Surgery, Horley.

In 2001, my mother was diagnosed as suffering from shingles. Since that time she has experienced continual pain down the sides of her body.

However, she recently received a letter informing her that she would no longer be able to attend the pain clinic at this surgery. She has been given no explanation as to the reasons for this decision from the health authority or from her doctor.

Since it is one of the NHS's officially stated core principles that it is committed to shaping its services around the needs and preferences of individual patients, I feel that you have a duty to ensure that she enjoys this later period of her life.

I would be glad to hear your comments on this case.

Yours faithfully

G. Glover

Gillian Glover

LETTERS OF COMPLAINT

● Complaining about financial services

 Tips

- You must complain to the firm before you go to the ombudsman.
- Remember to include important details like your customer number or your policy or account number. Put these details at the top of your letter.
- Remember to enclose copies of any relevant documents that you believe back up your case.
- Keep a copy of any letters between you and the firm. You may need to refer to them later.

4 Hove Lane
Newhaven
W Sussex BN12 6JL

24 October 2002

The Customer Relations Manager
Castle Building Society
Grove Street
Derby
DB5 4FY

Dear Sir/Madam

Complaint: savings acc. no. 9450001992

I wish to register my dissatisfaction with the service that I have received from the staff at your Brighton branch.

I opened a savings account, and arranged for a monthly standing order of £150 a month to be made from my current account, held at another bank. However, the last time I asked for a mini-statement, I noticed that there had not been a credit to my savings account for the previous two months, despite the fact that the money had been debited from my current account. Enclosed are copies of both the relevant statements. I brought this to the attention of your Brighton staff, but they dismissed the problem as being outside their remit.

I am therefore appealing to you for a thorough investigation into this matter, and look forward to hearing from you.

Yours faithfully

Patrick Horton

Patrick Horton

45

SOCIAL CORRESPONDENCE

● Formal invitations

 Tips

- Use good quality stationery that reflects your personal style, and the nature of the occasion.
- Issue your invitation well in advance of the occasion, so that the recipient will be able to make space in his or her calendar for your event.
- Include details of the nature of the event, the address, date and time, and indicate whether or not food and drink will be provided if the time is near to a usual meal time. If a dress code or special parking arrangements are required, give these details in as clear and brief a manner as possible.
- Include the line "RSVP" with a telephone number or address, so that guests can tell you whether or not they will be able to attend. You may want to include an RSVP card for the recipient's use.

● A wedding invitation

John and Angela Shaw
are delighted to invite
Jeremy Kempton and Kay Whitcroft
to the wedding of their daughter

Catharine

to

Matthew Tibbits

on Saturday 5th April 2003

at 2pm
at Hemel Methodist Church, Bristol
and afterwards to a
Reception
at Austen Place, Keynsham

RSVP
Cathy Shaw
89 Caird Drive
Brighton
BN1 9TQ

SOCIAL CORRESPONDENCE

● Refusing invitations

 Tips

- Begin by thanking the person for the invitation.
- Then show regret and give reasons.
- Finally, express desire to see them at a future date.

Useful phrases

- Thank you so much for the invitation to …
- Many thanks for your invitation to …
- I'm afraid I'm not going to be able to come.
- Unfortunately we're not going to be able to make it.
- Unfortunately I already have something arranged for that day.
- It's our 30th wedding anniversary, and we're going out for a meal that night.
- It's the day we get back from our holiday, so I don't know if we'll be home in time.
- Harry's got his school concert that night.
- What a shame!
- I'm really sorry, as I'd have loved to see you all.
- I hope we can get together soon, though.
- I hope you all have a really great time.

● Declining a formal invitation to a wedding

 Use the same style as that used in the invitation.

> 25 Dean Avenue
> Yeovil
> Somerset
> YO3 8LR
>
> 23 March 2003
>
> Mr and Mrs K Forbes thank Mr and Mrs O'Neill for their kind invitation to their daughter's wedding, and to the reception afterwards, but regret that a prior engagement prevents them from attending.

LANGUAGE IN ACTION

● Declining a formal invitation to dinner

> 8 Holmes Close
> Eskbank
> Midlothian
> EH16 3BV
>
> 14 May 2003
>
> Dear Caroline
>
> Many thanks for your kind invitation to dinner on 1st August. Unfortunately, Jeff is away on business that week, and I've arranged to go and visit Jackie and the children, so I'm afraid we won't be able to be with you.
>
> We are both very sorry, and hope to see you soon.
>
> Thank you again.
>
> *Fiona*

● An informal letter or email declining an invitation

> 67 Hawthornevale
> Gosforth
> Newcastle
> N7 5GD
>
> 24 April 2003
>
> Dear Nicola
>
> Thanks ever so much for the invitation to Gordon's party, but I'm afraid I'm not going to be able to make it. It's our 30th wedding anniversary that day, and we're going out for a meal in the evening. What a shame! I hope we'll be able to get together again soon.
>
> Hope you all have a great time.
>
> love,
>
> *Teresa*
>
> xxx

LANGUAGE IN ACTION

SOCIAL CORRESPONDENCE

● Writing a letter of apology

 Tips

- Make it clear from the start that you are apologizing, and state what you are apologizing for.
- Explain how the mistake came about, accepting responsibility if you are at fault.
- Think about how you can put the problem right, and suggest your solution tentatively.
- At the end of the letter, reiterate your apology.

Useful phrases

- I am writing to apologize for …
- I've just realized that …
- I can't tell you how sorry I am.
- I am sorry that …
- Due to …, I was unable to …
- I know it's no excuse, but …
- Unfortunately …
- I hope you will accept …
- Can I suggest …?
- Would you agree to …?
- Again, please accept my apologies (for …).
- In the meantime, many apologies again.

● Letters wishing a speedy recovery

FAQ

Q. *What sort of tone should I use?*
A. It is acceptable to use a fairly informal tone if you know that the person will recover quickly. If the illness is serious, you will need to use a slightly more formal tone.
Q. *Should I send a card or a letter?*
A. For informal wishes, a card is most appropriate. For more formal wishes, or if the illness is serious, you may like to write a letter.

● Informal wishes (card)

Useful phrases

- Hoping you get well very soon.
- Wishing you a speedy recovery.
- Sorry to hear you're not well. We're thinking of you.

SOCIAL CORRESPONDENCE

● Formal wishes (letter)

Useful phrases

- I was very sorry to hear of …
- Please accept my sympathies …
- … and best wishes for a speedy recovery.
- It must be an anxious time for you.
- You have our deepest sympathy.
- Is there any way in which we can help?
- If there's anything I can do, please don't hesitate to let me know.
- We hope and trust you will soon be better.
- We are feeling for you.

● Formal letter wishing someone a speedy recovery

Upper Steading, 17 June, 2003

Dear Mr Grierson

We were very sorry to hear of your wife's sudden illness. Please accept our sympathies and give her our best wishes for a speedy recovery.

It must be a very anxious time for you. If there's anything we can do, please don't hesitate to let us know. In the meantime, we are thinking of you both.

Yours sincerely

Mary Fawkes

✓ If the recipient is unlikely to make a full recovery, it is unwise to suggest that this might be the case.

● Letters of condolence

FAQ

Q. *What form should a letter of condolence take?*

A. A letter of condolence should normally be handwritten. However, you need to use your own discretion, depending on your relationship with the recipient.

Q. *I never know what to say at such times. Don't letters of condolence require flowery language and literary turns of phrase?*

A. No. Try to express yourself simply, and speak from the heart.

Q. *Should I make reference to God and religion?*

A. Only if you know that your recipient shares your beliefs.

LANGUAGE IN ACTION

SOCIAL CORRESPONDENCE

 Tips

A simple and effective structure for a condolence letter might be as follows:

- Express your shock or regret and the person's death.
- Briefly point out the deceased's qualities, and any achievements you may want to mention.
- Say how much the deceased will be missed.
- Offer any help that you are genuinely willing to give.

• An informal letter of condolence

Useful phrases

- We were very sad to hear of ...'s death.
- It came as a terrible shock to us all.
- Everyone who knew him found him a warm and affectionate person.
- She was such a good friend to us.
- We will all miss him terribly.
- We're thinking of you all.
- Please don't hesitate to call on us at any time.
- Is there anything we can do to help?

Littleton, 24 March 2003

Dear Pat,

We were terribly sad to hear the tragic news of Ken's death. It 's been a great shock, and we want you to know that you are in our thoughts.

Everyone who knew Ken found him an exceptional person, with his great talent for painting and his kindness and warmth. We will miss him greatly.

You know that you can call on us any time. Please don't hesitate if there is anything we can do to help.

All our love

Leonie and Andrew

LANGUAGE IN ACTION

● A more formal letter of condolence

Useful phrases

- I was deeply saddened to hear of ...'s death last ...
- I have just heard of the sad death of ...
- It has come to us as a great shock.
- Please accept my sincerest condolences.
- I am sure you know how much he was liked and respected by everyone.
- We will all miss him greatly.
- He will be greatly missed.
- It must be a comfort to you to know that ...

Taunton, 14 April 2003

Dear Mrs Morrison

I was very sad to hear of your husband's death last week, and I write to offer sincere condolences to you and your family.

I am sure you know how much Mr Morrison was liked and respected in the community. We will all miss him greatly.

If there is anything I can do to help, please don't hesitate to get in touch.

Kindest regards

Yvonne Tullis

WRITING SPEECHES

● Writing your speech

 Tips

- When writing your speech, if you're unsure of what to say, look at other people's speeches in books and on websites. Reading what others have said can help you decide what's appropriate for you.
- Think about who will be in the audience. What would *they* appreciate? How formal is the setting? What kind of jokes are likely to go down well?
- Brainstorm on topics.
- Select topic(s).
- Gather your material.
- Organize your material.
- Draft your speech.
- Practise your delivery.

● Delivering your speech

FAQ

Q. *Is it OK to read my speech or should I try to memorize it?*

A. It's best not to trust everything to memory. Try to thoroughly familiarise yourself with your speech and then reduce it to a set of brief notes on cue cards. This way your speech will not sound as if it is being read word for word.

Q. *Should I practise my speech, or might too much practice make it sound contrived?*

A. You should rehearse it, then rehearse it again. And then again, until you have had enough of it. Get a friend or family member to help by listening and ask them to tell you honestly how your voice sounds.

Q. *I tend to gabble when I'm nervous. How can I avoid this?*

A. Always pause to let your points sink in and wait for the laughs you want. Take your time. What will seem like an age to you will really only be a few seconds to your audience. Use pauses to gather your thoughts, glance at your notes and breathe in and out. Don't give in to the urge to speed up.

Q. *Is it advisable to have a few drinks beforehand?*

A. Don't drink too much before speaking. You might think it helps, but your audience won't.

Q. *How can I give an impression of confidence, even when I'm nervous?*

A. When delivering your speech, be conscious of your body language from the start. Stand with your weight equal on both feet, and look around at your audience for a few seconds before you start to speak. Try to make eye contact with the audience. Try to make everyone feel included.

WRITING SPEECHES

● Wedding speeches

There are three main speeches that are usually given at a wedding reception. They are:

- the bride's father's speech
- the bridegroom's speech
- the best man's speech

Other speeches are possible. For example, the bridegroom's father may give a short speech of thanks to the host and hostess for the occasion, or the bride may wish to give a speech. Here, though, we will look at the three principal speeches.

 Tips

- Once you have completed all the formalities, you may wish to expand your speech a little. When drafting your speech, start by considering some of the following points:
- When did you first meet the bride/groom?
- Who brought you together? (for bridegroom only)
- How did she/he come across to you then?
- Can you remember anything unusual that happened when you first met?
- What are her/his best qualities?
- Think of three words describing the way you feel about him/her.
- Do you have any plans or wishes for your future together? (for bridegroom only)

● The bride's father

The bride's father is called upon by the best man to propose a toast of health and happiness to the bride and bridegroom.

Before doing so, he should welcome the groom's parents, and the relatives of both families. He should say a few words about his daughter, and then the groom, welcoming him into the family.

Useful phrases

- On behalf of (name of wife) and myself, I would like to start by saying what a pleasure it is to welcome, on this very happy occasion (names of groom's parents), (named close relatives), together with all relatives and friends of both families.
- As father of the bride, it is my privilege to make the first speech, and I would like to start by …
- First I would like to welcome everybody here today to join (bride) and (groom) on this special day.
- To (name of officiator), our thanks for officiating at the ceremony,

and to his 'boss' for keeping the weather at bay.

- I know some people have travelled quite some distance, and I would like to express our gratitude and thanks for the effort they have made.
- I would like to thank (bride) and (groom) for organizing such a splendid occasion. I am sure you will agree that it is a tremendous success.
- I'd like to take this opportunity to thank especially, (wife), for not only being a tolerant wife but more importantly an outstanding mother.
- (Groom) is attentive, caring, hard-working, intelligent, and informed on most subjects, except football (he supports ......). I am very pleased and proud to welcome him as a son-in-law.
- During the time we've known him, we've come to realize how special he is to her. I would like to welcome my new son-in-law into our family.
- (Bride's name) and (groom's name),
    Here's to the past
    Here's to the present
    And here's to the future, for all that you can look forward to together.
- Ladies and gentlemen, please be upstanding, and raise your glasses to (bride) and (groom).
- The bride and groom.
- Thank you.
- It is now my pleasant duty to propose a toast to the happy couple. Please join me in wishing them a long and happy life together. Ladies and Gentlemen fill your glasses and join in the toast to the happy couple, (bride) and (groom).

● The bridegroom

The bridegroom replies on behalf of himself and his bride, thanking his parents for their love and care, and for the start they gave him in life.
He will also take this opportunity to thank all those present for their gifts.
Any members of the family who could not attend the wedding because of illness should be mentioned and wished a speedy recovery.
He would normally then say a few words about his new wife.
The bridegroom should propose a toast to the bridesmaids, and thank them for doing such a good job.

LANGUAGE IN ACTION

LANGUAGE IN ACTION

Useful phrases

- I'd like to thank (bride's father) for those kind words, I am very proud to be your son-in-law; I hope I can live up to your expectations.
- I would sincerely like to thank you and (bride's mother) for welcoming me into your family.
- Thank you again to (bride's father) and (bride's mother) for your daughter's hand. Julia is the most special person I've ever known, and I promise I'll take good care of her.
- To our parents, thank you for your love and support over the years, for the advice you have given us, for putting up with us and pointing us in the right direction.
- On behalf of my new wife and myself, I would like to say thank you to a few people:
- Firstly, to (bride)'s parents and to my own parents … We could never thank you enough for all your very generous help and the tremendous love and support you've always given us, but in particular in the last few months.
- To our two lovely bridesmaids for taking such good care of (bride) and getting her to the church on time.
- To my ushers, (names), for looking after me so well today.
- To (name of Master of Ceremonies), for keeping us all in line today as Master of Ceremonies.
- To my best man (name), for calming my nerves on the run-up to the wedding and for looking after me so well today.
- To everybody for all your cards, kind thoughts and presents. We've been quite staggered by your generosity.
- I would like to say thanks very much for all of you for sharing this special day with us.
- It's been an amazing day and having you all here has helped to make this the most memorable and happiest day of our lives.
- In conclusion, I would also like to thank my best friend for agreeing to marry me today.
- The one person in this room to which I owe the most thanks is (bride), my wife. I am sure you will all agree how stunning she looks today.
- She is beautiful, intelligent, hard-working – the list is endless, but unfortunately I can't read her handwriting …

● The best man

It is the best man's duty to respond to this toast on behalf of the bridesmaids. His speech should be light-hearted and fun.

WRITING SPEECHES

Useful phrases

- Firstly on behalf of the bridesmaid(s), (names), I'd like to thank (groom) for his kind words. I'm sure you'd agree with me that they look beautiful and that they have done an excellent job today.
- Firstly on behalf of the bridesmaid(s), (bridesmaids' names), I would like to thank (groom) for his kind words.
- I am sure you will all agree she does/they do look marvellous.
- The bride, well, we all agree how wonderful she looks today, and (groom) scrubs up well himself …
- I must say she is one of the nicest people you could ever wish to meet.
- On a serious note, can you all be up standing and charge your glasses while I propose a toast:
- To the bride – may she share everything with her husband, including the housework!
- To the bride and groom – may the roof above you never fall in and may you both never fall out!
- Please stay upstanding and join me in a toast to the bride and groom's parents … and those who were sadly unable to be here today.
- It gives me great pleasure to invite you to all stand and raise your glasses in a toast for (bride) and (groom). We wish them well for the future and hope they enjoy a long and happy marriage together.

● Writing a eulogy

FAQ

Q. *What sort of tone should I adopt when writing a eulogy?*

A. Generally, a eulogy should be written in an informal, conversational tone. Humour is acceptable if it fits the personality of the deceased. When delivering your eulogy, talk to the audience as though you were talking to a friend.

Q. *Should I just speak about my own experiences of the deceased, or should I try to include other people's experiences?*

A. A eulogy should convey the feelings and experiences of the person giving it. Don't try to objectively summarize the person's life or speak for all present. Having said that, it can be a good idea to write about memories that the audience can remember, and to get the audience involved in what you are saying.

Q. *How long should I speak for?*

A. Keep it brief. Five to ten minutes is the norm, but it's a good idea to verify that with the officiator.

WRITING SPEECHES

 Tips

- Be yourself.
- Be honest, and focus on the person's positive qualities.
- You may want to include the deceased's favourite poems, book passages, scripture verses, quotes, expressions or lines from songs.
- You could interview family and friends when preparing your draft.
- Some of the simplest thoughts are deeply touching and easy for those congregated to identify with. For example, 'I'll miss her laughter' is just as good as 'I admired her courage.'
- Here are some questions to ask yourself:
- How did you and the deceased become close?
- Is there a humorous or touching event that represents the essence of the deceased?
- What did you and others love and admire about the deceased?
- What will you miss most about him or her?

Useful phrases

- When I think of ..., I think of laughter and love.
- I can remember ...ing with ...
- One time ...
- ... even made it into the newspaper about it.
- ... taught me how to ...
- ... was involved in so many activities; she/he was very popular.
- I can see her/him now: ...ing, ...ing and ...
- ... was like a ray of sunshine.
- ... gave me so much wisdom.
- She/he always showed loyalty, courtesy and consideration for others.
- I am so lucky to have had ... as a friend.
- And in spirit she/he joins us today.
- I will miss her/him very much.

WRITING SPEECHES

● Leaving and retirement speeches

 Tips

- Remember that your approach may be slightly different depending on whether the employee is leaving under happy or more regrettable circumstances.
- Make sure you get your facts right, for example how long the employee has been working for the company.
- Remember that your main aim is to thank the employee and to praise them for any achievements you want to mention.
- On the whole, this kind of speech should be short, as people are usually standing at such occasions.
- Even if your relationship with the employee was not very warm, try to concentrate on their good points.
- Try to think of at least one anecdote, humorous if possible, that you can recount about the person who is leaving.

Useful phrases

- This is both a time to look back and a time to look forward.
- Some people here may remember the time when …
- When Jack first arrived at the company, there was … Now, there are …
- Thank you for all your hard work, especially …
- You have certainly made my job easier.
- The company has a lot to thank you for.
- We respect the decision you have made, and wish you all the best in your future career.
- We are sorry you had to leave under these circumstances, but we wish you every success in the future.
- Your future is looking very exciting, and we wish you great happiness in your new job.
- We are all going to miss you very much, and hope that the rest will do you the good your deserve.
- Everyone joins me in wishing you well.
- Please accept this gift as a mark of our respect and gratitude for all you have done.

L A N G U A G E   I N   A C T I O N

Tips

The rules of polite behaviour for email conversation are known as 'netiquette'. Some rules of netiquette are:

- Do not write in capital letters. This is considered to be the equivalent of shouting in speech.
- Use asterisks (*) before and after a word if you want to emphasize it.
- Be careful about using irony or sarcasm. Readers cannot see facial expressions or hear the tone of voice, and so statements intended as jokes may be taken seriously.
- Jokes can be shown by using a 'smiley' or 'emoticon' such as :-). On the other hand, do not use too many of these.
- Avoid 'flames'. A flame is an angry response to a message, especially on a newsgroup. An exchange of flames or a 'flame war' can be very annoying for other newsgroup readers.
- Always include the subject of a message in the subject line.
- Messages should be relatively short and to the point.
- Do not forward other people's messages without the author's permission.
- Include the parts of the message being responded to in new emails or posts to newsgroups.

● Emoticons

Emoticons or 'smileys' are often used to indicate tone. These symbols are read with the head tilted on the left shoulder. The basic smiley is :-). It may mean 'I'm happy to hear from you', or it may be used after a jokey statement. Tongue-in-cheek remarks might use a winking smiley ;-). Below is a list of emoticons in common use, both in email and text messaging:

o:-)	angel
;/	confused
>:-)	devil
:-%	Get lost!
:-s	I'm not making sense.
:-p	naughty
:@)	pig
:-(	sad
:-O	shouting
:o	surprised
:-@!	swearing
;&	tongue-tied

EMAILS

● Net abbreviations

Net abbreviations have developed to shorten messages and speed up typing. It is best to avoid using them if you are not sure that your recipient will understand them. Some of the more common ones are:

AFK	away from keyboard	IMHO	in my humble opinion
BAK	back at keyboard	IOW	in other words
BTW	by the way	NRN	no reply necessary
FAQ	frequently asked question(s) (or a web page containing frequently asked questions)	OTOH	on the other hand
		ROFL	rolling on the floor laughing
FWIW	for what it's worth	RSN	real soon now (often used ironically)
FYI	for your information	SITD	still in the dark
FUA	frequently used acronym	TIA	thanks in advance
IAE	in any event	TIC	tongue in cheek
IMO	in my opinion	TLA	three letter acronym
IMCO	in my considered opinion		

Useful phrases

Generally, email avoids the use of the more formal opening and closing conventions used in traditional letter writing. Below are the most common ones used:

more formal

Dear George   All the best
Dear Mr Thomas   Best wishes
                 Kind regards
                 Regards

more informal

Hi Jenny
Jenny
Hi there!
    See you soon
    All the best
    Best wishes
    Take care
    Love
    Lots of love

LANGUAGE IN ACTION

● A more formal email

> To: frankcollins@planet.co.uk, viviankaye@planet.co.uk
> Cc: robertwestwood@planet.co.uk
> Bcc:
> Subject: sales review meeting
> Attachments: salesfigures_jan_to_march2003.doc
>
> Dear Frank, Vivian
>
> I've just been looking at the sales figures for the last quarter, and I think it would be beneficial for us all to get together to discuss them.
>
> I'm attaching a copy of the document, and would be grateful for any comments you may have, especially with regard to the post-Christmas sale period.
>
> Would Thursday afternoon suit you both, say, 2.30pm? Please let me know if this is not convenient. Thanks.
>
> Regards
>
> Brian

● An informal email

> To: jennymartin@viking.net
> Cc:
> Bcc:
> Subject: Friday night
> Attachments:
>
> Hi Jenny
>
> How're things? Hope all's well, and that you had a riveting time last night at the committee meeting ;-)
>
> I was wondering what you and Will are up to on Friday? We're thinking of going out for something to eat – maybe an Indian. Do you fancy coming too?
>
> BTW, I've just heard that Kate's taken that new job. IMHO it's not going to be an easy job, but good for her anyway.
>
> Let us know what you think about Friday night.
>
> Lots of love
>
> Tamsin xxx

LANGUAGE IN ACTION

● Response to an informal email

To: tforbes@pgl.com
Cc:
Bcc:
Subject: Re: Friday night
Attachments:

Hi Tamsin

You wrote:

>Hope all's well, and that you had a riveting time last night at the >committee meeting ;-)

I nearly died of boredom, as you can well imagine!

>I was wondering what you and Will are up to on Friday? We're thinking of going out for >something to eat – maybe an Indian. Do you fancy coming too?

Sounds great! I'll have been paid by then, so I'll be up for a big night :-)

>BTW, I've just heard that Kate's taken that new job. IMHO it's not going to be an easy >job, but good for her anyway.

I'm amazed, but I suppose our Kate's always up for a challenge. Rather her than me though …

Looking forward to seeing you. Will give you a ring about meeting up on Friday.

Love

Jenny

xx

LANGUAGE IN ACTION

● Text messaging

Since most mobile phones do not have keyboards, senders of messages have to key through the letters marked on the numeric keypad. This can be tedious, and so text messages tend to be short, using a large number of short cuts. As with email, emoticon are also used. Some of the more common abbreviations are listed below:

1CE	once	NETHING	anything
2DAY	today	NO1	no one
2MOR	tomorrow	NP	no problem
2NITE	tonight	OIC	oh, I see
ASAP	as soon as possible	OMG	oh, my God
B	be	PLS	please
BCNU	be seeing you	PPL	people
BRB	be right back	R	are
BTDT	been there, done that	RTFM	read the flippin' manual
BTW	by the way	RU	are you
C	see	RUOK	are you okay
CID	consider it done	SOZ	sorry
COZ	because	STFU	shut up
CU	see you	SUM1	someone
DA	the	THANQ	thank you
EZ	easy	THX	thanks
F2T	free to talk	TMB	text me back
FOTFLOL	falling on the floor, laughing out loud	TTYL	talk to you later
GAL	get a life	TXT BAC	text back
GR8	great	TYVM	thank you very much
GTG	got to go	U	you
H8	hate	W/O	without
K	okay	WAN2	want to
L8	late	WBS	write back soon
L8ER	later	WIV	with
LOL	laughing out loud *or* loads of love	WKND	weekend
		WUD?	what you doing?
LV	love	XLNT	excellent
M8	mate	Y	why
MMFU	my mate fancies you	YR	your
NE	any	YYSSW	yeah yeah sure whatever
NE1	anyone		